Oct 22nd 1837.

"What are you doing now?" he asked, "Do you keep a Journal?" —— So I make my first entry to-day.

Solitude ——

To be alone I find it necessary to escape the present — I avoid myself. How could I be alone in the Roman emperor's chamber of mirrors? I seek a garret. The spiders must not be disturbed, nor the floor swept, nor the lumber arranged. ————

———— The Germans say —— Es ist alles wahr wodurch du besser wirst. ——

The first page of the manuscript of Thoreau's Journal, reproduced same size.
Courtesy of the Pierpont Morgan Library.

THE JOURNAL OF
HENRY D. THOREAU

Edited by Bradford Torrey and Francis H. Allen

With a Foreword By Walter Harding
Secretary, The Thoreau Society

In Fourteen Volumes Bound as Two
Vols. I - VII
(1837 - October, 1855)

DOVER PUBLICATIONS, INC.
NEW YORK   NEW YORK

Published in Canada by General Publishing Company, Ltd., 30 Lesmill Road, Don Mills, Toronto, Ontario.
Published in the United Kingdom by Constable and Company, Ltd., 10 Orange Street, London, WC 2.

This new Dover edition, first published in 1962, is an unabridged republication of the work first published by the Houghton Mifflin Company in 1906. The work originally appeared in fourteen volumes, and now appears in two volumes in this redesigned format.

This edition also contains a new Foreword, written especially for this Dover Edition by Walter Harding, Secretary, The Thoreau Society, and a photographic reproduction of one page of the manuscript journal.

Library of Congress Catalog Card Number: 63-3123

Manufactured in the United States of America

Dover Publications, Inc.
180 Varick Street
New York 14, N. Y.

A FOREWORD

Henry David Thoreau is the most erinaceous of American authors. Ideas stick out from his writings in all directions like porcupine quills, and they are guaranteed to prick the hide of even the most thick-skinned reader. One may not always agree with what Thoreau has to say, but there are few who do not find this prickly non-conformist stimulating. And with every passing year more and more are finding his thoughts more and more pertinent.

When Thoreau began his journal in the fall of 1837, it is doubtful that he had any idea of its ever being published. He began it, it is believed, at the suggestion of his neighbor and mentor Ralph Waldo Emerson. Emerson himself kept a journal primarily as an exercise book and source book for ideas for his lectures and essays. Therein he could jot down those nuggets of insight as they occurred to him. Later they could be quarried and polished at leisure for use in his more finished works.

Thoreau *began* his journal with the same idea in mind. The abbreviated version we now have left of its first thirteen years is ample evidence of how much he quarried and polished from it. Even as late as November 11, 1851, he wrote, " 'Says I to myself' should be the motto of my journal." But gradually, almost imperceptibly, and perhaps almost unconsciously the purpose changed. He began polishing and refining *before* he made his journal entries —a fact proved by the existence of many preliminary drafts of the later journal texts. It became no longer a means but an end in itself—a consciously created work of art.

Thoreau was perfectly aware of the minute chance of the complete journal's ever being published. He had difficulty enough in getting *Walden, A Week on the Concord and Merrimack Rivers,* and the few short essays that were published in his lifetime into print. But he had that faith in himself and in his work so characteristic of the truly great artist and kept working away at the journal right up until the time of his final illness a few months before his death, amassing therein the astounding total of more than two million words.

He had one brief flurry of hope that at least a small portion of his journal might see print during his lifetime. In 1853 Emerson hired Thoreau's boon companion Ellery Channing to edit a volume of excerpts from the journals of Thoreau, Emerson, and Channing himself. Channing completed the task, but the volume was never published. (Perhaps it is just as well, for Channing's manuscript—now in the Morgan Library in New York City—shows that he had thoroughly botched up what he had edited.)

v

16202

Walter Harding

After Thoreau's death various friends, including both Emerson and Bronson Alcott, borrowed the manuscript volumes of the journal from Thoreau's sister Sophia to read for their own personal pleasure. Thomas Wentworth Higginson, inspired by such a reading, made an effort to have the journal published, but he ran into the determined opposition of Sophia Thoreau who thought it too personal to be opened to the gaze of the general public. When Higginson attempted to enlist the aid of Judge Hoar, Concord's leading citizen, in persuading her otherwise, he met with the withering reply, "Why should any one care to have Thoreau's journals put into print?"

In 1872, however, Bronson Alcott suggested in his *Concord Days* that "a delightful volume might be compiled from Thoreau's Journals by selecting what he wrote at a certain date annually, thus giving a calendar of his thoughts on that day from year to year." And when Thoreau's Worcester friend H. G. O. Blake inherited the manuscript journal from Sophia Thoreau, he edited and published four volumes of such excerpts, one for each season of the year. These volumes, issued in the 1880's and 1890's, whetted the appetite of a growing number of Thoreauvians and in 1906 the complete journal (the present text) was published for the first time. Its publication even at that time was a real act of faith, for Thoreau was then still widely considered a minor writer who, in James Russell Lowell's words, picked most of his ideas from "Neighbor Emerson's orchards." (It will be noted that even Bradford Torrey's introduction to that 1906 edition, reprinted herein, excellent as it is, has a certain tone of condescension, labeling Thoreau an escapist and apologizing for his weaknesses as a natural scientist.) But the faith was justified. The entire edition, high priced as it necessarily was under the circumstances, was over-subscribed before publication and became almost immediately a speculator's item on the second-hand book market. A small reprint edition in 1949 solved the problem only briefly, for it too soon went out of print.

This complete* journal offers a unique opportunity to the thoughtful student. Henry Seidel Canby once aptly described it as "one of the most complete records extant of the inner life of an individual." In it we can watch Thoreau's interests focus variously on birds, on writing as an art, on flowers, on Oriental literature, on mammals, on the Greek classics, on grasses, on early Americana, on insects, on slavery. We can observe the conception, the embryonic development, and the birth of his ideas on subjects as various as the succession of forest trees or the relation of the individual to the state.

---

*Technically we should say "almost complete," for two of Thoreau's smaller manuscript journal volumes are not included in this text. The first, covering the period from July 30, 1840, to January 22, 1841, has been recently edited by Perry Miller and published under the title of *Consciousness in Concord* (Boston, 1958). The second, covering portions of the years 1845 and 1846 and devoted in a large part to a record of a trip to the Maine Woods, is still unpublished. Its manuscript is now in the Berg Collection of the New York Public Library.

There are several other minor omissions which Torrey and Allen point out in their "Editor's Preface" below. The careful student should also consult Perry Miller's "A Note on the Editing" in *Consciousness in Concord* (pp. 128-130) for a modern evaluation of the Torrey and Allen editorial practices. But for all but the most specialized student of Thoreau this edition can be considered complete. The original manuscripts of the journal (with the one exception mentioned above) are in the Morgan Library where they are readily accessible to qualified students. A complete microfilm of the manuscripts is in the Thoreau Society Archives in the Concord Free Public Library.

A Foreword

Here is an unmatched opportunity to observe the operation of a thinking man's mind.

Equally fascinating it is to watch the development of Thoreau's prose style through these years. The early entries tend to be comparatively diffuse and abstract. But gradually they become more concrete and develop the crisp cutting edge that is so characteristic of his writing at its best. So much and so clearly did his literary style develop that the astute student can identify most passages from the journal as to approximate date of composition without bothering to check on the entry date.

The journal offers us more than an insight into Thoreau's mind and style. It is also a massive sourcebook of facts and ideas. Although Mr. Torrey in his introduction belittled Thoreau's contributions as an ornithologist (Without question Thoreau did make some rather elementary errors, but Torrey overlooks the fact that in Thoreau's lifetime American science was still in an embryonic stage and that he had available none of the accurate ornithological tools and handbooks that by Torrey's time were commonplace.), Ludlow Griscom, half a century later than Torrey, found Thoreau's journal records so valuable that he used them as the foundation for his superb study of changing bird populations (*Birds of Concord*, Cambridge, 1949). Similar source material in a score of other fields of natural science lies here waiting for the researcher. No one has as yet made an adequate study of the journal as a sourcebook of mid-nineteenth century American word usage or as a compendium of folk-lore and regional proverbs. Still unmined is a wealth of material on political and social attitudes of the time. The journal is a veritable gold mine with its ore still virtually untouched.

Above all, however, the journal is a work of art. It contains character sketches, tales, descriptions, humor, pathos, argumentation, exposition—God's plenty of it and incomparably good. Up to now, because of the comparative unavailability of these complete journals, many have had to be satisfied with the samplings provided by the anthologizers, but now they can do their own sampling for themselves—a much more satisfactory and rewarding procedure.

In this day of accelerated living the sheer bulk of this journal may frighten some of the faint-hearted. They will think themselves too busy to attempt reading it in its entirety. But the connoisseur will read through in proper sequence the whole two million words. Its sheer massiveness can thus make an impression that can never be obtained by dipping here and there. The fascinating pattern of Thoreau's intellectual development can be observed clearly in no other way. And as I can personally testify after having read it through in its entirety a number of times, its greatness as a work of art grows on one with each new reading.

It is therefore a particular source of delight to know that once more the complete journal of this cosmic Yankee will be available and, thanks to advances in printing technology and the resourcefulness of the Dover Publications, Inc., it will be for the first time within the reach of the pocketbook of the most ardent advocate of Thoreau's simple life.

State University College
Geneseo, New York
August, 1962

WALTER HARDING
Secretary, The Thoreau Society

CONTENTS

Contents

The Journal of Henry D. Thoreau

VOLUME I

(1837 — 1847)

PUBLISHER'S NOTE
to the 1906 Edition

Aside from the use Thoreau himself made of his Journal in writing his more formal works, the first extensive publication of the Journal material began in 1881 with "Early Spring in Massachusetts." This volume consisted of extracts covering the month of March and parts of February and April, arranged according to the days of the month, the entries for the successive years following one another under each day. It was edited by Thoreau's friend Mr. H. G. O. Blake, to whom the Journal was bequeathed by Miss Sophia Thoreau, who died in 1876. It was succeeded in 1884 by a volume entitled "Summer," which in reality covered only the early summer, and that, in turn, by "Winter" in 1887 and "Autumn" in 1892, all made by Mr. Blake on the same principle. These volumes, from the first to the last, were received with delight by the ever-increasing body of Thoreau's admirers, but they have served to whet rather than satisfy the appetite of readers, and it has long been evident that they ought not to stand alone as representing this important phase of *Vol. I* Thoreau's activity. The publishers therefore gladly seized the opportunity afforded, when the Journal, on the death of Mr. Blake, passed into the hands of Mr. E. H. Russell of Worcester, who was desirous of giving it to the public in its entirety, and they at once made arrangements with him to bring it out *in extenso* as soon as the long labor of copying and comparing the manuscripts could be completed. As editor the publishers have been so fortunate as to secure Mr. Bradford Torrey, who is eminently qualified to consider Thoreau both as a writer and as an observer of nature.

EDITOR'S PREFACE
to the 1906 Edition

Concerning this first practically complete printing of Thoreau's Journal it seems proper to make the following explanations, in addition to those contained in the Publishers' Note:—

1. It has been found necessary, if the Journal was to be of comfortable use by ordinary readers, to punctuate it throughout. Otherwise each reader would have been compelled to do the work for himself. A literal reproduction, like the literal reproduction of Milton's minor poems, for example, may some day be of interest to antiquaries and special students; but such an edition could never be adapted, more than the literal reproduction of Milton's manuscripts, to the needs of those who read for pleasure and general profit.

2. Certain things have been omitted; *i.e.*, incomplete sentences, where parts of pages have been torn out by the writer; long quotations, especially from Latin authors, entered without comment, as in a commonplace-book; Maine woods matter — "Chesuncook" and "The Allegash and East Branch" — already printed *in extenso* in the volume entitled "The Maine Woods;" a few long lists of plants, etc., recapitulating matter contained in the preceding pages; the word *ultimo,* or *ult.,* which in hundreds of instances is written where the context makes it plain that *instant* was the word intended; a proper name here and there, out of regard for the feelings of possible relatives or descendants of the persons mentioned; guesses at the identification of particular plants, — willows, goldenrods, and the like, — often accompanied by tediously minute technical descriptions, the whole evidently meant as mere memoranda for the writer's possible future guidance, and believed to be of no interest now, even to the botanical reader.

3. In the case of passages which Thoreau had revised, mostly in pencil, the editors have commonly printed the original form when the amended one has been followed in already printed volumes. In other cases the amended version has been given. Corrections of error have always been allowed to stand, except that, where it is plain that the correction must have been made at a date later than that of the original entry, the correction has been printed as a footnote, without brackets.

4. The footnotes of the editors are always in brackets.

5. Where parts of the Journal have been printed in the author's books, the editors, as far as their knowledge has gone, have indicated the fact, citing first the present and then the Riverside edition, — thus: "*Week,* p. 305; Riv. 379." References to "Channing" are to "Thoreau, the Poet-Naturalist," by William Ellery Channing, new edition, edited by Mr. F. B. Sanborn. References to "Sanborn" are to "Henry D. Thoreau," by F. B. Sanborn, in the American Men of Letters.

6. The earlier manuscript volumes of the Journal, as we now have them, are evidently not the originals, but are made up of selections from volumes that appear to have been destroyed by the author.

It remains only to add the editor's very hearty acknowledgements to his associate, Mr. Francis H. Allen, who has overseen and verified the copying of the manuscript, an onerous task, and in every way, by counsel and labor, has facilitated, not to say made possible, the completion of the work.

Vol. I

CONTENTS

Vol. I

THOREAU was a man of his own kind. Many things may be said of him, favorable and unfavorable, but this must surely be said first,—that, taken for all in all, he was like nobody else. Taken for all in all, be it remarked. Other men have despised common sense; other men have chosen to be poor, and, as between physical comfort and better things, have made light of physical comfort; other men, whether to their credit or discredit, have held and expressed a contemptuous opinion of their neighbors and all their neighbors' doings; others, a smaller number, believing in an absolute goodness and in a wisdom transcending human knowledge, have distrusted the world as evil, accounting its influence degrading, its prudence no better than cowardice, its wisdom a kind of folly, its morality a compromise, its religion a bargain, its possessions a defilement and a hindrance, and so judging of the world, have striven at all cost to live above it and apart. And some, no doubt, have loved Nature as a mistress, fleeing to her from less congenial company, and devoting a lifetime to the observation and enjoyment of her ways. In no one of these particulars was the hermit of Walden without forerunners; but taken for all that he was, poet, idealist, stoic, cynic, naturalist, spiritualist, lover of purity, seeker of perfection, panegyrist of friendship and dweller in a hermitage, freethinker and saint, where shall we look to find his fellow? It seems but the plainest statement of

fact to say that, as there was none before him, so there is scanty prospect of any to come after him.

His profession was literature; as to that there is no sign that he was ever in doubt; and he understood from the first that for a writing man nothing could take the place of practice, partly because that is the one means of acquiring ease of expression, and partly because a man often has no suspicion of his own thoughts until his pen discovers them; and almost from the first — a friend (Emerson or another) having given him the hint — he had come to feel that no practice is better or readier than the keeping of a journal, a daily record of things thought, seen, and felt. Such a record he began soon after leaving college, and (being one of a thousand in this respect as in others) he continued it to the end. By good fortune he left it behind him, and, to complete the good fortune, it is at last printed, no longer in selections, but as a whole; and if a man is curious to know what such an original, plain-spoken, perfection-seeking, convention-despising, dogma-disbelieving, wisdom-loving, sham-hating, Nature-worshipping, poverty-proud genius was in the habit of confiding to so patient a listener at the close of the day, he has only to read the book.

The man himself is there. Something of him, indeed, is to be discovered, one half imagines, in the outward aspect of the thirty-nine manuscript volumes: ordinary "blank-books" of the sort furnished by country shopkeepers fifty or sixty years ago, larger or smaller as might happen, and of varying shapes (a customer seeking such wares must not be too particular; one remembers Thoreau's complaint that the universal preoccupation

with questions of money rendered it difficult for him to find a blank-book that was not ruled for dollars and cents), still neatly packed in the strong wooden box which their owner, a workman needing not to be ashamed, made with his own hands on purpose to hold them.

A pretty full result of a short life they seem to be, as one takes up volume after volume (the largest are found to contain about a hundred thousand words) and turns the leaves: the handwriting strong and rapid, leaning well forward in its haste, none too legible, slow reading at the best, with here and there a word that is almost past making out; the orthography that of a naturally good speller setting down his thoughts at full speed and leaving his mistakes behind him; and the punctuation, to call it such, no better than a makeshift, — after the model of Sterne's, if one chooses to say so: a spattering of dashes, and little else.[1]

As for the matter, it is more carefully considered, less strictly improvised, than is customary with diarists. It is evident, in fact, from references here and there, that many of the entries were copied from an earlier pencilled draft, made presumably in the field, " with the eye on the

[1] In many cases the punctuation seems to be absolutely without significance ; as if the writer had simply fallen into the habit of dropping dashes in an absent-minded way as he passed along. The following examples (the longest an extreme case) will show what is meant:—

"I heard from time to time — a new note."

"The *Equisetum sylvaticum* — there is now of a reddish cast."

"It is very difficult — to find a suitable place to camp near the road — affording — water — a good — prospect and retirement."

"Another alighted near — by — and a third a little further off."

object," while the work as a whole has been more or less carefully revised, with erasures, emendations, and suggested alternative readings.

As we have said, if a man wishes to know Thoreau as he was, let him read the book. One thing he may be sure of: he will find himself in clean, self-respecting company, with no call to blush, as if he were playing the eavesdropper. Of confessions, indeed, in the spicy sense of the word, Thoreau had none to make. He was no Montaigne, no Rousseau, no Samuel Pepys. How should he be? He was a Puritan of Massachusetts, though he kept no Sabbath, was seen in no church, — being very different from Mr. Pepys in more ways than one, — and esteemed the Hebrew scriptures as a good book like any other. Once, indeed, when he was thirty-four years old, he went to a "party." For anything we know, that (with a little sowing of wild oats in the matter of smoking dried lily-stems when a boy) was as near as he ever came to dissipation. And he did not like it. "It is a bad place to go to," he says, — "thirty or forty persons, mostly young women, in a small room, warm and noisy." One of the young women was reputed to be "pretty-looking;" but he scarcely looked at her, though he was "introduced," and he could not hear what she said, because there was "such a clacking." "I could imagine better places for conversation," he goes on, "where there should be a certain degree of silence surrounding you, and less than forty talking at once. Why, this afternoon, even, I did better. There was old Mr. Joseph Hosmer and I ate our luncheon of cracker and cheese together in the woods. I heard all he said, though

it was not much, to be sure, and he could hear me. And then he talked out of such a glorious repose, taking a leisurely bite at the cracker and cheese between his words; and so some of him was communicated to me, and some of me to him, I trust."

He entertains a shrewd suspicion that assemblies of this kind are got up with a view to matrimonial alliances among the young people! For his part, at all events, he does n't understand "the use of going to see people whom yet you never see, and who never see you." Some of his friends make a singular blunder. They go out of their way to talk to pretty young women *as such.* Their prettiness may be a reason for looking at them, so much he will concede, — for the sake of the antithesis, if for nothing else, — but why is it any reason for talking to them? For himself, though he may be "lacking a sense in this respect," he derives "no pleasure from talking with a young woman half an hour simply because she has regular features."

How crabbed is divine philosophy! After this we are not surprised when he concludes by saying: "The society of young women is the most unprofitable I have ever tried." No, no; he was nothing like Mr. Samuel Pepys.

The sect of young women, we may add, need not feel deeply affronted by this ungallant mention. It is perhaps the only one of its kind in the journal (by its nature restricted to matters interesting to the author), while there are multitudes of passages to prove that Thoreau's aversion to the society of older people taken as they run, men and women alike, was hardly less pronounced. In

truth (and it is nothing of necessity against him), he was not made for "parties," nor for clubs, nor even for general companionship. "I am all without and in sight," said Montaigne, "born for society and friendship." So was not Thoreau. He was all within, born for contemplation and solitude. And what we are born for, that let us be, — and so the will of God be done. Such, for good or ill, was Thoreau's philosophy. "We are constantly invited to be what we are," he said. It is one of his memorable sentences; an admirable summary of Emerson's essay on Self-Reliance.

His fellow mortals, as a rule, did not recommend themselves to him. His thoughts were none the better for their company, as they almost always were for the company of the pine tree and the meadow. Inspiration, a refreshing of the spiritual faculties, as indispensable to him as daily bread, that his fellow mortals did not furnish him. For this state of things he sometimes (once or twice at least) mildly reproaches himself. It may be that he is to blame for so commonly skipping humanity and its affairs; he will seek to amend the fault, he promises. But even at such a moment of exceptional humility, his pen, reversing Balaam's rôle, runs into left-handed compliments that are worse, if anything, than the original offense. Hear him: "I will not avoid to go by where those men are repairing the stone bridge. I will see if I cannot see poetry in that, if that will not yield me a reflection. It is narrow to be confined to woods and fields and grand aspects of nature only. . . . Why not see men standing in the sun and casting a shadow, even as trees? . . . I will try to enjoy them as animals, at least."

This is in 1851. A year afterward we find him concerned with the same theme, but in a less hesitating mood. Now he is on his high horse, with apologies to nobody. "It appears to me," he begins, "that to one standing on the heights of philosophy mankind and the works of man will have sunk out of sight altogether." Man, in his opinion, is "too much insisted upon." "The poet says, 'The proper study of mankind is man.' I say, Study to forget all that. Take wider views of the universe. . . . What is the village, city, state, nation, aye, the civilized world, that it should concern a man so much? The thought of them affects me, in my wisest hours, as when I pass a woodchuck's hole."

A high horse, indeed! But his comparison is really by no means so disparaging as it sounds; for Thoreau took a deep and lasting interest in woodchucks. At one time and another he wrote many good pages about them; for their reappearance in the spring he watched as for the return of a friend, and once, at least, he devoted an hour to digging out a burrow and recording with painstaking minuteness the course and length of its ramifications. A novelist, describing his heroine's boudoir, could hardly have been more strict with himself. In fact, to have said that one of Thoreau's human neighbors was as interesting to him as a woodchuck would have been to pay that neighbor a rather handsome compliment. None of the brute animals, so called, — we have it on his own authority, — ever vexed his ears with pomposity or nonsense.

But we have interrupted his discourse midway. "I do not value any view of the universe into which man and

the institutions of man enter very largely," he continues.
. . . "Man is a past phenomenon to philosophy."
Then he descends a little to particulars. "Some rarely
go outdoors, most are always at home at night," —
Concord people being uncommonly well brought up, it
would appear, — "very few indeed have stayed out all
night once in their lives; fewer still have gone behind the
world of humanity and seen its institutions like toadstools by the wayside."

And then, having, with this good bit of philosophical
"tall talk," brushed aside humanity as a very little thing,
he proceeds to chronicle the really essential facts of the
day: that he landed that afternoon on Tall's Island, and
to his disappointment found the weather not cold or
windy enough for the meadow to make "its most serious
impression;" also, that the staddles from which the hay
had been removed were found to stand a foot or two
above the water; besides which, he saw cranberries on
the bottom (although he forgot to mention them in their
proper place), and noticed that the steam of the engine
looked very white that morning against the hillside.

All which setting of ordinary valuations topsy-turvy,
the lords of creation below the beasts that perish, may
lead an innocent reader to exclaim with one of old,
"Lord, what is man, that thou art mindful of him? and
the son of man, that thou visitest him?"

Nevertheless, we must not treat the matter too lightly,
easily as it lends itself to persiflage. Even in this extreme
instance it is not to be assumed that Thoreau was talking for the sake of talking, or merely keeping his hand
in with his favorite rhetorical weapon, a paradox. That

desiderated "serious impression," at all events, was no
laughing matter; rather it was to have been the chief
event of the day; of more account to Thoreau than dinner and supper both were likely to be to his farmer
neighbor. As for the woodchuck, its comparative rank
in the scale of animal existence, be it higher or lower,
is nothing to the purpose. For Thoreau it was simple
truth that, on some days, and in some states of mind,
he found the society of such a cave-dweller more acceptable, or less unacceptable, than that of any number of his highly civilized townsmen. Nor is the
statement one to be nervously concerned about. Any
inveterate stroller, the most matter-of-fact man alive
(though matter-of-fact men are not apt to be strollers),
might say the same, in all soberness, with no thought
of writing himself down a misanthrope, or of setting
himself up as a philosopher.

For one thing, the woodchuck is sure to be less intru-
sive, less distracting, than the ordinary human specimen;
he fits in better with solitude and the solitary feeling.
He is never in the way. Moreover, you can say to a
woodchuck anything that comes into your head, without
fear of giving offense; a less important consideration
than the other, no doubt, woodchucks as a class not being
remarkably conversable, but still worthy of mention.
For, naturally enough, an outspoken freethinker like
Thoreau found the greater number of men not so very
different from "ministers," of whom he said, in a tone
of innocent surprise, that they "could not bear all kinds
of opinions," — "as if any sincere thought were not the
best sort of truth!"

Vol. I

He walked one afternoon with Alcott, and spent an
agreeable hour, though for the most part he preferred
having the woods and fields to himself. Alcott was an
ineffectual genius, he remarks, "forever feeling about
vainly in his speech, and touching nothing" (one thinks
of Arnold's characterization of Shelley as a "beautiful
and ineffectual angel, beating in the void his luminous
wings in vain," which, in its turn, may call to mind
Lowell's comparison of Shelley's genius to a St. Elmo's
fire, "playing in ineffectual flame about the points of
his thought"), but after all, he was good company; not
quite so good as none, of course, but on the whole, as
men go, rather better than most. At least, he would
listen to what you had to offer. He was open-minded;
he was n't shut up in a creed; an honest man's thought
would not shock him. You could talk to him without
running up against "some institution." In a word, —
though Thoreau does n't say it, — he was something
like a woodchuck.

With all his passion for "that glorious society called
solitude," and with all his feeling that mankind, as a
"past phenomenon," thought far too highly of itself, it
is abundantly in evidence that Thoreau, in his own time
and on his own terms, was capable of a really human
delight in familiar intercourse with his fellows. Channing, who should have known, speaks, a little vaguely,
to be sure, of his "fine social qualities." "Always a
genial and hospitable entertainer," he calls him. And
Mr. Ricketson, who also should have known, assures us
that "no man could hold a finer relationship with his
family than he." But of this aspect of his character,

it must be acknowledged, there is comparatively little
in the journal. What is very constant and emphatic
there — emphatic sometimes to the point of painful-
ness — is the hermit's hunger and thirst after friendship;
a friendship the sweets of which, so far as appears, he
was very sparingly to enjoy. For if he was at home in
the family group and in huckleberry excursions with
children, if he relished to the full a talk with a stray fisherman, a racy-tongued woodchopper, or a good Indian,
something very different seems to have been habitual
with him when it came to intercourse with equals and
friends.

Here, even more than elsewhere, he was an uncompromising idealist. His craving was for a friendship
more than human, friendship such as it was beyond any
one about him to furnish, if it was not, as may fairly be
suspected, beyond his own capacity to receive. In respect
to outward things, his wealth, he truly said, was to want
little. In respect to friendship, his poverty was to want
the unattainable. It might have been retorted upon him
in his own words, that he was like a man who should
complain of hard times because he could not afford to
buy himself a crown. But the retort would perhaps have
been rather smart than fair. He, at least, would never
have acquiesced in it. He confided to his journal again
and again that he asked nothing of his friends but honesty, sincerity, a grain of real appreciation, "an opportunity once in a year to speak the truth;" but in the
end it came always to this, that he insisted upon perfection, and, not finding it, went on his way hungry. Probably it is true — one seems to divine a reason for it —

that idealists, claimers of the absolute, have commonly found their fellow men a disappointment.

In Thoreau's case it was his best friends who most severely tried his patience. They invite him to see them, he complains, and then "do not show themselves." He "pines and starves near them." All is useless. They treat him so that he "feels a thousand miles off." "I leave my friends early. I go away to cherish my idea of friendship." Surely there is no sentence in all Thoreau's books that is more thoroughly characteristic than that. And how neatly it is turned! Listen also to this, which is equally bitter, and almost equally perfect in the phrasing: "No fields are so barren to me as the men of whom I expect everything, but get nothing. In their neighborhood I experience a painful yearning for society."

It is all a mystery to him. "How happens it," he exclaims, "that I find myself making such an enormous demand on men, and so constantly disappointed? Are my friends aware how disappointed I am? Is it all my fault? Am I incapable of expansion and generosity? I shall accuse myself of anything else sooner." And again he goes away sorrowful, consoling himself, as best he can, with his own paradox, —

"I might have loved him, had I loved him less."

Strange that he should have suffered in this way, many will think, with Emerson himself for a friend and neighbor! Well, the two men were friends, but neither was in this relation quite impeccable (which is as much as to say that both were human), and to judge by such hints as are gatherable on either side, their case was not

entirely unlike that of Bridget Elia and her cousin, — "generally in harmony, with occasional bickerings, as it should be among near relations;" though "bickerings" is no doubt an undignified term for use in this connection. It is interesting, some may deem it amusing, to put side by side the statements of the two men upon this very point; Emerson's communicated to the public shortly after his friend's death, Thoreau's intrusted nine years before to the privacy of his journal.

Emerson's speech is the more guarded, as, for more reasons than one, it might have been expected to be. His friend, he confesses, "was somewhat military in his nature . . . always manly and able, but rarely tender, as if he did not feel himself except in opposition. He wanted a fallacy to expose, a blunder to pillory, I may say required a little sense of victory, a roll of the drum, to call his powers into full exercise. . . . It seemed as if his first instinct on hearing a proposition was to controvert it, so impatient was he of the limitations of our daily thought. This habit, of course, is a little chilling to the social affections; and though the companion would in the end acquit him of any malice or untruth, yet it mars conversation. Hence no equal companion stood in affectionate relations with one so pure and guileless."

Thoreau's entry is dated May 24, 1853. "Talked, or tried to talk, with R. W. E. Lost my time, nay, almost my identity. He, assuming a false opposition where there was no difference of opinion, talked to the wind, told me what I knew, and I lost my time trying to imagine myself somebody else to oppose him."

It is the very same picture, drawn by another pencil,

Vol. I

with a different placing of the shadows; and since the two sketches were made so many years apart and yet seem to be descriptive of the same thing, it is perhaps fair to conclude that this particular interview, which appears to have degenerated into something like a dispute about nothing (a very frequent subject of disputes, by the way), was not exceptional, but rather typical. Without doubt this was one of the occasions when Thoreau felt himself treated as if he were "a thousand miles off," and went home early to "cherish his idea of friendship." Let us hope that he lost nothing else along with his time and identity.

But here, again, we are in danger of an unseasonable lightness. Friendship, according to Thoreau's apprehension of it, was a thing infinitely sacred. A *friend* might move him to petulance, as the best of friends sometimes will; but *friendship*, the ideal state shown to him in dreams, for speech concerning that there was nowhere in English, nor anywhere else, a word sufficiently noble and unsoiled. And even his friends he loved, although, tongue-tied New-Englander that he was, he could never tell them so. He loved them best (and this, likewise, was no singularity) when they were farthest away. In company, even in their company, he could never utter his truest thought. So it is with us all. It was a greater than Thoreau who said, "We descend to meet;" and a greater still, perhaps (and he also a Concord man), who confessed at fifty odd: "I doubt whether I have ever really talked with half a dozen persons in my life."

As for Thoreau, he knew at times, and owned as much

to himself, that his absorption in nature tended to unfit him for human society. But so it was; he loved to be alone. And in this respect he had no thought of change, — no thought nor wish. Whatever happened, he would still belong to no club but the true "country club," which dined "at the sign of the Shrub Oak." The fields and the woods, the old road, the river, and the pond, these were his real neighbors. Year in and year out, how near they were to him! — a nearness unspeakable; till sometimes it seemed as if their being and his were not two, but one and the same. With them was no frivolity, no vulgarity, no changeableness, no prejudice. With them he had no misunderstandings, no meaningless disputes, no disappointments. They knew him, and were known of him. In their society he felt himself renewed. There he lived, and loved his life. There, if anywhere, the Spirit of the Lord came upon him. Hear him, on a cool morning in August, with the wind in the branches and the crickets in the grass, and think of him, if you can, as a being too cold for friendship!

"My heart leaps out of my mouth at the sound of the wind in the woods. I, whose life was but yesterday so desultory and shallow, suddenly recover my spirits, my spirituality, through my hearing. . . . Ah! if I could so live that there should be no desultory moments . . . I would walk, I would sit and sleep, with natural piety. What if I could pray aloud, or to myself, as I went along by the brookside, a cheerful prayer, like the birds! For joy I could embrace the earth. I shall delight to be buried in it. And then, to think of those I love among men, who will know that I love them, though I tell them not. . . . I thank you, God. I do not deserve anything; I am unworthy of the least regard; and yet the world is gilded for my delight, and holidays are prepared for me, and my path is strewn with flowers. . . . O keep my senses pure!"

Highly characteristic is that concluding ejaculation. For Thoreau the five senses were not organs or means of sensuous gratification, but the five gateways of the soul. He would have them open and undefiled. Upon that point no man was ever more insistent. Above all, no sense must be pampered; else it would lose its native freshness and delicacy, and so its diviner use. That way lay perdition. When a woman came to Concord to lecture, and Thoreau carried her manuscript to the hall for her, wrapped in its owner's handkerchief, he complained twenty-four hours afterward that his pocket "still exhaled cologne." Faint, elusive outdoor odors were not only a continual delight to him, but a positive means of grace.

So, too, he would rather not see any of the scenic wonders of the world. Only let his sense of beauty remain uncorrupted, and he could trust his Musketaquid meadows, and the low hills round about, to feed and satisfy him forever.

Because of his jealousy in this regard, partly, — and partly from ignorance, it may be, just as some of his respectable village acquaintances would have found the Iliad, of which he talked so much, duller than death in comparison with the works of Mr. Sylvanus Cobb, — he often spoke in slighting terms of operas and all the more elaborate forms of music. The ear, he thought, if it

were kept innocent, would find satisfaction in the very simplest of musical sounds. For himself, there was no language extravagant enough to express his rapturous delight in them. Now "all the romance of his youthfulest moment" came flooding back upon him, and anon he was carried away till he "looked under the lids of Time," — all by the humming of telegraph-wires or, at night especially, by the distant baying of a hound.

To the modern "musical person" certain of his confessions under this head are of a character to excite mirth. He is "much indebted," for instance, to a neighbor "who will now and then, in the intervals of his work, draw forth a few strains from his accordion." The neighbor is only a learner, but, says Thoreau, "I find when his strains cease that I have been elevated." His daily philosophy is all of a piece, one perceives: plain fare, plain clothes, plain company, a hut in the woods, an old book, — and for inspiration the notes of a neighbor's accordion.

More than once, too, he acknowledges his obligation to that famous rural entertainer and civilizer, the handorgan. "All Vienna" could not do more for him, he ventures to think. "It is perhaps the best instrumental music that we have," he observes; which can hardly have been true, even in Concord, one prefers to believe, while admitting the possibility. If it is heard far enough away, he goes on, so that the creaking of the machinery is lost, "it serves the grandest use for me, — it deepens my existence."

We smile, of course, as in duty bound, at so artless an avowal; but, having smiled, we are bound also to render

Vol. I

our opinion that the most *blasé* concert-goer, if he be a man of native sensibility, will readily enough discern what Thoreau has in mind, and with equal readiness will concede to it a measure of reasonableness; for he will have the witness in himself that the effect of music upon the soul depends as much upon the temper of the soul as upon the perfection of the instrument. One day a simple air, simply sung or played, will land him in heaven; and another day the best efforts of the full symphony orchestra will leave him in the mire. And after all, it is possibly better, albeit in "poorer taste," to be transported by the wheezing of an accordion than to be bored by finer music. As for Thoreau, he studied to be a master of the art of living; and in the practice of that art, as of any other, it is the glory of the artist to achieve extraordinary results by ordinary means. To have one's existence deepened — there cannot be many things more desirable than that; and as between our unsophisticated recluse and the average "musical person" aforesaid, the case is perhaps not so one-sided as at first sight it looks; or, if it be, the odds are possibly not always on the side of what seems the greater opportunity.

His life, the quality of his life, that for Thoreau was the paramount concern. To the furthering of that end all things must be held subservient. Nature, man, books, music, all for him had the same use. This one thing he did, — he cultivated himself. If any, because of his so doing, accused him of selfishness, preaching to him of philanthropy, almsgiving, and what not, his answer was already in his mouth. Mankind, he was prepared to maintain, was very well off without such helps, which

oftener than not did as much harm as good (though the concrete case at his elbow — half-clad Johnny Riordan, a fugitive slave, an Irishman who wished to bring his family over — appealed to him as quickly as to most, one is glad to notice); and, however that might be, the world needed a thousand times more than any so-called charity the sight of a man here and there living for higher ends than the world itself knows of. His own course, at any rate, was clear before him: "What I am, I am, and say not. Being is the great explainer."

His life, his *own* life, that he must live; and he must be in earnest about it. He was no indifferent, no littlecarer, no skeptic, as if truth and a lie were but varying shades of the same color, and virtue, according to the old phrase, "a mean between vices." You would never catch him sighing, "Oh, well!" or "Who knows?" Qualifications, reconciliations, *rapprochements*, the two sides of the shield, and all that, — these were considerations not in his line. Before everything else he was a believer, — an idealist, that is, — the last person in the world to put up with half-truths or half-way measures. If "existing things" were thus and so, that was no reason why, with the sect of the Sadducees, he should make the best of them. What if there *were* no best of them? What if they were all bad? And anyhow, why not begin new? It was conceivable, was it not, that a man should set his own example, and follow his own copy. General opinion, — what was that? Was a thing better established because ten thousand fools believed it? Did folly become wisdom by being raised to a higher power? And antiquity, tradition, — what were they? Could a blind man of fifteen centuries ago see farther than a blind man of the present time? And if the blind led the blind, then or now, would not both fall into the ditch?

Yes, he was undoubtedly peculiar. As to that there could never be anything but agreement among practical people. In a world where shiftiness and hesitation are the rule, nothing looks so eccentric as a straight course. It must be acknowledged, too, that a man whose goodness has a strong infusion of the bitter, and whose opinions turn out of the way for nobody, is not apt to be the most comfortable kind of neighbor. We were not greatly surprised, lately, to hear an excellent lady remark of Thoreau that, from all she had read about him, she thought he must have been "a very disagreeable gentleman." It could hardly be said of him, as Mr. Birrell says of Matthew Arnold, who was himself a pretty serious person, and, after a way of his own, a preacher of righteousness, that he "conspired and contrived to make things pleasant."

Being a consistent idealist, he was of course an extremist, falling in that respect little behind the man out of Nazareth, whose hard sayings, by all accounts, were sometimes less acceptable than they might have been, and of whom Thoreau asserted, in his emphatic way, that if his words were really read from any pulpit in the land, "there would not be left one stone of that meeting-house upon another." Thoreau worshipped purity, and the every-day ethical standards of the street were to him an abomination. "There are certain current expressions and blasphemous moods of viewing things," he declares, "as when we say 'he is doing a good busi-

ness,' more profane than cursing and swearing. There is death and sin in such words. Let not the children hear them." That innocent-sounding phrase about "a good business" — as if a business might be taken for granted as good because it brought in money — was as abhorrent to him as the outrageous worldly philosophy of an old castaway like Major Pendennis is to the ordinarily sensitive reader.

He was constitutionally earnest. There are pages of the journal, indeed, which make one feel that perhaps he was in danger of being too much so for his own profit. Possibly it is not quite wholesome, possibly, if one dares to say it, it begets a something like priggishness, for the soul to be keyed up continually to so strenuous a pitch. In Thoreau's case, at all events, one is glad for every sign of a slackening of the tension. "Set the red hen to-day;" "Got green grapes to stew;" "Painted the bottom of my boat;" trivialities like these, too far apart (one is tempted to colloquialize, and call them "precious few," finding them so infrequent and so welcome), strike the reader with a sudden sensation of relief, as if he had been wading to the chin, and all at once his feet had touched a shallow.

So, too, one is thankful to come upon a really amusing dissertation about the tying of shoe-strings, or rather about their too easy untying; a matter with which, it appears, Thoreau had for years experienced "a great deal of trouble." His walking companion (Channing, presumably) and himself had often compared notes about it, concluding after experiments that the duration of a shoe-tie might be made to serve as a reasonably

accurate unit of measure, as accurate, say, as a stadium or a league. Channing, indeed, would sometimes go without shoe-strings, rather than be plagued so incessantly by their dissolute behavior. Finally Thoreau, being then thirty-six years old, and always exceptionally clever with his hands, set his wits seriously at work upon knots, and by a stroke of good fortune (or a stroke of genius) hit upon one which answered his end; only to be told, on communicating his discovery to a third party, that he had all his life been tying "granny knots," never having learned, at school or elsewhere, the secret of a square one! It might be well, he concludes, if all children were "taught the accomplishment." Verily, as Hosea Biglow did not say, they did n't know everything down in Concord.

More refreshing still are entries describing hours of serene communion with nature, hours in which, as in an instance already cited, the Spirit of the Lord blessed him, and he forgot even to be good. These entries, likewise, are less numerous than could be wished, though perhaps as frequent as could fairly be expected; since ecstasies, like feasts, must in the nature of things be somewhat broadly spaced; and it is interesting, not to say surprising, to see how frankly he looks upon them afterward as subjects on which to try his pen. In these "seasons when our genius reigns we may be powerless for expression," he remarks; but in calmer hours, when talent is again active, "the memory of those rarer moods comes to color our picture, and is the permanent paint-pot, as it were, into which we dip our brush." But, in truth, the whole journal, some volumes of which are carefully indexed

in his own hand, is quite undisguisedly a collection of thoughts, feelings, and observations, out of which copy is to be extracted. In it, he says, "I wish to set down such choice experiences that my own writings may inspire me, and at last I may make wholes of parts. . . . Each thought that is welcomed and recorded is a nest-egg by the side of which more will be laid."

A born writer, he is "greedy of occasions to express" himself. He counts it "wise to write on many subjects, that so he may find the right and inspiring one." "There are innumerable avenues to a perception of the truth," he tells himself. "Improve the suggestion of each object, however humble, however slight and transient the provocation. What else is there to be improved?"

The literary diarist, like the husbandman, knows not which shall prosper. Morning and evening, he can only sow the seed. So it was with Thoreau. "A strange and unaccountable thing," he pronounces his journal. "It will allow nothing to be predicated of it; its good is not good, nor its bad bad. If I make a huge effort to expose my innermost and richest wares to light, my counter seems cluttered with the meanest homemade stuffs; but after months or years I may discover the wealth of India, and whatever rarity is brought overland from Cathay, in that confused heap, and what seemed a festoon of dried apple or pumpkin will prove a string of Brazilian diamonds, or pearls from Coromandel."

Well, we make sure that whoever tumbles the heap over now, more than forty years after the last object was laid upon it, will be rewarded with many and many a jewel. Here, for his encouragement, are half a dozen out of the goodly number that one customer has lately turned up, in a hasty rummaging of the counter: —

"When a dog runs at you, whistle for him."

"We must be at the helm at least once a day; we must feel the tiller rope in our hands, and know that if we sail, we steer."

"In composition I miss the hue of the mind."

"After the era of youth is past, the knowledge of ourselves is an alloy that spoils our satisfactions."

"How vain it is to sit down to write when you have not stood up to live."

"Silence is of various depths and fertility, like soil."

"Praise should be spoken as simply and naturally as a flower emits its fragrance."

Here, again, is a mere nothing, a momentary impression caught, in ball-players' language, on the fly; nothing like a pearl from Coromandel, if you will, but at the worst a toothsome bite out of a wild New England apple. It is winter. "I saw a team come out of a path in the woods," says Thoreau, "as though it had never gone in, but belonged there, and only came out like Elisha's bears." There will be few country-bred Yankee boys, we imagine, who will not remember to have experienced something precisely like that, under precisely the same circumstances, though it never occurred to them to put the feeling into words, much less to preserve it in a drop of ink. That is one of the good things that a writer does for us. And our country-bred boy, if we mistake not, is likely to consider this one careless sentence of Thoreau, which adds not a cent's worth to the sum of what is called human knowledge, as of

more value than any dozen pages of his painstaking botanical records.

Thoreau the naturalist appears in the journal, not as a master, but as a learner. It could hardly be otherwise, of course, a journal being what it is. There we see him conning by himself his daily lesson, correcting yesterday by to-day, and to-day by to-morrow, progressing, like every scholar, over the stepping-stones of his own mistakes. Of the branches he pursued, as far as the present writer can presume to judge, he was strongest in botany; certainly it was to plants that he most persistently devoted himself; but even there he had as many uncertainties as discoveries to set down; and he set them down with unflagging zeal and unrestrained particularity. The daily account is running over with question-marks. His patience was admirable; the more so as he worked entirely by himself, with few of the helps that in this better-furnished time almost belie the old proverb, and make even the beginner's path a kind of royal road to learning. The day of "How-to-Know" handbooks had not yet dawned.

Of his bird-studies it would be interesting, if there were room, to speak at greater length. Here, even more than in botany, if that were possible, he suffered for lack of assistance, and even in his later entries leaves the present-day reader wondering how so eager a scholar could have spent so many years in learning so comparatively little. The mystery is partly cleared, however, when it is found that until 1854 — say for more than a dozen years — he studied without a glass. He does not buy things, he explains, with characteristic self-satisfac-

tion, till long after he begins to want them, so that when he does get them he is "prepared to make a perfect use of them." It was wasteful economy. He might as well have botanized without a pocket-lens.

But glass or no glass, how could an ornithological observer, whose power — so Emerson said — "seemed to indicate additional senses," be in the field daily for ten or fifteen years before setting eyes upon his first rose-breasted grosbeak? — which memorable event happened to Thoreau on the 13th of June, 1853! How could a man who had made it his business for at least a dozen years to "name all the birds without a gun," stand for a long time within a few feet of a large bird, so busy that it could not be scared far away, and then go home uncertain whether he had been looking at a woodcock or a snipe? How could he, when thirty-five years old, see a flock of sparrows, and hear them sing, and not be sure whether or not they were chipping sparrows? And how could a man so strong in times and seasons, always marking dates with an almanac's exactness, how could he, so late as '52, inquire concerning the downy woodpecker, one of the more familiar and constant of year-round birds, "Do we see him in the winter?" and again, a year later, be found asking whether he, the same downy woodpecker, is not the first of our woodland birds to arrive in the spring? At thirty-six he is amazed to the extent of double exclamation points by the sight of a flicker so early as March 29.

It fills one with astonishment to hear him (May 4, 1853) describing what he takes to be an indigo-bird after this fashion: "Dark throat and light beneath, and white

spot on wings," with hoarse, rapid notes, a kind of *twee, twee, twee*, not musical. The stranger may have been — most likely it was — a black-throated blue warbler; which is as much like an indigo-bird as a bluebird is like a blue jay, — or a yellow apple like an orange. And the indigo-bird, it should be said, is a common New-Englander, such as one of our modern schoolboy bird-gazers would have no difficulty in getting into his "list" any summer day in Concord; while the warbler in question, though nothing but a migrant, and somewhat seclusive in its habits, is so regular in its passage and so unmistakably marked (no bird more so), that it seems marvellous how Thoreau, prowling about everywhere with his eyes open, should year after year have missed it.

The truth appears to be that even of the commoner sorts of birds that breed in eastern Massachusetts or migrate through it, Thoreau — during the greater part of his life, at least — knew by sight and name only a small proportion, wonderful as his knowledge seemed to those who, like Emerson, knew practically nothing.[1]

Not that the journal is likely to prove less interesting to bird-loving readers on this account. On the contrary, it may rather be more so, as showing them the means and methods of an ornithological amateur fifty years

[1] Under date of June 9, 1854, we find him writing : "I should like to know the birds of the woods better. What birds inhabit our woods ? I hear their various notes ringing through them. What musicians compose our woodland quire? They must be forever strange and interesting to me." Even the glass that he finally bought was not an opera-glass, but a "spy-glass" (monocular) so called, and must have been of comparatively little help in the identification of woodland species.

ago, and, especially, as providing for them a desirable store of ornithological nuts to crack on winter evenings. Some such reader, by a careful collation of the data which the publication of the journal as a whole puts at his disposal, will perhaps succeed in settling the identity of the famous "night-warbler;" a bird which some, we believe, have suspected to be nothing rarer than the almost superabundant oven-bird, but which, so far as we ourselves know, may have been almost any one (or any two or three) of our smaller common birds that are given to occasional ecstatic song-flights.[1] Whatever it was, it was of use to Thoreau for the quickening of his imagination, and for literary purposes; and Emerson was well advised in warning him to beware of booking it, lest life henceforth should have so much the less to show him.

It must be said, however, that Thoreau stood in slight need of such a caution. He cherished for himself a pretty favorable opinion of a certain kind and measure of ignorance. With regard to some of his ornithological mysteries, for example, — the night-warbler, the seringo-bird (which with something like certainty we may conjecture to have been the savanna sparrow), and others, — he flatters himself that his good genius had withheld their names from him that he might the better learn their character, — whatever such an expression may be supposed to mean.

He maintained stoutly, from beginning to end, that

[1] Once he saw it (August 3, 1858), and then it proved to be a Maryland yellow throat. At other times it was almost certainly an oven-bird.

he was not of the ordinary school of naturalists, but "a mystic, a transcendentalist, and a natural philosopher in one;" though he believed himself, in his own words, "by constitution as good an observer as most." He will not be one of those who seek facts as facts, studying nature as a dead language. He studies her for purposes of his own, in search of the "raw material of tropes and figures." "I pray for such experience as will make nature significant," he declares; and then, with the same penful of ink, he asks: "Is that the swamp gooseberry of Gray now just beginning to blossom at Saw-Mill Brook? It has a divided style and stamens, etc., as yet not longer than the calyx, though my slip has no thorns nor prickles," and so on, and so on. Pages on pages of the journal are choke-full, literally, of this kind of botanical interrogation, till the unsympathetic reader will be in danger of surmising that the mystical searcher after tropes and symbols is sometimes not so utterly unlike the student of the dead language of fact. But then, it is one of the virtues of a journal that it is not a work of art, that it has no form, no fashion (and so does not go *out* of fashion), and is always at liberty to contradict itself. As Thoreau said, he tumbled his goods upon the counter; no single customer is bound to be pleased with them all; different men, different tastes; let each select from the pile the things that suit his fancy.

For our own part, we acknowledge, — and the shrewd reader may already have remarked the fact, — we have not been disinclined to choose here and there a bit of some less rare and costly stuff. The man is so sternly virtuous, so inexorably in earnest, so heart-set upon per-

fection, that we almost like him best when for a moment he betrays something that suggests a touch of human frailty. We prick up our ears when he speaks of a woman he once in a while goes to see, who tells him to his face that she thinks him self-conceited. Now, then, we whisper to ourselves, how will this man who despises flattery, and, boasting himself a "commoner," professes that for him "there is something devilish in manners," — how will this candor-loving, truth-speaking, truth-appreciating man enjoy the rebuke of so unmannered a mentor? And we smile and say Aha! when he adds that the lady wonders why he does not visit her oftener.

We smile, too, when he brags, in early February, that he has not yet put on his winter clothing, amusing himself the while over the muffs and furs of his less hardy neighbors, his own "simple diet" making him so tough in the fibre that he "flourishes like a tree;" and then, a week later, writes with unbroken equanimity that he is down with bronchitis, contenting himself to spend his days cuddled in a warm corner by the stove.

Trifles of this kind encourage a pleasant feeling of brotherly relationship. He is one of us, after all, with like passions. But of course we really like him best when he is *at* his best, — as in some outpouring of his love for things natural and wild. Let us have one more such quotation: "Now I yearn for one of those old, meandering, dry, uninhabited roads, which lead away from towns, which lead us away from temptation, which conduct us to the outside of earth, over its uppermost crust; where you may forget in what country you are travelling; where your head is more in heaven than your feet are on

earth; where you can pace when your breast is full, and cherish your moodiness. . . . There I can walk and recover the lost child that I am without any ringing of a bell."

For real warmth, when once the fire burns, who can exceed our stoic?

We like, also, his bits of prettiness, things in which he is second to nobody, though prettiness, again, is not supposed to be the stoic's "note;" and they are all the prettier, as well as ten times more welcome, because he has the grace — and the sound literary sense — to drop them here and there, as it were casually, upon a ground of simple, unaffected prose. Here, now, is a sentence that by itself is worth a deal of ornithology: "The song sparrow is heard in fields and pastures, setting the mid-summer day to music, — as if it were the music of a mossy rail or fence-post." Of dragon-flies he says: "How lavishly they are painted! How cheap was the paint! How free was the fancy of their Creator!" In early June, when woods are putting forth leaves, "the summer is pitching its tent." He finds the dainty fringed polygala (whose ordinary color is a lovely rose-purple) sporting white blossoms, and remarks: "Thus many flowers have their nun sisters, dressed in white." Soaring hawks are "kites without strings;" and when he and his companion are travelling across country, keeping out of the sight of houses, yet compelled to traverse here and there a farmer's field, they "shut every window with an apple tree."

Gems like these one need not be a connoisseur to appreciate, and they are common upon his counter. It was a good name that Channing gave him: "The Poet-Naturalist."

But there are better things than flowers and jewels to be found in Thoreau's stock. There are cordials and tonics there, to brace a man when he is weary; eye-washes, to cleanse his vision till he sees the heights above him and repents the lowness of his aims and the vulgarity of his satisfactions; blisters and irritant plasters in large variety and of warranted strength; but little or nothing, so far as the present customer has noticed, in the line of anodynes and sleeping-powders. There we may buy moral wisdom, which is not only the "foundation and source of good writing," as one of the ancients said, but of the arts in general, especially the art of life. If the world is too much with us, if wealth attracts and the "rust of copper" has begun to eat into the soul, if we are in danger of selling our years for things that perish with the using, here we may find correctives, and go away thankful, rejoicing henceforth to be rich in a better coinage than any that bears the world's stamp. The very exaggerations of the master — if we call them such — may do us good like a medicine; for there are diseased conditions which yield to nothing so quickly as to a shock.

As for Thoreau himself, life might have been smoother for him had he been less exacting in his idealism, more tolerant of imperfection in others and in himself; had he taken his studies, and even his spiritual aspirations, a grain or two less seriously. A bit of boyish play now and then, the bow quite unbent, or a dose of novel-reading of the love-making, humanizing (Trollopean) sort, could

one imagine it, with a more temperate cherishing of his moodiness, might have done him no harm. It would have been for his comfort, so much may confidently be said, whether for his happiness is another question, had he been one of those gentler humorists who can sometimes see themselves, as all humorists have the gift of seeing other people, funny side out. But then, had these things been so, had his natural scope been wider, his genius, so to say, more tropical, richer, freer, more expansive, more various and flexible, more like the spreading banyan and less like the soaring, sky-pointing spruce, — why, then he would no longer have been Thoreau; for better or worse, his speech would have lost its distinctive tang; and in the long run the world, which likes a touch of bitter and a touch of sour, would almost certainly have found the man himself less interesting, and his books less rememberable. And made as he was, "born to his own affairs," what else could he do but stick to himself? "We are constantly invited to be what we are," he said. The words might fittingly have been cut upon his gravestone.

B. T.

HENRY D. THOREAU

GLEANINGS
OR WHAT TIME
HAS NOT REAPED
OF MY
JOURNAL

[The small manuscript volume bearing on its first fly-leaf the legend printed on the preceding page is evidently a transcript of unused passages in the early journals, and this is also the case with several succeeding small volumes. See note on page 342. The following mottoes occupy the next three pages of the book.]

"By all means use sometimes to be alone.
Salute thyself: see what thy soul doth wear.
Dare to look in thy chest; for 't is thine own:
And tumble up and down what thou find'st there.
Who cannot rest till he good fellows find,
He breaks up house, turns out of doors his mind."
HERBERT, *The Church Porch.*

"Friends and companions, get you gone!
'T is my desire to be alone;
Ne'er well, but when my thoughts and I
Do domineer in privacy."
BURTON, *Anatomy of Melancholy.*

"Two Paradises are in one,
To live in Paradise alone."
MARVELL, *The Garden.*

I

1837

(ÆT. 20)

Oct. 22. "What are you doing now?" he asked. "Do you keep a journal?" So I make my first entry to-day.

SOLITUDE

To be alone I find it necessary to escape the present, — I avoid myself. How could I be alone in the Roman emperor's chamber of mirrors? I seek a garret. The spiders must not be disturbed, nor the floor swept, nor the lumber arranged.

The Germans say, "Es ist alles wahr wodurch du besser wirst."

THE MOULD OUR DEEDS LEAVE

Oct. 24. Every part of nature teaches that the passing away of one life is the making room for another. The oak dies down to the ground, leaving within its rind a rich virgin mould, which will impart a vigorous life to an infant forest. The pine leaves a sandy and sterile soil, the harder woods a strong and fruitful mould.

So this constant abrasion and decay makes the soil of my future growth. As I live now so shall I reap. If

I grow pines and birches, my virgin mould will not sustain the oak; but pines and birches, or, perchance, weeds and brambles, will constitute my second growth.[1]

SPRING

Oct. 25. She appears, and we are once more children; we commence again our course with the new year. Let the maiden no more return, and men will become poets for very grief. No sooner has winter left us time to regret her smiles, than we yield to the advances of poetic frenzy. "The flowers look kindly at us from the beds with their child eyes, and in the horizon the snow of the far mountains dissolves into light vapor." — GOETHE, *Torquato Tasso.*

THE POET

"He seems to avoid — even to flee from us, —
To seek something which we know not,
And perhaps he himself after all knows not." — *Ibid.*

Oct. 26.
"His eye hardly rests upon the earth;
His ear hears the one-clang of nature;
What history records, — what life gives, —
Directly and gladly his genius takes it up:
His mind collects the widely dispersed,
And his feeling animates the inanimate.
Often he ennobles what appeared to us common,
And the prized is as nothing to him.
In his own magic circle wanders

[1] [*Week,* p. 375; Riv. 464.]

The wonderful man, and draws us
With him to wander, and take part in it:
He seems to draw near to us, and remains afar from us:
He seems to be looking at us, and spirits, forsooth,
Appear to him strangely in our places." — *Ibid.*

HOW MAN GROWS

"A noble man has not to thank a private circle for his culture. Fatherland and world must work upon him. Fame and infamy must he learn to endure. He will be constrained to know himself and others. Solitude shall no more lull him with her flattery. The foe *will* not, the friend *dares* not, spare him. Then, striving, the youth puts forth his strength, feels what he is, and feels himself soon a man."

"A talent is builded in solitude,
A character in the stream of the world."

"He only fears man who knows him not, and he who avoids him will soonest misapprehend him." — *Ibid.*

ARIOSTO

"As nature decks her inward rich breast in a green variegated dress, so clothes he all that can make men honorable in the blooming garb of the fable. . . . The well of superfluity bubbles near, and lets us see variegated wonder-fishes. The air is filled with rare birds, the meads and copses with strange herds, wit lurks half concealed in the verdure, and wisdom from time to time lets sound from a golden cloud sustained words, while frenzy wildly seems to sweep the well-toned lute, yet holds itself measured in perfect time."

BEAUTY

"That beauty is transitory which alone you seem to honor." — GOETHE, *Torquato Tasso.*

THE FOG

Oct. 27. The prospect is limited to Nobscot and Annursnack. The trees stand with boughs downcast like pilgrims beaten by a storm, and the whole landscape wears a sombre aspect.

So when thick vapors cloud the soul, it strives in vain to escape from its humble working-day valley, and pierce the dense fog which shuts out from view the blue peaks in its horizon, but must be content to scan its near and homely hills.

DUCKS AT GOOSE POND

Oct. 29. Two ducks, of the summer or wood species, which were merrily dabbling in their favorite basin, struck up a retreat on my approach, and seemed disposed to take French leave, paddling off with swan-like majesty. They are first-rate swimmers, beating me at a round pace, and — what was to me a new trait in the duck character — dove every minute or two and swam several feet under water, in order to escape our attention. Just before immersion they seemed to give each other a significant nod, and then, as if by a common understanding, 't was heels up and head down in the shaking of a duck's wing. When they reappeared, it was amus-

Vol. I

be, proved a most perfect arrowhead, as sharp as if just from the hands of the Indian fabricator ! ! !

SUNRISE

Oct. 30. First we have the gray twilight of the poets, with dark and barry clouds diverging to the zenith. Then glows the intruding cloud in the east, as if it bore a precious jewel in its bosom; a deep round gulf of golden gray indenting its upper edge, while slender rules of fleecy vapor, radiating from the common centre, like light-armed troops, fall regularly into their places.

SAILING WITH AND AGAINST THE STREAM

Nov. 3. If one would reflect, let him embark on some placid stream, and float with the current. He cannot resist the Muse. As we ascend the stream, plying the paddle with might and main, snatched and impetuous thoughts course through the brain. We dream of conflict, power, and grandeur. But turn the prow down stream, and rock, tree, kine, knoll, assuming new and varying positions, as wind and water shift the scene, favor the liquid lapse of thought, far-reaching and sublime, but ever calm and gently undulating.

TRUTH

Nov. 5. Truth strikes us from behind, and in the dark, as well as from before and in broad daylight.

STILL STREAMS RUN DEEPEST

Nov. 9. It is the rill whose "silver sands and pebbles sing eternal ditties with the spring." The early frosts bridge its narrow channel, and its querulous note

ing to observe with what a self-satisfied, darn-it-how-he-nicks-'em air they paddled off to repeat the experiment.

THE ARROWHEAD

A curious incident happened some four or six weeks ago which I think it worth the while to record. John and I had been searching for Indian relics, and been successful enough to find two arrowheads and a pestle, when, of a Sunday evening, with our heads full of the past and its remains, we strolled to the mouth of Swamp Bridge Brook. As we neared the brow of the hill forming the bank of the river, inspired by my theme, I broke forth into an extravagant eulogy on those savage times, using most violent gesticulations by way of illustration. "There on Nawshawtuct," said I, "was their lodge, the rendezvous of the tribe, and yonder, on Clamshell Hill, their feasting ground. This was, no doubt, a favorite haunt; here on this brow was an eligible lookout post. How often have they stood on this very spot, at this very hour, when the sun was sinking behind yonder woods and gilding with his last rays the waters of the Musketaquid, and pondered the day's success and the morrow's prospects, or communed with the spirit of their fathers gone before them to the land of shades!

"Here," I exclaimed, "stood Tahatawan; and there" (to complete the period) "is Tahatawan's arrowhead."

We instantly proceeded to sit down on the spot I had pointed to, and I, to carry out the joke, to lay bare an ordinary stone which my whim had selected, when lo! the first I laid hands on, the grubbing stone that was to

is hushed. Only the flickering sunlight on its sandy bottom attracts the beholder. But there are souls whose depths are never fathomed, — on whose bottom the sun never shines. We get a distant view from the precipitous banks, but never a draught from their mid-channels. Only a sunken rock or fallen oak can provoke a murmur, and their surface is a stranger to the icy fetters which bind fast a thousand contributory rills.[1]

DISCIPLINE

Nov. 12. I yet lack discernment to distinguish the whole lesson of to-day; but it is not lost, — it will come to me at last. My desire is to know *what* I have lived, that I may know *how* to live henceforth.

SIN DESTROYS THE PERCEPTION OF THE BEAUTIFUL

Nov. 13. This shall be the test of innocence — if I can hear a taunt, and look out on this friendly moon, pacing the heavens in queen-like majesty, with the accustomed yearning.

TRUTH

Truth is ever returning into herself. I glimpse one feature to-day, another to-morrow; and the next day they are blended.

GOETHE

Nov. 15. "And now that it is evening, a few clouds in the mild atmosphere rest upon the mountains, more stand still than move in the heavens, and immediately after sunset the chirping of crickets begins to increase; then feels one once more at home in the world, and not

[1] [*Week*, p. 314 ; Riv. 390.]

as an alien, — an exile. I am contented as though I had been born and brought up here, and now returned from a Greenland or whaling voyage. Even the dust of my Fatherland, as it is whirled about the wagon, which for so long a time I had not seen, is welcome. The clock-and-bell jingling of the crickets is very agreeable, penetrating, and not without a meaning. Pleasant is it when roguish boys whistle in emulation of a field of such songstresses. One imagines that they really enhance each other. The evening is perfectly mild as the day. Should an inhabitant of the south, coming from the south, hear of my rapture, he would deem me very childish. Alas! what I here express have I long felt under an unpropitious heaven. And now this joy is to me an exception, which I am henceforth to enjoy, — a necessity of my nature." — *Italiänische Reise.*[1]

PONKAWTASSETT

Nov. 16. There goes the river, or rather is, "in serpent error wandering," the jugular vein of Musketaquid. Who knows how much of the proverbial moderation of the inhabitants was caught from its dull circulation?

The snow gives the landscape a washing-day appearance, — here a streak of white, there a streak of dark; it is spread like a napkin over the hills and meadows. This must be a rare drying day, to judge from the vapor that floats over the vast clothes-yard.

A hundred guns are firing and a flag flying in the village in celebration of the whig victory. Now a short dull report, — the mere disk of a sound, shorn of its

[1] [*Week*, p. 352 ; Riv. 435, 436.]

beams, — and then a puff of smoke rises in the horizon to join its misty relatives in the skies.

GOETHE

He gives such a glowing description of the old tower, that they who had been born and brought up in the neighborhood must needs look over their shoulders, "that they might behold with their eyes, what I had praised to their ears, . . . and I added nothing, not even the ivy which for centuries had decorated the walls." — *Italiänische Reise.*[1]

SUNRISE

Nov. 17. Now the king of day plays at bo-peep round the world's corner, and every cottage window smiles a golden smile, — a very picture of glee. I see the water glistening in the eye. The smothered breathings of awakening day strike the ear with an undulating motion; over hill and dale, pasture and woodland, come they to me, and I am at home in the world.

THE SKY

If there is nothing new on earth, still there is something new in the heavens. We have always a resource in the skies. They are constantly turning a new page to view. The wind sets the types in this blue ground, and the inquiring may always read a new truth.[2]

VIRGIL

Nov. 18. " Pulsae referunt ad sidera valles "[3] is such

[1] [*Week*, p. 348 ; Riv. 430.]　　[2] [*Week*, p. 383 ; Riv. 473.]
[3] [*Week*, p. 417 ; Riv. 515.]

Vol. I

a line as would save an epic; and how finely he concludes his " agrestem musam," now that Silenus has done, and the stars have heard his story, —

> " Cogere donec oves stabulis, numerumque referre
> Jussit, et invito processit Vesper Olympo."

HARMONY

Nature makes no noise. The howling storm, the rustling leaf, the pattering rain are no disturbance, there is an essential and unexplored harmony in them. Why is it that thought flows with so deep and sparkling a current when the sound of distant music strikes the ear? When I would muse I complain not of a rattling tune on the piano — a Battle of Prague even — if it be harmony, but an irregular, discordant drumming is intolerable.

SHADOWS

When a shadow flits across the landscape of the soul, where is the substance? Has it always its origin in sin? and is that sin in me?

VIRGIL

Nov. 20. I would read Virgil, if only that I might be reminded of the identity of human nature in all ages. I take satisfaction in " jam laeto turgent in palmite gemmae," or "Strata jacent passim sua quaeque sub arbore poma." It was the same world, and the same men inhabited it.[1]

NAWSHAWTUCT

Nov. 21. One must needs climb a hill to know what a world he inhabits. In the midst of this Indian sum-

[1] [*Week*, p. 93 ; Riv. 116. *Excursions*, p. 138 ; Riv. 169.]

mer I am perched on the topmost rock of Nawshawtuct, a velvet wind blowing from the southwest. I seem to feel the atoms as they strike my cheek. Hills, mountains, steeples stand out in bold relief in the horizon, while I am resting on the rounded boss of an enormous shield, the river like a vein of silver encircling its edge, and thence the shield gradually rises to its rim, the horizon. Not a cloud is to be seen, but villages, villas, forests, mountains, one above another, till they are swallowed up in the heavens.[1] The atmosphere is such that, as I look abroad upon the length and breadth of the land, it recedes from my eye, and I seem to be looking for the threads of the velvet.

Thus I admire the grandeur of my emerald carriage, with its border of blue, in which I am rolling through space.

THOUGHTS

Nov. 26. I look around for thoughts when I am overflowing myself. While I live on, thought is still in embryo, — it stirs not within me. Anon it begins to assume shape and comeliness, and I deliver it, and clothe it in its garment of language. But alas! how often when thoughts choke me do I resort to a spat on the back, or swallow a crust, or do anything but expectorate them!

HOAR FROST AND GREEN RIVER

Nov. 28. Every tree, fence, and spire of grass that could raise its head above the snow was this morning covered with a dense hoar frost. The trees looked like airy creatures of darkness caught napping. On this side

[1] [*Week*, p. 373 ; Riv. 461.]

they were huddled together, their gray hairs streaming, in a secluded valley which the sun had not yet penetrated, and on that they went hurrying off in Indian file by hedgerows and watercourses, while the shrubs and grasses, like elves and fairies of the night, sought to hide their diminished heads in the snow.

The branches and taller grasses were covered with a wonderful ice-foliage, answering leaf for leaf to their summer dress. The centre, diverging, and even more minute fibres were perfectly distinct and the edges regularly indented.

These leaves were on the side of the twig or stubble opposite to the sun (when it was not bent toward the east), meeting it for the most part at right angles, and there were others standing out at all possible angles upon these, and upon one another.

It struck me that these ghost leaves and the green ones whose forms they assume were the creatures of the same law. It could not be in obedience to two several laws that the vegetable juices swelled gradually into the perfect leaf on the one hand, and the crystalline particles trooped to their standard in the same admirable order on the other.

The river, viewed from the bank above, appeared of a yellowish-green color, but on a nearer approach this phenomenon vanished; and yet the landscape was covered with snow.[1]

ICE-HARP

Dec. 5. My friend tells me he has discovered a new note in nature, which he calls the Ice-Harp. Chancing

[1] [*Excursions*, pp. 126, 127 ; Riv. 155, 156.]

Vol. I

way through the underwood of words to the clear blue beyond;

> "O'er bog, or steep, through strait, rough, dense, or rare,
> With head, hands, wings, or feet, pursues *her* way,
> And swims, or sinks, or wades, or creeps, or flies; . . ."

but let her don her cumbersome working-day garment, and each sparkling dewdrop will seem a "slough of despond."

PECULIARITY

When we speak of a peculiarity in a man or a nation, we think to describe only one part, a mere mathematical point; but it is not so. It pervades all. Some parts may be further removed than others from this centre, but not a particle so remote as not to be either shined on or shaded by it.

THORNS

No faculty in man was created with a useless or sinister intent; in no respect can he be wholly bad, but the worst passions have their root in the best, — as anger, for instance, may be only a perverted sense of wrong which yet retains some traces of its origin.[1] So a spine is proved to be only an abortive branch, "which, notwithstanding, even as a spine, bears leaves, and, in *Euphorbia heptagona*, sometimes flowers and fruit."

JACK FROST

Dec. 15. As further confirmation of the fact that vegetation is a kind of crystallization, I observe that upon

[1] [Later.] We must consider war and slavery, with many other institutions and even the best existing governments, notwithstanding their apparent advantages, as the abortive rudiments of nobler institutions such as distinguish man in his savage and half-civilized state.

to throw a handful of pebbles upon the pond where there was an air chamber under the ice, it discoursed a pleasant music to him.

Herein resides a tenth muse, and as he was the man to discover it probably the extra melody is in him.

GOETHE

Dec. 8. He is generally satisfied with giving an exact description of objects as they appear to him, and his genius is exhibited in the points he seizes upon and illustrates. His description of Venice and her environs as seen from the Marcusthurm is that of an unconcerned spectator, whose object is faithfully to describe what he sees, and that, too, for the most part, in the order in which he saw it. It is this trait which is chiefly to be prized in the book; even the reflections of the author do not interfere with his descriptions.

It would thus be possible for inferior minds to produce invaluable books.[1]

MEASURE

Dec. 10. Not the carpenter alone carries his rule in his pocket. Space is quite subdued to us. The meanest peasant finds in a hair of his head, or the white crescent upon his nail, the unit of measure for the distance of the fixed stars. His middle finger measures how many *digits* into space; he extends a few times his thumb and finger, and the continent is *spanned ;* he stretches out his arms, and the sea is *fathomed.*

THOUGHT

Dec. 12. There are times when thought elbows her

[1] [*Week*, pp. 347, 348 ; Riv. 429, 430.]

the edge of the melting frost on the windows, Jack is playing singular freaks, — now bundling together his needle-shaped leaves so as to resemble fields waving with grain, or shocks of wheat rising here and there from the stubble. On one side the vegetation of the torrid zone is presented you, — high-towering palms, and widespread banyans, such as we see in pictures of Oriental scenery; on the other are arctic pines, stiff-frozen, with branches downcast, like the arms of tender men in frosty weather.[1] In some instances the panes are covered with little feathery flocks, where the particles radiate from a common centre, the number of radii varying from three to seven or eight. The crystalline particles are partial to the creases and flaws in the glass, and, when these extend from sash to sash, form complete hedgerows, or miniature watercourses, where dense masses of crystal foliage "high over-arched imbower."

FROZEN MIST

Dec. 16. The woods were this morning covered with thin bars of vapor, — the evaporation of the leaves according to Sprengel, — which seemed to have been suddenly stiffened by the cold. In some places it was spread out like gauze over the tops of the trees, forming extended lawns, where elves and fairies held high tournament;

> "before each van
> Prick forth the aery knights, and couch their spears,
> Till thickest legions close." [2]

[1] [*Excursions*, pp. 127, 128 ; Riv. 157.]
[2] [*Week*, p. 186; Riv. 231. *The Service*, Boston, 1902, p. 21].

The east was glowing with a narrow but ill-defined crescent of light, the blue of the zenith mingling in all possible proportions with the salmon-color of the horizon. And now the neighboring hilltops telegraph to us poor crawlers of the plain the Monarch's golden ensign in the east, and anon his "long levelled rules" fall sectorwise, and humblest cottage windows greet their lord.

FACTS

How indispensable to a correct study of Nature is a perception of her true meaning. The fact will one day flower out into a truth. The season will mature and fructify what the understanding had cultivated. Mere accumulators of facts — collectors of materials for the master-workmen — are like those plants growing in dark forests, which "put forth only leaves instead of blossoms."

DRUIDS

Dec. 17. In all ages and nations we observe a leaning towards a right state of things. This may especially be seen in the history of the priest, whose life approaches most nearly to that of the ideal man. The Druids paid no taxes, and "were allowed exemption from warfare and all other things." The clergy are even now a privileged class.

In the last stage of civilization Poetry, Religion, and Philosophy will be one; and this truth is glimpsed in the first. The druidical order was divided into Druids, Bards, and Ouates. "The Bards were the poets and musicians, of whom some were satirists, and some encomiasts. The Ouates sacrificed, divined, and contem-

plated the nature of things. The Druids cultivated physiology and moral philosophy; or, as Diodorus says, were their philosophers and theologians."

GOETHE

Dec. 18. He required that his heroine, Iphigenia, should say nothing which might not be uttered by the holy Agathe, whose picture he contemplated.

IMMORTALITY POST

The nations assert an immortality *post* as well as *ante*. The Athenians wore a golden grasshopper as an emblem that they sprang from the earth, and the Arcadians pretended that they were τροσέληνοι, or before the moon.

The Platos do not seem to have considered this back-reaching tendency of the human mind.

THE PRIDE OF ANCESTRY

Men are pleased to be called the sons of their fathers — so little truth suffices them, — and whoever addresses them by this or a similar title is termed a poet. The orator appeals to the sons of Greece, of Britannia, of France, or of Poland; and our fathers' homely name acquires some interest from the fact that Sakai-suna means sons-of-the-Sakai.[1]

HELL

Dec. 19. Hell itself may be contained within the compass of a spark.

[1] [A fanciful derivation of the word "Saxons"?]

Vol. I

SAXONS

The fact seems at first an anomalous one that the less a people have to contend for the more tenacious they are of their rights. The Saxons of Ditmarsia contended for a principle, not for their sterile sands and uncultivated marshes.

We are on the whole the same Saxons that our fathers were, when it was said of them, "They are emulous in hospitality, because to plunder and to lavish is the glory of an Holsatian; not to be versed in the science of depredation is, in his opinion, to be stupid and base."

The French are the same Franks of whom it is written, "Francis familiare est ridendo fidem frangere;" "Gens Francorum infidelis est. Si perjeret Francus quid novi faciet, qui perjuriam ipsam sermonis genus putat esse non criminis."

CRYSTALS

I observed this morning that the ice at Swamp Bridge was checkered with a kind of mosaic-work of white creases or channels; and when I examined the under side, I found it to be covered with a mass of crystallizations from three to five inches deep, standing, or rather depending, at right angles to the true ice, which was about an eighth of an inch thick. There was a yet older ice six or eight inches below this. The crystals were for the most part triangular prisms with the lower end open, though, in some cases, they had run into each other so as to form four or five sided prisms. When the ice was laid upon its smooth side, they resembled the

roofs and steeples of a Gothic city, or the vessels of a crowded haven under a press of canvas.

I noticed also that where the ice in the road had melted and left the mud bare, the latter, as if crystallized, discovered countless rectilinear fissures, an inch or more in length — a continuation, as it were, of the checkered ice.[1]

Dec. 22. About a year ago, having set aside a bowl which had contained some rhubarb grated in water, without wiping it, I was astonished to find, a few days afterward, that the rhubarb had crystallized, covering the bottom of the bowl with perfect cubes, of the color and consistency of glue, and a tenth of an inch in diameter.

CRYSTALS

Dec. 23. Crossed the river to-day on the ice. Though the weather is raw and wintry and the ground covered with snow, I noticed a solitary robin, who looked as if he needed to have his services to the Babes in the Woods speedily requited.

In the side of the high bank by the Leaning Hemlocks, there were some curious crystallizations. Wherever the water, or other causes, had formed a hole in the bank, its throat and outer edge, like the entrance to a citadel of the olden time, bristled with a glistening ice armor. In one place you might see minute ostrich feathers, which seemed the waving plumes of the warriors filing into the fortress, in another the glancing fan-shaped banners of the Lilliputian host, and in an-

[1] [*Excursions*, p. 128; Riv. 158.]

other the needle-shaped particles, collected into bundles resembling the plumes of the pine, might pass for a phalanx of spears.[1] The whole hill was like an immense quartz rock, with minute crystals sparkling from innumerable crannies. I tried to fancy that there was a disposition in these crystallizations to take the forms of the contiguous foliage.

REVOLUTIONS

Dec. 27. Revolutions are never sudden. Not one man, nor many men, in a few years or generations, suffice to regulate events and dispose mankind for the revolutionary movement. The hero is but the crowning stone of the pyramid, — the keystone of the arch. Who was Romulus or Remus, Hengist or Horsa, that we should attribute to them Rome or England? They are famous or infamous because the progress of events has chosen to make them its stepping-stones. But we would know where the avalanche commenced, or the hollow in the rock whence springs the Amazon. The most important is apt to be some silent and unobtrusive fact in history. In 449 three Saxon cyules arrived on the British coast, — "Three scipen gode comen mid than flode, three hundred cnihten." [2] The pirate of the British coast was no more the founder of a state than the scourge of the German shore.

HEROES

The real heroes of minstrelsy have been ideal, even when the names of actual heroes have been perpetuated.

[1] [*Excursions*, p. 128; Riv. 157, 158.]
[2] [*Familiar Letters*, Sept. 8, 1841.]

Vol. I

shade. The fact that Edwin of Northumbria "caused stakes to be fixed in the highways where he had seen a clear spring," and that "brazen dishes were chained to them, to refresh the weary sojourner, whose fatigues Edwin had himself experienced," is worth all Arthur's twelve battles.[1] The sun again shines along the highway, the landscape presents us sunny glades and occasional cultivated patches as well as dark primeval forests, and it is *merry* England after all.

Dec. 31. As the least drop of wine tinges the whole goblet, so the least particle of truth colors our whole life. It is never isolated, or simply added as treasure to our stock. When any real progress is made, we unlearn and learn anew what we thought we knew before. We go picking up from year to year and laying side by side the *disjecta membra* of truth, as he who picked up one by one a row of a hundred stones, and returned with each separately to his basket.

[1] [*Week*, p. 163; Riv. 203.]

The real Arthur, who "not only excelled the experienced past, but also the possible future," of whom it was affirmed for many centuries that he was not dead, but "had withdrawn from the world into some magical region; from which at a future crisis he was to reappear, and lead the Cymri in triumph through the island," whose character and actions were the theme of the bards of Bretagne and the foundation of their interminable romances, was only an ideal impersonation.

Men claim for the ideal an actual existence also, but do not often expand the actual into the ideal. "If you do not believe me, go into Bretagne, and mention in the streets or villages, that Arthur is really dead like other men; you will not escape with impunity; you will be either hooted with the curses of your hearers, or stoned to death."

HOMESICKNESS

The most remarkable instance of homesickness is that of the colony of Franks transplanted by the Romans from the German Ocean to the Euxine, who at length resolving to a man to abandon the country, seized the vessels which carried them out, and reached at last their native shores, after innumerable difficulties and dangers upon the Mediterranean and Atlantic.

THE INTERESTING FACTS IN HISTORY

How cheering is it, after toiling through the darker pages of history, — the heartless and fluctuating crust of human rest and unrest, — to alight on the solid earth where the sun shines, or rest in the checkered

II

1838

(ÆT. 20–21)

HEAVEN ON EARTH

Jan. 6. As a child looks forward to the coming of the summer, so could we contemplate with quiet joy the circle of the seasons returning without fail eternally. As the spring came round during so many years of the gods, we could go out to admire and adorn anew our Eden, and yet never tire.

SAXONS

Jan. 15. After all that has been said in praise of the Saxon race, we must allow that our blue-eyed and fair-haired ancestors were originally an ungodly and reckless crew.

WE MAKE OUR OWN FORTUNE

Jan. 16. Man is like a cork which no tempest can sink, but it will float securely to its haven at last. The world is never the less beautiful though viewed through a chink or knot-hole.

Jan. 21. Man is the artificer of his own happiness. Let him beware how he complains of the disposition of circumstances, for it is his own disposition he blames. If this is sour, or that rough, or the other steep, let him think if it be not his work. If his look curdles all hearts,

Frost Crystals at the Mouth of a Hole in a Bank

let him not complain of a sour reception; if he hobble
in his gait, let him not grumble at the roughness of the
way; if he is weak in the knees, let him not call the hill
steep. This was the pith of the inscription on the wall
of the Swedish inn: "You will find at Trolhate excellent bread, meat, and wine, provided you bring them
with you!" [1]

HOAR FROST

Every leaf and twig was this morning covered with
a sparkling ice armor; even the grasses in exposed
fields were hung with innumerable diamond pendants,
which jingled merrily when brushed by the foot of the
traveller. It was literally the wreck of jewels and the
crash of gems. It was as though some superincumbent
stratum of the earth had been removed in the night,
exposing to light a bed of untarnished crystals. The
scene changed at every step, or as the head was inclined to the right or the left. There were the opal and
sapphire and emerald and jasper and beryl and topaz
and ruby.[2]

Such is beauty ever, — neither here nor there, now
nor then, — neither in Rome nor in Athens, but wherever
there is a soul to admire. If I seek her elsewhere because
I do not find her at home, my search will prove a fruitless
one.

ZENO

Feb. 7. Zeno, the Stoic, stood in precisely the same
relation to the world that I do now. He is, forsooth,
bred a merchant — as how many still! — and can trade
and barter, and perchance higgle, and moreover he can

[1] [*Excursions*, p. 141; Riv. 173.]　　[2] [*Excursions*, p. 127; Riv. 156.]

be shipwrecked and cast ashore at the Piræus, like one
of your Johns or Thomases.

He strolls into a shop and is charmed by a book by
Xenophon — and straightway he becomes a philosopher.
The sun of a new life's day rises to him, — serene
and unclouded, — which looks over στοά. And still the
fleshly Zeno sails on, shipwrecked, buffeted, tempest-
tossed; but the true Zeno sails ever a placid sea. Play
high, play low, — rain, sleet, or snow, — it's all the
same with the Stoic. "Propriety and decorum" were
his Palinurus, — not the base progeny of fashion, but
the suggestions of an experienced taste.

When evening comes he sits down unwearied to the
review of his day, — what's done that's to be undone, —
what not done at all still to be done. Himself Truth's
unconcerned helpmate. Another system of book-keeping
this than that the Cyprian trader to Phœnicia practiced!

This was he who said to a certain garrulous young
man, "On this account have we two ears and but one
mouth, that we may hear more, and speak less."

That he had talked concerned not our philosopher,
but his audience; and herein we may see how it is more
noble to hear than to speak. The wisest may apologize
that he only said so to hear himself talk, for if he *heard*
not, as well for him had he never spoken. What is all
this gabble to the gabbler? Only the silent reap the
profit of it.

SOCIETY

Feb. 9. It is wholesome advice, — "to be a man
amongst folks." Go into society if you will, or if you
are unwilling, and take a human interest in its affairs.

Vol. I

If you mistake these Messieurs and Mesdames for so
many men and women, it is but erring on the safe side, —
or, rather, it is their error and not yours. Armed with a
manly sincerity, you shall not be trifled with, but drive
this business of life. It matters not how many men are
to be addressed, — rebuked, — provided one man rebuke them.

SMALL TALK

To manage the small talk of a party is to make an
effort to do what was at first done, admirably because
naturally, at your fireside.

INFLUENCE

Feb. 13. It is hard to subject ourselves to an influence.
It must steal upon us when we expect it not, and its
work be all done ere we are aware of it. If we make
advances, it is shy; if, when we feel its presence, we
presume to pry into its free-masonry, it vanishes and
leaves us alone in our folly, — brimful but stagnant, —
a full channel, it may be, but no inclination.

FEAR

All fear of the world or consequences is swallowed
up in a manly anxiety to do Truth justice.

OLD BOOKS

Feb. 15. The true student will cleave ever to the
good, recognizing no Past, no Present; but wherever
he emerges from the bosom of time, his course is not
with the sun, — eastward or westward, — but ever
towards the seashore. Day and night pursues he his

devious way, lingering by how many a Pierian spring,
how many an Academus grove, how many a sculptured
portico! — all which — spring, grove, and portico —
lie not so wide but he may take them conveniently in his
way.

GREECE

Feb. 16. In imagination I hie me to Greece as to
enchanted ground. No storms vex her coasts, no clouds
encircle her Helicon or Olympus, no tempests sweep
the peaceful Tempe or ruffle the bosom of the placid
Ægean; but always the beams of the summer's sun
gleam along the entablature of the Acropolis, or are
reflected through the mellow atmosphere from a thousand consecrated groves and fountains; always her sea-
girt isles are dallying with their zephyr guests, and the
low of kine is heard along the meads, and the landscape
sleeps — valley and hill and woodland — a dreamy sleep.
Each of her sons created a new heaven and a new earth
for Greece.

SUNDAY

Feb. 18. Rightly named Sune-day, or day of the sun.
One is satisfied in some angle by wood-house and garden
fence to bask in his beams — to exist barely — the livelong day.

SPRING

I had not been out long to-day when it seemed that a
new Spring was already born, — not quite weaned, it is
true, but verily entered upon existence. Nature struck
up "the same old song in the grass," despite eighteen
inches of snow, and I contrived to smuggle away a grin
of satisfaction by a smothered "Pshaw! and is that all?"

Feb. 19.   Each summer sound
        Is a summer round.[1]

GOETHE

Feb. 27. He jogs along at a snail's pace, but ever mindful that the earth is beneath and the heavens above him. His Italy is not merely the fatherland of lazzaroni and maccaroni but a solid turf-clad soil, daily illumined by a genial sun and nightly gleaming in the still moonshine, — to say nothing of the frequent showers which are so faithfully recorded. That sail to Palermo was literally a plowing through of the waves from Naples to Trinacria, — the sky overhead, and the sea with its isles on either hand.

His hearty good-will to all men is most amiable; not one cross word has he spoken, but on one occasion, the post boy snivelling, "Signore, perdonate! quésta è la mia patria," he confesses, "to me poor northerner came something tear-like into the eyes." [2]

SPRING

March 1. March fans it, April christens it, and May puts on its jacket and trousers. It never grows up, but Alexandrian-like "drags its slow length along," ever springing, bud following close upon leaf, and when winter comes it is not annihilated, but creeps on mole-like under the snow, showing its face nevertheless occasionally by fuming springs and watercourses.

So let it be with man, — let his manhood be a more

[1] [*Excursions*, p. 112; Riv. 138.]
[2] [*Week*, pp. 347, 348; Riv. 429–431.]

advanced and still advancing youth, bud following hard upon leaf. By the side of the ripening corn let's have a second or third crop of peas and turnips, decking the fields in a new green. So amid clumps of *sere* herd's-grass sometimes flower the violet and buttercup spring-born.

HOMER

March 3. Three thousand years and the world so little changed! The Iliad seems like a natural sound which has reverberated to our days. Whatever in it is still freshest in the memories of men was most childlike in the poet. It is the problem of old age, — a second childhood exhibited in the life of the world. Phœbus Apollo went like night, — ὁ δ' ἤιε νυκτὶ ἐοικώς. This either refers to the gross atmosphere of the plague darkening the sun, or to the crescent of night rising solemn and stately in the east while the sun is setting in the west.

Then Agamemnon darkly lowers on Calchas, prophet of evil, — ὄσσε δέ οἱ πυρὶ λαμπετόωντε ἐίκτην, — such a fire-eyed Agamemnon as you may see at town meetings and elections, as well here as in Troy neighborhood.

A SUNDAY SCENE

March 4. Here at my elbow sit five notable, or at least noteworthy, representatives of this nineteenth century, — of the gender feminine. One a sedate, indefatigable knitter, not spinster, of the old school, who had the supreme felicity to be born in days that tried men's souls, who can, and not unfrequently does, say with Nestor, another of the old school: "But you are younger than I. For time was when I conversed with greater

men than you. For not at any time have I seen such men, nor shall see them, as Perithous, and Dryas, and ποιμένα λαῶν," or, in one word, sole "shepherd of the people," Washington.

And when Apollo has now six times rolled westward, or seemed to roll, and now for the seventh time shows his face in the east, eyes well-nigh glazed, long glassed, which have fluctuated only between lamb's wool and worsted, explore ceaseless some good sermon book. For six days shalt thou labor and do all thy knitting, but on the seventh, forsooth, thy reading.[1]

Opposite, across this stone hearth, sits one of no school, but rather one who schools, a spinster who spins not, with elbow resting on the book of books, but with eyes turned towards the vain trumpery of that shelf, — trumpery of sere leaves, blossoms, and waxwork, built on sand, that presumes to look quite as gay, smell quite as earthy, as though this were not by good rights the sun's day. I marked how she spurned that innocent every-day book, "Germany by De Staël," as though a viper had stung her; — better to rest the elbow on The Book than the eye on such a page. Poor book! this is thy last chance.

Happy I who can bask in this warm spring sun which illumines all creatures, as well when they rest as when they toil, not without a feeling of gratitude! whose life is as blameless — how blameworthy soever it be — on the Lord's Mona-day as on his Suna-day! [2]

Thus much at least a man may do: he may not impose on his fellows, — perhaps not on himself. Thus

[1] [*Week*, p. 66; Riv. 82, 83.]   [2] [*Week*, p. 66; Riv. 83.]

much *let* a man do: confidently and heartily live up to his thought; for its error, if there be any, will soonest appear in practice, and if there be none, so much he may reckon as actual progress in the way of living.

HOMER

The poet does not leap, even in imagination, from Asia to Greece through mid-air, neglectful of the fair sea and still fairer land beneath him, but jogs on humanly observant over the intervening segment of a sphere, —

ἐπειὴ μάλα πολλὰ μεταξύ
Οὔρεά τε σκιόεντα, θάλασσά τε ἠχήεσσα, —

for there are very many
Shady mountains, and resounding seas between.[1]

March 5. How often, when Achilles like one διάνδιχα μερμήριξεν whether to retaliate or suppress his wrath, has his good Genius, like Pallas Athene, gliding down from heaven, θυμῷ φιλέουσά τε, κηδομένη τε, stood behind him, and whispered peace in his ear! [2]

Men may dispute about the fact whether a goddess did actually come down from heaven, calling it a poet's fancy, but was it not, considering the stuff that gods are made of, a very truth?

THE AGE OF HONEY

"And to them rose up the sweet-worded Nestor, the shrill orator of the Pylians,
And words *sweeter than honey* flowed from his tongue." [3]

[1] [*Week*, p. 96; Riv. 119, 120.]   [2] [*Week*, p. 65; Riv. 81.]
[3] [*Week*, p. 96; Riv. 120.]

E'en in old Homer's day was honey sweet, — not yet is sour, — tickling the palate of the blind old man, forsooth, with fresher sweet; then, as now, whene'er from leaky jar or drivelling lips it daubed the festive board, proving a baneful lure to swarms of parasites, Homer's cotemporaries, but alas! like Phthian hero, vulnerable in heel.

WHAT TO DO

But what does all this scribbling amount to? What is now scribbled in the heat of the moment one can contemplate with somewhat of satisfaction, but alas! to-morrow — aye, to-night — it is stale, flat, and unprofitable, — in fine, is not, only its shell remains, like some red parboiled lobster-shell which, kicked aside never so often, still stares at you in the path.

What may a man do and not be ashamed of it? He may not do nothing surely, for straightway he is dubbed Dolittle — aye! christens himself first — and reasonably, for he was first to duck. But let him do something, is he the less a Dolittle? Is it actually something done, or not rather something undone; or, if done, is it not badly done, or at most well done comparatively?

Such is man, — toiling, heaving, struggling ant-like to shoulder some stray unappropriated crumb and deposit it in his granary; then runs out, complacent, gazes heavenward, earthward (for even pismires can look down), heaven and earth meanwhile looking downward, upward; there seen of men, world-seen, deed-delivered, vanishes into all-grasping night. And is he doomed ever to run the same course? Can he not, wriggling, screwing, self-exhorting, self-constraining,

wriggle or screw out something that shall live, — respected, intact, intangible, not to be sneezed at?[1]

March 6. How can a man sit down and quietly pare his nails, while the earth goes gyrating ahead amid such a din of sphere music, whirling him along about her axis some twenty-four thousand miles between sun and sun, but mainly in a circle some two millions of miles actual progress? And then such a hurly-burly on the surface — wind always blowing — now a zephyr, now a hurricane — tides never idle, ever fluctuating — no rest for Niagara, but perpetual ran-tan on those limestone rocks — and then that summer simmering which our ears are used to, which would otherwise be christened confusion worse confounded, but is now ironically called "silence audible," and above all the incessant tinkering named "hum of industry," the hurrying to and fro and confused jabbering of men. Can man do less than get up and shake himself?

COMPOSITION

March 7. We should not endeavor coolly to analyze our thoughts, but, keeping the pen even and parallel with the current, make an accurate transcript of them. Impulse is, after all, the best linguist, and for his logic, if not conformable to Aristotle, it cannot fail to be most convincing. The nearer we approach to a complete but simple transcript of our thought the more tolerable will be the piece, for we can endure to consider ourselves in a state of passivity or in involuntary action, but rarely our efforts, and least of all our rare efforts.

[1] ("Carlyleish" is written in the margin against this passage.]

SCRAPS FROM A LECTURE ON "SOCIETY" WRITTEN MARCH 14TH, 1838, DELIVERED BEFORE OUR LYCEUM, APRIL 11TH

Every proverb in the newspapers originally stood for a truth. Thus the proverb that man was made for society, so long as it was not allowed to conflict with another important truth, deceived no one; but, now that the same words have come to stand for another thing, it may be for a lie, we are obliged, in order to preserve its significance, to write it anew, so that properly it will read, Society was made for man.

Man is not at once born into society, — hardly into the world. The world that he is hides for a time the world that he inhabits.

That which properly constitutes the life of every man is a profound secret. Yet this is what every one would give most to know, but is himself most backward to impart.

Hardly a rood of land but can show its fresh wound or indelible scar, in proof that earlier or later man has been there.

The mass never comes up to the standard of its best member, but on the contrary degrades itself to a level with the lowest. As the reformers say, it is a levelling down, not up. Hence the mass is only another name for the mob. The inhabitants of the earth assembled in one place would constitute the greatest mob. The mob is spoken of as an insane and blinded animal;

magistrates say it must be humored; they apprehend it may incline this way or that, as villagers dread an inundation, not knowing whose land may be flooded, nor how many bridges carried away.

One goes to a cattle-show expecting to find many men and women assembled, and beholds only working oxen and neat cattle. He goes to a commencement thinking that there at least he may find the men of the country; but such, if there were any, are completely merged in the day, and have become so many walking commencements, so that he is fain to take himself out of sight and hearing of the orator, lest he lose his own identity in the nonentities around him.

But you are getting all the while further and further from true society. Your silence was an approach to it, but your conversation is only a refuge from the encounter of men; as though men were to be satisfied with a meeting of heels, and not heads.

Nor is it better with private assemblies, or meetings together, with a sociable design, of acquaintances so called, — that is to say of men and women who are familiar with the lineaments of each other's countenances, who eat, drink, sleep, and transact the business of living within the circuit of a mile.

With a beating heart he fares him forth, by the light of the stars, to this meeting of gods. But the illusion speedily vanishes; what at first seemed to him nectar and ambrosia, is discovered to be plain bohea and short gingerbread.

Then with what speed does he throw off his strait-jacket of a godship, and play the one-eared, two-mouthed mortal, thus proving his title to the epithet applied to him of old by Homer of μέροψ ἄνθρωπος, or that possesses an articulating voice. But unfortunately we have as yet invented no rule by which the stranger may know when he has culminated. We read that among the Finlanders when one "has succeeded in rendering himself agreeable, it is a custom at an assemblage for all the women present to give him on the back a sudden slap, when it is least expected; and the compliment is in proportion to the weight of the blow."

It is provoking, when one sits waiting the assembling together of his neighbors around his hearth, to behold merely their clay houses, for the most part newly shingled and clapboarded, and not unfrequently with a fresh coat of paint, trundled to his door. He has but to knock slightly at the outer gate of one of these shingle palaces, to be assured that the master or mistress is not at home.

After all, the field of battle possesses many advantages over the drawing-room. There at least is no room for pretension or excessive ceremony, no shaking of hands or rubbing of noses, which make one doubt your sincerity, but hearty as well as hard hand-play. It at least exhibits one of the faces of humanity, the former only a mask.

The utmost nearness to which men approach each other amounts barely to a mechanical contact. As

If thy neighbor hail thee to inquire how goes the world, feel thyself put to thy trumps to return a true and explicit answer. Plant the feet firmly, and, will he nill he, dole out to him with strict and conscientious impartiality his modicum of a response.

Let not society be the element in which you swim, or are tossed about at the mercy of the waves, but be rather a strip of firm land running out into the sea, whose base is daily washed by the tide, but whose summit only the spring tide can reach.

But after all, such a morsel of society as this will not satisfy a man. But like those women of Malamocco and Pelestrina, who when their husbands are fishing at sea, repair to the shore and sing their shrill songs at evening, till they hear the voices of their husbands in reply borne to them over the water, so go we about indefatigably, chanting our stanza of the lay, and awaiting the response of a kindred soul out of the distance.

THE INDIAN AXE

April 1. The Indian must have possessed no small share of vital energy to have rubbed industriously stone upon stone for long months till at length he had rubbed out an axe or pestle, — as though he had said in the face of the constant flux of things, I at least will live an enduring life.

April 8.   FRIENDSHIP

I think awhile of Love, and, while I think,
Love is to me a world,

when you rub two stones together, though they emit an audible sound, yet do they not actually touch each other.

In obedience to an instinct of their nature men have pitched their cabins and planted corn and potatoes within speaking distance of one another, and so formed towns and villages, but they have not associated, they have only assembled, and society has signified only a *convention* of men.

When I think of a playhouse, it is as if we had not time to appreciate the follies of the day in detail as they occur, and so devoted an hour of our evening to laughing or crying at them in the lump. Despairing of a more perfect intercourse, or perhaps never dreaming that such is desirable, or at least possible, we are contented to act our part in what deserves to be called the great farce, not drama, of life, like pitiful and mercenary stock actors whose business it is to keep up the semblance of a stage.

Our least deed, like the young of the land crab, wends its way to the sea of cause and effect as soon as born, and makes a drop there to eternity.

Let ours be like the meeting of two planets, not hastening to confound their jarring spheres, but drawn together by the influence of a subtle attraction, soon to roll diverse in their respective orbits, from this their perigee, or point of nearest approach.

Sole meat and sweetest drink,
And close connecting link
'Tween heaven and earth.

I only know it is, not how or why,
My greatest happiness;
However hard I try,
Not if I were to die,
Can I explain.

I fain would ask my friend how it can be,
But, when the time arrives,
Then Love is more lovely
Than anything to me,
And so I'm dumb.

For, if the truth were known, Love cannot speak,
But only thinks and does;
Though surely out 't will leak
Without the help of Greek,
Or any tongue.

A man may love the truth and practice it,
Beauty he may admire,
And goodness not omit,
As much as may befit
To reverence.

But only when these three together meet,
As they always incline,
And make one soul the seat

And favorite retreat
Of loveliness;

When under kindred shape, like loves and hates
And a kindred nature,
Proclaim us to be mates,
Exposed to equal fates
Eternally;

And each may other help, and service do,
Drawing Love's bands more tight,
Service he ne'er shall rue
While one and one make two,
And two are one;

In such case only doth man fully prove,
Fully as man can do,
What power there is in Love
His inmost soul to move
Resistlessly.

———————

Two sturdy oaks I mean, which side by side
Withstand the winter's storm,
And, spite of wind and tide,
Grow up the meadow's pride,
For both are strong.

Above they barely touch, but, undermined
Down to their deepest source,
Admiring you shall find

Their roots are intertwined
Insep'rably.

CONVERSATION

April 15. Thomas Fuller relates that "in Merioneth-shire, in Wales, there are high mountains, whose hanging tops come so close together that shepherds on the tops of several hills may audibly talk together, yet will it be a day's journey for their bodies to meet, so vast is the hollowness of the valleys betwixt them." As much may be said in a moral sense of our intercourse in the plains, for, though we may audibly converse together, yet is there so vast a gulf of hollowness between that we are actually many days' journey from a veritable communication.

STEAMSHIPS

April 24. Men have been contriving new means and modes of motion. Steamships have been westering during these late days and nights on the Atlantic waves, — the fuglers of a new evolution to this generation. Meanwhile plants spring silently by the brooksides, and the grim woods wave indifferent; the earth emits no howl, pot on fire simmers and seethes, and men go about their business.

April 26.   THE BLUEBIRDS

In the midst of the poplar that stands by our door
We planted a bluebird box,
And we hoped before the summer was o'er
A transient pair to coax.

Vol. I

One warm summer's day the bluebirds came
And lighted on our tree,
But at first the wand'rers were not so tame
But they were afraid of me.

They seemed to come from the distant south,
Just over the Walden wood,
And they skimmed it along with open mouth
Close by where the bellows stood.

Warbling they swept round the distant cliff,
And they warbled it over the lea,
And over the blacksmith's shop in a jiff
Did they come warbling to me.

They came and sat on the box's top
Without looking into the hole,
And only from this side to that did they hop,
As 't were a common well-pole.

Methinks I had never seen them before,
Nor indeed had they seen me,
Till I chanced to stand by our back door,
And they came to the poplar tree.

In course of time they built their nest
And reared a happy brood,
And every morn they piped their best
As they flew away to the wood.

Thus wore the summer hours away
To the bluebirds and to me,

And every hour was a summer's day,
So pleasantly lived we.

They were a world within themselves,
And I a world in me,
Up in the tree — the little elves —
With their callow family.

One morn the wind blowed cold and strong,
And the leaves went whirling away;
The birds prepared for their journey long
That raw and gusty day.

Boreas came blust'ring down from the north,
And ruffled their azure smocks,
So they launched them forth, though somewhat loth,
By way of the old Cliff rocks.

Meanwhile the earth jogged steadily on
In her mantle of purest white,
And anon another spring was born
When winter was vanished quite.

And I wandered forth o'er the steamy earth,
And gazed at the mellow sky,
But never before from the hour of my birth
Had I wandered so thoughtfully.

For never before was the earth so still,
And never so mild was the sky,
The river, the fields, the woods, and the hill
Seemed to heave an audible sigh.

I felt that the heavens were all around,
And the earth was all below,
As when in the ears there rushes a sound
Which thrills you from top to toe.

I dreamed that I was a waking thought,
A something I hardly knew,
Not a solid piece, nor an empty nought,
But a drop of morning dew.

'T was the world and I at a game of bo-peep,
As a man would dodge his shadow,
An idea becalmed in eternity's deep,
'Tween Lima and Segraddo.

Anon a faintly warbled note
From out the azure deep
Into my ears did gently float
As is the approach of sleep.

It thrilled but startled not my soul;
Across my mind strange mem'ries gleamed,
As often distant scenes unroll
When we have lately dreamed.

The bluebird had come from the distant South
To his box in the poplar tree,
And he opened wide his slender mouth
On purpose to sing to me.

JOURNEY TO MAINE

May 3–4. Boston to Portland.
What, indeed, is this earth to us of New England

but a field for Yankee speculation? The Nantucket whaler goes a-fishing round it, and so knows it, — what it is, how long, how broad, and that no tortoise sustains it. He who has visited the confines of his real estate, looking out on all sides into space, will feel a new inducement to *be* the lord of creation.

We must all pay a small tribute to Neptune; the chief engineer must once have been seasick.

Midnight — head over the boat's side — between sleeping and waking — with glimpses of one or more lights in the vicinity of Cape Ann. Bright moonlight — the effect heightened by seasickness. Beyond that light yonder have my lines hitherto been cast, but now I know that there lies not the whole world, for I can say it is there and not here.

May 4. Portland. There is a proper and only right way to enter a city, as well as to make advances to a strange person; neither will allow of the least forwardness nor bustle. A sensitive person can hardly elbow his way boldly, laughing and talking, into a strange town, without experiencing some twinges of conscience, as when he has treated a stranger with too much familiarity.

May 5. Portland to Bath *via* Brunswick; Bath to Brunswick.

Each one's world is but a clearing in the forest, so much open and inclosed ground. When the mail coach rumbles into one of these, the villagers gaze after you with a compassionate look, as much as to say: "Where have you been all this time, that you make your début in the world at this late hour? Nevertheless, here we

are; come and study us, that you may learn men and manners."

May 6. Brunswick to Augusta *via* Gardiner and Hallowell.

May 7. We occasionally meet an individual of a character and disposition so entirely the reverse of our own that we wonder if he can indeed be another man like ourselves. We doubt if we ever could draw any nearer to him, and understand him. Such was the old English gentleman whom I met with to-day in H. Though I peered in at his eyes I could not discern myself reflected therein. The chief wonder was how we could ever arrive at so fair-seeming an intercourse upon so small ground of sympathy. He walked and fluttered like a strange bird at my side, prying into and making a handle of the least circumstance. The bustle and rapidity of our communication were astonishing; we skated in our conversation. All at once he would stop short in the path, and, in an abstracted air, query whether the steamboat had reached Bath or Portland, addressing me from time to time as his familiar genius, who could understand what was passing in his mind without the necessity of uninterrupted oral communication.

May 8. Augusta to Bangor *via* China.

May 10. Bangor to Oldtown.

The railroad from Bangor to Oldtown is civilization shooting off in a tangent into the forest. I had much conversation with an old Indian at the latter place, who sat dreaming upon a scow at the waterside and striking his deer-skin moccasins against the planks, while his

arms hung listlessly by his side. He was the most communicative man I had met. Talked of hunting and fishing, old times and new times. Pointing up the Penobscot, he observed, "Two or three mile up the river one beautiful country!" and then, as if he would come as far to meet me as I had gone to meet him, he exclaimed, "Ugh! one very hard time!" But he had mistaken his man.

May 11. Bangor to Belfast *via* Saturday Cove.

May 12. Belfast.

May 13. To Castine by sailboat "Cinderilla [*sic*]."

May 14. Castine to Belfast by packet, Captain Skinner. Found the Poems of Burns and an odd volume of the "Spectator" in the cabin.

May 15. Belfast to Bath *via* Thomaston.

May 16. To Portland.

May 17. To Boston and Concord.

May 21.   MAY MORNING

The school-boy loitered on his way to school,
Scorning to live so rare a day by rule.
So mild the air a pleasure 't was to breathe,
For what seems heaven above was earth beneath.

Soured neighbors chatted by the garden pale,
Nor quarrelled who should drive the needed nail;
The most unsocial made new friends that day,
As when the sun shines husbandmen make hay.

How long I slept I know not, but at last
I felt my consciousness returning fast,

For Zephyr rustled past with leafy tread,
And heedlessly with one heel grazed my head.

My eyelids opened on a field of blue,
For close above a nodding violet grew;
A part of heaven it seemed, which one could scent,
Its blue commingling with the firmament.

June 3.   WALDEN

True, our converse a stranger is to speech;
Only the practiced ear can catch the surging words
That break and die upon thy pebbled lips.
Thy flow of thought is noiseless as the lapse of thy own
        waters,
Wafted as is the morning mist up from thy surface,
So that the passive Soul doth breathe it in,
And is infected with the truth thou wouldst express.

E'en the remotest stars have come in troops
And stoopèd low to catch the benediction
Of thy countenance. Oft as the day came round,
Impartial has the sun exhibited himself
Before thy narrow skylight; nor has the moon
For cycles failed to roll this way
As oft as elsewhither, and tell thee of the night.
No cloud so rare but hitherward it stalked,
And in thy face looked doubly beautiful.
O! tell me what the winds have writ for the last thou-
        sand years
On the blue vault that spans thy flood,
Or sun transferred and delicately reprinted

For thy own private reading. Somewhat
Within these latter days I've read,
But surely there was much that would have thrilled the
        Soul,
Which human eye saw not.
I would give much to read that first bright page,
Wet from a virgin press, when Eurus, Boreas,
And the host of airy quill-drivers
First dipped their pens in mist.

June 14.
Truth, Goodness, Beauty, — those celestial thrins,[1]
Continually are born; e'en now the Universe,
With thousand throats, and eke with greener smiles,
Its joy confesses at their recent birth.

Strange that so many fickle gods, as fickle as the weather,
Throughout Dame Nature's provinces should always
        pull together.

June 16.
In the busy streets, domains of trade,
Man is a surly porter, or a vain and hectoring bully,
Who can claim no nearer kindredship with me
Than brotherhood by law.

July 8.   CLIFFS

The loudest sound that burdens here the breeze
Is the wood's whisper; 't is, when we choose to list,
Audible sound, and when we list not,

[1] [The word seems to be a new one, but its meaning is clear.]

It is calm profound. Tongues were provided
But to vex the ear with superficial thoughts.
When deeper thoughts upswell, the jarring discord
Of harsh speech is hushed, and senses seem
As little as may be to share the ecstasy.

HEROISM

July 13. What a hero one can be without moving a
finger! The world is not a field worthy of us, nor can
we be satisfied with the plains of Troy. A glorious strife
seems waging within us, yet so noiselessly that we but
just catch the sound of the clarion ringing of victory,
borne to us on the breeze. There are in each the seeds
of a heroic ardor, which need only to be stirred in with
the *soil where they lie*, by an inspired voice or pen, to
bear fruit of a divine flavor.[1]

SUSPICION

July 15. What though friends misinterpret your conduct, if it is right in sight of God and Nature. The
wrong, if there be any, pertains only to the wrongdoer,
nor is the integrity of your relations to the universe
affected, but you may gather encouragement from their
mistrust. If the friend withhold his favor, yet does
greater float gratuitous on the zephyr.

TRUTH

Aug. 4. Whatever of past or present wisdom has
published itself to the world, is palpable falsehood till
it come and utter itself by my side.

[1] [*Week*, p. 129; Riv. 161.]

SPHERE MUSIC

Aug. 5. Some sounds seem to reverberate along the
plain, and then settle to earth again like dust; such
are Noise, Discord, Jargon. But such only as spring
heavenward, and I may catch from steeples and hilltops
in their upward course, which are the more refined
parts of the former, are the true sphere music, — pure,
unmixed music, — in which no wail mingles.

DIVINE SERVICE IN THE ACADEMY HALL

In dark places and dungeons these words might
perhaps strike root and grow, but utter them in the daylight and their dusky hues are apparent. From this
window I can compare the written with the preached
word: within is weeping, and wailing, and gnashing of
teeth; without, grain fields and grasshoppers, which
give those the lie direct.

THE TIME OF THE UNIVERSE

Aug. 10. Nor can all the vanities that so vex the world
alter one whit the measure that night has chosen, but
ever it must be short particular metre. The human soul
is a silent harp in God's quire, whose strings need only
to be swept by the divine breath to chime in with the
harmonies of creation. Every pulse-beat is in exact time
with the cricket's chant, and the tickings of the death-
watch in the wall. Alternate with these if you can.[1]

CONSCIOUSNESS

Aug. 13. If with closed ears and eyes I consult con-

[1] [*Excursions*, p. 108; Riv. 133.]

sciousness for a moment, immediately are all walls and barriers dissipated, earth rolls from under me, and I float, by the impetus derived from the earth and the system, a subjective, heavily laden thought, in the midst of an unknown and infinite sea, or else heave and swell like a vast ocean of thought, without rock or headland, where are all riddles solved, all straight lines making there their two ends to meet, eternity and space gambolling familiarly through my depths. I am from the beginning, knowing no end, no aim. No sun illumines me, for I dissolve all lesser lights in my own intenser and steadier light. I am a restful kernel in the magazine of the universe.

RESOURCE

Men are constantly dinging in my ears their fair theories and plausible solutions of the universe, but ever there is no help, and I return again to my shoreless, islandless ocean, and fathom unceasingly for a bottom that will hold an anchor, that it may not drag.

SABBATH BELL

Aug. 19. The sound of the Sabbath bell, whose farthest waves are at this instant breaking on these cliffs, does not awaken pleasing associations alone. Its muse is wonderfully condescending and philanthropic. One involuntarily leans on his staff to humor the unusually meditative mood. It is as the sound of many catechisms and religious books twanging a canting peal round the world, and seems to issue from some Egyptian temple, and echo along the shore of the Nile, right opposite to

Pharaoh's palace and Moses in the bulrushes, startling a multitude of storks and alligators basking in the sun. Not so these larks and pewees of Musketaquid. One is sick at heart of this pagoda worship. It is like the beating of gongs in a Hindoo subterranean temple.[1]

HOLY WAR

Aug. 21. Passion and appetite are always an unholy land in which one may wage most holy war. Let him steadfastly follow the banner of his faith till it is planted on the enemy's citadel. Nor shall he lack fields to display his valor in, nor straits worthy of him. For when he has blown his blast, and smote those within reach, invisible enemies will not cease to torment him, who yet may be starved out in the garrisons where they lie.

SCRIPTURE

Aug. 22. How thrilling a noble sentiment in the oldest books, — in Homer, the Zendavesta, or Confucius! It is a strain of music wafted down to us on the breeze of time, through the aisles of innumerable ages. By its very nobleness it is made near and audible to us.

EVENING SOUNDS

Aug. 26. How strangely sounds of revelry strike the ear from over cultivated fields by the woodside, while the sun is declining in the west. It is a world we had not known before. We listen and are capable of no mean act or thought. We tread on Olympus and participate in the councils of the gods.

[1] [*Week*, p. 78; Riv. 97.]

HOMER

It does one's heart good if Homer but say the sun sets, — or, "As when beautiful stars accompany the bright moon through the serene heavens; and the woody hills and cliffs are discerned through the mild light, and each star is visible, and the shepherd rejoices in his heart." [1]

THE LOSS OF A TOOTH

Aug. 27. Verily I am the creature of circumstances. Here I have swallowed an indispensable tooth, and so am no whole man, but a lame and halting piece of manhood. I am conscious of no gap in my soul, but it would seem that, now the entrance to the oracle has been enlarged, the more rare and commonplace the responses that issue from it. I have felt cheap, and hardly dared hold up my head among men, ever since this accident happened. Nothing can I do as well and freely as before; nothing do I undertake but I am hindered and balked by this circumstance. What a great matter a little spark kindleth! I believe if I were called at this moment to rush into the thickest of the fight, I should halt for lack of so insignificant a piece of armor as a tooth. Virtue and Truth go undefended, and Falsehood and Affectation are thrown in my teeth, — though I am toothless. One does not need that the earth quake for the sake of excitement, when so slight a crack proves such an impassable moat. But let the lame man shake his leg, and match himself with the fleetest in the race. So shall he do what is in him to do. But let him who has lost a tooth open his mouth wide and gabble, lisp, and sputter never so resolutely.

[1] [*Week*, pp. 94, 95; Riv. 117, 119.]

DEFORMITY

Aug. 29. Here at the top of Nawshawtuct, this mild August afternoon, I can discern no deformed thing. The prophane hay-makers in yonder meadow are yet the hay-makers of poetry, — forsooth Faustus and Amyntas. Yonder schoolhouse of brick, than which, near at hand, nothing can be more mote-like to my eye, serves even to heighten the picturesqueness of the scene. Barns and outbuildings, which in the nearness mar by their presence the loveliness of nature, are not only endurable, but, observed where they lie by some waving field of grain or patch of woodland, prove a very cynosure to the pensive eye. Let man after infinite hammering and din of crows uprear a deformity in the plain, yet will Nature have her revenge on the hilltop. Retire a stone's throw and she will have changed his base metal into gold.

CRICKETS

The crackling flight of grasshoppers is a luxury; and pleasant is it when summer has once more followed in the steps of winter to hear scald cricket piping a Nibelungenlied in the grass. It is the most infinite of singers. Wiselier had the Greeks chosen a golden cricket, and let the grasshopper eat grass. One opens both his ears to the invisible, incessant quire, and doubts if it be not earth herself chanting for all time.

GENII

In the vulgar daylight of our self-conceit, good genii are still overlooking and conducting us; as the stars look down on us by day as by night — and we observe them not.

SPHERE MUSIC

Sept. 2. The cocks chant a strain of which we never tire. Some there are who find pleasure in the melody of birds and chirping of crickets, — aye, even the peeping of frogs. Such faint sounds as these are for the most part heard above the weeping and wailing and gnashing of teeth which so unhallow the Sabbath among us. The moan the earth makes is after all a very faint sound, infinitely inferior in volume to its creakings of joy and gleeful murmurs; so that we may expect the next balloonist will rise above the utmost range of discordant sounds into the region of pure melody. Never so loud was the wail but it seemed to taper off into a piercing melody and note of joy, which lingered not amid the clods of the valley.

CREEDS

Sept. 3. The only faith that men recognize is a creed. But the true creed which we unconsciously live by, and which rather adopts us than we it, is quite different from the written or preached one. Men anxiously hold fast to their creed, as to a straw, thinking this does them good service because their sheet anchor does not drag.[1]

RIVERS

Sept. 5. For the first time it occurred to me this afternoon what a piece of wonder a river is, — a huge volume of matter ceaselessly rolling through the fields and meadows of this substantial earth, making haste from the high places, by stable dwellings of men and Egyptian Pyramids, to its restless reservoir. One would think

[1] [*Week*, p. 79; Riv. 98, 99. *The Service*, p. 4.]

that, by a very natural impulse, the dwellers upon the headwaters of the Mississippi and Amazon would follow in the trail of their waters to see the end of the matter.[1]

HOMER

Sept. 7. When Homer's messengers repair to the tent of Achilles, we do not have to wonder how they get there, but step by step accompany them along the shore of the resounding sea.[2]

FLOW OF SPIRITS IN YOUTH

Sept. 15. How unaccountable the flow of spirits in youth. You may throw sticks and dirt into the current, and it will only rise the higher. Dam it up you may, but dry it up you may not, for you cannot reach its source. If you stop up this avenue or that, anon it will come gurgling out where you least expected and wash away all fixtures. Youth grasps at happiness as an inalienable right. The tear does no sooner gush than glisten. Who shall say when the tear that sprung of sorrow first sparkled with joy?

ALMA NATURA

Sept. 20. It is a luxury to muse by a wall-side in the sunshine of a September afternoon, — to cuddle down under a gray stone, and hearken to the siren song of the cricket. Day and night seem henceforth but accidents, and the time is always a still eventide, and as the close of a happy day. Parched fields and mulleins gilded with the slanting rays are my diet. I know of no word so fit to express this disposition of Nature as Alma Natura.

[1] [*Week*, pp. 9-11; Riv. 11, 13.]   [2] [*Week*, p. 96; Riv. 120.]

Vol. I

COMPENSATION

Sept. 23. If we will be quiet and ready enough, we shall find compensation in every disappointment. If a shower drives us for shelter to the maple grove or the trailing branches of the pine, yet in their recesses with microscopic eye we discover some new wonder in the bark, or the leaves, or the fungi at our feet. We are interested by some new resource of insect economy, or the chickadee is more than usually familiar. We can study Nature's nooks and corners then.[1]

Oct. 16.   MY BOOTS

Anon with gaping fearlessness they quaff
The dewy nectar with a natural thirst,
Or wet their leathern lungs where cranberries lurk,
With sweeter wine than Chian, Lesbian, or Falernian
        far.
Theirs was the inward lustre that bespeaks
An open sole — unknowing to exclude
The cheerful day — a worthier glory far
Than that which gilds the outmost rind with darkness
        visible —
Virtues that fast abide through lapse of years,
Rather rubbed in than off.

HOMER

Oct. 21. Hector hurrying from rank to rank is likened to the moon wading in majesty from cloud to cloud. We are reminded of the hour of the day by the fact that the woodcutter spreads now his morning meal in the

[1] [*Week*, p. 319; Riv. 395.]

recesses of the mountains, having already laid his axe at the root of many lofty trees.[1]

Oct. 23. Nestor's simple repast after the rescue of Machaon is a fit subject for poetry. The woodcutter may sit down to his cold victuals, the hero to soldier's fare, and the wild Arab to his dried dates and figs, without offense; but not so a modern gentleman to his dinner.

Oct. 24. It matters not whether these strains originate there in the grass or float thitherward like atoms of light from the minstrel days of Greece.

"The snowflakes fall thick and fast on a winter's day. The winds are lulled, and the snow falls incessant, covering the tops of the mountains, and the hills, and the plains where the lotus tree grows, and the cultivated fields. And they are falling by the inlets and shores of the foaming sea, but are silently dissolved by the waves."[2]

SPECULATION

Dec. 7. We may believe it, but never do we live a quiet, free life, such as Adam's, but are enveloped in an invisible network of speculations. Our progress is only from one such speculation to another, and only at rare intervals do we perceive that it is no progress. Could we for a moment drop this by-play, and simply wonder, without reference or inference!

[1] [See *Week*, p. 95 (Riv. 118), where the passages referred to appear in translation.]
[2] [*Excursions*, pp. 181, 182; Riv. 221, 222.]

BYRON

Dec. 8. Nothing in nature is sneaking or chapfallen, as somewhat maltreated and slighted, but each is satisfied with its being, and so is as lavender and balm. If skunk-cabbage is offensive to the nostrils of men, still has it not drooped in consequence, but trustfully unfolded its leaf of two hands' breadth. What was it to Lord Byron whether England owned or disowned him, whether he smelled sour and was skunk-cabbage to the English nostril or violet-like, the pride of the land and ornament of every lady's boudoir? Let not the oyster grieve that he has lost the race; he has gained as an oyster.

Dec. 15.   FAIR HAVEN [1]

When winter fringes every bough
With his fantastic wreath,
And puts the seal of silence now
Upon the leaves beneath;

When every stream in its penthouse
Goes gurgling on its way,
And in his gallery the mouse
Nibbleth the meadow hay;

Methinks the summer still is nigh,
And lurketh there below,
As that same meadow mouse doth lie
Snug underneath the snow.

[1] [All but the last stanza, somewhat revised and without title, appears in *Excursions*, pp. 176, 177 ; Riv. 215, 216.]

Vol. I

And if perchance the chickadee
Lisp a faint note anon,
The snow is summer's canopy,
Which she herself put on.

Rare blossoms deck the cheerful trees,
And dazzling fruits depend,
The north wind sighs a summer breeze,
The nipping frosts to fend,

Bringing glad tidings unto me,
While that I stand all ear,
Of a serene eternity,
That need not winter fear.

Out on the silent pond straightway
The restless ice doth crack,
And pond sprites merry gambols play
Amid the deaf'ning rack.

Eager I press me to the vale
As I had heard brave news,
How nature held high festival,
Which it were hard to lose.

I crack me with my neighbor ice,
And sympathizing quake,
As each new rent darts in a trice
Across the gladsome lake.

One with the cricket in the ground,
And fuel on the hearth,

Resounds the rare domestic sound
Along the forest path.

Fair Haven is my huge tea-urn
That seethes and sings to me,
And eke the crackling fagots burn, —
A homebred minstrelsy.

SOME SCRAPS FROM AN ESSAY ON "SOUND AND SILENCE" WRITTEN IN THE LATTER HALF OF THIS MONTH, — DECEMBER, 1838 [1]

As the truest society approaches always nearer to solitude, so the most excellent speech finally falls into silence. We go about to find Solitude and Silence, as though they dwelt only in distant glens and the depths of the forest, venturing out from these fastnesses at midnight. Silence *was*, say we, before ever the world was, as if creation had displaced her, and were not her visible framework and foil. It is only favorite dells that she deigns to frequent, and we dream not that she is then imported into them when we wend thither, as Selden's butcher busied himself with looking after his knife, when he had it in his mouth. For where man is, there is Silence.

Silence is the communing of a conscious soul with itself. If the soul attend for a moment to its own infinity, then and there is silence. She is audible to all men, at all times, in all places, and if we will we may always hearken to her admonitions.

[1] [Cf. *Week*, pp. 417–420 ; Riv. 515–518.]

Silence is ever less strange than noise, lurking amid the boughs of the hemlock or pine just in proportion as we find ourselves there. The nuthatch, tapping the upright trunks by our side, is only a partial spokesman for the solemn stillness.

She is always at hand with her wisdom, by roadsides and street corners; lurking in belfries, the cannon's mouth, and the wake of the earthquake; gathering up and fondling their puny din in her ample bosom.

Those divine sounds which are uttered to our inward ear — which are breathed in with the zephyr or reflected from the lake — come to us noiselessly, bathing the temples of the soul, as we stand motionless amid the rocks.

The halloo is the creature of walls and masonwork; the whisper is fittest in the depths of the wood, or by the shore of the lake; but silence is best adapted to the acoustics of space.

All sounds are her servants and purveyors, proclaiming not only that their mistress is, but is a rare mistress, and earnestly to be sought after. Behind the most distinct and significant hovers always a more significant silence which floats it. The thunder is only our signal gun, that we may know what communion awaits us. Not its dull sound, but the infinite expansion of our being which ensues, we praise and unanimously name sublime.

All sound is nearly akin to Silence; it is a bubble on her surface which straightway bursts, an emblem of the strength and prolificness of the undercurrent. It is a faint utterance of Silence, and then only agreeable to our auditory nerves when it contrasts itself with the former. In proportion as it does this, and is a heightener and intensifier of the Silence, it is harmony and purest melody.

Every melodious sound is the ally of Silence, — a help and not a hindrance to abstraction.

Certain sounds more than others have found favor with the poets only as foils to silence.

ANACREON'S ODE TO THE CICADA [1]

We pronounce thee happy, cicada,
For on the tops of the trees,
Sipping a little dew,
Like any king thou singest,
For thine are they all,
Whatever thou seest in the fields,
And whatever the woods bear.
Thou art the friend of the husbandmen,
In no respect injuring any one;
And thou art honored among men,
Sweet prophet of summer.
The Muses love thee,
And Phœbus himself loves thee,
And has given thee a shrill song;

[1] [*Excursions*, p. 108; Riv. 133. "Drinking" for "Sipping" in l. 3 is the only change.]

Age does not wrack thee,
Thou skillful, earth-born, song-loving,
Unsuffering, bloodless one;
Almost thou art like the gods.

Silence is the universal refuge, the sequel of all dry discourses and all foolish acts, as balm to our every chagrin, as welcome after satiety as [after] disappointment; that background which the painter may not daub, be he master or bungler, and which, however awkward a figure he may have made in the foreground, remains ever our inviolable asylum.

With what equanimity does the silent consider how his world goes, settles the awards of virtue and justice, is slandered and buffeted never so much and views it all as a phenomenon. He is one with Truth, Goodness, Beauty. No indignity can assail him, no personality disturb him.

The orator puts off his individuality, and is then most eloquent when most silent. He listens while he speaks, and is a hearer along with his audience.

Who has not hearkened to her infinite din? She is Truth's speaking trumpet, which every man carries slung over his shoulder, and when he will may apply to his ear. She is the sole oracle, the true Delphi and Dodona, which kings and courtiers would do well to consult, nor will they be balked by an ambiguous answer. Through her have all revelations been made. Just as

Vol. I

far as men have consulted her oracle, they have obtained a clear insight, and their age been marked for an enlightened one. But as often as they have gone gadding abroad to a strange Delphi and her mad priestess, they have been benighted, and their age Dark or Leaden. — These are garrulous and noisy eras, which no longer yield any sound; but the Grecian, or *silent* and melodious, Era is ever sounding on the ears of men.

A good book is the plectrum with which our silent lyres are struck. In all epics, when, after breathless attention, we come to the significant words " He said," then especially our inmost man is addressed. We not unfrequently refer the interest which belongs to our own unwritten sequel to the written and comparatively lifeless page. Of all valuable books this same sequel makes an indispensable part. It is the author's aim to say once and emphatically, " He said." This is the most the bookmaker can attain to. If he make his volume a foil whereon the waves of silence may break, it is well. It is not so much the sighing of the blast as that pause, as Gray expresses it, " when the gust is recollecting itself," that thrills us, and is infinitely grander than the importunate howlings of the storm.

At evening Silence sends many emissaries to me, some navigating the subsiding waves which the village murmur has agitated.

It were vain for me to interpret the Silence. She cannot be done into English. For six thousand years have

men translated her, with what fidelity belonged to each; still is she little better than a sealed book. A man may run on confidently for a time, thinking he has her under his thumb, and shall one day exhaust her, but he too must at last be silent, and men remark only how brave a beginning he made; for, when he at length dives into her, so vast is the disproportion of the told to the untold that the former will seem but the bubble on the surface where he disappeared.

Nevertheless will we go on, like those Chinese cliff swallows, feathering our nests with the froth, so they may one day be bread of life to such as dwell by the seashore.

ANACREONTICS

Dec. 23.   RETURN OF SPRING [1]

Behold, how, spring appearing,
The Graces send forth roses;
Behold, how the wave of the sea
Is made smooth by the calm;
Behold, how the duck dives;
Behold, how the crane travels;
And Titan shines constantly bright.
The shadows of the clouds are moving;
The works of man shine;
The earth puts forth fruits;
The fruit of the olive puts forth.
The cup of Bacchus is crowned.

[1] [*Excursions*, pp. 109, 110; Riv. 135.]

Along the leaves, along the branches,⁻
The fruit, bending them down, flourishes.

CUPID WOUNDED [1]

Love once among roses
A sleeping bee
Did not see, but was stung;
And, being wounded in the finger
Of his hand, cried for pain.
Running as well as flying
To the beautiful Venus,
I am killed, mother, said he,
I am killed, and I die.
A little serpent has stung me,
Winged, which they call
A bee, — the husbandmen.
And she said, If the sting
Of a bee afflicts you,
How, think you, are they afflicted,
Love, whom you smite?

[*Dated only* 1838.] Sometimes I hear the veery's silver clarion, or the brazen note of the impatient jay, or in secluded woods the chickadee doles out her scanty notes, which sing the praise of heroes, and set forth the loveliness of virtue evermore. — *Phe-be.*[2]

[1] [*Week*, p. 244 ; Riv. 302. Lines 2 and 3 are altered.]
[2] [*Excursions*, p. 112 ; Riv. 138.]

III

1839

(ÆT. 21–22)

Jan. 11.   THE THAW [1]

I saw the civil sun drying earth's tears,
Her tears of joy, that only faster flowed.

Fain would I stretch me by the highway-side,
To thaw and trickle with the melting snow,
That, mingled soul and body with the tide,
I too may through the pores of nature flow.

But I, alas, nor trickle can nor fume,
One jot to forward the great work of Time,
'T is mine to hearken while these ply the loom,
So shall my silence with their music chime.

THE DREAM VALLEY

Jan. 20. The prospect of our river valley from Tahatawan Cliff appeared to me again in my dreams.

Last night, as I lay gazing with shut eyes
Into the golden land of dreams,
I thought I gazed adown a quiet reach
Of land and water prospect,
Whose low beach

[1] [*Excursions, and Poems*, pp. 120 and 409 ; *Excursions*, Riv. 147.]

Vol. I

Was peopled with the now subsiding hum
Of happy industry whose work is done.

And as I turned me on my pillow o'er,
I heard the lapse of waves upon the shore,
Distinct as it had been at broad noonday,
And I were wandering at Rockaway.

LOVE

We two that planets erst had been
Are now a double star,
And in the heavens may be seen,
Where that we fixèd are.

Yet, whirled with subtle power along,
Into new space we enter,
And evermore with spheral song
Revolve about one centre.

Feb. 3.

The deeds of king and meanest hedger
Stand side by side in heaven's ledger.

'T will soon appear if we but look
At evening into earth's day-book,
Which way the great account doth stand
Between the heavens and the land.

THE EVENING WIND

The eastern mail comes lumbering in,
With outmost waves of Europe's din;

The western sighs adown the slope,
Or 'mid the rustling leaves doth grope,
Laden with news from Californ',
Whate'er transpired hath since morn,
How wags the world by brier and brake,
From hence to Athabasca lake.[1]

POETIZING

Feb. 8. When the poetic frenzy seizes us, we run and scratch with our pen, delighting, like the cock, in the dust we make, but do not detect where the jewel lies, which perhaps we have in the meantime cast to a distance, or quite covered up again.[2]

Feb. 9. It takes a man to make a room silent.

Feb. 10.   THE PEAL OF THE BELLS [3]

When the world grows old by the chimney-side,
Then forth to the youngling rocks I glide,
Where over the water, and over the land,
The bells are booming on either hand.

Now up they go ding, then down again dong,
And awhile they swing to the same old song,
And the metal goes round at a single bound,
A-lulling the fields with its measured sound,
Till the tired tongue falls with a lengthened boom
As solemn and loud as the crack of doom.

[1] [*Week*, p. 180 ; Riv. 224.]
[2] [*Week*, pp. 364, 365 ; Riv. 451, 452.]
[3] [This poem will be found in *Excursions, and Poems*, p. 417, under the title "Ding Dong," somewhat revised and without the last stanza.]

Then changed is their measure to tone upon tone,
And seldom it is that one sound comes alone,
For they ring out their peals in a mingled throng,
And the breezes waft the loud ding-dong along.

When the echo has reached me in this lone vale,
I am straightway a hero in coat of mail,
I tug at my belt and I march on my post,
And feel myself more than a match for a host.

I am on the alert for some wonderful Thing
Which somewhere's a-taking place;
'T is perchance the salute which our planet doth ring
When it meeteth another in space.

Feb. 25. THE SHRIKE

    Hark! hark! from out the thickest fog
    Warbles with might and main
    The fearless shrike, as all agog
    To find in fog his gain.

    His steady sails he never furls
    At any time o' year,
    And, perchèd now on Winter's curls,
    He whistles in his ear.[1]

THE POET

March 3. He must be something more than natural, — even supernatural. Nature will not speak through but along with him. His voice will not proceed from her

[1] [*Excursions*, p. 109; Riv. 134.]

---

midst, but, breathing on her, will make her the expression of his thought. He then poetizes when he takes a fact out of nature into spirit. He speaks without reference to time or place. His thought is one world, hers another. He is another Nature, — Nature's brother. Kindly offices do they perform for one another. Each publishes the other's truth.

MORNING

April 4. The atmosphere of morning gives a healthy hue to our prospects. Disease is a sluggard that overtakes, never encounters, us. We have the start each day, and may fairly distance him before the dew is off; but if we recline in the bowers of noon, he will come up with us after all. The morning dew breeds no cold. We enjoy a diurnal reprieve in the beginning of each day's creation. In the morning we do not believe in expediency; we will start afresh, and have no patching, no temporary fixtures. The afternoon man has an interest in the past; his eye is divided, and he sees indifferently well either way.

DRIFTING

Drifting in a sultry day on the sluggish waters of the pond, I almost cease to live and begin to be. A boatman stretched on the deck of his craft and dallying with the noon would be as apt an emblem of eternity for me as the serpent with his tail in his mouth. I am never so prone to lose my identity. I am dissolved in the haze.

DISAPPOINTMENT

April 7. Sunday. The tediousness and detail of execution never occur to the genius projecting; it always

Vol. I

---

antedates the completion of its work. It condescends to give time a few hours to do its bidding in.

RESOLVE

Most have sufficient contempt for what is mean to resolve that they will abstain from it, and a few virtue enough to abide by their resolution, but not often does one attain to such lofty contempt as to require no resolution to be made.

THE TEAMSTER

April 8. There goes a six-horse team, and a man by its side. He has rolled out of his cradle into a Tom-and-Jerry, and goes about his business while Nature goes about hers, without standing agape at his condition. As though sixty years were not enough for these things! What have death, and the cholera, and the immortal destiny of man, to do with the shipping interests? There is an unexplained bravery in this. What with bare astonishment one would think that man had his hands full for so short a term. But this is no drawback on the lace-working and cap-making interests. Some attain to such a degree of sang-froid and nonchalance as to be weavers of toilet cushions and manufacturers of pinheads, without once flinching or the slightest affection of the nerves, for the period of a natural life.[1]

FAT PINE FOR SPEARING

April 9. Fat roots of pine lying in rich veins as of gold or silver, even in old pastures where you would least expect it, make you realize that you live in the

[1] [*Walden*, p. 8; Riv. 14, 15.]

---

youth of the world, and you begin to know the wealth of the planet. Human nature is still in its prime, then. Bring axe, pickaxe, and shovel, and tap the earth here where there is most sap. The marrowy store gleams like some vigorous sinew, and you feel a new suppleness in your own limbs. These are the traits that conciliate man's moroseness, and make him civil to his fellows; every such pine root is a pledge of suavity. If he can discover absolute barrenness in any direction there will be some excuse for peevishness.

SOCIETY

April 14. There is a *terra firma* in society as well as in geography, some whose ports you may make by dead reckoning in all weather. All the rest are but floating and fabulous Atlantides which sometimes skirt the western horizon of our intercourse. They impose only on seasick mariners who have put into some Canary Island on the frontiers of society.

CIRCUMSTANCES

April 24. Why should we concern ourselves with what has happened to us, and the unaccountable fickleness of events, and not rather [with] how we have happened to the universe, and it has demeaned itself in consequence? Let us record in each case the judgment we have awarded to circumstances.

ACQUAINTANCE

Cheap persons will stand upon ceremony, because there is no other ground; but to the great of the earth we need no introduction, nor do they need any to us.

THE KINGDOMS OF THE EARTH

April 25. If we see the reality in things, of what moment is the superficial and apparent? Take the earth and all the interests it has known, — what are they beside one deep surmise that pierces and scatters them? The independent beggar disposes of all with one hearty, significant curse by the roadside. 'T is true they are not worth a "tinker's damn."

PICTURE

April 30. Of some illuminated pictures which I saw last evening, one representing the plain of Babylon, with only a heap of brick-dust in the centre, and an uninterrupted horizon bounding the desert, struck me most. I would see painted a boundless expanse of desert, prairie, or sea, without other object than the horizon. The heavens and the earth, — the first and last painting, — where is the artist who shall undertake it?

May 11. The farmer keeps pace with his crops and the revolutions of the seasons, but the merchant with the fluctuations of trade. Observe how differently they walk in the streets.

VICE AND VIRTUE

May 16. Virtue is the very heart and lungs of vice: it cannot stand up but it lean on virtue.

Who has not admired the twelve labors? And yet nobody thinks if Hercules had sufficient motive for

racking his bones to that degree. Men are not so much virtuous as patrons of virtue, and every one knows that it is easier to deal with the real possessor of a thing than the temporary guardian of it.

THE FORM OF STRENGTH

May 17. We say justly that the weak person is flat; for, like all flat substances, he does not stand in the direction of his strength, that is on his edge, but affords a convenient surface to put upon. He slides all the way through life. Most things are strong in one direction, — a straw longitudinally, a board in the direction of its edge, a knee transversely to its grain, — but the brave man is a perfect sphere, which cannot fall on its flat side, and is equally strong every way. The coward is wretchedly spheroidal at best, too much educated or drawn out on one side commonly and depressed on the other; or he may be likened to a hollow sphere, whose disposition of matter is best when the greatest bulk is intended.[1]

SELF-CULTURE

May 21. Who knows how incessant a surveillance a strong man may maintain over himself, — how far subject passion and appetite to reason, and lead the life his imagination paints? Well has the poet said, —

> " By manly mind
> Not e'en in sleep is will resigned."

By a strong effort may he not command even his brute body in unconscious moments?

[1] [*Cape Cod, and Miscellanies*, p. 278 ; *Misc.*, Riv. 36, 37. *The Service*, pp. 5, 6.]

MY ATTIC

June 4. I sit here this fourth of June, looking out on men and nature from this that I call my perspective window, through which all things are seen in their true relations. This is my upper empire, bounded by four walls, viz., three of boards yellow-washed, facing the north, west, and south, respectively, and the fourth of plaster, likewise yellow-washed, fronting the sunrise, — to say nothing of the purlieus and outlying provinces, unexplored as yet but by rats.

The words of some men are thrown forcibly against you and adhere like burs.

RENCOUNTER

June 22. Saturday. I have within the last few days come into contact with a pure, uncompromising spirit, that is somewhere wandering in the atmosphere, but settles not positively anywhere. Some persons carry about them the air and conviction of virtue, though they themselves are unconscious of it, and are even backward to appreciate it in others. Such it is impossible not to love; still is their loveliness, as it were, independent of them, so that you seem not to lose it when they are absent, for when they are near it is like an invisible presence which attends you.

That virtue we appreciate is as much ours as another's. We see so much only as we possess.

June 24.   SYMPATHY [1]

Lately, alas, I knew a gentle boy,
Whose features all were cast in Virtue's mould,

[1] [*Week*, pp. 276, 277; Riv. 343, 344.]

As one she had designed for Beauty's toy,
But after manned him for her own stronghold.

On every side he open was as day,
That you might see no lack of strength within,
For walls and ports do only serve alway
For a pretense to feebleness and sin.

Say not that Cæsar was victorious,
With toil and strife who stormed the House of Fame;
In other sense this youth was glorious,
Himself a kingdom wheresoe'er he came.

No strength went out to get him victory,
When all was income of its own accord;
For where he went none other was to see,
But all were parcel of their noble lord.

He forayed like the subtle haze of summer,
That stilly shows fresh landscapes to our eyes,
And revolutions works without a murmur,
Or rustling of a leaf beneath the skies.

So was I taken unawares by this,
I quite forgot my homage to confess;
Yet now am forced to know, though hard it is,
I might have loved him, had I loved him less.

Each moment, as we nearer drew to each,
A stern respect withheld us farther yet,
So that we seemed beyond each other's reach,
And less acquainted than when first we met.

We two were one while we did sympathize,
So could we not the simplest bargain drive;
And what avails it now that we are wise,
If absence doth this doubleness contrive?

Eternity may not the chance repeat,
But I must tread my single way alone,
In sad remembrance that we once did meet,
And know that bliss irrevocably gone.

The spheres henceforth my elegy shall sing,
For elegy has other subject none;
Each strain of music in my ears shall ring
Knell of departure from that other one.

Make haste and celebrate my tragedy;
With fitting strain resound, ye woods and fields;
Sorrow is dearer in such case to me
Than all the joys other occasion yields.

Is't then too late the damage to repair?
Distance, forsooth, from my weak grasp hath reft
The empty husk, and clutched the useless tare,
But in my hands the wheat and kernel left.

If I but love that virtue which he is,
Though it be scented in the morning air,
Still shall we be truest acquaintances,
Nor mortals know a sympathy more rare.

July 4.   THE "BOOK OF GEMS"

With cunning plates the polished leaves were decked,
Each one a window to the poet's world,

So rich a prospect that you might suspect
In that small space all paradise unfurled.

It was a right delightful road to go,
Marching through pastures of such fair herbage,
O'er hill and dale it led, and to and fro,
From bard to bard, making an easy stage;

Where ever and anon I slaked my thirst
Like a tired traveller at some poet's well,
Which from the teeming ground did bubbling burst,
And tinkling thence adown the page it fell.
Still through the leaves its music you might hear,
Till other springs fell faintly on the ear.

ANNURSNACK

July 11. At length we leave the river and take to
the road which leads to the hilltop, if by any means we
may spy out what manner of earth we inhabit. East,
west, north, and south, it is farm and parish, this world
of ours. One may see how at convenient, eternal intervals men have settled themselves, without thought for
the universe. How little matters it all they have built
and delved there in the valley! It is after all but a feature in the landscape. Still the vast impulse of nature
breathes over all. The eternal winds sweep across the
interval *to-day*, bringing mist and haze to shut out their
works. Still the crow caws from Nawshawtuct to
Annursnack, as no feeble tradesman nor smith may do.
And in all swamps the hum of mosquitoes drowns this
modern hum of industry.

Vol. I

EVERY MAN IS A ROMAN FORUM

All things are up and down, east and west, to *me*.
In me is the forum out of which go the Appian and
Sacred ways, and a thousand beside, to the ends of
the world. If I forget my centralness, and say a bean
winds with or against the *sun*, and not right or left, it
will not be true south of the equator.

July 18.   THE ASSABET

Up this pleasant stream let's row
    For the livelong summer's day,
Sprinkling foam where'er we go
In wreaths as white as driven snow.
    Ply the oars! away! away!¹

Now we glide along the shore,
    Chucking lilies as we go,
While the yellow-sanded floor
Doggedly resists the oar,
    Like some turtle dull and slow.

Now we stem the middle tide,
    Plowing through the deepest soil;
Ridges pile on either side,
While we through the furrow glide,
    Reaping bubbles for our toil.

Dew before and drought behind,
    Onward all doth seem to fly;
Naught contents the eager mind,
Only rapids now are kind,
    Forward are the earth and sky.

[*Week*, p. 188; Riv. 234.]

Sudden music strikes the ear,
    Leaking out from yonder bank,
Fit such voyagers to cheer.
Sure there must be Naiads here,
    Who have kindly played this prank.

There I know the cunning pack
    Where yon self-sufficient rill
All its telltale hath kept back,
Through the meadows held its clack,
    And now bubbleth its fill.

Silent flows the parent stream,
    And if rocks do lie below
Smothers with her waves the din,
As it were a youthful sin,
    Just as still and just as slow.

But this gleeful little rill,
    Purling round its storied pebble,
Tinkles to the selfsame tune
From December until June,
    Nor doth any drought enfeeble.

See the sun behind the willows,
    Rising through the golden haze,
How he gleams along the billows,
Their white crests the easy pillows
    Of his dew-besprinkled rays.

Forward press we to the dawning,
    For Aurora leads the way,

Sultry noon and twilight scorning;
In each dewdrop of the morning
  Lies the promise of a day.

Rivers from the sun do flow,
  Springing with the dewy morn;
Voyageurs 'gainst time do row,
Idle noon nor sunset know,
  Ever even with the dawn.[1]

Since that first "Away! away!"
  Many a lengthy league we've rowed,
Still the sparrow on the spray
Hastes to usher in the day
  With her simple stanza'd ode.[2]

July 20.   THE BREEZE'S INVITATION

Come, let's roam the breezy pastures,
  Where the freest zephyrs blow,
Batten on the oak tree's rustle,
And the pleasant insect bustle,
  Dripping with the streamlet's flow.

What if I no wings do wear,
  Thro' this solid-seeming air
I can skim like any swallow;
Whoso dareth let her follow,
  And we'll be a jovial pair.

Like two careless swifts let's sail,
  Zephyrus shall think for me;

[1] [*Week*, p. 188; Riv. 234.]   [2] [*Week*, p. 200; Riv. 248.]

Over hill and over dale,
  Riding on the easy gale,
    We will scan the earth and sea.

Yonder see that willow tree
  Winnowing the buxom air;
You a gnat and I a bee,
With our merry minstrelsy
  We will make a concert there.

One green leaf shall be our screen,
  Till the sun doth go to bed,
I the king and you the queen
Of that peaceful little green,
  Without any subject's aid.

To our music Time will linger,
  And earth open wide her ear,
Nor shall any need to tarry
To immortal verse to marry
  Such sweet music as he'll hear.

July 24.

Nature doth have her dawn each day,
But mine are far between;
Content, I cry, for, sooth to say,
Mine brightest are, I ween.

For when my sun doth deign to rise,
Though it be her noontide,
Her fairest field in shadow lies,
Nor can my light abide.

Sometimes I bask me in her day,
Conversing with my mate;
But if we interchange one ray,
Forthwith her heats abate.

Through his discourse I climb and see,
As from some eastern hill,
A brighter morrow rise to me
Than lieth in her skill.

As 't were two summer days in one,
Two Sundays come together,
Our rays united make one sun,
With fairest summer weather.[1]

July 25. There is no remedy for love but to love more.

Aug. 31. Made seven miles, and moored our boat on the west side of a little rising ground which in the spring forms an island in the river, the sun going down on one hand, and our eminence contributing its shadow to the night on the other.[2] In the twilight so elastic is the air that the sky seems to tinkle [*sic*] over farmhouse and wood. Scrambling up the bank of our *terra incognita* we fall on huckleberries, which have slowly ripened here, husbanding the juices which the months have distilled, for our peculiar use this night.[3] If they had been rank poison, the entire simplicity and confidence with which we plucked them would have

[1] [*Week*, pp. 302, 303; Riv. 375, 376.]   [2] [*Week*, p. 38; Riv. 47.]
[3] [*Week*, p. 38; Riv. 47.]

insured their wholesomeness. The devout attitude of the hour asked a blessing on that repast. It was fit for the setting sun to rest on.

From our tent here on the hillside, through that isosceles door, I see our lonely mast on the shore, it may be as an eternity fixture, to be seen in landscapes henceforth, or as the most temporary standstill of time, the boat just come to anchor, and the mast still rocking to find its balance.[1]

No human life is in night, — the woods, the boat, the shore, — yet is it lifelike.[2] The warm pulse of a young life beats steadily underneath all. This slight wind is where one artery approaches the surface and is skin deep.

While I write here, I hear the foxes trotting about me over the dead leaves, and now gently over the grass, as if not to disturb the dew which is falling. Why should we not cultivate neighborly relations with the foxes? As if to improve upon our seeming advances, comes one to greet us nosewise under our tent-curtain. Nor do we rudely repulse him. Is man powder and the fox flint and steel? Has not the time come when men and foxes shall lie down together?

Hist! there, the musquash by the boat is taking toll of potatoes and melons. Is not this the age of a community of goods? His presumption kindles in me

[1] [*Week*, p. 39; Riv. 48.]   [2] [*Week*, p. 39; Riv. 48, 49.]

View from Annursnack Hill

a brotherly feeling. Nevertheless. I get up to reconnoitre, and tread stealthily along the shore to make acquaintance with him. But on the riverside I can see only the stars reflected in the water, and now, by some ripple ruffling the disk of a star, I discover him.

In the silence of the night the sound of a distant alarm bell is borne to these woods. Even now men have fires and extinguish them, and, with distant horizon blazings and barking of dogs, enact the manifold drama of life.[1]

We begin to have an interest in sun, moon, and stars. What time riseth Orion? Which side the pole gropeth the bear? East, West, North, and South, — where are they? What clock shall tell the hours for us? — Billerica, midnight.

Sept. 1. *Sunday.* Under an oak on the bank of the canal in Chelmsford.

From Ball's Hill to Billerica meeting-house the river is a noble stream of water, flowing between gentle hills and occasional cliffs, and well wooded all the way. It can hardly be said to flow at all, but rests in the lap of the hills like a quiet lake. The boatmen call it a dead stream. For many long reaches you can see nothing to indicate that men inhabit its banks.[2] Nature seems to hold a sabbath herself to-day, — a still warm sun on river and wood, and not breeze enough to ruffle the water. Cattle stand up to their bellies in the river, and you think Rembrandt should be here.

[1] [*Week*, p. 39; Riv. 49.]   [2] [*Week*, p. 43; Riv. 54.]

Camped under some oaks in Tyngsboro, on the east bank of the Merrimack, just below the ferry.[1]

Sept. 2. Camped in Merrimack, on the west bank, by a deep ravine.[2]

Sept. 3. In Bedford, on the west bank, opposite a large rock, above Coos Falls.[3]

Sept. 4. *Wednesday.* Hooksett, east bank, two or three miles below the village, opposite Mr. Mitchel's.[4]

Sept. 5. Walked to Concord [N. H.], 10 miles.[5]

Sept. 6. By stage to Plymouth, 40 miles, and on foot to Tilton's inn, Thornton. The scenery commences on Sanbornton Square, whence the White Mountains are first visible. In Campton it is decidedly mountainous.

Sept. 7. Walked from Thornton through Peeling[6] and Lincoln to Franconia. In Lincoln visited Stone Flume and Basin, and in Franconia the Notch, and saw the Old Man of the Mountain.

Sept. 8. Walked from Franconia to Thomas J. Crawford's.

Sept. 9. At Crawford's.

Sept. 10. Ascended the mountain and rode to Conway.

Sept. 11. Rode to Concord.

Sept. 12. Rode to Hooksett and rowed to Bedford, N. H., or rather to the northern part of Merrimack, near the ferry, by a large island, near which we camped.[7]

[1] [*Week*, p. 118; Riv. 147.]   [3] [*Week*, p. 248; Riv. 307.]
[2] [*Week*, p. 179; Riv. 222.]   [4] [*Week*, p. 309; Riv. 383.]
[5] [See *Week*, pp. 318–322; Riv. 394–399.]
[6] [The original name of Woodstock, N. H.]
[7] [See *Week*, pp. 335–353; Riv. 414–437.]

Vol. I

Sept. 13. Rowed and sailed to Concord, about 50 miles.[1]

THE WISE REST

Sept. 17. Nature never makes haste; her systems revolve at an even pace. The bud swells imperceptibly, without hurry or confusion, as though the short spring days were an eternity.[2] All her operations seem separately, for the time, the single object for which all things tarry. Why, then, should man hasten as if anything less than eternity were allotted for the least deed? Let him consume never so many æons, so that he go about the meanest task well, though it be but the paring of his nails.[3] If the setting sun seems to hurry him to improve the day while it lasts, the chant of the crickets fails not to reassure him, even-measured as of old, teaching him to take his own time henceforth forever. The wise man is restful, never restless or impatient. He each moment abides there where he is, as some walkers actually rest the whole body at each step, while others never relax the muscles of the leg till the accumulated fatigue obliges them to stop short.

As the wise is not anxious that time wait for him, neither does he wait for it.

Oct. 22. Nature will bear the closest inspection. She invites us to lay our eye level with her smallest leaf, and take an insect view of its plain.[4]

[1] [See *Week*, pp. 356–420; Riv. 442–518.]
[2] [*Week*, pp. 110, 111; Riv. 137.]
[3] [*Week*, p. 110; Riv. 137.]
[4] [*Excursions*, p. 107; Riv. 132.]

ÆSCHYLUS

Nov. 5. There was one man lived his own healthy Attic life in those days. The words that have come down to us evidence that their speaker was a seer in his day and generation. At this day they owe nothing to their dramatic form, nothing to stage machinery, and the fact that they were spoken under these or those circumstances. All display of art for the gratification of a factitious taste is silently passed by to come at the least particle of absolute and genuine thought they contain. The reader will be disappointed, however, who looks for traits of a rare wisdom or eloquence, and will have to solace himself, for the most part, with the poet's humanity and what it was in him to say. He will discover that, like every genius, he was a solitary liver and worker in his day.

We are accustomed to say that the common sense of this age belonged to the seer of the last, — as if time gave him any vantage ground. But not so: I see not but Genius must ever take an equal start, and all the generations of men are virtually at a standstill for it to come and consider of them. Common sense is not so familiar with any truth but Genius will represent it in a strange light to it. Let the seer bring down his broad eye to the most stale and trivial fact, and he will make you believe it a new planet in the sky.

As to criticism, man has never to make allowance to man; there is naught to excuse, naught to bear in mind.

All the past is here present to be tried; let it approve itself if it can.

GROWTH

We are not apt to remember that we grow. It is curious to reflect how the maiden waiteth patiently, confiding as the unripe houstonia of the meadow, for the slow moving years to work their will with her, — perfect and ripen her, — like it to be fanned by the wind, watered by the rain, and receive her education at the hands of nature.

These young buds of manhood in the streets are like buttercups in the meadows, — surrendered to nature as they.

Nov. 7. I was not aware till to-day of a rising and risen generation. Children appear to me as raw as the fresh fungi on a fence rail. By what degrees of consanguinity is this succulent and rank-growing slip of manhood related to me? What is it but another herb, ranging all the kingdoms of nature, drawing in sustenance by a thousand roots and fibres from all soils.

LACONICISM

Nov. 8. Prometheus' answer to Io's question, who has bound him to the rock, is a good instance: —

Βούλουμα μὲν τὸ δῖον, Ἡφαίστου δὲ χείρ.
(The will indeed of Zeus, of Vulcan the hand.)

Also: —

Πταίσας δὲ τῷδε πρὸς κακῷ, μαθήσεται,
Ὅσον τό, τ' ἄρχειν καὶ τὸ δουλούειν δίχα.

Such naked speech is the standing aside of words to make room for thoughts.

Vol. I

fish, flower, and bird, quadruped and biped. The quiet bravery of the man is admirable. These facts have even a *novel* interest.[1]

Nov. 29. Many brave men have there been, thank Fortune, but I shall never grow brave by comparison. When I remember myself I shall forget them.

BRAVERY

Dec. 2. A rare landscape immediately suggests a suitable inhabitant, whose breath shall be its wind, whose moods its seasons, and to whom it will always be fair. To be chafed and worried, and not as serene as Nature, does not become one whose nature is as steadfast as she. We do all stand in the front ranks of the battle every moment of our lives; where there is a brave man there is the thickest of the fight, there the post of honor. Not he who procures a substitute to go to Florida is exempt from service; he gathers his laurels in another field. Waterloo is not the only battle-ground: as many and fatal guns are pointed at my breast now as are contained in the English arsenals.

[*Undated.*] [2]   NOON

Straightway dissolved,
Like to the morning mists — or rather like the subtler
    mists of noon —

---

[1] [*Excursions*, p. 107; Riv. 131, 132.]
[2] [This comes at the end of the first book of Journal transcripts (1837–39) and follows immediately a bit of verse dated Oct. 16, 1838, which has been included in its proper chronological place.]

REGRET

Nov. 13. Make the most of your regrets; never smother your sorrow, but tend and cherish it till it come to have a separate and integral interest. To regret deeply is to live afresh. By so doing you will be astonished to find yourself restored once more to all your emoluments.

DESPONDENCY

Nov. 14. There is nowhere any apology for despondency. Always there is life which, rightly lived, implies a divine satisfaction. I am soothed by the rain-drops on the door-sill; every globule that pitches thus confidently from the eaves to the ground is my life insurance. Disease and a rain-drop cannot coexist. The east wind is not itself consumptive, but has enjoyed a rare health from of old. If a fork or brand stand erect, *good* is portended by it. They are the warrant of universal innocence.

Nov. 19.   FAREWELL

Light-hearted, thoughtless, shall I take my way,
When I to thee this being have resigned,
Well knowing where, upon a future day,
With us'rer's craft more than myself to find.

LINNÆUS

Nov. 22. Linnæus, setting out for Lapland, surveys his "comb" and "spare shirt," "leather breeches," and "gauze cap to keep off gnats," with as much complacency as Buonaparte would a park of artillery to be used in the Russian Campaign. His eye is to take in

Stretched I far up the neighboring mountain's sides,
Adown the valleys, through the nether air,
Bathing, with fond expansiveness of soul,
The tiniest blade as the sublimest cloud.

What time the bittern, solitary bird,
Hides now her head amid the whispering fern,
And not a paddock vexes all the shore,
Nor feather ruffles the incumbent air,
Save where the wagtail interrupts the noon.

FROM A CHAPTER ON BRAVERY. — *Script*

Dec. Bravery deals not so much in resolute action, as in healthy and assured rest. Its palmy state is a staying at home, and compelling alliance in all directions.[1]

The brave man never heareth the din of war; he is trustful and unsuspecting, so observant of the least trait of good or beautiful that, if you turn toward him the dark side of anything, he will still see only the bright.

One moment of serene and confident life is more glorious than a whole campaign of daring. We should be ready for all issues, not daring to die but daring to live. To the brave even danger is an ally.

In their unconscious daily life all are braver than they know. Man slumbers and wakes in his twilight with the confidence of noonday; he is not palsied nor struck

---

[1] [*Cape Cod, and Miscellanies*, p. 277; *Misc.*, Riv. 35. *The Service*, p. 1.]

dumb by the inexplicable riddle of the universe. A mere surveyor's report or clause in a preëmption bill contains matter of quite extraneous interest, of a subdued but confident tone, evincing such a steadiness in the writer as would have done wonders at Bunker's Hill or Marathon. Where there is the collected eye, there will not fail the effective hand; χεὶρ δ' ὁρᾷ τὸ δράσιμον.

Science is always brave, for to know is to know good; doubt and danger quail before her eye. What the coward overlooks in his hurry, she calmly scrutinizes, breaking ground like a pioneer for the array of arts in her train. Cowardice is unscientific, for there cannot be a science of ignorance. There may be a science of war, for that advances, but a retreat is rarely well conducted; if it is, then is it an orderly advance in the face of circumstances.[1]

If his fortune deserts him, the brave man in pity still abides by her. Samuel Johnson and his friend Savage, compelled by poverty to pass the night in the streets, resolve that they will stand by their country.

The state of complete manhood is virtue, and virtue and bravery are one. This truth has long been in the languages. All the relations of the subject are hinted at in the derivation and analogies of the Latin words *vir* and *virtus*, and the Greek ἀγαθός and ἄριστος. Language in its settled form is the record of men's second thoughts, a more faithful utterance than they can mo-

[1] [*Excursions*, p. 107 ; Riv. 132.]

mentarily give. What men say is so sifted and obliged to approve itself as answering to a common want, that nothing absolutely frivolous obtains currency in the language. The analogies of words are never whimsical and meaningless, but stand for real likenesses. Only the ethics of mankind, and not of any particular man, give point and vigor to our speech.

The coward was born one day too late, for he has never overtaken the present hour. He is the younger son of creation, who now waiteth till the elder decease.[1] He does not dwell on the earth as though he had a deed of the land in his pocket, — not as another lump of nature, as imperturbable an occupant as the stones in the field. He has only rented a few acres of time and space, and thinks that every accident portends the expiration of his lease. He is a non-proprietor, a serf, in his moral economy nomadic, having no fixed abode. When danger appears, he goes abroad and clings to straws.

Bravery and Cowardice are kindred correlatives with Knowledge and Ignorance, Light and Darkness, Good and Evil.

If you let a single ray of light through the shutter, it will go on diffusing itself without limit till it enlighten the world, but the shadow that was never so wide at first as rapidly contracts till it comes to naught. The shadow of the moon when it passes nearest the sun is lost in

[1] [*Cape Cod, and Miscellanies*, p. 277; *Misc.*, Riv. 35. *The Service*, p. 1.]

space ere it can reach our earth to eclipse it. Always the *system* shines with uninterrupted light, for, as the sun is so much larger than any planet, no shadow can travel far into space. We may bask always in the light of the system, always may step back out of the shade. No man's shadow is as large as his body, if the rays make a right angle with the reflecting surface. Let our lives be passed under the equator, with the sun in the meridian.

There is no ill which may not be dissipated like the dark, if you let in a stronger light upon it. Overcome evil with good. Practice no such narrow economy as they whose bravery amounts to no more light than a farthing candle, before which most objects cast a shadow wider than themselves.[1]

It was a conceit of Plutarch, accounting for the preferences given to signs observed on the left hand, that men may have thought "things terrestrial and mortal directly over against heavenly and divine things, and do conjecture that the things which to us are on the left hand, the gods send down from their right hand."[2] If we are not blind, we shall see how a right hand is stretched over all, as well the unlucky as lucky, [and that the ordering soul is only right-handed, distributing with one palm all our fates.[3]

Men have made war from a deeper instinct than peace. War is but the compelling of peace.[4]

[1] [*Week*, p. 376 ; Riv. 465. *The Service*, pp. 8, 9.]
[2] [Plutarch's *Morals*, "Roman Questions," lxviii.]
[3] [*The Service*, p. 9.]   [4] [*The Service*, p. 12.]

When the world is declared under martial law, every Esau retakes his birthright, and what there is in him does not fail to appear. He wipes off all old scores and commences a new account. The world is interested to know how any soul will demean itself in so novel a position. But when war too, like commerce and husbandry, gets to be a routine, and men go about it as indented apprentices, the hero degenerates into a marine, and the standing army into a standing jest.

No pains are spared to do honor to the brave soldier. All guilds and corporations are taxed to provide him with fit harness and equipment. His coat must be red as the sunset, or blue as the heavens. Gold or silver, pinchbeck or copper, solid or superficial, mark him for fortune's favorite. The skill of a city enchases and tempers his sword-blade; the Tyrian dye confounds him with emperors and kings. Wherever he goes, music precedes and prepares the way for him. His life is a holiday, and the contagion of his example unhinges the universe. The world puts by work and comes out to stare. He is the one only man. He recognizes no time-honored casts and conventions, no fixtures but transfixtures, no governments at length settled on a permanent basis. One tap of the drum sets the political and moral harmonies all ajar. His ethics may well bear comparison with the priest's. He may rally, charge, retreat in an orderly manner, but never flee nor flinch.[1]

[1] [A pencil interlineation in this paragraph is as follows:] The soldier is the degenerate hero, as the priest is the degenerate saint; and the soldier and the priest are related as the hero and [the] saint. The

Each more melodious note I hear
Brings sad reproach to me,
That I alone afford the ear,
Who would the music be.[1]

The brave man is the sole patron of music;[2] he recognizes it for his mother-tongue, — a more mellifluous and articulate language than words, in comparison with which speech is recent and temporary. It is his voice. His language must have the same majestic movement and cadence that philosophy assigns to the heavenly bodies. The steady flux of his thought constitutes time in music. The universe falls in and keeps pace with it, which before proceeded singly and discordant. Hence are poetry and song. When Bravery first grew afraid and went to war, it took music along with it. The soul delighted still to hear the echo of its own voice. Especially the soldier insists on agreement and harmony always. Indeed, it is that friendship there is in war that makes it chivalrous and heroic. It was the dim sentiment of a noble friendship for the purest soul the world has seen, that gave to Europe a crusading era.[3]

The day of tilts and tournaments has gone by, but no herald summons us to the tournament of love.

one's virtue is bravery, the other's bravery virtue. Mankind still pay to the soldier the honors due only to the hero. They delight to do him honor. He is adorned with silver and gold and the colors of the rainbow, invested with outward splendor; music is for him especially, and his life is a holiday.

[1] [*The Service*, p. 11.]   [2] [*Week*, p 183; Riv. 228.]
[3] [*The Service*, p. 11.]

Vol. I

The brave warrior must have harmony if not melody at any sacrifice. Consider what shifts he makes. There are the bagpipe, the gong, the trumpet, the drum, — either the primitive central African or Indian, or the brass European. Ever since Jericho fell down before a blast of rams' horns, the martial and musical have gone hand in hand. If the soldier marches to the sack of a town, he must be preceded by drum and trumpet, which shall as it were identify his cause with the accordant universe. All woods and walls echo back his own spirit, and the hostile territory is then preoccupied for him. He is no longer insulated, but infinitely related and familiar. The roll-call musters for him all the forces of nature.[1]

All sounds, and more than all, silence, do fife and drum for us.[2] The least creaking doth whet all our senses and emit a tremulous light, like the aurora borealis, over things. As polishing expresses the vein in marble and the grain in wood, so music brings out what of heroic lurks anywhere.[3]

To the sensitive soul, the universe has its own fixed measure, which is its measure also, and, as a regular pulse is inseparable from a healthy body, so is its healthiness dependent on the regularity of its rhythm. In all sounds the soul recognizes its own rhythm, and seeks to express its sympathy by a correspondent movement of the limbs. When the body marches to the

[1] [*The Service*, p. 12.]   [2] [*Week*, p. 183; Riv. 228.]
[3] [*Week*, p. 183; Riv. 227. *The Service*, p. 13.]

measure of the soul, then is true courage and invincible strength.[1]

The coward would reduce this thrilling sphere music to a universal wail, this melodious chant to a nasal cant. He thinks to conciliate all hostile influences by compelling his neighborhood into a partial concord with himself, but his music is no better than a jingle which is akin to a jar, — jars regularly recurring.[2]

He blows a feeble blast of slender melody, because nature can have no more sympathy with such a soul than it has of cheerful melody in itself. Hence hears he no accordant note in the universe, and is a coward, or consciously outcast and deserted man. But the brave man, without drum or trumpet, compels concord everywhere by the universality and tunefulness of his soul.[3]

"Take a metallic plate," says Coleridge, "and strew sand on it; sound a harmonic chord over the sand, and the grains will whirl about in circles, and other geometrical figures, all, as it were, depending on some point

[1] [*Week*, p. 183; Riv. 228. *The Service*, p. 14.]
[2] [*The Service*, p. 14. See also p. 151 of this volume.]
[3] [*The Service*, p. 15.] [In pencil on a fly-leaf of the Journal:] The coward substitutes for this thrilling sphere music a universal wail, for this melodious chant a nasal cant, and but whistles to keep his courage up. He blows a feeble blast of slender melody and can compel his neighborhood only into a partial concord with himself, because nature has but little sympathy with such a soul. Hence he hears no accordant note in the universe, and is a coward, or consciously outcast and deserted man. But the brave man, without drum or trumpet, compels concord everywhere by the universality and tunefulness of his soul.

relatively at rest. Sound a discord, and every grain will whisk about without any order at all, in no figures, and with no points of rest." The brave man is such a point of relative rest, over which the soul sounds ever a harmonic chord.

Music is either a sedative or a tonic to the soul.[1] I read that "Plato thinks the gods never gave men music, the science of melody and harmony, for mere delectation or to tickle the ear; but that the discordant parts of the circulations and beauteous fabric of the soul, and that of it that roves about the body, and many times, for want of tune and air, breaks forth into many extravagances and excesses, might be sweetly recalled and artfully wound up to their former consent and agreement."[2]

By dint of wind and stringed instruments the coward endeavors to put the best face on the matter, — whistles to keep his courage up.

There are some brave traits related by Plutarch; *e. g.*: "Homer acquaints us how Ajax, being to engage in a single combat with Hector, bade the Grecians pray to the gods for him; and while they were at their devotions, he was putting on his armor."

On another occasion, a storm arises, "which as soon as the pilot sees, he falls to his prayers, and invokes

[1] [*The Service*, p. 13.]
[2] [*Week*, pp. 183, 184; Riv. 228. *The Service*, p. 13. The quotation is from Plutarch's *Morals*, "Of Superstition."]

his tutelar dæmons, but neglects not in the meantime to hold to the rudder and let down the main yard."

"Homer directs his husbandman, before he either plow or sow, to pray to the terrestrial Jove and the venerable Ceres, but with his hand upon the plow-tail."

Ἀρχὴ γὰρ ὄντως τοῦ νικᾷν τὸ θαῤῥεῖν. (Verily, to be brave is the beginning of victory.)

The Romans "made Fortune surname to Fortitude," for fortitude is that alchemy that turns all things to good fortune. The man of fortitude, whom the Latins called *fortis*, is no other than that lucky person whom *fors* favors, or *vir summae fortis*. If we will, every bark may "carry Cæsar and Cæsar's fortune." The brave man stays at home. For an impenetrable shield, stand inside yourself; he was an arrant coward who first made shields of brass. For armor of proof, *mea virtute me involvo* (I wrap myself in my virtue);

"Tumble me down, and I will sit
Upon my ruins, smiling yet." [1]

The bravest deed, which for the most part is left quite out of history, which alone wants the staleness of a deed done and the uncertainty of a deed doing, is the life of a great man. To perform exploits is to be temporarily bold, as becomes a courage that ebbs and flows, the soul quite vanquished by its own deed subsiding into indifference and cowardice; but the exploit of a brave life consists in its momentary completeness. [2]

[1] [*The Service*, pp. 7, 8. See p. 154 of this volume.]
[2] [*The Service*, pp. 23, 24.]

Commonly we degrade Love and Friendship by presenting them under the aspect of a trivial dualism.

What matter a few words more or less with my friend, — with all mankind; — they will still be my friends in spite of themselves. Let them stand aloof if they can! As though the most formidable distance could rob me of any real sympathy or advantage! No, when such interests are at stake, time, and distance, and difference fall into their own places.

But alas! to be actually separated from that parcel of heaven we call our friend, with the suspicion that we shall no more meet in nature, is source enough for all the elegies that ever were written. But the true remedy will be to recover our friend again piecemeal, wherever we can find a feature, as Æetes gathered up the members of his son, which Medea had strewn in her path.

The more complete our sympathy, the more our senses are struck dumb, and we are repressed by a delicate respect, so that to indifferent eyes we are least his friend, because no vulgar symbols pass between us. On after thought, perhaps, we come to fear that we have been the losers by such seeming indifference, but in truth that which withholds us is the bond between us.

My friend will be as much better than myself as my aspiration is above my performance.

FRIENDSHIP [1]

Fall of 1839. Then first I conceive of a true friendship, when some rare specimen of manhood presents itself. It seems the mission of such to commend virtue to mankind, not by any imperfect preaching of her word, but by their own carriage and conduct. We may then worship moral beauty without the formality of a religion.

They are some fresher wind that blows, some new fragrance that breathes. They make the landscape and the sky for us.

The rules of other intercourse are all inapplicable to this.

We are one virtue, one truth, one beauty. All nature is our satellite, whose light is dull and reflected. She is subaltern to us, — an episode to our poem; but we are primary, and radiate light and heat to the system.

I am only introduced once again to myself.

Conversation, contact, familiarity are the steps to it and instruments of it, but it is most perfect when these are done, and distance and time oppose no barrier.

I need not ask any man to be my friend, more than the sun the earth to be attracted by him. It is not his to give, nor mine to receive. I cannot pardon my enemy; let him pardon himself.

[1] [Cf. *Week*, pp. 274–307; Riv. 341–381.]

Vol. I

This is most serene autumn weather. The chirp of crickets may be heard at noon over all the land. As in summer they are heard only at nightfall, so now by their incessant chirp they usher in the evening of the year. [1] The lively decay of autumn promises as infinite duration and freshness as the green leaves of spring.

[1] [*Excursions*, p. 108 ; Riv. 133.]

IV

1840

(ÆT. 22–23)

Jan. 10.   THE FISHER'S SON [1]

I know the world where land and water meet,
By yonder hill abutting on the main;
One while I hear the waves incessant beat,
Then, turning round, survey the land again.

Within a humble cot that looks to sea,
Daily I breathe this curious warm life;
Beneath a friendly haven's sheltering lee
My noiseless day with myst'ry still is rife.

'T is here, they say, my simple life began;
And easy credit to the tale I lend,
For well I know 't is here I am a man.
But who will simply tell me of the end?

These eyes, fresh opened, spied the far-off Sea,
Which like a silent godfather did stand,
Nor uttered one explaining word to me,
But introducèd straight Godmother Land.

And yonder still stretches that silent main,
With many glancing ships besprinkled o'er;

[1] [Stanzas 8, 10, 11, 12, with revision, *Week*, p. 255; Riv. 317. Stanzas 2–5, 9, 13, *Familiar Letters*, Introduction.]

And earnest still I gaze and gaze again
Upon the selfsame waves and friendly shore,

Till like a watery humor on the eye
It still appears whichever way I turn,
Its silent waste and mute o'erarching sky
With close-shut eyes I clearly still discern.

And yet with lingering doubt I haste each morn
To see if ocean still my gaze will greet,
And with each day once more to life am born,
And tread once more the earth with infant feet.

———————

My years are like a stroll upon the beach,
As near the ocean's edge as I can go;
My tardy steps its waves do oft o'erreach,
Sometimes I stay to let them overflow.

Infinite work my hands find there to do,
Gathering the relics which the waves upcast;
Each storm doth scour the deep for something new,
And every time the strangest is the last.

My sole employment 't is, and scrupulous care,
To place my gains beyond the reach of tides,
Each smoother pebble, and each shell more rare,
Which ocean kindly to my hand confides.

I have no fellow-laborer on the shore;
They scorn the strand who sail upon the sea;
Sometimes I think the ocean they've sailed o'er
Is deeper known upon the strand to me.

The middle sea can show no crimson dulse,
Its deeper waves cast up no pearls to view,
Along the shore my hand is on its pulse,
Whose feeble beat is elsewhere felt by few.

My neighbors come sometimes with lumb'ring carts,
As it would seem my pleasant toil to share,
But straightway take their loads to distant marts,
For only weeds and ballast are their care.

———————

'T is by some strange coincidence, if I
Make common cause with ocean when he storms,
Who can so well support a separate sky,
And people it with multitude of forms.

Oft in the stillness of the night I hear
Some restless bird presage the coming din,
And distant murmurs faintly strike my ear
From some bold bluff projecting far within.

My stillest depths straightway do inly heave
More genially than rests the summer's calm;
The howling winds through my soul's cordage grieve,
Till every shelf and ledge gives the alarm.

Far from the shore the swelling billows rise,
And gathering strength come rolling to the land,
And, as each wave retires, and murmur dies,
I straight pursue upon the streaming sand,

Till the returning surge with gathered strength
Compels once more the backward way to take,

And, creeping up the beach a cable's length,
In many a thirsty hollow leaves a lake.

Oft as some ruling star my tide has swelled
The sea can scarcely brag more wrecks than I;
Ere other influence my waves has quelled,
The stanchest bark that floats is high and dry.

Jan. 19.
By a strong liking we prevail
Against the stoutest fort;
At length the fiercest heart will quail,
And our alliance court.

FRIENDS

Jan. 26. They are like air bubbles on water, hastening to flow together.

History tells of Orestes and Pylades, Damon and Pythias, but why should not we put to shame those old reserved worthies by a community of such?

Constantly, as it were through a remote skylight, I have glimpses of a serene friendship-land, and know the better why brooks murmur and violets grow.

This conjunction of souls, like waves which meet and break, subsides also backward over things, and gives all a fresh aspect.

I would live henceforth with some gentle soul such a life as may be conceived, double for variety, single for harmony, — two, only that we might admire at our oneness, — one, because indivisible. Such community to be a pledge of holy living. How could aught unworthy be admitted into our society? To listen with one ear to each summer sound, to behold with one eye each summer scene, our visual rays so to meet and mingle with the object as to be one bent and doubled; with two tongues to be wearied, and thought to spring ceaselessly from a double fountain.

POETRY

Jan. No definition of poetry is adequate unless it be poetry itself. The most accurate analysis by the rarest wisdom is yet insufficient, and the poet will instantly prove it false by setting aside its requisitions.[1] It is indeed all that we do not know.

The poet does not need to see how meadows are something else than earth, grass, and water, but how they are thus much. He does not need discover that potato blows are as beautiful as violets, as the farmer thinks, but only how good potato blows are.

The poem is drawn out from under the feet of the poet, his whole weight has rested on this ground.

It has a logic more severe than the logician's.

You might as well think to go in pursuit of the rainbow, and embrace it on the next hill, as to embrace the whole of poetry even in thought. The best book is

[1] [*Week*, p. 93; Riv. 116.]

only an advertisement of it, such as is sometimes sewed in with its cover.[1]

Its eccentric and unexplored orbit embraces the system.

Jan. 27. What a tame life we are living! How little heroic it is! Let us devise never so perfect a system of living, and straightway the soul leaves it to shuffle along its own way alone. It is easy enough to establish a durable and harmonious routine; immediately all parts of nature consent to it.[2] The sun-dial still points to the noon mark, and the sun rises and sets for it. The neighbors are never fatally obstinate when such a scheme is to be instituted; but forthwith all lend a hand, and ring the bell, and bring fuel and lights, and put by work and don their best garments, with an earnest conformity which matches the operations of nature. There is always a present and extant life which all combine to uphold, though its insufficiency is manifest enough.[3] Still the sing-song goes on.

Jan. 29. A friend in history looks like some premature soul. The nearest approach to a community of love in these days is like the distant breaking of waves on the seashore. An ocean there must be, for it washes our beach.

This alone do all men sail for, trade for, plow for, preach for, fight for.

[1] [*Week*, p. 93; Riv. 116.]   [2] [*Week*, p. 132; Riv. 164.]
[3] [*Week*, p. 132; Riv. 165.]

ÆSCHYLUS

The Greeks, as the Southerns generally, expressed themselves with more facility than we in distinct and lively images, and as to the grace and completeness with which they treated the subjects suited to their genius they must be allowed to retain their ancient supremacy. But a rugged and uncouth array of thought, though never so modern, may rout them at any moment. It remains for other than Greeks to write the literature of the next century.

Æschylus had a clear eye for the commonest things. His genius was only an enlarged common sense. He adverts with chaste severity to all natural facts. His sublimity is Greek sincerity and simpleness, naked wonder which mythology had not helped to explain.
Tydeus' shield had for device
  "An artificial heaven blazing with stars;
   A bright full moon in the midst of the shield,
   Eldest of stars, eye of night, is prominent."

The Greeks were stern but simple children in their literature. We have gained nothing by the few ages which we have the start of them. This universal wondering at those old men is as if a matured grown person should discover that the aspirations of his youth argued a diviner life than the contented wisdom of his manhood.

He is competent to express any of the common manly feelings. If his hero is to make a boast, it does not lack fullness, it is as boastful as could be desired; he has a flexible mouth, and can fill it readily with strong, round

words, so that you will say the man's speech wants nothing, he has left nothing unsaid, but he has actually wiped his lips of it.

Whatever the common eye sees at all and expresses as best it may, he sees uncommonly and describes with rare completeness. The multitude that thronged the theatre could no doubt go along with him to the end. The Greeks had no transcendent geniuses like Milton and Shakespeare, whose merit only posterity could fully appreciate.

The social condition of genius is the same in all ages. Æschylus was undoubtedly alone and without sympathy in his simple reverence for the mystery of the universe.

Feb. 10. CRITICISM ON AULUS PERSIUS FLACCUS [1]

Feb. 11. "Truth," says Lord Bacon, "may perhaps come to the price of a pearl, that sheweth best by day; but it will not rise to the price of a diamond or carbuncle, which sheweth best in varied lights." Like the pearl, truth shines with a steady but pale light which invites to introspection; it is intrinsically bright, not accidentally as the diamond. We seem to behold its rear always, as though it were not coming toward us but retiring from us. Its light is not reflected this way, but we see the sombre and wrong side of its rays. As the dust in his beams makes known that the sun shines.

[1] [The criticism was not transcribed here. The title was inserted doubtless as a memorandum and to record the date of its composition. See *Week*, p. 327; Riv. 405.]

Falsehoods that glare and dazzle are sloped toward us, reflecting full in our faces even the light of the sun. Wait till sunset, or go round them, and the falsity will be apparent.

It is never enough that our life is an easy one. We must live on the stretch; not be satisfied with a tame and undisturbed round of weeks and days, but retire to our rest like soldiers on the eve of a battle, looking forward with ardor to the strenuous sortie of the morrow.[1] "Sit not down in the popular seats and common level of virtues, but endeavor to make them heroical. Offer not only peace offerings but holocausts unto God." To the brave soldier the rust and leisure of peace are harder than the fatigues of war. As our bodies court physical encounters, and languish in the mild and even climate of the tropics, so our souls thrive best on unrest and discontent.[2]

He enjoys true leisure who has time to improve his soul's estate.

Feb. 12. Opposition is often so strong a likeness as to remind us of the difference.

Truth has properly no opponent, for nothing gets so far up on the other side as to be opposite. She looks broadcast over the field and sees no opponent.

The ring-leader of the mob will soonest be admitted into the councils of state.

[1] [*Cape Cod, and Miscellanies*, p. 279 ; *Misc.*, Riv. 37.]
[2] [*The Service*, p. 20.]

Vol. I

A very meagre natural history suffices to make me a child. Only their names and genealogy make me love fishes. I would know even the number of their fin-rays, and how many scales compose the lateral line. I fancy I am amphibious and swim in all the brooks and pools in the neighborhood, with the perch and bream, or doze under the pads of our river amid the winding aisles and corridors formed by their stems, with the stately pickerel. I am the wiser in respect to all knowledges, and the better qualified for all fortunes, for knowing that there is a minnow in the brook. Methinks I have need even of his sympathy, and to be his fellow in a degree. I do like him sometimes when he balances himself for an hour over the yellow floor of his basin.[1]

Feb. 15. The good seem to inhale a more generous atmosphere and be bathed in a more precious light than other men. Accordingly Virgil describes the *sedes beatas* thus : —

> "Largior hic campos aether et lumine vestit
> Purpureo : Solemque suum, sua sidera nôrunt."[2]

Feb. 16. Divination is prospective memory.

There is a kindred principle at the bottom of all affinities. The magnet cultivates a steady friendship with the pole, all bodies with all others. The friendliness of nature is that goddess Ceres who presides over every sowing and harvest, and we bless the same in sun and

[1] [*Excursions*, p. 118 ; Riv. 146.]   [2] [*Week*, p. 406 ; Riv. 501.]

Knavery is more foolish than folly, for that, half knowing its own foolishness, it still persists. The knave has reduced folly to a system, is the prudent, common-sense fool. The witling has the simplicity and directness of genius, is the inspired fool. His incomprehensible ravings become the creed of the dishonest of a succeeding era.

Feb. 13. An act of integrity is to an act of duty what the French verb *être* is to *devoir*. Duty is *ce que devrait être*.

Duty belongs to the understanding, but genius is not dutiful, the highest talent is dutiful. Goodness results from the wisest use of talent.

The perfect man has both genius and talent. The one is his head, the other his foot; by one he is, by the other he lives.

The unconsciousness of man is the consciousness of God, the end of the world.[1]

The very thrills of genius are disorganizing. The body is never quite acclimated to *its* atmosphere, but how often succumbs and goes into a decline!

Feb. 14. Beauty lives by rhymes. Double a deformity is a beauty. Draw this blunt quill over the paper, and fold it once transversely to the line, pressing it suddenly before the ink dries, and a delicately shaded and regular figure is the result, which art cannot surpass.[2]

[1] [*Week*, p. 351; Riv. 434.]
[2] [*Week*, p. 351; Riv. 434. A sheet with specimens of this familiar school-boy amusement is slipped into one of the manuscript Journal volumes.]

rain. The seed in the ground tarries for a season with its genial friends there; all the earths and grasses and minerals are its hosts, who entertain it hospitably, and plenteous crops and teeming wagons are the result.

Feb. 18. All romance is grounded on friendship. What is this rural, this pastoral, this poetical life but its invention? Does not the moon shine for Endymion? Smooth pastures and mild airs are for some Corydon and Phyllis. Paradise belongs to Adam and Eve. Plato's republic is governed by Platonic love.

Feb. 20. The coward's hope is suspicion, the hero's doubt a sort of hope. The gods neither hope nor doubt.

Feb. 22. The river is unusually high, owing to the melting of the snow. Men go in boats over their gardens and potato-fields, and all the children of the village are on tiptoe to see whose fence will be carried away next. Great numbers of muskrats, which have been driven out of their holes by the water, are killed by the sportsmen.

They are to us instead of the beaver. The wind from over the meadows is laden with a strong scent of musk, and by its racy freshness advertises us of an unexplored wildness. Those backwoods are not far off. I am affected by the sight of their cabins of mud and grass, raised four or five feet, along the river, as when I read of the Pyramids, or the barrows of Asia.[1]

People step brisker in the street for this unusual

[1] [*Excursions*, p. 114 ; Riv. 141.]

movement of the waters. You seem to hear the roar of a waterfall and the din of factories where the river breaks over the road.

Who would have thought that a few feet might not have been spared from the trunks of most trees? Such as grow in the meadows, and are now surrounded by that depth of water, have a dwarfish appearance. No matter whether they are longer or shorter, they are now equally out of proportion.

Feb. 24.   THE FRESHET

> A stir is on the Worcester hills,
> And Nobscot too the valley fills;
> Where scarce you 'd fill an acorn cup
> In summer when the sun was up,
> No more you 'll find a cup at all,
> But in its place a waterfall.
>
> O that the moon were in conjunction
> To the dry land's extremest unction,
> Till every dike and pier were flooded,
> And all the land with islands studded,
> For once to teach all human kind,
> Both those that plow and those that grind,
> There is no fixture in the land,
> But all unstable is as sand.
>
> The river swelleth more and more,
> Like some sweet influence stealing o'er
> The passive town; and for a while
> Each tussock makes a tiny isle,

> Where, on some friendly Ararat,
> Resteth the weary water-rat.
>
> No ripple shows Musketaquid,
> Her very current e'en is hid,
> As deepest souls do calmest rest
> When thoughts are swelling in the breast;
> And she, that in the summer's drought
> Doth make a rippling and a rout,
> Sleeps from Nawshawtuct to the Cliff,
> Unruffled by a single skiff;
> So like a deep and placid mind
> Whose currents underneath it wind,
> For by a thousand distant hills
> The louder roar a thousand rills,
> And many a spring which now is dumb,
> And many a stream with smothered hum,
> Doth faster well and swifter glide,
> Though buried deep beneath the tide.
>
> Our village shows a rural Venice,
> Its broad lagunes where yonder fen is,
> Far lovelier than the Bay of Naples
> Yon placid cove amid the maples,
> And in my neighbor's field of corn
> I recognize the Golden Horn.
>
> Here Nature taught from year to year,
> When only red men came to hear,
> Methinks 't was in this school of art
> Venice and Naples learned their part,

Vol. I

> But still their mistress, to my mind,
> Her young disciples leaves behind.[1]

Feb. 26. The most important events make no stir on their first taking place, nor indeed in their effects directly. They seem hedged about by secrecy. It is concussion, or the rushing together of air to fill a vacuum, which makes a noise. The great events to which all things consent, and for which they have prepared the way, produce no explosion, for they are gradual, and create no vacuum which requires to be suddenly filled; as a birth takes place in silence, and is whispered about the neighborhood, but an assassination, which is at war with the constitution of things, creates a tumult immediately.

Corn grows in the night.[2]

Feb. 27. Some geniuses seem to hover in the horizon, like heat lightning, which is not accompanied with fertilizing rain to us, but we are obliged to rest contented with the belief that it is purifying the air somewhere. Others make known their presence by their effects, like that vivid lightning which is accompanied by copious rain and thunder and, though it clears our atmosphere, sometimes destroys our lives. Others still impart a steady and harmless light at once to large tracts, as the aurora borealis; and this phenomenon is hardest to be accounted for, some thinking it to be a reflection of the polar splendor, others a subtle fluid which pervades all

[1] [*Excursions*, pp. 120, 121; Riv. 148, 149.]
[2] [See pp. 174 and 263.]

things and tends always to the zenith. All are agreed that these are equally electrical phenomena, as some clever persons have shown by drawing a spark with their knuckles. Modern philosophy thinks it has drawn down lightning from the clouds.

Feb. 28. On the death of a friend, we should consider that the fates through confidence have devolved on us the task of a double living, that we have henceforth to fulfill the promise of our friend's life also, in our own, to the world.

Feb. 29. A friend advises by his whole behavior,[1] and never condescends to particulars; another chides away a fault, he loves it away. While he sees the other's error, he is silently conscious of it, and only the more loves truth himself, and assists his friend in loving it, till the fault is expelled and gently extinguished.

March 2. Love is the burden of all Nature's odes. The song of the birds is an epithalamium, a hymeneal. The marriage of the flowers spots the meadows and fringes the hedges with pearls and diamonds. In the deep water, in the high air, in woods and pastures, and the bowels of the earth, this is the employment and condition of all things.

March 4. I learned to-day that my ornithology had done me no service. The birds I heard, which fortunately did not come within the scope of my science,

[1] [*Week*, p. 300; Riv. 373.]

sung as freshly as if it had been the first morning of creation, and had for background to their song an untrodden wilderness, stretching through many a Carolina and Mexico of the soul.[1]

March 6. There is no delay in answering great questions; for them all things have an answer ready. The Pythian priestess gave her answers instantly, and ofttimes before the questions were fairly propounded. Great topics do not wait for past or future to be determined, but the state of the crops or Brighton market no bird concerns itself about.

March 8. The wind shifts from northeast and east to northwest and south, and every icicle which has tinkled on the meadow grass so long trickles down its stem and seeks its water level unerringly with a million comrades. In the ponds the ice cracks with a busy and inspiriting din and down the larger streams is whirled, grating hoarsely and crashing its way along, which was so lately a firm field for the woodman's team and the fox, sometimes with the tracks of the skaters still fresh upon it, and the holes cut for pickerel. Town committees inspect the bridges and causeways, as if by mere eye-force to intercede with the ice and save the treasury.

In the brooks the slight grating sound of small cakes of ice, floating with various speed, is full of content and promise, and where the water gurgles under a natural bridge, you may hear these hasty rafts hold conversa-

[1] [*Excursions*, p. 114; Riv. 140.]

tion in an undertone. Every rill is a channel for the juices of the meadow.[1] Last year's grasses and flowerstalks have been steeped in rain and snow, and now the brooks flow with meadow tea, — thoroughwort, mint, flagroot, and pennyroyal, all at one draught.

In the ponds the sun makes incroachments around the edges first, as ice melts in a kettle on the fire, darting his rays through this crevice, and preparing the deep water to act simultaneously on the under side.

> Two years and twenty now have flown;
> Their meanness time away has flung;
> These limbs to man's estate have grown,
> But cannot claim a manly tongue.
>
> Amidst such boundless wealth without
> I only still am poor within;
> The birds have sung their summer out,
> But still my spring does not begin.
>
> In vain I see the morning rise,
> In vain observe the western blaze,
> Who idly look to other skies,
> Expecting life by other ways.
>
> The sparrow sings at earliest dawn,
> Building her nest without delay;
> All things are ripe to hear her song,
> And now arrives the perfect day.

[1] [*Excursions*, pp. 119, 120; Riv. 147, 148.]

Vol. I

> Shall I then wait the autumn wind,
> Compelled to seek a milder ray,
> And leave no empty nest behind,
> No wood still echoing to my lay?[1]

March 16. The cabins of the settlers are the points whence radiate these rays of green and yellow and russet over the landscape; out of these go the axes and spades with which the landscape is painted. How much is the Indian summer and the budding of spring related to the cottage? Have not the flight of the crow and the gyrations of the hawk a reference to that roof?

The ducks alight at this season on the windward side of the river, in the smooth water, and swim about by twos and threes, pluming themselves and diving to peck at the root of the lily and the cranberries which the frost has not loosened. It is impossible to approach them within gunshot when they are accompanied by the gull, which rises sooner and makes them restless. They fly to windward first, in order to get under weigh, and are more easily reached by the shot if approached on that side. When preparing to fly, they swim about with their heads erect, and then, gliding along a few feet with their bodies just touching the surface, rise heavily with much splashing and fly low at first, if not suddenly aroused, but otherwise rise directly to survey the danger. The cunning sportsman is not in haste to desert

[1] [Stanzas 3, 2, and 5, in this order, with slight alterations, are printed in *Week*, p. 366 (Riv. 453), under the title of "The Poet's Delay."]

his position, but waits to ascertain if, having got themselves into flying trim, they will not return over the ground in their course to a new resting-place.

March 20. In society all the inspiration of my lonely hours seems to flow back on me, and then first have expression.

Love never degrades its votaries, but lifts them up to higher walks of being. They *over-look* one another. All other charities are swallowed up in this; it is gift and reward both.

We will have no vulgar Cupid for a go-between, to make us the playthings of each other, but rather cultivate an irreconcilable hatred instead of this.

March 21. The world is a fit theatre to-day in which any part may be acted. There is this moment proposed to me every kind of life that men lead anywhere, or that imagination can paint. By another spring I may be a mail-carrier in Peru, or a South African planter, or a Siberian exile, or a Greenland whaler, or a settler on the Columbia River, or a Canton merchant, or a soldier in Florida, or a mackerel-fisher off Cape Sable, or a Robinson Crusoe in the Pacific, or a silent navigator of any sea. So wide is the choice of parts, what a pity if the part of Hamlet be left out!

I am freer than any planet; no complaint reaches round the world. I can move away from public opinion, from government, from religion, from education, from society. Shall I be reckoned a ratable poll in the county of Middlesex, or be rated at one spear under the palm trees of Guinea? Shall I raise corn and potatoes in Massachusetts, or figs and olives in Asia Minor? sit out the day in my office in State Street, or ride it out on the steppes of Tartary? For my Brobdingnag I may sail to Patagonia; for my Lilliput, to Lapland. In Arabia and Persia, my day's adventures may surpass the Arabian Nights' Entertainments. I may be a logger on the head waters of the Penobscot, to be recorded in fable hereafter as an amphibious river-god, by as sounding a name as Triton or Proteus; carry furs from Nootka to China, and so be more renowned than Jason and his golden fleece; or go on a South Sea exploring expedition, to be hereafter recounted along with the periplus of Hanno. I may repeat the adventures of Marco Polo or Mandeville.

These are but few of my chances, and how many more things may I do with which there are none to be compared!

Thank Fortune, we are not rooted to the soil, and here is not all the world. The buckeye does not grow in New England; the mockingbird is rarely heard here. Why not keep pace with the day, and not allow of a sunset nor fall behind the summer and the migration of birds? Shall we not compete with the buffalo, who keeps pace with the seasons, cropping the pastures of the Colorado till a greener and sweeter grass awaits him by the Yellowstone? The wild goose is more a cosmopolite than we; he breaks his fast in Canada, takes a luncheon in the Susquehanna, and plumes himself for the night in a Louisiana bayou. The pigeon

carries an acorn in his crop from the King of Holland's to Mason and Dixon's line. Yet we think if rail fences are pulled down and stone walls set up on our farms, bounds are henceforth set to our lives and our fates decided. If you are chosen town clerk, forsooth, you can't go to Tierra del Fuego this summer.[1]

But what of all this? A man may gather his limbs snugly within the shell of a mammoth squash, with his back to the northeastern boundary, and not be unusually straitened after all. Our limbs, indeed, have room enough, but it is our souls that rust in a corner. Let us migrate interiorly without intermission, and pitch our tent each day nearer the western horizon. The really fertile soils and luxuriant prairies lie on this side the Alleghanies. There has been no Hanno of the affections. Their domain is untravelled ground, to the Mogul's dominions.

March 22. While I bask in the sun on the shores of Walden Pond, by this heat and this rustle I am absolved from all obligation to the past. The council of nations may reconsider their votes; the grating of a pebble annuls them.[2]

March 27. How many are now standing on the European coast whom another spring will find located on the Red River, or Wisconsin! To-day we live an antediluvian life on our quiet homesteads, and to-morrow are transported to the turmoil and bustle of a crusading era.

[1] [*Walden*, p. 352; Riv. 493.]   [2] [*Week*, p. 383; Riv. 474.]

Think how finite after all the known world is. Money coined at Philadelphia is a legal tender over how much of it! You may carry ship biscuit, beef, and pork quite round to the place you set out from. England sends her felons to the other side for safe keeping and convenience.

March 30. Pray, what things interest me at present? A long, soaking rain, the drops trickling down the stubble, while I lay drenched on a last year's bed of wild oats, by the side of some bare hill, ruminating. These things are of moment. To watch this crystal globe just sent from heaven to associate with me. While these clouds and this sombre drizzling weather shut all in, we two draw nearer and know one another. The gathering in of the clouds with the last rush and dying breath of the wind, and then the regular dripping of twigs and leaves the country o'er, the impression of inward comfort and sociableness, the drenched stubble and trees that drop beads on you as you pass, their dim outline seen through the rain on all sides drooping in sympathy with yourself. These are my undisputed territory. This is Nature's English comfort. The birds draw closer and are more familiar under the thick foliage, composing new strains on their roosts against the sunshine.

April 4. We look to windward for fair weather.

April 8. How shall I help myself? By withdrawing into the garret, and associating with spiders and mice,

determining to meet myself face to face sooner or later. Completely silent and attentive I will be this hour, and the next, and forever. The most positive life that history notices has been a constant retiring out of life, a wiping one's hands of it, seeing how mean it is, and having nothing to do with it.

April 9. I read in Cudworth how "Origen determines that the stars do not make but signify; and that the heavens are a kind of divine volume, in whose characters they that are skilled may read or spell out human events." Nothing can be truer, and yet astrology is possible. Men seem to be just on the point of discerning a truth when the imposition is greatest.

April 17. Farewell, etiquette! My neighbor inhabits a hollow sycamore, and I a beech tree. What then becomes of morning calls with cards, and deference paid to door-knockers and front entries, and presiding at one's own table?[1]

April 19. The infinite bustle of Nature of a summer's noon, or her infinite silence of a summer's night, gives utterance to no dogma. They do not say to us even with a seer's assurance, that this or that law is immutable and so ever and only can the universe exist. But they are the indifferent occasion for all things and the annulment of all laws.

April 20. The universe will not wait to be explained. Whoever seriously attempts a theory of it is already

[1] [*Walden*, p. 247; Riv. 347, 348.]

behind his age. His yea has reserved no nay for the morrow.

The wisest solution is no better than dissolution. Already the seer *whispers* his *convictions* to bare walls; no audience in the land can attend to them.

An early morning walk is a blessing for the whole day. To my neighbors who have risen in mist and rain I tell of a clear sunrise and the singing of birds as some traditionary mythus. I look back to those fresh but now remote hours as to the old dawn of time, when a solid and blooming health reigned and every deed was simple and heroic.

April 22. Thales was the first of the Greeks who taught that souls are immortal, and it takes equal wisdom to discern this old fact to-day. What the first philosopher taught, the last will have to repeat. The *world* makes no progress.

I cannot turn on my heel in a carpeted room. What a gap in the morning is a breakfast! A supper supersedes the sunset.

Methinks I hear the *ranz des vaches* and shall soon be tempted to desert.

Will not one thick garment suffice for three thin ones? Then I shall be less compound, and can lay my hand on myself in the dark.

May 14. A kind act or gift lays us under obligation not so much to the giver as to Truth and Love. We

must then be truer and kinder ourselves. Just in proportion to our sense of the kindness, and pleasure at it, is the debt paid. What is it to be *grateful* but to be *gratified*, — to be *pleased?* The nobly poor will dissolve all obligations by nobly accepting a kindness.

If we are not sensible of kindness, then indeed we incur a debt. Not to be pleased by generous deeds at any time, though done to another, but to sit crabbedly silent in a corner, what is it but a voluntary imprisonment for debt? It is to see the world through a grating. Not to let the light of virtuous actions shine on us at all times, through every crevice, is to live in a dungeon.

War is the sympathy of concussion. We would fain rub one against another. Its rub may be friction merely, but it would rather be titillation. We discover in the quietest scenes how faithfully war has copied the moods of peace. Men do not peep into heaven but they see embattled hosts there. Milton's heaven was a camp. When the sun bursts through the morning fog I seem to hear the din of war louder than when his chariot thundered on the plains of Troy. Every man is a warrior when he aspires. He marches on his post. The soldier is the practical idealist; he has no sympathy with matter, he revels in the annihilation of it. So do we all at times. When a freshet destroys the works of man, or a fire consumes them, or a Lisbon earthquake shakes them down, our sympathy with persons is swallowed up in a wider sympathy with the universe. A crash is apt to grate agreeably on our ears.

Let not the faithful sorrow that he has no ear for the more fickle harmonies of creation, if he is awake to the slower measure of virtue and truth. If his pulse does not beat in unison with the musician's quips and turns, it accords with the pulse-beat of the ages.[1]

June 11. We had appointed Saturday, August 31st, 1839, for the commencement of our White Mountain expedition. We awake to a warm, drizzling rain which threatens delay to our plans, but at length the leaves and grass are dried, and it comes out a mild afternoon, of such a sober serenity and freshness that Nature herself seems maturing some greater scheme of her own. All things wear the aspect of a fertile idleness. It is the eventide of the soul. After this long dripping and oozing from every pore Nature begins to respire again more healthily than ever. So with a vigorous shove we launch our boat from the bank, while the flags and bulrushes curtsy a God-speed, and drop silently down the stream.[2] As if we had launched our bark in the sluggish current of our thoughts, and were bound nowhither.

Gradually the village murmur subsides, as when one falls into a placid dream and on its Lethe tide is floated from the past into the future, or as silently as fresh thoughts awaken us to new morning or evening light.[3]

Our boat[4] was built like a fisherman's dory, with

[1] [*The Service*, p. 15.]   [2] [*Week*, p. 12; Riv. 15.]
[3] [*Week*, p. 17; Riv. 21.]
[4] [T. finally sold this boat to Hawthorne, who changed the name from Musketaquid to Pond-Lily; and later it passed into Channing's hands. See Hawthorne's *American Note-Books*, Riv. pp. 318–321, and Channing, p. 13.]

thole-pins for four oars. Below it was green with a border of blue, as if out of courtesy [to] the green sea and the blue heavens. It was well calculated for service, but of consequence difficult to be dragged over shoal places or carried round falls.

A boat should have a sort of life and independence of its own. It is a sort of amphibious animal, a creature of two elements, a fish to swim and a bird to fly, related by one half of its structure to some swift and shapely fish and by the other to some strong-winged and graceful bird. The fins of the fish will tell where to set the oars, and the tail give some hint for the form and position of the rudder. And so may we learn where there should be the greatest breadth of beam and depth in the hold. The bird will show how to rig and trim the sails, and what form to give to the prow, that it may balance the boat and divide the air and water best.

The boat took to the water; from of old there had been a tacit league struck between these two, and now it gladly availed itself of the old law that the heavier shall float the lighter.

Two masts we had provided, one to serve for a tent-pole at night, and likewise other slender poles, that we might exchange the tedium of rowing for poling in shallow reaches. At night we lay on a buffalo-skin under a tent of drilled cotton eight feet high and as many in diameter, which effectually defended from dampness, so short a step is it from tiled roofs to drilled cotton, from carpeted floors to a buffalo-skin.[1]

[1] [*Week*, pp. 12, 13; Riv. 15–17.]

There were a few berries left still on the hills, hanging with brave content by the slenderest threads.[1]

As the night stole over, such a freshness stole across the meadow that every blade of cut-grass seemed to teem with life.[2]

We stole noiselessly down the stream, occasionally driving a pickerel from the covert of the pads, or a bream from her nest, and the small green bittern would now and then sail away on sluggish wings from some recess of the shore.[3] With its patient study by rocks and sandy capes, has it wrested the whole of her secret from Nature yet? It has looked out from its dull eye for so long, standing on one leg, on moon and stars sparkling through silence and dark, and now what a rich experience is its! What says it of stagnant pools, and reeds, and damp night fogs? It would be worth while to look in the eye which has been open and seeing at such hours and in such solitudes. When I behold that dull yellowish green, I wonder if my own soul is not a bright, invisible green. I would fain lay my eye side by side with its and learn of it.[4]

End of my Journal of 546 pages.[5]

[1] [*Week*, p. 19; Riv. 24.]
[2] [*Week*, p. 37; Riv. 47.]
[3] [*Week*, p. 17; Riv. 21.]
[4] [*Week*, p. 250; Riv. 310, 311.]
[5] [This was Thoreau's first journal, from which he made the transcripts which are now the only representatives of his early diarizing. See p. 188, where Journal of 396 pages ends.]

June 14.

Λόγος τοῦ ἔργου ἄνευ ὕλης. — *Aristotle's definition of art.*[1]

Ὁ χρή σε νοεῖν νόου ἄνθει. — *Chaldaic Oracles.*

Ἐγώ εἰμι πᾶν τὸ γεγονὸν, καὶ ὂν, καὶ ἐσόμενον, καὶ τὸν ἐμὸν πέπλον οὐδείς πω θνητὸς ἀπεκάλυψεν. — *Inscription upon the temple at Sais.*

Plotinus aimed at ἐπαφήν, and παρουσίαν ἐπιστήμης κρείττονα, and τὸ ἑαυτὸν κέντρον τῷ οἷον πάντων κέντρῳ συνάπτειν.

Μέλλει τὸ Θεῖον δ' ἐστὶ τοιοῦτον φύσει. — EURIPIDES in *Orestes.*

"The right Reason is in part divine, in part human; the second can be expressed, but no language can translate the first." — EMPEDOCLES.

"In glory and in joy,
Behind his plough, upon the mountain-side!"[2]

I seemed to see the woods wave on a hundred mountains, as I read these lines, and the distant rustling of their leaves reached my ear.

June 15. I stood by the river to-day considering the forms of the elms reflected in the water. For every oak

[1] [*Week*, p. 386; Riv. 476.]
[2] [Wordsworth, incorrectly quoted. The line reads, —
"Following his plough, along the mountain-side."]

and birch, too, growing on the hilltop, as well as for elms and willows, there is a graceful ethereal tree making down from the roots, as it were the original idea of the tree, and sometimes Nature in high tides brings her mirror to its foot and makes it visible.[1] Anxious Nature sometimes reflects from pools and puddles the objects which our grovelling senses may fail to see relieved against the sky with the pure ether for background.

It would be well if we saw ourselves as in perspective always, impressed with distinct outline on the sky, side by side with the shrubs on the river's brim. So let our life stand to heaven as some fair, sunlit tree against the western horizon, and by sunrise be planted on some eastern hill to glisten in the first rays of the dawn.

Why always insist that men incline to the moral side of their being? Our life is not all moral. Surely, its actual phenomena deserve to be studied impartially. The science of Human Nature has never been attempted, as the science of Nature has. The dry light has never shone on it. Neither physics nor metaphysics have touched it.

We have not yet met with a sonnet, genial and affectionate, to prophane swearing, breaking on the still night air, perhaps, like the hoarse croak of some bird. Noxious weeds and stagnant waters have their lovers, and the utterer of oaths must have honeyed lips, and be another Attic bee after a fashion, for only prevalent and essential harmony and beauty can employ the laws of sound and of light.

[1] [*Week*, pp. 44, 45; Riv. 56.]

June 16. The river down which we glided for that long afternoon was like a clear drop of dew with the heavens and the landscape reflected in it. And as evening drew on, faint purple clouds began to be reflected in its water, and the cow-bells tinkled louder and more incessantly on the banks, and like shy water-rats we stole along near the shore, looking out for a place to pitch our camp.[1]

It seems insensibly to grow lighter as night shuts in; the furthest hamlet begins to be revealed, which before lurked in the shade of the noon.[2] It twinkles now through the trees like some fair evening star darting its ray across valley and wood.

Would it not be a luxury to stand up to one's chin in some retired swamp for a whole summer's day, scenting the sweet-fern and bilberry blows, and lulled by the minstrelsy of gnats and mosquitoes? A day passed in the society of those Greek sages, such as described in the "Banquet" of Xenophon, would not be comparable with the dry wit of decayed cranberry vines, and the fresh Attic salt of the moss beds. Say twelve hours of genial and familiar converse with the leopard frog. The sun to rise behind alder and dogwood, and climb buoyantly to his meridian of three hands' breadth, and finally sink to rest behind some bold western hummock. To hear the evening chant of the mosquito from a thousand green chapels, and the bittern begin to boom from his concealed fort like a sunset gun! Surely, one may as profitably be soaked in the juices of a marsh for

[1] [*Week*, pp. 37, 38; Riv. 47.]   [2] [*Week*, p. 38; Riv. 47, 48.]

one day, as pick his way dry-shod over sand. Cold and damp, — are they not as rich experience as warmth and dryness?[1]

So is not shade as good as sunshine, night as day? Why be eagles and thrushes always, and owls and whippoor-wills never?

I am pleased to see the landscape through the bottom of a tumbler, it is clothed in such a mild, quiet light, and the barns and fences checker and partition it with new regularity. These rough and uneven fields stretch away with lawn-like smoothness to the horizon. The clouds are finely distinct and picturesque, the light-blue sky contrasting with their feathery whiteness. They are fit drapery to hang over Persia.[2] The smith's shop, resting in such a Grecian light, is worthy to stand beside the Parthenon. The potato and grain fields are such gardens as he imagines who has schemes of ornamental husbandry.

If I were to write of the dignity of the farmer's life, I would behold his farms and crops through a tumbler. All the occupations of men are ennobled so.

Our eyes, too, are convex lenses, but we do not learn with the eyes; they introduce us, and we learn after by converse with things.

June 17. Our lives will not attain to be spherical by lying on one or the other side forever; but only by resigning ourselves to the law of gravity in us, will our axis become coincident with the celestial axis, and

[1] [*Week*, pp. 319, 320; Riv. 395, 396.]   [2] [*Week*, p. 45; Riv. 56, 57.]

Think of the Universal History, and then tell me, — when did burdock and plantain sprout first?[1]

A fair land, indeed, do books spread open to us, from the Genesis down; but alas! men do not take them up kindly into their own being, and breathe into them a fresh beauty, knowing that the grimmest of them belongs to such warm sunshine and still moonlight as the present.

Of what consequence whether I stand on London bridge for the next century, or look into the depths of this bubbling spring which I have laid open with my hoe?

June 19. The other day I rowed in my boat a free, even lovely young lady, and, as I plied the oars, she sat in the stern, and there was nothing but she between me and the sky.[2] So might all our lives be picturesque if they were free enough, but mean relations and prejudices intervene to shut out the sky, and we never see a man as simple and distinct as the man-weathercock on a steeple.

The faint bugle notes which I hear in the west seem to flash on the horizon like heat lightning.[3] Cows low in the street more friendly than ever, and the note of the whip-poor-will, borne over the fields, is the voice with which the woods and moonlight woo me.

I shall not soon forget the sounds which lulled me when falling asleep on the banks of the Merrimack.

[1] [*Week*, p. 163; Riv. 203.]   [2] [*Week*, p. 45; Riv. 57.]
[3] [*The Service*, p. 14.]

[only] by revolving incessantly through all circles, shall we acquire a perfect sphericity.[1]

Men are inclined to lay the chief stress on likeness and not on difference. We seek to know how a thing is related to us, and not if it is strange. We call those bodies warm whose temperature is many degrees below our own, and never those cold which are warmer than we. There are many degrees of warmth below blood heat, but none of cold above it.[2]

Even the motto "Business before friends" admits of a high interpretation. No interval of time can avail to defer friendship. The concerns of time must be attended to in time. I need not make haste to explore the whole secret of a star; if it were vanished quite out of the firmament, so that no telescope could longer discover it, I should not despair of knowing it entirely one day.

We meet our friend with a certain awe, as if he had just lighted on the earth, and yet as if we had some title to be acquainted with him by our old familiarity with sun and moon.

June 18. I should be pleased to meet man in the woods. I wish he were to be encountered like wild caribou and moose.

I am startled when I consider how little I am *actually* concerned about the things I write in my journal.

[1] [*The Service*, p. 6.]   [2] [*Week*, p. 280; Riv. 347.]

Far into night I hear some tyro beating a drum incessantly with a view to some country muster, and am thrilled by an infinite sweetness as of a music which the breeze drew from the sinews of war. I think of the line, —

"When the drum beat at dead of night."

How I wish it would wake the whole world to march to its melody, but still it drums on alone in the silence and the dark. Cease not, thou drummer of the night, thou too shalt have thy reward. The stars and the firmament hear thee, and their aisles shall echo thy beat till its call is answered, and the forces are mustered. The universe is attentive as a little child to thy sound, and trembles as if each stroke bounded against an elastic vibrating firmament. I should be contented if the night never ended, for in the darkness heroism will not be deferred, and I see fields where no hero has couched his lance.[1]

June 20. Perfect sincerity and transparency make a great part of beauty, as in dewdrops, lakes, and diamonds. A spring is a cynosure in the fields. All Muscovy glitters in the minute particles of mica on its bottom, and the ripples cast their shadows flickeringly on the white sand, as the clouds which flit across the landscape.

Something like the woodland sounds will be heard to echo through the leaves of a good book. Sometimes I hear the fresh emphatic note of the oven-bird, and am

[1] [*Week*, p. 181; Riv. 224, 225.]

Trees Reflected in the River

tempted to turn many pages; sometimes the hurried chuckling sound of the squirrel when he dives into the wall.

If we only see clearly enough how mean our lives are, they will be splendid enough. Let us remember not to strive upwards too long, but sometimes drop plumb down the other way, and wallow in meanness. From the deepest pit we may see the stars, if not the sun. Let us have presence of mind enough to sink when we can't swim. At any rate, a carcass had better lie on the bottom than float an offense to all nostrils. It will not be falling, for we shall ride wide of the earth's gravity as a star, and always be drawn upward still, — *semper cadendo nunquam cadit*, — and so, by yielding to universal gravity, at length become fixed stars.

Praise begins when things are seen partially. We begin to praise when we begin to see that a thing needs our assistance.

When the heavens are obscured to us, and nothing noble or heroic appears, but we are oppressed by imperfection and shortcoming on all hands, we are apt to suck our thumbs and decry our fates. As if nothing were to be done in cloudy weather, or, if heaven were not accessible by the upper road, men would not find out a lower. Sometimes I feel so cheap that I am inspired, and could write a poem about it, — but straightway I cannot, for I am no longer mean. Let me know that I am ailing, and I am well. We should not always

beat off the impression of trivialness, but make haste to welcome and cherish it. Water the weed till it blossoms; with cultivation it will bear fruit. There are two ways to victory, — to strive bravely, or to yield. How much pain the last will save we have not yet learned.

June 21. I shall not soon forget my first night in a tent, — how the distant barking of dogs for so many still hours revealed to me the riches of the night. Who would not be a dog and bay the moon? [1]

I never feel that I am inspired unless my body is also. It too spurns a tame and commonplace life. They are fatally mistaken who think, while they strive with their minds, that they may suffer their bodies to stagnate in luxury or sloth. The body is the first proselyte the Soul makes. Our life is but the Soul made known by its fruits, the body. The whole duty of man may be expressed in one line, — Make to yourself a perfect body.

June 22. What a man knows, that he does.

It is odd that people will wonder how Shakespeare could write as he did without knowing Latin, or Greek, or geography, as if these were of more consequence than to know how to whistle. They are not backward to recognize Genius, — how it dispenses with those furtherances which others require, leaps where they

[1] [*Week*, pp. 39. 40 ; Riv. 49, 50.]

Vol. I

crawl, — and yet they never cease to marvel that so it was, — that it was Genius, and helped itself.

Nothing can shock a truly brave man but dullness. One can tolerate many things. What mean these sly, suspicious looks, as if you were an odd fish, a piece of crockery-ware to be tenderly handled? Surely people forget how many rebuffs every man has experienced in his day, — perhaps has fallen into a horsepond, eaten freshwater clams, or worn one shirt for a week without washing. Cannot a man be as calmly tolerant as a potato field in the sun, whose equanimity is not disturbed by Scotch thistles over the wall, but there it smiles and waxes till the harvest, let thistles mount never so high? You cannot receive a shock, unless you have an electric affinity for that which shocks you. Have no affinity for what is shocking.[1]

Do not present a gleaming edge to ward off harm, for that will oftenest attract the lightning, but rather be the all-pervading ether which the lightning does not strike but purify. Then will the rudeness or profanity of your companion be like a flash across the face of your sky, lighting up and revealing its serene depths.[2] Earth cannot shock the heavens; but its dull vapor and foul smoke make a bright cloud spot in the ether, and anon the sun, like a cunning artificer, will cut and paint it, and set it for a jewel in the breast of the sky.[3]

[1] [*Week*, p. 304 ; Riv. 378.]
[2] [*Cape Cod, and Miscellanies*, p. 277 ; *Misc.*, Riv. 35.]
[3] [*The Service*, p. 2.]

When we are shocked at vice we express a lingering sympathy with it. Dry rot, rust, and mildew shock no man, for none is subject to them.

June 23. We Yankees are not so far from right, who answer one question by asking another. Yes and No are lies. A true answer will not aim to establish anything, but rather to set all well afloat. All answers are in the future, and day answereth to day. Do we think we can anticipate them?

In Latin, to respond is to pledge one's self before the gods to do faithfully and honorably, as a man should, in any case. This is good.

Music soothes the din of philosophy and lightens incessantly over the heads of sages.[1]

How can the language of the poet be more expressive than nature? He is content that what he has already read in simple characters, or indifferently in all, be translated into the same again.

He is the true artist whose life is his material; every stroke of the chisel must enter his own flesh and bone and not grate dully on marble.[2]

The Springs. — What is any man's discourse to me if I am not sensible of something in it as steady and cheery as the creak of the crickets? In it the woods must be relieved against the sky. Men tire me when I am not

[1] [*The Service*, p. 13.]   [2] [*The Service*, p. 24.]

constantly greeted and cheered in their discourse, as it were by the flux of sparkling streams.

I cannot see the bottom of the sky, because I cannot see to the bottom of myself. It is the symbol of my own infinity. My eye penetrates as far into the ether as that depth is inward from which my contemporary thought springs.

Not by constraint or severity shall you have access to true wisdom, but by abandonment, and childlike mirthfulness. If you would know aught, be gay before it.

June 24. When I read Cudworth I find I can tolerate all, — atomists, pneumatologists, atheists, and theists, — Plato, Aristotle, Leucippus, Democritus, and Pythagoras. It is the attitude of these men, more than any communication, which charms me. It is so rare to find a man musing. But between them and their commentators there is an endless dispute. But if it come to that, that you compare notes, then you are all wrong. As it is, each takes me up into the serene heavens, and paints earth and sky. Any sincere thought is irresistible; it lifts us to the zenith, whither the smallest bubble rises as surely as the largest.

Dr. Cudworth does not consider that the belief in a deity is as great a heresy as exists. Epicurus held that the gods were "of human form, yet were so thin and subtile, as that, comparatively with our terrestrial bodies, they might be called incorporeal; they having not so much *carnem* as *quasi-carnem*, nor *sanguinem* as *quasi-sanguinem*, a certain kind of aerial or ethereal

flesh and blood." This, which Cudworth pronounces "romantical," is plainly as good doctrine as his own. As if any sincere thought were not the best sort of truth!

There is no doubt but the highest morality in the books is rhymed or measured, — is, in form as well as substance, poetry. Such is the scripture of all nations. If I were to compile a volume to contain the condensed wisdom of mankind, I should quote no rhythmless line.[1]

Not all the wit of a college can avail to make one harmonious line. It never *happens*. It may get so as to jingle, but a jingle is akin to a jar, — jars regularly recurring.[2]

So delicious is plain speech to my ears, as if I were to be more delighted by the whistling of the shot than frightened by the flying of the splinters, I am content, I fear, to be quite battered down and made a ruin of. I outgeneral myself when I direct the enemy to my vulnerable points.

The loftiest utterance of Love is, perhaps, sublimely satirical. Sympathy with what is sound makes sport of what is unsound.

Cliffs. Evening. — Though the sun set a quarter of an hour ago, his rays are still visible, darting half-way to the zenith. That glowing morrow in the west flashes on me like a faint presentiment of morning when I am

[1] [*Week*, pp. 93, 94; Riv. 116, 117.]   [2] [See p. 104.]

falling asleep. A dull mist comes rolling from the west, as if it were the dust which day has raised. A column of smoke is rising from the woods yonder, to uphold heaven's roof till the light comes again. The landscape, by its patient resting there, teaches me that all good remains with him that waiteth, and that I shall sooner overtake the dawn by remaining here, than by hurrying over the hills of the west.

Morning and evening are as like as brother and sister. The sparrow and thrush sing and the frogs peep for both.

The woods breathe louder and louder behind me. With what hurry-skurry night takes place! The wagon rattling over yonder bridge is the messenger which day sends back to night; but the dispatches are sealed. In its rattle the village seems to say, This one sound, and I have done.

Red, then, is Day's color; at 'least it is the color of his heel. He is 'stepping westward.' We only notice him when he comes and when he goes.

With noble perseverance the dog bays the stars yonder. I too, like thee, walk alone in this strange, familiar night, my voice, like thine, beating against its friendly concave; and barking I hear only my own voice. 10 o'clock.

June 25. Let me see no other conflict but with prosperity. If my path run on before me level and smooth, it is all a mirage; in reality it is steep and arduous as a chamois pass. I will not let the years roll over me like a Juggernaut car.

We will warm us at each other's fire. Friendship is not such a cold refining process as a double sieve, but a glowing furnace in which all impurities are consumed.

Men have learned to touch before they scrutinize, — to shake hands, and not to stare.

June 26. The best poetry has never been written, for when it might have been, the poet forgot it, and when it was too late remembered it; or when it might have been, the poet remembered it, and when it was too late forgot it.

The highest condition of art is artlessness.

Truth is always paradoxical.

He will get to the goal first who stands stillest.

There is one let better than any help, and that is, — *Let-alone.*

By sufferance you may escape suffering.

He who resists not at all will never surrender.

When a dog runs at you, whistle for him.

Say, Not so, and you will outcircle the philosophers.

Stand outside the wall, and no harm can reach you. The danger is that you be walled in with it.

June 27. I am living this 27th of June, 1840, a dull, cloudy day and no sun shining. The clink of the smith's hammer sounds feebly over the roofs, and the wind is sighing gently, as if dreaming of cheerfuler days. The farmer is plowing in yonder field, craftsmen are busy in the shops, the trader stands behind the counter, and all works go steadily forward. But I will have nothing to do; I will tell fortune that I play no game with her, and she may reach me in my Asia of serenity and indolence if she can.

For an impenetrable shield, stand inside yourself.[1]

He was no artist, but an artisan, who first made shields of brass.[2]

Unless we meet religiously, we prophane one another. What was the consecrated ground round the temple, we have used as no better than a domestic court.

Our friend's is as holy a shrine as any God's, to be approached with sacred love and awe. Veneration is the measure of Love. Our friend answers ambiguously, and sometimes before the question is propounded, like the oracle of Delphi. He forbears to ask explanation, but doubts and surmises darkly with full faith, as we silently ponder our fates.

In no presence are we so susceptible to shame. Our hour is a sabbath, our abode a temple, our gifts peace offerings, our conversation a communion, our silence a prayer. In prophanity we are absent, in holiness near, in sin estranged, in innocence reconciled.

June 28. The prophane never hear music; the holy ever hear it. It is God's voice, the divine breath audible. Where it is heard, there is a sabbath. It is omnipotent; all things obey it as they obey virtue. It is the herald of virtue.[3] It passes by sorrow, for grief hangs its harp on the willows.

  [1] [See p. 106.]   [2] [See p. 106.]   [3] [*The Service,* p. 12.]

June 29. Of all phenomena, my own race are the most mysterious and undiscoverable. For how many years have I striven to meet one, even on common manly ground, and have not succeeded!

June 30. I sailed from Fair Haven last evening as gently and steadily as the clouds sail through the atmosphere. The wind came blowing blithely from the southwest fields, and stepped into the folds of our sail like a winged horse, pulling with a strong and steady impulse. The sail bends gently to the breeze, as swells some generous impulse of the heart, and anon flutters and flaps with a kind of human suspense. I could watch the motions of a sail forever, they are so rich and full of meaning. I watch the play of its pulse, as if it were my own blood beating there. The varying temperature of distant atmospheres is graduated on its scale. It is a free, buoyant creature, the bauble of the heavens and the earth. A gay pastime the air plays with it. If it swells and tugs, it is because the sun lays his windy finger on it. The breeze it plays with has been outdoors so long. So thin is it, and yet so full of life; so noiseless when it labors hardest, so noisy and impatient when least serviceable.[1] So am I blown on by God's breath, so flutter and flap, and fill gently out with the breeze.

In this fresh evening each blade and leaf looks as if it had been dipped in an icy liquid greenness. Let eyes that ache come here and look, — the sight will be a sovereign eyewater, — or else wait and bathe them in the dark.

  [1] [*Week,* pp. 384, 385; Riv. 475.]

Vol. I

We go forth into the fields, and there the wind blows freshly onward, and still on, and we must make new efforts not to be left behind. What does the dogged wind intend, that, like a willful cur, it will not let me turn aside to rest or content? Must it always reprove and provoke me, and never welcome me as an equal?

The truth shall prevail and falsehood discover itself, as long as the wind blows on the hills.

A man's life should be a stately march to a sweet but unheard music, and when to his fellows it shall seem irregular and inharmonious, he will only be stepping to a livelier measure, or his nicer ear hurry him into a thousand symphonies and concordant variations. There will be no halt ever, but at most a marching on his post, or such a pause as is richer than any sound, when the melody runs into such depth and wildness as to be no longer heard, but implicitly consented to with the whole life and being. He will take a false step never, even in the most arduous times, for then the music will not fail to swell into greater sweetness and volume, and itself rule the movement it inspired.[1]

I have a deep sympathy with war, it so apes the gait and bearing of the soul.

Value and effort are as much coincident as weight and a tendency to fall. In a very wide but true sense, effort is the deed itself, and it is only when these sensible stuffs intervene, that our attention is distracted from

  [1] [*The Service,* pp. 15, 16.]

the deed to the accident. It is never the deed men praise, but some marble or canvas which are only a staging to the real work.[1]

July 1. To be a man is to do a man's work; always our resource is to endeavor. We may well say, Success to our endeavors. Effort is the prerogative of virtue.[2]

The true laborer is recompensed by his labor, not by his employer. Industry is its own wages. Let us not suffer our hands to lose one jot of their handiness by looking behind to a mean recompense, knowing that our true endeavor cannot be thwarted, nor we be cheated of our earnings unless by not earning them.[3]

The true poem is not that which the public read. There is always a poem not printed on paper, coincident with the production of this, which is stereotyped in the poet's life, is what he has become through his work. Some symbol of value may shape itself to the senses in wood, or marble, or verse, but this is fluctuating as the laborer's hire, which may or may not be withheld. His very material is not material but supernatural. Perhaps the hugest and most effective deed may have no sensible result at all on earth, but paint itself in the heavens in new stars and constellations. Its very material lies out of nature. When, in rare moments, we strive wholly with one consent, which we call a yearning, we may not hope that our work will stand in any artist's gallery.[4]

  [1] [*The Service,* p. 23.]   [3] [*The Service,* p. 23.]
  [2] [*The Service,* p. 23.]   [4] [*The Service,* p. 23.]

Let not the artist expect that his true work will stand in any prince's gallery.

July 2. I am not taken up, like Moses, upon a mountain to learn the law, but lifted up in my seat here, in the warm sunshine and genial light.

They who are ready to go are already invited.

Neither men nor things have any true mode of invitation but to be inviting.

Can that be a task which all things abet, and to postpone which is to strive against nature? [1]

July 3. When Alexander appears, the Hercynian and Dodonean woods seem to wave a welcome to him.

Do not thoughts and men's lives enrich the earth and change the aspect of things as much as a new growth of wood?

What are Godfrey and Gonsalvo unless we breathe a life into them, and reënact their exploits as a prelude to our own? The past is only so heroic as we see it; it is the canvas on which our conception of heroism is painted, the dim prospectus of our future field. We are dreaming of what we are to do. [2]

The last sunrise I witnessed seemed to outshine the

[1] [*The Service*, p. 23.]   [2] [*The Service*, pp. 25, 26.]

Vol. I

splendor of all preceding ones, and I was convinced that it behooved man to dawn as freshly, and with equal promise and steadiness advance into the career of life, with as lofty and serene a countenance to move onward through his midday to a yet fairer and more promising setting. Has the day grown old when it sets? and shall man wear out sooner than the sun? In the crimson colors of the west I discern the budding hues of dawn. To my western brother it is rising pure and bright as it did to me, but the evening exhibits in the still rear of day the beauty which through morning and noon escaped me. [1] When we are oppressed by the heat and turmoil of the noon, let us remember that the sun which scorches us with brazen beams is gilding the hills of morning and awaking the woodland quires for other men.

We will have a dawn, and noon, and serene sunset in ourselves.

What we call the gross atmosphere of evening is the accumulated deed of the day, which absorbs the rays of beauty, and shows more richly than the naked promise of the dawn. By earnest toil in the heat of the noon, let us get ready a rich western blaze against the evening of our lives. [2]

Low-thoughted, plodding men have come and camped in my neighbor's field to-night, with camp music and bustle. Their bugle instantly finds a sounding board in the heavens, though mean lips blow it. The sky is delighted with strains which the connois-

[1] [*The Service*, pp. 21, 22.]   [2] [*The Service*, p. 22.]

seur rejects. It seems to say, Now is this my own earth. [1]

In music are the centripetal and centrifugal forces. The universe needed only to hear a divine harmony that every star might fall into its proper place and assume a true sphericity. [2]

July 4. 4 o'clock, A. M. The Townsend Light Infantry encamped last night in my neighbor's inclosure.

The night still breathes slumberously over field and wood, when a few soldiers gather about one tent in the twilight, and their band plays an old Scotch air, with bugle and drum and fife attempered to the season. It seems like the morning hymn of creation. The first sounds of the awakening camp, mingled with the chastened strains which so sweetly salute the dawn, impress me as the morning prayer of an army. [3]

And now the morning gun fires. The soldier awakening to creation and awakening it. I am sure none are cowards now. These strains are the roving dreams which steal from tent to tent, and break forth into distinct melody. They are the soldier's morning thought. Each man awakes himself with lofty emotions, and would do some heroic deed. You need preach no homily to him; he is the stuff they are made of.

[1] [*The Service*, p. 14.]   [2] [*The Service*, p. 12.]

[3] I have heard a strain of music issuing from a soldiers' camp in the dawn, which sounded like the morning hymn of creation. The birches rustling in the breeze and the slumberous breathing of the crickets seemed to hush their murmuring to attend to it. [Written in pencil on a fly-leaf of the Journal.]

The whole course of our lives should be analogous to one day of the soldier's. His Genius seems to whisper in his ear what demeanor is befitting, and in his bravery and his march he yields a blind and partial obedience.

The fresher breeze which accompanies the dawn rustles the oaks and birches, and the earth respires calmly with the creaking of crickets. Some hazel leaf stirs gently, as if anxious not to awake the day too abruptly, while the time is hastening to the distinct line between darkness and light. And soldiers issue from their dewy tents, and as if in answer to expectant nature, sing a sweet and far-echoing hymn.

We may well neglect many things, provided we overlook them.

When to-day I saw the "Great Ball" rolled majestically along, it seemed a shame that man could not move like it. All dignity and grandeur has something of the undulatoriness of the sphere. It is the secret of majesty in the rolling gait of the elephant, and of all grace in action and in art. The line of beauty is a curve. Each man seems striving to imitate its gait, and keep pace with it, but it moves on regardless and conquers the multitude with its majesty. What shame that our lives, which should be the source of planetary motion and sanction the order of the spheres, are full of abruptness and angularity, so as not to roll, nor move majestically. [1]

[1] [*The Service*, p. 7. Mr. Sanborn, in a note to this passage, says, "The allusion here is to the extraordinary sight of the gravest citizens

July 5. Go where we will, we discover infinite change in particulars only, not in generals.

You cannot rob a man of anything which he will miss.

July 6. All this worldly wisdom was once the unamiable heresy of some wise man.[1]

I observe a truly wise practice on every hand, in education, in religion, and the morals of society, — enough embodied wisdom to have set up many an ancient philosopher.[2]

This society, if it were a person to be met face to face, would not only be tolerated but courted, with its so impressive experience and admirable acquaintance with things.

Consider society at any epoch, and who does not see that heresy has already *prevailed* in it? [3]

Have no mean hours, but be grateful for every hour, and accept what it brings. The reality will make any sincere record respectable. No day will have been wholly misspent, if one sincere, thoughtful page has been written.

of Concord, in that summer [1840], . . . turning out to roll a huge ball, emblematic of the popular movement against President Van Buren, from the battle-ground of Concord to that of Bunker Hill, singing as they rolled: —

'It is the Ball a-rolling on
For Tippecanoe and Tyler too.' "

[1] [*Week*, p. 129; Riv. 161.]   [2] [*Week*, p. 129; Riv. 160, 161.]
[3] [*Week*, p. 129; Riv. 161.]

though, to a distant and plodding planet, it is the uttermost extreme, yet, when that planet's year is complete, it will be found central.[1] They who are alarmed lest virtue run into extreme good, have not yet wholly embraced her, but described only a slight arc about her, and from so small a curvature you can calculate no centre whatever; but their mean is no better than meanness, nor their medium than mediocrity.

The brave man, while he observes strictly this golden mean, seems to run through all extremes with impunity; like the sun, which now appears in the zenith, now in the horizon, and again is faintly reflected from the moon's disk, and has the credit of describing an entire great circle, crossing the equinoctial and solstitial colures, without detriment to his steadfastness or mediocrity.[2]

Every planet asserts its own to be the centre of the system.

Only *meanness* is mediocre, *moderate;* but the true *medium* is not contained within any *bounds*, but is as wide as the ends it connects.

When Solon endeavored to prove that Salamis had formerly belonged to the Athenians and not to the Megarians, he caused the tombs to be opened, and showed that the inhabitants of Salamis turned the faces of their dead to the same side with the Athenians, but the Megarians to the opposite side.[3]

[1] [*Cape Cod, and Miscellanies*, p. 277; *Misc.*, Riv. 36.]
[2] [*The Service*, pp. 3, 4.]   [3] [*Week*, p. 265; Riv. 329.]

Let the daily tide leave some deposit on these pages, as it leaves sand and shells on the shore. So much increase of *terra firma*. This may be a calendar of the ebbs and flows of the soul; and on these sheets as a beach, the waves may cast up pearls and seaweed.

July 7. I have experienced such simple joy in the trivial matters of fishing and sporting, formerly, as might inspire the muse of Homer and Shakespeare. And now, when I turn over the pages and ponder the plates of the "Angler's Souvenir," I exclaim with the poet, —

" Can such things be,
And overcome us like a summer's cloud ? " [1]

When I hear a sudden burst from a horn, I am startled, as if one had provoked such wildness as he could not rule nor tame. He dares to wake the echoes which he cannot put to rest.[2]

July 8. Doubt and falsehood are yet good preachers. They affirm roundly, while they deny partially.

I am pleased to learn that Thales was up and stirring by night not unfrequently, as his astronomical discoveries prove.

It was a saying of Solon that "it is necessary to observe a medium in all things."

The golden mean, in ethics as in physics, is the centre of the system, and that about which all revolve; and

[1] [*Excursions*, p. 119; Riv. 146.]   [2] [*The Service*, p. 13.]

Vol. I

So does each part bear witness to all, and the history of all the past may be read in a single grain of its ashes.

July 9. In most men's religion the ligature which should be its muscle and sinew is rather like that thread which the accomplices of Cylon held in their hands, when they went abroad from the temple of Minerva, the other end being attached to the statue of the goddess. But frequently, as in their case, the thread breaks, being stretched, and they are left without an asylum.[1]

The value of many traits in Grecian history depends not so much on their importance as history, as [on] the readiness with which they accept a wide interpretation, and illustrate the poetry and ethics of mankind. When they announce no particular truth, they are yet central to all truth. They are like those examples by which we improve, but of which we never formally extract the moral. Even the isolated and unexplained facts are like the ruins of the temples which in imagination we restore, and ascribe to some Phidias, or other master.

The Greeks were boys in the sunshine, the Romans were men in the field, the Persians women in the house, the Egyptians old men in the dark.

He who receives an injury is an accomplice of the wrong-doer.

July 10. To myself I am as pliant as osier, and my
[1] [*Week*, p. 79; Riv. 99. *The Service*, p. 5.]

courses seem not so easy to be calculated as Encke's comet; but I am powerless to bend the character of another; he is like iron in my hands. I could tame a hyena more easily than my friend. I contemplate him as a granite boulder. He is material which no tool of mine will work. A naked savage will fell an oak with a firebrand, and wear a hatchet out of the rock, but I cannot hew the smallest chip out of my fellow. There is a character in every one which no art can reach to beautify or deform.[1]

Nothing was ever so unfamiliar and startling to me as my own thoughts.

We know men through their eyes. You might say that the eye was always original and unlike another. It is the feature of the individual, and not of the family, — in twins still different. All a man's privacy is in his eye, and its expression he cannot alter more than he can alter his character. So long as we look a man in the eye, it seems to rule the other features, and make them, too, original. When I have mistaken one person for another, observing only his form, and carriage, and inferior features, the unlikeness seemed of the least consequence; but when I caught his eye, and my doubts were removed, it seemed to pervade every feature.

The eye revolves on an independent pivot which we can no more control than our own will. Its axle is the axle of the soul, as the axis of the earth is coincident with the axis of the heavens.

[1] [*Week*, p. 301; Riv. 374.]

Vol. I

It is the man determines what is said, not the words. If a mean person uses a wise maxim, I bethink me how it can be interpreted so as to commend itself to his meanness; but if a wise man makes a commonplace remark, I consider what wider construction it will admit. When Pittacus says, "It is necessary to accommodate one's self to the time and take advantage of the occasion," I assent. He might have considered that to accommodate one's self to all times, and take advantage of all occasions, was really to be independent, and make our own opportunity.

July 12. What first suggested that necessity was grim, and made fate so fatal? The strongest is always the least violent. Necessity is a sort of Eastern cushion on which I recline. I contemplate its mild, inflexible countenance, as the haze in October days. When I am vexed I only ask to be left alone with it. Leave me to my fate. It is the bosom of time and the lap of eternity; since to be necessary is to be needful, it is only another name for inflexibility of good. How I welcome my grim fellow and aspire to be such a necessity as he! He is so flexible, and yields to me as the air to my body! I leap and dance in his midst, and play with his beard till he smiles. I greet thee, my elder brother, who with thy touch ennoblest all things. Must it be so, then is it good. Thou commendest even petty ills by thy countenance.

Over Greece hangs the divine necessity, ever a mellower heaven of itself, whose light too gilds the Acropolis and a thousand fanes and groves.[1]

[1] [*The Service*, p. 10.]

July 11. The true art is not merely a sublime consolation and holiday labor which the gods have given to sickly mortals, to be wrought at in parlors, and not in stithies amid soot and smoke, but such a masterpiece as you may imagine a dweller on the table-lands of Central Asia might produce, with threescore and ten years for canvas, and the faculties of a man for tools, — a human life, wherein you might hope to discover more than the freshness of Guido's Aurora, or the mild light of Titian's landscapes; not a bald imitation or rival of Nature, but the restored original of which she is the reflection. For such a work as this, whole galleries of Greece and Italy are a mere mixing of colors and preparatory quarrying of marble.[1]

Not how is the idea expressed in stone or on canvas, is the question, but how far it has obtained form and expression in the life of the artist.

There is much covert truth in the old mythology which makes Vulcan a brawny and deformed smith, who sweat more than the other gods. His stithy was not like a modern studio.

Let us not wait any longer, but step down from the mountains on to the plain of earth. Let our delay be like the sun's, when he lingers on the dividing line of day and night a brief space when the world is grateful for his light. We will make such haste as the morning and such delay as the evening.[2]

It concerns us rather to be something here present than to leave something behind us.[3]

[1] [*The Service*, p. 24.] [2] [*The Service*, p. 26.] [3] [*The Service*, p. 23.]

Pittacus said there was no better course than to endeavor to do well what you are doing at any moment.

Go where he will, the wise man is proprietor of all things. Everything bears a similar inscription, if we could but read it, to that on the vase found in the stomach of a fish in old times, — "To the most wise."

When his impious fellow-passengers invoked the gods in a storm, Bias cried, "Hist! hist! lest the gods perceive that you are here, for we should all be lost."

A wise man will always have his duds picked up, and be ready for whatever may happen, as the prudent merchant, notwithstanding the lavish display of his wares, will yet have them packed or easy to be removed in emergencies. In this sense there is something sluttish in all finery. When I see a fine lady or gentleman dressed to the top of the fashion, I wonder what they would do if an earthquake should happen, or a fire suddenly break out, for they seem to have counted only on fair weather, and that things will go on smoothly and without jostling. Those curls and jewels, so nicely adjusted, expect an unusual deference from the elements.

Our dress should be such as will hang conveniently about us, and fit equally well in good and in bad fortune; such as will approve itself of the right fashion and fabric, whether for the cotillion or the earthquake. In the sack of Priene, when the inhabitants with much hurry and bustle were carrying their effects to a place of safety, some one asked Bias, who remained tranquil amid the confusion, why he was not thinking how he should save something, as the others were. "I do so," said Bias, "for I carry all my effects with me."

July 14. Our discourse should be *ex tempore*, but not *pro tempore*.

July 16. We are as much refreshed by sounds as by sights, or scents, or flavors, — as the barking of a dog heard in the woods at midnight, or the tinklings which attend the dawn.

As I picked blackberries this morning, by starlight, the distant yelping of a dog fell on my inward ear, as the cool breeze on my cheek.

July 19. These two days that I have not written in my Journal, set down in the calendar as the 17th and 18th of July, have been really an æon in which a Syrian empire might rise and fall. How many Persias have been lost and won in the interim? Night is spangled with fresh stars.

July 26. When I consider how, after sunset, the stars come out gradually in troops from behind the hills and woods, I confess that I could not have contrived a more curious and inspiring night.

July 27. Some men, like some buildings, are bulky but not great. The Pyramids any traveller may measure with his line, but the dimensions of the Parthenon

in feet and inches will seem to dangle from its entablature like an elastic drapery.[1]

Much credit is due to a brave man's eye. It is the focus in which all rays are collected. It sees from within, or from the centre, just as we scan the whole concave of the heavens at a glance, but can compass only one side of the pebble at our feet.[2]

The grandeur of these stupendous masses of clouds, tossed into such irregular greatness across the sky, seems thrown away on the meanness of my employment. The drapery seems altogether too rich for such poor acting.[3]

In vain the sun challenges man to equal greatness in his career. We look in vain over earth for a Roman greatness to answer the eternal provocation.[4]

We look up to the gilded battlements of the eternal city, and are contented to be suburban dwellers outside the walls.[5]

By the last breath of the May air I inhale I am reminded that the ages never got so far down as this before. The wood thrush is a more modern philosopher than Plato and Aristotle. They are now a dogma, but he preaches the doctrine of this hour.

[1] [*Cape Cod, and Miscellanies*, p. 277; *Misc.*, Riv. 36. *The Service*, p. 3.]
[2] [*The Service*, p. 3.]
[3] [*Week*, p. 407; Riv. 502. *The Service*, p. 17.]
[4] [*The Service*, p. 17.]
[5] [*Week*, p. 407; Riv. 502. *The Service*, p. 17.]

Vol. I

This systole-diastole of the heart, the circulation of the blood from the centre to the extremities, the chylification which is constantly going on in our bodies are a sort of military evolution, a struggle to outgeneral the decay of time by the skillfulest tactics.

When bravery is worsted, it joins the peace society.

A word is wiser than any man, than any series of words. In its present received sense it may be false, but in its inner sense by descent and analogy it approves itself. Language is the most perfect work of art in the world. The chisel of a thousand years retouches it.

Nature refuses to sympathize with our sorrow. She seems not to have provided for, but by a thousand contrivances against, it. She has bevelled the margins of the eyelids that the tears may not overflow on the cheek.[1]

We can conceive of a Bravery so wide that nothing can meet to befall it, so omnipresent that nothing can lie in wait for it, so permanent that no obstinacy can reduce it. The stars are its silent sentries by night, and the sun its pioneer by day. From its abundant cheerfulness spring flowers and the rainbow, and its infinite humor and wantonness produce corn and vines.[2]

[1] [*The Service*, p. 9.]
[2] [The last two sentences appear also in pencil on a fly-leaf, preceded by, "It sleeps securely within its camp, not even dreaming of a foe."]

V

1841

(ÆT. 23–24)

Jan. 23. A day is lapsing. I hear cockerels crowing in the yard, and see them stalking among the chips in the sun. I hear busy feet on the floors, and the whole house jars with industry. Surely the day is well spent, and the time is full to overflowing. Mankind is as busy as the flowers in summer, which make haste to unfold themselves in the forenoon, and close their petals in the afternoon.

The momentous topics of human life are always of secondary importance to the business in hand, just as carpenters discuss politics between the strokes of the hammer while they are shingling a roof.[1]

The squeaking of the pump sounds as necessary as the music of the spheres.

The solidity and apparent necessity of this routine insensibly recommend it to me. It is like a cane or a cushion for the infirm, and in view of it all are infirm. If there were but one erect and solid-standing tree in the woods, all creatures would go to rub against it and make sure of their footing. Routine is a ground to stand on, a wall to retreat to; we cannot draw on our boots without bracing ourselves against it.[2] It is the fence over which neighbors lean when they talk. All this

[1] [*Week*, p. 230; Riv. 285.]   [2] [*Week*, p. 229; Riv. 284, 285.]

cockcrowing, and hawing and geeing, and business in the streets, is like the spring-board on which tumblers perform and develop their elasticity. Our health requires that we should recline on it from time to time. When we are in it, the hand stands still on the face of the clock, and we grow like corn in the genial dankness and silence of the night.[1] Our weakness wants it, but our strength uses it. Good for the body is the work of the body, good for the soul the work of the soul, and good for either the work of the other. Let them not call hard names, nor know a divided interest.

When I detect a beauty in any of the recesses of nature, I am reminded, by the serene and retired spirit in which it requires to be contemplated, of the inexpressible privacy of a life, — how silent and unambitious it is. The beauty there is in mosses will have to be considered from the holiest, quietest nook.[2]

The gods delight in stillness; they say, 'St — 'st. My truest, serenest moments are too still for emotion; they have woollen feet. In all our lives we live under the hill, and if we are not gone we live there still.

Jan. 24. Sunday. I almost shrink from the arduousness of meeting men erectly day by day.

Be resolutely and faithfully what you are; be humbly what you aspire to be. Be sure you give men the best of your wares, though they be poor enough, and the gods will help you to lay up a better store for the future.

[1] [*Week*, p. 229; Riv. 285. See also p. 124 of this volume.]
[2] [*Excursions*, p. 106; Riv. 131.]

fool, I have been driven to exchange the old for a more liberal and catholic philosophy.

Jan. 25. Monday. To-day I feel the migratory instinct strong in me, and all my members and humors anticipate the breaking up of winter. If I yielded to this impulse, it would surely guide me to summer haunts. This indefinite restlessness and fluttering on the perch do, no doubt, prophesy the final migration of souls out of nature to a serene summer, in long harrows and waving lines[1] in the spring weather, over what fair uplands and fertile Elysian meadows winging their way at evening and seeking a resting-place with loud cackling and uproar!

Wealth, no less than knowledge, is power. Among the Bedouins the richest man is the sheik, among savages he who has most iron and wampum is chief, and in England and America he is the merchant prince.

We should strengthen, and beautify, and industriously mould our bodies to be fit companions of the soul, — assist them to grow up like trees, and be agreeable and wholesome objects in nature. I think if I had had the disposal of this soul of man, I should have bestowed it sooner on some antelope of the plains than upon this sickly and sluggish body.

Jan. 26. Tuesday. I have as much property as I can command and use. If by a fault in my character I do

[1] [See *Excursions*, p. 110; Riv. 135.]

Man's noblest gift to man is his sincerity, for it embraces his integrity also. Let him not dole out of himself anxiously, to suit their weaker or stronger stomachs, but make a clean gift of himself, and empty his coffers at once. I would be in society as in the landscape; in the presence of nature there is no reserve, nor effrontery.

Coleridge says of the "*ideas* spoken out everywhere in the Old and New Testament," that they "resemble the fixed stars, which appear of the same size to the naked as to the armed eye; the magnitude of which the telescope may rather seem to diminish than to increase."

It is more proper for a spiritual fact to have suggested an analogous natural one, than for the natural fact to have preceded the spiritual in our minds.

By spells seriousness will be forced to cut capers, and drink a deep and refreshing draught of silliness; to turn this sedate day of Lucifer's and Apollo's, into an all fools' day for Harlequin and Cornwallis. The sun does not grudge his rays to either, but they are alike patronized by the gods. Like overtasked schoolboys, all my members and nerves and sinews petition Thought for a recess, and my very thigh-bones itch to slip away from under me, and run and join the mêlée. I exult in stark inanity, leering on nature and the soul. We think the gods reveal themselves only to sedate and musing gentlemen. But not so; the buffoon in the midst of his antics catches unobserved glimpses, which he treasures for the lonely hour. When I have been playing tom-

not derive my just revenues, there is virtually a mortgage on my inheritance. A man's wealth is never entered in the registrar's office. Wealth does not come in along the great thoroughfares, it does not float on the Erie or Pennsylvania canal, but is imported by a solitary track without bustle or competition, from a brave industry to a quiet mind.

I had a dream last night which had reference to an act in my life in which I had been most disinterested and true to my highest instinct but completely failed in realizing my hopes; and now, after so many months, in the stillness of sleep, complete justice was rendered me. It was a divine remuneration. In my waking hours I could not have conceived of such retribution; the presumption of desert would have damned the whole. But now I was permitted to be not so much a subject as a partner to that retribution. It was the award of divine justice, which will at length be and is even now accomplished.[1]

Good writing as well as good acting will be obedience to conscience. There must not be a particle of will or whim mixed with it. If we can listen, we shall hear. By reverently listening to the inner voice, we may reinstate ourselves on the pinnacle of humanity.

Jan. 27. Wednesday. In the compensation of the dream, there was no implied loss to any, but immeasurable advantage to all.[2]

[1] [*Week*, p. 315; Riv. 390, 391. See also below.]   [2] [See above.]

The punishment of sin is not positive, as is the reward of virtue.

For a flower, I like the name pansy, or *pensée*, best of any.

Jan. 28. No innocence can quite stand up under suspicion, if it is conscious of being suspected. In the company of one who puts a wrong construction upon your actions, they are apt really to deserve a mean construction. While in that society I can never retrieve myself. Attribute to me a great motive, and I shall not fail to have one; but a mean one, and the fountain of virtue will be poisoned by the suspicion. Show men unlimited faith as the coin with which you will deal with them, and they will invariably exhibit the best wares they have. I would meet men as the friends of all their virtue, and the foes of all their vice, for no man is the partner of his guilt. If you suspect me you will never see me, but all our intercourse will be the politest leave-taking; I shall constantly defer and apologize, and postpone myself in your presence. The self-defender is accursed in the sight of gods and men; he is a superfluous knight, who serves no lady in the land. He will find in the end that he has been fighting windmills, and battered his mace to no purpose. The injured man with querulous tone resisting his fate is like a tree struck by lightning, which rustles its sere leaves the winter through, not having vigor enough [to] cast them off.

As for apologies, I must be off with the dew and the

frost, and leave mankind to repair the damage with their gauze screens and straw.

Resistance is a very wholesome and delicious morsel at times. When Venus advanced against the Greeks with resistless valor, it was by far the most natural attitude into which the poet could throw his hero to make him resist heroically. To a devil one might yield gracefully, but a god would be a worthy foe, and would pardon the affront.

It would be worth while, once for all, fairly and cleanly to tell how we are to be used, as vendors of lucifer matches send directions in the envelope, both how light may be readily procured and no accident happen to the user.

Let your mood determine the form of salutation, and approach the creature with a natural nonchalance, as though he were anything but what he is, and you were anything but what you are, — as though he were he, and you were you; in short, as though he were so insignificant that it did not signify, and so important that it did not import. Depend upon it, the timber is well seasoned and tough, and will bear rough usage; and if it should crack, there is plenty more where it came from. I am no piece of china-ware that cannot be jostled against my neighbor, without danger of rupture from the collision, and must needs ring a scrannel strain to the end of my days when once I am cracked; but rather one of the old-fashioned wooden trenchers, which one

Vol. I

while stands at the head of the table, and at another is a milking-stool, and at another a seat for children, and finally goes down to its grave not unadorned with honorable scars, and does not die till it is *worn* out. Use me, for I am useful in my way. I stand as one of many petitioners, from toadstool and henbane up to dahlia and violet, supplicating to be put to my use, if by any means ye may find me serviceable; whether for a medicated drink or bath, as balm and lavender; or for fragrance, as verbena and geranium; or for sight, as cactus; or for thoughts, as pansy.[1]

Jan. 29. There is something proudly thrilling in the thought that this obedience to conscience and trust in God, which is so solemnly preached in extremities and arduous circumstances, is only to retreat to one's self, and rely on our own strength. In trivial circumstances I find myself sufficient to myself, and in the most momentous I have no ally but myself, and must silently put by their harm by my own strength, as I did the former. As my own hand bent aside the willow in my path, so must my single arm put to flight the devil and his angels. God is not our ally when we shrink, and neuter when we are bold. If by trusting in God you lose any particle of your vigor, trust in Him no longer. When you trust, do not lay aside your armor, but put it on and buckle it tighter. If by reliance on the gods I have disbanded one of my forces, then was it poor policy. I had better have retained the most inexperienced tyro who had straggled into the camp, and let go

[1] [*Week*, p. 304; Riv. 377, 378. See also p. 205.]

the heavenly alliance. I cannot afford to relax discipline because God is on my side, for He is on the side of discipline. And if the gods were only the heavens I fought under, I would not care if they stormed or were calm. I do not want a countenance, but a help. And there is more of God and divine help in a man's little finger than in idle prayer and trust.

The best and bravest deed is that which the whole man — heart, lungs, hands, fingers, and toes — at any time prompts. Each hanger-on in the purlieus of the camp, must strike his standard at the signal from the Prætorian tent, and fall into the line of march; but if a single sutler delay to make up his pack, then suspect the fates and consult the omens again. This is the meaning of integrity; this is to be an integer, and not a fraction. Be even for all virtuous ends, but odd for all vice. Be a perfect power, so that any of your roots multiplied into itself may give the whole again.

Beauty is compared, not measured, for it is the creature of proportions, not of size. Size must be subdued to it. It is hard for a tall or a short person to be beautiful.

To graft the Persian lilac on the ash, is as if you were to splice the thigh-bones of the Venus de Medici.

Friends will have to be introduced each time they meet. They will be eternally strange to one another, and when they have mutually appropriated their value for the last hour, they will go and gather a new measure of strangeness for the next. They are like two boughs crossed in the wood, which play backwards and forwards upon one another in the wind, and only wear into each other, but never the sap of the one flows into the pores of the other, for then the wind would no more draw from them those strains which enchanted the wood. They are not two united, but rather one divided.

Of all strange and unaccountable things this journalizing is the strangest. It will allow nothing to be predicated of it; its good is not good, nor its bad bad. If I make a huge effort to expose my innermost and richest wares to light, my counter seems cluttered with the meanest homemade stuffs; but after months or years I may discover the wealth of India, and whatever rarity is brought overland from Cathay, in that confused heap, and what perhaps seemed a festoon of dried apple or pumpkin will prove a string of Brazilian diamonds, or pearls from Coromandel.

Men lie behind the barrier of a relation as effectually concealed as the landscape by a mist; and when at length some unforeseen accident throws me into a new attitude to them, I am astounded, as if for the first time I saw the sun on the hillside. They lie out before me like a new order of things. As, when the master meets his pupil as a man, then first do we stand under the same heavens, and master and pupil alike go down the resistless ocean stream together.

Jan. 30. Saturday. Far over the fields, between the

Vol. I

When the wind blows, the fine snow comes filtering down through all the aisles of the wood in a golden cloud.

The trees covered with snow admit a very plain and clean light, but not brilliant, as if through windows of ground glass; a sort of white darkness it is, all of the sun's splendor that can be retained.

The fashions of the wood are more fluctuating than those of Paris; snow, rime, ice, green and dry leaves incessantly make new patterns. There are all the shapes and hues of the kaleidoscope and the designs and ciphers of books of heraldry in the outlines of the trees. Every time I see a nodding pine-top, it seems as if a new fashion of wearing plumes had come into vogue.

I saw a team come out of a path in the woods, as though it had never gone in, but belonged there, and only came out like Elisha's bears. It was wholly of the village, and not at all of the wood.

These particles of snow which the early wind shakes down are what is stirring, or the morning news of the wood. Sometimes it is blown up above the trees, like the sand of the desert.

You glance up these paths, closely imbowered by bent trees, as through the side aisles of a cathedral, and expect to hear a choir chanting from their depths. You are never so far in them as they are far before you.

tops of yonder wood, I see a slight cloud not larger than the vapor from a kettle, drifting by its own inward purpose in a direction contrary to the planet. As it flits across the dells and defiles of the tree-tops, now seen, then lost beyond a pine, I am curious to know wherein its will resides, for to my eye it has no heart, nor lungs, nor brain, nor any interior and private chamber which it may inhabit.

Its motion reminds me of those lines of Milton: —

"As when far off at sea a fleet descried
Hangs in the clouds, by equinoctial winds
Close sailing from Bengala, or the isles
Of Ternate and Tidore, whence merchants bring
Their spicy drugs; they on the trading flood,
Ply stemming nightly toward the pole."

The snow collects upon the plumes of the pitch pine in the form of a pineapple, which if you divide in the middle will expose three red kernels like the tamarind-stone. So does winter with his mock harvest jeer at the sincerity of summer. The tropical fruits, which will not bear the rawness of our summer, are imitated in a thousand fantastic shapes by the whimsical genius of winter.

In winter the warmth comes directly from the sun, and is not radiated from the earth. In summer I forget to bless the sun for his heat; but when I feel his beams on my back as I thread some snowy dale, I am grateful as for a special kindness which would not be weary of well doing but had pursued me even into that by-place.

Their secret is where you are not and where your feet can never carry you.

I tread in the tracks of the fox which has gone before me by some hours, or which perhaps I have started, with such a tiptoe of expectation as if I were on the trail of the Spirit itself which resides in these woods, and expected soon to catch it in its lair.[1]

The snow falls on no two trees alike, but the forms it assumes are as various as those of the twigs and leaves which receive it. They are, as it were, predetermined by the genius of the tree. So one divine spirit descends alike on all, but bears a peculiar fruit in each. The divinity subsides on all men, as the snowflakes settle on the fields and ledges and takes the form of the various clefts and surfaces on which it lodges.

Here is the distinct trail of a fox stretching [a] quarter of a mile across the pond. Now I am curious to know what has determined its graceful curvatures, its greater or less spaces and distinctness, and how surely they were coincident with the fluctuations of some mind, why they now lead me two steps to the right, and then three to the left. If these things are not to be called up and accounted for in the Lamb's Book of Life, I shall set them down for careless accountants. Here was one expression of the divine mind this morning. The pond was his journal, and last night's snow made a *tabula rasa* for him. I know which way a mind wended this

1 [*Excursions*, p. 117; Riv. 144.]

morning, what horizon it faced, by the setting of these tracks; whether it moved slowly or rapidly, by the greater or less intervals and distinctness, for the swiftest step leaves yet a lasting trace.[1]

Sometimes I come out suddenly upon a high plain, which seems to be the upper level and true surface of the earth, and by its very baldness aspires and lies up nearer to the stars, — a place where a decalogue might be let down or a saint translated.

I take a horse and oxen, standing among the wood-piles in the forest, for one of them, and when at length the horse pricks his ears, and I give him another name, where's the difference? I am startled by the possibility of such errors, and the indifference with [which] they are allowed to occur.

Fair Haven Pond is *scored* with the trails of foxes, and you may see where they have gambolled and gone through a hundred evolutions, which testify to a singular listlessness and leisure in nature.

Suddenly, looking down the river, I saw a fox some sixty rods off, making across to the hills on my left. As the snow lay five inches deep, he made but slow progress, but it was no impediment to me. So, yielding to the instinct of the chase, I tossed my head aloft and bounded away, snuffing the air like a fox-hound, and spurning the world and the Humane Society at each bound. It seemed the woods rang with the hunter's

[1] [*Excursions*, p. 117; Riv. 144.]

horn, and Diana and all the satyrs joined in the chase and cheered me on. Olympian and Elean youths were waving palms on the hills. In the meanwhile I gained rapidly on the fox; but he showed a remarkable presence of mind, for, instead of keeping up the face of the hill, which was steep and unwooded in that part, he kept along the slope in the direction of the forest, though he lost ground by it. Notwithstanding his fright, he took no step which was not beautiful. The course on his part was a series of most graceful curves. It was a sort of leopard canter, I should say, as if he were nowise impeded by the snow, but were husbanding his strength all the while. When he doubled I wheeled and cut him off, bounding with fresh vigor, and Antæus-like, recovering my strength each time I touched the snow. Having got near enough for a fair view, just as he was slipping into the wood, I gracefully yielded him the palm. He ran as though there were not a bone in his back, occasionally dropping his muzzle to the snow for a rod or two, and then tossing his head aloft when satisfied of his course. When he came to a declivity he put his fore feet together and slid down it like a cat. He trod so softly that you could not have heard it from any nearness, and yet with such expression that it would not have been quite inaudible at any distance. So, hoping this experience would prove a useful lesson to him, I returned to the village by the highway of the river.[1]

There is all the romance of my youthfulest moment in music. Heaven lies about us, as in our infancy. There

[1] [*Excursions*, pp. 117, 118 ; Riv. 144, 145.]

Vol. I

is nothing so wild and extravagant that it does not make true. It makes a dream my only real experience, and prompts faith to such elasticity that only the incredible can satisfy it. It tells me again to trust the remotest and finest, as the divinest, instinct. All that I have imagined of heroism, it reminds and reassures me of. It is a life unlived, a life beyond life, where at length my years will pass. I look under the lids of Time.

Jan. 31. Sunday. At each step man measures himself against the system. If he cannot actually belay the sun and make it fast to this planet, yet the British man alone spins a yarn in one year which will reach fifty-one times the distance from the earth to the sun. So, having his cable ready twisted and coiled, the fixed stars are virtually within his grasp. He carries his lasso coiled at his saddle bow, but is never forced to cast it.

All things are subdued to me by virtue of that coiled lasso I carry, and I lead them without the trouble of a cast. It is the rope that lies coiled on the deck, which moors my ship, and I have never to bend a cable.

In God's hall hang cables of infinite length, and in His entries stand bars of infinite strength; but those cables were never bent, nor those bars ever poised, for all things have been subdued to the divinity from the first, and these are the seals of His power.

The guilty never escape, for a steed stands ever ready saddled and bridled at God's door, and the sinner surrenders at last.

End of my Journal of 396 *pages.*

Feb. 2. Tuesday. It is easy to repeat, but hard to originate. Nature is readily made to repeat herself in a thousand forms, and in the daguerreotype her own light is amanuensis, and the picture too has more than a surface significance, — a depth equal to the prospect, — so that the microscope may be applied to the one as the spy-glass to the other. Thus we may easily multiply the forms of the outward; but to give the within outwardness, that is not easy.

That an impression may be taken, perfect stillness, though but for an instant, is necessary. There is something analogous in the birth of all rhymes.

Our sympathy is a gift whose value we can never know, nor when we impart it. The instant of communion is when, for the least point of time, we cease to oscillate, and coincide in rest by as fine a point as a star pierces the firmament.

The stars are the mountain peaks of celestial countries.

A child asked its father what became of the old moon, and he said it was cut up into stars.

There is always a single ear in the audience, to which we address ourselves.

How much does it concern you, the good opinion of your friend? Therein is the measure of fame. For the herd of men multiplied many times will never come up to the value of one friend. In this society there is no fame but love; for as our name may be on the lips of men, so are we in each other's hearts. There is no ambition but virtue; for why should we go round about, who may go direct?

All those contingences which the philanthropist, statesman, and housekeeper write so many books to meet are simply and quietly settled in the intercourse of friends.

For our aspirations there is no expression as yet, but if we obey steadily, by another year we shall have learned the language of last year's aspirations.

When I read the other day the weight of some of the generals of the Revolution, it seemed no unimportant fact in their biography. It is at least one other means of comparing ourselves with them. Tell me how much Milton or Shakespeare weighed, and I will get weighed myself, that I may know better what they are to me.

Weight has something very imposing in it, for we cannot get rid of it. Once in the scales we must weigh. And are we not always in the scales, and weighing just our due, though we kick the beam, and do all we can to heavy or lighten ourselves?

Feb. 3. Wednesday. The present seems never to get its due; it is the least obvious, — neither before, nor behind, but within us. All the past plays into this moment, and we are what we are. My aspiration is one thing, my reflection another, but, over all, myself and condition is and does. To men and nature I am each

moment a finished tool, — a spade, a barrow, or a pickaxe. This immense promise is no *efficient* quality. For all practical purposes I am done.

When we do a service to our neighbor, we serve our next neighbor.

We are constantly invited to be what we are; as to something worthy and noble. I never waited but for myself to come round; none ever detained me, but I lagged or tagged after myself.

It steads us to be as true to children and boors as to God himself. It is the only attitude which will suit all occasions; it only will make the earth yield her increase, and by it do we effectually expostulate with the wind. If I run against a post, this is the remedy. I would meet the morning and evening on very sincere ground. When the sun introduces me to a new day, I silently say to myself, "Let us be faithful all round; we will do justice and receive it." Something like this is the secret charm of Nature's demeanor toward us, strict conscientiousness [?] and disregard of us when we have ceased to have regard for ourselves. So she can never offend us. How true she is! — and never swerves. In her most genial moment her laws are as steadfastly and relentlessly fulfilled — though the decalogue is rhymed and set to sweetest music — as in her sternest.

Any exhibition of affection — as an inadvertent word, or act, or look — seems premature, as if the time

were not ripe for it; like the buds which the warm days near the end of winter cause to push out and unfold before the frosts are yet gone.

My life must seem as if it were passing at a higher level than that which I occupy. It must possess a dignity which will not allow me to be familiar.

The unpretending truth of a simile implies sometimes such distinctness in the conception as only experience could have supplied. Homer could not improve the simile of a soldier who was careful enough to tell the truth. If he knows what it was, he will know what it was like.

As the ancient Britons were exhibited in Rome in their native costume, and the Dacian came to display his swordsmanship in the arena, so Tyrolese peasants have come farther yet, even from the neighborhood of Rome to Concord, for our entertainment this night.

Feb. 4. Thursday. When you are once comfortably seated at a public meeting, there is something unmanly in the sitting on tiptoe and *qui vive* attitude, — the involuntarily rising into your throat, as if gravity had ceased to operate, — when a lady approaches, with quite godlike presumption, to elicit the miracle of a seat where none is.

Music will make the most nervous chord vibrate healthily.

Such a state of unrest becomes only a fluttered virtue. When once I have learned my place in the sphere, I will fill it once for all, rather like a fixed star than a planet. I will rest as the mountains do, so that your ladies might as well walk into the midst of the Tyrol, and look for Nature to spread them a green lawn for their disport in the midst of those solemn fastnesses, as that I should fly out of my orbit at their approach and go about eccentric, like a comet, to endanger other systems. No, be true to your instincts, and sit; wait till you can be genuinely polite, if it be till doomsday, and not lose your chance everlastingly by a cowardly yielding to young etiquette. By your look say unto them, The lines have fallen to me in pleasant places, and I will fill that station God has assigned me. As well Miss Cassiopeia up there might ask the brazen-fronted Taurus to draw in his horns, that she might shine in his stead. No, no! not till my cycle is completed.

How is it that motion will always find space to move in, and rest a seat? Men hate antagonism, and the weaker will always yield to the stronger. If a stranger enter with sufficient determination into a crowded assembly, as if commissioned by the gods to find a seat there, as the falling stone by a divine impulse seeks a resting-place, each one will rise without thinking to offer his place. Now we have only to be commissioned to sit, and depend upon it the gods will not balk their own work. Ye came one day too late, as did the poet after the world had been divided, and so returned to dwell with the god that sent him. When presumptuous womanhood demands to surrender my position, I bide my time, — though it be with misgiving, — and yield to no mortal shove, but expect a divine impulse. Produce your warrant, and I will retire; for not now can I give you a clear seat, but must leave part of my manhood behind and wander a diminished man, who at length will not have length and breadth enough to fill any seat at all. It was very kind in the gods who gave us a now condition, or condition of rest, in which we might unhurriedly deliberate before taking a step. When I give up my now and here without having secured my then and there, I am the prodigal son of a kind father and deserve no better than the husks which the swine eat, nor that the fatted calf be killed for me.

Rest forever. When instinct comes to the rescue of your politeness, it will seat you securely still, though it be to hang by a rail or poise yourself on a stick. To do otherwise is to be polite only as the soldier who runs away when the enemy demands his post. Politeness is rather when the generals interchange civilities before the fight, not when one returns a sword after the victory.

Not only in his cunning hand and brain, but when he speaks, too, does man assert his superiority. He conquers the spaces with his voice, as well as the lion. The voice of a strong man modulated to the cadence of some tune is more imposing than any natural sound. The keeper's is the most commanding, and is heard over all the din of the menagerie. A strong, musical voice imposes a new order and harmony upon nature; from it as a centre the law is promulgated to the universe. What it lacks in volume and loudness may

always be made up in musical expression and distinctness. The brute growls to secure obedience; he threatens. The man speaks as though obedience were already secured.

Brave speaking is the most entire and richest sacrifice to the gods.

Feb. 5. Friday. Only on rare occasions am I reminded that man too has a voice, as well as birds and quadrupeds, which breaks on the stillness of nature with its peculiar accent. The least sound pervades and subdues all space to it as long as it fills my ear. Contrasted single with the silence, it is as wide as it. Music is the crystallization of sound. There is something in the effect of a harmonious voice upon the disposition of its neighborhood analogous to the law of crystals; it centralizes itself and sounds like the published law of things. If the law of the universe were to be audibly promulgated, no mortal lawgiver would suspect it, for it would be a finer melody than his ears ever attended to. It would be sphere music.[1]

When by tutoring their voices singers enhance one another's performance, the harmony is more complete and essential than is heard. The quire is one family held together by a very close bond. Hence the romance we associate with Gypsies and circus companies and strolling musicians. The idea of brotherhood is so strong in them. Their society is ideal for that one end.

[1] [*Week*, p. 184; Riv. 228.]

Vol. I

There is something in this brotherhood — this feeling of kind, or kindness — which insensibly elevates the subjects of it in our eyes. However poor or mean, they have something which counterbalances our contempt. This is that in the strolling pauper *family* which does not court our charity but can even bless and smile on us and make the kindness reciprocal. It sanctifies the place and the hour.

These Rainers, if they are not brothers and sisters, must be uncles and cousins at least. These Swiss who have come to sing to us, we have no doubt are the flower of the Tyrol.[1] Such is the instinctive kindness with which the foreigner is always received, that he is ever presumed to be the fairest and noblest of his race. The traveller finds that it is not easy to move away from his friends, after all, but all people whom he visits are anxious to supply the place to him of his parents and brothers and sisters. To these Swiss I find that I have attributed all Tell's patriotism and the devotion of Arnold Winkelried and whatever goodness or greatness belongs to the nation.

All costume off a man, when not simply doffed, is grotesque. There must be a heart inside it. When these Swiss appear before me in gaiters and high-crowned hats with feathers, I am disposed to laugh, but soon I see that their serious eye becomes these and they it. It is the sincere life passed within it which consecrates the costume of any people. A sufficiently sober eye will

[1] [See Emerson's Journal (1841), quoted in E. W. Emerson's *Emerson in Concord*, p. 99.]

retrieve itself and subordinate any grotesqueness. Let Harlequin be taken with a fit of the colic in the midst of his buffoonery, and his trappings and finery will serve that mood too and with their drooping sympathy enhance the sincerity of his misfortune. When the soldier is hit by a cannon-ball, rags are as becoming as purple.[1] So soon as a man engages to eat, drink, sleep, walk, and sit, and meet all the contingencies of life therein, his costume is hallowed and a theme for poetry, whether it be a bear's skin or ermine, a beaver hat or a Turkish turban. He will not wear anything because it is blue, or black, or round, or square, but from a necessity which cannot be superseded.

I look into the face and manners for something familiar and homely even, to be assured that the costume of the foreigner is not whimsical or finical.

In all emergencies there is always one step which you may take on firm ground where gravity will assure you footing. So you hold a draft on Fate payable at sight.

Feb. 6. Saturday. One may discover a new side to his most intimate friend when for the first time he hears him speak in public. He will be stranger to him as he is more familiar to the audience. The longest intimacy could not foretell how he would behave then. When I observe my friend's conduct toward others, then chiefly I learn the traits in his character, and in each case I am unprepared for the issue.

When one gets up to address briefly a strange audi-

[1] [*Walden*, p. 28; Riv. 43.]

ence, in that little he may have opportunity to say he will not quite do himself injustice. For he will instantly and instinctively average himself to his audience, and while he is true to his own character still, he will in a few moments make that impression which a series of months and years would but expand. Before he answers, his thought like lightning runs round the whole compass of his experiences, and he is scrupulous to speak from that which he is and with a more entire truthfulness than usual. How little do we know each other then! Who can tell how his friend would behave on any occasion?

As for those Swiss, I think of the fields their hands have plowed and reaped, and respect their costume as the memorial or rather cotemporary and witness of this. What is there in a toga but a Roman? What but a Quaker in a broad-brimmed hat? He who describes the dress of a Janizary going to war does me a similar service as when he paints the scenery of the battle-field. It helps make his exploit picturesque.

Costume is not determined by whim, not even the tattooing and paint of the savage. Sun, wind, rain, and the form of our bodies shape our hats and coats for us, more even than taste. Good taste secures the utmost gratification without sacrificing any conveniences. If all nations derived their fashions from Paris or London, the world would seem like a Vanity Fair or all fools' day, and the Tartar and Bedouin ride in it like jesters in a circus, and the Pawnee and Esquimau hunt in masquerade. What I am must make you forget what I

wear. The fashionable world is content to be eclipsed by its dress, and never will bear the contrast. Only industry will reform *their* dress. They are idle, — *exostrious*, building without.

The value of the recess in any public entertainment consists in the opportunity for self-recovery which it offers. We who have been swayed as one heart, expanding and contracting with the common pulse, find ourselves in the interim, and set us up again, and feel our own hearts beating in our breasts. We are always a little astonished to see a man walking across the room, through an attentive audience, with any degree of self-possession. He makes himself strange to us. He is a little stubborn withal, and seems to say, "I am self-sustained and independent as well as the performer, and am not to be swallowed up in the common enthusiasm. No, no, there are two of us, and John's as good as Thomas." In the recess the audience is cut up into a hundred little coteries, and as soon as each individual life has recovered its tone and the purposes of health have been answered, it is time for the performances to commence again.

In a public performer, the simplest actions, which at other times are left to unconscious nature, as the ascending a few steps in front of an audience, acquire a fatal importance and become arduous deeds.

When I select one here and another there, and strive to join sundered thoughts, I make but a partial heap

after all. Nature strews her nuts and flowers broadcast, and never collects them into heaps. A man does not tell us all he has thought upon truth or beauty at a sitting, but, from his last thought on the subject, wanders through a varied scenery of upland, meadow, and woodland to his next. Sometimes a single and casual thought rises naturally and inevitably with a queenly majesty and escort, like the stars in the east. Fate has surely enshrined it in this hour and circumstances for some purpose. What she has joined together, let not man put asunder. Shall I transplant the primrose by the river's brim, to set it beside its sister on the mountain? *This* was the soil it grew in, *this* the hour it bloomed in. If sun, wind, and rain came *here* to cherish and expand it, shall not we come here to pluck it? Shall we require it to grow in a conservatory for our convenience?

I feel slightly complimented when Nature condescends to make use of me without my knowledge, as when I help scatter her seeds in my walk, or carry burs and cockles on my clothes from field to field.[1] I feel as though I had done something for the commonweal, and were entitled to board and lodging. I take such airs upon me as the boy who holds a horse for the circus company, whom all the spectators envy.

"Lu ral lu ral lu" may be more impressively sung than very respectable wisdom talked. It is well-timed, as wisdom is not always.

[1] [*Week*, p. 415; Riv. 512.]

All things prophesy but the prophet. In augury and divination nature is put to the torture. In Ben Jonson's tragedy of "Catiline," Lentulus makes answer to Catiline, who has bribed the augurs to say that he is that third Cornelius who is to be king of Rome, "All prophecies, you know, suffer the torture." He who inspects the entrails is *always* bribed, but they are unbribable. He who seeks to know the future by unlawful means has unavoidably subjected the oracle to the torture of *private* and *partial* interests. The oracles of God serve the public interest without fee. To the just and benevolent mind nature *declares*, as the sun lights the world.

Feb. 7. *Sunday.* Without greatcoat or drawers I have advanced thus far into the snow-banks of the winter, without thought and with impunity.[1] When I meet my neighbors in muffs and furs and tippets, they look as if they had retreated into the interior fastnesses from some foe invisible to me. They remind me that this is the season of winter, in which it becomes a man to be cold. For feeling, I am a piece of clean wood of this shape, which will do service till it rots, and though the cold has its physical effect on me, it is a kindly one, for it "finds its acquaintance there." My diet is so little stimulating, and my body in consequence so little heated, as to excite no antagonism in nature, but flourishes like a tree, which finds even the winter genial to its expansion and the secretion of sap. May not the body defend itself against cold by its very nakedness, and its elements be so simple and single that they cannot congeal? Frost

[1] [See p. 214, — bronchitis!]

does not affect one but several. My body now affords no more pasture for cold than a leafless twig.[1] I call it a protestant warmth. My limbs do not tire as formerly, but I use myself as any other piece of nature, and from mere indifference and thoughtlessness may break the timber.

It is the vice of the last season which compels us to arm ourselves for the next. If man always conformed to Nature, he would not have to defend himself against her, but find her his constant nurse and friend, as do plants and quadrupeds.

In the sunshine and the crowing of cocks I feel an illimitable holiness, which makes me bless God and myself. The warm sun casts his incessant gift at my feet as I walk along, unfolding his yellow worlds. Yonder sexton with a few cheap sounds makes me richer than these who mind his summons. The true gift is as wide as my gratitude, and as frequent, and the donor is as grateful as the recipient. There would be a New Year's gift indeed, if we would bestow on each other our sincerity. We should communicate our wealth, and not purchase that which does not belong to us for a sign. Why give each other a sign to keep? If we gave the thing itself, there would be no need of a sign.

I am not sure I should find out a really great person soon. He would be simple Thomas or Oliver for some centuries first. The lesser eminences would hide

[1] [*Excursions*, p. 167; Riv. 203, 204.]

the higher, and I should at last reach his top by a gentle acclivity. I felt it would be necessary to remain some weeks at the Notch to be impressed by the grandeur of the scenery. We do not expect that Alexander will conquer Asia the first time we are introduced to him. A great man accepts the occasion the fates offer him. Let us not be disappointed. We stand at first upon the pampas which surround him. It is these mountains round about which make the valleys here below. He is not a dead level, so many feet above low-water mark. Greatness is in the ascent. But there is no accounting for the little men.

> "They must sweat no less
> To fit their properties, than t' express their parts."

Or the line before this: —

> "Would you have
> Such an Herculean actor in the scene,
> And not his hydra?" — JONSON.

The eaves are running on the south side of the house; the titmouse lisps in the poplar; the bells are ringing for church; while the sun presides over all and makes his simple warmth more obvious than all else.[1] What shall I do with this hour, so like time and yet so fit for eternity? Where in me are these russet patches of ground, and scattered logs and chips in the yard? I do not feel cluttered. I have some notion what the John's-wort and life-everlasting may be thinking about when the sun shines on me as on them and turns my prompt thought into just such a seething shimmer. I lie out in-

[1] [*Excursions*, p. 173; Riv. 211.]

distinct as a heath at noonday. I am evaporating and ascending into the sun.

Nothing stands in the way to success, but to failure. To victory is all the way up hill; to defeat the simplest wight that weighs may soon slide down. Cowards would not have victory but the fruits of victory; but she it is that sweetens all the spoil. Thus, by a just fate, the booty cannot fall to him who did not win it. There is victory in every effort. In the least swing of the arm, in indignant thought, in stern content, we conquer our foes.

Great thoughts make great men. Without these no heraldry nor blood will avail.

The blood circulates to the feet and hands, but the thought never descends from the head.

The most I can do for my friend is simply to be his friend. I have no wealth to bestow on him. If he knows that I am happy in loving him, he will want no other reward. Is not Friendship divine in this?

I have myself to respect, but to myself I am not amiable; but my friend is my amiableness personified.

And yet we walk the stage indifferent actors, not thinking what a sublime drama we might enact if we would be joint workers and a mutual material. Why go to the woods to cut timber to display our art upon, when here are men as trees walking? The world has never learned what men can build each other up to be, when both master and pupil work in love.

He that comes as a stranger to my house will have to stay as a stranger. He has made his own reception. But persevering love was never yet refused.

> "The vicious count their years, virtuous their acts."
> JONSON.

The former consider the length of their service, the latter its quality.

> Wait not till I invite thee, but observe
> I'm glad to see thee when thou com'st.[1]

The most ardent lover holds yet a private court, and his love can never be so strong or ethereal that there will not be danger that judgment may be rendered against the beloved.

I would have men make a *greater* use of me.[2] Now I must belittle myself to have dealings with them. My friend will show such a noble confidence that I shall aspire to the society of his good opinion. Never presume men less that you may make them more. So far as we respond to our ideal estimate of each other do we have profitable intercourse.

A brave man always knows the way, no matter how intricate the roads.

Feb. 8. All we have experienced is so much gone within us, and there lies. It is the company we keep. One day,

[1] [*Week*, p. 289; Riv. 359.]   [2] [See p. 180.]

in health or sickness, it will come out and be remembered. Neither body nor soul forgets anything. The twig always remembers the wind that shook it, and the stone the cuff it received. Ask the old tree and the sand.

To be of most service to my brother I must meet him on the most equal and even ground, the platform on which our lives are passing. But how often does politeness permit this?

I seek a man who will appeal to me when I am in fault. We will treat as gods settling the affairs of men. In his intercourse I shall be always a god to-day, who was a man yesterday. He will never confound me with my guilt, but let me be immaculate and hold up my skirts. Differences he will make haste to clear up, but leave agreements unsettled the while.

As time is measured by the lapse of ideas, we may grow of our own force, as the mussel adds new circles to its shell. My thoughts secrete the lime. We may grow old with the vigor of youth. Are we not always in youth so long as we face heaven? We may always live in the morning of our days. To him who seeks early, the sun never gets over the edge of the hill, but his rays fall slanting forever. His wise sayings are like the chopping of wood and crowing of cocks in the dawn.

My Journal is that of me which would else spill over and run to waste, gleanings from the field which in action I reap. I must not live for it, but in it for the gods.

They are my correspondent, to whom daily I send off this sheet postpaid. I am clerk in their counting-room, and at evening transfer the account from day-book to ledger. It is as a leaf which hangs over my head in the path. I bend the twig and write my prayers on it; then letting it go, the bough springs up and shows the scrawl to heaven. As if it were not kept shut in my desk, but were as public a leaf as any in nature. It is papyrus by the riverside; it is vellum in the pastures; it is parchment on the hills. I find it everywhere as free as the leaves which troop along the lanes in autumn. The crow, the goose, the eagle carry my quill, and the wind blows the leaves as far as I go. Or, if my imagination does not soar, but gropes in slime and mud, then I write with a reed.

It is always a chance scrawl, and commemorates some accident, — as great as earthquake or eclipse. Like the sere leaves in yonder vase, these have been gathered far and wide. Upland and lowland, forest and field have been ransacked.

In our holiest moment our devil with a leer stands close at hand. He is a very busy devil. It gains vice some respect, I must confess, thus to be reminded how indefatigable it is. It has at least the merit of industriousness. When I go forth with zeal to some good work, my devil is sure to get his robe tucked up the first and arrives there as soon as I, with a look of sincere earnestness which puts to shame my best intent. He is as forward as I to a good work, and as disinterested. He has a winning way of recommending himself by mak-

ing himself useful. How readily he comes into my best project, and does his work with a quiet and steady cheerfulness which even virtue may take pattern from.

I never was so rapid in my virtue but my vice kept up with me. It always came in by a hand, and never panting, but with a curried coolness halted, as if halting were the beginning not the end of the course. It only runs the swifter because it has no rider. It never was behind me but when I turned to look and so fell behind myself. I never did a charitable thing but there he stood, scarce in the rear, with hat in hand, partner on the same errand, ready to share the smile of gratitude. Though I shut the door never so quick and tell it to stay at home like a good dog, it will out with me, for I shut in my own legs so, and it escapes in the meanwhile and is ready to back and reinforce me in most virtuous deeds. And if I turn and say, " Get thee behind me," he then indeed turns too and takes the lead, though he seems to retire with a pensive and compassionate look, as much as to say, " Ye know not what ye do."

Just as active as I become to virtue, just so active is my remaining vice. Every time we teach our virtue a new nobleness, we teach our vice a new cunning. When we sharpen the blade it will stab better as well as whittle. The scythe that cuts will cut our legs. We are double-edged blades, and every time we whet our virtue the return stroke straps our vice. And when we cut a clear descending blow, our vice on tother edge rips up the work. Where is the skillful swordsman that can draw his blade straight back out of the wound?[1]

[1] [Week, p. 236; Riv. 293.]

Every man proposes fairly, and does not willfully take the devil for his guide; as our shadows never fall between us and the sun. Go towards the sun and your shadow will fall behind you.

Feb. 9. Tuesday.

"*Cato.* Good Marcus Tullius (which is more than great),
    Thou hadst thy education with the gods."
                                                    JONSON.

Better be defamed than overpraised. Thou canst then justly praise thyself. What notoriety art thou that can be defamed? Who can be praised for what they are not deserve rather to be damned for what they are. It is hard to wear a dress that is too long and loose without stumbling.
                    " Whoe'er is raised,
    For wealth he has not, he is tax'd, not prais'd,"
says Jonson. If you mind the flatterer, you rob yourself and still cheat him. The fates never exaggerate; men pass for what they are. The state never fails to get a revenue out of you without a direct tax. Flattery would lay a direct tax. What I am praised for what I am not I put to the account of the gods. It needs a skillful eye to distinguish between their coin and my own. But however there can be no loss either way, for what meed I have earned is equally theirs. Let neither fame nor infamy hit you, but the one go as far beyond as the other falls behind. Let the one glance past you to the gods, and the other wallow where it was engendered. The home thrusts are at helmets upon blocks, and my worst foes but stab an armor through.

My life at this moment is like a summer morning when birds are singing. Yet that is false, for nature's is an idle pleasure in comparison: my hour has a more solid serenity. I have been breaking silence these twenty-three years and have hardly made a rent in it. Silence has no end; speech is but the beginning of it. My friend thinks I *keep* silence, who am only choked with letting it out so fast. Does he forget that new mines of secrecy are constantly opening in me?

If any scorn your love, let them see plainly that you serve not them but another. If these bars are up, go your way to other of God's pastures, and browse there the while. When your host shuts his door on you he incloses you in the dwelling of nature. He thrusts you over the threshold of the world. My foes restore me to my friends.

I might say friendship had no ears as love has no eyes, for no word is evidence in its court. The least act fulfills more than all words profess. The most gracious speech is but partial kindness, but the least genuine deed takes the whole man. If we had waited till doomsday it could never have been uttered.

Feb. 10. *Wednesday.* That was fine praise which Ben Jonson gave to Thomas, Lord Chancellor: —

> "Whilst thou art certain to thy words, once gone,
> As is thy conscience, which is always one."

Words do not lose their truth by time or misinterpretation, but stand unscathed longer than he who spoke them.

Let our words be such as we may unblushingly behold sculptured in granite on the walls to the least syllable. Our thoughts and actions may be very private for a long time, for they demand a more catholic publicity to be displayed in than the world can afford. Our best deeds shun the narrow walks of men, and are not ambitious of the faint light the world can shed on them, but delight to unfold themselves in that public ground between God and conscience.

Truth has for audience and spectator all the world. Within, where I resolve and deal with principles, there is more space and room than anywhere without, where my hands execute. Men should hear of your virtue only as they hear the creaking of the earth's axle and the music of the spheres. It will fall into the course of nature and be effectually concealed by publicness.

I asked a man to-day if he would rent me some land, and he said he had four acres as good soil "as any outdoors." It was a true poet's account of it. He and I, and all the world, went outdoors to breathe the free air and stretch ourselves. For the world is but outdoors, — and we duck behind a panel.

Feb. 11. True help, for the most part, implies a greatness in him who is to be helped as well as in the helper. It takes a god to be helped even. A great person, though unconsciously, will constantly give you great opportunities to serve him, but a mean one will quite preclude all active benevolence. It needs but simply and *greatly* to want it for once, that all true men may contend who

shall be foremost to render aid. My neighbor's state must pray to heaven so devoutly yet disinterestedly as he never prayed in words, before my ears can hear. It must ask divinely. But men so cobble and botch their request, that you must stoop as low as they to give them aid. Their meanness would drag down your deed to be a compromise with conscience, and not leave it to be done on the high table-land of the benevolent soul. They would have you doff your bright and knightly armor and drudge for them, — serve *them* and not God. But if I am to serve them I must not serve the devil.

What is called charity is no charity, but the interference of a third person. Shall I interfere with fate? Shall I defraud man of the opportunities which God gave him, and so take away his life? Beggars and silent poor cry — how often! — "Get between me and my god." I will not stay to cobble and patch God's rents, but do clean, new work when he has given me my hands full. This almshouse charity is like putting new wine into old bottles, when so many tuns in God's cellars stand empty. We go about mending the times, when we should be building the eternity.

I must serve a strong master, not a weak one. Help implies a sympathy of energy and effort, else no alleviation will avail.

Feb. 12. *Friday.* Those great men who are unknown to their own generation are already famous in the society of the great who have gone before them. All worldly fame but subsides from their high estimate beyond the

Vol. I

stars. We may still keep pace with those who have gone out of nature, for we run on as smooth ground as they.

The early and the latter saints are separated by no eternal interval.

The child may soon stand face to face with the best father.

Feb. 13. By the truthfulness of our story to-day we help explain ourselves for all our life henceforth. How we hamper and belay ourselves by the least exaggeration! The truth is God's concern; He will sustain it; but who can afford to maintain a lie? We have taken away one of the Pillars of Hercules, and must support the world on our shoulders, who might have walked freely upon it.

My neighbor says that his hill-farm is poor stuff and "only fit to hold the world together." [1] He deserves that God should give him better for so brave a treating of his gifts, instead of humbly putting up therewith. It is a sort of stay, or gore, or gusset, and he will not be blinded by modesty or gratitude, but sees it for what it is; knowing his neighbor's fertile land, he calls his by its right name. But perhaps my farmer forgets that his lean soil has sharpened his wits. This is a crop it was good for. [2] And beside, you see the heavens at a lesser angle from the hill than from the vale.

We have nothing to fear from our foes; God keeps a standing army for that service; but we have no ally

---

[1] [*Week*, p. 50; Riv. 63.]　　　[2] [*Week*, first edition, p. 71.]

against our friends, those ruthless vandals whose kind intent is a subtler poison than the Colchian, a more fatal shaft than the Lydian.[1]

Feb. 14. *Sunday.* I am confined to the house by bronchitis, and so seek to content myself with that quiet and serene life there is in a warm corner by the fireside, and see the sky through the chimney-top. Sickness should not be allowed to extend further than the body. We need only to retreat further within us to preserve uninterrupted the continuity of serene hours to the end of our lives.

As soon as I find my chest is not of tempered steel, and heart of adamant, I bid good-by to these and look out a new nature. I will be liable to no accidents.

I shall never be poor while I can command a still hour in which to take leave of my sin.

The jingling team which is creaking past reminds me of that verse in the Bible which speaks of God being heard in the bells of the horses.

Feb. 15. There is elevation in every hour. No part of the earth is so low and withdrawn that the heavens cannot be seen from it, but every part supports the sky. We have only to stand on the eminence of the hour, and look out thence into the empyrean, allowing no pinnacle above us, to command an uninterrupted horizon. The moments will lie outspread around us like a blue ex-

[1] [*Week*, p. 305 ; Riv. 379.]

panse of mountain and valley, while we stand on the summit of our hour as if we had descended on eagle's wings. For the eagle has stooped to his perch on the highest cliff and has never climbed the rock; he stands by his wings more than by his feet. We shall not want a foothold, but wings will sprout from our shoulders, and we shall walk securely, self-sustained.

For how slight an accident shall two noble souls wait to bring them together!

Feb. 17. Our work should be fitted to and lead on the time, as bud, flower, and fruit lead the circle of the seasons.

The mechanic works no longer than his labor will pay for lights, fuel, and shop rent. Would it not be well for us to consider if our deed will warrant the expense of nature? Will it maintain the sun's light?

Our actions do not use time independently, as the bud does. They should constitute its lapse. It is their room. But they shuffle after and serve the hour.

Feb. 18. *Thursday.* I do not judge men by anything they can do. Their greatest deed is the impression they make on me. Some serene, inactive men can do everything. Talent only indicates a depth of character in some direction. We do not acquire the ability to do new deeds, but a new capacity for all deeds. My recent growth does not appear in any visible new talent, but

its deed will enter into my gaze when I look into the sky, or vacancy. It will help me to consider ferns and everlasting. Man is like a tree which is limited to no age, but grows as long as it has its root in the ground. We have only to live in the alburnum and not in the old wood. The gnarled stump has as tender a bud as the sapling.

Sometimes I find that I have frequented a higher society during sleep, and my thoughts and actions proceed on a higher level in the morning.

A man is the hydrostatic paradox, the counterpoise of the system. You have studied flowers and birds cheaply enough, but you must lay yourself out to buy him.

Feb. 19. A truly good book attracts very little favor to itself. It is so true that it teaches me better than to read it. I must soon lay it down and commence living on its hint. I do not see how any can be written more, but this is the last effusion of genius. When I read an indifferent book, it seems the best thing I can do, but the inspiring volume hardly leaves me leisure to finish its latter pages. It is slipping out of my fingers while I read. It creates no atmosphere in which it may be perused, but one in which its teachings may be practiced. It confers on me such wealth that I lay it down with the least regret. What I began by reading I must finish by acting. So I cannot stay to hear a *good* sermon and applaud at the conclusion, but shall be half-way to Thermopylæ before that.

When any joke or hoax traverses the Union in the newspapers it apprises me of a fact which no geography or guide-book contains, of a certain leisure and nonchalance pervading society. It is a piece of information from over the Alleghanies, which I know how to prize, though I did not expect it. And it is just so in Nature. I sometimes observe in her a strange trifling, almost listlessness, which conducts to beauty and grace, — the fantastic and whimsical forms of snow and ice, the unaccountable freaks which the tracks of rabbits exhibit. I know now why all those busy speculators do not die of fever and ague.

Coleridge observed the "landscapes made by damp on a whitewashed wall," and so have I.

We seem but to linger in manhood to tell the dreams of our childhood, and they vanish out of memory ere we learn the language.[1]

It is the unexplored grandeur of the storm which keeps up the spirits of the traveller.[2] When I contemplate a hard and bare life in the woods, I find my last consolation in its untriviality. Shipwreck is less distressing because the breakers do not trifle with us. We are resigned as long as we recognize the sober and solemn mystery of nature. The dripping mariner finds consolation and sympathy in the infinite sublimity of the storm. It is a moral force as well as he. With courage he can lay down his life on the strand, for it never

[1] [*Week*, p. 406 ; Riv. 501.]   [2] [*Excursions*, p. 182 ; Riv. 222.]

turned a deaf ear to him, nor has he ever exhausted its sympathy.

In the love of narrow souls I make many short voyages, but in vain; I find no sea-room. But in great souls I sail before the wind without a watch, and never reach the shore.

You demand that I be less your friend that you may know it.

Nothing will reconcile friends but love. They make a fatal mistake when they go about like foes to explain and treat with one another. It is a mutual mistake. None are so unmanageable.

Feb. 20. Saturday. I suspect the moral discrimination of the oldest and best authors. I doubt if Milton distinguished greatly between his Satan and his Raphael. In Homer and Æschylus and Dante I miss a nice discrimination of the *important* shades of character.

When I am going out for an evening I arrange the fire in my stove so that I do not fail to find a good one when I return, though it would have engaged my frequent attention present. So that, when I know I am to be at home, I sometimes make believe that I may go out, to save trouble. And this is the art of living, too, — to leave our life in a condition to go alone, and not to require a constant supervision. We will then sit down serenely to live, as by the side of a stove.

When I sit in earnest, nothing must stand, all must be sedentary with me.

I hear the faint sound of a viol and voices from the neighboring cottage, and think to myself, "I will believe the Muse only for evermore." It assures me that no gleam which comes over the serene soul is deceptive. It warns me of a reality and substance, of which the best that I see is but the phantom and shadow. O music, thou tellest me of things of which memory takes no heed; thy strains are whispered aside from memory's ear.

This is the noblest plain of earth, over which these sounds are borne, the plain of Troy or Eleusis.

Thou openest all my senses to catch thy least hint, and givest me no thought. It would be good to sit at my door of summer evenings forever and hear thy strains. Thou makest me to toy with speech, or walk content without it, not regretting its absence. I am pleased to think how ignorant and shiftless the wisest are. My imperfect sympathies with my friend are cheerful, glimmering light in the valley.

Feb. 21. Sunday. It is hard to preserve equanimity and greatness on that debatable ground between love and esteem. There is nothing so stable and unfluctuating as love. The waves beat steadfast on its shore forever, and its tide has no ebb. It is a resource in all extremities, and a refuge even from itself. And yet love will not be leaned on.

Feb. 22. Love is the tenderest mood of that which is tough — and the toughest mood of that which is tender. It may be roughly handled as the nettle, or gently as the violet. It has its holidays, but is not made for them.

The whole of the day should not be daytime, nor of the night night-time, but some portion be rescued from time to oversee time in. All our hours must not be current; all our time must not lapse. There must be one hour at least which the day did not bring forth, — of ancient parentage and long-established nobility, — which will be a serene and lofty platform overlooking the rest. We should make our notch every day on our characters, as Robinson Crusoe on his stick. We must be at the helm at least once a day; we must feel the tiller-rope in our hands, and know that if we sail, we steer.

Friends will be much apart; they will respect more each other's privacy than their communion, for therein is the fulfillment of our high aims and the conclusion of our arguments. That we know and would associate with not only has high intents, but goes on high errands, and has much private business. The hours he devotes to me were snatched from higher society. He is hardly a gift level to me, but I have to reach up to take it. My imagination always assigns him a nobler employment in my absence than ever I find him engaged in.[1]

We have to go into retirement religiously, and en-

[1] [*Week,* p. 288; Riv. 358.]

hance our meeting by rarity and a degree of unfamiliarity. Would you know why I see thee so seldom, my friend? In solitude I have been making up a packet for thee.

The actions which grow out of some common but natural relations affect me strangely, as sometimes the behavior of a mother to her children. So quiet and noiseless an action often moves me more than many sounding exploits.

Feb. 23. Tuesday. Let all our stores and munitions be provided for the lone state.

The care of the body is the highest exercise of prudence. If I have brought this weakness on my lungs, I will consider calmly and disinterestedly how the thing came about, that I may find out the truth and render justice. Then, after patience, I shall be a wiser man than before.

Let us apply all our wit to the repair of our bodies, as we would mend a harrow, for the body will be dealt plainly and implicitly with. We want no moonshine nor surmises about it. This matter of health and sickness has no fatality in it, but is a subject for the merest prudence. If I know not what ails me, I may resort to amulets and charms and, moonstruck, die of dysentery.

We do wrong to slight our sickness and feel so ready to desert our posts when we are harassed. So much the more should we rise above our condition, and make the most of it, for the fruit of disease may be as good as that of health.[1]

There is a subtle elixir in society which makes it a fountain of health to the sick. We want no consolation which is not the overflow of our friend's health. We will have no condolence who are not dolent ourselves. We would have our friend come and respire healthily before us, with the fragrance of many meadows and heaths in his breath, and we will inhabit his body while our own recruits.

Nothing is so good medicine in sickness as to witness some nobleness in another which will advertise us of health. In sickness it is our faith that ails, and noble deeds reassure us.

That anybody has thought of you on some indifferent occasion frequently implies more good will than you had reason to expect. You have henceforth a higher motive for conduct. We do not know how many amiable thoughts are current.

Feb. 26. Friday. My prickles or smoothness are as much a quality of your hand as of myself. I cannot tell you what I am, more than a ray of the summer's sun. What I am I am, and say not. Being is the great explainer. In the attempt to explain, shall I plane away all the spines, till it is no thistle, but a cornstalk?

[1] [See his sister's account of his last sickness in Sanborn's *Thoreau*, pp. 310–313.]

fragrance comes in at all my senses which proclaims that I am still of Nature the child. The threshing in yonder barn and the tinkling of the anvil come from the same side of Styx with me. If I were a physician I would try my patients thus. I would wheel them to a window and let Nature feel their pulse. It will soon appear if their sensuous existence is sound. These sounds are but the throbbing of some pulse in me.[1]

Nature seems to have given me these hours to pry into her private drawers. I watch the shadow of the insensible perspiration rising from my coat or hand on the wall. I go and feel my pulse in all the recesses of the house and see if I am of force to carry a homely life and comfort into them.

Feb. 27. Saturday. Life looks as fair at this moment as a summer's sea, or a blond dress in a saffron light, with its sun and grass and walled towns so bright and chaste, as fair as my own virtue which would adventure therein. Like a Persian city or hanging gardens in the distance, so washed in light, so untried, only to be thridded by clean thoughts. All its flags are flowing, and tassels streaming, and drapery flapping, like some gay pavilion. The heavens hang over it like some low screen, and seem to undulate in the breeze.

Through this pure, unwiped hour, as through a crystal glass, I look out upon the future, as a smooth lawn for my virtue to disport in. It shows from afar as unrepulsive as the sunshine upon walls and cities, over

[1] [*Excursions*, p. 182; Riv. 223.]

If my world is not sufficient without thee, my friend, I will wait till it is and then call thee. You shall come to a palace, not to an almshouse.

My homeliest thought, like the diamond brought from farthest within the mine, will shine with the purest lustre.

Though I write every day, yet when I say a good thing it seems as if I wrote but rarely.

To be great, we do as if we would be tall merely, be longer than we are broad, stretch ourselves and stand on tiptoe. But greatness is well proportioned, unstrained, and stands on the soles of the feet.

How many are waiting for health and warm weather! But they wait for none.

In composition I miss the hue of the mind. As if we could be satisfied with the dews of the morning and evening without their colors, or the heavens without their azure.[1]

This good book helps the sun shine in my chamber. The rays fall on its page as if to explain and illustrate it.[2]

I who have been sick hear cattle low in the street, with such a healthy ear as prophesies my cure. These sounds lay a finger on my pulse to some purpose. A

[1] [*Week*, p. 106; Riv. 132.]   [2] [*Week*, p. 157; Riv. 195.]

which the passing life moves as gently as a shadow. I see the course of my life, like some retired road, wind on without obstruction into a country maze.[1]

I am attired for the future so, as the sun setting presumes all men at leisure and in contemplative mood, — and am thankful that it is thus presented blank and indistinct. It still o'ertops my hope. My future deeds bestir themselves within me and move grandly towards a consummation, as ships go down the Thames. A steady onward motion I feel in me, as still as that, or like some vast, snowy cloud, whose shadow first is seen across the fields. It is the material of all things loose and set afloat that makes my sea.

These various words are not without various meanings. The combined voice of the race makes nicer distinctions than any individual. There are the words "diversion" and "amusement." It takes more to amuse than to divert. We must be surrendered to our amusements, but only turned aside to our diversions. We have no will in the former, but oversee the latter. We are oftenest diverted in the street, but amused in our chambers. We are diverted from our engagements, but amused when we are listless. We may be diverted from an amusement, and amused by a diversion. It often happens that a diversion becomes our amusement, and our amusement our employment.

Feb. 28. Nothing goes by luck in composition. It allows of no tricks. The best you can write will be the

[1] [See *Week*, p. 45; Riv. 57.]

best you are. Every sentence is the result of a long probation. The author's character is read from title-page to end. Of this he never corrects the proofs. We read it as the essential character of a handwriting without regard to the flourishes. And so of the rest of our actions; it runs as straight as a ruled line through them all, no matter how many curvets about it. Our whole life is taxed for the least thing well done; it is its net result. How we eat, drink, sleep, and use our desultory hours, now in these indifferent days, with no eye to observe and no occasion [to] excite us, determines our authority and capacity for the time to come.

March 3. I hear a man blowing a horn this still evening, and it sounds like the plaint of nature in these times. In this, which I refer to some man, there is something greater than any man. It is as if the earth spoke. It adds a great remoteness to the horizon, and its very distance is grand, as when one draws back the head to speak. That which I now hear in the west seems like an invitation to the east. It runs round the earth as a whisper gallery. It is the spirit of the West calling to the spirit of the East, or else it is the rattling of some team lagging in Day's train. Coming to me through the darkness and silence, all things great seem transpiring there. It is friendly as a distant hermit's taper. When it is trilled, or undulates, the heavens are crumpled into time, and successive waves flow across them.

It is a strangely healthy sound for these disjointed times. It is a rare soundness when cow-bells and horns are heard from over the fields. And now I see the beauty

and full meaning of that word "sound." Nature always possesses a certain sonorousness, as in the hum of insects, the booming of ice, the crowing of cocks in the morning, and the barking of dogs in the night, which indicates her sound state.[1] God's voice is but a clear bell sound. I drink in a wonderful health, a cordial, in sound. The effect of the slightest tinkling in the horizon measures my own soundness. I thank God for sound; it always mounts, and makes me mount. I think I will not trouble myself for any wealth, when I can be so cheaply enriched. Here I contemplate to drudge that I may own a farm — and may have such a limitless estate for the listening. All good things are cheap: all bad are very dear.

As for these communities, I think I had rather keep bachelor's hall in hell than go to board in heaven. Do you think your virtue will be boarded with you? It will never live on the interest of your money, depend upon it. The boarder has no home. In heaven I hope to bake my own bread and clean my own linen. The tomb is the only boarding-house in which a hundred are served at once. In the catacomb we may dwell together and prop one another without loss.

March 4. Ben Jonson says in his epigrams, —

"He makes himself a thorough-fare of Vice."

This is true, for by vice the substance of a man is not changed, but all his pores, and cavities, and avenues are

[1] [*Week*, p. 40 ; Riv. 50.]

Vol. I

prophaned by being made the thoroughfares of vice. He is the highway of his vice. The searching devil courses through and through him. His flesh and blood and bones are cheapened. He is all trivial, a place where three highways of sin meet. So is another the thoroughfare of virtue, and virtue circulates through all his aisles like a wind, and he is hallowed.

We reprove each other unconsciously by our own behavior. Our very carriage and demeanor in the streets should be a reprimand that will go to the conscience of every beholder. An infusion of love from a great soul gives a color to our faults, which will discover them, as lunar caustic detects impurities in water.

The best will not seem to go contrary to others, but, as if *they* could afford to travel the same way, they go a parallel but higher course, a sort of upper road. Jonson says, —

"That to the vulgar canst thyself apply,
Treading a better path not contrary."

Their way is a mountain slope, a river valley's course, a tide which mingles a myriad lesser currents.

March 5. *Friday.* How can our love increase, unless our loveliness increase also? We must securely love each other as we love God, with no more danger that our love be unrequited or ill-bestowed. There is that in my friend before which I must first decay and prove untrue. Love is the least moral and the most. Are the best good in their love? or the worst, bad?

March 6. An honest misunderstanding is often the ground of future intercourse.

"THE SPHINX"[1]

March 7, 8, 9, 10. The Sphinx is man's insatiable and questioning spirit, which still, as of old, stands by the roadside in us and proposes the riddle of life to every passer. The ancients represented this by a monster who was a riddle of herself, having a body composed of various creatures, as if to hint that she had no individual existence, but was nearly allied to and brooded over all. They made her devour those who were unable to explain her enigmas, as we are devoured by doubt, and struggle towards the light, as if to be assured of our lives. For we live by confidence, and our bravery is in some moment when we are certain to that degree that our certainty cannot be increased; as, when a ray bursts through a gap in a cloud, it darts as far, and reaches the earth as surely, as the whole sun would have done.

1. In the first four lines is described the mood in which the Sphinx bestirs herself in us. We must look on the world with a drowsy and half-shut eye, that it may not be too much in our eye, and rather stand aloof from than within it. When we are awake to the real world, we are asleep to the actual. The sinful drowse to eternity, the virtuous to time. Menu says that the "supreme omnipresent intelligence" is "a spirit which can only be conceived by a mind *slumbering.*" Wisdom

[1] [An interpretation of Emerson's poem. The numbers refer to the stanzas.]

and holiness always slumber; they are never active in the ways of the world. As in our night-dreams we are nearest to awakening, so in our day-dreams we are nearest to a supernatural awakening, and the plain and flat satisfactoriness of life becomes so significant as to be questioned.

The Sphinx hints that in the ages her secret is kept, but in the annihilation of ages alone is it revealed. So far from solving the problem of life, Time only serves to propose and keep it in. Time waits but for its solution to become eternity. Its lapse is measured by the successive failures to answer the incessant question, and the generations of men are the unskillful passengers devoured.

2. She hints generally at man's mystery. He knows only that he is, not what, nor whence. Not only is he curiously and wonderfully wrought, but with Dædalian intricacy. He is lost in himself as a labyrinth and has no clue to get out by. If he could get out of his humanity, he would have got out of nature. "Dædalian" expresses both the skill and the inscrutable design of the builder.

The insolubleness of the riddle is only more forcibly expressed by the lines, —

> "Out of sleeping a waking,
> Out of waking a sleep."

They express the complete uncertainty and renunciation of knowledge of the propounder.

3, 4, 5, 6. In these verses is described the integrity of all animate and inanimate things but man, — how each is a problem of itself and not the solution of one

and presides over and uses the mystery of the universe as unhesitatingly as if it were the partner of God; how, by a sort of *essential and practical faith*, each understands all, for to see that we understand is to know that we misunderstand. Each natural object is an end to itself. A brave, undoubting life do they all live, and are content to be a part of the mystery which is God, and throw the responsibility on man of explaining them and himself too.

3. The outlines of the trees are as correct as if ruled by God on the sky. The motions of quadrupeds and birds Nature never thinks to mend, but they are a last copy and the flourishes of His hand.

4. The waves lapse with such a melody on the shore as shows that they have long been at one with Nature. Theirs is as perfect play as if the heavens and earth were not. They meet with a sweet difference and independently, as old playfellows. Nothing do they lack more than the world. The ripple is proud to be a ripple and balances the sea. The atoms, which are in such a continual flux, notwithstanding their minuteness, have a certain essential valor and independence. They have the integrity of worlds, and attract and repel firmly as such. The least has more manhood than Democritus.

5. So also in Nature the perfection of the whole is the perfection of the parts, and what is itself perfect serves to adorn and set off all the rest. Her distinctions are but reliefs. Night veileth the morning for the morning's sake, and the vapor adds a new attraction to the hill. Nature looks like a conspiracy for the advantage

of all her parts; when one feature shines, all the rest seem suborned to heighten its charm. In her circle each gladly gives precedence to the other. Day gladly alternates with night. Behind these the vapor atones to the hill for its interference, and this harmonious scene is the effect of that at-one-ment.

6. In a sense the babe takes its departure from Nature as the grown man his departure out of her, and so during its nonage is at one with her, and as a part of herself. It is indeed the very flower and blossom of Nature.

> "Shines the peace of all being
> Without cloud, in its eyes;
> And the *sum* of the world
> In soft *miniature* lies." [1]

To the charming consistency of the palm and thrush, this universal and serene beauty is added, as all the leaves of the tree flower in the blossom.

7. But alas, the fruit to be matured in these petals is fated to break the stem which holds it to universal consistency. It passes *through Nature* to manhood, and becomes unnatural, without being as yet quite supernatural. Man's most approved life is but conformity, not a simple and independent consistency, which would make all things conform to it. His actions do not adorn Nature nor one another, nor does she exist in harmony but in contrast with them. She is not their willing scenery. We conceive that if a true action were to be performed it would·be assisted by Nature, and perhaps be fondled and reflected many times as the rainbow. The sun is a true light for the trees in a picture, but not

---

[1] [The italics are Thoreau's.]

for the actions of men. They will not bear so strong a light as the stubble; the universe has little sympathy with them, and sooner or later they rebound hollowly on the memory. The April shower should be as reviving to our life as to the garden and the grove, and the scenery in which we live reflect our own beauty, as the dewdrop the flower. It is the actual man, not the actual Nature, that hurts the romance of the landscape. "He poisons the ground." The haymakers must be lost in the grass of the meadow. They may be Faustus and Amyntas here, but near at hand they are Reuben and Jonas. The woodcutter must not be better than the wood, lest he be *worse*. Neither will bear to be considered as a distinct feature. Man's works must lie in the bosom of Nature, cottages be buried in trees, or under vines and moss, like rocks, that they may not outrage the landscape. The hunter must be dressed in Lincoln green, with a plume of eagle's feathers, to imbosom him in Nature. So the skillful painter secures the distinctness of the whole by the indistinctness of the parts. We can endure best to consider our repose and silence. Only when the city, the hamlet, or the cottage is viewed from a distance does man's life seem in harmony with the universe; but seen closely his actions have no eagle's feathers or Lincoln green to redeem them. The sunlight on cities at a distance is a deceptive beauty, but foretells the final harmony of man with Nature.

Man as he is, is not the subject of any art, strictly speaking. The naturalist pursues his study with love, but the moralist persecutes his with hate. In man is the material of a picture, with a design partly sketched, but Nature is such a picture drawn and colored. He is a studio, Nature a gallery. If men were not idealists, no sonnets to beautiful persons nor eulogies on worthy ones would ever be written. We wait for the preacher to express *such* love for his congregation as the botanist for his herbarium.

8. Man, however, detects something in the lingering ineradicable sympathy of Nature which seems to side with him against the stern decrees of the soul. Her essential friendliness is only the more apparent to his waywardness, for disease and sorrow are but a rupture with her. In proportion as he renounces his will, she repairs his hurts, and, if she burns, does oftener warm, if she freezes, oftener refreshes. This is the motherliness which the poet personifies, and the Sphinx, or wisely inquiring man, makes express a real concern for him. Nature shows us a stern kindness, and only we are unkind. She endures long with us, and though the severity of her law is unrelaxed, yet its evenness and impartiality look relenting, and almost sympathize with our fault.

9, 10, 11, 12, 13, 14. But to the poet there are no riddles. They are "pleasant songs" to him; his faith solves the enigmas which recurring wisdom does not fail to repeat. Poetry is the only solution time can offer. But the poet is soonest a pilgrim from his own faith. Our brave moments may still be distinguished from our wise. Though the problem is always solved for the soul, still does it remain to be solved by the intellect. Almost faith puts the question, for only in her light can it be answered. However true the answer, it does not pre-

vent the question; for the best answer is but plausible, and man can only tell his relation to truth, but render no account of truth to herself.

9. Believe, and ask not, says the poet.

> "Deep love lieth under
>   These pictures of time;
> They fade in the light of
>   Their meaning sublime."

Nothing is plain but love.

10, 11, 12, 13. Man comes short, because he seeks perfection. He adorns no world, while he is seeking to adorn a better. His best actions have no reference to their actual scenery. For when our actions become of that worth that they might confer a grace on Nature, they pass out of her into a higher arena, where they are still mean and awkward. So that the world beholds only the rear of great deeds, and mistakes them often for inconsistencies, not knowing with what higher they consist. Nature is beautiful as in repose, not promising a higher beauty to-morrow. Her actions are level to one another, and so are never unfit or inconsistent. Shame and remorse, which are so unsightly to her, have a prospective beauty and fitness which redeem them. We would have our lover to be nobler than we, and do not fear to sacrifice our love to his greater nobleness. Better the disagreement of noble lovers than the agreement of base ones. In friendship each will be nobler than the other, and so avoid the cheapness of a level and idle harmony. Love will have its chromatic strains, — discordant yearnings for higher chords, — as well as symphonies. Let us expect no finite satisfaction.

Vol. I

13. Who looks in the sun will see no light else; but also he will see no shadow. Our life revolves unceasingly, but the centre is ever the same, and the wise will regard only the seasons of the soul.

14. The poet concludes with the same trust he began with, and jeers at the blindness which could inquire. But our sphinx is so wise as to put no riddle that can be answered. It is a great presumption to answer conclusively a question which any sincerity has put. The wise answer no questions, — nor do they ask them. She silences his jeers with the conviction that she is the eye-beam of his eye. Our proper eye never quails before an answer. To rest in a reply, as a response of the oracle, that is error; but to suspect time's reply, because we would not degrade one of God's meanings to be intelligible to us, that is wisdom. We shall never arrive at his meaning, but it will ceaselessly arrive to us. The truth we seek with ardor and devotion will not reward us with a cheap acquisition. We run unhesitatingly in our career, not fearing to pass any goal of truth in our haste. We career toward her eternally. A truth rested in stands for all the vice of an age, and revolution comes kindly to restore health.

16. The cunning Sphinx, who had been hushed into stony silence and repose in us, arouses herself and detects a mystery in all things, — in infancy, the moon, fire, flowers, sea, mountain, — and,

(17) in the spirit of the old fable, declares proudly, —

> "Who telleth one of my meanings
> Is master of all I am."

When some Œdipus has solved one of her enigmas, she will go dash her head against a rock.

You may find this as enigmatical as the Sphinx's riddle. Indeed, I doubt if she could solve it herself.

March 11. Thursday. Every man understands why a fool sings.

March 13. Saturday. There is a sort of homely truth and naturalness in some books, which is very rare to find, and yet looks quite cheap. There may be nothing lofty in the sentiment, or polished in the expression, but it is careless, countrified talk. The scholar rarely writes as well as the farmer talks. Homeliness is a great merit in a book; it is next to beauty and a high art. Some have this merit only. A few homely expressions redeem them. Rusticity is pastoral, but affectation merely civil. The scholar does not make his most familiar experience come gracefully to the aid of his expression, and hence, though he live in it, his books contain no tolerable pictures of the country and simple life. Very few men can speak of Nature with any truth. They confer no favor; they do not speak a good word for her. Most cry better than they speak. You can get more nature out of them by pinching than by addressing them. It is naturalness, and not simply good nature, that interests. I like better the surliness with which the woodchopper speaks of his woods, handling them as indifferently as his axe, than the mealy-mouthed enthusiasm of the lover of nature. Better that the primrose by the river's brim be a yellow primrose and nothing more, than the victim of his bouquet or herbarium, to shine with the flickering dull light of his imagination, and not the golden gleam of a star.

Aubrey relates of Thomas Fuller that his was "a very working head, in so much, that walking and meditating before dinner, he would eat up a penny loaf, not knowing that he did it. His natural memory was very great, to which he added the art of memory. He would repeat to you forwards and backwards all the signs from Ludgate to Charing-cross." These are very good and wholesome facts to know of a man, as copious as some modern volumes.

He also says of Mr. John Hales, that, "he loved Canarie" and was buried "under an altar monument of black marble . . . with a too long epitaph;" of Edmund Halley, that he "at sixteen could make a dial, and then he said he thought himself a brave fellow;" of William Holder, who wrote a book upon his curing one Popham, who was deaf and dumb, "He was beholding to no author; did only consult with nature." For the most part an author but consults with all who have written before upon any subject, and his book is but the advice of so many. But a true book will never have been forestalled, but the topic itself will be new, and, by consulting with nature, it will consult not only with those who have gone before, but with those who may come after. There is always room and occasion enough for a true book on any subject, as there is room for more light the brightest day, and more rays will not interfere with the first.[1]

[1] [*Week*, pp. 111, 112; Riv. 138–140.]

Vol. I

almost a prophane levity to such as understood them not, but their religion had the broader basis in proportion as it was less prominent. The religion I love is very laic. The clergy are as diseased, and as much possessed with a devil, as the reformers. They make their topic as offensive as the politician, for our religion is as unpublic and incommunicable as our poetical vein, and to be approached with as much love and tenderness.

March 17. *Wednesday.* The stars go up and down before my only eye. Seasons come round to me alone. I cannot lean so hard on any arm as on a sunbeam. So solid men are not to my sincerity as is the shimmer of the fields.

March 19. *Friday.* No true and brave person will be content to live on such a footing with his fellow and himself as the laws of every household now require. The house is the very haunt and lair of our vice. I am impatient to withdraw myself from under its roof as an unclean spot. There is no circulation there; it is full of stagnant and mephitic vapors.

March 20. Even the wisest and best are apt to use their lives as the occasion to do something else in than to live greatly. But we should hang as fondly over this work as the finishing and embellishment of a poem.

It is a great relief when for a few moments in the day we can retire to our chamber and be completely true to

How alone must our life be lived! We dwell on the seashore, and none between us and the sea. Men are my merry companions, my fellow-pilgrims, who beguile the way but leave me at the first turn in the road, for none are travelling *one* road so far as myself.

Each one marches in the van. The weakest child is exposed to the fates henceforth as barely as its parents. Parents and relations but entertain the youth; they cannot stand between him and his destiny. This is the one bare side of every man. There is no fence; it is clear before him to the bounds of space.

What is fame to a living man? If he live aright, the sound of no man's voice will resound through the aisles of his secluded life. His life is a hallowed silence, a fane. The loudest sounds have to thank my little ear that they are heard.

March 15. When I have access to a man's barrel of sermons, which were written from week to week, as his life lapsed, though I now know him to live cheerfully and bravely enough, still I cannot conceive what interval there was for laughter and smiles in the midst of so much sadness. Almost in proportion to the sincerity and earnestness of the life will be the sadness of the record. When I reflect that twice a week for so many years he pondered and preached such a sermon, I think he must have been a splenetic and melancholy man, and wonder if his food digested well. It seems as if the fruit of virtue was never a careless happiness.

A great cheerfulness have all great wits possessed,

ourselves. It leavens the rest of our hours. In that moment I will be nakedly as vicious as I am; this false life of mine shall have a being at length.

March 21. *Sunday.* To be associated with others by my friend's generosity when he bestows a gift is an additional favor to be grateful for.

March 27. *Saturday.* Magnanimity, though it look expensive for a short course, is always economy in the long run. Be generous in your poverty, if you would be rich. To make up a great action there are no subordinate mean ones. We can never afford to postpone a true life to-day to any future and anticipated nobleness. We think if by tight economy we can manage to arrive at independence, then indeed we will begin to be generous without stay. We sacrifice all nobleness to a little present meanness. If a man charges you eight hundred pay him eight hundred and fifty, and it will leave a clean edge to the sum. It will be like nature, overflowing and rounded like the bank of a river, not close and precise like a drain or ditch.

It is always a short step to peace — of mind.

Under this line there is or has been life; as, when I see the mole's raised gallery in the meadow, I know that he has passed underneath.

I must not lose any of my freedom by being a farmer and landholder. Most who enter on any profession are doomed men. The world might as well sing a dirge over them forthwith. The farmer's muscles are rigid. He can do one thing long, not many well. His pace seems determined henceforth; he never quickens it. A very rigid Nemesis is his fate. When the right wind blows or a star calls, I can leave this arable and grass ground, without making a will or settling my estate. I would buy a farm as freely as a silken streamer. Let me not think my front windows must face east henceforth because a particular hill slopes that way. My life must undulate still. I will not feel that my wings are clipped when once I have settled on ground which the law calls my own, but find new pinions grown to the old, and talaria to my feet beside.

March 30. *Tuesday.* I find my life growing slovenly when it does not exercise a constant supervision over itself. Its duds accumulate. Next to having lived a day well is a clear and calm overlooking of all our days.

FRIENDSHIP

Now we are partners in such legal trade,
We 'll look to the beginnings, not the ends,
Nor to pay-day, knowing true wealth is made
For current stock and not for dividends.

I am amused when I read how Ben Jonson engaged that the ridiculous masks with which the royal family and nobility were to be entertained should be "grounded upon antiquity and solid learning." [1]

[1] [*Week*, p. 108; Riv. 134.]

April 1. ON THE SUN COMING OUT IN THE AFTERNOON

Methinks all things have travelled since you shined,
But only Time, and clouds, Time's team, have moved;
Again foul weather shall not change my mind,
But in the shade I will believe what in the sun I loved.

In reading a work on agriculture, I skip the author's moral reflections, and the words "Providence" and "He" scattered along the page, to come at the profitable level of what he has to say. There is no science in men's religion; it does not teach me so much as the report of the committee on swine. My author shows he has dealt in corn and turnips and can worship God with the hoe and spade, but spare me his morality. [1]

April 3. Friends will not only live in harmony, but in melody. [2]

April 4. *Sunday.* The rattling of the tea-kettle below stairs reminds me of the cow-bells I used to hear when berrying in the Great Fields many years ago, sounding distant and deep amid the birches. That cheap piece of tinkling brass which the farmer hangs about his cow's neck has been more to me than the tons of metal which are swung in the belfry.

They who prepare my evening meal below
Carelessly hit the kettle as they go,
With tongs or shovel,
And, ringing round and round,

[1] [*Week*, p. 79; Riv. 98.]   [2] [*Week*, p. 283; Riv. 351.]

Vol. I

Out of this hovel
It makes an Eastern temple by the sound.

At first I thought a cow-bell, right at hand
'Mid birches, sounded o'er the open land,
Where I plucked flowers
Many years ago,
Speeding midsummer hours
With such secure delight they hardly seemed to flow.

April 5. This long series of desultory mornings does not tarnish the brightness of the prospective days. Surely faith is not dead. Wood, water, earth, air are essentially what they were; only society has degenerated. This lament for a golden age is only a lament for golden men.

I only ask a clean seat. I will build my lodge on the southern slope of some hill, and take there the life the gods send me. Will it not be employment enough to accept gratefully all that is yielded me between sun and sun? [1] Even the fox digs his own burrow. If my jacket and trousers, my boots and shoes, are fit to worship God in, they will do. Won't they, Deacon Spaulding? [2]

April 7. *Wednesday.* My life will wait for nobody, but is being matured still irresistibly while I go about the streets and chaffer with this man and that to secure it a living. It will cut its own channel, like the mountain stream, which by the longest ridges and by level

[1] [See p. 299.]   [2] [*Walden*, p. 25; Riv. 39.]

prairies is not kept from the sea finally. So flows a man's life, and will reach the sea water, if not by an earthy channel, yet in dew and rain, overleaping all barriers, with rainbows to announce its victory. It can wind as cunningly and unerringly as water that seeks its level; and shall I complain if the gods make it meander? This staying to buy me a farm is as if the Mississippi should stop to chaffer with a clamshell.

What have I to do with plows? I cut another furrow than you see. Where the off ox treads, there is it not, it is farther off; where the nigh ox walks, it will not be, it is nigher still. If corn fails, my crop fails not. What of drought? What of rain? Is not my sand well clayed, my peat well sanded? Is it not underdrained and watered? [1]

My ground is high,
But 't is not dry,
What you call dew
Comes filtering through;
Though in the sky,
It still is nigh;
Its soil is blue
And virgin too.

If from your price ye will not swerve,
Why, then I 'll think the gods reserve
A greater bargain there above,
Out of their sup'rabundant love

[1] [*Week*. p. 54; Riv. 67, 68.]

Have meantime better for me cared,
And so will get my stock prepared,
Plows of new pattern, hoes the same,
Designed a different soil to tame,
And sow my seed broadcast in air,
Certain to reap my harvest there.

April 8. Friends are the ancient and honorable of the earth. The oldest men did not begin friendship. It is older than Hindostan and the Chinese Empire. How long has it been cultivated, and is still the staple article! It is a divine league struck forever. Warm, serene days only bring it out to the surface. There is a friendliness between the sun and the earth in pleasant weather; the gray content of the land is its color.

You can tell what another's suspicions are by what you feel forced to become. You will wear a new character, like a strange habit, in their presence.

April 9. *Friday.* It would not be hard for some quiet brave man to leap into the saddle to-day and eclipse Napoleon's career by a grander, — show men at length the meaning of war. One reproaches himself with supineness, that he too has sat quiet in his chamber, and not treated the world to the sound of the trumpet; that the indignation which has so long rankled in his breast does not take to horse and to the field. The bravest warrior will have to fight his battles in his dreams, and no earthly war note can arouse him. There are who would not run with Leonidas. Only the third-rate Napoleons

and Alexanders does history tell of. The brave man does not mind the call of the trumpet nor hear the idle clashing of swords without, for the infinite din within. War is but a training, compared with the active service of his peace. Is he not at war? Does he not resist the ocean swell within him, and walk as gently as the summer's sea? Would you have him parade in uniform, and manœuvre men, whose equanimity is his uniform and who is himself manœuvred?

The times have no heart. The true reform can be undertaken any morning before unbarring our doors. It calls no convention. I can do two thirds the reform of the world myself. When two neighbors begin to eat corn bread, who before ate wheat, then the gods smile from ear to ear, for it is very pleasant to them. When an individual takes a sincere step, then all the gods attend, and his single deed is sweet.[1]

April 10. *Saturday.* I don't know but we should make life all too tame if we had our own way, and should miss these impulses in a happier time.

How much virtue there is in simply seeing! We may almost say that the hero has striven in vain for his preeminency, if the student oversees him. The woman who sits in the house and *sees* is a match for a stirring captain. Those still, piercing eyes, as faithfully exercised on their talent, will keep her even with Alexander or Shakespeare. They may go to Asia with parade, or to

[1] [See *Week*, p. 131; Riv. 163.]

fairyland, but not beyond her ray. We are as much as we see. Faith is sight and knowledge. The hands only serve the eyes. The farthest blue streak in the horizon I can see, I may reach before many sunsets. What I saw alters not; in my night, when I wander, it is still steadfast as the star which the sailor steers by.

Whoever has had one thought quite lonely, and could contentedly digest that in solitude, knowing that none could accept it, may rise to the height of humanity, and overlook all living men as from a pinnacle.

Speech never made man master of men, but the eloquently refraining from it.

April 11. *Sunday.* A greater baldness my life seeks, as the crest of some bare hill, which towns and cities do not afford. I want a directer relation with the sun.

FRIENDSHIP'S STEADFASTNESS

True friendship is so firm a league
That's maintenance falls into the even tenor
Of our lives, and is no tie,
But the continuance of our life's thread.

If I would safely keep this new-got pelf,
I have no care henceforth but watch myself,
For lo! it goes untended from my sight,
Waxes and wanes secure with the safe star of night.

See with what liberal step it makes its way,
As we could well afford to let it stray

Throughout the universe, with the sun and moon,
Which would dissolve allegiance as soon.

Shall I concern myself for fickleness,
And undertake to make my friends more sure,
When the great gods out of sheer kindliness,
Gave me this office for a sinecure?

Death cannot come too soon
Where it can come at all,
But always is too late
Unless the fates it call.

April 15. *Thursday.* The gods are of no sect; they side with no man. When I imagine that Nature inclined rather to some few earnest and faithful souls, and specially existed for them, I go to see an obscure individual who lives under the hill, letting both gods and men alone, and find that strawberries and tomatoes grow for him too in his garden there, and the sun lodges kindly under his hillside, and am compelled to acknowledge the unbribable charity of the gods.

Any simple, unquestioned mode of life is alluring to men. The man who picks peas steadily for a living is more than respectable. He is to be envied by his neighbors.

April 16. I have been inspecting my neighbors' farms to-day and chaffering with the landholders, and I must confess I am startled to find everywhere the old system of things so grim and assured. Wherever I go the farms are run out, and there they lie, and the youth must buy old land and bring it to. Everywhere the relentless opponents of reform are a few old maids and bachelors, who sit round the kitchen fire, listening to the singing of the tea-kettle and munching cheese-rinds.[1]

April 18. *Sunday.* We need pine for no office for the sake of a certain culture, for all valuable experience lies in the way of a man's duty. My necessities of late have compelled me to study Nature as she is related to the farmer, — as she simply satisfies a want of the body. Some interests have got a footing on the earth which I have not made sufficient allowance for. That which built these barns and cleared the land thus had some valor.[2]

We take little steps, and venture small stakes, as if our actions were very fatal and irretrievable. There is no swing to our deeds. But our life is only a retired valley where we rest on our packs awhile. Between us and our end there is room for any delay. It is not a short and easy southern way, but we must go over snow-capped mountains to reach the sun.

April 20. You can't beat down your virtue; so much goodness it must have.

When a room is furnished, comfort is not furnished.

Great thoughts hallow any labor. To-day I earned

[1] [*Week*, p. 131; Riv. 163.]   [2] [*Week*, p. 129; Riv. 161.]

seventy-five cents heaving manure out of a pen, and made a good bargain of it. If the ditcher muses the while how he may live uprightly, the ditching spade and turf knife may be engraved on the coat-of-arms of his posterity.

There are certain current expressions and blasphemous moods of viewing things, as when we say "he is doing a good business," more prophane than cursing and swearing. There is death and sin in such words. Let not the children hear them.[1]

April 22. *Thursday.* There are two classes of authors: the one write the history of their times, the other their biography.

April 23. *Friday.* Any greatness is not to be mistaken. Who shall cavil at it? It stands once for all on a level with the heroes of history. It is not to be patronized. It goes alone.

When I hear music, I flutter, and am the scene of life, as a fleet of merchantmen when the wind rises.

April 24. Music is the sound of the circulation in nature's veins. It is the flux which melts nature. Men dance to it, glasses ring and vibrate, and the fields seem to undulate. The healthy ear always hears it, nearer or more remote.

It has been a cloudy, drizzling day, with occasional

[1] [*Week*, first edition, pp. 70, 71.]

brightenings in the mist, when the trill of the tree sparrow seemed to be ushering in sunny hours.[1]

April 25. A momentous silence reigns always in the woods, and their meaning seems just ripening into expression. But alas! they make no haste. The rush sparrow,[2] Nature's minstrel of serene hours, sings of an immense leisure and duration.

When I hear a robin sing at sunset, I cannot help contrasting the equanimity of Nature with the bustle and impatience of man. We return from the lyceum and caucus with such stir and excitement, as if a crisis were at hand; but no natural scene or sound sympathizes with us, for Nature is always silent and unpretending as at the break of day. She but rubs her eyelids.

I am struck with the pleasing friendships and unanimities of nature in the woods, as when the moss on the trees takes the form of their leaves.

There is all of civilized life in the woods. Their wildest scenes have an air of domesticity and homeliness, and when the flicker's cackle is heard in the clearings, the musing hunter is reminded that civilization has imported nothing into them.[3] The ball-room is represented

[1] [*Week*, pp. 318, 319; Riv. 395. Tree sparrow = chipping sparrow? The "hair-bird" of *Week*, p. 317 (Riv. 393), is called tree sparrow in the commonplace-book referred to on p. 438.]
[2] [Field sparrow, Nuttall's *Fringilla juncorum.* Nuttall gives both field sparrow and rush sparrow as its vernacular names.]
[3] [*Week*, p. 336; Riv. 416.]

by the catkins of the alder at this season, which hang gracefully like a lady's ear-drops.

All the discoveries of science are equally true in their deepest recesses; nature there, too, obeys the same laws. Fair weather and foul concern the little red bug upon a pine stump; for him the wind goes round the right way and the sun breaks through the clouds.[1]

April 26. *Monday.* At R. W. E.'s.

The charm of the Indian to me is that he stands free and unconstrained in Nature, is her inhabitant and not her guest, and wears her easily and gracefully. But the civilized man has the habits of the house. His house is a prison, in which he finds himself oppressed and confined, not sheltered and protected. He walks as if he sustained the roof; he carries his arms as if the walls would fall in and crush him, and his feet remember the cellar beneath. His muscles are never relaxed. It is rare that he overcomes the house, and learns to sit at home in it, and roof and floor and walls support themselves, as the sky and trees and earth.

It is a great art to saunter.

April 27. It is only by a sort of voluntary blindness, and omitting to see, that we know ourselves, as when we see stars with the side of the eye. The nearest approach to discovering what we are is in dreams. It is as hard to see one's self as to look backwards without turning round. And foolish are they that look in glasses with that intent.

[1] [*Week*, p. 336; Riv. 416.]

The porters have a hard time, but not so hard as he that carries his own shoulders. That beats the Smyrna Turks. Some men's broad shoulders are load enough. Even a light frame can stand under a great burden, if it does not have to support itself. Virtue is buoyant and elastic; it stands without effort and does not feel gravity; but sin plods and shuffles. Newton needed not to wait for an apple to fall to discover the attraction of gravitation; it was implied in the fall of man.

April 28. Wednesday. We falsely attribute to men a determined character; putting together all their yesterdays and averaging them, we presume we know them. Pity the man who has a character to support. It is worse than a large family. He is silent poor indeed. But in fact character is never explored, nor does it get developed in time, but eternity is its development, time its envelope. In view of this distinction, a sort of divine politeness and heavenly good breeding suggests itself, to address always the enveloped character of a man. I approach a great nature with infinite expectation and uncertainty, not knowing what I may meet. It lies as broad and unexplored before me as a scraggy hillside or pasture. I may hear a fox bark, or a partridge drum, or some bird new to these localities may fly up. It lies out there as old, and yet as new. The aspect of the woods varies every day, what with their growth and the changes of the seasons and the influence of the elements, so that the eye of the forester never twice rests upon the same prospect. Much more does a character show newly and variedly, if directly seen. It is the highest

compliment to suppose that in the intervals of conversation your companion has expanded and grown. It may be a deference which he will not understand, but the nature which underlies him will understand it, and your influence will be shed as finely on him as the dust in the sun settles on our clothes. By such politeness we may educate one another to some purpose. So have I felt myself educated sometimes; I am expanded and enlarged.

April 29. Birds and quadrupeds pass freely through nature, without prop or stilt. But man very naturally carries a stick in his hand, seeking to ally himself by many points to nature, as a warrior stands by his horse's side with his hand on his mane. We walk the gracefuler for a cane, as the juggler uses a leaded pole to balance him when he dances on a slack wire.

Better a monosyllabic life than a ragged and muttered one; let its report be short and round like a rifle, so that it may hear its own echo in the surrounding silence.

April 30. Where shall we look for standard English but to the words of any man who has a depth of feeling in him? Not in any smooth and leisurely essay. From the gentlemanly windows of the country-seat no sincere eyes are directed upon nature, but from the peasant's horn windows a true glance and greeting occasionally. "For summer being ended, all things," said the Pilgrim, "stood in appearance with a weather-beaten face,

and the whole country full of woods and thickets represented a wild and savage hue." Compare this with the agricultural report.

May 1. Saturday. Life in gardens and parlors is unpalatable to me. It wants rudeness and necessity to give it relish. I would at least strike my spade into the earth with as good will as the woodpecker his bill into a tree.[1]

May 2.   WACHUSETT [2]
Especial I remember thee,
Wachusett, who like me
Standest alone without society.
Thy far blue eye,
A remnant of the sky,
Seen through the clearing or the gorge,
Or from the windows of the forge,
Doth leaven all it passes by.
Nothing is true
But stands 'tween me and you,
Thou western pioneer,
Who know'st not shame nor fear,
By venturous spirit driven
Under the eaves of heaven;
And canst expand thee there,
And breathe enough of air?

[1] [*Week*, p. 54 ; Riv. 67.]
[2] [In *Excursions*, p. 135 (Riv. 165), these lines are printed as part of a poem beginning, "With frontier strength ye stand your ground." The poem appears also, in extended form, in *Week*, pp. 170–173; Riv. 212–215.]

Upholding heaven, holding down earth,
Thy pastime from thy birth,
Not steadied by the one, nor leaning on the other;
May I approve myself thy worthy brother!

May 3. Monday. We are all pilots of the most intricate Bahama channels. Beauty may be the sky overhead, but Duty is the water underneath. When I see a man with serene countenance in the sunshine of summer, drinking in peace in the garden or parlor, it looks like a great inward leisure that he enjoys; but in reality he sails on no summer's sea, but this steady sailing comes of a heavy hand on the tiller. We do not attend to larks and bluebirds so leisurely but that conscience is as erect as the attitude of the listener. The man of principle gets never a holiday. Our true character silently underlies all our words and actions, as the granite underlies the other strata. Its steady pulse does not cease for any deed of ours, as the sap is still ascending in the stalk of the fairest flower.

May 6. Thursday. The fickle person is he that does not know what is true or right absolutely, — who has not an ancient wisdom for a lifetime, but a new prudence for every hour. We must sail by a sort of dead reckoning on this course of life, not speak any vessel nor spy any headland, but, in spite of all phenomena, come steadily to port at last. In general we must have a catholic and universal wisdom, wiser than any particular, and be prudent enough to defer to it always. We are literally wiser than we know. Men do not fail for want of knowledge, but for want of prudence to give wisdom the preference.[1] These low weathercocks on barns and fences show not which way the general and steady current of the wind sets, — which brings fair weather or foul, — but the vane on the steeple, high up in another stratum of atmosphere, tells that. What we need to know in any case is very simple.[2] I shall not mistake the direction of my life; if I but know the high land and the main, — on this side the Cordilleras, on that the Pacific, — I shall know how to run. If a ridge intervene, I have but to seek, or make, a gap to the sea.

May 9. Sunday. The pine stands in the woods like an Indian, — untamed, with a fantastic wildness about it, even in the clearings. If an Indian warrior were well painted, with pines in the background, he would seem to blend with the trees, and make a harmonious expression. The pitch pines are the ghosts of Philip and Massasoit. The white pine has the smoother features of the squaw.

The poet speaks only those thoughts that come unbidden, like the wind that stirs the trees, and men cannot help but listen. He is not listened to, but heard. The weathercock might as well dally with the wind as a man pretend to resist eloquence. The breath that inspires the poet has traversed a whole Campagna, and this new climate here indicates that other latitudes are chilled or heated.

Speak to men as to gods and you will not be insincere.

[1] [*Week*, p. 132; Riv. 164.]   [2] [*Week*, p. 132; Riv. 164.]

WESTWARD, HO!
The needles of the pine
All to the west incline.[1]

THE ECHO OF THE SABBATH BELL HEARD IN
THE WOODS[2]

Dong, sounds the brass in the east,
As if for a civic feast,
But I like that sound the best
Out of the fluttering west.

The steeple rings a knell,
But the fairies' silvery bell
Is the voice of that gentle folk,
Or else the horizon that spoke.

Its metal is not of brass,
But air, and water, and glass,
And under a cloud it is swung,
And by the wind is rung,
With a slim silver tongue.

When the steeple tolls the noon,
It soundeth not so soon,
Yet it rings an earlier hour,
And the sun has not reached its tower.

May 10. Monday. A good warning to the restless

[1] [*Excursions*, p. 133; Riv. 163.]
[2] [This poem appears in *Week*, p. 50 (Riv. 62), with some variations and without title.]

tourists of these days is contained in the last verses of Claudian's "Old Man of Verona."

" Erret, et extremos alter scrutetur Iberos.
Plus habet hic vitae, plus habet ille viae." [1]

May 23. Sunday. Barn. — The distant woods are but the tassels of my eye.

Books are to be attended to as new sounds merely. Most would be put to a sore trial if the reader should assume the attitude of a listener. They are but a new note in the forest. To our lonely, sober thought the earth is a wild unexplored. Wildness as of the jay and muskrat reigns over the great part of nature. The oven-bird and plover are heard in the horizon. Here is a new book of heroes, come to me like the note of the chewink from over the fen, only over a deeper and wider fen. The pines are unrelenting sifters of thought; nothing petty leaks through them. Let me put my ear close, and hear the sough of this book, that I may know if any inspiration yet haunts it. There is always a later edition of every book than the printer wots of, no matter how recently it was published. All nature is a new impression every instant.

The aspects of the most simple object are as various as the aspects of the most compound. Observe the same sheet of water from different eminences. When I have travelled a few miles I do not recognize the profile of the hills of my native village.

May 27. Thursday. I sit in my boat on Walden, playing the flute this evening, and see the perch, which I

[1] [*Walden*, p. 354; Riv. 496.]

seem to have charmed, hovering around me, and the moon travelling over the bottom, which is strewn with the wrecks of the forest, and feel that nothing but the wildest imagination can conceive of the manner of life we are living. Nature is a wizard. The Concord nights are stranger than the Arabian nights.

We not only want elbow-room, but eye-room in this gray air which shrouds all the fields. Sometimes my eyes see over the county road by daylight to the tops of yonder birches on the hill, as at others by moonlight.

Heaven lies above, because the air is deep.

In all my life hitherto I have left nothing behind.

May 31. Monday. That title, "The Laws of Menu[1] with the Gloss of Culluca," comes to me with such a volume of sound as if it had swept unobstructed over the plains of Hindostan; and when my eye rests on yonder birches, or the sun in the water, or the shadows of the trees, it seems to signify the laws of them all. They are the laws of you and me, a fragrance wafted down from those old times, and no more to be refuted than the wind.

When my imagination travels eastward and backward to those remote years of the gods, I seem to draw near to the habitation of the morning, and the dawn at length has a place. I remember the book as an hour before sunrise.

We are height and depth both, a calm sea at the foot of a promontory. Do we not overlook our own depths?

[1] [See *Week*, p. 154; Riv. 192.]

June 1. To have seen a man out of the East or West is sufficient to establish their reality and locality. I have seen a Mr. Wattles to-day, from Vermont, and now know where that is and that it is; a reformer, with two soldier's eyes and shoulders, who began to belabor the world at ten years, a ragged mountain boy, as fifer of a company, with set purpose to remould it from those first years.

The great person never wants an opportunity to be great, but makes occasion for all about him.

June 2. Wednesday. I am brought into the near neighborhood and am become a silent observer of the moon's paces to-night, by means of a glass, while the frogs are peeping all around me on the earth, and the sound of the accordion seems to come from some bright saloon yonder. I am sure the moon floats in a human atmosphere. It is but a distant scene of the world's drama. It is a wide theatre the gods have given us, and our actions must befit it. More sea and land, mountain and valley, here is, — a further West, a freshness and wildness in reserve when all the land shall be cleared.

I see three little lakes between the hills near its edge, reflecting the sun's rays. The light glimmers as on the water in a tumbler. So far off do the laws of reflection hold. I seem to see the ribs of the creature. This is the aspect of their day, its outside, — their heaven above their heads, towards which they breathe their prayers. So much is between me and them. It is noon there, perchance, and ships are at anchor in the havens or

sailing on the seas, and there is a din in the streets, and in this light or that shade some leisurely soul contemplates.

But now dor-bugs fly over its disk and bring me back to earth and night.

June 7. Monday. The inhabitants of those Eastern plains seem to possess a natural and hereditary right to be conservative and magnify forms and traditions. "Immemorial custom is transcendent law," says Menu. That is, it was the custom of gods before men used it. The fault of our New England custom is that it is memorial. What is morality but immemorial custom? It is not manner but character, and the conservative conscience sustains it.[1]

We are accustomed to exaggerate the immobility and stagnation of those eras, as of the waters which levelled the steppes; but those slow revolving "years of the gods" were as rapid to all the needs of virtue as these bustling and hasty seasons. Man stands to revere, he kneels to pray. Methinks history will have to be tried by new tests to show what centuries were rapid and what slow. Corn grows in the night.[2] Will this bustling era detain the future reader longer? Will the earth seem to have conversed more with the heavens during these times? Who is writing better Vedas? How science and art spread and flourished, how trivial conveniences were multiplied, that which is the gossip of the world is not recorded in them; and if they are left out of our scripture, too, what will remain?

[1] [*Week*, p. 140 ; Riv. 174, 175.]   [2] [See pp. 124 and 174.]

Since the Battle of Bunker Hill we think the world has *not* been at a standstill.

When I remember the treachery of memory and the manifold accidents to which tradition is liable, how soon the vista of the past closes behind, — as near as night's crescent to the setting day, — and the dazzling brightness of noon is reduced to the faint glimmer of the evening star, I feel as if it were by a rare indulgence of the fates that any traces of the past are left us, — that my ears which do not hear across the interval over which a crow caws should chance to hear this far-travelled sound. With how little coöperation of the societies, after all, is the past remembered!

I know of no book which comes to us with grander pretensions than the "Laws of Menu;" and this immense presumption is so impersonal and sincere that it is never offensive or ridiculous. Observe the modes in which modern literature is advertised, and then consider this Hindoo prospectus. Think what a reading public it addresses, what criticism it expects. What wonder if the times were not ripe for it?[1]

June 8. Having but one chair, I am obliged to receive my visitors standing, and, now I think of it, those old sages and heroes must always have met erectly.

July 10 *to* 12. This town, too, lies out under the sky, a port of entry and departure for souls to and from heaven.[2]

[1] [*Week*, p. 155 ; Riv. 193.]   [2] [*Week*, p. 12 ; Riv. 15.]

A slight sound at evening lifts me up by the ears, and makes life seem inexpressibly serene and grand. It may be in Uranus, or it may be in the shutter. It is the original sound of which all literature is but the echo. It makes all fear superfluous. Bravery comes from further than the sources of fear.

Aug. 1. *Sunday.* I never met a man who cast a free and healthy glance over life, but the best live in a sort of Sabbath light, a Jewish gloom. The best thought is not only without sombreness, but even without morality. The universe lies outspread in floods of white light to it. The moral aspect of nature is a jaundice reflected from man. To the innocent there are no cherubim nor angels. Occasionally we rise above the necessity of virtue into an unchangeable morning light, in which we have not to choose in a dilemma between right and wrong, but simply to live right on and breathe the circumambient air.[1] There is no name for this life unless it be the very vitality of *vita*. Silent is the preacher about this, and silent must ever be, for he who knows it will not preach.

Aug. 4. *Wednesday.* My pen is a lever which, in proportion as the near end stirs me further within, the further end reaches to a greater depth in the reader.

Nawshawtuct. — Far in the east I read *Nature's Corn Law Rhymes*. Here, in sight of Wachusett and these rivers and woods, my mind goes singing to itself of other themes than taxation. The rush sparrow sings

[1] [*Week*, p. 394 ; Riv. 486.]

still unintelligible, as from beyond a depth in me which I have not fathomed, where my future lies folded up. I hear several faint notes, quite outside me, which populate the waste.

This is such fresh and flowing weather, as if the waves of the morning had subsided over the day.

Aug. 6. If I am well, then I see well. The bulletins of health are twirled along my visual rays, like pasteboards on a kite string.

I cannot read a sentence in the book of the Hindoos without being elevated as upon the table-land of the Ghauts. It has such a rhythm as the winds of the desert, such a tide as the Ganges, and seems as superior to criticism as the Himmaleh Mounts. Even at this late hour, unworn by time, with a native and inherent dignity it wears the English dress as indifferently as the Sanscrit. The great tone of the book is of such fibre and such severe tension that no time nor accident can relax it.[1] The great thought is never found in a mean dress, but is of virtue to ennoble any language. Let it issue from the lips of the Wolofs, or from the forum of Rome, the nine Muses will seem to have been purveyors for it. Its education is always liberal; it has all the graces of oratory and of poetry. The lofty tone which is its indispensable breath is grace to the eye and music to the ear. It can endow a college.[2]

So supremely religious a book imposes with authority on the latest age. The very simplicity of style of the

[1] [*Week*, p. 155 ; Riv. 193.]   [2] [*Week*, p. 109 ; Riv. 136.]

ancient lawgiver, implying all in the omission of all, proves an habitual elevation of thought, which the multiplied glosses of later days strive in vain to slope up to. The whole book by noble gestures and inclinations seems to render words unnecessary. The abbreviated sentence points to the thing for explanation. As the sublimest thought is most faithfully printed in the face, and needs the fewest interpreting words. The page nods toward the fact and is silent.

As I walk across the yard from the barn to the house through the fog, with a lamp in my hand, I am reminded of the Merrimack nights, and seem to see the sod between tent-ropes. The trees, seen dimly through the mist, suggest things which do not at all belong to the past, but are peculiar to my fresh New England life. It is as novel as green peas. The dew hangs everywhere upon the grass, and I breathe the rich, damp air in slices.

Aug. 7. Saturday. The impression which those sublime sentences made on me last night has awakened me before any cockcrowing. Their influence lingers around me like a fragrance, or as the fog hangs over the earth late into the day.

The very locusts and crickets of a summer day are but later or older glosses on the Dherma Sástra of the Hindoos, a continuation of the sacred code.[1]

Aug. 9. It is vain to try to write unless you feel strong in the knees.

[1] [*Week*, p. 157 ; Riv. 195, 196.]

Any book of great authority and genius seems to our imagination to permeate and pervade all space. Its spirit, like a more subtle ether, sweeps along with the prevailing winds of the country. Its influence conveys a new gloss to the meadows and the depths of the wood, and bathes the huckleberries on the hills, as sometimes a new influence in the sky washes in waves over the fields and seems to break on some invisible beach in the air. All things confirm it. It spends the mornings and the evenings.[1]

Everywhere the speech of Menu demands the widest apprehension and proceeds from the loftiest plateau of the soul. It is spoken unbendingly to its own level, and does not imply any contemporaneous speaker.

I read history as little critically as I consider the landscape, and am more interested in the atmospheric tints and various lights and shades which the intervening spaces create than in its groundwork and composition. It is the morning now turned evening and seen in the west, — the same sun, but a new light and atmosphere. Its beauty is like the sunset; not a fresco painting on a wall, flat and bounded, but atmospheric and roving, or free. But, in reality, history fluctuates as the face of the landscape from morning to evening. What is of moment in it is its hue and color. Time hides no treasures; we want not its *then*, but its *now*. We do not complain that the mountains in the horizon are blue and indistinct; they are the more like the heavens.

[1] [*Week*, p. 157 ; Riv. 195.]

Of what moment are facts that can be lost, — which need to be commemorated? The monument of death will outlast the memory of the dead. The Pyramids do not tell the tale confided to them. The living fact commemorates itself. Why look in the dark for light? Look in the light rather. Strictly speaking, the Societies have not recovered one fact from oblivion, but they themselves are instead of the fact that is lost. The researcher is more memorable than the researched. The crowd stood admiring the mist and the dim outline of the trees seen through it, and when one of their number advanced to explore the phenomenon, with fresh admiration all eyes were turned on his dimly retreating figure. Critical acumen is exerted in vain to uncover the past; the *past* cannot be *presented;* we cannot know what we are not. But one veil hangs over past, present, and future, and it is the province of the historian to find out, not what was, but what is. Where a battle has been fought, you will find nothing but the bones of men and beasts; where a battle is being fought, there are hearts beating. We will sit on a mound and muse, and not try to make these skeletons stand on their legs again. Does Nature remember, think you, that they *were* men, or not rather that they *are* bones?

Ancient history has an air of antiquity. It should be more modern. It is written as if the spectator should be thinking of the back side of the picture on the wall, as if the author expected the dead would be his readers, and wished to detail to them their own experience. Men seem anxious to accomplish an orderly retreat through the centuries, earnestly rebuilding the works behind, as they are battered down by the incroachments of time; but while they loiter, they and their works both fall a prey to the enemy.

Biography is liable to the same objection; it should be autobiography. Let us not leave ourselves empty that, so vexing our bowels, we may go abroad and be somebody else to explain him. If I am not I, who will be? As if it were to dispense justice to all. But the time has not come for that.[1]

Aug. 12. We take pleasure in beholding the form of a mountain in the horizon, as if by retiring to this distance we had then first conquered it by our vision, and were made privy to the design of the architect; so when we behold the shadow of our earth on the moon's disk. When we climb a mountain and observe the lesser irregularities, we do not give credit to the comprehensive and general intelligence which shaped them; but when we see the outline in the horizon, we confess that the hand which moulded those opposite slopes, making one balance the other, worked round a deep centre, and was privy to the plan of the universe. The smallest of nature's works fits the farthest and widest view, as if it had been referred in its bearings to every point in space.[2] It harmonizes with the horizon line and the orbits of the planets.

Aug. 13. Friday. I have been in the swamp by Charles Miles's this afternoon, and found it so bosky and sylvan that Art would never have freedom or cour-

[1] [*Week*, pp. 161–163 ; Riv. 200–204.]
[2] [*Excursions*, p. 148 ; Riv. 181.]

age to imitate it. It can never match the luxury and superfluity of Nature. In Art all is seen; she cannot afford concealed wealth, and in consequence is niggardly; but Nature, even when she is scant and thin outwardly, contents us still by the assurance of a certain generosity at the roots. Surely no stinted hand has been at work here for these centuries to produce these particular tints this summer. The double spruce attracts me here, which I had hardly noticed in the gardens, and now I understand why men try to make them grow about their houses.[1]

Nature has her luxurious and florid style as well as Art. Having a pilgrim's cup to make, she gives to the whole — stem, bowl, handle, and nose — some fantastic shape, as if it were to be the car of a fabulous marine deity, — a Nereus or Triton. She is mythical and mystical always, and spends her whole genius upon the least work.[2]

Aug. 16. There is a double virtue in the sound that can wake an echo, as in the lowing of the cows this morning. Far out in the horizon that sound travels quite round the town, and invades each recess of the wood, advancing at a grand pace and with a sounding Eastern pomp.

Aug. 18. I sailed on the North River last night with

[1] [*Week*, p. 339; Riv. 419. The "double spruce" is now generally known as the black spruce. Thoreau makes it "single spruce" (*i. e.*, white spruce) in the book, but the tree he was familiar with was the black. He confused these two species for a time, but eventually discovered his error.]
[2] [*Excursions*, pp. 125, 126 ; Riv. 154, 155.]

my flute, and my music was a tinkling stream which meandered with the river, and fell from note to note as a brook from rock to rock. I did not hear the strains after they had issued from the flute, but before they were breathed into it, for the original strain precedes the sound by as much as the echo follows after, and the rest is the perquisite of the rocks and trees and beasts.[1] Unpremeditated music is the true gauge which measures the current of our thoughts, the very undertow of our life's stream.

Of all the duties of life it is hardest to be in earnest; it implies a good deal both before and behind. I sit here in the barn this flowing afternoon weather, while the school bell is ringing in the village, and find that all the things immediate to be done are very trivial. I could postpone them to hear this locust sing. The cockerels crow and the hens cluck in the yard as if time were dog-cheap. It seems something worth detaining time, — the laying of an egg. Cannot man do something to comfort the gods, and not let the world prove such a piddling concern? No doubt they would be glad to sell their shares at a large discount by this time. Eastern Railroad stock promises a better dividend.

The best poets, after all, exhibit only a tame and civil side of nature. They have not seen the west side of any mountain.

Day and night, mountain and wood, are visible from the wilderness as well as the village. They have their

[1] [*Week*, p. 363 ; Riv. 449.]

primeval aspects, sterner, savager than any poet has sung. It is only the white man's poetry. We want the Indian's report. Wordsworth is too tame for the Chippeway.[1]

The landscape contains a thousand dials which indicate the natural divisions of time; the shadows of a thousand styles point to the hour. The afternoon is now far advanced, and a fresh and leisurely wind is blowing on the river, causing long reaches of serene ripples. It has done its stent, and seems not to flow but lie at its length reflecting the light. The haze over the woods seems like the breath of all nature, rising from a myriad pores into the attenuated atmosphere.[2] It is sun smoke, the woof he has woven, his day's toil displayed.[3]

If I were awaked from a deep sleep, I should know which side the meridian the sun might be by the chirping of the crickets. Night has already insidiously set her foot in the valley in many places, where the shadows of the shrubs and fences begin to darken the landscape. There is a deeper shading in the colors of the afternoon landscape. Perhaps the forenoon is brighter than the afternoon, not only because of the greater transparency of the atmosphere then, but because we naturally look most into the west, — as we look forward into the day, — and so in the forenoon see the sunny side of things, but in the afternoon the shadow of every tree.

What a drama of light and shadow from morning to night! Soon as the sun is over the meridian, in deep

[1] [*Week*, p. 56 ; Riv. 70.]   [2] [*Week*, p. 341; Riv. 422.]
[3] [*Week*, p. 229 ; Riv. 284.]

ravines under the east side of the cliffs night forwardly plants her foot, and, as day retreats, steps into his trenches, till at length she sits in his citadel. For long time she skulks behind the needles of the pine, before she dares draw out her forces into the plain. Sun, moon, wind, and stars are the allies of one side or the other.[1]

How much will some officious men give to preserve an old book, of which perchance only a single [copy] exists, while a wise God is already giving, and will still give, infinitely more to get it destroyed!

Aug. 20. Friday. It seems as if no cock lived so far in the horizon but a faint vibration reached me here, spread the wider over earth as the more distant.

In the morning the crickets snore, in the afternoon they chirp, at midnight they dream.

Aug. 24. Let us wander where we will, the universe is built round about us, and we are central still. By reason of this, if we look into the heavens, they are concave, and if we were to look into a gulf as bottomless, it would be concave also. The sky is curved downward to the earth in the horizon, because I stand in the plain. I draw down its skirts. The stars so low there seem loth to go away from me, but by a circuitous path to be remembering and returning to me.[2]

Aug. 28. Saturday. A great poet will write for his peers alone, and indite no line to an inferior. He will

[1] [*Week*, p. 341; Riv. 421, 422.]   [2] [*Week*, p. 353; Riv. 436, 437.]

remember only that he saw truth and beauty from his position, and calmly expect the time when a vision as broad shall overlook the same field as freely.[1]

Johnson can no more criticise Milton than the naked eye can criticise Herschel's map of the sun.

The art which only gilds the surface and demands merely a superficial polish, without reaching to the core, is but varnish and filigree. But the work of genius is rough-hewn from the first, because it anticipates the lapse of time and has an ingrained polish, which still appears when fragments are broken off, an essential quality of its substance. Its beauty is its strength. It breaks with a lustre, and splits in cubes and diamonds. Like the diamond, it has only to be cut to be polished, and its surface is a window to its interior splendors.

True verses are not counted on the poet's fingers, but on his heart-strings.

> My life hath been the poem I would have writ,
> But I could not both live and live to utter it.[2]

In the Hindoo scripture the idea of man is quite illimitable and sublime. There is nowhere a loftier conception of his destiny. He is at length lost in Brahma himself, "the divine male." Indeed, the distinction of races in this life is only the commencement of a series of degrees which ends in Brahma.

The veneration in which the Vedas are held is itself

[1] [*Week*, p. 363; Riv. 450.]   [2] [*Week*, p. 365; Riv. 453.]

a remarkable fact. Their code embraced the whole moral life of the Hindoo, and in such a case there is no other truth than sincerity. Truth is such by reference to the heart of man within, not to any standard without. There is no creed so false but faith can make it true.

In inquiring into the origin and genuineness of this scripture it is impossible to tell when the divine agency in its composition ceased, and the human began. "From fire, from air, and from the sun" was it "milked out."

There is no grander conception of creation anywhere. It is peaceful as a dream,[1] and so is the annihilation of the world. It is such a beginning and ending as the morning and evening, for they had learned that God's methods are not violent. It was such an awakening as might have been heralded by the faint dreaming chirp of the crickets before the dawn.

The very indistinctness of its theogony implies a sublime truth. It does not allow the reader to rest in any supreme first cause, but directly hints of a supremer still which created the last. The creator is still behind, increate.[2] The divinity is so fleeting that its attributes are never expressed.

Aug. 30. What is a day, if the day's work be not done? What are the divisions of time to them who have nothing to do? What is the present or the future to him who has no occasion for them, who does not create them by his industry?

[1] [*Week*, p. 159; Riv. 198.]   [2] [*Week*, p. 159; Riv. 199.]

It is now easy to apply to this ancient scripture such a catholic criticism as it will become the part of some future age to apply to the Christian, — wherein the design and idea which underlies it is considered, and not the narrow and partial fulfillment.

These verses are so eminently textual, that it seems as if those old sages had concentrated all their wisdom in little fascicles, of which future times were to be the commentary; as the light of this lower world is only the dissipated rays of the sun and stars.[1] They seem to have been uttered with a sober morning prescience, in the dawn of time.[2] There is a sort of holding back, or withdrawal of the full meaning, that the ages may follow after and explore the whole. The sentence opens unexpensively and almost unmeaningly, as the petals of a flower.[3]

To our nearsightedness this mere outward life seems a constituent part of us, and we do not realize that as our soul expands it will cast off the shell of routine and convention, which afterward will only be an object for the cabinets of the curious. But of this people the temples are now crumbled away, and we are introduced to the very hearth of Hindoo life and to the primeval conventicle where how to eat and to drink and to sleep were the questions to be decided.[4]

The simple life herein described confers on us a degree of freedom even in the perusal. We throw down

[1] [*Week*, p. 155; Riv. 194.]   [3] [*Week*, p. 155; Riv. 194.]
[2] [*Week*, p. 155; Riv. 193.]   [4] [*Week*, p. 156; Riv. 195.]

our packs and go on our way unencumbered. Wants so easily and gracefully satisfied that they seem like a more refined pleasure and repleteness.[1]

Sept. 1. *Wednesday.* When I observe the effeminate taste of some of my contemporaries in this matter of poetry, and how hardly they bear with certain incongruities, I think if this age were consulted it would not choose granite to be the backbone of the world, but Bristol spar or Brazilian diamonds. But the verses which have consulted the refinements even of a golden age will be found weak and nerveless for an iron one. The poet is always such a Cincinnatus in literature as with republican simplicity to raise all to the chiefest honors of the state.

Each generation thinks to inhabit only a west end of the world, and have intercourse with a refined and civilized Nature, not conceiving of her broad equality and republicanism. They think her aristocratic and exclusive because their own estates are narrow. But the sun indifferently selects his rhymes, and with a liberal taste weaves into his verse the planet and the stubble.[2]

Let us know and conform only to the fashions of eternity.

The very austerity of these Hindoos is tempting to the devotional as a more refined and nobler luxury.[3] They seem to have indulged themselves with a certain moderation and temperance in the severities which their

[1] [*Week*, p. 159; Riv. 198.]   [2] [*Week*, p. 402; Riv. 496.]
[3] [*Week*, p. 159; Riv. 198.]

code requires, as divine exercises not to be excessively used as yet. One may discover the root of a Hindoo religion in his own private history, when, in the silent intervals of the day or the night, he does sometimes inflict on himself like austerities with a stern satisfaction.

The "Laws of Menu" are a manual of private devotion, so private and domestic and yet so public and universal a word as is not spoken in the parlor or pulpit in these days.[1] It is so impersonal that it exercises our sincerity more than any other. It goes with us into the yard and into the chamber, and is yet later spoken than the advice of our mother and sisters.[2]

Sept. 2. *Thursday.* There is but one obligation, and that is the obligation to obey the highest dictate. None can lay me under another which will supersede this. The gods have given me these years without any incumbrance; society has no mortgage on them. If any man assist me in the way of the world, let him derive satisfaction from the deed itself, for I think I never shall have dissolved my prior obligations to God. Kindness repaid is thereby annulled. I would let his deed lie as fair and generous as it was intended. The truly beneficent never relapses into a creditor; his great kindness is still extended to me and is never done. Of those noble deeds which have me for their object I am only the most fortunate spectator, and would rather be the abettor of their nobleness than stay their tide with the obstructions of impatient gratitude. As true as action and reaction are equal, that nobleness which was as wide as the

[1] [*Week*, p. 156; Riv. 194.]   [2] [*Week*, p. 156; Riv. 195.]

universe will rebound not on him the individual, but on the world. If any have been kind to me, what more do they want? I cannot make them richer than they are. If they have not been kind, they cannot take from me the privilege which they have not improved. My obligations will be my lightest load, for that gratitude which is of kindred stuff in me, expanding every pore, will easily sustain the pressure. We walk the freest through the air we breathe.

The sublime sentences of Menu carry us back to a time when purification and sacrifice and self-devotion had a place in the faith of men, and were not as now a superstition. They contain a subtle and refined philosophy also, such as in these times is not accompanied with so lofty and pure a devotion.

I saw a green meadow in the midst of the woods to-day which looked as if Dame Nature had set her foot there, and it had bloomed in consequence. It was the print of her moccasin.

Sometimes my thought rustles in midsummer as if ripe for the fall.[1] I anticipate the russet hues and the dry scent of autumn, as the feverish man dreams of balm and sage.

I was informed to-day that no Hindoo tyranny presided at the framing of the world, — that I am a freeman of the universe, and not sentenced to any caste.[2]

[1] [*Week*, p. 358; Riv. 443.]   [2] [*Week*, p. 155; Riv. 193.]

When I write verses I serve my thoughts as I do tumblers; I rap them to see if they will ring.

Sept. 3. *Friday.* Next to Nature, it seems as if man's actions were the most natural, they so gently accord with her. The small seines of flax or hemp stretched across the shallow and transparent parts of the river are no more intrusion than the cobweb in the sun. It is very slight and refined outrage at most. I stay my boat in mid-current and look down in the running water to see the civil meshes of his nets, and wonder how the blustering people of the town could have done this elvish work. The twine looks like a new river-weed and is to the river like a beautiful memento of man, man's presence in nature discovered as silently and delicately as Robinson discovered that there [were] savages on his island by a footprint in the sand.[1]

Moonlight is the best restorer of antiquity. The houses in the village have a classical elegance as of the best days of Greece, and this half-finished church reminds me of the Parthenon, or whatever is most famous and excellent in art.[2] So serene it stands, reflecting the moon, and intercepting the stars with its rafters, as if it were refreshed by the dews of the night equally with me. By day Mr. Hosmer, but by night Vitruvius rather. If it were always to stand in this mild and sombre light it would be finished already. It is in progress by day but completed by night, and already its

[1] [*Excursions*, p. 119; Riv. 146, 147.]
[2] [*Excursions*, pp. 331, 332; Riv. 408.]

designer is an old master. The projecting rafter so carelessly left on the tower, holding its single way through the sky, is quite architectural, and in the unnecessary length of the joists and flooring of the staging around the walls there is an artistic superfluity and grace. In these fantastic lines described upon the sky there is no trifling or conceit. Indeed, the staging for the most part is the only genuine native architecture and deserves to stand longer than the building it surrounds. In this obscurity there are no fresh colors to offend, and the light and shade of evening adorn the new equally with the old.

Sept. 4. Saturday. I think I could write a poem to be called "Concord." For argument I should have the River, the Woods, the Ponds, the Hills, the Fields, the Swamps and Meadows, the Streets and Buildings, and the Villagers. Then Morning, Noon, and Evening, Spring, Summer, Autumn, and Winter, Night, Indian Summer, and the Mountains in the Horizon.

A book should be so true as to be intimate and familiar to all men, as the sun to their faces, — such a word as is occasionally uttered to a companion in the woods in summer, and both are silent.

As I pass along the streets of the village on the day of our annual fair, when the leaves strew the ground, I see how the trees keep just such a holiday all the year. The lively spirits of their sap mount higher than any plowboy's let loose that day. A walk in the autumn woods, when, with serene courage, they are preparing for their

winter campaign, if you have an ear for the rustling of their camp or an eye for the glancing of their armor, is more inspiring than the Greek or Peninsular war.[1] Any grandeur may find society as great as itself in the forest.

Pond Hill. — I see yonder some men in a boat, which floats buoyantly amid the reflections of the trees, like a feather poised in mid-air, or a leaf wafted gently from its twig to the water without turning over. They seem very delicately to have availed themselves of the natural laws, and their floating there looks like a beautiful and successful experiment in philosophy. It reminds me how much more refined and noble the life of man might be made, how its whole economy might be as beautiful as a Tuscan villa,[2] — a new and more catholic art, the art of life, which should have its impassioned devotees and make the schools of Greece and Rome to be deserted.

Sept. 5. Saturday. Barn.

> Greater is the depth of sadness
> Than is any height of gladness.

I cannot read much of the best poetry in prose or verse without feeling that it is a partial and exaggerated plaint, rarely a carol as free as Nature's. That content which the sun shines for between morning and evening is unsung. The Muse solaces herself; she is not delighted but consoled.[3] But there are times when we feel a vigor in our limbs, and our thoughts are like a

[1] [*Week*, p. 358; Riv. 443.]   [2] [*Week*, p. 48; Riv. 60.]
[3] [*Week*, p. 393; Riv. 486.]

flowing morning light, and the stream of our life without reflection shows long reaches of serene ripples. And if we were to sing at such an hour, there would be no catastrophe contemplated in our verse, no tragic element in it,[1] nor yet a comic. For the life of the gods is not in any sense dramatic, nor can be the subject of the drama; it is epic without beginning or end, an eternal interlude without plot, — not subordinate one part to another, but supreme as a whole, at once leaf and flower and fruit. At present the highest strain is Hebraic. The church bell is the tone of all religious thought, the most musical that men consent to sing. In the youth of poetry, men love to praise the lark and the morning, but they soon forsake the dews and skies for the nightingale and evening shades. Without instituting a wider comparison I might say that in Homer there is more of the innocence and serenity of youth than in the more modern and moral poets. The Iliad is not Sabbath but morning reading, and men cling to this old song, because they have still moments of unbaptized and uncommitted life which give them an appetite for more. There is no cant in him, as there is no religion. We read him with a rare sense of freedom and irresponsibleness, as though we trod on native ground, and were autochthones of the soil.[2]

Through the fogs of this distant vale we look back and upward to the source of song, whose crystal stream still ripples and gleams in the clear atmosphere of the mountain's side.

[1] [*Week*, pp. 393, 394; Riv. 486.]   [2] [*Week*, p. 394; Riv. 486.]

Some hours seem not to be occasion for anything, unless for great resolves to draw breath and repose in, so religiously do we postpone all action therein. We do not straight go about to execute our thrilling purpose, but shut our doors behind us, and saunter with prepared mind, as if the half were already done.[1]

Sometimes a day serves only to hold time together.[2]

Sept. 12. Sunday.

> Where I have been
> There was none seen.

Sept. 14. No bravery is to be named with that which can face its own deeds.

In religion there is no society.

Do not dissect a man till he is dead.

Love does not analyze its object.

We do not know the number of muscles in a caterpillar dead; much less the faculties of a man living.

You must believe that I know before you can tell me.

To the highest communication I can make no reply; I lend only a silent ear.

[1] [*Week*, p. 111; Riv. 138.]
[2] [See p. 213 for the possible origin of this figure.]

Sept. 18. *Saturday.* Barn. — It is a great event, the hearing of a bell ring in one of the neighboring towns, particularly in the night. It excites in me an unusual hilarity, and I feel that I am in season wholly and enjoy a prime and leisure hour.

Sept. 20. *Monday.* Visited Sampson Wilder of Boston. His method of setting out peach trees is as follows: —

Dig a hole six feet square and two deep, and remove the earth; cover the bottom to the depth of six inches with lime and ashes in equal proportions, and upon this spread another layer of equal thickness, of horn parings, tips of horns, bones, and the like, then fill up with a compost of sod and strong animal manure, say four bushels of hog manure to a cartload of sod. Cover the tree — which should be budded at two years old — but slightly, and at the end of two years dig a trench round it three feet from the tree and six inches deep, and fill it with lime and ashes.

For grapes: —

Let your trench be twelve feet wide and four deep, cover the bottom with paving-stones six inches, then old bricks with mortar attached or loose six inches more, then beef-bones, horns, etc., six more (Captain Bobadil), then a compost similar to the preceding. Set your roots one foot from the north side, the trench running east and west, and bury eight feet of the vine crosswise the trench, not more than eight inches below the surface. Cut it down for three or four years, that root may accumulate, and then train it from the sun up an inclined plane.

Vol. I

selves more than you, — not by your ingratitude, but by sympathy and congratulation.

The twenty-first volume of Chalmers's English Poets contains Hoole's and Mickle's Translations. In the shape of a note to the Seventh Book of the Lusiad, Mickle has written a long "Inquiry into the Religious Tenets and Philosophy of the Bramins."

Nov. 30. *Tuesday.* Cambridge. — When looking over the dry and dusty volumes of the English poets, I cannot believe that those fresh and fair creations I had imagined are contained in them. English poetry from Gower down, collected into one alcove, and so from the library window compared with the commonest nature, seems very mean. Poetry cannot breathe in the scholar's atmosphere. The Aubreys and Hickeses, with all their learning, prophane it yet indirectly by their zeal. You need not envy his feelings who for the first time has cornered up poetry in an alcove. I can hardly be serious with myself when I remember that I have come to Cambridge after poetry; and while I am running over the catalogue and collating and selecting, I think if it would not be a shorter way to a complete volume to step at once into the field or wood, with a very low reverence to students and librarians. Milton did not foresee what company he was to fall into.[1] On running over the titles of these books, looking from time to time at their first pages or farther, I am oppressed by an inevitable sadness. One must have come into a

[1] [*Week*, p. 363; Riv. 450.]

Sept. 28. *Tuesday.* I anticipate the coming in of spring as a child does the approach of some pomp through a gate of the city.

Sept. 30.   Better wait
                  Than be too late.[1]

Nov. 29. Cambridge. — One must fight his way, after a fashion, even in the most civil and polite society. The most truly kind and gracious have to be won by a sort of valor, for the seeds of suspicion seem to lurk in every spadeful of earth, as well as those of confidence. The president and librarian turn the cold shoulder to your application, though they are known for benevolent persons. They wonder if you can be anything but a thief, contemplating frauds on the library. It is the instinctive and salutary principle of self-defense; that which makes the cat show her talons when you take her by the paw.[2]

Certainly that valor which can open the hearts of men is superior to that which can only open the gates of cities.[3]

You must always let people see that they serve them-

[1] [On the back lining-page of the manuscript Journal volume which ends with this date are the following sentences in pencil:]

There is another young day let loose to roam the earth.

Happiness is very unprofitable stock.

The love which is preached nowadays is an ocean of new milk for a man to swim in. I hear no surf nor surge, but the winds coo over it.

[2] [See *Week*, pp. xx, xxi; *Misc.*, Riv. 8, 9 (Emerson's Biographical Sketch of Thoreau).]

[3] [*Week*, p. 291; Riv. 361.]

library by an oriel window, as softly and undisturbed as the light which falls on the books through a stained window, and not by the librarian's door, else all his dreams will vanish. Can the Valhalla be warmed by steam and go by clock and bell?

Good poetry seems so simple and natural a thing that when we meet it we wonder that all men are not always poets. Poetry is nothing but healthy speech. Though the speech of the poet goes to the heart of things, yet he is that one especially who speaks civilly to Nature as a second person and in some sense is the patron of the world. Though more than any he stands in the midst of Nature, yet more than any he can stand aloof from her. The best lines, perhaps, only suggest to me that that man simply saw or heard or felt what seems the commonest fact in my experience.

One will know how to appreciate Chaucer best who has come down to him the natural way through the very meagre pastures of Saxon and ante-Chaucerian poetry. So human and wise he seems after such diet that we are as liable to misjudge him so as usually.[1]

The Saxon poetry extant seems of a more serious and philosophical cast than the very earliest that can be called English. It has more thought, but less music. It translates Boëthius, it paraphrases the Hebrew Bible, it solemnly sings of war, of life and death, and chronicles events. The earliest English poetry is tinctured with romance through the influence of the Normans, as the Saxon was not. The ballad and metrical romance

[1] [*Week*, p. 395; Riv. 488.]

belong to this period. Those old singers were for the most part imitators or translators.[1] Or will it not appear, when viewed at a sufficient distance, that our brave new poets are also secondary as they, and refer the eye that reads them and their poetry, too, back and backward without end?

Nothing is so attractive and unceasingly curious as character. There is no plant that needs such tender treatment, there is none that will endure so rough. It is the violet and the oak. It is the thing we mean, let us say what we will. We mean our own character, or we mean yours. It is divine and related to the heavens, as the earth is by the flashes of the Aurora. It has no acquaintance nor companion. It goes silent and un-observed longer than any planet in space, but when at length it does show itself, it seems like the flowering of all the world, and its before unseen orbit is lit up like the trail of a meteor. I hear no good news ever but some trait of a noble character. It reproaches me plaintively. I am mean in contrast, but again am thrilled and elevated that I can see my own mean-ness, and again still, that my own aspiration is realized in that other. You reach me, my friend, not by your kind or wise words to me here or there; but as you retreat, perhaps after years of vain familiarity, some gesture or unconscious action in the distance speaks to me with more emphasis than all those years. I am not concerned to know what eighth planet is wander-ing in space up there, or when Venus or Orion rises,

[1] [*Week*, p. 395 ; Riv. 488.]

but if, in any cot to east or west and set behind the woods, there is any planetary character illuminating the earth.

Packed in my mind lie all the clothes
Which outward nature wears,
For, as its hourly fashions change,
It all things else repairs.

My eyes look inward, not without,
And I but hear myself,
And this new wealth which I have got
Is part of my own pelf.

For while I look for change abroad,
I can no difference find,
Till some new ray of peace uncalled
Lumines my inmost mind,

As, when the sun streams through the wood,
Upon a winter's morn,
Where'er his silent beams may stray
The murky night is gone.

How could the patient pine have known
The morning breeze would come,
Or simple flowers anticipate
The insect's noonday hum,

Till that new light with morning cheer
From far streamed through the aisles,

Vol. I

And nimbly told the forest trees
For many stretching miles?[1]

[*Dec.*] 12. *Sunday.* All music is only a sweet striving to express character. Now that lately I have heard of some traits in the character of a fair and earnest maiden whom I had only known superficially, but who has gone hence to make herself more known by distance, they sound like strains of a wild harp music. They make all persons and places who had thus forgotten her to seem late and behindhand. Every maiden conceals a fairer flower and more luscious fruit than any calyx in the field, and if she go with averted face, confiding in her own purity and high resolves, she will make the heavens retrospective, and all nature will humbly con-fess its queen.[2]

There is apology enough for all the deficiency and shortcoming in the world in the patient waiting of any bud of character to unfold itself.

Only character can command our reverent love. It is all mysteries in itself.

What is it gilds the trees and clouds
And paints the heavens so gay,
But yonder fast-abiding light
With its unchanging ray?

[1] [This poem, with the four additional stanzas of the next date, appears in the *Week*, pp. 313, 314 (Riv. 388, 389) under the title of "The Inward Morning." The second stanza is there omitted and there are other alterations.]

[2] [*Familiar Letters*, Sept., 1852.]

I've felt within my inmost soul
Such cheerful morning news,
In the horizon of my mind
I've seen such morning hues,

As in the twilight of the dawn,
When the first birds awake,
Is heard within some silent wood
Where they the small twigs break;

Or in the eastern skies is seen
Before the sun appears,
Foretelling of the summer heats
Which far away he bears.

P. M. Walden. — I seem to discern the very form of the wind when, blowing over the hills, it falls in broad flakes upon the surface of the pond, this subtle element obeying the same law with the least subtle. As it falls it spreads itself like a mass of lead dropped upon an anvil. I cannot help being encouraged by this blithe activity in the elements in these degenerate days of men. Who hears the rippling of the rivers will not utterly despair of anything. The wind in the wood yonder sounds like an incessant waterfall, the water dashing and roaring among rocks.

[*Dec.*] 13. *Monday.* We constantly anticipate repose. Yet it surely can only be the repose that is in entire and healthy activity. It must be a repose without rust. What is leisure but opportunity for more complete and entire action? Our energies pine for exercise. That time we spend in our duties is so much leisure, so that there is no man but has sufficient of it.

I make my own time, I make my own terms. I cannot see how God or Nature can ever get the start of me.

This ancient Scotch poetry, at which its contemporaries so marvelled, sounds like the uncertain lisping of a child. When man's speech flows freest it but stutters and stammers. There is never a free and clear deliverance; but, read now when the illusion of smooth verse is destroyed by the antique spelling, the sense is seen to stammer and stumble all the plainer. To how few thoughts do all these sincere efforts give utterance! An hour's conversation with these men would have done more. I am astonished to find how meagre that diet is which has fed so many men. The music of sound, which is all-sufficient at first, is speedily lost, and then the fame of the poet must rest on the music of the sense. A great philosophical and moral poet would give permanence to the language by making the best sound convey the best sense.

[*Dec.*] 14. *Tuesday.* To hear the sunset described by the old Scotch poet Douglas as I have seen it repays me for many weary pages of antiquated Scotch. Nothing so restores and humanizes antiquity and makes it blithe as the discovery of some natural sympathy between it and the present. Why is it that there is something melancholy in antiquity? We forget that it had any other future than our present. As if it were not as

near to *the* future as ourselves! No, thank heavens, these ranks of men to right and left, posterity and ancestry, are not to be thridded by any earnest mortal. The heavens stood over the heads of our ancestors as near as to us. Any living word in their books abolishes the difference of time. It need only be considered from the present standpoint.

[*Dec.*] 15. *Wednesday.* A mild summer sun shines over forest and lake. The earth looks as fair this morning as the Valhalla of the gods. Indeed our spirits never go beyond nature. In the woods there is an inexpressible happiness. Their mirth is but just repressed. In winter, when there is but one green leaf for many rods, what warm content is in them! They are not rude, but tender, even in the severest cold. Their nakedness is their defense. All their sounds and sights are elixir to my spirit. They possess a divine health. God is not more well. Every sound is inspiriting and fraught with the same mysterious assurance, from the creaking of the boughs in January to the soft sough of the wind in July.

How much of my well-being, think you, depends on the condition of my lungs and stomach, — such cheap pieces of Nature as they, which, indeed, she is every day reproducing with prodigality. Is the arrow indeed fatal which rankles in the breast of the bird on the bough, in whose eye all this fair landscape is reflected, and whose voice still echoes through the wood?

The trees have come down to the bank to see the river go by. This old, familiar river is renewed each instant;

only the channel is the same.[1] The water which so calmly reflects the fleeting clouds and the primeval trees I have never seen before. It may have washed some distant shore, or framed a glacier or iceberg at the north, when I last stood here. Seen through a mild atmosphere, the works of the husbandman, his plowing and reaping, have a beauty to the beholder which the laborer never sees.[2]

I seem to see somewhat more of my own kith and kin in the lichens on the rocks than in any books. It does seem as if mine were a peculiarly wild nature, which so yearns toward all wildness. I know of no redeeming qualities in me but a sincere love for some things, and when I am reproved I have to fall back on to this ground.[3] This is my argument in reserve for all cases. My love is invulnerable. Meet me on that ground, and you will find me strong. When I am condemned, and condemn myself utterly, I think straightway, "But I rely on my love for some things." Therein I am whole and entire. Therein I am God-propped.

When I see the smoke curling up through the woods from some farmhouse invisible, it is more suggestive of the poetry of rural and domestic life than a nearer inspection can be. Up goes the smoke as quietly as the dew exhales in vapor from these pine leaves and oaks; as busy, disposing itself in circles and in wreaths, as the housewife on the hearth below. It is cotemporary with a piece of human biography, and waves as a feather in some *man's* cap. Under that rod of sky there is some

¹ [See p. 347.]   ² [*Week*, p. 373; Riv. 461.]
³ [*Week*, p. 54; Riv. 67.]

plot a-brewing, some ingenuity has planted itself, and we shall see what it will do. It tattles of more things than the boiling of the pot. It is but one of man's breaths. All that is interesting in history or fiction is transpiring beneath that cloud. The subject of all life and death, of happiness and grief, goes thereunder.

When the traveller in the forest, attaining to some eminence, descries a column of smoke in the distance, it is a very gentle hint to him of the presence of man. It seems as if it would establish friendly relations between them without more ado.[1]

[*Dec.*] 18. *Saturday.* Some men make their due impression upon their generation, because a petty occasion is enough to call forth all their energies; but are there not others who would rise to much higher levels, whom the world has never provoked to make the effort? I believe there are men now living who have never opened their mouths in a public assembly, in whom nevertheless there is such a well of eloquence that the appetite of any age could never exhaust it; who pine for an occasion worthy of them, and will pine till they are dead; who can admire, as well as the rest, at the flowing speech of the orator, but do yet miss the thunder and lightning and visible sympathy of the elements which would garnish their own utterance.

If in any strait I see a man fluttered and his ballast gone, then I lose all hope of him, he is undone; but if he reposes still, though he do nothing else worthy of him, if he is still a man in reserve, then is there every-

¹ [*Excursions*, p. 174; Riv. 212.]

Winter Landscape from Fair Haven Hill

thing to hope of him. The age may well go pine itself that it cannot put to use this gift of the gods. He lives on, still unconcerned, not needing to be used. The greatest occasion will be the slowest to come.

Sometimes a particular body of men do unconsciously assert that their will is fate, that the right is decided by their fiat without appeal, and when this is the case they can never be mistaken; as when one man is quite silenced by the thrilling eloquence of another, and submits to be neglected as to his fate, because such is not the willful vote of the assembly, but their instinctive decision.

Dec. 23. Thursday. Concord. — The best man's spirit makes a fearful sprite to haunt his tomb. The ghost of a priest is no better than that of a highwayman. It is pleasant to hear of one who has blest whole regions after his death by having frequented them while alive, who has prophaned or tabooed no place by being buried in it.[1] It adds not a little to the fame of Little John that his grave was long "celebrous for the yielding of excellent whetstones."[2]

A forest is in all mythologies a sacred place, as the oaks among the Druids and the grove of Egeria; and even in more familiar and common life a celebrated wood is spoken of with respect, as "Barnsdale Wood"

---

[1] [Written in pencil on a fly-leaf of the Journal:] A man might well pray that he may not taboo or curse any portion of nature by being buried in it.
[2] [Channing, p. 241.]

and "Sherwood." Had Robin Hood no Sherwood to resort [to], it would be difficult to invest his story with the charms it has got. It is always the tale that is untold, the deeds done and the life lived in the unexplored secrecy of the wood, that charm us and make us children again, — to read his ballads, and hear of the greenwood tree.

Dec. 24. Friday. I want to go soon and live away by the pond, where I shall hear only the wind whispering among the reeds. It will be success if I shall have left myself behind. But my friends ask what I will do when I get there. Will it not be employment enough to watch the progress of the seasons?[1]

Dec. 25. Saturday. It does seem as if Nature did for a long time gently overlook the prophanity of man. The wood still kindly echoes the strokes of the axe, and when the strokes are few and seldom, they add a new charm to a walk. All the elements strive to *naturalize* the sound.[2]

Such is our sympathy with the seasons that we experience the same degree of heat in the winter as in the summer.

It is not a true apology for any coarseness to say that it is natural. The grim woods can afford to be very delicate and perfect in the details.

I don't want to feel as if my life were a sojourn any longer. That philosophy cannot be true which so paints it. It is time now that I begin to live.

[1] [See p. 244.]   [2] [*Excursions*, p. 173; Riv. 212.]

Vol. I

Dec. 26. Sunday. He is the rich man and enjoys the fruits of riches, who, summer and winter forever, can find delight in the contemplation of his soul. I could look as unweariedly up to that cope as into the heavens of a summer day or a winter night. When I hear this bell ring, I am carried back to years and Sabbaths when I was newer and more innocent, I fear, than now, and it seems to me as if there were a world within a world. Sin, I am sure, is not in overt acts or, indeed, in acts of any kind, but is in proportion to the time which has come behind us and displaced eternity, — that degree to which our elements are mixed with the elements of the world. The whole duty of life is contained in the question how to respire and aspire both at once.

Dec. 29. Wednesday. One does not soon learn the trade of life. That one may work out a true life requires more art and delicate skill than any other work. There is need of the nice fingers of the girl as well as the tough hand of the farmer. The daily work is too often toughening the pericarp of the heart as well as the hand. Great familiarity with the world must be nicely managed, lest it win away and bereave us of some susceptibility. Experience bereaves us of our innocence; wisdom bereaves us of our ignorance. Let us walk in the world without learning its ways. Whole weeks or months of my summer life slide away in thin volumes like mist or smoke, till at length some warm morning, perchance, I see a sheet of mist blown down the brook to the swamp, its shadow flitting across the fields, which have caught a new significance from that accident; and as that

vapor is raised above the earth, so shall the next weeks be elevated above the plane of the actual;[1] or when the setting sun slants across the pastures, and the cows low to my inward ear and only enhance the stillness, and the eve is as the dawn, a beginning hour and not a final one, as if it would never have done, with its clear western amber inciting men to lives of as limpid purity. Then do other parts of my day's work shine than I had thought at noon, for I discover the real purport of my toil, as, when the husbandman has reached the end of the furrow and looks back, he can best tell where the pressed earth shines most.[2]

All true greatness runs as level a course, and is as unaspiring, as the plow in the furrow. It wears the homeliest dress and speaks the homeliest language. Its theme is gossamer and dew lines, johnswort and loosestrife, for it has never stirred from its repose and is most ignorant of foreign parts. Heaven is the inmost place. The good have not to travel far. What cheer may we not derive from the thought that our courses do not diverge, and we wend not asunder, but as the web of destiny is woven it [is] fulled, and we are cast more and more into the centre! And our fates even are social.[3] There is no wisdom which can take [the] place of humanity, and I find that in old Chaucer that love rings longest which rhymes best with some saw of Milton's or Edmunds's. I wish I could be as still as God is. I can recall to my mind the stillest summer hour,

[1] [*Week*, p. 314; Riv. 389.]   [2] [*Week*, p. 133; Riv. 166.]
[3] [*Week*, p. 280; Riv. 347.]

in which the grasshopper sings over the mulleins, and there is a valor in that time the memory of which is armor that can laugh at any blow of fortune. A man should go out [of] nature with the chirp of the cricket or the trill of the veery ringing in his ear. These earthly sounds should only die away for a season, as the strains of the harp rise and swell. Death is that expressive pause in the music of the blast.[1] I would be as clean as ye, O woods. I shall not rest till I be as innocent as you. I know that I shall sooner or later attain to an unspotted innocence, for when I consider that state even now I am thrilled.

If we were wise enough, we should see to what virtue we were indebted for any happier moment we might have, nor doubt we had earned this at some time.

These motions everywhere in nature must surely [be] the circulations of God. The flowing sail, the running stream, the waving tree, the roving wind, — whence else their infinite health and freedom?[2] I can see nothing so proper and holy as unrelaxed play and frolic in this bower God has built for us. The suspicion of sin never comes to this thought. Oh, if men felt this they would never build temples even of marble or diamond, but it would be sacrilege and prophane, but disport them forever in this paradise.

In the coldest day it melts somewhere.

It seems as if only one trait, one little incident in human biography, need to be said or written in some era, that all readers may go mad after it, and the man who did the miracle is made a demigod henceforth.

[1] [Week, p. 314; Riv. 390.]   [2] [Week, p. 384; Riv. 474.]

nothing better in its kind. The poets seem to be only more frank and plain-spoken than other men. Their verse is but confessions. They always confide in the reader, and speak privily with him, keeping nothing back.[1]

I know of no safe rule by which to judge of the purity of a former age but that I see that the impure of the present age are not apt to rise to noble sentiments when they speak or write, and suspect, therefore, that there may be more truth than is allowed in the apology that such was the manner of the age.[2]

Within the circuit of this plodding life,
There are moments of an azure hue
And as unspotted fair as is the violet
Or anemone, when the spring strews them
By some south woodside; which make untrue
The best philosophy which has so poor an aim
But to console man for his grievance here.
I have remembered when the winter came,
High in my chamber in the frosty nights,
How in the summer past some
Unrecorded beam slanted across
Some upland pasture where the Johnswort grew,
Or heard, amidst the verdure of my mind, the bee's
     long-smothered hum,
So by the cheap economy of God made rich to go upon
     my wintry work again.
In the still, cheerful cold of winter nights,
When, in the cold light of the moon,

[1] [Week, p. 397; Riv. 490.]   [2] [Week, p. 398; Riv. 491, 492.]

What we all do, not one can tell; and when some lucky speaker utters a truth of our experience and not of our speculation, we think he must have had the nine Muses and the three Graces to help him. I can at length stretch me when I come to Chaucer's breadth; and I think, "Well, I could be *that* man's acquaintance,"[1] for he walked in that low and retired way that I do, and was not too good to live. I am grieved when they hint of any unmanly submissions he may have made, for that subtracts from his breadth and humanity.

Dec. 30. Thursday. I admire Chaucer for a sturdy English wit. The easy height he speaks from in his Prologue to the Canterbury Tales is as good as anything in it, — as if he were indeed better than any of the company there assembled.[2]

The poet does not have to go out of himself and cease to tattle of his domestic affairs, to win our confidence, but is so broad that we see no limits to his sympathy.

Great delicacy and gentleness of character is constantly displayed in Chaucer's verse. The simplest and humblest words come readily to his lips. The natural innocence of the man appears in the simple and pure spirit in which "The Prioresses Tale" is conceived, in which the child sings *O alma redemptoris mater*, and in the account of the departure of Custance with her child upon the sea, in "The Man of Lawes Tale."[3] The whole story of Chanticleer and Dame Partlet in "The Nonnes Preestes Tale" is genuine humanity. I know

[1] [Week, p. 396; Riv. 489.]   [2] [Week, p. 397; Riv. 490.]
[3] [Week, p. 398; Riv. 491.]

On every twig and rail and jutting spout
The icy spears are doubling their length
Against the glancing arrows of the sun,
And the shrunk wheels creak along the way,
Some summer accident long past
Of lakelet gleaming in the July beams,
Or hum of bee under the blue flag,
Loitering in the meads, or busy rill
which now stands dumb and still,
its own memorial, purling at its play along the slopes,
and through the meadows next, till that its sound was
quenched in the staid current of its parent stream.

In memory is the more reality. I have seen how the furrows shone but late upturned, and where the fieldfare followed in the rear, when all the fields stood bound and hoar beneath a thick integument of snow.[1]

When the snow is falling thick and fast, the flakes nearest you seem to be driving straight to the ground, while the more distant seem to float in the air in a quivering bank, like feathers, or like birds at play, and not as if sent on any errand. So, at a little distance, all the works of Nature proceed with sport and frolic. They are more in the eye and less in the deed.

Dec. 31. Friday. Books of natural history make the most cheerful winter reading. I read in Audubon with a thrill of delight, when the snow covers the ground, of the magnolia, and the Florida keys, and their warm sea breezes; of the fence-rail, and the cotton-tree, and

[1] [Excursions, pp. 103, 104; Riv. 127, 128.]

the migrations of the rice-bird; or of the breaking up of winter in Labrador. I seem to hear the melting of the snow on the forks of the Missouri as I read. I imbibe some portion of health from these reminiscences of luxuriant nature.

There is a singular health for me in those words Labrador and East Main which no desponding creed recognizes. How much more than federal are these States! If there were no other vicissitudes but the seasons, with their attendant and consequent changes, our interest would never flag. Much more is a-doing than Congress wots of in the winter season. What journal do the persimmon and buckeye keep, or the sharp-shinned hawk? What is transpiring from summer to winter in the Carolinas, and the Great Pine Forest, and the Valley of the Mohawk? The merely political aspect of the land is never very cheering. Men are degraded when considered as the members of a political organization. As a nation the people never utter one great and healthy word. From this side all nations present only the symptoms of disease. I see but Bunker's Hill and Sing Sing, the District of Columbia and Sullivan's Island, with a few avenues connecting them. But paltry are all these beside one blast of the east or south wind which blows over them all.

In society you will not find health, but in nature. You must converse much with the field and woods, if you would imbibe such health into your mind and spirit as you covet for your body. Society is always diseased, and the best is the sickest. There is no scent in it so wholesome as that of the pines, nor any fragrance so

VI

1842

(ÆT. 24-25)

Jan. 1. Virtue is the deed of the bravest. It is that art which demands the greatest confidence and fearlessness. Only some hardy soul ventures upon it. Virtue is a bravery so hardy that it deals in what it has no experience in. The virtuous soul possesses a fortitude and hardihood which not the grenadier nor pioneer can match. It never shrunk. It goes singing to its work. Effort is its relaxation. The rude pioneer work of this world has been done by the most devoted worshippers of beauty.[1] Their resolution has possessed a keener edge than the soldier's. In winter is their campaign; they never go into quarters. They are elastic under the heaviest burden, under the extremest physical suffering.

Methinks good courage will not flag here on the Atlantic border as long as we are outflanked by the *Fur Countries*. There is enough in that sound to cheer one under any circumstances. The spruce, the hemlock, and the pine will not countenance despair. Methinks some creeds in vestries and churches do forget the hunter wrapped in furs by the Great Slave Lake, or how the Esquimaux sledges are drawn by dogs, and in the twilight of the northern night the hunter does not give over to follow the seal and walrus over the

[1] [*Week*, p. 362 ; Riv. 449.]

penetrating and restorative as that of everlasting in high pastures. Without that our feet at least stood in the midst of nature, all our faces would be pale and livid.

I should like to keep some book of natural history always by me as a sort of elixir, the reading of which would restore the tone of my system and secure me true and cheerful views of life. For to the sick, nature is sick, but to the well, a fountain of health. To the soul that contemplates some trait of natural beauty no harm nor disappointment can come. The doctrines of despair, of spiritual or political servitude, no priestcraft nor tyranny, was ever [*sic*] taught by such as drank in the harmony of nature.[1]

[1] [*Excursions*, pp. 103–105 ; Riv. 127-129.]

Vol. I

ice. These men are sick and of diseased imaginations who would toll the world's knell so soon. Cannot these sedentary sects do better than prepare the shrouds and write the epitaphs of those other busy living men? The practical faith of men belies the preacher's consolation. This is the creed of the hypochondriac.[1]

There is no infidelity so great as that which prays, and keeps the Sabbath, and founds churches. The sealer of the South Pacific preaches a truer doctrine. The church is the hospital for men's souls, but the reflection that he may one day occupy a ward in it should not discourage the cheerful labors of the able-bodied man. Let him remember the sick in their extremities, but not look thither as to his goal.[2]

Jan. 2. *Sunday.* The ringing of the church bell is a much more melodious sound than any that is heard within the church. All great values are thus public, and undulate like sound through the atmosphere. Wealth cannot purchase any great private solace or convenience. Riches are only the means of sociality. I will depend on the extravagance of my neighbors for my luxuries, for they will take care to pamper me if I will be overfed. The poor man who sacrificed nothing for the gratification seems to derive a safer and more natural enjoyment from his neighbor's extravagance than he does himself. It is a new natural product, from the contemplation of which he derives new vigor and solace as from a natural phenomenon.

[1] [*Excursions*, p. 105 ; Riv. 129, 130.]
[2] [*Week*, pp. 77, 78 ; Riv. 96, 97.]

In moments of quiet and leisure my thoughts are more apt to revert to some natural than any human relation.

Chaucer's sincere sorrow in his latter days for the grossness of his earlier works, and that he " cannot recall and annul " what he had " written of the base and filthy love of men towards women; but alas they are now continued from man to man," says he, "and I cannot do what I desire," is all very creditable to his character.

Chaucer is the make-weight of his century, — a worthy representative of England while Petrarch and Boccaccio lived in Italy, and Tell and Tamerlane in Switzerland and Asia, and Bruce and Rienzi in Europe, and Wickliffe and Gower in his own land. Edward III and John of Gaunt and the Black Prince complete the company. The fame of Roger Bacon came down from the preceding century, and Dante, though just departed, still exerted the influence of a living presence.[1]

With all his grossness he is not undistinguished for the tenderness and delicacy of his muse. A simple pathos and feminine gentleness is peculiar to him which not even Wordsworth can match.[2] And then his best passages of length are marked by a happy and healthy wit which is rather rare in the poetry of any nation. On the whole, he impresses me as greater than his reputation, and not a little like Homer and Shakespeare, for he would have held up his head in their company. Among the earliest English poets he is their landlord and host, and has the authority of such. We read him with affec-

[1] [Week, p. 396; Riv. 489.]   [2] [Week, p. 398; Riv. 492.]

tion and without criticism, for he pleads no cause, but speaks for us, his readers, always. He has that greatness of trust and reliance which compels popularity. He is for a whole country and country [sic] to know and to be proud of. The affectionate mention which succeeding early poets make of him, coupling him with Homer and Virgil, is also to be taken into the account in estimating his character. King James and Dunbar of Scotland speak with more love and reverence of him than any cotemporary poet of his predecessors of the last century. That childlike relation, indeed, does not seem to exist now which was then.[1]

Jan. 3. Monday. It is pleasant when one can relieve the grossness of the kitchen and the table by the simple beauty of his repast, so that there may be anything in it to attract the eye of the artist even. I have been popping corn to-night, which is only a more rapid blossoming of the seed under a greater than July heat. The popped corn is a perfect winter flower, hinting of anemones and houstonias. For this little grace man has, mixed in with the vulgarness of his repast, he may well thank his stars. The law by which flowers unfold their petals seems only to have operated more suddenly under the intense heat. It looks like a sympathy in this seed of the corn with its sisters of the vegetable kingdom, as if by preference it assumed the flower form rather than the crystalline. Here has bloomed for my repast such a delicate blossom as will soon spring by the wall-sides. And this is as it should be. Why should not Nature revel sometimes, and

[1] [Week, p. 396; Riv. 489, 490.]

genially relax and make herself familiar at my board? I would have my house a bower fit to entertain her. It is a feast of such innocence as might have snowed down. By my warm hearth sprang these cerealious blossoms; here was the bank where they grew.

Methinks some such visible token of approval would always accompany the simple and healthy repast. There would be such a smiling and blessing upon it. Our appetite should always be so related to our taste, and the board we spread for its gratification be an epitome of the universal table which Nature sets by hill and wood and stream for her dumb pensioners.[1]

Jan. 5. Wednesday. I find that whatever hindrances may occur I write just about the same amount of truth in my Journal; for the record is more concentrated, and usually it is some very real and earnest life, after all, that interrupts. All flourishes are omitted. If I saw wood from morning to night, though I grieve that I could not observe the train of my thoughts during that time, yet, in the evening, the few scrannel lines which describe my day's occupations will make the creaking of the saw more musical than my freest fancies could have been. I find incessant labor with the hands, which engrosses the attention also, the best method to remove palaver out of one's style. One will not dance at his work who has wood to cut and cord before the night falls in the short days of winter; but every stroke will be husbanded, and ring soberly through the wood; and so will his lines ring and tell on the ear, when at evening he settles the

[1] [Week, pp. 237, 238; Riv. 294, 295.]

accounts of the day. I have often been astonished at the force and precision of style to which busy laboring men, unpracticed in writing, easily attain when they are required to make the effort. It seems as if their sincerity and plainness were the main thing to be taught in schools, — and yet not in the schools, but in the fields, in actual service, I should say. The scholar not unfrequently envies the propriety and emphasis with which the farmer calls to his team, and confesses that if that lingo were written it would surpass his labored sentences.

Who is not tired of the weak and flowing periods of the politician and scholar, and resorts not even to the Farmer's Almanac, to read the simple account of the month's labor, to restore his tone again? I want to see a sentence run clear through to the end, as deep and fertile as a well-drawn furrow which shows that the plow was pressed down to the beam. If our scholars would lead more earnest lives, we should not witness those lame conclusions to their ill-sown discourses, but their sentences would pass over the ground like loaded rollers, and not mere hollow and wooden ones, to press in the seed and make it germinate.

A well-built sentence, in the rapidity and force with which it works, may be compared to a modern corn-planter, which furrows out, drops the seed, and covers it up at one movement.[1]

The scholar requires hard labor as an impetus to his pen. He will learn to grasp it as firmly and wield it as gracefully and effectually as an axe or a sword. When

[1] [Week, pp. 108–110; Riv. 134–136.]

I consider the labored periods of some gentleman scholar, who perchance in feet and inches comes up to the standard of his race, and is nowise deficient in girth, I am amazed at the immense sacrifice of thews and sinews. What! these proportions and these bones, and this their work! How these hands hewed this fragile matter, mere filagree or embroidery fit for ladies' fingers! Can this be a stalwart man's work, who has marrow in his backbone and a tendon Achilles in his heel? They who set up Stonehenge did somewhat, — much in comparison, — if it were only their strength was once fairly laid out, and they stretched themselves.[1]

I discover in Raleigh's verses the vices of the courtier. They are not equally sustained, as if his noble genius were warped by the frivolous society of the court. He was capable of rising to a remarkable elevation. His poetry has for the most part a heroic tone and vigor as of a knight errant. But again there seems to have been somewhat unkindly in his education, and as if he had by no means grown up to be the man he promised. He was apparently too genial and loyal a soul, or rather he was incapable of resisting temptations from that quarter. If to his genius and culture he could have added the temperament of Fox or Cromwell, the world would have had cause longer to remember him. He was the pattern of nobility. One would have said it was by some lucky fate that he and Shakespeare flourished at the same time in England, and yet what do we know of their acquaintanceship?

[1] [Week, p. 110; Riv. 136, 137.]

Jan. 7. Friday. I am singularly refreshed in winter when I hear tell of service-berries, pokeweed, juniper. Is not heaven made up of these cheap summer glories?[1]

The great God is very calm withal. How superfluous is any excitement in his creatures! He listens equally to the prayers of the believer and the unbeliever. The moods of man should unfold and alternate as gradually and placidly as those of nature. The sun shines for aye! The sudden revolutions of these times and this generation have acquired a very exaggerated importance. They do not interest me much, for they are not in harmony with the longer periods of nature. The present, in any aspect in which it can be presented to the smallest audience, is always mean. God does not sympathize with the popular movements.

Jan. 8. Saturday. When, as now, in January a south wind melts the snow, and the bare ground appears, covered with sere grass and occasionally wilted green leaves which seem in doubt whether to let go their greenness quite or absorb new juices against the coming year, — in such a season a perfume seems to exhale from the earth itself and the south wind melts my integuments also. Then is she my mother earth. I derive a real vigor from the scent of the gale wafted over the naked ground, as from strong meats, and realize again how man is the pensioner of Nature. We are always conciliated and cheered when we are fed by [such] an influence, and our needs are felt to be part of the domestic economy of Nature.

[1] [Excursions, p. 104; Riv. 128.]

Vol. I

What offends me most in my compositions is the moral element in them. The repentant say never a brave word. Their resolves should be mumbled in silence. Strictly speaking, morality is not healthy. Those undeserved joys which come uncalled and make us more pleased than grateful are they that sing.

One music seems to differ from another chiefly in its more perfect time, to use this word in a true sense. In the steadiness and equanimity of music lies its divinity. It is the only assured tone.[1] When men attain to speak with as settled a faith and as firm assurance, their voices will sing and their feet march as do the feet of the soldier. The very dogs howl if time is disregarded. Because of the perfect time of this music-box — its harmony with itself — is its greater dignity and stateliness. This music is more nobly related for its more exact measure. So simple a difference as this more even pace raises it to the higher dignity.

Man's progress through nature should have an accompaniment of music. It relieves the scenery, which is seen through it as a subtler element, like a very clear morning air in autumn. Music wafts me through the clear, sultry valleys, with only a slight gray vapor against the hills.

Of what manner of stuff is the web of time wove, when these consecutive sounds called a strain of music can be wafted down through the centuries from Homer to me, and Homer have been conversant with that same unfathomable mystery and charm which so newly

[1] [Week, p. 184; Riv. 228.]

tingles my ears?[1] These single strains, these melodious cadences which plainly proceed out of a very deep meaning and a sustained soul, are the interjections of God. They are perhaps the expression of the perfect knowledge which the righteous at length attain to. Am I so like thee, my brother, that the cadence of two notes affects us alike? Shall I not some time have an opportunity to thank him who made music? I feel a sad cheer when I hear these lofty strains,[2] because there must be something in me as lofty that hears. But ah, I hear them but rarely! Does it not rather hear me? If my blood were clogged in my veins, I am sure it would run more freely. God must be very rich, who, for the turning of a pivot, can pour out such melody on me. It is a little prophet; it tells me the secrets of futurity. Where are its secrets wound up but in this box?[3] So much hope had slumbered. There are in music such strains as far surpass any faith in the loftiness of man's destiny.[4] He must be very sad before he can comprehend them. The clear, liquid notes from the morning fields beyond seem to come through a vale of sadness to man, which gives all music a plaintive air. It hath caught a higher pace than any virtue I know. It is the arch-reformer. It hastens the sun to his setting. It invites him to his rising. It is the sweetest reproach, a measured satire.

[1] [Week, p. 182; Riv. 226.]   [2] [Week, p. 183; Riv. 227.]
[3] [It was about a year after the date of this entry that Richard F. Fuller made Thoreau a present of a music-box (see *Familiar Letters*, March 2, 1842, and Jan. 16 and 24, 1843), which a few months later, on departing for Staten Island, he lent to Hawthorne (*American Note-Books*, Riv. pp. 333, 338).]
[4] [Week, p. 184; Riv. 228.]

I know there is a people somewhere [where] this heroism has place. Or else things are to be learned which it will be sweet to learn.[1] This cannot be all rumor. When I hear this, I think of that everlasting and stable something which is not sound, but to be a thrilling reality, and can consent to go about the meanest work for as many years of time as it pleases even the Hindoo penance, for a year of the gods were as nothing to that which shall come after. What, then, can I do to hasten that other time, or that space where there shall be no time, and these things be a more living part of my life, — where there will be no discords in my life?

Jan. 9. Sunday. One cannot too soon forget his errors and misdemeanors; for [to] dwell long upon them is to add to the offense, and repentance and sorrow can only be displaced by somewhat better, and which is as free and original as if they had not been. Not to grieve long for any action, but to go immediately and do freshly and otherwise, subtracts so much from the wrong. Else we may make the delay of repentance the punishment of the sin. But a great nature will not consider its sins as its own, but be more absorbed in the prospect of that valor and virtue for the future which is more properly it, than in those improper actions which, by being sins, discover themselves to be not it.

Sir W. Raleigh's faults are those of a courtier and a soldier. In his counsels and aphorisms we see not

[1] [*Week*, p. 184; Riv. 228.]

Vol. I

unfrequently the haste and rashness of a boy. His philosophy was not wide nor deep, but continually giving way to the generosity of his nature. What he touches he adorns by his greater humanity and native nobleness, but he touches not the true nor original. He thus embellishes the old, but does not unfold the new. He seems to have been fitted by his genius for short flights of impulsive poetry, but not for the sustained loftiness of Shakespeare or Milton. He was not wise nor a seer in any sense, but rather one of nature's nobility; the most generous nature which can be spared to linger in the purlieus of the court.

His was a singularly perverted genius, with such an inclination to originality and freedom, and yet who never steered his own course. Of so fair and susceptible a nature, rather than broad or deep, that he delayed to slake his thirst at the nearest and even more turbid wells of truth and beauty. Whose homage to the least fair or noble left no space for homage to the all fair. The misfortune of his circumstances, or rather of the man, appears in the fact that he was the author of " Maxims of State " and " The Cabinet Council " and " The Soul's Errand."

Feb. 19. Saturday. I never yet saw two men sufficiently great to meet as two. In proportion as they are great the differences are fatal, because they are felt not to be partial but total. Frankness to him who is unlike me will lead to the utter denial of him. I begin to see how that the preparation for all issues is to do virtuously. When two approach to meet, they incur no petty dan-

gers, but they run terrible risks. Between the sincere there will be no civilities. No greatness seems prepared for the little decorum, even savage unmannerliness, it meets from equal greatness.

Feb. 20. Sunday. " Examine animal forms geometrically, from man, who represents the perpendicular, to the reptile which forms the horizontal line, and then applying to those forms the rules of the exact sciences, which God himself cannot change, we shall see that visible nature contains them all; that the combinations of the seven primitive forms are entirely exhausted, and that, therefore, they can represent all possible varieties of morality." — From " The True Messiah; or the Old and New Testaments, examined according to the Principles of the Language of Nature. By G. Segger," translated from French by Grater.

I am amused to see from my window here how busily man has divided and staked off his domain. God must smile at his puny fences running hither and thither everywhere over the land.

My path hitherto has been like a road through a diversified country, now climbing high mountains, then descending into the lowest vales. From the summits I saw the heavens; from the vales I looked up to the heights again. In prosperity I remember God, or memory is one with consciousness; in adversity I remember my own elevations, and only hope to see God again.

It is vain to talk. What do you want? To bandy words, or deliver some grains of truth which stir within you? Will you make a pleasant rumbling sound after feasting, for digestion's sake, or such music as the birds in springtime?

The death of friends should inspire us as much as their lives. If they are great and rich enough, they will leave consolation to the mourners before the expenses of their funerals.[1] It will not be hard to part with any worth, because it is worthy. How can any good depart? It does not go and come, but we. Shall we wait for it? Is it slower than we?

Feb. 21. I must confess there is nothing so strange to me as my own body. I love any other piece of nature, almost, better.

I was always conscious of sounds in nature which my ears could never hear, — that I caught but the prelude to a strain. She always retreats as I advance. Away behind and behind is she and her meaning. Will not this faith and expectation make to itself ears at length? I never saw to the end, nor heard to the end; but the best part was unseen and unheard.

I am like a feather floating in the atmosphere; on every side is depth unfathomable.

I feel as if years had been crowded into the last month,[2] and yet the regularity of what we call time has been so far preserved as that I[3] . . . will be

[1] [*Week*, p. 303; Riv. 377.]
[2] [Thoreau's brother John died Jan. 11, 1842.]
[3] [Two lines missing from the manuscript here.]

welcome in the present. I have lived ill for the most part because too near myself. I have tripped myself up, so that there was no progress for my own narrowness. I cannot walk conveniently and pleasantly but when I hold myself far off in the horizon. And the soul dilutes the body and makes it passable. My soul and body have tottered along together of late, tripping and hindering one another like unpracticed Siamese twins. They two should walk as one, that no obstacle may be nearer than the firmament.

There must be some narrowness in the soul that compels one to have secrets.

Feb. 23. Wednesday. Every poet's muse is circumscribed in her wanderings, and may be well said to haunt some favorite spring or mountain. Chaucer seems to have been the poet of gardens. He has hardly left a poem in which some retired and luxurious retreat of the kind is not described, to which he gains access by some secret port, and there, by some fount or grove, is found his hero and the scene of his tale. It seems as if, by letting his imagination riot in the matchless beauty of an ideal garden, he thus fed [*sic*] his fancy on to the invention of a tale which would fit the scene. The muse of the most universal poet retires into some familiar nook, whence it spies out the land as the eagle from his eyrie, for he who sees so far over plain and forest is perched in a narrow cleft of the crag. Such pure childlike love of Nature is nowhere to be matched.[1] And it is

[1] [*Week*, p. 398 ; Riv. 492.]

not strange that the poetry of so rude an age should contain such polished praise of Nature; for the charms of Nature are not enhanced by civilization, as society is, but she possesses a permanent refinement, which at last subdues and educates men.

The reader has great confidence in Chaucer. He tells no lies. You read his story with a smile, as if it were the circumlocution of a child, and yet you find that he has spoke with more directness and economy of words than a sage. He is never heartless. So new was all his theme in those days, that [he] had not to invent, but only to tell.[1]

The language of poetry is *infantile*. It cannot talk.

It is the charm and greatness of all society, from friendship to the drawing-room, that it takes place on a level slightly higher than the actual characters of the parties would warrant;[2] it is an expression of faith. True politeness is only hope and trust in men. It never addresses a fallen or falling man, but salutes a rising generation. It does not flatter, but only congratulates. The rays of light come to us in such a curve that every fellow in the street appears higher than he really is. It is the innate civility of nature.[3]

I am glad that it was so because it could be.

March 1. Whatever I learn from any circumstances, that especially I needed to know. Events come out of

[1] [*Week*, p. 397 ; Riv. 490.]   [2] [*Week*, p. 288 ; Riv. 357.]
[3] [*Week*, p. 288 ; Riv. 358.]

Vol. I

God, and our characters determine them and constrain fate, as much as they determine the words and tone of a friend to us. Hence are they always acceptable as experience, and we do not see how we could have done without them.

March 2. The greatest impression of character is made by that person who consents to have no character. He who sympathizes with and runs through the whole circle of attributes cannot afford to be an individual. Most men stand pledged to themselves, so that their narrow and confined virtue has no suppleness. They are like children who cannot walk in bad company and learn the lesson which even it teaches, without their guardians, for fear of contamination. He is a fortunate man who gets through the world without being burthened by a name and reputation, for they are at any rate but his past history and no prophecy, and as such concern him no more than another. Character is Genius settled. It can maintain itself against the world, and if it relapses it repents. It is as a dog set to watch the property of Genius. Genius, strictly speaking, is not responsible, for it is not moral.

March 8. I live in the perpetual verdure of the globe. I die in the annual decay of nature.

We can understand the phenomenon of death in the animal better if we first consider it in the order next below us, the vegetable.

The death of the flea and the elephant are but phenomena of the life of nature.

Most lecturers preface their discourses on music with a history of music, but as well introduce an essay on virtue with a history of virtue.[1] As if the possible combinations of sound, the last wind that sighed, or melody that waked the wood, had any history other than a perceptive ear might hear in the least and latest sound of nature! A history of music would be like the history of the future; for so little past is it, and capable of record, that it is but the hint of a prophecy. It is the history of gravitation. It has no history more than God. It circulates and resounds forever, and only flows like the sea or air. There might be a history of men or of hearing, but not of the unheard. Why, if I should sit down to write its story, the west wind would rise to refute me. Properly speaking, there can be no history but natural history, for there is no past in the soul but in nature. So that the history of anything is only the true account of it, which will be always the same. I might as well write the history of my aspirations. Does not the last and highest contain them all? Do the lives of the great composers contain the facts which interested them? What is this music? Why, thinner and more evanescent than ether; subtler than sound, for it is only a disposition of sound. It is to sound what color is to matter. It is the color of a flame, or of the rainbow, or of water. Only one sense has known it. The least profitable, the least tangible fact, which cannot be

[1] [At the head of this paragraph appears the following in pencil:] What has music to do with the lives of the Great Composers? It is the great composer who is not yet dead whose life should be written. Shall we presume to write such a history as the former while the winds blow?

bought or cultivated but by virtuous methods, and yet our ears ring with it like shells left on the shore.

March 11. *Friday.* Chaucer's familiar, but innocent, way of speaking of God is of a piece with his character. He comes readily to his thoughts without any false reverence. If Nature is our mother, is not God much more? God should come into our thoughts with no more parade than the zephyr into our ears. Only strangers approach him with ceremony. How rarely in our English tongue do we find expressed any affection for God! No sentiment is so rare as love of God, — universal love. Herbert is almost the only exception. "Ah, my dear God," etc. Chaucer's was a remarkably affectionate genius. There is less love and simple trust in Shakespeare. When he sees a beautiful person or object, he almost takes a pride in the "maistry" of his God.[1] The Protestant Church seems to have nothing to supply the place of the Saints of the Catholic calendar, who were at least channels for the affections. Its God has perhaps too many of the attributes of a Scandinavian deity.

We can only live healthily the life the gods assign us. I must receive my life as passively as the willow leaf that flutters over the brook. I must not be for myself, but God's work, and that is always good. I will wait the breezes patiently, and grow as Nature shall determine. My fate cannot but be grand so. We may live the life of a plant or an animal, without living an animal life. This constant and universal content of the

[1] [*Week*, pp. 398, 399; Riv. 492.]

Vol. I

continuance of death. It is a transient phenomenon. Nature presents nothing in a state of death.

March 13. *Sunday.* The sad memory of departed friends is soon incrusted over with sublime and pleasing thoughts, as their monuments are overgrown with moss.[1] Nature doth thus kindly heal every wound. By the mediation of a thousand little mosses and fungi, the most unsightly objects become radiant of beauty. There seem to be two sides to this world, presented us at different times, as we see things in growth or dissolution, in life or death. For seen with the eye of a poet, as God sees them, all are alive and beautiful; but seen with the historical eye, or the eye of the memory, they are dead and offensive. If we see Nature as pausing, immediately all mortifies and decays; but seen as progressing, she is beautiful.

I am startled that God can make me so rich even with my own cheap stores. It needs but a few wisps of straw in the sun, or some small word dropped, or that has long lain silent in some book. When heaven begins and the dead arise, no trumpet is blown; perhaps the south wind will blow. What if you or I be dead! God is alive still.

March 14. Chaucer's genius does not soar like Milton's, but is genial and familiar. It is only a greater portion of humanity, with all its weakness. It is not heroic, as Raleigh, or pious, as Herbert, or philosophical,

[1] [*Week*, p. 303; Riv. 377.]

animal comes of resting quietly in God's palm. I feel as if [I] could at any time resign my life and the responsibility of living into God's hands, and become as innocent, free from care, as a plant or stone.

My life, my life! why will you linger? Are the years short and the months of no account? How often has long delay quenched my aspirations! Can God afford that I should forget him? Is he so indifferent to my career? Can heaven be postponed with no more ado? Why were my ears given to hear those everlasting strains which haunt my life, and yet to be prophaned much more by these perpetual dull sounds?

Our doubts are so musical that they persuade themselves.

Why, God, did you include me in your great scheme? Will you not make me a partner at last? Did it need there should be a conscious material?

My friend, my friend, I'd speak so frank to thee that thou wouldst pray me to keep back some part, for fear I robbed myself. To address thee delights me, there is such cleanness in the delivery. I am delivered of my tale, which, told to strangers, still would linger on my lips as if untold, or doubtful how it ran.

March 12. Consider what a difference there is between living and dying. To die is not to *begin* to die, and *continue*; it is not a state of continuance, but of transientness; but to live is a condition of continuance, and does not mean to be born merely. There is no

as Shakespeare, but the child of the English nation, but that child that is "father of the man." His genius is only for the most part an exceeding naturalness. It is perfect sincerity, though with the behavior of a child rather than of a man.[1] He can complain, as in the "Testament of Love," but yet so truly and unfeignedly that his complaint does not fail to interest. All England has his case at heart.

He shows great tenderness and delicacy, but not the heroic sentiment. His genius was feminine, not masculine, — not but such is rarest to find in woman (though the appreciation of it is not), — but less manly than the manliest.[2]

It is not easy to find one brave enough to play the game of love quite alone with you, but they must get some third person, or world, to countenance them. They thrust others between. Love is so delicate and fastidious that I see not how [it] can ever begin. Do you expect me to love with you, unless you make my love secondary to nothing else? Your words come tainted, if the thought of the world darted between thee and the thought of me. You are not venturous enough for love. It goes alone unscared through wildernesses.

As soon as I see people loving what they see merely, and not their own high hopes that they form of others, I pity, and do not want their love. Such love delays me. Did I ask thee to love me who hate myself? No! Love that I love, and I will love thee that lovest it.

[1] [*Week*, pp. 397, 398; Riv. 491.]
[2] [*Week*, pp. 397, 398; Riv. 491, 492.]

The love is faint-hearted and short-lived that is contented with the past history of its object. It does not prepare the soil to bear new crops lustier than the old.

"I would I had leisure for these things," sighs the world. "When I have done my quilting and baking, then I will not be backward."

Love never stands still, nor does its object. It is the revolving sun and the swelling bud. If I know what I love, it is because I *remember* it.

Life is grand, and so are its environments of Past and Future. Would the face of nature be so serene and beautiful if man's destiny were not equally so? What am I good for now, who am still marching after high things, but to hear and tell the news, to bring wood and water, and count how many eggs the hens lay? In the meanwhile, I expect my life will begin. I will not aspire longer. I will see what it is I would be after. I will be unanimous.

March 15. *Tuesday.* It is a new day; the sun shines. The poor have come out to employ themselves in the sunshine, the old and feeble to scent the air once more. I hear the bluebird and the song sparrow and the robin, and the note of the lark leaks up through the meadows, as if its bill had been thawed by the warm sun.

As I am going to the woods I think to take some small book in my pocket whose author has been there already, whose pages will be as good as my thoughts, and will eke them out or show me human life still gleaming in the horizon when the woods have shut out the town. But I

can find none. None will sail as far forward into the bay of nature as my thought. They stay at home. I would go home. When I get to the wood their thin leaves rustle in my fingers. They are bare and obvious, and there is no halo or haze about them. Nature lies far and fair behind them all.[1] I should like to meet the great and serene sentence, which does not reveal itself, — only that it is great, — which I may never with my utmost intelligence pierce through and beyond (more than the earth itself), which no intelligence can understand. There should be a kind of life and palpitation to it; under its rind a kind of blood should circulate forever, communicating freshness to its countenance.[2]

Cold Spring. — I hear nothing but a phœbe, and the wind, and the rattling of a chaise in the wood. For a few years I stay here, not knowing, taking my own life by degrees, and then I go. I hear a spring bubbling near, where I drank out of a can in my earliest youth. The birds, the squirrels, the alders, the pines, they seem serene and in their places. I wonder if my life looks as serene to them too. Does no creature, then, see with the eyes of its own narrow destiny, but with God's? When God made man, he reserved some parts and some rights to himself. The eye has many qualities which belong to God more than man. It is his lightning which flashes in it. When I look into my companion's eye, I think it is God's private mine. It is a noble feature; it cannot be degraded; for God can look on all things undefiled.

[1] [*Week*, p. 156; Riv. 195.]   [2] [*Week*, p. 157; Riv. 196.]

Vol. I

Pond. — Nature is constantly original and inventing new patterns, like a mechanic in his shop. When the overhanging pine drops into the water, by the action of the sun, and the wind rubbing it on the shore, its boughs are worn white and smooth and assume fantastic forms, as if turned by a lathe.[1] All things, indeed, are subjected to a rotary motion, either gradual and partial or rapid and complete, from the planet and system to the simplest shellfish and pebbles on the beach; as if all beauty resulted from an object turning on its own axis, or others turning about it. It establishes a new centre in the universe. As all curves have reference to their centres or foci, so all beauty of character has reference to the soul, and is a graceful gesture of recognition or waving of the body toward it.

The great and solitary heart will love alone, without the knowledge of its object. It cannot have society in its love. It will expend its love as the cloud drops rain upon the fields over which [it] floats.

The only way to speak the truth is to speak lovingly; only the lover's words are heard. The intellect should never speak; it is not a natural sound. How trivial the best actions are! I am led about from sunrise to sunset by an ignoble routine, and yet can find no better road. I must make a part of the planet. I must obey the law of nature.

March 16. *Wednesday.* Raleigh's Maxims are not true and impartial, but yet are expressed with a certain mag-

[1] [*Week*, pp. 339, 340; Riv. 420.]

nanimity, which was natural to the man, as if this selfish policy could easily afford to give place in him to a more human and generous. He gives such advice that we have more faith in his conduct than his principles.

He seems to have carried the courtier's life to the highest pitch of magnanimity and grace it was capable of. He is liberal and generous as a prince, — that is, within bounds; brave, chivalrous, heroic, as the knight in armor and not as a defenseless man. His was not the heroism of Luther, but of Bayard. There was more of grace than of truth in it. He had more taste than character. There may be something petty in a refined taste; it easily degenerates into effeminacy; it does not consider the broadest use. It is not content with simple good and bad, and so is fastidious and curious, or nice only.

The most attractive sentences are not perhaps the wisest, but the surest and soundest. He who uttered them had a right to speak. He did not stand on a rolling stone, but was well assured of his footing, and naturally breathed them without effort. They were spoken in the nick of time. With rare fullness were they spoken, as a flower expands in the field; and if you dispute their doctrine, you will say, "But there is truth in their assurance." Raleigh's are of this nature, spoken with entire satisfaction and heartiness. They are not philosophy, but poetry.

With him it was always well done and nobly said.

That is very true which Raleigh says about the equal necessity of war and law, — that "the necessity of war, which among human actions is most lawless, hath some kind of affinity and near resemblance with the necessity of law;" for both equally rest on force as their basis, and war is only the resource of law, either on a smaller or larger scale, — its authority asserted. In war, in some sense, lies the very genius of law. It is law creative and active; it is the first principle of the law. What is human warfare but just this, — an effort to make the laws of God and nature take sides with one party. Men make an arbitrary code, and, because it is not right, they try to make it prevail by might. The moral law does not want any champion. Its asserters do not go to war. It was never infringed with impunity. It is inconsistent to decry war and maintain law, for if there were no need of war there would be no need of law.

I must confess I see no resource but to conclude that conscience was not given us to no purpose, or for a hindrance, but that, however flattering order and expediency may look, it is but the repose of a lethargy; and we will choose rather to be awake, though it be stormy, and maintain ourselves on this earth and in this life as we may, without signing our death-warrant in the outset. What does the law protect? My rights? or any rights? My right, or the right? If I avail myself of it, it may help my sin; it cannot help my virtue. Let us see if we cannot stay here, where God has put us, on his own conditions. Does not his law reach to the earth? While the law holds fast the thief and murderer for my protection (I should say its own), it lets itself go loose. Expediencies differ. They may clash. English law may go to war with Amer-

ican law, that is English interest with American interest, but what is expedient for the whole world will be absolute right, and synonymous with the law of God. So the law is only partial right. It is selfish, and consults for the interest of the few.[1]

Somehow, strangely, the vice of men gets well represented and protected, but their virtue has none to plead its cause, nor any charter of immunities and rights. The Magna Charta is not chartered rights, but chartered wrongs.

March 17. *Thursday.* I have been making pencils all day, and then at evening walked to see an old schoolmate who is going to help make the Welland Canal navigable for ships round Niagara. He cannot see any such motives and modes of living as I; professes not to look beyond the securing of certain "creature comforts." And so we go silently different ways, with all serenity, I in the still moonlight through the village this fair evening to write these thoughts in my journal, and he, forsooth, to mature his schemes to ends as good, maybe, but different. So are we two made, while the same stars shine quietly over us. If I or he be wrong, Nature yet consents placidly. She bites her lip and smiles to see how her children will agree. So does the Welland Canal get built, and other conveniences, while I live. Well and good, I must confess. Fast sailing ships are hence not detained.

What means this changing sky, that now I freeze and contract and go within myself to warm me, and now I

[1] [*Week*, p. 138; Riv. 172, 173.]

say it is a south wind, and go all soft and warm along the way? I sometimes wonder if I do not breathe the south wind.

March 18. *Friday.* Whatever book or sentence will bear to be read twice, we may be sure was thought twice. I say this thinking of Carlyle, who writes pictures or first impressions merely, which consequently will only bear a first reading. As if any transient, any *new*, mood of the best man deserved to detain the world long. I should call Carlyle's writing essentially dramatic, excellent acting, entertaining especially to those who see rather than those who hear, not to be repeated more than a joke. If he did not think who made the joke, how shall we think who hear it? He never consults the oracle, but thinks to utter oracles himself. There is nothing in his books for which he is not, and does not feel, responsible. He does not retire behind the truth he utters, but stands in the foreground. I wish he would just think, and tell me what he thinks, appear to me in the attitude of a man with his ear inclined, who comes as silently and meekly as the morning star, which is unconscious of the dawn it heralds, leading the way up the steep as though alone and unobserved in its observing, without looking behind. He is essentially a humorist. But humors will not feed a man; they are the least satisfactory morsel to the healthy appetite. They circulate; I want rather to meet that about which they circulate. The heart is not a humor, nor do they go to the heart, as the blood does.[1]

[1] [*Cape Cod, and Miscellanies*, p. 336; *Misc.*, Riv. 106, 107.]

March 19. *Saturday.* When I walk in the fields of Concord and meditate on the destiny of this prosperous slip of the Saxon family, the unexhausted energies of this new country, I forget that this which is now Concord was once Musketaquid, and that the *American race* has had its destiny also. Everywhere in the fields, in the corn and grain land, the earth is strewn with the relics of a race which has vanished as completely as if trodden in with the earth. I find it good to remember the eternity behind me as well as the eternity before. Wherever I go, I tread in the tracks of the Indian. I pick up the bolt which he has but just dropped at my feet. And if I consider destiny I am on his trail. I scatter his hearthstones with my feet, and pick out of the embers of his fire the simple but enduring implements of the wigwam and the chase. In planting my corn in the same furrow which yielded its increase to his support so long, I displace some memorial of him.

I have been walking this afternoon over a pleasant field planted with winter rye, near the house, where this strange people once had their dwelling-place. Another species of mortal men, but little less wild to me than the musquash they hunted. Strange spirits, dæmons, whose eyes could never meet mine; with another nature and another fate than mine. The crows flew over the edge of the woods, and, wheeling over my head, seemed to rebuke, as dark-winged spirits more akin to the Indian than I. Perhaps only the present disguise of the Indian. If the new has a meaning, so has the old.[1]

Nature has her russet hues as well as green. Indeed,

[1] [See pp. 443, 444.]

our eye splits on every object, and we can as well take one path as the other. If I consider its history, it is old; if its destiny, it is new. I may see a part of an object, or the whole. I will not be imposed on and think Nature is old because the season is advanced. I will study the botany of the mosses and fungi on the decayed [wood], and remember that decayed wood is not old, but has just begun to be what it is. I need not think of the pine almond [1] or the acorn and sapling when I meet the fallen pine or oak, more than of the generations of pines and oaks which have fed the young tree. The new blade of the corn, the third leaf of the melon, these are not green but gray with time, but sere in respect of time.

The pines and the crows are not changed, but instead that Philip and Paugus stand on the plain, here are Webster and Crockett. Instead of the council-house is the legislature. What a new aspect have new eyes given to the land! Where is this country but in the hearts of its inhabitants? Why, there is only so much of Indian America left as there is of the American Indian in the character of this generation.

A blithe west wind is blowing over all. In the fine flowing haze, men at a distance seem shadowy and gigantic, as ill-defined and great as men should always be. I do not know if yonder be a man or a ghost.

What a consolation are the stars to man! — so high and out of his reach, as is his own destiny. I do not know

[1] [See *Journal*, vol. ii, p. 128.]

but my life is fated to be thus low and grovelling always. I cannot discover its use even to myself. But it is permitted to see those stars in the sky equally useless, yet highest of all and deserving of a fair destiny. My fate is in some sense linked with that of the stars, and if they are to persevere to a great end, shall I die who could conjecture it? It surely is some encouragement to know that the stars are my fellow-creatures, for I do not suspect but they are reserved for a high destiny. Has not he who discovers and names a planet in the heavens as long a year as it? I do not fear that any misadventure will befall *them*. Shall I not be content to disappear with the missing stars? Do I mourn their fate?

Man's moral nature is a riddle which only eternity can solve.

I see laws which never fail, of whose failure I never conceived. Indeed I cannot detect failure anywhere but in my fear. I do not fear that right is not right, that good is not good, but only the annihilation of the present existence. But only that can make me incapable of fear. My fears are as good prophets as my hopes.

March 20. *Sunday*. My friend is cold and reserved because his love for me is waxing and not waning. These are the early processes; the particles are just beginning to shoot in crystals. If the mountains came to me, I should no longer go to the mountains. So soon as that consummation takes place which I wish, it will be past. Shall I not have a friend in reserve? Heaven is to come. I hope this is not it.

Vol. I

Words should pass between friends as the lightning passes from cloud to cloud. I don't know how much I assist in the economy of nature when I declare a fact. Is it not an important part in the history of the flower that I tell my friend where I found it? We do [not] wish friends to feed and clothe our bodies, — neighbors are kind enough for that, — but to do the like offices to ourselves.[1] We wish to spread and publish ourselves, as the sun spreads its rays; and we toss the new thought to the friend, and thus it is dispersed. Friends are those twain who feel their interests to be one. Each knows that the other might as well have said what he said. All beauty, all music, all delight springs from apparent dualism but real unity. My friend is my real brother. I see his nature groping yonder like my own. Does there go one whom I know? then I go there.

The field where friends have met is consecrated forever. Man seeks friendship out of the desire to realize a home here. As the Indian thinks he receives into himself the courage and strength of his conquered enemy, so we add to ourselves all the character and heart of our friends. He is my creation. I can do what I will with him. There is no possibility of being thwarted; the friend is like wax in the rays that fall from our own hearts.

The friend does not take my word for anything, but he takes me. He trusts me as I trust myself. We only need be as true to others as we are to ourselves, that there may be ground enough for friendship. In the beginnings of friendship, — for it does not grow, — we realize such love and justice as are attributed to God.

[1] [*Week*, p. 283; Riv. 351.]

Very few are they from whom we derive any *information*. The most only announce and tell tales, but the friend *in*-forms.

What is all nature and human life at this moment, what the scenery and vicinity of a human soul, but the song of an early sparrow from yonder fences, and the cackling hens in the barn? So for one while my destiny loiters within ear-shot of these sounds. The great busy Dame Nature is concerned to know how many eggs her hens lay. The Soul, the proprietor of the world, has an interest in the stacking of hay, the foddering of cattle, and the draining of peat meadows. Away in Scythia, away in India, they make butter and cheese for its larder.[1] I wish that in some page of the Testament there were something like Charlemagne's egg account. Was not Christ interested in the setting hens of Palestine?

Nature is very ample and roomy. She has left us plenty of space to move in. As far as I can see from this window, how little life in the landscape! The few birds that flit past do not crowd; they do not fill the valley. The traveller on the highway has no fellow-traveller for miles before or behind him. Nature was generous and not niggardly, certainly.

How simple is the natural connection of events. We complain greatly of the want of flow and sequence in books, but if the journalist only move himself from Boston to New York, and speak as before, there is link enough. And so there would be, if he were as careless of connection and order when he stayed at home, and

[1] [*Week*, pp. 130, 131; Riv. 163.]

let the incessant progress which his life makes be the apology for abruptness. Do I not travel as far away from my old resorts, though I stay here at home, as though I were on board the steamboat? Is not my life riveted together? Has not it sequence? Do not my breathings follow each other naturally?

March 21.[1] Who is old enough to have learned from experience?

March 22. Tuesday. Nothing can be more useful to a man than a determination not to be hurried.

I have not succeeded if I have an antagonist who fails. It must be humanity's success.

I cannot think nor utter my thought unless I have infinite room. The cope of heaven is not too high, the sea is not too deep, for him who would unfold a great thought. It must feed me and warm and clothe me. It must be an entertainment to which my whole nature is invited. I must know that the gods are to be my fellow-guests.

We cannot well do without our sins; they are the highway of our virtue.

March 23. Wednesday. Plain speech is always a desideratum. Men write in a florid style only because they

[1] Set the red hen, Sunday, March 21st [=20th]. [This memorandum is written in the margin. It is pretty good proof that by now we have come to the original Journal. Just where the transcripts end, however, it seems to be impossible to determine.]

times, to chew mallows and pick the apple tree buds? It is not hard to discover an instinct for the opium and betel and tobacco chewers.[1]

After all, I believe it is the style of thought entirely, and not the style of expression, which makes the difference in books. For if I find any thought worth extracting, I do not wish to alter the language. Then the author seems to have had all the graces of eloquence and poetry given him.

I am pleased to discover myself as much a pensioner in Nature as moles and titmice. In some very direct and simple uses to which man puts Nature he stands in this relation to her. Oriental life does not want this grandeur. It is in Sadi and the Arabian Nights and the Fables of Pilpay. In the New England noontide I have discovered more materials of Oriental history than the Sanskrit contains or Sir W. Jones has unlocked. I see why it is necessary there should be such history at all. Was not Asia mapped in my brain before it was in any geography? In my brain is the Sanskrit which contains the history of the primitive times. The Vedas and their Angas are not so ancient as my serenest contemplations.[2] My mind contemplates them, as Brahma his scribe.

I occasionally find myself to be nothing at all, because the gods give me nothing to do. I cannot brag; I can only congratulate my masters.

In idleness I am of no thickness, I am thinnest wafer. I never compass my own ends. God schemes for me.

[1] [*Week*, p. 130; Riv. 162.]   [2] [*Week*, p. 160; Riv. 199.]

would match the simple beauties of the plainest speech. They prefer to be misunderstood, rather than come short of its exuberance. Hussein Effendi praises the epistolary style of Ibrahim Pasha to the French traveller Botta, because of "the difficulty of understanding it: there was, he said, but one person at Jidda who was capable of understanding and explaining the Pasha's correspondence." A plain sentence, where every word is rooted in the soil, is indeed flowery and verdurous. It has the beauty and variety of mosaic with the strength and compactness of masonry. All fullness looks like exuberance. We are not rich without superfluous wealth; but the imitator only copies the superfluity. If the words were sufficiently simple and answering to the thing to be expressed, our sentences would be as blooming as wreaths of evergreen and flowers.[1] You cannot fill a wine-glass quite to the brim without heaping it. Simplicity is exuberant.

When I look back eastward over the world, it seems to be all in repose. Arabia, Persia, Hindostan are the land of contemplation. Those Eastern nations have perfected the luxury of idleness. Mount Sabér, according to the French traveller and naturalist Botta, is celebrated for producing the Kát tree. "The soft tops of the twigs and tender leaves are eaten," says his reviewer, "and produce an agreeable soothing excitement, restoring from fatigue, banishing sleep, and disposing to the enjoyment of conversation." What could be more dignified than to browse the tree-tops with the camelopard? Who would not be a rabbit or partridge some-

[1] [*Week*, p. 107; Riv. 133.]

We have our times of action and our times of reflection. The one mood caters for the other. Now I am Alexander, and then I am Homer. One while my hand is impatient to handle an axe or hoe, and at another to [*sic*] pen. I am sure I write the tougher truth for these calluses on my palms. They give firmness to the sentence. The sentences of a laboring man are like hardened thongs, or the sinews of the deer, or the roots of the pine.[1]

March 24. Thursday. Those authors are successful who do not *write down* to others, but make their own taste and judgment their audience. By some strange infatuation we forget that we do not approve what yet we recommend to others. It is enough if I please myself with writing; I am then sure of an audience.

If hoarded treasures can make me rich, have I not the wealth of the planet in my mines and at the bottom of the sea?

It is always singular to meet common sense in very old books, as the Veeshnoo Sarma, — as if they could have dispensed with the experience of later times.[2] We had not given space enough to *their* antiquity for the accumulation of wisdom. We meet even a trivial wisdom in them, as if truth were already hackneyed. The present is always younger than antiquity. A playful wisdom, which has eyes behind as well as before and oversees itself. This pledge of sanity cannot be spared

[1] [*Week*, p. 109; Riv. 135, 136.]   [2] [*Week*, p. 153; Riv. 191.]

in a book, that it sometimes reflect upon itself, that it pleasantly behold itself, that it hold the scales over itself.[1] The wise can afford to doubt in his wisest moment. The easiness of doubt is the ground of his assurance. Faith keeps many doubts in her pay. If I could not doubt, I should not believe.

It is seen in this old scripture how wisdom is older than the talent of composition. It is a simple and not a compound rock. The story is as slender as the thread on which pearls are strung; it is a spiral line, growing more and more perplexed till it winds itself up and dies like the silkworm in its cocoon. It is an interminable labyrinth. It seems as if the old philosopher could not talk without moving, and each motion were made the apology or occasion for a sentence, but, this being found inconvenient, the fictitious progress of the tale was invented. The story which winds between and around these sentences, these barrows in the desert, these oases, is as indistinct as a camel track between Mourzuk and Darfur, between the Pyramids and the Nile, from Gaza to Jaffa.[2]

The great thoughts of a wise man seem to the vulgar who do not generalize to stand far apart like isolated mounts; but science knows that the mountains which rise so solitary in our midst are parts of a great mountain-chain, dividing the earth, and the eye that looks into the horizon toward the blue Sierra melting away in the distance may detect their flow of thought. These sentences which take up your common life so easily are not seen to run into ridges, because they are the table-land on

[1] [*Week*, p. 153; Riv. 191.]   [2] [*Week*, p. 153; Riv. 191.]

which the spectator stands.[1] I do not require that the mountain-peaks be chained together, but by the common basis on which they stand, nor that the path of the muleteer be kept open at so much pains, when they may be bridged by the Milky Way. That they stand frowning upon one another, or mutually reflecting the sun's rays, is proof enough of their common basis.

The book should be found where the sentence is, and its connection be as inartificial. It is the inspiration of a day and not of a moment. The links should be gold also. Better that the good be not united than that a bad man be admitted into their society. When men can select they will. If there be any stone in the quarry better than the rest, they will forsake the rest because of it. Only the good will be quarried.

In these fables the story goes unregarded, while the reader leaps from sentence to sentence, as the traveller leaps from stone to stone while the water rushes unheeded between them.[2]

March 25. Friday. Great persons are not soon learned, not even their outlines, but they change like the mountains in the horizon as we ride along.

A man's life should be as fresh as a river. It should be the same channel, but a new water every instant.[3] Some men have no inclination; they have no rapids nor cascades, but marshes, and alligators, and miasma instead.[4]

[1] [*Week*, p. 105; Riv. 130.]   [3] [See pp. 295, 296.]
[2] [*Week*, p. 153; Riv. 191.]   [4] [*Week*, p. 137; Riv. 170.]

How insufficient is all wisdom without love! There may be courtesy, there may be good will, there may be even temper, there may be wit, and talent, and sparkling conversation, — and yet the soul pine for life. Just so sacred and rich as my life is to myself will it be to another. Ignorance and bungling with love are better than wisdom and skill without. Our life without love is like coke and ashes, — like the cocoanut in which the milk is dried up. I want to see the sweet sap of living wood in it. Men may be pure as alabaster and Parian marble, elegant as a Tuscan villa, sublime as Terni, but if they are not in society as retiring and inexperienced as children, we shall go join Alaric and the Goths and Vandals. There is no milk mixed with the wine at the entertainment.[1]

Enthusiasm which is the formless material of thought. Comparatively speaking, I care not for the man or his designs who would make the highest use of me short of an all-adventuring friendship. I wish by the behavior of my friend toward me to be led to have such regard for myself as for a box of precious ointment. I shall not be so cheap to myself if I see that another values me.

We talk much about education, and yet none will assume the office of an educator. I never gave any one the whole advantage of myself. I never afforded him the culture of my love. How can I talk of charity, who at last withhold the kindness which alone makes charity desirable? The poor want nothing less than me myself, and I shirk charity by giving rags and meat.

[1] [*Week*, p. 301; Riv. 374, 375.]

Very dangerous is the talent of composition, the striking out the heart of life at a blow, as the Indian takes off a scalp. I feel as if my life had grown more outward since I could express it.[1]

What can I give or what deny to another but myself?

The stars are God's dreams, thoughts remembered in the silence of his night.

In company, that person who alone can understand you you cannot get out of your mind.

The artist must work with indifferency. Too great interest vitiates his work.

March 26. Saturday. The wise will not be imposed on by wisdom. You can tell, but what do you know?

I thank God that the cheapness which appears in time and the world, the trivialness of the whole scheme of things, is in my own cheap and trivial moment. I am time and the world. I assert no independence. In me are summer and winter, village life and commercial routine, pestilence and famine and refreshing breezes, joy and sadness, life and death. How near is yesterday! How far to-morrow! I have seen nails which were driven before I was born. Why do they look old and rusty? Why does not God make some mistake to show to us that time is a delusion? Why did I invent time but to destroy it?

Did you ever remember the moment when you were not mean?

Is it not a satire to say that life is organic?

[1] [*Week*, p. 351; Riv. 434.]

Where is my heart gone? They say men cannot part with it and live.

Are setting hens troubled with ennui? Nature is very kind; does she let them reflect? These long March days, setting on and on in the crevice of a hayloft, with no active employment![1] Do setting hens sleep?

A book should be a vein of gold ore, as the sentence is a diamond found in the sand, or a pearl fished out of the sea.

He who does not borrow trouble does not lend it.

I must confess I have felt mean enough when asked how I was to act on society, what errand I had to mankind. Undoubtedly I did not feel mean without a reason, and yet my loitering is not without defense. I would fain communicate the wealth of my life to men, would really give them what is most precious in my gift. I would secrete pearls with the shellfish and lay up honey with the bees for them. I will sift the sunbeams for the public good. I know no riches I would keep back. I have no private good, unless it be my peculiar ability to serve the public. This is the only individual property. Each one may thus be innocently rich. I inclose and foster the pearl till it is grown. I wish to communicate those parts of my life which I would gladly live again myself.

It is hard to be a good citizen of the world in any great sense; but if we do render no interest or increase to mankind out of that talent God gave us, we can at

[1] [Week, p. 130; Riv. 163.]

strange for joy. One while it looks as shallow, though as intricate, as a Cretan labyrinth, and again it is a pathless depth. I ask for bread incessantly, — that my life sustain me, as much as meat my body. No man knoweth in what hour his life may come. Say not that Nature is trivial, for to-morrow she will be radiant with beauty. I am as old — as old as the Alleghanies. I was going to say Wachusett, but it excites a youthful feeling, as I were but too happy to be so young.

March 28. Monday. How often must one feel, as he looks back on his past life, that he has gained a talent but lost a character! My life has got down into my fingers. My inspiration at length is only so much breath as I can breathe.

Society affects to estimate men by their talents, but really feels and knows them by their characters. What a man does, compared with what he is, is but a small part. To require that our friend possess a certain skill is not to be satisfied till he is something less than our friend.

Friendship should be a great promise, a perennial springtime.

I can conceive how the life of the gods may be dull and tame, if it is not disappointed and insatiate.

One may well feel chagrined when he finds he can do nearly all he can conceive.

Some books ripple on like a stream, and we feel that the author is in the full tide of discourse. Plato and Jamblichus and Pythagoras and Bacon halt beside

least preserve the principle unimpaired. One would like to be making large dividends to society out [of] that deposited capital in us, but he does well for the most part if he proves a secure investment only, without adding to the stock.

In such a letter as I like there will be the most naked and direct speech, the least circumlocution.

March 27. Sunday. The eye must be firmly anchored to this earth which beholds birches and pines waving in the breeze in a certain light, a serene rippling light.

Cliffs. — Two little hawks have just come out to play, like butterflies rising one above the other in endless alternation far below me. They swoop from side to side in the broad basin of the tree-tops, with wider and wider surges, as if swung by an invisible pendulum. They stoop down on this side and scale up on that.

Suddenly I look up and see a new bird, probably an eagle, quite above me, laboring with the wind not more than forty rods off. It was the largest bird of the falcon kind I ever saw. I was never so impressed by any flight. She sailed the air, and fell back from time to time like a ship on her beam ends, holding her talons up as if ready for the arrows. I never allowed before for the grotesque attitudes of our national bird.[1]

The eagle must have an educated eye.

See what a life the gods have given us, set round with pain and pleasure. It is too strange for sorrow; it is too

[1] [In *Excursions*, p. 110 (Riv. 136), what appears to be the same bird is described, and is called the fish hawk.]

them. Long, stringy, slimy thoughts which flow or run together. They read as if written for military men or men of business, there is such a dispatch in them, and a double-quick time, a Saratoga march with beat of drum. But the grave thinkers and philosophers seem not to have got their swaddling-clothes off; they are slower than a Roman army on its march, the rear encampment to-night where the van camped last night. The wise Jamblichus eddies and gleams like a watery slough.

But the reviewer seizes the pen and shouts, "Forward! Alamo and Fanning!" and after rolls the tide of war. Immediately the author discovers himself launched, and if the slope was easy and the grease good, does not go to the bottom.

They flow as glibly as mill-streams sucking under a race-way. The flow is ofttimes in the poor reader who makes such haste over their pages, as to the traveller the walls and fences seem to travel. But the most rapid trot is no flow after all.[1]

If I cannot chop wood in the yard, can I not chop wood in my journal? Can I not give vent to that appetite so? I wish to relieve myself of superfluous energy. How poor is the life of the best and wisest! The petty side will appear at last. Understand once how the best in society live, — with what routine, with what tedium and insipidity, with what grimness and defiance, with what chuckling over an exaggeration of the sunshine. Altogether, are not the actions of your great man poor, even pitiful and ludicrous?

[1] [Week, pp. 105, 106; Riv. 131, 132.]

I am astonished, I must confess, that man looks so respectable in nature, considering the littlenesses Socrates must descend to in the twenty-four hours, that he yet wears a serene countenance and even adorns nature.

March 29. Tuesday.

March 30. Wednesday. Though Nature's laws are more immutable than any despot's, yet to our daily life they rarely seem rigid, but we relax with license in summer weather. We are not often nor harshly reminded of the things we may not do. I am often astonished to see how long, and with what manifold infringements of the natural laws, some men I meet in the highway maintain life. She does not deny them quarter; they do not die without priest. All the while she rejoices, for if they are not one part of her they are another. I am convinced that consistency is the secret of health. How many a poor man, striving to live a pure life, pines and dies after a life of sickness, and his successors doubt if Nature is not pitiless; while the confirmed and consistent sot, who is content with his rank life like mushrooms, a mass of corruption, still dozes comfortably under a hedge. He has made his peace with himself; there is no strife. Nature is really very kind and liberal to all persons of vicious habits. They take great licenses with her. She does not exhaust them with many excesses.[1]

How hard it is to be greatly related to mankind! They are only my uncles and aunts and cousins. I hear

[1] [*Week*, pp. 34, 35; Riv. 42, 43.]

of some persons greatly related, but only he is so who has all mankind for his friend. Our intercourse with the best grows soon shallow and trivial. They no longer inspire us. After enthusiasm comes insipidity and blankness. The sap of all noble schemes drieth up, and the schemers return again and again in despair to "common sense and labor." If I could help infuse some life and heart into society, should I not do a service? Why will not the gods mix a little of the wine of nobleness with the air we drink? Let virtue have some firm foothold in the earth. Where does she dwell? Who are the salt of the earth? May not Love have some resting-place on the earth as sure [as] the sunshine on the rock? The crystals imbedded in the cliff sparkle and gleam from afar, as if they did certainly enrich our planet; but where does any virtue permanently sparkle and gleam? She was sent forth over the waste too soon, before the earth was prepared for her.

Rightfully we are to each other the gate of heaven and redeemers from sin, but now we overlook these lowly and narrow ways. We will go over the bald mountain-tops without going through the valleys.

Men do not after all meet on the ground of their real acquaintance and actual understanding of one another, but degrade themselves immediately into the puppets of convention. They do as if, in given circumstances, they had agreed to know each other only so well. They rarely get to that [point] that they inform one another gratuitously, and use each other like the sea and woods for what is new and inspiring there.

Vol. I

The best intercourse and communion they have is in silence above and behind their speech. We should be very simple to rely on words. As it is, what we knew before always interprets a man's words. I cannot easily remember what any man has said, but how can I forget what he is to me? We know each other better than we are aware; we are admitted to startling privacies with every person we meet, and in some emergency we shall find how well we knew him. To my solitary and distant thought my neighbor is shorn of his halo, and is seen as privately and barely as a star through a glass.

March 31. Thursday. I cannot forget the majesty of that bird at the Cliff. It was no sloop or smaller craft hove in sight, but a ship of the line, worthy to struggle with the elements. It was a great presence, as of the master of river and forest. His eye would not have quailed before the owner of the soil; none could challenge his rights. And then his retreat, sailing so steadily away, was a kind of advance. How is it that man always feels like an interloper in nature, as if he had intruded on the domains of bird and beast?[1]

The really efficient laborer will be found not to crowd his day with work, but will saunter to his task surrounded by a wide halo of ease and leisure. There will be a wide margin for relaxation to his day. He is only earnest to secure the kernels of time, and does not exaggerate the value of the husk. Why should the hen set all day? She can lay but one egg, and besides she will

[1] [*Excursions*, p. 110; Riv. 136.]

not have picked up materials for a new one. Those who work much do not work hard.[1]

Nothing is so rare as sense. Very uncommon sense is poetry, and has a heroic or sweet music. But in verse, for the most part, the music now runs before and then behind the sense, but is never coincident with it. Given the metre, and one will make music while another makes sense. But good verse, like a good soldier, will make its own music, and it will march to the same with one consent. In most verse there is no inherent music. The man should not march, but walk like a citizen. It is not time of war but peace. Boys study the metres to write Latin verses, but it does not help them to write English.

Lydgate's "Story of Thebes," intended for a Canterbury Tale, is a specimen of most unprogressive, unmusical verse. Each line rings the knell of its brother, as if it were introduced but to dispose of him. No mortal man could have breathed to that cadence without long intervals of relaxation; the repetition would have been fatal to the lungs. No doubt there was much healthy exercise taken in the meanwhile. He should forget his rhyme and tell his story, or forget his story and breathe himself.

In Shakespeare and elsewhere the climax may be somewhere along the line, which runs as varied and meandering as a country road, but in Lydgate it is nowhere but in the rhyme. The couplets slope headlong to their confluence.

[1] [*Week*, p. 110; Riv. 137.]

April 2. Saturday.[1] The Prologue to the Canterbury Tales is full of good sense and humanity, but is not transcendent poetry. It is so good that it seems like faultfinding to esteem it second to any other. For picturesque description of persons it is without a parallel. It did not need inspiration, but a cheerful and easy wit. It is essentially humorous, as no inspired poetry is. Genius is so serious as to be grave and sublime rather. Humor takes a narrower vision — however broad and genial it may be — than enthusiasm. Humor delays and looks back.[2]

April 3. Sunday. I can remember when I was more enriched by a few cheap rays of light falling on the pond-side than by this broad sunny day. Riches have wings, indeed. The weight of present woe will express the sweetness of past experience. When sorrow comes, how easy it is to remember pleasure! When, in winter, the bees cannot make new honey, they consume the old.

Experience is in the fingers and head. The heart is inexperienced.

Sorrow singeth the sweetest strain: "The Daughters of Zion," "The Last Sigh of the Moor."

Joy is the nectar of flowers, sorrow the honey of bees.

I thank God for sorrow. It is hard to be abused. Is not He kind still, who lets this south wind blow, this warm sun shine on me?

[1] [On the margin of this page appears the memorandum: "Set the gray hen April 1st."]
[2] [*Week*, p. 397 ; Riv. 490, 491.]

Vol. I

On one side of man is the actual, and on the other the ideal. The former is the province of the reason; it is even a divine light when directed upon it, but it cannot reach forward into the ideal without blindness. The moon was made to rule by night, but the sun to rule by day. Reason will be but a pale cloud, like the moon, when one ray of divine light comes to illumine the soul.

How rich and lavish must be the system which can afford to let so many moons burn all the day as well as the night, though no man stands in need of their light! There is none of that kind of economy in Nature that husbands its stock, but she supplies inexhaustible means to the most frugal methods. The poor may learn of her frugality, and the rich generosity. Having carefully determined the extent of her charity, she establishes it forever; her almsgiving is an annuity. She supplies to the bee only so much wax as is necessary for its cell, so that no poverty could stint it more; but the little economist which fed the Evangelist in the desert still keeps in advance of the immigrant, and fills the cavities of the forest for his repast.

I have just heard the flicker among the oaks on the hillside ushering in a new dynasty. It is the age and youth of time. Why did Nature set this lure for sickly mortals? Eternity could not begin with more security and momentousness than the spring. The summer's eternity is reëstablished by this note.[1] All sights and sounds are seen and heard both in time and eternity. And when the eternity of any sight or sound strikes the eye or ear, they are intoxicated with delight.

Sometimes, as through a dim haze, we see objects in their eternal relations; and they stand like Stonehenge and the Pyramids, and we wonder who set them up and what for.

The destiny of the soul can never be studied by the reason, for its modes are not ecstatic. In the wisest calculation or demonstration I but play a game with myself. I am not to be taken captive by myself.

I cannot convince myself. God must convince. I can calculate a problem in arithmetic, but not any morality.

Virtue is incalculable, as it is inestimable. Well, man's destiny is but virtue, or manhood. It is wholly moral, to be learned only by the life of the soul. God cannot calculate it. He has no moral philosophy, no ethics. The reason, before it can be applied to such a subject, will have to fetter and restrict it. How can he, step by step, perform that long journey who has not conceived whither he is bound? How can he expect to perform an arduous journey without interruption who has no passport to the end?

[1] [*Excursions*, p. 111 ; Riv. 137.]

VII

1845–1846

(ÆT. 27–29)

July 5. Saturday. Walden. — Yesterday I came here to live. My house makes me think of some mountain houses I have seen, which seemed to have a fresher auroral atmosphere about them, as I fancy of the halls of Olympus. I lodged at the house of a saw-miller last summer, on the Caatskill Mountains, high up as Pine Orchard, in the blueberry and raspberry region, where the quiet and cleanliness and coolness seemed to be all one, — which had their ambrosial character. He was the miller of the Kaaterskill Falls. They were a clean and wholesome family, inside and out, like their house. The latter was not plastered, only lathed, and the inner doors were not hung. The house seemed high-placed, airy, and perfumed, fit to entertain a travelling god. It was so high, indeed, that all the music, the broken strains, the waifs and accompaniments of tunes, that swept over the ridge of the Caatskills, passed through its aisles. Could not man be man in such an abode? And would he ever find out this grovelling life?[1] It was the very light and atmosphere in which the works of Grecian art were composed, and in which they rest. They have appropriated to themselves a loftier hall than mortals ever occupy, at least on a level with the moun-

[1] [*Walden*, p. 94 ; Riv. 134.]

tain-brows of the world. There was wanting a little of the glare of the lower vales, and in its place a pure twilight as became the precincts of heaven. Yet so equable and calm was the season there that you could not tell whether it was morning or noon or evening. Always there was the sound of the morning cricket.

July 6. I wish to meet the facts of life — the vital facts, which are the phenomena or actuality the gods meant to show us — face to face, and so I came down here. Life! who knows what it is, what it does? If I am not quite right here, I am less wrong than before; and now let us see what they will have. The preacher, instead of vexing the ears of drowsy farmers on their day of rest, at the end of the week, — for Sunday always seemed to me like a fit conclusion of an ill-spent week and not the fresh and brave beginning of a new one, — with this one other draggletail and postponed affair of a sermon, from thirdly to fifteenthly, should teach them with a thundering voice pause and simplicity. "Stop! Avast! Why so fast?"[1] In all studies we go not forward but rather backward with redoubled pauses. We always study *antiques* with silence and reflection. Even time has a depth, and below its surface the waves do not lapse and roar. I wonder men can be so frivolous almost as to attend to the gross form of negro slavery, there are so many keen and subtle masters who subject us both. Self-emancipation in the West Indies of a man's thinking and imagining provinces, which should be more than his island territory, — one emancipated heart

[1] [*Walden*, p. 106; Riv. 150.]

and intellect! It would knock off the fetters from a million slaves.

July 7. I am glad to remember to-night, as I sit by my door, that I too am at least a remote descendant of that heroic race of men of whom there is tradition. I too sit here on the shore of my Ithaca, a fellow-wanderer and survivor of Ulysses. How symbolical, significant of I know not what, the pitch pine stands here before my door! Unlike any glyph I have seen sculptured or painted yet, one of Nature's later designs, yet perfect as her Grecian art. There it is, a done tree. Who can mend it? And now where is the generation of heroes whose lives are to pass amid these our northern pines, whose exploits shall appear to posterity pictured amid these strong and shaggy forms? Shall there be only arrows and bows to go with these pines on some pipe-stone quarry at length? There is something more respectable than railroads in these simple relics of the Indian race. What hieroglyphs shall we add to the pipe-stone quarry?

If we can forget, we have done somewhat; if we can remember, we have done somewhat. Let us remember this.

The Great Spirit makes indifferent all times and places. The place where he is seen is always the same, and indescribably pleasant to all our senses. We had allowed only neighboring and transient circumstances to make our occasions. They were, in fact, the causes of our distractions. But nearest to all things is that power

Vol. I

which fashions their being. Next to us the grandest laws are being enacted and administered. Next to us is not the workman whom we have hired, but ever the workman whose work we are. He is at work, not in my backyard, but inconceivably nearer than that. We are the subjects of an experiment how singular! Can we not dispense with the society of our gossips a little while under these circumstances?

My auxiliaries are the dews and rains, — to water this dry soil, — and genial fatness in the soil itself, which for the most part is lean and effete. My enemies are worms, cool days, and most of all woodchucks. They have nibbled for me an eighth of an acre clean. I plant in faith, and they reap. This is the tax I pay for ousting johnswort and the rest. But soon the surviving beans will be too tough for woodchucks, and then they will go forward to meet new foes.[1]

July 14. What sweet and tender, the most innocent and divinely encouraging society there is in every natural object, and so in universal nature, even for the poor misanthrope and most melancholy man! There can be no really black melan-choly to him who lives in the midst of nature and has still his senses. There never was yet such a storm but it was Æolian music to the innocent ear. Nothing can compel to a vulgar sadness a simple and brave man. While I enjoy the sweet friendship of the seasons I trust that nothing can make life a burden to me. This rain which is now watering my

[1] [*Walden*, pp. 171, 172; Riv. 242.]

beans and keeping me in the house waters me too. I needed it as much. And what if most are not hoed! Those who send the rain, whom I chiefly respect, will pardon me.[1]

Sometimes, when I compare myself with other men, methinks I am favored by the gods. They seem to whisper joy to me beyond my deserts, and that I do have a solid warrant and surety at their hands, which my fellows do not. I do not flatter myself, but if it were possible *they* flatter me. I am especially guided and guarded.[2]

What was seen true once, and sanctioned by the flash of Jove, will always be true, and nothing can hinder it. I have the warrant that no fair dream I have had need fail of its fulfillment.

Here I know I am in good company; here is the world, its centre and metropolis, and all the palms of Asia and the laurels of Greece and the firs of the Arctic Zone incline thither. Here I can read Homer, if I would have books, as well as in Ionia, and not wish myself in Boston, or New York, or London, or Rome, or Greece. In such place as this he wrote or sang. Who should come to my lodge just now but a true Homeric boor, one of those Paphlagonian men? Alek Therien, he called himself; a Canadian now, a woodchopper, a post-maker; makes fifty posts — holes them, *i. e.* — in a day; and who made his last supper on a woodchuck which his dog caught. And he too has heard of Homer, and *if it were not for books, would not know what to do* rainy days. Some priest once, who could read glibly

[1] [*Walden*, p. 145; Riv. 205.]   [2] [*Walden*, pp. 145, 146; Riv. 206.]

from the Greek itself, taught him reading in a measure — his verse, at least, in his turn — away by the Trois Rivières, at Nicolet. And now I must read to him, while he holds the book, Achilles' reproof of Patroclus on his sad countenance.

"Why are you in tears, Patroclus, like a young child (girl) ? " etc., etc.

"Or have you only heard some news from Phthia?
They say that Menœtius lives yet, son of Actor,
And Peleus lives, son of Æacus, among the Myrmidons,
Both of whom having died, we should greatly grieve."

He has a neat [1] bundle of white oak bark under his arm for a sick man, gathered this Sunday morning. "I suppose there's no harm in going after such a thing to-day." [2] The simple man. May the gods send him many woodchucks.

And earlier to-day came five Lestrigones, railroad men who take care of the road, some of them at least. They still represent the bodies of men, transmitting arms and legs and bowels downward from those remote days to more remote. They have some got a rude wisdom withal, thanks to their dear experience. And one with them, a handsome younger man, a sailor-like, Greek-like man, says: "Sir, I like your notions. I think I shall live so myself. Only I should like a wilder country, where there is more game. I have been among the Indians near Appalachicola. I have lived with them. I like your kind of life. Good day. I wish you success and happiness."

[1] [Plainly "neat" in Journal, though *Walden* has "great."]
[2] [*Walden*, pp. 159, 160 ; Riv. 224, 225.]

Therien said this morning (July 16th, Wednesday), "If those beans were mine, I should n't like to hoe them till the dew was off." He was going to his woodchopping. "Ah!" said I, "that is one of the notions the farmers have got, but I don't believe it." "How thick the pigeons are!" said he. "If working every day were not my trade, I could get all the meat I should want by hunting, — pigeons, woodchucks, rabbits, partridges, — by George! I could get all I should want for a week in one day." [1]

I imagine it to be some advantage to live a primitive and frontier life, though in the midst of an outward civilization. Of course all the improvements of the ages do not carry a man backward nor forward in relation to the great facts of his existence. [2]

Our furniture should be as simple as the Arab's or the Indian's. [3] At first the thoughtful, wondering man plucked in haste the fruits which the boughs extended to him, and found in the sticks and stones around him his implements ready to crack the nut, to wound the beast, and build his house with. And he still remembered that he was a sojourner in nature. When he was refreshed with food and sleep he contemplated his journey again. He dwelt in a tent in this world. He was either threading the valleys, or crossing the plains, or climbing the mountain-tops. [4]

Now the best works of art serve comparatively but

[1] [*Walden*, p. 161 ; Riv. 227.] [3] [*Walden*, p. 39 ; Riv. 59.]
[2] [*Walden*, pp. 12, 13 ; Riv. 21.] [4] [*Walden*, p. 41 ; Riv. 61.]

to dissipate the mind, for they themselves represent transitionary and paroxysmal, not free and absolute, thoughts.

Men have become the tools of their tools. The man who independently plucked the fruits when he was hungry is become a farmer. [1]

There are scores of pitch pines in my field, from one to three inches in diameter, girdled by the mice last winter. A Norwegian winter it was for them, for the snow lay long and deep, and they had to mix much pine meal with their usual diet. Yet these trees have not many of them died, even in midsummer, and laid bare for a foot, but have grown a foot. They seem to do all their gnawing beneath the snow. There is not much danger of the mouse tribe becoming extinct in hard winters, for their granary is a cheap and extensive one. [2]

Here is one has had her nest under my house, and came when I took my luncheon to pick the crumbs at my feet. It had never seen the race of man before, and so the sooner became familiar. It ran over my shoes and up my pantaloons inside, clinging to my flesh with its sharp claws. It would run up the side of the room by short impulses like a squirrel, which [it] resembles, coming between the house mouse and the former. Its belly is a little reddish, and its ears a little longer. At length, as I leaned my elbow on the bench, it ran over my arm and round the paper which contained my dinner. And when I held it a piece of cheese, it came and

[1] [*Walden*, p. 41 ; Riv. 61.] [2] [*Walden*, p. 309 ; Riv. 433.]

nibbled between my fingers, and then cleaned its face and paws like a fly. [1]

There is a memorable interval between the written and the spoken language, the language read and the language heard. The one is transient, a sound, a tongue, a dialect, and all men learn it of their mothers. It is loquacious, fragmentary, — raw material. The other is a reserved, select, matured expression, a deliberate word addressed to the ear of nations and generations. The one is natural and convenient, the other divine and instructive. The clouds flit here below, genial, refreshing with their showers and gratifying with their tints, — alternate sun and shade, a grosser heaven adapted to our trivial wants; but above them repose the blue firmament and the stars. The stars are written words and stereotyped on the blue parchment of the skies; the fickle clouds that hide them from our view, which we on this side need, though heaven does not, these are our daily colloquies, our vaporous, garrulous breath.

Books must be read as deliberately and reservedly as they were written. The herd of men, the generations who speak the Greek and Latin, are not entitled by the accident of birth to read the works of genius, whose mother tongue speaks everywhere, and is learned by every child who hears. The army of the Greeks and Latins are not coæternal, though contemporary, with Homer and Plato, Virgil and Cicero. In the transition ages, nations who loudest spoke the Greek and Latin tongues, whose mother's milk they were, learned not

[1] [*Walden*, p. 250 ; Riv. 351.]

their nobler dialects, but a base and vulgar speech. The men of the Middle Ages who spoke so glibly the language of the Roman and, in the Eastern Empire, of the Athenian mob, prized only a cheap contemporary learning. The classics of both languages were virtually lost and forgotten. When, after the several nations of Europe had acquired in some degree rude and original languages of their own, sufficient for the arts of life and conversation, then the few scholars beheld with advantage from this more distant standpoint the treasures of antiquity, and a new Latin age commenced, the era of reading. Those works of genius were then first classical. All those millions who had spoken Latin and Greek had not read Latin and Greek. The time had at length arrived for the written word, the *scripture*, to be heard. What the multitude could not *hear*, after the lapse of centuries a few scholars *read*. This is the matured thought which was not spoken in the market-place, unless it be in a market-place where the free genius of mankind resorts to-day. There is something very choice and select in a written word. No wonder Alexander carried his Homer in a precious casket on his expeditions. A word which may be translated into every dialect, and suggests a truth to every mind, is the most perfect work of human art; and as it may be breathed and taken on our lips, and, as it were, become the product of our physical organs, as its sense is of our intellectual, it is the nearest to life itself.[1] It is the simplest and purest channel by which a revelation may be transmitted from age to age. How it subsists itself whole and undiminished till the

[1] [*Walden*, pp. 112–114 ; Riv. 159–161.]

intelligent reader is born to decipher it! There are the tracks of Zoroaster, of Confucius and Moses, indelible in the sands of the remotest times.

There are no monuments of antiquity comparable to the classics for interest and importance. It does not need that the scholar should be an antiquarian, for these works of art have such an immortality as the works of nature, and are modern at the same time that they are ancient, like the sun and stars, and occupy by right no small share of the present. This palpable beauty is the treasured wealth of the world and the proper inheritance of each generation. Books, the oldest and the best, stand rightfully on the shelves of every cottage. They have not to plead their cause, but they enlighten their readers and it is gained. When the illiterate and scornful rustic earns his imagined leisure and wealth, he turns inevitably at last — he or his children — to these still higher and yet inaccessible circles; and even when his descendant has attained to move in the highest rank of the wise men of his own age and country, he will still be sensible only of the imperfection of his culture and the vanity and inefficiency of his intellectual wealth, if his genius will not permit him to listen with somewhat of the equanimity of an equal to the fames of godlike men, which yet, as it were, form an invisible upper class in every society.[1]

I have carried an apple in my pocket to-night — a sopsivine, they call it — till, now that I take my hand-

[1] [*Walden*, p. 114 ; Riv. 162.]

Vol. I

kerchief out, it has got so fine a fragrance that it really seems like a friendly trick of some pleasant dæmon to entertain me with.[1] It is redolent of sweet-scented orchards, of innocent, teeming harvests. I realize the existence of a goddess Pomona, and that the gods have really intended that men should feed divinely, like themselves, on their own nectar and ambrosia. They have so painted this fruit, and freighted it with such a fragrance, that it satisfies much more than an animal appetite. Grapes, peaches, berries, nuts, etc., are likewise provided for those who will sit at their sideboard. I have felt, when partaking of this inspiring diet, that my appetite was an indifferent consideration; that eating became a sacrament, a method of communion, an ecstatic exercise, a mingling of bloods, and [a] sitting at the communion table of the world; and so have not only quenched my thirst at the spring but the health of the universe.

The indecent haste and grossness with which our food is swallowed have cast a disgrace on the very act of eating itself. But I do believe that, if this process were rightly conducted, its aspect and effects would be wholly changed, and we should receive our daily life and health, Antæus-like, with an ecstatic delight, and, with upright front, an innocent and graceful behavior, take our strength from day to day. This fragrance of the apple in my pocket has, I confess, deterred me from eating of it. I am more effectually fed by it another way.

It is, indeed, the common notion that this fragrance

[1] [See *Excursions*, p. 295 ; Riv. 362.]

is the only food of the gods, and inasmuch as we are partially divine we are compelled to respect it.

> Tell me, ye wise ones, if ye can,
> Whither and whence the race of man.
> For I have seen his slender clan
> Clinging to hoar hills with their feet,
> Threading the forest for their meat.
> Moss and lichens, bark and grain
> They rake together with might and main,
> And they digest them with anxiety and pain.
> I meet them in their rags and unwashed hair,
> Instructed to eke out their scanty fare —
> Brave race — with a yet humbler prayer.
> Beggars they are, aye, on the largest scale.
> They beg their daily bread at heaven's door,
> And if their this year's crop alone should fail,
> They neither bread nor begging would know more.
> They are the titmen of their race,
> And hug the vales with mincing pace
> Like Troglodytes, and fight with cranes.
> We walk 'mid great relations' feet.
> What they let fall alone we eat.
> We are only able
> To catch the fragments from their table.
> These elder brothers of our race,
> By us unseen, with larger pace
> Walk o'er our heads, and live our lives,
> Embody our desires and dreams,
> Anticipate our hoped-for gleams.
> We grub the earth for our food.

We know not what is good.
Where does the fragrance of our orchards go,
Our vineyards, while we toil below?
A finer race and finer fed
Feast and revel above our head.
The tints and fragrance of the flowers and fruits
Are but the crumbs from off their table,
While we consume the pulp and roots.
Sometimes we do assert our kin,
And stand a moment where once they have been.
We hear their sounds and see their sights,
And we experience their delights.
But for the moment that we stand
Astonished on the Olympian land,
We do discern no traveller's face,
No elder brother of our race,
To lead us to the monarch's court
And represent our case;
But straightway we must journey back,
Retracing slow the arduous track,
Without the privilege to tell,
Even, the sight we know so well.[1]

In my father's house are many mansions.

Who ever explored the mansions of the air? Who knows who his neighbors are? We seem to lead our human lives amid a concentric system of worlds, of realm on realm, close bordering on each other, where dwell the unknown and the imagined races, as various in degree as our own thoughts are, — a system of in-

[1] [Eight lines, somewhat altered, *Week*, pp. 407, 408; Riv. 503.]

Vol. I

visible partitions more infinite in number and more inconceivable in intricacy than the starry one which science has penetrated.

When I play my flute to-night, earnest as if to leap the bounds [of] the narrow fold where human life is penned, and range the surrounding plain, I hear echo from a neighboring wood, a stolen pleasure, occasionally not rightfully heard, much more for other ears than ours, for 't is the reverse of sound. It is not our own melody that comes back to us, but an amended strain. And I would only hear myself as I would hear my echo, corrected and repronounced for me. It is as when my friend reads my verse.

The borders of our plot are set with flowers, whose seeds were blown from more Elysian fields adjacent. They are the pot-herbs of the gods, which our laborious feet have never reached, and fairer fruits and unaccustomed fragrance betray another realm's vicinity. There, too, is Echo found, with which we play at evening. There is the abutment of the rainbow's arch.[1]

Aug. 6. Walden. — I have just been reading a book called "The Crescent and the Cross,"[2] till now I am somewhat ashamed of myself. Am I sick, or idle, that I can sacrifice my energy, America, and to-day to this man's ill-remembered and indolent story? Carnac and Luxor are but names, and still more desert sand and at length a wave of the great ocean itself are needed to wash away the filth that attaches to their grandeur.

[1] [*Week*, p. 407; Riv. 503.]
[2] [By Eliot Warburton, London, 1844, and New York, 1845.]

Carnac! Carnac! this is Carnac for me, and I behold the columns of a larger and a purer temple.[1] May our childish and fickle aspirations be divine, while we descend to this mean intercourse. Our reading should be heroic, in an unknown tongue, a dialect always but imperfectly learned, through which we stammer line by line, catching but a glimmering of the sense, and still afterward admiring its unexhausted hieroglyphics, its untranslated columns. Here grow around me nameless trees and shrubs, each morning freshly sculptured, rising new stories day by day, instead of hideous ruins, — their myriad-handed worker uncompelled as uncompelling. This is my Carnac; that its unmeasured dome. The measuring art man has invented flourishes and dies upon this temple's floor, nor ever dreams to reach that ceiling's height. Carnac and Luxor crumble underneath. Their shadowy roofs let in the light once more reflected from the ceiling of the sky.

Behold these flowers! Let us be up with Time, not dreaming of three thousand years ago. Erect ourselves and let those columns lie, not stoop to raise a foil against the sky. Where is the *spirit* of that time but in this present day, this present line? Three thousand years ago are not agone; they are still lingering here this summer morn.

And Memnon's mother sprightly greets us now;
Wears still her youthful blushes on her brow.
And Carnac's columns, why stand they on the plain?
T' enjoy our opportunities they would fain remain.

[1] [*Week*, pp. 266, 267; Riv. 331.]

This is my Carnac, whose unmeasured dome
Shelters the measuring art and measurer's home,
Whose propylæum is the system high [?]
And sculptured façade the visible sky.

Where there is memory which compelleth Time, the Muses' mother, and the Muses nine, there are all ages, past and future time, — unwearied memory that does not forget the actions of the past, that does not forego to stamp them freshly, that Old Mortality, industrious to retouch the monuments of time, in the world's cemetery throughout every clime.[1]

The student may read Homer or Æschylus in the original Greek; for to do so implies to emulate their heroes, — the consecration of morning hours to their pages.

The heroic books, though printed in the character of our mother tongue, are always written in a foreign language, dead to idle and degenerate times, and we must laboriously seek the meaning of each word and line, conjecturing a larger sense than the text renders us, at last, out of our own valor and generosity.[2]

A man must find his own occasion in himself. The natural day is very calm, and will hardly reprove our indolence. If there is no elevation in our spirits, the pond will not seem elevated like a mountain tarn, but a low pool, a silent muddy water, a place for fishermen. I sit here at my window like a priest of Isis, and ob-

[1] [*Week*, pp. 266, 267; Riv. 330-332.]
[2] [*Walden*, p. 111; Riv. 157, 158.]

serve the phenomena of three thousand years ago, yet unimpaired. The tantivy of wild pigeons, an ancient race of birds, gives a voice to the air, flying by twos and threes athwart my view or perching restless on the white pine boughs occasionally; a fish hawk dimples the glassy surface of the pond and brings up a fish; and for the last half-hour I have heard the rattle of railroad cars conveying travellers from Boston to the country.[1]

After the evening train has gone by and left the world to silence and to me, the whip-poor-will chants her vespers for half an hour. And when all is still at night, the owls take up the strain, like mourning women their ancient ululu. Their most dismal scream is truly Ben-Jonsonian. Wise midnight hags! It is no honest and blunt tu-whit tu-who of the poets, but, without jesting, a most solemn graveyard ditty, — but the mutual consolations of suicide lovers remembering the pangs and the delights of supernal love in the infernal groves. And yet I love to hear their wailing, their doleful responses, trilled along the woodside, reminding me sometimes of music and singing birds, as if it were the dark and tearful side of music, the regrets and sighs, that would fain be sung. The spirits, the *low* spirits and melancholy forebodings, of fallen spirits who once in human shape night-walked the earth and did the deeds of darkness, now expiating with their wailing hymns, threnodiai, their sins in the very scenery of, their transgressions. They give me a new sense of the vastness and mystery of that nature which is the common dwelling of us both.

[1] [*Walden*, p. 127; Riv. 179, 180.]

paunched, that there be no mistake; and the bowl goes round again, until the sun dispels the morning mist, and only the patriarch is not under the pond, but vainly bellowing *troonk* from time to time, pausing for a reply.[1]

All nature is classic and akin to art. The sumach and pine and hickory which surround my house remind me of the most graceful sculpture. Sometimes their tops, or a single limb or leaf, seems to have grown to a distinct expression as if it were a symbol for me to interpret. Poetry, painting, and sculpture claim at once and associate with themselves those perfect specimens of the art of nature, — leaves, vines, acorns, pine cones, etc. The critic must at last stand as mute though contented before a true poem as before an acorn or a vine leaf. The perfect work of art is received again into the bosom of nature whence its material proceeded, and that criticism which can only detect its unnaturalness has no longer any office to fulfill. The choicest maxims that have come down to us are more beautiful or integrally wise than they are wise to our understandings. This wisdom which we are inclined to pluck from their stalk is the point only of a single association. Every natural form — palm leaves and acorns, oak leaves and sumach and dodder — are [*sic*] untranslatable aphorisms.

Twenty-three years since, when I was five years old, I was brought from Boston to this pond, away in the country, — which was then but another name for the extended world for me, — one of the most ancient scenes

[1] [*Walden*, pp. 139, 140; Riv. 197, 198.]

"Oh-o-o-o-o that I never had been bor-or-or-or-orn!" sighs one on this side of the pond, and circles in the restlessness of despair to some new perch in the gray oaks. Then, "That I never had been bor-or-or-or-orn!" echoes one on the further side, with a tremulous sincerity, and "Bor-or-or-or-orn" comes faintly from far in the Lincoln woods.[1]

And then the frogs, bullfrogs; they are the more sturdy spirits of ancient wine-bibbers and wassailers, still unrepentant, trying to sing a catch in their Stygian lakes. They would fain keep up the hilarious good fellowship and all the rules of their old round tables, but they have waxed hoarse and solemnly grave and serious their voices, mocking at mirth, and their wine has lost its flavor and is only liquor to distend their paunches, and never comes sweet intoxication to drown the memory of the past, but mere saturation and water-logged dullness and distension. Still the most aldermanic, with his chin upon a pad, which answers for a napkin to his drooling chaps, under the eastern shore quaffs a deep draught of the once scorned water, and passes round the cup with the ejaculation *tr-r-r-r-r-oonk, tr-r-r-r-r-oonk, tr-r-r-r-oonk!* and straightway comes over the water from some distant cove the selfsame password, where the next in seniority and girth has gulped down to his mark; and when the strain has made the circuit of the shores, then ejaculates the master of ceremonies with satisfaction *tr-r-r-r-oonk!* and each in turn repeats the sound, down to the least distended, leakiest, flabbiest

[1] [*Walden*, pp. 137, 138; Riv. 194–196.]

Vol. I

stamped on the tablets of my memory, the oriental Asiatic valley of my world, whence so many races and inventions have gone forth in recent times. That woodland vision for a long time made the drapery of my dreams. That sweet solitude my spirit seemed so early to require that I might have room to entertain my thronging guests, and that speaking silence that my ears might distinguish the significant sounds. Somehow or other it at once gave the preference to this recess among the pines, where almost sunshine and shadow were the only inhabitants that varied the scene, over that tumultuous and varied city, as if it had found its proper nursery.

Well, now, to-night my flute awakes the echoes over this very water, but one generation of pines has fallen, and with their stumps I have cooked my supper, and a lusty growth of oaks and pines is rising all around its brim and preparing its wilder aspect for new infant eyes. Almost the same johnswort springs from the same perennial root in this pasture. Even I have at length helped to clothe that fabulous landscape of my imagination, and one result of my presence and influence is seen in these bean leaves and corn blades and potato vines.[1]

As difficult to preserve is the tenderness of your nature as the bloom upon a peach.

Most men are so taken up with the cares and rude practice of life that its finer fruits cannot be plucked by them. Literally, the laboring man has not leisure for

[1] [*Walden*, p. 172 (Riv. 242), where he makes his age four instead of five at the time of this early visit.]

a strict and lofty integrity day by day; he-cannot afford to sustain the fairest and noblest relations. His labor will depreciate in the market.

How can he remember well his ignorance who has so often to use his knowledge.

Aug. 15. The sounds heard at this hour, 8.30, are the distant rumbling of wagons over bridges, — a sound farthest heard of any human at night, — the baying of dogs, the lowing of cattle in distant yards.[1]

What if we were to obey these fine dictates, these divine suggestions, which are addressed to the mind and not to the body, which are certainly true, — not to eat meat, not to buy, or sell, or barter, etc., etc., etc. ?

I will not plant beans another summer, but sincerity, truth, simplicity, faith, trust, innocence, and see if they will not grow in this soil with such manure as I have, and sustain me.[2] When a man meets a man, it should not be some uncertain appearance and falsehood, but the personification of great qualities. Here comes truth, perchance, personified, along the road.[3] Let me see how Truth behaves. I have not seen enough of her. He shall utter no foreign word, no doubtful sentence, and I shall not make haste to part with him.

I would not forget that I deal with infinite and divine qualities in my fellow. All men, indeed, are divine in their core of light, but that is indistinct and distant to me, like the stars of the least magnitude, or the galaxy

[1] [*Walden*, p. 139 ; Riv. 197.]   [2] [*Walden*, p. 181 ; Riv. 255.]
[3] [*Walden*, p. 182 ; Riv. 256.]

Vol. I

knowing that it was the last of a noble line and the hope and cynosure of the world. An honest, hard-working, but shiftless man plainly was John Field; and his wife, she too was brave to cook so many succeeding dinners in the recesses of that lofty stove; with round, greasy face and bare breast, still thinking to improve her condition one day; with the never absent mop in hand, and yet no effects of it visible anywhere. The chickens, like members of the family, stalked about the room, too much humanized to roast well. They stood and looked in my eye or pecked at my shoe. He told me his story, how hard he worked bogging for a neighbor, at ten dollars an acre and the use of the land with manure for one year, and the little broad-faced son worked cheerfully at his father's side the while, not knowing, alas! how poor a bargain he had made. Living, John Field, alas! without arithmetic; failing to live.

"Do you ever fish?" said I. "Oh yes, I catch a mess when I am lying by; good perch I catch." "What's your bait?" "I catch shiners with fishworms, and bait the perch with them." "You'd better go now, John," said his wife, with glistening, hopeful face. But poor John Field disturbed but a couple of fins, while I was catching a fair string, and he said it was his luck; and when he changed seats luck changed seats too. Thinking to live by some derivative old-country mode in this primitive new country, *e. g.* to catch perch with shiners.[1]

I find an instinct in me conducting to a mystic spiritual life, and also another to a primitive savage life.

[1] [*Walden*, pp. 225–227, 229, 231 ; Riv. 317–320, 322, 325, 326.]

itself, but my kindred planets show their round disks and even their attendant moons to my eye.

Even the tired laborers I meet on the road, I really meet as travelling gods, but it is as yet, and must be for a long season, without speech.

Aug. 23. Saturday. I set out this afternoon to go a-fishing for pickerel to eke out my scanty fare of vegetables. From Walden I went through the woods to Fair Haven, but by the way the rain came on again, and my fates compelled me to stand a half-hour under a pine, piling boughs over my head, and wearing my pocket handkerchief for an umbrella; and when at length I had made one cast over the pickerel-weed, the thunder gan romblen in the heven with that grisly steven that Chaucer tells of.[1] (The gods must be proud, with such forked flashes and such artillery to rout a poor unarmed fisherman.) I made haste to the nearest hut for a shelter. This stood a half a mile off the road, and so much the nearer to the pond. There dwelt a shiftless Irishman, John Field, and his wife, and many children, from the broad-faced boy that ran by his father's side to escape the rain to the wrinkled and sibyl-like, crone-like infant, not knowing whether to take the part of age or infancy, that sat upon its father's knee as in the palaces of nobles, and looked out from its home in the midst of wet and hunger inquisitively upon the stranger, with the privilege of infancy; the young creature not knowing but it might be the last of a line of kings instead of John Field's poor starveling brat, or, I should rather say, still

[1] [*The Legend of Good Women*, ll. 1218, 1219.]

Toward evening, as the world waxes darker, I am permitted to see the woodchuck stealing across my path, and tempted to seize and devour it. The wildest, most desolate scenes are strangely familiar to me.[1]

Why not live a hard and emphatic life, not to be avoided, full of adventures and work, learn much in it, travel much, though it be only in these woods? I sometimes walk across a field with unexpected expansion and long-missed content, as if there were a field worthy of me. The usual daily boundaries of life are dispersed, and I see in what field I stand.

When on my way this afternoon, Shall I go down this long hill in the rain to fish in the pond? I ask myself. And I say to myself: Yes, roam far, grasp life and conquer it, learn much and live. Your fetters are knocked off; you are really free. Stay till late in the night; be unwise and daring. See many men far and near, in their fields and cottages before the sun sets, though as if many more were to be seen. And yet each *rencontre* shall be so satisfactory and simple that no other shall seem possible. Do not repose every night as villagers do. The noble life is continuous and unintermitting. At least, live with a longer radius. Men come home at night only from the next field or street, where their household echoes haunt, and their life pines and is sickly because it breathes its own breath. Their shadows morning and evening reach farther than their daily steps. But come home from far, from ventures and perils, from enterprise and discovery and crusading, with faith

[1] [*Walden*, p. 232 ; Riv. 327.]

and experience and character.[1] Do not rest much. Dismiss prudence, fear, conformity. Remember only what is promised. Make the day light you, and the night hold a candle, though you be falling from heaven to earth "from morn to dewy eve a summer's day."

For Vulcan's fall occupied a day, but our highest aspirations and performances fill but the interstices of time.

Are we not reminded in our better moments that we have been needlessly husbanding somewhat, perchance our little God-derived capital, or title to capital, guarding it by methods we know? But the most diffuse prodigality a better wisdom teaches, — that we *hold* nothing. We are not what we were. By usurers' craft, by Jewish methods, we strive to retain and increase the divinity in us, when infinitely the greater part of divinity is out of us.

Most men have forgotten that it was ever morning; but a few serene memories, healthy and wakeful natures, there are who assure us that the sun rose clear, heralded by the singing of birds, — this very day's sun, which rose before Memnon was ready to greet it.

In all the dissertations on language, men forget the language that is, that is really universal, the inexpressible meaning that is in all things and everywhere, with which the morning and evening teem. As if language were especially of the tongue of course. With a more

[1] [*Walden*, pp. 230, 231; Riv. 323–325.]

copious learning or understanding of what is published, the present *languages*, and all that they express, will be forgotten.

The rays which streamed through the crevices will be no more remembered when the shadow is wholly removed.

Left house on account of plastering, Wednesday, November 12th, at night; returned Saturday, December 6th.[1]

Though the race is not so degenerated but a man might possibly live in a cave to-day and keep himself warm by furs, yet, as caves and wild beasts are not plenty enough to accommodate all at the present day, it were certainly better to accept the advantages which the invention and industry of mankind offer. In thickly settled civilized communities, boards and shingles, lime and brick, are cheaper and more easily come by than suitable caves, or the whole logs, or bark in sufficient quantity, or even well-tempered clay or flat stones.[2] A tolerable house for a rude and hardy race that lived much out of doors was once made here without any of these last materials. According to the testimony of the first settlers of Boston, an Indian wigwam was as comfortable in winter as an English house with all its wainscotting, and they had advanced so far as to regulate the effect of the wind by a mat suspended over the hole

[1] [See *Walden*, pp. 271, 272; Riv. 380, 381.]
[2] [*Walden*, p. 44; Riv. 65, 66.]

Vol. I

in the roof, which was moved by a string. Such a lodge was, in the first instance, constructed in a day or two and taken down and put up again in a few hours, and every family had one.[1]

Thus, to try our civilization by a fair test, in the ruder states of society every family owns a shelter as good as the best, and sufficient for its ruder and simpler wants; but in modern civilized society, though the birds of the air have their nests, and woodchucks and foxes their holes, though each one is commonly the owner of his coat and hat though never so poor, yet not more than one man in a thousand owns a shelter, but the nine hundred and ninety-nine pay an annual tax for this outside garment of all, indispensable summer and winter, which would buy a village of Indian wigwams and contributes to keep them poor as long as they live. But, answers one, by simply paying this annual tax the poorest man secures an abode which is a palace compared to the Indian's. An annual rent of from twenty to sixty or seventy dollars entitles him to the benefit of all the improvements of centuries, — Rumford fireplace, back plastering, Venetian blinds, copper pump, spring lock, etc., etc.[2] But while civilization has been improving our houses, she has not equally improved the men who should occupy them. She has created palaces, but it was not so easy to create noblemen and kings. The mason who finishes the cornice of the palace returns at night, perchance, to a hut no better than a

[1] [*Walden*, pp. 32, 33; Riv. 48, 49.]
[2] [*Walden*, pp. 33, 34; Riv. 50, 51.]

wigwam.[1] If she claims to have made a real advance in the welfare of man, she must show how she has produced better dwellings without making them more costly. And the cost of a thing, it will be remembered, is the amount of life it requires to be exchanged for it, immediately or in the long run. An average house costs perhaps from one thousand to fifteen hundred dollars, and to earn this sum will require from fifteen to twenty years of the day laborer's life, even if he is not incumbered with a family; so that he must spend more than half his life before a wigwam can be earned; and if we suppose he pays a rent instead, this is but a doubtful choice of evils. Would the savage have been wise to exchange his wigwam for a palace on these terms?[2]

When I consider my neighbors, the farmers of Concord, for instance, who are at least as well off as the other classes, what are they about? For the most part I find that they have been toiling ten, twenty, or thirty years to pay for their farms, and we may set down one half of that toil to the cost of their houses; and commonly they have not yet paid for them.[3] This is the reason they are poor; and for similar reasons we are all poor in respect to a thousand savage comforts, though surrounded by luxuries.[4]

But most men do not know what a house is, and the mass are actually poor all their days because they think they must have such an one as their neighbor's. As if one were to wear any sort of coat the tailor might cut

[1] [*Walden*, pp. 37, 38; Riv. 56.]
[2] [*Walden*, p. 34; Riv. 51, 52.]
[3] [*Walden*, p. 35; Riv. 53.]
[4] [*Walden*, p. 36; Riv. 55.]

out for him, or, gradually leaving off palm-leaf hat and cap of woodchuck-skin, should complain of hard times because he could not buy him a crown![1]

It reflects no little dignity on Nature, the fact that the Romans once inhabited her, — that from this same unaltered hill, forsooth, the Roman once looked out upon the sea, as from a signal station. The vestiges of military roads, of houses and tessellated courts and baths, — Nature need not be ashamed of these relics of her children. The hero's cairn, — one doubts at length whether his relations or Nature herself raised the hill. The whole earth is but a hero's cairn. How often are the Romans flattered by the historian and antiquary! Their vessels penetrated into this frith and up that river of some remote isle. Their military monuments still remain on the hills and under the sod of the valleys. The oft-repeated Roman story is written in still legible characters in every quarter of the old world, and but to-day a new coin is dug up whose inscription repeats and confirms their fame. Some "Judæa Capta," with a woman mourning under a palm tree, with silent argument and demonstration puts at rest whole pages of history.[2]

The Earth
Which seems so barren once gave birth
To heroes, who o'erran her plains,
Who plowed her seas and reaped her grains.

Some make the mythology of the Greeks to have

[1] [*Walden*, p. 39; Riv. 58.]   [2] [*Week*, p. 264; Riv. 328.]

been borrowed from that of the Hebrews, which however is not to be proved by analogies, — the story of Jupiter dethroning his father Saturn, for instance, from the conduct of Cham towards his father Noah, and the division of the world among the three brothers. But the Hebrew fable will not bear to be compared with the Grecian. The latter is infinitely more sublime and divine. The one is a history of mortals, the other a history of gods and heroes, therefore not so ancient. The one god of the Hebrews is not so much of a gentleman, not so gracious and divine, not so flexible and catholic, does not exert so intimate an influence on nature as many a one of the Greeks. He is not less human, though more absolute and unapproachable. The Grecian were youthful and living gods, but still of godlike or divine race, and had the virtues of gods. The Hebrew had not all of the divinity that is in man, no real love for man, but an inflexible justice. The attribute of the one god has been infinite power, not grace, not humanity, nor love even, — wholly masculine, with no sister Juno, no Apollo, no Venus in him. I might say that the one god was not yet apotheosized, not yet become the current material of poetry.[1]

The wisdom of some of those Greek fables is remarkable. The god Apollo (Wisdom, Wit, Poetry) condemned to serve, keep the sheep of *King* Admetus. So is poetry allied to the state.

To Æacus, Minos, Rhadamanthus, judges in hell,

[1] [*Week*, p. 65; Riv. 81.]

only naked men came to be judged. As Alexander Ross comments, "In this world we must not look for Justice; when we are stript of all, then shall we have it. For here something will be found about us that shall corrupt the Judge." When the island of Ægina was depopulated by sickness at the instance of Æacus, Jupiter turned the ants into men, *i. e.* made men of the inhabitants who lived meanly like ants.[1]

The hidden significance of these fables which has been detected, the ethics running parallel to the poetry and history, is not so remarkable as the readiness with which they may be made to express any truth. They are the skeletons of still older and more universal truths than any whose flesh and blood they are for the time made to wear. It is like striving to make the sun and the wind and the sea signify. What signifies it?[2]

Piety, that carries its father on its shoulders.[3]

Music was of three kinds, — mournful, martial, and effeminate, — Lydian, Doric, and Phrygian. Its inventors Amphion, Thamyris, and Marsyas. Amphion was bred by shepherds. He caused the stones to follow him and built the walls of Thebes by his music. All orderly and harmonious or beautiful structures may be said to be raised to a slow music.
Harmony was begotten of Mars and Venus.

[1] [*Week*, p. 58; Riv. 72.]   [2] [*Week*, p. 61; Riv. 76.]
[3] [*Week*, p. 136; Riv. 169.]

Antæus was the son of Neptune and the Earth. All physical bulk and strength is of the earth and mortal. When it loses this *point d'appui* it is weakness; it cannot soar. And so, *vice versa*, you can interpret this fable to the credit of the earth.

They all provoked or challenged the gods, — Amphion, Apollo and Diana, and was killed by them; Thamyris, the Muses, who conquered him in music, took away his eyesight and melodious voice, and broke his lyre. Marsyas took up the flute which Minerva threw away, challenged Apollo, was flayed alive by him, and his death mourned by Fauns, Satyrs, and Dryads, whose tears produced the river which bears his name.

The fable which is truly and naturally composed, so as to please the imagination of a child, harmonious though strange like a wild-flower, is to the wise man an apothegm and admits his wisest interpretation.
When we read that Bacchus made the Tyrrhenian mariners mad, so that they leaped into the sea, mistaking it for "a meadow full of flowers," and so became dolphins, we are not concerned about the historical truth of this, but rather a higher, poetical truth. We seem to hear the music of a thought, and care not if our intellect be not gratified.[1]

The mythologies, those vestiges of ancient poems, the world's inheritance, still reflecting some of their original hues, like the fragments of clouds tinted by the

[1] [*Week*, p. 58; Riv. 72, 73.]

departed sun, the wreck of poems, a retrospect as [of] the loftiest fames, — what survives of oldest fame, — some fragment will still float into the latest summer day and ally this hour to the morning of creation. These are the materials and hints for a history of the rise and progress of the race. How from the condition of ants it arrived at the condition of men, how arts were invented gradually, — let a thousand surmises shed some light on this story. We will not be confined by historical, even geological, periods, which would allow us to doubt of a progress in human events. If we rise above this wisdom for the day, we shall expect that this morning of the race, in which they have been supplied with the simplest necessaries, — with corn and wine and honey and oil and fire and articulate speech and agricultural and other arts, — reared up by degrees from the condition of ants to men, will be succeeded by a day of equally progressive splendor; that, in the lapse of the divine periods, other divine agents and godlike men will assist to elevate the race as much above its present condition.

Aristæus "found out honey and oil." "He obtained of Jupiter and Neptune, that the pestilential heat of the dog-days, wherein was great mortality, should be mitigated with wind."[1]

Dec. 12. Friday. The pond skimmed over on the night of this day, excepting a strip from the bar to the northwest shore. Flint's Pond has been frozen for some time.[2]

[1] [*Week*, p. 57; Riv. 72.]   [2] [*Walden*, p. 275; Riv. 386.]

Dec. 16, 17, 18, 19, 20. Pond *quite free* from ice, not yet having been frozen quite over.

Dec. 23. Tuesday. The pond froze over last night entirely for the first time, yet so as not to be safe to walk upon.[1]

I wish to say something to-night not of and concerning the Chinese and Sandwich-Islanders, but *to* and concerning you who hear me, who are said to live in New England; something about your condition, especially your outward condition or circumstances in this world, in this town; what it is, whether it is necessarily as bad as it is, whether it can't be improved as well as not.[2]

It is generally admitted that some of you are poor, find it hard to get a living, have n't always something in your pockets, have n't paid for all the dinners you 've actually eaten, or all your coats and shoes, some of which are already worn out. All this is very well known to all by hearsay and by experience. It is very evident what a mean and sneaking life you live, always in the hampers, always on the limits, trying to get into business and trying to get out of debt, a very ancient slough, called by the Latins *aes alienum*, another's brass, — some of their coins being made of brass, — and still so many living and dying and buried to-day by another's brass; always promising to pay, promising to pay, with interest, to-morrow perhaps, and die to-day, insolvent; seeking to curry favor, to get custom, lying, flattering,

[1] [*Walden*, p. 275; Riv. 386.]   [2] [*Walden*, p. 4; Riv. 9.]

Vol. I

voting, contracting yourselves into a nutshell of civility or dilating into a world of thin and vaporous generosity, that you may persuade your neighbor to let you make his [shoes, or his hat, or his coat, or his carriage, etc.].[1]

There is a civilization going on among brutes as well as men. Foxes are forest dogs. I hear one barking raggedly, wildly, demoniacally in the darkness to-night, seeking expression, laboring with some anxiety, striving to be a dog outright that he may carelessly run in the street, struggling for light. He is but a faint man, before pygmies; an imperfect, burrowing man. He has come up near to my window, attracted by the light, and barked a vulpine curse at me, then retreated.[2]

Reading suggested by Hallam's History of Literature.
1. "Abelard and Heloise."
2. Look at Luigi Pulci. His "Morgante Maggiore," published in 1481, "was to the poetical romances of chivalry what Don Quixote was to their brethren in prose."
3. Leonardo da Vinci. The most remarkable of his writings still in manuscript. For his universality of genius, "the first name of the fifteenth century."
4. Read Boiardo's "Orlando Innamorato," published between 1491 and 1500, for its influence on Ariosto and its intrinsic merits. Its sounding names repeated by Milton in "Paradise Regained."

[1] [*Walden*, p. 7; Riv. 12, 13.]   [2] [*Walden*, p. 301; Riv. 422.]

Landor's works are: —
A small volume of poems, 1793, out of print.
Poems of "Gebir," "Chrysaor," the "Phoceans," etc. The "Gebir" eulogized by Southey and Coleridge.
Wrote verses in Italian and Latin.
The dramas "Andrea of Hungary," "Giovanna of Naples," and "Fra Rupert."
"Pericles and Aspasia."
"Poems from the Arabic and Persian," 1800, pretending to be translations.
"A Satire upon Satirists, and Admonition to Detractors," printed 1836, not published.
Letters called "High and Low Life in Italy."
"Imaginary Conversations."
"Pentameron and Pentalogia."
"Examination of William Shakspeare before Sir Thomas Lucy, Knt., touching Deer-stealing."

Vide again Richard's sail in "Richard First and the Abbot."[1]
Phocion's remarks in conclusion of "Eschines and Phocion."
"Demosthenes and Eubulides."
In Milton and Marvel, speaking of the Greek poets, he says, "There is a sort of refreshing odor flying off it perpetually; not enough to oppress or to satiate; nothing is beaten or bruised; nothing smells of the stalk; the flower itself is half-concealed by the Genius of it hovering round."
Pericles and Sophocles.

[1] [See *Journal*, vol. vii, Feb. 1, 1855.]

Marcus Tullius Cicero and his brother Quintus. In this a sentence on Sleep and Death.

Johnson and Tooke, for a criticism on words.

It is worth the while to have lived a primitive wilderness life at some time, to know what are, after all, the necessaries of life and what methods society has taken to supply them. I have looked over the old day-books of the merchants with the same view, — to see what it was shopmen bought. They are the grossest groceries.[1] Salt is perhaps the most important article in such a list, and most commonly bought at the stores, of articles commonly thought to be necessaries, — salt, sugar, molasses, cloth, etc., — by the farmer. You will see why stores or shops exist, not to furnish tea and coffee, but salt, etc. Here's the rub, then.

I see how I could supply myself with every other article which I need, without using the shops, and to obtain this might be the fit occasion for a visit to the seashore. Yet even salt cannot strictly speaking be called a necessary of human life, since many tribes do not use it.

"Have you seen my hound, sir? I want to know — what! a lawyer's office? law books? — if you've seen anything of a hound about here. Why, what do you do here?" "I live here. No, I haven't." "Haven't you heard one in the woods anywhere?" "Oh, yes, I heard one this evening." "What do you do here?" "But he was some way off." "Which side did he seem to be?"

[1] [*Walden*, pp. 12, 13; Riv. 21.]

Vol. I

"Well, I should think he [was] the other side of the pond." "This is a large dog; makes a large track. He's been out hunting from Lexington for a week. How long have you lived here?" "Oh, about a year." "Somebody said there was a man up here had a camp in the woods somewhere, and he'd got him." "Well, I don't know of anybody. There's Britton's camp over on the other road. It may be there." "Isn't there anybody in these woods?" "Yes, they are chopping right up here behind me." "How far is it?" "Only a few steps. Hark a moment. There, don't you hear the sound of their axes?"[1]

Therien, the woodchopper, was here yesterday, and while I was cutting wood, some chickadees hopped near pecking the bark and chips and the potato-skins I had thrown out. "What do you call them," he asked. I told him.

"What do *you* call them," asked I. "*Mezezence* [?]," I think he said. "When I eat my dinner in the woods," said he, "sitting very still, having kindled a fire to warm my coffee, they come and light on my arm and peck at the potato in my fingers. I like to have the little fellers about me."[2] Just then one flew up from the snow and perched on the wood I was holding in my arms, and pecked it, and looked me familiarly in the face. *Chicadee-dee-dee-dee-dee*, while others were whistling phebe, — *phe-bee*, — in the woods behind the house.[3]

[1] [*Walden*, p. 306; Riv. 429.]   [2] [*Walden*, p. 162; Riv. 228.]
[3] [*Walden*, p. 304; Riv. 426.]

March 26, 1846. The change from foul weather to fair, from dark, sluggish hours to serene, elastic ones, is a memorable crisis which all things proclaim. The change from foulness to serenity is instantaneous. Suddenly an influx of light, though it was late, filled my room. I looked out and saw that the pond was already calm and full of hope as on a summer evening, though the ice was dissolved but yesterday. There seemed to be some intelligence in the pond which responded to the unseen serenity in a distant horizon. I heard a robin in the distance, — the first I had heard this spring, — repeating the assurance. The green pitch [pine] suddenly looked brighter and more erect, as if now entirely washed and cleansed by the rain. I knew it would not rain any more. A serene summer-evening sky seemed darkly reflected in the pond, though the clear sky was nowhere visible overhead. It was no longer the end of a season, but the beginning. The pines and shrub oaks, which had before drooped and cowered the winter through with myself, now recovered their several characters and in the landscape revived the expression of an immortal beauty. Trees seemed all at once to be fitly grouped, to sustain new relations to men and to one another. There was somewhat cosmical in the arrangement of nature. O the evening robin, at the close of a New England day! If I could ever find the twig he sits upon! Where does the minstrel really roost? We perceive it is not the bird of the ornithologist that is heard, — the *Turdus migratorius*.

The signs of fair weather are seen in the bosom of ponds before they are recognized in the heavens. It

is easy to tell by looking at any twig of the forest whether its winter is past or not.[1]

We forget how the sun looks on our fields, as on the forests and the prairies, as they reflect or absorb his rays. It matters not whether we stand in Italy or on the prairies of the West, in the eye of the sun the earth is all equally cultivated like a garden, and yields to the wave of an irresistible civilization.

This broad field, which I have looked on so long, looks not to me as the farmer, looks away from me to the sun, and attends to the harmony of nature. These beans have results which are not harvested in the autumn of the year. They do not mind, if I harvest them, who waters and makes them grow? Our grain-fields make part of a beautiful picture which the sun beholds in his daily course, and it matters little comparatively whether they fill the barns of the husbandman. The true husbandman will cease from anxiety and labor with every day, and relinquish all claim to the produce of his fields.[2]

The avaricious man would fain plant by himself.

A flock of geese has just got in late, now in the dark flying low over the pond. They came on, indulging at last like weary travellers in complaint and consolation, or like some creaking evening mail late lumbering in with regular anserine clangor. I stood at my door and could hear their wings when they suddenly spied my light and, ceasing their noise, wheeled to the east and apparently settled in the pond.[3]

[1] [*Walden*, pp. 344, 345; Riv. 481, 482.]
[2] [*Walden*, pp. 183, 184; Riv. 258, 259.]
[3] [*Walden*, p. 345; Riv. 482.]

March 27. This morning I saw the geese from the door through the mist sailing about in the middle of the pond, but when I went to the shore they rose and circled round like ducks over my head, so that I counted them, — twenty-nine. I after saw thirteen ducks.[1]

[1] [*Walden*, p. 345; Riv. 482, 483.]

VIII

1845–1847

(ÆT. 27–30)

[THE small and much mutilated journal which begins here appears to belong to the Walden period (1845–47), but the entries are undated.]

THE HERO[1]

What doth he ask?
Some worthy task,
Never to run
Till that be done,
That never done
Under the sun.
Here to begin
All things to win
By his endeavor
Forever and ever.
Happy and well
On this ground to dwell,
This soil subdue,
Plant, and renew.
By might and main
Health and strength gain,
So to give nerve

[1] [Twenty-six lines of this, somewhat revised, appear under the title of "Pilgrims" in *Excursions, and Poems*, p. 413.]

Vol. I

To his slenderness;
Yet some mighty pain
He would sustain,
So to preserve
His tenderness.
Not be deceived,
Of suff'ring bereaved,
Not lose his life
By living too well,
Nor escape strife
In his lonely cell,
And so find out heaven
By not knowing hell.
Strength like the rock
To withstand any shock,
Yet some Aaron's rod,
Some smiting by God,
Occasion to gain
To shed human tears
And to entertain
Still demonic fears.
Not once for all, forever, blest,
Still to be cheered out of the west;
Not from his heart to banish all sighs;
Still be encouraged by the sunrise;
Forever to love and to love and to love,
Within him, around him, beneath him, above.
To love is to know, is to feel, is to be;
At once 't is his birth and his destiny.
    Having sold all,
    Something would get,

Furnish his stall
With better yet, —
For earthly pleasures
Celestial pains,
Heavenly losses
For earthly gains.
Still to begin — unheard-of sin
A fallen angel — a risen man
Never returns to where he began.
Some childlike labor
Here to perform,
Some baby-house
To keep out the storm,
And make the sun laugh
While he doth warm,
And the moon cry
To think of her youth,
The months gone by,
And wintering truth.

How long to morning?
Can any tell?
How long since the warning
On our ears fell?
The bridegroom cometh
Know we not well?
Are we not ready,
Our packet made,
Our hearts steady,
Last words said?
Must we still eat

The bread we have spurned?
Must we rekindle
The faggots we've burned?
Must we go out
By the poor man's gate?
Die by degrees,
Not by new fate?
Is there no road
This way, my friend?
Is there no road
Without any end?
Have you not seen
In ancient times
Pilgrims go by here
Toward other climes,
With shining faces
Youthful and strong
Mounting this hill
With speech and with song?
Oh, my good sir,
I know not the ways;
Little my knowledge,
Though many my days.
When I have slumbered,
I have heard sounds
As travellers passing
Over my grounds.
'T was a sweet music
Wafted them by;
I could not tell
If far off or nigh.

Unless I dreamed it,
This was of yore,
But I never told it
To mortal before;
Never remembered
But in my dreams
What to me waking
A miracle seems.
If you will give of your pulse or your grain,
We will rekindle those flames again.
Here will we tarry, still without doubt,
Till a miracle putteth that fire out.

———————

At midnight's hour I raised my head.
The owls were seeking for their bread;
The foxes barked, impatient still
At their wan [?] fate they bear so ill.
I thought me of eternities delayed
And of commands but half obeyed.
The night wind rustled through the glade,
As if a force of men there staid;
The word was whispered through the ranks,
And every hero seized his lance.
The word was whispered through the ranks,
Advance!

To live to a good old age such as the ancients reached, serene and contented, dignifying the life of man, leading a simple, epic country life in these days of confusion and turmoil, — that is what Wordsworth has done.

Vol. I

Retaining the tastes and the innocence of his youth. There is more wonderful talent, but nothing so cheering and world-famous as this.

The life of man would seem to be going all to wrack and pieces, and no instance of permanence and the ancient natural health, notwithstanding Burns, and Coleridge, and Carlyle. It will not do for men to die young; the greatest genius does not die young. Whom the gods love most do indeed die young, but not till their life is matured, and their years are like those of the oak, for they are the products half of nature and half of God. What should nature do without old men, not children but men?

The life of men, not to become a mockery and a jest, should last a respectable term of years. We cannot spare the age of those old Greek Philosophers. They live long who do not live for a near end, who still forever look to the immeasurable future for their manhood.

All dramas have but one scene. There is but one stage for the peasant and for the actor, and both on the farm and in the theatre the curtain rises to reveal the same majestic scenery. The globe of earth is poised in space for his stage under the foundations of the theatre, and the cope of heaven, out of reach of the scene-shifter, overarches it. It is always to be remembered by the critic that all actions are to be regarded at last as performed from a distance upon some rood of earth and amid the operations of nature.

Rabelais, too, inhabited the soil of France in sunshine and shade in those years; and his life was no "farce" after all.

I seek the present time,
No other clime,
Life in to-day, —
Not to sail another way, —
To Paris or to Rome,
Or farther still from home.
That man, whoe'er he is,
Lives but a moral death
Whose life is not coeval
With his breath.
My feet forever stand
On Concord fields,
And I must live the life
Which their soil yields.
What are deeds done
Away from home?
What the best essay
On the Ruins of Rome?
The love of the new,
The unfathomed blue,
The wind in the wood,
All future good,
The sunlit tree,
The small chickadee,
The dusty highways,
What Scripture says,
This pleasant weather,
And all else together,
The river's meander,
All things, in short,
Forbid me to wander

In deed or in thought.
In cold or in drouth,
Not seek the sunny South,
But make my whole tour
In the sunny present hour.

For here if thou fail,
Where can'st thou prevail?
If you love not
Your own land most,
You'll find nothing lovely
On a distant coast.
If you love not
The latest sunset,
What is there in pictures
Or old gems set?
If no man should travel
Till he had the means,
There'd be little travelling
For kings or for queens.
The means, what are they?
They are the wherewithal
Great expenses to pay,
Life got, and some to spare,
Great works on hand,
And freedom from care,
Plenty of time well spent
To use,
Clothes paid for and no rent
In your shoes,
Something to eat

And something to burn,
And above all no need to return.
Then they who come back,
Say, have they not failed,
Wherever they've ridden,
Or steamed it, or sailed?

All your grass hay'd,
All your debts paid,
All your wills made;
Then you might as well have stay'd,
For are you not dead,
Only not buried?

The way unto "to-day,"
The railroad to "here,"
They never'll grade that way
Nor shorten it, I fear.
There are plenty of depots
All the world o'er,
But not a single station
At a man's door.
If he would get near
To the secret of things,
He'll not have to hear
When the engine bell rings.

Exaggeration! was ever any virtue attributed to a man without exaggeration? was ever any vice, without infinite exaggeration? Do we not exaggerate ourselves to ourselves, or do we often recognize ourselves for the

Vol. I

actual men we are? The lightning is an exaggeration of light. We live by exaggeration. Exaggerated history is poetry, and is truth referred to a new standard. To a small man every greater one is an exaggeration. No truth was ever expressed but with this sort of emphasis, so that for the time there was no other truth. The value of what is really valuable can never be exaggerated. You must speak loud to those who are hard of hearing; so you acquire a habit of speaking loud to those who are not. In order to appreciate any, even the humblest, man, you must not only understand, but you must first love him; and there never was such an exaggerator as love. Who are we? Are we not all of us great men? And yet what [are] we actually? Nothing, certainly, to speak of. By an immense exaggeration we appreciate our Greek poetry and philosophy, Egyptian ruins, our Shakespeares and Miltons, our liberty and Christianity. We give importance to this hour over all other hours. We do not live by justice, but [by grace.] [1]

Love never perjures itself, nor is it mistaken.

He is not the great writer, who is afraid to let the world know that he ever committed an impropriety. Does it not know that all men are mortal?

Carlyle told R. W. E. that he first discovered that he was not a jackass on reading "Tristram Shandy" and Rousseau's "Confessions," especially the last. His first essay is an article in *Fraser's Magazine* on two boys quarrelling.

[1] [*Cape Cod, and Miscellanies*, pp. 352, 353 ; *Misc.*, Riv. 127, 128.]

Youth wants something to look up to, to look forward to; as the little boy who inquired of me the other day, "How long do those old-agers live?" and expressed the intention of compassing two hundred summers at least. The old man who cobbles shoes without glasses at a hundred, and cuts a handsome swath at a hundred and five, is indispensable to give dignity and respectability to our life.

From all points of the compass, from the earth beneath and the heavens above, have come these inspirations and been entered duly in the order of their arrival in the journal. Thereafter, when the time arrived, they were winnowed into lectures, and again, in due time, from lectures into essays. And at last they stand, like the cubes of Pythagoras, firmly on either basis; like statues on their pedestals, but the statues rarely take hold of hands. There is only such connection and series as is attainable in the galleries. And this affects their immediate practical and popular influence.

Carlyle, we should say, more conspicuously than any other, though with little enough expressed or even conscious sympathy, represents the Reformer class. In him the universal plaint is most settled and serious. Until the thousand named and nameless grievances are righted, there will be no repose for him in the lap of Nature or the seclusion of science and literature. And all the more for not being the visible acknowledged leader of any class.[1]

[1] [*Cape Cod, and Miscellanies*, p. 344 ; *Misc.*, Riv. 116, 117.]

All places, all positions — all things in short — are a medium happy or unhappy. Every realm has its centre, and the nearer to that the better while you are in it. Even health is only the happiest of all mediums. There may be excess, or there may be deficiency; in either case there is disease. A man must only be *virtuous* enough.

I had one neighbor within half a mile for a short time when I first went to the woods, Hugh Quoil, an Irishman who had been a soldier at Waterloo, Colonel Quoil, as he was called, — I believe that he had killed a colonel and ridden off his horse, — who lived from hand — sometimes to mouth, — though it was commonly a glass of rum that the hand carried. He and his wife awaited their fate together in an old ruin in Walden woods. What life he got — or what means of death — he got by ditching.

I never was much acquainted with Hugh Quoil, though sometimes I met him in the path, and now do believe that a solid shank-bone, and skull which no longer aches, lie somewhere, and can still be produced, which once with garment of flesh and broadcloth were called and hired to do work as Hugh Quoil. He was a man of manners and gentlemanlike, as one who had seen the world, and was capable of more civil speech than you could well attend to. At a distance he had seemingly a ruddy face as of biting January, but nearer at hand it was bright carmine. It would have burnt your finger to touch his cheek. He wore a straight-bodied snuff-colored coat which had long been familiar with him, and carried a turf-knife in his hand — in-

Vol. I

stead of a sword. He had fought on the English side before, but he fought on the Napoleon side now. Napoleon went to St. Helena; Hugh Quoil came to Walden Pond. I heard that he used to tell travellers who inquired about myself that —— and Thoreau owned the *farm* together, but Thoreau lived on the *place* and carried it on.[1]

He was thirstier than I, and drank more, probably, but not out of the pond. That was never the lower for him. Perhaps I ate more than he. The last time I met him, the only time I spoke with him, was at the foot of the hill on the highway as I was crossing to the spring one summer afternoon, the pond water being too warm for me. I was crossing the road with a pail in my hand, when Quoil came down the hill, wearing his snuff-colored coat, as if it were winter, and shaking with delirium tremens. I hailed him and told him that my errand was to get water at a spring close by, only at the foot of the hill over the fence. He answered, with stuttering and parched lips, bloodshot eye, and staggering gesture, he'd like to see it. "Follow me there, then." But I had got my pail full and back before he scaled the fence. And he, drawing his coat about him, to warm him, or to cool him, answered in delirium-tremens, hydrophobia dialect, which is not easy to be written here, he'd heard of it, but had never seen it; and so shivered his way along to town, — to liquor and to oblivion.

On Sundays, brother Irishmen and others, who had gone far astray from steady habits and the village, crossed my bean-field with empty jugs toward Quoil's.

[1] [*Walden*, pp. 288, 289; Riv. 405.]

But what for? Did they sell rum there? I asked. "Respectable people they," "Know no harm of them," "Never heard that they drank too much," was the answer of all wayfarers. They went by sober, stealthy, silent, skulking (no harm to get elm bark Sundays); returned loquacious, sociable, having long intended to call on you.

At length one afternoon Hugh Quoil, feeling better, perchance, with snuff-colored coat, as usual, paced solitary and soldier-like, thinking [of] Waterloo, along the woodland road to the foot of the hill by the spring; and there the Fates met him, and threw him down in his snuff-colored coat on the gravel, and got ready to cut his thread; but not till travellers passed, who would raise him up, get him perpendicular, then settle, settle quick; but legs, what are they? "Lay me down," says Hugh hoarsely. "House locked up — key — in pocket — wife in town." And the Fates cut, and there he lay by the wayside, five feet ten, and looking taller than in life.

He has gone away; his house here "all tore to pieces." What kind of fighting or ditching work he finds to do now, how it fares with him, whether his thirst is quenched, whether there is still some semblance of that carmine cheek, struggles still with some liquid demon — perchance on more equal terms — till he swallow him completely, I cannot by any means learn. What his salutation is now, what his January-morning face, what he thinks of Waterloo, what start he has gained or lost, what work still for the ditcher and forester and soldier now, there is no evidence. He was here, the likes of him,

for a season, standing light in his shoes like a faded gentleman, with gesture almost learned in drawing-rooms; wore clothes, hat, shoes, cut ditches, felled wood, did farm work for various people, kindled fires, worked enough, ate enough, drank too much. He was one of those unnamed, countless sects of philosophers who founded no school.

Now that he was gone, and his wife was gone too, — for she could not support the solitude, — before it was too late and the house was torn down, I went over to make a call. Now that Irishmen with jugs avoided the old house, I visited it, — an "unlucky castle now," said they. There lay his old clothes curled up by habit, as if it were himself, upon his raised plank bed. His pipe lay broken on the hearth; and scattered about were soiled cards — king of diamonds, hearts, spades — on the floor. One black chicken, which they could not catch, still went to roost in the next apartment, stepping silent over the floor, frightened by the sound of its own wings, black as night and as silent, too, not even croaking; awaiting Reynard, its god actually dead. There was the dim outline of a garden which had been planted, but had never received its first hoeing, now overrun with weeds, with burs and cockles, which stick to your clothes; as if in the spring he had contemplated a harvest of corn and beans before that strange trembling of the limbs overtook him. Skin of woodchuck fresh-stretched, never to be cured, met once in bean-field by the Waterloo man with uplifted hoe; no cap, no mittens wanted. Pipe on hearth no more to be lighted, best buried with him.[1]

[1] [*Walden*, p. 289; Riv. 405, 406.]

No thirst for glory, only for strong drink.

Only the convalescent are conscious of the health of nature.

In case of an embargo there will be found to be old clothes enough in everybody's garret to last till the millennium. We are fond of news, novelties, new things. The bank-bill that is torn in two will pass if you save the pieces, if you have only got the essential piece with the signatures. Lowell and Manchester and Fall River think you will let go their broadcloth currency when it is torn; but hold on, have an eye to the signature about the back of it, and endorse the man's name from whom you received it, and they will be the first to fail and find nothing at all in their garrets. Every day our garments become more assimilated to the man that wears them, more near and dear to us, and not finally to be laid aside but with such delay and medical appliance and solemnity as our other mortal coil.[1] We know, after all, but few men, a great many coats and breeches. Dress a scarecrow with your last shift, you standing shiftless by, who would not soonest address the scarecrow and salute it?[2]

King James loved his old shoes best. Who does not? Indeed these new clothes are often won and worn only after a most painful birth. At first movable prisons, oyster-shells which the tide only raises, opens, and shuts, washing in what scanty nutriment may be afloat. How many men walk over the limits, carrying their

[1] [*Walden*, pp. 24, 26; Riv. 36, 40.]   [2] [*Walden*, p. 24; Riv. 37.]

limits with them? In the stocks they stand, not without gaze of multitudes, only without rotten eggs, in torturing boots, the last wedge but one driven. Why should we be startled at death? Life is constant putting off of the mortal coil, — coat, cuticle, flesh and bones, all old clothes.

Not till the prisoner has got some rents in his prison walls, possibility of egress without lock and key some day, — result of steel watch-spring rubbing on iron grate, or whatever friction and wear and tear, — will he rest contented in his prison.

Clothes brought in sewing, a kind of work you may call endless.[1]

A man who has at length found out something important to do will not have to get a new suit to do it in. For him the old will do, lying dusty in the garret for an indefinite period. Old shoes will serve a hero longer than they have served his valet. Bare feet are the oldest of shoes, and he can make them do. Only they who go to legislature and soirées, — they must have new coats, coats to turn as often as the man turns in them. Who ever saw his old shoes, his old coat, actually worn out, returned to their original elements, so that it was not [a] deed [of] charity to bestow them on some poorer boy, and by him to be bestowed on some poorer still, or shall we say on some richer who can do with less?[2]

Over eastward of my bean-field lived Cato Ingraham, slave, born slave, perhaps, of Duncan Ingraham, Esquire, gentleman, of Concord village, who built him a house

[1] [*Walden*, p. 25; Riv. 38.]   [2] [*Walden*, p. 25; Riv. 38, 39.]

and gave him permission to live in Walden Woods, for which no doubt he was thanked; and then, on the northeast corner, Zilpha, colored woman of fame; and down the road, on the right hand, Brister, colored man, on Brister's Hill, where grow still those little wild apples he tended, now large trees, but still wild and ciderish to my taste; and farther still you come to Breed's location, and again on the left, by well and roadside, Nutting lived. Farther up the road, at the pond's end, Wyman, the potter, who furnished his townsmen with earthenware, — the squatter.[1]

Now only a dent in the earth marks the site of most of these human dwellings; sometimes the well-dent where a spring oozed, now dry and tearless grass, or covered deep, — not to be discovered till late days by accident, — with a flat stone under the sod. These dents, like deserted fox-burrows, old holes, where once was the stir and bustle of human life overhead, and man's destiny, "fate, free-will, foreknowledge absolute," were all by turns discussed.

Still grows the vivacious lilac for a generation after the last vestige else is gone, unfolding still its early sweet-scented blossoms in the spring, to be plucked only by the musing traveller; planted, tended, weeded [?], watered by children's hands in front-yard plot, — now by wall-side in retired pasture, or giving place to a new rising forest. The last of that stirp, sole survivor of that family. Little did the dark children think that that weak slip with its two eyes which they watered would root itself so, and outlive them, and house in the rear that shaded

[1] [*Walden*, pp. 283, 284, 287, 288; Riv. 397–400, 404.]

it, and grown man's garden and field, and tell their story to the retired wanderer a half-century after they were no more, — blossoming as fair, smelling as sweet, as in that first spring. Its still cheerful, tender, civil lilac colors.[1]

The woodland road, though once more dark and shut in by the forest, resounded with the laugh and gossip of inhabitants, and was notched and dotted here and there with their little dwellings. Though now but a humble rapid passage to neighboring villages or for the woodman's team, it once delayed the traveller longer, and was a lesser village in itself.[2]

You still hear from time to time the whinnering of the raccoon, still living as of old in hollow trees, washing its food before it eats it. The red fox barks at night. The loon comes in the fall to sail and bathe in the pond, making the woods ring with its wild laughter in the early morning, at rumor of whose arrival all Concord sportsmen are on the alert, in gigs, on foot, two by two, three [by three], with patent rifles, patches, conical balls, spyglass or open hole over the barrel. They seem already to hear the loon laugh; come rustling through the woods like October leaves, these on this side, those on that, for the poor loon cannot be omnipresent; if he dive here, must come up somewhere. The October wind rises, rustling the leaves, ruffling the pond water, so that no loon can be seen rippling the surface. Our sportsmen scour, sweep the pond with spy-glass in vain, making the woods ring with rude [?] charges of powder, for the

[1] [*Walden*, pp. 289–291; Riv. 406–408.]
[2] [*Walden*, pp. 282, 283; Riv. 396, 397.]

loon went off in that morning rain with one loud, long, hearty laugh, and our sportsmen must beat a retreat to town and stable and daily routine, shop work, unfinished jobs again.[1]

Or in the gray dawn the sleeper hears the long ducking gun explode over toward Goose Pond, and, hastening to the door, sees the remnant of a flock, black duck or teal, go whistling by with outstretched neck, with broken ranks, but in ranger order. And the silent hunter emerges into the carriage road with ruffled feathers at his belt, from the dark pond-side where he has lain in his bower since the stars went out.

And for a week you hear the circling clamor, clangor, of some solitary goose through the fog, seeking its mate, peopling the woods with a larger life than they can hold.[2]

For hours in fall days you shall watch the ducks cunningly tack and veer and hold the middle of the pond, far from the sportsman on the shore, — tricks they have learned and practiced in far Canada lakes or in Louisiana bayous.[3]

The waves rise and dash, taking sides with all waterfowl.[4]

Then in dark winter mornings, in short winter afternoons, the pack of hounds, threading all woods with hounding cry and yelp, unable to resist the instinct of

[1] [*Walden*, pp. 258, 259 ; Riv. 363, 364.]
[2] [*Walden*, p. 345 ; Riv. 483.]
[3] [*Walden*, p. 262 ; Riv. 368.]
[4] [*Walden*, p. 259 ; Riv. 364.]

Vol. I

the chase, and note of hunting-horn at intervals, showing that man too is in the rear. And the woods ring again, and yet no fox bursts forth on to the open level of the pond, and no following pack after their Actæon.[1]

But this small village, germ of something more, why did it fail while Concord grows apace? No natural advantages, no water privilege, only the deep Walden Pond and cool Brister's Spring, — privileges to drink long, healthy, pure draughts, alas, all unimproved by those men but to dilute their glass. Might not the basket-making, stable-broom, mat-making, corn-parching, potters' business have thrived here, making the wilderness to blossom as the rose? Now, all too late for commerce, this waste, depopulated district has its railroad too. And transmitted the names of unborn Bristers, Catos, Hildas,[2] Zilphas to a remote and grateful posterity.

Again Nature will try, with me for a first settler, and my house raised last spring to be the oldest in the settlement.

The sterile soil would have been proof against any lowland degeneracy.[3]

Farmers far and near call it the paradise of beans.

And here, too, on winter days, while yet is cold January, and snow and ice lie thick, comes the prudent, foreseeing landlord or housekeeper (anticipating thirst) from the village, to get ice to cool his summer drink, —

[1] [*Walden*, p 305 ; Riv. 428.]
[2] ["Hilda" was originally written where "Nutting" appears on p. 420.]
[3] [*Walden*, p. 292 ; Riv. 408, 409.]

a grateful beverage if he should live, if time should endure so long. How few so wise, so industrious, to lay up treasures which neither rust nor melt, "to cool their summer drink" one day!

And cut off the solid pond, the element and air of fishes, held fast with chain and stake like corded wood, all through favoring, willing, kind, permitting winter air to wintery cellar, to underlie the summer there. And cut and saw the cream of the pond, unroof the house of fishes.[1]

And in early mornings come men with fishing-reels and slender lunch, men of real faith, and let down their fine lines and live minnows through the snowy field to hook the pickerel and perch.[2]

With buried well-stones, and strawberries, raspberries, thimble-berries growing on the sunny sward there; some pitchy pine or gnarled oak in the chimney-nook, or the sweet-scented black birch where the doorstone was.[3]

Breed's, — history must not yet tell the tragedies enacted there. Let time intervene to assuage and lend an azure atmospheric tint to them.[4]

There is something pathetic in the sedentary life of men who have travelled. They must naturally die when they leave the road.

[1] [*Walden*, pp. 323, 324 ; Riv. 452, 453.]
[2] [*Walden*, p. 313 ; Riv. 438.]
[3] [*Walden*, pp. 289, 290 ; Riv. 406, 407.]
[4] [*Walden*, p. 285 ; Riv. 400.]

What seems so fair and poetic in antiquity — almost fabulous — is realized, too, in Concord life. As poets and historians brought their work to the Grecian games, and genius wrestled there as well as strength of body, so have we seen works of kindred genius read at our Concord games, by their author, in their own Concord amphitheatre. It is virtually repeated by all ages and nations.[1]

Moles nesting in your cellar and nibbling every third potato.[2] A whole rabbit-warren only separated from you by the flooring. To be saluted when you stir in the dawn by the hasty departure of Monsieur, — thump, thump, thump, striking his head against the floor-timbers.[3] Squirrels and field mice that hold to a community of property in your stock of chestnuts.

The blue jays suffered few chestnuts to reach the ground, resorting to your single tree in flocks in the early morning, and picking them out of the burs at a great advantage.

The crop of blackberries small; berries not yet grown. Ground-nuts not dug.

One wonders how so much, after all, was expressed in the old way, so much here depends upon the emphasis, tone, pronunciation, style, and spirit of the reading. No writer uses so profusely all the aids to intelligibility which the printer's art affords. You wonder

[1] [See *Week*, p. 102 ; Riv. 127.]
[2] [*Walden*, p. 280 ; Riv. 392, 393.]
[3] [*Walden*, p. 309 ; Riv. 434.]

how others had contrived to write so many pages without emphatic, italicized words, they are so expressive, so natural and indispensable, here. As if none had ever used the demonstrative pronoun demonstratively. In another's sentences the thought, though immortal, is, as it were, embalmed and does not *strike* you, but here it is so freshly living, not purified by the ordeal of death, that it stirs in the very extremities, the smallest particles and pronouns are all alive with it. — You must not say it, but *it*. It is not simple it, your it or mine, but *it*. His books are solid, workmanlike, like all that England does. They tell of endless labor done, well done, and all the rubbish swept away, like this bright cutlery which glitters in the windows, while the coke and ashes, turnings, filings, borings, dust lie far away at Birmingham, unheard of. The words did not come at the command of grammar but of a tyrannous, inexorable meaning; not like the standing soldiers, by vote of Parliament, but any able-bodied countryman pressed into the service. It is no China war, but a revolution. This style is worth attending to as one of the most important features of the man that we at this distance know.[1]

What are the men of New England about? I have travelled some in New England, especially in Concord, and I found that no enterprise was on foot which it would not disgrace a man to take part in. They seemed to be employed everywhere in shops and offices and fields. They seemed, like the Brahmins of the East, to

[1] [*Cape Cod, and Miscellanies*, pp. 325–327; *Misc.*, Riv. 93–95 ("Thomas Carlyle and his Works").]

be doing penance in a thousand curious, unheard-of ways, their endurance surpassing anything I had ever seen or heard of, — Simeon Stylites, Brahmins looking in the face of the sun, standing on one leg, dwelling at the roots of trees, nothing to it; any of the twelve labors of Hercules to be matched, — the Nemean lion, Lernæan hydra, Œnœan stag, Erymanthian boar, Augean stables, Stymphalian birds, Cretan bull, Diomedes' mares, Amazonian girdle, monster Geryon, Hesperian apples, three-headed Cerberus, nothing at all in comparison, being only twelve and having an end. For I could never see that these men ever slew or captured any of their monsters, or finished any of their labors. They have no "friend Iolaus to burn, with a hot iron, the root" of the hydra's head; for as soon as one head is crushed, two spring up.[1]

Men labor under a mistake; they are laying up treasures which moth and rust will corrupt and thieves break through and steal. Northern Slavery, or the slavery which includes the Southern, Eastern, Western, and all others.[2]

It is hard to have a Southern overseer; it is worse to have a Northern one; but worst of all when you are yourself the slave-driver. Look at the lonely teamster on the highway, wending to market by day or night; is he a son of the morning, with somewhat of divinity in him, fearless because immortal, going to receive his birthright, greeting the sun as his fellow, bounding with youthful, gigantic strength over his mother earth? See

[1] [*Walden*, pp. 4, 5; Riv. 9, 10.]
[2] [*Walden*, pp. 6, 8; Riv. 11, 14.]

Vol. I

how he cowers and sneaks, how vaguely, indefinitely all the day he fears, not being immortal, not divine, the slave and prisoner of his own opinion of himself, fame which he has earned by his own deeds. Public opinion is a weak tyrant compared with private opinion. What I think of myself, that determines my fate.[1]

I see young men, my equals, who have inherited from their spiritual father a soul, — broad, fertile, uncultivated, — from their earthly father a farm, — with cattle and barns and farming tools, the implements of the picklock and the counterfeiter. Better if they had been born in the open pasture and suckled by a wolf, or perhaps cradled in a manger, that they might have seen with clear eye what was the field they were called to labor in. The young man has got to live a man's life, then, in this world, pushing all these things before him, and get on as well as he can. How many a poor immortal soul I have met, well-nigh crushed and smothered, creeping slowly down the road of life, pushing before it a barn seventy-five by forty feet and one hundred acres of land, — tillage, pasture, wood-lot! This dull, opaque garment of the flesh is load enough for the strongest spirit, but with such an earthly garment superadded the spiritual life is soon plowed into the soil for compost. It's a fool's life, as they will all find when they get to the end of it. The man that goes on accumulating property when the bare necessaries of life are cared for is a fool and knows better.[2]

There is a stronger desire to be respectable to one's neighbors than to one's self.

[1] [*Walden*, p. 8; Riv. 14, 15.]   [2] [*Walden*, pp. 5, 6; Riv. 10, 11.]

However, such distinctions as poet, philosopher, literary man, etc., do not much assist our final estimate. We do not lay much stress on them; "a man's a man for a' that." Any writer who interests us much is all and more than these.

It is not simple dictionary it.[1]

Talent at making books solid, workmanlike, graceful, which may be read.[2]

Some idyllic chapter or chapters are needed.

In the French Revolution are Mirabeau, king of men; Danton, Titan of the Revolution; Camille Desmoulins, poetic editor; Roland, heroic woman; Dumouriez, first efficient general: on the other side, Marat, friend of the people; Robespierre; Tinville, infernal judge; St. Just; etc., etc.

Nutting and Le Gros by the wall-side. The Stratten house and barn where the orchard covered all the slope of Brister's Hill, — now killed out by the pines.

Brister Freeman, a handy negro, slave once of Squire Cummings (?), and Fenda, his hospitable, pleasant wife, large, round, black, who told fortunes, blacker than all the children of night, such a dusky orb as had never risen on Concord before.

Zilpha's little house where "she was spinning linen," making the Walden woods ring with her shrill singing, — a loud, shrill, remarkable voice, — when once she

[1] [*Cape Cod, and Miscellanies*, p. 327; *Misc.*, Riv. 95 ("Thomas Carlyle and his Works").]
[2] [*Cape Cod, and Miscellanies*, p. 325; *Misc.*, Riv. 93 ("Thomas Carlyle and his Works").]

was away to town, set on fire by English soldiers on parole, in the last war, and cat and dog and hens all burned up. Boiling her witch's dinner, and heard muttering to herself over the gurgling pot by silent traveller, "Ye are all bones, bones."

And Cato, the Guinea negro, — his house and little patch among the walnuts, — who let the trees grow up till he should be old, and Richardson got them.

Where Breed's house stood tradition says a tavern once stood, the well the same, and all a swamp between the woods and town, and road made on logs.[1]

Bread I made pretty well for awhile, while I remembered the rules; for I studied this out methodically, going clear back to the primitive days and first invention of the unleavened kind, and coming gradually down through that lucky accidental souring of the dough which taught men the leavening process, and all the various fermentations thereafter, till you get to "good, sweet, wholesome bread," the staff of life. I went on very well, mixing rye and flour and Indian and potato with success, till one morning I had forgotten the rules, and thereafter scalded the yeast, — killed it out, — and so, after the lapse of a month, was glad after all to learn that such palatable staff of life could be made out of the dead and scalt creature and risings that lay flat.

I have hardly met with the housewife who has gone so far with this mystery. For all the farmers' wives pause at yeast. Given this and they can make bread.

¹ [*Walden*, pp. 283–285, 287, 288 ; Riv. 397–400, 404.]

a far more intense life; seeks to realize a divine life; his affections and intellect equally developed. Has advanced farther, and a new heaven opens to him. Love and Friendship, Religion, Poetry, the Holy are familiar to him. The life of an Artist; more variegated, more observing, finer perception; not so robust, elastic; practical enough in his own field; faithful, a judge of men. There is no such general critic of men and things, no such trustworthy and faithful man. More of the divine realized in him than in any. A poetic critic, reserving the unqualified nouns for the gods.

Alcott is a geometer, a visionary, the Laplace of ethics, more intellect, less of the affections, sight beyond talents, a substratum of practical skill and knowledge unquestionable, but overlaid and concealed by a faith in the unseen and impracticable. Seeks to realize an entire life; a catholic observer; habitually takes in the farthest star and nebula into his scheme. Will be the last man to be disappointed as the ages revolve. His attitude is one of greater faith and expectation than that of any man I know; with little to show; with undue share, for a philosopher, of the weaknesses of humanity. The most hospitable intellect, embracing high and low. For children how much that means, for the insane and vagabond, for the poet and scholar![1]

Emerson has special talents unequalled. The divine in man has had no more easy, methodically distinct expression. His personal influence upon young per-

¹ [*Walden*, p. 296 ; Riv. 415, 416.]

It is the axiom of the argument. What it is, where it came from, in what era bestowed on man, is wrapped in mystery. It is preserved religiously, like the vestal fire, and its virtue is not yet run out. Some precious bottleful, first brought over in the Mayflower, did the business for America, and its influence is still rising, swelling, spreading like Atlantic billows over the land, — the soul of bread, the spiritus, occupying its cellular tissue.[1]

The way to compare men is to compare their respective ideals. The actual man is too complex to deal with.

Carlyle is an earnest, honest, heroic worker as literary man and sympathizing brother of his race.

Idealize a man, and your notion takes distinctness at once.

Carlyle's talent is perhaps quite equal to his genius.[2]

Striving [?] to live in reality, — not a general critic, philosopher, or poet.

Wordsworth, with very feeble talent, has not so great and admirable as unquestionable and persevering genius.

Heroism, heroism is his word, — his thing.

He would realize a brave and adequate human life, and die hopefully at last.

Emerson again is a critic, poet, philosopher, with talent not so conspicuous, not so adequate to his task; but his field is still higher, his task more arduous. Lives

¹ [*Walden*, pp. 68, 69 ; Riv. 99, 100.]
² [*Cape Cod, and Miscellanies*, p. 348 ; *Misc.*, Riv. 121 ("Thomas Carlyle and his Works").]

sons greater than any man's. In his world every man would be a poet, Love would reign, Beauty would take place, Man and Nature would harmonize.

When Alcott's day comes, laws unsuspected by most will take effect,[1] the system will crystallize according to them, all seals and falsehood will slough off, everything will be in its place.

Feb. 22 [no year]. Jean Lapin sat at my door to-day, three paces from me, at first trembling with fear, yet unwilling to move; a poor, wee thing, lean and bony, with ragged ears and sharp nose, scant tail and slender paws. It looked as if nature no longer contained the breed of nobler bloods, the earth stood on its last legs. Is nature, too, unsound at last? I took two steps, and lo, away he scud with elastic spring over the snowy crust into the bushes, a free creature of the forest, still wild and fleet; and such then was his nature, and his motion asserted its vigor and dignity. Its large eye looked at first young and diseased, almost dropsical, unhealthy. But it bound[ed] free, the venison, straightening its body and its limbs into graceful length, and soon put the forest between me and itself.[2]

Emerson does not consider things in respect to their essential utility, but an important partial and relative one, as works of art perhaps. His probes pass one side of their centre of gravity. His exaggeration is of a part, not of the whole.

¹ [*Walden*, p. 296 ; Riv. 415.]   ² [*Walden*, p. 310 ; Riv. 434, 435.]

How many an afternoon has been stolen from more profitable, if not more attractive, industry, — afternoons when a good run of custom might have been expected on the main street, such as tempt the ladies out a-shopping, — spent, I say, by me away in the meadows, in the well-nigh hopeless attempt to set the river on fire or be set on fire by it, with such tinder as I had, with such flint as I was. Trying at least to make it flow with milk and honey, as I had heard of, or liquid gold, and drown myself without getting wet, — a laudable enterprise, though I have not much to show for it.

So many autumn days spent outside the town, trying to hear what was in the wind, to hear it and carry it express. I well-nigh sunk all my capital in it, and lost my own breath into the bargain, by running in the face of it. Depend upon it, if it had concerned either of the parties, it would have appeared in the yeoman's gazette, the *Freeman*, with other earliest intelligence.

For many years I was self-appointed inspector of snow-storms and rain-storms, and did my duty faithfully, though I never received one cent for it.

Surveyor, if not of higher ways, then of forest paths and all across-lot routes, keeping many open ravines bridged and passable at all seasons, where the public heel had testified to the importance of the same, all not only without charge, but even at considerable risk and inconvenience. Many a mower would have forborne to complain had he been aware of the invisible public good that was in jeopardy.

So I went on, I may say without boasting, I trust, faithfully minding my business without a partner, till

it became more and more evident that my townsmen would not, after all, admit me into the list of town officers, nor make the place a sinecure with moderate allowance.

I have looked after the wild stock of the town, which pastures in common, and every one knows that these cattle give you a good deal of trouble in the way of leaping fences. I have counted and registered all the eggs I could find at least, and have had an eye to all nooks and corners of the farm, though I did n't always know whether Jonas or Solomon worked in a particular field to-day; that was none of my business. I only knew him for one of the men, and trusted that he was as well employed as I was. I had to make my daily entries in the general farm book, and my duties may sometimes have made me a little stubborn and unyielding.

Many a day spent on the hilltops waiting for the sky to fall, that I might catch something, though I never caught much, only a little, manna-wise, that would dissolve again in the sun.

My accounts, indeed, which I can swear to have been faithfully kept, I have never got audited, still less accepted, still less paid and settled. However, I have n't set my heart upon *that*.

I have watered the red huckleberry and the sand cherry and the hoopwood [?] tree, and the cornel and spoonhunt and yellow violet, which might have withered else in dry seasons. The white grape.

To find the bottom of Walden Pond, and what inlet and outlet it might have.

Vol. I

I found at length that, as they were not likely to offer me any office in the court-house, any curacy or living anywhere else, I must shift for myself, I must furnish myself with the necessaries of life.

Now watching from the observatory of the Cliffs or Annursnack to telegraph any new arrival, to see if Wachusett, Watatic, or Monadnock had got any nearer. Climbing trees for the same purpose. I have been reporter for many years to one of the journals of no very wide circulation, and, as is too common, got only my pains for my labor. Literary contracts are little binding.[1]

The unlimited anxiety, strain, and care of some persons is one very incurable form of disease. Simple arithmetic might have corrected it; for the life of every man has, after all, an epic integrity, and Nature adapts herself to our weaknesses and deficiencies as well as talents.

No doubt it is indispensable that we should do *our* work between sun and sun, but only a wise man will know what that is. And yet how much work will be left undone, put off to the next day, and yet the system goes on!

We presume commonly to take care of ourselves, and trust as little as possible. Vigilant more or less all our days, we say our prayers at night and commit ourselves to uncertainties, as if in our very days and most vigilant moments the great part were not a necessary trust still.[2] How serenity, anxiety, confidence, fear paint the heavens for us.

[1] [*Walden*, pp. 19–21 ; Riv. 30–33.]
[2] [*Walden*, p. 12 ; Riv. 19, 20.]

All the laws of nature will bend and adapt themselves to the least motion of man.

All change is a miracle to contemplate, but it is a miracle which is taking place unobserved every instant; when all is ready it takes place, and only a miracle could stay it.

We [are] compelled to live so thoroughly and sincerely, reflecting on our steps, reverencing our life, that we never make allowance for the possible changes.

We may waive just so much care of ourselves as we devote of care elsewhere.[1]

[1] [*Walden*, p. 12 ; Riv. 20.]

1837–1847

(ÆT. 20–30)

[THIS chapter consists of paragraphs (chiefly undated) taken from a large commonplace-book containing transcripts from earlier journals. Thoreau drew largely from this book in writing the "Week," and to a less extent in writing "Walden." Passages used in these volumes (as far as noted), and those duplicating earlier journal entries already printed in the preceding pages, have been omitted. All the matter in the book appears to have been written before 1847.]

I was born upon thy bank, river,
My blood flows in thy stream,
And thou meanderest forever
At the bottom of my dream.

This great but silent traveller which had been so long moving past my door at three miles an hour, — might I not trust myself under its escort?

In friendship we worship moral beauty without the formality of religion.

Consider how much the sun and the summer, the buds of spring and the sered leaves of autumn, are re-

The robin is seen flying directly and high in the air at this season, especially over rivers, where in the morning they are constantly passing and repassing in company with the blackbird.

I have never insisted enough on the nakedness and simplicity of friendship, the result of all emotions, their subsidence, a fruit of the temperate zone. The friend is an unrelated man, solitary and of distinct outline.

Must not our whole lives go unexplained, without regard to us, notwithstanding a few flourishes of ours, which themselves need explanation?

Yet a friend does not afford us cheap contrasts or encounters. He forbears to ask explanations, but doubts and surmises with full faith, as we silently ponder our fates. He is vested with full powers, plenipotentiary, all in all.

"Plato gives science sublime counsels, directs her toward the regions of the ideal; Aristotle gives her positive and severe laws, and directs her toward a practical end." — DEGERANDO.

All day the dark blue outline of Crotched Mountain in Goffstown skirted the horizon. We took pleasure in beholding its outline, because at this distance our vision could so easily grasp the design of the founder. It was a pretty victory to conquer the distance and dimensions so easily with our eyes, which it would take our feet so long to traverse.

lated to the cabins of the settlers which we discover on the shore, — how all the rays which paint the landscape radiate from them. The flight of the crow and the gyrations of the hawk have reference to their roofs.

Friends do not interchange their common wealth, but each puts his finger into the private coffer of the other. They will be most familiar, they will be most unfamiliar, for they will be so one and single that common themes will not have to be bandied between them, but in silence they will digest them as one mind; but they will at the same time be so two and double that each will be to the other as admirable and as inaccessible as a star. He will view him as it were through "optic glass," — "at evening from the top of Fesolé." And after the longest earthly period, he will still be in apogee to him.

It [the boat] had been loaded at the door the evening before, half a mile from the river, and provided with wheels against emergencies, but, with the bulky cargo which we stevedores had stowed in it, it proved but an indifferent land carriage. For water and water-casks there was a plentiful supply of muskmelons from our patch, which had just begun to be ripe, and chests and spare spars and sails and tent and guns and munitions for the galleon. And as we pushed it through the meadows to the river's bank, we stepped as lightly about it as if a portion of our own bulk and burden was stored in its hold. We were amazed to find ourselves outside still, with scarcely independent force enough to push or pull effectually.

Notwithstanding the unexplained mystery of nature, man still pursues his studies with confidence, ever ready to grasp the secret, as if the truth were only contained, not withheld; as one of the three circles on the cocoanut is always so soft that it may be pierced with a thorn, and the traveller is grateful for the thick shell which held the liquor so faithfully.

Gracefulness is undulatory like these waves, and perhaps the sailor acquires a superior suppleness and grace through the planks of his ship from the element on which he lives.

The song sparrow, whose voice is one of the first heard in the spring, sings occasionally throughout the season, — from a greater depth in the summer, as it were behind the notes of other birds.

As the temperature and density of the atmosphere, so the aspects of our life vary.

In this bright and chaste light the world seemed like a pavilion made for holidays and washed in light. The ocean was a summer's lake, and the land a smooth lawn for disport, while in the horizon the sunshine seemed to fall on walled towns and villas, and the course of our lives was seen winding on like a country road over the plain.[1]

When we looked out from under our tent, the trees were seen dimly through the mist, and a cool dew hung

[1] [*Week*, p. 45; Riv. 57.]

upon the grass, and in the damp air we seemed to inhale a solid fragrance.

Communicating with the villas and hills and forests on either hand, by the glances we sent them, or the echoes we awakened. We glanced up many a pleasant ravine with its farmhouse in the distance, where some contributory stream came in; again the site of a saw-mill and a few forsaken eel-pots were all that greeted us.[1]

While we sail here we can remember unreservedly those friends who dwell far away on the banks and by the sources of this very river, and people this world for us, without any harsh and unfriendly interruptions.

At noon his horn[2] is heard echoing from shore to shore to give notice of his approach to the farmer's wife with whom he is to take his dinner, frequently in such retired scenes that only muskrats and kingfishers seem to hear.

If ever our idea of a friend is realized it will be in some broad and generous natural person, as frank as the day-light, in whose presence our behavior will be as simple and unconstrained as the wanderer amid the recesses of these hills.

I who sail now in a boat, have I not sailed in a thought ? *Vide* Chaucer.

[1] [This follows matter used on p. 81 of *Week* (Riv. 101).]
[2] [The boatman's. See *Week*, p. 222 ; Riv. 276.]

The hardest material obeys the same law with the most fluid. Trees are but rivers of sap and woody fibre flowing from the atmosphere and emptying into the earth by their trunks, as their roots flow upward to the surface. And in the heavens there are rivers of stars and milky ways. There are rivers of rock on the surface and rivers of ore in the bowels of the earth. And thoughts flow and circulate, and seasons lapse as tributaries of the current year.

Consider the phenomena of morn, or eve, and you will say that Nature has perfected herself by an eternity of practice, — evening stealing over the fields, the stars coming to bathe in retired waters, the shadows of the trees creeping farther and farther into the meadows, and a myriad phenomena beside.

Occasionally we had to muster all our energy to get round a point where the river broke rippling over rocks and the maples trailed their branches in the stream.

The future reader of history will associate this genera-tion with the red man in his thoughts, and give it credit for some sympathy with that race. Our history will have some copper tints and reflections, at least, and be read as through an Indian-summer haze; but such were not our associations. But the Indian is absolutely for-gotten but by some persevering poets.

The white man has commenced a new era. What do our anniversaries commemorate but white men's ex-ploits ? For Indian deeds there must be an Indian mem-

ory; the white man will remember his own only. We have forgotten their hostility as well as friendship. Who can realize that, within the memory of this generation, the remnant of an ancient and dusky race of mortals called the Stockbridge Indians, within the limits of this very State, furnished a company for the war, on condition only that they should not be expected to fight white man's fashion, or to train, but Indian fashion. And occasionally their wigwams are seen on the banks of this very stream still, solitary and inobvious, like the cabins of the muskrats in the meadows.

They seem like a race who have exhausted the se-crets of nature, tanned with age, while this young and still fair Saxon slip, on whom the sun has not long shone, is but commencing its career.

.   .   .   .

Their memory is in harmony with the russet hue of the fall of the year.[1]

For the Indian there is no safety but in the plow. If he would not be pushed into the Pacific, he must seize hold of a plow-tail and let go his bow and arrow, his fish-spear and rifle. This the only Christianity that will save him.[2]

His fate says sternly to him, "Forsake the hunter's life and enter into the agricultural, the second, state of man. Root yourselves a little deeper in the soil, if you would continue to be the occupants of the country."

[1] [See p. 337.]
[2] [This and the succeeding paragraphs on the Indian were written in pencil on loose sheets of paper and slipped between the pages of the Journal.]

But I confess I have no little sympathy with the Indians and hunter men. They seem to me a distinct and equally respectable people, born to wander and to hunt, and not to be inoculated with the twilight civilization of the white man.

Father Le Jeune, a French missionary, affirmed "that the Indians were superior in intellect to the French peasantry of that time," and advised "that laborers should be sent from France in order to work for the Indians."

The Indian population within the present bounda-ries of New Hampshire, Massachusetts, Rhode Island, and Connecticut has been estimated not to have ex-ceeded 40,000 "before the epidemic disease which preceded the landing of the Pilgrims," and it was far more dense here than elsewhere; yet they had no more land than they wanted. The present white population is more than 1,500,000 and two thirds of the land is unimproved.

The Indian, perchance, has not made up his mind to some things which the white man has consented to; he has not, in all respects, stooped so low; and hence, though he too loves food and warmth, he draws his tattered blanket about him and follows his fathers, rather than barter his birthright. He dies, and no doubt his Genius judges well for him. But he is not worsted in the fight; he is not destroyed. He only migrates beyond the Pacific to more spacious and happier hunting-grounds.

A race of hunters can never withstand the inroads of a race of husbandmen. The latter burrow in the night into their country and undermine them; and [even] if the hunter is brave enough to resist, his game is timid and has already fled. The rifle alone would never exterminate it, but the plow is a more fatal weapon; it wins the country inch by inch and holds all it gets.

What detained the Cherokees so long was the 2923 plows which that people possessed; and if they had grasped their handles more firmly, they would never have been driven beyond the Mississippi. No sense of justice will ever restrain the farmer from plowing up the land which is only hunted over by his neighbors. No hunting-field was ever well fenced and surveyed and its bounds accurately marked, unless it were an English park. It is a property not held by the hunter so much as by the game which roams it, and was never well secured by warranty deeds. The farmer in his treaties says only, or means only, "So far will I plow this summer," for he has not seed corn enough to plant more; but every summer the seed is grown which plants a new strip of the forest.

The African will survive, for he is docile, and is patiently learning his trade and dancing at his labor; but the Indian does not often dance, unless it be the war dance.

In whatever moment we awake to life, as now I this evening, after walking along the bank and hearing the same evening sounds that were heard of yore, it seems to have slumbered just below the surface, as in the spring the new verdure which covers the fields has never retreated far from the winter.

Vol. I

All actions and objects and events lose their *distinct* importance in this hour, in the brightness of the vision, as, when sometimes the pure light that attends the setting sun falls on the trees and houses, the light itself is the phenomenon, and no single object is so distinct to our admiration as the light itself.

If criticism is liable to abuse, it has yet a great and humane apology. When my sentiments aspire to be universal, then my neighbor has an equal interest to see that the expression be just, with myself.

> My friends, why should we live?
>   Life is an idle war, a toilsome peace;
> To-day I would not give
>   One small consent for its securest ease.
>
> Shall we outwear the year
>   In our pavilions on its dusty plain,
> And yet no signal hear
>   To strike our tents and take the road again?
>
> Or else drag up the slope
>   The heavy ordnance of religion's train?
> Useless, but in the hope
>   Some far remote and heavenward hill to gain.

The tortoises rapidly dropped into the water, as our boat ruffled the surface amid the willows. We glided along through the transparent water, breaking the reflections of the trees.

Not only are we late to find our friends, but mankind are late, and there is no record of a great success in history.

My friend is not chiefly wise or beautiful or noble. At least it is not for me to know it. He has no visible form nor appreciable character. I can never praise him nor esteem him praiseworthy, for I should sunder him from myself and put a bar between us. Let him not think he can please me by any behavior or even treat me well enough. When he treats, I retreat.[1]

I know of no rule which holds so true as that we are always paid for our suspicion by finding what we suspect. There can be no fairer recompense than this. Our suspicions exercise a demoniacal power over the subject of them. By some obscure law of influence, when we are perhaps unconsciously the subject of another's suspicion, we feel a strong impulse, even when it is contrary to our nature, to do that which he expects but reprobates.

No man seems to be aware that his influence is the result of his entire character, both that which is subject and that which is superior to his understanding, and what he really means or intends it is not in his power to explain or offer an apology for.

No man was ever party to a secure and settled friendship. It is no more a constant phenomenon than

[1] [See *Week*, pp. 286, 287; Riv. 356.]

meteors and lightning. It is a war of positions, of silent tactics.

> I mark the summer's swift decline;
> The springing sward its grave-clothes weaves.[1]
>
> Oh, could I catch the sounds remote!
> Could I but tell to human ear
> The strains which on the breezes float
> And sing the requiem of the dying year!

Sept. 29, 1842. To-day the lark sings again down in the meadow, and the robin peeps, and the bluebirds, old and young, have revisited their box, as if they would fain repeat the summer without the intervention of winter, if Nature would let them.

Beauty is a finer utility whose end we do not see.

Oct. 7, 1842. A little girl has just brought me a purple finch or American linnet. These birds are now moving south. It reminds me of the pine and spruce, and the juniper and cedar on whose berries it feeds. It has the crimson hues of the October evenings, and its plumage still shines as if it had caught and preserved some of their tints (beams?). We know it chiefly as a traveller. It reminds me of many things I had forgotten. Many a serene evening lies snugly packed under its wing.

[1] *Vide* the Fall of the Leaf poem. [This note is written in pencil between this line and the following stanza. The poem referred to is reprinted (without these lines) in *Excursions, and Poems*, p. 407.]

Gower writes like a man of common sense and good parts who has undertaken with steady, rather than high, purpose to do narrative with rhyme. With little or no invention, following in the track of the old fablers, he employs his leisure and his pen-craft to entertain his readers and speak a good word for the right. He has no fire, or rather blaze, though occasionally some brand's end peeps out from the ashes, especially if you approach the heap in a dark day, and if you extend your hands over it you experience a slight warmth there more than elsewhere. In fair weather you may see a slight smoke go up here and there. He narrates what Chaucer sometimes sings. He tells his story with a fair understanding of the original, and sometimes it gains a little in blunt plainness and in point in his hands. Unlike the early Saxon and later English, his poetry is but a plainer and directer speech than other men's prose. He might have been a teamster and written his rhymes on his wagon-seat as he went to mill with a load of plaster.

The banks by retired roadsides are covered with asters, hazels, brakes, and huckleberry bushes, emitting a dry, ripe scent.[1]

Facts must be learned directly and personally, but principles may be deduced from information. The collector of facts possesses a perfect physical organization, the philosopher a perfect intellectual one. One

[1] [This refers to the middle of September and follows matter used in *Week*, on p. 357 (Riv. 443).]

can walk, the other sit; one acts, the other thinks. But the poet in some degree does both, and uses and generalizes the results of both; he generalizes the widest deductions of philosophy.[1]

Oct. 21, 1842. The atmosphere is so dry and transparent and, as it were, inflammable at this season that a candle in the grass shines white and dazzling, and purer and brighter the farther off it is. Its heat seems to have been extracted and only its harmless refulgent light left. It is a star dropped down. The ancients were more than poetically true when they called fire Vulcan's flower. Light is somewhat almost moral. The most intense — as the fixed stars and our own sun — has an unquestionable preëminence among the elements. At a certain stage in the generation of all life, no doubt, light as well as heat is developed. It guides to the first rudiments of life. There is a vitality in heat and light.

Men who are felt rather than understood are being most rapidly developed. They stand many deep.

In many parts the Merrimack is as wild and natural as ever, and the shore and surrounding scenery exhibit only the revolutions of nature. The pine stands up erect on its brink, and the alders and willows fringe its edge; only the beaver and the red man have departed.

My friend knows me face to face, but many only

[1] [*Week*, p. 387; Riv. 478.]

Vol. I

venture to meet me under the shield of another's authority, backed by an invisible *corps du réserve* of wise friends and relations. To such I say, "Farewell, we cannot dwell alone in the world."

Sometimes, by a pleasing, sad wisdom, we find ourselves carried beyond all counsel and sympathy. Our friends' words do not reach us.

The truly noble and settled character of a man is not put forward, as the king or conqueror does not march foremost in a procession.

Among others I have picked up a curious spherical stone, probably an implement of war, like a small paving-stone about the size of a goose egg, with a groove worn quite round it, by which it was probably fastened to a thong or a withe and answered to strike a severe blow like a shotted colt. I have since seen larger ones of the same description.

These arrowheads are of every color and of various forms and materials, though commonly made of a stone which has a conchoidal fracture. Many small ones are found, of white quartz, which are mere equilateral triangles, with one side slightly convex. These were probably small shot for birds and squirrels. The chips which were made in their manufacture are also found in large numbers wherever a lodge stood for any length of time. And these slivers are the surest indication of Indian ground, since the geologists tell us that this stone is not to be found in this vicinity.

The spear-heads are of the same form and material only larger.

Some are found as perfect and sharp as ever, for time has not the effect of blunting them, but when they break they have a ragged and cutting edge. Yet they are so brittle that they can hardly be carried in the pocket without being broken.

It is a matter of wonder how the Indians made even those rude implements without iron or steel tools to work with. It is doubtful whether one of our mechanics, with all the aids of Yankee ingenuity, could soon learn to copy one of the thousands under our feet. It is well known the art of making flints with a cold chisel, as practiced in Austria, requires long practice and knack in the operator, but the arrowhead is of much more irregular form, and, like the flint, such is the nature of the stone, must be struck out by a succession of skillful blows.

An Indian to whom I once exhibited some, but to whom they were objects of as much curiosity as [to] myself, suggested that, as white men have but one blacksmith, so Indians had one arrowhead-maker for many families. But there are the marks of too many forges — unless they were like travelling cobblers — to allow of this.

I have seen some arrowheads from the South Seas which were precisely similar to those from here, so necessary, so little whimsical is this little tool.

So has the steel hatchet its prototype in the stone one of the Indian, as the stone hatchet in the necessities of man.

Venerable are these ancient arts, whose early history is lost in that of the race itself.

Here, too, is the pestle and mortar, — ancient forms and symbols older than the plow or the spade.

The invention of that plow which now turns them up to the surface marks the era of their burial. An era which can never have its history, which is older than history itself. These are relics of an era older than modern civilization, compared with which Greece and Rome and Egypt are modern. And still the savage retreats and the white man advances.

I have the following account of some relics in my possession which were brought from Taunton [?] in Bristol County. A field which had been planted with corn for many years. The sod being broken, the wind began to blow away the soil and then the sand, for several years, until at length it was blown away to the depth of several feet, where it ceased, and the ground appeared strewed with the remains of an Indian village, with regular circles of stones which formed the foundation of their wigwams, and numerous implements beside.

Commonly we use life sparingly, we husband it as if it were scarce, and admit the right of prudence; but occasionally we see how ample and inexhaustible is the stock from which we so scantily draw, and learn that we need not be prudent, that we may be prodigal, and all expenses will be met.

Am I not as far from those scenes, though I have wandered a different route, as my companion who has

Vol. I

But it is in the order of destiny that whatever is remote shall be near. Whatever the eyes see, the hands shall touch. The sentinels upon the turret and at the window and on the wall behold successively the approaching traveller whom the host will soon welcome in the hall.

It is not to be forgotten that the poet is innocent; but he is young, he is not yet a parent or a brother to his race. There are a thousand degrees of grace and beauty before absolute humanity and disinterestedness.

The meanest man can easily test the noblest. Is he embraced? Does he find him a brother?

I am sometimes made aware of a kindness which may have long since been shown, which surely memory cannot retain, which reflects its light long after its heat. I realize, my friend, that there have been times when thy thoughts of me have been of such lofty kindness that they passed over me like the winds of heaven unnoticed, so pure that they presented no object to my eyes, so generous and universal that I did not detect them. Thou hast loved me for what I was not, but for what I aspired to be. We shudder to think of the kindness of our friend which has fallen on us cold, though in some true but tardy hour we have awakened. There has just reached me the kindness of some acts, not to be forgotten, not to be remembered. I wipe off these scores at midnight, at rare intervals, in moments of insight and gratitude.

finished the voyage of life? Am I not most dead who have not life to die, and cast off my sere leaves?

It seemed the only right way to enter this country, borne on the bosom of the flood which receives the tribute of its innumerable vales. The river was the only key adequate to unlock its maze. We beheld the hills and valleys, the lakes and streams, in their natural order and position.

A state should be a complete epitome of the earth, a natural principality, and by the gradations of its surface and soil conduct the traveller to its principal marts. Nature is stronger than law, and the sure but slow influence of wind and water will balk the efforts of restricting legislatures. Man cannot set up bounds with safety but where the revolutions of nature will confirm and strengthen, not obliterate, them.

Every man's success is in proportion to his *average* ability. The meadow flowers spring and bloom where the waters annually deposit their slime, not where they reach in some freshet only. We seem to do ourselves little credit in our own eyes for our performance, which all know must ever fall short of our aspiration and promise, which only we can know entirely; as a stick will avail to reach further than it will strike effectually, since its greatest momentum is a little short of its extreme end. But we do not disappoint our neighbors. A man is not his hope nor his despair, nor his past deed.[1]

[1] [*Week*, p. 133; Riv. 166.]

> Far o'er the bow,
>   Amid the drowsy noon,
> Souhegan, creeping slow,
>   Appeareth soon.[1]

> Methinks that by a strict behavior
> I could elicit back the brightest star
> That hides behind a cloud.

> I have rolled near some other spirit's path,
> And with a pleased anxiety have felt
> Its purer influence on my opaque mass,
> But always was I doomed to learn, alas!
> I had scarce changèd its sidereal time.

Gray sedulously cultivated poetry, but the plant would not thrive. His life seems to have needed some more sincere and ruder experience.

Occasionally we rowed near enough to a cottage to see the sunflowers before the door, and the seed-vessels of the poppy, like small goblets filled with the waters of Lethe, but without disturbing the sluggish household.
Driving the small sandpiper before us.

FOG [2]

> Thou drifting meadow of the air,
>   Where bloom the daisied banks and violets,

[1] [The first four lines of a poem the rest of which appears on pp. 234, 235 of *Week* (Riv. 290, 291).]

[2] [This poem appears, slightly abridged and altered, in *Week*, p. 201 (Riv. 249).]

And in whose fenny labyrinths
The bittern booms and curlew peeps,
The heron wades and boding rain-crow clucks;
Low-anchored cloud,
Newfoundland air,
Fountain-head and source of rivers,
Ocean branch that flowest to the sun,
Diluvian spirit, or Deucalion shroud,
Dew-cloth, dream drapery,
And napkin spread by fays,
Spirit of lakes and seas and rivers,
Sea-fowl that with the east wind
Seek'st the shore, groping thy way inland,
By whichever name I please to call thee,
Bear only perfumes and the scent
Of healing herbs to just men's fields.

I am amused with the manner in which Quarles and his contemporary poets speak of Nature, — with a sort of gallantry, as a knight of his lady, — not as lovers, but as having a thorough respect for her and some title to her acquaintance. They speak manfully, and their lips are not closed by affection.

"The pale-faced lady of the black-eyed night."

Nature seems to have held her court then, and all authors were her gentlemen and esquires and had ready an abundance of courtly expressions.

Quarles is never weak or shallow, though coarse and untasteful. He presses able-bodied and strong-backed words into his service, which have a certain rustic fragrance and force, as if now first devoted to literature

after having served sincere and stern uses. He has the pronunciation of a poet though he stutters. He certainly speaks the English tongue with a right manly accent. To be sure his poems have the [1] musty odor of a confessional.

How little curious is man,
Who hath not searched his mystery a span,
But dreams of mines of treasure
Which he neglects to measure,
For threescore years and ten
Walks to and fro amid his fellow men
O'er this small tract of continental land,
His fancy bearing no divining wand.
Our uninquiring corpses lie more low
Than our life's curiosity doth go;
Our most ambitious steps climb not so high
As in their hourly sport the sparrows fly.
Yonder cloud 's blown farther in a day
Than our most vagrant feet may ever stray.
Surely, O Lord, he hath not greatly erred
Who hath so little from his birthplace stirred.
He wanders through this low and shallow world,
Scarcely his bolder thoughts and hopes unfurled,
Through this low wallèd world, which his huge sin
Hath hardly room to rest and harbor in.
Bearing his head just o'er some fallow ground,
Some cowslip'd meadows where the bitterns sound,
He wanders round until his end draws nigh,

[1] [There is a blank space here before "musty," as if Thoreau had sought another adjective to go with it.]

Vol. I

And then lays down his aged head to die.
And this is life! this is that famous strife!
His head doth court a fathom from the land,
Six feet from where his grovelling feet do stand.

What is called talking is a remarkable though I believe universal phenomenon of human society. The most constant phenomenon when men or women come together is talking. A chemist might try this experiment in his laboratory with certainty, and set down the fact in his journal. This characteristic of the race may be considered as established. No doubt every one can call to mind numerous conclusive instances. Some nations, it is true, are said to articulate more distinctly than others; yet the rule holds with those who have the fewest letters in their alphabet. Men cannot stay long together without talking, according to the rules of polite society. (As all men have two ears and but one tongue, they must spend the extra and unavoidable hours of silence in listening to the whisperings of genius, and this fact it is that makes silence always respectable in my eyes.) Not that they have anything to communicate, or do anything quite natural or important to be done so, but by common consent they fall to using the invention of speech, and make a conversation, good or bad. They say things, first this one and then that. They express their "opinions," as they are called.

By a well-directed silence I have sometimes seen threatening and troublesome people routed. You sit musing as if you were in broad nature again. They cannot stand it. Their position becomes more and

more uncomfortable every moment. So much humanity over against one without any disguise, — not even the disguise of speech! They cannot stand it nor sit against it.

Not only must men talk, but for the most part must talk about talk, — even about books, or dead and buried talk. Sometimes my friend expects a few periods from me. Is he exorbitant? He thinks it is my turn now. Sometimes my companion thinks he has said a good thing, but I don't see the difference. He looks just as he did before. Well, it is no loss. I suppose he has plenty more.

Then I have seen very near and intimate, very old friends introduced by very old strangers, with liberty given to talk. The stranger, who knows only the countersign, says, "Jonas — Eldred," giving those names which will make a title good in a court of law. (It may be presumed that God does not know the Christian names of men.) Then Jonas, like a ready soldier, makes a remark, — a benediction on the weather it may be, — and Eldred swiftly responds, and unburdens his breast, and so the action begins. They bless God and nature many times gratuitously, and part mutually well pleased, leaving their cards. They did not happen to be present at each other's christening.

Sometimes I have listened so attentively and with so much interest to the whole expression of a man that I did not hear one word he was saying, and saying too with the more vivacity observing my attention.

But a man may be an object of interest to me though his tongue is pulled out by the roots.

Men sometimes do as if they could eject themselves like bits of pack-thread from the end of the tongue.

Scholars have for the most part a diseasèd way of looking at the world. They mean by it a few cities and unfortunate assemblies of men and women, who might all be concealed in the grass of the prairies. They describe this world as old or new, healthy or diseased, according to the state of their libraries, — a little dust more or less on their shelves. When I go abroad from under this shingle or slate roof, I find several things which they have not considered. Their conclusions seem imperfect.

As with two eyes we see and with two ears we hear, with the like advantage is man added to man. Making no complaint, offering no encouragement, one human being is made aware of the neighboring and contemporaneous existence of another. Such is the tenderness of friendship. We never recognize each other as finite and imperfect beings, but with a smile and as strangers. My intercourse with men is governed by the same laws with my intercourse with nature.

Buonaparte said that the three-o'clock-in-the-morning courage was the rarest, but I cannot agree with him.[1] Fear does not awake so early. Few men are so degenerate as to balk nature by not beginning the day well.

I hold in my hands a recent volume of essays and

[1] [See *Excursions*, p. 208; Riv. 255; and *Walden*, pp. 131, 132; Riv. 186.]

odor. There is something in the refined and elastic air which reminds us of a work of art. It is like a verse of Anacreon or a tragedy of Æschylus.

All parts of nature belong to one head, as the curls of a maiden's hair. How beautifully flow the seasons as one year, and all streams as one ocean!

I hate museums; there is nothing so weighs upon my spirits. They are the catacombs of nature. One green bud of spring, one willow catkin, one faint trill from a migrating sparrow would set the world on its legs again. The life that is in a single green weed is of more worth than all this death. They are dead nature collected by dead men. I know not whether I muse most at the bodies stuffed with cotton and sawdust or those stuffed with bowels and fleshy fibre outside the cases.
Where is the proper herbarium, the true cabinet of shells, and museum of skeletons, but in the meadow where the flower bloomed, by the seaside where the tide cast up the fish, and on the hills and in the valleys where the beast laid down its life and the skeleton of the traveller reposes on the grass? What right have mortals to parade these things on their legs again, with their wires, and, when heaven has decreed that they shall return to dust again, to return them to sawdust? Would you have a dried specimen of a world, or a pickled one?
Embalming is a sin against heaven and earth, — against heaven, who has recalled the soul and set free the servile elements, and against the earth, which is

poems, in its outward aspect like the thousands which the press sends forth, and, if the gods permitted their own inspiration to be breathed in vain, this might be forgotten in the mass, but the accents of truth are as sure to be heard on earth as in heaven. The more I read it the more I am impressed by its sincerity, its depth and grandeur. It already seems ancient and has lost the traces of its modern birth. It is an evidence of many virtues in the writer. More serenely and humbly confident, this man has listened to the inspiration which all may hear, and with greater fidelity reported it. It is therefore a true prophecy, and shall at length come to pass. It has the grandeur of the Greek tragedy, or rather its Hebrew original, yet it is not necessarily referred to any form of faith. The slumbering, heavy depth of its sentences is perhaps without recent parallel. It lies like the sward in its native pasture, where its roots are never disturbed, and not spread over a sandy embankment.

On fields o'er which the reaper's hand has passed,
Lit by the harvest moon and autumn sun,
My thoughts like stubble floating in the wind
And of such fineness as October airs,
There, after harvest, could I glean my life,
A richer harvest reaping without toil,
And weaving gorgeous fancies at my will,
In subtler webs than finest summer haze.

In October the air is really the fine element the poets describe.[1] The fields emit a dry and temperate

[1] [*Week*, p. 377; Riv. 465.]

thus robbed of her dust. I have had my right-perceiving senses so disturbed in these haunts as to mistake a veritable living man for a stuffed specimen, and surveyed him with dumb wonder as the strangest of the whole collection. For the strangest is that which, being in many particulars most like, is in some essential particular most unlike.

It is one great and rare merit in the old English tragedy that it says something. The words slide away very fast, but toward some conclusion. It has to do with things, and the reader feels as if he were advancing. It does not make much odds what message the author has to deliver at this distance of time, since no message can startle us, but how he delivers it, — that it be done in a downright and manly way. They come to the point and do not waste the time.

They say that Carew was a laborious writer, but his poems do not show it. They are finished, but do not show the marks of the chisel. Drummond was indeed a quiddler, with little fire or fibre, and rather a taste *for* poetry than a taste *of* it.

After all, we draw on very gradually in English literature to Shakespeare, through Peele and Marlowe, to say nothing of Raleigh and Spenser and Sidney. We hear the same great tone already sounding to which Shakespeare added a serener wisdom and clearer expression. Its chief characteristics of reality and unaffected manliness are there. The more we read of the literature of those times, the more does acquaintance divest the genius of Shakespeare of the in some measure false mystery which has thickened around it, and leave it shrouded in the grander mystery of daylight. His critics have for the most part made their [*sic*] contemporaries less that they might make Shakespeare more.

The distinguished men of those times had a great flow of spirits, a cheerful and elastic wit far removed from the solemn wisdom of later days. What another thing was fame and a name then than now! This is seen in the familiar manner in which they were spoken of by each other and the nation at large, — *Kit* Marlowe, and *George* (Peele), and *Will* Shakespeare, and *Ben* Jonson, — great *fellows*, — *chaps*.

We pass through all degrees of life from the least organic to the most complex. Sometimes we are mere pudding-stone and scoriæ.

The present is the instant work and near process of living, and will be found in the last analysis to be nothing more nor less than digestion. Sometimes, it is true, it is indigestion.

Daniel deserves praise for his moderation, and sometimes has risen into poetry before you know it. Strong sense appears in his epistles, but you have to remember too often in what age he wrote, and yet that Shakespeare was his contemporary. His style is without the tricks of the trade and really in advance of his

age. We can well believe that he was a retired scholar, who would keep himself shut up in his house two whole months together.

Donne was not a poet, but a man of strong sense, a sturdy English thinker, full of conceits and whimsicalities, hammering away at his subject, be it eulogy or epitaph, sonnet or satire, with the patience of a day laborer, without taste but with an occasional fine distinction or poetic phrase. He was rather *Doctor* Donne, than the *poet* Donne. His letters are perhaps best.

Lovelace is what his name expresses, — of slight material to make a poet's fame. His goings and comings are of no great account. His taste is not so much love of excellence as fear of failure, though in one instance he has written fearlessly and memorably.

How wholesome are the natural laws to contemplate, as gravity, heat, light, moisture, dryness. Only let us not interfere. Let the soul withdraw into the chambers of the heart, let the mind reside steadily in the labyrinth of the brain, and not interfere with hands or feet more than with other parts of nature.

Thomson was a true lover of nature and seems to have needed only a deeper human experience to have taken a more vigorous and lofty flight. He is deservedly popular, and has found a place on many shelves and in many cottages. There are great merits in "The Seasons"—and the almanac. In "Autumn:"—

Vol. I

> "Attemper'd suns arise,
>
> . . . .
>
> . . . while broad and brown, below,
> Extensive harvests hang the heavy head.
> Rich, silent, deep, they stand."

The moon in "Autumn:"—

> "Her spotted disk,
> Where mountains rise, umbrageous dales descend,
>
> . . . .
>
> . . . gives all his blaze again,
> Void of its flame, and sheds a softer day.
> Now through the passing cloud she seems to stoop,
> Now up the pure cerulean rides sublime.
>
> . . . .
>
> The whole air whitens with a boundless tide
> Of silver radiance, trembling round the world."

My friend, thou art not of some other race and family of men;—thou art flesh of my flesh, bone of my bone. Has not nature associated us in many ways?[1] Water from the same fountain, lime from the same quarry, grain from the same field compose our bodies. And perchance our elements but reassert their ancient kindredship. Is it of no significance that I have so long partaken of the same loaf with thee, have breathed the same air summer and winter, have felt the same heat and cold, the same fruits of summer have been pleased to refresh us both, and thou hast never had a thought of different fibre from my own?[2]

Our kindred, of one blood with us. With the favor and not the displeasure of the gods, we have partaken the same bread.

[1] [*Week*, p. 302; Riv. 375.]   [2] [*Week*, p. 302; Riv. 375.]

It is hard to know rocks. They are crude and inaccessible to our nature. We have not enough of the stony element in us.

It is hard to know men by rumor only. But to stand near somewhat living and conscious. Who would not sail through mutiny and storm farther than Columbus, to reach the fabulous retreating shores of some continent man?

My friend can only be in any measure my foe, because he is fundamentally my friend; for everything is after all more nearly what it should rightfully be, than that which it is simply by failing to be the other.

It [friendship] cannot be the subject of reconciliation or the theme of conversation ever between friends. The true friend must in some sense disregard all professions of friendship and forget them.

It is as far from pity as from contempt. I should hesitate even to call it the highest sympathy, since the word is of suspicious origin and suggests suffering rather than joy. It was established before religion, for men are not friends in religion, but over and through it; and it records no apostasy or repentance, but there is a certain divine and innocent and perennial health about it.

Its charity is generosity, its virtue nobleness, its religion trust. We come nearer to friendship with flowers and inanimate objects than with merely affectionate and loving men. It is not for the friend to be just even, — at least he is not to be lost in this attribute, — but to be only a large and free existence, representative of humanity, its general court. Admirable to us as the heavenly bodies, but like them affording rather a summer heat and daylight, — the light and fire of sunshine and stars, — rather than the intense heats and splendors which our weakness and appetite require.

Yesterday I skated after a fox over the ice. Occasionally he sat on his haunches and barked at me like a young wolf. It made me think of the bear and her cubs mentioned by Captain Parry, I think. All brutes seem to have a genius for mystery, an Oriental aptitude for symbols and the language of signs; and this is the origin of Pilpay and Æsop. The fox manifested an almost human suspicion of mystery in my actions. While I skated directly after him, he cantered at the top of his speed; but when I stood still, though his fear was not abated, some strange but inflexible law of his nature caused him to stop also, and sit again on his haunches. While I still stood motionless, he would go slowly a rod to one side, then sit and bark, then a rod to the other side, and sit and bark again, but did not retreat, as if spellbound. When, however, I commenced the pursuit again, he found himself released from his durance.

Plainly the fox belongs to a different order of things from that which reigns in the village. Our courts, though they offer a bounty for his hide, and our pulpits, though they draw many a moral from his cunning, are in few senses contemporary with his free forest life.

Vol. I

To the poet considered as an artist, his words must be as the relation of his oldest and finest memory, and wisdom derived from the remotest experience.

I have thought, when walking in the woods through a certain retired dell, bordered with shrub oaks and pines, far from the village and affording a glimpse only through an opening of the mountains in the horizon, how my life might pass there, simple and true and natural, and how many things would be impossible to be done there. How many books I might not read!

Why avoid my friends and live among strangers? Why not reside in my native country?

Many a book is written which does not necessarily suggest or imply the phenomenon or object to explain which it professes to have been written.

Every child should be encouraged to study not man's system of nature but nature's.

Giles Fletcher knew how to write, and has left English verses behind. He is the most valuable imitator of the Spenserian stanza, and adds a moral tone of his own.

TO A MARSH HAWK IN SPRING

There is health in thy gray wing,
Health of nature's furnishing.
Say, thou modern-winged antique,
Was thy mistress ever sick?

In each heaving of thy wing
Thou dost health and leisure bring,
Thou dost waive disease and pain
And resume new life again.

Man walks in nature still alone,
    And knows no one,
Discovers no lineament nor feature
    Of any creature.

Though all the firmament
    Is o'er me bent,
Yet still I miss the grace
    Of an intelligent and kindred face.

I still must seek the friend
Who does with nature blend.
Who is the person in her mask,
He is the friend I ask;

Who is the expression of her meaning,
Who is the uprightness of her leaning,
Who is the grown child of her weaning.

We twain would walk together
    Through every weather,
And see this aged Nature
    Go with a bending stature.

The centre of this world,
The face of Nature,

The site of human life,
Some sure foundation
And nucleus of a nation,
At least, a private station.

It is the saddest thought of all, that what we are to others, that we are much more to ourselves, — avaricious, mean, irascible, affected, — we are the victims of these faults. If our pride offends our humble neighbor, much more does it offend ourselves, though our lives are never so private and solitary.

If the Indian is somewhat of a stranger in nature, the gardener is too much a familiar. There is something vulgar and foul in the latter's closeness to his mistress, something noble and cleanly in the former's distance. Yet the hunter seems to have a property in the moon which even the farmer has not. Ah! the poet knows uses of plants which are not easily reported, though he cultivates no parterre. See how the sun smiles on him while he walks in the gardener's aisles, rather than on the gardener.

Not only has the foreground of a picture its glass of transparent crystal spread over it, but the picture itself is a glass or transparent medium to a remoter background. We demand only of all pictures that they be perspicuous, that the laws of perspective have been truly observed. It is not the fringed foreground of the desert nor the intermediate oases that detain the eye and the imagination, but the infinite, level, and roomy horizon, where the sky meets the sand, and heavens and earth, the ideal and actual, are coincident, the background into which leads the path of the pilgrim.

All things are in revolution; it is the one law of nature by which order is preserved, and time itself lapses and is measured. Yet some things men will do from age to age, and some things they will not do.

"Fisherman's Acct. for 1805 [1]   Began March 25

		cts.
D^d Mr. Saml Potter 2 q^{ts} W I 3/ 1 lb sugar 10^d		$0.64
One Cod line 5/		84
April 8 Q^t W I 1/6 & 1 lb Sugar 10^d & Brown Mug		48
9 Q^t N E rum 1/ 10th D^o. of D^o 1/		33
13 Q^t N E rum & 1 lb Sugar 15th 2 Q^{ts} N E rum 2/		62
17 Q^t W I 1/6 D^o N E 1/ lb Sugar 9^d & Q^t N E Rum		71
22 Q^t N E rum 1/ lb sugar 9^d & Q^t N E rum 1/ ...		44½
23 Q^t N E rum 1/ D^o of D^o & sugar 5^d		39
24 Q^t N E rum 1/ lb sugar 9^d		28½
29 Q^t N E rum 1/ & lb sugar 9^d—30th Rum 1/ ...		44½
May first Q^t rum ½ lb Sugar 1/5^d		22
Q^t N E rum 1/ & ½ lb Loaf Sugar 9^d		29
4 Q^t rum 1/ Sugar 5^d		22
6 Q^t N E rum 1/ & lb good sugar 11^d		31
7 Q^t N E rum 1/8th Q^t N E rum 1/ & ½ lb Sugar 5^d.		40
11 Q^t N E rum 11^d lb Sugar 10^d		29
15 Q^t rum & lb Sugar 1/9 & Q^t N E rum		44
16 To a Line for the Sceene 3/		0.50
20 To Q^t N E rum 11^d lb Sugar 10^d		0.29
21 To Q^t N E rum 11^d & lb Sugar 10^d		0.29
27 To Q^t W I 1/6 & lb Sugar 10^d		0.39
June 5th 1805 Settled this acc^t by Recev.g Cash in Full ..		$8.82½

How many young finny contemporaries of various character and destiny, form and habits, we have even

[1] [See *Week*, pp. 33, 34; Riv. 41, 42.]

---

in this water! And it will not be forgotten by some memory that we *were* contemporaries. It is of *some* import. We shall be some time friends, I trust, and know each other better. Distrust is too prevalent now. We are so much alike! have so many faculties in common! I have not yet met with the philosopher who could, in a quite conclusive, undoubtful way, show me *the*, and, if not *the*, then how *any*, difference between man and a fish. We are so much alike! How much could a really tolerant, patient, humane, and truly great and natural man make of them, if he should try? For they are to be understood, surely, as all things else, by no other method than that of sympathy. It is easy to say what they are not to us, *i. e.*, what we are not to them; but what we might and ought to be is another affair.

In the tributaries the brook minnow and the trout. Even in the rills emptying into the river, over which you stride at a step, you may see small trout not so large as your finger glide past or hide under the bank.

The character of this [the horned pout], as indeed of all fishes, depends directly upon that of the water it inhabits, those taken in clear and sandy water being of brighter hue and cleaner and of firmer and sweeter flesh. It makes a peculiar squeaking noise when drawn out, which has given it the name of the minister or preacher.

The bream is the familiar and homely sparrow, which makes her nest everywhere, and is early and late.

Vol. I

The pickerel is the hawk, a fish of prey, hovering over the finny broods.

The pout is the owl, which steals so noiselessly about at evening with its clumsy body.

The shiner is the summer yellowbird, or goldfinch, of the river.

The sucker is the sluggish bittern, or stake-driver.

The minnow is the hummingbird.

The trout is the partridge woodpecker.

The perch is the robin.[1]

We read Marlowe as so much poetical pabulum. It is food for poets, water from the Castalian Spring, some of the atmosphere of Parnassus, raw and crude indeed, and at times breezy, but pure and bracing. Few have so rich a phrase! He had drunk deep of the Pierian Spring, though not deep enough, and had that fine madness, as Drayton says,

"Which justly should possess a poet's brain."

We read his "Dr. Faustus," "Dido, Queen of Carthage," and "Hero and Leander," especially the last, without being wearied. He had many of the qualities of a great poet, and was in some degree worthy to precede Shakespeare. But he seems to have run to waste for want of seclusion and solitude, as if mere pause and deliberation would have added a new element of greatness to his poetry. In his unquestionably fine, heroic tone it would seem as if he had the rarest part of genius, and education could have added the rest. The "Hero

[1] [This appears in pencil on a loose sheet of paper inclosed between the pages of the Journal.]

---

and Leander" tells better for his character than the anecdotes which survive.

> I fain would stretch me by the highway-side,
>   To thaw and trickle with the melting snow,
> That mingled soul and body with the tide
>   I too might through the pores of Nature flow,[1]
>
> Might help to forward the new spring along,
>   If it were mine to choose my toil or day,
> Scouring the roads with yonder sluice-way throng,
>   And so work out my tax on *Her* highway.

> Yet let us thank the purblind race
>   Who still have thought it good
> With lasting stone to mark the place
>   Where braver men have stood.
>
> In Concord, town of quiet name
>   And quiet fame as well, . . .

> I've seen ye, sisters, on the mountain-side,
> When your green mantles fluttered in the wind;
> I've seen your footprints on the lake's smooth shore,
> Lesser than man's, a more ethereal trace;
> I have heard of ye as some far-famed race,
> Daughters of gods, whom I should one day meet,
> Or mothers, I might say, of all our race.
> I reverence your natures, so like mine
> Yet strangely different, like but still unlike.
> Thou only stranger that hast crossed my path,

[1] [*Excursions, and Poems*, p. 409. See also p. 71.]

Accept my hospitality; let me hear
The message which thou bring'st.
      Made different from me,
   Perchance thou 'rt made to be
   The creature of a different destiny.
I know not who ye are that meekly stand
Thus side by side with man in every land.
When did ye form alliance with our race,
Ye children of the moon, who in mild nights
Vaulted upon the hills and sought this earth?
Reveal that which I fear ye cannot tell,
Wherein ye are not I, wherein ye dwell
Where I can never come.
What boots it that I do regard ye so?
Does it make suns to shine or crops to grow?
What boots [it] that I never should forget
That I have sisters sitting for me yet?
And what are sisters?
The robust man, who can so stoutly strive,
In this bleak world is hardly kept alive.
And who is it protects *ye*, smooths *your* way?

We can afford to lend a willing ear occasionally to those earnest reformers of the age. Let us treat them hospitably. Shall we be charitable only to the poor? What though they are fanatics? Their errors are likely to be generous errors, and these may be they who will put to rest the American Church and the American government, and awaken better ones in their stead.

Let us not meanly seek to maintain our delicate lives in chambers or in legislative halls by a timid watchful-

ness of the rude mobs that threaten to pull down our baby-houses. Let us not think to raise a revenue which shall maintain our domestic quiet by an impost on the liberty of speech. Let us not think to live by the principle of self-defense. Have we survived our accidents hitherto, think you, by virtue of our good swords, — that three-foot lath that dangles by your side, or those brazen-mouthed pieces under the burying hill which the trainers keep to hurrah with in the April and July mornings? Do our protectors burrow under the burying-ground hill, on the edge of the bean-field which you all know, gorging themselves once a year with powder and smoke, and kept bright and in condition by a chafing of oiled rags and rotten stone? Have we resigned the protection of our hearts and civil liberties to that feathered race of wading birds and marching men who drill but once a month? — and I mean no reproach to our Concord train-bands, who certainly make a handsome appearance —and dance well. Do we enjoy the sweets of domestic life undisturbed, because the naughty boys are all shut up in that whitewashed "stone-yard," as it is called, and see the Concord meadows only through a grating.

No, let us live amid the free play of the elements. Let the dogs bark, let the cocks crow, and the sun shine, and the winds blow!

Ye do commend me to all virtue ever,
And simple truth, the law by which we live.
Methinks that I can trust your clearer sense
And your immediate knowledge of the truth.
I would obey your influence, one with fate.

There is a true march to the sentence, as if a man or a body of men were actually making progress there step by step, and these are not the mere *disjecta membra*, the dispersed and mutilated members though it were of heroes, which can no longer walk and join themselves to their comrades. They are not perfect nor liberated pieces of art for the galleries, yet they stand on the natural and broad pedestal of the living rock, but have a principle of life and growth in them still, as has that human nature from which they spring.[1]

It is a marvel how the birds contrive to survive in this world. These tender sparrows that flit from bush to bush this evening, though it is so late, do not seem improvident, [but appear] to have found a roost for the night. They must succeed by weakness and reliance, for they are not bold and enterprising, as their mode of life would seem to require, but very weak and tender creatures. I have seen a little chipping sparrow, come too early in the spring, shivering on an apple twig, drawing in its head and striving to warm it in its muffled feathers; and it had no voice to intercede with nature, but peeped as helpless as an infant, and was ready to yield up its spirit and die without any effort. And yet this was no new spring in the revolution of the seasons.

Our offense is rank, it smells to heaven. In the midst of our village, as in most villages, there is a slaughter-house, and throughout the summer months, day and

[1] [Here follows matter printed on pp. 105, 106 of *Week* (Riv. 130–

night, to the distance of half a mile, which embraces the greater part of the village, the air [is] filled with such scents as we instinctively avoid in a woodland walk; and doubtless, if our senses were once purified and educated by a simpler and truer life, we should not consent to live in such a neighborhood.

George Melvin, our Concord trapper, told me that in going to the spring near his house, where he kept his minnows for bait, he found that they were all gone, and immediately suspected that a mink had got them; so he removed the snow all around and laid open the trail of a mink underneath, which he traced to his hole, where were the fragments of his booty. There he set his trap, and baited it with fresh minnows. Going again soon to the spot, he found one of the mink's fore legs in the trap gnawed off near the body, and, having set it again, he caught the mink with his three legs, the fourth having only a short bare bone sticking out.

When I expressed some surprise at this, and said that I heard of such things but did not know whether to believe them, and was now glad to have the story confirmed, said he: "Oh, the muskrats are the greatest fellows to gnaw their legs off. Why, I caught one once that had just gnawed his third leg off, this being the third time he had been trapped; and he lay dead by the trap, for he could n't run on one leg."[1] Such tragedies are enacted even in this sphere and along our peaceful streams, and dignify at least the hunter's trade. Only courage does anywhere prolong life, whether of man or beast.

[1] [See *Walden*, p. 73; Riv. 105.]

When they are caught by the leg and cannot get into the water to drown themselves, they very frequently gnaw the limb off. They are commonly caught under water or close to the edge, and dive immediately with the trap and go to gnawing and are quackled and drowned in a moment, though under other circumstances they will live several minutes under water. They prefer to gnaw off a fore leg to a hind leg, and do not gnaw off their tails. He says the wharf rats are very common on the river and will swim and cross it like a muskrat, and will gnaw their legs and even their tails off in the trap.

These would be times that tried men's souls, if men had souls to be tried; aye, and the souls of brutes, for they must have souls as well as teeth. Even the water-rats lead sleepless nights and live Achillean lives. There are the strong will and the endeavor. Man, even the hunter, naturally has sympathy with every brave effort, even in his game, to maintain that life it enjoys. The hunter regards with awe his game, and it becomes at last his medicine.[1]

Of Cadew or Case worms there are the Ruff-coats or Cockspurs, whose cases are rough and made of various materials, and the Piper Cadis or Straw-worm, made of reed or rush, and straight and smooth.

Carlyle's works are not to be studied, — hardly re-read. Their first impression is the truest and the deepest. There is no reprint. If you look again, you will be dis-

[1] [See *Journal*, vol. vi, Feb. 5, 1854.]

appointed and find nothing answering to the mood they have excited. They are true natural products in this respect. All things are but once, and never repeated. The first faint blushes of the morning gilding the mountain-tops, with the pale phosphorus and saffron-colored clouds, — they verily transport us to the morning of creation; but what avails it to travel eastward, or look again there an hour hence. We should be as far in the day ourselves, mounting toward our meridian. There is no *double entendre* for the alert reader; in fact the work was designed for such complete success that it serves but for a single occasion. It is the luxury of wealth and art when for every deed its own instrument is manufactured. The knife which sliced the bread of Jove ceased to be a knife when that service was rendered.

For every inferior, earthly pleasure we forego, a superior, celestial one is substituted.

To purify our lives requires simply to weed out what is foul and noxious and the sound and innocent is supplied, as nature purifies the blood if we will but reject impurities.

Nature and human life are as various to our several experiences as our constitutions are various. Who shall say what prospect life offers to another? Could a greater miracle take place than if we should look through each other's eyes for an instant? We should live in all the ages of the world in an hour, — aye, in all the worlds of the ages. What I have read of rhapsodists. of the primitive poets, Argonautic expeditions, the life of demigods and heroes, Eleusinian mysteries, etc., sug-

Vol. I

gests nothing so ineffably grand and informing as this would be.

The phœbe came into my house to find a place for its nest, flying through the windows.

It was a bright thought, that of man's to have bells; no doubt the birds hear them with pleasure.

To compete with the squirrels in the chestnut harvest, picking ofttimes the nuts that bear the mark of their teeth.

I require of any lecturer that he will read me a more or less simple and sincere account of his own life, of what he has done and thought, — not so much what he has read or heard of other men's lives and actions, but some such account as he would send to his kindred from a distant land, — and if he has lived sincerely, it must have been in a distant land to me, — describing even his outward circumstances and what adventures he has had, as well as his thoughts and feelings about them. He who gives us only the results of other men's lives, though with brilliant temporary success, we may in some measure justly accuse of having defrauded us of our time. We want him to give us that which was most precious to him, — not his life's blood but even that for which his life's blood circulated, what he has got by living. If anything ever yielded him pure pleasure or instruction, let him communicate it. Let the money-getter tell us how much he loves wealth, and what means he takes

to accumulate it. He must describe those facts which he knows and loves better than anybody else. He must not write on foreign missions. The mechanic will naturally lecture about his trade, the farmer about his farm, and every man about that which he, compared with other men, knows best. Yet incredible mistakes are made. I have heard an owl lecture with perverse show of learning upon the solar microscope, and chanticleer upon nebulous stars, when both ought to have been sound asleep, the one in a hollow tree, the other on his roost.

After I lectured here before, this winter, I heard that some of my townsmen had expected of me some account of my life at the pond. This I will endeavor to give to-night.

I know a robust and hearty mother who thinks that her son, who died abroad, came to his end by living too low, as she had since learned that he drank only water. Men are not inclined to leave off hanging men to-day, though they will be to-morrow. I heard of a family in Concord this winter which would have starved, if it had not been for potatoes — and tea and coffee.

It has not been my design to live cheaply, but only to live as I could, not devoting much time to getting a living. I made the most of what means were already got.

To determine the character of our life and how adequate it is to its occasion, just try it by any test, as for instance that this same sun is seen in Europe and in

America at the same time, that these same stars are visible in twenty-four hours to two thirds the inhabitants of the globe, and who knows how many and various inhabitants of the universe. What farmer in his field lives according even to this somewhat trivial material fact.

I just looked up at a fine twinkling star and thought that a voyager whom I know, now many days' sail from this coast, might possibly be looking up at that same star with me. The stars are the apexes of what triangles! There is always the possibility — the possibility, I say — of being *all*, or remaining a particle, in the universe.

In these days and in this country, a few implements, as the axe, shovel, etc., and, to the studious, light and stationery and access to a few books, will rank next to necessaries, but can all be obtained at a very trifling cost. Under the head of clothing is to be ranked bedding, or night-clothes.

We are very anxious to keep the animal heat in us. What pains we take with our beds! robbing the nests of birds and their breasts, this shelter within a shelter, as the mole has a bed of leaves and grass at the end of its burrow.

In the summer I caught fish occasionally in the pond, but since September have not missed them.

In a man or his work, over all special excellence or failure, prevails the general authority or value.

Vol. I

heard to-day. The snow going off. The ice in the pond one foot thick.

END OF VOLUME I

Almost any man knows how to earn money, but not one in a million knows how to spend it. If he had known so much as this, he would never have earned it.

All matter, indeed, is capable of entertaining thought.

The complete subjugation of the body to the mind prophesies the sovereignty of the latter over the whole of nature. The instincts are to a certain extent a sort of independent nobility, of equal date with the mind, or crown, — ancient dukes and princes of the regal blood. They are perhaps the mind of our ancestors subsided in us, the experience of the race.

A small sum would really do much good, if the donor spent himself with it and did not merely relinquish it to some distant society whose managers do the good or the evil with it. How much might be done for this town with a hundred dollars! I could provide a select course of lectures for the summer or winter with that sum, which would be an incalculable benefit to every inhabitant. With a thousand dollars I could purchase for this town a more complete and select library than exists in the State out of Cambridge and Boston, perhaps a more available one than any. Men sit palsied and helpless by the side of their buried treasures.[1]

After all, those who do most good with money, do it with the least, because they can do better than to acquire it.

March 13, 1846.   The song sparrow and blackbird

[1] [See *Walden*, pp. 120, 121; Riv. 171, 172.]

The Journal of Henry D. Thoreau

VOLUME II

(1850 — September, 1851)

First Snow

CONTENTS

Vol. II

Vol. II

THE JOURNAL OF
HENRY DAVID THOREAU

VOLUME II

I

1850 (ÆT. 32–33)[1]

THE Hindoos are more serenely and thoughtfully religious than the Hebrews. They have perhaps a purer, more independent and impersonal knowledge of God. Their religious books describe the first inquisitive and contemplative access to God; the Hebrew bible a conscientious return, a grosser and more personal repentance. Repentance is not a free and fair highway to God. A wise man will dispense with repentance. It is shocking and passionate. God prefers that you approach him thoughtful, not penitent, though you are the chief of sinners. It is only by forgetting yourself that you draw near to him.

The calmness and gentleness with which the Hindoo philosophers approach and discourse on forbidden themes is admirable.

[1] [A new book is begun here, but the first date is that of May 12, 1850, on p. 7 (p. 8 of the original). The first entries may or may not belong to this year.]

What extracts from the Vedas I have read fall on me like the light of a higher and purer luminary, which describes a loftier course through a purer stratum, — free from particulars, simple, universal. It rises on me like the full moon after the stars have come out, wading through some far summer stratum of the sky.

The Vedant teaches how, "by forsaking religious rites," the votary may "obtain purification of mind."

One wise sentence is worth the state of Massachusetts many times over.

The Vedas contain a sensible account of God.

The religion and philosophy of the Hebrews are those of a wilder and ruder tribe, wanting the civility and intellectual refinements and subtlety of the Hindoos.

Man flows at once to God as soon as the channel of purity, physical, intellectual, and moral, is open.

With the Hindoos virtue is an intellectual exercise, not a social and practical one. It is a knowing, not a doing.

I do not prefer one religion or philosophy to another. I have no sympathy with the bigotry and ignorance which make transient and partial and puerile distinctions between one man's faith or form of faith and another's, — as Christian and heathen. I pray to be delivered from narrowness, partiality, exaggeration, bigotry. To the philosopher all sects, all nations, are alike. I like Brahma, Hari, Buddha, the Great Spirit, as well as God.

[Part of leaf missing here.]

A page with as true and inevitable and deep a meaning as a hillside, a book which Nature shall own as her own flower, her own leaves; with whose leaves her own shall rustle in sympathy imperishable and russet; which shall push out with the skunk-cabbage in the spring. I am not offended by the odor of the skunk in passing by sacred places.[1] I am invigorated rather. It is a reminiscence of immortality borne on the gale. O thou partial world, when wilt thou know God? I would as soon transplant this vegetable to Polynesia or to heaven with me as the violet.

Shoes are commonly too narrow. If you should take off a gentleman's shoes, you would find that his foot was wider than his shoe. Think of his wearing such an engine! walking in it many miles year after year! A shoe which presses against the sides of the foot is to be condemned. To compress the foot like the Chinese is as bad as to compress the head like the Flatheads, for the head and the foot are one body. The narrow feet, — they greet each other on the two sides of the Pacific. A sensible man will not follow fashion in this respect, but reason. Better moccasins, or sandals, or even bare feet, than a tight shoe. A wise man will wear a shoe wide and large enough, shaped somewhat like the foot, and tied with a leather string, and so go his way in peace, letting his foot fall at every step.

When your shoe chafes your feet, put in a mullein leaf.

When I ask for a garment of a particular form, my tailoress tells me gravely, "They do not make them so

[1] [See *Excursions*, p. 228 ; Riv. 280.]

now," and I find it difficult to get made what I want, simply because she cannot believe that I mean what I say; it surpasses her credulity. Properly speaking, my style is as fashionable as theirs. "They do not make them so now," as if she quoted the Fates! I am for a moment absorbed in thought, thinking, wondering who *they* are, where *they* live. It is some Oak Hall, O call, O. K., all correct establishment which she knows but I do not. Oliver Cromwell. I emphasize and in imagination italicize each word separately of that sentence to come at the meaning of it.[1]

Or you may walk into the foreign land of Bedford, where not even yet, after four or five, or even seven or eight, miles, does the sky shut down, but the airy and crystal dome of heaven arches high over all, when you did not suspect that there was so much daylight under its crystal dome, and from the hill eastward perchance see the small town of Bedford standing stately on the crest of a hill like some city of Belgrade with one hundred and fifty thousand inhabitants. I wonder if Mr. Fitch lives there among them.

How many noble men and women must have their abode there! So it seems, — I trust that so it is, — but I did not go into Bedford that time. But alas! I have been into a village before now, and there was not a man of a large soul in it. In what respect was it better than a village of prairie-dogs.[2] I mean to hint no reproach even by implica- [part of leaf torn off].

[1] [*Walden*, p. 27; Riv. 41, 42.]
[2] [See *Walden*, p. 185; Riv. 262.]

Vol. II

one, by stooping slightly, and looked up at the sky. Ayer said jokingly that some said they were so made to shoot wild geese as they flew over. The chains and hooks were suspended from a wooden bar high in the chimney. The timbers were of immense size.

Fourteen vessels in or to be in the port of Haverhill, laden with coal, lumber, lime, wood, and so forth. Boys go [to] the wharf with their fourpences to buy a bundle of laths to make a hen-house; none elsewhere to be had.

Saw two or three other garrison-houses. Mrs. Dustin was an Emerson, one of the family for whom I surveyed.

Measured a buttonwood tree in Haverhill, one of twenty and more set out about 1739 on the banks of the Merrimack. It was thirteen and eight twelfths feet in circumference at three and a half feet from the ground.

Jewett's steam mill is profitable, because the planing machine alone, while that is running, makes shavings and waste enough to feed the engine, to say nothing of the sawdust from the sawmill; and the engine had not required the least repair for several years. Perhaps, as there is not so much sawing and planing to be done in England, they therefore may not find steam so cheap as water.

A single gentle rain in the spring makes the grass look many shades greener.

It is wisest to live without any definite and recognized object from day to day, — any particular object, — for the world is round, and we are not to live on a tangent or

Sunday, May 12, 1850, visited the site of the Dustin house in the northwest part of Haverhill, now but a slight indentation in a corn-field, three or four feet deep, with an occasional brick and cellar-stone turned up in plowing. The owner, Dick Kimball, made much of the corn grown in this hole, some ears of which were sent to Philadelphia. The apple tree which is said to have stood north from the house at a considerable distance is gone. A brick house occupied by a descendant is visible from the spot, and there are old cellar-holes in the neighborhood, probably the sites of some of the other eight houses which were burned on that day. It is a question with some which is the site of the true Dustin house.

Also visited the same day an ancient garrison-house now occupied by Fred. Ayer, who said it was built one hundred and fifty or one hundred and sixty years ago by one Emerson, and that several oxen were killed by lightning while it was building. There was also a pear tree nearly as old as the house. It was built of larger and thicker and harder brick than are used nowadays, and on the whole looked more durable and still likely to stand a hundred years. The hard burnt blue-black ends of some of the bricks were so arranged as to checker the outside. He said it was considered the handsomest house in Haverhill when it was built, and people used to come up from town some two miles to see it. He thought that they were the original doors which we saw. There were but few windows, and most of them were about two feet and a half long and a foot or more wide, only to fire out of. The oven originally projected outside. There were two large fireplaces. I walked into

a radius to the sphere. As an old poet says, "though man proposeth, God disposeth all."

Our thoughts are wont to run in muddy or dusty ruts.

I too revive as does the grass after rain. We are never so flourishing, our day is never so fair, but that the sun may come out a little brighter through mists and we yearn to live a better life. What have we to boast of? We are made the very sewers, the cloacæ, of nature.

If the hunter has a taste for mud turtles and muskrats and skunks and other such savage titbits, the fine lady indulges a taste for some form of potted cheese, or jelly made of a calf's foot, or anchovies from over the water, and they are even. He goes to the mill-pond, she to her preserve pot. I wonder how he, I wonder how I, can live this slimy, beastly kind of life, eating and drinking.[1]

The fresh foliage of the woods in May, when the leaves are about as big as a mouse's ear, putting out like taller grasses and herbs.

In all my rambles I have seen no landscape which can make me forget Fair Haven. I still sit on its Cliff in a new spring day, and look over the awakening woods and the river, and hear the new birds sing, with the same delight as ever. It is as sweet a mystery to me as ever, what this world is. Fair Haven Lake in the south, with its pine-covered island and its meadows, the hickories putting out fresh young yellowish leaves, and the oaks light-grayish ones, while the oven-bird thrums his sawyer-like strain, and the chewink rustles through the

[1] [*Walden*, p. 241; Riv. 340.]

dry leaves or repeats his jingle on a tree-top, and the wood thrush, the genius of the wood, whistles for the first time his clear and thrilling strain, — it sounds as it did the first time I heard it. The sight of these budding woods intoxicates me, — this diet drink.

The strong-colored pine, the grass of trees, in the midst of which other trees are but as weeds or flowers, — a little exotic.

In the row of buttonwood trees on the banks of the Merrimack in Haverhill, I saw that several had been cut down, probably because of their unsightly appearance, they all suffering from the prevalent disease which has attacked the buttonwood of late years, and one large one still resting on its stump where it had fallen. It seemed like a waste of timber or of fuel, but when I inquired about it, they answered that the millers did not like to saw it. Like other ornamental trees which have stood by the roadside for a hundred years, the inhabitants have been accustomed to fasten their horses to them, and have driven many spikes into them for this purpose. One man, having carried some buttonwood logs to mill, the miller agreed to saw them if he would make good the injury which might be done to his saw. The other agreed to it, but almost at the first clip they ran on to a spike and broke the saw, and the owner of the logs cried, "Stop!" he would have no more sawed. They are difficult to split, beside, and make poor timber at best, being very liable to warp.

The "itinerary distance" between two points, a convenient expression.

Humboldt says, "It is still undetermined where life is most abundant: whether on the earth or in the fathomless depths of the ocean."

It was a *mirage*, what in Sanscrit, according to Humboldt, is called "the thirst of the gazelle."

Nothing memorable was ever accomplished in a prosaic mood of mind. The heroes and discoverers have found true more than was previously believed, only when they were expecting and dreaming of something more than their contemporaries dreamed of, — when they were in a frame of mind prepared in some measure for the truth.

Referred to the world's standard, the hero, the discoverer, is insane, its greatest men are all insane. At first the world does not respect its great men. Some rude and simple nations go to the other extreme and reverence all kinds of insanity. Humboldt says, speaking of Columbus approaching the New World: "The grateful coolness of the evening air, the ethereal purity of the starry firmament, the balmy fragrance of flowers, wafted to him by the land breeze, all led him to suppose (as we are told by Herrera, in the Decades (5)), that he was approaching the garden of Eden, the sacred abode of our first parents. The Orinoco seemed to him one of the four rivers which, according to the venerable tradition of the ancient world, flowed from Paradise, to water and divide the surface of the earth, newly adorned with plants."

Expeditions for the discovery of El Dorado, and also

Vol. II

of the Fountain of Youth, led to real, though perhaps not compensatory, discoveries.[1]

I have heard my brother playing on his flute at evening half a mile off through the houses of the village, every note with perfect distinctness. It seemed a more beautiful communication with me than the sending up of a rocket would have been. So, if I mistake not, the sound of blasting rocks has been heard from down the river as far as Lowell, — some twenty miles by its course, — where they were making a deep cut for the railroad.

The sand cherry (*Prunus depressa* Pursh., *Cerasus pumila* Mx.) grew about my door, and near the end of May enlivened my yard with its umbels arranged cylindrically about its short branches. In the fall, weighed down with the weight of its large and handsome cherries, it fell over in wreath-like rays on every side. I tasted them out of compliment to nature, but I never learned to love them.[2]

If the long-continued rains cause the seeds to rot in the ground and destroy the potatoes in the low lands, they are good for the grass on the uplands, though the farmers say it is not so sweet.[3]

As I walked, I was intoxicated with the slight spicy odor of the hickory buds and the bruised bark of the black birch, and, in the fall, the pennyroyal.

[1] [*Cape Cod*, p. 121; Riv. 143, 144.]   [2] [*Walden*, p. 126; Riv. 178.]
[3] [*Walden*, p. 145; Riv. 206.]

Many a time I have expected to find a woodchuck, or rabbit, or a gray squirrel, when it was the ground-robin rustling the leaves.

I have been surprised to discover the amount and the various kinds of life which a single shallow swamp will sustain. On the south side of the pond, not more than a quarter of a mile from it, is a small meadow of ten or a dozen acres in the woods, considerably lower than Walden, and which by some is thought to be fed by the former by a subterranean outlet, — which is very likely, for its shores are quite springy and its supply of water is abundant and unfailing, — indeed tradition says that a sawmill once stood over its outlet, though its whole extent, including its sources, is not more than I have mentioned, — a meadow through which the Fitchburg Railroad passes by a very high causeway, which required many a carload of sand, where the laborers for a long time seemed to make no progress, for the sand settled so much in the night that by morning they were where they were the day before, and finally the weight of the sand forced upward the adjacent crust of the meadow with the trees on it many feet, and cracked it for some rods around. It is a wet and springy place throughout the summer, with a ditch-like channel, and in one part water stands the year round, with cat-o'-nine-tails and tussocks and muskrats' cabins rising above it, where good cranberries may be raked if you are careful to anticipate the frost which visits this cool hollow unexpectedly early. Well, as I was saying, I heard a splashing in the shallow and muddy water and stood awhile to observe the cause of it. Again and again I heard and saw the commotion, but could not guess the cause of it, — what kind of life had its residence in that insignificant pool. We sat down on the hillside. Ere long a muskrat came swimming by as if attracted by the same disturbance, and then another and another, till three had passed, and I began to suspect that they were at the bottom of it. Still ever and anon I observed the same commotion in the waters over the same spot, and at length I observed the snout of some creature slyly raised above the surface after each commotion, as if to see if it were observed by foes, and then but a few rods distant I saw another snout above the water and began to divine the cause of the disturbance. Putting off my shoes and stockings, I crept stealthily down the hill and waded out slowly and noiselessly about a rod from the firm land, keeping behind the tussocks, till I stood behind the tussock near which I had observed the splashing. Then, suddenly stooping over it, I saw through the shallow but muddy water that there was a mud turtle there, and thrusting in my hand at once caught him by the claw, and, quicker than I can tell it, heaved him high and dry ashore; and there came out with him a large pout just dead and partly devoured, which he held in his jaws. It was the pout in his flurry and the turtle in his struggles to hold him fast which had created the commotion. There he had lain, probably buried in the mud at the bottom up to his eyes, till the pout came sailing over, and then this musky lagune had put forth in the direction of his ventral fins, expanding suddenly under the influence of a more than vernal heat, — there

are sermons in stones, aye and mud turtles at the bottoms of the pools, — in the direction of his ventral fins, his tender white belly, where he kept no eye; and the minister squeaked his last.[1] Oh, what an eye was there, my countrymen! buried in mud up to the lids, meditating on what? sleepless at the bottom of the pool, at the top of the bottom, directed heavenward, in no danger from motes. Pouts expect their foes not from below. Suddenly a mud volcano swallowed him up, seized his midriff; he fell into those relentless jaws from which there is no escape, which relax not their hold even in death.[2] There the pout might calculate on remaining until nine days after the head was cut off. Sculled through Heywood's shallow meadow, not thinking of foes, looking through the water up into the sky. I saw his [the turtle's] brother sunning and airing his broad back like a ship bottom up which had been scuttled, — foundered at sea. I had no idea that there was so much going on in Heywood's meadow.

The pickerel commonly lie perfectly still at night, like sticks, in very shallow water near the shore near a brook's mouth. I have seen a large one with a deep white wound from a spear, cutting him half in two, unhealed and unhealable, fast asleep, and forked him into my boat. I have struck a pickerel sound asleep and knew that I cut him almost in two, and the next moment heard him go ashore several rods off; for being thus awakened in their dreams they shoot off with one impulse, intending only to abandon those parts, without considering exactly to what places they

[1] [See *Journal*, vol. i, p. 475.]   [2] [Channing, p. 298.]

Vol. II

shall go. One night a small pickerel, which the boat had probably struck in his sleep, leaped into the boat and so was secured without a wound.

The chub is a soft fish and tastes like boiled brown paper salted.

I was as interested in the discovery of limestone as if it had been gold, and wondered that I had never thought of it before. Now all things seemed to radiate round limestone, and I saw how the farmers lived near to, or far from, a locality of limestone. I detected it sometimes in walls, and surmised from what parts it was probably carted; or when I looked down into an old deserted well, I detected it in the wall, and found where the first settlers had quarried it extensively. I read a new page in the history of these parts in the old limestone quarries and kilns where the old settlers found the materials of their houses; and I considered that, since it was found so profitable even at Thomaston to burn lime with coal dust, perchance these quarries might be worked again.[1]

When the rocks were covered with snow, I even uncovered them with my hands, that I might observe their composition and strata, and thought myself lucky when the sun had laid one bare for me; but [now] that they are all uncovered I pass by without noticing them. There is a time for everything.

We are never prepared to believe that our ancestors lifted large stones or built thick walls. I find that I must have supposed that they built their bank walls of such as a single man could handle. For since we have put

[1] [See *Journal*, vol. v, June 10, 1853.]

their lives behind us we can think of no sufficient motive for such exertion. How can their works be so visible and permanent and themselves so transient? When I see a stone which it must have taken many yoke of oxen to move, lying in a bank wall which was built two hundred years ago, I am curiously surprised, because it suggests an energy and force of which we have no memorials. Where are the traces of the corresponding moral and intellectual energy? I am not prepared to believe that a man lived here so long ago who could elevate into a wall and properly aline a rock of great size and fix it securely, — such an Archimedes. I walk over the old corn-fields, it is true, where the grassy corn-hills still appear in the woods, but there are no such traces of them there. Again, we are wont to think that our ancestors were all stalwart men, because only their most enduring works have come down to us. I think that the man who lifted so large a rock in the course of his ordinary work should have had a still larger for his monument.

I noticed a singular instance of ventriloquism to-day in a male chewink singing on the top of a young oak. It was difficult to believe that the last part of his strain, the concluding jingle, did not proceed from a different quarter, a woodside many rods off. *Hip-you, he-he-he-he.* It was long before I was satisfied that the last part was not the answer of his mate given in exact time. I endeavored to get between the two; indeed, I seemed to be almost between them already.

I have not seen Walden so high for many years; it is within four feet of the pond-hole in Hubbard's woods.

The river is higher than it has been at this season for many years.

When the far mountains are invisible, the near ones look the higher.

The oldest nature is elastic. I just felt myself raised upon the swell of the eternal ocean, which came rolling this way to land.

When my eye ranges over some thirty miles of this globe's surface, — an eminence green and waving, with sky and mountains to bound it, — I am richer than Crœsus.

The variously colored blossoms of the shrub oaks now, in May, hanging gracefully like ear-drops, or the similar blossoms of the large oaks.

I have noticed the effect of a flag set up on a hill in the country. It tames the landscape, subdues it to itself. The hill looks as if it were a military post. Our green, wild country landscape is gathered under the folds of a flag.

A lively appearance is imparted to the landscape as seen from Nawshawtuct, by the flood on the meadows, — by the alternation of land and water, of green and of light colors. The frequent causeways, and the hedge-rows (?) jutting into the meadows, and the islands, have an appearance full of light and life.

To-day, May 31st, a red and white cow, being uneasy, broke out of the steam-mill pasture and crossed the bridge and broke into Elijah Wood's grounds. When he endeavored to drive her out by the bars, she boldly took to the water, wading first through the meadows

full of ditches, and swam across the river, about forty rods wide at this time, and landed in her own pasture again. She was a buffalo crossing her Mississippi. This exploit conferred some dignity on the herd in my eyes, already dignified, and reflectedly on the river, which I looked on as a kind of Bosphorus.

I love to see the domestic animals reassert their native rights, — any evidence that they have not lost their original wild habits and vigor.[1]

There is a sweet wild world which lies along the strain of the wood thrush — the rich intervales which border the stream of its song — more thoroughly genial to my nature than any other.[2]

The blossoms of the tough and vivacious shrub oak are very handsome.

I visited a retired, now almost unused, graveyard in Lincoln to-day, where five British soldiers lie buried who fell on the 19th April, '75. Edmund Wheeler, grandfather of William, who lived in the old house now pulled down near the present, went over the next day and carted them to this ground. A few years ago one Felch, a phrenologist, by leave of the selectmen dug up and took away two skulls. The skeletons were very large, probably those of grenadiers. William Wheeler, who was present, told me this. He said that he had heard old Mr. Child, who lived opposite, say that when one soldier was shot he leaped right up his full length out of the ranks and fell dead; and he, William Wheeler, saw a bullet-hole through and through one of the skulls.

[1] [*Excursions*, p. 234; Riv. 287.]   [2] [*Excursions*, p. 225; Riv. 276.]

Vol. II

Close by stood a stone with this inscription: —

In memory of
Sippio Brister
a man of Colour
who died
Nov 1. 1820
Æt. 64.

But that is not telling us that he lived.[1]

There was one Newell, a tailor, his neighbor, who became a Universalist minister. Breed put on his sign:—

Tailoring and barbering done with speed
By John C Newell & John C Breed.[2]

The water was over the turnpike below Master Cheney's when I returned (May 31st, 1850).

[A third of a page torn out here.]

that these fences, to a considerable extent, will be found to mark natural divisions, especially if the land is not very minutely divided, — mowing (upland and meadow) pasture, woodland, and the different kinds of tillage. There will be found in the farmer's motive for setting a fence here or there some conformity to natural limits. These artificial divisions no doubt have the effect of increasing the area and variety to the traveller. These various fields taken together appear more extensive than a single prairie of the same size would. If the divisions corresponded [A third of a page torn out here.]

[1] [*Walden*, p. 284; Riv. 399.]
[2] [This in regard to Breed and Newell is written in a fine hand at the top of the page, and probably belonged with something on the part torn out.]

The year has many seasons more than are recognized in the almanac. There is that time about the first of June, the beginning of summer, when the buttercups blossom in the now luxuriant grass and I am first reminded of mowing and of the dairy. Every one will have observed different epochs. There is the time when they begin to drive cows to pasture, — about the 20th of May, — observed by the farmer, but a little arbitrary year by year. Cows spend their winters in barns and cow-yards, their summers in pastures. In summer, therefore, they may low with emphasis, "To-morrow to fresh woods and pastures new." I sometimes see a neighbor or two united with their boys and hired men to drive their cattle to some far-off country pasture, fifty or sixty miles distant in New Hampshire, early in the morning, with their sticks and dogs. It is a memorable time with the farmers' boys, and frequently their first journey from home. The herdsman in some mountain pasture is expecting them. And then in the fall, when they go up to drive them back, they speculate as to whether Janet or Brindle will know them. I heard such a boy exclaim on such an occasion, when the calf of the spring returned a heifer, as he stroked her side, "She knows me, father; she knows me." Driven up to be the cattle on a thousand hills.

I once set fire to the woods. Having set out, one April day, to go to the sources of Concord River in a boat with a single companion, meaning to camp on the bank at night or seek a lodging in some neighboring country inn or farmhouse, we took fishing tackle with us that we might fitly procure our food from the stream, Indian-like. At the shoemaker's near the river, we obtained a match, which we had forgotten. Though it was thus early in the spring, the river was low, for there had not been much rain, and we succeeded in catching a mess of fish sufficient for our dinner before we had left the town, and by the shores of Fair Haven Pond we proceeded to cook them. The earth was uncommonly dry, and our fire, kindled far from the woods in a sunny recess in the hillside on the east of the pond, suddenly caught the dry grass of the previous year which grew about the stump on which it was kindled. We sprang to extinguish it at first with our hands and feet, and then we fought it with a board obtained from the boat, but in a few minutes it was beyond our reach; being on the side of a hill, it spread rapidly upward, through the long, dry, wiry grass interspersed with bushes.

"Well, where will this end?" asked my companion. I saw that it might be bounded by Well Meadow Brook on one side, but would, perchance, go to the village side of the brook. "It will go to town," I answered. While my companion took the boat back down the river, I set out through the woods to inform the owners and to raise the town. The fire had already spread a dozen rods on every side and went leaping and crackling wildly and irreclaimably toward the wood. That way went the flames with wild delight, and we felt that we had no control over the demonic creature to which we had given birth. We had kindled many fires in the woods before, burning a clear space in the grass, without ever kindling such a fire as this.

As I ran toward the town through the woods, I could

see the smoke over the woods behind me marking the spot and the progress of the flames. The first farmer whom I met driving a team, after leaving the woods, inquired the cause of the smoke. I told him. "Well," said he, "it is none of my stuff," and drove along. The next I met was the owner in his field, with whom I returned at once to the woods, running all the way. I had already run two miles. When at length we got into the neighborhood of the flames, we met a carpenter who had been hewing timber, an infirm man who had been driven off by the fire, fleeing with his axe. The farmer returned to hasten more assistance. I, who was spent with running, remained. What could I do alone against a front of flame half a mile wide?

I walked slowly through the wood to Fair Haven Cliff, climbed to the highest rock, and sat down upon it to observe the progress of the flames, which were rapidly approaching me, now about a mile distant from the spot where the fire was kindled. Presently I heard the sound of the distant bell giving the alarm, and I knew that the town was on its way to the scene. Hitherto I had felt like a guilty person, — nothing but shame and regret. But now I settled the matter with myself shortly. I said to myself: "Who are these men who are said to be the owners of these woods, and how am I related to them? I have set fire to the forest, but I have done no wrong therein, and now it is as if the lightning had done it. These flames are but consuming their natural food." (It has never troubled me from that day to this more than if the lightning had done it. The trivial fishing was all that disturbed me and disturbs me still.) So shortly I

settled it with myself and stood to watch the approaching flames.[1] It was a glorious spectacle, and I was the only one there to enjoy it. The fire now reached the base of the cliff and then rushed up its sides. The squirrels ran before it in blind haste, and three pigeons dashed into the midst of the smoke. The flames flashed up the pines to their tops, as if they were powder.

When I found I was about to be surrounded by the fire, I retreated and joined the forces now arriving from the town. It took us several hours to surround the flames with our hoes and shovels and by back fires subdue them. In the midst of all I saw the farmer whom I first met, who had turned indifferently away saying it was none of his stuff, striving earnestly to save his corded wood, his stuff, which the fire had already seized and which it after all consumed.

It burned over a hundred acres or more and destroyed much young wood. When I returned home late in the day, with others of my townsmen, I could not help noticing that the crowd who were so ready to condemn the individual who had kindled the fire did not sympathize with the owners of the wood, but were in fact highly elate and as it were thankful for the opportunity which had afforded them so much sport; and it was only half a dozen owners, so called, though not all of them, who looked sour or grieved, and I felt that I had a deeper interest in the woods, knew them better and should feel their loss more, than any or all of them. The farmer whom I had first conducted to the woods was obliged to ask me the shortest way back, through his own lot.

[1] [See p. 40.]

Why, then, should the half-dozen owners [and] the individuals who set the fire alone feel sorrow for the loss of the wood, while the rest of the town have their spirits raised? Some of the owners, however, bore their loss like men, but other some declared behind my back that I was a "damned rascal;" and a flibbertigibbet or two, who crowed like the old cock, shouted some reminiscences of "burnt woods" from safe recesses for some years after. I have had nothing to say to any of them. The locomotive engine has since burned over nearly all the same ground and more, and in some measure blotted out the memory of the previous fire. For a long time after I had learned this lesson I marvelled that while matches and tinder were contemporaries the world was not consumed; why the houses that have hearths were not burned before another day; if the flames were not as hungry now as when I waked them. I at once ceased to regard the owners and my own fault, — if fault there was any in the matter, — and attended to the phenomenon before me, determined to make the most of it. To be sure, I felt a little ashamed when I reflected on what a trivial occasion this had happened, that at the time I was no better employed than my townsmen.

That night I watched the fire, where some stumps still flamed at midnight in the midst of the blackened waste, wandering through the woods by myself; and far in the night I threaded my way to the spot where the fire had taken, and discovered the now broiled fish, — which had been dressed, — scattered over the burnt grass.

This has been a cool day, though the first of summer.

The prospect of the meadows from Lee's Hill was very fine. I observe that the shadows of the trees are very distinct and heavy in such a day, falling on the fresh grass. They are as obvious as the trees themselves by mid-afternoon. Commonly we do not make much account of the distinct shadows of objects in the landscape.

What is bare and unsightly is covered by the water now. The verdure seems to spring directly from its bosom; there are no stems nor roots. The meadows are so many mirrors reflecting the light, — toward sunset dazzlingly bright.

I visited this afternoon (June 3d) Goodman's Hill in Sudbury, going through Lincoln over Sherman's Bridge and Round Hill, and returning through the Corner. It probably affords the best view of Concord River meadows of any hill. The horizon is very extensive as it is, and if the top were cleared so that you could get the western view, it would be one of the most extensive seen from any hill in the county. The most imposing horizons are those which are seen from tops of hills rising out of a river valley. The prospect even from a low hill has something majestic in it in such a case. The landscape is a vast amphitheatre rising to its rim in the horizon. There is a good view of Lincoln lying high up in among the hills. You see that it is the highest town hereabouts, and hence its fruit. The river at this time looks as large as the Hudson. I think that a river-valley town is much the handsomest and largest-featured, — like Concord and Lancaster, for instance, natural centres. Upon the

hills of Bolton, again, the height of land between the Concord and Nashua, I have seen how the peach flourishes. Nobscot, too, is quite imposing as seen from the west side of Goodman's Hill. On the western side of a continuation of this hill is Wadsworth's battle-field.[1]

Returning, I saw in Sudbury twenty-five nests of the new (cliff?) swallow under the eaves of a barn. They seemed particularly social and loquacious neighbors, though their voices are rather squeaking. Their nests, built side by side, looked somewhat like large hornets' nests, enough so to prove a sort of connection. Their activity, sociability, and chattiness make them fit pensioners and neighbors of man — summer companions — for the barn-yard.

The last of May and the first of June the farmers are everywhere planting their corn and beans and potatoes.

To-day, June 4th, I have been tending a burning in the woods. Ray was there. It is a pleasant fact that you will know no man long, however low in the social scale, however poor, miserable, intemperate, and worthless he may appear to be, a mere burden to society, but you will find at last that there is something which he understands and can do better than any other. I was pleased to hear that one man had sent Ray as the one who had had the most experience in setting fires of any man in Lincoln. He had experience and skill as a burner of brush.

[1] [Where Captain Samuel Wadsworth fell in a battle with the Indians, April 18, 1676.]

Vol. II

You must burn against the wind always, and burn slowly. When the fire breaks over the hoed line, a little system and perseverance will accomplish more toward quelling it than any man would believe. It fortunately happens that the experience acquired is oftentimes worth more than the wages. When a fire breaks out in the woods, and a man fights it too near and on the side, in the heat of the moment, without the systematic coöperation of others, he is disposed to think it a desperate case, and that this relentless fiend will run through the forest till it is glutted with food; but let the company rest from their labors a moment, and then proceed more deliberately and systematically, giving the fire a wider berth, and the company will be astonished to find how soon and easily they will subdue it. The woods themselves furnish one of the best weapons with which to contend with the fires that destroy them, — a pitch pine bough. It is the best instrument to thrash it with. There are few men who do not love better to give advice than to give assistance.

However large the fire, let a few men go to work deliberately but perseveringly to rake away the leaves and hoe off the surface of the ground at a convenient distance from the fire, while others follow with pine boughs to thrash it with when it reaches the line, and they will finally get round it and subdue it, and will be astonished at their own success.

A man who is about to burn his field in the midst of woods should rake off the leaves and twigs for the breadth of a rod at least, making no large heaps near the outside, and then plow around it several furrows and

break them up with hoes, and set his fire early in the morning, before the wind rises.

As I was fighting the fire to-day, in the midst of the roaring and crackling, — for the fire seems to snort like a wild horse, — I heard from time to time the dying strain, the last sigh, the fine, clear, shrill scream of agony, as it were, of the trees breathing their last, probably the heated air or the steam escaping from some chink. At first I thought it was some bird, or a dying squirrel's note of anguish, or steam escaping from the tree. You sometimes hear it on a small scale in the log on the hearth. When a field is burned over, the squirrels probably go into the ground. How foreign is the yellow pine to the green woods — and what business has it here?

The fire stopped within a few inches of a partridge's nest to-day, June 4th, whom we took off in our hands and found thirteen creamy-colored eggs. I started up a woodcock when I went to a rill to drink, at the westernmost angle of R. W. E.'s wood-lot.

To-night, June 5th, after a hot day, I hear the first peculiar summer breathing of the frogs.

When all is calm, a small whirlwind will suddenly lift up the blazing leaves and let them fall beyond the line, and set all the woods in a blaze in a moment. Or some slight almost invisible cinder, seed of fire, will be wafted from the burnt district on to the dry turf which covers the surface and fills the crevices of many rocks, and there it will catch as in tinder, and smoke and smoulder, perchance, for half an hour, heating several square yards of ground where yet no fire is visible, until it spreads to the leaves and the wind fans it into a blaze.

Men go to a fire for entertainment. When I see how eagerly men will run to a fire, whether in warm or in cold weather, by day or by night, dragging an engine at their heels, I am astonished to perceive how good a purpose the love of excitement is made to serve. What other force, pray, what offered pay, what disinterested neighborliness could ever effect so much? No, these are boys who are to be dealt with, and these are the motives that prevail. There is no old man or woman dropping into the grave but covets excitement.

Yesterday, when I walked to Goodman's Hill, it seemed to me that the atmosphere was never so full of fragrance and spicy odors. There is a great variety in the fragrance of the apple blossoms as well as their tints. Some are quite spicy. The air seemed filled with the odor of ripe strawberries, though it is quite too early for them. The earth was not only fragrant but sweet and spicy to the smell, reminding us of Arabian gales and what mariners tell of the spice islands. The first of June, when the lady's-slipper and the wild pink have come out in sunny places on the hillsides, then the summer is begun according to the clock of the seasons.

Here it is the 8th of June, and the grass is growing apace. In the front yards of the village they are already beginning to cut it. The fields look luxuriant and verdurous, but, as the weather is warmer, the atmosphere is not so clear. In distant woods the partridge sits on

her eggs, and at evening the frogs begin to dream and boys begin to bathe in the river and ponds.

Cultivate the habit of early rising. It is unwise to keep the head long on a level with the feet.

The cars come and go with such regularity and precision, and the whistle and rumble are heard so far, that town clocks and family clocks are already half dispensed with, and it is easy to foresee that one extensive well-conducted and orderly institution like a railroad will keep time and order for a whole country. The startings and arrivals of the cars are the epochs in a village day.[1]

Not till June can the grass be said to be waving in the fields. When the frogs dream, and the grass waves, and the buttercups toss their heads, and the heat disposes to bathe in the ponds and streams, then is summer begun.

June 9th, 1850, Walden is still rising, though the rains have ceased and the river has fallen very much. I see the pollen of the pitch pine now beginning to cover the surface of the pond. Most of the pines at the north-northwest end have none, and on some there is only one pollen-bearing flower.

I saw a striped snake which the fire in the woods had killed, stiffened and partially blackened by the flames, with its body partly coiled up and raised from the ground,

[1] [*Walden*, p. 130; Riv. 184, 185.]

and its head still erect as if ready to dart out its tongue and strike its foe. No creature can exhibit more venom than a snake, even when it is not venomous, strictly speaking.

The fire ascended the oak trees very swiftly by the moss which fringed them.

It has a singular effect on us when we hear the geologist apply his terms to Judea, — speak of "limestone" and "blocks of trap and conglomerate, boulders of sandstone and quartz" there. Or think of a chemical analysis of the water of the Dead Sea!

The pitch and white pines are two years or more maturing their seed.

Certain rites are practiced by the Smrities (among the Hindoos) at the digging of wells.

In early times the Brahmans, though they were the legislators of India, possessed no executive power and lived in poverty; yet they were for the most part independent and respected.

Galbraith's Math. Tables, Edinburgh, 1834. For descriptions of instruments he refers to Jones's edition of Adam's Geom. and Graphical Essays, Biot's Traité d'Astronomie Physique, Base du Système Métrique, Woodhouse's, Vince's, and Pearson's Treatises of Astronomy. For problems connected with trigonometrical surveying, to the third volume of Hutton's Course of Math. by Dr. O. Gregory, Baron Zach's work on the Attraction of Mountains, the Base du Système de Métrique Décimal, and Puissant's Géodesie.

Olive or red seems the fittest color for a man, a deni-

zen of the woods. The *pale white man!* I do not wonder that the African pitied him.[1]

The white pine cones are now two inches long, curved sickle-like from the topmost branches, reminding you of the tropical trees which bear their fruit at their heads.[2]

The life in us is like the water in the river; it may rise this year higher than ever it was known to before and flood the uplands — even this may be the eventful year — and drown out all our muskrats.[3]

There [are] as many strata at different levels of life as there are leaves in a book. Most men probably have lived in two or three. When on the higher levels we can remember the lower levels, but when on the lower we cannot remember the higher.

My imagination, my love and reverence and admiration, my sense of the miraculous, is not so excited by any event as by the remembrance of my youth. Men talk about Bible miracles because there is no miracle in their lives. Cease to gnaw that crust. There is ripe fruit over your head.

Woe to him who wants a companion, for he is unfit to be the companion even of himself.

We inspire friendship in men when we have contracted friendship with the gods.

When we cease to sympathize with and to be personally related to men, and begin to be universally related, then we are capable of inspiring others with the sentiment of love for us.

[1] [*Excursions*, p. 226; Riv. 277.]
[2] I find that they are last year's. The white pine has not blossomed.
[3] [*Walden*, p. 366; Riv. 513.]

We hug the earth. How rarely we mount! How rarely we climb a tree! We might get a little higher, methinks. That pine would make us dizzy. You can see the mountains from it as you never did before.[1]

Shall not a man have his spring as well as the plants?

The halo around the shadow is visible both morning and evening.[2]

After this and some other fires in the woods which I helped to put out, a more effectual system by which to quell them occurred to me. When the bell rings, hundreds will run to a fire in the woods without carrying any implement, and then waste much time after they get there either in doing nothing or what is worse than nothing, having come mainly out of curiosity, it being as interesting to see it burn as to put it out. I thought that it would be well if forty or fifty men in every country town should enroll themselves into a company for this purpose and elect suitable officers. The town should provide a sufficient number of rakes, hoes, and shovels, which it should be the duty of certain of the company to convey to [the] woods in a wagon, together with the drum, on the first alarm, people being unwilling to carry their own tools for fear they will be lost. When the captain or one of the numerous vice-captains arrives, having inspected the fire and taken his measures, let him cause the roll to be called, however the men may be engaged, and just take a turn or two with his men to form them into sections and see where they are. Then

[1] [*Excursions*, pp. 244, 245; Riv. 300.]
[2] [*Walden*, pp. 224, 225; Riv. 316.]

he can appoint and equip his rake-men and his hoe-men and his bough-men, and drop them at the proper places, always retaining the drummer and a scout; and when he has learned through his scout that the fire has broken out in a new place, he, by beat of drum, can take up one or two men of each class — as many as can be spared — and repair to the scene of danger.

One of my friends suggests instead of the drum some delicious music, adding that then he would come. It might be well, to refresh the men when wearied with work, and cheer them on their return. Music is the proper regulator.

So, far in the East, among the Yezidis, or Worshippers of the Devil, so called, and the Chaldæans, and so forth, you may hear these remarkable disputations on doctrinal points.[1]

Any reverence, even for a material thing, proceeds from an elevation of character. Layard, speaking of the reverence for the sun exhibited by the Yezidis, or Worshippers of the Devil, says: "They are accustomed to kiss the object on which its first beams fall; and I have frequently, when travelling in their company at sunrise, observed them perform this ceremony. For fire, as symbolic, they have nearly the same reverence; they never spit into it, but frequently pass their hands through the flame, kiss them, and rub them over their right eyebrow, or sometimes over the whole face."

Who taught the oven-bird to conceal her nest? It is

[1] [*Cape Cod*, p. 54; Riv. 62.]

Vol. II

on the ground, yet out of sight. What cunning there is in nature! No man could have arranged it more artfully for the purpose of concealment. Only the escape of the bird betrays it.

I observe to-night, June 15th, the air over the river by the Leaning Hemlocks filled with myriads of newly fledged insects drifting and falling as it were like snowflakes from the maples, only not so white. Now they drift up the stream, now down, while the river below is dimpled with the fishes rising to swallow the innumerable insects which have fallen [into] it and are struggling with it. I saw how He fed his fish. They, swimming in the dark nether atmosphere of the river, rose lazily to its surface to swallow such swimmers of the light upper atmosphere as sank to its bottom.[1]

I picked up to-day the lower jaw of a hog, with white and sound teeth and tusks, which reminded me that there was an animal health and vigor distinct from the spiritual health. This animal succeeded by other means than temperance and purity.[2]

There are thirty-eight lighthouses in Massachusetts. The light on the Highlands of Neversink is visible the greatest distance, *viz.* thirty miles. There are two there, one revolving, one not.

The fantastic open light crosses which the limbs of the larch make, seen against the sky, of the sky-blue color its foliage.

In a swamp where the trees stand up to their knees, two or three feet deep, in the fine bushes as in a moss bed.

[1] *Vide* Kirby and Spence, vol. i.   [2] [*Walden*, p. 242; Riv. 341.]

The arbor-vitæ fans, rich, heavy, elaborate, like bead-work.

June 20. I can see from my window three or four cows in a pasture on the side of Fair Haven Hill, a mile and a half distant. There is but one tree in the pasture, and they are all collected and now reposing in its shade, which, as it is early though sultry, is extended a good way along the ground. It makes a pretty landscape. That must have been an epoch in the history of the cow when they discovered to stand in the shadow of a tree. I wonder if they are wise enough to recline on the north side of it, that they may not be disturbed so soon. It shows the importance of leaving trees for shade in the pastures as well as for beauty. There is a long black streak, and in it the cows are collected. How much more they will need this shelter at noon! It is a pleasant life they lead in the summer, — roaming in well-watered pastures, grazing, and chewing the cud in the shade, — quite a philosophic life and favorable for contemplation, not like their pent-up winter life in close and foul barns. If only they could say as on the prairies, "To-morrow to fresh woods and pastures new."

Cattle and horses, however, retain many of their wild habits or instincts wonderfully. The seeds of instinct are preserved under their thick hides, like seeds in the bowels of the earth, an indefinite period.[1] I have heard of a horse which his master could not catch in his pasture when the first snowflakes were falling, who persisted in wintering out. As he persisted in keeping out

[1] [*Excursions*, p. 234; Riv. 287.]

of his reach, his master finally left him. When the snow had covered the ground three or four inches deep, the horse pawed it away to come at the grass, — just as the wild horses of Michigan do, who are turned loose by their Indian masters, — and so he picked up a scanty subsistence. By the next day he had had enough of free life and pined for his stable, and so suffered himself to be caught.

A blacksmith, my neighbor, heard a great clattering noise the other day behind his shop, and on going out found that his mare and his neighbor the pumpmaker's were fighting. They would run at one another, then turn round suddenly and let their heels fly. The rattling of their hoofs one against the other was the noise he heard. They repeated this several times with intervals of grazing, until one prevailed. The next day they bore the marks of some bruises, some places where the skin was rucked up, and some swellings.

And then for my afternoon walks I have a garden, larger than any artificial garden that I have read of and far more attractive to me, — mile after mile of embowered walks, such as no nobleman's grounds can boast, with animals running free and wild therein as from the first, — varied with land and water prospect, and, above all, so retired that it is extremely rare that I meet a single wanderer in its mazes. No gardener is seen therein, no gates nor [sic]. You may wander away to solitary bowers and brooks and hills.

The ripple marks on the sandy bottom of Flint's Pond, where the rushes grow, feel hard to the feet of

the wader, though the sand is really soft, — made firm perchance by the weight of the water.[1]

The rushes over the water are white with the exuviæ, the skeletons, of insects, — like blossoms, — which have deposited their eggs on their tops. The skeletons looked like those of shad-flies, though some living insects were not.

I have seen crimson-colored eggs painting the leaves of the black birch quite beautifully.

And now the ascending sun has contracted the shadow of the solitary tree, and they are compelled to seek the neighboring wood for shelter.

June 21. The flowers of the white pine are now in their prime, but I see none of their pollen on the pond.

This piece of rural pantomime, this bucolic, is enacted before me every day. Far over the hills on that fair hillside, I look into the pastoral age.

But these are only the disadvantages of a fire. It is without doubt an advantage on the whole. It sweeps and ventilates the forest floor, and makes it clear and clean. It is nature's besom. By destroying the punier underwood it gives prominence to the larger and sturdier trees, and makes a wood in which you can go and come. I have often remarked with how much more comfort and pleasure I could walk in woods through which a fire had run the previous year. It will clean the forest floor like a broom perfectly smooth and clear, — no twigs

[1] [*Walden*, p. 216; Riv. 305.]

left to crackle underfoot, the dead and rotten wood removed, — and thus in the course of two or three years new huckleberry fields are created for the town, — for birds and men.

When the lightning burns the forest its Director makes no apology to man, and I was but His agent. Perhaps we owe to this accident partly some of the noblest natural parks. It is inspiriting to walk amid the fresh green sprouts of grass and shrubbery pushing upward through the charred surface with more vigorous growth.

Wherever a man goes men will pursue and paw him with their dirty institutions.[1]

Sometimes an arrowhead is found with the mouldering shaft still attached. (*Vide* Charles Hubbard.) A little boy from Compton, R. I., told me that his father found an arrowhead sticking in a dead tree and nearly buried in it. Where is the hand that drew that bow? The arrow shot by the Indian is still found occasionally, sticking in the trees of our forest.

It is astonishing how much information is to be got out of very unpromising witnesses. A wise man will avail himself of the observation of all. Every boy and simpleton has been an observer in some field, — so many more senses they are, differently located. Will inquire of eyes what they have seen, of ears what they have heard, of hands what they have done, of feet where they have been.

July 16. I have not yet been able to collect half a

[1] [*Walden*, p. 190; Riv. 268.]

thimbleful of the pollen of the pine on Walden, abundant as it was last summer.

There is in our yard a little pitch pine four or five years old and not much more than a foot high, with small cones on it but no male flowers; and yet I do not know of another pitch pine tree within half a mile.

Many men walk by day; few walk by night. It is a very different season. Instead of the sun, there are the moon and stars; instead of the wood thrush, there is the whip-poor-will; instead of butterflies, fireflies, winged sparks of fire! who would have believed it? What kind of life and cool deliberation dwells in a spark of fire in dewy abodes? Every man carries fire in his eye, or in his blood, or in his brain. Instead of singing birds, the croaking of frogs and the intenser dream of crickets. The potatoes stand up straight, the corn grows, the bushes loom, and, in a moonlight night, the shadows of rocks and trees and bushes and hills are more conspicuous than the objects themselves. The slightest inequalities in the ground are revealed by the shadows; what the feet find comparatively smooth appears rough and diversified to the eye. The smallest recesses in the rocks are dim and cavernous; the ferns in the wood appear to be of tropical size; the pools seen through the leaves become as full of light as the sky. "The light of day takes refuge in their bosom," as the Purana says of the ocean. The woods are heavy and dark. Nature slumbers. The rocks retain the warmth of the sun which they have absorbed all night.[1]

[1] [*Excursions*, pp. 326–328; Riv. 401–403.]

The names of those who bought these fields of the red men, the wild men of the woods, are Buttrick, Davis, Barrett, Bulkley, etc., etc. (*Vide* History.) Here and there still you will find a man with Indian blood in his veins, an eccentric farmer descended from an Indian chief; or you will see a solitary pure-blooded Indian, looking as wild as ever among the pines, one of the last of the Massachusetts tribes, stepping into a railroad car with his gun.

Still here and there an Indian squaw with her dog, her only companion, lives in some lone house, insulted by school-children, making baskets and picking berries her employment. You will meet her on the highway, with few children or none, with melancholy face, history, destiny; stepping after her race; who had stayed to tuck them up in their long sleep. For whom berries condescend to grow. I have not seen one on the Musketaquid for many a year, and some who came up in their canoes and camped on its banks a dozen years ago had to ask me where it came from. A lone Indian woman without children, accompanied by her dog, wearing the shroud of her race, performing the last offices for her departed race. Not yet absorbed into the elements again; a daughter of the soil; one of the nobility of the land. The white man an imported weed, — burdock and mullein, which displace the ground-nut.

As a proof that oysters do not move, I have been told by a Long Island oysterman that they are found in large clusters surrounding the parent oyster in the position in which they must have grown, the young being several years old.

I find the actual to be far less real to me than the imagined. Why this singular prominence and importance is given to the former, I do not know. In proportion as that which possesses my thoughts is removed from the actual, it impresses me. I have never met with anything so truly visionary and accidental as some actual events. They have affected me less than my dreams. Whatever actually happens to a man is wonderfully trivial and insignificant, — even to death itself, I imagine. He complains of the fates who drown him, that they do not touch *him*. They do not deal directly with him. I have in my pocket a button which I ripped off the coat of the Marquis of Ossoli [1] on the seashore the other day. Held up, it intercepts the light and casts a shadow, — an *actual* button so called, — and yet all the life it is connected with is less substantial to me than my faintest dreams. This stream of events which we consent to call actual, and that other mightier stream which alone carries us with it, — what makes the difference? On the one our bodies float, and we have sympathy with it through them; on the other, our spirits. We are ever dying to one world and being born into another, and possibly no man knows whether he is at any time dead in the sense in which he affirms that phenomenon of another, or not. Our thoughts are the epochs of our life: all else is but as a journal of the winds that blew while we were here. [2]

[1] [In July, 1850, Thoreau went to Fire Island with other friends of Margaret Fuller to search for her remains. See *Cape Cod*, pp. 107, 108; Riv. 126, 127. See also next page.]

[2] [Part of draft of a letter to H. G. O. Blake, dated Aug. 9, 1850. Other parts follow. *Familiar Letters.*]

Vol. II

I do not think much of the actual. It is something which we have long since done with. It is a sort of vomit in which the unclean love to wallow.

There was nothing at all remarkable about them. They were simply some bones lying on the beach. They would not detain a walker there more than so much seaweed. I should think that the fates would not take the trouble to show me any bones again, I so slightly appreciate the favor. [1]

Do a little more of that work which you have sometime confessed to be good, which you feel that society and your justest judge rightly demands of you. Do what you reprove yourself for not doing. Know that you are neither satisfied nor dissatisfied with yourself without reason. Let me say to you and to myself in one breath, Cultivate the tree which you have found to bear fruit in your soil. Regard not your past failures nor successes. All the past is equally a failure and a success; it is a success in as much as it offers you the present opportunity. Have you not a pretty good thinking faculty, worth more than the rarest gold watch? Can you not pass a judgment on something? Does not the stream still rise to its fountain-head in you? Go to the devil and come back again. Dispose of evil. Get punished once for all. Die, if you can. Depart. Exchange your salvation for a glass of water. If you know of any risk to run, run it. If you don't know of any, enjoy confidence. Do not trouble yourself to be religious; you will never get a thank-you for it. If you can drive a nail and have any nails to drive, drive them. If you have any experiments

[1] [See *Cape Cod*, p. 108; Riv. 127. See also p. 80 of this volume.]

you would like to try, try them; now's your chance. Do not entertain doubts, if they are not agreeable to you. Send them to the tavern. Do not eat unless you are hungry; there's no need of it. Do not read the newspapers. Improve every opportunity to be melancholy. Be as melancholy as you can be, and note the result. Rejoice with fate. As for health, consider yourself well, and mind your business. Who knows but you are dead already? Do not stop to be scared yet; there are more terrible things to come, and ever to come. Men die of fright and live of confidence. Be not simply obedient like the vegetables; set up your own Ebenezer. Of man's "*dis*obedience and the fruit," etc. Do not engage to find things as you think they are. Do what nobody can do for you. Omit to do everything else. [1]

According to Lieutenant Davis, the forms, extent, and distribution of sand-bars and banks are principally determined by tides, not by winds and waves. [2] On sand-bars recently elevated above the level of the ocean, fresh water is obtained by digging a foot or two. It is very common for wells near the shore to rise and fall with the tide. It is an interesting fact that the low sand-bars in the midst of the ocean, even those which are laid bare only at low tide, are reservoirs of fresh water at which the thirsty mariner can supply himself. Perchance, like huge sponges, they hold the rain and dew which falls on them, and which, by capillary attraction, is prevented from mingling with the surrounding brine. [3]

[1] [*Familiar Letters*, Aug. 9, 1850.]   [2] [*Cape Cod*, p. 155; Riv. 185.]

[3] [*Cape Cod*, p. 225; Riv. 271.]

It is not easy to make our lives respectable to ourselves by any course of activity. We have repeatedly to withdraw ourselves into our shells of thought like the tortoise, somewhat helplessly; and yet there is even more than philosophy in that. I do not love to entertain doubts and questions.

I am sure that my acquaintances mistake me. I am not the man they take me for. On a little nearer view they would find me out. They ask my advice on high matters, but they do not even know how poorly on't I am for hats and shoes. I have hardly a shift. Just as shabby as I am in my outward apparel, — aye, and more lamentably shabby, for nakedness is not so bad a condition after all, — am I in my inward apparel. If I should turn myself inside out, my rags and meanness would appear. I am something to him that made me, undoubtedly, but not much to any other that he has made.[1] All I can say is that I live and breathe and have my thoughts.

What is peculiar in the life of a man consists not in his obedience, but his opposition, to his instincts. In one direction or another he strives to live a supernatural life.

Would it not be worth the while to discover Nature in Milton?[2] Be native to the universe. I, too, love Concord best, but I am glad when I discover, in oceans and wildernesses far away, the materials out of which a million Concords can be made, — indeed, unless I discover them, I am lost myself, — that there too I am at

[1] [*Familiar Letters*, Aug. 9, 1850.]
[2] [Blake was at the time living in Milton, Mass.]

Do not waste any reverence on my attitude. I manage to sit up where I have dropped. Except as you reverence the evil one, — or rather the evil *myriad*. As for missing friends, — fortunate perhaps is he who has any to miss, whose place a thought will not supply. I have an ideal friend in whose place actual persons sometimes stand for a season. The last I may often miss, but the first I recover when I am myself again. What if we do miss one another? have we not agreed upon a rendezvous? While each travels his own way through the wood with serene and inexpressible joy, though it be on his hands and knees over the rocks and fallen trees, he cannot but be on the right way; there is no wrong way to him. I have found myself as well off when I have fallen into a quagmire, as in an armchair in the most hospitable house. The prospect was pretty much the same. Without anxiety let us wander on, admiring whatever beauty the woods exhibit.[1]

Do you know on what bushes a little peace, faith, and contentment grow? Go a-berrying early and late after them.[2] Miss our friends! It is not easy to get rid of them. We shall miss our bodies directly.

As to conforming outwardly, and living your own life inwardly, I have not a very high opinion of that course. Do not let your right hand know what your left hand does in that line of business. I have no doubt it will prove a failure.[3]

[1] [*Familiar Letters*, Aug. 9, 1850.]
[2] [Channing, p. 78.]
[3] [*Familiar Letters*, Aug. 9, 1850.]

home. Nature is as far from me as God, and sometimes I have thought to go West after her. Though the city is no more attractive to me than ever, yet I see less difference between a city and some dismallest swamp than formerly. It is a swamp too dismal and dreary, however, for me. I would as lief find a few owls and frogs and mosquitoes less. I prefer even a more cultivated place, free from miasma and crocodiles, and I will take my choice.[1]

From time to time I overlook the promised land, but I do not feel that I am travelling toward it. The moment I begin to look there, men and institutions get out of the way that I may see. I see nothing permanent in the society around me, and am not quite committed to any of its ways.

The heaven-born Numa, or Lycurgus, or Solon, gravely makes laws to regulate the exportation of tobacco. Will a divine legislator legislate for slaves, or to regulate the exportation of tobacco? What shall a State say for itself at the last day, in which this is a principal production?

What have grave, not to say divine, legislators — Numas, Lycurguses, Solons — to do with the exportation or the importation of tobacco. There was a man appealed to me the other day, "Can you give me a chaw of tobacco?" I *legislated* for him. Suppose you were to submit the question to any *son of God*, in what State would you get it again?[2]

[1] [*Familiar Letters*, Aug. 9, 1850.]
[2] [*Cape Cod, and Miscellanies*, p. 478; *Misc.*, Riv. 282, 283.]

The wind through the blind just now sounded like the baying of a distant hound, — somewhat plaintive and melodious.

The railroad cuts make cliffs for swallows.

Getting into Patchogue late one night in an oyster-boat, there was a drunken Dutchman aboard whose wit reminded me of Shakespeare. When we came to leave the beach, our boat was aground, and we were detained three hours waiting for the tide. In the meanwhile two of the fishermen took an extra dram at the beach house. Then they stretched themselves on the seaweed by the shore in the sun to sleep off the effects of their debauch. One was an inconceivably broad-faced young Dutchman, — but oh! of such a peculiar breadth and heavy look, I should not know whether to call it more ridiculous or sublime. You would say that he had humbled himself so much that he was beginning to be exalted. An indescribable mynheerish stupidity. I was less disgusted by their filthiness and vulgarity, because I was compelled to look on them as animals, as swine in their sty. For the whole voyage they lay flat on their backs on the bottom of the boat, in the bilge-water and wet with each bailing, half insensible and wallowing in their vomit. But ever and anon, when aroused by the rude kicks or curses of the skipper, the Dutchman, who never lost his wit nor equanimity, though snoring and rolling in the vomit produced by his debauch, blurted forth some happy repartee like an illuminated swine. It was the earthiest, slimiest wit I ever heard. The countenance was one of a million. It was unmistakable Dutch. In the midst of a million faces of other races it could not be mistaken. It told of Amsterdam. I kept racking my brains to conceive how he could have been born in America, how lonely he must feel, what he did for fellowship. When we were groping up the narrow creek of Patchogue at ten o'clock at night, keeping our boat off, now from this bank, now from that, with a pole, the two inebriates roused themselves betimes. For in spite of their low estate they seemed to have all their wits as much about them as ever, aye, and all the self-respect they ever had. And the Dutchman gave wise directions to the steerer, which were not heeded. Suddenly rousing himself up where the sharpest-eyed might be bewildered in the darkness, he leaned over the side of the boat and pointed straight down into the creek, averring that that identical hole was a first-rate place for eels. And again he roused himself at the right time and declared what luck he had once had with his pots (not his cups) in another place, which we were floating over in the dark. At last he suddenly stepped on to another boat which was moored to the shore, with a divine ease and sureness, saying, "Well, good-night, take care of yourselves, I can't be with you any longer." He was one of the few remarkable men whom I have met. I have been impressed by one or two men in their cups. There was really a divinity stirred within them, so that in their case I have reverenced the drunken, as savages the insane, man. So stupid that he could never be intoxicated. When I said, "You have had a hard time of it to-day," he answered with indescribable good humor out of the

very midst of his debauch, with watery eyes, "Well, it does n't happen every day." It was happening then.[1] He had taken me aboard on his back, the boat lying a rod from the shore, before I knew his condition. In the darkness our skipper steered with a pole on the bottom, for an oysterman knows the bottom of his bay as well as the shores, and can tell where he is by the soundings.[2]

There was a glorious lurid sunset to-night, accompanied with many sombre clouds, and when I looked into the west with my head turned, the grass had the same fresh green, and the distant herbage and foliage in the horizon the same dark blue, and the clouds and sky the same bright colors beautifully mingled and dissolving into one another, that I have seen in pictures of tropical landscapes and skies. Pale saffron skies with faint fishes of rosy clouds dissolving in them. A blood-stained sky. I regretted that I had an impatient companion. What shall we make of the fact that you have only to stand on your head a moment to be enchanted with the beauty of the landscape?

I met with a man on the beach who told me that when he wanted to jump over a brook he held up one leg a certain height, and then, if a line from his eye through his toe touched the opposite bank, he knew that he could jump it. I asked him how he knew when he held his leg at the right angle, and he said he knew the hitch very well. An Irishman told me that he held up one leg and if he could bring his toe in a range with his eye and the opposite bank he knew that he could

[1] [Channing, pp. 36, 37.]   [2] [See pp. 78, 79.]

Vol. II

jump it. Why, I told him, I can blot out a star with my toe, but I would not engage to jump the distance. It then appeared that he knew when he had got his leg at the right height by a certain hitch there was in it. I suggested that he should connect his two ankles with a string.[1]

I knew a clergyman who, when any person died, was wont to speak of that portion of mankind who survived as living monuments of God's mercy. A negative kind of life to live!

I can easily walk ten, fifteen, twenty, any number of miles, commencing at my own door, without going by any house, without crossing a road except where the fox and the mink do. Concord is the oldest inland town in New England, perhaps in the States, and the walker is peculiarly favored here. There are square miles in my vicinity which have no inhabitant. First along by the river, and then the brook, and then the meadow and the woodside. Such solitude! From a hundred hills I can see civilization and abodes of man afar. These farmers and their works are scarcely more obvious than woodchucks.[2]

As I was going by with a creaking wheelbarrow, one of my neighbors, who heard the music, ran out with his grease-pot and brush and greased the wheels.

[1] [An example of Thoreau's practice work, — the same story told in two forms. For its final form see *Cape Cod*, p. 88; Riv. 103, 104.]
[2] [*Excursions*, p. 212; Riv. 260.]

That is a peculiar season when about the middle of August the farmers are getting their meadow-hay. If you sail up the river, you will see them in all meadows, raking hay and loading it on to carts, great towering [?] teams, under which the oxen stand like beetles, chewing the cud, waiting for men to put the meadow on. With the heaviest load they dash aside to crop some more savory grass, — the half-broken steers.

There was reason enough for the first settler's selecting the elm out of all the trees of the forest with which to ornament his villages. It is beautiful alike by sunlight and moonlight, and the most beautiful specimens are not the largest. I have seen some only twenty-five or thirty years old, more graceful and healthy, I think, than any others. It is almost become a villageous tree, — like martins and bluebirds.

The high blueberry has the wildest flavor of any of the huckleberry tribe. It is a little mithridatic. It is like eating a poisonous berry which your nature makes harmless. I derive the same pleasure as if I were eating dog-berries, nightshade, and wild parsnip with impunity.

Man and his affairs, — Church and State and school, trade and commerce and agriculture, — Politics, — for that is the word for them all here to-day, — I am pleased to see how little space it occupies in the landscape. It is but a narrow field. That still narrower highway yonder leads to it. I sometimes direct the traveller [1] [Two pages missing.]

[1] [*Excursions*, pp. 212, 213; Riv. 260, 261.]

And once again,
When I went a-maying,
And once or twice more
I had seen thee before,
For there grow the mayflower
 (*Epigæa repens*)
And the mountain cranberry
 And the screech owl *strepens*.

O whither dost thou go?
Which way dost thou flow?
Thou art the way.
Thou art a road
Which Dante never trode.
Not many they be
Who enter therein,
Only the guests of the
Irishman Quin.[1]

There was a cross-eyed fellow used to help me survey, — he was my stake-driver, — and all he said was, at every stake he drove, "There, I should n't like to undertake to pull *that* up with my teeth."

It sticks in my *crop*. That's a good phrase. Many things stick there.

The man of wild habits,
Partridges and rabbits,
Who has no cares
Only to set snares,

[1] [*Excursions*, p. 215; Riv. 263.]

Vol. II

They 're a great endeavor
To be something for ever.
They are a monument to somebody,
To some selectman
Who thought of the plan.
What king
Did the thing,
I am still wondering.
Cenotaphs of the towns
Named on their crowns;
Huge as Stonehenge;
Set up how or when,
By what selectmen?
Gourgas or Lee,
Clark or Darby?
Blank tablets of stone,
Where a traveller might groan,
And in one sentence
Grave all that is known;
Which another might read,
In his extreme need.
I know two or three
Sentences, *i. e.*,
That might there be.
Literature that might stand
All over the land.
Which a man might remember
Till after December,
And read again in the spring,
After the thawing.[1]

[1] [*Excursions*, pp. 214–216; Riv. 263, 264.]

Who liv'st all alone,
Close to the bone,
And where life is sweetest
Constantly eatest.

Where they once dug for money,
But never found " ony."

To market fares
With early apples and pears.
When the spring stirs my blood
 With the instinct to travel,
 I can get enough gravel
On the Old Marlborough Road.

If you'll leave your abode
 With your fancy unfurled,
 You may go round the world
By the Old Marlborough Road.

Nobody repairs it,
For nobody wears it.
It is a living way,
As the Christians say.
What is it, what is it,
 But a direction out there
And the bare possibility
 Of going somewhere?
Great guide-*boards* of stone,
But travellers none.
It is worth going there to see
Where you might be.

Old meeting-house bell,
I love thy music well.
It peals through the air,
Sweetly full and fair,
As in the early times,
When I listened to its chimes.

I walk over the hills, to compare *great* things with *small*, as through a gallery of pictures, ever and anon looking through a gap in the wood, as through the frame of a picture, to a more distant wood or hillside, painted with several more coats of air. It is a cheap but pleasant effect. To a landscape in picture, glassed with air.

What is a horizon without mountains?

A field of water betrays the spirit that is in the air. It has new life and motion. It is intermediate between land and sky. On land, only the grass and trees wave, but the water itself is *rippled* by the wind. I see the breeze dash across it in streaks and flakes of light. It is somewhat singular that we should *look down* on the surface of water. We shall look down on the surface of air next, and mark where a still subtler spirit sweeps over *it*.[1]

Without inlet it lies,
Without outlet it flows.
From and to the skies
It comes and it goes.
I am its source,
And my life is its course.

[1] [*Walden*, pp. 209, 210; Riv. 296.]

I am its stony shore
And the breeze that passes o'er.[1]

[Two thirds of a page missing.]

All that the money-digger had ever found was a pine-tree shilling, once as he was dunging out. He was paid much more for dunging out, but he valued more the money which he found. The boy thinks most of the cent he found, not the cent he earned; for it suggests to him that he may find a great deal more, but he knows that he can't earn *much*, and perhaps did not deserve that.

[Two pages missing.]

Among the worst of men that ever lived.
However, we did seriously attend,
A little space we let our thoughts ascend,
Experienced our religion and confessed
'T was good for us to be there, — be anywhere.
Then to a heap of apples we addressed,
And cleared a five-rail fence with hand on the topmost
     rider *sine* care.
Then our Icarian thoughts returned to ground,
And we went on to heaven the long way round.

What's the railroad to me?
I never go to see
Where it ends.
It fills a few hollows,
And makes banks for the swallows;

[1] [*Walden*, p. 215; Riv. 303.]

'T is very fit the ambrosia of the gods
Should be a weed on earth, as nectar is
The morning dew which our shoes brush aside;
For the gods are simple folks, and we should pine upon
     their humble fare.

The purple flowers of the humble trichostema mingled with the wormwood, smelling like it; and the spring-scented, dandelion-scented primrose, yellow primrose. The swamp-pink (*Azalea viscosa*), its now withered pistils standing out.

The odoriferous sassafras, with its delicate green stem, its three-lobed leaf, tempting the traveller to bruise it, it sheds so rare a perfume on him, equal to all the spices of the East. Then its rare-tasting root bark, like nothing else, which I used to dig. The first navigators freighted their ships with it and deemed it worth its weight in gold.

The alder-leaved clethra (*Clethra alnifolia*), sweet-smelling queen of the swamp; its long white racemes.

We are most apt to remember and cherish the flowers which appear earliest in the spring. I look with equal affection on those which are the latest to bloom in the fall. The choke-berry (*Pyrus arbutifolia*).

The beautiful white waxen berries of the cornel, either *Cornus alba* or *paniculata*, white-berried or panicled, beautiful both when full of fruit and when its cymes are naked; delicate red cymes or stems of berries; spreading its little fairy fingers to the skies, its little palms; fairy palms they might be called.

One of the viburnums, *Lentago* or *pyrifolium* or

It sets the sand a-flowing,
And blackberries a-growing.[1]

Aug. 31.   TALL AMBROSIA

Among the signs of autumn I perceive
The Roman wormwood (called by learned men
Ambrosia elatior, food for gods,
For by impartial science the humblest weed
Is as well named as is the proudest flower)
Sprinkles its yellow dust over my shoes
As I brush through the now neglected garden.
We trample under foot the food of gods
And spill their nectar in each drop of dew.
My honest shoes, fast friends that never stray
Far from my couch, thus powdered, countrified,
Bearing many a mile the marks of their adventure,
At the post-house disgrace the Gallic gloss
Of those well-dressed ones who no morning dew
Nor Roman wormwood ever have gone through,
Who never walk, but are *transported* rather,
For what old crime of theirs I do not gather.

The gray blueberry bushes, venerable as oaks, — why is not their fruit poisonous? Bilberry called *Vaccinium corymbosum*; some say *amœnum*, or blue bilberry, and *Vaccinium disomorphum* Mx., black bilberry. Its fruit hangs on into September, but loses its wild and sprightly taste.

Th' ambrosia of the Gods 's a weed on earth,
Their nectar is the morning dew which on-
Ly our shoes taste, for they are simple folks.

[1] [*Walden*, pp. 135, 136; Riv. 192.]

Vol. II

nudum, with its poisonous-looking fruit in cymes, first greenish-white, then red, then purple, or all at once.

The imp-eyed, red, velvety-looking berry of the swamps.[1]

The spotted polygonum (*Polygonum Persicaria*), seen in low lands amid the potatoes now, wild prince's-feather (?), slight flower that does not forget to grace the autumn.

The late whortleberry — dangleberry — that ripens now that other huckleberries and blueberries are shrivelled and spoiling, September 1st; dangle down two or three inches; can rarely find many. They have a more transparent look, large, blue, long-stemmed, dangling, fruit of the swamp concealed.

I detect the pennyroyal which my feet have bruised. Butter-and-eggs still hold out to bloom.

I notice that cows never walk abreast, but in single file commonly, making a narrow cow-path, or the herd walks in an irregular and loose wedge. They retain still the habit of all the deer tribe, acquired when the earth was all covered with forest, of travelling from necessity in narrow paths in the woods.

At sundown a herd of cows, returning homeward from pasture over a sandy knoll, pause to paw the sand and challenge the representatives of another herd, raising a cloud of dust between the beholder and the setting sun. And then the herd boys rush to mingle in the fray and separate the combatants, two cows with horns interlocked, the one pushing the other down the bank.

[1] Wild holly?

My grandmother called her cow home at night from the pasture over the hill, by thumping on a mortar out of which the cow was accustomed to eat salt.

At Nagog I saw a hundred bushels of huckleberries in one field.

The Roman wormwood, pigweed, a stout, coarse redtopped (?) weed (*Amaranthus hybridus*), and spotted polygonum; these are the lusty growing plants now, September 2d.

Tall, slender, minute white-flowered weed in gardens, annual fleabane (*Erigeron Canadensis*).

One of my neighbors, of whom I borrowed a horse, cart, and harness to-day, which last was in a singularly dilapidated condition, considering that he is a wealthy farmer, did not know but I would make a book about it.

As I was stalking over the surface of this planet in the dark to-night, I started a plover resting on the ground and heard him go off with whistling wings.

My friends wonder that I love to walk alone in solitary fields and woods by night. Sometimes in my loneliest and wildest midnight walk I hear the sound of the whistle and the rattle of the cars, where perchance some of those very friends are being whirled by night over, as they think, a well-known, safe, and public road. I see that men do not make or choose their own paths, whether they are railroads or trackless through the wilds, but what the powers permit each one enjoys. My solitary

Vol. II

course has the same sanction that the Fitchburg Railroad has. If they have a charter from Massachusetts and — what is of much more importance — from Heaven, to travel the course and in the fashion they do, I have a charter, though it be from Heaven alone, to travel the course I do, — to take the necessary lands and pay the damages. It is by the grace of God in both cases.

Now, about the first of September, you will see flocks of small birds forming compact and distinct masses, as if they were not only animated by one spirit but actually held together by some invisible fluid or film, and will hear the sound of their wings rippling or fanning the air as they flow through it, flying, the whole mass, ricochet like a single bird, — or as they flow over the fence. Their mind must operate faster than man's, in proportion as their bodies do.

What a generation this is! It travels with some brains in its hat, with a couple of spare cigars on top of them. It carries a heart in its breast, covered by a lozenge in its waistcoat pocket.

John Garfield brought me this morning (September 6th) a young great heron (*Ardea Herodias*), which he shot this morning on a pine tree on the North Branch. It measured four feet, nine inches, from bill to toe and six feet in alar extent, and belongs to a different race from myself and Mr. Frost. I am glad to recognize him for a native of America, — why not an American citizen?

In the twilight, when you can only see the outlines of the trees in the horizon, the elm-tops indicate where the houses are. I have looked afar over fields and even over distant woods and distinguished the conspicuous graceful, sheaf-like head of an elm which shadowed some farmhouse. From the northwest (?) part of Sudbury you can see an elm on the Boston road, on the hilltop in the horizon in Wayland, five or six miles distant. The elm is a tree which can be distinguished farther off perhaps than any other. The wheelwright still makes his hubs of it, his spokes of white oak, his fellies of yellow oak, which does not crack on the corners. In England, 't is said, they use the ash for fellies.

There is a little grove in a swampy place in Conantum where some rare things grow, — several bass trees, two kinds of ash, sassafras, maidenhair fern, the whiteberried plant (ivory?), etc., etc., and the sweet viburnum (?) in the hedge near by.

This will be called the wet year of 1850. The river is as high now, September 9th, as in the spring, and hence the prospects and the reflections seen from the village are something novel.

Roman wormwood, pigweed, amaranth, polygonum, and one or two coarse kinds of grass reign now in the cultivated fields.

Though the potatoes have man with all his implements on their side, these rowdy and rampant weeds completely bury them, between the last hoeing and the digging. The potatoes hardly succeed with the utmost care: these weeds only ask to be *let alone* a little

while. I judge that they have not got the rot. I sympathize with all this luxuriant growth of weeds. Such is the year. The weeds grow as if in sport and frolic.

You might say green as green-briar.

I do not know whether the practice of putting indigoweed about horses' tackling to keep off flies is well founded, but I hope it is, for I have been pleased to notice that wherever I have occasion to tie a horse I am sure to find indigo-weed not far off, and therefore this, which is so universally dispersed, would be the fittest weed for this purpose.

The thistle is now in bloom, which every child is eager to clutch once, — just a child's handful.

The prunella, self-heal, small purplish-flowered plant of low grounds.

Charles [1] grew up to be a remarkably eccentric man. He was of large frame, athletic, and celebrated for his feats of strength. His lungs were proportionally strong. There was a man who heard him named once, and asked if it was the same Charles Dunbar whom he remembered when he was a little boy walking on the coast of Maine. A man came down to the shore and hailed a vessel that was sailing by. He should never forget that man's name.

It was well grassed, and delicate flowers grew in the middle of the road.

[1] [Charles Dunbar was Thoreau's uncle. See Sanborn, pp. 21–23, 92, 93; also *Journal*, vol. iv, Jan. 1, 1853, and vol. viii, Apr. 3, 1856.]

I saw a delicate flower had grown up two feet
   high
Between the horses' path and the wheel-track,
Which Dakin's and Maynard's wagons had
Passed over many a time.
An inch more to right or left had sealed its fate,
Or an inch higher. And yet it lived and flourished
As much as if it had a thousand acres
Of untrodden space around it, and never
Knew the danger it incurred.
It did not borrow trouble nor invite an
Evil fate by apprehending it.[1]
For though the distant market-wagon
Every other day inevitably rolled
This way, it just as inevitably rolled
In those ruts. And the same
Charioteer who steered the flower
Upward guided the horse and cart aside from it.
There were other flowers which you would say
Incurred less danger, grew more out of the way,
Which no cart rattled near, no walker daily passed,
But at length one rambling deviously —
For no rut restrained — plucked them,
And then it appeared that they stood
Directly in his way, though he had come
From farther than the market-wagon.

And then it appeared that this brave flower which
grew between the wheel and horse did actually stand
farther out of the way than that which stood in the wide
prairie where the man of science plucked it.

[1] [Channing, p. 293 (as prose).]

To-day I climbed a handsome rounded hill
Covered with hickory trees, wishing to see
The country from its top, for low hills
Show unexpected prospects. I looked
Many miles over a woody lowland
Toward Marlborough, Framingham, and Sudbury;
And as I sat amid the hickory trees

And the young sumachs, enjoying the prospect, a neat herd of cows approached, of unusually fair proportions and smooth, clean skins, evidently petted by their owner, who must have carefully selected them. One more confiding heifer, the fairest of the herd, did by degrees approach as if to take some morsel from our hands, while our hearts leaped to our mouths with expectation and delight. She by degrees drew near with her fair limbs progressive, making pretense of browsing; nearer and nearer, till there was wafted toward us the bovine fragrance, — cream of all the dairies that ever were or will be, — and then she raised her gentle muzzle toward us, and snuffed an honest recognition within hand's reach. I saw 't was possible for his herd to inspire with love the herdsman. She was as delicately featured as a hind. Her hide was mingled white and fawn-color, and on her muzzle's tip there was a white spot not bigger than a daisy, and on her side toward me the map of Asia plain to see.

Farewell, dear heifer! Though thou forgettest me, my prayer to heaven shall be that thou may'st not forget thyself. There was a whole bucolic in her snuff. I saw her name was Sumach. And by the kindred spots I knew her mother, more sedate and matronly,

with full-grown bag; and on her sides was Asia, great and small, the plains of Tartary, even to the pole, while on her daughter it was Asia Minor. She not disposed to wanton with the herdsman.

And as I walked, she followed me, and took an apple from my hand, and seemed to care more for the hand than apple. So innocent a face as I have rarely seen on any creature, and I have looked in face of many heifers. And as she took the apple from my hand, I caught the apple of her eye. She smelled as sweet as the clethra blossom. There was no sinister expression. And for horns, though she had them, they were so well disposed in the right place, bent neither up nor down, I do not now remember she had any. No horn was held toward me.[1]

Sept. 11. *Wednesday.* The river higher than I ever knew it at this season, as high as in the spring.

Yesterday, September 14, walked to White Pond in Stow, on the Marlborough road, having passed one pond called sometimes Pratt's Pond, sometimes Bottomless Pond, in Sudbury. Saw afterward another pond beyond Willis's also called Bottomless Pond, in a thick swamp. To name two ponds bottomless when both of them have a bottom! Verily men choose darkness rather than light.[2]

The farmers are now cutting — topping — their corn, gathering their early fruit, raking their cranberries, digging their potatoes, etc.

[1] [Channing, pp. 76, 77; Sanborn, pp. 258, 259.]
[2] [See *Walden*, p. 315; Riv. 441.]

Everything has its use, and man seeks sedulously for the best article for each use. The watchmaker finds the oil of the porpoise's jaw the best for oiling his watches. Man has a million eyes, and the race knows infinitely more than the individual. Consent to be wise through your race.

Autumnal mornings, when the feet of countless sparrows are heard like rain-drops on the roof by the boy who sleeps in the garret.

Villages with a single long street lined with trees, so straight and wide that you can see a chicken run across it a mile off.[1]

Sept. 19. The gerardia, yellow trumpet-like flower. Veiny-leaved hawkweed (leaves handsome, radical excepting one or two; know them well) (*Hieracium venosum*), flower like a dandelion. Canada snapdragon, small pea-like blue flower in the wood-paths, (*Antirrhinum Canadense*). Pine-weed, thickly branched low weed with red seed-vessels, in wood-paths and fields, (*Sarothra gentianoides*). Cucumber-root (*Medeola*). Tree-primrose. Red-stemmed cornel. The very minute flower which grows now in the middle of the Marlborough road.

I am glad to have drunk water so long, as I prefer the natural sky to an opium-eater's heaven, — would keep sober always, and lead a sane life not indebted to stimulants. Whatever my practice may be, I believe that it

[1] [*Excursions*, p. 4; Riv. 4.]

is the only drink for a wise man, and only the foolish habitually use any other. Think of dashing the hopes of a morning with a cup of coffee, or of an evening with a dish of tea! Wine is not a noble liquor, except when it is confined to the pores of the grape. Even music is wont to be intoxicating. Such apparently slight causes destroyed Greece and Rome, and will destroy England and America.[1]

I have seen where the rain dripped from the trees on a sand-bank on the Marlborough road, that each little pebble which had protected the sand made the summit of a sort of basaltic column of sand, — a phenomenon which looked as if it might be repeated on a larger scale in nature.

The goldenrods and asters impress me not like individuals but great families covering a thousand hills and having a season to themselves.

The indigo-weed turns black when dry, and I have been interested to find in each of its humble seed-vessels a worm.

The Deep Cut is sometimes excited to productiveness by a rain in midsummer. It impresses me somewhat as if it were a cave, with all its stalactites turned wrong side outward. Workers in bronze should come here for their patterns.

Those were carrots which I saw naturalized in Wheeler's field. It was four or five years since he planted there.

To-day I saw a sunflower in the woods.

It is pleasant to see the *Viola pedata* blossoming again

[1] [*Walden*, p. 240; Riv. 338.]

Vol. II

Oh, if I could be intoxicated on air and water![1] on hope and memory! and always see the maples standing red in the midst of the waters on the meadow!

Those have met with losses, who have lost their children. I saw the widow this morning whose son was drowned.

That I might never be blind to the beauty of the landscape! To hear music without any vibrating cord!

A family in which there was singing in the morning. To hear a neighbor singing! All other speech sounds thereafter like profanity. A man cannot sing falsehood or cowardice; he must sing truth and heroism to attune his voice to some instrument. It would be noblest to sing with the wind. I have seen a man making himself a viol, patiently and fondly paring the thin wood and shaping it, and when I considered the end of the work he was ennobled in my eyes. He was building himself a ship in which to sail to new worlds. I am much indebted to my neighbor who will now and then in the intervals of his work draw forth a few strains from his accordion. Though he is but a learner, I find when his strains cease that I have been elevated.

The question is not whether you drink, but what liquor.

Plucked a wild rose the 9th of October on Fair Haven Hill.

Butter-and-eggs, which blossomed several months ago, still freshly [in] bloom (October 11th).

He knew what shrubs were best for withes.

[1] [*Walden*, p. 240; Riv. 338.]

now, in September, with a beauty somewhat serener than that of these yellow flowers.

The trees on the bank of the river have white furrows worn about them, marking the height of the freshets, at what levels the water has stood.

Water is so much more fine and sensitive an element than earth. A single boatman passing up or down unavoidably shakes the whole of a wide river, and disturbs its every reflection. The air is an element which our voices shake still further than our oars the water.

The red maples on the river, standing far in the water when the banks are overflown and touched by the earliest frosts, are memorable features in the scenery of the stream at this season.

Now you can scent the ripe grapes far off on the banks as you row along. Their fragrance is finer than their flavor.

My companion said he would drink when the boat got under the bridge, because the water would be cooler in the shade, though the stream quickly passes through the piers from shade to sun again. It is something beautiful, the act of drinking, the stooping to imbibe some of this widespread element, in obedience to instinct, without whim. We do not so simply drink in other influences.

It is pleasant to have been to a place by the way a river went.

The forms of trees and groves change with every stroke of the oar.

It seems hardly worth the while to risk the dangers of the sea between Leghorn and New York for the sake of a cargo of juniper berries and bitter almonds.

This is a remarkable year. Huckleberries are still quite abundant and fresh on Conantum. There have been more berries than pickers or even worms. (October 9th.)

I am always exhilarated, as were the early voyagers, by the sight of sassafras (*Laurus Sassafras*). The green leaves bruised have the fragrance of lemons and a thousand spices. To the same order belong cinnamon, cassia, camphor.

Hickory is said to be an Indian name. (Nuttall's continuation of Michaux.)

The seed vessel of the sweet-briar is a very beautiful glossy elliptical fruit. What with the fragrance of its leaves, its blossom, and its fruit, it is thrice crowned.

I observed to-day (October 17th) the small blueberry bushes by the path-side, now blood-red, full of white blossoms as in the spring, the blossoms of spring contrasting strangely with the leaves of autumn. The former seemed to have expanded from sympathy with the maturity of the leaves.

Walter Colton in his "California"[1] says, "Age is no certain evidence of merit, since folly runs to seed as fast as wisdom."

The imagination never forgives an insult.

Left Concord, Wednesday morning, September 25th, 1850, for Quebec. Fare $7.00 to and fro. Obliged to leave Montreal on return as soon as Friday, October 4th. The country was new to me beyond Fitchburg.

[1] [*Three Years in California*, 1850.]

In Ashburnham and afterwards I noticed the wood-bine.[1]

[Eighty-four pages missing, — doubtless the Canada journal.]

However mean your life is, meet it and live; do not shun it and call it hard names. It is not so bad as you are. It looks poorest when you are richest. The fault-finder will find faults even in paradise. Love your life, poor as it is. You may perchance have some pleasant, thrilling, glorious hours, even in a poorhouse. The set-ting sun is reflected from the windows of the almshouse as brightly as from the rich man's house. The snow melts before its door as early in the spring. I do not see but a quiet mind may live as contentedly there, and have as cheering thoughts as anywhere, and, indeed, the town's poor seem to live the most independent lives of any. They are simply great enough to receive without misgiving. Cultivate poverty like sage, like a garden herb. Do not trouble yourself to get new things, whether clothes or friends. That is dissipation. Turn the old; return to them. Things do not change; we change. If I were confined to a corner in a garret all my days, like a spider, the world would be just as large to me while I had my thoughts.[2]

In all my travels I never came to the abode of the present.

I live in the angle of a leaden wall, into whose alloy was poured a little bell-metal. Sometimes in the repose of my mid-day there reaches my ears a confused tintin-

[1] [*Excursions*, p. 3; Riv. 3.]   [2] [*Walden*, p. 361; Riv. 505, 506.]

nabulum from without. It is the noise of my contem-poraries.[1]

That the brilliant leaves of autumn are not withered ones is proved by the fact that they wilt when gathered as soon as the green.

But now, October 31st, they are all withered. This has been the most perfect afternoon in the year. The air quite warm enough, perfectly still and dry and clear, and not a cloud in the sky. Scarcely the song of a cricket is heard to disturb the stillness. When they ceased their song I do not know. I wonder that the impetus which our hearing had got did not hurry us into deafness over a precipitous silence. There must have been a thick web of cobwebs on the grass this morning, promising this fair day, for I see them still through the afternoon, covering not only the grass but the bushes and the trees. They are stretched across the unfrequented roads from weed to weed, and broken by the legs of the horses.

I thought to-day that it would be pleasing to study the dead and withered plants, the ghosts of plants, which now remain in the fields, for they fill almost as large a space to the eye as the green have done. They live not in memory only, but to the fancy and imagina-tion.

As we were passing through Ashburnham, by a new white house which stood at some distance in a field, one passenger exclaimed so that all the passengers could hear him, "There, there's not so good a house as that in all Canada." And I did not much wonder at his remark. There is a neatness as well as thrift and elastic

[1] [*Walden*, p. 362; Riv. 507.]

comfort, a certain flexible easiness of circumstance when not rich, about a New England house which the Cana-dian houses do not suggest. Though of stone, they were no better constructed than a stone barn would be with us. The only building on which money and taste are expended is the church.[1] At Beauport we examined a magnificent cathedral, not quite completed, where I do not remember that there were any but the meanest houses in sight around it.

Our Indian summer, I am tempted to say, is the finest season of the year. Here has been such a day as I think Italy never sees.

Though it has been so warm to-day, I found some of the morning's frost still remaining under the north side of a wood, to my astonishment.

Why was this beautiful day made, and no man to improve it? We went through Seven-Star (?) Lane to White Pond.

Looking through a stately pine grove, I saw the western sun falling in golden streams through its aisles. Its west side, opposite to me, was all lit up with golden light; but what was I to it? Such sights remind me of houses which we never inhabit, — that commonly I am not at home in the world. I see somewhat fairer than I enjoy or possess.

A fair afternoon, a celestial afternoon, cannot occur but we mar our pleasure by reproaching ourselves that we do not make all our days beautiful. The thought of what I am, of my pitiful conduct, deters me from receiv-ing what joy I might from the glorious days that visit me.

[1] [*Excursions*, p. 100; Riv. 124.]

After the era of youth is passed, the knowledge of our-selves is an alloy that spoils our satisfactions.

I am wont to think that I could spend my days con-tentedly in any retired country house that I see; for I see it to advantage now and without incumbrance; I have not yet imported my humdrum thoughts, my pro-saic habits, into it to mar the landscape. What is this beauty in the landscape but a certain fertility in me? I look in vain to see it realized but in my own life. If I could wholly cease to be ashamed of myself, I think that all my days would be fair.

When I asked at the principal bookstore in Montreal to see such books as were published there, the answer was that none were published there but those of a sta-tistical character and the like, that their books came from the States.[1]

[Two thirds of a page missing]

As once he was riding past Jennie Dugan's, was invited by her boys to look into their mother's spring-house. He looked in. It *was* a delectable place to keep butter and milk cool and sweet in dog-days, — but there was a leopard frog swimming in the milk, and another sitting on the edge of the pan.

[Half a page missing.]

Thou art a personality so vast and universal that I have never seen one of thy features. I am suddenly very near to another land than can be bought and sold; this is not Charles Miles's swamp. This is a far, far-

[1] [*Excursions*, p. 15; Riv. 18.]

away field on the confines of the actual Concord, where nature is partially present. These farms I have myself surveyed; these lines I have run; these bounds I have set up; they have no chemistry to fix them; they fade from the surface of the glass (the picture); this light is too strong for them.

[Four and two thirds pages missing.]

My dear, my dewy sister, let thy rain descend on me. I not only love thee, but I love the best of thee; that is to love thee rarely. I do not love thee every day. Commonly I love those who are less than thou. I love thee only on great days. Thy dewy words feed me like the manna of the morning. I am as much thy sister as thy brother. Thou art as much my brother as my sister. It is a portion of thee and a portion of me which are of kin. Thou dost not have to woo me. I do not have to woo thee. O my sister! O Diana, thy tracks are on the eastern hills. Thou surely passedst that way. I, the hunter, saw them in the morning dew. My eyes are the hounds that pursue thee. Ah, my friend, what if I do not answer thee? I hear thee. Thou canst speak; I cannot. I hear and forget to answer. I am occupied with hearing. I awoke and thought of thee; thou wast present to my mind. How camest thou there? Was I not present to thee likewise? [1]

The oystermen had anchored their boat near the shore without regard to the state of the tide, and when we came to it to set sail, just after noon, we found that it was aground. Seeing that they were preparing to

[1] [Channing, pp. 70, 71; Sanborn, pp. 259, 260.]

Vol. II

that it was about the turn of the tide and we must wait some hours longer.[1]

I once went in search of the relics of a human body — a week after a wreck — which had been cast up the day before on to the beach, though the sharks had stripped off the flesh. I got the direction from a lighthouse. I should find it a mile or two distant over the sand, a dozen rods from the water, by a stick which was stuck up covered with a cloth. Pursuing the direction pointed out, I expected that I should have to look very narrowly at the sand to find so small an object, but so completely smooth and bare was the beach — half a mile wide of sand — and so magnifying the mirage toward the sea that when I was half a mile distant the insignificant stick or sliver which marked the spot looked like a broken mast in the sand. As if there was no other object, this trifling sliver had puffed itself up to the vision to fill the void; and there lay the relics in a certain state, rendered perfectly inoffensive to both bodily and spiritual eye by the surrounding scenery, — a slight inequality in the sweep of the shore. Alone with the sea and the beach, attending to the sea, whose hollow roar seemed addressed to the ears of the departed, — articulate speech to them. It was as conspicuous on that sandy plain as if a generation had labored to pile up a cairn there. Where there were so few objects, the least was obvious as a mausoleum. It reigned over the shore. That dead body possessed the shore as no living one could. It showed a title to the sands which no living ruler could.[2]

[1] [See pp. 49-51.]

[2] [*Cape Cod*, pp. 107, 108; Riv. 126, 127. See also pp. 49-51 of this volume.]

push it off, I was about to take off my shoes and stockings in order to wade to it first, but a Dutch sailor with a singular bullfrog or trilobite expression of the eyes, whose eyes were like frog ponds in the broad platter of his cheeks and gleamed like a pool covered with frog-spittle, immediately offered me the use of his back. So mounting, with my legs under his arms, and hugging him like one of [the] family, he set me aboard of the periauger?

They then leaned their hardest against the stern, bracing their feet against the sandy bottom in two feet of water, the Dutchman with his broad back among them. In the most Dutch-like and easy way they applied themselves to this labor, while the skipper tried to raise the bows, never jerking or hustling but silently exerting what vigor was inherent in them, doing, no doubt, their utmost endeavor, while I pushed with a spike pole; but it was all in vain. It was decided to be unsuccessful; we did not disturb its bed by a grain of sand. "Well, what now?" said I. "How long have we got to wait?" "Till the tide rises," said the captain. But no man knew of the tide, how it was. So I went in to bathe, looking out for sharks and chasing crabs, and the Dutchman waded out among the mussels to spear a crab. The skipper stuck a clamshell into the sand at the water's edge to discover if it was rising, and the sailors, — the Dutchman and the other, — having got more drink at Oakes's, stretched themselves on the seaweed close to the water's edge [and] went to sleep. After an hour or more we could discover no change in the shell even by a hair's breadth, from which we learned

My father was commissary at Fort Independence in the last war. He says that the baker whom he engaged returned eighteen ounces of bread for sixteen of flour, and was glad of the job on those terms.

In a pleasant spring morning all men's sins are forgiven. You may have known your neighbor yesterday for a drunkard and a thief, and merely pitied or despised him, and despaired of the world; but the sun shines bright and warm this first spring morning, and you meet him quietly, serenely at any work, and see how even his exhausted, debauched veins and nerves expand with still joy and bless the new day, feel the spring influence with the innocence [1] [Two thirds of a page missing.]

There is a good echo from that wood to one standing on the side of Fair Haven. It was particularly good to-day. The woodland lungs seemed particularly sound to-day; they echoed your shout with a fuller and rounder voice than it was given in, seeming to *mouth* it. It was uttered with a sort of sweeping intonation half round a vast circle, *ore rotundo*, by a broad dell among the tree-tops passing it round to the entrance of all the aisles of the wood. You had to choose the right key or pitch, else the woods would not echo it with any spirit, and so with eloquence. Of what significance is any sound if Nature does not echo it? It does not prevail. It dies away as soon as uttered. I wonder that wild men have not made more of echoes, or that we do

[1] [*Walden*, pp. 346, 347; Riv. 484, 485.]

not hear that they have made more. It would be a pleasant, a soothing and cheerful mission to go about the country in search of them, — articulating, speaking, vocal, oracular, resounding, sonorous, hollow, prophetic places; places wherein to found an oracle, sites for oracles, sacred ears of Nature.

I used to strike with a paddle on the side of my boat on Walden Pond, filling the surrounding woods with circling and dilating sound, awaking the woods, "stirring them up," as a keeper of a menagerie his lions and tigers, a growl from all. All melody is a sweet echo, as it were coincident with [the] movement of our organs. We wake the echo of the place we are in, its slumbering music.

I should think that savages would have made a god of echo.

I will call that Echo Wood.

Crystal Water for White Pond.

There was a sawmill once on Nut Meadow Brook, near Jennie's Road. These little brooks have their history. They once turned sawmills. They even used their *influence* to destroy the primitive [forests] which grew on their banks, and now, for their reward, the sun is let in to dry them up and narrow their channels. Their crime rebounds against themselves. You still find the traces of ancient dams where the simple brooks were taught to use their influence to destroy the primitive forests on their borders, and now for penalty they flow in shrunken channels, with repentant and plaintive tinkling through the wood, being by an evil spirit turned against their neighbor forests.

What does education often do? It makes a straight-cut ditch of a free, meandering brook.

You must walk like a camel, which is said to be the only beast which ruminates when it walks.

The actual life of men is not without a dramatic interest to the thinker. It is not in all its respects prosaic. Seventy thousand pilgrims proceed annually to Mecca from the various nations of Islam.

I was one evening passing a retired farmhouse which had a smooth green plat before it, just after sundown, when I saw a hen turkey which had gone to roost on the front fence with her wings outspread over her young now pretty well advanced, who were roosting on the next rail a foot or two below her. It completed a picture of rural repose and happiness such as I had not seen for a long time. A particularly neat and quiet place, where the very ground was swept around the wood-pile. The neighboring fence of roots, agreeable forms for the traveller to study, like the bones of marine monsters and the horns of mastodons or megatheriums.

You might say of a philosopher that he was in this world as a spectator.

A squaw came to our door to-day with two pappooses, and said, "Me want a pie." Theirs is not common begging. You are merely the rich Indian who shares his goods with the poor. They merely offer you an opportunity to be generous and hospitable.

Vol. II

Equally simple was the observation which an Indian made at Mr. Hoar's door the other day, who went there to sell his baskets. "No, we don't want any," said the one who went to the door. "What! do you mean to starve us?" asked the Indian in astonishment, as he was going out [*sic*] the gate. The Indian seems to have said: I too will do like the white man; I will go into business. He sees his white neighbors well off around him, and he thinks that if he only enters on the profession of basket-making, riches will flow in unto him as a matter of course; just as the lawyer weaves arguments, and by some magical means wealth and standing follow. He thinks that when he has made the baskets he has done his part, now it is yours to buy them. He has not discovered that it is necessary for him to make it worth your while to buy them, or make some which it will be worth your while to buy. With great simplicity he says to himself: I too will be a man of business; I will go into trade. It is n't enough simply to make baskets. You have got to sell them.[1]

I have an uncle who once, just as he stepped on to the dock at New York from a steamboat, saw some strange birds in the water and called to [a] Gothamite to know what they were. Just then his hat blew off into the dock, and the man answered by saying, "Mister, your hat is off," whereupon my uncle, straightening himself up, asked again with vehemence, "Blast you, sir, I want to know what those birds are." By the time that he had got this information, a sailor had recovered his hat.

[1] [*Walden*, pp. 20, 21; Riv. 32.]

Nov. 8. The stillness of the woods and fields is remarkable at this season of the year. There is not even the creak of a cricket to be heard. Of myriads of dry shrub oak leaves, not one rustles. Your own breath can rustle them, yet the breath of heaven does not suffice to. The trees have the aspect of waiting for winter. The autumnal leaves have lost their color; they are now truly sere, dead, and the woods wear a sombre color. Summer and harvest are over. The hickories, birches, chestnuts, no less than the maples, have lost their leaves. The sprouts, which had shot up so vigorously to repair the damage which the choppers had done, have stopped short for the winter. Everything stands silent and expectant. If I listen, I hear only the note of a chickadee, — our most common and I may say native bird, most identified with our forests, — or perchance the scream of a jay, or perchance from the solemn depths of these woods I hear tolling far away the knell of one departed. Thought rushes in to fill the vacuum. As you walk, however, the partridge still bursts away. The silent, dry, almost leafless, certainly fruitless woods. You wonder what cheer that bird can find in them. The partridge bursts away from the foot of a shrub oak like its own dry fruit, immortal bird! This sound still startles us. Dry goldenrods, now turned gray and white, lint our clothes as we walk. And the drooping, downy seed-vessels of the epilobium remind us of the summer. Perchance you will meet with a few solitary asters in the dry fields, with a little color left. The sumach is stripped of everything but its cone of red berries.

This is a peculiar season, peculiar for its stillness. The crickets have ceased their song. The few birds are well-nigh silent. The tinted and gay leaves are now sere and dead, and the woods wear a sombre aspect. A carpet of snow under the pines and shrub oaks will make it look more cheerful. Very few plants have now their spring. But thoughts still spring in man's brain. There are no flowers nor berries to speak of. The grass begins to die at top. In the morning it is stiff with frost. Ice has been discovered in somebody's tub very early this morn, of the thickness of a dollar. The flies are betwixt life and death. The wasps come into the houses and settle on the walls and windows. All insects go into crevices. The fly is entangled in a web and struggles vainly to escape, but there is no spider to secure him; the corner of the pane is a deserted camp. When I lived in the woods the wasps came by thousands to my lodge in November, as to winter quarters, and settled on my windows and on the walls over my head, sometimes deterring visitors from entering. Each morning, when they were numbed with cold, I swept some of them out. But I did not trouble myself to get rid of them. They never molested me, though they bedded with me, and they gradually disappeared into what crevices I do not know, avoiding winter.[1] I saw a squash-bug go slowly behind a clapboard to avoid winter. As some of these melon seeds come up in the garden again in the spring, so some of these squash-bugs come forth. The flies are for a long time in a somnambulic state. They

[1] [*Walden*, p. 265 (Riv. 372, 373), where October is the month named.]

have too little energy or *vis vitæ* to clean their wings or heads, which are covered with dust. They buzz and bump their heads against the windows two or three times a day, or lie on their backs in a trance, and that is all, — two or three short spurts. One of these mornings we shall hear that Mr. Minott had to break the ice to water his cow. And so it will go on till the ground freezes. If the race had never lived through a winter, what would they think was coming?

Walden Pond has at last fallen a little. It has been so high over the stones — quite into the bushes — that walkers have been excluded from it.[1] There has been no accessible shore. All ponds have been high. The water stood higher than usual in the distant ponds which I visited and had never seen before. It has been a peculiar season. At Goose Pond, I notice that the birches of one year's growth from the stumps standing in the water are all dead, apparently killed by the water, unless, like the pine, they die down after springing from the stump.

It is warm somewhere any day in the year. You will find some nook in the woods generally, at mid-forenoon of the most blustering day, where you may forget the cold. I used to resort to the northeast side of Walden, where the sun, reflected from the pine woods on the stony shore, made it the fireside of the pond. It is so much pleasanter and wholesomer to be warmed by the sun when you can, than by a fire.

I saw to-day a double reflection on the pond of the

[1] It reached its height in '52, and has now fallen decidedly in the fall of '53.

cars passing, one beneath the other, occasioned by a bright rippled streak on the surface of the water, from which a second reflection sprang.

One who would study lichens must go into a new country where the rocks have not been burned.

Therien says that the Canadians say *marche-donc* to their horses; and that the acid fruit must be spelled *painbéna*.[1] He says that the French acre or *arpent* is ten perches by ten, of eighteen feet each.

Nov. 9. It is a pleasant surprise to walk over a hill where an old wood has recently been cut off, and, on looking round, to see, instead of dense ranks of trees almost impermeable to light, distant well-known blue mountains in the horizon and perchance a white village over an expanded open country. I now take this in preference to all my old familiar walks. So a new prospect and walks can be created where we least expected it. The old men have seen other prospects from these hills than we do. There was the old Kettell place, now Watts's, which I surveyed for him last winter and lotted off, where twenty-five years ago I played horse in the paths of a thick wood and roasted apples and potatoes in an old pigeon-place [2] and gathered fruit at the pie-apple tree. A week or two after I surveyed it, it now being rotten and going to waste, I walked there and was surprised to find the place and prospect which I have described.

[1] [See *Excursions*, p. 48; Riv. 59.]   [2] [See pp. 499, 500.]

I found many fresh violets (*Viola pedata*) to-day (November 9th) in the woods.

Saw a cat on the Great Fields, wilder than a rabbit, hunting artfully. I remember to have seen one once walking about the stony shore at Walden Pond. It is not often that they wander so far from the houses. I once, however, met with a cat with young kittens in the woods, quite wild.[1]

The leaves of the larch are now yellow and falling off. Just a month ago, I observed that the white pines were parti-colored, green and yellow, the needles of the previous year now falling. Now I do not observe any yellow ones, and I expect to find that it is only for a few weeks in the fall after the new leaves have done growing that there are any yellow and falling, — that there is a season when we may say the old pine leaves are now yellow, and again, they are fallen. The trees were not so tidy then; they are not so full now. They look best when contrasted with a field of snow.

A rusty sparrow or two only remains to people the drear spaces. It goes to roost without neighbors.

It is pleasant to observe any growth in a wood. There is the pitch pine field northeast of Beck Stow's Swamp, where some years ago I went a-blackberrying and observed that the pitch pines were beginning to come in, and I have frequently noticed since how fairly they grew, dotting the plain as evenly as if dispersed by art. To-day I was aware that I walked in a pitch pine wood, which ere long, perchance, I may survey and lot off for a wood auction and see the chop-

[1] [*Walden*, p. 257; Riv. 361, 362.]

Fair Haven Pond from the Cliffs

November Woods

pers at their work. There is also the old pigeon-place field by the Deep Cut. I remember it as an open grassy field. It is now one of our most pleasant woodland paths. In the former place, near the edge of the old wood, the young pines line each side of the path like a palisade, they grow so densely. It never rains but it pours, and so I think when I see a young grove of pitch pines crowding each other to death in this wide world. These are destined for the locomotive's maw. These branches, which it has taken so many years to mature, are regarded even by the woodman as "trash."

Delicate, dry, feathery (perchance fescue) grasses growing out of a tuft, gracefully bending over the pathway. I do not know what they are, but they belong to the season.

The chickadees, if I stand long enough, hop nearer and nearer inquisitively, from pine bough to pine bough, till within four or five feet, occasionally lisping a note.

The pitcher-plant, though a little frost-bitten and often cut off by the mower, now stands full of water in the meadows. I never found one that had not an insect in it.

I sometimes see well-preserved walls running straight through the midst of high and old woods, built, of course, when the soil was cultivated many years ago, and am surprised to see slight stones still lying one upon another, as the builder placed them, while this huge oak has grown up from a chance acorn in the soil.

Though a man were known to have only one acquaintance in the world, yet there are so many men in

the world, and they are so much alike, that when he spoke what might be construed personally, no one would know certainly whom he meant. Though there were but two on a desolate island, they would conduct toward each other in this respect as if each had intercourse with a thousand others.

I saw in Canada two or three persons wearing homespun gray greatcoats, with comical and conical hoods which fell back on their backs between the shoulders, like small bags ready to be turned up over the head when need was, though then a hat usurped that place. I saw that these must be what are called capots. They looked as if they would be convenient and proper enough as long as the coats were new and tidy, but as if they would soon come to look like rags and unsightly.[1]

Nov. 11. Gathered to-day the autumnal dandelion(?) and the common dandelion.

Some farmers' wives use the white ashes of corn-cobs instead of pearlash.

I am attracted by a fence made of white pine roots. There is, or rather was, one (for it has been tipped into the gutter this year) on the road to Hubbard's Bridge which I can remember for more than twenty years. It is almost as indestructible as a wall and certainly requires fewer repairs. It is light, white, and dry withal, and its fantastic forms are agreeable to my eye. One would not have believed that any trees had such snarled

[1] [*Excursions*, p. 99; Riv. 123.]

Vol. II

and gnarled roots. In some instances you have a coarse network of roots as they interlaced on the surface perhaps of a swamp, which, set on its edge, really looks like a fence, with its paling crossing at various angles, and root repeatedly growing into root, — a rare phenomenon above ground, — so as to leave open spaces, square and diamond-shaped and triangular, quite like a length of fence. It is remarkable how white and clean these roots are, and that no lichens, or very few, grow on them; so free from decay are they. The different branches of the roots continually grow into one another, so as to make grotesque figures, sometimes rude harps whose resonant strings of roots give a sort of musical sound when struck, such as the earth spirit might play on. Sometimes the roots are of a delicate wine-color here and there, an evening tint. No line of fence could be too long for me to study each individual stump. Rocks would have been covered with lichens by this time. Perhaps they are grown into one another that they may stand more firmly.

Now is the time for wild apples. I pluck them as a wild fruit native to this quarter of the earth, fruit of old trees that have been dying ever since I was a boy and are not yet dead. From the appearance of the tree you would expect nothing but lichens to drop from it, but underneath your faith is rewarded by finding the ground strewn with spirited fruit. Frequented only by the woodpecker, deserted now by the farmer, who has not faith enough to look under the boughs.[1] Food for walkers. Sometimes apples red inside, perfused with a

[1] [*Excursions*, p. 309; Riv. 379.]

beautiful blush, faery food, too beautiful to eat, — apple of the evening sky, of the Hesperides.[1]

This afternoon I heard a single cricket singing, chirruping, in a bank, the only one I have heard for a long time, like a squirrel or a little bird, clear and shrill, — as I fancied, like an evening robin, singing in this evening of the year. A very fine and poetical strain for such a little singer. I had never before heard the cricket so like a bird. It is a remarkable note. The earth-song.

That delicate, waving, feathery dry grass which I saw yesterday is to be remembered with the autumn. The dry grasses are not dead for me. A beautiful form has as much life at one season as another.

I notice that everywhere in the pastures minute young fragrant life-everlasting, with only four or five flat-lying leaves and thread-like roots, all together as big as a fourpence, spot the ground, like winter rye and grass which roots itself in the fall against another year. These little things have bespoken their places for the next season. They have a little pellet of cotton or down in their centres, ready for an early start in the spring.

The autumnal (?) dandelion is still bright.

I saw an old bone in the woods covered with lichens, which looked like the bone of an old settler, which yet some little animal had recently gnawed, and I plainly saw the marks of its teeth, so indefatigable is Nature to strip the flesh from bones and return it to dust again. No little rambling beast can go by some dry and ancient bone but he must turn aside and try his teeth upon it.

[1] [*Excursions*, p. 315; Riv. 387.]

An old bone is knocked about till it becomes dust; Nature has no mercy on it. It was quite too ancient to suggest disagreeable associations. It was like a piece of dry pine root. It survives like the memory of a man. With time all that was personal and offensive wears off. The tooth of envy may sometimes gnaw it and reduce it more rapidly, but it is much more a prey to forgetfulness. Lichens grow upon it, and at last, in what moment no man knows, it has completely wasted away and ceases to be a bone any longer.

The fields are covered now with the empty cups of the *Trichostema dichotomum*, all dry.

We had a remarkable sunset to-night. I was walking in the meadow, the source of Nut Meadow Brook.[1]

[Two pages missing.]

We walked in so pure and bright a light, so softly and serenely bright, I thought I had never bathed in such a golden flood, without a ripple or a murmur to it. The west side of every wood and rising ground gleamed like the boundary of Elysium.[2] An adventurous spirit turns the evening into morning. A little black brook in the midst of the marsh, just beginning to meander, winding slowly round a decaying stump,— an artery of the meadow.[3]

Some circumstantial evidence is very strong, as when you find a trout in the milk.

A people who would begin by burning the fences and let the forest stand! I saw the fences half consumed,

[1] [*Excursions*, p. 246; Riv. 302.]
[2] [*Excursions*, p. 247; Riv. 303.]
[3] [*Excursions*, p. 247; Riv. 303.]

Vol. II

inches in diameter though the rock was uneven, and was handsomely shaded by a darker stripe of older leaves, an inch or more wide, just within its circumference, like a rich lamp-mat. The recent growth on the outside, half an inch in width, was a sort of tea-green or bluish-green color.

The ivy berries are now sere and yellowish, or sand-colored, like the berries of the dogwood.

The farmers are now casting out their manure, and removing the muck-heap from the shore of ponds where it will be inaccessible in the winter; or are doing their fall plowing, which destroys many insects and mellows the soil. I also see some pulling their turnips, and even getting in corn which has been left out notwithstanding the crows. Those who have wood to sell, as the weather grows colder and people can better appreciate the value of fuel, lot off their woods and advertise a wood auction.

You can tell when a cat has seen a dog by the size of her tail.

Nov. 16. I found three good arrowheads to-day behind Dennis's. The season for them began some time ago, as soon as the farmers had sown their winter rye, but the spring, after the melting of the snow, is still better.

I am accustomed to regard the smallest brook with as much interest for the time being as if it were the Orinoco or Mississippi. What is the difference, I would like to know, but mere size? And when a tributary rill empties in, it is like the confluence of famous rivers I have read

their ends lost in the middle of the prairie, and some worldly miser with a surveyor looking after his bounds, while heaven had taken place around him, and he did not see the angels around, but was looking for an old post-hole in the midst of paradise. I looked again and saw him standing in the middle of a boggy Stygian fen, surrounded by devils, and he had found his bounds without a doubt, three little stones where a stake had been driven, and, looking nearer, I saw that the Prince of Darkness was his surveyor.[1]

Nov. 14. Saw to-day, while surveying in the Second Division woods, a singular round mound in a valley, made perhaps sixty or seventy years ago. Cyrus Stow thought it was a pigeon-bed, but I soon discovered the coal and that it was an old coal-pit. I once mistook one in the Maine woods for an Indian mound. The indestructible charcoal told the tale. I had noticed singular holes and trenches in the former wood, as if a fox had been dug out. The sun has probably been let in here many times, and this has been a cultivated field; and now it is clothed in a savage dress again. The wild, rank, luxuriant place is where mosses and lichens abound. We find no heroes' cairns except those of heroic colliers, who once sweated here begrimed and dingy, who lodged here, tending their fires, who lay on a beetle here, perchance, to keep awake.

Nov. 15. I saw to-day a very perfect lichen on a rock in a meadow. It formed a perfect circle about fifteen

[1] [*Excursions*, p. 212; Riv. 259, 260.]

of. When I cross one on a fence, I love to pause in mid-passage and look down into the water, and study its bottom, its little mystery. There is none so small but you may see a pickerel regarding you with a wary eye, or a pygmy trout glance from under the bank, or in spring, perchance, a sucker will have found its way far up its stream. You are sometimes astonished to see a pickerel far up some now shrunken rill, where it is a mere puddle by the roadside. I have stooped to drink at a clear spring no bigger than a bushel basket in a meadow, from which a rill was scarcely seen to dribble away, and seen lurking at its bottom two little pickerel not so big as my finger, sole monarchs of this their ocean, and who probably would never visit a larger water.

In literature it is only the wild that attracts us. Dullness is only another name for tameness. It is the untamed, uncivilized, free, and wild thinking in Hamlet, in the Iliad, and in all the scriptures and mythologies that delights us, — not learned in the schools, not refined and polished by art. A truly good book is something as wildly natural and primitive, mysterious and marvellous, ambrosial and fertile, as a fungus or a lichen.[1] Suppose the muskrat or beaver were to turn his views [*sic*] to literature, what fresh views of nature would he present! The fault of our books and other deeds is that they are too humane, I want something speaking in some measure to the condition of muskrats and skunk-cabbage as well as of men, — not merely to a pining and complaining coterie of philanthropists.

I discover again about these times that cranberries are

[1] [*Excursions*, p. 231; Riv. 283.]

good to eat in small quantities as you are crossing the meadows.

I hear deep amid the birches some row among the birds or the squirrels, where evidently some mystery is being developed to them. The jay is on the alert, mimicking every woodland note. What *has* happened? Who's dead? The twitter retreats before you, and you are never let into the secret. Some tragedy surely is being enacted, but murder will out. How many little dramas are enacted in the depth of the woods at which man is not present!

When I am considering which way I will walk, my needle is slow to settle, my compass varies by a few degrees and does not always point due southwest; and there is good authority for these variations in the heavens. It pursues the straighter course for it at last, like the ball which has come out of a rifle, or the quoit that is twirled when cast. To-day it is some particular wood or meadow or deserted pasture in that direction that is my southwest.[1]

I love my friends very much, but I find that it is of no use to go to see them. I hate them commonly when I am near them. They belie themselves and deny me continually.

Somebody shut the cat's tail in the door just now, and she made such a caterwaul as has driven two whole worlds out of my thoughts. I saw unspeakable things in the sky and looming in the horizon of my mind, and now they are all reduced to a cat's tail. Vast films of thought floated through my brain, like clouds pregnant

[1] [*Excursions*, p. 217; Riv. 266.]

with rain enough to fertilize and restore a world, and now they are all dissipated.

There is a place whither I should walk to-day. Though oftenest I fail to find, when by accident I ramble into it, great is my delight. I have stood by my door sometimes half an hour, irresolute as to what course I should take.[1]

Apparently all but the evergreens and oaks have lost their leaves now. It is singular that the shrub oaks retain their leaves through the winter. Why do they?

The walnut trees spot the sky with black nuts. Only catkins are seen on the birches.

I saw the other day a dead limb which the wind or some other cause had broken nearly off, which had lost none of its leaves, though all the rest of the tree, which was flourishing, had shed them.

There seems to be in the fall a sort of attempt at a spring, a rejuvenescence, as if the winter were not expected by a part of nature. Violets, dandelions, and some other flowers blossom again, and mulleins and innumerable other plants begin again to spring and are only checked by the increasing cold. There is a slight uncertainty whether there will be any winter this year.

I was pleased to-day to hear a great noise and trampling in the woods produced by some cows which came running toward their homes, which apparently had been scared by something unusual, as their ancestors might have been by wolves. I have known sheep to be scared in the same [way] and a whole flock to run bleating to me for protection.

[1] [*Excursions*, p. 217; Riv. 265, 266.]

Vol. II

What shall we do with a man who is afraid of the woods, their solitude and darkness? What salvation is there for him? God is silent and mysterious.

Some of our richest days are those in which no sun shines outwardly, but so much the more a sun shines inwardly. I love nature, I love the landscape, because it is so sincere. It never cheats me. It never jests. It is cheerfully, musically earnest. I lie and relie [*sic*] on the earth.

Land where the wood has been cut off and is just beginning to come up again is called sprout land.

The sweet-scented life-everlasting has not lost its scent yet, but smells like the balm of the fields.

The partridge-berry leaves checker the ground on the side of moist hillsides in the woods. Are *they* not properly called *checker*-berries?

The era of wild apples will soon be over. I wander through old orchards of great extent, now all gone to decay, all of native fruit which for the most part went to the cider-mill. But since the temperance reform and the general introduction of grafted fruit, no wild apples, such as I see everywhere in deserted pastures, and where the woods have grown up among them, are set out. I fear that he who walks over these hills a century hence will not know the pleasure of knocking off wild apples. Ah, poor man! there are many pleasures which he will be debarred from! Notwithstanding the prevalence of the Baldwin and the Porter, I doubt if as extensive orchards are set out to-day in this town as there were a century ago, when these vast straggling cider-orchards were planted. Men stuck in a tree then by every wall-

side and let it take its chance. I see nobody planting trees to-day in such out of the way places, along almost every road and lane and wall-side, and at the bottom of dells in the wood. Now that they have grafted trees and pay a price for them, they collect them into a plot by their houses and fence them in.[1]

My Journal should be the record of my love. I would write in it only of the things I love, my affection for any aspect of the world, what I love to think of. I have no more distinctness or pointedness in my yearnings than an expanding bud, which does indeed point to flower and fruit, to summer and autumn, but is aware of the warm sun and spring influence only. I feel ripe for something, yet do nothing, can't discover what that thing is. I feel fertile merely. It is seedtime with me. I have lain fallow long enough.

Notwithstanding a sense of unworthiness which possesses me, not without reason, notwithstanding that I regard myself as a good deal of a scamp, yet for the most part the spirit of the universe is unaccountably kind to me, and I enjoy perhaps an unusual share of happiness. Yet I question sometimes if there is not some settlement to come.

Nov. 17. It is a strange age of the world this, when empires, kingdoms, and republics come a-begging to our doors and utter their complaints at our elbows. I cannot take up a newspaper but I find that some wretched government or other, hard pushed and on its last legs, is interceding with me, the reader, to vote for it, —

[1] [*Excursions*, p. 321; Riv. 394, 395.]

more importunate than an Italian beggar. Why does it not keep its castle in silence, as I do? The poor President, what with preserving his popularity and doing his duty, does not know what to do. If you do not read the newspapers, you may be impeached for treason. The newspapers are the ruling power. What Congress does is an afterclap. Any other government is reduced to a few marines at Fort Independence. If a man neglects to read the Daily Times, government will go on its knees to him; this is the only treason in these days. The newspapers devote some of their columns specially to government and politics without charge, and this is all that saves it, but I never read those columns.[1]

I found this afternoon, in a field of winter rye, a snapping turtle's egg, white and elliptical like a pebble, mistaking it for which I broke it. The little turtle was perfectly formed, even to the dorsal ridge, which was distinctly visible.

"Chesipooc Sinus" is on Wytfliet's Map of 159–.

Even the Dutch were forward to claim the great river of Canada. In a map of New Belgium in Ogilby's "America," 1670, the St. Lawrence is also called "De Groote Rivier van Niew Nederlandt."[2]

On this same map, east of Lake Champlain, called "Lacus Irocoisiensis" or in Dutch "Meer der Irocoisen," is a chain of mountains answering to the Green Mountains of Vermont, and "Irocoisia," or the country of the Iroquois, between the mountains and the lake.

[1] [Cape Cod, and Miscellanies, pp. 480, 481; Misc., Riv. 285, 286.]
[2] [Excursions, p. 91; Riv. 113.]

Vol. II

again as if for another spring. They had sprung up freshly a foot or more, and were budded to blossom, fresh and green. And sometimes on the same stem were old and dry and white downy flowers, and fresh green blossom-buds not yet expanded. I saw there some *pale* blue asters still bright, and the mullein leaves still large and green, one green to its top. And I discovered that when I put my hand on the mullein leaves they felt decidedly warm, but the radical leaves of the goldenrods felt cold and clammy. There was also the columbine, its leaves still alive and green; and I was pleased to smell the pennyroyal which I had bruised, though this dried up long ago. Each season is thus drawn out and lingers in certain localities, as the birds and insects know very well. If you penetrate to some warm recess under a cliff in the woods, you will be astonished at the amount of summer life that still flourishes there. No doubt more of the summer's life than we are aware thus slips by and outmanœuvres the winter, gliding from fence to fence. I have no doubt that a diligent search in proper places would discover many more of our summer flowers thus lingering till the snow came, than we suspect. It is as if the plant made no preparation for winter.

Now that the grass is withered and the leaves are withered or fallen, it begins to appear what is evergreen: the partridge[-berry] and checkerberry, and wintergreen leaves even, are more conspicuous.

The old leaves have been off the pines now for a month.

I once found a kernel of corn in the middle of a deep wood by Walden, tucked in behind a lichen on a pine,

Nov. 19. The first really cold day. I find, on breaking off a shrub oak leaf, a little life at the foot of the leafstalk, so that a part of the green comes off. It has not died quite down to the point of separation, as it will do, I suppose, before spring. Most of the oaks have lost their leaves except on the lower branches, as if they were less exposed and less mature there, and felt the changes of the seasons less. The leaves have either fallen or withered long since, yet I found this afternoon, cold as it is, — and there has been snow in the neighborhood, — some sprouts which had come up this year from the stump of a young black-looking oak, covered still with handsome fresh red and green leaves, very large and unwithered and unwilted. It was on the south side of Fair Haven in a warm angle, where the wood was cut last winter and the exposed edge of the still standing wood running north and south met the cliff at right angles and served for a fence to keep off the wind. There were one or two stumps here whose sprouts had fresh leaves which transported me back to October. Yet the surrounding shrub oak leaves were as dry and dead as usual. There were also some minute birches only a year old, their leaves still freshly yellow, and some young wild apple trees apparently still growing, their leaves as green and tender as in summer. The goldenrods, one or more species of the white and some yellow ones, were many of them still quite fresh, though elsewhere they are all whitish and dry. I saw one whose top rose above the edge of a rock, and so much of it was turned white and dry; but the lower part of its raceme was still yellow. Some of the white species seemed to have started

about as high as my head, either by a crow or a squirrel. It was a mile at least from any corn-field.

Several species plainly linger till the snow comes.

Nov. 20. It is a common saying among country people that if you eat much fried hasty pudding it will make your hair curl. My experience, which was considerable, did not confirm this assertion.

Horace Hosmer was picking out to-day half a bushel or more of a different and better kind of cranberry, as he thought, separating them from the rest. They are very dark red, shaded with lighter, harder and more oblong, somewhat like the fruit of the sweet-briar or a Canada red plum, though I have no common cranberry to compare with them. He says that they grow apart from the others. I must see him about it. It may prove to be one more of those instances in which the farmer detects a new species and makes use of the knowledge from year to year in his profession, while the botanist expressly devoted to such investigation has failed to observe it.

The farmer, in picking over many bushels of cranberries year after year, finds at length, or has forced upon his observation, a new species of that berry, and avails himself thereafter of his discovery for many years before the naturalist is aware of the fact.

Desor, who has been among the Indians at Lake Superior this summer, told me the other day that they had a particular name for each species of tree, as of the maple, but they had but one word for flowers; they did not distinguish the species of the last.

It is often the unscientific man who discovers the new species. It would be strange if it were not so. But we are accustomed properly to call that only a scientific discovery which knows the relative value of the thing discovered, uncovers a fact to mankind.

Nov. 21. For a month past the grass under the pines has been covered with a new carpet of pine leaves. It is remarkable that the old leaves turn and fall in so short a time.

Some of the densest and most impenetrable clumps of bushes I have seen, as well on account of the closeness of their branches as of their thorns, have been wild apples. Its [*sic*] branches as stiff as those of the black spruce on the tops of mountains.[1]

I saw a herd of a dozen cows and young steers and oxen on Conantum this afternoon, running about and frisking in unwieldy sport like huge rats. Any sportiveness in cattle is unexpected. They even played like kittens, in their way; shook their heads, raised their tails, and rushed up and down the hill.[2]

The witch-hazel blossom on Conantum has for the most part lost its ribbons now.

Some distant angle in the sun where a lofty and dense white pine wood, with mingled gray and green, meets a hill covered with shrub oaks, affects me singularly, reinspiring me with all the dreams of my youth. It is a place far away, yet actual and where we have been. I saw the sun falling on a distant white pine wood whose gray and

[1] [*Excursions*, p. 304; Riv. 373.]
[2] [*Excursions*, p. 235; Riv. 287, 288.]

moss-covered stems were visible amid the green, in an angle where this forest abutted on a hill covered with shrub oaks. It was like looking into dreamland. It is one of the avenues to my future. Certain coincidences like this are accompanied by a certain flash as of hazy lightning, flooding all the world suddenly with a tremulous serene light which it is difficult to see long at a time.

I saw Fair Haven Pond with its island, and meadow between the island and the shore, and a strip of perfectly still and smooth water in the lee of the island, and two hawks, fish hawks perhaps, sailing over it. I did not see how it could be improved. Yet I do not see what these things can be. I begin to see such an object when I cease to *understand* it and see that I did not realize or appreciate it before, but I get no further than this. How adapted these forms and colors to my eye! A meadow and an island! What are these things? Yet the hawks and the ducks keep so aloof! and Nature is so reserved! I am made to love the pond and the meadow, as the wind is made to ripple the water.[1]

As I looked on the Walden woods eastward across the pond, I saw suddenly a white cloud rising above their tops, now here, now there, marking the progress of the cars which were rolling toward Boston far below, behind many hills and woods.

October must be the month of ripe and tinted leaves. Throughout November they are almost entirely withered and sombre, the few that remain. In this month the sun is valued. When it shines warmer or brighter we are sure to observe it. There are not so many colors to attract

[1] [See p. 161.]

the eye. We begin to remember the summer. We walk fast to keep warm. For a month past I have sat by a fire.

Every sunset inspires me with the desire to go to a *West* as distant and as fair as that into which the sun goes down.[1]

I get nothing to eat in my walks now but wild apples, sometimes some cranberries, and some walnuts. The squirrels have got the hazelnuts and chestnuts.

Nov. 23. To-day it has been finger-cold.[2] Unexpectedly I found ice by the side of the brooks this afternoon nearly an inch thick. Prudent people get in their barrels of apples to-day.[3] The difference of the temperature of various localities is greater than is supposed. If I was surprised to find ice on the sides of the brooks, I was much more surprised to find quite a pond in the woods, containing an acre or more, quite frozen over so that I walked across it. It was in a cold corner, where a pine wood excluded the sun. In the larger ponds and the river, of course, there is no ice yet. It is a shallow, weedy pond. I lay down on the ice and looked through at the bottom. The plants appeared to grow more uprightly than on the dry land, being sustained and protected by the water. Caddis-worms were everywhere crawling about in their handsome quiver-like sheaths or cases.

The wild apples, though they are more mellow and edible, have for some time lost their beauty, as well as

[1] [*Excursions*, p. 219; Riv. 268.]   [3] [*Ibid.*]
[2] [*Excursions*, p. 319; Riv. 392.]

the leaves, and now too they are beginning to freeze. The apple season is well-nigh over. Such, however, as are frozen while sound are not unpleasant to eat when the spring sun thaws them.[1]

I find it to be the height of wisdom not to endeavor to oversee myself and live a life of prudence and common sense, but to see over and above myself, entertain sublime conjectures, to make myself the thoroughfare of thrilling thoughts, live all that can be lived. The man who is dissatisfied with himself, what can he not do?

Nov. 24. Plucked a buttercup on Bear Hill to-day.

I have certain friends whom I visit occasionally, but I commonly part from them early with a certain bitter-sweet sentiment. That which we love is so mixed and entangled with that we hate in one another that we are more grieved and disappointed, aye, and estranged from one another, by meeting than by absence. Some men may be my acquaintances merely, but one whom I have been accustomed to regard, to idealize, to have dreams about as a friend, and mix up intimately with myself, can never degenerate into an acquaintance. I must know him on that higher ground or not know him at all. We do not confess and explain, because we would fain be so intimately related as to understand each other without speech. Our friend must be broad. His must be an atmosphere coextensive with the universe, in which we can expand and breathe. For the most part we are smothered and stifled by one another. I go and see my friend and try his atmosphere. If our

[1] [*Excursions*, p. 319; Riv. 392.]

Vol. II

atmospheres do not mingle, if we repel each other strongly, it is of no use to stay.

Nov. 25. I feel a little alarmed when it happens that I have walked a mile into the woods bodily, without getting there in spirit. I would fain forget all my morning's occupation, my obligations to society. But sometimes it happens that I cannot easily shake off the village; the thought of some work, some surveying, will run in my head, and I am not where my body is, I am out of my senses. In my walks I would return to my senses like a bird or a beast. What business have I in the woods, if I am thinking of something out of the woods?[1]

This afternoon, late and cold as it is, has been a sort of Indian summer. Indeed, I think that we have summer days from time to time the winter through, and that it is often the snow on the ground makes the whole difference. This afternoon the air was indescribably clear and exhilarating, and though the thermometer would have shown it to be cold, I thought that there was a finer and purer warmth than in summer; a wholesome, intellectual warmth, in which the body was warmed by the mind's contentment. The warmth was hardly sensuous, but rather the satisfaction of existence.

I found Fair Haven skimmed entirely over, though the stones which I threw down on it from the high bank on the east broke through. Yet the river was open. The landscape looked singularly clean and pure and dry, the air, like a pure glass, being laid over the picture,

[1] [*Excursions*, p. 211; Riv. 258, 259.]

Vol. II

---

the trees so tidy, stripped of their leaves; the meadows and pastures, clothed with clean dry grass, looked as if they had been swept; ice on the water and winter in the air, but yet not a particle of snow on the ground. The woods, divested in great part of their leaves, are being ventilated. It is the season of perfect works, of hard, tough, ripe twigs, not of tender buds and leaves. The leaves have made their wood, and a myriad new withes stand up all around pointing to the sky, able to survive the cold. It is only the perennial that you see, the iron age of the year.

These expansions of the river skim over before the river itself takes on its icy fetters. What is the analogy?

I saw a muskrat come out of a hole in the ice. He is a man wilder than Ray or Melvin. While I am looking at him, I am thinking what he is thinking of me. He is a different sort of a man, that is all. He would dive when I went nearer, then reappear again, and had kept open a place five or six feet square so that it had not frozen, by swimming about in it. Then he would sit on the edge of the ice and busy himself about something, I could not see whether it was a clam or not. What a cold-blooded fellow! thoughts at a low temperature, sitting perfectly still so long on ice covered with water, mumbling a cold, wet clam in its shell. What safe, low, moderate thoughts it must have! It does not get on to stilts. The generations of muskrats do not fail. They are not preserved by the legislature of Massachusetts.

Boats are drawn up high which will not be launched again till spring.

There is a beautiful fine wild grass which grows in the path in sprout land, now dry, white, and waving, in light beds soft to the touch.

I experience such an interior comfort, far removed from the sense of cold, as if the thin atmosphere were rarefied by heat, were the medium of invisible flames, as if the whole landscape were one great hearthside, that where the shrub oak leaves rustle on the hillside, I seem to hear a crackling fire and see the pure flame, and I wonder that the dry leaves do not blaze into yellow flames.

I find but little change yet on the south side of the Cliffs; only the leaves of the wild apple are a little frostbitten on their edges and curled dry there; but some wild cherry leaves and blueberries are still fresh and tender green and red, as well as all the other leaves and plants which I noticed there the other day.

When I got up so high on the side of the Cliff the sun was setting like an Indian-summer sun. There was a purple tint in the horizon. It was warm on the face of the rocks, and I could have sat till the sun disappeared, to dream there. It was a mild sunset such as is to be attended to. Just as the sun shines into us warmly and serenely, our Creator breathes on us and re-creates us.

Nov. 26. An inch of snow on ground this morning, — our first.

Went to-night to see the Indians, who are still living in tents. Showed the horns of the moose, the black moose they call it, that goes in lowlands. Horns three

---

or four feet wide. (The red moose they say is another kind; runs on mountains and has horns six feet wide.) Can move their horns. The broad, flat side portions of the horns are covered with hair, and are so soft when the creature is alive that you can run a knife through them.[1] They color the lower portions a darker color by rubbing them on alders, etc., to harden them. Make *kee-nong-gun* or pappoose cradle, of the broad part of the horn, putting a rim on it. Once scared, will run all day. A dog will hang to their lips and be carried along and swung against a tree and drop off. Always find two or three together. Can't run on glare ice, but can run in snow four feet deep. The caribou can run on ice.[2] Sometimes spear them with a sharp pole, sometimes with a knife at the end of a pole. Signs, good or bad, from the turn of the horns. Their caribou-horns had been gnawed by mice in their wigwams. The moose-horns and others are not gnawed by mice while the creature is alive. Moose cover themselves with water, all but noses, to escape flies.[3] About as many now as fifty years ago.

Imitated the sounds of the moose, caribou, and deer with a birch-bark horn, which last they sometimes make very long. The moose can be heard eight or ten miles sometimes, — a loud sort of bellowing sound, clearer, more sonorous than the looing of cattle. The caribou's, a sort of snort; the small deer, like a lamb.

Made their clothes of the young moose-skin. Cure the meat by smoking it; use no salt in curing it, but when they eat it.

[1] [*Maine Woods*, p. 153; Riv. 187.]   [2] [*Ibid.*]   [3] [*Ibid.*]

Their spear very serviceable. The inner, pointed part, of a hemlock knot; the side spring pieces, of hickory. Spear salmon, pickerel, trout, chub, etc.; also by birch-bark light at night, using the other end of spear as pole.

Their sled, *jeborgon* or *jebongon* (?), one foot wide, four or five long, of thin wood turned up in front; draw by a strong rope of basswood bark.

Canoe of moose-hide. One hide will hold three or four. Can be taken apart and put together very quickly. Can take out cross-bars and bring the sides together. A very convenient boat to carry and cross streams with. They say they did not make birch canoes till they had edge tools. The birches the lightest. They think our birches the same, only second growth.

Their *kee-nong-gun*, or cradle, has a hoop to prevent the child being hurt when it falls. Can't eat dirt; can be hung up out of way of snakes.

Aboak-henjo [?], a birch-bark vessel for water. Can boil meat in it with hot stones; takes a long time. Also a vessel of birch bark, shaped like a pan. Both ornamented by scratching the bark, which is wrong side out. Very neatly made. Valued our kettles much.

Did not know use of eye in axe. Put a string through it and wore it round neck. Cut toes.

Did not like gun. Killed one moose; scared all the rest.

The *squaw-heegun* for cooking, a mere stick put

through the game and stuck in the ground slanted over the fire, a spit. Can be eating one side while the other is doing.

The *ar-tu-e-se*, a stick, string, and bunch of leaves, which they toss and catch on the point of the stick. Make great use of it. Make the clouds go off the sun with it.

Snowshoes of two kinds; one of same shape at both ends so that the Mohawks could not tell which way they were going. (Put some rags in the heel-hole to make a toe-mark?)

Log trap to catch many kinds of animals. Some for bears let the log fall six or seven feet. First there is a frame, then the little stick 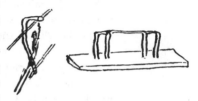 which the animal moves, presses down, as he goes through under the log; then the crooked stick is hung over the top of the frame, and holds up the log by a string; the weight of the log on this keeps the little stick up.

Side View

A drizzling and misty day this has been, melting the snow. The mist, divided into a thousand ghostly forms, was blowing across Walden. Mr. Emerson's Cliff Hill, seen from the railroad through the mist, looked like a dark, heavy, frowning New Hampshire mountain. I do not understand fully why hills look so much larger

Vol. II

at such a time, unless, being the most distant we see and in the horizon, we suppose them farther off and so magnify them. I think there can be no looming about it.

Nov. 28. Thursday. Cold drizzling and misty rains, which have melted the little snow. The farmers are beginning to pick up their dead wood. Within a day or two the walker finds gloves to be comfortable, and begins to think of an outside coat and of boots. Embarks in his boots for the winter voyage.

The Indian talked about "our folks" and "your folks," "my grandfather" and "my grandfather's cousin," Samoset.

It is remarkable, but nevertheless true, as far as my observation goes, that women, to whom we commonly concede a somewhat finer and more sibylline nature, yield a more implicit obedience even to their animal instincts than men. The nature in them is stronger, the reason weaker. There are, for instance, many young and middle-aged men among my acquaintance — shoemakers, carpenters, farmers, and others — who have scruples about using animal food, but comparatively few girls or women. The latter, even the most refined, are the most intolerant of such reforms. I think that the reformer of the severest, as well as finest, class will find more sympathy in the intellect and philosophy of man than in the refinement and delicacy of woman. It is, perchance, a part of woman's conformity and easy nature. Her savior must not be too strong, stern, and intellectual, but charitable above all things.

The thought of its greater independence and its close-

ness to nature diminishes the pain I feel when I see a more interesting child than usual destined to be brought up in a shanty. I see that for the present the child is happy and is not puny, and has all the wonders of nature for its toys. Have I not faith that its tenderness will in some way be cherished and protected, as the buds of the spring in the remotest and wildest wintry dell no less than in the garden plot and summer-house?

> I am the little Irish boy
>   That lives in the shanty.
> I am four years old to-day
>   And shall soon be one and twenty.
>
>   I shall grow up
>   And be a great man,
>   And shovel all day
>   As hard as I can.
>
>   Down in the Deep Cut,
>   .   .   .   .   .
>   Where the men lived
>   Who made the railroad.
>
> For supper
>   I have some potato
>   And sometimes some bread,
>   And then, if it's cold,
>   I go right to bed.
>
>   I lie on some straw
>   Under my father's coat.

At recess I play
With little Billy Gray,
And when school is done,
Then home I run.

And if I meet the cars,
    I get on the other track,
And then I know whatever comes
    I need n't look back.

My mother does not cry,
    And my father does not scold,
For I am a little Irish boy,
    And I 'm four years old.

Every day I go to school
    Along the railroad.
It was so cold it made me cry
    The day that it snowed.

And if my feet ache
    I do not mind the cold,
For I am a little Irish boy,
    And I 'm four years old.[1]

Nov. 29. Still misty, drizzling weather without snow
or ice. The puffballs, with their open rays, checker
the path-side in the woods, but they are not yet dry
enough to make much dust. Damp weather in the fall
seems to cause them to crack open, *i. e.* their outer skin.

[1] [See *Journal*, vol. iii, pp. 149, 150, 241–244.]

Vol. II

II

DECEMBER, 1850

(ÆT. 33)

Dec. 1. It is quite mild and pleasant to-day. I saw a
little green hemisphere of moss which looked as if it
covered a stone, but, thrusting my cane into it, I found
it was nothing but moss, about fifteen inches in diameter
and eight or nine inches high. When I broke it up, it
appeared as if the annual growth was marked by successive layers half an inch deep each. The lower ones
were quite rotten, but the present year's quite green,
the intermediate white. I counted fifteen or eighteen.
It was quite solid, and I saw that it continued solid as it
grew by branching occasionally, just enough to fill the
newly gained space, and the tender extremities of each
plant, crowded close together, made the firm and compact surface of the bed. There was a darker line separating the growths, where I thought the surface had been
exposed to the winter. It was quite saturated with
water, though firm and solid.

Dec. 2. The woodpeckers' holes in the apple trees are
about a fifth of an inch deep or just through the bark and
half an inch apart. They must be the decaying trees that
are most frequented by them, and probably their work
serves to relieve and ventilate the tree and, as well, to
destroy its enemies.

They look white like the shells of five-fingers on the
shore.

The trees and shrubs look larger than usual when seen
through the mist, perhaps because, though near, yet
being in the visible horizon and there being nothing
beyond to compare them with, we naturally magnify
them, supposing them further off.

It is very still yet in the woods. There are no leaves to
rustle, no crickets to chirp, and but few birds to sing.

The pines standing in the ocean of mist, seen from
the Cliffs, are trees in every stage of transition from the
actual to the imaginary. The near are more distinct, the
distant more faint, till at last they are a mere shadowy
cone in the distance. What, then, are these solid pines
become? You can command only a circle of thirty or
forty rods in diameter. As you advance, the trees gradually come out of the mist and take form before your
eyes. You are reminded of your dreams. Life looks like
a dream. You are prepared to see visions. And now,
just before sundown, the night wind blows up more mist
through the valley, thickening the veil which already
hung over the trees, and the gloom of night gathers early
and rapidly around. Birds lose their way.

The barberries are shrivelled and dried. I find yet
cranberries hard and not touched by the frost.

Dec. 4. *Wednesday.* Fair Haven Pond is now open,
and there is no snow. It is a beautiful, almost Indian-
summer, afternoon, though the air is more pure and
glassy. The shrub oak fire burns briskly as seen from
the Cliffs. The evergreens are greener than ever. I notice
the row of dwarf willows advanced into the water in
Fair Haven, three or four rods from the dry land, just
at the lowest water-mark. You can get no disease but
cold in such an atmosphere.

Though the sun is now an hour high, there is a peculiar
bright light on the pines and on their stems. The lichens
on their bark reflect it. In the horizon I see a succession
of the brows of hills, bare or covered with wood, — look
over the eyebrows of the recumbent earth. These are
separated by long valleys filled with vapory haze.

If there is a little more warmth than usual at this
season, then the beautiful air which belongs to winter is
perceived and appreciated.

Dec. 6. Being at Newburyport this evening, Dr.
(H. C.?) Perkins showed me the circulations in the
nitella, which is slightly different from the chara, under
a microscope. I saw plainly the circulation, looking like
bubbles going round in each joint, up one side and down
the other of a sort of white line, and sometimes a dark-
colored mote appeared to be carried along with them.
He said that the circulation could be well seen in the
common celandine, and moreover that when a shade

was cast on it by a knife-blade the circulation was reversed. Ether would stop it, or the death of the plant.

He showed me a green clamshell, — *Anodon fluviatilis*, — which he said was a *female* with young, found in a pond near by.

Also the head of a Chinook or Flathead.

Also the humerus of a mylodon (of Owen) from Oregon. Some more remains have been found in Missouri, and a whole skeleton in Buenos Ayres. A digging animal.

He could not catch his frogs asleep.

Dec. 8. It snowed in the night of the 6th, and the ground is now covered, — our first snow, two inches deep. A week ago I saw cows being driven home from pasture. Now they are kept at home. Here's an end to their grazing. The farmer improves this first slight snow to accomplish some pressing jobs, — to move some particular rocks on a drag, or the like. I perceive how quickly he has seized the opportunity. I see no tracks now of cows or men or boys beyond the edge of the wood. Suddenly they are shut up. The remote pastures and hills beyond the woods are now closed to cows and cowherds, aye, and to cowards. I am struck by this sudden solitude and remoteness which these places have acquired. The dear privacy and retirement and solitude which winter makes possible! carpeting the earth with snow, furnishing more than woolen feet to all walkers, cronching the snow only. From Fair Haven I see the hills and fields, aye, and the icy woods in the corner

shine, gleam with the dear old wintry sheen. Those are not surely the cottages I have seen all summer. They are some cottages which I have in my mind.

Now Fair Haven Pond is open and ground is covered with snow and ice; a week or two ago the pond was frozen and the ground was still bare.

Still those particular red oak leaves which I had noticed are quite unwilted under the cliffs, and the apple leaves, though standing in snow and ice and incrusted with the latter, still ripe red, and *tender* fresh green leaves.

It is interesting to observe the manner in which the plants bear their snowy burden. The dry calyx leaves, like an oblong cup, of the *Trichostema dichotomum* have caught the rain or melting snow, and so this little butter-boat is filled with a frozen pure drop which stands up high above the sides of the cup, — so many pearly drops covering the whole plant, — in the wood-paths. The pennyroyal there also retains its fragrance under the ice and snow.

I find that the indigo-weed, whose *shade* still stands and holds its black seed-vessels, is not too humble to escape enemies. Almost every seed-vessel, which contains half a dozen seeds or more, contains also a little black six-legged bug about as big as a bug [*sic*], which gnaws the seeds; and sometimes I find a grub, though it is now cold weather and the plant is covered with ice. Not only our peas and grain have their weevils, but the fruit of the indigo-weed!

This evening for the first time the new moon is reflected from the frozen snow-crust.

Vol. II

Dec. 13. The river froze over last night, — skimmed over.

Dec. 16. Walden is open still. The river is probably open again.

There are wild men living along the shores of the Frozen Ocean. Who shall say that there is not as great an interval between the civilized man and the savage as between the savage and the brute? The undiscovered polar regions are the home of men.

I am struck with the difference between my feet and my hands. My feet are much nearer to foreign or inanimate matter or nature than my hands; they are more brute, they are more like the earth they tread on, they are more clod-like and lumpish, and I scarcely animate them.

Last Sunday, or the 14th, I walked on Loring's Pond to three or four islands there which I had never visited, not having a boat in the summer. On one containing an acre or two, I found a low, branching shrub frozen into the edge of the ice, with a fine spicy scent somewhat like sweet-fern and a handsome imbricate bud. When I rubbed the dry-looking fruit in my hands, it felt greasy and stained them a permanent yellow, which I could not wash out; it lasted several days, and my fingers smelled medicinal. I conclude that it is sweet-gale, and we named the island Myrica Island.

On those unfrequented islands, too, I noticed the red osier or willow, that common hard-berried plant with small red buds,[1] apparently two kinds of swamp-pink buds, some yellow, some reddish, a brittle, rough yellow-

[1] Panicled andromeda.

ish bush with handsome pinkish shoots; in one place in the meadow the greatest quantity of wild rose hips of various forms that I ever saw, now slightly withered; they were as thick as winterberries.

I noticed a bush covered with cocoons which were artfully concealed by two leaves wrapped round them, one still hanging by its stem, so that they looked like a few withered leaves left dangling. The worm, having first encased itself in another leaf for greater protection, folded more loosely around itself one of the leaves of the plant, taking care, however, to encase the leaf-stalk and the twig with a thick and strong web of silk, so far from depending on the strength of the stalk, which is now quite brittle. The strongest fingers cannot break it, and the cocoon can only be got off by slipping it up and off the twig. There they hang themselves secure for the winter, proof against cold and the birds, ready to become butterflies when new leaves push forth.[1]

The snow everywhere was covered with snow-fleas like pepper. When you hold a mass in your hand, they skip and are gone before you know it. They are so small that they go through and through the new snow. Sometimes when collected they look like some powder which the hunter has spilled in the path.

Dec. 17. Flint's Pond apparently froze completely over last night. It is about two inches thick. Walden is only slightly skimmed over a rod from the shore. I noticed, where it had been frozen for some time near the shore of Flint's Pond and the ice was thicker and

[1] [Evidently cocoons of the Promethea moth.]

whiter, there were handsome spider-shaped dark places, where the under ice had melted, and the water had worn it running through, — a handsome figure on the icy carpet.

I noticed when the snow first came that the days were very sensibly lengthened by the light being reflected from the snow. Any work which required light could be pursued about half an hour longer. So that we may well pray that the ground may not be laid bare by a thaw in these short winter days.

Dec. 19. Yesterday I tracked a partridge in the new-fallen snow, till I came to where she took to flight, and I could track her no further. I see where the snowbirds have picked the seeds of the Roman wormwood and other weeds and have covered the snow with the shells and husks. The smilax berries are as plump as ever. The catkins of the alders are as tender and fresh-looking as ripe mulberries. The dried choke-cherries so abundant in the swamp are now quite sweet. The witch-hazel is covered with fruit and drops over gracefully like a willow, the yellow foundation of its flowers still remaining. I find the sweet-gale (*Myrica*) by the river also. The wild apples are frozen as hard as stones, and rattle in my pockets, but I find that they soon thaw when I get to my chamber and yield a sweet cider.[1] I am astonished that the animals make no more use of them.

Dec. 22. The apples are now thawed. This is their first thawing. Those which a month ago were sour,

[1] [*Excursions*, p. 320; Riv. 393.]

Vol. II

crabbed, and uneatable are now filled with a rich, sweet cider which I am better acquainted with than with wine. And others, which have more substance, are a sweet and luscious food, — in my opinion of more worth than the pineapples which are imported from the torrid zone. Those which a month ago I tasted and repented of it, which the farmer willingly left on the tree, I am now glad to find have the property of hanging on like the leaves of the shrub oak. It is a way to keep cider sweet without boiling. Let the frost come to freeze them first solid as stones, and then the sun or a warm winter day — for it takes but little heat — to thaw them, and they will seem to have borrowed a flavor from heaven through the medium of the air in which they hang. I find when I get home that they have thawed in my pocket and the ice is turned to cider. But I suspect that after the second freezing and thawing they will not be so good. I bend to drink the cup and save my lappets. What are the half-ripe fruits of the torrid south, to this fruit matured by the cold of the frigid north. There are those crabbed apples with which I cheated my companion, and kept a smooth face to tempt him to eat. Now we both greedily fill our pockets with them, and grow more social with their wine. Was there one that hung so high and sheltered by the tangled branches that our sticks could not dislodge it? It is a fruit never brought to market that I am aware of, — quite distinct from the apple of the markets, as from dried apple and cider. It is not every winter that produces it in perfection.[1]

In winter I can explore the swamps and ponds. It is

[1] [*Excursions*, pp. 319, 320; Riv. 392–394.]

a dark-aired winter day, yet I see the summer plants still peering above the snow. There are but few tracks in all this snow. It is the Yellow Knife River or the Saskatchewan. The large leafy lichens on the white pines, especially on the outside of the wood, look almost a golden yellow in the light reflected from the snow, while deeper in the wood they are ash-colored. In the swamps the dry, yellowish-colored fruit of the poison dogwood hangs like jewelry on long, drooping stems. It is pleasant to meet it, it has so much character relatively to man. Here is a stump on which a squirrel has sat and stripped the pine cones of a neighboring tree. Their cores and scales lie all around. He knew that they contained an almond[1] before the naturalist did. He has long been a close observer of Nature; opens her caskets. I see more tracks in the swamps than elsewhere.

Dec. 23. Here is an old-fashioned snow-storm. There is not much passing on railroads. The engineer says it is three feet deep above. Walden is frozen, one third of it, though I thought it was all frozen as I stood on the shore on one side only. There is no track on the Walden road. A traveller might cross it in the woods and not be sure it was a road. As I pass the farmers' houses I observe the cop [*sic*] of the sled propped up with a stick to prevent its freezing into the snow. The needles of the pines are drooping like cockerels' feathers after a rain, and frozen together by the sleety snow. The pitch pines now bear their snowy fruit.

[1] [See *Journal*, vol. i, p. 338.]

I can discern a faint foot or sled path sooner when the ground is covered with snow than when it is bare. The depression caused by the feet or the wheels is more obvious; perhaps the light and shade betray it, but I think it is mainly because the grass and weeds rise above it on each side and leave it blank, and a blank space of snow contrasts more strongly with the woods or grass than bare or beaten ground.

Even the surface of the snow is wont to be in waves like billows of the ocean.

Dec. 24. In walking across the Great Meadows to-day on the snow-crust, I noticed that the fine, dry snow which was blown over the surface of the frozen field, when I [looked] westward over it or toward the sun, looked precisely like steam curling up from its surface, as sometimes from a wet roof when the sun comes out after a rain.

The snow catches only in the hollows and against the reeds and grass, and never rests there, but when it has formed a broad and shallow drift or a long and narrow one like a winrow on the ice, it blows away again from one extremity, and leaves often a thin, tongue-like projection at one end, some inches above the firm crust.

I observe that there are many dead pine-needles sprinkled over the snow, which had not fallen before.

Saw a shrike pecking to pieces a small bird, apparently a snowbird. At length he took him up in his bill, almost half as big as himself, and flew slowly off with his prey dangling from his beak. I find that I had not associated such actions with my idea of birds. It was not birdlike.

It is never so cold but it melts somewhere. Our mason well remarked that he had sometimes known it to be melting and freezing at the same time on a particular side of a house; while it was melting on the roof the icicles [were] forming under the eaves. It is always melting and freezing at the same time when icicles are formed.

Our thoughts are with those among the dead into whose sphere we are rising, or who are now rising into our own. Others we inevitably forget, though they be brothers and sisters. Thus the departed may be nearer to us than when they were present. At death our friends and relations either draw nearer to us and are found out, or depart further from us and are forgotten. Friends are as often brought nearer together as separated by death.

Dec. 26. Thursday. The pine woods seen from the hilltops, now that the ground is covered with snow, are not green but a dark brown, greenish-brown perhaps. You see dark patches of wood. There are still half a dozen fresh ripe red and glossy oak leaves left on the bush under the Cliffs.

Walden not yet more than half frozen over.

Dec. 30. In R. Gordon Cumming's "Hunter's Life in South Africa," [1] I find an account of the honey-bird,

[1] [*Five Years of a Hunter's Life in the Far Interior of South Africa,* 1850.]

which will lead a person to a wild bees' nest and, having got its share of the spoil, will sometimes lead to a second and third. (Vol. I, page 49.)

He saw dry sheep's dung burning, and after eighteen months it was burning still. One heap was said to have burned seven years. Remarkable for burning slowly. (Page 62.)

He came across a Boer who manufactured ashes by burning a particular bush and sold it to the richer Boers. (Page 71.)

He says that the oryx or gemsbok, a kind of antelope, never tastes water. Lives on the deserts. (Page 94.)

The Bushmen conceal water in ostrich eggs at regular intervals across the desert, and so perform long journeys over them safely. (Page 101.)

The hatching of ostrich eggs not left to heat of sun. (Page 105.) The natives empty them by a small aperture at one end, fill with water, and cork up the hole with grass. (Page 106.)

The Hottentots devoured the marrow of a koodoo raw as a matter of course. [1]

The Bechuanas use "the assagai," "a sort of light spear or javelin" with a shaft six feet long, which they will send through a man's body at a hundred yards. (Page 201.)

The Bakatlas smelt and work in iron quite well; make spears, battle-axes, knives, needles, etc., etc. (Page 207.)

The skin of the eland just killed, like that of most

[1] [*Excursions,* p. 225; Riv. 275, 276.]

Vol. II

other antelopes, emits the most delicious perfume of trees and grass. (Page 218.) [1]

When waiting by night for elephants to approach a fountain, he "heard a low rumbling noise . . . , caused (as the Bechuanas affirmed) by the bowels of the elephants which were approaching the fountain." (Page 261.)

"A child can put a hundred of them [elephants] [2] to flight by passing at a quarter of a mile to windward." (Page 263.)

It is incredible how many "goodly" trees an elephant will destroy, sometimes wantonly. (265.)

An elephant's friend will protect its wounded companion at the risk of its own life. (268.)

The rhinoceros-birds stick their bills in the ear of the rhinoceros and wake him up when the hunter is approaching. They live on ticks and other parasitic insects on his body. He perfectly understands their warning. He has chased a rhinoceros many miles on horseback and fired many shots before he fell, and all the while the birds remained by him, perched on his back and sides, and as each bullet struck him they ascended about six feet into the air, uttering a cry of alarm, and then resumed their position. Sometimes they were swept off his back by branches of trees. When the rhinoceros was shot at midnight, they have remained by his body thinking him asleep, and on the hunter's approaching in the morning have tried to wake him up. (Page 293.)

[1] [*Excursions,* p. 225; Riv. 276.]
[2] [Thoreau supplies the word.]

The Bechuanas make a pipe in a few moments by kneading moistened earth with their knuckles on a twig, until a hole is established, then one end of the aperture is enlarged with their fingers for a bowl. (Page 306.)

Dec. 31. I observe that in the cut by Walden Pond the sand and stones fall from the overhanging bank and rest on the snow below; and thus, perchance, the stratum deposited by the side of the road in the winter can permanently be distinguished from the summer one by some faint seam, to be referred to the peculiar conditions under which it was deposited.

The pond has been frozen over since I was there last.

Certain meadows, as Heywood's, contain warmer water than others and are slow to freeze. I do not remember to have crossed this with impunity in all places. The brook that issues from it is still open completely, though the thermometer was down to eight below zero this morning.

The blue jays evidently notify each other of the presence of an intruder, and will sometimes make a great chattering about it, and so communicate the alarm to other birds and to beasts.

III

JANUARY – APRIL, 1851

(ÆT. 33)

Jan. 2. Saw at Clinton last night a room at the gingham-mills which covers one and seven-eighths acres and contains 578 looms, not to speak of spindles, both throttle and mule. The rooms all together cover three acres. They were using between three and four hundred horse-power, and kept an engine of two hundred horse-power, with a wheel twenty-three feet in diameter and a band ready to supply deficiencies, which have not often occurred. Some portion of the machinery — I think it was where the cotton was broken up, lightened up, and mixed before being matted together — revolved eighteen hundred times in a minute.

I first saw the pattern room where patterns are made by a hand loom. There were two styles of warps ready for the woof or filling. The operator must count the threads of the woof, which in the mill is done by the machinery. It was the ancient art of weaving, the shuttle flying back and forth, putting in the filling. As long as the warp is the same, it is but one " style," so called.

The cotton should possess a long staple and be clean and free from seed. The Sea Island cotton has a long staple and is valuable for thread. Many bales are thoroughly mixed to make the goods of one quality. The cotton is then torn to pieces and thoroughly light-

ened up by cylinders armed with hooks and by fans; then spread, a certain weight on a square yard, and matted together, and torn up and matted together again two or three times over; then the matted cotton fed to a cylindrical card, a very thin web of it, which is gathered into a copper trough, making six (the six-card machines) flat, rope-like bands, which are united into one at the railway head and drawn. And this operation of uniting and drawing or stretching goes on from one machine to another until the thread is spun, which is then dyed (calico is printed after being woven), — having been wound off on to reels and so made into skeins, — dyed and dried by steam; then, by machinery, wound on to spools for the warp and the woof. From a great many spools the warp is drawn off over cylinders and different-colored threads properly mixed and arranged. Then the ends of the warp are drawn through the harness of the loom by hand. The operator knows the succession of red, blue, green, etc., threads, having the numbers given her, and draws them through the harness accordingly, keeping count. Then the woof is put in, or it is *woven!!* Then the inequalities or nubs are picked off by girls. If *they* discover any imperfection, they tag it, and if necessary the wages of the weaver are reduced. Now, I think, it is passed over a red-hot iron cylinder, and the fuzz singed off, then washed with wheels with cold water; then the water forced out by centrifugal force within horizontal wheels. Then it is starched, the ends stitched together by machinery; then stretched smooth, dried, and ironed by machinery; then measured, folded, and packed.

This the agent, Forbes, says is the best gingham-mill in this country. The goods are better than the imported. The English have even stolen their name Lancaster Mills, calling them " Lancasterian."

The machinery is some of it peculiar, part of the throttle spindles (?) for instance.

The coach-lace-mill, only place in this country where it is made by machinery; made of thread of different materials, as cotton, worsted, linen, as well as colors, the raised figure produced by needles inserted woof fashion. Well worth examining further. Also pantaloon stuffs made in same mill and dyed after being woven, the woolen not taking the same dye with the cotton; hence a slight parti-colored appearance. These goods are sheared, *i. e.* a part of the nap taken off, making them smoother. Pressed between pasteboards.

The Brussels carpets made at the carpet-factory said to be the best in the world. Made like coach lace, only wider.

Erastus (?) Bigelow inventor of what is new in the above machinery; and, with his brother and another, owner of the carpet-factory.

I am struck by the fact that no work has been shirked when a piece of cloth is produced. Every thread has been counted in the finest web; it has not been matted together. The operator has succeeded only by patience, perseverance, and fidelity.

The direction in which a railroad runs, though intersecting another at right angles, may cause that one will be blocked up with snow and the other be

comparatively open even for great distances, depending on the direction of prevailing winds and valleys. There are the Fitchburg and Nashua & Worcester.

Jan. 4. The longest silence is the most pertinent question most pertinently put. Emphatically silent. The most important question, whose answers concern us more than any, are never put in any other way.

It is difficult for two strangers, mutually well disposed, so truly to bear themselves toward each other that a feeling of falseness and hollowness shall not soon spring up between them. The least anxiety to behave truly vitiates the relation. I think of those to whom I am at the moment truly related, with a joy never expressed and never to be expressed, before I fall asleep at night, though I am hardly on speaking terms with them these years. When I think of it, I am truly related to them.

Jan. 5. The catkins of the alders are now frozen stiff!!

Almost all that my neighbors call good I believe in my soul to be bad. If I repent of anything, it is of my good behavior. What demon possessed me that I behaved so well? You may say the wisest thing you can, old man, — you who have lived seventy years, not without honor of a kind, — I hear an irresistible voice, the voice of my destiny, which invites me away from all that.[1]

Jan. 7. The snow is sixteen inches deep at least, but [it] is a mild and genial afternoon, as if it were the

[1] *[Walden,* p. 11; Riv. 19.]

beginning of a January thaw. Take away the snow and it would not be winter but like many days in the fall. The birds acknowledge the difference in the air; the jays are more noisy, and the chickadees are oftener heard.

Many herbs are not crushed by the snow.

I do not remember to have seen fleas except when the weather was mild and the snow damp.

I must live above all in the present.

Science does not embody all that men know, only what is for men of science. The woodman tells me how he caught trout in a box trap, how he made his trough for maple sap of pine logs, and the spouts of sumach or white ash, which have a large pith. He can relate his facts to human life.

The knowledge of an unlearned man is living and luxuriant like a forest, but covered with mosses and lichens and for the most part inaccessible and going to waste; the knowledge of the man of science is like timber collected in yards for public works, which still supports a green sprout here and there, but even this is liable to dry rot.

I felt my spirits rise when I had got off the road into the open fields, and the sky had a new appearance. I stepped along more buoyantly. There was a warm sunset over the wooded valleys, a yellowish tinge on the pines. Reddish dun-colored clouds like dusky flames stood over it. And then streaks of blue sky were seen here and there. The life, the joy, that is in blue sky after a storm! There is no account of the blue sky in

history. Before I walked in the ruts of travel; now I adventured. This evening a fog comes up from the south.

If I have any conversation with a scamp in my walk, my afternoon is wont to be spoiled.

The squirrels and apparently the rabbits have got all the frozen apples in the hollow behind Miles's. The rabbits appear to have devoured what the squirrels dropped and left. I see the tracks of both leading from the woods on all sides to the apple trees.

Jan. 8. The smilax (green-briar) berries still hang on like small grapes. The thorn of this vine is very perfect, like a straight dagger.

The light of the setting sun falling on the snow-banks to-day made them glow almost yellow.

The hills seen from Fair Haven Pond make a wholly new landscape; covered with snow and yellowish green or brown pines and shrub oaks, they look higher and more massive. Their white mantle relates them to the clouds in the horizon and to the sky. Perchance what is light-colored looks loftier than what is dark.

You might say of a very old and withered man or woman that they hung on like a shrub oak leaf, almost to a second spring. There was still a little life in the heel of the leaf-stalk.

Jan. 10. The snow shows how much of the mountains in the horizon are covered with forest. I can also see plainer as I stand on a hill what proportion of the township is in forest.

Vol. II

Got some excellent frozen-thawed apples off of Annursnack, soft and luscious as a custard and free from worms and rot. Saw a partridge budding, but they did not appear to have pecked the apples.

There was a remarkable sunset; a mother-of-pearl sky seen over the Price farm; some small clouds, as well as the edges of large ones, most brilliantly painted with mother-of-pearl tints through and through. I never saw the like before. Who can foretell the sunset, — what it will be?

The near and bare hills covered with snow look like mountains, but the mountains in the horizon do not look higher than hills.

I frequently see a hole in the snow where a partridge has squatted, the mark or form of her tail very distinct.

The chivalric and heroic spirit, which once belonged to the chevalier or rider only, seems now to reside in the walker. To represent the chivalric spirit we have no longer a knight, but a walker, errant.[1] I speak not of pedestrianism, or of walking a thousand miles in a thousand successive hours.

The Adam who daily takes a turn in his garden.

Methinks I would not accept of the gift of life, if I were required to spend as large a portion of it sitting foot up or with my legs crossed, as the shoemakers and tailors do. As well be tied neck and heels together and cast into the sea. Making acquaintance with my extremities.

I have met with but one or two persons in the course of my life who understood the art of taking walks daily, — not [to] exercise the legs or body merely, nor barely to

[1] [*Excursions*, p. 206; Riv. 253.]

recruit the spirits, but positively to exercise both body and spirit, and to succeed to the highest and worthiest ends by the abandonment of all specific ends, — who had a genius, so to speak, for sauntering. And this word "saunter," by the way, is happily derived "from idle people who roved about the country [in the Middle Ages][1] and asked charity under pretence of going *à la Sainte Terre*," to the Holy Land, till, perchance, the children exclaimed, "There goes a *Sainte-Terrer*," a Holy-Lander. They who never go to the Holy Land in their walks, as they pretend, are indeed mere idlers and vagabonds.[2]

[Four pages missing.]

[Perhaps I am more] than usually jealous of my freedom. I feel that my connections with and obligations to society are at present very slight and transient. Those slight labors which afford me a livelihood, and by which I am serviceable to my contemporaries, are as yet a pleasure to me, and I am not often reminded that they are a necessity. So far I am successful, and only he is successful in his business who makes that pursuit which affords him the highest pleasure sustain him. But I foresee that if my wants should be much increased the labor required to supply them would become a drudgery. If I should sell both my forenoons and afternoons to society, neglecting my peculiar calling, there would be nothing left worth living for. I trust that I shall never thus sell my birthright for a mess of pottage.[3]

[1] [The brackets are Thoreau's.]   [2] [*Excursions*, p. 205; Riv. 251.]
[3] [*Cape Cod, and Miscellanies*, pp. 460, 461; *Misc.*, Riv. 260.]

F. Andrew Michaux says that "the species of large trees are much more numerous in North America than in Europe: in the United States there are more than one hundred and forty species that exceed thirty feet in height; in France there are but thirty that attain this size, of which eighteen enter into the composition of the forests, and seven only are employed in building." [1]

The perfect resemblance of the chestnut, beech, and hornbeam in Europe and the United States rendered a separate figure unnecessary.

He says the white oak "is the only oak on which a few of the dried leaves persist till the circulation is renewed in the spring."

Had often heard his father say that "the fruit of the common European walnut, in its natural state, is harder than that of the American species just mentioned [the pacane-nut hickory] [2] and inferior to it in size and quality."

The arts teach us a thousand lessons. Not a yard of cloth can be woven without the most thorough fidelity in the weaver. The ship must be made *absolutely* tight before it is launched.

It is an important difference between two characters that the one is satisfied with a happy but level success but the other as constantly elevates his aim. Though my life is low, if my spirit looks upward habitually at an elevated angle, it is as it were redeemed. When the

[1] [*Excursions*, p. 220; Riv. 269, 270.]
[2] [The bracketed words are Thoreau's.]

desire to be better than we are is really sincere we are instantly elevated, and so far better already.

I lose my friends, of course, as much by my own ill treatment and ill valuing of them, prophaning of them, cheapening of them, as by their cheapening of themselves, till at last, when I am prepared to [do] them justice, I am permitted to deal only with the memories of themselves, their ideals still surviving in me, no longer with their actual selves. We exclude ourselves, as the child said of the stream in which he bathed head or foot. (*Vide* Confucius.)

It is something to know when you are addressed by Divinity and not by a common traveller. I went down cellar just now to get an armful of wood and, passing the brick piers with my wood and candle, I heard, methought, a commonplace suggestion, but when, as it were by accident, I reverently attended to the hint, I found that it was the voice of a god who had followed me down cellar to speak to me. How many communications may we not lose through inattention!

I would fain keep a journal which should contain those thoughts and impressions which I am most liable to forget that I have had; which would have in one sense the greatest remoteness, in another, the greatest nearness to me.

'T is healthy to be sick sometimes.

I do not know but the reason why I love some Latin verses more than whole English poems is simply in the elegant terseness and conciseness of the language,

an advantage which the individual appears to have shared with his nation.

When we can no longer ramble in the fields of nature, we ramble in the fields of thought and literature. The old become readers. Our heads retain their strength when our legs have become weak.

English literature from the days of the minstrels to the Lake Poets, Chaucer and Spenser and Shakspeare and Milton included, breathes no quite fresh and, in this sense, wild strain. It is an essentially tame and civilized literature, reflecting Greece and Rome. Her wilderness is a greenwood, her wild man a Robin Hood. There is plenty of genial love of nature in her poets, but [not so much of nature herself.] Her chronicles inform us when her wild animals, but not when the wild man in her, became extinct.[1] There was need of America. I cannot think of any poetry which adequately expresses this yearning for the Wild, the *wilde*.[2]

Ovid says: —

Nilus in extremum fugit perterritus orbem,
Occuluitque caput, quod adhuc latet.
(Nilus, terrified, fled to the extremity of the globe,
And hid his head, which is still concealed.)

And we moderns must repeat, "*Quod adhuc latet.*" Phaëton's epitaph: —

Hic situs est Phaëton, currûs auriga paterni;
Quem si non tenuit, magnis tamen excidit ausis.

[1] [*Excursions*, p. 231; Riv. 283, 284.]
[2] [*Excursions*, p. 232; Riv. 284.]

His sister Lampetie *subitâ radice retenta est*. All the sisters were changed to trees while they were in vain beseeching their mother not to break their branches. *Cortex in verba novissima venit.*

His brother Cycnus, lamenting the death of Phaëton killed by Jove's lightning, and the metamorphosis of his sisters, was changed into a swan, —

nec se coeloque, Jovique
Credit, ut injustè missi memor ignis ab illo.

(Nor trusts himself to the heavens
Nor to Jove, as if remembering the fire unjustly sent by him),

i. e. against Phaëton. (Reason why the swan does not fly.)

. . . precibusque minas regaliter addit.
([Jove] royally adds threats to prayers.)

Callisto *miles erat Phoebes, i. e.* a huntress.

. . (neque enim coelestia tingi
Ora decet lachrymis).

(For it is not becoming that the faces of the celestials be tinged with tears, — keep a stiff upper lip.)

How much more fertile a nature has Grecian mythology its root in than English literature! The nature which inspired mythology still flourishes. Mythology is the crop which the Old World bore before its soil was exhausted. The West is preparing to add its fables to those of the East.[1] A more fertile nature than the Mississippi Valley.

None of your four-hour nights for me. The wise man

[1] [*Excursions*, pp. 232, 233; Riv. 285.]

will take a fool's allowance. The corn would not come to much if the nights were but four hours long.

The soil in which those fables grew is deep and inexhaustible.

Lead cast by the Balearian sling: —

> Volat illud, et incandescit eundo;
> Et, quos non habuit, sub nubibus invenit ignes.
> (That flies and grows hot with going,
> And fires which it had not finds amid the clouds.)

I went some months ago to see a panorama of the Rhine. It was like a dream of the Middle Ages. I floated down its historic stream in something more than imagination, under bridges built by the Romans and repaired by later heroes, past cities and castles whose very names were music to me, — made my ears tingle, — and each of which was the subject of a legend. There seemed to come up from its waters and its vine-clad hills and valleys a hushed music as of crusaders departing for the Holy Land. There were Ehrenbreitstein and Rolandseck and Coblentz, which I knew only in history. I floated along through the moonlight of history under the spell of enchantment. It was as if I remembered a glorious dream, — as if I had been transported to a heroic age and breathed an atmosphere of chivalry. Those times appeared far more poetic and heroic than these.

Soon after I went to see the panorama of the Mississippi, and as I fitly worked my way upward in the light of to-day, and saw the steamboats wooding up, and looked up the Ohio and the Missouri, and saw its

unpeopled cliffs, and counted the rising cities,[1] and saw the Indians removing west across the stream, and heard the legends of Dubuque and of Wenona's Cliff, — still thinking more of the future than of the past or present, — I saw that this was a Rhine stream of a different kind.[2]

The Old World, with its vast deserts and its arid and elevated steppes and table-lands, contrasted with the New World with its humid and fertile valleys and savannas and prairies and its boundless primitive forests, is like the exhausted Indian corn lands contrasted with the peat meadows. America requires some of the sand of the Old World to be carted on to her rich but as yet unassimilated meadows.

Guyot says, "The Baltic Sea has a depth of only 120 feet between the coasts of Germany and those of Sweden " (page 82). "The Adriatic, between Venice and Trieste, has a depth of only 130 feet." "Between France and England, the greatest depth does not exceed 300 feet." The most extensive forest, "the most gigantic wilderness," on the earth is in the basin of the Amazon, and extends almost unbroken more than fifteen hundred miles. South America the kingdom of palms; nowhere a greater number of species. "This is a sign of the preponderating development of leaves over every other part of the vegetable growth; of that expansion of foliage, of that *leafiness*, peculiar to warm and moist climates.

[1] The fresh ruins of Nauvoo, the bright brick towns. Davenport?
[2] [*Excursions*, pp. 223, 224; Riv. 274.]

America has no plants with slender, shrunken leaves, like those of Africa and New Holland. The Ericas, or heather, so common, so varied, so characteristic of the flora of the Cape of Good Hope, is a form unknown to the New World. There is nothing resembling those Metrosideri of Africa, those dry Myrtles (Eucalyptus) and willow-leaved acacias, whose flowers shine with the liveliest colors, but their narrow foliage, turned edgewise to the vertical sun, casts no shadow." [1]

The white man derives his nourishment from the earth, — from the roots and grains, the potato and wheat and corn and rice and sugar, which often grow in fertile and pestilential river bottoms fatal to the life of the cultivator. The Indian has but a slender hold on the earth. He derives his nourishment in great part but indirectly from her, through the animals he hunts.[2]

"Compared with the Old World, the New World is the humid side of our planet, the *oceanic, vegetative* world, the passive element awaiting the excitement of a livelier impulse from without." [3]

"For the American, this task is to work the virgin soil."

"Agriculture here already assumes proportions unknown everywhere else." [4]

[1] [Arnold Guyot, *The Earth and Man.* Translated by C. C. Felton.]
[2] My own.
[3] [Guyot, *op. cit.*]
[4] [Guyot, *op. cit.*]

Feb. 9. The last half of January was warm and thawy. The swift streams were open, and the muskrats were seen swimming and diving and bringing up clams, leaving their shells on the ice. We had now forgotten summer and autumn, but had already begun to anticipate spring. Fishermen improved the warmer weather to fish for pickerel through the ice. Before it was only the autumn landscape with a thin layer of snow upon it; we saw the withered flowers through it; but now we do not think of autumn when we look on this snow. That earth is effectually buried. It is midwinter. Within a few days the cold has set in stronger than ever, though the days are much longer now. Now I travel across the fields on the crust which has frozen since the January thaw, and I can cross the river in most places. It is easier to get about the country than at any other season, — easier than in summer, because the rivers and meadows are frozen and there is no high grass or other crops to be avoided; easier than in December before the crust was frozen.

Sir John Mandeville says, "In fro what partie of the earth that men dwell, outher aboven or benethen, it seemeth always to hem that dwellen there, that they gon more right than any other folk." Again, "And yee shulle undirstonde, that of all theise contrees, and of all theise yles, and of all the dyverse folk, that I have spoken of before, and of dyverse laws and of dyverse beleeves that thei have, yit is there non of hem alle, but that thei have sum resoun within hem and understondinge, but gif it be the fewere."

I have heard that there is a Society for the Diffusion of Useful Knowledge. It is said that knowledge is power and the like. Methinks there is equal need of a Society for the Diffusion of Useful Ignorance, for what is most of our boasted so-called knowledge but a conceit that we know something, which robs us of the advantages of our actual ignorance.[1]

For a man's ignorance sometimes is not only useful but beautiful, while his knowledge is oftentimes worse than useless, beside being ugly.[2] In reference to important things, whose knowledge amounts to more than a consciousness of his ignorance? Yet what more refreshing and inspiring knowledge than this?

How often are we wise as serpents without being harmless as doves!

Donne says, "Who are a little wise the best fools be." Cudworth says, "We have all of us by nature μάντευμά τε (as both Plato and Aristotle call it), a certain divination, presage and parturient vaticination in our minds, of some higher good and perfection than either power or knowledge." Aristotle himself declares, that there is λόγου τι κρεῖττον, which is λόγου ἀρχή, — (something better than reason and knowledge, which is the principle and original of all). Lavater says, "Who finds the clearest not clear, thinks the darkest not obscure."

My desire for knowledge is intermittent; but my desire to commune with the spirit of the universe, to

[1] [*Excursions*, p. 239; Riv. 293.]
[2] [*Excursions*, p. 240; Riv. 294.]

Vol. II

exclusively toward men, or society.[1] The young men of Concord and in other towns do not walk in the woods, but congregate in shops and offices. They suck one another. Their strongest attraction is toward the mill-dam. A thousand assemble about the fountain in the public square, — the town pump, — be it full or dry, clear or turbid, every morning, but not one in a thousand is in the meanwhile drinking at that fountain's head. It is hard for the young, aye, and the old, man in the outskirts to keep away from the mill-dam a whole day; but he will find some excuse, as an ounce of cloves that might be wanted, or a *New England Farmer* still in the office, to tackle up the horse, or even go afoot, but he will go at some rate. This is not bad comparatively; this is because he cannot do better. In spite of his hoeing and chopping, he is unexpressed and undeveloped.

I do not know where to find in any literature, whether ancient or modern, any adequate account of that Nature with which I am acquainted. Mythology comes nearest to it of any.[2]

The actual life of men is not without a dramatic interest at least to the thinker. It is not always and everywhere prosaic. Seventy thousand pilgrims proceed annually to Mecca from the various nations of Islam. But this is not so significant as the far simpler and more unpretending pilgrimage to the shrines of some obscure individual, which yet makes no bustle in the world.

I believe that Adam in paradise was not so favorably situated on the whole as is the backwoodsman

[1] [*Excursions*, p. 241; Riv. 296.]
[2] [*Excursions*, p. 232; Riv. 284, 285.]

be intoxicated even with the fumes, call it, of that divine nectar, to bear my head through atmospheres and over heights unknown to my feet, is perennial and constant.[1]

It is remarkable how few events or crises there are in our minds' histories, how little *exercised* we have been in our minds, how few experiences we have had.[2]

[Four pages missing.]

The story of Romulus and Remus being suckled by a wolf is not a mere fable; the founders of every state which has risen to eminence have drawn their nourishment and vigor from a similar source. It is because the children of the empire were not suckled by wolves that they were conquered and displaced by the children of the northern forests who were.[3]

America is the she wolf to-day, and the children of exhausted Europe exposed on her uninhabited and savage shores are the Romulus and Remus who, having derived new life and vigor from her breast, have founded a new Rome in the West.

It is remarkable how few passages, comparatively speaking, there are in the best literature of the day which betray any intimacy with Nature.

It is apparent enough to me that only one or two of my townsmen or acquaintances — not more than one in many thousand men, indeed — feel or at least obey any strong attraction drawing them toward the forest or to Nature, but all, almost without exception, gravitate

[1] [*Excursions*, p. 240; Riv. 294.]
[2] [*Excursions*, p. 241; Riv. 295.]
[3] [*Excursions*, pp. 224, 225; Riv. 275.]

in America.[1] You all know how miserably the former turned out, — or was turned out, — but there is some consolation at least in the fact that it yet remains to be seen how the western Adam in the wilderness will turn out.

> In Adam's fall
> We sinned all.
> In the new Adam's rise
> We shall all reach the skies.

An infusion of hemlock in our tea, if we must drink tea, — not the poison hemlock, but the hemlock spruce, I mean,[2] — or perchance the Arbor-Vitæ, the tree of life, — is what we want.

Feb. 12. *Wednesday.* A beautiful day, with but little snow or ice on the ground. Though the air is sharp, as the earth is half bare the hens have strayed to some distance from the barns. The hens, standing around their lord and pluming themselves and still fretting a little, strive to fetch the year about.

A thaw has nearly washed away the snow and raised the river and the brooks and flooded the meadows, covering the old ice, which is still fast to the bottom.

I find that it is an excellent walk for variety and novelty and wildness, to keep round the edge of the meadow, — the ice not being strong enough to bear and transparent as water, — on the bare ground or snow, just between the highest water mark and the present water line, — a narrow, meandering walk, rich in unex-

[1] [*Excursions*, p. 223; Riv. 273.]
[2] [*Excursions*, p. 225; Riv. 275.]

Midwinter

pected views and objects. The line of rubbish which marks the higher tides — withered flags and reeds and twigs and cranberries — is to my eyes a very agreeable and significant line, which Nature traces along the edge of the meadows. It is a strongly marked, enduring natural line, which in summer reminds me that the water has once stood over where I walk. Sometimes the grooved trees tell the same tale. The wrecks of the meadow, which fill a thousand coves, and tell a thousand tales to those who can read them. Our prairial, mediterranean shore. The gentle rise of water around the trees in the meadow, where oaks and maples stand far out in the sea, and young elms sometimes are seen standing close around some rock which lifts its head above the water, as if protecting it, preventing it from being washed away, though in truth they owe their origin and preservation to it. It first invited and detained their seed, and now preserves the soil in which they grow. A pleasant reminiscence of the rise of waters, to go up one side of the river and down the other, following this way, which meanders so much more than the river itself. If you cannot go on the ice, you are then gently compelled to take this course, which is on the whole more beautiful, — to follow the sinuosities of the meadow. Between the highest water mark and the present water line is a space generally from a few feet to a few rods in width. When the water comes over the road, then my spirits rise, — when the fences are carried away. A prairial walk. Saw a caterpillar crawling about on the snow.

The earth is so bare that it makes an impression on me as if it were catching cold.

I saw to-day something new to me as I walked along the edge of the meadow. Every half-mile or so along the channel of the river I saw at a distance where apparently the ice had been broken up while freezing by the pressure of other ice, — thin cakes of ice forced up on their edges and reflecting the sun like so many mirrors, whole fleets of shining sails, giving a very lively appearance to the river, — where for a dozen rods the flakes of ice stood on their edges, like a fleet beating up-stream against the sun, a fleet of ice-boats.

It is remarkable that the cracks in the ice on the meadows sometimes may be traced a dozen rods from the water through the snow in the neighboring fields.

It is only necessary that man should start a fence that Nature should carry it on and complete it. The farmer cannot plow quite up to the rails or wall which he himself has placed, and hence it often becomes a hedgerow and sometimes a coppice.

I found to-day apples still green under the snow, and others frozen and thawed, sweeter far than when sound, — a sugary sweetness.[1]

There is something more than association at the bottom of the excitement which the roar of a cataract produces. It is allied to the circulation in our veins. We have a waterfall which corresponds even to Niagara somewhere within us.[2] It is astonishing what a rush and tumult a slight inclination will produce in a swollen brook. How it proclaims its glee, its boisterousness, rushing headlong in its prodigal course as if it would exhaust itself in half an hour! How it spends itself! I

[1] [See *Excursions*, p. 319; Riv. 392.]   [2] [See p. 300.]

Vol. II

would say to the orator and poet, Flow freely and *lavishly* as a brook that is full, — without stint. Perchance I have stumbled upon the origin of the word "lavish." It does not hesitate to tumble down the steepest precipice and roar or tinkle as it goes, for fear it will exhaust its fountain. The impetuosity of descending water even by the slightest inclination! It seems to flow with ever increasing rapidity.

It is difficult to believe what philosophers assert, that it is merely a difference in the form of the elementary particles — as whether they are square or globular — which makes the difference between the steadfast, everlasting, and reposing hillside and the impetuous torrent which tumbles down it.

It is refreshing to walk over sprout-lands, where oak and chestnut sprouts are mounting swiftly up again into the sky, and already perchance their sere leaves begin to rustle in the breeze and reflect the light on the hillsides.

"Heroic underwoods that take the air
With freedom, nor respect their parents' death." [1]

I trust that the walkers of the present day are conscious of the blessings which they enjoy in the comparative freedom with which they can ramble over the country and enjoy the landscape, anticipating with compassion that future day when possibly it will be partitioned off into so-called pleasure-grounds, where only a few may enjoy the narrow and exclusive pleasure which is compatible with ownership, — when walking over the surface of God's earth shall be construed to

[1] [W. E. Channing, "Walden Spring."]

mean trespassing on some gentleman's grounds, when fences shall be multiplied and man traps and other engines invented to confine men to the public road. I am thankful that we have yet so much room in America.[1]

Feb. 13. Skated to Sudbury. A beautiful, summer-like day. The meadows were frozen just enough to bear. Examined now the fleets of ice-flakes close at hand. They are a very singular and interesting phenomenon, which I do not remember to have seen. I should say that when the water was frozen about as thick as pasteboard, a violent gust had here and there broken it up, and while the wind and waves held it up on its edge, the increasing cold froze it in firmly. So it seemed, for the flakes were for the most part turned one way; *i. e.* standing on one side, you saw only their edges, on another — the northeast or southwest — their sides. They were for the most part of a triangular form, like a shoulder[*sic*]-of-mutton sail, slightly scalloped, like

shells. They looked like a fleet of a thousand mackerel-fishers under a press of sail careering before a smacking breeze. Sometimes the sun and wind had reduced them to the thinness of writing-paper, and they fluttered and rustled and tinkled merrily. I skated through them and strewed their wrecks around. They appear to have been elevated expressly to reflect the sun like mirrors, to adorn the river and attract the eye of the skater. Who will say

[1] [*Excursions*, p. 216; Riv. 264, 265.]

that their principal end is not answered when they excite the admiration of the skater? Every half-mile or mile, as you skate up the river, you see these crystal fleets. Nature is a great imitator and loves to repeat herself. She wastes her wonders on the town. It impresses me as one superiority in her art, if art it may be called, that she does not require that man appreciate her, takes no steps to attract his attention.

The trouble is in getting on and off the ice; when you are once on you can go well enough. It melts round the edges.

Again I saw to-day, half a mile off in Sudbury, a sandy spot on the top of a hill, where I prophesied that I should find traces of the Indians. When within a dozen rods, I distinguished the foundation of a lodge, and merely passing over it, I saw many fragments of the arrowhead stone. I have frequently distinguished these localities half a mile [off], gone forward, and picked up arrowheads.

Saw in a warm, muddy brook in Sudbury, quite open and exposed, the skunk-cabbage spathes above water. The tops of the spathes were frost-bitten, but the fruit [*sic*] sound. There was one partly expanded. The first flower of the season; for it is a flower. I doubt if there is [a] month without its flower. Examined by the botany all its parts, — the first flower I have seen. The *Ictodes fœtidus.*

Also mosses, mingled red and green. The red will pass for the blossom.

As for antiquities, one of our old deserted country roads, marked only by the parallel fences and cellar-hole

with its bricks where the last inhabitant died, the victim of intemperance, fifty years ago, with its bare and exhausted fields stretching around, suggests to me an antiquity greater and more remote from the America of the newspapers than the tombs of Etruria. I insert the rise and fall of Rome in the interval. This is the decline and fall of the Roman Empire.

It is important to observe not only the subject of our pure and unalloyed joys, but also the secret of any dissatisfaction one may feel.

In society, in the best institutions of men, I remark a certain precocity. When we should be growing children, we are already little men. Infants as we are, we make haste to be weaned from our great mother's breast, and cultivate our parts by intercourse with one another.

I have not much faith in the method of restoring impoverished soils which relies on manuring mainly and does not add some virgin soil or muck.

Many a poor, sore-eyed student that I have heard of would grow faster, both intellectually and physically, if, instead of sitting up so very late to study, he honestly slumbered a fool's allowance.[1]

I would not have every man cultivated, any more than I would have every acre of earth cultivated. Some must be preparing a mould by the annual decay of the forests which they sustain.[2]

Saw half a dozen cows let out and standing about in a retired meadow as in a cow-yard.

[1] [*Excursions*, p. 238; Riv. 291.]
[2] [*Excursions*, p. 238; Riv. 292.]

Vol. II

Feb. 14. Consider the farmer, who is commonly regarded as the healthiest man. He may be the toughest, but he is not the healthiest. He has lost his elasticity; he can neither run nor jump. Health is the free use and command of all our faculties, and equal development. His is the health of the ox, an overworked buffalo. His joints are stiff. The resemblance is true even in particulars. He is cast away in a pair of cowhide boots, and travels at an ox's pace. Indeed, in some places he puts his foot into the skin of an ox's shin. It would do him good to be thoroughly shampooed to make him supple. His health is an insensibility to all influence. But only the healthiest man in the world is sensible to the finest influence; he who is affected by more or less of electricity in the air.

We shall see but little way if we require to understand what we see. How few things can a man measure with the tape of his understanding! How many greater things might he be seeing in the meanwhile!

One afternoon in the fall, November 21st, I saw Fair Haven Pond with its island and meadow; between the island and the shore, a strip of perfectly smooth water in the lee of the island; and two hawks sailing over it; and something more I saw which cannot easily be described, which made me say to myself that the landscape could not be improved. I did not see how it could be improved. Yet I do not know what these things can be; I begin to see such objects only when I leave off understanding them, and afterwards remember that I did not appreciate them before. But I get no further than this. How adapted these forms and colors to our

eyes, a meadow and its islands! What are these things? Yet the hawks and the ducks keep so aloof, and nature is so reserved! We are made to love the river and the meadow, as the wind to ripple the water.[1]

There is a difference between eating for strength and from mere gluttony. The Hottentots eagerly devour the marrow of the koodoo and other antelopes raw, as a matter of course, and herein perchance have stolen a march on the cooks of Paris. The eater of meat must come to this. This is better than stall-fed cattle and slaughter-house pork. Possibly they derive a certain wild-animal vigor therefrom which the most artfully cooked meats do not furnish.[2]

We learn by the January thaw that the winter is intermittent and are reminded of other seasons. The back of the winter is broken.

Feb. 15. Fatal is the discovery that our friend is fallible, that he has prejudices. He is, then, only prejudiced in our favor. What is the value of his esteem who does not justly esteem another?

Alas! Alas! when my friend begins to deal in confessions, breaks silence, makes a theme of friendship (which then is always something past), and descends to merely human relations! As long as there is a spark of love remaining, cherish that alone. Only *that* can be kindled into a flame. I thought that friendship, that love was still possible between [us]. I thought that we had not withdrawn very far asunder. But now that my friend rashly, thoughtlessly, profanely speaks, *recogniz-*

[1] [See p. 107.]		[2] [*Excursions*, p. 225; Riv. 275, 276.]

ing the distance between us, that distance seems infinitely increased.

Of our friends we do not incline to speak, to complain, to others; we would not disturb the foundations of confidence that may still be.

Why should we not still continue to live with the intensity and rapidity of infants? Is not the world, are not the heavens, as unfathomed as ever? Have we exhausted any joy, any sentiment?

The author of Festus well exclaims: —

> "Could we but think with the intensity
> We love with, we might do great things, I think."

Feb. 16. Do we call this the land of the free? What is it to be free from King George the Fourth and continue the slaves of prejudice? What is it [to] be born free and equal, and not to live? What is the value of any political freedom, but as a means to moral freedom? Is it a freedom to be slaves or a freedom to be free, of which we boast? We are a nation of politicians, concerned about the outsides of freedom, the means and outmost defenses of freedom. It is our children's children who may perchance be essentially free. We tax ourselves unjustly. There is a part of us which is not represented. It is taxation without representation. We quarter troops upon ourselves. In respect to virtue or true manhood, we are essentially provincial, not metropolitan, — mere Jonathans. We are provincial, because we do not find at home our standards; because

we do not worship truth but the reflection of truth; because we are absorbed in and narrowed by trade and commerce and agriculture, which are but means and not the end. We are essentially provincial, I say, and so is the English Parliament. Mere country bumpkins they betray themselves, when any more important question arises for them to settle. Their natures are subdued to what they work in!

The finest manners in the world are awkwardness and fatuity when contrasted with a finer intelligence. They appear but as the fashions of past days, — mere courtliness, small-clothes, and knee-buckles, — have the vice of getting out of date; an attitude merely. The vice of manners is that they are continually deserted by the character; they are cast-off clothes or shells, claiming the respect of the living creature. You are presented with the shells instead of the meat, and it is no excuse generally that, in the case of some fish, the shells are of more worth than the meat. The man who thrusts his manners upon me does as if he were to insist on introducing me to his cabinet of curiosities, when I wish to see himself. Manners are conscious; character is unconscious.[1]

My neighbor does not recover from his formal bow so soon as I do from the pleasure of meeting him.

Feb. 18. *Tuesday.* Ground nearly bare of snow. Pleasant day with a strong south wind. Skated, though the ice was soft in spots. Saw the skunk-cabbage in flower. Gathered nuts and apples on the bare ground,

[1] [*Cape Cod, and Miscellanies*, pp. 476–478; *Misc.*, Riv. 280–282.]

Vol. II

still sound and preserving their colors, red and green, many of them.

Yesterday the river was over the road by Hubbard's Bridge.

Surveyed White Pond yesterday, February 17th.

There is little or nothing to be remembered written on the subject of getting an honest living. Neither the New Testament nor Poor Richard speaks to our condition. I cannot think of a single page which entertains, much less answers, the questions which I put to myself on this subject. How to make the getting our living poetic! for if it is not poetic, it is not life but death that we get. Is it that men are too disgusted with their experience to speak of it? or that commonly they do not question the common modes? The most practically important of all questions, it seems to me, is how shall I get my living, and yet I find little or nothing said to the purpose in any book. Those who are living on the interest of money inherited, or dishonestly, *i. e.* by false methods, acquired, are of course incompetent to answer it. I consider that society with all its arts, has done nothing for us in this respect. One would think, from looking at literature, that this question had never disturbed a solitary individual's musings. Cold and hunger seem more friendly to my nature than those methods which men have adopted and advise to ward them off.[1] If it were not that I desire to do something here, — accomplish some work, — I should certainly prefer to suffer and die rather than be at the pains to get a living by the modes men propose.

[1] [*Cape Cod, and Miscellanies*, p. 462; *Misc.*, Riv. 262.]

There may be an excess even of informing light.

Niepce, a Frenchman, announced that "no substance can be exposed to the sun's rays without undergoing a chemical change." Granite rocks and stone structures and statues of metal, etc., "are," says Robert Hunt, "all alike destructively acted upon during the hours of sunshine, and, but for provisions of nature no less wonderful, would soon perish under the delicate touch of the most subtile of the agencies of the universe." But Niepce showed, says Hunt, "that those bodies which underwent this change during daylight possessed the power of restoring themselves to their original conditions during the hours of night, when this excitement was no longer influencing them." So, in the case of the daguerreotype, "the picture which we receive to-night, unless we adopt some method of securing its permanency, fades away before the morning, and we try to restore it in vain." (Infers) "the hours of darkness are as necessary to the inorganic creation as we know night and sleep are to the organic kingdom." Such is the influence of "actinism," that power in the sun's rays which produces a chemical effect.[1]

Feb. 25. A very windy day. A slight snow which fell last night was melted at noon. A strong, gusty wind; the waves on the meadows make a fine show. I saw at Hubbard's Bridge that all the ice had been blown up-stream from the meadows, and was collected over the channel against the bridge in large

[1] [*Excursions*, p. 238; Riv. 292.]

cakes. These were covered and intermingled with a remarkable quantity of the meadow's crust. There was no ice to be seen up-stream and no more down-stream.

The meadows have been flooded for a fortnight, and this water has been frozen barely thick enough to bear once only. The old ice on the meadows was covered several feet deep. I observed from the bridge, a few rods off northward, what looked like an island directly over the channel. It was the crust of the meadow afloat. I reached [it] with a little risk and found it to be four rods long by one broad, — the surface of the meadow with cranberry vines, etc., all connected and in their natural position, and no ice visible but around its edges. It appeared to be the frozen crust (which was separated from the unfrozen soil as ice is from the water beneath), buoyed up (?), perchance, by the ice around its edges frozen to the stubble. Was there any pure ice under it? Had there been any above it? Will frozen meadow float? Had ice which originally supported it from above melted except about the edges? When the ice melts or the soil thaws, of course it falls to the bottom, wherever it may be. Here is another agent employed in the distribution of plants. I have seen where a smooth shore which I frequented for bathing was in one season strewn with these hummocks, bearing the button-bush with them, which have now changed the character of the shore. There were many rushes and lily-pad stems on the ice. Had the ice formed about them as they grew, broken them off when it floated away, and so they were strewn about on it?

Vol. II

best to deal with? I do not know that knowledge amounts to anything more definite than a novel and grand surprise, or a sudden revelation of the insufficiency of all that we had called knowledge before; an indefinite sense of the grandeur and glory of the universe. It is the lighting up of the mist by the sun. But man cannot be said to know in any higher sense, [any more] than he can look serenely and with impunity in the face of the sun.[1]

A culture which imports much muck from the meadows and deepens the soil, not that which trusts to heating manures and improved agricultural implements only.

How, when a man purchases a thing, he is determined to get and get hold of it, using how many expletives and how long a string of synonymous or similar terms signifying possession, in the legal process! What's mine's my own. An old deed of a small piece of swamp land, which I have lately surveyed at the risk of being mired past recovery, says that "the said Spaulding his Heirs and Assigns, shall and may from this (?) time, and at all times forever hereafter, by force and virtue of these presents, lawfully, peaceably and quietly have, hold, use, occupy, possess and enjoy the said swamp," etc.

Magnetic iron, being anciently found in *Magnesia*, — hence *magnes*, or magnet, — employed by Pliny and others. Chinese appear to have discovered the magnet very early, A. D. 121 and before (?); used by them to

[1] [*Excursions*, p. 240; Riv. 294.]

Feb. 26. Wednesday. Examined the floating meadow again to-day. It is more than a foot thick, the under part much mixed with ice, — ice and muck. It appeared to me that the meadow surface had been heaved by the frost, and then the water had run down and under it, and finally, when the ice rose, lifted it up, wherever there was ice enough mixed with it to float it. I saw large cakes of ice with other large cakes, the latter as big as a table, on top of them. Probably the former rose while the latter were already floating about. The plants scattered about were bulrushes and lily-pad stems.

Saw five red-wings and a song sparrow(?) this afternoon.

Feb. 27. Saw to-day on Pine Hill behind Mr. Joseph Merriam's house a Norway pine, the first I have seen in Concord. Mr. Gleason pointed it out to me as a singular pine which he did not know the name of. It was a very handsome tree, about twenty-five feet high. E. Wood thinks that he has lost the surface of two acres of his meadow by the ice. Got fifteen cartloads out of a hummock left on another meadow. Blue-joint was introduced into the first meadow where it did not grow before.

Of two men, one of whom knows nothing about a subject, and, what is extremely rare, knows that he knows nothing, and the other really knows something about it, but thinks that he knows all, — what great advantage has the latter over the former? which is the

steer ships in 419; mentioned by an Icelander, 1068; in a French poem, 1181; in Torfæus' History of Norway, 1266. Used by De Gama in 1427. Leading stone, hence loadstone.

The peroxide of hydrogen, or ozone, at first thought to be a chemical curiosity merely, is found to be very generally diffused through nature.

The following bears on the floating ice which has risen from the bottom of the meadows. Robert Hunt says: "Water conducts heat downward but very slowly; a mass of ice will remain undissolved but a few inches under water on the surface of which ether or any other inflammable body is burning. If ice swam beneath the surface, the summer sun would scarcely have power to thaw it; and thus our lakes and seas would be gradually converted into solid masses."

The figures of serpents, of griffins, flying dragons, and other embellishments of heraldry, the eastern idea of the world on an elephant, that on a tortoise, and that on a serpent again, etc., usually regarded as mythological in the common sense of that word, are thought by some to "indicate a faint and shadowy knowledge of a previous state of organic existence," such as geology partly reveals.

The fossil tortoise has been found in Asia large enough to support an elephant.

Ammonites, snake-stones, or petrified snakes have been found from of old, often decapitated.

In the northern part of Great Britain the fossil remains of encrinites are called "St. Cuthbert's beads." "Fiction dependent on truth."

Westward is heaven, or rather heavenward is the west. The way to heaven is from east to west round the earth. The sun leads and shows it. The stars, too, light it.

Nature and man; some prefer the one, others the other; but that is all *de gustibus*. It makes no odds at what well you drink, provided it be a well-head.

Walking in the woods, it may be, some afternoon, the shadow of the wings of a thought flits across the landscape of my mind, and I am reminded how little eventful are our lives. What have been all these wars and rumors of wars, and modern discoveries and improvements so-called? A mere irritation in the skin. But this shadow which is so soon past, and whose substance is not detected, suggests that there are events of importance whose interval is to us a true historic period.[1]

The lecturer is wont to describe the Nineteenth Century, the American [of] the last generation, in an off-hand and triumphant strain, wafting him to paradise, spreading his fame by steam and telegraph, recounting the number of wooden stopples he has whittled. But who does not perceive that this is not a sincere or pertinent account of any man's or nation's life? It is the hip-hip-hurrah and mutual-admiration-society style. Cars go by, and we know their substance as well as their shadow. They stop and we get into them. But those sublime thoughts passing on high do not stop, and we never get into them. Their conductor is not like one of us.

I feel that the man who, in his conversation with me

[1] [*Excursions*, p. 244; Riv. 299.]

about the life of man in New England, lays much stress on railroads, telegraphs, and such enterprises does not go below the surface of things. He treats the shallow and transitory as if it were profound and enduring. In one of the mind's avatars, in the interval between sleeping and waking, aye, even in one of the interstices of a Hindoo dynasty, perchance, such things as the Nineteenth Century, with all its improvements, may come and go again. Nothing makes a deep and lasting impression but what is weighty.

Obey the law which reveals, and not the law revealed.

I wish my neighbors were wilder.

A wildness whose glance no civilization could endure.[1]

He who lives according to the highest law is in one sense lawless. That is an unfortunate discovery, certainly, that of a law which binds us where we did not know that we were bound. Live free, child of the mist! He for whom the law is made, who does not obey the law but whom the law obeys, reclines on pillows of down and is wafted at will whither he pleases, for man is superior to all laws, both of heaven and earth, when he takes his liberty.[2]

Wild as if we lived on the marrow of antelopes devoured raw.[3]

There would seem to be men in whose lives there have been no events of importance, more than in the beetle's which crawls in our path.

[1] [*Excursions*, p. 225; Riv. 276.]
[2] [*Excursions*, p. 240; Riv. 295.]
[3] [*Excursions*, p. 225; Riv. 276.]

Vol. II

March 19. The ice in the pond is now soft and will not bear a heavy stone thrown from the bank. It is melted for a rod from the shore. The ground has been bare of snow for some weeks, but yesterday we had a violent northeast snow-storm, which has drifted worse than any the past winter. The spring birds — ducks and geese, etc. — had come, but now the spring seems far off.

No good ever came of obeying a law which you had discovered.

March 23. For a week past the elm buds have been swollen. The willow catkins have put out. The ice still remains in Walden, though it will not bear. Mather Howard saw a large meadow near his house which had risen up but was prevented from floating away by the bushes.

March 27. Walden is two-thirds broken up. It will probably be quite open by to-morrow night.

March 30. Spring is already upon us. I see the tortoises, or rather I hear them drop from the bank into the brooks at my approach. The catkins of the alders have blossomed. The pads are springing at the bottom of the water. The pewee is heard, and the lark.

"It is only the squalid savages and degraded boschmen of creation that have their feeble teeth and tiny stings steeped in venom, and so made formidable," — ants, centipedes, and mosquitoes, spiders, wasps, and scorpions. — HUGH MILLER.

To attain to a true relation to one human creature is enough to make a year memorable.

The man for whom law exists — the man of forms, the conservative — is a tame man.

CARRYING OFF SIMS

A recent English writer (De Quincey),[1] endeavoring to account for the atrocities of Caligula and Nero, their monstrous and anomalous cruelties, and the general servility and corruption which they imply, observes that it is difficult to believe that "the descendants of a people so severe in their habits" as the Romans had been "could thus rapidly" have degenerated and that, "in reality, the citizens of Rome were at this time a new race, brought together from every quarter of the world, but especially from Asia." A vast "proportion of the ancient citizens had been cut off by the sword," and such multitudes of emancipated slaves from Asia had been invested with the rights of citizens "that, in a single generation, Rome became almost transmuted into a baser metal." As Juvenal complained, "the Orontes . . . had mingled its impure waters with those of the Tiber." And "probably, in the time of Nero, not one man in six was of pure Roman descent." Instead of such, says another, "came Syrians, Cappadocians, Phrygians, and other enfranchised slaves." "These in half a century had sunk so low, that Tiberius pronounced her [Rome's][2] very senators to be *homines ad servitutem natos*, men born to be slaves."[3]

[1] [In *The Cæsars*.]   [2] [Supplied by Thoreau.]
[3] [Blackwell, *Court of Augustus*; quoted by De Quincey in a note.]

So one would say, in the absence of particular genealogical evidence, that the vast majority of the inhabitants of the city of Boston, even those of senatorial dignity, — the Curtises, Lunts, Woodburys, and others, — were not descendants of the men of the Revolution, — the Hancocks, Adamses, Otises, — but some "Syrians, Cappadocians, and Phrygians," merely, *homines ad servitutem natos*, men born to be slaves. But I would have done with comparing ourselves with our ancestors, for on the whole I believe that even they, if somewhat braver and less corrupt than we, were not men of so much principle and generosity as to go to war in behalf of another race in their midst. I do not believe that the North will soon come to blows with the South on this question. It would be too bright a page to be written in the history of the race at present.

There is such an officer, if not such a man, as the Governor of Massachusetts. What has he been about the last fortnight? He has probably had as much as he could do to keep on the fence during this moral earthquake. It seems to me that no such keen satire, no such cutting insult, could be offered to that man, as the absence of all inquiry after him in this crisis. It appears to [have] been forgotten that there was such a man or such an office. Yet no doubt he has been filling the gubernatorial chair all the while. One Mr. Boutwell, — so named, perchance, because he goes about well to suit the prevailing wind.[1]

In '75 two or three hundred of the inhabitants of

[1] [*Cape Cod, and Miscellanies*, p. 390; *Misc.*, Riv. 174.]

Concord assembled at one of the bridges with arms in their hands to assert the right of three millions to tax themselves, to have a voice in governing themselves. About a week ago the authorities of Boston, having the sympathy of many of the inhabitants of Concord, assembled in the gray of the dawn, assisted by a still larger armed force, to send back a perfectly innocent man, and one whom they knew to be innocent, into a slavery as complete as the world ever knew. Of course it makes not the least difference — I wish you to consider this — who the man was, — whether he was Jesus Christ or another, — for inasmuch as ye did it unto the least of these his brethren ye did it unto him. Do you think *he* would have stayed here in liberty and let the black man go into slavery in his stead? They sent him back, I say, to live in slavery with other three millions — mark that — whom the same slave power, or slavish power, North and South, holds in that condition, — three millions who do not, like the first mentioned, assert the right to govern themselves but simply to run away and stay away from their prison.

Just a week afterward, those inhabitants of this town who especially sympathize with the authorities of Boston in this their deed caused the bells to be rung and the cannon to be fired to celebrate the courage and the love of liberty of those men who assembled at the bridge. As if *those* three millions had fought for the right to be free themselves, but to hold in slavery three million others. Why, gentlemen, even consistency, though it is much abused, is sometimes a virtue. Every humane and intelligent inhabitant of Concord, when he

Vol. II

or she heard those bells and those cannon, thought not so much of the events of the 19th of April, 1775, as of the event of the 12th of April, 1851.

I wish my townsmen to consider that, whatever the human law may be, neither an individual nor a nation can ever deliberately commit the least act of injustice without having to pay the penalty for it. A government which deliberately enacts injustice, and persists in it! — it will become the laughing-stock of the world.

Much as has been said about American slavery, I think that commonly we do not yet realize what slavery is. If I were seriously to propose to Congress to make mankind into sausages, I have no doubt that most would smile at my proposition and, if any believed me to be in earnest, they would think that I proposed something much worse than Congress had ever done. But, gentlemen, if any of you will tell me that to make a man into a sausage would be much worse — would be any worse — than to make him into a slave, — than it was then to enact the fugitive slave law, — I shall here accuse him of foolishness, of intellectual incapacity, of making a distinction without a difference. The one is just as sensible a proposition as the other.[1]

When I read the account of the carrying back of the fugitive into slavery, which was read last Sunday evening, and read also what was not read here, that the man who made the prayer on the wharf was Daniel Foster of *Concord*, I could not help feeling a slight degree of pride because, of all the towns in the Commonwealth,

[1] [*Cape Cod, and Miscellanies*, pp. 392–394; *Misc.*, Riv. 177–179.]

Concord was the only one distinctly named as being represented in that new tea-party, and, as she had a place in the first, so would have a place in this, the last and perhaps next most important chapter of the History of Massachusetts. But my second feeling, when I reflected how short a time that gentleman has resided in this town, was one of doubt and shame, because the *men* of Concord in recent times have done nothing to entitle them to the honor of having their town named in such a connection.

I hear a good deal said about trampling this law under foot. Why, one need not go out of his way to do that. This law lies not at the level of the head or the reason. Its natural habitat is in the dirt. It was bred and has its life only in the dust and mire, on a level with the feet; and he who walks with freedom, unless, with a sort of quibbling and Hindoo mercy, he avoids treading on every venomous reptile, will inevitably tread on it, and so trample it under foot.

It has come to this, that the friends of liberty, the friends of the slave, have shuddered when they have understood that his fate has been left to the legal tribunals, so-called, of the country to be decided. The people have no faith that justice will be awarded in such a case. The judge may decide this way or that; it is a kind of accident at best. It is evident that he is not a competent authority in so important a case. I would not trust the life of my friend to the judges of all the Supreme Courts in the world put together, to be sacrificed or saved by precedent. I would much rather trust to the sentiment of the people, which would itself be a precedent to posterity. In their vote you would get something worth having at any rate, but in the other case only the trammelled judgment of an individual, of no significance, be it which way it will.

I think that recent events will be valuable as a criticism on the administration of justice in our midst, or rather as revealing what are the true sources of justice in any community. It is to some extent fatal to the courts when the people are compelled to go behind the courts. They learn that the courts are made for fair weather and for very civil cases.[1]

[Two pages missing.]

let us entertain opinions of our own;[2] let us be a town and not a suburb, as far from Boston in this sense as we were by the old road which led through Lexington; a place where tyranny may ever be met with firmness and driven back with defeat to its ships.

Concord has several more bridges left of the same sort, which she is taxed to maintain. Can she not raise men to defend them?

As for measures to be adopted, among others I would advise abolitionists to make as earnest and vigorous and persevering an assault on the press, as they have already made, and with effect too, on the church. The church has decidedly improved within a year or two, aye, even within a fortnight; but the press is, almost without exception, corrupt. I believe that in this country the press exerts a greater and a more pernicious

1 [*Cape Cod, and Miscellanies*, pp. 394, 395; *Misc.*, Riv. 179, 180.]
2 [*Cape Cod, and Miscellanies*, p. 397; *Misc.*, Riv. 183.]

influence than the church. We are not a religious people, but we are a nation of politicians. We do not much care for, we do not read, the Bible, but we do care for and we do read the newspaper. It is a bible which we read every morning and every afternoon, standing and sitting, riding and walking. It is a bible which every man carries in his pocket, which lies on every table and counter, which the mail and thousands of missionaries are continually dispersing. It is the only book which America has printed, and is capable of exerting an almost inconceivable influence for good or for bad. The editor is [a] preacher whom you voluntarily support. Your tax is commonly one cent, and it costs nothing for pew hire. But how many of these preachers preach the truth? I repeat the testimony of many an intelligent traveller, as well as my own convictions, when I say that probably no country was ever ruled by so mean a class of tyrants as are the editors of the periodical press in *this* country. Almost without exception the tone of the press is mercenary and servile. The *Commonwealth*, and the *Liberator*, are the only papers, as far as I know, which make themselves heard in condemnation of the cowardice and meanness of the authorities of Boston as lately exhibited. The other journals, almost without exception, — as the *Advertiser*, the *Transcript*, the *Journal*, the *Times*, *Bee*, *Herald*, etc., — by their manner of referring to and speaking of the Fugitive Slave Law or the carrying back of the slave, insult the common sense of the country. And they do this for the most part, because they think so to secure the approbation of their patrons, and also, one would

Vol. II

think, because they are not aware that a sounder sentiment prevails to any extent.

But, thank fortune, this preacher can be more easily reached by the weapons of the reformer than could the recreant priest. The *free* men of New England have only to refrain from purchasing and reading these sheets, have only to withhold their cents, to kill a score of them at once.[1]

Mahomet made his celestial journey in so short a time that "on his return he was able to prevent the complete overturn of a vase of water, which the angel Gabriel had struck with his wing on his departure."

When he took refuge in a cave near Mecca, being on his flight (Hegira) to Medina, "by the time that the Koreishites [who were close behind][2] reached the mouth of the cavern, an acacia tree had sprung up before it, in the spreading branches of which a pigeon had made its nest, and laid its eggs, and over the whole a spider had woven its web."

He said of himself, "I am no king, but the son of a Koreishite woman, who ate flesh dried in the sun."

He exacted "a tithe of the productions of the earth, where it was fertilized by brooks and rain; and a twentieth part where its fertility was the result of irrigation."

April 22. Had mouse-ear in blossom for a week. Observed the crowfoot on the Cliffs in abundance, and

1 [*Cape Cod, and Miscellanies*, pp. 397–399; *Misc.*, Riv. 183–185.]
2 [The brackets are Thoreau's.]

the saxifrage. The wind last Wednesday, April 16th, blew down a hundred pines on Fair Haven Hill.

Having treated my friend ill, I wished to apologize; but, not meeting him, I made an apology to myself.

It is not the invitation which I hear, but which I feel, that I obey.

April 26. The judge whose words seal the fate of a man for the longest time and furthest into eternity is not he who merely pronounces the verdict of the law, but he, whoever he may be, who, from a love of truth and unprejudiced by any custom or enactment of men, utters a true opinion or *sentence* concerning him. He it is that *sentences* him.[1] More fatal, as affecting his good or ill fame, is the utterance of the least inexpugnable truth concerning him, by the humblest individual, than the sentence of the supremest court in the land.

Gathered the mayflower and cowslips yesterday, and saw the houstonia, violets, etc. Saw a dandelion in blossom.

Are they Americans, are they New-Englanders, are they inhabitants of Concord, — Buttricks and Davises and Hosmers by name, — who read and support the Boston *Herald*, *Advertiser*, *Traveller*, *Journal*, *Transcript*, etc., etc., *Times?* Is that the *Flag of our Union?* Could slavery suggest a more complete servility? Is there any dust which such conduct does not lick and make fouler still with its slime? Has not the Boston

1 [*Cape Cod, and Miscellanies*, p. 396; *Misc.*, Riv. 181.]

Herald acted its part well, served its master faithfully? How could it have gone lower on its belly? How can a man stoop lower than he is low? do more than put his extremities in the place of that head he has? than make his head his *lower* extremity? And when I say the Boston *Herald* I mean the Boston press, with such few and slight exceptions as need not be made. When I have taken up this paper or the Boston *Times*, with my cuffs turned up, I have heard the gurgling of the sewer through every column; I have felt that I was handling a paper picked out of the public sewers, a leaf from the gospel of the gambling-house, the groggery, and the brothel, harmonizing with the gospel of the Merchants' Exchange.[1]

I do not know but there are some who, if they were tied to the whipping-post and could but get one hand free, would use it to ring the bells and fire the cannon to celebrate their liberty. It reminded me of the Roman Saturnalia, on which even the slaves were allowed to take some liberty. So some of you took the liberty to ring and fire. That was the extent of your freedom; and when the sound of the bells died away, your liberty died away also, and when the powder was all expended, your liberty went off with the smoke. Nowadays men wear a fool's-cap and call it a liberty-cap. The joke could be no broader if the inmates of the prisons were to subscribe for all the powder to be used in such salutes, and hire their jailors to do the firing and ringing for them.[2]

[1] [*Cape Cod, and Miscellanies*, pp. 399, 400; *Misc.*, Riv. 185, 186.]
[2] [*Cape Cod, and Miscellanies*, p. 393; *Misc.*, Riv. 177, 178.]

Vol. II

Every one experiences that, while his relation to another actually may be one of distrust and disappointment, he may still have relations to him ideally and so really, in spite of both. He is faintly conscious of a confidence and satisfaction somewhere, and all further intercourse is based on this experience of success.

The very dogs and cats incline to affection in their relation to man. It often happens that a man is more humanely related to a cat or dog than to any human being. What bond is it relates us to any animal we keep in the house but the bond of affection? In a degree we grow to love one another.

April 30. What is a chamber to which the sun does not rise in the morning? What is a chamber to which the sun does not set at evening? Such are often the chambers of the mind, for the most part.

Even the cat which lies on a rug all day commences to prowl about the fields at night, resumes her ancient forest habits. The most tenderly bred grimalkin steals forth at night, — watches some bird on its perch for an hour in the furrow, like a gun at rest. She catches no cold; it is her nature. Caressed by children and cherished with a saucer of milk. Even she can erect her back and expand her tail and spit at her enemies like the wild cat of the woods. Sweet Sylvia!

What is the singing of birds, or any natural sound, compared with the voice of one we love?

To one we love we are related as to nature in the spring. Our dreams are mutually intelligible. We take the census, and find that there is one.

April 29. Every man, perhaps, is inclined to think his own situation singular in relation to friendship. Our thoughts would imply that other men *have* friends, though we have not. But I do not know of two whom I can speak of as standing in this relation to one another. Each one makes a standing offer to mankind, "On such and such terms I will give myself to you;" but it is only by a miracle that his terms are ever accepted.

We have to defend ourselves even against those who are nearest to friendship with us.

What a difference it is! — to perform the pilgrimage of life in the society of a mate, and not to have an acquaintance among all the tribes of men!

What signifies the census — this periodical numbering of men — to one who has no friend?

I distinguish between my *actual* and my *real* communication with individuals. I *really* communicate with my friends and congratulate myself and them on our relation and rejoice in their presence and society oftenest when they are personally absent. I remember that not long ago, as I laid my head on my pillow for the night, I was visited by an inexpressible joy that I was permitted to know and be related to such mortals as I was then actually related to; and yet no special event that I could think of had occurred to remind me of any with whom I was connected, and by the next noon, perchance, those essences that had caused me joy would have receded somewhat. I experienced a remarkable gladness in the thought that they existed. Their existence was then blessed to me. Yet such has never been my actual waking relation to any.

Love is a mutual confidence whose foundations no one knows. The one I love surpasses all the laws of nature in sureness. Love is capable of any wisdom.

> "He that hath love and judgment too
> Sees more than any other doe."

By our very mutual attraction, and our attraction to all other spheres, kept properly asunder. Two planets which are mutually attracted, being at the same time attracted by the sun, preserve equipoise and harmony.

Does not the history of chivalry and knight-errantry suggest or point to another relation to woman than leads to marriage, yet an elevating and all-absorbing one, perchance transcending marriage? As yet men know not one another, nor does man know woman.

I am sure that the design of my maker when he has brought me nearest to woman was not the propagation, but rather the maturation, of the species. Man is capable of a love of woman quite transcending marriage.

I observe that the *New York Herald* advertises situations wanted by "respectable young women" by the column, but never by respectable young men, rather "intelligent" and "smart" ones; from which I infer that the public opinion of New York does not require young men to be respectable in the same sense in which it requires young women to be so.

May it consist with the health of some bodies to be impure?

IV

MAY, 1851

(ÆT. 33)

May 1. Observed the *Nuphar advena*, yellow water-lily, in blossom; also the *Laurus Benzoin*, or fever-bush, spice-wood, near William Wheeler's in Lincoln, resembling the witch-hazel. It is remarkable that this aromatic shrub, though it grows by the roadside and does not hide itself, may be, as it were, effectually concealed, though it blossoms every spring. It may be observed only once in many years.

The blossom-buds of the peach have expanded just enough to give a slight peach tint to the orchards.

In regard to purity, I do not know whether I am much worse or better than my acquaintances. If I confine my thought to myself, I appear, whether by constitution or by education, irrevocably impure, as if I should be shunned by my fellow-men if they knew me better, as if I were of two inconsistent natures; but again, when I observe how the mass of men speak of woman and of chastity, — with how little love and reverence, — I feel that so far I am unaccountably better than they. I think that none of my acquaintances has a greater love and admiration for chastity than I have. Perhaps it is necessary that one should actually stand low himself in order to reverence what is high in others.

All distant landscapes seen from hilltops are veritable pictures, which will be found to have no actual existence to him who travels to them. "'T is distance lends enchantment to the view." It is the bare landscape without this depth of atmosphere to glass it. The distant river-reach seen in the north from the Lincoln Hill, high in the horizon, like the ocean stream flowing round Homer's shield, the rippling waves reflecting the light, is unlike the same seen near at hand. Heaven intervenes between me and the object. By what license do I call it Concord River. It redeems the character of rivers to see them thus. They were worthy then of a place on Homer's shield.

As I looked to-day from Mt. Tabor in Lincoln to the Waltham hill, I saw the same deceptive slope, the near hill melting into the further inseparably, indistinguishably; it was one gradual slope from the base of the near hill to the summit of the further one, a succession of copse-woods, but I knew that there intervened a valley two or three miles wide, studded with houses and orchards and drained by a considerable stream. When the shadow of a cloud passed over the nearer hill, I could distinguish its shaded summit against the side of the other.

I had in my mind's eye a silent gray tarn which I had seen the summer before high up on the side of a mountain, Bald Mountain, where the half-dead spruce trees stood far in the water draped with wreathy mist as with usnea moss, made of dews, where the mountain spirit bathed; whose bottom was high above the sur-

Vol. II

face of other lakes. Spruces whose dead limbs were more in harmony with the mists which draped them.

The forenoon that I moved to my house, a poor old lame fellow who had formerly frozen his feet hobbled off the road, came and stood before my door with one hand on each door-post, looking into the house, and asked for a drink of water. I knew that rum or something like it was the only drink he loved, but I gave him a dish of warm pond water, which was all I had, nevertheless, which to my astonishment he drank, being used to drinking.

Nations! What are nations? Tartars! and Huns! and Chinamen! Like insects they swarm. The historian strives in vain to make them memorable. It is for want of a man that there are so many men. It is individuals that populate the world.

THE SPIRIT OF LODIN

"I look down from my height on nations,
And they become ashes before me;
Calm is my dwelling in the clouds;
Pleasant are the great fields of my rest." [1]

Man is as singular as God.

There is a certain class of unbelievers who sometimes ask me such questions as, if I think that I can live on vegetable food alone; and to strike at the root of the matter at once, I am accustomed to answer such, "Yes, I can live on board nails." If they cannot understand that, they cannot understand much that I

[1] [*Cape Cod, and Miscellanies*, p. 473; *Misc.*, Riv. 275, 276.]

have to say. That cuts the matter short with them. For my own part, I am glad to hear of experiments of this kind being tried; as that a young man tried for a fortnight to see if he could live on hard, raw corn on the ear, using his tooth for his only mortar. The squirrel tribe tried the same and succeeded. The human race is interested in these experiments, though a few old women may be alarmed, who own their thirds in mills. [1]

Khaled would have his weary soldiers vigilant still; apprehending a midnight sally from the enemy, "Let no man sleep," said he. "We shall have rest enough after death." Would such an exhortation be understood by Yankee soldiers?

Omar answered the dying Abu Beker: "O successor to the apostle of God! spare me from this burden. I have no need of the Caliphat." "But the Caliphat has need of you!" replied the dying Abu Beker.

"Heraclius had heard of the mean attire of the Caliph Omar, and asked why, having gained so much wealth by his conquests, he did not go richly clad like other princes? They replied, that he cared not for this world, but for the world to come, and sought favor in the eyes of God alone. 'In what kind of a palace does he reside?' asked the emperor. 'In a house built of mud.' 'Who are his attendants?' 'Beggars and the poor.' 'What tapestry does he sit upon?' 'Justice and equity.'

[1] [*Walden*, p. 72; Riv. 103.]

'What is his throne?' 'Abstinence and true knowledge.' 'What is his treasure?' 'Trust in God.' 'And who are his guard?' 'The bravest of the Unitarians.'"

It was the custom of Ziyad, once governor of Bassora, "wherever he held sway, to order the inhabitants to leave their doors open at night, with merely a hurdle at the entrance to exclude cattle, engaging to replace any thing that should be stolen: and so effective was his police, that no robberies were committed."

Abdallah was "so fixed and immovable in prayer, that a pigeon once perched upon his head mistaking him for a statue."

May 6. Monday. The Harivansa describes a "substance called *Poroucha*, a spiritual substance known also under the name of Mahat, spirit united to the five elements, soul of being, now enclosing itself in a body like ours, now returning to the eternal body; it is mysterious wisdom, the perpetual sacrifice made by the virtue of the *Yoga*, the fire which animates animals, shines in the sun, and is mingled with all bodies. Its nature is to be born and to die, to pass from repose to movement. The spirit led astray by the senses, in the midst of the creation of Brahma, engages itself in works and knows birth, as well as death. The organs of the senses are its paths, and its work manifests itself in this creation of Brahma. Thought tormented by desires, is like the sea agitated by the wind. Brahma has said: the heart filled with strange affections is to be here below purified by wisdom. Here below even, clothed already as it were in a luminous form, let the spirit,

Vol. II

Like some other preachers, I have added my texts — derived from the Chinese and Hindoo scriptures — long after my discourse was written.

A commentary on the Sankhya Karika says, "By external knowledge worldly distinction is acquired; by internal knowledge, liberation."

The Sankhya Karika says, "By attainment of perfect knowledge, virtue and the rest become causeless; yet soul remains awhile invested with body, as the potter's wheel continues whirling from the effect of the impulse previously given to it."

I rejoice that horses and steers have to [be] *broken* before they can be made the slaves of men, and that men themselves have some wild oats still left to sow before they become submissive members of society. Undoubtedly all men are not equally fit subjects for civilization, and because the majority, like dogs and sheep, are tame by inherited disposition, is no reason why the others should have their natures broken, that they may be reduced to the same level. Men are in the main alike, but they were made several in order that [they] might be various. If a low use is to be served, one man will do nearly or quite as well as another; if a high one, individual excellence is to be regarded. Any man can stop a hole to keep the wind away, but no other man can serve that use which the author of this illustration did. Confucius says, "The skins of the tiger and the leopard when they are tanned, are as the skins of the dog and the

though clogged by the bonds of the body, prepare for itself an abode sure and permanent.

"He who would obtain final emancipation must abstain from every exterior action. The operation which conducts the pious and penitent Brahman to the knowledge of the truth, is all interior, intellectual, mental. They are not ordinary practices which can bring light into the soul.

"The Mouni who desires his final emancipation will have care evening and morning to subdue his senses, to fix his mind on the divine essence, and to transport himself by the force of his soul to the eternal abode of Vichnou. Although he may have engaged in works, he does not wear the clog of them, because his soul is not attached to them. A being returns to life in consequence of the affection which he has borne for terrestrial things: he finds himself emancipated, when he has felt only indifference for them.

"The Richis mingle with nature, which remains strange to their senses. Luminous and brilliant they cover themselves with a humid vapor, under which they seem no more to exist, although existing always, like the thread which is lost and confounded in the woof.

"Free in this world, as the birds in the air, disengaged from every kind of chain.

"Thus the Yogin, absorbed in contemplation, contributes for his part to creation: he breathes a divine perfume, he hears wonderful things. Divine forms traverse him without tearing him, and united to the nature which is proper to him, he goes, he acts, as animating original matter."

sheep tanned." But it is not the part of a true culture to tame tigers, any more than it is to make sheep ferocious. It is evident, then, that tanning their skins for shoes and the like is not the best use to which they can be put.[1]

How important is a constant intercourse with nature and the contemplation of natural phenomena to the preservation of moral and intellectual health! The discipline of the schools or of business can never impart such serenity to the mind. The philosopher contemplates human affairs as calmly and from as great a remoteness as he does natural phenomena. The ethical philosopher needs the discipline of the natural philosopher. He approaches the study of mankind with great advantages who is accustomed to the study of nature.

The Brahman Saradwata, says the Dharma Sacontala, was at first confounded on entering the city, "but now," says he, "I look on it as the freeman on the captive, as a man just bathed in pure water on a man smeared with oil and dust."

May 10. Heard the snipe over the meadows this evening.

May 12. Heard the golden robin and the bobolink. But where she has her seat, — whether in Westford or in Boxboro, — not even the assessors know. Inquire perchance of that dusky family on the cross-road, which is said to have Indian blood in their veins. Or perchance where this old cellar-hole now grassed over is faintly

[1] [*Excursions*, pp. 235, 236; Riv. 288, 289.]

visible, Nature once had her dwelling. Ask the crazy old woman who brings huckleberries to the village, but who lives nobody knows where.

If I have got false teeth, I trust that I have not got a false conscience. It is safer to employ the dentist than the priest to repair the deficiencies of nature.

By taking the ether the other day I was convinced how far asunder a man could be separated from his senses. You are told that it will make you unconscious, but no one can imagine what it is to be unconscious — how far removed from the state of consciousness and all that we call " this world " — until he has experienced it. The value of the experiment is that it does give you experience of an interval as between one life and another, — a greater space than you ever travelled. You are a sane mind without organs, — groping for organs, — which if it did not soon recover its old senses would get new ones. You expand like a seed in the ground. You exist in your roots, like a tree in the winter. If you have an inclination to travel, take the ether; you go beyond the furthest star.

It is not necessary for them to take ether, who in their sane and waking hours are ever translated by a thought; nor for them to see with their hindheads, who sometimes see from their foreheads; nor listen to the spiritual knockings, who attend to the intimations of reason and conscience.

May 16. Heard the whip-poor-will this evening. A splendid full moon to-night. Walked from 6.30 to

10 P. M. Lay on a rock near a meadow, which had absorbed and retained much heat, so that I could warm my back on it, it being a cold night. I found that the side of the sand-hill was cold on the surface, but warm two or three inches beneath.[1]

If there is a more splendid moonlight than usual, only the belated traveller observes it. When I am outside, on the outskirts of the town, enjoying the still majesty of the moon, I am wont to think that all men are aware of this miracle, that they too are silently worshipping this manifestation of divinity elsewhere. But when I go into the house I am undeceived; they are absorbed in checkers or chess or novel, though they may have been advertised of the brightness through the shutters.

In the moonlight night what intervals are created! The rising moon is related to the near pine tree which rises above the forest, and we get a juster notion of distance. The moon is only somewhat further off and on one side. There may be only three objects, — myself, a pine tree, and the moon, nearly equidistant.

Talk of demonstrating the rotation of the earth on its axis, — see the moon rise, or the sun!

The moonlight reveals the beauty of trees. By day it is so light and in this climate so *cold* commonly, that we do not perceive their shade. We do not know when we are beneath them.

According to Michaux, the canoe birch (*Betula papyracea*) ceases below the forty-third degree of latitude. Sections of the wood from just below the first

[1] [*Excursions*, p. 328; Riv. 403.]

ramification are used to inlay mahogany, in these parts It is brought from Maine for fuel.

Common white birch (*B. populifolia*) not found south of Virginia. Its epidermis incapable of being divided like the canoe birch and the European white.

The common alder (*Alnus serrulata*) blooms in January.

The locust (*Robinia Pseudacacia*) was one of the earliest trees introduced into Europe from America (by one Robin, about 1601); now extensively propagated in England, France, and Germany. Used for trunnels to the exclusion of all others in the Middle and Southern States. Instead of decaying, acquire hardness with time.

May 18. *Sunday.* Lady's-slipper almost fully blossomed. The log of a canoe birch on Fair Haven, cut down the last winter, more than a foot in diameter at the stump; one foot in diameter at ten feet from the ground. I observed that all parts of the epidermis exposed to the air and light were white, but the inner surfaces, freshly exposed, were a buff or salmon-color. Sinclair says that in winter it is white throughout. But this was cut before the sap flowed ? ?! Was there any sap in the log ? I counted about fifty rings. The shrub oaks are now blossoming. The scarlet tanagers are come. The oak leaves of all colors are just expanding, and are more beautiful than most flowers. The hickory buds are almost leaves. The landscape has a new life and light infused into it. The deciduous trees are springing, to countenance the pines, which are evergreen. It seems to take but one summer day to fetch the summer in. The turning-point between

winter and summer is reached. The birds are in full blast. There is a peculiar freshness about the landscape; you scent the fragrance of new leaves, of hickory and sassafras, etc. And to the eye the forest presents the tenderest green. The blooming of the apple trees is becoming general.

I think that I have made out two kinds of poplar, — the *Populus tremuloides*, or American aspen, and the *P. grandidentata*, or large American aspen, whose young leaves are downy.

Michaux says that the locust begins to convert its sap into perfect wood from the third year; which is not done by the oak, the chestnut, the beech, and the elm till after the tenth or the fifteenth year.

He quotes the saying, " The foot of the owner is the best manure for his land." " He " is Augustus L. Hillhouse, who writes the account of the olive at the request of Michaux.

The elder Michaux found the balsam poplar (*P. balsamifera*) very abundant on Lake St. John and the Saguenay River, where it is eighty feet high and three feet in diameter. This, however, is distinct from the *P. candicans*, heart-leaved balsam poplar, which M. finds hereabouts, though never in the woods, and does not know where it came from.

He praises the Lombardy poplar because, its limbs being compressed about the trunk, it does not interfere with the walls of a house nor obstruct the windows.

No wood equal to our black ash for oars, so pliant and

elastic and strong, second only to hickory for hand-spikes; used also for chair-bottoms and riddles.

The French call the nettle-tree *bois inconnu*.

Our white elm (*Ulmus Americana*) "the most magnificent vegetable of the temperate zone."

The *Pinus mitis*, yellow pine, or spruce pine, or short-leaved pine. A two-leaved pine widely diffused, but not found northward beyond certain districts of Connecticut and Massachusetts. In New Jersey fifty or sixty feet high and fifteen to eighteen inches in diameter. Sometimes three leaves on fresh shoots; smallest of pine cones; seeds cast first year. Very excellent wood for houses, masts, decks, yards, beams, and cabins, next in durability to the long-leaved pine. Called at Liverpool New York pine. Its regular branches make it to be called spruce pine sometimes.

Pinus australis, or long-leaved pine, an invaluable tree, called yellow pine, pitch pine, and broom pine where it grows; in the North, Southern pine and red pine; in England, Georgia pitch pine. First appears at Norfolk, Virginia; thence stretches six hundred miles southwest. Sixty or seventy feet high, by fifteen to eighteen inches; leaves a foot long, three in a sheath; negroes use them for brooms. Being stronger, more compact and durable, because the resin is equally distributed, and also fine-grained and susceptible of a bright polish, it is preferred to every other pine. In naval architecture, most esteemed of all pines, — keels, beams, side-planks, trunnels, etc. For decks preferred to yellow pine, — and flooring houses. Sold for more at Liverpool than any other pine. Moreover it supplies

nearly all the resinous matter used and exported. Others which contain much pitch are more dispersed. At present (1819) this business is confined to North Carolina.

M. says the branches of resinous trees consist almost wholly of *wood*, of which the organization is even more perfect than in the body of the tree. They use dead wood for the tar, etc., in which it has accumulated.

Says the vicinity of Brunswick, Me., and Burlington, Vt., are the most northerly limits of the pitch pine or *P. rigida*. (I saw what I should have called a pitch pine at Montmorency.)

White pine (*P. Strobus*) most abundant between forty-third and forty-seventh degrees, one hundred and eighty feet by seven and eight twelfths the largest. "The loftiest and most valuable" of the productions of the New Hampshire forest.

The black spruce is called *épinette noire* and *épinette à la bière* in Canada. From its strength best substitute for oak and larch. Used here for rafters and preferred to hemlock; tougher than white pine, but more liable to crack.

The white spruce (*Abies alba*) called *épinette blanche* in Canada. Not so large as the last and wood inferior.

Hemlock spruce (*Abies Canadensis*) called *pérusse* in Canada. In Maine, Vermont, and upper New Hampshire, three fourths of the evergreen woods, the rest being black spruce. Belongs to cold regions; begins to appear about Hudson's Bay. Its fibre makes the circuit of stocks fifteen or twenty inches in diameter in ascending five or six feet. Old trees have their circles separated, and the boards are *shaky*. Decays

rapidly when exposed to the air. It is firmer, though coarser, than the white pine; affords tighter hold to nails. Used in Maine for threshing-floors, resisting indentation. Most common use sheathing of houses, to be covered with clapboards. Used for laths.

White cedar (*Cupressus thyoides*). "The perfect wood resists the succession of dryness and moisture longer than that of any other species;" hence for shingles.

Larch (*Larix Americana*); in Canada *épinette rouge; tamarack* by the Dutch. Male aments appear before the leaves. Wood superior to any pine or spruce in strength and durability. Used in Maine for knees.

Cedar of Lebanon (*Larix cedrus*) largest and most majestic of resinous trees of the Old World and one of the finest vegetable productions of the globe.

Cedar Island in Lake Champlain northern limit of red cedar (*Juniperus Virginiana*). Eastward, not beyond Wiscasset. Seeds mature at beginning of fall and *sown at once;* shoot next spring. Gin made from them.

Arbor-vitæ (*Thuya occidentalis*), the only species of *Thuya* in the New World. Lake St. John in Canada its northern limit; abounds between 48° 50′ and 45°. The posts last thirty-five or forty years, and the rails sixty, or three or four times as long as those of any other species. In northern New England States the best for fences; last longer in clay than sand.

The superiority of mahogany in the fineness of its grain and its hardness, which make it susceptible of a brilliant polish. Native trees in Northern States used in cabinet making are black, yellow, and canoe birches,

red-flowering curled maple, bird's-eye maple, wild cherry, and sumach.

The circle[s] of peck and other measures made at Hingham of black, red, or gray oak are "always of a dull blue color, produced by the gallic acid of the wood acting upon the iron vessel in which it is boiled."

White ash used for sieve rims, rake heads and handles, scythe handles, pulleys, etc. Rake teeth of the mockernut hickory.

In New York and Philadelphia "the price [of wood for fuel] [1] nearly equals and sometimes exceeds that of the best wood in Paris, though this immense capital annually requires more than 300,000 cords, and is surrounded to the distance of 300 miles by cultivated plains." Said in book of 1819.

May 19. Found the *Arum triphyllum* and the nodding trillium, or wake-robin, in Conant's Swamp. An ash also in bloom there, and the sassafras quite striking. Also the fringed polygala by Conantum wood.

Sinclair says the hornbeam is called "swamp beech" in Vermont.

May 20. *Tuesday.* There is, no doubt, a perfect analogy between the life of the human being and that of the vegetable, both of the body and the mind. The botanist Gray says: —

"The organs of plants are of two sorts: — 1. Those of *Vegetation*, which are concerned in growth, — by

[1] [Supplied by Thoreau.]

which the plant takes in the aërial and earthy matters on which it lives, and elaborates them into the materials of its own organized substance; 2. Those of *Fructification* or *Reproduction*, which are concerned with the propagation of the species."

So is it with the human being. I am concerned first to come to my *Growth*, intellectually and morally (and physically, of course, as a means to this, for the body is the symbol of the soul), and then to bear my *Fruit*, do my *Work*, *propagate* my kind, not only physically but *morally*, not only in body but in mind.

"The organs of vegetation are the *Root, Stem,* and *Leaves*. The *Stem* is the axis and original basis of the plant."

"The first point of the stem preëxists in the embryo (*i. e.* in the rudimentary plantlet contained within the seed): it is here called the radicle." Such is the rudiment of mind, already partially developed, more than a bud, but pale, having never been exposed to the light, and slumbering coiled up, packed away in the seed, unfolded [*sic*].

Consider the still pale, rudimentary, infantine, radicle-like thoughts of some students, which who knows what they might expand to, if they should ever come to the light and air, if they do not become rancid and perish in the seed. It is not every seed that will survive a thousand years. Other thoughts further developed, but yet pale and languid, like shoots grown in a cellar.

"The plant . . . develops from the first in two opposite directions, *viz.* upwards [to expand in the light and air] to produce and continue the stem (or

ascending axis), and downwards [avoiding the light][1] to form the root (or *descending* axis). The former is ordinarily or in great part aërial, the latter subterranean."

So the mind develops from the first in two opposite directions: upwards to expand in the light and air; and downwards avoiding the light to form the root. One half is aërial, the other subterranean. The mind is not well balanced and firmly planted, like the oak, which has not as much root as branch, whose roots like those of the white pine are slight and near the surface. One half of the mind's development must still be root, — in the embryonic state, in the womb of nature, more unborn than at first. For each successive new idea or bud, a new rootlet in the earth. The growing man penetrates yet deeper by his roots into the womb of things. The infant is comparatively near the surface, just covered from the light; but the man sends down a tap-root to the centre of things.

The mere logician, the mere reasoner, who weaves his arguments as a tree its branches in the sky, — nothing equally developed in the roots, — is overthrown by the first wind.

As with the roots of the plant, so with the roots of the mind, the branches and branchlets of the root "are mere repetitions for the purpose of multiplying the absorbing points, which are chiefly the growing or newly formed extremities, sometimes termed *spongelets*. It bears no other organs."

So this organ of the mind's development, the *Root*, bears no organs but spongelets or absorbing points.

[1] [The bracketed portions in both cases are Thoreau's.]

Vol. II

Annuals, which perish root and all the first season, especially have slender and thread-like fibrous roots. But biennials are particularly characterized by distended, fleshy roots containing starch, a stock for future growth, to be consumed during their second or flowering season, — as carrots, radishes, turnips. Perennials frequently have many thickened roots clustered together, tuberous or palmate roots, fasciculated or clustered as in the dahlia, pæony, etc.

Roots may spring from any part of the stem under favorable circumstances; "that is to say in darkness and moisture, as when covered by the soil or resting on its surface."

That is, the most clear and ethereal ideas (Antæus-like) readily ally themselves to the earth, to the primal womb of things. They put forth roots as soon as branches; they are eager to be *soiled*. No thought soars so high that it sunders these apron-strings of its mother. The thought that comes to light, that pierces the empyrean on the other side, is wombed and rooted in darkness, a moist and fertile darkness, — its roots in Hades like the tree of life. No idea is so soaring but it will readily put forth roots. Wherever there is an air-and-light-seeking bud about to expand, it may become in the earth a darkness-seeking root. Even swallows and birds-of-paradise *can* walk on the ground. To quote the sentence from Gray entire: "Roots not only spring from the root-end of the primary stem in germination, but also from any subsequent part of the stem under favorable circumstances, that is to say, in darkness and moisture, as when covered by the soil or resting on its surface."

No thought but is connected as strictly as a flower, with the earth. The mind flashes not so far on one side but its rootlets, its spongelets, find their way instantly on the other side into a moist darkness, uterine, — a low bottom in the heavens, even miasma-exhaling to such immigrants as are not acclimated. A cloud is uplifted to sustain its roots. Imbosomed in clouds as in a chariot, the mind drives through the boundless fields of space. Even there is the dwelling of Indra.

I might here quote the following, with the last — of roots: "They may even strike in the open air and light, as is seen in the copious aërial rootlets by which the Ivy, the Poison Ivy, and the Trumpet Creeper climb and adhere to the trunks of trees or other bodies; and also in Epiphytes or Air-plants, of most warm regions, which have no connection whatever with the soil, but germinate and grow high in air on the trunks or branches of trees, etc.; as well as in some terrestrial plants, such as the Banian and Mangrove, that send off aërial roots from their trunks or branches, which finally reach the ground."

So, if our light-and-air-seeking tendencies extend too widely for our original root or stem, we must send downward new roots to ally us to the earth.

Also there are parasitic plants which have their roots in the branches or roots of other trees, as the mistletoe, the beech-drops, etc. There are minds which so have their roots in other minds as in the womb of nature, — if, indeed, most are not such?!

May 21. *Wednesday*. Yesterday I made out the black

and the white ashes. A double male white ash in Miles's Swamp, and two black ashes with sessile leaflets. A female white ash near railroad, in Stow's land. The white ashes by Mr. Prichard's have no blossoms, at least as yet.

If I am right, the *black* ash is improperly so called, from the color of its bark being lighter than the white. Though it answers to the description in other respects, even to the elder-like odor of the leaves, I should like still to see a description of the yellow ash which grows in made [*sic*].

The day before yesterday I found the male sassafras in abundance but no female.

The leaves of my new pine on Merriam's or Pine Hill are of intermediate length between those of the yellow pine and the Norway pine. I can find no cone to distinguish the tree by; but, as the leaves are *semicylindrical* and not *hollowed* I think it must be the red or Norway Pine, though it does not look very red, and is *spruce !* answering perhaps to the description of the yellow pine, which is sometimes called spruce pine.

To-day examined the flowers of the *Nemopanthes Canadensis*, — a genus of a single species, says Emerson. It bears the beautiful crimson velvety berry of the swamps, and is what I have heard called the cornel. Common name wild holly.

I have heard now within a few days that peculiar dreaming sound of the frogs [1] which belongs to the summer, — their midsummer night's dream.

[1] [Toads. See p. 250.]

swamp to his fellow, what was his joy and consolation to find that he too had seen the same sights in the heavens, he too had dreamed the same dreams!

From nature we turn astonished to this *near* but supernatural fact.

I think that the existence of man in nature is the divinest and most startling of all facts. It is a fact which few have realized.

I can go to my neighbors and meet on ground as elevated as we could expect to meet upon if we were now in heaven.

> "And we live,
> We of this mortal mixture, in the same law
> As the pure colorless intelligence
> Which dwells in Heaven, and the dead Hadean shades."

I do not think that man can understand the *importance* of man's existence, its bearing on the other phenomena of life, until it shall become a remembrance to him the survivor that such a being or such a race once existed on the earth. Imagine yourself alone in the world, a musing, wondering, reflecting spirit, *lost* in thought, and imagine thereafter the creation of man! — man made in the image of God!

Looking into a book on dentistry the other day, I observed a list of authors who had written on this subject. There were Ran and Tan and Yungerman, and I was impressed by the fact that there was nothing in a name. It was as if they had been named by the child's rigmarole of *Iery* [*wiery*] *ichery van, tittle-tol-tan*, etc. I saw in my mind a herd of wild creatures swarming over the earth, and to each one its own herdsman had affixed

Only that thought and that expression are good which are musical.

I think that we are not commonly aware that man is our contemporary, — that in this strange, outlandish world, so barren, so prosaic, fit not to live in but merely to pass through, that even here so divine a creature as man does actually live. Man, the crowning fact, the god we know. While the earth supports so rare an inhabitant, there is somewhat to cheer us. Who shall say that there is no God, if there is a *just* man. It is only within a year that it has occurred to me that there is such a being actually existing on the globe. Now that I perceive that it is so, many questions assume a new aspect. We have not only the idea and vision of the divine ourselves, but we have brothers, it seems, who have this idea also. Methinks my neighbor is better than I, and his thought is better than mine. There is a representative of the divinity on earth, of [whom] all things fair and noble are to be expected. We have the material of heaven here. I think that the standing miracle to man is man. Behind the paling yonder, come rain or shine, hope or doubt, there dwells a man, an actual being who can sympathize with our sublimest thoughts.

The revelations of nature are infinitely glorious and cheering, hinting to us of a remote future, of possibilities untold; but startlingly near to us some day we find a fellow-man.

The frog had eyed the heavens from his marsh, until his mind was filled with visions, and he saw more than belongs to this fenny earth. He mistrusted that he was become a dreamer and visionary. Leaping across the

some barbarous name, or sound, or syllables, in his own dialect, — so in a thousand languages. Their names were seen to be as meaningless exactly as Bose or Tray, the names of dogs.[1] Men get named no better.

We seem to be distinct ourselves, never repeated, and yet we bear no names which express a proportionate distinctness; they are quite accidental. Take away their names, and you leave men a wild herd, distinguished only by their individual qualities. It is as if you were to give names in the Caffre dialect to the individuals in a herd of spring-boks or gnus.

We have but few patronymics, but few Christian names, in proportion to the number of us. Is it that men ceased to be original when genuine and original names ceased to be given. Have we not enough character to establish a new patronymic.

Methinks it would be some advantage to philosophy if men were *named* merely in the gross, as they are known. It would only be necessary to know the genus and, perchance, the species and variety, to know the individual.

I will not allow *mere names* to make distinctions for me, but still see men in herds for all *them*. A familiar name cannot make a man less strange to me. It may be given to a savage who retains in secret his own wild title earned in the woods. I see that the neighbor who wears the familiar epithet of William or Edwin takes it off with his jacket. It does not adhere to him when asleep or when in anger, or aroused by any passion or inspiration. I seem to hear pronounced by some of his

[1] [*Excursions*, p. 236; Riv. 289.]

kin at such a time his original wild name in some jaw-breaking or else melodious tongue. As the names of the Poles and Russians are to us, so are ours to them.

Our names are as cheap as the names given to dogs. We know what are dogs' names; we know what are men's names. Sometimes it would be significant and truer, it would lead to generalization, it would avoid exaggeration, to say, "*There was a man* who said or did —," instead of designating him by some familiar, but perchance delusive, name.

We hardly believe that every private soldier in a Roman army had a name of his own.[1]

It is interesting to see how the names of famous men are repeated, — even of great poets and philosophers. The poet is not known to-day even by his neighbors to be more than a common man. He is perchance the butt of many. The proud farmer looks down [on] and boorishly ignores him, or regards him as a loafer who treads down his grass, but perchance in course of time the poet will have so succeeded that some of the farmer's posterity, though equally boorish with their ancestor, will bear the poet's name. The boor names his boy Homer, and so succumbs unknowingly to the bard's victorious fame. Anything so fine as poetic genius he cannot more directly recognize. The unpoetic farmer names his child Homer.

You have a wild savage in you, and a savage name is perchance somewhere recorded as yours.[2]

[1] [*Excursions*, pp. 236, 237; Riv. 289–291.]
[2] *Excursions*, p. 237; Riv. 290.]

May 23. Friday. And wilder still there grows elsewhere, I hear, a native and aboriginal crab-apple, *Malus* (as Michaux, or, as Emerson has it, *Pyrus*) *coronaria* in Southern States, and also *angustifolia* in the Middle States; whose young leaves "have a bitter and slightly aromatic taste" (Michaux), whose beautiful flowers perfume the air to a great distance. "The apples ... are small, green, intensely acid, and very odoriferous. Some farmers make cider of them, which is said to be excellent: they make very fine sweet-meats also, by the addition of a large quantity of sugar" (Michaux). Celebrated for "the beauty of its flowers, and for the sweetness of its perfume" (Michaux).[1]

Michaux says that the wild apple of Europe has yielded to cultivation nearly three hundred species in France alone. Emerson says, referring to Loudon, "In 1836, the catalogue and the gardens of the London Horticultural Society contained upwards of 1400 distinct sorts, and new ones are every year added."

But here are species which they have not in their catalogue, not to mention the varieties which the crab might yield to cultivation.[2]

This genus, so kind to the human race, the *Malus* or *Pyrus*; *Rosaceæ* the family, or others say *Pomaceæ*. Its flowers are perhaps the most beautiful of any tree. I am frequently compelled to turn and linger by some more than usually beautiful two-thirds-expanded blossoms.[3] If such were not so common, its fame would be

[1] [*Excursions*, p. 301; Riv. 370.]
[2] [*Excursions*, p. 316; Riv. 388.]
[3] [*Excursions*, p. 294; Riv. 361.]

Vol. II

loud as well as wide. Its most copious and delicious blossoms.

But our wild apple is wild perchance like myself, who belong not to the aboriginal race here, but have strayed into the woods from the cultivated stock,[1] — where the birds, where winged thoughts or agents, have planted or are planting me. Even these at length furnish hardy stocks for the orchard.

You might call one *Malus oculata;* another *M. Iridis; M. cum parvuli dæmonis oculis,* or Imp-eyed: Blue-Jay Apple, or *M. corvi cristati;* Wood-Dell Apple (*M. silvestri-vallis*); Field-Dell Apple (*M. campestri-vallis*); Meadow Apple (*M. pratensis*); Rock Meadow Apple (*saxopratensis*); Partridge or Grouse Apple or bud [*sic*]; Apple of the Hesperides (*Malus Hesperidum*); Woodside Apple; Wood Apple (*M. silvatica*); the Truant's Apple (*M. cessatoris*); Saunterer's Apple (*M. erronis vel vagabundi*); the Wayside Apple (*M. trivialis*); Beauty of the Air (*decus aëris*); December-eating; Frozen-thawed (*gelato-soluta* or *gelata regelata*); the Concord Apple (*M. Concordiensis*); the Brindled Apple; Wine of New England (*M. vinosa*); the Chickaree Apple; the Green Apple (*M. viridis*); the Dysentery or Cholera-morbus Apple.[2]

Distinctly related things are strangely near in *fact*, brush one another with their jackets. Perchance this window-seat in which we sit discoursing Transcendentalism, with only Germany and Greece stretching behind our minds, was made so deep because this was a few

[1] [*Excursions*, p. 301; Riv. 369.]
[2] [*Excursions*, p. 316; Riv. 388, 389.]

years ago a garrison-house, with thick log walls, bullet-proof, behind which men sat to escape the wild red man's bullet and the arrow and the tomahawk, and bullets fired by Indians are now buried in its walls. Pythagoras seems near compared with them.

May 24. Saturday. Our most glorious experiences are a kind of regret. Our regret is so sublime that we may mistake it for triumph. It is the painful, plaintively sad surprise of our Genius remembering our past lives and contemplating what is possible. It is remarkable that men commonly never refer to, never hint at, any crowning experiences when the common laws of their being were unsettled and the divine and eternal laws prevailed in them. Their lives are not revolutionary; they never recognize any other than the local and temporal authorities. It is a regret so divine and inspiring, so genuine, based on so true and distinct a contrast, that it surpasses our proudest boasts and the fairest expectations.

My most sacred and memorable life is commonly on awaking in the morning. I frequently awake with an atmosphere about me as if my unremembered dreams had been divine, as if my spirit had journeyed to its native place, and, in the act of reëntering its native body, had diffused an elysian fragrance around.

The Genius says: "Ah! That is what you were! That is what you may yet be!" It is glorious for us to be able to regret even such an existence.

A sane and growing man revolutionizes every day. What institutions of man can survive a morning experience? A single night's sleep, if we have indeed slumbered and forgotten anything and grown in our sleep, puts them behind us like the river Lethe: It is no unusual thing for him to see the kingdoms of this world pass away.[1]

It is an interesting inquiry to seek for the medicines which will cure our ails in the plants which grow around us. At first we are not disposed to believe that man and plants are so intimately related. Very few plants have been medically examined. And yet this is the extent of most men's botany; and it is more extensive than would at first be supposed. The botanist is startled by some countryman's familiarity with an obscure plant to him rare and strange. He, who has been an observer for some years, knows not what it is, but the unobserving countryman, who sees nothing but what is thrust upon him, or the old woman who rarely goes out of the house, shows an easy familiarity with it and can call it by name.

I am struck by the fact that, though any important individual experience is rare, though it is so rare that the individual is conscious of a relation to his maker transcending time and space and earth, though any knowledge of, or communication from, "Providence" is the rarest thing in the world, yet men very easily, regarding themselves in the gross, speak of carrying out the designs of Providence as nations. How often the Saxon man talks of carrying out the designs of Providence, as if he had some knowledge of Providence

[1] *Vide* [p. 286].

and His designs. Men allow themselves to associate Providence and designs of Providence with their dull, prosaic, every-day thoughts of things. That language is usurped by the stalest and deadest prose, which can only report the most choice poetic experience. This "Providence" is the stalest jest in the universe. The office-boy sweeps out his office "by the leave of Providence."

May 25. A fine, freshening air, a little hazy, that bathes and washes everything, saving the day from extreme heat. Walked to the hills south of Wayland by the road by Deacon Farrar's. First vista just beyond Merron's (?), looking west down a valley, with a verdant-columned elm at the extremity of the vale and the blue hills and horizon beyond. These are the resting-places in a walk. We love to see any part of the earth tinged with blue, cerulean, the color of the sky, the celestial color. I wonder that houses are not oftener located mainly that they may command particular rare prospects, every convenience yielding to this. The farmer would never suspect what it was you were buying, and such sites would be the cheapest of any. A site where you might avail yourself of the art of Nature for three thousand years, which could never be materially changed or taken from you, a noble inheritance for your children. The true sites for human dwellings are unimproved. They command no price in the market. Men will pay something to look into a travelling showman's box, but not to look upon the fairest prospects on the earth. A vista where you have the near green horizon contrasted with

the distant blue one, terrestrial with celestial earth. The prospect of a vast horizon must be accessible in our neighborhood. Where men of enlarged views may be educated. An unchangeable kind of wealth, a *real* estate.

There we found the celandine in blossom and the *Ranunculus bulbosus*, which we afterwards saw *double* in Wayland, having nine petals.

The *Pyrus arbutifolia*, variety *melanocarpa*. Gray makes also the variety *erythrocarpa*. Is this the late red choke-berry of the swamps? and is the former the earlier black one of the swamps?

By Farrar's the *Nepeta Glechoma*, a kind of mint. Linnæus calls it *Glechoma hederacea*. Looks somewhat like catnep.

The marsh-marigold, *Caltha palustris*, improperly called cowslip.

The white oak, *Quercus alba*. And the commonest scrub oak, the bear or black oak, *Q. ilicifolia*.

The chinquapin, or dwarf chestnut, oak, the smallest of our oaks, *Q. prinoides*.

The *Cratægus coccinea* (?), or scarlet-fruited thorn (?)

Another glorious vista with a wide horizon at the yellow Dutch house, just over the Wayland line, by the black spruce, heavy and dark as night, which we could see two or three miles as a landmark. Now at least, before the deciduous trees have fully expanded their leaves, it is remarkably black. It is more stoutly and irregularly branched than Holbrook's spruces — has a much darker foliage; but the cone scales of both are slightly waved or notched. Are they, then, both

black spruce? The cones are enough like, and the thickness of the leaves; their color enough unlike. Here is a view of the Jenkins house, the fish-pole house, and Wachusett beyond.

Noticed what I think must be a young poison sumach[1] abundant by the roadside in woods, with last year's berries, with small greenish-yellow flowers, but leaves not pinnatifid, three together; from one to two feet high. What is it?

Alnus serrulata, the common alder, with a grayish stem, leaves smooth on both sides.

Alnus incana, the speckled alder, downy on under side of leaves.

The hard-berried plant seems to be *Andromeda ligustrina* (?) of Gray, *A. paniculata* of Bigelow, *Lyonia paniculata* of Emerson.

Thyme-leaved veronica, little bluish-white, streak-petalled flower by road sides. *Silene Pennsylvanica.*

What is the orange-yellow aster-like flower of the meadows now in blossom with a sweet-smelling stem when bruised?[2]

What the delicate pinkish and yellowish flower with hoary-green stem and leaves, of rocky hills.[3]

Saw Bunker Hill Monument and Charlestown from the Wayland hills, and across the valleys to Milton Hill.[4] Westward, or west by south, an island in a pond or in the river (!which see!) A grand horizon. Probably saw the elm between Wayland and Weston which is seen so

[1] Ivy?   [2] Golden senecio.   [3] Corydalis.
[4] [Doubtless Blue Hill is meant, not the lower eminence known as Milton Hill.]

far in the horizon from the northwest part of Sudbury. A good, a rare place this must be to view the Sudbury or Wayland meadows a little earlier.

Came back across lots to the black spruce.

Now, at 8.30 o'clock P. M., I hear the dreaming of the frogs.[1] So it seems to me, and so significantly passes my life away. It is like the dreaming of frogs in a summer evening.

May 27. I saw an organ-grinder this morning before a rich man's house, thrilling the street with harmony, loosening the very paving-stones and tearing the routine of life to rags and tatters, when the lady of the house shoved up a window and in a semiphilanthropic tone inquired if he wanted anything to eat. But he, very properly it seemed to me, kept on grinding and paid no attention to her question, feeding her ears with melody unasked for. So the world shoves up its window and interrogates the poet, and sets him to gauging ale casks in return. It seemed to me that the music suggested that the recompense should be as fine as the gift. It would be much nobler to enjoy the music, though you paid no money for it, than to presume always a beggarly relation. It is after all, perhaps, the best instrumental music that we have.

May 28. The trees now begin to shade the streets. When the sun gets high in the sky the trees give shade. With oppressive heats come refreshing shadows.

The buttercups spot the churchyard.

[1] [Toads. See p. 250.]

May 29. It is evident that the virtues of plants are almost completely unknown to us, and we esteem the few with which we are better acquainted unreasonably above the many which are comparatively unknown to us. Bigelow says: "It is a subject of some curiosity to consider, if the knowledge of the present Materia Medica were by any means to be lost, how many of the same articles would again rise into notice and use. Doubtless a variety of new substances would develop unexpected powers, while perhaps the poppy would be shunned as a deleterious plant, and the cinchona might grow unmolested upon the mountains of Quito." Sawyer regards *Nux vomica* among the most valuable. B. says (1817): "We have yet to discover our anodynes and our emetics, although we abound in bitters, astringents, aromatics, and demulcents. In the present state of our knowledge we could not well dispense with opium and ipecacuanha, yet a great number of foreign drugs, such as gentian, columbo, chamomile, kino, catechu, cascarilla, canella, etc., for which we pay a large annual tax to other countries, might in all probability be superseded by the indigenous products of our own. It is certainly better that our own country people should have the benefit of collecting such articles, than that we should pay for them to the Moors of Africa, or the Indians of Brazil."

The thorn-apple (*Datura Stramonium*) (apple of Peru, devil's-apple, Jamestown-weed) "emigrates with great facility, and often springs up in the ballast of ships, and in earth carried from one country to another." It secretes itself in the hold of vessels and migrates. It

Vol. II

is a sort of cosmopolitan weed, a roving weed. What adventures! What historian knows when first it came into a country! He quotes Beverly's "History of Virginia" as saying that some soldiers in the days of Bacon's rebellion, having eaten some of this plant, which was boiled for salad by mistake, were made natural fools and buffoons by it for eleven days, without injury to their bodies (? ?).

The root of a biennial or perennial will accumulate the virtues of the plant more than any other part.

B. says that Pursh states that the sweet-scented goldenrod (*Solidago odora*) "has for some time [*i. e.* before 1817][1] been an article of exportation to China, where it fetches a high price." And yet it is known to very few New-Englanders.

"No botanist," says B., "even if in danger of starving in a wilderness, would indulge his hunger on a root or fruit taken from an unknown plant of the natural order *Luridæ*, of the *Multisiliquæ*, or the *umbelliferous aquatics*. On the contrary he would not feel a moment's hesitation in regard to any of the *Gramina*, the fruit of the *Pomaceæ*, and several other natural families of plants, which are known to be uniformly innocent in their effects."

The aromatic flavor of the checkerberry is also perceived in the *Gaultheria hispidula*, in *Spiræa ulmaria* and the root of *Spiræa lobata*, and in the birches.

He says ginseng, spigelia, snake-root, etc., form considerable articles of exportation.

The odor of skunk-cabbage is perceived in some

[1] [Supplied by Thoreau.]

North American currants, as *Ribes rigens* of Michaux on high mountains.

At one time the Indians about Quebec and Montreal were so taken up with searching for ginseng that they could not be hired for any other purpose. It is said that both the Chinese and the Indians named this plant from its resemblance to the figure of a man.[1]

The Indians use the bark of *Dirca palustris*, or leather-wood, for their cordage. It was after the long-continued search of many generations that these qualities were discovered.

Of tobacco (*Nicotiana Tabacum*) B. says, after speaking of its poisonous qualities: "Yet the first person who had courage and patience enough to persevere in its use, until habit had overcome his original disgust, eventually found in it a pleasing sedative, a soother of care, and a material addition to the pleasures of life. Its use, which originated among savages, has spread into every civilized country; it has made its way against the declamations of the learned, and the prohibitions of civil and religious authority, and it now gives rise to an extensive branch of agriculture, or of commerce, in every part of the globe." Soon after its introduction into Europe, "the rich indulged in it as a luxury of the highest kind; and the poor gave themselves up to it, as a solace for the miseries of life." Several varieties are cultivated.

In return for many foreign weeds, we have sent abroad, says B., "the *Erigeron Canadensis* and the prolific families of *Ambrosia* and *Amaranthus*."

[1] Bigelow got this from Kalm. *Vide* extract from Kalm.

"The Indians were acquainted with the medicinal properties of more than one species of Euphorbia."

I noticed the button-bush, May 25th, around an elevated pond or mud-hole, its leaves just beginning to expand. This slight amount of green contrasted with its dark, craggly [sic], naked-looking stem and branches — as if subsiding waters had left them bare — looked Dantesque and infernal. It is not a handsome bush at this season, it is so slow to put out its leaves and hide its naked and unsightly stems.

The *Andromeda ligustrina* is late to leave out.

Malus excelsa; amara; florida; palustris; gratissima; ramosa; spinosa; ferruginea; aromatica; aurea; rubiginosa; odorata; tristis; officinalis!! herbacea; vulgaris; æstivalis; autumnalis; riparia; versicolor; communis; farinosa; super septa pendens;[1] *Malus sepium; vinum Novæ-Angliæ; succosa; sæpe formicis præoccupata; vermiculosa aut verminosa aut a vermibus corrupta vel erosa; Malus semper virens et viridis; cholera-morbifera or dysenterifera; M. sylvestripaludosa, excelsa et ramosa superne, difficilis conscendere, (fructus difficillimus stringere, parvus et durus); Cortex picis perforata or perterebata; rupestris; agrestis; arvensis; Assabettia;* Railroad Apple; *Musketaquidensis;* Dew Apple (*rorifera*); the apple whose fruit we tasted in our youth which grows *passim et nusquam,* (*Malus cujus fructum ineunte ætate gustavi quæ passim et nusquam viget*); our own particular apple; *Malus numquam legata vel stricta; cortice muscosâ; Malus viæ-ferreæ; sylvatica in sylvis densissimis.*[2]

[1] *Parietes, sepes, sepimenta* [alternatives for *septa*].
[2] [*Excursions,* p. 316; Riv. 388, 389.]

V

JUNE, 1851

(ÆT. 33)

June 3. Tuesday. Lectured in Worcester last Saturday, and walked to *As-* or *Has*nebumskit Hill in Paxton the next day. Said to be the highest land in Worcester County except Wachusett.

Met Mr. Blake, Brown, Chamberlin, Hinsdale, Miss Butman (?), Wyman, Conant.

Returned to Boston yesterday. Conversed with John Downes, who is connected with the Coast Survey, is printing tables for astronomical, geodesic, and other uses. He tells me that he once saw the common sucker in numbers piling up stones as big as his fist (like the piles which I have seen), taking them up or moving them with their mouths.

Dr. Harris suggests that the mountain cranberry which I saw at Ktaadn was the *Vaccinium Vitis-Idæa,* cowberry, because it was edible and not the *Uva-Ursi,* or bear-berry, which we have in Concord.

Saw the *Uvularia perfoliata,* perfoliate bellwort, in Worcester near the hill; an abundance of mountain laurel on the hills, now budded to blossom and the fresh lighter growth contrasting with the dark green; an abundance of very large checkerberries, or partridgeberries, as Bigelow calls them, on Hasnebumskit. Sugar maples about there. A very extensive view, but

May 30. Friday. There was a Concord man once who had a foxhound named Burgoyne. He called him Bugïne. A good name.[1]

May 31. Pedestrium solatium in apricis locis; nodosa.[2]

[1] [*Walden,* p. 308; Riv. 432.]
[2] [*Excursions,* p. 316; Riv. 389.]

the western view not so much wilder as I expected. See Barre, about fifteen miles off, and Rutland, etc., etc. Not so much forest as in our neighborhood; high, swelling hills, but less shade for the walker. The hills are green, the soil springier; and it is written that water is more easily obtained on the hill than in the valleys. Saw a Scotch fir, the pine so valued for tar and naval uses in the north of Europe.

Mr. Chamberlin told me that there was no corporation in Worcester except the banks (which I suspect may not be literally true), and hence their freedom and independence. I think it likely there is a gas company to light the streets at least.

John Mactaggart finds the ice thickest not in the largest lakes in Canada, nor in the smallest, where the surrounding forests melt it. He says that the surveyor of the boundary-line between England and United States on the Columbia River saw pine trees which would require sixteen feet in the blade to a cross-cut saw to do anything with them.

I examined to-day a large swamp white oak in Hubbard's meadow, which was blown down by the same storm which destroyed the lighthouse. At five feet from the ground it was nine and three fourths feet in circumference; the first branch at eleven and a half feet from ground; and it held its size up to twenty-three feet from the ground. Its whole height, measured on the ground, was eighty feet, and its breadth about sixty-six feet. The roots on one side were turned up with the soil on them, making an object very conspicuous a great distance off, the highest root being eighteen feet from the ground and fourteen feet above centre of trunk. The roots, which were small and thickly interlaced, were from three to nine inches beneath the surface (in other trees I saw them level with the surface) and thence extended fifteen to eighteen inches in depth (*i. e.* to this depth they occupied the ground). They were broken off at about eleven feet from the centre of the trunk and were there on an average one inch in diameter, the largest being three inches in diameter. The longest root was broken off at twenty feet from the centre, and was there three quarters of an inch in diameter. The tree was rotten within. The lower side of the soil (what was originally the lower), which clothed the roots for nine feet from the centre of the tree, was white and clayey to appearance, and a sparrow was sitting on three eggs within the mass. Directly under where the massive trunk had stood, and within a foot of the surface, you could apparently strike in a spade and meet with no obstruction to a free cultivation. There was no tap-root to be seen. The roots were encircled with dark, nubby rings. The tree, which still had a portion of its roots in the ground and held to them by a sliver on the leeward side, was alive and had leaved out, though on many branches the leaves were shrivelled again. *Quercus bicolor* of Bigelow, *Q. Prinus discolor* Mx. f.

I observed the grass waving to-day for the first time, — the swift Camilla on it. It might have been noticed before. You might have seen it now for a week past on grain-fields.

Clover has blossomed.

I noticed the indigo-weed a week or two ago pushing up like asparagus. Methinks it must be the small andromeda (?), that dull red mass of leaves in the swamp, mixed perchance with the rhodora, with its dry fruit-like appendages, as well as the *Andromeda paniculata*, else called *ligustrina*, and the clethra. It was the golden senecio (*Senecio aureus*) which I plucked a week ago in a meadow in Wayland. The earliest, methinks, of the aster and autumnal-looking yellow flowers. Its bruised stems enchanted me with their indescribable sweet odor, like I cannot think what.

The *Phaseolus vulgaris* includes several kinds of bush beans, of which those I raised were one.

June 6. Friday. Gathered last night the strong, rank, penetrating-scented angelica.

Under the head of the *Cicuta maculata*, or American hemlock, — "It is a rule sanctioned by the observations of medical botanists, that umbelliferous plants, which grow in or about the water, are of a poisonous nature." [1] He does not say that the angelica is poisonous, but I suppose that it is. It has such a rank, offensive, and killing odor as makes me think of the ingredients of the witches' cauldron. It did not leave my hands, which had carried it, long after I had washed them. A strong, penetrating, lasting, and sickening odor.

Gathered to-night the *Cicuta maculata*, American hemlock, the veins of the leaflets ending in the notches and the root fasciculated.

[1] [Bigelow, *American Medical Botany*, vol. i.]

Vol. II

Bigelow says, "The leaves of the *Solidago odora* have a delightfully fragrant odor, partaking of that of anise and sassafras, but different from either." [1]

June 7. My practicalness is not to be trusted to the last. To be sure, I go upon my legs for the most part, but, being hard-pushed and dogged by a superficial common sense which is bound to near objects by beaten paths, I am off the handle, as the phrase is, — I begin to be transcendental and show where my heart is. I am like those guinea-fowl which Charles Darwin saw at the Cape de Verd Islands. He says, "They avoided us like partridges on a rainy day in September, running with their heads cocked up; and if pursued, they readily took to the wing." Keep your distance, do not infringe on the interval between us, and I will pick up lime and lay real terrestrial eggs for you, and let you know by cackling when I have done it.

When I have been asked to speak at a temperance meeting, my answer has been, "I am too transcendental to serve you in your way." They would fain confine me to the rum-sellers and rum-drinkers, of whom I am not one, and whom I know little about.

It is a certain faeryland where we live. You may walk out in any direction over the earth's surface, lifting your horizon, and everywhere your path, climbing the convexity of the globe, leads you between heaven and earth, not away from the light of the sun and stars and the habitations of men. I wonder that I ever get five miles on my way, the walk is so crowded with events and

[1] [Bigelow, *American Medical Botany*, vol. i.]

phenomena. How many questions there are which I have not put to the inhabitants!

But how far can you carry *your* practicalness? How far does your knowledge really extend? When I have read in deeds only a hundred years old the words "to enjoy and possess, he and his assigns, *forever*," I have seen how short-sighted is the sense which conducts from day to day. When I read the epitaphs of those who died a century ago, they seem deader even than they expected. A day seems proportionally a long part of your "forever and a day."

There are few so temperate and chaste that they can afford to remind us even at table that they have a palate and a stomach.

We believe that the possibility of the future far exceeds the accomplishment of the past. We review the past with the common sense, but we anticipate the future with transcendental senses. In our sanest moments we find ourselves naturally expecting or prepared for far greater changes than any which we have experienced within the period of distinct memory, only to be paralleled by experiences which are forgotten. Perchance there are revolutions which create an interval impassable to the memory.

With reference to the near past, we all occupy the region of common sense, but in the prospect of the future we are, by instinct, transcendentalists.

We affirm that all things are possible, but only these things have been to our knowledge. I do not even infer the future *from what I know of the past*. I am hardly better acquainted with the past than with the future.

What is new to the individual may be familiar to the experience of his race. It must be rare indeed that the experience of the individual transcends that of his race. It will be perceived that there are two kinds of change, — that of the race, and that of the individual within the limits of the former.

One of those gentle, straight-down rainy days, when the rain begins by spotting the cultivated fields as if shaken from a pepper-box; a fishing day, when I see one neighbor after another, having donned his oil-cloth suit, walking or riding past with a fish-pole, having struck work, — a day and an employment to make philosophers of them all.

When introduced to high life I cannot help perceiving how it is as a thing jumped at, and I find that I do not get on in my enjoyment of the fine arts which adorn it, because my attention is wholly occupied with the jump, remembering that the greatest genuine leap on record, due to human muscles alone, is that of certain wandering Arabs who cleared twenty-five feet on level ground. The first question which I am tempted to put to the proprietor of such great impropriety is, "Who boosts you?" Are you one of the ninety-nine who fail or the hundredth, who succeeds?

June 8. *Sunday.* In F. A. Michaux's, *i. e.* the younger Michaux's, "Voyage à l'ouest des Monts Alléghanys, 1802," printed at Paris, 1808: —

He says the common inquiry in the newly settled

West was, "'From what part of the world have you come?' As if these vast and fertile regions would naturally be the point of union (*réunion*, meeting) and the common country of all the inhabitants of the globe."[1]

The current of the Ohio is so swift in the spring that it is not necessary to row. Indeed rowing would do more harm than good, since it would tend to turn the ark out of the current on to some isle or sand-bar, where it would be entangled amid floating trees. This has determined the form of the bateaux, which are not the best calculated for swiftness but to obey the current. They are from fifteen to fifty feet long by ten to twelve and fifteen, with square ends, and roof of boards like a house at one end. The sides are about four and a half feet above the water. "I was alone on the shore of the Monongahela, when I perceived, for the first time, in the distance, five or six of these bateaux which were descending this river. I could not conceive what those great square boxes were, which, abandoned to the current, presented alternately their ends, their sides, and even (or also (?), *et même*) their angles. As they came nearer, I heard a confused noise but without distinguishing anything, on account of the elevation of the sides. It was only on ascending the bank of the river that I perceived, in these bateaux, many families carrying with them their horses, cows, poultry, dismounted carts (*charrettes*), plows, harnesses, beds, agricultural implements, in short all that constitute the movables of a household (*ménage*) and the carrying

[1] [*Excursions*, p. 221; Riv. 271.]

on (*exploitation*) of a farm." But he was obliged to paddle his log canoe "*sans cesse*" because of the sluggishness of the current of the Ohio in April, 1802.

A Vermonter told him that the expense of clearing land in his State was always defrayed by the potash obtained from the ashes of the trees which were burnt, and sometimes people took land to clear on condition that they should have what potash they could make.

After travelling more than three thousand miles in North America, he says that no part is to be compared for the "*force végétative des forêts*" to the region of the Ohio between Wheeling and Marietta. Thirty-six miles above the last place he measured a plane tree on the bank of the Ohio which, at four feet from the ground, was forty-seven in circumference. It is true it was "*renflé d'une manière prodigieuse.*" Tulip and plane trees, his father had said, attained the greatest diameter of North American trees.

Ginseng was then the only "territorial" production of Kentucky which would pay the expense of transportation *by land* to Philadelphia. They collected it from spring to the first frosts. Even hunters carried for this purpose, beside their guns, a bag and a little "*pioche.*" From twenty-five to thirty "*milliers pesant*" were then transported annually, and this commerce was on the increase. Some transported it themselves from Kentucky to China, *i. e.* without selling it [to] the merchants of the seaboard. Traders in Kentucky gave twenty to twenty-four "sous" the pound for it.

They habituated their wild hogs to return to the house from time to time by distributing corn for them

once or twice a week. So I read that in Buenos Ayres they collect the horses into the corral twice a week to keep them tame in a degree.

Gathered the first strawberries to-day.

Observed on Fair Haven a tall pitch pine, such as some call yellow pine, — very smooth, yellowish, and destitute of branches to a great height. The outer and darker-colored bark appeared to have scaled off, leaving a fresh and smooth surface. At the ground, all round the tree, I saw what appeared to be the edges of the old surface scales, extending to two inches more in thickness. The bark was divided into large, smooth plates, one to two feet long and four to six inches wide.

I noticed that the cellular portion of the bark of the canoe birch log from which I stripped the epidermis a week or two ago was turned a complete brick-red color very striking to behold and reminding me of the red man and all strong, natural things, — the color of our blood somewhat. Under the epidermis it was still a sort of buff. The different colors of the various parts of this bark, at various times, fresh or stale, are extremely agreeable to my eye.

I found the white-pine-top full of staminate blossom-buds not yet fully grown or expanded, with a rich red tint like a tree full of fruit, but I could find no pistillate blossom.

The fugacious-petalled cistus, and the pink, and the lupines of various tints are seen together.

Our outside garments, which are often thin and fanciful and merely for show, are our epidermis, hanging loose and fantastic like that of the yellow birch, which may be cast off without harm, stripped off here and there without fatal injury; sometimes called cuticle and false skin. The vital principle wholly wanting in it; partakes not of the life of the plant. Our thicker and more essential garments are our cellular integument. When this is removed, the tree is said to be girdled and dies. Our shirt is the cortex, liber, or true bark, beneath which is found the alburnum or sap-wood, while the heart in old stocks is commonly rotten or has disappeared. As if we grew like trees, and were of the exogenous kind.[1]

June 9. James Wood, Senior, told me to-day that Asa (?) Melvin's father told him that he had seen alewives caught (many of them) in the meadow which we were crossing, on the west of Bateman's Pond, where now there is no stream, and though it is wet you can walk everywhere; also one shad. He thinks that a great part of the meadow once belonged to the pond.

Gathered the *Linnæa borealis*.

June 11. *Wednesday*. Last night a beautiful summer night, not too warm, moon not quite full, after two or three rainy days. Walked to Fair Haven by railroad, returning by Potter's pasture and Sudbury road. I feared at first that there would be too much white light, like the pale remains of daylight, and not a yellow, gloomy, dreamier light; that it would be like a candlelight by day; but when I got away from the town and deeper into the night, it was better. I hear whip-poor-wills, and see a few fireflies in the meadow.

[1] [*Walden*, p. 26; Riv. 40.]

I saw by the shadows cast by the inequalities of the clayey sand-bank in the Deep Cut that it was necessary to see objects by moonlight as well as sunlight, to get a complete notion of them. This bank had looked much more flat by day, when the light was stronger, but now the heavy shadows revealed its prominences. The prominences are light, made more remarkable by the dark shadows which they cast.

When I rose out of the Deep Cut into the old pigeon-place field, I rose into a warmer stratum of air, it being lighter. It told of the day, of sunny noontide hours, — an air in which work had been done, which men had breathed. It still remembered the sunny banks, — of the laborer wiping his brow, of the bee humming amid flowers, the hum of insects. Here is a puff of warmer air which has taken its station on the hills; which has come up from the sultry plains of noon.[1]

I hear the nighthawks uttering their squeaking notes high in the air now at nine o'clock P. M., and occasionally — what I do not remember to have heard so late — their booming note. It sounds more as if under a cope than by day. The sound is not so fugacious, going off to be lost amid the spheres, but is echoed hollowly to earth, making the low roof of heaven vibrate. Such a sound is more confused and dissipated by day.

The whip-poor-will suggests how wide asunder [are] the woods and the town. Its note is very rarely heard by those who live on the street, and then it is thought to be of ill omen. Only the dwellers on the outskirts of the village hear it occasionally. It sometimes comes

[1] [*Excursions*, p. 328; Riv. 403.]

Vol. II

into their yards. But go into the woods in a warm night at this season, and it is the prevailing sound. I hear now five or six at once. It is no more of ill omen therefore here than the night and the moonlight are. It is a bird not only of the woods, but of the night side of the woods.

New beings have usurped the air we breathe, rounding Nature, filling her crevices with sound. To sleep where you may hear the whip-poor-will in your dreams!

I hear from this upland, from which I see Wachusett by day, a wagon crossing one of the bridges. I have no doubt that in some places to-night I should be sure to hear every carriage which crossed a bridge over the river within the limits of Concord, for in such an hour and atmosphere the sense of hearing is wonderfully assisted and asserts a new dignity, and [we] become the Hearalls of the story. The late traveller cannot drive his horse across the distant bridge, but this still and resonant atmosphere tells the tale to my ear. Circumstances are very favorable to the transmission of such a sound. In the first place, planks so placed and struck like a bell swung near the earth emit a very resonant and penetrating sound; add that the bell is, in this instance, hung over water, and that the night air, not only on account of its stillness, but perhaps on account of its density, is more favorable to the transmission of sound. If the whole town were a raised planked floor, what a din there would be!

I hear some whip-poor-wills on hills, others in thick wooded vales, which ring hollow and cavernous, like an apartment or cellar, with their note. As when I hear

the working of some artisan from within an apartment.

I now descend round the corner of the grain-field, through the pitch pine wood into a lower field, more inclosed by woods, and find myself in a colder, damp and misty atmosphere, with much dew on the grass. I seem to be nearer to the origin of things. There is something creative and primal in the cool mist. This dewy mist does not fail to suggest music to me, unaccountably; fertility, the origin of things. An atmosphere which has forgotten the sun, where the ancient principle of moisture prevails. It is laden with the condensed fragrance of plants and, as it were, distilled in dews.

The woodland paths are never seen to such advantage as in a moonlight night, so embowered, still opening before you almost against expectation as you walk; you are so completely in the woods, and yet your feet meet no obstacles. It is as if it were not a path, but an open, winding passage through the bushes, which your feet find.

Now I go by the spring, and when I have risen to the same level as before, find myself in the warm stratum again.

The woods are about as destitute of inhabitants at night as the streets. In both there will be some night-walkers. There are but few wild creatures to seek their prey. The greater part of its inhabitants have retired to rest.

Ah, that life that I have known! How hard it is to remember what is most memorable! We remember how we itched, not how our hearts beat. I can sometimes recall to mind the quality, the immortality, of my youthful life, but in memory is the only relation to it.

The very cows have now left their pastures and are driven home to their yards. I meet no creature in the fields.

I hear the night-warbler [1] breaking out as in his dreams, made so from the first for some mysterious reason.

Our spiritual side takes a more distinct form, like our shadow which we see accompanying us.

I do not know but I feel less vigor at night; my legs will not carry me so far; as if the night were less favorable to muscular exertion, — weakened us, somewhat as darkness turns plants pale. But perhaps my experience is to be referred to being already exhausted by the day, and I have never tried the experiment fairly. Yet sometimes after a hard day's work I have found myself unexpectedly vigorous. It was so hot summer before last that the Irish laborers on the railroad worked by night instead of day for a while, several of them having been killed by the heat and cold water. I do not know but they did as much work as ever by day. Yet methinks Nature would not smile on such labors.

Only the Hunter's and Harvest moons are famous, but I think that each full moon deserves to be and has its own character well marked. One might be called the Midsummer-Night Moon.

[1] [The first mention in the Journal of a bird the identity of which Thoreau seems never to have made out. See *Journal*, vol. i, Introduction, p. xlvi.]

The wind and water are still awake. At night you are sure to hear what wind there is stirring. The wind blows, the river flows, without resting. There lies Fair Haven Lake, undistinguishable from fallen sky. The pines seem forever foreign, at least to the civilized man, — not only their aspect but their scent, and their turpentine.

So still and moderate is the night! No scream is heard, whether of fear or joy. No great comedy nor tragedy is being enacted. The chirping of crickets is the most universal, if not the loudest, sound. There is no French Revolution in Nature, no excess. She is warmer or colder by a degree or two.

By night no flowers, at least no variety of colors. The pinks are no longer pink; they only shine faintly, reflecting more light. Instead of flowers underfoot, stars overhead.

My shadow has the distinctness of a second person, a certain black companion bordering on the imp, and I ask, "Who is this?" which I see dodging behind me as I am about to sit down on a rock.

No one, to my knowledge, has observed the minute differences in the seasons. Hardly two nights are alike. The rocks do not feel warm to-night, for the air is warmest; nor does the sand particularly. A book of the seasons, each page of which should be written in its own season and out-of-doors, or in its own locality wherever it may be.

When you get into the road, though far from the town, and feel the sand under your feet, it is as if you had reached your own gravel walk. You no longer

hear the whip-poor-will, nor regard your shadow, for here you expect a fellow-traveller. You catch yourself walking merely. The road leads your steps and thoughts alike to the town. You see only the path, and your thoughts wander from the objects which are presented to your senses. You are no longer in place. It is like conformity, — walking in the ways of men.

In Charles Darwin's "Voyage of a Naturalist round the World," commenced in 1831: —

He gave to Ehrenberg some of an impalpably fine dust which filled the air at sea near the Cape de Verd Islands, and he found it to consist in great part of "infusoria with siliceous shields, and of the siliceous tissue of plants;" found in this sixty-seven different organic forms. The infusoria with two exceptions inhabitants of fresh water. Vessels have even run on shore owing to the obscurity. Is seen a thousand miles from Africa. Darwin found particles of stone above a thousandth of an inch square.

Speaking of St. Paul's Rocks, Lat. 58' N., Long. 29° 15' W., "Not a single plant, not even a lichen, grows on this islet; yet it is inhabited by several insects and spiders. The following list completes, I believe, the terrestrial fauna: a fly (Olfersia) living on the booby, and a tick which must have come here as a parasite on the birds; a small brown moth, belonging to a genus that feeds on feathers; a beetle (Quedius), and a woodlouse from beneath the dung; and lastly numerous spiders, which I suppose prey on these small attendants and scavengers of the waterfowl. The often-repeated description of the stately palm and other noble tropical

plants, then birds, and lastly man, taking possession of the coral islets as soon as formed, in the Pacific, is probably not quite correct; I fear it destroys the poetry of this story, that feather and dirt-feeding and parasitic insects and spiders should be the first inhabitants of newly-formed oceanic land."

At Bahia or San Salvador, Brazil, took shelter under a tree "so thick that it would never have been penetrated by common English rain," but not so there.

Of a partridge near the mouth of the Plata, "A man on horseback, by riding round and round in a circle, or rather in a spire, so as to approach closer each time, may knock on the head as many as he pleases." Refers to Hearne's Journey, page 383, for "In Arctic North America the Indians catch the Varying Hare by walking spirally round and round it, when on its form: the middle of the day is reckoned the best time, when the sun is high, and the shadow of the hunter not very long."

In the same place, "General Rosas is also a perfect horseman — an accomplishment of no small consequence in a country where an assembled army elected its general by the following trial: A troop of unbroken horses being driven into a corral, were let out through a gateway, above which was a cross-bar: it was agreed whoever should drop from the bar on one of these wild animals, as it rushed out, and should be able, without saddle or bridle, not only to ride it, but also to bring it back to the door of the corral, should be their general. The person who succeeded was accordingly elected, and doubtless made a general fit for such an army. This extraordinary feat has also been performed by Rosas."

Speaks of the Gaucho sharpening his knife on the back of the armadillo before he kills him.

Alcide d'Orbigny, from 1825 to 1833 in South America, now (1846) publishing the results on a scale which places him second to Humboldt among South American travellers.

Hail in Buenos Ayres as large as small apples; killed thirteen deer, beside ostriches, which last also it blinded, etc., etc. Dr. Malcomson told him of hail in India, in 1831, which "much injured the cattle." Stones flat, one ten inches in circumference; passed through windows, making round holes.

A difference in the country about Montevideo and somewhere else attributed to the manuring and grazing of the cattle. Refers to Atwater as saying that the same thing is observed in the prairies of North America, "where coarse grass, between five and six feet high, when grazed by cattle, changes into common pasture land." (*Vide* Atwater's words in Silliman's *North American Journal*, vol. i, p. 117.)

I would like to read Azara's Voyage.

Speaks [1] of the fennel and the cardoon (*Cynara cardunculus*), introduced from Europe, now very common in those parts of South America. The latter occurs now on both sides the Cordilleras across the continent. In Banda Oriental alone "very many (probably several hundred) square miles are covered by one mass of these prickly plants, and are impenetrable by man or beast. Over the undulating plains, where these great beds occur, nothing else can now live. . . . I doubt whether

[1] [That is, Darwin.]

any case is on record of an invasion on so grand a scale of one plant over the aborigines."

Horses first landed at the La Plata in 1535. Now these, with cattle and sheep, have altered the whole aspect of the country, — vegetation, etc. "The wild pig in some parts probably replaces the peccari; packs of wild dogs may be heard howling on the wooded banks of the less frequented streams; and the common cat, altered into a large and fierce animal, inhabits rocky hills."

At sea, eye being six feet above level, horizon is two and four fifths miles distant. "In like manner, the more level the plain, the more nearly does the horizon approach within these narrow limits; and this, in my opinion, entirely destroys that grandeur which one would have imagined that a vast level plain would have possessed."

Darwin found a tooth of a *native horse* contemporary with the mastodon, on the Pampas of Buenos Ayres, though he says there is good evidence against any horse living in America at the time of Columbus. He speaks of their remains being common in North America. Owen has found Darwin's tooth similar to one Lyell brought from the United States, but unlike any other, fossil or living, and named this American horse *Equus curvidens*, from a slight but peculiar curvature in it.

The great table-land of southern Mexico makes the division between North and South America with reference to the migration of animals.

Quotes Captain Owen's "Surveying Voyage" for saying that, at the town of Benguela on the west coast of

Vol. II

Africa in a time of great drought, a number of elephants entered in a body to possess themselves of the wells. After a desperate conflict and the loss of one man, the inhabitants — three thousand — drove them off. During a great drought in India, says Dr. Malcomson, "a hare drank out of a vessel held by the adjutant of the regiment."

The guanacos (wild llama) and other animals of this genus have the habit of dropping their dung from day to day in the same heap. The Peruvian Indians use it for fuel, and are thus aided in collecting it.

Rowing up a stream which takes its rise in a mountain, you meet at last with pebbles which have been washed down from it, when many miles distant. I love to think of this kind of introduction to it.

The only quadruped native to the Falkland Islands is a large wolf-like fox. As far as he is aware, "there is no other instance in any part of the world of so small a mass of broken land, distant from a continent, possessing so large an aboriginal quadruped peculiar to itself."

In the Falkland Isles, where other fuel is scarce, they frequently cook their beef with the bones from which the meat has been scraped. Also they have "a green little bush about the size of common heath, which has the useful property of burning while fresh and green."

Saw a cormorant play with its fishy prey as a cat with a mouse, — eight times let it go and dive after it again.

Seminal propagation produces a more original individual than that by buds, layers, and grafts.

Some inhabitants of Tierra del Fuego having got some putrid whale's blubber in time of famine, "an old man cut off thin slices and muttering over them, broiled them for a minute, and distributed them to the famished party, who during this time preserved a profound silence." This was the only evidence of any religious worship among them. It suggests that even the animals may have something divine in them and akin to revelation, — some inspirations allying them to man as to God.

"Nor is it easy to teach them our superiority except by striking a fatal blow. Like wild beasts, they do not appear to compare numbers; for each individual, if attacked, instead of retiring, will endeavor to dash your brains out with a stone, as certainly as a tiger under similar circumstances would tear you."

"We were well clothed, and though sitting close to the fire, were far from too warm; yet these naked savages, though further off, were observed, to our great surprise, to be streaming with perspiration at undergoing such a roasting." [1]

Ehrenberg examined some of the white paint with which the Fuegians daub themselves, and found it to be composed of infusoria, including fourteen polygastrica, and four phytolitharia, inhabitants of fresh water, all old and known forms! !

Again of the Fuegians: "Simple circumstances — such as the beauty of scarlet cloth or blue beads, the absence of women, our care in washing ourselves — excited their admiration far more than any grand or

[1] [*Walden*, p. 14; Riv. 22.]

complicated object, such as our ship. Bougainville has well remarked concerning these people, that they treat the 'chef-d'œuvres de l'industrie humaine, comme ils traitent les loix de la nature es ses phénomènes.'"

He was informed of a tribe of foot Indians now changing into horse Indians apparently in Patagonia.

"With the exception of a few berries, chiefly of a dwarf arbutus, the natives [*i. e.* of Tierra del Fuego][1] eat no vegetable food besides this fungus" (*Cyttaria Darwinii*). The "only country . . . where a cryptogamic plant affords a staple article of food."

No reptiles in Tierra del Fuego nor in Falkland Islands.

Describes a species of kelp there, — *Macrocystis pyrifera*. "I know few things more surprising than to see this plant growing and flourishing amidst those great breakers of the Western Ocean, which no mass of rock, let it be ever so hard, can long resist. . . . A few [stems][2] taken together are sufficiently strong to support the weight of the large loose stones to which, in the inland channels, they grow attached; and yet some of these stones were so heavy that, when drawn to the surface, they could scarcely be lifted into a boat by one person." Captain Cook thought that some of it grew to the length of three hundred and sixty feet. "The beds of this sea-weed, even when not of great breadth," says D., "make excellent natural floating breakwaters. It is quite curious to see, in an exposed

[1] [The brackets are Thoreau's.]
[2] [The word is supplied by Thoreau.]

Vol. II

harbor, how soon the waves from the open sea, as they travel through the straggling stems, sink in height, and pass into smooth water."

Number of living creatures of all orders whose existence seems to depend on the kelp; a volume might be written on them. If a forest were destroyed anywhere, so many species would not perish as if this weed were, and with the fish would go many birds and larger marine animals, and hence the Fuegian himself perchance.

Tree ferns in Van Diemen's Land (lat. 45°) six feet in circumference.

Missionaries encountered icebergs in Patagonia in latitude corresponding to the Lake of Geneva, in a season corresponding to June in Europe. In Europe, the most southern glacier which comes down to the sea is on coast of Norway, latitude 67°, — 20°, or 1230 [geographical miles] nearer the pole.

Erratic boulders not observed in the intertropical parts of the world; due to icebergs or glaciers.

Under soil perpetually frozen in North America in 56° at three feet; in Siberia in 62° at twelve to fifteen feet.

In an excursion from Valparaiso to the base of the Andes: "We unsaddled our horses near the spring, and prepared to pass the night. The evening was fine, and the atmosphere so clear that the masts of the vessels at anchor in the bay of Valparaiso, although no less than twenty-six geographical miles distant, could be distinguished clearly as little black streaks." Anson had been surprised at the distance at which his vessels

were discovered from the coast without knowing the reason, — the great height of the land and the transparency of the air.

Floating islands from four to six feet thick in Lake Tagua-tagua in central Chile; blown about.

June 12. Listen to music religiously, as if it were the last strain you might hear.[1]

There would be this advantage in travelling in your own country, even in your own neighborhood, that you would be so thoroughly prepared to understand what you saw you would make fewer travellers' mistakes.

Is not he hospitable who entertains thoughts?

June 13. Walked to Walden last night (moon not quite full) by railroad and upland wood-path, returning by Wayland road. Last full moon the elms had not leaved out, — cast no heavy shadows, — and their outlines were less striking and rich in the streets at night.

I noticed night before night before last from Fair Haven how valuable was some water by moonlight, like the river and Fair Haven Pond, though far away, reflecting the light with a faint glimmering sheen, as in the spring of the year. The water shines with an inward light like a heaven on earth. The silent depth and serenity and majesty of water! Strange that men should distinguish gold and diamonds, when these precious elements are so common. I saw a distant river by moonlight, making no noise, yet flowing, as by day, still to the sea, like melted silver reflecting the moon-

[1] [Channing, p. 78.]

light. Far away it lay encircling the earth. How far away it may look in the night, and even from a low hill how miles away down in the valley! As far off as paradise and the delectable country! There is a certain glory attends on water by night. By it the heavens are related to the earth, undistinguishable from a sky beneath you. And I forgot to say that after I reached the road by Potter's bars, — or further, by Potter's Brook, — I saw the moon suddenly reflected full from a pool. A puddle from which you may see the moon reflected, and the earth dissolved under your feet. The magical moon with attendant stars suddenly looking up with mild lustre from a window in the dark earth.

I observed also the same night a halo about my shadow in the moonlight, which I referred to the accidentally lighter color of the surrounding surface; I transferred my shadow to the darkest patches of grass, and saw the halo there equally. It serves to make the outlines of the shadow more distinct.

But now for last night. A few fireflies in the meadow. Do they shine, though invisibly, by day? Is their candle lighted by day? It is not nightfall till the whip-poor-wills begin to sing.

As I entered the Deep Cut, I was affected by beholding the first faint reflection of genuine and unmixed moonlight on the eastern sand-bank while the horizon, yet red with day, was tingeing the western side. What an interval between those two lights! The light of the moon, — in what age of the world does that fall upon the earth? The moonlight was as the earliest and dewy morning light, and the daylight tinge reminded me much more of the night. There were the old and new dynasties opposed, contrasted, and an interval between, which time could not span. Then is night, when the daylight yields to the nightlight. It suggested an interval, a distance not recognized in history. Nations have flourished in that light.

When I had climbed the sand-bank on the left, I felt the warmer current or stratum of air on my cheek, like a blast from a furnace.

The white stems of the pines, which reflected the weak light, standing thick and close together while their lower branches were gone, reminded me that the pines are only larger grasses which rise to a chaffy head, and we the insects that crawl between them. They are particularly grass-like.

How long do the gales retain the heat of the sun? I find them retreated high up the sides of hills, especially on open fields or cleared places. Does, perchance, any of this pregnant air survive the dews of night? Can any of it be found remembering the sun of yesterday even in the morning hours. Does, perchance, some puff, some blast, survive the night on elevated clearings surrounded by the forest?

The bullfrog belongs to summer. The different frogs mark the seasons pretty well, — the peeping hyla, the dreaming frog,[1] and the bullfrog. I believe that all may be heard at last occasionally together.

I heard partridges drumming to-night as late as 9 o'clock. What singularly space penetrating and filling sound! Why am I never nearer to its source?

[1] Toad.

We do not commonly live our life out and full; we do not fill all our pores with our blood; we do not inspire and expire fully and entirely enough, so that the wave, the comber, of each inspiration shall break upon our extremest shores, rolling till it meets the sand which bounds us, and the sound of the surf come back to us. Might not a bellows assist us to breathe? That our breathing should create a wind in a calm day! We live but a fraction of our life. Why do we not let on the flood, raise the gates, and set all our wheels in motion? He that hath ears to hear, let him hear. Employ your senses.

The newspapers tell us of news not to be named even with that in its own kind which an observing man can pick up in a solitary walk, as if it gained some importance and dignity by its publicness. Do we need to be advertised each day that such is still the routine of life?[1]

The tree-toad's, too, is a summer sound.

I hear, just as the night sets in, faint notes from time to time from some sparrow (?) falling asleep, — a vesper hymn, — and later, in the woods, the chuckling, rattling sound of some unseen bird on the near trees. The nighthawk booms wide awake.

By moonlight we see not distinctly even the surface of the earth, but our daylight experience supplies us with confidence.

As I approached the pond down Hubbard's Path, after coming out of the woods into a warmer air, I saw the shimmering of the moon on its surface, and, in the

[1] [See *Cape Cod, and Miscellanies*, pp. 471, 472 ; *Misc.*, Riv. 274.]

near, now flooded cove, the water-bugs, darting, circling about, made streaks or curves of light. The moon's inverted pyramid of shimmering light commenced about twenty rods off, like so much micaceous sand. But I was startled to see midway in the dark water a bright flamelike, more than phosphorescent light crowning the crests of the wavelets, which at first I mistook for fireflies, and thought even of cucullos.[1] It had the appearance of a pure, smokeless flame a half-dozen inches long, issuing from the water and bending flickeringly along its surface. I thought of St. Elmo's lights and the like. But, coming near to the shore of the pond itself, these flames increased, and I saw that even this was so many broken reflections of the moon's disk, though one would have said they were of an intenser light than the moon herself; from contrast with the surrounding water they were. Standing up close to the shore and nearer the rippled surface, I saw the reflections of the moon sliding down the watery concave like so many lustrous burnished coins poured from a bag with inexhaustible lavishness, and the lambent flames on the surface were much multiplied, seeming to slide along a few inches with each wave before they were extinguished; and I saw how farther and farther off they gradually merged in the general sheen, which, in fact, was made up of a myriad little mirrors reflecting the disk of the moon with equal brightness to an eye rightly placed. The pyramid or sheaf of light which we see springing from near where we stand only, in fact, is the outline of that portion of the shimmering surface which

[1] [Otherwise spelled "cucuyo," a West Indian firefly.]

an eye takes in. To myriad eyes suitably placed, the whole surface of the pond would be seen to shimmer, or rather it would be seen, as the waves turned up their mirrors, to be covered with those bright flame-like reflections of the moon's disk, like a myriad candles everywhere issuing from the waves; *i. e.* if there were as many eyes as angles presented by the waves, the whole surface would appear as bright as the moon; and these reflections are dispersed in all directions into the atmosphere, flooding it with light. No wonder that water reveals itself so far by night; even further in many states of the atmosphere than by day. I thought at first it [was] some unusual phosphorescence. In some positions these flames were star-like points, brighter than the brightest stars. Suddenly a flame would show itself in a near and dark space, precisely like some inflammable gas on the surface, — as if an inflammable gas made its way up from the bottom.

I heard my old musical, simple-noted owl. The sound of the *dreaming* frogs[1] prevails over the others. Occasionally a bullfrog near me made an obscene noise, a sound like an eructation, near me. I think they must be imbodied eructations. They suggest flatulency.

The pond is higher than ever, so as to hinder fishermen, and I could hardly get to the true shore here on account of the bushes. I pushed out in a boat a little and heard the chopping of the waves under its bow. And on the bottom I saw the moving reflections of the shining waves, faint streaks of light revealing the shadows of the waves or the opaqueness of the water.

[1] [Toads. See p. 250.]

As I climbed the hill again toward my old bean-field, I listened to the ancient, familiar, immortal, dear cricket sound under all others, hearing at first some distinct chirps; but when these ceased I was aware of the general earth-song, which my hearing had not heard, amid which these were only taller flowers in a bed, and I wondered if behind or beneath this there was not some other chant yet more universal. Why do we not hear when this begins in the spring? and when it ceases in the fall? Or is it too gradual?

After I have got into the road I have no thought to record all the way home, — the walk is comparatively barren. The leafy elm sprays seem to droop more by night (? ?).

June 14. *Saturday.* Full moon last night. Set out on a walk to Conantum at 7 p. m. A serene evening, the sun going down behind clouds, a few white or slightly shaded piles of clouds floating in the eastern sky, but a broad, clear, mellow cope left for the moon to rise into. An evening for poets to describe. Met a man driving home his cow from pasture and stopping to chat with his neighbor; then a boy, who had set down his pail in the road to stone a bird most perseveringly, whom I heard afterward behind me telling his pail to be quiet in a tone of assumed anger, because it squeaked under his arm. As I proceed along the back road I hear the lark still singing in the meadow, and the bobolink, and the gold robin on the elms, and the swallows twittering about the barns. A small bird chasing a crow high in the air, who is going home at night. All nature is in an

expectant attitude. Before Goodwin's house, at the opening of the Sudbury road, the swallows are diving at a tortoise-shell cat, who curvets and frisks rather awkwardly, as if she did not know whether to be scared or not. And now, having proceeded a little way down this road, the sun having buried himself in the low cloud in the west and hung out his crimson curtains,[1] I hear, while sitting by the wall, the sound of the stake-driver at a distance, — like that made by a man pumping in a neighboring farmyard, watering his cattle, or like chopping wood before his door on a frosty morning,[2] and I can imagine like driving a stake in a meadow. The pumper. I immediately went in search of the bird, but, after going a third of a mile, it did not sound much nearer, and the two parts of the sound did not appear to proceed from the same place. What is the peculiarity of these sounds which penetrate so far on the keynote of nature? At last I got near to the brook in the meadow behind Hubbard's wood, but I could not tell if [it] were further or nearer than that. When I got within half a dozen rods of the brook, it ceased, and I heard it no more. I suppose that I scared it. As before I was further off than I thought, so now I was nearer than I thought. It is not easy to understand how so small a creature can make so loud a sound by merely sucking in or throwing out water with pump-like lungs.[3] As

[1] How quietly we entertain the possibility of joy, of recreation, of light into [*sic*] our souls! We should be more excited at the pulling of a tooth.

[2] [*Excursions*, p. 111; Riv. 137.]

[3] [No water is used in producing the sound. Thoreau had been misinformed by one of his neighbors. See *Excursions*, p. 111; Riv. 137.]

yet no moon, but downy piles of cloud scattered here and there in the expectant sky.

Saw a blue flag blossom in the meadow while waiting for the stake-driver.

It was a sound as of gulping water.

Where my path crosses the brook in the meadow there is a singularly sweet scent in the heavy air bathing the brakes, where the brakes grow, — the fragrance of the earth, as if the dew were a distillation of the fragrant essences of nature. When I reach the road, the farmer going home from town invites me to ride in his high-set wagon, not thinking why I walk, nor can I shortly explain. He remarks on the coolness of the weather. The angelica is budded, a handsome luxuriant plant. And now my senses are captivated again by a sweet fragrance as I enter the embowered willow causeway, and I know not if it be from a particular plant or all together, — sweet-scented vernal grass or sweet-briar. Now the sun is fairly gone, I hear the dreaming frog,[1] and the whip-poor-will from some *darker* wood, — it is not far from eight, — and the cuckoo. The song sparrows sing quite briskly among the willows, as if it were spring again, and the blackbird's harsher note resounds over the meadows, and the veery's comes up from the wood. Fishes are dimpling the surface of the river, seizing the insects which alight. A solitary fisherman in his boat inhabits the scene. As I rose the hill beyond the bridge, I found myself in a cool, fragrant, dewy, up-country, mountain morning air, a new region. (When I had issued from the willows on to the bridge,

[1] Toad?

it was like coming out of night into twilight, the river reflected so much light.) The moon was now seen rising over Fair Haven and at the same time reflected in the river, pale and white like a silvery cloud, barred with a cloud, not promising how it will shine anon. Now I meet an acquaintance coming from a remote field in his hay-rigging, with a jag of wood; who reins up to show me how large a woodchuck he has killed, which he found eating his clover. But now he must drive on, for behind comes a boy taking up the whole road with a huge roller drawn by a horse, which goes lumbering and bouncing along, getting out of the way of night, — while the sun has gone the other way, — and making such a noise as if it had the contents of a tinker's shop in its bowels, and rolls the whole road smooth like a newly sown grain-field.

In Conant's orchard I hear the faint cricket-like song of a sparrow saying its vespers, as if it were a link between the cricket and the bird. The robin sings now, though the moon shines silverly, and the veery jingles its trill. I hear the fresh and refreshing sound of falling water, as I have heard it in New Hampshire. It is a sound we do not commonly hear. I see that the whiteweed is in blossom, which, as I had not walked by day for some time, I had not seen before.

How moderate, deliberate, is Nature! How gradually the shades of night gather and deepen, giving man ample leisure to bid farewell to-day, conclude his day's affairs, and prepare for slumber! The twilight seems out of proportion to the length of the day. Perchance it saves our eyes. Now for some hours the farmers have been getting home.

Since the alarm about mad dogs a couple of years ago there are comparatively few left to bark at the traveller and bay the moon. All nature is abandoned to me.

You feel yourself — your body, your legs, — more at night, for there is less beside to be distinctly known, and hence perhaps you think yourself more tired than you are. I see indistinctly oxen asleep in the fields, silent in majestic slumber, like the sphinx, — statuesque, Egyptian, reclining. What solid rest! How their heads are supported! A sparrow or a cricket makes more noise. From Conant's summit I hear as many as fifteen whip-poor-wills — or whip-or-I-wills — at once, the succeeding cluck sounding strangely foreign, like a hewer at work elsewhere.

The moon is accumulating yellow light and triumphing over the clouds, but still the west is suffused here and there with a slight red tinge, marking the path of the day. Though inexperienced ones might call it night, it is not yet. Dark, heavy clouds lie along the western horizon, exhibiting the forms of animals and men, while the moon is behind a cloud. Why do we detect these forms so readily? — whales or giants reclining, busts of heroes, Michael-Angelic. There is the gallery of statuary, the picture gallery of man, — not a board upon an Italian's head, but these dark figures along the horizon, — the board some Titan carries on his head. What firm and heavy outlines for such soft and light material!

How sweet and encouraging it is to hear the sound of some artificial music from the midst of woods or from the top of a hill at night, borne on the breeze from some distant farmhouse, — the human voice or a flute! That is a civilization one can endure, worth having. I could go about the world listening for the strains of music. Men use this gift but sparingly, methinks. What should we think of a bird which had the gift of song but used it only once in a dozen years, like the tree which blossoms only once in a century?

Now the dorbug comes humming by, the first I have heard this year. In three months it will be the Harvest Moon. I cannot easily believe it. Why not call this the Traveller's Moon? It would be as true to call the last (the May) the Planter's Moon as it is to call September's the Harvest Moon, for the farmers use one about as little as the other. Perhaps this is the Whip-poor-will's Moon. The bullfrog now, which I have not heard before, this evening. It is nearly nine. They are much less common and their note more intermittent than that of the dreamers. I scared up a bird on a *low* bush, perchance on its nest. It is rare that you start them at night from such places.

Peabody says that the nighthawk retires to rest about the time the whip-poor-will begins its song. The whip-poor-will begins now at 7.30. I hear the nighthawk after 9 o'clock. He says it flies low in the evening, but it also flies high, as it must needs do to make the booming sound.

I hear the lowing of cows occasionally, and the barking of dogs. The pond by moonlight, which may make

Vol. II

the object in a walk, suggests little to be said. Where there was only one firefly in a dozen rods, I hastily ran to one which had crawled up to the top of a grass-head and exhibited its light, and instantly another sailed in to it, showing its light also; but my presence made them extinguish their lights. The latter retreated, and the former crawled slowly down the stem. It appeared to me that the first was a female who thus revealed her place to the male, who was also making known his neighborhood as he hovered about, both showing their lights that they might come together. It was like a mistress who had climbed to the turrets of her castle and exhibited there a blazing taper for a signal, while her lover had displayed his light on the plain. If perchance she might have any lovers abroad.

Not much before 10 o'clock does the moonlight night begin. When man is asleep and day fairly forgotten, then is the beauty of moonlight seen over lonely pastures where cattle are silently feeding.[1] Then let me walk in a diversified country, of hill and dale, with heavy woods one side, and copses and scattered trees and bushes enough to give me shadows. Returning, a mist is on the river. The river is taken into the womb of Nature again.

Now is the clover month, but haying is not yet begun.

Evening. — Went to Nawshawtuct by North Branch. Overtaken by a slight shower. The same increased fragrance from the ground — sweet-fern, etc. — as in the night, and for the like reason probably. The houstonias

[1] [*Excursions*, p. 326 ; Riv. 401.]

still blossom freshly, as I believe they continue to do all summer. The fever-root in blossom; pictured in Bigelow's "Medical Botany." *Triosteum perfoliatum*, near the top of Hill, under the wall, looks somewhat like a milkweed. The *Viburnum dentatum*, very regularly toothed, just ready to blossom; sometimes called arrow-wood.

Nature seems not [to] have designed that man should be much abroad by night, and in the moon proportioned the light fitly. By the faintness and rareness of the light compared with that of the sun, she expresses her intention with regard to him.

June 15. Sunday. Darwin still: —

Finds runaway sailors on the Chonos Archipelago, who he thought "had kept a very good reckoning of time," having lost only four days in fifteen months.

Near same place, on the islands of the archipelago, he found wild potato, the tallest four feet high, tubers generally small but one two inches in diameter; "resembled in every respect, and had the same smell as English potatoes; but when boiled they shrunk much, and were watery and insipid, without any bitter taste."

Speaking of the surf on the coast of Chiloe, "I was assured that, after a heavy gale, the roar can be heard at night even at Castro, a distance of no less than twenty-one sea-miles, across a hilly and wooded country."

Subsidence and elevation of the west coast of South America and of the Cordilleras. "Daily it is forced home on the mind of the geologist, that nothing, not even the wind that blows, is so unstable as the level of the crust of this earth."

Would like to see Sir Francis Head's travels in South America, — Pampas perhaps.[1] Also Chambers' "Sea Levels." Also travels of Spix and Von Martius.

It is said that hydrophobia was first known in South America in 1803.

At the Galapagos, the tortoises going to any place travel night and day and so get there sooner than would be expected, — about eight miles in two or three days. He rode on their backs.

The productions of the Galapagos Archipelago, from five to six hundred miles from America, are still of the American type. "It was most striking to be surrounded by new birds, new reptiles, new shells, new insects, new plants, and yet, by innumerable trifling details of structure, and even by the tones of voice and plumage of the birds, to have the temperate plains of Patagonia, or the hot, dry deserts of Northern Chile, vividly brought before my eyes." What is most singular, not only are the plants, etc., to a great extent peculiar to these islands, but each for the most part has its own kinds, though they are within sight of each other.

Birds so tame that they can be killed with a stick. *I* would suggest that, from having dealt so long with the inoffensive and slow-moulded tortoise, they have not yet acquired an instinctive fear of man, who is a new-comer. Methinks tortoises, lizards, etc., for wild creatures are remarkable for the nearness to which man approaches them and handles them, as logs, — cold-

[1] [*Rough Notes of Journeys in the Pampas and Andes.*]

that "the great continents are, for the most part, rising areas; and . . . the central parts of the great oceans are sinking areas."

Not a *private* person on the island of Ascension; the inhabitants are paid and victualled by the British government. Springs, cisterns, etc., are managed by the same. "Indeed, the whole island may be compared to a huge ship kept in first-rate order."

Vide "Circumnavigation of Globe up to Cook."
Vide "Voyages Round the World since Cook."

The author of the article on Orchids in the *Eclectic* says that "a single plant produced three different flowers of genera previously supposed to be quite distinct."

Saw the first wild rose to-day on the west side of the railroad causeway. The whiteweed has suddenly appeared, and the clover gives whole fields a rich and florid appearance, — the rich red and the sweet-scented white. The fields are blushing with the red species as the western sky at evening. The blue-eyed grass, well named, looks up to heaven. And the yarrow, with its persistent dry stalks and heads, is now ready to blossom again. The dry stems and heads of last year's tansy stand high above the new green leaves.

I sit in the shade of the pines to hear a wood thrush at noon. The ground smells of dry leaves; the heat is oppressive. The bird begins on a low strain, *i. e.* it first delivers a strain on a lower key, then a moment after another a little higher, then another still varied from the others, — no two successive strains alike, but

blooded, lumpish forms of life, — only taking care not to step into their mouths. An alligator has been known to have come out of the mud like a mud volcano where was now the floor of a native's hut.

"The common dock is . . . widely disseminated, [in New Zealand][1] and will, I fear, forever remain a proof of the rascality of an Englishman, who sold the seeds for those of the tobacco plant."

The New-Hollanders a little higher in the scale of civilization than the Fuegians.

Puzzled by a "well rounded fragment of greenstone, rather larger than a man's head," which a captain had found on a small coral circle or atoll near Keeling Island, "where every other particle of matter is calcareous," about six hundred miles from Sumatra. D. agrees with Kotzebue (*vide* Kotzebue) who states that (Darwin's words) "the inhabitants of the Radack Archipelago, a group of lagoon-islands in the midst of the Pacific, obtained stones for sharpening their instruments by searching the roots of trees which are cast upon the beach," and "laws have been established that such stones belong to the chief, and a punishment is inflicted on any one who attempts to steal them." Let geologists look out. "Some natives carried by Kotzebue to Kamtschatka collected stones to take back to their country."

Found no bottom at 7200 feet, and 2200 yards from shore of Keeling Island, a coral isle.

His theory of the formation of coral isles by the subsidence of the land appears probable. He concludes

[1] [Supplied by Thoreau.]

either ascending or descending. He confines himself to his few notes, in which he is unrivalled, as if his kind had learned this and no more anciently.

I perceive, as formerly, a white froth dripping from the pitch pines, just at the base of the new shoots. It has no taste. The pollywogs in the pond are now full-tailed. The hickory leaves are blackened by a recent frost, which reminds me that this is near their northern limit.

It is remarkable the rapidity with which the grass grows. The 25th of May I walked to the hills in Wayland, and when I returned across lots do not remember that I had much occasion to think of the grass, or to go round any fields to avoid treading on it; but just a week afterward, at Worcester, it was high and waving in the fields, and I was to some extent confined to the road; and the same was the case here. Apparently in one month you get from fields which you can cross without hesitation, to haying time. It has grown you hardly know when, be the weather what it may, sunshine or storm. I start up a solitary woodcock in the shade, in some copse; goes off with a startled, rattling, hurried note.

After walking by night several times I now walk by day, but I am not aware of any crowning advantage in it. I see small objects better, but it does not enlighten me any. The day is more trivial.

What a careful gardener Nature is! She does not let the sun come out suddenly with all his intensity after rain and cloudy weather, but graduates the change to suit the tenderness of plants.

I see the tall crowfoot now in the meadows (*Ranunculus acris*), with a smooth stem. I do not notice the *bulbosus*, which was so common a fortnight ago. The rose-colored flowers of the *Kalmia angustifolia*, lambkill, just opened and opening. The *Convallaria bifolia* growing stale in the woods. The *Hieracium venosum*, veiny-leaved hawkweed, with its yellow blossoms in the woodland path. The *Hypoxis erecta*, yellow Bethlehem-star, where there is a thick, wiry grass in open paths; should be called yellow-eyed grass, methinks. The *Pyrola asarifolia*, with its pagoda-like stem of flowers, *i. e.* broad-leaved wintergreen. The *Trientalis Americana*, like last, in the woods, with its star-like white flower and pointed whorled leaves. The prunella too is in blossom, and the rather delicate *Thesium umbellatum*, a white flower. The Solomon's-seal, with a greenish drooping raceme of flowers at the top, I do not identify.

I notice to-day the same remarkable bushy growth on the fir (in Wheildon's garden) that I have noticed on the pines and cedars. The leaves are not so thickly set and are much stiffer.

I find that I postpone all actual intercourse with my friends to a certain real intercourse which takes place commonly when we are actually at a distance from one another.

June 22. Sunday. Is the shrub with yellow blossoms which I found last week near the Lincoln road while surveying for E. Hosmer and thought to be *Xylosteum ciliatum*, or fly honeysuckle, the same

with the yellow diervilla which I find in Laurel Glen to-day?

The birch is the surveyor's tree. It makes the best stakes to look at through the sights of a compass, except when there is snow on the ground. Their white bark was not made in vain. In surveying wood-lots I have frequent occasion to say this is what they were made for.

I see that Dugan has trimmed off and peeled the limbs of the willows on the Turnpike to sell at the Acton powder-mill. I believe they get eight dollars a cord for this wood.

I. Hapgood of Acton got me last Friday to compare the level of his cellar-bottom with his garden, for, as he says, when Robbins & Wetherbee keep the water of Nashoba Brook back so as to flood his garden, it comes into my cellar. I found that part of the garden five inches lower than the cellar-bottom. Men are affected in various ways by the actions of others. If a man far away builds a dam, I have water in my cellar. He said that the water was sometimes a foot deep in the garden.

We are enabled to criticise others only when we are different from, and in a given particular superior to, them ourselves. By our aloofness from men and their affairs we are enabled to overlook and criticise them. There are but few men who stand on the hills by the roadside. I am sane only when I have risen above my common sense, when I do not take the foolish view of things which is commonly taken, when I do not live for the low ends for which men commonly live. Wisdom is not common. To what purpose have I senses, if I

am thus absorbed in affairs? My pulse must beat with Nature. After a hard day's work without a thought, turning my very brain into a mere tool, only in the quiet of evening do I so far recover my senses as to hear the cricket, which in fact has been chirping all day. In my better hours I am conscious of the influx of a serene and unquestionable wisdom which partly unfits, and if I yielded to it more rememberingly would wholly unfit me, for what is called the active business of life, for that furnishes nothing on which the eye of reason can rest. What is that other kind of life to which I am thus continually allured? which alone I love? Is it a life for this world? Can a man feed and clothe himself gloriously who keeps only the truth steadily before him? who calls in no evil to his aid? Are there duties which necessarily interfere with the serene perception of truth? Are our serene moments mere foretastes of heaven, — joys gratuitously vouchsafed to us as a consolation, — or simply a transient realization of what might be the whole tenor of our lives?

To be calm, to be serene! There is the calmness of the lake when there is not a breath of wind; there is the calmness of a stagnant ditch. So is it with us. Sometimes we are clarified and calmed healthily, as we never were before in our lives, not by an opiate, but by some unconscious obedience to the all-just laws, so that we become like a still lake of purest crystal and without an effort our depths are revealed to ourselves. All the world goes by us and is reflected in our deeps. Such clarity! obtained by such pure means! by simple living, by honesty of purpose. We live and

rejoice. I awoke into a music which no one about me heard. Whom shall I thank for it? The luxury of wisdom! the luxury of virtue! Are there any intemperate in these things? I feel my Maker blessing me. To the sane man the world is a musical instrument. The very touch affords an exquisite pleasure.

As I walk the railroad causeway, I notice that the fields and meadows have acquired various tinges as the season advances, the sun gradually using all his paints. There is the rosaceous evening red tinge of red clover, — like an evening sky gone down upon the grass, — the whiteweed tinge, the white clover tinge, which reminds me how sweet it smells. The tall buttercup stars the meadow on another side, telling of the wealth of dairies. The blue-eyed grass, so beautiful near at hand, imparts a kind of slate or clay blue tinge to the meads.

It is hot noon. The white pines are covered with froth at the base of the new shoots, as I noticed the pitch pines were a week ago; as if they perspired. I am threading an open pitch and white pine wood, easily traversed, where the pine-needles redden all the ground, which is as smooth as a carpet. Still the blackberries love to creep over this floor, for it is not many years since this was a blackberry-field. And I hear around me, but never in sight, the many wood thrushes whetting their steel-like notes. Such keen singers! It takes a fiery heat, many dry pine leaves added to the furnace of the sun, to temper their strains! Always they are either rising or falling to a new strain. After what a moderate pause they deliver themselves again! saying ever a new thing, avoiding repetition, methinks answering one another. While most other birds take their siesta, the wood thrush discharges his song. It is delivered like a bolas, or a piece of jingling steel.

The domestic ox has his horns tipped with brass. This and his shoes are the badges of servitude which he wears; as if he would soon get to jacket and trousers. I am singularly affected when I look over a herd of reclining oxen in their pasture, and find that every one has these brazen balls on his horns. They are partly humanized so. It is not pure brute; there is art added. Where are these balls sold? Who is their maker? The bull has a ring in his nose.

The *Lysimachia quadrifolia* exhibits its small yellow blossoms now in the wood-path. Butter-and-eggs has blossomed. The *Uvularia vulgaris*, or bladderwort, a yellow pea-like flower, has blossomed in stagnant pools.

June 23. It is a pleasant sound to me, the squeaking and the booming of nighthawks flying over high open fields in the woods. They fly like butterflies, not to avoid birds of prey but, apparently, to secure their own insect prey. There is a particular part of the railroad just below the shanty where they may be heard and seen in greatest numbers. But often you must look a long while before you can detect the mote in the sky from which the note proceeds.

The common cinquefoil (*Potentilla simplex*) greets me with its simple and unobtrusive yellow flower in the grass. The *P. argentea*, hoary cinquefoil, also is now in blossom. *P. sarmentosa*, running cinquefoil, we had common enough in the spring.

sown for many years at least, it is more abundant than the red, and the heads are nearly as large. Also pastures which are close cropped, and where I think there was little or no clover last year, are spotted white with a humbler growth. And everywhere, by roadsides, garden borders, etc., even where the sward is trodden hard, the small white heads on short stems are sprinkled everywhere. As this is the season for the swarming of bees, and this clover is very attractive to them, it is probably the more difficult to secure them; at any rate it is the more important to secure their services now that they can make honey so fast. It is an interesting inquiry why this year is so favorable to the growth of clover!

I am interested to observe how old-country methods of farming resources are introduced among us. The Irish laborer, for instance, seeing that his employer is contemplating some agricultural enterprise, as ditching or fencing, suggests some old-country mode with [which] he has been familiar from a boy, which is often found to be cheaper as well as more ornamental than the common; and Patrick is allowed to accomplish the object his own way, and for once exhibits some skill and has not to be shown, but, working with a will as well as with pride, does better than ever in the old country. Even the Irishman exhibits what might be mistaken for a Yankee knack, exercising a merely inbred skill derived from the long teachings and practice of his ancestors.

I saw an Irishman building a bank of sod where his employer had contemplated building a bank wall, pil-

June 26. Thursday. The slight reddish-topped grass (red-top?) now gives a reddish tinge to some fields, like sorrel.

Visited a menagerie this afternoon. I am always surprised to see the same spots and stripes on wild beasts from Africa and Asia and also from South America, — on the Brazilian tiger and the African leopard, — and their general similarity. All these wild animals — lions, tigers, chetas, leopards, etc. — have one hue, — tawny and commonly spotted or striped, — what you may call pard-color, a color and marking which I had not associated with America. These are wild beasts. What constitutes the difference between a wild beast and a tame one? How much more human the one than the other! Growling, scratching, roaring, with whatever beauty and gracefulness, still untamable, this royal Bengal tiger or this leopard. They have the character and the importance of another order of men. The majestic lion, the king of beasts, — he must retain his title.

I was struck by the gem-like, changeable, greenish reflections from the eyes of the grizzly bear, so glassy that you never saw the surface of the eye. They [were] quite demonic. Its claws, though extremely large and long, look weak and made for digging or pawing the earth and leaves. It is unavoidable, the idea of transmigration; not merely a fancy of the poets, but an instinct of the race.

June 29. There is a great deal of white clover this year. In many fields where there has been no clover seed

ing up very neatly and solidly with his spade and a line the sods taken from the rear, and coping the face at a very small angle from the perpendicular, intermingling the sods with bushes as they came to hand, which would grow and strengthen the whole. It was much more agreeable to the eye, as well as less expensive, than stone would have been, and he thought that it would be equally effective as a fence and no less durable. But it is true only experience will show when the same practice may be followed in this climate and in Ireland, — whether our atmosphere is not too dry to admit of it. At any rate it was wise in the farmer thus to avail himself of any peculiar experience which his hired laborer possessed. That was what he *should* buy.

Also I noticed the other day where one who raises seeds, when his ropes and poles failed, had used ropes twisted of straw to support his plants, — a resource probably suggested and supplied by his foreign laborers. It is only remarkable that so few improvements or resources are or are to be adopted from the Old World.

I look down on rays of prunella by the roadsides now. The panicled or privet andromeda with its fruit-like white flowers. Swamp-pink I see for the first time this season.

The tree-primrose (scabish)[1] (*Œnothera biennis*), a rather coarse yellow flower with a long tubular calyx,

[1] [Bigelow, in his *Florula Bostoniensis*, says of this plant, now generally called the evening-primrose, "In the country it is vulgarly known by the name of *Scabish*, a corruption probably of *Scabious*, from which however it is a very different plant." Josselyn gives a quaint description of it under the name of Lysimachus or Loose-strife in his *Two Voyages*, and says it "is taken by the English for Scabious."]

naturalized extensively in Europe. The clasping bell-flower (*Campanula perfoliata*, from the heart-shaped leaves clasping the stalk), an interesting flower.

The *Convolvulus sepium*, large bindweed, make a fresh morning impression as of dews and purity. The adder's-tongue arethusa, a delicate pink flower.

How different is day from day! Yesterday the air was filled with a thick fog-like haze, so that the sun did not once shine with ardor, but everything was so tempered under this thin veil that it was a luxury merely to be outdoors, — you were less out for it. The shadows of the apple trees even early in the afternoon were remarkably distinct. The landscape wore a classical smoothness. Every object was as in [a] picture with a glass over it. I saw some hills on this side the river, looking from Conantum, on which, the grass being of a yellow tinge, though the sun did not shine out on them, they had the appearance of being shone upon peculiarly. It was merely an unusual yellow tint of the grass. The mere surface of water was an object for the eye to linger on.

The panicled cornel, a low shrub, in blossom by wall-sides now.

I thought that one peculiarity of my " Week " was its *hypæthral* character, to use an epithet applied to those Egyptian temples which are open to the heavens above, *under the ether.* I thought that it had little of the atmosphere of the house about it, but might wholly have been written, as in fact it was to a considerable extent, out-of-doors. It was only at a late period in writing it, as it happened, that I used any phrases implying that

I lived in a house or led a *domestic* life. I trust it does not smell [so much] of the study and library, even of the poet's attic, as of the fields and woods; that it is a hypæthral or unroofed book, lying open under the ether and permeated by it, open to all weathers, not easy to be kept on a shelf.

The potatoes are beginning to blossom.

Riding to survey a wood-lot yesterday, I observed that a dog accompanied the wagon. Having tied the horse at the last house and entered the woods, I saw no more of the dog while there; but when riding back to the village, I saw the dog again running by the wagon, and in answer to my inquiry was told that the horse and wagon were hired and that the dog always accompanied the horse. I queried whether it might happen that a dog would accompany the wagon if a strange horse were put into it; whether he would ever attach himself to an inanimate object. Methinks the driver, though a stranger, as it were added intellect to the mere animality of the horse, and the dog, not making very nice distinctions, yielded respect to the horse and equipage as if it were human. If the horse were to trot off alone without a wagon or driver, I think it doubtful if the dog would follow; if with the wagon, then the chances of his following would be increased; but if with a driver, though a stranger, I have found by experience that he would follow.

At a distance in the meadow I hear still, at long intervals, the hurried commencement of the bobolink's strain, the bird just dashing into song, which is as suddenly checked, as it were, by the warder of the

Vol. II

seasons, and the strain is left incomplete forever. Like human beings they are inspired to sing only for a short season.[1]

That little roadside pea-like-blossomed blue flower [2] is interesting to me. The mulleins are just blossoming.

The voice of the crickets, heard at noon from deep in the grass, allies day to night. It is unaffected by sun and moon. It is a midnight sound heard at noon, a midday sound heard at midnight.

I observed some mulleins growing on the western slope of the sandy railroad embankment, in as warm a place as can easily be found, where the heat was reflected from the sand oppressively at 3 o'clock P. M. this hot day; yet the green and living leaves felt rather cool than otherwise to the hand, but the dead ones at the root were quite warm. The living plant thus preserves a cool temperature in the hottest exposure, as if it kept a cellar below, from which cooling liquors were drawn up.

Yarrow is now in full bloom, and elder, and a small many-headed white daisy like a small whiteweed. The epilobium, too, is out.

The night-warbler sings the same strain at noon. The song sparrow still occasionally reminds me of spring.

I observe that the high water in the ponds, which have been rising for a year, has killed most of the pitch pines and alders which it had planted and merely watered at its edge during the years of dryness. But now it comes to undo its own work.

[1] I have since heard some complete strains. [2] Pale lobelia.

How awful is the least unquestionable meanness, when we cannot deny that we have been guilty of it. There seem to be no bounds to our unworthiness.

June 30. Haying has commenced. I see the farmers in distant fields cocking their hay now at six o'clock. The day has been so oppressively warm that some workmen have lain by at noon, and the haymakers are mowing now in the early twilight.

The blue flag (*Iris versicolor*) enlivens the meadow. The lark sings at sundown off in the meadow. It is a note which belongs to a New England summer evening. Though so late, I hear the summer hum of a bee in the grass, as I am on my way to the river behind Hubbard's to bathe. After hoeing in a dusty garden all this warm afternoon, — so warm that the baker says he never knew the like and expects to find his horses dead in the stable when he gets home, — it is very grateful to wend one's way at evening to some pure and cool stream and bathe therein.

The cranberry is now in blossom. Their fresh shoots have run a foot or two over the surface.

I have noticed an abundance of poison sumach this season. It is now in blossom. In some instances it has the size and form of a healthy peach tree.

The cuckoo is faintly heard from a neighboring grove. Now that it is beginning to be dark, as I am crossing a pasture I hear a happy, cricket-like, shrill little lay from a sparrow, either in the grass or else on that distant tree, as if it were the vibrations of a watch-spring; its vespers. The tree-primrose, which was so abundant in one field last Saturday, is now all gone. The cattle on Bear Garden Hill, seen through the twilight, look monstrously large. I find abounding in the meadows the adder's-tongue arethusa and occasionally with it the *Cymbidium tuberosum* of the same tint. The obtuse galium is a delicate vine-like plant with a minute white blossom in the same places. The St. John's-wort has blossomed. The *Œnothera pumila*, or dwarf tree-prim-rose, a neat yellow flower, abounds in the meadows; which the careless would mistake at a distance for buttercups. The white buds of the clethra (alder-leaved) rise above their recent shoots. The narrow-leaved cotton-grass spots the meadow with white, seeming like loose down, its stems are so slight. The carrot growing wild which I observed by the railroad is now blossoming, with its dishing blossom. I found by the railroad, a quarter of a mile from the road, some common garden catch-fly, the pink flower, grow-ing wild. Angelica is now in blossom, with its large umbels. Swamp rose, fugacious-petalled. The prinos, or winterberry, budded, with white clustered berry-like flower-buds, is a pretty contrast to itself in the winter, — wax-like. While bathing I plucked the common floating plant like a small yellow lily, the yellow water ranunculus (*R. multifidus*). What I suppose is the *Aster miser*, small-flowered aster, like a small many-headed whiteweed, has now for a week been in bloom; a humble weed, but one of the earliest of the asters.[1] The umbelled thesium, a simple white flower, on the

[1] [Evidently not *Aster miser*, or, as it is now called *A. lateriflorus*, which flowers much later in the season.]

edge of the woods. *Erysimum officinale*, hedge mustard, with its yellow flowers.

I first observed about ten days ago that the fresh shoots of the fir balsam (*Abies balsamifera*), found under the tree wilted, or plucked and kept in the pocket or in the house a few days, emit the fragrance of strawberries, only it is somewhat more aromatic and spicy. It was to me a very remarkable fragrance to be emitted by a pine. A very rich, delicious, aromatic, spicy fragrance, which if the fresh and living shoots emitted, they would be still more to be sought after.

Saw a brood of young partridges yesterday, a little larger than robins.

VI

JULY, 1851

(ÆT. 33–34)

July 2. It is a fresh, cool summer morning. From the road at N. Barrett's, on my way to P. Blood's at 8.30 A. M., the Great Meadows have a slight bluish misty tinge in part; elsewhere a sort of hoary sheen like a fine downiness, inconceivably fine and silvery far away, — the light reflected from the grass blades, a sea of grass hoary with light, the counterpart of the frost in spring. As yet no mower has profaned it; scarcely a footstep since the waters left it. Miles of waving grass adorning the surface of the earth.

Last night, a sultry night which compelled to leave all windows open, I heard two travellers talking aloud, was roused out of my sleep by their loud, day-like, and somewhat unearthly discourse at perchance one o'clock. From the country, whiling away the night with loud discourse. I heard the words "Theodore Parker" and "Wendell Phillips" loudly spoken, and so did half a dozen of my neighbors, who also were awakened. Such is fame. It affected [me] like Dante talking of the men of this world in the infernal regions. If the travellers had called my own name I should equally have thought it an unearthly personage which it would take me some hours into daylight to realize. O traveller, have n't you got any further than that? My genius hinted before

I fairly awoke, "Improve your time." What is the night that a traveller's voice should sound so hollow in it? that a man speaking aloud in the night, speak-ing in regions under the earth, should utter the words "Theodore Parker"?

A traveller! I love his title. A traveller is to be re-verenced as such. His profession is the best symbol of our life. Going from —— toward ——; it is the history of every one of us. I am interested in those that travel in the night.

It takes but little distance to make the hills and even the meadows look blue to-day. That principle which gives the air an azure color is more abundant.

To-day the milkweed is blossoming. Some of the raspberries are ripe, the most innocent and simple of fruits, the purest and most ethereal. Cherries are ripe. Strawberries in the gardens have passed their prime.

Many large trees, especially elms, about a house are a surer indication of old family distinction and worth than any evidence of wealth. Any evidence of care bestowed on these trees secures the traveller's respect as for a nobler husbandry than the raising of corn and potatoes.

I passed a regular country dooryard this forenoon, the unpainted one-story house, long and low with pro-jecting stoop, a deep grass-plot unfenced for yard, hens and chickens scratching amid the chip dirt about the door, — this last the main feature, relics of wood-piles, sites of the wooden towers.

The nightshade has bloomed and the prinos, or winterberry.

July 5. The vetch-like flower by the Marlborough road, the *Tephrosia Virginica*, is in blossom, with mixed red and yellowish blossoms. Also the white fine-flowered Jersey tea (*Ceanothus Americana*), and, by the side of wood-paths, the humble cow-wheat (*Apocynum*, etc.). The blue flower by the roadside, slender but pretty spike, is the pale lobelia (*L. pallida*). The reddish blossoms of the umbelled wintergreen (*Pyrola umbellata*) are now in perfection and are exceedingly beautiful. Also the white sweet-scented flowers of the *P. rotundifolia.*

It is a remarkably cool, clear, breezy atmosphere to-day. One would say there were fewer flowers just now than there have been and are to be; *i. e.* we do not look so much for the blossoming of new flowers. The earliest small fruits are just beginning to be ripe, — the raspberry, thimble-berry, blueberry, etc. We have no longer the blossoms of those which must ripen their fruits in early autumn.

I am interested in those fields in the woods where the potato is cultivated, growing in the light, dry, sandy soil, free from weeds; now in blossom, the slight vine not crowded in the hill. I think they do not promise many potatoes, though mealy and wholesome like nuts. Many fields have now received their last hoeing, and the farmers' work seems to be soon over with them. What a pleasant interview he must have had with them! What a liberal education with these professors! Better than a university. It is pleasing to consider man's cultivating this plant thus assiduously, without reference to any crop it may yield him, as if he were to cultivate

johnswort in like manner. What influences does he receive from this long intercourse.

The flowers of the umbelled pyrola, or common wintergreen, are really very handsome now, dangling red from their little umbels like jewelry, — especially the unexpanded buds with their red calyx-leaves against the white globe of petals.

There is a handsome wood-path on the east side of White Pond. The shadows of the pine stems and branches falling across the path, which is perfectly red with pine-needles, make a very handsome carpet. Here is a small road running north and south along the edge of the wood, which would be a good place to walk by moonlight.

The calamint grows by the lane beyond Seven-Star Lane; now in blossom.

As we come over Hubbard's Bridge between 5 and 6 P. M., the sun getting low, a cool wind blowing up the valley, we sit awhile on the rails which are destined for the new railing. The light on the Indian hill is very soft and glorious, giving the idea of the most wonderful fertility. The most barren hills are gilded like waving grain-fields. What a paradise to sail by! The cliffs and woods up the stream are nearer and have more shadow and actuality about them. This retired bridge is a favorite spot with me. I have witnessed many a fair sunset from it.

July 6. Sunday. I walked by night last moon, and saw its disk reflected in Walden Pond, the broken disk, now here, now there, a pure and memorable flame

unearthly bright, like a cucullo [1] of a water-bug. Ah! but that first faint tinge of moonlight on the gap! (seen some time ago),[2] — a silvery light from the east before day had departed in the west. What an immeasurable interval there is between the first tinge of moonlight which we detect, lighting with mysterious, silvery, poetic light the western slopes, like a paler grass, and the last wave of daylight on the eastern slopes! It is wonderful how our senses ever span so vast an interval, how from being aware of the one we become aware of the other. And now the night wind blows, — from where? What gave it birth? It suggests an interval equal to that between the most distant periods recorded in history. The silver age is not more distant from the golden than moonlight is from sunlight. I am looking into the west, where the red clouds still indicate the course of departing day. I turn and see the silent, spiritual, contemplative moonlight shedding the softest imaginable light on the western slopes of the hills, as if, after a thousand years of polishing, their surfaces were just beginning to be bright, — a pale whitish lustre. Already the crickets chirp to the moon a different strain, and the night wind rustles the leaves of the wood. A different dynasty has commenced. Yet moonlight, like daylight, is more valuable for what it suggests than for what it actually is. It is a long past season of which I dream. And the reason is perchance because it is a more sacred and glorious season, to which I instantly refer all glorious actions in past time. Let a nobler landscape present itself, let a purer air blow, and I locate all the worthies

[1] [See p. 252.]   [2] [Night of June 12. See p. 249.]

of the world. Ah, there is the mysterious light which for some hours has illustrated Asia and the scene of Alexander's victories, now at length, after two or three hours spent in surmounting the billows of the Atlantic, come to shine on America. There, on that illustrated sand-bank, was revealed an antiquity beside which Nineveh is young. Such a light as sufficed for the earliest ages. From what star has it arrived on this planet? Yet even at midday I see the full moon shining in the sky. What if, in some vales, only its light is reflected? What if there are some spirits which walk in its light alone still? who separate the moonlight from the sunlight, and are shined on by the former only? I passed from dynasty to dynasty, from one age of the world to another age of the world, from Jove perchance back to Saturn. What river of Lethe was there to run between? I bade farewell to that light setting in the west and turned to salute the new light rising in the east.

There is some advantage in being the humblest, cheapest, least dignified man in the village, so that the very stable boys shall damn you. Methinks I enjoy that advantage to an unusual extent. There is many a coarsely well-meaning fellow, who knows only the skin of me, who addresses me familiarly by my Christian name. I get the whole good of him and lose nothing myself. There is "Sam," the jailer, — whom I never call Sam, however, — who exclaimed last evening: "Thoreau, are you going up the street pretty soon? Well, just take a couple of these handbills along and drop one in at Hoar's piazza and one at Holbrook's, and I'll do as much for you another time." I am not above being used, aye abused, sometimes.

The red clover heads are now turned black. They no longer impart that rosaceous tinge to the meadows and fertile fields. It is but a short time that their rich bloom lasts. The white is black or withering also. Whiteweed still looks white in the fields. Blue-eyed grass is now rarely seen. The grass in the fields and meadows is not so fresh and fair as it was a fortnight ago. It is dryer and riper and ready for the mowers. Now June is past. June is the month for grass and flowers. Now grass is turning to hay, and flowers to fruits. Already I gather ripe blueberries on the hills. The red-topped grass is in its prime, tingeing the fields with red.

It is a free, flowing wind, with wet clouds in the sky, though the sun shines. The distant hills look unusually near in this atmosphere. Acton meeting-houses seen to stand on the side of some hills, Nagog or Nashoba, beyond, as never before. Nobscot looks like a high pasture in the sunlight not far off. From time to time I hear a few drops of rain falling on the leaves, but none is felt and the sun does not cease to shine. All serious showers go round me and get out of my way.

The clasping harebell is certainly a pretty flower, and so is the tephrosia. The poke has blossomed and the indigo-weed.

July 7. The intimations of the night are divine, methinks. Men might meet in the morning and report the news of the night, — what divine suggestions have been made to them. I find that I carry with me into

the day often some such hint derived from the gods, — such impulses to purity, to heroism, to literary effort even, as are never day-born.[1]

One of those mornings which usher in no day, but rather an endless morning, a protracted auroral season, for clouds prolong the twilight the livelong day.

And now that there is an interregnum in the blossoming of the flowers, so is there in the singing of the birds. The golden robin is rarely heard, and the bobolink, etc.

I rejoice when in a dream I have loved virtue and nobleness.

Where is Grecian history? It is when in the morning I recall the intimations of the night.

The moon is now more than half full. When I come through the village at 10 o'clock this cold night, cold as in May, the heavy shadows of the elms covering the ground with their rich tracery impress me as if men had got so much more than they had bargained for, not only trees to stand in the air, but to checker the ground with their shadows. At night they lie along the earth. They tower, they arch, they droop over the streets like chandeliers of darkness. In my walk the other afternoon, I saw the sun shining into the depths of a thick pine wood, checkering the ground like moonlight and illuminating the lichen-covered bark of a large white pine, from which it was reflected through the surrounding thicket as from another sun. This was so deep in the woods that you would have said no sun could penetrate thither.

[1] [See pp. 213, 214.]

I have been to-night with Anthony Wright to look through Perez Blood's telescope a second time. A dozen of Blood's neighbors were swept along in the stream of our curiosity. One who lived half a mile this side said that Blood had been down that way within a day or two with his terrestrial, or day, glass, looking into the eastern horizon [at] the hills of Billerica, Burlington, and Woburn. I was amused to see what sort of respect this man with a telescope had obtained from his neighbors, something akin to that which savages award to civilized men, though in this case the interval between the parties was very slight. Mr. Blood, with his skull-cap on, his short figure, his north European figure, made me think of Tycho Brahe. He did not invite us into his house this cool evening, — men nor women, — nor did he ever before to my knowledge. I am still contented to see the stars with my naked eye. Mr. Wright asked him what his instrument cost. He answered, "Well, that is something I don't like to tell." (Stuttering or hesitating in his speech a little as usual.) "It is a very proper question, however." "Yes," said I, "and you think that you have given a very proper answer."

Returning, my companion, Wright, the sexton, told me how dusty he found it digging a grave that afternoon, — for one who had been a pupil of mine. For two feet, he said, notwithstanding the rain, he found the soil as dry as ashes.

With a certain wariness, but not without a slight shudder at the danger oftentimes, I perceive how near I had come to admitting into my mind the details of

some trivial affair, as a case at court; and I am astonished to observe how willing men are to lumber their minds with such rubbish, — to permit idle rumors, tales, incidents, even of an insignificant kind, to intrude upon what should be the sacred ground of the thoughts. Shall the temple of our thought be a public arena where the most trivial affairs of the market and the gossip of the tea-table is discussed, — a dusty, noisy, trivial place? Or shall it be a quarter of heaven itself, a place consecrated to the service of the gods, a hypæthral temple? I find it so difficult to dispose of the few facts which to me are significant, that I hesitate to burden my mind with the most insignificant, which only a divine mind could illustrate. Such is, for the most part, the news, — in newspapers and conversation. It is important to preserve the mind's chastity in this respect. Think of admitting the details of a single case of the criminal court into the mind, to stalk profanely through its very *sanctum sanctorum* for an hour, aye, for many hours! to make a very bar-room of your mind's inmost apartment, as if for a moment the dust of the street had occupied you, aye, the very street itself, with all its travel, passed through your very mind of minds, your thoughts' shrine, with all its filth and bustle! Would it not be an intellectual suicide? By all manner of boards and traps, threatening the extreme penalty of the divine law, excluding trespassers from these grounds, it behooves us to preserve the purity and sanctity of the mind.[1] It is so hard to forget what it is worse than useless to remember. If I am to be a channel or thor-

[1] [Channing, p. 85.]

oughfare, I prefer that it be of the mountain springs, and not the town sewers, — the Parnassian streams. There is inspiration, the divine gossip which comes to the ear of the attentive mind from the courts of heaven; there is the profane and stale revelation of the bar-room and the police court. The same ear is fitted to receive both communications. Only the character of the individual determines to which source chiefly it shall be open and to which closed. I believe that the mind can be profaned by the habit of attending to trivial things, so that all our thoughts shall be tinged with triviality. They shall be dusty as stones in the street. Our very minds shall be paved and macadamized, as it were, their foundation broken into fragments for the wheels of travel to roll over. If we have thus desecrated ourselves, the remedy will be, by circumspection and wariness, by our aspiration and devotion, to consecrate ourselves, to make a fane of the mind. I think that we should treat our minds as innocent and ingenuous children whose guardians we are, — be careful what objects and what subjects we thrust on their attention. Even the facts of science may dust the mind by their dryness, unless they are in a sense effaced each morning, or rather rendered fertile by the dews of fresh and living truth. Every thought that passes through the mind helps to wear and tear it, and to deepen the ruts, which, as in the streets of Pompeii, evince how much it has been used. How many things there are concerning which we might well deliberate whether we had better know them![1] Routine, conven-

[1] [*Cape Cod, and Miscellanies*, pp. 473-476; *Misc.*, Riv. 276-279.]

---

tionality, manners, etc., etc., — how insensibly an undue attention to these dissipates and impoverishes the mind, robs it of its simplicity and strength, emasculates it!

Knowledge does not come to us by details but by *lieferungs* from the gods. What else is it to wash and purify ourselves? Conventionalities are as bad as impurities.[1] Only thought which is expressed by the mind in repose — as it were, lying on its back and contemplating the heavens — is adequately and fully expressed. What are sidelong, transient, passing half-views? The writer expressing his thought must be as well seated as the astronomer contemplating the heavens; he must not occupy a constrained position. The facts, the experience, we are well poised upon! which secures our whole attention!

The senses of children are unprofaned. Their whole body is one sense; they take a physical pleasure in riding on a rail, they love to teeter. So does the unviolated, the unsophisticated mind derive an inexpressible pleasure from the simplest exercise of thoughts.

I can express adequately only the thought which I *love* to express. All the faculties in repose but the one you are using, the whole energy concentrated in that. Be ever so little distracted, your thoughts so little confused, your engagements so few, your attention so free, your existence so mundane, that in all places and in all hours you can hear the sound of crickets in those seasons when they are to be heard. It is a mark of serenity and health of mind when a person hears this sound much.

[1] [*Cape Cod, and Miscellanies*, pp. 475, 476; *Misc.*, Riv. 279.]

Vol. II

— in streets of cities as well as in fields. Some ears never hear this sound; are called deaf. Is it not because they have so long attended to other sounds?

July 8. *Tuesday.* Walked along the Clamshell bank after sundown. A cloudy sky. The heads of the grass in the pasture behind Dennis's have a reddish cast, but another grass, with a lighter-colored stem and leaves, on the higher parts of the field gives a yellowish tinge to those parts, as if they reflected a misty sunlight. Even much later in the night these light spots were distinguishable. I am struck by the cool, juicy, pickled-cucumber green of the potato-fields now. How lusty these vines look! The pasture naturally exhibits at this season no such living green as the cultivated fields. I perceive that flower of the lowlands now, with a peculiar leaf and conspicuous white umbels.[1]

Here are mulleins covering a field (the Clamshell field) where three years [ago] were none noticeable, but a smooth uninterrupted pasture sod. Two years ago it was plowed for the first time for many years, and millet and corn and potatoes planted, and now *where the millet grew* these mulleins have sprung up. Who can write the history of these fields? The millet does not perpetuate itself, but the few seeds of the mullein, which perchance were brought here with it, are still multiplying the race.

The thick heads of the yellow dock warn me of the lapse of time.

[1] Rue [*i. e.* meadow-rue].

Here are some rich rye-fields waving over all the land, their heads nodding in the evening breeze with an apparently alternating motion; *i. e.* they do not all bend at once by ranks, but separately, and hence this agreeable alternation. How rich a sight this cereal fruit, now yellow for the cradle, — *flavus!* It is an impenetrable phalanx. I walk for half a mile beside these Macedonians, looking in vain for an opening. There is no Arnold Winkelried to gather these spear-heads upon his breast and make an opening for me. This is food for man. The earth labors not in vain; it is bearing its burden. The yellow, waving, rustling rye extends far up and over the hills on either side, a kind of pinafore to nature, leaving only a narrow and dark passage at the bottom of a deep ravine. How rankly it has grown! How it hastes to maturity! I discover that there is such a goddess as Ceres. These long grain-fields which you must respect, — must go round, — occupying the ground like an army. The small trees and shrubs seen dimly in its midst are overwhelmed by the grain as by an inundation. They are seen only as indistinct forms of bushes and green leaves mixed with the yellow stalks. There are certain crops which give me the idea of bounty, of the *Alma Natura*.[1] They are the grains. Potatoes do not so fill the lap of earth. This rye excludes everything else and takes possession of the soil. The farmer says, "Next year I will raise a crop of rye;" and he proceeds to clear away the brush, and either plows it, or, if it is too uneven or stony, burns and harrows it only, and scatters the seed with faith. And all winter

[1] [See *Journal*, vol. i, p. 59.]

the earth keeps his secret, — unless it did leak out somewhat in the fall, — and in the spring this early green on the hillsides betrays him. When I see this luxuriant crop spreading far and wide in spite of rock and bushes and unevenness of ground, I cannot help thinking that it must have been unexpected by the farmer himself, and regarded by him as a lucky accident for which to thank fortune. This, to reward a transient faith, the gods had given. As if he must have forgotten that he did it, until he saw the waving grain inviting his sickle.

July 9. When I got out of the cars at Porter's, Cambridge, this morning, I was pleased to see the handsome blue flowers of the succory or endive (*Cichorium Intybus*), which reminded me that within the hour I had been whirled into a new botanical region. They must be extremely rare, if they occur at all, in Concord. This weed is handsomer than most garden flowers. Saw there also the *Cucubalus Behen*, or bladder campion, also the autumnal dandelion (*Apargia autumnalis*).

Visited the Observatory. Bond said they were cataloguing the stars at Washington (?), or trying to. They do not at Cambridge; of no use with their force. Have not force enough now to make mag[netic] obs[ervations]. When I asked if an observer with the small telescope could find employment, he said, Oh yes, there was employment enough for observation with the naked eye, observing the changes in the brilliancy of stars, etc., etc., if they could only get some good observers. One is glad to hear that the naked eye still retains some importance in the estimation of astronomers.

Vol. II

How many times I have seen this kind of sunset, — the most gorgeous sight in nature! From the hill behind Minott's I see the birds flying against this red sky, the sun having set; one looks like a bat. Now between two stupendous mountains of the low stratum under the evening red, clothed in slightly rosaceous amber light, through a magnificent gorge, far, far away, as perchance may occur in pictures of the Spanish coast viewed from the Mediterranean, I see a city, the eternal city of the west, the phantom city, in whose streets no traveller has trod, over whose pavements the horses of the sun have already hurried, some Salamanca of the imagination. But it lasts only for a moment, for now the changing light has wrought such changes in it that I see the resemblance no longer.

A softer amber sky than in any picture. The swallows are improving this short day, twittering as they fly, and the huckleberry-bird [1] repeats his jingling strain, and the song sparrow, more honest than most.

I am always struck by the centrality of the observer's position. He always stands fronting the middle of the arch, and does not suspect at first that a thousand observers on a thousand hills behold the sunset sky from equally favorable positions.

And now I turn and observe the dark masses of the trees in the east, not green but black. While the sun was setting in the west, the trees were rising in the east.

I perceive that the low stratum of dark clouds under

[1] [Thoreau's name for the field sparrow (*Spizella pusilla*, or, as it was called by Nuttall, *Fringilla juncorum*). He had the name from his old friend Minott.]

Coming out of town, — willingly as usual, — when I saw that reach of Charles River just above the depot, the fair, still water this cloudy evening suggesting the way to eternal peace and beauty, whence it flows, the placid, lake-like fresh water, so unlike the salt brine, affected me not a little. I was reminded of the way in which Wordsworth so coldly speaks of some natural visions or scenes "giving him pleasure." This is perhaps the first vision of elysium on this route from Boston. And just then I saw an encampment of Penobscots, their wigwams appearing above the railroad fence, they, too, looking up the river as they sat on the ground, and enjoying the scene. What can be more impressive than to look up a noble river just at evening, — one, perchance, which you have never explored, — and behold its placid waters, reflecting the woods and sky, lapsing inaudibly toward the ocean; to behold as a lake, but know it as a river, tempting the beholder to explore it and his own destiny at once? Haunt of waterfowl. This was above the factories, — all that I saw. That water could never have flowed under a factory. How *then* could it have reflected the sky?

July 10. A gorgeous sunset after rain, with horizontal bars of clouds, red sashes to the western window, barry clouds hanging like a curtain over the window of the west, damask. First there is a low arch of the storm clouds in the west, under which is seen the clearer, fairer, serener sky and more distant sunset clouds, and under all, on the horizon's edge, heavier, massive dark clouds, not to be distinguished from the mountains.

the red sky all dips one way, and to a remarkable degree presents the appearance of the butt ends of cannons slanted toward the sky, thus: —

Such uniformity on a large scale is unexpected and pleasant to detect, evincing the simplicity of the laws of their formation. Uniformity in the shapes of clouds of a single stratum is always to be detected, the same wind shaping clouds of the like consistency and in like positions. No doubt an experienced observer could discover the states of the upper atmosphere by studying the forms and characters of the clouds. I traced the distinct form of the cannon in seven instances, stretching over the whole length of the cloud, many a mile in the horizon.

And the nighthawk dashes past in the twilight with mottled (?) wing, within a rod of me.

July 11. *Friday.* At 7.15 P. M. with W. E. C. go forth to see the moon, the glimpses of the moon. We think she is not quite full; we can detect a little flatness on the eastern side. Shall we wear thick coats? The day has been warm enough, but how cool will the night be? It is not sultry, as the last night. As a general rule, it is best to wear your thickest coat even in a July night. Which way shall we walk? Northwest, that we may see the moon returning? But on that side the river prevents our walking in the fields, and on other accounts that direction is not so attractive. We go toward Bear

Garden Hill. The sun is setting. The meadow-sweet has bloomed. These dry hills and pastures are the places to walk by moonlight. The moon is silvery still, not yet inaugurated. The tree-tops are seen against the amber west. I seem to see the outlines of one spruce among them, distinguishable afar. My thoughts expand and flourish most on this barren hill, where in the twilight I see the moss spreading in rings and prevailing over the short, thin grass, carpeting the earth, adding a few inches of green to its circle annually while it dies within.

As we round the sandy promontory, we try the sand and rocks with our hands. The sand is cool on the surface but warmer a few inches beneath, though the contrast is not so great as it was in May. The larger rocks are perceptibly warm. I pluck the blossom of the milkweed in the twilight and find how sweet it smells. The white blossoms of the Jersey tea dot the hillside, with the yarrow everywhere. Some woods are black as clouds; if we knew not they were green by day, they would appear blacker still. When we sit, we hear the mosquitoes hum. The woodland paths are not the same by night as by day; if they are a little grown up, the eye cannot find them, but must give the reins to the feet, as the traveller to his horse. So we went through the aspens at the base of the Cliffs, their round leaves reflecting the lingering twilight on the one side, the waxing moonlight on the other. Always the path was unexpectedly open.

Now we are getting into moonlight. We see it reflected from particular stumps in the depths of the darkest woods, and from the stems of trees, as if it

selected what to shine on,[1] — a silvery light. It is a light, of course, which we have had all day, but which we have not appreciated, and proves how remarkable a lesser light can be when a greater has departed. How simply and naturally the moon presides! 'T is true she was eclipsed by the sun, but now she acquires an almost equal respect and worship by reflecting and representing him, with some new quality, perchance, added to his light, showing how original the disciple may be who still in midday is seen, though pale and cloud-like, beside his master. Such is a worthy disciple. In his master's presence he still is seen and preserves a distinct existence; and in his absence he reflects and represents him, not without adding some new quality to his light, not servile and never rival. As the master withdraws himself, the disciple, who was a pale cloud before, begins to emit a silvery light, acquiring at last a tinge of golden as the darkness deepens, but not enough to scorch the seeds which have been planted or to dry up the fertilizing dews which are falling.

Passing now near Well Meadow Head toward Baker's orchard. The sweet-fern and indigo-weed fill the path up to one's middle, wetting us with dews so high. The leaves are shining and flowing.[2] We wade through the luxuriant vegetation, seeing no bottom. Looking back toward the Cliffs, some dead trees in the horizon, high on the rocks, make a wild New Hampshire prospect. There is the faintest possible mist over the pond-holes, where the frogs are eructating, like the falling of huge drops, the bursting of mephitic air-bubbles rising from

[1] [Excursions, p. 327; Riv. 402.]   [2] [Excursions, p. 327; Riv. 402.]

Vol. II

the bottom, a sort of blubbering, — such conversation as I *have* heard between men, a belching conversation, expressing a sympathy of stomachs and abdomens. The peculiar appearance of the indigo-weed, its misty massiveness, is striking. In Baker's orchard the thick grass looks like a sea of mowing in this weird moonlight, a bottomless sea of grass. Our feet must be imaginative, must know the earth in imagination only, as well as our heads. We sit on the fence, and, where it is broken and interrupted, the fallen and slanting rails are lost in the grass (really thin and wiry) as in water. We even see our tracks a long way behind, where we have brushed off the dew. The clouds are peculiarly wispy to-night, somewhat like fine flames, not massed and dark nor downy, not thick, but slight, thin wisps of mist.

I hear the sound of Heywood's Brook falling into Fair Haven Pond, inexpressibly refreshing to my senses. It seems to flow through my very bones. I hear it with insatiable thirst. It allays some sandy heat in me. It affects my circulations; methinks my arteries have sympathy with it. What is it I hear but the pure waterfalls within me, in the circulation of my blood, the streams that fall into my heart? What mists do I ever see but such as hang over and rise from my blood? The sound of this gurgling water, running thus by night as by day, falls on all my dashes, fills all my buckets, overflows my float-boards, turns all the machinery of my nature, makes me a flume, a sluice-way, to the springs of nature. Thus I am washed; thus I drink and quench my thirst.[1] Where the streams fall

[1] [See p. 155.]

into the lake, if they are only a few inches more elevated, all walkers may hear.

On the high path through Baker's wood I see, or rather feel, the tephrosia. Now we come out into the open pasture. And under those woods of elm and buttonwood, where still no light is seen, repose a family of human beings. By night there is less to distinguish this locality from the woods and meadows we have threaded. We might go very near to farmhouses covered with ornamental trees and standing on a highroad, thinking that [we] were in the most retired woods and fields still. Having yielded to sleep, man is a less obtrusive inhabitant of nature. Now, having reached the dry pastures again, we are surrounded by a flood of moonlight. The dim cart-path over the sward curves gracefully through the pitch pines, ever to some more fairy-like spot. The rails in the fences shine like silver. We know not whether we are sitting on the ruins of a wall, or the materials which are to compose a new one. I see, half a mile off, a phosphorescent arc on the hillside, where Bartlett's Cliff reflects the moonlight. Going by the shanty, I smell the excrements of its inhabitants, which I had never smelt before.

And now, at half-past 10 o'clock, I hear the cockerels crow in Hubbard's barns, and morning is already anticipated. It is the feathered, wakeful thought in us that anticipates the following day. This sound is wonderfully exhilarating at all times. These birds are worth far more to me for their crowing and cackling than for their drumsticks and eggs.[1] How singular the connec-

[1] [See *Walden*, pp. 140, 141; Riv. 199.]

tion of the hen with man, — that she leaves her eggs in his barns always! She is a domestic fowl, though still a little shyish of him. I cannot [help] looking at the whole as an experiment still and wondering that in each case it succeeds. There is no doubt at last but hens may be kept. They will put their eggs in your barn by a tacit agreement. They will not wander far from your yard.

July 12. 8 p. m. — Now at least the moon is full, and I walk alone, which is best by night, if not by day always. Your companion must sympathize with the present mood. The conversation must be located where the walkers are, and vary exactly with the scene and events and the contour of the ground. Farewell to those who will talk of nature unnaturally, whose presence is an interruption. I know but one with whom I can walk. I might as well be sitting in a bar-room with them as walk and talk with most. We are never side by side in our thoughts, and we cannot hear each other's silence. Indeed, we cannot be silent. We are forever breaking silence, that is all, and mending nothing. How can they keep together who are going different ways!

I start a sparrow from her three eggs in the grass, where she had settled for the night. The earliest corn is beginning to show its tassels now, and I scent it as I walk, — its peculiar dry scent.[1] (This afternoon I gathered ripe blackberries, and felt as if the autumn had commenced.) Now perchance many sounds and sights only remind me that they once said something to

[1] [*Excursions*, p. 327; Riv. 403.]

me, and are so by association interesting. I go forth to be reminded of a previous state of existence, if perchance any memento of it is to be met with hereabouts. I have no doubt that Nature preserves her integrity. Nature is in as rude health as when Homer sang. We may at last by our sympathies be well. I see a skunk on Bear Garden Hill stealing noiselessly away from me, while the moon shines over the pitch pines, which send long shadows down the hill. Now, looking back, I see it shining on the south side of farmhouses and barns with a weird light, for I pass here half an hour later than last night. I smell the huckleberry bushes. I hear a human voice, — some laborer singing after his day's toil, — which I do not often hear. Loud it must be, for it is far away. Methinks I should know it for a white man's voice. Some strains have the melody of an instrument. Now I hear the sound of a bugle in the "Corner," reminding me of poetic wars; a few flourishes and the bugler has gone to rest. At the foot of the Cliff hill I hear the sound of the clock striking nine, as distinctly as within a quarter of a mile usually, though there is no wind. The moonlight is more perfect than last night; hardly a cloud in the sky, — only a few fleecy ones. There is more serenity and more light. I hear that sort of throttled or chuckling note as of a bird flying high, now from this side, then from that.[1] Methinks when I turn my head I see Wachusett from the side of the hill. I smell the butter-and-eggs as I walk. I am startled by the rapid transit of some wild animal across my path, a rabbit or a fox, — or you hardly

[1] [See *Excursions*, p. 326; Riv. 401.]

know if it be not a bird. Looking down from the cliffs, the leaves of the tree-tops shine more than ever by day. Here and there a lightning-bug shows his greenish light over the tops of the trees.

As I return through the orchard, a foolish robin bursts away from his perch unnaturally, with the habits of man. The air is remarkably still and unobjectionable on the hilltop, and the whole world below is covered as with a gossamer blanket of moonlight. It is just about as yellow as a blanket. It is a great dimly burnished shield with darker blotches on its surface. You have lost some light, it is true, but you have got this simple and magnificent stillness, brooding like genius.[1]

July 13. Observed yesterday, while surveying near Gordon's, a bittern flying over near Gordon's, with moderate flight and outstretched neck, its breastbone sticking out sharp like the bone in the throats of some persons, its anatomy exposed. The evergreen is very handsome in the woods now, rising somewhat spirally in a round tower of five or six stories, surmounted by a long bud. Looking across the river to Conantum from the open plains, I think how the history of the hills would read, since they have been pastured by cows, if every plowing and mowing and sowing and chopping were recorded. I hear, 4 p. m., a pigeon woodpecker on a dead pine near by, uttering a harsh and scolding scream, spying me. The chewink jingles on the tops of the bushes, and the rush

[1] *Vide* [p. 337].

sparrow,[1] the vireo, and oven-bird at a distance; and a robin sings, superior to all; and a barking dog has started something on the opposite side of the river; and now the wood thrush surpasses them all. These plains are covered with shrub oaks, birches, aspens, hickories, mingled with sweet-fern and brakes and huckleberry bushes and epilobium, now in bloom, and much fine grass. The hellebore by the brooksides has now fallen over, though it is not broken off. The cows now repose and chew the cud under the shadow of a tree, or crop the grass in the shade along the side of the woods, and when you approach to observe them they mind you just enough. I turn up the *Juniperus repens*, and see the lighter color of its leaves on the under sides, and its berries with three petal-like divisions in one end. The sweet-scented life-everlasting is budded.

This might be called the Hayer's or Haymaker's Moon, for I perceive that when the day has been oppressively warm the haymakers rest at noon and resume their mowing after sunset, sometimes quite into evening.

July 14. Passing over the Great Fields (where I have been surveying a road) this forenoon, where were some early turnips, the county commissioners plucked and pared them with their knives and ate them. I, too, tried hard to chew a mouthful of raw turnip and realize the life of cows and oxen, for it might be a useful habit in extremities. These things occur as the seasons revolve. These are things which travellers will do. How many

[1] [The field sparrow. See *Journal*, vol. i, p. 252, note.]

men have tasted a raw turnip! How few have eaten a whole one! Some bovine appetites, which find some fodder in every field. For like reasons we sometimes eat sorrel and say we love it, that we may return the hospitality of Nature by exhibiting a good appetite.

The citizen looks sharp to see if there is any dogwood or poison sumach in the swamp before he enters.

If I take the same walk by moonlight an hour later or earlier in the evening, it is as good as a different one. I love the night for its novelty; it is less prophaned than the day.[1]

The creaking of the crickets seems at the very foundation of all sound. At last I cannot tell it from a ringing in my ears. It is a sound from within, not without. You cannot dispose of it by listening to it. In proportion as I am stilled I hear it. It reminds me that I am a denizen of the earth.

July 16. *Wednesday.* Methinks my present experience is nothing; my past experience is all in all. I think that no experience which I have to-day comes up to, or is comparable with, the experiences of my boyhood. And not only this is true, but as far back as I can remember I have unconsciously referred to the experiences of a previous state of existence. "For life is a forgetting," etc. Formerly, methought, nature developed as I developed, and grew up with me. My life was ecstasy. In youth, before I lost any of my senses, I can remember that I was all alive, and inhabited my body with inexpressible satisfaction; both its weari-

[1] [*Excursions,* p. 323; Riv. 398.]

ness and its refreshment were sweet to me. This earth was the most glorious musical instrument, and I was audience to its strains. To have such sweet impressions made on us, such ecstasies begotten of the breezes! I can remember how I was astonished. I said to myself, — I said to others, — "There comes into my mind such an indescribable, infinite, all-absorbing, divine, heavenly pleasure, a sense of elevation and expansion, and [I] have had nought to do with it. I perceive that I am dealt with by superior powers.[1] This is a pleasure, a joy, an existence which I have not procured myself. I speak as a witness on the stand, and tell what I have perceived." The morning and the evening were sweet to me, and I led a life aloof from society of men. I wondered if a mortal had ever known what I knew. I looked in books for some recognition of a kindred experience, but, strange to say, I found none. Indeed, I was slow to discover that other men had had this experience, for it had been possible to read books and to associate with men on other grounds. The maker of me was improving me. When I detected this interference I was profoundly moved. For years I marched as to a music in comparison with which the military music of the streets is noise and discord. I was daily intoxicated, and yet no man could call me intemperate. With all your science can you tell how it is, and whence it is, that light comes into the soul?

Set out at 3 P. M. for Nine-Acre Corner Bridge *via* Hubbard's Bridge and Conantum, returning *via* Dashing Brook, rear of Baker's, and railroad at 6.30 P. M.

[1] [Channing, p. 84.]

The song sparrow, the most familiar and New England bird, is heard in fields and pastures, setting this midsummer day to music, as if it were the music of a mossy rail or fence post; a little stream of song, cooling, rippling through the noon, — the usually unseen songster usually unheard like the cricket, it is so common, — like the poet's song, unheard by most men, whose ears are stopped with business, though perchance it sang on the fence before the farmer's house this morning for an hour. There are little strains of poetry in our animals.

Berries are just beginning to ripen, and children are planning expeditions after them. They are important as introducing children to the fields and woods, and as wild fruits of which much account is made. During the berry season the schools have a vacation, and many little fingers are busy picking these small fruits. It is ever a pastime, not a drudgery. I remember how glad I was when I was kept from school a half a day to pick huckleberries on a neighboring hill all by myself to make a pudding for the family dinner. Ah, they got nothing but the pudding, but I got invaluable experience beside! A half a day of liberty like that was like the promise of life eternal. It was emancipation in New England. O, what a day was there, my countrymen!

I see the yellow butterflies now gathered in fleets in the road, and on the flowers of the milkweed (*Asclepias pulchra*) by the roadside, a really handsome flower; also the smaller butterfly, with reddish wings, and a larger, black or steel-blue, with wings spotted red on edge, and one of equal size, reddish copper-colored. Now you may

see a boy stealing after one, hat in hand. The earliest corn begins to tassel out, and my neighbor has put his hand in the hill some days ago and abstracted some new potatoes as big as nuts, then covered up again. Now they will need — or will get — no more weeding. The lark sings in the meadow; the very essence of the afternoon is in his strain. This is a New England sound, but the cricket is heard under all sounds. Still the cars come and go with the regularity of nature, of the sun and moon. (If a hen puts her eggs elsewhere than in the barns, — in woods or among rocks, — she is said to *steal* her nest!) The twittering of swallows is in the air, reminding me of water. The meadow-sweet is now in bloom, and the yarrow prevails by all roadsides. I see the hardhack too, homely but dear plant, just opening its red clustered flowers. The small aster, too, now abounds (*Aster miser*),[1] and the tall buttercup still. After wading through a swamp the other day with my shoes in my hand, I wiped my feet with sassafras leaves, which reminded me of some Arabian practices, the bruised leaves perfuming the air and by their softness being adapted to this purpose. The tree-primrose, or scabish, still is seen over the fence. The red-wings and crow blackbirds are heard chattering on the trees, and the cow troopials are accompanying the cows in the pastures for the sake of the insects they scare up. Oftentimes the thoughtless sportsman has lodged his charge of shot in the cow's legs or body in his eagerness to obtain the birds. St. John's-wort, one of the first of yellow flowers, begins to shine along the roadside. The mul-

[1] [This is queried in pencil. See p. 278.]

lein for some time past. I see a farmer cradling his rye,
John Potter. Fields are partly mown, — some English
grass on the higher parts of the meadow next to the road.
The farmer's work comes not all at once. In haying
time there is a cessation from other labors to a considerable extent. Planting is done, and hoeing mainly;
only some turnip seed is to be scattered amid the corn.
I hear the kingbird twittering or chattering like a stout-
chested swallow. The prunella sends back a blue ray
from under my feet as I walk; the pale lobelia too. The
plaintive, spring-restoring peep of a bluebird is occasionally heard. I met loads of hay on the road, which
the oxen draw indifferently, swaggering in their gait, as
if it were not fodder for them. Methinks they should
testify sometimes that they are working for themselves.
The whiteweed is turning black. Grapes are half grown
and lead the mind forward to autumn. It is an air this
afternoon that makes you indifferent to all things, —
perfect summer, but with a comfortable breeziness.
You know not heat nor cold. What season of the year
is this? The balls of the button-bush are half formed,
with its fine, glossy, red-stemmed leaf atoning for its
nakedness in the spring. My eye ranges over green
fields of oats, for which there is a demand then somewhere. The wild rose peeps from amid the alders and
other shrubs by the roadside. The elder-blow fills the
air with its scent. The angelica, with its large umbels, is
gone to seed. On it I find one of those slow-moving
green worms, with rings spotted black and yellow, like
an East Indian production. What if these grew as large
as elephants? The honest and truly fair is more mod-

estly colored. Notwithstanding the drifting clouds,
you fear no rain to-day. As you walk, you smell some
sweet herbage, but detect not what it is. Hay is sticking to the willows and the alders on the causeway, and
the bridge is sprinkled with it. The hemlock (*Cicuta
Americana*) displays its white umbels now. The yellow
lilies reign in the river. The painted tortoises drop off
the willow stumps as you go over the bridge. The river
is now so low that you can see its bottom, shined on by
the sun, and travellers stop to look at fishes as they go
over, leaning on the rails. The pickerel-weed sends
up its heavenly blue. The color of the cows on Fair
Haven Hill, how fair a contrast to the hillside! How
striking and wholesome their clean brick-red! When
were they painted? How carelessly the eye rests on
them, or passes them by as things of course! The tansy
is budded. The devil's-needles seem to rest in air over
the water. There is nothing New-English about them.

Now, at 4 P. M., I hear the pewee in the woods, and
the cuckoo reminds me of some silence among the birds
I had not noticed. The vireo (red-eyed?) sings like a
robin at even, incessantly, — for I have now turned
into Conant's woods. The oven-bird helps fill some
pauses. The poison sumach shows its green berries,
now unconscious of guilt. The heart-leaved loosestrife
(*Lysimachia ciliata*) is seen in low open woods. The
breeze displays the white under sides of the oak leaves
and gives a fresh and flowing look to the woods. The
river is a dark-blue winding stripe amid the green of the
meadow. What is the color of the world? Green mixed
with yellowish and reddish for hills and ripe grass, and

Vol. II

darker green for trees and forests; blue spotted with
dark and white for sky and clouds, and dark blue for
water. Beyond the old house I hear the squirrel chirp
in the wall like a sparrow; so Nature merges her creations into one. I am refreshed by the view of Nobscot
and the southwestern vales, from Conantum, seething
with the blue element. Here comes a small bird with a
ricochet flight and a faint twittering note like a messenger from Elysium. The rush sparrow jingles her
small change, pure silver, on the counter of the pasture.
From far I see the rye stacked up. A few dead trees
impart the effect of wildness to the landscape, though
it is a feature rare in an old settled country.

Methinks this is the first of dog-days. The air in the
distance has a peculiar blue mistiness, or furnace-like
look, though, as I have said, it is not sultry yet. It is
not the season for distant views. Mountains are not
clearly blue now. The air is the opposite to what it is
in October and November. You are not inclined to
travel. It is a world of orchards and small-fruits now,
and you can stay at home if the well has cool water in
it. The black thimble-berry is an honest, homely berry,
now drying up as usual. I used to have a pleasant time
stringing them on herd's-grass stems, tracing the wall-
sides for them. It is pleasant to walk through these
elevated fields, terraced upon the side of the hill so that
the eye of the walker looks off into the blue cauldron
of the air at his own level. Here the haymakers have
just gone to tea, — at 5 o'clock, the farmer's hour, before the afternoon is ended, while he still thinks much
work may still be done before night. He does not wait

till he is strongly reminded of the night. In the distance
some burdened fields are black with haycocks. Some
thoughtless and cruel sportsman has killed twenty-two
young partridges not much bigger than robins, against
the laws of Massachusetts and humanity. At the Corner Bridge the white lilies are budded. Green apples
are now so large as to remind me of coddling and the
autumn again.[1] The season of fruits is arrived. The
dog's-bane has a pretty, delicate bell-like flower. The
Jersey tea abounds. I see the marks of the scythes
in the fields, showing the breadth of each swath the
mowers cut. Cool springs are now a desideratum. The
geranium still hangs on. Even the creeping vines love
the brooks, and I see where one slender one has struggled down and dangles into the current, which rocks it
to and fro. Filberts are formed, and you may get the
berry stains out of your hands with their husks, if you
have any. Nightshade is in blossom. Came through the
pine plains behind James Baker's, where late was open
pasture, now open pitch pine woods, only here and there
the grass has given place to a carpet of pine-needles.
These are among our pleasantest woods, — open, level,
with blackberry vines interspersed and flowers, as lady's-
slippers, earlier, and pinks on the outskirts. Each tree
has room enough. And now I hear the wood thrush
from the shade, who loves these pine woods as well as
I. I pass by Walden's scalloped shore. The epilobium
reflects a pink gleam up the vales and down the hills.
The chewink jingles on a bush's top. Why will the
Irishman drink of a puddle by the railroad instead of

[1] [*Excursions*, p. 294; Riv. 361.]

digging a well? How shiftless! What death in life! He cannot be said to live who does not get pure water.

The milkweeds, or silkweeds, are rich flowers, now in blossom. The *Asclepias syriaca*, or common milkweed; its buds fly open at a touch. But handsomer much is *Asclepias pulchra*, or water silkweed. The thin green bark of this last, and indeed of the other, is so strong that a man cannot break a small strip of it by pulling. It contains a mass of fine silken fibres, arranged side by side like the strings of a fiddle-bow, and may be bent short without weakening it.

What more glorious condition of being can we imagine than from impure to be becoming pure? It is almost desirable to be impure that we may be the subject of this improvement. That I am innocent to myself! That I love and reverence my life! That I am better fitted for a lofty society to-day than I was yesterday! To make my life a sacrament! What is nature without this lofty tumbling? May I treat myself with more and more respect and tenderness. May I not forget that I am impure and vicious. May I not cease to love purity. May I go to my slumbers as expecting to arise to a new and more perfect day. May I so live and refine my life as fitting myself for a society ever higher than I actually enjoy. May I treat myself tenderly as I would treat the most innocent child whom I love; may I treat children and my friends as my newly discovered self. Let me forever go in search of myself; never for a moment think that I have found myself; be as a stranger to myself, never a familiar, seeking

acquaintance still. May I be to myself as one is to me whom I love, a dear and cherished object. What temple, what fane, what sacred place can there be but the innermost part of my own being? The possibility of my own improvement, that is to be cherished. As I regard myself, so I am. O my dear friends, I have not forgotten you. I will know you to-morrow. I associate you with my ideal self. I had ceased to have faith in myself. I thought I was grown up and become what I was intended to be, but it is earliest spring with me. In relation to virtue and innocence the oldest man is in the beginning spring and vernal season of life. It is the love of virtue makes us young ever. That is the fountain of youth, the very aspiration after the perfect. I love and worship myself with a love which absorbs my love for the world. The lecturer suggested to me that I might become better than I am. Was it not a good lecture, then? May I dream not that I shunned vice; may I dream that I loved and practiced virtue.

July 18. It is a test question affecting the youth of a person, — Have you knowledge of the morning? Do you sympathize with that season of nature? Are you abroad early, brushing the dews aside? If the sun rises on you slumbering, if you do not hear the morning cock-crow, if you do not witness the blushes of Aurora, if you are not acquainted with Venus as the morning star, what relation have you to wisdom and purity? You have then forgotten your Creator in the days of your youth! Your shutters were darkened till noon!

Vol. II

You rose with a sick headache! In the morning sing, as do the birds. What of those birds which should slumber on their perches till the sun was an hour high? What kind of fowl would they be and new kind of bats and owls, — hedge sparrows or larks? then took a dish of tea or hot coffee before they began to sing?

I might have added to the list of July 16th the *Aralia hispida*, bristling aralia; the heart-leaved loosestrife (*Lysimachia ciliata*); also the upright loosestrife (*L. racemosa*), with a rounded terminal raceme; the tufted vetch (*Vicia cracca*). Sweet-gale fruit now green.

I first heard the locust sing, so dry and piercing, by the side of the pine woods in the heat of the day.

July 19. Here I am thirty-four years old,[1] and yet my life is almost wholly unexpanded. How much is in the germ! There is such an interval between my ideal and the actual in many instances that I may say I am unborn. There is the instinct for society, but no society. Life is not long enough for one success. Within another thirty-four years that miracle can hardly take place. Methinks my seasons revolve more slowly than those of nature; I am differently timed. I am contented. This rapid revolution of nature, even of nature in me, why should it hurry me? Let a man step to the music which he hears, however measured. Is it important that I should mature as soon as an apple tree? aye, as soon as an oak? May not my life in nature, in proportion as it is supernatural, be only the spring and infantile por-

[1] [His birthday was July 12.]

tion of my spirit's life? Shall I turn my spring to summer? May I not sacrifice a hasty and petty completeness here to entireness there? If my curve is large, why bend it to a smaller circle? My spirit's unfolding observes not the pace of nature. The society which I was made for is not here. Shall I, then, substitute for the anticipation of that this poor reality? I would [rather] have the unmixed expectation of that than this reality. If life is a waiting, so be it. I will not be shipwrecked on a vain reality. What were any reality which I can substitute? Shall I with pains erect a heaven of blue glass over myself, though when it is done I shall be sure to gaze still on the true ethereal heaven far above, as if the former were not, — that still distant sky o'erarching that blue expressive eye of heaven?[1] I am enamored of the blue-eyed arch of heaven.

I did not *make* this demand for a more thorough sympathy. This is not my idiosyncrasy or disease. He that made the demand will answer the demand.

My blood flows as slowly as the waves of my native Musketaquid; yet they reach the ocean sooner, perchance, than those of the Nashua.

Already the goldenrod is budded, but I can make no haste for that.

2 P. M. — The weather is warm and dry, and many leaves curl. There is a threatening cloud in the southwest. The farmers dare not spread their hay. It remains cocked in the fields. As you walk in the woods nowadays, the flies striking against your hat sound

[1] [*Walden*, pp. 358, 359; Riv. 502.]

like rain-drops. The stump or root fences on the Corner road remind me of fossil remains of mastodons, etc., exhumed and bleached in sun and rain. To-day I met with the first orange flower of autumn. What means this doubly torrid, this Bengal, tint? Yellow took sun enough, but this is the fruit of a dog-day sun. The year has but just produced it. Here is the Canada thistle in bloom, visited by butterflies and bees. The butterflies have swarmed within these few days, especially about the milkweeds. The swamp-pink still fills the air with its perfume in swamps and by the causeways, though it is far gone. The wild rose still scatters its petals over the leaves of neighboring plants. The wild morning-glory or bindweed, with its delicate red and white blossoms. I remember it ever as a goblet full of purest morning air and sparkling with dew, showing the dew-point, winding round itself for want of other support. It grows by the Hubbard Bridge causeway, near the angelica. The cherry-birds are making their *seringo* sound as they flit past. They soon find out the locality of the cherry trees. And beyond the bridge there is a goldenrod partially blossomed. Yesterday it was spring, and to-morrow it will be autumn. Where is the summer then? First came the St. John's-wort and now the goldenrod to admonish us. I hear, too, a cricket amid these stones under the blackberry vines, singing as in the fall. Ripe blackberries are multiplying. I see the red-spotted berries of the small Solomon's-seal in my path. I notice, in the decayed end of an oak post, that the silver grain is not decayed, but remains sound in thin flakes, alternating with the decayed por-

tions and giving the whole a honeycombed look. Such an object supramundane, as even a swallow may descend to light on, a dry mullein stalk for instance. I see that hens, too, follow the cows feeding near the house, like the cow troopial, and for the same object. They cannot so well scare up insects for themselves. This is the dog the cowbird uses to start up its insect game. I see yellow butterflies in pairs, pursuing each other a rod or two into the air, and now, as he had bethought himself of the danger of being devoured by a passing bird, he descends with a zigzag flight to the earth, and the other follows. The black huckleberries are now so thick among the green ones that they no longer incur suspicion of being worm-eaten.

When formerly I was looking about to see what I could do for a living, some sad experience in conforming to the wishes of friends being fresh in my mind to tax my ingenuity, I thought often and seriously of picking huckleberries; that surely I could do, and its small profits might suffice, so little capital it required, so little distraction from my wonted thoughts, I foolishly thought. While my acquaintances went unhesitatingly into trad_ or the professions, I thought of this occupation as most like theirs; ranging the hills all summer to pick the berries which came in my way, which I might carelessly dispose of; so to keep the flocks of King Admetus. My greatest skill has been to want but little. I also dreamed that I might gather the wild herbs, or carry evergreens to such villagers as loved to be reminded of the woods, and so find my living got. But I have since learned that trade curses everything it handles; and though you

trade in messages from heaven, the whole curse of trade attaches to the business.[1]

The wind rises more and more. The river and the pond are blacker than the threatening cloud in the south. The thunder mutters in the distance. The surface of the water is slightly rippled. Where the pads grow is a light green border. The woods roar. Small white clouds are hurrying across the dark-blue ground of the storm, which rests on all the woods of the south horizon. But still no rain now for some hours, as if the clouds were dissipated as fast as they reached this atmosphere.

The barberry's fruit hangs yellowish-green. What pretty covers the thick bush makes, so large and wide and drooping! The *Fringilla juncorum* sings still, in spite of the coming tempest, which, perchance, only threatens.

The woodchuck is a good native of the soil. The distant hillside and the grain-fields and pastures are spotted yellow or white with his recent burrows, and the small mounds remain for many years. Here where the clover has lately been cut, see what a yellow mound is brought to light!

Heavily hangs the common yellow lily (*Lilium Canadense*) in the meadows. In the thick alder copses by the causeway-side I find the *Lysimachia hybrida*. Here is the *Lactuca sanguinea* with its runcinate leaves, tall stem, and pale-crimson ray. And that green-stemmed one higher than my head, resembling the last in its leaves, is perchance the "tall lettuce," or fireweed. Can that [sketch] fine white-flowered meadow-plant with the [sketch] leaf be a thalictrum?

[1] [*Walden*, p. 77; Riv. 110, 111.]

July 20. Sunday morning. A thunder-shower in the night. Thunder near at hand, though louder, is a more trivial and earthly sound than at a distance; likened to sounds of men. The clap which waked me last night was as if some one was moving lumber in an upper apartment, some vast hollow hall, tumbling it down and dragging it over the floor; and ever and anon the lightning filled the damp air with light, like some vast glow-worm in the fields of ether opening its wings.

The river, too, steadily yields its crop. In louring days it is remarkable how many villagers resort to it. It is of more worth than many gardens. I meet one, late in the afternoon, going to the river with his basket on his arm and his pole in hand, not ambitious to catch pickerel this time, but he thinks he may perhaps get a mess of small fish. These [*sic*] kind of values are real and important, though but little appreciated, and he is not a wise legislator who underrates them and allows the bridges to be built low so as to prevent the passage of small boats. The town is but little conscious how much interest it has in the river, and might vote it away any day thoughtlessly. There is always to be seen either some unshaven wading man, an old mower of the river meadows, familiar with water, vibrating his long pole over the lagoons of the off-shore pads, or else some solitary fisher, in a boat behind the willows, like a mote in the sunbeams reflecting the light; and who can tell how many a mess of river fish is daily cooked in the town? They are an important article of food to many a poor family.

Some are poets, some are not, — as in relation to

getting a living, so to getting a wife. As their ideals of life vary, so do their ideals of love.

4 P. M. Annursnack. — The under sides of the leaves, exposed by the breeze, give a light bluish tinge to the woods as I look down on them. Looking at the woods west of this hill, there is a grateful dark shade under their eastern sides, where they meet the meadows, their cool night side, — a triangular segment of night, to which the sun has set. The mountains look like waves on a blue ocean tossed up by a stiff gale. The *Rhexia Virginica* is in bloom.

July 21. 8 A. M. — The forenoon is fuller of light. The butterflies on the flowers look like other and frequently larger flowers themselves. Now I yearn for one of those old, meandering, dry, uninhabited roads, which lead away from towns, which lead us away from temptation, which conduct to the outside of earth, over its uppermost crust; where you may forget in what country you are travelling; where no farmer can complain that you are treading down his grass, no gentleman who has recently constructed a seat in the country that you are trespassing; on which you can go off at half-cock and wave adieu to the village; along which you may travel like a pilgrim, going nowhither; where travellers are not too often to be met; where my spirit is free; where the walls and fences are not cared for; where your head is more in heaven than your feet are on earth; which have long reaches where you can see the approaching traveller half a mile off and be pre-

pared for him; not so luxuriant a soil as to attract men; some root and stump fences which do not need attention; where travellers have no occasion to stop, but pass along and leave you to your thoughts; where it makes no odds which way you face, whether you are going or coming, whether it is morning or evening, mid-noon or midnight; where earth is cheap enough by being public; where you can walk and think with least obstruction, there being nothing to measure progress by; where you can pace when your breast is full, and cherish your moodiness; where you are not in false relations with men, are not dining nor conversing with them; by which you may go to the uttermost parts of the earth. It is wide enough, wide as the thoughts it allows to visit you. Sometimes it is some particular half-dozen rods which I wish to find myself pacing over, as where certain airs blow; then my life will come to me, methinks; like a hunter I walk in wait for it. When I am against this bare promontory of a huckleberry hill, then forsooth my thoughts will expand. Is it some influence, as a vapor which exhales from the ground, or something in the gales which blow there, or in all things there brought together agreeably to my spirit? The walls must not be too high, imprisoning me, but low, with numerous gaps. The trees must not be too numerous, nor the hills too near, bounding the view, nor the soil too rich, attracting the attention to the earth. It must simply be the way and the life, — a way that was never known to be repaired, nor to need repair, within the memory of the oldest inhabitant. I cannot walk habitually in those ways that are liable to

Vol. II

be mended; for sure it was the devil only that wore them. Never by the heel of thinkers (of thought) were they worn; the zephyrs could repair that damage. The saunterer wears out no road, even though he travel on it, and therefore should pay no highway, or rather *low* way, tax. He may be taxed to construct a higher way than men travel. A way which no geese defile, nor hiss along it, but only sometimes their wild brethren fly far overhead; which the kingbird and the swallow twitter over, and the song sparrow sings on its rails; where the small red butterfly is at home on the yarrow, and no boys threaten it with imprisoning hat. There I can walk and stalk and pace and plod. Which nobody but Jonas Potter travels beside me; where no cow but his is tempted to linger for the herbage by its side; where the guide-board is fallen, and now the hand points to heaven significantly, — to a Sudbury and Marlborough in the skies. That's a road I can travel, that the particular Sudbury I am bound for, six miles an hour, or two, as you please; and few there be that enter thereon. There I can walk, and recover the lost child that I am without any ringing of a bell; where there was nothing ever discovered to detain a traveller, but all went through about their business; where I never passed the time of day with any, — indifferent to me were the arbitrary divisions of time; where Tullus Hostilius might have disappeared, — at any rate has never been seen. The road to the Corner! the ninety and nine acres that you go through to get there! I would rather see it again, though I saw it this morning, than Gray's churchyard. The road whence

you may hear a stake-driver, a whip-poor-will, a quail in a midsummer day, a — yes, a quail comes nearest to the *gum-c* [1] bird heard there; where it would not be sport for a sportsman to go. And the mayweed looks up in my face, — not there; the pale lobelia, the Canada snapdragon, rather. A little hardhack and meadowsweet peep over the fence, — nothing more serious to obstruct the view, — and thimble-berries are the food of thought, before the drought, along by the walls. [2]

It is they who go to Brighton and to market that wear out the roads, and they should pay all the tax. The deliberate pace of a thinker never made a road the worse for travelling on.

There I have freedom in my thought, and in my soul am free. Excepting the omnipresent butcher with his calf-cart, followed by a distracted and anxious cow. [3]

Be it known that in Concord, where the first forcible resistance to British aggression was made in the year 1775, they chop up the young calves and give them to the hens to make them lay, it being considered the cheapest and most profitable food for them, and they sell the milk to Boston.

On the promenade deck of the world, an outside passenger. The inattentive, ever strange baker, whom no weather detains, that does not bake his bread in this hemisphere, — and therefore it is dry before it

---

[1] [So Channing (p. 128), who calls it "one of Thoreau's names for some bird, so named by the farmers." The word as written is far from clear.]

[2] *Vide* p. [373].   [3] [Channing, pp. 126–128.]

gets here. Ah! there is a road where you might advertise to fly, and make no preparations till the time comes; where your wings will sprout if anywhere, where your feet are not confined to earth. An airy head makes light walking.

Where I am not confined and balked by the sight of distant farmhouses which I have not gone past. In roads the obstructions are not under my feet, — I care not for rough ground or wet even, — but they are in my vision and in the thoughts or associations which I am compelled to entertain. I must be fancy-free; I must feel that, wet or dry, high or low, it is the genuine surface of the planet, and not a little chip-dirt or a compost-heap, or made land or redeemed. Where I can sit by the wall-side and not be peered at by any old ladies going a-shopping, not have to bow to one whom I may have seen in my youth, — at least, not more than once. I am engaged and cannot be polite. Did you ever hear of such a thing as a man sitting in the road, and then have four eyes levelled at you? Have we any more right sometimes to look at one than to point a revolver at him; it might go off; and so, perchance, we might *see* him, — though there is not so much danger of *that*, — which would be equally fatal, if it *should* ever happen, though perhaps it never has.

A thinker's weight is in his thought, not in his tread: when he thinks freely, his body weighs nothing. He cannot tread down your grass, farmers.[1]

I thought to walk this forenoon instead of this afternoon, for I have not been in the fields and woods much

[1] [Channing, pp. 128, 129.]

Vol. II

this and afternoon, though it is positive and decided enough, as my instincts know. By 2 o'clock it will be warmer and hazier, obscuring the mountains, and the leaves will curl, and the dust will rise more readily. Every herb is fresher now, has recovered from yesterday's drought. The cooler air of night still lingers in the fields, as by night the warm air of day. The noon is perchance the time to stay in the house.

There is no glory so bright but the veil of business can hide it effectually. With most men life is postponed to some trivial business, and so therefore is heaven. Men think foolishly they may abuse and misspend life as they please and when they get to heaven turn over a new leaf.

I see the track of a bare human foot in the dusty road, the toes and muscles all faithfully imprinted. Such a sight is so rare that it affects me with surprise, as the footprint on the shore of Juan Fernandez did Crusoe. It is equally rare here. I am affected as if some Indian or South-Sea-Islander had been along, some man who had a foot. I am slow to be convinced that any of my neighbors — the judge on the bench, the parson in the pulpit — might have made that or something like it, however irregular. It is pleasant as it is to see the tracks of cows and deer and birds. I am brought so much nearer to the tracker — when again I think of the sole of my own foot — than when I behold that of his shoe merely, or am introduced to him and converse with him in the usual way. I am disposed to say to the judge whom I meet, "Make tracks."

Men are very generally spoiled by being so civil and

of late except when surveying, but the least affair of that kind is as if you had [a] black veil drawn over your face which shut out nature, as that eccentric and melancholy minister whom I have heard of.[1] It may be the fairest day in all the year and you shall not know it. One little chore to do, one little commission to fulfill, one message to carry, would spoil heaven itself. Talk about a lover being engaged! He is the only man in all the world who is free. And all you get is your dollars. To go forth before the heat is intolerable, and see what is the difference between forenoon and afternoon. It seems there is a little more coolness in the air; there is still some dew, even on this short grass in the shade of the walls and woods; and a feeling of vigor the walker has. There are few sounds but the slight twittering of swallows, and the *springy* note of the sparrow in the grass or trees, and a lark in the meadow (now at 8 A. M.), and the cricket under all to ally the hour to night. Day is, in fact, about as still as night. Draw the veil of night over this landscape, and these sounds would not disturb nor be inconsistent for their loudness with the night. It is a difference of white and black. Nature is in a white sleep. It threatens to be a hot day, and the haymakers are whetting their scythes in the fields, where they have been out since 4 o'clock. When I have seen them in the twilight commencing their labors, I have been impressed as if it were last night. There is something ghastly about such very early labor. I cannot detect the whole and characteristic difference between

[1] [See Hawthorne's story "The Minister's Black Veil" and footnote to the title, *Twice-Told Tales*, Riverside Edition, p. 52.]

well-disposed. You can have no profitable conversation with them, they are so conciliatory, determined to agree with you. They exhibit such long-suffering and kindness in a short interview. I would meet with some provoking strangeness, so that we may be guest and host and refresh one another. It is possible for a man wholly to disappear and be merged in his manners. The thousand and one gentlemen whom I meet, I meet despairingly and but to part from them, for I am not cheered by the hope of any rudeness from them. A cross man, a coarse man, an eccentric man, a silent, a man who does not drill well, — of him there is some hope. Your gentlemen, they are all alike. They utter their opinions as if it was not a man that uttered them. It is "just as you please;" they are indifferent to everything. They will talk with you for nothing. The interesting man will rather avoid [you], and it is a rare chance if you get so far as talk with him. The laborers whom I know, the loafers, fishers, and hunters, I can spin yarns with profitably, for it is hands off; they are they and I am I still; they do not come to me and quarter themselves on me for a day or an hour to be treated politely, they do not cast themselves on me for entertainment, they do not approach me with a flag of truce. They do not go out of themselves to meet me. I am never electrified by my gentleman; he is not an electric eel, but one of the common kind that slip through your hands, however hard you clutch them, and leave them covered with slime. He is a man, every inch of him; is worth a groom.

To eat berries on the dry pastures of Conantum, as if

they were the food of thought, dry as itself! Berries are now thick enough to pick.

9 A. M. On Conantum. — A quarter of a mile is distance enough to make the atmosphere look blue now. This is never the case in spring or early summer. It was fit that I should see an indigo-bird here, concerned about its young, a perfect embodiment of the darkest blue that ever fills the valleys at this season. The meadow-grass reflecting the light has a bluish cast also.

Remember thy Creator in the days of thy youth; *i. e.*, lay up a store of natural influences. Sing while you may, before the evil days come. He that hath ears, let him hear. See, hear, smell, taste, etc., while these senses are fresh and pure.

There is always a kind of fine æolian harp music to be heard in the air. I hear now, as it were, the mellow sound of distant horns in the hollow mansions of the upper air, a sound to make all men divinely insane that hear it, far away overhead, subsiding into my ear. To ears that are expanded what a harp this world is! The occupied ear thinks that beyond the cricket no sound can be heard, but there is an immortal melody that may be heard morning, noon, and night, by ears that can attend, and from time to time this man or that hears it, having ears that were made for music. To hear this the hardhack and the meadow-sweet *aspire*. They are thus beautifully painted, because they are tinged in the lower stratum of that melody.

I eat these berries as simply and naturally as thoughts come to my mind.

Never yet did I chance to sit in a house, except my own house in the woods, and hear a wood thrush sing. Would it not be well to sit in such a chamber within sound of the finest songster of the grove?

The quail, invisible, whistles, and who attends?

10 A. M. — The white lily has opened. How could it stand these heats? It has pantingly opened, and now lies stretched out by its too long stem on the surface of the shrunken river. The air grows more and more blue, making pretty effects when one wood is seen from another through a little interval. Some pigeons here are resting in the thickest of the white pines during the heat of the day, migrating, no doubt. They are unwilling to move for me. Flies buzz and rain about my hat, and the dead twigs and leaves of the white pine, which the choppers have left here, exhale a dry and almost sickening scent. A cuckoo chuckles, half throttled, on a neighboring tree, and now, flying into the pine, scares out a pigeon, which flies with its handsome tail spread, dashes this side and that between the trees helplessly, like a ship carrying too much sail in midst of a small creek, some great ammiral having no room to manœuvre, — a fluttering flight.

The mountains can scarcely be seen for the blue haze, — only Wachusett and the near ones. The thorny apple bush on Conantum has lately sent up branches from its top, resolved to become a tree; and these spreading (and bearing fruit), the whole has the form of a vast hour-glass. The lower part being the most dense by far, you would say the sand had run out.[1]

[1] [*Excursions*, p. 305; Riv. 375.]

Vol. II

I now return through Conant's leafy woods by the spring, whose floor is sprinkled with sunlight, — low trees which yet effectually shade you.

The dusty mayweed now blooms by the roadside, one of the humblest flowers. The rough hawkweed, too, by the damp roadside, resembling in its flower the autumnal dandelion. That was probably the *Verbena hastata*, or common blue vervain, which I found the other day by Walden Pond.

The *Antirrhinum Canadense*, Canada snapdragon, in the Corner road; and the ragged orchis on Conantum.

8.30 P. M. — The streets of the village are much more interesting to me at this hour of a summer evening than by day. Neighbors, and also farmers, come a-shopping after their day's haying, are chatting in the streets, and I hear the sound of many musical instruments and of singing from various houses. For a short hour or two the inhabitants are sensibly employed. The evening is devoted to poetry, such as the villagers can appreciate.

How rare to meet with a farmer who is a man of sentiment! Yet there was one, Gen. Joshua Buttrick, who died the other day, who is said to have lived in his sentiments. He used to say that the smell of burning powder excited him.

It is said that Mirabeau took to highway robbery "to ascertain what degree of resolution was necessary in order to place one's self in formal opposition to the most sacred laws of society." He declared that "a soldier who fights in the ranks does not require half so much courage as a foot-pad." "Honor and religion have

never stood in the way of a well-considered and a firm resolve.[1] Tell me, Du Saillant, when you lead your regiment into the heat of battle, to conquer a province to which he whom you call your master has no right whatever, do you consider that you are performing a better action than mine, in stopping your friend on the king's highway, and demanding his purse?"

"I obey without reasoning," replied the count.

"And I reason without obeying, when obedience appears to me to be contrary to reason," rejoined Mirabeau.[2]

This was good and manly, as the world goes; and yet it was desperate. A saner man would have found opportunities enough to put himself in formal opposition to the most sacred laws of society, and so test his resolution, in the natural course of events, without violating the laws of his own nature. It is not for a man to *put himself* in such an attitude to society, but to *maintain* himself in whatever attitude he finds himself through obedience to the laws of his being, which will never be one of opposition to a just government.[3] Cut the leather only where the shoe pinches. Let us not have a rabid virtue that will be revenged on society, — that falls on it, not like the morning dew, but like the fervid noonday sun, to wither it.

July 22. The season of morning fogs has arrived. I think it is connected with dog-days. Perhaps it is owing

[1] [*Walden*, p. 355; Riv. 497.]
[2] *Harper's New Monthly*, vol. i, p. 648, from *Chambers' Edinburgh Journal*.
[3] [*Walden*, p. 355; Riv. 497.]

to the greater contrast between the night and the day, the nights being nearly as cold, while the days are warmer? Before I rise from my couch, I see the ambrosial fog stretched over the river, draping the trees. It is the summer's vapor bath. What purity in the color! It is almost musical; it is positively fragrant. How faery-like it has visited our fields. I am struck by its firm outlines, as distinct as a pillow's edge, about the height of my house. A great crescent over the course of the river from southwest to northeast. Already, 5.30 A.M., some parts of the river are bare. It goes off in a body down the river, before this air, and does not rise into the heavens. It retreats, and I do not see how it is dissipated. This slight, thin vapor which is left to curl over the surface of the still, dark water, still as glass, seems not [to] be the same thing, — of a different quality. I hear the cockerels crow through it, and the rich crow of young roosters, that sound indicative of the bravest, rudest health, hoarse without cold, hoarse with rude health. That crow is all-nature-compelling; famine and pestilence flee before it. These are our fairest days, which are born in a fog.

I saw the tall lettuce yesterday (*Lactuca elongata*), whose top or main shoot had been broken off, and it had put up various stems, with entire and lanceolate, not runcinate leaves as usual, thus making what some botanists have called a variety, *β. linearis*. So I have met with some geniuses who, having met with some such accident maiming them, have been developed in some such *monstrous* and partial, though original, way. They were original in being less than themselves.

Yes, your leaf is peculiar, and some would make of you a distinct variety, but to me you appear like the puny result of an accident and misfortune, for you have lost your main shoot, and the leaves which would have grown runcinate are small and lanceolate.

The last Sunday afternoon I smelled the clear pork frying for a farmer's supper thirty rods off (what a Sunday supper!), the windows being open, and could imagine the *clear* tea without milk which usually accompanies it.

Now the cat-o'-nine-tails are seen in the impenetrable meadows, and the tall green rush is perfecting its tufts. The spotted polygonum .(*P. Persicaria*) by the roadside.

I scare up a woodcock from some moist place at midday.

The pewee and kingbird are killing bees, perched on a post or a dead twig.

I bathe me in the river. I lie down where it is shallow, amid the weeds over its sandy bottom; but it seems shrunken and parched; I find it difficult to get *wet* through. I would fain be the channel of a mountain brook. I bathe, and in a few hours I bathe again, not remembering that I was wetted before. When I come to the river, I take off my clothes and carry them over, then bathe and wash off the mud and continue my walk. I would fain take rivers in my walks endwise.

There was a singular charm for me in those French names, — more than in the things themselves. The names of Italian and Grecian cities, villages, and natural features are not more poetic to me than the

names of those humble Canadian villages. To be told by a habitant, when I asked the name of a village in sight, that is St. Féréol or St. Anne's! But I was quite taken off my feet when, running back to inquire what river we were crossing, and thinking for a long time he said *la rivière d'océan*, it flashed upon me at last that it was *La Rivière du Chien*.[1]

There was so much grace and sentiment and refinement in the names, how could they be coarse who took them so often on their lips, — St. Anne's, St. Joseph's; the holy Anne's, the holy Joseph's! Next to the Indian, the French missionary and voyageur and Catholic habitant have named the natural features of the land. The *prairie*, the *voyageur*! Or does every man think his neighbor is the richer and more fortunate man, his neighbor's fields the richest?

It needed only a little outlandishness in the names, a little foreign accent, a few more vowels in the words, to make me locate all my ideals at once. How prepared we are for another world than this! We are no sooner over the line of the States than we expect to see men leading poetic lives, — nothing so natural, that is the presumption. The names of the mountains, and the streams, and the villages reel with the intoxication of poetry — Longueuil, Chambly, Barthillon (?), Montilly (?).[2]

Where there were books only, to find realities. Of course we assign to the place the idea which the written

[1] [*Excursions*, pp. 56, 57; Riv. 69, 70.]
[2] [*Excursions*, p. 57; Riv. 71.]

history or poem suggested. Quebec, of course, is never seen for what it simply is to practical eyes, but as the local habitation of those thoughts and visions which we have derived from reading of Wolfe and Montcalm, Montgomery and Arnold. It is hard to make me attend to the geology of Cape Diamond or the botany of the Plains of Abraham.[1] How glad we are to find that there is another race of men! for they may be more successful and fortunate than we.

Canada is not a place for railroads to terminate in, or for criminals to run to.[2]

July 23. Wednesday. I remember the last moon, shining through a creamy atmosphere, with a tear in the eye of Nature and her tresses dishevelled and drooping, sliding up the sky, the glistening air, the leaves shining with dew, pulsating upward; an atmosphere unworn, unprophaned by day. What self-healing in Nature! — swept by the dews.

For some weeks past the roadsides and the dry and trivial fields have been covered with the field trefoil (*Trifolium arvense*), now in bloom.

8 A.M. — A comfortable breeze blowing. Methinks I can write better in the afternoon, for the novelty of it, if I should go abroad this morning. My genius makes distinctions which my understanding cannot, and which my senses do not report. If I should reverse the usual, — go forth and saunter in the fields all the

[1] [*Excursions*, p. 88; Riv. 109, 110.]
[2] [*Excursions*, p. 57; Riv. 71.]

forenoon, then sit down in my chamber in the afternoon, which it is so unusual for me to do, — it would be like a new season to me, and the novelty of it [would] inspire me. The wind has fairly blown me outdoors; the elements were so lively and active, and I so sympathized with them, that I could not sit while the wind went by. And I am reminded that we should especially improve the summer to live out-of-doors. When we may so easily, it behooves us to break up this custom of sitting in the house, for it is but a custom, and I am not sure that it has the sanction of common sense. A man no sooner gets up than he sits down again. Fowls leave their perch in the morning, and beasts their lairs, unless they are such as go abroad only by night. The cockerel does not take up a new perch *in the barn*, and he is the embodiment of health and common sense. Is the literary man to live always or chiefly sitting in a chamber through which nature enters by a window only ? What is the use of the summer ?

You must walk so gently as to hear the finest sounds, the faculties being in repose. Your mind must not perspire. True, out of doors my thought is commonly drowned, as it were, and shrunken, pressed down by stupendous piles of light ethereal influences, for the pressure of the atmosphere is still fifteen pounds to a square inch. I can do little more than preserve the equilibrium and resist the pressure of the atmosphere. I can only nod like the rye-heads in the breeze. I expand more surely in my chamber, as far as expression goes, as if that pressure were taken off; but here outdoors is the place to store up influences.

a few inches' depth of transparent water rippling over yellow sand and pebbles, the pure blood of nature. How miraculously crystal-like, how exquisite, fine, and subtle, and liquid this element, which an imperceptible inclination in the channel causes to flow thus surely and swiftly! How obedient to its instinct, to the faintest suggestion of the hills! If inclined but a hair's breadth, it is in a torrent haste to obey. And all the revolutions of the planet — nature is so exquisitely adjusted — and the attraction of the stars do not disturb this equipoise, but the rills still flow the same way, and the water levels are not disturbed.

We are not so much like debauchees as in the afternoon.

The mind is subject to moods, as the shadows of clouds pass over the earth. Pay not too much heed to them. Let not the traveller stop for them. They consist with the fairest weather. By the mood of my mind, I suddenly felt dissuaded from continuing my walk, but I observed at the same instant that the shadow of a cloud was passing over [the] spot on which I stood, though it was of small extent, which, if it had no connection with my mood, at any rate suggested how transient and little to be regarded that mood was. I kept on, and in a moment the sun shone on my walk within and without.

The button-bush in blossom. The tobacco-pipe in damp woods. Certain localities only a few rods square in the fields and on the hills, sometimes the other side of a wall, attract me as if they had been the scene of pleasure in another state of existence.

The swallow's twitter is the sound of the lapsing waves of the air, or when they break and burst, as his wings represent the ripple. He has more air in his bones than other birds; his feet are defective. The fish of the air. His note is the voice of the air. As fishes may hear the sound of waves lapsing on the surface and see the outlines of the ripples, so we hear the note and see the flight of swallows.

The influences which make for one walk more than another, and one day more than another, are much more ethereal than terrestrial. It is the quality of the air much more than the quality of the ground that concerns the walker, — cheers or depresses him. What he may find in the air, not what he may find on the ground.

On such a road (the Corner) I walk securely, seeing far and wide on both sides, as if I were flanked by light infantry on the hills, to rout the provincials, as the British marched into Concord, while my grenadier thoughts keep the main road. That is, my light-armed and wandering thoughts scour the neighboring fields, and so I know if the coast is clear. With what a breadth of van I advance! I am not bounded by the walls. I think more than the road full. (Going southwesterly.)

While I am abroad, the ovipositors plant their seeds in me; I am fly-blown with thought, and go home to hatch and brood over them.

I was too discursive and rambling in my thought for the chamber, and must go where the wind blows on me walking.

A little brook crossing the road (the Corner road),

Vol. II

But this habit of close observation, — in Humboldt, Darwin, and others. Is it to be kept up long, this science ? Do not tread on the heels of your experience. Be impressed without making a minute of it. Poetry puts an interval between the impression and the expression, — waits till the seed germinates naturally.

July 24. 5 A. M. — The street and fields betray the drought and look more parched than at noon; they look as I feel, — languid and thin and feeling my nerves. The potatoes and the elms and the herbage by the roadside, though there is a slight dew, seem to rise out of an arid and thirsty soil into the atmosphere of a furnace slightly cooled down. The leaves of the elms are yellow. Ah! now I see what the noon was and what it may be again. The effects of drought are never more apparent than at dawn. Nature is like a hen panting with open mouth, in the grass, as the morning after a debauch.

July 25. *Friday.* Started for Clark's Island at 7 A. M.

At 9 A. M. took the Hingham boat and was landed at Hull. There was a pleasure party on board, apparently boys and girls belonging to the South End, going to Hingham. There was a large proportion of ill-dressed and ill-mannered boys of Irish extraction. A sad sight to behold! Little boys of twelve years, prematurely old, sucking cigars! I felt that if I were their mothers I should whip them and send them to bed. Such children should be dealt with as for stealing or impurity. The opening of this valve for the safety of the city!

Oh, what a wretched resource! What right have parents to beget, to bring up, and attempt to *educate* children in a city? I thought of infanticide among the Orientals with complacency. I seemed to hear infant voices lisp, "Give us a fair chance, parents." There is no such squalidness in the country. You would have said that they must all have come from the house of correction and the farm-school, but such a company do the boys in Boston streets make. The birds have more care for their young, — where they place their nests. What are a city's charities? She cannot be charitable any more than the old philosopher could move the earth, unless she has a resting-place without herself. A true culture is more possible to the savage than to the boy of average intellect, born of average parents, in a great city. I believe that they perish miserably. How can they be kept clean, physically or morally? It is folly to attempt to educate children within a city; the first step must be to remove them out of it. It seemed a groping and helpless philanthropy that I heard of.

I heard a boy telling the story of Nix's Mate to some girls, as we passed that spot, how "he said, 'If I am guilty, this island will remain; but if I am innocent, it will be washed away,' and now it is all washed away." [1] This was a simple and strong expression of feeling suitable to the occasion, by which he committed the evidence of his innocence to the dumb isle, such as the boy could appreciate, a proper sailor's legend; and I was reminded that it is the illiterate and unimaginative class that seizes on and transmits the legends in which

[1] [*Cape Cod*, p. 267; Riv. 323.]

the more cultivated delight. No fastidious poet dwelling in Boston had tampered with it, — no narrow poet, but broad mankind, sailors from all ports sailing by. They, sitting on the deck, were the literary academy that sat upon its periods.

On the beach at Hull, and afterwards all along the shore to Plymouth, I saw the datura, the variety (red-stemmed), methinks, which some call *Tatula* instead of *Stramonium*. I felt as if I was on the highway of the world, at sight of this cosmopolite and veteran traveller. It told of commerce and sailors' yarns without end. It grows luxuriantly in sand and gravel. This Captain Cook among plants, this Norseman or sea pirate, viking or king of the bays, the beaches. It is not an innocent plant; it suggests commerce, with its attendant vices. [1]

Saw a public house where I landed at Hull, made like some barns which I have seen, of boards with a cleat nailed over the cracks, without clapboards or paint, evidently very simple and cheap, yet neat and convenient as well as airy. It interested me, as the New House at Long Island did not, as it brought the luxury and comfort of the seashore within reach of the less wealthy. It was such an exhibition of good sense as I was not prepared for and do not remember to have seen before. Ascended to the top of the hill, where is the old French fort, with the well said to be ninety feet deep, now covered. [2] I saw some horses standing on the very top of the ramparts, the highest part of Hull, where

[1] [*Cape Cod*, p. 14; Riv. 15.]
[2] [*Cape Cod*, p. 16; Riv. 17.]

there was hardly room to turn round, for the sake of the breeze. [1] It was excessively warm, and their instincts, or their experience perchance, guided them as surely to the summit as it did me. Here is the telegraph, nine miles from Boston, whose State-House was just visible, — movable signs on a pole with holes in them for the passage of the wind. A man about the telegraph station thought it the highest point in the harbor; said they could tell the kind of vessel thirty miles off, the number at masthead ten or twelve miles, name on hull six or seven miles. They can see furthest in the fall. There is a mist summer and winter, when the contrast between the temperature of the sea and the air is greatest. I did not see why this hill should not be fortified as well as George's Island, it being higher and also commanding the main channel. However, an enemy could go by all the forts in the dark, as Wolfe did at Quebec. [2] They are bungling contrivances.

Here the bank is rapidly washing away. On every side, in Boston Harbor, the evidences of the wasting away of the islands are so obvious and striking that they appear to be wasting faster than they are. You will sometimes see a springing hill, showing by the interrupted arch of its surface against the sky how much space [it] must have occupied where there is now water, as at Point Allerton, — what botanists call premorse. Hull looks as if it had been two is- lands, since connected by a beach. I was struck by the gracefully curving

[1] [*Cape Cod*, p. 14; Riv. 15.]
[2] [See *Excursions*, p. 79; Riv. 98.]

and fantastic shore of a small island (Hog Island) inside of Hull, be gently laps- inhabitants for device on where everything seemed to ing into futurity, as if the should bear a ripple their coat-of-arms, a wave passing over them, with the datura growing on their shores. The wrecks of isles fancifully arranged into a new shore. To see the sea nibbling thus voraciously at the continents! [1] A man at the telegraph told me of a white oak pole a foot and a half in diameter, forty feet high, and four feet or more in the rock at Minot's Ledge, with four guys, which stood only one year. Stone piled up cob-fashion near same place stood eight years.

Hull pretty good land, but bare of trees — only a few cherries for the most part — and mostly uncultivated, being owned by few. I heard the voices of men shouting aboard a vessel half a mile from the shore, which sounded as if they were in a barn in the country, they being between the sails. It was not a sea sound. It was a purely rural sound. [2]

Man needs to know but little more than a lobster in order to catch him in his traps. Here were many lobster traps on the shore. The beds of dry seaweed or eel-grass on the beach remind me of narrow shavings. On the farther hill in Hull, I saw a field full of Canada thistles close up to the fences on all sides, while beyond them there was none. So much for these fields having been subjected to different culture. So a differ-

[1] [*Cape Cod*, p. 15; Riv. 15, 16.]
[2] [*Cape Cod*, pp. 14, 15; Riv. 15.]

ent culture in the case of men brings in different weeds. As are the virtues, so are the vices. Weeds come in with the seeds, though perhaps much more in the manure. Each kind of culture will introduce its own weeds.

I am bothered to walk with those who wish to keep step with me. It is not necessary to keep step with your companion, as some endeavor to do.

They told me at Hull that they burned the *stem* of the kelp chiefly for potash. Chemistry is not a splitting hairs when you have got half a dozen raw Irishmen in the laboratory.

As I walked on the beach (Nantasket), panting with thirst, a man pointed to a white spot on the side of a distant hill (Strawberry Hill he called it) which rose from the gravelly beach, and said that there was a pure and cold and unfailing spring; and I could not help admiring that in this town of Hull, of which I had heard, but now for the first time saw, a single spring should appear to me and should be of so much value. I found Hull indeed, but there was also a spring on that parched, unsheltered shore; the spring, though I did not visit it, made the deepest impression on my mind. Hull, the place of the spring and of the well. This is what the traveller would remember. All that he remembered of Rome was a spring on the Capitoline Hill! [1]

It is the most perfect seashore I have seen.[2] The rockweed falls over you like the *tresses* of mermaids,

[1] [*Cape Cod*, pp. 15, 16; Riv. 16.]
[2] [*Cape Cod*, pp. 16, 17; Riv. 17, 18.]

for three years, which sunk several boats and caused some vessels to drag their anchors and come near going ashore; proving that the gust which struck the water there must have been of very limited breadth, for I was or might have been overlooking the spot and felt no wind. This rocky shore is called Pleasant Cove on large maps; on the map of Cohasset alone, the name seems to be confined to the cove where I first saw the wreck of the St. John alone.[1]

Brush Island, opposite this, with a hut on it, not permanently inhabited. It takes but little soil to tempt men to inhabit such places. I saw here the American holly (*Ilex opaca*), which is not found further north than Massachusetts, but south and west. The yellow gerardia in the woods.

July 26. At Cohasset. — Called on Captain Snow, who remembered hearing fishermen say that they "fitted out at Thoreau's;" remembered him. He had commanded a packet between Boston or New York and England. Spoke of the wave which he sometimes met on the Atlantic coming against the wind, and which indicated that the wind was blowing from an opposite quarter at a distance, the undulation travelling faster than the wind. They see Cape Cod loom here. Thought the Bay between here and Cape Ann thirty fathoms deep; between here and Cape Cod, sixty or seventy fathoms. The "Annual of Scientific Discovery" for 1851 says, quoting a Mr. A. G. Findley, "Waves travel very great distances, and are often raised by distant

[1] [*Cape Cod*, pp. 16, 18; Riv. 17, 19.]

and you see the propriety of that epithet. You cannot swim among these weeds and pull yourself up by them without thinking of mermen and mermaids.

The barnacles on the rocks, which make a whitish strip a few feet in width just above the weeds, remind me of some vegetable growth which I have seen, — surrounded by a circle of calyx-like or petal-like shells like some buds or seed-vessels. They, too, clinging to the rocks like the weeds; lying along the seams of the rock like buttons on a waistcoat.

I saw in Cohasset, separated from the sea only by a narrow beach, a very large and handsome but shallow lake, of at least four hundred acres, with five rocky islets in it; which the sea had tossed over the beach in the great storm in the spring, and, after the alewives had passed into it, stopped up its outlet; and now the alewives were dying by thousands, and the inhabitants apprehended a pestilence as the water evaporated. The water was very foul.[1]

The rockweed is considered the best for manure. I saw them drying the Irish moss in quantities at Jerusalem Village in Cohasset. It is said to be used for sizing calico. Finding myself on the edge of a thunder-storm, I stopped a few moments at the Rock House in Cohasset, close to the shore. There was scarcely rain enough to wet one, and no wind. I was therefore surprised to hear afterward, through a young man who had just returned from Liverpool, that there was a severe squall at quarantine ground, only seven or eight miles northwest of me, such as he had not experienced

[1] [*Cape Cod*, pp. 16, 17; Riv. 17–19.]

Vol. II

hurricanes, having been felt simultaneously at St. Helena and Ascension, though 600 miles apart, and it is probable that ground swells often originate at the Cape of Good Hope, 3000 miles distant." Sailors tell of tide-rips. Some are thought to be occasioned by earthquakes.

The ocean at Cohasset did not look as if any were ever shipwrecked in it. Not a vestige of a wreck left. It was not grand and sublime now, but beautiful. The water held in the little hollows of the rocks, on the receding of the tide, is so crystal-pure that you cannot believe it salt, but wish to drink it.[1]

The architect of a Minot Rock lighthouse might profitably spend a day studying the worn rocks of Cohasset shore, and learn the power of the waves, see what kind of sand the sea is using to grind them down.

A fine delicate seaweed, which some properly enough call sea-green. Saw here the staghorn, or velvet, sumach (*Rhus typhina*), so called from form of young branches, a size larger than the *Rhus glabra* common with us. The *Plantago maritima*, or sea plantain, properly named. I guessed its name before I knew what it was called by botanists. The American sea-rocket (*Bunias edentula*) I suppose it was that I saw, — the succulent plant with much cut leaves and small pinkish (?) flowers.

July 27. *Sunday.* Walked from Cohasset to Duxbury and sailed thence to Clark's Island.

Visited the large tupelo tree (*Nyssa multiflora*) in

[1] [*Cape Cod*, pp. 17, 18; Riv. 18, 19.]

Scituate, whose rounded and open top, like some umbelliferous plant's, I could see from Mr. Sewal's, the
tree which George Emerson went twenty-five miles to
see, called sometimes snag-tree and swamp hornbeam,
also pepperidge and gum-tree. Hard to split. We have
it in Concord. Cardinal-flower in bloom. Scituate
meeting-houses on very high ground; the principal one
a landmark for sailors. Saw the buckthorn, which is
naturalized. One of Marshfield meeting-houses on the
height of land on my road. The country generally descends westerly toward the sources of Taunton River.

After taking the road by Webster's beyond South
Marshfield, I walked a long way at noon, hot and
thirsty, before I could find a suitable place to sit and
eat my dinner, — a place where the shade and the
sward pleased me. At length I was obliged to put up
with a small shade close to the ruts, where the only
stream I had seen for some time crossed the road. Here,
also, numerous robins came to cool and wash themselves and to drink. They stood in the water up to their
bellies, from time to time wetting their wings and tails
and also ducking their heads and sprinkling the water
over themselves; then they sat on a fence near by to dry.
Then a goldfinch came and did the same, accompanied by the less brilliant female. These birds evidently
enjoyed their bath greatly, and it seemed indispensable
to them.

A neighbor of Webster's told me that he had hard
on to sixteen hundred acres and was still buying more,
— a farm and factory within the year; cultivated a
hundred and fifty acres. I saw twelve acres of potatoes

together, the same of rye and wheat, and more methinks of buckwheat. Fifteen or sixteen men, Irish
mostly, at ten dollars a month, doing the work of fifty,
with a Yankee overseer, long a resident of Marshfield, named Wright. Would eat only the produce of his
farm during the few weeks he was at home, — brown
bread and butter and milk, — and sent out for a pig's
cheek to eat with his greens. Ate only what grew on
his farm, but drank more than ran on his farm.

Took refuge from the rain at a Mr. Stetson's in
Duxbury.

I forgot to say that I passed the Winslow House, now
belonging to Webster. This land was granted to the
family in 1637.

Sailed with tavern-keeper Winsor, who was going
out mackereling. Seven men, stripping up their clothes,
each bearing an armful of wood and one some new
potatoes, walked to the boats, then shoved them out a
dozen rods over the mud, then rowed half a mile to the
schooner of forty-three tons. They expected [to] be
gone about a week, and to begin to fish perhaps the
next morning. Fresh mackerel which they carried to
Boston. Had four dories, and commonly fished from
them. Else they fished on the starboard side aft, where
their lines hung ready with the old baits on, two to a
man. I had the experience of going on a mackerel
cruise.

They went aboard their schooner in a leisurely way
this Sunday evening, with a fair but very slight wind,
the sun now setting clear and shining on the vessel after
several thunder-showers. I was struck by the small

quantity of supplies which they appeared to take. We
climbed aboard, and there we were in a mackerel
schooner. The baits were not dry on the hooks. Winsor
cast overboard the foul juice of mackerels mixed with
rain-water which remained in his trough. There was
the mill in which to grind up the mackerel for bait, and
the trough to hold it, and the long-handled dipper to
cast it overboard with; and already in the harbor we
saw the surface rippled with schools of small mackerel.
They proceeded leisurely to weigh anchor, and then to
raise their two sails. There was one passenger, going
for health or amusement, who had been to California.
I had the experience of going a-mackereling, though I
was landed on an island before we got out of the harbor.
They expected to commence fishing the next morning.
It had been a very warm day with frequent thunder-
showers. I had walked from Cohasset to Duxbury, and
had walked about the latter town to find a passage to
Clark's Island, about three miles distant, but no boat
could stir, they said, at that state of the tide.[1] The
tide was down, and boats were left high and dry. At
length I was directed to Winsor's tavern, where perchance I might find some mackerel-fishers, who were
going to sail that night to be ready for fishing in the
morning, and, as they would pass near the island, they
would take me. I found it so. Winsor himself was
going. I told him he was the very man for me; but I
must wait an hour. So I ate supper with them. Then
one after another of his crew was seen straggling to the

---

[1] [Here he tells the story in a different form, showing an intention
of using it later.]

shore, for the most part in high boots, — some made
of india-rubber, — some with their pants stripped up.
There were seven for this schooner, beside a passenger
and myself. The leisurely manner in which they proceeded struck me. I had taken off my shoes and stockings and prepared to wade. Each of the seven took an
armful of pine wood and walked with it to the two boats,
which lay at high-water mark in the mud; then they
resolved that each should bring one more armful and
that would be enough. They had already got a barrel
of water and had some more in the schooner, also a
bucket of new potatoes. Then, dividing into two parties, we pulled and shoved the boats a dozen rods over
the mud and water till they floated, then rowed half a
mile or more over the shallow water to the little schooner
and climbed aboard. Many seals had their heads out.
We gathered about the helmsman and talked about the
compass, which was affected by the iron in the vessel,
etc., etc.[1]

Clark's Island, Sunday night. — On Friday night
December 8th, O. S., the Pilgrims, exploring in the shal-
lop, landed on Clark's Island (so called from the master's mate of the May-Flower), where they spent three
nights and kept their first Sabbath. On Monday, or
the 11th, O. S., they landed on the Rock. This island
contains about eighty-six acres and was once covered
with red cedars which were sold at Boston for gate-posts.
I saw a few left, one, two feet in diameter at the ground,
which was probably standing when the Pilgrims came.

---

[1] [Cape Cod, pp. 182–184; Riv. 219–221.]

Ed. Watson, who could remember them nearly fifty years, had observed but little change in them. Hutchinson calls this one of the best islands in Massachusetts Bay. The town kept it at first as a sacred place, but finally sold it in 1690 to Samuel Lucas, Elkanah Watson, and George Morton. Saw a stag's-horn sumach five or six inches in diameter and eighteen feet high. Here was the marsh goldenrod (*Solidago lœvigata*) not yet in blossom; a small bluish flower in the marshes, which they called rosemary; a kind of chenopodium which appeared distinct from the common; and a short oval-leaved, set-looking plant which I suppose is *Glaux maritima*, sea milkwort, or saltwort. Skates' eggs, called in England skate-barrows from their form, on the sand. The old cedars were flat-topped, spreading, the stratum of the wind drawn out.

July 28. Monday morning. Sailed [to] the Gurnet, which runs down seven miles into the bay from Marshfield. Heard the *peep* of the *beach-bird.* Saw some ring-necks in company with peeps. They told of eagles which had flown low over the island lately. Went by Saquish. Gathered a basketful of Irish moss bleached on the beach. Saw a field full of pink-blossomed potatoes at the lighthouse, remarkably luxuriant and full of blossoms; also some French barley. Old fort and barracks by lighthouse. Visited lobster houses or huts there, where they use lobsters to catch bait for lobsters. Saw on the shanties signs from ships, as " Justice Story " and "Margueritta." To obtain bait is sometimes the

main thing. Samphire (*Salicornia*), which they pickle; also a kind of prickly samphire, which I suppose is saltwort, or *Salsola Caroliniana*. Well at Clark's Island twenty-seven and three quarters feet deep. Cut the rock-weed on the rocks at low tide once in two or three years. Very valuable; more than they have time to save.

Uncle Ned told of a man who went off fishing from back of Wellfleet in calm weather, and with great difficulty got ashore through the surf. Those in the other boat, who had landed, were unwilling to take the responsibility of telling them when to pull for shore; the one who had the helm was inexperienced. They were swamped at once. So treacherous is this shore. Before the wind comes, perchance, the sea may run so as to upset and drown you on the shore. At first they thought to pull for Provincetown, but night was coming on, and that was distant many a long mile. Their case was a desperate one. When they came near the shore and saw the terrific breakers that intervened, they were deterred. They were thoroughly frightened.[1]

Were troubled with skunks on this island; they must have come over on the ice. Foxes they had seen; had killed one woodchuck; even a large *mud turtle*, which they *conjectured some bird must have dropped.* Musk-rats they had seen, and killed two raccoons once. I went a-clamming just before night. This the clam-digger, borrowed of Uncle Bill (Watson) in his schooner home. The clams nearly a foot deep, but I broke many in digging. Said not to be good now, but we found them good eaten fresh. No sale for

[1] [*Cape Cod*, p. 157; Riv. 187, 188.]

them now; fetch twenty-five cents a bucket in their season. Barry caught squids as bait for bass. We found many dead clams, — their shells full of sand, — called sand clams.[1] By a new clam law any one can dig clams here. Brown's Island, so called, a shoal off the Gurnet, thought to have been an isle once, a dangerous place. Saw here fences, the posts set in cross sleepers, made to be removed in winter.

The finest music in a menagerie, its wildest strains, have something in them akin to the cries of the tigers and leopards heard in their native forests. Those strains are not unfitted to the assemblage of wild beasts. They express to my ear what the tiger's stripes and the leopard's spots express to my eye; and they appear to grin with satisfaction at the sound. That nature has any place at all for music is very good.

July 29. Tuesday. A northeast wind with rain, but the sea is the wilder for it. I heard the surf roar on the Gurnet [in] the night, which, as Uncle Ned and Freeman said, showed that the wind would work round east and we should have rainy weather. It was the wave reaching the shore before the wind. The ocean was heaped up somewhere to the eastward, and this roar was occasioned by its effort to preserve its equilibrium. The rut of the sea.[2] In the afternoon I sailed to Plymouth, three miles, notwithstanding the drizzling rain, or " drisk," as Uncle Ned called it. We passed round the head of Plymouth beach, which is three miles long. I did not know till

[1] [*Cape Cod*, pp. 109, 110; Riv. 129.]
[2] [See *Cape Cod*, pp. 97, 98; Riv. 115.]

afterward that I had landed where the Pilgrims did and passed over the Rock on Hedge's Wharf. Returning, we had more wind and tacking to do.

Saw many seals together on a flat. Singular that these strange animals should be so abundant here and yet the man who lives a few miles inland never hear of them. To him there is no report of the sea, though he may read the Plymouth paper. The Boston papers do not tell us that they have seals in the Harbor. The inhabitants of Plymouth do not seem to be aware of it. I always think of seals in connection with Esquimaux or some other outlandish people, not in connection with those who live on the shores of Boston and Plymouth harbors. Yet from their windows they may daily see a family [of] seals, the real *Phoca vitulina*, collected on a flat or sporting in the waves. I saw one dashing through the waves just ahead of our boat, going to join his companions on the bar, — as strange to me as the merman. No less wild, essentially, than when the Pilgrims came is this harbor.

It being low tide, we landed on a flat which makes out from Clark's Island, to while away the time, not being able to get quite up yet. I found numerous *large* holes of the sea clam in this sand (no small clams), and dug them out easily and rapidly with my hands. Could have got a large quantity in a short time; but here they do not eat them; think they will make you sick. They were not so deep in the sand, not more than five or six inches. I saw where one had squirted full ten feet before the wind, as appeared by the marks of the drops on the sand. Some small ones I found not more than a quarter of an inch in length. Le Baron brought me [a] round clam or quahog alive, with a very thick shell, and not so nearly an isosceles triangle as the sea clam, — more like this: ◯   ◯ with a protuberance on the back. The sea clam: ◯   A small, narrow clam ⬯ which ◯ they called the bank clam; also crab-cases, handsomely spotted. Small crab always in a cockle-shell if not in a case of his own. A cockle as large as my fist. Mussels, small ones, empty shells; an extensive bank where they had died. Occasionally a large deep-sea mussel, which some kelp had brought up. We caught some sand eels seven or eight inches long, — *Ammodytes tobianus*, according to Storer, and not the *A. lancea* of Yarrell, though the size of the last comes nearer. They were in the shallow pools left on the sand (the flat was here pure naked yellowish sand), and quickly buried themselves when pursued. They are used as bait for bass. Found some sand-circles or sandpaper, like top of a stone jug cut off, with a large nose; said to be made by the foot of the large cockle, which has some glutinous matter on it.[1] A circle of sand about as thick as thick pasteboard. It reminded me of the caddis-worm cases, skate-barrows, etc., etc. I observed the shell of a sea clam one valve of which was filled exactly even full with sand, — evenly as if it had been heaped and then scraped off, as when men measure by the peck. This was a fresher one of the myriad sand-clams, and it suggested to me how the stone clams which I had seen on Cape Cod might have been formed.

[1] The nidus of the animal of *Natica*, — cells with eggs in sand.

Perchance a clamshell was the mould in which they were cast, and a slight hardening of the level surface, before the whole is turned to stone, causes them to split in two. The sand was full of stone clams in the mould.[1] I saw the kelp attached to stones half as big as my head, which it had transported. I do not think I ever saw the kelp *in situ*. Also attached to a deep-sea mussel. The kelp is like a broad ruffled belt. The middle portion is thicker and flat, the edges for two or three inches thinner and fuller, so that it is fulled or ruffled, as if the edges had been hammered. The extremity is generally worn and ragged from the lashing of the waves. It is the prototype of a fringed belt. Uncle Ned said that the cows ate it.[2] We saw in the shallow water a long, *round* green grass, six or eight feet long, clogging up the channel. Round grass, I think they called it. We caught a lobster, as you might catch a mud turtle in the country, in the shallow water, pushing him ashore with the paddle, taking hold of his tail to avoid being bitten. They are obliged to put wooden plugs or wedges beside their claws to prevent their tearing each other to pieces. All weeds are bleached on the beach.

This sailing on salt water was something new to me. The boat is such a living creature, even this clumsy one sailing within five points of the wind. The sailboat is an admirable invention, by which you compel the wind to transport you even against itself. It is easier to guide than a horse; the slightest pressure on the tiller suffices. I think the inventor must have been greatly

[1] [*Cape Cod*, pp. 109, 110 ; Riv. 129.]
[2] [*Cape Cod*, pp. 68, 69 ; Riv. 79.]

Vol. II

surprised, as well as delighted, at the success of his experiment. It is so contrary to expectation, as if the elements were disposed to favor you. This deep, unfordable sea! but this wind ever blowing over it to transport you! At 10 P. M. it was perfectly fair and bright starlight.

July 30. Wednesday. The house here stands within a grove of balm-of-Gileads, horse-chestnuts, cherries, apples, and plums, etc. Uncle Bill, who lives in his schooner, — not turned up Numidian fashion, but anchored in the mud, — whom I meant to call on yesterday morn, lo! had run over to "the Pines" last evening, fearing an easterly storm. He outrode the great gale in the spring alone in the harbor, dashing about. He goes after rockweed, lighters vessels, and saves wrecks. Now I see him lying in the mud over at the Pines in the horizon, which place he cannot leave if he will, till flood-tide; but he will not, it seems. This waiting for the tide is a singular feature in the life by the shore. In leaving your boat to-day you must always have reference to what you are going to do the next day. A frequent answer is, " Well, you can't start for two hours yet." It is something new to a landsman, and at first he is not disposed to wait.[1] I saw some heaps of shells left by the Indians near the northern end of the island. They were a rod in diameter and a foot or more high in the middle, and covered with a shorter and greener grass than the surrounding field. Found one imperfect arrowhead.

At 10 A. M. sailed to Webster's, past Powder Point in

[1] [*Cape Cod*, pp. 141, 142 ; Riv. 168, 169.]

Duxbury. We could see his land from the island. I was steersman and learned the meaning of some nautical phrases, — "luff," to keep the boat close to the wind till the sails begin to flap; "bear away," to put the sail more at right angles with the wind; a "close haul," when the sails are brought and belayed nearly or quite in a line with the vessel. On the marshes we saw patches of a "*black* grass." A large field of wheat at Webster's, — half a dozen acres at least, — many apple trees, three-thorned acacias, tulip-trees; cranberry experiment; seaweed spread under his tomatoes. Wild geese with black and gray heads and necks, not so heavy and clumsy as the tame Bremens. Large, noisy Hongkong geese. Handsome calves. Three thousand (?) acres of marsh.

Talked with Webster's nearest neighbor, Captain Hewit, whose small farm he surrounds and endeavors in vain to buy. A fair specimen of a retired Yankee sea-captain turned farmer. Proud of the quantity of carrots he had raised on a small patch. It was better husbandry than Webster's. He told a story of his buying a cargo for his owners at St. Petersburg just as peace was declared in the last war. These men are not so remarkable for anything as the quality of hardness. The very fixedness and rigidity of their jaws and necks express a sort of adamantine hardness. This is what they have learned by contact with the elements. The man who does not grow rigid with years and experience! Where is he? What avails it to grow hard merely? The harder you are, the more brittle really, like the bones of the old. How much rarer and better to grow mellow! A sort of stone fruit the man bears commonly; a bare stone it is, without any sweet and mellow pericarp around it. It is like the peach which has dried to the stone as the season advanced; it is dwindled to a dry stone with its almond. In presence of one of these hard men I think: "How brittle! How easily you would crack! What a poor and lame conclusion!" I can think of nothing but a stone in his head. Truly genial men do not grow [hard]. It is the result of despair, this attitude of resistance. They behave like men already driven to the wall. Notwithstanding that the speaker trembles with infirmity while he speaks, — his hand on the spade, — it is such a trembling as betrays a stony nature. His hand trembles so that the full glass of cider which he prizes to a drop will have lost half its contents before it reaches his lips, as if a tempest had arisen in it. Hopelessly hard. But there is another view of him. He is somebody. He has an opinion to express, if you will wait to hear him. A certain manliness and refreshing resistance is in him. He generally makes Webster a call, but Webster does not want to see you more than twenty minutes. It does not take him long to say all he has got to say. He had not seen him to speak to him since he had come home this time. He had sent him over a couple of fine cod the night before. Such a man as Hewit sees not finely but coarsely.

The eagle given by Lawrence on the hill in the buckwheat field.

July 31. *Thursday.* Those same round shells (*Scutella parma* (*placenta*) ?) on the sand as at Cape Cod, the

live ones reddish, the dead white. Went off early this morning with Uncle Ned to catch bass with the small fish I had found on the sand the night before. Two of his neighbor Albert Watson's boys were there, — not James, the oldest, but Edward, the sailor, and Mortimer (or Mort), — in their boat. They killed some striped bass (*Labrax lineatus*) with paddles in a shallow creek in the sand, and caught some lobsters. I remarked that the seashore was singularly clean, for, notwithstanding the spattering of the water and mud and squirting of the clams and wading to and fro the boat, my best black pants retained no stains nor dirt, as they would acquire from walking in the country. I caught a bass with a young — haik? (perchance), trailing thirty feet behind while Uncle Ned paddled. They catch them in England with a "trawl-net." Sometimes they weigh seventy-five pounds here.

At 11 A. M. set sail to Plymouth. We went somewhat out of a direct course, to take advantage of the tide, which was coming in. Saw the site of the first house, which was burned, on Leyden Street. Walked up the same, parallel with the Town Brook. Hill from which Billington Sea was discovered hardly a mile from the shore, on Watson's grounds. Watson's Hill, where treaty was made, across brook south of Burying Hill. At Watson's,[1] the oriental plane, *Abies Douglasii*, ginkgo tree (*q. v.* on Common), a foreign hardhack, English oak (dark-colored, small leaf), Spanish chest-

[1] [Marston Watson, Thoreau's friend and correspondent. See *Familiar Letters, passim*, and especially note to letter of April 25, 1858.]

nut, Chinese arbor-vitæ, Norway spruce (like our fir balsam), a new kind of fir balsam. Black eagle one of the good cherries. Fuchsias in hothouse. Earth bank covered with cement.

Mr. Thomas Russell, who cannot be seventy, at whose house on Leyden Street I took tea and spent the evening, told me that he remembered to have seen Ebenezer Cobb, a native of Plymouth, who died in Kingston in 1801, aged one hundred and seven, who remembered to have had personal knowledge of Peregrine White, saw him an old man riding on horseback (he lived to be eighty-three). White was born at Cape Cod Harbor before the Pilgrims got to Plymouth. C. Sturgis's mother told me the same of herself at the same time. She remembered Cobb sitting in an arm chair like the one she herself occupied, with his silver locks falling about his shoulders, twirling one thumb over the other. Lyell in first volume, "Second Visit," page 97, published 1849,[1] says: "Colonel Perkins, of Boston, . . . informed me, in 1846, that there was but one link wanting in the chain of personal communication between him and Peregrine White, the first white child born in Massachusetts, a few days after the Pilgrims landed. White lived to an advanced age, and was known to a man of the name of Cobb, whom Colonel Perkins visited, in 1807, with some friends who yet survive. Cobb died in 1808, the year after Colonel Perkins saw him."

Russell told me that he once bought some *primitive* woodland in Plymouth which was sold at auction —

[1] [Sir Charles Lyell, *A Second Visit to the United States.*]

the biggest pitch pines two feet diameter — for *eight shillings* an acre. If he had bought enough, it would have been a fortune. There is still forest in this town which the axe has not touched, says George Bradford. According to Thacher's History of Plymouth, there were 11,662 acres of woodland in 1831, or twenty square miles. Pilgrims first saw Billington Sea about January 1st; visited it January 8th. The oldest stone in the Plymouth Burying Ground, 1681. (Coles (?) Hill, where those who died the first winter were buried, is said to have been levelled and sown to conceal loss from Indians.) Oldest on our hill, 1677. In Mrs. Plympton's garden on Leyden Street, running down to Town Brook, saw an abundance of pears, gathered excellent June-eating apples, saw a large lilac about eight inches diameter. Methinks a soil may improve when at length it has shaded itself with vegetation.

William S. Russell, the registrar at the court-house, showed the oldest town records, for all are preserved. On first page a plan of Leyden Street dated December, 1620, with names of settlers. They have a great many folios. The writing plain. Saw the charter granted by the Plymouth Company to the Pilgrims, signed by Warwick, dated 1629, and the box in which it was brought over, with the seal.

Pilgrim Hall. They used to crack off pieces of the Forefathers' Rock for visitors with a cold chisel, till the town forbade it. The stone remaining at wharf is about seven feet square. Saw two old armchairs that came over in the Mayflower, the large picture by Sargent, Standish's sword, gun-barrel with which Philip was killed, mug and pocket-book of Clark the mate, iron pot of Standish, old pipe-tongs. Indian relics: a flayer; a pot or mortar of a kind of fire-proof stone, very hard, only seven or eight inches long. A commission from Cromwell to Winslow (?), his signature torn off. They talk of a monument on the Rock. The Burying Hill 165 feet high. Manomet 394 feet high by State map. Saw more pears at Washburn's garden. No graves of Pilgrims.

Seaweed generally used along shore. Saw the *Prinos glabra*, ink-berry, at Billington Sea. Sandy plain with oaks of various kinds cut in less than twenty years. No communication with Sandwich. Plymouth end of world; fifty miles thither by railroad. Old Colony road poor property. Nothing saves Plymouth but the Rock. Fern-leaved beach.

Saw the king crab (*Limulus polyphemus*), horseshoe and saucepan fish, at the Island, covered with sea-green and buried in the sand for concealment.

In Plymouth the *Convolvulus arvensis*, small bindweed.

VII

AUGUST, 1851

(ÆT. 34)

Left [Plymouth] at 9 a. m., August 1st. After Kingston came Plympton, Halifax, and Hanson, all level with frequent cedar swamps, especially the last, — also in Weymouth.

Desor and Cabot think the jellyfish *Oceania tubulosa* are buds from a polyp of genus *Syncoryne*. Desor, accounting for suspended moisture or fogs over sandbanks (or shoals), says, the heat being abstracted by radiation, the moisture is condensed in form of fog.

Lieutenant Walsh lost his lead and wire when 34,200 [feet], or more than six statute miles, had run out perpendicularly.

I could make a list of things ill-managed. We Yankees do not deserve our fame. *Viz.* [*sic*]: —

I went to a menagerie the other day, advertised by a flaming show-bill as big as a barn-door. The proprietors had taken wonderful pains to collect rare and interesting animals from all parts of the world, and then placed by them a few stupid and ignorant fellows, coachmen or stablers, who knew little or nothing about the animals and were unwilling even to communicate the little they knew. You catch a rare creature, interesting to all mankind, and then place the first biped

that comes along, with but a grain more reason in him, to exhibit and describe the former. At the expense of millions, this rare quadruped from the sun [*sic*] is obtained, and then Jack Halyard or Tom Coach-whip is hired to explain it. Why all this pains taken to catch in Africa, and no pains taken to exhibit in America? Not a cage was labelled. There was nobody to tell us how or where the animals were caught, or what they were. Probably the proprietors themselves do not know, — or what their habits are. They told me that a hyena came from South America. But hardly had we been ushered into the presence of this choice, this admirable collection, than a ring was formed for Master Jack and the pony! Were they *animals*, then, who had caught and exhibited these, and who had come to see these? Would it not be worth the while to learn something? to have some information imparted? The absurdity of importing the behemoth, and then, instead of somebody appearing [to] tell which it is, to have to *while away the time*, — though your curiosity is growing desperate to learn one fact about the creature, — to have Jack and the pony introduced ! ! ! Why, I expected to see some descendant of Cuvier there, to improve this opportunity for a lecture on natural history!

That is what they should do, — make this an occasion for communicating some solid information. That would be fun alive! that would be a sunny day, a sun day, in one's existence, not a secular day of Shetland ponies. Not Jack and his pony and a tintamarre of musical instruments, and a man with his head in the lion's mouth. First let him prove that he has got a

head on his shoulders. I go not there to see a man hug a lion or fondle a tiger, but to learn how he is related to the wild beast. There'll be All-Fools' days enough without our creating any intentionally. The presumption is that men wish to behave like reasonable creatures; that they do not need, and are not seeking, relaxation; that they are not dissipated. Let it be a travelling zoölogical garden, with a travelling professor to accompany it. At present, foolishly, the professor goes alone with his poor painted illustrations of animals, while the menagerie takes another road, without its professor, — only its keepers, stupid coachmen.

I. M. June [?] & Co., or Van Amburgh & Co., are engaged in a pecuniary speculation in which certain wild beasts are used as the counters. Cuvier & Co. are engaged in giving a course of lectures on Natural History. Now why could they not put head and means together for the benefit of mankind, and still get their living? The present institution is imperfect precisely because its object is to enrich Van Amburgh & Co., and their low aim unfits them for rendering any more valuable service; but no doubt the most valuable course would also be the most valuable in a pecuniary sense. No doubt a low self-interest is a better motive force to these enterprises than no interest at all; but a high self-interest, which consists with the greatest advantage of all, would be a better still.

Item 2nd: Why have we not a decent pocket-map of the State of Massachusetts? There is the large map. Why is it not cut into half a dozen sheets and folded into a small cover for the pocket? Are there no travellers

Town Brook, Plymouth

to use it? Well, to tell the truth, there are but few, and that's the reason why. Men go by railroad, and State maps hanging in bar-rooms are small enough. The State has been admirably surveyed at a great cost, and yet Dearborn's Pocket-Map is the best one we have!

Aug. 4. Now the hardhack and meadow-sweet reign, the former one of our handsomest flowers, I think. The mayweed, too, dusty by the roadside, and in the fields I scent the sweet-scented life-everlasting, which is half expanded. The grass is withered by the drought. The potatoes begin generally to flat down. The corn is tasselled out; its crosses show in all fields above the blades. The turnips are growing in its midst.

As my eye rested on the blossom of the meadow-sweet in a hedge, I heard the note of an autumnal cricket, and was penetrated with the sense of autumn. Was it sound? or was it form? or was it scent? or was it flavor? It is now the royal month of August. When I hear this sound, I am as dry as the rye which is everywhere cut and housed, though I am drunk with the season's wine.

The farmer is the most inoffensive of men, with his barns and cattle and poultry and grain and grass. I like the smell of his hay well enough, though as grass it may be in my way.

The yellow Bethlehem-star still, and the yellow gerardia, and a bluish "savory-leaved aster."

Aug. 5. 7.30 p. m. — Moon half full. I sit beside Hubbard's Grove. A few level red bars above the horizon;

a dark, irregular bank beneath them, with a streak of red sky below, on the horizon's edge. This will describe many a sunset. It is 8 o'clock. The farmer has driven in his cows, and is cutting an armful of green corn fodder for them. Another is still patching the roof of his barn, making his hammer heard afar in the twilight, as if he took a satisfaction in his elevated work, — sitting astride the ridge, — which he wished to prolong. The robin utters a sort of cackling note, as if he had learned the ways of man. The air is still. I hear the voices of loud-talking boys in the early twilight, it must be a mile off. The swallows go over with a watery twittering.

When the moon is on the increase and half full, it is already in mid-heavens at sunset, so that there is no marked twilight intervening. I hear the whip-poor-will at a distance, but they are few of late.

It is almost dark. I hear the voices of berry-pickers coming homeward from Bear Garden. Why do they go home, as it were defeated by the approaching night? Did it never occur to them to stay overnight? The wind now rising from over Bear Garden Hill falls gently on my ear and delivers its message, the same that I have so often heard passing over bare and stony mountain-tops, so uncontaminated and untamed is the wind. The air that has swept over Caucasus and the sands of Arabia comes to breathe on New England fields. The dogs bark; they are not as much stiller as man. They are on the alert, suspecting the approach of foes. The darkness perchance affects them, makes them mad and wild. The mosquitoes hum about me. I distinguish the modest moonlight on my paper.

Vol. II

As the twilight deepens and the moonlight is more and more bright, I begin to distinguish myself, who I am and where; as my walls contract, I become more collected and composed, and sensible of my own existence, as when a lamp is brought into a dark apartment and I see who the company are. With the coolness and the mild silvery light, I recover some sanity, my thoughts are more distinct, moderated, and tempered. Reflection is more possible while the day goes by. The intense light of the sun unfits me for meditation, makes me wander in my thought; my life is too diffuse and dissipated; routine succeeds and prevails over us; the trivial has greater power then, and most at noonday, the most trivial hour of the twenty-four. I am sobered by the moonlight. I bethink myself. It is like a cup of cold water to a thirsty man. The moonlight is more favorable to meditation than sunlight.

The sun lights this world from without, shines in at a window, but the moon is like a lamp within an apartment. It shines for us. The stars themselves make a more visible, and hence a nearer and more domestic, roof at night. Nature broods us, and has not left our germs of thought to be hatched by the sun. We feel her heat and see her body darkening over us. Our thoughts are not dissipated, but come back to us like an echo.

The different kinds of moonlight are infinite. This is not a night for contrasts of light and shade, but a faint diffused light in which there is light enough to travel, and that is all.

A road (the Corner road) that passes over the height

of land between earth and heaven, separating those streams which flow earthward from those which flow heavenward.

Ah, what a poor, dry compilation is the "Annual of Scientific Discovery!" I trust that observations are made during the year which are not chronicled there, — that some mortal may have caught a glimpse of Nature in some corner of the earth during the year 1851. One sentence of perennial poetry would make me forget, would atone for, volumes of mere science. The astronomer is as blind to the significant phenomena, or the significance of phenomena, as the wood-sawyer who wears glasses to defend his eyes from sawdust. The question is not what you look at, but what you see.

I hear now from Bear Garden Hill — I rarely walk by moonlight without hearing — the sound of a flute, or a horn, or a human voice. It is a performer I never see by day; should not recognize him if pointed out; but you may hear his performance in every horizon. He plays but one strain and goes to bed early, but I know by the character of that single strain that he is deeply dissatisfied with the manner in which he spends his day. He is a slave who is purchasing his freedom. He is Apollo watching the flocks of Admetus on every hill, and this strain he plays every evening to remind him of his heavenly descent. It is all that saves him, — his one redeeming trait. It is a reminiscence; he loves to remember his youth. He is sprung of a noble family. He is highly related, I have no doubt; was tenderly nurtured in his infancy, poor hind as he is. That noble strain he utters, instead of any jewel on his finger, or precious locket fastened to his breast, or purple garments that came with him. The elements recognize him, and echo his strain. All the dogs know him their master, though lords and ladies, rich men and learned, know him not. He is the son of a rich man, of a famous man who served his country well. He has heard his sire's stories. I thought of the time when he would discover his parentage, obtain his inheritance and sing a strain suited to the morning hour. He cherishes hopes. I never see the man by day who plays that clarionet.

The distant lamps in the farmhouse look like fires. The trees and clouds are seen at a distance reflected in the river as by day. I see Fair Haven Pond from the Cliffs, as it were through a slight mist. It is the wildest scenery imaginable, — a Lake of the Woods. I just remembered the wildness of St. Anne's. That's the Ultima Thule of wildness to me.

What an entertainment for the traveller, this incessant motion apparently of the moon traversing the clouds! Whether you sit or stand, it is always preparing new developments for you. It is event enough for simple minds. You all alone, the moon all alone, overcoming with incessant victory whole squadrons of clouds above the forests and the lakes and rivers and the mountains. You cannot always calculate which one the moon will undertake next.[1]

I see a solitary firefly over the woods.

The moon wading through clouds; though she is eclipsed by this one, I see her shining on a more distant

[1] [*Excursions*, pp. 329, 330; Riv. 405. See also pp. 383–385 of this volume.]

but lower one. The entrance into Hubbard's Wood above the spring, coming from the hill, is like the entrance to a cave; but when you are within, there are some streaks of light on the edge of the path.

All these leaves so still, none whispering, no birds in motion, — how can I be else than still and thoughtful?

Aug. 6. The motions of circus horses are not so expressive of music, do not harmonize so well with a strain of music, as those of animals of the cat kind. An Italian has just carried a hand-organ through the village. I hear it even at Walden Wood. It is as if a cheeta had skulked, howling, through the streets of the village, with knotted tail, and left its perfume there.

Neglected gardens are full of fleabane (?) now, not yet in blossom. Thoroughwort has opened, and goldenrod is gradually opening. The smooth sumach shows its red fruit. The berries of the bristly aralia are turning dark. The wild holly's scarlet fruit is seen and the red cherry (*Cerasus*). After how few steps, how little exertion, the student stands in pine woods above the Solomon's-seal and the cow-wheat, in a place still unaccountably strange and wild to him, and to all civilization! This so easy and so common, though our literature implies that it is rare! We in the country make no report of the seals and sharks in our neighborhood to those in the city. We send them only our huckleberries, not free wild thoughts.

Why does not man sleep all day as well as all night,

it seems so very natural and easy? For what is he awake?

A man must generally get away some hundreds or thousands of miles from home before he can be said to begin his travels. Why not begin his travels at home? Would he have to go far or look very closely to discover novelties? The traveller who, in this sense, pursues his travels at home, has the advantage at any rate of a long residence in the country to make his observations correct and profitable. Now the American goes to England, while the Englishman comes to America, in order to describe the country. No doubt there [are] some advantages in this kind of mutual criticism. But might there not be invented a better way of coming at the truth than this scratch-my-back-and-I-'ll-scratch-yours method? Would not the American, for instance, who had himself, perchance, travelled in England and elsewhere make the most profitable and accurate traveller in his own country? How often it happens that the traveller's principal distinction is that he is one who knows less about a country than a native! Now if he should begin with all the knowledge of a native, and add thereto the knowledge of a traveller, both natives and foreigners would be obliged to read his book; and the world would be absolutely benefited. It takes a man of genius to travel in his own country, in his native village; to make any progress between his door and his gate. But such a traveller will make the distances which Hanno and Marco Polo and Cook and Ledyard went over ridiculous. So worthy a traveller as William Bartram heads his first chapter with the words, "The author

sets sail from Philadelphia, and arrives at Charleston, from whence he begins his travels."

I am, perchance, most and most profitably interested in the things which I already know a little about; a mere and utter novelty is a mere monstrosity to me. I am interested to see the yellow pine, which we have not in Concord, though Michaux says it grows in Massachusetts; or the Oriental plane, having often heard of it and being well acquainted with its sister, the Occidental plane; or the English oak, having heard of the royal oak and having oaks ourselves; but the new Chinese flower, whose cousin I do not happen to know, I pass by with indifference. I do not know that I am very fond of novelty. I wish to get a clearer notion of what I have already some inkling.

These Italian boys with their hand-organs remind me of the keepers of wild beasts in menageries, whose whole art consists in stirring up their beasts from time to time with a pole. I am reminded of bright flowers and glancing birds and striped pards of the jungle; these delicious harmonies tear me to pieces while they charm me. The tiger's musical smile.

How some inventions have spread! Some, brought to perfection by the most enlightened nations, have been surely and rapidly communicated to the most savage. The gun, for instance. How soon after the settlement of America were comparatively remote Indian tribes, most of whose members had never seen a white man, supplied with guns! The gun is invented by the civilized man, and the savage in remote wildernesses on the other side of the globe throws away his bow and arrows and takes up this arm. Bartram, travelling in the Southern States between 1770 and 1780, describes the warriors as so many gun-men.

Ah, yes, even here in Concord horizon Apollo is at work for King Admetus! Who is King Admetus? It is Business, with his four prime ministers Trade and Commerce and Manufactures and Agriculture. And this is what makes mythology true and interesting to us.

Aug. 8. 7.30 P. M. — To Conantum.

The moon has not yet quite filled her horns. I perceive why we so often remark a dark cloud in the west at and after sunset. It is because it is almost directly between us and the sun, and hence we see the dark side, and moreover it is much darker than it otherwise would be, because of the little light reflected from the earth at that hour. The same cloud at midday and overhead might not attract attention. There is a pure amber sky beneath the present bank, thus framed off from the rest of the heavens, which, with the outlines of small dead elms seen against it, — I hardly know if far or near, — make picture enough. Men will travel far to see less interesting sights than this. Turning away from the sun, we get this enchanting view, as when a man looks at the landscape with inverted head. Under shadow of the dark cloud which I have described, the cricket begins his strain, his ubiquitous strain. Is there a fall cricket distinct from the species we hear in spring and summer? I smell the corn-field over the brook a dozen rods off, and it reminds me of the green-corn feasts of the Indians. The evening train comes rolling

in, but none of the passengers jumping out in such haste attend to the beautiful, fresh picture which Nature has unrolled in the west and surmounted with that dark frame. The circular platter of the carrot's blossom is now perfect.

Might not this be called the Invalid's Moon, on account of the warmth of the nights? The principal employment of the farmers now seems to be getting their meadow-hay and cradling some oats, etc.

The light from the western sky is stronger still than that of the moon, and when I hold up my hand, the west side is lighted while the side toward the moon is comparatively dark. But now that I have put this dark wood (Hubbard's) between me and the west, I see the moonlight plainly on my paper; I am even startled by it. One star, too, — is it Venus? — I see in the west. Starlight! that would be a good way to mark the hour, if we were precise. Hubbard's Brook. How much the beauty of the moon is enhanced by being seen shining between two trees, or even by the neighborhood of clouds! I hear the clock striking eight faintly. I smell the late shorn meadows.

One will lose no music by not attending the oratorios and operas. The really inspiring melodies are cheap and universal, and are as audible to the poor man's son as to the rich man's. Listening to the harmonies of the universe is not allied to dissipation. My neighbors have gone to the vestry to hear "Ned Kendal," the bugler, to-night, but I am come forth to the hills to hear my bugler in the horizon. I can forego the seeming advantages of cities without misgiving. No heavenly strain is

Vol. II

lost to the ear that is fitted to hear it, for want of money or opportunity. I am convinced that for instrumental music all Vienna cannot serve me more than the Italian boy who seeks my door with his organ.

And now I strike the road at the causeway. It is hard, and I hear the sound of my steps, a sound which should never be heard, for it draws down my thoughts. It is more like the treadmill exercise. The fireflies are not so numerous as they have been. There is no dew as yet. The planks and railing of Hubbard's Bridge are removed. I walk over on the string-pieces, resting in the middle until the moon comes out of a cloud, that I may see my path, for between the next piers the string-pieces also are removed and there is only a rather narrow plank, let down three or four feet. I essay to cross it, but it springs a little and I mistrust myself, whether I shall not plunge into the river. Some demonic genius seems to be warning me. Attempt not the passage; you will surely be drowned. It is very real that I am thus affected. Yet I am fully aware of the absurdity of minding such suggestions. I put out my foot, but I am checked, as if that power had laid a hand on my breast and chilled me back. Nevertheless, I cross, stooping at first, and gain the other side. (I make the most of it on account of the admonition, but it was nothing to remark on. I returned the same way two hours later and made nothing of it.) It is easy to see how, by yielding to such feelings as this, men would reëstablish all the superstitions of antiquity. It is best that reason should govern us, and not these blind intimations, in which we exalt our fears into a genius.

On Conantum I sit awhile in the shade of the woods and look out on the moonlit fields. White rocks are more remarkable than by day.[1]

The air is warmer than the rocks now. It is perfectly warm and I am tempted to stay out all night and observe each phenomenon of the night until day dawns. But if I should do so, I should not wonder if the town were raised to hunt me up. I could lie out here on this pinnacle rock all night without cold. To lie here on your back with nothing between your eye and the stars, — nothing but space, — they your nearest neighbors on that side, be they strange or be they tame, be they other worlds or merely ornaments to this, who could ever go to sleep under these circumstances? Sitting on the door-step of Conant house at 9 o'clock, I hear a pear drop. How few of all the apples that fall do we hear fall! I hear a horse *sneeze* (?) from time to time in his pasture. He sees me and knows me to be a man, though I do not see him. I hear the nine o'clock bell ringing in Bedford. An unexpectedly musical sound that of a bell in the horizon always is. Pleasantly sounds the voice of one village to another. It is sweet as it is rare. Since I sat here a bright star has gone behind the stem of a tree, proving that my machine is moving, — proving it better for me than a rotating pendulum. I hear a solitary whip-poor-will, and a bullfrog on the river, — fewer sounds than in spring. The gray cliffs across the river are plain to be seen.

And now the star appears on the other side of the tree, and I must go. Still no dew up here. I see three

[1] [*Excursions,* p. 327; Riv. 402.]

scythes hanging on an apple tree. There is the wild apple tree where hangs the forgotten scythe,[1] — the rock where the shoe was left. The woods and the separate trees cast longer shadows than by day, for the moon goes lower in her course at this season. Some dew at last in the meadow. As I recross the string-pieces of the bridge, I see the water-bugs swimming briskly in the moonlight. I scent the Roman wormwood in the potato-fields.

Aug. 9. Saturday. Tansy now in bloom and the fresh white clethra. Among the pines and birches I hear the invisible locust. As I am going to the pond to bathe, I see a black cloud in the northern horizon and hear the muttering of thunder, and make haste. Before I have bathed and dressed, the gusts which precede the tempest are heard roaring in the woods, and the first black, gusty clouds have reached my zenith. Hastening toward town, I meet the rain at the edge of the wood, and take refuge under the thickest leaves, where not a drop reaches me, and, at the end of half an hour, the renewed singing of the birds alone advertises me that the rain has ceased, and it is only the dripping from the leaves which I hear in the woods. It was a splendid sunset that day, a celestial light on all the land, so that all people went to their doors and windows to look on the grass and leaves and buildings and the sky, and it was equally glorious in whatever quarter you looked; a sort of fulgor as of stereotyped lightning[2] filled the air. Of which this is my solution. We were in the westernmost edge of

[1] [*Excursions*, p. 317; Riv. 389.]   [2] [See vol. iii, p. 439.]

in his behalf. What cloud will enter the lists with her next, this employs his thoughts; and when she enters on a clear field of great extent in the heavens, and shines unobstructedly, he is glad. And when she has fought her way through all the squadrons of her foes, and rides majestic in a clear sky, he cheerfully and confidently pursues his way, and rejoices in his heart. But if he sees that she has many new clouds to contend with, he pursues his way moodily, as one disappointed and aggrieved; he resents it as an injury to himself. It is his employment to watch the moon, the companion and guide of his journey, wading through clouds, and calculate what one is destined to shut out her cheering light. He traces her course, now almost completely obscured, through the ranks of her foes, and calculates where she will issue from them.[1] He is disappointed and saddened when he sees that she has many clouds to contend with.

Sitting on the sleepers of Hubbard's Bridge, which is being repaired, now, 3 o'clock A. M., I hear a cock crow. How admirably adapted to the dawn is that sound! as if made by the first rays of light rending the darkness, the creaking of the sun's axle heard already over the eastern hills.

Though man's life is trivial and handselled, Nature is holy and heroic. With what infinite faith and promise and moderation begins each new day! It is only a little after 3 o'clock, and already there is evidence of morning in the sky.

He rejoices when the moon comes forth from the

[1] [*Excursions*, pp. 329, 330; Riv. 405, 406. See also p. 374 of this volume.]

the shower at the moment the sun was setting, and its rays shone through the cloud and the falling rain. We were, in fact, in a rainbow and it was here its arch rested on the earth. At a little distance we should have seen all the colors.[1]

The *Œnothera biennis* along the railroad now. Do the cars disperse seeds? The *Trichostema dichotomum* is quite beautiful now in the cool of the morning. The epilobium in the woods still. Now the earliest apples begin to be ripe, but none are so good to eat as some to smell. Some knurly apple which I pick up in the road reminds me by its fragrance of all the wealth of Pomona.[2]

Aug. 12. Tuesday. 1.30 A. M. — Full moon. Arose and went to the river and bathed, stepping very carefully not to disturb the household, and still carefully in the street not to disturb the neighbors. I did not walk naturally and freely till I had got over the wall. Then to Hubbard's Bridge at 2 A. M. There was a whip-poor-will in the road just beyond Goodwin's, which flew up and lighted on the fence and kept alighting on the fence within a rod of me and circling round me with a slight squeak as if inquisitive about me. I do not remember what I observed or thought in coming hither.

The traveller's whole employment is to calculate what cloud will obscure the moon and what she will triumph over. In the after-midnight hours the traveller's sole companion is the moon. All his thoughts are centred in her. She is waging continual war with the clouds

[1] [See *Walden*, p. 224; Riv. 316.]
[2] [*Excursions*, p. 295; Riv. 362.]

squadrons of the clouds unscathed and there are no more any obstructions in her path, and the cricket also seems to express joy in his song. It does not concern men who are asleep in their beds, but it is very important to the traveller, whether the moon shines bright and unobstructed or is obscured by clouds. It is not easy to realize the serene joy of all the earth when the moon commences to shine unobstructedly, unless you have often been a traveller by night.[1]

The traveller also resents it if the wind rises and rustles the leaves or ripples the water and increases the coolness at such an hour.

A solitary horse in his pasture was scared by the sudden sight of me, an apparition to him, standing still in the moonlight, and moved about, inspecting with alarm, but I spoke and he heard the sound of my voice; he was at once reassured and expressed his pleasure by wagging his stump of a tail, though still half a dozen rods off. How wholesome the taste of huckleberries, when now by moonlight I feel for them amid the bushes!

And now the first signs of morning attract the traveller's attention, and he cannot help rejoicing, and the moon begins gradually to fade from his recollection. The wind rises and rustles the copses. The sand is cool on the surface but warm two or three inches beneath, and the rocks are quite warm to the hand, so that he sits on them or leans against them for warmth, though indeed it is not cold elsewhere.[2] As I walk along the side of Fair Haven Hill, I see a ripple on the river, and

[1] [*Excursions*, pp. 329, 330; Riv. 405, 406.]
[2] [See *Excursions*, p. 328; Riv. 403.]

now the moon has gone behind a large and black mass of clouds, and I realize that I may not see her again in her glory this night, that perchance ere she rises from this obscurity, the sun will have risen, and she will appear but as a cloud herself, and sink unnoticed into the west (being a little after full (a day?)). As yet no sounds of awakening men; only the more frequent crowing of cocks, still standing on their perches in the barns. The milkmen are the earliest risers, — though I see no lanthorns carried to their barns in the distance, — preparing to carry the milk of cows in their tin cans for men's breakfasts, even for those who dwell in distant cities. In the twilight now, by the light of the stars alone, the moon being concealed, they are pressing the bounteous streams from full udders into their milk-pails, and the sound of the streaming milk is all that breaks the sacred stillness of the dawn; distributing their milk to such as have no cows. I perceive no mosquitoes now. Are they vespertinal, like the singing of the whip-poor-will? I see the light of the obscured moon reflected from the river brightly. With what mild emphasis Nature marks the spot! — so bright and serene a sheen that does not more contrast with the night.

4 A. M. — It adds a charm, a dignity, a glory, to the earth to see the light of the moon reflected from her streams. There are but us three, the moon, the earth which wears this jewel (the moon's reflection) in her crown, and myself. Now there has come round the Cliff (on which I sit), which faces the west, all unobserved and mingled with the dusky sky of night, a lighter and more ethereal living blue, whispering of the sun

still far, far away, behind the horizon. From the summit of our atmosphere, perchance, he may already be seen by soaring spirits that inhabit those thin upper regions, and they communicate the glorious intelligence to us lower ones. The real *divine*, the heavenly, blue, the Jove-containing air, it is, I see through this dusky lower stratum. The sun gilding the summits of the air. The broad artery of light flows over all the sky. Yet not without sadness and compassion I reflect that I shall not see the moon again in her glory. (Not far from four, still in the night, I heard a nighthawk squeak and *boom*, high in the air, as I sat on the Cliff. What is said about this being less of a night bird than the whippoor-will is perhaps to be questioned. For neither do I remember to have heard the whip-poor-will *sing* at 12 o'clock, though I met one sitting and flying between two and three this morning. I believe that both may be heard at midnight, though very rarely.) Now at *very earliest* dawn the nighthawk booms and the whip-poorwill sings. Returning down the hill by the path to where the woods [are] cut off, I see the signs of the day, the morning red. There is the lurid morning star, soon to be blotted out by a cloud.

There is an early redness in the east which I was not prepared for, changing to amber or saffron, with clouds beneath in the horizon and also above this clear streak.

The birds utter a few languid and yawning notes, as if they had not left their perches, so sensible to light to wake so soon, — a faint peeping sound from I know not what kind, a slight, innocent, half-awake sound, like the sounds which a quiet housewife makes in the

earliest dawn. Nature preserves her innocence like a beautiful child. I hear a wood thrush even now, long before sunrise, as in the heat of the day. And the pewee and the catbird and the vireo, red-eyed? I do not hear — or do not mind, perchance — the crickets now. Now whip-poor-wills commence to sing in earnest, considerably *after* the wood thrush. The wood thrush, that beautiful singer, inviting the day once more to enter his pine woods. (So you may hear the wood thrush and whip-poor-will at the same time.) Now go by two whip-poor-wills, in haste seeking some coverts from the eye of day. And the bats are flying about on the edge of the wood, improving the last moments of their day in catching insects. The moon appears at length, not yet as a cloud, but with a frozen light, ominous of her fate. The early cars sound like a wind in the woods. The chewinks make a business now of waking each other up with their low *yorrick* in the neighboring low copse. The sun would have shown before but for the cloud. Now, on his rising, not the clear sky, but the cheeks of the clouds high and wide, are tinged with red, which, like the sky before, turns gradually to saffron and then to the white light of day.

The nettle-leaved vervain (*Verbena urticifolia*) by roadside at Emerson's. What we have called hemp answers best to *Urtica dioica*, large stinging nettle? Now the great sunflower's golden disk is seen.

The days for some time have been sensibly shorter; there is time for music in the evening.

I see polygonums in blossom by roadside, white and red.

A eupatorium from Hubbard's Bridge causeway answers to *E. purpureum*, except in these doubtful points, that the former has four leaves in a whorl, is unequally serrate, the stem is *nearly* filled with a thin pith, the corymb is not merely terminal, florets eight and nine. Differs from *verticillatum* in the stem being not solid, and I perceive no difference between calyx and corolla in color, if I know what the two are. It may be one of the intermediate varieties referred to.

Aug. 15. Friday. *Hypericum Canadense*, Canadian St. John's-wort, distinguished by its red capsules. The petals shine under the microscope, as if they had a golden dew on them.

Cnicus pumilus, pasture thistle. How many insects a single one attracts! While you sit by it, bee after bee will visit it, and busy himself probing for honey and loading himself with pollen, regardless of your overshadowing presence. He sees its purple flower from afar, and that use there is in its color.

Oxalis stricta, upright wood-sorrel, the little yellow ternate-leaved flower in pastures and corn-fields.

Sagittaria sagittifolia, or arrowhead. It has very little root that I can find to eat.

Campanula crinoides, var. 2nd, slender bellflower, vine-like like a galium, by brook-side in Depot Field.

Impatiens, noli-me-tangere, or touch-me-not, with its dangling yellow pitchers or horns of plenty, which I have seen for a month by damp causeway thickets, but the whole plant was so tender and drooped so soon I could not get it home.

May I love and revere myself above all the gods that men have ever invented. May I never let the vestal fire go out in my recesses.

Aug. 16. *Agrimonia Eupatoria*, small-flowered (yellow) plant with hispid fruit, two or three feet high, Turnpike, at Tuttle's peat meadow. Hemp (*Cannabis sativa*), said by Gray to have been introduced; not named by Bigelow. Is it not a native?

It is true man can and does live by preying on other animals, but this is a miserable way of sustaining himself, and he will be regarded as a benefactor of his race, along with Prometheus and Christ, who shall teach men to live on a more innocent and wholesome diet. Is it not already acknowledged to be a reproach that man is a carnivorous animal? [1]

Aug. 17. For a day or two it has been quite cool, a coolness that was felt even when sitting by an open window in a thin coat on the west side of the house in the morning, and you naturally sought the sun at that hour. The coolness concentrated your thought, however. As I could not command a sunny window, I went abroad on the morning of the 15th and lay in the sun in the fields in my thin coat, though it was rather cool even there. I feel as if this coolness would do me good. If it only makes my life more pensive! Why should pensiveness be akin to sadness? There is a certain fertile sadness which I would not avoid, but rather earnestly seek. It is positively joyful to me. It saves my life from

[1] [*Walden*, p. 238 ; Riv. 336.]

now I have occasion to be grateful for the flood of life that is flowing over me. I am not so poor: I can smell the ripening apples; the very rills are deep; the autumnal flowers, the *Trichostema dichotomum*, — not only its bright blue flower above the sand, but its strong wormwood scent which belongs to the season, — feed my spirit, endear the earth to me, make me value myself and rejoice; the quivering of pigeons' wings reminds me of the tough fibre of the air which they rend. I thank you, God. I do not deserve anything, I am unworthy of the least regard; and yet I am made to rejoice. I am impure and worthless, and yet the world is gilded for my delight and holidays are prepared for me, and my path is strewn with flowers. But I cannot thank the Giver; I cannot even whisper my thanks to those human friends I have. It seems to me that I am more rewarded for my expectations than for anything I do or can do. Ah, I would not tread on a cricket in whose song is such a revelation, so soothing and cheering to my ear! Oh, keep my senses pure! And why should I speak to my friends? for how rarely is it that I am I; and are they, then, they? We will meet, then, far away. The seeds of the summer are getting dry and falling from a thousand nodding heads. If I did not know you through thick and thin, how should I know you at all? Ah, the very brooks seem fuller of reflections than they were! Ah, such provoking sibylline sentences they are! The shallowest is all at once unfathomable. How can that depth be fathomed where a man may see himself reflected? The rill I stopped to drink at I drink in more than I expected. I satisfy and still provoke the thirst

being trivial. My life flows with a deeper current, no longer as a shallow and brawling stream, parched and shrunken by the summer heats. This coolness comes to condense the dews and clear the atmosphere. The stillness seems more deep and significant. Each sound seems to come from out a greater thoughtfulness in nature, as if nature had acquired some character and mind. The cricket, the gurgling stream, the rushing wind amid the trees, all speak to me soberly yet encouragingly of the steady onward progress of the universe. My heart leaps into my mouth at the sound of the wind in the woods. I, whose life was but yesterday so desultory and shallow, suddenly recover my spirits, my spirituality, through my hearing. I see a goldfinch go twittering through the still, louring day, and am reminded of the peeping flocks which will soon herald the thoughtful season. Ah! if I could so live that there should be no desultory moment in all my life! that in the trivial season, when small fruits are ripe, my fruits might be ripe also! that I could match nature always with my moods! that in each season when some part of nature especially flourishes, then a corresponding part of me may not fail to flourish! Ah, I would walk, I would sit and sleep, with natural piety! What if I could pray aloud or to myself as I went along by the brooksides a cheerful prayer like the birds! For joy I could embrace the earth; I shall delight to be buried in it. And then to think of those I love among men, who will know that I love them though I tell them not! I sometimes feel as if I were rewarded merely for expecting better hours. I did not despair of worthier moods, and

of thirsts. Nut Meadow Brook where it crosses the road beyond Jenny Dugan's that was. I do not drink in vain. I mark that brook as if I had swallowed a water snake that would live in my stomach. I have swallowed something worth the while. The day is not what it was before I stooped to drink. Ah, I shall hear from that draught! It is not in vain that I have drunk. I have drunk an arrowhead. It flows from where all fountains rise.

How many ova have I swallowed? Who knows what will be hatched within me? There were some seeds of thought, methinks, floating in that water, which are expanding in me. The man must not drink of the running streams, the living waters, who is not prepared to have all nature reborn in him, — to suckle monsters. The snake in my stomach lifts his head to my mouth at the sound of running water. When was it that I swallowed a snake? I have got rid of the snake in my stomach. I drank of stagnant waters once. That accounts for it. I caught him by the throat and drew him out, and had a well day after all. Is there not such a thing as getting rid of the snake which you have swallowed when young, when thoughtless you stooped and drank at stagnant waters, which has worried you in your waking hours and in your sleep ever since, and appropriated the life that was yours? Will he not ascend into your mouth at the sound of running water? Then catch him boldly by the head and draw him out, though you may think his tail be curled about your vitals.

The farmers are just finishing their meadow-haying. (To-day is Sunday.) Those who have early potatoes may be digging them, or doing any other job which the haying has obliged them to postpone. For six weeks or more this has been the farmer's work, to shave the surface of the fields and meadows clean. This is done all over the country. The razor is passed over these parts of nature's face the country over. A thirteenth labor which methinks would have broken the back of Hercules, would have given him a memorable sweat, accomplished with what sweating of scythes and early and late! I chance [to] know one young man who has lost his life in this season's campaign, by overdoing. In haying time some men take double wages, and they are engaged long before in the spring. To shave all the fields and meadows of New England clean! If men did this but once, and not every year, we should never hear the last of that labor; it would be more famous in each farmer's case than Buonaparte's road over the Simplon. It has no other bulletin but the truthful "Farmer's Almanac." Ask them where scythe-snaths are made and sold, and rifles too, if it is not a real labor. In its very weapons and its passes it has the semblance of war. Mexico was won with less exertion and less true valor than are required to do one season's haying in New England. The former work was done by those who played truant and ran away from the latter. Those Mexicans were mown down more easily than the summer's crop of grass in many a farmer's fields. Is there not some work in New England men? This haying is no work for marines, nor for deserters; nor for United States troops, so called, nor for West Point cadets. It would wilt them, and they would desert. Have they not deserted? and run off to

West Point? Every field is a battle-field to the mower, — a pitched battle too, — and whole winrows of dead have covered it in the course of the season. Early and late the farmer has gone forth with his formidable scythe, weapon of time, Time's weapon, and fought the ground inch by inch. It is the summer's enterprise. And if we were a more poetic people, horns would be blown to celebrate its completion. There might be a Haymakers' Day. New England's peaceful battles. At Bunker Hill there were some who stood at the railfence and behind the winrows of new-mown hay.[1] They have not yet quitted the field. They stand there still; they alone have not retreated.

The *Polygala sanguinea*, caducous polygala, in damp ground, with red or purple heads. The dandelion still blossoms, and the lupine still, belated.

I have been to Tarbell's Swamp by the Second Division this afternoon, and to the Marlborough road.

It has promised rain all day; cloudy and still and rather cool; from time to time a few drops gently spitting, but no shower. The landscape wears a sober autumnal look. I hear a drop or two on my hat. I wear a thick coat. The birds seem to know that it will not rain just yet. The swallows skim low over the pastures, twittering as they fly near me with forked tail, dashing near me as if I scared up insects for them. I see where a squirrel has been eating hazelnuts on a stump.

Tarbell's Swamp is mainly composed of low and even but dense beds of *Andromeda calyculata*, or dwarf andromeda, which bears the early flower in the spring.

[1] Stark and his companions met the enemy in the hay-field.

Vol. II

Here and there, mingled with it, is the water (?) andromeda; also pitch pines, birches, hardhack, and the common alder (*Alnus serrulata*), and, in separate and lower beds, the cranberry; and probably the *Rhodora Canadensis* might be found.

The lead-colored berries of the *Viburnum dentatum* now. Cow-wheat and indigo-weed still in bloom by the dry wood-path-side, and Norway cinquefoil. I detected a wild apple on the Marlborough road by its fragrance, in the thick woods; small stems, four inches in diameter, falling over or leaning like rays on every side; a clean white fruit, the ripest yellowish, a pleasant acid. The fruit covered the ground. It is unusual to meet with an early apple thus wild in the thickest woods. It seemed admirable to me. One of the noblest of fruits. With green specks under the skin.

Prenanthes alba, white-flowering prenanthes, with its strange halbert and variously shaped leaves; neottia; and hypericum.

I hear the rain (11 P. M.) distilling upon the ground, wetting the grass and leaves. The melons needed it. Their leaves were curled and their fruit stinted.

I am less somnolent for the cool season. I wake to a perennial day.

The hayer's work is done, but I hear no boasting, no firing of guns nor ringing of bells. He celebrates it by going about the work he had postponed "till after haying"! If all this steadiness and valor were spent upon some still worthier enterprise!!

All men's employments, all trades and professions, in some of their aspects are attractive. Hence the boy I

knew, having sucked cider at a minister's cider-mill, resolved to be a minister and make cider, not thinking, boy as he was, how little fun there was in being a minister, willing to purchase that pleasure at any price. When I saw the carpenters the other day repairing Hubbard's Bridge, their bench on the new planking they had laid over the water in the sun and air, with no railing yet to obstruct the view, I was almost ready to resolve that I would be a carpenter and work on bridges, to secure a pleasant place to work. One of the men had a fish-line cast round a sleeper, which he looked at from time to time.

John Potter told me that those root fences on the Corner road were at least sixty or seventy years old.[1] I see a solitary goldfinch now and then.

Hieracium Marianum or *scabrum*; *H. Kalmii* or *Canadense*; Marlborough road. *Leontodon autumnale* passim.

Aug. 18. It plainly makes men sad to think. Hence *pensiveness* is akin to sadness.

Some dogs, I have noticed, have a propensity to worry cows. They go off by themselves to distant pastures, and ever and anon, like four-legged devils, they worry the cows, — literally full of the devil. They are so full of the devil they know not what to do. I come to interfere between the cows and their tormentors. Ah, I grieve to see the devils escape so easily by their swift

[1] Some were drawn out of the swamp behind Abiel Wheeler's. Old lady Potter tells me she cannot remember when they were not there.

limbs, imps of mischief! They are the dog state of those boys who pull down hand-bills in the streets. Their next migration perchance will be into such dogs as these, ignoble fate! The dog, whose office it should be to guard the herd, turned its tormentor. Some courageous cow endeavoring in vain to toss the nimble devil.

Those soldiers in the Champ de Mars [1] at Montreal convinced me that I had arrived in a foreign country under a different government, where many are under the control of one. Such perfect drill could never be in a republic. Yet it had the effect on us as when the keeper shows his animals' claws. It was the English leopard showing his claws. The royal something or other.[2] I have no doubt that soldiers well drilled, as a class, are peculiarly destitute of originality and independence. The men were dressed above their condition; had the bearing of gentlemen without a corresponding intellectual culture.[3]

The Irish was a familiar element, but the Scotch a novel one. The St. Andrew's Church was prominent, and sometimes I was reminded of Edinburgh, — indeed, much more than of London.

Warburton remarked, soon after landing at Quebec, that everything was cheap in that country but men. My thought, when observing how the wooden pavements were sawed by hand in the streets, instead of by machinery, because labor was cheap, how cheap men are here![4]

[1] [See *Excursions*, pp. 16, 17; Riv. 20.]
[2] [*Excursions*, p. 79; Riv. 98.]
[3] [*Excursions*, p. 27; Riv. 32, 33.]
[4] [*Excursions*, pp. 29, 30; Riv. 36.]

Vol. II

It is evident that a private man is not worth so much in Canada as in the United States, and if that is the bulk of a man's property, *i. e.* the being private and peculiar, he had better stay here. An Englishman, methinks, not to speak of other nations, habitually regards himself merely as a constituent part of the English nation; he holds a recognized place as such; he is a member of the royal regiment of Englishmen. And he is proud of his nation. But an American cares very little about such, and greater freedom and independence are possible to him. He is nearer to the primitive condition of man. Government lets him alone, and he lets government alone.[1]

I often thought of the Tories and refugees who settled in Canada at [the time of] the Revolution. These English were to a considerable extent their descendants.

Quebec began to be fortified in a more regular manner in 1690.

The most modern fortifications have an air of antiquity about them; they have the aspect of ruins in better or worse repair, — ruins kept in repair from the day they were built, though they were completed yesterday, — because they are not in a true sense the work of this age. I couple them with the dismantled Spanish forts to be found in so many parts of the world. They carry me back to the Middle Ages, and the siege of Jerusalem, and St. Jean d'Acre, and the days of the Bucaniers. Such works are not consistent with the development of the intellect. Huge stone structures of all kinds, both by their creation and their influence,

[1] [*Excursions*, pp. 82, 83; Riv. 102.]

rather oppress the intellect than set it free. A little thought will dismantle them as fast as they are built. They are a bungling contrivance. It is an institution as rotten as the church. The sentinel with his musket beside a man with his umbrella is spectral. There is not sufficient reason for his existence. My friend there, with a bullet resting on half an ounce of powder, does he think that he needs that argument in conversing with me? Of what use this fortification, to look at it from the soldier's point of view? General Wolfe sailed by it with impunity, and took the town of Quebec without experiencing any hindrance from its fortifications. How often do we have to read that the enemy occupied a position which commanded the old, and so the fort was evacuated![1]

How impossible it is to give that soldier a good education, without first making him virtually a deserter.[2]

It is as if I were to come to a country village surrounded with palisadoes in the old Indian style, — interesting as a relic of antiquity and barbarism. A fortified town is a man cased in the heavy armor of antiquity, and a horse-load of broadswords and small-arms slung to him, endeavoring to go about his business.

The idea seemed to be that some time the inhabitants of Canada might wish to govern themselves, and this was to hinder. But the inhabitants of California succeed well without any such establishment.[3] There would be the same sense in a man's wearing a breastplate all his days for fear somebody should fire a bullet

[1] [*Excursions*, pp. 77–79; Riv. 95–98.]
[2] [*Excursions*, p. 27; Riv. 33.]   [3] [*Excursions*, p. 78; Riv. 97.]

at his vitals. The English in Canada seem to be everywhere prepared and preparing for war. In the United States they are prepared for anything; they may even be the aggressors. This is a ruin kept in a remarkably good repair. There are some eight hundred or a thousand men there to exhibit it. One regiment goes barelegged to increase the attraction. If you wish to study the muscles of the leg about the knee, repair to Quebec.[1]

Aug. 19. *Clematis Virginiana;* calamint; *Lycopus Europeus*, water horehound.

This is a world where there are flowers. Now, at 5 A. M., the fog, which in the west looks like a wreath of hard-rolled cotton-batting, is rapidly dispersing. The echo of the railroad whistle is heard the horizon round; the gravel train is starting out. The farmers are cradling oats in some places. For some days past I have noticed a *red* maple or two about the pond, though we have had no frost. The grass is very wet with dew this morning.

The way in which men cling to old institutions after the life has departed out of them, and out of themselves, reminds me of those monkeys which cling by their tails, — aye, whose tails contract about the limbs, even the dead limbs, of the forest, and they hang suspended beyond the hunter's reach long after they are dead. It is of no use to argue with such men. They have not an apprehensive intellect, but merely, as it were, a prehensile tail. Their intellect possesses merely the quality of a prehensile tail. The tail itself contracts around the dead

[1] [*Excursions*, p. 79; Riv. 98.]

limb even after they themselves are dead, and not till sensible corruption takes place do they fall. The black howling monkey, or caraya. According to Azara, it is extremely difficult to get at them, for "when mortally wounded they coil the tail round a branch, and hang by it with the head downwards for days after death, and until, in fact, decomposition begins to take effect." The commenting naturalist says, "A singular peculiarity of this organ is to contract at its extremity of its own accord as soon as it is extended to its full length." I relinquish argument, I wait for decomposition to take place, for the subject is dead; as I value the hide for the museum. They say, "Though you've got my soul, you sha'n't have my carcass."

P. M. — To Marlborough Road *via* Clamshell Hill, Jenny Dugan's, Round Pond, Canoe Birch Road (Deacon Dakin's), and White Pond.

How many things concur to keep a man at home, to prevent his yielding to his inclination to wander! If I would extend my walk a hundred miles, I must carry a tent on my back for shelter at night or in the rain, or at least I must carry a thick coat to be prepared for a change in the weather. So that it requires some resolution, as well as energy and foresight, to undertake the simplest journey. Man does not travel as easily as the birds migrate. He is not everywhere at home, like flies. When I think how many things I can conveniently carry, I am wont to think it most convenient to stay at home. My home, then, to a certain extent is the place where I keep my thick coat and my tent and some books which

I cannot carry; where, next, I can depend upon meeting some friends; and where, finally, I, even I, have established myself in business. But this last in my case is the least important qualification of a home.

The poet must be continually watching the moods of his mind, as the astronomer watches the aspects of the heavens. What might we not expect from a long life faithfully spent in this wise? The humblest observer would see some stars shoot. A faithful description as by a disinterested person of the thoughts which visited a certain mind in threescore years and ten, as when one reports the number and character of the vehicles which pass a particular point. As travellers go round the world and report natural objects and phenomena, so faithfully let another stay at home and report the phenomena of his own life, — catalogue stars, those thoughts whose orbits are as rarely calculated as comets. It matters not whether they visit my mind or yours, — whether the meteor falls in my field or in yours, — only that it come from heaven. (I am not concerned to express that kind of truth which Nature has expressed. Who knows but I may suggest some things to her? Time was when she was indebted to such suggestions from another quarter, as her present advancement shows. I deal with the truths that recommend themselves to me, — please me, — not those merely which any system has voted to accept.) A meteorological journal of the mind. You shall observe what occurs in your latitude, I in mine.

Some institutions — most institutions, indeed — have had a divine origin. But of most that we see pre-

vailing in society nothing but the form, the shell, is left; the life is extinct, and there is nothing divine in them. Then the reformer arises inspired to reinstitute life, and whatever he does or causes to be done is a reëstablishment of that same or a similar divineness. But some, who never knew the significance of these instincts, are, by a sort of false instinct, found clinging to the shells. Those who have no knowledge of the divine appoint themselves defenders of the divine, as champions of the church, etc. I have been astonished to observe how long some audiences can endure to hear a man speak on a subject which he knows nothing about, as religion for instance, when one who has no ear for music might with the same propriety take up the time of a musical assembly with putting through his opinions on music. This young man who is the main pillar of some divine institution, — does he know what he has undertaken? If the saints were to come again on earth, would they be likely to stay at his house? would they meet with his approbation even? *Ne sutor ultra crepidam.* They who merely have a talent for affairs are forward to express their opinions. A Roman soldier sits there to decide upon the righteousness of Christ. The world does not long endure such blunders, though they are made every day. The weak-brained and pusillanimous farmers would fain abide by the institutions of their fathers. Their argument is they have not long to live, and for that little space let them not be disturbed in their slumbers; blessed are the peacemakers; let this cup pass from me, etc.

How vain it is to sit down to write when you have not stood up to live! Methinks that the moment my legs

begin to move, my thoughts begin to flow, as if I had given vent to the stream at the lower end and consequently new fountains flowed into it at the upper. A thousand rills which have their rise in the sources of thought burst forth and fertilize my brain. You need to increase the draught below, as the owners of meadows on Concord River say of the Billerica Dam. Only while we are in action is the circulation perfect. The writing which consists with habitual sitting is mechanical, wooden, dull to read.

The grass in the high pastures is almost as dry as hay. The seasons do not cease a moment to revolve, and therefore Nature rests no longer at her culminating point than at any other. If you are not out at the right instant, the summer may go by and you not see it. How much of the year is spring and fall! how little can be called summer! The grass is no sooner grown than it begins to wither. How much Nature herself suffers from drought! It seems quite as much as she can do to produce these crops.

The most inattentive walker can see how the science of geology took its rise. The inland hills and promontories betray the action of water on their rounded sides as plainly as if the work were completed yesterday. He sees it with but half an eye as he walks, and forgets his thought again. Also the level plains and more recent meadows and marine shells found on the tops of hills. The geologist painfully and elaborately follows out these suggestions, and hence his fine-spun theories.

The goldfinch, though solitary, is now one of the commonest birds in the air

What if a man were earnestly and wisely to set about recollecting and preserving the thoughts which he has had! How many perchance are now irrecoverable! Calling in his neighbors to aid him.

I do not like to hear the name of particular States given to birds and flowers which are found in all equally, — as Maryland yellow-throat, etc., etc. The *Canadenses* and *Virginicas* may be suffered to pass for the most part, for there is historical as well as natural reason at least for them. Canada is the peculiar country of some and the northern limit of many more plants. And Virginia, which was originally the name for all the Atlantic shore, has some right to stand for the South.

The fruit of the sweet-gale by Nut Meadow Brook is of a yellowish green now and has not yet its greasy feel.

The little red-streaked and dotted excrescences on the shrub oaks I find as yet no name for.

Now for the pretty red capsules or pods of the *Hypericum Canadense*.

White goldenrod is budded along the Marlborough road.

Chickadees and jays never fail. The cricket's is a note which does not attract you to itself. It is not easy to find one.

I fear that the character of my knowledge is from year to year becoming more distinct and scientific; that, in exchange for views as wide as heaven's cope, I am being narrowed down to the field of the microscope. I see details, not wholes nor the shadow of the whole. I count some parts, and say, "I know." The cricket's chirp now fills the air in dry fields near pine woods.

Vol. II

Lespedeza capitata, shrubby lespedeza, White Pond road and Marlborough road.

L. polystachya, hairy lespedeza, Corner road beyond Hubbard's Bridge.

Aug. 20. 2 P. M. — To Lee's Bridge *via* Hubbard's Wood, Potter's field, Conantum, returning by Abel Minott's house, Clematis Brook, Baker's pine plain, and railroad.

I hear a cricket in the Depot Field, walk a rod or two, and find the note proceeds from near a rock. Partly under a rock, between it and the roots of the grass, he lies concealed, — for I pull away the withered grass with my hands, — uttering his night-like creak, with a vibratory motion of his wings, and flattering himself that it is night, because he has shut out the day. He was a black fellow nearly an inch long, with two long, slender feelers. They plainly avoid the light and hide their heads in the grass. At any rate they regard this as the evening of the year. They are remarkably secret and unobserved, considering how much noise they make. Every milkman has heard them all his life; it is the sound that fills his ears as he drives along. But what one has ever got off his cart to go in search of one? I see smaller ones moving stealthily about, whose note I do not know. Who ever distinguished their various notes, which fill the crevices in each other's song? It would be a curious ear, indeed, that distinguished the species of the crickets which it heard, and traced even the earth-song home, each part to its particular performer. I am afraid to be so knowing. They are shy as birds, these little bodies. Those nearest

Gathered our first watermelon to-day. By the Marlborough road I notice the richly veined leaves of the *Neottia pubescens*, or veined neottia, rattlesnake-plantain. I like this last name very well, though it might not be easy to convince a quibbler or proser of its fitness. We want some name to express the mystic wildness of its rich leaves. Such work as men imitate in their embroidery, unaccountably agreeable to the eye, as if it answered its end only when it met the eye of man; a reticulated leaf, visible only on one side; little things which make one pause in the woods, take captive the eye.

Here is a bees' or wasps' nest in the sandy, mouldering bank by the roadside, four inches in diameter, as if made of scales of striped brown paper. It is singular if indeed man first made paper and then discovered its resemblance to the work of the wasps, and did not derive the hint from them.

Canoe birches by road to Dakin's. Cuticle stripped off; inner bark dead and scaling off; new (inner) bark formed.

The Solomon's-seals are fruited now, with finely red-dotted berries.

There was one original name well given, *Buster* Kendal.[1] The fragrance of the clethra fills the air by watersides. In the hollows where in winter is a pond, the grass is short, thick, and green still, and here and there are tufts pulled up as if by the mouth of cows.

Small rough sunflower by side of road between canoe birch and White Pond, — *Helianthus divaricatus*.

[1] [See *Excursions*, p. 290; also *Journal*, vol. iii, p. 117.]

me continually cease their song as I walk, so that the singers are always a rod distant, and I cannot easily detect one. It is difficult, moreover, to judge correctly whence the sound proceeds. Perhaps this wariness is necessary to save them from insectivorous birds, which would otherwise speedily find out so loud a singer. They are somewhat protected by the universalness of the sound, each one's song being merged and lost in the general concert, as if it were the creaking of earth's axle. They are very numerous in oats and other grain, which conceals them and yet affords a clear passage. I never knew any drought or sickness so to prevail as to quench the song of the crickets; it fails not in its season, night or day.

The *Lobelia inflata*, Indian-tobacco, meets me at every turn. At first I suspect some new bluish flower in the grass, but stooping see the inflated pods. Tasting one such herb convinces me that there are such things as drugs which may either kill or cure.[1]

The *Rhexia Virginica* is a showy flower at present.

How copious and precise the botanical language to describe the leaves, as well as the other parts of a plant! Botany is worth studying if only for the precision of its terms, — to learn the value of words and of system. It is wonderful how much pains has been taken to describe a flower's leaf, compared for instance with the care that is taken in describing a psychological fact. Suppose as much ingenuity (perhaps it would be needless) in making a language to express the sentiments! We are armed

[1] A farmer tells me that he knows when his horse has eaten it, because it makes him slobber badly.

with language adequate to describe each leaf in the field, or at least to distinguish it from each other, but not to describe a human character. With equally wonderful indistinctness and confusion we describe men. The precision and copiousness of botanical language applied to the description of moral qualities!

The neottia, or ladies'-tresses, behind Garfield's house. The golden robin is now a rare bird to see. Here are the small, lively-tasting blackberries, so small they are not commonly eaten. The grasshoppers seem no drier than the grass. In Lee's field are two kinds of plantain. Is the common one found there?

The willow reach by Lee's Bridge has been stripped for powder. None escapes. This morning, hearing a cart, I looked out and saw George Dugan going by with a horse-load of his willow toward Acton powder-mills, which I had seen in piles by the turnpike. Every traveller has just as particular an errand which I might likewise chance to be privy to.

Now that I am at the extremity of my walk, I see a threatening cloud blowing up from the south, which however, methinks, will not compel me to make haste.

Apios tuberosa, or *Glycine Apios*, ground-nut. The prenanthes now takes the place of the lactucas, which are gone to seed.

In the dry ditch, near Abel Minott's house that was, I see cardinal-flowers, with their red artillery, reminding me of soldiers, — red men, war, and bloodshed. Some are four and a half feet high. Thy sins shall be as scarlet. Is it my sins that I see? It shows how far a little color can go; for the flower is not large, yet it makes

itself seen from afar, and so answers the purpose for which it was colored completely. It is remarkable for its intensely brilliant scarlet color. You are slow to concede to it a high rank among flowers, but ever and anon, as you turn your eyes away, it dazzles you and you pluck it. *Scutellaria lateriflora*, side-flowering skullcap, here. This brook deserves to be called Clematis Brook (though that name is too often applied), for the clematis is very abundant, running over the alders and other bushes on its brink. Where the brook issues from the pond, the nightshade grows profusely, spreading five or six feet each way, with its red berries now ripe. It grows, too, at the upper end of the pond. But if it is the button-bush that grows in the now low water, it should rather be called the Button-Bush Pond. Now the tall rush is in its prime on the shore here, and the clematis abounds by this pond also.

I came out by the leafy-columned elm under Mt. Misery, where the trees stood up one above another, higher and higher, immeasurably far to my imagination, as on the side of a New Hampshire mountain.

On the pitch pine plain, at first the pines are far apart, with a wiry grass between, and goldenrod and hardhack and St. John's-wort and blackberry vines, each tree merely keeping down the grass for a space about itself, meditating to make a forest floor; and here and there younger pines are springing up. Further in, you come to moss-covered patches, dry, deep white moss, or almost bare mould, half covered with pine needles. Thus begins the future forest floor.

The sites of the shanties that once stood by the rail-

road in Lincoln when the Irish built it, the still remaining hollow square mounds of earth which formed their embankments, are to me instead of barrows and druidical monuments and other ruins. It is a sufficient antiquity to me since they were built, their material being earth. Now the Canada thistle and the mullein crown their tops. I see the stones which made their simple chimneys still left one upon another at one end, which were surmounted with barrels to eke them out; and clean boiled beef bones and old shoes are strewn about. Otherwise it is a clean ruin, and nothing is left but a mound, as in the graveyard.

Sium lineare, a kind of water-parsnip, whose blossom resembles the *Cicuta maculata*. The flowers of the blue vervain have now nearly reached the summit of their spikes.

A traveller who looks at things with an impartial eye may see what the oldest inhabitant has not observed.

Aug. 21. To a great extent the feudal system still prevails there (in Canada), and I saw that I should be a bad citizen, that any man who thought for himself and was only reasonably independent would naturally be a rebel. You could not read or hear of their laws without seeing that it was a legislating for a few and not for all. That certainly is the best government where the inhabitants are least often reminded of the government. (Where a man cannot be a poet even without danger of being made poet-laureate! Where he cannot be healthily neglected, and grow up a man, and not an Englishman merely!) Where it is the most natural thing

in the world for a government that does not understand you, to let you alone. Oh, what a government were there, my countrymen! It is a government, that English one, — and most other European ones, — that cannot afford to be forgotten, as you would naturally forget them, that cannot let you go alone, having learned to walk. It appears to me that a true Englishman can only speculate within bounds; he has to pay his respects to so many things that before he knows it he has paid all he is worth. The principal respect in which our government is more tolerable is in the fact that there is so much less of government with us. In the States it is only once in a dog's age that a man need remember his government, but here he is reminded of it every day. Government parades itself before you. It is in no sense the servant but the master.[1]

What a faculty must that be which can paint the most barren landscape and humblest life in glorious colors! It is pure and invigorated senses reacting on a sound and strong imagination. Is not that the poet's case? The intellect of most men is barren. They neither fertilize nor are fertilized. It is the marriage of the soul with Nature that makes the intellect fruitful, that gives birth to imagination. When we were dead and dry as the highway, some sense which has been healthily fed will put us in relation with Nature, in sympathy with her; some grains of fertilizing pollen, floating in the air, fall on us, and suddenly the sky is all one rainbow, is full of music and fragrance and flavor. The man of intellect only, the prosaic man, is a barren,

[1] [*Excursions*, p. 83; Riv. 102, 103.]

staminiferous flower; the poet is a fertile and perfect flower. Men are such confirmed arithmeticians and slaves of business that I cannot easily find a blank-book that has not a red line or a blue one for the dollars and cents, or some such purpose.[1]

As is a man's intellectual character, is not such his physical after all? Can you not infer from knowing the intellectual characters of two which is most tenacious of life, which would die the hardest and will live the longest, which is the toughest, which has most brute strength, which the most passive endurance? Methinks I could to some extent infer these things.

1 P. M. — Round Flint's Pond *via* railroad, my old field, Goose Pond, Wharf Rock, Cedar Hill, Smith's, and so back.

Bigelow, speaking of the spikes of the blue vervain (*Verbena hastata*), says, "The flowering commences at their base and is long in reaching their summit." I perceive that only one circle of buds, about half a dozen, blossoms at a time, — and there are about thirty circles in the space of three inches, — while the next circle of buds above at the same time shows the blue. Thus this triumphant blossoming circle travels upward, driving the remaining buds off into space.[2] I think it was the 16th of July when I first noticed them (on another plant), and now they are all within about half an inch of the top of the spikes. Yet the blossoms have got no nearer the top on long [*sic*] spikes, which had many buds, than on short ones only an inch long. Per-

[1] [Channing, pp. 85, 86.]   [2] [Channing, p. 214.]

haps the blossoming commenced enough earlier on the long ones to make up for the difference in length. It is very pleasant to measure the progress of the season by this and similar clocks. So you get, not the absolute time, but the true time of the season.[1] But I can measure the progress of the seasons only by observing a particular plant, for I notice that they are by no means equally advanced.

The prevailing conspicuous flowers at present are: The early goldenrods, tansy, the life-everlastings, fleabane (though not for its flower), yarrow (rather dry), hardhack and meadow-sweet (both getting dry, also mayweed), *Eupatorium purpureum*, scabish, clethra (really a fine, sweet-scented, and this year particularly fair and fresh, flower, some unexpanded buds at top tinged with red), *Rhexia Virginica*, thoroughwort, *Polygala sanguinea*, prunella, and dog's-bane (getting stale), etc., etc. Touch-me-not (less observed), Canada snapdragon by roadside (not conspicuous). The purple gerardia now, horsemint, or *Mentha borealis*, *Veronica scutellata* (marsh speedwell), *Ranunculus acris* (tall crowfoot) still. Mowing to some extent improves the landscape to the eye of the walker. The aftermath, so fresh and green, begins now to recall the spring to my mind. In some fields fresh clover heads appear. This is certainly better than fields of lodged and withered grass. I find ground-nuts by the railroad causeway three quarters of an inch long by a third of an inch. The epilobium still. Cow-wheat (*Melampyrum Americanum*) still flourishes as much if not more than ever, and, shrubby-

[1] [Channing, p. 214.]

looking, helps cover the ground where the wood has recently been cut off, like huckleberry bushes.

There is some advantage, intellectually and spiritually, in taking wide views with the bodily eye and not pursuing an occupation which holds the body prone. There is some advantage, perhaps, in attending to the general features of the landscape over studying the particular plants and animals which inhabit it. A man may walk abroad and no more see the sky than if he walked under a shed. The poet is more in the air than the naturalist, though they may walk side by side. Granted that you are out-of-doors; but what if the outer door *is* open, if the inner door is shut! You must walk sometimes perfectly free, not prying nor inquisitive, not bent upon seeing things. Throw away a whole day for a single expansion, a single inspiration of air.

Any anomaly in vegetation makes Nature seem more real and present in her working, as the various red and yellow excrescences on young oaks. I am affected as if it were a different Nature that produced them. As if a poet were born who had designs in his head.[1]

It is remarkable that animals are often obviously, manifestly, related to the plants which they feed upon or live among, — as caterpillars, butterflies, tree-toads, partridges, chewinks, — and this afternoon I noticed a yellow spider on a goldenrod; as if every condition might have its expression in some form of animated being.[2]

Spear-leaved goldenrod in path to northeast of Flint's Pond. *Hieracium paniculatum*, a very delicate and

[1] [Channing, p. 74.]   [2] [Channing, p. 215.]

slender hawkweed. I have now found all the hawkweeds. Singular these genera of plants, plants manifestly related yet distinct. They suggest a history to nature, a natural *history* in a new sense.[1]

At Wharf Rock found water lobelia in blossom. I saw some smilax vines in the swamp, which were connected with trees ten feet above the ground whereon they grew and four or five feet above the surrounding bushes. This slender vine, which cannot stand erect, how did it establish that connection? Have the trees and shrubs by which it once climbed been cut down? Or perchance do the young and flexible shoots blow up in high winds and fix themselves?[2] On Cedar Hill, south side pond, I still hear the locust, though it has been so much colder for the last week. It is quite hazy in the west, though comparatively clear in other directions. The barberry bushes, with their drooping wreaths of fruit now turning red, bushed up with some other shrub or tree.

Aug. 22. I found last winter that it was expected by my townsmen that I would give some account of Canada because I had *visited* it, and because many of them had, and so felt interested in the subject, — visited it as the bullet visits the wall at which it is fired, and from which it rebounds as quickly, and flattened (somewhat damaged, perchance)! Yes, a certain man contracted to take fifteen hundred live Yankees through Canada, at a certain rate and within a certain time. It did not matter to him what the commodity was, if only it would pack

[1] [Channing, p. 74.]   [2] [Channing, p. 214.]

well and were delivered to him according to agreement at the right place and time and rightly ticketed, so much in bulk, wet or dry, on deck or in the hold, at the option of the carrier how to stow the cargo and not always right side up. In the meanwhile, it was understood that the freight was not to be willfully and intentionally debarred from seeing the country if it had eyes. It was understood that there would be a country to be seen on either side, though that was a secret advantage which the contractors seemed not to be aware of. I fear that I have not got much to say, not having seen much, for the very rapidity of the motion had a tendency to keep my eyelids closed. What I *got* by going to Canada was a cold, and not till I get a fever, which I never had, shall I know how to appreciate it.[1]

It is the fault of some excellent writers — De Quincey's first impressions on seeing London suggest it to me — that they express themselves with too great fullness and detail. They give the most faithful, natural, and lifelike account of their sensations, mental and physical, but they lack moderation and sententiousness. They do not affect us by an ineffectual earnestness and a reserve of meaning, like a stutterer; they say all they mean. Their sentences are not concentrated and nutty. Sentences which suggest far more than they say, which have an atmosphere about them, which do not merely report an old, but make a new, impression; sentences which suggest as many things and are as durable as a Roman aqueduct; to frame these, that is the *art* of writing. Sentences which are expensive, towards which

[1] [*Excursions*, p. 3; Riv. 3.]

so many volumes, so much life, went; which lie like boulders on the page, up and down or across; which contain the seed of other sentences, not mere repetition, but creation; which a man might sell his grounds and castles to build. If De Quincey had suggested each of his pages in a sentence and passed on, it would have been far more excellent writing. His style is nowhere kinked and knotted up into something hard and significant, which you could swallow like a diamond, without digesting.[1]

Aug. 23. Saturday. To Walden to bathe at 5.30 A. M. Traces of the heavy rains in the night. The sand and gravel are beaten hard by them. Three or four showers in succession. But the grass is not so wet as after an ordinary dew. The *Verbena hastata* at the pond has reached the top of its spike, a little in advance of what I noticed yesterday; only one or two flowers are adhering. At the commencement of my walk I saw no traces of fog, but after detected fogs over particular meadows and high up some brooks' valleys, and far in the Deep Cut the wood fog. First muskmelon this morning.

I rarely pass the shanty in the woods, where human beings are lodged, literally, no better than pigs in a sty, — little children, a grown man and his wife, and an aged grandmother living this squalid life, squatting on the ground, — but I wonder if it can be indeed true that little Julia Riordan calls this place home, comes here to rest at night and for her daily food, — in whom

[1] [Channing, pp. 229, 230.]

ladies and gentlemen in the village take an interest. Of what significance are charity and almshouses? That there they live unmolested! in one sense so many degrees below the almshouse! beneath charity! It is admirable, — Nature against almshouses. A certain wealth of nature, not poverty, it suggests. Not to identify health and contentment, aye, and independence, with the possession of this world's goods! It is not wise to waste compassion on them.

As I go through the Deep Cut, I hear one or two early humblebees, come out on the damp sandy bank, whose low hum sounds like distant horns from far in the horizon over the woods. It was long before I detected the bees that made it, so far away and musical it sounded, like the shepherds in some distant eastern vale greeting the king of day.[1]

The farmers now carry — those who have got them — their early potatoes and onions to market, starting away early in the morning or at midnight. I see them returning in the afternoon with the empty barrels.

Perchance the copious rain of last night will trouble those who had not been so provident as to get their hay from the Great Meadows, where it is often lost.

P. M. — Walk to Annursnack and back over stone bridge.

I sometimes reproach myself because I do not find anything attractive in certain mere trivial employments of men, — that I skip men so commonly, and their affairs, — the professions and the trades, — do not

[1] [Channing, p. 77.]

elevate them at least in my thought and get some material for poetry out of them directly. I will not avoid, then, to go by where these men are repairing the stone bridge, — see if I cannot see poetry in that, if that will not yield me a reflection. It is narrow to be confined to woods and fields and grand aspects of nature only. The greatest and wisest will still be related to men. Why not see men standing in the sun and casting a shadow, even as trees? May not some light be reflected from them as from the stems of trees? I will try to enjoy them as animals, at least. They are perhaps better animals than men. Do not neglect to speak of men's low life and affairs with sympathy, though you ever so speak as to suggest a contrast between them and the ideal and divine. You may be excused if you are always pathetic, but do not refuse to recognize.

Resolve to read no book, to take no walk, to undertake no enterprise, but such as you can endure to give an account of to yourself. Live thus deliberately for the most part.

When I stopped to gather some blueberries by the roadside this afternoon, I heard the shrilling of a cricket or a grasshopper close to me, quite clear, almost like a bell, a stridulous sound, a clear ring, incessant, not intermittent, like the song of the black fellow I caught the other day, and not suggesting the night, but belonging to day. It was long before I could find him, though all the while within a foot or two. I did not know whether to search amid the grass and stones or amid the leaves. At last, by accident I saw him, he shrilling all the while under an alder leaf two feet from the ground, — a slender green fellow with long feelers and transparent wings. When he shrilled, his wings, which opened on each other in the form of a heart perpendicularly to his body like the wings of fairies, vibrated swiftly on each other. The apparently wingless female, as I thought, was near.

We experience pleasure when an elevated field or even road in which we may be walking holds its level toward the horizon at a tangent to the earth, is not convex with the earth's surface, but an absolute level.

On or under east side of Annursnack, *Epilobium coloratum*, colored willow-herb, near the spring. Also *Polygonum sagittatum*, scratch-grass.

The Price Farm road, one of those everlasting roads which the sun delights to shine along in an August afternoon, playing truant; which seem to stretch themselves with terrene jest as the weary traveller journeys on; where there are three white sandy furrows (*liræ*), two for the wheels and one between them for the horse, with endless green grass borders between and room on each side for huckleberries and birches; where the walls indulge in freaks, not always parallel to the ruts, and goldenrod yellows all the path; which some elms began to border and shade once, but left off in despair, it was so long; from no point on which can you be said to be at any definite distance from a town.

I associate the beauty of Quebec with the steel-like and flashing air.[1]

Our little river reaches are not to be forgotten. I noticed that seen northward on the Assabet from the

[1] [*Excursions*, p. 88; Riv. 109.]

Causeway Bridge near the second stone bridge. There was [a] man in a boat in the sun, just disappearing in the distance round a bend, lifting high his arms and dipping his paddle as if he were a vision bound to land of the blessed, — far off, as in picture. When I see Concord to purpose, I see it as if it were not real but painted, and what wonder if I do not speak to *thee?* I saw a snake by the roadside and touched him with my foot to see if he were alive. He had a toad in his jaws, which he was preparing to swallow with his jaws distended to three times his width, but he relinquished his prey in haste and fled; and I thought, as the toad jumped leisurely away with his slime-covered hind-quarters glistening in the sun, as if I, his deliverer, wished to interrupt his meditations, — without a shriek or fainting, — I thought what a healthy indifference he manifested. Is not this the broad earth still? he said.[1]

Aug. 24. *Mollugo verticillata*, carpet-weed, flat, whorl-leaved weed in gardens, with small white flowers. *Portulaca oleracea*, purslane, with its yellow blossoms. *Chelone glabra*. I have seen the small mulleins as big as a ninepence in the fields for a day or two.[2]

The weather is warmer again after a week or more of cool days. There is greater average warmth, but not such intolerable heats as in July. The nights especially are more equably warm now, even when the day has been comparatively rather cool. There are few days now, fewer than in July, when you cannot lie at your length on the grass. You have now forgotten winter

[1] [Channing, pp. 287, 288.]
[2] [The word "mulleins" is queried in pencil.]

and its fashions, and have learned new summer fashions. Your life may be out-of-doors now mainly.

Rattlesnake grass is ripe. The pods of the *Asclepias pulchra* stand up pointedly like slender vases on a salver, — an open salver truly! Those of the *Asclepias Syriaca* hang down. The interregnum in the blossoming of flowers being *well* over, many small flowers blossom now in the low grounds, having just reached their summer. It is now dry enough, and they feel the heat their tenderness required. The autumnal flowers, — goldenrods, asters, and johnswort, — though they have made demonstrations, have not yet commenced to reign. The tansy is already getting stale; it is perhaps the first conspicuous yellow flower that passes from the stage.[1]

In Hubbard's Swamp, where the blueberries, dangleberries, and especially the pyrus or choke-berries were so abundant last summer, there is now perhaps not one (unless a blueberry) to be found. Where the chokeberries held on all last winter, the black and the red.

The common skullcap (*Scutellaria galericulata*), quite a handsome and middling-large blue flower. *Lobelia pallida* still. Pointed cleavers or clivers (*Galium asprellum*). Is that the naked viburnum, so common, with its white, red, then purple berries, in Hubbard's meadow?[2]

Did I find the dwarf tree-primrose in Hubbard's meadow to-day? *Stachys aspera*, hedge-nettle or woundwort, a rather handsome purplish flower. The capsules of the *Iris versicolor*, or blue flag, are now ready for humming [?]. Elderberries are ripe.

[1] [Channing, p. 215.]   [2] Yes.

Aug. 25. Monday. What the little regular, rounded, light-blue flower in Heywood Brook which I make Class V, Order 1? Also the small purplish flower growing on the mud in Hubbard's meadow, perchance C. XIV, with one pistil? What the bean vine in the garden, Class VIII, Order 1? I do not find the name of the large white polygonum of the river. Was it the filiform ranunculus which I found on Hubbard's shore? *Hypericum Virginicum*, mixed yellow and purple. The black rough fruit of the skunk-cabbage, though green within, barely rising above the level of the ground; you see where it has been cut in two by the mowers in the meadows. *Polygonum amphibium*, red, in river. *Lysimachia hybrida* still. Checkerberry in bloom. Blue-eyed grass still. *Rhus copallina*, mountain or dwarf sumach. I now know all of the *Rhus* genus in Bigelow. We have all but the staghorn in Concord. What a miserable name has the *Gratiola aurea*, hedge hyssop! Whose hedge does it grow by, pray, in this part of the world?[1]

Aug. 26. A cool and even piercing wind blows to-day, making all shrubs to bow and trees to wave; such as we could not have had in July. I speak not of its coolness but its strength and steadiness. The wind and the coldness increased as the day advanced, and finally the wind went down with the sun. I was compelled to put on an extra coat for my walk. The ground is strewn with windfalls, and much fruit will consequently be lost.

The wind roars amid the pines like the surf. You can hardly hear the crickets for the din, or the cars. I think

[1] [Channing, p. 215.]

the last must be considerably delayed when their course is against it. Indeed it is difficult to enjoy a quiet thought. You sympathize too much with the commotion and restlessness of the elements. Such a blowing, stirring, bustling day, — what does it mean? All light things decamp; straws and loose leaves change their places. Such a blowing day is no doubt indispensable in the economy of nature. The whole country is a sea-shore, and the wind is the surf that breaks on it. It shows the white and silvery under sides of the leaves. Do plants and trees need to be thus tried and twisted? Is it a first intimation to the sap to cease to ascend, to thicken their stems? The *Gerardia pedicularia*, bushy gerardia, I find on the White Pond road.

I perceive that some farmers are cutting turf now. They require the driest season of the year. There is something agreeable to my thoughts in thus burning a part of the earth, the stock of fuel is so inexhaustible. Nature looks not mean and niggardly, but like an ample loaf. Is not he a rich man who owns a peat meadow? It is to enjoy the luxury of wealth. It must be a luxury to sit around the fire in winter days and nights and burn these dry slices of the meadow which contain roots of all herbs. You dry and burn the very earth itself. It is a fact kindred with salt-licks. The meadow is strewn with the fresh bars, bearing the marks of the fork, and the turf-cutter is wheeling them out with his barrow. To sit and see the world aglow and try to imagine how it would seem to have it so destroyed!

Woodchucks are seen tumbling into their holes on all sides.

Aug. 27. I see the volumes of smoke — not quite the blaze — from burning brush, as I suppose, far in the western horizon. I believe it is at this season of the year chiefly that you see this sight. It is always a question with some whether it is not a fire in the woods, or some building. It is an interesting feature in the scenery at this season. The farmer's simple enterprises.

The vervain which I examined by the railroad the other day has still a quarter of an inch to the top of its spikes. Hawkweed groundsel (*Senecio hieracifolius*) (fireweed). *Rubus sempervirens*, evergreen raspberry, the small low blackberry, is now in fruit. The *Medeola Virginica*, cucumber-root, the whorl-leaved plant, is now in green fruit. *Polygala cruciata*, cross-leaved polygala, in the meadow between Trillium Woods and railroad. This is rare and new to me. It has a very sweet, but as it were intermittent, fragrance, as of checkerberry and mayflowers combined. The handsome calyx-leaves.[1]

Aug. 28. The pretty little blue flower in the Heywood Brook, Class V, Order 1. Corolla about one sixth of an inch in diameter, with five rounded segments; stamens and pistil shorter than corolla; calyx with five acute segments and acute sinuses; leaves not opposite, lanceolate, spatulate, blunt, somewhat hairy on upper side with a midrib only, sessile; flowers in a loose raceme on rather long pedicels. Whole plant decumbent, curving upward. Wet ground. Said to be like the forget-me-not.

[1] [Channing, p. 216.]

Raphanus Raphanistrum, or wild radish, in meadows.

I find three or four ordinary laborers to-day putting up the necessary outdoor fixtures for a magnetic telegraph from Boston to Burlington. They carry along a basket full of simple implements, like travelling tinkers, and, with a little rude soldering, and twisting, and straightening of wires, the work is done. It is a work which seems to admit of the greatest latitude of ignorance and bungling, and as if you might set your hired man with the poorest head and hands to building a magnetic telegraph. All great inventions stoop thus low to succeed, for the understanding is but little above the feet. They preserve so low a tone; they are simple almost to coarseness and commonplaceness. Somebody had told them what he wanted, and sent them forth with a coil of wire to make a magnetic telegraph. It seems not so wonderful an invention as a common cart or a plow.

Evening. — A new moon visible in the east [*sic*]. How unexpectedly it always appears! You easily lose it in the sky. The whip-poor-will sings, but not so commonly as in spring. The bats are active.

The poet is a man who lives at last by watching his moods. An old poet comes at last to watch his moods as narrowly as a cat does a mouse.

I omit the unusual — the hurricanes and earthquakes — and describe the common. This has the greatest charm and is the true theme of poetry. You may have the extraordinary for your province, if you will let me have the ordinary. Give me the obscure life, the cot-

tage of the poor and humble, the workdays of the world, the barren fields, the smallest share of all things but poetic perception. Give me but the eyes to see the things which you possess.[1]

Aug. 29. Though it is early, my neighbor's hens have strayed far into the fog toward the river. I find a wasp in my window, which already appears to be taking refuge from winter and unspeakable fate.

Those who first built it, coming from old France, with the memory and tradition of feudal days and customs weighing on them, were unquestionably behind their age, and those who now inhabit it and repair it are behind their ancestors. It is as if the inhabitants of Boston should go down to Fort Independence, or the inhabitants of New York should go over to Castle William, to live. I rubbed my eyes to be sure that I was in the Nineteenth Century. That would be a good place to read Froissart's Chronicles, I thought. It is a specimen of the Old World in the New. It is such a reminiscence of the Middle Ages as one of Scott's novels. Those old chevaliers thought they could transplant the feudal system to America. It has been set out, but it has not thriven.[2]

Might I not walk a little further, till I hear new crickets, till their creak has acquired some novelty, as if they were a new species whose habitat I had reached?[3]

The air is filled with mist, yet a transparent mist, a principle in it you might call *flavor*, which ripens fruits.

[1] [Channing, p. 87.] [2] [*Excursions*, p. 81; Riv. 100, 101.]
[3] [Channing, p. 70.]

Vol. II

This haziness seems to confine and concentrate the sunlight, as if you lived in a halo. It is August.

A flock of forty-four young turkeys with their old [*sic*], half a mile from a house on Conantum by the river, the old faintly gobbling, the half-grown young peeping. Turkey-men!

Gerardia glauca (*quercifolia*, says one), tall gerardia, one flower only left; also *Corydalis glauca*.

Aug. 30. Saturday. I perceive in the Norway cinquefoil (*Potentilla Norvegica*), now nearly out of blossom, that the alternate five leaves of the calyx are closing over the seeds to protect them. This evidence of forethought, this simple *reflection* in a double sense of the term, in this flower, is affecting to me, as if it said to me: "Even I am doing my appointed work in this world faithfully. Not even do I, however obscurely I may grow among the other loftier and more famous plants, shirk my work, humble weed as I am. Not even when I have blossomed, and have lost my painted petals and am preparing to die down to my root, do I forget to fall with my arms around my babe, faithful to the last, that the infant may be found preserved in the arms of the frozen mother." That thus all the Norway cinquefoils in the world had curled back their calyx leaves, their warm cloaks, when now their flowering season was past, over their progeny, from the time they were created! There is one door closed, of the closing year. Nature ordered this bending back of the calyx leaves, and every year since this plant was created her order has been faithfully obeyed, and this plant acts

not an obscure, but essential, part in the revolution of the seasons. I am not ashamed to be contemporary with the Norway cinquefoil. May I perform my part as well! [1] There is so much done toward closing up the year's accounts. It is as good as if I saw the great globe go round. It is as if I saw the Janus doors of the year closing. The fall of each humblest flower marks the annual period of some phase of human life, experience. I can be said to note the flower's fall only when I see in it the symbol of my own change. When I experience this, then the flower appears to me.

Drosera rotundifolia in Moore's new field ditch. The *Viola pedata* and the houstonia now. What is the peculiarity of these flowers that *they* blossom again? Is it merely because they blossomed so early in the spring, and now are ready for a new spring? They impress me as so much more native or naturalized here.

We love to see Nature fruitful in whatever kind. It assures us of her vigor and that she may equally bring forth the fruits which we prize. I love to see the acorns plenty, even on the shrub oaks, aye, and the nightshade berries. I love to see the potato balls numerous and large, as I go through a low field, poisonous though they look, the plant thus, as it were, bearing fruit at both ends, saying ever and anon, "Not only these tubers I offer you for the present, but if you will have new varieties, — if these do not satisfy you, — plant these seeds." [2] What abundance! what luxuriance! what bounty! The potato balls, which are worth-

[1] [Channing, p. 74.]   [2] [Channing, pp. 74, 215.]

less to the farmer, combine to make the general impression of the year's fruitfulness. It is as cheering to me as the rapid increase of the population of New York.

Aug. 31. *Proserpinaca palustris*, spear-leaved proserpinaca, mermaid-weed. (This in Hubbard's Grove on my way to Conantum.) A hornets' (?) nest in a rather tall huckleberry bush, the stems projecting through it, the leaves spreading over it. How these fellows avail themselves of the vegetables! They kept arriving, the great fellows, but I never saw whence they came, but only heard the buzz just at the entrance. (With whitish abdomens.) At length, after I have stood before the nest five minutes, during which time they had taken no notice of me, two seemed to be consulting at the entrance, and then one made a threatening dash at me and returned to the nest. I took the hint and retired. They spoke as plainly as man could have done. [1]

I see that the farmers have begun to top their corn.

Examined my old friend the green locust (?), shrilling on an alder leaf.

What relation does the fall dandelion bear to the spring dandelion? There is a rank scent of tansy now on some roads, disagreeable to many people from being associated in their minds with funerals, where it is sometimes put into the coffin and about the corpse. I have not observed much St. John's-wort yet. *Galium triflorum*, three-flowered cleavers, in Conant's Spring Swamp; also fever-bush there, now budded for next

[1] [Channing, p. 249.]

year. Tobacco-pipe (*Monotropa uniflora*) in Spring Swamp Path. I came out of the thick, dark, swampy wood as from night into day. Having forgotten the daylight, I was surprised to see how bright it was. I had light enough, methought, and here was an afternoon sun illumining all the landscape. It was a surprise to me to see how much brighter an ordinary afternoon is than the light which penetrates a thick wood.

One of these drooping clusters of potato balls would be as good a symbol, emblem, of the year's fertility as anything, — better surely than a bunch of grapes. Fruit of the strong soil, containing potash (?). The vintage is come; the olive is ripe.

"I come to pluck your berries harsh and crude;
    And with forc'd fingers rude,
        Shatter your leaves before the mellowing year;"

Why not for my coat-of-arms, for device, a drooping cluster of potato balls, — in a *potato* field? [1]

What right has a New England poet to sing of wine, who never saw a vineyard, who obtains his liquor from the grocer, who would not dare, if he could, tell him what it is composed of. A Yankee singing in praise of wine! It is not sour grapes in this case, it is sweet grapes; the more inaccessible they are the sweeter they are. It seemed to me that the year had nothing so much to brag of as these potato balls. Do they not concern New-Englanders a thousand times more than all her grapes? In Moore's new field they grow, cultivated with the bog hoe, manured with ashes and sphagnum. How they take to the virgin soil! [2] Shannon tells me that he took

[1] [Channing, pp. 75, 216.]   [2] [Channing, p. 216.]

a piece of bog land of Augustus Hayden, cleared, turned up the stumps and roots and burned it over, making a coat of ashes six inches deep, then planted potatoes. He never put a hoe to it till he went to dig them; then between 8 o'clock A. M. and 5 P. M. he and another man dug and housed seventy-five bushels apiece!!

Cohush now in fruit, ivory-white berries tipped *now* with black on stout red pedicels, — *Actœa alba. Collinsonia Canadensis*, horseweed. I had discovered this singular flower there new to me, and, having a botany by me, looked it out. What a surprise and disappointment, what an insult and impertinence to my curiosity and expectation, to have given me the name "horseweed!"

Cohush Swamp is about twenty rods by three or four. Among rarer plants it contains the basswood, the black (as well as white) ash, the fever-bush, the cohush, the collinsonia, not to mention sassafras, poison sumach, ivy, agrimony, *Arum triphyllum*, (sweet viburnum (?) in hedges near by), ground-nut, touch-me-not (as high as your head), and *Eupatorium purpureum* (eight feet, eight inches high, with a large convex corymb (hemispherical) of many stories, fourteen inches wide; width of plant from tip of leaf to tip of leaf two feet, diameter of stalk one inch at ground, leaves seven in a whorl). Rare plants seem to love certain localities. As if the original Conant had been a botanist and endeavored to form an arboretum. A natural arboretum?

The handsome sweet viburnum berries, now red on one cheek.

It was the filiform crowfoot (*Ranunculus filiformis*)

that I saw by the riverside the other day and to-day. The season advances apace. The flowers of the nettle-leaved vervain are now near the ends of the spike, like the blue. *Utricularia inflata*, whorled bladderwort, floating on the water at same place. *Gentiana Saponaria* budded. *Gerardia flava* at Conant's Grove.

Half an hour before sunset I was at Tupelo Cliff, when, looking up from my botanizing (I had been examining the *Ranunculus filiformis*, the *Sium latifolium* (? ?), and the obtuse galium on the muddy shore), I saw the seal of evening on the river. There was a quiet beauty in the landscape at that hour which my senses were prepared to appreciate. The sun going down on the west side, that hand being already in shadow for the most part, but his rays lighting up the water and the willows and pads even more than before. His rays then fell at right angles on their stems. I sitting on the old brown geologic rocks, their feet submerged and covered with weedy moss (utricularia roots?). Sometimes their tops are submerged. The cardinal-flowers standing by me. The trivialness of the day is past. The greater stillness, the *serenity* of the air, its coolness and transparency, the mistiness being condensed, are favorable to thought. (The pensive eve.) The coolness of evening comes to condense the haze of noon and make the air transparent and the outline of objects firm and distinct, and chaste (chaste eve); even as I am made more vigorous by my bath, am more *continent* of thought. After bathing, even at noonday, a man realizes a morning or evening life.[1] The evening air is such a bath

[1] [Channing, pp. 301, 302.]

Vol. II

for both mind and body. When I have walked all day in vain under the torrid sun, and the world has been all trivial, — as well field and wood as highway, — then at eve the sun goes down westward, and the wind goes down with it, and the dews begin to purify the air and make it transparent, and the lakes and rivers acquire a glassy stillness, reflecting the skies, the reflex of the day. I too am at the top of my condition for perceiving beauty. Thus, long after feeding, the diviner faculties begin to be fed, to feel their oats, their nutriment, and are not oppressed by the belly's load. It is abstinence from loading the belly anew until the brain and divine faculties have felt their vigor. Not till some hours does my food invigorate my brain, — ascendeth into the brain. We practice at this hour an involuntary abstinence. We are comparatively chaste and temperate as Eve herself; the nutriment is just reaching the brain. Every sound is music now. The grating of some distant boat which a man is launching on the rocky bottom, — though here is no man nor inhabited house, nor even cultivated field, in sight, — this is heard with such distinctness that I listen with pleasure as if it was [*sic*] music. The attractive point is that line where the water meets the land, not distinct, but known to exist. The willows are not the less interesting because of their nakedness below. How rich, like what we love to read of South American primitive forests, is the scenery of this river! What luxuriance of weeds, what depth of mud along its sides! These old antehistoric, geologic, antediluvian rocks, which only primitive wading birds, still lingering among us, are worthy to tread. The season

which we seem to *live* in anticipation of is arrived. The water, indeed, reflects heaven because my mind does; such is its own serenity, its transparency and stillness.

With what sober joy I stand to let the water drip from me and feel my fresh vigor, who have been bathing in the same tub which the muskrat uses! Such a medicated bath as only nature furnishes. A fish leaps, and the dimple he makes is observed now. How ample and generous was nature! My inheritance is not narrow.[1] Here is no other this evening. Those resorts which I most love and frequent, numerous and vast as they are, are as it were given up to me, as much as if I were an autocrat or owner of the world, and by my edicts excluded men from my territories. Perchance there is some advantage here not enjoyed in older countries. There are said to be two thousand inhabitants in Concord, and yet I find such ample space and verge, even miles of walking every day in which I do not meet nor see a human being, and often not very recent traces of them. So much of man as there is in your mind, there will be in your eye. Methinks that for a great part of the time, as much as it is possible, I walk as one possessing the advantages of human culture, fresh from society of men, but turned loose into the woods, the only man in nature, walking and meditating to a great extent as if man and his customs and institutions were not. The catbird, or the jay, is sure of the whole of your ear now. Each noise is like a stain on pure glass. The rivers now, these great blue subterranean heavens, reflecting the supernal skies and red-tinted clouds.

[1] [Channing, p. 301.]

A fly (or gnat?) will often buzz round you and persecute you like an imp. How much of imp-like, pestering character they express! (I hear a boy driving home his cows.) What unanimity between the water and the sky! — one only a little denser element than the other. The grossest part of heaven. Think of a mirror on so large a scale! Standing on distant hills, you see the heavens reflected, the evening sky, in some low lake or river in the valley, as perfectly as in any mirror they could be. Does it not prove how intimate heaven is with earth?

We commonly sacrifice to supper this serene and sacred hour. Our customs turn the hour of sunset to a trivial time, as at the meeting of two roads, one coming from the noon, the other leading to the night. It might be [well] if our repasts were taken out-of-doors, in view of the sunset and the rising stars; if there were two persons whose pulses beat together, if men cared for the κόσμος, or *beauty* of the world; if men were *social* in a high and rare sense; if they associated on high levels; if we took in with our tea a draught of the transparent, dew-freighted evening air; if, with our bread and butter, we took a slice of the red western sky; if the smoking, steaming urn were the vapor on a thousand lakes and rivers and meads.

The air of the valleys at this hour is the distilled essence of all those fragrances which during the day have been filling and have been dispersed in the atmosphere. The fine fragrances, perchance, which have floated in the upper atmospheres have settled to these low vales!

Vol. II

VIII

SEPTEMBER, 1851

(ÆT. 34)

Sept. 1. *Mikania scandens*, with its purplish white flowers, now covering the button-bushes and willows by the side of the stream. *Bidens chrysanthemoides*, large-flowered bidens, edge of river. Various-colored polygonums standing high among the bushes and weeds by riverside, — white and reddish and red.

Is not disease the rule of existence? There is not a lily pad floating on the river but has been riddled by insects. Almost every shrub and tree has its gall, oftentimes esteemed its chief ornament and hardly to be distinguished from the fruit. If misery loves company, misery has company enough. Now, at midsummer, find me a perfect leaf or fruit.

The fruit of the trilliums is very handsome. I found some a month ago, a singular *red*, angular-cased pulp, drooping, with the old anthers surrounding it three quarters of an inch in diameter; and now there is another kind, a dense crowded cluster of many ovoid berries turning from green to scarlet or bright brick-color. Then there is the mottled fruit of the clustered Solomon's-seal, and also the greenish (with blue meat) fruit of the *Convallaria multiflora* dangling from the axils of the leaves.

I talked of buying Conantum once, but for want of money we did not come to terms. But I have farmed it in my own fashion every year since.

I have no objection to giving the names of some naturalists, men of flowers, to plants, if by their lives they have identified themselves with them. There may be a few Kalmias. But it must be done very sparingly, or, rather, discriminatingly, and no man's name be used who has not been such a lover of flowers that the flowers themselves may be supposed thus to reciprocate his love.

Sept. 2. The dense fog came into my chamber early this morning, freighted with light, and woke me. It was, no doubt, lighter at that hour than if there had been no fog.

Not till after several months does an infant find its hands, and it may be seen looking at them with astonishment, holding them up to the light; and so also it finds its toes. How many faculties there are which we have never found![1] Some men, methinks, have found only their hands and feet. At least I have seen some who appeared never to have found their heads, but used them only instinctively, as the negro who butts with his,[2] or the water-carrier who makes a pack-horse of his. They have but partially found their heads.

We cannot write well or truly but what we write with gusto. The body, the senses, must conspire with the mind. Expression is the act of the whole man, that our speech may be vascular. The intellect is powerless to express thought without the aid of the heart and liver and of every member. Often I feel that my head stands out too dry, when it should be immersed. A writer, a man writing, is the scribe of all nature; he is the corn and the grass and the atmosphere writing. It is always essential that we love to do what we are doing, do it with a heart. The maturity of the mind, however, may perchance consist with a certain dryness.

There are flowers of thought, and there are leaves of thought; most of our thoughts are merely leaves, to which the thread of thought is the stem.

What affinity is it brings the goldfinch to the sun-

[1] [Channing, p. 203.]   [2] [Channing, p. 86.]

flower — both yellow — to pick its seeds? Whatever things I perceive with my entire man, those let me record, and it will be poetry. The sounds which I hear with the consent and coincidence of all my senses, these are significant and musical; at least, they only are heard.[1]

In a day or two the first message will be conveyed or transmitted over the magnetic telegraph through this town, as a thought traverses space, and no citizen of the town shall be aware of it. The atmosphere is full of telegraphs equally unobserved. We are not confined to Morse's or House's or Bain's line.

Raise some sunflowers to attract the goldfinches, to feed them as well as your hens. What a broad and loaded, bounteously filled platter of food is presented this *bon-vivant!*

Here is one of those thick fogs which last well into the day. While the farmer is concerned about the crops which his fields bear, I will be concerned about the fertility of my human farm. I will watch the winds and the rains as they affect the crop of thought, — the crop of crops, ripe thoughts, which glow and rustle and fill the air with fragrance for centuries. Is it a drought? How long since we had a rain? What is the state of the springs? Are the low springs high?

I now begin to pluck wild apples.

The difference is not great between some fruits in which the worm is always present and those gall fruits which were produced by the insect.

Old Cato says well, "*Patremfamilias vendacem, non*

[1] [Channing, p. 87.]

emacem, esse oportet." These Latin terminations express better than any English that I know the greediness, as it were, and tenacity of purpose with which the husbandman and householder is required to be a seller and not a buyer, — with mastiff-like tenacity, — these *lipped* words, which, like the lips of moose and browsing creatures, gather in the herbage and twigs with a certain greed. This termination *cious* adds force to a word, like the lips of browsing creatures, which greedily collect what the jaw holds; as in the word "tenacious" the first half represents the kind of jaw which holds, the last the lips which collect. It can only be pronounced by a certain opening and protruding of the lips; so "avaricious." These words express the sense of their simple roots with the addition, as it were, of a certain lip greediness. Hence "capacious" and "capacity," "emacity." When these expressive words are used, the hearer gets something to chew upon. To be a seller with the tenacity and firmness and steadiness of the jaws which hold and the greediness of the lips which collect. The audacious man not only dares, but he greedily collects more danger to dare. The avaricious man not only desires and satisfies his desire, but he collects ever new browse in anticipation of his ever-springing desires. What is *luscious* is especially enjoyed by the lips. The mastiff-mouthed are tenacious. To be a seller with mastiff-mouthed tenacity of purpose, with moose-lipped greediness, — ability to browse! To be edacious and voracious is to be not nibbling and swallowing merely, but eating and swallowing while the lips are greedily collecting more food.

Vol. II

There is a reptile in the throat of the greedy man always thirsting and famishing. It is not his own natural hunger and thirst which he satisfies.

The more we know about the ancients, the more we find that they were like the moderns. When I read Marcus Cato De Re Rustica, a small treatise or Farmer's Manual of those days, fresh from the field of Roman life, all reeking with and redolent of the life of those days, containing more indirect history than any of the histories of Rome of direct, — all of that time but that time, — *here* is a simple, direct, pertinent word addressed to the Romans. And where are *the Romans?* Rome and the Romans are commonly a piece of rhetoric. As if New England had disappeared poetically and there were left Buel's "Farmer's Companion," or the letters of Solon Robinson, or a volume of extracts from the *New England Farmer.* Though the Romans are no more but a fable and an ornament of rhetoric, we have here their *New England Farmer,* the very manual those Roman farmers read, speaking as if they were to hear it, its voice not silenced, as if Rome were still the mistress of the world, — as fresh as a dripping dish-cloth from a Roman kitchen.[1] As when you overhaul the correspondence of a man who died fifty years ago, with like surprise and feelings you overhaul the manuscripts of the Roman nation. There exist certain old papers, manuscripts, either the originals or faithful and trustworthy old copies of the originals, which were left by the Roman people. They have gone their way, but these old papers of all sorts remain. Among them there are some

[1] [Channing, pp. 60, 61.]

farm journals, or farm books; just such a collection of diary and memorandum — as when the cow calved, and the dimensions, with a plan, of the barn, and how much paid to Joe Farrar for work done on the farm, etc., etc. — as you might find in an old farmer's pocket-book to-day.

Indeed the farmer's was pretty much the same routine then as now. Cato says: "Sterquilinium magnum stude ut habeas. Stercus sedulo conserva, cum exportabis purgato et comminuito. Per autumnum evehito." (Study to have a great dungheap. Carefully preserve your dung, when you carry it out, make clean work of it and break it up fine. Carry it out during the autumn.) Just such directions as you find in the "Farmer's Almanack" to-day. It reminds me of what I see going on in our fields every autumn. As if the farmers of Concord were obeying Cato's directions. And Cato but repeated the maxims of a remote antiquity. Nothing can be more homely and suggestive of the every-day life of the Roman agr culturalists, thus supplying the very deficiencies in what is commonly called Roman history, *i. e.* revealing to us the actual life of the Romans, the how they got their living and what they did from day to day.[1]

They planted *rapa, raphanos, milium,* and *panicum* in low foggy land, *ager nebulosus.*

I see the farmer now — *i. e.* I shall in autumn — on every side carting out his manure and sedulously making his compost-heap, or scattering it over his grass ground and breaking it up with a mallet; and it reminds me of Cato's advice. He died one hundred and fifty

[1] [Channing, pp. 60, 61.]

years before Christ.[1] Before Christianity was heard of, this was done. A Roman family appears to have had a great supply of tubs and kettles.

A fire in the sitting-room to-day. Walk in the afternoon by Walden road and railroad to Minn's place, and round it to railroad and home. The first coolness is welcome, so serious and fertile of thought. My skin contracts, and I become more continent. Carried umbrellas, it mizzling. As in the night, now in the rain, I smell the fragrance of the woods. The prunella leaves have turned a delicate claret or lake color by the roadside. I am interested in these revolutions as much as in those of kingdoms. Is there not tragedy enough in the autumn? Walden seems to be going down at last. The pines are dead and leaning, red and half upset, about its shore. Thus, by its rising once in twenty-five years, perchance, it keeps an open shore, as if the ice had heaved them over. Found the succory at Minn's Bridge on railroad and beyond. Query: May not this and the tree-primrose and other plants be distributed from Boston on the rays of the railroads, the seeds mixing with the grains and all kinds of dirt and being blown from the passing freight-cars? The feathery-tailed fruit of the fertile flowers of the clematis conspicuous now.

The shorn meadows looked of a living green as we came home at eve, even greener than in spring. The *faenum cordum*, the aftermath, *sicilimenta de prato*, the second mowings of the meadow, this reminds me of, in Cato.[2]

[1] [Channing, p. 60.]   [2] [Channing, p. 220.]

is conceded to them, but to the horse none. Now and forever he is man's slave. The more I considered, the more the man seemed akin to the horse; only his was the stronger will of the two. For a little further on I saw an Irishman shovelling, who evidently was as much tamed as the horse. He had stipulated that to a certain extent his independence be recognized, and yet really he was but little more independent. I had always instinctively regarded the horse as a free people somewhere, living wild. Whatever has not come under the sway of man is wild. In this sense original and independent men are wild, — not tamed and broken by society. Now for my part I have such a respect for the horse's nature as would tempt me to let him alone; not to interfere with him, — his walks, his diet, his loves. But by mankind he is treated simply as if he were an engine which must have rest and is sensible of pain. Suppose that every squirrel were made to turn a coffee-mill! Suppose that the gazelles were made to draw milk-carts!

There he was with his tail cut off, because it was in the way, or to suit the taste of his owner; his mane trimmed, and his feet shod with iron that he might wear longer. What is a horse but an animal that has lost its liberty? What is it but a system of slavery? and do you not thus by *insensible* and unimportant degrees come to human slavery? Has lost its liberty! — and has man got any more liberty himself for having robbed the horse, or has he lost just as much of his own, and become more like the horse he has robbed? Is not the other end of the bridle in this case, too, coiled round his own neck? Hence stable-boys, jockeys, all

Sept. 3. Why was there never a poem on the cricket? Its creak seems to me to be one of the most prominent and obvious facts in the world, and the least heeded. In the report of a man's contemplations I look to see somewhat answering to this sound.[1] When I sat on Lee's Cliff the other day (August 29th), I saw a man working with a horse in a field by the river, carting dirt; and the horse and his relation to him struck me as very remarkable. There was the horse, a mere animated machine, — though his tail was brushing off the flies, — his whole existence subordinated to the man's, with no tradition, perhaps no instinct, in him of independence and freedom, of a time when he was wild and free, — completely humanized. No compact made with him that he should have the Saturday afternoons, or the Sundays, or any holidays. His independence never recognized, it being now quite forgotten both by men and by horses that the horse was ever free. For I am not aware that there are any wild horses known surely not to be descended from tame ones. Assisting that man to pull down that bank and spread it over the meadow; only keeping off the flies with his tail, and stamping, and catching a mouthful of grass or leaves from time to time, on his own account, — all the rest for man. It seemed hardly worth while that he should be *animated* for this. It was plain that the man was not educating the horse; not trying to develop his nature, but merely getting work out of him. That mass of animated matter seemed more completely the servant of man than any inanimate. For slaves have their holidays; a heaven

[1] [Channing, p. 78.]

that class that is daily transported by fast horses. There he stood with his oblong square figure (his tail being cut off) seen against the water, brushing off the flies with his tail and stamping, braced back while the man was filling the cart.[1]

It is a very remarkable and significant fact that, though no man is quite well or healthy, yet every one believes practically that health is the rule and disease the exception, and each invalid is wont to think himself in a minority, and to postpone somewhat of endeavor to another state of existence. But it may be some encouragement to men to know that in this respect they stand on the same platform, that disease is, in fact, the *rule* of our terrestrial life and the prophecy of a *celestial* life. Where is the coward who despairs because he is sick? Every one may live either the life of Achilles or of Nestor. Seen in this light, our life with all its diseases will look healthy, and in one sense the more healthy as it is the more diseased. Disease is not the accident of the individual, nor even of the generation, but of life itself. In some form, and to some degree or other, it is one of the permanent conditions of life. It is, nevertheless, a cheering fact that men affirm health unanimously, and esteem themselves miserable failures. Here was no blunder. They gave us life on exactly these conditions, and methinks we shall live it with more heart when we perceive clearly that these are the terms on which we have it. Life is a warfare, a struggle, and the diseases of the body answer to the troubles and defeats of the spirit. Man begins by quarrelling with the animal in him, and

[1] [Channing, pp. 173–175.]

the result is immediate disease. In proportion as the spirit is the more ambitious and persevering, the more obstacles it will meet with. It is as a seer that man asserts his disease to be exceptional.[1]

2 P. M. — To Hubbard's Swimming-Place and Grove in rain.

As I went under the new telegraph-wire, I heard it vibrating like a harp high overhead. It was as the sound of a far-off glorious life, a supernal life, which came down to us, and vibrated the lattice-work of this life of ours.[2]

The melons and the apples seem at once to feed my brain.

Here comes a laborer from his dinner to resume his work at clearing out a ditch notwithstanding the rain, remembering as Cato says, *per ferias potuisse fossas veteres tergeri*, that in the holidays old ditches might have been cleared out. One would think that I were the paterfamilias come to see if the steward of my farm has done his duty.

The ivy leaves are turning red. Fall dandelions stand thick in the meadows.

How much the Roman must have been indebted to his agriculture, dealing with the earth, its clods and stubble, its dust and mire. Their farmer consuls were their glory, and they well knew the farm to be the nursery of soldiers. Read Cato to see what kind of legs the Romans stood on.

The leaves of the hardhack are somewhat appressed,

¹ [Channing, p. 164.]   ² [Channing, p. 199.]

clothing the stem and showing their downy under sides like white, waving wands. Is it peculiar to the season, or the rain, — or the plant?

Walk often in drizzly weather, for then the small weeds (especially if they stand on bare ground), covered with rain-drops like beads, appear more beautiful than ever, — the hypericums, for instance. They are equally beautiful when covered with dew, fresh and adorned, almost spirited away, in a robe of dewdrops.[1]

Some farmers have begun to thresh and winnow their oats.

Identified spotted spurge (*Euphorbia maculata*), apparently out of blossom. Shepherd's-purse and chickweed.

As for walking, the inhabitants of large English towns are confined almost exclusively to their parks and to the highways. The few footpaths in their vicinities "are gradually vanishing," says Wilkinson, "under the encroachments of the proprietors." He proposes that the people's right to them be asserted and defended and that they be kept in a passable state at the public expense. "This," says he, "would be easily done by means of asphalt laid upon a good foundation" ! ! ! So much for walking, and the prospects of walking, in the neighborhood of English large towns.

Think of a man — he may be a genius of some kind — being confined to a highway and a park for his world to range in! I should die from mere nervousness at the thought of such confinement. I should hesitate before I were born, if those terms could be made known to me

¹ [Channing, p. 216.]

Vol. II

beforehand. Fenced in forever by those green barriers of fields, where gentlemen are seated! Can they be said to be inhabitants of this globe? Will they be content to inhabit heaven thus partially?

Sept. 4. 8 A. M. — A clear and pleasant day after the rain. Start for Boon's Pond in Stow with C. Every sight and sound was the more interesting for the clear atmosphere. When you are starting away, leaving your more familiar fields, for a little adventure like a walk, you look at every object with a traveller's, or at least with historical, eyes; you pause on the first bridge, where an ordinary walk hardly commences, and begin to observe and moralize like a traveller. It is worth the while to see your native village thus sometimes, as if you were a traveller passing through it, commenting on your neighbors as strangers.[1] We stood thus on Wood's Bridge, the first bridge, in the capacity of pilgrims and strangers to its familiarity, giving it one more chance with us, though our townsmen who passed may not have perceived it.

There was a pretty good-sized pickerel poised over the sandy bottom close to the shore and motionless as a shadow. It is wonderful how they resist the slight current of our river and remain thus stationary for hours. He, no doubt, saw us plainly on the bridge, — in the sunny water, his whole form distinct and his shadow, — motionless as the steel trap which does not spring till the fox's foot has touched it.

—— ——'s dog sprang up, ran out, and growled at

¹ [Channing, p. 222.]

us, and in his eye I seemed to see the eye of his master. I have no doubt but that, as is the master, such in course of time tend to become his herds and flocks as well as dogs. One man's oxen will be clever and solid, another's mischievous, another's mangy, — in each case like their respective owners. No doubt man impresses his own character on the beasts which he tames and employs; they are not only humanized, but they acquire his particular human nature.[1] How much oxen are like farmers generally, and cows like farmers' wives! and young steers and heifers like farmers' boys and girls! The farmer acts on the ox, and the ox reacts on the farmer. They do not meet half-way, it is true, but they do meet at a distance from the centre of each proportionate to each one's intellectual power.[2] The farmer is ox-like in his thought, in his walk, in his strength, in his trustworthiness, in his taste.[3]

Hosmer's man was cutting his millet, and his buckwheat already lay in *red* piles in the field.

The first picture we noticed was where the road turned among the pitch pines and showed the Hadley house, with the high wooded hill behind with dew and sun on it, the gracefully winding road path, and a more distant horizon on the right of the house. Just beyond, on the left, it was pleasant walking where the road was shaded by a high hill, as it can be only in the morning. Even in the morning that additional coolness and early-dawn-like feeling of a more sacred and earlier season are agreeable.

¹ [Channing, p. 76.]   ² [*Ibid.*]
³ [Channing, p. 175.]

The lane in front of Tarbell's house, which is but little worn and appears to lead nowhere, though it has so wide and all-engulfing an opening, suggested that such things might be contrived for effect in laying out grounds. (Only those things are sure to have the greatest and best effect, which like this were not contrived for the sake of effect.) An open path which would suggest walking and adventuring on it, the going to some place strange and far away. It would make you think of or imagine distant places and spaces greater than the estate.

It was pleasant, looking back just beyond, to see a heavy shadow (made by some high birches) reaching quite across the road. Light and shadow are sufficient contrast and furnish sufficient excitement when we are well.

Now we were passing the vale of Brown and Tarbell, a sunshiny mead pastured by cattle and sparkling with dew, the sound of crows and swallows heard in the air, and leafy-columned elms seen here and there shining with dew. The morning freshness and unworldliness of that domain![1] The vale of Tempe and of Arcady is not farther off than are the conscious lives of men from their opportunities. Our life is as far from corresponding to its scenery as we are distant from Tempe and Arcadia; that is to say, they are far away because we are far from living natural lives. How absurd it would be to insist on the vale of Tempe in particular when we have such vales as we have!

In the Marlborough road, in the woods, I saw a pur-

[1] [Channing, p. 222.]

ple streak like a stain on the red pine leaves and sand under my feet, which I was surprised to find was made by a dense mass of purple fleas, somewhat like snow-fleas, — a faint purple stain as if some purple dye had been spilt. What is that slender pink flower that I find in the Marlborough road, — smaller than a snap-dragon? The slender stems of grass which hang over the ruts and horses' path in this little-frequented road are so laden with dew that I am compelled to hold a bush before me to shake it off. The jays scream on the right and left and are seen flying further off as we go by.

We drink in the meadow at Second Division Brook, then sit awhile to watch its yellowish pebbles and the cress (?) in it and other weeds. The ripples cover its surface like a network and are faithfully reflected on the bottom. In some places, the sun reflected from ripples on a flat stone looks like a golden comb. The whole brook seems as busy as a loom: it is a woof and warp of ripples; fairy fingers are throwing the shuttle at every step, and the long, waving brook is the fine product. The water is wonderfully clear.

To have a hut here, and a footpath to the brook! For roads, I think that a poet cannot tolerate more than a footpath through the fields; that is wide enough, and for purposes of winged poesy suffices. It is not for the muse to speak of cart-paths. I would fain travel by a footpath round the world.[1] I do not ask the railroads of commerce, not even the cart-paths of the farmer. Pray, what other path would you have than a footpath? What

[1] [Channing, p. 69.]

else should wear a path? This is the track of man alone. What more suggestive to the pensive walker?[1] One walks in a wheel-track with less emotion; he is at a greater distance from man; but this footpath was, perchance, worn by the bare feet of human beings, and he cannot but think with interest of them.

The grapes, though their leaves are withering and falling, are yet too sour to eat.

In the summer we lay up a stock of experiences for the winter, as the squirrel of nuts, — something for conversation in winter evenings. I love to think then of the more distant walks I took in summer.[2]

At the powder-mills the carbonic acid gas in the road from the building where they were making charcoal made us cough for twenty or thirty rods.

Saw some gray squirrels whirling their cylinder by the roadside. How fitted that cylinder to this animal! "A squirrel is easily taught to turn his cylinder" might be a saying frequently applicable. And as they turned, one leaped over or dodged under another most gracefully and unexpectedly, with interweaving motions. It was the circus and menagerie combined. So human they were, exhibiting themselves.

In the Marlborough road, I forgot to say, we brushed the *Polygonum articulatum* with its spikes of reddish-white flowers, a slender and tender plant which loves the middle of dry and sandy not-much-travelled roads. To find that the very atoms bloom, that there are

[1] *Vide* last journal for bare foot track in Corner road [p. 328 of this volume].
[2] [Channing, p. 70.]

flowers we rudely brush against which only the microscope reveals!

It is wise to write on many subjects, to try many themes, that so you may find the right and inspiring one. Be greedy of occasions to express your thought. Improve the opportunity to draw analogies. There are innumerable avenues to a perception of the truth. Improve the suggestion of each object however humble, however slight and transient the provocation. What else is there to be improved? ·Who knows what opportunities he may neglect? It is not in vain that the mind turns aside this way or that: follow its leading; apply it whither it inclines to go. Probe the universe in a myriad points. Be avaricious of these impulses. You must try a thousand themes before you find the right one, as nature makes a thousand acorns to get one oak. He is a wise man and experienced who has taken many views; to whom stones and plants and animals and a myriad objects have each suggested something, contributed something.[1]

And now, methinks, this wider wood-path[2] is not bad, for it admits of society more conveniently. Two can walk side by side in it in the ruts, aye, and one more in the horse-track.[3] The Indian walked in single file, more solitary, — not side by side, chatting as he went. The woodman's cart and sled make just the path two walkers want through the wood.

Beyond the powder-mills we watched some fat oxen,

[1] [Channing, p. 86.]
[2] By Second Division Brook.
[3] [Channing, p. 70.]

elephantine, behemoths, — one Rufus-Hosmer-eyed, with the long lash and projecting eye-ball.

Now past the paper-mills, by the westernmost road east of the river, the first new ground we've reached.

Not only the prunella turns *lake*, but the *Hypericum Virginicum* in the hollows by the roadside, — a handsome blush. A part of the autumnal tints, ripe leaves. Leaves acquire red blood. Red colors touch our blood, and excite us as well as cows and geese.

And now we leave the road and go through the woods and swamps toward Boon's Pond, crossing two or three roads and by Potter's house in Stow; still on east of river. The fruit of the *Pyrola rotundifolia* in the damp woods. Larch trees in Stow about the houses. Beyond Potter's we struck into the extensive wooded plain where the ponds are found in Stow, Sudbury, and Marlborough. Part of it called Boon's Plain.[1] Boon said to have lived on or under Bailey's Hill at west of pond. Killed by Indians between Boon['s Pond] and White's Pond as he was driving his ox-cart. The oxen ran off to Marlborough garrison-house. His remains have been searched for. A sandy plain, a large level tract. The pond shores handsome enough, but water shallow and muddy looking. Well-wooded shores. The maples begin to show red about it. Much fished.

Saw a load of sunflowers in a farmers [*sic*]. Such is the destiny of this large, coarse flower; the farmers gather it like pumpkins.

Returned by railroad down the Assabet. A potato-field yellow with wild radish. But no good place to

[1] *Vide* hawks [p. 480].

bathe for three miles, Knight's new dam has so raised the river. A permanent freshet, as it were, the fluviatile trees standing dead for fish hawk perches, and the water stagnant for weeds to grow in. You have only to dam up a running stream to give it the aspect of a dead stream, and to some degree restore its primitive wild appearance. Tracts made inaccessible to man and at the same time more fertile. Some speculator comes and dams up the stream below, and lo! the water stands over all meadows, making impassable morasses and dead trees for fish hawks, — a wild, stagnant, fenny country, the last gasp of wildness before it yields to the civilization of the factory, — to cheer the eyes of the factory people and educate them. It makes a little wilderness above the factories.

The woodbine now begins to hang red about the maples and other trees.

As I looked back up the stream from near the bridge (I suppose on the road from Potter's house to Stow), I on the railroad, I saw the ripples sparkling in the sun, reminding me of the sparkling icy fleets which I saw last winter; and I saw how one corresponded to the other, ice waves to water ones; the erect ice-flakes were the waves stereotyped. It was the same sight, the reflection of the sun sparkling from a myriad slanting surfaces at a distance, a rippled water surface or a crystallized frozen one.

Here crossed the river and climbed the high hills on the west side. The walnut trees con- formed in their branches to the slope of the hill, being just as high from the ground on the upper side as on the lower.

On all sides now I see and smell the withering leaves of brush that has been cut to clear the land. I see some blackened tracts which have been burnt over. It is remarkable, for it is rare to see the surface of the earth black. And in the horizon I can see the smokes of several fires. The farmers improve this season, which is the driest, their haying being done and their harvest not begun, to do these jobs, — burn brush, build walls, dig ditches, cut turf. This is what I find them doing all over the country now; also topping corn and digging potatoes.

Saw quite a flock, for the first time, of goldfinches.

On the high, round hills in the east and southeast of Stow, — perchance they are called the Assabet Hills, — rising directly from the river. They are the highest I know rising thus. The rounded hills of Stow. A hill and valley country. Very different from Concord.

It had been a warm day, especially warm to the head. I do not perspire as in the early summer, but am sensible of the ripening heat, more as if by contact. Suddenly the wind changed to east, and the atmosphere grew more and more hazy and thick on that side, obstructing the view, while it was yet clear in the west. I thought it was the result of the cooler air from over the sea meeting and condensing the vapor in the warm air of the land. That was the haze, or thin, dry fog which some call smoke. It gradually moved westward and affected the prospect on that side somewhat. It was a very thin fog invading all the east. I felt the cool air from the ocean, and it was very refreshing. I opened my bosom

and my mouth to inhale it. Very delicious and invigorating.

We sat on the top of those hills looking down on the new brick ice-house. Where there are several hills near together, you cannot determine at once which is the highest, whether the one you are on or the next. So, when great men are assembled, each yields an uncertain respect to the other, as if it were not certain whose crown rose highest.

Under the nut trees on these hills, the grass is short and green as if grazed close by cattle who had stood there for shade, making a distinct circular yard. Yet, as there is no dung and the form corresponds so closely to the tree, I doubt if that can be the cause.

On hillside north of river above powder-mills the *Pycnanthemum incanum* (mountain mint, calamint) and the *Lespedeza violacea*.

Saw what I thought a small red dog in the road, which cantered along over the bridge this side the powder-mills and then turned into the woods. This decided me — this turning into the woods — that it was a fox. The dog of the woods, the dog that is more at home in the woods than in the roads and fields. I do not often see a dog turning into the woods.

Some large white (?) oak acorns this side the last-named bridge. A few oaks stand in the pastures still, great ornaments. I do not see any young ones springing up to supply their places. Will there be any a hundred years hence? These are the remnants of the primitive wood, methinks. We are a young people and have not learned by experience the consequence of cutting off the forest. One day they will be planted, methinks, and nature reinstated to some extent.

I love to see the yellow knots and their lengthened stain on the dry, unpainted pitch [?]-pine boards on barns and other buildings, — the Dugan house, for instance. The indestructible yellow fat! it fats my eyes to see it; worthy for art to imitate, telling of branches in the forest once.

Sept. 5. No doubt, like plants, we are fed through the atmosphere, and the varying atmospheres of various seasons of the year feed us variously. How often we are sensible of being thus fed and invigorated! And all nature contributes to this aerial diet its food of finest quality. Methinks that in the fragrance of the fruits I get a finer flavor, and in beauty (which is appreciated by sight — the taste and smell of the eye) a finer still. As Wilkinson says, "the physical man himself is the builded aroma of the world. This then, at least, is the office of the lungs — to drink the atmosphere with the planet dissolved in it." "What is the import of *change of air*, and how each pair of lungs has a *native air* under some one dome of the sky."

Wilkinson's book to some extent realizes what I have dreamed of, — a return to the primitive analogical and derivative senses of words. His ability to trace analogies often leads him to a truer word than more remarkable writers have found; as when, in his chapter on the human skin, he describes the papillary cutis as "an encampment of small conical tents coextensive with the surface of the body." The faith he puts in old and cur-

rent expressions as having sprung from an instinct wiser than science, and safely to be trusted if they can be interpreted. The man of science discovers no world for the mind of man with all its faculties to inhabit. Wilkinson finds a *home* for the imagination, and it is no longer outcast and homeless. All perception of truth is the detection of an analogy; we reason from our hands to our head.

It is remarkable that Kalm says in 1748 (being in Philadelphia): "Coals have not yet been found in Pennsylvania; but people pretend to have seen them higher up in the country among the natives. Many people however agree that they are met with in great quantity more to the north, near Cape Breton."

As we grow old we live more coarsely, we relax a little in our disciplines, and, to some extent, cease to obey our finest instincts. We are more careless about our diet and our chastity. But we should be fastidious to the extreme of sanity.[1] All wisdom is the reward of a discipline, conscious or unconscious.

By moonlight at Potter's Field toward Bear Garden Hill, 8 P. M. The whip-poor-wills sing.

Cultivate reverence. It is as if you were so much more respectable yourself. By the quality of a man's writing, by the elevation of its tone, you may measure his self-respect. How shall a man continue his culture after manhood?

Moonlight on Fair Haven Pond seen from the Cliffs. A sheeny lake in the midst of a boundless forest, the

[1] [*Cape Cod, and Miscellanies*, p. 468; *Misc.*, Riv. 270.]

Vol. II

windy surf sounding freshly and wildly in the single pine behind you; the silence of hushed wolves in the wilderness, and, as you fancy, moose looking off from the shore of the lake. The stars of poetry and history and unexplored nature looking down on the scene. This is my world now, with a dull whitish mark curving northward through the forest marking the outlet to the lake. Fair Haven by moonlight lies there like a lake in the Maine wilderness in the midst of a primitive forest untrodden by man. This light and this hour take the civilization all out of the landscape. Even in villages dogs bay the moon; in forests like this we listen to hear wolves howl to Cynthia.

Even at this hour in the evening the crickets chirp, the small birds peep, the wind roars in the wood, as if it were just before dawn. The moonlight seems to linger as if it were giving way to the light of coming day.

The landscape seen from the slightest elevation by moonlight is seen remotely, and flattened, as it were, into mere light and shade, open field and forest, like the surface of the earth seen from the top of a mountain.

How much excited we are, how much recruited, by a great many particular fragrances! A field of ripening corn, now at night, that has been topped, with the stalks stacked up to dry, — an inexpressibly dry, rich, sweet, ripening scent.[1] I feel as if I were an ear of ripening corn myself. Is not the whole air then a compound of such odors undistinguishable? Drying corn-stalks in a field; what an herb-garden![2]

[1] [See *Excursions*, p. 327; Riv. 403.]
[2] [Channing, pp. 251, 252.]

Sept. 6. The other afternoon I met Sam H—— walking on the railroad between the depot and the back road. It was something quite novel to see him there, though the railroad there is only a short thoroughfare to the public road. It then occurred to me that I had never met Mr. H. on the railroad, though he walks every day, and moreover that it would be quite impossible for him to walk on the railroad, such a formalist as he is, such strait-jackets we weave for ourselves. He could do nothing that was not sanctioned by the longest use of men, and as men had voted in all their assemblies from the first to travel on the public way, he would confine himself to that. It would no doubt seem to him very improper, not to say undignified, to walk on the railroad; and then, is it not forbidden by the railroad corporations? I was sure he could not keep the railroad, but was merely using the thoroughfare here which a thousand pioneers had prepared for him. I stood to see what he would do. He turned off the rails directly on to the back road and pursued his walk. A passing train will never meet him on the railroad causeway. How much of the life of certain men *goes* to sustain, to make respected, the institutions of society. They are the ones who pay the heaviest tax. Here are certain valuable institutions which can only be sustained by a wonderful strain which appears all to come upon certain Spartans who volunteer. Certain men are always to be found — especially the children of our present institutions — who are born with an instinct to perceive them. They are, in effect, supported by a fund which society possesses for that end, or they receive a pension and their life *seems* to be a sinecure, — but it is not. The unwritten laws are the most stringent. They are required to wear a certain dress. What an array of gentlemen whose sole employment — and it is no sinecure — is to support their dignity, and with it the dignity of so many indispensable institutions!

The use of many vegetables — wild plants — for food, which botanists relate, such as Kalm at Cap aux Oyes on the St. Lawrence, *viz.* the sea plantain, sea-rocket, sweet-gale, etc., etc., making us feel the poorer at first because we never use them, really advertises us of our superior riches, and shows to what extremities men have been driven in times of scarcity. No people that fare as well as we will grub these weeds out of the seashore.

2 P. M. — To Hapgood's in Acton direct, returning *via* Strawberry Hill and Smith's Road.

The ripening grapes begin to fill the air with their fragrance. The vervain will hardly do for a clock, for I perceive that some later and smaller specimens have not much more than begun to blossom, while most have done. Saw a tall pear tree by the roadside beyond Harris's in front of Hapgood's. Saw the lambkill (*Kalmia angustifolia*) in blossom — a few fresh blossoms at *the ends* of the fresh twigs — on Strawberry Hill, beautiful bright flowers. Apparently a new spring with it, while seed vessels, apparently of this year, hung dry below.

From Strawberry Hill the first, but a very slight, glimpse of Nagog Pond by standing up on the wall. That is enough to relate of a hill, methinks, that its

elevation gives you the first sight of some distant lake. The horizon is remarkably blue with mist this afternoon. Looking from this hill over Acton, successive valleys filled with blue mist appear, and divided by darker lines of wooded hills. The shadows of the elms are deepened, as if the whole atmosphere were permeated by floods of ether. Annursnack never looked so well as now seen from this hill. The ether gives a velvet softness to the whole landscape. The hills float in it. A blue veil is drawn over the earth.

The elecampane (*Inula Helenium*), with its broad leaves wrinkled underneath and the remains of sunflower-like blossoms, in front of Nathan Brooks's, Acton, and near J. H. Wheeler's. *Prenanthes alba;* this Gray calls *Nabalus albus*, white lettuce or rattlesnake-root. Also I *seem* (?) to have found *Nabalus Fraseri*, or lion's-foot.

Every morning for a week there has been a fog which all disappeared by seven or eight o'clock.

A large field of sunflowers for hens now in full bloom at Temple's, surrounding the house, and now, at 6 o'clock P. M., facing the east.

The larches in the front yards, both Scotch and American, have turned red. Their fall has come.

Sept. 7. We sometimes experience a mere fullness of life, which does not find any channels to flow into. We are stimulated, but to no obvious purpose. I feel myself uncommonly prepared for *some* literary work, but I can select no work. I am prepared not so much for contemplation, as for forceful expression. I am braced

Vol. II

both physically and intellectually. It is not so much the music as the marching to the music that I feel. I feel that the juices of the fruits which I have eaten, the melons and apples, have ascended to my brain and are stimulating it. They give me a heady force. Now I can write nervously. Carlyle's writing is for the most part of this character.

Miss Martineau's last book is not so bad as the timidity which fears its influence. As if the popularity of this or that book would be so fatal, and man would not still be man in the world. Nothing is so much to be feared as fear. Atheism may comparatively be popular with God himself.[1]

What shall we say of these timid folk who carry the principle of thinking nothing and doing nothing and being nothing to such an extreme? As if, in the absence of thought, that vast yearning of their natures for something to fill the vacuum made the least traditionary expression and shadow of a thought to be clung to with instinctive tenacity. They atone for their producing nothing by a brutish respect for something. They are as simple as oxen, and as guiltless of thought and reflection. Their reflections are reflected from other minds. The creature of institutions, bigoted and a conservatist, can say nothing hearty. He cannot meet life with life, but only with words. He rebuts you by avoiding you. He is shocked like a woman.

Our ecstatic states, which appear to yield so little fruit, have this value at least: though in the seasons when our genius reigns we may be powerless for ex-

[1] [Channing, p. 90.]

pression, yet, in calmer seasons, when our talent is active, the memory of those rarer moods comes to color our picture and is the permanent paint-pot, as it were, into which we dip our brush. Thus no life or experience goes unreported at last; but if it be not solid gold it is gold-leaf, which gilds the furniture of the mind. It is an experience of infinite beauty on which we unfailingly draw, which enables us to exaggerate ever truly. Our moments of inspiration are not lost though we have no particular poem to show for them; for those experiences have left an indelible impression, and we are ever and anon reminded of them. Their truth subsides, and in cooler moments we can use them as paint to gild and adorn our prose. When I despair to sing them, I will remember that they will furnish me with paint with which to adorn and preserve the works of talent one day. They are like a pot of pure ether. They lend the writer when the moment comes a certain superfluity of wealth, making his expression to overrun and float itself. It is the difference between our river, now parched and dried up, exposing its unsightly and weedy bottom, and the same when, in the spring, it covers all the meads with a chain of placid lakes, reflecting the forests and the skies.

We are receiving our portion of the infinite. The art of life! Was there ever anything memorable written upon it? By what disciplines to secure the most life, with what care to watch our thoughts. To observe what transpires, not in the street, but in the mind and heart of me! I do not remember any page which will tell me how to spend this afternoon. I do not so much wish to know how to economize time as how to spend it, by what means to grow rich, that the day may not have been in vain.

What if one moon has come and gone with its world of poetry, its weird teachings, its oracular suggestions? So divine a creature, freighted with hints for me, and I not use her! One moon gone by unnoticed ! ! Suppose you attend to the hints, to the suggestions, which the moon makes for one month, — commonly in vain, — will they not be very different from anything in literature or religion or philosophy?[1]

The scenery, when it is truly seen, reacts on the life of the seer. How to live. How to get the most life. As if you were to teach the young hunter how to entrap his game. How to extract its honey from the flower of the world. That is my every-day business. I am as busy as a bee about it. I ramble over all fields on that errand, and am never so happy as when I feel myself heavy with honey and wax. I am like a bee searching the livelong day for the sweets of nature. Do I not impregnate and intermix the flowers, produce rare and finer varieties by transferring my eyes from one to another? I do as naturally and as joyfully, with my own humming music, seek honey all the day. With what honeyed thought any experience yields me I take a bee line to my cell. It is with flowers I would deal. Where is the flower, there is the honey, — which is perchance the nectareous portion of the fruit, — there is to be the fruit, and no doubt flowers are thus colored and painted to attract and guide the bee. So by the dawning or radi-

[1] [*Excursions*, p. 324; Riv. 398.]

ance of beauty are we advertised where is the honey and the fruit of thought, of discourse, and of action. We are first attracted by the beauty of the flower, before we discover the honey which is a foretaste of the future fruit. Did not the young Achilles (?) spend his youth learning how to hunt? The art of spending a day. If it is possible that we may be addressed, it behooves us to be attentive. If by watching all day and all night I may detect some trace of the Ineffable, then will it not be worth the while to watch? Watch and pray without ceasing, but not necessarily in sadness. Be of good cheer. Those Jews were too sad: to another people a still deeper revelation may suggest only joy. Don't I know what gladness is? Is it but the reflex of sadness, its back side? In the Hebrew gladness, I hear but too distinctly still the sound of sadness retreating. Give me a gladness which has never given place to sadness.

I am convinced that men are not well employed, that this is not the way to spend a day. If by patience, if by watching, I can secure one new ray of light, can feel myself elevated for an instant upon Pisgah, the world which was dead prose to me become living and divine, shall I not watch ever? shall I not be a watchman henceforth? If by watching a whole year on the city's walls I may obtain a communication from heaven, shall I not do well to shut up my shop and turn a watchman? Can a youth, a man, do more wisely than to go where his life is to [be] found? As if I had suffered that to be rumor which may be verified. We are surrounded by a rich and fertile mystery. May we not probe it, pry into it, employ ourselves about it, a little? To devote your life

to the discovery of the divinity in nature or to the eating of oysters, would they not be attended with very different results?

I cannot *easily* buy a blank-book to write thoughts in; they are all ruled for dollars and cents.[1]

If the wine, the water, which will nourish me grows on the surface of the moon, I will do the best I can to go to the moon for it.

The discoveries which we make abroad are special and particular; those which we make at home are general and significant. The further off, the nearer the surface. The nearer home, the deeper. Go in search of the springs of life, and you will get exercise enough. Think of a man's swinging dumb-bells for his health, when those springs are bubbling in far-off pastures unsought by him! The seeming necessity of swinging dumb-bells proves that he has lost his way.[2]

To watch for, describe, all the divine features which I detect in Nature.

My profession is to be always on the alert to find God in nature, to know his lurking-places, to attend all the oratorios, the operas, in nature.

The mind may perchance be persuaded to act, to energize, by the action and energy of the body. Any kind of liquid will fetch the pump.

We all have our states of fullness and of emptiness, but we overflow at different points. One overflows through the sensual outlets, another through his heart, another through his head, and another perchance only

[1] [*Cape Cod, and Miscellanies*, p. 456; *Misc.*, Riv. 254, 255.]
[2] [*Excursions*, p. 209; Riv. 257.]

through the higher part of his head, or his poetic faculty. It depends on where each is tight and open. We can, perchance, then direct our nutriment to those organs we specially use.

How happens it that there are few men so well employed, — so much to their mind, — but that a little money or fame would buy them off from their present pursuits?

To Conantum *via* fields, Hubbard's Grove, and grain-field, to Tupelo Cliff and Conantum and returning over peak same way. 6 P. M.

I hear no larks sing at evening as in the spring, nor robins; only a few distressed notes from the robin. In Hubbard's grain-field beyond the brook, now the sun is down. The air is very still. There is a fine sound of crickets, not loud. The woods and single trees are heavier masses in the landscape than in the spring. Night has more allies. The heavy shadows of woods and trees are remarkable now. The meadows are green with their second crop. I hear only a tree-toad or song sparrow singing as in spring, at long intervals. The Roman wormwood is beginning to yellow-green my shoes, — intermingled with the blue-curls over the sand in this grain-field. Perchance some poet likened this yellow dust to the ambrosia of the gods. The birds are remarkably silent. At the bridge perceive the bats are out. And the yet silvery moon, not quite full, is reflected in the water. The water is perfectly still, and there is a red tinge from the evening sky in it.

The sky is singularly marked this evening. There are bars or rays of nebulous light springing from the western horizon where the sun has disappeared, and alternating with beautiful blue rays, more blue by far than any other portion of the sky. These continue to diverge till they have reached the middle, and then converge to the eastern horizon, making a symmetrical figure like the divisions of a muskmelon, not very bright, yet distinct, though growing less and less bright toward the east. It was a quite remarkable phenomenon encompassing the heavens, as if you were to behold the divisions of a muskmelon thus alternately colored from within it. A proper vision, a colored mist. The most beautiful thing in nature is the sun reflected from a tearful cloud. These white and blue ribs embraced the earth. The two outer blues much the brightest and matching one another.

You hear the hum of mosquitoes.

Going up the road. The sound of the crickets is now much more universal and loud. Now in the fields I see the white streak of the neottia in the twilight. The whip-poor-wills sing far off. I smell burnt land somewhere. At Tupelo Cliff I hear the sound of singers on the river, young men and women, — which is unusual here, — returning from their row. Man's voice, thus uttered, fits well the spaces. It fills nature. And, after all, the singing of men is something far grander than any natural sound. It is wonderful that men do not oftener sing in the fields, by day and night. I bathe at the north side the Cliff, while the moon shines round the end of the rock. The opposite Cliff is reflected in the water. Then sit on the south side of the Cliff in the woods. One or two fireflies. Could it be a glow-worm?

I thought I saw one or two in the air. That is all in this walk. I hear a whip-poor-will uttering a cluck of suspicion in my rear. He is suspicious and inquisitive. The river stretches off southward from me. I see the sheeny portions of its western shore interruptedly for a quarter of a mile, where the moonlight is reflected from the pads, a strong, gleaming light while the water is lost in the obscurity. I hear the sound from time to time of a leaping fish, or a frog, or a muskrat, or turtle. It is even warmer, *methinks*, than it was in August, and it is perfectly clear, — the air. I know not how it is that this universal crickets' creak should sound thus regularly intermittent, as if for the most part they fell in with one another and creaked in time, making a certain pulsing sound, a sort of breathing or panting of all nature. You sit twenty feet above the still river; see the sheeny pads, and the moon, and some bare tree-tops in the distant horizon. Those bare tree-tops add greatly to the wildness.

Lower down I see the moon in the water as bright as in the heavens; only the water-bugs disturb its disk; and now I catch a faint glassy glare from the whole river surface, which before was simply dark. This is set in a frame of double darkness on the east, *i. e.* the reflected shore of woods and hills and the reality, the shadow and the substance, bipartite, answering to each.

I see the northern lights over my shoulder, to remind me of the Esquimaux and that they are still my contemporaries on this globe, that they too are taking their walks on another part of the planet, in pursuit

Vol. II

of seals, perchance.[1] The stars are dimly reflected in the water. The path of water-bugs in the moon's rays is like ripples of light. It is only when you stand fronting the sun or moon that you see their light reflected in the water. I hear no frogs these nights, — bullfrogs or others, — as in the spring. It is not the season of sound.

At Conantum end, just under the wall. From this point and at this height I do not perceive any bright or yellowish light on Fair Haven, but an oily and glass-like smoothness on its southwestern bay, through a very slight mistiness. Two or three pines appear to stand in the moonlit air on this side of the pond, while the enlightened portion of the water is bounded by the heavy reflection of the wood on the east. It was so soft and velvety a light as contained a thousand placid days sweetly put to rest in the bosom of the water. So looked the North Twin Lake in the Maine woods. It reminds me of placid lakes in the mid-noon of Indian summer days, but yet more placid and civilized, suggesting a higher cultivation, as the wild ever does, which æons of summer days have gone to make. Like a summer day seen far away. All the effects of sunlight, with a softer tone; and all this stillness of the water and the air superadded, and the witchery of the hour. What gods are they that require so fair a vase of gleaming water to their prospect in the midst of the wild woods by night? Else why this beauty allotted to night, a gem to sparkle in the zone of night? They are strange gods now out; methinks their names are not in any

¹ [Channing, p. 115.]

mythology.[1] I can faintly trace its zigzag border of sheeny pads even here. If such is then to be seen in remotest wildernesses, does it not suggest its own nymphs and wood gods to enjoy it? As when, at middle of the placid noon in Indian-summer days, all the surface of a lake is as one cobweb gleaming in the sun, which heaves gently to the passing zephyr. There was the lake, its glassy surface just distinguishable, its sheeny shore of pads, with a few pines bathed in light on its hither shore, just as in the middle of a November day, except that this was the chaster light of the moon, the cooler temperature of the night, and there were the deep shades of night that fenced it round and imbosomed. It tells of a far-away, long-passed civilization, of an antiquity superior to time, unappreciable by time.

Is there such virtue in raking cranberries that those men's industry whom I now see on the meadow shall reprove my idleness? Can I not go over those same meadows after them, and rake still more valuable fruits? Can I not rake with my mind? Can I not rake a thought, perchance, which shall be worth a bushel of cranberries?

A certain refinement and civilization in nature which increases with the wildness. The civilization that consists with wildness, the light that is in night. A smile as in a dream on the face of the sleeping lake. There is light enough to show what we see, what *night* has to exhibit. Any more would obscure these objects. I am not advertised of any deficiency of light.[2] The actual

¹ [Channing, p. 116.]   ² [Channing, p. 116.]

is fair as a vision or a dream. If ever we have attained
to any nobleness, even in our imagination and intentions, that will surely ennoble the features of nature
for us, that will clothe them with beauty. Of course no
jeweller ever dealt with a gem so fair and suggestive
as this actual lake, the scene, it may be, of so much
noble and poetic life, and not merely [to] adorn some
monarch's crown.

It is remarkably still at this hour and season. No
sound of bird or beast for the most part. This has none
of the reputed noxious qualities of night.

On the peak. The faint sounds of birds, dreaming
aloud in the night, the fresh, cool air, and sound of the
wind rushing over the rocks remind me of the tops of
mountains. That is, all the earth is but the outside
of the planet bordering on the hard-eyed sky. Equally
withdrawn and near to heaven is this pasture as the
summit of the White Mountains. All the earth's surface like a mountain-top, for I see its relation to heaven
as simply, and am not imposed upon by a difference of
a few feet in elevation. In this faint, hoary light, all
fields are like a mossy rock and remote from the cultivated plains of day. All is equally savage, equally
solitary and cool-aired, and the slight difference in
elevation is felt to be unimportant. It is all one with
Caucasus, the slightest hill pasture.

The basswood had a singularly solid look and
sharply defined, as by a web or film, as if its leaves
covered it like scales.

Scared up a whip-poor-will on the ground on the hill.
Will not my townsmen consider me a benefactor if

I conquer some realms from the night, if I can show
them that there is some beauty awake while they are
asleep, if I add to the domains of poetry,[1] if I report to
the gazettes anything transpiring in our midst worthy
of man's attention? I will say nothing now to the dis-
paragement of Day, for he is not here to defend himself.

The northern lights now, as I descend from the
Conantum house, have become a crescent of light
crowned with short, shooting flames, — or the shadows
of flames, for sometimes they are dark as well as white.
There is scarcely any dew even in the low lands.

Now the fire in the north increases wonderfully,
not shooting up so much as creeping along, like a fire
on the mountains of the north seen afar in the night.
The Hyperborean gods are burning brush, and it
spread, and all the hoes in heaven could n't stop it.
It spread from west to east over the crescent hill. Like
a vast fiery worm it lay across the northern sky, broken
into many pieces; and each piece, with rainbow colors
skirting it, strove to advance itself toward the east,
worm-like, on its own annular muscles. It has spread
into their choicest wood-lots. Now it shoots up like a
single solitary watch-fire or burning bush, or where it
ran up a pine tree like powder, and still it continues
to gleam here and there like a fat stump in the burning,
and is reflected in the water. And now I see the gods
by great exertions have got it under, and the stars have
come out without fear, in peace.

Though no birds sing, the crickets vibrate their
shrill and stridulous cymbals, especially on the alders

[1] [*Excursions*, p. 323; Riv. 397, 398.]

of the causeway, those minstrels especially engaged
for Night's quire.[1]

It takes some time to wear off the trivial impression
which the day has made, and thus the first hours of
night are sometimes lost.

There were two hen-hawks soared and circled for
our entertainment, when we were in the woods on that
Boon Plain the other day, crossing each other's orbits
from time to time, alternating like the squirrels of the
morning, till, alarmed by our imitation of a hawk's
shrill cry, they gradually inflated themselves, made
themselves more aerial, and rose higher and higher into
the heavens, and were at length lost to sight; yet all
the while earnestly looking, scanning the surface of the
earth for a stray mouse or rabbit.[2]

Sept. 8. No fog this morning. Shall I not have words
as fresh as my thoughts? Shall I use any other man's
word? A genuine thought or feeling can find expression for itself, if it have to invent hieroglyphics. It has
the universe for type-metal. It is for want of original
thought that one man's style is like another's.

Certainly the voice of no bird or beast can be compared with that of man for true melody. All other sounds
seem to be hushed, as if their possessors were attending,
when the voice of man is heard in melody. The air
gladly bears the burden. It is infinitely significant.
Man only sings in concert. The bird's song is a mere

[1] [Channing, pp. 116, 117.]
[2] *Vide* back [p. 458].

interjectional shout of joy; man's a glorious expression
of the foundations of his joy.

Do not the song of birds and the fireflies go with the
grass? While the grass is fresh, the earth is in its vigor.
The greenness of the grass is the best symptom or evidence of the earth's youth or health. Perhaps it will be
found that when the grass ceases to be fresh and green,
or after June, the birds have ceased to sing, and that
the fireflies, too, no longer in *myriads* sparkle in the
meadows. Perhaps a history of the year would be a
history of the grass, or of a leaf, regarding the grass-
blades as leaves, for it is equally true that the leaves
soon lose their freshness and soundness, and become
the prey of insects and of drought. Plants commonly
soon cease to grow for the year, unless they may have
a fall growth, which is a kind of second spring. In the
feelings of the man, too, the year is already past, and
he looks forward to the coming winter. His occasional
rejuvenescence and faith in the current time is like the
aftermath, a scanty crop. The enterprise which he has
not already undertaken cannot be undertaken this year.
The period of youth is past. The year may be in its
summer, in its manhood, but it is no longer in the flower
of its age. It is a season of withering, of dust and heat,
a season of small fruits and trivial experiences. Summer thus answers to manhood. But there is an aftermath in early autumn, and some spring flowers bloom
again, followed by an Indian summer of finer atmosphere and of a pensive beauty. May my life be not
destitute of its Indian summer, a season of fine and clear,
mild weather in which I may prolong my hunting be-

fore the winter comes, when I may once more lie on the ground with faith, as in spring, and even with more serene confidence. And then I will [wrap the] drapery of summer about me and lie down to pleasant dreams. As one year passes into another through the medium of winter, so does this our life pass into another through the medium of death.

De Quincey and Dickens have not moderation enough. They never stutter; they flow too readily.

The tree-primrose and the dwarf ditto and epilobium still. Locust is heard. *Aster amplexicaulis*, beautiful blue, purplish blue (?), about twenty-four rayed. *Utricularia vulgaris*, bladderwort. Dandelion and houstonia.

Sept. 9. 2 A. M. — The moon not quite full. To Conantum *via* road.

There is a low vapor in the meadows beyond the depot, dense and white, though scarcely higher than a man's head, concealing the stems of the trees. I see that the oaks, which are so dark and distinctly outlined, are illumined by the moon on the opposite side. This as I go up the back road. A few thin, ineffectual clouds in the sky. I come out thus into the moonlit night, where men are not, as if into a scenery anciently deserted by men. The life of men is like a dream. It is three thousand years since night has had possession. Go forth and hear the crickets chirp at midnight. Hear if their dynasty is not an ancient one and well founded. I feel the antiquity of the night. She surely repossesses herself of her realms, as if her dynasty were uninter-

rupted, or she had underlain the day. No sounds but the steady creaking of crickets and the occasional crowing of cocks.

I go by the farmer's houses and barns, standing there in the dim light under the trees, as if they lay at an immense distance or under a veil. The farmer and his oxen now all asleep. Not even a watch-dog awake. The human slumbers. There is less of man in the world.

The fog in the lowlands on the Corner road is never still. It now advances and envelops me as I stand to write these words, then clears away, with ever noiseless step. It covers the meadows like a web. I hear the clock strike three.

Now at the clayey bank. The light of Orion's belt seems to show traces of the blue day through which it came to us. The sky at least is lighter on that side than in the west, even about the moon. Even by night the sky is blue and not black, for we see through the veil of night into the distant atmosphere of day. I see to the plains of the sun, where the sunbeams are revelling. The cricket's (?) song, on the alders of the causeway, not quite so loud at this hour as at evening. The moon is getting low. I hear a wagon cross one of the bridges leading into the town. I see the moonlight at this hour on a different side of objects. I smell the ripe apples many rods off beyond the bridge. A sultry night; a thin coat is enough.

On the first top of Conantum. I hear the farmer harnessing his horse and starting for the distant market, but no man harnesses himself, and starts for worthier

Vol. II

enterprises. One cock-crow tells the whole story of the farmer's life. The moon is now sinking into clouds in the horizon. I see the glow-worms deep in the grass by the little brookside in midst of Conantum. The moon shines dun and red. A solitary whip-poor-will sings.

The clock strikes four. A few dogs bark. A few more wagons start for market, their faint rattling heard in the distance. I hear my owl without a name; the murmur of the slow-approaching freight-train, as far off, perchance, as Waltham; and one early bird.

The round, red moon disappearing in the west. I detect a whiteness in the east. Some dark, massive clouds have come over from the west within the hour, as if attracted by the approaching sun, and have arranged themselves raywise about the eastern portal, as if to bar his coming. They have moved suddenly and almost unobservedly quite across the sky (which before was clear) from west to east. No trumpet was heard which marshalled and advanced these dark masses of the west's forces thus rapidly against the coming day. Column after column the mighty west sent forth across the sky while men slept, but all in vain.

The eastern horizon is now grown dun-colored, showing where the advanced guard of the night are already skirmishing with the vanguard of the sun, a lurid light tingeing the atmosphere there, while a dark-columned cloud hangs imminent over the broad portal, untouched by the glare. Some bird flies over, making a noise like the barking of a puppy.[1] It is yet so dark that I have dropped my pencil and cannot find it.

[1] It was a cuckoo.

The sound of the cars is like that of a rushing wind. They come on slowly. I thought at first a morning wind was rising. And now (perchance at half-past four) I hear the sound of some far-off factory-bell arousing the operatives to their early labors. It sounds very sweet here. It is very likely some factory which I have never seen, in some valley which I have never visited; yet now I hear this, which is its only matin bell, sweet and inspiring as if it summoned holy men and maids to worship and not factory girls and men to resume their trivial toil, as if it were the summons of some religious or even poetic community. My first impression is that it is the matin bell of some holy community who in a distant valley dwell, a band of spiritual knights, — thus sounding far and wide, sweet and sonorous, in harmony with their own morning thoughts. What else could I suppose fitting this earth and hour? Some man of high resolve, devoted soul, has touched the rope; and by its peals how many men and maids are waked from peaceful slumbers to fragrant morning thoughts! Why should I fear to tell that it is Knight's factory-bell at Assabet? A few melodious peals and all is still again.

The whip-poor-wills now begin to sing in earnest about half an hour before sunrise, as if making haste to improve the short time that is left them. As far as my observation goes, they sing for several hours in the early part of the night, are silent commonly at midnight, — though you may meet [them] then sitting on a rock or flitting silently about, — then sing again just before sunrise. It grows more and more red in the east — a fine-grained red under the overhanging cloud — and lighter too, and the threatening clouds are falling off to southward of the sun's passage, shrunken and defeated, leaving his path comparatively clear. The increased light shows more distinctly the river and the fog.

5 o'clock. — The light now reveals a thin film of vapor like a gossamer veil cast over the lower hills beneath the Cliffs and stretching to the river, thicker in the ravines, thinnest on the even slopes. The distant meadows towards the north beyond Conant's Grove, full of fog, appear like a vast lake out of which rise Annursnack and Ponkawtasset like rounded islands. Nawshawtuct is a low and wooded isle, scarcely seen above the waves. The heavens are now clear again. The vapor, which was confined to the river and meadows, now rises and creeps up the sides of the hills. I see it in transparent columns advancing down the valley of the river, ghost-like, from Fair Haven, and investing some wooded or rocky promontory, before free. So ghosts are said to advance.

Annursnack is exactly like some round, steep, distant hill on the opposite shore of a large lake (and Tabor on the other side), with here and there some low Brush Island in middle of the waves (the tops of some oaks or elms). Oh, what a sail I could take, if I had the right kind of bark, over to Annursnack! for there she lies four miles from land as sailors say. And all the farms and houses of Concord are at bottom of that sea. So I forget them, and my thought sails triumphantly over them. As I looked down where the village of Concord lay buried in fog, I thought of nothing but the surface of

a lake, a summer sea over which to sail; no more than a voyager on the Dead Sea who had not read the Testament would think of Sodom and Gomorrah, once cities of the plain. I only wished to get off to one of the low isles I saw in midst of the [sea] (it may have been the top of Holbrook's elm), and spend the whole summer day there.

Meanwhile the redness in the east had diminished and was less deep. (The fog over some meadows looked green.) I went down to Tupelo Cliff to bathe. A great bittern, which I had scared, flew heavily across the stream. The redness had risen at length above the dark cloud, the sun approaching. And next the redness became a sort of yellowish or fawn-colored light, and the sun now set fire to the edges of the broken cloud which had hung over the horizon, and they glowed like burning turf.

Sept. 10. As I watch the groves on the meadow opposite our house, I see how differently they look at different hours of the day, *i. e.* in different lights, when the sun shines on them variously. In the morning, perchance, they seem one blended mass of light green. In the afternoon, distinct trees appear, separated by heavy shadows, and in some places I can see quite through the grove.

3 P. M. — To the Cliffs and the Grape Cliff beyond.

Hardhack and meadow-sweet are now all dry. I see the smoke of burning brush in the west horizon this dry and sultry afternoon, and wish to look off from some hill. It is a kind of work the farmer cannot do

Vol. II

without discovery. Sometimes I smell these smokes several miles off, and by the odor know it is not a burning building, but withered leaves and the rubbish of the woods and swamp. As I go through the woods, I see that the ferns have turned brown and give the woods an autumnal look. The boiling spring is almost completely dry. Nothing flows (I mean without the shed), but there are many hornets and yellow wasps apparently buzzing and circling about in jealousy of one another, either drinking the stagnant water, which is the most accessible this dry parching day, or it may be collecting something from the slime, — I think the former.

As I go up Fair Haven Hill, I see some signs of the approaching fall of the white pine. On some trees the old leaves are already somewhat reddish, though not enough to give the trees a parti-colored look, and they come off easily on being touched, — the old leaves on the lower part of the twigs.

Some farmers are sowing their winter rye? I see the fields smoothly rolled. (I hear the locust still.) I see others plowing steep rocky and bushy fields, apparently for the same purpose. How beautiful the sprout-land (burnt plain) seen from the Cliff! No more cheering and inspiring sight than a young wood springing up thus over a large tract, when you look down on it, the light green of the maples shaded off into the darker oaks; and here and there a maple blushes quite red, enlivening the scene yet more. Surely this earth is fit to be inhabited, and many enterprises may be undertaken with hope where so many young plants are pushing up. In the spring I burned over a hundred acres till the

earth was sere and black, and by midsummer this space was clad in a fresher and more luxuriant green than the surrounding even. Shall man then despair? Is he not a sprout-land too, after never so many searings and witherings?[1] If you witness growth and luxuriance, it is all the same as if you grew luxuriantly.

I see three smokes in Stow. One sends up dark volumes of wreathed smoke, as if from the mouth of Erebus. It is remarkable what effects so thin and subtile a substance as smoke produces, even at a distance, — dark and heavy and powerful as rocks at a distance.

The woodbine is red on the rocks.

The poke is a very rich and striking plant. Some which stand under the Cliffs quite dazzled me with their now purple stems gracefully drooping each way, their rich, somewhat yellowish, purple-veined leaves, their bright purple racemes, — peduncles, and pedicels, and calyx-like petals from which the birds have picked the berries (these racemes, with their petals now turned to purple, are more brilliant than anything of the kind), — flower-buds, flowers, ripe berries and dark purple ones, and calyx-like petals which have lost their fruit, all on the same plant. I love to see any redness in the vegetation of the temperate zone. It is the richest color. I love to press these berries between my fingers and see their rich purple wine staining my hand. It asks a bright sun on it to make it show to best advantage, and it must be seen at this season of the year. It speaks to my blood. Every part of it is flower, such is its superfluity of color, — a feast of color. That is the richest flower which

[1] [Channing, p. 217]

most abounds in color. What need to taste the fruit, to drink the wine, to him who can thus taste and drink with his eyes? Its boughs, gracefully drooping, offering repasts to the birds. It is cardinal in its rank, as in its color. Nature here is full of blood and heat and luxuriance. What a triumph it appears in Nature to have produced and perfected such a plant, — as if this were enough for a summer.[1]

The downy seeds of the groundsel are taking their flight here. The calyx has dismissed them and quite curled back, having done its part. *Lespedeza sessiliflora*, or reticulated lespedeza on the Cliffs now out of bloom. At the Grape Cliff, the few bright-red leaves of the tupelo contrast with the polished green ones. The tupelos with drooping branches.

The grape-vines overrunning and bending down the maples form little arching bowers over the meadow, five or six feet in diameter, like parasols held over the ladies of the harem, in the East. *Cuscuta Americana*, or dodder, in blossom still. The *Desmodium paniculatum* of De Candolle and Gray (*Hedysarum paniculatum* of Linnæus and Bigelow), tick-trefoil, with still one blossom, by the path-side up from the meadow. The rhomboidal joints of its loments adhere to my clothes. One of an interesting family that thus disperse themselves. The oak-ball of dirty drab now.[2]

Sept. 11. Every artisan learns positively something by his trade. Each craft is familiar with a few simple,

[1] [*Excursions*, pp. 253–255; Riv. 311, 312.]
[2] [Channing, pp. 216, 217.]

well-known, well-established facts, not requiring any genius to discover, but mere use and familiarity. You may go by the man at his work in the street every day of your life, and though he is there before you, carrying into practice certain essential information, you shall never be the wiser. Each trade is in fact a craft, a cunning, a covering an ability; and its methods are the result of a long experience. There sits a stone-mason, splitting Westford granite for fence-posts. Egypt has perchance taught New England something in this matter. His hammer, his chisels, his wedges, his shims or half-rounds, his iron spoon, — I suspect that these tools are hoary with age as with granite dust. He learns as easily where the best granite comes from as he learns how to erect that screen to keep off the sun. He knows that he can drill faster into a large stone than a small one, because there is less jar and yielding. He deals in stone as the carpenter in lumber. In many of his operations only the materials are different. His work is slow and expensive. Nature is here hard to be overcome. He wears up one or two drills in splitting a single stone. He must sharpen his tools oftener than the carpenter. He fights with granite. He knows the temper of the rocks. He grows stony himself. His tread is ponderous and steady like the fall of a rock. And yet by patience and art he splits a stone as surely as the carpenter or woodcutter a log. So much time and perseverance will accomplish. One would say that mankind had much less moral than physical energy, that any day you see men following the trade of splitting rocks, who yet shrink from undertaking apparently less

Vol. II

arduous moral labors, the solving of moral problems. See how surely he proceeds. He does not hesitate to drill a dozen holes, each one the labor of a day or two for a savage; he carefully takes out the dust with his iron spoon; he inserts his wedges, one in each hole, and protects the sides of the holes and gives resistance to his wedges by thin pieces of half-round iron (or shims); he marks the red line which he has drawn, with his chisel, carefully cutting it straight; and then how carefully he drives each wedge in succession, fearful lest he should not have a good split!

The habit of looking at men in the gross makes their lives have less of human interest for us. But though there are crowds of laborers before us, yet each one leads his little epic life each day. There is the stone-mason, who, methought, was simply a stony man that hammered stone from breakfast to dinner, and dinner to supper, and then went to his slumbers. But he, I find, is even a man like myself, for he feels the heat of the sun and has raised some boards on a frame to protect him. And now, at mid-forenoon, I see his wife and child have come and brought him drink and meat for his lunch and to assuage the stoniness of his labor, and sit to chat with him.

There are many rocks lying there for him to split from end to end, and he will surely do it. This only at the command of luxury, since stone posts are preferred to wood. But how many moral blocks are lying there in every man's yard, which he surely will not split nor earnestly endeavor to split. There lie the blocks which will surely get split, but here lie the blocks which will

surely not get split. Do we say it is too hard for human faculties? But does not the mason dull a basketful of steel chisels in a day, and yet, by sharpening them again and tempering them aright, succeed? Moral effort! Difficulty to be overcome!!! Why, men work in stone, and sharpen their drills when they go home to dinner!

Why should Canada, wild and unsettled as it is, impress one as an older country than the States, except that her institutions are old. All things seem to contend there with a certain rust of antiquity, such as forms on old armor and iron guns, the rust of conventions and formalities. If the rust was not on the tinned roofs and spires, it was on the inhabitants.[1]

2 P. M. — To Hubbard's Meadow Grove.

The skunk-cabbage's checkered fruit (spadix), one three inches long; all parts of the flower but the anthers left and enlarged. *Bidens cernua*, or nodding burr-marigold, like a small sunflower (with rays) in Heywood Brook, *i. e.* beggar-tick. *Bidens connata* (?), without rays, in Hubbard's Meadow. Blue-eyed grass still. Drooping neottia very common. I see some yellow butterflies and others occasionally and singly only. The smilax berries are mostly turned dark. I started a great bittern from the weeds at the swimming-place.

It is very hot and dry weather. We have had no rain for a week, and yet the pitcher-plants have water in them. Are they ever quite dry? Are they not replenished by the dews always, and, being shaded by the

[1] [*Excursions*, pp. 80, 81; Riv. 100.]

grass, saved from evaporation? What wells for the birds!

The white-red-purple-berried bush in Hubbard's Meadow, whose berries were fairest a fortnight ago, appears to be the *Viburnum nudum*, or withe-rod. Our cornel (the common) with berries blue one side, whitish the other, appears to be either the *Cornus sericea* or *C. stolonifera* of Gray, *i. e.* the silky, or the red-osier cornel (*osier rouge*), though its leaves are neither silky nor downy nor rough.

This and the last four or five nights have been perhaps the most sultry in the year thus far.

Sept. 12. Not till after 8 A. M. does the fog clear off so much that I see the sun shining in patches on Nawshawtuct. This is the season of fogs.

Like knight, like esquire. When Benvenuto Cellini was attacked by the constables in Rome, his boy Cencio assisted him, or at least stood by, and afterward related his master's exploits; "and as they asked him several times whether he had been afraid, he answered that they should propose the question to me, for he had been affected upon the occasion just in the same manner that I was."

Benvenuto Cellini relates in his memoirs that, during his confinement in the castle of St. Angelo in Rome, he had a terrible dream or vision in which certain events were communicated to him which afterward came to pass, and he adds: "From the very moment that I beheld the phenomenon, there appeared (strange to relate!) a resplendent light over my head, which has dis-

played itself conspicuously to all that I have thought proper to show it to, but those were very few. This shining light is to be seen in the morning over my shadow till two o'clock in the afternoon, and it appears to the greatest advantage when the grass is moist with dew: it is likewise visible in the evening at sunset. This phenomenon I took notice of when I was at Paris, because the air is exceedingly clear in that climate, so that I could distinguish it there much plainer than in Italy, where mists are much more frequent; but I can still see it even here, and show it to others, though not to the same advantage as in France." This reminds me of the halo around my shadow which I notice from the causeway in the morning, — also by moonlight, — as if, in the case of a man of an excitable imagination, this were basis enough for his superstition.[1]

After I have spent the greater part of a night abroad in the moonlight, I am obliged to sleep enough more the next night to make up for it, — *Endymionis somnum dormire* (to sleep an Endymion sleep), as the ancients expressed it.[2] And there is something gained still by thus turning the day into night. Endymion is said to have obtained of Jupiter the privilege of sleeping as much as he would. Let no man be afraid of sleep, if his weariness comes of obeying his Genius. He who has spent the night with the gods sleeps more innocently by day than the sluggard who has spent the day with the satyrs sleeps by night. He who has travelled to fairyland in the night sleeps by day more innocently

[1] [*Walden*, pp. 224, 225; Riv. 316, 317.]
[2] [*Excursions*, p. 331; Riv. 407.]

than he who is fatigued by the merely trivial labors of the day sleeps by night. That kind of life which, sleeping, we dream that we live awake, in our walks by night, we, waking, live, while our daily life appears as a dream.

2 P. M. — To the Three Friends' Hill beyond Flint's Pond, *via* railroad, R. W. E.'s wood-path south side Walden, George Heywood's cleared lot, and Smith's orchard; return *via* east of Flint's Pond, *via* Goose Pond and my old home to railroad.

I go to Flint's Pond for the sake of the mountain view from the hill beyond, looking over Concord. I have thought it the best, especially in the winter, which I can get in this neighborhood. It is worth the while to see the mountains in the horizon once a day. I have thus seen some earth which corresponds to my least earthly and trivial, to my most heavenward-looking, thoughts. The earth seen through an azure, an ethereal, veil. They are the natural *temples*, elevated brows, of the earth, looking at which, the thoughts of the beholder are naturally elevated and sublimed, — etherealized. I wish to see the earth through the medium of much air or heaven, for there is no paint like the air. Mountains thus seen are worthy of worship. I go to Flint's Pond also to see a rippling lake and a reedy island in its midst, — Reed Island. A man should feed his senses with the best that the land affords.[1]

At the entrance to the Deep Cut, I heard the telegraph-wire vibrating like an æolian harp. It reminded me suddenly, — reservedly, with a beautiful paucity

[1] [Channing, p. 163.]

of communication, even silently, such was its effect on my thoughts, — it reminded me, I say, with a certain pathetic moderation, of what finer and deeper stirrings I was susceptible, which grandly set all argument and dispute aside, a triumphant though transient exhibition of the truth. It told me by the faintest imaginable strain, it told me by the finest strain that a human ear can hear, yet conclusively and past all refutation, that there were higher, infinitely higher, planes of life which it behooved me never to forget. As I was entering the Deep Cut, the wind, which was conveying a message to me from heaven, dropped it on the wire of the telegraph which it vibrated as it passed. I instantly sat down on a stone at the foot of the telegraph-pole, and attended to the communication. It merely said: "Bear in mind, Child, and never for an instant forget, that there are higher planes, infinitely higher planes, of life than this thou art now travelling on. Know that the goal is distant, and is upward, and is worthy all your life's efforts to attain to." And then it ceased, and though I sat some minutes longer I heard nothing more.

There is every variety and degree of inspiration from mere fullness of life to the most rapt mood. A human soul is played on even as this wire, which now vibrates slowly and gently so that the passer can hardly hear it, and anon the sound swells and vibrates with such intensity as if it would rend the wire, as far as the elasticity and tension of the wire permits, and now it dies away and is silent, and though the breeze continues to sweep over it, no strain comes from it, and the traveller hearkens in vain. It is no small gain to have this wire stretched through Concord, though there may be no office here. Thus I make my own use of the telegraph, without consulting the directors, like the sparrows, which I perceive use it extensively for a perch. Shall I not go to this office to hear if there is any communication for me, as steadily as to the post-office in the village? [1]

I can hardly believe that there is so great a difference between one year and another as my journal shows. The 11th of this month last year, the river was as high as it commonly is in the spring, over the causeway on the Corner road. It is now quite low. Last year, October 9th, the huckleberries were fresh and abundant on Conantum. They are now already dried up.

We yearn to see the mountains daily, as the Israelites yearned for the promised land, and we daily live the fate of Moses, who only looked into the promised land from Pisgah before he died.

On Monday, the 15th instant, I am going to perambulate the bounds of the town. As I am partial to across-lot routes, this appears to be a very proper duty for me to perform, for certainly no route can well be chosen which shall be more across-lot, since the roads in no case run round the town but ray out from its centre, and my course will lie across each one. It is almost as if I had undertaken to walk round the town at the greatest distance from its centre and at the same time from the surrounding villages. There is no public house near the line. It is a sort of reconnoissance of its frontiers authorized by the central government of the town,

[1] [Channing, pp. 199, 200.]

which will bring the surveyor in contact with whatever wild inhabitant or wilderness its territory embraces.

This appears to be a very ancient custom, and I find that this word "perambulation" has exactly the same meaning that it has at present in Johnson and Walker's dictionary. A hundred years ago they went round the towns of this State every three years. And the old selectmen tell me that, before the present split stones were set up in 1829, the bounds were marked by a heap of stones, and it was customary for each selectman to add a stone to the heap.

Saw a pigeon-place on George Heywood's cleared lot, — the six dead trees set up for the pigeons to alight on, and the brush house close by to conceal the man. I was rather startled to find such a thing going now in Concord. The pigeons on the trees looked like fabulous birds with their long tails and their pointed breasts. I could hardly believe they were alive and not some wooden birds used for decoys, they sat so still; and, even when they moved their necks, I thought it was the effect of art. As they were not catching then, I approached and scared away a dozen birds who were perched on the trees, and found that they were freshly baited there, though the net was carried away, perchance to some other bed. The smooth sandy bed was covered with buckwheat, wheat or rye, and acorns. Sometimes they use corn, shaved off the ear in its present state with a knife. There were left the sticks with which they fastened the nets. As I stood there, I heard a rushing sound and, looking up, saw a flock of thirty or forty pigeons dashing toward the *trees*, who suddenly

whirled on seeing me and circled round and made a new dash toward the bed, as if they would fain alight if I had not been there, then steered off. I crawled into the bough house and lay awhile looking through the leaves, hoping to see them come again and feed, but they did not while I stayed. This net and bed belong to one Harrington of Weston, as I hear. Several men still take pigeons in Concord every year; by a method, methinks, extremely old and which I seem to have seen pictured in some old book of fables or symbols, and yet few in Concord know exactly how it is done. And yet it is all done for money and because the birds fetch a good price, just as the farmers raise corn and potatoes. I am always expecting that those engaged in such a pursuit will be somewhat less grovelling and mercenary than the regular trader or farmer, but I fear that it is not so.

Found a violet, apparently *Viola cucullata*, or hood-leaved violet, in bloom in Baker's Meadow beyond Pine Hill; also the *Bidens cernua*, nodding burr-marigold, with five petals, in same place. Went through the old corn-field on the hillside beyond, now grown up to birches and hickories, — woods where you feel the old corn-hills under your feet; for these, not being disturbed or levelled in getting the crop, like potato-hills, last an indefinite while; and by some they are called Indian corn-fields, though I think erroneously, not only from their position in rocky soil frequently, but because the squaws probably, with their clamshells or thin stones or wooden hoes, did not hill their corn more than many now recommend.

What we call woodbine is the *Vitis hederacea*, or common creeper, or American ivy.

When I got into the Lincoln road, I perceived a singular sweet scent in the air, which I suspected arose from some plant now in a peculiar state owing to the season, but though I smelled everything around, I could not detect it, but the more eagerly I smelled, the further I seemed to be from finding it; but when I gave up the search, again it would be wafted to me. It was one of the sweet scents which go to make the autumn air, which fed my sense of smell rarely and dilated my nostrils. I felt the better for it. Methinks that I possess the sense of smell in greater perfection than usual, and have the habit of smelling of every plant I pluck. How autumnal is the scent of ripe grapes now by the roadside! [1]

From the pond-side hill I perceive that the forest leaves begin to look rather rusty or brown. The pendulous, drooping barberries are pretty well reddened. I am glad when the berries look fair and plump. I love to gaze at the low island in the pond, — at any island or inaccessible land. The isle at which you look always seems fairer than the mainland on which you stand.

I had already bathed in Walden as I passed, but now I forgot that I had been wetted, and wanted to embrace and mingle myself with the water of Flint's Pond this warm afternoon, to get wet inwardly and deeply.

Found on the shore of the pond that singular willow-like herb in blossom, though its petals were gone. It grows up two feet from a large woody horizontal root,

[1] [Channing, p. 217.]

and droops over to the sand again, meeting which, it puts out a myriad rootlets from the side of its stem, fastens itself, and curves upward again to the air, thus spanning or looping itself along. The bark just above the ground thickens into a singular cellular or spongy substance, which at length appears to crack nearer the earth, giving that part of the plant a winged and somewhat four-sided appearance. It appears to be the cellular tissue, or what is commonly called the green bark, and likewise invests the root to a great thickness, somewhat like a fungus, and is of a fawn-color. The *Lythrum verticillatum*, or swamp loosestrife, or grass poly, but I think better named, as in Dewey, swamp-willow-herb.

The prinos berries are pretty red. Any redness like cardinal-flowers, or poke, or the evening sky, or cheronæa, excites us as a red flag does cows and turkeys.

Sept. 13. Railroad causeway, before sunrise.

Here is a morning after a warm, clear, moonlight night almost entirely without dew or fog. It has been a little breezy through the night, it is true; but why so great a difference between this and other mornings of late? I can walk in any direction in the fields without wetting my feet.

I see the same rays in the dun, buff, or fawn-colored sky now, just twenty minutes before sunrise, though they do not extend quite so far as at sundown the other night. Why these rays? What is it divides the light of the sun? Is it thus divided by distant inequalities in the surface of the earth, behind which the other parts are concealed, and since the morning atmosphere is

clearer they do not reach so far? Some small island clouds are the first to look red.

The cross-leaved polygala emits its fragrance as if at will. You are quite sure you smelled it and are ravished with its sweet fragrance, but now it has no smell. You must not hold it too near, but hold it on all sides and at all distances, and there will perchance be wafted to you sooner or later a very sweet and penetrating fragrance. What it is like you cannot surely tell, for you do not enjoy it long enough nor in volume enough to compare it. It is very likely that you will not discover any fragrance while you are rudely smelling at it; you can only remember that you once perceived it. Both this and the caducous polygala are now somewhat faded.

Now the sun is risen. The sky is almost perfectly clear this morning; not a cloud in the horizon. The morning is not pensive like the evening, but joyous and youthful, and its blush is soon gone. It is unfallen day. The Bedford sunrise bell rings sweetly and musically at this hour, when there is no bustle in the village to drown it. Bedford deserves a vote of thanks from Concord for it. It is a great good at these still and sacred hours, when towns can hear each other. It would be nought at noon.

Sept. 14. A great change in the weather from sultry to cold, from one thin coat to a thick coat or two thin ones.

2 P. M. — To Cliffs.

The dry grass yields a crisped sound to my feet. The

white oak which appears to have made part of a hedge fence once, now standing in Hubbard's fence near the Corner road, where it stretches along horizontally, is (one of its arms, for it has one running each way) two and a half feet thick, with a sprout growing perpendicularly out of it eighteen inches in diameter. The corn-stalks standing in stacks, in long rows along the edges of the corn-fields, remind me of stacks of muskets.

As soon as berries are gone, grapes come. The chalices of the *Rhexia Virginica*, deer-grass or meadow-beauty, are literally little reddish chalices now, though many still have petals, — little cream pitchers.[1] The caducous polygala in cool places is faded almost white. I see the river at the foot of Fair Haven Hill running up-stream before the strong cool wind, which here strikes it from the north. The cold wind makes me shudder after my bath, before I get dressed.

Polygonum aviculare — knot-grass, goose-grass, or door-grass — still in bloom.

Sept. 15. *Monday.* Ice in the pail under the pump, and quite a frost.

Commenced perambulating the town bounds. At 7.30 A. M. rode in company with —— and Mr. —— to the bound between Acton and Concord near Paul Dudley's. Mr. —— told a story of his wife walking in the fields somewhere, and, to keep the rain off, throwing her gown over her head and holding it in her mouth, and so being poisoned about her mouth from the skirts of her dress having come in contact with poisonous plants.

[1] [Channing, p. 222.]

At Dudley's, which house is handsomely situated, with five large elms in front, we met the selectmen of Acton, —— —— and —— ——. Here were five of us. It appeared that we weighed, — —— I think about 160, —— 155, —— about 140, —— 130, myself 127. —— described the wall about or at Forest Hills Cemetery in Roxbury as being made of stones upon which they were careful to preserve the moss, so that it cannot be distinguished from a very old wall.

Found one intermediate bound-stone near the powder-mill drying-house on the bank of the river. The workmen there wore shoes without iron tacks. He said that the kernel-house was the most dangerous, the drying-house next, the press-house next. One of the powder-mill buildings in Concord? The potato vines and the beans which were still green are now blackened and flattened by the frost.

END OF VOLUME II

The Journal of Henry D. Thoreau

VOLUME III

(September, 1851 — April, 1852)

Large Boulder at Nonesuch Pond

CONTENTS

Vol. III

Vol. III

THE JOURNAL OF
HENRY DAVID THOREAU

VOLUME III

I

SEPTEMBER AND OCTOBER, 1851 (ÆT. 34)

Sept. 16. Met the selectmen of Sudbury, —— and ——. I trust that towns will remember that they are supposed to be fairly represented by their *select* men. From the specimen which Acton sent, I should judge that the inhabitants of that town were made up of a mixture of quiet, respectable, and even gentlemanly farmer people, well to do in the world, with a rather boisterous, coarse, and a little self-willed class; that the inhabitants of Sudbury are farmers almost exclusively, exceedingly rough and countrified and more illiterate than usual, very tenacious of their rights and dignities and difficult to deal with; that the inhabitants of Lincoln yield sooner than usual to the influence of the rising generation, and are a mixture of rather simple but clever with a well-informed and trustworthy people; that the inhabitants of Bedford are mechanics, who aspire to keep up with the age, with some of the polish of society, mingled with substantial and rather intelligent farmers.

—— of Sudbury thinks the river would be still lower now if it were not for the water in the reservoir pond in Hopkinton running into it.

Sept. 17. Perambulated the Lincoln line.

Was it the small rough sunflower which I saw this morning at the brook near Lee's Bridge?[1]

Saw at James Baker's a buttonwood tree with a swarm of bees now three years in it, but honey and all inaccessible.

John W. Farrar tells of sugar maples behind Miles's in the Corner.

Did I see privet in the swamp at the Bedford stone near Giles's house?

Swamp all dry now; could not wash my hands.

Sept. 18. Perambulated Bedford line.

Sept. 19. Perambulated Carlisle line.

Large-flowered bidens, or beggar-ticks, or bur-marigold, now abundant by riverside. Found the bound-stones on Carlisle by the river all or mostly tipped over by the ice and water, like the pitch pines about Walden Pond. Grapes very abundant along that line. The soapwort gentian now. In an old pasture, now grown up to birches and other trees, followed the cow-paths to the old apple trees.

Mr. Isaiah Green of Carlisle, who lives nearest to the Kibbe Place, can remember when there were three or four houses around him (he is nearly eighty years old

[1] Probably great bidens.

and has always lived there and was born there); now he is quite retired, and the nearest road is scarcely used at all. He spoke of one old field, now grown up, which [we] were going through, as the "hog-pasture," formerly. He found the meadows so dry that it was thought to be a good time to burn out the moss.

Sept. 20. 3 P. M. — To Cliffs *via* Bear Hill.

As I go through the fields, endeavoring to recover my tone and sanity and to perceive things truly and simply again, after having been perambulating the bounds of the town all the week, and dealing with the most commonplace and worldly-minded men, and emphatically *trivial* things, I feel as if I had committed suicide in a sense. I am again forcibly struck with the truth of the fable of Apollo serving King Admetus, its universal applicability. A fatal coarseness is the result of mixing in the trivial affairs of men. Though I have been associating even with the *select* men of this and the surrounding towns, I feel inexpressibly begrimed. My Pegasus has lost his wings; he has turned a reptile and gone on his belly. Such things are compatible only with a cheap and superficial life.

The poet must keep himself unstained and aloof. Let him perambulate the bounds of Imagination's provinces, the realms of faery, and not the insignificant boundaries of towns.[1] The excursions of the imagination are so boundless, the limits of towns are so petty.

I scare up the great bittern in meadow by the Heywood Brook near the ivy. He rises buoyantly as he flies

[1] [Channing, p. 86.]

against the wind, and sweeps south over the willow with outstretched neck, surveying.

The ivy here is reddened. The dogwood, or poison sumach, by Hubbard's meadow is also turned reddish. Here are late buttercups and dwarf tree-primroses still. Methinks there are not many goldenrods this year. The river is remarkably low. There is a rod wide of bare shore beneath the Cliff Hill.

Last week was the warmest perhaps in the year. On Monday of the present week water was frozen in a pail under the pump. Yet to-day I hear the locust sing as in August. This week we have had most glorious autumnal weather, — cool and cloudless, bright days, filled with the fragrance of ripe grapes, preceded by frosty mornings. All tender herbs are flat in gardens and meadows. The cranberries, too, are touched.

To-day it is warmer and hazier, and there is, no doubt, some smoke in the air, from the burning of the turf and moss in low lands, where the smoke, seen at sunset, looks like a rising fog. I fear that the autumnal tints will not be brilliant this season, the frosts have commenced so early. Butter-and-eggs on Fair Haven. The cleared plateau beneath the Cliff, now covered with sprouts, shows red, green, and yellow tints, like a rich rug. I see ducks or teal flying silent, swift, and straight, the wild creatures. White pines on Fair Haven Hill begin to look parti-colored with the falling leaves, but not at a distance.

Sept. 21. *Sunday.* It is remarkably dry weather. The neighbors' wells are failing. The watering-places

greenness, though it may be a mile or more off. I doubt if a man can drive his cows to that part of their pasture where is the best feed for them, so soon as they will find it for themselves. The man tries in vain to drive them to the best part of the meadow. As soon as he is gone, they seek their own parts.

The light of the moon, sufficient though it is for the pensive walker, and not disproportionate to the inner light we have, is very inferior in quantity and intensity to that of the sun.[1] The Cyclopedia says that Dr. Hooke has calculated that "it would require 104,368 full moons to give a light and heat equal to that of the sun at noon," and Dr. Smith says, "The light of the full moon is but equal to a 90,900th part of the common light of the day, when the sun is hidden by a cloud."[2]

But the moon is not to be judged alone by the quantity of light she sends us, but also by her influence on the earth. No thinker can afford to overlook the influence of the moon any more than the astronomer can. "The moon gravitates towards the earth, and the earth reciprocally towards the moon." This statement of the astronomer would be bald and meaningless, if it were not in fact a symbolical expression of the value of all lunar influence on man. Even the astronomer admits that "the notion of the moon's influence on terrestrial things was confirmed by her manifest effect upon the ocean," but is not the poet who walks by night conscious of a tide in his thought which is to be referred to lunar influence, in which the ocean within him over-

[1] [*Excursions*, p. 325; Riv. 399.]
[2] *Vide* next page.

for cattle in pastures, though they have been freshly scooped out, are dry. People have to go far for water to drink, and then drink it warm. The river is so low that rocks which are rarely seen show their black heads in mid-channel. I saw one which a year or two ago upset a boat and drowned a girl. You see the nests of the bream on the dry shore. I perceive that many of the leaves of shrub oaks and other bushes have been killed by the severe frosts of last week, before they have got ripe and acquired the tints of autumn, and they now look as [if] a fire had run through them, dry and crispy and brown. So far from the frost painting them, it has withered them. I notice new cabins of the muskrats in solitary swamps. The chestnut trees have suffered severely from the drought; already their leaves look withered.

Moonlight is peculiarly favorable to reflection. It is a cold and dewy light in which the vapors of the day are condensed, and though the air is obscured by darkness, it is more clear. Lunacy must be a cold excitement, not such insanity as a torrid sun on the brain would produce. In Rees's Cyclopedia it is said, "The light of the moon, condensed by the best mirrors, produces no sensible heat upon the thermometer."

I see some cows on the new Wheeler's Meadow, which a man is trying to drive to certain green parts of the meadow next to the river to feed, the hill being dried up, but they seem disinclined and not to like the coarse grass there, though it is green. And now one cow is steering for the edge of the hill, where is some greenness. I suppose that herds are attracted by a distant

flows its shores and bathes the dry land?[1] Has he not his spring-tides and his neap-tides, the former sometimes combining with the winds of heaven to produce those memorable high tides of the calendar which leave their marks for ages, when all Broad Street is submerged, and incalculable damage is done to the ordinary shipping of the mind?

Burritt in his "Geography of the Heavens" says, "The quantity of light which we derive from the Moon when full, is at least three hundred thousand times less than that of the Sun." This is M. Bouguer's inference as stated by Laplace. Professor Leslie makes it one hundred and fifty thousand times less, older astronomers less still.

Rees says: "It is remarkable, that the moon during the week in which she is full in harvest, rises sooner after sun-setting than she does in any other full moon week in the year. By doing so she affords an immediate supply of light after sunset, which is very beneficial to the farmers for reaping and gathering in the fruits of the earth; and therefore they distinguish this full moon from all the others in the year, by calling it the harvest moon." Howitt places the Harvest Moon in August.

The retirement in which Green has lived for nearly eighty years in Carlisle is a retirement very different from and much greater than that in which the pioneer dwells at the West; for the latter dwells within sound of the surf of those billows of migration which are breaking on the shores around him, or near him, of the West, but those billows have long since swept over the spot

[1] [*Excursions*, p. 325; Riv. 399, 400.]

which Green inhabits, and left him in the calm sea. There is somewhat exceedingly pathetic to think of in such a life as he must have lived, — with no more to redeem it, — such a life as an average Carlisle man may be supposed to live drawn out to eighty years. And he has died, perchance, and there is nothing but the mark of his cider-mill left. Here was the cider-mill, and there the orchard, and there the hog-pasture; and so men lived, and ate, and drank, and passed away, — like vermin. Their long life was mere duration. As respectable is the life of the woodchucks, which perpetuate their race in the orchard still. That is the life of these *selectmen* (!) spun out. They will be forgotten in a few years, even by such as themselves, like vermin. They will be known only like Kibbe, who is said to have been a large man who weighed two hundred and fifty, who had five or six heavy daughters who rode to Concord meeting-house on horseback, taking turns, — they were so heavy that only one could ride at once. What, then, would redeem such a life? We only know that they ate, and drank, and built barns, and died and were buried, and still, perchance, their tombstones cumber the ground.[1] But if I could know that there was ever entertained over their cellar-hole some divine thought, which came as a messenger of the gods, that he who resided here acted once in his life from a noble impulse, rising superior to his grovelling and penurious life, if only a single verse of poetry or of poetic prose had ever been written or spoken or conceived here beyond a doubt, I should not think it in vain that man had lived here. It would to

[1] [Channing, pp. 176, 177.]

some extent be true then that God had lived here. That all his life he lived only as a farmer — as the most valuable stock only on a farm — and in no moments as a man!

Sept. 22. To the Three Friends' Hill over Bear Hill.

Yesterday and to-day the stronger winds of autumn have begun to blow, and the telegraph harp has sounded loudly. I heard it especially in the Deep Cut this afternoon, the tone varying with the tension of different parts of the wire. The sound proceeds from near the posts, where the vibration is apparently more rapid. I put my ear to one of the posts, and it seemed to me as if every pore of the wood was filled with music, labored with the strain, — as if every fibre was affected and being seasoned or timed, rearranged according to a new and more harmonious law. Every swell and change or inflection of tone pervaded and seemed to proceed from the wood, the divine tree or wood, as if its very substance was transmuted. What a recipe for preserving wood, perchance, — to keep it from rotting, — to fill its pores with music! How this wild tree from the forest, stripped of its bark and set up here, rejoices to transmit this music! When no music proceeds from the wire, on applying my ear I hear the hum within the entrails of the wood, — the oracular tree acquiring, accumulating, the prophetic fury.

The resounding wood! how much the ancients would have made of it! To have a harp on so great a scale, girdling the very earth, and played on by the winds of

Vol. III

every latitude and longitude, and that harp were, as it were, the manifest blessing of heaven on a work of man's! Shall we not add a tenth Muse to the immortal Nine? And that the invention thus divinely honored and distinguished — on which the Muse has condescended to smile — is this magic medium of communication for mankind!

To read that the ancients stretched a wire round the earth, attaching it to the trees of the forest, by which they sent messages by one named Electricity, father of Lightning and Magnetism, swifter far than Mercury, the stern commands of war and news of peace, and that the winds caused this wire to vibrate so that it emitted a harp-like and æolian music in all the lands through which it passed, as if to express the satisfaction of the gods in this invention. Yet this is fact, and we have yet attributed the invention to no god.[1]

I am astonished to see how brown and sere the groundsel or "fire-weed" on hillside by Heywood's Meadow, which has been touched by frost, already is, — as if it had died long months ago, or a fire had run through it. It is a very tender plant.

Standing on Bear Hill in Lincoln. The black birches (I think they are), now yellow, on the south side of Flint's Pond, on the hillside, look like flames. The chestnut trees are brownish-yellow as well as green. It is a beautifully clear and bracing air, with just enough coolness, full of the memory of frosty mornings, through which all things are distinctly seen and the fields look as smooth as velvet. The fragrance of grapes is on the

[1] [Channing, pp. 201, 202.]

breeze and the red drooping barberries sparkle amid the leaves. From the hill on the south side of the pond, the forests have a singularly rounded and bowery look, clothing the hills quite down to the water's edge and leaving no shore; the ponds are like drops of dew amid and partly covering the leaves. So the great globe is luxuriously crowded without margin.

The *Utricularia cornuta*, or horned utricularia, on the sandy pond-shore, not affected by the frost.

Sept. 23. Notwithstanding the fog, the fences this morning are covered with so thick a frost that you can write your name anywhere with your nail.

The partridge and the rabbit, — they still are sure to thrive like true natives of the soil, whatever revolutions occur. If the forest is cut off, many bushes spring up which afford them concealment, and they become more numerous than ever.

The sumach are among the reddest leaves at present. The telegraph harp sounds strongly to-day, in the midst of the rain. I put my ear to the trees and I hear it working terribly within, and anon it swells into a clear tone, which seems to concentrate in the core of the tree, for all the sound seems to proceed from the wood. It is as if you had entered some world-famous cathedral, resounding to some vast organ. The fibres of all things have their tension, and are strained like the strings of a lyre. I feel the very ground tremble under my feet as I stand near the post. This wire vibrates with great power, as if it would strain and rend the wood. What an awful and fateful music it must be to the worms in the wood! No better vermifuge were needed.[1] No danger that worms will attack this wood; such vibrating music would thrill them to death. I scare up large flocks of sparrows in the garden.

Sept. 24. Returning over the causeway from Flint's Pond the other evening (22d), just at sunset, I observed that while the west was of a bright golden color under a bank of clouds, — the sun just setting, — and not a tinge of red was yet visible there, there was a distinct purple tinge in the nearer atmosphere, so that Annursnack Hill, seen through it, had an exceedingly rich empurpled look. It is rare that we perceive this purple tint in the air, telling of the juice of the wild grape and poke-berries. The empurpled hills! Methinks I have only noticed this in cooler weather.

Last night was exceedingly dark. I could not see the sidewalk in the street, but only felt it with my feet. I was obliged to whistle to warn travellers of my nearness, and then I would suddenly find myself abreast of them without having seen anything or heard their footsteps. It was cloudy and rainy weather combined with the absence of the moon. So dark a night that, if a farmer who had come in a-shopping had spent but an hour after sunset in some shop, he might find himself a prisoner in the village for the night. Thick darkness.

8 A. M. — To Lee's Bridge *via* Conantum.

It is a cool and windy morning, and I have donned a thick coat for a walk. The wind is from the north, so that the telegraph harp does not sound where I cross.

[1] [Channing, p. 202.]

This windy autumnal weather is very exciting and bracing, clear and cold, after the rain of yesterday, it having cleared off in the night. I see a small hawk, a pigeon (?) hawk, over the Depot Field, which can hardly fly against the wind. At Hubbard's Grove the wind roars loudly in the woods. Grapes are ripe and already shrivelled by frost; barberries also. It is cattle-show day at Lowell.

Yesterday's wind and rain has strewn the ground with leaves, especially under the apple trees. Rain coming after frost seems to loosen the hold of the leaves, making them rot off. Saw a woodchuck disappearing in his hole. The river washes up-stream before the wind, with white streaks of foam on its dark surface, diagonally to its course, showing the direction of the wind. Its surface, reflecting the sun, is dazzlingly bright. The outlines of the hills are remarkably distinct and firm, and their surfaces bare and hard, not clothed with a thick air. I notice one red tree, a red maple, against the green woodside in Conant's meadow. It is a far brighter red than the blossoms of any tree in summer and more conspicuous. The huckleberry bushes on Conantum are all turned red.

What can be handsomer for a picture than our river scenery now? Take this view from the first Conantum Cliff. First this smoothly shorn meadow on the west side of the stream, with all the swaths distinct, sprinkled with apple trees casting heavy shadows black as ink, such as can be seen only in this clear air, this strong light, one cow wandering restlessly about in it and lowing; then the blue river, scarcely darker than

and not to be distinguished from the sky, its waves driven southward, or up-stream, by the wind, making it appear to flow that way, bordered by willows and button-bushes; then the narrow meadow beyond, with varied lights and shades from its waving grass, which for some reason has not been cut this year, though so dry, now at length each grass-blade bending south before the wintry blast, as if bending for aid in that direction; then the hill rising sixty feet to a terrace-like plain covered with shrub oaks, maples, etc., now variously tinted, clad all in a livery of gay colors, every bush a feather in its cap; and further in the rear the wood-crowned Cliff some two hundred feet high, where gray rocks here and there project from amidst the bushes, with its orchard on the slope; and to the right of the Cliff the distant Lincoln hills in the horizon. The landscape so handsomely colored, the air so clear and wholesome; and the surface of the earth is so pleasingly varied, that it seems rarely fitted for the abode of man.

In Cohush Swamp the sumach leaves have turned a very deep red, but have not lost their fragrance. I notice wild apples growing luxuriantly in the midst of the swamp, rising red over the colored, painted leaves of the sumach, and reminding me that they were ripened and colored by the same influences, — some green, some yellow, some red, like the leaves.

Fell in with a man whose breath smelled of spirit which he had drunk. How could I but feel that it was his own spirit that I smelt?[1] Behind Miles's, Darius Miles's, that was, I asked an Irishman how many po-

[1] [Channing, p. 217.]

tatoes he could dig in a day, wishing to know how well they yielded. "Well, I don't keep any account," he answered; "I scratch away, and let the day's work praise itself." Aye, there's the difference between the Irishman and the Yankee; the Yankee keeps an account. The simple honesty of the Irish pleases me. A sparrow hawk, hardly so big as a nighthawk, flew over high above my head, — a pretty little graceful fellow, too small and delicate to be rapacious.

Found a grove of young sugar maples (*Acer saccharinum*) behind what was Miles's. How silently and yet startlingly the existence of these sugar maples was revealed to me, — which I had not thought grew in my immediate neighborhood, — when first I perceived the entire edges of its leaves and their obtuse sinuses.

Such near hills as Nobscot and Nashoba have lost all their azure in this clear air and plainly belong to earth. Give me clearness nevertheless, though my heavens be moved further off to pay for it.

I perceive from the hill behind Lee's that much of the river meadows is not cut, though they have been very dry. The sun-sparkle on the river is dazzlingly bright in this atmosphere, as it has not been, perchance, for many a month. It is so cold I am glad to sit behind the wall. Still the great bidens blooms by the causeway-side beyond the bridge.[1]

At Clematis Brook I perceive that the pods or follicles of the *Asclepias Syriaca* now point upward. Did they before all point down? Have they turned up? They are already bursting. I release some seeds with

[1] [Channing, pp. 217, 218.]

Saw Mill Brook

From Conantum Cliff in September

the long, fine silk attached. The fine threads fly apart at once, open with a spring, and then ray themselves out into a hemispherical form, each thread freeing itself from its neighbor and all reflecting prismatic or rainbow tints. The seeds, besides, are furnished with wings, which plainly keep them steady and prevent their whirling round. I let one go, and it rises slowly and uncertainly at first, now driven this way, then that, by currents which I cannot perceive, and I fear it will make shipwreck against the neighboring wood; but no, as it approaches it, it surely rises above it, and then, feeling the strong north wind, it is borne off rapidly in the opposite direction, ever rising higher and higher and tossing and heaved about with every fluctuation of the air, till, at a hundred feet above the earth and fifty rods off, steering south, I lose sight of it. How many myriads go sailing away at this season, high over hill and meadow and river, on various tacks until the wind lulls, to plant their race in new localities, who can tell how many miles distant! And for this end these silken streamers have been perfecting all summer, snugly packed in this light chest, — a perfect adaptation to this end, a prophecy not only of the fall but of future springs. Who could believe in prophecies of Daniel or of Miller that the world would end this summer, while one milkweed with faith matured its seeds?[1]

On Mt. Misery some very rich yellow leaves — clear yellow — of the *Populus grandidentata*, which still love to wag, and tremble in my hands. Also canoe birches there.

[1] [Channing, pp. 204, 205.]

shaped seeds (or like a steelyards poise), which have derived their nutriment through a band of extremely fine silken threads attached by their extremities to the core. At length, when the seeds are matured and cease to require nourishment from the parent plant, being weaned, and the pod with dryness and frost bursts, the extremities of the silken threads detach themselves from the core, and from being the conduits of nutriment to the seed become the buoyant balloon which, like some spiders' webs, bear the seeds to new and distant fields. They merely serve to buoy up the full-fed seed. Far finer than the finest thread. Think of the great variety of balloons which at this season are buoyed up by similar means! I am interested in the fate or success of every such venture which the autumn sends forth.[1]

I am astonished to find how much travellers, both in the East and West, permit themselves to be imposed on by a name, — that the traveller in the East, for instance, presumes so great a difference between one Asiatic and another because one bears the title of a Christian and the other not. At length he comes to a sect of Christians, — Armenians or Nestorians, — and predicates of them a far greater civilization, civility, and humanity than of their neighbors, I suspect not with much truth. At that distance and so impartially viewed, I see but little difference between a Christian and a Mahometan; and so I perceive that European and American Christians, so called, are precisely like these heathenish Armenian and Nestorian Christians,

[1] [Channing, p. 205.]

The river and pond from the side of the sun look comparatively dark. As I look over the country westward and northwestward, the prospect looks already bleak and wintry. The surface of the earth between the forests is no longer green, but russet and hoary. You see distinctly eight or ten miles the russet earth and even houses, and then its outline is distinctly traced against the further blue mountains, thirty or thirty-five miles distant. You see distinctly perhaps to the height of land between the Nashua and Concord, and then the convexity of the earth conceals the further hills, though high, and your vision leaps a broad valley at once to the mountains.

Get home at noon.

At sundown the wind has all gone down.

Sept. 25. I was struck by the fitness of the expression chosen by the Irishman yesterday, — "I let the day's work praise itself." It was more pertinent than a scholar could have selected. But the Irishman does not trouble himself to inquire if the day's work has not reason to blame itself.

Some men are excited by the smell of burning powder, but I thought in my dream last night how much saner to be excited by the smell of new bread.

I did not see but the seeds of the milkweed would be borne many hundred miles, and those which were ripened in New England might plant themselves in Pennsylvania. Densely packed in a little oblong chest armed with soft downy prickles and lined with a smooth silky lining, lie some one or two hundreds such pear-

Vol. III

— not Christians, of course, in any true sense, but one other heathenish sect in the West, the difference between whose religion and that of the Mahometans is very slight and unimportant. Just such, not Christians but, as it were, heathenish Nestorian Christians, are we Americans. As if a Christian's dog were something better than a Mahometan's! I perceive no triumphant superiority in the so-called Christian over the so-called Mahometan. That nation is not Christian where the principles of humanity do not prevail, but the prejudices of race. I expect the Christian not to be superstitious, but to be distinguished by the clearness of his knowledge, the strength of his faith, the breadth of his humanity. A man of another race, an African for instance, comes to America to travel through it, and he meets with treatment exactly similar to, or worse than, that which the American meets with among the Turks, and Arabs, and Tartars. He is kicked out of the cars and hotels, or only admitted to the poorest place in them. The traveller, in both cases, finds the religion to be a mere superstition and frenzy, or rabidness.

The season of flowers may be considered as past now that the frosts have come. Fires have become comfortable. The evenings are pretty long.

2 P. M. — To bathe in Hubbard's meadow, thence to Cliffs.

It is beautiful weather, the air wonderfully clear and all objects bright and distinct. The air is of crystal purity. Both air and water are so transparent that the fisherman tries in vain to deceive the fish with his baits. Even our commonly muddy river looks clear to-day.

I find the water suddenly cold, and that the bathing days are over.

I see numerous butterflies still, yellow and small red, though not in fleets. Examined the hornets' nest near Hubbard's Grove, suspended from contiguous huckleberry bushes. The tops of the bushes appearing to grow out of it, little leafy sprigs, had a pleasing effect. An inverted cone eight or nine inches by seven or eight. I found no hornets now buzzing about it. Its entrance appeared to have been enlarged; so I concluded it had been deserted, but, looking nearer I discovered two or three dead hornets, men of war, in the entryway. Cutting off the bushes which sustained it, I proceeded to open it with my knife. First there were half a dozen layers of waved brownish paper resting loosely on one another, occupying nearly an inch in thickness, for a covering. Within were the six-sided cells in three stories, suspended from the roof and from one another by one or two suspension rods only, the lower story much smaller than the rest. And in what may be called the attic garret of the structure were two live hornets apparently partially benumbed with cold, which in the sun seemed rapidly recovering themselves, — their faculties. Most of the cells were empty, but in some were young hornets still, their heads projecting, apparently still-born, perhaps overtaken unexpectedly by cold weather. These insects appear to be very sensible to cold. The inner circles of cells were made of whitish, the outer of grayish, paper. It was like a deserted castle of the Mohawks, a few dead ones at the entrance of their castle.[1]

[1] [Channing, pp. 249, 250.]

landscape would be glorious to me, if I were assured that its sky was arched over a single hero. Hornets, hyenas, and baboons are not so great a curse to a country as men of a similar character. It is a charmed circle which I have drawn around my abode, having walked not with God but with the devil. I am too well aware when I have crossed this line.

Most New England biographies and journals — John Adams's not excepted — affect me like opening of the tombs.

The prudent and seasonable farmers are already plowing against another year.

Sept. 27. Here is a cloudy day, and now the fisherman is out. Some tall, many-flowered, bluish-white asters are still abundant by the brook-sides.

I never found a pitcher-plant without an insect in it. The bristles about the nose of the pitcher all point inward, and insects which enter or fall in appear for this reason unable to get out again. It is some obstacle which our senses cannot appreciate. Pitcher-plants more obvious now.

We of Massachusetts boast a good deal of what we do for the education of our people, of our district-school system; and yet our district schools are as it were but infant-schools, and we have no system for the education of the great mass who are grown up. I have yet to learn that one cent is spent by this town, this political community called Concord, directly to educate the great mass of its inhabitants who have long since left the district school; for the Lyceum, impor-

I watched the seeds of the milkweed rising higher and higher till lost in the sky, with as much interest as his friends did Mr. Lauriat.[1] I brought home two of the pods which were already bursting open, and amused myself from day to day with releasing the seeds and watching [them] rise slowly into the heavens till they were lost to my eye. No doubt the greater or less rapidity with which they rose would serve as a natural barometer to test the condition of the air.

The hornets' nest not brown but gray, two shades, whitish and dark, alternating on the outer layers or the covering, giving it a waved appearance.

In these cooler, windier, crystal days the note of the jay sounds a little more native. Standing on the Cliffs, I see them flitting and screaming from pine to pine beneath, displaying their gaudy blue pinions. Hawks, too, I perceive, sailing about in the clear air, looking white against the green pines, like the seeds of the milkweed. There is almost always a pair of hawks. Their shrill scream, that of the owls, and wolves are all related.

Sept. 26. Since I perambulated the bounds of the town, I find that I have in some degree confined myself, — my vision and my walks. On whatever side I look off I am reminded of the mean and narrow-minded men whom I have lately met there. What can be uglier than a country occupied by grovelling, coarse, and low-lived men? No scenery will redeem it. What can be more beautiful than any scenery inhabited by heroes? Any

[1] [Channing, p. 204.]

tant as it is comparatively, though absolutely trifling, is supported by individuals. There are certain refining and civilizing influences, as works of art, journals and books, and scientific instruments, which this community is amply rich enough to purchase, which would educate this village, elevate its tone of thought, and, if it alone improved these opportunities, easily make it the centre of civilization in the known world, put us on a level as to opportunities at once with London and Arcadia, and secure us a culture at once superior to both. Yet we spend sixteen thousand dollars on a Town House, a hall for our political meetings mainly, and nothing to educate ourselves who are grown up. Pray is there nothing in the market, no advantages, no intellectual food worth buying? Have Paris and London and New York and Boston nothing to dispose of which this village might try and appropriate to its own use? Might not this great villager adorn his villa with a few pictures and statues, enrich himself with a choice library as available, without being cumbrous, as any in the world, with scientific instruments for such as have a taste to use them? Yet we are contented to be countrified, to be provincial. I am astonished to find that in this Nineteenth Century, in this land of free schools, we spend absolutely nothing as a town on our own education, cultivation, civilization. Each town, like each individual, has its own character, — some more, some less, cultivated. I know many towns so mean-spirited and benighted that it would be a disgrace to belong to them. I believe that some of our New England villages within thirty miles of Boston are as boorish and barbarous communities as there are on the face of the earth. And how much superior are the best of them? If London has any refinement, any information to sell, why should we not buy it? Would not the town of Carlisle do well to spend sixteen thousand dollars on its own education at once, if it could only find a schoolmaster for itself? It has one man, as I hear, who takes the *North American Review*. That will never civilize them, I fear. Why should not the town itself take the London and Edinburgh Reviews, and put itself in communication with whatever sources of light and intelligence there are in the world? Yet Carlisle is very little behind Concord in these respects. I do not know but it spends its proportional part on education. How happens it that the only libraries which the towns possess are the district school libraries, — books for children only, or for readers who must needs be written down to? Why should they not have a library, if not so extensive, yet of the same stamp and more select than the British Museum? It is not that the town cannot well afford to buy these things, but it is unaspiring and ignorant of its own wants. It sells milk, but it only builds larger barns with the money which it gets for its milk. Undoubtedly every New England village is as able to surround itself with as many civilizing influences of this kind [as] the members of the English nobility; and here there need be no peasantry. If the London *Times* is the best newspaper in the world, why does not the village of Concord take it, that its inhabitants may read it, and not the second best? If the South Sea explorers have at length got their story ready, and Congress has

neglected to make it accessible to the people, why does not Concord purchase one for its grown-up children? [1]

Parrot in his "Journey to Ararat," speaking of the difficulty of reaching it owing to the lateness of the season, says of the surrounding country, "As early even as the month of June vegetable life becomes in a manner extinct, from the combined influence of the sun's rays, and the aridity of the atmosphere and soil: the plains and mountain-sides, being destitute of both wood and water, have no covering but a scanty and burnt herbage, the roots of which are so rarely visited by a refreshing shower that the reparatory power of nature is all but lost, while the active animal kingdom seeks protection against the heat and drought either by burrowing in the earth, or retiring to the cool and inaccessible retreats in Caucasus and the mountains of Asia Minor."

This reminds me of what I have observed even in our own summers. With us, too, "vegetable life becomes in a manner extinct" by the end of June, and the beholder is impressed as if "the reparatory power of nature [were] all but lost."

2 P. M. — Rowed down the river to Ball's Hill.

The maples by the riverside look very green yet, — have not begun to blush, nor are the leaves touched by frost. Not so on the uplands. The river is so low that, off N. Barrett's shore, some low islands are exposed, covered with a green grass like mildew. There are all

[1] [See *Journal*, vol. iv, Aug. 29, 1852; also *Walden*, pp. 120–122; Riv. 171–173.]

Vol. III

kinds of boats chained to trees and stumps by the riverside, — some from Boston and the salt [water], — but I think that none after all is so suitable and convenient as the simple flat-bottomed and light boat that has long been made here by the farmers themselves. They are better adapted to the river than those made in Boston.

From Ball's Hill the Great Meadows, now smoothly shorn, have a quite imposing appearance, so spacious and level. There is so little of this level land in our midst. There is a shadow on the sides of the hills surrounding (a cloudy day), and where the meadow meets them it is darkest. The shadow deepens down the woody hills and is most distinctly dark where they meet the meadow line. Now the sun in the west is coming out and lights up the river a mile off, so that it shines with a white light like a burnished silver mirror. The poplar tree seems quite important to the scene. The pastures are so dry that the cows have been turned on to the meadow, but they gradually desert it, all feeding one way. The patches of sunlight on the meadow look luridly yellow, as if flames were traversing it. It is a day for fishermen. The farmers are gathering in their corn. The *Mikania scandens* and the button-bushes and the pickerel-weed are sere and flat with frost. We looked down the long reach toward Carlisle Bridge. The river, which is as low as ever, still makes a more than respectable appearance here and is of generous width. Rambled over the hills toward Tarbell's. The huckleberry bushes appear to be unusually red this fall, reddening these hills. We scared a calf out of the meadow, which ran like a ship tossed on the waves, over the hills toward Tarbell's.

They run awkwardly, red oblong squares tossing up and down like a vessel in a storm, with great commotion.[1] We fell into the path, printed by the feet of the calves, with no cows' tracks. The note of the yellow-hammer is heard from the edges of the fields. The soapwort gentian looks like a flower prematurely killed by the frost. The soil of these fields looks as yellowish-white as the corn-stalks themselves. Tarbell's hip-roofed house looked the picture of retirement, — of cottage size, under its noble elm, with its heap of apples before the door and the wood coming up within a few rods, — it being far off the road. The smoke from his chimney so white and vapor-like, like a winter scene. The lower limbs of the willows and maples and button-bushes are covered with the black and dry roots of the water-marigold and the ranunculi, plants with filiform, capillary, root-like submerged leaves.

Sept. 28. A considerable part of the last two nights and yesterday, a steady and rather warm rain, such as we have not had for a long time. This morning it is still completely overcast and drizzling a little. Flocks of small birds — apparently sparrows, bobolinks (or some bird of equal size with a pencilled breast which makes a musical clucking), and piping goldfinches — are flitting about like leaves and hopping up on to the bent grass stems in the garden, letting themselves down to the heavy heads, either shaking or picking out a seed or two, then alighting to pick it up. I am amused to see them hop up on to the slender, drooping grass stems;

[1] [Channing, p. 221.]

then slide down, or let themselves down, as it were foot over foot, with great fluttering, till they can pick at the head and release a few seeds; then alight to pick them up. They seem to prefer a coarse grass which grows like a weed in the garden between the potato-hills, also the amaranth.[1]

It is an ill wind that blows nobody any good. They say that this has been a good year to raise turkeys, it has been so dry. So that we shall have something to be thankful for.

Hugh Miller, in his "Old Red Sandstone," speaking of "the consistency of style which obtains among the ichthyolites of this formation" and the "microscopic beauty of these ancient fishes," says: "The artist who sculptured the cherry stone consigned it to a cabinet, and placed a microscope beside it; the microscopic beauty of these ancient fish was consigned to the twilight depths of a primeval ocean. There is a feeling which at times grows upon the painter and the statuary, as if the perception and love of the beautiful had been sublimed into a kind of moral sense. Art comes to be pursued for its own sake; the exquisite conception in the mind, or the elegant and elaborate model, becomes all in all to the worker, and the dread of criticism or the appetite of praise almost nothing. And thus, through the influence of a power somewhat akin to conscience, but whose province is not the just and the good, but the fair, the refined, the exquisite, have works prosecuted in solitude, and never intended for the world, been found fraught with loveliness." The hesitation with

[1] [See p. 83.]

which this is said — to say nothing of its simplicity — betrays a latent infidelity more fatal far than that of the "Vestiges of Creation," which in another work this author endeavors to correct. He describes that as an exception which is in fact the rule. The supposed want of harmony between "the perception and love of the beautiful" and a delicate moral sense betrays what kind of beauty the writer has been conversant with. He speaks of his work becoming all in all to the worker, his rising above the dread of criticism and the appetite of praise, as if these were the very rare exceptions in a great artist's life, and not the very definition of it.

2 P. M. — To Conantum.

A warm, damp, mistling day, without much wind. The white pines in Hubbard's Grove have now a pretty distinct parti-colored look, — green and yellow mottled, — reminding me of some plants like the milkweed, expanding with maturity and pushing off their downy seeds. They have a singularly soft look. For a week or ten days I have ceased to look for new flowers or carry my botany in my pocket. The fall dandelion is now very fresh and abundant in its prime.

I see where the squirrels have carried off the ears of corn more than twenty rods from the corn-field into the woods. A little further on, beyond Hubbard's Brook, I saw a gray squirrel with an ear of yellow corn a foot long sitting on the fence, fifteen rods from the field. He dropped the corn, but continued to sit on the rail, where I could hardly see him, it being of the same color with himself, which I have no doubt he was well

aware of. He next took to a red maple, where his policy was to conceal himself behind the stem, hanging perfectly still there till I passed, his fur being exactly the color of the bark. When I struck the tree and tried to frighten him, he knew better than to run to the next tree, there being no continuous row by which he might escape; but he merely fled higher up and put so many leaves between us that it was difficult to discover him. When I threw up a stick to frighten him, he disappeared entirely, though I kept the best watch I could, and stood close to the foot of the tree. They are wonderfully cunning.[1]

The *Eupatorium purpureum* is early killed by frost and stands now all dry and brown by the sides of other herbs like the goldenrod and tansy, which are quite green and in blossom.

The railroads as much as anything appear to have unsettled the farmers. Our young Concord farmers and their young wives, hearing this bustle about them, seeing the world all going by as it were, — some daily to the cities about their business, some to California, — plainly cannot make up their minds to live the quiet, retired, old-fashioned, country-farmer's life. They are impatient if they live more than a mile from a railroad. While all their neighbors are rushing to the road, there are few who have character or bravery enough to live off the road. He is too well aware what is going on in the world not to wish to take some part in it. I was reminded of this by meeting S. Tuttle in his wagon.

The pontederia, which apparently makes the mass of

[1] [Channing, pp. 175, 176.]

the weeds by the side of the river, is all dead and brown and has been for some time; the year is over for it.

The mist is so thin that it is like haze or smoke in the air, imparting a softness to the landscape.

Sitting by the spruce swamp in Conant's Grove, I am reminded that this is a perfect day to visit the swamps, with its damp, mistling, mildewy air, so solemnly still. There are the spectre-like black spruces hanging with usnea moss, and in the rear rise the dark green pines and oaks on the hillside, touched here and there with livelier tints where a maple or birch may stand, this so luxuriant vegetation standing heavy, dark, sombre, like mould in a cellar. The peculiar tops of the spruce are seen against this.

I hear the barking of a red squirrel, who is alarmed at something, and a great scolding or ado among the jays, who make a great cry about nothing. The swamp is bordered with the red-berried alder, or prinos, and the button-bush. The balls of the last appear not half grown this season, — probably on account of the drought, — and now they are killed by frost.

This swamp contains beautiful specimens of the sidesaddle-flower (*Sarracenia purpurea*), better called pitcher-plant. They ray out around the dry scape and flower, which still remain, resting on rich uneven beds of a coarse reddish moss, through which the small-flowered andromeda puts up, presenting altogether a most rich and luxuriant appearance to the eye. Though the moss is comparatively dry, I cannot walk without upsetting the numerous pitchers, which are now full of water, and so wetting my feet. I once accidentally sat down on such a bed of pitcher-plants, and found an uncommonly wet seat where I expected a dry one. These leaves are of various colors from plain green to a rich striped yellow or deep red. No plants are more richly painted and streaked than the inside of the broad lips of these. Old Josselyn called this "Hollow-leaved Lavender." No other plant, methinks, that we have is so remarkable and singular.

Here was a large hornets' nest, which when I went to take and first knocked on it to see if anybody was at home, out came the whole swarm upon me lively enough. I do not know why they should linger longer than their fellows whom I saw the other day, unless because the swamp is warmer. They were all within and not working, however.

I picked up two arrowheads in the field beyond.

What honest, homely, earth-loving, unaspiring houses they used to live in! Take that on Conantum for instance, — so low you can put your hand on the eaves behind. There are few whose pride could stoop to enter such a house to-day. And then the broad chimney, built for comfort, not for beauty, with no coping of bricks to catch the eye, no alto or basso relievo.

The mist has now thickened into a fine rain, and I retreat.

Sept. 29. Van der Donck says of the water-beech (buttonwood), "This tree retains the leaves later than any other tree of the woods."

P. M. — To Goose Pond *via* E. Hosmer's; return by Walden.

Found Hosmer carting out manure from under his barn to make room for the winter. He said he was tired of farming, he was too old. Quoted Webster as saying that he had never eaten the bread of idleness for a single day, and thought that Lord Brougham might have said as much with truth while he was in the opposition, but he did not know that he could say as much of himself. However, he did not wish to be idle, he merely wished to rest.

Looked on Walden from the hill with the sawed pine stump on the north side. Scared up three black ducks, which rose with a great noise of their wings, striking the water. The hills this fall are unusually red, not only with the huckleberry, but the sumach and the blackberry vines.

Walden plainly can never be spoiled by the woodchopper, for, do what you will to the shore, there will still remain this crystal well. The intense brilliancy of the red-ripe maples scattered here and there in the midst of the green oaks and hickories on its hilly shore is quite charming. They are unexpectedly and incredibly brilliant, especially on the western shore and close to the water's edge, where, alternating with yellow birches and poplars and green oaks, they remind me of a line of soldiers, redcoats and riflemen in green mixed together.[1]

The pine is one of the richest of trees to my eye. It stands like a great moss, a luxuriant mildew, — the pumpkin pine, — which the earth produces without effort.

[1] [See *Excursions*, p. 283; Riv. 347; *Journal*, Oct. 31, 1858.]

Vol. III

The poet writes the history of his body.

Query: Would not the cellular tissue of the grass poly make good tinder? I find that, when I light it, it burns up slowly and entirely, without blaze, like spunk.

Sept. 30. To powder-mills, and set an intermediate bound-stone on the new road there.

Saw them making hoops for powder-casks, of alder and the sprouts of the white birch, which are red with whitish spots. How interesting it is to observe a particular use discovered in any material! I am pleased to find that the artisan has good reason for preferring one material to another for a particular purpose. I am pleased to learn that a man has detected any *use* in wood or stone or any material, or, in other words, its relation to man.

The white ash has got its autumnal mulberry hue. What is the autumnal tint of the black ash? The former contrasts strongly with the other shade-trees on the village street — the elms and buttonwoods — at this season, looking almost black at the first glance. The different characters of the trees appear [more clearly] at this season, when their leaves, so to speak, are ripe, than at any other, — than in the winter, for instance, when they are little remarkable and almost uniformly gray or brown, or in the spring and summer, when they are undistinguishably green. Now a red maple, an ash, a white birch, a *Populus grandidentata*, etc., is distinguished almost as far as they are visible. It is with leaves as with fruits and woods, and animals and men; when they are mature their different characters appear.

The sun has been obscured much of the day by passing clouds, but now, at 5 P. M., the sun comes out and by the very clear and brilliant light, — though the shadows begin to fall long from the trees, — it is proved how remarkably clear or pure the atmosphere is. According to all accounts, an hour of such a light would be something quite memorable in England.

As the wood of an old Cremona, its very fibre, perchance, harmoniously transposed and educated to resound melody, has brought a great price, so methinks these telegraph-posts should bear a great price with musical instrument makers. It is prepared to be the material of harps for ages to come, as it were put asoak in and seasoning in music.[1]

Saw a hornets' nest on a tree over the road near the powder-mills, thirty or forty feet high.

Even the pearl, like the beautiful galls on the oaks, is said to be the production of diseases, or rather obstruction, the fish covering as with a tear some rough obstruction that has got into his shell.

Oct. 1. 5 P. M. — Just put a fugitive slave, who has taken the name of Henry Williams, into the cars for Canada. He escaped from Stafford County, Virginia, to Boston last October; has been in Shadrach's place at the Cornhill Coffee-House; had been corresponding through an agent with his master, who is his father, about buying himself, his master asking $600, but he having been able to raise only $500. Heard that there were writs out for two Williamses, fugitives, and was informed by his fellow-servants and employer that Auger-

[1] [Channing, p. 202.]

hole Burns and others of the police had called for him when he was out. Accordingly fled to Concord last night on foot, bringing a letter to our family from Mr. Lovejoy of Cambridge and another which Garrison had formerly given him on another occasion. He lodged with us, and waited in the house till funds were collected with which to forward him. Intended to dispatch him at noon through to Burlington, but when I went to buy his ticket, saw one at the depot who looked and behaved so much like a Boston policeman that I did not venture that time. An intelligent and very well-behaved man, a mulatto.

There is art to be used, not only in selecting wood for a withe, but in using it. Birch withes are twisted, I suppose in order that the fibres may be less abruptly bent; or is it only by accident that they are twisted?

The slave said he could guide himself by many other stars than the north star, whose rising and setting he knew. They steered for the north star even when it had got round and appeared to them to be in the south. They frequently followed the telegraph when there was no railroad. The slaves bring many superstitions from Africa. The fugitives sometimes superstitiously carry a turf in their hats, thinking that their success depends on it.

These days when the trees have put on their autumnal tints are the gala days of the year, when the very foliage of trees is colored like a blossom. It is a proper time for a yearly festival, an agricultural show.

Candle-light. — To Conantum.
The moon not quite half full. The twilight is much

other bird. At 8 o'clock the fogs have begun, which, with the low half-moon shining on them, look like cobwebs or thin white veils spread over the earth. They are the dreams or visions of the meadow.

The second growth of the white pine is probably softer and more beautiful than the primitive forest ever afforded. The primitive forest is more grand with its bare mossy stems and ragged branches, but exhibits no such masses of green needles trembling in the light.

The elms are generally of a dirty or brownish yellow now.

Oct. 2. P. M. — Some of the white pines on Fair Haven Hill have just reached the acme of their fall; others have almost entirely shed their leaves, and they are scattered over the ground and the walls. The same is the state of the pitch pines. At the Cliffs, I find the wasps prolonging their short lives on the sunny rocks, just as they endeavored to do at my house in the woods. It is a little hazy as I look into the west to-day. The shrub oaks on the terraced plain are now almost uniformly of a deep red.

Oct. 4. Saturday. The emigrant has for weeks been tossing on the Atlantic and perchance as long ascending the St. Lawrence with contrary winds, conversant as yet in the New World only with the dreary coast of Newfoundland and Labrador and the comparatively wild shores of the river below the Isle of Orleans. It is said that, under these circumstances, the sudden

shorter now than a month ago, probably as the atmosphere is clearer and there is less to reflect the light. The air is cool, and the ground also feels cold under my feet, as if the grass were wet with dew, which is not yet the case. I go through Wheeler's corn-field in the twilight, where the stalks are bleached almost white, and his tops are still stacked along the edge of the field. The moon is not far up above the southwestern horizon. Looking west at this hour, the earth is an unvaried, undistinguishable black in contrast with the twilight sky. It is as if you were walking in night up to your chin. There is no wind stirring. An oak tree in Hubbard's pasture stands absolutely motionless and dark against the sky. The crickets sound farther off or fainter at this season, as if they had gone deeper into the sod to avoid the cold. There are no crickets heard on the alders on the causeway. The moon looks colder in the water, though the water-bugs are still active. There is a great change between this and my last moonlight walk. I experience a comfortable warmth when I approach the south side of a dry wood, which keeps off the cooler air and also retains some of the warmth of day. The voices of travellers in the road are heard afar over the fields, even to Conantum house. The stars are brighter than before. The moon is too far west to be seen reflected in the river at Tupelo Cliff, but the stars are reflected. The river is a dark mirror with bright points feebly fluctuating. I smell the bruised horsemint, which I cannot see, while I sit on the brown rocks by the shore. I see the glow-worm under the damp cliff. No whippoor-wills are heard to-night, and scarcely a note of any

apparition of Quebec on turning Point Levi makes a memorable impression on the beholder.[1]

Minott was telling me to-day that he used to know a man in Lincoln who had no floor to his barn, but waited till the ground froze, then swept it clean in his barn and threshed his grain on it. He also used to see men threshing their buckwheat in the field where it grew, having just taken off the surface down to a hard-pan.

Minott used the word "gavel" to describe a parcel of stalks cast on the ground to dry. His are good old English words, and I am always sure to find them in the dictionary, though I never heard them before in my life.

I was admiring his corn-stalks disposed about the barn to dry, over or astride the braces and the timbers, of such a fresh, clean, and handsome green, retaining their strength and nutritive properties so, unlike the gross and careless husbandry of speculating, money-making farmers, who suffer their stalks to remain out till they are dry and dingy and black as chips.

Minott is, perhaps, the most poetical farmer — who most realizes to me the poetry of the farmer's life — that I know. He does nothing with haste and drudgery, but as if he loved it. He makes the most of his labor, and takes infinite satisfaction in every part of it. He is not looking forward to the sale of his crops or any pecuniary profit, but he is paid by the constant satisfaction which his labor yields him. He has not too much land to trouble him, — too much work to do, — no hired man nor

[1] [*Excursions*, p. 88; Riv. 109.]

boy, — but simply to amuse himself and live. He cares not so much to raise a large crop as to do his work well. He knows every pin and nail in his barn. If another linter is to be floored, he lets no hired man rob him of that amusement, but he goes slowly to the woods and, at his leisure, selects a pitch pine tree, cuts it, and hauls it or gets it hauled to the mill; and so he knows the history of his barn floor.

Farming is an amusement which has lasted him longer than gunning or fishing. He is never in a hurry to get his garden planted and yet [it] is always planted soon enough, and none in the town is kept so beautifully clean.

He always prophesies a failure of the crops, and yet is satisfied with what he gets. His barn floor is fastened down with oak pins, and he prefers them to iron spikes, which he says will rust and give way. He handles and amuses himself with every ear of his corn crop as much as a child with its playthings, and so his small crop goes a great way. He might well cry if it were carried to market. The seed of weeds is no longer in his soil.

He loves to walk in a swamp in windy weather and hear the wind groan through the pines. He keeps a cat in his barn to catch the mice. He indulges in no luxury of food or dress or furniture, yet he is not penurious but merely simple. If his sister dies before him, he may have to go to the almshouse in his old age; yet he is not poor, for he does not want riches. He gets out of each manipulation in the farmers' operations a fund of entertainment which the speculating drudge hardly knows. With never-failing rheumatism and trembling hands,

he seems yet to enjoy perennial health. Though he never reads a book, — since he has finished the "Naval Monument," — he speaks the best of English.

Oct. 5. Sunday. I noticed on Friday, October 3d, that the willows generally were green and unchanged. The red maples varied from green through yellow to bright red. The black cherry was green inclining to yellow. (I speak of such trees as I chanced to see.) The apple trees, green but shedding their leaves like most of the trees. Elm, a dingy yellow. White ash, from green to dark purple or mulberry. White oak, green inclining to yellow. Tupelo, reddish yellow and red; tree bushed about the head, limbs small and slanting downward. Some maples when ripe are yellow or whitish yellow, others reddish yellow, others bright red, by the accident of the season or position, — the more or less light and sun, being on the edge or in the midst of the wood; just as the fruits are more or less deeply colored. Birches, green and yellow. Swamp white oak, a yellowish green. Black ash, greenish yellow and now sered by frost. Bass, sered yellowish.

Color in the maturity of foliage is as variable and little characteristic as naturalists have found it to be for distinguishing fishes and quadrupeds, etc.

Observed that the woodchuck has two or more holes, a rod or two apart: one, or the front door, where the excavated sand is heaped up; another, not so easily discovered, very small, round, without any sand about it, — being that by which he emerged, — smaller directly at the surface than beneath, on the principle by which

a well is dug,[1] making as small a hole as possible at the surface to prevent caving. About these holes is now seen their manure, apparently composed chiefly of the remains of crickets, which are seen crawling over the sand. Saw a very fat woodchuck on a wall, evidently prepared to go into winter quarters.[2]

Still purplish asters, and late goldenrods, and fragrant life-everlasting, and purple gerardia, great bidens, etc., etc. The dogwood by the Corner road has lost every leaf, its bunches of dry greenish berries hanging straight down from the bare stout twigs as if their peduncles were broken. It has assumed its winter aspect, — a mithridatic look. The prinos berries are quite red.[3] The panicled hawkweed is one of those yellowish spherical or hemispherical fuzzy-seeded plants which you see about the wood-paths and fields at present, which however only a strong wind can blow far. Saw by the pathside beyond the Conant spring that singular jelly-like sort of mushroom which I saw last spring while surveying White's farm; now red, globular, three quarters of an inch in diameter, covering the coarse moss by the ruts on the path-side with jelly-covered seeds(?).

2 p. m. — To the high open land between Bateman's Pond and the lime-kiln.

It is a still, cloudy afternoon, rather cool. As I go past Cheney's boat-house, the river looks lighter than the sky. The butternuts have shed nearly all their leaves, and their nuts are seen black against the sky. The white oaks are turned a reddish brown in some valleys. The

Norway cinquefoil and a smaller cinquefoil are still in blossom, and also the late buttercup. My companion remarked that the land (for the most part consisting of decayed orchards, huckleberry pastures, and forests) on both sides of the old Carlisle road, uneven and undulating like the road, appeared to be all in motion like the traveller, travelling on with him. Found a wild russet apple, very good, of peculiar form, flattened at the poles. Some red maples have entirely lost their leaves. The black birch is straw-colored.[1]

The rocks in the high open pasture are peculiar and interesting to walk over, for, though presenting broad and flat surfaces, the strata are perpendicular, producing a grained and curled appearance, — this rocky crown like a hoary head covered with curly hair, — or it is like walking over the edges of the leaves of a vast book. I wonder how these rocks were ever worn even thus smooth by the elements. The strata are remarkably serpentine or waving. It appears as if you were upon the axis of elevation, geologically speaking. I do not remember any other pasture in Concord where the rocks are so remarkable for this.

What is that fleshy or knot-fleshy [?] root which we found in the soil on the rocks by Bateman's Pond, which looked so edible? All meadows and swamps have been remarkably dry this year, and are still, notwithstanding the few showers and rainy days. Witch-hazel now in bloom. I perceive the fragrance of ripe grapes in the air, and after a little search discover the ground covered with them, — where the frost has stripped the vines

---

¹ [Channing, p. 221.]   ² [*Ibid.*]   ³ [Channing, p. 250.]

¹ [Channing, p. 250.]

of leaves, — still fresh and plump and perfectly ripe. The little conical burs of the agrimony stick to my clothes. The pale lobelia still blooms freshly. The rough hawkweed holds up its globes of yellowish fuzzy seeds as well as the panicled. The clouds have cleared away, the sun come out, and it is warmer and very pleasant. The declining sun, falling on the willows, etc., below Mrs. Ripley's and on the water, produces a rare, soft light, such as I do not often see, a greenish yellow.[1] The milkweed seeds are in the air. I see one in the river, which a minnow occasionally jostles.

Stood near a small rabbit, hardly half grown, by the old Carlisle road.

I hear the red-wing blackbirds by the riverside again, as if it were a new spring. They appear to have come to bid farewell. The birds appear to depart with the coming of the frosts, which kill vegetation and, directly or indirectly, the insects on which they feed. The American bittern (*Ardea minor*) flew across the river, trailing his legs in the water, scared up by us. This, according to Peabody, is the boomer (stake-driver). In their sluggish flight they can hardly keep their legs up. Wonder if they can soar.

8 P. M. — To Cliffs.

Moon three-quarters full. The nights now are very still, for there is hardly any noise of birds or of insects. The whip-poor-will is not heard, nor the mosquito; only the occasional lisping of some sparrow. The moon gives not a creamy but white, cold light, through which

[1] [Channing, p. 250.]

you can see far distinctly. About villages you hear the bark of dogs instead of the howl of wolves. When I descend into the valley by Wheeler's grain-field, I find it quite cold. The sand slopes in the Deep Cut gleam coldly as if covered with rime. As I go through the Spring Woods I perceive a sweet, dry scent from the underwoods like that of the fragrant life-everlasting. I suppose it is that. To appreciate the moonlight you must stand in the shade and see where a few rods or a few feet distant it falls in between the trees. It is a "milder day," made for some inhabitants whom you do not see. The fairies are a quiet, gentle folk, invented plainly to inhabit the moonlight. I frequently see a light on the ground within thick and dark woods where all around is in shadow, and haste forward, expecting to find some decayed and phosphorescent stump, but find it to be some clear moonlight that falls in between some crevice in the leaves. As moonlight is to sunlight, so are the fairies to men.

Standing on the Cliffs, no sound comes up from the woods. The earth has gradually turned more northward; the birds have fled south after the sun, and this impresses me, as well by day as by night, as a deserted country. There is a down-like mist over the river and pond, and there are no bright reflections of the moon or sheeniness from the pond in consequence, all the light being absorbed by the low fog.

Oct. 6. *Monday.* 12 M. — To Bedford line to set a stone by river on Bedford line.

The reach of the river between Bedford and Carlisle,

seen from a distance in the road to-day, as formerly, has a singularly ethereal, celestial, or elysian look. It is of a light sky-blue, alternating with smoother white streaks, where the surface reflects the light differently, like a milk-pan full of the milk of Valhalla partially skimmed, more gloriously and heavenly fair and pure than the sky itself. It is something more celestial than the sky above it. I never saw any water look so celestial. I have often noticed it. I believe I have seen this reach from the hill in the middle of Lincoln. We have names for the rivers of hell, but none for the rivers of heaven, unless the Milky Way be one. It is such a smooth and shining blue, like a panoply of sky-blue plates.[1] Our dark and muddy river has such a tint in this case as I might expect Walden or White Pond to exhibit, if they could be seen under similar circumstances, but Walden seen from Fair Haven is, if I remember, of a deep blue color tinged with green. Cerulean? Such water as that river reach appears to me of quite incalculable value, and the man who would blot that out of his prospect for a sum of money does not otherwise than to sell heaven.

George Thatcher, having searched an hour in vain this morning to find a frog, caught a pickerel with a mullein leaf.

The white ash near our house, which the other day was purple or mulberry-color, is now much more red.

7.30 P. M. — To Fair Haven Pond by boat, the moon four-fifths full, not a cloud in the sky; paddling all the way.

[1] [Channing, p. 251.]

The water perfectly still, and the air almost, the former gleaming like oil in the moonlight, with the moon's disk reflected in it.

When we started, saw some fishermen kindling their fire for spearing by the riverside. It was a lurid, reddish blaze, contrasting with the white light of the moon, with dense volumes of black smoke from the burning pitch pine roots rolling upward in the form of an inverted pyramid. The blaze reflected in the water, almost as distinct as the substance. It looked like tarring a ship on the shore of the Styx or Cocytus. For it is still and dark, notwithstanding the moon, and no sound but the crackling of the fire. The fishermen can be seen only near at hand, though their fire is visible far away; and then they appear as dusky, fuliginous figures, half enveloped in smoke, seen only by their enlightened sides. Like devils they look, clad in old coats to defend themselves from the fogs, one standing up forward holding the spear ready to dart, while the smoke and flames are blown in his face, the other paddling the boat slowly and silently along close to the shore with almost imperceptible motion.

The river appears indefinitely wide; there is a mist rising from the water, which increases the indefiniteness. A high bank or moonlit hill rises at a distance over the meadow on the bank, with its sandy gullies and clamshells exposed where the Indians feasted. The shore line, though close, is removed by the eye to the side of the hill. It is at high-water mark. It is continued till it meets the hill. Now the fisherman's fire, left behind, acquires some thick rays in the distance and becomes a star. As surely as sunlight falling through an irregular chink makes a round figure on the opposite wall, so the blaze at a distance appears a star. Such is the effect of the atmosphere. The bright sheen of the moon is constantly travelling with us, and is seen at the same angle in front on the surface of the pads; and the reflection of its disk in the rippled water by our boat-side appears like bright gold pieces falling on the river's counter. This coin is incessantly poured forth as from some unseen horn of plenty at our side.

(I hear a lark singing this morn (October 7th), and yesterday saw them in the meadows. Both larks and blackbirds are heard again now occasionally, seemingly after a short absence, as if come to bid farewell.)

I do not know but the weirdness of the gleaming oily surface is enhanced by the thin fog. A few water-bugs are seen glancing in our course.

I shout like a farmer to his oxen, — a short barking shout, — and instantly the woods on the eastern shore take it up, and the western hills a little up the stream; and so it appears to rebound from one side the river valley to the other, till at length I hear a farmer call to his team far up as Fair Haven Bay, whither we are bound.

We pass through reaches where there is no fog, perhaps where a little air is stirring. Our clothes are almost wet through with the mist, as if we sat in water. Some portions of the river are much warmer than others. In one instance it was warmer in the midst of the fog than in a clear reach.

In the middle of the pond we tried the echo again.

First the hill to the right took it up; then further up the stream on the left; and then after a long pause, when we had almost given it up, — and the longer expected, the more in one sense unexpected and surprising it was, — we heard a farmer shout to his team in a distant valley, far up on the opposite side of the stream, much louder than the previous echo; and even after this we heard one shout faintly in some neighboring town. The third echo seemed more loud and distinct than the second. But why, I asked, do the echoes always travel up the stream? I turned about and shouted again, and then I found that they all appeared equally to travel down the stream, or perchance I heard only those that did so.

As we rowed to Fair Haven's eastern shore, a moonlit hill covered with shrub oaks, we could form no opinion of our progress toward it, — not seeing the water-line where it met the hill, — until we saw the weeds and sandy shore and the tall bulrushes rising above the shallow water [like] the masts of large vessels in a haven. The moon was so high that the angle of excidence [sic] did not permit of our seeing her reflection in the pond.

As we paddled down the stream with our backs to the moon, we saw the reflection of every wood and hill on both sides distinctly. These answering reflections — shadow to substance — impress the voyager with a sense of harmony and symmetry, as when you fold a blotted paper and produce a regular figure, — a dualism which nature loves. What you commonly see is but half. Where the shore is very low the actual and reflected trees

Vol. III

appear to stand foot to foot, and it is but a line that separates them, and the water and the sky almost flow into one another, and the shore seems to float. As we paddle up or down, we see the cabins of muskrats faintly rising from amid the weeds, and the strong odor of musk is borne to us from particular parts of the shore. Also the odor of a skunk is wafted from over the meadows or fields. The fog appears in some places gathered into a little pyramid or squad by itself, on the surface of the water. Home at ten.

Oct. 7. This morning the fog over the river and the brooks and meadows running into it has risen to the height of forty or fifty feet.

1 P. M. — To river; by boat to Corner Bridge.

A very still, warm, bright, clear afternoon. Our boat so small and low that we are close to the water.[1]

The muskrats all the way are now building their houses, about two thirds done. They are of an oval form (looking down on them), sloping upward from the smaller end, by which the rat apparently ascends, and composed of mouthfuls of pontederia leaf-stems (now dead), the capillaceous roots or leaves of the water-marigold (?) and other capillaceous-leaved water-plants, flag-root, a plant which looks like a cock's tail or a peacock's feather in form,[2] clamshells, etc., sometimes rising from amidst the dead pontederia stems or resting on the button-bushes or the willows. The mouthfuls are disposed in layers successively smaller, forming a somewhat conical mound. Seen at this stage they show some art and a

[1] *Vide* forward, Nov. 9th. [2] The *Potamogeton Robbinsii.*

good deal of labor. We pulled one to pieces to examine the inside. There was a small cavity, which might hold two or three full-grown muskrats, just above the level of the water, quite wet and of course dark and narrow, communicating immediately with a gallery under water. There were a few pieces of the white root of some water-plant — perhaps a pontederia or a lily root — in it. There they dwell, in close contiguity to the water itself, always in a wet apartment, in a wet coat never changed, with immeasurable water in the cellar, through which is the only exit. They have reduced life to a lower scale than Diogenes. Certainly they do not fear cold, ague, or consumption. Think of bringing up a family in such a place, — worse than a Broad Street cellar. But probably these are not their breeding-places. The muskrat and the fresh-water mussel are very native to our river. The Indian, their human compeer, has departed. There is a settler whom our lowlands and our fogs do not hurt. One of the fishermen speared one last night. How long has the muskrat dined on mussels? The river mud itself will have the ague as soon as he. What occasion has he for a dentist? Their unfinished, rapidly rising nests look now like truncated cones. They seem to be all building at once in different parts of the river, and to have advanced equally far.

The weeds being dead and the weather cooler, the water is more transparent. Now is the time to observe such weeds as have not been destroyed. The fishes are plainly seen. Saw a pickerel which had swallowed a smaller fish, with the tail projecting from his mouth. There is a dirty-looking weed quite submerged, with short, densely crowded, finely divided leaves, in dense masses atop, like the tops of spruce trees, more slender below. The shores for a great width are occupied by the dead leaves and stems of the pontederia, which give the river a very wild look. There is a strong-scented, green plant which looks like a fresh-water sponge or coral, clumsy-limbed like a dead tree, or a cactus. A long narrow grass like a fresh-water eel-grass.

The swamp white oak on the meadow, which was blown down in the spring, is still alive, as if it had been supported by the sap in its trunk. The dirt still adheres to its roots, which are of the color of an elephant's skin.

I suppose it is the *Nuphar Kalmiana* which I find in blossom in deep water, though its long stem, — four feet or more, — round and gradually tapering toward the root with no leaves apparent, makes me doubt a little. Apparently five sepals, greenish and yellow without, yellow within, eight small petals, many stamens, stigma eight-rayed.

Saw the *Ardea minor* walking along the shore, like a hen with long green legs. Its pencilled throat is so like the reeds and shore, amid which it holds its head erect to watch the passer, that it is difficult to discern it. You can get very near it, for it is unwilling to fly, preferring to hide amid the weeds. The lower parts of the willows and the button-bushes are black with the capillaceous leaves and stems of the water-marigold, etc.[1]

The raw edge of the rushes (common *Juncus militaris* I think it is), two to four feet high, in dense fields along

[1] [This is queried in pencil.]

Vol. III

Oct. 8. Wednesday. A slight wind now fills the air with elm leaves. The nights have been cool of late, so that a fire has been comfortable, but the last was quite warm.

2 P. M. — To the Marlborough road.

This day is very warm, yet not bright like the last, but hazy. Picked up an Indian gouge on Dennis's Hill. The foliage has lost its very bright tints now; it is more dull, looks dry, or as if burnt, even. The very ground or grass is crisped with drought, and yields a crispy sound to my feet. The woods are brownish, reddish, yellowish merely, excepting of course the evergreens. It is so warm that I am obliged to take off my neck-handkerchief and laborers complain of the heat.

By the side of J. P. Brown's grain-field I picked up some white oak acorns in the path by the wood-side, which I found to be unexpectedly sweet and palatable, the bitterness being scarcely perceptible. To my taste they are quite as good as chestnuts. No wonder the first men lived on acorns. Such as these are no mean food, such as they are represented to be. Their sweetness is like the sweetness of bread, and to have discovered this palatableness in this neglected nut, the whole world is to me the sweeter for it. I am related again to the first men. What can be handsomer, wear better to the eye, than the color of the acorn, like the leaves on which they fall polished, or varnished? To find that acorns are edible, — it is a greater addition to one's stock of life than would be imagined. I should be at least equally pleased if I were to find that the grass tasted sweet and nutritious. It increases the number of my friends; it diminishes the

the shore, in various stages of decay, looks like a level rainbow skirting the water's edge and reflected in the water, though a single one, or a few near at hand, do not exhibit very marked or distinct colors. But [at] a distance from a shore which is lined with them, the colors are very distinct and produce a pleasing effect, — first, next the water, a few inches of pink; then a faint narrow line, or halo, of yellowish; then a broad and lively green, the proper color of the rush; then a sunny yellow, passing into the brown of the dead and sered tops. The different parts of the plant from the surface of the water to its tip, when you look at the edge of a large and dense field of them, produce five distinct horizontal and parallel bars of different colors like a level rainbow, — a rainbow-like effect, — making a pleasing border to the river in a bright day like this; and occasionally the sunlight from the rippled surface produced by our boat, reflected on them, enhances the effect. The colors pass into each other so gradually and indefinitely, as if it were the reflection of the sun falling on a mist.

The rounded hills beyond the clamshells look velvety smooth as we are floating down the stream, covered with the now red blackberry vines. The oaks look light against the sky, rising story above story. I see small whitish and pinkish polygonums along the waterside.

There is a great difference between this season and a month ago, — warm as this happens to be, — as between one period of your life and another. A little frost is at the bottom of it.

It is a remarkable difference between night and day on the river, that there is no fog by day.

number of my foes. How easily at this season I could feed myself in the woods! There is mast for me too, as well as for the pigeon and the squirrel. This Dodonean fruit.

The goldfinches are in the air. I hear a blackbird also, and see a downy woodpecker, and see and hear a hairy one. The seeds of the pasture thistle are not so buoyed up by their down as the milkweed.

In the forenoon commonly I see nature only through a window; in the afternoon my study or apartment in which I sit is a vale.

The farmers are ditching, — redeeming more meadow, — getting corn, collecting their apples, threshing, etc.

I cannot but believe that acorns were intended to be the food of man. They are agreeable to the palate, as the mother's milk to the babe. The sweet acorn tree is famous and well known to the boys. There can be no question respecting the wholesomeness of this diet.

This warm day is a godsend to the wasps. I see them buzzing about the broken windows of deserted buildings, as Jenny Dugan's, — the yellow-knotted. I smell the dry leaves like hay from the woods. Some elms are already bare. The basswood here is quite sere. The pines are still shedding their leaves. This brook by Jenny's is always a pleasant sight and sound to me. In the spring I saw the sucker here. It is remarkable through what narrow and shallow brooks a sucker will be seen to dart, and a trout. I perceive that some white oaks are quite red. The black oaks are yellowish. I know not surely whether the brighter red and more divided leaf is that of the red or the scarlet oak. The jointed polygonum in the Marlborough road is an interesting flower, it is so late, so bright a red, — though inobvious from its minuteness, — without leaves, above the sand like sorrel, mixed with other minute flowers and the empty chalices of the trichostema. I saw one blue curl still adhering. The puffballs are split open and rayed out on the sand like five or *ten* (!) fingers. The milkweed seeds must be carried far, for it is only when a strong wind is blowing that they are loosened from their pods. An arrowhead at the desert. *Spergula arvensis* — corn-spurry (some call it tares) — at the acorn tree. Filled my pockets with acorns. Found another gouge on Dennis's Hill. To have found the Indian gouges and tasted sweet acorns, — is it not enough for one afternoon?

The sun set red in haze, visible fifteen minutes before setting, and the moon rose in like manner at the same time.

This evening, I am obliged to sit with my door and window open, in a thin coat, which I have not done for three weeks at least.

A warm night like this at this season produces its effect on the village. The boys are heard at play in the street now, at 9 o'clock, in greater force and with more noise than usual. My neighbor has got out his flute.

There is more fog than usual. The moon is full. The tops of the woods in the horizon seen above the fog look exactly like long, low black clouds, the fog being the color of the sky.

Oct. 9. Heard two screech owls in the night. Boiled a quart of acorns for breakfast, but found them not so palatable as raw, having acquired a bitterish taste, per-

chance from being boiled with the shells and skins; yet one would soon get accustomed to this.

The sound of foxhounds in the woods, heard now, at 9 A. M., in the village, reminds me of mild winter mornings.

2 P. M. — To Conantum.
In the maple woods the ground is strewn with new-fallen leaves. I hear the green locust again on the alders of the causeway, but he is turned a straw-color. The warm weather has revived them. All the acorns on the same tree are not equally sweet. They appear to dry sweet. From Conantum I see them getting hay from the meadow below the Cliffs. It must have been quite dry when cut. The black ash has lost its leaves, and the white here is dry and brownish yellow, not having turned mulberry. I see half a dozen snakes in this walk, green and striped (one very young striped one), who appear to be out enjoying the sun. They appear to make the most of the last warm days of the year. The hills and plain on the opposite side of the river are covered with deep warm red leaves of shrub oaks. On Lee's hillside by the pond, the old leaves of some pitch pines are almost of a golden-yellow hue, seen in the sunlight, — a rich autumnal look. The green are, as it were, set in the yellow.

The witch-hazel here is in full blossom on this magical hillside, while its broad yellow leaves are falling. Some bushes are completely bare of leaves, and leather-colored they strew the ground. It is an extremely interesting plant, — October and November's child, and yet

Vol. III

reminds me of the very earliest spring. Its blossoms smell like the spring, like the willow catkins; by their color as well as fragrance they belong to the saffron dawn of the year, suggesting amid all these signs of autumn, falling leaves and frost, that the life of Nature, by which she eternally flourishes, is untouched. It stands here in the shadow on the side of the hill, while the sunlight from over the top of the hill lights up its topmost sprays and yellow blossoms. Its spray, so jointed and angular, is not to be mistaken for any other. I lie on my back with joy under its boughs. While its leaves fall, its blossoms spring. The autumn, then, is indeed a spring. All the year is a spring. I see two blackbirds high overhead, going south, but I am going north in my thought with these hazel blossoms. It is a faery place. This is a part of the immortality of the soul. When I was thinking that it bloomed too late for bees or other insects to extract honey from its flowers, — that perchance they yielded no honey, — I saw a bee upon it. How important, then, to the bees this late-blossoming plant!

The circling hawk steers himself through the air like the skater, without a visible motion.

The hoary cinquefoil in blossom.

A large sassafras tree behind Lee's, two feet diameter at ground. As I return over the bridge, I hear a song sparrow singing on the willows exactly as in spring. I see a large sucker rise to the surface of the river. I hear the crickets singing loudly in the walls as they have not done (so loudly) for some weeks, while the sun is going down shorn of his rays by the haze.

There is a thick bed of leaves in the road under Hubbard's elms. This reminds me of Cato, as if the ancients made more use of nature. He says, "Stramenta si deerunt, frondem iligneam legito, eam substernito ovibus bubusque." (If litter is wanting, gather the leaves of the holm oak and strew them under your sheep and oxen.) In another place he says, "Circum vias ulmos serito, et partim populos, uti frondem ovibus et bubus habeas." I suppose they were getting that dry meadow grass for litter. There is little or no use made by us of the leaves of trees, not even for beds, unless it be sometimes to rake them up in the woods and cast into hog-pens or compost-heaps.

Cut a stout purple cane of pokeweed.

Oct. 10. The air this morning is full of bluebirds, and again it is spring. There are many things to indicate the renewing of spring at this season. The blossoming of spring flowers, — not to mention the witch-hazel, — the notes of spring birds, the springing of grain and grass and other plants.

Ah, I yearn toward thee, my friend, but I have not confidence in thee. We do not believe in the same God. I am not thou; thou art not I. We trust each other to-day, but we distrust to-morrow. Even when I meet thee unexpectedly, I part from thee with disappointment. Though I enjoy thee more than other men, yet I am more disappointed with thee than with others. I know a noble man; what is it hinders me from knowing him better? I know not how it is that our distrust, our hate, is stronger than our love. Here I have been on

what the world would call friendly terms with one fourteen years, have pleased my imagination sometimes with
loving him; and yet our hate is stronger than our love.
Why are we related, yet thus unsatisfactorily? We
almost are a sore to one another. Ah, I am afraid
because thy relations are not my relations. Because I
have experienced that in some respects we are strange
to one another, strange as some wild creature. Ever and
anon there will come the consciousness to mar our love
that, change the theme but a hair's breadth, and we are
tragically strange to one another. We do not know what
hinders us from coming together. But when I consider
what my friend's relations and acquaintances are, what
his tastes and habits, then the difference between us gets
named. I see that all these friends and acquaintances
and tastes and habits are indeed my friend's self. In the
first place, my friend is prouder than I am, — and I am
very proud, perchance.

2 P. M. — To Flint's Pond.

It was the seed-vessel of the Canada snapdragon in
the Marlborough road that I mistook for a new flower.
This is still in bloom in the Deep Cut. The chickadee,
sounding all alone, now that birds are getting scarce, reminds me of the winter, in which it almost alone is heard.

How agreeable to the eye at this season the color of
new-fallen leaves (I am going through the young woods
where the locusts grow near Goose Pond), sere and crisp!
When freshly fallen, with their forms and their veins
still distinct, they have a certain life in them still. The
chestnut leaves now almost completely cover the ground

under the trees, lying up light and deep, so clean and
wholesome, whether to look at or handle or smell, — the
tawny leaves, nature's color. They look as if they might
all yield a wholesome tea. They are rustling down fast
from the young chestnuts, leaving their bare and black-
ish-looking stems. You make a great noise now walking in the woods, on account of the dry leaves, especially
chestnut and oak and maple, that cover the ground. I
wish that we might make more use of leaves than we do.
We wait till they are reduced to virgin mould. Might
we not fill beds with them? or use them for fodder or
litter? After they have been flattened by the snow and
rain, they will be much less obvious. Now is the time
to enjoy the dry leaves. Now all nature is a dried herb,
full of medicinal odors. I love to hear of a preference
given to one kind of leaves over another for beds. Some
maples which a week ago were a mass of yellow foliage
are now a fine gray smoke, as it were, and their leaves
cover the ground.

Plants have two states, certainly, — the green and the
dry. The lespedeza and primrose heads, etc., etc., —
I look on these with interest, as if they were newly blossoming plants.

Going through Britton's clearing, I find a black snake
out enjoying the sun. I perceive his lustrous greenish
blackness. He holds up his head and threatens; then
dashes off into the woods, making a great rustling among
the leaves. This might be called snake summer or snakes'
week.

Our Irish washwoman, seeing me playing with the
milkweed seeds, said they filled beds with that down in

her country. They are not indigenous in Europe, at any
rate.

The horned utricularia by Flint's Pond still. There
a gunner has built his bower to shoot ducks from, far
out amid the rushes. The nightshade leaves have turned
a very dark purple, almost steel-blue, lighter, more like
mulberry, underneath, with light glossy, viscid or sticky
spots above, as if covered with dew. I do not think of
any other leaf of this color. The delicate pinkish leaves
of the *Hypericum Virginicum* about the shore of the
pond. The yellow leaves of the clethra mixed with the
green.

The stones of Flint's Pond shore are comparatively
flat, as the pond is flatter than Walden. The young trees
and bushes — perhaps the birches particularly — are
covered now with a small yellowish insect like a louse,
spotted with green above, which cover the hat and
clothes of him who goes through them. Now certainly
is the season for rushes, for, most other weeds being
dead, these are the more obvious along the shore of the
ponds and rivers. A very fair canoe birch near Flint's
Pond.

The witch-hazel loves a hillside with or without wood
or shrubs. It is always pleasant to come upon it unexpectedly as you are threading the woods in such places.
Methinks I attribute to it some elvish quality apart from
its fame. It affects a hillside partially covered with
young copsewood. I love to behold its *gray speckled
stems*. The leaf first green, then yellow for a short season, then, when it touches the ground, tawny leather-
color. As I stood amid the witch-hazels near Flint's

Pond, a flock of a dozen chickadees came flitting and
singing about me with great ado, — a most cheering
and enlivening sound, — with incessant *day-day-day* and
a fine wiry strain betweenwhiles, flitting ever nearer
and nearer and nearer, inquisitively, till the boldest was
within five feet of me; then suddenly, their curiosity
satiated, they flit by degrees further away and disappear,
and I hear with regret their retreating *day-day-days*.

Saw a smooth sumach beyond Cyrus Smith's, very
large.

The elms in the village have lost many of their leaves,
and their shadows by moonlight are not so heavy as last
month.

Another warm night.

Oct. 12. Sunday. Yesterday afternoon, saw by the
brook-side above Emerson's the dwarf primrose in blossom, the Norway cinquefoil and fall dandelions which
are now drying up, the houstonia, buttercups, small
goldenrods, and various asters, more or less purplish.

The seeds of the bidens, — without florets, — or
beggar-ticks, with four-barbed awns like hay-hooks,
now adhere to your clothes, so that you are all bristling
with them. Certainly they adhere to nothing so readily
as to woolen cloth, as if in the creation of them the invention of woolen clothing by man had been foreseen.
How tenacious of its purpose to spread and plant its
race! By all methods nature secures this end, whether
by the balloon, or parachute, or hook, or barbed spear
like this, or mere lightness which the winds can waft.
What are those seeds, big as skunk-cabbage seeds,

amid leafless stalks like pontederia in the brooks, now bending their stems ready to plant themselves at the bottom?

The swamp-pink buds begin to show.

Blackbirds and larks are about, and the flicker or yellow-hammer, so beautifully spotted (in the hand), and the goldfinches. I see a cow in the meadow with a new-dropped calf by her side.

The *Anemone nemorosa* in bloom and the *Potentilla sarmentosa*, or running cinquefoil, which springs in April, now again springing.

I love very well this cloudy afternoon, so sober and favorable to reflection after so many bright ones. What if the clouds shut out the heavens, provided they concentrate my thoughts and make a more celestial heaven below! I hear the crickets plainer; I wander less in my thoughts, am less dissipated; am aware how shallow was the current of my thoughts before. Deep streams are dark, as if there were a cloud in their sky; shallow ones are bright and sparkling, reflecting the sun from their bottoms. The very wind on my cheek seems more fraught with meaning.

Many maples around the edges of the meadows are now quite bare, like smoke.

I seem to be more constantly merged in nature; my intellectual life is more obedient to nature than formerly, but perchance less obedient to spirit. I have less memorable seasons. I exact less of myself. I am getting used to my meanness, getting to accept my low estate. O if I could be discontented with myself! If I could feel anguish at each descent!

The sweet-fern is losing its leaves. I see where a field of oats has been cradled, by the railroad, — alternate white and dark green stripes, the width of a swath, running across the field. I find it arises from the stubble being bent a particular way by the cradle, as the cradler advanced, and accordingly reflecting the light but one way, and if I look over the field from the other side, the first swath will be dark and the latter white.

Minott shells all his corn by hand. He has got a boxful ready for the mill. He will not winnow it, for he says the chaff (?) makes it lie loose and dry faster. He tells me that Jacob Baker, who raises as fair corn as anybody, gives all the corn of his own raising to his stock, and buys the flat yellow corn of the South for bread; and yet the Northern corn is worth the most per bushel. Minott did not like this kind of farming any better than I. Baker also buys a great quantity of "shorts" below for his cows, to make more milk. He remembers when a Prescott, who lived where E. Hosmer does, used to let his hogs run in the woods in the fall, and they grew quite fat on the acorns, etc., they found, but now there are few nuts, and it is against the law. He tells me of places in the woods which to his eyes are unchanged since he was a boy, as natural as life. He tells me, then, that in some respects he is still a boy. And yet the gray squirrels were ten then to one now. But for the most part, he says, the world is turned upside down.

P. M. — To Cliffs.

I hear Lincoln bell tolling for church. At first I thought of the telegraph harp. Heard at a distance,

the sound of a bell acquires a certain vibratory hum, as it were from the air through which it passes, like a harp. All music is a harp music at length, as if the atmosphere were full of strings vibrating to this music. It is not the mere sound of the bell, but the humming in the air, that enchants me, just [as the] azure tint which much air or distance imparts delights the eye. It is not so much the object, as the object clothed with an azure veil. All sound heard at a great distance thus tends to produce the same music, vibrating the strings of the universal lyre. There comes to me a melody which the air has strained, which has conversed with every leaf and needle of the woods. It is by no means the sound of the bell as heard near at hand, and which at this distance I can plainly distinguish, but its vibrating echoes, that portion of the sound which the elements take up and modulate, — a sound which is very much modified, sifted, and refined before it reaches my ear. The echo is to some extent an independent sound, and therein is the magic and charm of it. It is not merely a repetition of my voice, but it is in some measure the voice of the wood.[1]

A cloudy, misty day with rain more or less steady. This gentle rain is fast loosening the leaves, — I see them filling the air at the least puff, — and it is also flattening down the layer which has already fallen. The pines on Fair Haven have shed nearly all their leaves. Butter-and-eggs still blooms. Barrels of apples lie under the trees. The Smiths have carried their last load of peaches to market.

[1] [*Walden*, pp. 136, 137; Riv. 192, 193.]

To-day no part of the heavens is so clear and bright as Fair Haven Pond and the river. Though the air [is] quite misty, yet the island wood is distinctly reflected. Ever and anon I see the mist thickening in the southwest and concealing trees which were before seen, and revealing the direction and limits of the valleys, — precursor of harder rain which soon passes again.

Minott calls the stake-driver "belcher-squelcher." Says he has seen them when making the noise. They go *slug-toot, slug-toot, slug-toot.* Told me of his hunting gray squirrels with old Colonel Brooks's hound. How the latter came into the yard one day, and he spoke to him, patted him, went into the house, took down his gun marked London, thought he would go a-squirrel-hunting. Went over among the ledges, away from Brooks's, for Tige had a dreadful strong voice and could be heard as far as a cannon, and he was plaguy afraid Brooks would hear him. How Tige treed them on the oaks on the plain below the Cliffs. He could tell by his bark when he had treed one; he never told a lie. And so he got six or seven. How Tige told him from a distance that he had got one, but when he came up he could see nothing; but still he knew that Tige never told a lie, and at length he saw his head, in a crotch high up in the top of a very tall oak, and though he did n't expect to get him, he knocked him over.

Oct. 13. Drizzling, misty showers still, with a little misty sunshine at intervals. The trees have lost many of their leaves in the last twenty-four hours. The sun has got so low that it will do to let his rays in on the earth; the cattle do not need their shade now, nor men. Warmth is more desirable now than shade.

The alert and energetic man leads a more intellectual life in winter than in summer. In summer the animal and vegetable in him are perfected as in a torrid zone; he lives in his senses mainly. In winter cold reason and not warm passion has her sway; he lives in thought and reflection; he lives a more spiritual, a less sensual, life. If he has passed a merely sensual summer, he passes his winter in a torpid state like some reptiles and other animals.

The mind of man in the two seasons is like the atmosphere of summer compared with the atmosphere of winter. He depends more on himself in winter, — on his own resources, — less on outward aid. Insects, it is true, disappear for the most part, and those animals which depend upon them; but the nobler animals abide with man the severity of winter. He migrates into his mind, to perpetual summer. And to the healthy man the winter of his discontent never comes.

Mr. Pratt told me that Jonas (?) Melvin found a honey-bees' nest lately near Beck Stow's swamp with twenty-five pounds of honey in it, in the top [of] a maple tree which was blown down. There is now a large swarm in the meeting-house chimney, in a flue not used. Many swarms have gone off that have not been heard from.

Oct. 14. Down the railroad before sunrise.

A freight-train in the Deep Cut. The sun rising over the woods. When the vapor from the engine rose above the woods, the level rays of the rising sun fell on it. It

presented the same redness, — morning red, — inclining to saffron, which the clouds in the eastern horizon do.

There was but little wind this morning, yet I heard the telegraph harp. It does not require a strong wind to wake its strings; it depends more on its direction and the tension of the wire apparently. A gentle but steady breeze will often call forth its finest strains, when a strong but unsteady gale, blowing at the wrong angle withal, fails to elicit any melodious sound.

In the psychological world there are phenomena analogous to what zoölogists call *alternate reproduction*, in which it requires several generations unlike each other to evolve the perfect animal. Some men's lives are but an aspiration, a yearning toward a higher state, and they are wholly misapprehended, until they are referred to, or traced through, all their metamorphoses. We cannot pronounce upon a man's intellectual and moral state until we foresee what metamorphosis it is preparing him for.

It is said that "the working bees . . . are barren females. The attributes of their sex . . . seem to consist only in their solicitude for the welfare of the new generation, of which they are the natural guardians, but not the parents." (Agassiz and Gould.[1]) This phenomenon is paralleled in man by maiden aunts and bachelor uncles, who perform a similar function.

"The muskrat," according to Agassiz and Gould, "is found from the mouth of Mackenzie's River to Florida." It is moreover of a type peculiar to temperate America. He is a native American surely. He neither dies of con-

[1] [*Principles of Zoölogy*, Boston, 1851.]

Vol. III

sumption in New England nor of fever and ague at the South and West. Thoroughly acclimated and naturalized.

"The hyenas, wild-boars, and rhinoceroses of the Cape of Good Hope have no analogues on the American continent." At the last menagerie I visited they told me that one of the hyenas came from South America!

There is something significant and interesting in the fact that the fauna of Europe and that of the United States are very similar, pointing to the fitness of this country for the settlement of Europeans.

They say, "There are . . . many species of animals whose numbers are daily diminishing, and whose extinction may be foreseen; as the Canada deer (Wapiti), the Ibex of the Alps, the Lämmergeyer, the bison, the beaver, the wild turkey, etc." With these, of course, is to be associated the Indian.

They say that the house-fly has followed man in his migrations.

One would say that the Yankee belonged properly to the *northern* temperate fauna, the region of the pines.

Oct. 15. *Wednesday.* 8.30 A. M. — Up the river in a boat to Pelham's Pond with W. E. C.

(But first a neighbor sent in a girl to inquire if I knew where worm-seed grew, otherwise called "Jerusalem-oak" (so said the recipe which she brought cut out of a newspaper), for her mistress's hen had the "gapes." But I answered that this was a Southern plant and [I] knew not where it was to be had. Referred her to the poultry book. Also the next proprietor commenced

stoning and settling down the stone for a new well, an operation which I wished to witness, purely beautiful, simple, and necessary. The stones laid on a wheel, and continually added to above as it is settled down by digging under the wheel. Also Goodwin, with a partridge and a stout mess of large pickerel, applied to me to dispose of a mud turtle which he had found moving the mud in a ditch. Some men will be in the way to see such movements.)

The muskrat-houses appear now for the most part to be finished. Some, it is true, are still rising. They line the river all the way. Some are as big as small haycocks. The river is still quite low, though a foot or more higher than when I was last on it. There is quite a wind, and the sky is full of flitting clouds, so that sky and water are quite unlike that warm, bright, transparent day when I last sailed on the river, when the surface was of such oily smoothness. You could not now study the river bottom for the black waves and the streaks of foam. When the sun shines brightest to-day, its pyramidal-shaped sheen (when for a short time we are looking up-stream, for we row) is dazzling and blinding. It is pleasant to hear the sound of the waves and feel the surging of the boat, — an inspiriting sound, as if you were bound on adventures. It is delightful to be tossed about in such a harmless storm, and see the waves look so angry and black. We see objects on shore — trees, etc., — much better from the boat, — from a low point of view. It brings them against the sky, into a novel point of view at least. The otherwise low on the meadows, as well as the hills, is conspicuous. I perceive that the bulrushes are nibbled along the shore, as if they had been cut by a scythe, yet in such positions as no mower could have reached, even outside the flags. Probably the muskrat was the mower, — for his houses. In this cool sunlight, Fair Haven Hill shows to advantage. Every rock and shrub and protuberance has justice done it, the sun shining at [an] angle on the hill and giving each a shadow. The hills have a hard and distinct outline, and I see into their very texture. On Fair Haven I see the sunlit light-green grass in the hollows where snow makes water sometimes, and on the russet slopes. Cut three white pine boughs opposite Fair Haven, and set them up in the bow of our boat for a sail. It was pleasant [to] hear the water begin to ripple under the prow, telling of our easy progress. We thus without a tack made the south side of Fair Haven, then threw our sails overboard, and the moment after mistook them for green bushes or weeds which had sprung from the bottom unusually far from shore. Then to hear the wind sough in your sail, — that is to be a sailor and hear a land sound. The grayish-whitish mikania, all fuzzy, covers the endless button-bushes, which are now bare of leaves. Observed the verification of the Scripture saying "as a dog returneth to his vomit." Our black pup, sole passenger in the stern, perhaps made seasick, vomited, then cleaned the boat again most faithfully and with a bright eye, licking his chops and looking round for more.

We comment on the boats of different patterns, — dories (?), punts, bread-troughs, flatirons, etc., etc., — which we pass, the prevailing our genuine dead-river boats, not to be matched by Boston carpenters. One

farmer blacksmith whom we know, whose boat we pass in Sudbury, has got a horseshoe nailed about the sculling-hole; — keeps off the witches too? The water carriages of various patterns and in various conditions, — some for pleasure (against the gentleman's seat?); some for ducking, small and portable; some for honest fishing, broad and leaky but not cranky; some with spearing fixtures; some stout and square-endish for hay boats; one canal-boat or mud-scow in the weeds, not worth getting down the stream, like some vast pike that could swallow all the rest, proper craft for our river.

In some places in the meadows opposite Bound Rock, the river seemed to have come to an end, it was so narrow suddenly. After getting in sight of Sherman's Bridge, counted nineteen birches on the right-hand shore in one whirl.

Now commenced the remarkable meandering of the river, so that we seemed for some [time] to be now running up, then running down parallel with a long, low hill, tacking over the meadow in spite of ourselves. Landed at Sherman's Bridge. An apple tree, made scrubby by being browsed by cows. Through what early hardships it may attain to bear a sweet fruit![1] No wonder it is prompted to grow thorns at last, to defend itself from such foes.[2] The pup nibbles clams, or plays with a bone no matter how dry. Thus the dog can be taken on a river voyage, but the cat cannot. She is too set in her ways. Now again for the Great Meadows. What meandering! The Serpentine, our river should be called.

[1] [*Excursions*, p. 306; Riv. 376.]
[2] [*Excursions*, p. 304; Riv. 373.]

What makes the river love to delay here? Here come to study the law of meandering. We see the vast meadow studded with haycocks. We suspect that we have got to visit them all. It proves even so. Now we run down one haycock, now another. The distance made is frequently not more than a third the distance gone. Between Sherman's Bridge and Causeway Bridge is about a mile and three quarters in a straight line, but we judged that we went more than three miles. Here the "pipes" (at first) line the shore, and muskrat-houses still. A duck (a loon?) sails within gunshot, unwilling to fly; also a stake-driver (*Ardea minor*) rises with prominent breast or throat bone, as if badly loaded, his ship. Now no button-bushes line the stream, the changeable (?) stream; no rocks exist; the shores are lined with, first, in the water, still green polygonum, then wide fields of dead pontederia, then great bulrushes, then various reeds, sedges, or tall grasses, also dead thalictrum(?), — or is it cicuta? Just this side the causeway bridges a field, like a tall corn-field, of tall rustling reeds (?), ten feet high with broadish leaves and large, now seedy tufts, standing amid the button-bushes and great bulrushes.[1] I remember to have seen none elsewhere in this vicinity, unless at Fresh Pond, and there are they not straighter? Also, just beyond the bridges, very tall flags from six to eight feet high, leaves like the cat-tail but no tail. What are they?[2] We pass under two bridges above the Causeway Bridge. After passing under the first one of these two, — at the mouth of Larnum Brook, which is fed from Blandford's Pond,

[1] *Arundo Phragmites?*   [2] Yes, a tall kind of cat-tail.

comes from Marlborough through Mill Village, and has a branch, Hop Brook, from south of Nobscot, — we see Nobscot, very handsome in a purplish atmosphere in the west, over a *very* deep meadow, which makes far up. A good way to skate to Nobscot, or within a mile or two. To see a distant hill from the surface of water over a low and very broad meadow, much better than to see it from another hill. This perhaps the most novel and so memorable prospect we got.

Walked across half a mile to Pelham's Pond, whose waves were dashing quite grandly. A house near, with two grand elms in front. I have seen other elms in Wayland. This pond a good point to skate to in winter, when it is easily accessible. Now we should have to draw our boat.

On the return, as in going, we expended nearly as much time and labor in counteracting the boat's tendency to whirl round, it is so miserably built. Now and then, — aye, aye, almost an everlasting *now*, — it will take the bits in its mouth and go round in spite of us, though we row on one side only, for the wind fills the after part of the boat, which is nearly out of water, and we therefore get along best and fastest when the wind is strong and dead ahead. That's the kind of wind we advertise to race in. To row a boat thus all the day, with an hour's intermission, making fishes of ourselves as it were, putting on these long fins, realizing the finny life! Surely oars and paddles are but the fins which a man may use.

The very pads stand perpendicular (on their edges) before this wind, — which appears to have worked more to the north, — showing their red under sides. The muskrats have exposed the clamshells to us in heaps all along the shore; else most [would] not know that a clam existed. If it were not for muskrats, how little would the fisherman see or know of fresh-water clamshells or clams! In the Great Meadows again the loon (?) rises, and again alights, and a heron (?) too flies sluggishly away, with vast wings, and small ducks which seem to have no tails, but their wings set quite aft. The crows ashore are making an ado, perchance about some carrion. We taste some swamp white oak acorns at the south end of Bound Rock Meadow.

The sun sets when we are off Israel Rice's. A few golden coppery clouds, intensely glowing, like fishes in some molten metal of the sky, and then the small scattered clouds grow blue-black above, or one half, and reddish or pink the other half, and after a short twilight the night sets in. We think it is pleasantest to be on the water at this hour. We row across Fair Haven in the thickening twilight and far below it, steadily and without speaking. As the night draws on her veil, the shores retreat; we only keep in the middle of this low stream of light; we know not whether we float in the air or in the lower regions. We seem to recede from the trees on shore or the island very slowly, and yet a few reaches make all our voyage. Nature has divided it agreeably into reaches. The reflections of the stars in the water are dim and elongated like the zodiacal light straight down into the depths, but no mist rises to-night. It is pleasant not to get home till after dark, — to steer by the lights of the villagers. The lamps in the houses twinkle now like stars; they shine doubly bright.

Vol. III

trees, to distinguish a natural disease or scar from the "blazing" of an axe.

Has the aspen (?) poplar any more of a red heart than the other? The powder man does not want the red-hearted. Even this poor wood has its use.

Observed an oak, — a red or black, — at a pigeon-place, whose top limbs were cut off perhaps a month ago; the leaves had dried a sort of snuff-yellow and rather glossy.

Oct. 22. The pines, both white and pitch, have now shed their leaves, and the ground in the pine woods is strewn with the newly fallen needles. The fragrant life-everlasting is still fresh, and the Canada snapdragon still blooms bluely by the roadside. The rain and damp-ness have given birth to a new crop of mushrooms. The small willow-like shrub (sage willow (?), *Salix longi-rostris*, Mx.) is shedding its small leaves, which turn black in drying and cover the path.

Oct. 23. It is never too late to learn. I observed to-day the Irishman who helped me survey *twisting* the branch of a birch for a withe, and *before* he cut it off; and also, wishing to stick a tall, smooth pole in the ground, cut a notch in the side of it by which to drive it with a hatchet.

Oct. 26. I awoke this morning to infinite regret. In my dream I had been riding, but the horses bit each other and occasioned endless trouble and anxiety, and it was my employment to hold their heads apart. Next I sailed over the sea in a small vessel such as the North-

Rowed about twenty-four miles, going and coming. In a straight line it would be fifteen and one half.

Oct. 16. The new moon, seen by day, reminds me of a poet's cheese. Surveying for Loring to-day. Saw the Indian Ditch, so called. A plant newly leaving out, a shrub; looks somewhat like shad blossom. To-night the spearers are out again.

Oct. 17. Surveying for Loring. A severe frost this morning, which puts [us] one remove further from summer.

Oct. 19. The Indian (?)' Ditch crosses the road be-yond Loring's, running south seven and one half west, or within about two and a half degrees of the true me-ridian. According to Stephen Hosmer's plan of Thomas Jones's woodland, made in 1766, the ditch where Derby and Loring bound on it must be about eighty-four rods from old town line.

To the northern voyager who does not see the sun for three months, night is expanded into winter, and day into summer.

Observed to-day on the edge of a wood-lot of Lor-ing's, where his shrub oaks bounded on a neighbor's small pitch pines, which grew very close together, that the line of separation was remarkably straight and dis-tinct, neither a shrub oak nor a pine passing its limit, the ground where the pines grew having apparently been cultivated so far, and its edges defined by the plow.

A surveyor must be curious in studying the wounds of

men used, as it were to the Bay of Fundy, and thence overland I sailed, still over the shallows about the sources of rivers toward the deeper *channel* of a stream which emptied into the Gulf beyond, — the Miramichi, was it? Again I was in my own small pleasure-boat, learning to sail on the sea, and I raised my sail before my anchor, which I dragged far into the sea. I saw the buttons which had come off the coats of drowned men, and suddenly I saw my dog — when I knew not that I had one — standing in the sea up to his chin, to warm his legs, which had been wet, which the cool wind numbed. And then I was walking in a meadow, where the dry season permitted me to walk further than usual, and there I met Mr. Alcott, and we fell to quoting and referring to grand and pleasing couplets and single lines which we had read in times past; and I quoted one which in my waking hours I have no knowledge of, but in my dream it was familiar enough. I only know that those which I quoted expressed regret, and were like the following, though they were not these, *viz.:* —

> "The short parenthesis of life was sweet,"
> "The remembrance of youth is a sigh," etc.

It had the word "memory" in it!! And then again the instant that I awoke, methought I was a musical instru-ment from which I heard a strain die out, — a bugle, or a clarionet, or a flute. My body was the organ and channel of melody, as a flute is of the music that is breathed through it. My flesh sounded and vibrated still to the strain, and my nerves were the chords of the lyre. I awoke, therefore, to an infinite regret, — to find myself, not the thoroughfare of glorious and world-stirring inspirations, but a scuttle full of dirt, such a thoroughfare only as the street and the kennel, where, perchance, the wind may sometimes draw forth a strain of music from a straw.

I can partly account for this. Last evening I was reading Laing's account of the Northmen, and though I did not write in my Journal, I remember feeling a fertile regret, and deriving even an inexpressible satisfaction, as it were, from my ability to feel regret, which made that evening richer than those which had preceded it. I heard the last strain or flourish, as I woke, played on my body as the instrument. Such I knew I had been and might be again, and my regret arose from the consciousness how little like a musical instrument my body was now.

Oct. 27. This morning I wake and find it snowing and the ground covered with snow; quite unexpectedly, for last night it was rainy but not cold.

The obstacles which the heart meets with are like granite blocks which one alone cannot move. She who was as the morning light to me is now neither the morning star nor the evening star. We meet but to find each other further asunder, and the oftener we meet the more rapid our divergence. So a star of the first magnitude pales in the heavens, not from any fault in the observer's eye nor from any fault in itself, perchance, but because its progress in its own system has put a greater distance between.

The night is oracular. What have been the intimations of the night? I ask. How have you passed the night? Good-night!

My friend will be bold to conjecture; he will guess bravely at the significance of my words.

The cold numbs my fingers this morning. The strong northwest wind blows the damp snow along almost horizontally. The birds fly about as if seeking shelter.

Perhaps it was the young of the purple finch that I saw sliding down the grass stems some weeks ago; or was it the white-throated finch?[1]

Winter, with its *inwardness*, is upon us. A man is constrained to sit down, and to think.

The *Ardea minor* still with us. Saw a woodcock[2] feeding, probing the mud with its long bill, under the railroad bridge within two feet of me for a long time. Could not scare it far away. What a disproportionate length of bill! It is a sort of badge they [wear] as a punishment for greediness in a former state.

The highest arch of the stone bridge is six feet eight inches above the present surface of the water, which I should think was more than a foot higher than it has been this summer, and is four inches below the long stone in the east abutment.

Oct. 31. The wild apples are now getting palatable. I find a few left on distant trees, which the farmer thinks it not worth his while to gather. He thinks that he has better in his barrels, but he is mistaken, unless he has a walker's appetite and imagination, neither of which can he have.[3] These apples cannot be too knurly and rusty and crabbed (to look at). The knurliest will have some redeeming traits, even to the eyes.

[1] [See p. 29.]   [2] Or snipe?   [3] [*Excursions*, p. 308; Riv. 378.]

Vol. III

II

NOVEMBER, 1851

(ÆT. 34)

Nov. 1. Saturday. R. W. E. says that Channing calls [   ][1] "seven feet of sandstone with a spoonful of wit."

It is a rare qualification to be able to state a fact simply and adequately, to digest some experience cleanly, to say "yes" and "no" with authority, to make a square edge, to conceive and suffer the truth to pass through us living and intact, even as a waterfowl an eel, as it flies over the meadows, thus stocking new waters. First of all a man must see, before he can say. Statements are made but partially. Things are said with reference to certain conventions or existing institutions, not absolutely. A fact truly and absolutely stated is taken out of the region of common sense and acquires a mythologic or universal significance. Say it and have done with it. Express it without expressing yourself. See not with the eye of science, which is barren, nor of youthful poetry, which is impotent. But taste the world and digest it. It would seem as if things got said but rarely and by chance. As you *see*, so at length will you *say*. When facts are seen superficially, they are seen as they lie in relation to certain institutions, perchance. But I would have them expressed as more deeply seen, with deeper

[1] [Name scratched out.]

You will discover some evening redness dashed or sprinkled on some protuberance or in some cavity. It is rare that the summer lets an apple go without streaking or spotting it on some part of its sphere, though perchance one side may only seem to betray that it has once fallen in a brick-yard, and the other have been bespattered from a roily ink-bottle.[1] Some red stains it will have, commemorating the mornings and evenings it has witnessed; some dark and rusty blotches, in memory of the clouds and foggy mildewy days that have passed over it; and a spacious field of green, reflecting the general face of nature, — green even as the fields; or yellowish ground, if it has a sunny flavor, — yellow as the harvests, or russet as the hills.[2] The saunterer's apple not even the saunterer can eat in the house.[3] The noblest of fruits is the apple. Let the most beautiful or swiftest have it.[4]

The robins now fly in flocks.

[1] [*Excursions*, p. 314; Riv. 385, 386.]
[2] [*Excursions*, p. 314; Riv. 386.]
[3] [*Excursions*, p. 311; Riv. 382.]
[4] [*Excursions*, p. 297; Riv. 364, 365.]

references; so that the hearer or reader cannot recognize them or apprehend their significance from the platform of common life, but it will be necessary that he be in a sense translated in order to understand them; when the truth respecting his things shall naturally exhale from a man like the odor of the muskrat from the coat of the trapper. At first blush a man is not capable of reporting truth; he must be drenched and saturated with it first. What was *enthusiasm* in the young man must become *temperament* in the mature man. Without excitement, heat, or passion, he will survey the world which excited the youth and threw him off his balance. As all things are significant, so all words should be significant. It is a fault which attaches to the speaker, to speak flippantly or superficially of anything. Of what use are words which do not move the hearer, — are not oracular and fateful? A style in which the matter is all in all, and the manner nothing at all.

In your thoughts no more than in your walks do you meet men. In moods I find such privacy as in dismal swamps and on mountain-tops.

Man recognizes laws little enforced, and he condescends to obey them. In the moment that he feels his superiority to them as compulsatory, he, as it were, courteously reënacts them but to obey them.

This on my way to Conantum, 2.30 P. M. It is a bright, clear, warm November day. I feel blessed. I love my life. I warm toward all nature. The woods are now much more open than when I last observed them; the leaves have fallen, and they let in light, and I see the sky through them as through a crow's wing in every direction. For

the most part only the pines and oaks (white?) retain their leaves. At a distance, accordingly, the forest is green and reddish. The crickets now sound faintly and from very deep in the sod.

Minott says that G. M. Barrett told him that Amos Baker told him that during Concord Fight he went over behind the hill to the old Whittaker place (Sam Buttrick's) and stayed. Yet he was described as the only survivor of Concord Fight. Received a pension for running away?

Fall dandelions look bright still. The grass has got a new greenness in spots. At this season there are stranger sparrows or finches about. The skunk-cabbage is already pushing up again. The alders have lost their leaves, and the willows except a few shrivelled ones.

It is a remarkable day for fine gossamer cobwebs. Here in the causeway, as I walk toward the sun, I perceive that the air is full of them streaming from off the willows and spanning the road, all stretching across the road, and yet I cannot see them in any other direction, and feel not one. It looks as if the birds would be incommoded. They have the effect of a shimmer in the air. This shimmer, moving along them as they are waved by the wind, gives the effect of a drifting storm of light. It is more like a fine snow-storm which drifts athwart your path than anything else. What is the peculiar condition of the atmosphere, to call forth this activity? If there were no sunshine, I should never find out that they existed, I should not know that I was bursting a myriad barriers. Though you break them

with your person, you feel not one. Why should this day be so distinguished?

The rain of night before last has raised the river at least two feet, and the meadows wear a late-fall look. The naked and weedy stems of the button-bush are suddenly submerged; you no longer look for pickerel from the bridges. The shallow and shrunken shore is also submerged. I see so far and distinctly, my eyes seem to slide in this clear air. The river is peculiarly sky-blue to-day, not dark as usual. It is all in the air. The cinquefoil on Conantum. Counted one hundred and twenty-five crows in one straggling flock moving westward. The red shrub oak leaves abide on the hills. The witch-hazels have mostly lost their blossoms, perhaps on account of the snow. The ground wears its red carpet under the pines. The pitch pines show new buds at the end of their plumes. How long this?

Saw a canoe birch by road beyond the Abel Minott house; distinguished it thirty rods off by the chalky whiteness of its limbs. It is of a more unspotted, transparent, and perhaps pinkish white than the common, has considerable branches as well as white ones, and its branches do not droop and curl downward like that. There will be some loose curls of bark about it. The common birch is *finely* branched and has frequently a *snarly* head; the former is a more open and free-growing tree. If at a distance you see the birch near its top forking into two or more white limbs, you may know it for a canoe birch. You can tell where it has grown after the wood has turned to mould by a small fragment of its bark still left, — if it divides readily. The common

birch is more covered with moss, has the aspect of having grown more slowly, and has many more branches. I have heard of a man in Maine who copied the whole Bible on to birch bark. It was so much easier than to write that sentence which the birch tree stands for.

Nov. 2. Sunday. The muskrat-houses are mostly covered by the rise of the river! — not a very unexpected one either. Old wells as well as walls must be among the oldest monuments of civilized man here. How old may be the most ancient well which men use to-day. Saw a canoe birch beyond Nawshawtuct, growing out of the middle of a white pine stump, which still showed the mark of the axe, sixteen inches in diameter at its bottom, or two feet from the ground, or where it had first taken root on the stump.

Nov. 4. To Saw Mill Brook by Turnpike; return by Walden.

I see why the checkerberry was so called, — *Mitchella repens* (we call it falsely partridge-berry), — for its leaves, variegated, *checker* the ground, now mingled with red berries and partially covered with the fallen leaves of the forest.

Saw Mill Brook is peculiar among our brooks as a mountain brook. For a short distance it reminds me of runs I have seen in New Hampshire. A brawling little stream tumbling through a rocky wood, ever down and down. Where the wood has been cleared, it is almost covered with the rubbish which the woodchoppers have left, the fine tree-tops, which no one cared to make into fagots. It was quite a discovery when I first came upon this brawling mountain stream in Concord woods. Rising out of an obscure meadow in the woods, for some fifty or sixty rods of its course it is a brawling mountain stream in our quiet Concord woods, as much obstructed by rocks — rocks out of all proportion to its tiny stream — as a brook can well be. And the rocks are bared throughout the wood on either side, as if a torrent had anciently swept through here; so unlike the after character of the stream. Who would have thought that, on tracing it up from where it empties into the larger Mill Brook in the open peat meadows, it would conduct him to such a headlong and impetuous youth. Perchance it should be called a "force." [1] It suggests what various moods may attach to the same character. Ah, if I but knew that some minds which flow so muddily in the lowland portion of their course, when they cross the highways, tumbled thus impetuously and musically, mixed themselves with the air in foam, but a little way back in the woods! that these dark and muddy pools, where only the pout and the leech are to be found, issued from pure trout streams higher up! that the man's thoughts ever flowed as sparkling mountain water, that trout there loved to glance through his dimples, where the witch-hazel hangs over his stream!

This stream is here sometimes quite lost amid the rocks, which appear as if they had been arched over it, but which, in fact, it has undermined and found its way beneath, and they have merely fallen together archwise, as they were undermined.

[1] No, a force is a fall.

It is truly a raw and gusty day, and I hear a tree creak sharply like a bird, a phœbe. The hypericums stand red or lake over the brook. The jays with their scream are at home in the scenery. I see where trees have spread themselves over the rocks in a scanty covering of soil, been undermined by the brook, then blown over and, as they fell, lifted and carried over with them all the soil, together with considerable rocks. So from time to time, by these natural levers, rocks are removed from the middle of the stream to the shore. The slender chestnuts, maples, elms, and white ash trees, which last are uncommonly numerous here, are now all bare of leaves, and a few small hemlocks, with their now thin but unmixed and fresh green foliage, stand over and cheer the stream and remind me of winter, the snows which are to come and drape them and contrast with their green, and the chickadees that are to flit and lisp amid them.

Ah, the beautiful tree, the hemlock, with its green canopy, under which little grows, not exciting the cupidity of the carpenter, whose use most men have not discovered! I know of some memorable ones worth walking many miles to see. These little cheerful hemlocks, — the lisp of chickadees seems to come from them now, — each standing with its foot on the very edge of the stream, reaching sometimes part way over its channel, and here and there one has lightly stepped across. These evergreens are plainly as much for shelter for the birds as for anything else. The fallen leaves are so thick they almost fill the bed of the stream and choke it. I hear the runnel gurgling underground. As if this puny rill had ever tossed these rocks about! these storied rocks with their

fine lichens and sometimes red stains as of Indian blood on them! There are a few bright-green ferns lying flat by the sides of the brook, but it is cold, cold, withering to all else. A whitish lichen on the witch-hazel rings it here. I glimpse the frizzled tail of a red squirrel with a chestnut in its mouth on a white pine.

The ants appear to be gone into winter quarters. Here are two bushels of fine gravel, piled up in a cone, overpowering the grass, which tells of a corresponding cavity.

Nov. 6. I had on my "bad-weather clothes" at Quebec like Olaf Trygvesson, the Northman, when he went to Thing in England.[1]

Nov. 7. 8 A. M. — To Long Pond with W. E. C. [Four fifths of a page missing.] From there we looked over the lower land and westward to the Jenkins house and Wachusett; the latter to-day a very faint blue, almost lost in the atmosphere. Entering Wayland, the sluggish country town, C. remarked that we might take the town if we had a couple of oyster-knives. We marvelled as usual at the queer-looking building which C. thought must be an engine-house, but which a boy told us was occupied as a shoemaker's shop but was built for a library. C. was much amused here by a bigger schoolboy whom we saw on the common, one of those who stretch themselves on the back seats and can chew up a whole newspaper into a spitball to plaster the wall with when the master's back

[1] [*Excursions*, p. 28; Riv. 34.]

is turned; made considerable fun of him, and thought this the *event* of Wayland. Soon got into a country new to us, in Wayland, opposite to Pelham or Heard's Pond, going across lots. Cedar hills and valleys near the river. A well-placed farmhouse with great old chestnuts near it, the greatest collection of large chestnuts which I remember to have seen. It is a tree full and well outlined at top, being bushy with short twigs at top, — a firm outline. Some long, moraine-like hills covered with cedars, with the hill country of Wayland on our left. The white oaks still thick with leaves turned pinkish? From a pretty high hill on the left of the road, after passing a very large field which was being plowed, a glorious view of the meadows and Nobscot, now red or purplish with its shrub oaks in this air; and Wachusett here seen in perfection, and Dudley Pond first seen on the south.

Dudley Pond is revealed due south now at noon (twelve), by its sparkling water, on both sides its promontory. The sparkles are even like fireflies in a meadow. This is not far above the opening to Pelham Pond, which also we fairly see. The white pines now look uncommonly soft. Their foliage, indeed, is not so thick as it was, but, the old leaves being fallen, and none left which are a year old, it is perchance more bright and fair. Dudley Pond, beyond the promontory, appears to be revealed by such a mirage as the coin in a basin. The sun-sparkles seen through the leafless woods on both sides this promontory, over its neck, are very large and innumerable; when one goes out, up flashes another, like a meadow full of fireflies, — dancing sparkles. When we reach the pond we find much beech wood just cut down, last winter, and still standing on its shores. Where young beeches have been cut off four feet from the ground, to cord the wood against, I see that they have put out sprouts this summer in a dense bunch at its top; and also all those stumps which are clothed with short sprouts still covered with curled and crisped leaves are beeches. These large sparkles are magic lanterns by daylight. It is the game of " Go away Jack, come again Gill," played by the Genius of the lake, with the sun on his nail instead of a piece of paper, to amuse Nature's children with. Should it not be called Sparkle Pond? Buttonwood trees are frequent about its shores, its handsome hilly shores. This side, cedars also, on its pleasant hilly shores; and opposite, dark, dense hemlocks. Thus, in the form of its shores and, above all, in the trees which prevail about it, it is peculiar or at least wilder than the Concord ponds, and is exceedingly handsome. It has, perhaps, greater variety than any pond I know. Let it be called Peninsula Pond, nevertheless. The willow herb is there abundant, with its arching stem and its calyces, or dried flowers, still attached. No tree has so fair a bole and so handsome an *instep* as the beech. The lower leaves, which are an orange (?) red, hang on (dry) while the rest of the tree is bare. Chased by an ox, whom we escaped over a fence while he gored the trees instead of us, — the first time I was ever chased by his kind. It is a clear water without weeds. There is a handsomely sloping grassy shore on the west.

Close by we found Long Pond, in Wayland, Framingham, and Natick, a great body of water with singularly sandy, shelving, caving, undermined banks; and there we

ate our luncheon. The mayflower leaves we saw there, and the *Viola pedata* in blossom. We went down it a mile or two on the east side through the woods on its high bank, and then dined, looking far down to what seemed the Boston outlet (opposite to its natural outlet), where a solitary building stood on the shore. It is a wild and stretching loch, where yachts might sail, — Cochituate. It was not only larger but wilder and more novel than I had expected. In some respects unlike New England. I could hardly have told in what part of the world I was, if I had been carried there blindfolded. Yet some features, at least the composition of the soil, were familiar. The glorious sandy banks far   and near, caving and sliding, — far sandy   slopes, the forts of the land, — where you see   the naked flesh of New England, her garment being blown aside like that of the priests (of the Levites?) when they ascend to the altar. Seen through this November sky, these sands are dear to me, worth all the gold of California, suggesting Pactolus, while the Saxonville factory-bell sounds o'er the woods. That sound perchance it is that whets my vision. The shore suggests the seashore, and two objects at a distance near the shore look like seals on a sand-bar. Dear to me to lie in, this sand; fit to preserve the bones of a race for thousands of years to come. And this is my home, my native soil; and I am a New-Englander. Of thee, O earth, are my bone and sinew made; to thee, O sun, am I brother. It must be the largest lake in Middlesex. To this dust my body will gladly return as to its origin. Here have I my habitat. I am of thee.

Returned by the south side of Dudley Pond, which looked fairer than ever, though smaller, — now so still, the afternoon somewhat advanced, Nobscot in the west in a purplish light, and the scalloped peninsula before us. When we held our heads down, this was thrown far off. This shore was crowded with hemlocks, which elsewhere I do not remember to have seen so numerous. Outside the wood there are little rounded clumps of smaller ones about. This pond must have been dear to the Indians.

At Nonesuch Pond, in Natick, we saw a boulder some thirty-two feet square by sixteen high, with a large rock leaning against it, — under which we walked, — forming a triangular frame, through which we beheld the picture of the pond. How   many white men and Indians have passed   under it! Boulder Pond! Thence across   lots by the Weston elm, to the bounds of Lincoln at the railroad. Saw a delicate fringed purple flower, *Gentiana crinita*, between those Weston hills, in a meadow, and after on higher land.

C. kept up an incessant strain of wit, banter, about my legs, which were so springy and unweariable, declared I had got my double legs on, that they were not cork but steel, that I should let myself to Van Amburgh, should have sent them to the World's Fair, etc., etc.; wanted to know if I could not carry my father Anchises.

The sun sets while we are perched on a high rock in the north of Weston. It soon grows finger cold. At Walden are three reflections of the bright full (or nearly) moon, one moon and two sheens further off.

Nov. 8. The dark spruce tree at Sherman's; its vicinity the site for a house.

Ah, those sun-sparkles on Dudley Pond in this November air! what a heaven to live in! Intensely brilliant, as no artificial light I have seen, like a dance of diamonds. Coarse mazes of a diamond dance seen through the trees. All objects shine to-day, even the sportsmen seen at a distance, as if a cavern were unroofed, and its crystals gave entertainment to the sun. This great seesaw of brilliants, the ἀνήριθμον γέλασμα. You look several inches into the sod. The cedarn hills. The squirrels that run across the road sport their tails like banners. The gray squirrels in their cylinders are set out in the sun. When I saw the bare sand at Cochituate I felt my relation to the soil. These are *my* sands not yet run out. Not yet will the fates turn the glass. This air have I title to taint with my decay. In this clean sand my bones will gladly lie. Like *Viola pedata*, I shall be ready to bloom again here in my Indian summer days. Here ever springing, never dying, with perennial root I stand; for the winter of the land is warm to me. While the flowers bloom again as in the spring, shall I pine? When I see her sands exposed, thrown up from beneath the surface, it touches me inwardly, it reminds me of my origin; for I am such a plant, so native to New England, methinks, as springs from the sand cast up from below.

4 P. M. — I find ice under the north side of woods nearly an inch thick, where the acorns are frozen in, which have dropped from the overhanging oaks and been saved from the squirrels, perchance by the water.[1] W. E. C.

[1] Must be rotten if they float.

says he found a ripe strawberry last week in Berkshire. Saw a frog at the Swamp Bridge on back road.

Nov. 9. The boat which we paddled that elysian day, Oct. 7th, was made of three distinct boxes shaped like bread-troughs, excepting the bow piece, which was rounded, ⬜ fastened together by screws and nuts, with stout round leather handles by which to carry the separate parts. It was made of the thinnest and lightest material, without seats or thole-pins, for portability. So that three passengers could sit in three different boats which, by turning the hand-nuts(?), they might separate and steer different ways.

The river has fallen more than a foot since I last observed it.[1] I see minute yellow cocoons on the grass, as I go across the field behind Dennis's, reminding me of some late flower, as the cinquefoil. What is the insect? I hear a cricket singing the requiem of the year under the Clamshell Bank. Soon all will be frozen up, and I shall hear no cricket chirp in the land. The very rabbit-forms and squirrel-holes will be snowed up, and walking in the winter days, in the sunny forenoons after a light snow has fallen in the night, covering up the old snow, already deep, and [when] the gentle wind from time to time shakes down a golden dust from above, I shall see still the gray squirrel or the red, still cheery and lifesome, making tiny tracks over the snow-covered rails and riders, when the sun shines aslant between the stems of the pines.

In our walks C. takes out his note-book sometimes

[1] *Vide* Oct. 27.

and tries to write as I do, but all in vain. He soon puts it up again, or contents himself with scrawling some sketch of the landscape. Observing me still scribbling, he will say that he confines himself to the ideal, purely ideal remarks; he leaves the facts to me. Sometimes, too, he will say a little petulantly, "*I* am universal; I have nothing to do with the particular and definite."[1] He is the moodiest person, perhaps, that I ever saw. As naturally whimsical as a cow is brindled, both in his tenderness and his roughness he belies himself. He can be incredibly selfish and unexpectedly generous. He is conceited, and yet there is in him far more than usual to ground conceit upon.[2]

I, too, would fain set down something beside facts. Facts should only be as the frame to my pictures; they should be material to the mythology which I am writing; not facts to assist men to make money, farmers to farm profitably, in any common sense; facts to tell who I am, and where I have been or what I have thought: as now the bell rings for evening meeting, and its volumes of sound, like smoke which rises from where a cannon is fired, make the tent in which I dwell. My facts shall be falsehoods to the common sense. I would so state facts that they shall be significant, shall be myths or mythologic. Facts which the mind perceived, thoughts which the body thought, — with these I deal. I, too, cherish vague and misty forms, vaguest when the cloud at which I gaze is dissipated quite and naught but the skyey depths are seen.

James P. Brown's retired pond, now shallow and

[1] [Channing, p. 66.]   [2] [Channing, p. 332.]

more than half dried up, seems far away and rarely visited, known to few, though not far off. It is encircled by an amphitheatre of low hills, on two opposite sides covered with high pine woods, the other sides with young white oaks and white pines respectively. I am affected by beholding there reflected this gray day, so unpretendingly, the gray stems of the pine wood on the hillside and the sky, — that mirror, as it were a permanent picture to be seen there, a permanent piece of idealism. What were these reflections to the cows alone! Were these things made for cows' eyes mainly? You shall go over behind the hills, where you would suppose that otherwise there was no eye to behold, and find this piece of magic a constant phenomenon there. It is not merely a few favored lakes or pools that reflect the trees and skies, but the obscurest pond-hole in the most unfrequented dell does the same.

These reflections suggest that the sky underlies the hills as well as overlies them, and in another sense than in appearance. I am a little surprised on beholding this reflection, which I did not perceive for some minutes after looking into the pond, as if I had not regarded this as a constant phenomenon. What has become of Nature's common sense and love of facts, when in the very mud-puddles she reflects the skies and trees? Does that procedure recommend itself entirely to the common sense of men? Is that the way the *New England Farmer* would have arranged it?

I think it is not true, what De Quincey says of himself, that he read Greek as easily and copiously as other men do French; for as murder will out, so will a man's read-

ing, and in this author's writings the amount of reference to Greek literature does not at all correspond to such a statement.

I knew that this pond was early to freeze; I had forgotten that it reflected the hills around it. So retired! which I must think even the sordid owner does not know that he owns. It is full of little pollywogs now. Pray, when were they born?

To-day the mountains seen from the pasture above are dark blue, so dark that they look like new mountains and make a new impression, and the intervening town of Acton is seen against them in a new relation, a new neighborhood.

The new monument in Acton, rising by the side of its mountain houses, like a tall and slender chimney, looking black against the sky! I cannot associate that tall and slender column, or any column in fact, with the death of Davis and Hosmer, and Concord Fight, and the American Revolution. It should have been a large, flat stone rather, covered with lichens like an old farmer's door-step, which it took all the oxen in the town to draw. Such a column this as might fitly stand perchance in Abyssinia or Nubia, but not here in Middlesex County, where the genius of the people does not soar after that fashion. It is the Acton flue, to carry off the vapors of patriotism into the upper air, which, confined, would be deleterious to animal and vegetable health. The Davis and Hosmer Monument might have been a doorstep to the Town House, and so the Concord Monument.

Pitch pine cones very beautiful, not only the fresh leather-colored ones but especially the dead gray ones covered with lichens, the scales so regular and close, like an impenetrable coat of mail. These are very handsome to my eye; also those which have long since opened regularly and shed their seeds.

An abundance of the rattlesnake plantain in the woods by Brown's Pond, now full of a fine chaffy seed (?).

Now the leaves are gone the birds' nests are revealed, the brood being fledged and flown. There is a perfect adaptation in the material used in constructing a nest. There is one which I took from a maple on the causeway at Hubbard's Bridge. It is fastened to the twigs by white woolen strings (out of a shawl?), which it has picked up in the road, though it is more than half a mile from a house; and the sharp eyes of the bird have discovered plenty of horsehairs out of the tail or mane, with which to give it form by their spring; with fine meadow hay for body, and the reddish woolly material which invests the ferns in the spring (apparently) for lining.

Nov. 10. This morning the ground is once more whitened with snow, but it will apparently be gone in an hour or two. I live where the *Pinus rigida* grows, with its firm cones, almost as hard as iron, armed with recurved spines.

In relation to politics, to society, aye, to the whole outward world, I am tempted to ask, Why do *they* lay such stress on a particular experience which you have had? — that, after twenty-five years, you should meet Cyrus Warren again on the sidewalk! Have n't I budged an inch, then? This daily routine should go on, then, like

them, — but ever a petty reference to man, to society, aye, often to Christianity. What these things are when men are asleep. I come from the funeral of mankind to attend to a natural phenomenon. The so much grander significance of any fact — of sun and moon and stars — when not referred to man and his needs but viewed absolutely! Sounds that are wafted from over the confines of time.

Nov. 11. When, pointing toward Cap Tourmente, I asked the name of a *habitant* whom we met, he hazarded[?] the name of Belange, or fair angel, — or perchance he referred to some other sort. At any rate, my interrogations of this nature gave vent to such a musical catalogue of sweet names — though I did not know which one to fix on — that I continued to put them to every *habitant* I met, if only for this pleasure.

Living much out-of-doors in the air, in the sun and wind, will, no doubt, produce a certain roughness of character, will cause a thicker cuticle to grow over some of the finer sensibilities of a man's nature, as on his face and hands, or those parts of his body which are exposed to the weather; as staying in the house, on the other hand, may produce a softness and smoothness, not to say thinness, of skin, accompanied by an increased sensibility to certain impressions. And no doubt it is a nice matter to proportion rightly the thick and thin skin. Perhaps we should be more susceptible to some influences important to our intellectual growth, if the sun had shone and the wind blown on us a little less. As too much manual labor callouses the hand and deprives

those — it must be conceded — vital functions of digestion, circulation of the blood, etc., which in health we know nothing about. A wise man is as unconscious of the movements in the body politic as he is of the process of digestion and the circulation of the blood in the natural body. These processes are *infra*-human. I sometimes awake to a half-consciousness of these things going on about me, — as politics, society, business, etc., etc., — as a man may become conscious of some of the processes of digestion, in a morbid state, and so have the dyspepsia, as it is called. It appears to me that those things which most engage the attention of men, as politics, for instance, are vital functions of human society, it is true, but should [be] unconsciously performed, like the vital functions of the natural body. It is as if a thinker submitted himself to be rasped by the great gizzard of creation. Politics is, as it were, the gizzard of society, full of grit and gravel, and the two political parties are its two opposite halves, which grind on each other. Not only individuals but states have thus a confirmed dyspepsia, which expresses itself, you can imagine by what sort of eloquence. Our life is not altogether a forgetting, but also, alas, to a great extent a remembering, of that which perchance we should never have been conscious of, — the consciousness of what should not be permitted to disturb a man's waking hours. As for society, why should we not meet, not always as dyspeptics, but sometimes as eupeptics?[1]

No true and absolute account of things, — of the evening and the morning and all the phenomena between

[1] [*Cape Cod, and Miscellanies*, pp. 472, 481, 482; *Misc.*, Riv. 274, 286, 287.]

it of the exquisiteness of the touch. But then methinks that is a scurf that will fall off fast enough, — that the natural remedy is to be found in the proportion which the night bears to the day, the winter to the summer, etc., thought to experience.[1]

2 P. M. — A bright, but cold day, finger-cold. One must next wear gloves, put his hands in winter quarters. There is a cold, silvery light on the white pines as I go through J. P. Brown's field near Jenny Dugan's. I am glad of the shelter of the thick pine wood on the Marlborough road, on the plain. The roar of the wind over the pines sounds like the surf on countless beaches, an endless shore; and at intervals it sounds like a gong resounding through halls and entries, *i. e.* there is a certain resounding woodiness in the tone. How the wind roars among the shrouds of the wood! The sky looks mild and fair enough from this shelter. Every withered blade of grass and every dry weed, as well as pine-needle, reflects light. The lately dark woods are open and light; the sun shines in upon the stems of trees which it has not shone on since spring. Around the edges of ponds the weeds are dead, and there, too, the light penetrates. The atmosphere is less moist and gross, and light is universally dispersed. We are greatly indebted to these transition seasons or states of the atmosphere, which show us thus phenomena which belong not to the summer or the winter of any climate. The brilliancy of the autumn is wonderful, this flashing brilliancy, as if the atmosphere were phosphoric.

[1] [*Excursions*, p. 210; Riv. 257.]

When I have been confined to my chamber for the greater part of several days by some employment, or perchance by the ague, till I felt weary and house-worn, I have been conscious of a certain softness to which I am otherwise and commonly a stranger, in which the gates were loosened to some emotions; and if I were to become a confirmed invalid, I see how some sympathy with mankind and society might spring up. Yet what is my softness good for, even to tears. It is not I, but nature in me. I laughed at myself the other day to think that I cried while reading a pathetic story. I was no more affected in spirit than I frequently am, methinks. The tears were merely a phenomenon of the bowels, and I felt that that expression of my sympathy, so unusual with me, was something mean, and such as I should be ashamed to have the subject of it understand. I had a cold in my head withal, about those days. I found that I had some bowels, but then it was because my bowels were out of order.

The *fall* of the year is over, and now let us see if we shall have any Indian summer.

White Pond is prepared for winter. Now that most other trees have lost their leaves, the evergreens are more conspicuous about its shores and on its capes. The view of the southern horizon from the lane this side still attracts me, but not so much as before I had explored those Wayland hills, which look so much fairer, perhaps, than they are. To-day you may write a chapter on the advantages of travelling, and to-morrow you may write another chapter on the advantages of not travelling. The horizon has one kind of beauty and attraction to him

who has never explored the hills and mountains in it, and another, I fear a less ethereal and glorious one, to him who has. That blue mountain in the horizon is certainly the most heavenly, the most elysian, which we have not climbed, on which we have not camped for a night. But only our horizon is moved thus further off, and if our whole life should prove thus a failure, the future which is to atone for all, where still there must be some success, will be more glorious still.

"Says I to myself" should be the motto of my journal.

It is fatal to the writer to be too much possessed by his thought. Things must lie a little remote to be described.

Nov. 12. Write often, write upon a thousand themes, rather than long at a time, not trying to turn too many feeble somersets in the air, — and so come down upon your head at last. Antæus-like, be not long absent from the ground. Those sentences are good and well discharged which are like so many little resiliencies from the spring floor of our life, — a distinct fruit and kernel itself, springing from terra firma. Let there be as many distinct plants as the soil and the light can sustain. Take as many bounds in a day as possible. Sentences uttered with your back to the wall. Those are the admirable bounds when the performer has lately touched the springboard. A good bound into the air from the air [*sic*] is a good and wholesome experience, but what shall we say to a man's leaping off precipices in the attempt to fly? He comes down like lead. In the meanwhile, you have got your feet planted upon the rock, with the rock also

at your back, and, as in the case of King James and Roderick Dhu, can say, —

> "Come one, come all! this rock shall fly
> From its firm base as soon as I."

Such, uttered or not, is the strength of your sentence. Sentences in which there is no strain. A fluttering and inconstant and *quasi* inspiration, and ever memorable Icarian fall, in which your helpless wings are expanded merely by your swift descent into the *pelagos* beneath.

C. is one who will not stoop to rise (to change the subject). He wants something for which he will not pay the going price. He will only learn slowly by failure, — not a noble, but disgraceful, failure.[1] This is not a noble method of learning, to be educated by inevitable suffering, like De Quincey, for instance. Better dive like a muskrat into the mud, and pile up a few weeds to sit on during the floods, a foundation of your own laying, a house of your own building, however cold and cheerless.

Methinks the hawk that soars so loftily and circles so steadily and apparently without effort has earned this power by faithfully creeping on the ground as a reptile in a former state of existence. You must creep before you can run; you must run before you can fly. Better one effective bound upward with elastic limbs from the valley than a jumping from the mountain-tops in the attempt to fly. The observatories are not built high but deep; the foundation is equal to the superstructure. It is more important to a distinct vision that it be steady than that it be from an elevated point of view.

Walking through Ebby Hubbard's wood this after-

[1] [Channing, pp. 332, 333.]

noon, with Minott, who was actually taking a walk for amusement and exercise, he said, on seeing some white pines blown down, that you might know that ground had been cultivated, by the trees being torn up so, for otherwise they would have rooted themselves more strongly. Saw some very handsome canoe birches there, the largest I know, a foot in diameter and forty or fifty feet high. The large ones have a reddish cast, perhaps from some small lichen. Their fringes and curls give them an agreeable appearance. Observed a peculiarity in some white oaks. Though they had a firm and close bark near the ground, the bark was very coarse and scaly, in loose flakes, above. Much coarser than the swamp white oak. Minott has a story for every woodland path. He has hunted in them all. Where we walked last, he had once caught a partridge by the *wing!*

7 P. M. — To Conantum.

A still, cold night. The light of the rising moon in the east. Moonrise is a faint sunrise. And what shall we name the faint aurora that precedes the moonrise? The ground is frozen and echoes to my tread. There are absolutely no crickets to be heard now. They are heard, then, till the ground freezes. To-day I heard for the first time this season the crackling, vibrating sound which resounds from thin ice when a stone is cast upon it. So far have we got toward winter. It is doubtful if they who have not pulled their turnips will have a chance to get them. It is not of much use to drive the cows to pasture. I can fancy that I hear the booming of ice in the ponds. I hear no sound of any bird now at night, but sometimes some creature stirring, — a rabbit, or skunk, or fox, — betrayed now by the dry leaves which lie so thick and light. The openness of the leafless woods is particularly apparent now by moonlight; they are nearly as bright as the open field. It is worth the while always to go to the waterside when there is but little light in the heavens and see the heavens and the stars reflected. There is double the light that there is elsewhere, and the reflection has the force of a great silent companion. There is no fog now o' nights. I thought to-night that I saw glow-worms in the grass, on the side of the hill; was almost certain of it, and tried to lay my hand on them, but found it was the moonlight reflected from (apparently) the fine frost crystals on the withered grass, and they were so fine that they went and came like glow-worms. It had precisely the effect of twinkling glow-worms. They gleamed just long enough for glow-worms.

Nov. 13. To Fair Haven Hill.

A cold and dark afternoon, the sun being behind clouds in the west. The landscape is barren of objects, the trees being leafless, and so little light in the sky for variety. Such a day as will almost oblige a man to eat his own heart. A day in which you must hold on to life by your teeth. You can hardly ruck up any skin on Nature's bones. The sap is down; she won't peel. Now is the time to cut timber for yokes and ox-bows, leaving the tough bark on, — yokes for your own neck. Finding yourself yoked to Matter and to Time. Truly a hard day, hard times these! Not a mosquito left. Not an insect to hum. Crickets gone into winter quarters. Friends

for for him no fodder is stored in barns. He relies upon his instinct, which teaches him to paw away the snow to come at the withered grass.

Methinks man came very near being made a dormant creature, just as some of these animals. The ground squirrel, for instance, which lays up vast stores, is yet found to be half dormant, if you dig him out. Now for the oily nuts of thought which you have stored up.

The mountains are of an uncommonly dark blue to-day. Perhaps this is owing, not only to the greater clearness of the atmosphere, which brings them nearer, but to the absence of the leaves! They are many miles nearer for it. A little mistiness occasioned by warmth would set them further off and make them fainter.

I see snow on the Peterboro hills, reflecting the sun. It is pleasant thus to look from afar into winter. We look at a condition which we have not reached. Notwithstanding the poverty of the immediate landscape, in the horizon it is simplicity and grandeur. I look into valleys white with snow and now lit up by the sun, while all this country is in shade. This accounts for the cold northwest wind.

There is a great gap in the mountain range just south of the two Peterboro hills. Methinks I have been through it, and that a road runs there. At any rate, humble as these mountains are compared with some, yet at this distance I am convinced that they answer the purpose of Andes; and, seen in the horizon, I know of nothing more grand and stupendous than this great mountain gate or pass, a great cleft or sinus in the blue banks, as in a dark evening cloud, fit portal to lead

long since gone there, and you left to walk on frozen ground, with your hands in your pockets. Ah, but is not this a glorious time for your deep inward fires? And will not your green hickory and white oak burn clear in this frosty air? Now is not your manhood taxed by the great Assessor? Taxed for having a soul, a ratable soul. A day when you cannot pluck a flower, cannot dig a parsnip, nor pull a turnip, for the frozen ground! What do the thoughts find to live on? What avails you now the fire you stole from heaven? Does not each thought become a vulture to gnaw your vitals? No Indian summer have we had this November. I see but few traces of the perennial spring. Now is there nothing, not even the cold beauty of ice crystals and snowy architecture, nothing but the echo of your steps over the frozen ground, no voice of birds nor frogs. You are dry as a farrow cow. The earth will not admit a spade. All fields lie fallow. Shall not your mind? True, the freezing ground is being prepared for immeasurable snows, but there are brave thoughts within you that shall remain to rustle the winter through like white oak leaves upon your boughs, or like scrub oaks that remind the traveller of a fire upon the hillsides; or evergreen thoughts, cold even in midsummer, by their nature shall contrast the more fairly with the snow. Some warm springs shall still tinkle and fume, and send their column of vapor to the skies.

The walker now fares like cows in the pastures, where is no grass but hay; he gets nothing but an appetite. If we must return to hay, pray let us have that which has been stored in barns, which has not lost its sweetness. The poet needs to have more stomachs than the cow,

from one country, from one quarter of the earth, to another, where the children of the Israelites may file through. Little does the New Hampshire farmer who drives over that road realize through what a sublime gap he is passing. You would almost as soon think of a road to wind through and over a dark evening cloud. This prospect of the mountains from our low hills is what I would rather have than pastures on the mountainsides such as my neighbors own, aye, than townships at their base. Instead that I drive my cattle up in May, I turn my eyes that way. My eyes pasture there, and straightway the yearling thoughts come back. The grass they feed on never withers, for though they are not evergreen, they 're ever blue to me. For though not evergreen to you, to me they 're ever blue.

> I do not fear my thoughts will die,
> For never yet it was so dry
> As to scorch the azure of the sky.
> It knows no withering and no drought,
> Though all eyes crop, it ne'er gives out.
> My eyes my flocks are;
> Mountains my crops are.
> I do not fear my flocks will stray,
> For they were made to roam the day,
> For they can wander with the latest light,
> Yet be at home at night.

Just spent a couple of hours (eight to ten) with Miss Mary Emerson at Holbrook's. The wittiest and most vivacious woman that I know, certainly that woman among my acquaintance whom it is most profitable to meet, the least frivolous, who will most surely provoke to good conversation and the expression of what is in you. She is singular, among women at least, in being really and perseveringly interested to know what thinkers think. She relates herself surely to the intellectual where she goes. It is perhaps her greatest praise and peculiarity that she, more surely than any other woman, gives her companion occasion to utter his best thought. In spite of her own biases, she can entertain a large thought with hospitality, and is not prevented by any intellectuality in it, as women commonly are. In short, she is a genius, as woman seldom is, reminding you less often of her sex than any woman whom I know. In that sense she is capable of a masculine appreciation of poetry and philosophy. I never talked with any other woman who I thought accompanied me so far in describing a poetic experience. Miss Fuller is the only woman I think of in this connection, and of her rather from her fame than from any knowledge of her. Miss Emerson expressed to-night a singular want of respect for her own sex, saying that they were frivolous almost without exception, that woman was the weaker vessel, etc.; that into whatever family she might go, she depended more upon the "clown" for society than upon the lady of the house. Men are more likely to have opinions of their own.

The cattle-train came down last night from Vermont with snow nearly a foot thick upon it. It is as if, in the fall of the year, a swift traveller should come out of the north with snow upon his coat. So it snows. Such, some years, may be our first snow.

Just in proportion to the outward poverty is the in-

ward wealth. In cold weather fire burns with a clearer flame.

Nov. 14. Friday. Surveying the Ministerial Lot in the southwestern part of the town. Unexpectedly find Hayward's Pond frozen over thinly, it being shallow and coldly placed.

In the evening went to a party. It is a bad place to go to, — thirty or forty persons, mostly young women, in a small room, warm and noisy. Was introduced to two young women. The first one was as lively and loquacious as a chickadee; had been accustomed to the society of watering-places, and therefore could get no refreshment out of such a dry fellow as I. The other was said to be pretty-looking, but I rarely look people in their faces, and, moreover, I could not hear what she said, there was such a clacking, — could only see the motion of her lips when I looked that way. I could imagine better places for conversation, where there should be a certain degree of silence surrounding you, and less than forty talking at once. Why, this afternoon, even, I did better. There was old Mr. Joseph Hosmer and I ate our luncheon of cracker and cheese together in the woods. I heard all he said, though it was not much, to be sure, and he could hear me. And then he talked out of such a glorious repose, taking a leisurely bite at the cracker and cheese between his words; and so some of him was communicated to me, and some of me to him, I trust.

These parties, I think, are a part of the machinery of modern society, that young people may be brought together to form marriage connections.

What is the use of going to see people whom yet you never see, and who never see you? I begin to suspect that it is not necessary that we should see one another.

Some of my friends make singular blunders. They go out of their way to talk with certain young women of whom they think, or have heard, that they are pretty, and take pains to introduce me to them. That may be a reason why they should look at them, but it is not a reason why they should talk with them. I confess that I am lacking a sense, perchance, in this respect, and I derive no pleasure from talking with a young woman half an hour simply because she has regular features. The society of young women is the most unprofitable I have ever tried. They are so light and flighty that you can never be sure whether they are there or not there. I prefer to talk with the more staid and settled, *settled for life*, in every sense.

I met a man yesterday afternoon in the road who behaved as if he was deaf, and I talked with him in the cold in a loud tone for fifteen minutes, but that uncertainty about his ears, and the necessity I felt to talk loudly, took off the fine edge of what I had to say and prevented my saying anything satisfactory. It is bad enough when your neighbor does not understand you, but if there is any uncertainty as to whether he hears you, so that you are obliged to become your own auditor, you are so much the poorer speaker, and so there is a double failure.

Nov. 15. Here is a rainy day, which keeps me in the house.

Asked Therien this afternoon if he had got a new idea

this summer. "Good Lord!" says he, "a man that has to work as I do, if he does not forget the ideas he has had, he will do well. Maybe the man you work with is inclined to race; then, by gorry, your mind must be there; you think of weeds." [1]

I am pleased to read in Stoever's Life of Linnæus (Trapp's translation) that his father, being the first learned man of his family, changed his family name and borrowed that of Linnæus (Linden-tree-man) from a lofty linden tree which stood near his native place, — "a custom," he says, "not unfrequent in Sweden, to take fresh appellations from natural objects." What more fit than that the advent of a new man into a family should acquire for it, and transmit to his posterity, a new patronymic? Such a custom suggests, if it does not argue, an unabated vigor in the race, relating it to those primitive times when men did, indeed, acquire a name, as memorable and distinct as their characters. It is refreshing to get to a man whom you will not be satisfied to call John's son or Johnson's son, but a new name applicable to himself alone, he being the first of his kind. We may say there have been but so many men as there are surnames, and of all the John-Smiths there has been but one true John Smith, and he of course is dead. Get yourself therefore a name, and better a nickname than none at all. There was one enterprising boy came to school to me whose name was "Buster," and an honorable name it was. He was the only boy in the school, to my knowledge, who was named. [2]

[1] [*Walden*, p. 165; Riv. 233.]

[2] [*Excursions*, pp. 236, 237; Riv. 290. See also *Journal*, vol. ii, p. 407.]

What shall we say of the comparative intellectual vigor of the ancients and moderns, when we read of Theophrastus, the father of botany, that he composed more than two hundred treatises in the third century before Christ and the seventeenth before printing, about twenty of which remain, and that these fill six volumes in folio printed at Venice? Among the last are two works on natural history and the generation of plants. What a stimulus to a literary man to read his works! They *were* *opera*, not an essay or two, which you can carry between your thumb and finger.

Dioscorides (according to Stoever), who lived in the first century after Christ, was the first to inquire into the medicinal properties of plants, "the literary father of the *materia medica*." His work remains. And next comes Pliny the Elder, and "by his own avowal (?), his natural history is a compilation from about twenty-five hundred (?) different authors." Conrad Gesner, of the Sixteenth Century, the first botanist of note among the moderns; also a naturalist generally. In this century botany first "became a regular academical study."

I think it would be a good discipline for Channing, who writes poetry in a sublimo-slipshod style, to write Latin, for then he would be compelled to say something always, and frequently have recourse to his grammar and dictionary. Methinks that what a man might write in a dead language could be more surely translated into good sense in his own language, than his own language could be translated into good Latin, or the dead language.

Vol. III

reason is convinced long before the life is. They may see the Church and the Sabbath to be false, but nothing else to be true. One woman in the neighborhood says, "Nobody can hear Mr. —— preach, — hear him through, — without seeing that he is a good man." "Well, is there any truth in what he says?" asks another. "Oh, yes, it's true enough, but then it won't do; you know it won't do. Now there's our George, he's got the whole of it; and when I say, 'Come, George, put on your things and go along to meeting,' he says, 'No, Mother, I'm going out into the fields.' It won't do." The fact is, this woman has not character and religion enough to exert a controlling influence over her children by her example, and knows of no such police as the Church and the minister.

If it were not for death and funerals, I think the institution of the Church would not stand longer. The necessity that men be decently buried — our fathers and mothers, brothers and sisters and children (notwithstanding the danger that they be buried alive) — will long, if not forever, prevent our laying violent hands on it. If salaries were stopped off, and men walked out of this world bodily at last, the minister and his vocation would be gone. What is the churchyard but a graveyard? Imagine a church at the other end of the town, without any carrion beneath or beside it, but all the dead regularly carried to the bone-mill! The cry that comes up from the churches in all the great cities in the world is, "How they stink!"

What more fatal vengeance could Linnæus have taken than to give the names of his enemies to pernicious and unsightly plants, thus simply putting upon record

Nov. 16. Sunday. It is remarkable that the highest intellectual mood which the world tolerates is the perception of the truth of the most ancient revelations, now in some respects out of date; but any direct revelation, any original thoughts, it hates like virtue. The fathers and the mothers of the town would rather hear the young man or young woman at their tables express reverence for some old statement of the truth than utter a direct revelation themselves. They don't want to have any prophets born into their families, — damn them! So far as thinking is concerned, surely original thinking is the divinest thing. Rather we should reverently watch for the least motions, the least scintillations, of thought in this sluggish world, and men should run to and fro on the occasion more than at an earthquake. We check and repress the divinity that stirs within us, to fall down and worship the divinity that is dead without us. I go to see many a good man or good woman, so called, and utter freely that thought which alone it was given to me to utter; but there was a man who lived a long, long time ago, and his name was Moses, and another whose name was Christ, and if your thought does not, or does not appear to, coincide with what they said, the good man or the good woman has no ears to hear you. They think they love God! It is only his old clothes, of which they make scarecrows for the children. Where will they come nearer to God than in those very children?

A man lately preached here against the abuse of the Sabbath and recommended to walk in the fields and dance on that [day], — good advice enough, which may take effect after a while. But with the mass of men the

for as long as the Linnæan system shall prevail who were his friends and foes? It was enough to record the fact that they were opposed to him. To this they could not themselves have objected, nor could he have taken a more fatal vengeance. (*Vide* Scraps.)

Noticed this afternoon that where a pitch pine three inches in diameter had been cut down last winter, it had sent out more than a hundred horizontal plumes about a foot long close together and on every side. Plenty of ripe checkerberries now. Do they blossom again in the spring?[1] The ferns, which are almost the only green things left now, love the crevices and seams of moist cliffs and boulders and adorn them very much. They become more conspicuous now than at any season.

I had a thought this morning before I awoke. I endeavored to retain it in my mind's grasp after I became conscious, yet I doubted, while I lay on my back, whether my mind could apprehend it when I should stand erect. It is a far more difficult feat to get up without spilling your morning thought, than that which is often practiced of taking a cup of water from behind your head as you lie on your back and drinking from it. It was the thought I endeavored to express on the first page of to-day.

Thinkers and writers are in foolish haste to come before the world with crude works. Young men are persuaded by their friends, or by their own restless ambition, to write a course of lectures in a summer against the ensuing winter; and what it took the lecturer a summer to write, it will take his audience but an hour to

[1] Only once.

forget. If time is short, then you have no time to waste.

That sounds like a fine mode of expressing gratitude referred to by Linnæus. Hermann was a botanist who gave up his place to Tournefort, who was unprovided for. "Hermann," says Linnæus, "came afterwards to Paris, and Tournefort in honor of him ordered the fountains to play in the royal garden."

Nov. 17. All things tend to flow to him who can make the best use of them, even away from their legal owner. A thief, finding with the property of the Italian naturalist Donati, whom he had robbed abroad, a collection of rare African seeds, forwarded them to Linnæus from Marseilles. Donati suffered shipwreck and never returned.

Nov. 18. Surveying these days the Ministerial Lot.

Now at sundown I hear the hooting of an owl, — *hoo hoo hoo, hoorer hoo.*[1] It sounds like the hooting of an idiot or a maniac broke loose. This is faintly answered in a different strain, apparently from a greater distance, almost as if it were the echo, *i. e.* so far as the *succession* is concerned. This is my music each evening. I heard it last evening. The men who help me call it the "hooting owl" and think it is the cat owl. It is a sound admirably suited [to] the swamp and to the twilight woods, suggesting a vast undeveloped nature which men have not recognized nor satisfied. I rejoice that there are owls. They represent the stark, twilight, unsatisfied thoughts

[1] [*Walden*, p. 139; Riv. 196.]

I have. Let owls do the idiotic and maniacal hooting for men. This sound faintly suggests the infinite roominess of nature, that there is a world in which owls live. Yet how few are seen, even by the hunters! The sun has shone for a day over this savage swamp, where the single spruce stands covered with usnea moss, which a Concord merchant mortgaged once to the trustees of the ministerial fund and lost, but now for a different race of creatures a new day dawns over this wilderness, which one would have thought was sufficiently dismal before. Here hawks also circle by day, and chickadees are heard, and rabbits and partridges abound.[1]

The chopper who works in the woods all day for many weeks or months at a time becomes intimately acquainted with them in his way. He is more open in some respects to the impressions they are fitted to make than the naturalist who goes to see them. He is not liable to exaggerate insignificant features. He really forgets himself, forgets to observe, and at night he *dreams* of the swamp, its phenomena and events. Not so the naturalist; enough of his unconscious life does not pass there.

A man can hardly be said to be *there* if he *knows* that he is there, or to go there if he knows where he is going. The man who is bent upon his work is frequently in the best attitude to observe what is irrelevant to his work. (*Mem.* Wordsworth's observations on relaxed attention.) You must be conversant with things for a long time to know much about them, like the moss which has hung from the spruce, and as the partridge and the rabbit are acquainted with the thickets and at length have acquired

[1] [*Walden*, pp. 138, 139; Riv. 196, 197.]

Vol. III

the color of the places they frequent. If the man of science can put all his knowledge into propositions, the woodman has a great deal of incommunicable knowledge.

Deacon Brown told me to-day of a tall, raw-boned fellow by the name of Hosmer who used to help draw the seine behind the Jones house, who once, when he had hauled it without getting a single shad, held up a little perch in sport above his face, to show what he had got. At that moment the perch wiggled and dropped right down his throat head foremost, and nearly suffocated him; and it was only after considerable time, during which the man suffered much, that he was extracted or forced down. He was in a worse predicament than a fish hawk would have been.

In the woods south of the swamp are many great holes made by digging for foxes.

Nov. 19. Old Mr. Joseph Hosmer, who helped me to-day, said that he used to know all about the lots, but since they've chopped off so much, and the woods have grown up, he finds himself lost. Thirty or forty years ago, when he went to meeting, he knew every face in the meeting-house, even the boys and girls, they looked so much like their parents; but after ten or twelve years they would have outgrown his knowledge entirely (they would have altered so), but he knew the old folks still, because they held their own and did n't alter. Just so he could tell the boundaries of the old wood which had n't been cut down, but the young wood altered so much in a few years that he could n't tell anything about it. When

I asked him why the old road which went by this swamp was so roundabout, he said he would answer me as Mr. —— —— did him in a similar case once, — "Why, if they had made it straight, they would n't have left any room for improvement."

Standing by Harrington's pond-hole in the swamp, which had skimmed over, we saw that there were many holes through the thin black ice, of various sizes, from a few inches to more than a foot in diameter, all of which were *perfectly* circular. Mr. H. asked me if I could account for it. As we stood considering, we jarred the boggy ground and made a dimple in the water, and this accident, we thought, betrayed the cause of it; *i. e.* the circular wavelets so wore off the edges of the ice when once a hole was made. The ice was very thin, and the holes were perfect disks. But what jarred the ground and shook the water? Perhaps the wind which shook the spruce and pine trees which stood in the quaking ground, as well as the little life in the water itself, and the wind on the ice and water itself. There was a more permanent form created by the dimple, but not yet a shellfish.

Nov. 20. It is often said that melody can be heard farther than noise, and the finest melody farther than the coarsest. I think there is truth in this, and that accordingly those strains of the piano which reach me here in my attic stir me so much more than the sounds which I should hear if I were below in the parlor, because they are so much purer and diviner melody. They who sit farthest off from the noisy and bustling world are not at pains to distinguish what is sweet and musical, for that alone can reach them; that chiefly comes down to posterity.

Hard and steady and engrossing labor with the hands, especially out of doors, is invaluable to the literary man and serves him directly. Here I have been for six days surveying in the woods, and yet when I get home at evening, somewhat weary at last, and beginning to feel that I have nerves, I find myself more susceptible than usual to the finest influences, as music and poetry. The very air can intoxicate me, or the least sight or sound, as if my finer senses had acquired an appetite by their fast.

As I was riding to the Ministerial Lot this morning, about 8.30 A. M., I observed that the white clouds were disposed raywise in the west and also in the east, — as if the sun's rays had split and so arranged them? A striking symmetry in the heavens. What its law? Mr. J. Hosmer tells me that one spring he saw a red squirrel gnaw the bark of a maple and then suck the juice, and this he repeated many times.

What is the bush where we dined in Poplar Hollow? Hosmer tells of finding a kind of apple, with an apple seed (?) to it, on scabish which had been injured or cut off. Thinks plowed ground more moist than grass ground. That there are more leaves on the ground on the north side of a hill than on the other sides, and that the trees thrive more there, perhaps because the winds cause the leaves to fall there.

Nov. 21. My mother says that, visiting once at Captain Pulsifer's at the North End, two sea-captains' wives told the girl, when the things were carried out to

be replenished, not to turn out their slops, as it would drown their husbands who were at sea.

Frank Brown showed me to-day the velvet duck (white-winged coot) and the surf duck. These two, as well as the scaup (?) duck, he says are called coots. Saw also a fine brant, a shore lark, a pine grosbeak, kittiwake gull and Bonaparte's ditto (the last very like the first but smaller), all shot at Clark's Island; also a little brown creeper with a woodpecker tail and curved bill, killed here.

Old Mr. Joseph Hosmer, who lives where Hadley did, remembers when there were two or three times as many inhabitants in that part of the town as there are now: a blacksmith with his shop in front where he now lives, a goldsmith (Oliver Wheeler?) at the fork in the road just beyond him, one *in front* of Tarbell's, one in the orchard on the south side of the lane in front of Tarbell's, one, Nathan Wheeler, further on the right of the old road by the balm-of-Gilead, three between Tarbell's and J. P. Brown's, a tavern at Loring's, a store at the Dodge cottage that was burnt, also at Derby's (?), etc., etc. The farms were smaller then. One man now often holds two or three old farms. We walk in a deserted country.

The Major Heywood and mill roads together turn out of the Marlborough road just beyond the Desert. The former keeps the left to the powder-mills, the latter the right to the sawmill. The main road beyond Loring's used to be called Law's Path, where is Law's Brook (south branch of Nagog, *i. e.* Fort Pond?). The old roads furrow the Second Division woods like trenches.

Better men never lecture than they hire to come here. Why don't they ask Edmund Hosmer or George Minott? I would rather hear them decline than most of these hirelings lecture.

Nov. 22. The milkweed pods by the roadside are yet but half emptied of their silky contents. For months the gales are dispersing their seeds, though we have had snow.

Saw E. Hosmer this afternoon making a road for himself along a hillside (I being on my way to Saw Mill Brook). He turned over a stone, and I saw under it many crickets and ants still lively, which had gone into winter quarters there apparently. There were many little galleries leading under the stone, indenting the hardened earth like veins. (*Mem.* Turn over a rock in midwinter and see if you can find them.) That is the reason, then, that I have not heard the crickets lately. I have frequently seen them lurking under the eaves or portico of a stone, even in midsummer.

At the brook the partridge-berries checker the ground with their leaves, now interspersed with red berries. The cress at the bottom of the brook is doubly beautiful now, because it is green while most other plants are sere. It rises and falls and waves with the current. There are many young hornbeams there which still retain their withered leaves. As I returned through Hosmer's field, the sun was setting just beneath a black cloud by which it had been obscured, and as it had been a cold and windy afternoon, its light, which fell suddenly on some white pines between me and it, lighting them up like a shim-

mering fire, and also on the oak leaves and chestnut stems, was quite a circumstance. It was from the contrast between the dark and comfortless afternoon and this bright and cheerful light, almost fire. The eastern hills and woods, too, were clothed in a still golden light. The light of the setting sun, just emerged from a cloud and suddenly falling on and lighting up the needles of the white pine between you and it, after a raw and louring afternoon near the beginning of winter, is a memorable phenomenon. A sort of Indian summer in the day, which thus far has been denied to the year. After a cold gray day this cheering light almost warms us by its resemblance to fire.

Nov. 23. *Sunday.* The trees (counting all three inches in diameter) in Conantum Swamp are: —

Bass	6
Black ash	8
Elm	16 (See if all are really elms.)
Red (?) oak	2
White ash	2
Walnut	3
Apple	5
Maple	9
Hornbeam	2
Swamp white (?) oak	1

Dogwood also there is, and cone-bearing willow, and what kind of winterberry with a light-colored bark?

Another such a sunset to-night as the last, while I was on Conantum.

Nov. 24. Setting stakes in the swamp (Ministerial). Saw seven black ducks fly out of the peat-hole. Saw there also a tortoise still stirring, the painted tortoise, I believe.

Found on the south side of the swamp the *Lygodium palmatum*, which Bigelow calls the only climbing fern in our latitude, an evergreen, called (with others) snake-tongue, as I find in Loudon.

The Irishman who helped me says, when I ask why his countrymen do not learn trades, — do something but the plainest and hardest work, — they are too old to learn trades when they come here.

Nov. 25. This morning the ground is again covered with snow, deeper than before.

In the afternoon walked to the east part of Lincoln. Saw a tree on the turnpike full of hickory-nuts which had an agreeable appearance. Saw also quite a flock of the pine grosbeak, a plump and handsome bird as big as a robin. When returning between Bear Hill and the rail-road, the sun had set and there was a very clear amber light in the west, and, turning about, we were surprised at the darkness in the east, the crescent of night, almost as if the air were thick, a thick snow-storm were gathering, which, as we had faced the west, we were not prepared for; yet the air was clear.

That kind of sunset which I witnessed on Saturday and Sunday is perhaps peculiar to the late autumn. The sun is unseen behind a hill. Only this bright white light like a fire falls on the trembling needles of the pine.

When surveying in the swamp on the 20th last, at

sundown, I heard the owls. Hosmer said: "If you ever minded it, it is about the surest sign of rain that there is. Don't you know that last Friday night you heard them and spoke of them, and the next day it rained?" This time there were other signs of rain in abundance. "But night before last," said I, "when you were not here, they hooted louder than ever, and we have had no rain yet." At any rate, it rained hard the 21st, and by that rain the river was raised much higher than it has been this fall.

Nov. 30. Sunday. A rather cold and windy afternoon, with some snow not yet melted on the ground. Under the south side of the hill between Brown's and Tarbell's, in a warm nook, disturbed three large gray squirrels and some partridges, who had all sought out this bare and warm place. While the squirrels hid themselves in the tree-tops, I sat on an oak stump by an old cellar-hole and mused. This squirrel is always an unexpectedly large animal to see frisking about. My eye wanders across the valley to the pine woods which fringe the opposite side, and in their aspect my eye finds something which addresses itself to my nature. Methinks that in my mood I was asking Nature to give me a sign. I do not know exactly what it was that attracted my eye. I experienced a transient gladness, at any rate, at something which I saw. I am sure that my eye rested with pleasure on the white pines, now reflecting a silvery light, the infinite stories of their boughs, tier above tier, a sort of basaltic structure, a crumbling precipice of pine horizontally stratified. Each pine is like a great green feather stuck in the ground. A myriad white pine

boughs extend themselves horizontally, one above and behind another, each bearing its burden of silvery sun-light, with darker seams between them, as if it were a great crumbling piny precipice thus stratified. On this my eyes pastured, while the squirrels were up the trees behind me. That, at any rate, it was that I got by my afternoon walk, a certain recognition from the pine, some congratulation. Where is my home? It is indistinct as an old cellar-hole, now a faint indentation merely in a farmer's field, which he has plowed into and rounded off its edges years ago, and I sit by the old site on the stump of an oak which once grew there. Such is the nature where we have lived. Thick birch groves stand here and there, dark brown (?) now with white lines more or less distinct.

The *Lygodium palmatum* is quite abundant on that side of the swamp, twining round the goldenrods, etc., etc.

III

DECEMBER, 1851

(ÆT. 34)

Dec. 12. In regard to my friends, I feel that I know and have communion with a finer and subtler part of themselves which does not put me off when they put me off, which is not cold to me when they are cold, not till I am cold. I hold by a deeper and stronger tie than absence can sunder.

Ah, dear nature, the mere remembrance, after a short forgetfulness, of the pine woods! I come to it as a hungry man to a crust of bread.

I have been surveying for twenty or thirty days, living coarsely, even as respects my diet, — for I find that that will always alter to suit my employment, — indeed, leading a quite trivial life; and to-night, for the first time, had made a fire in my chamber and endeavored to return to myself. I wished to ally myself to the powers that rule the universe. I wished to dive into some deep stream of thoughtful and devoted life, which meandered through retired and fertile meadows far from towns. I wished to do again, or for once, things quite congenial to my highest inmost and most sacred nature, to lurk in crystalline thought like the trout under verdurous banks, where stray mankind should only see my bubble come to the surface. I wished to live, ah! as far away as a man can think. I wished for leisure and quiet to let my life flow in its proper channels, with its proper currents;

when I might not waste the days, might establish daily prayer and thanksgiving in my family; might do my own work and not the work of Concord and Carlisle, which would yield me better than money. (How much forbearance, aye, sacrifice and loss, goes to every accomplishment! I am thinking by what long discipline and at what cost a man learns to speak simply at last.) I bethought myself, while my fire was kindling, to open one of Emerson's books, which it happens that I rarely look at, to try what a chance sentence out of that could do for me; thinking, at the same time, of a conversation I had with him the other night, I finding fault with him for the stress he had laid on some of Margaret Fuller's whims and superstitions, but he declaring gravely that she was one of those persons whose experience warranted her attaching importance to such things, — as the *Sortes Virgilianae*, for instance, of which her numerous friends could tell remarkable instances. At any rate, I saw that he was disposed [to] regard such things more seriously than I. The first sentence which I opened upon in his book was this: "If, with a high trust, he can thus submit himself, he will find that ample returns are poured into his bosom out of what seemed hours of obstruction and loss. Let him not grieve too much on account of unfit associates. . . . In a society of perfect sympathy, no word, no act, no record, would be. He will learn that it is not much matter what he reads, what he does. Be a scholar, and he shall have the scholar's part of everything," etc., etc.[1]

[1] [*Nature, Addresses, and Lectures*, Centenary Ed., p. 184; Riv. 177, 178.]

Vol. III

plumb and went to get it, then he showed the red soles of his boots.

Nothing is so sure to make itself known as the truth, for what else waits to be known?

Dec. 13. Saturday. While surveying to-day, saw much mountain laurel for this neighborhood in Mason's pasture, just over the line in Carlisle. Its bright yellowish-green shoots are agreeable to my eye. We had one hour of almost Indian summer weather in the middle of the day. I felt the influence of the sun. It melted my stoniness a little. The pines looked like old friends again. Cutting a path through a swamp where was much brittle dogwood, etc., etc., I wanted to know the name of every shrub. This varied employment, to which my necessities compel me, serves instead of foreign travel and the lapse of time. If it makes me forget some things which I ought to remember, it no doubt enables me to forget many things which it is well to forget. By stepping aside from my chosen path so often, I see myself better and am enabled to criticise myself. Of this nature is the only true lapse of time. It seems an age since I took walks and wrote in my journal, and when shall I revisit the glimpses of the moon? To be able to see ourselves, not merely as others see us, but as we are, that service a *variety* of absorbing employments does us.

I would not be rude to the fine intimations of the gods for fear of incurring the reproach of superstition.

When I think of the Carlisle man whom I saw to-day and the filthiness of his house, I am reminded that there are all degrees of barbarism, even in this so-called civil-

Most of this responded well enough to my mood, and this would be as good an instance of the *Sortes Virgilianae* as most to quote. But what makes this coincidence very little if at all remarkable to me is the fact of the obviousness of the moral, so that I had, perhaps, *thought* the same thing myself twenty times during the day, and yet had not been *contented* with that account of it, leaving me thus to be amused by the coincidence, rather than impressed as by an intimation out of the deeps.

The Irishman (MacCarty) who helped me survey day before yesterday would not sit on a rock with me to eat his dinner (there being snow on the ground), from a notion that there was nothing so deadly as sitting on a rock, — sure to give you a cold in the back. He would rather stand. So the doctors said, down in the Province of New Brunswick. But I warranted him that he would not get a cold in his back, which was half as broad again as mine, and so he minded me as a new doctor. A gray-headed boy, good for nothing but to eat his dinner. These Irishmen have no heads. Let me inquire strictly into a man's descent, and if his remotest ancestors were Erse, let me not have him to help me survey. One or two I have seen, handy men, but I learned that their fathers, who came from Ireland, were of the Scotch-Irish. This fellow was sure to do the wrong thing from the best motives, and the only time he was spry was when he was running to correct his own blunders out of his own head — and make them worse than before, but I could not stop him; then I saw the broad red soles of his new cowhide boots alternately rising and falling like the buckets of a dasher or water-wheel. When he had lost his

ized community. Carlisle, too, belongs to the Nineteenth Century.

Saw Perez Blood in his frock, — a stuttering, sure, unpretending man, who does not speak without thinking, does not guess. When I reflected how different he was from his neighbors, Conant, Mason, Hodgman, I saw that it was not so much outwardly, but that I saw an inner form. We do, indeed, see through and through each other, through the veil of the body, and see the real form and character in spite of the garment. Any coarseness or tenderness is seen and felt under whatever garb. How nakedly men appear to us! for the spiritual assists the natural eye.

Dec. 14. The boys have been skating for a week, but I have had no time to skate for surveying. I have hardly realized that there was ice, though I have walked over it about this business. As for the weather, all seasons are pretty much alike to one who is actively at work in the woods. I should say that there were two or three remarkably warm days and as many cold ones in the course of a year, but the rest are all alike in respect to temperature. This is my answer to my acquaintances who ask me if I have not found it very cold being out all day.

McKean tells me of hardy horses left to multiply on the Isle of Sable. His father had one (for the shipwrecked to eat). Can they be descendants of those beasts Champlain or Lescarbot refers to?

I hear the small woodpecker whistle as he flies toward the leafless wood on Fair Haven, doomed to be cut this winter. The chickadees remind me of Hudson's Bay for some reason. I look on them as natives of a more northern latitude.

The now dry and empty but clean-washed cups of the blue-curls spot the half snow-covered grain-fields. Where lately was a delicate blue flower, now all the winter are held up these dry chalices. What mementos to stand above the snow!

The fresh young spruces in the swamp are free from moss, but it adheres especially to the bare and dead masts of spruce trees oftentimes half destitute of bark. They look like slanting may-poles with drooping or withered garlands and festoons hanging to them. For an emblem of stillness, a spruce swamp with hanging moss now or at any season.

I notice that hornets' nests are hardly deserted by the insects than they look as if a truant boy had fired a charge of shot through them, — all ragged and full of holes. It is the work either of the insects themselves or else of other insects or birds.

It is the andromeda (panicled?) that has the fine-barked stem and the green wood, in the swamps.

Why not live out more yet, and have my friends and relations altogether in nature, only my acquaintances among the villagers? That way diverges from this I follow, not at a sharp but a very wide angle. Ah, nature is serene and immortal! Am I not one of the Zincali?

There is a beautifully pure greenish-blue sky under the clouds now in the southwest just before sunset. I hear the ice along the edge of the river cracking as the water settles. It has settled about two feet, leaving

ice for the most part without water on the meadows, all uneven and cracked over the hummocks, so that you cannot run straight for sliding. The ice takes the least hint of a core to eke out a perfect plant; the wrecks of bulrushes and meadow grass are expanded into palm leaves and other luxuriant foliage. I see delicate-looking green pads frozen into the ice, and, here and there, where some tender and still green weeds from the warm bottom of the river have lately been cast up on to the ice.

There are certain places where the river will always be open, where perchance warmer springs come in. There are such places in every character, genial and open in the coldest seasons.

I come from contact with certain acquaintances, whom even I am disposed to look toward as possible friends. It oftenest happens that I come from them wounded. Only they can wound me seriously, and that perhaps without their knowing it.

Dec. 17. The pitch pine woods on the right of the Corner road. A piercing cold afternoon, wading in the snow. R. Rice was going to Sudbury to put his bees into the cellar for fear they would freeze. He had a small hive; not enough to keep each other warm. The pitch pines hold the snow well. It lies now in balls on their plumes and in streaks on their branches, their low branches rising at a small angle and meeting each other. A certain dim religious light comes through this roof of pine leaves and snow. It is a sombre twilight, yet in some places the sun streams in, producing the strongest contrasts of light and shade.

Vol. III

The winter morning is the time to see the woods and shrubs in their perfection, wearing their snowy and frosty dress. Even he who visits them half an hour after sunrise will have lost some of their most delicate and fleeting beauties. The trees wear their snowy burden but coarsely after midday, and it no longer expresses the character of the tree. I observed that early in the morning every pine-needle was covered with a frosty sheath, but soon after sunrise it was all gone. You walk in the pitch pine wood as under a penthouse. The stems and branches of the trees look black by contrast. You wander zigzag through the aisles of the wood, where stillness and twilight reign.

Improve every opportunity to express yourself in writing, as if it were your last.

I do not know but a pine wood is as substantial and as memorable a fact as a friend. I am more sure to come away from it cheered, than from those who come nearest to being my friends. It is unfortunate for the chopper and the walker when the cold wind comes from the same side with the sun, for then he cannot find a warm recess in which to sit. It is pleasant to walk now through open and stately white pine woods. Their plumes do not hold so much snow commonly, unless where their limbs rest or are weighed down on to a neighboring tree. It is cold but still in their midst, where the snow is untracked by man, and ever and anon you see the snow-dust, shone on by the sun, falling from their tops and, as it strikes the lower limbs, producing innumerable new showers. For, as after a rain there is a second rain in the woods, so after a light snow there is a second snow in the woods,

when the wind rises. The branches of the white pine are more horizontal than those of the pitch, and the white streaks of snow on them look accordingly. I perceive that the young black oaks and the red oaks, too, methinks, still keep their leaves as well as the white. This piercing wind is so nearly from the west this afternoon that, to stand at once in a sheltered and a sunny place, you must seek the south-southeast side of the woods.

What slight but important distinctions between one creature and another! What little, but essential, advantages one enjoys over another! I noticed this afternoon a squirrel's nest high in the fork of a white pine. Thither he easily ascends, but many creatures strive in vain to get at him.

The lower branches of the hemlock point down, and even trail on the ground, the whole tree making a perfect canopy.

When they who have aspired to be friends cease to sympathize, it is the part of religion to keep asunder.

One of the best men I know often offends me by uttering made words — the very best words, of course, or dinner speeches, most smooth and gracious and fluent repartees, a sort of talking to Buncombe, a dash of polite conversation, a graceful bending, as if I were Master Slingsby of promising parts, from the University. O would you but be simple and downright! Would you but cease your palaver! It is the misfortune of being a gentleman and famous. The conversation of gentlemen after dinner! One of the best of men and wisest, to whom this diabolical formality will adhere. Repeating himself, shampooing himself! Passing the time of day, as if he were just introduced! No words are so tedious. Never a natural or simple word or yawn. It produces an appearance of phlegm and stupidity in me the auditor. I am suddenly the closest and most phlegmatic of mortals, and the conversation comes to naught. Such speeches as an ex-Member of Congress might make to an ex-Member of Parliament.

To explain to a friend is to suppose that you are not intelligent of one another. If you are not, to what purpose will you explain?

My acquaintances will sometimes wonder why I will impoverish myself by living aloof from this or that company, but greater would be the impoverishment if I should associate with them.

Dec. 19. In all woods is heard now far and near the sound of the woodchopper's axe, a twilight sound, now in the night of the year, men having come out for fuel to the forests, — as if men had stolen forth in the arctic night to get fuel to keep their fires a-going. Men go to the woods now for fuel who never go there at any other time. Why should it be so pleasing to look into a thick pine wood where the sunlight streams in and gilds it? The sound of the axes far in the horizon sounds like the dropping of the eaves. Now the sun gets suddenly without a cloud, and with scarcely any redness following, so pure is the atmosphere, — only a faint rosy blush along the horizon.

Dec. 20. *Saturday.* 2 P. M. — To Fair Haven Hill and plain below.

Saw a large hawk circling over a pine wood below me, and screaming, apparently that he might discover his prey by their flight. Travelling ever by wider circles. What a symbol of the thoughts, now soaring, now descending, taking larger and larger circles, or smaller and smaller! It flies not directly whither it is bound, but advances by circles, like a courtier of the skies. No such noble progress! How it comes round, as with a wider sweep of thought! But the majesty is in the imagination of the beholder, for the bird is intent on its prey. Circling and ever circling, you cannot divine which way it will incline, till perchance it dives down straight as an arrow to its mark. It rises higher above where I stand, and I see with beautiful distinctness its wings against the sky, — primaries and secondaries, and the rich tracery of the outline of the latter (?), its inner wings, or wing-linings, within the outer, — like a great moth seen against the sky. A will-o'-the-wind. Following its path, as it were through the vortices of the air. The poetry of motion. Not as preferring one place to another, but enjoying each as long as possible. Most gracefully so surveys new scenes and revisits the old. As if that hawk were made to be the symbol of my thought, how bravely he came round over those parts of the wood which he had not surveyed, taking in a new segment, annexing new territories! Without "heave-yo!" it trims its sail. It goes about without the creaking of a block. That America yacht of the air that never makes a tack, though it rounds the globe itself, takes in and shakes out its reefs without a flutter, — its sky-scrapers all under its control. Holds up one wing, as if to admire, and sweeps off this way,

then holds up the other and sweeps that. If there are two concentrically circling, it is such a regatta as Southampton waters never witnessed.

Flights of imagination, Coleridgean thoughts. So a man is said to soar in his thought, ever to fresh woods and pastures new. Rises as in thought.

Snow-squalls pass, obscuring the sun, as if blown off from a larger storm.

Since last Monday the ground has [been] covered half a foot or more with snow; and the ice also, before I have had a skate. Hitherto we had had mostly bare, frozen ground. Red, white, green, and, in the distance, dark brown are the colors of the winter landscape. I view it now from the cliffs. The red shrub oaks on the white ground of the plain beneath make a pretty scene. Most walkers are pretty effectually shut up by the snow.

I observe that they who saw down trees in the woods with a cross-cut saw carry a mat to kneel on.

It is no doubt a good lesson for the woodchopper, the long day alone in the woods, and he gets more than his half dollar a cord.

Say the thing with which you labor. It is a waste of time for the writer to use his talents merely. Be faithful to your genius. Write in the strain that interests you most. Consult not the popular taste.

The red oak leaves are even more fresh and glossy than the white.

A clump of white pines, seen far westward over the shrub oak plain, which is now lit up by the setting sun, a soft, feathery grove, with their gray stems indistinctly seen, like human beings come to their cabin door, stand-

ing expectant on the edge of the plain, impress me with a mild humanity. The trees indeed have hearts. With a certain affection the sun seems to send its farewell ray far and level over the copses to them, and they silently receive it with gratitude, like a group of settlers with their children. The pines impress me as human. A slight vaporous cloud floats high over them, while in the west the sun goes down apace behind glowing pines, and golden clouds like mountains skirt the horizon.

Nothing stands up more free from blame in this world than a pine tree.

The dull and blundering behavior of clowns will as surely polish the writer at last as the criticism of men of thought.

It is wonderful, wonderful, the unceasing demand that Christendom makes on you, that you speak *from a moral point of view.* Though you be a babe, the cry is, Repent, repent. The Christian world will not admit that a man has a just perception of any truth, unless at the same time he cries, "Lord be merciful to me a sinner."

What made the hawk mount? Did you perceive the manœuvre? Did he fill himself with air? Before you were aware of it, he had mounted by his spiral path into the heavens.

Our country is broad and rich, for here, within twenty miles of Boston, I can stand in a clearing in the woods and look a mile or more, over the shrub oaks, to the distant pine copses and horizon of uncut woods, without a house or road or cultivated field in sight.

Sunset in winter from a clearing in the woods, about Well Meadow Head.

They say that the Indians of the Great Basin live on the almonds of the pine. Have not I been fed by the pine for many a year?

Go out before sunrise or stay out till sunset.

Dec. 21. Sunday. My difficulties with my friends are such as no frankness will settle. There is no precept in the New Testament that will assist me. My nature, it may [be], is secret. Others can confess and explain; I cannot. It is not that I am too proud, but that is not what is wanted. Friendship is the unspeakable joy and blessing that results to two or more individuals who from constitution sympathize; and natures are liable to no mistakes, but will know each other through thick and thin. Between two by nature alike and fitted to sympathize there is no veil and there can be no obstacle. Who are the estranged? Two friends explaining.

I feel sometimes as if I could say to my friends, "My friends, I am aware how I have outraged you, how I have seemingly preferred hate to love, seemingly treated others kindly and you unkindly, sedulously concealed my love, and sooner or later expressed all and more than all my hate." I can imagine how I might utter something like this in some moment never to be realized. But let me say frankly that at the same time I feel, it may be with too little regret, that I am under an awful necessity to be what I am. If the truth were known, which I do not know, I have no concern with those friends whom I misunderstand or who misunderstand me.

The fates only are unkind that keep us asunder, but

my friend is ever kind. I am of the nature of stone. It takes the summer's sun to warm it.

My acquaintances sometimes imply that I am too cold; but each thing is warm enough of its kind. Is the stone too cold which absorbs the heat of the summer sun and does not part with it during the night? Crystals, though they be of ice, are not too cold to melt, but it was in melting that they were formed. Cold! I am most sensible of warmth in winter days. It is not the warmth of fire that you would have, but everything is warm and cold according to its nature. It is not that I am too cold, but that our warmth and coldness are not of the same nature; hence when I am absolutely warmest, I may be coldest to you. Crystal does not complain of crystal any more than the dove of its mate. You who complain that I am cold find Nature cold. To me she is warm. My heat is latent to you. Fire itself is cold to whatever is not of a nature to be warmed by it. A cool wind is warmer to a feverish man than the air of a furnace. That I am cold means that I am of another nature.

The dogwood and its berries in the *swamp* by the railroad, just above the red house, pendent on long stems which hang short down as if broken, betwixt yellowish (?) and greenish (?), white, ovoid, pearly (?) or waxen (?) berries. What is the color of them? Ah, give me to walk in the dogwood swamp, with its few coarse branches! Beautiful as Satan. The prinos or black alder berries appear to have been consumed; only the skins left, for the most part, sticking to the twigs, so that I thought there were fewer than usual. Is it that our woods have

Vol. III

had to entertain arctic visitors in unusual numbers, who have exhausted their stores?

Sunlight on pine-needles is the phenomenon of a winter day.

Who ever saw a partridge soar over the fields? To every creature its own nature. They are very wild; but are they scarce? or can you exterminate them for that?

As I stand by the edge of the swamp (Ministerial), a heavy-winged hawk flies home to it at sundown, just over my head, in silence. I cross some mink or muskrat's devious path in the snow, with mincing feet and trailing body.

To-night, as so many nights within the year, the clouds arrange themselves in the east at sunset in long converging bars, according to the simple tactics of the sky. It is the melon-rind jig. It would serve for a permanent description of the sunset. Such is the morning and such the evening, converging bars inclose the day at each end as within a melon rind, and the morning and evening are one day. Long after the sun has set, and downy clouds have turned dark, and the shades of night have taken possession of the east, some rosy clouds will be seen in the upper sky over the portals of the darkening west.

How swiftly the earth appears to revolve at sunset, which at midday appears to rest on its axle!

Dec. 22. If I am thus seemingly cold compared with my companion's warm, who knows but mine is a less transient glow, a steadier and more equable heat, like that of the earth in spring, in which the flowers spring and expand? It is not words that I wish to hear or

to utter, but relations that I seek to stand in; and it oftener happens, methinks, that I go away unmet, unrecognized, ungreeted in my offered relation, than that you are disappointed of words. If I can believe that we are related to one another as truly and gloriously as I have imagined, I ask nothing more, and words are not required to convince me of this. I am disappointed of relations, you of words.

I have seen, in the form, in the expression of face, of a child three years old, the tried magnanimity and grave nobility of ancient and departed worthies. Just saw a little Irish boy, come from the distant shanty in the woods over the bleak railroad to school this morning, take his last step from his last snow-drift on to the schoolhouse door-step, floundering still; saw not his face or his profile, only his mien, and imagined, saw clearly in imagination, his old-worthy face behind the sober visor of his cap. Ah! this little Irish boy, I know not why, revives to my mind the worthies of antiquity. He is not drawn, he never was drawn, in a willow wagon; he progresses by his own brave steps. Has not the world waited for such a generation? Here he condescends to his a-b-c without one smile, who has the lore of worlds uncounted in his brain. He speaks not of the adventures of the causeway. What was the bravery of Leonidas and his three hundred boys at the pass of Thermopylæ to this infant's? They but dared to die; he dares to live, — and take his "reward of merit," perchance without relaxing his face into a smile, that overlooks his unseen and unrewardable merits. Little Johnny Riordan, who faces cold and routs it like a Persian army, who, yet innocent, carries in his knees the strength of a thousand Indras. That does not reward the thousandth part of his merit. While the charitable waddle about cased in furs, he, lively as a cricket, passes them on his way to school. I forget for the time Kossuth and his Hungarians. Here's a Kossuth for you![1]

An innocent child is a man who has repented once for all, and is born again, — has entered into the joy of his Lord.

Almost the whole world is orthodox and looks upon you as in a state of nature. In conversation with people of more than average wit, I find that the common assumption is that they have experienced a new birth, but you are in a state of nature.

Dec. 23. It would give me such joy to know that a friend had come to see me, and yet that pleasure I seldom if ever experience.

It is a record of the mellow and ripe moments that I would keep. I would not preserve the husk of life, but the kernel.

When the cup of life is full and flowing over, preserve some drops as a specimen, sample. When the intellect enlightens the heart and the heart warms the intellect.

Thoughts will sometimes possess our heads when we are up and about our business which are the exact counterpart of the bad dreams which we sometimes have by night, and I think that the intellect is equally inert in both cases. Very frequently, no doubt, the thoughts men have are the consequence of something which they have

[1] [See pp. 241–244; also *Journal*, vol. ii, pp. 117, 118.]

days has been remarkably light and dry. It is pleasant walking in the woods now, when the sun is just coming out and shining on the woods freshly covered with snow. At a distance the oak woods look very venerable. A fine, hale, wintry aspect things wear, and the pines, all snowed up, even suggest comfort. Where boughs cross each other much snow is caught, which now in all woods is gradually tumbling down.

By half past three the sun is fairly out. I go to the Cliffs. There is a narrow ridge of snow, a white line, on the storm side of the stem of every exposed tree. I see that there is to be a fine, clear sunset, and make myself a seat in the snow on the Cliff to witness it. Already a few clouds are glowing like a golden sierra just above the horizon. From a low arch the clear sky has rapidly spread eastward over the whole heavens, and the sun shines serenely, and the air is still, and the spotless snow covers the fields. The snow-storm is over, the clouds have departed, the sun shines serenely, the air is still, a pure and trackless white napkin covers the ground, and a fair evening is coming to conclude all. Gradually the sun sinks, the air grows more dusky, and I perceive that if it were not for the light reflected from the snow it would be quite dark. The woodchopper has started for home. I can no longer distinguish the color of the red oak leaves against the snow, but they appear black. The partridges have come forth to bud on the apple trees. Now the sun has quite disappeared, but the afterglow, as I may call it, apparently the reflection from the cloud beyond which the sun went down on the thick atmosphere of the horizon, is unusually bright and lasting.

eaten or done. Our waking *moods* and *humors* are our dreams, but whenever we are truly awake and serene, and healthy in all our senses, we have memorable visions. Who that takes up a book wishes for the report of the clogged bowels or the impure blood?

Yesterday afternoon I walked to the stone bridge over the Assabet, and thence down the river on the ice to the Leaning Hemlocks, and then crossed the other branch to the house. Do I not see two kinds of black alder, one blotched, the other lighter-colored, the former with many small berries crowded, the latter larger and single? Scared up partridges into the tops of the hemlocks, where they thought to conceal themselves.

Observed where a woodchopper had come to the river and cut a hole for water some days before. The river, frozen unexpectedly even, — but few open places, — had gone down since it froze, and the ice was accordingly bulged up over the rocks in its channel, with many fine cracks in all directions. It was a good opportunity to examine the fluviatile trees. I was struck by the amount of small interlaced roots — making almost a solid mass — of some red (?) oaks on the bank which the water had undermined, opposite Sam Barrett's. Observed by a wall beneath Nawshawtuct where many rabbits appeared to have played and nearly half a pint of dung was dropped in one pile on the snow.

This morning, when I woke, I found it snowing, the snow fine and driving almost horizontally, as if it had set in for a long storm, but a little after noon it ceased snowing and began to clear up, and I set forth for a walk. The snow which we have had for the last week or ten

Long, broken clouds in the horizon, in the dun atmosphere, — as if the fires of day were still smoking there, — hang with red and golden edging like the saddle-cloths of the steeds of the sun. Now all the clouds grow black, and I give up to-night; but unexpectedly, half an hour later when I look out, having got home, I find that the evening star is shining brightly, and, beneath all, the west horizon is glowing red, — that dun atmosphere instead of clouds reflecting the sun, — and I detect, just above the horizon, the narrowest imaginable white sickle of the new moon.

Dec. 24. It spits snow this afternoon. Saw a flock of snowbirds on the Walden road. I see them so commonly when it is beginning to snow that I am inclined to regard them as a sign of a snow-storm. The snow bunting (*Emberiza nivalis*) methinks it is, so white and arctic, not the slate-colored. Saw also some pine grosbeaks, magnificent winter birds, among the weeds and on the apple trees; like large catbirds[1] at a distance, but, nearer at hand, some of them, when they flit by, are seen to have gorgeous heads, breasts, and rumps (?), with red or crimson reflections, more beautiful than a steady bright red would be. The note I heard, a rather faint and innocent whistle of two bars.

Now and long since the birds' nests have been full of snow.

I had looked in vain into the west for nearly half an hour to see a red cloud blushing in the sky. The few clouds were dark, and I had given up all to night, but

[1] Rice calls them winter larks. Perhaps he means another.

when I had got home and chanced to look out the window from the supper [table], I perceived that all the west horizon was glowing with a rosy border, and that dun atmosphere had been the cloud this time which made the day's adieus. But half an hour before, that dun atmosphere hung over all the western woods and hills, precisely as if the fires of the day had just been put out in the west, and the burnt territory was sending out volumes of dun and lurid smoke to heaven, as if Phaëton had again driven the chariot of the sun so near as to set fire to earth.

Dec. 25. Thursday. Via spruce swamp on Conantum to hilltop, returning across river over shrub oak plain to Cliffs.

A wind is now blowing the light snow which fell a day or two ago into drifts, especially on the lee, now the south, side of the walls, the outlines of the drifts corresponding to the chinks in the walls and the eddies of the wind. The snow glides, unperceived for the most part, over the open fields without rising into the air (unless the ground is elevated), until it reaches an opposite wall, which it sifts through and is blown over, blowing off from it like steam when seen in the sun. As it passes through the chinks, it does not drive straight onward, but curves gracefully upwards into fantastic shapes, somewhat like the waves which curve as they break upon the shore; that is, as if the snow that passes through a chink were one connected body, detained by the friction of its lower side. It takes the form of saddles and shells and porringers. It builds up a fantastic alabaster wall

behind the first, — a snowy sierra. It is wonderful what sharp turrets it builds up, — builds up, *i. e.* by accumulation though seemingly by attrition, though the curves upward to a point like the prows of ancient vessels look like sharp carving, or as if the material had been held before the blowpipe. So what was blown up into the air gradually sifts down into the road or field, and forms the slope of the sierra. Astonishingly sharp and thin overhanging eaves it builds, even this dry snow, where it has the least suggestion from a wall or bank, — less than a mason ever springs his brick from. This is the architecture of the snow. On high hills exposed to wind and sun, it curls off like the steam from a damp roof in the morning. Such sharply defined forms it takes as if the core had been the flames of gaslights.

I go forth to see the sun set. Who knows how it will set, even half an hour beforehand? whether it will go down in clouds or a clear sky? I feel that it is late when the mountains in the north and northwest have ceased to reflect the sun. The shadow is not partial but universal.

In a winter day the sun is almost all in all.

I witness a beauty in the form or coloring of the clouds which addresses itself to my imagination, for which you account scientifically to my understanding, but do not so account to my imagination. It is what it suggests and is the symbol of that I care for, and if, by any trick of science, you rob it of its symbolicalness, you do me no service and explain nothing. I, standing twenty miles off, see a crimson cloud in the horizon. You tell me it is a mass of vapor which absorbs all other rays and reflects the red, but that is nothing to the purpose, for

Vol. III

this red vision excites me, stirs my blood, makes my thoughts flow, and I have new and indescribable fancies, and you have not touched the secret of that influence. If there is not something mystical in your explanation, something unexplainable to the understanding, some elements of mystery, it is quite insufficient. If there is nothing in it which speaks to my imagination, what boots it? What sort of science is that which enriches the understanding, but robs the imagination? not merely robs Peter to pay Paul, but takes from Peter more than it ever gives to Paul? That is simply the way in which it speaks to the understanding, and that is the account which the understanding gives of it; but that is not the way it speaks to the imagination, and that is not the account which the imagination gives of it. Just as inadequate to a pure mechanic would be a poet's account of a steam-engine.

If we knew all things thus mechanically merely, should we know anything really?

It would be a truer discipline for the writer to take the least film of thought that floats in the twilight sky of his mind for his theme, about which he has scarcely one idea (that would be teaching his ideas how to shoot), faintest intimations, shadowiest subjects, make a lecture on this, by assiduity and attention get perchance two views of the same, increase a little the stock of knowledge, clear a new field instead of manuring the old; instead of making a lecture out of such obvious truths, hackneyed to the minds of all thinkers. We seek too soon to ally the perceptions of the mind to the

experience of the hand, to prove our gossamer truths practical, to show their connection with our every-day life (better show their distance from our every-day life), to relate them to the cider-mill and the banking institution. Ah, give me pure mind, pure thought! Let me not be in haste to detect the *universal law;* let me see more clearly a particular instance of it! Much finer themes I aspire to, which will yield no satisfaction to the vulgar mind, not one sentence for them. Perchance it may convince such that there are more things in heaven and earth than are dreamed of in their philosophy. Dissolve one nebula, and so destroy the nebular system and hypothesis. Do not seek expressions, seek thoughts to be expressed. By perseverance you get two views of the same rare truth.

That way of viewing things you know of, least insisted on by you, however, least remembered, — take that view, adhere to that, insist on that, see all things from that point of view. Will you let these intimations go unattended to and watch the door-bell or knocker? That is your text. Do not speak for other men; speak for yourself. They show you as in a vision the kingdoms of the world, and of all the worlds, but you prefer to look in upon a puppet-show. Though you should only speak to one kindred mind in all time, though you should not speak to one, but only utter aloud, that you may the more completely realize and live in the idea which contains the reason of your life, that you may build yourself up to the height of your conceptions, that you may remember your Creator in the days of your youth and justify His ways to man, that the end of life may not be its amusement, speak — though your thought presupposes the non-existence of your hearers — thoughts that transcend life and death. What though mortal ears are not fitted to hear absolute truth! Thoughts that blot out the earth are best conceived in the night, when darkness has already blotted it out from sight.

We look upward for inspiration.

Dec. 26. I observed this afternoon that when Edmund Hosmer came home from sledding wood and unyoked his oxen, they made a business of stretching and scratching themselves with their horns and rubbing against the posts, and licking themselves in those parts which the yoke had prevented their reaching all day. The human way in which they behaved affected me even pathetically. They were too serious to be glad that their day's work was done; they had not spirits enough left for that. They behaved as a tired woodchopper might. This was to me a new phase in the life of the laboring ox. It is painful to think how they may sometimes be overworked. I saw that even the ox could be weary with toil.

Dec. 27. Saturday. Sunset from Fair Haven Hill. This evening there are many clouds in the west into which the sun goes down so that we have our visible or apparent sunset and red evening sky as much as fifteen minutes before the real sunset. You must be early on the hills to witness such a sunset, — by half past four at least. Then all the vales, even to the horizon, are full of a purple vapor, which half veils the distant moun-

tains, and the windows of undiscoverable farmhouses shine like an early candle or a fire. After the sun has gone behind a cloud, there appears to be a gathering of clouds around his setting, and for a few moments his light in the amber sky seems more intense, brighter, and purer than at noonday.

I think you never see such a brightness in the noonday heavens as in the western sky sometimes, just before the sun goes down in clouds, like the ecstasy which we [are] told sometimes lights up the face of a dying man. That is a *serene* or evening death, like the end of the day. Then, at last, through all the grossness which has accumulated in the atmosphere of day, is seen a patch of serene sky fairer by contrast with the surrounding dark than midday, and even the gross atmosphere of the day is gilded and made pure as amber by the setting sun, as if the day's sins were forgiven it. The man is blessed who every day is permitted to behold anything so pure and serene as the western sky at sunset, while revolutions vex the world.

There is no winter necessarily in the sky, though the snow covers the earth. The sky is always ready to answer to our moods; we can see summer there or winter. Snow and drifts on the earth; it swiftly descends from the heavens and leaves them pure. The heavens present, perhaps, pretty much the same aspect summer and winter.

It is remarkable that the sun rarely goes down without a cloud.

Venus — I suppose it is — is now the evening star, and very bright she is immediately after sunset in the early twilight.

Dec. 28. All day a drizzling rain, ever and anon holding up with driving mists. A January thaw. The snow rapidly dissolving; in all hollows a pond forming; unfathomable water beneath the snow. Went into Tommy Wheeler's house, where still stands the spinning-wheel, and even the loom, home-made. Great pitch pine timbers overhead, fifteen or sixteen inches in diameter, telling of the primitive forest here. The white pines look greener than usual in this gentle rain, and every needle has a drop at the end of it. There is a mist in the air which partially conceals them, and they seem of a piece with it. Some one has cut a hole in the ice at Jenny's Brook, and set a steel trap under water, and suspended a large piece of meat over it, for a bait for a mink, apparently.

Dec. 29. The sun just risen. The ground is almost entirely bare. The puddles are not skimmed over. It is warm as an April morning. There is a sound as of bluebirds in the air, and the cocks crow as in the spring. The steam curls up from the roofs and the ground. You walk with open cloak. It is exciting [to] behold the smooth, glassy surface of water where the melted snow has formed large puddles and ponds, and to see it running in the sluices. In the clear atmosphere I saw, far in the eastern horizon, the steam from the steam-engine, like downy clouds above the woods, I think even beyond Weston. By school-time you see the boys in the streets playing with the sluices, and the whole population is inspired with new life.

In the afternoon to Saw Mill Brook with W. E. C.

Snow all gone from Minott's hillside. The willow at the red house shines in the sun. The boys have come out under the hill to pitch coppers. Watts sits on his door-step. It is like the first of April. The wind is west. At the turnpike bridge, water stands a foot or two deep over the ice. Water spiders have come out and are skating against the stream. How much they depend on January thaws! Now for the frozen-thawed apples! This is the first chance they have had to thaw this winter. It feels as warm as in summer; you sit on any fence-rail and vegetate in the sun, and realize that the earth may produce peas again. Yet they say that this open and mild weather is unhealthy; that is always the way with them. How admirable it is that we can never foresee the weather, — that that is always novel! Yesterday nobody dreamed of to-day; nobody dreams of to-morrow. Hence the weather is ever the news. What a fine and measureless joy the gods grant us thus, letting us know nothing about the day that is to dawn! This day, yesterday, was as incredible as any other miracle. Now all creatures feel it, even the cattle chewing stalks in the barn-yards; and perchance it has penetrated even to the lurking-places of the crickets under the rocks.

The artist is at work in the Deep Cut. The telegraph harp sounds.

Dec. 30. Tuesday. Mem.: Go to the Deep Cut.[1]
The flies now crawl forth from the crevices all covered with dust, dreaming of summer, without life or energy enough to clean their wings.

[1] [See next date.]

This afternoon, being on Fair Haven Hill, I heard the sound of a saw, and soon after from the Cliff saw two men sawing down a noble pine beneath, about forty rods off. I resolved to watch it till it fell, the last of a dozen or more which were left when the forest was cut and for fifteen years have waved in solitary majesty over the sprout-land. I saw them like beavers or insects gnawing at the trunk of this noble tree, the diminutive manikins with their cross-cut saw which could scarcely span it. It towered up a hundred feet as I afterward found by measurement, one of the tallest probably in the township and straight as an arrow, but slanting a little toward the hillside, its top seen against the frozen river and the hills of Conantum. I watch closely to see when it begins to move. Now the sawers stop, and with an axe open it a little on the side toward which it leans, that it may break the faster. And now their saw goes again. Now surely it is going; it is inclined one quarter of the quadrant, and, breathless, I expect its crashing fall. But no, I was mistaken; it has not moved an inch; it stands at the same angle as at first. It is fifteen minutes yet to its fall. Still its branches wave in the wind, as if it were destined to stand for a century, and the wind soughs through its needles as of yore; it is still a forest tree, the most majestic tree that waves over Musketaquid. The silvery sheen of the sunlight is reflected from its needles; it still affords an inaccessible crotch for the squirrel's nest; not a lichen has forsaken its mast-like stem, its raking mast, — the hill is the hulk. Now, now 's the moment! The manikins at its base are fleeing from their crime. They have

dropped the guilty saw and axe. How slowly and majestically it starts! as if it were only swayed by a summer breeze, and would return without a sigh to its location in the air. And now it fans the hillside with its fall, and it lies down to its bed in the valley, from which it is never to rise, as softly as a feather, folding its green mantle about it like a warrior, as if, tired of standing, it embraced the earth with silent joy, returning its elements to the dust again. But hark! there you only saw, but did not hear. There now comes up a deafening crash to these rocks, advertising you that even trees do not die without a groan. It rushes to embrace the earth, and mingle its elements with the dust. And now all is still once more and forever, both to eye and ear.

I went down and measured it. It was about four feet in diameter where it was sawed, about one hundred feet long. Before I had reached it the axemen had already half divested it of its branches. Its gracefully spreading top was a perfect wreck on the hillside as if it had been made of glass, and the tender cones of one year's growth upon its summit appealed in vain and too late to the mercy of the chopper. Already he has measured it with his axe, and marked off the mill-logs it will make. And the space it occupied in upper air is vacant for the next two centuries. It is lumber. He has laid waste the air. When the fish hawk in the spring revisits the banks of the Musketaquid, he will circle in vain to find his accustomed perch, and the hen-hawk will mourn for the pines lofty enough to protect her brood. A plant which it has taken two centuries to

Vol. III

perfect, rising by slow stages into the heavens, has this afternoon ceased to exist. Its sapling top had expanded to this January thaw as the forerunner of summers to come. Why does not the village bell sound a knell? I hear no knell tolled. I see no procession of mourners in the streets, or the woodland aisles. The squirrel has leaped to another tree; the hawk has circled further off, and has now settled upon a new eyrie, but the woodman is preparing [to] lay his axe at the root of that also.

Dec. 31. The third warm day; now overcast and beginning to drizzle. Still it is inspiriting as the brightest weather. Though the sun surely is not a-going to shine, there is a latent light in the mist, as if there were more electricity than usual in the air. There are warm, foggy days in winter which excite us.

It reminds me, this thick, spring-like weather, that I have not enough valued and attended to the pure clarity and brilliancy of the winter skies. Consider in what respects the winter sunsets differ from the summer ones. Shall I ever in summer evenings see so celestial a reach of blue sky contrasting with amber as I have seen a few days since. The day sky in winter corresponds for clarity to the night sky, in which the stars shine and twinkle so brightly in this latitude.

I am too late, perhaps, to see the sand foliage in the Deep Cut; should have been there day before yesterday; it is now too wet and soft. Yet in some places it is perfect. I see some perfect leopards' paws.[1] These

[1] [*Walden*, pp. 336, 337; Riv. 470.]

things suggest that there is motion in the earth as well as on the surface; it lives and grows. It is warmed and influenced by the sun, just as my blood by my thoughts. I seem to see some of the life that is in the spring bud and blossom more intimately, nearer its fountainhead, the fancy sketches and designs of the artist. It is more simple and primitive growth; as if for ages sand and clay might have thus flowed into the forms of foliage, before plants were produced to clothe the earth. The earth I tread on is not a dead, inert mass. It is a body, has a spirit, is organic, and fluid to the influence of its spirit, and to whatever particle of that spirit is in me. She is not dead, but sleepeth. It is more cheering than the fertility and luxuriance of vineyards, this fundamental fertility near to the principle of growth. To be sure it is somewhat fœcal and stercoral.[1] So the poet's creative moment is when the frost is coming out in the spring, but, as in the case of some too easy poets, if the weather is too warm and rainy or long continued it becomes mere diarrhœa, mud and clay relaxed. The poet must not have something pass his bowels merely; that is women's poetry. He must have something pass his brain and heart and bowels, too, it may be, all together. So he gets delivered. There is no end to the fine bowels here exhibited, — heaps of liver, lights, and bowels. Have you no bowels? Nature has some bowels. And there again she is mother of humanity.[2] Concord is a worthier place to live in, the globe is a worthier place, for these creations, this slumbering life that may wake. Even the solid globe is permeated by the living

[1] [*Walden*, p. 340; Riv. 475.]   [2] [*Ibid.*]

law. It is the most living of creatures. No doubt all creatures that live on its surface are but parasites.

I observed this afternoon the old Irishwoman at the shanty in the woods, sitting out on the hillside, bareheaded, in the rain and on the icy though thawing ground, knitting. She comes out, like the ground squirrel, at the least intimation of warmer weather. She will not have to go far to be buried, so close she lives to the earth, while I walk still in a greatcoat and under an umbrella. Such Irish as these are naturalizing themselves at a rapid rate, and threaten at last to displace the Yankees, as the latter have the Indians. The process of acclimation is rapid with them; they draw long breaths in the American sick-room. What must be the philosophy of life to that woman, ready to flow down the slope with the running sand! Ah, what would I not give for her point of view! She does not use any *th*'s in her style. Yet I fear that even she may have learned to lie.

There is a low mist in the woods. It is a good day to study lichens. The view so confined it compels your attention to near objects, and the white background reveals the disks of the lichens distinctly. They appear more loose, flowing, expanded, flattened out, the colors brighter for the damp. The round greenish-yellow lichens on the white pines loom through the mist (or are seen dimly) like shields whose devices you would fain read. The trees appear all at once covered with their crop of lichens and mosses of all kinds, — flat and tearful are some, distended by moisture. This is their solstice, and your eyes run swiftly through the mist to these things only. On every fallen twig, even,

that has lain under the snows, as well as on the trees, they appear erect and now first to have attained their full expansion. Nature has a day for each of her creatures, her creations. To-day it is an exhibition of lichens at Forest Hall, the livid green of some, the fruit of others. They eclipse the trees they cover. And the red, club-pointed (baobab-tree-like) on the stumps, the *erythrean* stumps! Ah, beautiful is decay! True, as Thales said, the world was made out of water. That is the principle of all things.

I do not lay myself open to my friends!? The owner of the casket locks it, and unlocks it. Treat your friends for what you know them to be. Regard no surfaces. Consider not what they did, but what they intended. Be sure, as you know them you are known of them again. Last night I treated my dearest friend ill. Though I could find some excuse for myself, it is not such excuse as under the circumstances could be pleaded in so many words. Instantly I blamed myself, and sought an opportunity to make atonement, but the friend avoided me, and, with kinder feelings even than before, I was obliged to depart. And now this morning I feel that it is too late to speak of the trifle, and, besides, I doubt now in the cool morning, if I have a right to suppose such intimate and serious relations as afford a basis for the apology I had conceived, for even magnanimity must ask this poor earth for a field. The virtues even wait for invitation. Yet I am resolved to know that one centrally, through thick and thin, and though we should be cold to one another, though we should never speak to one another, I will know that inward

and essential love may exist even under a superficial cold, and that the law of attraction speaks louder than words. My true relation this instant shall be my apology for my false relation the last instant. I made haste to cast off my injustice as scurf. I own it least of anybody, for I have absolutely done with it. Let the idle and wavering and apologizing friend appropriate it. Methinks our estrangement is only like the divergence of the branches which unite in the stem.

This night I heard Mrs. S—— lecture on womanhood. The most important fact about the lecture was that a woman said it, and in that respect it was suggestive. Went to see her afterward, but the interview added nothing to the previous impression, rather subtracted. She was a woman in the too common sense after all. You had to fire small charges: I did not have a finger in once, for fear of blowing away all her works and so ending the game. You had to substitute courtesy for sense and argument. It requires nothing less than a chivalric feeling to sustain a conversation with a lady. I carried her lecture for her in my pocket wrapped in her handkerchief; my pocket exhales cologne to this moment. The championess of woman's rights still asks you to be a ladies' man. I can't fire a salute, even, for fear some of the guns may be shotted. I had to unshot all the guns in truth's battery and fire powder and wadding only. Certainly the heart is only for rare occasions; the intellect affords the most unfailing entertainment. It would only do to let her feel the wind of the ball. I fear that to the last woman's lectures will demand mainly courtesy from man.

(To go on with walk, this written next morning.) How deceptive the size of a large pine! still, as you approach it, even within a rod or two, it looks only like a reasonable stick, fit for a string-piece, perchance, the average size of trees one foot in diameter, — big as a keg or a half-barrel, it may be, — fit for the sill or the beams of an old-fashioned house. This you think is a generous appreciation and allowance. Not till you stand close to its foot, upon one of its swelling insteps, and compare its diameter with the diameter of your own eyeballs, do you begin to discover its width. Stand by its side, and see how it shuts out a hemisphere from you. Why, it is as wide as a front door. What a slender arrow, a light shaft, now that you stand a rod or two off! What a ballista, a battering ram, a mighty vegetable monster, a cannon, near at hand! Now set a barrel, aye, a hogshead beside it. You apply your measures. The foot rule seems suddenly shrunk. Your umbrella is but half as long as it was.

The pine I saw fall yesterday measured to-day one hundred and five feet, and was about ninety-four years old. There was one still larger lying beside it, one hundred and fifteen feet long, ninety-six years old, four feet diameter the longest way. The tears were streaming from the sap-wood — about twenty circles — of each, pure amber or pearly tears.

Through the drizzling fog, now just before nightfall, I see from the Cliffs the dark cones of pine trees that rise above the level of the tree-tops, and can trace a few elm tree tops where a farmhouse hides beneath.

Denuded pines stand in the clearings with no old

cloak to wrap about them, only the apexes of their cones entire, telling a pathetic story of the companions that clothed them. So stands a man. It is clearing around him. He has no companions on the hills. The lonely traveller, looking up, wonders why he was left when his companions were taken.

IV

JANUARY, 1852

(ÆT. 34)

Jan. 1. Mr. Frost did not like Mrs. S——'s lecture last night; did not like what she said about the clergy. Said it was too *transcendental* for him. This is the profane swearing of such men.

I have observed that one mood is the natural critic of another. When possessed with a strong feeling on any subject foreign to the one I may be writing on, I know very well what of good and what of bad I have written on the latter. It looks to me now as it will ten years hence. My life is then earnest and will tolerate no makeshifts nor nonsense. What is tinsel or euphuism or irrelevant is revealed to such a touchstone. In the light of a strong feeling, all things take their places, and truth of every kind is seen for such. Now let me read my verses, and I will tell you if the god has had a hand in them. I wish to survey my composition for a moment from the least favorable point of view. I wish to be translated to the future, and look at my work as it were at a structure on the plain, to observe what portions have crumbled under the influence of the elements.

9.30 P. M. — To Fair Haven.
Moon little more than half full. Not a cloud in the

Vol. III

sky. It is a remarkably warm night for the season, the ground almost entirely bare. The stars are dazzlingly bright. The fault may be in my own barrenness, but methinks there is a certain poverty about the winter night's sky. The stars of higher magnitude are more bright and dazzling, and therefore appear more near and numerable, while those that appear indistinct and infinitely remote in the summer, imparting the impression of unfathomability to the sky, are scarcely seen at all. The front halls of heaven are so brilliantly lighted that they quite eclipse the more remote. The sky has fallen many degrees.

The river has risen and flooded the meadows again. The white pines, now seen against the moon, with their *single* foliage, look thin.

These are some of the differences between this and the autumn or summer nights: the stiffened glebe under my feet, the dazzle and seeming nearness of the stars, the duller gleam from ice on rivers and ponds, the white spots in the fields and streaks by the wall-sides where are the remains of drifts, yet unmelted. Perhaps the only thing that spoke to me on this walk was the bare, lichen-covered gray rock at the Cliff, in the moonlight, naked and almost warm as in summer.

I have so much faith in the power of truth to communicate itself, that I should not believe a friend if he should tell me that he had given credit to an unjust rumor concerning me. Suspect! Ah! yes, you may suspect a thousand things, but I well know that that which you suspect most confidently of all, is just the

truth. Your other doubts but flavor this your main suspicion; they are the condiments which, taken alone, do simply bite the tongue.

McKean has sawed another of the pines under Fair Haven. He says it made eighty-two feet in length of mill-logs, and was so straight that it would have made a first-rate mast eighty feet long. I told him that Nathan Hosmer had told me that he once helped saw down a pine three feet in diameter, that they sawed it clean through and it still stood on the stump, and it took two men to push it over. McKean could understand how this might be done by wedging. He says that he often runs his saw straight through a tree without wedges and without its pinching to within an eighth of an inch of the other side before it breaks. To do this you must begin on the side toward which the tree leans. Of course it does not lean any more so as to pinch the saw till you have got beyond the heart. It will then make room for itself and be relieved by the tipping of the tree. A green hand would begin on the other side and so split the tree up the middle.

The worst kind of *chigo*, or tick, to get under your skin is yourself in an irritable mood.

I believe it was Chalmers who said, speaking of Coleridge, that for his part he wanted ideas which he could see all round and not such as he must look at away up in the heavens. Such a man, one would say, would never look at the moon, because she never turns her other side to us, but holds it steadily toward the heavens beyond; and the light which comes from ideas which have their orbit as distant from the earth, and which is no less cheering and enlightening to the benighted traveller than that of the moon and stars, is naturally reproached or nicknamed as moonshine by such. Ideas that soar above the earth cannot be seen all round, but ever have one side turned toward the heavens. They are moonshine, are they? Very well, then, do your night travelling when there is no moon to light you; but I will be thankful for the light that reaches me from the star of least magnitude. I will be thankful that I see so much as one side of a celestial idea, one side of the rainbow and the sunset sky, the *face* of God alone.[1]

Jan. 3. Oak-apples are a winter fruit. The leaves being gone, they are now conspicuous and shine in the sun. Some trees are quite full of them. Do they not suggest that all vegetable fruit is but the albumen about young animal life?

The ground has been bare for some days, and the weather warm. The river has risen, and now the meadows are frozen so as to bear, — a dark, thin, but rather opaque ice, as if covered with steam, — and I see now travelling, sweeping, coursing over it, in long winrows, fine pellets of snow, like cotton, fine, round, and dry, which I do not detect in the air before they fall. They lodge against a rail and make a small drift. So once more the skating will be spoiled.

A spirit sweeps the string of the telegraph harp, and strains of music are drawn out endlessly like the wire

[1] [*Excursions*, p. 324; Riv. 398, 399.]

itself. We have no need to refer music and poetry to Greece for an origin now. What becomes of the story of a tortoise-shell on the seashore now? The world is young, and music is its infant voice. I do not despair of such a world where you have only to stretch an ordinary wire from tree to tree to hear such strains drawn from it by New England breezes as make Greece and all antiquity seem poor in melody. Why was it made that man should be thrilled to his inmost being by the vibrating of a wire? Are not inspiration and ecstasy a more rapid vibration of the nerves swept by the inrushing excited spirit, whether zephyral or boreal in its character.

Jan. 4. To Fair Haven on the ice partially covered with snow.

The cracks in the ice showing a white cleavage. What is their law? Somewhat like foliage, but too rectangular, like the characters of some Oriental language. I feel as if I could get grammar and dictionary and go into it. They are of the form which a thin flake of ice takes in melting, somewhat rectangular with an irregular edge.

The pond is covered, — dappled or sprinkled, — more than half covered, with flat drifts or patches of snow which has lodged, of graceful curving outlines. One would like to skim over it like a hawk, and detect their law.

Jan. 5. To-day the trees are white with snow — I mean their stems and branches — and have the true

wintry look, on the storm side. Not till this has the winter come to the forest. They look like the small frostwork in the path and on the windows now, especially the oak woods at a distance, and you see better the form which their branches take. That is a picture of winter, and now you may put a cottage under them and roof it with snow-drifts, and let the smoke curl up amid the boughs in the morning.

Sitting on the Cliffs, I see plainly for the first time that the island in Fair Haven is the triangular point of a hill cut off, and forty or fifty rods west, on the mainland, I see the still almost raw and shelving edge of the bank, the raw sand-scar as if sodded over the past summer, — as a man cuts off a piece of pudding on his plate, — as if the intermediate portion of the hill had sunk and left a cranberry meadow.

It is with singular emotions that I stand on this Cliff and reflect in what age of the world this revolution, the evidence of which is of to-day, was evidenced by a raw and shelving sand-bank.

After this revolution how long came the settlers out of England to Musketaquid, came our political revolution and Concord Fight? After the natural elements were quiet, perchance.

It was a dark day, the heavens shut out with dense snow-clouds and the trees wetting me with the melting snow, when I went through Brown's wood on Fair Haven, which they are cutting off, and suddenly looking through the woods between the stems of the trees, I thought I saw an extensive fire in the western horizon. It was a bright coppery-yellow fair-weather cloud along

the edge of the horizon, gold with some alloy of copper, in such contrast with the remaining clouds as to suggest nothing less than fire. On that side the clouds which covered our day, low in the horizon with a dun and smoke-like edge, were rolled up like a curtain with heavy folds, revealing this further bright curtain beyond.

Jan. 7. Last evening, walked to Lincoln to lecture in a driving snow-storm, but the invisible moon gave light through the thickest of it. I observed how richly the snow lay on the cedars.

This afternoon, in dells of the wood and on the lee side of the woods, where the wind has not disturbed it, the snow still lies on the trees as richly as I ever saw it. It was just moist enough to stick. The pitch pines wear it best, their plumes hang down like the feathers of the ostrich or the tail of the cassowary, so purely white, — I am sorry that I cannot say *snowy* white, for in purity it is like nothing but itself. From contrast with the dark needles and stems of the trees, whiter than ever on the ground. Even the bare apple tree limbs and twigs in the hollows support each a little ridge of snow, a collar of snow, five or six inches high. The trees are bent under the weight into a great variety of postures, — arches, etc. Their branches and tops are so consolidated by the burden of snow, and they stand in such new attitudes, the tops often like canopies or parasols, agglomerated, that they remind me of the pictures of palms and other Oriental trees. In some places bent to the ground on each side, quite closing the path, bowed

not with grief but in a contented wintry sleep; looking often, when the tops or branches or plumes only are
bent, like travellers facing the storm, whose heads and
shoulders are covered with a white mantle and whose
drapery falls about them revealing protuberances here
and there, — forehead or elbows. Travellers bending
to the storm under white mantles through which you
can tell where their heads and elbows **are**. Sometimes
the lower limbs of the pitch pine, divested of plumes,
under such plumes and canopies, bear each their ridge
of snow, crossing and interlacing each other like lattice-
work, so that you cannot look more than a rod into
the rich tracery. The sunlight, breaking forth at sundown on these snowed [*sic*] trees, is faint and uncertain
like a sprinkling of red oak leaves, — a whitish glow
on the snow and the oak leaves. I hardly know if it is
shining on the oak leaves or not.

Now from the shanty plain I see the sun descending
into the west. There is something new, a *snow*-bow, in
the east, on the snow-clouds, merely a *white* bow, hardly
any color distinguishable. But in the west what inconceivable crystalline purity of blue sky! (C. says it is
color of a robin's egg); and I see feathery clouds on
this ground, some travelling north, others directly in
the opposite direction, though apparently close together.
Some of these cloudlets are waifs and droppings from
rainbows, clear rainbow through and through, spun
out of the fibre of the rainbow, or, rather, as if the children of the west had been pulling rainbow (instead of
tow) that had done service, old junk of rainbow, and
cast it into flox.

And then such fantastic feathery scrawls of gauze-
like vapor on this elysian ground! We never tire of the
drama of sunset. I go forth each afternoon and look
into the west a quarter of an hour before sunset, with
fresh curiosity, to see what new picture will be painted
there, what new panorama exhibited, what new dissolving views. Can Washington Street or Broadway show
anything as good? Every day a new picture is painted
and framed, held up for half an hour, in such lights as
the Great Artist chooses, and then withdrawn, and the
curtain falls.

And then the sun goes down, and long the afterglow
gives light. And then the damask curtains glow along
the western window. And now the first star is lit, and
I go home.

Jan. 8. I notice that almost every track which I
made yesterday in the snow — perhaps ten inches deep
— has got a dead leaf in it, though none is to be seen
on the snow around.

Even as early as 3 o'clock these winter afternoons
the axes in the woods sound like nightfall, like the
sound of a twilight labor.

Reading from my manuscripts to Miss Emerson this
evening and using the word "god," in one instance,
in perchance a merely heathenish sense, she inquired
hastily in a tone of dignified anxiety, "Is that god spelt
with a little *g* ?" Fortunately it was. (I had brought
in the word "god" without any solemnity of voice or
connection.) So I went on as if nothing had happened.

Vol. III

I perceive that the livid lettuce-leaved lichen which
I gathered the other day has dried almost an ash or
satin, with no green about [it], — has bleached.

Jan. 9. The sky shut out by snow-clouds. It spits
a little snow and then holds up. Where a path has been
shovelled through drifts in the road, and the cakes of
snow piled up, I see little azures, little heavens, in the
crannies and crevices. The deeper they are, and the
larger masses they are surrounded by, the darker-blue
they are. Some are a very light blue with a tinge of
green. Methinks I oftenest see this when it is snowing.
At any rate the atmosphere must be in a peculiar state.
Apparently the snow absorbs the other rays and reflects
the blue. It has strained the air, and only the blue rays
have passed through the sieve. Is, then, the blue water
of Walden snow-water? I see the heaven hiding in
nooks and crevices in the snow. Into every track which
the teamster makes, this elysian, empyrean atmosphere
rushes. The blue of my eye sympathizes with this blue
in the snow.

The great pine woods have a peculiar appearance
this afternoon. This rather fine snow has lodged in
their limbs and given them a grayish look, but as it
lies thicker along the core of the limb, it has the appearance, at a distance, of dim white lines lying at various
angles like a vast network over the woods, or, rather,
like cobwebs seen on the grass in summer mornings.
A kind of film over them.

I never saw the pitch pines better snowed up. They
look like Chinese pagodas.

"The majestic prerogative which Linnæus was possessed of," says Stoever, "to confer titles in the vegetable kingdom," did not escape the criticism of Haller,
who says: "We would reserve all those garlands for
those alone who are real and experienced botanists.
Nor would we ever assign such a denomination to the
mere hopes conceived of men who have not passed the
ordeal of merit."

Jan. 11. What need to travel? There are no sierras
equal to the clouds in the sunset sky. And are not these
substantial enough? In a low or level country, perchance,
the forms of the clouds supply the place of mountains
and precipices to the eye, the grosser atmosphere makes
a mountainous country in the sky.

The glory of these afternoons, though the sky may be
mostly overcast, is in the ineffably clear blue, or else
pale greenish-yellow, patches of sky in the west just
before sunset. The whole cope of heaven seen at once
is never so elysian. Windows to heaven, the heavenward windows of the earth. The end of the day is
truly Hesperian.

R. W. E. showed me yesterday a letter from H. Greenough, the sculptor, on architecture, which he liked very
much. Greenough's idea was to make architectural ornaments have a core of truth, a necessity and hence a
beauty. All very well, as I told R. W. E., from Greenough's point of view, but only a little better than the
common dilettantism.[1] I was afraid I should say hard
things if I said more.

¹ [*Walden*, p. 51; Riv. 75.]

We sometimes find ourselves living fast, — unprofitably and coarsely even, — as we catch ourselves eating our meals in unaccountable haste. But in one sense we cannot live too leisurely. Let me not live as if time was short. Catch the pace of the seasons; have leisure to attend to every phenomenon of nature, and to entertain every thought that comes to you. Let your life be a leisurely progress through the realms of nature, even in guest-quarters.

This reminds me that the old Northman kings did in fact board round a good part of the time, as schoolmasters sometimes with us.

But as for Greenough, I felt as if it was dilettantism, and he was such a reformer in architecture as Channing in social matters. He began at the cornice. It was only how to put a core of truth within the ornaments, that every sugar-plum might in fact have an almond or carroway seed in it, and not how the inhabitant, the indweller, might be true and let the ornaments take care of themselves. He seemed to me to lean over the cornice and timidly whisper this half truth to the rude indwellers, who really knew it more interiorly than he. What of architectural beauty I now see, I know has gradually grown from within outward, out of the character and necessities of the indweller and builder, without even a thought for mere ornament, but an unconscious nobleness and truthfulness of character and life; and whatever additional beauty of this kind is destined to be produced will be preceded and accompanied, aye, created, by a like unconscious beauty of life. One of the most beautiful buildings in this country is a logger's

hut in the woods, and equally beautiful will be the citizen's suburban box, when the life of the indweller shall be as simple and as agreeable to the imagination, and there is as little straining after effect in the style of his dwelling. Much it concerns a man, forsooth, how a few sticks are slanted under him or over him, what colors are daubed upon his box! One man says, in his despair, "Take up a handful of the earth at your feet, and paint your house that color!" What an abundance of leisure he must have on his hands! An enterprise to improve the style of cottage architecture! Grow your own house, I say. Build it after an Orphean fashion. When R. W. E. and Greenough have got a few blocks finished and advertised, I will look at them. When they have got my ornaments ready I will wear them. What do you take up a handful of dirt for? Why don't you paint your house with your blood? with your sweat? Thin not the paint with *spirits* of turpentine. There's a deal of nonsense abroad.[1]

The question is not where did the traveller go? what places did he see? — it would be difficult to choose between places — but who was the traveller? how did he travel? how genuine an experience did he get? For travelling is, in the main, like as if you stayed at home, and then the question is how do you live and conduct yourself at home? What I mean is that it might be hard to decide whether I would travel to Lake Superior, or Labrador, or Florida. Perhaps none would be worth the while, if I went by the usual mode. But if I travel in a simple, primitive, original manner, standing in a

[1] [*Walden*, pp. 51–53; Riv. 75–78.]

truer relation to men and nature, travel away from the old and commonplace, get some honest experience of life, if only out of my feet and homesickness, then it becomes less important whither I go or how far. I so see the world from a new and more commanding point of view. Perhaps it is easier to live a true and natural life while travelling, — as one can move about less awkwardly than he can stand still.

Jan. 12. *Monday.* C. says that he studied lichens a little while, but he found that if you pursued that study you must give up man. It was so thin, and there was so little of man in it! Why, the whole of it was n't more than an inch thick.

He went to hear Noggs [?] the other night. It was the poorest lecture he ever heard. Did n't know why he did n't come out. But then he found himself in a handsome hall well lighted and warmed, and thought it would be cheaper to spend the evening there than to go home.

I sometimes think that I may go forth and walk hard and earnestly, and live a more substantial life and get a glorious experience; be much abroad in heat and cold, day and night; live more, expend more atmospheres, be weary often, etc., etc. But then swiftly the thought comes to me, Go not so far out of your way for a truer life; keep strictly onward in that path alone which your genius points out. Do the things which lie nearest to you, but which are difficult to do. Live a purer, a more thoughtful and laborious life, more true to your friends and neighbors, more noble and mag-

nanimous, and that will be better than a wild walk. To live in relations of truth and sincerity with men is to dwell in a frontier country. What a wild and unfrequented wilderness that would be! What Saguenays of magnanimity that might be explored! Men talk about travelling this way or that, as if seeing were all in the eyes, and a man could sufficiently report what he stood bodily before, when the seeing depends ever on the being. All report of travel is the report of victory or defeat, of a contest with every event and phenomenon and how you came out of it. A blind man who possesses inward truth and consistency will see more than one who has faultless eyes but no serious and laborious astronomer to look through them. As if the eyes were the only part of a man that travelled! Men convert their property into cash, ministers fall sick to obtain the assistance of their parishes, all chaffer with sea-captains, etc., as if the whole object were to get conveyed to some part of the world a pair of eyes merely. A telescope conveyed to and set up at the Cape of Good Hope at great expense, and only a Bushman to look through it. Nothing like a little internal activity called life — if it were only walking much in a day — to keep the eyes in good order; no such collyrium.

Jan. 13. James Wood, Jr., told me this afternoon of a white pine in Carlisle which the owner was offered thirty dollars for and refused. He had bought the lot for the sake of the tree, which he left standing.

Here I am on the Cliffs at half past three or four o'clock. The snow more than a foot deep over all the land. Few if any leave the beaten paths. A few clouds are floating overhead, downy and dark. Clear sky and bright sun, and yet no redness. Remarkable, yet admirable, moderation that this should be confined to the morning and evening. Greeks were they who did it. A mother-o'-pearl tint is the utmost they will give you at midday, and this but rarely. Singular enough, twenty minutes later, looking up, I saw a long, light-textured cloud stretching from north to south, with a dunnish mass and an enlightened border, with its under edge toward the west all beautiful mother-o'-pearl, as remarkable as a rainbow, stretching over half the heavens; and underneath it, in the west, were flitting mother-o'-pearl clouds, which change their loose-textured form and melt rapidly away, never any so fast, even while I write. Before I can complete this sentence, I look up and they are gone, like smoke or rather the steam from the engine in the winter air. Even a considerable cloud, like a fabulous Atlantis or unfortunate isle in the Hesperian sea, is dissolved and dispersed in a minute or two, and nothing is left but the pure ether. Then another comes by magic, is born out of the pure blue empyrean, with beautiful mother-o'-pearl tints, where not a shred of vapor was to be seen before, not enough to stain a glass or polished steel blade. It grows more light and porous; the blue deeps are seen through it here and there; only a few flocks are left; and now these too have disappeared, and no one knows whither it is gone. You are compelled to look at the sky, for the earth is invisible.

Would not snow-drifts be a good study, — their

philosophy and poetry? Are they not worthy of a chapter? Are they always built up, or not rather carved out of the heaps of snow by the wind passing through the chinks in the walls? I do not see yet but they are builded. They are a sort of ripple-marks which the atmospheric sea makes on the snow-covered bottom.

Why can't I go to his office and talk with James Wood and learn his facts? But I should impose a certain restraint on him. We are strictly confined to our men; to whom we give liberty. I saw him with E. Wood snaking trees out of the woods on Fair Haven, — rude Northman work, with their chains and skids, in which Elijah Wood took the lead. If a tree stood in the way it was cut down, and pushed aside as it fell that it might not strike the oxen, though it might scare the horse, who began to dash through the woods with his rattling harness on, reckless and horse-like, ready to harm himself if not others, instinctively apprehending harm from that operation, — ready to impale himself upon the first stake and expose his bloody bowels to the air and spoil that piece of workmanship that he is, — a ghastly sight. So little prudence have horses, like some men. I knew one once, tied to a post, that, when a cannon [was] fired, reared and came down upon the post's sharp top, which pierced clean through and came out at his back, impaling him; and so he met his fate, and his equine spirit departed. As reckless as a horse that is "started."

We forget to strive and aspire, to do better ever than is expected of us. I cannot stay to be congratulated. I would leave the world behind me. We must with-

Vol. III

draw from our flatterers, even from our friends. They drag us down. It is rare that we use our thinking faculty as resolutely as an Irishman his spade. To please our friends and relatives we turn out our silver ore in cartloads, while we neglect to work our mines of gold known only to ourselves far up in the Sierras, where we pulled up a bush in our mountain walk, and saw the glittering treasure. Let us return thither. Let it be the price of our freedom to make that known.

Jan. 14. When I see the dead stems of the tansy, goldenrod, johnswort, asters, hardhack, etc., etc., rising above the snow by the roadside, sometimes in dense masses, which carry me back in imagination to their green summer life, I put faintly a question which I do not yet hear answered, Why stand they there? Why should the dead corn-stalks occupy the field longer than the green and living did? Many of them are granaries for the birds. It suggests that man is not an annual. He sees the annual plants wither. Nor does his sap cease to flow in the winter as does that of the trees, though, perhaps, even he may be slightly dormant at that season. It is to most a season to some extent of inactivity. He lays up his stores, and is perhaps a little chilled. On the approach of spring there is an increased flow of spirits, of blood, in his veins.

Here is a dense mass of dry tansy stems, attached still to the same roots which sustained them in summer, but what an interval between these and those. Here are no yellow disks; here are no green leaves; here is no strong odor to remind some of funerals.

Here is a change as great as can well be imagined. Bare, brown, scentless stalks, with the dry heads still adhering. Color, scent, and flavor gone.

We are related to all nature, animate and inanimate, and accordingly we share to some extent the nature of the dormant creatures. We all feel somewhat confined by the winter; the nights are longer, and we sleep more. We also wear more clothes. Yet the thought is not less active; perhaps it is more so.

What an effect the sight of green grass in the winter has on us! as at the spring by the Corner road.

Clouds are our mountains, and the child who had lived in a plain always and had never seen a mountain would find that he was prepared for the sight of them by his familiarity with clouds.

This dark, dull veil which shuts out the sky makes a favorable light and a frame under which to view those sailing island clouds in the clearer west.

I love to see now a cock of deep-reddish meadow-hay full of ferns and other meadow plants of the coarsest kind. My imagination supplies the green and the hum of bees. What a memento of summer such a haycock! To stand beside a haycock covered with snow in winter, through which the dry meadow plants peep out! And yet our hopes survive.

The snow flowing over the walls and across the road looks like a mist before me. In some places the wind passing through the chinks of the walls appears to have burst or cut through old snow-heaps, and so carved out these fantastic forms.[1]

[1] *Vide* forward to the 17th [p. 199].

Standing on the hill on the Baker Farm to-day, the level shrub oak plain under Fair Haven appeared as if Walden and other smaller ponds, and perhaps Fair Haven, had anciently sunk down in it, and the Cliffs been pushed up, for the level is continued in many cases even over extensive hollows. The shrub oaks here have lost their leaves, i. e. the small scrubby kind on this hill. I can see at a distance above the level of the snow a few bushes and grasses which mark the edge of the river. They seem to write the word *rivus* there. That is all or most to indicate that there is a river there. It is betrayed by that thin sedgy and willowy line or border marking the snow yonder.

As usual, there was no blueness in the ruts and crevices in the snow to-day. What kind of atmosphere does this require? When I observed it the other day, it was a rather moist air, some snow falling, the sky completely overcast, and the weather not very cold. It is one of the most interesting phenomena of the winter.

I noticed to-night, about sundown, that the clouds in the eastern horizon were the deepest indigo-blue of any I ever saw. Commencing with a pale blue or slate in the west, the color deepened toward the east.

The Governor, Bout*well* (?), lectured before the Lyceum to-night. Quite democratic. He wore no badge of his office. I believe that not even his brass buttons were official, but, perchance, worn with some respect to his station. If he could have divested himself a little more completely in his tone and manner of a sense of the dignity which belonged to his office, it would have been better still.

Vol. III

Jan. 15. We have heard a deal about English comfort. But may you not trace these stories home to some wealthy Sardanapalus who was able to pay for obsequious attendance and for every luxury? How far does it describe merely the tact and selfishness of the wealthy class? Ask the great mass of Englishmen and travellers, whose vote alone is conclusive, concerning the comfort they enjoyed in second and third class accommodations in steamboats and railroads and eating and lodging houses. Lord Somebody-or-other may have made himself comfortable, but the very style of his living makes it necessary that the great majority of his countrymen should be uncomfortable.

Are the second-class cars, the second-class accommodations on board steamboats, etc., i. e. the only class that can be compared with our own, remarkable for their comfort?

I do not know but the poet is he who generates poems. By continence he rises to creation on a higher level, a supernatural level.

When King Olaf the Saint was about to fight with the bonders to recover his lost kingdom, his scalds, who stood about him, composed songs about the events which would soon be taking place. Thormod's song concluded thus, —

> "One viking cheer! — then, stead of words,
> We'll speak with our death-dealing swords."

"These songs," says the chronicler, "were immediately got by heart by the army." Surely the scald's office was a significant and an honorable one then.

"This night the king lay with his army around him

on the field, — and lay long awake in prayer to God, and slept but little. Towards morning a slumber fell on him, and when he awoke daylight was shooting up. The king thought it too early to awaken the army, and asked where Thormod the scald was. Thormod was at hand, and asked what was the king's pleasure. 'Sing us a song,' said the king. Thormod raised himself up, and sang so loud that the whole army could hear him. He began to sing the old Biarkamal [composed and sung by Biarke before an old battle].[1]

. . . .

"Then the troops awoke, and when the song was ended the people thanked him for it; and it pleased many, as it was suitable to the time and occasion, and they called it the house-carle's whet."

For the first time this winter I notice snow-fleas this afternoon in Walden Wood. Wherever I go they are to be seen, especially in the deepest ruts and foot-tracks. Their number is almost infinite. It is a rather warm and moist afternoon, and feels like rain. I suppose that some peculiarity in the weather has called them forth from the bark of the trees.

It is good to see Minott's hens pecking and scratching the ground. What never-failing health they suggest! Even the sick hen is so naturally sick — like a green leaf turning to brown. No wonder men love to have hens about them and hear their creaking note. They are even laying eggs from time to time still — the undespairing race!

[1] [The brackets are Thoreau's.]

Minott was telling me to-day about his going across lots on snow-shoes. Why do they not use them now? He thinks the snows are not so deep.

It is a good school the farmers' sons go to these afternoons, loading and hauling great mill-logs bigger than any cannon, — a sort of battle in the forest. I think there must be an excitement derived from their labor such as they cannot tell. After reading of the life and battles of the Northmen in Snorro Sturleson's Chronicle, these labors most remind me of that. Some of these logs are for pumps; most are for boards and timbers and spiles for bridges. I met one old pupil of mine stretched at his length upon a vast ballista, or battering-ram, of a log, while one yoke and loaded sled went on alone before and another followed behind. How they renew and wear out the paths through the woods! They think I 'm loafing. I think they are drudging for gain. But no doubt our employment is more alike than we suspect, and we are each serving the great Master's ends more than our own. I have my work in the woods where I meet them, though my logs do not go to the same mill. I make a different use of skids. These men, too, who are sledding wood and sawing the logs into lengths in the woods, appear to me employed more after the old Northman fashion than the mechanics in their shops or the merchants behind their counters. There are many more men now in the woods than in summer.

The weather has been moderate for a fortnight. The overlapping snow-drifts by the path-sides remind me of some marble tombs and carving I have seen. I see where from time to time the teamster has laid his whip in them. He stains the spotless purity of the snow with his tobacco-juice.

In an account of a Chinese funeral, it is said the friends who attended "observed no particular order in their march." That seems a more natural and fitter way, more grief-like. The ranks should be broken. What must be the state of morals in that country where custom requires the chief mourner to put on the outward signs of extreme grief when he does not feel it, to throw himself on the ground and sob and howl though not a tear is shed, and require the support of others as he walks! What refuge can there be for truth in such a country?

Jan. 16. I see that to some men their relation to mankind is all-important. It is fatal in their eyes to outrage the opinions and customs of their fellow-men. Failure and success are, therefore, never proved by them by absolute and universal tests. I feel myself not so vitally related to my fellow-men. I impinge on them but by a point on one side. It is not a Siamese-twin ligature that binds me to them. It is unsafe to defer so much to mankind and the opinions of society, for these are always and without exception heathenish and barbarous, seen from the heights of philosophy. A wise man sees as clearly the heathenism and barbarity of his own countrymen as those of the nations to whom his countrymen send missionaries. The Englishman and American are subject to equally many national superstitions with the Hindoo and Chinese. My countrymen are to me foreigners. I have but little

more sympathy with them than with the mob of India or of China.

All nations are remiss in their duties and fall short of their standards. Madame Pfeiffer says of the Parsees, or Fire-Worshippers, in Bombay, who should all have been on hand on the esplanade to greet the first rays of the sun, that she found only a few here and there, and some did not make their appearance till 9 o'clock.

I see no important difference between the assumed gravity and the bought funeral sermon of the parish clergyman and the howlings and strikings of the breast of the hired mourning women of the East.

Bill Wheeler had two clumps for feet and progressed slowly, by short steps, having frozen his feet once, as I understood. Him I have been sure to meet once in five years, progressing into the town on his stubs, holding the middle of the road as if he drove an invisible herd before him, especially on a military day, — out of what confines, whose hired man having been, I never knew, — in what remote barn having quartered all these years. He seemed to belong to a different caste from other men, and reminded me of both the Indian Pariah and martyr. I understood that somebody was found to give him his drink for the few chores he could do. His meat was never referred to, he had so sublimed his life. One day since this, not long ago, I saw in my walk a kind of shelter such as woodmen might use, in the woods by the Great Meadows, made of meadow-hay cast over a rude frame. Thrusting my head in at

Vol. III

a hole, as I am wont to do in such cases, I found Bill Wheeler there curled up asleep on the hay, who, being suddenly wakened from a sound sleep, rubbed his eyes and inquired if I found any game, thinking I was sporting. I came away reflecting much on that man's life, — how he communicated with none; how now, perchance, he did chores for none; how low he lived, perhaps from a deep principle, that he might be some mighty philosopher, greater than Socrates or Diogenes, simplifying life, returning to nature, having turned his back on towns; how many things he had put off, — luxuries, comforts, human society, even his feet, — wrestling with his thoughts. I felt even as Diogenes when he saw the boy drinking out of his hands, and threw away his cup. Here was one who went alone, did no work, and had no relatives that I knew of, was not ambitious that I could see, did not depend on the good opinion of men. Must he not see things with an impartial eye, disinterested, as a toad observes the gardener? Perchance here is one of a sect of philosophers, the only one, so simple, so abstracted in thought and life from his contemporaries, that his wisdom is indeed foolishness to them. Who knows but in his solitary meadow-hay bunk he indulges, in thought, only in triumphant satires on men? Who knows but here is a superiority to literature and such things, unexpressed and inexpressible? Who has resolved to humble and mortify himself as never man was humbled and mortified. Whose very vividness of perception, clear knowledge, and insight have made him dumb, leaving no common consciousness and ground of parlance with

his kind, — or, rather, his unlike kindred! Whose news plainly is not my news nor yours. I was not sure for a moment but here was a philosopher who had left far behind him the philosophers of Greece and India, and I envied him his advantageous point of view. I was not to be deceived by a few stupid words, of course, and apparent besottedness. It was his position and career that I contemplated.

Channing has great respect for McKean, he stands on so low a level. Says he's great for conversation. He never says anything, hardly answers a question, but keeps at work; never exaggerates, nor uses an exclamation, and does as he agrees to. He appears to have got his shoulder to the wheel of the universe. But the other day he went greater lengths with me, as he and Barry were sawing down a pine, both kneeling of necessity. I said it was wet work for the knees in the snow. He observed, looking up at me, "We pray without ceasing."

But to return to Bill. I would have liked to know what view he took of life. A month or two after this, as I heard, he was found dead among the brush over back of the hill, — so far decomposed that his coffin was carried to his body and it was put into it with pitchforks. I have my misgivings still that he may have died a Brahmin's death, dwelling at the roots of trees at last, and been absorbed into the spirit of Brahm; though I have since been assured that he suffered from disappointed love, — was what is called love-cracked, — than which can there be any nobler suffering, any fairer death, for a human creature? — that that made him to drink, froze his feet, and did all the rest for him. Why have not the world the benefit of his long trial?

Jan. 17. One day two young women — a Sunday — stopped at the door of my hut and asked for some water. I answered that I had no cold water but I would lend them a dipper.[1] They never returned the dipper, and I had a right to suppose that they came to steal. They were a disgrace to their sex and to humanity. Pariahs of the moral world. Evil spirits that thirsted not for water but threw the dipper into the lake. Such as Dante saw. What the lake to them but liquid fire and brimstone? They will never know peace till they have returned the dipper. In all the worlds this is decreed.

"Evergreens" would be a good title for some of my things, — or "Gill-go-over-the-Ground," or "Wintergreen," or "Checkerberry," or "Usnea Lichens," etc., etc. "Iter Canadense."

One day an inoffensive, simple-minded pauper from the almshouse, who, with others, I often saw used as fencing-stuff, standing or sitting on a bushel in the fields to keep cattle from straying, visited me, and expressed a wish to live as I did. He told me in the simplest manner (and therefore quite superior to anything that is called humility — it was too simple and truthful for that) that he was "deficient in intellect." These were his words. The Lord had made him so, and yet he supposed that the Lord cared for him as much as for another. Said he: "I have always been so from my childhood; I never had much mind. It was the Lord's

[1] [See *Walden*, p. 167; Riv. 234.]

will, I suppose. I am weak in the head. I was not like other children." I have rarely been so fortunate as to meet a fellow-man on such promising ground. It was so solemnly true all that he said.[1]

The other day, the 14th, as I was passing the further Garfield house beyond Holden's, with my pantaloons, as usual, tucked into my boots (there was no path beyond Holden's), I heard some persons in Garfield's shed, but did not look round, and when I had got a rod or two beyond, I heard some one call out impudently from the shed, quite loud, something like "Holloa, mister! what do you think of the walking?" I turned round directly, and saw three men standing in the shed. I was resolved to discomfit them, — that they should prove their manhood, if they had any, and find something to say, though they had nothing before, that they should make amends to the universe by feeling cheap. They should either say to my face and eye what they had said to my back, or they should feel the meanness of having to change their tone. So I called out, looking at one, "Do you wish to speak to me, sir?" No answer. So I stepped a little nearer and repeated the question, when one replied, "Yes, sir." So I advanced with alacrity up the path they had shovelled. In the meanwhile one ran into the house. I thought I had seen the nearest one [before]. He called me by name, faintly and with hesitation, and held out his hand half unconsciously, which I did not decline, and I inquired gravely if he wished to say anything to me. He could only wave me to the other and

[1] [*Walden*, pp. 167, 168; Riv. 235, 236.]

mutter, "My brother." I approached *him* and repeated the question. He looked as if he were shrinking into a nutshell; a pitiable object he was. He looked away from me while he began to frame some business, some surveying, that he might wish to have done. I saw that he was drunk, that his brother was ashamed of him, and I turned my back on him in the outset of this indirect but drunken apology.

When Madame Pfeiffer arrived in Asiatic Russia, she felt the necessity of wearing other than a travelling dress, when she went to meet the authorities, for, as she remarks, she "was now in a civilized country, where . . . people are judged of by their clothes." This is another barbarous trait.[1]

It seemed that from such a basis as the poor weak-headed pauper had laid, — such a basis of truth and frankness, — an intercourse might go forward to something better than the intercourse of sages.[2]

It was on the 4th of July[3] that I put a few articles of furniture into a hay-rigging, some of which I had made myself, and commenced housekeeping.

There is the world-wide fact that, from the mass of men, the appearance of wealth, dress, and equipage alone command respect. They who yield it are the heathen who need to have missionaries sent to them;[4] and they who cannot afford to live and travel but in this *respectable* way are, if possible, more pitiable still.

In proportion as I have celestial thoughts, is the necessity for me to be out and behold the western sky

[1] [*Walden*, p. 25; Riv. 38.]   [2] [*Walden*, p. 168; Riv. 236.]
[3] [See *Walden*, p. 94; Riv. 133.]   [4] [*Walden*, p. 25; Riv. 38.]

before sunset these winter days. That is the symbol of the unclouded mind that knows neither winter nor summer. What is your thought like? That is the hue, that the purity, and transparency, and distance from earthly taint of my inmost mind, for whatever we see without is a symbol of something within, and that which is farthest off is the symbol of what is deepest within. The lover of contemplation, accordingly, will gaze much into the sky. Fair thoughts and a serene mind make fair days. The rainbow is the symbol of the triumph which succeeds to a grief that has tried us to our advantage, so that at last we can smile through our tears. It is the aspect with which we come out of the house of mourning. We have found our relief in tears. As the skies appear to a man, so is his mind. Some see only clouds there; some, prodigies and portents; some rarely look up at all; their heads, like the brutes', are directed toward earth. Some behold there serenity, purity, beauty ineffable. The world run to see the panorama, when there is a panorama in the sky which few go out to see.

Methinks there might be a chapter, when I speak of hens in the thawy days and spring weather on the chips, called "Chickweed" or "Plantain."

To seagoing men the very mountains are but boats turned upside down, as the Northmen in Norway speak of the "keel-ridge of the country," *i. e.* the ridge of the mountains which divide the waters flowing east and west[1] — as if they were a boat turned bottom up.

Those western vistas through clouds to the sky show

[1] [See *Journal*, vol. iv, p. 353.]

the clearest heavens, clearer and more elysian than if the whole sky is comparatively free from clouds, for then there is wont to be a vapor more generally diffused, especially near the horizon, which, in cloudy days, is absorbed, as it were, and collected into masses; and the vistas are clearer than the unobstructed cope of heaven.

The endless variety in the forms and texture of the clouds! — some fine, some coarse grained. I saw to-night overhead, stretching two thirds across the sky, what looked like the backbone, with portions of the ribs, of a fossil monster. Every form and creature is thus shadowed forth in vapor in the heavens.

Saw a teamster coming up the Boston road this afternoon, sitting on his load, which was bags of corn or salt, apparently, behind two horses and beating his hands for warmth. He finally got off and walked behind, to make his blood circulate faster, and I saw that he was a large man. But when I came near him, I found that he was a monstrous man and dwarfed all whom he stood by, so that I did not know whether he was large or they were small. Yet, though he stood so high, he stooped considerably, more than anybody I think of, and he wore a flat glazed cap to conceal his height, and when he got into the village he sat down on his bags again. I heard him remark to a boy that it was a cold day, and it was; but I wondered that he should feel the cold so sensibly, for I thought it must take a long time to cool so large a body.

I learned that it was Kimball of Littleton, that probably he was not twenty. The family was not *large*.

Wild, who took the census, said so, and that his sister said he could n't do much, — health and strength not much. It troubled him that he was so large, for people looked at him. There is at once something monstrous, in the bad sense, suggested by the sight of such a man. Great size is inhuman. It is as if a man should be born with the earth attached to him. I saw him standing up on a sled, talking with the driver, while his own team went on ahead; and I supposed from their comparative height that his companion was sitting, but he proved to be standing. Such a man is so much less human; that is what may make him sad.

Those old Northmen were not like so many men in these days, whom you can pass your hand through because they have not any backbone. When Asmund was going to kill Harek of Thiottö with a thin hatchet, King Magnus said, "'Rather take this axe of mine.' It was thick, and made like a club. 'Thou must know, Asmund,' added he, 'that there are hard bones in the old fellow.'" Asmund struck Harek on the head, and gave him his death-wound, but when he returned to the king's house, it appeared that "the whole edge of the axe was turned with the blow."

It appears to me that at a very early age the mind of man, perhaps at the same time with his body, ceases to be elastic. His intellectual power becomes something defined and limited. He does not think expansively, as he would stretch himself in his growing days. What was flexible sap hardens into heart-wood, and there is no further change. In the season of youth,

Vol. III

methinks, man is capable of intellectual effort and performance which surpass all rules and bounds; as the youth lays out his whole strength without fear or prudence and does not feel his limits. It is the transition from poetry to prose. The young man can run and leap; he has not learned exactly how far, he knows no limits. The grown man does not exceed his daily labor. He has no strength to waste.

Jan. 18. Sunday. E. Hosmer tells me that his daughter, walking with Miss Mary Emerson to some meeting or lecture, — perhaps it was Mrs. Smith's, — the latter was saying that she did not want to go, she did not think it was worth while to be running after such amusements, etc., etc. Whereupon Miss Hosmer asked, "What do you go for, then?" "None of your business," was the characteristic reply. Sometimes, when a woman was speaking where gentlemen were present, she put her hand on her and said, "Be still. I want to hear the men talk."

I still remember those wonderful sparkles at Pelham Pond. The very sportsmen in the distance, with their guns and dogs, presented some surfaces on which a sparkle could impinge, such was the transparent, flashing air. It was a most exhilarating, intoxicating air, as when poets sing of the sparkling wine.

I have seen some men in whom the usually posthumous decay appeared to have commenced. They impressed me as actually nothing alive; as if there was not salt enough in their composition to preserve them. I could not approach them without a smelling-bottle

at my nose, — not till the Fates strengthened the pickle in which they were.

While the snow is falling, the telegraph harp is resounding across the fields. As if the telegraph approached so near an attribute of divinity that music naturally attended it.

To-day, again, I saw some of the *blue* in the crevices of the snow. It is snowing, but not a moist snow. Perhaps the snow in the air, as well as on the ground, takes up the white rays and reflects the blue. There is no blue to be seen overhead, and it has as it were taken refuge in the chinks and crevices in the snow.

What is like the peep or whistle of a bird in the midst of a winter storm?

The pines, some of them, seen through this fine driving snow, have a bluish hue.

Barbarous as we esteem the Chinese, they have already built their steamboat. Swiftly the arts spread in these days. Madame Pfeiffer visited the garden of a mandarin in Canton, "in which," says she, "I was the more interested because it was the birthplace of the first Chinese steamboat, built by order of the mandarin and by Chinese workmen. The mandarin had gone through his studies in North America, where he remained for thirteen years." She was there after 1846.

Jan. 19. I felt a little wonder the other night that the large man went so as a matter of course with the human race, that he did not suspect that he belonged to some other genus, that he did not go off with some menagerie, with the elephant or the camelopard. You do not have to go far, to grow much, to get beyond the sphere of humanity. Why he should exist as a sort of attaché to the human race. Where was the rest of his family? He was, as it were, astray. There is something comically pathetic about it. What made him think that he belonged to the human race? Did he gradually grow up to that faith? His was a vegetable growth. His face lacked expression. When his large features were done, his face still bulged out and grew this way and that, just like a mammoth squash which magnifies all its warts. Great growth of body suggests the vegetable. He was pumpkin pine, sycamore. The extra growth was squash and pumpkin all. It was more flesh than his soul could animate. There is something monstrous even about his thoughts.

The snow, which has drifted badly, ceasing about 2 o'clock, I went forth by way of Walden road, whither no sleigh or sled had passed this day, the fine, dry snow blowing and drifting still. It was pleasant to make the first tracks in this road through the woods, where all the road, except a faint depression, two long slight valleys, marking the ruts, was obliterated, — a smooth, white plain between the bordering woods, which only a few dry oak leaves coursed over. I sank into the snow for long distances more than three feet at each step. From Bare Hill I looked into the west, the sun still fifteen minutes high. The snow blowing far off in the sun, high as a house, looked like the mist that rises from rivers in the morning. I came across lots through the dry white powder from Britton's camp. Very cold on the causeway and on the hilltops. The

low western sky an Indian red, after the sun was gone.

Jan. 20. Walked down the Boston road. It was good to look off over the great unspotted fields of snow, the walls and fences almost buried in it and hardly a turf or stake left bare for the starving crows to light on. There is no track nor mark to mar its purity beyond the single sled track, except where, once in half a mile, some traveller has stepped aside for a sleigh to pass.

The farmers nowadays can cart out peat and muck over the frozen meadows. Somewhat analogous, methinks, the scholar does; drives in with tight-braced energy and winter cheer on to his now firm meadowy grounds, and carts, hauls off, the virgin loads of fertilizing soil which he threw up in the warm, soft summer. We now bring our muck out of the meadows, but it was thrown up first in summer. The scholar's and the farmer's work are strictly analogous. Easily he now conveys, sliding over the snow-clad ground, great loads of fuel and of lumber which have grown in many summers, from the forest to the town. *He* deals with the dry hay and cows, the spoils of summer meads and fields, stored in his barns, doling it out from day to day, and manufactures milk for men. When I see the farmer driving into his barn-yard with a load of muck, whose blackness contrasts strangely with the white snow, I have the thoughts which I have described. He is doing like myself. My barn-yard is my journal.

I do not know but it is too much to read one newspaper in a week, for I now take the weekly *Tribune,* and for a few days past, it seems to me, I have not dwelt in Concord; the sun, the clouds, the snow, the trees say not so much to me. You cannot serve two masters. It requires more than a day's devotion to know and to possess the wealth of a day.[1] To read of things distant and sounding betrays us into slighting these which are then apparently near and small. We learn to look abroad for our mind and spirit's daily nutriment, and what is this dull town to me? what are these plain fields and the aspects of this earth and these skies? All summer and far into the fall I unconsciously went by the newspapers and the news, and now I find it was because the morning and the evening were full of news to me. My walks were full of incidents. I attended not to the affairs of Europe, but to my own affairs in Concord fields.[2]

To see the sun rise or go down every day would preserve us sane forever, — so to relate ourselves, for our mind's and body's health, to a universal fact.[3]

Last spring our new stone bridge was said to be about to fall. The selectmen got a bridge architect to look at it and, acting on his advice, put up a barrier and warned travellers not to cross it. Of course, I believed with the rest of my neighbors that there was no *immediate* danger, for there it was standing, and the barrier knocked down, that travellers might go over,

---

[1] [*Cape Cod, and Miscellanies*, p. 471; *Misc.*, Riv. 247.]
[2] [*Cape Cod, and Miscellanies*, p. 472; *Misc.*, Riv. 275.]
[3] [*Cape Cod, and Miscellanies*, pp. 472, 473; *Misc.*, Riv. 275.]

as they did with few exceptions. But one day, riding that way with another man, and reflecting that I had never looked into the condition of the bridge myself, and if it should fall with us on it, I should have reason to say what a fool I was to go over when I was warned, I made him stop on this side, merely for principle's sake, and walked over while he rode before, and I got in again at the other end. I paid that degree of respect to the advice of the bridge architect and the warning of the selectmen. It was my companion's daily thoroughfare.

Greeley says of London, "The morning to sleep, the afternoon to business, and the evening to enjoyment, seems the usual routine with the favored classes." They have no morning life then. They are afternoon men. To begin the day at noon!

The days are now sensibly longer, and half past five is as light as five was.

Jan. 21. One day, when I went out to my wood-pile, or rather my pile of stumps, I observed two large ants, the one red, the other much larger and black, fiercely contending with one another, and rolling over on the chips. It was evidently a struggle for life and death which had grown out of a serious feud. Having once got hold, they never let go of each other, but struggled and wrestled and rolled on the chips, each retaining his hold with mastiff-like pertinacity. Looking further, I found to my astonishment that the chips were covered with such combatants, that it was not a *duellum* but a *bellum*, a war between two races of ants, the red always pitted against the black, and frequently two red ones to one black.[1] They covered all the hills and vales of my wood-yard, and, indeed, the ground was already strewn with the dead, both red and black. It was the only war I had ever witnessed, the only battle-field I ever trod while the battle was raging; internecine war; the red republicans and the black despots or imperialists. On every side they were engaged in deadly combat, yet without any noise that I could hear, and never human soldiers fought so resolutely. I watched a couple, in a little sunny valley amid the chips, that were fast locked in each other's embraces, now at noonday prepared to fight till the sun went down. The smaller red champion had fastened himself like a vise to his adversary's front, and through all the tumblings on that field never for an instant ceased to gnaw at one of his feelers near the root, having already caused the other to go by the board, while the stronger black one dashed him from side to side, and, as I saw on looking nearer, had divested him of several of his members. None manifested a disposition to retreat from the combat equal or unequal. It was evident that their battle-cry was conquer or die. They fought like mastiffs or bulldogs, who will not let go though all their legs are cut off. In the meanwhile there came along a single red ant on the side-hill of this valley, evidently full of excitement, who either had dispatched his foe or had not yet taken part in the battle; probably the latter, for he had lost none of his limbs. He

[1] [The story of this battle is told in *Walden*, pp. 253-256; Riv. 355-360.]

saw this unequal combat from afar, — for the blacks were nearly twice the size of the red, — he drew near with rapid pace till he stood on his guard within half an inch of the combatants, then, watching his opportunity, he sprang upon the black warrior and commenced his operations near the root of his right fore leg, leaving the other to select among his own members, and so there were three united for life and death apparently, — united for life until death, — as if a new kind of attraction had been invented, which put all other locks and cements to shame.

I should not wonder if they had their respective musical bands stationed on some chip and playing their national airs the while to cheer the dying combatants. (Whose mother had charged him to return with his shield or upon it.) I was myself excited somewhat, even as if they had been men. The more you think of it, the less the difference. And certainly there is no other fight recorded in Concord that will bear a moment's comparison with this. I have no doubt they had as just a cause, one or even both parties, as our forefathers, and that the results will be as important and memorable. And there was far more patriotism and heroism. For numbers and for carnage it was an Austerlitz or Dresden. I saw no disposition to retreat.

I took up the chip on which the three I have particularly described were struggling, carried it into my house, and placed it under a tumbler on my window-sill, wishing [to] see the issue. Holding a microscope to the first-mentioned red ant, I saw that though he

was assiduously gnawing at the near fore leg of his enemy, having severed his remaining feeler, his own breast was all torn away, exposing what vitals he had there to the jaws of the black warrior, whose own breastplate was apparently too thick for him; and the dark carbuncles of his eyes shone with ferocity such as wars only could excite. They struggled for half an hour longer under the tumbler, and when I looked again, the black soldier had severed the heads of his foes from their bodies, and the former were hanging on either side of him still apparently as firmly fastened as ever, and he was endeavoring, with feeble struggles, being without feelers and with only one or two legs, and I know not how many other wounds, to divest himself of them; which at length, after half an hour more, he had accomplished. I raised the tumbler, and he went off over the window-sill in that crippled state. Whether he finally survived that combat and had a pension settled on him, I do not know. But I thought that his industry would not be worth much thereafter.

Which party was victorious I never learned, nor the cause of the war. But I felt for the rest of that day as if I had had my feelings harrowed and excited by witnessing the struggle, the ferocity and carnage, of a human battle before my door.

To record truths which shall have the same relation and value to the next world, *i. e.* the world of thought and of the soul, that political news has to this.

This winter they are cutting down our woods more seriously than ever, — Fair Haven Hill, Walden, Lin-

næa Borealis Wood, etc., etc. Thank God, they cannot cut down the clouds!

History used to be the history of successive kings or their reigns, — the Williams, Henrys, Johns, Richards, etc., etc., all of them great in somebody's estimation. But we have altered that considerably. Hereafter it is to be to a greater extent the history of peoples. You do not hear some King Louis or Edward or Leopold referred to now by sensible men with much respect.

Heard Higginson lecture to-night on Mohammed. Why did I not like it better? Can I deny that it was good? Perhaps I am bound to account to *myself* at least for any lurking dislike for what others admire and I am not *prepared* to find fault with. Well, I did not like it, then, because it did not make me like it, it did not carry me away captive. He is not simple enough. For the most part the manner overbore, choked off, and stifled, put out of sight and hearing, the matter. I was inclined to forget that he was speaking, conveying ideas; thought there had been an intermission. Never endeavor consciously to supply the tone which you think proper for certain sentences. It is as if a man whose mind was at ease should supply the tones and gestures for a man in distress who found only the words; as when one makes a speech and another behind him makes gestures. Then he reminded me of Emerson, and I could not afford to be reminded of Christ himself. Yet who can deny that it was good? But it was that intelligence, that way of viewing things (combined with much peculiar *talent*), which is the common property of this generation. A man does best when he is most himself.

I never realized so distinctly as this moment that I am peacefully parting company with the best friend I ever had, by each pursuing his proper path. I perceive that it is possible that we may have a better *understanding* now than when we were more at one. Not expecting such essential agreement as before. Simply our paths diverge.

Jan. 22. Having occasion to get up and light a lamp in the middle of a sultry night, — perhaps it was to exterminate the mosquito race, — I observed a stream of large black ants passing up and down one of the bare corner posts, those descending having their large white larvæ in their mouths, the others making haste up for another load. I supposed that they had found the heat so great just under the roof as to compel them to remove their offspring to a cooler place by night. They had evidently taken and communicated the resolution to improve the coolness of the night to remove their young to a cooler and safer locality. One stream running up, another down, with great industry.

But why I changed? why I left the woods? I do not think that I can tell. I have often wished myself back. I do not know any better how I ever came to go there. Perhaps it is none of my business, even if it is yours. Perhaps I wanted a change. There was a little stagnation, it may be. About 2 o'clock in the afternoon the world's axle creaked as if it needed greasing, as if the oxen labored with the wain and could hardly get their

load over the ridge of the day. Perhaps if I lived there much longer, I might live there forever. One would think twice before he accepted heaven on such terms. A ticket to Heaven must include tickets to Limbo, Purgatory, and Hell. Your ticket to the boxes admits you to the pit also. And if you take a cabin passage, you can smoke, at least forward of the engine, — you have the liberty of the whole boat. But no, I do not wish for a ticket to the boxes, nor to take a cabin passage. I will rather go before the mast and on the deck of the world. I have no desire to go "abaft the engine."[1]

What is it that I see from one mile to two miles distant in the horizon on all sides from my window, but the woods, which still, almost without exception, encircle our New England towns. They still bound almost every view. They have been driven off only so far. Where still wild creatures haunt. How long will these last? Is this a universal and permanent feature? Have the oldest countries retained it? Is it not an interesting and important question whether these are decreasing or not? Look out what window I will, my eyes rest in the distance on a forest! Is this fact of no significance? Is this circumstance of no value? Why such pains in old countries to plant gardens and parks? A certain sample of wild nature, a certain primitiveness.

One man proposed a book in which visitors should write their names; said he would be at the expense of it!!! Did he consider what the expense of it would be? As if it were of any use, when a man failed to make any memorable impression on you, for him to leave his name.

[1] [*Walden*, p. 356; Riv. 498.]

But it may be that he writes a good hand, who had not left any fame. No! I kept a book to put their fames in. I was at the expense of it.[1]

The milkman is now filling his ice-house.

The towns thus bordered, with a fringed and tasselled border, each has its preserves. Methinks the town should have more supervision and control over its parks than it has. It concerns us all whether these proprietors choose to cut down all the woods this winter or not.

I must say that I do not know what made me leave the pond. I left it as unaccountably as I went to it. To speak sincerely, I went there because I had got ready to go; I left it for the same reason.

How much botany is indebted to the Arabians! A great part of our common names of plants would appear to be Arabic.

Was it not fit that I should live on rice mainly, who loved so well to read the philosophy of India?[2]

The pleasures of the intellect are permanent, the pleasures of the heart are transitory.

My friend invites me to read my papers to him. Gladly would I read, if he would hear. He must not hear coarsely but finely, suffering not the *least* to pass through the sieve of hearing. To associate with one for years with joy who never met you thought with thought! An overflowing sympathy while yet there is no intellectual communion. Could we not meet on higher ground with the same heartiness? It is dull work reading to one who does not apprehend you.

[1] [*Walden*, p. 169; Riv. 237, 238.]   [2] [*Walden*, p. 67; Riv. 97.]

How can it go on? I will still abide by the truth in my converse and intercourse with my friends, whether I am so brought nearer to or removed further from them. I shall not be the less your friend for answering you truly though coldly. Even the estrangement of friends is a fact to be serenely contemplated, as in the course of nature. It is of no use to lie either by word or action. Is not the everlasting truth agreeable to you?

To set down such choice experiences that my own writings may inspire me and at last I may make wholes of parts. Certainly it is a distinct profession to rescue from oblivion and to fix the sentiments and thoughts which visit all men more or less generally, that the contemplation of the unfinished picture may suggest its harmonious completion. Associate reverently and as much as you can with your loftiest thoughts. Each thought that is welcomed and recorded is a nest egg, by the side of which more will be laid. Thoughts accidentally thrown together become a frame in which more may be developed and exhibited. Perhaps this is the main value of a habit of writing, of keeping a journal, — that so we remember our best hours and stimulate ourselves. My thoughts are my company. They have a certain individuality and separate existence, aye, personality. Having by chance recorded a few disconnected thoughts and then brought them into juxtaposition, they suggest a whole new field in which it was possible to labor and to think. Thought begat thought.

One mother-o'-pearl tint is common to the winter sky half an hour before sundown.

I love to look at Ebby Hubbard's oaks and pines on the hillside from Brister's Hill. Am thankful that there is one old miser who will not sell nor cut his woods, though it is said that they are wasting. It is an ill wind that blows nobody any good.

It is a sharp, cutting cold day, stiffening the face. Thermometers have lately sunk to 20°.

When a man asks me a question, I look him in the face. If I do not see any inquiry there, I cannot answer it. A man asked me about the coldness of this winter compared with others last night. I looked at him. His face expressed no more curiosity or relationship to me than a custard pudding. I made him a random answer. I put him off till he was in earnest. He wanted to make conversation.

The surface of the snow in the fields is that of pretty large waves on a sea over which a summer breeze is sweeping.

That in the preaching or mission of the Jesuits in Canada which converted the Indians was their sincerity. They could not be suspected of sinister motives. The savages were not poor observers and reasoners. The priests were, therefore, sure of success, for they had paid the price of it.

We resist no true invitations; they are irresistible. When my friend asks me to stay, and I do not, unless I have another engagement it is because I do not find myself invited. It is not in his will to invite me. We should deal with the real mood of our friends. I visited my friend constantly for many years, and he postponed our friendship to trivial engagements, so that I saw him

not at all. When in after years he had leisure to meet me, I did not find myself invited to go to him.

Jan. 23. The snow is so deep and the cold so intense that the crows are compelled to be very bold in seeking their food, and come very near the houses in the village. One is now walking about and pecking the dung in the street in front of Frank Monroe's. They remind me, as they sail along over the street, of the turkey buzzards of the South, and perhaps many hard winters in succession would make them as tame.

There is a vegetable life, as well as a spiritual and animal life, in us, for the hair and nails continue to grow after the *anima* has left the body, and the spiritual and animal life is dead. There is also probably an inorganic mineral life.

The surface of the snow on the 20th was not yet disturbed, or rippled even, by the wind.

P. M. — Deep Cut, going to Fair Haven Hill.

No music from the telegraph harp on the causeway, where the wind is strong, but in the Cut this cold day I hear memorable strains. What must the birds and beasts think where it passes through woods, who heard only the squeaking of the trees before! I should think that these strains would get into their music at last. Will not the mockingbird be heard one day inserting this strain in his medley? It intoxicates me. Orpheus is still alive. All poetry and mythology revive. The spirits of all bards sweep the strings. I hear the clearest silver, lyre-like tones, Tyrtæan tones. I think of Menander and the rest. It is the most glorious music I ever heard.

Vol. III

All those bards revive and flourish again in that five minutes in the Deep Cut. The breeze came through an oak still wearing its dry leaves. The very fine clear tones seemed to come from the very core and pith of the telegraph-pole. I know not but it is my own chords that tremble so divinely. There are barytones and high sharp tones, etc. Some come sweeping seemingly from further along the wire. The latent music of the earth had found here a vent. Music Æolian. There were two strings, in fact, one each side. I do not know but this will make me read the Greek poets. Thus, as ever, the finest uses of things are the accidental. Mr. Morse did not invent this music.

I see where the squirrels have torn the pine cones in pieces to come at their seeds. And in some cases the mice (?) have nibbled the buds of the pitch pines, where the plumes have been bent down by the snow.

The Blue Hills of Milton are now white.

Lindley, in Loudon, dismisses the winterberries by saying, "The species are low shrubs of little beauty." Says nothing of the berry.

There are some whose ears help me so that my things have a rare significance when I read to them. It is almost too good a hearing, so that for the time I regard my own writing from too favorable a point of view.

Just before sunset there were few clouds or specks to be seen in the western sky, but the sun gets down lower, and many dark clouds are made visible, their sides toward us being darkened. In the bright light they were but floating feathers of vapor; now they swell into dark evening clouds.

It is a fair sunset, with many purplish fishes in the horizon, pinkish and golden with bright edges; like a school of purplish whales, they sail or float down from the north; or like leopards' skins they hang in the west. If the sun goes behind a cloud, it is still reflected from the least haziness or vapor in that part of the sky, the air is so clear; and the afterglow is remarkably long. And now the blaze is put out, and only a few glowing clouds, like the flickering light of the fire, skirt the west. And now only the brands and embers, mixed with smoke, make an Indian red along the horizon. And the new moon and the evening star, close together, preside over the twilight scene.

The thermometer was at 21° this morning.

Some botanical names have originated in a mere blunder. Thus the *Citharexylum melanocardium* of the West Indies, "called by the French *fidèle*, from its faithfulness or durability in building," the English have corrupted into fiddle-wood, and so the genus goes. It is unfit for musical instruments. (Lindley.)

Jan. 24. If thou art a writer, write as if thy time were short, for it is indeed short at the longest. Improve each occasion when thy soul is reached. Drain the cup of inspiration to its last dregs. Fear no intemperance in that, for the years will come when otherwise thou wilt regret opportunities unimproved. The spring will not last forever. These fertile and expanding seasons of thy life, when the rain reaches thy root, when thy vigor shoots, when thy flower is budding, shall be fewer and farther between. Again I say,

Remember thy Creator in the days of thy youth. Use and commit to life what you cannot commit to memory. I hear the tones of my sister's piano below. It reminds me of strains which once I heard more frequently, when, possessed with the inaudible rhythm, I sought my chamber in the cold and communed with my own thoughts. I feel as if I then received the gifts of the gods with too much indifference. Why did I not cultivate those fields they introduced me to? Does nothing withstand the inevitable march of time? Why did I not use my eyes when I stood on Pisgah? Now I hear those strains but seldom. My rhythmical mood does not endure. I cannot draw from it and return to it in my thought as to a well all the evening or the morning. I cannot dip my pen in it. I cannot work the vein, it is so fine and volatile. Ah, sweet, ineffable reminiscences!

In thy journal let there never be a jest! To the earnest there is nothing ludicrous.

P. M. — Down the Flint's Pond road and return across.

Where the mountains in the horizon are well wooded and the snow does not lodge, they still look blue. All but a narrow segment of the sky in the northwest and southeast being suddenly overcast by a passing kind of snow-squall, though no snow falls, I look into the clear sky with its floating clouds in the northwest as from night into day, now at 4 P. M. The sun sets about five.

Walden and White Ponds are a vitreous greenish

blue, like patches of the winter sky seen in the west before sundown.[1]

Even the dry leaves are gregarious, and they collect in little heaps in the hollows in the snow, or even on the plane surfaces, driven in flocks by the wind. How like shrinking maidens wrapping their scarfs about them they flutter along! The oaks are made thus to retain their leaves, that they may play over the snow-crust and add variety to the winter landscape. If you wished to collect leaves, you would only have to make holes in the snow for traps. I see that my tracks are often filled two feet deep with them. They are blown quite across Walden on the wavy snow. Two flitting along together by fits and starts, now one running ahead, then another, remind me of squirrels. Mostly white oak leaves, but the other oaks, i. e. especially red oaks, also. There is a certain refinement or cultivation, even feminineness, suggested by the rounded lobes, the scalloped edge, of the white oak leaf, compared with the wild, brusque points of the red and black and scarlet and shrub oaks.

Now I see a faint bluish tinge in the ruts, but it is warmer and there is a snow-bearing cloud over all.

When the cars passed, I being on the pond (Walden), the sun was setting and suffusing the clouds far and near with rosy light. Even the steam from the engine, as its flocks or wreaths rose above the shadow of the woods, became a rosy cloud even fairer than the rest, but it was soon dissipated.

I see in the woods the woodman's embers, which

[1] [*Walden*, p. 197; Riv. 277, 278.]

have melted a circular hole in the snow, where he warms his coffee at noon. But these days the fire does not melt the snow over a space three feet across.

These woods! Why do I not feel their being cut more sorely? Does it not affect me nearly? The axe can deprive me of much. Concord is sheared of its pride. I am certainly the less attached to my native town in consequence. One, and a main, link is broken. I shall go to Walden less frequently.

When the telegraph harp trembles and wavers, I am most affected, as if it were approaching to articulation. It sports so with my heart-strings. When the harp dies away a little, then I revive for it. It cannot be too faint. I almost envy the Irish, whose shanty in the Cut is so near, that they can hear this music daily standing at their door. How strange to think that a sound so soothing, elevating, educating, telling of Greece and the Muses, might have been heard sweeping other strings when only the red man ranged these fields! might, perchance, in course of time have civilized him!

If an Indian brave will not fear torture and aids his enemies to torment him, what become of pity and a hundred other Christian virtues? The charitable are suddenly without employment.

When I come out on to the causeway, I behold a splendid picture in the west. The damask-lined clouds, like rifts from a coal mine, which sparkle beneath, seen diving into the west. When clouds rise in mid-afternoon, you cannot foresee what sunset picture they are preparing for us. A single elm by Hayden's is re-

lieved against the amber and golden border, deepening into dusky but soon to be red, in the horizon.

And now the crescent of the moon is seen, and her attendant star is farther off than last night.

Jan. 25. Sunday. The snow has been for some time more than a foot deep on a level, and some roads drifted quite full; and the cold for some weeks has been intense, as low as twenty and twenty-one degrees in the early morning. A Canadian winter. Some say that we have not had so long a spell of cold weather since '31, when they say it was not seen to thaw for six weeks. But last night and to-day the weather has moderated. It is glorious to be abroad this afternoon. The snow melts on the surface. The warmth of the sun reminds me of summer. The dog runs before us on the railroad causeway and appears to enjoy it as much as ourselves. C. remarks truly that most people do not distinguish between a pup and a dog, and treat both alike, though the former may not yet have a tooth in his head.

When Sophia told R. Rice that Dr. B. said that Foster was an infidel and was injuring the young men, etc., "Did he?" he observed. "Well, he is a great man. He swims in pretty deep water, but it is n't very extensive." When she added, "Mr. Frost says that Garrison had to apologize for printing Foster's sermon," he said, "Did he? Well, they may set as many back fires as they please; they won't be of any use; they'll soon go out." She said the selectmen were going to ask seven dollars instead of five for the hall. But he said that he would build them a hall, if they would engage to give him five dollars steadily. To be sure, it would not be quite so handsome as the present, but it should have the same kind of seats.

The clay in the Deep Cut is melting and streaming down, glistening in the sun. It is I that melts, while the harp sounds on high, and the snow-drifts on the west side look like clouds.

We turned down the brook at Heywood's meadow. It was worth the while to see how the water, even in the marsh where the brook is almost stagnant, sparkled in this atmosphere, for though warm it is remarkably clear. Water which in summer would look dark and perhaps turbid now sparkles like the lakes in November. This water is the more attractive, since all around is deep snow. The brook here is full of cat-tails (*Typha latifolia*, reed-mace). I found, on pulling open or breaking in my hand, as one would break bread, the still nearly perfect spikes of this fine reed, that the flowers were red or crimson at their base, where united to the stem. When I rubbed off thus what was at first but a thimbleful of these dry flowerets, they suddenly took in air and flushed up like powder, expanding like feathers and foam, filling and overflowing my hand, to which they imparted a sensation of warmth quite remarkable. I was astonished to see how a small quantity was expanded and inflated on being released and given to the air, and I could not be tired with repeating the experiment. I think a single one would more than fill a half-peck measure if they lay as light as at first in the air. It is something magical to one

who tries it for the first time. Like a puff of powder it flashes up. You do not know at first where they all come from. It is the conjurer's trick in nature, equal to taking feathers enough to fill a bed out of a hat. When you had done, but still will scrape the almost bare stem, still they overflow your hand as before. See it again, and try the combustibility of the pollen. As the flowerets are opening and liberating themselves, showing their red extremities, it has the effect of a changeable color.

Ah, then, the brook beyond, its rippling waters and its sunny sands! They made me forget that it was winter. Where springs oozed out of the soft bank over the dead leaves and the green sphagnum, they had melted the snow, or the snow had melted as it fell perchance, and the rabbits had sprinkled the mud about on the snow. The sun reflected from the sandy, gravelly bottom sometimes a bright sunny streak no bigger than your finger, reflected from a ripple as from a prism, and the sunlight, reflected from a hundred points of the surface of the rippling brook, enabled me to realize summer. But the dog partly spoiled the transparency of the water by running in the brook. A pup that had never seen a summer brook.

I am struck and attracted by the parallelism of the twigs of the hornbeam, *fine* parallelism.

Having gone a quarter of a mile beyond the bridge, where C. calls this his Spanish Brook, I looked back from the top of the hill on the south into this deep dell. Where the white pines stood thick, rising one above another, reflecting the sunlight, so soft and warm by

Vol. III

contrast with the snow, as never in summer, — for the idea of warmth prevailed over the cold which the snow suggested, though I saw through and between them to a distant snow-clad hill, and also to oaks red with their dry leaves, — and maple limbs were mingled with the pines, I was on the verge of seeing something, but I did not. If I had been alone and had had more leisure, I might have seen something to report.

Now we are on Fair Haven, still but a snow plain. Far down the river the shadows on Conantum are bluish, somewhat like the holes in the snow, perchance. The sun is half an hour high, perhaps. Standing near the outlet of the pond, I look up and down the river with delight, it is so warm and the air is, notwithstanding, so clear. When I invert my head and look at the woods half a mile down the stream, they suddenly sink lower in the horizon and are removed full two miles off; yet the air is so clear that I seem to see every stem and twig with beautiful distinctness. The fine tops of the trees are so relieved against the sky that I never cease to admire the minute subdivisions. It is the same when I look up the stream. A bare hickory under Lee's Cliff, seen against the sky, becomes an interesting, even beautiful, object to behold. I think where have I been staying all these days. I will surely come here again.

When I first paddled a boat on Walden, it was completely surrounded by thick and lofty pine and oak woods, and in some of its coves grape-vines had run over the trees and formed bowers under which a boat could pass. The hills which form its shores are so steep, and the woods on them were then so high, that, as you

looked down the pond from west to east, it looked like an amphitheatre for some kind of sylvan spectacle. I have spent many an hour, when I was younger, floating over its surface as the zephyr willed, having paddled to the middle, lying on my back across the seats of my boat, in a summer forenoon, and looking into the sky above, dreaming awake, until I was aroused by my boat touching the sand, and I arose to see what shore my fates had impelled me to; when idleness was the most attractive and productive industry. Many a forenoon have I stolen away thus, preferring thus to spend the most valued part of the day. For I was rich, if not in money, in sunny hours and summer days, and spent them lavishly. Nor do I regret that I did not spend more of them behind a counter or in the workshop or the teacher's desk, in which last two places I have spent so many of them.[1]

Jan. 26. Men have ever associated the verdure of evergreen trees — hemlocks, firs, spruces, etc. — with the moisture and coolness of mountains. Our word pine is from the Celtic "*pin* or *pen*, a rock or mountain," from which is derived the name of this genus in many languages. Hence the name "Apennines" (*Alpes pennines*). "*Pinaster* is Pliny's name for the wild pine." (All this from Lindley in Loudon.) But *Pinus* does not include hemlock or larch or fir.

Foster's success is in reaching such men as Houghton, Goodwin, Rice, McKean, Pratt, E. Hubbard, S. Barrett, and others, — Wilson, and even Dillingham;

[1] [*Walden*, pp. 212, 213; Riv. 300, 301.]

some of whom are men of sterling worth and probity, the salt of the earth, and confessedly the very best of our citizens, though the Church may have called them infidels. They were only more faithful than the rest. They did not go off at half-cock. I do not know more honest or trustworthy men than Rice, Pratt, Barrett, McKean, etc. Frost and Anger [?] might preach forever; they would never reach these men. Houghton never realized before that the design of any preacher was to do good to men. In this movement of the waters, the sectarians and formalists are left floating on chips and slivers of doctrine. In preaching to the men whom I have named they make the mistake of preaching or writing on the letter and not the meaning of the letter, the creed and not the life. When a truer man comes, the assembly see the difference at last between his life and the life of his predecessors, and the doctrines of the latter properly pass for *wind*. They say of the former, "He hits the nail on the head." Every shade and degree of hypocrisy will affect the tone of the voice, and the audience will laugh. The rumseller likes Foster better than Manning, though he is strenuously opposed to his traffic, because he is frank and manly with him and not all things to all men. Those men I have named represent the healthy mind of the generation, who have ears to hear. The man may be proud who satisfies them.

A tree seen against other trees is a mere dark mass, but against the sky it has parts, has symmetry and expression.

Whatever wit has been produced on the spur of the moment will bear to be reconsidered and reformed with

phlegm. The arrow had best not be loosely shot. The most transient and passing remark must be reconsidered by the writer, made sure and warranted, as if the earth had rested on its axle to back it, and all the natural forces lay behind it. The writer must direct his sentences as carefully and leisurely as the marksman his rifle, who shoots sitting and with a rest, with patent sights and conical balls beside. He must not merely seem to speak the truth. He must really speak it. If you foresee that a part of your essay will topple down after the lapse of time, throw it down now yourself.[1]

The thousand fine points and tops of the trees delight me; they are the plumes and standards and bayonets of a host that march to victory over the earth. The trees are handsome towards the heavens as well as up their boles; they are good for other things than boards and shingles.

Obey the spur of the moment. These accumulated it is that make the impulse and the impetus of the life of genius. These are the spongioles or rootlets by which its trunk is fed. If you neglect the moments, if you cut off your fibrous roots, what but a languishing life is to be expected? Let the spurs of countless moments goad us incessantly into life. I feel the spur of the moment thrust deep into my side. The present is an inexorable rider. The moment always spurs either with a sharp or a blunt spur. Are my sides calloused? Let us trust the rider, that he knows the way, that he knows when speed and effort are required. What other impulse do we wait for? Let us preserve religiously, secure, pro-

[1] [Channing, p. 248.]

tect the coincidence of our life with the life of nature. Else what are heat and cold, day and night, sun, moon, and stars to us? Was it not from sympathy with the present life of nature that we were born at this epoch rather than at another?

The truest account of heaven is the fairest, and I will accept none which disappoints expectation. It is more glorious to expect a better, than to enjoy a worse.

My life as essentially belongs to the present as that of a willow tree in the spring. Now, now, its catkins expand, its yellow bark shines, its sap flows; now or never must you make whistles of it. Get the day to back you; let it back you and the night.

When the thermometer is down to 20°, the streams of thought tinkle underneath like the rivers under the ice. Thought like the ocean is nearly of one temperature. Ideas, — are they the fishes of thought?

Poetry *implies* the whole truth. Philosophy *expresses* a particle of it.

Would you see your mind, look at the sky. Would you know your own moods, be weather-wise. He whom the weather disappoints, disappoints himself.

Let all things give way to the impulse of expression. It is the bud unfolding, the perennial spring. As well stay the spring. Who shall resist the thaw?

What if all the ponds were shallow? Would it not react on the minds of men? If there were no physical deeps. I thank God that he made this pond deep and pure for a symbol.[1]

The word is well naturalized or rooted that can be

[1] [*Walden*, p. 316; Riv. 442.]

traced back to a Celtic original. It is like getting out stumps and fat pine roots.

While men believe in the infinite some ponds will be thought bottomless.[1]

In winter we will think brave and hardy and most native thoughts. Then the tender summer birds are flown.

In few countries do they enjoy so fine a contrast of summer and winter. We really have four seasons, each incredible to the other. Winter cannot be mistaken for summer here. Though I see the boat turned up on the shore and half buried under snow, as I walk over the invisible river, summer is far away, with its rustling reeds. It only suggests the want of thrift, the carelessness, of its owner.

Nature never indulges in exclamations, never says Ah! or Alas! She is not of French descent. She is a plain writer, uses few gestures, does not add to her verbs, uses few adverbs, uses no expletives. I find that I use many words for the sake of emphasis which really add nothing to the force of my sentences, and they look relieved the moment I have cancelled these. Words by which I express my mood, my conviction, rather than the simple truth.

Yesterday, though warm, it was clear enough for water and windows to sparkle.

Youth supplies us with colors, age with canvas. How rare it must be that in age our life receives a new coloring! The heavens were blue when I was young, and that is their color still. Paint is costly. Nevertheless,

[1] [*Walden*, p. 316; Riv. 442.]

let thy report be colorless as it respects the hue of the reporter's mind; only let it have the colors of the thing reported. I think the heavens have had but one coat of paint since I was a boy, and their blue is paled and dingy and worn off in many places. I cannot afford to give them another coat. Where is the man so rich that he can give the earth a second coat of green in his manhood, or the heavens a second coat of blue? Our paints are all mixed when we are young. Methinks the skies need a new coat. Have our eyes any blue to spare? To see some men's heavens you would not suspect they had ever been azure or celestial, but that their painter had cheated them, had taken up a handful of the dirt at their feet and painted them that color, more in harmony with their lives. At least the color must have come out in a shower, in which they had the "blues."

I hear of one good thing Foster said in his sermon the other day, the subject being Nature: "Thank God, there is no doctrine of election with regard to Nature! We are all admitted to her."

To-day I see a few snow-fleas on the Walden road and a slight blueness in the chinks, it being cloudy and melting.

It is good to break and smell the black birch twigs now. The lichens look rather bright to-day, near the town line, in Heywood's wood by the pond. When they are bright and expanded, is it not a sign of a thaw or of rain? The beauty of lichens, with their scalloped leaves, the small attractive fields, the crinkled edge! I could study a single piece of bark for hours. How they flourish! I sympathize with their growth.

The woodpeckers work in Emerson's wood on the Cliff-top, the trees being partly killed by the top, and the grubs having hatched under the bark. The woodpeckers have stripped a whole side of some trees, and in a sound red oak they have dug out a mortise-hole with squarish shoulders, as if with a chisel. I have often seen these holes.

From these cliffs at this moment, the clouds in the west have a singular brassy color, and they are arranged in an unusual manner. A new disposition of the clouds will make the most familiar country appear foreign, like Tartary or Arabia Felix.

About 2 o'clock P. M. these days, after a fair forenoon, there is wont to blow up from the northwest a squally cloud, spanning the heavens, but before it reaches the southeast horizon it has lifted above the northwest, and so it leaves the sky clear there for sunset, while it has sunk low and dark in the southeast.

The men on the freight-train, who go over the whole length of the road, bow to me as to an old acquaintance, they pass me so often, and I think they take me for an "employé;" and am I not?[1]

The flowing clay on the east side is still richer to-day. I know of nothing so purgative of winter fumes and indigestions.[2] And then there is heard the harp high overhead, a new Orpheus modulating, moulding the earth and making the sands to follow its strains. Who is not young again? What more wonderful than that a simple string or wire stretched between two posts, on which the breezes play, can so excite the race

[1] [*Walden*, p. 128; Riv. 181.]   [2] [*Walden*, p. 340; Riv. 476.]

of man with its vibrations, producing sounds kindred with the song of bards and the most admirable works of art?

Thaw with his gentle persuasion is more powerful than Thor with his hammer. The one melts, the other but breaks in pieces.[1] In these fresh designs there is more than the freedom of Grecian art, more than acanthus leaves. It flows even over the snow.

The vibrations of that string will surely remind a man of all that is most glorious in his experience, will more than realize to him the stories of the Delphic Oracle, will take him captive, make him mad. The distant is brought near to him through hearing. He abides in the body still, his soul is not quite ravished away, but news from other spheres than he lives in reaches him. It is evident that his life does not pass on that level.

Jan. 27. The peculiarity of a work of genius is the absence of the speaker from his speech. He is but the medium. You behold a perfect work, but you do not behold the worker. I read its page, but it is as free from any man that can be remembered as an impassable desert.

I think that the one word which will explain the Shakespeare miracle is "unconsciousness." If he had known his own comparative eminence, he would not have failed to publish it incessantly, though Bacon did not. There probably has been no more conscious age than the present.

[1] [*Walden*, p. 341; Riv. 477.]

Mill road south of Ministerial Swamp, 3 P. M.

As I stand under the hill beyond J. Hosmer's and look over the plains westward toward Acton and see the farmhouses nearly half a mile apart, few and solitary, in these great fields between these stretching woods, out of the world, where the children have to go far to school; the still, stagnant, heart-eating, life-everlasting, and gone-to-seed country, so far from the post-office where the weekly paper comes, wherein the new-married wife cannot live for loneliness, and the young man has to depend upon his horse for society; see young J. Hosmer's house, whither he returns with his wife in despair after living in the city, — I standing in Tarbell's road, which he alone cannot break out, — the world in winter for most walkers reduced to a sled track winding far through the drifts, all springs sealed up and no digressions; where the old man thinks he may possibly afford to rust it out, not having long to live, but the young man pines to get nearer the post-office and the Lyceum, is restless and resolves to go to California, because the depot is a mile off (he hears the rattle of the cars at a distance and thinks the world is going by and leaving him); where rabbits and partridges multiply, and muskrats are more numerous than ever, and none of the farmer's sons are willing to be farmers, and the apple trees are decayed, and the cellar-holes are more numerous than the houses, and the rails are covered with lichens, and the old maids wish to sell out and move into the village, and have waited twenty years in vain for this purpose and never finished but one room in the house, never plastered nor painted, inside or out, lands which the Indian was long since dispossessed [of], and now the farms are run out, and what were forests are grain-fields, what were grain-fields, pastures; dwellings which only those Arnolds of the wilderness, those *coureurs de bois*, the baker and the butcher visit, to which at least the latter penetrates for the annual calf, — and as he returns the cow lows after; — whither the villager never penetrates, but in huckleberry time, perchance, and if he does not, who does? — where some men's breaths smell of rum, having smuggled in a jugful to alleviate their misery and solitude; where the owls give a regular serenade; — I say, standing there and seeing these things, I cannot realize that this is that hopeful young America which is famous throughout the world for its activity and enterprise, and this is the most thickly settled and Yankee part of it. What must be the condition of the *old* world! The *sphagnum* must by this time have concealed it from the eye.

In new countries men are scattered broadcast; they do not wait for roads to place their houses on, but roads seek out the houses, and each man is a prince in his principality and depends on himself. Perchance when the virgin soil is exhausted, a reaction takes place, and men concentrate in villages again, become social and commercial, and leave the steady and moderate few to work the country's mines.

The snow has been slowly melting, without rain or mist, the last two or three days. It has settled very much, though the eaves have not been heard to run by me. In going across lots, I walk in the woods, where

the snow is not so deep, part having been caught in the trees and dissipated in the air, and a part melted by the warmth of the wood and the reflection.

The poison sumach, with its stems hanging down on every side, is a very agreeable object now, seen against the snow.

I do not know but thoughts written down thus in a journal might be printed in the same form with greater advantage than if the related ones were brought together into separate essays. They are now allied to life, and are seen by the reader not to be far-fetched. It is more simple, less artful. I feel that in the other case I should have no proper frame for my sketches. Mere facts and names and dates communicate more than we suspect. Whether the flower looks better in the nosegay than in the meadow where it grew and we had to wet our feet to get it! Is the scholastic air any advantage?

Jan. 28. Perhaps I can never find so good a setting for my thoughts as I shall thus have taken them out of. The crystal never sparkles more brightly than in the cavern. The world have always loved best the fable with the moral. The children could read the fable alone, the grown-up read both. The truth so told has the best advantages of the most abstract statement, for it is not the less universally applicable. Where else will you ever find the true cement for your thoughts? How will you ever rivet them together without leaving the marks of the file? Yet Plutarch did not so; Montaigne did not so. Men have written travels in this

Vol. III

form, but perhaps no man's daily life has been rich enough to be journalized.

Our life should be so active and progressive as to be a journey. Our meals should all be of journey-cake and hasty pudding. We should be more alert, see the sun rise, not keep fashionable hours, enter a house, our own house, as a khan, a caravansary. At noon I did not dine; I ate my journey-cake. I quenched my thirst at a spring or a brook. As I sat at the table, the hospitality was so perfect and the repast so sumptuous that I seemed to be breaking my fast upon a bank in the midst of an arduous journey, that the water seemed to be a living spring, the napkins grass, the conversation free as the winds; and the servants that waited on us were our simple desires.

Cut off from Pilpay and Æsop the moral alone at the bottom, would that content you?

There will be no more rambling through the aisles of the wood, with occasional vistas through which you see the pond.

In those days when how to get my living honestly, with freedom left for my proper pursuits, was a question which vexed me even more than it does now, I used to see a large box by the railroad, six feet long by three wide, in which the workmen locked up their tools at night; and it suggested to me that every man who was hard pushed might get him such a one for a dollar, and, having bored a few auger-holes in it, to admit the air at least, get into it when it rained and at night, and shut the lid and hook it, and so have free-

dom in his mind, and in his soul be free. This did not seem the worst alternative, nor by any means a despicable resource. You could sit up as late as you pleased; and, whenever you got up in the morning, you would not have any creditor dogging you for rent. I should not be in a bad box. Many a man is harassed to death to pay the rent of a larger and more luxurious box, who would not have frozen to death in such a box as this. I should not be in so bad a box as many a man is in now.[1]

If you mean by hard times, times, not when there is no bread, but when there is no cake, I have no sympathy with you.

Economy is a subject that admits of being treated with levity, but it is not a subject that can be so disposed of.[2]

"Why don't you put on your overalls?" "Why, these are overalls and underalls, being all I have got. These are over all I have got."

They showed me Johnny Riordan to-day, with one thickness of ragged cloth over his little shirt for all this cold weather, with shoes with large holes in the toes, into which the snow got, as he said, without an outer garment, to walk a mile to school every day over the bleakest of causeways, — the clothes with countless patches, which hailed from, claimed descent from, were originally identical with, pantaloons of mine, which set as if his mother had fitted them to a tea-kettle first. This little mass of humanity, this tender gobbet

---

[1] [*Walden*, pp. 31, 32; Riv. 47, 48.]
[2] [*Walden*, p. 32; Riv. 48.]

for the fates, cast into a cold world with a torn lichen leaf wrapped about him, — Oh, I should rather hear that America's first-born were all slain than that his little fingers and toes should feel cold while I am warm. Is man so cheap that he cannot be clothed but with a mat, a rag, that we should bestow on him our *cold* victuals? Are there any fellow-creatures to whom we abandon our rags, to whom we give our old clothes and shoes when they will not fend the weather from ourselves? Let the mature rich wear the rags and insufficient clothing; let the infant poor wear the purple and fine linen. I shudder when I think of the fate of innocency. Our charitable institutions are an insult to humanity. A charity which dispenses the crumbs that fall from its overloaded tables, which are left after its feasts! [1]

[1] [See *Journal*, vol. ii, pp. 117, 118; vol. iii, pp. 149, 150. Some loose sheets of manuscript inclosed between the leaves of one of the journals contain the following more complete sketch of the little Irish boy, made up, with some revision, from the original entries: —

"They showed me little Johnny Riordan the other day, as bright a boy of five years as ever trod our paths, whom you could not see for five minutes without loving and honoring him. He *lives* in what they call the *shanty* in the woods. He had on, in the middle of January of the coldest winter we have had for twenty years, one thickness only of ragged cloth sewed on to his pantaloons over his little shirt, and shoes with large holes in the toes, into which the snow got, as he was obliged to confess, he who had trodden five winters under his feet! Thus clad he walked a mile to school every day, over the bleakest of railroad causeways, where I know by experience the grown man would frequently freeze his ears or nose if they were not well protected, — for his parents have no thermometer, — all to get learning and warmth and there sit at the head of his bench. These clothes, with countless patches, which had for vehicle — O shame! shame! — pantaloons

3 P. M. — Went round by Tuttle's road, and so out on to the Walden road.

that had been mine, they whispered to me, set as if his mother had fitted them to a tea-kettle first.

"I glimpsed him the other morning taking his last step from his last snow-drift on to the schoolhouse door-step, floundering still; saw not his face nor his profile, only his mien, but saw clearly in imagination his 'old-worthy' face behind the sober visor of his cap, and he revived to my mind the grave nobility and magnanimity of ancient heroes. He never was drawn in a willow wagon, but progresses by his own brave steps. Has not the world waited for such a generation? Here he condescends to his a-b-c without one smile, who has the lore of worlds uncounted in his brain. He speaks not of the adventures of the causeway. What was the bravery of Leonidas and his three hundred boys at the pass of Thermopylæ to this infant's? They dared but to die; he dares to live, and takes his reward of merit, perchance, without relaxing his face into a smile, that does not reward a thousandth part of his merits, that overlooks his unseen and unrewardable merits, — Little Johnny Riordan, who faces cold and routs it like a Persian army, who, yet innocent, carries in his knees the strength of a thousand Indras. Not to be so tenderly nurtured as you and I forsooth? All day he plays with his coevals and equals, and then they go to their several homes.

> "I am the little Irish boy,
>   That lives in the shanty.
> I am five years old to-day,
>   And shall soon be one and twenty.
>
> "At recess I play
> With little Billy Gray,
> And when school is done,
> Then away I run.
>
> "And if I meet the cars,
>   I get on the other track,
> And then I know, whatever comes,
>   I need n't look back.

Vol. III

These warmer days the woodchopper finds that the wood cuts easier than when it had the frost in its sapwood, though it does not split so readily. Thus every change in the weather has its influence on him, and is appreciated by him in a peculiar way. The woodcutter and his practices and experiences are more to be attended to; his accidents, perhaps more than any other's, should mark the epochs in the winter day. Now that the Indian is gone, he stands nearest to nature. Who has written the history of his day? How far still is the writer of books from the man, his old playmate it may

"Having carried off the palm in the intellectual contest with the children of luxury, how bravely he contemplates his destiny: —

> "I shall grow up
> And be a great man,
> And shovel all day
> As hard as I can.

"This tender gobbet for the fates, cast into a cold world, with a torn lichen leaf wrapped about him! I would rather hear that America's first-born were all slain than that his little fingers and toes should feel cold while I am warm. Is man so cheap that he cannot be clothed but with a mat or a rag? that we should abandon to him our *worn-out* clothes or our *cold* victuals? Infancy pleads with equal eloquence from all platforms. Rather let the mature rich wear the rags and insufficient clothing, the infant poor and rich, if any, wear the costly furs, the purple and fine linen. Our charitable institutions are an insult to humanity, — a charity which dispenses the crumbs that fall from its overloaded tables! whose waste and whose example helped to produce that poverty!

"While the charitable waddle about cased in furs and finery, this boy, lively as a cricket, passes them on his way to school. I see that, for the present, the child is happy, is not puny, and has all the wonders of nature for his toys. Have I not faith that his tenderness will in some way be cherished and protected, as the buds of spring in the remotest wintry dell no less than in the garden and summer-house?"]

be, who chops in the woods! There are ages between them. Homer refers to the progress of the woodcutter's work, to mark the time of day on the plains of Troy, and the inference from such passages commonly is that he lived in a more primitive state of society than the present. But I think that this is a mistake. Like proves like in all ages, and the fact that I myself should take pleasure in referring to just such simple and peaceful labors which are always proceeding, that the contrast itself always attracts the civilized poet to what is rudest and most primitive in his contemporaries, all this rather proves a certain interval between the poet and the chopper whose labor he refers to, than an unusual nearness to him, on the principle that familiarity breeds contempt. Homer is to be subjected to a very different kind of criticism from any he has received.

That reader who most fully appreciates the poet, and derives the greatest pleasure from his works, himself lives in circumstances most like those of the poet himself.

About Brister's Spring the ferns, which have been covered with snow, and the grass are still quite green. The skunk-cabbage in the water is already pushed up, and I find the pinkish head of flowers within its spathe bigger than a pea.

It is remarkable that no pains is taken to teach children to distinguish colors. I am myself uncertain about the names of many.

Jan. 29. We must be very active if we would be clean and live our own life, and not a languishing and scurvy one. The trees, which are stationary, are covered with parasites, especially those which have grown slowly. The air is filled with the fine sporules of countless mosses, algæ, lichens, fungi, which settle and plant themselves on all quiet surfaces. Under the nails and between the joints of the fingers of the idle, flourish crops of mildew, algæ, and fungi, and other vegetable sloths, though they may be invisible, — the lichens where life still exists, the fungi where decomposition has begun to take place. And the sluggard is soon covered with sphagnum. Algæ take root in the corners of his eyes, and lichens cover the bulbs of his fingers and his head, etc., etc., the lowest forms of vegetable life. This is the definition of dirt. We fall a prey to others of nature's tenants, who take possession of the unoccupied house. With the utmost inward activity we have to wash and comb ourselves beside, to get rid of the adhering seeds. Cleanliness is by activity not to give any quiet shelf for the seeds of parasitic plants to take root on.

If he cuts pines, the woodchopper's hands are covered with pitch.

The names of plants are for the most part traced to Celtic and Arabian roots.

The forcible writer does not go far for his themes. His ideas are not far-fetched. He derives inspiration from his chagrins and his satisfactions. His theme being ever an instant one, his own gravity assists him, gives impetus to what he says. He minds his business. He does not speculate while others drudge for him.

I am often reminded that if I had bestowed on me

the wealth of Crœsus, my aims must still be the same and my means essentially the same.[1]

It still melts. I observed this afternoon that the ground where they are digging for some scales near the depot was frozen about nine inches where the snow has lain most and sixteen inches where the road was. I begin to see the tops of the grasses and stubble in the fields, which deceive me as if it were the ground itself.

That point where the sun goes down is the cynosure which attracts all eyes at sundown and half an hour before. What do all other parts of the horizon concern us? Our eyes follow the path of that great luminary. We watch for his rising, and we observe his setting. He is a companion and fellow-traveller we all have. We pity him who has his cheerless dwelling elsewhere, even in the northwest or southwest, off the high road of nature.

The snow is nearly gone from the railroad causeway.

Few are the days when the telegraph harp rises into a pure, clear melody. Though the wind may blow strong or soft, in this or that direction, naught will you hear but a low hum or murmur, or even a buzzing sound; but at length, when some undistinguishable zephyr blows, when the conditions not easy to be detected arrive, it suddenly and unexpectedly rises into melody, as if a god had touched it, and fortunate is the walker who chances to be within hearing. So is it with the lyres of bards, and for the most part it is only a feeble and ineffectual hum that comes from them, which leads you to expect the melody you do not hear. When the

[1] [Walden, p. 362; Riv. 507.]

gale is modified, when the favorable conditions occur, and the indescribable coincidence takes place, then there is music. Of a thousand buzzing strings, only one yields music. It is like the hum of the shaft, or other machinery, of a steamboat, which at length might become music in a divine hand. I feel greatly enriched by this telegraph.

I have come to see the clay and sand in the Cut. A reddish tinge in the earth, stains. An Indian hue is singularly agreeable, even exciting, to the eye. Here the whole bank is sliding. Even the color of the subsoil excites me, as if I were already getting near to life and vegetation. This clay is fæcal in its color also. It runs off at bottom into mere shoals, shallows, vasa, vague sand-bars, like the mammoth leaves, — makes strands.[1]

Perhaps those mother-o'-pearl clouds I described some time ago might be called rainbow flocks. The snow on the slope of the Cliffs is dotted with black specks, the seeds of the mullein which the wind has shaken out. When I strike the dry stalks, the seeds fall in a shower and color the snow black like charcoal dust or powder.

The green mosses on the rocks are evidently nourished and kept bright by the snows lying on them a part of the year.

Day before yesterday, I saw the hunters out with a dozen dogs, but only two pussies, one white and one little gray one, did I see, for so many men and dogs, who seem to set all the village astir as if the fox's trail led through it. And Stedman Buttrick, with whom I

[1] [See Walden, p. 337; Riv. 471.]

was walking, was excited as if in the heyday of his youth.

Heard C. lecture to-night. It was a bushel of nuts. Perhaps the most original lecture I ever heard. Ever so unexpected, not to be foretold, and so sententious that you could not look at him and take his thought at the same time. You had to give your undivided attention to the thoughts, for you were not assisted by set phrases or modes of speech intervening. There was no sloping up or down to or from his points. It was all genius, no talent. It required more close attention, more abstraction from surrounding circumstances, than any lecture I have heard. For, well as I know C., he more than any man disappoints my expectation. When I see him in the desk, hear him, I cannot realize that I ever saw him before. He will be strange, unexpected, to his best acquaintance. I cannot associate the lecturer with the companion of my walks. It was from so original and peculiar a point of view, yet just to himself in the main, that I doubt if three in the audience apprehended a tithe that he said. It was so hard to hear that doubtless few made the exertion. A thick succession of mountain passes and no intermediate slopes and plains. Other lectures, even the best, in which so much space is given to the elaborate development of a few ideas, seemed somewhat meagre in comparison. Yet it would be how much more glorious if talent were added to genius, if there [were] a just arrangement and development of the thoughts, and each step were not a leap, but he ran a space to take a yet higher leap!

Most of the spectators sat in front of the performer,

but here was one who, by accident, sat all the while on one side, and his report was peculiar and startling.

Jan. 30. Friday. I feel as if I were gradually parting company with certain friends, just as I perceive familiar objects successively disappear when I am leaving my native town in the cars.

It is an encouraging piece of news, when I read in the *Weekly Tribune*, appended to an article on "The Liquor Groceries" which had appeared in the Daily, close as the moral to the fable or its operation to the medicine, that the worst of those establishments had refused to receive the *Tribune*, being offended by its disclosures; showing that the arrow has already reached its mark before we distant readers have heard its whiz.

One must not complain that his friend is cold, for heat is generated between them.

I doubt if Emerson could trundle a wheelbarrow through the streets, because it would be out of character. One needs to have a comprehensive character.

Channing's lecture was full of wise, acute, and witty observations, yet most of the audience did not know but it was mere incoherent and reckless verbiage and nonsense. I lose my respect for people who do not know what is good and true. I know full well that readers and hearers, with the fewest exceptions, ask me for my second best.

Lindley (apparently) in Loudon asks, when you have referred a plant to its class and order in the Linnæan system, "What more has been acquired than the bare knowledge that the plant in question pos-

sesses a certain number of stamens and styles? No possible notion can be formed of the relation it bears to other plants of the same nature, of the qualities it probably possesses, or of the structure of those parts not under examination, the fruit for example; and, finally, if it were wished to convey an idea of the plant to a stranger, no means would be in the possession of the Linnæan botanist of doing so, except by stating that the plant belonged to Pentandria Monogynia, for example, which is stating nothing. But what would be the condition of the student of the natural affinities of plants in a similar case? It is true he would be obliged to consult more characters than the two uninfluential ones of Linnæus — it would be necessary to ascertain if his subject was Vascular or Cellular; if Vascular, whether it was Monocotyledonous or Dicotyledonous; if Dicotyledonous, whether the leaves were opposite or alternate, stipulate or exstipulate, whether the flowers were monopetalous, polypetalous, or apetalous, the nature and station of the stamens, the condition of the ovarium, and so on. But when he *has* ascertained thus much, only let it be remembered, for a moment, how much he has gained indirectly as well as directly. Perhaps he has discovered that his plant belongs to Rubiaceæ; he will then have learned that all vegetables with opposite entire stipulate leaves, and a monopetalous superior corolla, are also Rubiaceous; if a fragment of the leaves and stem only of such a plant were afterwards submitted to him for examination, he would recognize its affinities, and remember that it was Rubiaceous, and being aware of that fact, he

would be able safely to infer that its calyx and corolla would be of a particular nature, that if the roots afforded any color for dyeing, it would be red; that the medicinal properties of the bark, if any, would be tonic, astringent, and febrifugal, and that its seeds would be of the same nature as those of coffee, and finally, its geographical position would be tolerably certain to him."

No good introduction to the study of the natural system, but such a work expected from Lindley in 1829.

But after all, where is the flower lore? for the first book, and not the last, should contain the poetry of flowers. The natural system may tell us the value of a plant in medicine or the arts or for food, but neither it nor the Linnæan, to any great extent, tells us its chief value and significance to man, which in any measure accounts for its beauty, its flower-like properties. There will be pages about some fair flower's qualities as food or medicine, but perhaps not a sentence about its significance to the eye, as if the cowslip were better for greens than for yellows. Not about what children and all flower-lovers gather flowers for. Are they emissaries sent forth by the arts to purvey and explore for them? Not how good they are to wear on the bosom, or to smell, how much they are to the eye and the sentiments, not how much to the palate and the sensations, — flowers as flowers. Not addressed to the cook or the physician or the dyer merely, but to the lovers of flowers, young and old. The most poetical of books. It should have the beauty

and the fragrance of flowers, some of their color. A keepsake! What a keepsake a manual of botany! In which is uttered, breathed, man's love of flowers. It is dry as a *hortus siccus*. Flowers are pressed into the botanist's service.[1]

Do nothing merely out of good resolutions. Discipline yourself only to yield to love; suffer yourself to be attracted. It is in vain to write on chosen themes. We must wait till they have kindled a flame in our minds. There must be the copulating and generating force of love behind every effort destined to be successful. The cold resolve gives birth to, begets, nothing. The theme that seeks me, not I it. The poet's relation to his theme is the relation of lovers. It is no more to be courted. Obey, report.

Though they are cutting off the woods at Walden, it is not all loss. It makes some new and unexpected prospects. We read books about logging in the Maine woods as if it were wholly strange to these parts. But I here witness almost exactly the same things, scenes that might be witnessed in Maine or New Hampshire: the logger's team, his oxen on the ice chewing the cud, the long pine tree, stripped of its branches, chained upon his sled, resting on a stout cross-bar or log and trailing behind, the smoke of his fire curling up blue amid the trees, the sound of the axe and of the teamsters' voices. A pretty forest scene, seeing oxen, so patient and stationary, good for pictures, standing on the ice, — a piece of still life. Oh, it is refreshing to see, to think of, these things after hearing of the dis-

[1] *Vide* forward about child plucking flower.

cussions and politics of the day! The smoke I saw was quite blue. As I stood on the partially cleared bank at the east end of the pond, I looked south over the side of the hill into a deep dell still wooded, and I saw, not more than thirty rods off, a chopper at his work. I was half a dozen rods distant from the standing wood, and I saw him through a vista between two trees (it was now mainly an oak wood, the pine having been cut), and he appeared to me apparently half a mile distant, yet charmingly distinct, as in a picture of which the two trees were the frame. He was seen against the snow on the hillside beyond. I could distinguish each part of his dress perfectly, and the axe with distinct outline as he raised it above his head, the black iron against the snow, and could hear every stroke distinctly. Yet I should have deemed it ridiculous to have called to him, he appeared so distant. He appeared with the same distinctness as objects seen through a pinhole in a card. This was the effect rather than by comparison of him, his size, with the nearer trees, between which I saw him and which made the canopied roof of the grove far above his head. It was, perhaps, one of those coincidences and effects which have made men painters. I could not behold him as an actual man; he was more ideal than in any picture I have seen. He refused to be seen as actual. Far in the hollow, yet somewhat enlightened, aisles of this wooded dell. Some scenes will thus present themselves as picture. Those scenes which are picture, subjects for the pencil, are distinctly marked; they do not require the aid of genius to idealize them. They must be seen as ideal.

Nature allows of no universal secrets. The more carefully a secret is kept on one side of the globe, the larger the type it is printed in on the other. Nothing is too pointed, too personal, too immodest, for her to blazon. The relations of sex, transferred to flowers, become the study of ladies in the drawing-room. While men wear fig leaves, she grows the *Phallus impudicus* and *P. caninus* and other phallus-like fungi.

The rhymes which I used to see on the walls of privies, scribbled by boys, I have lately seen, word for word the same; in spite [of] whitewash and brick walls and admonitions they survive. They are no doubt older than Orpheus, and have come down from an antiquity as remote as mythology or fable. So, too, no doubt corporations have ever struggled in vain to obtain cleanliness in those provinces. Filth and impurity are as old as cleanliness and purity. To correspond to man completely, Nature is even perhaps unchaste herself. Or perchance man's impurity begets a monster somewhere, to proclaim his sin. The poetry of the jakes, — it flows as perennially as the gutter.

I am afraid to travel much or to famous places, lest it might completely dissipate the mind. Then I am sure that what we observe at home, if we observe anything, is of more importance than what we observe abroad. The far-fetched is of the least value. What we observe in travelling are to some extent the accidents of the body, but [what] we observe when sitting at home are, in the same proportion, phenomena of the mind itself. A wakeful night will yield as much thought as a long journey. If I try thoughts by their quality, not their

quantity, I may find that a restless night will yield more than the longest journey.

I live in an age when men have agreed to say "God" instead of "Jove."

It is remarkable that there is no man so coarse and insensible but he can be profane, can pronounce the word "God" with emphasis in the woods when anything happens to disturb, as a spoiled child loves to see what liberties he can presume to take. I am only astonished that B—— should think it any daring; that he should believe in God so much. Then look round to see if the auditors appreciated his boldness.

Jan. 31. We hear the sounds of screech owls in our nostrils, and the snoring of men is perhaps not to be distinguished from that of pigs.

—— [*sic*] is too grand for me. He belongs to the nobility and wears their cloak and manners; is attracted to Plato, not to Socrates, I fear partly because the latter's life and associates were too humble. I am a commoner. To me there is something devilish in manners. The best manners is nakedness of manners. I should value E.'s praise more, which is always so discriminating, if there were not some alloy of patronage and hence of flattery about [it]. In that respect he is like —— [*sic*];[1] they flatter you, but themselves more. Praise should be spoken as simply and naturally as a flower emits its fragrance.

I am repeatedly astonished by the coolness and ob-

[1] [The first dash (made in pencil) stands for a single initial carefully scratched out; the second, for a full name, also erased.]

tuse bigotry with which some will appropriate the New Testament in conversation with you. It is as if they were to appropriate the sun and stand between you and it, because they understood that you had walked once by moonlight, though that was in the reflected light of the sun, which you could not get directly. I have seen two persons conversing at a tea-table, both lovers of the New Testament, each in his own way, the one a lover of all kindred expression of truth also; and yet the other appropriated the New Testament wholly to herself, and took it for granted, with singular or rather lamentable blindness and obtuseness, that the former neither knew nor cared anything about it. Horace Greeley found some fault with me to the world because I presumed to speak of the New Testament using my own words and thoughts, and challenged me to a controversy. The one thought I had was that it would give me real pleasure to know that he loved it as sincerely and enlightenedly as I did; but I felt that he did not care so much about it as I.

Botanies, instead of being the poetry, are the prose, of flowers. I do not mean to underrate Linnæus's admirable nomenclature, much of which is itself poetry.

Moreover, if you [are] restricted in your range by poverty, if you cannot buy books and newspapers, you are but confined to the most significant and vital experiences, you are compelled to deal with the material which yields the most sugar and the most starch. You are defended from being a trifler. No man loses, even on a lower level, by magnanimity on a higher. Super-

Snow-Laden Pitch Pines

fluous wealth can buy superfluities only. Money is not required to buy one necessary of the soul.[1]

Not the same things are great to all men. Many of the words which we write with capital letters are not so distinguished by those who live at a distance.

That work of man's must be vast indeed which, like the Pyramids, looks blue in the horizon, as mountains. Few works of man rise high enough, and with breadth enough, to be blued by the air between them and the spectator.

In the East, women religiously conceal that they have faces; in the West, that they have legs. In both cases they make it evident that they have but little brains.

I hear my friend say, "I have lost my faith in men; there are none true, magnanimous, holy," etc., etc., meaning, all the while, that I do not possess those unattainable virtues; but, worm as I am, this is not wise in my friend, and I feel simply discouraged so far as my relation to him is concerned. We must have infinite faith in each other. If we have not, we must never let it leak out that we have not. He erects his want of faith as a barrier between us. When I hear grown man or woman say, "Once I had faith in men; now I have not," I am inclined to ask, "Who are you whom the world has disappointed? Have not you rather disappointed the world? There is the same ground for faith now that ever there was. It needs only a little love in you who complain so to ground it on." For my own part, I am thankful that there are those who come

¹ [*Walden*, p. 362; Riv. 507.]

so near being my friends that they can be estranged from me. I had faith before they would destroy the little I have. The mason asks but a narrow shelf to spring his brick from; man requires only an infinitely narrower one to spring the arch of faith from.

What can I do? There is one whom I would fain call my friend. I feel disposed to practice any virtue. I am at liberty to do so. But it chances that at present I feel no sympathy with, no warmth toward, him. I am capable of sympathy and of warmth. What can I do? The universal laws will work; I must condemn what is wrong in him as well as in another. I cannot act a part. I submit myself. Do what you will with us, O ye gods!

See what a swift penalty you have to pay. If you say to your friend that he is less than an angel, he is your friend no longer.

The only ledge I can spring the arch of friendship from is the ground of infinite faith. If you have lost any of your faith in me, you might as well have lost it all. How can you renounce and retain at the same time?

One woman whom I visit sometimes thinks I am conceited, and yet wonders that I do not visit her oftener. If I were sure she was right perhaps I should. Now this is a sad obstacle in the way of hearty communications. As, naturally enough, we are not agreed on that point, our sympathy is lessened. Another with whom I converse a good deal allows that sometimes my actions are better than my principles as expressed in conversation.

I am not sure that I have any right to address to you the words I am about to write. The reason I have not visited you oftener and more earnestly is that I am offended by your pride, your sometime assumption of dignity, your manners, which come over me like waves of Lethe. I know that if I stood in that relation to you which you seem to ask, I should not be met. Perhaps I am wiser than you think. Do you never for an instant treat me as a thing, flatter me? You treat me with politeness, and I make myself scarce. We have not sympathy enough. We do not always apprehend each other. You talk to me often as if I were Mr. Tompkins of the firm of —— ——, retired merchant. If I had never thought of you as a friend, I could make much use of you as an acquaintance.

I observed this afternoon, on the Turnpike, that where it drifts over the edge of a brook or a ditch, the snow being damp as it falls, what does not adhere to the sharp edge of the drift falls on the dead weeds and shrubs and forms a drapery like a napkin or a white table-cloth hanging down with folds and tassels or fringed border. Or perhaps the fresh snow merely rounds and whitens thus the old cores. It was like looking from one side of a rich white counterpane or table-cloth where it hangs over the side of the bed or table.

The value of the pitch pine in winter is that it holds the snow so finely. I see it now afar on the hillsides decking itself with it, its whited towers forming coverts where the rabbit and the gray squirrel lurk. It makes the most cheerful winter scenery beheld from the window, you know so well the nature of the coverts and

the sombre light it makes. The young oaks, with their red leaves, covering so many acres, are also an indispensable feature of the winter landscape, and the limbs of oak woods where some of the trees have been cut off.

V

FEBRUARY, 1852

(ÆT. 34)

Feb. 1. When I hear that a friend on whom I relied has spoken of me, not with cold words perhaps, but even with a cold and indifferent tone, to another, ah! what treachery I feel it to be! — the sum of all crimes against humanity. My friend may cherish a thousand suspicions against me, and they may but represent his faith and expectations, till he cherishes them so heartlessly that he can speak of them.

If I have not succeeded in my friendships, it was because I demanded more of them and did not put up with what I could get; and I got no more partly because I gave so little.

I must be dumb to those who, I have not faith, appreciate my actions, not knowing the springs of them.

While we preach obedience to human laws and to that portion of the divine laws set forth in the New Testament, the natural laws of genius, of love and friendship, we do not preach nor insist upon. How many a seeming heartlessness is to be explained by the very abundance of the heart! How much of seeming recklessness, even selfishness, is to be explained by obedience to this code of the divine laws! It is evident that as buyers and sellers we obey a very different law from what we do as lovers and friends. The Hindoo is

Vol. III

not to be tried in all things by the Christian standard, nor the Christian by the Hindoo. How much fidelity to law of a kind not commonly recognized, how much magnanimity even, may be thrown away on mankind! is like pearls cast before swine! The hero obeys his own law, the Christian his, the lover and friend theirs; they are to some extent different codes. What incessant tragedy between men when one silently obeys the code of friendship, the other the code of philanthropy, in their dealings with one another. As our constitutions, our geniuses, are different, so are our standards, and we are amenable to different codes. My neighbor asks me in vain to be good as he is good. I must be good as I am made to be good, whether I am heathen or Christian. Every man's laws are hard enough to obey. The Christian falls as far short of obeying the heathen's moral law as the heathen does. One of little faith looks for his rewards and punishments to the next world, and, despairing of this world, behaves accordingly in it; another thinks the present a worthy occasion and arena, sacrifices to it, and expects to hear sympathizing voices. The man who believes in another world and not in this is wont to put me off with Christianity. The present moment in which we talk is of a little less value to him than the next world. So we are said to hope in proportion as we do not realize. It is all hope deferred. But one grain of realization, of instant life, on which we stand, is equivalent to acres of the leaf of hope hammered out to gild our prospect. The former so qualifies the vision that it gilds all that we look upon with the foil of truth. We must meet the hero

on heroic grounds. Some tribes inhabit the mountains; some dwell on the plain. We discourage one another. We obey different laws.

Is not the midnight like Central Africa to most? Are we not tempted to explore it, to penetrate to the shores of its Lake Tchad, to discover the sources of its Nile, perchance in the Mountains of the Moon? Who knows what fertility, what beauty in the animal and vegetable kingdom, are there to be found,[1] what primeval simplicity and reflection of the truth among its dusky inhabitants? We illuminate only the first hours of the night. The light behind the face of the clock on the State-House in Philadelphia extinguished at 11 o'clock P. M. with punctuality, to save oil. Those hours are resigned to a few watchmen in the cities, watching for the disgrace of humanity. Shall we never have watchmen on the country's hills, of another sort, watching for the glory of God? Watch on city walls for a foe, not on country hills for a friend!

In the Mountains of the Moon, in the Central Africa of the night, — there is where all Niles hide their heads. The expeditions up the Niles extend but to the Cataracts, past the ruins of Thebes, or perchance to the mouth of the White Nile; but it is the Black Nile that concerns us.[2] Of some of the great rivers, like the Nile and the Orinoco (?), men still only conjecture the sources.

Shall we put our heads out the chamber window and ask the watchmen, the city police, to tell us of the night, — what its signs of gladness are? Are these the

[1] [*Excursions*, p. 323; Riv. 397.]   [2] [*Ibid.*]

questions we shall put to the watchmen? Who, then, shall we put them to? Or is there none who can answer them?

Each thing is attracted to each, and running to coalesce like drops of water. The fingers incline to be webbed and run together. When I hold mine up to the light and bring them near together, such are the laws of light that, just before they touch, a web appears to grow on them and unite them. So of objects seen through imperfections in glass.

It depends upon how a man has spent his day, whether he has any right to be in his bed. So spend some hours that you may have a right to sleep in the sunshine.

My friends! my friends! it does not cheer me to see them. They but express their want of faith in me or in mankind; their coldest, cruelest thought comes clothed in polite and easy-spoken words at last. I am silent to their invitations, because I do not *feel* invited, and we have no reasons to give for what we do *not* do. One says, "Love me out of this mire;" the other says, "Come out of it and be lovely." One speaks with scorn of the scorners.

In the winter the botanist can study lichens.

The recent rush to California and the attitude of the world, even of its philosophers and prophets, in relation to it appears to me to reflect the greatest disgrace on mankind. That so many are ready to get their living by the lottery of gold-digging without contributing any value to society, and that the great majority who stay at home justify them in this both by precept and example! It matches the infatuation of the Hindoos who have cast themselves under the car of Juggernaut. I know of no more startling development of the morality of trade and all the modes of getting a living than the rush to California affords. Of what significance the philosophy, or poetry, or religion of a world that will rush to the lottery of California gold-digging on the receipt of the first news, to live by luck, to get the means of commanding the labor of others less lucky, *i. e.* of slaveholding, without contributing any value to society? And that is called enterprise, and the devil is only a little more enterprising! The philosophy and poetry and religion of such a mankind are not worth the dust of a puffball. The hog that *roots* his own living, and so makes manure, would be ashamed of such company. If I could command the wealth of all the worlds by lifting my finger, I would not pay such a price for it. It makes God to be a moneyed gentleman who scatters a handful of pennies in order to see mankind scramble for them. Going to California. It is only three thousand miles nearer to hell. I will resign my life sooner than live by luck. The world's raffle. A subsistence in the domains of nature a thing to be raffled for! No wonder that they gamble there. I never heard that they did anything else there. What a comment, what a satire, on our institutions! The conclusion will be that mankind will hang itself upon a tree. And who would interfere to cut it down. And have all the precepts in all the bibles taught men only this? and is the last and most admirable invention of the Yankee race only an improved muck-rake? — patented too!

If one came hither to sell lottery tickets, bringing satisfactory credentials, and the prizes were seats in heaven, this world would buy them with a rush.[1]

Did God direct us so to get our living, digging where we never planted, — and He would perchance reward us with lumps of gold?[2] It is a text, oh! for the Jonahs of this generation, and yet the pulpits are as silent as immortal Greece [?], silent, some of them, because the preacher is gone to California himself. The gold of California is a touchstone which has betrayed the rottenness, the baseness, of mankind. Satan, from one of his elevations, showed mankind the kingdom of California, and they entered into a compact with him at once.

God gave a man a certificate of righteousness which entitled him to food and raiment, but the rest were discontented and envied him. But at last news came that one had discovered a depository of like certificates, intended also for the righteous in times to come, and a cry went up from all lands, and sinners rushed thither from all parts and appropriated them.

God gave the righteous man a certificate entitling him to food and raiment, but the unrighteous man found a facsimile of the same in God's coffers, and appropriated it, and obtained food and raiment like the former.[3]

There are some things which God may afford to smile at; man cannot.

[1] [*Cape Cod, and Miscellanies*, pp. 463, 464; *Misc.*, Riv. 263, 264.]
[2] [*Cape Cod, and Miscellanies*, p. 464; *Misc.*, Riv. 264.]
[3] [*Ibid.*]

Feb. 2. Sir Francis Head says that in America "the moon looks larger" than in Europe. Here, then, more moonshine is to be expected. Perhaps the sun looks larger also. Such are the advantages of the New World.

The same writer says, "the heavens of America appear infinitely higher," "the stars are brighter." These, too, are encouraging facts, symbolical of the height to which the philosophy and poetry and religion of her inhabitants may one day soar. At length, perchance, the immaterial heaven will appear as much higher to the American mind, and the intimations that star it will appear as much brighter. For I believe that climate does thus react on man, and that there is something in the mountain air that feeds the spirit and inspires. We shall be more imaginative; we shall be clearer, as our sky, bluer, fresher; broader and more comprehensive in our understanding, like our plains; our intellect on a grander scale, like our thunder and lightning, our rivers and our lakes, and mountains and forests. Are not these advantages? Will not man grow to greater perfection intellectually as well as physically under these influences? Or is it unimportant how many foggy days there are in his life?[1]

Sir F. Head thinks that the greater cold — equal to thirteen degrees of latitude — in this country is owing to the extensive forests, which prevent the sun and wind from melting the snows, which therefore accumulate on the ground and create a cold stratum of air, which, blown to warmer ones by the northwest wind, condenses the last into snow. But, in Concord woods at

[1] [*Excursions*, p. 222; Riv. 272, 273.]

any rate, the snow (in the winter) melts faster, and beside is not so deep as in the fields. Not so toward spring, on the north sides of hills and in hollows. At any rate I think he has not allowed enough for the warmth of the woods.

The moose (and beaver?) will, perchance, one day become extinct, but how naturally would a future poet imagine or sculptor carve a fabulous animal with such branching and leafy horns, when this will in fact exist as a fossil relic! His horns a sort of fucus in bone, or a lichen. The elk (moose) may stand with the gryphon and dragon and dodo, etc., etc.

The fireflies and bright-plumaged birds! do not they too indicate the peculiarities of the future American?

Head "felt that there was something indescribably awful and appalling in all these bestial, birdal, and piscal precautions" at the approach of winter, — going into winter quarters, migrating, etc.

Head, coming to Canada in the winter, to a house in the fields covered with snow, did not know that he was surrounded by a lawn and garden, with gravelled walks, flowers, and shrubbery, till the spring thawed the snow.

The race that settles and clears the land has got to deal with every tree in the forest in succession. It must be resolute and industrious, and even the stumps must be got out, — or are. It is a thorough process, this war with the wilderness, — breaking nature, taming the soil, feeding it on oats. The civilized man regards the pine tree as his enemy. He will fell it and let in the light, grub it up and raise wheat or rye there. It is no better than a fungus to him.

Vol. III

It is natural that we should be enterprising, for we are descended from the enterprising, who sought to better their fortunes in the New World.

The Yankee has no leisure to touch his hat to you, even if he were so disposed.[1]

Feb. 3. When I review the list of my acquaintances from the most impartial point of view, and consider each one's excesses and defects of character, — which are the subject of mutual ridicule, astonishment, and pity, — and I class myself among them, — I cannot help asking myself, "If this is the sane world, what must a madhouse be?" It is only by a certain flattery and an ignoring of their faults that even the best are made available for society.

I have been to the libraries (yesterday) at Cambridge and Boston. It would seem as if all things compelled us to originality. How happens it that I find not in the country, in the fields and woods, the *works* even of like-minded naturalists and poets. Those who have expressed the purest and deepest love of nature have not recorded it on the bark of the trees with the lichens; they have left no memento of it there; but if I would read their books I must go to the city, — so strange and repulsive both to them and to me, — and deal with men and institutions with whom I have no sympathy. When I have just been there on this errand, it seems too great a price to pay for access even to the works of Homer, or Chaucer, or Linnæus. Greece and Asia Minor should henceforth bear Iliads and Odysseys as their trees lichens.

[1] [*Excursions*, p. 47; Riv. 59.]

Vol. III

But no! if the works of nature are to any extent collected in the forest, the works of man are to a still greater extent collected in the city. I have sometimes imagined a library, *i. e.* a collection of the works of true poets, philosophers, naturalists, etc., deposited not in a brick or marble edifice in a crowded and dusty city, guarded by cold-blooded and methodical officials and preyed on by bookworms, in which you own no share, and are not likely to, but rather far away in the depths of a primitive forest, like the ruins of Central America, where you can trace a series of crumbling alcoves, the older books protecting the most modern from the elements, partially buried by the luxuriance of nature, which the heroic student could reach only after adventures in the wilderness amid wild beasts and wild men. That, to my imagination, seems a fitter place for these interesting relics, which owe no small part of their interest to their antiquity, and whose occasion is nature, than the well-preserved edifice, with its well-preserved officials on the side of a city's square. More terrible than lions and tigers these Cerberuses.

Access to nature for original observation is secured by one ticket, by one kind of expense, but access to the works of your predecessors by a very different kind of expense. All things tend to cherish the originality of the original. Nature, at least, takes no pains to introduce him to the works of his predecessors, but only presents him with her own *Opera Omnia*.

Is it the lover of nature who has access to all that has been written on the subject of his favorite studies? No; he lives far away from this. It is the lover of

books and systems, who knows nature chiefly at second hand.

The botanists have a phrase, *mantissa*, as *Mantissa Plantarum* (Linnæus), which I suppose means an over-measure or additional matter about. A convenient term.[1] Also *prodromus*, as a forerunner, or preparer of the way.

"Suent" is an expressive word, applied to machinery whose joints are worn, which has got into working order, — apparently from *sueo*, to be accustomed. So of the writer's faculties.

About 6 P. M. walked to Cliffs *via* railroad.

Snow quite deep. The sun had set without a cloud in the sky, — a rare occurrence, but I missed the clouds, which make the glory of evening. The sky must have a few clouds, as the mind a few moods; nor is the evening the less serene for them. There is only a tinge of red along the horizon. The moon is nearly full to-night, and the moment is passed when the light in the east (*i. e.* of the moon) balances the light in the west. With the Latins, apparently, there was afternoon, *tempus pomeridianum* or *post meridiem;* then perhaps sunset, *sole occidente*, when *sol inclinat vel decedit;* then perhaps evening, when the evening star reigns, *vespera* (ἕως πέρας).[2] *Vesperascit*, the evening approaches. (By the way, a studying, or working, by candle-light is a *lucubratio a luce* — study all night is *elucubratio* — also *labor vespertinus*. *Serotinus* also means "in the

[1] [Channing, p. 299.]
[2] [Ἕως πέρας signifies "until the end," and is evidently given as the derivation of the Greek ἑσπέρα and Latin *vespera*.]

evening," and more than that, for Pliny says, *Praecocibus brevior [vita]*[1] *quam serotinis*, which cannot be expressed so elegantly in English.) After sundown I should have put twilight, *crepusculum* (*crepera lux* or doubtful light). Then comes decided night or *nox*, *multa nox*. Staying up all night, *pervigilium* or *pervigilatio*. The night far spent, *nox adulta*. Midnight, *nox silens vel profunda*, *meridies noctis*. A starlight night, *nox sideria*. Night-shining, *noctu lucens*. I would not be a mere *tenebrio* or *lucifugus*, shunning the daylight and delighting to skulk in darkness, but simply I am a *noctivagus*. My walk may be *pernox* but not *perniciosus*. They are *Vigiliae Nocturnae*. That little bird that I hear and call the night-warbler may be translated, *Noctu suave canens*. When the moon does not shine all night, it is not a *pernox luna*.

Selenite "is a stone (as is said) in Arabia, wherein is a white, which decreases and increases with the moon" (Dictionary). My summer journal was selenitic in this sense.[2] It had this white spot in it.

Venus is now like a little moon in the west, and the lights in the village twinkle like stars. It is perfectly still and not very cold. The shadows of the trees on the snow are more minutely distinct than at any other season, not dark masses merely, but finely reticulated, each limb and twig represented, as cannot be in summer, both from the leaves and the inequality and darkness of the ground. The heavens appear less thickly starred and less habitable than in summer, — rather

[1] [The brackets are Thoreau's.]
[2] [*Excursions*, p. 323; Riv. 397.]

a few bright stars, brought nearer by this splendid twinkling in the cold sky, than countless points in the warm deeps. I hear my old acquaintance, the owl, from the causeway.

The reflector of the cars, as I stand over the Deep Cut, makes a large and dazzling light in this air. The cars do not make much noise, or else I am used to it; and now whizzes the boiling, sizzling kettle by me, in which the passengers make me think of potatoes, which a fork would show to be done by this time. The steam is denser for the cold, and more white; like the purest downy clouds in the summer sky, its volumes roll up between me and the moon, and far behind, when the cars are a mile off, it still goes shading the fields with its wreaths, — the breath of the panting traveller. I now cross from the railroad to the road. This snow, the last of which fell day before yesterday, is two feet deep, pure and powdery. There is but little on the trees except the pitch pines. From a myriad little crystal mirrors the moon is reflected, which is the untarnished sparkle of its surface. I hear a gentle rustling of the oak leaves as I go through the woods, but this snow has yet no troops of leaves on its surface. The snow evidently by its smooth crust assists in the more equal dispersion and distribution of the leaves which course over it, blown by the [wind], and perchance for this reason the oak leaves and some others hang on.

Now through the Spring Woods and up Fair Haven Hill. Here, in the midst of a clearing where the choppers have been leaving the woods in pieces to-day, and the tops of the pine trees are strewn about half buried

in snow, only the saw-logs being carried off, it is stiller and milder than by day, and I think the chopper might work here more comfortably in some respects now, but he is at home in the village, getting rest or recreation. Instead of the sound of his axe, I hear the hooting of an owl, *nocturnus ululatus*, whose haunts he is laying waste. The ground is all pure white powdery snow, which his sled, etc., has stirred up, except the scattered twigs and pine plumes. I can see every track distinctly where the teamster drove his oxen to the choppers' piles and loaded his sled, and even the tracks of his dog in the moonlight, and plainly to write this.

The moonlight now is very splendid in the untouched pine woods above the Cliffs, alternate patches of shade and light. The light has almost the brightness of sunlight, the fulgor. The stems of the trees are more obvious than by day, being simple black against the moonlight and the snow. The sough of the breeze in the pine-tops sounds far away, like the surf on a distant shore, and for all sound beside there is only the rattling or chafing of little dry twigs, — perchance a little snow falling on them, or they are so brittle that they break and fall with the motion of the trees.

My owl sounds $h\overline{oo}$ $h\breve{oo}$ $h\overline{oo}$, $h\overline{oo}$.

The landscape covered with snow, seen by moonlight from these Cliffs, encased in snowy armor two feet thick, gleaming in the moon and of spotless white. Who can believe that this is the habitable globe? The scenery is wholly arctic. Fair Haven Pond is a Baffin's Bay. Man must have ascertained the limits of the winter before he ventured to withstand it and not migrate

Vol. III

with the birds. No cultivated field, no house, no candle. All is as dreary as the shores of the Frozen Ocean. I can tell where there is wood and where open land for many miles in the horizon by the darkness of the former and whiteness of the latter. The trees, especially the young oaks covered with leaves, stand out distinctly in this bright light from contrast with the snow. It looks as if the snow and ice of the arctic world, travelling like a glacier, had crept down southward and overwhelmed and buried New England. And see if a man can think his summer thoughts now. But the evening star is preparing to set, and I will return. Floundering through snow, sometimes up to my middle.

Is not the sky unusually blue to-night? dark blue? Is it not always bluer when the ground is covered with snow in the winter than in summer?

The forcible writer stands bodily behind his words with his experience. He does not make books out of books, but he has been *there* in person.

Head calls the "sough" an "æolian murmur."

That is a good mythological incident told of the wounded farmer who, his foot being lacerated and held fast between his plow and a fallen tree in a forest clearing, drew his oxen to him, with difficulty smeared their horns with blood which the mosquitoes had drawn from his bare arms, and, cutting the reins [*sic*], sent them home as an advertisement to his family.

Feb. 4. Wednesday. A mild, thawy day. The needles of the pine are the touchstone for the air; any change in that element is revealed to the practiced eye

by their livelier green or increased motion. They are the telltales. Now they are (the white pine) a cadaverous, misty blue; anon a lively, silvery light plays on them, and they seem to erect themselves unusually; while the pitch pines are a brighter yellowish-green than usual. The sun loves to nestle in the boughs of the pine and pass rays through them.

The scent of bruised pine leaves where a sled has passed is a little exciting to me now. I saw this afternoon such lively blood-red colors on a white pine stump recently cut that at first I thought the chopper had cut himself. The heart of the tree was partly decayed, and here and there the sounder parts were of this vermilion (?) color, alternating with the ordinary white of the wood. Here it was apparently in the earlier stages of decay. The color was the livelier for being wet with the melting snow.

11 P. M. — Coming home through the village by this full moonlight, it seems one of the most glorious nights I ever beheld. Though the pure snow is so deep around, the air, by contrast perhaps with the recent days, is mild and even balmy to my senses, and the snow is still sticky to my feet and hands. And the sky is the most glorious blue I ever beheld, even a light blue on some sides, as if I actually saw into day, while small white, fleecy clouds, at long intervals, are drifting from west-north-west to south-southeast. If you would know the direction of the wind, look not at the clouds, which are such large bodies and confuse you, but consider in what direction the moon appears to be wading through them. The outlines of the elms were never more distinctly seen

than now. It seems a slighting of the gifts of God to
go to sleep now; as if we could better afford to close
our eyes to daylight, of which we see so much. Has not
this blueness of the sky the same cause with the blueness in the holes in the snow, and in some distant shadows on the snow ? — if, indeed, it is true that the sky is
bluer in winter when the ground is covered with snow.

Heard Professor Blasius lecture on the tornado this
evening. He said that nine vessels were wrecked daily
in the world on an average; that Professor Dove of
Berlin was the best meteorologist in his opinion, but
had not studied the effects of wind in the fields so much
as some here.

These nights are warmer than the days; but by morning it is colder.

Head's theory of American cold, founded on the
unmelted snows of our forests, reminds me of the fish
and bucket of water dispute. Is it a fact that such vast
quantities of snow are slow to melt in our forests ?

The audience are never tired of hearing how far the
wind carried some man, woman, or child, or family
Bible, but they are immediately tired if you undertake
to give them a scientific account of it.

Feb. 5. Suppose that an equal ado were made about
the *ornaments* of style in literature (as in architecture),
should we be any more likely to attain to a truly beautiful and forcible style ? Buonaparte said pretty truly,
"Speak plain; the rest will follow." I do not believe
that any writer who considered the ornaments, and
not the truth simply, ever succeeded. So are made the

Vol. III

belles lettres and the *beaux arts* and their *professors*,
which we can do without.[1]

The sky last night was a deeper, more cerulean blue
than the far lighter and whiter sky of to-day.

The national flag is the emblem of patriotism, and
whether that floats over the Government House or not
is, even in times of peace, an all-absorbing question.
The hearts of millions flutter with it. Men do believe
in symbols yet and can understand some. When Sir
F. Head left his Government in Upper Canada and
the usual farewell had been said as the vessel moved off,
he, standing on the deck, pointed for all reply to the
British flag floating over his head, and a shriek, rather
than a cheer, went up from the crowd on the pier, who
had observed his gesture. One of the first things he
had done was to run it up over the Government House
at Toronto, and it made a great sensation.

Time never passes so rapidly and unaccountably
as when I am engaged in recording my thoughts. The
world may perchance reach its end for us in a profounder thought, and Time itself run down.

I suspect that the child plucks its first flower with
an insight into its beauty and significance which the
subsequent botanist never retains.

The trunks and branches of the trees are of different colors at different times and in different lights and
weathers, — in sun, rain, and in the night. The oaks
bare of leaves on Hubbard's hillside are now a light
gray in the sun, and their boughs, seen against the
pines behind, are a very agreeable maze. The stems

[1] [*Walden*, pp. 52, 53; Riv. 77.]

of the white pines also are quite gray at this distance,
with their lichens. I am detained to contemplate the
boughs, feathery boughs, of the white pines, tier above
tier, reflecting a silvery light, with intervals between
them through which you look, if you so intend your
eye, into the darkness of the grove. That is, you can
see both the silvery-lighted and greenish bough and the
shadowy intervals as belonging to one tree, or, more
truly, refer the latter to the shade behind.

Read the Englishman's history of the French and
Indian wars, and then read the Frenchman's, and see
how each awards the meed of glory to the other's monsters of cruelty or perfidy.

We have all sorts of histories of wars. One omits
the less important skirmishes altogether, another condescends to give you the result of these and the number of killed and wounded, and if you choose to go
further and consult tradition and old manuscripts or
town and local histories, you may learn whether the
parson was killed by a shot through the door or toma-
hawked at the well.

Feb. 6. If the woodchopper rises early, shall not
the scholar sit up late ?

I have been told at the pattern-room of certain print-
works that the taste of the public in respect to these
things was singularly whimsical, and that it was impossible to foretell what would most take with it. Of two
patterns which differed only by a few threads more or
less of a particular color, the one would be sold readily,
the other would be unsalable, thus occasioning great

loss to the manufacturer; though it frequently happened
that after the lapse of a season the unsalable goods
became the most fashionable.[1]

If a poor man returns to a gentleman his purse, which
he has found, the bystanders are astonished at his honesty, and if the gentleman does not reward him munifi-
cently, they make up a purse for him themselves.

Tuckerman very well refers science to the medicine-
man of the savages. He took the first step toward science.

Dioscorides, "the second father of Botany," — what
a flowery name!

The artificial system has been very properly called
the dictionary, and the natural method, the grammar,
of the science of botany, by botanists themselves. But
are we to have nothing but grammars and dictionaries
in this literature ? Are there no works written in the
language of the flowers ?

I asked a learned and accurate naturalist, who is
at the same time the courteous guardian of a public
library, to direct me to those works which contained
the more particular *popular* account, or *biography*,
of particular flowers, from which the botanies I had
met with appeared to draw sparingly, — for I trusted
that each flower had had many lovers and faithful
describers in past times, — but he informed me that
I had read all; that no one was acquainted with them,
they were only catalogued like his books.

3 P. M. Round by C. Miles's place.

It is still thawy. A mistiness makes the woods look
denser, darker, and more imposing. Seen through this

[1] [*Walden*, p. 29; Riv. 44.]

veil, they are more grand and primitive. Near the C. Miles house there are some remarkably yellow lichens (parmelias?) on the rails, — ever as if the sun were about to shine forth clearly. Methinks I would have lichens on some of my rails, [even] if it were not consistent with good husbandry.

Some of our days, in June perchance, may be styled all-saints' days.

Who will not confess that the necessity to get money has helped to ripen some of his schemes?

The historian of Haverhill[1] commences his account of the attack on that town in 1708 by the French and Indians, by saying that one [of] the French commanders was "the infamous Hertel de Rouville, the sacker of Deerfield," that the French of that period equalled, if they did not exceed, the Indians in acts of wantonness and barbarity, and "when the former were weary of murdering 'poor, helpless women and children,' — when they were glutted with blood, it is said that M. Vaudreuil, then Governor of Canada, employed the latter to do it." He then goes on to describe the sudden and appalling attack before sunrise, the slaughter of women and infants and the brave or cowardly conduct of the inhabitants. Rolfe and Wainwright and many others were killed. The French historian Charlevoix says of Rouville that he supplied his father's place worthily and that the Governor, Vaudreuil, called him one of the two best partisans in Canada. He tells us that Rouville made a short speech to the French

[1] [B. L. Mirick, *The History of Haverhill, Massachusetts*, Haverhill, 1832.]

before they commenced the attack, exhorting them to forget their differences and embrace one another. "And then they said their prayers" and marched to the assault. And after giving an account of the attack, and of the subsequent actions almost totally different from the former, not having said a word about the barbarities of the savages, he proceeds to enumerate the "belles actions" of some officers who showed humanity to the prisoners on the retreat.

Feb. 7. The warmer weather we have had for a few days past was particularly pleasant to the poor whose wood-piles were low, whose clothes were ragged and thin. I think how the little boy must enjoy it whom I saw a week ago with his shoes truncated at the toes. Hard are the times when the infants' shoes are secondfoot.

The French historian speaks of both French and Indians as "our braves (*nos Braves*)." The village historian takes you into the village graveyard and reads the inscriptions on the monuments of the slain. Takes you to the grave of the parish priest, his wife, and child, which is honored with a Latin inscription. The French historian, who signs himself *de la Compagnie de Jésus*, who was at the waterside at Montreal when the expedition disembarked, and so heard the freshest news. To show the discrepancies, I will compare the two accounts in relation to one part of the affair alone.

The Haverhill historian says, "The retreat [of the French and Indians][1] commenced about the rising of the

[1] [The brackets are Thoreau's.]

Vol. III

sun." "The town, by this time, was generally alarmed. Joseph Bradley collected a small party, . . . and secured the medicine-box and packs of the enemy, which they had left about three miles from the village. Capt. Samuel Ayer, a fearless man, and of great strength, collected a body of about twenty men, and pursued the retreating foe. He came up with them just as they were entering the woods, when they faced about, and though they numbered thirteen or more to one, still Capt. Ayer did not hesitate to give them battle. These gallant men were soon reinforced by another party, under the command of his son; and after a severe skirmish, which lasted about an hour, they retook some of the prisoners, and the enemy precipitately retreated, leaving nine of their number dead.

"The French and Indians continued their retreat, and so great were their sufferings, arising from the loss of their packs, and their consequent exposure to famine, that many of the Frenchmen returned and surrendered themselves prisoners of war; and some of the captives were dismissed, with a message that, if they were pursued, the others should be put to death. Perhaps, if they had been pursued, nearly the whole of their force might have been conquered. . . . As it was, they left thirty of their number dead, in both engagements, and many were wounded, whom they carried with them."

One Joseph Bartlett, a soldier who was carried away captive but returned after some years and published a narrative of his captivity, says that after the retreat commenced, "they then marched on together,

when Capt. Eaires [Ayer], with a small company, waylaid and shot upon them, which put them to flight, so that they did not get together again until three days after."[1] His party, says the historian, had nothing to eat for four days "but a few sour grapes and thorn plums. They then killed a hawk and divided it among fifteen — the head fell to the share of Mr. Bartlett, which, he says, 'was the largest meal I had these four days.'" The historian concludes that between thirty and forty New-Englanders in all were either killed or taken prisoners.

Now for Charlevoix's account, who happened to be at the waterside at Montreal when the French party disembarked and so got the most' direct and freshest news. He says: "There were about a hundred English slain in these different attacks; many others . . . were burned (in the houses), and the number of prisoners was considerable." (This was before the retreat.) "As for booty there was none at all, they did not think of it, till it had all been consumed in the flames." Speaking of the retreat, he says: "It was made with much order, each one having taken so many provisions only as was needed for the return. This precaution was even (*encore*) more necessary than they thought. Our men had hardly made half a league, when, on entering a wood, they fell into an ambuscade, which seventy men had prepared for them, who, before discovering themselves, fired each his shot. Our braves met this discharge without wavering, and fortunately it produced no great effect. Meanwhile all the rear was already full

[1] [As quoted by Mirick.]

of people on foot and on horseback, who followed them closely, and there was no other course to take but to force their way through those (*que de passer sur le ventre à ceux*) who had just fired upon them."

"They took it without hesitating, each threw away his pack of provisions, and almost all his apparel (*hardes*), and without amusing themselves with firing they came at once to a hand-to-hand contest (with them) (*sans s'amuser à tirer ils en vinrent d'abord aux armes blanches*). The English, astonished at so vigorous an assault made by men whom they thought they had thrown into disorder, found themselves in that condition (*y*, there) and could not recover (themselves). So that, excepting ten or twelve who saved themselves by flight, all were killed or taken."

"We had in the two actions eighteen men wounded, three savages and five French killed, and in the number of the dead were two young officers of great promise, Hertel de Chambly, brother of Rouville, and Verchères. Many prisoners made in the attack on Haverhill saved themselves during the last combat."

Tuckerman says that Fries "states formally the *quaqua*versal affinity of plants, and hence rejects once more the notion of a single series in nature. He declares species 'unica in natura fixe circumscripta idea,' and hence all superior sections are more or less indefinite." Just as true is this of man, even of an individual man. He is not to be referred to, or classed with, any company. He is truly singular, and, so far as systems are concerned, in a sense abnormal ever.

Tuckerman says of Linnæus, "Who, while he indi-

cated the affinities of nature, and pronounced their explication the true end of the science of plants, yet constructed also an artificial system, which so surpassed every other, that it seemed nigh to overwhelming that very knowledge of affinities, to which, as just said, he had consecrated the whole design of Botany." Again, "Fries may be said to represent that higher school of Linnæans, which started from the great naturalist's *natural doctrine*."

The English did not come here from a mere love of adventure, to truck with the savages, or to convert the savages, or to hold offices under the crown, as the French did, but to live in earnest and with freedom. The French had no *busy-ness* here. They ran over an immense extent of country, selling strong water, and collecting its furs and converting its inhabitants, — or at least baptizing its dying infants, — without improving it. The New England youth were not *coureurs de bois*.

It was freedom to hunt and fish, not to work, that they sought. Hontan says the *coureurs de bois* lived like sailors ashore.[1]

Feb. 8. Mrs. Buttrick says that she has five cents for making a shirt, and that if she does her best she can make one in a day.

It is interesting to see loads of hay coming down from the country nowadays, — within a week. They make them very broad and low. They do not carry hay by railroad yet. The spoils of up-country fields. A mountain of dried herbs. I had forgotten that there

[1] [*Excursions*, pp. 66, 67; Riv. 83, 84.]

ever was so much grass as they prove. And all these horses and oxen and cows, then, are still fed on the last summer's grass which has been dried! They still roam in the meads.

One would think that some people regarded character in man as the botanist regards character in flowers, who says, "Character characterem non antecellit nisi constantia," but this is well explained, and so that it becomes applicable to man, by this parallel aphorism of Linnæus, "Character non est, ut genus fiat, sed ut genus noscatur."

It is apparently Fries who is made to say of his own system — or it may be Tuckerman who says it — that "By this key, I have not yet found that any plants, manifestly and by consent of all allied, are sundered."

Tuckerman says cunningly, "If the rapt admirer of the wonders and the beauties of life and being might well come to learn of our knowledge the laws and the history of what he loves, let us remember that we have the best right to all the pleasure that he has discovered, and that we are not complete if we do not possess it all. Linnæus was as hearty a lover and admirer of nature as if he had been nothing more."

Night before last, our first rain for a long time; this afternoon, the first crust to walk on. It is pleasant to walk over the fields raised a foot or more above their summer level, and the prospect is altogether new.

Is not all music a hum more or less divine? I hear something new at every telegraph-post. I have not got out of hearing of one before I hear a new harp.

Thoughts of different dates will not cohere.

Carried a new cloak to Johnny Riordan. I found that the shanty was warmed by the simple social relations of the Irish. On Sunday they come from the town and stand in the doorway and so keep out the cold. One is not cold among his brothers and sisters. What if there is less fire on the hearth, if there is more in the heart!

These Irish are not succeeding so ill after all. The little boy goes to the primary school and proves a forward boy there, and the mother's brother, who has let himself in the village, tells me that he takes the *Flag of our Union* (if that is the paper edited by an Irishman). It is musical news to hear that Johnny does not love to be kept at home from school in deep snows.

In this winter often no apparent difference between rivers, ponds, and fields.

The French respected the Indians as a separate and independent people, and speak of them and contrast themselves with them, as the English have never done. They not only went to war with them, but they lived at home with them. There was a much less interval between them.[1]

Feb. 9. I am interested to see the seeds of the poke, about a dozen, shiny black with a white spot, somewhat like a saba bean in shape. The still full granary of the birds.

At 9 A. M. up river to Fair Haven Pond.

This is our month of the crusted snow. Was this the Indians'? I get over the half-buried fences at a stride, and the drifts slope up to the tops of the walls

[1] [*Excursions*, p. 66; Riv. 82.]

on each side. The crust is melted on the south slopes and lets me in, or where the sun has been reflected (yesterday) from a wood-side and rotted it, but the least inclination to the north is evidence of a hard surface. On the meadows and in level open fields away from the reflection of pines and oak leaves, it will generally bear.

Met Sudbury Haines on the river before the Cliffs, come a-fishing. Wearing an old coat, much patched, with many colors. He represents the Indian still. The very patches in his coat and his improvident life do so. I feel that he is as essential a part, nevertheless, of our community as the lawyer in the village. He tells me that he caught three pickerel here the other day that weighed seven pounds all together. It is the old story. The fisherman is a natural story-teller. No man's imagination plays more pranks than his, while he is tending his reels and trotting from one to another, or watching his cork in summer. He is ever waiting for the sky to fall. He has sent out a venture. He has a ticket in the lottery of fate, and who knows what it may draw? He ever expects to catch a bigger fish yet. He is the most patient and believing of men. Who else will stand so long in wet places? When the haymaker runs to shelter, he takes down his pole and bends his steps to the river, glad to have a leisure day. He is more like an inhabitant of nature. The weather concerns him. He is an observer of her phenomena.

They say that the Pasha, by some improvements in cutting down trees, has banished rain from Egypt altogether for some years past.

Men tell about the mirage to be seen in certain deserts

and in peculiar states of the atmosphere. The mirage is constant. The state of the atmosphere is continually varying, and, to a keen observer, objects do not twice present exactly the same appearance. If I invert my head this morning and look at the woods in the horizon, they do not look so far off and elysian-like as in the afternoon. If I am not mistaken, it is late in the afternoon that the atmosphere is in such a state that we derive the most pleasure from and are most surprised by this experiment. The prospect is thus actually a constantly varying mirage, answering to the condition of our perceptive faculties and our fluctuating imaginations. If we incline our heads never so little, the most familiar things begin to put on some new aspect. If we invert our heads completely our desecrated wood-lot appears far off, incredible, elysian, unprofaned by us. As you cannot swear through glass, no more can you swear through air, the thinnest section of it. It paints and glasses everything. When was not the air as elastic as our spirits? I cannot well conceive of greater variety than it produces by its changes from hour to hour of every day. It is a new glass placed over the picture every hour.

I did not know that the world was suffering for want of gold. The discovery of a mountain of gold would only derange the currency. I have seen a little of it. I know it is very malleable, but not so malleable as wit. A grain of it will gild a great surface, but not so much as a grain of wisdom. I do not care if the goldsmiths and jewellers find these hard times.[1]

[1] [Cape Cod, and Miscellanies, p. 464; Misc., Riv. 265.]

Vol. III

A man goes to the end of his garden, inverts his head, and does not know his own cottage. The novelty is in us, and it is also in nature.

When I break off a twig of green-barked sassafras, as I am going through the woods now, and smell it, I am startled to find it fragrant as in summer. It is an importation of all the spices of Oriental summers into our New England winter. Very foreign to the snow and the oak leaves. I find that the wood on the Island in Fair Haven Pond has been cut off this winter, but as the young [wood] and underwood is left, I am surprised to see so much witch-hazel there, — more than anywhere else that I know of. It shall be called Witch-Hazel Island. The spray of this shrub is remarkably recurved in some instances; on one whole side of a large bush.

For the first time this many a year, I tasted there some of the sweet froth which had issued from the sap of a walnut or hickory lately cut. It is always cheering and somewhat unexpected to meet in nature with anything so agreeable to the human palate. So innocent a sweet. It reminded me of the days when I used to scrape this juice off the logs in my father's wood-pile.

Respecting lichens, perhaps the first question which the mass of men put is, "What ones are good to eat?" And the meagre answer is rock-tripe (*Umbilicaria*) and Iceland moss (*Cetraria Islandica*). They may next inquire which are the most beautiful. The most scientific will only assist to answer similar questions. How they

concern man, — the most elaborate and driest system must tell us better at last how they concern man.

Feb. 10. Now if there are any who think that I am vainglorious, that I set myself up above others and crow over their low estate, let me tell them that I could tell a pitiful story respecting myself as well as them, if my spirits held out to do it; I could encourage them with a sufficient list of failures, and could flow as humbly as the very gutters themselves; I could enumerate a list of as rank offenses as ever reached the nostrils of heaven; that I think worse of myself than they can possibly think of me, being better acquainted with the man. I put the best face on the matter. I will tell them this secret, if they will not tell it to anybody else.

Write while the heat is in you. When the farmer burns a hole in his yoke, he carries the hot iron quickly from the fire to the wood, for every moment it is less effectual to penetrate (pierce) it. It must be used instantly, or it is useless. The writer who postpones the recording of his thoughts uses an iron which has cooled to burn a hole with. He cannot inflame the minds of his audience.

We have none of those peculiar clear, vitreous, crystalline vistas in the western sky before sundown of late. There is perchance more moisture in the air. Perhaps that phenomenon does not belong to this part of the winter.

I saw yesterday on the snow on the ice, on the south side of Fair Haven Pond, some hundreds of honey-bees, dead and sunk half an inch below the crust. They had evidently come forth from their hive (perhaps in a large hemlock on the bank close by), and had fallen on the snow chilled to death. Their bodies extended from the tree to about three rods from it toward the pond. Pratt says he would advise me to remove the dead bees, lest somebody else should be led to discover their retreat, and I may get five dollars for the swarm, and perhaps a good deal of honey.

Feb. 11. *Wednesday.* When the thermometer is down to 20° in the morning, as last month, I think of the poor dogs who have no masters. If a poor dog has no master, everybody will throw a billet of wood at him. It never rains but it pours.

It now rains, — a drizzling rain mixed with mist, which ever and anon fills the air to the height of fifteen or twenty feet. It makes what they call an old-fashioned mill privilege in the streets, *i. e.* I suppose, a privilege on a small stream good only for a part of the year.

Perhaps the best evidence of an amelioration of the climate — at least that the snows are less deep than formerly — is the snow-shoes which still lie about in so many garrets, now useless, though the population of this town has not essentially increased for seventy-five years past, and the travelling within the limits of the town accordingly not much facilitated. No man ever uses them now, yet the old men used them in their youth.

I have lived some thirty-odd years on this planet, and I have yet to hear the first syllable of valuable or even earnest advice from my seniors. They have told

Vol. III

me nothing, and probably can tell me nothing to the purpose. There is life, an experiment untried by me, and it does not avail me that you have tried it. If I have any valuable experience, I am sure to reflect that this my mentors said nothing about. What were mysteries to the child remain mysteries to the old man.[1]

It is a mistake to suppose that, in a country where railroads and steamboats, the printing-press and the church, and the usual evidences of what is called civilization exist, the condition of a very large body of the inhabitants cannot be as degraded as that of savages. Savages have their high and their low estate, and so have civilized nations. To know this I should not need to look further than to the shanties which everywhere line our railroads, that last improvement in civilization. But I will refer you to Ireland, which is marked as one of the white or enlightened spots on the map. Yet I have no doubt that that nation's rulers are as wise as the average of civilized rulers.[2]

Feb. 12. Living all winter with an open door for light and no visible wood-pile, the forms of old and young permanently contracted through long shrinking from cold, and their faces pinched by want. I have seen an old crone sitting bareheaded on the hillside, then in the middle of January, while it was raining and the ground was slowly thawing under her, knitting there. Their undeveloped limbs and faculties, buds that cannot expand on account of the severity of the season. There

[1] [*Walden*, p. 10; Riv. 17.]
[2] [*Walden*, pp. 38, 39; Riv. 56–58.]

is no greater squalidness in any part of the world![1] Contrast the physical condition of the Irish with that of the North American Indian, or the South Sea Islander, or any other savage race before they were degraded by contact with the civilized man.[2]

Feb. 13. Talking with Rice this afternoon about the bees which I discovered the other day, he told me something about his bee-hunting. He and Pratt go out together once or twice a year. He takes a little tin box with a little refined sugar and water about the consistency of honey, or some honey in the comb, which comes up so high only in the box as to let the lid clear a bee's back, also some little bottles of paint — red, blue, white, etc. — and a compass properly prepared to line the bees with, the sights perhaps a foot apart. Then they ride off (this is in the fall) to some extensive wood, perhaps the west side of Sudbury. They go to some buckwheat-field or a particular species of late goldenrod which especially the bees frequent at that season, and they are sure to find honey-bees enough. They catch one by putting the box under the blossoms and then covering him with the lid, at the same time cutting off the stalk of the flower. They then set down the box, and after a while raise the lid slightly to see if the bee is feeding; if so, they take off the lid, knowing that he will not fly away till he gets ready, and catch another; and so on till they get a sufficient number. Then they thrust sticks into their little paint-bot-

[1] [*Walden*, p. 58; Riv. 57.]
[2] [*Walden*, pp. 38, 39; Riv. 57, 58.]

tles, and, with these, watching their opportunity, they give the bees each a spot of a particular color on his body, — they spot him distinctly, — and then, lying about a rod off, not to scare them, and watching them carefully all the while, they wait till one has filled his sac, and prepares to depart to his hive. They are careful to note whether he has a red or a blue jacket or what color. He rises up about ten feet and then begins to circle rapidly round and round with a hum, sometimes a circle twenty feet in diameter before he has decided which way to steer, and then suddenly shoots off in a bee-line to his hive. The hunters lie flat on their backs and watch him carefully all the while. If blue-jacket steers toward the open land where there are known to be hives, they forthwith leave out of the box all the blue-jackets, and move off a little and open the box in a new place to get rid of that family. And so they work till they come to a bee, red-jacket perhaps, that steers into the wood or swamp or in a direction to suit them. They take the point of compass exactly, and wait perhaps till red-jacket comes back, that they may ascertain his course more exactly, and also judge by the time it has taken for him to go and return, using their watches, how far off the nest is, though sometimes they are disappointed in their calculations, for it may take the [bee] more or less time to crawl into its nest, depending on its position in the tree. By the third journey he will commonly bring some of his companions. Our hunters then move forward a piece, from time to time letting out a bee to make sure of their course. After the bees have gone and come once, they generally steer straight to their nest at once without circling round first. Sometimes the hunters, having observed this course carefully on the compass, go round a quarter of a circle and, letting out another bee, observe the course from that point, knowing that where these two lines intersect must be the nest. Rice thinks that a bee-line does not vary more than fifteen or twenty feet from a straight one in going half a mile. They frequently trace the bees thus to their hives more than a mile.

He said that the last time he went out the wind was so strong that the bees made some leeway just as a bullet will, and he could not get the exact course to their hives. He has a hive of bees over in Sudbury, and he every year sows some buckwheat for them. He has visited this buckwheat when in blossom when there was more than one bee to every six inches square, and out of curiosity has caught a number of the bees and, letting them out successively, has calculated by the several courses they took whose hives they came from in almost every instance, though some had come more than two miles and others belonged to his own hive close by.

He has seen a dozen hogsheads of honey from South America on the wharf at Boston. Says they manufacture honey now from maple syrup, which you cannot tell from bee honey, taking care to throw some dead bees and bees' wings and a little honeycomb into it.

He was repaid if he found the nest, even if he did not get any honey. I am glad to know that there are such grown children left. He says the mountain honeysuckle (columbine) has a good deal of honey at the

bottom of the flower which the bee cannot get at in the usual way; it therefore gnaws a hole in it from the outside.

The actual bee-hunter and pigeon-catcher is familiar with facts in the natural history of bees and pigeons which Huber and even Audubon are totally ignorant of. I love best the unscientific man's knowledge; there is so much more humanity in it. It is connected with true *sports*.

9 A. M. — To Conantum.

The rain has diminished the snow and hardened the crust, and made bare ground in many places. A yellow water, a foot or two deep, covers the ice on the meadows, but is not frozen quite hard enough to bear. As the river swells, the ice cracks along both sides over the edge of its channel, often defined by willows, and that part over the river rises with the water, but that over the meadow is held down apparently by the grass and bushes (and moreover feels the force of the freshet less), and is, accordingly, covered with water.

I sat by the little brook in Conant's meadow, where it falls over an oak rail between some boards which partially dam it, — eight or nine inches, — the bubbles on the surface making a coarse foam, the surface of which I perceive has frozen in the night, forming an irregular shell-like covering which is now partly worn away at top. These bubbles which so closely push up and crowd one another, each making haste to expand and burst (forming coarse frothy heaps), impinging on each other, remind me of the cells of honeycomb,

Vol. III

as if they inclined to take the same hexagonal form, — four-sided, five-sided, but the most perfect, methinks, six-sided, — but it is difficult to count them, they are so restless and burst so soon. In one place this froth had been frozen into the form of little hollow towers larger at top than at bottom, six inches high, and the bubbles were now incessantly rising through and bursting at their top, — overflowing with bubbles. I saw the ruined shells of many similar towers that had been washed down the stream.

Air being carried down by the force of this little fall and mixed with the water, deeper bubbles were formed, which rose up further down and were flattened against the transparent ice, through which they appeared like coins of all sizes from a pin-head to a dollar, poured out of a miser's pot, hesitating at first which way to troop, seeming sometimes to be detained by some inequality in the ice which they so closely hugged. The coin-like bubbles of the brook.

I traced this rill further up, to where it comes under the road, and heard its rumbling like a mill privilege from afar, but it was quite bridged over there with snow; but here and there the foam was frothing up through a hole in the snow like a little geyser, and in some places it was frozen in the form of beehives eighteen inches high and a foot wide, the most delicate flocculent masses which could not be handled, regularly formed, layer on layer, sometimes of a downy white, sometimes tinged with a delicate fawn-color, in which you could detect a slight trembling, showing that the geyser was still at work in its core. Nature handled

the froth more delicately than the spinner's machinery his roping.

Color, which is the poet's wealth, is so expensive that most take to mere outline or pencil sketches and become men of science.

Feb. 14. But this points to a distinction between the civilized man and the savage; and, no doubt, they have designs on us in making (of the life of a civilized people) an institution in which the life of the individual is to a great extent absorbed, in order, perchance, to preserve and perfect the race. But I wish to show at what a sacrifice this advantage is at present obtained, and to suggest that we may possibly so live as to secure all the advantage without suffering any of the disadvantage. What mean ye by saying that the fathers have eaten sour grapes, and the children's teeth are set on edge?

"As I live, saith the Lord God, ye shall not have occasion any more to use this proverb in Israel.

"Behold, all souls are mine; as the soul of the father, so also the soul of the son is mine: the soul that sinneth, it shall die." [1]

3 P. M. — Walden road to pond, thence to Cliffs.

The slight snow of last night, lodging on the limbs of the oaks, has given them the wintry and cobwebbed appearance which distinguishes them so plainly from the pines. They are great cladonias, perchance.

Met Joshua Brown returning from the pond (Walden)

[1] [*Walden*, pp. 34, 35; Riv. 52, 53.]

without having caught a fish. Has had no luck there this winter, he thinks because of the woodcutters' falling trees on to the ice. He, too, tells how many weighed a certain number of pounds. Four pounds and three quarters is the heaviest he ever caught, but the pickerel that ran off with his reel (before he got to it), which he did not see, he set at ten pounds.

I noticed a white pine, rotten within, near the pond, — or, rather, eaten out, honeycombed, by the ants, as I think, — and I was struck by the regular cellular character of the cavities they had made, separated by thin partitions, each cell about an inch and a half long, reminding me of Chinese puzzles carved in wood.

The seeds or seed-vessels of wintergreen are conspicuous above the snow.

The winter has had its seasons somewhat in this order, as near as I now remember: First there were a few glowing sunsets after raw and blustering days, setting the pines and oaks on fire with their blaze, when the summer and fall had set, — the afterglow of the year. Then, if I remember, came the snows, and true winter began, the snow growing gradually deeper and the cold more intense. I think it was before the first thaw, which this winter came before the end of December, that the main attraction in my afternoon walks (at any rate when the days were shortest and the cold most intense) was the western sky at and before sunset, when, through the vistas there between the clouds, you saw a singularly crystalline, vitreous sky, which perhaps is not seen at any other season of the year, at least not in such perfection. I will see if

Vol. III

we have any more this winter. Well, then there was the thaw, January thaw, which this year came in December, for it is the first thaw after long-continued cold weather and snow, when we have fairly forgotten summer. This winter was remarkable for the long continuance of severe cold weather after it had once set in. Latterly we have had, *i. e.* within a week, crusted snow, made by thaw and rain, but now I do not see the crystalline sky.

In the January thaw I should have mentioned the sand foliage in the Cut.

Now we have the swollen river, and yellow water over the meadow ice to some extent. Other epochs I might find described in my Journal.

At the Cliffs, the rocks are in some places covered with ice; and the least inclination beyond a perpendicular in their faces is betrayed by the formation of icicles at once, which hang perpendicularly, like organ pipes, in front of the rock. They are now conducting downward the melting ice and snow, which drips from their points with a slight clinking and lapsing sound, but when the sun has set will freeze there and add to the icicles' length. Where the icicles have reached the ground and are like thick pillars, they have a sort of annular appearance, somewhat like the successive swells on the legs of tables and on bed-posts. There is perhaps a harmony between the turner's taste and the law of nature in this instance. The shadow of the water flowing or pulsating behind this transparent icy crust or these stalactites in the sun imparts a semblance of life to the whole.

The traveller's is so apt to be a progress more or less rapid toward his home (I have read many a voyage round the world more than half of which, certainly, was taken up with the return voyage; he no sooner is out of sight of his native hills than he begins to tell us how he got home again) that I wonder he did not stay at home in the first place.

The laws of nature always furnish us with the best excuse for going and coming. If we do not go now, we shall find our fire out.

I hate that my motive for visiting a friend should be that I want society; that it should lie in my poverty and weakness, and not in his and my riches and strength. His friendship should make me strong enough to do without him.

Feb. 15. Perhaps I am descended from that Northman named "Thorer the Dog-footed." Thorer Hund — "he was the most powerful man in the North" — to judge from his name belonged to the same family. Thorer is one of the most, if not the most, common name in the chronicles of the Northmen.

Feb. 16. Laing says that "the Heimskringla has been hardly used by the learned men of the period in which it was first published. It appeared first in the literary world in 1697, frozen into the Latin of the Swedish antiquary, Peringskiold."

Snorro Sturleson says, "From Thor's name comes Thorer, also Thorarinn." Again: "Earl Rognvald was King Harald's dearest friend, and the king had the

greatest regard for him. He was married to Hilda, a daughter of Rolf Naefia, and their sons were Rolf and Thorer. . . . Rolf became a great viking, and was of so stout a growth that no horse could carry him, and wheresoever he went he must go on foot; and therefore he was called Gange-Rolf." (Laing says in a note, what Sturleson also tells in the text, Gange-Rolf, Rolf Ganger, Rolf the Walker, was the conqueror of Normandy.) "Gange-Rolf's son was William, father to Richard, and grandfather to another Richard, who was the father of Richard Longspear, and grandfather of William the Bastard, from whom all the following English kings are descended."

King Harald "set Earl Rognvald's son Thorer over Möre, and gave him his daughter Alof in marriage. Thorer, called the Silent, got the same territory his father Rognvald had possessed." His brother Einar, going into battle to take vengeance on his father's murderers, sang a kind of reproach against his brothers Rollang and Rolf for their slowness and concludes, —

"And silent Thorer sits and dreams
At home, beside the mead-bowl's streams."

Of himself it is related that he cut a spread eagle on the back of his enemy Halfdan.

So it seems that from one branch of the family were descended the kings of England, and from the other myself.

Down Turnpike.

It is interesting to meet an ox with handsomely spreading horns. There is a great variety of sizes and forms, though one horn commonly matches the other. I am willing to turn out for those that spread their branches wide. Large and spreading horns methinks indicate a certain vegetable force and naturalization in the wearer; it softens and eases off the distinction between the animal and vegetable, the unhorned animals and the trees. I should say that the horned animals approached nearer to the vegetable. The deer that run in the woods, as the moose for instance, carry perfect trees on their heads. The French call them *bois*. No wonder there are fables of centaurs and the like. No wonder there is a story of a hunter who, when his bullets failed, fired cherry-stones into the heads of his game and so trees sprouted out of them, and the hunter refreshed himself with the cherries. It is a perfect piece of mythology which belongs to these days. Oxen, which are de-animalized to some extent, approach nearer to the vegetable, perchance, than bulls and cows, and hence their bulky bodies and large and spreading horns. Nothing more natural than that the deer should appear with a tree growing out of his head. Thus is the animal allied to the vegetable kingdom and passes into it by insensible degrees. These appendages are indispensable to the beauty of the animal, as appears from the great calf look of a cow without horns, or a "bunter."

Man's relation to oxen is the same that it was in primitive ages. It is equally primitive. He has got no nearer to them. If his ox breaks through the ice, he knows no better how to get him out than if it had never happened. The helpless unwieldiness of the oxen is remarkable. I was told yesterday that when a man had got his ox out of Bateman's Pond, the latter gave a

spring, and, coming down, his hind legs slipped and spread apart on the ice, and he was split up so that he had to be killed.

This afternoon there is a clear, bright air, which, though cold and windy, I love to inhale. I see mother-o'-pearl tints, and I am not sure but this will be such a sunset as we had a month ago. The sky is a much fairer and [more] undimmed blue than usual.

The surface of the snow which fell last night is coarse like bran, with shining flakes. I see the steam-like snow-dust curling up and careering along over the fields. As I walk the bleak Walden road, it blows up over the highest drifts in the west, lit by the westering sun like the spray on a beach before the northwest wind. This drifting snow-dust has formed long, flattish drifts a few feet wide by some rods [long], with a rounded, swelling surface where it has lodged. The intermediate spaces, a rod or two wide, being swept clean and left uneven and naked, over these rollers it sweeps on to fill the road.

By the artificial system we learn the names of plants, by the natural their relations to one another; but still it remains to learn their relation to man. The poet does more for us in this department.

Linnæus says *elementa* are simple, *naturalia* composed by divine art. And these two embrace all things on earth. Physics treats of the properties of *elementa*, natural science of *naturalia*.

Feb. 17. Perhaps the peculiarity of those western vistas was partly owing to the shortness of the days.

Vol. III

when we naturally look to the heavens and make the most of the little light, when we live an arctic life, when the woodchopper's axe reminds us of twilight at 3 o'clock P. M., when the morning and the evening literally make the whole day, when I travelled, as it were, between the portals of the night, and the path was narrow as well as blocked with snow. Then, too, the sun has the last opportunity to fill the air with vapor.

I see on the Walden road that the wind through the wall is cutting *through* the drifts, leaving a portion adhering to the stones.

It is hard for the traveller when, in a cold and blustering day, the sun and wind come from the same side. To-day the wind is northwest, or west by north, and the sun from the southwest.

The apothecium of lichens appears to be a fungus, — all fruit.

I saw Patrick Riordan carrying home an armful of fagots from the woods to his shanty, on his shoulder. How much more interesting an event is that man's supper who has just been forth in the snow to hunt, or perchance to steal, the fuel to cook it with! His bread and meat must be sweet.[1]

It was something to hear that the women of Waltham used the *Parmelia saxatilis* (?) in dyeing.

If you would read books on botany, go to the fathers of the science. Read Linnæus at once, and come down from him as far as you please. I lost much time reading the florists. It is remarkable how little the mass of those

[1] [*Walden*, p. 275; Riv. 386.]

interested in botany are acquainted with Linnæus. His "Philosophia Botanica," which Rousseau, Sprengel, and others praised so highly, — I doubt if it has ever been translated into English. It is simpler, more easy to understand, and more comprehensive, than any of the hundred manuals to which it has given birth. A few pages of cuts representing the different parts of plants, with the botanical names attached, is worth whole volumes of explanation.

According to Linnæus's classification, I come under the head of the *Miscellaneous* Botanophilists, — "Botanophili sunt, qui varia de vegetabilibus tradiderunt, licet ea non proprie de scientiam Botanicam spectant," — either one of the *Biologi* (*Panegyrica plerumque exclamarunt*) or *Poetæ*.

Feb. 18. When Eystein the Bad ravaged the land of Drontheim, "he then offered the people either his slave Thorer Faxe, or his dog, whose name was Sauer, to be their king. They preferred the dog, as they thought they would sooner get rid of him. Now the dog was, by witchcraft, gifted with three men's wisdom; and when he barked, he spoke one word and barked two. A collar and chain of gold and silver were made for him, and his courtiers carried him in their hands when the weather or ways were foul. A throne was erected for him, and he sat upon a high place, as kings are used to sit. . . . It is told that the occasion of his death was that the wolves one day broke into his fold, and his courtiers stirred him up to defend his cattle; but when he ran down from his mound, and attacked the wolves, they tore him to pieces." Now I think if he had spoken two words and barked only one, he would have been wiser still and never fallen into the clutches of the wolves.

By some traits in the saga concerning King Hakon the Good, I am reminded of the concessions which some politicians and religionists, who are all things to all men, make. Hakon was unpopular on account of his attempts to spread Christianity, and to conciliate his subjects he drank out of the horn which had been blessed in Odin's name at a festival of sacrifice, but as he drank he made the sign of the cross over it. And one of his earls told the people that he was making the sign of Thor's hammer over it. "On this," it is said, "there was quietness for the evening. The next day, when the people sat down to table, the bonders pressed the king strongly to eat of horse flesh [this was an evidence of paganism]; [1] and as he would on no account do so, they wanted him to drink of the soup; and as he would not do this, they insisted he should at least taste the gravy; and on his refusal they were going to lay hands on him. Earl Sigurd came and made peace among them, by asking the king to hold his mouth over the handle of the kettle, upon which the fat smoke of the boiled horse flesh had settled itself; and the king first laid a linen cloth over the handle, and then gaped over it, and returned to the throne; but neither party was satisfied with this." On another day the Earl "brought it so far that the king took some bits of horse liver, and emptied all the goblets the bonders filled for him." This Hakon had a daughter *Thora*.

[1] [The brackets are Thoreau's.]

Vol. III

others arrive in middle age by the decay of their poetic faculties.

Feb. 19. The sky appears broader now than it did. The day has opened its eyelids wider. The lengthening of the days, commenced a good while ago, is a kind of forerunner of the spring. Of course it is then that the ameliorating cause begins to work.

To White Pond.

Considering the melon-rind arrangement of the clouds, by an ocular illusion the bars appearing to approach each other in the east and west horizons, I am prompted to ask whether the melons will not be found to lie in this direction oftenest.

The strains from my muse are as rare nowadays, or of late years, as the notes of birds in the winter, — the faintest occasional tinkling sound, and mostly of the woodpecker kind or the harsh jay or crow. It never melts into a song. Only the *day-day-day* of an inquisitive titmouse.

Everywhere snow, gathered into sloping drifts about the walls and fences, and, beneath the snow, the frozen ground, and men are compelled to deposit the summer's provision in burrows in the earth like the ground squirrel. Many creatures, daunted by the prospect, migrated in the fall, but man remains and walks over the frozen snow-crust and over the stiffened rivers and ponds, and draws now upon his summer stores. Life is reduced to its lowest terms. There is no home for you now, in this freezing wind, but in that shelter which you prepared in the summer. You steer straight across

Thorer Klakke was one "who had been long on Viking expeditions."

Thorer Hiort "was quicker on foot than any man."

I have a commonplace-book for facts and another for poetry, but I find it difficult always to preserve the vague distinction which I had in my mind, for the most interesting and beautiful facts are so much the more poetry and that is their success. They are *translated* from earth to heaven. I see that if my facts were sufficiently vital and significant, — perhaps transmuted more into the substance of the human mind, — I should need but one book of poetry to contain them all.

P. M. — To Fair Haven Hill.

One discovery in meteorology, one significant observation, is a good deal. I am grateful to the man who introduces order among the clouds. Yet I look up into the heavens so fancy free, I am almost glad not to know any law for the winds.

I find the partridges among the fallen pine-tops on Fair Haven these afternoons, an hour before sundown, ready to commence budding in the neighboring orchard.

The mosses on the rocks look green where the snow has melted. This must be one of the spring signs, when spring comes.

It is impossible for the same person to see things from the poet's point of view and that of the man of science. The poet's second love may be science, not his first, — when use has worn off the bloom. I realize that men may be born to a condition of mind at which

the fields to that in season. I can with difficulty tell when I am over the river. There is a similar crust over my heart. Where I rambled in the summer and gathered flowers and rested on the grass by the brook-side in the shade, now no grass nor flowers, no brook nor shade, but cold, unvaried snow, stretching mile after mile, and no place to sit.

Look at White Pond, that crystal drop that was, in which the umbrageous shore was reflected, and schools of fabulous perch and shiners rose to the surface, and with difficulty you made your way along the pebbly shore in a summer afternoon to the bathing-place. Now you stalk rapidly across where it was, muffled in your cloak, over a more level snow-field than usual, furrowed by the wind, its finny inhabitants and its pebbly shore all hidden and forgotten, and you would shudder at the thought of wetting your feet in it.

Returning across the river just as the sun was setting behind the Hollowell place, the ice eastward of me a few rods, where the snow was blown off, was as green as bottle glass, seen at the right angle, though all around, above and below, was one unvaried white, — a vitreous glass green. Just as I have seen the river green in a winter morning. This phenomenon is to be put with the blue in the crevices of the snow.

So, likewise, give me leave, or require me, to mend my work, and I will chip down the vessel on both sides to a level with the notches which I have made.

A fine display of the northern lights after 10 P. M., flashing up from all parts of the horizon to the zenith, where there was a kind of core formed, stretching south-

southeast [and] north-northwest, surrounded by what looked like a permanent white cloud, which, however, was very variable in its form. The light flashes or trembles upward, as if it were the light of the sun reflected from a frozen mist which undulated in the wind in the upper atmosphere.

Feb. 20. Erling had a son Thorer. It is said of the former that "both winter and summer it was the custom in his house to drink at the mid-day meal according to a measure, but at the night meal there was no measure in drinking."

Kings are not they who go abroad to conquer kingdoms, but who stay at home and mind their business, proving first their ability to govern their families and themselves. "King Sigurd Syr was standing in his corn-field when the messengers came to him. . . . He had many people on his farm. Some were then shearing corn, some bound it together, some drove it to the building, some unloaded it and put it in stack or barn; but the king and two men with him went sometimes into the field, sometimes to the place where the corn was put into the barn." He "attended carefully to his cattle and husbandry, and managed his housekeeping himself. He was nowise given to pomp and was rather taciturn. But he was a man of the best understanding in Norway." After hearing the messengers, he replied: "The news ye bring me is weighty, and ye bring it forward in great heat. Already before now Aasta has been taken up much with people who were not so near to her; and I see she is still of the same disposition.

She takes this up with great warmth; but can she lead her son out of the business with the same splendor she is leading him into it?"

Fate will go all lengths to aid her protégés. When the Swedish king and Olaf, king of Norway, threw lots for the possession of a farm, "the Swedish king threw two sixes, and said King Olaf need scarcely throw. He replied, while shaking the dice in his hand, 'Although there be two sixes on the dice, it would be easy, sire, for God Almighty to let them turn up in my favor.' Then he threw, and had sixes also. Now the Swedish king threw again, and had again two sixes. Olaf, king of Norway, then threw, and had six upon one dice, and the other split in two, so as to make seven eyes in all upon it; and the farm was adjudged to the king of Norway."

There was a Thorer Sel, who "was a man of low birth, but had swung himself up in the world as an active man."

There was a Northman named "Rane Thin-nose."

There is a long story about Thorer Hund's expedition to Biarmeland.

"*Ludr*, the lure," says Laing in note, "is a long tube or roll of birch-bark used as a horn by the herdboys in the mountains of Norway."

There was a "Thorer the Low."

There was a giant of a man named Ganka-Thorer and his brother, who joined King Olaf's army. The king inquired if they were Christians.

"Ganka-Thorer replies, that he is neither Christian nor heathen. 'I and my comrades have no faith but on

Vol. III

ourselves, our strength, and the luck of victory; and with this faith we slip through sufficiently well.'

"The king replies, 'A great pity it is that such brave slaughtering fellows do not believe in Christ their Creator.'

"Thorer replies, 'Is there any Christian man, king, in thy following, who stands so high in the air as we two brothers?'"

In King Olaf's last battle, he "hewed at Thorer Hund, and struck him across the shoulders; but the sword would not cut, and it was as if dust flew from his reindeer-skin coat." There are some verses about it. But Thorer, having had a hand in the death of the king, left the country. "He went all the way to Jerusalem, and many people say he never came back."

Poeta nascitur non fit, but under what conditions is the poet born? Perchance there is such a thing as a perpetual propagation or reproduction of the human without any recreation, as all botanists assert respecting plants, and as Meyer in particular concerning lichens, who says that "the pulverulent matter of Lichens is that which is subject to this kind of indefinite propagation, while the sporules lying in the shields are the only part that will really multiply the species."

Every gardener practices budding and grafting, but only Van Mons and his equals cultivate seedlings and produce new and valuable varieties. The genius is a seedling, often precocious or made to bear fruit early, as Van Mons treated his pears. The common man is the Baldwin, propagated by mere offshoots or repetitions of the parent stock. At least, if all men are to be

regarded as seedlings, the greater part are exceedingly like the parent stock.

The slope from the last generation to this seems steeper than any part of history. I hear with surprise this afternoon that the ox-wagon was rarely seen fifty years ago; they used the ox-cart here almost exclusively then, even to team wood to Boston.

The law requires wood to be four feet long from the middle of the carf to the middle of the carf, yet the honest deacon and farmer directs his hired men to cut his wood "four feet a little scant." He does it as naturally as he breathes.

We love to see nature clad, whether in earth or a human body. Nobody likes to set his house under that part of the hill where the sod is broken and the sand is flowing.

P. M. — To Flint's Pond.

The last two or three days have been *among* the coldest in the winter, though not so cold as a few weeks ago. I notice, in the low ground covered with bushes near Flint's Pond, many little rabbit-paths in the snow, where they have travelled in each other's tracks, or many times back and forth, six inches wide. This, too, is probably their summer habit. The rock by the pond is remarkable for its umbilicaria (?).

I saw a mole (?) run along under the bank by the edge of the pond, but it was only by watching long and sharply that I glimpsed him now and then, he ran so close to the ground and under rather than over anything, as roots and beds of leaves and twigs, and yet without making any noise. No wonder that we so rarely see these animals, though their tracks are so common. I have been astonished to observe before, after holding them in my hand, how quickly they will bury themselves and glide along just beneath the surface, whatever it may be composed of, — grass or leaves or twigs or earth or snow. So some men are sly and subterranean in their ways, and skulk, though often they raise a mound of earth or snow above their backs, which betrays rather than conceals them. For privacy they prefer to travel in a gallery like the mole, though it sometimes happens that it is arched above the ground when they think themselves deep in the sod. The mole goes behind and beneath, rather than before and above.

Feb. 21. "As fat as a hen in the forehead," — a saying which I heard my father use this morning.

Feb. 22. Went to Plymouth to lecture or preach all day.

Bæomyces roseus (βαιός, small, and μύκης, a fungus).

Saw in Plymouth, near Billington Sea, the *Prinos glaber*, or evergreen winterberry. It must be the same with the black-berried bush behind Provincetown.

A mild, misty day. The red (?) oaks about Billington Sea fringed with usneas, which in this damp air appear in perfection. The trunks and main stems of the trees have, as it were, suddenly leaved out in the winter, — a very lively light green, — and these ringlets and ends of usnea are so expanded and puffed out

with light and life, with their reddish or rosaceous fruit, it is a true lichen day. They take the place of leaves in the winter. The clusters dripping with moisture, expanded as it were by electricity, sometimes completely investing the stem of the tree.

I understood that there were two only of the sixth generation from the Pilgrims still alive (in Plymouth ?).

Every man will take such views as he can afford to take. Views one would think were the most expensive guests to entertain. I perceive that the reason my neighbor cannot entertain certain views is the narrow limit within which he is obliged to live, on account of the smallness of his means. His instinct tells him that it will not do to relax his hold here and take hold where he cannot keep hold.

Feb. 24. P. M. — Railroad causeway.

I am reminded of spring by the quality of the air. The cock-crowing and even the telegraph harp prophesy it, though the ground is for the most part covered with snow. It is a natural resurrection, an experience of immortality. Observe the poplar's swollen buds and the brightness of the willow's bark.[1]

The telegraph harp reminds me of Anacreon. That is the glory of Greece, that we are reminded of her only when in our best estate, our elysian days, when our senses are young and healthy again. I could find a name for every strain or intonation of the harp from one or other of the Grecian bards. I often hear Mimnermus, often Menander.

[1] Probably not.

Vol. III

I am too late by a day or two for the sand foliage on the east side of the Deep Cut. It is glorious to see the soil again, here where a shovel, perchance, will enter it and find no frost. The frost is partly come out of this bank, and it is become dry again in the sun.

The very sound of men's work reminds, advertises, me of the coming of spring. As I now hear at a distance the sound of the laborer's sledge on the rails.

The *empressement* of a little dog when he starts any wild thing in the woods! The woods ring with his barking as if the tragedy of Actæon were being acted over again.

Talked with two men and a boy fishing on Fair Haven, just before sunset. (Heard the dog bark in Baker's wood as I came down the brook.) They had caught a fine parcel of pickerel and perch. The perch especially were full of spawn. The boy had caught a large bream which had risen to the surface, in his hands. They had none of them ever seen one before in the winter, though they sometimes catch chivins. They had also kicked to death a muskrat that was crossing the southwest end of the pond on the snow. They told me of two otters being killed in Sudbury this winter, beside some coons near here.

As we grow older, is it not ominous that we have more to write about evening, less about morning? We must associate more with the early hours.

Feb. 26. The east side of Deep Cut nearly dry; sand has ceased flowing; west side just beginning. Now

begin to see the *Cladonia rangiferina* ("reindeer moss") in the dry pastures. Observed for the first time on and about Bear Hill in Lincoln the *Parmelia conspersa* (?), "greenish straw-colored," and what I suppose is *P. saxatilis*, "glaucous-cinerescent." The *P. conspersa* is a very handsome and memorable lichen, which every child has admired. I love to find it where the rocks will split into their laminæ so that I can easily carry away a specimen. The low hills in the northeast beyond Bedford, seen from Bear Hill about 4.30 P. M., were remarkably dark blue, much more blue than the mountains in the northwest. The sky was in great part concealed by white clouds. Had this blue the same cause with the blue in the crevices of the snow?

Returned across Flint's Pond and the wood-lot, where some Irishman must have tried his first experiment in chopping, his first winter, where the trees were hacked off two feet from the ground, as if with a hatchet, — standing on every side of the tree by turns, and crossing the carf a hundred ways. The owner can commonly tell when an Irishman has trespassed on his wood-lot.

We are told to-day that civilization is making rapid progress; the tendency is ever upward; substantial justice is done even by human courts; you may trust the good intentions of mankind. We read to-morrow in the newspapers that the French nation is on the eve of going to war with England to give employment to her army. What is the influence of men of principle, or how numerous are they? How many moral teachers has society? This Russian war is popular. Of course so many as she has will resist her. How many resist her? How many have I heard speak with warning voice? utter wise warnings? The preacher's standard of morality is no higher than that of his audience. He studies to conciliate his hearers and never to offend them. Does the threatened war between France and England evince any more enlightenment than a war between two savage tribes, as the Iroquois and the Hurons? Is it founded in better reason?

Feb. 27. The mosses now are in fruit — or have sent up their filaments with calyptræ.

The main river is not yet open but in very few places, but the North Branch, which is so much more rapid, is open near Tarbell's and Harrington's, where I walked to-day, and, flowing with full tide bordered with ice on either side, sparkles in the clear, cool air, — a silvery sparkle as from a stream that would not soil the sky.

Half the ground is covered with snow. It is a moderately cool and pleasant day near the end of winter. We have almost completely forgotten summer. This restless and now swollen stream has burst its icy fetters, and as I stand looking up it westward for half a mile, where it winds slightly under a high bank, its surface is lit up here and there with a fine-grained silvery sparkle which makes the river appear something celestial, — more than a terrestrial river, — which might have suggested that which surrounded the shield in Homer. If rivers come out of their icy prison thus bright and immortal, shall not I too resume my spring life with joy

and hope? Have I no hopes to sparkle on the surface of life's current?

It is worth the while to have our faith revived by seeing where a river swells and eddies about a half-buried rock, — dimples on the surface of water.

This has truly been a month of crusted snow. Now the snow-patches, which partially melt one part of the day or week, freeze at another, so that the walker traverses them with tolerable ease.

Crossed the river on ice.

To-night a circle round the moon. The buds of the aspen show a part of their down or silky catkins (?). The bank by Tarbell's road is a grand place for *Cladonia Scyphiferæ*[1] of various kinds.

Feb. 28. To-day it snows again, covering the ground.

To get the value of the storm we must be out a long time and travel far in it, so that it may fairly penetrate our skin, and we be as it were turned inside out to it, and there be no part in us but is wet or weather-beaten, — so that we become storm men instead of fair-weather men. Some men speak of having been wetted to the skin once as a memorable event in their lives, which, notwithstanding the croakers, they survived.

The snow is finally turned to a drenching rain.

Feb. 29. High winds last night and this morning, which made some tremble for their roofs and kept them awake half the night. Before which it cleared off in the night. The house shakes, and the beds and tables

[1] [The *Scyphiferæ* form a subdivision of the genus *Cladonia*.]

Vol. III

rock. This morning is clear and cold. Our neighbor's chimney was blown down last night.

Simplicity is the law of nature for men as well as for flowers. When the tapestry (corolla) of the nuptial bed (calyx) is excessive, luxuriant, it is unproductive. Linnæus says, "Luxuriant flowers are none natural but all monsters," and so for the most part abortive, and when *proliferous* "they but increase the monstrous deformity." "Luxurians flos tegmenta fructificationis ita multiplicat, ut essentiales equidem partes destruantur." "Oritur luxurians flos plerumque ab alimento luxuriante."

Such a flower has no true progeny and can only be *reproduced* by the humble mode of cuttings from its stem or roots. "Anthophilorum et Hortulanorum deliciæ sunt flores pleni," not of nature. The fertile flowers are single, not double.

P. M. — To Pine Hill across Walden.

The high wind takes off the oak leaves. I see them scrambling up the slopes of the Deep Cut, hurry-scurry over the slippery snow-crust, like a flock of squirrels. The ice on Walden is of a dull white as I look directly down on it, but not half a dozen rods distant on every side it is a light-blue color.

For the past month there has been more sea-room in the day, without so great danger of running aground on one of those two promontories that make it arduous to navigate the winter day, the morning or the evening. It is a narrow pass, and you must go through with the tide. Might not some of my pages be called "The Short Days of Winter"?

From Pine Hill, looking westward, I see the snow-crust shine in the sun as far as the eye can reach, — snow which fell but yesterday morning. Then, before night, came the rain; then, in the night, the freezing northwest wind, and where day before yesterday was half the ground bare, is this sheeny snow-crust to-day.

VI

MARCH, 1852

(ÆT. 34)

March 1. Linnæus, speaking of the necessity of precise and adequate terms in any science, after naming some which he invented for botany, says, "Termini praeservarunt Anatomiam, Mathesin, Chemiam, ab idiotis; Medicinam autem eorum defectus conculcavit." (Terms (well defined) have preserved anatomy, mathematics, and chemistry from idiots; but the want of them has ruined medicine.) But I should say that men generally were not enough interested in the first-mentioned sciences to meddle with and degrade them. There is no interested motive to induce them to listen to the quack in mathematics, as they have to attend to the quack in medicine; yet chemistry has been converted into alchemy, and astronomy into astrology.

However, I can see that there is a certain advantage in these hard and precise terms, such as the lichenist uses, for instance. No one masters them so as to use them in writing on the subject without being far better informed than the rabble about it. New books are not written on chemistry or cryptogamia of as little worth comparatively as are written on the *spiritual* phenomena of the day. No man writes on lichens, using the terms of the science intelligibly, without having something to say, but every one thinks himself competent to write

on the relation of the soul to the body, as if that were a *phænogamous* subject.

After having read various books on various subjects for some months, I take up a report on Farms by a committee of Middlesex Husbandmen, and read of the number of acres of bog that some farmer has redeemed, and the number of rods of stone wall that he has built, and the number of tons of hay he now cuts, or of bushels of corn or potatoes he raises there, and I feel as if I had got my foot down on to the solid and sunny earth, the basis of all philosophy, and poetry, and religion even. I have faith that the man who redeemed some acres of land the past summer redeemed also some parts of his character. I shall not expect to find him ever in the almshouse or the prison. He is, in fact, so far on his way to heaven. When he took the farm there was not a grafted tree on it, and now he realizes something handsome from the sale of fruit. These, in the absence of other facts, are evidence of a certain moral worth.

March 2. If the sciences are protected from being carried by assault by the mob, by a palisade or *chevaux-de-frise* of technical terms, so also the learned man may sometimes ensconce himself and conceal his little true knowledge behind hard names. Perhaps the value of any statement may be measured by its susceptibility to be expressed in popular language. The greatest discoveries can be reported in the newspapers. I thought it was a great advantage both to speakers and hearers when, at the meetings of scientific gentlemen at the

Marlborough Chapel, the representatives of all departments of science were required to speak intelligibly to those of other departments, therefore dispensing with the most peculiarly technical terms. A man may be permitted to state a very meagre truth to a fellow-student, using technical terms, but when he stands up before the mass of men, he must have some distinct and important truth to communicate; and the most important it will always be the most easy to communicate to the vulgar.

If anybody thinks a thought, how sure we are to hear of it! Though it be only a half-thought or half a delusion, it gets into the newspapers, and all the country rings with it. But how much clearing of land and plowing and planting and building of stone wall is done every summer without being reported in the newspapers or in literature! Agricultural literature is not as extensive as the fields, and the farmer's almanac is never a big book. And yet I think that the history (or poetry) of one farm from a state of nature to the highest state of cultivation comes nearer to being the true subject of a modern epic than the siege of Jerusalem or any such paltry and ridiculous resource to which some have thought men reduced. Was it Coleridge? The Works and Days of Hesiod, the Eclogues and Georgics of Virgil, are but leaves out of that epic.

The turning a swamp into a garden, though the poet may not think it an improvement, is at any rate an enterprise interesting to all men.

A wealthy farmer who has money to let was here yesterday, who said that fourteen years ago a man came

to him to hire two hundred dollars for thirty days. He told him that he should have it if he would give proper security, but the other, thinking it exorbitant to require security for so short a term, went away. But he soon returned and gave the security. "And," said the farmer, "he has punctually paid me twelve dollars a year ever since. I have never said a word to him about the principle."

It will soon be forgotten, in these days of stoves, that we used to roast potatoes in the ashes, after the Indian fashion of cooking.

The farmer increases the extent of the habitable earth. He makes soil. That is an honorable occupation.

March 3. *Wednesday.* Moore's larch trees beyond Sleepy Hollow cut this winter. They were much decayed. The woodpeckers had stripped many of bark in pursuit of grubs. When the woodpeckers visit your woods in great numbers, you may suspect that it is time to cut them. The chopper does not complain of cutting the larch, but when he comes to the splitting there's the rub. The grain runs almost round a four-foot stick sometimes. They make good posts.

Are those poplars whose buds I have seen so much expanded for a week or more a new species to me? The river poplar?[1]

March 4. The gold-digger in the ravines of the mountains is as much a gambler as his fellow in the saloons of San Francisco. What difference does it

[1] No.

make whether you shake dirt or shake dice? If you win, society is the loser. The gold-digger is the enemy of the honest laborer, whatever checks and compensations a kind fate (?) has provided. The humblest thinker who has been to the mines sees and says that gold-digging is of the character of a lottery, that the reward is not proportionate to the labor, that the gold has not the same look, is not the same thing, with the wages of honest toil; but he practically forgets what he has seen, for he has seen only the fact, not the principle. He looks out for "the main chance" still; he buys a ticket in another lottery, nevertheless, where the fact is not so obvious. It is remarkable that among all the teachers and preachers there are so few moral teachers. I find the prophets and preachers employed in excusing the ways of men. My most reverend seniors — doctors, deacons, and the illuminated — tell me with a reminiscent smile, betwixt an aspiration and a shudder, not to be so tender about these things, — to lump all that, *i. e.* make a lump of gold of it. I was never refreshed by any advice on this subject; the highest I have heard was grovelling. It is not worth the while for you to undertake to reform the world in this particular. They tell me not to ask how my bread is buttered, — it will make me sick if I do, — and the like.[1]

It is discouraging to talk with men who will recognize no principles. How little use is made of reason in this world! You argue with a man for an hour, he

[1] [*Cape Cod, and Miscellanies*, pp. 464, 465, 468; *Misc.*, Riv. 265, 269, 270.]

agrees with you step by step, you are approaching a triumphant conclusion, you think that you have converted him; but ah, no, he has a habit, he takes a pinch of snuff, he remembers that he entertained a different opinion at the commencement of the controversy, and his reverence for the past compels him to reiterate it now. You began at the butt of the pole to curve it, you gradually bent it round according to rule, and planted the other end in the ground, and already in imagination saw the vine curling round this segment of an arbor, under which a new generation was to recreate itself; but when you had done, just when the twig was bent, it sprang back to its former stubborn and unhandsome position like a bit of whalebone.

This world is a place of business. What an infinite bustle! I am awaked almost every night by the panting of the steam-engine. It interrupts my dreams. There is no sabbath. It would be glorious to see mankind at leisure for once.[1]

Concord Fight! Two killed on the patriots' side, and Luther Blanchard wounded! Why, here every ant was a Buttrick, — "Fire! for God's sake, fire!" — and thousands shared the fate of Davis and Hosmer. I have no doubt it was a principle they fought for as much as our ancestors, and not a threepenny tax on their tea.[2]

10 A. M. — Up river on ice to Fair Haven Pond.
The steam of the steam-engine rises to heaven this

[1] [*Cape Cod, and Miscellanies*, p. 456; *Misc.*, Riv. 254.]
[2] [*Walden*, p. 255; Riv. 358. See also pp. 209–212 of this volume.]

clear morning. The other day, when the weather was thick, I observed that it hugged the earth. Was the air lighter then? Some refer the music of the telegraph harp to the electricity passing along the wire! others, to the air passing through the glasses. The air is fresher and the sky clearer in the morning. We have this morning the clear, cold, continent sky of January. The river is frozen solidly, and I do not have to look out for openings. Now I can take that walk along the river highway and the meadow which leads me under the boughs of the maples and the swamp white oaks, etc., which in summer overhang the water. There I can now stand at my ease, and study their phenomena, amid the sweet-gale and button-bushes projecting above the snow and ice. I see the shore from the waterside. A liberal walk, so level and wide and smooth, without underbrush. I easily approach and study the boughs which usually overhang the water. In some places where the ice is exposed, I see a kind of crystallized, chaffy snow like little bundles of asbestos on its surface. I seek some sunny nook on the south side of a wood, which keeps off the cold wind, among the maples and the swamp white oaks which are frozen in, and there sit and anticipate the spring, and hear the chickadees and the belching of the ice. The sun has got a new power in his rays after all, cold as the weather is. He could not have warmed me so much a month ago, nor should I have heard such rumblings of the ice in December. I see where a maple has been wounded the sap is flowing out. Now, then, is the time to make sugar.

If I were to paint the short days of winter, I should

represent two towering icebergs, approaching each other like promontories, for morning and evening, with cavernous recesses, and a solitary traveller, wrapping his cloak about him and bent forward against a driving storm, just entering the narrow pass. I would paint the light of a taper at midday, seen through a cottage window half buried in snow and frost, and some pale stars in the sky, and the sound of the woodcutter's axe. The icebergs with cavernous recesses. In the foreground should appear the harvest, and far in the background, through the pass, should be seen the sowers in the fields and other evidences of spring. The icebergs should gradually approach, and on the right and left the heavens should be shaded off from the light of midday to midnight with its stars. The sun low in the sky.

I look between my legs up the river across Fair Haven. Subverting the head, we refer things to the heavens; the sky becomes the ground of the picture, and where the river breaks through low hills which slope to meet each other a quarter of a mile off, appears a mountain pass, so much nearer is it to heaven. We are compelled to call it something which relates it to the heavens rather than the earth. But I think that the mirage is not so great in the morning. Perhaps there is some advantage in looking at the landscape thus at this season, since it is a plain white field hence to the horizon.

I cut my initials on the bee tree. Now, at 11.30 perhaps, the sky begins to be slightly overcast. The northwest is the god of the winter, as the southwest of the summer. Interesting the forms of clouds, often, as now, like flames, or more like the surf curling before it breaks, reminding me of the prows of ancient vessels, which have their pattern or prototype again in the surf, as if the wind made a surf of the mist. Thus, as the fishes look up at the waves, we look up at the clouds. It is pleasant to see the reddish-green leaves of the lambkill still hanging with fruit above the snow, for I am now crossing the shrub oak plain to the Cliffs.

I find a place on the south side of this rocky hill, where the snow is melted and the bare gray rock appears, covered with mosses and lichens and beds of oak leaves in the hollows, where I can sit, and an invisible flame and smoke seems to ascend from the leaves, and the sun shines with a genial warmth, and you can imagine the hum of bees amid flowers. That is a near approach to summer. A summer heat reflected from the dry leaves, which reminds you of the sweet-fern and those summer afternoons which are longer than a winter day. Though you sit on a mere oasis in the snow.

I love that the rocks should appear to have some spots of blood on them, Indian blood at least; to be convinced that the earth has been crowded with men, living, enjoying, suffering, that races passed away have stained the rocks with their blood, that the mould I tread on has been animated, aye, humanized. I am the more at home. I farm the dust of my ancestors, though the chemist's analysis may not detect it. I go forth to redeem the meadows they have become. I compel them to take refuge in turnips.

The snow is melting on the rocks; the water trickles down in shining streams; the mosses look bright; the first awakening of vegetation at the root of the saxi-

frage. As I go by the farmer's yard, the hens cackle more solidly, as if eggs were the burden of the strain.

A horse's fore legs are handier than his hind ones; the latter but fall into the place which the former have found. They have the advantage of being nearer the head, the source of intelligence. He strikes and paws with them. It is true he kicks with the hind legs, but that is a very simple and unscientific action, as if his whole body were a whip-lash and his heels the snapper.

The constant reference in our lives, even in the most trivial matters, to the superhuman is wonderful. If a portrait is painted, neither the wife's opinion of the husband, nor the husband's of the wife, nor either's opinion of the artist — not man's opinion of man — is final and satisfactory. Man is not the final judge of the humblest work, though it be piling wood. The queen and the chambermaid, the king and the hired man, the Indian and the slave, alike appeal to God.

Each man's mode of speaking of the sexual relation proves how sacred his own relations of that kind are. We do not respect the mind that can jest on this subject.

If the husband and wife quarrel over their coffee, if the pie is underdone, if your partner treads on your toes, there is a silent appeal to the just and eternal gods, — or to time and posterity, at least.

March 5. It is encouraging to know that, though every kernel of truth has been carefully swept out of our churches, there yet remains the dust of truth on their walls, so that if you should carry a light into

them they would still, like some powder-mills, blow up at once.

The only man in Concord who has interested himself in the spiritual knockers, who has had them at his house, is Dr. Dillingham!!

3 P. M. — To the beeches.

A misty afternoon, but warm, threatening rain. Standing on Walden, whose eastern shore is laid waste, men walking on the hillside a quarter of a mile off are singularly interesting objects, seen through this mist, which has the effect of a mirage. The persons of the walkers black on the snowy ground, and the horizon limited, makes them the more important in the scene. This kind of weather is very favorable to our landscape. I must not forget the lichen-painted boles of the beeches.

So round even to the Red Bridge, where the red maple buds are already much expanded, foretelling summer, though our eyes see only winter as yet. As I sit under their boughs, looking into the sky, I suddenly see the myriad black dots of the expanded buds against the sky. Their sap is flowing. The elm buds, too, I find are expanded, though on earth are no signs of spring.

I find myself inspecting little granules, as it were, on the bark of trees, little shields or apothecia springing from a thallus, such is the mood of my mind, and I call it studying lichens. That is merely the prospect which is afforded me. It is short commons and innutritious. Surely I might take wider views. The habit of looking at things microscopically, as the lichens on the trees and rocks, really prevents my seeing aught

else in a walk. Would it not be noble to study the shield of the sun on the thallus of the sky, cerulean, which scatters its infinite sporules of light through the universe? To the lichenist is not the shield (or rather the apothecium) of a lichen disproportionately large compared with the universe? The minute apothecium of the pertusaria, which the woodchopper never detected, occupies so large a space in my eye at present as to shut out a great part of the world.

March 6. La Hontan, hunting moose (*orignal*) in Canada in 1686, says, facing a cruel north wind in winter, "One of my soldiers told me that it was necessary to have blood of *eau-de-vie*, body of brass, and eyes of glass, to resist a cold so sharp (*âpre*)."

3 P. M. — To Harrington's.

Old Mr. Joe Hosmer chopping wood at his door. He is full of meat. Had a crack with him. I told him I was studying lichens, pointing to his wood. He thought I meant the wood itself. Well, he supposed he'd had more to do with wood than I had. "Now," said he, "there are two kinds of white oak. Most people would n't notice it. When I've been chopping, say along in March, after the sap begins to start, I'll sometimes come to an oak that will color my axe steel-blue like a sword-blade. Well, that oak is fine-grained and heavier than the common, and I call it blue white oak, for no other blues my axe so. Then there are two kinds of black oak, or yellow-bark. One is the mean black oak, or bastard. Then there's a kind of red oak smells like urine three or four days old." It was really respectable in him that he avoided using the vulgar name of this oak. In an old man like him it was a true delicacy. Of this red oak he told me a story. There was old Mr. Joe Derby. He came after houses were built. He settled near the present Derby place. Well, his manteltree was very large, of red oak hewn square, — they used wood in those days, — and in course of time it had become charred with heat, and you could break coals off it. He could remember the house; it was more than a hundred years old. Well, when they pulled it down, old Mr. Derby told him that he split it up and put

[The rest of the page (a half) cut out.]

been the track of an otter near the Clamshell Hill, for it looks too large for a mink, — nearly an inch and a half in diameter and nearly round. Occasionally it looked as if a rail had been drawn along through the thin snow over the ice, with faint footprints at long intervals. I saw where he came out of a hole in the ice, and tracked him forty rods, to where he went into another. Saw where he appeared to have been sliding.

Found three or four parmelias (*caperata*) in fruit on a white oak on the high river-bank between Tarbell's and Harrington's.

[The rest of the page (a half) cut out.]

I remember a few words that I had with a young Englishman in the citadel, who politely undertook to do the honors of Quebec to me, whose clear, glowing Eng

lish complexion I can still see. Perhaps he was a chaplain in the army. In answer to his information, I looked round with a half-suppressed smile at those preparations for war, Quebec all primed and cocked for it, and at length expressed some of my surprise. "Perhaps you hold the opinions of the Quakers," he replied. I thought, if there was any difference between us, it might be that I was born in modern times.

March 7. Sunday. A very pleasant, spring-promising day. Yet I walked up the river on the ice to Fair Haven Pond. As I cross the snow (2 P. M.) where it lies deepest in hollows, its surface honeycombed by the sun, I hear it suddenly sink under and around me with a crash, and look about for a tree or roof from which it may have fallen. It has melted next the earth, and my weight makes it fall. In one instance, when I jumped over a wall on to snow nearly three feet deep, I heard this loud and startling crash and looked round in vain to discover the cause of it. I hear it settle over many rods.

At 9 o'clock P. M. to the woods by the full moon.

The ground is thinly covered with a crusted snow, through which the dead grass and weeds appear, telling the nearness of spring. Though the snow-crust between me and the moon reflects the moon at a distance, westward it is but a dusky white; only where it is heaped up into a drift, or a steep bank occurs, is the moonlight reflected to me as from a phosphorescent place. I distinguish thus large tracts an eighth of a mile distant in the west, where a steep bank sloping

Vol. III

toward the moon occurs, which glow with a white, phosphorescent light, while all the surrounding snow is comparatively dark, as if shaded by the woods. I looked to see if these white tracts in the distant fields corresponded to openings in the woods, and found that they were places where the crystal mirrors were so disposed as to reflect the moon's light to me.

Going through the high field beyond the lone graveyard, I see the track of a boy's sled before me, and his footsteps shining like silver between me and the moon. And now I come to where they have coasted in a hollow in this upland bean-field, and there are countless tracks of sleds, and I forget that the sun shone on them in their sport, as if I had reached the region of perpetual twilight, and their sport appears more significant and symbolical now, more earnest. For what a man does abroad by night requires and implies more deliberate energy than what he is encouraged to do in the sunshine. He is more spiritual, less animal or vegetable, in the former case.

The student of lichens has his objects of study brought to his study on his fuel without any extra expense.

It is rather mild to-night. I can walk without gloves. As I look down the railroad, standing on the west brink of the Deep Cut, I seem to see in the manner in which the moon is reflected from the west slope covered with snow, in the sort of misty light as if a fine vapor were rising from it, a promise or sign of spring. This stillness is more impressive than any sound, — the moon, the stars, the trees, the snow, the sand when bare, —

a monumental stillness, whose void must be supplied by thought. It extracts thought from the beholder, as the void under a cupping-glass raises a swelling. How much a silent mankind might suggest! There is no snow on the trees. The moon appears to have waned a little, yet, with this snow on the ground, I can plainly see the words I write. What a contrast there may be between this moon and the next!

I do not know why such emphasis should be laid on certain events that transpire, why my news should be so trivial; considering what one's dreams and expectations are, why the developments should be so paltry. The news I hear for the most part is not news to my genius. It is the stalest repetition. These facts appear to float in the atmosphere, insignificant as the sporules of fungi, and impinge on my thallus; some neglected surface of my mind affords a basis for them, and hence a parasitic growth. We should wash ourselves clean of such news. Methinks I should hear with indifference if a trustworthy messenger were to inform me that the sun drowned himself last night.[1]

March 9. A warm spring rain in the night.

3 P. M. — Down the railroad.

Cloudy but springlike. When the frost comes out of the ground, there is a corresponding thawing of the man. The earth is now half bare. These March winds, which make the woods roar and fill the world with life and bustle, appear to wake up the trees out of their

[1] [*Cape Cod, and Miscellanies*, pp. 471, 472; *Misc.*, Riv. 274.]

winter sleep and excite the sap to flow. I have no doubt they serve some such use, as well as to hasten the evaporation of the snow and water.

The railroad men have now their hands full. I hear and see bluebirds, come with the warm wind. The sand is flowing in the Deep Cut. I am affected by the sight of the moist red sand or subsoil under the edge of the sandy bank, under the pitch pines. The railroad is perhaps our pleasantest and wildest road. It only makes deep cuts into and through the hills. On it are no houses nor foot-travellers. The travel on it does not disturb me. The woods are left to hang over it. Though straight, is wild in its accompaniments. All is raw edges. Even the laborers on it are not like other laborers. Its houses, if any, are shanties, and its ruins the ruins of shanties, shells where the race that built the railroad dwelt, and the bones they gnawed lie about. I am cheered by the sound of running water now down the wooden troughs on each side the cut. Then it is the driest walking in wet weather, and the easiest in snowy. This road breaks the surface of the earth. Even the sight of smoke from the shanty excites me to-day. Already these puddles on the railroad, reflecting the pine woods, remind me of summer lakes.

When I hear the telegraph harp, I think I must read the Greek poets. This sound is like a brighter color, red, or blue, or green, where all was dull white or black. It prophesies finer senses, a finer life, a golden age. It is the poetry of the railroad, the heroic and poetic thoughts which the Irish laborers had at their toil now got expression, — that which has made the world mad

Vol. III

so long. Or is it the gods expressing their delight at this invention?

The flowing sand bursts out through the snow and overflows it where no sand was to be seen. I see where the banks have deposited great heaps, many cartloads, of clayey sand, as if they had relieved themselves of their winter's indigestions, and it is not easy to see where they came from.[1]

Again it rains, and I turn about.

The sound of water falling on rocks and of air falling on trees are very much alike.

Though cloudy, the air excites me. Yesterday all was tight as a stricture on my breast; to-day all is loosened. It is a different element from what it was. The sides of bushy hills where the snow is melted look, through this air, as if I were under the influence of some intoxicating liquor. The earth is not quite steady nor palpable to my sense, a little idealized. I see that the new chestnut sleepers that have been put down this winter are turned a very dark blue or blue black, and smell like dyestuff. The pond is covered with puddles. I see one farmer trimming his trees.

March 10. I was reminded, this morning before I rose, of those undescribed ambrosial mornings of summer which I can remember, when a thousand birds were heard gently twittering and ushering in the light, like the argument to a new canto of an epic and heroic poem. The serenity, the infinite promise, of such a morning! The song or twitter of birds drips from the

[1] [*Walden*, pp. 336, 340; Riv. 470, 476.]

leaves like dew. Then there was something divine and immortal in our life. When I have waked up on my couch in the woods and seen the day dawning, and heard the twittering of the birds.

P. M. — Through Deep Cut to Cliffs.

The mingled sand and water flowing down the bank, the water inclines ever to separate from the sand, and while the latter is detained by its weight and by friction beneath and on the sides, the water flows in a semicylindrical channel which it makes for itself, still carrying much sand with it. When the flowing drop of sand and water in front meets with new resistance, or the impetus of the water is diminished, perhaps by being absorbed, the drop of sand suddenly swells out laterally and dries, while the water, accumulating, pushes out a new sandy drop on one side and forms a new leafy lobe, and by other streams one is piled upon another. I have not observed any cylindrical canals this year. Did I ever? In some places when the sand has gone as far as it can flow, or the water prevails, the latter makes a true rivulet, which wears a channel through the sand it has washed down.

I see flocks of a dozen bluebirds together. The warble of this bird is innocent and celestial, like its color. Saw a sparrow, perhaps a song sparrow, flitting amid the young oaks where the ground was covered with snow. I think that this is an indication that the ground is quite bare a little further south. Probably the spring birds never fly far over a snow-clad country. A woodchopper tells me he heard a robin this morning. I see the reticulated leaves of the rattlesnake-plantain in the

woods, quite fresh and green. What is the little chickweed-like plant already springing up on the top of the Cliffs? There are some other plants with bright-green leaves which have either started somewhat or have never suffered from the cold under the snow. Summer clenches hands with summer under the snow. I am pretty sure that I heard the chuckle of a ground squirrel among the warm and bare rocks of the Cliffs. The earth is perhaps two thirds bare to-day. The mosses are now very handsome, like young grass pushing up. Heard the phœbe note of the chickadee to-day for the first time. I had at first heard their *day-day-day* ungratefully, — ah! you but carry my thoughts back to winter, — but anon I found that they too had become spring birds; they had changed their note. Even they feel the influence of spring.

I see cup lichens (cladonias) with their cups beset inside and out with little leafets like shellwork.

The *Populus grandidentata* on the Cliffs, in a warm position, shows no cotton yet like that on Harrington's road.

March 11. 2 P. M. — To White Pond to sound it.

That dull-gray-barked willow shows the silvery down of its forthcoming catkins. I believe that I saw blackbirds yesterday. The ice in the pond is soft on the surface, but it is still more than a foot thick. Is that slender green weed which I draw up on my sounding-stone where it is forty feet deep and upward *Nitella gracilis* (allied to *Chara*), described in Loudon?

The woods I walked in in my youth are cut off. Is

it not time that I ceased to sing? My groves are invaded. Water that has been so long detained on the hills and uplands by frost is now rapidly finding its level in the ocean. All lakes without outlet are oceans, larger or smaller.

March 12. According to Linnæus, very many plants become perennial and arborescent in warm regions which with us are annual, as *Tropæolum, Beta, Majorana,*[1] *Malva arborea,* etc., for duration often depends more on the locality than on the plant. So is it with men. Under more favorable conditions the human plant that is short-lived and dwarfed becomes perennial and arborescent.

Linnæus thus classifies *solum* as it respects plants (I omit the explanation, etc.):[2] —

1. *Mare.*
2. *Littora maris.*
3. *Fontes.*
4. *Fluvii.*
5. *Ripae Fluviorum et Lacuum.*
6. *Lacus aqua pura repleti, fundo consistenti gaudent.* (Walden and others?)
7. *Stagna et Fossae fundo limoso et aqua quieta sunt repleta.*
8. *Paludes humo lutosa laxa et aqua referta, aestate siccescunt.* (Very wet meadows?)
9. *Cespitosae Paludes, refertae humo mixta Sphagno, tectae tuberibus* (hummocks?), *cinctae aqua limosa, profunda.* (Peat meadows?)
10. *Inundata loca hyeme repleta aqua, aestate putrida exsiccata, imbribus interdum suffusa.* (Round Pond on Marlborough road and Goose Pond?)

[1] [Now *Origanum.*]   [2] [In *Philosophia Botanica.*]

11. *Uliginosa mihi sunt loca spongiosa, aqua putrida laborantia, colonis invisa, nec segetis, nec foeni proventui apta, innotescentia propriis plantis.* (Swamps?)
12. *Alpes.*
13. *Rupes.* (Cliffs, etc.?)
14. *Montes et Colles sabulosi, aridi, steriles, aquam vix admittunt.*
15. *Campi aprici ventis expositi, sicci, asperi sunt.* (Most of our pastures? Parts of Cape Cod?)
16. *Sylvae umbrosae terra sabulosa sterili refertae.* (Most of our woods?)
17. *Nemora ad radices Montium, inter Lucos, humo spongiosa tecta, umbrosa semper, exhalantia continuo aerem humidiusculum, ventis minime expositum, Plantas Vernales, frigoris et caloris impatientes, alunt.* (Our primitive woods?)
18. *Prata Herbis luxuriantia, campis depressis, convallibusque constant.* (Low rich grass grounds?)
19. *Pascua differunt a pratis, quod steriliora, sicciora et magis sabulosa.* (A low pasture?)
20. *Arva.* (Fields at rest.)
21. *Agri terra subacta laeta gaudent.* (Cultivated fields?)
22. *Versurae s. Margines agrorum, tanquam prata* (! !) *stercorata considerantur.*
23. *Culta.* (Rich soil in gardens?)
24. *Fimeta.* (Dung-heaps?)
25. *Ruderata.*

He gives examples of the plants which grow in each locality.

I have learned in a shorter time and more accurately the meaning of the scientific terms used in botany from a few plates of figures at the end of the " Philosophia Botanica," with the names annexed, than a volume of explanations or glossaries could teach. And, that the alternate pages to the plates may not be left blank, he has given on them very concise and important in-

struction to students of botany. This lawgiver of science, this systematizer, this methodist, carries his system into his studies in the field. On one of these little pages he gives some instruction concerning *herbatio,* or what the French called *herborisations,* — we say botanizing. Into this he introduces law and order and system, and describes with the greatest economy of words what some would have required a small volume to tell, all on a small page; tells what dress you shall wear, what instruments you shall carry, what season and hour you shall observe, — *viz.* "from the leafing of the trees, Sirius excepted, to the fall of the leaf, twice a week in summer, once in spring, from seven in the morning till seven at night," — when you shall dine and take your rest, etc., in a crowd or dispersed, etc., how far you shall go, — two miles and a half at most, — what you shall collect and what kind of observations make, etc., etc.

Railroad to Walden, 3 P. M.

I see the *Populus* (apparently *tremuloides,* not *grandidentata*) at the end of the railroad causeway, showing the down of its ament. Bigelow makes it flower in April, the *grandidentata* in May.

I see the sand flowing in the Cut and hear the harp at the same time. Who shall say that the primitive forces are not still at work? Nature has not lost her pristine vigor, neither has he who sees this. To see the first dust fly is a pleasant sight. I saw it on the east side of the Deep Cut.

These heaps of sand foliage remind me of the lacini-

ated, lobed, and imbricated thalluses of some lichens, — somewhat linear-laciniate. It cannot make much odds what the sand is, for I have seen it in the soil of our garden. They come out from the interior of the earth like bowels — a rupture in the spring — and bury the snow. The crust of the snow is completely concealed with the sand for an eighth of a mile. They also remind me sometimes of masses of rockweed on the rocks. At any moment the creative stream will be seen flowing in a restricted channel or artery, but it is forming new lobes, and at last, in the ditch, it forms sands, as at the mouths of rivers, in which the outlines of the different lobes are almost lost, are dissipated into mere shaded outlines on the flat floor.[1]

Bent has left the chestnuts about Walden till the sap is well up, that the bark may peel. He has cut the other trees. I saw the ants crawling about torpidly on the stump of an oak which had been sawed this winter. The choppers think they have seen them a fortnight.

The whistling of the wind, which makes one melancholy, inspires another.

The little grain of wheat, *triticum,* is the noblest food of man. The lesser grains of other grasses are the food of passerine birds at present. Their diet is like man's.

The gods can never afford to leave a man in the world who is privy to any of their secrets. They cannot have a spy here. They will at once send him packing. How can you walk on ground when you see through it?

The telegraph harp has spoken to me more distinctly and effectually than any man ever did.

[1] [*Walden*, pp. 336, 337; Riv. 470, 471.]

March 14. *Sunday*. Rain, rain, rain; but even this is fair weather after so much snow. The ice-on Walden has now for some days looked white like snow, the surface being softened by the sun. I see a flock of blackbirds and hear their *conqueree*. The ground is mostly bare now. Again I hear the chickadee's spring note. I remember that one spring, when I travelled in Maine, the woods were ringing with it, as I rode in the stage, *phœ-be*.[1]

Charlevoix baptized a dying infant on the bank of the Illinois River, 1721. He writes, "I confess to you, Madame, that though my travels should be altogether useless else, I should not regret the fatigues and dangers of it, since, according to all appearances, if I had not come to Pimiteouy, this infant would never have entered heaven, where I do not doubt it will be presently." [2] Celebrated historian.

March 15. This afternoon I throw off my outside coat. A mild spring day. I must hie to the Great Meadows. The air is full of bluebirds. The ground almost entirely bare. The villagers are out in the sun, and every man is happy whose work takes him outdoors. I go by Sleepy Hollow toward the Great Fields. I lean over a rail to hear what is in the air, liquid with the bluebirds' warble. My life partakes of infinity. The air is as deep as our natures. Is the drawing in of this vital air attended with no more glorious results than I witness? The air is a velvet cushion against which I press my

[1] Probably white-throat sparrow.
[2] [*Histoire de la Nouvelle France*.]

Vol. III

on the bottom in white sheets. And now one great cake rises amid the bushes (behind Peter's). I see no ducks.

Most men find farming unprofitable; but there are some who can get their living anywhere. If you set them down on a bare rock they will thrive there. The true farmer is to those who come after him and take the benefit of his improvements, like the lichen which plants itself on the bare rock, and grows and thrives and cracks it and makes a vegetable mould, to the garden vegetable which grows in it.

March 16. Before sunrise.

With what infinite and unwearied expectation and proclamation the cocks usher in every dawn, as if there had never been one before! And the dogs bark still, and the thallus of lichens springs, so tenacious of life is nature.

Spent the day in Cambridge Library. Walden is not yet melted round the edge. It is, perhaps, more suddenly warm this spring than usual. Mr. Bull thinks that the pine grosbeaks, which have been unusually numerous the past winter, have killed many branches of his elms by budding them, and that they will die and the wind bring them down, as heretofore. Saw a large flock of geese go over Cambridge and heard the robins in the College Yard.

The Library a wilderness of books. Looking over books on Canada written within the last three hundred years, could see how one had been built upon another, each author consulting and referring to his predecessors. You could read most of them without changing

ear. I go forth to make new demands on life. I wish to begin this summer well; to do something in it worthy of it and of me; to transcend my daily routine and that of my townsmen; to have my immortality now, that it be in the *quality* of my daily life; to pay the greatest price, the greatest tax, of any man in Concord, and enjoy the most!! I will give all I am for *my* nobility. I will pay all my days for *my* success. I pray that the life of this spring and summer may ever lie fair in my memory. May I dare as I have never done! May I persevere as I have never done! May I purify myself anew as with fire and water, soul and body! May my melody not be wanting to the season! May I gird myself to be a hunter of the beautiful, that naught escape me! May I attain to a youth never attained! I am eager to report the glory of the universe; may I be worthy to do it; to have got through with regarding human values, so as not to be distracted from regarding divine values. It is reasonable that a man should be something worthier at the end of the year than he was at the beginning.

Yesterday's rain, in which I was glad to be drenched, has advanced the spring, settled the ways, and the old footpath and the brook and the plank bridge behind the hill are suddenly uncovered, which have [been] buried so long; as if we had returned to our earth after an absence, and took pleasure in finding things so nearly in the state in which we left them.

We go out without our coats, saunter along the street, look at the aments of the willow beginning to appear and the swelling buds of the maple and the elm. The Great Meadows are water instead of ice. I see the ice

your leg on the steps. It is necessary to find out exactly what books to read on a given subject. Though there may be a thousand books written upon it, it is only important to read three or four; they will contain all that is essential, and a few pages will show which they are. Books which are books are all that you want, and there are but half a dozen in any thousand. I saw that while we are clearing the forest in our westward progress, we are accumulating a forest of books in our rear, as wild and unexplored as any of nature's primitive wildernesses. The volumes of the Fifteenth, Sixteenth, and Seventeenth Centuries, which lie so near on the shelf, are rarely opened, are effectually forgotten and not implied by our literature and newspapers. When I looked into Purchas's Pilgrims, it affected me like looking into an impassable swamp, ten feet deep with sphagnum, where the monarchs of the forest, covered with mosses and stretched along the ground, were making haste to become peat. Those old books suggested a certain fertility, an Ohio soil, as if they were making a humus for new literatures to spring in. I heard the bellowing of bullfrogs and the hum of mosquitoes reverberating through the thick embossed covers when I had closed the book. Decayed literature makes the richest of all soils.

March 17. I catch myself philosophizing most abstractly when first returning to consciousness in the night or morning. I make the truest observations and distinctions then, when the will is yet wholly asleep and the mind works like a machine without friction.

I am conscious of having, in my sleep, transcended the limits of the individual, and made observations and carried on conversations which in my waking hours I can neither recall nor appreciate. As if in sleep our individual fell into the infinite mind, and at the moment of awakening we found ourselves on the confines of the latter. On awakening we resume our enterprise, take up our bodies and become limited mind again. We meet and converse with those bodies which we have previously animated. There is a moment in the dawn, when the darkness of the night is dissipated and before the exhalations of the day commence to rise, when we see things more truly than at any other time. The light is more trustworthy, since our senses are purer and the atmosphere is less gross. By afternoon all objects are seen in mirage.

Frank Brown showed me the pintail duck day before yesterday, which he had received from Duxbury. To-day the fox-colored sparrow on its way to Hudson's Bay.

March 18. This morning the ground is again covered with snow, and the storm still continues.

That is a pretty good story told of a London citizen just retired to country life on a fortune, who, wishing, among other novel rustic experiments, to establish a number of bee communities, would not listen to the advice of his under steward, but, asking fiercely "how he could be so thoughtless as to recommend a purchase of what might so easily be procured on the Downs, ordered him to hire ten women to go in quest of bees the next morning, and to prepare hives for the reception

of the captives. Early the next day the detachment started for the Downs, each furnished with a tin canister to contain the spoil; and after running about for hours, stunning the bees with blows from their straw bonnets, and encountering stings without number, secured about thirty prisoners who were safely lodged in a hive. But, as has been the fate of many arduous campaigns, little advantage accrued from all this fatigue and danger. Next morning the Squire sallied forth to visit his new colony. As he approached, a loud humming assured him that they were hard at work, when to his infinite disappointment, it was found that the bees had made their escape through a small hole in the hive, leaving behind them only an unfortunate humblebee, whose bulk prevented his squeezing himself through the aperture, and whose loud complaints had been mistaken for the busy hum of industry." You must patiently study the method of nature, and take advice of the under steward, in the establishment of all communities, both insect and human.

This afternoon the woods and walls and the whole face of the country wear once more a wintry aspect, though there is more moisture in the snow and the trunks of the trees are whitened now on a more southerly or southeast side. These slight falls of snow which come and go again so soon when the ground is partly open in the spring, perhaps helping to open and crumble and prepare it for the seed, are called "the poor man's manure." They are, no doubt, more serviceable still to those who are rich enough to have some manure spread on their grass ground, which the melting snow

Vol. III

helps dissolve and soak in and carry to the roots of the grass. At any rate, it is all the poor man has got, whether it is good or bad. There is more rain than snow now falling, and the lichens, especially the *Parmelia conspersa*, appear to be full of fresh fruit, though they are nearly buried in snow. The *Evernia jubata* might now be called even a *very* dark olive-green. I feel a certain sympathy with the pine or oak fringed with lichens in a wet day. They remind me of the dewy and ambrosial vigor of nature and of man's prime. The pond is still very little melted around the shore. As I go by a pile of red oak recently split in the woods and now wet with rain, I perceive its strong urine-like scent. I see within the trunks solid masses of worm or ant borings, turned to a black or very dark brown mould, purest of virgin mould, six inches in diameter and some feet long, within the tree, — the tree turned to mould again before its fall. But this snow has not driven back the birds. I hear the song sparrow's simple strain, most genuine herald of the spring, and see flocks of chubby northern birds with the habit of snowbirds, passing north.

A wise man will not go out of his way for information. He might as well go out of nature, or commit suicide.

I am glad to hear that naked eyes are of any use, for I cannot afford to buy a Munich telescope.

Probably the bees could not make industry attractive under the circumstances described above.

March 19. Observed as I stood with Channing on the brink of the rill on Conantum, where, falling a few

inches, it produced bubbles, our images, three quarters of an inch long and black as imps, appearing to lean toward each other on account of the convexity of the bubble. There was nothing but these two distinct black manikins and the branch of the elm over our heads to be seen. The bubbles rapidly burst and succeeded one another.

March 20. As to the winter birds, — those which came here in the winter, — I saw first that rusty sparrow-like bird flying in flocks with the smaller sparrows early in the winter and sliding down the grass stems to their seeds, which clucked like a hen, and F. Brown thought to be the young of the purple finch; then I saw, about Thanksgiving time and later in the winter, the pine grosbeaks, large and carmine, a noble bird; then, in midwinter, the snow bunting, the white snowbird, sweeping low like snowflakes from field to field over the walls and fences. And now, within a day or two, I have noticed the chubby slate-colored snowbird (*Fringilla hyemalis?*), and I drive the flocks before me on the railroad causeway as I walk. It has two white feathers in its tail.

It is cold as winter to-day, the ground still covered with snow, and the stars twinkle as in winter nights.

The fox-colored sparrow is about now.

March 21. Railroad causeway at Heywood's meadow. The ice no sooner melts than you see the now red and yellow pads of the yellow lily beginning to shoot up from the bottom of the pools and ditches, for there they yield to the first impulses of the heat and feel not the chilling blasts of March.

This evening a little snow falls. The weather about these days is cold and wintry again.

March 23. I heard, this forenoon, a pleasant jingling note from the slate-colored snowbird on the oaks in the sun on Minott's hillside. Apparently they sing with us in the pleasantest days before they go northward.

Minott thinks that the farmers formerly used their meadow-hay better, gave it more sun, so that the cattle liked it as well as the English now.

As I cannot go upon a Northwest Passage, then I will find a passage round the actual world where I am. Connect the Behring Straits and Lancaster Sounds of thought; winter on Melville Island, and make a chart of Banks Land; explore the northward-trending Wellington Inlet, where there is said to be a perpetual open sea, cutting my way through floes of ice.

March 24. The night of the 24th, quite a deep snow covered the ground.

March 26. Walden not melted about shore.

March 28. Sunday. A pleasant afternoon; cool wind but warm sun. Snow almost all gone. The yellow lily leaves are pushing up in the ditch beyond Hubbard's Grove (this is not so warm a place as Heywood's meadow under the causeway), hard-rolled and triangular, with a sharp point with which to pierce the mud;

larger circle, less distinct, extending to the east of this, cutting the former and having the moon on its circumference or at least where its circumference would be. The inner circle is very contracted and more distinct on its eastern side, included within the larger, and it appears to shed a luminous mist from all sides.[1]

10.15 P. M. — The geese have just gone over, making a great cackling and awaking people in their beds. They will probably settle in the river. Who knows but they had expected to find the pond open?

March 29. An Esquimau, one of a littoral people, inquired with surprise of Sir John Richardson, "Are not all lands islands?"

Observed yesterday that Fair Haven Pond was covered with ice. Many plants which have been covered with snow now begin to show green about the roots, and so they push forward till the green prevails over the withered portion of their leaves. There are many of which you are doubtful whether they have been kept fresh and green under the snow, or have recently put forth their leaves in the spring. I observe to-day the buttercup, very common, the pasture thistle, etc., etc., what perhaps are chickweeds? The radical leaves of some, like sorrel, appear never to wither. Saw sportsmen out this morning, a boat on the meadows, men who heard the

<hr/>

[1] [If the drawing shows the way the moon and circles actually appeared, the letters W and E should evidently be transposed and "east" and "eastern" in the description should read "west" and "western."]

green at the tips and yellow below. The leaf is rolled in from both sides to the midrib. This is, perhaps, to be regarded as the most obvious sign of advancing spring, for the skunk-cabbage may be seen in warm weather in January. The latter is the first conspicuous growth on the surface. It now shows its agreeably variegated, not yet unfolded, leaves in the meadows. Saw dead frogs, and the mud stirred by a living one, in this ditch, and afterward in Conantum Brook a living frog, the first of the season; also a yellow-spotted tortoise by the causeway side in the meadow near Hubbard's Bridge. Fresh-looking caddis-worm cases in the ditch.

The smoky maple swamps have now got a reddish tinge from their expanding buds.

I have not noticed any new movements among the farmers, unless a little more activity in carting out manure and spreading it on their grass grounds.

Observed a singular circle round the moon to-night between nine and ten, the moon being about half full,

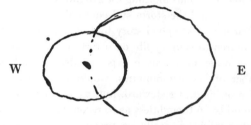

or in its first quarter, and the sky *pretty* clear, — a very bright and distinct circle about the moon, and a second,

geese last night. It is but a day or two that I have seen a boat on the meadows. The water on them has looked very dark from the street. Their color depends on the position of the beholder in relation to the direction of the wind. There is more water and it is more ruffled at this season than at any other, and the waves look quite angry and black.

Going to the Second Division Brook.

There is an evident spring in the grass about springs and brooks, as at Tarbell's. Some mosses now in fruit. Icicles still form under the banks at night on the north side of hills, from the dripping of the melting snow during the day. The leaves of the rattlesnake-plantain continue green but not so distinctly reticulated. Struck Second Division Brook at the old dam. It is as deep as wide, three feet or more, with a very handsome sandy bottom, rapidly flowing and meandering. A very attractive brook, to trout, etc., as well as men. It not only meanders as you look down on it, but the line of its bottom is very serpentine, in this wise, ⁓⁓⁓ successively deep and shallow. There is a great volume of water for so small a show as it makes. The sands, where they are rippled, are agreeably diversified with the black sediment of decayed wood and leaves in the ripple-marks. This apparently is not a deep or a peat meadow, but has a sandy foundation. The only obvious signs of spring in the vegetation of this meadow are the just expanding downy buds of a rather late kind of slender willow that stands in the brook and, if this can be regarded as a spring phenomenon, the green leaves of the cowslip everywhere. Saw two wood tortoises at the bottom of the brook, one upon another. The upper and larger one was decidedly bronze on the back; the under one, with more sharply grooved scales. The former, perhaps the male, with a decided depression of the sternum. Their legs a reddish orange. In the deeper parts of the brook, where, in the elbow of a meander, it had gullied under the bank, the surface was narrowest, and the dead grass almost met, making coverts for the trout. These tortoises crawled off very clumsily on the bottom. The flippers on one side were not both put forward at the same time, but one moved up to the other. Found the mayflower budded, though mostly covered with snow. There commenced to fall, not hail, but cotton-like pellets of snow, or like crispy snow broken up into triangular prismical [sic] pieces.

The *Populus tremuloides*, the round fine-toothed leaved aspen, shows the influence of the spring, this and some of the willows, more than any other trees or shrubs. Over a sandy bottom the brook water has one color; over the black sediment of decayed leaves another.

What animal more clumsy than the tortoise? If it wishes to get into the brook, it crawls to its edge and then tumbles, lets itself fall, turning a somerset, perhaps, from the bank to the water, — resigns itself to mere gravity, drawing in its head and members.

March 30. Dug some parsnips this morning. They break off about ten inches from the surface, the ground being frozen there.

The Greek word ἔαρ runs in my head in connection with the season and Richardson's Book.

The Cliffs remind me of that narrow place in the brook where two meadows nearly meet, with floating grass, though the water is deeper there under the bank than anywhere. So the Cliffs are a place where two summers nearly meet. Put up a bluebird-box, and found a whole egg in it. Saw a pewee from the railroad causeway.

Having occasion to-day to put up a long ladder against the house, I found, from the trembling of my nerves with the exertion, that I had not exercised that part of my system this winter. How much I may have lost! It would do me good to go forth and work hard and sweat. Though the frost is nearly out of the ground, the winter has not broken up in me. It is a backward season with me. Perhaps we grow older and older till we no longer sympathize with the revolution of the seasons, and our winters never break up.

To-day, as frequently for some time past, we have a raw east wind, which is rare in winter. I see as yet very little, perhaps no, new growth in the plants in open fields, but only the green radical leaves which have been kept fresh under the snow; but if I should explore carefully about their roots, I should find some expanding buds and even new-rising shoots. The farmers are making haste to clear up their wood-lots, which they have cut off the past winter, to get off the tops and brush, that they may not be too late and injure the young sprouts and lose a year's growth in the operation, also that they may be ready for their spring work.

Vol. III

From the Cliffs I see that Fair Haven Pond is open over the channel of the river, — which is in fact thus only revealed, of the same width as elsewhere, running from the end of Baker's Wood to the point of the Island. The slight current there has worn away the ice. I never knew before exactly where the channel was. It is pretty central. I perceive the hollow sound from the rocky ground as I tread and stamp about the Cliffs, and am reminded how much more sure children are to notice this peculiarity than grown persons. I remember when I used to make this a regular part of the entertainment when I conducted a stranger to the Cliffs. On the warm slope of the Cliffs the radical (?) leaves of the St. John's-wort (somewhat spurge-like), small on slender sprigs, have been evergreen under the snow. In this warm locality there is some recent growth nearest the ground. The leaves of the *Saxifraga vernalis* on the most mossy rocks are quite fresh. That large evergreen leaf sometimes mistaken for the mayflower is the *Pyrola rotundifolia* and perhaps some other species. What are those leaves in rounded beds, curled and hoary beneath, reddish-brown above, looking as if covered with frost? It is now budded, — a white, downy bud.[1]

March 31. Intended to get up early this morning and commence a series of spring walks, but clouds and drowsiness prevented. Early, however, I saw the clouds in the west, — for my window looks west, — suffused with rosy light, but that "flattery" is all forgotten

[1] The *Gnaphalium plantaginifolium* and *G. purpureum*.

now. How can one help being an early riser and walker in that season when the birds begin to twitter and sing in the morning?

The expedition in search of Sir John Franklin in 1850 landed at Cape Riley on the north side of Lancaster Sound, and one vessel brought off relics of Franklin, viz. "five pieces of beef, mutton, and pork bones, together with a bit of rope, a small rag of canvas, and a chip of wood cut by an ax." Richardson says: "From a careful examination of the beef bones, I came to the conclusion that they had belonged to pieces of salt-beef ordinarily supplied to the Navy, and that probably they and the other bones had been exposed to the atmosphere and to friction in rivulets of melted snow for four or five summers. The rope was proved by the ropemaker who examined it to have been made at Chatham, of Hungarian hemp, subsequent to 1841. The fragment of canvas, which seemed to have been part of a boat's swab, had the Queen's broad arrow painted on it; and the chip of wood was of ash, a tree which does not grow on the banks of any river that falls into the Arctic Sea. It had, however, been long exposed to the weather, and was likely to have been cut from a piece of drift-timber found lying on the spot, as the mark of the ax was recent compared to the surface of the wood, which might have been exposed to the weather for a century." "The grounds of these conclusions were fully stated in a report made to the Admiralty by Sir Edward Parry, myself, and other officers." Is not here an instance of the civilized man detecting the traces of a friend or foe with a skill at least equal to that of the savage? Indeed it is in both cases but a common sense applied to the objects, and in a manner most familiar to the parties. The skill of the savage is just such a science, though referred sometimes to instinct.

Perhaps after the thawing of the trees their buds universally swell before they can be said to spring.

Perchance as we grow old we cease to spring with the spring, and we are indifferent to the succession of years, and they go by without epoch as months. Woe be to us when we cease to form new resolutions on the opening of a new year!

A cold, raw day with alternating hail-like snow and rain.

According to Gilpin, a copse is composed of forest trees mixed with brushwood, which last is periodically cut down in twelve or fourteen years.

What Gilpin says about copses, glens, etc., suggests that the different places to which the walker resorts may be profitably classified and suggest many things to be said. Gilpin prefers the continuous song of the insects in the shade of a copse to the buzzing vagrant fly in the glare of day. He says the pools in the forest must receive their black hue from clearness. I suppose he means they may have a muddy bottom or covered with dark dead leaves, but the water above must be clear to reflect the trees.

It would be worth the while to tell why a swamp pleases us, what kinds please us, also what weather, etc., etc., — analyze our impressions. Why the moaning of the storm gives me pleasure. Methinks it is be-

cause it puts to rout the triviality of our fair-weather life and gives it at least a tragic interest. The sound has the effect of a pleasing challenge, to call forth our energy to resist the invaders of our life's territory. It is musical and thrilling, as the sound of an enemy's bugle. Our spirits revive like lichens in the storm. There is something worth living for when we are resisted, threatened. As at the last day we might be thrilled with the prospect of the grandeur of our destiny, so in these *first* days our destiny appears grander. What would the days, what would our life, be worth, if some nights were not dark as pitch, — of darkness tangible or that you can cut with a knife? How else could the light in the mind shine? How should we be conscious of the light of reason? If it were not for physical cold, how should we have discovered the warmth of the affections? I sometimes feel that I need to sit in a far-away cave through a three weeks' storm, cold and wet, to give a tone to my system. The spring has its windy March to usher it in, with many soaking rains reaching into April. Methinks I would share every creature's suffering for the sake of its experience and joy. The song sparrow and the transient fox-colored sparrow, — have they brought me no message this year? Do they go to lead heroic lives in Rupert's Land? They are so small, I think their destinies must be large. Have I heard what this tiny passenger has to say, while it flits thus from tree to tree? Is not the coming of the fox-colored sparrow something more earnest and significant than I have dreamed of? Can I forgive myself if I let it go to Rupert's Land before

Vol. III

I have appreciated it? God did not make this world in jest; no, nor in indifference. These migrating sparrows all bear messages that concern my life. I do not pluck the fruits in their season. I love the birds and beasts because they are mythologically in earnest. I see that the sparrow cheeps and flits and sings adequately to the great design of the universe; that man does not communicate with it, understand its language, because he is not at one with nature. I reproach myself because I have regarded with indifference the passage of the birds; I have thought them no better than I.

What philosopher can estimate the different values of a waking thought and a dream?

I hear late to-night the unspeakable rain, mingled with rattling snow against the windows, preparing the ground for spring.

VII

APRIL, 1852

(ÆT. 34)

April 1. Gilpin says well that the object of a light mist is a "*nearer distance.*"

Among winter plants, regarded as component parts of the forest, he thinks the fern the most picturesque. He says: "We are often at a loss to distinguish in pictures, the rising from the setting sun; though their characters are very different, both in the lights and shadows. The ruddy lights indeed of the evening are more easily distinguished: but it is not perhaps always sufficiently observed, that the shadows of the evening are much less opaque, than those of the morning."

This morning, the ground was completely covered with snow, and the water on the meadows looked dark and stormy and contrasted well with the white landscape. Now, at noon, the ground is once more as bare as before.

He is in the lowest scale of laborers who is merely an able-bodied man and can compete with others only in physical strength. Woodchoppers in this neighborhood get but fifty cents a cord, but, though many can chop two cords in a day in pleasant weather and under favorable circumstances, yet most do not average more than seventy-five cents a day, take the months together. But one among them of only equal physical strength and skill as a chopper, having more wit, buys a cross-cut saw for four dollars, hires a man to help him at a dollar a day, and saws down trees all winter at ten cents apiece and thirty or forty a day, and clears two or more dollars a day by it. Yet as long as the world may last few will be found to buy the cross-cut saw, and probably the wages of the sawyer will never be reduced to a level with those of the chopper.

2 P. M. — To Flint's Pond cedar woods *via* railroad, returning by C. Smith's orchard.

Saw the first bee of the season on the railroad causeway, also a small red butterfly and, later, a large dark one with buff-edged wings.

Gilpin's "Forest Scenery" is a pleasing book, so moderate, temperate, graceful, roomy, like a gladed wood; not condensed; with a certain religion in its manners and respect for all the good of the past, rare in more recent books; and it is grateful to read after them. Somewhat spare indeed in the thoughts as in the sentences. Some of the cool wind of the copses converted into grammatical and graceful sentences, without heat. Not one of those humors come to a head which some modern books are, but some of the natural surface of a healthy mind.

Walden is all white ice, but little melted about the shores. The very sight of it, when I get so far on the causeway, though I hear the *spring* note of the chickadee from over the ice, carries my thoughts back at once some weeks toward winter, and a chill comes over them.

There is an early willow on sand-bank of the rail-

road, against the pond, by the fence, grayish below and yellowish above. The railroad men have dug around the sleepers that the sun may thaw the ground and let them down. It is not yet out. Cut across near Baker's barn. The swollen buds of some trees now give a new tint to their tops seen at a distance, — to the maples at least. Baker's peach orchard looks at this distance purplish below and red above, the color of the last year's twigs. The geranium (?) [1] is the most common green leaf to be seen everywhere on the surface now the snow is gone.

They have been shooting great numbers of muskrats the last day or two. Is that the red osier (cornel or viburnum) near the grape-vine on the Bare Hill road? How sure the farmer is to find out what bush affords the best withes, little of a botanist as he is! The mountains seen from Bare Hill are very fine now in the horizon, so evanescent, being broadly spotted white and blue like the skins of some animals, the white predominating. The Peterboro Hills to the north are almost all white. The snow has melted more on the more southern mountains. With their white mantles, notwithstanding the alternating dark patches, they melt into the sky. Yet perhaps the white portions may be distinguished by the peculiar light of the sun shining on them. They are like a narrow strip of broadly spotted leopard-skin, the saddle-cloth of the sun spread along the horizon.

I am surprised to find Flint's Pond frozen still, which should have been open a week ago. The Great Sud-

[1] Cowslip.

Vol. III

bury Meadows covered with water are revealed. Blue they look over the woods. Each part of the river seen further north shines like silver in the sun, and the little pond in the woods west of this hill is half open water. Cheering, that water with its reflections, compared with this opaque dumb pond. How unexpectedly dumb and poor and cold does Nature look, when, where we had expected to find a glassy lake reflecting the skies and trees in the spring, we find only dull, white ice! Such am I, no doubt, to many friends. But, now that I have reached the cedar hill, I see that there is about an acre of open water, perhaps, over Bush Island in the middle of the pond, and there are some water-fowl there on the edge of the ice, — mere black spots, though I detect their character by discovering a relative motion, — and some are swimming about in the water. The pond is, perhaps, the handsomer, after all, for this distant patch only of blue water, in the midst of the field of white ice. Each enhances the other. It is an azure spot, an elysian feature, in your cold companion, making the imagined concealed depths seem deeper and rarer. This pond is worth coming to, if only because it is larger than Walden. I can so easily fancy it indefinitely large. It represents to me that Icy Sea of which I have been reading in Sir J. Richardson's book.

The prevailing color of the woods at present, excepting the evergreens, is russet, a little more red or grayish, as the case may be, than the earth, for those are the colors of the withered leaves and the branches; the earth has the lighter hue of withered grass. Let me

see how soon the woods will have acquired a new color. Went over the hill toward the eastern end of the pond. What is the significance of odors, of the odoriferous woods? Sweet and yellow birch, sassafras, fever-bush, etc., are an interesting clan to me. When we bruise them in our walk, we are suddenly exhilarated by their odor. This sweet scent soon evaporates, and you must break the twig afresh. If you cut it, it is not as if you break it. Some, like the sassafras, have brought a great price as articles of commerce. No wonder that men thought they might have some effect toward renovating their lives. Gosnold, the discoverer of Cape Cod, carried home a cargo of sassafras. What could be more grateful to the discoverer of a new country than a new fragrant wood?

Gilpin's is a book in which first there is nothing to offend, and secondly something to attract and please.

The branches of the young black birch grow very upright, as it were appressed to the main stem. Their buds appear a little expanded now. Saw the fox-colored sparrows and slate-colored snowbirds on Smith's Hill, the latter singing in the sun, — a pleasant jingle.

The mountains, which an hour ago were white, are now all blue, the mistiness has increased so much in the horizon, and crept even into the vales of the distant woods. The mist is in wreaths or stripes because we see the mist of successive vales. There could not easily be a greater contrast than between this morning's and this evening's landscapes. The sun now an hour high.

Now I see the river-reach, far in the north. The more distant river is ever the most ethereal.

Sat awhile before sunset on the rocks in Saw Mill Brook. A brook need not be large to afford us pleasure by its sands and meanderings and falls and their various accompaniments. It is not so much size that we want as picturesque beauty and harmony. If the sound of its fall fills my ear it is enough. I require that the rocks over which it falls be agreeably disposed, and prefer that they be covered with lichens. The height and volume of the fall is of very little importance compared with the appearance and disposition of the rocks over which it falls, the agreeable diversity of still water, rapids, and falls, and of the surrounding scenery. I require that the banks and neighboring hillsides be not cut off, but excite a sense of at least graceful wildness. One or two small evergreens, especially hemlocks, standing gracefully on the brink of the rill, contrasting by their green with the surrounding deciduous trees when they have lost their leaves, and thus enlivening the scene and betraying their attachment to the water. It would be no more pleasing to me if the stream were a mile wide and the hemlocks five feet in diameter. I believe that there is a harmony between the hemlock and the water which it overhangs not explainable. In the first place, its green is especially grateful to the eye the greater part of the year in any locality, and in the winter, by its verdure overhanging and shading the water, it concentrates in itself the beauty of all fluviatile trees. It loves to stand with its foot close to the water, its roots running over the rocks of the shore, and two or more on opposite sides of a brook make the most beautiful frame to a waterscape, especially

in deciduous woods, where the light is sombre and not too glaring. It makes the more complete frame because its branches, particularly in young specimens such as I am thinking of, spring from so near the ground, and it makes so dense a mass of verdure. There are many larger hemlocks covering the steep side-hill forming the bank of the Assabet, where they are successively undermined by the water, and they lean at every angle over the water. Some are almost horizontally directed, and almost every year one falls in and is washed away. The place is known as the "Leaning Hemlocks."

But to return to Saw Mill Run. I love that the green fronds of the fern, pressed by the snow, lie on its rocks. It is a great advantage to take in so many parts at one view. We love to see the water stand, or seem to stand, at many different levels within a short distance, while we sit in its midst, some above, some below us, and many successive falls in different directions, meandering in the course of the fall, rather than one "chute," — rather spreading and shoaling than contracting and deepening at the fall. In a small brook like this, there are many adjuncts to increase the variety which are wanting in a river, or, if present, cannot be attended to; even dead leaves and twigs vary the ripplings and increase the foam. And the very lichens on the rocks of the run are an important ornament, which in the great waterfall are wont to be overlooked. I enjoy this little fall on Saw Mill Run more than many a large one on a river that I have seen. The hornbeams and witch-hazel and canoe birches all come in for their share of

attention. We get such a complete idea of the small rill with its overhanging shrubs as only a bird's-eye view from some eminence could give us of the larger stream. Perhaps it does not fall more than five feet within a rod and a half. I should not hear Niagara a short distance off. The never-ending refreshing sound! It suggests more thoughts than Montmorenci. A stream and fall which the woods imbosom. They are not in this proportion to a larger fall. They lie in a more glaring and less picturesque light. Even the bubbles are a study. It can be completely examined in its details. The consciousness of there being water about you at different levels is agreeable. The sun can break through and fall on it and vary the whole scene infinitely.

Saw the freshly (?) broken shells of a tortoise's eggs — or were they a snake's? — in Hosmer's field. I hear a robin singing in the woods south of Hosmer's, just before sunset. It is a sound associated with New England village life. It brings to my thoughts summer evenings when the children are playing in the yards before the doors and their parents conversing at the open windows. It foretells all this now, before those summer hours are come.

As I come over the Turnpike, the song sparrow's jingle comes up from every part of the meadow, as native as the tinkling rills or the blossoms of the spirea, the meadow-sweet, soon to spring. Its cheep is like the sound of opening buds. The sparrow is continually singing on the alders along the brook-side, while the sun is continually setting.

We have had a good solid winter, which has put the

previous summer far behind us; intense cold, deep and lasting snows, and clear, tense winter sky. It is a good experience to have gone through with.

April 2. 6 A. M. — To the riverside and Merrick's pasture.

The sun is up. The water on the meadows is perfectly smooth and placid, reflecting the hills and clouds and trees. The air is full of the notes of birds, — song sparrows, red-wings, robins (singing a strain), bluebirds, — and I hear also a lark, — as if all the earth had burst forth into song. The influence of this April morning has reached them, for they live out-of-doors all the night, and there is no danger that they will oversleep themselves such a morning. A few weeks ago, before the birds had come, there came to my mind in the night the twittering sound of birds in the early dawn of a spring morning, a semiprophecy of it, and last night I attended mentally as if I heard the spray-like dreaming sound of the midsummer frog and realized how glorious and full of revelations it was. Expectation may amount to prophecy. The clouds are *white* watery, not such as we had in the winter. I see in this fresh morning the shells left by the muskrats along the shore, and their galleries leading into the meadow, and the bright-red cranberries washed up along the shore in the old water-mark. Suddenly there is a blur on the placid surface of the waters, a rippling mistiness produced, as it were, by a slight morning breeze, and I should be sorry to show it to the stranger now. So is it with our minds.

As a fair day is promised, and the waters are falling, decide to go to the Sudbury meadows with C., 9 A. M. Started some woodcocks in a wet place in Hi Wheeler's stubble-field. Saw six spotted tortoises (*Emys guttata*), which had crawled to the shore by the side of the Hubbard Bridge causeway. Too late now for the morning influence and inspiration. The birds sing not so earnestly and joyously; there is a blurring ripple on the surface of the lake. How few valuable observations can we make in youth! What if there were united the susceptibility of youth with the discrimination of age? Once I was part and parcel of Nature; now I am observant of her.

What ails the pewee's tail? It is loosely hung, pulsating with life. What mean these wag-tail birds? Cats and dogs, too, express some of their life through their tails.

The bridges are a station at this season. They are the most advantageous positions. There I would take up my stand morning and evening, looking over the water.

The Charles Miles Run full and rumbling. The water is the color of ale, here dark-red ale over the yellow sand, there yellowish frothy ale where it tumbles down. Its foam, composed of large white bubbles, makes a kind of arch over the rill, snow white and contrasting with the general color of the stream, while the latter ever runs under it carrying the lower bubbles with it and new ones ever supply their places. At least eighteen inches high, this stationary arch. I do not remember elsewhere such highly colored water. It drains a

swamp near by and is dry the greater part of the year. Coarse bubbles continually bursting. A striped snake by the spring, and a black one. The grass there is delightfully green while there is no fresh green anywhere else to be seen. It is the most refreshing of all colors. It is what all the meadows will soon be. The color of no flower is so grateful to the eye. Why is the dog black and the grass green? If all the banks were suddenly painted green and spotted with yellow, white, red, blue, purple, etc., we should more fully realize the miracle of the summer's coloring.

Now the snow is off, it is pleasant to visit the sandy bean-fields covered with last year's blue-curls and sorrel and the flakes of arrowhead stone. I love these sandy fields which melt the snows and yield but small crops to the farmer. Saw a striped squirrel in the wall near Lee's. Brigham, the wheelwright, building a boat. At the sight of all this water, men build boats if ever. Are those large scarred roots at the bottom of the brooks now, three inches in diameter, the roots of the pickerel-weed? What vigor! What vitality! The yellow spots of the tortoise (*Emys guttata*) on his dark shell, seen bright through clear water, remind me of flowers, the houstonias, etc., when there are no colors on the land.

Israel Rice's dog stood stock-still so long that I took him at a distance for the end of a bench. He looked much like a fox, and his fur was as soft. Rice was very ready to go with us to his boat, which we borrowed, as soon as he had driven his cow into the barn where her calf was, but she preferred to stay out in the yard

this pleasant morning. He was very obliging, persisted, without regard to our suggestions that we could help ourselves, in going with us to his boat, showed us after a larger boat and made no remark on the miserableness of it. Thanks and compliments fell off him like water off a rock. If the king of the French should send him a medal, he would have to look in many dictionaries to know what the sending of a medal meant, and then he would appreciate the abstract fact merely, and it would fail of its intended effect.

Steered across for the oaks opposite the mouth of the Pantry. For a long distance, as we paddle up the river, we hear the two-stanza'd lay of the pewee on the shore, — pee-wet, pee-wee, etc. Those are the two obvious facts to eye and ear, the river and the pewee. After coming in sight of Sherman's Bridge, we moored our boat by sitting on a maple twig on the east side, to take a leisurely view of the meadow. The eastern shore here is a fair specimen of New England fields and hills, sandy and barren but agreeable to my eye, covered with withered grass on their rounded slopes and crowned with low reddish bushes, shrub oaks. There is a picturesque group of eight oaks near the shore, and through a thin fringe of wood I see some boys driving home an ox-cartload of hay. I have noticed black oaks within a day or two still covered with oak-balls. In upsetting the boat, which has been newly tarred, I have got some tar on my hands, which imparts to them on the whole an agreeable fragrance. This exercise of the arms and chest after a long winter's stagnation, during which only the legs have la-

bored, this pumping off the Lincolnshire fens, the Haarlem lakes, of wintry fumes and damps and foul blood, is perhaps the greatest value of these paddling excursions. I see, far in the south, the upright black piers of the bridge just rising above the water. They are more conspicuous than the sleepers and rails. The occasional patches of snow on the hillsides are unusually bright by contrast; they are landmarks to steer by.

It appears to me that, to one standing on the heights of philosophy, mankind and the works of man will have sunk out of sight altogether; that man is altogether too much insisted on. The poet says the proper study of mankind is man. I say, study to forget all that; take wider views of the universe. That is the egotism of the race. What is this our childish, gossiping, social literature, mainly in the hands of the publishers? When another poet says the world is too much with us, he means, of course, that man is too much with us. In the promulgated views of man, in institutions, in the common sense, there is narrowness and delusion. It is our weakness that so exaggerates the virtues of philanthropy and charity and makes it the highest human attribute. The world will sooner or later tire of philanthropy and all religions based on it mainly. They cannot long sustain my spirit. In order to avoid delusions, I would fain let man go by and behold a universe in which man is but as a grain of sand. I am sure that those of my thoughts which consist, or are contemporaneous, with social personal connections, however humane, are not the wisest and widest, most universal. What is the village, city, State, nation, aye the civilized world, that it should concern a man so much? the thought of them affects me in my wisest hours as when I pass a woodchuck's hole. It is a comfortable place to nestle, no doubt, and we have friends, some sympathizing ones, it may be, and a hearth, there; but I have only to get up at midnight, aye to soar or wander a little in my thought by day, to find them all slumbering. Look at our literature. What a poor, puny, social thing, seeking sympathy! The author troubles himself about his readers, — would fain have one before he dies. He stands too near his printer; he corrects the proofs. Not satisfied with defiling one another in this world, we would all go to heaven together. To be a good man, that is, a good neighbor in the widest sense, is but little more than to be a good citizen. Mankind is a gigantic institution; it is a community to which most men belong. It is a test I would apply to my companion, — can he forget man? can he see this world slumbering?

I do not value any view of the universe into which man and the institutions of man enter very largely and absorb much of the attention. Man is but the place where I stand, and the prospect hence is infinite. It is not a chamber of mirrors which reflect me. When I reflect, I find that there is other than me. Man is a past phenomenon to philosophy. The universe is larger than enough for man's abode. Some rarely go outdoors, most are always at home at night, very few indeed have stayed out all night once in their lives, fewer still have gone behind the world of humanity, seen its institutions like toadstools by the wayside.

Landed on Tall's Island. It is not cold or windy enough, perchance, for the meadow to make its most serious impression. The staddles, from which the hay has been removed, rise a foot or two above the water. Large white gulls are circling over the water. The shore of this meadow lake is quite wild, and in most places low and rather inaccessible to walkers. On the rocky point of this island, where the wind is felt, the waves are breaking merrily, and now for half an hour our dog has been standing in the water under the small swamp white oaks, and ceaselessly snapping at each wave as it broke, as if it were a living creature. He, regardless of cold and wet, thrusts his head into each wave to gripe it. A dog snapping at the waves as they break on a rocky shore. He then rolls himself in the leaves for a napkin. We hardly set out to return, when the water looked sober and rainy. There was more appearance of rain in the water than in the sky, — April weather look. And soon we saw the dimples of drops on the surface. I forgot to mention before the cranberries seen on the bottom, as we pushed over the meadows, and the red beds of pitcher-plants.

We landed near a corn-field in the bay on the west side, below Sherman's Bridge, in order to ascend Round Hill, it still raining gently or with drops far apart. From the top we see smoke rising from the green pine hill in the southern part of Lincoln. The steam of the engine looked very white this morning against the oak-clad hillsides. The clouds, the showers, and the breaking away now in the west, all belong to the summer side of the year and remind me of long-past

days. The prospect is often best from two thirds the way up a hill, where, looking directly down at the parts of the landscape — the fields and barns — nearest the base, you get the sense of height best, and see how the land slopes up to where you stand. From the top, commonly, you overlook all this, and get a sense of *distance* merely, with a break in the landscape by which the most interesting point is concealed. This hill with its adjuncts is now almost an island, surrounded by broad lakes. The south lakes reflect the most light at present, but the sober surface of the northern is yet more interesting to me.

How novel and original must be each new man's view of the universe! for though the world is so old, and so many books have been written, each object appears wholly undescribed to our experience, each field of thought wholly unexplored. The whole world is an America, a *New World*. The fathers lived in a dark age and throw no light on any of our subjects. The sun climbs to the zenith daily, high over all literature and science. Astronomy, even, concerns us worldlings only, but the sun of poetry and of each new child born into the planet has never been astronomized, nor brought nearer by a telescope. So it will be to the end of time. The end of the world is not yet. Science is young by the ruins of Luxor, unearthing the Sphinx, or Nineveh, or between the Pyramids. The parts of the meadows nearly surrounded by water form interesting peninsulas and promontories.

Return to our boat. We have to go ashore and upset it every half-hour, it leaks so fast, for the leak in-

creases as it sinks in the water in geometrical progression. I see, among the phenomena of spring, here and there a dead sucker floating on the surface, perhaps dropped by a fish hawk or a gull, for the gulls are circling this way overhead to reconnoitre us. They will come sailing overhead to observe us. On making the eastward curve in the river, we find a strong wind against us. Pushing slowly across the meadow in front of the Pantry, the waves beat against the bows and sprinkle the water half the length of the boat. The froth is in long white streaks before the wind, as usual striping the surface.

We land in a steady rain and walk inland by R. Rice's barn, regardless of the storm, toward White Pond. Overtaken by an Irishman in search of work. Discovered some new oaks and pine groves and more New England fields. At last the drops fall wider apart, and we pause in a sandy field near the Great Road of the Corner, where it was agreeably retired and sandy, drinking up the rain. The rain was soothing, so still and sober, gently beating against and amusing our thoughts, swelling the brooks. The robin now peeps with scared note in the heavy overcast air, among the apple trees. The hour is favorable to thought. Such a day I like a sandy road, snows that melt and leave bare the corn and grain fields, with Indian relics shining on them, and prepare the ground for the farmer. Saw a cow or ox in a hollow in the woods, which had been skinned and looked red and striped, like those Italian anatomical preparations. It scared the dog. Went through a reddish andromeda swamp, where still a little icy stiffness in the crust under the woods keeps us from slumping. The rain now turns to snow with large flakes, so soft many cohere in the air as they fall. They make us white as millers and wet us through, yet it is clear gain. I hear a solitary hyla for the first time. At Hubbard's Bridge, count eight ducks going over. Had seen one with outstretched neck over the Great Meadows in Sudbury. Looking up, the flakes are black against the sky. And now the ground begins to whiten. Get home at 5.30 P. M.

At the bend of the river above the river [*sic*], I noticed many ferns on the bank where there was much snow, very green.

April 3. They call that northernmost sea, thought to be free from ice, "Polina," — whither the musk oxen migrate. The coldest natures, persevere with them, go far enough, are found to have open sea in the highest latitudes.

It is a clear day with a cold westerly wind, the snow of yesterday being melted. When the sun shines unobstructedly the landscape is full of light, for it is reflected from the withered fawn-colored grass, as it cannot be from the green grass of summer. (On the back of the hill behind Gourgas's.)

The bluebird carries the sky on his back.

I am going over the hills in the rear of the windmill site and along Peter's path. This path through the rolling stubble-fields, with the woods rather distant and the horizon distant in front on account of the intervention of the river and meadow, reminds me a little of the downs of Cape Cod, of the Plains of Nau-

set. This is the only walk of the kind that we have in Concord. Perhaps it should be called Cæsar's Path. The maple at the brook by this path has not expanded its buds, though that by the Red Bridge had so long ago. What the cause? Are they different species?

I have observed much snow lately on the north slopes where shrub oaks grow, where probably the ground is frozen, more snow, I think, than lies in the woods in such positions. It is even two or three feet deep in many such places, though few villagers would believe it. One side of the village street, which runs east and west, appears a month in advance of the other. I go down the street on the wintry side; I return through summer. How agreeable the contrasts of light and shade, especially when the successive swells of a hillside produce the shade! The clouds are important to-day for their shadows. If it were not for them, the landscape would be one glare of light without variety. By their motion they still more vary the scene.

Man's eye is so placed as to look straight forward on a level best, or rather down than up. His eye demands the sober colors of the earth for its daily diet. He does not look up at a great angle but with an effort. Many clouds go over without our noticing them, for it would not profit us much to notice it, but few cattle pass by in the street or the field without our knowing it.

The moon appears to be full to-night. About 8.30 P. M. I walked to the Clamshell Hill. It is very cold and windy, and I miss my gloves, left at home. Colder than the last moon. The sky is two-thirds covered with great four or more sided downy clouds, drifting

Vol. III

from the north or northwest, with dark-blue partitions between them. The moon, with a small brassy halo, seems travelling ever through them toward the north. The water is dull and dark, except close to the windward shore, where there is a smooth strip a rod or more in width protected from the wind, which reflects a faint light. When the moon reaches a clear space, the water is suddenly lit up quite across the meadows, for half a mile in length and several rods in width, while the woods beyond are thrown more into the shade, or seen more in a mass and indistinctly, than before. The ripples on the river, seen in the moonlight, those between the sunken willow lines, have this form: the arc of a circle, as if their extremities were retarded by the friction of the banks. I noticed this afternoon that bank below Cæsar's, now partially flooded, higher than the neighboring meadow, so that sometimes you can walk down on it a mile dry-shod with water on both sides of you. Like the banks of the Mississippi. There always appears to be something phosphorescent in moonlight reflected from water. Venus is very bright now in the west, and Orion is there, too, now. I came out mainly to see the light of the moon reflected from the meadowy flood. It is a pathway of light, of sheeny ripples, extending across the meadow toward the moon, consisting of a myriad little bent and broken moons. I hear one faint peep from a bird on its roost. The clouds are travelling very fast into the south. I would not have believed the heavens could be cleared so soon. They consist of irregularly

margined, wide whitish bars, *apparently* converging, rendezvousing, toward one point far in the south horizon. Like the columns of a host in the sky, each being conducted by its own leader to one rendezvous in the southern heavens. Such is the illusion, for we are deceived when we look up at this concave sphere, as when we look on a plane map representing the convex globe, — not by Mercator's projection. But what a grand incident of the night — though hardly a night passes without many such — that, between the hours of nine and ten, a battalion of downy clouds many miles in length and several in width were observed sailing noiselessly like a fleet from north to south over land and water, town and cottage, at the height of half a dozen miles above the earth! Over woods and over villages they swept along, intercepting the light of the moon, and yet perchance no man observed them. Now they are all gone. The sky is left clear and cold and but thinly peopled at this season. It is of a very light blue in all the horizon, but darker in the zenith, darkest of all in the crevice between two downy clouds. It is particularly light in the western horizon. Who knows but light is reflected from snow lying on the ground further inland? The water, as I look at it in the north or northeast, is a very dark blue, the moon being on my right; afterwards, crossing the railroad bridge, is a deep sea-green. The evenings are now much shortened, suggesting that ours is to be henceforth a daylight life.

April 4. Sunday. I have got to that pass with my friend that our words do not pass with each other for what they are worth. We speak in vain; there is none to hear. He finds fault with me that I walk alone, when I pine for want of a companion; that I commit my thoughts to a diary even on my walks, instead of seeking to share them generously with a friend; curses my practice even. Awful as it is to contemplate, I pray that, if I am the cold intellectual skeptic whom he rebukes, his curse may take effect, and wither and dry up those sources of my life, and my journal no longer yield me pleasure nor life.

P. M. — Going across Wheeler's large field beyond Potter's, saw a large flock of small birds go by, I am not sure what kind, the near ones continually overtaking the foremost, so that the whole flock appeared to roll over as it went forward. When they lit on a tree, they appeared at a distance to clothe it like dead leaves. Went round Bear Garden Hill to the bank of the river. I am interested by the line of deposits which form the high-water mark. If you were to examine a bushel of it, how much you might learn of the productions of the shores above. I notice that the highest and driest lines, some months old, are composed mainly of sticks and coarse stems of plants; the most recent, which the water has but just left, have a large proportion of leaves, having been formed since the March winds have blown off so many dry leaves. So you can tell the season of the year when it was formed. It makes a manure in which the grass, etc., springs earlier and more luxuriantly than elsewhere. The water has plainly stood comparatively still at a few levels, for there are but two or three lines of deposit or drift. So that in this

respect, too, nature is self-registering. Is it the columbine or the anemone leaf that I now see grown a few inches among the rocks under the Cliffs?

It is refreshing to stand on the face of the Cliff and see the water gliding over the surface of the almost perpendicular rock in a broad thin sheet, pulsing over it. It reflects the sun for half a mile like a patch of snow, — as you stand close by, bringing out the colors of the lichens like polishing or varnish. It is admirable, regarded as a dripping fountain. You have lichens and moss on the surface, and starting saxifrage, ferns still green, and huckleberry bushes in the crevices. The rocks never appear so diversified, and cracked, as if the chemistry of nature were now in full force. Then the drops, falling perpendicularly from a projecting rock, have a pleasing geometrical effect.

I see the snow lying thick on the south side of the Peterboro Hills, and though the ground is bare from the seashore to their base, I presume it is covered with snow from their base to the Icy Sea. I feel the northwest air cooled by the snow on my cheek. Those hills are probably the dividing line at present between the bare ground and the snow-clad ground stretching three thousand miles to the Saskatchewan and Mackenzie and the Icy Sea.

The shrub oaks on the plateau below the Cliffs have now lost so many of their leaves that I see much more of the grass ground between them. I see the old circular shore of Fair Haven, where the tops of the button-bushes, willows, etc., rise above the water. This pond

is now open; only a little ice against the Pleasant Meadow. There are three great gulls sailing in the middle. Now my shouting (perchance) raises one, and, flying low and heavily over the water, with heavy shoulders and sharp beak, it utters its loud mewing or squeaking notes, some of them like a squeaking pump-handle, which sound very strange to our woods. It gives a different character to the pond. To the south of the Island there is a triangular strip of smooth water many rods wide in its lee, contrasting with the waved surface elsewhere. No obvious signs of spring as yet except in the buds of a few trees and the slight greenness of the grass in some places.

April 6. Last night a snow-storm, and this morning we find the ground covered again six or eight inches deep — and drifted pretty badly beside. The conductor in the cars, which have been detained more than an hour, says it is a dry snow up-country. Here it is very damp.

April 8. To-day I hear the croak of frogs in small pond-holes in the woods, and see dimples on the surface, which I suppose that they make, for when I approach they are silent and the dimples are no longer seen. They are very shy. I notice the alder, the *A. serrulata*,[1] in blossom, its reddish-brown catkins now lengthened and loose. What mean the apparently younger small red (catkins?)?[2]

---

[1] [The name is queried in pencil.]
[2] *They* are the female aments.

I see a light, of fishermen, I suppose, spearing to-night on the river, though half the ground is covered with snow.

April 9. I frequently detect the Canadian in New England by his coarse gray homespun capote, with a picturesque red sash round his waist, and his well-furred cap made to protect his ears and face against the severities of his winter.[1] Observe the *Alnus incana*, which is distinguished from the common by the whole branchlet hanging down, so that the sterile aments not only are but appear terminal, and by the brilliant polished reddish green of the bark, and by the leaves. The snow now disappearing, I observe the Mill Brook suddenly inclosed between two lines of green. Some kind of grass rises above the surface in deep water, like two faint lines of green drawn with a brush, betraying the sun's chemistry. Perhaps three days ago it was not. Answering to the dotted lines.

Went into the old Hunt house, which they said Uncle Abel said was built one hundred and fifty years ago. The second story projects five or six inches over the first, the garret a foot over the second at the gables. There are two large rooms, one above the other, though the walls are low. The fireplace in the lower room rather large, with a high shelf of wood painted or stained to represent mahogany. That whole side the room panelled. The main timbers about fifteen inches square, of pine or oak, and for the most part the frame

---

[1] [*Excursions*, p. 45; Riv. 55.]

exposed. Where cased, in the best rooms, sixteen inches or more in width. The sills of the house appearing in the lower rooms all round the house, and cased, making a low shelf to put your feet on. No weather-boards on the corners outside; the raw edges of the clapboards.

The maple by the bridge in bloom.

April 10. 8 A. M. — Down river to half a mile below Carlisle Bridge, the river being high, yet not high for the spring.

Saw and heard the white-bellied swallows this morning for the first time. Took boat at Stedman Buttrick's, a gunner's boat, smelling of muskrats and provided with slats for bushing the boat. Having got into the Great Meadows, after grounding once or twice on low spits of grass ground, we begin to see ducks which we have scared, flying low over the water, always with a striking parallelism in the direction of their flight. They fly like regulars. They are like rolling-pins with wings. A few gulls, sailing like hawks, seen against the woods; crows; white-bellied swallows even here, already, which, I suppose, proves that their insect food is in the air. The water on our left, *i. e.* the northwest, is now dark; on our right, has a silvery brightness on the summits of the waves, scarcely yellowish. Waves here do not break. Ducks most commonly seen flying by twos or threes.

From Ball's Hill the Great Meadow looks more light; perhaps it is the medium between the dark and light above mentioned. (*Mem.* Try this experiment again; *i. e.* look not toward nor from the sun but athwart

this line.) Seen from this hill in this direction, there are, here and there, dark shadows spreading rapidly over the surface, where the wind strikes the water. The water toward the sun, seen from this height, shows not the broad silvery light but a myriad fine sparkles. The sky is full of light this morning, with different shades of blue, lighter below, darker above, separated perhaps by a thin strip of white vapor; thicker in the east. The first painted tortoise (*Emys picta*) at the bottom on the meadow. Look now toward Carlisle Bridge. See ahead the waves running higher in the middle of the meadow, and here they get the full sweep of the wind and they break into whitecaps; but we, yet in the lee of the land, feel only the long smooth swells, as the day after a storm. It is pleasant, now that we are in the wind, to feel [*sic*] the chopping sound when the boat seems to fall upon the successive waves which it meets at right angles or in the eye of the wind. Why are some maples now in blossom so much redder than others? I have seen, then, the maples and the alders in blossom, but not yet the maple keys.

From Carlisle Bridge we saw many ducks a quarter of a mile or more northward, black objects on the water, and heard them laugh something like a loon. Might have got near enough to shoot them. A fine sight to see them rise at last, about fifty of them, apparently black ducks. While they float on the water they appear to preserve constantly their relative distance. Their note not exactly like that of a goose, yet resembling some domestic fowl's cry, you know not what one; like a new species of goose. See very red

Vol. III

cranberry vines now budded. The now brownish-red shrub growing everywhere in and about bogs (originally green), with fine-dotted leaf, is probably the dwarf andromeda.[1]

When we go ashore and ramble inland below Carlisle Bridge, find here and there the freshly cut woodpiles which the choppers have not yet carted off, the ground strewn with chips. A field lately cleared (last fall perhaps), with charred stumps, and grain now greening the sandy and uneven soil, reminds me agreeably of a new country. Found a large bed of *Arbutus Uva-Ursi with fruit* in Carlisle half a mile below bridge. Some of the berries were turned black, as well as the berried stems and leaves next the ground at bottom of the thick beds — an inky black. This vine red in the sunniest places. Never saw its fruit in this neighborhood before. As we ate our luncheon on the peninsula off Carlisle shore, saw a large ring round the sun. The aspect of the sky varies every hour. About noon I observed it in the south, composed of short clouds horizontal and parallel to one another, each straight and

 dark below with a slight cumulus resting on it, a little marsh-wise; again, in the north, I see a light but rather watery-looking flock of clouds; at mid-afternoon, slight wisps and thin veils of whitish clouds also. This meadow is about two miles long at one view from Carlisle Bridge southward, appearing to wash the base of Pine Hill,[2] and it is about as much longer northward

[1] *Vide* April 15.   [2] Can it be the hill near C. Smith's?

and from a third to a half a mile wide. We sailed this whole distance with two or three pitch pine boughs for a sail, though we made leeway the whole width of the meadow. If the bridge and its causeway were gone, there would not be so long a reach to my knowledge on this river. There is a large swamp on the east above the bridge, maples and birches in front, with pines in the rear, making a low, wild shore, the shore opening farther south to one or two solitary farmhouses; on the west, low hills covered with woods, but no house. The young trees and bushes, now making apparent islands on the meadows, are there nearly in this proportion, I should think; *i. e.* in deep water, young maples, willows, button-bushes, red osier; where less water, alder, sweet-gale, and dwarf (?) andromeda, etc.

We lay to in the lee of an island a little north of the bridge, where the surface is quite smooth, and the woods shelter us completely, while we hear the roar of the wind behind them, with an agreeable sense of protection, and see the white caps of the waves on either side. When there is a ripple merely in our calm port, we see the sunny reflections of the waves on the bottom, and the cranberries, etc. It is warm here in the sun, and the dog is drying his wet coat after so many voyages, and is drowsily nodding.

April 11. 2.30 P. M. — To Second Division Brook.

The ground is now for the most part bare, though I went through drifts three feet deep in some places. I hear that Simmonds had planted his potatoes (!!)

before the snow a week ago. As I go over the railroad bridge, I hear the pewee singing *pewet pewee, pee-wet pee-wee*. The last time rising on the last syllable, sometimes repeating it thus many times, *pe-wee*. The maple beyond the railroad bridge is not yet in blossom, though that at the Red Bridge is.[1]

The sight of Nut Meadow Brook in Brown's land reminds me that the attractiveness of a brook depends much on the character of its bottom. I love just now to see one flowing through soft sand like this, where it wears a deep but irregular channel, now wider and shallower with distinct ripple-marks, now shelving off suddenly to indistinct depths, meandering as much up and down as from side to side, deepest where narrowest, and ever gullying under this bank or that, its bottom lifted up to one side or the other, the current inclining to one side. I stop to look at the circular shadows of the dimples over the yellow sand, and the dark-brown clams on their edges in the sand at the bottom. (I hear the sound of the piano below as I write this, and feel as if the winter in me were at length beginning to thaw, for my spring has been even more backward than nature's. For a month past life has been a thing incredible to me. None but the kind gods can make me sane. If only they will let their south winds blow on me! I ask to be melted. You can only ask of the metals that they be tender to the fire that *melts* them. To naught else can they be tender.) The sweet flags are now starting up under water two inches high, and minnows dart. A pure brook is a very beau-

[1] Different species.

Vol. III

tiful object to study minutely. It will bear the closest inspection, even to the fine air-bubbles, like minute globules of quicksilver, that lie on its bottom. The minute particles or spangles of golden mica in these sands, when the sun shines on them, remind one of the golden sands we read of. Everything is washed clean and bright, and the water is the best glass through which to see it.

I asked W. E. C. yesterday if he had acquired fame. He answered that, giving his name at some place, the bystanders said: "Yes, sir, we have heard of you. We know you here, sir. Your name is mentioned in Mr. ——'s book." That's all the fame I have had, — to be made known by another man.

Great flocks of slate-colored snowbirds still about and uttering their jingling note in the sun. In the brook behind Jenny Dugan's I was pleased to find the *Alnus incana* (?) in bloom in the water, its long sterile aments, yellowish-brown, hanging in panicles or clusters at the ends of the drooping branchlets, while all the twigs else are bare and the well-cased and handsome leaf-buds are not yet expanded at all. It is a kind of resurrection of the year, these pliant and pendulous blossoms on this apparently dead bush, while all is sere and tawny around, withered and bleached grass. A sort of harbinger of spring, this and the maple blossoms especially, and also the early willow catkins. Even these humble and inconspicuous aments are as grateful now as the most beautiful flowers will be a month hence. They are two and a half inches long and more. This appears to be more forward, and the

aments larger, than what I take to be the common alder hereabouts. This and the maple and the earliest willow are the most flower-like now. The skunk-cabbage is not yet fairly in blossom, nor the mayflower. In all the brooks I see the spotted tortoise (*Emys guttata*) now, and in some fields and on some hillsides have seen holes apparently dug by turtles, but I have not yet noticed their tracks over the sand. The neat compact catkins of the hazel, — fawn-colored? The birches still rather hard.

If I am too cold for human friendship, I trust I shall not soon be too cold for natural influences. It appears to be a law that you cannot have a deep sympathy with both man and nature. Those qualities which bring you near to the one estrange you from the other.

Second Division Brook. — This is of similar character, but deeper than Nut Meadow Brook. It is pleasant that there be on a brook the remains of an old flume or dam or causeway, as here, overgrown with trees, and whose rocks make stepping-stones. Large skaters and small black water-bugs are out now on the surface. Now, then, migrating fishes may come up the streams. The expanding mayflower buds show a little pinkish tint under the snow. The cress is apparently all last year's. The cowslip does not yet spring. Very little change in anything since I was last here. Is that the *Viburnum Lentago* with the spear-shaped buds? They have cut down the black aspens that used to stand on the White Pond road, the Dantean trees. Thought I heard a snipe or

an owl. White Pond about a fourth or a fifth open at the north end. A man who passed Walden to-day says it is melted two rods wide on north side. Here are large flocks of *Fringilla hyemalis* in the stubble.

Every man will be a poet if he can; otherwise a philosopher or man of science. This proves the superiority of the poet.

It is hard for a man to take money from his friends, or any service. This suggests how all men should be related.

Ah! when a man has travelled, and robbed the horizon of his native fields of its mystery and poetry, its indefinite promise, tarnished the blue of distant mountains with his feet!! When he has done this he may begin to think of another world. What is this longer to him?

I see now the mosses in pastures, bearing their light-colored capsules on the top of red filaments. When I reach the bridge, it is become a serene evening; the broad waters are more and more smooth, and everything is more beautiful in the still light. The view toward Fair Haven, whose woods are now cut off, is beautiful. No obvious sign of spring. The hill now dimly reflected; the air not yet quite still. The wood on Conantum abuts handsomely on the water and can ill be spared. The ground on which it stands is not level as seen from this point, but pleasantly varied and swelling, which is important. (Before my neighbor's pig is cold his boys have made a football of his bladder! So goes the world. No matter how much the boy snivels at first, he kicks the bladder with ecstasy.) This is the

Nut Meadow Brook

still evening hour. Insects in the air. The blackbirds whistle and sing *conqueree;* the robin peeps and sings; the bluebird warbles. The light of the setting sun on the pitch pines on Fair Haven and Bear Hill lights them up warmly, for the rays fall horizontally on them through the *mellow* evening atmosphere. They do not appear so bright to us at noon, nor do they now to the hawk that comes soaring sluggishly over them, — the brown and dusky bird seen even from beneath. Of course the pines seen from above have now more of the evening shades in them than seen from the earth on one side. The catkins of the willow are silvery. The shadow of the wood named above at the river end is indispensable in this scene; and, what is remarkable, I see where it has reached across the river and is creeping up the hill with dark pointed spears, though the intermediate river is all sunny, the reflection of the sunny hill covered with withered grass being seen through the invisible shadow. A river is best seen breaking through highlands, issuing from some narrow pass. It imparts a sense of power. The shadow at the end of the wood makes it appear grander in this case. The serenity and warmth are the main thing after the windy and cool days we have had. You may even hear a fish leap in the water now. The lowing of a cow advances me many weeks towards summer. The reflections grow more distinct every moment. At last the outline of the hill is as distinct below as above. And every object appears rhymed by reflection. By partly closing my eyes and looking through my eyelashes, the wood end appears thus: —

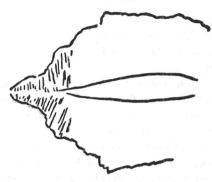

Now the shadow, reaching across the river, has crept so far up the hill that I see its reflection on the hillside in the water, and in this way it may at length connect itself with its source. Clouds are now distinctly seen in the water. The bridge is now a station for walkers. I parted with my companion here; told him not to wait for me. Maple in the swamp answers to maple, birch to birch. There is one clump of three birches particularly picturesque. In a few minutes the wind has thus gone down. At this season the reflections of deciduous trees are more picturesque and remarkable than when they are in leaf, because, the branches being seen, they make with their reflections a more wonderful rhyme. It is not mere mass or outline corresponding to outline, but a kind of geometrical figure. The maples look thus: The twilight must to the

Vol. III

extent above mentioned be earlier to birds soaring in the sky; *i. e.* they see more decided shades of evening than a man looking east. The frogs peep thinly.

My nature may be as still as this water, but it is not so pure, and its reflections are not so distinct. The snow has turned yellow the opening leaves of the nuphar. The song of a robin on an oak in Hubbard's Grove sounds far off. So I have heard a robin within three feet in a cage in a dark barroom (how unstained by all the filth of that place?) with a kind of ventriloquism, so singing that his song sounded far off on the elms. It was more pathetic still for this. The robins are singing now on all hands while the sun is setting. At what an expense any valuable work is performed! At the expense of a life! If you do one thing well, what else are you good for in the meanwhile?

April 12. Gilpin says that our turkey was domesticated in Windsor Forest at one time, and from its size was an object of consequence to lovers of the picturesque, as most birds are not, and, in its form and color and actions, more picturesque than the peacock or indeed any other bird. Being recently reclaimed from the woods, its habits continue wilder than those of other domestic fowls. "It strays widely for its food, it flies well considering its apparent inactivity, and it perches and roosts on trees." He says of the leaf of the beech: "On handling, it feels as if it were fabricated with metallic rigor. . . . For this reason, I suppose, as its rigor gives it an elastic quality, the common people in France and Switzerland use it for their beds."

I have heard thus far two sounds from two kinds of frogs, I suppose, the hyla's peep and a rather faint croak in pond-holes.

2 P. M. — To the powder-mills *via* Harrington's, returning by railroad.

The road through the pitch pine woods beyond J. Hosmer's is very pleasant to me, curving under the pines, without a fence, — the sandy road, with the pines close abutting on it, yellow in the sun and low-branched, with younger pines filling up all to the ground. I love to see a sandy road like this curving through a pitch pine wood where the trees closely border it without fences, a great cart-path merely. That is a pleasant part of the North River, under the black birches. The dog does not hesitate to take to the water for a stick, but the current carries him rapidly down. The lines of sawdust left at different levels on the shore is just hint enough of a sawmill on the stream above.

Saw the first blossoms (bright-yellow stamens or pistils) on the willow catkins to-day. The speckled alders and the maples are earlier then. The yellow blossom appears first on one side of the ament and is the most of bright and sunny color the spring has shown, the most decidedly flower-like that I have seen. It flowers, then, I should say, without regard to the skunk-cabbage, *q. v.* First the speckled alder, then the maple without keys, then this earliest, perhaps swamp, willow with its bright-yellow blossoms on one side of the ament. It is fit that this almost earliest spring flower should be yellow, the color of the sun.

Saw a maple in the water with yellowish flowers. Is it the water brings them forward? But I believe that these are all the barren flowers, and the perfect flowers appear afterward.

When I look closely, I perceive the sward beginning to be green under my feet, very slightly. It rains with sleet and hail, yet not enough to color the ground. At this season I can walk in the fields without wetting my feet in grass. Observed in the stonework of the railroad bridge — I think it must be in Acton — many large stones more or less disintegrated and even turned to a soft soil into which I could thrust my finger, threatening the destruction of the bridge. A geologist is needed to tell you whether your stones will continue stones and not turn to earth. It was very pleasant to come out on the railroad in this gentle rain. The track, laid in gray sand, looks best at such a time, with the rails all wet. The factory bridge, seen through the mist, is agreeably indistinct, seen against a dark-grayish pine wood. I should not know there was a bridge there, if I had not been there. The dark line made by its shaded under side is most that I see here spanning the road; the rails are quite indistinct. We love to see things thus with a certain indistinctness.

I am made somewhat sad this afternoon by the coarseness and vulgarity of my companion, because he is one with whom I have made myself intimate. He inclines latterly to speak with coarse jesting of facts which should always be treated with delicacy and reverence. I lose my respect for the man who can make the mystery of sex the subject of a coarse jest, yet, when you speak

earnestly and seriously on the subject, is silent. I feel that this is to be truly irreligious. Whatever may befall me, I trust that I may never lose my respect for purity in others. The subject of sex is one on which I do not wish to meet a man at all unless I *can* meet him on the most inspiring ground, — if his view degrades, and does not elevate. I would preserve purity in act and thought, as I would cherish the memory of my mother. A companion can possess no worse quality than vulgarity. If I find that *he* is not habitually reverent of the fact of sex, I, even I, will not associate with [him]. I will cast this first stone. What were life without some religion of this kind? Can I walk with one who by his jests and by his habitual tone reduces the life of men and women to a level with that of cats and dogs? The man who uses such a vulgar jest describes his relation to his dearest friend. Impure as I am, I could protect and worship purity. I can have no really serious conversation with my companion. He seems not capable of it. The men whom I most esteem, when they speak at all on this subject, do not speak with sufficient reverence. They speak to men with a coarseness which they would not use in the presence of women, and I think they would feel a slight shame if a woman coming in should hear their remarks. A man's speech on this subject should, of course, be ever as reverent and chaste and simple as if it were to be heard by the ears of maidens.

In the New Forest in Hampshire they had a chief officer called the Lord Warden and under him two distinct officers, one to preserve the *venison* of the forest,

another to preserve its *vert*, *i. e.* woods, lawns, etc. Does not our Walden need such? The Lord Warden was a person of distinction, as the Duke of Gloucester.

Walden Wood was my forest walk.

The English forests are divided into "walks," with a keeper presiding over each. My "walk" is ten miles from my house every way. Gilpin says, "It is a forest adage of ancient date, *Non est inquirendum unde venit venison*," *i. e.* whether stolen or not.

"The incroachments of trespassers, and the houses and fences thus raised on the borders of the forest" by forest borderers, were "considered as great nuisances by the old forest law, and were severely punished under the name of *purprestures*, as tending *ad terrorem ferarum — ad nocumentum forestae*, etc." [1]

There is, this afternoon and evening, a rather cool April rain. Pleasant to hear its steady dripping.

April 13. *Tuesday.* A driving snow-storm in the night and still raging; five or six inches deep on a level at 7 A. M. All birds are turned into snowbirds. Trees and houses have put on the aspect of winter. The traveller's carriage wheels, the farmer's wagon, are converted into white disks of snow through which the spokes hardly appear. But it is good now to stay in the house and read and write. We do not now go wandering all abroad and dissipated, but the imprisoning storm condenses our thoughts. I can hear the clock tick as not in pleasant weather. My life is enriched. I love to hear the wind howl. I have a fancy for sitting

[1] [*Walden*, p. 276; Riv. 387, 388.]

with my book or paper in some mean and apparently unfavorable place, in the kitchen, for instance, where the work is going on, rather a little cold than comfortable. My thoughts are of more worth in such places than they would be in a well furnished and warmed studio.

Windsor, according to Gilpin, is contracted from wind-shore, the Saxons not sounding the *sh*.

The robin is the only bird as yet that makes a business of singing, steadily singing, — sings continuously out of pure joy and melody of soul, carols. The jingle of the song sparrow, simple and sweet as it is, is not of sufficient volume nor sufficiently continuous to command and hold attention, and the bluebird's is but a transient warble, from a throat overflowing with azure and serene hopes; but the song of the robin on the elms or oaks, loud and clear and heard afar through the streets of a village, makes a fit conclusion to a spring day. The larks are not yet in sufficient numbers or sufficiently musical. The robin is the prime singer as yet. The blackbird's *conqueree*, when first heard in the spring, is pleasant from the associations it awakens, and is best heard by one boating on the river. It belongs to the stream. The robin is the only bird with whose song the groves can be said to be now *vocal* morning and evening, for, though many other notes are heard, none fill the air like this bird. As yet no other thrushes.

Snowed all day, till the ground was covered eight inches deep. Heard the robin singing as usual last night, though it was raining. The elm buds begin to show their blossoms. As I came home through the streets at 11 o'clock last night through the snow, it cheered me to think that there was a little bit of a yellow blossom by warm sandy watersides which had expanded its yellow blossom on the sunny side amid the snows. I mean the catkins of the earliest willow. To think of those little sunny spots in nature, so incredibly contrasting with all this white and cold.

April 14. Going down the railroad at 9 A. M., I hear the lark singing from over the snow. This for steady singing comes next to the robin now. It will come up very sweet from the meadows ere long. I do not hear those peculiar tender die-away notes from the pewee yet. Is it another pewee, or a later note? The snow melts astonishingly fast. The whole upper surface, when you take it up in your hand, is heavy and dark with water. The slate-colored snowbird's (for they are still about) is a somewhat shrill jingle, like the sound of ramrods when the order has been given to a regiment to "return ramrods" and they obey stragglingly. It is oppressively hot in the Deep Cut, the sun is now so high and reflected from the snow on both sides. When I inquire again of Riordan where he gets his water now, seeing that the ditch by the railroad is full of rain-water and sand, he answers cheerfully as ever: "I get it from the ditch, sir. It is good spr-ring water,"—with a good deal of burr to the *r*. Certainly it will not poison him so soon for his contentedness. Walden is only melted two or three rods from the north shore yet. It is a good thermometer of the annual heats,

because, having no outlet nor inlet on the surface, it has no stream to wear it away more or less rapidly or early as the water may be higher or lower, and also, being so deep, it is not warmed through by a transient change of temperature. Is that *Cornus florida* at the Howard's Meadow dam? Many red oak leaves have fallen since yesterday, for now they lie on the surface of the snow, perchance loosened by the moisture. The white oak leaves are more bleached and thinner than the red. The squarish-leaved shrub oak appears to bear the winter still better. The leaves of the hornbeam are well withered. The snow in the sunshine is more white and dazzling now than in the winter; at least this is the effect on our eyes. Haynes told me of breams caught through the ice. The surface of the meadow is very attractive now, seen through a foot or more of calm water while the neighboring fields are covered with snow. The evenings have for a long time been grievously shortened. The pond-holes are filled with snow which looks like ice. With snow on the ground, the sky appears once more to wear the peculiar blue of winter, and contrasts in like manner with small whitish cumulus; but there is not yet in the air the vapor you would expect from the evaporation of so much snow.

On the Cliffs. — If it were not for the snow it would be a remarkably pleasant, as well as warm, day. It is now perfectly calm. The different parts of Fair Haven Pond — the pond, the meadow beyond the button-bush and willow curve, the island, and the meadow between the island and mainland with its own defining lines — are all parted off like the parts of a mirror.

Vol. III

A fish hawk is calmly sailing over all, looking for his prey. The gulls are all gone now, though the water is high, but I can see the motions of a muskrat on the calm sunny surface a great way off. So perfectly calm and beautiful, and yet no man looking at it this morning but myself. It is pleasant to see the zephyrs strike the smooth surface of the pond from time to time, and a darker shade ripple over it.

The streams break up; the ice goes to the sea. Then sails the fish hawk overhead, looking for his prey. I saw the first white-bellied swallows (about the house) on the morning of the 10th, as I have said, and, that day also, I saw them skimming over the Great Meadows, as if they had come to all parts of the town at once.

Can we believe when beholding this landscape, with only a few buds visibly swollen on the trees and the ground covered eight inches deep with snow, that the grain was waving in the fields and the apple trees were in blossom April 19, 1775? It may confirm this story, however, what Grandmother said, — that she carried ripe cherries from Weston to her brother in Concord Jail [1] the 17th of June the same year. It is probably true, what E. Wood, senior, says, that the grain was just beginning to wave, and the apple blossoms beginning to expand.

Abel Hunt tells me to-night that he remembers that the date of the old Hunt house used to be on the chim-

[1] [Mr. Sanborn informs the editors that this Mr. Jones was a Tory, who fled to Halifax and later, in trying to bring in supplies for the British soldiers in Boston during the siege, was captured with his vessel and sent to Concord Jail as prisoner.]

ney, and it was 1703, or 1704, within a year or two; that Governor Winthrop sold the farm to a Hunt, and they have the deed now. There is one of the old-fashioned diamond squares set in lead still, in the back part of the house.

The snow goes off fast, for I hear it melting [?] and the eaves dripping all night as well as all day.

I have been out every afternoon this past winter, as usual, in sun and wind, snow and rain, without being particularly tanned. This *forenoon* I walked in the woods and felt the heat reflected from the snow so sensibly in some parts of the cut on the railroad that I was reminded of those oppressive days two or three summers ago, when the laborers were obliged to work by night. Well, since I have come home, this afternoon and evening, I find that I am suddenly tanned, even to making the skin of my nose sore. The sun, reflected thus from snow in April, perhaps especially in the forenoon, possesses a tanning power.

April 15. My face still burns with yesterday's sunning. It rains this morning, as if the vapor from the melting snow were falling again. There is so much sun and light reflected from the snow at this season that it is not only remarkably white and dazzling but tans in a few moments. It is fortunate, then, that the sun on the approach of the snows, the season of snow, takes his course so many degrees lower in the heavens; else he might burn us up, even at that season. The face comes from the house of winter, tender and white, to the house of summer, and these late snows convey the sun to it with sudden and scorching power. It was not the March winds or others. It was a still, warm, beautiful day. I was out but three hours. It was the sun suddenly and copiously applied to a face from winter quarters.

The broad flat brown buds on Mr. Cheney's elm, containing twenty or thirty yellowish-green *threads*, surmounted with little brownish-mulberry cups, which contain the stamens and the two styles, — these are just expanding or blossoming now. The flat imbricated buds, which open their scales both ways, have had a rich look for some weeks past. Why so few elms so advanced, so rich now? Are the staminiferous and pistilliferous flowers ever on different trees?

It is, according to Emerson, the dwarf cassandra (*C. calyculata* of D. Don) that is so common on the river meadows and in swamps and bogs; formerly called an andromeda, of the *Ericaceæ*, or Heath Family, with the uva-ursi (*Arctostaphylos*). Now well flower-budded. I had forgotten the aspen in my latest enumeration of flowers. *Vide* if its flowers have not decidedly appeared.

I think that the largest early-catkined willow in large bushes in sand by water now blossoming — the fertile catkins with paler blossoms, the sterile covered with pollen, a pleasant lively bright yellow — [is] the brightest flower I have seen thus far.

Gilpin says of the stags in the New Forest, if one "be hunted by the king, and escape; or have his life given him for the sport he has afforded, he becomes from thence forward a *hart-royal*. — If he be hunted

out of the forest, and there escape, the king hath sometimes honoured him with a royal proclamation; the purport of which is, to forbid any one to molest him, that he may have free liberty of returning to his forest. From that time he becomes a *hart-royal proclaimed*." As is said of Richard the First, that, having pursued a hart a great distance, "the king in gratitude for the diversion he had received, ordered him immediately to be proclaimed at Tickill, and at all the neighbouring towns." [1] (A hart is a stag in his fifth or sixth year and upward.)

Think of having such a fellow as that for a king, causing his proclamation to be blown about your country towns at the end of his day's sport, at Tickill or elsewhere, that you hinds may not molest the hart that has afforded him such an ever-memorable day's sport. Is it not time that his subjects whom he has so sorely troubled and so long, be *harts-royal proclaimed* themselves, — who have afforded him such famous sport? It will be a finer day's-sport when the hinds shall turn and hunt the royal hart himself beyond the bounds of his forest and his kingdom, and in perpetual banishment alone he become a royal hart proclaimed. Such is the magnanimity of royal hearts that, through a whimsical prick of generosity, spares the game it could not kill, and fetters its equals with its arbitrary will. Kings love to say "shall" and "will."

Rain, rain, rain, all day, carrying off the snow. It appears, then, that if you go out at this season and walk in the sun in a clear, warm day like yesterday,

[1] [William Gilpin, *Remarks on Forest Scenery*, London, 1794.]

Vol. III

while the earth is covered with snow, you may have your face burnt in a few moments. The rays glance off from the snowy crystals and scorch the skin.

Thinking of the value of the gull to the scenery of our river in the spring, when for a few weeks they are seen circling about so deliberately and heavily yet gracefully, without apparent object, beating like a vessel in the air, Gilpin says something to the purpose, that water-fowl "discover in their flight some determined aim. They eagerly coast the river, or return to the sea; bent on some purpose, of which they never lose sight. But the evolutions of the gull appear capricious, and undirected, both when she flies alone, and, as she often does, in large companies. — The more however her character suffers as a loiterer, the more it is raised in picturesque value, by her continuing longer before the eye; and displaying, in her elegant sweeps along the air, her sharp-pointed wings, and her bright silvery hue. — She is beautiful also, not only on the wing, but when she floats, in numerous assemblies on the water; or when she rests on the shore, dotting either one, or the other with white spots; which, minute as they are, are very picturesque: . . . giving life and spirit to a view." [1]

He seems to be describing our very bird. I do not *remember* to have seen them over or in our river meadows when there was not ice there. They come annually a-fishing here like royal hunters, to remind us of the sea and that our town, after all, lies but further up a creek of the universal sea, above the head of the tide.

[1] [*Op. cit.*]

So ready is a deluge to overwhelm our lands, as the gulls to circle hither in the spring freshets. To see a gull beating high over our meadowy flood in chill and windy March is akin to seeing a mackerel schooner on the coast. It is the nearest approach to sailing vessels in our scenery. I never saw one at Walden. Oh, how it salts our fresh, our sweet watered Fair Haven all at once to see this sharp-beaked, greedy sea-bird beating over it! For a while the water is brackish to my eyes. It is merely some herring pond, and if I climb the eastern bank I expect to see the Atlantic there covered with countless sails. We are so far maritime, do not dwell beyond the range of the seagoing gull, the littoral birds. Does not the gull come up after those suckers which I see? He is never to me perfectly in harmony with the scenery, but, like the high water, something unusual.

What a novel life, to be introduced to a dead sucker floating on the water in the spring! Where was it spawned, pray? The sucker is so recent, so unexpected, so unrememberable, so unanticipatable a creation. While so many institutions are gone by the board, and we are despairing of men and of ourselves, there seems to be life even in a dead sucker, whose fellows at least are alive. The world never looks more recent or promising — religion, philosophy, poetry — than when viewed from this point. To see a sucker tossing on the spring flood, its swelling, imbricated breast heaving up a bait to not-despairing gulls! It is a strong and a strengthening sight. Is the world coming to an end? Ask the chubs. As long as fishes spawn, glory and honor to the cold-blooded who despair! As long as ideas are expressed, as long as friction makes bright, as long as vibrating wires make music of harps, we do not want redeemers. What a volume you might [write] on the separate virtues of the various animals, the black duck and the rest!

How indispensable our one or two flocks of geese in spring and autumn! What would be a spring in which that sound was not heard? Coming to unlock the fetters of northern rivers. Those annual steamers of the air.

Would it not be a fine office to preserve the *vert* of this forest in which I ramble?

Channing calls our walks along the banks of the river, taking a boat for convenience at some distant point, *riparial* excursions. It is a pleasing epithet, but I mistrust such, even as good as this, in which the mere name is so agreeable, as if it would ring hollow ere long; and rather the thing should make the true name poetic at last. Alcott wished me to name my book *Sylvania!* But he and C. are two men in these respects. We make a good many prairial excursions. We take a boat four or five miles out, then paddle up the stream as much further, meanwhile landing and making excursions inland or further along the banks.

Walden is but little more melted than yesterday.

I see that the grass, which, unless in the most favored spots, did not show any evidence of spring to the casual glance before the snow, will look unexpectedly green as soon as it has gone. It has actually grown beneath it. The lengthened spires about our pump remind me

of flame, as if it were a kind of green flame allied to fire, as it is the product of the sun.

The aspen on the railroad is beginning to blossom, showing the purple or mulberry in the terminal catkins, though it droops like dead cats' tails in the rain. It appears about the same date with the elm.

Is it the chickweed so forward by our back doorstep?

Vide that sentence in Gilpin about "*Lawing*, or *expeditation*, was a forest term for disqualifying a dog to exert such speed, as was necessary to take a deer. It was performed either by cutting out the sole of his foot, or by taking off two of his claws by a chisel, and mallet." [1] A gentleman might keep a greyhound within ten miles of the forest if he was *lawed*. It reminds me of the majority of human hounds that tread the forest paths of this world; they go slightly limping in their gait, as if disqualified by a cruel fate to overtake the nobler game of the forest, their natural quarry. Most men are such dogs. Ever and anon starting a quarry, with perfect scent, which, from this cruel maiming and disqualification of the fates, he is incapable of coming up with. Does not the noble dog shed tears?

Gilpin on the subject of docking horses' tails; thinks that leaving the tail may even help the racer to fly toward the goal.

I notice that the sterile blossoms of that large-catkined early willow begin to open on the side of the catkin, like a tinge of golden light, gradually spreading and

[1] Poet laureate lawed.

expanding over the whole surface and lifting their anthers far and wide. The stem of these sterile catkins is more reddish, smoother, and slenderer than that of the female ones (pale-flowered), which is darker and downy.

April 16. That large early swamp (?) willow catkin (the sterile blossom) opens on one side like a tinge of golden sunlight, the yellow anthers bursting through the down that invests the scales.

2 P. M. — To Conantum.

It clears up (the rain) at noon, with a rather cool wind from the northwest and flitting clouds. The ground about one third covered with snow still. What variety in the trunks of oaks! How expressive of strength are some! There is one behind Hubbard's which expresses a sturdy strength, thus: with a protuberant ridge and seam toward the north. There is a still more remarkable one in a different style near Derby's Bridge. The very emblem of sturdy resistance to tempests.

How many there are who advise you to print! How few who advise you to lead a more interior life! In the one case there is all the world to advise you, in the other there is none to advise you but yourself. Nobody ever advised me not to print but myself. The public persuade the author to print, as the meadow invites the brook to fall into it. Only he can be trusted with gifts who can present a face of bronze to expectations.

As I turned round the corner of Hubbard's Grove, saw a woodchuck, the first of the season, in the middle

of the field, six or seven rods from the fence which bounds the wood, and twenty rods distant. I ran along the fence and cut him off, or rather overtook him, though he started at the same time. When I was only a rod and a half off, he stopped, and I did the same; then he ran again, and I ran up within three feet of him, when he stopped again, the fence being between us. I squatted down and surveyed him at my leisure. His eyes were dull black and rather inobvious, with a faint chestnut (?) iris, with but little expression and that more of resignation than of anger. The general aspect was a coarse grayish brown, a sort of grisel (?). A lighter brown next the skin, then black or very dark brown and tipped with whitish rather loosely. The head between a squirrel and a bear, flat on the top and dark brown, and darker still or black on the tip of the nose. The whiskers black, two inches long. The ears very small and roundish, set far back and nearly buried in the fur. Black feet, with long and slender claws for digging. It appeared to tremble, or perchance shivered with cold. When I moved, it gritted its teeth quite loud, sometimes striking the under jaw against the other chatteringly, sometimes grinding one jaw on the other, yet as if more from instinct than anger. Whichever way I turned, that way it headed. I took a twig a foot long and touched its snout, at which it started forward and bit the stick, lessening the distance between us to two feet, and still it held all the ground it gained. I played with it tenderly awhile with the stick, trying to open its gritting jaws. Ever its long incisors, two above and two below, were presented. But I thought it would go to sleep if I stayed long enough. It did not sit upright as sometimes, but *standing* on its fore feet with its head down, *i. e.* half sitting, half standing. We sat looking at one another about half an hour, till we began to feel mesmeric influences. When I was tired, I moved away, wishing to see him run, but I could not start him. He would not stir as long as I was looking at him or could see him. I walked round him; he turned as fast and fronted me still. I sat down by his side within a foot. I talked to him *quasi* forest lingo, baby-talk, at any rate in a conciliatory tone, and thought that I had some influence on him. He gritted his teeth less. I chewed checkerberry leaves and presented them to his nose at last without a grit; though I saw that by so much gritting of the teeth he had worn them rapidly and they were covered with a fine white powder, which, if you measured it thus, would have made his anger terrible. He did not mind any noise I might make. With a little stick I lifted one of his paws to examine it, and held it up at pleasure. I turned him over to see what color he was beneath (darker or more purely brown), though he turned himself back again sooner than I could have wished. His tail was also all brown, though not very dark, rat-tail like, with loose hairs standing out on all sides like a caterpillar brush. He had a rather mild look. I spoke kindly to him. I reached checkerberry leaves to his mouth. I stretched my hands over him, though he turned up his head and still gritted a little. I laid my hand on him, but immediately took it off again, instinct not being wholly overcome. If I had had

a few fresh bean leaves, thus in advance of the season, I am sure I should have tamed him completely. It was a frizzly tail. His is a humble, terrestrial color like the partridge's, well concealed where dead wiry grass rises above darker brown or chestnut dead leaves, — a modest color. If I had had some food, I should have ended with stroking him at my leisure. Could easily have wrapped him in my handkerchief. He was not fat nor particularly lean. I finally had to leave him without seeing him move from the place. A large, clumsy, burrowing squirrel. *Arctomys*, bear-mouse. I respect him as one of the natives. He lies there, by his color and habits so naturalized amid the dry leaves, the withered grass, and the bushes. A sound nap, too, he has enjoyed in his native fields, the past winter. I think I might learn some wisdom of him. His ancestors have lived here longer than mine. He is more thoroughly acclimated and naturalized than I. Bean leaves the red man raised for him, but he can do without them.

The streaked mahogany spathes of the skunk-cabbage, which for some time have pushed up and stood above the naked ground where is no leaf yet, of this or other plant, inclosing the now perfect flower and for some time perfect, are like bent spear-heads ("ovate swelling," "incurved," "cucullate") appearing above the ground, a sort of device in nature. The foremost of the summer's phalanx. This is the earliest flower that I know.

How inconspicuous the blossoms of the woods are! How many have seen the pistillate flowers of the hazel,

"star-like tufts of crimson stigmas?" All boys know the nuts, yet man nor boy the flower, though, minute [as it is,] it is interesting. They turn dark and shrivel soon in the pocket; cannot be brought home so. Their catkins also are perfect now. They may be mentioned immediately after the alders.

The red stems of the cornel (?) are conspicuous at this season. I think that the tassels of the *Alnus incana* are rather earlier, longer, and more yellow, with smaller scales, than those of the *A. serrulata*, which are not yellow but green, mixed with the purplish or reddish brown scales. It is pleasant to walk the windy causeways where the tassels of the alders are dangling and swinging now.

The water on the meadows is now quite high on account of the melting snow and the rain. It makes a lively prospect when the wind blows, where our summer meads spread, — a tumultuous sea, a myriad waves breaking with whitecaps, like gambolling sheep, for want of other comparison in the country. Far and wide a sea of motion, schools of porpoises, lines of Virgil realized. One would think it a novel sight for inland meadows. Where the cranberry and andromeda and swamp white oak and maple grow, here is a mimic sea, with its gulls. At the bottom of the sea, cranberries.

We love to see streams colored by the earth they have flown over, as well as pure.

Saxifrage, well named, budded but not risen (its stem) on Conantum Cliff. It there grows in the seams of the rocks, where is no earth apparent. The radical leaves of the columbine are also well advanced. Flight

of ducks and partridges earnest but not graceful. I see many nests of squirrels in the trees, which appear to have been made and used the past winter only.

Is that a black ash in Conant's orchard by the riverside? Stand half-way down the hill north of Fair Haven Pond, the sun in clouds, the wind pretty strong from the northward, the pond and meadow on the south (at 4 or 5 o'clock) are of dark and sad aspect as in a rainy day, with streaks of foam at intervals of six or eight feet, stretching quite across from north to south. Eastward the water is lighter; northeastward it is a very dark, deep blue, yet full of light; northward it is a dark and angry flood, with one or two white-capped waves in the distance.

I saw two or three large white birds in middle of pond, probably gulls (!),[1] though the ice has long been gone.

The two states of the meadow are to be remembered: first in a March or April wind, as I have described it; second in a perfectly calm and beautiful mild morning or evening or midday, as lately, at the same season, such as I have also partially described, when there are no gulls circling over it. What different thoughts it suggests! Would it not be worth the while to describe the different states of our meadows which cover so large a portion of the town? It is not as if we had a few acres only of water surface. From every side the milkman rides over long causeways into the village, and carries the vision of much meadow's surface with him into his dreams. They answer to moods of the Concord

[1] Whistlers.

mind. There might be a chapter: The Sudbury Meadows, the Humors of the Town.

Might I not write on sunshine as well as moonshine? Might I not observe the sun, at least when the moon does not show her crescent?

Saw a red squirrel, or a tawny one rather.

I think our overflowing river far handsomer and more abounding in soft and beautiful contrasts than a merely broad river would be. A succession of bays it is, a chain of lakes, an endlessly scalloped shore, rounding wood and field. Cultivated field and wood and pasture and house are brought into ever new and unexpected positions and relations to the water. There is just stream enough for a flow of thought; that is all. Many a foreigner who has come to this town has worked for years on its banks without discovering which way the river runs.

I see where moles have been at work near the river on the sides of hills, probably under the snow.

Hawks sail over dry (?) meadows now, because the frogs are out.

April 17. Gilpin says, "As the wheeling motion of the gull is beautiful, so also is the figured flight of the goose, the duck, and the widgeon; all of which are highly ornamental to coast-views, bays, and estuaries." [1] A flight of ducks adds to the wildness of our wildest river scenery. Undoubtedly the soaring and sailing of the hen-hawk, the red-shouldered buzzard (?), is the most ornamental, graceful, stately, beautiful to contemplate,

[1] [*Remarks on Forest Scenery.*]

of all the birds that ordinarily frequent our skies. The eagle is but a rare and casual visitor. The goose, the osprey, the great heron, though interesting, are either transient visitors or rarely seen; they either move through the air as passengers or too exclusively looking for their prey, but the hen-hawk soars like a creature of the air. The flight of martins is interesting in the same way. When I was young and compelled to pass my Sunday in the house without the aid of interesting books, I used to spend many an hour till the wished-for sundown, watching the martins soar, from an attic window; and fortunate indeed did I deem myself when a hawk appeared in the heavens, though far toward the horizon against a downy cloud, and I searched for hours till I had found his mate. They, at least, took my thoughts from earthly things.

Gilpin says that the black-cock, scarce in the New Forest, "has the honour, which no other bird can boast, of being protected as royal-game." [1]

Stood by the riverside early this morning. The water has been rising during the night. The sun has been shining on it half an hour. It is quite placid. The village smokes are seen against the long hill. And now I see the river also is awakening, a slight ripple beginning to appear on its surface. It wakens like the village.

It proves a beautiful day, and I see that glimmering or motion in the air just above the fields, which we associate with heat. I noticed yesterday that some of those early staminate catkins had apparently been blasted on one side by the snow. The waters are, after

[1] [*Op. cit.*]

all, as quiet at noon as in the morning, and I see the reflections with rare distinctness from my window.

Up the east bank of river to Fair Haven at 2 P. M.

The farmers are in haste beginning their plowing. The season is remarkably backward. The wind is rising at last, and it is somewhat from the east-south-east, but it is the more fresh and life-giving. The water is over the Corner road since last night, higher than before this season, so that we (I and C.) go not that way. In that little pasture of Potter's under the oak, I am struck with the advantage of the fence in landscapes. Here is but a half-acre inclosed, but the fence has the effect of confining the attention to this little undulation of the land and to make you consider it by itself, and the importance of the oak is proportionally increased. This formation of the surface would be lost in an unfenced prairie, but the fence, which nearly enough defines it, frames it and presents it as a picture.

Sat on the smooth river-bank under Fair Haven, the sunlight in the wood across the stream. It proves a breezy afternoon. There are fresh cobwebs on the alders in the sun. The atmosphere grows somewhat misty and blue in the distance. The sun-sparkle on the water, — is it not brighter now than it will be in summer? In this freshet and overflow, the permanent shore and shore-marks are obliterated, and the wooded point making into the water shows no gradations, no naked stems beneath, but the pine boughs and the bushes actually rest gently on the water. There is no shore. The waters steal so gently and noiselessly

over the land amid the alders and the copses, so soft, so placid a shore, which would not wreck a cranberry! The groves are simply immersed, as when you raise the water in a wine-glass by dropping pins into it. What is that large hawk with a pure white belly and slender long black wings (a goshawk?) [1] which I see sailing over the Cliffs, — a pair of them looking for prey? From this burnt shrub oak plain beneath the Cliff, where in spots not even the grass has caught again, I see the pond southward through the hazy atmosphere, a blue rippled water surrounded mistily by red shrub oak woods and on one side green pines and tawny grass, — a blue rippled water surrounded by low reddish shrub oak hills, — the whole invested, softened, and made more remote and indistinct by a bluish mistiness. I am not sure but the contrast is more exciting and lastingly satisfactory than if the woods were green. A meadow must not be deep nor have well-defined shore. The more indented and finely divided and fringed and shallow and copsy its shore, the more islanded bushes and cranberry vines appear here and there above the surface, the more truly it answers to the word meadow or prairie.

These deep withdrawn bays, like that toward Well Meadow, are resorts for many a shy flock of ducks. They are very numerous this afternoon. We scare them up every quarter of a mile. Mostly the whitish duck which Brown thinks the golden-eye (we call them whistlers), and also black ducks, perchance also sheldrakes. They are quite shy; swim rapidly

[1] Or fish hawk (?).

away far into the pond. A flock which we surprised in the smooth bay of Well Meadow divided and showed much cunning, dodging under the shore to avoid us.

Struck upon a wild maple swamp a little northwest (?) of Well Meadow Head, where the ground had the appearance of a wild ravine running up from the swamp water here, even to the rocks of the Cliffs which from no other point would be associated with this place. Here is a very retired wild swamp, now drowned land, with picturesque maples in it, and the leaves and sticks on the bottom seen through the transparent water, the yellowish bottom, yellow with decayed leaves, etc. Found within the just swelling buds of the amelanchier [1] evidences of the coming blossom.

Observed in the second of the chain of ponds between Fair Haven and Walden a large (for the pond) island patch of the dwarf andromeda, I sitting on the east bank; its fine brownish-red color very agreeable and memorable to behold. In the last long pond, looking at it from the south, I saw it filled with a slightly grayish shrub which I took for the sweet-gale, but when I had got round to the east side, chancing to turn round, I was surprised to see that all this pond-hole also was filled with the same warm brownish-red-colored andromeda. The fact was I was opposite to the sun, but from every other position I saw only the sun reflected from the surface of the andromeda leaves, which gave the whole a grayish-brown hue tinged with red; but from this position alone I saw, as it were, through

[1] Or was it *Pyrus arbutifolia*, choke-berry?

Vol. III

the leaves which the opposite sun lit up, giving to the whole this charming warm, what I call *Indian*, red color, — the mellowest, the ripest, red imbrowned color; but when I looked to the right or left, *i. e.* north or south, the more the swamp had the mottled light or grayish aspect where the light was reflected from the surfaces of the leaves. And afterward, when I had risen higher up the hill, though still opposite the sun, the light came reflected upward from the surfaces, and I lost that warm, rich red tinge, surpassing cathedral windows. Let me look again at a different hour of the day, and see if it is really so. It is a very interesting piece of magic. It is the autumnal tints in spring, only more subdued and mellow. These leaves are so slow to decay. *Vide* when they fall. Already these ponds are greened with frog-spittle.[1] I see the tracks of muskrats through it. Hear the faint croak of frogs and the still rather faint peeping of hylas. It is about 4.30 p. m.

The form of the surface hereabouts is very agreeable. There are many dry hollows and valleys hereabouts connecting these two ponds. The undulating ground.

A fisherman, making change the other day, gave a ninepence whose pillars were indistinct. Some of the women returned it, whereupon he took it and, taking off his hat, rubbed it on his hair, saying he guessed he could make the pillars appear. The pond is still half covered with ice, and it will take another day like this to empty it. It is clear up tight to the shore on the south side, — dark-gray cold ice, com-

[1] [This sentence is queried in pencil.]

pletely saturated with water. The air from over it is very cold.

The scent of the earliest spring flowers! I smelt the willow catkins to-day, tender and innocent after this rude winter, yet slightly sickening, yet full of vernal promise. This odor, — how unlike anything that winter affords, or nature has afforded this six months! A mild, sweet, vernal scent, not highly spiced and intoxicating, as some ere long, but attractive to bees, — that early yellow smell. The odor of spring, of life developing amid buds, of the earth's epithalamium. The first flowers are not the highest-scented, — as catkins, — as the first birds are not the finest singers, — as the blackbirds and song sparrows, etc. The beginnings of the year are humble. But though this fragrance is not rich, it contains and prophesies all others in it.

The leaves of the *Veratrum viride*, American hellebore, now just pushing up.

April 18.[1] The ground is now generally bare of snow, though it lies along walls and on the north sides of valleys in the woods pretty deep. We have had a great deal of foul weather this season, scarcely two fair days together.

Gray refers the cone-like excrescences on the ends of willow twigs to the punctures of insects. I think that both these and the galls of the oak, etc., are to be regarded as something more normal than this implies. Though it is impossible to draw the line between disease and health at last.

[1] Storm begins this morning and continues five days incessantly.

Day before yesterday I brought home some twigs of that earliest large oval-catkined willow just over Hubbard's Bridge on the right hand, a male tree. The anthers just beginning to show themselves; not *quite* so forward as those above the Deacon Hosmer house, which I have thought to be the same. They looked much the worse for the rain. Catkins about one inch long, not being much expanded yet, opening a little below the apex, two stamens to a scale. There are smaller female bushes further on, on the left, catkins about the same size, with greenish ovaries stalked and rather small and slightly reddish stigmas, fourdivided. I thought this the other sex of the same tree. There is also the very gray hardwood-like willow at the bars just beyond Hubbard's Brook, with long, cylindrical, caterpillar-like catkins, which do not yet show their yellow. And, thirdly, opposite the firstnamed, *i. e.* the other side the way, a smaller-catkined willow not yet showing its yellow. Fourthly, near the Conantum Swamp, sterile catkins *in blossom* on a bush willow an inch and a quarter long, more forward than any, but the stamens one to a bract or scale and bifid or trifid or quatrifid toward the top!! Fifthly, what I should think the *Salix humilis*, *i. e. S. Muhlenbergiana*, shows its small catkins now, but not yet blossoms.

I still feel stiff places in the swamps where there is ice still. Saw yesterday on an apple tree, in company with the *Fringilla hyemalis*, an olivaceous-backed [bird], yellow-throated, and yellow, brown-spotted breast, about the same size or a little less than they, — the first of the late coming or passing, or the summer, birds? When we have got to these colors, the olivaceous and yellow, then the sun is high in the sky. The *Fringilla hyemalis* is the most common bird at present.

Was pleased to observe yesterday in the woods a new method (to me) which the woodchopper had invented to keep up his corded wood where he could not drive a stake on account of the frost. He had set up the stake on the surface, then looped several large birch withes once about it, resting the wood on their ends, as he carried up the pile, or else he used a forked stick, thus:

2 P. M. — To river.

A driving rain, *i. e.* a rain with easterly wind and driving mists. River higher than before this season, about eighteen inches of the highest arch of the stone bridge above water.

Going through Dennis's field with C., saw a flock of geese on east side of river near willows. Twelve great birds on the troubled surface of the meadow, delayed by the storm. We lay on the ground behind an oak and our umbrella, eighty rods off, and watched them. Soon we heard a gun go off, but could see no smoke in the mist and rain. And the whole flock rose, spreading their great wings and flew with clangor [1] a few rods and lit in the water again, then swam swiftly toward our shore with outstretched necks. I knew them first from ducks by their long necks. Soon ap-

[1] The "honk" of the goose.

peared the man, running toward the shore in vain, in his greatcoat; but he soon retired in vain. We remained close under our umbrella by the tree, ever and anon looking through a peep-hole between the umbrella and the tree at the birds. On they came, sometimes in two, sometimes in three, squads, warily, till we could see the steel-blue and green reflections from their necks. We held the dog close the while, — C., lying on his back in the rain, had him in his arms, — and thus we gradually edged round on the ground in this cold, wet, windy storm, keeping our feet to the tree, and the great wet calf of a dog with his eyes shut so meekly in our arms. We laughed well at our adventure. They swam fast and warily, seeing our umbrella. Occasionally one expanded a gray wing. They showed white on breasts. And not till after half an hour, sitting cramped and cold and wet on the ground, did we leave them.

Ducks also were on the meadow. I have seen more ducks within a few days than ever before. They are apparently delayed here by the backwardness of the season. Yesterday the river was full of them. It proves a serious storm. The point of pines left by Britton on Hubbard's meadow looks very dark in the mist. We cannot see more than eighty rods before as we walk. Saw a sizable hawk in the meadow at N[ut] Meadow crossing, with a white rump, — the hen-harrier (?). The catkins of the *Alnus incana* at Jenny's Brook are longer than ever, — three or four inches. Somebody keeps his minnows there in a barrel. Observed a thistle just springing up in the meadow, a disk of

Vol. III

green a few inches in diameter in the midst of the old decayed leaves, which, now being covered with rain-drops, beaded and edged — the close-packed leaves — *with purple*, made a very rich sight, not to be seen in dry weather. The green leaves of the thistle in a dense disk, edged with purple and covered with bead-like rain-drops, just springing from the meadow. It re-minded me of some delicious fruit, all ripe, quite flat. We sought the desert, it is so agreeable to cross the sand in wet weather. You might dig into the sand for dryness. I saw where somebody appeared to have dug there for turtles' eggs. The catkins of some willows, silvery and not yet blossomed, covered with rain-like dew, look like snow or frost, sleet, adhering to the twigs. The andromeda in Tarbell's Swamp does not look so fresh nor red now. Does it require a sunny day? The buds of the balm-of-Gilead, coated with a gummy sub-stance, mahogany(?)-colored, have already a fragrant odor.

Heard the cackling of geese from over the Ministerial Swamp, and soon appeared twenty-eight geese that flew over our heads toward the other river we had left, we now near the black birches. With these great birds in it, the air seems for the first time inhabited. We detect holes in their wings. Their clank expresses anxiety.

The most interesting fact, perhaps, at present is these few tender yellow blossoms, these half-expanded sterile aments of the willow, seen through the rain and cold, — signs of the advancing year, pledges of the sun's return. Anything so delicate, both in struc-

ture, in color and in fragrance, contrasts strangely with surrounding nature and feeds the faith of man. The fields are acquiring a greenish tinge.

The birds which I see and hear in the midst of the storm are robins, song sparrows, blackbirds, and crows occasionally.

This is the spring of the year. Birds are migrating northward to their breeding-places; the melted snows are escaping to the sea. We have now the unspeakable rain of the Greek winter. The element of water pre-vails. The river has far overflowed its channel. What a conspicuous place Nature has assigned to the skunk-cabbage, first flower to show itself above the bare ground! What occult relation is implied between this plant and man? Most buds have expanded perceptibly, — show some greenness or yellowness. Universally Nature relaxes somewhat of her rigidity, yields to the influence of heat. Each day the grass springs and is greener. The skunk-cabbage is inclosed in its spathe, but the willow catkin expands its bright-yellow blos-soms without fear at the end of its twigs, and the fer-tile flower of the hazel has elevated its almost invisible crimson star of stigmas above the sober and barren earth.

The sight of the sucker floating on the meadow at this season affects me singularly, as if it were a fabu-lous or mythological fish, realizing my *idea* of a fish. It reminds me of pictures of dolphins or of Proteus. I see it for what it is, — not an actual terrene fish, but the fair symbol of a divine idea, the design of an artist. Its color and form, its gills and fins and scales, are perfectly beautiful, because they completely express to my mind what they were intended to express. It is as little fishy as a fossil fish. Such a form as is sculptured on ancient monuments and will be to the end of time; made to point a moral. I am serene and satisfied when the birds fly and the fishes swim as in fable, for the moral is not far off; when the migration of the goose is significant and has a moral to it; when the events of the day have a mythological character, and the most trivial is symbolical.

For the first time I perceive this spring that the year is a circle. I see distinctly the spring arc thus far. It is drawn with a firm line. Every incident is a parable of the Great Teacher. The cranberries washed up in the meadows and into the road on the causeways now yield a pleasant acid.

Why should just these sights and sounds accompany our life? Why should I hear the chattering of blackbirds, why smell the skunk each year? I would fain explore the mysterious relation between myself and these things. I would at least know what these things unavoidably are, make a chart of our life, know how its shores trend, that butterflies reappear and when, know why just this circle of creatures completes the world. Can I not by expectation affect the revolutions of nature, make a day to bring forth something new?

As Cowley loved a garden, so I a forest.

Observe all kinds of coincidences, as what kinds of birds come with what flowers.

An east wind. I hear the clock strike plainly ten or eleven P. M.

Vol. III

April 19. 6 A. M. — Rain still, a fine rain. The robin sang early this morning over the bare ground, an hour ago, nevertheless, ushering in the day. Then the guns were fired and the bells rung to commemorate the anniversary of the birth of a nation's liberty. The birds must live on expectation now. There is nothing in nature to cheer them yet.

That last flock of geese yesterday is still in my eye. After hearing their clangor, looking southwest, we saw them just appearing over a dark pine wood, in an irregular waved line, one abreast of the other, as it were breasting the air and pushing it before them. It made you think of the streams of Cayster, etc., etc. They carry weight, such a weight of metal in the air. Their dark waved outline as they disappear. The grenadiers of the air. Man pygmifies himself at sight of these inhabitants of the air. These stormy days they do not love to fly; they alight in some retired marsh or river. From their lofty pathway they can easily spy out the most extensive and retired swamp. How many there must be, that one or more flocks are seen to go over almost every farm in New England in the spring!

That oak by Derby's is a grand object, seen from any side. It stands like an athlete and defies the tempests in every direction. It has not a weak point. It is an agony of strength. Its branches look like stereotyped gray lightning[1] on the sky. But I fear a price is set upon its sturdy trunk and roots for ship-timber, for knees to make stiff the sides of ships against the Atlantic billows. Like an athlete, it shows its well-developed muscles.

[1] [See vol. ii, p. 382.]

I saw yesterday that the farmers had been out to save their fencing-stuff from the flood, and everywhere it was drawn above high-water mark. The North River had fallen nearly a foot, which I cannot account for, unless some of the dams above had broken away or been suddenly raised [*sic*]. This slight difference in the character of the tributaries of a river and their different histories and adventures is interesting, — all making one character at last.

The willow catkin might be the emblem of spring.

The buds of the lilac look ready to take advantage of the first warm day.

The skin of my nose has come off in consequence of that burning of the sun reflected from the snow.

A stormy day.

2 P. M. — With C. over Wood's Bridge to Lee's and back by Baker Farm.

It is a violent northeast storm, in which it is very difficult and almost useless to carry an umbrella. I am soon wet to my skin over half my body. At first, and for a long time, I feel cold and as if I had lost some vital heat by it, but at last the water in my clothes feels warm to me, and I know not but I am dry. It is a wind to turn umbrellas. The meadows are higher, more wild and angry, and the waves run higher with more white to their caps than before this year. I expect to hear of shipwrecks and of damage done by the tide. This wind, too, keeps the water in the river. It is worth the while to walk to-day to hear the rumbling roar of the wind, as if it echoed through the hollow chambers of the air. It even sounds like thunder some-

times, and when you pass under trees, oaks or elms, that overhang the road, the sound is more grand and stormy still. The wind sounds even in open fields as if on a roof over our heads. It sounds as if amid sails. The mists against the woods are seen driving by in upright columns or sections, as if separated by waves of air. Drifting by, they make a dimly mottled landscape.

What comes flapping low with heavy wing over the middle of the flood? Is it an eagle or a fish hawk? Ah, now he is betrayed, I know not by what motion, — a great gull, right in the eye of the storm. He holds not a steady course, but suddenly he dashes upward even like the surf of the sea which he frequents, showing the under sides of his long, pointed wings, on which do I not see two white spots? He suddenly beats upward thus as if to surmount the airy billows by a slanting course, as the teamster surmounts a slope. The swallow, too, plays thus fantastically and luxuriously and leisurely, doubling some unseen corners in the sky. Here is a gull, then, long after ice in the river. It is a fine sight to see this noble bird leisurely advancing right in the face of the storm.

How sweet is the perception of a new natural fact! suggesting what worlds remain to be unveiled. That phenomenon of the andromeda seen against the sun cheers me exceedingly. When the phenomenon was not observed, it was not at all. I think that no man ever takes an original [*sic*], or detects a principle, without experiencing an inexpressible, as quite infinite and sane, pleasure, which advertises him of the dignity of that truth he has perceived. The thing that pleases me most within these three days is the discovery of the andromeda phenomenon. It makes all those parts of the country where it grows more attractive and elysian to me. It is a natural magic. These little leaves are the stained windows in the cathedral of my world. At sight of any redness I am excited like a cow.

To-day you can find arrowheads, for every stone is washed bright in the rain.

On the Miles road, the *Bæomyces roseus* is now in perfection. Seen on the clay-like surface, amid the dark dead birch and pine leaves, it looks like a minute dull-pinkish bloom, a bloom on the earth, and passes for a terrene flower. It impresses me like a mildew passing into a higher type. It covers large tracts of ground there [with] a pink color. C. calls it flesh-colored, but it is high-colored for that.

Observed the thistle again covered with the beads of rain-drops and tinged with purple on the edges of the leaves. It impressed me again as some rich fruit of the tropics ready to be eaten with a spoon. It suggests pineapples, custard-apples, or what is it? The pasture thistle. All the farmers' cart-paths (for their meadow-hay) are now seen losing themselves in the water. In the midst of this storm I see and hear the robin still and the song sparrow, and see the bluebird also, and the crow, and a hawk a-hunting (a marsh hawk?), and a blue woodpecker, I thought about the size of the hairy. The meadow from Lee's causeway, looking northeast against the storm, looks dark

and, as C. says, slate-colored. I observe that, to get the dark color of the waves, you must not only look in the direction whence they come, but stand as low and nearly on a level with them as possible. If you are on the top of a hill, light is reflected upward to you from their surface. In all this storm and wet, see a muskrat's head in the meadow, as if some one thrust up a mop from below, — literally a drowned rat. Such independence of the moods of nature! He does not care, if he knows, when it rains. Saw a woodchuck out in the storm. The elder buds are forward. I stood by Clematis Brook, hearing the wind roar in the woods and the water in the brook; and, trying to distinguish between these sounds, I at last concluded that the first was a drier sound, the last a wetter. There is a slight dry hum to the wind blowing on the twigs of the forest, a softer and more liquid splashing sound to the water falling on rocks.

Scared up three blue herons in the little pond close by, quite near us. It was a grand sight to see them rise, so slow and stately, so long and limber, with an undulating motion from head to foot, undulating also their large wings, undulating in two directions, and looking warily about them. With this graceful, limber, undulating motion they arose, as if so they got under way, their two legs trailing parallel far behind like an earthy residuum to be left behind. They are large, like birds of Syrian lands, and seemed to oppress the earth, and hush the hillside to silence, as they winged their way over it, looking back toward us. It would affect our

Vol. III

thoughts, deepen and perchance darken our reflections, if such huge birds flew in numbers in our sky. Have the effect of magnetic passes. They are few and rare. Among the birds of celebrated flight, storks, cranes, geese, and ducks. The legs hang down like a weight which they [?] raise, to pump up as it were with its [*sic*] wings and convey out of danger.

The mist to-day makes those near distances which Gilpin tells of. I saw, looking from the railroad to Fair Haven Hill soon after we started, four such, — the wood on E. Hubbard's meadow, dark but open; that of Hubbard's Grove, showing the branches of the trees; Potter's pitch pines, perhaps one solid black mass with outline only distinct; Brown's on the Cliff, but dimly seen through the mist, — one above and beyond the other, with vales of mist between.

To see the larger and wilder birds, you must go forth in the great storms like this. At such times they frequent our neighborhood and trust themselves in our midst. A life of fair-weather walks *might* never show you the goose sailing on our waters, or the great heron feeding here. When the storm increases, then these great birds that carry the mail of the seasons lay to. To see wild life you must go forth at a wild season. When it rains and blows, keeping men indoors, then the lover of Nature must forth. Then returns Nature to her wild estate. In pleasant sunny weather you may catch butterflies, but only when the storm rages that lays prostrate the forest and wrecks the mariner, do you come upon the feeding-grounds of wildest fowl, — of heron and geese.

The light buff(?)-colored hazel catkins, some three inches long, are conspicuous now.

Beside the direct and steady rain, large drops fall from the trees and dimple the water.

Stopped in the barn on the Baker Farm. Sat in the dry meadow-hay, where the mice nest. To sit there, rustling the hay, just beyond reach of the rain while the storm roars without, it suggested an inexpressible dry stillness, the quiet of the haymow in a rainy day; such stacks of quiet and undisturbed thought, when there is not even a cricket to stir in the hay, but all without is wet and tumultuous, and all within is dry and quiet. Oh, what reams of thought one might have here! The crackling of the hay makes silence audible. It is so deep a bed, it makes one dream to sit on it, to think of it. The never-failing jay still screams. Standing in Pleasant Meadow, Conantum shore, seen through the mist and rain, looks dark and heavy and without perspective, like a perpendicular upon its edge.

Crossed by the chain of ponds to Walden. The first, looking back, appears elevated high above Fair Haven between the hills above the swamp, and the next higher yet. Each is distinct, a wild and interesting pond with its musquash house. The second the simplest perhaps, with decayed spruce (?) trees, rising out of the island of andromeda in its midst, draped with usnea, and the mists now driving between them. Saw the *Veratrum viride*, seven or eight inches high, in Well Meadow Swamp, — the greatest growth of the season, at least above water, if not above or below. I doubt if there is so much recent vegetable matter pushed above ground elsewhere; certainly there is not unless of pads under water. Yet it did not start so early as it has grown fast. Walden is clear of ice. The ice left it yesterday, then, the 18th. Trillium Woods make a lee thirty or forty rods off, though you are raised twenty feet on the causeway.

April 20. Morning. — Storms still. The robin sings unfailingly each morning at the time the sun should rise, in spite of dreary rain. Some storms have much more wet in them than others, though they look the same to one in the house, and you cannot walk half an hour without being wet through, while in the others you may keep pretty dry a whole afternoon. Turned up the *Juniperus repens* on Conantum yesterday with my foot, which above had a reddish and rusty look; beneath it was of an unexpectedly fine glaucous tinge with a bright green inmixed. Like many things, it looks best in the rain.

They have many birds for sale in Quincy Market next the fish-market. I observe that one cage bears permanently the label "A good singer" tied to it. Every passer's eye rests on it, and he thinks if he were to buy a bird it would be the occupant of that cage. When I go to Boston the next year I perceive that this cage still wears its label, and I suppose that they put a new bird into this cage without changing the label, as fast as they sell the old one. Any bird that is without a home goes into the cage thus labelled, whatever may be his vocal powers. No deception, no falsehood

seems too stale to succeed. The bird-fancier who recommends his bird as "a good singer" finds customers by the means.

Saw yesterday apparently freshly broken shells of tortoise eggs.

April 21. The storm still continues. When I walked in the storm day before yesterday, I felt very cold when my clothes were first wet through, but at last they, being saturated with water, were tight and kept out the air and fresh wet like a thicker and closer garment, and, the water in them being warmed by my person, I felt warmer and even drier.

The color of the water changes with the sky. It is as dull and sober as the sky to-day.

The woodchuck has not far to go to his home. In foul weather, if he chooses, he can turn in anywhere. He lives on and in the earth. A little parasite on the skin of the earth, that knows the taste of clover and bean leaves and beetles.

2 P. M. — Another walk in the rain.

The river is remarkably high. Nobody remembers when the water came into so many cellars. The water is up to the top of the easternmost end of the easternmost iron truss on the south side of the stone bridge. It is over the Union Turnpike that was west of the bridge, so that it is impassable to a foot-traveller, and *just over* the road west of Wood's Bridge. Of eight carriage roads leading into Concord, the water to my knowledge is now over six, *viz.*, Lee's Bridge, the Corner road, Wood's Bridge, Stone Bridge, Red

Bridge (on both sides, full half a mile in all, over the walls), and the Turnpike. All of these are impassable to foot-travellers except Wood's Bridge, where only a lady would be stopped. I should think that nine inches more would carry it over Flint's Bridge road. How it is at the East Quarter schoolhouse I don't know, nor at the further stone bridge and above, nor at Derby's Bridge. It is probably over the road near Miles's in the Corner, and in two places on the Turnpike, perhaps between J. P. Brown's and C. Miles's. This may suggest how low Concord is situated. Most of the cellars on both sides of the main street east of our house have water in them, and some that are on high ground. All this has been occasioned by the repeated storms of snow and rain for a month or six weeks past, especially the melting of the deep snow of April 13th, and, added to this, the steady rain from Sunday morning, April 18th, to this moment, 8 P. M., April 21st. The element of water is in the ascendant. From the Poplar Hill, the expanse of water looks about as large on the southwest as the northeast. Many new islands are made, — of grassy and sometimes rocky knolls, and clumps of trees and bushes where there is no dry land. Straight willow hedges rising above the water in some places, marking the boundaries of some man's improvements, look prettily. Some of the bushy islands on the Great Meadows are distinctly red at· this distance, even a mile off, from the stems of some bush not red (distinctly) in fair weather, wet now. Is it cornel?

In front of Peter's. — The grass has been springing in spite of the snow and rain, and the earth has an

increased greenish tinge, though it is still decidedly tawny. Men are out in boats in the rain for muskrats, ducks, and geese. It appears to me, as I stand on this hill, that the white houses of the village, seen through the whitish misty storm and rain, are a very suitable color and harmonize well with the scenery, like concentrations of the mist. It is a cheerful color in stormy weather. A few patches of snow are still left. The robins sing through the ceaseless rain, and the song sparrows, and I hear a lark's plaintive strain. I am glad that men are so dispersed over the earth. The need of fuel causes woods to be left, and the use of cattle and horses requires pastures, and hence men live far apart and the walkers of every town have this wide range over forest and field. Sitting behind the wall on the height of the road beyond N. Barrett's (for we have come down the north bank of the river), I love in this weather to look abroad and let my eye fall on some sandy hill clothed with pitch pines on its sides, and covered on its top with the whitish cladonia lichen, usually so dry but now saturated with water. It reminds me of northern regions. I am thinking of the hill near Tarbell's, three quarters of a mile from me. They are agreeable colors to my eye, the green pine and, on the summit, the patches of whitish moss like mildew seen through the mist and rain, for I think, perhaps, how much moisture that soil can bear, how grateful it is to it.

Proceed toward Hubbard's black birch hill. The grass is greenest in the hollows where some snow and ice are still left melting, showing by its greenness how much space they recently covered.

On the east side of Ponkawtasset I hear a robin singing cheerily from some perch in the wood, in the midst of the rain, where the scenery is now wild and dreary. His song a singular antagonism and offset to the storm. As if Nature said, "Have faith, these *two* things I can do." It sings with power, like a bird of great faith that sees the bright future through the dark present, to reassure the race of man, like one to whom many talents were given and who will improve its talents. They are sounds to make a dying man live. They sing not their despair. It is a pure, immortal melody.

The side of the hill is covered first with tall birches rising from a reddish ground, just above a small swamp; then comes a white pine wood whose needles, covered with the fine rain-drops, have a light sheen on them. I see one pine that has been snapped off half-way up in the storm, and, seen against the misty background, it is a distinct yellow mark. The sky is not one homogeneous color, but somewhat mottled with darker clouds and white intervals, and anon it rains harder than before. (I saw the other day the rootlets which spring from the alder above the ground, so tenacious of the earth is it.) Was that a large shad-bush where Father's mill used to be? There is quite a waterfall beyond where the old dam was. Where the rapids commence, at the outlet of the pond, the water is singularly creased as it rushes to the fall, like braided hair, as the poet has it. I did not see any inequalities in the rock it rushed over which could make it so plaited. Here is enough of that suds which in warm weather disperses such a sense of coolness through the

air. Sat under the dark hemlocks, gloomy hemlocks, on the hillside beyond. In a stormy day like this there is the gloom of night beneath them. The ground beneath them almost bare, with wet rocks and fine twigs, without leaves (but hemlock leaves) or grass.

The birds are singing in the rain about the small pond in front, the inquisitive chickadee that has flown at once to the alders to reconnoitre us, the blackbirds, the song sparrow, telling of expanding buds. But above all the robin sings here too, I know not at what distance in the wood. "Did he sing thus in Indian days?" I ask myself; for I have always associated this sound with the village and the clearing, but now I do detect the aboriginal wildness in his strain, and can imagine him a woodland bird, and that he sang thus when there was no civilized ear to hear him, a pure forest melody even like the wood thrush. Every genuine thing retains this wild tone, which no true culture displaces. I heard him even as he might have sounded to the Indian, singing at evening upon the elm above his wigwam, with which was associated in the red man's mind the events of an Indian's life, his childhood. Formerly I had heard in it only those strains which tell of the white man's village life; now I heard those strains which remembered the red man's life, such as fell on the ears of Indian children,— as he sang when these arrowheads, which the rain has made shine so on the lean stubble-field, were fastened to their shaft. Thus the birds sing round this piece of water, some on the alders which fringe, some farther off and higher up the hills; it is a centre to them. Here stand

Vol. III

buttonwoods, an uncommon tree in the woods, naked to look at, and now covered with little tufts of twigs on the sides of the branches in consequence of the disease which has attacked them. The singing of birds implies fair weather.

I see where some farmer has been at pains to knock to pieces the manure which his cattle have dropped in the pasture, so to spread it over the sward. The yellow birch is to me an interesting tree from its remarkable and peculiar color, like a silvery gold. In the pasture beyond the brook, where grow the barberries, huckleberries,— creeping juniper, etc., are half a dozen huge boulders, which look grandly now in the storm, covered with greenish-gray lichens, alternating with the slatish-colored rock. Slumbering, silent, like the exuviæ of giants; some of their cattle left. From a height I look down on some of them as on the backs of oxen. A certain personality, or at least brute life, they seem to have. C. calls it Boulder Field. There is a good prospect southward over the pond, between the two hills, even to the *river meadows* now.

As we stand by the monument on the Battle-Ground, I see a white pine dimly in the horizon just north of Lee's Hill, at 5.30 P. M., its upright stem and straight horizontal feathered branches, while at the same time I hear a robin sing. Each enhances the other. That tree seems the emblem of my life; it stands for the west, the wild. The sight of it is grateful to me as to a bird whose perch it is to be at the end of a weary flight. I [am] not sure whether the music I hear is most in the robin's song or in its boughs. My wealth should

be all in pine-tree shillings. The pine tree that stands on the verge of the clearing, whose boughs point westward; which the village does not permit to grow on the common or by the roadside; which is banished from the village; in whose boughs the crow and the hawk have their nests.

We have heard enough nonsense about the Pyramids. If Congress should vote to rear such structures on the prairies to-day, I should not think it worth the while, nor be interested in the enterprise. It was the foolish undertaking of some tyrant. "But," says my neighbor, "when they were built, all men believed in them and were inspired to build them." Nonsense! nonsense! I believe that they were built essentially in the same spirit in which the public works of Egypt, of England, and America are built to-day,— the Mahmoudi Canal, the Tubular Bridge, Thames Tunnel, and the Washington Monument. The inspiring motive in the actual builders of these works is garlic, or beef, or potatoes. For meat and drink and the necessaries of life men can be hired to do many things. "Ah," says my neighbor, "but the stones are fitted with such nice joints!" But the joints were nicer yet before they were disjointed in the quarry. Men are wont to speak as if it were a noble work to build a pyramid,— to set, forsooth, a hundred thousand Irishmen at work at fifty cents a day to piling stone. As if the good joints could ennoble it, if a noble motive was wanting! To ramble round the world to see that pile of stones which ambitious Mr. Cheops, an Egyptian booby, like some Lord Timothy Dexter, caused a hundred thousand poor devils to pile up for low wages, which contained for all treasure the thigh-bone of a cow. The tower of Babel has been a good deal laughed at. It was just as sensible an undertaking as the Pyramids, which, because they were completed and have stood to this day, are admired. I don't believe they made a better joint than Mr. Crab, the joiner, can.[1]

I have not this season heard more robins sing than this rainy day.

April 22. It still rains. The water is over the road at Flint's Bridge, and, as I am told, has been for some time over the J. Miles road in the Corner, and near the further stone bridge. So that there is now only the Boston road open, unless we regard the Walden road as coming from Wayland and not from Lee's Bridge. At 9 A. M. it was five and one half inches higher than the east end of the eastern truss, horizontal part, on the south side of the stone bridge. Up to the top of the lowest stone step on the north side east end of railroad bridge. Mr. Stacy thinks it was higher thirty years ago, when a man, horse, and sleigh were washed off the Red Bridge road and lodged against a tree in the meadow. And Sam Barrett thinks it was about one foot higher some thirty-five years ago. Water a foot deep on Wood's Bridge road. Abel Hunt saw a flock of geese this morning.

This flood tempts men to build boats. I saw two on the stocks this morning. It is pleasant work to see progressing.

[1] [See *Walden*, p. 64; Riv. 93.]

Vol. III

ing his tail too all the while. I thought of what Gilpin says, that he sailed and steered by means of his tail. Sat under Potter's oak, the ground thickly strewn with broken acorn shells and cups and twigs, the short, close-nibbled sward of last year. Our dog sends off a partridge with a whir, far across the open field and the river, like a winged bullet. From Cliffs see much snow on the mountains. The pine on Lee's shore of the pond, seen against the light water this cloudy weather from part way down the Cliff, is an agreeable object to me. When the outline and texture of white pine is thus seen against the water or the sky, it is an affecting sight. The shadow of the Cliff on Conantum in the semi-sunshine, with indistinct edge and a reddish tinge from bushes here and there!

I want things to be incredible, — too good to appear true. C. says, "After you have been to the post-office once you are damned!" But I answer that it depends somewhat on whether you get a letter or not. If you should not get a letter there is some hope for you. If you would be wise, learn science and then forget it. A boat on the river, on the white surface, looks black, and the boatman like Charon. I see swarms of gnats in the air. What is that grass with a yellow blossom which I find now on the Cliff?[1] It is the contrast between sunshine and storm that is most pleasing; the gleams of sunshine in the midst of the storm are the most memorable. Saw that winkle-like fungus, *fresh and green*, covering an oak stump to-day with concentric marks, spirally

[1] *Carex marginata* (?), early sedge, the earliest grass [*sic*] that flowers.

P. M. — Up river on east side.

It takes this day to clear up gradually; successive sun-showers still make it foul. But the sun feels very warm after the storm. This makes five stormy days. Sunday, Monday, Tuesday, Wednesday, Thursday. The water, slightly agitated, looks bright when the sun shines. Saw four hawks soaring high in the heavens over the Swamp Bridge Brook. At first saw three; said to myself there must be four, and found the fourth. Glad are they, no doubt, to be out after being confined by the storm. I hear bees (?) humming near the brook, which reminded me of the telegraph harp.

I love to see the dull gravity, even stolidity, of the farmer opposed to the fluency of the lawyer or official person. The farmer sits silent, not making any pretensions nor feeling any responsibility even to apprehend the other, while the Judge or Governor talks glibly and with official dispatch, all lost on the farmer, who minds it not, but looks out for the main chance, with his great inexpressive face and his two small eyes, looking the first in the face and rolling a quid in the back part of his mouth. The lawyer is wise in deeds, but the farmer, who buys land, puts the pertinent questions respecting the title.

I observe the *Parmelia saxatilis* in many places, now turned a pinkish. The yellow lily leaves appear no more advanced than when I first observed them. A strange dog accompanied us to-day, a hunting dog, gyrating about us at a great distance, beating every bush and barking at the birds, with great speed, gyrat-

arranged, sometimes in a circle, very handsome. I love this apparent exuberance of nature.

The maples in the side swamp near Well Meadow are arranged nearly in a circle in the water. This stranger dog has good habits for a companion, he keeps so distant. He never trusts himself near us, though he accompanies us for miles. On the most retired, the wildest and craggiest, most precipitous hillside you will find some old road by which the teamster carted off the wood. It is pleasant sometimes looking thirty or forty rods into an open wood, where the trunks of the trees are plainly seen, and patches of soft light on the ground. The hylas peep now in full chorus, but are silent on my side of the pond. The water at 6 P. M. is one and a half inches higher than in the morning, *i. e.* seven inches above the iron truss. The strain of the red-wing on the willow spray over the water to-night is liquid, bubbling, watery, almost like a tinkling fountain, in perfect harmony with the meadow. It oozes, trickles, tinkles, bubbles from his throat, — *bob-y-lee-e-e*, and then its shrill, fine whistle.

The villagers walk the streets and talk of the great rise of waters.

At 10 P. M. the northern lights are flashing, like some grain sown broadcast in the sky. I hear the hylas peep on the meadow as I stand at the door.

The early sedge (?) grows on the side of the Cliffs in little tufts with small yellow blossoms, *i. e.* with yellow anthers, low in the grass.

Mr. Holbrook tells me he heard and saw martins (?) yesterday.[1]

[1] Storm ends this evening.

April 23. The water has risen one and a half inches at six this morning since last night. It is now, then, eight and a half inches above the iron truss, *i. e.* the horizontal part of it.[1] There is absolutely no passing, in carriages or otherwise, over Hubbard's and the Red Bridge roads, and over *none* [*sic*] of the bridges for foot-travellers. Throughout this part of the country most people do not remember so great a flood, but, judging from some accounts, it was probably as high here thirty-five years ago. The willow catkins have made but little progress for a week. They have suffered from the cold rain and wind, and are partly blasted. It is a pleasant sight, among the pleasantest, at this season, to see the at first reddish anthers of the sterile catkins of our earliest willow bursting forth on their upper sides like rays of sunshine from amidst the *downy* fog, turning a more and more lively yellow as the pollen appears, — like a flash of sulphur. It is like the sun bursting out of a *downy* cloud or mists. I hear this morning, in the pine woods above the railroad bridge, for the first time, that delicious cool-sounding *wetter-wetter-wetter-wetter-wet'* from that small bird (pine warbler?) in the tops of the pines.[2] I associate it with the *cool, moist, evergreen spring* woods.

The wood pewee[3] on an elm sings now *peer-r-weet peer-r-weet, peer-wee'.* It is not the simple *peer-r-wet*

[1] *Greatest height. Vide* Aug. 23d, when apparently it was as low as any time that year.

[2] *Vide* April 24 [p. 464].

[3] [This is queried in pencil after the word "wood." The bird must have been a phœbe.]

peer-r-wee' that I heard at first. Will it not change next to that more tender strain?

Vegetation starts when the earth's axis is sufficiently inclined; *i. e.* it follows the sun. Insects and all the smaller animals (as well as many larger) follow vegetation. The fishes, the small fry, start probably for this reason; worms come out of the trees; buffaloes finally seek new pastures; water-bugs appear on the water, etc., etc. Next, the large fish and fish hawks, etc., follow the small fry; flycatchers follow the insects and worms. (The granivorous birds, who can depend on the supplies of dry seeds of last year, are to some extent independent of the seasons, and can remain through the winter or come early in the spring, and they furnish food for a few birds of prey at that season.) Indians follow the buffaloes; trout, suckers, etc., follow the water-bugs, etc.; reptiles follow vegetation, insects, and worms; birds of prey, the flycatchers, etc. Man follows all, and all follow the sun. The greater or less abundance of food determines migrations. If the buds are deceived and suffer from frost, then are the birds. The great necessary of life for the brute creation is food; next, perhaps, shelter, *i. e.* a suitable climate; thirdly, perhaps, security from foes.

The storm may be said to have fairly ended last night. I observed yesterday that it was drier in most fields, pastures, and even meadows that were not reached by the flood, *immediately* after this remarkable fall of water than at the beginning. The condition of the fields has been steadily improving for walkers.

Vol. III

I think one reason is that there was some frost in the ground which the rain melted, so that the ground soaked up the water. But no doubt it goes to prove the dryness of our sandy soil and absence of springs.

At 6 P. M. the water has fallen an inch and a half.

Heard the pigeon woodpecker to-day, that long-continued unmusical note, — somewhat like a robin's, heard afar, — yet pleasant to hear because associated with a more advanced stage of the season. Saw the *Fringilla hyemalis* to-day, lingering still.

April 24. 6 A. M. — Water has fallen an inch and a half since last night, — which is at a regular rate.

I know two species of men. The vast majority are men of society. They live on the surface; they are interested in the transient and fleeting; they are like driftwood on the flood. They ask forever and only the news, the froth and scum of the eternal sea. They use policy; they make up for want of matter with manner. They have many letters to write. Wealth and the approbation of men is to them success. The enterprises of society are something final and sufficing for them. The world advises them, and they listen to its advice. They live wholly an evanescent life, creatures of circumstance. It is of prime importance to them who is the president of the day. They have no knowledge of truth, but by an exceedingly dim and transient instinct, which stereotypes the church and some other institutions. They dwell, they are ever, right in my face and eyes like gnats; they are like motes, so near the eyes that, looking beyond, they appear like blurs;

they have their being between my eyes and the end of my nose. The *terra firma* of my existence lies far beyond, behind them and their improvements. If they write, the best of them deal in "elegant literature." Society, man, has no prize to offer me that can tempt me; not one. That which interests a town or city or any large number of men is always something trivial, as politics. It is impossible for me to be interested in what interests men generally. Their pursuits and interests seem to me frivolous. When I am most myself and see the clearest, men are least to be seen; they are like *muscae volitantes*, and that they are seen at all is the proof of imperfect vision. These affairs of men are so narrow as to afford no vista, no distance; it is a shallow foreground only, no large extended views to be taken. Men put to me frivolous questions: When did I come? where am I going? That was a more pertinent question, — what I lectured for? — which one auditor put once to another.[1] What an ordeal it were to make men pass through, to consider how many ever put to you a vital question! Their knowledge of something better gets no further than what is called religion and spiritual knockings.

Now that the sun shines and the sky is blue, the water is a dark blue which in the storm was light or whitish. It follows the sky's, though the sky is a lighter blue.

The lilac buds have looked as forward as any for many weeks.

2 P. M. — To Carlisle Bridge *via* Flint's Bridge, bank

[1] [*Cape Cod, and Miscellanies,* p. 470; *Misc.,* Riv. 272.]

of river, rear of Joel Barrett's, returning by bridle-road.

The elms are now fairly in blossom. It is one of those clear, *washing* days, — though the air is cold, — such as succeed a storm, when the air is clear and flowing, and the cultivated ground and the roads shine. Passed Flint's road on the wall. Sorrel is well under weigh, and cinquefoil. White oaks still hold their leaves. The pitch pine is a cheerful tree at this season, with its lively yellow-green in the sunshine, while the landscape is still russet and dead-grass colored.

Sitting by the road beyond N. Barrett's, the colors of the world are: overhead a very light blue sky, darkest in the zenith, lightest in the horizon, with scattered white clouds *seeming* thickest in the horizon; all around the undulating earth a very light tawny color, from the dead grass, with the reddish and gray of forests mingled with evergreen; and, in the lap of earth, very dark blue rippled water, answering to the light blue above; the shadows of clouds flitting over all below; the spires of woods fringing the horizon on every side, and, nearer, single trees here and there seen with dark branches against the sky. This tawny ground divided by walls and houses, white, light slate, and red sprinkled here and there.

Ball's Hill and the rest are deep sunk in the flood. The level water-line appears to best advantage when it appears thus to cut the trees and hills. It looks as if the water were just poured into its basin and simply stood so high. No permanent shore gives you this pleasure.

Vol. III

Saw the honey-bees on the staminate flowers of the willow catkins by the roadside (such as I described April 23d), with little bottles of the yellow pollen, apparently, as big as pin-heads on their thighs. With these flowers, then, come bees. Is there honey in staminate flowers? The innocent odor of spring flowers, flavorless, as a breakfast. They will be more spiced by and by.

Went over the cladonia hills toward Tarbell's. A small tree, an oak for instance, looks large on a bare hilltop. The farmers, whom the storm has delayed, are busily plowing and overhauling their manure. Observed the ants at work on a large ant-heap. They plainly begin as soon as the snow is off and the ground thawed. Gold-thread, an evergreen, still bright in the swamps. The rattlesnake-plantain has fresh leaves. A wall running over the top of a rocky hill, with the light seen through its chinks, has a pretty effect. The sparrows, frogs, rabbits, etc., are made to resemble the ground for their protection; but so is the hawk that preys on them; but he is of a lighter color beneath, that creeping things over which he hovers may confound him with the sky. The marsh hawk is not easily distinguished from the meadow or the stems of the maples. The water is still over the causeway on both sides of Carlisle Bridge for a long distance. It is a straight flood now for about four miles. Fortunately for the bridge the wind has not been very high since the flood was at its height. The leaves of the hardhack, curled up, show their white under sides. On the bridle-road observed the interesting light-crim-

son star-like flowers of the hazel, the catkins being now more yellowish. This is a singular and interesting part of Concord, extensive and rather flat rocky pastures without houses or cultivated fields on any but this unused bridle-road, from which I hear the frogs peep. These are Channing's "moors." He went in on this road to chop, and this is the scene of his "Woodman."

Heard again (*in the village*) that *vetter-vetter-vetter-vetter-vet'*, or *tchi-tchi-tchi-tchi-tchi-tchi-tchi'* very rapidly repeated, which I heard April 23d,[1] and perhaps the same that I saw April 17th (described April 18th).[2] I am pretty sure it is the pine warbler, yellow beneath, with faint olivaceous marks on the sides, olivaceous above, tail forked, about the size of a yellow-bird.

I have not seen the fox-colored sparrow for some weeks. Thought I saw a loon on Walden yesterday.

April 25. It is related that Giorgio Barbarelli, Titian's friend, defending painting against the charge of being an incomplete art because it could exhibit but one side of a picture, laid a wager with some sculptor that he could represent the back, face, and both profiles of a man, without the spectator being obliged to walk round it as a statue. He painted "a warrior, who, having his back turned towards the spectator, stood looking at himself in a fountain, in whose limpid waters his full front figure was reflected. At the left

[1] [See p. 458.]
[2] [See p. 433, where the bird described would seem to be a yellow palm, or yellow redpoll, warbler.]

of the warrior was suspended his suit of polished steel armor, in which was mirrored, with exact fidelity, the whole of his left side. At the right was painted a looking-glass, which reflected that side;" and thus he won the wager. So I would fain represent some truths as roundly and solidly as a statue, or as completely and in all their relations as Barbarelli his warrior, — so that you may see round them.

1.30 P. M. — Up railroad, returning through Acton *via* powder-mills and Second Division.

The frogs peep at midday. The bees are on the pistillate flowers of the early willows, — the honey-bee, a smaller, fly-like bee with very transparent wings and bright-yellow marks on the abdomen, and also a still smaller bee, more like the honey-bee. They all hum like summer. The water in the meadow beyond J. Hosmer's is still and transparent, and I hear the more stertorous sound or croak of frogs from it, such as you associate with sunny, warmer, calm, placid spring weather. The tortoises are out sunning. The painted tortoise on a tussock. A spotted tortoise on the railroad *hisses* when I touch it with my foot and draws its [head] in. What is that bird on the willows, size of a vireo, yellow below, with darker lines, chestnut crown, whitish (?) line over eye, two white feathers in tail, yellow-olive back, darker tail?[1] Yarrow is started. Saw the first kingfisher, and heard his most unmusical note. That warmer, placid pool and stertorous sound of frogs must not be forgotten, — beneath the railroad causeway. The bees hum on the early willows that

[1] It must have been the yellow redpoll warbler (*Sylvia petechia*).

grow in the sand. They appear to have nearly stripped the sterile flowers of their pollen, and each has its little yellow parcel. The year is stretching itself, is waking up.

If a small oak on a bare hilltop looks large, a large one looks small. That one by Derby's stand, two rods off, looks no bigger than a corpulent man; go close up to it, and it dwarfs an ox, it is as broad as a cart or a wood-shed door. That is a handsome elm by Derby's Bridge, with nine branches springing from near the ground. Near the factory, a willow with small reddish catkins just beginning to expand looks like a peach tree with its blossom-buds.

Found in the midst of the woods in Acton, on the Concord line, a small shanty or shed, whitewashed, which I mistook at first, through the trees, for a white marble tomb with a slight clearing about it. Is it a bowling-alley? Is it a pigeon-place? What means this sign on the tree, "O. B. Trask"? that rocking-chair under a pine? Went through a kind of gate into a little green patch which had been *spaded* up the previous year, about a quarter of an acre cleared, and winter rye coming up on a part of it. The shed was locked; no trace of a recent inhabitant or visitor; window a bit of glass no bigger than your hand, flat against a joist; sign on the roof, "Any pirson who shall Burn or distroy this bilding is liable to 15 years imprisonment;" one or two herbs, catnip or balm, about the door, protected with sticks; a sunken barrel to catch the drip of the eaves; the stones picked up and thrown into heaps; a kind of small truck; another sign, "O. B. Trask T. line," cut on a board and nailed to a pine.

It makes a sad impression, like a poorhouse or hospital. Is he insane or of sound, serene mind? Is he weak, or is he strong? If I knew that the occupant was a cheerful, strong, serene man, how rejoiced I should be to see his shanty!

That steep hill west of the Concord line, from which the autumnal view is got, is covered on the top with that short moss now in fruit. The filaments, seen singly and close to, are of a varnished-mahogany color, but seen in dense masses, as you approach the summit in the ascent, with the sunlight on them, they are a light crimson surmounted with the whitish capsules. It has a very rich effect like a sort of crimson mould or mildew, flower-like. The bare top of the hill is covered with sere tufts of fine grass, this crimson moss, that reddish frosted (?) saxifrage (?) in patches, and with cladonias, with much bare pebbly earth.

In the rear of the Major Heywood house, lay on the sere grass in a long pasture bounded by a pitch pine wood and heard the robin sing. What different tints of blue in the same sky! It requires to be parted by white clouds that the delicacy and depth of each part may appear. Beyond a narrow wisp or feather of mist, how different the sky! Sometimes it is full of light, especially toward the horizon. The sky is never seen to be of so deep and delicate a blue as when it is seen between downy clouds.

The mayflower is well budded and ready to blossom, but not yet out; nor the andromeda, nor saxifrage, nor violet, that I can find. I am surprised to find the cowslip in full bloom at Second Division Meadow,

numerous flowers. Growing in the water, it is not, comparatively, so backward this year perhaps. Its heart or kidney shaped, crenate green leaves, which had not freshly grown when I was here before, have suddenly pushed up. The snows soon melted on this meadow. The horse-tail[1] too is in flower.[2] And what is that low, regular, red-leaved and red-rooted plant in the meadow with the cowslip?[3] Yet we walk over snow and ice a long distance in the road here. I hear the first wood thrush singing faintly and at a distance. The hills are yet the color of a Roxbury russet, *i. e.* a russet without the red. Heard from a chickadee a note like one of the notes of a brown thrasher. Saw a dandelion in blossom at Jenny's in the water. Water over the road still, beyond J. P. Brown's, toward C. Miles.

We have reached the Clamshell Hill. The setting sun, which we do not see behind Loring's wood, which we have not seen for an hour or two behind dark dull clouds in the west, is falling bright and warm at last on the eastern hills and woods, and the windows of the village, which are as bright as itself. It is best to see it thus from the shade. Now the sun is set, and we have turned the point of Loring's wood and see a long, low gilded cloud just above the horizon, so low that the fluctuating, seething (?) over the fields produces a tremulous motion which the beholder refers to the gilded edge of that far-distant cloud. I do not remember to have seen this watery trembling in the horizon before.

[1] Field (?) [horse-tail].
[2] Sheds its pollen in the house the 27th, abundant and pea-green.
[3] Meadow saxifrage.

April 26. Chickweed (*Stellaria media*), naturalized, shows its humble star-like white flowers now on rather dirty weather-worn branches in low, damp gardens. Also the smaller white flowers of the shepherd's-purse, which is already six or eight inches high, in the same places, *i. e.* Cheney's garden. Both, according to Dewey, introduced and naturalized.

What they call April weather, threatening rain notwithstanding the late long-continued rains.

P. M. — Rambled amid the shrub oak hills beyond Hayden's.

Lay on the dead grass in a cup-like hollow sprinkled with half-dead low shrub oaks. As I lie flat, looking close in among the roots of the grass, I perceive that its endless ribbon has pushed up about one inch and is green to that extent, — such is the length to which the spring has gone here, — though when you stand up the green is not perceptible. It is a dull, rain dropping and threatening afternoon, inclining to drowsiness. I feel as if I could go to sleep under a hedge. The landscape wears a subdued tone, quite soothing to the feelings; no glaring colors. I begin now to leave off my greatcoat.

The frogs at a distance are now so numerous that, instead of the distinct shrill peeps, it is one dreamy sound. It is not easy to tell where or how far off they are. When you have reached their pool, they seem to recede as you advance. As you squat by the side of the pool, you still see no motion in the water, though your ears ring with the sound, seemingly and probably within three feet. I sat for ten minutes on the watch, waving my hand over the water that they might betray themselves, a tortoise, with his head out, a few feet off, watching me all the while, till at last I caught sight of a frog under a leaf, and caught and pocketed him; but when I looked afterward, he had escaped. The moment the dog stepped into the water they stopped. They are very shy. Hundreds filled the air with their shrill peep. Yet two or three could be distinguished by some peculiarity or variation in their note. Are these different?

The *Viola ovata* budded. Saw pollywogs two or three inches long.

April 27. Heard the field or rush sparrow this morning (*Fringilla juncorum*), George Minott's "huckleberry-bird." It sits on a birch and sings at short intervals, apparently answered from a distance. It is clear and sonorous heard afar; but I found it quite impossible to tell from which side it came; sounding like *phe, phe, phe, pher-pher-tw-tw-tw-t-t-t-t*, — the first three slow and loud, the next two syllables quicker, and the last part quicker and quicker, becoming a clear, sonorous trill or rattle, like a spoon in a saucer. Heard also a chipping sparrow (*F. socialis*).

It has rained a little in the night. The landscape is still dark and wet. The hills look very dank, but I notice that some houses, one yellow one especially, look much better in this light.

The aments of the balm-of-Gilead are just beginning to appear (are they the male or female?),[1] with the

[1] [This is altered in pencil to read, "they are female."]

That smallest willow, sage-like, and another, reddish osier-like, are just beginning to show their catkins in rather dry places. I see another similar to last, with female catkins already in bloom; also another, low and yellowish, with half-inch elliptical catkins showing red anthers within the down. *Bæomyces roseus* does not show in dry weather. The *Viola pedata* is advancing. What is that weed the under side of whose radical leaves is now a claret-color, by a sandy path-side?[1] At the spring by the Corner road, the grass is now of [what] I must call a fiery green. It is an eye-salve, a collyrium, to behold it. Here, where the snow cannot lie long on the ground, vegetation has made great progress. The common angelica is a foot high, the skunk-cabbage leaves five inches broad, the wood anemone is budded, and a thimble-berry or rose leaved out; and several smaller green weeds there are. It is not only warmer for the water, but it is sheltered from the wind. Saw what I take to be the barn swallow. Some of the mosses bear now a green fruit.

On Conantum Cliffs, whose seams dip to the northwest at an angle of 50° (?) and run northeast and southwest, I find to-day for the first time the early saxifrage (*Saxifraga vernalis*) in blossom, growing high and dry in the narrow seams, where there is no soil for it but a little green moss. Following thus early after the bare rock, it is one of the first flowers, not only in the spring of the year, but in the spring of the world. It can take advantage of a perpendicular cliff where

[1] *Aster undulatus?*

large leaf-bud in the centre. The leaves in the last are larger and more developed than those of any tree which I have noticed this season. The bud is filled with "a fragrant, viscid balsam," which is yellowish and difficult to wash from the fingers. It is an agreeable fragrance at this season. A nearer approach to leaves than in any tree?

Is that a golden willow by the stone bridge, with bright-yellow twigs (the most westerly on the south) and reddish-tipped catkins, five eighths of an inch long, just appearing before leaves (male or female?)?

The balsam of the balm-of-Gilead buds appears to protect the early expanding leaves from the wet.

Should I not have mentioned the butcher-bird, the downy woodpecker or sapsucker, and the white-breasted nuthatch among the winter birds? Also the quail and partridge, etc.

2.30 P. M. — To Conantum *via* railroad bridge.

The Corner road still impassable to foot-travellers. Water eighteen or twenty inches deep; must have been two feet deeper. Observed the spotted tortoise in the water of the meadow on J. Hosmer's land, by riverside. Bright-yellow spots on both shell and head, yet not regularly disposed, but as if, when they were finished in other respects, the maker had sprinkled them with a brush. This fact, that the yellow spots are common to the shell and the head, affected me considerably, as evincing the action of an artist from without; spotted with reference to my eyes. One, I suppose the male, was larger than the other, with a depressed and lighter-colored sternum.

the snow cannot lie and fronting the south. In exactly the same places grows the columbine, now well budded and seven or eight inches high. The higher up the rock and the more sheltered and sunny the location, the earlier they are. Also the first plantain-leaved everlasting (Gray's *Antennaria plantaginifolia*) is in blossom in a sheltered place in the grass at the top of the rock. The thimble-berry and the sweet-briar are partly leaved out in the crevices of the rock, and the latter emits its fragrance. The half-open bud of the saxifrage, showing the white of the petals in a corymb or cyme, on a short stem, surrounded by its new leaves mingled with the purplish tips of the calyx-leaves, is handsomer than when it is fully expanded. This is a place to look for early blossoms of the saxifrage, columbine, and plantain-leaved everlasting, — the first two especially. The crevices of the rock (cliff) make natural hothouses for them, affording dryness, warmth, and shelter.

It is astonishing how soon and unexpectedly flowers appear, when the fields are scarcely tinged with green. Yesterday, for instance, you observed only the radical leaves of some plants; to-day you pluck a flower.

See the first downy woodpecker, or sapsucker, tapping an elm. He taps very rapidly, then turns his head as if listening to hear the worm; plainly is not now making a hole. Do we see him in the winter? What is that alarmed, loud, short, whistling note that I hear? A woodpecker?

Found the first *Gnaphalium purpureum*, purplish cudweed, on Conantum by the edge of a rock. Its humble, woolly, purplish-white flower, close to the ground amid its greenish leaves, downy and white on the under side, is the more interesting for appearing at this time, especially if it is seen with the dew on it, though it bears transportation. A little purplish button, the larger central shoot or bud being surrounded by five others smaller. Its leaves have not three nerves. The hickory buds show a little yellow; the black birch buds and the bass-wood look fresh. There are large clouds and extensive shadows on land and the broad water, and a cheerful bright light on the russet grass (I am still on Conantum), which all together make our landscape appear larger-featured than usual. Gooseberry bushes in the garden have leaved out partly.

April 28. I scarcely know why I am excited when, in M. Huc's book, I read of the country of the Mongol Tartars as the "Land of Grass," but I am, as much as if I were a cow.[1]

2.30 P. M. — To Cliffs and Heywood's Brook.

Are not the flowers which appear earliest in the spring the most primitive and simplest? They have been in this town thus far, as I have observed them this spring, putting them down in the order in which I think they should be named, using Gray's names: —

[1] *Symplocarpus fœtidus* (well advanced Feb. 13th, '51)[2]
[2] *Alnus incana* April 11
[3] " *serrulata* 8

[1] Drive about the 10th of May to Ashburnham.
[2] N. B. Spring of '51 ten days or more earlier.

[4] *Acer rubrum* [1] April 9 one by Red Bridge
[5] *Salix*, willow, earliest 12
[6] *Ulmus Americana* [2] 15 one, Cheney's (others ten days or fourteen later)
[7] *Populus tremuloides* 15
[8] *Corylus* " 16 perhaps before the last[3]
[9] *Carex Pennsylvanica* [4] 22
[10] *Caltha palustris* 25 many
[11] *Stellaria media* [5] 26 Cheney's garden
[12] *Capsella Bursa-pastoris* 26 " "
[13] *Taraxacum Dens-leonis* 25 one in water (seen by another the 20th)
[14] *Equisetum arvense* 25 in water
[15] *Gnaphalium purpureum* 27 (about April 16th, '51)
[16] *Saxifraga Virginiensis* 27 (April 22d, '51)
[17] *Antennaria plantaginifolia* 27
[18] *Ranunculus fascicularis* 28 only two (abundant April 22d, '51)

All but the 3d, 8th, 11th, 12th observed in the very best season, and these within a day (?) of their flowering.[6]

I observe that the first six are decidedly water or water-loving plants, and the 10th, 13th, and 14th were found in the water and are equally if not more confined to that element. The 7th and 8th belong to the cooler zones of the earth, the 7th, according to Emerson, as far north as 64° and comes up (is it this?) on burnt lands first and will grow in dry, cool, dreary places. The 9th on a dry, warm rocky hillside, — the earliest (?) grass to blossom, — also the 18th; the 11th and 12th in cold, damp gardens, like the earth first

[1] [*Rubrum* crossed out in pencil and *dasycarpum* substituted.]
[2] [Queried in pencil.] [3] *Corylus rostrata* when?
[4] [Queried in pencil.] [5] [Queried in pencil.]
[6] N. B. Is the *Hepatica triloba* found here?

Vol. III

made dry land; the 15th and 17th on dry (scantily clad with grass) fields and hills, hardy; the 16th, sunny bare rocks, in seams on moss, where also in a day or two the columbine will bloom. The 18th is also indebted to the warmth of the rocks.

This may, perhaps, be nearly the order of the world's creation. Thus we have in the spring of the year the spring of the world represented. — Such were the first localities afforded for plants, — water-bottoms, bare rocks, and scantily clad lands, and land recently bared of water.

The spotted tortoise is spotted on shell, head, tail, and legs. Fresh leaves of a neottia pale and not distinctly veined. Red Solomon's-seal berries on their short stems prostrate on the dead leaves, some of them plump still. One man has turned his cows out to pasture. Have not seen the slate-colored snowbird for a few days. I am getting my greatcoat off, but it is a cold and wintry day, with snow-clouds appearing to draw water, but cold water, surely, or out of the north side of the well; a few flakes in the air; drawing snow as well as water. From Fair Haven the landscape all in shadow, apparently to the base of the mountains, but the Peterboro hills are in sunshine and unexpectedly are white with snow (no snow here, unless in some hollows in the woods), reflecting the sun, more obvious for the sunshine. I never saw them appear so near. It is startling thus to look into winter.

How suddenly the flowers bloom! Two or three days ago I could not, or did not, find the leaves of the crowfoot. To-day, not knowing it well, I looked in vain, till

at length, in the very warmest nook in the grass above the rocks of the Cliff, I found two bright-yellow blossoms, which betrayed the inconspicuous leaves and all. The spring flowers wait not to perfect their leaves before they expand their blossoms. The blossom in so many cases precedes the leaf; so with poetry? They flash out. In the most favorable locality you will find flowers earlier than the May goers will believe. This year, at least, one flower (of several) hardly precedes another, but as soon as the storms were over and pleasant weather came, all blossomed at once, having been retarded so long. This *appears* to be particularly true of the herbaceous flowers. How much does this happen every year?

There is no important change in the color of the woods yet. There are fewer dry leaves; buds color the maples; and, perhaps, the bark on some last year's shoots, as the willows, is brighter; and some willows, covered with catkins, and even alders, maples, elms, and poplars show at a distance. The earth has now a greenish tinge, and the ice, of course, has universally given place to water for a long time past. These are general aspects. The *Veratrum viride* at Well Meadow is fifteen or sixteen inches high, the most of a growth this year. The angelica (?) at the Corner Spring is pretty near it.

I suppose the geese are all gone. And the ducks? Did the snowbirds go off with the pleasant weather?

Standing above the first little pond east of Fair Haven, this bright reflecting water surface is seen plainly at a higher level than the distant pond. It has a singular but pleasant effect on the beholder to see considerable sheets of water standing at different levels. Pleasant to see lakes like platters full of water. Found a large cockle(?)-shell by the shore of this little pond. It reminds me that all the earth is seashore, — the sight of these little shells inland. It is a beach I stand on. Is the male willow on the east end of this pondlet — catkins about three quarters of an inch long and just bursting, commonly on the side and always before any leaves — the brittle gray willow (*Salix grisea*)? That small, flat, downy gnaphalium in sandy paths, — is it the fragrant life-everlasting? The andromeda requires the sun. It is now merely a dull reddish brown with light (grayish?) from the upper surface of the leaves. Frog-spawn a mass of transparent jelly bigger than the two fists, composed of contiguous globules or eyes, with each a little squirming pollywog (?) in the centre, a third of an inch long.

Walden is yellowish (apparently) next the shore, where you see the sand, then green in still shallow water, then, or generally, deep-blue.[1] This as well under the railroad, and now that the trees have not leaved out, as under pines.[2]

That last long storm brought down a coarse, elephantine sand foliage in the Cut. Slumbrous ornaments for a cave or subterranean temple, such as at Elephantium? I see no willow leaves yet. A maple by Heywood's meadow has opened its sterile blossoms.

[1] [A pencilled interrogation-point in parentheses follows the word "blue."]
[2] [*Walden*, p. 196 ; Riv. 276.]

Why is this (and maples generally) so much later than the Red Bridge one?[1]

A week or more ago I made this list of early willows in Massachusetts, according to Gray, putting Emerson in brackets : —

Salix tristis (sage willow).
S. *humilis* (low bush willow); S. *Muhlenbergiana ; S. conifera.*
S. *discolor* (glaucous willow) ; [two-colored willow, bog willow]; S. *sensitiva.*
S. *eriocephala* (silky-headed willow) ; S. *prinoides* (?) ; S. *crassa;* "closely resembles the last," *i. e.* S. *discolor ;* [woolly-headed swamp].
S. *sericea* (silky-leaved willow) ; S. *grisea ;* [brittle gray].

April 29. Observed a fire yesterday on the railroad, — Emerson's Island that was. The leaves are dry enough to burn; and I see a smoke this afternoon in the west horizon. There is a slight haziness on the woods, as I go to Mayflower Road at 2.30 P. M., which advances me further into summer. Is that the arrowhead, so forward with its buds, in the Nut Meadow ditch? The ground is dry. I smell the dryness of the woods. Their shadows look more inviting, and I am reminded of the hum of bees. The pines have an appearance which they have not worn before, yet not easy to describe. The mottled light (sunlight) and shade, seen looking into the woods, is more like summer. But the season is most forward at the Second Division Brook, where the cowslip is in blossom, —

[1] [The Red Bridge one (see vol. iv of the *Journal*, p. 6, and list, p. 475 *ante*) was a white maple, which species regularly blooms earlier than the red.]

and nothing yet planted at home, — these bright-yellow *suns* of the meadow, in rich clusters, their flowers contrasting with the green leaves, from amidst the all-producing, dark-bottomed water. A flower-fire bursting up, as if through crevices in the meadow. They are very rich, seen in the meadow where they grow, and the most conspicuous flower at present, but held in the hand they are rather coarse. But their yellow and green are really rich, and in the meadow they are the most delicate objects. Their bright yellow is something incredible when first beheld. There is still considerable snow in the woods, where it has not melted since winter. Here is a small reddish-topped rush (is it the *Juncus effusus*, common or soft rush?[1]), now a foot high, in the meadow with the cowslips. It is the greatest growth of the grass form I have seen. The butterflies are now more numerous, red and blue-black or dark velvety. The art of life, of a poet's life, is, not having anything to do, to do something. People are going to see Kossuth, but the same man does not attract me and George Loring. If he could come openly to Boston without the knowledge of Boston, it might be worth my while to go and see him.

The mayflower on the point of blossoming. I think I may say that it will blossom to-morrow. The blossoms of this plant are remarkably concealed beneath the leaves, perhaps for protection. It is singularly unpretending, not seeking to exhibit or display its simple beauty. It is the most delicate flower, both to eye and to scent, as yet. Its weather-worn leaves do not adorn

[1] No.

it. If it had fresh spring leaves it would be more famous and sought after. Observed two thrushes arrived which I do not know. I discover a hawk over my head by his shadow on the ground; also small birds. The acorns among·the leaves have been sprouted for a week past, the shells open and the blushing (red) meat exposed at the sprout end, where the sprout is already turning toward the bowels of the earth, already thinking of the tempests which it is destined as an oak to withstand, if it escapes worm and squirrel. Pick these up and plant them, if you would make a forest.

Old Mr. Francis Wheeler thinks the river has not risen so high as recently for sixty-three years; that was in June!! that it was then higher. Noah Wheeler never saw it so high as lately. I think it doubtful if it was higher in 1817.

F. Wheeler, Jr., saw dandelions in bloom the 20th of April. Garfield's folks used them for greens. They grew in a springy place behind Brigham's in the Corner.

The *Fringilla hyemalis* still here, though apparently not so numerous as before. The *Populus grandidentata* in blossom, the sterile (?) flowers, though I cannot count, at most, more than five or six stamens. I observe the light-green leaves of a pyrola (?) standing high on the stem in the woods, with the last year's fruit; the "one-sided" or else the "oval-leaved," I think.

As I come home over the Corner road, the sun, now getting low, is reflected very bright and silvery from the water on the meadows, seen through the pines of Hubbard's Grove. The causeway will be passable on foot to-morrow.

April 30. 2 p. m. — Down the Boston road and across to Turnpike, etc., etc.

The elms are now generally in blossom and Cheney's elm still also. The last has leaf-buds which show the white. Now, before any leaves have appeared, their blossoms clothe the trees with a rich, warm brown color, which serves partially for foliage to the street-walker, and makes the tree more obvious. Held in the hand, the blossoms of some of the elms are quite rich and variegated, now purple and yellowish specked with the dark anthers and two light styles. I know not why some should be so much earlier than others. It is a beautiful day, — a mild air, — and all farmers and gardeners out and at work. Now is the time to set trees and consider what things you will plant in your garden. Yesterday I observed many fields newly plowed, the yellow soil looking very warm and dry in the sun; and one boy had fixed his handkerchief on a stick and elevated it on the yoke, where it flapped or streamed and rippled gayly in the wind, as he drove his oxen dragging a harrow over the plowed field. I see now what I should call a small-sized bullfrog in the brook in front of Alcott's house that was. The sweet-gale is in blossom. Its rich reddish-brown buds have expanded into yellowish and brown blossoms, all male blossoms that I see. Those handsome buds that I have observed are the male blossom buds then. This has undoubtedly been in bloom a day or two in some places. I saw yesterday a large-sized water-bug; to-day many in the brook; yesterday a trout; to-day shiners, I think. The huckleberry-bird sings. When I look

hence to the hills on the Boston road under which the inhabitants are beginning to plant in their gardens, the air is so fine and peculiar that I seem to see the hills and woods through a mirage. I am doubtful about their distance and exact form and elevation. The sound of a spade, too, sounds musical on the spring air. (To-night for the first time I sit without a fire.) One plower in a red flannel shirt, who looks pictur-esquely under the hill, suggests that our dress is not commonly of such colors as to adorn the landscape. (To-night and last night the spearer's light is seen on the meadows; he has been delayed by the height of the water.) I like very well to walk here on the low ground on the meadow; to see the churches and houses in the horizon against the sky and the now very blue Mt. Wachusett seeming to rise from amid them. When you get still further off on the lowest ground, you see distant barns and houses against the horizon, and the mountain appears to preside over this vale alone, which the adjacent hills on right and left fence in.

The season advances by fits and starts; you would not believe that there could be so many degrees to it. If you have had foul and cold weather, still some advance has been made, as you find when the fair weather comes, — new *lieferungs* of warmth and sum-meriness, which make yesterday seem far off and the dog-days or midsummer incredibly nearer. Yester-day I would not have believed that there could have been such an improvement on that day as this is, short of midsummer or June.

My pocket being full of the flowers of the maple,

elm, etc., my handkerchief by its fragrance reminded me of some fruitful or flowery bank, I know not where.

A pleasant little green knoll north of the Turnpike near the Lincoln line. I thought that the greenness of the sward there on the highest ground was occasioned by the decay of the roots of two oaks, whose old stumps still remained. The greenness covered a circle about two rods in diameter. It was too late to feel the influence of the drip of the trees. We have had no such summer heat this year (unless when I was burned in the Deep Cut), yet there is an agreeable balmy wind. I see here, while looking for the first violet, those little heaps made by the mole cricket (?), or by worms (?). I observe to-day the bright-crimson (?) perfect flowers of the maple, — crimson styles, sepals, and petals (crimson or scarlet?), — whose leaves are not yet very handsome in the rain as you look to the sky; and the hum of small bees from them. So much color have they.

Crossing the Turnpike, we entered Smith's high-lands. Dodging behind a swell of land to avoid the men who were plowing, I saw unexpectedly (when I looked to see if we were concealed by the field) the blue mountains' line in the west (the whole intermedi-ate earth and towns being concealed), this greenish field for a foreground sloping upward a few rods, and then those grand mountains seen over it in the background, so blue, — seashore, earth-shore, — and, warm as it is, covered with snow which reflected the sun. Then when I turned, I saw in the east, just over the woods, the modest, pale, cloud-like moon, two-

thirds full, looking spirit-like on these daylight scenes. Such a sight excites me. The earth is worthy to in-habit. The far river-reach from this hill. It is not so placid a blue — as if with a film of azure over it — to-day, however. The more remote the water, the lighter the blue, perchance. It is like a lake in Tar-tary; there our camels will find water. Here is a rock made to sit on, — large and inviting, which you do not fear to crush. I hear the flicker and the huckleberry-bird. Yet no leaves apparent. This in some measure corresponds to the fine afternoon weather after the leaves have fallen, though there is a different kind of promise now than then. We are now going out into the field to work; then we were going into the house to think. I love to see alders and dogwood instead of peach trees. May we not see the melted snow lapsing over the rocks on the mountains in the sun, as well as snow? The white surfaces appear declivitous. While we sit here, I hear for the first time the flies buzz so dronishly in the air. I see travellers like mere dark objects in the yellow road afar, — the Turnpike. Hosmer's house and cottage under its elms and on the summit of green smooth slopes looks like a terrestrial paradise, the abode of peace and domestic happiness. Far over the woods westward, a shining vane, glimmering in the sun.

At Saw Mill Run the swamp (?) gooseberry (is it?) is partly leaved out.[1] This, being in the shade of the woods, and not, like the thimble-berry, in a warm and sunny place, methinks is the earliest shrub or tree that

[1] I think it is Gray's *Ribes hirtellum*, short-stalked wild goose-berry.

shows leaves.¹ The neatly and closely folded, plaited, leaves of the hellebore are rather handsome objects now. As you pull them apart, they emit a slight marshy scent, somewhat like the skunk-cabbage. They are tender and dewy within, folded fan-like.

I hear a wood thrush here, with a fine metallic ring to his note. This sound most adequately expresses the immortal beauty and wildness of the woods. I go in search of him. He sounds no nearer. On a low bough of a small maple near the brook in the swamp, he sits with ruffled feathers, singing more low or with less power, as it were ventriloquizing; for though I am scarcely more than a rod off, he seems further off than ever.

Caught three little peeping frogs. When I approached, and my shadow fell on the water, I heard a peculiarly trilled and more rapidly vibrated note, somewhat, in kind, like that which a hen makes to warn her chickens when a hawk goes over, and most stopped peeping; another trill, and all stopped. It seemed to be a note of alarm. I caught one. It proved to be two coupled. They remained together in my hand. This sound has connection with their loves probably. (I hear a trilled sound from a frog this evening. It is my dreaming midsummer frog, and he seems to be toward the depot.) I find them generally sitting on the dead leaves near the water's edge, from which they leap into the water.

On the hill behind Hosmer's, half an hour before

---

¹ The Missouri currant in gardens is equally forward; the cultivated gooseberry nearly so; the lilac not so.

Vol. III

sunset. — The hill on the Boston road is very handsome with its regular promontories, and the smokes now seen against it rising from the chimneys, what time the laborer takes his tea. The robins sing powerfully on the elms; the little frogs peep; the woodpecker's harsh and long-continued cry is heard from the woods; the huckleberry-bird's simple, sonorous trill. The plowed land shines where a drag has passed over it. It is a pleasant place for a house, because you overlook the road, and the near land seems to run into the meadow.

Saw male willow catkins in Tuttle's lane, now just out of bloom, about two inches long. The flower of some of the earliest elms is by no means to be despised at this season. It is conspicuous and rich in any nosegay that can now be made. The female plants of the sweet-gale are rare (?) here. The scales of the male catkins are "set with amber-colored resinous dots" (Emerson).

END OF VOLUME III

The Journal of Henry D. Thoreau

VOLUME IV

(May, 1852 — February, 1853)

Cows in Emerson's Pasture

CONTENTS

Vol. IV

THE JOURNAL OF
HENRY DAVID THOREAU

VOLUME IV

I

MAY, 1852 (ÆT. 34)

May 1. 5 A. M. — To Cliffs.

A smart frost in the night, the plowed ground and platforms white with it. I hear the little forked-tail chipping sparrow (*Fringilla socialis*) shaking out his rapid *tchi-tchi-tchi-tchi-tchi-tchi*, a little jingle, from the oak behind the Depot. I hear the note of the shy Savannah sparrow (*F. Savanna*),[1] that plump bird with a dark-streaked breast that runs and hides in the grass, whose note sounds so like a cricket's in the grass. (I used to hear it when I walked by moonlight last sum-

[1] Probably have seen it before, — seringo. [Though here, where the "seringo-bird" makes its first appearance in the *Journal*, its identity with the savanna sparrow seems to have been unquestioned by Thoreau, it proved afterwards (see p. 8., *et seq.*) to be almost as puzzling to him as the ever elusive "night-warbler." The probability is that the "seringo" in this and most other cases was the savanna sparrow, but it may sometimes have been the yellow-winged, or grasshopper, sparrow, or even, as Thoreau once suspected, the grass finch, or vesper sparrow. It is quite likely that at times the bird he saw was not the bird he heard.]

mer.) I hear it now from deep in the sod, — for there is hardly grass yet. The bird keeps so low you do not see it. You do not suspect how many there are till at length their heads appear. The word *seringo* reminds me of its note, — as if it were produced by some kind of fine metallic spring. It is an earth-sound. It is a moist, lowering morning for the mayers. The sun now shines under a cloud in the horizon, and his still yellow light falls on the western fields, as sometimes on the eastern after a shower in a summer afternoon. Nuttall says the note of the chipping sparrow is "given from time to time in the night like the reverie of a dream." Have I not heard it when spearing? Is not that the tree sparrow which I have heard in the fall (in company with the *F. hyemalis*), which also clucks like a hen? Nuttall says they sing *s'weedit s'weedit weet.* I hear a lark in the meadow.

Hayden is sowing his oats. There is not much rye sown in the spring. There is the old picture in the fables, the sower stepping over plowed ground and the yellowish grain in a regularly formed shower in the air. I do not hear the peep of the frogs at this time. Found the first violet, which would open to-day, — either *V. sagittata* var. *ovata*,[1] or *V. cucullata*, for the leaves are not toothed at base nor arrow-shaped as in the first, yet they are hairy and I should say petiole-margined. Still, like the latter, they are rolled in at base and the scape is four-angled (??). I found this violet under a bank by a pool-side. I think it *cucullata*. The woods have a

[1] ["Either" and "or *V. cucullata*" crossed out in pencil. See p. 33.]

damp smell this morning. I hear a robin amid them, yet there are fewer singers to be heard than on a very pleasant morning some weeks ago. The low early blueberry, June berry, is now well budded. The grass ground, low ground at least, wears a good green tinge now. There are no leaves on the woods. The river is high over the meadows. There is a thin gauze-like veil over the village (I am on Fair Haven Hill), probably formed of the smokes. As yet we have had no morning fogs to my knowledge.

I hear the first towhee finch. He says *to-wee*, *to-wee*, and another, much farther off than I supposed when I went in search of him, says *whip your ch-r-r-r-r-r*, with a metallic ring. I hear the first catbird also, mewing, and the wood thrush, which still thrills me, — a sound to be heard in a new country, — from one side of a clearing. I think I heard an oven-bird just now, — *wicher wicher whicher wich*.[1] I am on the Cliff. It is about six. The flicker cackles. I hear a woodpecker tapping. The tinkle of the huckleberry-bird comes up from the shrub oak plain. He commonly lives away from the habitations of men, in retired bushy fields and sprout-lands. A partridge bursts away from under the rock below me on quivering wings, like some moths I have seen. We have, then, flowers, and the song of birds before the woods leave out, — like poetry. When leaving the woods I heard the hooting of an owl, which sounded very much like a clown calling to his team. Saw two large woodpeckers on

[1] ["Think" is crossed out in pencil, and "black and white creeper" substituted for "oven-bird."]

an oak. I am tempted to say that they were other and larger than the flicker, but I have been deceived in him before.

5 P. M. — To Red Bridge.

The smell of our fresh meadows, from which the flood has in some measure receded, reminds me of the scent of salt marshes, to which it corresponds. A coarse grass is starting up, all the greener and more luxuriant for the freshet, one foot high. I hear a new kind of stertorous sound from the meadow; a new frog? The flowers (male) of the maple by the bridge are all dried up, and its buds are just expanding into leaves, while red maples are in their flowering prime. I find by the leaves that this is probably a white maple. The purple finch is come to Minott's neighborhood. I saw it. I rarely see it elsewhere than about R. W. E.'s. Are they not attracted hither by his fir trees? (I think it was not the tree sparrow which I used to hear in rainy weather.)

E. Wood, Senior, says it was in 1818 the river was so high, and that Sted. Buttrick marked it, but thinks the last flood an inch or two higher. Wood has observed that the North River will rise first, and he has seen the South Branch flowing up-stream faster than ever he saw it flowing down. Tells a story of barrels that floated once from where Loring's factory is to the old Lee or Barrett house meadow.

The little peeping frogs which I got last night resemble the description of the *Hylodes Pickeringii* and in some respects the peeping hyla, but they are probably

Vol. IV

May 2. 6 A. M. — Is not the chipping sparrow the commonest heard in the village streets in the mornings now, sitting on an elm or apple tree? Was it the black and white warbler that I saw this morning? It did not stop to creep round the trunks; was very shy. Or was it the myrtle-bird? Might it have been the log-cock woodpecker that I saw yesterday morning? Reptiles must not be omitted, especially frogs; their croaking is the most earthy sound now, a rustling of the scurf of the earth, not to be overlooked in the awakening of the year. It is such an earth-sound.

The flowers of Cheney's elm are not only much earlier and larger than others, but the peduncles are in separate bundles proceeding from a common *short* peduncle. There appears to be such a difference, the tree is made of a different form and appearance. I can easily break off a twig from its branches, which hang very low. *Vide* the rough-barked elm in the swamp, — if it is not the corky elm. The balm-of-Gilead begins to show its male (?) catkins.

The commonplaces of one age or nation make the poetry of another. I think that my seringo-bird has not the marks of the Savannah sparrow. Looks like a chip-bird; or did I see a spot on its breast? That white maple, methinks, has a smoother bark than the red ones.

P. M. — To Conantum.

The handsome blood-red lacquered marks on the edge and under the edge of the painted tortoise's shell, like the marks on a waiter, concentric, few colors like

the former, though every way considerably smaller (*vide* pencil mark in report). Mine are about three quarters of an inch long as they sit, seven eighths if stretched; thigh five sixteenths, leg same; tarsus and toes one half; four-fingered and five-toed with *small* tubercles on the ends of them. Some difference in their color; one is like a pale oak leaf at this season, streaked with brown; two others more ashy. Two have crosses like this on back, of dark brown. On the head thus, with transverse bands on the legs. I keep them in a tumbler. Peep at twilight and evening, occasionally at other times. One that got out in the evening on to the carpet was found soon after by his peeping *on the piano.* They easily ascend the glass of the window; jump eighteen inches and more. When they peep, the loose wrinkled skin of the throat is swelled up into a globular bubble, very large and transparent and quite round, except on the throat side, behind which their little heads are lost, mere protuberances on the side of this sphere; and the peeping wholly absorbs them; their mouths shut, or apparently so. Will sit half a day on the side of a smooth tumbler. Made that trilling note in the house. Remain many hours at the bottom of the water in the tumbler, or sit as long on the leaves above. A pulse in the throat always, except in one for an hour or two apparently asleep. They change their color to a darker or lighter shade, chameleon-like.

it in nature. This tortoise, too, like the *guttata*, painted on these parts of its shell and on legs and tail in this style, but throat bright yellow stripes, sternum dull yellowish or buff. It hisses like the spotted. Tortoises everywhere coupling. Is the male the large and flatter, with depressed sternum? It so seems? There is *some* regularity in the *guttata's* spots, — generally a straight row on back. Some of the spots are orange sometimes on the head.

Brought home two little frogs which I have described in the Report (*q. v.*) but cannot make out. Are they young? The andromeda is ready to bloom. The yellow lily is budded. The little frogs peep more or less during the day, but chiefly at evening twilight, rarely in the morning. They peep at intervals. One begins, then all join in over the whole pond, and they suddenly stop all together.

If you would obtain insight, avoid anatomy.

I am pretty sure that is the myrtle-bird I see and hear on the Corner road, picking the blossoms of the maple, with the yellow crown and black throat or cheeks. It sings *pe-te-te-te-ter twe'*, emphasizing the last and repeating the second, third, and fourth fast.

The little frogs I kept three days in the house peeped at evening twilight, though they had been silent all day; never failed; swelled up their little bagpipes, transparent, and as big as a small cherry or a *large* pea. Saw a bird on the willows, very shy, which may be the indigo-bird, but I am not sure. The *Equisetum arvense* is now in bloom (the male flowers) all over the railroad embankment, coloring it yellowish (?).

May 3. 5 A. M. — To Cliffs.

A great brassy moon going down in the west. A flock of neat sparrows, small, striped-throated, whitish over eye, on an apple tree by J. Potter's. At Hayden's orchard, quite a concert from some small sparrows, forked-tailed, many jingling together like canaries. Their note still somewhat like the chip-sparrow's. Can it be this?

Fair Haven. How cheering and glorious any landscape viewed from an eminence! For every one has its horizon and sky. It is so easy to take wide views. Snow on the mountains. The wood thrush reminds me of cool mountain springs and morning walks.

That oven-birdish note which I heard here on May 1st I now find to have been uttered by the black and white warbler or creeper. He has a habit of looking under the branches. The towhee finch is the loudest singer here now.

Does that long-drawn, interesting note, something like *ha, ha, tull-a-lull tull-a-lull*, proceed from the chickadee?[1]

Looking from the Cliff, now, about 6 A. M., the landscape is as if seen in a mirage, the Cliff being in shadow, and that in the fresh and dewy sunshine (not much dew yet). Cool sunlight. The landscape lies in a fresh morning light; the earth and water smell fresh and new; the water is marked by a few smooth streaks. The atmosphere suits the grayish-brown landscape, — the still ashy maple swamps and now nearly bare shrub

[1] [Probably the song of the white-throated sparrow, whose voice Thoreau mistook for the chickadee's in the Maine woods.]

oaks. The white pine, left here and there over the sprout-land, is never more beautiful than with the morning light — the early sunlight and the dew — on it. (Dew comes with grass? and for it?) Before the water is rippled and the morning song of the birds is quenched.

Hear the first brown thrasher, — two of them. Minott says he heard one yesterday, but does he know it from a catbird? They drown all the rest. He says *cherruwit, cherruwit; go ahead, go ahead; give it to him, give it to him;* etc., etc., etc. Plenty of birds in the woods this morning. The huckleberry birds and the chickadees are as numerous, if not as loud, as any. The flicker taps a dead tree as some what [*sic*] uses a knocker on a door in the village street. In his note he begins low, rising higher and higher. Is it a wood pewee or a vireo that I hear, something like *pewit pewit chowy chow?* It requires so much closer attention to the habits of the birds, that, if for that reason only, I am willing to omit the gun.[1]

P. M. — Cinquefoil or five-finger (*Potentilla Canadensis*). Also the golden saxifrage (what a name!) (*Chrysosplenium Americanum*), in the meadow at Brister's Hill, in the water, in moss-like beds. It may have been in bloom some time; an obscure flower.

A cold wind from the northwest. How much are our summers retarded by the snow on the mountains? Annursnack looks green three miles off. This is an important epoch, when the distant bare hills begin to show

[1] [*Walden*, p. 234; Riv. 330.]

green or verdurous to the eye. The earth wears a new aspect. Not tawny or russet now, but green, are such hills.

Some of the notes, the trills, of the lark sitting amid the tussocks and stubble are like my seringo-bird. May these birds that live so low in the grass be called the cricket birds? and does their song resemble the cricket's, an earth-song?

Was that a flying squirrel which the Emerson children found in his nest on the 1st of May? Heard some kind of dor-bug approaching with a hum, as I sat in a meadow this afternoon, and it struck the ground near me with as much noise as a bullet, as if some one had fired at me with an air-gun.

Evening. — The moon is full. The air is filled with a certain luminous, liquid, white light. You can see the moonlight, as it were reflected from the atmosphere, which some might mistake for a haze, — a glow of mellow light, somewhat like the light I saw in the afternoon sky some weeks ago; as if the air were a very thin but transparent liquid, not dry, as in winter, nor gross, as in summer. It has depth, and not merely distance (the sky).

Going through the Depot Field, I hear the dream frog at a distance. The little peeping frogs make a background of sound in the horizon, which you do not hear unless you attend. The former is a trembling note, some higher, some lower, along the edge of the earth, an all-pervading sound. Nearer, it is a blubbering or rather bubbling sound, such as children, who

stand nearer to nature, can and do often make, — this and many others, remembering the frog state.[1] There is no dew (I have observed none yet). The dream of the frog sounds best at a distance, — most dreamy. The little peeper prefers a pool on the edge of a wood, which mostly dries up at midsummer, whose shore is covered with leaves and [where] twigs lie in the water, as where choppers have worked. Theirs is a clear, sharp, ear-piercing peep, not shrill, — sometimes a squeak from one whose pipe is out of order, frequently a quavering, curving (?) trill, as if of alarm (?). The sound of the dreamer frog does not fail, for one no sooner ceases than another in a different part of the landscape takes up the strain.

The sky is not so withdrawn, clear, tight, and cold as last moon. It is quite comfortable, more than during the day. No crickets are heard. The river in the west looks blue, exactly like the sky reflecting it. Is not the sky a lighter blue than in winter? The dogs bark. The rocks have not been enough warmed by day to feel decidedly warm at night.

At Hubbard's Bridge. The river still quite high. The water is calm. I hear a stertorous sound from some frog. This makes three frogs' notes that I hear. There is the moon in the south, with one bright star just beneath it, which, when the moon is in clouds, is its representative. Looking from bridge to hill, above is the moon, separated from attendant star by a bar of white clouds, below which the star shines brightly in a clearing; beneath this, bars of white clouds to the

[1] [The last four words crossed out in pencil.]

horizon. The hill and opposite woods are dark with fine effect. The little peepers have much the greatest

apparatus for peeping of any frogs that I know. Frogs are the birds of the night.

I go along the side of Fair Haven Hill. The clock strikes distinctly, showing the wind is easterly. There is a grand, rich, musical echo trembling on the air long after the clock has ceased to strike, like a vast organ, filling the air with a trembling music like a flower of sound. Nature adopts it. Beautiful is sound. The water is so calm the woods and single trees are doubled by the reflection, and in this light you cannot divide them as you walk along the river. See the spearers' lights, one northeast, one southwest, toward Sudbury, beyond Lee's Bridge, — scarlet-colored fires. From the hill the river is a broad blue stream exactly the color of the heavens which it reflects. Sit on the Cliff with comfort, in greatcoat. All the tawny and russet earth — for no green is seen on the *ground* at this hour — sending only this faint multitudinous sound (of frogs) to heaven. The vast, wild earth. The first whip-or-u-will startles me. Hear three.

thought, or the want of thought, of the multitude. No man stands on truth. They are merely banded together as usual, one leaning on another and all together on nothing; as the Hindoos made the world rest on an elephant, and the elephant on a tortoise, and had nothing to put under the tortoise.[1] You can pass your hand under the largest mob, a nation in revolution even, and, however solid a bulk they may make, like a hail-cloud in the atmosphere, you may not meet so much as a cobweb of support. They may not rest, even by a point, on eternal foundations. But an individual standing on truth you cannot pass your hand under, for his foundations reach to the centre of the universe. So superficial these men and their doings, it is life on a leaf or a chip which has nothing but air or water beneath. I love to see a man with a tap-root, though it make him difficult to transplant.[2] It is unimportant what these men do. Let them try forever, they can effect nothing. Of what significance the things you can forget?

A little thought is sexton to all the world.

I see the slate-colored snowbird still, — a few. What was that large olive-yellow bird on Heywood's apple trees? The female flower of the sweet-gale, red, like so many female flowers. The meadow-sweet begins to leave out. The male flowers of the maple look yellowish-scarlet, looking up to the sky. The elms are still in full blossom. The cowslip's is a vigorous growth and makes at present the most show of any flower. Leaf,

[1] [*Cape Cod, and Miscellanies*, pp. 470, 471; *Misc.*, Riv. 273.]
[2] *Vide* [pp. 54, 55].

Summer is coming apace. Within three or four days the birds have come so fast I can hardly keep the run of them, — much faster than the flowers. I did not watch for the *very earliest*, however.

My little peepers — when they slept, the pulsation in their throats stopped. There was a wrinkled bag there. They begin to peep in earnest at or before sundown, and they keep it up now at 10 P. M. But I rarely hear any numbers in the morning, when they probably sleep. Heard the dreaming frogs close at hand, in the pool in the road by Hubbard's, a loud, liquid *ringing*, bubbling. One plainly answers another. Almost put my hand on one while bubbling. There is more ring to it close by, but on the whole it is not as poetic.

The salutations and commonplaces of all nations, which sound to us formal often, are always adapted to their circumstances, and grow out of their necessities. The Tartar inquires, "Has the rain been abundant? Are your flocks in prosperity? Have your mares been fruitful?" and the answer is, "All is at peace in our pastures." Serene and Biblical, and no man's invention.

M. Huc met with a family in China remarkable for hospitality.

May 4. R. W. E. tells me he does not like Haynes as well as I do. I tell him that he makes better manure than most men.

This excitement about Kossuth is not interesting to me, it is so superficial. It is only another kind of dancing or of politics. Men are making speeches to him all over the country, but each expresses only the

stem, bud, and flower are all very handsome in their place and season. It has no scent, but speaks wholly to the eye. The petals are covered at base with a transparent, dewy (dew-like), apparently golden nectar. Better for yellows than for greens. I hear trees creak here (at Saw Mill Brook) like inn signs in the street. The singularly rough winged (?) barked elms here, which run up so high, blossom only at top. They are *very* easy to climb, the bark is so rough and furrowed and soft, affording a support to the clothes. The bark on the twigs strips up long. A kind of corky bark, but flower like the common.

The little frogs begin to peep in good earnest *toward* sundown.

May 5. 5 A. M. — Frost in night; hence the grass is wet. Hear the seringo-bird on an apple tree. I think it must be one of the species of song sparrow. Hear on the elms in the street, for the first time that I remember, the purple finch (without the crimson) singing loud, like a warbling vireo but with more variety. Hear also this morning in the village the chickadees' fine, ringing, air-possessing *tull-a-lull tull-a-lull.* Is this the third note of this bird, and confined to this season?[1] Heard it the morning of the brown thrasher. The other afternoon I could not hear the birds sing, the wind in the woods made such a noise.

3 P. M. — To little ponds.

A really warm day. I perspire in my thick coat. Hear

[1] [See p. 10.]

the dream frogs, but fainter than by night. The aspect of the woods half a mile distant shows the state of the atmosphere. There is a very slight transparent haze on them, just enough to glass them; somewhat such a reflection and seething in the air as I have described by moonlight. The maple-tops show red with their blossoms against the higher trees. What is the color of their tops in winter? The red maples and the elms, now covered with full rich [sic], are now on the whole the most common and obvious blossoms. It is their season, and they are worthy of it. The one has the woods and swamps and causeways; the other, the village. My seringo-bird sounds now from the railroad like the dropping of a file, or any bit of steel, on an anvil. Saw a shad-fly. The white-bellied (?) swallow soars and sails like a hawk. Leave the Cut. The woods are now dry, and the ground feels crisp under my feet. Fires in the woods will now rage. I see their traces by the railroad. I smell the dry leaves. Nature invites fire to sweep her floors, for purification. From the high field, see smokes toward Wachusett. The shade is even agreeable to-day. I smell the pines lately; is it because they are starting? Oh, the huckleberry-bird! The *Viola pedata* budded, ready to blossom. In Stow's clearing. Every part of the world is beautiful to-day; the bright, shimmering water; the fresh, light-green grass springing up on the hills, tender, firm, moss-like before it waves; — the very faint blue sky, without distinct clouds, is least beautiful of all, having yielded its beauty to the earth; —and the fine light smokes, sometimes blue against the woods; and the tracts where the woods have been

cut the past winter. The beautiful, ethereal, not misty, blue of the horizon and its mountains, as if painted. Now all buds may swell, methinks; now the summer may begin for all creatures. The wind appears to be a little north of west. The waters, still high, have a fine shimmering sparkle over a great part of their surface, not so large nor quite so bright as in the fall.

As I can throw my voice into my head and sing very loud and clear there, so I can throw my thought into a higher chamber, and think louder and clearer above the earth than men will understand.

The maple woods *half a mile* distant are not a bright red, but a little brighter than the oak leaves have been. It looks best from a hilltop a quarter of a mile distant, seen rising amid pines, with a light rosaceous tint in the sun, in Holden's Swamp. I can see them of a dull red a mile and a half distant. The blossom (male) of the maple has *very little* fragrance, but that agreeable. This and the elm may go together, possessing the season to careless eyes.

Now the flies are heard to buzz about you, as you sit on a rock on the hillside. How long is it since I saw geese and ducks? Methinks ever since the Great Freshet. They are swept northward with the storms, — a transient wildness. Is that a hop-hornbeam under the Cliffs which looks like a black birch? There is red-stemmed moss on the earth-covered rocks half-way down. The male flowers of the *grandidentata* begin to dry up. The young oaks on the plain have suddenly, I think within a day or two, lost all their leaves, being about to put forth new.

In its America of enterprise and active life, does not the mind lose its adipose tissue that Knox tells of?

A tree-toad again. The outlines of Fair Haven Pond begin to appear, and the two arms that claim the island. Few birds are heard from the Cliffs now at 4 P. M. Sunrise is already their hour.

I succeed best when I *recur* to my experience not too late, but within a day or two; when there is some distance, but enough of freshness.

Saxifrage and crowfoot abundant, though I have found but one violet. The crowfoot has a sweet spring-like fragrance, like the dandelion, if you have many, but very little of it. A gloss like varnish on its thin petals. It makes a show here in the grass over warm rocks. Saxifrage still less scent.

Heard the first cricket singing, on a lower level than any bird, observing a lower tone — the sane, wise one — than all the singers. He came not from the south, but from the depths. He has felt the heats at last, — that migrates downward. The smallest of birds. The myrtle-bird again, rather tame. A pretty little crimson willow, *i. e.* its four-divided stigmas, either the *Salix tristis* or *humilis*, one to two feet high, catkins a third of an inch long, recurved. I have seen no female willow so handsome, but neither Gray nor Emerson describes its beauty. It turns greenish as it grows old. Dotted with minute crimson stigmas. In the small ponds I hear a slight bullfroggy note. The andromeda is now a brownish-green; very little of the redness left. Seen from the sun side, now the sun is getting low, it looks like a large bed of greenish-gray moss, reflecting

the light. What has become of its red leaves? Does it shed them, and the present fresher ones not till next spring? These leaves show their under sides appressed to the stem. The sweet-fern now begins to shed its yellow pollen. The first anemones on a warm hillside west of the Island Pond. *Thalictrum anemonoides* (rue-leaved). What the shrub now leaving out at the east of the Long Pond, with sticky buds? A cherry or plum?[1] There is a dust on Walden, — where I come to drink, —which I think is the pollen of such trees and shrubs as are now in blossom, — aspens, maples, sweet-fern, etc., — food for fishes. I did not see any when I last drank here, a short time ago.

A fine scarlet sunset. As I sit by my window and see the clouds reflected in the meadow, I think it is important to have water, because it multiplies the heavens.

Evening. — To the Lee place rock.

Moon not up. The dream frog's is such a sound as you can make with a quill on water, a bubbling sound. Behind Dodd's. The spearers are out, their flame a bright yellow, reflected in the calm water. Without noise it is slowly carried along the shores. It reminds me of the light which Columbus saw on approaching the shores of the New World. There goes a shooting star down towards the horizon, like a rocket, appearing to describe a curve. The water sleeps with stars in its bosom. I see another light in the far southwest. To a stranger in the dark they would appear like light-houses on low points, lighting voyagers to our shores.

[1] Wild red cherry.

This might be called the spearer's moon this year, if it were of use to him. Hear a pout-like sound of frogs. (The chickadee [1] says now in morning, *har* (long), *pe-e-e pe-e-e p-e-e-e*, the last trill something like *tull-a-lull lull-a-lull*.) The dream of the frogs [2] is very indistinct at a distance. Venus, the evening star, high in the sky. The spearers' light reveals the forms of trees and bushes near which it passes. When it is not seen, it makes a pillar of reddish or rosy light on the twigs above it. I see even the lamps of the village in the water, the river is so high.

As I went up the Groton road, I saw a dim light at a distance, where no house was, which appeared to come from the earth. Could it be a traveller with a lanthorn? Could it be a will-o'-the-wisp? (Who ever saw one? Are not they a piece of modern mythology?) You wonder if you will ever reach it; already it seems to recede. Is it the reflection of the evening star in water? or what kind of phosphorescence? But now I smell the burning. I see the sparks go up in the dark. — It is a heap of stumps half covered with earth, left to smoulder and consume in the newly plowed meadow, now burst forth into dull internal flames. Looks like a gipsy encampment. I sit on the untouched end of a stump, and warm me by it, and write by the light, the moon not having risen. What a strange, Titanic thing this Fire, this Vulcan, here at work in the night in this bog, far from men, dangerous to them, consuming earth,

[1] ["Myrtle-bird" is substituted in pencil for "chickadee." Thoreau afterward learned that the bird was the white-throated sparrow!]
[2] ["Toads" substituted in pencil for "frogs."]

Vol. IV

herself from the clouds of earth and reached the clear and serene heavens.

No nighthawks heard yet.

I stand by the bubbling frogs (dreamers at a distance). They are sometimes intermittent, with a quavering. I hear betweenwhiles a little bird-like conversation between them. It is evidently their wooing.

May 6. 3 p. m. — To Conantum.

Heard the first warbling vireo this morning on the elms. This almost makes a summer. Heard also, as I sat at my desk, the unusual low of cows being driven to their country pastures. Sat all day with the window open, for the outer air is the warmest. The balm-of-Gilead was well blossomed out yesterday, and has been for three or four days probably. The woods seen a mile off in the horizon are more indistinct yesterday and to-day, these two summer-like days (it is a summer heat), the green of the pines being blended with the gray or ash of the deciduous trees; partly, perhaps, because the fine haze in the air is the color of the twigs, and partly because the buds are expanded into leaves on many; but this last cause is hardly admissible. Now the wasps have come.

My dream frog turns out to be a toad. I watched half a dozen a long time at 3.30 this afternoon in Hubbard's Pool, where they were frogging(?) lustily. They sat in the shade, either partly in the water, or on a stick; looked darker and narrower in proportion to their length than toads usually do, and moreover are aquatic. I see them jump into the ditches as I walk. After an

gnawing at its vitals! The heap glows within. Here sits hungry Fire with the forest in his mouth. On the one side is the solid wood; on the other, smoke and sparks. Thus he works. The farmer designs to consume, to destroy, this wood, remains of trees. He gives them to his dog or vulture Fire. They burn like spunk, and I love the smell of the smoke. The frogs peep and dream around. Within are fiery caverns, incrusted with fire as a cave with saltpetre. No wonder at salamanders. It suggests a creature that lives in it, generated by it. The glass men are nearer the truth than the men of science.

I hear Barrett's sawmill [1] running by night to improve the high water. Then water is at work, another devourer of wood. These two wild forces let loose against nature. It is a hollow, galloping sound; makes tearing work, taming timber, in a rude Orphean fashion preparing it for dwellings of men and musical instruments, perchance. I can imagine the sawyer, with his lanthorn and his bar in hand, standing by, amid the shadows cast by his light. There is a sonorous vibration and ring to it, as if from the nerves of the tortured log. Tearing its entrails.

I go forward. The rabbit goes off from the wood-side with a squeak and bounce. I hear him strike the ground each time. He squeaks once like an alarmed bird. The rocks are very slightly warm, perhaps because it is not cold enough to-night, and it is a very little colder in the hollows.

The moon is just rising (9.30). She has not yet freed

[1] *Vide* p. [151].

interval of silence, one appeared to be gulping the wind into his belly, inflating himself so that he was considerably expanded; then he discharged it all into his throat while his body or belly collapsed suddenly, expanding his throat to a remarkable size. Was nearly a minute inflating itself; then swelled out its sac, which is rounded and reminded me of the bag to a worktable, holding its head up the while. It is whitish specked (the bag) on a dull bluish or slate ground, much bigger than all the rest of the head, and nearly an inch in diameter. It was a ludicrous sight, with their so serious prominent eyes peering over it; and a deafening sound, when several were frogging at once, as I was leaning over them. The mouth [seemed] to be shut always, and perhaps the air was expelled through the nostrils. The strain appeared prolonged as long as the air lasted, and was sometimes quavered or made intermittent, apparently by closing the orifice, whatever it was, or the blast. One, which I brought home, answers well enough to the description of the common toad (*Bufo Americanus*), though it is hardly so gray. Their piping(?) was evidently connected with their loves. Close by, it is an unmusical monotonous deafening sound, a steady blast, — not a peep nor a croak, but a *kind* of piping, — but, far away, it is a dreamy, lulling sound, and fills well the crevices of nature. Out of its place, as very near, it would be as intolerable as the thrumming of children. The plower yesterday disturbed a toad in the garden, the first I have heard of. I must catch him and compare them. Their heads are well above the water when they pipe.

Saw a striped snake lying by the roadside as if watching for toads, though they must be scarce now, his head just on the edge of the road. The most flexible of creatures, it is so motionless it appears the most rigid, in its waving line.

The yellow willows on the causeways are now fairly leaving out. They are more forward in this respect than that early willow, or any other that I see. The trees are already a mass of green, partly concealing the yellow stems, — a tender, fresh light green. No *trees* look so forward in this respect, and, being in rows, they make the more show, their branches are so thick and numerous, close together. If some have leaves as large, they are much more scattered and make no such show. I did not observe what time the willow bark would strip and make whistles. The female maple is more crimson, the male more scarlet. The horse-chestnut buds are so advanced that they are larger than the leaves of any tree. The elder, the wild cherry, thimble-berries, sweet-briars, cultivated cherry, and early apples, etc., white birches, hazels, aspens, hornbeams, maples, etc., etc., — not quite the hickory and alder, — are opening their buds; the alders are beginning to.

It is pleasant when the road winds along the side of a hill with a thin fringe of wood through which to look into the low land. It furnishes both shade and frame for your pictures, — as this Corner road. The first *Anemone nemorosa*, wind-flower or wood anemone, its petals more slightly tinged with purple than the rue-leaved. See the ferns here at the spring curling up like the proboscis of the sphinx moth. The first *Viola*

blanda (sweet-scented white), in the moist ground, also, by this spring. It is pretty numerous and may have been out a day or two. I think I could not find so many blue ones. It has a rather strong scent like heliotrope (?). The *Convallaria bifolia* budded. Sometimes the toad reminds me of the cricket, its note also proceeding from the ground. See now the woodchuck rollicking across a field toward his hole and tumbling into it. See where he has just dug a new hole. Their claws long and rather weak-looking for digging. The woodpeckers tapping. The first columbine (*Aquilegia Canadensis*) to-day, on Conantum. Shade is grateful, and the walker feels a desire to bathe in some pond or stream for coolness and invigoration.

Cowslips show at a distance in the meadows (Miles's). The new butter is white still, but with these *cows' lips* in the grass it will soon be yellow, I trust. This yellowness in the spring, derived from the sun, affects even the cream in the cow's bag, and flowers in yellow butter at last. Who has not turned pale at the sight of hay butter? These are the cows' lips.

The music of all creatures has to do with their loves, even of toads and frogs. Is it not the same with man?

There are odors enough in nature to remind you of everything, if you had lost every sense but smell. The fever-bush is an apothecary's shop.

The farmers are very busily harrowing and rolling in their grain. The dust flies from their harrows across the field. The tearing, toothed harrow and the ponderous cylinder, which goes creaking and rumbling over the surface, heard afar, and vying with the sphere.

Vol. IV

The cylinder is a simple machine, and must go into the new symbols. It is an interesting object, seen drawn across a grain-field. The willows are now suddenly of a light, fresh, tender yellowish-green. A green bittern, a gawky bird. As I return over the bridge, shadflies very numerous. Many insects now in the evening sunshine, especially over the water.

Houstonia (*Hedyotis cærulea*), bluets, now just begun. Dewey calls it Venus' Pride. Gray says truly, " a very delicate little herb, . . . producing in spring a profusion of handsome bright blue blossoms fading to white, with a yellow eye." I should say bluish-white. The dwarf andromeda (*A. calyculata*) just begun; leaves called evergreen; flowers on " one-sided leafy racemes." Methinks its leaves remain two years, and fall in the spring, the small ones continuing to grow.[1] The ground is now strewn with the old red-brown lower leaves, and only the smaller and fresher green ones remain.

The common toad, with which I compared the dream toad I brought home, has two horn-like dark marks reaching over the eyes. It is not depressed, but rather has a tubercle, on the top of the head between the eyes. It is also much wider in proportion to length, and is triangular, as I have drawn in report. Yet they are probably the same. The garden toad made the same faint chicken-like, musical croak, when I held him in my hand, with the other, and in the same manner swelling his bag. The garden toad was yellowish beneath, the other white with some small spots. The latter turned much lighter-colored, — from brown to a

[1] [This sentence is queried in the margin.]

yellowish and light-brown green, or rather greenish-brown, — while I had him. They have a bright eye, with coppery or golden-coppery iris. It is their redeeming feature. But why do I not hear them in the garden? They appear to frequent the water first, and breed there, then hop to the gardens, and turn lighter and grow thicker.

May 7. Friday. 4.30 A. M. — To Cliffs.

Has been a dew, which wets the feet, and I see a very thin fog over the low ground, the first fog, which must be owing to the warm weather. Heard a robin singing powerfully an hour ago, and song sparrows, and the cocks. No peeping frogs in the morning, or rarely.

The toads sing (?), but not as at evening. I walk half a mile (to Hubbard's Pool, in the road), before I reach those I heard, — only two or three. The sound is uttered so low and over water; still it is wonderful that it should be heard so far. The traveller rarely perceives when he comes near the source of it, nor when he is farthest away from it. Like the will-o'-the-wisp, it will lead one a long chase over the fields and meadows to find one. They dream more or less at all hours now. I see the relation to the frogs in the throat of many a man. The full throat has relation to the distended paunch.

I would fain see the sun as a moon, more weird. The sun now rises in a rosaceous amber. Methinks the birds sing more some mornings than others, when I cannot see the reason. I smell the damp path, and derive vigor from the earthy scent between Potter's and

Hayden's. Beginning, I may say, with robins, song sparrows, chip-birds, bluebirds, etc., I walked through larks, pewees, pigeon woodpeckers, chickadee *tull-a-lulls*, to towhees, huckleberry-birds, wood thrushes, brown thrasher, jay, catbird, etc., etc. Entered a cool stratum of air beyond Hayden's after the warmth of yesterday. The *Viola pedata* still in bud only, and the other (*q. v.*). Hear the first partridge drum. The first oven-bird. A wood thrush which I thought a dozen rods off, was only two or three, to my surprise, and betrayed himself by moving, like a large sparrow with ruffled feathers, and quirking his tail like a pewee,[1] on a low branch. Blackbirds are seen going over the woods with a chattering bound to some meadow.

A rich bluish mist now divides the vales in the eastern horizon mile after mile. (I am ascending Fair Haven.) An oval-leaved pyrola (evergreen) in Brown's pines on Fair Haven.

Cliffs. — This is the gray morning; the sun risen; a very thin mist on the landscape; the falling water smooth. Far below, a screaming jay seen flying, against the bare stems of the pines. The young oaks on the plain, the pines standing here and there, the walls in Conantum pastures seen in the sun, the little groves on the opposite side of the river lit up by it while I am [in] shade, these are memorable and belong to the hour.

Here at this hour the brown thrasher often drowns the other birds. The towhee has been a main bird for

---

[1] [Probably the bird was a hermit thrush, this motion of the tail being almost a proof positive. Probably, too, all the "wood thrushes" seen by Thoreau in April (see *ante*) were hermits.]

regular morning singing in the woods for a little while. The creeper is regularly heard, too. Found the first strawberry blossoms (*Fragaria Virginiana*) on Fair Haven. The sedge grass blossom is now quite large and showy on the dry hillside where the wood has recently been cut off.

I think that birds vary their notes considerably with the seasons. When I hear a bird singing, I cannot think of any words that will imitate it. What word can stand in place of a bird's note? You would have to bury [?] it, or surround it with a *chevaux de frise* of accents, and exhaust the art of the musical composer besides with your different bars, to represent it, and finally get a bird to sing it, to perform it. It has so little relation to words. The wood thrush says *ah-tully-tully* for one strain. There appear to be one or more little warblers in the woods this morning which are new to the season, about which I am in doubt, myrtle-birds among them. For now, before the leaves, they begin to people the trees in this warm weather. The first wave of summer from the south. The purple finch (sober-colored) is a rich singer. As I said the other day, something like the warbling vireo, only louder, clearer, mellower, and more various. Bank swallows at Hayden's.

I fear that the dream of the toads will not sound so musical now that I know whence it proceeds. But I will not fear to *know*. They will awaken new and more glorious music for me as I advance, still farther in the horizon, not to be traced to toads and frogs in slimy pools.

P. M. — To Nawshawtuct.

The vireo comes with warm weather, midwife to the leaves of the elms. I see little ant-hills in the path, already raised. How long have they been? The first small pewee sings now *che-vet*, or rather chirrups *chevet, tche-vet* — a rather delicate bird with a large head and two white bars on wings. The first summer yellow-birds on the willow causeway. The birds I have lately mentioned come not singly, as the earliest, but all at once, *i. e.* many yellowbirds all over town. Now I remember the yellowbird comes when the willows begin to leave out. (And the small pewee on the willows also.) So yellow. They bring summer with them and the sun, *tche-tche-tche-tcha tcha-tchar*. Also they haunt the oaks, white and swamp white, where are not leaves. On the hill I sit in the shadow of the locust trunks and branches, for want of other shade. This is a mistake in Nature, to make shade necessary before she has expanded the leaves.

The catnep is now up, with a lustrous purple tinge to the under side of its leaves. (Why should so many leaves be so painted on the under side, concealed from men's eye — only not from the insects — as much as the sculptures on the tops of columns?) There is something in its fragrance as soothing as balm to a sick man. It advances me ever to the autumn and beyond it. How full of reminiscence is any fragrance! If it were not for virtuous, brave, generous actions, could there be any sweet fragrance?

> "Only the actions of the just
> Smell sweet and blossom in the dust."

Now you may say the trees generally are *beginning* to leave out, excepting the oaks, celtis, late water willow, etc., etc. But only the willows and the balm-of-Gileads make any show in our landscape yet, — of native or wild trees, — the latter where they grow in clumps. Its catkins are five inches long.

Top of hill. — The haze is remarkably thick to-day as if all the distant western woods were on fire. (The wind west and what coolness in it most grateful.) The haze makes the western view quite rich, so many edges of woodland ridges where you see the pine tops against the white mist of the vale beyond. I count five or six such ridges rising partly above the mist, but successively more indistinct, the first only a quarter of a mile off. Of course there are no mountains. It belongs to this warm weather. The lower part of the sky is white, like a fog; only in the zenith do I see any blue. It makes the outlines of the blue water on the meadow eastward agreeably indistinct, being more nearly the color of the water itself than the land. A maple swamp in bloom, westward from this hill, is a rich sight, even like a rosy orchard in bloom. The dust flies.

I am not sure whether my first violet was the *cucullata* or *ovata*,[1] or the same with that minute one which I found prepared to blossom by the Spring Path this morning. A fern, one of the osmundas, beyond the celtis, one foot high, covered with reddish wool, unfolding its blossom (?) as it rises. The wool used for birds' nests. Might be used for other purposes? It is such weather as in summer we expect a thunder-shower after.

---

[1] ["I . . . whether" and "*cucullata* or" crossed out in pencil.]

Is this smoke-like haze produced by the warm west wind meeting the still cool earth? Or is it smoke? The ground under the walnuts is richly strewn with nutshells, broken and gnawed by squirrels, like an unswept dining-hall in early times. That little early violet close to the ground in dry fields and hillsides, which only children's eyes detect, with buds showing purple but lying so low, as if stooping to rise, or rather its stems actually bent to hide its head amid the leaves, quite unpretending. The gnaphalium, though without scent, is now a pure, dry, enduring flower and bears inspection. The first peetweet; myrtle-birds numerous. The catbird does not make the corn-planting sounds. The toads dream loudly these first warm days. A yellow-throated green frog in the river, by the hemlocks, — bright silk-green the fore part of the body, tiger-striped legs. The eyes of toads and frogs are remarkably bright and handsome, — oval pupils (?) or blacks and golden or coppery irides. The hop-hornbeam is almost in bloom. The red-wing's shoulder, seen in a favorable light, throws all epaulets into the shade. It is General Abercrombie, methinks, when they wheel partly with the red to me. The crow blackbirds make a noise like crows, and also a singular and rarely heard scream or screech. They fly with lark-like wings. We require just so much acid as the cranberries afford in the spring. The first humblebee, that prince of hummers, — *bombyle* [*sic*], looking now over the ground as if he could find something. He follows after flowers. To have your existence depend on flowers, like the bees and hummingbirds! The willow twigs now may make

wreaths so pretty and graceful with their expanding leaves. They afford the only chaplets yet, fit to crown the fairest. The horse-chestnuts in the yards have opened their parasol-like leaves to-day, reminding me of tropical palms; and the rock maples' large buds are almost open. Such a haze as this makes a dark night.

May 8. 4.30. — The robin and the bluebird have sung for some time. The haziness is now like a sea-turn, through which the sun, shorn of beams, looks claret, and at length, when half an hour high, scarlet. You thought it might become rain. Many swallows flying in flocks *high* over the river, — the chimney swallow for one. What is the other? They sustain themselves sometimes on quivering wings, making little progress, as if to catch insects. A pretty little blossom on a willow, male and female sometimes on one catkin. The female catkins of the early willows are now expanded to two or three inches in length, making the otherwise backward tree look green. The male catkins have lost all their anthers for some time. The female maples are lengthening their stems for the keys. Some are a quite yellowish green (?), stigmas and all. A singular noise from a jay this morning. Hear the yellowbird, the creeper, and the myrtle-bird this morning, all together; they are much alike. The creeper, a faint oven-bird note; the myrtle-bird, a little more of the *s* or ψ in it than the yellowbird and more various. I hear the *wit er che*,[1] Maryland yellow-throat. Two gold robins; they chatter like blackbirds; the fire bursts

[1] *Vide* p. [40].

forth on their backs when they lift their wings. A fresh scent blows off from the meadows, the river rapidly going down. The leaves of the young rock maples, which have first expanded this morning, make little crosses against the sky, — four leaves, — or stars, the leaves being finely cut. The ground was found frozen still to-day, in the shade behind Aunt's house.

P. M. — Down river to Red Bridge.

The blackbirds have a rich *sprayey* warble now, sitting on the top [of] a willow or an elm. They possess the river now, flying back and forth across it. The high-backed, elliptical stinkpot covered with leeches. They lie near the shore with their backs out of water, dry in the sun. The spotted, and especially the painted, how they love to lie in the sun on rails and rocks!

No tarts that I ever tasted at any table possessed such a refreshing, cheering, encouraging acid that literally put the heart in you and set you on edge for this world's experiences, bracing the spirit, as the cranberries I have plucked in the meadows in the spring. They cut the winter's phlegm, and now I can swallow another year of this world without other sauce. Even on the Thanksgiving table they are comparatively insipid, have lost as much flavor as beauty, are never so beautiful as in water.

The warm weather (looking back over the past days) has [come] very suddenly. One day I had a fire (which day? *Vide* back a week or two), and the next night, and each night since, I slept with my window open, as I have sat with it all day. Everything has taken a sud-

den start within three or four days, and our thoughts are equally affected. The air has been remarkably hazy or smoky. The weather has been delightfully warm; not what you would call sultry, for there is, after all, a grateful coolness in the breeze. The haze is so thick that only the zenith is blue to-day and yesterday.

The aspens, with their young leaves, now make a show in the woods like light-green fires amid the other trees. Martins are heard over the meadows — their rich warble — and in one place they make the street alive. The white maple is covered with small leaves now, as forward or perhaps more so than the sugar maple. The cross they make is more irregular, two of the leaves being longer than the others. Is that female maple higher up the river a white one? Horse-mint is up (above ground).

The blackbirds fly in flocks and sing in concert on the willows, — what a lively, chattering concert! a great deal of chattering with many liquid and rich warbling notes and clear whistles, — till now a hawk sails low, beating the bush: and they are silent or off, but soon begin again. Do any other birds sing in such deafening concert? The red-wings, male and female. The red maple in blossom is most beautiful near to. Here too, on Red Bridge causeway, I find the yellow-birds *on the willows*. The *Salix alba* has bloomed to-day and fills the causeway with sweet fragrance, though there are yet but few flowers. Here are boys making whistles. Now no instrumental music should be heard in the streets more youthful and innocent than willow whistles. Its sound has something soft in it as the wood of the willow. A rather rich scent has this willow blossom.

Sundown. — To Cliffs. (No moon.)

I am most impressed by the rapidity of the changes within a week. Saw a load of rock maples on a car from the country. Their buds have not yet started, while ours are leaved out. They must have been brought from the northern part of Vermont, where is winter still. A tree, with all its roots, which has not felt the influence of spring is a most startling evidence of winter, — of the magic worked by the railroad. The young sugar maples in our streets are now green with young leaves. These trees from the north are whirled into their midst from a region of ice and snow, with not a bud yet started, at least a fortnight or three weeks more backward, not fairly awaked from their winter's sleep.

Children are digging dandelions by the roadside with a pan and a case-knife. For the first time, this evening I observe the twittering of swallows about the barns. The sun has set *in the haze.* Methinks I have heard the snipe. Now hear the lark, the song sparrow, etc. The peeper, is he not lord of sound? so tiny, yet heard farther than a man! A cool but an agreeable wind. (Going by Bear Garden.) The sounds of peeping frogs (*Hylodes*) and dreaming toads are mingled into a sort of indistinct universal evening lullaby to creation, while the wind roars in the woods for a background or sea of sound, in which — on whose bosom — these others float.

little peepers have been so thick all together as to hinder his cattle from drinking, — a hundred together. It was when the weather was cooler. Was it not for warmth, and when they were asleep in the morning?

Methinks the scent is a more primitive inquisition than the eye, more oracular and trustworthy. When I criticise my own writing, I go by the scent, as it were. The scent reveals, of course, what is concealed from the other senses. By it I detect earthiness.[1]

May 9. Sunday Morning. — To Trillium Woods.

Apples and cherry trees begin to look green at a distance. I see the catkin of a female *Populus tremuloides* far advanced, *i. e.* become large like the willows. These low woods are full of the *Anemone nemorosa*, half opened at this hour and gracefully drooping, — sepals with a purple tinge on the under side, now exposed. They are in beds and look like hail on the ground; their now globular flowers spot the ground white. Saw a Maryland yellow-throat, whose note I have heard before, — the little restless bird that sits low, *i. e.* on low bushes. The golden senecio, ragwort, or squaw-weed (*Senecio aureus*), whose lower or radical leaves, roundish and crenate, somewhat resemble the cowslip early in the meadows, has now got up six inches high and shows purple buds. It is the plant whose stem when broken yields that sweet scent. Low blueberry bushes and high are well budded to bloom. The bluet (sometimes at least?) begins with a kind of lilac-blue, fading through white, delicately tinged with blue, to white.

¹ [Channing, p. 299.]

The young birch leaves, very neatly plaited, small triangular light-green leaves, yield an agreeable sweet fragrance, just expanded and sticky, — sweet-scented as innocence. The song sparrow and the robin sing early and late. The night-warbler while it is yet pretty light. It is that kind of mirage now in which the slope of the hills appears not a position but a motion. The hills ascend, the earth rocks. Do I not hear the veery's *yorick?* The "whipp-or-u-wills" begin. When I heard the first one the other night, feeling myself on the verge of winter, I was startled as if I had heard a summer sound in the midst of winter. I hear a catbird singing within a rod among the alders, but it is too dark to see him. Now he stops and half angrily, half anxiously and inquisitively, inquires *char-char*, sounding like the caw of a crow, not like a cat.

Venus is the evening star and the only star yet visible. Starlight marks conveniently a stage in the evening, *i. e.* when the first star can be seen. Does it not coincide with the whip-poor-wills' beginning? I am struck by the blackness of the small pines at this hour, two or three feet high, on the plain below Fair Haven Hill. It is already midnight behind or within them. Is there as great a contrast in the summer, when the grass in this field is more green? Such trees are, as it were, nuclei of the night. A strong but not cold southwest wind is blowing against the rocks mercilessly, an aerial surf, having been ordered to do so. The twilight seems long this evening. Is it not made so by the haze?

Hayden tells me that when he has been to water his cattle some time since in the pool behind his house, the

P. M. — To hill north of Walden.

I smell the blossoms of the willows, the row of *Salix alba* on Swamp Bridge Brook, a quarter of a mile to windward, the wind being strong. There is a delightful coolness in the wind. Reduce neck-cloth. Nothing so harmonizes with this condition of the atmosphere — warm and hazy — as the dream of the toad. The samaræ on Cheney's elms now give it a leafy appearance, or as if covered with hops, before the buds are expanded. Other elms are nearly as forward. The gray, misty-looking deciduous woods now appear to imbosom the evergreens, which before stood out distinct. It is partly to be referred now, I think, to the expanding leaves as well as the haze. They are closing in around them, and there is an indescribable change in the appearance of the evergreens. Now and for some days the west and southwest winds have prevailed. The early blueberry is almost in flower. The arbutus (?) pyrus shows red scales (?). The barren plants of the *Equisetum arvense* now shoot up rapidly on the railroad bank and make it suddenly green. *Viola ovata* in bloom. The shrub oak buds are expanding, red of various hues and mixtures, quite rich. There is a *positive* sweetness in the air from flowers and expanding leaves, a universal sweetness. A longish yellow-abdomened bee. Chickadee's phœbe note is common now, the *tull-a-lull* more rare and in mornings.

It is impossible to remember a week ago. A river of Lethe flows with many windings the year through, separating one season from another. The heavens for a few days have been lost. It has been a sort of *para-*

dise instead. As with the seashore, so is it with the universal earth-shore, not in summer can you look far into the ocean of the ether. They who come to this world as to a watering-place in the summer for coolness and luxury never get the far and fine November views of heaven. Is not all the summer akin to a paradise? We have to bathe in ponds to brace ourselves. The earth is blue now, — the near hills, in this haze.

The yellowish-white birch catkins are now opened. The buds of the white oak are now well swollen; they are later than the black and red oaks, which are beginning to leave out. The oaks, excepting the white, are quite as early if not earlier than the hickory. A choke (?) cherry well budded by Brooks's clearing; will blossom to-morrow or next day.

The cinquefoil, which so much resembles a strawberry, comes yellow not white. Do yellow flowers often bear an edible fruit? The *Viola ovata* is one of the minutest of spring flowers, — two leaves and a blossom-bud showing the blue close to the earth. What haste to push up and open its lesser azure to the greater above! Such a disproportion of blossom to the leaves! Almost literally a pretty delicate blue flower bursting forth from the scurf of the earth. The rue-leaved anemone not for scent, but a pretty leaf. The chair flag is six or eight inches high in the water, bluish-green. Swarms of little gnats with two plumes on their heads just born on the edge of the pond. The chestnuts are perhaps more advanced than oaks. Bees know what flowers have bloomed, but they must depend mainly on the willows as yet. I am not sure but the pond is higher

than ever. Some rich young oak buds I see, young and tender reddish leaves under scales, making buds [two] or three inches long, making a kind of cross with a fifth in the middle, — red oak, I think. There is also the number five in the form of the wood, when you cut the end of a twig. Some of the female catkins on cone-bearing willows are now more than three inches long. Tortoises out sunning, on rails, etc. Some young trees very forward in a warm place. The leaves of the maple are sharply recurved, partly so as to protect the tender parts, apparently. In such a place the scales have recurved from the hickory buds, revealing already developed branches. Saw a green snake, twenty or more inches long, on a bush, hanging over a twig with its head held forward six inches into the air, without support and motionless. What there for? Leaves generally are most beautiful when young and tender, before insects or weather has defaced them.

These are the warm-west-wind, dream-frog, leafing-out, willowy, haze days. Is not this summer, whenever it occurs, the vireo and yellowbird and golden robin being here? The young birch leaves reflect the light in the sun.

Mankind seen in a dream. The gardener asks what kind of beans he shall plant. Nobody is looking up into the sky. *In our woods* it is the aspens now and the birches that show their growth at a distance. It was in such a season and such a wind that the crow brought the corn from the southwest.[1] Our eyes are turned to the west and southwest. It grows somewhat clearer; a cloud, threatening rain, coming up in the west. The

[1] [See *Walden*, p. 264; Riv. 371.]

veiny leaves of the hawkweed appear. The *Salix tristis* is in bloom. Saw pigeons in the woods, with their inquisitive necks and long tails, but few representatives of the great flocks that once broke down our forests. Heard the night warbler. Our moods vary from week to week, with the winds and the temperature and the revolution of the seasons. The first shad-bush, June-berry, or service-berry (*Amelanchier Canadensis*), in blossom. The first *Viola pedata* and also, in a low place, the first *Viola cucullata*. That I observed the first of May was a *V. ovata*, a variety of *sagittata*. Saw one of the peeping frogs this afternoon, sitting on a dead leaf on the surface of the water. The color of a white oak leaf at present, so that it is hard to detect one, — much lighter and more decidedly fawn-colored than those I had. They will peep on the sideboard. The clumps of alders now look greenish with expanding leaves. The haze is now going off before a coming shower. The bluebird's warble is soon in a great measure drowned by the notes of new birds.

May 10. This Monday the streets are full of cattle being driven up-country, — cows and calves and colts. The rain is making the grass grow apace. It appears to stand upright, — its blades, — and you can almost see it grow. For some reason I now remember the autumn, — the succory and the goldenrod. We remember autumn to best advantage in the spring; the finest aroma of it reaches us then. Are those the young keys of sugar maples that I see? The Canada (?) (N. Brooks's) plum in bloom, and a cherry tree. How

closely the flower follows upon, if it does not precede, the leaf! The leaves are but calyx and escort to the flower. Some beds of clover wave.

Some look out only for the main chance, and do not regard appearances nor manners; others — others regard these mainly. It is an immense difference. I feel it frequently. It is a theme I must dwell upon. There is an aurora borealis to-night, and I hear a snoring, praying sound from frogs in the river, baser and less ringing and sonorous than the dreamers.

May 11. Sunrise, — merely a segment of a circle of rich amber in the east, growing brighter and brighter at one point. There is no rosy color at this moment and not a speck in the sky, and now comes the sun without pomp, a bright liquid gold. Dews come with the grass. There is, I find on examining, a small, clear drop at the end of each blade, quite at the top on one side.

The *Salix alba* has a *spicier* fragrance than the earliest willows. We have so much causeway planted with willows, — set with them on each side to prevent its washing away, — that they make a great show, and are obvious now before other trees are so advanced. The birches at a distance appear as in a thin green veil, in their expanding leaves.

P. M. — *Kossuth here.*

The hand-organ, when I am far enough off not to hear the friction of the machinery, not to see or be reminded of the performer, serves the grandest use for me, deepens my existence. Heard best through walls and obstructions. These performers, too, have come with the pleasant weather and the birds.

I think I saw a female yellowbird yesterday; its note different from the male's, somewhat like the night warbler's. They come a little later than the males. The larches are leafing out.

May 12. Morning. — Swallows (I suppose barn) flying low over the Depot Field, a barren field, and sitting on the mulleins. Bobolinks.

Currants and gooseberries are in bloom in the garden. The mountain-ash leafed out as much as two days ago. The elms have been leafing out for two or three days. Sugar maples on the common are in blossom. Hear the peepers in the rain to-night (9.30), but not the dream toads.

May 13. The best men that I know are not serene, a world in themselves. They dwell in form. They flatter and study effect, only more finely than the rest. The world to me appears uninhabited. My neighbors select granite for the underpinning of their houses and barns; they build their fences of stone; but they do not themselves rest on an underpinning of granite. Their sills are rotten. What stuff is the man made of who is not coexistent in your thought with the purest and subtlest truth? While there are manners and compliments we do not meet. I accuse my finest acquaintances of an immense frivolity. They do not teach me the lessons of honesty and sincerity that the brute beasts do, or of

steadiness and solidity that the rocks do.[1] I cannot associate with those who do not understand me.

Rain to-day and yesterday, with fires in house. The birds — sparrows and yellowbirds — seeking shelter in the wood-pile.

Where are the men who dwell in thought? Talk, — that is palaver! at which men hurrah and clap! The manners of the bear are so far good that he does not pay you any compliments.

P. M. — To Walden in rain.

A May storm, yesterday and to-day; rather cold. The fields are green now, and the cows find good feed. The female *Populus grandidentata*, whose long catkins are now growing old, is now leafing out. The flowerless (male?) ones show half-unfolded silvery leaves. Both these and the aspens are quite green (the bark) in the rain. A young, slender maple-like bush from four to ten feet high just leafing out and in blossom, their few scarlet or crimson blossoms in the rain very handsome. It answers to the description of the red maple, but is it not different? I see an oak against the pines, apparently a red oak, now decidedly in the gray, — a light breaking through mist. All these expanding leaves and flower-buds are much more beautiful in the rain, — covered with clear drops. They have lost some of their beauty when I have shaken the drops off. They who do not walk in the woods in the rain never behold them in their freshest, most radiant and blooming beauty. The white birch is a very handsome object, with its golden tassels three inches long, hanging directly down,

[1] [*Cape Cod, and Miscellanies*, p. 470 ; *Misc.*, Riv. 272.]

amid the just expanding yellowish-green leaves, their perpendicularity contrasting with the direction of the branches, geometry mixed with nature. The catkins, beaten down by the rain, also strew the ground. The shrub oaks, covered with rain-drops, are very handsome, masses of variegated red-budded tassels and opening leaves, some redder, some lighter green or yellowish. They appear more forward than the oak trees. The red and black oaks are more forward than the white, which last is just opening its buds. The sweet-fern shows minute green leaves expanding. The shad-blossom with pinkish scales, or Emerson calls them "purple or faint crimson" "stipules." Botryapium (?). The amelanchiers (*Botryapium*, June-berry, which I suppose is the taller, and *ovalis* (Emerson), swamp sugar-pear, the shorter and more crowded) are now the prevailing flowers in the woods and swamps and sprout-lands, and a very beautiful, delicate flower the former is, with its purplish stipules and delicate drooping white blossoms, — so large and graceful a tree or bush. The shad-blossom days in the woods. The pines have started, white pines the most. These last are in advance of the white oak. The low early blueberry (*Vaccinium Pennsylvanicum*) (*V. tenellum* Big.) is just in blossom, and the *Cerasus Virginiana*, dwarf choke-cherry.

The birds are silent and in their coverts, excepting the black and white creepers and the jay and a brown thrasher. You know not what has become of all the rest. Channing heard the quail yesterday. The cowslips, in rounded bunches a foot in diameter, make a

splendid show, even fresher and brighter, methinks, in the rain. The *Viola pedata* and *ovata* now begin to be abundant on warm, sandy slopes. The leaves of the lupine, six inches high, are handsome, covered with rain-drops.

May 14. *Hastily* reviewing this Journal, I find the flowers to have appeared in this order since the 28th of April (perhaps *some note* in my Journal has escaped me):[1] —

Acer rubrum	April 28	male ; a female 30th ; first date is perhaps early enough for both.
Populus grandidentata	29	
Epigœa repens	30	(April 25, '51).
Sweet-gale	30	probably a *day* or *two* before.
Viola ovata	May 1	(April 25, '51).
Potentilla Canadensis	3	
Chrysosplenium Americanum	3	this may have bloomed *two* or *three* days before.
Salix tristis or *humilis*	5	
Sweet-fern	5	
Thalictrum anemonoides	5	
Populus balsamifera	5	two inches long.
Anemone nemorosa	6	
Viola blanda	6	perhaps the day before.
Aquilegia Canadensis	6	
Hedyotis cœrulea	6	(April 25, '51).
Andromeda calyculata	6	
Fragaria Virginiana	7	
Benzoin odoriferum	7	probably now (May 1, '51).
Ostrya	8	begins.

[1] The Latin Gray's. By last of June, '51 is apparently three or four days earlier than '52.

Salix alba	May 8	
Betula populifolia	9	
Amelanchier Canadensis	9	
Viola pedata	9	probably a *day* or *two* before.
V. cucullata	9	did not examine where they grow.
Acer saccharinum	10	probably some days earlier.
Canada (?) plum in gardens	10	
Rubus triflorus?	10	probably about this (ripe July 1).
Cultivated cherry	10	
Fraxinus Americana when?		
Currants	12	
Gooseberries in garden	12	
Ribes hirtellum? The wild; are they one?		
Vaccinium Pennsylvanicum	13	
Cerasus Pennsylvanica?	13	
Betula papyracea ⎫		
B. excelsa ⎬ when?		
B. lenta ⎭		

Did not observe so *very* carefully the first common elm and first red maple, but Cheney's and white (?) maple at bridge instead; yet accurately enough. *Perhaps* the wild gooseberry and some Solomon's-seal and other violets and birches and the hornbeam and the yellow lily in some places are in bloom now!

BIRDS SINCE 28TH APRIL

Saw the last *Fringilla hyemalis* May 4.
First
Savannah (?) [1] sparrow   May 1 or a day or two before.

[1] ["Seringo" in pencil written over "Savannah" and "Bay-winged" under.]

Ground robin	May 1	
Catbird	1	
Black and white creeper	1	
Purple finch	1	
Myrtle-bird	2	
Chipping sparrow	2	
Indigo-bird (?)	2	
Brown thrasher	3	
Whip-poor-will	3	
Warbling vireo	6	
Green bittern	6	
Oven-bird	7	
Bank swallow	7	
Small pewee	7	
Summer yellowbird	7	
Peetweet	7	
Chimney swallow	8	
Maryland yellow-throat	8	
Golden robin	8	
Martins	8	probably long before.
Snipe (?)	8	
Night-warbler	8	
Yorrick (?)	8	
Pigeon or turtle dove	9	
Female yellowbird	10	
Bobolink	12	
Quail	12	

Snow in hollows?	April 28	
Saw frog spawn	28	
Rushes at Second Division one foot high, highest of grass-like herbs	29	
A *large* water-bug	29	
Heard toad (dreaming)	30	
Bull(?)frog (saw him)	30	
Flies buzz outdoors		

Gooseberry leaves (earliest of leaves?)	April 30	
Sit without fire to-night. Spearing.		
Chickadee's *tull-a-lull*	May 4	
First cricket on Cliff	5	
Shad-fly	5	
Toad in garden	5	
Wasps	6	
Willows suddenly green	6	
Cows going up-country		
Many trees *just beginning* to expand leaves	6	
First fog, very slight		
Ant-hills	7	
Humblebee	7	
Partridge drums	7	
Stinkpot tortoise	8	How much earlier?
Birch leaves, sweet-scented	8	
Ground still frozen in some places	8	
Barn swallows twitter	8	
Apple and cherry trees begin to show green	9	
Elms darkened with samaræ		
A green snake	9	
Reduce neck-cloth		
Clover waves	10	
Frogs snore in the river	10	
One oak in the gray	13	
Pines start	13	
A May storm	13	

These pages do not contain the earliest phenomena of the spring, for which see the previous journal, as far as observed.

P. M. — To Second Division.
A foul day. One scent of golden senecio recalls the

meadows of my golden age. It is like sweet-briar a little.

First kingbird. Its voice and flight relate it to the swallow. The maple-keys are already formed, though the male blossoms (on different trees) are not withered. Going over the Corner causeway, the willow blossoms fill the air with a sweet fragrance, and I am ready to sing, Ah! willow, willow! These willows have yellow bark, bear yellow flowers and yellowish-green leaves, and are now haunted by the summer yellowbird and Maryland yellow-throat. They see this now conspicuous mass of yellowish verdure at a distance and fly to it. Single large willows at distance are great nosegays of yellow. This orchard precedes the peach and apple weeks. The *Salix nigra* (?) is leafing out now with its catkins appearing. The sounds and sights — as birds and flowers — heard and seen at those seasons when there are fewest are most memorable and suggestive of poetic associations. The trillium is budded. The *Uvularia sessilifolia*, a drooping flower with tender stems and leaves; the latter curled so as to show their under sides hanging about the stems, as if shrinking from the cold. The *Ranunculus bulbosus* shows its yellow by this spring thus early (Corner Spring). Apparently it is the leaves of this, and not the geranium, that are so common and early. Here is half an acre of skunk-cabbage leaves. It looks like a garden in the midst of the trees of the swamp. The cowslip even smells a little like the skunk-cabbage with which it grows. The grass is now whitened with bluets; the fields are green, and the roadsides. (I am on the C. Miles road.) Now is the season to travel. The deciduous trees are rapidly investing the evergreens, making the woods rich and bosky by degrees. The robin sings this louring day. They sang most in and about that great freshet storm. The song of the robin is most suggestive in cloudy weather. I have not heard any toads during this rain (of which this is the third day), and very few peepers. A man wishes me to find a lead mine for him somewhere within three miles from this point (Marshal Miles's). The discoverer died suddenly about seven years ago, a month after the discovery, and revealed not the locality. Wanted to know where it grew! The beautiful birch catkins hang down four inches. Saw a whip-poor-will sitting in the path in woods on the mill road, — the brown mottled bird. It flutters off blindly, with slow, soft flight. Most birds are silent in the storm. Hear the robin, oven-bird, night warbler, and, at length, the towhee's *towee*, chickadee's *phœbe*, and a preluding thrasher and a jay. The *Saxifraga Pennsylvanica* with the golden saxifrage and cowslip. The mayflowers, which I plucked to-day, surpass all flowers hitherto in fragrance; peeping up from amid the leaves, they perfume the roadside. A strawberry by the meadow-side, probably the other species. This weather has produced fungi in the path. Anemones now in their prime. The bear-berry (*Arbutus Uva-Ursi*) in bloom, a neat bell-like white flower with a red contracted rim, clear pearly and red, a reddish tinge and red lips, transparent at base.

Most men can be easily transplanted from here there, for they have so little root, — no tap-root, — or their

roots penetrate so little way, that you can thrust a shovel quite under them and take them up, roots and all.[1]

On the 11th, when Kossuth was here, I looked about for shade, but did not find it, the trees not being leaved out. Nature was not prepared for great heats.

The barren flowers of the gnaphalium (*plantagineum?* no nerve to leaves), now three or four inches high, white, dotted with reddish anthers, like a diamond set in pearls, — very dry and pure and pearly like a breastpin.

That early willow at end of Corner Bridge has now female catkins on particular branches[2] at same time with leaves expanding. These are already serrulate and lighter beneath. The catkins are about an inch long (longer than the male were); ovaries stalked; rather downy scales, brown, rounded; stigmas distinctly two-divided and indistinctly four-divided; stem downy. Is it Bigelow's swamp willow?

Found four or five early grass-like plants or grasses or sedges. I think one the field rush (*Juncus campestris*).

May 16. The last four days have been a May storm, and this day is not quite fair yet. As I remember, there was the long storm and freshet near the end of April, then the warm, pleasant, hazy days, then this May storm, cooler but not cold as the first.

P. M. — To Conantum.

I think I may say that the buttercup (bulbous crow-

[1] [See p. 16.]   [2] Another tree?

foot) which I plucked at the Corner Spring would have blossomed to-day. The *Gnaphalium plantagineum* has a tender, springlike scent. The clustered purple buds of the senecio are very common in the meadows. The bees on the *Salix alba*, the prevailing one now in blossom, hum a further advance into summer. The American water cress (*Cardamine Pennsylvanica*) in blossom. The dwarf andromeda's leaf-buds are just starting. The dense beds of this plant resound with the hum of honey-bees. There is enough of this early flower to make up for deficiencies elsewhere at this season. The meadows ring with the bobolink's strain. I do not observe the female yet. Here is a bird's nest by the ditch-side which some animal has robbed, and an egg is fallen into the water. The first I have found this season. The air is sweet with fragrance. I have not seen any speckled frogs before to-day. The bobolink sits on a hardhack, swaying to and fro, uncertain whether to begin his strain, — dropping a few bubbling notes by way of prelude, — with which he overflows. There are many insects now. I was ready to say that I had seen no more beautiful flower than the dandelion. That has the vernal scent. How many flowers have no peculiar, but only this simple vernal, fragrance?

The sessile-leaved bellwort, with three or four delicate pale-green leaves with reflexed edges, on a tender-looking stalk, the single modest-colored flower gracefully drooping, neat, with a fugacious, richly spiced fragrance, facing the ground, the dry leaves, as if unworthy to face the heavens. It is a beautiful sight, a pleasing discovery, the first of the season, — growing in

a little straggling company, in damp woods or swamps. When you turn up the drooping flower, its petals make a perfect geometrical figure, a six-pointed star. These faint, fugacious fragrances are pleasing. You are not always quite sure that you perceive any. In the swamp at end of Hubbard's Grove. Here are a million *Anemone nemorosa*. The inconspicuous white blossom of the gold-thread is detected amid them, but you are more struck by the bright-golden thread of its root when you pull it up. The *Viola ovata* is now very common, but rather indistinct in the grass, in both high and low land, in the sod where there is yet but little grass. The earth reflects the heavens in violets. The whole earth is fragrant as a bouquet held to your nose. I distinguish Bigelow's *Pyrus ovalis* (swamp) and *Botryapium* (wood), the former now downy, with smaller racemes, a shorter shrub, the other larger in most respects, if not all, with smooth aspen-colored leaves. Think it was the last I first plucked, though they apparently came together. *Vide* back. Peach trees in blossom. I have not walked to Lincoln lately; so have not watched their opening. It must have been some days ago. The apple buds show red. The trees are gradually leafing out and investing the evergreens. The high blueberry on high land will blossom fully in a day or two. Pretty sure I heard a hummingbird about the columbines. Can now pluck a sprig of fresh sweet-briar and feed my senses with that. I begin to hesitate about walking through some fields on account of the grass. Rye has been five or six inches high for some time. Methinks the columbine *here* is more remarkable for growing out of the seams of the rocks than the saxifrage, and perhaps better deserves the latter name. It is now in its prime, ornamental for nature's rockwork. It is a beautiful sight to see large clusters of splendid scarlet and yellow flowers growing out of a seam in the side of this gray cliff. I observe some very *pale* blue *Viola cucullata* in the meadows. The *Arum triphyllum* in bloom and the nodding trillium budded. The black ash is now in flower (and some out of flower), and the male white ash in Miles's swamp. Is the fever-bush dead, that its wood looks so dry and its flower-buds do not expand?[1] Some of the *Gnaphalium plantagineum* have a yellow tip to the blossoms. Which is it? Male or female?

I hear few peepers to-day and no toads. The *Anemone nemorosa* are half closed, showing the purple under sides of the petals, but all the rue-leaved are open; but they are not so handsome open, notwithstanding their pretty leaves and yellow stamens, as the purple buds of the other. Some of these are wholly purple and their leaves a rich brown.

The muskrat has piled his shells high up the bank this year, on account of the freshet. Even our river shells will have some black, purple, or green tints, telling of distant skies, like shells from the Indies. How did these beautiful rainbow tints get into the shell of the fresh-water clam buried in the mud at the bottom of our dark river? Even the sea-bottom tells of the upper skies.

The tupelo tree is as late as, or later than, the white

[1] Yes, dead.

oak to leaf out. What is that grass in Conant's orchard in bloom? Early sedge? Here a woodchuck has dug out a bushel of sharp stones on a hillside, as big as your fist. The thrasher has a sort of laugh in his strain which the catbird has not. The sun comes out in patches somewhat like the expanding oak leaves. This gleam of sunshine, an hour or more before sundown (I am on the top of Conantum), on the tender foliage of Garfield's elms and of other trees, from behind a dark cloud in the west. Nature letting her sun shine by degrees, holding a veil of cloud before her tender plants. The patches of ground plowed and planted look fresh after the rain and of a dark-brown color. Even this nakedness is agreeable.

This will be the week of the oaks in the gray, when the farmers must plant away [?]. The bass is very conspicuous now, with its light yellow-green leaves, more forward than most. I see a hundred young apple trees come up in cow-dung. The flower-like leaves of the shrub oaks now, so red! A young of the painted tortoise, almost exactly circular and one inch in diameter, run over by a wheel in the road on the causeway.

Here on this causeway is the sweetest fragrance I have perceived this season, blown from the newly flooded meadows. I cannot imagine what there is to produce it. No nosegay can equal it. It is ambrosially, nectareally, fine and subtile, for you can see naught but the water, with green spires of meadow grass rising above it. Yet no flower from the Islands of the Blessed could smell sweeter. Yet I shall never know whence it

comes. Is it not all water-plants combined? A fine, delicious fragrance, which will come to the senses only when it will, — willful as the gales. I would give something to know of it. How it must attract all birds and insects! Can it be the willow over my head? I think not.

I hear the peepers *and toads again* this evening. It *gradually* clears up at the end of this May storm.

May 17. My seringo-bird is reddish-brown with a spot on the breast and other marks, two whitish lines on back, and some white in tail; runs in the grass, so that you see nothing of it where the grass is very low; and sings standing on a tuft of grass and holding its head up the while.

P. M. — To Loring's Pond.

Decidedly fair weather at last; a bright, breezy, flowing, *washing* day. I see that dull-red grass whose blades, having risen above the surface of the water, lie flat on it in close and conspicuous flakes, making a right angle with the part in the water. Perhaps a slightly rosaceous tint to it.

The different color of the water at different times would be worth observing. To-day it is full of light and life, the breeze presenting many surfaces to the sun. There is a sparkling shimmer on it. It is a deep, dark blue, as the sky is clear. The air everywhere is, as it were, full of the rippling of waves. This pond is the more interesting for the islands in it. The water is seen running behind them, and it is pleasant to know that it penetrates quite behind and isolates the land you

see, or to see it apparently flowing out from behind an island with shining ripples.

To-day the cinquefoils (the earliest one) on the hillsides shine in the sun. Their brightness becomes the day. That is a beautiful footpath through the pitch pines on the hillside north of this pond, over a carpet of tawny pine leaves, so slippery under your feet. Why do not men sprinkle these over their floors instead of sand? The sun on the young foliage of birches, alders, etc., on the opposite side of the pond has an enchanting effect. The sunshine has a double effect. The new leaves abet it, so fresh and tender, not apprehending their insect foes. Now the sun has come out after the May storm, how bright, how full of freshness and tender promise and fragrance is the new world! The woods putting forth new leaves; it is a memorable season. So hopeful! These young leaves have the beauty of flowers. The shrub oaks are just beginning to blossom. The forward leaves and shoots of the meadow-sweet, beneath the persistent dead flowers, make a very rich and conspicuous green now along the fences and walls. The conspicuous white flowers of the two kinds of shad-blossom spot the hillsides at a distance. This is the only bush or tree whose flowers are sufficiently common and large at this time (to-day), except the *Salix alba* and the peach (the choke-cherry is rare), to make a show now, as the apples will soon. I see dark pines in the distance in the sunshine, contrasting with the light fresh green of the deciduous trees.

There is life in these fresh and varied colors, life in the motion of the wind and the waves; all make it a flowing, washing day. It is a good day to saunter. The female crimson flowers of the sweet-gale are still conspicuous. Is that the shepherd's-purse and the speedwell[1] that I found in blossom? Those commonest cockle(?)-shells are holding on to the rocks under water by their feet in Fort Pond Brook. Wood tortoises are numerous in the fields to-day. Saw a young one two and a half inches diameter. Do I smell the young birch leaves at a distance? Most trees are beautiful when leafing out, but especially the birch. After a storm at this season, the sun comes out and lights up the tender expanding leaves, and all nature is full of light and fragrance, and the birds sing without ceasing, and the earth is a fairyland. The birch leaves are so small that you see the landscape through the tree, and they are like silvery and green spangles in the sun, fluttering about the tree. Bridged the brook with help of an alder loop and a rider. Are they not grandidentatas on Annursnack which show so white at this distance like shad-blossoms? Does not summer begin after the May storm? What is that huckleberry with sticky leaf-buds and just expanding leaves covered with a yellow waxy matter? The first *veery* note.

Methinks they were turtle doves which I saw this afternoon baited to a pigeon-place. They fly like a pigeon, — a slender, darting bird. I do not surely know them apart.

To-night I hear a new dreamer, a frog, — that sprayey note which perhaps I have referred to the midsummer frog. That praying or snoring sound also I hear.

[1] It is either the smooth or the procumbent, probably the first.

Vol. IV

— like a fire flaming up from the earth. The earth proves itself well alive even in the skin. No scurf on it, only a browner color on the barren tops of hills. Fourthly, the forest, the dark-green pines, wonderfully distinct, near and erect, with their distinct dark stems, spiring tops, regularly disposed branches, and silvery light on their needles. They seem to wear an aspect as much fresher and livelier as the other trees, — though their growth can hardly be perceptible yet, — as if they had been washed by the rains and the air. They are now being invested with the light, sunny, yellowish-green of the deciduous trees. This tender foliage, putting so much light and life into the landscape, is the remarkable feature at this date. The week when the deciduous trees are generally and conspicuously expanding their leaves. The various tints of gray oaks and yellowish-green birches and aspens and hickories, and the red or scarlet tops where maple keys are formed (the blossoms are now over), — these last the high color (rosaceous?) in the bouquet. And fifthly, I detect a great stretch of high-backed, mostly bare, grassy pasture country between this and the Nashua, spotted with pines and forests, which I had formerly taken for forest uninterrupted. And finally, sixthly, Wachusett rising in the background, slightly veiled in bluish mist, — toward which all these seem to slope gradually upward, — and those grassy hillsides in the foreground, seen but as patches of bare grassy ground on a spur of that distant mountain.

This afternoon the brown thrashers are very numerous and musical. They plunge downward when they

May 18. The rhodora in blossom, a delicate-colored flower.

P. M. — To Cliffs.

Frog or toad spawn in a pool in long worm-like or bowel-like strings, sometimes coiled up spirally.

It is fine clear atmosphere, only the mountains blue. A slight seething but no haze. Shall we have much of *this* weather after this? There is scarcely a flock of cloud in the sky. The heaven is now broad and open to the earth in these longest days. The world can never be more beautiful than now, for, combined with the tender fresh green, you have this remarkable clearness of the air. I doubt if the landscape will be any greener.

The landscape is most beautiful looking towards the sun (in the orchard on Fair Haven) at four. First, there is this green slope on which I sit, looking down between the rows of apple trees just being clothed with tender green, — sometimes underneath them to the sparkling water, or over through them, or seeing them against the sky. Secondly, the outline of this bank or hill is drawn against the water far below; the river still high, a beautifully bright sheen on the water there, though it is elsewhere a dull slaty-blue color, a sober rippled surface. A fine sparkling shimmer in front, owing to the remarkable clearness of the atmosphere (clarified by the May storm?). Thirdly, on either side of the wood beyond the river are patches of bright, tender, yellowish, velvety green grass in meadows and on hillsides. It is like a short furred mantle now and bright as if it had the sun on it. Those great fields of green affect me as did those early green blades by the Corner Spring,

leave their perch, in a peculiar way. It is a bird that appears to make a business of singing for its own amusement. There is great variety in its strains. It is not easy to detect any repetition. The wood thrush, too, is pretty sure to be heard in a walk. Some shrub oaks are beginning to blossom. I hear my second cricket on the face of the Cliffs, clear and distinct, — only one. The shrub oaks on the plain show a little red with their buds and young leaves. The crowfoot shines on the rocks.

At evening the water is quite white, reflecting the white evening sky, and oily smooth. I see the willows reflected in it, when I cannot see their tops in the twilight against the dark hillside. The first bat by the riverside. The praying or snoring frog, the peepers (not so common as lately), the toads (not many), and sometimes my midsummer frog, — all together. The spearers are out to-night.

These days the golden robin is the important bird in the streets, on the elms.

May 19. Up to about the 14th of May I watched the progress of the season very closely, — though not so carefully the earliest birds, — but since that date, both from poor health and multiplicity of objects, I have noted little but what fell under my observation. The pear trees are in bloom before the apples. The cherries appear to have been blasted by the winter. The lilac has begun to blossom. There was the first lightning we have noticed this year, last Sunday evening, and a thunder-storm in Walpole, N. H. Lightning here this evening and an aurora in form of a segment of a circle.

May 20. P. M. — To Corner Spring.

So many birds that I have not attended much to any of late. A barn swallow accompanied me across the Depot Field, methinks attracted by the insects which I started, though I saw them not, wheeling and tacking incessantly on all sides and repeatedly dashing within a rod of me. It is an agreeable sight to watch one. Nothing lives in the air but is in rapid motion.

Now is the season of the leafing of the trees and of planting. The fields are white with houstonias, as they will soon be yellow with buttercups. Perchance the beginning of summer may be dated from the fully formed leaves, when dense shade (?) begins. I will see. High blueberries at length. It is unnecessary to speak of them. All flowers are beautiful. The *Salix alba* is about out of bloom. Pads begin to appear, though the river is high over the meadows.[1] A caterpillars' nest on a wild cherry. Some apple trees in blossom; most are just ready to burst forth, the leaves being half formed. I find the fever-bush in bloom, but apparently its blossoms are now stale. I must observe it next year. They were fresh perhaps a week ago. Currants in bloom by Conant's Spring. Are they natives of America? A lady's-slipper well budded and now white. The *Viola ovata* is of a deep purple blue, is darkest and has most of the *red* in it; the *V. pedata* is smooth and pale-blue, delicately tinged with purple reflections; the *cucullata*

[1] *Vide* p. [71]

is more decidedly blue, slaty-blue, and darkly striated. The white violets by the spring are rather scarce now. The red oak leaves are very pretty and finely cut, about an inch and three quarters long. Like most young leaves, they are turned back around the twig, parasol-like. The farmers apprehend frosts these nights. A purplish gnaphalium with three-nerved leaves.

May 21. Morning by river.

A song sparrow's nest and eggs so placed in a bank that none could tread on it; bluish-white, speckled. Also a robin's nest and eggs in the crotch of a maple. Methinks birds that build amid the small branches of trees wait for the leaves to expand.[1] The dew hangs on the grass like globules of quicksilver. Can I tell by it if it has rained in the night? I *hear that it has*.

P. M. — The black oak is just beginning to blossom. The earlier apple trees are in bloom, and resound with the hum of bees of all sizes and other insects. To sit under the first apple tree in blossom is to take another step into summer. The apple blossoms are so abundant and full, white tinged with red; a rich-scented Pomona fragrance, telling of heaps of apples in the autumn, perfectly innocent, wholesome, and delicious. On hillsides cut off two years ago, the red oaks now contrast at a little distance with the yellowish-green birches. The latter are covered with green lice, which cover me.

The catbird sings like a robin sometimes, sometimes

[1] [This sentence is queried in the margin.]

Vol. IV

like a blackbird's sprayey warble. There is more of squeak or mew, and also of clear *whistle*, than in the thrasher's note.

Nemopanthes in bloom; leaves three quarters of an inch. Sand cherry also, fully. Young blueberries everywhere in bloom, and *Viola pedata* along the woodland paths, in high land. Sorrel in bloom, beginning. I am eager to taste a handful.

May 22. Saturday. On my way to Plymouth, looked at Audubon in the State-House. Saw painted the *red* berries of the *Arum triphyllum*. The pigeon is more red on the breast and more blue than the turtle dove. The female (and male?) wood thrush spotted the whole length of belly; the hermit thrush not so. The seringo-bird cannot be the Savannah sparrow. The piping plover has a big head, white breast, and ring neck.

Two kinds of bluets in New York Report.

5 P. M. — Plymouth.

The hill whence Billington discovered the pond. The field plantain in blossom and abundant here. A chickweed in bloom in Watson's garden. Is it the same that was so early? A yellow flower, apparently a hieraceum, just ready to blossom. The four-leaved loosestrife, with dark leaves, shows its flower-buds on the ends of its threads. The mayweed is ready to blossom.[1] The German forget-me-not reminded me of my little blue flower in the brook.

[1] Was it not whiteweed?

May 23. To Billington Sea at sunrise.

The purple finch sings like a canary and like a robin. Huckleberry leaves here, too, are sticky, and yellow my fingers. *Pyrus arbutifolia* in bloom. The low, spreading red cedars which come abruptly to naught at top suggest that they be used for posts with the stubs of branches left, as they often are. The bayberry is late, just beginning to leaf. The buttercup season has arrived here. Mrs. Watson says they have no bluets nor wild pinks (catchfly) here. Some ponds have outlets; some have not. So some men. Singular that so many ponds should have connection with the sea. The inkberry is late. The red-eyed vireo is a steady singer, sitting near the top of a tree a long time alone, — the robin of the woods, — as the robin sings at morning and evening on an elm in the village.

It is worth the while to go a little south to anticipate nature at home. I am now covered with down from the tender foliage, walking in the woods in the morning. Hear the hollow, spitting, *tunk tunk* sound of frogs in the morning, which tells of sultry nights, though we have not had them yet. The *Viola lanceolata* here. *Corema Conradii* in the cemetery, just out of bloom, — broom crowberry, from κόρημα, a broom, — a rare plant which I have seen at Provincetown. The *Empetrum nigrum*, or black crowberry, is found at the White Mountains. The buck-bean in bloom. What is that linear-leaved, small pink-purple flower which they say grows about the stones in a walk? Beach plum ready to bloom. Young oak leaves red above and light below, with a red edge only, handsome as flowers.

P. M. — To Great South Pond.

A brown spotted snake, two feet or more long, light-colored beneath, with blotchy dark-brown spots above like this:[1] —

The trientalis in bloom. The dandelions close at eve, so that you cannot find those that starred the meadow. Woods extensive but small and low, soil sandy; no variety in the landscape. Woods and deer because the soil is sandy and unfit for cultivation.

May 24. The cooing of a dove reminded me of an owl this morning. Counted just fifty violets (*pedata*) in a little bunch, three and a half by five inches, and as many buds, there being six plants close together; on the hill where Billington climbed a tree.

A calabash at Pilgrim Hall nearly two feet high, in the form of a jar, showed what these fruits were made for. Nature's jars and vases.

Holbrook says the *Bufo Americanus* is the most common in America and is our representative of the *Bufo communis* of Europe; speaks of its trill; deposits its spawn in pools.

Found in College Yard *Trifolium procumbens*, or yellow clover.

Concord. — Celandine in blossom, and horse-chestnut.

May 25. Tuesday. P. M. — To Saw Mill Brook and Flint's Pond.

[1] The *Tropidonotus sipedon*, water snake, of Holbrook.

Vol. IV

The *Rhodora Canadensis* is not yet out of blossom, and its leaves are not expanded. It is important for its contrast with the surrounding green, — so much high-colored blossom. The *Pyrus arbutifolia* now. The ferns are grown up large, and some are in fruit, a dark or blackish fruit part way down the stem, with a strong scent, — quite a rich-looking fruit, of small dark-greenish globules clustered together. The female red maples bearing keys are later to put forth leaves. The catkins of the willows on the Turnpike, now fallen, cover the water. The water has subsided so that the pads lie on the surface. The chinquapin shrub oak is blossoming. The pincushion galls appear on the oak. The oak apples are forming. Those galls first named, a sparkling frosted cotton, are very beautiful. The veronica is everywhere in bloom, in the grass by the roadside. It is blossom week with the apples. The shad-blossoms are gone. Apple trees on distant hillsides look like whitish rocks, or like a snow imperfectly covering the ground, or like the reindeer mosses. The sarsaparilla in bloom; and trientalis, its white star. Some call bluets innocence. The reddish buds of the *Pyrus arbutifolia* are handsomer than the flower. What a *sunny* yellow in the early cinquefoil, which now spots the grass! The red oak sprouts have grown ten inches before their leaves are expanded. Some late willows have fresh green catkins now. Clustered Solomon's-seal. *Polygonatum pubescens* ready to bloom. Is that an aralia near the brook? Medeola or cucumber-root in bud, with its two-storied whorl of leaves. The trilliums (*T. cernuum*, wake-robin) in bloom, and the geraniums show great

leaves. Mosquitoes have come. (They say there are none in Plymouth village.) Consider the fugacious fragrance of many flowers. The dark striped flowers of the arums now, some whitish. Cress in flower. The veratrums by this brook have run up so high they make a tropical scenery on the edge of the water, like young palms. Yellow butterflies one at a time. The large yellow woods violet (*V. pubescens*) by this brook now out. The *Rana palustris*, or pickerel frog, is abundant in the meadows. I hear the first troonk of a bull-frog. The fringed polygala (*P. paucifolia*), flowering wintergreen. What bird was that whose wild note I heard at Goose Pond to-night? A loon or a bittern? First nighthawks squeak and boom. Grasshoppers appear.

May 26. Wednesday. Surveying the Brooks farm.

The early thalictrum has been in bloom some time. Perceive the rank smell of brakes. Observe the yellow bark of the barberry.

When the cows and bullocks were lively in the pasture about my compass, Bigelow said the grubs were working in their backs. He had that morning taken out three or four from the back of a young bull he has. They have black heads, which appear and are three quarters of an inch long; are natural to the creature; lie right in the meat, and when they begin to squirm, then the cattle toss their tails and are lively. Great corporations are the cattle, and their vermin are large. This is a new version of the œstrus, — a sudden stampede among the steers when the grubs

squirm in their backs!! He had also seen the grub in their tails. They are occupied as parts of the earth.

The air is full of the odor of apple blossoms, yet the air is fresh as from the salt water. The meadow smells sweet as you go along low places in the road at sundown. To-night I hear many crickets. They have commenced their song. They bring in the summer.

Walking home from surveying. — The fields are *just beginning* to be reddened with sorrel. I hear the pea-wai, the tender note. Is it not the small pewee? Channing says he has seen a red clover blossom and heard a stake-driver. Lousewort (*Pedicularis Canadensis*), very badly named. Pipes (*Equisetum uliginosum*) in blossom. The *Geranium maculatum*(?). One of the large flowering ferns, — part way up the stalk, — (*Osmunda*?); and an early *Thalictrum* (*dioicum*?). The meadows are full of saxifrage.

May 27. At Corner Spring.

A wet day. The veery sings nevertheless. The road is white with the apple blossoms fallen off, as with snowflakes. The dogwood is coming out. Ladies'-slippers out. They perfume the air. *Ranunculus recurvatus*, hooked crowfoot, by the spring. *Prunus maritima*, beach plum, by Hubbard's. Dwarf cornel. *Smilacina racemosa*, clustered Solomon's-seal. The nodding trillium has a faint, rich scent; the *Convallaria bifolia* a strong but not very pleasant scent. *Ranunculus acris*, or tall crowfoot, before the first buttercup shows much.

Viola lanceolata, white. (I did not distinguish it before.) My early willow is either the swamp willow or the bog willow of Bigelow. The *Salix nigra*, or black willow, of Gray, in bloom. *Myosotis laxa*, water mouse-ear, by Depot Field Brook. The fruit of the sweet flag is now just fit to eat, and reminds me of childhood, — the critchicrotches. They would help sustain a famished traveller. The inmost tender leaf, also, near the base, is quite palatable, as children know. I love it as well as muskrats (?). The smooth speedwell, the minute pale-blue striated flower by the roadsides and in the short sod of fields, common now. I hear but few toads and peepers now. The sweetness which appears to be wafted from the meadow (I am on the Corner causeway) is indescribably captivating, Sabean odors, such as voyageurs tell of when approaching a coast. Can it be the grape so early? I think not. May it be the mint in the meadow, just left bare by the receding waters? It appears to come from the ditch by the roadside. Methinks the tree-toad croaks more this wet weather. The tall crowfoot out. The fringed polygala near the Corner Spring is a delicate flower, with very fresh tender green leaves and red-purple blossoms; beautiful from the contrast of its clear red-purple flowers with its clear green leaves. The cuckoo. Caught a wood frog (*Rana sylvatica*), the color of a dead leaf. He croaked as I held him, perfectly frog-like. A humblebee is on my bunch of flowers laid down.

May 28. White thorn and yellow Bethlehem-star (*Hypoxis erecta*).

May 29. Fogs this and yesterday morning. I hear the quails nowadays while surveying. Barberry in bloom, wild pinks, and blue-eyed grass.

May 30. Sunday. Now is the summer come. A breezy, washing day. A day for shadows, even of moving clouds, over fields in which the grass is beginning to wave. Senecio in bloom. A bird's nest in grass, with coffee-colored eggs. Cinquefoil and houstonia cover the ground, mixed with the grass and contrasting with each other. Strong lights and shades now. Wild cherry on the low shrubs, but not yet the trees, a rummy scent. Violets everywhere spot the meadows, some more purple, some more lilac. The tall pipe-grass (*Equisetum uliginosum*). The *Drosera rotundifolia* now glistens with its dew at midday, a beautiful object closely examined. The dwarf andromeda is about out of bloom. Its new shoots from the side of the old stem are an inch or more long. The little leaves appear to be gradually falling off, after all. See again if they do not all fall off in the summer. Distinguished the *Viola palmata* in Hubbard's meadow, near the sidesaddle-flowers, which last are *just beginning* to blossom. The last are quite showy flowers when the wind turns them so as to show their under sides.

It is a day of shadows, the leaves have so grown, and of wind, — a washing day, — and the shadows of the clouds are observed flitting over the landscape. I do not yet observe a difference between the two kinds of *Pyrus arbutifolia*, if, indeed, I have compared the two, *i. e.* my early black and later red-fruited, which last

Vol. IV

holds on all winter. The fruit of the amelanchier is as big as *small* peas. I have not noticed any other berry so large yet. The anemones appear to be nearly gone. Yellow lilies are abundant. The bulbous arethusa, the most splendid, rich, and high-colored flower thus far, methinks, all flower and color, almost without leaves, and looking much larger than it is, and more conspicuous on account of its intense color. A flower of mark. It appeared two or three times as large as reality when it flashed upon me from the meadow. Bigelow calls it a "crystalline purple." (Saw some the 6th of June, but no longer fresh.) [1] What kind of blackberry did I find in blossom in Hubbard's Swamp? Passed a cow that had just dropped her calf in the meadow. The sumach (*glabra*) is well under weigh now. The yellow water ranunculus by the Corner causeway. There are young robins in nests. To what sparrow belong the coffee-colored eggs in Hubbard's field by the brook? White cohush in bloom; also *Smilacina stellata*. The branches or branchlets of the maidenhair fern are so disposed as to form two thirds of a cup around the stem. The flowers of the sassafras have not such a fragrance as I perceived last year. High blueberry flowers are quite conspicuous. The bass leaf is now large and handsome. The geranium is a delicate flower and belongs especially to shady places under trees and shrubs, — better if about springs, — in by-nooks, so modest. The early gnaphaliums are gone to seed, having run

[1] [In this case, as not infrequently happened, Thoreau was evidently writing up his Journal — or copying his pencilled field-notes into it — some days after the event.]

up seven or ten inches. The field plantain, which I saw in Plymouth a week ago, abundant there. The narrow-leaved cotton-grass. The *Equisetum sylvaticum*, or wood horse-tail in the meadows. The lupine, which I saw almost in blossom a week ago at Plymouth, I hear is in blossom here. The river is my own highway, the only wild and unfenced part of the world hereabouts. How much of the world is widow's thirds, with a hired man to take negligent care of it! The apple trees are about out of blossom. It is but a week they last.

Israel Rice thinks the first half of June is not commonly so warm as May, and that the reason is that vegetation is so advanced that the earth is shaded and protected from the sun by the grass also, so that it is delayed in being warmed by the summer sun.

II

JUNE, 1852

(ÆT. 34)

June 1. Evening. — To the Lee place, the moon about full.

The sounds I hear by the bridge: the midsummer frog (I think it is not the toad), the nighthawk, crickets, the peetweet (it is early), the hum of dor-bugs, and the whip-poor-will. The boys are coming home from fishing, for the river is down at last. The moving clouds are the drama of the moonlight nights, and never-failing entertainment of nightly travellers. You can never foretell the fate of the moon, — whether she will prevail over or be obscured by the clouds half an hour hence. The traveller's sympathy with the moon makes the drama of the shifting clouds interesting. The fate of the moon will disappoint all expectations. Her own light creates the shadows in the coming (advancing) clouds, and exaggerates her destiny.[1] I do not perceive much warmth in the rocks.

June 2. *Wednesday.* Measured C. Davis's elm at the top of his fence, just built, five feet from the ground. It is fifteen and two twelfths feet in circumference and much larger many feet higher. Buttercups now spot the churchyard. The elms now hold a good deal of

[1] [*Excursions*, pp. 329, 330; Riv. 405.]

children may now see if " your mother wants you." The golden alexanders is called *Zizia aurea.* The cistus is out. Lupines in prime. The Canada snapdragon, that little blue flower that lasts so long, grows with the lupines under Fair Haven. The early chickweed[1] with the star-shaped flower is common in fields now.

June 5. The medeola has blossomed in a tumbler. I seem to perceive a pleasant fugacious fragrance from its rather delicate but inconspicuous green flower. Its whorls of leaves of two stages are the most remarkable. I do not perceive the smell of the cucumber in its root.

To Harrington's, P. M. The silver cinquefoil (*Potentilla argentea*) now, a delicate spring-yellow, sunny-yellow (before the dog-days) flower; none of the fire of autumnal yellows in it. Its silvery leaf is as good as a flower. Whiteweed.

The constant inquiry which nature puts is: " Are you virtuous? Then you can behold me." Beauty, fragrance, music, sweetness, and joy of all kinds are for the virtuous. That I thought when I heard the telegraph harp to-day.

Raspberry some days since. The leaves of young oaks are full-grown. The *Viburnum lentago*, if that edged petiole marks it enough. The *Veratrum viride*, with its green and yellowish flower. Umbelled thesium, which has shown its buds so long. The *Viola lanceolata* now, instead of the *V. blanda.* In some places the

[1] Cerastium?

shade and look rich and heavy with foliage. You see darkness in them. Golden alexanders — looks like a parsnip — near or beyond the East Quarter schoolhouse. The barberry blossoms are now abundant. They fill the air with a disagreeable, buttery fragrance. Low blackberry in bloom. Hazy days now. Milkweed, elecampane, butter-and-eggs, etc., etc., are getting up. The dried brown petals of apple blossoms spot the sod in pastures. Measured a chestnut stump on Asa White's land, twenty-three and nine twelfths feet in circumference, eight and one half feet one way, seven feet the other, at one foot from ground. Nest of Wilson's thrush with bluish-green eggs. Female sassafras in bloom. I think I may say the umbelled thesium has begun to bloom. The pincushion galls appear on the oaks.

I found a plant whose name I know not; somewhat fern-like; leaves in a whorl of five, two double, one single; the whole nine inches high; no flower.

June 3. The nepeta by Deacon Brown's, a pretty blue flower. It has been a sultry day, and a slight thunder-shower, and now I see fireflies in the meadows at evening.

June 4. *Friday.* The birds sing at dawn. What sounds to be awakened by! If only our sleep, our dreams, are such as to harmonize with the song, the warbling, of the birds, ushering in the day! They appear comparatively silent an hour or two later.

The dandelions are now almost all gone to seed, and

leaves of the last are grown quite large. The sidesaddleflowers. The *Thalictrum anemonoides* still. The dwarf cornel by Harrington's road looks like large snowflakes on the hillside, it is so thick. It is a neat, geometrical flower, of a pure white, sometimes greenish, or green. The white[1] spruce cones are an inch and a half long. The larch cones appear not so red yet as they will be. Can it be that earliest potentilla that now stands up so high in open pine woods and wood-paths, — a foot high? The *simplex* variety? There is now froth on the white and pitch pines, at the base of the new shoots, which are from three to six inches long. Some meadows are quite white with the cotton-grass. White clover now. Some rye-fields are almost fully grown, where it appears to have sown itself. It is commonly two feet high. Those great roots belong to the yellow lily. Some poet must sing in praise of the bulbous arethusa.

The lupine is now in its glory. It is the more important because it occurs in such extensive patches, even an acre or more together, and of such a pleasing variety of colors, — purple, pink, or lilac, and white, — especially with the sun on it, when the transparency of the flower makes its color changeable. It paints a whole hillside with its blue, making such a field (if not meadow) as Proserpine might have wandered in. Its leaf was made to be covered with dewdrops. I am quite excited by this prospect of blue flowers in clumps with narrow intervals. Such a profusion of the heavenly, the elysian, color, as if these were the Elysian

[1] [" Black" is substituted in pencil.]

Fields. They say the seeds look like babies' faces, and hence the flower is so named. No other flowers exhibit so much blue. That is the value of the lupine. The earth is blued with them. Yet a third of a mile distant I do not detect their color on the hillside. Perchance because it is the color of the air. It is not *distinct* enough. You passed along here, perchance, a fortnight ago, and the hillside was comparatively barren, but now you come and these glorious redeemers appear to have flashed out here all at once. Who planted the seeds of lupines in the barren soil? Who watereth the lupines in the fields?

Distinguished the *Geum rivale*, water avens, in James P. Brown's meadow, a drooping, half-closed, purplish-brown flower, with a strawberry-looking fruit. The *Erigeron bellidifolius*, robin's-plantain (may it be the *E. Philadelphicus?*), that rather rose-purple flower which looks like an early aster. A rather delicate and interesting flower, flesh-colored.

Pray let us live without being drawn by dogs, Esquimaux-fashion, a scrambling pack tearing over hill and vale and biting each other's ears. What a despicable mode of progressing, to be drawn by a pack of dogs! Why not by a flock of mice?[1]

De Kay, of the New York Report, says the bream "is of no value as an article of food, but is often caught for amusement!" I think it is the sweetest fish in our river.

Richardson says that white bears and arctic foxes frequent the most northern land discovered.

[1] [*Cape Cod, and Miscellanies,* p. 473; *Misc.,* Riv. 276.]

June 6. Sunday. First devil's-needles in the air, and some smaller, bright-green ones on flowers. The earliest blueberries are now forming as greenberries. The wind already injures the just-expanded leaves, tearing them and making them turn black. I see the effects of recent frosts on the young oaks in hollows in the woods. The leaves are turned dry, black, and crisp. The side-flowering sandwort, an inconspicuous white flower like a chickweed.

June 7. Surveying for Sam. Pierce. Found piece of an Indian soapstone pot.

June 9. The buck-bean in Hubbard's meadow just going out of blossom. The yellow water ranunculus is an important flower in the river now, rising above the white lily pads, whose flower does not yet appear. I perceive that their petals, washed ashore, line the sand conspicuously. The green-briar in flower.

For a week past we have had *washing* days. The grass waving, and trees having leaved out, their boughs wave and feel the effect of the breeze. Thus new life and motion is imparted to the trees. The season of waving boughs; and the lighter under sides of the new leaves are exposed. This is the first half of June. Already the grass is not so fresh and liquid-velvety a green, having much of it blossom[ed] and some even gone to seed, and it is mixed with reddish ferns and other plants, but the general leafiness, shadiness, and waving of grass and boughs in the breeze characterize the season. The wind is not quite agreeable, because it

Vol. IV

prevents your hearing the birds sing. Meanwhile the crickets are strengthening their quire. The weather is very clear, and the sky bright. The river shines like silver. Methinks this is a traveller's month. The locust in bloom. The waving, undulating rye. The deciduous trees have filled up the intervals between the evergreens, and the woods are bosky now.

Is that the *Thalictrum Cornuti* that shows green stamens, at the Corner Spring? Gathered strawberries on Fair Haven. Rather acid yet.

The priests of the Germans and Britons were druids. They had their sacred oaken groves. Such were their steeple houses. Nature was to some extent a fane to them. There was fine religion in that form of worship, and Stonehenge remains as evidence of some vigor in the worshippers, as the Pyramids, perchance, of the vigor of the Egyptians, derived from the slime of the Nile. Evelyn says of the oak, which he calls "these robust sons of the earth," "It is reported that the very shade of this tree is so wholesome, that the sleeping, or lying under it, becomes a present remedy to paralytics, and recovers those whom the mistaken malign influence of the Walnut-tree has smitten."[1] Which we may take for a metaphorical expression of the invigorating influence of rude, wild, robust nature, compared with the effeminating luxury of civilized life. Evelyn has collected the fine exaggerations of antiquity respecting the virtues and habits of trees and added some himself. He says, "I am told that those small young acorns which we find in the stock-doves' craws are a delicious

[1] [John Evelyn, *Silva: or a Discourse of Forest Trees.*]

fare, as well as those incomparable salads, young herbs taken out of the maws of partridges at a certain season of the year, which gives them a preparation far exceeding all the art of cookery." If the oft-repeated glorification of the forest from age to age smacks of religion, is even druidical, Evelyn is as good as several old druids, and his "Silva" is a new kind of prayer-book, a glorifying of the trees and enjoying them forever, which was the chief end of his life.

A child loves to strike on a tin pan or other ringing vessel with a stick, because, its ears being fresh, sound, attentive, and percipient, it detects the finest music in the sound, at which all nature assists. Is not the very cope of the heavens the sounding-board of the infant drummer? So clear and unprejudiced ears hear the sweetest and most soul-stirring melody in tinkling cowbells and the like (dogs baying the moon), not to be referred to association, but intrinsic in the sound itself; those cheap and simple sounds which men despise because their ears are dull and debauched. Ah, that I were so much a child that I could unfailingly draw music from a quart pot! Its little ears tingle with the melody. To it there is music in sound alone.

Evelyn speaks of "mel-dews" attracting bees. Can mildews be corrupted from this? Says that the alder, laid under water, "will harden like a very stone," and speaks of their being used "for the draining of grounds by placing them . . . in the trenches," which I have just seen done here under Clamshell Hill.

Evelyn's love of his subject teaches him to use many expressive words, some imported from the Latin, which

I wonder how we can do without. He says of the "oziers or aquatic salix," "It likewise yields more limber and flexible twigs for baskets, flaskets, hampers, cages, lattices, cradles, . . . the bodies of coaches and waggons, . . . for chairs, hurdles, stays, bands," etc.; "likewise for fish-weirs, and to support the banks of impetuous rivers: In fine, for all wicker and *twiggy* works;

'Viminibus Salices' — Virg."

Many of his words show a poetic genius.

The above-mentioned is the reason that children are fond of and make what grown people call a *noise*, because of the music which their young ears detect in it.

Peaches are the principal crop in Lincoln, and cherries a very important one; yet Evelyn says, "We may read that the peach was at first accounted so tender and delicate a tree, as that it was believed to thrive only in Persia; and even in the days of Galen, it grew no nearer than Egypt, of all the Roman Provinces, but was not seen in the city till about thirty years before Pliny's time;" but now it is the principal crop cultivated in Lincoln in New England, and it is also cultivated extensively in the West and on lands not half a dozen years vacated by the Indians. Also, "It was 680 years after the foundation of Rome, ere Italy had tasted a cherry of their own, which being then brought thither out of Pontus, did after 120 years, travel ad ultimos Britannos," and I may add *Lincolnos*. As Evelyn says, "Methinks this should be a wonderful incitement."

Evelyn well says "a *sobbing* rain."

Vol. IV

Trees live so long that Evelyn in Milton's day tells anecdotes of old trees, and recent writers tell the same or similar anecdotes of the same trees still standing. They have stood to have the stories repeated and enlarged concerning them. He tells of "*Neustadt an der grossen Linden*, or Neustadt by the great Lime-tree." After quoting at length some of the inscriptions on the stone columns placed under this famous tree by noble persons, proving its age, he adds, "Together with several more too tedious to recite; and even these might have [been] spared the reader, but that I found the instance so particular and solemn."

What means that custom of parents planting a tree or a forest at the birth of an heir, to be an inheritance or a dower, but a sort of regrafting the man on the vegetable? If a forest were planted at the birth of every man, nations would not be likely to become effete. It has ever been regarded as a crime, even among warriors, to cut down a nation's woods.

He, Evelyn, speaks of pines "pearling out into gums." Things raised in a garden he calls "*hortular furniture*." He talks of modifying the air as well as the soil, about plants, "and make the remedy as well regional as topical." This suggests the propriety of Shakespeare's expression the "*region* cloud," region meaning then oftener upper regions relatively to the earth.

He speaks of a "dewie *sperge* or brush," to be used instead of a watering-pot, which "gluts" the earth. He calls the kitchen-garden the "olitory garden." In a dedication of his "Kalendarium Hortense" to Cowley, he inserts two or three good sentences or quotations,

viz.: "As the philosopher in Seneca desired only bread and herbs to dispute felicity with Jupiter," so of Cowley's simple retired life. "Who would not, like you, *cacher sa vie?*" "Delivered from the gilded impertinences of life."

June 11. *Friday.* 3 p. m. — Down railroad.

I hear the bobolink, though he does not sing so much as he did, and the lark and my seringo, as I go down the railroad causeway. The cricket sings. The red clover does not yet cover the fields. The whiteweed is more obvious. It commonly happens that a flower is considered more beautiful that is not followed by fruit. It must culminate in the flower. The cistus is a delicate flower in sandy woods now, with a slight, innocent spring fragrance, — one of those, like the pink, which you cannot bring home in good condition. June-grass is ripe. The red-eye sings now in the woods, perhaps more than any other bird. (In the shanty field.) The mountains are misty and blue. It has been quite windy for ten days, and cold a part of the time. The maple-leaved viburnum at Laurel Glen; the round-leaved cornel, and the mountain laurel, all budded.[1] The yellow diervilla (*D. trifida*) ready to blossom there. The low blueberry leaves and flowers (*Vaccinium vacillans* of Gray) have a sweet scent. Froth on the pigeon-plain pines. A robin sings (3.30 p. m.) and wood thrush amid the pines; flies hum, and mosquitoes; and the earth feels under the feet as if it were going to be dry. The air in this pitch pine wood is filled with the hum of

[1] [A pencilled interrogation-point in parenthesis follows here.]

gnats, flies, and mosquitoes. High blackberries a day or two since. The bullfrogs in Walden (some of them at least) are a light-colored greenish brown. The huckleberry-bird is heard. I perceived that untraceable odor by the shore of Walden near railroad, where there are grape-vines, and yet the vines do not smell, and I have perceived it for two or three weeks. The vines appear but just in flower. Bittersweet, woody nightshade (*Solanum Dulcamara*). It has a singular strong odor. Everywhere the leaves of goldenrods from the old roots; also, in some places, epilobium. The veery reminds me of the wood thrush in its note, as well as form and color. You must attend to the birds in the spring.

As I climbed the Cliffs, when I jarred the foliage, I perceived an exquisite perfume which I could not trace to its source. Ah, those fugacious universal fragrances of the meadows and woods! Odors rightly mingled!

The snapdragon, a slight blue flower, in dry places. Interesting. The oak balls lie about under the black oaks. The shrub oaks on the plain are so covered with foliage that, when I looked down on it from the Cliff, I am impressed as if I looked down on a forest of oaks. The oven-bird and the thrasher sing. The last has a sort of chuckle. The crickets began to sing in warm dry places.

Another little veronica (?) on the Cliffs, just going out of bloom, *V. arvensis* (?), with crenately cut leaves and hairy. The first was the smooth. The pines are budded. I do not see the female flower yet. There is froth at the base of the new shoots even at the top of the highest pines. Yarrow, with a strong tansy scent. Lupines, their pods and seeds. First the profusion of color, spikes of flowers rising above and prevailing over the leaves; then the variety in different clumps, rose(?)-purple, blue, and white; then the handsome palmate leaf, made to hold dew. Gray says from *lupus* (wolf) because they " were thought to devour the fertility of the soil." This is scurrilous. Under Fair Haven. First grew the *Viola pedata* here, then lupines, mixed with the delicate snapdragon. This soil must abound with the blue principle. Is that the tephrosia, so forward? The fruit of the *Cerasus pumila* is puffed up like How's plums. The *Aralia nudicaulis* already shows small green berries. The lupine has no pleasant fragrance. The cistus a slight enlargement of the cinquefoil, the June (?) cinquefoil, what the summer can do.

It was probably the *Thalictrum Cornuti*, meadow-rue, which I saw at the Corner Spring, though it has no white stamens. The red (Indian (?) red) huckleberry and the white and red blueberry blossoms (the *Gaylussacia resinosa*, black huckleberry, and *Vaccinium vacillans*) are very handsome and interesting now and would attract more attention if the prospect of their fruit did not make us overlook them. Moon-seed is a good name for a plant. I should know it.

The Jones elm is fifteen and three twelfths feet circumference at five or six feet from ground, or at the smallest place; much more at twelve or fourteen feet from ground, — larger, then, than C. Davis's elm at the smallest place.

The pyrolas now ready to blossom. Shin-leaf is a good name for one. *Scleranthus annuus*, common knawel, in the paths; inconspicuous and moss-like. *Utricularia vulgaris*, common bladderwort, a dirty-conditioned flower, like a sluttish woman with a gaudy yellow bonnet. Is the grape out? Solomon's-seal, two-leaved, with a third. *Sanicula Marylandica*, black snake-root, without color at first, glows [?] like a buttercup, leaf and stem. Those spotted maple leaves, — what mean their bright colors? Yellow with a greenish centre and a crimson border on the green leaves, as if the Great Chemist had dropped some strong acid by chance from a phial designed for autumnal use! Very handsome. Decay and disease are often beautiful, like the pearly tear of the shellfish and the hectic glow of consumption.

The ivy or *Rhus Toxicodendron* (*radicans* when climbing trees), budded to blossom, looks like an aralia.

June 12. Saturday. P. M. — To Lupine Hill *via* Depot Field Brook.

For some time I have noticed the grass whitish and killed at top by worms (?). The meadows are yellow with golden senecio. Marsh speedwell (*Veronica scutellata*), lilac-tinted, rather pretty. The mouse-ear forget-me-not (*Myosotis laxa*) has now extended its racemes (?) very much, and hangs over the edge of the brook. It is one of the most interesting minute flowers. It is the more beautiful for being small and unpretending, for even flowers must be modest. The blue flag (*Iris versi-*

color). Its buds are a dark indigo-blue tip beyond the green calyx. It is rich but hardly delicate and simple enough; a very handsome sword-shaped leaf. The blue-eyed grass is one of the most beautiful of flowers. It might have been famous from Proserpine down. It will bear to be praised by poets. The blue flag, notwithstanding its rich furniture, its fringed recurved parasols over its anthers, and its variously streaked and colored petals, is loose and coarse in its habit. How completely all character is expressed by flowers! This is a little too showy and gaudy, like some women's bonnets. Yet it belongs to the meadow and ornaments it much. The critchicrotches are going to seed. I love the sweet-flag as well as the muskrat (?). Its tender inmost leaf is very palatable below. *Œnothera pumila*, dwarf tree-primrose. Ever it will be some obscure small and modest flower that will most please us. Some of the ferns have branches wholly covered with fruit.

How difficult, if not impossible, to do the things we have done! as fishing and camping out. They seem to me a little fabulous now.

Boys are bathing at Hubbard's Bend, playing with a boat (I at the willows). The color of their bodies in the sun at a distance is pleasing, the not often seen flesh-color. I hear the sound of their sport borne over the water. As yet we have not man in nature. What a singular fact for an angel visitant to this earth to carry back in his note-book, that men were forbidden to expose their bodies under the severest penalties! A pale pink, which the sun would soon tan. White men!

There are no white men to contrast with the red and the black; they are of such colors as the weaver gives them. I wonder that the dog knows his master when he goes in to bathe and does not stay by his clothes.

Small white-bellied (?) swallows in a row (a dozen) on the telegraph-wire over the water by the bridge. This perch is little enough departure from unobstructed air to suit them. Pluming themselves. If you could furnish a perch aerial enough, even birds of paradise would alight. Swallows have forked tails, and wings and tails are about the same length. They do not alight on trees, methinks, unless on dead and bare boughs, but stretch a wire over water and they perch on it. This is among the phenomena that cluster about the telegraph.

Hedge-mustard. (Turned into the lane beyond Dennis's.) Some fields are almost wholly covered with sheep's-sorrel, now turned red, — its valves (?). It helps thus agreeably to paint the earth, contrasting even at a distance with the greener fields, blue sky, and dark or downy clouds. It is red, marbled, watered, mottled, or waved with greenish, like waving grain, — three or four acres of it. To the farmer or grazier it is a troublesome weed, but to the landscape-viewer an agreeable red tinge laid on by the painter. I feel well into summer when I see this redness. It appears to be avoided by the cows.

The petals of the sidesaddle-flower, fully expanded, hang down. How complex it is, what with flowers and leaves! It is a wholesome and interesting plant to me, the leaf especially. Rye that has sown itself and come up scatteringly in bunches is now nearly ripe. They are beginning to cut rank grass on the village street. I should say the summer began with the leafiness, — umbrageous summer! The glory of Dennis's lupines is departed, and the white now shows in abundance beneath them. So I cannot walk longer in those fields of Enna in which Proserpine amused herself gathering flowers.

The steam whistle at a distance sounds even like the hum of a bee in a flower. So man's works fall into nature.

The flies hum at mid-afternoon, as if peevish and weary of the length of the days. The river is shrunk to summer width; on the sides smooth whitish water, — or rather it is the light from the pads; — in the middle, dark blue or slate, rippled.

The color of the earth at a distance where a wood has been cut off is a reddish brown. Nature has put no large object on the face of New England so glaringly white as a white house.

The *Ranunculus filiformis* on the muddy shore of the river. The locusts' blossoms in the graveyard fill the street with their sweet fragrance.

It is day, and we have more of that same light that the moon sent us, but not reflected now, but shining directly. The sun is a fuller moon. Who knows how much lighter day there may be?

June 13. *Sunday.* 3 P. M. — To Conantum.
A warm day. It has been cold, and we have had fires the past week sometimes. Clover begins to show

Vol. IV

red in the fields, and the wild cherry is not out of blossom. The river has a summer midday look, smooth to a cobweb, with green shores, and shade from the trees on its banks. The *Viburnum nudum.* The oblong-leaved sundew, but not its flower. Do the bulbous arethusas last long?

What a sweetness fills the air now in low grounds or meadows, reminding me of times when I went strawberrying years ago! It is as if all meadows were filled with some sweet mint. The *Dracæna borealis* (Bigelow) (*Clintonia borealis* (Gray)) amid the Solomon's-seals in Hubbard's Grove Swamp, a very neat and handsome liliaceous flower with three large, regular, spotless, green convallaria leaves, making a triangle from the root, and sometimes a fourth from the scape, linear, with four drooping, greenish-yellow, bell-shaped (?) flowers. Not in sun. In low shady woods. It is a handsome and perfect flower, though not high-colored. I prefer it to some more famous. But Gray should not name it from the Governor of New York.[1] What is he to the lovers of flowers in Massachusetts? If named after a man, it must be a man of flowers. Rhode Island botanists may as well name the flowers after their governors as New York. Name your canals and railroads after Clinton, if you please, but his name is not associated with flowers. Mosquitoes now trouble the walker in low shady woods. No doubt woodchucks in their burrows hear the steps of walkers through the earth and come not forth. Yellow wood sorrel (*Oxalis stricta*), which, according to Gray, closes its leaves and droops at nightfall. The

[1] [It was named by Rafinesque.]

woolly aphides on alders whiten one's clothes now. What is that palmate(?)-leaved water-plant by the Corner causeway? The buck-bean grows in Conant's meadow. Lambkill is out. I remember with what delight I used to discover this flower in dewy mornings. All things in this world must be seen with the morning dew on them, must be seen with youthful, early-opened, hopeful eyes. Saw four cunning little woodchucks nibbling the short grass, about one third grown, that live under Conant's old house. Mistook one for a piece of rusty iron. The *Viburnum Lentago* is about out of bloom; shows young berries. The *Smilax herbacea*, carrion-flower, a rank green vine with long-peduncled umbels, with small greenish or yellowish flowers just opening, and tendrils, at the Miles swamp. It smells exactly like a dead rat in the wall, and apparently attracts flies (I find small gnats on it) like carrion. A very remarkable odor; a single minute flower in an umbel open will scent a whole room. Nature imitates all things in flowers. They are at once the most beautiful and the ugliest objects, the most fragrant and the most offensive to the nostrils, etc., etc. The compound-racemed convallaria, being fully out, is white. I put it down too early, perhaps by a week. The great leaves of the bass attract you now, six inches in diameter. The delicate maidenhair fern forms a cup or dish, very delicate and graceful. Beautiful, too, its glossy black stem and its wave-edged fruited leafets. I hear the feeble plaintive note of young bluebirds, just trying their wings or getting used to them. Young robins peep.

I think I know four kinds of cornel beside the dog-

wood and bunchberry: one now in bloom, with *rather* small leaves with a smooth, silky feeling beneath, a greenish-gray spotted stem, in older stocks all gray (*Cornus alternifolia?* or *sericea?*); the broad-leaved cornel in Laurel Glen, yet green in the bud (*C. circinata?*); the small-leaved cornel with a small cyme or corymb, as late to be [*sic*] as the last, in Potter's hedge and on high hills (*C. paniculata*); and the red osier by the river (*C. stolonifera*), which I have not seen this year.

Mosquitoes are first troublesome in the house with sultry nights.

Orobanche uniflora, single-flowered broom-rape (Bigelow), [or] *Aphyllon uniflorum*, one-flowered cancer-root (Gray). C. found it June 12 at Clematis Brook. Also the common fumitory (?), methinks; it is a fine-leaved small plant.

Captain Jonathan Carver commences his Travels with these words: "In June, 1766, I set out from Boston, and proceeded by way of Albany and Niagara, to Michillimackinac; a Fort situated between the Lakes Huron and Michigan, and distant from Boston 1300 miles. This being the uttermost of our factories towards the northwest, I considered it as the most convenient place from whence I could begin my intended progress, and enter at once into the Regions I designed to explore." [1] So he gives us no information respecting the intermediate country, nor much, I fear, about the country beyond.

Holbrook says the *Emys picta* is the first to be seen in the spring.

[1] [*Travels through the Interior Parts of North America.*]

June 14. There are various new reflections now of the light, *viz.* from the under sides of leaves (fresh and white) turned up by the wind, and also from the bent blades (horizontal tops) of rank grass in the meadows, — a sort of bluish sheeny light, this last. Saw a wild rose from the cars in Weston. The early red roses are out in gardens at home.

June 15. *Tuesday. Silene Antirrhina,* sleepy catch-fly, or snapdragon catch-fly, the ordinarily curled-up petals scarcely noticeable at the end of the large oval calyx. Gray says opening only by night or cloudy weather. Bigelow says probably nocturnal, for he never found it expanded by day. (I found it June 16th at 6 A. M. expanded, two of its flowers, — and they remained so for some hours, in my chamber.) By railroad near Badger's.

Yesterday we smelt the sea strongly; the sea breeze alone made the day tolerable. This morning, a shower! The robin only sings the louder for it. He is inclined to sing in foul weather.

To Clematis Brook, 1.30 P. M.

Very warm. Now for a thin coat. This melting weather makes a stage in the year. The crickets creak louder and more steadily; the bullfrogs croak in earnest. The drouth begins. The dry z-ing of the locust is heard. The potatoes are of that height to stand up at night. Bathing cannot be omitted. The conversation of all boys in the streets is whether they will or not or who will go in a-swimming, and how they will not tell their parents. You lie with open windows and hear the sounds in the streets.

The seringo sings now *at noon* on a post; has a light streak over eye.

The autumnal dandelion (*Leontodon,* or *Apargia*). *Erigeron integrifolius* of Bigelow (*strigosus, i. e.* narrow-leaved daisy fleabane, of Gray) very common, like a white aster.

I will note such birds as I observe in this walk, beginning on the railroad causeway in middle of this hot day. The chuckling warble of martins heard over the meadow, from a village box. The lark. The fields are blued with blue-eyed grass, — a slaty blue. The epilobium shows some color in its spikes.

How rapidly new flowers unfold! as if Nature would get through her work too soon. One has as much as he can do to observe how flowers successively unfold. It is a flowery revolution, to which but few attend. Hardly too much attention can be bestowed on flowers. We follow, we march after, the highest color; that is our flag, our standard, our " color." Flowers were made to be seen, not overlooked. Their bright colors imply eyes, spectators. There have been many flower men who have rambled the world over to see them. The flowers robbed from an Egyptian traveller were at length carefully boxed up and forwarded to Linnæus, the man of flowers. The common, early cultivated red roses are certainly very handsome, so rich a color and so full of blossoms; you see why even blunderers have introduced them into their gardens.

Ascending to pigeon-place plain, the reflection of the heat from the dead pine-needles and the boughs strewn about, combined with the dry, suffocating scent, is

Vol. IV

oppressive and reminds me of the first settlers of Concord. The oven-bird, chewink, pine warbler (?), thrasher, swallows on the wire, cuckoo, phœbe, redeye, robin, veery. The maple-leaved viburnum is opening with a purplish tinge. Wood thrush.

Is not that the *Prunus obovata,* which I find in fruit, a mere shrub, in Laurel Glen, with oval fruit and long pedicels in a raceme? And have I not mistaken the *P. Virginiana,* or northern red cherry, for this? *Vide Virginiana* and also *vide* the *P. depressa.* Golden and coppery reflections from a yellow dor-bug's coat of mail in the water. Is it a yellowbird or myrtle-bird? Huckleberry-bird.

Walden is two inches above my last mark. It must be four or five feet, at least, higher than when I sounded it. Men are inclined to be amphibious, to sympathize with fishes, now. I desire to get wet and saturated with water. The North River, Assabet, by the old stone bridge, affords the best bathing-place I think of, — a pure sandy, uneven bottom, — with a swift current, a grassy bank, and overhanging maples, with transparent water, deep enough, where you can see every fish in it. Though you stand still, you feel the rippling current about you.

First locust. The *pea-wai.*

There is considerable pollen on the pond; more than last year, notwithstanding that all the white pines near the pond are gone and there are very few pitch. It must all come from the pitch pine, whose sterile blossoms are now dry and empty, for it is earlier than the white pine. Probably I have never observed it in the

river because it is carried away by the current. The umbelled pyrola is just ready to bloom.

Young robins, dark-speckled, and the pigeon woodpecker flies up from the ground and darts away. I forget that there are lichens at this season.

The farmhouses under their shady trees (Baker's) look as if the inhabitants were taking their siesta at this hour. I pass it [*sic*] in the rear, through the open pitch pine wood. Why does work go forward now? No scouring of tubs or cans now. The cat and all are gone to sleep, preparing for an early tea, excepting the indefatigable, never-resting hoers in the corn-field, who have carried a jug of molasses and water to the field and will wring their shirts to-night. I shall ere long hear the horn blow for their early tea. The wife or the hired Irishwoman steps to the door and blows the long tin horn, a cheering sound to the laborers in the field.

The motive of the laborer should be not to get his living, to get a good job, but to perform well a certain work. A town must pay its engineers so well that they shall not feel that they are working for low ends, as for a livelihood merely, but for scientific ends. Do not hire a man who does your work for money, but him who does it for love, and pay him well.[1]

On Mt. Misery, panting with heat, looking down the river. The haze an hour ago reached to Wachusett; now it obscures it. Methinks there is a male and female shore to the river, one abrupt, the other flat and meadowy. Have not all streams this contrast more or less, on the one hand eating into the bank, on the other depos-

[1] [*Cape Cod, and Miscellanies,* p. 459; *Misc.,* Riv. 258, 259.]

iting their sediment? The year is in its manhood now. The very river looks warm, and there is none of that light celestial blue seen in far reaches in the spring. I see fields a mile distant reddened with sorrel. The very sight of distant water is refreshing, though a bluish steam appears to rest on it. Catbird. The waxwork is just in blossom and groves [of] hickories on the south of Mt. Misery.

How refreshing the sound of the smallest waterfall in hot [weather]! I sit by that on Clematis Brook and listen to its music. The very sight of this half-stagnant pond-hole, drying up and leaving bare mud, with the pollywogs and turtles making off in it, is agreeable and encouraging to behold, as if it contained the seeds of life, the liquor rather, boiled down. The foulest water will bubble purely. They speak to our blood, even these stagnant, slimy pools. It, too, no doubt, has its falls nobler than Montmorenci, grander than Niagara, in the course of its circulations. Here is the primitive force of Egypt and the Nile, where the lotus grows.

Some geraniums are quite rose-colored, others pale purplish-blue, others whitish. The blossom of the *Lentago* is rather sweet smelling. *Orobanche uniflora*, single-flowered broom-rape (Bigelow), [or] *Aphyllon uniflorum*, one-flowered cancer-root (Gray), grows by this brook-side, — a naked, low, bluish-white flower, even reminding you of the tobacco-pipe. Cattle walk along in a brook or ditch now for coolness, lashing their tails, and browse the edges; or they stand concealed for shade amid thick bushes. How perfectly acquainted they are with man, and never run from him! Thorn

bushes appear to be just out of blossom. I have not observed them well. Woodchucks and squirrels are seen and heard in a walk. How much of a tortoise is shell! But little is gone with its spirit. It is well cleaned out, I trust. It is emptied of the reptile. It is not its exuviæ.

I hear the scream of a great hawk, sailing with a ragged wing against the high wood-side, apparently to scare his prey and so detect it, — shrill, harsh, fitted to excite terror in sparrows and to issue from his split and curved bill. I see his open bill the while against the sky. Spit with force from his mouth with an undulatory quaver imparted to it from his wings or motion as he flies. A hawk's ragged wing will grow whole again, but so will not a poet's.

By half past five, robins more than before, crows, of course, and jays. Dogsbane is just ready to open. Swallows. It is pleasant walking through the June-grass (in Pleasant Meadow), so thin and offering but little obstruction. The nighthawk squeaks and booms. The *Veratrum viride* top is now a handsome green cluster, two feet by ten inches.

Here also, at Well Meadow Head, I see the fringed purple orchis, unexpectedly beautiful, though a pale lilac purple, — a large spike of purple flowers. I find two, — the *grandiflora* of Bigelow and *fimbriata* of Gray. Bigelow thinks it the most beautiful of all the orchises. I am not prepared to say it is the most beautiful wild flower I have found this year. Why does it grow there only, far in a swamp, remote from public view? It is somewhat fragrant, reminding me of the lady's-slipper.

Is it not significant that some rare and delicate and beautiful flowers should be found only in unfrequented wild swamps? There is the mould in which the orchis grows. Yet I am not sure but this is a fault in the flower. It is not quite perfect in all its parts. A beautiful flower must be simple, not spiked. It must have a fair stem and leaves. This stem is rather naked, and the leaves are for shade and moisture. It is fairest seen rising from amid brakes and hellebore, its lower part or rather naked stem concealed. Where the most beautiful wild-flowers grow, there man's spirit is fed, and poets grow. It cannot be high-colored, growing in the shade. Nature has taken no pains to exhibit [it], and few that bloom are ever seen by mortal eyes. The most striking and handsome large wild-flower of the year thus far that I have seen.

Disturbed a company of tree-toads amid the bushes. They seemed to bewilder the passer by their croaking; when he went toward one, he was silent, and another sounded on the other side. The hickory leaves are fragrant as I brush past them. Quite a feast of strawberries on Fair Haven, — the upland strawberry. The largest and sweetest on sand. The *first fruit*. The night-warbler. There are few really cold springs. I go out of my way to go by the Boiling Spring. How few men can be believed when they say the spring is cold! There is one cold as the coldest well water. What a treasure is such a spring! Who *divined* it? The cistuses are all closed. Is it because of the heat, and will they be open in the morning? C. found common hound's-tongue (*Cynoglossum officinale*) by railroad.

8 p. m. — On river.

No moon. A deafening sound from the toads, and intermittingly from bullfrogs. What I have thought to be frogs prove to be toads, sitting by thousands along the shore and trilling short and loud, — not so long a quaver as in the spring, — and I have not heard them in those pools, now, indeed, mostly dried up, where I heard them in the spring. (I do not know what to think of my midsummer frog now.) The bullfrogs are very loud, of various degrees of baseness and sonorousness, answering each other across the river with two or three grunting croaks. They are not nearly so numerous as the toads.

It is candle-light. The fishes leap. The meadows sparkle with the coppery light of fireflies. The evening star, multiplied by undulating water, is like bright sparks of fire continually ascending. The reflections of the trees are grandly indistinct. There is a low mist slightly enlarging the river, through which the arches of the stone bridge are just visible, as a vision. The mist is singularly bounded, collected here, while there is none there; close up to the bridge on one side and none on the other, depending apparently on currents of air. A dew in the air it is, which in time will wet you through. See stars reflected in the bottom of our boat, it being a quarter full of water. There is a low crescent of northern light and shooting stars from time to time. (We go only from Channing's to the ash above the railroad.) I paddle with a bough, the Nile boatman's oar, which is rightly pliant, and you do not labor much. Some dogs bay. A sultry night.

June 16. Wednesday. 4.30 A. M. — A low fog on the meadows, but not so much as last night, — a low incense frosting them. The clouds scattered wisps in the sky, like a squadron thrown into disorder at the approach of the sun. The sun now gilds an eastern cloud a broad, bright, coppery-golden edge, fiery bright, notwithstanding which the protuberances of the cloud cast dark shadows ray-like up into the day. The curled dock (*Rumex crispus*) and the *Malva*,[1] the cheese mallows. A new season. The earth looks like a debauchee after the sultry night. Birds sing at this hour as in the spring. You hear that spitting, *dumping* frog and the bullfrogs occasionally still, for the heat is scarcely less than the last night. *No toads now.* The white lily is budded.

Paddle from the ash tree to the swimming-place. The further shore is crowded with polygonums (leaves) and pontederia leaves. There seems to have intervened no night. The heat of the day is unabated. You perspire before sunrise. The bullfrogs boom still. The river appears covered with an almost imperceptible blue film. The sun is not yet over the bank. What wealth in a stagnant river! There is music in every sound in the morning atmosphere. As I look up over the bay, I see the reflections of the meadow woods and the Hosmer hill at a distance, the tops of the trees cut off by a slight ripple. Even the fine grasses on the near bank are distinctly reflected. Owing to the reflections of the distant woods and hills, you seem to be paddling into a vast hollow country, doubly novel and interesting. Thus the voyageur is lured onward to fresh pastures.

[1] [A blank space left for the specific name.]

The melting heat begins again as soon as the sun gets up. My shoes are covered with the reddish seeds of the grass, for I have been walking in the dew. I hear a stake-driver, like a man at his pump, which sucks, — fit sound for our sluggish river. What is the devil's-needle about? He hovers about a foot above the pads on humming wings thus early, from time to time darting one side as if in pursuit of some invisible prey. Most would suppose the stake-driver the sound of a farmer at a distance at his pump, watering his cattle. It oftener sounds like this than like a stake, but sometimes exactly like a man driving a stake in the meadow. Mistook a crow blackbird, on a dark-brown rock rising out of the water, for a crow or a bittern, referring it to a greater distance than the actual, by some mirage. It had a boat tail, conspicuous when it flew. The bullfrogs lie on the very surface of the pads, showing their great yellow throats, color of the yellow breeches of the old school, and protuberant eyes. His whole back out, revealing a vast expanse of belly. His eyes like ranunculus or yellow lily buds, winking from time to time and showing his large dark-bordered tympanum. Imperturbable-looking. His yellow throat swells up like a small moon at a distance over the pads when he croaks. The floating pondweed (*Potamogeton natans*), with the oblong oval leaf floating on the surface, now in bloom. The yellow water ranunculus still yellows the river in the middle, where shallow, in beds many rods long. It is one of the capillary-leaved plants.

It is Bigelow's spotted geranium (*G. maculatum*), or crane's-bill, that we have.

Vol. IV

The fisherman offers you mackerel this sultry weather.

By and by the bidens (marigold) will stand in the river, as now the ranunculus. The summer's fervor will have sunk into it. The spring yellows are faint, cool, innocent as the saffron of the morning compared with the blaze of noon. The autumnal, methinks, are the fruit of the dog-days, heats of manhood or age, not of youth. The former are pure, transparent, crystalline, *viz.* [sic] the willow catkins and the early cinquefoils. This ranunculus, too, standing two or three inches above the water, is of a light yellow, especially at a distance. This, I think, is the rule with respect to spring flowers, though there are exceptions.

P. M. — To Great Meadows, 4 o'clock.

All but dogs and Englishmen are housed. It has been quite breezy, even windy, this month. The new foliage has rustled. Already leaves are eaten by insects. I see their excrement in the path; even the pads on the river have many holes in them. The *Viola pedata* and the columbines last into June, but now they are scarce. The *Lysimachia thyrsiflora*, tufted loosestrife, by the Depot Field Brook.

9 P. M. — Down railroad.

Heat lightning in the horizon. A sultry night. A flute from some villager. How rare among men so fit a thing as the sound of a flute at evening! Have not the fireflies in the meadow relation to the stars above, *étincelant?* When the darkness comes, we see stars

beneath also. The sonorous note of bullfrogs is heard a mile off in the river, the loudest sound this evening. Ever and anon the sound of his trombone comes over the meadows and fields, a-lulling all Concord to sleep. Do not the stars, too, show their light for love, like the fireflies? There are northern lights, shooting high up withal.

Even the botanist calls your fine new flower "a troublesome weed," — hound's-tongue.

June 17. Thursday. 4 A. M. — To Cliffs.

No fog this morning. At early dawn, the windows being open, I hear a steady, breathing, cricket-like sound from the chip-bird (?), ushering in the day. Perhaps these mornings are the most memorable in the year, — after a sultry night and before a sultry day, — when, especially, the morning is the most glorious season of the day, when its coolness is most refreshing and you enjoy the glory of the summer gilded or silvered with dews, without the torrid summer's sun or the obscuring haze. The sound of the crickets at dawn after these first sultry nights seems like the dreaming of the earth still continued into the daylight. I love that early twilight hour when the crickets still creak right on with such dewy faith and promise, as if it were still night, — expressing the innocence of morning, — when the creak of the cricket is fresh and bedewed. While the creak of the cricket has that ambrosial sound, no crime can be committed. It buries Greece and Rome past resurrection. The earth-song of the cricket! Before Christianity was, it is. Health! health!

health! is the burden of its song. It is, of course, that man, refreshed with sleep, is thus innocent and healthy and hopeful. When we hear that sound of the crickets in the sod, the world is not so much with us.

I hear the universal cock-crowing with surprise and pleasure, as if I never heard it before. What a tough fellow! How native to the earth! Neither wet nor dry, cold nor warm, kills him.

Is there any fog in a sultry night? The prudent farmer improves the early morning to do some of his work before the heat becomes too oppressive, while he can use his oxen. As yet no whetting of the scythe. The morning is ambrosial, but the day is a terrestrial *paradise*. Ah, the refreshing coolness of the morning, full of all kinds of fragrance! What is that *little* olivaceous-yellowish bird, whitish beneath, that followed me cheeping under the bushes? The birds sing well this morning, well as ever. The brown thrasher drowns the rest. Lark first, and, in the woods, the red-eye, veery, chewink, oven-bird, wood thrush.

The cistus is well open now, with its broad cup-like flower. One of the most delicate yellow flowers, with large spring-yellow petals and its stamens laid one way. It is hard to get home fresh; is caducous and inclined to droop. The amelanchier berries begin to be red and edible; perhaps they should be quite purple to be ripe. They will be the second berry of the year. The yellow Bethlehem-star is of a deeper yellow than the cistus, a very neat flower, grass-like. The *Viburnum dentatum*.

Vol. IV

P. M. — On the river by Hubbard's meadow.

Looking at a clump of trees and bushes on the meadow, which is commonly flooded in the spring, I saw a middling-sized rock concealed by the leaves lying in the midst, and perceived that this had obtained a place, had made good the locality, for the maples and shrubs which had found a foothold about it. Here the reeds or tender plants were detained and protected. Now concealed by the beneficiaries it had protected? The boulder dropped once on a meadow makes at length a clump of trees there.

Kalm's lily (*Nuphar lutea* var. *Kalmiana* (Gray)) appears to be more abundant on the river than the large one. The polygonum leaves make a dense leafy reddish or red edge to the river. The carrion-flower is very abundant on this river meadow. How many times I must have mistaken it for carrion.

A small thunder-shower came up in the southwest. The thunder sounded like moving a pile of boards in the attic. We could see the increasing outline of the slate-colored falling rain from the black cloud. It passed mainly to the south. We felt only the wind of it at first, but after it appeared to back up and we got some rain. You see large hummocks, one two rods long by one wide, lying high on the bank, as if the farmers had thrown up mud there, and perhaps detect a corresponding hollow, now an open bay amid the pads, from which it was scooped out.

In the damp, warm evening after the rain, the fireflies appear to be more numerous than ever.

June 18. The hornet's nest is built with many thin layers of his paper, with an interval of about an eighth of an inch between them, so that his wall is one or two inches thick. This probably for warmth, dryness, and lightness. So sometimes the carpenter has learned to build double walls.

When I attended to the lichens last winter, I made out: —

First, the *Umbilicaria Muhlenbergii*, which Tuckerman says was the favorite rock-tripe in Franklin's Journey.

Second, *U. pustulata.*

Third, *U. Dillenii.*

All common on our rocks. The first like a cinder beneath, the second pustuled, the third like an old dried felt hat.

Parmelia perforata (with great shields).

P. caperata (wrinkled sulphur (H.)).

P. saxatilis (gray rock (Hooker)).

P. conspersa (greenish chestnut shielded (Hooker)).

One of the *Parmelia Citrinæ* (Is it the *P. chrysophthalma* on the apple trees of the Cape? In Loudon, *Borreri chrysophthalma?* What is that on the elm?).

P. stellaris (?).

P. hypoleuca (?), very handsome on black oak.

P. perlata (?).

P. orcina, crustaceous on rocks, yellow and fine.

P. albella.

P. Borreri.

P. scruposa (?), on the ground.

Sticta pulmonaria, on rocks.

S. glomerulifera (?), at the foot of oaks.

Cetraria lacunosa, perforated, very common. (*C. Islandica* famous. Some kinds dark-colored, some greenish.)

Evernia jubata, on the pitch pine, dark brown.

E. prunastri, stag's-horn, very handsome.

Ramalinas of two or more kinds, especially on red oaks.

Usneas of several kinds, some fine, some coarse, some long, some short, some ferruginous.

Cladonias, as *C. Cocciferæ*, the red-fruited, on the earth and on stumps.

Cladonias, *Scyphiferæ*, cup lichens of various kinds, on ground under banks and on stumps.

Cladonias, various cladonias of the reindeer moss kind (which last I have not identified), very common on dry pastures and hills.

Endocarpon miniatum, on moist rocks, Conantum.

Pertusaria papillata (*Porina* Ach.), minute, black, crustaceous.

On a small piece of bark, *Pertusaria faginea, Parmelia subfusca*, and *Lecidea parasema* (with the black border).

What is that very common greenish (when wet), pliant, leathery or gelatinous (?) lichen, very common on the earth and amid moss on rocks, with the shield on the under side? There is another, flat, small-leaved, and ash-colored when dry. The dead black birch bark is covered with many handsome small crustaceous lichens.

With roses rose-bugs have come.

Concord River in June

Anemones

7 P. M. — To Cliffs. No moon.

Methinks I saw and heard goldfinches. Pyrolas are beginning to blossom. The four-leaved loosestrife. The longest days in the year have now come. The sun goes down now (this moment) behind Watatic, from the Cliffs. St. John's-wort is beginning to blossom; looks yellow.

I hear a man playing a clarionet far off. Apollo tending the flocks of King Admetus. How cultivated, how sweet and glorious, is music! Men have brought this art to great perfection, the art of modulating sound, by long practice since the world began. What superiority over the rude harmony of savages! There is something glorious and flower-like in it. What a contrast this evening melody with the occupations of the day! It is perhaps the most admirable accomplishment of man.

June 19. Saturday. 8.30 A. M. — To Flag Hill — on which Stow, Acton, and Boxboro corner — with C., with bread and butter and cheese in pocket.

A comfortable breezy June morning. No dust to-day. To explore a segment of country between the Stow hills and the railroad in Acton, west to Boxboro. A fine, clear day, a journey day. A very small blue veronica in the bank by the roadside at Mrs. Hosmer's, apparently the same with that I saw on the Cliffs with toothed leaves. Interesting from being blue. The traveller now has the creak of the cricket to encourage him on all country routes, out of the fresh sod, still fresh as in the dawn, not interrupting his thoughts.

Very cheering and refreshing to hear so late in the day, this morning sound. The whiteweed colors some meadows as completely as the frosting does a cake. The waving June grass shows watered colors like grain. No mower's scythe is heard. The farmers are hoeing their corn and potatoes. Some low blackberry leaves are covered with a sort of orange-colored mildew or fungus. The clover is now in its glory. Whole fields are *rosed* with it, mixed with sorrel, and looking deeper than it is. It makes fields look luxuriant which are really thinly clad. The air is full of its sweet fragrance. I cannot find the linnæa in Loring's; perhaps because the woods are cut down; perhaps I am too late. The robins sing more than usual, maybe because of the coolness. Buttercups and geraniums cover the meadows, the latter appearing to float on the grass, — of various tints. It has lasted long, this rather tender flower. Methinks there are most *tall* buttercups now. These and the senecio, now getting stale, prevail in the meadows. Green early blueberries on hillsides *passim* remind you of the time when berries will be ripe. This is the ante-huckleberry season, when fruits are green. The green fruit of the thorn is conspicuous, and of the wild cherry and the amelanchiers and the thimble-berry. These are the clover days. The small white-starred flowers of the stitchwort (*Stellaria longifolia*), amid grass and bushes by the meadow-sides. Some grass may perchance be well named bent, if from its bended blade. The light of June is not golden but silvery, not a torrid but somewhat temperate heat. See it reflected from the bent grass and the under sides of leaves.

Vol. IV

Also I perceive faint silvery gleaming ripples where there is a rapid in the river (from railroad bridge at Darby's), without sun on it.

At the pond on Lord's land saw the *Villarsia lacunosa* (Bigelow), common villarsia, with its small rounded heart-shaped leaves like a small pond-lily leaf, and its transparent frosty white flowers, spotting the whole surface like the white petals of some flower which had fallen on it. It belongs to a stagnant pond like this. What is that smooth elliptical leaf, three or four inches long, of the texture of the white lily leaf, peltate and almost, if not quite, vermilion on the under side? I do not see its flower.

The mullein out, with a disagreeable scent, and the dogsbane, with a quite handsome bell-shaped flower, beautifully striped with red (rose red?) within.

Facts collected by a poet are set down at last as winged seeds of truth, samaræ, tinged with his expectation. Oh, may my words be verdurous and sempiternal as the hills! Facts fall from the poetic observer as ripe seeds.

At Willis's Spring under the railroad, a cocoanut shell from the other side of the globe to drink at a New England spring. Water kept cool in the bowels of the earth, the cellar of the earth. The meadow thalictrum there. *Aralia hispida.* The river has a June look, dark, smooth, reflecting surfaces in shade, and the water is refreshing as suggesting coolness. The shadows in and under elms and other trees have not been so rich hitherto. It is grateful to look forward half a mile into some dark umbrageous elm or ash. Is

that the common puffball, now white, convex, nubby? The panicled cornel (under which Gray puts Bigelow's white cornel), with pure white flowers. This and the *Viburnum dentatum*, now out, show handsome corymbs (and the *V. nudum*) in copses, both in sun and *shade*, against and amid the green leaves of the shrubs or trees. Grape in bloom; agreeable perfume to many, to me not so. This is not the meadow fragrance, then, which I have perceived. I hear the wiry phœbe note of the chickadee. Maybe the huckleberry-bird best expresses the season, or the red-eye. The four-leaved loosestrife covers large sandy tracts by the side of the railroad. The new shoots of the oaks are long enough to droop gracefully.

What subtile differences between one season and another! The warmest weather has, perchance, arrived and the longest days, but not the driest. When I remember gathering ripe blackberries on sandy fields or stones by the roadside, the very berries warmed by the sun, I am convinced of this. The seasons admit of infinite degrees in their revolutions.

Found one of the purple orchises in an open meadow.

Left the railroad near Ford Brook Fall and went over a hill on the left at South Acton. The veiny-leaved hawkweed out. A large swelling pasture hill with hickories left for shade and cattle now occupying them. The bark is rubbed smooth and red with their hides. Pleasant to go over the hills, for there there is most air stirring, but you must look out for bulls in the pastures. Saw one here reclining in the shade amid the cows. His short, sanguinary horns betrayed him, and we gave him a wide berth, for they are not to be reasoned with.

On our right is Acton, on our left is Stow, and forward, Boxboro. Thus King Richard sailed the Ægean and passed kingdoms on his right and left. Now we are on one of the breezy hills that make the west horizon from Concord, from which we see our familiar Concord hills much changed and reduced in height and breadth. We are in a country very different from Concord, — of swelling hills and long vales, on the bounds of these three towns, more up-countryish. Some clovers are of a beautiful rich transparent (?) red color with their conical heads. A wild rose with large pale-pinkish blossom.

There rose a higher wooded hill on the north side of South Acton. From this hill, on the south side, we selected one from the west (it proved to be Flag Hill on the edge of Boxboro), which we decided to reach by striking more southerly and then following the *ridge* along [?] northwest, so we thought.

It requires considerable skill in crossing a country to avoid the houses and too cultivated parts, — somewhat of the engineer's or gunner's skill, — so to pass a house, if you must go near it through high grass, — pass the enemy's lines where houses are thick, — as to make a hill or wood screen you, — to shut every window with an apple tree. For that route which most avoids the houses is not only the one in which you will be least molested, but it is by far the most agreeable. Saw the handsomest large maple [1] west of this hill that I ever saw. We crawled through the end of a swamp on our

[1] White maple ?

bellies, the bushes were so thick, to screen us from a house forty rods off whose windows completely commanded the open ground, leaping some broad ditches, and when we emerged into the grass ground, some apple trees near the house beautifully screened us. It is rare that you cannot avoid a grain-field or piece of English mowing by skirting a corn-field or nursery near by, but if you must go through high grass, then step lightly and in each other's tracks.

We soon fell into a swamp where we smelt the *Viburnum nudum* rather strong and unpleasant; a dry swamp filled with high bushes and trees and, beneath, tall ferns, one large pinnate leaf, five or six feet high and one foot broad, making a dense undergrowth in tufts at bottom, spreading every way, — two species of this size, one more compound; these we opened with our hands, making a path through. Completely in cool shade. I steered by the sun, though it was so high now at noon that I observed which way my short shadow fell before I entered the swamp, — for in it we could see nothing of the country around, — and then, by keeping my shadow on a particular side of me, I steered surely, standing still sometimes till the sun came out of a cloud to be sure of our course. Came out at length on a side-hill very near the South Acton line in Stow, another large pasture hill smelling of strawberries, where I saw a large sugar maple, the nearest large one, wild, that I know, and some large ash trees. You could see no more of the surrounding country from the swamp than you could of a village street if you were in the cellars of the houses.

On this second hill we sat under another walnut, where the ants on and about the tree ran over us as we were eating our dinner. No water had we seen fit to drink since we started. The farmers of Stow and Acton, we fancied, were now taking a nooning. Now our further hill, which had appeared to be but a continuation of a ridge from this, proved to lie west-north-west across a broad valley some one and one half or two miles. So we dashed down the west side of this toward Heather Meadow Brook, where we found the swamp pink in blossom, a most cool refreshing fragrance to travellers in hot weather. I should place this with, if not before, the mayflower. Its flowers, just opened, have caught but few insects. *This* brook we could not drink, it was so tepid and stagnant. In these meadows, I forgot to say, we saw the beautiful wild rose of a deep red color, in blossom, — a rich sight; islands of rose bushes with a profusion of flowers and buds. How suddenly they have expanded! They are first seen in abundance in meadows. Is not this the carnival of the year, when the swamp rose and wild pink are in bloom, the last stage before blueberries come? We were obliged to choose a shallow place and wade Heather Meadow Brook, but we could not drink it. A cooler rill that emptied in smelt and tasted too strongly of muskrats. Then we threaded more swamp, very tangled, where we had to stoop continually, and full of brakes which we could more easily part, but not so wide as the last. And at length we reached the last hillside, but it proved a long way to its top. Still we could find no water fit to drink, and

were thinking of cool springs gushing from the hillsides under the shade of some maples.

The cow-wheat. The huckleberry-bird still. You see, on distant hills, cows everywhere standing in the shade; sometimes a woodchuck by the side of a clover-field standing up on his hind quarters like a short post. The strawberries are small and dried up.

Now, half-way up this hill, we struck into a thick wood, which, descending, turned into a thicker swamp, sometimes with trees, sometimes high bushes only, which completely shaded us, blueberries, etc.; and I saw the *Prinos lævigatus* (?), smooth winterberry, though the flowers, *in clusters*, appeared fertile and the pedicels were rather long, a half-inch all of them; beneath and around, brakes; under foot, sphagnum and gold-thread and decaying logs. This was the most intricate swamp of all, high on the side of a hill and wide. I climbed a yellow birch covered with lichens, looking as if dead, and another, whence I saw a larch red with cones, but could not see out; but, steering by the sun, at length came out right, on Flag Hill, in the southeast corner of Boxboro, where the three towns corner, and looked west to Harvard and Bolton hills. The country wore a New Hampshire aspect.

Returned by road and railroad to South Acton, crossed the side of the South Acton Hill, and cut across to Ford Brook at the Boxboro road. The *Juncus militaris* [1] in bloom. The prunella already, with few flowers. The adder's-tongue arethusa, with the bulbous. Thus we returned as we went, skirting meadows, threading

[1] *Scirpus lacustris?*

woods and swamps, and climbing hills, and occasionally skirting or crossing dusty cultivated fields between the rows of corn or potatoes. In the meadows the senecio, bruised, yields the prevailing smell. Saw some canoe (?) birches, probably, which looked like whitewashed trees, so large.

Can that hairy potentilla (but not dichotomous) be the Norway potentilla, already?

The orchis keeps well. One put in my hat this morning, and carried all day, will last fresh a day or two at home. These are peculiar days when you find the purple orchis and the arethusa, too, in the meadows. The fields a walker loves best to strike into are bare, extended, rolling, bordered by copses, with brooks and meadows in sight, sandy beneath the thin sod, where now blackberries and pinks grow, erst rye or oats, — perchance these and stony pastures, where is no high grass nor grain nor cultivated ground nor houses near.

Bathed in the North River by the old stone bridge just before sundown.

Flag Hill is about eight miles *by the road* from Concord. We went much further, going and returning both; but by how much nobler road! Suppose you were to ride to Boxboro, what then? You pass a few teams with their dust, drive through many farmers' barn-yards, between two walls, see where Squire Tuttle lives and barrels his apples, bait your horse at White's Tavern, and so return, with your hands smelling of greasy leather and horsehair and the squeak of a chaise body in your ears, with no new flower nor agreeable experience. But, going as we did, before you got to Boxboro line,

you often went much further, many times ascended New Hampshire hills, taking the noble road from hill to hill, across swamps and valleys, not regarding political courses and boundaries, many times far west in your thought. It is a journey of a day and a picture of human life.

It was a very good day on the whole, for it was cool in the morning, and there were just clouds enough to shade the earth in the hottest part of the day, and at evening it was comfortably cool again.

The prinos-like shrub in the southwest of Acton swamp, on side of Flag Hill, has from six to nine petals and the same number of stamens on the monopetalous flower, which all comes off together and leaves a distinct calyx of six or seven lanceolate segments and, within, the germ, with apparently three sessile stigmas or short divisions at its apex. All on slender peduncles about five eighths of an inch long, proceeding from nearly a common centre (with leaves).

June 20. 7 p. m. — To Hubbard Bathing-Place.
The blue-eyed grass is shut up. When does it open? Some blue flags are quite a red purple, — dark wine-color. Identified the *Iris prismatica*, Boston iris, with linear leaves and round stem.

The stake-driver is at it in his favorite meadow. I followed the sound. At last I got within two rods, it seeming always to recede and drawing you like a will-o'-the-wisp further away into the meadows. When thus near, I heard some lower sounds at the beginning, much more like striking on a stump or a stake, a dry,

hard sound; and then followed the gurgling, pumping notes, fit to come from a meadow. This was just within the blueberry and *Pyrus arbutifolia* (choke-berry) bushes, and when the bird flew up alarmed, I went to the place, but could see no water, which makes me doubt if water is necessary to it in making the sound. Perhaps it thrusts its bill so deep as to reach the water where it is dry on the surface. It sounds the more like wood-chopping or pumping, because you seem to hear the echo of the stroke or the reverse motion of the pump-handle. I hear them morning and evening. After the warm weather has come, both morning and evening you hear the bittern pumping in the fens. It does not sound loud near at hand, and it is remarkable that it should be heard so far. Perhaps it is pitched on a favorable key. Is it not a call to its mate? Methinks that in the resemblance of this note to rural sounds, to sounds made by farmers, the protection, the security, of the bird is designed. Minott says: "I call them belcher-squelchers. They go *slug-toot, slug-toot, slug-toot.*"

Dry fields have now a reddish tinge from the seeds of the grass.

Lying with my window open, these warm, even sultry nights, I hear the sonorously musical trump of the bullfrogs from time to time, from some distant shore of the river, as if the world were given up to them. By those villagers who live on the street they are never seen and rarely heard by day, but in the quiet sultry nights their notes ring from one end of the town to another. It is as if you had waked up in the infernal regions. I do not know for a time in what world I am.

It affects my morals, and all questions take a new aspect from this sound. At night bullfrogs lie on the pads and answer to one another all over North America; undoubtedly there is an incessant and uninterrupted chain of sound, *troomp, troomp, troomp,* from the Atlantic to the Pacific (*vide* if they reach so far west), further than Britain's morning gun. It is the snoring music of nature at night. When you wake thus at midnight and hear this sonorous trump from far in the horizon, you need not go to Dante for an idea of the infernal regions. It requires the night air, this sound. How allied to a pad in place, in color, — for his greenish back is the leaf and his yellow throat the flower, — even in form, with his sesquipedality of belly! (And other, white-bellied frogs are white lilies.) Through the summer he lies on the pads, or with his head out, and in the winter buries himself at their roots (?). The bull-paddock! His eyes like the buds of the *Nuphar Kalmiana*. Methinks his skin would stand water without shrinking forever. Gloves made of it for rainy weather, for trout-fishers!! Frogs appear slow to make up their minds, but then they act precipitately. As long as they are here, they are here, and express no intention of removing; but the idea of removing fills them instantaneously, as nature, abhorring, fills a vacuum. Now they are fixed and imperturbable like the Sphinx, and now they go off with short, squatty leaps over the spatter-dock, on the irruption of the least idea.

June 21. Monday. 7 p. m. — To Cliffs *via* Hubbard Bathing-Place.

Cherry-birds. I have not seen, though I think I have heard them before,—their *fine* seringo note, like a vibrating spring in the air. They are a handsome bird, with their crest and chestnut breasts. There is no keeping the run of their goings and comings, but they will be ready for the cherries when they shall be ripe.

The adder's-tongue arethusa smells exactly like a snake. How singular that in nature, too, beauty and offensiveness should be thus combined! In flowers, as well as men, we demand a beauty pure and fragrant, which perfumes the air. The flower which is showy but has no, or an offensive, odor expresses the character of too many mortals.

The swamp-pink bushes have many whitish spongy excrescences. Elder is blossoming; flowers opening now where black berries will be by and by. Panicled andromeda, or privet andromeda.

Nature has looked uncommonly bare and dry to me for a day or two. With our senses applied to the surrounding world we are reading our own physical and corresponding moral revolutions. Nature was so shallow all at once I did not know what had attracted me all my life. I was therefore encouraged when, going through a field this evening, I was unexpectedly struck with the beauty of an apple tree. The perception of beauty is a moral test.

When, in bathing, I rush hastily into the river the clamshells cut my feet.

It is dusky now. Men are fishing on the Corner Bridge. I hear the veery and the huckleberry-bird and the catbird. It is a cool evening, past 8 o'clock. I

see the tephrosia out through the dusk; a handsome flower.

What rich crops this dry hillside has yielded! First I saw the *Viola pedata* here, and then the lupines and the snapdragon covered it; and now the lupines are done and their pods are left, the tephrosia has taken their place. This small dry hillside is thus a natural garden. I omit other flowers which grow here, and name only those which to some extent cover it or possess it. No eighth of an acre in a cultivated garden would be better clothed, or with a more pleasing variety, from month to month, and while one flower is in bloom you little suspect that which is to succeed and perchance eclipse it. It is a warmly placed dry hillside beneath a wall, very thinly clad with grass. Such spots there are in nature, natural flower gardens. Of this succession I hardly know which to admire the most. It would be pleasant to write the history of one hillside for one year. First and last you have the colors of the rainbow and more, and the various fragrances, which it has not. Blackberries, roses, and dogsbane also are now in bloom here.

I hear neither toads nor bullfrogs at present; they want a warmer night. I hear the sound of distant thunder, though no cloud is obvious, muttering like the roar of artillery. That is a phenomenon of this season. As you walk at evening, you see the light of the flashes in the horizon and hear the muttering of distant thunder, where some village is being refreshed with the rain denied to Concord. We say that showers avoid us, that they go down the river, *i. e.* go off down the Merrimack,

or keep to the south. Thunder and lightning are remarkable accompaniments to our life, as if to remind us that there always is or should be a kind of battle waging. The thunder is signal guns to us.

The dwarf orchis (*O. herbiola* (Bigelow), *Platanthera flava* (Gray)) at the bathing-place in Hubbard's meadow, not remarkable. The purple orchis is a good flower to bring home. It will keep fresh many days, and its buds open at last in a pitcher of water. Obtuse galium. I observe a rose (called by some moss rose), with a bristly reddish stem; another, with a smooth red stem and but a few prickles; another, with many prickles and bristles. Found the single-flowered broom-rape in Love Lane, under the oak.

June 22. 8 p. m. — Up the Union Turnpike.
We have had a succession of thunder-showers today and at sunset a rainbow. How moral the world is made! This bow is not utilitarian. Methinks men are great in proportion as they are moral. After the rain He sets his bow in the heavens! The world is not destitute of beauty. Ask of the skeptic who inquires, *Cui bono?* why the rainbow was made. While men cultivate flowers below, God cultivates flowers above; he takes charge of the parterres in the heavens. Is not the rainbow a faint vision of God's face? How glorious should be the life of man passed under this arch! What more remarkable phenomenon than a rainbow, yet how little it is remarked!

Near the river thus late, I hear the peetweet, with white-barred wings. The scent of the balm-of-Gilead

leaves fills the road after the rain. There are the amber skies of evening, the colored skies of both morning and evening! Nature adorns these seasons. Unquestionable truth is sweet, though it were the announcement of our dissolution.

More thunder-showers threaten, and I still can trace those that are gone by. The fireflies in the meadows are very numerous, as if they had replenished their lights from the lightning. The far-retreated thunder-clouds low in the southeast horizon and in the north, emitting low flashes which reveal their forms, appear to lift their wings like fireflies; or it is a steady glare like the glow-worm. Wherever they go, they make a meadow. I hear no toads this cool evening.

June 23. 5 a. m. — To Laurel Glen.
The bobolink still sings, though not as in May. The tall buttercups do not make so much show in the meadows, methinks, as the others did. Or are they beaten down by last night's rain? The small Solomon's-seal is going out of flower and shows small berries. The pretty little *Mitchella repens*, with its twin flowers, spots the ground under the pines with its downy-petalled, cross-shaped flowers and its purplish buds. Gray's *Pyrola asarifolia*[1] for some days, with small roundish thick leaves, and his *P. secunda*, or one-sided pyrola, apparently a little later. Another ripe amelanchier berry, red inclining to purple, with a still downy peduncle, so I suppose it is Bigelow's *Pyrus ovalis*. This is the next fruit after the strawberry. I

¹ [Queried in pencil.]

suppose the June berry (blue berry) [*sic*] will be the next. The first amelanchier berry I tasted corresponded in leaf to Bigelow's *P. sanguinea*, which is a tree, though that was a low shrub. The grass is not nearly so wet after thunder-showers in the night as after an ordinary dew. Apparently the rain falls so swiftly and hard that it does not rest on the leaves, and then there is no more moisture to be deposited in dew. Yellow diervilla must have been in bloom about a week. Round-leaved cornel resembles the panicled in flower. The mountain laurel, with its milk-white flower, in cool and shady woods, reminds one of the vigor of nature. It is perhaps a first-rate flower, considering its size and ever-greenness. Its flower-buds, curiously folded in a ten-angled pyramidal form, are remarkable. A profusion of flowers, with an innocent fragrance. It reminds me of shady mountain-sides where it forms the underwood. I hear my old Walden owl. Its first note is almost like a somewhat peevish scream or squeal of a child shrugging its shoulders, and then succeed two more moderate and musical ones. The wood thrush sings at all hours. I associate it with the cool morning, sultry noon, and serene evening. At this hour it suggests a cool vigor.

What I have called the dwarf choke-cherry is the *Cerasus Pennsylvanica* of Gray, *i. e.* wild red cherry. We have also the *C. Virginiana* (or *obovata* of Bigelow), the true choke-cherry, with a raceme. Both their fruits are now the size of small peas. When does the last blossom? Bigelow says a fortnight before the *serotina*. The herd's-grass shows its tops.

P. M. — To the mountain laurel in Mason's pasture in Carlisle *via* old Carlisle road.

I hear the trilled dream of many toads from a roadside pool, though not quite so loud, perchance, as in the spring, and from time to time, when very near, a sound somewhat like a hoarse chicken. It is what I call a *washing* day, such as we sometimes have when buttercups first appear in the spring, an agreeably cool and clear and breezy day, when all things appear as if washed bright and shine, and, at this season especially, the sound of the wind rustling the leaves is like the rippling of a stream, and you see the light-colored under side of the still fresh foliage, and a sheeny light is reflected from the bent grass in the meadows. Haze and sultriness are far off. The air is cleared and cooled by yesterday's thunder-storms. The river too has a fine, cool, silvery sparkle or sheen on it. You can see far into the horizon, and you can hear the sound of crickets with such feelings as in the cool morning.

The Canada thistles begin to show their purple. What great thistle is that by the wall near Dakin's, not yet in bloom? In the Carlisle road, the rather slender veiny-leaved hawkweed. Rattlesnake-weed is in blossom quite commonly, like a small elevated dandelion on a slender stalk taking the place of the true. These slight yellow flowers to cheer the traveller here; also a *Hieraceum scabrum* (rough) or else *Gronovii* (hairy) of Gray. I saw one of *these last the 19th*. These little hawkweeds are to me a rather interesting family, so unpretending, or if only because they make so distinct or marked a family by themselves. Also the

barberry bushes hang now with small reddish-green fruit, and green huckleberries grow in this grassy road. Cheered by these promises, the traveller holds on his way. But I travel chiefly in the fields or pastures parallel with the road.

These are very agreeable pastures to me; no house in sight, no cultivation. I sit under a large white oak, upon its swelling instep, which makes an admirable seat, and look forth over these pleasant rocky and bushy pastures, where for the most part there are not even cattle to graze them, but patches of huckleberry bushes, and birches, and pitch pines, and barberry bushes, and creeping juniper in great circles, its edges curving upward, and wild roses spotting the green with red, and numerous tufts of indigo-weed, and, above all, great gray boulders lying about far and near, with some barberry bush, perchance, growing half-way up them; and, between all, the short sod of the pasture here and there appears.

The beauty and fragrance of the wild rose are wholly agreeable and wholesome and wear well, and I do not wonder much that men have given the preference to this family of flowers, notwithstanding their thorns. It is hardy and more complete in its parts than most flowers, — its color, buds, fragrance, leaves, the whole bush, frequently its stem in particular, and finally its red or scarlet hips. Here is the sweet-briar in blossom, which to a fragrant flower adds more fragrant leaves. I take the wild rose buds to my chamber and put them in a pitcher of water, and they will open there the next day, and a single flower will perfume a room; and

then, after a day, the petals drop off, and new buds open.

I am inclined to think that my hat, whose lining is gathered in midway so as to make a shelf, is about as good a botany-box as I could have and far more convenient, and there is something in the darkness and the vapors that arise from the head — at least if you take a bath — which preserves flowers through a long walk. Flowers will frequently come fresh out of this botany-box at the end of the day, though they have had no sprinkling.

As I walk through these old deserted wild orchards, half pasture, half huckleberry-field, the air is filled with fragrance from I know not what source. How much purer and sweeter it must be than the atmosphere of the streets, rendered impure by the filth about our houses! It is quite offensive often when the air is heavy at night. The roses in the front yard do not atone for the sink and pigsty and cow-yard and jakes in the rear.

I sit on one of these boulders and look south to Ponkawtasset. Looking west, whence the wind comes, you do not see the under sides of the leaves, but, looking east, every bough shows its under side; those of the maples are particularly white. All leaves tremble like aspen leaves. Perhaps on those westward hills where I walked last Saturday the fields are somewhat larger than commonly with us, and I expand with a sense of freedom. The side of the hill commonly makes but one field. They begin to partake of the character of up-country pastures a little more. Two or three large boulders, fifteen or twenty feet square, make a good foreground in this landscape, for the gray color of the rock contrasts well with the green of the surrounding and more distant hills and woods and fields. They serve instead of cottages for a wild landscape as perches or *points d'appui* for the eye.

The red color of cattle, also, is agreeable in a landscape; or let them be what color they may, — red, black, white, or mouse-color, or spotted, all which I have seen this afternoon. The cows which, confined to the barn or barn-yard all winter, were covered with filth, after roaming in flowery pastures possess now clean and shining coats, and the cowy odor is without alloy. Indeed they make such an impression of neatness (I think of a white cow, spotted with red, and her two sizable calves of like color, which I saw this afternoon) that one who was unacquainted with etymology might be excused if he gave a new signification to the word neat as applied to cattle, and did not refer it to *knittan*, to butt (*i. e.* horned cattle).

It seems natural that rocks which have lain under the heavens so long should be gray, as it were an intermediate color between the heavens and the earth. The air is the thin paint in which they have been dipped and brushed with the wind. Water, which is more fluid and like the sky in its nature, is still more like it in color. Time will make the most discordant materials harmonize.

I see the silk-green-abdomened fly on cow-dung in the road.

There are some very handsome white pines and pine

groves on the left of the road just before you enter the woods. They are of second growth, of course, broad and perfect, with limbs almost to the ground, and almost as broad as they are high, their fine leaves trembling with silvery light, very different from the tall masts of the primitive wood, naked of limbs beneath and crowded together. So soft, and with such a mass of foliage through which the wind soughs. But you must be careful how you sit beneath them on account of pitch. Somewhat of a conical form.

This grassy road now dives into the wood, as if it were entering a cellar or bulkhead, the shadow is so deep. June is the first month for shadows. How is it in July? And now I scent the pines. I plucked a blue geranium in a meadow near the Kibbe Place, which appeared to me remarkably fragrant, like lilies and strawberries combined. The path I cut through the swamp late last fall is much more grown up than I expected. The sweet fragrance of swamp-pinks fills all the swamps, and when I look down, I see commonly the leaf of the gold-thread. The mountain laurels in Mason's pasture have not a blossom. They appear to have been partly killed by the winter or else late frosts; the leaves many of them are turned red and dead. And yet they sometimes blossom, for I see the remains of former flowers. They grow in the open pasture. Here is another pasture, with fields of sweet-fern bushes, and the humble but beautiful red lambkill everywhere, alone or mingled with other shrubs. Ever the walker will be attracted by some deeper red blossom than usual. You cannot bring it home in good condition;

else, perchance, it would be better known. With white pines and birches, beginning to prevail over the grass.

There are interesting groves of young soft white pines eighteen feet high, whose vigorous yellowish-green shoots of this season, from three to eighteen inches long, at the extremities of all the branches, contrast remarkably with the dark green of the old leaves. I observe that these shoots are bent and, what is more remarkable, all one way, *i. e.* to the east, almost at a right angle the topmost ones, and I am reminded of the observation in Henry's Adventures, that the Indians guided themselves in cloudy weather by this mark. All these shoots, excepting those low down on the east side, are bent toward the east. I am very much pleased with this observation, confirming that of the Indians. I was singularly impressed when I first observed that all the young pines in this pasture obeyed this law, without regard to the direction of the wind or the shelter of other trees. To make myself more sure of the direction, as it was not easy to determine it exactly, standing on one side, where so many shoots were bent in the air, I went behind the trees on the west till the bent shoot appeared as a straight line, and then, by observing my shadow and guessing at the time of day, I decided that their direction was due east. This gives me more satisfaction than any observation which I have made for a long time. This is true of the rapidly growing shoots. How long will this phenomenon avail to guide the traveller? How soon do they become erect? A natural compass. How few civilized men probably have ever made this observation, so important to the

savage! How much may there have been known to his woodcraft which has not been detected by science! At first I remarked the shoots of a distinct yellowish green, contrasting with the rest of the tree, then that they were not upright but bent more or less, and next that they were all inclined one way, as if bent by the wind, and finally that they were all bent east, without regard to the wind.

On the side of this pasture, I hear the red-eye in the swamp and the cool peep of a robin who has young, amid the pines. How quick are cattle and horses to hear the step of a walker! I pass much nearer to men at work in a field without being observed than to cattle or horses feeding. The latter hear me or, perchance, scent me if they do not look up. I observed a bullock this afternoon, when all his companions on a side-hill were already looking at me, suddenly whirl round to stare, as if he had detected from their attitude that some object engaged them. Then how curiously a whole herd will leave off grazing, and stare till you have passed, and if you have a dog, will think of their calves and make demonstrations of tossing him!

I returned to the bridle road and thence over Hubbard's oak grove hill. We have few handsome open oak groves left, but how handsome and cool and bosky they look in this breezy weather!

From N. Barrett's road I look over the Great Meadows. The meadows are the freshest, the greenest green in the landscape, and I do not (at this hour, at any rate) see any bent grass light. The river is a singularly deep living blue, the bluest blue, such as I rarely observe, and its shore is silvered with white maples, which show the under sides of their leaves, stage upon stage, in leafy towers. Methinks the leaves continue to show their under sides some time after the wind has done blowing. The southern edge of the meadow is also silvered with (I suppose) the red maple. Then there is the darker green of the forest, and the reddish, brownish, and bluish green of grass-lands and pastures and grain-fields, and the light-blue sky. There are not clouds enough in the sky to attract you to-day.

The sweet-briar bud which I brought home opened in the night. Is that the habit of roses?

June 24. P. M. — To White Pond.

The keys of the white ash cover the trees profusely, a sort of mulberry brown, an inch and a half long, handsome. The *Vaccinium macrocarpon*, probably for some days.

The *Calopogon pulchellus* (*Cymbidium* of Bigelow), grass pink of some, a pretty purple arethusa-like flower in a shady low copse on Corner road, near the *Asclepias quadrifolia*, a rather striking flower with two umbels of small pink and white flowers standing above the surrounding herbage. *Spiræa salicifolia* by the roadsides. *Archangelica atropurpurea*, interesting for its great umbels and vigorous growth of its purplish but rank-smelling stem. It is one of the most forward early leaves in warm springy places. I perceive excrescences on the grape leaves and vines, resembling in their form and disposition the grape clusters that are to be.

The drifting white downy clouds are to the landsman

what sails on the sea are to him that dwells by the shore, — objects of a large, diffusive interest. When the laborer lies on the grass or in the shade for rest, they do not too much tax or weary his attention. They are unobtrusive. I have not heard that white clouds, like white houses, made any one's eyes ache. They are the flitting sails in that ocean whose bounds no man has visited. They are like all great themes, always at hand to be considered, or they float over us unregarded. Far away they float in the serene sky, the most inoffensive of objects, or, near and low, they smite us with their lightnings and deafen us with their thunder. We know no Ternate nor Tidore grand enough whither we can imagine them bound. There are many mare's-tails to-day, if that is the name. What could a man learn by watching the clouds? The objects which go over our heads unobserved are vast and indefinite. Even those clouds which have the most distinct and interesting outlines are commonly below the zenith, somewhat low in the heavens, and seen on one side. They are among the most glorious objects in nature. A sky without clouds is a meadow without flowers, a sea without sails. Some days we have the mackerel fleet. But our devilishly industrious laborers rarely lie in the shade. How much better if they were to take their nooning like the Italians, relax and expand and never do any work in the middle of the day, enjoy a little sabbath in the middle of the day.

I still perceive that wonderful fragrance from the meadow (?) on the Corner causeway, intense as ever. It is one of those effects whose cause it

Vol. IV

is best not to know, perchance. Uncommonly cool weather now, after warm days and nights for a week or more. I see *many* grasshoppers for the first time (only single ones before), in the grass in the White Pond road. They describe a thousand little curves as I walk, ⌒ ⌒ ⌒ ⌐ ⌒ with an ominous dry rustling of their wings, about three quarters of an inch long. Come to eat the grass? It is the biggest game our dog starts. Much of the June-grass is dead; *most* of it in dry fields.

White Pond very handsome to-day. The shore alive with pollywogs of large size, which ripple the water on our approach. There is a fine sparkle on the water, though not equal to the fall one quite. The water is very high, so that you cannot walk round it, but it is the more pleasant while you are swimming to see how the trees *actually* rise out of it on all sides. It bathes their feet. The pines now hold somewhat of a subordinate rank amid the flourishing evergreens.

The dog worried a woodchuck, half grown, which did not turn its back and run into its hole, but backed into it and faced him and us, gritting its teeth and prepared to die. But even this little fellow was able to defend himself against the dog with his sharp teeth. That fierce gritting of their teeth is a remarkable habit with these animals.

I am disappointed to notice to-day that most of the pine-tops incline to the west, as if the wind had to do with it. The panicled andromeda has froth on it. The *Linnæa borealis* just going out of blossom. I should

have found it long ago. Its leaves densely cover the ground.

June 25. Just as the sun was rising this morning, under clouds, I saw a rainbow in the west horizon, the lower parts quite bright.

> "Rainbow in the morning,
> Sailors take warning;
> Rainbow at night
> Sailors' delight."

A few moments after, it rained heavily for a half-hour; and it has continued cloudy as well as cool most of the day. I observe that young birds are usually of a duller color and more speckled than old ones, as if for their protection in their tender state. They have not yet the markings (and the beauty) which distinguish their species, and which betray it often, but by their colors are merged in the variety of colors of the season.

P. M. — To Cliffs, 4 P. M.

It is cool and cloudy weather in which the crickets, still heard, remind you of the fall, — a clearer ring to their creak. Also the prunella, cool in the grass, and the johnswort make you think it late in the year. *Maruta Cotula*, or mayweed, — why so named? — just begins, with its strong-scented leaf. It has taken up its position by the roadside close to the ruts, — in bad taste. The *Prinos verticillatus*, with its small, neat, scentless white flower. Dogwood (*Rhus venenata*). The bobolink and golden robin are occasionally heard nowadays. Sometimes the lambkill flowers form a very even rounded, close cylinder, six inches long and two and a half in diameter, of rich red saucer-like flowers, the counterpart of the *latifolia* in flowers and flower-buds, but higher colored. I regard it as a beautiful flower neglected. It has a slight but not remarkable scent. The *Convolvulus sepium*, bindweed; morning-glory is the best name. It always refreshes me to see it. Some saw it the 19th. In the morning and cloudy weather, says Gray. I associate it with holiest morning hours. It may preside over my morning walks and thoughts. There is a flower for every mood of the mind.

Methinks roses oftenest display their high colors, colors which invariably attract all eyes and betray them, against a dark ground, as the dark green or the shady recesses of the bushes and copses, where they show to best advantage. Their enemies do not spare the open flower for an hour. Hence, if for no other reason, their buds are most beautiful. Their promise of perfect and dazzling beauty, when their buds are just beginning to expand, — beauty which they can hardly contain, — as in most youths, commonly surpasses the fulfillment of their expanded flowers. The color shows fairest and brightest in the bud. The expanded flower has no higher or deeper tint than the swelling bud exposed. This raised a dangerous expectation. The season when wild roses are in bloom should have some preëminence, methinks.

Agreeable is this cool cloudy weather, favorable to thought, after the sultry days. *Linaria vulgaris*, butter-and-eggs. toad-flax, on Fair Haven. (Was seen the 19th.) It is rather rich-colored, with a not disagreeable

scent. It is called a troublesome weed. Flowers must not be too profuse nor obtrusive; else they acquire the reputation of weeds. It grows almost like a cotton-grass, so above and distinct from its leaves, in wandering patches higher and higher up the side of the hill. I see no reddish ferns in the meadows now (looking from the hill), but much of the grass and the ferns, perhaps, is of a yellowish green, as if retaining the sunlight in this cloudy weather. Grateful the coolness which compels me to wear a thick coat.

One man lies in his words, and gets a bad reputation; another in his manners, and enjoys a good one.

The air is clear, as if a cool, dewy brush had swept the vales and meadows of all haze. A liquid coolness invests them, as if their midnight aspect were suddenly revealed to midday. The mountain outline is remarkably distinct, and the intermediate earth appears more than usually scooped out, like a vast saucer sloping upward to its sharp mountain rim. The mountains are washed in air. The sunshine, now seen far away on fields and hills in the northwest, looks cool and wholesome, like the yellow grass in the meadows.

I am too late for the white pine flowers. The cones are half an inch long and greenish, and the male flowers effete.

The sun now comes out bright, though westering, and shines on Fair Haven, which, rippled by the wind, is of an unusual clay-muddy color. The *Specularia perfoliata*, clasping bellflower, on the Cliffs is very pretty, and has apparently been out several days. There are little recesses, a rod or two square, in bosky woods

which have not grown fast, where a fine, wiry grass invites to lie down in the shade, under the shrub oaks, on the edge of the Well Meadow Head field.

8.30 P. M. — To Conantum.

Moon half full. Fields dusky; the evening star and one other bright one near the moon. It is a cool but pretty still night. Methinks I am less thoughtful than I was last year at this time. The flute I now hear from the Depot Field does not find such caverns to echo and resound in in my mind, — no such answering depths. Our minds should echo at least as many times as a Mammoth Cave to every musical sound. It should awaken reflections in us. I hear not many crickets. Some children calling their kitten home by some endearing name. Now his day's work is done, the laborer plays his flute, — only possible at this hour. Contrasted with his work, what an accomplishment! Some drink and gamble. He plays some well-known march. But the music is not in the tune; it is in the sound. It does not proceed from the trading nor political world. He practices this ancient art. There are light, vaporous clouds overhead; dark, fuscous ones in the north. The trees are turned black. As candles are lit on earth, stars are lit in the heavens. I hear the bullfrog's trump from afar.

Now I turn down the Corner road. At this quiet hour the evening wind is heard to moan in the hollows of your face, mysterious, spirit-like, conversing with you. It can be heard now only. The whip-poor-will sings. I hear a laborer going home, coarsely singing to

himself. Though he has scarcely had a thought all day, killing weeds, at this hour he sings or talks to himself. His humble, earthy contentment gets expression. It is kindred in its origin with the notes or music of many creatures. A more fit and natural expression of his mood, this humming, than conversation is wont to be. The fireflies appear to be flying, though they may be stationary on the grass stems, for their perch and the nearness of the ground are obscured by the darkness, and now you see one here and then another there, as if it were one in motion. Their light is singularly bright and glowing to proceed from a living creature. Nature loves variety in all things, and so she adds glow-worms to fireflies, though I have not noticed any this year. The great story of the night is the moon's adventures with the clouds. What innumerable encounters she has had with them! When I enter on the moonlit causeway, where the light is reflected from the glistening alder leaves, and their deep, dark, liquid shade beneath strictly bounds the firm damp road and narrows it, it seems like autumn. The rows of willows completely fence the way and appear to converge in perspective, as I had not noticed by day. The bullfrogs are of various tones. Some horse in a distant pasture whinnies; dogs bark; there is that dull, dumping sound of frogs, as if a bubble containing the lifeless sultry air of day burst on the surface, a belching sound. When two or more bullfrogs trump together, it is a ten-pound-ten note. In Conant's meadow I hear the gurgling of unwearied water, the trill of a toad, and go through the cool, primordial liquid air that has settled there.

As I sit on the great door-step, the loose clapboards on the old house rattle in the wind weirdly, and I seem to hear some wild mice running about on the floor, and sometimes a loud crack from some weary timber trying to change its position.

On Conantum-top, all white objects like stones are observed, and dark masses of foliage, at a distance even. How distant is day and its associations! The light, dry cladonia lichens on the brows of hills reflect the moon-light well, looking like rocks. The night wind comes cold and whispering, murmuring weirdly from distant mountain-tops. No need to climb the Andes or Hima-layas, for brows of lowest hills are highest mountain-tops in cool moonlight nights. Is it a cuckoo's chuckling note I heard? Occasionally there is something enor-mous and monstrous in the size and distance of objects. A rock, is it? or an elephant asleep? Are these trees on an upland or a lowland? Or do they skirt the brink of a sea-beach? When I get there, shall I look off over the sea? The whiteweed is the only obvious flower. I see the tops of the rye wave, and grain-fields are more interesting than by day. The water is dull-colored, hardly more bright than a rye-field. There is dew only in the low grounds. What were the firefly's light, if it were not for darkness? The one implies the other.

You may not suspect that the milk of the cocoanut which is imported from the other side of the world is mixed. So pure do some truths come to us, I trust.

What a mean and wretched creature is man! By and by some Dr. Morton may be filling your cranium with white mustard seed to learn its internal capacity. Of

all ways invented to come at a knowledge of a living man, this seems to me the worst, as it is the most be-lated. You would learn more by once paring the toe-nails of the living subject. There is nothing out of which the spirit has more completely departed, and in which it has left fewer significant traces.

June 26. I have not put darkness, duskiness, enough into my night and moonlight walks. Every sentence should contain some twilight or night. At least the light in it should be the yellow or creamy light of the moon or the fine beams of stars, and not the white light of day. The peculiar dusky serenity of the sentences must not allow the reader to forget that it is evening or night, without my saying that it is dark. Otherwise he will, of course, presume a daylight atmosphere.

The earliest water surfaces, as I remember, as soon as the ice is melted, present as fair and matured scenes, as soft and warm, reflecting the sky through the clear atmosphere, as in midsummer, — far in advance of the earth. The earliest promise of the summer, — is it not in the smooth reflecting surface of woodland lakes in which the ice is just melted? Those liquid eyes of na-ture, blue or black or even hazel, deep or shallow, clear or turbid; green next the shore, the color of their iris.

P. M. — Boated up the Assabet.

The *Nymphœa odorata*, water nymph, sweet water-lily, pond-lily, in bloom. A superb flower, our lotus, queen of the waters. Now is the solstice in still waters. How sweet, innocent, wholesome its fragrance! How pure its white petals, though its root is in the mud! It

Vol. IV

must answer in my mind for what the Orientals say of the lotus flower. Probably the first a day or two since. To-morrow, then, will be the first Sabbath when the young men, having bathed, will walk slowly and so-berly to church in their best clothes, each with a lily in his hand or bosom, — with as long a stem as he could get. At least I used to see them go by and come into church smelling a pond-lily, when I used to go myself. So that the flower is to some extent associated with bathing in Sabbath mornings and going to church, its odor contrasting and atoning for that of the sermon. We now have roses on the land and lilies on the water, — both land and water have done their best, — now *just* after the longest day. Nature says, " You be-hold the utmost I can do." And the young women carry their finest roses on the other hand. Roses and lilies. The floral days. The red rose, with the intense color of many suns concentrated, spreads its tender petals perfectly fair, its flower not to be overlooked, modest yet queenly, on the edges of shady copses and meadows, against its green leaves, surrounded by blush-ing buds, of perfect form; not only beautiful, but right-fully commanding attention; unspoiled by the admira-tion of gazers. And the water-lily floats on the smooth surface of slow waters, amid rounded shields of leaves, bucklers, red beneath, which simulate a green field, perfuming the air. Each instantly the prey of the spoiler, — the rose-bug and water-insects. How transi-tory the perfect beauty of the rose and lily! The high-est, intensest color belongs to the land, the purest, perchance, to the water. The lily is perhaps the only

flower which all are eager to pluck; it may be partly because of its inaccessibility to most. The farmers' sons will frequently collect every bud that shows itself above the surface within half a mile. They are so in-fested by insects, and it is so rare you get a perfect one which has opened itself, — though these only are per-fect, — that the buds are commonly plucked and opened by hand. I have a faint recollection of pleasure derived from smoking dried lily stems before I was a man. I had commonly a supply of these. I have never smoked anything more noxious. I used to amuse myself with making the yellow drooping stamens rise and fall by blowing through the pores of the long stem.

I see the nests of the bream, with each its occu-pant, hollowed, scooped in the sunny water, and partly shaded by the leaves of the limnanthemum, or floating heart, now in blossom, and the *Potamogeton natans*, or pondweed. Under the cool, glossy green leaves of small swamp white oaks, and leaning against their scaly bark near the water, you see the wild roses, five or six feet high, looking forth from the shade; but al-most every bush or copse near the river or in low land which you approach these days emits the noisome odor of the carrion-flower, so that you would think that all the dead dogs had drifted to that shore. All things, both beautiful and ugly, agreeable and offensive, are expressed in flowers, — all kinds and degrees of beauty and all kinds of foulness. For what purpose has nature made a flower to fill the lowlands with the odor of car-rion? Just so much beauty and virtue as there is in the world, and just so much ugliness and vice, you see expressed in flowers. Each human being has his flower, which expresses his character. In them nothing is concealed, but everything published. Many a villager whose garden bounds on the river, when he approaches the willows and cornels by the river's edge, thinks that some carrion has lodged on his shore, when it is only the carrion-flower he smells.

Though the water is many feet deep, I hear very plainly the grating sound of the pole on the sandy bottom communicated through the wood. Some of the hemlock twigs, especially those that hang low about the trunks, broad, flat, and triangular like fans, edged with the recent yellowish green leaves about an inch deep, are very handsome and rich, shaped, the whole, like a fan or reticule, a foot base by eight or nine inches altitude. So many rich green drooping fans edged with yellowish hanging about the trunk. All shadows or shadowlets on the sandy bottom of the river are interesting. All are circular, or nearly so, almost lenticular, for they appear to have thickness; even the shadows of grass blades are broken into several separate circles of shade. Such is the fabulous or Protean character of the water lights. A skater insect casts seven flat globular shades, — four smaller in front, two larger be- hind, and the small- est of all in the centre. From the shadow on the bottom you cannot guess the form on the surface; everything is transmuted by the water. The shadow, however small, is black within, edged with a sunny halo, corresponding to the day's twilights; and a certain liquidness is imparted to

Vol. IV

the whole by the incessant motion from the undulation of the surface. The oblong leaves of the *Potamogeton hybridus*,[1] now in seed, make a circular shadow also, — somewhat coin-like. A halo produced by the thick atmosphere which the water is. These bright, sparkling brook and river bottoms are the true gold washings, — where the stream has washed the pebbly earth so long.

It is pleasant to walk in sprout-lands now in June, there is so much light reflected from the under side of the new foliage. The rich meadows, too, reflect much of the bluish light from the *bent* grass. We land on the south side opposite S. Barrett's, where the innocent forest trees, become dead logs, are unceasingly and relentlessly, I know not for what crime, drawn and quartered and sawn asunder (after being torn limb from limb), with an agony of sound. There are some interesting retired natural meadows here, concealed by the woods near the river-bank, which are never cut, long, narrow, and winding, full of a kind of stiff, dry cut-grass and tender meadow-sweet and occasional cranberry patches (now in bloom), with a high border, almost as high as the meadows are wide, of maples, birches, swamp white oaks, and alders, etc. The flashing, silvery light from the under sides of the maple leaves, — high, rippling, washing towers, far and near, — such a cool, refreshing, breezy, light-flashing look, they are very memorable. When you think you have reached the end of such a winding meadow, you pass between two alders where the copses meet, and emerge into another meadow beyond. I suppose that these

[1] [Queried in pencil.]

meadows are as nearly in their primitive state as any; that we see there how this country looked (in one of its aspects) a thousand years ago. What difference to the meadow-sweet or the swamp white oak, or to the silver-flashing maple leaves, a thousand years ago or to-day? We noticed two or three large wood tortoises, showing but little of their orange-skins, there. The meadows, for the most part, dry enough for walking. The prevalence of the meadow-sweet (at least) distinguishes these meadows from the ordinary ones. Picked two blue blueberries where they lay over a rock.

Forded the river with our clothes on our heads. The rounded heaps of stones, whether made by suckers or lamprey eels, are among the curiosities of the river.

From the sand-bank we looked at the arched bridge while a traveller in a simple carriage with a single pair of wheels went over it. It interested me because the stratum of earth beneath him was so thin that he appeared quite in the air, while he sat with his elbows on his knees, entertaining all earthly thoughts, or thoughtless, while [we] looked directly beneath him through much air to a fair and distant landscape beyond. Channing says that is what men go to Italy to see. I love to see the firm earth mingled with the sky, like the spray of the sea tossed up. Is there not always, whenever an arch is constructed, a latent reference to its beauty? The arch supports itself, like the stars, by gravity, — by always falling never falls (*semper cadendo nunquam cadit*). But it should not be by their architecture but by their abstract thoughts that a nation should seek to commemorate itself. How much more

admirable the Bhagavat Geeta than all the ruins of the East! Methinks there are few specimens of architecture so perfect as a verse of poetry. Architectural remains are beautiful not intrinsically and absolutely, but from association. They are the luxury of princes. A simple and independent mind does not toil at the bidding of any prince, nor is its material silver and gold, or marble. The American's taste for architecture, whether Grecian or Gothic, is like his taste for olives and wine, though the last may be made of logwood. Consider the beauty of New York architecture, — and there is no very material difference between this and Baalbec, — a vulgar adornment of what is vulgar. To what end pray is so much stone hammered? An insane ambition to perpetuate the memory of themselves by the amount of hammered stone they leave. Such is the glory of nations. What if equal pains were taken to smooth and polish their manners? Is not the builder of more consequence than the material? One sensible act will be more memorable than a monument as high as the moon. I love better to see stones in place. The grandeur of Thebes was a vulgar grandeur. She was not simple, and why should I be imposed on by the hundred gates of her prison? More sensible is a rod of stone wall that bounds an honest man's field than a hundred-gated Thebes that has mistaken the true end of life, that places hammered marble before honesty. The religion and civilization which are barbaric and heathenish build splendid temples, but Christianity does not. It needs no college-bred architect. All the stone a nation hammers goes toward its tomb only. It buries itself alive.[1] The too exquisitely cultured I avoid as I do the theatre. Their life lacks reality. They offer me wine instead of water. They are surrounded by things that can be bought.

The alders, birches, etc., are covered with white *winged* aphides (?), which whiten my clothes, — perfect showers of them.

In some shallow parts of the North River, as at the Leaning Hemlocks, where some large rocks partially bridge the stream, I notice smaller stones strewn between in a low wall, as if they had helped form an Indian weir once.

Some names are to be retained, not because they are descriptive, but because they strike the fancy and suggest ideas in harmony with the flower.

June 27. Sunday. P. M. — To Bear Hill, Lincoln.

The epilobium, spiked willow herb, shows its showy pale-purple spikes (pinkish?). It showed some color the 15th. I will set it down to the 20th. *Epilobium angustifolium*, one of the most conspicuous flowers at this season on dry open hillsides in the woods, sproutlands. That tree-like cornel by the Heywood Meadow Brook, now showing green fruit, must be the alternate-leaved cornel. I perceive the morning-glory open at midday, but the worse for the wear. I still perceive that ambrosial sweetness from the meadows in some places. Give me the strong, rank scent of ferns in the spring for vigor; just blossoming late in the spring.

[1] [*Walden*, pp. 63, 64; Riv. 92, 93.]

A healthy and refined nature would always derive pleasure from the landscape. As long as the bodily vigor lasts, man sympathizes with nature.

Looking from Bear Hill, I am struck by the yellowish green of meadows, almost like an ingrained sunlight. Perhaps they have that appearance because the fields generally incline now to a reddish-brown green. The freshness of the year in most fields is already past. The tops of the early grass are white, killed by the worm. It is somewhat hazy, yet I can just distinguish Monadnock. It is a good way to describe the density of a haze to say how distant a mountain can be distinguished through it, or how near a hill is obscured by it.

Saw a very large white ash tree, three and a half feet in diameter, in front of the house which White formerly owned, under this hill, which was struck by lightning the 22d, about 4 p. m. The lightning apparently struck the top of the tree and scorched the bark and leaves for ten or fifteen feet downward, then began to strip off the bark and enter the wood, making a ragged narrow furrow or crack, till, reaching one of the upper limbs, it apparently divided, descending on both sides and entering deeper and deeper into the wood. At the first general branching, it had got full possession of the tree in its centre and tossed off the main limbs butt foremost, making holes in the ground where they struck; and so it went down in the midst of the trunk to the earth, where it apparently exploded, rending the trunk into six segments, whose tops, ten or twenty feet long, were rayed out on every side at an angle of about

30° from a perpendicular, leaving the ground bare directly under where the tree had stood, though they were still fastened to the earth by their roots. The lightning appeared to have gone off through the roots, furrowing them as the branches, and through the earth, making a furrow like a plow, four or five rods in one direction, and in another passing through the cellar of the neighboring house, about thirty feet distant, scorching the tin milk-pans and throwing dirt into the milk, and coming out the back side of the house in a furrow, splitting some planks there. The main body of the tree was completely stripped of bark, which was cast in every direction two hundred feet; and large pieces of the inside of the tree, fifteen feet long, were hurled with tremendous force in various directions, one into the side of [a] shed, smashing it, another burying itself in a wood-pile. The heart of the tree lay by itself. Probably a piece as large as [a] man's leg could not have been sawn out of the trunk which would not have had a crack in it, and much of it was very finely splintered. The windows in the house were broken and the inhabitants knocked down by the concussion. All this was accomplished in an instant by a kind of fire out of the heavens called lightning, or a thunderbolt, accompanied by a crashing sound. For what purpose? The ancients called it Jove's bolt, with which he punished the guilty, and we moderns understand it no better. There was displayed a Titanic force, some of that force which made and can unmake the world. The brute forces are not yet wholly tamed. Is this of the character of a wild beast, or is it guided by intelligence

and mercy? If we trust our natural impressions, it is a manifestation of brutish force or vengeance, more or less tempered with justice. Yet it is our own consciousness of sin, probably, which suggests the idea of vengeance, and to a righteous man it would be merely sublime without being awful.

This is one of those instances in which a man hesitates to refer his safety to his prudence, as the putting up of a lightning-rod. There is no lightning-rod by which the sinner can finally avert the avenging Nemesis. Though I should put up a rod if its utility were satisfactorily demonstrated to me, yet, so mixed are we, I should feel myself safe or in danger quite independently of the senseless rod. Yet there is a degree of faith and righteousness in putting up a rod, as well as trusting without one, though the latter, which is the rarest, I feel to be [the] most effectual rod of the two. It only suggests that impunity in respect to all forms of death or disease, whether sickness or casualty, is only to be attained by moral integrity. It is the faith with which we take medicine that cures us. Otherwise we may be cured into greater disease. In a violent tempest, we both fear and trust. We are ashamed of our fear, for we know that a righteous man would not suspect danger, nor incur any. Wherever a man feels fear, there is an avenger. The savage's and the civilized man's instincts are right. Science affirms too much. Science assumes to show *why* the lightning strikes a tree, but it does not show us the moral *why* any better than our instincts did. It is full of presumption. Why should trees be struck? It is not enough to say because they are in the way. Science answers, *Non scio,* I am ignorant. All the phenomena of nature need [to] be seen from the point of view of wonder and awe, like lightning; and, on the other hand, the lightning itself needs to [be] regarded with serenity, as the most familiar and innocent phenomena are. There runs through the righteous man's moral spinal column a rod with burnished points to heaven, which conducts safely away into the earth the flashing wrath of Nemesis, so that it merely clarifies the air. This moment the confidence of the righteous man erects a sure conductor within him; the next, perchance, a timid staple diverts the fluid to his vitals. If a mortal be struck with a thunderbolt *coelo sereno*, it is naturally felt to be more awful and vengeful. Men are probably nearer to the essential truth in their superstitions than in their science. Some places are thought to be particularly exposed to lightning, some oaks on hilltops, for instance.

I meet the partridge with her brood in the woods, a perfect little hen. She spreads her tail into a fan and beats the ground with her wings fearlessly within a few feet of me, to attract my attention while her young disperse; but they keep up a faint, wiry kind of peep, which betrays them, while she mews and squeaks as if giving them directions.

Chestnut trees are budded.

I picked a handful or two of blueberries, though strawberries are now in their prime. They follow hard upon the first red amelanchier berries. Blueberries and huckleberries deserve to be celebrated, such simple, wholesome, universal fruits, food for the gods and for

aboriginal men. They are so abundant that they concern our race much. Tournefort called some of this genus, at least, *Vitis Idæa*, which apparently means the vine of Mount Ida. I cannot imagine any country without this kind of berry. Berry of berries. On which men live like birds. Still covering our hills as when the red men lived here. Are they not the principal wild fruit? Huckleberry puddings and pies, and huckleberries and milk, are regular and important dishes.

Hedyotis longifolia, a smaller-flowered houstonia, rather interesting, on the top of Bear Hill.

Have I not omitted to mention the star-flowered cerastium, like the early *Stellaria media*. I saw it at least as early as the last week of May.

June 28. *Œnothera biennis*, evening-primrose, with its conspicuous flowers but rather unsightly stem and leaves. The *Rubus odoratus*, purple flowering raspberry, in gardens. Potatoes for some time.

Evening. 7 P. M. — Moon more than half.

There are meteorologists, but who keeps a record of the fairer sunsets? While men are recording the direction of the wind, they neglect to record the beauty of the sunset or the rainbow. The sun not yet set. The bobolink sings ~ ~ ____ descending to the meadow as I go along ____ ~ the railroad to the pond. The seringo-bird and the common song sparrow, — and the swallows twitter. The plaintive strain of the lark, coming up from the meadow, is perfectly adapted to the hour. When I get nearer the wood, the veery is heard, and the oven-bird, or whet-saw, sounds hollowly

from within the recesses of the wood.[1] The clouds in the west are edged with fiery red. A few robins faintly sing. The huckleberry-bird in more open fields in the woods. The thrasher? The sun is down. The nighthawks are squeaking in the somewhat dusky air and occasionally making the ripping sound; the chewinks sound; the bullfrogs begin, and the toads; also tree-toads more numerously.

Walden imparts to the body of the bather a remarkably chalky-white appearance, whiter than natural, tinged with blue, which, combined with its magnifying and distorting influence, produces a monstrous and ogre-like effect, proving, nevertheless, the purity of the water. The river water, on the other hand, imparts to the bather a yellowish tinge.[2]

There is a very low mist on the water close to the shore, a few inches high. The moon is brassy or golden now, and the air more dusky; yet I hear the pea-wai and the wood thrush, and now a whip-poor-will before I have seen a star. The walker in the woods at this hour takes note of the different veins of air through which he passes, — the fresher and cooler in the hollows, laden with the condensed fragrance of plants, as it were distilled in dews; and yet the warmer veins in a cool evening like this do not fail to be agreeable, though in them the air is comparatively lifeless or exhausted of its vitality. It circulates about from pillar to post, from wood-side to side-hill, like a dog that has lost its master, now the sun is gone.

Now it is starlight; perhaps that dark cloud in the

[1] [There is a marginal query against this sentence.]
[2] [*Walden*, p. 197; Riv. 278.]

west has concealed the evening star before. Yet I hear a chewink, veery, and wood thrush. Nighthawks and whip-poor-wills, of course. A whip-poor-will whose nest, perchance, I am near, on the side of the Cliff, hovers in the dusky air about ten feet from me, now on this side, then on that, on quivering wings, inspecting me, showing the white on its wings. It holds itself stationary for a minute. It is the first warm night for a week, and I hear the toads by the river very numerous. First there was sundown, then starlight. Starlight! That would be a good way to mark the hour, if we were precise. That is an epoch, when the last traces of daylight have disappeared and the night (*nox*) has fairly set in. Is not the moon a mediator? She is a light-giver that does not dazzle me.

I have camped out all night on the tops of four mountains, — Wachusett, Saddle-back, Ktaadn, and Monadnock, — and I usually took a ramble over the summit at midnight by moonlight. I remember the moaning of the wind on the rocks, and that you seemed much nearer to the moon than on the plains. The light is then in harmony with the scenery. Of what use the sunlight to the mountain-summits? From the cliffs you looked off into vast depths of illumined air.

June 29. P. M. — On North River.

Leonurus Cardiaca, motherwort, a nettle-like plant by the street-side.

The *Rana halecina* (?), shad frog, is our handsomest frog, bronze striped, with brown spots, edged and intermixed with *bright* green; does not regard the fly that sits on him. The frogs and tortoises are striped and spotted for their concealment. The painted tortoise's throat held up above the pads, streaked with yellowish, makes it the less obvious. The mud turtle is the color of the mud, the wood frog and the hylodes of the dead leaves, the bullfrogs of the pads, the toad of the earth, etc., etc. The tree-toad of the bark.

In my experience nothing is so opposed to poetry — not crime — as business.[1] It is a negation of life.

The wind exposes the red under sides of the white lily pads. This is one of the aspects of the river now. The bud-bearing stem of this plant is a little larger, but otherwise like the leaf-stem, and coming like it directly from the long, large root. It is interesting to pull up the lily root with flowers and leaves attached and see how it sends its buds upward to the light and air to expand and flower in another element. How interesting the bud's progress from the water to the air! So many of these stems are leaf-bearing, and so many flower-bearing. Then consider how defended these plants against drought, at the bottom of the water, at most their leaves and flowers floating on its surface. How much mud and water are required to support their vitality! It is pleasant to remember those quiet Sabbath mornings by remote stagnant rivers and ponds, when pure white water-lilies, just expanded, not yet infested by insects, float on the waveless water and perfume the atmosphere. Nature never appears more serene and innocent and fragrant. A hundred white lilies, open to the sun, rest on the surface smooth as

[1] [Cape Cod, and Miscellanies, p. 456; Misc., Riv. 255.]

oil amid their pads, while devil's-needles are glancing over them. It requires some skill so to pull a lily as to get a long stem. The great yellow lily, the spatter-dock, expresses well the fertility of the river.

The *Sparganium ramosum*, or bur-reed, amid the flags now. It is associated with the reed-mace by systematists. One flower on a spike of the *Pontederia cordata* just ready to expand. Children bring you the early blueberry to sell now. It is considerably earlier on the tops of hills which have been recently cut off than on the plains or in vales. The girl that has Indian blood in her veins and picks berries for a living will find them out as soon as they turn. The yellow water ranunculus is hardly to be seen in the river now. The *Anemone Virginiana*, tall anemone, looking like a white buttercup, on Egg Rock, cannot have been long in bloom. I see the columbine lingering still.

June 30. Nature must be viewed humanly to be viewed at all; that is, her scenes must be associated with humane affections, such as are associated with one's native place, for instance. She is most significant to a lover. A lover of Nature is preëminently a lover of man. If I have no friend, what is Nature to me? She ceases to be morally significant.

7.30 P. M. — To stone bridge over Assabet. Moon nearly full; rose a little before sunset.

Cat-mint (*Nepeta cataria*) in bloom. The lower shoots of the *Andromeda calyculata* are now six inches long, the upper from two to four.[1] The fruit is on the

[1] [This sentence is queried in the margin.]

Vol. IV

extremities of last year's shoots in the midst of the persistent small leaves. The shrub oak acorns are as big as peas; principally cup.

The moon appears full. At first a mere white cloud. As soon as the sun sets, begins to grow brassy or obscure golden in the gross atmosphere. It is starlight about half an hour after sunset to-night; i. e. the first stars appear. The moon is now brighter, but not so yellowish. Ten or fifteen minutes after, the fireflies are observed, at first about the willows on the Causeway, where the evening is further advanced. Sparrows quite generally, and occasionally a robin sings. (I heard a bobolink this afternoon.) The creak of the crickets is more universal and loud, and becomes a distinct sound. The oily surface of the river in which the moon is reflected looks most attractive at this hour. I see the bright curves made by the water-bugs in the moonlight, and a muskrat crossing the river, now at 9 o'clock. Finally the last traces of day disappear, about 9.30 o'clock, and the night fairly sets in. The color of the moon is more silvery than golden, or silvery with a slight admixture of golden, a *sort of burnished cloud*.

The bass tree is budded. Haying has commenced. Some think the foliage of the trees is not so thick as last year, that the leaves have suffered from the wind.

Is not this period more than any distinguished for flowers, when roses, swamp-pinks, morning-glories, arethusas, pogonias, orchises, blue flags, epilobiums, mountain laurel, and white lilies are all in blossom at once?

III

JULY, 1852

(ÆT. 34–35)

July 1. *Thursday.* 9.30 A. M. — To Sherman's Bridge by land and water.

A cloudy and slightly showery morning, following a thunder-shower the previous afternoon. One object to see the white lilies in blossom. The *Trifolium arvense*, or rabbit's-foot clover, is just beginning to show its color, and in the same state is the (I think) *Lysimachia stricta*, or upright loosestrife (?), by the back road. The mulleins generally now begin to show their pure yellow in roadside fields, and the white cymes of the elder are conspicuous on the edges of the copses. I perceive the meadow fragrance still. From the bridge I see a bream's nest in soft sand on the edge of deeper water, scooped out quite deep, with very sharp edges sloping both ways. Some peetweets, which probably have eggs in Conant's corn-field, make a great ado twittering and circling about the dog. The path by the wood-side is red with the effete staminiferous flowers of the white pine. It is more agreeable walking this cloudy day, with a few harmless sun-showers, than it would be in a glaring sunny day. It is pleasant to behold so much of the landscape in the shadow of the clouds, especially to look off from the top of Conantum, under shady walnut boughs, to larger shades in valleys,

— all Nine-Acre Corner in the cool shade of a cloud. Roses are in their prime now, growing amid huckleberry bushes, ferns, and sweet-ferns, especially about some dry pond-hole; some paler, some more red. Methinks they must have bloomed in vain while only wild men roamed, yet now they only adorn these cows' pasture.

How well-behaved are cows! When they approach me reclining in the shade, from curiosity, or to receive a whisp of grass, or to share the shade, or to lick the dog held up, like a calf, — though just now they ran at him to toss him, — they do not obtrude. Their company is acceptable, for they can endure the longest pause; they have not got to be entertained. They occupy the most eligible lots in the town. I love to see some pure white about them; they suggest the more neatness.

Borrowed Brigham the wheelwright's boat at the Corner Bridge. He was quite ready to lend it, and took pains to shave down the handle of a paddle for me, conversing the while on the subject of spiritual knocking, which he asked if I had looked into, — which made him the slower. An obliging man, who understands that I am abroad viewing the works of Nature and not loafing, though he makes the pursuit a semi-religious one, as are all more serious ones to most men. All that is not sporting in the field, as hunting and fishing, is of a religious or else love-cracked character. Another hard-featured but talkative character at the bridge inquired, as I was unlocking the boat, if I knew anything that was good for the rheumatism; but I answered that I

had heard of so many and had so little faith in any that I had forgotten them all. (On Conantum I had found *Krigia Virginica*, one of the smallest compound flowers.) The white lilies were in all their splendor, fully open, sometimes their lower petals lying flat on the surface. The largest appeared to grow in the shallower water, where some stood five or six inches out of water, and were five inches in diameter. Two which I examined had twenty-nine petals each. We pushed our boat into the midst of some shallow bays, where the water, not more than a foot deep, was covered with pads and spotted white with many hundreds of lilies which had just expanded. Yet perhaps there was not one open which had not an insect in it, and most had some hundreds of small gnats, which, however, we shook out without much trouble, instead of drowning them out, which makes the petals close.

The freshly opened lilies were a pearly white, and though the water amid the pads was quite unrippled, the passing air gave a slight oscillating, boat-like motion to and fro to the flowers, like boats held fast by their cables. Some of the lilies had a beautiful rosaceous tinge, most conspicuous in the half-opened flower, extending through the calyx to the second row of petals, on those parts of the petals between the calyx-leaves which were most exposed to the influence of the light. They were tinged with red, as they are very commonly tinged with green, as if there were a gradual transition from the stamens to the petals. It seemed to be referred to the same coloring principle which is seen in the under sides of the pads as well as the calyx-leaves.

Yet these rosaceous ones are chiefly interesting to me for variety, and I am contented that lilies should be white and leave those higher colors to the land. I wished to breathe the atmosphere of lilies, and get the full impression which lilies are fitted to make. The form of this flower is also very perfect, the petals are so distinctly arranged at equal intervals and at all angles, from nearly a perpendicular to horizontal about the centre. And buds that were half expanded were interesting, showing the regularly notched outline of the points of the petals above the erect green calyx-leaves.

Some of these bays contained a quarter of an acre, through which we with difficulty forced our boat. First there is the low smooth green surface of the pads, — some of the kalmianas purplish, — then the higher level of the pickerel-weed just beginning to blossom, and, rising a little higher in the rear, often extensive fields of pipes (*Equisetum*), making a very level appearance. Mingled with the white lilies were the large yellow ones and the smaller and, here at least, much more common *Nuphar lutea* var. *Kalmiana*, and the floating heart also, still in blossom, and the *Brasenia peltata*, water target or shield, not yet in bloom, the petiole attached to its leaf like a boy's string to his sucking-leather. The rich violet purple of the ponte-derias was the more striking, as the blossoms were still rare. Nature will soon be very lavish of this blue along the riversides. It is a rich spike of blue flowers with yellowish spots. Over all these flowers hover devil's-needles in their zigzag flight. On the edge of the

meadow I see blushing roses and cornels (probably the panicled). The woods ring with the veery this cloudy day, and I also hear the red-eye, oven-bird, Maryland yellow-throat, etc. In shallow places the river is for long distances filled, quite bridged over, with the leaves of the *Potamogeton natans*, the direction of whose stems, at least, may show which way the sluggish water is inclined. You frequently see a blue devil's-needle resting on a potamogeton flower (raceme?). You will see one red-wing in the midst of many dusky females making a great chattering over some particular part of the meadow, or else chasing a female in *zigzag* (?) *curves*. What are those taller grasses, now headed, in the meadow?

After eating our luncheon at Rice's landing, we observed that every white lily in the river was shut, — and they remained so all the afternoon, though it was no more sunny nor cloudy than the forenoon, — except some which I had plucked before noon and cast into the river, which, floating down, lodged amid the pondweed, which continued fresh but had not the power to close their petals. It would be interesting to observe how instantaneously these lilies close at noon. I only observed that, though there were myriads fully open before I ate my lunch at noon, after dinner I could not find one open anywhere for the rest of the day.

Continuing up the river, we saw the *Comarum palustre*, marsh cinquefoil, in blossom. Its leaf is more noticeable than its flower. The last incloses a strawberry-like fruit. These leaves make very rich and rare-looking beds, alternating with the pontederia and button-bush.

It is so foreign-looking a leaf. Opposite the mouth of the Pantry Brook, or a little more west, I saw the leaves and flower-buds of the *Peltandra Virginica* (calla), — though Gray says its leaves have "shorter and more obtuse lobes" than the sagittaria.

Being made thirsty with our herring, we left our boat at the great bend and went inland to the fine cool spring near the Jenkins house. Found the *Polygonum sagittatum*, scratch-grass, just blossoming in the meadows, and an abundance of the marsh speedwell and of pogonias (adder's-tongue arethusas). The erect-scaped pyrola. The Jersey tea almost in bloom and, close by the Jenkins house in Wayland, the privet (*Ligustrum vulgare*). At the spring, where much forget-me-not now in bloom, I found ripe — of a dark red color — what I think must be Gray's *Rubus triflorus*, dwarf raspberry, though it was in *a meadow*, — a pleasant lively acid fruit. It was running over some sand cast out in digging a ditch, and I observed none so large or edible elsewhere. This is the fourth kind of berry I have found ripe this season. I must see it again. It tastes and looks like a cross between a raspberry and a blackberry. It may be this whose flowers I observed so early in Hubbard's Grove Swamp. I drank some high-colored water from a little stream in the meadow; for I love to drink the water of the meadow or the river I pass the day on, and so get eyes to see it with. The potamogeton leaves redden the stream in shoal places and retard the progress of our boat. The lowest front ranks of the riparial plants beyond the pads are the smaller-leaved polygonum beds,

not yet in bloom; then the pontederia, or, perchance (in some places), the marsh cinquefoil; then the meadow-grass, or pipes, or sweet flag, or button-bushes, with their lower limbs and stems covered — is it with a parasitic, moss-like plant? This might be called the Potamogeton River. The leaves now, both on land and in water, are eaten by insects and have been for some weeks. There is hardly a whole pad or potamogeton leaf. They are curiously eaten, often only half through, often in direct straight lines across the pads, as it were skippingly, or as if they had been raked with shot. Their under sides are covered with eggs of insects, as on land. Counted twenty-one fishes' nests by the shallow shore just beyond Sherman's Bridge, within less than half a rod, edge to edge, with each a bream poised in it. In some cases the fish had just cleared away the mud or frog-spittle, exposing the yellow sand or pebbles, — sixteen to twenty-four inches in diameter. My early rubus has a much-wrinkled leaf. The morning-glory which I bring home opens the next morning in a pitcher. Is it the *Hypericum ellipticum* now in blossom in the river meadows, about a foot high?[1] The *Lobelia spicata*, pale lobelia, like a snapdragon. Is it the *Erigeron annuus* (*strigosus* of Bigelow) now beginning?

Rice says the earliest flower the honey-bee is found on is that of the skunk-cabbage, before the frost is out of the meadows; also he gets his first honey from the maple and walnut stumps that have been cut in the winter, as soon as the sap begins to flow.

[1] Yes (in June).

Vol. IV

A young man in Sudbury told me he had heard woodchucks whistle.

July 2. Bigelow tells me that saddlers sometimes use the excrescence, the whitish fungus, on the birch to stick their awls in. Men find a use for everything at last. I saw one nailed up in his shop with an awl in it.

Last night, as I lay awake, I dreamed of the muddy and weedy river on which I had been paddling, and I seemed to derive some vigor from my day's experience, like the lilies which have their roots at the bottom.

I have plucked a white lily bud just ready to expand, and, after keeping it in water for two days,[1] have turned back its sepals with my hand and touched the lapped points of the petals, when they sprang open and rapidly expanded in my hand into a perfect blossom, with the petals as perfectly disposed at equal intervals as on their native lakes, and in this case, of course, untouched by an insect. I cut its stem short and placed it in a broad dish of water, where it sailed about under the breath of the beholder with a slight undulatory motion. The breeze of his half-suppressed admiration it was that filled its sail. It was a rare-tinted one. A kind of popular aura that may be trusted, methinks. Men will travel to the Nile to see the lotus flower, who have never seen in their glory the lotuses of their native streams.

The *Mollugo verticillata*, carpet-weed, is just beginning in the garden, and the *Polygonum convolvulus*, black bindweed. The spikes of the pale lobelia, some

[1] Till July 3d.

blue, some white, passing insensibly from one to the other, and especially hard to distinguish in the twilight, are quite handsome now in moist ground, rising above the grass. The prunella has various tints in various lights, now blue, now lilac. As the twilight deepens into night, its color changes. It always suggests freshness and coolness, from the places where it grows. I see the downy heads of the senecio gone to seed, thistle-like but small. The gnaphaliums and this are among the earliest to present this appearance.

On my way to the Hubbard Bathing-Place, at sundown.

The blue-eyed grass shuts up before night, and methinks it does not open *very early* the next morning. The *Cornus stolonifera*, red osier, *osier rouge*, well out, and probably has been *a day or two*. I have got the order of the cornels, I think, pretty well. I see plenty of the *Peltandra Virginica* coming forward in Hubbard's meadow, and its lobes are more blunt than the sagittaria. Pogonias are very common in the meadows now. The seed-vessels of the *Iris Virginica* are formed.

At the bathing-place there is [a] hummock which was floated on to the meadow some springs ago, now densely covered with the handsome red-stemmed wild rose, a full but irregular clump, from the ground, showing no bare stems below, but a dense mass of shining leaves and small red stems above in their midst, and on every side now, in the twilight, more than usually beautiful they appear. Countless roses, partly closed, of a very deep rich color, as if the rays of the departed sun still shone through them; a more spiritual rose at this hour, beautifully blushing; and then the unspeakable beauty and promise of those fair swollen buds that spot the mass, which will blossom to-morrow, and the more distant promise of the handsomely formed green ones, which yet show no red, for few things are handsomer than a rosebud in any stage; these mingled with a few pure white elder blossoms and some rosaceous or pinkish meadow-sweet heads. I am confident that there can be nothing so beautiful in any cultivated garden, with all their varieties, as this wild clump. I afterwards found a similar though not so large and dense a clump of sweet-briars. Methinks their flowers are not so fragrant, and perhaps never of so deep a red. Perhaps they are more sure to open in a pitcher than the last.

It is starlight. Near woods the veery is a steady singer at this hour.[1] I notice that the lowest leaves of my potamogeton are pellucid and wavy, which, combined with their purplish tinge on the surface, makes me doubt if it be not the *pulcher*.

Do the hardhack leaves stand up and hug the stem at night, that they show their under sides so?

Nature is reported not by him who goes forth consciously as an observer, but in the fullness of life. To such a one she rushes to make her report. To the full heart she is all but a figure of speech. This is my year of observation, and I fancy that my friends are also more devoted to outward observation than ever before, as if it were an epidemic. I cross the brook by Hubbard's little bridge. Now nothing but the cool invigo-

[1] [This sentence is queried in the margin.]

Vol. IV

rating scent which is perceived at night in these low meadowy places where the alder and ferns grow can restore my spirits. (I made it an object to find a new *Parmelia caperata* in fruit in each walk.) At this season, methinks, we do not regard the larger features of the landscape, as in the spring, but are absorbed in details. Then, when the meadows were flooded, I looked far over them to the distant woods and the outlines of hills, which were more distinct. I should not have so much to say of extensive water or landscapes at this season. You are a little bewildered by the variety of objects. There must be a certain meagreness of details and nakedness for wide views.

(The obtuse galium shows its minute white flowers in the meadows.) If I remember, the early part of June was cool, as also the latter, though we had some hot weather, perhaps, toward the middle. The clover heads are drying up except in meadows.

9 o'clock. — The full moon rising (or full last night) is revealed first by some slight clouds above the eastern horizon looking white, — the first indication that she is about to rise, the traces of day not yet gone in the west. In the west, similar clouds, seen against a lighter sky, look dark and heavy. Now a lower cloud in the east reflects a more yellowish light. The moon, far over the round globe travelling this way, sends her light forward to yonder cloud, from which the news of her coming is reflected to us. The moon's aurora! it is without redness or fulgidness, like the dawn of philosophy, — and its noon, too. At her dawning no cocks crow. How few creatures to hail her rising! Only some

belated travellers that may be abroad this night. What graduated information of her coming! More and more yellow glows the low cloud, with concentrating light, and now the moon's edge suddenly appears above a low bank of cloud not seen before, and she seems to come forward apace without introduction, after all; and the steadiness with which she rises with undisturbed serenity, like a queen who has learned to walk before her court, is glorious, and she soon reaches the open sea of the heavens. She seems to advance (so, perchance, flows the blood in the veins of the beholder) by graceful sallying essays, trailing her garment up the sky.

July 3. From Deep Cut over Fair Haven; back by Potter's path; 5 P. M.

The yellow lily (*Lilium Canadense*) is out, rising above the meadow-grass, sometimes one, sometimes two. Young woodchucks, sitting in their holes, allow me to come quite near. Clover is mostly dried up. The *Chimaphila umbellata*, wintergreen, must have been in blossom some time. The back side of its petals, "cream colored tinged with purple," which is turned toward the beholder, while the face is toward the earth, is the handsomest. It is a very pretty little chandelier of a flower, fit to adorn the forest floor. Its buds are nearly as handsome. (They appear long in unfolding.) *Polygonum Persicaria* just beginning.

The pickers have quite thinned the crop of early blueberries where Stow cut off winter before last. When the woods on some hillside are cut off, the *Vac-*

cinium Pennsylvanicum springs up, or grows more luxuriantly, being exposed to light and air, and by the second year its stems are weighed to the ground with clusters of blue berries covered with bloom, and much larger than they commonly grow, also with a livelier taste than usual, as if remembering some primitive mountain-side given up to them anciently. Such places supply the villagers with the earliest berries for two or three years, or until the rising wood overgrows them and they withdraw into the bosom of Nature again. They flourish during the few years between one forest's fall and another's rise. Before you had prepared your mind or made up your mouth for berries, thinking only of crude green ones, earlier by ten days than you had expected, some child of the woods is at your door with ripe blueberries; for did n't you know that Mr. Stow cut off his wood-lot winter before last? It is an ill wind that blows nobody any good, and thus it happens that when the owner lays bare and deforms a hillside, and alone appears to reap any advantage from it by a crop of wood, all the villagers and the inhabitants of distant cities obtain some compensation in the crop of berries that it yields. They glean after the woodchopper, not fagots, but full baskets of blueberries. I am surprised to see how suddenly, when the sun and air and rain are let in, these bushes, which, in the shade of the forest, scarcely yielded the walker a berry, will suddenly be weighed down with fruit. Let alone your garden, cease your cultivation, and in how short a time will blueberries and huckleberries grow there!

I have not noticed a violet for some time.

Bathed beneath Fair Haven.

How much food the muskrats have at hand! They may well be numerous. At this place the bottom in shallow water at a little distance from the shore is thickly covered with clams, half buried and on their ends, generally a little aslant. Sometimes there are a dozen or more side by side within a square foot, and I [sic] that, over a space twenty rods long and one wide (I know not how much farther they reach into the river), they would average three to a square foot, which would give 16,335 clams to twenty rods of shore (on one side of the river), and I suspect that there are many more. No wonder that muskrats multiply, and that the shores are covered with their shells left by the musk-rats. In bathing here I can hardly step without tread-ing on them, sometimes half a dozen at once, and often I cut my feet pretty severely on their shells. They are partly covered with mud and the short weeds at the bottom, and they are of the same color themselves; but, stooping down over them, when the roil has sub-sided, I can see them now (at 5.30 P. M.) with their mouths (?) open, — an inch long and a quarter of an inch wide, with a waving fringe about it, and another smaller opening close to it without any fringe, through both of which I see distinctly into the white interior of the fish. When I touch one, he instantly closes his shell and, if taken out, quickly spurts water like a salt-water clam. Evidently taking in their food and strain-ing it with that waving motion of the ciliæ. There they lie, both under the pads and in the sun.

Ceanothus Americanus, New Jersey tea. The last

month has been very breezy and on the whole a cold one, I remember; rippling leaves, showing their light under sides. *Rubus strigosus*, wild red raspberry. I can hardly find a geranium now. The common carrot by the roadside (*Daucus Carota*) is in some respects an interesting plant, for its umbel, as Bigelow says, is shaped like a bird's nest, and its large pinnatifid in-volucre, interlacing by its fine segments, resembles a fanciful ladies' work-basket. *Asclepias purpurascens.* I find a potamogeton to-day over the clams, which ap-pears to correspond to the *P. pulcher.* I am not sure that it is what *I have called* the *natans*, but *this* cannot be the *natans*, for the leaves are not all long-petioled, but the lower ones waved and quite pellucid.

July 4. Sunday. 3 A. M. — To Conantum, to see the lilies open.

I hear an occasional crowing of cocks in distant barns, as has been their habit for how many thousand years. It was so when I was young; and it will be so when I am old. I hear the croak of a tree-toad as I am crossing the yard. I am surprised to find the dawn so far advanced. There is a yellowish segment of light in the east, paling a star and adding sensibly to the light of the waning and now declining moon. There is very little dew on the uplands. I hear a little twittering and some clear singing from the seringo and the song sparrow as I go along the back road, and now and then the note of a bullfrog from the river. The light in the east has acquired a reddish tinge near the hori-zon. Small wisps of cloud are already fuscous and

Vol. IV

dark, seen against the light, as in the west at evening. It being Sunday morning, I hear no early stirring farmer driving over a bridge. The crickets are not remarkably loud at this season. The sound of a whip-poor-will is wafted from the woods. Now, on the Corner road, the hedges are alive with twittering sparrows, a bluebird or two, etc. The daylight now balances the moonlight. How short the nights! The last traces of day have not disappeared much before 10 o'clock, or perchance 9.30, and before 3 A. M. you see them again in the east, — probably 2.30, — leaving about five hours of solid night, the sun so soon coming round again. The robins sing, but not so loud and long as in the spring. I have not been awakened by them latterly in the mornings. Is it my fault? Ah! those mornings when you are awakened in the dawn by the singing, the matins, of the birds! I hear the dumping sound of frogs now on the causeway. Some small clouds in the east are red-dish fuscous. There is no fog on the river nor in the meadows. The kingbird twitters (?) on the black wil-lows. Methinks I saw the not yet extinguished lights of one or two fireflies in the darker ruts in the grass, in Conant's meadow. The moon yields to the sun. She pales even in the presence of his *dawn*. It is chiefly the spring birds that I hear at this hour, and in each dawn the spring is thus revived. The notes of the sparrows and the bluebirds and the robin have a prominence now which they have not by day.

The light is more and more general, and some low bars begin to look bluish as well as reddish. (Else-where the sky wholly clear of clouds.) The dawn is at

this stage far lighter than the brightest moonlight. I write by it. Yet the sun will not rise for some time. Those bars are reddening more above one spot. They grow purplish, or lilac rather. White and whiter grows the light in the eastern sky. (And now, descending to the Cliff by the riverside, I cannot see the low horizon and its phenomena.) I love to go through these old apple orchards so irregularly set out. Sometimes two trees standing close together. The rows of grafted fruit will never tempt me to wander amid them like these. A bittern leaves the shore at my approach. I suppose it is he whose excrement has whitened the rocks, as if a mason had spilled his whitewash. A nighthawk squeaks and booms, before sunrise. The insects shaped like shad-flies (some which I see are larger and yellowish) begin to leave their cases (and selves?) on the stems of the grasses and the rushes in the water. I find them so weak they can hardly hold on. I hear the black-bird's *conqueree*, and the kingfisher darts away with his alarum and outstretched neck. Every lily is shut.

Sunrise. I see it gilding the top of the hill behind me, but the sun itself is concealed by the hills and woods on the east shore. A very slight fog begins to rise now in one place on the river. There is something serenely glorious and memorable to me in the sight of the first cool sunlight now gilding the eastern extremity of the bushy island in Fair Haven, that wild lake. The subdued light and the repose remind me of Hades. In such sunlight there is no fever. It is such an innocent pale yellow as the spring flowers. It is the pollen of the sun, fertilizing plants. The color of the earliest spring flowers is as cool and innocent as the first rays of the sun in the morning falling on woods and hills. The fog not only rises upward (about two feet), but at once there is a motion from the sun over the surface. What means this endless motion of water-bugs collected in little groups on the surface and ceaselessly circling about their centre, as if they were a family hatched from the eggs on the under side of a pad? Is not this motion intended partly to balk the fishes? Methinks they did not begin to move till sunrise. Where were they? And now I see an army of skaters advancing in loose array, — of chasseurs or scouts, as Indian allies are drawn in old books.

Now the rays of the sun have reached my seat, a few feet above the water; flies begin to buzz, mosquitoes to be less troublesome. A hummingbird hums by over the pads up the river, as if looking, like myself, to see if lilies have blossomed. The birds begin to sing generally, and, if not loudest, at least most noticeably on account of the quietness of the hour, just before — a few minutes before — sunrise. They do not sing so incessantly and earnestly, as a regular thing, half an hour later.

Carefully looking both up and down the river, I could perceive that the lilies began to open about fifteen minutes after the sun from over the opposite bank fell on them, which was perhaps three quarters of an hour after sunrise (which is about 4.30), and one was fully expanded about twenty minutes later. When I returned over the bridge about 6.15, there were perhaps a dozen open ones in sight. It was very difficult to find one

not injured by insects. Even the buds which were just about to expand were frequently bored quite through, and the water had rotted them. You must be on hand early to anticipate insects.

One thimble-berry which will be quite ripe by to-morrow. Indigo almost expanded. I perceive the meadow fragrance on the causeway. Bobolinks still.

I bring home a dozen *perfect* lily buds, — all I can find within many rods, — which have never yet opened; I prepare a large pan of water; I cut their stems quite short; I turn back their calyx-leaves with my fingers, so that they may float upright; I touch the points of their petals, and breathe or blow on them, and toss them in. They spring open rapidly, or gradually expand in the course of an hour, — all but one or two.

At 12.30 P. M., I perceive that the lilies in the river have begun to shut up. The water has gone down so much that I can stand on the shore and pluck as many as I want, and they are the fairest ones, concealed by the pickerel-weed, often the whole plant high and dry. I go again to the river at 2.30 P. M., and every lily is shut.

I will here tell the history of my rosaceous lilies plucked the 1st of July. They were buds at the bottom of a pitcher of water all the 2d, having been kept in my hat part of the day before. On the morning of the 3d I assisted their opening, and put them in water, as I have described; but they did not shut up at noon, like those in the river, but at dark, their petals, at least, quite tight and close. They all opened again in the course of the forenoon of the 4th, but had not shut up

at 10 o'clock P. M., though I found them shut in the morning of the 5th. May it be that they can bear only a certain amount of light, and these, being in the shade, remained open longer? (I think not, for they shut up in the river that quite cloudy day, July 1st.) Or is their vitality too little to permit [them] to perform their regular functions?

Can that meadow fragrance come from the purple summits of the eupatorium?

I looked down on the river behind Dodd's at 2.30 P. M., a slate-colored stream with a scarcely perceptible current, with a male and female shore; the former, more abrupt, of button-bushes and willows, the other, flat, of grass and pickerel-weed alone. Beyond the former, the water being deep, extends a border or fringe of green and purplish pads lying perfectly flat on the surface, but on the latter side the pads extend a half a rood or a rod beyond the pickerel-weed, — shining pads reflecting the light, dotted with white or yellow lilies. This sort of ruff does the river wear, and so the land is graduated off to water. A tender place in Nature, an exposed vein, and Nature making a feint to bridge it quite over with a paddy film, with red-winged blackbirds liquidly warbling and whistling on the willows, and kingbirds on the elms and oaks; these pads, if there is any wind, rippling with the water and helping to smooth and allay it. It looks tender and exposed, as if it were naturally subterranean, and now, with these shields of pads, held scale-like by long threads from the bottom, she makes a feint to bridge it. So floats the Musketaquid over its segment of the sphere.

Methinks there is not even a lily, white or yellow, in Walden.

I see perfectly formed pouts by the shore of the river, one inch long. The great spatterdock lily is a rich yellow at a little distance, and, seen lying on its great pads, it is an indispensable evidence of the fertility of the river. The gratiola begins to yellow the mud by the riverside. The *Lysimachia lanceolata* var. *hybrida* is out, in the meadows. The *Rosa nitida* (?) appears to be now out of bloom.

July 5. I know a man who never speaks of the sexual relation but jestingly, though it is a subject to be approached only with reverence and affection. What can be the character of that man's love? It is ever the subject of a stale jest, though his health or his dinner can be seriously considered. The glory of the world is seen only by a chaste mind. To whomsoever this fact is not an awful but beautiful mystery, there are no flowers in nature.

White lilies continue to open in the house in the morning and shut in the night for five or six days, until their stamens have shed their pollen and they turn rusty and begin to decay, and the beauty of the flower is gone, and its vitality, so that it no longer expands with the light.

How perfect an invention is glass! There is a fitness in glass windows which reflect the sun morning and evening, windows, the doorways of light, thus reflecting the rays of that luminary with a splendor only second to itself. This invention one would say was anticipated in the arrangement of things. The sun rises with a salute and leaves the world with a farewell to our windows. To have, instead of opaque shutters or dull horn or paper, a material like solidified air, which reflects the sun thus brightly! It is inseparable from our civilization and enlightenment. It is encouraging that this intelligence and brilliancy or splendor should belong to the dwellings of men, and not to the cliffs and micaceous rocks and lakes exclusively.

P. M. — To Second Division Brook.

The *Typha latifolia*, or reed-mace, sheds an abundance of sulphur-like pollen into the hand now. Its tall and handsome swords are seen waving above the bushes in low grounds now. What I suppose the *Vaccinium fuscatum*, or black blueberry, is now ripe here and there, quite small. Heard the blating or lowing of a calf. Sat in the shade of the locusts in front of J. Hosmer's cottage and heard a locust z-ing on them, but could not find him. This cottage and the landscape, seen through the frame made by the "Railroad Crossing" sign, as you approach it along the winding bushy road, is a pleasing sight. It is picturesque.

There is a meadow on the Assabet just above Derby's Bridge, — it may contain an acre, — bounded on one side by the river, on the other by alders and a hill, completely covered with small hummocks which have lodged on it in the winter, covering it like the mounds in a graveyard at pretty regular intervals. Their edges are rounded like [the] latter, and they and the paths

between are covered with a firm, short greensward, with here and there hardhacks springing out of them, so that they make excellent seats, especially in the shade of an elm that grows there. They are completely united with the meadow, forming little oblong hillocks from one to ten feet long, flat as a mole to the sward. I am inclined to call it the elfin burial-ground, or perchance it might be called the Indian burial-ground. It is a remarkably firm-swarded meadow, and convenient to walk on. And these hummocks have an important effect in elevating it. It suggests at once a burial-ground of the aborigines, where perchance lie the earthly remains of the rude forefathers of the race. I love to ponder the natural history thus written on the banks of the stream, for every higher freshet and intenser frost is recorded by it. The stream keeps a faithful and a true journal of every event in its experience, whatever race may settle on its banks; and it purls past this natural graveyard with a storied murmur, and no doubt it could find endless employment for an old mortality in renewing its epitaphs.

The progress of the season is indescribable. It is growing warm again, but the warmth is different from that we have had. We lie in the shade of locust trees. Haymakers go by in a hay-rigging. I am reminded of berrying. I scent the sweet-fern and the dead or dry pine leaves. Cherry-birds alight on a neighboring tree. The warmth is something more normal and steady, ripening fruits. *Campanula aparinoides*, slender bell-flower. The *Cicuta maculata*, American hemlock. It begins to be such weather as when people go a-huckle-

Vol. IV

berrying. Nature offers fruits now as well as flowers. We have become accustomed to the summer. It has acquired a certain eternity. The earth is dry. Perhaps the sound of the locust expresses the season as well as anything. The farmers say the abundance of the grass depends on wet in June. I might make a separate season of those days when the locust is heard. That is our torrid zone. This dryness and heat are necessary for the maturing of fruits.

How cheering it is to behold a full spring bursting forth directly from the earth, like this of Tarbell's, from clean gravel, copiously, in a thin sheet; for it descends at once, where you see no opening, cool from the caverns of the earth, and making a considerable stream. Such springs, in the sale of lands, are not valued for as much as they are worth. I lie almost flat, resting my hands on what offers, to drink at this water where it bubbles, at the very udders of Nature, for man is never weaned from her breast while this life lasts. How many times in a single walk does he stoop for a draught!

We are favored in having two rivers, flowing into one, whose banks afford different kinds of scenery, the streams being of different characters; one a dark, muddy, dead stream, full of animal and vegetable life, with broad meadows and black dwarf willows and weeds, the other *comparatively* pebbly and swift, with more abrupt banks and narrower meadows. To the latter I go to see the ripple, and the varied bottom with its stones and sands and shadows; to the former for the influence of its dark water resting on invisible mud,

and for its reflections. It is a factory of soil, depositing sediment.

How many virtues have cattle in the fields! They do not make a noise at your approach, like dogs; they rarely low, but are quiet as nature, — merely look up at you. In the Ministerial Swamp there is a great deal of the naked viburnum rising above the dwarf andromeda. The calopogon, or grass-pink, now fully open, is remarkably handsome in the grass in low grounds, by contrast — its four or five *open* purple flowers — with the surrounding green. It makes a much greater show than the pogonia. It is of the same character with that and the arethusa, with a slight fragrance, methinks. It is very much indebted to its situation, no doubt, in low ground, where it contrasts with the dark-green grass. All color, with only a grass-like leaf below; flowers eminently. If it grew on dry and barren hilltops, or in woods above the dead leaves, it would lose half its attractions. Buttercups have now almost disappeared, as well as clover. Some of the earliest roses are ceasing, but others remain. I see many devil's-needles zigzagging along the Second Division Brook, some green, some blue, both with black and perhaps velvety wings. They are confined to the brook. How lavishly they are painted! How cheap was the paint! How free the fancy of their creator! I caught a handful of small water-bugs, fifteen or twenty, about as large as apple seeds. Some country people call them apple seeds, it is said, from their scent. I perceived a strong scent, but I am not sure it was like apples. I should rather think they were so called from their shape.

Some birds are poets and sing all summer. They are the true singers. Any man can write verses during the love season. I am reminded of this while we rest in the shade on the Major Heywood road and listen to a wood thrush, now just before sunset. We are most interested in those birds who sing for the love of the music and not of their mates; who meditate their strains, and *amuse* themselves with singing; the birds, the strains, of deeper sentiment; not bobolinks, that lose their plumage, their bright colors, and their song so early.

The robin, the red-eye, the veery, the wood thrush, etc., etc.

The wood thrush's is no opera music; it is not so much the composition as the strain, the tone, — cool bars of melody from the atmosphere of everlasting morning or evening. It is the quality of the song, not the sequence. In the peawai's note there is some sultriness, but in the thrush's, though heard at noon, there is the liquid coolness of things that are just drawn from the bottom of springs. The thrush alone declares the immortal wealth and vigor that is in the forest. Here is a bird in whose strain the story is told, though Nature waited for the science of æsthetics to discover it to man. Whenever a man hears it, he is young, and Nature is in her spring. Wherever he hears it, it is a new world and a free country, and the gates of heaven are not shut against him. Most other birds sing from the level of my ordinary cheerful hours — a carol; but this bird never fails to speak to me out of an ether purer than that I breathe, of immortal beauty

and vigor. He deepens the significance of all things seen in the light of his strain. He sings to make men take higher and truer views of things. He sings to amend their institutions; to relieve the slave on the plantation and the prisoner in his dungeon, the slave in the house of luxury and the prisoner of his own low thoughts.

How fitting to have every day in a vase of water on your table the wild-flowers of the season which are just blossoming! Can any house [be] said to be furnished without them? Shall we be so forward to pluck the fruits of Nature and neglect her flowers? These are surely her finest influences. So may the season suggest the fine thoughts it is fitted to suggest. Shall we say, "A penny for your thoughts," before we have looked into the face of Nature? Let me know what picture she is painting, what poetry she is writing, what ode composing, now.

I hear my hooting owl now just before sunset. You can fancy it the most melancholy sound in Nature, as if Nature meant by this to stereotype and make permanent in her quire the dying moans of a human being, made more awful by a certain gurgling melodiousness. It reminds of ghouls and idiots and insane howlings. One answers from far woods in a strain made really sweet by distance. Some poor weak relic of mortality who has left hope behind, and howls like an animal, yet with human sobs, on entering the dark valley. I find myself beginning with the letters *gl* when I try to imitate it. Yet for the most part it is a sweet and melodious strain to me.[1]

[1] [*Walden*, pp. 138, 139; Riv. 196.]

Some fields are quite yellow with johnswort now, — a pleasing motley hue, which looks autumnal. What is that small chickweed-like plant on Clamshell Hill, now out of bloom?

The sun has set. We are in Dennis's field. The dew is falling fast. Some fine clouds, which have just escaped being condensed in dew, hang on the skirts of day and make the attraction in our western sky, — that part of day's gross atmosphere which has escaped the clutches of the night and is not enough condensed to fall to earth, — soon to be gilded by his parting rays. They are remarkably finely divided clouds, a very fine mackerel sky, or, rather, as if one had sprinkled that part of the sky with a brush, the outline of the whole being that of several large sprigs of fan coral. C., as usual, calls it a Mediterranean sky. They grow darker and darker, and now are reddened, while dark-blue bars of clouds of wholly different character lie along the northwest horizon.

The *Asclepias Cornuti* (*Syriaca*) and the *A. incarnata* (*pulchra*) (this hardly out). Considerable fog tonight.

July 6. 2.30 P. M. — To Beck Stow's, thence to Saw Mill Brook, and return by Walden.

Now for the shade of oaks in pastures. The witnesses attending court sit on the benches in the shade of the great elm. The cattle gather under the trees. The pewai is heard now in the heat of the day, and the red-eye (?). The pure white cymes (?) of the elder are very conspicuous now along the edges of meadows,

contrasting with the green above and around. Yarrow is another of those flat-cymed flowers, now common. Here are holes dug by cattle in the dry fields (the Great Fields), like the buffalo wallows. In the swamp I find no blueberries ripe. But few *old* leaves remain on the dwarf andromeda. Woodchucks are remarkably numerous this year. *Cirsium arvense*, Canada thistle, just begun.

From the lane in front of Hawthorne's I see dense beds of tufted vetch (*Vicia cracca*), for some time taking the place of the grass in the low grounds, blue inclining in spots to lilac like the lupines. This, too, was one of the flowers that Proserpine was gathering, and yellow lilies, too. It is affecting to see such an abundance of blueness in the grass. It affects the eyes, this celestial color. I see it afar (from Hosmer's) in masses on the hillsides near the meadow. So much blue, laid on with so heavy a hand!

In selecting a site in the country, let a lane near your house, grass-grown, cross a sizable brook where is a watering-place. I see a pickerel in the brook showing his whitish greedy upper lips projecting over the lower. How well concealed he is! He is generally of the color of the muddy bottom or the decayed leaves and wood that compose it, and the longitudinal white stripe on his back and the transverse ones on his sides are the color of the yellowish sand here and there exposed. He heads up-stream and keeps his body perfectly motionless, however rapid the current, chiefly by the motion of his narrow pectoral fins, though also by the waving of his other fins and tail as much as necessary, which a frog might mistake for that of weeds. Thus, concealed by his color and stillness, like a stake, he lies in wait [for] frogs or minnows. Now a frog leaps in, and he darts forward three or four feet.

Pastinaca sativa, parsnip. How wholesome and edible smells its sweet root! What is that succulent plant near Tuttle's? *Agrimonia Eupatoria* with a rather handsome spike of yellow flowers. Tansy (*Tanacetum vulgare*) just begins.

A quail. I associate its whistle with breezy weather.

Hosmer is haying, but inclined to talk as usual. I blowed on his horn at supper-time. I asked if I should do any harm if I sounded it. He said no, but I called Mrs. Hosmer back, who was on her way to the village, though I blowed it but poorly. I was surprised to find how much skill and breath it took, depending on the size of the throat. Let blow a horn, says Robin, that good fellowship may us know. Where could a man go to practice on the horn, unless he went round to the farmer's at meal-time?

I am disappointed that Hosmer, the most intelligent farmer in Concord, and perchance in Middlesex, who admits that he has property enough for his use without accumulating more, and talks of leaving off hard work, letting his farm, and spending the rest of his days easier and better, cannot yet think of any method of employing himself but in work with his hands; only he would have a little less of it. Much as he is inclined to speculation in conversation — giving up any work to it for the time — and long-headed as he is, he talks of working for a neighbor for a day now and then and taking

his dollar. He "would not like to spend his time sitting on the mill-dam." He has not even planned an essentially better life.

Lysimachia stricta, upright loosestrife, now well out, by Hosmer's Pond and elsewhere, a rather handsome flower or cylindrical raceme of flowers. The *Castanea vesca*, with cream-colored flowers, seen from far, and the small green burs just forming. This is before the bass, methinks. It is covered with insects, now that tree flowers are scarce, — rose-bugs, a kind of locust, and I see a milk-white spider with two reddish spots; — a rather disagreeable buttery scent. I saw the other day a spider on a dwarf primrose, yellow, like the flower, and shaped like a flower. The red lily (*Lilium Philadelphicum*). This has very open petals of a dark vermilion color, speckled within, and grows in rather dry places, by wood-paths, etc., and is very interesting and handsome.

Sometimes the swampy vigor in such doses proves rank poison to the sensitively bred man! — as where dogwood grows. How far he has departed from the rude vigor of Nature, that he cannot assimilate and transmute her elements! The morning air may make a debauchee sick; no herb is friendly to him; all, at last, are poisons, and yet none are medicines to him, and so he dies; the air kills him.

Saw five drooping lily buds — yellow lilies, I suppose — on one stem. I notice the handsome stages of leaves, whorl-like or spiral, of the ground pine (*Lycopodium dendroideum*), whose spike is budded now. The *Galium trifidum*, rough. Also the *Galium triflorum*, flat on the

Vol. IV

ground, raying out two feet each way with broad and pointed leaves.

Returning through Britton's peach-field, I see numerous caterpillars' nests on the shrub oaks, made of clustered leaves, as big as your fist. They are three quarters of an inch long within. Soon to strip the bushes.

The *Erigeron strigosus* (*integrifolius* of Bigelow) is very common now in the fields, the flowers on the branches generally higher than the middle ones, like small white asters. At Saw Mill Brook, *Circæa alpina*, enchanter's-nightshade, moist shady places, with thin tender leaves *somewhat* like the touch-me-not's, — a sounding name for so inconspicuous a flower. The *Rubus hispidus*, or running swamp blackberry, was just in bloom when I gathered my early red ones, and is still generally in bloom; also the *R. Canadensis* is still often in bloom.

The early blueberries ripen first on the hills, before those who confine themselves to the lowlands are aware of it. When the old folks find only one turned here and there, children, who are best acquainted with the localities of berries, bring pailfuls to sell at their doors. For birds' nests and berries, give me a child's eyes. But berries must be eaten on the hills, and then how far from the surfeiting luxury of an alderman's dinner!

I heard a solitary duck on Goose Pond making a doleful cry, though its ordinary one, just before sundown, as if caught in a trap or by a fox, and, creeping silently through the bushes, I saw it — probably a

wood duck — sailing rapidly away; but it still repeated its cry, as if calling for a mate.

When the hen hatches ducks they do not mind her clucking. They lead the hen. Chickens and ducks are well set on the earth. What great legs they have! This part is early developed. A perfect Antæus is a young duck in this respect, deriving a steady stream of health and strength, for he rarely gets off it, ready either for land or water. Nature is not on her last legs yet. A chick's stout legs! If they were a little larger they would injure the globe's tender organization with their scratching. Then, for digestion, consider their crops and what they put into them in the course of a day! Consider how well fitted to endure the fatigue of a day's excursion. A young chick will run all day in pursuit of grasshoppers and occasionally vary its exercise by scratching, go to bed at night with protuberant crop, and get up early in the morning ready for a new start.

We have all kinds of walks in the woods, if we follow the paths, — some quite embowered in old forests and carpeted with slippery pine leaves, some covered with fine grass, rarely used between glossy shrub oaks and locusts, winding away.

July 7. 4 A. M. — The first[1] really foggy morning. Yet before I rise I hear the song of birds from out it, like the bursting of its bubbles with music, the bead on liquids just uncorked. Their song gilds thus the frostwork of the morning. As if the fog were a great sweet froth

---

[1] [This is queried in pencil.]

on the surface of land and water, whose fixed air escaped, whose bubbles burst with music. The sound of its evaporation, the fixed air of the morning just brought from the cellars of the night escaping. The morning twittering of birds in perfect harmony with it. I came near awaking this morning. I am older than last year; the mornings are further between; the days are fewer. Any excess — to have drunk too much water, even, the day before — is fatal to the morning's clarity, but in health the sound of a cow-bell is celestial music. Oh, might I always wake to thought and poetry — regenerated ! Can [it] be called a morning, if our senses are not clarified so that we perceive more clearly, if we do not rise with elastic vigor ? How wholesome these fogs which some fear ! They are cool, medicated vapor baths, mingled by Nature, which bring to our senses all the medical properties of the meadows. The touchstones of health. Sleep with all your windows open, and let the mist embrace you.

To the Cliffs.

The fog condenses into fountains and streams of music, as into the strain of the bobolink which I hear, and runs off so. The music of the birds is the tinkling of the rills that flow from it. I cannot see twenty rods. The trees look darker through it, and their outlines more distinct, apparently because of the whiteness of the fog and the less light that comes through the trees. There is everywhere dew on the cobwebs, little gossamer veils or scarfs as big as your hand, dropped from fairy shoulders that danced on the grass the past night.

Even where the grass was cut yesterday and is now cocked up, these dewy webs are as thick as anywhere, promising a fair day. There is no sunrise.

Hayden says his old cow "split her bones" in giving birth to a calf, and lies now helpless and incurable in the pasture, where he feeds her. Thus Nature rends the old husks, careful only for the fruit. The old, no doubt, have their satisfactions as well as the young.

The cobwebs on the dead twigs in sprout-lands covered with fog or dew. Their geometry is very distinct, and I see where birds have flown through them. I noticed that the fog last night, just after sundown, was like a fine smoke in valleys between the woods. The, to me, beautiful rose-colored spikes of the hardhack (*Spiræa tomentosa*). One is out. I think it was this thin vapor that produced a kind of mirage when I looked over the meadow from the railroad last night toward Trillium Wood, giving to the level meadow a certain liquid, sea-like look. Now the heads of herd's-grass, seen through the dispersing fog, look like an ocean of grass. Yesterday I noticed some goldenrods by the Walden road whose sheafy tops were yellowish. I appear to have brought home last night the *Pyrola rotundifolia* and *elliptica*, or shin-leaf, and perhaps *chlorantha* (?), now quite abundant.

6 P. M. — To Hubbard's Bathing-Place.

Pogonias are still abundant in the meadows, but arethusas I have not lately seen. The drooping heads of rattlesnake grass look autumnal. The blue-eyed

grass shuts up before sunset. The blossom of the cranberry looks singularly dry and shaving-like, considering its locality. The very handsome " pink purple " flowers of the *Calopogon* (!) *pulchellus* enrich the grass all around the edge of Hubbard's blueberry swamp, and are now in their prime. The *Arethusa bulbosa*, " crystalline purple;" *Pogonia ophioglossoides*, snake-mouthed arethusa, " pale purple;" and the *Calopogon pulchellus*, grass pink, " pink purple," make one family in my mind, — next to the purple orchis, or with it, — being flowers *par excellence*, all flower, all color, with inconspicuous leaves, naked flowers, and difficult — at least the calopogon — to preserve. But they are flowers, excepting the first, at least, without a name. Pogonia! Calopogon!! They would blush still deeper if they knew what names man had given them. The first and the last interest me most, for the pogonia has a strong snaky odor. The first may perhaps retain its name arethusa, from the places in which it grows, and the other two deserve the names of nymphs, perhaps of the class called Naiades. How would the Naiad Ægle do for one? The calopogon, like so many flowers, looks lilac-colored in the twilight. (My hummock of roses is still full of flowers and buds.) To be sure, in a perfect flower there will be proportion between the flowers and leaves, but these are fair and delicate, nymph-like.

The flowers of the *Lysimachia lanceolata* var. *hybrida*, loosestrife, are of a particularly faint or saffron or spring (?) yellow. *Plantago major*, *Lepidium Virginicum*, pepper-grass, an inconspicuous weed, with seed-vessels

somewhat like shepherd's-purse. I find in Hubbard's meadow what may be the 17th, 18th, or 19th aster of Gray. *Vide* Dictionary.

When the yellow lily flowers in the meadows, and the red in dry lands and by wood-paths, then, methinks, the flowering season has reached its height. They surprise me as perhaps no more can. Now I am prepared for anything.

July 8. P. M. — Down river in boat to the Holt.

The small globose white flower in muddy places by river and elsewhere. The bass on Egg Rock is just ready to expand. It is perhaps the warmest day yet.

We held on to the abutments under the red bridge to cool ourselves in the shade. No better place in hot weather, the river rippling away beneath you and the air rippling through beneath the abutments, if only in sympathy with the river, while the planks afford a shade, and you hear all the travel and the travellers' talk without being seen or suspected. The bullfrog it is, methinks, that makes the dumping sound. There is generally a current of air circulating over water, always, methinks, if the water runs swiftly, as if it put the air in motion. There is quite a breeze here this sultry day. Commend me to the sub-pontean, the under-bridge, life.

I am inclined to think bathing almost one of the necessaries of life, but it is surprising how indifferent some are to it. What a coarse, foul, busy life we lead, compared even with the South-Sea-Islanders, in some respects. Truant boys steal away to bathe, but the farmers, who most need it, rarely dip their bodies into the streams or ponds. M—— was telling me last night that he had thought of bathing when he had done his hoeing,—of taking some soap and going down to Walden and giving himself a good scrubbing,—but something had occurred to prevent it, and now he will go unwashed to the harvesting, aye, even till the next hoeing is over. Better the faith and practice of the Hindoos who worship the sacred Ganges. We have not faith enough in the Musketaquid to wash in it, even after hoeing. Men stay on shore, keep themselves dry, and drink rum. Pray what were rivers made for? One farmer, who came to bathe in Walden one Sunday while I lived there, told me it was the first bath he had had for fifteen years. Now what kind of religion could his be? Or was it any better than a Hindoo's?

M—— said that Abel Heywood told him he had been down to the Great Meadows (river meadows) to look at the grass, and that there was n't a-going to be much of a crop; in some places there was n't any grass at all. The great freshet in the spring did n't do it any good.

Under the *Salix nigra* var. *falcata*, near that handsomest one, which now is full of scythe-shaped leaves, the larger six inches long by seven eighths wide, with remarkably broad lunar leafy appendages or stipules at their base, I found a remarkable moth lying flat on the still water as if asleep (they appear to sleep during the day), as large as the smaller birds. Five and a half inches in alar extent and about three inches long, some-

thing like the smaller figure in one position of the wings (with a remarkably narrow lunar-cut tail), of a sea-green color, with four conspicuous spots whitish within, then a red line, then yellowish border below or toward the tail, but brown, brown orange, and black above, toward head; a very robust body, covered with a kind of downy plumage, an inch  and a quarter long by five eighths thick. The sight affected me as tropical, and I suppose it is the northern verge of some species. It suggests into what productions Nature would run if all the year were a July. By night it is active, for, though I thought it dying at first, it made a great noise in its prison, a cigar-box, at night. When the day returns, it apparently drops wherever it may be, even into the water, and dozes till evening again. Is it called the emperor moth?[1]

Yesterday I observed the arrow-wood at Saw Mill Brook, remarkably tall, straight, and slender. It is quite likely the Indians made their arrows of it, for it makes just such shoots as I used to select for my own arrows. It appears to owe its straightness partly to its rapid growth, already two feet from the extremities chiefly. The pontederia begins to make a show now. The black willow has branches horizontal or curving downward to the water first,   branching at once at the ground. The ————   *Sium latifolium*, water parsnip,—except that the calyx-leaves *are* minute and the fruit *ribbed*,—close to the edge of the river.

[1] [The luna moth.]

Vol. IV

July 9. Friday. 4 A. M.—To Cliffs.

No dew; no dewy cobwebs. The sky looks mist-like, not clear blue. An aurora fading into a general saffron color. At length the redness travels over, partly from east to west, before sunrise, and there is little color in the east. The birds all unite to make the morning quire; sing rather faintly, not prolonging their strains. The crickets appear to have received a reinforcement during the sultry night. There is no name for the evening red corresponding to aurora. It is the blushing foam about the prow of the sun's boat, and at eve the same in its wake. I do not often hear the bluebird now except at dawn. Methinks we have had no clear winter skies—no skies the color of a robin's egg, and pure amber around—for some months. These blueberries on Fair Haven have a very innocent, ambrosial taste, as if made of the ether itself, as they plainly are colored with it. I hear the chickadee's two wiry notes. The jay's note, resounding along a raw wood-side, suggests a singular wildness. I hear many scarlet tanagers, the first I have seen this season, which some might mistake for a red-eye. A hoarse, rough strain, comparatively, but more easily caught owing to its simplicity and sameness; something like *heer chip-er-way-heer chory chay.* A bobolink. How handsome the leaves of the shrub oak, so clear and unspotted a green, so firm and enduring, like fame; glossy, uninjured by the wind, meed for mighty conquerors; and also lighter on the under side, which contrast is important. The wood thrush sings on a dead tree-top. There is an insect in the froth on the *Vaccinium vacillans.* I see the cistus

still. The amelanchier's is a handsome berry, purplish when ripe, though handsomest when red, and inkish [?] next the stem. It must be the cuckoo that makes that half-throttled sound at night, for I saw one while he made it this morning, as he flew from an apple tree when I disturbed him. Those white water-lilies, what boats ! I toss one into the pan half unfolded, and it floats upright like a boat. It is beautiful when half open and also when fully expanded. Methinks I have found the *Asclepias obtusifolia*, which has long horns and is quite fragrant.

Morton, in his "Crania Americana," says, referring to Wilkinson as his authority, that "vessels of porcelain of Chinese manufacture have of late been repeatedly found in the catacombs of Thebes, in Egypt," some as old as the Pharaonic period, and the inscriptions on them "have been read with ease by Chinese scholars, and in three instances record the following legend: The flower opens, and lo ! another year." There is something sublime in the fact that some of the oldest written sentences should thus celebrate the coming in of spring. How many times have the flowers opened and a new year begun ! Hardly a more cheering sentence could have come down to us. How old is spring, a phenomenon still so fresh ! Do we perceive any decay in Nature? How much evidence is contained in this short and simple sentence respecting the former inhabitants of this globe ! It is a sentence to be inscribed on vessels of porcelain. Suggesting that so many years had gone before. An observation as fit then as now.

3 p. m. —To Clematis Brook.

The heat to-day (as yesterday) is furnace-like. It produces a thickness almost amounting to vapor in the near horizon. The railroad men cannot work in the Deep Cut, but have come out on to the causeway, where there is a circulation of air. They tell with a shudder of the heat reflected from the rails. Yet a breezy wind, as it were born of the heat, rustles all leaves. Those drifting piles of clouds in the north, assuming interesting forms, of unmeasured rocky mountains or unfathomed precipices, light-colored and even downy above, but with watery bases, portend a thundershower before night. Well, I can take shelter in some haven or under a bridge. It shall not spoil my afternoon. I have scarcely heard one strain from the telegraph harp this season. Its string is rusted and slackened, relaxed, and now no more it encourages the walker. I miss it much. So is it with all sublunary things. Every poet's lyre loses its tension. It cannot bear the alternate contraction and expansion of the seasons. The *Lactuca elongata*, four or five feet high, with its small pale-yellow flowers now closed. How intense and suffocating the heat under some sunny wood-sides where no breeze circulates ! I go by Well Meadow Head. The tephrosia, which still lingers, is remarkable, perhaps, for the contrast of its light or clear purple with its cream-colored petals. The *Veratrum viride* in the swamp is already turned yellow and decaying and half prostrate. Its fall is already come. I observe that the fever-bush here, as on Conantum, died down last winter. The red lily, with its torrid

Vol. IV

color and sun-freckled spots, dispensing, too, with the outer garment of a calyx, its petals so open and wide apart that you can see through it in every direction, tells of hot weather. It is a handsome bell shape, so upright, and the *flower* prevails over every other part. It belongs not to spring. It grows in the path by the town bound. It is refreshing to see the surface of Fair Haven rippled with wind. The waves break here quite as on the seashore and with the like effects. This little brook makes great sands comparatively at its mouth, which the waves of the pond wash up and break upon like a sea. The *Ludwigia palustris*, water purslane, on mud in bottom of dry ditches.

Bathing is an undescribed luxury. To feel the wind blow on your body, the water flow on you and lave you, is a rare physical enjoyment this hot day. The water is remarkably warm here, especially in the shallows, — warm to the hand, like that which has stood long in a kettle over a fire. The pond water being so warm made the water of the brook feel very cold; and this kept close on the bottom of the pond for a good many rods about the mouth of the brook, as I could feel with my feet; and when I thrust my arm down where it was only two feet deep, my arm was in the warm water of the pond, but my hand in the cold water of the brook. The clams are, if possible, more numerous here, though perhaps smaller than at the shore under the Cliffs. I could collect many bushels of them.

The sandy shore just beyond this is quite yellow with the *Utricularia cornuta*, the small ranunculus, and

the gratiola, all growing together. They make quite a show. A black snake on the sand retreats not into the bushes, but into the pond, amid the pontederia. The *Rhus glabra* is out. At Clematis Pond, the small arrowhead in the mud is still bleeding where cows have cropped. In some places the mud is covered with the *Ilysanthes gratioloides*, false pimpernel. I think it is this, the *flower* shaped somewhat like a skull-cap (*Lindernia* of Bigelow). The bottom of this pond, now for the most part exposed, of dark virgin mud, soft and moist, is an invigorating sight. It is alive with hundreds of small bullfrogs (?) at my approach, which go skipping into the water. Perhaps they were outside for coolness. It is also recently tracked by minks or muskrats in all directions, and by birds. (I should have said that the sand washed down by the brook at Pleasant Meadow covered the muddy bottom of the pond, but where the sandy covering was thin I slumped through it into the mud. I saw there some golden or brownishgolden winged devil's-needles, and was struck by the manner in which they held to the tops of the rushes when they alighted, — just on one side. You would perhaps confound them with the spike (?) of flowers.) The *Corylus rostrata*, beaked hazel, with green fruit, by Clematis Brook. The milkweeds, *syriaca* chiefly, are now in full flower by the ditch just beyond and fill the air with a strong scent, — five or six feet high. The *Asclepias obtusifolia* has a handsome waved or curled leaf and, methinks, more fragrant flowers. By this ditch also grows the *Sisym-*

brium amphibium, amphibious cress, of Bigelow (apparently *Nasturtium palustre* of Gray, though the pods are tipped with a conspicuous style and are not to be compared for length with the pedicels). It has the aspect and the taste of mustard. A rather high plant in water. That large galium. Can it be the cardinalflower here in bud, a coarse plant with a leaf-like redtipped envelope to its united stamens ?

Nowadays I scare up the woodcock (?) by shaded brooks and springs in the woods. It has a carry-legs flight and goes off with a sort of whistle. As you walk now in wood-paths, your head is encompassed with a swarm of ravenous, buzzing flies. It seems almost too hot for locusts.

Low hills, or even hillocks, which are stone-capped, — have rocky summits, — as that near James Baker's, remind me of mountains, which, in fact, they are on a small scale. The brows of earth, round which the trees and bushes trail like the hair of eyebrows, outside bald places, *templa*, primitive places, where lichens grow. I have some of the same sensations as if I sat on the summit of the Rocky Mountains. Some low places thus give a sense of elevation.

Sleeman says that no boy in India ever robs a bird's nest. Are they heathenish in that ?

Walden and White Ponds have a brimful look at present, though the former is not quite so high as when I last observed it. The bare hills about it are reddened in spots where the pine leaves are sere on the ground. The *Vaccinium vacillans*, small glaucous blueberry, bears here and there a ripe one on the hills, and the *Rubus Canadensis*, low blackberry, bears already a few ripe ones on sandy banks like the railroad causeway, exposed to the sun. *Portulaca oleracea* (?), purslane, just in flower, bright yellow, in the garden.[1] Observed in the river yesterday a potamogeton with leaves half an inch wide and four or five long. The white spruce shoots when wilted have the same raspberry fragrance with those of the fir balsam, but not so much of it. *Galium asprellum*, pointed cleavers.

July 10. *Saturday.* Another day, if possible still hotter than the last. We have already had three or four such, and still no rain. The soil under the sward in the yard is dusty as an ash-heap for a foot in depth, and young trees are suffering and dying.

2 P. M. — To the North River in front of Major Barrett's.

It is with a suffocating sensation and a slight pain in the head that I walk the Union Turnpike where the heat is reflected from the road. The leaves of the elms on the dry highways begin to roll up. I have to lift my hat to let the air cool my head. But I find a refreshing breeze from over the river and meadow. In the hottest day you can be comfortable in the shade on the open shore of a pond or river where a zephyr comes over the water, sensibly cooled by it; that is, if the water is deep enough to cool it. I find the white melilot (*Melilotus leucantha*), a fragrant clover, in blossom by this roadside.

[1] This should have been in next day, 10th.

We turn aside by a large rye-field near the old Lee place. The rye-fields are now quite yellow and ready for the sickle. Already there are many flavous colors in the landscape, much maturity of small seeds. The nodding heads of the rye make an agreeable maze to the eye. I hear now the huckleberry-bird, the red-eye, and the oven-bird. The robin, methinks, is oftener heard of late, even at noon. There are but few travellers abroad, on account of the oppressive heat. This heat is at the same time ripening and drying up the berries.

The long, narrow open intervals in the woods near the Assabet are quite dry now, in some parts yellow with the upright loosestrife. One of these meadows, a quarter of a mile long by a few rods wide, narrow and winding and bounded on all sides by maples, showing the under sides of their leaves, swamp white oaks with their glossy dark-green leaves, and birches, etc., and full of meadow-sweet just coming into bloom and cranberry vines and a dry kind of grass, is a very attractive place to walk in. We undressed on this side, carried our clothes down in the stream a considerable distance, and finally bathed in earnest from the opposite side. The heat tempted us to prolong this luxury. I think that I never felt the water so warm, yet it was not disagreeably so, though probably bathing in [it] was the less bracing and exhilarating, not so good as when you have to make haste, shivering, to get your clothes on in the wind; when ice has formed in the morning. But this is certainly the most luxurious. The river has here a sandy bottom and is for the most part quite shallow.

Vol. IV

I made quite an excursion up and down it in the water, a fluvial, a water, walk. It seemed the properest highway for this weather. Now in water a foot or two deep, now suddenly descending through valleys up to my neck, but all alike agreeable. Sometimes the bottom looked as if covered with long, flat, sharp-edged rocks. I could break off cakes three or four inches thick and a foot or two square. It was a conglomeration and consolidation of sand and pebbles, as it were cemented with oxid of iron (?), quite red with it, iron-colored, to the depth of an inch on the upper side, — a hard kind of pan covering or forming the bottom in many places. When I had left the river and walked in the woods for some time, and jumped into the river again, I was surprised to find for the first time how warm it was, — as it seemed to me, almost warm enough to boil eggs, — like water that has stood a considerable while in a kettle over a fire. There are many interesting objects of study as you walk up and down a clear river like this in the water, where you can see every inequality in the bottom and every object on it. The breams' nests are interesting and even handsome, and the shallow water in them over the sand is so warm to my hand that I think their ova will soon be hatched. Also the numerous heaps of stones, made I know not certainly by what fish, many of them rising above the surface. There are weeds on the bottom which remind you of the sea. The radical leaves of the floating-heart, which I have never seen mentioned, very large, five inches long and four wide, dull claret (and green where freshest), pellucid, with waved edges, in large tufts or

dimples on the bottom, oftenest without the floating leaves, like lettuce or some kelps or carrageen moss (?). The bottom is also scored with furrows made by the clams moving about, sometimes a rod long; and always the clam lies at one end. So this fish can change its position and get into deeper and cooler water. I was in doubt before whether the clam made these furrows, for one apparently fresh that I examined had a "mud clam" at the end; but these, which were very numerous, had living clams.

There are but few fishes to be seen. They have, no doubt, retreated to the deepest water. In one somewhat muddier place, close to the shore, I came upon an old pout cruising with her young. She dashed away at my approach, but the fry remained. They were of various sizes from a third of an inch to an inch and a half long, quite black and pout-shaped, except that the head was most developed in the smallest. They were constantly moving about in a somewhat circular, or rather lenticular, school, about fifteen or eighteen inches in diameter, and I estimated that there were at least a thousand of them. Presently the old pout came back and took the lead of her brood, which followed her, or rather gathered about her, like chickens about a hen; but this mother had so many children she did n't know what to do. Her maternal yearnings must be on a great scale. When one half of the divided school found her out, they came down upon her and completely invested her like a small cloud. She was soon joined by another smaller pout, apparently her mate, and all, both old and young, began to be very familiar with me; they came round my legs and felt them with their feelers, and the old pouts nibbled my toes, while the fry half concealed my feet. Probably if I had been standing on the bank with my clothes on they would have been more shy. Ever and anon the old pouts dashed aside to drive away a passing bream or perch. The larger one kept circling about her charge, as if to keep them together within a certain compass. If any of her flock were lost or devoured she could hardly have missed them. I wondered if there was any calling of the roll at night, — whether she, like a faithful shepherdess, ever told her tale under some hawthorn in the river's dales. Ever ready to do battle with the wolves that might break into her fold. The young pouts are protected then for a season by the old. Some had evidently been hatched before the others. One of these large pouts had a large velvet-black spot which included the right pectoral fin, a kind of disease which I have often observed on them.

I wonder if any Roman emperor ever indulged in such luxury as this, — of walking up and down a river in torrid weather with only a hat to shade the head. What were the baths of Caracalla to this? Now we traverse a long water plain some two feet deep; now we descend into a darker river valley, where the bottom is lost sight of and the water rises to our armpits; now we go over a hard iron pan; now we stoop and go under a low bough of the *Salix nigra;* now we slump into soft mud amid the pads of the *Nymphœa odorata,* at this hour shut. On this road there is no other traveller to turn out for.

from a distant field did not accomplish it without some skill and effort of the lungs.

July 11. 4.30 A. M. — To the river.

The shore is strewn with quite a long grove of young red maples two inches high, with the samaræ attached. So they are dispersed. The heart-leaf flower is abundant more than ever, but shut up at this hour. The first lily I noticed opened about half an hour after sunrise, or at 5 o'clock. The *Polygonum hydropiperoides,* I think it is, now in blossom in the mud by the river. Morning-glories are in perfection now, some dense masses of this vine with very red flowers, very attractive and cool-looking in dry mornings. They are very tender and soon defaced in a nosegay. The large orange lily with sword-shaped leaves, strayed from cultivation, by the roadside beyond the stone bridge.

It is a sufficient reason for walking in the forenoon sometimes that some flowers shut up at noon and do not open again during the day, thus showing a preference for that portion of the day.

P. M. — To Conantum.

The wind makes it rather more comfortable to-day. That small globose white flower with glossy radical leaves is common now on the muddy shore of the river. The fishes' nests are left high and dry, and I perceive that they are distinctly hollowed, five or six inches deep, in the sand, *i. e.* below the surrounding surface. Here are some which still contain their panful of water, but are no longer connected with

When I first came out of the water, the short, dry grass was burning hot to my bare feet, and my skin was soon parched and dry in the sun.

We finally return to the dry land, and recline in the shade of an apple tree on a bank overlooking the meadow. I still hear the bobolink. (There are comparatively few clams in the sandy Assabet, but methinks there are more than usual everywhere this year.) The stones lying in the sun on this hillside where the grass has been cut are as hot to the hand as an egg just boiled, and very uncomfortable to hold, so do they absorb the heat. Every hour we expect a thundershower to cool the air, but none comes. We say they are gone down the river.

The skull-cap (*Scutellaria galericulata*) is open in this meadow, a pretty conspicuous blue flower. Also the *Drosera longifolia.* That sort of erigeron is open. *Sericocarpus conyzoides* (?), small, many-flowered, with few rays, has long been budded.

St. John's-wort is perhaps the prevailing flower now. Many fields are very yellow with it. In one such I was surprised to see rutabaga turnips growing well and showing no effects of drouth, and still more surprised when the farmer, a very worthy but perfect Don Quixote looking man, showed me with his hoe that the earth was quite fresh and moist there, only an inch beneath the surface. This, he thought, was the result of keeping the earth loose by cultivation. This man's farm is extremely long and narrow, so that he could hardly hear a dinner horn where he was then at work. I was pleased to find that the woman who called her husband

the river. They have a distinct raised edge of sand about one and a half inches high and three or four wide. The lilies I have tried in water this warmest weather have wilted the first day. Only the water can produce and sustain such flowers. Those which are left high and dry, or even in very shallow water, are wont to have a dwarfed growth. The Victoria lily is a water flower.

The river is low. Now is the time for meadow walking. (I am in the meadow north of Hubbard's Bridge.) You go dry-shod now through meadows which were comparatively impassable before, — those western reserves which you had not explored. We are thankful that the water has preserved them inviolate so long. There is a cheerful light reflected from the under sides of the ferns in the drier meadows now, and has been for some time, especially in breezy weather. It was so in June. The dusty roads and roadsides begin to show the effects of drouth. The corn rolls.

The bass on Conantum is now well in blossom. It probably commenced about the 9th. Its flowers are conspicuous for a tree, and a rather agreeable odor fills the air. The tree resounds with the hum of bees on the flowers. On the whole it is a rich sight. Is it not later than the chestnut? The elder is a very conspicuous and prevalent flower now, with its large flat cymes.

Pogonias and calopogons are very abundant in the meadows. They are interesting, if only for their high color. Any redness is, after all, rare and precious. It is the color of our blood. The rose owes its preëminence in great measure to its color. It is said to be from the Celtic *rhos*, red. It is nature's most precious color.

Impatiens fulva, by Corner Spring. I hear often nowadays the kingbird's chattering twitter. As you walk under oaks, you perceive from time to time a considerable twig come gently falling to the ground, whose stem has been weakened by a worm, and here and there lie similar twigs whose leaves are now withered and changed.

How valuable and significant is shade now! Trees appear valuable for shade mainly, and we observe their shadows as much as their form and foliage. The waving of the meadow-grass near Fair Haven Isle is very agreeable and refreshing to one looking down from an elevation. It appears not merely like a waving or undulation, but a progress, a creeping, as of an invisible army, over it, its flat curly head. The grass appears tufted, *watered*. On the river the ripple is continued into the pads, where it is smoother, — a longer undulation. Pines or evergreens do not attract so much attention now. They have retired on the laurels of the winter campaign.

What is called genius is the abundance of life or health, so that whatever addresses the senses, as the flavor of these berries, or the lowing of that cow, which sounds as if it echoed along a cool mountain-side just before night, where odoriferous dews perfume the air and there is everlasting vigor, serenity, and expectation of perpetual untarnished morning, — each sight and sound and scent and flavor, — intoxicates with a healthy

intoxication. The shrunken stream of life overflows its banks, makes and fertilizes broad intervals, from which generations derive their sustenances. This is the true overflowing of the Nile. So exquisitely sensitive are we, it makes us embrace our fates, and, instead of suffering or indifference, we enjoy and bless. If we have not dissipated the vital, the divine, fluids, there is, then, a circulation of vitality beyond our bodies. The cow is nothing. Heaven is not there, but in the condition of the hearer. I am thrilled to think that I owe a perception to the commonly gross sense of taste, that I have been inspired through the palate, that these berries have fed my brain.[1] After I had been eating these simple, wholesome, ambrosial fruits on this high hillside, I found my senses whetted, I was young again, and whether I stood or sat I was not the same creature.

The yellow lily is not open-petalled like the red, nor is its flower upright, but drooping. On the whole I am most attracted by the red. They both make freckles beautiful.

Fragrances must not be overpowering, however sweet. I love the sweet fragrance of melilot. The *Circæa alpina*, enchanter's-nightshade, by Corner Spring, low, weed-like, somewhat like touch-me-not leaves. Was it not the *C. Lutetiana* (a larger plant) that I found at Saw Mill Brook?

July 12. I observed this morning a row of several dozen swallows perched on the telegraph-wire by the bridge, and ever and anon a part of them would launch

[1] [*Walden*, p. 241; Riv. 339.]

Vol. IV

forth as with one consent, circle a few moments over the water or meadow, and return to the wire again.

2 P. M. — To the Assabet.

Still no rain. The clouds, cumuli, lie in high piles along the southern horizon, glowing, downy, or cream-colored, broken into irregular summits in the form of bears erect, or demigods, or rocking stones, infant Herculeses; and still we think that from their darker bases a thunder-shower may issue. In other parts of the heavens are long stratified whitish clouds, and in the northwest floating isles, white above and darker beneath. The kingbird is active over the causeway, notwithstanding the heat, and near the woods I hear the huckleberry-bird and the song sparrow. The turtle dove flutters before you in shady wood-paths, or looks out with extended neck, losing its balance, slow to leave its perch.

Now for another fluvial walk. There is always a current of air above the water, blowing up or down the course of the river, so that this is the coolest highway. Divesting yourself of all clothing but your shirt and hat, which are to protect your exposed parts from the sun, you are prepared for the fluvial excursion. You choose what depths you like, tucking your toga higher or lower, as you take the deep middle of the road or the shallow sidewalks. Here is a road where no dust was ever known, no intolerable drouth. Now your feet expand on a smooth sandy bottom, now contract timidly on pebbles, now slump in genial fatty mud — greasy, saponaceous — amid the pads. You scare out whole schools of small breams and perch, and some-

times a pickerel, which have taken shelter from the sun under the pads. This river is so clear compared with the South Branch, or main stream, that all their secrets are betrayed to you. Or you meet with and interrupt a turtle taking a more leisurely walk up the stream. Ever and anon you cross some furrow in the sand, made by a muskrat, leading off to right or left to their galleries in the bank, and you thrust your foot into the entrance, which is just below the surface of the water and is strewn with grass and rushes, of which they make their nests. In shallow water near the shore, your feet at once detect the presence of springs in the bank emptying in, by the sudden coldness of the water, and there, if you are thirsty, you dig a little well in the sand with your hands, and when you return, after it has settled and clarified itself, get a draught of pure cold water there. The fishes are very forward to find out such places, and I have observed that a frog will occupy a cool spring, however small.

The most striking phenomenon in this stream is the heaps of small stones about the size of a walnut, more or less, which line the shore in shallow water, one every rod or two, the recent ones frequently rising by more than half their height above the water, at present, *i. e.* a foot or a foot and a half, and sharply conical, the older flattened by the elements and greened over with the threadlike stem of *Ranunculus filiformis*, with its minute bright-yellow flower. Some of these heaps contain two cartloads of stones, and as probably the creature that raised them took up one at a time, it must have been a stupendous task. They are from the size of a hen's egg down to the smallest gravel, and some are so perfect that I cannot believe they were made before the river fell.

Now you walk through fields of the small potamogeton (*heterophyllus* or *hybridus*), now in flower; now through the glossy pads of the white or the yellow water-lily, stepping over the now closed buds of the latter; now pause in the shade of a swamp white oak (up to your middle in the cool element), to which the very skaters and water-bugs confine themselves for the most part. It is an objection to walking in the mud that from time to time you have to pick the leeches off you. The stinkpot's shell, covered with mud and fine green weeds, gives him exactly the appearance of a stone on the bottom, and I noticed a large snapping turtle on one of the dark-brown rocks in the middle of the river (apparently for coolness, in company with a painted tortoise), so completely the color of the rock that, if it had not been for his head curved upwards to a point from anxiety, I should not have detected him. Thus nature subjects them to the same circumstances with the stones, and paints them alike, as with one brush, for their safety.

What art can surpass the rows of maples and elms and swamp white oaks which the water plants along the river, — I mean in variety and gracefulness, — conforming to the curves of the river.

Excepting those fences which are mere boundaries of individual property, the walker can generally perceive the reason for those which he is obliged to get over. This wall runs along just on the edge of the hill and

following all its windings, to separate the more level and cultivatable summit from the slope, which is only fit for pasture or wood-lot, and that other wall below divides the pasture or wood-lot from the richer low grass ground or potato-field, etc. Even these crooked walls are not always unaccountable and lawless.

The mower, perchance, cuts some plants which I have never seen in flower.

I hear the toads still at night, together with bullfrogs, but not so universally nor loud as formerly. I go to walk at twilight, — at the same time that toads go to their walks, and are seen hopping about the sidewalks or the pump. Now, a quarter after nine, as I walk along the river-bank, long after starlight, and perhaps an hour or more after sunset, I see some of those high-pillared clouds of the day, in the southwest, still reflecting a downy light from the regions of day, they are so high. It is a pleasing reminiscence of the day in the midst of the deepening shadows of the night. The dor-bugs hum around me, as I sit on the river-bank beyond the ash tree. Warm as is the night, — one of the warmest in the whole year, — there is an aurora, a low arc of a circle, in the north. The twilight ends to-night apparently about a quarter before ten. There is no moon.

July 13. A journal, a book that shall contain a record of all your joy, your ecstasy.

4 P. M. — To R. W. E.'s wood-lot south of Walden.

The pool by Walden is now *quite yellow* with the common utricularia (*vulgaris*). This morning the hea-

vens were overcast with a fog, which did not clear off till late in the forenoon. I heard the muttering of thunder behind it about 5 A. M. and thought it would rain at last, but there were dewy cobwebs on the grass, and it did not rain, but we had another hot dry day after all.

The northern wild red cherry of the woods is ripe, handsome, bright red, but scarcely edible; also, sooner than I expected, huckleberries, both blue and black; the former, not described by Gray or Bigelow, in the greater abundance, and must have been ripe several days. They are thick enough to pick. The black only here and there. The former is apparently a variety of the latter, blue with bloom and a tough or thick skin. There are evidently several kinds of huckleberries and blueberries not described by botanists: of the very early blueberries at least two varieties, one glossy black with dark-green leaves, the other a rich light blue with bloom and yellowish-green leaves; and more kinds I remember. I found the *Vaccinium corymbosum* well ripe on an exposed hillside. Each day now I scare up woodcocks by shady springs and swamps. The dark-purple amelanchier are the sweetest berries I have tasted yet. One who walks the woods and hills daily, expecting to see the first berry that turns, will be surprised at last to find them ripe and thick before he is aware of it, ripened, he cannot tell how long before, in some more favorable situation. It is impossible to say what day — almost what week — the huckleberries begin to be ripe, unless you are acquainted with, and daily visit, every huckleberry bush in the town, at least every place where they grow.

Already the goldenrod, apparently *Solidago stricta*, willow-leaved goldenrod, preaches of the lapse of time, on the Walden road. How many a tale its yellow tells! The *Polygala sanguinea* and *P. cruciata* in Brister's meadow, both numerous and well out. The last has a fugacious (?) spicy scent, in which, methinks, I detect the scent of nutmegs. Afterward I find that it is the lower part of the stem and root which is most highly scented, like checkerberry, and not fugacious. The *Verbena urticifolia*, white vervain. Succory, or *Cichorium intybus*. It appears to shut up this hot weather. Is that nettle-like plant by the wall below Mrs. Heywood's *Urtica gracilis*? Now in blossom. *Polygonum aviculare*, goose-grass, about the door.

The weather has been remarkably warm for a week or ten days, the thermometer at ninety-five degrees, more or less; and we have had no rain. You have not thought of cold or of taking cold, night or day, but only how you should be cool enough. Such weather as this the only use of clothing is to cover nakedness and to protect the body from the sun. It is remarkable that, though it would be a great luxury to throw aside all clothing now except one thin robe to keep off the sun, yet throughout the whole community not one is found to do it.

July 14. A writer who does not speak out of a full experience uses torpid words, wooden or lifeless words, such words as "humanitary," which have a paralysis in their tails.

Is it not more attractive to be a sailor than a farmer?

The farmer's son is restless and wants to go to sea. Is it not better to plow the ocean than the land? In the former case the plow runs further in its furrow before it turns. You may go round the world before the mast, but not behind the plow.

Morton quotes Wafer as saying of some albinos among the Indians of Darien that "they are quite white, but their whiteness is like that of a horse, quite different from the fair or pale European, as they have not the least tincture of a blush or sanguine complexion. . . . Their eyebrows are milk-white, as is likewise the hair of their heads, which is very fine, inclining to a curl, and growing to the length of six or eight inches. . . . They seldom go abroad in the daytime, the sun being disagreeable to them, and causing their eyes, which are weak and poring, to water, especially if it shines towards them; yet they see very well by moonlight, from which we call them moon-eyed." In Drake's "Collection of Voyages." Neither in our thoughts in these moonlight walks, methinks, is there "the least tincture of a blush or sanguine complexion," but we are, perchance, intellectually and morally albinos, children of Endymion whose parents have walked much by moonlight. Walking much by moonlight, conversing with the moon, makes us, then, albinos. Methinks we should rather represent Endymion in colorless marble, or in the whiteness of marble, than painted of the ruddy color of ordinary youths.[1]

Saw to-day for the first time this season fleets of yellow butterflies dispersing before us, [as] we rode

[1] [*Excursions*, pp. 325, 326; Riv. 400.]

along berrying on the Walden road. Their yellow fleets are in the offing. Do I ever see them in numbers off the road? They are a yellow flower that blossoms generally about this time. Like a mackerel fleet, with their small hulls and great sails. Collected now in compact but gorgeous assembly in the road, like schooners in a harbor, a haven; now suddenly dispersing on our approach and filling the air with yellow snowflakes in their zigzag flight, or as when a fair wind calls those schooners out and disperses them over the broad ocean.

How deep or perhaps slaty sky-blue are those blueberries that grow in the shade! It is an unexpected and thrilling discovery to find such ethereal fruits in dense drooping clusters under the fresh green of oak and hickory sprouts. Those that grow in the sun appear to be the same species, only to have lost their bloom and freshness, and hence are darker.[1]

The youth gets together his materials to build a bridge to the moon, or perchance a palace or temple on the earth, and at length the middle-aged man concludes to build a wood-shed with them.

Trees have commonly two growths in the year, a spring and a fall growth, the latter sometimes equalling the former, and you can see where the first was checked whether by cold or drouth, and wonder what there was in the summer to produce this check, this blight. So is it with man; most have a spring growth only, and never get over this first check to their youthful hopes; but plants of hardier constitution, or perchance planted in a more genial soil, speedily recover

[1] *Vide* p. [283].

themselves, and, though they bear the scar or knot in remembrance of their disappointment, they push forward again and have a vigorous fall growth which is equivalent to a new spring. These two growths are now visible on the oak sprouts, the second already nearly equalling the first.

Murder will out. Morton detects the filthiness of the lower class of the ancient Peruvians by the hair of old mummies being "charged with desiccated vermin, which, though buried for centuries in the sand, could not possibly be mistaken for anything else."

July 16. *Chenopodium album*, pigweed. The common form of the arrowhead, with larger, clear-white flowers. Also an-   other arrowhead, with a leaf shaped   not   not in flower. Xyris, yellow-eyed   grass, with three pretty yellow pet-   als atop. The forget-me-not is still abundant.

There is sport in the boy's water-mill, which grinds no corn and saws no logs and yields no money, but not in the man's.

Pyrus arbutifolia melanocarpa fruit begins to be black. *Cephalanthus occidentalis*, button-bush.

The bass on Conantum is a very rich sight now, though the flowers are somewhat stale; a solid mass of verdure and of flowers with its massed and rounded outline. Its twigs are drooping, weighed down with pendulous flowers, so that, when you stand directly under it and look up, you see one mass of flowers, a flowery canopy. Its conspicuous leaf-like bracts, too,

have the effect of flowers. The tree resounds with the hum of bees, — bumblebees and honey-bees; rose-bugs and butterflies, also, are here, — a perfect susurrus, a sound, as C. says, unlike any other in nature, — not like the wind, as that is like the sea. The bees abound on the flowers of the smooth sumach now. The branches of this tree touch the ground, and it has somewhat the appearance of being weighed down with flowers. The air is full of sweetness. The tree is full of poetry.

I observe the yellow butterflies everywhere in the fields and on the pontederias, which now give a faint blue tinge to the sides of the rivers. I hear the *link link*, fall-like note of the bobolink (?) in the meadows; he has lost the *bobo* off. Is it the goldfinch that goes twittering over, but which I cannot see? This is a still, thoughtful day, the air full of vapors which shade the earth, preparing rain for the morrow. The sarsaparilla berries are black. The weeds begin to be high in low grounds and low wood-paths, — the *Eupatorium purpureum* and goldenrods, etc., — suggesting a certain fecundity and vigor in nature, so that we love to wade through their ranks. The *Rhexia Virginica*, the meadow-beauty, high-colored, more beautiful than you remembered. The *Stachys aspera*, or hedge-nettle, looking like a white prunella with a long spike, in the meadows. The *Platanthera lacera*, ragged orchis, an unpainted flower. Is that delicate rose-purple flower in the Miles Swamp, with a long slender panicle and large leaves in a sort of whorl with long petioles, the *Desmodium acuminatum*, pointed-leaved tick-trefoil or hedysarum? The *Lechea major*, larger pinweed, everywhere in dry fields. Is it open?

July 17. Saturday. Cooler weather; a gentle steady rain, not shower; such coolness as rain makes; not sharp and invigorating, exhilarating, as in the spring, but thoughtful, reminding of the fall; still, moist, unoppressive weather, in which corn and potatoes grow; not a vein of the northwest wind or the northeast. The coolness of the west tempered with rain and mist. As I walked by the river last evening, I heard no toads. A coolness as from an earth covered with vegetation, such as the toad finds in the high grass. A verdurous coolness, not a snowy or icy one, in the shadow of the vapors which the heat makes rise from the earth. Can this be dog-dayish?

P. M. — A summer rain. A gentle steady rain, long a-gathering, without thunder or lightning, — such as we have not, and, methinks, could not have had, earlier than this.

To Beck Stow's.

I pick raspberries dripping with rain beyond Sleepy Hollow. This weather is rather favorable to thought. On all sides is heard a gentle dripping of the rain on the leaves, yet it is perfectly warm. It is a day of comparative leisure to many farmers. Some go to the mill-dam and the shops; some go a-fishing. The *Antennaria margaritacea*, pearly everlasting, is out; and the thoroughworts, red and white, begin (?) to show their colors. Notwithstanding the rain, some children still pursue their blackberrying on the Great Fields.

Swamp-pink lingers still. Roses are not so numerous as they were. Some which I examine now have short, stout hooked thorns and narrow bracts. Is it the *Rosa Carolina?* I love to see a clear crystalline water flowing out of a swamp over white sand and decayed wood, spring-like. The year begins to have a husky look or scent in some quarters. I remark the green coats of the hazelnuts, and hear the permanent jay. Some fields are covered now with tufts or clumps of indigo-weed, yellow with blossoms, with a few dead leaves turned black here and there.

Beck Stow's Swamp! What an incredible spot to think of in town or city! When life looks sandy and barren, is reduced to its lowest terms, we have no appetite, and it has no flavor, then let me visit such a swamp as this, deep and impenetrable, where the earth quakes for a rod around you at every step, with its open water where the swallows skim and twitter, its meadow and cotton-grass, its dense patches of dwarf [1] andromeda, now brownish-green, with clumps of blueberry bushes, its spruces and its verdurous border of woods imbowering it on every side. The trees now in the rain look heavy and rich all day, as commonly at twilight, drooping with the weight of wet leaves.

That *Sericocarpus conyzoides* prevails now, and the entire-leaved erigeron still abounds everywhere. The meadows on the Turnpike are *white* with the meadow-rue *now more than ever*. They are filled with it many feet high. The *Lysimachia lanceolata* is very common too. All flowers are handsomer in rain. Methinks the

[1] [This word is queried in pencil.]

sweet-briar is done. The hardhack, whose spires are not yet abundant, stands to me for agreeable coarseness. Swallows are active throughout this rain. *Lobelia inflata*, Indian-tobacco. *Lappa major*, burdock. *Amaranthus hybridus*, though not yet red. *Verbena hastata*, blue vervain. *Gnaphalium uliginosum* by the roadside, cudweed. Again methinks I hear the goldfinch, but not for a day or two the bobolink. At evening the prunellas in the grass like the sky glow purple, which were blue all day. The vetch I looked for is mown, but I find it fresh elsewhere. The caducous polygala has the odor of checkerberry at its root, and hence I thought the flower had a fugacious, spicy fragrance. *Hypericum Canadense*. The slender bell-flower, galium-like, with a triangular stem in low grounds now.

July 18. Sunday. 8.30 A. M. — To the Sudbury meadows in boat.

Peter Robbins says that the rain of yesterday has not reached the potatoes, after all. Exorbitant potatoes! It takes a good deal to reach them, — serious preaching to convert them. The white lilies and the floating-heart are both well open at this hour, and more abundant than I have noticed them before. Like ducks, the former sit on the water as far as I can see on both sides. As we push away from Monroe's shore, the robins are singing and the swallows twittering. There is hardly a cloud in the sky. There are dewy cobwebs on the grass; so this is a fit morning for any adventure. It is one of those everlasting mornings, with

cobwebs on the grass, which are provided for long enterprises. It is a sabbath within the water as well as in the air and on the land, and even the little pickerels not half so long as your finger appear to be keeping it holy amid the pads. There is a sort of dusty or mealy light in the bream's tail and fins waving in clear water. The river is now in all its glory, adorned with water-lilies on both sides. Walkers and sailers ordinarily come hither in the afternoon, when the lilies are shut, and so never see the river in its pride. They come after the exhibition is over for the day, and do not suspect it. We are gliding swiftly up the river by Barrett's Bend. The surface of the water is the place to see the pontederia from, for now the spikes of flowers are all brought into a dense line, — a heavy line of blue, a foot or more in width, on one or both sides of the river. The pontederias are now in their prime, there being no withered heads. They are very freshly blue. In the sun, when you are looking west, they are of a violaceous blue. The lilies are in greater profusion than when we came to see them before. They appear to be too many for the insects, and we find enough untouched. Horsemint (*Mentha Canadensis*) is now out.

We take a bath at Hubbard's Bend. The water seems fresher, as the air, in the morning. Again under weigh, we scare up the great bittern amid the pontederia, and, rowing to where he alights, come within three feet of him and scare him up again. He flies sluggishly away plowing the air with the coulter of his breast-bone, and alighting ever higher up the stream.

We scare him up many times in the course of an hour. The surface of the river is spotted with the radical leaves of the floating-heart, large and thin and torn, rarely whole, which something has loosened from the bottom. The larks and blackbirds and kingbirds are heard in the meadows. But few button-bushes are in blossom yet. Are they dark-brown weed-like fibrous roots of the plant itself that invest its stems below? Harmless bright downy clouds form in the atmosphere on every side and sail the heavens.

After passing Hubbard's Bridge, looking up the smooth river between the rows of button-bushes, willows, and pads, we see the sun shining on Fair Haven Hill behind a sun-born cloud, while we are in shadow, — a misty golden light, yellow, fern-like, with shadows of clouds flitting across its slope, — and horses in their pasture standing with outstretched necks to watch us; and now they dash up the steep in single file, as if to exhibit their limbs and mettle. The carcass of a cow which has recently died lies on the sandy shore under Fair Haven, close to the water. Perhaps she was poisoned with the water parsnip, which is now in flower and abounds along the side of the river. We have left the dog in the middle of Fair Haven Bay swimming in our wake, while we are rowing past Lee's, and we see no more of him. How simple are the ornaments of a farmhouse! To one rowing past in the middle of a warm summer day, a well at a distance from the house in the shadow of an oak, as here, is a charming sight. The house, too, with no yard but an open lawn sloping to the river. And young turkeys seen wandering in the

grass, and ever and anon hopping up as if a snake had scared them. The ponderias are alive with butterflies. Here is a fisherman's willow pole left to mark a lucky place, with green shoots at the top. The other day I noticed that Neighbor Gorman's willow beanpoles had grown more than his beans. We now go through the narrow gut at the bend near the town bound. A comfortable day. Methinks we shall have no torrid blazing dry heats after this,[1] but muggy, dog-dayish weather, tempered by mists and shadows of fogs, the evaporation of vegetation? The nights, too, can be decidedly cool.

No one has ever put into words what the odor of water-lilies expresses. A sweet and innocent purity. The perfect purity of the flower is not to be surpassed. They now begin to shut up. Looking toward the sun, I cannot see them, cannot distinguish lilies from the sun reflected from the pads.

Thus we go on, into the Sudbury meadows, opening the hills. The near hills, even, have a misty blueness, — a liquid one, like a field of oats yet green. Both wish now to face up-stream and see the hills open. The *Peltandra Virginica* (*Calla*), which I saw well budded opposite the Pantry, July 1st, has flowered and curved downward into the water and mud, but I observe other flowers to come. The columbine lingers still. The red-eye sings at noon, and the song sparrow. The bobolink I do not hear of late, — not since this fall-like, late-feeling weather. Now the fogs have begun, in midsummer and mid-haying time. We go inland to

[1] [Two interrogation-points in the margin here.]

the Jenkins house spring, through the handsome oak grove, white and black (?), eight or nine of them, on the further edge of the meadow, where the haymakers' path comes in. Strawberries are still occasionally found in meadows. The *Cerasus Virginiana*, or choke-cherry, is turning, nearly ripe. We sit on the edge of the hill at the Jenkins house, looking northward over a retired dell in the woods, an unfrequented johnswort and blackberry field, surrounded by a deep forest — with several tall white pines against the horizon, a study of which you would never tire. The swallows twitter overhead, the locust, we know not where, is z-ing, and the huckleberry-bird is heard on the birches. The ground under the apple tree, where we lie, is strewn with small sun-baked apples, but we are not yet reminded of apples.

When I think of the London *Times* and the reviews here, the *Revue des Deux Mondes*, and of the kind of life which it is possible to live here, I perceive that this, the natural side, has not got into literature. Think of an essay on human life, through all which was heard the note of the huckleberry-bird still ringing, as here it rings ceaselessly. As if it were the muse invoked! The *Revue des Deux Mondes* does not embrace this view of things, nor imply it.

Which neottia have I found? In the front and lowest rank, the narrow-leaved polygonum, in the river, I see a flower or two beginning. The farmers have cut some meadow-hay here. In the broader meadows the river winds the most, where there are no iron-bound rocky hills to constrain it. Through all these Sudbury mead-

ows it is a perfect meander, where no wind will serve the sailer long. It is a luxury to sit sailing or rowing here and look off to the hills, at the deep shadows of the trees in which the cattle stand. We land on the left, half a mile above Sherman's Bridge, ramble to the " sand " and poplars, where I picked up two arrowheads. The *Spergula arvensis*, corn-spurry, which has long been in blossom; the *Raphanus Raphanistrum*, wild radish; the *Lycopus sinuatus*, horehound. Here is a horse who keeps the hilltop for the breeze.

We push still further up the river into the great meadow, scaring the bitterns, the largest and the next in size. In many parts of the river the pickerel-weed is several rods wide, its blueness akin to the misty blue air which paints the hills. You thin it by rising in the boat; you thicken or deepen it by sitting low. (When we looked from the hills, there was a general sheeny light from the broad, level meadow, from the bent grass, watered, as it were, with darker streaks where a darker grass, the pipes, etc., bordered the (for the most part) concealed river.) The lilies are shut. First on the edge of the bright river in the sun, in this great meadow, are the pads, then the pontederia or polygonum, then the bulrushes standing in dense squadrons, or pipes or meadow-grass, then the broad heavens, in which small downy clouds are constantly forming and dissolving. No fear of rain. The sky is a pretty clear blue, yet not such a skimmed-milk blue, methinks, as in winter; some cream left in the milk. I cannot believe that any of these dissolving cloudlets will be rainbow-tinged or mother-o'-pearled. I observe that even in these meadows, where no willows nor button-bushes line the shore, there is still a pretty constant difference between the shores. The border of pontederia is rarely of equal depth on both sides at once, but it keeps that side in the meander where the sediment is deposited, the shortest

course which will follow the shore, as I have dotted it, crossing from this side to that as the river meanders; for on the longest side the river is active, not passive, wearing into the bank, and runs there more swiftly. This is the longest line of blue that nature paints with flowers in our fields, though the lupines may have been more densely blue within a small compass. Thus by a natural law a river, instead of flowing straight through its meadows, meanders from side to side and fertilizes this side or that, and adorns its banks with flowers. The river has its active and its passive side, its right and left breast.

Return. There is a grand view of the river from the hill near Rice's. The outlines of this hill, as you ascend it, and its various swells are very grateful, closely grazed, with a few shade trees on its sides. You look far south over the gulf meadow, and north also. The meadow-grass seen from this side has no sheen on it. Round Hill is a mathematical curve. The petals of the rhexia have a beautiful clear purple with a violet tinge. The *Brasenia peltata*, or water-shield, which was budded July 1st, is now in blossom, — obscure reddish blossoms. To what plant does that elliptical pad belong whose lobes lap more than half an inch, three inches long,

and stem lenticular on a cross-section? Does the *Kalmiana* so vary? What kind of lettuce (or *Nabalus?*) is that, with triangular hastate leaves, reddish stem, and apparently whitish flowers, now budded?

When near home, just before sundown, the sun still inconveniently warm, we were surprised to observe on the uppermost point of each pontederia leaf a clear drop of dew already formed, or flowing down the leaf, where all seemed still warmth and dryness, also as often hanging from the lobes below. It appeared a wonderful chemistry by which the broad leaf had collected this pearly drop on its uppermost extremity. The sun had no sooner sunk behind the willows and the button-bushes, than this process commenced. And now we see a slight steam like smoke rising from amidst the pontederias. In half an hour the river and the meadows are white with fog, like a frosted cake. As you stand on the bank in the twilight, it suddenly moves up in sprayey clouds, moved by an unfelt wind, and invests you where you stand, its battalions of mists reaching even to the road.

But there is less in the morning.

Every poet has trembled on the verge of science.

Got green grapes to stew.

July 19. P. M. — R. W. E.'s cliff.

Phytolacca decandra, poke, in blossom. The *Cerasus pumila* ripe. The chestnuts on Pine Hill being in blossom reveals the rounded tops of the trees; separates them, and makes a richer and more varied scene.

July 20. To Assabet behind Lee Place.

Perceived a small weed, coming up all over the fields, which has an aromatic scent. Did not at first discover that it was blue-curls. It is a little affecting that the year should be thus solemn and regular, that this weed should have withheld itself so long, biding its appointed time, and now, without fail, be coming up all over the land, still extracting that well-known aroma out of the elements, to adorn its part of the year! I also perceive one of the coarse late fleabanes making itself conspicuous. The stinging nettle is not very obvious, methinks. Fields are yellow with grain, being cut and stacked, or still standing. Long rows I see from far, as they were left by the cradle. *Elodea Virginica*, marsh St. John's-wort. Dug open a muskrat's gallery. It was flat on the bottom, on sand, and quite regularly arched, and strewn with coarse meadow-grass or flags for a carpet. There was half of a critchicrotch in it.

Sunset. — To Cliffs.

The clouds, as usual, are arranged with reference to the sunset. The sun is gone. An amber light and golden glow. The first redness is on clouds in the east horizon. As we go by the farmhouses, the chickens are coming home to roost. The horns of the moon only three or four days old look very sharp, still cloud-like, in the midst of a blue space, prepared to shine a brief half-hour before it sets. The redness now begins to fade on eastern clouds, and the western cloudlets glow with burnished copper alloyed with gold. As we approach the woods, we perceive a fresh, cool evening

scent from them. The squeak of the nighthawk is heard; the hum of mosquitoes in the woods; the song sparrow and the huckleberry-bird. The bat seen flying over the path. The western clouds grow more red or fiery, by fits and starts, and now, as suddenly, their glory departs, and they remain gray or greenish. We see from the hill darkness infolding the village, collected first in the elm-tops. If it were not for the light-colored barns and white houses, it would already be dark there. The redness of the clouds, or the golden or coppery or fuscous glow, appears to endure almost till starlight. Then the cloudlets in the west turn rapidly dark, the shadow of night advances in the east, and the first stars become visible. Then, and before the western clouds, the light behind them having faded, do or appear to disperse and contract and leave a clear sky, when I invert my head (on Fair Haven Hill), the dark cloudlets in the west horizon are like isles, like the tops of mountains cut off by the gross atmosphere. The pitch pine woods are heavy and dark, but the river is full of golden light and more conspicuous than by day. It is starlight. You see the first star in the southwest, and know not how much earlier you might have seen it had you looked. Now the first whip-poor-will sings hollowly in the dark pitch pine wood on Bear Garden Hill, as if the night had never ceased, and it had never ceased to sing, only now we heard it. And now, when we had thought the day birds gone to roost, the wood thrush takes up the strain. The bullfrog trumps. We sit on the warm rocks (Cliffs). Now is the evening red; late into the night almost it reaches.

The gross atmosphere of day, closest to the heels of the sun, is the last to glow red, — this general low fuliginous, lurid redness, long after the sunset and the glowing of the clouds. The western sky is comparatively clear, the clouds that followed in day's train having swept by. Night is seen settling down with mists on Fair Haven Bay. The stars are few and distant; the fireflies fewer still. Will they again be as numerous as after the early thunder-showers?

Now there is a *second* fuscous glow, brassy (?) glow, on the few low western cloudlets, when we thought the sun had bid us a final adieu, — quite into evening. Those small clouds, the rearmost guard of day, which were wholly dark, are again lit up for a moment with a dull-yellowish glow and again darken; and now the evening redness deepens till all the west or northwest horizon is red; as if the sky were rubbed there with some rich Indian pigment, a permanent dye; as if the Artist of the world had mixed his red paints on the edge of the inverted saucer of the sky. An exhilarating, cheering redness, most wholesome. There should be a red race of men. I would look into the west at this hour till my face permanently reflects that red. It is like the stain of some berries crushed along the edge of the sky. The crescent moon, meanwhile, has grown more silvery, and, as it sank in [the] west, more yellowish, and the outline of the old moon in its arms was visible if you did not look directly at it. The first distinct moonlight was observed some time before this, like the first gray light of the dawn reflected from the tree-tops below us. Some dusky redness lasted almost

till the last traces of daylight disappeared. The last took place about 10 o'clock, and about the same time the moon went down.

At evening the eastern clouds, the western clouds, and the atmosphere of the west horizon have one history successively — a fainter glow and redness, gradually and by stages deepening till the darkness prevails.

This afternoon, in the gutter by roadside beyond S. Wheeler's, *Penthorum sedoides* (?), ditch stonecrop. Is that nettle-like but smooth and, I should say, obtusely four-angled plant in the low moist ground on the Assabet the *Boehmeria cylindrica*? *Alisma Plantago*, water-plantain, about out of flower, by the Assabet; small leaves like the plantain. What is that ternate-leaved vine with yellow dusty excrescences by the Assabet, not in bloom?[1] The *Vernonia Noveboracensis* is budded by the riverside.

July 21. 4 A. M. — Robins sing as loud as in spring, and the chip-bird breathes in the dawn. The eastern waters reflect the morning redness, and now it fades into saffron. And now the glow concentrates about one point. At this season the northeast horizon is lit up and glows red and saffron, and the sun sets so far northwest that but a small part of the north horizon is left unillustrated. The meadows are incrusted with low, flat, white, and apparently hard fog. Soon it begins to rise and disperse.

Walden Pond and Lake Superior are both uncommonly high this year.

[1] Ground-nut (?).

Vol. IV

At sunset to Corner Spring.

A broken strain from a bobolink. A golden robin once or twice to-day. The *Mimulus ringens*, or monkey-flower; one of the most noticeable of this class of flowers. Is that *Sium lineare*, with a *smooth, round* stem and *fringe-serrate* linear leaves, without bulblets?[1] *Eupatorium pubescens*, ovate-leaved eupatorium, not quite out, with a fastigiate corymb. All sunsets are not equally splendid. To-night there is not a cloud in the west, and the sun goes down without pomp or circumstance, — only a faint glow in the gross atmosphere next the earth after a warm day. Those first (not moss) roses appear to be out of bloom. Those I see now have stout, rather short, hooked prickles or thorns. This evening is remarkably serene. It is awfully still; not a bird now heard, only the *fine* sound of crickets. I see the earliest star fifteen or twenty minutes before the red is deepest in the horizon. I mean the atmospheric redness. It is not generally, *i. e.* conspicuously, starlight till that begins to fade. Perhaps it is not time to light a candle till then, for some duskiness should intervene to separate between day and night. This redness is at first intenser as reflected in the river, as, when you look into the horizon with inverted head, all colors are intensified. Methinks I hear my old friend the locust in the alders. The river is perfectly smooth, reflecting the golden sky and the red, for there is an unexpectedly bright and general golden or amber glow from the upper atmosphere in the west. At evening lakes and rivers become thus placid. Every

[1] [See p. 295.]

dimple made by a fish or insect is betrayed. Evening descends on the waters. There is not a breath of air. Now is the time to be on the water, for there is no mist rising and little evening coolness or damp. At morning and at evening this precious color suffuses the sky. Evening is the reverse of the day with all its stages intensified and exaggerated. The roads and bridges are strewn with hay which has dropped from the loads. The whip-poor-will began to sing at earliest twilight. Do we perceive such a deep Indian red after the first starlight at any other season as now in July? How far we smell carrion at night! A dead cow lies by the shore under Fair Haven nearly half a mile above this causeway. When I passed this way at earliest starlight I did not smell it, but now, returning half an hour later, it taints [the] atmosphere of the causeway from one end to the other, and I am obliged to hurry over, — borne down over the meadow on the damp air. The root of the caducous polygala has a checkerberry odor. Has the other?

It is midsummer, and, looking from the hills at midday, I see the waving blades of corn reflecting the light. The foliage of the trees looks green generally. The shrub oak leaves especially are not much injured, and the fields, though rather brown, are not so dry as I expected.

July 22. This morning, though perfectly fair except a haziness in the east, which prevented any splendor, the birds do not sing as yesterday. They appear to make distinctions which we cannot appreciate, and perhaps sing with most animation on the finest mornings.

1 p. m. — Lee's Bridge, *via* Conantum; return by Clematis Brook.

There men in the fields are at work thus indefatigably, more or less honestly getting bread for men. The writer should be employed with at least equal industry to an analogous though higher end.

Flocks of yellow-breasted, russet-backed female bobolinks are seen flitting stragglingly across the meadows. The bobolink loses his song as he loses his colors.

Tansy is now conspicuous by the roadsides, covered with small red butterflies. It is not an uninteresting plant. I probably put it down a little too early. Is that a slender bellflower with entire leaves by the Corner road? The green berries of the arum are seen, and the now *reddish* fruit of the trillium, and the round green-pea-sized green berries of the axil-flowering Solomon's-seal. Farmers have commenced their meadow-haying. The *Aster macrophyllus*, large-leafed, in Miles's Swamp. Is not that the *Lysimachia ciliata*, or hairy-stalked loosestrife, by the Corner road, not the *lanceolata? Eupatorium sessilifolium* now whitish. A strong west wind, saving us from intolerable heat, accompanied by a blue haze, making the mountains invisible. We have more of the furnace-like heat to-day, after all. The *Rhus glabra* flowers are covered with bees, *large* yellowish wasps, and butterflies; they are all alive with them. How much account insects make of some flowers! There are other botanists than I. The *Asclepias syriaca* is going to seed. Here is a kingfisher frequenting the

Corner Brook Pond. They find out such places. Huckleberrying and blackberrying have commenced. The round-leafed sundew. *Monotropa uniflora*, Indian-pipe. *Solidago Canadensis* (?) almost out. Either a smooth *Polygonum hydropiperoides* or a white *P. amphibium* var. *terrestre*. The spear thistle.[1] *Galium circæzans*, wild liquorice, in Baker Farm Swamp.

What is that minute whitish flower with an upright thread-like stem and thread-like linear leaves, with a kind of interrupted spike or raceme of small, whitish, erect, bell-like flowers, the corolla divided by a stout partition, from which projects the style, with three distinct segments in the edge of the bell each side of the partition?[2] Also found a very small narrow-leaved whitish aster (?).[3]

July 23. P. M. — To Annursnack.

Herbage is drying up; even weeds are wilted, and the corn rolls. Agriculture is a good school in which to drill a man. Successful farming admits of no idling. Now is the haying season. How active must these men be, all the country over, that they may get through their work in season! A few spoiled windrows, all black and musty, have taught them that they must make hay while the sun shines, and get it in before it rains.

Much that I had taken to be the lanceolate loosestrife is the heart-leaved, especially by the Corner road. *Pycnanthemum muticum*, mountain mint. Have I not

[1] *Cirsium lanceolatum.*   [2] Canada snapdragon.
[3] *Erigeron Canadensis.*

mistaken this for the other species heretofore? The dwarf choke-cherry is ripe now, long before the rum cherry. Also the *Pyrus arbutifolia. Cnicus pumilus*,[1] pasture thistle. *Chenopodium hybridum*, maple-leaved goose-foot.

What is that white hairy plant with lanceolate leaves and racemes now, with flat burs, one to three, and a long spine in the midst, and five ovate calyx-leaves left (these turned to one side of the peduncle), burs very adhesive, close to road in meadow just beyond stone bridge on right; long out of bloom? Every man says his dog will not touch you. Look out, nevertheless.

Twenty minutes after seven, I sit at my window to observe the sun set. The lower clouds in the north and southwest grow gradually darker as the sun goes down, since we now see the side opposite to the sun, but those high overhead, whose under sides we see reflecting the day, are light. The small clouds low in the western sky were at first dark also, but, as the sun descends, they are lit up and aglow all but their cores. Those in the east, though we see their sunward sides, are a dark blue, presaging night, only the highest faintly glowing. A roseate redness, clear as amber, suffuses the low western sky about the sun, in which the small clouds are mostly melted, only their golden edges still revealed. The atmosphere there is like some kinds of wine, perchance, or molten cinnabar, if that is red, in which also all kinds of pearls and precious stones are melted. Clouds generally near the horizon, except near the sun, are now a dark blue. (The sun sets.) It is half past seven.

[1] *Cirsium pumilum.*

The roseate glow deepens to purple. The low western sky is now, and has been for some minutes, a splendid map, where the fancy can trace islands, continents, and cities beyond compare. The glow forsakes the high eastern clouds, the uppermost clouds in the west now darken, the glow having forsaken them too; they become a dark blue, and anon their under sides reflect a deep red, like heavy damask curtains, after they had already been dark. The general redness gradually fades into a pale reddish tinge in the horizon, with a clear white light above it, in which the clouds grow more conspicuous and darker and darker blue, appearing to follow in the wake of the sun, and it is now a quarter to eight, or fifteen minutes after sunset, twenty-five minutes from the first. A quarter of an hour later, or half an hour after sunset, the white light grows cream-colored above the increasing horizon redness, passing through white into blue above. The western clouds, high and low, are now dark fuscous, not dark blue, but the eastern clouds are not so dark as the western. Now, about twenty minutes after the first glow left the clouds above the sun's place, there is a second faint fuscous or warm brown glow on the edges of the dark clouds there, sudden and distinct, and it fades again, and it is early starlight, but the tops of the eastern clouds still are white, reflecting the day. The cream-color grows more yellowish or amber. About three quarters of an hour after sunset the evening red is deepest, *i. e.* a general atmospheric redness close to the west horizon. There is more of it, after all, than I expected, for the day has been clear and rather cool, and the evening red is what was the blue haze by day. The moon, now in her first quarter, now begins to preside, — her light to prevail, — though for the most part eclipsed by clouds. As the light in the west fades, the sky there, seen between the clouds, has a singular clarity and serenity.

July 24. The cardinal-flower probably open to-day. The quails are heard whistling this morning near the village.

It would be well if the false preacher of Christianity were always met and balked by a superior, more living and elastic faith in his audience; just as some missionaries in India are balked by the easiness with which the Hindoos believe every word of the miracles and prophecies, being only surprised "that they are so much less wonderful than those of their own scripture, which also they implicitly believe."

3.30 P. M. — To Goose Pond.

Is that slender narrow-leaved weed which is just coming into flower everywhere the *Erigeron Canadensis* which has spread so far and wide? Not only blue-curls but wormwood, both aromatic herbs, are seen preparing for their reign: the former a few inches high now over all fields, which has reserved itself so long; and most do not recognize it, but you stoop and pluck it and are thankful for the reminiscence of autumn which its aroma affords; the latter, still larger, shows itself on all compost-heaps and in all gardens, where the chenopodium and amaranth are already rank. I sympathize with weeds perhaps more than with the crop they choke,

they express so much vigor. They are the truer crop which the earth more willingly bears. The ground is very dry, the berries are drying up. It is long since we have had any rain to speak of. Gardeners use the watering-pot. The sere and fallen leaves of the birches in many places redden the ground; this heat and drouth have the effect of autumn to some extent. The smooth sumach berries are red. However, there is a short, fresh green on the shorn fields, the aftermath. When the first crop of grass is off, and the aftermath springs, the year has passed its culmination.

7 P. M. — To the hills by Abel Hosmer's.

How dusty the roads! Wagons, chaises, loads of barrels, etc., all drive into the dust and are lost. The dust now, looking toward the sun, is white and handsome like a vapor in the morning, curling round the head and load of the teamster, while his dog walks obscured in it under the wagon. Even this dust is to one at a distance an agreeable object.

I heard this afternoon the cool water twitter of the goldfinch, and saw the bird. They come with the springing aftermath. It is refreshing as a cup of cold water to a thirsty man to hear them, now only one at a time. Walden has fallen about six inches from where it was a month or so ago. I found, by wading out on the bar, that it had been about six feet higher than the lowest stage I have known.

Just after sunrise this morning I noticed Hayden walking beside his team, which was slowly drawing a heavy hewn stone swung under the axle, surrounded

Vol. IV

by an atmosphere of industry, his day's work begun. Honest, peaceful industry, conserving the world, which all men respect, which society has consecrated. A reproach to all sluggards and idlers. Pausing abreast the shoulders of his oxen and half turning round, with a flourish of his merciful whip, while they gained their length on him. And I thought, such is the labor which the American Congress exists to protect, — honest, manly toil. His brow has commenced to sweat. Honest as the day is long. One of the sacred band doing the needful but irksome drudgery. Toil that makes his bread taste sweet, and keeps society sweet. The day went by, and at evening I passed a rich man's yard, who keeps many servants and foolishly spends much money while he adds nothing to the common stock, and there I saw Hayden's stone lying beside a whimsical structure intended to adorn this Lord Timothy Dexter's mansion, and the dignity forthwith departed from Hayden's labor, in my eyes.[1] I am frequently invited to survey farms in a rude manner, a very [*sic*] and insignificant labor, though I manage to get more out of it than my employers; but I am never invited by the community to do anything quite worth the while to do. How much of the industry of the boor, traced to the end, is found thus to be subserving some rich man's foolish enterprise! There is a coarse, boisterous, money-making fellow in the north part of the town who is going to build a bank wall under the hill along the edge of his meadow. The powers have put this into his head to keep him out of mischief, and he wishes

[1] [*Cape Cod, and Miscellanies*, pp. 457, 458; *Misc.*, Riv. 256, 257.]

me to spend three weeks digging there with him. The result will be that he will perchance get a little more money to hoard, or leave for his heirs to spend foolishly when he is dead. Now, if I do this, the community will commend me as an industrious and hardworking man; but, as I choose to devote myself to labors which yield more real profit, though but little money, they regard me as a loafer. But, as I do not need this police of meaningless labor to regulate me, and do not see anything absolutely praiseworthy in his undertaking, however amusing it may be to him, I prefer to finish my education at a different school.[1]

The corn now forms solid phalanxes, though the ears have not set, and, the sun going down, the shadows, even of corn-fields, fall long over the meadows, and a sweetness comes up from the shaven grass, and the crickets creak more loud in the new-springing grass. Just after sunset I notice that a thin veil of clouds, far in the east, beyond the nearer and heavier dark-gray masses, glows a fine rose-color, like the inner bark or lining of some evergreens. The clear, solemn western sky till far into night was framed by a dark line of clouds with a heavy edge, curving across the northwest sky, at a considerable height, separating the region of day from that of night. Lay on a lichen-covered hill which looked white in the moonlight.

July 25. 4 A. M. — To Cliffs.

This early twitter or breathing of chip-birds in the dawn sounds like something organic in the earth. This

[1] [*Cape Cod, and Miscellanies*, pp. 456, 457; *Misc.*, Riv. 255, 256.]

is a morning celebrated by birds. Our bluebird sits on the peak of the house and warbles as in the spring, but as he does not now by day. This morning is all the more glorious for a white fog, which, though not universal, is still very extensive over all lowlands, some fifty feet high or more, though there was none at ten last night. There are white cobwebs on the grass. The battalions of the fog are continually on the move.

How hardy are cows that lie in the fog chewing the cud all night! They wake up with no stiffness in their limbs. They are indifferent to fogs as frogs to water; like hippopotami, fitted are they to dwell ever on the river bank of this world, fitted to meadows and their vicissitudes. I see where, in pastures of short, firm turf, they have pulled up the grass by the roots, and it lies scattered in small tufts. To anticipate a little, when I return this way I find two farmers loading their cart with dirt, and they are so unmanly as to excuse themselves to me for working this Sunday morning by saying with a serious face that they are burying a cow which died last night after some months of sickness, — which, however, they unthinkingly admit that they killed last night, being the most convenient time for them, and I see that they are now putting more loads of soil over her body to save the manure. How often men will betray their sense of guilt, and hence their actual guilt, by their excuses, where no guilt necessarily was. I remarked that it must be cold for a cow lying in such fogs all night, but one answered, properly, " Well, I don't know how it may be with a sick cow, but it won't hurt a well critter any."

hills are seen as islands, great bays of the sea, many miles across, where the largest fleets would find ample room and in which countless farms and farmhouses are immersed. The fog rises highest over the channel of the river and over the ponds in the woods which are thus revealed. I clearly distinguish where White Pond lies by this sign, and various other ponds, methinks, to which I have walked ten or twelve miles distant, and I distinguish the course of the Assabet far in the west and southwest beyond the woods. Every valley is densely packed with the downy vapor. What levelling on a great scale is done thus for the eye! The fog rises to the top of Round Hill in the Sudbury meadows, whose sunburnt yellow grass makes it look like a low sand-bar in the ocean, and I can judge thus pretty accurately what hills are higher than this by their elevation above the surface of the fog. Every meadow and watercourse makes an arm of this bay. The primeval banks make thus a channel which only the fogs of late summer and autumn fill. The Wayland hills make a sort of promontory or peninsula like some Nahant. As I look across thither, I think of the sea monsters that swim in that sea and of the wrecks that strew the bottom, many fathom deep, where, in an hour, when this sea dries up, farms will smile and farmhouses be revealed. A certain thrilling vastness or wasteness it now suggests. This is one of those ambrosial, white, ever-memorable fogs presaging fair weather. It produces the most picturesque and grandest effects as it rises, and travels hither and thither, enveloping and concealing trees and forests and hills. It is lifted up

The ditch stonecrop is abundant in the now dry pool by the roadside near Hubbard's.

From Fair Haven Hill, the sun having risen, I see great wreaths of fog far northeast, revealing the course of the river, a noble sight, as it were the river elevated, or rather the ghost of the ample stream that once flowed to ocean between these now distant uplands in another geological period, filling the broad meadows, — the dews saved to the earth by this great Musketaquid condenser, refrigerator. And now the rising sun makes glow with downiest white the ample wreaths, which rise higher than the highest trees. The farmers that lie slumbering on this their day of rest, how little do they know of this stupendous pageant! The bright, fresh aspect of the woods glistening with moisture when the early sun falls on them. (As I came along, the whole earth resounded with the crowing of cocks, from the eastern unto the western horizon, and as I passed a yard, I saw a white rooster on the topmost rail of a fence pouring forth his challenges for destiny to come on. This salutation was travelling round the world; some six hours since had resounded through England, France, and Spain; then the sun passed over a belt of silence where the Atlantic flows, except a clarion here and there from some cooped-up cock upon the waves, till greeted with a general all-hail along the Atlantic shore.) Looking now from the rocks, the fog is a perfect sea over the great Sudbury meadows in the southwest, commencing at the base of this Cliff and reaching to the hills south of Wayland, and further still to Framingham, through which only the tops of the higher

now into quite a little white mountain over Fair Haven Bay, and, even on its skirts, only the tops of the highest pines are seen above it, and all adown the river it has an uneven outline like a rugged mountain ridge; in one place some rainbow tints, and far, far in the south horizon, near the further verge of the sea (over Saxonville?) it is heaved up into great waves, as if there were breakers there. In the meanwhile the wood thrush and the jay and the robin sing around me here, and birds are heard singing from the midst of the fog. And in one short hour this sea will all evaporate and the sun be reflected from farm windows on its green bottom.

It is a rare music, the earliest bee's hum amid the flowers, revisiting the flower-bells just after sunrise.

Of flowers observed before June 11th the following I know or think to be still in blossom, *viz.* : —

Stellaria media	⎫	Nuphars, both not numerous
Shepherd's-purse	⎬ probably	*Ranunculus Purshii* ? ?
Potentilla Cana-	⎭	Ribwort
densis [1]		Cotton-grass, common
Columbine ?		*Rubus Canadensis* ?
Hedyotis		Cistus, very scarce
Grasses and sedges		Canada snapdragon
Sorrel ? ?		*Potentilla argentea*, not very
Trifolium procumbens, yellow		common ?
clover		Whiteweed, may be here and there
Celandine		White clover
Red clover ⎫ in favorable moist		Meadow-rue, very common
Tall crowfoot ⎭ and shady places		High blackberry ?
Forget-me-not, common		Bitter-sweet, still
Hypoxis erecta		Yarrow, very common
Blue-eyed grass, scarce		Knawel ?
Sarracenia ? ? [2]		*Utricularia vulgaris* ?

[1] [Two interrogation points in pencil here.]   [2] No petals?

Gone out of blossom since June 10th (of those observed after June 10th before June 24th) the following: —

Iris versicolor	*Aralia hispida*
Broom-rape?	Grape-vines
Fumaria?	Moss rose and early straight-
Viburnums	thorned (?)
Dracæna	Pyrolas?
Carrion-flower	Swamp-pink? may linger some-
Cornels	where
Silene antirrhina??	*Prinos lævigatus*
Erigeron strigosus	Pogonia?
Waxwork?	*Iris Virginica*
Large purple orchises	Elder?
Hound's-tongue?	Mitchella?
Tufted loosestrife	Diervilla
Four-leaved loosestrife??	Mountain laurel
A veronica	Sweet-briar

Of those observed between June 10th and 24th the following are still *common* : —

Marsh speedwell	Butter-and-eggs
Floating-heart	Prunella
Mullein	Epilobium
Dogsbane	Some or most galiums
Cow-wheat	

July 26. By my intimacy with nature I find myself withdrawn from man. My interest in the sun and the moon, in the morning and the evening, compels me to solitude.

The grandest picture in the world is the sunset sky. In your higher moods what man is there to meet? You are of necessity isolated. The mind that perceives clearly any natural beauty is in that instant withdrawn

from human society. My desire for society is infinitely increased; my fitness for any actual society is diminished.

Went to Cambridge and Boston to-day. Dr. Harris says that my great moth is the *Attacus luna;* may be regarded as one of several emperor moths. They are rarely seen, being very liable to be snapped up by birds. Once, as he was crossing the College Yard, he saw the wings of one coming down, which reached the ground just at his feet. What a tragedy! The wings came down as the only evidence that such a creature had soared, — wings large and splendid, which were designed to bear a precious burthen through the upper air. So most poems, even epics, are like the wings come down to earth, while the poet whose adventurous flight they evidence has been snapped up [by] the ravenous vulture of this world. If this moth ventures abroad by day, some bird will pick out the precious cargo and let the sails and rigging drift, as when the sailor meets with a floating spar and sail and reports a wreck seen in a certain latitude and longitude. For what were such tender and defenseless organizations made? The one I had, being put into a large box, beat itself — its wings, etc. — all to pieces in the night, in its efforts to get out, depositing its eggs, nevertheless, on the sides of its prison. Perchance the entomologist never saw an entire specimen, but, as he walked one day, the wings of a larger species than he had ever seen came fluttering down. The wreck of an argosy in the air.

He tells me the glow-worms are first seen, he thinks, in the last part of August. Also that there is a large

Vol. IV

and brilliant glow-worm found here, more than an inch long, as he measured it to me on his finger, but rare.

Perhaps the sunset glows are sudden in proportion as the edges of the clouds are abrupt, when the sun finally reaches such a point that his rays can be reflected from them.

At 10 P. M. I see high columns of fog, formed in the lowlands and lit by the moon, preparing to charge this higher ground. It is as if the sky reached the solid ground there, for they shut out the woods.

July 27. *Tuesday.* 4 P. M. — To Assabet behind Lee place.

It is pleasing to behold at this season contrasted shade and sunshine on the side of neighboring hills. They are not so attractive to the eye when all in the shadow of a cloud or wholly open to the sunshine. Each must enhance the other.

That the luxury of walking in the river may be perfect it must be very warm, such as are few days even in July, so that the breeze on those parts of the body that have just been immersed may not produce the least chilliness. It cannot be too warm, so that, with a shirt to fend the sun from your back, you may walk with perfect indifference, or rather with equal pleasure, alternately in deep and in shallow water. Both water and air must be unusually warm; otherwise we shall feel no impulse to cast ourselves into and remain in the stream. To-day it is uncomfortably cool for such a walk. It is very pleasant to walk up and down the stream, however, studying the further bank, which is six

or seven feet high and completely covered with verdure of various kinds. I observe grape-vines with green clusters almost fully grown hanging over the water, and hazelnut husks are fully formed and are richly, autumnally, significant. *Viburnum dentatum*, elder, and red-stemmed cornel, all with an abundance of green berries, help clothe the bank, and the *Asclepias incarnata* and meadow-rue fill the crevices. Above all there is the cardinal-flower just opened, close to the water's edge, remarkable for its intense scarlet color, contrasting with the surrounding green.

I see young breams in small schools, only one inch long, light-colored and semitransparent as yet, long in proportion to their depth. Some two inches long are ludicrously deep already, like little halibuts, making the impression, by their form, of vast size like halibuts or whales. They appear to be attended and guarded still by their parents. What innumerable enemies they have to encounter!

The sun on the bottom is indispensable, and you must have your back to it.

Woodcocks have been common by the streams and springs in woods for some weeks.

Aster dumosus (?) by wood-paths.

A quarter before seven P. M. — To Cliffs.

It has been a clear, cool, breezy day for the season. There is only one white bar of cloud in the north. I now perceive the peculiar scent of the corn-fields. The corn is just high enough, and this hour is favorable. I should think the ears had hardly set yet. Half an hour before sundown, you perceive the cool, damp air in valleys surrounded by woods, where dew is already formed.

I am sure that if I call for a companion in my walk I have relinquished in my design some closeness of communion with Nature. The walk will surely be more commonplace. The inclination for society indicates a distance from Nature. I do not design so wild and mysterious a walk.

The bigoted and sectarian forget that without religion or devotion of some kind nothing great was ever accomplished.

On Fair Haven Hill. The slight distraction of picking berries is favorable to a mild, abstracted, poetic mood, to sequestered or transcendental thinking. I return ever more fresh to my mood from such slight interruptions.

All the clouds in the sky are now close to the west horizon, so that the sun is nearly down before they are reached and lighted or gilded. Wachusett, free of clouds, has a fine purplish tinge, as if the juice of grapes had been squeezed over it, darkening into blue. I hear the scratching sound of a worm at work in this hardwood-pile on which I sit.

We are most disturbed by the sun's dazzle when it is lowest. Now the upper edge of that low blue bank is gilt where the sun has disappeared, leaving a glory in the horizon through which a few cloudy peaks send raylike shadows. Now a slight rosy blush is spreading north and south over the horizon sky and tingeing a few small scattered clouds in the east. A blue tinge southward makes the very edge of the earth there a moun-

tain. That low bank of cloud in the west is now exactly the color of the mountains, a dark blue. We should think sacredly, with devotion. That is one thing, at least, we may do magnanimously. May not every man have some private affair which he can conduct greatly, unhurriedly? The river is silvery, as it were plated and polished smooth, with the slightest possible tinge of gold, to-night. How beautiful the meanders of a river, thus revealed! How beautiful hills and vales, the whole surface of the earth a succession of these great cups, falling away from dry or rocky edges to gelid green meadows and water in the midst, where night already is setting in! The thrush, now the sun is apparently set, fails not to sing. Have I heard the veery lately? All glow on the clouds is gone, except from one higher, small, rosy pink or flesh-colored isle. The sun is now probably set. There are no clouds on high to reflect a golden light into the river.

How cool and assuaging the thrush's note after the fever of the day! I doubt if they have anything so richly wild in Europe. So long a civilization must have banished it. It will only be heard in America, perchance, while our star is in the ascendant. I should be very much surprised if I were to hear in the strain of the nightingale such unexplored wildness and fertility, reaching to sundown, inciting to emigration. Such a bird must itself have emigrated long ago. Why, then, was I born in America? I might ask.

I should like to ask the assessors what is the value of that blue mountain range in the northwest horizon to Concord, and see if they would laugh or seriously

set about calculating it. How poor, comparatively, should we be without it! It would be descending to the scale of the merchant to say it is worth its weight in gold. The privilege of beholding it, as an ornament, a suggestion, a provocation, a heaven on earth. If I were one of the fathers of the town I would not sell this right which we now enjoy for all the merely material wealth and prosperity conceivable. If need were, we would rather all go down together.

The huckleberry-bird as usual, and the nighthawk squeaks and booms, and the bullfrog trumps, just before the earliest star. The evening red is much more remarkable than the morning red. The solemnity of the evening sky! I turn round, and there shines the moon, silvering the small clouds which have gathered; she makes nothing red.

New creaking or shrilling from crickets (?) for a long time past, more fine and piercing than the other. *Aster dumosus* (?) by wood-paths.

July 28. P. M. — To Yellow Pine Lake.

Epilobium coloratum, roadside just this side of Dennis's. Water lobelia, is it, that C. shows me? There is a yellowish light now from a low, tufted, yellowish, broad-leaved grass, in fields that have been mown. A June-like, breezy air. The large ⋀ shaped sagittaria out, a large crystalline-white ⋁ three-petalled flower. Enough has not been said of the beauty of the shrub oak leaf (*Quercus ilicifolia*), of a thick, firm texture, for the most part uninjured by insects, intended to last all winter; of a glossy green above

and now silky downy beneath, fit for a wreath or crown. The leaves of the chinquapin oak might be intermixed. Grasshoppers are very abundant, several to every square foot in some fields. I observed some leaves of woodbine which had not risen from the ground, turned a beautiful bright red, perhaps from heat and drought, though it was in a low wood. This *Ampelopsis quinquefolia* is in blossom. Is it identical with that about R. W. E.'s posts, which was in blossom July 13th? *Aster Radula* (?) in J. P. Brown's meadow. *Solidago altissima* (?) beyond the Corner Bridge, out some days at least, but not rough-hairy. Goldenrod and asters have *fairly* begun; *i. e.* there are several kinds of each out. What is that slender hieracium or aster-like plant in woods on Corner road with lanceolate, coarsely feather-veined leaves, sessile and remotely toothed; minute, clustered, imbricate buds (?) or flowers and buds? Paniced hieracium? [1]

The evenings are now sensibly longer, and the cooler weather makes them improvable.

July 29. P. M. — To Burnt Plain.

The forget-me-not still by the brook. Floating-heart was very common yesterday in J. P. Brown's woodland pond. *Gaultheria procumbens* in bloom on this year's plants. The *Mitchella repens* shows small green fruit, and the trientalis is gone to seed, black in a small white globule. *Proserpinaca palustris* for how long? *Euphorbia maculata* how long? I see a bluet still in damp ground. Apples now by their size remind me of

[1] Yes.

the harvest. I see a few roses in moist places with short curved thorns and narrow bracts. *Eupatorium perfoliatum* just beginning. The *Ranunculus repens* var. *filiformis* is still very abundant on the river-shore. I see a geranium leaf turned red in the shade of a copse; the same color with the woodbine seen yesterday. These leaves interest me as much as flowers. I should like to have a complete list of those that are the first to turn red or yellow. How attractive is color, especially red; kindred this with the color of fruits in the harvest and skies in the evening. The colors which some rather obscure leaves assume in the fall in dark copses or by the roadside, for the most part unobserved, interest me more than their flowers. There is also that plant with a lake or claret under side to its radical leaves in early spring. What is that?[1]

It did me good this afternoon to see the large soft-looking roots of alders occupying a small brook in a narrow shady swamp, laid bare at a distance from their base, covered with white warts sometimes on a green ground. With what rapacity they grasped, with what tenacity they held to life! also filling the wet soil with innumerable fibres, ready to resist the severest drought.

Blue-curls and wormwood springing up everywhere, with their aroma, — especially the first, — are quite restorative. It is time we had a little wormwood to flavor the somewhat tasteless or cloying summer, which palls upon the taste. That common rigid narrow-leaved faint-purplish aster in dry woods by shrub oak paths, *Aster linariifolius* of Bigelow, but it is not *savory-*

[1] *Aster undulatus?*

leaved. I do not find it in Gray. *Lespedeza violacea*, is that under Fair Haven? It must have been out a week. Can that be *Hypericum mutilum* grown so high in Potter's low field? That is apparently *Solidago nemoralis* in dry fields. *Lechea minor?*

It is commonly said that history is a history of war, but it is at the same time a history of development. Savage nations — any of our Indian tribes, for instance — would have enough stirring incidents in their annals, wars and murders enough, surely, to make interesting anecdotes without end, such a chronicle of startling and monstrous events as fill the daily papers and suit the appetite of barrooms; but the annals of such a tribe do not furnish the materials for history.

July 30. The fore part of this month was the warmest weather we have had; the last part, sloping toward autumn, has reflected some of its coolness, for we are very forward to anticipate the fall. Perhaps I may say the spring culminated with the commencement of haying, and the summer side of the year in mid-July.

3.30 P. M. — To Flint's Pond.

How long is it since I heard a veery? Do they go, or become silent, when the goldfinch heralds the autumn? Do not all flowers that blossom after mid-July remind us of the fall? After midsummer we have a belated feeling as if we had all been idlers, and are forward to see in each sight and hear in each sound some presage of the fall, just as in middle age man anticipates the end of life. Tansy is a prevalent flower now; dogsbane still common. Nighthawks squeak and

Vol. IV

fly low over Thrush Alley at 4 P. M. A small purple orchis (*Platanthera psycodes*), quite small, so that I perceive what I called by this name before must have been the *fimbriata*. The sand cherry is a handsome fruit but not very palatable. *Hedeoma pulegioides*, pennyroyal, is out of bloom apparently for some time; in the ruts of an old path through a copse. *Lobelia Dortmanna*, water lobelia, apparently for some time. A small kind of potamogeton which I have not examined before, most like the *P. hybridus*, but with a cylindrical spike.

The ripple-marks on the east shore of Flint's are nearly parallel firm ridges in the white sand, one inch or more apart. They are very distinctly felt by the naked feet of the wader. What are those remarkable spherical masses of fine grass or fibres looking like the nests of water mice, washing toward the shore at the bottom amid the weeds? Quite numerous over a long shore. I thought they must be nests of mice till I found some solid.

The *Clethra alnifolia* is just beginning, — as the swamp-pink shows its last white petals, — but August will have its beauty. It is important as one of the later flowers. High blackberries ripe, apparently for a day or two. That succulent plant by Tuttle's sluice appears to be *Sedum Telephium*, garden orpine, or live-forever, called also house-leek, since it will grow if only one end is tucked under a shingle.

What a gem is a bird's egg, especially a blue or a green one, when you see one broken or whole in the woods! I noticed a small blue egg this afternoon washed up by Flint's Pond and half buried by white

sand, and as it lay there, alternately wet and dry, no color could be fairer, no gem could have a more advantageous or favorable setting. Probably it was shaken out of some nest which overhung the water. I frequently meet with broken egg-shells where a crow, perchance, or some other thief has been marauding. And is not that shell something very precious that houses that winged life?

Caught in a thunder-shower, when south of Flint's Pond. Came back by C. Smith's road. Stood under thick trees. I care not how hard it rains, if it does not rain more than fifteen minutes. I can shelter myself effectually in the woods. It is a grand sound, that of the rain on the leaves of the forest a quarter of a mile distant, approaching. But I got wet through, after all, being caught where there were no trees.

July 31. P. M. — To Assabet over Nawshawtuct.

There is more shadow under the edges of woods and copses now. The foliage appears to have increased so that the shadows are heavier, and perhaps it is this that makes it cooler, especially morning and evening, though it may be as warm as ever at noon. Saw but one *Lysimachia stricta* left in the meadows, the meadow-sweet meadows. The green cranberries are half formed. The absence of flowers, the shadows, the wind, the green cranberries, etc., are autumnal. The river has risen a foot or so since its lowest early in the month. The water is quite cool. Methinks it cannot be so warm again this year. After that torrid season the river rises in the first rains and is much cooled.

The springs are mostly buried on its shore. The high blueberry has a singularly cool flavor. The alder locust again reminds me of autumn. Can that low blackberry which has, I think, a rather wrinkled leaf and bears dense masses of lively berries now, commonly in cool moist ground, be the same with the common? *Eupatorium purpureum* has just begun, and probably the *ovate*, etc., but I suspect no entire corymb is out.

IV

AUGUST, 1852

(ÆT. 35)

Aug. 1. P. M. — To Conantum.

Is not that the small-flowered hypericum? The berries of what I have called the alternate-leaved cornel are now ripe, a very dark blue — blue-black — and round, but dropping off prematurely, leaving handsome *red* cymes, which adorn the trees from a distance. *Chelone glabra* just out. Singing birds are scarce. I have not heard the catbird or the thrush for a long time. The peawai sings yet. *Early* apples are ripe, and the sopsivine scents my handkerchief before I have perceived any odor from the orchards.[1] The small rough sunflower (*Helianthus divaricatus*) tells of August heats; also *Helianthus annuus*, common sunflower. May it not stand for the character of August? Found a long, dense spike of the *Orchis psycodes*. Much later this than the great orchis. The same, only smaller and denser, not high-colored enough.

Aug. 2. At 5.30 this morning, saw from Nawshawtuct the trees on the Great Meadows against and rising out of the dispersing wreaths of fog, on which the sun was shining.

Just before sunset. At the window. — The clear sky

[1] [See *Excursions*, p. 295; Riv. 362.]

in the west, the sunset window, has a cloud both above and below. The edges of these clouds about the sun glow golden, running into fuscous. A dark shower is vanishing in the southeast. There will commonly be a window in the west. The sun enters the low cloud, but still is reflected brightly, though more brassily perhaps, from the edges of the upper cloud. There is as yet no redness in the heavens. Now the glow becomes redder, tingeing new edges of the clouds near and higher up the sky, as they were dipped in an invisible reddening stream of light, into a rosy bath. Far in the southwest, along the horizon, is now the fairer rose-tinted or flesh-colored sky, the west being occupied by a dark cloud mainly, and, still further south, a huge boulder shines like a chalk cliff tinged with pink. The rear of the departing shower is blushing.

Before this, at 2 P. M., walked to Burnt Plain.

I do not remember to have heard tree-toads for a long time. We have had a day or two (and here is another) of hanging clouds, not threatening rain, yet affording shade, so that you are but little incommoded by the sun in a long walk. Varied dark and downy cumulus, fair-weather clouds, well-nigh covering the sky, with dark bases and white glowing fronts and brows. You see the blue sky on every side between clouds. Is this peculiar to this season, early August? The whole cope equally divided into sky and cloud. Merely a rich drapery in the sky. Arras or curtains to adorn the gorgeous days. The midday is very silent. *Trichostema dichotomum* just out. The common St. John's-wort is now scarce. The reddening sumach

berries are of rare beauty. Are they crimson or vermilion? Some sumach leaves, where the stem has broken, have turned red. Blue-eyed grass lingers still. Is the dodder out of bloom, or merely budded? It is a new era with the flowers when the small purple fringed orchis, as now, is found in shady swamps standing along the brooks. It appears to be alone of its class. Not to be overlooked, it has so much flower, though not so high-colored as the arethusa. Together with the side-flowering skull-cap, etc. The arethusas, pogonias, calopogons all gone, and violets of all kinds.

We had a little rain after all, but I walked through a long alder copse, where the leafy tops of the alders spread like umbrellas over my head, and heard the harmless pattering of the rain on my roof.

Wachusett from Fair Haven Hill looks like this: —

the dotted line being the top of the surrounding forest. Even on the low principle that misery loves company and is relieved by the consciousness that it is shared by many, and therefore is not so insignificant and trivial, after all, this blue mountain outline is valuable. In many moods it is cheering to look across hence to that blue rim of the earth, and be reminded of the invisible towns and communities, for the most part also unremembered, which lie in the further and deeper hollows between me and those hills. Towns of sturdy uplandish fame, where some of the morning and primal vigor still lingers, I trust. Ashburnham, Rindge,

Jaffrey, etc., — it is cheering to think that it is with such communities that we survive or perish. Yes, the mountains do thus impart, in the mere prospect of them, some of the New Hampshire vigor. The melancholy man who had come forth to commit suicide on this hill might be saved by being thus reminded how many brave and contented lives are lived between him and the horizon. Those hills extend our plot of earth; they make our native valley or indentation in the earth so much the larger. There is a whitish line along the base of Wachusett more particularly, as if the reflection of bare cliffs there in the sun. Undoubtedly it is the slight vaporous haze in the atmosphere seen edgewise just above the top of the forest, though it is a clear day. It, this line, makes the mountains loom, in fact, a faint whitish line separating the mountains from their bases and the rest of the globe.

Aug. 3. The *Hypericum Sarothra* appears to be out.

12 M. At the east window. — A temperate noon. I hear a cricket creak in the shade; also the sound of a distant piano. The music reminds me of imagined heroic ages; it suggests such ideas of human life and the field which the earth affords as the few noblest passages of poetry. Those few interrupted strains which reach me through the trees suggest the same thoughts and aspirations that all melody, by whatever sense appreciated, has ever done. I am affected. What coloring variously fair and intense our life admits of! How a thought will mould and paint it! Impressed by some vague vision,

as it were, elevated into a more glorious sphere of life, we no longer know this, we can deny its existence. We say we are enchanted, perhaps. But what I am impressed by is the fact that this enchantment is no delusion. So far as truth is concerned, it is a fact such as what we *call* our actual existence, but it is a far higher and more glorious fact. It is evidence of such a sphere, of such possibilities. It is its truth and reality that affect me. A thrumming of piano-strings beyond the gardens and through the elms. At length the melody steals into my being. I know not when it began to occupy me. By some fortunate coincidence of thought or circumstance I am attuned to the universe, I am fitted to hear, my being moves in a sphere of melody, my fancy and imagination are excited to an inconceivable degree. This is no longer the dull earth on which I stood. It is possible to live a grander life here; already the steed is stamping, the knights are prancing; already our thoughts bid a proud farewell to the so-called actual life and its humble glories. Now this is the verdict of a soul in health. But the soul diseased says that its own vision and life alone is true and sane. What a different aspect will courage put upon the face of things! This suggests what a perpetual flow of spirit would produce.

Of course, no man was ever made so truly generous, was so expanded by any vile draught, but that he might be equally and more expanded by imbibing a saner and wholesomer draught than ever he has swallowed. There is a wine that does not intoxicate; there is a pure juice of the grape, and unfermented. What kind of draught is that which the aspirant soul imbibes?

Vol. IV

In every part of Great Britain are discovered the traces of the Romans, — their funereal urns, their lamps, their roads, their dwellings. But New England, at least, is not based on any Roman ruins. We have not to lay the foundation of our houses in the ashes of a former civilization.

P. M. — To Boulder Field.

Vernonia Noveboracensis, iron-weed, by Flint's Bridge, began to open by July 31st; a tall plant with a broad fastigiate corymb of rich dark-purple thistle-like flowers, the middle ones opening first. Saw two haycarts and teams cross the shallow part of the river in front of N. Barrett's, empty, to the Great Meadows. An interesting sight. The Great Meadows alive with farmers getting their hay. I could count four or five great loads already loaded in different parts. *Clematis Virginiana* just begun. Observed a low prostrate veronica with roundish, regularly opposite leaves, somewhat crenulate, and white flowers veined with purple, in damp, cool grass. Think I have not seen it before. A houstonia still. The huckleberries in the low ground by the river beyond Flint's are large and fresh. The black shine as with a gloss, and the blue are equally large.

Looking down into the singular bare hollows from the back of hill near here, the paths made by the cows in the sides of the hills, going round the hollows, made gracefully curving lines in the landscape, ribbing it. The curves, both the rising and falling of the path and its winding to right and left, are agreeable.

What remarkable customs still prevail at funerals! The chief mourner, though it may be a maiden who has lost her lover, consents to be made a sort of puppet and is by them put forward to walk behind the corpse in the street, before the eyes of all, at a time which should be sacred to grief; is, beside, compelled, as it were, to attend to the coarse and unfeeling, almost inevitably to her impertinent, words of consolation or admonition, so called, of whatever clerical gentleman may be in the neighborhood. Friends and neighbors of the family should bury their dead. It is fitting that they should walk in procession with parade and even assumed solemnity. It is for them to pay this kind of respect to the dead, that it be not left to hirelings alone. It is soothing to the feelings of the absent mourners. They may fitly listen to the words of the preacher, but the feelings of the mourners should be respected.

Spergularia rubra, spurry sandwort, a pretty, minute red flower spreading flat by roadside, nearly out of blossom. Apparently *Urtica dioica*, but not very stinging, may have been out some time. *Hypericum mutilum*, probably last part of July.

Took that interesting view from one of the boulder rocks toward Lincoln Hills, between Hubbard's Hill and Grove and Barrett's, whose back or north and wooded side is in front, a few oaks and elms in front and on the right, and some fine boulders slumbering in the foreground. It is a peculiar part of the town, — the old bridle-road plains further east. A great tract here of unimproved and unfrequented country, the boulders sometimes crowned with barberry bushes. I hear crows, the robin, huckleberry-birds, young bluebirds, etc.

The sun coming out of a cloud and shining brightly on patches of cudweed reminds me of frost on the grass in the morning. A splendid entire rainbow after a slight shower, with two reflections of it, outermost broad red, passing through yellow to green, then narrow red, then blue or indigo (not plain what), then faint red again. It is too remarkable to be remarked on.

Aug. 4. To Walden by poorhouse road.

Have had a gentle rain, and now with a lowering sky, but still I hear the cricket. He seems to chirp from a new depth toward autumn, new *lieferungs* of the fall. The singular thought-inducing stillness after a gentle rain like this. It has allayed all excitement. I hear the singular watery twitter of the goldfinch, *ter tweeter e et* or *e ee*, as it ricochets over, he and his russet (?) female. The chirp of the constant chip-bird and the plaintive strain of the lark, also. I must make a list of those birds which, like the lark and the robin, if they do not stay all the year, are heard to sing longest of those that migrate. The bobolink and thrasher, etc., are silent. English-haying is long since done, only meadow-haying going on now. I smell the fragrant life-everlasting, now almost out; another scent that reminds me of the autumn. The little bees have gone to sleep amid the clethra blossoms in the rain and are not yet aroused. What is that weed somewhat like wormwood and amaranth on the ditch by roadside

here?[1] What the vine now budded like clematis in the wall? Most huckleberries and blueberries and low blackberries are in their prime now.

A pleasant time to behold a small lake in the woods is in the intervals of a gentle rain-storm at this season, when the air and water are perfectly still, but the sky still overcast; first, because the lake is very smooth at such a time, second, as the atmosphere is so shallow and contracted, being low-roofed with clouds, the lake as a lower heaven is much larger in proportion to it. With its glassy reflecting surface, it is somewhat more heavenly and more full of light than the regions of the air above it. There is a pleasing vista southward over and through a wide indentation in the hills which form its shore, where their opposite sides slope to each other so as to suggest a stream flowing from it in that direction through a wooded valley, toward some distant blue hills in Sudbury and Framingham, Goodman's and Nobscot; that is, you look over and between the low near and green hills to the distant, which are tinged with blue, the heavenly color. Such is what is fair to mortal eyes. In the meanwhile the wood thrush sings in the woods around the lake.[2]

Pycnanthemum lanceolatum, probably as early as the other variety, *Hypericum corymbosum*. Spotted St. John's-wort, some time in July.

History has not been so truthfully or livingly, convincingly, written but that we still need the evidence, the oral testimony of an eye-witness. Hence I am sin-

[1] *Acalypha Virginica*, three-seeded mercury.
[2] [*Walden*, p. 96; Riv. 136, 137.]

gularly surprised when I read of the celebrated Henry Jenkins (who lived to be some one hundred and sixty nine years old), who used to preface his conversation in this wise, "About a hundred and thirty years ago, when I was butler to Lord Conyers," etc. I am surprised to find that I needed this testimony to be convinced of the reality of Lord Conyers's existence.

Aug. 5. I can tell the extent to which a man has heard music by the faith he retains in the trivial and mean, even by the importance he attaches to what is called the actual world. Any memorable strains will have unsettled so low a faith and substituted a higher. Men profess to be lovers of music, but for the most part they give no evidence in their opinions and lives that they have heard it. It would not leave them narrow-minded and bigoted.

Hearing that one with whom I was acquainted had committed suicide, I said I did not know when I had planted the seed of that fact that I should hear of it.

P. M. — To C. Miles's blueberry swamp.

There is a pond-hole there perfectly covered with the leaves of the floating-heart and whiter than ever with its small white flowers, as if a slight large-flaked snow had fallen on it. The ground rises gently on every side, and first by the edge grow a few gratiolas, then the *Lysimachia stricta*, with a few blossoms left, then, a rod or two distant, in the higher rows of this natural coliseum, the red-panicled racemes of the hardhack rise. That is a glorious swamp of Miles's, — the more open parts, where the dwarf andromeda prevails. Now, per-

haps, an olivaceous green is the tint, not at all reddish, the lambkill and the bluish or glaucous rhodora and the pyrus intermixed making an extensive rich moss-like bed, in which you sink three feet to a dry bottom of moss or dead twigs, or, if peaty ground, it is covered with cup lichens; surrounded all by wild-looking woods, with the wild white spruce advancing into it and the pitch pine here and there, and high blueberry and tall pyrus and holly and other bushes under their countenance and protection. These are the wildest and richest gardens that we have. Such a depth of verdure into which you sink. They were never cultivated by any. Descending wooded hills, you come suddenly to this beautifully level pasture, comparatively open, with a close border of high blueberry bushes. You cannot believe that this can possibly abut on any cultivated field. Some wood or pasture, at least, must intervene. Here is a place, at last, which no woodchopper nor farmer frequents and to which no cows stray, perfectly wild, where the bittern and the hawk are undisturbed. The men, women, and children who perchance come hither blueberrying in their season get more than the value of the berries in the influences of the scene. How wildly rich and beautiful hang on high there the blueberries which might so easily be poisonous, the cool blue clusters high in air. Choke-berries, fair to the eye but scarcely palatable, hang far above your head, weighing down the bushes. The wild holly berry, perhaps the most beautiful of berries, hanging by slender threads from its more light and open bushes and more delicate leaves. The bushes, eight feet high, are black with choke-berries, and there are no wild animals to eat them.

I cannot sufficiently admire the rhexia, one of the highest-colored purple flowers, but difficult to bring home in its perfection, with its fugacious petals. The *Hieracium scabrum* is just opening. Large spotted polygonum by the river, with white flowers on a slender spike. *Lechea racemulosa* (?) of Bigelow, — not in Gray, — a fine, almost leafless, bushy, sometimes reddish, low plant in dry fields.

Aug. 6. 5 A. M. — I do not hear this morning the breathing of chip-birds nor the song of robins. Are the mornings now thus ushered in? Are they as spring-like? Has not the year grown old? Methinks we do ourselves, at any rate, somewhat tire of the season and observe less attentively and with less interest the opening of new flowers and the song of the birds. It is the signs of the fall that affect us most. It is hard to live in the summer content with it.

To Cliffs.

How different the feeble twittering of the birds here at sunrise from the full quire of the spring! Only the wood thrush, a huckleberry-bird or two, or chickadee, the scream of a flicker or a jay, or the caw of a crow, and commonly only an alarmed note of a robin. A solitary peawai may be heard, perchance, or a red-eye, but no thrashers, or catbirds, or oven-birds, or the jingle of the chewink. I hear the ominous twittering of the goldfinch over all.

The village is seen through a thin veil of fog. I just

distinguish the tree-tops beneath me in the southwest, and the light-colored river through the mist, which is gathering and preparing to retreat before the sun. From a tree-top I see the surface of Walden, whose shores are laid bare, the sun being directly opposite, and therefore the surface of the lake is a bright sheen seen through some stately pines near the railroad. This bright, silvery sheen comes through the dispersing mists to me its shores being still concealed by fog, and a low white scudding mist is seen against the more distant dark clouds, drifting westward over all the forests before the sun.

Gathered some of those large, sometimes pear-shaped, sweet blue huckleberries which grow amid the rubbish where woods have just been cut.

A farmer told me that he lost a good many doves by their being trodden upon by oxen.

P. M. — To Saw Mill Brook and hill beyond.

I still remember how much bluer those early blueberries were that grew in the shade. Have just finished Gilpin's "Lakes of Cumberland." An elegant writer of English prose. I wish he would look at scenery sometimes not with the eye of an artist. It is all side screens and fore screens and near distances and broken grounds with him. I remark that in his tour through Wales, and afterward through Cumberland and Westmoreland, he never ascends to the top of a mountain, and if he gets up higher than usual, he merely says that the view is grand and amusing, as if because it was not easy to paint, or *picturesque*, it was not worth

Vol. IV

beholding, or deserving of serious attention. However, his elegant moderation, his discrimination, and real interest in nature excuse many things.

Milkweeds and trumpet-flowers are important now, to contrast with the cool, dark, shaded sides and recesses of moist copses. I see their red under the willows and alders everywhere against a dark ground. Methinks that blue, next to red, attracts us in a flower. Blue vervain is now very attractive to me, and then there is that interesting progressive history in its rising ring of blossoms. It has a story. Next to our blood is our prospect of heaven. Does not the blood in fact show blue in the covered veins and arteries, when distance lends enchantment to the view? The sight of it is more affecting than I can describe or account for.

The rainbow, after all, does not attract an attention proportionate to its singularity and beauty. Moses (?) was the last to comment on it. It is a phenomenon more aside from the common course of nature. Too distinctly a sign or symbol of something to be disregarded. What form of beauty could be imagined more striking and conspicuous? An arch of the most brilliant and glorious colors completely spanning [the] heavens before the eyes of men! Children look at it. It is wonderful that all men do not take pains to behold it. At some waterfalls it is permanent, as long as the sun shines. Plainly thus the Maker of the universe sets the seal to his covenant with men. Many articles are thus clinched. Designed to impress man. All men beholding it begin to understand the significance of the Greek epithet applied to the world, — name for the world, —

Kosmos, or beauty. It was designed to impress man. We live, as it were, within the calyx of a flower.

Methinks there are few new flowers of late. An abundance of small fruits takes their place. Summer gets to be an old story. Birds leave off singing, as flowers blossoming, *i. e.* perhaps in the same proportion. With the goldenrod comes the goldfinch. About the time his cool twitter was heard, did not the bobolink, thrasher, catbird, oven-bird, veery, etc., cease?

I see some delicate ferns, in the low damp woods by the brook, which have turned whitish at the extremity. Cohush berries have just begun to be white, as if they contained a pearly venom, — wax white with a black spot (or very dark brown), imp-eyed. The leaves of one of the cornels (alternate-leaved or else round-leaved) are, some of them, turned lake-color.

The weeds are now very high and rank in moist wood-paths and along such streams as this. I love to follow up the course of the brook and see the cardinal-flowers which stand in its midst above the rocks, their brilliant scarlet the more interesting in this open, but dark, cellar-like wood; the small purple fringed orchises with long dense spikes, all flower, — for that is often all that is seen above the leaves of other plants (is not this the last flower of this peculiar *flower* kind, — *i. e.* all flower and color, the leaves subordinated?); and the *Mimulus ringens*, abundant and handsome in these low and rather shady places. Many flowers, of course, like the last, are prominent, if you visit such scenes as this, though one who confines himself to the road may never see them.

From Smith's Hill beyond, there is as good a view of the mountains as from any place in our neighborhood, because you look across the broad valley in which Concord lies first of all. The foreground is on a larger scale and more proportionate. The Peterboro Hills are to us as good as mountains. Hence, too, I see that fair river-reach, in the north. I find a bumblebee asleep in a thistle blossom (a pasture thistle), the loiterer; having crowded himself in deep amid the dense florets, out of the reach of birds, while the sky was overcast. What a sweet couch!

As I always notice the tone of the bell when I go into a new town, so surely, methinks, I notice some peculiarity in the accent and manners of the inhabitants.

The bristly aralia berries are ripe; like the sarsaparilla, a blue black. The shorn fields are acquiring a late green or refresh [sic]. They are greener, much, than a month ago, before the grass was cut. For ten days the weather has been cool and the air full of moisture. Is it not because of the increase of vegetation, the leaves being multiplied, the weeds more rank, the shadows heavier? This is what is called dog-day weather. The water in the river and pond is quite cool, and it is more bracing and invigorating to bathe, though less luxurious. Methinks the water cannot again be as warm as it has been. *Erechthites hieracifolia*, apparently a day or two. *Lespedeza capitata. Aralia racemosa*, how long? — petty morel, spikenard, like a large sarsaparilla. *Hieracium paniculatum. Lycopus Virginicus* (with five calyx-teeth). Solidagos, *lanceolata* (?) and *puberula* (?). *Stellaria media* at R. W. E.'s. Is it the same, then,

which I saw in Cheney's garden so early? That clammy, hairy-leaved cerastium (?) I still see, with a starry white flower. Was it the *Urtica gracilis* I examined, or the common nettle? What is that plant at the brook with hairy under sides now budded?

Aug. 7. When I think of the thorough drilling to which young men are subjected in the English universities, acquiring a minute knowledge of Latin prosody and of Greek particles and accents, so that they can not only turn a passage of Homer into English prose or verse, but readily a passage of Shakespeare into Latin hexameters or elegiacs, — that this and the like of this is to be liberally educated, — I am reminded how different was the education of the actual Homer and Shakespeare. The worthies of the world and liberally educated have always, in this sense, got along with little Latin and less Greek.

At this season we have gentle rain-storms, making the aftermath green. The rich and moist English grass land looks very green after the rain, as if it were a second spring.

If I were to choose a time for a friend to make a passing visit to this world for the first time, in the full possession of all his faculties, perchance it would be at a moment when the sun was setting with splendor in the west, his light reflected far and wide through the clarified air after a rain, and a brilliant rainbow, as now, o'erarching the eastern sky. Would he be likely to think this a vulgar place to live [sic], where one would weary of existence, and be compelled to devote

his life to frivolity and dissipation? If a man travelling from world to world were to pass through this world at such a moment, would he not be tempted to take up his abode here?

We see the rainbow apparently when we are on the edge of the rain, just as the sun is setting. If we are too deep in the rain, then it will appear dim. Sometimes it is so near that I see a portion of its arch this side of the woods in the horizon, tingeing them. Sometimes we are completely within it, enveloped by it, and experience the realization of the child's wish. The obvious colors are red and green. Why green? It is astonishing how brilliant the red may be. What is the difference between that red and the ordinary red of the evening sky? Who does not feel that here is a phenomenon which natural philosophy alone is inadequate to explain? The use of the rainbow, who has described it?

Aug. 8. 5 a. m. — Awoke into a rosy fog. I was enveloped by the skirts of Aurora.

To the Cliffs.

The small dewdrops rest on the *Asclepias pulchra* by the roadside like gems, and the flower has lost half its beauty when they are shaken off. What mean these orange-colored toadstools that cumber the ground, and the citron-colored (ice-cream-like) fungus? Is the earth in her monthly courses? The fog has risen up before the sun around the summit of Fair Haven. It does not make such perfect seas as formerly. It is too general and wandering. It must have a core over the river —

as this has not — and be of sufficient density to keep down on the low lands in a clear white, not grayish, smoky mass, and there must be no wind to drift it about. However, the Bedford meeting-house, rising above it and dark toward the sun, looks like a ship far at sea with all sails set. Thus the clouds may be said to float low at this season, — rest on the ground in the morning, — so that you look down on them from the hills. The whole surface of the earth is now streaked with wreaths of fog over meadow and forest, alternating with the green. The sun, now working round the Cliffs, fires his rays into the battalions of fog which are collected over Fair Haven Pond and have taken refuge on the west side of the Hill; routs and disperses them. A dewy, cobwebbed morning. You observe the geometry of cobwebs, though most are of that gossamer character, close woven, as if a fairy had dropt her veil on the grass in the night.

Men have, perchance, detected every kind of flower that grows in this township, have pursued it with children's eyes into the thickest and darkest woods and swamps, where the painter's color has betrayed it. Have they with proportionate thoroughness plucked every flower of thought which it is possible for a man to entertain, proved every sentiment which it is possible for a man to experience, here? Men have circumnavigated this globe of land and water, but how few have sailed out of sight of common sense over the ocean of knowledge!

The entertaining a single thought of a certain elevation makes all men of one religion. It is always some base alloy that creates the distinction of sects. Thought greets thought over the widest gulfs of time with unerring freemasonry. I know, for instance, that Sadi entertained once identically the same thought that I do, and thereafter I can find no essential difference between Sadi and myself. He is not Persian, he is not ancient, he is not strange to me. By the identity of his thoughts with mine he still survives. It makes no odds what atoms serve us. Sadi possessed no greater privacy or individuality than is thrown open to me. He had no more interior and essential and sacred self than can come naked into my thought this moment. Truth and a true man is something essentially public, not private. If Sadi were to come back to claim a *personal* identity with the historical Sadi, he would find there were too many of us; he could not get a skin that would contain us all. The symbol of a personal identity preserved in this sense is a mummy from the catacombs, — a whole skin, it may [be], but no life within it. By living the life of a man is made common property. By sympathy with Sadi I have embowelled him. In his thought I have a sample of *him*, a slice from his core, which makes it unimportant where certain bones which the thinker once employed may lie; but I could not have got this without being equally entitled to it with himself. The difference between any man and that posterity amid whom he is famous is too insignificant to sanction that he should be set up again in any world as distinct from them. Methinks I can be as intimate with the essence of an ancient worthy as, so to speak, he was with himself.

meadows. In some places the ground is covered now with the black umbelled berries of the sarsaparilla. The naked viburnum berries are now greenish-white. *Nabalus albus*, white lettuce, perhaps a week? Varies in leaves. *Spiranthes gracilis*, slender neottia, for some time. *Goodyera repens*, white-veined rattlesnake-plantain, some days (?). *Bartonia tenella* (*Centaurella*), apparently leafless plant, in path in Ministerial Swamp. *Hieracium Gronovii* (?). An aster near the lygodium, with numerous small white flowers, apparently either the umbelled or spreading of Bigelow, just opening. No man ever makes a discovery, ever [sic] an observation of the least importance, but he is advertised of the fact by a joy that surprises him. The powers thus celebrate all discovery. The squirrels are now devouring the hazelnuts fast. A lupine blossomed again.

Aug. 11. Wednesday. Alcott here the 9th and 10th. He, the spiritual philosopher, is, and has been for some months, devoted to the study of his own genealogy, — he whom only the genealogy of humanity, the descent of man from God, should concern! He has been to his native town of Wolcott, Connecticut, on this errand, has faithfully perused the records of some fifteen towns, has read the epitaphs in as many churchyards, and, wherever he found the name Alcock, excerpted it and all connected with it, — for he is delighted to discover that the original name was All-*cock* and meant something, that some grandfather or great-grandfather bore it, Philip Alcock (though his son wisely enough changed it to Alcott). He who wrote of Human Culture, he who conducted

I only know myself as a human entity, the scene, so to speak, of thoughts and affections, and am sensible of a certain doubleness by which I can stand as remote from myself as from another. However intense my experience, I am conscious of the presence and criticism of a part of me which, as it were, is not a part of me, but spectator, sharing no experience, but taking note of it, and that is no more I than it is you. When the play — it may be the tragedy of life — is over, the spectator goes his way. It was a kind of fiction, a work of the imagination only, so far as he was concerned. A man *may* be affected by a theatrical exhibition; on the other hand, he *may not* be affected by an actual event which appears to concern him never so much.

P. M. — To Heywood's Pond.

Ambrosia artemisiæfolia. July was a month of dry, torrid heat and drouth, especially the fore part. August, thus far, of gentle rain-storms and fogs, dog-days. Things mildew now. The sun is warm, but it is damp and cool in shade. The colored willow-herb is an interesting small flower, pink (?) or white, with its long seed-vessel, in railroad gutter by red house. Dodder (*Cuscuta Americana*) just out. *Cerasus Virginiana* is now dark, almost quite black, and rather edible. It was only red before. Elder-berries almost ripe. I notice now, along the North River, horse-mint, arrowhead, cardinal-flower, trumpet-weed (just coming out), water parsnip, skull-cap (*lateriflora*), monkey-flower, etc., etc. Rattlesnake-plantain is budded. Rivers meander most not amid rugged mountains, but through soft level

Vol. IV

the Conversations on the Gospels, he who discoursed of Sleep, Health, Worship, Friendship, etc., last winter, now reading the wills and the epitaphs of the Alcocks with the zeal of a professed antiquarian and genealogist! He has discovered that one George Alcock (afterwards Deacon George) came over with Winthrop in 1630 and settled in Roxbury. Has read Eliot's account of him in the Church records and been caught by a passage in which [his] character is described by Eliot as being of "good savor." I think it is. But he has by no means made out his descent from him. Only knows that that family owned lands in Woodstock, Connecticut. Nevertheless the similarity of name is enough, and he pursues the least trace of it. Has visited a crockery-dealer in Boston who trades with Alcocks of Staffordshire (?), England, *great* potters who took a prize at the world's fair. Has through him obtained a cup or so with the name of the maker Alcock on it. Has it at his house. Has got the dealer to describe the persons of those Staffordshire Alcocks, and finds them to be of the right type, even to their noses. He knew they must be so. Has visited the tomb of Dr. John Alcock in the Granary Burying-Ground, read, and copied it. Has visited also the only bearer of the name in Boston, a sail-maker perchance, — though there is no evidence of the slightest connection except through Adam, — and communicated with him. He says I should survey Concord and put down every house exactly as it stands with the name. Admires the manuscript of the old records; more pleasing than print. Has some design to collect and print epitaphs.

Thinks they should be collected and printed *verbatim et literatim*, every one in every yard, with a perfect index added, so that persons engaged in such pursuits as himself might be absolutely sure, when they turned to the name Alcock, for instance, to find it if it was there, and not have to look over the whole yard. Talks of going to England — says it would be in his way — to visit the Alcocks of Staffordshire. Has gone now to find where lie the three thousand acres granted to the Roxbury family in 16— "on the Assabett," and has talked with a lawyer about the possibility of breaking the title, etc., etc., from time to time pulling out a long note-book from his bosom, with epitaphs and the like copied into it. Had copied into it the epitaph of my grand-mother-in-law which he came across in some graveyard (in Charlestown?), thinking "it would interest me!"

C. says he keeps a dog for society, to stir up the air of the room when it becomes dead, for he experiences awful solitudes. Another time thinks we must cultivate the social qualities, perhaps had better keep two dogs apiece.

P. M. — To Conantum.

The mountain-ash berries are turning. We had a ripe watermelon on the 7th. I see the great yellow flowers of the squash amid the potatoes in the garden, one of the largest yellow flowers we have. How fat and rich! Of course it is long since they blossomed. Green corn begins. The autumnal ring of the alder locust. White lilies are not very numerous now. The skunk-cabbage leaves are fallen and decaying, and their fruit

is black. Their fall is earlier than that of other plants. What is that tall plant now budded by the Corner Spring? [1] I am attracted by the clear dark-green leaves of the fever-bush. The rum cherry is ripe. The *Collinsonia Canadensis* just begun. The great trumpet-weeds now fairly out. Sumach berries now generally red. Some naked viburnum berries are red. The sweet viburnum turning. The larger skull-cap is quite an important and interesting flower. *Platanthera blephariglottis*, white fringed orchis. This side of Hubbard's Meadow Bridge, *Lespedeza hirta* (hairy), *Cannabis sativa*, apparently out. *Aster corymbosus*, path beyond Corner Spring and in Miles Swamp. *Cicuta bulbifera*, first seen July 21st and called *Sium lineare*. The true (?) *Sium lineare*, probably last month.[2]

Aug. 12. Walked to Walden and Fair Haven Hill with Mrs. Wilson and son, of Cincinnati. They tell me that the only men of thought in that part of the world are one young Goddard and Stallo the German. The subjects that engage the mass are theological dogmas and European politics. The man of the West is not yet.

Solidago bicolor, white goldenrod, apparently in good season.

Aug. 13. *Mikania scandens* well out; was not out July 18th. How long since, then? Perhaps not far from 1st August. The *Lactuca sanguinea* (var.) was perhaps as early as the other. Rhexia, very common

[1] *Chelone glabra.*   [2] *Vide* July 8 [p. 203.]

on those bare places on the river meadows from which the soil has been moved by the ice. Saw the head and neck of a great bittern projecting above the meadow-grass, exactly like the point of a stump, only I knew there could be no stump there. There are green lice now on the birches, but I notice no cotton on them. Pennyroyal abundant in bloom. I find it springing from the soil lodged on large rocks in sprout-lands, and gather a little bundle, which scents my pocket for many days. I hear that the *Corallorhiza odontorhiza*, coral-root, is out.

Aug. 14. *Viburnum dentatum* berries blue. Saw a rose still. There is such a haze that I cannot see the mountains.

Aug. 15. Some birds fly in flocks. I see a dense, compact flock of bobolinks going off in the air over a field. They cover the rails and alders, and go rustling off with a brassy, tinkling note like a ripe crop as I approach, revealing their yellow breasts and bellies. This is an autumnal sight, that small flock of grown birds in the afternoon sky.

Elder-berry ripe. The river was lowest early in July. Some time past I have noticed meadow-grass floating on the river, reminding me that they were getting the hay up the stream. Some naked viburnum berries are quite dark purple amid the red, while other bunches are wholly green yet. The red choke-berry is small and green still. I plainly distinguish it, also, by its woolly under side. In E. Hubbard's swamp I gather some

large and juicy and agreeable rum cherries. The birds make much account of them. They are much finer than the small ones on large trees; quite a good fruit. Some cranberries turned red on one cheek along the edges of the meadows. Now a sudden gust of wind blows from the northwest, cooled by a storm there, blowing the dust from roads far over the fields. The whole air, indeed, is suddenly filled with dust, and the outlines of the clouds are concealed. But it proves only the wind of the ball, which apparently passes north of us. That clear ring like an alder locust (is it a cricket?) for some time past is a sound which belongs to the season, — autumnal. Here is a second crop of clover almost as red as the first. The swamp blackberry begins. Saw a blue heron on the meadow. *Aster amplexicaulis* of Bigelow, apparently; probably for a day or two. An orchis by the brook under the Cliffs with only three white flowers, only smaller than the fringed white; spurs half an inch long. May it be another species?

Aug. 16. P. M. — Down river in boat with George Bradford.

Zizania aquatica, Indian or Canadian rice, or water oats, like slender corn. How long?

Hibiscus Moscheutos (?), marsh hibiscus, apparently, N. Barrett's. Perchance has been out a week. I think it must be the most conspicuous and showy and at the same time *rich*-colored flower of this month. It is not so conspicuous as the sunflower, but of a rarer color, — "pale rose-purple," they call it, — like a hollyhock. It is surprising for its amount of color, and, seen unexpectedly amid the willows and button-bushes, with the mikania twining around its stem, you can hardly believe it is a flower, so large and tender it looks, like the greatest effort of the season to adorn the August days, and reminded me of that great tender moth, the *Attacus luna*, which I found on the water near where it grows. I think it must be allied to southern species. It suggests a more genial climate and luxuriant soil. It requires these vaporous dog-days.

Galeopsis Tetrahit, common hemp-nettle, in roadside by Keyes's. How long? Flower like hedge-nettle. *Apios tuberosa*, ground-nut, a day or two. These are locust days. I hear them on the elms in the street, but cannot tell where they are. Loud is their song, drowning many others, but men appear not to distinguish it, though it pervades their ears as the dust their eyes. The river was exceedingly fair this afternoon, and there are few handsomer reaches than that by the leaning oak, the deep place, where the willows make a perfect shore.

At sunset, the glow being confined to the north, it tinges the rails on the causeway lake-color, but behind they are a dead dark blue. I must look for the rudbeckia which Bradford says he found yesterday behind Joe Clark's.

Aug. 17. Twenty minutes before 5 A. M. — To Cliffs and Walden.

Dawn. No breathing of chip-birds nor singing of robins as in spring, but still the cock crows lustily. The creak of the crickets sounds louder. As I go along

the back road, hear two or three song sparrows. This morning's red, there being a misty cloud there, is equal to an evening red. The woods are very still. I hear only a faint peep or twitter from one bird, then the never-failing wood thrush, it being about sunrise, and after, on the Cliff, the phœbe note of a chickadee, a night-warbler, a creeper (?), and a pewee (?), and, later still, the huckleberry-bird and red-eye, but all few and faint.

Cannot distinguish the steam of the engine toward Waltham from one of the morning fogs over hollows in woods. *Lespedeza violacea* var. (apparently) *angustifolia* (?), *sessiliflora* of Bigelow. Also another *L. violacea*, or at least violet, perhaps different from what I saw some time since. *Gerardia pedicularia*, bushy gerardia, almost ready. The white cornel berries are dropping off before they are fairly white.

Is not the hibiscus a very bright pink or even flesh-color? It is so delicate and peculiar. I do not think of any flower just like it. It reminds me of some of the wild geraniums most. It is a singular, large, delicate, high-colored flower with a tree-like leaf.

Gaylussacia frondosa, blue-tangle, dangle-berry, ripe perhaps a week. Weston of Lincoln thought there were more grapes, both cultivated and wild, than usual this year, because the rose-bugs had not done so much harm.

Aug. 18. 3 P. M. — To Joe Clark's and Hibiscus Bank.

I cannot conceive how a man can accomplish anything worthy of him, unless his very breath is sweet to

Vol. IV

him. He must be particularly alive. As if a man were himself and could work well only at a certain rare crisis.

The river is full of weeds. The *Hypericum mutilum*, small-flowered, has in some places turned wholly red on the shore. There is indeed something royal about the month of August. Its is a more ingrained and perhaps more tropical heat than that of July. Though hot, it is not so suffocating and unveiled a blaze. The vapors in the air temper it somewhat. But we have had some pretty cool weather within a week or two, and the evenings generally are cooler. As I go over the hill behind Hunt's, the North River has a glassy stillness and smoothness, seen through the smoky haze that fills the air and has the effect of a film on the water, so that it looks stagnant. No mountains can be seen. The locust is heard. The fruits are ripening. Ripe apples here and there scent the air. Huckleberries probably have begun to spoil. I see those minute yellow cocoons on the grass. Hazelnuts; methinks it is time to gather them if you would anticipate the squirrels. The clematis and mikania belong to this month, filling the crevices and rounding the outline of leafy banks and hedges.

Perceived to-day and some weeks since (August 3d) the strong invigorating aroma of green walnuts, astringent and bracing to the spirits, the fancy and imagination, suggesting a tree that has its roots well in amid the bowels of nature. Their shells are, in fact and from association, exhilarating to smell, suggesting a strong, nutty native vigor. A fruit which I am glad

that our zone produces, looking like the nutmeg of the East. I acquire some of the hardness and elasticity of the hickory when I smell them. They are among *our* spices. High-scented, aromatic, as you bruise one against another in your hand, almost like nutmegs, only more bracing and northern. Fragrant stones which the trees bear.

The hibiscus flowers are seen a quarter of a mile off over the water, like large roses, now that these high colors are rather rare. Some are exceedingly delicate and pale, almost white, just rose-tinted, others a brighter pink or rose-color, and all slightly plaited (the five large petals) and turned toward the sun, now in the west, trembling in the wind. So much color looks very rich in these localities. The flowers are some four inches in diameter, as large as water-lilies, rising amid and above the button-bushes and willows, with a large light-green tree-like leaf and a stem half an inch in diameter, apparently dying down to a perennial (?) root each year. A superb flower. Where it occurs it is certainly, next to the white lily, if not equally with it, the most splendid ornament of the river. Looking up the gleaming river, reflecting the August sun, the round-topped silvery *white* maples, the glossy-leaved swamp white oaks, the ethereal and buoyant *Salix Purshiana*, — the first and last resting on the water and giving the river a full appearance, — and the hibiscus flowers adorning the shores, contrasting with the green across the river, close to the water's edge, the meadows being just shorn, all make a perfect August scene. Here is the place where the hayers cross the river with their loads. As I made

excursions on the river when the white lilies were in
bloom, so now I should make a hibiscus excursion.

Rudbeckia laciniata, sunflower-like tall cone-flower,
behind Joe Clark's. *Symphytum officinale*, common
comfrey, by Dakin, pump-maker's. The *Cerastium viscosum* which I saw months ago, still. And the ovate
heads of the tall anemone gone to seed. *Linum usita-
tissimum*, common flax, with a pretty large and pretty
blue flower in the yard. *Rumex obtusifolius*, for weeks,
apparently.

Elizabeth Hoar shows me the following plants which
she brought from the White Mountains the 16th:
Chiogenes hispidula, creeping snow-berry, also called
Gaultheria and also *Vaccinium hispidulum*, *in fruit*,
with a partridge-berry scent and taste; *Taxus Canadensis*, ground hemlock, with red cup-shaped berries,
very handsome and remarkably like wax or red marble; *Platanthera orbiculata*, remarkable for its watery
shining leaves, flat on the ground, while its spike of
flowers rises perpendicular, suggesting, as she said, repose and steadiness amid the prostrate trunks, — and
you could not avoid seeing it any more than a child, —
in blossom; *Oxalis Acetosella*, in blossom; *Arenaria
Grœnlandica*, also in bloom, in tufts like houstonia;
Lonicera ciliata, probably, with a double red fruit. She
also brought lichens and mosses and convallaria berries
which she gathered at the Flume in Franconia. The
latter, red-ripe, hanging from the axils of the leaves,
affected me, reminding me of the progress of autumn
in the north; and the other two were a very fit importation, still dripping with the moisture, the water, of

the Flume. It carries you, indeed, into the primitive
wood. To think how, in those wild woods, now hang
these wild berries, in grim solitude as of yore, already scenting their autumn! A thousand years ago
this convallaria growing there, its berries turning red
as now and its leaves acquiring an autumnal tint.
Lichens and mosses enough to cover a waiter, still dripping with the water of the Flume, — is not that a true
specimen of it?

J. [?] Stacy says that fifty years ago his father used
to blow his fire with onion stems. Thinks there have
been great improvements. But then, as I hear, there
was a bellows-maker in the town. Is not that the *Aster
umbellatus* which I found by the lygodium?

Aug. 19. 2 p. m. — To Corner Spring, Burnt Plain,
and Brister Hill.

Forget-me-not Brook, *Epilobium lineare* (Bigelow),
molle (?) (Gray). The small fruits of most plants are
now generally ripe or ripening, and this is coincident
with the flying in flocks of such young birds now grown
as feed on them. The twittering, tinkling *link* notes of
the bobolinks occasionally border on the old bobolink
strain. The *Epilobium coloratum* is an interesting little
flower for its contrasted white and pink; the bud is
commonly pink. The *Viburnum dentatum* berries are
now blue. I still find the stitchwort (*Stellaria*). Many
leaves of the mountain sumach are red. What are the
checkerberry-scented plants? Checkerberry; black and
yellow birch; polygala, caducous and cross-leaved and
verticillata, at root; *Chiogenes hispidula*, creeping snow-

berry. I perceive the fragrance of the clethra on the
meadow gales. The checkerberries are in bloom, looking almost like snow-white berries. The dracæna berries, "amethystine blue," are almost all fallen. The
dangle-berry is a very handsome tangled berry, but
with a slightly astringent and to me not altogether
agreeable flavor. What is that large many-flowered
hieracium (I think I saw it at same time with the
veiny), with radical leaves and one sheathing leaflet
and a spreading panicle minutely downy? *Gronovii?*
or *Kalmii?* The trillium berries, six-sided, one inch
in diameter, like varnished and stained cherry wood,
glossy red, crystalline and ingrained, concealed under
its green leaves in shady swamps. It is already fall in
some of these shady, springy swamps, as at the Corner
Spring. The skunk-cabbages and the trilliums, both
leaves and fruit, are many flat prostrate, the former
decaying, and all looking as if early frosts had prevailed. Here, too, the bright scarlet berries of the
arum, perhaps premature.

Here is a little brook of very cold spring-water, rising a few rods distant, with a gray sandy and pebbly
bottom, flowing through this dense swampy thicket,
where, nevertheless, the sun falls in here and there
between the leaves and shines on its bottom, meandering exceedingly, and sometimes running underground.
The trilliums on its brink have fallen into it and bathe
their red berries in the water, waving in the stream.
The water has the coldness it acquired in the bowels
of the earth. Here is a recess apparently never frequented. Thus this rill flowed here a thousand years

ago, and with exactly these environments. It is a few
rods of primitive wood, such as the bear and the deer
beheld. It has a singular charm for me, carrying me
back in imagination to those days. Yet a fisherman
has once found out this retreat, and here is his box
in the brook to keep his minnows in, now gone to decay.
I love the rank smells of the swamp, its decaying
leaves. The clear dark-green leaves of the fever-bush
overhang the stream.

I name the shore under Fair Haven Hill the Cardinal
Shore from the abundance of cardinal-flowers there.
The red-stemmed (?) cornel berries are mingled whitish
and amethystine (?) blue. I see some bright red leaves
on the tupelo contrasting with its glossy green ones.
How sweet the fragrance where meadow-hay has been
brushed off a load in narrow paths in low woods! The
panicled (?) hedysarum apparently will blossom in
a week. *Gerardia purpurea* at Forget-me-not Brook.
Eupatorium pubescens, between this and the first of
August.

Aug. 20. That large galium still abundant and in
blossom, filling crevices. The *Corallorhiza multiflora*,
coral-root (not *odontorhiza*, I think, for it has twenty-
four flowers, and its germ is not roundish oval, and
its lip is three-lobed), by Brister's Spring. Found by
R. W. E., August 12; also *Goodyera pubescens* found
at same date. The purple gerardia is very beautiful
now in green grass, and the rhexia also, both difficult
to get home. I find raspberries still. An aster with a
smooth leaf narrowed below, somewhat like *A. amplexi-*

caulis (or *patens* (Gray)?). Is it var. *phlogifolius?* Is that smooth, handsome-stemmed goldenrod in Brown's Sleepy Hollow meadow *Solidago serotina?*

Bidens, either *connata* or *cernua*, by Moore's potato-field.

Aug. 21. Weeds in potato-fields are now very rank. What should we come to if the season were longer, and the reins were given to vegetation? Those savages that do not wither before the glance of civilization, that are waiting their turn to be cultivated, preparing a granary for the birds. The air within a day or two is quite cool, almost too cool for a thin coat, yet the alternate days are by some reckoned among the warmest in the year, *scalding* hot. That will apply very well to the greatest heat of August. Young turkeys are straying in the grass, which is alive with grasshoppers.

3 P. M. — To Bear Hill *via* railroad and Flint's.

The bees, wasps, etc., are on the goldenrods, impatient to be interrupted, improving their time before the sun of the year sets. A man killed by lightning would have a good answer ready in the next world to the question "How came *you* here?" which he need not hesitate to give. Can that be *Mulgedium leucophæum*, with the aspect of a lettuce but bluish flowers, seven feet high with a panicle two feet by ten inches? Cat-tails ripe. The common epilobium holds not a neat flower but rich-colored.

Moralists say of men, By their fruits ye shall know them, but botanists say of plants, By their flowers ye shall know them. This is very well generally, but they

must make exceptions sometimes when the fruit is fairer than the flower. They are to be compared at that stage in which they are most significant to man. I say that sometimes by their fruits ye shall know them. The bright red or scarlet fruit of the scarlet thorn (*Cratægus coccinea*) in the woods off Bear Hill road, Winn's woods. How handsomely they contrast with the green leaves! Are edible also. Fruits now take the place of flowers to some extent. These brilliant-colored fruits, flower-like. There are few flowers have such brilliant and remarkable colors as the fruit of the arum, trillium, convallarias, dracæna, cornels, viburnums, actæa, etc., etc. I must notice this kind of flowers now.

The leaves of the dogsbane are turning yellow. There are as few or fewer birds heard than flowers seen. The red-eye still occasionally. Agrimony still. "The dry, pearly, and almost incorruptible heads of the Life Everlasting." Ah! this is a truly elysian flower now, beyond change and decay, not lusty but immortal, — pure ascetics, suggesting a widowed virginity. *Bidens frondosa* in corn-fields under Bear Hill, west side. The large kind. *Polygonum arifolium*, a very large scratchweed, in the ditch in Baker's Swamp, reminding me of a boa-constrictor creeping over the plants' stems, a third of an inch in diameter. Some time earlier in this month. The sound of the crickets gradually prevails more and more. I hear the year falling asleep. When dry seeds come, then I hear these dry locust and cricket sounds. Berries are still abundant on Bear Hill, but how late when huckleberries begin to be wormy and pickers are deserting the fields?

Vol. IV

The high blackberries by the roadside are sweet though covered with dust. At this season, too, the farmers burn brush, and the smoke is added to the haziness of the atmosphere. From this hill I count five or six smokes, far and near, and am advertised of one species of industry over a wide extent of country. The mountains are just visible. The grass-poly by the Lincoln road, with its "fine purple" flowers. *Decodon verticillatus*, swamp loosestrife. Those in the water do not generally bloom. What stout, woody, perennial rootstocks! It is a handsome purple flower, falling over wreath-like on every side, with an epilobium look, a *lively* purple. The *Cardamine hirsuta* still. The bittersweet berries now bright red, still handsomer than the flowers. The barberries are turning. Many leaves of the pyrus, both kinds, are red, and some sweet-ferns. See the great umbels, lead-blue, of the *Aralia hispida*.

This coloring and reddening of the leaves toward fall is interesting; as if the sun had so prevailed that even the leaves, better late than never, were turning to flowers, — so filled with mature juices, the whole plant turns at length to one flower, and all its leaves are petals around its fruit or dry seed. A second flowering to celebrate the maturity of the fruit. The first to celebrate the age of puberty, the marriageable age; the second, the maturity of the parent, the age of wisdom, the fullness of years.

Aug. 22. *Sunday.* The ways by which men express themselves are infinite, — the literary through their writings, and often they do not mind with what

air they walk the streets, being sufficiently reported otherwise. But some express themselves chiefly by their gait and carriage, with swelling breasts or elephantine roll and elevated brows, making themselves moving and adequate signs of themselves, having no other outlet. If their greatness had signalized itself sufficiently in some other way, though it were only in picking locks, they could afford to dispense with the swagger.

P. M. — To Marlborough road and White Pond.

Dodder by railroad bridge. I am attracted by the deep purple (?) of some polygalas standing amid dark-green grass. Some of the leaves of the choke-cherry are the brightest scarlet that I have seen, or, at least, the clearest. *Eupatorium purpureum* fully out everywhere. Potamogetons still in flower (small ones) in brooks. Heart-leaves in Walden and water-target leaves in the overflowed meadow. The elder bushes are weighed down with fruit partially turned, and are still in bloom at the extremities of their twigs. The low downy gnaphalium leaves are already prepared for winter and spring again on dry hills and sprout-lands. I am struck by the handsome and abundant clusters of yet green shrub oak acorns. Some are whitish. How much food for some creatures! The sprouts, apparently of the *Populus grandidentata*, run up very fast the first year where the wood has been cut, and make great leaves nearly a foot long and nine or ten inches wide, — unlike those of the parent tree, downy. Just smelled an apple which carried me forward to those days when they will be heaped in the orchards and about the cider-mills. The fragrance of some fruits is not to be forgotten, along with that of flowers.[1] Is not the high black-berry our finest berry? I gather very sweet ones which weigh down the vines in sprout-lands. The arum berries are mostly devoured, apparently by birds. The two-leaved Solomon's-seal berries begin to be red. *Rumex Hydrolapathum* (?) by Jenny's Brook. *Hieracium Canadense*, apparently Bigelow's *Kalmiana*, which Gray says is not Linnæus's, Marlborough road. The oval maple-leaved viburnum berries have got to be yellowish. The panicled cornel berries now white. The bushy gerardia is abundant on the White Pond road, beyond pond. What is that thistle in Brown's and Tarbell's meadows with no stem, only radical leaves, very prickly and not pinnatifid? *Desmodium acuminatum* still in bloom, near the poplars on White Pond road. The *Smilacina racemosa* has a compound raceme of red-speckled berries now. *Polygonatum pubescens* berries are now green with a bluish bloom, and the leaves eaten up. Was not that which E. Hoar brought from the White Mountains *Polygonatum canaliculatum* with axillary large red berries, though Gray says of this genus, its berries are black or blue?[2] Perhaps fruits are colored like the trillium berry and the scarlet thorn to attract birds to them. Is that rather large lilac-purple aster by Jenny's Brook *A. puniceus*?[3]

Aug. 23. 3 p. m. — To Assabet.

The river is eight and one twelfth feet below top of

---

[1] [*Excursions*, p. 295; Riv. 362.]
[2] Probably the large convallaria.
[3] *Longifolius?*

Vol. IV

truss.[1] Add eight and a half inches for its greatest height this year, and you have eight feet nine and a half inches for the difference. It is apparently as low now as the first week in July.[2] That is, those are the limits of our river's expansibility; so much it may swell. Of course, the water now in it is but a small fraction of that which it contains in the highest freshets, for this additional eight and nine twelfths feet is much more than its present average depth, half as much again perhaps, beside averaging eight or ten times its present width.

The ferns in low shady woods are faded. *Hydrocotyle Americana*, marsh pennywort, by the Lee place path. It probably opened in June or July. Saw a new form of arrowhead leaf with linear lobes, but the flowers apparently the same, a crystalline white. The bank at the bathing-place has now a new kind of beauty. It is spotted with bright-scarlet cardinal-flowers and bright-purple vernonias. The profuse clusters of grapes, partially concealed under their leaves, are turning; have got a purple tinge. Dense clusters of elder-berries, some black, some turning, are hanging drooping by their weight over the water. The glassy or bead (amethystine?) blue berries of the red osier[3] cornel, mixed with whitish, are as abundant as any berries here; and the dull slaty-blue and smaller berries of the *Viburnum dentatum* fill the remaining crevices. These things I see as I swim beneath it.

---

[1] Horizontal part (probably).
[2] This I calculate to be two inches below my summer level for 1859.
[3] Silky.

About 8 p. m. — To Cliffs, moon half full.

As I go up the back road, I hear the loud ringing creak of crickets, louder singers on each apple tree by the roadside, with an intermittent pulsing creak. Not the sound of a bird all the way to the woods. How dark the shadows of the pines and oaks fall across the woodland path! There is a new tree, another forest in the shadow. It is pleasant walking in these forest paths, with heavy darkness on one side and a silvery moonlight on the oak leaves on the other, and again, when the trees meet overhead, to tread the checkered floor of finely divided light and shade. I hear a faint metallic titter from a bird, so faint that if uttered at noonday it would not be heard, — not so loud as a cricket. I cannot remember the last moon.

Now that birds and flowers fall off, fruits take their places, and young birds in flocks. What a list of bright-colored, sometimes venomous-looking berries spot the swamps and copses amid changing leaves! For colors they will surpass the flowers, methinks. There is something rare, precious, and gem-like about them. Now is their time, and I must attend to them. Some, like grapes, we gather and eat, but the fairest are not edible.

Now I sit on the Cliffs and look abroad over the river and Conantum hills. I live so much in my habitual thoughts, a routine of thought, that I forget there is any outside to the globe, and am surprised when I behold it as now, — yonder hills and river in the moonlight, the monsters. Yet it is salutary to deal with the surface of things. What are these rivers and hills, these hieroglyphics which my eyes behold? There is some-

thing invigorating in this air, which I am peculiarly sensible is a real wind, blowing from over the surface of a planet. I look out at my eyes, I come to my window, and I feel and breathe the fresh air. It is a fact equally glorious with the most inward experience. Why have we ever slandered the outward? The perception of surfaces will always have the effect of miracle to a sane sense. I can see Nobscot faintly.

Descend the rocks and return through woods to railroad. How picturesque the moonlight on rocks in the woods! To-night there are no fireflies, no nighthawks nor whip-poor-wills.

Aug. 24. How far we can be apart and yet attract each other! There is one who almost wholly misunderstands me and whom I too probably misunderstand, toward whom, nevertheless, I am distinctly drawn. I have the utmost human good-will toward that one, and yet I know not what mistrust keeps us asunder. I am so much and so exclusively the friend of my friend's virtue that I am compelled to be silent for the most part, because his vice is present. I am made dumb by this third party. I only desire *sincere* relations with the worthiest of my acquaintance, that they may give me an opportunity once in a year to speak the truth. They invite me to see them, and do not show themselves. Who *are* they, pray? I pine and starve near them. The hospitable man will invite me to an atmosphere where truth can be spoken, where a man can live and breathe. Think what crumbs we offer each other, — and think to make up the deficiency with our *roast meats!* Let us have a human creature's heart and let go the beef's heart. How happens it that I find myself making such an enormous demand on men and so constantly disappointed? Are my friends aware how disappointed I am? Is it all my fault? Have I no heart? Am I incapable of expansion and generosity? I shall accuse myself of everything else sooner. I have never met with a friend who furnished me sea-room. I have only tacked a few times and come to anchor, — not sailed, — made no voyage, carried no venture. Do they think me eccentric because I refuse this chicken's meat, this babe's food? Would not men have something to communicate if they were sincere? Is not my silent expectation an invitation, an offer, an opportunity offered? My friend has complained of me, cursed me even, but it did not affect me; I did not know the persons he talked about. I have been disappointed from first to last in my friends, but I have never complained of them, nor to them. I would have them know me, guess at me. It is not petty and trivial relations that I seek to establish with them. A world in which there is a demand for ice-creams but not for truth! I leave my friends early; I go away to cherish my idea of friendship. Is not friendship a great relation? My friend so treats me that I feel a thousand miles off; like the greatest possible stranger, speaking a different language; as if it would be the fittest thing in the world for us to be introduced. Persists in thinking me the opposite to what [I am], and so shuts my mouth. Intercourse with men! How little it amounts to! How rarely we love them! Do we not meet very much as Yankees

meet Arabs? It is remarkable if a man gives us a civil answer about the road. And how far from love still are even pretty intimate friends! How little it is that we can trust each other! It is the bravest thing we do for one moment to put so much confidence in our companion as to treat him for what he aspires to be, a confidence which we retract instantly.

Like cuttlefish we conceal ourselves, we darken the atmosphere in which we move; we are not transparent. I pine for one to whom I can speak my *first thoughts;* thoughts which represent me truly, which are no better and no worse than I; thoughts which have the bloom on them, which alone can be sacred and divine. Our sin and shame prevent our expressing even the innocent thoughts we have. I know of no one to whom I can be transparent instinctively. I live the life of the cuttlefish; another appears, and the element in which I move is tinged and I am concealed. My first thoughts are azure; there is a bloom and a dew on them; they are papillaceous feelers which I put out, tender, innocent. Only to a friend can I expose them. To all parties, though they be youth and maiden, if they are transparent to each other, and their thoughts can be expressed, there can be no further nakedness. I cannot be surprised by an intimacy which reveals the outside, when it has shown me the inside. The result of a full communication of our thoughts would be the immediate neglect of those coverings which a false modesty wears.

P. M. — To Saw Mill Brook.

The *Viburnum dentatum* berries, which are, methinks,

Vol. IV

the earliest of the viburnums, are a dead light blue, small. The *Viburnum nudum* shows now rich, variegated clusters amid its handsome, firm leaves, — bright rosy-cheeked ones mingled with dark-purple. All do not appear to turn purple. The *Lentago* I have not seen ripe yet. The *acerifolium* is merely yellowish, oval, flattish. Of cornels, have not seen the dwarf nor the dogwood berries. The alternate-leaved with red cymes and round dull (?) blue berries appeared first; then the red osier began to turn bright, glass-beady, amethystine (?) blue, mixed with white, and is still for the most part green; then the white-berried. But the round-leaved I have not seen.

Autumnal dandelions are more common now. I see a smooth [drawing] red-skinned gall on oak twigs.

Surely the high blackberry is the finest berry, — not by dusty roadsides, but when now the season is rather late, and you find them in some rocky sprout-land, far from any road, fully ripe, having escaped the pickers, weighing down their stems and half hidden amid the green leaves of other plants, black and shiny, ready to drop, with a spirited juice. Who will pretend that, plucked and eaten there, they are the same with those offered at the tea-table? These are among the berries that are eaten by men.

The *Neottia pubescens* is a rather interesting flower.

The ghost-horse on a goldenrod, a real caricature of Flying Childers, like a light-green seed-vessel, three or four inches long and one tenth of an inch in diameter, with four slender legs more than an inch long, in

two pairs, springing from within an inch of each other in the middle of his body, and an eye more than an inch behind its snout, — a caricature on the horse, one or more of its legs in the air as if arrested while taking a step. You can hardly believe it is an insect, and if you handle it, it is so sluggish in its motions that you might not discover it, if not bent on it. Thus I thought of it, till I disturbed it, took it into my hand; and then found it had six legs and no long snout at all but only two slender feelers, that it had laid its two fore legs and feelers together, so as exactly to resemble a long snout, and also a seed-vessel the more, with its eye far in the rear.

The year is but a succession of days, and I see that I could assign some office to each day which, summed up, would be the history of the year. Everything is done in season, and there is no time to spare. The bird gets its brood hatched in season and is off. I looked into the nest where I saw a vireo feeding its young a few days ago, but it is empty; it is fledged and flown.

Smoke is very like but still different from cloud: first, from its rapid motion, from being nearer commonly; secondly, from a certain fuliginous or yellowish color in its hollows, as if it had fire in its entrails, a darkness not to be referred to shadow.

At Saw Mill Brook, *Solidago latifolia* budded. Saw Mill Brook path, *Desmodium paniculatum*, perhaps a week. By red house on Turnpike, *Polygonum Careyi*. In R. W. E.'s garden, *Pilea pumila*, rich-weed, August, and *Sonchus oleraceus*, common sow-thistle with a small dandelion-like flower, and also *Amaranthus albus*, the last July (?).

Aug. 25. Cape Wrath, the northwest cape of Scotland. What a good name for a cape lying far away dark, over the water, under a lowering sky !

P. M. — To Conantum.

The dandelion blooms again.

One of the most noticeable wild fruits at present is the *Viburnum nudum* berries, their variegated cymes amid the green leaves in the swamps or low grounds, some whitish, some greenish, some red, some pink, some rose-purple and very beautiful, — not so beautiful, however, off the bush, — some dark purple or blue, and some black whose bloom is rubbed off, — a very rich sight. The silky cornel is the most common everywhere, bordering the river and swamps, its drooping cymes of amethystine (?) china or glass beads mingled with whitish. The fruit of the *Viburnum Lentago* is now very handsome, with its sessile cymes of large elliptical berries, green on one side and red with a purple bloom on the other or exposed side, not yet purple, blushing on one cheek. Many pyrus leaves are now red in the swamps, and some *Viburnum nudum*.

Yesterday was a hot day, but oh, this dull, cloudy, breezy, thoughtful weather in which the creak of the cricket sounds louder, preparatory to a cheerful storm ! How grateful to our feelings is the approach of autumn ! We have had no serious storm since spring. What a salad to my spirits is this cooler, darker day! Of late we have had several cloudy days without rain.

weather-wise will know themselves and find the signs of rain in their own moods, the aspect of their own skies or thoughts, and not consult swallows and spiders. I incline always [to] questions about the weather without thinking. Does a mind in sympathy with nature need a hygrometer?

Aug. 26. Rain. Rain.

Aug. 27. It still rains. I am struck by the ease and simplicity with which an Englishman expresses a sentiment of reverence for the Author and Ruler of the Universe. It is very manly, and appears to some extent to characterize the nation. Osborn, in his Arctic Journal, prints with much simplicity a prayer which had been prepared for the Arctic expedition.

P. M. — To Walden.

Storm drawing to a close. Crickets sound much louder after the rain in this cloudy weather. They are beginning to dig potatoes in earnest. Hips of the early roses are reddening. I have not seen a rose for a week or two. Lower leaves of the smooth sumach are red. Hear *chic-a-day-day-day* and crows; but, for music, reduced almost to the winter quire. Young partridges two thirds grown burst away. Globular galls on young oaks, green on one side, red on the other. *Elatine Americana*, small crypta [?], in Walden Pond.

Paddled *round* the pond. The shore is composed of a belt of smooth rounded white stones like paving-stones, a rod or two in width, excepting one or two short sand-beaches, and is so steep that much of the way a

I hear no birds sing these days, only the plaintive note of young bluebirds, or the peep of a robin, or the scream of a jay, to whom all seasons are indifferent, the mew of a catbird, the *link link* of a bobolink, or the twitter of a goldfinch, all faint and rare. The great bittern is still about, but silent and shy. I see where its roost on the pitch pines is betrayed at Tupelo Cliff by the lime-like ordure on the leaves of the bushes beneath. Or a hawk is occasionally seen, etc., etc.

The linear lespedeza is out of bloom at Tupelo Cliff. *Euphorbia hypericifolia* there (July). *Spiranthes cernua* in the meadows. That earliest one I saw was either the *gracilis* or *repens*, probably the first. Again and several times I have found a low hieracium, not a foot high, with radical leaves only and not veined, few-flowered; may be one form of *Gronovii*. That white polygonum of the river is apparently *P. hydropiperoides*, but faintly perforate-spotted; but I cannot find described the smaller, rose-colored one, also perforate-dotted. Some thorn berries, to the eyes similar to the scarlet-fruited, are hard. How many kinds have we? Some are already cutting rowen, which is sweetest and best for milch cows.

At length, before sundown, it begins to rain. You can hardly say when it began, and now, after dark, the sound of it dripping and pattering without is quite cheering. It is long since I heard it. One of those serious and normal storms, not a shower which you can see through, something regular, a fall (?) rain, coincident with a different mood or season of the mind, not a transient cloud that drops rain. Methinks the truly

single leap will carry you into water over your head. It is nowhere muddy, and the bottom is not to be touched, scarcely even seen again, except for the transparency of the water, till it rises on the other side. A casual observer would say that there were no weeds at all in it, and of noticeable plants a closer scrutiny detects only a few small heart-leaves and potamogetons, and perchance a water-target or two, which yet even a bather might not perceive. Both fishes and plants are clean and bright, like the element they live in.[1] Viewed from a hilltop, it is blue in the depths and green in the shallows, but from a boat it is seen to be a uniform dark green.[2] I can remember when it was four or five feet higher, also a foot or two lower, than when I lived there. There is a narrow sand-bar running into it in one place, with very deep water on one side, on which I boiled a kettle of chowder, at least six rods from the main shore, more than twenty years ago, which it has not been possible to do since; and my friends used to listen with incredulity when I told them, that a year or two later I was accustomed to fish from a boat in a deep cove in the woods, long since converted into a meadow. But since I left it the pond has risen steadily for a year past, apparently unaffected by drouth or rain, and now, in the summer of '52, is as high as it was twenty years ago, and fishing goes on again in the meadow; and yet the water shed by the surrounding hills is insignificant in amount, and this overflow must be referred to causes which affect the deep springs.[3]

[1] [*Walden*, p. 198; Riv. 279, 280.] [2] [*Walden*, p. 196; Riv. 276.]
[3] [*Walden*, pp. 200, 201; Riv. 283.]

The surrounding hills are from fifty to a hundred, and in one place perhaps two hundred, feet high, covered with wood.[1]

The bushy gerardia yellows the hilly side, where the wood is cut off on the north side of the pond. Among the effects of the high water, I observe that the alders have thrown out innumerable roots, two feet or more in length, with red extremities, for three feet or more up their stems, or as high as the water stands, which do not seek the ground, but collect sustenance from the water, forming a dense mass. Also the willows and the meadow-sweet in their proportion; but the pitch pines and many other trees are killed. The high blueberries standing in the water bear more and larger berries than usual, and they are still quite fresh.

The berries of the red pyrus are now red in some places. Apparently *Mulgedium leucophæum* by the railroad. *Aster longifolius* (?), handsome, large, bushy, lilac-tinted, apparently the same found the 22d at Jenny's Brook. The leaves of some young maples in the water about the pond are now quite scarlet, running into dark purple-red.

Aug. 28. Sicyos angulatus, one-seeded star-cucumber in Aunt's garden, probably in July. *Nepeta Glechoma*, ground ivy, or gill, probably May, now out of bloom. *Bidens chrysanthemoides*, perhaps a day. *Polygonum amphibium* var. *terrestre* with a small spike of large clear rose-colored flowers, flowers rare, probably

[1] [*Walden*, p. 195; Riv. 275.]

August. What I called by this name before was not this. Now the red osier[1] berries are very handsome along the river, overhanging the water, for the most part pale blue mixed with whitish, — part of the pendant jewelry of the season. The berries of the alternate-leaved cornel have dropped off mostly. The white-berried and red[2] osier are in their prime. The other three kinds I have not seen. The viburnums, *dentatum* and *nudum*, are in their prime. The sweet viburnum not yet purple, and the maple-leaved still yellowish. Hemp still in blossom.

Aug. 29. A warm rain-storm in the night, with wind, and to-day it continues. The first leaves begin to fall; a few yellow ones lie in the road this morning, loosened by the rain and blown off by the wind. The ground in orchards is covered with windfalls; imperfect fruits now fall.

We boast that we belong to the Nineteenth Century, and are making the most rapid strides of any nation. But consider how little this village does for its own culture. We have a comparatively decent system of common schools, schools for infants only, as it were, but, excepting the half-starved Lyceum in the winter, no school for ourselves. It is time that we had uncommon schools, that we did not leave off our education when we begin to be men. Comparatively few of my townsmen evince any interest in their own culture, however much they may boast of the school tax they pay. It is time that villages were universities, and their elder

[1] River cornel.   [2] Silky.

Vol. IV

inhabitants the fellows, with leisure — if they are indeed so well off — to pursue liberal studies as long as they live. In this country the village should in many respects take the place of the nobleman who has gone by the board. It should be the patron of the fine arts. It is rich enough; it only wants the refinement. It can spend money enough on such things as farmers value, but it is thought utopian to propose spending money for things which more intelligent men know to be of far more worth. If we live in the Nineteenth Century, why should we not enjoy the advantages which the Nineteenth Century has to offer? Why should our life be in any respect provincial? As the nobleman of cultivated taste surrounds himself with whatever conduces to his culture, — books, paintings, statuary, etc., — so let the village do. This town, — how much has it ever spent directly on its own culture? To act collectively is according to the spirit of our institutions, and I am confident that, as our circumstances are more flourishing, our means are greater. New England can hire all the wise men in the world to come and teach her, and board them round the while, and not be provincial at all. That is the uncommon school we want. The one hundred and twenty-five dollars which is subscribed in this town every winter for a Lyceum is better spent than any other equal sum. Instead of noblemen, let us have noble towns or villages of men. This town has just spent sixteen thousand dollars for a town-house. Suppose it had been proposed to spend an equal sum for something which will tend far more to refine and cultivate its inhabitants, a library, for instance. We have

sadly neglected our education. We leave it to Harper & Brothers and Redding & Co.[1]

Aug. 30. A cold storm still, — this the third day, — and a fire to keep warm by. This, methinks, is the most serious storm since spring. *Polygonum amphibium* var. *aquaticum*, which is rather rare. I have not seen it in flower. It is floating. Its broad heart-shaped leaves are purplish beneath, like white lily pads, heart-leaves, and water-targets. What is there in the water that colors them? The other variety, which [is] rough and upright, is more common, and its flowers very beautiful.

Aug. 31. Tuesday. 9 A. M. — Up river in boat to the bend above the Pantry.

It is pleasant to embark on a voyage, if only for a short river excursion, the boat to be your home for the day, especially if it is neat and dry. A sort of moving studio it becomes, you can carry so many things with you. It is almost as if you put oars out at your windows and moved your house along. A sailor, I see, easily becomes attached to his vessel. How continually we [are] thankful to the boat if it does not leak! We move now with a certain pomp and circumstance, with planetary dignity. The pleasure of sailing is akin to that which a planet feels. It seems a more complete adventure than a walk. We make believe embark our all, — our house and furniture. We are further from the earth than the rider; we receive no jar from it. We can carry many things with us.

[1] [*Walden*, pp. 120–122; Riv. 171–173.]

This high water will retard the blossoming of the *Bidens Beckii*, perhaps. The pads are covered for the most part; only those which have very long stems are on the surface, the white lilies oftenest. Here and there is seen a blue spike of a pontederia still, but I do not see a single white lily. I should think this would put an end to them. It is a bright and breezy day. I hear the note of goldfinches. The shore is whitened in some places with dense fields of the *Polygonum hydropiperoides*, now in its prime, but the smaller rose-colored polygonum, also in blossom, is covered. The mikania still covers the banks, and imparts its fragrance to the whole shore, but it is past its prime, as also is the trumpet-weed. The purple gerardias are very fresh and handsome next the water, behind Hubbard's or Dennis's. I see crows feeding on the meadow, large and black.

I rigged my mast by putting a post across the boat, and putting the mast through it and into a piece of a post at the bottom, and lashing and bracing it, and so sailed most of the way. The water, methinks, has a little of the fall sparkle on it after the rain. It has run over the meadows considerably and drowned the flowers. I feel as if it was a month later than it was a week ago.

A few days ago some saw a circular rainbow about the sun at midday. Singular phenomenon. Is not this the season when conventions are held? Or do they not appoint conventions, temperance or political, at such times as the farmers are most at leisure? There is a silvery light on the washed willows this morning, and the shadows under the wood-sides appear deeper, per-

chance by contrast, in the brilliant air. Is not the air a little more bracing than it was? Looking up the sparkling river, whose waves are flashing in the sun, it appears to be giving off its pure silver from the amalgam. The sky is more beautiful, a clearer blue, methinks, than for some time past, with light and downy clouds sailing all round a quarter of the way up it. The fields of bulrushes are now conspicuous, being left alone above the water. The balls of the button-bush have lost their bloom. From the shore I hear only the creak of crickets. The winds of autumn begin to blow. Now I can sail. The cardinal-flowers, almost drowned in a foot or two of water, are still very brilliant. The wind is Septemberish. That rush, reed, or sedge with the handsome head rises above the water. I pass boats now far from the shore and full of water. I see and hear the kingfisher with his disproportionate black [*sic*] head or crest. The pigeon woodpecker darts across the valley; a catbird mews in the alders; a great bittern flies sluggishly away from his pine tree perch on Tupelo Cliff, digging his way through the air. These and crows at long intervals are all the birds seen or heard.

How much he knows of the wind, its strength and direction, whose steed it is, — the sailor. With a good gale he advances rapidly; when it dies away he is at a standstill. The very sounds made by moving the furniture of my boat are agreeable, echoing so distinctly and sweetly over the water; they give the sense of being abroad. I find myself *at home* in new scenery. I carry more of myself with me; I am more entirely abroad, as when a man takes his children into the

fields with him. I carry so many me's with [me]. This large basket of melons, umbrella, flowers, hammer, etc., etc., all go with me to the end of the voyage without being the least incumbrance, and preserve their relative distances. Our capacity to carry our furniture with us is so much increased. There is little danger of overloading the steed. We can go completely equipped to fields a dozen miles off. The tent and the chest can be taken as easily as not. We embark; we go aboard a boat; we sit or we stand. If we sail, there is no exertion necessary. If we move in the opposite direction, we nevertheless progress. And if we row, we sit to an agreeable exercise, akin to flying. A student, of course, if it were perfectly convenient, would always move with his escritoire and his library about him. If you have a cabin and can descend into that, the charm is double.

Landed near the bee tree. A bumblebee on a cow-wheat blossom sounded like the engine's whistle far over the woods; then like an æolian harp. Then walked through the damp, cellar-like, fungus woods, with bare, damp, dead leaves and no bushes for their floor, where the corallorhiza grows, now out of bloom. The fall dandelion yellows the meadows. What is that bird like a large peetweet that flew away with a kind of whistle from a grass spit in the Sudbury meadows? A larger sandpiper? Probably a yellow-legs.

Lunched on Rice's Hill. I see some yellow pumpkins from afar in the field next his house. This sight belongs to the season. It has all clouded up again, so that I scarcely see the sun during the day. I find, on

bathing, that the water has been made very cold by the rain-storm, so that I soon come out. It must affect the fishes very much.

All the fields and meadows are shorn. I would like to go into perfectly new and wild country where the meadows are rich in decaying and rustling vegetation, present a wilder luxuriance. I wish to lose myself amid reeds and sedges and wild grasses that have not been touched. If haying were omitted for a season or two, a voyage up this river in the fall, methinks, would make a much wilder impression. I sail and paddle to find a place where the bank has a more neglected look. I wish to bury myself amid reeds. I pine for the luxuriant vegetation of the river-banks.

I ramble over the wooded hill on the right beyond the Pantry. The bushy gerardia is now very conspicuous with its great yellow trumpets, on hillsides on sprout-lands. Sometimes you come upon a large field of them. The buds or closed tubes are as handsome, at least, as the flowers. The various kinds of lespedezas are now in bloom. The panicled desmodium is going to seed and adheres to the clothes, with only a few flowers left. The strong contrast of the bright-pink (hard) and blue (soft and ripe) berries of the *Viburnum nudum*. Here are some irregularly globular or apple-shaped and larger than the common, which are more elliptical. The rustling of aspen leaves (*grandidentata*) this cloudy day startled me as if it were rain-drops on the leaves. Here are great pyrus berries in dense clusters falling over in wreaths and actually blackening the ground. I have rarely seen any kind of berries so thick. As big as small cherries. The great *Bidens chrysanthemoides*, now in blossom, like a sunflower, two inches in diameter, is for the most part far under water, blossoms and all. I see its drowned flowers far beneath the surface. Gunners out with their pants tucked into their boots. Pigeons fly over, and ducks. Poke berries ripe for some time. The various beauties of this plant now appear. Its stem is ripe, too, as if full of purple wine. It is so florid that the whole plant blossoms. In the fall, after so much sun, all leaves turn to petals and blossoms. The evening of the year is colored like the sunset. *Utricularia inflata*, or whorled bladderwort, numerous in Fair Haven Pond. I found it the same day of the month last year. I plucked a white lily pad above Lee's Bridge, nine inches in diameter.

Landed at Lee's Cliff, in Fair Haven Pond, and sat on the Cliff. Late in the afternoon. The wind is gone down; the water is smooth; a serene evening is approaching; the clouds are dispersing; the sun has shone once or twice, but is now in a cloud. The pond, so smooth and full of reflections after a dark and breezy day, is unexpectedly beautiful. There is a little boat on it, schooner-rigged, with three sails, a perfect little vessel and perfectly reflected now in the water. It is sufficient life for the pond. Being in the reflection of the opposite woods, the water on which it rests (for there is hardly a puff of air, and the boatman is only airing his sails after the storm) is absolutely invisible; only the junction of the reflections shows where it must be, and it makes an agreeable impression of buoyancy and lightness as of a feather. The broad, dense, and now

lower and flatter border of button-bushes, having water on both sides, is very rich and moss-like, seen from this height, with an irregular outline, being flooded while verdurous. The sky is reflected on both sides, and no finer edging can be imagined. A sail is, perhaps, the largest white object that can be admitted into the landscape. It contrasts well with the water, and is the most agreeable of regular forms. If they were shaped like houses, they would be disagreeable. The very mists which rise from the water are also white.

It is worth the while to have had a cloudy, even a stormy, day for an excursion, if only that you are out at the clearing up. The beauty of the landscape is the greater, not only by reason of the contrast with its recent lowering aspect, but because of the greater freshness and purity of the air and of vegetation, and of the repressed and so recruited spirits of the beholder. Sunshine is nothing to be observed or described, but when it is seen in patches on the hillsides, or suddenly bursts forth with splendor at the end of a storm. I derive pleasure now from the shadows of the clouds diversifying the sunshine on the hills, where lately all was shadow. The spirits of the cows at pasture on this very hillside appear excited. They are restless from a kind of joy, and are not content with feeding. The weedy shore is suddenly blotted out by this rise of waters.

I saw a small hawk fly along under the hillside and alight on the ground, its breast and belly pure downy white. It was a very handsome bird. Though they are not fitted to walk much on the ground, but to soar,

yet its feet, which are but claws to seize its prey and hold to its perch, are handsome appendages, and it is a very interesting sight on the ground. Yet there is a certain unfitness in so fair a breast, so pure white, made to breast nothing less pure than the sky or clouds, coming so nearly in contact with the earth. Never bespattered with the mud of earth. That was the impression made on me, — of a very pure breast, accustomed to float on the sky, in contact with the earth. It stood quite still, watching me, as if it was not easy for it to walk.

I forgot to say that I saw nighthawks sailing about in the middle of the day. The barberries are red in some places. Methinks I am in better spirits and physical health now that melons are ripe, *i. e.* for three weeks past. I hear the sound of a flail. The clouds do not entirely disperse, but, since it is decidedly fair and serene, I am contented.

I float slowly down from Fair Haven till I have passed the bridge. The sun, half an hour high, has come out again just before setting, with a brilliant, warm light, and there is the slightest undulation discernible on the water, from the boat or other cause, as it were its imitation in glass. The reflections are perfect. A bright, fresh green on fields and trees now after the rain, spring-like with the sense of summer past. The reflections are the more perfect for the blackness of the water. I see the down of a thistle, probably, in the air, descending to the water two or three rods off, which I mistake for a man in his shirt sleeves descending a distant hill, by an ocular delusion. How fair the smooth green swells

of those low grassy hills on which the sunlight falls! Indian hills.

This is the most glorious part of this day, the serenest, warmest, brightest part, and the most suggestive. Evening is fairer than morning. It is chaste eve, for it has sustained the trials of the day, but to the morning such praise was inapplicable. It is incense-breathing. Morning is full of promise and vigor. Evening is pensive. The serenity is far more remarkable to those who are on the water. That part of the sky just above the horizon seen reflected, apparently, some rods off from the boat is as light a blue as the actual, but it goes on deepening as your eye draws nearer to the boat, until, when you look directly down at the reflection of the zenith, it is lost in the blackness of the water. It passes through all degrees of dark blue, and the threatening aspect of a cloud is very much enhanced in the reflection. As I wish to be on the water at sunset, I let the boat float. I enjoy now the warmth of summer with some of the water prospect of spring. Looking westward, the surface of the water on the meadows in the sun has a slight dusty appearance, with clear black lines, as if some water nymph had written "slut" with her finger there.

A flock of half a dozen or more blue-winged teal, scared up down-stream behind me, as I was rowing, have circled round to reconnoitre and cross up-stream before me, quite close. I had seen another flock of ducks high in the air in the course of the day. Have ducks then begun to return?

I observe, on the willows on the east shore, the

shadow of my boat and self and oars, upside down, and, I believe, it is joined to the same right side up, but the branches are so thin there that that shadow is not perfect. There goes a great bittern *plodding* home over the meadows at evening, to his perch on some tree by the shore. The rain has washed the leaves clean where he perches. There stands another in the meadow just like a stake, or the point of a stump or root. Its security was consulted both in its form and color. The latter is a sober brown, pale on the breast, as the less exposed side of a root might be; and its attitude is accidental, too, bent forward and *perfectly* motionless. Therefore there is no change in appearance but such as can be referred to the motion of the sailor.

Eupatorium sessilifolium, not yet fully open, — a week or ten days ago must have been the earliest, — Lee's Cliff. *Solidago cæsia*, blue-stemmed, not long. Waxwork berries orange now, not open. What mean the different forms of apocynum leaves? Have we more than one species? The fruit of the triosteum is orange-colored now at Tupelo Cliff. *Polygonum tenue*, slender (I should say upright) knot-grass, there, too (July?). *Polygonum dumetorum*, climbing false-buckwheat. Apparently *Bidens cernua* (?), but is it nodding, and are not its leaves ever trifid? Its achenia are not obovate. Were the pods of my corallorhiza long enough to be the *multiflora*? *Vide* that small lespedeza-like plant at Tupelo Cliff.

V

SEPTEMBER, 1852

(ÆT. 35)

Sept. 1. Wednesday. Some tragedy, at least some dwelling on, or even exaggeration of, the tragic side of life is necessary for contrast or relief to the picture. The genius of the writer may be such a colored glass as Gilpin describes, the use of which is "to give a greater depth to the shades; by which the effect is shown with more force." The whole of life is seen by some through this darker medium, — partakes of the tragic, — and its bright and splendid lights become thus lurid.

4 P. M. — To Walden.

Paddling over it, I see large schools of perch only an inch long, yet easily distinguished by their transverse bars. Great is the beauty of a wooded shore seen from the water, for the trees have ample room to expand on that side, and each puts forth its most vigorous bough to fringe and adorn the pond. It is rare that you see so natural an edge to the forest. Hence a pond like this, surrounded by hills wooded down to the edge of the water, is the best place to observe the tints of the autumnal foliage. Moreover, such as stand in or near to the water change earlier than elsewhere.

This is a very warm and serene evening, and the surface of the pond is perfectly smooth except where

the skaters dimple it, for at equal intervals they are scattered over its whole extent, and, looking west, they make a fine sparkle in the sun. Here and there is a thistle(?)-down floating on its surface, which the fishes dart at, and dimple the water,[1] — delicate hint of approaching autumn, when the first thistle-down descends on some smooth lake's surface, full of reflections, in the woods, sign to the fishes of the ripening year. These white faery vessels are annually wafted over the cope of their sky. Bethink thyself, O man, when the first thistle-down is in the air. Buoyantly it floated high in air over hills and fields all day, and now, weighed down with evening dews, perchance, it sinks gently to the surface of the lake. Nothing can stay the thistle-down, but with September winds it unfailingly sets sail. The irresistible revolution of time. It but comes down upon the sea in its ship, and is still perchance wafted to the shore with its delicate sails. The thistle-down is in the air. Tell me, is thy fruit also there? Dost thou approach maturity? Do gales shake windfalls from thy tree? But I see no dust here as on the river.

Some of the leaves of the rough hawkweed are purple now, especially beneath.

I see a yet smoother, darker water, separated from this abruptly, as if by an invisible cobweb resting on the surface.[2] I view it from Heywood's Peak. How rich and autumnal the haze which blues the distant hills and fills the valleys. The lakes look better in this haze, which confines our view more to their reflected

¹ [*Walden*, pp. 197, 206, 207; Riv. 278, 291–293.]
² [*Walden*, p. 208; Riv. 293.]

heavens and makes the shore-line more indistinct. Viewed from the hilltop, it reflects the color of the sky. Some have referred the vivid greenness next the shores to the reflection of the verdure, but it is equally green there against the railroad sand-bank and in the spring before the leaves are expanded. Beyond the deep reflecting surface, near the shore, where the bottom is seen, it is a vivid green.[1] I see two or three small maples already scarlet, across the pond, beneath where the white stems of three birches diverge, at the point of a promontory next the water, a distinct scarlet tint a quarter of a mile off. Ah, many a tale their color tells of Indian times — and autumn wells [?] — primeval dells.[2] The beautifully varied shores of Walden, — the western indented with deep bays, the bold northern shore, the gracefully sweeping curve of the eastern, and above all the beautifully scalloped southern shore, where successive capes overlap each other and suggest unexplored coves between. Its shore is just irregular enough not to be monotonous. From this peak I can see a fish leap in almost any part of the pond, for not a pickerel or shiner picks an insect from this smooth surface but it manifestly disturbs the equilibrium of the lake. It is wonderful with what elaborateness this simple fact is advertised. This piscine murder will out, and from my distant perch I distinguish the circling undulations when they are now half a dozen rods in diameter.[3] Methinks I distinguish

¹ [*Walden*, p. 196; Riv. 276, 277.]
² [*Walden*, p. 265; Riv. 372.]
³ [*Walden*, p. 208; Riv. 293.]

Fair Haven Pond from this point, elevated by a mirage in its seething valley, like a coin in a basin.[1] They cannot fatally injure Walden with an axe, for they have done their worst and failed. We see things in the reflection which we do not see in the substance. In the reflected woods of Pine Hill there is a vista through which I see the sky, but I am indebted to the water for this advantage, for from this point the actual wood affords no such vista.

Bidens connata (?) not quite out. I see the *Hieracium venosum* still, but slightly veined. Have I not made another species of this variety? *Aster undulatus* (?), like a many-flowered *amplexicaulis*, with leaves narrowed below, a few days. *Amphicarpæa monoica*, like the ground-nut, but ternate, out of bloom; probably July or August. Pods just forming. *Desmodium rotundifolium* just going out of bloom. Last two, side of Heywood's Peak.

Gilpin, who is usually so correct, standing at the head of Loch Fyne in Scotland, which he describes as "a bay of salt water, sixty or seventy fathoms deep, four miles in breadth," and about fifty miles long, surrounded by mountains, observes: "If we could have seen it immediately after the diluvian crash, or whatever convulsion of nature occasioned it, before the waters gushed in, what a horrid chasm must it have appeared!

> "So high as heaved the tumid hills, so low
> Down sunk a hollow bottom broad and deep,
> Capacious bed of waters." [2]

[1] [This sentence is queried in the margin.]
[2] [William Gilpin, *Observations on the Highlands of Scotland.*]

But if we apply these proportions to Walden, which, as we have seen, appears already in a *transverse* section like a shallow plate, it will appear four times as shallow. So much for the increased horrors of the emptied chasm of Loch Fyne. No doubt many a smiling valley with its extended fields of corn occupies exactly such a "horrid chasm," from which the waters have receded, though it requires the insight of the geologist to convince the unsuspicious inhabitants of the fact. Most ponds, being emptied, would leave a meadow no more hollow than we frequently see. I have seen many a village situated in the midst of a plain which the geologist has at length affirmed must have been levelled by water, where the observing eye might still detect the shores of a lake in the horizon, and no subsequent elevation of the plain was necessary to conceal the fact.[1]

Thus it is only by emphasis and exaggeration that real effects are described. What Gilpin says in another place is perfectly applicable to this case; though he says that that which he is about to disclose is so bold a truth, "that it ought only, perhaps, to be opened to the initiated." "In the exhibition of distant mountains on paper, or canvas," says he, "unless you make them exceed their *real* or *proportional* size, they have no effect. It is inconceivable how objects lessen by distance. Examine any distance, closed by mountains, in a camera, and you will easily see what a poor, diminutive appearance the mountains make. By the power of perspective they are lessened to nothing. Should

[1] [*Walden*, pp. 317, 318; Riv. 443, 444.]

you represent them in your landscape in so diminutive a form, all dignity, and grandeur of idea would be lost."

Sept. 2. P. M. — To Walden.

The seringo, too, has long been silent like other birds. The red prinos berries ripe in sunny places. Rose hips begin to be handsome. Small flocks of pigeons are seen these days. Distinguished from doves by their sharper wings and bodies. August has been a month of berries and melons, small fruits. First in the descent from summer's culminating-point. There is a stillness in nature for want of singing birds, commenced a month or more ago; only the crickets' louder creak to supply their place. I have not heard a bullfrog this long time. The small cornel, or bunch-berry, is in bloom now (!!) near the pond. What great tuft-like masses the cow-wheat makes now in sprout-lands!

As I look over the pond now from the eastern shore, I am obliged to employ both my hands to defend my eyes against the reflected as well as the true sun, for they appear equally bright; and between my hands I look over the smooth and glassy surface of the lake. The skaters make the finest imaginable sparkle. Otherwise it is literally as smooth as glass, except where a fish leaps into the air or a swallow dips beneath its surface. Sometimes a fish describes an arc of three or four feet in the air, and there is a bright flash where it emerges and another where it strikes the water.[1] A slight haze at this season makes the shore-line so much

[1] [*Walden*, p. 207; Riv. 292, 293.]

the more indistinct. Looking across the pond from the Peak toward Fair Haven, which I seem to see, all the earth beyond appears insulated and floated, even by this small sheet of water, the heavens being seen reflected, as it were beneath it, so that it looks thin.

The scenery of this small pond is humble though very beautiful, and does not approach to grandeur, nor can it much concern one who has not long frequented it, or lived by its shore.[1]

Sept. 3. 1 A. M., moon waning, to Conantum.

A warm night. A thin coat sufficient. I hear an apple fall, as I go along the road. Meet a man going to market thus early. There are no mists to diversify the night. Its features are very simple. I hear no whippoor-will or other bird. See no fireflies. Saw a whippoor-will (?) flutter across the road. Hear the dumping sound of frogs on the river meadow, and occasionally a kind of croak as from a bittern there. It is very dewy, and I bring home much mud on my shoes. This is a peculiarity of night, — its dews, water resuming its reign. Return before dawn. Morning and evening are more attractive than midnight.

I will endeavor to separate the tide in my thoughts, or what is due to the influence of the moon, from the current distractions and fluctuations. The winds which the sun has aroused go down at evening, and the lunar influence may then perchance be detected.

Of late I have not heard the wood thrush.

[1] [*Walden*, p. 195; Riv. 275.]

Sept. 5. P. M. — To Cliffs.

The petals of the purple gerardia strew the brooks. The oval spikes of somewhat pear-shaped berries of the arum perhaps vermilion-color now; its scapes bent to the ground. These by their color must have caught an Indian's eye. The brooks are full of red rootlets of the alder, etc. The country begins to have a dry and *flavid* look, — corn-fields, grass-fields, etc., — and when winds blow, a slight rustling is heard. I observed minute red maples, on the shore near water, only an inch high, completely turned red. I have noticed the thistle-down now for some days in the air, not yet the milkweed, though some flowers of the thistle are still seen. Some galls on the oak an inch in diameter like Castile soap balls, quite handsome. Some smaller and redder, with watered zones. Interesting kind of parasitic fruits, not so handsome, perchance, as the pincushion galls of the spring. What is that bidens now just blossomed, rough-stemmed or bristly, with undivided, lanceolate, serrate, and strongly connate leaves, short but conspicuous rays, achenia four-awned and downwardly barbed?[1]

Sept. 6. Monday. To Peterboro. Railroad to Mason Village.

Observed from cars at 7.30 A. M. the dew, or fog rather, on the fine grass in meadows, — a dirty white, which, one of these mornings, will be frozen to a white frost. A woman who wished to go to Nashua was left behind at Groton Junction, — to which she said, "Why,

[1] *B. cernua.*

Vol. IV

I was *he-ar.*" Girls picking hops in Townsend. Some fields are completely yellow — one mass of yellow — from the solidago. It is the prevailing flower the traveller sees. Walked from Mason Village over the mountain-*tops* to Peterboro. Saw, sailing over Mason Village about 10 A. M., a white-headed and *white-tailed* eagle with black wings, — a grand sight. The "doubly compound racemed panicles" of the spikenard berries, varnish-colored berries, or color of varnished mahogany. Met a crazy man, probably being carried to a hospital, who must take us both by the hand and tell us how the spirit of God had descended on him and given him all the world, and he was going to make every man a present of half a million, etc., etc. High blackberries by the roadside abundant still, the long, sweet, mulberry-shaped ones, mostly confined to the road, and very grateful to the walker. A stone by the roadside in Temple, whitewashed, with an inscription in black, evincing the vulgarity of the Yankees, "Here Jesse Spofford was killed," etc., etc., not telling how. Thus we record only the trivial, not the important event, as the advent of a thought. Who cares whether Jesse Spofford was killed or not, if he does not know whether he was worthy to live?

The tavern-keeper at Temple said the summit just south of the Peterboro road, covered with wood, was the highest (probably a mistake), — 980 feet above Temple Common, which is itself very high. Went across lots from here toward this. When part way up, or on a lower part of the ridge, discovered it was not the highest, and turned northward across the road to what

is apparently the highest, first having looked south to Kidder's mountain, between New Ipswich and Temple and further west and quite near to Boundary Mountain between Sharon and Temple. Already we had had experience of a mountain-side covered with bare rocks, as if successive thunder [*sic*] spouts had burst over it and bleached timber lying across the rocks, the woodbine red as blood about a tall stump, and the strong, sweet, bracing scent of ferns between the rocks, the raspberry bushes still retaining a few berries. They usually tell you how many mountain-houses you can see from a mountain, but they are interesting to me in proportion to the number you cannot see. We went down the west side of this first mountain, from whose summit we could not see west on account of another ridge; descended far, and across the road, and up the southernmost of what I have called the Peterboro Hills. The raw edge of a forest of canoe birches on the side of this hill was remarkable on account of the wonderful contrast of the white stems with the green leaves; the former glaringly white, as if whitewashed and varnished or polished. You now hear that grating, creaking flight of the grasshopper. There is something in the aspect of the evergreens, the dwarfed forests and the bare rocks of mountain-tops, and the scent of the ferns, stern yet sweet to man. Hazy. Monadnock would probably look better toward evening. It was now two or three P. M. In the woods near the top, the *Viburnum lantanoides*, hobble-bush, American wayfaring-tree, in fruit, mostly large and red, but the ripe dark blue or black like the *V. nudum*, — what I have

formerly falsely called moose-berry. Probably it does not grow in Concord.

Went, still across lots, to Peterboro village, which we could not see from the mountain. But first we had seen the Lyndeboro Mountain, north of these two, — partly in Greenfield, — and further Crotched Mountain, and in the northeast Uncannunuc. Descended where, as usual, the forest had been burned formerly, — tall bleached masts still standing, making a very wild and agreeably [*sic*] scenery, — keeping on a westward spur or side, that we might see north and south. Saw the pond on the " embenchement " between the two mountains. Some sheep ran from us in great fear. Others put their heads down and together, and stood *perfectly still*, resembling rocks, so that I did not notice them at first. Did they not do it for concealment? After we got down, the prevailing trees were hemlock, spruce, black and yellow birch, and beech, the ground very cleanly and smoothly carpeted with the old leaves of the last two especially, without weeds. Saw some ground-hemlock with some fruit still. Had seen on the hill *Polygonum cilinode*, running polygonum, but no flower, — *alias* fringe-jointed false-buckwheat.

A man in Peterboro told me that his father told him that Monadnock used to be covered with forest, that fires ran through it and killed the turf; then the trees were blown down, and their roots turned up and formed a dense and impenetrable thicket in which the wolves abounded. They came down at night, killed sheep, etc., and returned to their dens, whither they could not be pursued, before morning; till finally they set fire to

this thicket, and it made the greatest fire they had
ever had in the county, and drove out all the wolves,
which have not troubled them since. He himself had
seen one wolf killed there when he was a boy. They
kill now raccoons, hedgehogs, and wildcats there. I
thought that I did not see so great a proportion of
forest from their hilltops as about Concord, to which
they agreed. I should say their hills were uncommonly
rocky, — more stone than soil.

Sept. 7. *Tuesday.* Went, across lots still, to Monadnock, the base some half-dozen miles in a straight line
from Peterboro, — six or seven miles. (It had been
eleven miles (*by road*) from Mason Village to Peterboro.) My clothes sprinkled with ambrosia pollen.
Saw near the mountain a field of turnips whose leaves,
all but the midribs, were eaten up by grasshoppers and
looked white over the field, and sometimes the turnips were eaten also. Joe Eavely's, the house nearest
the top, that we saw under the east side, a small red
house a little way up. The summit hardly more than
a mile distant in a straight line, but about two miles as
they go. Bunch-berries everywhere now. *Acer Pennsylvanicum,* striped maple or moosewood or striped dogwood, but no keys to be seen, — a very large-leaved,
three-lobed maple with a handsome striped bark.
This, I believe, the Indians smoke. Also *Acer spicatum,*
mountain maple, with upright racemes in fruit. Between the rocks on the summit, an abundance of large
and fresh blueberries still, apparently *Vaccinium Pennsylvanicum,* very large, fresh and cooling to eat, supply-

ing the place of water. They said they did not get ripe
so early as below, but at any rate they last much longer;
both, perhaps, because of the greater coolness of the
atmosphere. Though this vegetation was very humble,
yet it was very productive of fruit. In one little hollow between the rocks grew blueberries, choke-berries,
bunch-berries, *red* cherries, wild currants (*Ribes pro-
stratum,* with the berry the odor of skunk-cabbage,
but a not quite disagreeable wild flavor), a few raspberries still, holly berries, mountain cranberries (*Vaccinium Vitis-Idæa*), all close together. The little soil
on the summit between the rocks was covered with the
Potentilla tridentata, now out of bloom, the prevailing
plant at the extreme summit. Mountain-ash berries
also.

Descending toward Troy, a little after 1 P. M.,
plucked the *Trillium erythrocarpum* with the large red
berry, painted trillium. The *Aster acuminatus,* with
its leaves in a whorl, white; methinks we may have it.
When we had got down, we could see that the mountain had spurs or buttresses on every side, by whose
ridge you might ascend. It is an interesting feature in
a mountain. I have noticed that they will send out
these buttresses every way from their centre.

Were on the top of the mountain at 1 P. M. The
cars left Troy, four or five miles off, at three. We
reached the depot, by running at last, at the same instant the cars did, and reached Concord at a quarter
after five, *i. e.* four hours from the time we were picking blueberries on the mountain, with the plants of the
mountain fresh in my hat.

Vol. IV

Sept. 8. Grapes ripe on the Assabet for some days.
Gentiana saponaria out. Carrion-flower berries ripe for
some days. *Polygala verticillata* still, on left side of
road beyond Lee place. I put it with the other polygalas in July. Do I perceive the shadows lengthen
already?

Sept. 9. There are enough who will flatter me with
sweet words, and anon use bitter ones to balance
them, but they are not my friends. Simple sincerity
and truth are rare indeed. One acquaintance criticises
me to my face, expecting every moment that I will become his friend to pay for it. I hear my acquaintance
thinking his criticism aloud. We love to talk with those
who can make a good guess at us, not with those who
talk to us as if we were somebody else all the while.
Our neighbors invite us to be amiable toward their
vices. How simple is the law of love! One who loves
us acts accordingly, and anon we come together and
succeed together without let or hindrance.

Yesterday and to-day have felt about as hot as any
weather this year. The potato-balls lie ripe in the
fields. The groundsel down is in the air. The last day
of August I saw a sharp-nosed green grasshopper. The
goldenrods resound with the hum of bees and other insects. Methinks the little leaves now springing, which I
have called mullein, must be fragrant everlasting (?).
I believe that I occasionally hear a hylodes within a
day or two. In front of Cæsar's, the *Crotalaria sagittalis,*
rattle-pod, still in bloom, though the seeds are ripe;
probably began in July. Also by Cæsar's well, *Liatris*

scariosa, handsome rose-purple, with the aspect of a
Canada thistle at a distance, or a single vernonia. Referred to August. Ah! the beauty of the liatris bud
just bursting into bloom, the rich fiery rose-purple, like
that of the sun at his rising. Some call it button snake-
root. Those crotalaria pods would make pretty playthings for children.

Sept. 11. Genius is, like the snapping-turtle, born
with a great developed head. They say our brain at
birth is one sixth the weight of the body.

Cranberries are being raked for fear of frosts. These
fall rains are a peculiarity of the season. How much
fresher some flowers look in rainy weather! When I
thought they were about done, they appear to revive,
and moreover their beauty is enhanced, as if by the
contrast of the louring atmosphere with their bright
colors. Such are the purple gerardia and the *Bidens
cernua.* The purple gerardia and blue-curls are interesting for their petals strewn about, beaten down by
the rain. Many a brook I look into is strewn with the
purple petals of the gerardia, whose stalk is not obvious in the bank. Again the *Potentilla Canadensis* var.
pumila, and dandelions occasionally.

Sept. 13. Yesterday it rained all day, with considerable wind, which has strewn the ground with apples
and peaches, and, all the country over, people are busy
picking up the windfalls. More leaves also have fallen.
Rain has as much to do with it as wind. Rode round
through Lincoln and a part of Weston and Wayland.

The barberries, now red and reddening, begin to show. Asters, various shades of blue, and especially the smaller kinds of *dense-flowering white ones*, are more than ever by the roadsides. The great bidens in the sun in brooks affects me as the rose of the fall, the most *flavid* product of the water and the sun. They are low suns in the brook. The golden glow of autumn concentrated, more golden than the sun. How surely this yellow comes out along the brooks when you have applied the chemical test of autumn air to it! It yellows along the brook. The earth wears different colors or liveries at different seasons. If I come by at this season, a golden blaze will salute me here from a thousand suns.

How earnestly and rapidly each creature, each flower, is fulfilling its part while its day lasts! Nature never lost a day, nor a moment. As the planet in its orbit and around its axis, so do the seasons, so does time, revolve, with a rapidity inconceivable. In the moment, in the æon, well employed, time ever advances with this rapidity. To an idler the man employed is terribly rapid. He that is not behind his time is swift. The immortals are swift. Clear the track! The plant that waited a whole year, and then blossomed the instant it was ready and the earth was ready for it, without the conception of delay, was rapid. To the conscience of the idle man, the stillness of a placid September day sounds like the din and whirl of a factory. Only employment can still this din in the air.

In my ride I experienced the pleasure of coming into a landscape where there was more distance and a bluish

tinge in the horizon. I am not contented long with such narrow valleys that all is greenness in them. I wish to see the earth translated, the green passing into blue. How this heaven intervenes and tinges our more distant prospects! The farther off the mountain which is the goal of our enterprise, the more of heaven's tint it wears. This is the chief value of a distance in landscapes.

I must walk more with free senses. It is as bad to *study* stars and clouds as flowers and stones. I must let my senses wander as my thoughts, my eyes see without looking. Carlyle said that how to observe was to look, but I say that it is rather to see, and the more you look the less you will observe. I have the habit of attention to such excess that my senses get no rest, but suffer from a constant strain. Be not preoccupied with looking. Go not to the object; let it come to you. When I have found myself ever looking down and confining my gaze to the flowers, I have thought it might be well to get into the habit of observing the clouds as a corrective; but no! that study would be just as bad. What I need is not to look at all, but a true sauntering of the eye.

Sept. 14. This morning the first frost. Yet the 10th was one of the warmest days in the year. Methinks it is the *Amaranthus hypochondriacus*, prince's-feather, with "bright red-purple flowers" and sanguine stem, on Emerson's muck-heap in the Turnpike, and the *Polygonum orientale*, prince's-feather, in E. Hosmer's grounds. Blue vervain still. The grass is very green

after the rains, like a second spring, and, in my ride yesterday, the under sides of the willows, etc., in the wind, the leaves of the fall growth perhaps, reminded me of June. Is not the colder and frosty weather thus introduced by a rain? *i. e.* it clears up cold.

Sept. 16. *Thursday.* 8 A. M. — To Fair Haven Pond. Since the rains and the sun, great fungi, six inches in diameter, stand in the woods, warped upward on their edges, showing their gills, so as to hold half a gill of water.

The two-leaved convallaria berries are now decidedly red. The sweet-fern has a russet look. The jay screams; the goldfinch twitters; the barberries are red. I heard a warbling vireo in the village, which I have not heard for long, and the common *che-wink* note in the woods. Some birds, like some flowers, begin to sing again in the fall. The corn is topped.

The rippled blue surface of Fair Haven from the Cliffs, with its smooth white border where weeds preserve the surface smooth, a placid silver-plated rim. The pond is like the sky with a border of whitish clouds in the horizon. Yesterday it rained all day.

What makes this such a day for hawks? There are eight or ten in sight from the Cliffs, large and small, one or more with a white rump. I detected the transit of the first by his shadow on the rock, and I look toward the sun for him. Though he is made light beneath to conceal him, his shadow betrays him. A hawk must get out of the wood, must get above it, where he can sail. It is narrow dodging for him amid the boughs.

He cannot be a hawk there, but only perch gloomily. Now I see a large one — perchance an eagle, I say to myself! — down in the valley, circling and circling, higher and wider. This way he comes. How beautiful does he repose on the air, in the moment when he is directly over you, and you see the form and texture of his wings! How light he must make himself, how much earthy heaviness expel, before he can thus soar and sail! He carries no useless clogs there with him. They are out by families; while one is circling this way, another circles that. Kites without strings. Where is the boy that flies them? Are not the hawks most observed at this season?

Before this, probably no leaves have been affected by frost. The puffballs (?), five to eight fingered, now. Tobacco-pipe still, and the water parsnip. Discovered an excellent lively wild red grape. Why not propagate from it and call it the *Musketaquid?* Gathered some sound blueberries still. Mitchella berries ripe. Dogsbane still. What I have called the *Cornus circinata* is that of Emerson, if you call the fruit white tinged with blue (in Laurel Glen), but its cyme is not flat, as Gray says. Its berries to-day. I suspect that my *C. stolonifera* is the *sericea*. Maple-leaved viburnum berries, dark-bluish.

The Norwegians, the Normen [*sic*], were such inveterate mariners that they called the summit of the mountain chain which separates Norway from Sweden the Keel Ridge of the country, as if it were a vessel turned up.[1]

[1] [See *Journal*, vol. iii, p. 201.]

Sept. 17. What produces this flashing air of autumn? — a brightness as if there were not green enough to absorb the light, now that the first frosts wither the herbs. The corn-stalks are stacked like muskets along the fields. The pontederia leaves are sere and brown along the river. The fall is further advanced in the water, as the spring was earlier there. I should say that the vegetation of the river was a month further advanced in its decay than of the land generally. The yellow lily pads are apparently decayed generally; as I wade, I tread on their great roots only; and the white lily pads are thinned. Now, before any effects of the frost are obvious on the leaves, I observe two black rows of dead pontederia in the river. Is it the alder locust that rings so loud in low land now? The umbel-shaped smilax berry clusters are now ripe. Still the oxalis blows, and yellow butterflies are on the flowers. I hear the downy woodpecker whistle, and see him looking about the apple trees as if to bore him a hole. Are they returning south? Abundance of wild grapes.

I laid down some wild red grapes in front of the Cliffs, three united to a two-thirds-inch stock, many feet from the root, under an alder *marked* with two or three small sticks atop, and, ten feet north, two more of different stocks, one-half inch diameter, directly on the edge of the brook, their tops over the water, the shell of a five-inch log across them.

Sept. 18. I think it must be the *Cornus sericea* which I have called the *stolonifera. Vide* that red stem on the Bear Hill road. The poor student begins now to seek

the sun. In the forenoons I move into a chamber on the east side of the house, and so follow the sun round. It is agreeable to stand in a new relation to the sun. They begin to have a fire occasionally below-stairs.

3.30 P. M. — A-barberrying to Flint's Pond.

The goldenrods have generally lost their brightness. Methinks the asters were in their prime four or five days ago. Came upon a nighthawk on the ground in Thrush Alley. There are many large toadstools, pecked apparently by birds. I find the Castile soap gall still under the oaks. The robins of late fly in flocks, and I hear them oftener. The partridges, grown up, oftener burst away. Pennyroyal still in bloom. The crows congregate and pursue me through the half-covered woodland path, cawing loud and angrily above me, and when they cease, I hear the winnowing sound of their wings. What ragged ones! Water lobelia still in blossom. Gratiola, horned utricularia, and the white globose flower by Flint's still. Is that the *Cirsium muticum*, four feet high, in the blue-stemmed goldenrod path, with a glutinous involucre, but I should say spinous? The prinos berries now quite red. How densely they cover the bushes! Very handsome, contrasting with the leaves. The barberries are not wholly reddened yet. How much handsomer in fruit for being bent down in wreaths by the weight! The increasing weight of the fruits adds gracefulness to the form of the bush. I get my hands full of thorns, but my basket full of berries. How productive a barberry bush! On each the berries seem more abundant and plumper than on the last. They stand amid the cedars. Coming home by the

Vol. IV

pond road, I see and smell the grapes on trees, under the dense bowers made by their leaves in trees, three feet above the water or the road. The purple clusters hang at that height and scent the air. They impart a sense of tropical richness to our zone. I hear little warbling sparrows in the garden, which apparently have come from the north. Now-a-nights there are fogs pretty extensive in the evening.

Sophia has come from Bangor and brought the *Dalibarda repens*, white dalibarda, a little crenate-rounded-heart-shaped-leafed flower of damp woods; the small-leaved *Geranium Carolinianum;* etc.

Sept. 19. P. M. — To Great Meadows.

The red capsules of the sarothra. Many large crickets about on the sand. Observe the effects of frost in particular places. Some blackberry vines are very red. I see the oxalis and the tree primrose and the Norway cinquefoil and the prenanthes and the *Epilobium coloratum* and the cardinal-flower and the small hypericum and yarrow, and I think it is the *Ranunculus repens*, between Ripley Hill and river, with spotted leaves lingering still. The soapwort gentian cheers and surprises, — solid bulbs of blue from the shade, the stale grown purplish. It abounds along the river, after so much has been mown. The polygala and the purple gerardia are still common and attract by their high color. The small-flowering *Bidens cernua* (?) and the fall dandelion and the fragrant everlasting abound. The *Viola lanceolata* has blossomed again, and the lambkill. What pretty six-fingered leaves the three oxalis leafets make! I see

the effects of frost on the *Salix Purshiana*, imbrowning their masses; and in the distance is a maple or two by the water, beginning to blush.

That small, slender-leaved, rose-tinted (white petals, red calyx) polygonum by the river is perhaps in its prime now; slender spikes and slender lanceolate sessile leaves, with rent hairy and ciliate sheaths, eight stamens, and three styles united in middle. Not biting. I cannot find it described. And what is that white flower which I should call *Cicuta maculata*, except that the veins do not terminate in the sinuses?

Sept. 20. The smooth sumachs are turning conspicuously and generally red, apparently from frost, and here and there is a whole maple tree red, about water. In some hollows in sprout-lands, the grass and ferns are crisp and brown from frost. I suppose it is the *Aster undulatus*, or variable aster, with a large head of middle-sized blue flowers. The *Viola sagittata* has blossomed again. The *Galium circæzans* (?) still, and narrow-leaved johnswort.

On Heywood's Peak by Walden. — The surface is not *perfectly* smooth, on account of the zephyr, and the reflections of the woods are a little indistinct and blurred. How soothing to sit on a stump on this height, overlooking the pond, and study the dimpling circles which are incessantly inscribed and again erased on the smooth and otherwise invisible surface, amid the reflected skies! The reflected sky is of a deeper blue. How beautiful that over this vast expanse there can be no disturbance, but it is thus at once gently smoothed away and assuaged, as, when a vase of water is jarred, the trembling circles seek the shore and all is smooth again! Not a fish can leap or an insect fall on it but it is reported in lines of beauty, in circling dimples, as it were the constant welling up of its fountain, the gentle pulsing of its life, the heaving of its breast. The thrills of joy and those of pain are indistinguishable. How sweet the phenomena of the lake! Everything that moves on its surface produces a sparkle. The peaceful pond! The works of men shine as in the spring. The motion of an oar or an insect produces a flash of light; and if an oar falls, how sweet the echo![1]

The groundsel and hieracium down is in the air. The golden plover, they say, has been more than usually plenty here this year. Droves of cattle have for some time been coming down from up-country.

How distinctly each thing in nature is marked! as the day by a little yellow sunlight, so that the sluggard cannot mistake it.

Sept. 21. P. M. — To Conantum.

The small skull-cap and cress and the mullein still in bloom. I see pigeon woodpeckers oftener now, with their light rears. Birches and elms begin to turn yellow, and ferns are quite yellow or brown in many places. I see many tall clustered bluish asters by the brooks, like the *A. undulatus.* The blue-stemmed goldenrod is abundant, bright and in its prime. The maples begin to be ripe. How beautiful when a whole maple on the edge of a swamp is like one great scarlet

[1] [*Walden*, pp. 208, 209; Riv. 294, 295.]

Sept. 22. Sophia has in her herbarium and has found in Concord these which I have not seen this summer: —

Pogonia verticillata, Hubbard's Second Wood. Bigelow says July.
Trillium erythrocarpum, Bigelow says May and June.
Uvularia perfoliata, Bigelow says May.

P. M. — On river.

The *Polygonum amphibium* var. *terrestre* is a late flower, and now more common and the spikes larger, quite handsome and conspicuous, and more like a prince's-feather than any. Large woolly aphides are now clustered close together on the alder stems. Some of those I see are probably the sharp-shinned hawk. When was it I heard the upland plover? Has been a great flight of blue-winged teal this season. The soapwort gentian the flower of the river-banks now.

In love we impart, each to each, in subtlest immaterial form of thought or atmosphere, the best of ourselves, such as commonly vanishes or evaporates in aspirations, and mutually enrich each other. The lover alone perceives and dwells in a certain human fragrance. To him humanity is not only a flower, but an aroma and a flavor also.

Sept. 23. P. M. — Round by Clematis Brook.

The forget-me-not still. I observe the rounded tops of the dogwood bushes, scarlet in the distance, on the edge of the meadow (Hubbard's), more full and bright than any flower. The maples are mostly darker, the

fruit, full of ripe juices! A sign of the ripening. Every leaf, from lowest limb to topmost spire, is aglow.[1] The woodbine is red, too, and its berries are bluing. The flattened black berries of the cucumber-root, with the triangular bases of its leaves tinged red beneath, as a sort of cup for them. My red ball fungus *blossoms* in the path in the midst of its jelly.

As I was walking through the maple swamp by the Corner Spring, I was surprised to see apples on the ground, and at first supposed that somebody had dropped them, but, looking up, I detected a wild apple tree, as tall and slender as the young maples and not more than five inches in diameter at the ground. This had blossomed and borne fruit this year. The apples were quite mellow and of a very agreeable flavor, though they had a rusty-scraperish look, and I filled my pockets with them. The squirrels had found them out before me. It is an agreeable surprise to find in the midst of a swamp so large and edible a fruit as an apple.

Of late we have much cloudy weather without rain. Are not liable to showers, as in summer, but may have a storm. The *Lentago* berries appear to drop off before, or as soon as, they turn. There are few left on the bushes. Many that I bring home will turn in a single night. The sassafras leaves are red. The huckleberry bushes begin to redden. The white actæa berries still hang on, or their red pedicels remain.

My friend is he who can make a good guess at me, hit me on the wing.

[1] [*Excursions*, p. 259; Riv. 318.]

very few boughs that are turned, and the tupelo, which is reddening. The ash is just beginning to turn. The scarlet dogwood is the striking bush to-day. I find huckleberries on Conantum still sound and blackening the bushes.

How much longer a mile appears between two blue mountain peaks thirty or more miles off in the horizon than one would expect!

Some acorns and hickory nuts on the ground, but they have not begun to shell. Is it the nut of the *Carya amara*, with raised seams, but not bitter, that I perceive? I suppose that is the *Carya tomentosa*, or mockernut hickory, with large rounded nuts on Lee's land. The bitternuts (?), rubbed together, smell like varnish.

The sarothra in bloom. The wind from the north has turned the white lily pads wrong side up, so that they look red, and their stems are slanted up-stream. Almost all the yellow ones have disappeared. A blue-stemmed goldenrod, its stem and leaves red. The woodbine high on trees in the shade a delicate pink. I gathered some haws very good to eat to-day. I think they must be the senelles of the Canadians. *Hamamelis Virginiana* out, before its leaves fall. A woodchuck out. The waxwork not opened. The " feathery tails " of the clematis fruit conspicuous and interesting now. Yellow lily out (again ?) in the pond-holes.

Passing a corn-field the other day, close by a hat and coat on a stake, I recognized the owner of the farm. Any of his acquaintances would. He was only a trifle more weather[-beaten] than when I saw him last. His back being toward me, I missed nothing, and I thought to myself if I were a crow I should not fear the balance of him, at any rate.[1]

In northern latitudes, where other edible fruits are scarce, they make an account of haws and bunch-berries.

The barberry bushes in Clematis Hollow are very beautiful now, with their wreaths of red or scarlet fruit drooping over a rock.

Sept. 24. According to Emerson, *Lonicera hirsuta,* hairy honeysuckle, grows in Sudbury. Some hickories are yellow. Hazel bushes a brownish red. Most grapes are shrivelled. Pasture thistle still. The zizania ripe, shining black, cylindrical kernels, five eighths of an inch long. The fruit of the thorn trees on Lee's Hill is large, globular, and gray-dotted, but I cannot identify it certainly.

Sept. 25. *Polygonum dumetorum,* climbing false-buckwheat, still; also dodder. The fall dandelions are a prevailing flower on low turfy grounds, especially near the river. *Ranunculus reptans* still. The small galium (*trifidum*). A rose again, apparently *lucida* (?). This is always unexpected. The scarlet of the dogwood is the most conspicuous and interesting of the autumnal colors at present. You can now easily detect them at a distance; every one in the swamps you overlook is revealed. The smooth sumach and the mountain is a darker, deeper, bloodier red.

Found the *Bidens Beckii* (?) September 1st, and the fringed gentian November 7th, last year.

[1] [*Walden,* p. 24; Riv. 37.]

Sept. 26. Dreamed of purity last night. The thoughts seemed not to originate with me, but I was invested, my thought was tinged, by another's thought. It was not I that originated, but I that *entertained* the thought.

The river is getting to be too cold for bathing. There are comparatively few weeds left in it.

It is not in vain, perhaps, that every winter the forest is brought to our doors, shaggy with lichens. Even in so humble a shape as a wood-pile, it contains sermons for us.

P. M. — To Ministerial Swamp.

The small cottony leaves of the fragrant everlasting in the fields for some time, protected, as it were, by a little web of cotton against frost and snow, — a little dense web of cotton spun over it, — entangled in it, — as if to restrain it from rising higher.

The increasing scarlet and yellow tints around the meadows and river remind me of the opening of a vast flower-bud; they are the petals of its corolla, which is of the width of the valleys. It is the flower of autumn, whose expanding bud just begins to blush. As yet, however, in the forest there are very few changes of foliage.

The *Polygonum articulatum,* giving a rosy tinge to Jenny's Desert and elsewhere, is very interesting now, with its slender dense racemes of rose-tinted flowers, apparently without leaves, rising cleanly out of the sand. It looks warm and brave, a foot or more high, and mingled with deciduous blue-curls. It is much divided, into many spreading slender-racemed branches, with

inconspicuous linear leaves, reminding me, both by its form and its color, of a peach orchard in blossom, especially when the sunlight falls on it. Minute rose-tinted flowers that brave the frosts and advance the summer into fall, warming with their color sandy hillsides and deserts, like the glow of evening reflected on the sand. Apparently all flower and no leaf. A warm blush on the sands, after frosty nights have come. Perhaps it may be called the " evening red." Rising, apparently, with clean bare stems from the sand, it spreads out into this graceful head of slender rosy racemes, wisp-like. This little desert of less than [an] acre blushes with it.

I see now ripe, large (three-inch), very dark chocolate(?)-colored puffballs. Are then my five-fingers puffballs? The tree fern is in fruit now, with its delicate, tendril-like fruit climbing three or four feet over the asters, goldenrods, etc., on the edge of the swamp. The large ferns are yellow or brown now. Larks, like robins, fly in flocks. Dogsbane leaves a clear yellow. Succory in bloom at the Tommy Wheeler house. It bears the frost well, though we have not had much. Set out for use. The *Gnaphalium plantaginifolium* leaves, green above, downy beneath.

Sept. 27. Monday. P. M. — To C. Smith's Hill.

The flashing clearness of the atmosphere. More light appears to be reflected from the earth, less absorbed. Green lice are still on the birches.

At Saw Mill Brook many finely cut and flat ferns are faded whitish and very handsome, as if pressed, — very

delicate. White oak acorns edible. Everywhere the squirrels are trying the nuts in good season. The touch-me-not seed-vessels go off like pistols, — shoot their seeds off like bullets. They explode in my hat.

The arum berries are now in perfection, cone-shaped spikes an inch and a half long, of scarlet or vermilion-colored, irregular, somewhat pear-shaped berries springing from a purplish core. They are exactly the color of bright sealing-wax, or, I believe, the painted tortoise's shell; on club-shaped peduncles. The changed leaves of this are delicately white, especially beneath. Here and there lies prostrate on the damp leaves or ground this conspicuous red spike. The medeola berries are common now, and the large red berries of the panicled Solomon's-seal.

It must have been a turtle dove that eyed me so near, turned its head sideways to me for a fair view, looking with a St. Vitus twitching of its neck, as if to recover its balance on an unstable perch, — that is their way.

From Smith's Hill I looked toward the mountain line. Who can believe that the mountain peak which he beholds fifty miles off in the horizon, rising far and faintly blue above an intermediate range, while he stands on his trivial native hills or in the dusty highway, can be the same with that which he looked up at once near at hand from a gorge in the midst of primitive woods? For a part of two days I travelled across lots once, loitering by the way, through primitive wood and swamps over the highest peak of the Peterboro Hills to Monadnock, by ways from which all landlords and stage-drivers endeavored to dissuade us. It was not a month ago. But now that I look across the globe in an instant to the dim Monadnock peak, and these familiar fields and copsewoods appear to occupy the greater part of the interval, I cannot realize that Joe Eavely's house still stands there at the base of the mountain, and all that long tramp through wild woods with invigorating scents before I got to it. I cannot realize that on the tops of those cool blue ridges are in abundance berries still, bluer than themselves, as if they borrowed their blueness from their locality. From the mountains we do not discern our native hills; but from our native hills we look out easily to the far blue mountains, which seem to preside over them. As I look northwestward to that summit from a Concord cornfield, how little can I realize all the life that is passing between me and it, — the retired up-country farmhouses, the lonely mills, wooded vales, wild rocky pastures, and new clearings on stark mountain-sides, and rivers murmuring through primitive woods! All these, and how much more, I *overlook*. I see the very peak, — there can be no mistake, — but how much I do not see, that is between me and it! How much I overlook! In this way we see stars. What is it but a faint blue cloud, a mist that may vanish? But what is it, on the other hand, to one who has travelled to it day after day, has threaded the forest and climbed the hills that are between this and that, has tasted the raspberries or the blueberries that grow on it, and the springs that gush from it, has been wearied with climbing its rocky sides, felt the coolness of its summit, and been lost in the clouds there?

rising amid the maples and birches in a swamp the rounded tops of apple trees rosy with fair fruit.

A windy day. What have these high and roaring winds to do with the fall? No doubt they speak plainly enough to the sap that is in these trees, and perchance they check its upward flow.

A very handsome *gray dotted* thorn near the black birch grove, six inches in diameter, with a top large in proportion, as large as a small apple tree, bristling with many thorns from suckers about its trunk. This is a very handsome object, and the largest thorn I have seen in Concord, almost bare of leaves and one mass of red fruit, five eighths of an inch in diameter, causing its slender branches to spread and droop gracefully. It reminds me of a wisp of straws tied together, or a dust-brush upright on its handle. It must be the same I have seen in Canada. The same with that on Naw-shawtuct. Probably most beautiful in fruit, not only on account of its color, but because this causes the branches to spread and curve outward gracefully.

Ah, if I could put into words that music that I hear; that music which can bring tears to the eyes of marble statues! — to which the very muscles of men are obedient!

Sept. 30. Thursday. 10 A. M. — To Fair Haven Pond, bee-hunting, — Pratt, Rice, Hastings, and myself, in a wagon.

A fine, clear day after the coolest night and severest frost we have had. The apparatus was, first a simple round tin box about four and a half inches in diameter

When I could sit in a cold chamber muffled in a cloak each evening till Thanksgiving time, warmed by my own thoughts, the world was not so much with me.

Sept. 28. P. M. — To the Boulder Field.

I find the hood-leaved violet quite abundant in a meadow, and the *pedata* in the Boulder Field. I have now seen all but the *blanda*, *palmata*, and *pubescens* blooming again, and bluebirds and robins, etc., are heard again in the air. This is the commencement, then, of the second spring. Violets, *Potentilla Canadensis*, lambkill, wild rose, yellow lily, etc., etc., begin again.

Children are now gathering barberries, — just the right time. Speaking of the great fall flower which the valleys are at present, its brightest petal is still the scarlet one of dogwood, and in some places the redder red maple one is equally bright; then there is the yellow walnut one, and the broad dull red one of the huckleberry, and the hazel, high blueberry, and *Viburnum nudum* of various similar tints.

It has been too cold for the thinnest coat since the middle of September.

Grapes are still abundant. I have only to shake the birches to bring down a shower of plums. But the flavor of none is quite equal to their fragrance. Some soils, like this rocky one on the old Carlisle road, are so suited to the apple that they spring up wild and bear well in the midst of pines, birches, maples, and oaks, their red and yellow fruit harmonizing with the autumnal tints of the forest in which they grow. I am surprised to see

and one and a half inches deep, containing a piece of empty honeycomb of its own size and form, filling it within a third of an inch of the top; also another, *wooden* box about two and a half inches square every way, with a glass window occupying two thirds the upper side under a slide, with a couple of narrow slits in the wood, each side of the glass, to admit air, but too narrow for the bees to pass; the whole resting on a circular bottom a little larger than the lid of the tin box, with a sliding door in it. We were earnest to go this week, before the flowers were gone, and we feared the frosty night might make the bees slow to come forth.

After we got to the Baker Farm, to one of the open fields nearest to the tree I had marked, the first thing was to find some flowers and catch some honey-bees. We followed up the bank of the brook for some distance, but the goldenrods were all dried up there, and the asters on which we expected to find them were very scarce. By the pond-side we had no better luck, the frosts perhaps having made flowers still more scarce there. We then took the path to Clematis Brook on the north of Mt. Misery, where we found a few of the *Diplopappus linariifolius* (savory-leaved aster) and one or two small white (bushy?) asters, also *A. undulatus* and *Solidago nemoralis* rarely, on which they work in a sunny place; but there were only two or three bumblebees, wasps, and butterflies, yellow and small red, on them. We had no better luck at Clematis Brook. Not a honey-bee could we find, and we concluded that we were too late, — that the weather was too cold, and so repaired at once to the tree I had found, a hemlock two feet and a half in diameter on a side-hill a rod from the pond. I had cut my initials in the bark in the winter, for custom gives the first finder of the nest a right to the honey and to cut down the tree to get it and pay the damages, and if he cuts his initials on it no other hunter will interfere. Not seeing any signs of bees from the ground, one of the party climbed the tree to where the leading stem had formerly been broken off, leaving a crotch at about eighteen feet from the ground, and there he found a small hole into which he thrust a stick two or three feet down the tree, and dropped it to the bottom; and, putting in his hand, he took out some old comb. The bees had probably died.

After eating our lunch, we set out on our return. By the roadside at Walden, on the sunny hillside sloping to the pond, we saw a large mass of goldenrod and aster several rods square and comparatively fresh. Getting out of our wagon, we found it to be resounding with the hum of bees. (It was about 1 o'clock.) There were far more flowers than we had seen elsewhere. Here were bees in great numbers, both bumblebees and honey-bees, as well as butterflies and wasps and flies. So, pouring a mixture of honey and water into the empty comb in the tin box, and holding the lid of the tin box in one hand and the wooden box with the slides shut in the other, we proceeded to catch the honey-bees by shutting them in suddenly between the lid of the tin box and the large circular bottom of the wooden one, cutting off the flower-stem with the edge of the lid at

the same time. Then, holding the lid still against the wooden box, we drew the slide in the bottom and also the slide covering the window at the top, that the light might attract the bee to pass up into the wooden box. As soon as he had done so and was buzzing against the glass, the lower slide was closed and the lid with the flower removed, and more bees were caught in the same way. Then, placing the other, tin, box containing the comb filled with honeyed water close under the wooden one, the slide was drawn again, and the upper slide closed, making it dark; and in about a minute they went to feeding, as was ascertained by raising slightly the wooden box. Then the latter was wholly removed, and they were left feeding or sucking up the honey in broad daylight. In from two to three minutes one had loaded himself and commenced leaving the box. He would buzz round it back and forth a foot or more, and then, sometimes, finding that he was too heavily loaded, alight to empty himself or clean his feet. Then, starting once more, he would begin to circle round irregularly, at first in a small circle only a foot or two in diameter, as

if to examine the premises that he might know them again, till, at length, rising higher and higher and circling wider and wider and swifter and swifter, till his orbit was ten or twelve feet in diameter and as much from the ground, — though its centre might be moved to one side, — so that it was very difficult to follow him, especially if you looked against a wood or the hill,

Vol. IV

and you had to lie low to fetch him against the sky (you must operate in an open space, not in a wood); all this as if to ascertain the course to his nest; then, in a minute or less from his first starting, he darts off in a bee-line, that is, as far as I could see him, which might be eight or ten rods, looking against the sky (and you had to follow his whole career very attentively indeed to see when and where he went off at a tangent), in a waving or sinuous (right and left) line, toward his nest.

We sent forth as many as a dozen bees, which flew in about three directions, but all toward the village, or where we knew there were hives. They did not fly so almost absolutely straight as I had heard, but within three or four feet of the same course for half a dozen rods, or as far as we could see. Those belonging to one hive all had to digress to get round an apple tree. As none flew in the right direction for us, we did not attempt to line them. In less than half an hour the first returned to the box still lying on the wood-pile, — for not one of the bees on the surrounding flowers discovered it, — and so they came back, one after another, loaded themselves and departed; but now they went off with very little preliminary circling, as if assured of their course. We were furnished with little boxes of red, blue, green, yellow, and white paint, in dry powder, and with a stick we sprinkled a little of the red powder on the back of one while he was feeding, — gave him a little dab, — and it settled down amid the fuzz of his back and gave him a distinct red jacket. He went off like most of them toward some hives about three

quarters of a mile distant, and we observed by the watch the time of his departure. In just twenty-two minutes red jacket came back, with enough of the powder still on his back to mark him plainly. He may have gone more than three quarters of a mile. At any rate, he had a head wind to contend with while laden. They fly swiftly and surely to their nests, never resting by the way, and I was surprised — though I had been informed of it — at the distance to which the village bees go for flowers.

The rambler in the most remote woods and pastures little thinks that the bees which are humming so industriously on the rare wild flowers he is plucking for his herbarium, in some out-of-the-way nook, are, like himself, ramblers from the village, perhaps from his own yard, come to get their honey for his hives. All the honey-bees we saw were on the blue-stemmed goldenrod (*Solidago cæsia*), which is late, lasts long, which emitted a sweet agreeable fragrance, not on the asters. I feel the richer for this experience. It taught me that even the insects in my path are not loafers, but have their special errands. Not merely and vaguely in this world, but in this hour, each is about its business. If, then, there are any sweet flowers still lingering on the hillside, it is known to the bees both of the forest and the village. The botanist should make interest with the bees if he would know when the flowers open and when they close. Those I have named were the only common and prevailing flowers at this time to look for them on.

Our red jacket had performed the voyage in safety;

no bird had picked him up. Are the kingbirds gone? Now is the time to hunt bees and take them up, when the combs are full of honey and before the flowers are so scarce that they begin to consume the honey they have stored.

The common milkweed down has begun to fly; the desmodium, tick-trefoil, adheres now to my clothes. Saw by Clematis Brook extensive rootings of moles.

Forty pounds of honey was the most our company had got hereabouts.

We also caught and sent forth a bumblebee, who manœuvred like the others, though we thought he took time to eat some before he loaded himself, and then he was so overloaded and bedaubed that he had to alight after he had started, and it took him several minutes to clean himself.

It is not in vain that the flowers bloom, and bloom late too, in favored spots. To us they are a culture and a luxury, but to bees meat and drink. The tiny bee which we thought lived far away there in a flower-bell in that remote vale, he is a great voyager, and anon he rises up over the top of the wood and sets sail with his sweet cargo straight for his distant haven. How well they know the woods and fields and the haunt of every flower! The flowers, perchance, are widely dispersed, because the sweet which they collect from the atmosphere is rare but also widely dispersed, and the bees are enabled to travel far to find it. A precious burthen, like their color and fragrance, a crop which the heavens bear and deposit on the earth.

Rees's Cyclopædia says that " Philliscus retired into

a desert wood, that he might have the opportunity of observing them [bees][1] to better advantage." Paul Dudley wrote the Royal Society about 1723 that the Indians had no word for bee; called it " Englishman's fly."

[1] [The word is supplied by Thoreau.]

VI

OCTOBER, 1852

(ÆT. 35)

Oct. 1. *Friday.* Surveying in Lincoln. A severer frost last night. The young and tender trees begin to assume the autumnal tints more generally, plainly in consequence of the frost the last two mornings. The sides of the bushy hills present a rich variety of colors like rug work, but the forest generally is not yet changed.

Oct. 2. P. M. — To Cliffs.

The beggar-ticks (*Bidens*) now adhere to my clothes. I also find the desmodium sooner thus — as a magnet discovers the steel filings in a heap of ashes — than if I used my eyes alone. The river is as low, within an inch or two, as when I made my mark. A very warm day after the frosts, so that I wish — though I am afraid to wear — a thin coat. From Cliffs the shrub oak plain has now a bright-red ground, perhaps of maples. How much more beautiful the lakes now, like Fair Haven, surrounded by the autumn-tinted woods and hills, as in an ornamented frame! Some maples in sprout-lands are of a delicate, pure, clear, unspotted red, inclining to crimson, surpassing most flowers. I would fain pluck the whole tree and carry it home for a nosegay. The veiny-leaved hawkweed in blossom (again?).

Oct. 3. P. M. — To Flint's Pond.

I hear a hylodes (?) from time to time. Shrub oaks are red, some of them. Hear the loud laughing of a loon on Flint's, apparently alone in the middle. A wild sound, heard far and suited to the wildest lake. Many acorns strew the ground, and have fallen into the water.

Collected a parcel of grass (?) balls, some washed up high and dry, — part of the shore-line consists of the same material, — from a half-inch to four inches diameter. The sand indicates that they are formed on the sandy shore. The partly decomposed rushes composed of similar fibres.[1]

From Heywood's Peak at Walden, the shore is now more beautifully painted. The most prominent are the red maples and the yellowish aspens. The *Aster undulatus* is common and fresh, also the *Solidago nemoralis* of Gray.

The pine fall, *i. e.* change, is commenced, and the trees are mottled green and yellowish.

Oct. 5. Was told at Bunker Hill Monument to-day that Mr. Savage saw the White Mountains several times while working on the monument. It required very clear weather in the northwest and a storm clearing up here.

Oct. 7. P. M. — To Great Meadows.

I find no fringed gentian. Perhaps the autumnal tints are as bright and interesting now as they will be. Now is the time to behold the maple swamps, one mass of red and yellow, all on fire, as it were; these and the

[1] A *Scirpus*?

blood-red huckleberries are the most conspicuous; and then, in the village, the warm brownish-yellow elms, and there and elsewhere the dark-red ashes. The green pines springing out of huckleberries on the hillsides look as if surrounded by red or vermilion paint. I notice the *Viola ovata*, houstonia, *Ranunculus repens*, caducous polygala, small scratch-grass polygonum, autumnal dandelion (very abundant, yellowing the low turfy grounds and hills), small bushy white aster, a few goldenrods, *Polygonum hydropiperoides* and the unknown flowerless bidens, soapwort gentian (now turned dark purple), yarrow, the white erigeron, red clover, hedge-mustard. The muskrats have begun to erect their cabins. They begin soon after the pontederias are dead (??). Saw one done. Do they build them in the night? Hear and see larks, bluebirds, robins, song sparrows. Also see painted tortoises and shad frogs. There must be an abundance of mast this year. I could gather up nearly a bushel of acorns under one white oak, out of their cups, and, I think, quite good to eat. They are earlier to fall than the walnuts. It is encouraging to see a large crop of acorns, though we do not use them. The white maples turn yellowish, though some boughs are red.

I sit on Poplar Hill. It is a warm Indian-summerish afternoon. The sun comes out of clouds, and lights up and warms the whole scene. It is perfect autumn. I see a hundred smokes arising through the yellow elm-tops in the village, where the villagers are preparing for tea. It is the mellowing year. The sunshine harmonizes with the imbrowned and fiery foliage.

Did Russell call my red globular fungus geiropodium [?], etc.?

Oct. 8. P. M. — Walden.

Canada snapdragon, a few flowers at top. Everlastings, field trefoil, shepherd's-purse, door-grass, white goldenrod, fresh tansy, veiny-leaved hawkweed, also that which seems to run from this into *Gronovii* (probably the former). *Aster undulatus* (?), with delicate purplish or lilac-tinted flowers, has those heart-shaped, crenate leaves with a claret under surface. Bushy gerardia budded still.

The autumnal tints about the pond are now perfect. Nothing can exceed the brilliancy of some of the maples which stand by the shore and extend their red banners over the water. Why should so many be yellow? I see the browner yellow of the chestnuts on Pine Hill. The maples and hickories are a clearer yellow. Some white oaks are red. The shrub oaks are bloody enough for a ground. The red and black oaks are yet green.

As I was paddling along the north shore, after having looked in vain over the pond for a loon, suddenly a loon, sailing toward the middle, a few rods in front, set up his wild laugh and betrayed himself. I pursued with a paddle and he dived, but when he came up I was nearer than before. He dived again, but I miscalculated the direction he would take, and we were fifty rods apart when he came up, and again he laughed long and loud. He managed very cunningly, and I could not get within half a dozen rods of him. Some-

Vol. IV

times he would come up unexpectedly on the opposite side of me, as if he had passed directly under the boat. So long-winded was he, so unwearable, that he would immediately plunge again, and then no wit could divine where in the deep pond, beneath the smooth surface, he might be speeding his way like a fish, perchance passing under the boat. He had time and ability to visit the bottom of the pond in its deepest part. A newspaper authority says a fisherman — giving his name — has caught loon in Seneca Lake, N. Y., eighty feet beneath the surface, with hooks set for trout. Miss Cooper has said the same. Yet he appeared to know his course as surely under water as on the surface, and swam much faster there than he sailed on the surface. It was surprising how serenely he sailed off with unruffled bosom when he came to the surface. It was as well for me to rest on my oars and await his reappearing as to endeavor to calculate where he would come up. When I was straining my eyes over the surface, I would suddenly be startled by his unearthly laugh behind me. But why, after displaying so much cunning, did he betray himself the moment he came to the surface with that loud laugh? His white breast enough betrayed him. He was indeed a silly loon, I thought. Though he took all this pains to avoid me, he never failed to give notice of his whereabouts the moment he came to the surface. After an hour he seemed as fresh as ever, dived as willingly, and swam yet farther than at first. Once or twice I saw a ripple where he approached the surface, just put his head out to reconnoitre, and instantly dived again. I could commonly

hear the plash of the water when he came up, and so also detected him. It was commonly a demoniac laughter, yet somewhat like a water-bird, but occasionally, when he had balked me most successfully and come up a long way off, he uttered a long-drawn unearthly howl, probably more like a wolf than any other bird. This was his looning. As when a beast puts his muzzle to the ground and deliberately howls; perhaps the wildest sound I ever heard, making the woods ring; and I concluded that he laughed in derision of my efforts, confident of his own resources. Though the sky was overcast, the pond was so smooth that I could see where he broke the surface if I did not hear him. His white breast, the stillness of the air, the smoothness of the water, were all against [him]. At length, having come up fifty rods off, he uttered one of those prolonged unearthly howls, as if calling on the god of loons to aid him, and immediately there came a wind from the east and rippled the surface, and filled the whole air with misty rain. I was impressed as if it were the prayer of the loon and his god was angry with me. How surprised must be the fishes to see this ungainly visitant from another sphere speeding his way amid their schools![1]

I have never seen more than one at a time in our pond, and I believe that that is always a male.[2]

Oct. 9. Touch-me-not, self-heal, *Bidens cernua*, ladies'-tresses, cerastium, dwarf tree-primrose, butter-

[1] [*Walden*, pp. 259–262; Riv. 364–368.]
[2] *Vide* Oct. 11 [p. 382].

and-eggs (abundant), prenanthes, sium, silvery cinque-foil, mayweed. My rainbow rush must be the *Juncus militaris*, not yet colored.

Oct. 10. Burdock, *Ranunculus acris*, rough hawk-weed. A drizzling rain to-day. The air is full of fall-ing leaves. The streets are strewn with elm leaves. The trees begin to look thin. The butternut is perhaps the first on the street to lose its leaves. Rain, more than wind, makes the leaves fall. Glow-worms in the evening.

Oct. 11. *Monday.* Most leaves are already somewhat faded and withered. Their tints are not so bright. The chestnut leaves already rustle with a great noise as you walk through the woods, as they lie light, firm, and crisp. Now the chestnuts are rattling out. The burs are gaping and showing the plump nuts. They fill the ruts in the road, and are abundant amid the fallen leaves in the midst of the wood. The jays scream, and the red squirrels scold, while you are clubbing and shaking the trees. Now it is true autumn; all things are crisp and ripe.

I observed the other day (October 8) that those insects whose ripple I could see from the Peak were water-bugs. I could detect the progress of a water-bug over the smooth surface in almost any part of the pond, for they furrow the water slightly, making a conspicu-ous ripple bounded by two diverging lines, but the skaters slide over it without producing a perceptible ripple. In this clear air and with this glassy surface the motion of every water-bug, ceaselessly progressing

over the pond, was perceptible.[1] Here and there amid the skaters.

Oct. 12. I am struck by the superfluity of light in the atmosphere in the autumn, as if the earth absorbed none, and out of this profusion of dazzling light came the autumnal tints. Can it be because there is less vapor? The delicacy of the stratification in the white sand by the railroad, where they have been getting out sand for the brick-yards, the delicate stratification of this great globe like the leaves of the choicest volume just shut on a lady's table. The piled-up history! I am struck by the slow and delicate process by which the globe was formed.

Paddled on Walden. A rippled surface. Scared up ducks. Saw them first far over the surface, just risen, — two smaller, white-bellied, one larger, black. They circled round as usual, and the first went off, but the black one went round and round and over the pond five or six times at a considerable height and distance, when I thought several times he had gone to the river, and at length settled down by a slanting flight of a quarter of a mile into a distant part of the pond which I had left free; but what beside safety these ducks get by sailing in the middle of Walden I don't know.[2] That black rolling-pin with wings, circling round you half a mile off for a quarter of an hour, at that height, from which he sees the river and Fair Haven all the while, from which he sees so many things, while I see

[1] [*Walden*, p. 208; Riv. 294.]
[2] [*Walden*, p. 262; Riv. 368.]

almost him alone. Their wings set so far back. They are not handsome, but wild.

What an ample share of the light of heaven each pond and lake on the surface of the globe enjoys! No woods are so dark and deep but it is light above the pond. Its window or skylight is as broad as its surface. It lies out patent to the sky. From the mountain-top you may not be able to see out because of the woods, but on the lake you are bathed in light.

I can discern no skaters nor water-bugs on the sur-face of the pond, which is now rippled. Do they, then, glide forth to the middle in calm days only, by short impulses, till they have completely covered it?[1]

A new carpet of pine leaves is forming in the woods. The forest is laying down her carpet for the winter. The elms in the village, losing their leaves, reveal the birds' nests.

I dug some ground-nuts in the railroad bank with my hands this afternoon, the vine being now dead. They were nearly as large as hen's eggs, six inches or a foot beneath the surface, on the end of a root or strung along on it. I had them roasted and boiled at supper time. The skin came readily off like a potato. Roasted, they have an agreeable taste very much like a potato, though somewhat fibrous in texture. With my eyes shut, I should not know but I was eating a rather soggy potato. Boiled, they were unexpectedly quite dry, and though in this instance a little strong, had a more nutty flavor. With a little salt, a hungry man would make a very palatable meal on them. It

[1] [*Walden*, p. 208; Riv. 294.]

would not be easy to find them, especially now that the vines are dead, unless you knew beforehand where they grew.[1]

Oct. 13. P. M. — To Cliffs.

Many maples have lost all their leaves and are shrunk all at once to handsome clean gray wisps on the edge of the meadows, where, crowded together, at a distance they look like smoke. This is a sudden and important change, produced mainly, I suppose, by the rain of Sunday, 10th. The autumnal tints have commonly already lost their brightness. It lasts but a day or two. Corn-spurry and spotted polygonum and polygala.

Fair Haven Pond, methinks, never looks so hand-some as at this season. It is a sufficiently clear and warm, rather Indian-summer day, and they are gather-ing the apples in the orchard. The warmth is more required, and we welcome and appreciate it all. The shrub oak plain is now a deep red, with grayish, with-ered, apparently white oak leaves intermixed. The chickadees take heart, too, and sing above these warm rocks. Birches, hickories, aspens, etc., in the distance, are like innumerable small flames on the hillsides about the pond. The pond is now most beautifully framed with the autumn-tinted woods and hills. The water or lake, from however distant a point seen, is always the centre of the landscape. Fair Haven lies more open and can be seen from more distant points than any of our ponds. The air is singularly fine-grained; the sward looks short and firm. The mountains are more

[1] [*Walden*, p. 264; Riv. 371.]

distinct from the rest of the earth and slightly impurpled. Seeming to lie up more. How peaceful great nature! There is no disturbing sound, but far amid the western hills there rises a pure white smoke in constant volumes.

That handsome kind of sedge (?) which lasts through the winter must be the *Scirpus Eriophorum*, red cottongrass of Bigelow, and wool-grass (under bulrush and club-rush) of Gray.

Oct. 14. That coarse yellowish fungus is very common in the paths in woods of late, for a month, often picked by birds, often decayed, often mashed by the foot like a piece of pumpkin, defiling and yellowing the grass, as if a liquor (or dust) distilled from them. The pines are now two-colored, green and yellow, — the latter just below the ends of the boughs. The woods have lost so many leaves they begin to look bare, — maples, poplars, etc., chestnuts. Flowers are fast disappearing. Winter may be anticipated. But few crickets are heard. Jays and chickadees are oftener heard in the fall than in summer. It is apparently the *Eriophorum Virginicum*, Virginian cotton-grass, now nodding or waving with its white woolly heads over the greenish andromeda and amid the red isolated blueberry bushes in Beck Stow's Swamp. A thousand white woolly heads, one to two inches in diameter, suggesting winter. The lower or older leaves of the andromeda begin to redden. This plant forms extensive solid beds with a definite surface, level or undulating, like a moss bed. Not, like the huckleberry, irregular and independent each of the

other, but regular and in community, as if covered by a film.

Oct. 15. 9 A. M. — The first snow is falling (after not very cool weather), in large flakes, filling the air and obscuring the distant woods and houses, as if the inhabitants above were emptying their pillow-cases. Like a mist it divides the uneven landscape at a little distance into ridges and vales. The ground begins to whiten, and our thoughts begin to prepare for winter. Whiteweed. The Canada snapdragon is one of the latest flowers noticed, a few buds being still left to blossom at the tops of its spike or raceme. The snow lasted but half an hour. Ice a week or two ago.

P. M. — Walden.

The water of Walden is a light green next the shore, apparently because of the light rays reflected from the sandy bottom mingling with the rays which the water reflects. Just this portion it is which in the spring, being warmed by the heat reflected from the bottom and transmitted through the earth, melts first and forms a narrow canal about the still frozen pond.[1] The water appears blue when the surface is much disturbed, also in a single cake of ice; that is, perhaps, when enough light is mixed with it.

The flight of a partridge, leaving her lair (?) on the hillside only a few rods distant, with a gentle whirring sound, is like the blowing of rocks at a great distance. Perhaps it produces the same kind of undulations in the air.

[1] [*Walden*, p. 196; Riv. 277.]

Vol. IV

The rain of the night and morning, together with the wind, had strewn the ground with chestnuts. The burs, generally empty, come down with a loud sound, while I am picking the nuts in the woods. I have come out before the rain is fairly over, before there are any fresh tracks on the Lincoln road by Britton's shanty, and I find the nuts abundant in the road itself. It is a pleasure to detect them in the woods amid the firm, crispy, crackling chestnut leaves. There is somewhat singularly refreshing in the color of this nut, the chestnut color. No wonder it gives a name to a color. One man tells me he has bought a wood-lot in Hollis to cut, and has let out the picking of the chestnuts to women at the halves. As the trees will probably be cut for them, they will make rapid work of it.

How Father Le Jeune pestered the poor Indians with his God at every turn (they must have thought it his one idea), only getting their attention when they required some external aid to save them from starving! Then, indeed, they were good Christians.

Oct. 16. Saturday. The sidewalks are covered with the impressions of leaves which fell yesterday and were pressed into the soil by the feet of the passers, leaving a myriad dark spots — like bird-tracks or hieroglyphics to a casual observer.

What are the sparrow-like birds with striped breasts and two triangular chestnut-colored spots on the breasts which I have seen some time, picking the seeds of the weeds in the garden?

Oct. 18. Up river to Bittern Cliff.

A mild, still, but cloudy, or rather misty, afternoon. The water is at present perfectly smooth and calm, but covered with a kind of smoky or hazy film. Nevertheless, the reflections of distant woods, though less distinct, are softer, seen through this smoky and darkened atmosphere. I speak only of the reflections as seen in the broader bays and longer reaches of the river, as at the Willow End. The general impression made by the river landscape now is that of bareness and bleakness, the black willow (not yet the golden) and the button-bush having lost almost all their leaves (the latter perhaps all), and the last is covered with the fuzzy mikania blossoms gone to seed, a dirty white. There are a very few polygonums, *hydropiperoides* and perhaps the unknown rose-tinted one, but most have withered before the frosts. The vegetation of the immediate shore and the water is for the most part black and withered. A few muskrat-houses are going up, abrupt and precipitous on one side, sloped on the other. I distinguish the dark moist layer of weeds deposited last night on what had dried in the sun. The tall bulrush and the wool-grass are dry and yellow, except a few in deep water, but the rainbow rush (*Juncus militaris*) is still green. The autumnal tints, though less brilliant and striking, are perhaps quite as agreeable, now that the frosts have somewhat dulled and softened [them]. Now that the forest is universally imbrowned, they make a more harmonious impression. Wooded hillsides reflected in the water are particularly agreeable. The undulation which the boat creates gives them the appearance of being terraced. Chickadees and jays are heard from the shore as in winter. Saw two or three ducks, which fly up, before and alight far behind.

Oct. 19. I see the dandelion blossoms in the path. The buds of the skunk-cabbage already show themselves in the meadow, the pointed involucres (?).

At 5 p. m. I found the fringed gentian now somewhat stale and touched by frost, being in the meadow toward Peter's. (*Gentiana crinita* in September, Bigelow and Gray.) Probably on high, moist ground it is fresher. It may have been in bloom a month. It has been cut off by the mower, and apparently has put out in consequence a mass of short branches full of flowers. This may make it later. I doubt if I can find one naturally grown. At this hour the blossoms are tightly rolled and twisted, and I see that the bees have gnawed round holes in their sides to come at the nectar. They have found them, though I had not. "Full many a flower is born to blush unseen" by man. An hour ago I doubted if fringed gentians were in Concord now, but, having found these, they as it were surrender, and I hear of them at the bottom of N. Barrett's orchard toward the river, and by Tuttle's (?). They are now, at 8 a. m., opening a little in a pitcher. It is too remarkable a flower not to be sought out and admired each year, however rare. It is one of the errands of the walker, as well as of the bees, for it yields him a more celestial nectar still. It is a very singular and agreeable surprise to come upon this conspicuous

and handsome and withal blue flower at this season, when flowers have passed out of our minds and memories; the latest of all to begin to bloom, unless it be the witch-hazel, when, excepting the latter, flowers are reduced to that small Spartan cohort, hardy, but for the most part unobserved, which linger till the snow buries them, and those interesting reappearing flowers which, though fair and fresh and tender, hardly delude us with the prospect of a new spring, and which we pass by indifferent, as if they only bloomed to die. *Vide* Bryant's verses on the Fringed Gentian.

There are a few bulrushes, lances of the pigmies or the cranes, still green in the brooks. I brought home one big as my finger and almost six feet high. Most are now yellowed and dry.

It is remarkable how tightly the gentians roll and twist up at night, as if that were their constant state. Probably those bees were working late that found it necessary to perforate the flower.

Oct. 20. Canada snapdragon, tansy, white goldenrod, blue-stemmed ditto. *Aster undulatus*, autumnal dandelion, tall buttercup, yarrow, mayweed. Picking chestnuts on Pine Hill. A rather cold and windy, somewhat wintry afternoon, the heavens overcast. The clouds have lifted in the northwest, and I see the mountains in sunshine, all the more attractive from the cold I feel here, with a tinge of purple on them, a cold but memorable and glorious outline. This is an advantage of mountains in the horizon: they show you fair weather from the midst of foul. The small red Solomon's-seal

berries spot the ground here and there amid the dry leaves. The witch-hazel is bare of all but flowers.

Many a man, when I tell him that I have been on to a mountain, asks if I took a glass with me. No doubt, I could have seen further with a glass, and particular objects more distinctly, — could have counted more meeting-houses; but this has nothing to do with the peculiar beauty and grandeur of the view which an elevated position affords. It was not to see a few particular objects, as if they were near at hand, as I had been accustomed to see them, that I ascended the mountain, but to see an infinite variety far and near in their relation to each other, thus reduced to a single picture. The facts of science, in comparison with poetry, are wont to be as vulgar as looking from the mountain with a telescope. It is a counting of meeting-houses. At the public house, the mountain-house, they keep a glass to let, and think the journey to the mountain-top is lost, that you have got but half the view, if you have not taken a glass with you.

Oct. 21. Thursday. P. M. — To Second Division Brook and Ministerial Swamp.

Cerastium. Apparently some flowers yield to the frosts; others linger here and there till the snow buries them. Saw that the side-flowering skull-cap was killed by the frost. If they grow in some nook out of the way of frosts, they last so much the longer. Methinks the frost puts a period to a large class. The goldenrods, being dead, are now a dingy white along the brooks (white fuzz, dark-brown leaves), together with rusty,

fuzzy trumpet-weeds and asters in the same condition. This is a remarkable feature in the landscape now, the abundance of dead weeds. The frosts have done it. Winter comes on gradually. The red maples have lost their leaves before the rock maple, which is now losing its leaves at top first. All the country over, the frosts have come and seared the tenderer herbs along all brooksides. How unobserved this change until it has taken place! The birds that fly at the approach of winter are come from the north. Some time since I might have said some birds are leaving us, others, like ducks, are just arriving from the north, the herbs are withering along the brooks, the humming insects are going into winter quarters.

The deciduous trees are green but about four months in the year, — from June 1st to October 1st, perhaps.

Polygonum articulatum lingers still.[1] Silvery cinquefoil, hedge-mustard, and clover. I find caddis-cases with worms in Second Division Brook. And what mean those little piles of yellow sand on dark-colored stones at the bottom of the swift-running water, kept together and in place by some kind of gluten and looking as if sprinkled on the stones, one eighteenth of an inch in diameter? These caddis-worms just build a little case around themselves, and sometimes attach a few dead leaves to disguise it, and then fasten it (?) slightly to some swaying grass stem or blade at the bottom in swift water, and these are their quarters till next spring. This reminds me that winter does not put his rude fin-

[1] [An interrogation-point in the margin.]

gers in the bottom of the brooks. When you look into the brooks you see various dead leaves floating or resting on the bottom, and you do not suspect that some are the disguises which the caddis-worms have borrowed. Fresh *Bæomyces roseus* near Tommy Wheeler's. The cotton-woolly aphides on the alders.

Gilpin speaks of "floats of timber" on the river Wey, in 1775, as picturesque objects. Thus in the oldest settled and civilized country there is a resemblance or reminiscence still of the primitive new country, and more or less timber never ceases to grow on the head waters of its streams, and perchance the wild muskrat still perforates its banks. England may endure as long as she grows oaks for her navy.[1] Timber rafts still (?) annually come down the Rhine, like the Mississippi and St. Lawrence. But the forests of England are thin, for Gilpin says of the Isle of Wight in Charles II's time, "There were woods in the island so complete and extensive, that it is said a squirrel might have travelled in several parts, many leagues together, on the tops of the trees."

Oct. 22. To Walden.

Ebby Hubbard's oaks, now turned a sober and warm red and yellow, have a very rich crisp and curled look, especially against the green pines. This is when the ripe high-colored leaves have begun to curl and wither. Then they have a warm and harmonious tint. First they are ripened by the progress of the year, and the character of each appears in distinct colors. Then

[1] *Vide* Loudon on the extent of oak forest there.

come the severe frosts and, dulling the brilliancy of most, produce a harmony of warm brown or red and yellow tinges throughout the forest, something like marbling and painting over it, making one shade run into another. The forest is the more rug-like.

When I approached the pond over Heywood's Peak, I disturbed a hawk (a fish hawk?) on a white pine by the water watching for his prey, with long, narrow, sharp wings and a white belly. He flew slowly across the pond somewhat like a gull. He is the more picturesque object against the woods or water for being white beneath.

Now and for some time past, northwest winds prevail, wafting the air cooled by the snows that way, perhaps. This being the direction of the wind, I see again the clouds lifted in the northwest horizon. And methinks this phenomenon is very often repeated during the winter. The blue-stemmed goldenrod. *Aster undulatus* with a pinkish or lilac tinge, and humblebees on it. *Solidago altissima.* The bushy gerardia still with sticky stem and wrinkled radical leaves. Scarcely a skater insect to be seen. I see no water-bugs. It is getting too cool for them.

In consequence of the above winds and clouds, we have to-night a bright warm sunset (to me on the water) after a cool gray afternoon, lighting up the green pines at the northeast end of the pond; every yellow leaf of birch or aspen or hickory is doubly bright, and, looking over the forest on Pine Hill, I can hardly tell which trees are lit up by the sunshine and which are the yellow chestnut-tops. Thus both the spring and autumn

tints or aspect of the woods reminds me of the sunshine. The forest has never so good a setting and foreground as seen from the middle of a lake, rising from the water's edge. The water's edge makes the best frame for the picture and natural boundary to the forest.[1]

Oct. 23. P. M. — To Conantum.

This may be called an Indian-summer day. It is quite hazy withal, and the mountains invisible. I see a horehound turned lake or steel-claret color. The yellow lily pads in Hubbard's ditch are fresh, as if recently expanded. There are some white lily pads in river still, but very few indeed of the yellow lily. A pasture thistle on Conantum just budded, but flat with the ground. The fields generally wear a russet hue. A striped snake out. The milkweed (*Syriaca*) now rapidly discounting. The lanceolate pods having opened, the seeds spring out on the least jar, or when dried by the sun, and form a little fluctuating white silky mass or tuft, each held by the extremities of the fine threads, until a stronger puff of wind sets them free. It is a pleasant sight to see it dispersing its seeds. The bass has lost its leaves. I see where boys have gathered the mockernut, though it has not fallen out of its shells. The red squirrel chirrups in the walnut grove. The chickadees flit along, following me inquisitively a few rods with lisping, tinkling note, — flit within a few feet of me from curiosity, head downward on the pines. The white pines have shed their leaves, making a yellow carpet on the grass,

[1] [*Walden*, p. 291.]

but the pitch pines are yet parti-colored. Is it the procumbent speedwell (*Veronica agrestis*) still in flower on Lee's Cliff? But its leaves are neither heart-ovate nor shorter than the peduncles. The sprays of the witch-hazel are sprinkled on the air, and recurved. The pennyroyal stands brown and sere, though fragrant still, on the shelves of the Cliff. The elms in the street have nearly lost their leaves.

October has been the month of autumnal tints. The first of the month the tints began to be more general, at which time the frosts began, though there were scattered bright tints long before; but not till then did the forest begin to be painted. By the end of the month the leaves will either have fallen or be sered and turned brown by the frosts for the most part. Also the month of barberries and chestnuts.

My friend is one whom I meet, who takes me for what I am. A stranger takes me for something else than I am. We do not speak, we cannot communicate, till we find that we are recognized. The stranger supposes in our stead a third person whom we do not know, and we leave him to converse with that one. It is suicide for us to become abetters in misapprehending ourselves. Suspicion creates the stranger and substitutes him for the friend. I cannot abet any man in misapprehending myself.

What men call social virtues, good fellowship, is commonly but the virtue of pigs in a litter, which lie close together to keep each other warm. It brings men together in crowds and mobs in barrooms and elsewhere, but it does not deserve the name of virtue.

Oct. 24. Another Indian-summer day.

P. M. — Rode to Stow *via* powder-mills with W. E. C., returning *via* the fir tree house, Vose's Hill, and Corner.

The road through the woods this side the powder-mills was very gorgeous with the sun shining endwise through it, and the red tints of the deciduous trees, now somewhat imbrowned, mingled with the liquid green of the pines. The andromeda is already browned, has a grayish-brown speckled look. I see, far over the river, boys gathering walnuts. At the fall on the river at Parker's paper-mill, there is a bright sparkle on the water long before we get to it.

I saw in Stow some trees fuller of apples still than I remember to have ever seen. Small yellow apples hanging over the road. The branches were gracefully drooping with the weight of the fruit like a barberry bush, so that the whole tree acquired a new character. The topmost branches, instead of standing erect, spread and drooped in all directions.[1]

The larches in the swamps are now conspicuously yellow and ready for their fall. They can now be distinguished at a distance. There is an agreeable prospect from near the post-office in the northwest of Sudbury. The southeast (?) horizon is very distant, — but what perhaps makes it more agreeable, it is a low distance, — extending to the Weston elm in the horizon. You are more impressed with the extent of earth overlooked than if the view were bounded by mountains.

[1] [*Excursions*, p. 296; Riv. 364.]

Vol. IV

The sheen on the water blinds my eyes. The zizania stands still, with its slender spires empty of grain, by the water's edge. The *Polygonum hydropiperoides* is now all crisp and brown with frost. Mint is still green and wonderfully recreating to smell. I had put such things behind me. It is hard to remember lilies now. The savory-leaved aster in a sheltered place, and caducous polygala. Where large chestnuts were sawed down last winter by Walden, sprouts have come up six feet high on every side of the stump, very thick, so as to form perfect bowers in which a man might be concealed. Where a fire has run over such ground, I have noticed such shoots all dead and drawn or shrunk together at top.

The constitution of the Indian mind appears to be the very opposite to that of the white man. He is acquainted with a different side of nature. He measures his life by winters, not summers. His year is not measured by the sun, but consists of a certain number of moons, and his moons are measured not by days, but by nights. He has taken hold of the dark side of nature; the white man, the bright side.

Oct. 26. P. M. — Walden and Cliffs.

There are no skaters on the pond now. It is cool to-day and windier. The water is rippled considerably. As I stand in the boat, the farther off the water, the bluer it is. Looking straight down, it is a dark green. Hence, apparently, the celestial blueness of those distant river-reaches, when the water is agitated, so that their surfaces reflect the sky at the right angle. It is a

Oct. 25. *Monday*. P. M. — Down river to Ball's Hill in boat.

Another perfect Indian-summer day. One of my oars makes a creaking sound like a block in a harbor, such a sound as would bring tears into an old sailor's eyes. It suggests to me adventure and seeking one's fortune. Turtles are still seen dropping into the water (*Emys picta*). The white maples have mostly shed their leaves, but those which are beneath the level of the bank, protected by it, still hold on. This leafy stratum rises exactly to a level with the bank. The water for some time has been clear of weeds mostly, but looks cool for fishes. We get into the lee of the hill near Abner Buttrick's (?), where is smooth water, and here it is very warm and sunny under the pitch pines, and some small bushy white asters still survive.

The autumnal tints grow gradually darker and duller, but not less rich to my eye. And now a hillside near the river exhibits the darkest, crispy reds and browns of every hue, all agreeably blended. At the foot, next the meadow, stands a front rank of smoke-like maples bare of leaves, intermixed with yellow birches. Higher up, red oaks of various shades of dull red, with yellowish, perhaps black oaks intermixed, and walnuts, now brown, and near the hilltop, or rising above the rest, perhaps, a still yellowish oak, and here and there amid the rest or in the foreground on the meadow, dull ashy salmon-colored white oaks large and small, all these contrasting with the clear liquid, sempiternal green of pines.

darker blue than that of the sky itself.[1] When I look down on the pond from the Peak, it is far less blue.

The blue-stemmed and white goldenrod apparently survive till winter, — push up and blossom anew. And a few oak leaves in sheltered nooks do not wither. *Aster undulatus.* Very few crickets for a long time. At this season we seek warm sunny lees and hillsides, as that under the pitch pines by Walden shore, where we cuddle and warm ourselves in the sun as by a fire, where we may get some of its reflected as well as direct heat.

Coming by Hayden's, I see that, the sun setting, its rays, which yet find some vapor to lodge on in the clear cold air, impart a purple tinge to the mountains in the northwest. Methinks it is only in cold weather I see this.

Richard Harlan, M. D., in his "Fauna Americana" (1825), says of man that those parts are "most hairy, which in animals are most bare, *viz.* the axillæ and pubes."

Harlan says the vespertilio catch insects during the crepusculum.

Harlan says that when white is associated with another color on a dog's tail it is always terminal, and that the observations of Desmarest confirm it.

Oct. 28. Sunset from the Poplar Hill. A warm, moist afternoon. The clouds lift in the west, — indeed the horizon is now clear all around, — and suddenly the light of the setting sun yellows and warms all the

[1] [*Walden*, p. 196; Riv. 277.]

landscape. The air is filled with a remarkably vaporous haze. The shadows of the trees on the river's edge stretch straight a quarter of a mile into the level russet Great Meadows. The boys are gathering walnuts. Their leaves are a yellowish brown.

8 P. M. — To Cliffs.

The moon beginning to wane. It is a quite warm but moist night. As I cross the railroad I hear the telegraph harp again, the undecayed oracle. Its vibrations are communicated through the tall pole to the surrounding earth for a considerable distance, so that I feel them when I stand near. And when I put my ear to a fence-rail, it is all alive with them, though the post with which it is connected is planted two feet from the telegraph-post; yet the rail resounded with the harp music so that a deaf man might have heard it. I hear no sound of a bird as I go up the back road; only a few faint crickets to be heard, — these the birds we are reduced to. What a puny sound this for the great globe to make!

After whatever revolutions in my moods and experiences, when I come forth at evening, as if from years of confinement to the house, I see the few stars which make the constellation of the Lesser Bear in the same relative position, — the everlasting geometry of the stars. How incredible to be described are these bright points which appear in the blue sky as the darkness increases, said to be other worlds, like the berries on the hills when the summer is ripe! Even the ocean of birds, even the regions of the ether, are studded with isles. Far in this ethereal sea lie the Hesperian isles, unseen

by day, but when the darkness comes their fires are seen from this shore, as Columbus saw the fires of San Salvador (?). The dew in the withered grass reflects the moonlight like glow-worms. That star which accompanies the moon will not be her companion to-morrow.

The forest has lost so many leaves that its floor and paths are much more checkered with light. I hear no sound but the rustling of the withered leaves, which lulls the few and silent birds to sleep, and, on the wooded hilltops, the roar of the wind. Each tree is a harp which resounds all night, though some have but a few leaves left to flutter and hum. From the Cliffs, the river and pond are exactly the color of the sky. Though the latter is slightly veiled with a thin mist, the outline of the peninsula in it is quite distinct. Even the distant fields across the river are seen to be russet by moonlight as by day, and the young pines near by are green. The ground in the woods is light with fallen leaves. There is a certain tameness or civilization in the rounded lobe of the white oak leaf, very different from the wild, pointed black and red oak leaves, and in its uses and qualities the former is nearer to man. Those trees are comparatively wild whose bark alone is extensively used by man. Returning through Abiel Wheeler's hillside field toward the railroad, I see the springing mullein leaves more distinct than by day. Their leaves are remarkably warm to my hand, compared with the earth or a stone. I should be glad to make my bed of them some time.

Four months of the green leaf make all our summer,

Vol. IV

if I reckon from June 1st to October 1st, the growing season, and methinks there are about four months when the ground is white with snow. That would leave two months for spring and two for autumn. October the month of ripe or painted leaves; November the month of withered leaves and bare twigs and limbs.

As I was eating my dinner of rice to-day, with an open window, a small species of wild bee, with many yellow rings about the abdomen, came in and alighted on the molasses pitcher. It took up the molasses quite fast, and soon made quite bare and white a considerable space on the nose of the pitcher which was smeared with molasses; then, having loaded itself, it circled round the pitcher a few times, while I was helping myself to some molasses, and flew against a closed window, but ere long, finding the open one by which it had entered, it winged its way to its nest. Probably if I had been willing to leave the window open and wait awhile, it would have returned.

I heard one boy say to another in the street to-day, "You don't know much more than a piece of putty."

VII

NOVEMBER, 1852

(ÆT. 35)

Nov. 1. A warm, mizzling kind of rain for two days past and still. *Stellaria media* in Cheney's garden, as last spring, butter-and-eggs, that small white aster (*A. dumosus ?*), the small white fleabane, hedge-mustard.

Day before yesterday to the Cliffs in the rain, misty rain. As I approached their edge, I saw the woods beneath, Fair Haven Pond, and the hills across the river, — which, owing to the mist, was as far as I could see, and seemed much further in consequence. I saw these between the converging boughs of two white pines a rod or two from me on the edge of the rock; and I thought that there was no frame to a landscape equal to this, — to see, between two near pine boughs, whose lichens are distinct, a distant forest and lake, the one frame, the other picture. In November, a man will eat his heart, if in any month. The birches have almost all lost their leaves. On the river this afternoon, the leaves, now crisp and curled, when the wind blows them on to the water become rude boats which float and sail about awhile conspicuously before they go to the bottom, — oaks, walnuts, etc.

It is remarkable how native man proves himself to the earth, after all, and the completeness of his life in all its appurtenances. His alliances, how wide! He has domesticated not only beasts but fowl, not only hens and geese and ducks and turkeys, but his doves, winging their way to their dovecots over street and village and field, enhance the picturesqueness of his sky, to say nothing of his trained falcons, his beautiful scouts in the upper air. He is lord of the fowl and the brute. His allies are not only on the land, but in the air and water. The dove, the martin, the bluebird, the swallow, and, in some countries, the hawk have attached themselves to his fortunes. The doves that wing their way so near the clouds, they too are man's retainers.

Nov. 2. Tall buttercups, red clover, houstonias, *Polygonum aviculare*, still.

Those handsome red buds on often red-barked twigs, with some red leaves still left, appear to be blueberry buds. The prinos berries also now attract me in the scarcity of leaves, its own all gone; its berries are apparently a brighter red for it. The month of chickadees and new-swollen buds. At long intervals I see or hear a robin still.

To Walden.

In the latter part of October the skaters and waterbugs entirely disappear from the surface of the pond, and then and in November, when the weather is perfectly calm, it is almost absolutely as smooth as glass. This afternoon a three-days' rain-storm is drawing to an end, though still overcast. The air is quite still but misty, from time to time mizzling, and the pond is very smooth, and its surface difficult to distinguish, though

Vol. IV

it no longer reflects the *bright* tints of autumn but sombre colors only, — calm at the end of a storm, except here and there a slight glimmer or dimple, as if a few skaters which had escaped the frosts were still collected there, or a faint breeze there struck, or a few rain-drops fell there, or perchance the surface, being remarkably smooth, betrayed by circling dimples where a spring welled up from below. I paddled gently toward one of these places and was surprised to find myriads of small perch about five inches long sporting there, one after another rising to the surface and dimpling it, leaving bubbles on it. They were very handsome as they surrounded the boat, with their distinct transverse stripes, a rich brown color. There were many such schools in the pond, as it were improving the short season before the ice would close their window. When I approached them suddenly with noise, they made a sudden plash and rippling with their tails in fright, and then took refuge in the depths. Suddenly the wind rose, the mist increased, and the waves rose, and still the perch leaped, but much higher, half out of water, a hundred black points, three inches long, at once above the surface.[1] The pond, dark before, was now a glorious and indescribable blue, mixed with dark, perhaps the opposite side of the wave, a sort of changeable or watered-silk blue, more cerulean if possible than the sky itself, which was now seen overhead. It required a certain division of the sight, however, to discern this. Like the colors on a steel sword-blade.[2]

[1] [*Walden*, pp. 210, 211; Riv. 296–298.]
[2] [*Walden*, p. 196; Riv. 277.]

Slate-colored snowbirds (?) with a faint note.

The leaves which are not withered, whose tints are still fresh and bright, are now remarked in sheltered places. Plucked quite a handsome nosegay from the side of Heywood's Peak, — white and blue-stemmed goldenrods, asters (*undulatus* and ?).

I do not know whether the perch amuse themselves thus more in the fall than at any other time. In such transparent and apparently bottomless water their swimming impresses the beholder as a kind of flight or hovering, like a compact flock of birds passing below one, just beneath his level on the right or left.[1] What a singular experience must be theirs in their winter quarters, their long night, expecting when the sun will open their shutters!

If you look discerningly, so as to see the reflection only, you see a most glorious light blue, in comparison with which the original dark green of the opposite side of the waves is but muddy.[2]

Nov. 3. Shepherd's-purse abundant still in gardens.
3 P. M. — To Cliffs and Andromeda Ponds.

In the Heywood Brooks, many young pollywogs two inches long and more; also snails on the bottom. I find these water-bugs, large and small, not on the surface, but apparently sheltered amid the weeds, going into winter quarters. While collecting caddis-worms, of which there are many, whose cases are made of little pieces of weeds piled about them like well-stones, I disturbed

[1] [*Walden*, pp. 210, 211; Riv. 297.]
[2] [*Walden*, p. 196; Riv. 277.]

a good-sized fish, either a pout or a sucker, near the path. It swam rapidly down this shallow stream, creating a wave which reached from side to side and betrayed it. I followed it down till it concealed itself under some frog-spittle, and when I had dislodged it thence, it went down further, till, coming to where the stream was dammed, it buried itself in the mud above the dam in an instant, and I could not dig it out.

The landscape from Fair Haven Hill looks Novembery, bare gray limbs and twigs in the swamps; and where many young (or shrub) oaks have lost their leaves, you hear the rustling of oak and walnut leaves in the air. There is a ripple on the river from the cool northerly wind. The plants are sere. It is the month of withered oak leaves. The shrub oak plain is all withered. Only one or two butter-and-eggs left. At Andromeda Pond, started nine black (?) ducks just at sunset, as usual they circling far round to look at me. The andromeda is a dull brown like the shrub oak leaves now.

Or I was startled by the cracking of the ground in the coldest nights, which sounded as if it were my house that cracked, and in the morning I would find a crack in the earth a quarter of an inch wide and a quarter of a mile long.[1]

The sunsets begin to be interestingly warm.

Nov. 4. Autumnal dandelion and yarrow.

Must be out-of-doors enough to get experience of wholesome reality, as a ballast to thought and senti-

[1] [*Walden*, p. 301; Riv. 422.]

ment. Health requires this relaxation, this aimless life. This life in the present. Let a man have thought what he will of Nature in the house, she will still be novel outdoors. I keep out of doors for the sake of the mineral, vegetable, and animal in me.

How precious a fine day early in the spring! — less so in the fall; less still in the summer and winter. Chimaphila[1] sheds its pollen now. Saw witch-hazels out of bloom, some still fresh.

The winds of autumn draw a few strains from the telegraph, after all. At this post it is only a musical hum, but at the next it attains to clearness and reminds me of the isles of Greece. I put my ear to the post. Every fibre resounded with the increasing inflatus, but when it rose into a more melodious and tenser tone it seemed to retire and concentrate itself in the pith of the wood.

There was also Thorer of Steige, in Magnus Barefoot's reign, who was "old and heavy." He gained some victories, but when it went against him could not run. He told his foe, "I am well in hands, but ill on my feet." He "was a man exceedingly stout, both high of stature and thick." So that, when he was hung, his neck gave way and his body fell to the ground. The poet sings: —

> "How the king's thralls hung on the gallows
> Old Thorer and his traitor-fellows."

My thought is a part of the meaning of the world, and hence I use a part of the world as a symbol to express my thought.

[1] ["*Lycopodium dendroideum*" substituted for this in pencil.]

Nov. 9. Tuesday. Ranunculus repens, Bidens connata (flat in a brook), yarrow, dandelion, autumnal dandelion, tansy, *Aster undulatus*, etc. A late three-ribbed goldenrod, with large serratures in middle of the narrow leaves, ten or twelve rays. *Potentilla argentea.* Fore part of November time for walnutting.

All around Walden, both in the thickest wood and where the wood has been cut off, there can be traced a meandering narrow shelf on the steep hillside, the footpath worn by the feet of Indian hunters, and still occasionally trodden by the white man, probably as old as the race of man here. And the same trail may be found encircling all our ponds. Near the sandy eastern shore, where the water is eight or ten feet deep, I have seen from a boat, in calm weather, broad circular heaps of small stones on the bottom, half a dozen feet in diameter by a foot or more in height, where all around was bare sand, — probably the work of some kind of fish.[1]

The French call dragon-flies "demoiselles."

Nov. 11. Did Harris call the water-bug *Gyrinus* to-day?

Nov. 12. 4 P. M. — To Cliffs.

It clears up. A very bright rainbow. Three reds and greens. I see its foot within half a mile in the southeast, heightening the green of the pines. From Fair Haven Hill, I see a very distant, long, low dark-blue cloud, still left, in the northwest horizon beyond

[1] [*Walden*, pp. 199, 200, 205; Riv. 282, 290.]

Vol. IV

the mountains, and against this I see, apparently, a narrow white cloud resting on every mountain and conforming exactly to its outline, — as if the white *frilled* edge of the main cloud were turned up over them. In fact, the massive dark-blue cloud beyond revealed these distinct white caps resting on the mountains this side, for twenty miles along the horizon.

The sun having set, my long dark cloud has assumed the form of an alligator, and where the sun has just disappeared it is split into two tremendous jaws, between which glows the eternal city, its crenate lips all coppery golden, its serrate fiery teeth. Its body lies a slumbering mass along the horizon.

Nov. 13. Saturday. To Andromeda Ponds. Andromeda is a dull reddish brown, like oak leaves. Saw a flock of little passenger birds[1] by Walden, busily pecking at the white birch catkins; about the size of a chickadee; *distinct* white bar on wings; most with dark pencilled breast, some with whitish; forked tail; bright chestnut or crimson (?) frontlet; yellowish shoulders or sack. When startled, they went off with a jingling sound somewhat like emptying a bag of coin. Is it the yellow redpoll?

Nov. 14. Still yarrow, tall buttercup, and tansy.

Nov. 16. 9 A. M. — Sail up river to Lee's Bridge.
Colder weather and very windy, but still no snow. A very little ice along the edges of the river, which

[1] *Fringilla linaria* [now called *Acanthis linaria*, the redpoll].

does not all melt before night. Muskrat-houses completed. Interesting objects looking down a river-reach at this season, and our river should not be represented without one or two of these cones. They are quite conspicuous half a mile distant, and are of too much importance to be omitted in the river landscape. I still see the drowned white lily pads showing their red sides. On the meadow side the water is very much soiled by the dashing of the waves. I see one duck. The pines on shore look very cold, reflecting a silvery light. The waves run high, with white caps, and communicate a pleasant motion to the boat. At Lee's Cliff the *Cerastium viscosum*. We sailed up Well Meadow Brook. The water is singularly grayey, clear and cold. The bottom of the brook showing great nuphar roots, like its ribs, with some budding leaves. Returning, landed at Holden's Spruce Swamp. The water is frozen in the pitcher-plant leaf. The swamp-pink and blueberry buds attract.

Nov. 18. Measured a stick of round timber, probably white pine, on the cars this afternoon, — ninety-five feet long, nine and ten twelfths in circumference at butt, and six and two twelfths in circumference at small end, quite straight. From Vermont. Yarrow and tansy still. These are cold, gray days.

Nov. 21. I was surprised this afternoon to find the river skimmed over in some places, and Fair Haven Pond one-third frozen or skimmed over, though commonly there is scarcely any ice to be observed along the shores. The commonest bird I see and hear nowadays is that little red crowned or fronted bird I described the 13th. I hear now more music from them. They have a mewing note which reminds me of a canary-bird. They make very good forerunners of winter. Is it not the ruby-crowned wren?[1]

Nov. 23. This morning the ground is white with snow, and it still snows. This is the first time it has been fairly white this season, though once before, many weeks ago, it was slightly whitened for ten or fifteen minutes. It was so warm and still last night at sundown that I remarked to a neighbor that it was moderating to snow. It is, in some degree, also, warmer after the first snow has come and banked up the houses and filled the crevices in the roof. Already the landscape impresses me with a greater sense of fertility. I have not worn gloves yet, though it has been finger-cold. There is something genial even in the first snow, and Nature seems to relent a little of her November harshness. Men, too, are disposed to give thanks for the bounties of the year all over the land, and the sound of the mortar is heard in all houses, and the odor of summer savory reaches even to poets' garrets.

This, then, may be considered the end of the flower season for this year, though this snow will probably soon melt again.

Among the flowers which may be put down as lasting thus far, as I remember, in the order of their hardiness: yarrow, tansy (these very fresh and common),

[1] Lesser redpoll.

cerastium, autumnal dandelion, dandelion, and perhaps tall buttercup, etc., the last four scarce. The following seen within a fortnight: a late three-ribbed goldenrod of some kind, blue-stemmed goldenrod (these two perhaps within a week), *Potentilla argentea, Aster undulatus, Ranunculus repens, Bidens connata,* shepherd's-purse, etc., etc. N. B.: I have not looked for witch-hazel nor *Stellaria media* lately.

I had a thought in a dream last night which surprised me by its strangeness, as if it were based on an experience in a previous state of existence, and could not be entertained by my waking self. Both the thought and the language were equally novel to me, but I at once perceived it to be true and to coincide with my experience in this state.

3 P. M. — To Cliffs and Walden.

You must go forth early to see the snow on the twigs. The twigs and leaves are all bare now, and the snow half melted on the ground; where the trees are thick it has not reached the ground at all, except in the shape of water in the course of the day. But early this morning the woods presented a very different scene. The beauty and purity of new-fallen snow, lying just as it fell, on the twigs and leaves all the country over, afforded endless delight to the walker. It was a delicate and fairylike scene. But a few hours later the woods were comparatively lumpish and dirty. So, too, you must go forth very early to see a hoar frost, which is rare here; these crisped curls adorn only the forehead of the day. The air is full of low, heavy mist, almost rain. The pines, in this atmosphere and contrasted with the

snow, are suddenly many degrees darker, and the oaks redder. But still the tops of the dead grass rise above the snow in the fields, and give the country a yellow or russet look. The wetter meadows are quite russet. I am surprised to see Fair Haven entirely skimmed over.

Having descended the Cliff, I go along to the Andromeda Ponds. Sportsmen have already been out with their dogs, improving this first snow to track their game. The andromeda looks somewhat redder than before, a warm reddish brown, with an edging of yellowish sedge or coarse grass about the swamp, and red rustling shrub oak hills with a white ground rising around. These swamps, resorted to by the muskrat and ducks, most remind me of the Indian.

The mist so low is clouds close to the ground, and the steam of the engine also hugs the earth in the Cut, concealing all objects for a great distance.

Though the parents cannot determine whether the child shall be male or female, yet, methinks, it depends on them whether he shall be a worthy addition to the human family.

Nov. 24. At this time last year the andromeda in the Ministerial Swamp was red. Now it has not turned from brown.

Nov. 25. At Walden. — I hear at sundown what I mistake for the squawking of a hen, — for they are firing at chickens hereabouts, — but it proved to be a flock of wild geese going south. This proves how much the voices of all fowls are alike.

Nov. 27. Almost an Indian-summer day. The shrub oaks and the sprouts make woods you can look down on. They are now our rustling gardens. The leaves of the former are now a very handsome leather-color, whiter on the under side, clear and firm; smooth, and not shrivelled nor dimmed. It is a new color for a garden; something foreign and Oriental, even, it suggests. I find acorns which have sent a shoot down into the earth this fall.

Like many of my contemporaries I had rarely for many years used animal food, or tea or coffee, etc., etc., not so much because of any ill effects which I had traced to them in my own case, though I could theorize extensively in that direction, as because it was not agreeable to my imagination. It appeared more beautiful to live low and fare hard in many respects; and though I never did so, I went just far enough to please my imagination. But now I find myself somewhat less particular in these respects. I carry less religion to the table, ask no blessing, not because I am wiser than I was, but, I am obliged to confess, because, however much it is to be regretted, with years I have grown more coarse and indifferent. The repugnance to animal food and the rest is not the result of experience, but is an instinct.[1]

Nov. 29, 30, and *Dec.* 1. The snow which fell the 23d whitened the ground but a day or two. These have been the mildest and pleasantest days since November came in.

November 29th, walked in P. M. to old stone bridge and down bank of river by Sam Barrett's house.

[1] [*Walden,* pp. 237, 240; Riv. 334, 338.]

When I stood on the caving swallow banks by the bridge about 4 o'clock, the sun sank below some clouds, or they rose above it, and it shone out with that bright, calm, memorable light which I have elsewhere described, lighting up the pitch pines and everything. The patches of winter rye, at this season so green by contrast, are an interesting feature in the landscape. When I got out of the wood, going toward Barrett's, the softness of the sunlight on the russet landscape, the smooth russet grassy fields and meadows, was very soothing, the sun now getting low in a November day. The stems and twigs of the maples, etc., looking down the river, were beautifully distinct. You see distinctly the form of the various clumps of maples and birches. Geese in river swam as fast as I walked. Many broken but apparently rather recent turtles' eggs on the bank.

Nov. 30. To Pine Hill.

The buds of the *Populus tremuloides* show their down as in early spring, and the early willows. Woodchoppers have commenced some time since. This is another pleasant day. From Pine Hill, Wachusett is seen over Walden. The country seems to slope up from the west end of Walden to the mountain. Already, a little after 4 o'clock, the sparkling windows and vanes of the village, seen under and against the faintly purple-tinged, slate-colored mountains, remind me of a village in a mountainous country at twilight, where early lights appear. I think that this peculiar sparkle without redness, a cold glitter, is peculiar to this season.

VIII

DECEMBER, 1852

(ÆT. 35)

Dec. 1. To Cliffs.

The snow keeps off unusually. The landscape is the color of a russet apple which has no golden cheek. The sunset sky supplies that. But though it be crude to bite, it yields a pleasant acid flavor. The year looks back toward summer, and a summer smile is reflected in her face. There is in these days a coolness in the air which makes me hesitate to call them Indian summer. At this season I observe the form of the buds which are prepared for spring, — the large bright yellowish and reddish buds of the swamp-pink, the already downy once of the *Populus tremuloides* and the willows, the red ones of the blueberry, etc., the long, sharp ones of the amelanchier, the spear-shaped ones of the viburnum, etc.; also the catkins of the alders and birches.

Dec. 2. The pleasantest day of all.

Started in boat before 9 A. M. down river to Billerica with W. E. C.

Not wind enough for a sail. I do not remember when I have taken a sail or a row on the river in December before. We had to break the ice about the boat-house for some distance. Still no snow. The banks

are white with frost. The air is calm, and the water smooth. The distant sounds of cars, cocks, hounds, etc., as we glide past N. Barrett's farm, remind me of spring. It is an anticipation, a looking through winter to spring. There is a certain resonance and elasticity in the air that makes the least sound melodious as in spring. The old unpainted houses under their trees (Joel Barrett's?) look as if winter had come and gone. There is one side of Abner (?) Buttrick's, painted as if with the pumpkin pies left over after Thanksgiving, it is so singular a yellow. The river has risen since the last rain a few feet, and partially floods the meadow. See still two ducks on the meadow. Hear the jay in distant copses, and the ruby-crowned wren (?)[1] flies and mews over. Some parts of the meadow are covered with thin ice, through which we row, — which yet lasts all day, — and the waves we make in the river nibble and crumble its edge, and produce a rustling of the grass and reeds, as if a muskrat were stirring.

We land behind Tarbell's and walk inland. How warm in the hollows! The outline of the hills is very agreeable there; ridgy hills, with backs to them, and a perfect cow-path winds along the side of one. They have such weight to carry that they select the easiest course.

Again embark. It is remarkably calm and warm in the sun, now that we have brought a hill between us and the wind. There goes a muskrat. He leaves so long a ripple behind that in this light you cannot tell where his body ends, and think him longer than he is.

[1] *Fringilla linaria.*

This is a glorious river-reach. At length we pass the bridge. Everywhere the muskrat-houses line the shores, — or what *was* the shore, — some three feet high and regularly sharp as the Peak of Teneriffe.

C. says, "Let us land" (in an orchard by Atkins's (?) boathouse). "The angle of inci*dents* should be equal to the angle of reflection." We did so. By the island where I formerly camped, half a mile or more above the bridge on the road from Chelmsford to Bedford, we saw a mink, a slender black (at ten rods' distance; Emmons says they are a "dark glossy brown"), very like a weasel in form. He alternately ran along on the ice and swam in the water, now and then holding up his head and long neck and looking at us. Not so shy as a muskrat, but I should say very black. The muskrats would curl up into a ball on the ice, decidedly reddish brown. The ice made no show, being thin and dark. Mink's head is larger in proportion to body than the muskrat's, not so sharp and rat-like.

Left our boat just above the last-named bridge on west side. A bright dazzling sheen for miles on the river as you looked up it. Crossed the bridge, turned into a path on the left, and ascended a hill a mile and a half off, between us and Billerica, somewhat off from the river. The Concord affords the water prospects of a larger river, like the Connecticut even. Hereabouts I found a spear-head, by a mysterious little building. Dined on the hill, from which we saw Billerica centre, a mile and a half northerly. We had crossed what by the map must be the brook from Nutting's Pond. On the west side of the river in Billerica here, is a grand range of hills, somewhat cliffy, covered with young oaks, whose leaves now give it a red appearance, even when seen from Ball's Hill. It is one of the most interesting and novel features in the river scenery.

Men commonly talk as if genius were something proper to an individual. I esteem it but a common privilege, and if one does not enjoy it now, he may congratulate his neighbor that *he* does. There is no place for man-worship. We understand very well a man's relation, not to *his* genius, but to the genius.

Returning, the water is smoother and more beautiful than ever. The ripples we make produce ribbed reflections or shadows on the dense but leafless bushes on shore, thirty or forty rods distant, very regular, and so far that they seem motionless and permanent. Again we see the mink, plainer than ever. The smooth river-reaches, so calm and glorious in this light, " I see, not feel, how beautiful they are." All the water behind us as we row (and even on the right and left at a distance) is perfectly unrippled, we move so fast; but before us, down-stream, it is all in commotion from shore to shore. There are some fine shadows on those grand red oaken hills in the north. What a fine color to last through summer!

We look at Atkins's boathouse, ugly, like a barn carried off and lodged in the river. A muskrat had made his cabin in the bathing-apartment. Man's boat-house is a deformity, but the muskrats' cabins are an ornament to the river. The squareness of the former

building, roof and all, offend. Could not the architect take a hint from the pyramidal or conical form of the muskrat's house? Something of this form and color, like a large haycock in the meadow, would be in harmony with the scenery. The muskrat's house is made in the midst of weeds or bushes commonly, which protect it from the waves. When a muskrat comes to the surface too near you, how quickly and with what force he turns and plunges again, making a sound in the calm water as if you had thrown into it a large stone with violence!

Long did it take to sink the Carlisle Bridge. The reflections after sunset were distinct and glorious, — the heaven into which we unceasingly rowed. I thought now that the angle of reflection was greater than the angle of inci*dents*. It cooler grew. The stars came out soon after we turned Ball's Hill, and it became difficult to distinguish our course. The boatman knows a river by reaches. We ran part way into several holts, or *poke-logans*. Got home in the dark, our feet and legs numb and cold with sitting and inactivity, having been about eight miles by river, etc. It was some time before we recovered the full use of our cramped legs. I forgot to speak of the afterglows. The twilight, in fact, had several stages to it, and several times after it had grown dusky the twilight acquired a new transparency, and the trees on the hillsides were lit up again.

Dec. 5. P. M. — Rowed over Walden !
A dark, but warm, misty day, completely overcast. This great rise of the pond after an interval of many

years, and the water standing at this great height for a year or more, kills the shrubs and trees about its edge, — pitch pines, birches, alders, aspens, etc., — and, falling again, leaves an unobstructed shore. The rise and fall of the pond serves this use at least. This fluctuation, though it makes it difficult to walk round it when the water is highest, by killing the trees makes it so much the easier and more agreeable when the water is low. By this fluctuation, this rise of its waters after long intervals, it asserts its title to a shore, and the trees cannot hold it by right of possession. But unlike those waters which are subject to a daily tide, its shore is cleanest when the water is lowest. I have been surprised to observe how surely the water standing for a few months about such trees would kill them. On the side of the pond next my house a row of pitch pines fifteen feet high was killed and tipped over as if by a lever, and thus a stop put to their encroachments; and their size may indicate how many years had elapsed since the last rise.[1] I have been surprised to see what a rampart has been formed about many ponds, — in one place at Walden, but especially at Flint's Pond, where it occurs between the pond and a swamp, as if it were the remains of an Indian swamp fort, — apparently by the action of the waves and the ice, several feet in height and containing large stones and trees. These lips of the lake, on which no beard grows. It licks its chaps from time to time.[2]

I saw some dimples on the surface, and, thinking it

[1] [*Walden*, pp. 201, 202; Riv. 284, 285.]
[2] [*Walden*, p. 202; Riv. 285.]

was going to rain hard immediately, the air being full of mist, I made haste to take my place at the oars to row homeward. Already the rain seemed rapidly increasing, though I felt none on my cheek, and I anticipated a thorough soaking; but suddenly the dimples ceased, for they were produced by the perch which the noise of my oars had scared into the depths. I saw their schools dimly disappearing.[1]

I have said that Walden has no visible inlet nor outlet, but it is on the one hand distantly and indirectly related to Flint's Pond, which is more elevated, by a chain of small ponds coming from that quarter, and on the other hand directly and manifestly related to Concord River, which is lower, by a similar chain of ponds, through which in some other geological period it may have flowed thither, and by a little digging, which God forbid, could probably be made to flow thither again. If, by living thus " reserved and austere " like a hermit in the woods so long, it has acquired such wonderful depth and purity, who would not regret that the impure waters of Flint's Pond should be mingled with it, or itself should go waste its sweetness in the ocean wave?[2]

Dec. 6. Though foul weather yesterday, this is the warmest and pleasantest day yet. Cows are turned out to pasture again. On the Corner causeway fine cobwebs glimmer in the air, covering the willow twigs and the road, and sometimes stretching from side to side

[1] [*Walden*, p. 211; Riv. 298.]
[2] [*Walden*, p. 215; Riv. 303, 304.]

above my head. I see many little gnat-like insects in the air there. Tansy still fresh, and I saw autumnal dandelion a few days since. In the evening I see the spearer's light on the river. Saw a great slate-colored hawk sail away from the Cliffs.

Dec. 7. P. M. — Perhaps the warmest day yet. True Indian summer. The walker perspires. The shepherd's-purse is in full bloom: the andromeda not turned red. Saw a pile of snow-fleas in a rut in the wood-path, six or seven inches long and three quarters of an inch high, to the eye exactly like powder, as if a sportsman had spilled it from his flask; and when a stick was passed through the living and skipping mass, each side of the furrow preserved its edge as in powder.

Dec. 8. Another Indian-summer day. Saw some puffballs in the woods, wonderfully full of sulphur-like dust, which yellowed my shoes, greenish-yellow. The recent water-line at Walden is quite distinct, though like the limit of a shadow, on the alders about eighteen inches above the present level. One cannot burn or bury even his old shoes without a feeling of sadness and compassion; much more [*sic*] his old body, without a slight sense of guilt.

Dec. 9. P. M. — To C. Smith's Hill.
Those little ruby-crowned wrens (?)[1] still about. They suddenly dash away from this side to that in flocks, with a tumultuous note, half jingle, half rattle,

[1] Lesser redpolls.

like nuts shaken in a bag, or a bushel of nutshells, soon returning to the tree they had forsaken on some alarm. They are oftenest seen on the white birch, apparently feeding on its seeds, scattering the scales about.

A fresh dandelion.

The chestnuts are almost as plenty as ever, both in the fallen burs and out of them. There are more this year than the squirrels can consume. I picked three pints this afternoon, and though some bought at a store the other day were more than half mouldy, I did not find one mouldy one among these which I picked from under the wet and mouldy leaves, where they have been snowed on once. Probably they do not heat, though wet. These are also still plump and tender. I love to gather them, if only for the sense of the bountifulness of nature they give me.[1]

A few petals of the witch-hazel still hold on.

In the "Homes of American Authors" it is said of most that at one time they wrote for the *North American Review*. It is one of my qualifications that I have not written an article for the *North American Review*.

A man tells me he saw a violet to-day.

Very nice; as the old lady said when she had got a gravestone for her husband.

Dec. 12. Cold at last. Saw a violet on the C. Miles road where the bank had been burned in the fall. *Bæomyces roseus* also. Tansy still fresh yellow by the Corner Bridge. From Cliffs I see snow on the

[1] [*Excursions*, p. 197; Riv. 241. See also p. 462 (Jan. 10, 1853).]

Vol. IV

mountains. Last night's rain was snow there, then. They now have a parti-colored look, like the skin of a pard, as if they were spread with a saddle-cloth for Boreas to ride. I hear of a cultivated rose blossoming in a garden in Cambridge within a day or two. The buds of the aspen are large and show wool in the fall.

Dec. 13. Walk early through the woods to Lincoln to survey. Winter weather may be said to have begun yesterday. River and ponds all open. Goose Pond skimmed over. Why have I ever omitted early rising and a morning walk?

As we walked over the Cedar Hill, Mr. Weston asked me if I had ever noticed how the frost formed around a particular weed in the grass, and no other. It was a clear cold morning. We stooped to examine, and I observed, about the base of the *Lechea major* (?), or larger pinweed,[1] the frost formed into little flattened trumpets or bells, an inch or more long, with the mouth down about the base of the stem. They were very conspicuous, dotting the grass white. But what was most remarkable was that, though there were plenty of other dead weeds and grasses about, no other species exhibited this phenomenon. I think it can hardly be because of the form of its top, and that therefore the moisture is collected and condensed and flows down its stem particularly. It may have something to do with the life of the root, which I noticed was putting forth shoots *beneath*. Perhaps this growth generates heat

[1] ["*Lechea* . . . pinweed" crossed out in pencil and "cistus" substituted.]

and so steam. He said that his cows never touched that weed. I judge from his account of the rise and fall of Flint's Pond that, allowing for the disturbance occasioned by its inlets and outlet, it sympathizes with Walden.[1]

I observed a mouse run down a bush by the pond-side. I approached and found that he had neatly covered over a thrasher or other bird's nest (it was made partly of sticks like a thrasher's), about four or five feet from the ground, and lined it warmly with that common kind of green moss (?) which grows about the base of oaks, but chiefly with a kind [of] vegetable wool, perhaps from the wool-grass. He appeared to be a reddish brown above and cream-colored beneath, and ran swiftly down the stems. I think it must be the *Gerbillus Canadensis*, or perhaps the *Arvicola Emmonsii*, or maybe the *Arvicola hirsutus*, meadow mouse.[2]

Began to snow at noon. This the third snow; the first lasted half an hour on ground; the second, two or three days.

Dec. 14. *Tuesday.* P. M. — To Assabet Stone Bridge.

We have now the scenery of winter, though the snow is but an inch or two deep. The dried chalices of the *Rhexia Virginica* stand above the snow, and the cups of the blue-curls and the long sharp red capsules of the small (?) hypericum, etc., etc., johnswort; and a new era commences with the dried herbs.

[1] [*Walden*, p. 201; Riv. 284.]
[2] *Vide* forward to Dec. 30th.

Ah, who can tell the serenity and clarity of a New England winter sunset? This could not be till the cold and the snow came. Ah, what isles those western clouds! in what a sea! Just after sunset there is a broad pillar of light for many minutes in the west.

Dec. 15. Saw a small flock of geese go over.

One's *life*, the enterprise he is here upon, should certainly be a grand fact to consider, not a mean or insignificant one. A man should not live without a purpose, and that purpose must surely be a grand one. But is this fact of " our life " commonly but a puff of air, a flash in the pan, a smoke, a nothing? It does not afford arena for a tragedy.

Dec. 16. Observed the reflection of the snow on Pine Hill from Walden, extending far beyond the true

limits of a reflection, quite across the pond; also, less obviously, of pines. The sky overcast with thick scud, which, in the reflection, the snow ran into.

Dec. 18. P. M. — To Annursnack.

Sedum Telephium, garden orpine or live-for-ever; I think this is the plant with a sort of pineapple-leaved and sheathed bulbs, on a rock between Cox's and Heywood's.[1] Saw where a red squirrel (tinged gray) had

[1] No. *Sempervivum tectorum.*

Vol. IV

been eating the hips of a sweet-briar, which had apparently grown recently, leaves still fresh and green. Very cold, windy day. The crust of the slight snow covered in some woods with the scales (bird-shaped) of the birch, and their seeds. Loring's Pond beautifully frozen. So polished a surface, I mistook many parts of it for water. It was *waved* or *watered* with a slight dust nevertheless. Cracked into large squares like the faces of a reflector, it was so exquisitely polished that the sky and scudding dun-colored clouds, with mother-o'-pearl tints, were reflected in it as in the calmest water. I slid over it with a little misgiving, mistaking the ice before me for water. This is the first skating. Still the little ruby-crowned birds about.

Dec. 22. *Wednesday.* Surveying the Hunt Farm this and the 20th.

C. says that Flint's Pond was frozen *over* yesterday. A rambling, rocky, wild, moorish pasture, this of Hunt's, with two or three great white oaks to shade the cattle, which the farmer would not take fifty dollars apiece for, though the ship-builder wanted them. The snow balled so badly to-day while I was working in the swamp, that I was set up full four inches. It is pleasant, cutting a path through the bushes in a swamp, to see the color of the different woods, — the yellowish dogwood, the green prinos (?), and, on the upland, the splendid yellow barberry. The squirrel, rabbit, fox tracks, etc., attract the attention in the new-fallen snow; and the squirrel nests, bunches of grass and leaves high

in the trees, more conspicuous if not larger now, or the glimpse of a meadow (?) mouse, give occasion for a remark. You cannot go out so early but you will find the track of some wild creature. Returning home just after the sun had sunk below the horizon, I saw from N. Barrett's a fire made by boys on the ice near the Red Bridge, which looked like a bright reflection of a setting sun from the water under the bridge, so clear, so little lurid, in this winter evening air.

Dec. 27. *Monday.* Not a particle of ice in Walden to-day. Paddled across it. I took my new boat out. A black and white duck on it, Flint's and Fair Haven being frozen up. Ground bare. River open. Countless birches, white pines, etc., have been killed within a year or two about Goose Pond by the high water. The dead birches have broken in two in the middle and fallen over. In some coves where the water is shallow, their wrecks make quite a dense thicket. Found chestnuts quite plenty to-day.

Dec. 28. Brought my boat from Walden in rain. No snow on ground. Grass in the churchyard and elsewhere green as in the spring.

I omitted some observations apparently between the 18th and 22d, to the effect that the berries that hold on into winter are to be remarked, — the winterberry, alder and birch fruit, smilax, pyrus, hips, etc.

Both for bodily and mental health, court the present. Embrace health wherever you find her. A clump of birches raying out from one centre make a more agree-

able object than a single tree. The rosettes in the ice, as Channing calls them, now and for some time have attracted me.

It is worth the while to apply what wisdom one has to the conduct of his life, surely. I find myself oftenest wise in little things and foolish in great ones. That I may accomplish some particular petty affair well, I live my whole life coarsely. A broad margin of leisure is as beautiful in a man's life as in a book. Haste makes waste, no less in life than in housekeeping. Keep the time, observe the hours of the universe, not of the cars. What are threescore years and ten hurriedly and coarsely lived to moments of divine leisure in which your life is coincident with the life of the universe? We live too fast and coarsely, just as we eat too fast, and do not know the true savor of our food. We consult our will and understanding and the expectation of men, not our genius. I can impose upon myself tasks which will crush me for life and prevent all expansion, and this I am but too inclined to do.

One moment of life costs many hours, hours not of business but of preparation and invitation. Yet the man who does not betake himself at once and desperately to sawing is called a loafer, though he may be knocking at the doors of heaven all the while, which shall surely be opened to him. That aim in life is highest which requires the highest and finest discipline. How much, what infinite, leisure it requires, as of a lifetime, to appreciate a single phenomenon! You must camp down beside it as for life, having reached your land of promise, and give yourself wholly to it. It must stand for the whole world to you, symbolical of all things. The least partialness is your own defect of sight and cheapens the experience fatally. Unless the humming of a gnat is as the music of the spheres, and the music of the spheres is as the humming of a gnat, they are naught to me. It is not communications to serve for a history, — which are science, — but the great story itself, that cheers and satisfies us.

As I have not observed the rainbow on the *Juncus militaris* nor the andromeda red the past fall, it suggests a great difference in seasons.

Dec. 30. In Audubon's Animals: —
Sigmodon hispidum, Say and Ord.
Marsh-Rat of Lawson's Carolina.
Wood-Rat, Bartram's Travels in Florida.
Arvicola hispidus, Godman.
Arvicola hortensis of Griffith and of Cuvier.
The plate of this *resembles* my mouse of December 13th.

Dec. 31. I was this afternoon gathering chestnuts at Saw Mill Brook. I have within a few weeks spent some hours thus, scraping away the leaves with my hands and feet over some square rods, and have at least learned how chestnuts are planted and new forests raised. First fall the chestnuts with the severe frosts, the greater part of them at least, and then, at length, the rains and winds bring down the leaves which cover them with a thick coat. I have wondered sometimes how the nuts got planted which merely fell

on to the surface of the earth, but already I find the nuts of the present year partially mixed with the mould, as it were, under the decaying and mouldy leaves, where is all the moisture and manure they want. A large proportion of this year's nuts are now covered loosely an inch deep under mouldy leaves, though they are themselves sound, and are moreover concealed from squirrels thus.[1]

It is a sort of frozen rain this afternoon, which does not wet one, but makes the still bare ground slippery with a coating of ice, and stiffens your umbrella so that it cannot be shut. Will not the trees look finely in the morning?

[1] [*Excursions*, p. 196; Riv. 240, 241.]

IX

JANUARY, 1853

(ÆT. 35)

Jan. 1. *Saturday.* This morning we have something between ice and frost on the trees, etc. The whole earth, as last night, but much more, is encased in ice, which on the plowed fields makes a singular icy coat a quarter of an inch or more in thickness. About 9 o'clock A. M., I go to Lee's *via* Hubbard's Wood and Holden's Swamp and the riverside, for the middle is open. The stones and cow-dung, and the walls too, are all cased in ice on the north side. The latter look like alum rocks. This, not frozen mist or frost, but frozen drizzle, collected around the slightest cores, gives prominence to the least withered herbs and grasses. Where yesterday was a plain, smooth field, appears now a teeming crop of fat, *icy* herbage. The stems of the herbs on their north sides are enlarged from ten to a hundred times. The addition is so universally on the north side that a traveller could not lose the points of compass to-day, though it should [be] never so dark, for every blade of grass would serve to guide him, telling from which side the storm came yesterday. These straight stems of grasses stand up like white batons or sceptres, and make conspicuous foreground to the landscape, from six inches to three feet high. C. thought that these fat, icy branches on the withered grass and

herbs had no nucleus, but looking closer I showed him the fine black wiry threads on which they impinged, which made him laugh with surprise. The very cow-dung is incrusted, and the clover and sorrel send up a dull-green gleam through their icy coat, like strange plants. The pebbles in the plowed land are seen as through a transparent coating of gum. Some weeds bear the ice in masses, some, like the trumpet-weed and tansy, in balls for each dried flower. What a crash of jewels as you walk! The most careless walker, who never deigned to look at these humble weeds before, cannot help observing them now. This is why the herbage is left to stand dry in the fields all winter. Upon a solid foundation of ice stand out, pointing in all directions between northwest and northeast, or within the limits of ninety degrees, little spicula or crystallized points, half an inch or more in length.

Upon the dark, glazed plowed ground, where a mere wiry stem rises, its north side is thickly clad with these snow-white spears, like some Indian's head-dress, as if it had attracted all the frost. I saw a prinos bush full of large berries, by the wall in Hubbard's field. Standing on the west side, the contrast of the red berries with their white incrustation or prolongation on the north was admirable. I thought I had never seen the berries so dazzlingly bright. The whole north side of the bush, berries and stock, was beautifully incrusted. And when I went round to the north side, the redness of the berries came softened through and tingeing the allied snow-white bush, like an evening sky beyond. These adjoined snow or ice berries being beset, within the limits of ninety degrees on the north, with those icy prickles or spicula, between which the red glow and sometimes the clear red itself appeared, gave it the appearance of a raspberry bush full of over-ripe fruit.

Standing on the north side of a bush or tree, looking against the sky, you see only a white ghost of a tree, without a mote of earthiness, but as you go round it, the dark core comes into view. It makes all the odds imaginable whether you are travelling north or south. The drooping birches along the edges of woods are the most feathery, fairy-like ostrich plumes of the trees, and the color of their trunks increases the delusion. The weight of the ice gives to the pines the forms which northern trees, like the firs, constantly wear, bending and twisting the branches; for the twigs and plumes of the pines, being frozen, remain as the wind held them, and new portions of the trunk are exposed. Seen from the north, there is no greenness in the pines, and the character of the tree is changed. The willows along the edge of the river look like sedge in meadows. The sky is overcast, and a fine snowy hail and rain is falling, and these ghost-like trees make a scenery which reminds you of Spitzbergen. I see now the beauty of the causeway, by the bridge alders below swelling into the road, overtopped by willows and maples. The fine grasses and shrubs in the meadow rise to meet and mingle with the drooping willows, and the whole make an indistinct impression like a mist, and between this the road runs toward those white ice-clad ghostly or fairy trees in the distance, — toward spirit-land. The pines are as white as a counterpane, with raised em-

broidery and white tassels and fringes. Each fascicle of leaves or needles is held apart by an icy club surmounted by a little snowy or icy ball. Finer than the Saxon arch is this path running under the pines, roofed, not with crossing boughs, but drooping ice-covered twigs in irregular confusion. See in the midst of this stately pine, towering like the solemn ghost of a tree, the white ice-clad boughs of other trees appearing, of a different character; sometimes oaks with leaves incrusted, or fine-sprayed maples or walnuts. But finer than all, this red oak, its leaves incrusted like shields a quarter of an inch thick, and a thousand fine spicula, like long serrations at right angles with their planes, upon their edges. It has an indescribably rich effect, with color of the leaf coming softened through the ice, a delicate fawn-color of many shades. Where the plumes of the pitch pine are short and spreading close upon the trunk, sometimes perfect cups or rays are formed. Pitch pines present rough, massy grenadier plumes, with each a darker spot or cavity in the end, where you look in to the buds.

I listen to the booming of the pond as if it were a reasonable creature. I return at last in a rain, and am coated with a glaze, like the fields.

Being at Cambridge day before yesterday, Sibley told me that Agassiz told him that Harris was the greatest entomologist in the world, and gave him permission to repeat his remark. As I stood on the top of a ladder, he came along with his hand full of papers and inquired, " Do you value autographs ? " " No, I do not," I answered slowly and gravely. " Oh, I did n't know

but you did. I had some of Governor Dunlap," said he, retreating.

After talking with Uncle Charles the other night about the worthies of this country, Webster and the rest, as usual, considering who were geniuses and who not, I showed him up to bed, and when I had got into bed myself, I heard his chamber door opened, after eleven o'clock, and he called out, in an earnest, stentorian voice, loud enough to wake the whole house, " Henry! was John Quincy Adams a genius ? " " No, I think not," was my reply. " Well, I did n't think he was," answered he.

Jan. 2. 9 A. M. — Down railroad to Cliffs.

A clear day; a pure sky with cirrhi. In this clear air and bright sunlight, the ice-covered trees have a new beauty, especially the birches along under the edge of Warren's wood on each side of the railroad, bent quite to the ground   in every kind of curve. At a distance, as   you are approaching them endwise, they look like white tents of Indians under the edge of the wood. The birch is thus remarkable, perhaps, because from the feathery form of the tree, whose numerous small branches sustain so great a weight, bending it to the ground, and moreover because, from the color of the bark, the core is less observable. The oaks not only are less pliant in the trunk, but have fewer and stiffer twigs and branches. The birches droop over in all directions, like ostrich-feathers. Most wood-paths are impassable now to a carriage, almost to a foot traveller, from the number of saplings and boughs

bent over even to the ground in them. Both sides of the Deep Cut now shine in the sun, as if silver-plated, and the fine spray of a myriad bushes on the edge of the bank sparkle like silver. The telegraph-wire is coated to ten times its size, and looks like a slight fence scalloping along at a distance. Is merged in nature. When we climb the bank at Stow's wood-lot and come upon the piles of freshly split white pine wood (for he is ruthlessly laying it waste), the transparent ice, like a thick varnish, beautifully exhibits the color of the clear, tender, yellowish wood (pumpkin pine ?), and its grain, and we pick our way over a bed of pine boughs and twigs a foot or two deep, covering the ground, each twig and needle thickly incrusted with ice into one vast gelid mass, which our feet cronch as if we were walking through the cellar of some confectioner to the gods. The invigorating scent of the recently cut pines refreshes us, if that is any atonement for this devastation. The beauty of the oak-tops all silvered o'er. Especially now do I notice the hips, barberries, and winterberries, for their red. The red or purplish catkins of the alders are interesting as a winter fruit, and also of the birch. But few birds about. Apparently their granaries are locked up in ice, with which the grasses and buds are coated. Even far in the horizon the pine-tops are turned to firs or spruce by the weight of the ice bending them down, so that they look like a spruce swamp. No two trees wear the ice alike. The short plumes and needles of the spruce make a very pretty and peculiar figure. I see some oaks in the distance which, by their branches being curved or arched downward and massed, are turned into perfect elms, which suggests that that is the peculiarity of the elm. Few if any other trees are thus wisp-like, the branches gracefully drooping. I mean some slender red and white oaks which have recently been left in a clearing. Just apply a weight to the ends of the boughs, which will cause them to droop on all sides, and to each particular twig, which will mass them together, and you have perfect elms. Seen at the right angle, each ice-incrusted stubble shines like a prism with some color of the rainbow, — intense blue, or violet, and red. The smooth field, clad the other day with a low, wiry grass, is now converted into rough stubble-land, where you walk with cronching feet. It is remarkable that the trees ever recover from this burden which bends them to the ground. I should like to weigh a limb of this pitch pine. The character of the tree is changed.

I have now passed the bars and am approaching the Cliffs. The forms and variety of the ice are particularly rich here, there are so many low bushes and weeds before me as I ascend toward the sun, especially very small white pines almost merged in the ice-incrusted ground. All objects, even the apple trees and rails, are to the eye polished silver. It is a perfect land of faery. As if the world were a great frosted cake with its ornaments. The boughs gleam like silver candlesticks. Le Jeune describes the same in Canada, in 1636, as " *nos grands bois ne paroissoient qu'une forest de cristal.*" The silvery ice stands out an inch by three fourths [of] an inch in width on the north side of every twig of these apple trees, with rich irregularities of its own in

its edge. When I stoop and examine some fat icy stubble in my path, I find for all core a ridiculous wiry russet thread, scarce visible, not a hundredth part its size, which breaks with the ice under my feet; yet where this has a minute stub of a branch only a fortieth of an inch in length, there is a corresponding clumsy icy protuberance on the surface an eighth of an inch off. Nature works with such luxuriance and fury that she follows the least hint. And on the twigs of bushes, for each bud there is a corresponding icy swelling.

The bells are particularly sweet this morning. I hear more, methinks, than ever before. How much more religion in their sound, than they ever call men together to! Men obey their call and go to the stove-warmed church, though God exhibits himself to the walker in a frosted bush to-day, as much as in a burning one to Moses of old.

We build a fire on the Cliffs. When kicking to pieces a pine stump for the fat knots which alone would burn in this icy day, at the risk of spoiling my boots, having looked in vain for a stone, I thought how convenient would be an Indian stone axe to batter it with. The bark of white birch, though covered with ice, burned well. We soon had a roaring fire of fat pine on a shelf of rock, from which we overlooked the icy landscape. The sun, too, was melting the ice on the rocks, and the water was bubbling and pulsing downward in dark bubbles, exactly like pollywogs. What a good word is "flame," expressing the form and soul of fire, lambent with forked tongue! We lit a fire to see it rather than to feel it, it is so rare a sight these days. To have our

eyes ache once more with smoke! What a peculiar, perhaps indescribable color has this flame ! — a reddish or lurid yellow, not so splendid or full of light as of life and heat. These fat roots made much flame, and a very black smoke, commencing where the flame left off, which cast fine flickering shadows on the rocks. There was some bluish-white smoke from the rotten part of the wood. Then there was the fine white ashes, which farmers' wives sometimes use for pearlash. Fire is the most tolerable third party. I hear the wiry *phœbe* note of the chickadee, as if the spring were coming in. Brown thinks my ruby wren may be the lesser redpoll linnet.

Walden begins to freeze in the coves or shallower water on the north [1] side, where it was slightly skimmed over several weeks ago.

Jan. 3. Down railroad to Lincoln Bridge.

The evergreens appear to relieve themselves soonest of the ice, perhaps because of the reflection from their leaves. Those trees, like the maples and hickories, which have most spray and branches make the finest show of ice. This afternoon it snows, the snow lodging on the ice, which still adheres to the trees. The more completely the trees are changed to ice trees, to spirits of trees, the finer. Instead of the minute frostwork on a window, you have whole forests of silver boughs. I refer to the last two days. The " brattling " of the ice. Is not that the word? Along some causeway or fence in the meadow, the trees are changed into

[1] [Queried in pencil.]

silvery wisps. Nothing dark met the eye, but a silvery sheen, precisely as if the whole tree — trunk, boughs, and twigs — were converted into burnished silver. You exclaimed at every hedgerow. Sometimes a clump of birches fell over every way in graceful ostrich-plumes, all raying from one centre. You clambered over them like an ant in the grass. Then the beautifully checkered ice in the ruts, where the water had been soaked up, surpassing the richest tracery of watch-crystals! Suddenly all is converted to crystal. The world is a crystal palace. The trees, stiff and drooping and encased in ice, looked as if they were sculptured in marble, especially the evergreens.

I love Nature partly *because* she is not man, but a retreat from him. None of his institutions control or pervade her. There a different kind of right prevails. In her midst I can be glad with an entire gladness. If this world were all man, I could not stretch myself, I should lose all hope. He is constraint, she is freedom to me. He makes me wish for another world. She makes me content with this. None of the joys she supplies is subject to his rules and definitions. What he touches he taints. In thought he moralizes. One would think that no free, joyful labor was possible to him. How infinite and pure the least pleasure of which Nature is basis, compared with the congratulation of mankind! The joy which Nature yields is like [that] afforded by the frank words of one we love.

> Man, man is the devil,
> The source of all evil.

Methinks that these prosers, with their saws and their

laws, do not know how glad a man can be. What wisdom, what warning, can prevail against gladness? There is no law so strong which a little gladness may not transgress. I have a room all to myself; it is nature. It is a place beyond the jurisdiction of human governments. Pile up your books, the records of sadness, your saws and your laws. Nature is glad outside, and her merry worms within will ere long topple them down. There is a prairie beyond your laws. Nature is a prairie for outlaws. There are two worlds, the post-office and nature. I know them both. I continually forget mankind and their institutions, as I do a bank.

Well, now this afternoon the snow is lodging on all this ice. Is this the winter gnat I find on the snow, with six legs, a long, narrow, cylindrical body about one sixth of an inch, and the two narrow wings one third longer? Two feelers. Walden not yet frozen.

The red-crowns here still. They appear to frequent one clump of birches a long time, for here the snow beneath is covered with the seeds they have loosened, while elsewhere there are none. They hang by the twigs while they peck the catkins, and others are busy on the snow beneath, picking up what drops. They are continually in motion, with a jingling twitter and occasional mew, and suddenly, when disturbed, go off with a loud jingle like the motion of a whole bag of nuts.

The air is thick and darkened with falling snow, and the woods are being draped with it in white wreaths. This is winter. They are putting on their white greatcoats. The woodland road is spotless white.

The color of the pond depends on the light. It is now dark, in the storm. True to its nature, between earth and air, it is both green and blue. Let clear, serene weather come and illustrate its depth, and it is green; let the air descend on it and toss up its surface in waves, and it is blue like the sky.[1]

Jan. 4. To what I will call Yellow Birch Swamp, E. Hubbard's, in north part of town.

Still ice is left on the trees, but to-day is a windy and blustering day. The quantity of ice on the birches being reduced, they are still more wand- or faery-like. Tall ones, with no limbs for half their height, are gracefully bent over, and are now swaying from side to side in the wind, exactly like waving ostrich-plumes, as delicate as the spray on frosted windows. The color of these ice-clad trees at a distance is not white, but rather slightly grayish or hoary, which the better merges them in the landscape. This is the fourth day of the ice. The landscape is white, not only from the ice on the ground and trees, but from the snow which fell yesterday, though it is not an inch deep. In respect to snow, the winter appears to be just beginning.

I must call that swamp of E. Hubbard's west of the Hunt Pasture, Yellow Birch Swamp. There are more of those trees than anywhere else in town that I know. How pleasing to stand beside a new or rare tree! And few are so handsome as this. Singularly allied to the black birch in its sweet checkerberry scent and its form, and to the canoe birch in its peeling or fringed and

[1] [*Walden*, p. 196; Riv. 276.]

tasselled bark. The top is brush-like as the black birch; the bark an exquisite fine or delicate gold-color, curled off partly from the trunk, with vertical clear or smooth spaces, as if a plane had been passed up the tree. The sight of these trees affects me more than California gold. I measured one five feet and two inches in circumference at six feet from the ground. We have the silver and the golden birch. This is like a fair, flaxen-haired sister of the dark-complexioned black birch, with golden ringlets. How lustily it takes hold of the swampy soil, and braces itself! And here flows a dark cherry-wood or wine-colored brook over the iron-red sands in the sombre swamp, — swampy wine. In an undress, this tree. Ah, time will come when these will be all gone. Among the primitive trees. What sort of dryads haunt these? Blond nymphs.

Near by, the great pasture oaks with horizontal boughs. At Pratt's, the stupendous, boughy, branching elm, like vast thunderbolts stereotyped upon the sky; heaven-defying, sending back dark vegetable bolts, as if

flowing back in the channel of the lightning. The white oaks have a few leaves about the crown of the trunk in the lowest part of the tree, like a tree within a tree. The tree is thus less racked by the wind and ice.

In the twilight I went through the swamp, and yellow birches sent forth a dull-yellow gleam which each time made my heart beat faster. Occasionally you come to a dead and leaning white birch, beset with large fungi like ears or little shelves, with a rounded edge above.

I walked with the yellow birch. The prinos is green within. If there were Druids whose temples were the oak groves, my temple is the swamp. Sometimes I was in doubt about a birch whose vest was buttoned smooth and dark, till I came nearer and saw the yellow gleaming through, or where a button was off.

The animals do not use fire; man does. At first there was a pile of cold fat pine roots on the icy rock. A match was rubbed, fire elicited, and now this fire is the most emphatic and significant fact hereabouts. Fire slumbers never far off, and the friction of a match can awaken it.

Jan. 5. To Kibbe Place Swamp.

I see where probably a red squirrel had scratched along over the snow, and in one place a very perfect and delicate print of his feet. His five toes in separate sharp triangles distinctly raying off, or often only four visible. In one place I find a beaten track from a hole in the *ground* to [a] walnut a rod distant up which they have gone for nuts, which still hang on it. The whole print of the foot, etc., is about an inch and three quarters long, a part of the leg being impressed. Two of the tracks, when they are running, apparently, the two foremost, are wider apart; and perhaps with one pair they often make five marks, with the other four. Where there is a deep furrow in a chestnut tree between two swelling muscles, in two instances the squirrels, knowing it to be hollow, have gnawed a hole, enlarging the crack between two

Walden Pond in Winter

The Mountains from Ponkawtasset Hill

cheeks, and so made themselves a retreat. In one instance they have commenced to gnaw between the

cheeks, though no cavity appears, but I have no doubt the tree is hollow.

A large yellow birch — or black — has the main stem very short and branches very long, nearly from one centre.

There was a fine rosy sky in the west after sunset; and later an amber-colored horizon, in which a single tree-top showed finely.

Jan. 6. Walden apparently *froze over* last night. It is but little more than an inch thick, and two or three square rods by Hubbard's shore are still open. A dark, transparent ice. It would not have frozen entirely over, as it were in one night, or maybe a little more, and yet have been so thin next the shore as well as in the middle, if it had not been so late in the winter, and so ready to freeze. It is a dark, transparent ice, but will not bear me without much cracking. As I walked along the edge, I started out three little pickerel no longer than my finger from *close* to the shore, which went wiggling into deeper water like bloodsuckers or pollywogs. When I lie down on it and examine it closely, I find that the greater part of the bubbles which I had thought were within its own substance are against its under surface, and that they are continually rising up from the bottom, — perfect spheres, apparently, and very beautiful and clear, in which I see my face through this thin ice (perhaps an

inch and an eighth), from one eightieth of an inch in diameter, or a mere point, up to one eighth of an inch. There are thirty or forty of these, at least, to every square inch. These, probably, when heated by the sun, make it crack and whoop. There are, also, within the substance of the ice, oblong perpendicular bubbles half an inch long, more or less, by about one thirtieth of an inch, and these are commonly widest at the bottom (?), or, oftener, separate minute spherical bubbles of equal or smaller diameter, one directly above another, like a string of beads, perhaps the first stage of the former. But these internal bubbles are not nearly so numerous as those in the water beneath. It may be twenty-four hours since the ice began to form decidedly.

I see, on the sandy bottom a few inches beneath, the white cases of caddis-worms made of the white quartz sand or pebbles. And the bottom is very much creased or furrowed where some creature has travelled about and doubled on its tracks, — perhaps the caddis-worm, for I find one or two of the same in the furrows, though the latter are deep and broad for them to make.[1]

This morning the weeds and twigs and fences were covered with what I may call a leaf frost, the leaves a third of an inch long, shaped somewhat like this, with triangular points, but very thin. Another morning there will be no frost.

I forgot to say yesterday that I picked up four pignuts by the squirrel's hole, from which he had picked

[1] [*Walden*, pp. 382, 383.]

Vol. IV

the meat, having gnawed a hole about half the diameter of the nut in width on each side. After I got home I observed that in each case the holes were on the sides of the nut and not on the edges, and I cut into a couple with my knife in order to see certainly which was the best way to get at the meat. Cutting into the edge, I came upon the thick partition which runs the whole length of the nut, and then came upon the edges of the meats, and finally was obliged to cut away a good part of the nut on both edges before I could extract the meat, because it was held by the *neck* in the middle. But when I cut holes on the sides, not only the partitions I met with were thin and partial, but I struck the meats broadside and extracted them with less trouble. It may be that it is most convenient for the squirrel to hold the nut thus, but I think there is a deeper reason than that. I observe that, out of six whole pignuts which I picked from a tree, three are so cracked transversely to the division of the meat that I can easily pry them open with my knife. They hang on as food for animals.

Jan. 7. To Nawshawtuct.

This is one of those pleasant winter mornings when you find the river firmly frozen in the night, but still the air is serene and the sun feels gratefully warm an hour after sunrise, — though so fair, a healthy whitish vapor fills the lower stratum of the air, concealing the mountains, — the smokes go up from the village, you hear the cocks with immortal vigor, and the children shout on their way to school, and the sound made by the

railroad men hammering a rail is uncommonly musical. This promises a perfect winter day. In the heavens, except the altitude of the sun, you have, as it were, the conditions of summer. Perfect serenity and clarity and sonorousness in the earth. All nature is but braced by the cold. It gives tension to both body and mind.

Still the snow is strewn with the seeds of the birch, the small winged seeds or samaræ and the larger scales or bracts shaped like a bird in flight, — a hawk or dove. The least touch or jar shakes them off, and it is difficult to bring the female catkins home in your pocket. They cover the snow like coarse bran. On breaking the male catkins, I am surprised to see the yellow anthers so distinct, promising spring. I did not suspect that there was so sure a promise or prophecy of spring. These are frozen in December or earlier, — the anthers of spring, filled with their fertilizing dust.

About ten minutes before 10 A. M., I heard a very loud sound, and felt a violent jar, which made the house rock and the loose articles on my table rattle, which I knew must be either a powder-mill blown up or an earthquake. Not knowing but another and more violent might take place, I immediately ran down-stairs, but I saw from the door a vast expanding column of whitish smoke rising in the west directly over the powder-mills four miles distant. It was unfolding its volumes above, which made it widest there. In three or four minutes it had all risen and spread itself into a lengthening, somewhat copper-colored cloud parallel with the horizon from north to south, and about ten minutes after the explosion it passed over my head, being several miles long from north to south and distinctly dark and smoky toward the north, not nearly so high as the few cirrhi in the sky. I jumped into a man's wagon and rode toward the mills. In a few minutes more, I saw behind me, far in the east, a faint salmon-colored cloud carrying the news of the explosion to the sea, and perchance over [the] head of the absent proprietor.

Arrived probably before half past ten. There were perhaps thirty or forty wagons there. The kernel-mill had blown up first, and killed three men who were in it, said to be turning a roller with a chisel. In three seconds after, one of the mixing-houses exploded. The kernel-house was swept away, and fragments, mostly but a foot or two in length, were strewn over the hills and meadows, as if sown, for thirty rods, and the slight snow then on the ground was for the most part melted around. The mixing-house, about ten rods west, was not so completely dispersed, for most of the machinery remained, a total wreck. The press-house, about twelve rods east, had two thirds [of] its boards off, and a mixing-house next westward from that which blew up had lost some boards on the east side. The boards fell out (i. e. of those buildings which did not blow up), the air within apparently rushing out to fill up the vacuum occasioned by the explosions, and so, the powder being bared to the fiery particles in the air, another building explodes. The powder on the floor of the bared press-house was six inches deep in some places, and the crowd were thoughtlessly going into it. A few windows

were broken thirty or forty rods off. Timber six inches square and eighteen feet long was thrown over a hill eighty feet high at least, — a dozen rods; thirty rods was about the limit of fragments. The drying-house, in which was a fire, was perhaps twenty-five rods distant and escaped. Every timber and piece of wood which was blown up was as black as if it had been dyed, except where it had broken on falling; other breakages were completely concealed by the color. I mistook what had been iron hoops in the woods for leather straps. Some of the clothes of the men were in the tops of the trees, where undoubtedly their bodies had been and left them. The bodies were naked and black, some limbs and bowels here and there, and a head at a distance from its trunk. The feet were bare; the hair singed to a crisp. I smelt the powder half a mile before I got there. Put the different buildings thirty rods apart, and then but one will blow up at a time.

Brown thinks my red-headed bird of the winter the lesser redpoll. He has that fall snowbird, he thinks the young of the purple finch. What is my pine knot of the sea? Knot, or ash-colored sandpiper? or phalarope? Brown's pine knot looks too large and clumsy. He shows me the spirit duck of the Indians, of which Peabody says the Indians call it by a word meaning spirit, "because of the wonderful quickness with which it disappears at the twang of a bow."

I perceive (?) the increased length of the day on returning from my afternoon walk. Can it be? The sun sets only about five minutes later, and the day is about ten minutes longer.

Le Jeune thus describes the trees covered with ice in Canada in the winter of '35 and '36 (he *appears* to be at Quebec): "There was a great wind from the northeast, accompanied by a rain which lasted a very long time, and by a cold great enough to freeze these waters as soon as they touched anything, so that, as this rain fell on the trees from the summit (*cime*) to the foot, there was formed (*il s'y fit*) a crystal of ice, which enchased both trunk (*tige*) and branches, so that for a very long time all our great woods appeared only a forest of crystal; for in truth the ice which clothed them universally everywhere (*partout*) was thicker than a testoon (*épaisse de plus d'un teston*); in a word all the bushes and all that was above the snow was environed on all sides and enchased in (*avec*) ice; the savages have told me that it does not happen often so (*de même*)."

Jan. 8. I see what are probably the anther cells distinctly in the large buds of the poplar, which for a long time have shown their wool one sixth of an inch long. Also similar cells in the alder catkins, but greener and less springlike. The birch ones are the yellowest.

At Walden. — The bubbles which I made under the ice by casting on stones here night before last, or forty-eight hours ago, nearly half a foot in diameter, still remain. The last two days have been very warm, like an Indian summer or very early spring, yet about an inch more of ice has formed, making about two inches in all, and you can see the line of juncture distinctly. The ice is not now transparent, revealing the bottom

distinctly, and the dark-green color of the water, but whitish or gray, and, though twice as thick, is hardly stronger than before. The air-bubbles within it have greatly expanded in the heat, and run together and lost their regularity. I do not see that they are regularly superimposed, i. e. perpendicularly, but they have expanded off and run together at different angles, like silver coins poured from a bag and overlapping each other, and even form thin but wide flakes occasionally. It is too late to study the bottom. The beauty of the ice is gone. With a stone I broke the ice above one of my bubbles and let the air out, and water took its place. I then took out a cake of ice including two old bubbles, each about four inches in diameter, and was surprised to find that they were included between the two ices. I actually took the bubbles out between the ices and turned them bottom-upwards. These bubbles were a quarter of an inch thick and shaped like this: ⊏━━━▷ rounded on the edge. They appeared to be wholly within the new or lower ice, though the under surface of the upper was made rough; and I was surprised to find beneath them, on the under surface of the lower ice, which, like the upper, was, as I have said, about one inch thick, regular circular, saucer-like depressions, in this case five eighths of an inch deep, leaving the lower ice little more than an eighth of an inch thick directly above their middle. Thus: ————————— And this thin part of the ⎯⎯⎯⎯⎯ lower ice was almost perforated by large bubbles almost a quarter of an inch in diameter, which had burst out below. Probably there was no ice directly under my largest bubbles. I inferred, therefore, that all those infinite minute bubbles I had seen first on the under side of the ice were now frozen in with it, and that each, in its proportion or degree, like the large ones, had operated like a burning-glass on the ice beneath it to rot it. And probably it is the expanding and shrinking of the air in them, as well as in the water, which cracks the ice and makes the whooping sound.[1] Perhaps those minute bubbles that are seen one above another in the freshest ice have been frozen in like the largest, as they successively rose from the bottom while the ice was freezing. It has been supposed that Walden ice does not keep so well because it has more air in it, there being no outlet or stream to carry it off. There may be something in this. Let me look at the fresh ice of a pond that has a stream, and see if there are fewer bubbles under it. Of course, large bubbles would be very obvious under transparent or black ice.

Jan. 9. 3 p. m. — To Walden and Cliffs.

The telegraph harp again. Always the same unrememberable revelation it is to me. It is something as enduring as the worm that never dies. Before the [*sic*] it was, and will be after. I never hear it without thinking of Greece. How the Greeks *harped* upon the words immortal, ambrosial! They are what it says. It stings my ear with everlasting truth. It allies Concord to Athens, and both to Elysium. It always intoxicates me, makes me sane, reverses my views of things.

[1] [*Walden*, pp. 273, 274; Riv. 383–385.]

I am pledged to it. I get down the railroad till I hear that which makes all the world a lie. When the zephyr, or west wind, sweeps this wire, I rise to the height of my being. A period — a semicolon, at least — is put to my previous and habitual ways of viewing things. This wire is my redeemer. It always brings a special and a general message to me from the Highest. Day before yesterday I looked at the mangled and blackened bodies of men which had been blown up by powder, and felt that the lives of men were not innocent, and that there was an avenging power in nature. To-day I hear this immortal melody, while the west wind is blowing balmily on my cheek, and methinks a roseate sunset is preparing. Are there not two powers?

Where the brickmakers got their sand I measured the tap-root of a pitch pine, five inches in diameter at the surface, which extended straight downward into pure sand — excepting the usual thickness of soil — nine feet visibly, and undoubtedly three feet further than I could see.

This is the third warm day, the warmest of all. The Andromeda Ponds methinks look redder. I walked through one. The lowest growth is sphagnum, fresh, large, and handsome, some green, some red, into which occasionally I slumped nearly a foot. Some lambkill is mixed with the andromeda. A few islands of gray high blueberry bushes, with round red buds, rise here and there mixed with the panicled andromeda, large cotton-grass, now prostrate, etc. The pitcher-plant leaves are still for the most part green and uninjured here, though full of ice. Many have holes in their sides,

Vol. IV

through which insects appear to have eaten out. However, the external ear or handle is also eaten through, so the agent may have been without.

I see a dogbane sickle-shaped seed-vessel which has not discounted. I open it and let the seeds fly. As I walked the railroad this springlike day, I heard from time to time the sound of stones and earth falling and rolling down the bank in the cuts. The earth is almost entirely bare. We have not yet had snow more than one inch deep!!!

As I climbed the Cliff, I paused in the sun and sat on a dry rock, dreaming. I thought of those summery hours when time is tinged with eternity, — runs into it and becomes of one stuff with it. How much — how, perhaps, all — that is best in our experience in middle life may be resolved into the memory of our youth! I remember how I expanded. If the genius visits me now I am not quite taken off my feet, but I remember how this experience is like, but less than, that I had long since.

Pulling up the johnswort on the face of the Cliff, I am surprised to see the signs of unceasing growth about the roots, — fresh shoots two inches long, white with red leafets, and all the radical part quite green. The leaves of the crowfoot, also, are quite green, and carry me forward to spring. I dig one up with a stick, and, pulling it to pieces, I find deep in the centre of the plant, just beneath the ground, surrounded by all the tender leaves that are to precede it, the blossom-bud, about half as big as the head of a pin, perfectly white.[1] There it patiently sits, or slumbers, how full of

[1] I open one next day, and it is yellow.

faith, informed of a spring which the world has never seen, the promise and prophecy of it shaped somewhat like some Eastern temples, in which a bud-shaped dome o'ertops the whole. It affected me, this tender dome-like bud, within the bosom of the earth, like a temple upon the earth, resounding with the worship of votaries. Methought I saw the flamens in yellow robes within it. The crowfoot buds — and how many beside! — lie unexpanded just beneath the surface. May I lead my life the following year as innocently as they! May it be as fair and smell as sweet! I anticipate nature. Destined to become a fair yellow flower above the surface to delight the eyes of children and its Maker. It offered to my mind a little temple into which to enter and worship. It will go forth in April, this vestal now cherishing her fire, to be married to the sun. How innocent are Nature's purposes! How unambitious! Her elections are not Presidential. The springing and blossoming of this flower do not depend on the votes of men.

That first day of ice, when my coat and cap were glazed with a thick coat, the fine rain freezing as it fell, was not a cold day. I am pretty sure I have known it rain without freezing when colder. Had the fineness of the rain anything to do with it?

I saw to-day the reflected sunset sky in the river, but the colors in the reflection were different from those in the sky. The sky was dark clouds with coppery or dun-colored under sides. In the water were dun-colored clouds with bluish-green patches or bars.

Jan. 10. Went a-chestnutting this afternoon to Smith's wood-lot near the Turnpike. Carried four ladies. I raked. We got six and a half quarts,[1] the ground being bare and the leaves not frozen. The fourth remarkably mild day. I found thirty-five chestnuts in a little pile under the end of a stick under the leaves, near — within a foot of — what I should call a gallery of a meadow mouse. These galleries were quite common as I raked. There was no nest nor apparent cavity about this store. Aunt M. found another with sixteen in it. Many chestnuts are still in the burs on the ground. Aunt found a twig which had apparently fallen prematurely, with eight small burs, all within the compass of its five or six inches, and all but one full of nuts. The galleries above named were evidently permanent and not made by one trip.

Jan. 11 and 12. Surveying for John L——.

He says that he saw blackbirds about a week ago. He says that the most snow we have had this winter (it has not been more than one inch deep) has been only a "robin snow," as it is called, *i. e.* a snow which does not drive off the robins. By a bound of his wood-lot in Carlisle, observed a peculiar oak, very smooth and light-colored bark, which his brother, who knows them in Wayland, calls a chestnut oak. I am not quite sure. I did not see a chestnut oak leaf at any rate. *Vide* again. Says they will split like chestnut and are easy to cut. J. says they have both red and white huckleberries near his house. Described an "old

[1] [*Excursions*, p. 197; Riv. 241.]

Vol. IV

fort," about the size and shape of a cellar, which he saw in 1816 perhaps across the river near Heywood's sawmill. This man is continually drinking cider; thinks it corrects some mistake in him; wishes he had a barrel of it in the woods; if he had known he was to be out so long would have brought a jugful; will dun Captain Hutchinson for a drink on his way home. This, or rum, runs in his head, if not in his throat, all the time. Is interested in juniper berries, gooseberries, currants, etc., whether they will make wine; has recipes for this. Eats the juniper berries raw as he walks. Tobacco is another staff of life with him. Thinks, with others, that he has metals on his farm which the divining-rod might find, but is convertible on this point.

Jan. 13. A drifting snow-storm last night and to-day, the first of consequence; and the first sleighing this winter.

Jan. 14. Snows all day.
P. M. — To Walden and Andromeda Ponds.

The place of the sun appears through the storm about three o'clock, a sign that it is near its end, though it still snows as hard as ever. An intenser, whiter light is reflected from the west side of drifts and hills, like another day, in comparison with which the level snow is dark. There is this recognition of fair weather. The west side of abrupt drifts toward the lit clouds reflects quite a glow of light, many shades brighter than the levels. It is a very light snow, lying like down

or feathery scales. Examined closely, the flakes are beautifully regular six-rayed stars or wheels with a centre disk, perfect geometrical figures in thin scales like this : far more perfect than I can draw. These thin crystals are piled about a foot deep all over the country, but as light as bran. And now the snow has quite ceased, blue sky appears, and the sun goes down in clouds. The surface of fields, as I look toward the western light, appears waved or watered on a large scale, as if different kinds of flakes drifted together, some glistening scales, others darker; or perhaps the same reflected the light differently from different sides of slight drifts or undulations on the surface. Thus beautiful the snow. These starry crystals, descending profusely, have woven a pure garment, as of white watered satin, over all the fields. Snow freshly fallen is one thing, to-morrow it will be another. It is now pure and trackless. Walking three or four miles in the woods, I saw but one track of any kind, that of a rabbit, which was very large and indistinct, necessarily, and scared one partridge from a scrub oak. Most animals — almost all quadrupeds, at least — are now buried deep and still beneath it. Methinks it would not upbear a meadow mouse, but it would sink out of sight in it. There is not a trace of one of these, nor of a muskrat, on the Andromeda Ponds, yet by to-morrow morning there will be countless tracks of all sizes all over the country; which makes me think these creatures, even in the deepest woods and in winter, are far the most active by night. In the midst of the storm I saw the little chestnut or red frontleted bird on the birches. It

is warm, and the snow-fleas are about. White walls of snow rest on the boughs of trees, in height two or three times their thickness. These white irregular arms give the forest a wintry and picturesque look at a distance. The evergreens, especially the pitch pine, often bear large irregular white burdens, agreeably diversified and loopholed by the interstices of the plumes. But it is only when fresh that this snow on the trees is beautiful. Already, before the storm is over, the surface of the snow in the high woods is full of indentations and hollows where some of this burden has fallen.

I am often reminded that the farmer living far inland has not thought of plows and carts alone. Here, when getting his fuel, he cuts the roots or limbs of some sturdier [tree] with reference to the uses it may serve in the construction of a ship. The farmer not only gets out wood to burn, but ship-timber. It was he who decided the destiny [of] some mighty oak, that it should become the keel of a famous ship. It is he who says, "Ye shall become ships to plow the sea," when he says, "Ye shall become money to me." It is in the woods and in the farmer's yard that the vessel is first put upon the stocks. He burns the hewings in his ample fireplace; he teams the rest to Medford with the same yokes that plow his fields. With bars and chains he clutches and binds to wheels, and with numerous yokes drags it over the hills to the nearest port. He learns as well as the engineer what hills are steep, what ground ascends. By repeated strains and restings on the terraces, he at length surmounts every difficulty.

Think of the difficulties which the farmer silently overcomes, who conveys the keel or mast of a man-of-war from his woods to the nearest port, which would have defied the skill of a tribe of savages to overcome!

Men's ignorance is made as useful as their knowledge. If one knew more, he would admire less. In the winter how many farmers help build ships where men grow up who never saw the ocean.

I suppose that the meadow mouse can still pick up chestnuts under the snow. The nuts commonly lie as they fell from the bur, two or three together.

The bones of children soon turn to dust again.

Jan. 15. 9 A. M. — To woods.

The starry flakes or crystals, like everything that falls from heaven to earth, have partially melted, coalesced, and lost their regularity and beauty. A good part of the snow has fallen from the trees. See one or two short trails of meadow mice. Apparently they work now under the snow, but when the sun has melted and settled and the cold somewhat consolidated the snow, they come out on the surface? As you walk in the woods you hear the rustling sound of limbs and leaves that are relieved of their burden, and of the falling snow. Young evergreens look like statues partially covered with white veils.

Saw near L——'s, the 12th, a shrike. He told me about seeing Uncle Charles once, come to Barrett's mill with logs, leap over the yoke that drew them and back again. It amused the boys.

True words are those, as Trench says, — transport,

rapture, ravishment, ecstasy. These are the words I want. This is the effect of music. I am rapt away by it, out of myself. These are truly poetical words. I am inspired, elevated, expanded. I am on the mount.

Mrs. Ripley told me this afternoon that Russell had decided that that green (and sometimes yellow) dust on the under side of stones in walls was a decaying state of *Lepraria chlorina*, a lichen, — the yellow another species of *Lepraria*. Science suggests the value of mutual intelligence. I have long known this dust, but, as I did not know the name of it, *i. e.* what others called [it], and therefore could not conveniently speak of it, it has suggested less to me and I have made less use of it. I now first feel as if I had got hold of it.

In Carlisle and Boxboro they go to church as of old; they are still pagans (*pagani*), or villagers.

Jan. 16. Sunday. Cold, with blustering winds drifting the snow. Yesterday the hounds were heard. It was a hunter's day. All tracks were fresh, the snow deep and light. I met Melvin with his bag full.

Trench says that "' rivals,' in the primary sense of the word, are those who dwell on the banks of the same stream" or "on opposite banks," but as he says, in many words, since the use of water-rights is a fruitful source of contention between such neighbors, the word has acquired this secondary sense. My friends are my *rivals* on the Concord, in the primitive sense of the word. There is no strife between us respecting the use of the stream. The Concord offers many privileges, but none to quarrel about. It is a peaceful, not a

Vol. IV

brawling, stream. It has not made *rivals* out of neighbors *that lived on its banks*, but friends. My friends are my *rivals*; we dwell on opposite banks of the stream, but that stream is the Concord, which flows without a ripple or a murmur, without a rapid or a brawl, and offers no petty privileges to quarrel about.[1]

Jan. 20. P. M. — To Walden.

I see where snowbirds in troops have visited each withered chenopodium that rises above the snow in the yard — and some are large and bushlike — for its seeds, their well-filled granary now. There are a few tracks reaching from weed to weed, where some have run, but under the larger plants the snow is entirely trodden and blackened, proving that a large flock has been there and flown.

Ah, our indescribable winter sky, pure and continent and clear, between emerald (?) and amber (?), such as summer never sees! What more beautiful or soothing to the eye than those finely divided or minced clouds, like down or loose-spread cotton-batting, now reaching up from the west above my head! Beneath this a different stratum, all whose ends are curved like spray or wisps, All kinds of figures are drawn on the blue ground with this fibrous white paint.

No sooner has Walden frozen thick enough to bear than the fishermen have got out their reels and minnows, for he who fishes a pond first in the season expects to succeed best.

[1] Bailey, I find, has it: " Rival (*Rivalis* L. q. d. cui juxta eundem rivum pascit)." My friends my rivals are.

Jan. 21. A fine, still, warm moonlight evening. We have had one or two already. Moon not yet full.

To the woods by the Deep Cut at 9 o'clock.

The blueness of the sky at night — the color it wears by day — is an everlasting surprise to me, suggesting the constant presence and prevalence of light in the firmament, that we see through the veil of night to the constant blue, as by day. The night is not black when the air is clear, but blue still. The great ocean of light and ether is unaffected by our partial night. Night is not universal. At midnight I see into the universal day. Walking at that hour, unless it is cloudy, still the blue sky o'erarches me.

I am somewhat oppressed and saddened by the sameness and apparent poverty of the heavens, — that these irregular and few geometrical figures which the constellations make are no other than those seen by the Chaldean shepherds. The same simplicity and unchangeableness which commonly impresses me by wealth sometimes affects me as barrenness. I pine for a new world in the heavens as well as on the earth, and though it is some consolation to hear of the wilderness of stars and systems invisible to the naked eye, yet the sky does not make that impression of variety and wildness that even the forest does, as it ought. It makes an impression, rather, of simplicity and unchangeableness, as of eternal laws; this being the same constellation which the shepherds saw, and obedient still to the same law. It does not affect me as that unhandselled wilderness which the forest is. I seem to see it pierced with visual rays from a thousand observatories.

It is more the domain of science than of poetry. But it is the stars as not known to science that I would know, the stars which the lonely traveller knows.

The Chaldean shepherds saw not the same stars which I see, and if I am elevated in the least toward the heavens, I do not accept their classification of them. I am not to be distracted by the names which they have imposed. The sun which I know is not Apollo, nor is the evening star Venus. The heavens should be as new, at least, as the world is new. This classification of the stars is old and musty; it is as if a mildew had taken place in the heavens, as if the stars so closely packed had heated and moulded there. If they appear fixed, it is because that hitherto men have been thus necessitated to see them. I see not merely old but new testaments in the skies. Do not I stand as near the stars as the Chaldean shepherds? The heavens commonly look as dry and meagre as our astronomies are, — mere troops, as the latter are catalogues, of stars. The Milky Way yields no milk.

A few good anecdotes is our science, with a few imposing statements respecting distance and size, and little or nothing about the stars as they concern man; teaching how he may survey a country or sail a ship, and not how he may steer his life. Astrology contained the germ of a higher truth than this. It may happen that the stars are more significant and truly celestial to the teamster than to the astronomer. Nobody sees the stars now. They study astronomy at the district school, and learn that the sun is ninety-five millions [of miles] distant, and the like, — a statement which

never made any impression on me, because I never walked it, and which I cannot be said to believe. But the sun shines nevertheless. Though observatories are multiplied, the heavens receive very little attention. The naked eye may easily see farther than the armed. It depends on who looks through it. No superior telescope to this has been invented. In those big ones the recoil is equal to the force of the discharge. The poet's eye in a fine frenzy rolling ranges from earth to heaven, but this the astronomer's does not often do. It does not see far beyond the dome of the observatory.

Compared with the visible phenomena of the heavens, the anecdotes of science affect me as trivial and petty. Man's eye is the true star-finder, the comet-seeker. As I sat looking out the window the other evening just after dark, I saw the lamp of a freight-train, and, near by, just over the train, a bright star, which looked exactly like the former, as if it belonged to a different part of the same train. It was difficult to realize that the one was a feeble oil lamp, the other a world.

As I walk the railroad causeway I am, as the last two months, disturbed by the sound of my steps on the frozen ground. I wish to hear the silence of the night, for the silence is something positive and to be heard. I cannot walk with my ears covered. I must stand still and listen with open ears, far from the noises of the village, that the night may make its impression on me. A fertile and eloquent silence. Sometimes the silence is merely negative, an arid and barren waste in which I shudder, where no ambrosia grows. I must hear the whispering of a myriad voices.

Silence alone is worthy to be heard. Silence is of various depth and fertility, like soil. Now it is a mere Sahara, where men perish of hunger and thirst, now a fertile bottom, or prairie, of the West. As I leave the village, drawing nearer to the woods, I listen from time to time to hear the hounds of Silence baying the Moon, — to know if they are on the track of any game. If there's no Diana in the night, what is it worth? I hark the goddess Diana. The silence rings; it is musical and thrills me. A night in which the silence was audible. I hear the unspeakable.

I easily read the moral of my dreams. Yesterday I was influenced with the rottenness of human relations. They appeared full of death and decay, and offended the nostrils. In the night I dreamed of delving amid the graves of the dead, and soiled my fingers with their rank mould. It was *sanitarily*, *morally*, and *physically* true.

If night is the mere negation of day, I hear nothing but my own steps in it. Death is with me, and life far away. If the elements are not human, if the winds do not sing or sigh, as the stars twinkle, my life runs shallow. I measure the depth of my own being. I walk with vast alliances. I am the allied powers, the holy alliance, absorbing the European potentates. I do not get much from the blue sky, these twinkling stars, and bright snow-fields reflecting an almost rosaceous light. But when I enter the woods I am fed by the variety, — the forms of the trees above against the blue, with the stars seen through the pines like the lamps hung on them in an illumination, the somewhat indistinct and misty fineness of the pine-tops, and the

finely divided spray of the oaks, etc., and the shadows of all these on the snow. The first shadow I came to I thought was a black place where the woodchoppers had had a fire. These myriad shadows checker the white ground and enhance the brightness of the enlightened portions. See the shadows of these young oaks which have lost half their leaves, more beautiful than themselves, like the shadow of a chandelier, and motionless as if they were fallen leaves on the snow, — but shake the tree, and all is in motion.

In this stillness and at this distance, I hear the nine-o'clock bell in Bedford five miles off, which I might never hear in the village, but here its music surmounts the village din and has something very sweet and noble and inspiring in it, associated, in fact, with the hooting of owls.

Returning, I thought I heard the creaking of a wagon just starting from Hubbard's door, and rarely musical it sounded. It was the telegraph harp. It began to sound but at one spot only. It is very fitful, and only sounds when it is in the mood. You may go by twenty times, both when the wind is high and when it is low and let it blow which way it will, and yet hear no strain from it, but another time, at a particular spot, you may hear a strain rising and swelling on the string, which may at last ripen to something glorious. The wire will perhaps labor long with it before it attains to melody.

Even the creaking of a wagon in a frosty night has music in it which allies it to the highest and purest strain of the muse.

I think it was January 20th that I saw that which I think an otter track [1] in path under the Cliffs, — a deep trail in the snow, six or seven inches wide and two or three deep in the middle, as if a log had been drawn along, similar to a muskrat's only much larger, and the legs evidently short and the steps short, sinking three or four inches deeper still, ▬▬▬▬ ▪ ▪ as if it had waddled along. It finally ▬▬▬▪▪▪▪ turned into my old tracks and went toward the river and Fair Haven Pond. One was killed there last spring. Minott says his mother told him she had seen a deer come down the hill behind her house, where I. Moore's now is, and cross the road and the meadow in front; thinks it may have been eighty years ago. Otter are very rare here now. I have not heard of any killed hereabouts for twenty or thirty years till, within two years, two or three of them. In Sudbury and at Fair Haven Pond.

Jan. 23. Sunday. Rain, carrying off the snow and making slosh of the lower half of it. It is perhaps the wettest walking we ever have.

Jan. 25. P. M. — To Flint's Pond, down railroad.

There is something springlike in this afternoon. In winter, after middle, we are interested in what is springlike. The earth and sun appear to have approached some degrees. The banks seem to lie in the embrace

[1] No doubt it was. Israel Rice tells of one shot within the year in a ditch near White Pond ; probably the same. He says I saw an otter track.

of the sun. The ground is partly bare. The cress is fresh and green at the bottoms of the brooks. What is that long-leaved green plant in the brook in Hosmer's meadow on the Turnpike? The buttercup leaves appear everywhere when the ground is bare. There are temporary ponds in the fields made by the rain and melted snow, which hardly have time [to] freeze, they soak up so fast. As I go up Bare Hill, there being only snow enough there to whiten the ground, the last year's stems of the blueberry (*vacillans*) give a pink tinge to the hillside, reminding me of red snow, though they do not semble it. I am surprised to see Flint's Pond a quarter part open, — the middle. Walden, which froze much later, is nowhere open. But Flint's feels the wind and is shallow.

I noticed on a small pitch pine, in the axils close to the main stem, little spherical bunches of buds, an inch and more in diameter, with short, apparently abortive leaves from some. The leaves were nearly all single, as in the plants of one or two years' growth, and were finely serrate or toothed, *ʃ* pectinate (?). On the lot I surveyed for Weston I found the chestnut oak (though the teeth are sharper than E.'s plate), a handsome leaf, still on the young trees. I had taken it for a chestnut before. It is hard to distinguish them by the trunk alone. I found some barberry sprouts where the bushes had been cut down not long since, and they were covered with small withered leaves beset with stiff prickles on their edges, and you could see the thorns, as it were gradually passing into leaves, being, as one stage, the nerves of the leaf alone, —

Vol. IV

starlike and branched thorns, gradually, as you descended the stem, getting some pulp between them. I suppose it was owing to the shortening them in. I still pick chestnuts. Some larger ones proved to contain double meats, divided, as it were arbitrarily, as with a knife, each part having the common division without the brown skin transverse to this.

The pickerel of Walden! when I see them lying on the ice, or in the well which the fisherman cuts in the ice, I am always surprised by their rare beauty, as if they were a fabulous fish, they are so foreign to the streets, or even the woods; handsome as flowers and gems, golden and emerald, — a transcendent and dazzling beauty which separates [them] by a wide interval from the cadaverous cod and haddock, at least a day old, which we see. They are as foreign as Arabia to our Concord life, as if the two ends of the earth had come together. These are not green like the pines, or gray like the stones, or blue like the sky; but they have, if possible, to my eye, yet rarer colors, like precious stones. It is surprising that these fishes are caught here. They are something tropical. That in this deep and capacious spring, far beneath the rattling teams and chaises and tinkling sleighs that travel the Walden road, this great gold and emerald fish swims! They are true topazes, inasmuch as you can only conjecture what place they came from. The pearls of Walden, some animalized Walden water. I never chanced to see this kind of fish in any market. With

a few convulsive quirks they give up their diluted ghosts.[1]

I have noticed that leaves are green and violets bloom later where a bank has been burnt over in the fall, as if the fire warmed it. I saw to-day, where a creeping juniper had been burnt, radical leaves of johnswort, thistle, clover, dandelion, etc., as well as sorrel and veronica.

Young white oaks retain their leaves, and large ones on their lower parts.

> Swamp white oak (?)
> Very young rock chestnut oaks
> The little chinquapin (?)
> The bear oak
> The scarlet oak (?)
> The red
> The black (?), young trees
> The witch-hazel, more or less
> *Carpinus Americana*
> *Ostrya Virginica*, somewhat
> Sweet-fern, more or less
> Andromeda
> Andromeda, panicled (?)
> *Kalmia latifolia*
> *Kalmia angustifolia*
> Cranberry

The above are such as I think of which wear their leaves conspicuously now.

Jan. 26. Up river on ice 9 A. M., above Pantry. A sharp, cutting air. This is a pretty good winter

[1] [*Walden*, pp. 314, 315; Riv. 439, 440.]

morning, however. Not one of the rarer. There are from time to time mornings, both in summer and winter, when especially the world seems to begin anew, beyond which memory need not go, for not behind them is yesterday and our past life; when, as in the morning of a hoar frost, there are visible the effects of a certain creative energy, the world has visibly been recreated in the night. Mornings of creation, I call them. In the midst of these marks of a creative energy recently active, while the sun is rising with more than usual splendor, I look back,— I look back for the era of this creation, not into the night, but to a dawn for which no man ever rose early enough. A morning which carries us back beyond the Mosaic creation, where crystallizations are fresh and unmelted. It is the poet's hour. Mornings when men are new-born, men who have the seeds of life in them. It should be a part of my religion to [be] abroad then. This is not one of those mornings, but a clear, cold, airy winter day.

It is surprising how much room there is in nature,— if a man will follow his proper path. In these broad fields, in these extensive woods, on this stretching river, I never meet a walker. Passing behind the farmhouses, I see no man out. Perhaps I do not meet so many men as I should have met three centuries ago, when the Indian hunter roamed these woods. I enjoy the retirement and solitude of an early settler. Men have cleared some of the earth, which no doubt is an advantage to the walker. I see a man sometimes chopping in the woods, or planting or hoeing in a field, at a distance; and yet there may be a lyceum in the evening, and there

is a book-shop and library in the village, and five times a day I can be whirled to Boston within an hour.

There is a little thin ice on the meadows. I see the bubbles underneath, looking like coin. A slight, fine snow has fallen in the night and drifted before the wind. I observe that it is so distributed over the ice as [to] show equal spaces of bare ice and of snow at pretty regular distances. I have seen the same phenomenon on the surface of snow in fields, as if the surface of the snow disposed itself according to the same law that makes waves of water. There is now a fine steam-like snow blowing over the ice, which continually lodges here and there, and forthwith a little drift accumulates. But why does it lodge at such regular intervals? I see this fine drifting snow in the air ten or twelve feet high at a distance. Perhaps it may have to do with the manner in, or the angle at, which the wind strikes the earth.

Made a roaring fire on the edge of the meadow at Ware (?) Hill in Sudbury. A piece of paper, birch bark, and dry leaves started it, and then we depended on the dead maple twigs and limbs to kindle the large dead wood. Green wood will burn better than the damp and rotten wood that lies on the ground. We chose a place which afforded a prospect, but it turned out that we looked only at the fire. It made all places indifferent. The color of the coals, in a glowing heap or seen through the white ashes on the brands, like rubies. The shadows, coming and going, of the flame passing over the white ashes of the brands. I burnt off my eyelashes when the fire suddenly blazed up with the wind, without knowing that I had come very near it. Though

our fuel was dead and rotten wood found in the snow, it made very little smoke, which may have been owing to the state of the atmosphere, clear and cold. The sound of the air or steam escaping from a brand, its sighing or dying shriek, fine and sharp as a cambric needle, is the music we hear. One half the pleasure is in making the fire. But then we should have something to cook by it. Collecting fresh fuel from time to time is very pleasant. The smoke ever and anon compelled us to move round to the opposite side. The sap which flowed from some maple boughs which I cut froze in large drops at the end. How came sap there now?

It is remarkable that many men will go with eagerness to Walden Pond in the winter to fish for pickerel and yet not seem to care for the landscape. Of course it cannot be *merely* for the pickerel they may catch; there is some adventure in it; but any love of nature which they may feel is certainly very slight and indefinite. They call it going a-fishing, and so indeed it is, though, perchance, their natures know better. Now I go a-fishing and a-hunting every day, but omit the fish and the game, which are the least important part. I have learned to do without them. They were indispensable only as long as I was a boy. I am encouraged when I see a dozen villagers drawn to Walden Pond to spend a day in fishing through the ice, and suspect that I have more fellows than I knew, but I am disappointed and surprised to find that they lay all the stress on the fish which they catch or fail to catch, and on nothing else, as if there were nothing else to be caught.

When we got off at some distance from our fire, returning, we saw a light bluish smoke rising as high as the woods above it, though we had not perceived it before, and thought that no one could have detected us.

At the fall on Clematis Brook the forms of the ice were admirable. The coarse spray had frozen as it fell on the rocks, and formed shell-like crusts over them, with irregular but beautifully clear and sparkling surfaces like egg-shaped diamonds, each being the top of a club-shaped and branched fungus icicle. This spray had improved the least core — as the dead and slender rushes drooping over the water — and formed larger icicles about them, shaped exactly like horns, with the skulls often attached, or roots of horns. On similar slight limbs there were built out from the shore and rocks all sorts of fantastic forms, with broader and flatter bases, from which hung stalactites of ice; and on logs in the water were perfect ice fungi of all sizes, under which the water gurgled, flat underneath and hemispherical. A form like this would project over the water: six inches deep by four or five in width and a foot long, held by the rocks, but with a slight weed for core. You could take off the incrustations on the rocks, turn them up, and they were perfect shells.

These are the horns: a foot or two high. In the rock there were upright incrustations icicles, as I have club-shaped said, packed close together, three or four inches long, thus: and so on, right and left, with a homogeneous or undivided base. They appeared like crystallizations, as quartz crystals with rounded instead of flattened summits, built from below and, as they grew, widening or thickening to fill the space.

The only birds I have seen to-day were some jays, — one whistled clearly, — some of my mewing red frontlets, and some familiar chickadees. They are inquisitive, and fly along after the traveller to inspect him.

In civilized nations there are those answering to the rain-makers and sorcerers of savages. Also this office is universal among savage tribes. Bitter, cutting, cold northwest wind on causeway, stiffening the face, freezing the ears.

Jan. 27. Trench says a wild man is a *willed* man. Well, then, a man of will who does what he wills or wishes, a man of hope and of the future tense, for not only the obstinate is willed, but far more the constant and persevering. The obstinate man, properly speaking, is one who will not. The perseverance of the saints is positive willedness, not a mere passive willingness. The fates are wild, for they *will;* and the Almighty is wild above all, as fate is.

What are our fields but *felds* or *felled* woods. They

bear a more recent name than the woods, suggesting that previously the earth was covered with woods. Always in the new country a field is a clearing.

Jan. 28. Saw three ducks sailing in the river behind Prichard's this afternoon, black with white on wings, though these two or three have been the coldest days of the winter, and the river is generally closed. Observed a new wall, of stones recently dug out of the earth, all yellow and easily detected at a distance, not yet gray with lichens. Though somewhat cool, it has been remarkably pleasant to-day, and the sun-sparkles where the river is open are very cheerful to behold.

As I approached Bateman's Pond, the ice looked blue. Is it indeed blue like Walden ice?

I saw an improvement, I suppose by William Brown, on the shore of the pond this afternoon, which really is something to tell of. The exploits of the farmer are not often reported even in the agricultural paper, nor are they handed down by tradition from father to son, praiseworthy and memorable as so many of them are; though if he ran away from hard work once in his youth and enlisted, and chanced to be present at one short battle, he will even in his old age love to dwell on this, " shoulder his crutch and *show how fields are won*," with cruel satire, as if he had not far better shown this with his axe and spade and plow. Here was an extensive swamp, level of course as a floor, which first had been cut, then ditched broadly, then burnt over; then the surface paved off, stumps and all, in great slices; then these piled up every six feet, three

Vol. IV

or four feet high, like countless larger muskrat-cabins, to dry; then fire put to them; and so the soil was tamed. We witnessed the different stages in different parts of the swamp.

You can walk in the woods in no direction but you hear the sound of the axe.

I tasted some black shrivelled pyrus berries in a spruce swamp; rather sweet.

Jan. 29. To Walden.

Melvin calls the ducks which I saw yesterday sheldrakes; being small, then wood sheldrakes.[1] He never shot any at this season. Saw a woodcock last month; never before. Killed a goshawk (which was eating a rabbit) and a cat owl lately. Says I hear the cat owl. Has got only three or four minks this year. Never saw an otter track.

I saw a little grayish mouse frozen into Walden, three or four rods from the shore, its tail sticking out a hole. It had apparently run into this hole when full of water, as if on land, and been drowned and frozen. Headed downward, it was. The ice is eight inches thick. It is full of short, faint, flake-like perpendicular cleavages, an inch or two broad, or varying somewhat from the perpendicular. Melvin thinks that the " thundering " of the pond scares the pickerel.

Pickerel of at least three different forms and colors were lying on the ice of Walden this afternoon: first, a long and shallow kind most like those caught in the

[1] I judge from the plate they were velvet ducks, or white-winged coots.

river, steel-colored with greenish or brownish lines, darker on the back and white beneath; second, a bright-golden fish with greenish reflections, remarkably deep, with a shorter head; both of these are mottled on the sides with an irregular network of dark-brown lines, often extending over the back, the meshes three fourths of an inch long, more or less, producing longitudinal stripes more or less distinct and continuous, very pure white beneath; third, shaped like the last, but peppered on the sides with small dark-brown or black spots, intermixed with a few faint blood-red ones, very much like a trout. The specific name of *reticulatus* would not describe this. These are all very firm fish, and weigh more than their size promises.

The perch also, and indeed all the fishes which inhabit this pond, are as much handsomer than ordinary, as the water is purer than that of other ponds. Probably many ichthyologists would make new varieties, at least, of most of them.[1]

Jan. 30. The most common and conspicuous green leaf on the ground when the snow is off at this season, as at present, is that of the buttercup. Sorrel is also very common, and johnswort, and the purplish gnaphaliums. There is also the early crowfoot in some places, strawberry, mullein, and thistle leaves, and hawkweeds, etc., etc.

On Cliffs.

The westering sun is yet high above the horizon, but, concealed by clouds, shoots down to earth on every side

[1] [*Walden*, pp. 204, 205; Riv. 288, 289.]

vast misty rays like the frame of a tent, to which clouds perchance are the canvas, under which a whole country rests. The northern and southern rays appear very much slanted and long; those between us and the west, steeper and shorter.

What I have called the Shrub Oak Plain contains comparatively few shrub oaks, — rather, young red and white and, it may be, some scarlet (?). The shrub oak leaf is the firmest and best preserved. The white oak is the most sere and curled and brittle, frequently with discolored, mould-like spots.

Jan. 31. Found an Indian adze in the bridle-road at the brook just beyond Daniel Clark, Jr.'s house.

A man is wise with the wisdom of his time only, and ignorant with its ignorance. Observe how the greatest minds yield in some degree to the superstitions of their age.

De Quincey (whose pains to prove that [it] was not Christ's mission to teach men science, though he, *of course* (!), knew it all, suggested the above) says: —

"This downward direction of the eyes, however, must have been worse in former ages; because, else, it never *could* have happened that, until Queen Anne's days, nobody ever hinted in a book that there *was* such a thing, or *could* be such a thing, as the Aurora Borealis; and in fact, Halley had the credit of discovering it."

X

FEBRUARY, 1853

(ÆT. 35)

Feb. 1. Surveying the Hunt farm.

Saw a duck in the river; different kind from the last. Dr. Bartlett tells me that it was Adam Winthrop, a *grandson* of the *Governor*, who sold this farm to Hunt in 1701. I saw the old window, some eighteen inches square, of diamond squares, four or five inches across, set in lead, on the back side [of] the house.

Feb. 2. The *Stellaria media* is full of frost-bitten blossoms, containing stamens, etc., still and half-grown buds. Apparently it never rests.

Feb. 3. Saw three ducks in the river. They resort to those parts necessarily which are open, which are near the houses. I always see them in the fall as long as the river and ponds are open, and, that being the case all this winter (almost), they have not all gone further south. The shallow and curving part of the river behind Cheney's being open all this winter, they are confined for the most part to this, in this neighborhood.

The thickest ice I have seen this winter is full nine inches.

Feb. 5. To Walden, P. M.

A thick fog. The trees and woods look well through it. You are inclined to walk in the woods for objects. They are draped with mist, and you hear the sound of it dripping from them. It is a lichen day. Not a bit of rotten wood lies on the dead leaves, but it is covered with fresh, green cup lichens, etc., etc. All the world seems a great lichen and to grow like one to-day, — a sudden humid growth. I remember now that the mist was much thicker over the pond than elsewhere. I could not distinguish a man there more than ten rods off, and the woods, seen dimly across a bay, were mistaken for the opposite side of the pond. I could almost fancy a bay of an acre in extent the whole pond. Elsewhere, methinks, I could see twice as far. I felt the greater coolness of the air over the pond, which it was, I suppose, that condensed the vapor more there.

Somebody has been fishing in a rude way and left some of their lines, apparently by mistake. They have laid branches of alders over the holes, and, after tying their lines to a stick two feet long to prevent their being pulled through, have passed the slack line over a twig of the alder a foot or more above the ice and tied a dry oak leaf to it, which, being pulled down, will show when they have a bite. These sprigs or boughs are arranged all around the pond.[1]

At the eastern shore I see at last how those ridges or ramparts are formed along the edges of ponds. The sand has been recently cast up there, six or eight inches high, by a foot or two in width, just on the edge of the

[1] [*Walden*, p. 314; Riv. 439.]

ice, in the form of waves just breaking on the shore, as if the ice had crowded against the shore and forced it up, or it had been washed down by the rain and lodged against the edge of the ice. On a close examination, I found that apparently the ice had not moved, but rather had melted a foot or two, and left bare ground, the water having subsided since it froze, and its edge was exceedingly thin and rotten. The sand was forced or puffed up in the form of a pent roof for a long distance, and under this roof there was no frost in the ground, though all the shore above was still frozen, and even below, if the ice happened to be very thin and there was no water between it and the sand. Apparently the water of the pond, warmed by the rain which had run into it, especially next the shore, penetrating under the frozen shore, produced this expansion and puffing up of the shore there. Sometimes the ice itself, lying on the shore, was raised. The stones as big as one's fist, which for the most part compose the shore, were heaved up into a less conspicuous ridge, all loose, beneath which also there was no frost; also the dead wood, chips, twigs, and other rubbish. Within a limited space, just on the edge of the ice, was the phenomenon so common in the spring, of the frost coming out of the ground. No matter how large the rocks superimposed, or what the depth of sand that had accumulated, it was heaved up, so that the pitch pines by my shore were literally tipped or pried over by a force applied beneath, and many may now be seen slanted at an angle of forty-five degrees. Taking up some masses of this shore heaved up, which were still frozen,

I found that, as in stones a vein of a different kind often passes through and through them, so the frozen sand alternated with sparkling veins of clear ice. Where the water had stood over the sand and frozen, and then fresh sand been worked into it, these veins of ice surrounded by sand were black. The ice of Sam Barrett's pond has a greenish tinge. The bottom of the ice on the edge of the pond next the sand had a singularly reticulated appearance, like tripe or the coats of the stomach, and I thought I detected the effects of countless air-bubbles of all sizes which had melted it there.

The frost is out of the ground in many places. A *Stellaria media* in blossom in the garden, and were of course last month.

Feb. 6. Observed some buds on a young apple tree, partially unfolded at the extremity and apparently swollen. Probably blossom-buds.

Feb. 8. The warm rains have melted off the surface snow or white ice on Walden, down to the dark ice, the color of the water, only three or four inches thick; but I observe that still, for a rod or more in width around the shores, the ice is white as snow and apparently thicker, probably owing to the reflection from the bottom from the first filling it with air-bubbles.[1]

Feb. 9. At Cambridge to-day.

Dr. Harris thinks the Indians had no real hemp but

---

[1] [*Walden*, p. 332; Riv. 463, 464.]

---

their apocynum, and, he thinks, a kind of nettle, and an asclepias, etc. He doubts if the dog was indigenous among them. Finds nothing to convince him in the history of New England.[1] Thinks that the potato which is said to have been carried from Virginia by Raleigh was the ground-nut (which is described, I perceived, in Debry (Heriot?) among the fruits of Virginia), the potato not being indigenous in North America, and the ground-nut having been called wild potato in New England, the north part of Virginia, and not being found in England. Yet he allows that Raleigh cultivated the potato in Ireland.

Saw the grizzly bear near the Haymarket to-day, said (?) to weigh nineteen hundred, — apparently too much. He looked four feet and a few inches in height, by as much in length, not including his great head, and his tail, which was invisible. He looked gentle, and continually sucked his claws and cleaned between them with his tongue. Small eyes and funny little ears; perfectly bearish, with a strong wild-beast scent; fed on Indian meal and water. Hind paws a foot long. Lying down, with his feet up against the bars; often sitting up in the corner on his hind quarters.

Two sables also, that would not be waked up by day, with their faces in each other's fur. An American chinchilla, and a silver lioness said to be from California.

Feb. 11. *Friday*. While surveying for J. Moore to-day, saw a large wood tortoise stirring in the Mill

---

[1] Agassiz asked him what authority there was for it.

Brook, and several bodies of frogs[1] without their hind legs. But Sunday it snowed about a foot deep, — our second, only, important snow this winter, — and now the brook is not only frozen over, but almost completely concealed under drifts, and that reminiscence or prophecy of spring is also buried up.

While surveying on the Hunt farm the other day, behind Simon Brown's house I heard a remarkable echo. In the course of surveying, being obliged to call aloud to my assistant from every side and almost every part of a farm in succession, and at various hours of a day, I am pretty sure to discover an echo if any exists, and the other day it was encouraging and soothing to hear it. After so many days of comparatively insignificant drudgery with stupid companions, this leisure, this sportiveness, this generosity in nature, sympathizing with the better part of me; somebody I could talk with, — one degree, at least, better than talking with one's self. Ah! Simon Brown's premises harbor a hired man and a hired maid he wots not of. Some voice of somebody I pined to hear, with whom I could form a community. I did wish, rather, to linger there and call all day to the air and hear my words repeated, but a vulgar necessity dragged me along round the bounds of the farm, to hear only the stale answers of my chain-man shouted back to me.

I am surprised that we make no more ado about echoes. They are almost the only kindred voices that I hear. I wonder that the traveller does not oftener remark upon a remarkable echo, — he who observes

---

[1] *Rana palustris*. Channing saw some entire.

---

so many things. There needs some actual doubleness like this in nature, for if the voices which we commonly hear were all that we ever heard, what then? Has it to do with the season of the year? I have since heard an echo on Moore's farm.

It was the memorable event of the day, that echo I heard, not anything my companions said, or the travellers whom I met, or my thoughts, for they were all mere repetitions or echoes in the worst sense of what I had heard and thought before many times; but this echo was accompanied with novelty, and by its repetition of my voice it did more than double that. It was a profounder Socratic method of suggesting thoughts unutterable to me the speaker. There was one I heartily loved to talk with. Under such favorable auspices I could converse with myself, could reflect; the hour, the atmosphere, and the conformation of the ground permitted it.

Feb. 13. In the midst of the snow-storm on Sunday (to-day), I was called to window to see a dense flock of snowbirds on and under the pigweed in the garden.[1] It was so in the other storm. It is to be remarked that I have not observed them in the garden at any other time this winter. They come with the storm, the falling and driving snow. I *suspect* they were my chestnut-fronted ones.[2]

Feb. 23. *Wednesday*. Melvin tells me that he saw shiners while fishing in Walden yesterday. The ice-

---

[1] Probably tree sparrows.   [2] Not linarias.

men worked till midnight night before last at Loring's Pond, to improve the short cold.

I think myself in a wilder country, and a little nearer to primitive times, when I read in old books which spell the word savages with an *l* (salvages), like John Smith's "General Historie of Virginia, etc.," reminding me of the derivation of the word from *sylva*. There is some of the wild wood and its bristling branches still left in their language. The savages they described are really *salvages*, men of the *woods*.

Feb. 27. Frank Brown has killed, within a day or two, a tree sparrow (*Emberiza Canadensis*, Canada bunting, or tree sparrow, of Audubon's Synopsis). I think this must be my bright-chestnut-fronted bird of the winter,[1] though Peabody says it is distinguished by the spot on the breast, which reminds me of the larger, finch-like bird.

A week or two ago I brought home a handsome pitch pine cone which had freshly fallen and was closed perfectly tight. It was put into a table drawer. To-day I am agreeably surprised to find that it has there dried and opened with perfect regularity, filling the drawer, and from a solid, narrow, and sharp cone, has become a broad, rounded, open one, — has, in fact, expanded with the regularity of a flower's petals into a conical flower of rigid scales, and has shed a remarkable quantity of delicate-winged seeds. Each scale, which is very elaborately and perfectly constructed, is armed with a short spine, pointing downward, as if to protect

[1] A mistake. *Vide* [*Journal*, vol. v, p. 3].

Vol. IV

its seed from squirrels and birds. That hard closed cone, which defied all violent attempts to open it, and could only be cut open with [*sic*], has thus yielded to the gentle persuasion of warmth and dryness. The expanding [of] the pine cones, that, too, is a season.

Mr. Herbert is strenuous that I say "ruffed grouse" for "partridge" and "hare" for "rabbit." He says of the snipe, "I am myself satisfied that the sound is produced by the fact that the bird, by some muscular action or other, turns the quill-feathers edgewise, as he drops plumb through the air; and that while in this position, during his accelerated descent, the vibration of the feathers and the passage of the air between them gives utterance to this wild humming sound."

END OF VOLUME IV

The Journal of Henry D. Thoreau

VOLUME V

(March, 1853 — November, 1853)

Wild Roses

CONTENTS

Vol. V

March 5. F. Brown showed me to-day some lesser redpolls which he shot yesterday. They turn out to be my falsely-called chestnut-frontleted bird of the winter. "*Linaria minor*, Ray. Lesser Redpoll Linnet. From Pennsylvania and New Jersey to Maine, in winter; inland to Kentucky. Breeds in Maine, Nova Scotia, Newfoundland, Labrador, and the Fur Countries." — Audubon's Synopsis. They have a sharp bill, black legs and claws, and a bright-crimson crown or frontlet, in the male reaching to the base of the bill, with, in his case, a delicate rose or carmine on the breast and rump. Though this is described by Nuttall as an occasional visitor in the winter, it has been the prevailing bird here this winter.

Yesterday I got my grape cuttings. The day before went to the Corner Spring to look at the tufts of green grass. Got some of the very common leptogium (??). Is it one of the *Collemaceæ*? Was pleased with the sight of the yellow osiers of the golden willow, and the red

of the cornel, now colors are so rare. Saw the green fine-threaded conferva in a ditch, commonly called frog-spittle. Brought it home in my pocket, and it expanded again in a tumbler. It appeared quite a fresh growth, with what looked like filmy air-bubbles, as big as large shot, in its midst.

The secretary of the Association for the Advancement of Science requests me, as he probably has thousands of others, by a printed circular letter from Washington the other day, to fill the blank against certain questions, among which the most important one was what branch of science I was specially interested in, using the term science in the most comprehensive sense possible. Now, though I could state to a select few that department of human inquiry which engages me, and should be rejoiced at an opportunity to do so, I felt that it would be to make myself the laughing-stock of the scientific community to describe or attempt to describe to them that branch of science which specially interests me, inasmuch as they do not believe in a science which deals with the higher law. So I was obliged to speak to their condition and describe to them that poor part of me which alone they can understand. The fact is I am a mystic, a transcendentalist, and a natural philosopher to boot. Now I think of it, I should have told them at once that I was a transcendentalist. That would have been the shortest way of telling them that they would not understand my explanations.

How absurd that, though I probably stand as near to nature as any of them, and am by constitution as

good an observer as most, yet a true account of my relation to nature should excite their ridicule only! If it had been the secretary of an association of which Plato or Aristotle was the president, I should not have hesitated to describe my studies at once and particularly.

March 6. Sunday. Last Sunday I plucked some alder (apparently speckled) twigs, some (apparently *tremuloides*) aspen, and some swamp (?) willow, and put them in water in a warm room. Immediately the alder catkins were relaxed and began to lengthen and open, and by the second day to drop their pollen; like handsome pendants they hung round the pitcher, and at the same time the smaller female flower expanded and brightened. In about four days the aspens began to show their red anthers and feathery scales, being an inch in length and still extending. March 2d, I added the andromeda; March 3d, the rhodora. This morning, the ground being still covered with snow, there was quite a fog over the river and meadows, which I think owing to a warm atmosphere over the cold snow.

P. M. — To Lee's Hill.

I am pleased to cut the small woods with my knife to see their color. The high blueberry, hazel, and swamp-pink are green. I love to see the dear green sprouts of the sassafras and its large and fragrant buds and bark. The twigs or extremities of the branches of young trees twenty feet high look as if scorched and blackened. I gathered a pocketful of pignuts from a tree of Lee's Hill. Still sound, half of them. The water is pretty high on the meadows (though the ground is covered with snow), so that we get a little of the peculiar still lake view at evening when the wind goes down.

Two red squirrels made an ado about or above me near the North River, hastily running from tree to tree, leaping from the extremity of one bough to that of the nearest, or the next tree, until they gained and ascended a large white pine. I approached and stood under this, while they made a great fuss about me. One at length came part way down to reconnoitre me. It seemed that one did the barking — a faint, short, chippy bark, like that of a *toy* dog, — its tail vibrating each time, while its neck was stretched over a bough as it peered at me. The other, higher up, kept up a sort of gurgling whistle, more like a bird than a beast. When I made a noise they would stop a moment.

Scared up a partridge, which had crawled into a pile of wood. Saw a gray hare, a dirty yellowish gray, not trig and neat, but, as usual, apparently in a deshabille. As it frequently does, it ran a little way and stopped just at the entrance to its retreat; then, when I moved again, suddenly disappeared. By a slight obscure hole in the snow, it had access to a large and apparently deep woodchuck's (?) hole.

Stedman Buttrick calls the ducks which we see in the winter, widgeons and wood sheldrakes.

The hemlock cones have shed their seeds, but there

are some closed yet on the ground. Part of the pitch pine cones are yet closed. This is the form of one: —

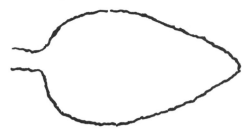

March 7. The lichen on the earth and stones amid mosses which I have thought a collema, is, I now think, a peltigera, perhaps *P. canina* (mad-dog peltigera of Hooker?). The catkins of the sweet-gale have now, after nine days, opened, and drop their sulphury pollen more perfectly than the alders and poplars, methinks, which soon dried up and the last turned black, *i. e.* the anthers. I doubt if the willow catkins gathered at the same time (February 27) will blossom, though they have expanded.

P. M. — To Walden, Goose, and Flint's Ponds, and chestnut wood by Turnpike.

The silk of the most forward willows does not generally project the length of the scale beyond the scale yet, and I am in doubt whether they give any indication of spring; but I saw one whose catkins projected more than the length of the scale, and revealed a tinge of red through their silk, which I think have felt the influence of the new year. Also the dark chocolate-colored alder catkins — what I have called *A. incana* — are not only

relaxed, but there is an obvious looseness and space between the scales. I doubt if I have detected the speckled alder in flower. I see, however, some with short thick reddish catkins and a dull opaque bark, others with a fresh glossy and speckled bark and long, rather more forward (?), dark-chocolate catkins. These may be only a more recent and vigorous growth of the other. There is one of these a few rods east of the Peak clearing, on the shore of Walden.

On the side of the Peak, I see now small radical (?) or lower leaves of a goldenrod, as fresh as anything, the dark mulberry, claret, or lake colored radical leaves of the hawkweed,[1] and the greenish radical leaves of the bushy gerardia.

What is the earliest sign of spring? The motion of worms and insects? The flow of sap in trees and the swelling of buds? Do not the insects awake with the flow of the sap? Bluebirds, etc., probably do not come till insects come out. Or are there earlier signs in the water? — the tortoises, frogs, etc.

The little cup and cocciferæ lichens, mixed with other cladonias of the reindeer moss kind, are full of fresh fruit to-day. The scarlet apothecia of the cocciferæ on the stumps and earth partly covered with snow, with which they contrast, I never saw more fresh and brilliant, but they shrivel up and lose their brightness by the time you get them home. The only birds I *see* to-day are the lesser redpolls. I have not seen a fox-colored sparrow or a *Fringilla hyemalis*. In the Flint's Pond Mill Brook ditch, I see where the green conferva is left

[1] *?? Was it not Aster undulatus?*

suspended vertically to the twigs, the water having gone down, and, being blanched, looks like very dense cobwebs. There are still a few pretty bright sumach berries left.

Gathered a few chestnuts. A good many, if not most, are now turned black and soured or spoiled and softened by the wet. Where they are less exposed to moisture, close to the base of the [*sic*], or on stumps where the ground is more elevated, or where they are protected under a very thick heap of light-lying leaves, they are perfectly sound and sweet and fresh yet, neither shrivelled nor soured (?). This peculiar condition is probably requisite to preserve their life for sprouting. I planted some in Sophia's pot. No doubt the mice and squirrels put many in secure, sufficiently dry and sufficiently moist places for this purpose, and so do a service. I find whitish grubs stretching themselves under the moist chestnut leaves, but they were in the same state in January.

Found the yellow bud of a *Nuphar advena* in the ditch on the Turnpike on E. Hosmer's land, bud nearly half an inch in diameter on a very thick stem, three fourths of an inch thick at base and ten inches long, four or five inches above the mud. This may have swollen somewhat during the warmest weather in the winter, after pushing up in the fall. And I see that it may, in such a case, in favorable locations, blossom at very early but irregular periods in the spring. What are the weeds in the water, — these which, together with the common cress, have been perfectly green and fresh all winter, one in regular beds of small roundish leaves very like the cress,[1] the other with a long, narrow, coarse leaf?[2]

I read an account the other day of a snipe, I think it was, which, though neither plucked nor drawn, underwent no change but that of drying up, becoming a natural mummy for some unknown reason, as has happened to other, larger bodies. Methinks that many, if not most, men are a sort of natural mummies. The life having departed out of them, decay and putrefaction, disorganization, has not taken place, but they still keep up a dry and withered semblance of life. What the salt is that saves them and robs the worms I do not know. Some bodies there are that, being dead and buried, do not decay, but after the lapse of years are found as fresh as if they had died but yesterday. So some men, though all true life was long ago extinct in them, wear this deceitful semblance of life. They seem to *live* on, without salt or season, from mere toughness or dryness or some antiseptic quality in their fibre. They do not mellowly dissolve and fatten the earth with their decay.

March 8. 10 A. M. — Rode to Saxonville with F. Brown to look at a small place for sale, *via* Wayland. Return by Sudbury.

On wheels in snow. A spring sheen on the snow. The melting snow, running and sparkling down-hill in the ruts, was quite springlike. The snow pure white, but full of water and dissolving through the heat of the sun. Saw a mink run across the road in Sudbury, a large

[1] *Chrysosplenium?*   [2] Probably forget-me-not.

black weasel, to appearance, worming its supple way over the snow. Where it ran, its tracks were thus: = = = = the intervals between the fore and hind feet sixteen or eighteen inches by two and a half.

The distant view of the open flooded Sudbury meadows, all dark blue, surrounded by a landscape of white snow, gave an impulse to the dormant sap in my veins. Dark-blue and angry waves, contrasting with the white but melting winter landscape. Ponds, of course, do not yet afford this water prospect; only the flooded meadows. There is no ice over or near the stream, and the flood has covered or broken up much of the ice on the meadows. The aspect of these waters at sunset, when the air is still, begins to be unspeakably soothing and promising. Waters are at length, and begin to reflect, and, instead of looking into the sky, I look into the placid reflecting water for the signs and promise of the morrow. These meadows are the most of ocean that I have fairly learned. Now, when the sap of the trees is probably beginning to flow, the sap of the earth, the river, overflows and bursts its icy fetters. This is the sap of which I make my sugar after the frosty nights, boiling it down and crystallizing it. I must be on the lookout now for the gulls and the ducks. That dark-blue meadowy revelation. It is as when the sap of the maple bursts forth early and runs down the trunk to the snow.

Saw two or three hawks sailing. Saw the remains of four cows and a horse that were burned in a barn a month ago. Where the paunch was, a large bag of coarse hay and stalks was seen in the midst of an indistinct circumference of ribs. Saw some very large willow

buds expanded (their silk) to thrice the length of their scales, indistinctly carved or waved with darker lines around them. They look more like, are more of, spring than anything I have seen. Heard the *phebe*, or spring note of the chickadee, now, before any spring bird has arrived.

I know of no more pleasing employment than to ride about the country with a companion very early in the spring, looking at farms with a view to purchasing if not paying for them.

Heard the first flies buzz in the sun on the south side of the house.

March 9. *Wednesday*. Rain, dissolving the snow and raising the river. I do not perceive that the early elm or the white maple buds have swollen yet. So the relaxed and loosened (?) alder catkins and the extended willow catkins and poplar catkins are the first signs of reviving vegetation which I have witnessed. Minott thinks, and quotes some old worthy as authority for saying, that the bark of the striped squirrel is the, or a, first sure sign of decided spring weather.

March 10. This is the first really spring day. The sun is brightly reflected from all surfaces, and the north side of the street begins to be a little more passable to foot-travellers. You do not think it necessary to button up your coat.

P. M. — To Second Division Brook.

As I stand looking over the swollen river, looking from the bridge into the flowing, eddying tide, — the

almost strange chocolate-colored water, — the sound of distant crows and cocks is full of spring. As Anacreon says "the works of men shine," so the sounds of men and birds are musical. Something analogous to the thawing of the ice seems to have taken place in the air. At the end of winter there is a season in which we are daily expecting spring, and finally a day when it arrives.

I see many middling-sized black spiders on the edge of the snow, very active. By John Hosmer's ditch by the riverside I see the skunk-cabbage springing freshly, the points of the spathes just peeping out of the ground, in some other places three inches high even. The radical leaves of innumerable plants (as here a dock in and near the water) are evidently affected by the spring influences. Many plants are to some extent evergreen, like the buttercup now beginning to start. Methinks the first obvious evidence of spring is the pushing out of the swamp willow catkins, then the relaxing of the earlier alder catkins, then the pushing up of skunk-cabbage spathes (and pads at the bottom of water). This is the order I am inclined to, though perhaps any of these may take precedence of all the rest in any particular case.[1]

What is that dark pickle-green alga (?) at the bottom of this ditch, looking *somewhat* like a decaying cress, with fruit like a lichen?

At Nut Meadow Brook crossing we rest awhile on the rail, gazing into the eddying stream. The ripple-marks on the sandy bottom, where silver spangles shine in the river with black wrecks of caddis-cases lodged under each shelving sand, the shadows of the invisible dimples

[1] *Vide* next page.

reflecting prismatic colors on the bottom, the minnows already stemming the current with restless, wiggling tails, ever and anon darting aside, probably to secure some invisible mote in the water, whose shadows we do not at first detect on the sandy bottom, — when detected so much more obvious as well as larger and more interesting than the substance, — in which each fin is distinctly seen, though scarcely to be detected in the substance; these are all very beautiful and exhilarating sights, a sort of diet drink to heal our winter discontent. Have the minnows played thus all winter? The equisetum at the bottom has freshly grown several inches. Then should I not have given the precedence on the last page to this and some other water-plants? I suspect that I should, and the flags appear to be starting.

I am surprised to find on the rail a young tortoise, an inch and one sixteenth long in the shell, which has crawled out to sun, or perchance is on its way to the water, which I think must be the *Emys guttata*, for there is a large and distinct yellow spot on each dorsal and lateral plate, and the third dorsal plate is hexagonal and not quadrangular, as the *E. picta* is described to be, though in my specimen I can't make it out to be so. Yet the edges of the plates are prominent, as is described in the *E. insculpta*, which, but for the spots and two yellow spots on each side of the hind head and one fainter on the top of the head, I should take it to be. It is about seven eighths of an inch wide. Very inactive. When was it hatched and where?

What is the theory of these sudden pitches, or steep shelving places, in the sandy bottom of the brook? It is

very interesting to walk along such a brook as this in the midst of the meadow, which you can better do now before the frost is quite out of the sod, and gaze into the deep holes in its irregular bottom and the dark gulfs under the banks. Where it rushes rapidly over the edge of a steep slope in the bottom, the shadow of the disturbed surface is like sand hurried forward in the water. The bottom, being of shifting sand, is exceedingly irregular and interesting.

What was that sound that came on the softened air? It was the warble of the first bluebird from that scraggy apple orchard yonder. When this is heard, then has spring arrived.

It must be that the willow twigs, both the yellow and green, are brighter-colored than before. I cannot be deceived. They shine as if the sap were already flowing under the bark; a certain lively and glossy hue they have. The early poplars are pushing forward their catkins, though they make not so much display as the willows.

Still in some parts of the woods it is good sledding. At Second Division Brook, the fragrance of the senecio, which is decidedly evergreen, which I have bruised, is very permanent and brings round the year again. It is a memorable sweet meadowy fragrance. I find a yellow-spotted tortoise (*Emys guttata*) in the brook. A very few leaves of cowslips, and those wholly under water, show themselves yet. The leaves of the water saxifrage, for the most part frost-bitten, are common enough. Near the caltha was also green frog-*spawn*, and Channing

says he saw pollywogs.[1] Perhaps it is a particularly warm place. The alder's catkins — the earliest of them — are very plainly expanding, or, rather, the scales are loose and separated, and the whole catkin relaxed.

Minott says that old Sam Nutting, the hunter, — Fox Nutting, Old Fox, he was called, — who died more than forty years ago (he lived in Jacob Baker's house, Lincoln; came from Weston) and was some seventy years old then, told him that he had killed not only bear about Fair Haven among the walnuts, but *moose!*

March 12. Last night it snowed, a sleety snow again, and now the ground is whitened with it, and where are gone the bluebirds whose warble was wafted to me so lately like a blue wavelet through the air?

The greater part of the alder catkins (as well as the willow) are still in their winter condition, but some have their scales conspicuously loosened and elevated, showing their lighter-colored edges and interstices. They are actually beginning to blossom, certainly in advance of the willows. The sweet-gale is the prettiest flower which I have [found] expanded yet.

It is essential that a man confine himself to pursuits — a scholar, for instance, to studies — which lie next to and conduce to his life, which do not go against the grain, either of his will or his imagination. The scholar finds in his experience some studies to be most fertile and radiant with light, others dry, barren, and dark. If he is wise, he will not persevere in the last, as a plant in a cellar will strive toward the light. He will confine

[1] Possibly lizards [*i. e.* newts, or salamanders].

the observations of his mind as closely as possible to the experience or life of his senses. His thought must live with and be inspired with the life of the body. The death-bed scenes and observations even of the best and wisest afford but a sorry picture of our humanity. Some men endeavor to live a constrained life, to subject their whole lives to their wills, as he who said he would give a sign if he were conscious after his head was cut off, — but he gave no sign. Dwell as near as possible to the channel in which your life flows. A man may associate with such companions, he may pursue such employments, as will darken the day for him. Men choose darkness rather than light.

P. M. — To Cliffs and Fair Haven.

The sleety snow has whitened the north sides of the oaks, giving a wintry aspect as well to the wood as to the ground.

Saw the first lark rise from the railroad causeway and sail on quivering wing over the meadow to alight on a heap of dirt. Was that a mink we saw at the Boiling Spring? The senecio was very forward there in the water, and it still scents my fingers; a very lasting odor it leaves. These melting snows, so saturated with water, their white contrasting so strongly with the dark spaces, wet the feet most of any. The farmer says that no composition will keep out snow-water. The snow rests on your feet to melt. There has been no regular breaking up of the river, it has been so transiently closed the past winter. Fair Haven Pond is nearly half open. But I see no gulls nor ducks. The young oaks on the plain under the Cliffs appear still full of leaves. It is a rare lichen day.

The usnea with its large fruit is very rich on the maples in the swamp, luxuriating in this moist, overcast, melting day, but it is impossible to get it home in good condition. Looking behind the bark of a dead white pine, I find plenty of small gnats quite lively and ready to issue forth as soon as the sun comes out. The grubs there are sluggish, buried in the *chankings*. I took off some pieces of bark more than three feet long and one foot wide. Between this and the wood, in the dust left by borers, the gnats were concealed, ready to swarm. This their hibernaculum. The rich red-brown leaves of the gnaphalium, downy white beneath in circles, begin to attract me where the snow is off.

If I were to make a study of the tracks of animals and represent them by plates, I should conclude with the track of man. Everywhere I see the track of the dog and within it that of the game he is pursuing.

March 13. 6 A. M. — To Cliffs.

There begins to be a greater depth of saffron in the morning sky. The morning and evening horizon fires are warmer to the eye. I go to the Cliffs to hear if any new spring birds have arrived, for not only they are more sure to sing in the morning, but it is stiller and you can hear them better then. I hear only crows and blue jays and chickadees lisping. Excepting a few blue-birds and larks, no spring birds have come, apparently. The woods are still. But what was that familiar spring sound from the pine wood across the river, a sharp *vetter vetter vetter vetter*, like some woodpecker, or possibly nuthatch? Yet I thought it the voice of the bird and

not a tapping. It reminds me of the pine warbler (?), if that is it. I see the nuphar pushing up faintly, and I see some of my little gnats of yesterday in the morning sun, somewhat mosquito-like.

P. M. — No sap flows yet from my hole in the white maple by the bridge. Found on the Great Fields a fragment of Indian soapstone ware, which, judging from its curve and thinness, for a vestige of the rim remains, was a dish of the form and size of a saucer, only three times as thick. Listening for early birds, I hear a faint tinkling sound in the leafless woods, as if a piece of glass rattled against a stone.

All enterprises must be self-supporting, must pay for themselves. The great art of life is how to turn the surplus life of the soul into life for the body, — that so the life be not a failure. For instance, a poet must sustain his body with his poetry. As is said of the merchants, in ninety-nine cases out of a hundred the life of men is a failure, and bankruptcy may be surely prophesied. You must get your living by loving. To be supported by the charity of friends or a government pension is to go into the almshouse. To inherit property is not to be born, — is to be still-born rather. And the other, as I said, provided you continue to breathe, is to go into the almshouse. On Sundays the poor debtor goes to church to take an account of stock, and finds his outgoes greater than his income. In the Catholic Church especially they go into chancery.[1] As is the sun to the vegetable, so is virtue to the bodily health.

[1] [*Cape Cod, and Miscellanies*, p. 461; *Misc.*, Riv. 261.]

Vol. V

March 14. P. M. — Repairing my boat.

High winds, growing colder and colder, ground stiffening again. My ears have not been colder the past winter. Lowell Fay tells me that he overtook with a boat and killed last July a woodchuck which was crossing the river at Hollowell Place. He also says that the blacksmith of Sudbury has two otter skins taken in that town. March is rightly famous for its winds.

March 15. There were few colder nights last winter than the last. The water in the flower-stand containing my pet tortoise froze solid, — completely enveloping him, though I had a fire in my chamber all the evening, — also that in my pail pretty thick. But the tortoise, having been thawed out on the stove, leaving the impression of his back shell in the ice, was even more lively than ever. His efforts at first had been to get under his chip, as if to go into the mud. To-day the weather is severely and remarkably cold. It is not easy to keep warm in my chamber. I have not taken a more blustering walk the past winter than this afternoon.

C. says he has heard a striped squirrel and seen a water-bug (*Gyrinus*), — it must have been on Saturday (12th). Ice froze just hard enough to bear last night, — about an inch thick. In the woods beyond Peter's we heard our dog, a large Newfoundland dog, barking at something, and, going forward, were amused to see him barking while he retreated with fear at that black oak with remarkable excrescence, which had been cut off just above it, leaving it like some misshapen idol about the height of a man. Though we set him on to it, he did not

venture within three or four rods. I would not have believed that he would notice any such strange thing.

Organization, — how it prevails! After a little discipline, we study with love and reverence the forms of disease as healthy organisms. The fungi have a department in the science of botany. Who can doubt but that they too are fungi lower in the scale which he sees on the wick of his lamp!

Notwithstanding this day is so cold that I keep my ears covered, the sidewalks melt in the sun, such is its altitude. The coldness of the air blown from the icy northwest prevails over the heat of the sun.

The Bermudas are said to have been first discovered by a Spanish ship of that name, which was wrecked on them, — "which till then for six thousand years had been nameless," says John Smith. "No place known hath better walls nor a broader ditch." The English did not stumble upon them in their first voyages to Virginia, and the first Englishman who was ever in them was wrecked on them in 1593; yet at the very first planting of them in 1612 with some sixty persons, the first Governor the same year "built and laid the foundations of eight or nine forts" (!!), to be ready, one would say, to entertain the first ship company that should be next shipwrecked on to them. It would have been more sensible to have built as many charity houses. These are the vex'd Bermoothes.

March 17. Channing says he saw blackbirds yesterday; F. C. Brown, that they were getting ice out of Loring's Pond yesterday.

P. M. — Rode to Lexington with Brown.

Saw, on the corner of a wall by a house about three quarters of a mile from the monument on the Bedford road, a stone apparently worn by water into the form of a rude bird-like idol, which I thought, as I rode by, to be the work of the Indians. It was probably discovered and used by them. It was as near as nature might come by accident to an eagle, with a very regular pedestal such as busts have, on which it stood, — in all about two and a half feet high. Whitewashed as well as the wall. Found not near water. It is one of those stones which Schoolcraft describes as found among the Chippeways.

The ways are mostly settled, frozen dry.

March 18. The season is so far advanced that the sun, every now and then promising to shine out through this rather warm rain, lighting up transiently with a whiter light the dark day and my dark chamber, affects me as I have not been affected for a long time. I must go forth.

P. M. — To Conantum.

I find it unexpectedly mild. It appears to be clearing up but will be wet underfoot.

Now, then, spring is beginning again in earnest after this short check. Is it not always thus? Is there not always an early promise of spring, something answering to the Indian summer, which succeeds the summer, so an Indian or false spring preceding the true spring, — first false promise which merely excites our expectations to disappoint them, followed by a short return of

winter? Yet all things appear to have made progress, even during these wintry days, for I cannot believe that they have thus instantaneously taken a start. I no sooner step out of the house than I hear the bluebirds in the air, and far and near, everywhere except in the woods, throughout the town you may hear them, — the blue curls of their warblings, — harbingers of serene and warm weather, little azure rills of melody trickling here and there from out the air, their short warble trilled in the air reminding of so many corkscrews assaulting and thawing the torpid mass of winter, assisting the ice and snow to melt and the streams to flow. Everywhere also, all over the town, within an hour or two have come out little black two-winged gnats with plumed or fuzzy shoulders. When I catch one in my hands, it looks like [a] bit of black silk ravelling. They have suddenly come forth everywhere.

How eagerly the birds of passage penetrate the northern ice, watching for a crack by which to enter! Forthwith the swift ducks will be seen winging their way along the rivers and up the coast. They watch the weather more sedulously than the teamster. All nature is thus forward to move with the revolution of the seasons. Now for some days the birds have been ready by myriads, a flight or two south, to invade our latitudes and, with this mild and serener weather, resume their flight.

Bells and the lowing of cows have acquired I know not what new melody in this air, for a change has come over all things, as well as our spirits. They sound more limpid, as, in this sun just bursting forth, the drops of

water on the sprays are prismatic. The geiropodium has bleached all white.

I stand still now to listen if I may hear the note of any new bird, for the sound of my steps hinders, and there are so few sounds at this season in a still afternoon like this that you are pretty sure to detect one within a considerable distance. Hark! Did I not hear the note of some bird then? Methinks it could not have been my own breathing through my nose. No, there it is again, — a robin; and we have put the winter so much further behind us. What mate does he call to in these deserted fields? It is, as it were, a scared note as he whisks by, followed by the familiar but still anxious *toot, toot, toot.* He does not sing as yet. There were one or two more fine bird-like tinkling sounds I could not trace home, not to be referred to my breathing.

It is decidedly clearing up. At Conantum Cliff the columbines have started and the saxifrage even, the former as conspicuously as any plant, particularly any on dry ground. Both these grow there in high and dry chinks in the face of the cliff, where no soil appears, and the sunnier the exposure the more advanced. Even if a fallen fragment of the rock is so placed as to reflect the heat upon it, it has the start of its neighbors. These plants waste not a day, not a moment, suitable to their development. I pluck dry sprigs of pennyroyal, which I love to put in my pocket, for it scents me thoroughly and reminds me of garrets full of herbs.

With regard to my seringo-bird (and others), I think that my good genius withheld his name that I might learn his character.

I came forth expecting to hear new birds, and I am not disappointed. We know well what to count upon. Their coming is more sure than the arrival of the sailing and steaming packets. Almost while I listen for this purpose, I hear the *chuck, chuck* of a blackbird in the sky, whom I cannot detect. So small an object is lost in the wide expanse of the heavens, though no obstacle intervenes. When your eye has detected it, you can follow it well enough, but it is difficult to bring your sight to bear on it, as to direct a telescope to a particular star. How many hawks may fly undetected, yet within sight, above our heads! And there 's the great gull I came to see, already fishing in front of Bittern Cliff. Now he stoops to the water for his prey, but sluggishly, methinks. He requires a high and perhaps a head wind to make his motions graceful. I see no mate. He must have come up, methinks, before the storm was over, unless he started when I did. I believe it is only an easterly wind or storm brings him up.

The ice in Fair Haven is more than half melted, and now the woods beyond the pond, reflected in its serene water where there has been opaque ice so long, affect me as they perhaps will not again this year.[1] The oaks have not yet lost their leaves. The thistles, which keep their heads so low they do not feel the wind, show their green faces everywhere. It grows more and more fair. Yesterday at this hour it was more raw and blustering than the past winter; to-day it seems more mild and balmy than summer. I have rarely known a greater contrast. There is a little cap of dark and angry cloud

[1] The tapping of the woodpecker about this time.

on Wachusett, not so wide as the mountain's base, while all the rest of the horizon there is clear.

Several times I hear and see blackbirds flying north singly, high overhead, chucking as if to find their mates, migrating; or are they even now getting near their own breeding-place? Perchance these are blackbirds that were hatched here, — that know me! I saw a silent sparrow lurking amid the hazels and other shrubs by a wall and picking worms or what-not, — brownish gray with a forked tail, two triangular black spots on the breast, and black stripes lengthwise there, altogether a gray, much striped bird, two brownish stripes with a lighter-colored one on the centre of the head. Soon after, I heard a song sparrow distinctly. Could it have been this?[1] I think not.

The bluebird and song sparrow sing immediately on their arrival, and hence deserve to enjoy some pre-eminence. They give expression to the joy which the season inspires. But the robin and blackbird only peep and chuck at first, commonly, and the lark is silent and flitting. The bluebird at once fills the air with his sweet warbling, and the song sparrow from the top of a rail pours forth his most joyous strain. Both express their delight at the weather which permits them to return to their favorite haunts. They are the more welcome to man for it.

Hearing a faint quack, I looked up and saw two apparently dusky ducks winging their swift way north-ward over the course of the river. Channing says he saw

[1] Think now (March 24) it must have been the song sparrow. *Vide* Apr. 1st.

some large white-breasted ducks to-day, and also a frog. I have seen dead frogs, as if killed while dormant.

The sun is now declining, with a warm and bright light on all things, a light which answers to the late after-glow of the year, when, in the fall, wrapping his cloak closer about him, the traveller goes home at night to pre-pare for winter. This the foreglow of the year, when the walker goes home at eve to dream of summer.

To-day first I smelled the earth.

March 19. This morning I hear the blackbird's fine clear whistle and also his sprayey note, as he is swayed back and forth on the twigs of the elm or of the black willow over the [river]. His first note may be a chuck, but his second is a rich gurgle or warble.

" Coelum non animum mutant, qui trans mare currunt."
(Marginal index in Benzo's " History of the West Indies.")

Observed the leaves of a dock in the water, more forward than any vegetation I have noticed.

March 20. Sunday. 8 a. m. — *Via* Walden, Goose, Flint's, and Beaver Ponds and the valley of Stony Brook to the south end of Lincoln.

A rather cool and breezy morning, which was fol-lowed by milder day. We go listening for early birds, with bread and cheese for our dinners.

(Yesterday I forgot to say I painted my boat. Spanish brown and raw oil were the ingredients. I found the painter had sold me the brown in hard lumps as big as peas, which I could not reduce with a stick: so I passed the whole when mixed through an old coffee-mill, which

Vol. V

made a very good paint-mill, catching it in an old coffee-pot, whose holes I puttied up, there being a lack of vessels; and then I broke up the coffee-mill and nailed a part over the bows to protect them, the boat is made so flat. I had first filled the seams with some grafting-wax I had, melted.)

It was a question whether we should not go to Fair Haven to see the gulls, etc. I notice the downy, swaddled plants now and in the fall, the fragrant life-everlasting and the ribwort, innocents born in a cloud. Those algæ I saw the other day in John Hosmer's ditch were the most like seaweed of anything I have seen in the county. They made me look at the whole earth as a seashore; reminded me of Nereids, sea nymphs, Triton, Proteus, etc., etc.; made the ditches fabulate in an older than the arrow-headed character. Better learn this strange character which nature speaks to-day than the Sanscrit. Books in the brooks. Saw a large dead water-bug on Walden. I suspect he came out alive.

Walden is melting apace. It has a canal two rods wide along the northerly side and the west end, wider at the east end, yet, after running round from west to east, it does not keep the south shore, but crosses in front of the deep cove in a broad crack to where it started, by the ice ground. It is glorious to behold the life and joy of this ribbon of water sparkling in the sun. The wind blows eastward over the opaque ice, unusually hard, owing to the recent severe though transient cold, all watered or waved like a tessellated floor, a figured car-pet; yet dead, yet in vain, till it slides on to the living water surface, where it raises a myriad brilliant sparkles

on the bare face of the pond, an expression of glee, of youth, of spring, as if it spoke the joy of the fishes within it and of the sands on its shore, a silvery sheen like the scales of a leuciscus, as if it were all one active fish in the spring. It is the contrast between life and death. There is the difference between winter and spring. The bared face of the pond sparkles with joy. How handsome the curves which the edge of the ice makes, answering some-what to those of the shore, but more regular, sweeping en-tirely round the pond, as if defined by a vast, bold sweep![1]

It is evident that the English do not enjoy that con-trast between winter and summer that we do, — that there is too much greenness and spring in the winter. There is no such wonderful resurrection of the year. Birds kindred with our first spring ones remain with them all winter, and flowers answering to our earliest spring ones put forth there in January. In one sense they have no winter but such as our spring. Our April is their March; our March, their February; our Feb-ruary, January, and December are not theirs at all under any name or sign.

Those alder catkins on the west side of Walden trem-ble and undulate in the wind, they are so relaxed and ready to bloom, — the most forward blossom-buds. Here and there, around the pond, within a rod of the water, is the fisherman's stone fireplace, with its charred brands, where he cheered and warmed himself and ate his lunch.

The peculiarity of to-day is that now first you per-ceive that dry, warm, summer-presaging scent from dry

[1] [*Walden*, pp. 343, 344; Riv. 480.]

oak and other leaves, on the sides of hills and ledges. You smell the summer from afar. The warm [*sic*] makes a man young again. There is also some dryness, almost dustiness, in the roads. The mountains are white with snow, and sure as the wind is northwest it is wintry; but now it is more westerly. The edges of the mountains now melt into the sky. It is affecting to be put into communication with such distant objects by the power of vision, — actually to look into rich lands of promise. In this spring breeze, how full of life the silvery pines, probably the under sides of their leaves. Goose Pond is wholly open. Unexpectedly dry and crispy the grass is getting in warm places.

At Flint's Pond, gathered a handful or two of chestnuts on a sloping bank under the leaves, *every one* sound and sweet, but mostly sprouting. There were none black as at C. Smith's, proving that in such places as this, somewhat warm and dry, they are all preserved the winter through. Now, then, new groves of chestnuts (and of oaks?) are being born. Under these wet leaves I find myriads of the snow-fleas, like powder. Some brooks are full of little wiggling creatures *somewhat* like caddis-worms, stemming the stream, — food for the early fishes. The canoe birch sprouts are red or salmon-colored like those of the common, but soon they cast off their salmon-colored jackets and come forth with a white but naked look, all dangling with ragged reddish curls. What is that little bird that makes so much use of these curls in its nest, lined with coarse grass? The snow still covers the ground on the north side of hills, which are hard and slippery with frost.

I am surprised to find Flint's Pond not more than half broken up. Probably it was detained by the late short but severe cold, while Walden, being deeper, was not. Standing on the icy side, the pond appears nearly all frozen; the breadth of open water is far removed and diminished to a streak; I say it is beginning to break up. Standing on the water side (which in Flint's is the middle portion), it appears to be but bordered with ice, and I say there is ice still left in the pond.

Saw a bluish-winged beetle or two.[1] In a stubble-field east of Mt. Tabor, started up a pack (though for numbers, about twenty, it may have been a bevy) of quail, which went off to some young pitch pines, with a whir like a shot, the plump, round birds. The redpolls are still numerous.[2] On the warm, dry cliff, looking south over Beaver Pond, I was surprised to see a large butterfly, black with buff-edged wings, so tender a creature to be out so early, and, when alighted, opening and shutting its wings. What does it do these frosty nights? Its chrysalis must have hung in some sunny nook of the rocks. Born to be food for some early bird.[3]

Cutting a maple for a bridge over Lily Brook, I was rejoiced to see the sap falling in large, clear drops from the wound.

March 21. Morning along the river.

The air full of song sparrows, — *swedit swedit swedit* and then a rapid jingle or trill, holding up its head with-

[1] *Vide* forward [p. 33].

[2] Have not seen them again, March 28.

[3] [This butterfly, the mourning-cloak (Antiopa), hibernates in the perfect state.]

out fear of me, the innocent, humble bird, or one pursuing another through the alders by the waterside. Why are the early birds found most along the water? These song sparrows are now first heard *commonly*. The blackbirds, too, create some melody. And the bluebirds, how sweet their warble in the soft air, heard over the water! The robin is heard further off, and seen flying rapidly, hurriedly through the orchard. And now the elms suddenly ring with the *chill-lill-lill* and canary-like notes of the *Fringilla hyemalis*, which fill the air more than those of any bird yet, — a little strange they sound because they do not tarry to breed with us, — a ringing sound. The Cheney elm buds appear to be beginning to open, and a few green blades of grass are shooting up on our bank.

I think that with my knife I can cut a pole that will bridge almost anything that can be called a *brook* even in New England.

Observed yesterday where a mass of ice in Walden of about an acre had cracked off from the main body and blown thirty or forty rods, crumbling up its edge against the eastern shore.[1]

Might not my Journal be called "Field Notes?"

I see a honey-bee about my boat, apparently attracted by the beeswax (if there is any) in the grafting-wax with which I have luted it. There are many; one is caught and killed in it.

P. M. — To Kibbe Place.

The *Stellaria media* is fairly in bloom in Mr. Cheney's

[1] [*Walden*, p. 343; Riv. 480.]

garden. This, then, is our earliest flower; though it is said to have been introduced. It may blossom under favorable circumstances in warmer weather any time in the winter. It has been so much opened that you could easily count its petals any month the past winter, and plainly blossoms with the first pleasant weather that brings the robins, etc., in numbers. I heard undoubtedly a frog jump into the river, though I did not see him. Conspicuous, now that the snow is almost entirely gone, are the fresh-looking evergreen leaves of the pyrola. What shall I name those run-out pastures, those arid downs, where the reindeer lichen fairly covers the whole surface, and your feet cronch it at every step? I see the *Fringilla hyemalis* on the old Carlisle road. How suddenly the newly arrived birds are dispersed over the whole town! How numerous they must be! Robins are now quite abundant, flying in flocks. One after another flits away before you from the trees, somewhat like grasshoppers in the grass, uttering their notes faintly, — ventriloquizing, in fact. I hear [one] meditating a bar to be sung anon, which sounds a quarter of a mile off, though he is within two rods. However, they do not yet get to melody. I thank the red-wing for a little bustle and commotion which he makes, trying to people the fields again. To-day, as well as yesterday, there is a slight warm haze before the day is over. A hawk looking about. Are they not more active now? Do they not, in fact, migrate? What is that lustrous green pestle-shaped beetle (common enough) with a waved buff spot on each wing-case? When he flew, I thought he showed blue beneath and was the same I saw yesterday in Lincoln, — the first beetle-insect I have seen. Insects and flies, both in air and water, come out in the spring sun. Just as flies buzz on the dry and sunny side of a bank or rock, those little wiggling insects come forth in the open and sunny water, and are no less active, though they do not hum. Saw two more of those large black and buff butterflies. The same degree of heat brings them out everywhere.

The bees this morning had access to no flower; so they came to my grafting-wax, notwithstanding it was mixed with tallow and covered with fresh paint. Often they essayed to light on it and retreated with disgust; yet one got caught. As they detected the beeswax concealed and disguised in this composition, so they will receive the earliest intelligence of the blossoming of the first flower which contains any sweet for them.

It is a genial and reassuring day; the mere warmth of the west wind amounts almost to balminess. The softness of the air mollifies our own dry and congealed substance. I sit down by a wall to see if I can muse again. We become, as it were, pliant and ductile again to strange but memorable influences; we are led a little way by our genius. We are affected like the earth, and yield to the elemental tenderness; winter breaks up within us; the frost is coming out of me, and I am heaved like the road; accumulated masses of ice and snow dissolve, and thoughts like a freshet pour down unwonted channels. A strain of music comes to solace the traveller over earth's downs and dignify his chagrins, the petty men whom he meets are the shadows of grander to come. Roads lead elsewhither than to Carlisle and Sudbury. The earth is uninhabited but fair to inhabit, like

the old Carlisle road. Is then the road so rough that it should be neglected? Not only narrow but rough is the way that leadeth to life everlasting. Our experience does not wear upon us. It is seen to be fabulous or symbolical, and the future is worth expecting. Encouraged, I set out once more to climb the mountain of the earth, for my steps are symbolical steps, and in all my walking I have not reached the top of the earth yet.

In two or three places I hear the ground squirrel's pert chirrup or *qui vive* in the wall, like a bird or a cricket. Though I do not see him, the sun has reached him too.

Ah! then, as I was rising this crowning road, just beyond the old lime-kiln, there leaked into my open ear the faint peep of a hyla from some far pool. One little hyla somewhere in the fens, aroused by the genial season, crawls up the bank or a bush, squats on a dry leaf, and essays a note or two, which scarcely rends the air, does no violence to the zephyr, but yet breaks through all obstacles, thick-planted maples, and far over the downs to the ear of the listening naturalist, who will never see that piper in this world, — nor even the next, it may be, — as it were the first faint cry of the new-born year, notwithstanding the notes of birds. Where so long I have heard only the brattling and moaning of the wind, what means this tenser, far-piercing sound? All nature rejoices with one joy. If the hyla has revived again, may not I? He is heard the first warm, hazy evening.

Came home through the Hunt pasture. A warmer sunset marks the season. Some oaks have lost their leaves.

Vol. V

Whatever your sex or position, life is a battle in which you are to show your pluck, and woe be to the coward. Whether passed on a bed of sickness or a tented field, it is ever the same fair play and admits no foolish distinction. Despair and postponement are cowardice and defeat. Men were born to succeed, not to fail.

J. Farmer saw a phœbe to-day. They build in his cellar. I hear a few peepers from over the meadows at my door in the evening.

March 22. As soon as the damp gardens are bared of snow and a really warm spring day arrives, the chickweed blossoms fairly.

As soon as those spring mornings arrive in which the birds sing, I am sure to be an early riser. I am waked by my genius. I wake to inaudible melodies and am surprised to find myself expecting the dawn in so serene and joyful and expectant a mood. I have an appointment with spring. She comes to the window to wake me, and I go forth an hour or two earlier than usual. It is by especial favor that I am waked, — not rudely but gently, as infants should be waked. Though as yet the trill of the chip-bird is not heard, — added, — like the sparkling bead which bursts on bottled cider or ale. When we wake indeed, with a double awakening, — not only from our ordinary nocturnal slumbers, but from our diurnal, — we burst through the thallus of our ordinary life with a proper exciple, we awake with emphasis.

6 A. M. — To Cliffs.

There is a white frost on the ground.

One robin really sings on the elms. Even the cockerel

crows with new lustiness. Already I hear from the railroad the plaintive strain of a lark or two. They sit now conspicuous on the bare russet ground. The tinkling bubbles of the song sparrow are wafted from distant fence-posts, — little rills of song that begin to flow and tinkle as soon as the frost is out of the ground. The blackbird tries to sing, as it were with a bone in his throat, or to whistle and sing at once. Whither so fast, the restless creature, — *chuck, chuck,* at every rod, and now and then *whistle-ter-ee?* The *chill-lill* of the blue snowbirds is heard again. A partridge goes off on Fair Haven Hill-side with a sudden whir like the wad of a sixpounder, keeping just level with the tops of the sprouts. These birds and quails go off like a report.

It affects one's philosophy, after so long living in winter quarters, to see the day dawn from some hill. Our effete lowland town is fresh as New Hampshire. It is as if we had migrated and were ready to begin life again in a new country, with new hopes and resolutions. See your town with the dew on it, in as wild a morning mist (though thin) as ever draped it. To stay in the house all day, such reviving spring days as the past have been, bending over a stove and gnawing one's heart, seems to me as absurd as for a woodchuck to linger in his burrow. We have not heard the news then! Sucking the claws of our philosophy when there is game to be had!

The tapping of the woodpecker, *rat-tat-tat,* knocking at the door of some sluggish grub to tell him that the spring has arrived, and his fate, this is one of the season sounds, calling the roll of birds and insects, the reveille.

The Cliff woods are comparatively silent. Not yet the woodland birds, except, perhaps, the woodpecker, so far as it migrates; only the orchard and river birds have arrived. Probably the improvements of men thus advance the season. This is the Bahamas and the tropics or turning-point to the redpoll. Is not the woodpecker (downy?) our first woodland bird? Come to see what effects the frost and snow and rain have produced on decaying trees, — what trunks will drum.

Fair Haven Pond will be open entirely in the course of the day. The oak plain is still red. There are no expanding leaves to greet and reflect the sun as it first falls over the hills. To see the first rays of the sun falling over an eastern wooded ridge on to a western wood and stream and lake! I go along the riverside to see the now novel reflections. The subsiding waters have left a thousand little isles, where willows and sweet-gale and the meadow itself appears. I hear the phœbe note of the chickadee, one taking it up behind another as in a catch, *phe-bee phe-bee.* The very earliest alder is in bloom and sheds its pollen. I detect a few catkins at a distance by their distinct yellowish color. This the first native flower. One of my willow catkins in the pitcher has opened at length.

That is an interesting morning when one first uses the warmth of the sun instead of fire; bathes in the sun, as anon in the river; eschewing fire, draws up to a garret window and warms his thoughts at nature's great central fire, as does the buzzing fly by his side. Like it, too, our muse, wiping the dust off her long-unused wings, goes blundering through the cobweb of criticism, more dusty

Vol. V

still, — what venerable cobweb is that, which has hitherto escaped the broom, whose spider is invisible, but the *North American Review?* — and carries away the half of it.

No sap flows from the maples I cut into, except that one in Lincoln. What means it? *Hylodes Pickeringii,* a name that is longer than the frog itself! A description of animals, too, from a dead specimen only, as if, in a work on man, you were to describe a dead man only, omitting his manners and customs, his institutions and divine faculties, from want of opportunity to observe them, suggesting, perchance, that the colors of the eye are said to be much more brilliant in the living specimen, and that some cannibal, your neighbor, who has tried him on his table, has found him to be sweet and nutritious, good on the gridiron. Having had no opportunity to observe his habits, because you do not live in the country. Only dindons and dandies. Nothing is known of his habits. Food: seeds of wheat, beef, pork, and potatoes.

P. M. — To Martial Miles Meadow, by boat to Nut Meadow Brook.

Launched my new boat. It is very steady, too steady for me; does not toss enough and communicate the motion of the waves. Beside, the seats are not well arranged; when there are two in it, it requires a heavy stone in the stern to trim. But it holds its course very well with a side wind from being so flat from stem to stern.

The cranberries now make a show under water, and I

always make it a point to taste a few. Fresh clamshells have been left by the muskrats at various heights. C. says he saw a painted tortoise yesterday. Very likely. We started two ducks feeding behind a low spit of meadow. From Brooks's plates I should think them widgeons.[1] They had the grayish-white breasts of the wood duck. They look as if they had dropped from heaven, motionless. Saw a green grasshopper and a common caterpillar, also another beetle similar to that of yesterday, except that this was a sort of slate-color with two or three fawn-colored marks on each wing-case.[2] The spear-heads of the skunk-cabbage are now quite conspicuous. I see that many flowers have been destroyed by the cold. In no case is the spathe unrolled, and I think it is not yet in blossom.

At Nut Meadow Brook, water-bugs and skaters are now plenty. I see the *Emys guttata* with red spots. Some which I think to be the same sex have striated scales, while others are smooth above. What I take to be the female has a flat-edged shell as well as depressed sternum. The yellow spots appear like some yellow wood let in. The spots are brightest when they are in the water. They are in couples. C. saw a frog. Some willows will be out in a day or two. Silvery catkins of all sizes shine afar. The two white feathers of the blue snowbird contrast prettily with the slate.

Returning to river, the water is blue as blue ink from this side. Hubbard's field a smooth russet bank lit by the setting sun and the pale skim-milk sky above.

[1] Brown thinks them sheldrakes. [See p. 65].
[2] *Vide* March 18, 1860.

I told Stacy the other day that there was another volume of De Quincey's Essays (wanting to see it in his library). "I know it," says he, "but I shan't buy any more of them, for nobody reads them." I asked what book in his library was most read. He said, "The Wide, Wide World."

In a little dried and bleached tortoise-shell about an inch and three quarters long, I can easily study his anatomy and the house he lives in. His ribs are now distinctly revealed under his lateral scales, slanted like rafters to the ridge of his roof, for his sternum is so large that his ribs are driven round upon his back. It is wonderful to see what a perfect piece of dovetailing his house is, the different plates of his shell fitting into each other by a thousand sharp teeth or serrations, and the scales always breaking joints over them so as to bind the whole firmly together, all parts of his abode variously interspliced and dovetailed. An architect might learn much from a faithful study of it. There are three large diamond-shaped openings down the middle of the sternum, covered only by the scales, through [which], perhaps, he feels, he breasts the earth. His roof rests on four stout posts. This young one is very deep in proportion to its breadth. The *Emys guttata* is first found in warm, muddy ditches.

The bæomyces is not yet dried up.

March 23. 5 A. M. — I hear the robin sing before I rise.

6 A. M. — Up the North River.

A fresh, cool spring morning. The white maple may

perhaps be said to begin to blossom to-day, — the male, — for the stamens, both anthers and filament, are conspicuous on some buds. It has opened unexpectedly, and a rich sight it is, looking up through the expanded buds to the sky. This and the aspen are the first trees that *ever grow large*, I believe, which show the influence of the season thus conspicuously. From Nawshawtuct I see the snow is off the mountains. A large aspen by the Island is unexpectedly forward. I already see the red anthers appearing. It will bloom in a day or two.

My boat is very good to float and go before the wind, but it has not *run* enough to it, — if that is the phrase, — but lugs too much dead water astern. However, it is all the steadier for it. Methinks it will not be a bad sailer.

I have seen for a week past fresh holes in the sand made by some early burrowing animal, probably the skunk.

One studies books of science merely to learn the language of naturalists, — to be able to communicate with them.

The frost in swamps and meadows makes it good walking there still. Away, away to the swamps, where the silver catkins of the swamp willow shine a quarter of a mile off, — those southward-penetrating vales of Rupert's Land.

The birds which are merely migrating or tarrying here for a season are especially gregarious now, — the redpoll, *Fringilla hyemalis*, fox-colored sparrow, etc. The white maples appear to be confined to the bank of the river.

I judge by the dead bodies of frogs, partially devoured, in brooks and ditches that many are killed in their hibernacula.

Evelyn and others wrote when the language was in a tender, nascent state and could be moulded to express the shades of meaning; when sesquipedalian words, long since cut and apparently dried and drawn to mill, — not yet to the dictionary lumber-yard, — put forth a fringe of green sprouts here and there along in the angles of their rugged bark, their very bulk insuring some sap remaining; some florid suckers they sustain at least. Which words, split into shingles and laths, will supply poets for ages to come.

A man can't ask properly for a piece of bread and butter without some animal spirits. A child can't cry without them.

P. M. — To Howard's meadow.

The telegraph harp sounds more commonly, now that westerly winds prevail. The winds of winter are too boisterous, too violent or rude, and do not strike it at the right angle when I walk, so that it becomes one of the spring sounds.

The ice went out of Walden this forenoon; of Flint's Pond day before yesterday, I have no doubt. Methinks I see a more reddish chestnut sparrow, with distinct whiter lines and two white feathers in tail, or is this the song sparrow? With a faint, tinkling *cheep*. Grass or bay-winged finch? or could it have been field sparrow? but not my seringo. The pads at Howard's meadow are very forward, more than a foot high, their tips above the water.

The cat-tail down puffs and swells in your hand like a mist, or the conjurer's trick of filling a hat with feathers,

Vol. V

for when you have rubbed off but a thimbleful, and can close and conceal the wound completely, the expanded down fills your hand to overflowing. Apparently there is a spring to the fine elastic threads which compose the down, which, after having been so long closely packed, on being the least relieved at the base, spring open apace into the form of parachutes to convey the seed afar. Where birds or the winds or ice have assaulted them, this has spread like an eruption.[1] Again, when I rub off the down of its spike with my thumb, I am surprised at the sensation of warmth it imparts to my hand, as it flushes over it magically, at the same time revealing a faint purplish-crimson tinge at the base of the down, as it rolls off and expands. It is a very pleasing experiment to try.

The buds of the shad-blossom look green. The crimson-starred flowers of the hazel begin to peep out, though the catkins have not opened. The alders are almost generally in full bloom, and a very handsome and interesting show they make with their graceful tawny pendants, inclining to yellow. They shake like ear-drops in the wind, perhaps the first completed ornaments with which the new year decks herself. Their yellow pollen is shaken down and colors my coat like sulphur as I go through them.

I go to look for mud turtles in Heywood's meadow. The alder catkins, just burst open, are prettily marked spirally by streaks of yellow, contrasting with alternate rows of rich reddish-brown scales, which make one revolution in the length of the catkin. I see trout glance

[1] *Vide* amount of seed in *Tribune*, Mar. 16, 1860.

along the brook, as indeed a month ago. I hear in Heywood's north meadow the most unmusical low croak from one or two frogs, though it is half ice there yet, — a remarkable note with which to greet the new year, as if one's teeth slid off with a grating sound in cracking a nut, — but not a frog nor a dimple is to be seen.

Man cannot afford to be a naturalist, to look at Nature directly, but only with the side of his eye. He must look through and beyond her. To look at her is fatal as to look at the head of Medusa. It turns the man of science to stone. I feel that I am dissipated by so many observations. I should be the magnet in the midst of all this dust and filings. I knock the back of my hand against a rock, and as I smooth back the skin, I find myself prepared to study lichens there. I look upon man but as a fungus. I have almost a slight, dry headache as the result of all this observing. How to observe is how to behave. O for a little Lethe! To crown all, lichens, which are so thin, are described in the *dry* state, as they are most commonly, not most truly, seen. Truly, they are *dryly* described.

Without being the owner of any land, I find that I have a civil right in the river, — that, if I am not a land-owner I am a water-owner. It is fitting, therefore, that I should have a boat, a cart, for this my farm. Since it is almost wholly given up to a few of us, while the other highways are much travelled, no wonder that I improve it. Such a one as I will choose to dwell in a township where there are most ponds and rivers and our range is widest. In relation to the river, I find my natural rights least infringed on. It is an extensive "common" still left. Certain savage liberties still prevail in the oldest and most civilized countries. I am pleased to find that, in Gilbert White's day, at least, the laborers in that part of England enjoyed certain rights of common in the royal forests, — so called, though no large wood, — where they cut their turf and other fuel, etc., etc., and obtained materials for broom-making, etc., when other labor failed. It is no longer so, according to his editor. Nobody legislates for me, for the way would be not to legislate at all.

I am surprised as well as delighted when any one wishes to know what I think. It is such a rare use they would make of me, as if they were acquainted with the tool. Commonly, if men want anything of me, it is only to know how many acres I make of their land, or, at most, what trivial news I have burdened myself with. They never will go to law for my meat. They prefer the shell.[1]

I saw probably a milkweed down in the air, the 20th.

March 24. 6 A. M. — By river to Hemlocks.

I see where the muskrats opened clams, probably last evening, close to the water's edge, or in the fork of a willow, or on a tussock just covered with water, the shells remaining, for they bring the clam to the air to eat it. The downy (?) woodpeckers are quite numerous this morning, the skirts of their coats barred with white and a large, long white spot on their backs. They have a smart, shrill peep or whistle, somewhat like

[1] [*Cape Cod, and Miscellanies*, p. 455; *Misc.*, Riv. 253.]

a robin, but more metallic. Saw two gray squirrels coursing over the trees on the Rock Island. The forest is to them a vast web over which they run with as little hesitation as a spider across his net. They appear to have planned or to be familiar with their course before they start. The Island has several bunches of leaves in its trees, probably their nests. For several mornings the water has been perfectly smooth at six o'clock, but by seven the wind has risen with the ascending sun and the waves with the wind, and the day assumed a new and less promising aspect.

I think I may consider the shepherd's-purse in bloom to-day, for its flowers are nearly as conspicuous as those of the stellaria, which had its spring opening some days since, both being the worse for the frost this morning. Since the cold snap of the 14th, 15th, etc., have walked for the most part with unbuttoned coat, and for the most part without mittens.

I find the arrow-headed character on our plains, older than the written character in Persia.

Now are the windy days of March drying up the superabundant moisture. The river does not yet preserve a smooth reflecting surface far into the day. The meadows are mostly bare, the water going down, but perchance the April rains will fill them again.

Last afternoon was moist and cloudy and still, and the robin sang faintly, as if to usher in a warm rainstorm, but it cleared off at evening.

There are very slight but white mists on the river these mornings.

It spits a little snow this afternoon.

P. M. — To Second Division Brook.

The white pine wood, freshly cut, piled by the side of the Charles Miles road, is agreeable to walk beside. I like the smell of it, all ready for the borers, and the rich light-yellow color of the freshly split wood and the purple color of the sap at the ends of the quarters, from which distill perfectly clear and crystalline tears, colorless and brilliant as diamonds, tears shed for the loss of a forest in which is a world of light and purity, its life oozing out. These beautiful accidents that attend on man's works! Fit pendants to the ears of the Queen of Heaven! How full of interest is one of these wrecks of a wood! C. declares that Miss Ripley spent one whole season studying the lichens on a stick of wood they were about to put on the fire. I am surprised to find that these terebinthine (?) tears have a hard (seemingly soft as water) not film but transparent skin over them. How many curiosities are brought to us with our wood! The trees and the lichens that clothe them, the forest warrior and his shield adhering to him.

I have heard of two skeletons dug up in Concord within twenty years, one, at least, undoubtedly an Indian. This was as they were digging away the bank directly behind I. Moore's house. Dr. Jarvis pronounced it an Indian. The other near the jail.

I tied a string round what I take to be the *Alnus incana*, two or three rods this side Jenny's Road, on T. Wheeler's ditch. The bark is of a more opaque and lighter color, the fruit more orbicular, but the most sure difference was that a part of the pistillate catkins were upright. It was not quite in bloom, but neither

were some of those whose fertile catkins drooped, nor could I yet see a difference in the color of the opened catkins.

At Second Division, saw pollywogs again, full grown with long tails. The cowslip leaves are in many places above water, and I see what I suppose is that slender rush two inches high at the bottom of the water like a fine grass. What is that foliaceous plant amid the mosses in the wet which resembles the algæ? I find nothing like it in Hooker under head of Algæ. In many cases I find that the willow cones are a mere dense cluster of loose leaves, suggesting that the scales of cones of all kinds are only modified leaves, a crowding and stinting of the leaves, as the stem becomes a thorn; and in this view those conical bunches of leaves of so many of the pine family have relation to the cones of the tree as well in origin as in form. The leaf, perchance, becomes calyx, cone, husk, and nutshell.

The past has been a remarkable winter; such a one as I do not remember. The ground has been bare almost all the time, and the river has been open about as much. I got but one chance to take a turn on skates over half an acre. The first snow more than an inch deep fell January 13th, but probably was not a foot deep and was soon gone. There was about as much more fell February 13th, and no more to be remembered, *i. e.* only two or three inches since. I doubt if there has been one day when it was decidedly better sleighing than wheeling. I have hardly heard the sound of sleigh-bells. A yellow lily bud already yellow at the Tortoise Ditch, Nut Meadow.

Those little holes in sandy fields and on the sides of hills, which I see so numerously as soon as the snow is off and the frost out of the ground, are probably made by the skunk in search of bugs and worms, as Rice says. His tracks in the winter are very numerous, considering how rarely he is seen at that season. Probably the tortoises do not lay their eggs so early as I thought. The skunk gets them too.

March 25. I forgot to say yesterday that several little groves of alders on which I had set my eye had been cut down the past winter. One in Trillium Woods was a favorite because it was so dense and regular, its outline rounded as if it were a moss bed; and another more than two miles from this, at Dugan's, which I went to see yesterday, was then being cut, like the former, to supply charcoal for powder. Dugan does most of this work about the town. The willow hedges by causeways are regularly trimmed and peeled. The small wood brings eight dollars a cord. Alders, also, and poplars are extensively used.

6 A. M. — To Brister's Hill.

The *Fringilla hyemalis* sing *most* in concert of any bird nowadays that I hear. Sitting near together on an oak or pine in the woods or an elm in the village, they keep up a very pleasant, enlivening, and incessant jingling and twittering *chill-lill-lill*, so that it is difficult to distinguish a single bird's note, — parts of it much like a canary. This sound advances me furthest toward summer, unless it be the note of the lark, who, by the way, is the most steady singer at present. Notwith-

standing the raw and windy mornings, it will sit on a low twig or tussock or pile of manure in the meadow and sing for hours, as sweetly and plaintively as in summer. I see the white-breasted nuthatch, head downward, on the oaks. First heard his rapid and, as it were, angry *gnah gnah gna*, and a *faint*, wiry creaking note about grubs as he moved round the tree. I thought I heard the note of a robin and of a bluebird from an oak. It proceeded from a small bird about as big as a blue-[bird], which did not perch like a woodpecker, uttering first some notes robin-like or like the golden robin, then perfect bluebird warbles,[1] and then it flew off with a flight like neither. From what I saw and heard afterward I suspected it *might* be a downy woodpecker. I see fine little green beds of moss peeping up at Brister's Spring above the water.

When I saw the fungi in my lamp, I was startled and awed, as if I were stooping too low, and should next be found classifying carbuncles and ulcers. Is there not sense in the mass of men who ignore and confound these things, and never see the cryptogamia on the one side any more than the stars on the other? Underfoot they catch a transient glimpse of what they call toadstools, mosses, and frog-spittle, and overhead of the heavens, but they can all read the pillars on a Mexican quarter. They ignore the worlds above and below, keep straight along, and do not run their boots down at the heel as I do. How to keep the heels up I have been obliged to study carefully, turning the nigh foot painfully on side-hills. I find that the shoemakers, to save

[1] Was it not the fox-colored sparrow?

a few iron heel-pegs, do not complete the rows on the inside by three or four, — the very place in the whole boot where they are most needed, — which has fatal consequences to the buyer. I often see the tracks of them in the paths. It is as if you were to put no underpinning under one corner of your house. I have managed to cross very wet and miry places dry-shod by moving rapidly on my heels. I always use leather strings tied in a hard knot; they untie but too easily even then.

The various lights in which you may regard the earth, *e. g.* the dry land as sea bottom, or the sea bottom as a dry down.

Those willow cones appear to be galls, for, cutting open one of the leafy ones, I found a hard core such as are often seen bare, the nucleus of the cone, and in it a grub. This gall had completely checked the extension of the twig, and the leaves had collected and overflowed it as the water at a dam. Perchance when the twig is vigorous and full of sap the cone is leafy; otherwise a hard cone.

11 A. M. — To Framingham.

A Lincoln man heard a flock of geese, he thinks it was day before yesterday.

Measured a white oak in front of Mr. Billings's new house, about one mile beyond Saxonville, — twelve and one twelfth feet in circumference at four feet from the ground (the smallest place within ten feet from the ground), fourteen feet circumference at ground, and a great spread.

Frank's place is on the Concord River within less than ten miles of Whitehall Pond in Hopkinton, one of [the sources], perhaps the principal source, of the river. I thought that a month hence the stream would not be twenty feet wide there. Mr. Wheeler, auctioneer, of Framingham, told me that the timber of the factory at Saxonville was brought by water to within about one mile of where the mill stands. There is a slight rapid.

Brown says that he saw the north end of Long Pond covered with ice the 22d, and that R. W. E. saw the south end entirely open. The red maple buds already redden the swamps and riverside. The winter rye greens the ground.

March 26. There is a large specimen of what I take to be the common alder by the poplar at Egg Rock, five inches in diameter. It may be considered as beginning to bloom to-day. Some white maples appear still as backward as the red.

Saw about 10 A. M. a gaggle of geese, forty-three in number, in a very perfect harrow flying northeasterly. One side [of] the harrow was a little longer than the other. They appeared to be four or five feet apart. At first I heard faintly, as I stood by Minott's gate, borne to me from the southwest through the confused sounds of the village, the indistinct honking of geese. I was somewhat surprised to find that Mr. Loring at his house should have heard and seen the same flock. I should think that the same flock was commonly seen and heard from the distance of a mile east and west. It is remarkable that we commonly see geese go over in the spring about 10 o'clock in the morning, as if they were accustomed to stop for the night at some place southward whence they reached us at that time. Goodwin saw six geese in Walden about the same time.

The scales of the alder run to leaves sometimes.

P. M. — Up Assabet to stone-heaps, in boat.

A warm, moist, April-like afternoon, with wet-looking sky, and misty. For the first time I take off my coat. Everywhere are hovering over the river and floating, wrecked and struggling, on its surface, a miller-like insect, without mealy wings, very long and narrow, six-legged with two long feelers and, I believe, two long slender grayish wings, from my harbor to the heaps, or a couple of miles at least, food for fishes. This was the degree and kind of warmth to bring them forth. The tortoises, undoubtedly painted, drop now in several instances from the limbs and floating rails on which they had come out to sun. I notice by the Island a yellow scum on the water close to the shore, which must be the pollen of the alders just above. This, too, is perhaps food for fishes.

Up the Assabet, scared from his perch a stout hawk, — the red-tailed undoubtedly, for I saw very plainly the cow-red when he spread his wings from off his tail (and rump?). I rowed the boat three times within gunshot before he flew, twice within four rods, while he sat on an oak over the water, — I think because I had two ladies with me, which was as good as bushing the boat. Each time, or twice at least, he made a motion to fly before he started. The ends of his primaries looked

very ragged against the sky. This is the hen-hawk of the farmer, the same, probably, which I have scared off from the Cliff so often. It was an interesting eagle-like object, as he sat upright on his perch with his back to us, now and then looking over his shoulder, the broad-backed, flat-headed, curve-beaked bird.

Heard a pewee. This, it seems to me, is the first true pewee day, though they have been here some time. What is that cress-like weed in and on the edge of the river opposite Prescott Barrett's? A fresher and more luxuriant growth of green leaf than I have seen yet; as if it had grown in winter.

I do not perceive any fresh additions to the stone-heaps, though perhaps I did not examine carefully enough.

Went forth just after sunset. A storm gathering, an April-like storm. I hear now in the dusk only the song sparrow along the fences and a few hylas at a distance. And now the rattling drops compel me to return.

March 27. Sunday. After a long spell of fair weather, the first April-like rain fell last night. But it is fair again this morning with a cool breeze, which will hardly permit the catkins to open. I miss very much the early willows along the railroad, which have been cut down the past winter to prevent catching fire from the engines and spreading to the woods. And hence my neighbor the switch-man has bean-poles to sell.

P. M. — To Martial Miles's.

The skunk-cabbage in full bloom under the Clamshell

Hill; undoubtedly was open yesterday afternoon. Perhaps I might have found one a day earlier still, had I looked here carefully. Call it the 26th. The spathes of those in bloom are open *at least* half an inch wide. Many are decaying, having been killed by that severe cold a fortnight ago, probably; else it would have blossomed earlier. Nevertheless, the spathes appear to furnish a remarkable protection to the spadix, they are so curved over it as well as involved about it, and so roomy. What meant those little pellets of the pollen in one of these vegetable shells? Had some bee left them yesterday? The inside of the shell-like vessel which the spathe makes contains considerable of the yellow pollen of the flower. I fear I may not have got so early a specimen of this as of the other plants thus far, after all. Clusters of stout, curved spear-heads about three inches high; in some the mahogany-color, in some the yellowish green prevails. Some are a very dark mahogany, others almost a clear light yellow. Also the thistles, johns-wort (radical leaves), buttercups, clover, mullein, have grown very decidedly. I see but one tortoise (*Emys guttata*) in Nut Meadow Brook now; the weather is too raw and gusty.

The hazel is fully out. The 23d was perhaps full early to date them. It is in some respects the most interesting flower yet, though so minute that only an observer of nature, or one who looked for them, would notice it. It is the highest and richest colored yet, — ten or a dozen little rays at the end of the buds which are [at] the ends and along the sides of the bare stems. Some of the flowers are a light, some a dark crimson. The high

color of this minute, unobserved flower, at this cold, leafless, and almost flowerless season! It is a beautiful greeting of the spring, when the catkins are scarcely relaxed and there are no signs of life in the bush. Moreover, they are so tender that I never get one home in good condition. They wilt and turn black.

Tried to see the faint-croaking frogs at J. P. Brown's Pond in the woods. They are remarkably timid and shy; had their noses and eyes out, croaking, but all ceased, dove, and concealed themselves, before I got within a rod of the shore. Stood perfectly still amid the bushes on the shore, before one showed himself; finally five or six, and all eyed me, gradually approached me within three feet to reconnoitre, and, though I waited about half an hour, would not utter a sound nor take their eyes off me, — were plainly affected by curiosity. Dark brown and some, perhaps, dark green, about two inches long; had their noses and eyes out when they croaked. If described at all, must be either young of *Rana pipiens* or the *R. palustris*.

That earliest willow I can find, behind Miles's, sheltered by a wood on the north but on high and dry land (!!), will bloom to-morrow if it is pleasant.[1] I see the yellow now. I see the earth freshly stirred and tracks about the woodchuck-holes. So they have been out. You hear that faint croak of frogs and, toward night, a few hylas regularly now. Did not see frog spawn in the pool by Hubbard's Wood. Still the hardhack and meadow-sweet tops are perfect.

The base of the pitch pine cone which, closed, was

[1] *Vide* [p. 80].

semicircular, after it has opened becomes more or less flat and horizontal by the crowding of the scales backward upon the smaller and imperfect ones next the stem, and, viewed on this flat end, they are handsomely arranged in curving rays.

March 28. My Aunt Maria asked me to read the life of Dr. Chalmers, which however I did not promise to do. Yesterday, Sunday, she was heard through the partition shouting to my Aunt Jane, who is deaf, " Think of it! He stood half an hour to-day to hear the frogs croak, and he would n't read the life of Chalmers."

6 A. M. — To Cliffs.

Too cold for the birds to sing much. There appears to be more snow on the mountains. Many of our spring rains are snow-storms there. The woods ring with the cheerful jingle of the *F. hyemalis*. This is a very trig and compact little bird, and appears to be in good condition. The straight edge of slate on their breasts contrasts remarkably with the white from beneath; the short, light-colored bill is also very conspicuous amid the dark slate; and when they fly from you, the two white feathers in their tails are very distinct at a good distance. They are very lively, pursuing each other from bush to bush. Could that be the fox-colored sparrow I saw this morning, — that reddish-brown sparrow? [1]

I do not now think of a bird that *hops* so distinctly, rapidly, and commonly as the robin, with its head up.

Why is the pollen of flowers commonly yellow?

[1] Probably.

I saw yesterday, on the warm pool by Hubbard's Wood, long, narrow blades of reddish grass, bent nearly at right angles and floating on the water, lighter-colored beneath (lake-colored?). The floating part was from six inches to ten or twelve in length. This is much the greatest growth of grass that I have seen, for it is scarcely anywhere yet visibly green. It is an agreeable surprise, flushing the cheek, this warm color on the surface of some warm pool.

P. M. — To Assabet.

Saw eleven black ducks near the bathing-place on the Assabet, flying up the stream. Came within three or four rods of me, then wheeled and went down. Their faint quack sounded much [like] the croak of the frogs occasionally heard now in the pools. As they wheeled and went off, made a very fine whistling sound, which yet I think was not made by their wings.

Opened an ant-hill about two and a half feet wide and eight inches high, in open land. It was light and dry, and apparently made by the ants; free from stones or sticks for about a foot in depth. The ants, which were red with black abdomens and were about a third of an inch long, crawled about sluggishly on being exposed. Their galleries, a quarter of an inch and more in diameter, with ants in them, extended to the depth of two feet in the yellow sand, and how much further I don't know. Opened another in the woods with black ants of the same size in the same condition.

This is a raw, cloudy, and disagreeable day. Yet I think you are most likely to see wild fowl this weather.

Vol. V

I saw in Dodd's yard and flying thence to the alders by the river what I think must be the tree sparrow,[1] — a ferruginous crowned, or headed, and partly winged bird, light beneath, with a few of the *F. hyemalis* in company. It sang sweetly, much like some notes of a canary. One pursued another. It was not large enough for the fox-colored sparrow. Perhaps I have seen it before within the month.

As near as I can make out, the hawks or falcons I am likely to see here are the American sparrow hawk, the fish hawk, the goshawk, the short-winged buzzard (if this is the same with Brown's stuffed sharp-shinned or slate-colored hawk, — not slate in his specimen; is not this the common small hawk that soars?), the red-tailed hawk (have we the red-shouldered hawk, about the same size and aspect with the last?), the hen-harrier. (I suppose it is the adult of this with the slate-color over meadows.)

March 29. 6 A. M. — To Leaning Hemlocks, by boat.

The sun has just risen, but there is only a now clear saffron belt next the east horizon; all the rest of the sky is covered with clouds, broken into lighter and darker shades. An agreeable yellow sunlight falls on the western fields and the banks of the river. Whence this yellow tinge? Probably a different light would be reflected if there were no dark clouds above. A somewhat milder morning than yesterday, and the river as usual quite smooth. From Cheney's boat-house I hear very distinctly the tapping of a woodpecker at the Island about

[1] No doubt of it.

a quarter of a mile. Undoubtedly could hear it twice as far at least, if still, over the water. At every stroke of my paddle, small silvery bubbles about the size of a pin-head, dashed from the surface, slide or roll over the smooth surface a foot or two. On approaching the Island, I am surprised to hear the scolding, cackle-like note of the pigeon woodpecker, a prolonged loud sound somewhat like one note of the robin. This was the tapper, on the old hollow aspen which the small woodpeckers so much frequent. Unless the latter make *exactly* the same sound with the former, then the pigeon woodpecker has come! ! But I could not get near enough to distinguish his size and colors. He went up the Assabet, and I heard him cackling and tapping far ahead.

The catkins of the *Populus tremuloides* are just beginning to open, — to curl over and downward like caterpillars. Yesterday proved too cold, undoubtedly, for the willow to open, and unless I learn better, I shall give the poplar the precedence, dating both, however, from to-day.[1]

It would be worth the while to attend more to the different notes of the blackbirds. Methinks I may have seen the female red-wing within a day or two; or what are these purely black ones without the red shoulder? It is pleasant to see them scattered about on the drying meadow. The red-wings will stand close to the water's edge, looking larger than usual, with their red shoulders very distinct and handsome in that position, and sing *okolee*, or *bob-y-lee*, or what-not. Others, on the tops of trees over your head, out of a fuzzy beginning spit forth a clear, shrill whistle incessantly, for what purpose I

[1] *Vide* [p. 70].

don't know. Others, on the elms over the water, utter still another note, each time lifting their wings slightly. Others are flying across the stream with a loud *char-r, char-r*.

Looking at the mouth of a woodchuck-hole and at low places, as on the moss, in the meadows, [I see] that those places are sprinkled with little pellets or sometimes salt-shaped masses of frost some inches apart, apparently like snow. This is one kind of frost.

There is snow and ice still along the edge of the meadows on the north side of woods; the latter even five or six inches thick in some places.

The female flowers of the white maple, crimson stigmas from the same rounded masses of buds with the male, are now quite abundant. I think they have not come out more than a day or two. I did not notice them the 26th, though I did not look carefully for them. The two sorts of flowers are not only on the same tree and the same twig and sometimes in the same bud, but also sometimes in the same little cup. The recent shoot of the white maple is now a yellowish brown, sprinkled with ashy dots.

I am in some uncertainty about whether I do not confound several kinds under the name of the downy woodpecker. It not only flies *volatu undoso*, but you hear, as it passes over you, the strong ripple of its wings.

Two or three times, when a visitor stayed into evening, and it proved a dark night, I was obliged to conduct him to the cart-path in the rear of my house and then point out to him the direction he was to pursue, and in keeping which he was to be guided rather by his feet

Vol. V

than his eyes. One very dark night I directed thus on their way two young men who had been fishing in the pond, who would otherwise have been at a loss what course to take. They lived about a mile off, and were quite used to the woods. A day or two after, one of them told me that they wandered about the greater part of the night, close by their own premises, and did not get home till toward morning, by which time, as there were several heavy showers in the course of the night, and the leaves were very wet, they were drenched to their skins. I have heard of many going astray, even in the village streets, when the darkness was so thick that you could cut it with a knife, as the phrase is. Some who lived in the outskirts, having come to town shopping with their wagons, have been obliged to put up for the night, and gentlemen and ladies making a call have gone half a mile out of their way, feeling the sidewalk only and not knowing when they turned, and were obliged to inquire the way at the first house they discovered. Even one of the village doctors was thus lost in the heart of the village on a nocturnal mission, and spent nearly the whole night feeling the fences and the houses, being, as he said, ashamed to inquire. If one with the vision of an owl, or as in broad daylight, could have watched his motions, they would have been ludicrous indeed. It is a novel and memorable acquaintance one may make thus with the most familiar objects. It is a surprising and memorable and, I may add, valuable experience to be lost in the woods, especially at night. Sometimes in a snow-storm, even by day, one will come out upon a well-known road and yet find it impossible

to tell which way leads to the village. Though your reason tells you that you have travelled it one hundred times, yet no object looks familiar, but it is as strange to you as if it were in Tartary. By night, of course, the perplexity is infinitely greater. We are constantly steering like pilots by certain well-known beacons and headlands, though we are not conscious of it, and if we go beyond our usual course we still preserve the bearing of some neighboring cape, and not till we are completely lost or turned round, — for a man needs only to be turned round once with his eyes shut in this world to be lost, — do we appreciate the vastness and strangeness of nature. Every man has once more to learn the points of compass as often as he awakes, whether from sleep or from any abstraction. In fact, not till we are lost do we begin to realize where we are, and the infinite extent of our relations.[1]

A pleasant short voyage is that to the Leaning Hemlocks on the Assabet, just round the Island under Nawshawtuct Hill. The river here has in the course of ages gullied into the hill, at a curve, making a high and steep bank, on which a few hemlocks grow and overhang the deep, eddying basin. For as long as I can remember, one or more of these has always been slanting over the stream at various angles, being undermined by it, until one after another, from year to year, they fall in and are swept away. This is a favorite voyage for ladies to make, down one stream and up the other, plucking the lilies by the way and landing on the Island, and concluding with a walk on Nawshawtuct Hill.

¹ [*Walden*, pp. 188–190; Riv. 266–268.]

This which Gilbert White says of the raven is applicable to our crow: "There is a peculiarity belonging to ravens that must draw the attention even of the most incurious — they spend all their leisure time in striking and cuffing each other on the wing in a kind of playful skirmish."

P. M. — To early willow behind Martial Miles's.

A bright, sunny, but yet rather breezy and cool afternoon. On the railroad I hear the telegraph. This is the lyre that is as old as the world. I put my ear to the post, and the sound seems to be in the core of the post, directly against my ear. This is all of music. The utmost refinements of art, methinks, can go no further. This is one of those days divided against itself, when there is a cool wind but a warm sun, when there is little or no coolness proper to this locality, but it is wafted to us probably from the snow-clad northwest, and hence in sheltered places it is very warm. However, the sun is rapidly prevailing over the wind, and it is already warmer than when I came out.

Four ducks, two by two, are sailing conspicuously on the river. There appear to be two pairs. In each case one two-thirds white and another grayish-brown and, I think, smaller. They are very shy and fly at fifty rods' distance. Are they whistlers? The white are much more white than those I saw the other day and at first thought summer ducks.[1] Would it not be well to carry a

¹ [See p. 40.] These were either mergansers or the golden-eye; I think the former, *i. e. Mergus serrator*, or red-breasted merganser (?), or sheldrake.

Fair Haven Bay through the Woods

Conantum Pool

spy-glass in order to watch these shy birds such as ducks and hawks? In some respects, methinks, it would be better than a gun. The latter brings them nearer dead, but the former alive. You can identify the species better by killing the bird, because it was a dead specimen that was so minutely described, but you can study the habits and appearance best in the living specimen. These ducks first flew north, or somewhat against the wind (was it to get under weigh?), then wheeled, flew nearer me, and went south up-stream, where I saw them afterward.

In one of those little holes which I refer to the skunk, I found part of the shell of a *reddish* beetle or dor-bug. Both hole and beetle looked quite fresh. Saw small ants there active.

Under the south side of Clamshell Hill, in the sun, the air is filled with those black fuzzy gnats, and I hear a fine hum from them. The first humming of insects — unless of those honey-bees the other day — of the season. I can find no honey-bees in the skunk-cabbage this pleasant afternoon. I find that many of the oak-balls are pierced, and their inhabitants have left them; they have a small round hole in them. The rest have still thirty or forty small white maggots about one twelfth of an inch long. Thus far I have not seen these balls but on the black oak, and some are still full of them, like apples.

Walking along near the edge of the meadow under Lupine Hill, I slumped through the sod into a muskrat's nest, for the sod was only two inches thick over it, which was enough when it was frozen. I laid it open with my hands. There were three or four channels or hollowed

paths, a rod or more in length, not merely worn but made in the meadow, and centring at the mouth of this burrow. They were three or four inches deep, and finally became indistinct and were lost amid the cranberry vines and grass toward the river. The entrance to the burrow was just at the edge of the upland, here a gently sloping bank, and was probably just beneath the surface of the water six weeks ago. It was about twenty-five rods distant from the true bank of the river. From this a straight gallery, about six inches in diameter every way, sloped upward about eight feet into the bank just beneath the turf, so that the end was about a foot higher than the entrance. There was a somewhat circular enlargement about one foot in horizontal diameter and the same depth with the gallery; and [in] it was nearly a peck of coarse meadow stubble, showing the marks of the scythe, with which was mixed accidentally a very little of the moss which grew with it. Three short galleries, only two feet long, were continued from this centre somewhat like rays toward the high land, as if they had been prepared in order to be ready for a sudden rise of the water, or had been actually made so far under such an emergency. The nest was of course thoroughly wet and, humanly speaking, uncomfortable, though the creature could breathe in it. But it is plain that the muskrat cannot be subject to the toothache. I have no doubt this was made and used last winter, for the grass was as fresh as that in the meadow (except that it was pulled up), and the sand which had been taken out lay partly in a flattened heap in the meadow, and no grass had sprung up through it.

Vol. V

In the course of the above examination I made a very interesting discovery. When I turned up the thin sod from over the damp cavity of the nest, I was surprised to see at this hour of a pleasant day what I took to be beautiful frost crystals of a rare form, — frost bodkins I was in haste to name them, for around the fine white roots of the grass, apparently the herd's-grass, which were from one to two or more inches long, reaching downward into the dark, damp cavern (though the green blades had scarcely made so much growth above; indeed, the growth was scarcely visible there), appeared to be lingering still into the middle of this warm afternoon rare and beautiful frost crystals exactly in the form of a bodkin, about one sixth of an inch wide at base and tapering evenly to the lower end, sometimes the upper part of the core being naked for half an inch, which last gave them a slight resemblance to feathers, though they were not flat but round, and at the abrupt end of the rootlet (as if cut off) a larger, clear drop. On examining them more closely, feeling and tasting them, I found that it was not frost but a clear, crystalline dew in almost invisible drops, concentrated from the dampness of the cavern, and perhaps melted frost still reserving by its fineness its original color, thus regularly arranged around the delicate white fibre; and, looking again, incredulous, I discerned extremely minute white threads or gossamer standing out on all sides from the main rootlet in this form and affording the core for these drops. Yet on those fibres which had lost their dew, none of these minute threads appeared. There they pointed downward somewhat

like stalactites, or very narrow caterpillar brushes. It impressed me as a wonderful piece of chemistry, that the very grass we trample on and esteem so cheap should be thus wonderfully nourished, that this spring greenness was not produced by coarse and cheap means, but in sod, out of sight, the most delicate and magical processes are going on. The half is not shown. The very sod is replete with mechanism far finer than that of a watch, and yet it is cast under our feet to be trampled on. The process that goes on in the sod and the dark, about the minute fibres of the grass, — the chemistry and the mechanics, — before a single green blade can appear above the withered herbage, if it could [be] adequately described, would supplant all other revelations. We are acquainted with but one side of the sod. I brought home some tufts of the grass in my pocket, but when I took it out I could not at first find those pearly white fibres and thought that they were lost, for they were shrunk to dry brown threads; and, as for the still finer gossamer which supported the roscid droplets, with few exceptions they were absolutely undiscoverable, — they no longer stood out around the core, — so fine and delicate was their organization. It made me doubt almost if there were not actual, substantial, though invisible cores to the leaflets and veins of the hoar frost. And can these almost invisible and tender fibres penetrate the earth where there is no cavern? Or is what we call the solid earth porous and cavernous enough for them?

A wood tortoise in Nut Meadow Brook.

I see a little three-spotted sparrow, — apparently

the same seen March 18th, — with its mate, not so spotted. The first apparently the female, quite tame. The male sings a regular song sparrow strain, and they must be that, I think. Keep up a faint chip. Apparently thinking of a nest.

The trout glances like a film from side to side and under the bank.

Saw a solid mass of green conferva at the bottom of the brook, waved with the sand which had washed into it, which made it look exactly like a rock partly covered with green lichens. I was surprised when I thrust a stick into it and was undeceived. Observe the shadow of water flowing rapidly over a shelving bottom in this brook, producing the appearance of sand washing along.

Tried several times to catch a skater. Got my hand close to him; grasped at him as quick as possible; was sure I had got him this time; let the water run out between my fingers; hoped I had not crushed him; opened my hand; and lo! he was not there. I never succeeded in catching one. What are those common snails in the mud in ditches, with their feet out, for some time past?

The early willow will bloom to-morrow. Its catkins have lost many of their scales. The crowded yellow anthers are already bursting out through the silvery down, like the sun of spring through the clouds of winter. How measuredly this plant has advanced, sensitive to the least change of temperature, its expanding not to be foretold, unless you can foretell the weather. This is the earliest willow that I know.

Yet it is on a dry upland. There is a great difference in localities in respect to warmth, and a corresponding difference in the blossoming of plants of the same species. But can this be the same species with that early one in Miles's Swamp? Its catkins have been picked off, by what?

Dugan tells me that three otter were dug out the past winter in Deacon Farrar's wood-lot, side of the swamp, by Powers and Willis of Sudbury. He has himself seen one in the Second Division woods. He saw two pigeons to-day. *Prated* [*sic*] for them; they came near and then flew away. He saw a woodchuck yesterday. I believe I saw the slate-colored marsh hawk to-day. I saw water-worn stones by the gates of three separate houses in Framingham the other day. The grass now looks quite green in those places where the water recently stood, in grassy hollows where the melted snow collects. Dugan wished to get some guinea-hens to keep off the hawks.

Those fine webs of the grass fibres stood out as if drawn out and held up by electricity.

March 30. April weather, alternate rain and brightening up. I am not sure my willow will bloom fairly to-day. How warily the flowers open! not to be caught out too early, not bursting into bloom with the first genial heat, but holding back as if foreseeing the transient checks, and yielding only to the absolute progress of the season. However, probably some hardy flowers which are quite ready will open just before a cold snap, while others, which were almost

equally advanced, may be retarded a week. Is it not the pollen which the bees seek in the earliest flowers, as the skunk-cabbage (?) and the willow, having occasion for bee-bread first? As usual, the robin sings more this cloudy and showery morning than I have heard it yet.

P. M. — To Cliffs.

The gooseberry leaves in the garden are just *beginning* to show a little green. Is this the same with the wild? Lilacs have buds equally advanced.

Seeing one of those little holes (which I have thought were made by beetles or dor-bugs) in Wheeler's upland rye-field near the Burying-Ground, the mouth walled about like a well with a raised curb with fragments of dried grass and little bits of wood, I resolved to explore it, but after the first shovelful I lost the trace of it, for I had filled it with sand. Finding another, I stuck a mullein stalk into it to a surprising depth, and then could dig with confidence. At fifteen or sixteen inches from the surface, I found a black spider, nearly three quarters of an inch long in the body, clasping the mullein, but very sluggish, only moving its legs, but not crawling away. In another hole I found another similar spider in exactly the same condition and at the same depth, but in this case my stick went down only one foot and was there stopped by ice, which filled the hole, but after digging through an inch of frozen ground, I found the spider in the dry cavity, three or four inches deeper. How the water stood so as to freeze above him I don't know. I could see nothing like a nest at the bottom, nor any

enlargement of the hole. The soil is very sandy and light. In the sand beneath the frost was a moving common red earthworm. I did not expect to find frost in such a place now.

Now commences the season for fires in the woods. The winter, and now the sun and winds, have dried the old leaves more thoroughly than ever, and there are no green leaves to shade the ground or to check the flames, and these high March winds are the very ones to spread them. It is a dry, windy, and withal hazy day, — that blue smoky haze that reminds of fires, which some have thought the effect of distant fires in the woods, which perhaps is only a finer mist, produced by the increased heat of the sun on an earth abounding in moisture. Is not this White's London smoke (*vide* Commonplace-Book), and followed by rain? The woods look peculiarly dry and russet. There is as yet no new greenness in the landscape. With these thoughts and impressions I had not gone far before I saw the smoke of a fire on Fair Haven Hill. Some boys were going *sassafrasing*, for boys will have some pursuit peculiar to every season. A match came in contact with a marble, nobody knew how, and suddenly the fire flashed up the broad open hillside, consuming the low grass and sweet-fern and leaving a smoking, blackened waste. A few glowing stumps, with spadefuls of fresh earth thrown on them, the white ashes here and there on the black ground, and the not disagreeable scent of smoke and cinders was all that was left when I arrived.

I see from the Cliffs that the young oaks look thin,

are losing their leaves. A warm, breezy wind roves in the woods. Dry leaves, which I at first mistake for birds, go sailing through the air in front of the Cliff. The distant highways, I perceive, begin to be dusty; sandy fields to be dry. There is an inspiriting strong ripple on the river, which seems to flow up-stream.

I see again that same kind of clouds that I saw the 10th of last April, low in the sky; higher and overhead those great downy clouds, equal to the intervals of celestial blue, with glowing edges and with wet bases. The sky is mapped with them as with New Hollands and Borneos. There are mares'-tails and rosettes in the west.

The motions of a hawk correcting the flaws in the wind by raising his shoulder from time to time, are much like those of a leaf yielding to them. For the little hawks are hunting now. You have not to sit long on the Cliffs before you see one. I still see fresh earth where the skunk, if it is he, has been probing last night for insects about the pines in pastures and any dead twigs that afford lurking-places. Saw a dead cricket in one. They make a hole sometimes so deep and pointed that only two fingers will fathom it. If dor-bugs make such holes as the spiders, they can easily find them.

I am surprised to find many of the early sedge already out. It may have been out a day or two. I should put it between the skunk-cabbage and the aspen, — at any rate, before the last. Little black ants in the pitchy-looking earth about the base of white pines in woods are still dormant.

Ah, those youthful days! are they never to return? when the walker does not too curiously observe particulars, but sees, hears, scents, tastes, and feels only himself, — the phenomena that show themselves in him, — his expanding body, his intellect and heart. No worm or insect, quadruped or bird, confined his view, but the unbounded universe was his. A bird is now become a mote in his eye.

Dug into what I take to be a woodchuck's burrow in the low knoll below the Cliffs. It was in the side of the hill and sloped gently downward at first, diagonally, into the hill about five feet, perhaps westerly, then turned and ran north into the hill about three feet, then northwest further into the hill four feet, then north again five feet, then northeast I know not how far, the last five feet perhaps ascending. It was the full length of the shovel from the surface of the ground to the bottom of the hole when I left off, owing, perhaps, to the rise of the hill. The hole was arched above and flat on the bottom like an oven, about five inches [in] diameter at base, and it seemed to have a pretty hard crust as I broke into it. There was a little enlargement, perhaps ten inches in diameter, in the angle at the end of twelve feet. It was thus. It was a wonder where the sand was conveyed to, for there was not a wheelbarrow-load at the entrance.

March 31. The robins sing at the very earliest dawn. I wake with their note ringing in my ear.

6 A. M. — To Island by boat.

The pickerels dart away from the shallows, where they have spent the night. It is spearing-time, then. The chickadee sings, not merely *phebe* but *phe-be-be*. Heard a note like that of the warbling vireo from a bird in Cheney's elm which I think must be a fox-colored sparrow. Should think it a vireo if it could be here now.

9 A. M. — To Lincoln, surveying for Mr. Austin.

The catkins of the hazel are now trembling in the wind and much lengthened, showing yellowish and beginning to shed pollen.

Saw and heard sing in a peach orchard my *warbling vireo* of the morning. It must be the fox-colored sparrow. It is plumper than a bluebird, tail fox-colored, a distinct spot on the breast, no bars visible on wings. Beginning with a clear, rich, deliberate note, jingling more rapidly at the end; much like the warbling vireo at the end.

I afterward heard a fine concert of little songsters along the edge of the meadow. Approached and watched and listened for more than half an hour. There were many little sparrows, difficult to detect, flitting and hopping along and scratching the ground like hens, under the alders, willows, and cornels in a wet leafy place, occasionally alighting on a low twig and preening themselves. They had bright-bay crowns, two rather indistinct white bars on wings, an ashy breast and dark tail. These twittered sweetly, some parts very much like a canary and many together, making it the fullest and sweetest I have heard yet, — like a

shopful of canaries. The blackbirds may make more noise. About the size of a song sparrow. I think these are the tree sparrow. Also, mixed with them, and puzzling me to distinguish for a long time, were many of the fox-colored (?) sparrows mentioned above, with a creamy cinnamon-tinged ashy breast, cinnamon shoulderlet, ashy about side head and throat, a fox-colored tail; a size larger than the others; the spot on breast very marked. Were evidently two birds intimately mixed. Did not Peabody confound them when he mentioned the mark on the breast of the tree sparrow? The rich strain of the fox-colored sparrow, as I think it is, added much to the quire. The latter solos, the former in concert. I kept off a hawk by my presence. These were for a long time invisible to me, except when they flitted past.

Heard the jingle of the rush sparrow.

A range-pole on the side of Mt. Tabor, twenty-odd feet long and ten or twelve from the ground, slanted upward on three forked posts like a rafter, a bower being opposite the lower end two rods off, and this end of the pole full of shot.

Mt. Tabor. — When the air is a little hazy, the mountains are particularly dark blue. It is affecting to see a distant mountain-top, like the summits of Uncannunuc, well seen from this hill, whereon you camped for a night in your youth, which you have never revisited, still as blue and ethereal to your eyes as is your memory of it. It lies like an isle in the far heavens, a part of earth unprophaned, which does not bear a price in the market, is not advertised by the real estate broker.

There is another fire in the horizon, and there was one also yesterday on the side of this hill. What is that forward weed, its narrow green leaves floating at end of a long stem, in springs for cattle south side this hill, somewhat potamogeton-like?[1]

Brown has these birds set up which I may wish to examine:—

Turtle-dove, green heron, *Ardea Herodias*, pileated woodpecker, fox-colored sparrow, young of purple finch, white-eyed vireo, goldfinch, brown creeper, scarlet tanager (male and female), white-breasted nuthatch, solitary vireo, red-eyed vireo, yellow redpoll warbler, hermit thrush (killed here), cardinal grosbeak, pine grosbeak, black-billed cuckoo, mockingbird, woodcock, *Totanus flavipes* (or small yellow-leg), (great ditto?), Bartram's tatler (or upland plover), golden ditto, *Falco sparverius*, sharp-shinned or slate-colored hawk, or *F. Pennsylvanicus* of Wilson, green-winged teal, blue-winged teal, wood duck (young drakes).

[1] *Callitriche verna. Vide* May 2d.

II

APRIL, 1853

(ÆT. 35)

April 1. Of the small and ambiguous sparrow family, methinks I have seen only the song sparrow, that one with white feathers in tail seen March 23d, the tree sparrow; and heard the field or rush sparrow. I have for some time noticed the large yellow lily roots. Thus far we have had very little if any freshet this year, — none since spring came in, I believe. The river has been going down a month, at least.

P. M. — To Dugan's.

The three spots on breast of the song sparrow seem to mark a difference of sex. At least, the three-spotted is the one I oftenest hear sing of late. The accompanying one is lighter beneath and one-spotted. One of the former by J. P. Brown's meadow-side, selecting the top of a bush, after lurking and feeding under the alders, sang *olit olit olit|* (faster) *chip chip chip che char|* (fast) *che wiss wiss wiss.*[1] The last bar was much varied, and sometimes one *olit* omitted in the first. This, I have no doubt, is my bird of March 18th. Another three-spotted sang *vit chit chit char| weeter char| tee chu.*

Saw ten black ducks at Clamshell. Had already started two, who probably occupied an outpost. They

[1] [*Walden,* p. 343; Riv. 480.]

all went off with a loud and disagreeable quacking like ducks in a poultry-yard, their wings appearing lighter beneath.

It has rained all night and this forenoon, and now begins to clear up. The rain rests on the downy leaves of the young mulleins in separate, irregular drops, from their irregularity and color looking like ice. The drops quite in the cup of the mullein have a peculiar translucent silveriness, apparently because, being upheld by the wool, it reflects the light which would otherwise be absorbed, as if cased in light. The fresh mullein leaves are pushing up amid the brown unsightly wreck of last fall, which strews the ground like old clothes, — these the new patches.

The gooseberry in Brown's pasture shows no green yet, though ours in the garden does. The former is on the north side of a hill. Many blackbirds in concert, like leaves on the trees. The hazel stigmas now more *fully* out, curving over and a third of an inch long, that the catkins begin to shed pollen. In a skunk's probing, several dead and bruised small black crickets with a brassy tinge or reflection.

That early willow by Miles's (which I have little doubt is Gray's *Salix eriocephala*[1]) has been injured by the rain. The drops rest on the catkins as on the mullein. Though this began to open only day before yesterday and was the earliest I could find, already I hear the well-known hum of a honey-bee, and one alights on it (also a fly or two), loads himself, circles round with a loud humming and is off. Where the first wil-

[1] [Two interrogation-points in pencil here.]

low catkin opens, there will be found the honey-bee also with it. He found this out as soon as I. The stamens have burst out on the side toward the top, like a sheaf of spears thrust forth to encounter the sun, so many spears as the garrison can spare, advanced into the spring. With this flower, so much more flower-like or noticeable than any yet, begins a new era in the flower season.

The early sedge is very fit to be the earliest grass that flowers here, appearing in the midst of dry tufts more than half hay.

Heard, I have very little doubt, the strain of my seringo[1] in the midst of the strain of a song sparrow, I believe with three spots.

Starlight by river up Assabet.

Now, at early starlight, I hear the snipe's hovering note as he circles over Nawshawtuct Meadow. Only once did I seem to see him; occasionally his squeak. He is now heard near, now farther, but is sure to circle round again. It sounds very much like a winnowing-machine increasing rapidly in intensity for a few seconds.

There will be no moon till toward morning. A slight mist is rising from the surface of the water. Hear what I should not hesitate to call the squeak of the nighthawk, — only Wilson makes them arrive early in May, — also over the meadow. Can it be the snipe? It is a little fainter than the nighthawk, perhaps, but it is further off.[2]

[1] [Two interrogation-points in pencil here.]
[2] It may be the squeak of the snipe mentioned by Nuttall. May be woodcock.

Without a mist the river appears indefinitely wide. Looking westward, the water, still reflecting the twilight, appears elevated, and the shore-line, being invisible, lost against the distant highland, is referred toward the highland against which it is seen, for the slope of the hill and the expanse of the meadow cannot be appreciated, appearing only edgewise as height. We therefore make the water, which extends but a rod or two, wash the base of hills a quarter of a mile distant. There are but three elements in the landscape now, — the star-studded sky, the water, reflecting the stars and the lingering daylight, and the dark but comparatively narrow land between. At first there was no fog.

Hear ducks, disturbed, make a quacking or loud croaking. Now, at night, the scent of muskrats is very strong in particular localities. Next to the skunk it is perceived further than that of any of our animals that I think of. I perceive no difference between this and the musk with which ladies scent themselves, though here I pronounce it a strong, rank odor. In the faint reflected twilight, I distinguish one rapidly swimming away from me, leaving a widening ripple behind, and now hear one plunge from some willow or rock. A faint croaking from over the meadow up the Assabet, exactly like frogs. Can it be ducks? They stop when I walk toward them. How happens it that I never found them on the water when spearing? Now and then, when I pass an opening in the trees which line the shore, I am startled by the reflection of some brighter star from a bay.

Ascend Nawshawtuct. See a fire in horizon toward Boston. The first spearer's fire I have noticed is floating along the meadow-side in the south. The mist is now all gone. The baying of dogs is borne to me with great loudness down the river. We still have the wolf in the village.

April 2. 5.30 A. M. — Down railroad.

Ground white with frost and slippery. Thin ice formed over pools. The beaked hazel pistillate blossoms (*i. e.* by Walden road). Do not find its flower described. Are not its catkins distinct from the common in not being stalked? The tree sparrows and a few blue snowbirds in company sing (the former) very sweetly in the garden this morning. I now see a faint spot on the breast. It says something like *a twee twee, chit chit, chit chit chee var-r.* Notice still plenty of sumach berries, *Juniperus repens* (those in shade green, in light turning purplish), green-briar, and a few barberries, etc., etc.

The farmers are trembling for their poultry nowadays. I heard the scream of hens, and a tumult among their mistresses (at Dugan's), calling them and scaring away the hawk, yesterday. They say they do not lose by hawks in midsummer. White quotes Linnæus as saying of hawks, "Paciscuntur inducias cum avibus, quamdiu cuculus cuculat," but White doubts it.

" 'Beetles, flies, worms, form part of the lion and tiger's food, as they do that of the fox.' See Jarrold's Dissert. on Man." [1] (Mitford, Note to White's "Selborne.")

[1] [*Dissertations on Man*, London, 1806, p. 232. Mitford's quotation, if it is from Jarrold, is inexact.]

Found twenty or thirty of the little brown nuts of the skunk-cabbage deposited on a shelf of the turf under an apple tree by E. Hubbard's close, as I have done before. What animal uses them?

The song sparrows, the three-spotted, away by the meadow-sides, are very shy and cunning: instead of flying will frequently trot along the ground under the bushes, or dodge through a wall like a swallow; and I have observed that they generally bring some object, as a rail or branch, between themselves and the face of the walker, — often with outstretched necks will peep at him anxiously for five or ten minutes.

P. M. — To Second Division Brook.

The rain cleared away yesterday afternoon, and today that haziness is all gone, and the air is remarkably clear. I can see houses with distinct and sharp outlines at a great distance, though there is a little seething shimmer in the air. Especially I can see far into the pine woods to tree behind tree and one tower behind another of silvery needles, stage above stage, relieved with shade. The edge of the wood is not a plane surface, but has depth. Was that *Rana fontinalis* or *pipiens* in the pool by E. Wood's railroad crossing? The first large frog I have seen. C. says a wasp lit on him.

A wood tortoise by river above Derby's Bridge; extreme length of shell seven and three eighths inches, extreme breadth five inches across the back part, fore part about one half inch less, and a trifle less still in middle. The orange-color of its inner parts. It was

sluggish, lean, and I judged old from the shell being worn beneath and it not resisting much when I drew out its claws; unlike [in] these respects to one I after found. Irides golden. A singularly flat and broad head with a beak slanting backward much like a snake's head. There were some hundreds of small dark-colored leeches in masses in the chink over his tail and under his hind quarters, a kind of vermin they are much infested by. The same was the case with second one.

Heard and saw what I call the pine warbler, — *vetter vetter vetter vetter vet,* — the cool woodland sound. The first this year of the higher-colored birds, after the bluebird and the blackbird's wing; is it not? It so affects me as something more tender. Together with the driftwood on the shore of the Assabet and the sawdust from Heywood's mill, I pick up teasel-heads from the factory with the wool still in them. How many tales the stream tells! The poplars by the railroad and near Harrington's, male aspens, begin to-day. A turtle dove. It sailed like a hawk. Heard the hooting owl in Ministerial Swamp. It sounded somewhat like the hounding or howling of some dogs, and as often as the whistle of the engine sounded, I noticed a resemblance in the tone. A singular kind of squealing introduced into its note. See the larger red-and-black-abdomen ants at work. See the fine moss in the pastures with beautiful red stems even crimsoning the ground. This is its season. The amelanchier buds look more forward than those of any shrub I notice. The cowslip at Second Division shows the yellow in its bud; will blossom in four or five days. I see the skins of many caddis-worms in the water there. Have not the ephemeræ already flown? Again I notice the sort of small green ova in the water there like frog's ova, on the weeds and even on the shells of the snails. The stem, so to speak, of a cocoon, — though it inclosed the leaf-stem of the plant (a viburnum) it was on, and so put on the guise of the leaf, — was still so strongly fastened about the main stem that I broke the latter in getting it off. Cheney's elm blossomed to-day. Many others scarcely a day behind it.

We cannot well afford not to see the geese go over a single spring, and so commence our year regularly.

Observed the first female willow just coming out, apparently *Salix eriocephala*, just beyond woods by Abel Hosmer's field by railroad. Apparently the female willows, as well as white maples and poplars, are a few days later than the males. The swollen red maple buds now conspicuously tinge the tops of the trees.

Methinks some birds are earlier this year because the ground has been bare so long. Observed some plowing yesterday.

April 3. Saturday. Nothing is more saddening than an ineffectual and proud intercourse with those of whom we expect sympathy and encouragement. I repeatedly find myself drawn toward certain persons but to be disappointed. No concessions which are not radical are the least satisfaction. By myself I can live and

thrive, but in the society of incompatible friends I starve. To cultivate their society is to cherish a sore which can only be healed by abandoning them. I cannot trust my neighbors whom I know any more than I can trust the law of gravitation and jump off the Cliffs.

The last two *Tribunes* I have not looked at. I have no time to read newspapers. If you chance to live and move and have your being in that thin stratum in which the events which make the news transpire, — thinner than the paper on which it is printed, — then these things will fill the world for you; but if you soar above or dive below that plane, you cannot remember nor be reminded of them.[1]

No fields are so barren to me as the men of whom I expect everything but get nothing. In their neighborhood I experience a painful yearning for society, which cannot be satisfied, for the hate is greater than the love.

P. M. — To Cliffs.
At Hayden's I hear hylas on two keys or notes. Heard one after the other, it might be mistaken for the varied note of one. The little croakers, too, are very lively there. I get close to them and witness a great commotion and half hopping, half swimming, about, with their heads out, apparently in pursuit of each other, — perhaps thirty or forty within a few square yards and fifteen or twenty within one yard. There is not only the incessant lively croaking of many

[1] [*Cape Cod, and Miscellanies*, p. 472; *Misc.*, Riv. 275.]

together, as usually heard, but a lower, hoarser, squirming, screwing kind of croak, perhaps from the other sex. As I approach nearer, they disperse and bury themselves in the grass at the bottom; only one or two remain outstretched on the surface, and, at another step, these, too, conceal themselves.

Looking up the river yesterday, in a direction opposite to the sun, not long before it set, the water was of a rich, dark blue — while looking at it in a direction diagonal to this, *i. e.* northeast, it was nearly slate-colored.

To my great surprise the saxifrage is in bloom. It was, as it were, by mere accident that I found it. I had not observed any particular forwardness in it, when, happening to look under a projecting rock in a little nook on the south side of a stump, I spied one little plant which had opened three or four blossoms high up the Cliff. Evidently you must look very sharp and faithfully to find the first flower, such is the advantage of position, and when you have postponed a flower for a week and are turning away, a little further search may reveal it. Some flowers, perhaps, have advantages one year which they have not the next. This spring, as well as the past winter, has been remarkably free from snow, and this reason, and the plant being hardy withal, may account for its early blossoming. With what skill it secures moisture and heat, growing commonly in a little bed of moss which keeps it moist, and lying low in some cleft of the rock! The sunniest and most sheltered exposures possible it secures. This faced the southeast, was nearly a foot under the eaves of the rock,

had not raised its little strawberry-like cluster of buds in the least above the level of its projecting, calyx-like leaves. It was shelter within shelter. The blasts sweep over it. Ready to shoot upward when it shall be warm. The leaves of those which have been more exposed are turned red. It is a very pretty, snug plant with its notched leaves, one of the neatest and prettiest leaves seen now.

A blackberry vine which lay over the rock was beginning to leave out, as much or more than the gooseberry in the garden, such was the reflected heat. The Missouri currant is perhaps more advanced than the early gooseberry in our garden. The female *Populus tremuliformis* catkins, narrower and at present more red and somewhat less downy than the male, west side of railroad at Deep Cut, quite as forward as the male in this situation. The male *P. grandidentata's* a little further west are nearly out.

I should have noticed the fact that the pistillate flower of the hazel peeps forth gradually.[1]

April 4. Last night, a sugaring of snow, which goes off in an hour or two in the rain. Rains all day. The steam-cloud from the engine rises but slowly in such an atmosphere, and makes a small angle with the earth. It is low, perhaps, for the same reason that the clouds are. The robins sang this morning, nevertheless, and now more than ever hop about boldly in the garden in the rain, with full, broad, light cow-colored breasts.

[1] *Vide* [p. 92].

P. M. — Rain, rain. To Clematis Brook *via* Lee's Bridge.

Again I notice that early reddish or purplish grass that lies flat on the pools, like a warm blush suffusing the youthful face of the year. A warm, dripping rain, heard on one's umbrella as on a snug roof, and on the leaves without, suggests comfort. We go abroad with a slow but sure contentment, like turtles under their shells. We never feel so comfortable as when we are abroad in a storm with satisfaction. Our comfort is positive then. We are all compact, and our thoughts collected. We walk under the clouds and mists as under a roof. Now we seem to hear the ground a-soaking up the rain, and not falling [*sic*] ineffectually on a frozen surface. We, too, are penetrated and revived by it. Robins still sing, and song sparrows more or less, and blackbirds, and the unfailing jay screams. How the thirsty grass rejoices! It has pushed up so visibly since morning, and fields that were completely russet yesterday are already tinged with green. We rejoice with the grass.

I hear the hollow sound of drops falling into the water under Hubbard's Bridge, and each one makes a conspicuous bubble which is floated down-stream. Instead of ripples there are a myriad dimples on the stream. The lichens remember the sea to-day. The usually dry cladonias, which are so crisp under the feet, are full of moist vigor. The rocks speak and tell the tales inscribed on them. Their inscriptions are brought out. I pause to study their geography.

At Conantum End I saw a red-tailed hawk launch

himself away from an oak by the pond at my approach, — a heavy flier, flapping even like the great bittern at first, — heavy forward. After turning Lee's Cliff I heard, methinks, more birds singing even than in fair weather, — tree sparrows, whose song has the character of the canary's, *F. hyemalis's chill-lill*, the sweet strain of the fox-colored sparrow, song sparrows, a nuthatch, jays, crows, bluebirds, robins, and a large congregation of blackbirds. They suddenly alight with great din in a stubble-field just over the wall, not perceiving me and my umbrella behind the pitch pines, and there feed silently; then, getting uneasy or anxious, they fly up on to an apple tree, where being reassured, commences a rich but deafening concert, *o-gurgle-ee-e, o-gurgle-ee-e*, some of the most liquid notes ever heard, as if produced by some of the water of the Pierian spring, flowing through some kind of musical water-pipe and at the same time setting in motion a multitude of fine vibrating metallic springs. Like a shepherd merely meditating most enrapturing glees on such a water-pipe. A more liquid bagpipe or clarionet, immersed like bubbles in a thousand sprayey notes, the bubbles half lost in the spray. When I show myself, away they go with a loud harsh *charr-r, charr-r*. At first I had heard an inundation of blackbirds approaching, some beating time with a loud *chuck, chuck*, while the rest played a hurried, gurgling fugue.

Saw a sucker washed to the shore at Lee's Bridge, its tail gone, large fins standing out, purplish on top of head and snout. Reminds me of spring, spearing, and gulls.

A rainy day is to the walker in solitude and retirement like the night. Few travellers are about, and they half hidden under umbrellas and confined to the highways. One's thoughts run in a different channel from usual. It is somewhat like the dark day; it is a light night.

How cheerful the roar of a brook swollen by the rain, especially if there is no sound of a mill in it!

A woodcock went off from the shore of Clematis or Nightshade Pond with a few slight rapid sounds like a watchman's rattle half revolved.

A clustering of small narrow leaves somewhat cone-like on the shrub oak. Some late, low, remarkably upright alders (*serrulata*), short thick catkins, at Clematis Brook. The hazel bloom is about one tenth of an inch long (the stigmas) now. A little willow (*Salix Muhlenbergiana?*) nearly ready to bloom, not larger than a sage willow.

All *our* early willows with catkins appearing before the leaves must belong to the group of "The Sallows. Cinereæ. Borrer," and that of the "Two-colored Willows. Discolores. Borrer," as adopted by Barratt; or, in other words, to the first § of Carey in Gray.

The other day, when I had been standing perfectly still some ten minutes, looking at a willow which had just blossomed, some rods in the rear of Martial Miles's house, I felt eyes on my back and, turning round suddenly, saw the heads of two men who had stolen out of the house and were watching me over a rising ground as fixedly as I the willow. They were study-

ing man, which is said to be the proper study of mankind, I nature, and yet, when detected, they felt the cheapest of the two.

I hear the twitter of tree sparrows from fences and shrubs in the yard and from alders by meadows and the riverside every day.

April 5. The bluebird comes to us bright in his vernal dress as a bridegroom. (Cleared up at noon, making a day and a half of rain.) Has he not got new feathers then? Brooks says "the greater number of birds renew their plumage in autumn only;" if they have two moults, spring and autumn, there is still but one of the wings and tail feathers. Also says that in the spring various "birds undergo a change of color unaccompanied by any moult."

I have noticed the few phœbes, not to mention other birds, mostly near the river. Is it not because of the greater abundance of insects there, those early moths or ephemeræ? As these and other birds are most numerous there, the red-tailed hawk is there to catch them?

April 6. 6 a. m. — To Cliffs.

The robin is the singer at present, such is its power and universality, being found both in garden and wood. Morning and evening it does not fail, perched on some elm or the like, and in rainy days it is one long morning or evening. The song sparrow is still more universal but not so powerful. The lark, too, is equally constant, morning and evening, but con-

Vol. V

fined to certain localities, as is the blackbird to some extent. The bluebird, with feebler but not less sweet warbling, helps fill the air, and the phœbe does her part. The tree sparrow, *F. hyemalis*, and fox-colored sparrows make the meadow-sides or gardens where they are flitting vocal, the first with its canary-like twittering, the second with its lively ringing trills or jingle. The third is a very sweet and more powerful singer, which would be memorable if we heard him long enough. The woodpecker's tapping, though not musical, suggests pleasant associations in the cool morning, — is inspiriting, enlivening.

I hear no hylas nor croakers in the morning. Is it too cool for them? The gray branches of the oaks, which have lost still more of their leaves, seen against the pines when the sun is rising and falling on them, how rich and interesting!

From Cliffs see on the still water under the hill, at the outlet of the pond, two ducks sailing, partly white. Hear the faint, swelling, far-off beat of a partridge.

Saw probably female red-wings (?), grayish or dark ashy-brown, on an oak in the woods, with a male (?) whose red shoulder did not appear.

How many walks along the brooks I take in the spring! What shall I call them? Lesser riparial excursions? Prairial? rivular? [1]

When I came out there was not a speck of mist in the sky, but the morning without a cloud is not the fairest. Now, 8.30 A. M., it rains. Such is April.

¹ [Channing, p. 97.]

Vol. V

They go off with a loud squeaking quack. Each pair is by itself. One pair on shore some rods from the water. Is not the object of the quacking to give notice of danger to the rest who cannot see it?

All along under the south side of this hill on the edge of the meadow, the air resounds with the hum of honey-bees, attracted by the flower of the skunk-cabbage. I first heard the fine, peculiarly sharp hum of the honey-bee before I thought of them. Some hummed hollowly within the spathes, perchance to give notice to their fellows that plant was occupied, for they repeatedly looked in, and backed out on finding another. It was surprising to see them, directed by their instincts to these localities, while the earth has still but a wintry aspect so far as vegetation is concerned, buzz around some obscure spathe close to the ground, well knowing what they were about, then alight and enter. As the cabbages were very numerous for thirty or forty rods, there must have been some hundreds of bees there at once, at least. I watched many when they entered and came out, and they all had little yellow pellets of pollen at their thighs. As the skunk-cabbage comes out before the willow, it is probable that the former is the first flower they visit. It is the more surprising, as the flower is for the most part invisible within the spathe. Some of these spathes are now quite large and twisted up like cows' horns, not curved over as usual. Commonly they make a pretty little crypt or shrine for the flower, like the overlapping door of a tent. It must be bee-bread (?), then, they are after. Lucky

A male willow, apparently same with that at H.'s Bridge, or No. 2, near end of second track on west. Another male by ring-post on east side, long cylindrical catkins, now dark with scales, which are generally more rounded than usual and reddish at base and not lanceolate, turning backwards in blossom and exposing their sides or breasts to the sun, from which side burst forth fifty or seventy-five long white stamens like rays, tipped with yellow anthers which at first were reddish above, — spears to be embraced by invisible Arnold Winkelrieds; — reddish twigs and clear gray beneath. These last colors, especially, distinguish it from Nos. 1 and 2. Also a female, four or five rods north of last, just coming into bloom, with very narrow tapering catkins, lengthening already, some to an inch and a half, ovaries conspicuously stalked; very downy twigs, more reddish and rough than last below.

If we consider the eagle as a large hawk, how he falls in our estimation!

Our new citizen Sam Wheeler has a brave new weathercock all gilt on his new barn. This morning at sunrise it reflected the sun so brightly that I thought it was a house on fire in Acton, though I saw no smoke, but that might well be omitted.

The flower-buds of the red maple have very red inner scales, now being more and more exposed, which color the tree-tops a great distance off.

P. M. — To Second Division Brook.

Near Clamshell Hill, I scare up in succession four pairs of good-sized brown or grayish-brown ducks.

that this flower does not flavor their honey. I have noticed for a month or more the bare ground sprinkled here and there with several kinds of fungi, now conspicuous, — the starred kind, puffballs, etc. Now it is fair, and the sun shines, though it shines and rains with short intervals to-day. I do not see so much greenness in the grass as I expected, though a considerable change. No doubt the rain exaggerates a little by showing all the greenness there is! The thistle is now ready to wear the rain-drops.

I see, in J. P. Brown's field, by Nut Meadow Brook, where a hen has been devoured by a hawk probably. The feathers whiten the ground. They cannot carry a large fowl very far from the farmyard, and when driven off are frequently baited and caught in a trap by the remainder of their quarry. The gooseberry has not yet started. I cannot describe the lark's song. I used these syllables in the morning to remember it by, — *heetar-su-e-oo*. The willow in Miles's Swamp which resembles No. 2 not fairly in blossom yet. Heard unusual notes from, I think, a chickadee in the swamp, elicited, probably, by the love season, — *che che vet*, accent on last syllable, and *vissa viss a viss*, the last sharp and fine. Yet the bird looked more slender than the common titmouse, with a longer tail, which jerked a little, but it seemed to be the same bird that sang *phebe* and *he-phebe* so sweetly. The woods rang with this. Nuttall says it is the young that *phebe* in winter. I noticed some aspens (*tremuliformis*) of good size there, which have no flowers! The first lightning I remember this year was in the rain last evening, quite bright; and the thunder followed very long after. A thunder-shower in Boston yesterday.

One cowslip, though it shows the yellow, is not *fairly* out, but will be by to-morrow. How they improve their time! Not a moment of sunshine lost. One thing I may depend on: there has been no idling with the flowers. They advance as steadily as a clock. Nature loses not a moment, takes no vacation. These plants, now protected by the water, just peeping forth. I should not be surprised to find that they drew in their heads in a frosty night. Returning by Harrington's, saw a pigeon woodpecker flash away, showing the rich golden under side of its glancing wings and the large whitish spot on its back, and presently I heard its familiar long-repeated loud note, almost familiar as that of a barn-door fowl, which it somewhat resembles. The robins, too, now toward sunset, perched on the old apple trees in Tarbell's orchard, twirl forth their evening lays unweariedly. Is that a willow, the low bush from the fireplace ravine which from the lichen oak, fifty or sixty rods distant, shows so red in the westering sunlight? More red, I find, by far than close at hand.

To-night for the first time I hear the hylas in full blast.

Is that pretty little reddish-leaved star-shaped plant by the edge of water a different species of hypericum from the *perforatum?*

April 7. 6 A. M. — I did not notice any bees on the willows I looked at yesterday, though so many on the cabbage.

The white-bellied swallows advertise themselves this morning, dashing up the street, and two have already come to disturb the bluebirds at our box. Saw and heard this morning, on a small elm and the wall by Badger's, a sparrow (?), seemingly somewhat slaty-brown and lighter beneath, whose note began loud and clear, *twee-tooai*, etc., etc., ending much like the field sparrow. Was it a female *F. hyemalis?* Or a field, or a swamp, sparrow? Saw no white in tail. Also saw a small, plain, warbler-like bird for a moment, which I did not recognize.

10 A. M. — Down river in boat to Bedford, with C.

A windy, but clear, sunny day; cold wind from northwest. Notice a white maple with almost all the staminate flowers above or on the top, most of the stamens now withered, before the red maple has blossomed. Another maple, all or nearly all female. The staminiferous flowers look light yellowish, the female dark crimson. These white maples' lower branches droop quite low, striking the head of the rower, and curve gracefully upward at the ends. Another sucker, the counterpart of the one I saw the other day, tail gone, but not purpled snout, being fresher. Is it the work of a gull or of the spearer? Do not the suckers chiefly attract the gulls at this season?

River has risen from last rains, and we cross the Great Meadows, scaring up many ducks at a great distance, some partly white, some apparently black, some brownish (?). It is Fast-Day, and many gunners are about the shore, which makes them shy.

Vol. V

I never cross the meadow at this season without seeing ducks. That is probably a marsh hawk, flying low over the water and then skirting the meadow's copsy edge, when abreast, from its apparently triangular wings, reminding me of a smaller gull. Saw more afterward. A hawk above Ball's Hill which, though with a distinct white rump, I think was not the harrier but sharp-shinned, from its broadish, mothlike form, light and slightly spotted beneath, with head bent downward, watching for prey. A great gull, though it is so fair and the wind northwest, fishing over the flooded meadow. He slowly circles round and hovers with flapping wings in the air over particular spots, repeatedly returning there and sailing quite low over the water, with long, narrow, pointed wings, trembling throughout their length. Hawks much about water at this season.

If you make the least correct observation of nature this year, you will have occasion to repeat it with illustrations the next, and the season and life itself is prolonged.

I am surprised to see how much in warm places the high blueberry buds are started, some reddish, some greenish, earlier now than any gooseberries I have noticed. Several painted tortoises; no doubt have been out a long time.

Walk in and about Tarbell's Swamp. Heard in two distinct places a slight, more prolonged croak, somewhat like the toad. This? Or a frog? It is a *warmer* sound than I have heard yet, as if dreaming outdoors were possible.

Many spotted tortoises are basking amid the dry leaves in the sun, along the side of a still, warm ditch cut through the swamp. They make a great rustling a rod ahead, as they make haste through the leaves to tumble into the water. The flower-buds of the andromeda here are ready to open, almost. Yet three or four rods off from all this, on the edge of the swamp, under a north hillside, is a long strip of ice five inches thick for ten or twelve rods. The first striped snake crawling off through leaves in the sun.

Crossed to Bedford side to see where [they] had been digging out (probably) a woodchuck. How handsome the river from those hills! The river southwest over the Great Meadows a sheet of sparkling molten silver, with broad lagoons parted from it by curving lines of low bushes; to the right or northward now, at 2 or 3 P. M., a dark blue, with small smooth, light edgings, firm plating, under the lee of the shore. Fly-like bees buzzing about, close to the dry, barren hillside.

The only large catkins I notice along the riverside are on the recent yellow-green shoots from the stump of what looks like the ordinary early swamp willow, which is common, — near by almost wholly grayish and stinted and scarcely opening yet. Small bee-like wasps (?) and flies are numerous on them, not flying when you stand never so close. A large leech in the water, serpentine this wise, ~~~ as the snake is not. Approach near to Simon Brown's ducks, on river. They are continually bobbing their heads under water in a shallow part of the meadow, more under water than above. I infer that the wild employ themselves likewise. You are most struck with the apparent ease with which they glide away, — not seeing the motion of their feet, — as by their wills.

As we stand on Nawshawtuct at 5 P. M., looking over the meadows, I doubt if there is a town more adorned by its river than ours. Now the sun is low in the west, the northeasterly water is of a peculiarly ethereal light blue, more beautiful than the sky, and this broad water with innumerable bays and inlets running up into the land on either side and often divided by bridges and causeways, as if it were the very essence and richness of the heavens distilled and poured over the earth, contrasting with the clear russet land and the paler sky from which it has been subtracted, — nothing can be more elysian. Is not the blue more ethereal when the sun is at this angle? The river is but a long chain of flooded meadows. I think our most distant extensive low horizon must be that northeast from this hill over Ball's Hill, — to what town is it? It is down the river valley, partly at least toward the Merrimack, as it should be.

What is that plant with a whorl of four, five, or six reddish cornel-like leaves, seven or eight inches from the ground, with the minute relics of small dried flowers left, and a large pink (?) bud now springing, just beneath the leaves?[1] It is a true evergreen, for it dries soon in the house, as if kept fresh by the root.

[1] Large cornel (*Canadensis*).

Vol. V

April 8. 6 A. M. — To Abel Hosmer's ring-post.

The ground sprinkled, salted, with little snowlike pellets one tenth of an inch in diameter, from half an inch to one inch apart, sometimes cohering starwise together. As if it had spit so much snow only. I think it one form of frost merely, or frozen dew. Noticed the like a week or two ago. It was gone in half an hour, when I came back. What is the peculiar state of the atmosphere that determines these things? The spearer's light last night shone into my chamber on the wall and awakened me.

Saw and heard my small pine warbler shaking out his trills, or jingle, even like money coming to its bearings. They appear much the smaller from perching high in the tops of white pines and flitting from tree to tree at that height.

Is not my night-warbler the white-eyed vireo?—not yet here. Heard the field sparrow again.

The male *Populus grandidentata* appears to open very gradually, beginning sooner than I supposed. It shows some of its red anthers long before it opens. There is a female on the left, on Warren's Path at Deep Cut.

Is not the pollen of the *P. tremuliformis* like rye meal? Are not female flowers of more sober and modest colors, as the willows for instance? The hylas have fairly begun now.

April 9. P. M. — To Second Division.

The chipping sparrow, with its ashy-white breast and white streak over eye and undivided chestnut

crown, holds up its head and pours forth its *che che che che che che*. On a pitch [pine] on side of J. Hosmer's river hill, a pine warbler, by ventriloquism sounding farther off than it was, which was seven or eight feet, hopping and flitting from twig to twig, apparently picking the small flies at and about the base of the needles at the extremities of the twigs. Saw two afterward on the walls by roadside.

A warm and hazy but breezy day. The sound of the laborers' striking the iron rails of the railroad with their sledges, is as in the sultry days of summer, — resounds, as it were, from the hazy sky as a roof, — a more confined and, in that sense, domestic sound echoing along between the earth and the low heavens. The same strokes would produce a very different sound in the winter. Men fishing for trout. Small light-brown lizards, about five inches long, with somewhat darker tails, and some a light line along back, are very active, wiggling off, in J. P. Brown's ditch, with pollywogs.

Beyond the desert, hear the hooting owl, which, as formerly, I at first mistook for the hounding of a dog, — a squealing *eee* followed by *hoo hoo hoo* deliberately, and particularly sonorous and ringing. This at 2 P. M. Now mated. Pay their addresses by day, says Brooks. Winkle lichens, some with greenish bases, on a small prostrate white oak, near base. Also large white earlike ones higher up. A middling-sized orange-copper butterfly on the mill road, at the clearing, with deeply scalloped leaves [*sic*]. You see the buff-edged and this, etc., in warm, sunny southern exposures on the edge of woods or sides of rocky hills and cliffs, above dry

leaves and twigs, where the wood has been lately cut and there are many dry leaves and twigs about. An ant-hill covered with a firm sward except at top. The cowslips are well out, — the first conspicuous herbaceous flower, for the cabbage is concealed in its spathe.

The *Populus tremuliformis*, just beyond, *resound* with the hum of honey-bees, flies, etc. These male trees are frequently at a great distance from the females. Do not the bees and flies alone carry the pollen to the latter? I did not know at first whence the humming of bees proceeded. At this comparatively still season, before the crickets begin, the hum of bees is a very noticeable sound, and the least hum or buzz that fills the void is detected. Here appear to be more bees than on the willows. On the last, where I can see them better, are not only bees with pellets of pollen, but more flies, small bees, and a lady-bug. What do flies get here on male flowers, if not nectar? Bees also in the female willows, of course without pellets. It must be nectar alone there. That willow by H.'s Bridge is very brittle at base of stem, but hard to break above. The more I study willows, the more I am confused. The epigæa will not be out for some days.

Elm blossoms now in prime. Their tops heavier against the sky, a rich brown; their outlines further seen. Most alders done. Some small upright ones still fresh.

Evening. — Hear the snipe a short time at early starlight.

I hear this evening for the first time, from the partially flooded meadow across the river, I standing on this side, at early starlight, a general faint, prolonged stuttering or stertorous croak, — probably same with that heard April 7th, — that kind of growling, like wild beasts or a coffee-mill, which you can produce in your throat. It seems too dry and wooden, not sonorous or pleasing enough, for the toad. I hear occasionally the bullfrog's note, croakingly and hoarsely but faintly imitated, in the midst of it, — which makes me think it may be they, though I have not seen any frogs so large yet, but that one by the railroad which I suspect may have been a *fontinalis*. What sound do the tortoises make beside hissing? There were the mutilated *Rana palustris* seen in the winter, the hylodes, the small or middling-sized croakers in pools (a shorter, less stuttering note than this to-night), and next the note of the 7th, and to-night the last, the first I have heard from the river. I occasionally see a little frog jump into a brook.

The whole meadow resounds, probably from one end of the river to the other, this evening, with this faint, stertorous breathing. It is the waking up of the meadows. Louder than all is heard the shrill peep of the hylodes and the hovering note of the snipe, circling invisible above them all.

Vide again in Howitt, pp. 31, 32, 33, 34, 35, 37, 49, 54, 95.

Is it the red-eye or white-eye whose pensile nest is so common?

April 10 (?). P. M. — To Cliffs.

A cold and windy day. Our earliest gooseberry is pretty green; next, probably the Mississippi [*sic*] cur-

rant, which is beginning to look green; next, the large buds of the lilac are opening; and next, our second or later gooseberry appears to be just beginning to expand or to show its green, and this appears to be the same with the wild one by J. P. Brown's. The male red maple buds now show eight or ten (ten counting everything) scales, alternately crosswise, and the pairs successively brighter red or scarlet, which will account for the gradual reddening of their tops. They are about ready to open.

From Fair Haven I see, in the northwestern and northern horizon and pretty high, the light reflected from falling rain, sleet, or hail, or all together, — a certain glow, almost sunny light, from the upright or nearly upright, but always straight, sides of clouds, defined by the falling rain or hail, — for hail and rain fell on me within an hour or two. The northern Peterboro Hill is concealed by a driving storm, while the southern one is distinct.

A small black dor-bug dead in the wood-path.

Two crowfoots out on the Cliff. A very warm and dry exposure, but no further sheltered were they. Pale-yellow offering of spring. The saxifrage is beginning to be abundant, elevating its flowers somewhat, pure, trustful, white, amid its pretty notched and reddish cup of leaves. The white saxifrage is a response from earth to the increased light of the year; the yellow crowfoot, to the increased heat of the sun. The buds of the thorn bushes are conspicuous. The chrysosplenium is open, a few of them, in Hubbard's meadow. I thought he had destroyed them all.

Vol. V

When the farmer cleans out his ditches, I mourn the loss of many a flower which he calls a weed. The main *charm* about the Corner road, just beyond the bridge, to me, has been in the little grove of locusts, sallows, and birches, etc., which has sprung up on the bank as you rise the hill. Yesterday I saw a man who is building a house near by cutting them down. I asked him if he was going to cut them all. He said he was. I said if I were in his place I would not have cut them for a hundred dollars, that they were the chief attraction of the place. "Why," said he, "they are nothing but a parcel of prickly bushes and are not worth anything. I'm going to build a new wall here." And so, to ornament the approach to his house, he substitutes a bare, ugly wall for an interesting grove.

I still feel the frost in the meadows firm under my feet.

Saw a pretty large narrow-winged hawk with a white rump and white spots or bars on under (?) side of wings. Probably the female or young of a marsh hawk. What was that smaller, broader-winged hawk with *white* rump of April 7th? For, after all, I do not find it described.

The sweet-gale will blossom very soon.

April 11. I hear the clear, loud whistle of a purple finch, somewhat like and nearly as loud as the robin, from the elm by Whiting's. The maple which I think is a red one, just this side of Wheildon's, is just out this morning.

9 A. M. — To Haverhill *via* Cambridge and Boston.

Dr. Harris says that that early black-winged, buff-edged butterfly is the *Vanessa Antiopa*, and is introduced from Europe, and is sometimes found in this state alive in winter. The orange-brown one with scalloped wings, and smaller somewhat, is *Vanessa Progne*. The early pestle-shaped bug or beetle is a cicindela, of which there are three species, one of them named from a semicolon-like mark on it. *Vide* Hassley on spiders in Boston *Journal of Natural History*.

At Natural History Rooms, saw the female red-wing, striped white and ash; female cow-bird, ashy-brown.

First. The swamp sparrow is ferruginous-brown (spotted with black) and ash above about neck; brownish-white beneath; undivided chestnut crown.

Second. The grass-bird, grayish-brown, mingled with ashy-whitish above; light, pencilled with dark brown beneath; no marked crown; outer tail feathers whitish, perhaps a faint bar on wing.

Third. Field sparrow, smaller than either; marked like first, with less black, and less distinct ash on neck, and less ferruginous and no distinct crown.

Fourth. Savannah sparrow, much like second, with more black, but not noticeable white in tail, and a little more brown; no crown marked.

Emberiza miliaria Gmel. (What is it in Nuttall?) appears to be my young of purple finch.

One Maryland yellow-throat, probably female, has no black on side head, and is like a summer yellow-bird except that the latter has ends of the wings and tail black.

The yellow-rump warbler (what is it in Nuttall?) is bluish-gray, with two white bars on wings, a bright yellow crown, side breasts, and rump. Female less distinct.

Blackburnian is orange-throated.

American redstart, male, is black forward, coppery-orange beneath and stripe on wings and near base of tail. Female dark ashy and fainter marks.

J. E. Cabot thought my small hawk might be Cooper's hawk. Says that Gould, an Englishman, is the best authority on birds.

April 13. Haverhill. — Pewee days and April showers.

First hear toads (and take off coat), a loud, ringing sound filling the air, which yet few notice. First shad caught at Haverhill to-day; first alewife 10th. Fishermen say that no fish can get above the dam at Lawrence. No shad, etc., were caught at Lowell last year. Were catching smelts with·a small seine. It says in deeds that brooks shall be opened or obstructions removed by the 20th of April, on account of fish.

April 15. Mouse-ear.

April 16. Either barn or bank swallows overhead. Birds loosen and expand their feathers and look larger in the rain.

April 17. *Sunday.* The elder leaf is the most forward of any shrub or tree I have seen; more than one inch long.

Vol. V

April 21. Haverhill. — A peach tree in bloom.

April 23. Haverhill. — Martins.

April 24. *Sunday.* To and around Creek Pond and back over Parsonage Hill, Haverhill.

Field horse-tail in bloom. Marsh (?) hawk, with black tips of wings. Alders about all done. Green leaves just beginning to expand. Houstonias. How affecting that, annually at this season, as surely as the sun takes a higher course in the heavens, this pure and simple little flower peeps out and spots the great globe with white in our America, its four little white or bluish petals on a slender stalk making a delicate flower about a third of an inch in diameter! What a significant, though faint, utterance of spring through the veins of earth!

I see, in a pool by the Creek Brook, pretty chains of toad-spawn in double parallel crenate or serpentine or sometimes corkscrewing lines of black ova, close together, immersed in a light-colored jelly a third of an inch in diameter, appearing as if the two strings were one, like a lace with two scalloped black borders. This is what they were singing about.

Haverhill is remarkably bare of trees and woods. The young ladies cannot tell where are the nearest woods. I saw the moon rise last night over great bare hills eastward, and it reminded me of Ossian. Saw a pretty islet in the Creek Pond on the east side covered with white pine wood, appearing from the south higher than wide and as if the trees grew out of the water. You saw the light-colored trunks six or eight feet

Visited two houses of refuge about one hundred and sixty years old, two miles or more east of Haverhill village, — the Peaslee houses, substantial brick houses some forty by twenty feet. Two rows of bricks project between the two stories; cavities left for the staging; marks of ovens (which projected outdoors) cut off; *white oak* timber, fifteen by twelve inches, sound; space in chimney above fireplace about three feet deep (see stars); two or three very narrow windows; large-sized bricks. These were the houses of Joseph and Nathaniel Peaslee, appointed houses of refuge by the town about 1690. The occupant of one, not a very old man, told me that his grandfather, Joseph Peaslee, was seventeen years old when the French and Indians attacked the town, killed Rolfe, etc. A Newcomb from Cape Cod lives in the other. There are as many as six garrison-houses and houses of refuge still standing in Haverhill. I have seen four still entire and one partly so, all brick.

Field sparrows common now. The Merrimack is yellow and turbid in the spring; will run clear anon. The red maple begins to show stamens here. A pleasant hilly country north of Great Pond. What were those five large gray ducks with white wing-coverts?

April 19. Haverhill. — Willow and bass strip freely. Surveying Charles White's long piece. Hear again that same nighthawk-like sound over a meadow at evening.

April 20. Saw a toad and a small snake.

beneath, and then the heavy green mass overhung the water a rod, under and beyond which you see the light surface of the pond, which gives the isle a peculiarly light and floating appearance. So much beauty does a wooded islet add to a pond. It is an object sufficiently central and *insular.* Dandelions. How surprising this bright-yellow disk! Why study other hieroglyphics? It is along the east side of this pond that the Indians are said to have taken their way with Hannah Dustin and her nurse in 1697 toward the Merrimack. I walked along it and thought how they might have been ambuscaded.

April 27. Haverhill. — The warbling vireo.

Talked with a fisherman at the Burrough [*sic*], who was cracking and eating walnuts on a post before his hut. He said he got twenty cents a stick for sawing marked logs, which were mostly owned at Lowell, but trees that fell in and whatever was not marked belonged to them. Much went by in the ice and could not be got. They haul it in and tie it. He called it Little Concord where I lived. They got some small stuff which came from that river, and said he knew the ice, it was blue (it is not) and was turned over by the falls. The Lawrence dam breaks up the ice so now that it will not be so likely to jam below and produce a freshet. Said a thousand dollars' damage was done by a recent freshet to the farm just above, at the great bend. The wind blowing on to the shore ate it away, trees and all. In the greatest freshet he could remember, methinks about ten years ago, the water came up to his window-sill. His family took refuge on the hillside. His barn was moved and tipped over, his well filled up, and it took him, with help, a day or more to clear a passage through the ice from his door to his well. His trees were all prostrated by the ice. This was apparently between twenty and thirty feet above the present level. Says the railroad bridge hurts the fishing by stopping the ice and wearing away and deepening the channel near the north shore, where they fish, — draw their seines. Call it sixty rods wide, — their seines being thirty rods long, — and twenty-five feet deep in the middle.

Interesting to me are their habits and conversation who live along the shores of a great river. The shore, here some seventy or eighty feet high, is broken by gullies, more or less sandy, where water has flowed down, and the cottages rise not more than one sixth or one seventh the way up.

April 29. Return to Concord. At Natural History Rooms in Boston. Have I seen the least bittern? It is so brown above and yellowish, woolly, white beneath. The American goshawk is slate above, gray beneath; the young spotted dark and white beneath, and brown above. Fish hawk, white beneath. Young of marsh hawk, reddish-brown above, iron-rusty beneath. Summer duck with a crest. Dusky duck, not black, but rather dark brown. The velvet ducks I saw, hardly large enough for this. My whiter ducks may be the *Merganser castor*, or the red-breasted.

III

MAY, 1853

(ÆT. 35)

May 1. *Sunday.* A cold northwest wind. Now, on my return to Concord, I am struck by the increased greenness of the country, or landscape.

I find that since I left Concord, April 11th, there have blossomed here, probably nearly in the following order, these plants, including those I saw in Haverhill: dandelion, field horse-tail, *Antennaria plantaginifolia*, sweet-gale, epigæa, *Populus grandidentata, Salix tristis, Viola ovata* (Ellen Emerson found it April 20th), *Potentilla Canadensis*, comptonia, *Thalictrum anemonoides, Anemone nemorosa, V. blanda, P. balsamifera, Aquilegia Canadensis, Hedyotis cærulea*, andromeda, *Fragaria Virginiana* (?) (distinguished from the other species in fruit), *Salix alba*, benzoin, *Amelanchier Canadensis* var. *Botryapium.* Peach, cultivated cherry, and the following apparently just begun: *Viola pedata, Ostrya Virginica, V. cucullata* (Ellen Emerson says she saw it the 30th *ult.;* it is to be looked for at Depot Field Brook). And *Rumex Acetosella* shows red and is eight inches high on Columbine Cliff.

The expanding leaves of the sugar maples now make small crosses against the sky. Other conspicuous green leaves are the gooseberry, currant, elder,

April 30. Concord. — Cultivated cherry in bloom.

Moses Emerson, the kind and gentlemanly man who assisted and looked after me in Haverhill, said that a good horse was worth $75, and all above was fancy, and that when he saw a man driving a fast horse he expected he would fail soon.

Vol. V

the willows just beginning, and alder, and apple trees and high blackberry, amelanchier, meadow-sweet, beside many herbaceous plants. Drosera (round-leaved) leaves now. Sedge-grass (early sedge) very abundant still. The *Vaccinium Pennsylvanicum* is just ready to bloom and also the *vacillans* nearly. These things observed on way—

To Cliffs.

The oak leaves on the plain are fallen. The colors are now: light blue above (where is my cyanometer? Saussure invented one, and Humboldt used it in his travels); landscape russet and greenish, spotted with fawn-colored plowed lands, with green pine and gray or reddish oak woods intermixed, and dark-blue or slate-colored water here and there. It is greenest in the meadows and where water has lately stood, and a strong, invigorating scent comes up from the fresh meadows. It is like the greenness of an apple faintly or dimly appearing through the russet.

A phœbe's nest and one cream-colored white egg at the spring-house; nest of mud, lined with grass and edged with hypnum. Channing has seen a robin's nest and eggs. I hear a black and white creeper at the Cliffs, and a chewink.

The shrub oaks are well budded. The young ivy leaves are red on Cliffs. Oaks and hickory buds just ready to open. How aromatic the balm-of-Gilead buds now!

The large woolly ferns and others stand up a foot on banks. The skunk-cabbage leaves green the warm, springy meads.

Was it not the black and yellow or spotted warbler [1] I saw by the Corner Spring? Apparently black, brown-striped, with a yellow rump and also yellow wing, shoulders, and sides of breast, with a large black spot on breast; size of phœbe nearly; note somewhat like yellowbird. Yet I think it much too dark for the myrtle-bird.

Columbine Cliff a place to look for early rue anemones and *nemorosa* and dandelions. The columbines have been out some days. How ornamental to these dark-colored perpendicular cliffs, nodding from the clefts and shelves!

The barn swallow is about.

Have we the *Viola lanceolata?* [2] Is not the *Botryapium* our earliest variety of amelanchier, and what difference in the fruit?

Channing says he has heard the wood thrush, brown thrasher, and stake-driver (?), since I have been gone. This and last page for birds which I find come in the interval. Did I not see the oven-bird yesterday?

May 2. Summer yellowbird on the opening *Salix alba*. Chimney swallows and the bank or else cliff ditto. Small pewee?

Our earliest gooseberry in garden has bloomed. What is that pondweed-like plant floating in a pool near Breed's, with a slender stem and linear leaves and a small whorl of minute leaves on the surface,

[1] *Vide* May 10th.
[2] Yes. *Vide* Hubbard's meadow, by willows.

Vol. V

and nutlets in the axils of the leaves, along the stem, as if now out of bloom? [1] Missouri currant.

May 4. Cattle are going up country. Hear the *tull-lull* of the chickadee (?). [2] The currant in bloom. The Canada plum just ready, probably to-day. [3]

8 A. M. — To Walden and Cliffs.

The sound of the oven-bird. Caterpillar nests two or three inches in diameter on wild cherries; caterpillars one third of an inch long.

The *Vaccinium Pennsylvanicum* appeared yesterday. The *vacillans*, *resinosum* (?), and early high blueberry will bloom in a few days. *Vide Cerasus pumila* by shanty path, and wild red ditto, as early. The white birch leaves are beginning to expand and are shining with some sticky matter. I must attend to their fragrance. In a warm place on the Cliffs one of their catkins shows its anthers, the golden pendant.

The woods and paths next them now ring with the silver jingle of the field sparrow, the medley of the brown thrasher, the honest *qui vive* of the chewink, or his jingle from the top of a low copse tree, while his

[1] *Callitriche verna.*
[2] [The word "chickadee" is crossed out and "myrtle-bird" substituted, which latter is in turn crossed out and replaced by "white-throat sparrow." The final correction would seem to have been made some years after the original entry, for in January, 1858, we find Thoreau getting what appears to be his first intimation as to the real authorship of this song (see *Journal*, vol. x.). In the manuscript notes of the excursion to the Maine Woods in 1857, the song of the white-throat is still attributed to the "myrtle-bird."]
[3] Not before the 7th.

mate scratches in the dry leaves beneath; the black and white creeper is hopping along the oak boughs, head downward, pausing from time to time to utter its note like a fine, delicate saw-sharpening; and ever and anon rises clear over all the smooth, rich melody of the wood thrush. Could that have been a jay? I think it was some large, uncommon woodpecker that uttered that very loud, strange, cackling note.

The dry woods have the smell of fragrant everlasting. I am surprised by the cool drops which now, at 10 o'clock, drop from the flowers of the amelanchier, while other plants are dry, as if these had attracted more moisture. The white pines have started.

The indigo-bird and mate; dark throat and light beneath, and white spot on wings, which is not described; a hoarse note, and rapid the first two or three syllables, — *twe twe twee*, dwelling on the last, or *twe twe twe twee-e*, or as if an *r* in it, *tre*, etc., not musical. The myrtle-bird, which makes me think the more that I saw the black and yellow warbler on Sunday.

I find apparently two varieties of the amelanchier, — the first I noticed, with *smooth* reddish delicate leaves and somewhat linear petals and loose racemes, petals sometimes pinkish; the second to-day, perhaps a little later than the first, leaves light-colored and downy and petals broader and perhaps not quite so long as the first, racemes more crowded. I am not sure that this is the variety *oblongifolium* of Gray. [1]

It is stated in the Life of Humboldt that he proved

[1] This appears to be the *Pyrus ovalis* or swamp pyrus of Bigelow and Willdeming.

"that the expression, 'the ocean reflects the sky,' was a purely poetical, but not a scientifically correct one, as the sea is often blue when the sky is almost totally covered with light white clouds." He used Saussure's cyanometer even to measure the color of the sea. This might probably be used to measure the intensity of the color of blue flowers like lupines at a distance. Humboldt speaks of its having been proved that pine pollen falls from the atmosphere.

May 6. P. M. — To Nut Meadow Brook and Corner Spring.

Choice plum in gardens. The *Salix alba* is conspicuous and interesting in the landscape now, some bright yellow, truly golden (staminate?), some greenish, filling the air of causeways with a sweet scent. The whole landscape is many shades greener for the rain, almost a blue green. The leafing of the trees has commenced, and the forms of some, accordingly, begin to be defined. Some, however, like the large maples, elms, etc., look heavy and are defined by their samaræ and not yet by their leaves, which are not comparatively forward. I perceive the strong odor of horse-mint, rising dark above the brooks. Hear the loud echoing note of the peet-weet-weet-weet-weet. *Viola cucullata* at John Hosmer's ditch by Clamshell Hill. Four large robin's eggs in an apple tree. A ground-bird's nest with eggs. *Equisetum sylvaticum* in front of Hosmer's Gorge. I have seen no ducks since I returned from Haverhill on the 29th April. There are pretty large leaves on the young red maples (which have no flowers), disposed crosswise, as well as on the sugar maple, but not so with larger flowering maples. The maple-tops begin to look red now with the growing keys, at a distance, — crescents of red. *Uvularia sessilifolia* just begun. Common knawel, apparently for some time, though Bigelow says July (?). Those long spear-shaped buds of the viburnum have expanded into dark but handsome leaves rather early; probably *Viburnum nudum*.

As I walk through the village at evening, when the air is still damp after the rainy morning, I perceive and am exhilarated by the sweet scent of expanding leaves. The woods are beginning to be in the gray now; leaves and flower-buds generally expanding, covered with a mealy or downy web (which now reminds me of those plants like gnaphalium, swathed in cotton), a clean dirt, which whitens the coat of the walker.

May 7. Forenoon. — Up North River to stone-heaps. The willows (*Salix alba*) where I keep my boat resound with the hum of bees and other insects. The leaves of the aspen are perhaps the most conspicuous of any, though the *Salix alba*, from its mass and its flowers in addition, makes the greater impression. I hear the loud cackling of the flicker about the aspen at the rock. A gray squirrel is stealing along beneath. Hundreds of tortoises, painted and wood, are heard hurrying through the dry leaves on the bank, and seen tumbling into the water as my boat approaches; sometimes half a dozen and more are sunning on a floating rail, and one will remain with outstretched neck, its head

moving slowly round in a semicircle, while the boat passes within a few feet. Fresh green meadow-grass is springing up, as the water goes down, and flags. The larch has grown a quarter of an inch or more, studded with green buds; not so forward as the Scotch larch. The hemlock and the pitch pine have also started.

The keys of the white maple are more than half an inch long, not including stem; a dull-purplish cottony white. They make no such show as the red. The keys of the red are longer-stemmed but as yet much smaller. The leaves of the white are perhaps most advanced, yet lost in the fruit. The catkins of the hop-hornbeam, yellow tassels hanging from the trees, which grow on the steep bank of the Assabet, give them a light, graceful, and quite noticeable appearance. It is among the more conspicuous growths now; yet the anthers shed no pollen yet. Smaller trees and limbs which have few or no catkins have leaves, elm-like, already an inch long. The black cherry leaves are among the more conspicuous, more than an inch long. One of the many cherries which have when bruised the strong cherry scent. But this is the strongest and most rummy of all. The black oak buds are considerably expanded, probably more than any oaks. Their catkins are more than half an inch long. The swamp white oak is late, but the tips of the buds show yellowish green. The sugar maple in blossom, probably for a day or two, but since April 30th, though the peduncles are not half their length yet. Apple trees are greened with opening leaves, and their blossom-buds show the red.

As I advance up the Assabet, the lively note of the

yellowbird is borne from the willows, and the creeper is seen busy amid the lichens of the maple, and the loud, jingling *tche tche tche tche*, etc., of the chip-bird rings along the shore occasionally. The chewink is seen and heard scratching amid the dry leaves like a hen. The woods now begin to ring with the woodland note of the oven-bird. I hear the mew of the first catbird, and, soon after, its rich and varied melody; and there sits on a tree over the water the ungainly kingfisher, who flies off with an apparently laborious flight, sounding his alarum.

A few yellow lily pads are already spread out on the surface, tender reddish leaves, with a still crenate or scalloped border like that of some tin platters on which turnovers are cooked, while the muddy bottom is almost everywhere spotted with the large reddish ruffle-like leaves, from the midst of which the flower-stems already stand up a foot, aiming toward the light and heat. That long reddish *bent* grass abounds on the river now. That small kind of pondweed, with a whorl of small leaves on the surface and nutlets already in the axils of the very common linear leaves, is common in the river.

I hear the *witter-che* of the Maryland yellow-throat, also, on the willows. The note of the peetweet resounds along the river, — standing on the rocks laid bare by the fallen water or running along the sandy shore. The rich medley of the thrasher is also heard.

In the frog-spawn (which looks like oats in a jelly, masses as big as the fist), I distinguish the form of the pollywog, which squirms a little. The female flowers

of the sweet-gale, somewhat like but larger and more crowded than the hazel, is now an interesting sight along the edge of the river. That early cross-like plant is a foot high and budded.

The stone-heaps have been formed since I was here before, methinks about a month ago, and for the most part of fresh stones; *i. e.*, piles several feet in diameter by a foot high have evidently been made (no doubt commonly on the ruins of old ones) within a month. The stones are less than the size of a hen's egg, down to a pebble; now all under water. The Haverhill fisherman found the young of the common eel in such, and referred them to it.

I take it to be the small pewee whose smart chirp I hear so commonly. The delicate cherry-like leaf, transparent red, of the shad-bush is now interesting, especially in the sun. Some have green leaves. There is one of the former, five inches in diameter and eighteen or twenty feet high, on the Island, with only four to six flowers to a raceme. Heard a stake-driver. Saw a large snake, I think a black one, drop into the river close by; pursued, and as he found me gaining, he dived when he had reached the middle, and that was the last I saw of him. Fishing has commenced in the river. A white-throated sparrow (*Fringilla Pennsylvanica*) died in R. W. E.'s garden this morning. Half the streak over eye yellow. A passer. The odor of the sweet-briar along the side of a house. Riding through Lincoln, found the peach bloom now in prime, generally a dark pink with a lighter almost white inmixed, more striking from the complete absence of leaves, and especially when seen against the green of pines. I can find no wild gooseberry in bloom yet. The barberry bushes are in some places now quite green.

Various grasses in bloom for a week.

With respect to leafing, the more conspicuous and forward trees and shrubs are the following, and nearly in this order, as I think, and these have formed *small* leaves: Gooseberry, aspens (not *grandidentata*), willows, *young* maples of all kinds, balm-of-Gilead (?), elder, meadow-sweet, back cherry, and is that Jersey tea on Island? or diervilla? ostrya, alder, white birch and the three others, *Pyrus arbutifolia* (?), apple, amelanchier, choke(?)-cherry, dwarf ditto, wild red, *Viburnum nudum* (?) and *Lentago*, barberry.

The following are bursting into leaf: Hazel, shrub oak, black oak and red, white pine, larch, cornel, thorns, etc., elms.

Yorrick.[1]

Some birds — pewees, ground birds, robins, etc. — have already built nests and laid their eggs, before the leaves are expanded or the fields fairly green. Heard to-day that more slumbrous stertorous sound (not the hoarse one of early frogs) as I paddled up the river. Is it tortoises? These are abundantly out.

The *Viola pedata* with the large pale-blue flower is now quite common along warm sandy banks. The *ovata* is a smaller and darker and striped violet.

May 8. P. M. — To Annursnack.

A long row of elms just set out by Wheeler from his

[1] [This was Thoreau's rendering of the veery's call-note.]

In color it matches Sophia's cactus blossoms exactly. It is all the more interesting for being a painted leaf and not petal, and its spidery leaves, pinnatifid with linear divisions, increase its strangeness. It is now from three to six inches high, rising from the moist base of the hill. It is wonderful what a variety of flowers may grow within the range of a walk, and how long some very conspicuous ones may escape the most diligent walker, if you do not chance to visit their localities the right week or fortnight, when their signs are out. It is a flaming leaf. The very leaf has flowered; not the ripe tints of autumn, but the rose in the cheek of infancy; a more positive flowering. Still more abundant on the same ground was the *Erigeron bellidifolius*, robin's-plantain,[1] with a pale-purple ray still erect, like a small thimble, not yet horizontal. This, then, its very earliest date. Neither of these did I see last year, and I was affected as if I had got into a new botanical district. A kind of mint,[2] shoots now six or eight inches high, with a velvety purple or lake under surface to leaves.

They have cut off the woods, and with them the shad-bush, on the top of Annursnack, but laid open new and wider prospects. The landscape is in some respects more interesting because of the overcast sky, threatening rain; a cold southwest wind. I am struck and charmed by the quantity of forest, especially in the southwest, after having witnessed the bareness of the Haverhill country. It is as if every farmer had a beautiful garden and boundless plantations of trees

[1] *Vide* May 15th.   [2] The soft-leaved calamint.

gate to the old Lee place. The planting of so long a row of trees which are so stately and may endure so long deserves to be recorded. In many localities a much shorter row, or even a few scattered trees, set out sixty or a hundred years since, is the most conspicuous as well as interesting relic of the past in sight. Nothing more proves the civility of one's ancestors.

The *Ribes floridum*, wild black currant, just begun by the wooden bridge just this side of the Assabet stone bridge, with dotted leaves. The thimble-berry and high blackberry leaves are among the *most* forward. That large reddish-stemmed cornel shows now narrow green buds tipped with reddish, three quarters of an inch long by one quarter wide.

Some thrashers are plainly better singers than others.

How surprising and interesting this cluster of leek buds on the rock in the Jesse Hosmer farm, composed of thick, succulent green leaves, cactus-like, tipped with dull purple, in buds from a half-inch to three inches in diameter! What tenacity of life! Its leaves so disposed (from circumference to centre) as to break joints. Some place it on a gate-post to grow high and dry above the earth for a curiosity. It may be a convenient symbol.

At the foot of Annursnack, rising from the Jesse Hosmer meadow, was surprised by the brilliant pale scarlet flowers of the painted-cup (*Castilleja coccinea*) just coming into bloom. Some may have been out a day or two. Methinks this the most high-colored and brilliant flower yet, not excepting the columbine.

and shrubs, such as no imperial wealth can surpass. The pyramidal pine-tops are now seen rising out of a reddish mistiness of the deciduous trees just bursting into leaf. A week ago the deciduous woods had not this misty look,[1] and the evergreens were more sharply divided from them, but now they have the appearance of being merged in or buoyed up in a mist. I am not [sic] sure what is the cause of the reddish line around the lower edges of the wood. It is plainly the red maple, and in many places, no doubt, the shrub oak. The oaks are plainly more gray already and some trees greenish. *Vide* again after a week.

The catkins of the black birch appear more advanced than those of the white birch. They are very large, four inches long, half a dozen gracefully drooping at the ends of the twigs bent down by their weight, conspicuous at a distance in wisps, as if dry leaves left on, very rich golden. The yellow birch is the first I have noticed fully in bloom, — considerably in advance of the others. Its flowers smell like its bark. Methinks the black and the paper birch next, and then the white, or all nearly together. The leaves of the *papyracea* unfold like a fan and are sticky. How fresh and glossy! And the catkins I gather shed pollen the next morning.

Some hickory buds are nearly two inches long. The handsome finely divided leaves of the pedicularis are conspicuous. It is now budded amid the painted-cups. The fruit of the *Populus grandidentata* appears puffed up and blasted into a large bright yellow [sic], like some

[1] [Two interrogation-points in pencil here.]

plums some seasons. The thorn bushes have so far leaved out on the north side of Annursnack as to reveal their forms, as I look up the hill and see them against the light. They are remarkably uniform, somewhat like this, the leading shoot finally rising above the rest, somewhat like a broad poplar.

May 9. Since I returned from Haverhill, not only I find the ducks are gone, but I no longer hear the *chill-lill* of the blue snowbird or the sweet strains of the fox-colored sparrow and the tree sparrow. The robin's strain is less remarkable.

I have devoted most of my day to Mr. Alcott. He is broad and genial, but indefinite; some would say feeble; forever feeling about vainly in his speech and touching nothing. But this is a very negative account of him, for he thus suggests far more than the sharp and definite practical mind. The feelers of his thought diverge, — such is the breadth of their grasp, — not converge; and in his society almost alone I can express at my leisure, with more or less success, my vaguest but most cherished fancy or thought. There are never any obstacles in the way of our meeting. He has no creed. He is not pledged to any institution. The sanest man I ever knew; the fewest crotchets, after all, has he.[1]

It has occurred to me, while I am thinking with pleasure of our day's intercourse, "Why should I not think aloud to you?" Having each some shingles of thought well dried, we walk and whittle them, trying our knives, and admiring the clear yellowish grain of the pump-

[1] [*Walden*, p. 296; Riv. 416.]

kin pine. We wade so gently and reverently, or we pull together so smoothly, that the fishes of thought are not scared from the stream, but come and go grandly, like yonder clouds that float peacefully through the western sky. When we walk it seems as if the heavens — whose mother-o'-pearl and rainbow tints come and go, form and dissolve — and the earth had met together, and righteousness and peace had kissed each other. I have an ally against the arch-enemy. A blue-robed man dwells under the blue concave. The blue sky is a distant reflection of the azure serenity that looks out from under a human brow.[1] We walk together like the most innocent children, going after wild pinks with case-knives. Most with whom I endeavor to talk soon fetch up against some institution or particular way of viewing things, theirs not being a universal view. They will continually bring their own roofs or — what is not much better — their own narrow skylights between us and the sky, when it is the unobstructed heavens I would view. Get out of the way with your old Jewish cobwebs. Wash your windows.[2]

Saw on Mr. Emerson's firs several parti-colored warblers, or finch creepers (*Sylvia Americana*), a small blue and yellow bird, *somewhat* like but smaller than the indigo-bird; quite tame, about the buds of the firs, now showing red; often head downward. Heard no note. He says it has been here a day or two.

At sundown paddled up the river.

[1] [*Walden*, p. 297; Riv. 416, 417.]
[2] [*Cape Cod, and Miscellanies*, p. 469; Misc. Riv. 271.]

Vol. V

The pump-like note of a stake-driver from the fenny place across the Lee meadow.

The greenest and rankest grass as yet is that in the water along the sides of the river. The hylodes are peeping. I love to paddle now at evening, when the water is smooth and the air begins to be warm. The rich warble of blackbirds about retiring is loud and incessant, not to mention the notes of numerous other birds. The black willow has started, but not yet the button-bush. Again I think I heard the night-warbler. Now, at starlight, that same nighthawk or snipe squeak is heard, but no hovering. The first bat goes suddenly zigzag overhead through the dusky air; comes out of the dusk and disappears into it. That slumbrous, snoring croak, far less ringing and musical than the toad's (which is occasionally heard), now comes up from the meadow's edge. I save a floating plank, which exhales and imparts to my hands the rank scent of the muskrats which have squatted on it. I often see their fresh green excrement on rocks and wood. Already men are fishing for pouts.

This has been almost the first warm day; none yet quite so warm. Walking to the Cliffs this afternoon, I noticed, on Fair Haven Hill, a season stillness, as I looked over the distant budding forest and heard the buzzing of a fly.

May 10. 5 A. M. — Up railroad.

The *veery* note after having heard the *yorrick* for some days, in the primitive-looking pine swamp. Heard also that peculiarly wild evergreen-forest note which

I heard May 6th, from a small, lisping warbler, — *er er ter re rer ree*, — from high in the pines, as if a chickadee (?); or was it the still smaller, slenderer white-bellied bird I saw? Female (?) yellowbird (?) this morning. All at once a strain which sounded like old times and recalled a hundred associations. Not at once did I remember that a year had elapsed since I heard it, and then the idea of the bobolink was formed in my mind, yet I afterward doubted if it was not the imitation of a catbird.[1] Saw a kingbird, looking like [a] large phœbe, on a willow by the river, and heard higher the clear whistle of the oriole. New days, then, have come, ushered in by the warbling vireo, yellowbird, Maryland yellow-throat, and small pewee, and now made perfect by the twittering of the king-bird and the whistle of the oriole amid the elms (for I hear the last in various parts of the town within a few hours), which are but just beginning to leaf out, thinking of his nest there, — if not already the bobolink. The warbling vireo promised warmer days, but the oriole ushers in summer heats.

There is an old pasture behind E. Wood's incrusted with the clay-like thallus of the bæomyces, which is unexpectedly thin. The fruit now large.

How far the woodpecker's tapping is heard! And no wonder, for he taps very hard as well as fast, to make a hole, and the dead, dry wood is very resounding withal. Now he taps on one part of the tree, and it yields one note; then on that side, a few inches distant, and it yields another key; propped on its tail the while.

[1] It was the bobolink.

The pear has blossomed. The butternut buds are more advanced than any hickories I have noticed.

P. M. — To Saw Mill Brook and Smith's Hill.

The *Nepeta Glechoma* is out under R. Brown's poles, a pretty deep-blue, half-concealed, violet-like flower. It is the earliest flower of this character. Warm days when you begin to *think* of thin coats.

I proceed down the Turnpike. The masses of the golden willow are seen in the distance on either side the way, twice as high as the road is wide, conspicuous against the distant, still half-russet hills and forests, for the green grass hardly yet prevails over the dead stubble, and the woods are but just beginning to gray. The female willow is a shade greener. At this season the traveller passes through a golden gate on causeways where these willows are planted, as if he were approaching the entrance to Fairyland; and there will surely be found the yellowbird, and already from a distance is heard his note, a *tche tche tche tcha tchar tcha*, — ah, willow, willow. Could not he truly arrange for us the difficult family of the willows better than Borrer, or Barratt of Middletown? And as he passes between the portals, a sweet fragrance is wafted to him; he not only breathes but scents and tastes the air, and he hears the low humming or susurrus of a myriad insects which are feeding on its sweets. It is, apparently, these that attract the yellowbird. The golden gates of the year, the *May*-gate. The traveller cannot pass out of Concord by the highways in any direction without passing between such portals, — graceful, curving,

Vol. V

drooping, wand-like twigs, on which leaves and blossoms appear together.

It is remarkable that I saw this morning for the first time the bobolink, gold robin, and kingbird, — and have since heard the first two in various parts of the town and am satisfied that they have just come, — and, in the woods, the veery note. I hear the ringing sound of the toads borne on the rippling wind as I keep down the causeway.

He is the richest who has most use for nature as raw material of tropes and symbols with which to describe his life. If these gates of golden willows affect me, they correspond to the beauty and promise of some experience on which I am entering. If I am overflowing with life, am rich in experience for which I lack expression, then nature will be my language full of poetry, — all nature will *fable*, and every natural phenomenon be a myth. The man of science, who is not seeking for expression but for a fact to be expressed merely, studies nature as a dead language. I pray for such inward experience as will make nature significant.

That sedum (?) by Tuttle's is now a foot high; has no great cactus-like buds, and is quite distinct from the house-leek in Jesse Hosmer's field. What is it? A gooseberry which has been in blossom for some time, by the roadside on the left, between Wright's and Hosmer's old place. It is apparently *Ribes hirtellum*. Is that the swamp gooseberry of Gray, now just beginning to blossom at Saw Mill Brook? It has a divided style and stamens, etc., as yet not longer than the

calyx, though my slip has no thorns nor prickles. The leaves are deeply divided and glossy. But what is the *stout, prickly* gooseberry in the garden, with *divided* style? It seems the *Cynosbati* of Bigelow, yet not of Gray. A cerastium, apparently *viscosum*, on right hand just beyond the Hosmer house. What kind? A wild red cherry (*Cerasus Pennsylvanica*) just out by the first-named gooseberry. I was surprised by the number of bees above this gooseberry's blossoms, small and inconspicuous as they are. Indeed there is scarcely a flower which is not immediately found out by insects, and their coming must be coincident with flowers and leaves. Some of the most forward plantain-leaved antennaria is already pinkish at top.

You hear the clear whistle and see the red or fiery orange of the oriole darting through Hosmer's orchard. But its note is not melodious and rich. It is at most a clear tone, the healthiest of your city beaux and belles.

When I heard the first bobolink strain this morning I could not at first collect myself enough to tell what it was I heard, — a reminiscence of last May in all its prime occurring in the midst of the experience of this in its unripe state. Suddenly, the season being sufficiently advanced, the atmosphere in the right condition, these flashing, scintillating notes are struck out from it where that dark mote disappears through it, as sparks by a flint, with a tinkling sound. This flashing, tinkling meteor bursts through the expectant meadow air, leaving a train of tinkling notes behind. Successive regiments of birds arrive and are disbanded in our fields, like soldiers still wearing their

regimentals. I doubted at first if it were not a strain brought on a few days in advance by an imitative catbird or thrush (?) from where he had been staying.

Within a day or more, a lower and decidedly downy and small racemed amelanchier has opened, and I think that the first and slightly downy and greenish-leaved ones are associated with the decidedly smooth and red-leaved *Botryapium*. Is not this now the most conspicuous native flower? The *Vaccinium vacillans* is out.

The three colored violets, as I observe them this afternoon, are thus distinguished: the *ovata*, a dark lilac, especially in sun; the *cucullata*, oftenest slaty-blue, sometimes lilac, deeper within, more or less pale and striped; the *pedata*, large, exposed, clear pale-blue with a white spot. None like the sky, but *pedata* most like it; lilac *ovata* least like it. Yet the last is the richest-colored. The *pedata* often pale to whiteness. It begins now to be quite obvious along the side of warm and sandy woodland paths.

Saw, quite near, a skunk, in a cloud of long, coarse black and white hair, within a rod and a half, sharply staring at me with head to the ground, with its black, shining, bead-like eyes. It was at the edge of its hole. Its head is so narrow, and snout long and pointed, that it can make those deep holes in the spring. By the way, what makes these innumerable little punctures just through the grass in woodland paths, as with a stick? Is this, too, by the skunk?

The chestnut leaves are now commonly as far unfolded as the larger maples and earlier oaks and more than the elm; yet perhaps it should come after the red and black oaks. The aspen *leaves* (*P. tremuli-formis*), at least a few days since, were decidedly the most forward and conspicuous of any tree, and are still, I think, being more than an inch in diameter, light-green, but open and trembling and not in dense masses. Only the rather rare paper birch and an occasional white birch in a favorable place (I see no black nor yellow ones this afternoon) can be compared with it, and such, indeed, make now, at last, a denser green; but in the case of the golden willow it is as much flowers as leaves that make the show. But the *P. grandidentata* which have flowered show no leaves yet; only very young ones, small downy leaves now. Of sizable wild trees which blossom, the most forward in respect to leafing, methinks, are the tremble, the willows, wild black cherry, the birches (the *papyracea* especially), balm-of-Gilead, *Ostrya*. The spring growth of the larch is the most conspicuous of evergreens [*sic*], though its buds have not pushed out so far as the white pines. As on the late willows, so on the oaks, catkins and leaves appearing together. Both leaf and flower buds of the oaks, especially shrub oaks and red and black, are reddish (the white and swamp white are not at present), and hence the *reddish* mistiness of the deciduous woods at present.

At Saw Mill Brook, I see the flower-buds of the nodding trillium. I sit on a rock in Saw Mill Brook.

The hornbeam (*Carpinus*) is just ready to bloom, its hop-like catkins, shorter than those of the *Ostrya*, do not shed pollen just yet.[1] I was in search of this,

[1] Does next morning in pitcher.

and, not observing it at first, and having forgotten it, I sat down on a rock, with the thought that if I sat there quietly a little while I might see some flower or other object about me; unexpectedly, as I cast my eyes upward, over my head stretched a spreading branch of the carpinus full of small catkins with anthers now reddish, spread like a canopy just over my head. As it is best to sit in a grove and let the birds come to you, so, as it were, even the flowers will come to you.

I sit here surrounded by hellebores eighteen inches high or more, with handsome, regular, plaited leaves, regularly arranged around the erect stems, and a multitude of ferns are unrolling themselves, altogether making the impression of a tropical vegetation.

I hear, and have for a week, in the woods, the note of one or more small birds somewhat like a yellow-bird's. What is it? Is it the redstart? I now see one of these. The first I have distinguished. And now I feel pretty certain that my black and yellow warbler of May 1st was this. As I sit, it inquisitively hops nearer and nearer. It is one of the election-birds of rare colors which I can remember, mingled dark and reddish. This reminds me that I supposed much more variety and fertility in nature before I had learned the numbers and the names of each order. I find that I had expected such fertility in our Concord woods alone as not even the completest museum of stuffed birds of all the forms and colors from all parts of the world comes up to. The neat and active creeper hops about the trunks, its note like a squeaking twig.

I leave the woods and begin to ascend Smith's

Vol. V

Hill along the course of the rill. The anemonies with reddish-pink buds stand thick amid the loose grass under protecting brush or fagots, about rocks and young trees.

From the hill, I look westward over the landscape. The deciduous woods are in their hoary youth, every expanding bud swaddled with downy webs. From this more eastern hill, with the whole breadth of the river valley on the west, the mountains appear higher still, the width of the blue border is greater, — not mere peaks, or a short and shallow sierra, but a high blue table-land with broad foundations, a deep and solid base or tablet, in proportion to the peaks that rest on it. As you ascend, the near and low hills sink and flatten into the earth; no sky is seen behind them; the distant mountains rise. The truly great are distinguished. Vergers, crests of the waves of earth, which in the highest break at the summit into granitic rocks over which the air beats. A part of their hitherto concealed base is seen blue. You see, not the domes only, but the body, the façade, of these terrene temples. You see that the foundation answers to the superstructure. Moral structures. (The sweet-fern leaves among odors now.) The successive lines of haze which divide the western landscape, deeper and more misty over each intervening valley, are not yet very dense; yet there is a light atmospheric line along the base of the mountains for their whole length, formed by this denser and grosser atmosphere through which we look next the earth, which almost melts them into the atmosphere, like the contact of

molten metal with that which is unfused; but their pure, sublimed tops and main body rise, palpable sky-land above it, like the waving signal of the departing who have already left these shores. It will be worth the while to observe carefully the direction and altitude of the mountains from the Cliffs. The value of the mountains in the horizon, — would not that be a good theme for a lecture? The text for a discourse on real values, and permanent; a sermon on the mount. They are stepping-stones to heaven, — as the rider has a horse-block at his gate, — by which to mount when we would commence our pilgrimage to heaven; by which we gradually take our departure from earth, from the time when our youthful eyes first rested on them, — from this bare actual earth, which has so little of the hue of heaven. They make it easier to die and easier to live. They let us off.

(With Alcott almost alone is it possible to put all institutions behind us. Every other man owns some stock in this or that one, and will not forget it.)

Whether any picture by a human master hung on our western wall could supply their place. Whether to shovel them away and level them would really smooth the way to the true west. Whether the skies would not weep over their scars. They are valuable to mankind as is the iris of the eye to a man. They are the path of the translated. The undisputed territory between earth and heaven. In our travels rising higher and higher, we at length got to where the earth was blue. Suggesting that this earth, unless our conduct curse it, is as celestial as that sky. They are the pastures to which we drive our thoughts on these 20ths of May. (George Baker told me the other day that he had driven cows to Winchendon, forty miles, in one day.) Men often spend a great deal on a border to their papered walls, of the costliest figure and colors, ultramarine (or what other?). This color bears a price like precious stones. We may measure our wealth, then, by the number of square rods of superficial *blue* earth in our earth border. Such proportion as it bears to the area of the visible earth, in such proportion are we heavenly-minded. Yet I doubt if I can find a man in this country who would not think it better if they were converted into solid gold, which could in no case be a blessing to all, but only a curse to a few, — and so they would be stepping-stones to hell.

Return by Mill Brook Ditch Path. There is now a multiplicity of sounds, in which the few faint spring ones are drowned. The birds are in full blast, singing, warbling, chirping, humming. Yet we do not receive more ideas through our ears than before. The storms and ducks of spring have swept by and left us to the repose of summer, the farmers to the ignoble pursuits of planting and hoeing corn and potatoes. The summer is not bracing, as when you hear the note of the jay in the cool air of October from the rustling chestnut woods. Hear the night-warbler now distinctly. It does not soon repeat its note, and disappears with the sound. I mistook a distant farmer's horn calling the men to early tea for the low hum of a bee in the grass. Heard a tree-toad. The pond, Walden, has risen considerably since the melting.

Vol. V

The late pipes (*limosum?*), now nearly a foot high, are very handsome, like Oriental work, their encircled columns of some precious wood or gem, or like small bamboos, from Oriental jungles. Very much like art. The gold-thread, apparently for a day or two, though few flowers compared with buds; not at once referred to its leaf, so distant on its thread-like peduncle. The water-saxifrage also for a day or two in some places, on its tall, straight stem, rising from its whorl of leaves. Sorrel now fairly out in some places. I will put it under May 8th. A high blueberry by Potter's heater piece. A yellow lily.

The red-eye at the spring; quite a woodland note. The different moods or degrees of wildness and poetry of which the song of birds is the keynote. The wood thrush Mr. Barnum never hired nor can, though he could bribe Jenny Lind and put her into his cage. How many little birds of the warbler family are busy now about the opening buds, while I sit by the spring! They are almost as much a part of the tree as its blossoms and leaves. They come and give it voice. Its twigs feel with pleasure their little feet clasping them.

I hear the distant drumming of a partridge. Its beat, however distant and low, falls still with a remarkably forcible, almost painful, impulse on the ear, like veritable little drumsticks on our tympanum, as if it were a throbbing or fluttering in our veins or brows or the chambers of the ear, and belonging to ourselves, — as if it were produced by some little insect which had made its way up into the passages of the ear, so penetrating is it. It is as palpable to the

May 11. 5 A. M. — In the morning and evening, when waters are still and smooth, and dimpled by innate currents only, not disturbed by foreign winds and currents of the air, and reflect more light than at noonday. [*Sic.*]

P. M. — To Corner Spring *via* Hubbard's Bathing-Place.

The buck-bean is budded, but hard to find now. The *Viola lanceolata* is now abundant thereabouts, methinks larger and quite as fragrant (which is not saying much) as the *blanda*. How long has it been open? It is a warm afternoon, and great numbers of painted and spotted tortoises are lying in the sun in the meadow. I notice that the thin scales are peeling off of one of the painted and curled up more than half an inch at the edges, and others look as if they had just lost them, the dividing-line being of a dull cream-color. Has this lying in the sun anything to do with it? I nearly stepped upon a song sparrow and a striped snake at the same time. The bird fluttered away almost as if detained. I thought it was a case of charming, without doubt, and should think so still if I had not found her nest with five eggs there, which will account for her being so near the snake that was about to devour her. The amelanchier has a sickish fragrance. It must be the myrtle-bird which is now so common in Hubbard's Meadow Woods or Swamp, with a note somewhat like a yellowbird's, striped olive-yellow and black on back or shoulders, light or white beneath, black dim; restless bird; sharp head. The catbird has a squeaking and split note with some clear whistles.

ear as the sharpest note of a fife. Of course, that bird can drum with its wings on a log which can go off with such a powerful whir, beating the air. I have seen a thoroughly frightened hen and cockerel fly almost as powerfully, but neither can sustain it long. Beginning slowly and deliberately, the partridge's beat sounds faster and faster from far away under the boughs and through the aisles of the wood until it becomes a regular roll, but is speedily concluded. How many things shall we not see and be and do, when we walk there where the partridge drums!

As I stand by the river in the truly warm sun, I hear the low trump of a bullfrog, but half sounded, — doubting if it be really July, — some bassoon sounds, as it were the tuning that precedes the summer's orchestra; and all is silent again. How the air is saturated with sweetness on causeways these willowy days! The willow alone of trees as yet makes light, often *rounded masses* of verdure in large trees, stage above stage. But oftenest they are cut down at the height of four or five feet and spread out thence. There appear to be most clouds in the horizon on [one] of these days of drifting downy clouds, because, when we look that way, more fall within our field of view, but when we look upward, overhead we see the true proportion of clear blue.

The mountains are something solid which is blue, a *terra firma* in the heavens; but in the heavens there is nothing but the air. Blue is the color of the day, and the sky is blue by night as well as by day, because it knows no night.

May 12. 5.30 A. M. — To Nawshawtuct by river.

The first considerable fog I have noticed, at first as high as the trees, curling gray over the water now beneath me, as I paddle my boat, and through it I see the welling dimples of the still stream. You are pretty sure now to hear the stake-driver farther or nearer, morning or evening. Thought I heard a tanager. What are those dark-brown striped sparrow-like birds, rather tame, on hickories, size of myrtle-bird, mottled with black on breast and more or less distinct yellowish on rump and wing shoulder, at least on male; somewhat brown-creeper-looking, without long bill? The fog has now risen up as high as the houses at 6.15 and mingled with the smokes of the town. The first [*sic*] are puffed up as if they were cold, to nearly twice their size, as they sit on willows. The yellowbird has another note, *tchut tchut tchar te tchit e war.*

P. M. — To Black Birch Woods and Yellow Birch Swamp.

Veronica serpyllifolia at Flint's and along the roadsides, apparently for some time, for not only are there some frost-bitten flowers, but pods alone as large as flowers, even as if they belonged to last year. Yet is it any earlier than May? A pretty but minute bluish flower.

Some grass is seen to wave in the distance on the side of N. Barrett's warm hill, showing the lighter under sides. That is a soft, soothing, June-like impression when the most forward grass is seen to wave and the sorrel looks reddish. The year has the down

of youth on its cheek. This, too, is the era of the bobolink, now, when apple trees are ready to burst into bloom. Now it is too late to retreat from the summer adventure. You have passed the Rubicon, and will spend your summer here. Lately, for a few days, the note of the pine warbler rang through the woods, but now it is lost in the notes of other birds. Then each song was solo. Its *vetter vetter vetter vetter* rang through silent woods. Now I rarely hear it. A yellow butterfly.

The river meadows from Barrett's wall are very green where the water has gone down. A wild pear in blossom on Ponkawtasset, detected by its uprightness and no large limbs; but the blossoms, being white, are not so handsome as the apple, but are earlier.

The *V. cucullata* are large and conspicuous on Barrett's side-hill. The *ovata* blue the ground in the Boulder Field. These and the *pedata* are all more or less lilac-colored, and it produces a pleasing bewilderment to pass from clump to clump, and one species to another, and say which is the most lilac. Putting one cluster beside another more lilac, the first no longer seems lilac at all. Has not violet then always some lilac in it?

The birches (white) are now rapidly and conspicuously greening. They make the first conspicuous mass of green amid the evergreens; not grayish or hoary like the oaks; a closer-woven light-green vest. The black birch is now a beautiful sight, its long, slender, bushy branches waving in the wind (the leaf-buds but just beginning to unfold), with countless little tassel-like bunches of five or six golden catkins, spotted with

brown and three inches long, one bunch at the end of each drooping twig, hanging straight down, or dangling like heads of rye, or blown off at various angles with the horizon. All these, seen against the sky on the otherwise bare trees, make an exceedingly graceful outline, the catkin is so large and conspicuous. (On the white birch the catkins are more slender, and are concealed by the more forward leaves.) The reddish long female flowers are detected in the axils lower down. I notice that the staminate ones are apparently torn by birds, pecking at insects. Not a bunch is perfect. The yellow birch is considerably the most forward, — its flowers, not, perhaps, its leaves, which last are only expanded on young trees, though here is one large one leaved out. The yellow birch first, then the black or the paper birch, then the white. The staminate flowers of the yellow birch are already imbrowned and dry, and the female flowers large and hop-like, one inch long. The twigs of this tree are, methinks, still longer and slenderer than those of the black birch, a yard long by one sixth of an inch diameter at base without a branch at the ends of the limbs, or a yard and a half by a third of an inch with a little fork near the end, or often three inches in diameter by more than twenty feet; and so is described the whole tree, of long slender branches springing from the height of five or six feet upward in the form of a great brush. I do not know another place in town where there are black birches enough to give you the effect of a forest of these trees, but in a swamp here. They are so slender and brushy that they yield to the wind, and their tops, with gracefully

drooping twigs bent down by dangling tassel-like catkins, are all inclined one way, sweeping the air, making a peculiarly light and graceful sight.

I am surprised to find the pedicularis, or lousewort, — a yellowish one, — out, on a warm bank near the meadow-edge. The hellebore is the most forward herb, two feet high.

The tupelo shows signs of life, but is later than the black willow; not so late, nearly, as the button-bush. The oaks are in the gray. Some in warm localities already have expanded small leaves, both black, red, and shrub oak. The large light-yellowish scales of the hickory buds, also, are turned back, revealing blossom-buds and little clusters of tender leaves ready to unfold, and the now [*sic*] web of verdure is spreading thick and palpable over the forest. Shade is being born; the summer is pitching its tent; concealment will soon be afforded to the birds in which to build their nests.

The robin nowadays betrays its great bare nest and blue eggs by its anxious peeping at your approach.

Is that the so-called Canada plum, now in bloom twenty rods this side the lime-kiln in the road? And is it ever indigenous here?

The farmers on all sides are mending their fences and turning out their cows to pasture. You see where the rails have been newly sharpened, and the leafing birches have been cut and laid over gaps in the walls, as if old fences were putting forth leaves.

The beautiful round red (?) buds of the grape now, like beads, at long intervals along the bare vine.

William Wheeler has raised a new staring house beyond the Corner Bridge, and so done irreparable injury to a large section of country for walkers. It obliges us to take still more steps after weary ones, to reach the secluded fields and woods. Channing proposes that we petition him to put his house out of sight; that we send it in to him in the form of a round-robin with his name on one side and mine on the other, — so to abate a nuisance.

May 13. Methinks I hear and see the tanager now. The middle of May is the time for many transient sylvias.

P. M. — To Conantum.

See a goldfinch glance by on the back road and hear its cool watery twitter. A little larger than a yellow-bird, more golden, or paler (?) yellow, with black [*sic*] and on wings. A robin's nest, with young, on the causeway. At Corner Spring, stood listening to a cat-bird, sounding a good way off. Was surprised to detect the singer within a rod and a half on a low twig, the ventriloquist. Should not have believed it was he, if I had not seen the movements of his throat, corresponding to each note, — looking at this near singer whose notes sounded so far away. There is a small bird or two I have not taken pains to identify; one's note, perhaps that of May 6th, *ee, ee, te ter twee,* like a fine squeaking amid the pines.

——'s peach trees in bloom, the richest, highest color of any tree's bloom, like wine compared to beer; the trees, bare of leaves, one mass of pink, some dark, some

Vol. V

light, almost flame-like seen against green hillsides or the red ground where the woods have just been cut. How much more beautiful than the life of the peach-raiser! No such rich pink bloom falling through cracks in the dark shutters irradiates his soul. If only such a peach-bloom hue suffused the dark chambers of his soul! Large masses of bloom with the delicate tint which commonly belongs to minute plants only.

The bass is suddenly as forward in leaf as the white birch; leaves one inch across, how varnished, thin, and transparent! It is apparently the *Myosotis stricta,* now just in flower at Columbine Cliff, scorpion grass, minute and white, three inches high, somewhat like a cerastium. An *Arum triphyllum,* but no signs of pollen yet. Probably was set down too early last year, *i. e.* before pollen. A thorn with expanded leaves, not deeply lobed, and large red scales and a beautifully shining or varnished ash-colored twig. The male sassafras just out, probably yesterday, but the twig end is the sweetest. A big woodpecker enlarging the entrance to its nest in an apple tree. I thought it the echo of carpenters at work on Wheeler's house three quarters of a mile off. It was within four or five rods. How well the woodpecker must know by the ring if the tree is hollow, by this time!

Most of the anthers of the black ash are black and withered or blasted, but the rest show no pollen yet. Still methinks it [is] now in bloom; leaf-buds not started. The white ash (male), with its male buds conspicuous but not ready yet, its leaf-buds partly expanded. So, if its flowers are a little later, which is not certain, its

leaves are earlier than the last. The sweet viburnum, apparently equally advanced with the *nudum,* but not so dark-colored, in advance of cornels. Hazelnuts next to birches.

Heard a stake-driver in Hubbard's meadow from Corner road. Thus far off, I hear only, or chiefly, the last dry, hard click or stroke part of the note, sounding like the echo from some near wood of a distant stake-driving. Here only this portion of the note, but close by it is more like pumping, when the dry stroke is accompanied by the incessant sound of the pump.

May 14. *Saturday.* 9 A. M. — To Wayland by boat.

E. Wood has added a pair of ugly wings to his house, bare of trees and painted white, particularly conspicuous from the river. You might speak of the alar extent of this house, monopolizing so much of our horizon; but alas! it is not formed for flight, after all.

The water is considerably rough to-day, and higher than usual at this season. The black willows have started, but make no show of green. The button-bushes are yet apparently dead. The green buds of yellow lilies are bobbing up and down, already showing more or less yellow; this the most forward sign in the water. The great scalloped platters of their leaves have begun to show themselves on the surface, and the red round leaves of the white lily, now red above as well as below. A myriad of polygonums, potamogetons, and pontederias are pushing up from the bottom, but have not yet reached the surface. Dande-

lions and houstonias, etc., spot the meadows with yellow and white.

The still dead-looking willows and button-bushes are alive with red-wings,[1] now perched on a yielding twig, now pursuing a female swiftly over the meadow, now darting across the stream. No two have epaulets equally brilliant. Some are small and almost white, and others a brilliant vermilion. They are handsomer than the golden robin, methinks. The yellowbird, kingbird, and pewee, beside many swallows, are also seen. But the rich colors and the rich and varied notes of the blackbirds surpass them all.

Passing Conantum under sail at 10 o'clock, the cows in this pasture are already chewing the cud in the thin shade of the apple trees, a picture of peace, already enjoying the luxury of their green pastures. I was not prepared to find the season so far advanced. The breeze which comes over the water, sensibly cooled or freshened by it, is already grateful. Suddenly there start up from the riverside at the entrance of Fair Haven Pond, scared by our sail, two great blue herons, — slate-color rather, — slowly flapping and undulating, their projecting breast-bones very visible, — or is it possibly their necks bent back? — their legs stuck out straight behind. Getting higher by their flight, they straight come back to reconnoitre us.

Land at Lee's Cliff, where the herons have preceded us and are perched on the oaks, conspicuous from afar, and again we have a fair view of their flight.

[1] *Vide* June 11.

We find here, unexpectedly, the warmth of June. The hot, dry scent, or say warm and balmy, from ground amid the pitch pines carpeted with red needles, where a wiry green grass is springing up, reminds us of June and of wild pinks. Under the south side of the Cliff, vegetation seems a fortnight earlier than elsewhere. Not only the beautiful little veronicas (*serpyllifolia*) are abundantly out, and cowslips past their prime, columbines past prime, and saxifrage gone to seed, some of it, and dandelions, and the sod sparkling with the pure, brilliant, spotless yellow of cinquefoil, also violets and strawberries, but the glossy or varnished yellow of buttercups (*bulbosus*, also abundant, some days out) spots the hillside. The south side of these rocks is like a hothouse where the gardener has removed his glass. The air, scented with sweetbriar, may almost make you faint in imagination. The nearer the base of the rock, the more forward each plant. The trees are equally forward, red and black; leaves an inch and a half long and shoots of three inches.

The prospect from these rocks is early-June-like. You notice the tender light green of the birches, both white and paper, and the brown-red tops of the maples where their keys are. Close under the lee of the button-bushes which skirt the pond, as I look south, there is a narrow smooth strip of water, silvery and contrasting with the darker rippled body of the pond. Its edge, or the separation between this, which I will call the polished silvery border of the pond, and the dark and ruffled body, is not a straight line or film,

but an ever-varying, irregularly and finely serrated or fringed border, ever changing as the breeze falls over the bushes at an angle more or less steep, so that this moment it is a rod wide, the next not half so much. Every feature is thus fluent in the landscape.

Again we embark, now having furled our sail and taken to our oars. The air is clear and fine-grained, and as we glide by the hills I can look into the very roots of the grass amid the springing pines in their deepest valleys. The wind rises, but still it is not a cold wind. There is nothing but slate-colored water and a few red pads appearing at Lily Bay.

After leaving Rice's harbor the wind is with us again. What a fine tender *yellow* green from the meadow-grass just pushed up, where the sun strikes it at the right angle! How it contrasts with the dark bluish-green of that rye, already beginning to wave, which covers that little rounded hill by Pantry Brook! Grain waves earlier than grass. How flat the top of the muskrat's head as he swims, and his back, even with it, and then when he dives he ludicrously shows his tail. They look gray and brown, like a rabbit, now. At Forget-me-not Spring the chrysosplenium beds are very large, rich and deep, almost out of bloom. I find none of the early blackberry in bloom. It is mostly destroyed. Already we pluck and eat the sweet flag and detect small critchicrotches. The handsome comandra leaves also are prominent. In the woods which skirt the river near

Deacon Farrar's swamp, the *Populus grandidentata*, just expanding its downy leaves, makes silvery patches in the sun. It is abundant and truly silvery.

The paper birch woods at Fair Haven present this aspect: there is the somewhat dense light green of aspens (*tremuliformis*) and paper birches in the foreground next the water, both of one tint, and occasionally a red maple with brownish-red top, with— equally advanced, aye, more fully expanded, intermixed or a little higher up—very tall and slender amelanchiers (*Botryapium?*), some twenty-five feet high, on which no signs of fruit, though I have seen them on some; some silvery *grandidentata*, and red and black oaks (some yellowish, some reddish, green), and still reddish-white oaks, just starting; and green pines for contrast, showing the silvery under sides of their leaves or the edges of their dark stages (contrasting with their shaded under sides). These are the colors of the forest-top, — the rug, looking down on it.

Tufts of coarse grass [1] are in full bloom along the riverside, — little islets big enough to support a fisherman.

Again we scare up the herons, who, methinks, will build hereabouts. They were standing by the waterside. And again they alight farther below, and we see their light-colored heads erect, and their bodies at various angles as they stoop to drink. And again they flap away with their great slate-blue wings, necks curled up (?) and legs straight out behind, and, having

[1] *Carex stricta.*

attained a great elevation, they circle back over our heads, now seemingly black as crows against the sky, — crows with long wings, they might be taken for, — but higher and higher they mount by stages in the sky, till heads and tails are lost and they are mere black wavelets amid the blue, one always following close behind the other. They are evidently mated. It would be worth the while if we could see them oftener in our sky.

Some apple trees are fairly out.

What is that small slate-colored hawk with black tips to wings?

May 15. Sunday. P. M. — To Annursnack.

Silvery cinquefoil now open. Its petals, perchance, show the green between them, but the beautiful under sides of the leaves more than make up for it. What was that bird beyond the Lee place, with a chickadee-like note, black head and throat, and light color round the neck and beneath; methinks longer and slenderer than the chickadee? The golden willow catkins begin to fall; their prime is past. And buttercups and silvery cinquefoil, and the first apple blossoms, and waving grass beginning to be tinged with sorrel, introduce us to a different season. The huckleberry, *resinosa*, its red flowers are open, in more favorable places several days earlier, probably; and the earliest shrub and red and black oaks in warm exposures may be set down to to-day. A red butterfly goes by. Methinks I have seen them before. The painted-cup is now abundantly and fully out. Six or eight inches high above its spidery leaves, almost like a red flame, it stands on edge of the hill just rising from the meadow, — on the instep of the hill. It tells of July with its fiery color. It promises a heat we have not experienced yet. This is a field which lies nearer to summer. Yellow is the color of spring; red, of midsummer. Through pale golden and green we arrive at the yellow of the buttercup; through scarlet, to the fiery July red, the red lily.

The first cricket's chirrup which I have chanced to hear now falls on my ear and makes me forget all else; all else is a thin and movable crust down to that depth where he resides eternally. He already foretells autumn. Deep under the dry border of some rock in this hillside he sits, and makes the finest singing of birds outward and insignificant, his own song is so much deeper and more significant. His voice has set me thinking, philosophizing, moralizing at once. It is not so wildly melodious, but it is wiser and more mature than that of the wood thrush. With this elixir I see clear through the summer now to autumn, and any summer work seems frivolous. I am disposed to ask this humblebee that hurries humming past so busily if he knows what he is about. At one leap I go from the just opened buttercup to the life-everlasting. This singer has antedated autumn. His strain is superior (inferior?) [1] to seasons. It annihilates time and space; the summer is for time-servers.

The *Erigeron bellidifolius* has now spread its rays out flat since last Sabbath. I may set it down to

---

[1] Exaltedly inferior.

May 10th, methinks. It is the first of what I may call the daisy family, sometimes almost white. What are those large conical-shaped fungi of which I see a dozen round an apple tree? I thought them pieces of a yellowish wasp-nest, they are so honeycombed.

I looked again on the forest from this hill, which view may contrast with that of last Sunday. The mist produced by the leafing of the deciduous trees has greatly thickened now and lost much of its reddishness in the lighter green of expanding leaves, has become a brownish or yellowish green, except where it has attained distinctness in the light-green foliage of the birch, the earliest distinct foliage visible in *extensive great* masses at a great distance, the aspen not being common. The pines and other evergreens are now fast being merged in a sea of foliage.

The weather has grown rapidly warm. Methinks I wore a greatcoat here last Sunday; now an undercoat is too much. I even think of bathing in the river. I love to sit in the wind on this hill and be blown on. We bathe thus first in air; then, when the air has warmed it, in water.

Here are ten cows feeding on the hill beside me. Why do they move about so fast as they feed? They have advanced thirty rods in ten minutes, and sometimes the [last] one runs to keep up. Is it to give the grass thus a chance to grow more equally and always get a fresh bite? The tall buttercup on the west edge of Painted-Cup Meadow for a day or two at least, and the fringed polygala as long. This side stone bridge, *Barbarea vulgaris*, or common winter cress. yellow rocket,

also as long. A thorn will blossom in a day or two, without varnished ashy twigs and with deep-cut lobes.

The following trees and shrubs methinks *leaf* out in nearly the following order. The more questionable, or which I have not seen, are marked — (?).

Gooseberry	Thorns	Swamp white oak
Currant	Waxwork	Chestnut oak
Trembles	Maples (??)	Hardhack (?)
Some willows	Shrub oak	*Salix nigra*
Young white, red, and	Chinquapin oak	Grape
sugar maples	Red "	White ash
Balm-of-Gilead	Black "	Black "
Elder	Scarlet " (?)	Sumach
Meadow-sweet	Hazel	Beech (?)
Diervilla	Larch	Swamp-pink
Black cherry	White pine	Witch-hazel
Ostrya	Elm	Nemopanthes } (?)
Alder	Hornbeam (??)	Prinos
Paper birch	Cornels (some later ?)	Clethra
Black "	Chestnut	Tupelo
Yellow "	Great-leaved poplar	Mountain laurel (??)
White "	Butternut	Panicled andromeda
Pyrus arbutifolia	Hickories	Dwarf
Apple	Bass	Rhodora
Amelanchier	Sassafras	Button-bush
Choke cherry	Locust (?)	Hemlock (?) ? (?)[1]
Dwarf "	Celtis(?)	White spruce [1]
Wild red "	Pitch pine	Black spruce [1]
Viburnum nudum	*Juniperus repens*	
" *Lentago*	Red cedar	} (?) The above list made
Maple leaved viburnum (?)	White "	May 20th.
Barberry	Arbor-vitæ	
	White oak	

---

[1] Seen a day or two after the button-bush started. The hemlock appeared later, but it may [be] because it is of slower growth.

May 16. E. Hoar saw the henbit (*Lamium amplexicaule*) a week ago from Mr. Pritchard's garden. Celandine is out a day or more, and rhodora, trillium, and yellow violets yesterday at least. Horse-chestnut to-day. What handsome long yellow, threadlike peduncles to the staminate flowers of the sugar maple! three inches long, tassel-like, appearing with the leaves.

A man is about town with a wagon-load of the *Rhododendron maximum* this evening from Gardiner, Maine. It is well budded; buds nearly an inch long; long, narrow, thick leaves, six inches long or more. He says it means the "rose of Dendrum" and will grow from a mere slip cut off and stuck in any soil, — only water it three times a day! ! ! No doubt of it.

It has been oppressively warm to-day, the first really warm, sultry-like weather, so that we were prepared for a thunder-storm at evening. At 5 P. M., dark, heavy, wet-looking clouds are seen in the northern horizon, perhaps over the Merrimack Valley, and we say it is going down the river and we shall not get a drop. The main body goes by, there is a shower in the north, and the western sky is suffused with yellow where its thin skirts are withdrawing. People stand at their doors in the warm evening, listening to the muttering of distant thunder and watching the forked lightning, now descending to the earth, now ascending to the clouds. This the first really warm day and thunder-shower. Had thunder-shower while I was in Haverhill in April. Nature appears to have passed a crisis. All slimy reptile life is wide awake. The sprayey dream of the toad has a new sound; from the meadow the hylodes are heard more distinctly; and the tree-toad chirrups often from the elms (?). The sultry warmth and moister air has called him into life. We smell the fresher and cooler air from where the storm has passed. And now that it has grown dark, the skirts of the cloud seem to promise us a shower. It lightens incessantly right in the west; the right wing of the rear guard of the storm is steadily advancing and firing, and every flash shows the outlines of the cloud. We look out into the dark, and ever and anon comes a sudden illumination blinding our eyes, like a vast glow-worm, succeeded ere long by the roll of thunder. The first pattering of drops is heard; all west windows are hastily shut. The weak-eyed sit with their backs to windows and close the blinds. But we are disappointed, after all, and each flash reveals a narrow strip of evening red through the thin drops below the advancing cloud.

May 17. 5 A. M. — To Island by boat.

Everything has sensibly advanced during the warm and moist night. Some trees, as the small maples in the street, already look verdurous. The air has not sensibly cooled much. The chimney swallows are busily skimming low over the river and just touching the water without regard to me, as a week ago they did, and as they circle back overhead to repeat the experiment, I hear a sharp snap or short rustling of their wings. The button-bush now shows the first signs of life, on a close inspection, in its small round, smooth, greenish buds. The polygonums and pontederias are getting

above water, the latter like spoons on long handles. The *Cornus florida* is blossoming; will be fairly out to-day.[1] The *Polygonatum pubescens;* one on the Island has just opened. This is the smaller Solomon's-seal. A thorn there will blossom to-day. The *Viola palmata* is out there, in the meadow. Everywhere the huckleberry's sticky leaves are seen expanding, and the *high blueberry* is in blossom. Now is the time to admire the very young and tender leaves. The blossoms of the red oak hang down under its young leaves as under a canopy. The petals have already fallen from the *Amelanchier Botryapium,* and young berries are plainly forming. I hear the wood pewee, — *pe-a-wai.* The heat of yesterday has brought him on.

P. M. — To Corner Spring and Fair Haven Cliffs.

Myosotis laxa is out a day or two. At first does not run; is short and upright like *M. stricta.* Golden senecio will be out by to-morrow at least. The early cinquefoil is now in its prime and spots the banks and hillsides and dry meadows with its dazzling yellow. How lively! It is one of the most interesting yellow flowers. The fields are also now whitened, perhaps as much as ever, with the houstonia. The buckbean is out, apparently to-day, the singularly fuzzy-looking blossom. How inconspicuous its leaves now! The rhodora is peculiar for being, like the peach, a profusion of pink blossoms on a leafless stem. This shrub is, then, a late one to leaf out. The bobolink skims by before the wind how far without motion

[1] Involucre not spread and true flowers not open till about May 20th.

of his wings! sometimes borne sidewise as he turns his head — for thus he can fly — and tinkling, *link-ing,* incessantly all the way. How very beautiful, like the fairest flowers, the young black oak shoots with leaves an inch long now! like red velvet on one side and downy white on the other, with only a red edge. Compare this with the pinker white oak. The *Salix nigra* just in bloom. The trientalis, properly called star-flower, is a white star, single, double, or treble. The fringed polygala surprises us in meadows or in low woods as a rarer, richer, and more delicate color, with a singularly tender or delicate-looking leaf. As you approach midsummer, the color of flowers is more intense and fiery. The reddest flower is the flower especially. Our blood is not white, nor is it yellow, nor even blue. The nodding trillium has apparently been out a day or two. Methinks it smells like the lady's-slipper. Also the *Ranunculus recurvatus* for a day or two. The small two or three leaved Solomon's-seal is just out. The *Viola cucullata* is sometimes eight inches high, and leaves in proportion. It must be the largest of the violets except perhaps the yellow. The *V. blanda* is almost entirely out of bloom at the spring.

Returning toward Fair Haven, I perceive at Potter's fence the first whiff of that ineffable fragrance from the Wheeler meadow, — as it were the promise of strawberries, pineapples, etc., in the aroma of their flowers, so blandly sweet, — aroma that fitly forerun the summer and the autumn's most delicious fruits. It would certainly restore all such sick as could

be conscious of it. The odors of no garden are to be named with it. It is wafted from the garden of gardens. It appears to blow from the river meadow from the west or southwest, here about forty rods wide or more. If the air here always possessed this bland sweetness, this spot would become famous and be visited by sick and well from all parts of the earth. It would be carried off in bottles and become an article of traffic which kings would strive to monopolize. The air of Elysium cannot be more sweet.

Cardamine hirsuta out some time by the ivy tree. The *Viola lanceolata* seems to pass into the *cucullata* insensibly, but can that small round-leaved white violet now so abundantly in blossom in open low ground be the same with that large round-leaved one now about out of blossom in shady low ground? *Arabis rhomboidea* just out by the willow on the Corner causeway. The *Ranunculus repens* perhaps yesterday, with its spotted leaves and its not recurved calyx though furrowed stem. Was that a very large *Veronica serpyllifolia* by the Corner Spring? Who shall keep with the lupines? They will apparently blossom within a week under Fair Haven. The *Viola sagittata,* of which *Viola ovata* is made a variety, is now very marked there. The *V. pedata* there presents the greatest array of blue of any flower as yet. The flowers are so raised above their leaves, and so close together, that they make a more indelible impression of blue on the eye; it is almost dazzling. I blink as I look at them, they seem to reflect the blue rays so forcibly, with a slight tinge of lilac. To be sure, there is no telling what the redder *ovata* might not do if they grew as densely, so many eyes or scales of blue side by side, forming small shields of that color four or five inches in diameter. The effect and intensity is very much increased by the numbers.

I hear the first unquestionable nighthawk squeak and see him circling far off high above the earth. It is now about 5 o'clock P. M. The tree-toads are heard in the rather moist atmosphere, as if presaging rain. I hear the dumping sound of bull(?)frogs, telling the weather is warm. The paddocks, as if too lazy to be disturbed, say now to the intruder, " don't, don't, don't, don't;" also in the morning after the first sultry night.

The chinquapin oak may be said to flower and leave out at the same time with the *ilicifolia*. It is distinguished as well by its yellow catkins as by its leaves. *Pyrus arbutifolia* is out, to-day or yesterday. A cratægus just out.

I sit now on a rock on the west slope of Fair Haven orchard, an hour before sunset, this warm, almost sultry evening, the air filled with the sweetness of apple blossoms (this is blossom week), — or I think it is mainly that meadow fragrance still, — the sun partly concealed behind a low cloud in the west, the air cleared by last evening's thunder-shower, the river now beautifully smooth (though a warm, bland breeze blows up here), full of light and reflecting the placid western sky and the dark woods which overhang it. I was surprised, on turning round, to behold the serene and everlasting beauty of the world, it was so soothing.

Vol. V

I saw that I could not go home to supper and lose it. It was so much fairer, serener, more beautiful, than my mood had been. The fields beyond the river have unexpectedly a smooth, lawn-like beauty, and in beautiful curves sweep round the edge of the woods. The rapidly expanding foliage of the deciduous [trees] (last evening's rain or moisture has started them) lights up with a lively yellow green the dark pines which we have so long been used to. Some patches (I speak of woods half a mile or more off) are a lively green, some gray or reddish-gray still, where white oaks stand. With the stillness of the air comes the stillness of the water. The sweetest singers among the birds are heard more distinctly now, as the reflections are seen more distinctly in the water, — the veery constantly now. Methinks this serene, ambrosial beauty could hardly have been but for last evening's thundershower, which, to be sure, barely touched us, but cleared the air and gave a start to vegetation. The elm on the opposite side of the river has now a thin but dark verdure, almost as dark as the pines, while, as I have said, the prevailing color of the deciduous woods is a light yellowish and sunny green. The woods rarely if ever present a more beautiful aspect from afar than now. Methinks the black oak at early leafing is more red than the red oak. Ah, the beauty of this last hour of the day — when a power stills the air and smooths all waters and all minds — that partakes of the light of the day and the stillness of the night!

Sit on Cliffs. The Shrub Oak Plain, where are so

many young white oaks, is now a faint rose-color, almost like a distant peach orchard in bloom and seen against sere red ground. What might at first be taken for the color of some sere leaves and bare twigs still left, its tender red expanding leaves. You might say of the white oaks and of many black oaks at least, "When the oaks are in the red." The perfect smoothness of Fair Haven Pond, full of light and reflecting the wood so distinctly, while still occasionally the sun shines warm and brightly from behind a cloud, giving the completest contrast of sunshine and shade, is enough to make this hour memorable. The red pincushion gall is already formed on the new black oak leaves, with little grubs in them, and the leaves, scarcely more than two inches long, are already attacked by other foes.

Looking down from these rocks, the black oak has a very light hoary or faint silvery color; the white oak, though much less advanced, has a yet more hoary color; but the red oaks (as well as the hickories) have a lively, glossy aspen green, a shade lighter than the birch now, and their long yellowish catkins appear further advanced than the black. Some black as well as white oaks are reddish still.

The new shoots now color the whole of the juniper (creeping) with a light yellow tinge. It appears to be just in blossom,[1] and those little green berries must be already a year old; and, as it is called diœcious, these must be the fertile blossoms. This must be *Krigia Virginica* now budded, close by the juniper,

[1] [This is queried in pencil.]

and will blossom in a day or two.[1] The low blackberry, apparently, on Cliffs is out, earlier than elsewhere, and *Veronica arvensis* (?), very small, obscure pale-blue flower, and, to my surprise, *Linaria Canadensis*.

Returning slowly, I sit on the wall of the orchard by the white pine. Now the cows begin to low, and the river reflects the golden light of the sun just before his setting. The sough of the wind in the pines is more noticeable, as if the air were otherwise more still and hollow. The wood thrush has sung for some time. He touches a depth in me which no other bird's song does. He has learned to sing, and no thrumming of the strings or tuning disturbs you. Other birds may whistle pretty well, but he is the master of a finer-toned instrument. His song is musical, not from association merely, not from variety, but the character of its tone. It is all divine, — a Shakespeare among birds, and a Homer too. This sweetness of the air, does it not always first succeed a thunder-storm? Is it not a general sweetness, and not to be referred to a particular plant?

He who cuts down woods beyond a certain limit exterminates birds. How red are the scales of some hickory buds, now turned back! The fragrance of the apple blossom reminds me of a pure and innocent and unsophisticated country girl bedecked for church. The purple sunset is reflected from the surface of the river, as if its surface were tinged with *lake*. Here is a field sparrow that varies his strain very sweetly.

[1] Out on Nobscot the 22d.

Coming home from Spring by Potter's Path to the Corner road in the dusk, saw a dead-leaf-colored hylodes; detected it by its expanding and relapsing bubble, nearly twice as big as its head, as it sat on an alder twig six inches from ground and one rod from a pool.

The beach plum is out to-day.[1] The whip-poor-will sings. Large insects now fly at night. This is a somewhat sultry night. We must begin now to look out for insects about the candles. The lilac out.

Genius rises above nature; in spite of heat, in spite of cold, works and lives.

May 18. The rhodora is one of the very latest-leafing shrubs, for its leaf-buds are but just expanding, making scarcely any show yet, but quite leafless amid the blossoms. The *Celtis occidentalis* in bloom, maybe a day. Its shoots have grown two inches. It is as forward as the hickory at least; more than the elm. A red clover in blossom. A geranium budded; will open in a day or two. Surprised to see a *Ranunculus Purshii* open. A choke-cherry blossomed in a tumbler yesterday,[2] and probably outdoors.

Finding the *Linaria Canadensis* yesterday at the Cliffs on a very close search for flowers makes me think that, by looking very carefully in the most favored and warmest localities, you may find most flowers out some weeks even in advance of the rest of their kind.

[1] Apparently same with that by red house and Jenny Dugan's and probably not beach plum.
[2] On Island, May 20th.

We have had no storm this spring thus far, but it mizzles to-night. Perchance a May storm is brewing. This day it has mizzled, — as it were a dewy atmosphere, through which for the most part the sun shines. Methinks this is common at this season of the tender foliage, which requires a moist air and protection against the sun.

A singular effect produced by a mass of ferns at a little distance, some rods square, their light yellow-green tops seen above the dark masses of their fruit. At first one is puzzled to account for it. White ash fully in bloom.

May 19. Thunder-showers in the night, and it still storms, with holdings-up. A May storm, gentle and rather warm. The days of the golden willow are over for this season; their withered catkins strew the causeways and cover the water and also my boat, which is moored beneath them. The locust has grown three inches and is blossom-budded. It may come just after the white ash at least, and before the celtis. The weather toward evening still cloudy and somewhat mizzling. The foliage of the young maples, elms, etc., in the street has become, since the rain commenced, several shades darker, changing from its tender and lighter green, as if the electricity of the thunder-storm may have had some effect on it. It is best observed while it is still cloudy; almost a bluish, no longer yellowish green, it is peculiarly rich. The very grass appears to have undergone a similar change.

Vol. V

May 20. The 18th and 19th a rather gentle and warm May storm, — more rain, methinks, than we have had before this spring at one time. Began with thunder-showers on the night of the 18th, the flashing van of the storm, followed by the long, dripping main body, with, at very long intervals, an occasional firing or skirmishing in the rear or on the flanks.

6 A. M. — To Island by river.

Probably a red-wing blackbird's nest, of grass, hung between two button-bushes; whitish eggs with irregular black marks. Sarsaparilla (*Aralia nudicaulis*), probably two days. White oak, swamp white, and chestnut oak probably will open by the 22d.

The white ashes are in full flower now, and how long?

8 A. M. — To Flint's Pond.

Cornus Canadensis just out. Probably the *C. florida* should be set down to-day, since it just begins to shed pollen and its involucre is more open. It is a fair but cool and windy day, a strong northwest wind, and the grass, to which the rain has given such a start, conspicuously waves, showing its lighter under side, and the buttercups toss in the wind. The pitch and white pines have grown from one to five inches.

On Pine Hill. — In this clear morning light and a strong wind from the northwest, the mountains in the horizon, seen against some low, thin clouds in the background, look darker and more like earth than usual; you distinguish forest and pasture on them. This in the clear, cool atmosphere in the morning after

a rain-storm, with the wind northwest. They will grow more ethereal, melting into the sky, as the day advances.

The beech is already one of the most densely clothed trees, or rather makes a great show of verdure from the size of its fully expanded light-green leaves, though some are later. The fresh shoots on low branches are five or six inches long. It is an interesting tree to me, with its neat, close, tight-looking bark, like the dress which athletes wear, its bare instep, and roots beginning to branch like bird's feet, showing how it is planted and holds by the ground. Not merely stuck in the ground like a stick. It gives the beholder the same pleasure that it does to see the timbers of a house above and around. Do they blossom here? I found nuts, but apparently not sound, at Haverhill the other day, — last year's. There are some slender, perfectly horizontal limbs which go zigzagging, as it were creeping through the air, only two or three feet above the ground, over the side-hill, as if they corresponded to concealed rills in the ground beneath.

Plenty of arums now in bloom. Probably my earliest one was in bloom, for I did not look within it. What is that pretty, transparent moss in the brooks, which holds the rain or dewdrops so beautifully on the under sides of the leafets, through which they sparkle crystallinely? Fresh checkerberry shoots now. The cedars are full of yellowish cedar apples and minute berries just formed, the effete staminiferous blossom still on. When did they begin to bloom? I find none of the rare hedyotis yet on Bare Hill. The peach bloom is now gone and the apple bloom come. Heard the seringo note, like a rattling watch-spring, from a flock passing swiftly overhead.

The wind makes such a din in the woods that the notes of birds are lost, and added to this is the sound of the waves of Flint's Pond breaking on the shore, — the fresh surf. The pond is spotted with whitecaps, five or six feet long by one foot, like a thin flock of sheep running toward the southeast shore. The smallest lakes can be lashed into a sort of fury by the wind, and are quite ocean-like then. These caps are a striving to dilute the water with air.

The barberry will probably blossom to-day.

Here, by the side of the pond, a fire has recently run through the young woods on the hillside. It is surprising how clean it has swept the ground, only the very lowest and dampest rotten leaves remaining, but uvularias and smilacinas have pushed up here and there conspicuously on the black ground, a foot high. At first you do not observe the full effect of the fire, walking amid the bare dead or dying trees, which wear a perfect winter aspect, which, as trees generally are not yet fully leaved out and you are still used to this, you do not notice, till you look up and see the still green tops everywhere above the height of fifteen feet. Yet the trees do not bear many marks of fire commonly; they are but little blackened except where the fire has run a few feet up a birch, or paused at a dry stump, or a young evergreen has been killed and reddened by it and is now dropping a shower of red leaves.

Hemlock will blossom to-morrow. The geranium is

just out, and the lady's-slipper. Some with old seed-vessels are still seen.

Hear again, what I have heard for a week or more sometimes, that rasping, springy note, a very hoarse chirp, — *ooh, twee twee twee*, — from a bluish bird as big as a bluebird, with some bright yellow about head, white beneath and lateral tail-feathers, and black cheeks (?). This and that sort of brown-creeper-like bird — of May 12 — and the chickadee-like bird (which may be the chickadee), and the *ah te ter twee* of deep pine woods (which also may be the chickadee), I have not identified.

Arbor-vitæ has been out some time and the butternut some days. Mountain-ash on the 18th. Larch apparently ten days. Nemopanthes several days. The swamp blueberry abundantly out.

Saw a tanager in Sleepy Hollow. It most takes the eye of any bird. You here have the red-wing reversed, — the deepest scarlet of the red-wing spread over the whole body, not on the wing-coverts merely, while the wings are black. It flies through the green foliage as if it would ignite the leaves.

Of deciduous trees and shrubs, the latest to leaf out, as I find by observation to-day, must be the panicled andromeda, rhodora, and button-bush. In some places, however, the first has perfectly formed leaves, the rhodora at most not half unfolded, the button-bush for the most part just bursting buds. But I have not seen the prinos and perhaps one or two other shrubs. I have no doubt that the button-bush may be called the latest of all.

Is that female ash by river at Lee's Hill a new kind? In bloom fully May 18th.

Even this remote forest, which stands so far away and innocent, has this terrible foe Fire to fear. Lightning may ignite a dead tree or the dry leaves, and in a few minutes a green forest be blackened and killed. This liability to accident from which no part of nature is exempt.

Plucked to-day a bunch of *Viola pedata*, consisting of four divisions or offshoots around a central or fifth root, all *united* and about one inch in diameter at the ground and four inches at top.

			Flowers	Buds
1st	division	contained	10	5
2d	"	"	11	4
3d	"	"	9	4
4th	"	"	8	4
5th	"	"	11	5
			49	22

And perhaps more buds would still make their appearance, and undoubtedly half a dozen more would have blown the next day. Forming a complex, close little testudo of violet scales above their leaves.

May 21. P. M. — Up Assabet to cress, with Sophia.

Land on Island. One of the most beautiful things to me now is the reddish-ash, and, higher, the silvery, canopies of half a dozen young white oak leaves over their catkins, — thousands of little tents pitched in the air for the May training of the flowers, so many

little parasols to their tenderer flowers. Young white oaks and shrub oaks have a reddish look quite similar to their *withered* leaves in the winter.

It is still windy weather, and while I hear the bobolink strain dying away in the distance through the maples, I can [*sic*] the falling apple blossoms which I do not see, as if they were his falling notes. Yet the water is quite still and smooth by the Hemlocks, and as the weather is warm, it is a soothing sight to see it covered with dust there over the Deep Eddy.

Landed beyond the grape vine bower and cleared out the spring of leaves and sticks and mud, and deepened it, making an outlet, and it soon ran clear and cold. The cress, which proves to be the rock cress, or herb of St. Barbara, is now luxuriant and in bloom in many places along the river, looking like mustard.

Found the *Ranunculus abortivus*, apparently some time in blossom, in the woods opposite to the cress. Put it after the *repens*.

There are, apparently, two kinds of thorns close together on Nawshawtuct, — one now and for some days in blossom, both bushes and the largest tree, — which are evidently varieties of the *Cratægus coccinea*, or scarlet-fruited thorn. The tree one is about eleven feet high by ten feet, and would be taken for an apple tree; is crowded full with white bloom very compact and handsome; the most showy of any native tree in these parts when in bloom. Its thorns are stout. But there is another kind, thin, wisp-shaped trees, not yet in bloom, with very long, slender, straight needle-shaped thorns and two or three stipules to each peduncle. As it has the usual petioles, is not the cockspur, but may be a variety of the first-named.

The grass begins to be conspicuously reddened with sorrel. The white maple keys are nearly two inches long by a half-inch wide, in pairs, with waved inner edges like green moths ready to bear off their seeds.[1] The red maple keys are not half so large now, and are a dull red, of a similar form. The hickories are budded and show the red anthers.

May 22. Sunday. To Nobscot with W. E. C.

This is the third windy day following the two days' rain. A washing day, such as we always have at this season, methinks. The grass has sprung up as by magic since the rains. The birds are heard through the pleasant dashing wind, which enlivens everything.

It is clear June, the first day of summer. The rye, which, when I last looked, was one foot high, is now three feet high and waving and tossing its heads in the wind. We ride by these bluish-green waving rye-fields in the woods, as if an Indian juggler had made them spring up in a night. Why, the sickle and cradle will soon be taken up. Though I walk every day I am never prepared for this magical growth of the rye. I am advanced by whole months, as it were, into summer. Sorrel reddens the fields. Cows are preparing the milk for June butter. Already the falling apple blossoms fill the air and spot the roads and fields, and some are already turned dark with decay on the ground. With this warmth and wind the air is full of haze, such

[1] *Vide* May 29, 1854.

as we have not had before. The lilac is scented at every house. The wood pewee's warm note is heard. We ride through warm, sandy shrub oak roads, where the *Viola pedata* blues the edge of the path, and the sand cherry and the choke-cherry whiten it. The crickets now first are generally heard. Houstonias whiten the fields and are now in their prime. The thorn bushes are full of bloom. Observed a *large* sassafras tree in bloom, — a rich lemon (?) yellow.

Left our horse at the Howe tavern. The oldest date on the sign is "D. H. 1716." An old woman, who had been a servant in the family and said she was ninety-one, said this was the first house built on the spot. Went on to Nobscot. Very warm in the woods, — and hear the hoarse note of the tanager and the sweet *pe-a-wai*, — but pleasantly breezy on the bare hilltops. Can't see the mountains. Found an abundance of the *Viola Muhlenbergii*[1] (*debilis* of Bigelow), a stalked violet, pale blue and bearded.

The krigia out, a redder, more July, yellow than the dandelion; also a yellow Bethlehem-star and ribwort; and the mountain cranberry still here and there in blossom, though for the most part small berries formed. An abundance of saxifrage going to seed, and in their midst two or three looking densely white like the pearly everlasting — round dense white heads, apparently an abortion, an abnormal state, without stamens, etc., which I cannot find described.

The pastures on this hill and its spurs are sprinkled profusely with thorny pyramidal apple scrubs, very

[1] Also Holden farm and Pinxter-Flower Brook.

Vol. V

thick and stubborn, first planted by the cows, then browsed by them and kept down stubborn and thorny for years, till, as they spread, their centre is protected and beyond reach and shoots up into a tree, giving a wine-glass form to the whole; and finally perchance the bottom disappears and cows come in to stand in the shade and rub against and redden the trunk. They must make fine dark shadows, these shrubs, when the sun is low; perfectly pyramidal they are now, many of them. You see the cow-dung everywhere now with a hundred little trees springing up in it. Thus the cows create their own shade and food.[1]

This hill, Nobscot, is the summit of the island (?) or cape between the Assabet and Musketaquid — perhaps the best point from which to view the Concord River valley. The Wayland hills bound it on the east; Berlin, Bolton, [and] Harvard hills on the west. The Sudbury meadows, seen here and there in distance, are of a peculiar bluish green. This is the first truly lively *summer* Sunday, what with lilacs, warm weather, waving rye, slight[ly] dusty sandy roads in some places, falling apple blossoms, etc., etc., and the wood pewee. The country people walk so quietly to church, and at five o'clock the farmer stands reading the newspaper while his cows go through the bars. I ought perhaps to have measured the great white oak by Howe's. A remarkably thick white pine wood this side of Willis's Pond!!

When yesterday Sophia and I were rowing past Mr. Prichard's land, where the river is bordered by a

[1] [See *Excursions*, p. 305; Riv. 374, 375.]

row of elms and low willows, at 6 P. M., we heard a singular note of distress as it were from a catbird — a loud, vibrating, catbird sort of note, as if the catbird's mew were imitated by a smart vibrating spring. Blackbirds and others were flitting about, apparently attracted by it. At first, thinking it was merely some peevish catbird or red-wing, I was disregarding it, but on second thought turned the bows to the shore, looking into the trees as well as over the shore, thinking some bird might be in distress, caught by a snake or in a forked twig. The hovering birds dispersed at my approach; the note of distress sounded louder and nearer as I approached the shore covered with low osiers. The sound came from the ground, not from the trees. I saw a little black animal making haste to meet the boat under the osiers. A young muskrat? a mink? No, it was a little dot of a kitten. It was scarcely six inches long from the face to the base — or I might as well say the tip — of the tail, for the latter was a short, sharp pyramid, perfectly perpendicular but not swelled in the least. It was a very handsome and very precocious kitten, in perfectly good condition, its breadth being considerably more than one third of its length. Leaving its mewing, it came scrambling over the stones as fast as its weak legs would permit, straight to me. I took it up and dropped it into the boat, but while I was pushing off it ran the length of the boat to Sophia, who held it while we rowed homeward. Evidently it had not been weaned — was smaller than we remembered that kittens ever were — almost infinitely small; yet it had hailed a boat, its life being in danger, and saved itself. Its performance, considering its age and amount of experience, was more wonderful than that of any young mathematician or musician that I have read of. Various were the conjectures as to how the kitten came there, a quarter of a mile from a house. The possible solutions were finally reduced to three: first, it must either have been born there, or, secondly, carried there by its mother, or, thirdly, by human hands. In the first case, it had possibly brothers and sisters, one or both, and its mother had left them to go a-hunting on her own account and might be expected back. In the second, she might equally be expected to return. At any rate, not having thought of all this till we got home, we found that we had got ourselves into a scrape; for this kitten, though exceedingly interesting, required one nurse to attend it constantly for the present, and, of course, another to spell the first; and, beside, we had already a cat well-nigh grown, who manifested such a disposition toward the young stranger that we had no doubt it would have torn it in pieces in a moment if left alone with it. As nobody made up his or her mind to have it drowned, and still less to drown it, — having once looked into its innocent extremely pale blue eyes (as of milk thrice skimmed) and had his finger or his chin sucked by it, while, its eyes being shut, its little paws played a soothing tune, — it was resolved to keep it till it could be suitably disposed of. It rested nowhere, in no lap, under no covert, but still faintly cried for its mother and its accustomed supper. It ran toward every sound

or movement of a human being, and whoever crossed the room it was sure to follow at a rapid pace. It had all the ways of a cat of the maturest years; could purr divinely and raised its back to rub all boots and shoes. When it raised its foot to scratch its ear, which by the way it never hit, it was sure to fall over and roll on the floor. It climbed straight up the sitter, faintly mewing all the way, and sucked his chin. In vain, at first, its head was bent down into saucers of milk which its eyes did not see, and its chin was wetted. But soon it learned to suck a finger that had been dipped in it, and better still a rag; and then at last it slept and rested. The street was explored in vain to find its owner, and at length an Irish family took it into their cradle. Soon after we learned that a neighbor who had heard the mewing of kittens in the partition had sent for a carpenter, taken off a board, and found two the very day at noon that we sailed. That same hour it was first brought to the light a coarse Irish cook had volunteered to drown it, had carried it to the river, and without bag or sinker had cast it in! It saved itself and hailed a boat! What an eventful life! What a precocious kitten! We feared it owed its first plump condition to the water. How strong and effective the instinct of self-preservation!

Our quince blossomed yesterday. Saw many low blackberries in bloom to-day.

May 23. P. M. — To Ministerial Swamp.

The poet must bring to Nature the smooth mirror in which she is to be reflected. He must be something

superior to her, something more than natural. He must furnish equanimity. No genius will excuse him from importing the ivory which is to be his material.

That small veronica (*V. arvensis*) by Mrs. Hosmer's is the same with that on the Cliffs; there is also the smooth or *V. serpyllifolia* by her path at the brook. This is the fifth windy day. A May wind — a washing wind. Do we not always have after the early thunder-showers a May storm? The first windy weather which it is agreeable to walk or ride in — creating a lively din. That must be the *Arenaria serpyllifolia,* thyme-leaved sandwort, now for some days (weeks?) out on the Clamshell Hill. Put it with viscid myosotis. To-day I am surprised by the dark orange-yellow of the senecio. At first we had the lighter, paler spring yellows of willows (cowslips even, for do they not grow a little darker afterward?), dandelion, cinquefoil, then the darker (methinks it is a little darker than the cowslip) and deeper yellow of the buttercup; and then this broad distinction between the buttercup and the krigia and senecio, as the seasons revolve toward July. Every new flower that opens, no doubt, expresses a new mood of the human mind. Have I any dark or ripe orange-yellow thoughts to correspond? The *flavor* of my thoughts begins to correspond. Lupines now for some days, probably about the 19th. Whiteweed will open perhaps to-morrow or next day. For some time dandelions and mouse-ear have been seen gone to seed — autumnal sights. I have not yet seen a white oak (and put with it swamp white and chestnut) fairly in bloom.

The 20th, when at Flint's Pond I raked away the leaves for acorns, I found many dor-bugs either just ready to issue forth or which had taken refuge from the storm.

The geum is out, maybe one day.

As I rise the hill beyond Geum Meadow I perceive the sweet fragrance of the season from over the turf; as if the vales were vast saucers full of strawberries, as if our walks were on the rim of such a saucer. With this, couple ·the fact that directly the fresh shoots of the firs and spruces will have the fragrance of strawberries. White clover. I see the light purple of the rhodora enlivening the edges of swamps — another color the sun wears. It is a beautiful shrub seen afar, and makes a great show from the abundance of its bloom unconcealed by leaves, rising above the andromeda. Is it not the most showy *high-colored* flower or shrub? Flowers are the different colors of the sunlight.

Saw a great silvery-grayish cocoon, perchance of an emperor moth, on a scrub apple six inches from the ground, reminding me of a hornet's or wasp's nest — the great silk bag — two and one half inches long by nearly two inches, with a hole by which, apparently, the perfect insect had flown. What a rich stuff the shining silky, silvery bag!

At the Ministerial Swamp I find the spruce leaf-buds have not yet burst their envelopes except at the tops of the trees where they have pushed out and are perfect handsome cones containing a bundle of leaves. The large staminate blossoms are now dry and effete, and the young cones more than one half inch long.

Perhaps they should come between the red cedar and the larch. Put the first the last of May; the spruce, both white and black, end of the first week of May, and larch directly after, till I know better. It is glorious to stand in the midst of the andromeda, which so level and thick fills the swamp, and look up at the blue spruce trees. The edges of the scales of the young cones, which are at the tops of the trees (where the branches make light and open crosses), seen against the sunlit sky or against the light merely, being transparent, are a splendid crimson color, as if the condensed fire of all sunsets were reflected from them, like the richest damask or ruby-throated hummingbird's breast. They glow with the crimson fires of the sunset sky, reflected over the swamp — unspeakably rare and precious rubies as you thus look up at them; but climb the tree and look down on them, and they are comparatively dull and opaque. These are the rubies of the swamp. Already the just bursting leaf-buds emit that rare strawberry fragrance. It is one of the most glowing, beautiful, brilliant effects in nature, exactly like the reflections from the breast of the ruby-throated hummingbird; as if a hundred ruby-throated hummingbirds sat on the topmost crosses of the trees, their breasts turned to the sun. The dwarf andromeda is for the most part just prepared to leave out, though some twigs have grown an inch.

How different the ramrod jingle of the chewink or any bird's note sounds now at 5 P. M. in the cooler, stiller air, when also the humming of insects is more distinctly heard, and perchance some impurity has

begun to sink to earth strained by the air! Or is it, perchance, to be referred to the cooler, more clarified and pensive state of the mind, when dews have begun to descend in it and clarify it? Chaste eve! A certain lateness in the sound, pleasing to hear, which releases me from the obligation to return in any particular season. I have passed the Rubicon of staying out. I have said to myself, that way is not homeward; I will wander further from what I have called my home — to the home which is forever inviting me. In such an hour the freedom of the woods is offered me, and the birds sing my dispensation. In dreams the links of life are united: we forget that our friends are dead; we know them as of old.

An abundance of pure white fringed polygalas, very delicate, by the path at Harrington's mud-hole. Thus many flowers have their nun sisters, dressed in white. At Loring's Wood heard and saw a tanager. That contrast of a *red* bird with the green pines and the blue sky! Even when I have heard his note and look for him and find the bloody fellow, sitting on a dead twig of a pine, I am always startled. (They seem to love the darkest and thickest pines.) That incredible red, with the green and blue, as if these were the trinity we wanted. Yet with his hoarse note he pays for his color. I am transported; these are not the woods I ordinarily walk in. He sunk Concord in his thought. How he enhances the wildness and wealth of the woods! This and the emperor moth make the tropical phenomena of our zone. There is warmth in the pewee's strain, but this bird's colors and his note tell of Brazil.

Vol. V

Even in remotest woods the trivial noon has its rule and its limit. When the chaste and pensive eve draws on, suddenly the walker begins to reflect.

When I listened this evening at the door, I heard no hylodes;[1] but methinks I did hear toads on the river, — unless they were frogs.[2]

May 24. The smooth speedwell is in its prime now, whitening the sides of the back road, above the Swamp Bridge and front of Hubbard's. Its sweet little pansy-like face looks up on all sides. This and the *Myosotis laxa* are the two most beautiful *little* flowers yet, if I remember rightly.

P. M. — Talked, or tried to talk, with R. W. E. Lost my time — nay, almost my identity. He, assuming a false opposition where there was no difference of opinion, talked to the wind — told me what I knew — and I lost my time trying to imagine myself somebody else to oppose him.

The wild pink was out day before yesterday.

May 25. Wednesday. Election day. — Rain yesterday afternoon and to-day. Heard the popping of guns last night and this morning, nevertheless.

I quarrel with most botanists' description of different species, say of willows. It is a difference without a distinction. No stress is laid upon the peculiarity of the species in question, and it requires a very careful examination and comparison to detect any difference in the description. Having described you one species, he begins

[1] Heard a few next evening, also the 27th.   [2] *Vide* May 30th.

again at the beginning when he comes to the next and describes it *absolutely*, wasting time; in fact does not describe the species, but rather the genus or family; as if, in describing the particular races of men, you should say of each in its turn that it is but dust and to dust it shall return. The object should be to describe not those particulars in which a species resembles its genus, for they are many and that would be but a negative description, but those in which it is peculiar, for they are few and positive.

Steady fisherman's rain, without wind, straight down, flooding the ground and spattering on it, beating off the blossoms of apples and thorns, etc. Within the last week or so the grass and leaves have grown many shades darker, and if we had leaped from last Wednesday to this, we should have been startled by the change — the dark bluish green of rank grass especially. How rapidly the young twigs shoot — the herbs, trees, shrubs no sooner leaf out than they shoot forward surprisingly, as if they had acquired a head by being repressed so long. The[y] do not grow nearly so rapidly at any [other] season. Many do most of their growing for the year in a week or two at this season. They *shoot* — they *spring* — and the rest of the year they harden and mature, and perhaps have a second spring in the latter part of summer or in the fall. The hedge-mustard is just out.

Two young men who borrowed my boat the other day returned from the riverside through Channing's yard, quietly. It was almost the only way for them. But, as they passed out his gate, C. boorishly walked out his house behind them in his shirt-sleeves, and shut his gate again behind them as if to shut them out. It was just that sort of behavior which, if he had met with it in Italy or France, he would have complained of, whose meanness he would have condemned.

May 26. P. M. — To Lee's Cliff.

No breaking away, but the clouds have ceased to drop rain awhile and the birds are very lively. The waters are dark, and our attention is confined to earth. Saw two striped snakes deliberately drop from the stone bank wall into the river at Hubbard's Bridge and remain under water while we looked. Do not perceive the meadow fragrance in this wet weather. A high blueberry bush by roadside beyond the bridge very full of blossoms. It has the more florid and blossoming effect because the leaves are few and quite distinct, or standing out from the flowers — the countless inverted white mugs (in rows and everywhere as on counters or shelves) with their peculiar green calyxes. If there are as many berries as blossoms we shall fare well.

Now is the time to walk in low, damp maple copses and see the tender, luxuriant foliage that has pushed up, mushroom-like, before the sun has come to harden it — the ferns of various species and in various stages, some now in their most perfect and beautiful condition, completely unfolded, tender and delicate, but perfect in all their details, far more than any lace work — the most elaborate leaf we have. So flat, just from the laundry, as if pressed by some invisible flat-

iron in the air. Unfolding with such mathematical precision in the free air, — green, starched and pressed, — might they not be transferred, patterns for Mechlin and Brussels? Skunk-cabbage, nodding trillium with concealed flowers, sarsaparilla, and arums, uvularias in thick-sown regiments now past their prime — a rank growth of these, forming an almost uninterrupted counter of green leaves a foot or two above the damp ground. *Actæa alba* some time. Maidenhair — frames of basins spirally arranged. The pitch pines just out, with crowded bunches of staminate blossoms about the new shoots.

That barberry bush near the bars on Conantum is methinks now the most beautiful, light, and graceful bush that I ever saw in bloom. It is shaped like a haycock, broad and dense, yet light as if some leaven had raised it. But how orientally beautiful now, seen through this dark mizzling air, its parallel or rather concentric wreaths composed of leaves and flowers keeping each other apart and lightening the whole mass, each wreath above composed of rich dark-green leaves, below of drooping racemes of lively yellow flowers! Its beauty consists in a great measure in this intimate mixture of flowers and leaves, the small rich-colored flowers not being too much massed. It suggests the yellow-robed priests perchance of Thibet (?). The lowest wreaths lie on the ground. But go not so near as to be disturbed by that sickening buttery odor, as of an underdone batter pudding, all eggs but no spice. Who would think this would bake into such a red acid fruit?

Woodchucks seen tumbling into their holes.

The *Galium aparine*, common cleavers, a new one and the earliest, several days out, perhaps, high up at the base of the rocks under Lee's Cliff. In the same place *Turritis stricta*, straight tower-mustard, a slender towering plant with a delicate whitish or purplish-white blossom; not in Bigelow, nor located in New England by Gray. Side-flowering sandwort is abundant, for some time, by wall of Lee's field near Garfield's. The *Cratægus Crus-Galli* is all ready to blossom close by the barberry bush on Conantum. It is distinguished by its leaves, which are wedge-obovate with a short petiole and shining on the upper side, as if varnished and the varnish had soaked in in spots. What is that soft-leaved rubus (?), three-leaved with the odd one wedge-based, now in bloom? I see no thorns on my slip.

May 27. 5.30 A. M. — To Island.

The *Cornus florida* now fairly out, and the involucres are now not greenish-white but white tipped with reddish — like a small flock of white birds passing — three and a half inches in diameter, the larger ones, as I find by measuring. It is something quite novel in the tree line. That needle-shaped variety of thorn is now almost *fully* out on Lee's Hill; *i. e.* half the flowers open. Amelanchier berries are as large as small peas. How beautiful the geranium flower-buds just opening! — little purple cylindrical tubes or hoods — cigaritos — with the petals lapped over and round each other. One opens visibly in a pitcher before me. Heard

a stake-driver yesterday in the rain. It sounded exactly like a man pumping, while another man struck on the head of the pump with an axe, the last strokes sounding peculiarly dry and hard like a forcible echo from the wood-side. One would think all Concord would be built on piles by this time. Very deliberately they drive, and in the intervals are considering the progress of the pile into the soft mud. They are working by the day. He is early and late at his work, building his stake[?]-house, yet did anybody ever see the pile he had driven? He has come back from his Southern tour to finish that job of spile-driving which he undertook last year. It is heavy work — not to be hurried. Only green hands are overhasty.

A turtle walking is as if a man were to try to walk by sticking his legs and arms merely out the windows.

P. M. — To Saw Mill Brook.

Cleared up last night after two and a half days' rain. This, with the two days' rain the 18th and 19th, makes our May rain — and more rain either of the two than at any other time this spring. Coming out into the sun after this rain, with my thick clothes, I find it unexpectedly and oppressively warm. Yet the heat seems tempered by a certain moisture still lingering in the air. (Methinks I heard a cuckoo yesterday and a quail (?) to-day.) A new season has commenced — summer — leafy June. The elms begin to droop and are heavy with shade. The buttercups in the churchyard are now in perfection, and it is surprising what a fairyland they make on some hillsides, looking more glossy and bright than ever after the rain. The vireo, too, is heard more than ever on the elms; his note begins to prevail. The broad pads lying on the surface of the ditches on the Turnpike seem to reflect a fierce heat upon the traveller. Yellow clover is out — how long? Hellebore a day or two at Saw Mill Brook — its great spike of green flowers with yellow anthers. Its great plaited leaves look like a green shirt bosom; drawn out smooth they prove to be basins. Was that *Stellaria longifolia* in bloom in the low ground at Saw Mill Brook? The crickets, which I have heard for a week now more and more, as much as anything mark a new season. They are importers of thought into the world — the poor trivial world; wholesale dealers in that article. Blue-eyed grass has been out some time, as I judge by the size of its seed-vessel. The river does not look blue from Smith's Hill, — nor has it from any point for some time past, — but indistinctly slaty and rippling, as through a mistiness. Is it not getting to be too warm? A gray down or lint comes off of the leaves and shoots, which have grown so rapidly during the warm wet weather, and whitens the clothes with clean dirt. This is the state of the woods — the beardless woods, with downy cheek as yet. Sit in shade nowadays. The bullfrogs lie spread out on the surface of Flint's Pond. Holding down my head, the young rushes begin to look thick and green in the shallow water advancing into the deep.

8 P. M. — Up Union Turnpike.

The reign of insects commences this warm evening

after the rains. They could not come out before. I hear from the pitch pine woods beyond E. Wood's a vast faint hum, as of a factory far enough off to be musical. I can fancy it something ambrosial from starlit mansions, a faint murmuring harp music rising from all groves; and soon insects are felt on the hands and face, and dor-bugs are heard humming by, or entangled in the pines, like winged bullets. I suppose that those dor-bugs which I saw the other day just beginning to stir under the dead leaves have now first issued forth. They never mistake their time. Between the pines here, white and pitch, whose outlines are dimly seen, — the rising grass cool and damp beneath, — they are heard like a thousand bullets. The toads, too, completely fill the air with their dreamy snore; so that I wonder that everybody does not remark upon it and, the first time they hear it, do not rush to the riverside and the pools and capture a thousand; but hardly the naturalists know whence the sound proceeds, and nobody else seems to hear it at all. The whole air trembles with it, and hearing has no other pillow but this rippling one. Tree-toads, too, keep up an incessant din from elms (?) — when near, drowning the common toads.

The toads gradually ceased after midnight and I heard not one in the morning. They want much muggy warmth.

May 28. A rose in a garden.

5 P. M. — To Lupine Hill by boat.

The carnival of the year commencing — a warm, moist,

hazy air, the water already smooth and uncommonly high, the river overflowing, and yellow lilies all drowned, their stems not long enough to reach the surface. I see the boat-club, or three or four in pink shirts, rowing at a distance. Beech-drops out apparently some days, the old bridge landing at Nawshawtuct; also just out green-briar. Already the ringing croak of a toad *begins* to be heard here and there along the river, and the *troonk* of a bullfrog from time to time. What is peculiar now, beginning yesterday, after rains, is the sudden heat, and the more general sound of insects by day, and the loud ringing croak of common toads and tree-toads at evening and in the night. Our river has so little current that when the wind has gone down, as at present, it is dark and perfectly smooth, and at present dusty as a stagnant pool in every part of it; far from there being any murmur, there is no ripple nor eddy for the most part. Hubbard has plowed up the low-lying field at the bathing-place and planted it with potatoes; and now we find that the field we resort to was equally used by the Indians, for their arrowheads are now exposed by the plow. The sidesaddle-flower conspicuous, but no pollen yet. The bulbous arethusa out a day or two — probably yesterday. Though in a measure prepared for it, still its beauty surprised me; it is by far the highest and richest color yet. Its intense color in the midst of the green meadow made it look twice as large as reality; it looks very foreign in the midst of our plants — its richly speckled, curled, and bearded lip. Devil's-needles begin to fly; saw one the 14th. Thesium just

out. This hazy afternoon the sun is shorn of his beams now at six o'clock, and the lupines do not look so well for it; their lilac tints show best looking at them towards the sun, for they are transparent. Last night in the dark they were all a pale, whitish color like the moon by day — a mere dull luminousness, as if they reflected light absorbed by day. Seen from this point now, the pitch pines on Bear Garden Hill, the fresh green foliage of the deciduous trees now so prevails, the pitch pines, which lately looked green, are of a dark-brownish or mulberry color by contrast, and the white pines almost as dark, but bluer. In this haziness no doubt they are a *little* darker than usual. The grass on pretty high ground is wet with dew an hour before sunset. Whiteweed now, and cotton-grass. For three quarters of an hour the sun is a great round red ball in the west, reflected in the water; at first a scarlet, but as it descends growing more purple and crimson and larger, with a blue bar of a cloud across it; still reflected in the water, two suns, one above the other, below the hilly bank; as if it were a round hole in the cope of heaven, through which we looked into a crimson atmosphere. If such scenes were painted faithfully they would be pronounced unnatural. It is remarkable at how little distance a hillside covered with lupines looks blue, while a house or board painted blue is seen so great a distance.

A sprig of wilted fir now grown an inch emits that rich fragrance somewhat like strawberries and pineapples, yet peculiar.

Mayhew, in his "London Labour and London

Poor," treating of the costermongers, or those who get their living in the streets of London, speaks of "the muscular irritability begotten by continued wandering," making one "unable to rest for any time in one place." Mentions the instance of a girl who had been accustomed to sell sprats in the streets, who having been taken into a gentleman's house out of charity, "the pressure of shoes was intolerable to her." "But no sooner did she hear from her friends, that sprats were again in the market, than as if there were some magical influence in the fish, she at once requested to be freed from the confinement, and permitted to return to her old calling." I am perhaps equally accustomed to a roaming field-life, experience a good deal of that muscular irritability, and have a good many friends who let me know when sprats are in the market.

May 29. These last two days, with their sultry, hazy air, are the first that suggest the expression "the furnace-like heat." Bathing has begun. In the evening and during the night the ring of the toads fills the air, so that some have to shut the windows toward the river, but when you awake in the morning not one is to be heard. As it grows warmer in the forenoon I hear a few again; but still I do not hear them numerously and loudly as earlier in the season at that hour, though far more numerously and loudly at night.

P. M. — To Hosmer's Holden place.

Thimble-berry two or three days. Cattle stand in

white, pigeon-egg fungi in the grass since the rains. Do they become puffballs? The thyme-leaved veronica shows its modest face in little crescent-shaped regiments in every little hollow in the pastures where there is moisture, and around stumps and in the road ditches. The *Cratægus Crus-Galli* this side the Holden place on left, probably yesterday, thorns three inches long, flowers with anthers not conspicuously red. The *Viola debilis* near west end of Holden farm in meadow south side of road.

May 30. The morning wind forever blows; the poem of the world is uninterrupted, but few are the ears that hear it. Forever that strain of the harp which soothed the Cerberus and called me back to life is sounding. Olympus is the outside of the earth everywhere.

5 A. M. — To Cliffs.

High blackberry out. As I go by Hayden's in the still cool morning, the farmer's door is open — probably his cattle have been attended to — and the odor of the bacon which is being fried for his breakfast fills the air. The dog lies with his paws hanging over the door-sill this agreeably cool morning. The cistus out, probably yesterday, — a simple and delicate flower, its stamens all swept to one side. It upholds a delicate saffron-golden (?) basin about nine inches from the ground.

As I look off from Fair Haven I perceive that that downy, silvery hoariness has mostly left the leaves (it now comes off on to the clothes), and they are of

the river by the bridge for coolness. Place my hat lightly on my head that the air may circulate beneath. Wild roses budded before you know it — will be out often before you know they are budded. Fields are whitened with mouse-ear gone to seed — a mass of white fuzz blowing off one side — and also with dandelion globes of seeds. Some plants have already reached their fall. How still the hot noon; people have retired behind blinds. Yet the kingbird — lively bird, with white belly and tail edged with white, and with its lively twittering — stirs and keeps the air brisk. I see men and women through open windows in white undress taking their Sunday-afternoon nap, overcome with heat. At A. Hosmer's hill on the Union Turnpike I see the tanager hoarsely warbling in the shade; the surprising red bird, a small morsel of Brazil, advanced picket of that Brazilian army, — parrot-like. But no more shall we see; it is only an affair of outposts. It appears as if he loved to contrast himself with the green of the forest. These are afternoons when you expect a thunder-shower before night; the outlines of cloudy cumuli are dimly seen through the hazy, furnace-like air rising in the west. *Spergularia rubra*, spurry sandwort, in the roadside ditch on left just beyond A. Hosmer's hill; also *Veronica peregrina* (?) a good while. The last also in Great Fields in the path.

Raspberry out. That exceedingly neat and interesting little flower blue-eyed grass now claims our attention. The barrenest pastures wear now a green and luxuriant aspect. I see many of those round,

a uniform smooth light green, while the pines are a dirty dark brown, almost purple, and are mostly merged and lost in the deciduous trees. The *Erigeron bellidifolius* is a tender-looking, pale-purple, aster-like flower a foot high in little squads, nodding in the wind on the bare slopes of hill pastures. Young bush-like black cherries a day or two, on Cliffs and in such favorable places. The hylodes were about done peeping before those last few warm days, — when the toads began in earnest in the river, — but last night being somewhat cooler they were not so loud.

P. M. — To Carlisle Bridge by boat.

A strong but somewhat gusty southerly wind, before which C. and I sailed all the way from home to Carlisle Bridge in not far from an hour; the river unusually high for the season. Very pleasant to feel the strong, fresh southerly wind from over the water. There are no clouds in the sky, but a high haziness, as if the moisture drawn up by yesterday's heat was condensed by to-day's comparative coolness. The water a dull slate-color and waves running high, — a dirty yellow where they break, — and long streaks of white foam, six or eight feet apart, stretching north and south between Concord and Bedford, — without end. The common blue flag just out at Ball's Hill. The white maples, especially those shaped like large bushes, on the banks are now full of foliage, showing the white under sides of the leaves in the wind, and the swamp white oak, having similar silvery under sides to its leaves, and both growing abundantly and prevailing here along the river, make or impart a peculiar flashing light to the scenery in windy weather, all bright, flashing, and cheerful. On the meadows are large yellow-green patches of ferns beginning to prevail. Passed a large boat anchored off in the meadows not far from the boundary of Concord. It was quite a piece of ocean scenery, we saw it so long before reaching it and so long after; and it looked larger than reality, what with the roaring of the wind in our shrouds and the dashing of the waves. The incessant drifting about of a boat so anchored by a long cable, playing with its halter, now showing more, now less, of its side, is a pleasing sight. Landed at a high lupine bank by Carlisle Bridge. How many such lupine banks there are! — whose blue you detect many rods off. There I found, methinks, minute *Specularia perfoliata*, with small crenate clasping leaves alternate at some distance apart, on upright stems about three inches high, but apparently *fruiting in the bud*. Also the *Silene antirrhina* very abundant there. The *Viola palmata*, which is later, and therefore, methinks, fresher than most, is now quite prevalent, one of the most common, in fact, in low ground and a very handsome purple, with more red than usual in its violet. The pines now dotted with white shoots, the pitch pines a little reddish, are an interesting sight now. Whence came all those dead suckers, a dozen at least, which we saw floating to-day, some on their sides, transversely barred, some on their backs with their white bellies up and dark fins on each side? Why are they suckers only that we see? Can it be because the spearers have

thrown them away? Or has some bird of prey dropped them? I rarely see other fish floating. Melvin gave George Brooks some pink azaleas yesterday, said to have grown in the north part of the town.[1] The white maple keys falling and covering the river.

May 31. Some incidents in my life have seemed far more allegorical than actual; they were so significant that they plainly served no other use. That is, I have been more impressed by their allegorical significance and fitness; they have been like myths or passages in a myth, rather than mere incidents or history which have to wait to become significant. Quite in harmony with my subjective philosophy. This, for instance: that, when I thought I knew the flowers so well, the beautiful purple azalea or pinxter-flower should be shown me by the hunter who found it. Such facts are lifted quite above the level of the actual. They are all just such events as my imagination prepares me for, no matter how incredible. Perfectly in keeping with my life and characteristic. Ever and anon something will occur which my philosophy has not dreamed of. The limits of the actual are set some thoughts further off. That which had seemed a rigid wall of vast thickness unexpectedly proves a thin and undulating drapery. The boundaries of the actual are no more fixed and rigid than the elasticity of our imaginations. The fact that a rare and beautiful flower which we never saw, perhaps never heard [of], for which therefore there was no place in our thoughts,

[1] *Vide* forward [next page].

Vol. V

may at length be found in our immediate neighborhood, is very suggestive.

P. M. — A change in the weather. It is comparatively cool since last night, and the air is very clear accordingly; none of that haze in it occasioned by the late heat. Yesterday was another very windy day, making the sixth, I believe, of this May, the 23d having been the last. The leaves are now fairly expanded — that has been the work of May — and are of a dark summer greenness. Some have even begun to cut the rankest grass in front yards. May has been, on the whole, a pleasant month, with a few days of gentle rain-storm, — fishermen's rains, — straight down and spattering on the earth, — and the last week quite warm, even somewhat sultry and summer-like. The bulk of the planting has been done this month, and there have been half a dozen days of strong, breezy and gusty, but not cold, winds, — northwest and then southwest and south. It is surprising to see how many leaves are already attacked by insects, — leaf-rollers, pincushion galls, one kind of oak-balls, etc., etc.; and many a shrub and tree, black cherry and shrub oak, is no sooner leaved out than it is completely stripped by its caterpillar foes.

I am going in search of the *Azalea nudiflora*. Sophia brought home a single flower without twig or leaf from Mrs. Brooks's last evening. Mrs. Brooks, I find, has a large twig in a vase of water, still pretty fresh, which she says George Melvin gave to her son George. I called at his office. He says that Melvin came in to

Mr. Gourgas's office, where he and others were sitting Saturday evening, with his arms full and gave each a sprig, but he does n't know where he got it. Somebody, I heard, had seen it at Captain Jarvis's; so I went there. I found that they had some still pretty fresh in the house. Melvin gave it to them Saturday night, but they did not know where he got it. A young man working at Stedman Buttrick's said it was a secret; there was only one bush in the town; Melvin knew of it and Stedman knew; when asked, Melvin said he got it in the swamp, or from a bush, etc. The young man thought it grew on the Island across the river on the Wheeler farm. I went on to Melvin's house, though I did not expect to find him at home at this hour, so early in the afternoon. (Saw the wood-sorrel out, a day or two perhaps, by the way.) At length I saw his dog by the door, and knew he was at home.

He was sitting in the shade, bareheaded, at his back door. He had a large pailful of the azalea recently plucked and in the shade behind his house, which he said he was going to carry to town at evening. He had also a sprig set out. He had been out all the forenoon and said he had got seven pickerel, — perhaps ten [?]. Apparently he had been drinking and was just getting over it. At first he was a little shy about telling me where the azalea grew, but I saw that I should get it out of him. He dilly-dallied a little; called to his neighbor Farmer, whom he called "Razor," to know if he could tell me where that flower grew. He called it, by the way, the "red honeysuckle." This was to prolong the time and make the most of his secret. I felt pretty sure the plant was to be found on Wheeler's land beyond the river, as the young man had said, for I had remembered how, some weeks before this, when I went up the Assabet after the yellow rocket, I saw Melvin, who had just crossed with his dog, and when I landed to pluck the rocket he appeared out of the woods, said he was after a fish-pole, and asked me the name of my flower. Did n't think it was very handsome, — "not so handsome as the honeysuckle, is it?" And now I knew it was his "red honeysuckle," and not the columbine, he meant. Well, I told him he had better tell me where it was; I was a botanist and ought to know. But he thought I could n't possibly find it by his directions. I told him he 'd better tell me and have the glory of it, for I should surely find it if he did n't; I 'd got a clue to it, and should n't give it up. I should go over the river for it. I could smell it a good way, you know. He thought I could smell it half a mile, and he wondered that I had n't stumbled on it, or Channing. Channing, he said, came close by it once, when it was in flower. He thought he 'd surely find it then; but he did n't, and he said nothing to him.

He told me he found it about ten years ago, and he went to it every year. It blossomed at the old election time, and he thought it "the handsomest flower that grows." Yarrow just out.

In the meanwhile, Farmer, who was hoeing, came up to the wall, and we fell into a talk about Dodge's Brook, which runs through his farm. A man in Cambridge, he said, had recently written to Mr. Monroe about it, but he did n't know why. All he knew about

the brook was that he had seen it dry and then again, after a week of dry weather in which no rain fell, it would be full again, and either the writer or Monroe said there were only two such brooks in all North America. One of its sources — he thought the principal one — was in his land. We all went to it. It was in a meadow, — rather a dry one, once a swamp. He said it never ceased to flow at the head now, since he dug it out, and never froze there. He ran a pole down eight or nine feet into the mud to show me the depth. He had minnows there in a large deep pool, and cast an insect into the water, which they presently rose to and swallowed. Fifteen years ago he dug it out nine feet deep and found spruce logs as big as his leg, which the beavers had gnawed, with the marks of their teeth very distinct upon them; but they soon crumbled away on coming to the air. Melvin, meanwhile, was telling me of a pair of geese he had seen which were breeding in the Bedford Swamp. He had seen them within a day. Last year he got a large brood (11?) of black ducks there.

We went on down the brook, — Melvin and I and his dog, — and crossed the river in his boat, and he conducted me to where the *Azalea nudiflora* grew, — it was a little past its prime, perhaps, — and showed me how near Channing came. ("You won't tell him what I said; will you?" said he.) I offered to pay him for his trouble, but he would n't take anything. He had just as lief I 'd know as not. He thought it first came out last Wednesday, on the 25th.

Azalea nudiflora, — purple azalea, pinxter-flower,

— but Gray and Bigelow say nothing about its *clamminess*. It is a conspicuously beautiful flowering shrub, with the sweet fragrance of the common swamp-pink, but the flowers are larger and, in this case, a fine lively rosy pink, not so clammy as the other, and, being earlier, it is free from the insects which often infest and spoil the first, though I find a very few little flies on them. With a broader, somewhat downy pale-green leaf. Growing in the shade of large wood, like the laurel. The flowers, being in naked umbels, are so much the more conspicuous. (The *Viola debilis* by the brook, near the azalea.) It is a flower with the fragrance of the swamp[-pink], without its extreme clamminess and consequent insects, and with a high and beautiful color and larger segments to the corolla, with very much exserted stamens and pistil. Eaton says the *nudiflora* is "not viscous;" names half a dozen varieties and among them *A. partita* (flesh-colored flowers, 5-parted to the base), but then this is viscous. And it cannot be his species *A. nitida*, with glabrous and shining and small leaves. It must be an undescribed variety — a viscous one — of *A. nudiflora*.

Melvin says the gray squirrel nests are made of leaves, the red squirrel of pine stuff. Jarvis tells me that Stedman Buttrick once hired Melvin to work for him on condition that he should not take his gun into the field, but he had known him to do so when Buttrick was away and earn two or three dollars with his game beside his day's work, but of course the last was neglected.

There is a little danger of a frost to-night.

IV

JUNE, 1853

(ÆT. 35)

June 1. Quite a fog this morning. Does it not always follow the cooler nights after the first really warm weather about the end of May? Saw a water snake yesterday, with its tail twisted about some dead weed stubble and quite dry and stiff for an inch, as if it were preparing to shed its skin. A wilted sprig of creeping juniper has a little, a very little, of sweet fragrance, somewhat like that of the fir and spruce. It seems to be just coming into bloom. Bees are swarming now, and those who keep them often have to leave their work in haste to secure them.

P. M. — To Walden.

Summer begins now about a week past, with the expanded leaves, the shade and warm weather. Cultivated fields also are *leaving* out, *i. e.* corn and potatoes coming up. Most trees have bloomed and are now forming their fruit. Young berries, too, are forming, and birds are being hatched. Dor-bugs and other insects have come forth the first warm evening after showers.

The birds have now all (?) come and no longer fly in flocks. The hylodes are no longer heard. The bullfrogs begin to trump. Thick and extensive fogs in the morning begin. Plants are rapidly growing, — *shooting*.

Hoeing corn has commenced (June 1st). It is now the season of growth. The first bloom of the year is over. Have not wild animals now henceforth (?) their young? and fishes too?

The pincushion galls on young white oaks are now among the most beautiful objects in the woods, coarse woolly white to appearance, spotted with bright red or crimson on the exposed side. It is remarkable that a mere gall, which at first we are inclined to regard as something abnormal, should be made so beautiful, as if it were the *flower* of the tree; that a disease, an excrescence, should prove, perchance, the greatest beauty, — as the tear of the pearl. Beautiful scarlet sins they may be. Through our temptations, — aye, and our falls, — our virtues appear. As in many a character, — many a poet, — we see that beauty exhibited in a gall, which was meant to have bloomed in a flower, unchecked. Such, however, is the accomplishment of the world. The poet cherishes his chagrins and sets his sighs to music. This gall is the tree's "Ode to Dejection." How oft it chances that the apparent fruit of a shrub, its apple, is merely a gall or blight! How many men meet with some blast in the moist growing days of their youth, and what should have been a sweet and palatable fruit in them becomes a mere puff and excrescence, ripening no kernel, and they say that they have experienced religion! For the hardening of the seed is the crisis. Their fruit is a gall, a puff, an excrescence, for want of moderation and continence. So many plants never ripen their fruit.

I see the effects of a frost last night and earlier in

the hollow west of Laurel Glen. The young white oaks have suffered especially, their leaves shrivelled and now drying up, and the hickories are turned quite black. These effects are most noticeable, not in the deepest hollows, if they are shady, but in those where the wood has been cut off a year or two, next to standing wood which reflected the sun, and which were the warmest during the day. Are not those trees which are latest to leave out generally the most tender in this respect?

I notice that most of the *Smilacina racemosa* has had its tip or flower-bud nipped off. Eggs in oven-bird's nest. The water-target leaves are conspicuous on the pond meadows now. The heart-leaves already on the river. A little of the pollen now along the shore of the still coves. The pitch pines near by have shed theirs.

The news of the explosion of the powder-mills was not only carried seaward by the cloud which its smoke made, but more effectually, though more slowly, by the fragments which were floated thither by the river. Melvin yesterday showed me quite a pile of fragments, — some short pieces of large timber, — still black with powder, which he had saved as they were drifting by. Nobody takes the trouble to record all the consequences of such an event. And some, no doubt, were carried down to the Merrimack, and by the Merrimack to the ocean, till perchance they got into the Gulf Stream and were cast up the coast of Norway, covered with barnacles, or who can tell what more distant strand? — still bearing some traces of burnt

Vol. V

powder, still capable of telling how and where they were launched, to those who can read their signs. To see a man lying all bare, lank, and tender on the rocks, like a skinned frog or lizard! We did not suspect that he was made of such cold, tender, clammy substance before.

Mingling with wrecks of vessels, which communicated a different tale, this wreck of a powder-mill was cast up on some outlandish strand, and went to swell the pile of driftwood collected by some native. Shouldered by whales. Alighted on at first by the muskrat and the peetweet, — and finally perhaps the stormy petrel and the beach-birds. It is long before Nature forgets it. How slowly the ruins are being dispersed!

Viola pedata past its prime; and are not the *sagittata*, and run to leaf? and also the *cucullata* (?) (?), so that the *palmata* take their places? I am as white as a miller, — a rye-miller, at least, — with the lint from the young leaves and twigs. The tufts of pinks on the side of the peak by the pond grow raying out somewhat from a centre, somewhat like a cyme, on the warm dry side-hill, — some a lighter, some a richer and darker, shade of pink. With what a variety of colors we are entertained! Yet most colors are rare or in small doses, presented us as a condiment or spice. Much of green, blue, black, and white, but of yellow and the different shades of red far less. The eye feasts on the colors of flowers as on titbits; they are its spices.

I hear now, at five o'clock, from this hill, a farmer's

horn calling his hands in from the field to an early tea. Heard afar by the walker, over the woods at this hour or at noon, bursting upon the stillness of the air, putting life into some portion of the horizon, this is one of the most suggestive and pleasing of the country sounds produced by man. I know not how far it is peculiar to New England or the United States. I hear two or three prolonged blasts, as I am walking alone some sultry noon in midst of the still woods, — a sound which I know to be produced by human breath, the most sonorous parts of which alone reach me, — and I see in my mind the hired men and master dropping the implements of their labor in the field and wending their way with a sober satisfaction toward the house; I see the well-sweep rise and fall; I see the preparatory ablutions and the table laden with the smoking meal. It is a significant hum in a distant part of the hive. Often it tells me [the] time of day.

How much lupine is now in full bloom on bare sandy brows or promontories running into meadows, where the sod is half worn away and the sand exposed! The geraniums are now getting to be common. *Hieracium venosum* just out on this peak. And the snapdragon catchfly is here abundantly in blossom, a little after 5 p. m., — a pretty little flower, the petals dull crimson beneath or varnished mahogany-color, and rose-tinted white within or above. It closed on my way home, but opened again in water in the evening. Its opening in the night chiefly is a fact which interests and piques me. Do any insects visit it then?

Lambkill just beginning, the very earliest. A purple (!) Canada snapdragon.

New, bright, and glossy light-green leaves of the umbelled wintergreen are shooting on this hillside, but the old leaves are particularly glossy and shining, as if varnished and not yet dry, or most highly polished. Did they look thus in the winter? I do not know any leaf so wet-glossy.

Walking up this side-hill, I disturbed a nighthawk eight or ten feet from me, which went, half fluttering, half hopping, the mottled creature, like a winged toad, as Nuttall says the French of Louisiana (?) call them, down the hill as far as I could see. Without moving, I looked about and saw its two eggs on the bare ground, on a slight shelf of the hill, on the dead pine-needles and sand, without any cavity or nest whatever, very obvious when once you had detected them, but not easily detected from their color, a coarse gray formed of white spotted with a bluish or slaty brown or umber, — a stone — granite — color, like the places it selects. I advanced and put my hand on them, and while I stooped, seeing a shadow on the ground, looked up and saw the bird, which had fluttered down the hill so blind and helpless, circling low and swiftly past over my head, showing the white spot on each wing in true nighthawk fashion. When I had gone a dozen rods, it appeared again higher in the air, with its peculiar flitting, limping kind of flight, all the while noiseless, and suddenly descending, it dashed at me within ten feet of my head, like an imp of darkness, then swept away high over the pond, dashing

ticleer in the morning, with all the lustiness that the new day imparts, without thinking of the evening, when I and all of us shall go to roost, — with all the humility of the cock, that takes his perch upon the highest rail and wakes the country with his clarion.[1] Shall not men be inspired as much as cockerels? My feet are soon wet with fog. It is, indeed, a vast dew. And are not the clouds another kind of dew? Cool nights produce them.

Now I have reached the hilltop above the fog at a quarter to five, about sunrise, and all around me is a sea of fog, level and white, reaching nearly to the top of this hill, only the tops of a few high hills appearing as distant islands in the main. Wachusett is a more distant and larger island, an Atlantis in the west; there is hardly one to touch at between me and it. It is just like the clouds beneath you as seen from a mountain. It is a perfect level in some directions, cutting the hills near their summits with a geometrical line, but puffed up here and there, and more and more toward the east, by the influence of the sun. An early freight-train of cars is heard, not seen, rushing through the town beneath it. It resembles nothing so much as the ocean. You can get here the impression which the ocean makes, without ever going to the shore. Men — poor simpletons as they are — will go to a panorama by families, to see a Pilgrim's Progress, perchance, who never yet made progress so far as to the top of such a hill as this at the dawn of a foggy morning. All the fog they know is in their brains. The seashore exhibits nothing more grand or on a

[1] [See *Walden*, pp. 2 and 94; Riv. 133 and title-page.]

now to this side now to that, on different tacks, as if, in pursuit of its prey, it had already forgotten its eggs on the earth. I can see how it might easily come to be regarded with superstitious awe. A cuckoo very plainly heard.

June 2. 3.30 A. M. — When I awake I hear the low universal chirping or twittering of the chip-birds, like the bursting bead on the surface of the uncorked day. First come, first served! You must taste the first glass of the day's nectar, if you would get all the spirit of it. Its fixed air begins to stir and escape. Also the robin's morning song is heard as in the spring, earlier than the notes of most other birds, thus bringing back the spring; now rarely heard or noticed in the course of the day.

4 A. M. — To Nawshawtuct.

I go to the river in a fog through which I cannot see more than a dozen rods, — three or four times as deep as the houses. As I row down the stream, the dark, dim outlines of the trees on the banks appear, coming to meet me out of the mist on the one hand, while they retreat and are soon concealed in it on the other. My strokes soon bury them behind me. The birds are wide awake, as if knowing that this fog presages a fair day. I ascend Nawshawtuct from the north side. I am aware that I yield to the same influence which inspires the birds and the cockerels, whose hoarse courage I hear now vaunted. So men should crow in the morning. I would crow like chan-

larger scale. How grand where it rolls off northeastward (?) over Ball's Hill like a glorious ocean after a storm, just lit by the rising sun! It is as boundless as the view from the highlands of Cape Cod. They are exaggerated billows, the ocean on a larger scale, the sea after some tremendous and unheard-of storm, for the actual sea never appears so tossed up and universally white with foam and spray as this now far in the northeastern horizon, where mountain billows are breaking on some hidden reef or bank. It is tossed up toward the sun and by it into the most boisterous of seas, which no craft, no ocean steamer, is vast enough to sail on.

Meanwhile my hands are numb with cold and my wet feet ache with it. Now, at 5.15, before this southwest wind, it is already grown thin as gossamer in that direction, and woods and houses are seen through it, while it is heaped up toward the sun, and finally becomes so thick there that for a short time it appears in one place a dark, low cloud, such as else can only be seen from mountains; and now long, dark ridges of wood appear through it, and now the sun reflected from the river makes a bright glow in the fog, and now, at 5.30, I see the green surface of the meadows and the water through the trees, sparkling with bright reflections. Men will go further and pay more to see a tawdry picture on canvas, a poor painted scene, than to behold the fairest or grandest scene that nature ever displays in their immediate vicinity, though they may have never seen it in their lives.

The triosteum a day or two. Cherry-birds are the

River Fog from Nawshawtuct Hill

only ones I see in flocks now. I can tell them afar by their peculiar fine springy note. The hickory is not yet blossomed. Sanicle and waxwork just out. On Monday saw apparently fresh-broken tortoise eggs. Locust tree just opening.

4 P. M. — To Conantum.

Equisetum limosum out some days. Look for it at Myosotis Brook, bottom of Wheildon's field. Side-saddle-flower — purple petals (?) now begin to hang down. Arethusas are abundant in what I may call Arethusa Meadow. They are the more striking for growing in such green localities, — in meadows where their brilliant purple, more or less red, contrasts with the green grass. Found four perfect arrowheads and one imperfect in the potato-field, just plowed up for the first time that I remember, at the Hubbard Bathing-Place. Each hill of potatoes (they are now just out of the ground) has been probed by some animal, and a great many of the potatoes, planted not long since, abstracted. Some are left on the surface. Almost every hill in the field which bounds on the river has been disturbed. Was it a muskrat, or a mink, or a woodchuck, or a skunk? The tracks are of the right size for any of these.

Viburnum Lentago in the hedge on west side of Arethusa Meadow. It is all fully out. It must be three or four days or more, then, some of it. *Clintonia borealis*, a day or two. This is perhaps the most interesting and neatest of what I may call the liliaceous (?) plants we have. Its beauty at present consists chiefly

in its commonly three very handsome, rich, clear dark-green leaves, which Bigelow describes truly as "more than half a foot long, oblanceolate, smooth and shining." They are perfect in form and color, broadly oblanceolate with a deep channel down the middle, uninjured by insects, arching over from a centre at the ground, sometimes very symmetrically disposed in a triangular fashion; and from their midst rises the scape [a] foot high, with one or more umbels of "green bell-shaped flowers," yellowish-green, nodding or bent downward, but without fragrance. In fact, the flower is all green, both leaves and corolla. The leaves alone — and many have no scape — would detain the walker. Its berries are its flower. A single plant is a great ornament in a vase, from the beauty of its form and the rich, unspotted green of its leaves.

The sorrel now reddens the fields far and wide. As I look over the fields thus reddened in extensive patches, now deeper, now passing into green, and think of the season now in its prime and heyday, it looks as if it were the blood mantling in the cheek of the youthful year, — the rosy cheek of its health, its rude June health. The medeola has been out a day or two, apparently, — another green flower. The *Cornus alternifolia* at Conantum also apparently a day or two; and there is near by it a cockspur thorn. I hear the pine warbler note from a sparrow-like bird on pitch pines, employed like the pine warbler. Is it the female? The pinxter-flower growing as it does as an underwood in the shade of larger trees, the naked

Vol. V

umbels of its lively rose-pink flowers are seen flashing out against a background of green or of dark shaded recesses. The lobes of the corolla are of a lively rose pink, the tubes and stamens of a deeper red. My sleepy catchflies open each night in a pitcher. An abundance of this flower as a weed in Mr. Prichard's garden.

June 3. *Friday.* P. M. — To Annursnack.

By way of the linnæa, which I find is not yet out. That thick pine wood is full of birds. Saw a large moth or butterfly exactly like a decayed withered leaf, — a rotten yellowish or buff. The small-leaved pyrola will open in a day or two. Two or three ripe strawberries on the south slope of a dry hill. I was thinking that they had set, when, seeking a more favorable slope, I found ripe fruit.

The painted-cup is in its prime. It reddens the meadow, — Painted-Cup Meadow. It is a splendid show of brilliant scarlet, the color of the cardinal-flower, and surpassing it in *mass* and *profusion*. They first appear on the side of the hill in drier ground, half a dozen inches high, and their color is most striking then, when it is most rare and precious; but they now cover the meadow, mingled with buttercups, etc., and many are more than eighteen inches high. I do not like the name; it does not remind me of a cup, rather of a flame, when it first appears. It might be called flame-flower, or scarlet-tip. Here is a large meadow full of it, and yet very few in the town have ever seen it. It is startling to see a leaf thus brilliantly

painted, as if its tip were dipped into some scarlet tincture, surpassing most flowers in intensity of color. Seen from Annursnack the woods now appear full-leafed, smooth green, no longer hoary, and the pines a dark mulberry, not green. But you are still covered with lint as you go through the copses. Summer begins when the hoariness disappears from the forest as you look down on it, and gives place thus to smooth green, full and universal.

Butter-and-eggs just out. A small thorn with deep cut-lobed leaves, no flower, on this hill. May be a variety of the scarlet? White cedar now out of bloom. Is that rank grass by the Red Bridge, already between three and four feet high, wild oats?

The song of the robin and the chirp (?) of the chip-bird now begin prominently to usher in and to conclude the day. The robin's song seems not so loud as in the early spring, perhaps because there are so many other sounds at present.

June 4. *Saturday.* The date of the introduction of the *Rhododendron maximum* into Concord is worth preserving, May 16th, '53. They were small plants, one to four feet high, some with large flower-buds, twenty-five cents apiece; and I noticed next day one or more in every front yard on each side of the street, and the inhabitants out watering them. Said to be the most splendid native flower in Massachusetts; in a swamp in Medfield. I hear to-day that one in town has blossomed.

George Minott says he saw many lightning-bugs a

warm evening the fore part of this week, after the rains. Probably it was the 29th.

P. M. — To Hubbard's Close Swamp.

The vetch just out by Turnpike, — dark violet-purple. Horse-radish fully out (some time). The great ferns are already two or three feet high in Hubbard's shady swamp. The clintonia is abundant there along by the foot of the hill, and in its prime. Look there for its berries. Commonly four leaves there, with an obtuse point, — the lady's-slipper leaf not so rich, dark green and smooth, having several channels. The bullfrog now begins to be heard at night regularly; has taken the place of the hylodes.

Looked over the oldest town records at the clerk's office this evening, the old book containing grants of land. Am surprised to find such names as "Walden Pond" and "Fair Haven" as early as 1653, and apparently 1652; also, under the first date at least, "Second Division," the rivers as North and South Rivers (no Assabet at that date), "Swamp bridge," apparently on back road, "Goose Pond," "Mr. Flints Pond," "Nutt Meadow," "Willow Swamp," "Spruce Swamp," etc., etc. "Dongy," "Dung Hole," or what-not, appears to be between Walden and Fair Haven. Is Rocky Hill Mr. Emerson's or the Cliffs? Where are South Brook, Frog Ponds, etc., etc., etc.? It is pleasing to read these evergreen wilderness names, i. e. of particular swamps and woods, then applied to now perchance cleared fields and meadows said to be redeemed. The Second Division appears to have been a very large tract between the two rivers.

Vol. V

blossom on the gill I looked at yesterday; its prime is probably past. Now see those great green, half fruit, half flower like, excrescences on blueberry and huckleberry bushes. The hemlocks, whose fresh light-green shoots have now grown half an inch or an inch, spotting the trees, contrasting with the dark green of last year's foliage, the fan-like sprays looking like bead bags.

P. M. — To Mason's pasture.

The world now full of *verdure* and *fragrance* and the air *comparatively* clear (not yet the constant haze of the dog-days), through which the distant fields are seen, reddened with sorrel, and the meadows wet-green, full of fresh grass, and the trees in their first beautiful, bright, untarnished and unspotted green. May is the bursting into leaf and early flowering, with much coolness and wet and a few decidedly warm days, ushering in summer; June, *verdure* and *growth* with not intolerable, but agreeable, heat.

The river meadows from N. Barrett's have for some time lost their early yellow look. Nightshade out, maybe some days. The young pitch pines in Mason's pasture are a glorious sight, now most of the shoots grown six inches, so soft and blue-green, nearly as wide as high. It is nature's front yard. The mountain laurel shows its red flower-buds, but many shoots have been killed by frost. A *Polygonatum pubescens* there two and a half feet long. The large thorn by Yellow Birch Swamp must be a *Cratœgus coccinea*. Though full of fruit last year, it has not blossomed

June 5. Sunday. 5 A. M. — By river to Nawshawtuct.

For the most part we are inclined to doubt the prevalence of gross superstition among the civilized ancients, — whether the Greeks, for instance, accepted literally the mythology which we accept as matchless poetry, — but we have only to be reminded of the kind of respect paid to the Sabbath as a *holy* day here in New England, and the fears which haunt those who *break* it, to see that our neighbors are the creatures of an equally gross superstition with the ancients. I am convinced that there is no very important difference between a New-Englander's religion and a Roman's. We both worship in the shadow of our sins: they erect the temples for us. Jehovah has no superiority to Jupiter. The New-Englander is a pagan suckled in a creed outworn. Superstition has always reigned. It is absurd to think that these farmers, dressed in their Sunday clothes, proceeding to church, differ essentially in this respect from the Roman peasantry. They have merely changed the names and number of their gods. Men were as good then as they are now, and loved one another as much — or little.

The sweet flag has been out some days. The *Smilacina racemosa*. The river has now assumed a summer aspect, the water gone down somewhat. The pickerel-weed is more conspicuous, a foot high or more, and potamogetons and polygonums appear, and pads are quite abundant. I see green flower-buds [1] on the tupelo. The hickory is fairly out. The azalea about done. The carrion-flower just out. Saw no

[1] They are flowers; also the 9th.

this year. There is a tract of pasture, woodland, orchard, and swamp in the north part of the town, through which the old Carlisle road runs, which is nearly two miles square, without a single house and scarcely any cultivated land in it, — four square miles. I perceive some black birch leaves with a beautiful crimson kind of sugaring along the furrows of the nerves, giving them wholly a bright-crimson color, — either a fungus or the deposit of an insect. Seen through a microscope it sparkles like a ruby.

Nature is fair in proportion as the youth is pure. The heavens and the earth are one flower. The earth is the calyx, the heavens the corolla.

June 6. 4.30 A. M. — To Linnæa Woods.

Famous place for tanagers. Considerable fog on river. Few sights more exhilarating than one of these banks of fog lying along a stream. The linnæa just out. *Corydalis glauca*, a delicate glaucous plant rarely met with, with delicate flesh-colored and yellow flowers, covered with a glaucous bloom, on dry, rocky hills. Perhaps it suggests gentility. Set it down as early as middle of May or earlier. *Viburnum nudum;* may be Bigelow's *pyrifolium* (which Gray makes a variety), except that its scales are not *black*, though the peduncle of its cyme is short. That is apparently *Pyrola chlorantha*, so well budded now. *Galium triflorum* (?) there on the dry hillside; peduncles two-flowered as well as three, green or no petals.

Is that blackberry mixed with the linnæa swamp blackberry? It will open to-day or to-morrow. Begin to observe and to admire the forms of trees with shining foliage and each its shadow on the hillside. This morning I hear the note of young bluebirds in the air, which have recently taken wing, and the old birds keep up such a warbling and twittering as remind me of spring.

According to Sophia's account she must have seen an emperor moth, "pea-green with a sort of maple keys for tail," in a lady's hand in Cambridge to-day. So it may have come out of the chrysalid seen May 23d.

P. M. — To Conantum by boat.

The *Potamogeton* [a blank space] out two or three days, probably. The small primrose out at Hubbard's Swimming-Place, drooping at top like a smilacina's leaves. Blue-eyed grass now begins to give that slaty-blue tint to meadows. A breezy day, a June wind showing the under sides of leaves. The *now red* round white lily pads are now very numerous and conspicuous, red more or less on both sides and, with the yellow lily pads, turned up by the wind. In May and June we have breezes which, for the most part, are not too cold but exhilarating. I see the breams' nests and breams in them. The larger rushes are conspicuously above water. The *Viburnum dentatum*, that very conspicuously and regularly tooth-leafed shrub, like a saw with coarse teeth, as yet *very few* flowers in its cymes. This is at edge of Hubbard's Woods, opposite Hollowell place. As I sit looking over the side of the boat there, I see the bottom covered with small hypericums springing up in the yellowish water,

and in the axils of the leaves under water are little sparkling, silvery beads of air, as are sometimes seen on plants covered with dew out of water, but I do not perceive them on the adjacent plants. The deep shadow of Conantum Cliff and of mere prominences in the hills, now at mid-afternoon as we row by, is very interesting. It is the most pleasing effect of the kind, or contrast of light and shade, that I notice. Methinks that in winter a shadow is not attractive. The air is very clear, — at least, as we look from the river valley, — and the landscape all swept and brushed. We seem to see to some depth into the side of Fair Haven Hill. *Rhus Toxicodendron*, the shrub, out at Bittern Cliff. The sidesaddle-flowers are now in their prime. There are some very large ones hereabouts, five inches in diameter when you flatten out their petals, like great dull-red roses. Their petals are of a peculiar but agreeable red, but their upper sides, — *i. e.* of their calyx-leaves, — shiny leather-red or brown-red, are agreeable. A slippery elm (*Ulmus fulva*) on Lee's Cliff, — red elm. Put it with the common, It has large, rough leaves and straggling branches — a rather small, much-spreading tree, with an appearance between the common elm and iron-wood.

The aspect of the dry rocky hills already indicates the rapid revolution of the seasons. The spring, that early age of the world, following hard on the reign of water and the barren rocks yet dripping with it, is past. How many plants have already dried up ! — lichens and algæ, which we can still remember, as if belonging to a former epoch, saxifrage, crowfoot,

Vol. V

anemone, columbine for the most part, etc. It is Lee's Cliff I am on. There is a growth confined to the damp and early spring. How dry and crisp the turf feels there now, not moist with melted snows, remembering, as it were, when it was the bottom of the sea. How wet-glossy the leaves of the red oak, now fully expanded! They shine when the sun comes out as after rain. I find on a shelf of the rock the *Turritis stricta*, now gone to seed; but two feet two inches high (Gray allows but one foot?); pods upright and nearly three inches long, linear; and flat leaves decidedly lanceolate or linear; but some minute imperfect unexpanded flowers still on it appear as if they would have been yellowish.

In the very open park in rear of the Rocks on the hilltop, where lambkill and huckleberries and grass alternate, came to one of those handsome, round, mirror-like pools a rod or two in diameter and surrounded with a border of fine weeds, such as you frequently meet with on the top of springy hills. Though warm and muddy at bottom, they are very beautiful and glassy and look as if they were cool springs; so high, exposed to the light, yet so wild and fertile, as if the fertility of the lowland was transferred to the summit of the hills. These are the kind of mirrors at which the huntresses in the golden age arranged their toilets, which the deer frequented and contemplated their branching horns in.

June 7. P. M. — To Walden.
Huckleberry-apples, which are various stages of a

monstrous and abortive development of the flower, common now. Clover begins to redden the fields generally. The horsetail has for some time covered the causeway with a close, dense green, like moss. The quail is heard at a distance. The marsh speedwell has been out apparently some days. A little mowing begins in the gardens and front yards. The grass is in full vigor now, yet it is already parti-colored with whitish withered stems which worms have cut. Buttercups, of various kinds mingled, yellow the meadows, — the tall, the bulbous, and the *repens*. Probably a *Prinos lævigatus* in Trillium Woods, ready to blossom. Observe its berries in the fall. The cinquefoil in its ascending state, keeping pace with the grass, is now abundant in the fields. Saw it one or two weeks ago. This is a feature of June. Still both high and low blueberry and huckleberry blossoms abound. The hemlock woods, their fan-like sprays edged or spotted with short yellowish-green shoots, tier above tier, shelf above shelf, look like a cool bazar of rich embroidered goods. How dense their shade, dark and cool beneath them as in a cellar! No plants grow there, but the ground is covered with fine red leaves. It is oftenest on a side-hill they grow. The oven-bird runs from her covered nest, so close to the ground under the lowest twigs and leaves, even the loose leaves on the ground, like a mouse, that I cannot get a fair view of her. She does not fly at all. Is it to attract me, or partly to protect herself? The *Viburnum acerifolium* will open to-morrow or next day.

Going through Thrush Alley, see the froth on the

base of the shoots of the pitch pine, now three or four to ten inches long.

Visited my nighthawk on her nest. Could hardly believe my eyes when I stood within seven feet and beheld her sitting on her eggs, her head to me. She looked so Saturnian, so one with the earth, so sphinx-like, a relic of the reign of Saturn which Jupiter did not destroy, a riddle that might well cause a man to go dash his head against a stone. It was not an actual living creature, far less a winged creature of the air, but a figure in stone or bronze, a fanciful production of art, like the gryphon or phœnix. In fact, with its breast toward me, and owing to its color or size no bill perceptible, it looked like the end [of] a brand, such as are common in a clearing, its breast mottled or alternately waved with dark brown and gray, its flat, grayish, weather-beaten crown, its eyes nearly closed, purposely, lest those bright beads should betray it, with the stony cunning of the sphinx. A fanciful work in bronze to ornament a mantel. It was enough to fill one with awe. The sight of this creature sitting on its eggs impressed me with the venerableness of the globe. There was nothing novel about it. All the while, this seemingly sleeping bronze sphinx, as motionless as the earth, was watching me with intense anxiety through those narrow slits in its eyelids. Another step, and it fluttered down the hill close to the ground, with a wabbling motion, as if touching the ground now with the tip of one wing, now with the other, so ten rods to the water, which [it] skimmed close over a few rods, then rose and soared in the air above me. Wonder-

ful creature, which sits motionless on its eggs on the barest, most exposed hills, through pelting storms of rain or hail, as if it were a rock or a part of the earth itself, the outside of the globe, with its eyes shut and its wings folded, and, after the two days' storm, when you think it has become a fit symbol of the rheumatism, it suddenly rises into the air a bird, one of the most aerial, supple, and graceful of creatures, without stiffness in its wings or joints! It was a fit prelude to meeting Prometheus bound to his rock on Caucasus.

Autumnal dandelion out. For a long time the cows, having been turned out to pasture, have looked clean and sleek. How many plants and flowers smell like strawberries, — a wild moss rose bud to-day; and the acanthus [sic] flower is strongly like strawberries partly decayed in the box. Perhaps the flower was stale.

June 8. Wednesday. P. M. — To Well Meadow.

Nest of a Maryland yellow-throat by Utricularia Pool in a tuft of sedge ; made of dry sedge, grass, and a few dry leaves ; about four small eggs, a delicate white with reddish-brown spots on larger end ; the nest well concealed. At the last small pond near Well Meadow, a frog, apparently a small bullfrog, on the shore enveloped by a swarm of small, almost invisible insects, some resting on him, attracted perhaps by the slime which shone on him. He appeared to endure the persecution like a philosopher. *Utricularia vulgaris* out, how long?

As I stood by this pond, I heard a hawk scream,

and, looking up, saw a pretty large one circling not far off and incessantly screaming, as I at first supposed to scare and so discover its prey, but its screaming was so incessant and it circled from time to time so near me, as I moved southward, that I began to think it had a nest near by and was angry at my intrusion into its domains. As I moved, the bird still followed and screamed, coming sometimes quite near or within gunshot, then circling far off or high into the sky. At length, as I was looking up at it, thinking it the only living creature within view, I was singularly startled to behold, as my eye by chance penetrated deeper into the blue, — the abyss of blue above, which I had taken for a solitude, — its mate silently soaring at an immense height and seemingly indifferent to me. We are surprised to discover that there can be an eye on us on that side, and so little suspected, that the heavens are full of eyes, though they look so blue and spotless. Then I knew it was the female that circled and screamed below. At last the latter rose gradually to meet her mate, and they circled together there, as if they could not possibly feel any anxiety on my account. When I drew nearer to the tall trees where I suspected the nest to be, the female descended again, swept by screaming still nearer to me just over the tree-tops, and finally, while I was looking for the orchis in the swamp, alighted on a white pine twenty or thirty rods off. (The great fringed orchis just open.) At length I detected the nest about eighty feet from the ground, in a very large white pine by the edge of the swamp. It was about three feet in diameter,

of dry sticks, and a young hawk, apparently as big as its mother, stood on the edge of the nest looking down at me, and only moving its head when I moved. In its imperfect plumage and by the slow motion of its head it reminded me strongly of a vulture, so large and gaunt. It appeared a tawny brown on its neck and breast, and dark brown or blackish on wings. The mother was light beneath, and apparently lighter still on rump.

The *Pyrola chlorantha*, — if the style can be said to be "scarcely exserted," — under Cliffs, a day or more. The *Aralia hispida* at the foot of the rocks higher up, earlier than elsewhere. White pine in flower, — all the female flowers on the very tops of the trees, a small crimson cone upright on the ends of its peduncles, while the last year's, now three or four inches long and green, are curved downward like scythes. Best seen looking down on the tops of lower pines from the top of a higher one. Apparently just beginning.

June 9. 4.30 A. M. — To Nawshawtuct by boat.

A prevalent fog, though not quite so thick as the last described. It is a little more local, for it is so thin southwest of this hill that I can see the earth through it, but as thick as before northeast. Yet here and there deep valleys are excavated in it, as painters imagine the Red Sea for the passage of Pharaoh's host, wherein trees and houses appear as it were at the bottom of the sea. What is peculiar about it is that it is the tops of the trees which you see first and most distinctly, before you see their trunks or where they stand on earth. Far in the northeast there is, as before, apparently a tremendous surf breaking on a distant shoal. It is either a real shoal, *i. e.* a hill over which the fog breaks, or the effect of the sun's rays on it.

I was amused by the account which Mary, the Irish girl who left us the other day, gave of her experience at —— ——, the milkman's, in the north part of the town. She said that twenty-two lodged in the house the first night, including two pig men, that Mr. —— kept ten men, had six children and a deaf wife, and one of the men had his wife with him, who helped sew, beside taking care of her own child. Also all the cooking and washing for his father and mother, who live in another house and whom he is bound to carry through, is done in his house, and she, Mary, was the only girl they hired; and the workmen were called up at four by an alarm clock which was set a quarter of an hour ahead of the clock downstairs, — and that more than as much ahead of the town clock, — and she was on her feet from that hour till nine at night. Each man had two pairs of overalls in the wash, and the cans to be scalded were countless. Having got through washing the breakfast dishes by a quarter before twelve, Sunday noon, by ——'s time, she left, no more to return. He had told her that the work was easy, that girls had lived with him to recover their health, and then went away to be married. He is regarded as one of the most enterprising and thrifty farmers in the county, and takes the premiums of the Agricultural Society. He probably exacts too much of his hands.

The steam of the engine streaming far behind is regularly divided, as if it were the vertebræ of a serpent, probably by the strokes of the piston. The reddish seeds or glumes of grasses cover my boots now in the dewy or foggy morning. The diervilla out apparently yesterday. The first white lily bud. White clover is abundant and very sweet on the common, filling the air, but not yet elsewhere as last year.

8 A. M. — To Orchis Swamp; Well Meadow.

Hear a goldfinch; this the second or third only that I have heard. Whiteweed now whitens the fields. There are many *star* flowers. I remember the anemone, especially the rue anemone, — which is not yet all gone, lasting longer than the true one, — above all the trientalis, and of late the yellow Bethlehem-star, and perhaps others.

I have come with a spy-glass to look at the hawks. They have detected me and are already screaming over my head more than half a mile from the nest. I find no difficulty in looking at the young hawk (there appears to be one only, standing on the edge of the nest), resting the glass in the crotch of a young oak. I can see every wink and the color of its iris. It watches me more steadily than I it, now looking straight down at me with both eyes and outstretched neck, now turning its head and looking with one eye. How its eye and its whole head express anger! Its anger is more in its eye than in its beak. It is quite hoary over the eye and on the chin. The mother meanwhile is incessantly circling about and above its charge and me, farther or nearer,

Vol. V

sometimes withdrawing a quarter of a mile, but occasionally coming to alight for a moment almost within gunshot, on the top of a tall white pine; but I hardly bring my glass fairly to bear on her, and get sight of her angry eye through the pine-needles, before she circles away again. Thus for an hour that I lay there, screaming every minute or oftener with open bill. Now and then pursued by a kingbird or a blackbird, who appear merely to annoy it by dashing down at its back. Meanwhile the male is soaring, apparently quite undisturbed, at a great height above, evidently not hunting, but amusing or recreating himself in the thinner and cooler air, as if pleased with his own circles, like a geometer, and enjoying the sublime scene. I doubt if he has his eye fixed on any prey, or the earth. He probably descends to hunt.

Got two or three handfuls of strawberries on Fair Haven. They are already drying up. The huckleberry bedbug-smelling bug is on them. It is natural that the first fruit which the earth bears should emit and be as it were an embodiment of that vernal fragrance with which the air has teemed. Strawberries are its manna, found ere long where that fragrance has filled the air. Little natural beds or patches on the sides of dry hills, where the fruit sometimes reddens the ground. But it soon dries up, unless there is a great deal of rain. Well, are not the juices of early fruit distilled from the air?

Prunella out. The meadows are now yellow with the golden senecio, a more orange yellow, mingled with the light glossy yellow of the buttercup. The

green fruit of the sweet-fern now. The *Juniperus repens* appears, though now dry and effete, to have blossomed recently.

The tall white *Erigeron annuus* (?), for this is the only one described as white tinged with purple, just out.[1]

The bullfrogs are in full blast to-night. I do not hear a toad from my window; only the crickets beside. The toads I have but rarely heard of late.[2] So there is an evening for the toads and another for the bullfrogs.

June 10. *Friday.* Another great fog this morning. Haying commencing in front yards.

P. M. — To Mason's pasture in Carlisle.

Cool but agreeable easterly wind. Streets now beautiful with verdure and shade of elms, under which you look, through an air clear for summer, to the woods in the horizon. By the way, I amused myself yesterday afternoon with looking from my window, through a spy-glass, at the tops of the woods in the horizon. It was pleasant to bring them so near and individualize the trees, to examine in detail the tree-tops which before you had beheld only in the mass as the woods in the horizon. It was an exceedingly rich border, seen thus against [*sic*], and the imperfections in a particular tree-top more than two miles off were quite apparent. I could easily have seen a hawk sailing over the top of the wood, and possibly his nest in some higher tree. Thus to contemplate, from my attic in the village, the

[1] I think it is *strigosus*, but tinged with purple sometimes.
[2] *Vide* [p. 241].

hawks circling about their nests above some dense forest or swamp miles away, almost as if they were flies on my own premises! I actually distinguished a taller white pine with which I am well acquainted, with a double top rising high above the surrounding woods, between two and three miles distant, which, with the naked eye, I had confounded with the nearer woods.

But to return, as C. and I go through the town, we hear the cool peep of the robin calling to its young, now learning to fly. The locust bloom is now perfect, filling the street with its sweetness, but it is more agreeable to my eye than my nose. The curled dock out. The fuzzy seeds or down of the black (?) willows is filling the air over the river and, falling on the water, covers the surface. By the 30th of May, at least, white maple keys were falling. How early, then, they had matured their seed! Cow-wheat out, and *Iris Virginica*, and the grape. The mountain laurel will begin to bloom to-morrow. The frost some weeks since killed most of the buds and shoots, except where they were protected by trees or by themselves, and now new shoots have put forth and grow four or five inches from the sides of what were the leading ones. It is a plant which plainly requires the protection of the wood. It is stunted in the open pasture. We continued on, round the head of "Cedar Swamp," and *may* say that we drank at the source of it or of Saw Mill Brook, where a spring is conducted through a hollow log to a tub for cattle. Crossed on to the old Carlisle road by the house north of Isaiah Green's, and then across

the road through the woods to the Paul Adams house by Bateman's Pond. Saw a hog-pasture of a dozen acres in the woods, with thirty or forty large hogs and a shelter for them at night, a half-mile east of the last house, — something rare in these days hereabouts.

What shall this great wild tract over which we strolled be called? Many farmers have pastures there, and wood-lots, and orchards. It consists mainly of rocky pastures. It contains what I call the Boulder Field, the Yellow Birch Swamp, the Black Birch Hill, the Laurel Pasture, the Hog-Pasture, the White Pine Grove, the Easterbrooks Place, the Old Lime-Kiln, the Lime Quarries, Spruce Swamp, the Ermine Weasel Woods; also the Oak Meadows, the Cedar Swamp, the Kibbe Place, and the old place northwest of Brooks Clark's. Ponkawtasset bounds it on the south. There are a few frog-ponds and an old mill-pond within it, and Bateman's Pond on its edge. What shall the whole be called? The old Carlisle road, which runs through the middle of it, is bordered on each side with wild apple pastures, where the trees stand without order, having, many if not most of them, sprung up by accident or from pomace sown at random, and are for the most part concealed by birches and pines. These orchards are very extensive, and yet many of these apple trees, growing as forest trees, bear good crops of apples. It is a paradise for walkers in the fall. There are also boundless huckleberry pastures as well as many blueberry swamps. Shall we call it the Easterbrooks Country? It would make a princely

estate in Europe, yet it is owned by farmers, who live by the labor of their hands and do not esteem it much. Plenty of huckleberries and barberries here.

A second great uninhabited tract is that on the Marlborough road, stretching westerly from Francis Wheeler's to the river, and beyond about three miles, and from Harrington's on the north to Dakin's on the south, more than a mile in width. A third, the Walden Woods. A fourth, the Great Fields. These four are all in Concord.

There are one or two in the town who probably have Indian blood in their veins, and when they exhibit any unusual irascibility, their neighbors say they have got their Indian blood roused.

C. proposes to call the first-named wild the Melvin Preserve, for it is favorite hunting-ground with George Melvin. It is a sort of Robin Hood Ground. Shall we call it the Apple Pastures?

Now, methinks, the birds begin to sing less tumultuously, with, as the weather grows more constantly warm, morning and noon and evening songs, and suitable recesses in the concert.

High blackberries conspicuously in bloom, whitening the side of lanes.

Mention is made in the Town Records, as quoted by Shattuck, page 33, under date of 1654, of "the Hogepen-walke about Annursnake," and reference is at the same time made to "the old hogepen." The phrase is " *in* the Hogepen-walke about Annursnake," *i. e.* in the hog-pasture. There is some propriety in calling such a tract a walk, methinks, from the habit

which hogs have of walking about with an independent air and pausing from time to time to look about from under their flapping ears and snuff the air. The hogs I saw this afternoon, all busily rooting without holding up their heads to look at us, — the whole field looked as if it had been most miserably plowed or scarified with a harrow, — with their shed to retreat to in rainy weather, affected me as more human than other quadrupeds. They are comparatively clean about their lodgings, and their shed, with its litter bed, was on the whole cleaner than an Irishman's shanty. I am not certain what there was so very human about them.

In 1668 the town had a pasture near Silas Holden's and a herd of fifty cattle constantly watched by a "herdsman," etc. (page 43). In 1672 there is an article referring to the "crane field and brickil field."

June 11. *Saturday.* Another fog this morning.

The mosquitoes first troubled me a little last night. On the river at dusk I hear the toads still, with the bullfrogs. The black willow, having shed its fuzzy seeds and expanded its foliage, now begins to be handsome, so light and graceful.

The upland fields are already less green where the June-grass is ripening its seeds. They are greenest when only the blade is seen. In the sorrel-fields, also, what lately was the ruddy, rosy cheek of health, now that the sorrel is ripening and dying, has become the tanned and imbrowned cheek of manhood.

Probably blackbirds were never less numerous along our river than in these years. They do not depend on the clearing of the woods and the cultivation of orchards, etc. Streams and meadows, in which they delight, always existed. Most of the towns, soon after they were settled, were obliged to set a price upon their heads. In 1672, according to the town records of Concord, instruction was given to the selectmen, "That incorrigent be given for the destroying of blackbirds and jaies." (Shattuck, page 45.)

Murder will out. I find, in the dry excrement of a fox left on a rock, the vertebræ and talons of a partridge (?) which he has consumed. They are *mémoires pour servir*.

I remember Helen's telling me that John Marston of Taunton told her that he was on board a vessel during the Revolution, which met another vessel,—and, as I think, one hailed the other,—and a French name being given could not be understood, whereupon a sailor, probably aboard his vessel, ran out on the bowsprit and shouted "La Sensible," [1] and that sailor's name was Thoreau. My father tells me that, when the war came on, my grandfather, being thrown out of business and being a young man, went a-privateering. I find from his Diary that John Adams set sail from Port Louis at L'Orient in the French frigate Sensible, Captain Chavagnes, June 17th, 1779, the Bonhomme Richard, Captain Jones, and four other vessels being in company at first, and the Sensible arrived at Boston the 2d of August. On

[1] The vessel in which John Adams was being brought back from or carried out to France. My father has an idea that he stood on the wharf and cried this to the bystanders.

the 13th of November following, he set out for France again in the same frigate from Boston, and he says that a few days before the 24th, being at the last date "on the Grand Bank of Newfoundland," "we spoke an American privateer, the General Lincoln, Captain Barnes." If the above-mentioned incident occurred at sea, it was probably on this occasion.

June 12. Sunday. P. M. — To Bear Hill.

Maple-leaved viburnum well out at Laurel Glen, probably 9th.[1] The laurel probably by day after to-morrow. The note of the wood thrush answers to some cool unexhausted morning vigor in the hearer. The leaf of the rattlesnake-plantain now surprises the walker amid the dry leaves on cool hillsides in the woods; of very simple form, but richly veined with longitudinal and transverse white veins. It looks like art. Crows, like hawks, betray the neighborhood of their nests by harsh scolding at the intruder while they circle over the top of the wood. The red-eyed vireo is the bird most commonly heard in the woods. The wood thrush and the cuckoo also are heard now at noon. The round-leaved cornel fully out on Heywood Peak, but not in the woods. Did I mention that the sawed stump of the chestnut made a seat within the bower formed by its sprouts?

Going up Pine Hill, disturbed a partridge and her brood. She ran in deshabille directly to me, within four feet, while her young, not larger than a chicken just hatched, dispersed, flying along a foot or two

[1] *Vide* 6th.

Vol. V

from the ground, just over the bushes, for a rod or two. The mother kept close at hand to attract my attention, and mewed and clucked and made a noise as when a hawk is in sight. She stepped about and held her head above the bushes and clucked just like a hen. What a remarkable instinct that which keeps the young so silent and prevents their peeping and betraying themselves! The wild bird will run almost any risk to save her young. The young, I believe, make a fine sound at first in dispersing, something like a cherry-bird.

I find beechnuts already about fully grown for size, where a tree overhangs Baker's hillside, and there are old nuts on the ground. Were they sound? This tree must have blossomed early, then. A light-green excrescence three inches in diameter on a panicled andromeda. The lint still comes off the bushes on to my clothes. The hedyotis long leaved out; only two or three plants to be found; probably some days.

Visited the great orchis which I am waiting to have open completely. It is emphatically a flower (within gunshot of the hawk's nest); its great spike, six inches by two, of delicate pale-purple flowers, which begin to expand at bottom, rises above and contrasts with the green leaves of the hellebore and skunk-cabbage and ferns (by which its own leaves are concealed) in the cool shade of an alder swamp. It is the more interesting for its rarity and the secluded situations in which it grows, owing to which it is seldom seen, not thrusting itself on the observation of men. It is a pale purple, as if from growing in the shade. It is not

remarkable in its stalk and leaves, which indeed are commonly concealed by other plants.

Norway cinquefoil. A wild moss rose in Arethusa Meadow, where are arethusas lingering still. The sidesaddle-flowers are partly turned up now and make a great show, with their broad red petals flapping like saddle *ears* (?). The tree-climbing ivy. Was it out as early as the other? Apparently so.

I forgot to say that I visited my hawk's nest, and the young hawk was perched now four or five feet above the nest, still in the shade. It will soon fly. Now, then, in secluded pine woods, the young hawks sit high on the edges of their nests or on the twigs near by in the shade, waiting for their pinions to grow, while their parents bring to them their prey. Their silence also is remarkable, not to betray themselves, nor will the old bird go to the nest while you are in sight. She pursues me half a mile when I withdraw.

The buds of young white oaks which have been frost-bitten are just pushing forth again. Are these such as were intended for next year at the base of the leaf-stalk?

June 13. 9 A. M. — To Orchis Swamp.

Find that there are two young hawks; one has left the nest and is perched on a small maple seven or eight rods distant. This one appears much smaller than the former one. I am struck by its large, naked head, so vulture-like, and large eyes, as if the vulture's were an inferior stage through which the hawk passed. Its feet, too, are large, remarkably developed, by which it holds to its perch securely like an old bird, before its wings can perform their office. It has a buff breast, striped with dark brown. Pratt, when I told him of this nest, said he would like to carry one of his rifles down there. But I told him that I should be sorry to have them killed. I would rather save one of these hawks than have a hundred hens and chickens. It was worth more to see them soar especially now that they are so rare in the landscape. It is easy to buy eggs, but not to buy hen-hawks. My neighbors would not hesitate to shoot the last pair of hen-hawks in the town to save a few of their chickens! But such economy is narrow and grovelling. It is unnecessarily to sacrifice the greater value to the less. I would rather never taste chickens' meat nor hens' eggs than never to see a hawk sailing through the upper air again. This sight is worth incomparably more than a chicken soup or a boiled egg. So we exterminate the deer and substitute the hog. It was amusing to observe the swaying to and fro of the young hawk's head to counterbalance the gentle motion of the bough in the wind.

Violets appear to be about done, generally. Four-leaved loosestrife just out; also the smooth wild rose yesterday. The pogonia at Forget-me-not Brook.

What was that rare and beautiful bird in the dark woods under the Cliffs, with black above and white spots and bars, a large triangular blood-red spot on breast, and sides of breast and beneath white? Note a warble like the oriole, but softer and sweeter. It was quite tame. I cannot find this bird described.

Vol. V

I think it must be a grosbeak.[1] At first I thought I saw a chewink, [as] it sat within a rod sideways to me, and I was going to call Sophia to look at it, but then it turned its breast full toward me and I saw the blood-red breast, a *large* triangular painted spot occupying the greater part of the breast. It was in the cool, shaded underwood by the old path just under the Cliff. It is a memorable event to meet with so rare a bird. Birds answer to flowers, both in their abundance and their rareness. The meeting with a rare and beautiful bird like this is like meeting with some rare and beautiful flower, which you may never find again, perchance, like the great purple fringed orchis, at least. How much it enhances the wildness and the richness of the forest to see in it some beautiful bird which you never detected before!

June 14. P. M. — To White Pond.
Herd's-grass heads. The warmest afternoon as yet. Ground getting dry, it is so long since we had any rain to speak of.

C. says he saw a "lurker" yesterday in the woods on the Marlborough road. He heard a distressing noise like a man sneezing but long continued, but at length found it was a man wheezing. He was oldish and grizzled, the stumps of his grizzled beard about an inch long, and his clothes in the worst possible condition, — a wretched-looking creature, an escaped convict hiding in the woods, perhaps. He appeared holding on to his paunch, and wheezing as if it would

[1] Probably a rose-breasted grosbeak.

kill him. He appeared to have come straight through the swamp, and — what was most interesting about him, and proved him to be a lurker of the first class, — one of our party, as C. said, — he kept straight through a field of rye which was fully grown, not regarding it in the least; and, though C. tried to conceal himself on the edge of the rye, fearing to hurt his feelings if the man should mistake him for the proprietor, yet they met, and the lurker, giving him a short bow, disappeared in the woods on the opposite side of the road. He went through everything.

Went to the Harrington Bathing-Place. Drank at the Tarbell Spring first. The swamp-pink by to-morrow. The *Allium Canadense* in Tarbell's meadow. Wild meadow garlic, with its head of bulbs and a few flower-buds, not yet; apparently with cultivated onion.

The desert at Dugan's is all scored over with tortoise-tracks, — two parallel dotted lines four or five inches apart, the impressions being nearly a half-inch deep, with the distinct mark of the tail making a waving line between. It looks as if twenty tortoises had spent a night travelling over it; and here and there there were marks of a slight digging, but I found no eggs. They came out of the brook near by. Perhaps they select such a bare sandy tract for their encounters, where there is no grass to impede them. Perhaps it makes the most remarkable track of any creature. Sometimes the sand appeared as if dabbled and patted for a foot or more in diameter.

Heard the first locust from amid the shrubs by the roadside. He comes with heat. Snake-sloughs are

found nowadays; whitish and bleached they are. Beyond the rye-field on the Marlborough road, the oaks were extensively cut off by the frost some weeks ago. They are all dry and red for half a mile, — young trees eight or ten feet high, — as if a fire had run through them after they had grown two or three inches; and young red leaves are beginning to appear on them. Since the maples and birches are untouched (sometimes a maple!), it looks as if the fire had run in veins. Yet most travellers, if they did not ride close to them, would not notice them, perhaps being used as yet even to a wintry landscape. Is that the indigo-bird that sings, between here and White Pond, a-chit chit-chit awee? Perhaps the andromeda swamp on this path is as handsome as any, appearing so far down from the hills and still so level. I observed the cotton of aphides on the alders yesterday and to-day. How regularly these phenomena appear! — even the stains or spots or galls on leaves, as that bright yellow on blackberry leaves, now common, and those crimson ring-spots on maple leaves I see to-day, exactly the same pattern with last year's, and the crimson frosting on the black birch leaves I saw the other day. Then there are the huckleberry-apples, and the large green puffs on the panicled andromeda, and also I see now the very light or whitish solid and juicy apples on the swamp-pink, with a fungus-like smell when broken. *Erigeron annuus* (?),[1] some white, some purplish, common now and daisylike. I put it rather early on the 9th.

[1] [*Strigosus.*]

On the Strawberry Hill on the further side of White Pond, about fifty feet above the pond and a dozen rods from it, found a painted tortoise laying her eggs. Her posterior was inserted into a slight cavity she had dug in the sandy hillside. There were three eggs already laid, the top of them hardly two inches below the surface. She had dug down about one and a half or two inches, somewhat in the form of the hind part of her shell, and then under the turf up the hill about two and a half inches, enlarging the cavity slightly within, leaving a neck of an oval form about seven eighths of an inch by one and a quarter inches, apparently packing the eggs with her tail. She lay still where I put her, while I examined her eggs, and I replaced her in the hole. A little further on, I saw where such a deposit had been broken up, apparently by a skunk, and the egg-shells strewn about. The *whole* hole about three inches deep. The three eggs already laid, about one inch long, cream-colored or slightly flesh-color, easily indented with the finger, but a little elastic, not exactly elliptical, but slightly larger at one end.

C. says his dog chased a woodchuck yesterday, and it climbed up into an oak and sat on a limb ten or twelve feet high. He killed a young rabbit. Took another bath at the cove in White Pond. We had already bathed in the North River at Harrington's.

It is about 5 P. M. The pond is perfectly smooth and very beautiful now. Its shores are still almost entirely uninjured by the axe. While we are dressing, the bullfrogs in this cove, it is so late in the day, are

beginning to trump. They utter a short, laughable, belching sound from time to time and then break into a powerful trump as the whim takes them. The dog lies flat on his belly the while to cool him. We took an old leaky boat and a forked stick which had made part of a fence, and pushed out to see the shores from the middle of the pond. There sit the great paddocks in their yellow vests, imperturbable by the sides of the boat. See now the great stems of trees on the bottom and the stones curiously strewn about. Now we cross the bar to this cove; now we are leaving the edge of the heart-leaves, whose long, clean, slender, thread-like stems rise from the bottom still where six feet deep; and now the stones on the bottom grow dim, as if a mildew formed about them, and now the bottom is lost in the dim greenness of the water.

How beautifully the northeast (?) shore curves! The pines and other trees so perfect on their water side. There is no rawness nor imperfection to the edge of the wood in this case, as where an axe has cleared, or a cultivated field abuts on it; but the eye rises by natural gradations from the low shrubs, the alders, of the shore to the higher trees. It is a natural selvage. It is comparatively unaffected by man. The water laves the shore as it did a thousand years ago.[1] Such curves in a wood bordering on a field do not affect us as when it is a winding shore of a lake. This is a firmer edge. It will not be so easily torn.

Our boat leaked so, — faster and faster as it sank deeper and tipped with the water in it, — that we were

[1] [*Walden*, p. 206; Riv. 291.]

Vol. V

obliged to turn to the shore. The blue flag (*Iris versicolor*) grows in this pure water, rising from the stony bottom all around the shores, and is very beautiful, — not too high-colored, — especially its reflections in the water. There was something [in] its bluish blade which harmonized with the greenish water.[1] The pollen of the pine yellowed the driftwood on the shore and the stems of bushes which stood in the water, and in little flakes extended out some distance on the surface, until at four or five rods in this cove it was suddenly and distinctly bounded by an invisible fence on the surface; but in the middle, as deep down as you could [see], there appeared some fine white particles in the water, either this or something else and perhaps some ova of fishes. Instead of the white lily, which requires mud, or the sweet flag, here grows the blue flag in the water, thinly about the shore. The color of the flower harmonizes singularly with the water.[2]

With our boat's prow to the shore, we sat half an hour this evening listening to the bullfrogs. Their belching is my dumping sound more hoarsely heard near at hand. What imperturbable fellows! One sits perfectly still behind some blades of grass while the dog is chasing others within two feet. Some are quite handsome, large, spotted fellows. We see here and there light-colored greenish-white spots on the bottom where a fish, a bream perhaps, has picked away all the dead wood and leaves for her nest over a space of eighteen inches or more. Young breams from one to three

[1] [*Walden*, p. 221; Riv. 312.]   [2] [*Ibid.*]

inches long, light-colored and transparent, are swimming about, and here and there a leech in the shallow water, moving ⁓⁓ as serpents are represented to do. Large devil's-needles are buzzing back and forth. They skim along the edge of the blue flags, apparently quite round this cove or further, like hen-harriers beating the bush for game. And now comes a hummingbird humming from the woods and alights on the blossom of a blue flag: The bullfrogs begin with one or two notes and with each peal add another trill to their trump, — *er-roonk, er-er-roonk, er-er-er-roonk*, etc. I am amused to hear one after another, and then an unexpectedly deep and confident bass, as if he had charged himself with more wind than the rest. And now, as if by a general agreement, they all trump together, making a deafening noise. Sometimes one jumps up a foot out of water in the midst of these concerts. What are they about? Suddenly a tree-toad in the overhanging woods begins, and another answers, and another, with loud, ringing notes such as I never heard before, and in three minutes they are all silent again. A red-eye sings on a tree-top, and a cuckoo is heard far in the wood. These are the evening sounds.

As we look over the water now, the opposite woods are seen dimly through what appears not so much the condensing dew and mist as the dry haziness of the afternoon, now settled and condensed. The woods on the opposite shore have not the distinctness they had an hour before, but perhaps a more agreeable dimness, a sort of gloaming or settling and thickening of the haze over the water, which melts tree into tree and masses them agreeably. The trees no longer bright and distinct, — a bluish mistiness. This appears to be an earlier gloaming before sunset, such as by and by is universal.

Went through the woods along the old canal to Haynes's pasture, from the height of which we looked down on the rich New Hampshire wood we had come out of. The ground rising within the wood gave it the appearance of woods rising by successive stages from a smaller growth on the edge to stately trees in the middle, and Nobscot was seen in the southwest through the blue furnace mist. This seems the true hour to be abroad sauntering far from home. Your thoughts being already turned toward home, your walk in one sense ended, you are in that favorable frame of mind described by De Quincey, open to great impressions, and you see those rare sights with the unconscious side of the eye, which you could not see by a direct gaze before. Then the dews begin to descend in your mind, and its atmosphere is strained of all impurities; and home is farther away than ever. Here is home; the beauty of the world impresses you. There is a coolness in your mind as in a well. Life is too grand for supper.

The wood thrush launches forth his evening strains from the midst of the pines. I admire the moderation of this master. There is nothing tumultuous in his song. He launches forth one strain with all his heart and life and soul, of pure and unmatchable melody, and then he pauses and gives the hearer and himself time to digest this, and then another and another at

Vol. V

suitable intervals. Men talk of the *rich* song of other birds, — the thrasher, mockingbird, nightingale. But I doubt, I doubt. They know not what they say! There is as great an interval between the thrasher and the wood thrush as between Thomson's "Seasons" and Homer. The sweetness of the day crystallizes in this morning coolness.

Probably the tortoise leaves her eggs thus near the surface and in sand that they may receive the greatest heat from the sand, being just deep enough for the sand to receive and retain it and not part with it at night, — not so deep as to be cool.

June 15. A great fog this morning.

P. M. — To Trillium Woods.

Clover now in its prime. What more luxuriant than a clover-field? The poorest soil that is covered with it looks incomparably fertile. This is perhaps the most characteristic feature of June, resounding with the hum of insects. It is so massive, such a blush on the fields. The rude health of the sorrel cheek has given place to the blush of clover. Painters are wont, in their pictures of Paradise, to strew the ground too thickly with flowers. There should be moderation in all things. Though we love flowers, we do not want them so thick under our feet that we cannot walk without treading on them. But a clover-field in bloom is some excuse for them.

The *Prinos lævigatus*, it seems to be, probably the 14th, though it seems to have three or four pistils, if any, and six to nine stamens and petals. A small

wheel-shaped white flower. The peduncles are sometimes branched and have two flowers. *Mitchella repens* just bursting, say to-day. Rose-bugs for a day or two. Here is one on a *Viburnum nudum* var. *pyrifolium* (?). A strong southerly wind blows.

Here are many wild roses northeast of Trillium Woods. We are liable to underrate this flower on account of its commonness. Is it not the queen of our flowers? How ample and high-colored its petals, glancing half concealed from its own green bowers! There is a certain noble and delicate civility about it, — not wildness. It is properly the type of the *Rosaceæ*, or flowers among others of most wholesome fruits. It is at home in the garden, as readily cultivated as apples. It is the pride of June. In summing up its attractions I should mention its rich color, size, and form, the rare beauty of its bud, its fine fragrance, and the beauty of the entire shrub, not to mention the almost innumerable varieties it runs into. I bring home the buds ready to expand, put them in a pitcher of water, and the next morning they open and fill my chamber with fragrance. This, found in the wilderness, must have reminded the Pilgrim of home.

Strawberries in the meadow now ready for the picker. They lie deep at the roots of the grass in the shade; else they are dried up. You spread aside the tall grass, and deep down in little cavities by the roots of the grass you find this rich fruit. But it is only a taste we get here. 5 P. M., I hear distinctly the sound of thunder in the northwest, but not a cloud is in sight, only a little thickness or mistiness in that horizon, and

we get no shower. For a week past I have heard the cool, watery note of the goldfinch, from time to time, as it twittered past.

June 16. 4 A. M. — To Nawshawtuct by boat.

No fog this morning and scarcely any dew except in the lowest ground. There is a little air stirring, too; the breeze in the night must have been the reason. It threatens to be a hot, as well as dry, day, and gardens begin to suffer.

Before 4 A. M., or sunrise, the sound of chip-birds and robins and bluebirds, etc., fills the air and is incessant. It is a crowing on the roost, methinks, as the cock crows before he goes abroad. They do not sing deliberately as at eve, but greet the morning with an incessant twitter. Even the crickets seem to join the concert. Yet I think it is not the same every morning, though it may be fair. An hour or two later it is comparative silence. The awaking of the birds, a tumultuous twittering.

At sunrise, however, a slight mist curls along the surface of the water. When the sun falls on it, it looks like a red dust.

What is that tall rank grass now in bloom, four or five feet high, with an upright pyramidal spike, which some time ago I mistook for wild rice?[1] It stands amid the button-bushes on the edge of the river; leafy except the upper foot.

From top of the hill, the sun, just above the horizon, red and shorn of beams, is somewhat pear-shaped,

[1] Canary grass.

owing to some irregularity in the refraction of the lower strata, produced, as it were, by the dragging of the lower part; and then it becomes a broad ellipse, the lower half a dun red, owing to the grossness of the air. It appears as if it rose in the northeast, — over Ball's Hill at any rate. The distant river is like molten silver at this hour; it merely reflects the *light*, not the blue. I hear the *meow* of Shaw's peacock here, very loud. What shall I name that small cloud that attends the sun's rising, that hangs over the portals of the day like an embroidered banner and heralds his coming, though sometimes it proves a portcullis which falls and cuts off the new day in its birth?

Bathed in Assabet at Leaning Hemlocks and examined the stone-heaps, now partly exposed to the air, but found nothing. Found four tortoises' deposits on the high bank there just robbed and the eggs devoured. He had not emptied the yolk out of one. The holes had been made exactly in all respects like that I have described. Some were put in pure sand. There were others which had been robbed some days. Apparently about three eggs to each. Presently I saw a skunk making off, — undoubtedly the robber, — with an undulating motion, a white streak above and a parallel and broader black one below (?). A tick in woods by White Pond yesterday. A sweet-briar, apparently yesterday. The locusts on the hill are still white with blossoms, which also strew the ground far and wide as if a sleety snow had fallen, and also adhere to the trees. They resound with the hum of insects even at 5 A. M.

Coming along near the celtis I heard a singular sound as of a bird in distress amid the bushes, and turned to relieve it. Next thought it a squirrel in an apple tree barking at me. Then found that it came from a hole in the ground under my feet, a loud sound between a grunting and a wheezing, yet not unlike the sound a red squirrel sometimes makes, but louder. Looking down the hole, I saw the tail and hind quarters of a woodchuck, which seemed to be contending with another further down. Reaching down carefully, I took hold of the tail, and, though I had to pull very hard indeed, I drew him out between the rocks, a bouncing great fat fellow, and tossed him a little way down the hill. As soon as he recovered from his bewilderment he made for the hole again, but, I barring the way, he ran off elsewhere.

Coming down the river, heard opposite the new houses, where I stopped to pluck the tall grass, a sound as of young blackbirds amid the button-bushes. After a long while gazing, standing on the roots of the button-bushes, I detected a couple of meadow or mud hens (*Rallus Virginianus*) gliding about under the button-bushes over the mud and through the shallow water, and uttering a squeaking or squawking note, as if they had a nest there or young. Bodies about the size of a robin; short tail; wings and tail white-edged; bill about one and a half inches long, orange beneath in one bird; brown, deepening into black spots above; turtle-dove color on breasts and beneath; ashy about eyes and cheeks. Seemed not willing to fly, and for a long time unwilling to pass

me, because it must come near to keep under the button-bushes.

An old man who used to frequent Walden fifty-five years ago, when it was dark with surrounding forests, tells me that in those days he sometimes saw it all alive with ducks and other game. He went there to fish and used an old log canoe, made of two white pine logs dug out and pinned together and pitched, which he found on the shore. It was very clumsy but durable and belonged to the pond. He did not know whom it belonged to; it belonged to the pond. He used to make a cable for his anchor of hickory bark tied together. An old man, a potter, who lived in these woods before the Revolution, told him that there was an iron chest at the bottom of the pond, and he had seen it. It would sometimes come floating up toward the shore, and, when you went toward it, go back into deep water and disappear.[1]

P. M. — To Baker Farm by boat.

The yellowish or greenish orchis out, maybe a day or two. It would be a very warm afternoon, if there were not so good a breeze from the southwest. The *Ranunculus Purshii* begins to show now in large fields in shallow water, both on shore and in middle, the river having gone down lately. The *Ranunculus filiformis* is out a day or two, delayed by the height of the water. *Comarum palustre*, some time; *vide* twenty or thirty rods above the Hubbard Bridge; an interesting leaf.

[1] [*Walden*, pp. 211, 212; Riv. 298, 299.]

Was that a smaller bittern or a meadow-hen that we started from out the button-bushes? What places for the mud-hen beneath the wild stems of the button-bushes along the shore, all shaggy with rootlets, as if all the weeds the river produced — all the ranunculus at least — had drifted and lodged against them. Their stems are so nearly horizontal near the mud and water that you can clamber along on them over the water many rods. It is one of the wildest features in our scenery. There is scarcely any firm footing on the ground except where a muskrat has made a heap of clamshells. Picture the river at a low stage of the water, the pads shrivelled in the sun hanging from the dark-brown stems of the button-bush, which are all shaggy with masses of dark rootlets, an impenetrable thicket, and a stake-driver, or *Ardea minor*, sluggishly winging his way up the stream.

The breams' nests, like large deep milk-pans, are left high and dry on the shore. They are not only deepened within, but have raised edges. In some places, as at the boat place at the Baker Farm, they are as close together as they can stick, with each a great bream in it, whose waving fins and tail are tipped with a sort of phosphorescent luminousness.

Saw in the meadow there a more than double side-saddle-flower, — a monster, though not in size. The exterior calyx was of five or six small greenish leaves of different sizes, and others smaller were continued irregularly nearly two inches down the stem. The interior calyx consisted of, not one only, but four, rows of narrower leaves than usual. Petals were none, *now* at least, it being late, and the stigma, instead of being one, broad and flat, was of half a dozen erectish crimped green leaves. I should have mentioned the rich salmon-brown (is it?), sort of iron-rust color, of the fields of potamogeton, now that the river is low, with its spikes of flowers just rising above the water and the large, semitransparent radical leaves now floating on the surface, here and there. What a rapid and luxuriant growth of weeds along the shore! overtopped by that tall rank grass I mentioned yesterday, now in flower (?).[1] The polygonums are reddish.

We sailed all the way back from the Baker Farm, though the wind blew very nearly at right angles with the river much of the way. By sitting on one side of the boat we made its edge serve for a keel, so that she would mind her helm. The dog swam for long distances behind us. Each time we passed under the lee of a wood we were becalmed and then met with contrary and flawy winds till we got fairly beyond its influence. But you can always sail either up or down the river, for the wind inclines to blow with the stream, especially where the banks are high. We taste at each cool spring with which we are acquainted in the bank, making haste to reach it before the dog, who otherwise is sure to be found cooling himself in it. We sometimes use him on board to sit in the stern and trim the boat while we both row, for he is heavy, and otherwise we sink the bows too much in the water. But he has a habit of standing too near the rower, and each time receiving a fillip under the chin from the

[1] *Phalaris.*

rower's fists. So at last he tumbles himself overboard and takes a riparial excursion. And we are amused to see how judiciously he selects his points for crossing the river from time to time, in order to avoid long circuits made by bays and meadows and keep as near us as possible.

At Bittern Cliff, on the south side, the little earth on the rocks is already parched and the shrubs are withering with drought. The spring is long since past there. Found there the *Potentilla arguta*, — crowded cinquefoil, — well out, *our* only white cinquefoil; stem and leaves somewhat like the *Norvegica*, but more woolly, a yellowish white. According to Bigelow, rare. Also there a *Galium trifidum* var. *tinctorium* (?). I see some red maple leaves with the points of the three principal lobes covered with that crimson frosting which I saw some time since on the black birch.

June 17. *Friday.* Another breezy night and no fog this morning. The pogonias, adder's-tongue arethusas, I see nowadays, getting to be numerous, are far too pale to compete with the *A. bulbosa*, and then their snake-like odor is much against them.

Fresh mackerel for some days past.

Here have been three ultra-reformers, lecturers on Slavery, Temperance, the Church, etc., in and about our house and Mrs. Brooks's the last three or four days, — A. D. Foss, once a Baptist minister in Hopkinton, N. H.; Loring Moody, a sort of travelling pattern-working chaplain; and H. C. Wright, who shocks all the old women with his infidel writings.

Though Foss was a stranger to the others, you would have thought them old and familiar cronies. (They happened here together by accident.) They addressed each other constantly by their Christian names, and rubbed you continually with the greasy cheeks of their kindness. They would not keep their distance, but cuddle up and lie spoon-fashion with you, no matter how hot the weather nor how narrow the bed,[1] — chiefly[2] ——. I was awfully pestered with his benignity; feared I should get greased all over with it past restoration; tried to keep some starch in my clothes. He wrote a book called "A Kiss for a Blow," and he behaved as if there were no alternative between these, or as if I had given him a blow. I would have preferred the blow, but he was bent on giving me the kiss, when there was neither quarrel nor agreement between us. I wanted that he should straighten his back, smooth out those ogling wrinkles of benignity about his eyes, and, with a healthy reserve, pronounce something in a downright manner. It was difficult to keep clear of his slimy benignity, with which he sought to cover you before he swallowed you and took you fairly into his bowels.[3] It would have been far worse than the fate of Jonah. I do not wish to get any nearer to a man's bowels than usual. They lick you as a cow her calf. They would fain wrap you about with their bowels. —— addressed me as "Henry" within one minute from the time I first laid eyes on

[1] [Channing, p. 29.]
[2] ["Chiefly" is crossed out in pencil and "wholly" substituted.]
[3] [Channing, p. 29.]

him, and when I spoke, he said with drawling, sultry sympathy, "Henry, I know all you would say; I understand you perfectly; you need not explain anything to me;"[1] and to another, "I am going to dive into Henry's inmost depths." I said, "I trust you will not strike your head against the bottom." He could tell in a dark room, with his eyes blinded and in perfect stillness, if there was one there whom he loved. One of the most attractive things about the flowers is their beautiful reserve. The truly beautiful and noble puts its lover, as it were, at an infinite distance, while it attracts him more strongly than ever. I do not like the men who come so near me with their bowels. It is the most disagreeable kind of snare to be caught in. Men's bowels are far more slimy than their brains. They must be ascetics indeed who approach you by this side. What a relief to have heard the ring of one healthy reserved tone! With such a forgiving disposition, as if he were all the while forgiving you for existing. Considering our condition or *habit* of soul, — maybe corpulent and asthmatic, — maybe dying of atrophy, with all our bones sticking out, — is it kindness to embrace a man? They lay their sweaty hand on your shoulder, or your knee, to magnetize you.

I loved to hear of the old log canoe, which perchance had first been a tree on its brink, and then, as it were, fell into the water, to float there for a generation as the only proper vessel for it, — very thick and at length water-logged. So primitive a vessel! I remember that when I first paddled on it there were more large trunks

[1] [Channing, p. 29.]

of trees to be seen indistinctly lying on the bottom, which had probably blown over formerly, when the trees were larger, or had been left on the ice at the last cutting, when wood was cheaper; but now for the most part they have disappeared. The old log canoe, which took the place of a more graceful one of Indian construction.[1]

Now the trunks of trees on the bottom and the old log canoe are gone, the dark surrounding woods are gone, and the villagers, who scarcely know how it lies, instead of going to the pond to bathe or drink, are thinking to bring its water to the village in a pipe, to form a reservoir as high as the roofs of the houses, to wash their dishes and be their scullion, — which should be more sacred than the Ganges, — to earn their Walden by the turning of a cock or drawing of a plug, as they draw cider from a cask. The Boiling Spring is turned into a tank for the Iron Horse to drink at, and the Walden woods have been cut and dried for his fodder. That devilish Iron Horse, whose ear-rending whinner is heard throughout the town, has defiled the Boiling Spring with his feet and drunk it up, and browsed off all the wood around the pond. He has got a taste for berries even, and with unnatural appetite he robs the country babies of milk, with the breath of his nostrils polluting the air. That Trojan horse, with a thousand men in his belly, insidiously introduced by mercenary Greeks. With the scream of a hawk he beats the bush for men, the man-harrier, and carries them to his infernal home by thousands for

[1] [*Walden*, p. 212; Riv. 299, 300.]

his progeny. Where is the country's champion, the Moore of Moore Hall, to meet him at the Deep Cut and throw a victorious and avenging lance against this bloated pest? [1]

The dense fields of blue-eyed grass now blue the meadows, as if, in this fair season of the year, the clouds that envelop the earth were dispersing, and blue patches began to appear, answering to the blue sky. The eyes pass from these blue patches into the surrounding green as from the patches of clear sky into the clouds.

If a man walks in the woods for love of them and [to] see his fellows with impartial eye afar, for half his days, he is esteemed a loafer; but if he spends his whole day as a speculator, shearing off those woods, he is esteemed industrious and enterprising — making earth bald before its time.[2]

Amelanchier berries begin to be red, and softer and eatable, though not ripe.

P. M. — To Walden.

I did not mention yesterday the great devil's-needle with his humped back, which hovered over the boat and, though headed across its course, and not appearing to fly in the direction in which the boat was moving, yet preserved his relation to the boat perfectly. What steamer can reverse its paddle-wheels as he can?

A remarkably strong south wind this afternoon, and cool. The greenness about the edge of Walden is very

[1] [*Walden*, pp. 213, 214; Riv. 301, 302.]
[2] [*Cape Cod, and Miscellanies*, p. 457; *Misc.*, Riv. 256.]

Vol. V

striking when seen from the Peak nowadays. Is it in the fall?

One of the nighthawk's eggs is hatched. The young is unlike any that I have seen, exactly like a pinch of rabbit's fur or down of that color dropped on the ground, not two inches long, with a dimpling or geometrical or somewhat regular arrangement of minute feathers in the middle, destined to become the wings and tail. Yet even it half opened its eye, and peeped if I mistake not. Was ever bird more completely protected, both by the color of its eggs and of its own body that sits on them, and of the young bird just hatched? Accordingly the eggs and young are rarely discovered. There was one egg still, and by the side of it this little pinch of down, flattened out and not observed at first, and a foot down the hill had rolled a half of the egg it came out of. There was no callowness, as in the young of most birds. It seemed a singular place for a bird to begin its life, — to come out of its egg, — this little pinch of down, — and lie still on the exact spot where the egg lay, on a flat exposed shelf on the side of a bare hill, with nothing but the whole heavens, the broad universe above, to brood it when its mother was away.

How happens it that the tortoises frequently drop their eggs on the surface of the ground? I believe they are sometimes a bluish white. The leaves of some young oaks — red apparently and perhaps black — are a very rich dark green now, so dark that, if we had seen them a month ago and contrasted them with those then expanding, we should have exclaimed at

the difference. Our eyes are gradually prepared for it. The huckleberry-apple is sometimes a red shoot, with tender and *thick* red leaves and branchlets, in all three inches long. It is, as it were, a monstrous precocity, and what should have waited to become fruit is a merely bloated or puffed-up flower. A child with a great dropsical head, and prematurely bright, is a huckleberry-apple. The really sweet and palatable huckleberry is not matured before July, and incurs the risk of drying up rather in droughts and never attaining its proper size. The indigo out. There are some fine large clusters of lambkill close to the shore of Walden under the Peak, fronting the south. They are early there and large, apparently both on account of the warmth and the vicinity of the water. These flowers are in perfect cylinders, sometimes six inches long by two wide, and three such raying out or upward from one centre, *i. e.* three branches clustered together. Examined close by, I think this handsomer than the mountain laurel which we have; the color is richer, but they do not show so well at a little distance, and the corymbs are somewhat concealed by the green shoot and leaves rising above them, and also injured by the mixture of the dry remains of last year's flowers.

The mountain laurel by Walden in its prime. It is a splendid flower, and more red than that in Mason's pasture. Its dry, dead-looking, brittle stems, as it were leaning over other bushes or each other, bearing at the ends great dense corymbs five inches in diameter of rose or pink (?) tinged flowers, without an interstice between them, overlapping each other, each often more than an inch in diameter. A single one of which would be esteemed very beautiful. It is a highlander wandered down into the plain. The *Lactuca elongata*, with a reddish stem.

June 18. *Saturday.* 4 A. M. — By boat to Nawshawtuct; to Azalea Spring, or Pinxter Spring.

No fog and very little dew, or perhaps it was a slight rain in the night. I find always some dew in low ground. There is a broad crescent of clear sky in the west, but it looks rainy in the east. As yet we are disappointed of rain. Almost all birds appear to join the early morning chorus before sunrise on the roost, the matin hymn. I hear now the robin, the chip-bird, the blackbird, the martin, etc., etc., but I see none flying, or, at last, only one wing in the air, not yet illustrated by the sun.

As I was going up the hill, I was surprised to see rising above the June-grass, near a walnut, a whitish object, like a stone with a white top, or a skunk erect, for it was black below. It was an enormous toadstool, or fungus, a sharply conical parasol in the form of a sugar loaf, slightly turned up at the edges, which were rent half an inch in every inch or two. The whole height was sixteen inches. The pileus or cap was six inches long by seven in width at the rim, though it appeared longer than wide. There was no veil, and the stem was about one inch in diameter and naked. The top of the cap was quite white within and without, hoariest at top of the cone like a mountain-top, not smooth but with [a] stringy kind of scales turned up-

ward at the edge, which declined downward, *i. e.* down the cap, into a coarse hoariness, as if the compact white fibres had been burst by the spreading of the gills and showed the black. As you looked up within, the light was transmitted between the trembling gills. It looked much like an old felt hat [that] is pushed up into a cone and its rim all ragged and with some meal shaken on to it; in fact, it was almost big enough for a child's head. It was so delicate and fragile that its whole cap trembled on the least touch, and, as I could not lay it down without injuring it, I was obliged to carry it home all the way in my hand and erect, while I paddled my boat with one hand. It was a wonder how its soft cone ever broke through the earth. Such growths ally our age to former periods, such as geology reveals. I wondered if it had not some relation to the skunk, though not in odor, yet in its colors and the general impression it made. It suggests a vegetative force which may almost make man tremble for his dominion. It carries me back to the era of the formation of the coal-measures — the age of the saurus and pleiosaurus and when bullfrogs were as big as bulls. Its stem had something massy about it like an oak, large in proportion to the weight it had to support (though not perhaps to the size of the cap), like the vast hollow columns under some piazzas, whose caps have hardly weight enough to hold their tops together. It made you think of parasols of Chinese mandarins; or it might have been used by the great fossil bullfrog in his walks. What part does it play in the economy of the world?

I see the curled fragments of some larger turtle's egg-shells on the high bank of the North River, near a cavity, proportionally large, in the black earth, where was once a coal pit. Was it not a mud turtle? They are more dusky-spotted. The panicled andromeda. The mullein yesterday. It bears inspection; is a rich yellow flower with dark-orange anthers, opening now in rings of five or six large flowers one inch in diameter around the spike, the next row of buds above just showing yellowish through downy floral leaves, like the saffron dawn through twilight clouds.

I have just been out (7.30 A. M.) to show my fungus. The milkman and the butcher followed me to inquire what it was, and children and young ladies addressed me in the street who never spoke to me before. It is so fragile I was obliged to walk at a funereal pace for fear of jarring it. It is so delicately balanced on its stem that it falls to one side across it on the least inclination; falls about like an umbrella that has lost its stays. It is rapidly curling up on the edge, and the rents increasing, until it is completely fringed, and is an inch wider there. It is melting in the sun and light, and black drops and streams falling on my hand and fragments of the black fringed rim falling on the sidewalk. Evidently such a plant can only be seen in perfection in the early morning. It is a creature of the night, like the great moths. They wish me to send it to the first of a series of exhibitions of flowers and fruits to be held at the court-house this afternoon, which I promise to do if it is presentable then. Perhaps it might be placed in the court-house cellar and the

company be invited at last to walk down and examine it. Think of placing this giant parasol fungus in the midst of all their roses; yet they admit that it would overshadow and eclipse them all. It is to be remarked that this grew, not in low and damp soil, but high up on the open side of a dry hill, about two rods from a walnut and one from a wall, in the midst of and rising above the thin June-grass. The last night was warm; the earth was very dry, and there was a slight sprinkling of rain.

I believe the 14th was the first day I began to wear my single thin sack in my walk and at night sleep with both windows open; say, when the swamp-pink opens. The locust is done, and its shrivelled dirty-white petals cover the ground between the blades of grass like a crusting or sugaring of snow. Meadow-rue, with a rank, offensive smell like a strong-smelling dog. The floating-heart in river like a minute white lily, now at 5 A. M. Swamp blackberry probably now.

I think the blossom of the sweet-briar, now in prime, — eglantine, — is more delicate and interesting than that of the common roses, though smaller and paler and without their spicy fragrance; but its fragrance is in its leaves all summer, and the form of the bush is handsomer, curving over from a considerable height in wreaths sprinkled with numerous flowers. They open out flat soon after sunrise. Flowers whitish in middle, then pinkish-rose inclining to purple toward the edges.

The laurel of many varieties. I have now three

differently marked or colored. Some a delicate calico, — a new print just washed and starched for a morning dress.

Carrion-flower now abundant. At first this morning there was no mist whatever, even on the water, but it was all smooth and dark; but when the sun fell on it a very slight vapor curled along it.

How far from our minds now the early blossoms of the spring, the willow catkins, for example !

I put the parasol fungus in the cellar to preserve it, but it went on rapidly melting and wasting away from the edges upward, spreading as it dissolved, till it was shaped like a dish cover. By night, though kept in the cellar all the day, there was not more than two of the six inches of the height of the cap left, and the barrel-head beneath it and its own stem looked as if a large bottle of ink had been broken there. It defiled all it touched. The next morning the hollow stem was left perfectly bare, and only the hoary apex of the cone, spreading about two inches in diameter, lay on the ground beneath. Probably one night produced it, and in one day, with all our pains, it wasted away. Is it not a giant mildew or mould? In the warm, muggy night the surface of the earth is mildewed. The mould, which is the flower of humid darkness and ignorance. The Pyramids and other monuments of Egypt are a vast mildew or toadstools which have met with no light of day sufficient to waste them away. Slavery is such a mould, and superstition, — which are most rank in the warm and humid portions of the globe. Luxor sprang up one night out of the slime

of the Nile. The humblest, puniest weed that can endure the sun is thus superior to the largest fungus, as is the peasant's cabin to those foul temples. It is a temple consecrated to Apis. All things flower, both vices and virtues, but the one is essentially foul, the other fair. In hell, toadstools should be represented as overshadowing men. The priest is the fungus of the graveyard, the mildew of the tomb. In the animal world there are toads and lizards.

P. M. — To Island by boat.

The first white lily to-day perhaps. It is the only *bud* I have seen. The river has gone down and left it nearly dry. On the Island, where a month ago plants were so fresh and early, it is now parched and crisp under my feet, and I feel the heat reflected from the ground and the dry scent of grass and leaves. So universally on dry and rocky hills where the spring was earliest, the autumn has already commenced. The panicled cornel, a day or two. Cranberry also a day or two, with its dry-looking curled flower. Found the nest of a cuckoo, — a long, slender, handsome bird, probably St. Domingo cuckoo, — at the edge of the meadow on a bent sallow, not in a crotch, covered by the broad, shining leaves of a swamp white oak, whose boughs stretched over it, two feet or more from the ground. The nest was made of dry twigs and was small for the size of the bird and very shallow, but handsomely lined with an abundance of what looked like the dry yellowish-brown (?) catkins of the hickory, which made a pleasing contrast with the

surrounding grayish twigs. There were some worm-eaten green leaves inwoven. It contained a single greenish-white elliptical egg, an inch or more long. The bird flew off a little way and *clow-clow-clowed*.

At the Flower Exhibition, saw the rhododendron plucked yesterday in Fitzwilliam, N. H. It was the earliest to be found there, and only one bud yet fully open. They say it is in perfection there the 4th of July, nearer Monadnock than the town. Bigelow says "the flowers form a terminal cluster or thyrsus immediately above the leaves," and, before expansion, form "a large compound bud, resembling a strobilus or cone." These buds are very remarkable. *These* flowers were, I should say, a very pale rose-color, with permanent greenish spots on one side, as of fallen pollen. In the midst of such a profusion of roses, etc., I could not discriminate its odor well. It cannot be very remarkable in this respect.

This unexpected display of flowers culled from the gardens of the village suggests how many virtues also are cultivated by the villagers, more than meet the eye.

It would be an interesting subject, — the materials with which different birds line their nests, or, more generally, *construct* them. The hickory catkins, etc., of the cuckoo, the hypnum and large nest of the phœbe.

Saw to-night Lewis the blind man's horse, which works on the sawing-machine at the depot, now let out to graze along the road, but at each step he lifts his hind legs convulsively high from the ground, as

if the whole earth were a treadmill continually slipping away from under him while he climbed its convex surface. It was painful to witness, but it was symbolical of the moral condition of his master and of all artisans in contradistinction from artists, all who are engaged in any routine; for to them also the whole earth is a treadmill, and the routine results instantly in a similar painful deformity. The horse may bear the mark of his servitude on the muscles of his legs, the man on his brow.

8.30 p. m. — To Cliffs.

Moon not quite full. Going across Depot Field. The western sky is now a crescent of saffron inclining to salmon, a little dunnish, perhaps. The grass is wet with dew. The evening star has come out, but no other. There is no wind. I see a nighthawk in the twilight, flitting near the ground. I hear the hum of a beetle going by. The greenish fires of lightning-bugs are already seen in the meadow. I almost lay my hand on one amid the leaves as I get over the fence at the brook. I pass through Hubbardston [*sic*] along the side of a field of oats, which wet one leg. I perceive the smell of a burning far off by the river, which I saw smoking two days ago. The moon is laboring in a mackerel cloud, and my hopes are with her. Why do I hear no bullfrogs yet? Do they ever trump as early and as universally as on that their first evening? I hear the whip-poor-wills on different sides. White flowers alone show much at night, — white clover and whiteweed. It is commonly still at night, as now. The day has gone by with its wind like the wind of a cannon-ball, and now far in the west it blows. By that dun-colored sky you may track it. There is no motion nor sound in the woods (Hubbard's Grove) along which I am walking. The trees stand like great screens against the sky. The distant village sounds are the barking of dogs, that animal with which man has allied himself, and the rattling of wagons, for the farmers have gone into town a-shopping this Saturday night. The dog is the tamed wolf, as the villager is the tamed savage. But near, the crickets are heard in the grass, chirping from everlasting to everlasting, a mosquito sings near my ear, and the humming of a dor-bug drowns all the noise of the village, so roomy is the universe.[1] The moon comes out of the mackerel cloud, and the traveller rejoices. How can a man write the same thoughts by the light of the moon, resting his book on a rail by the side of a remote potato-field, that he does by the light of the sun, on his study table? The light is but a luminousness. My pencil seems to move through a creamy, mystic medium. The moonlight is rich and somewhat opaque, like cream, but the daylight is thin and blue, like skimmed milk. I am less conscious than in the presence of the sun; my instincts have more influence. I love the smell of that burning as a man may his pipe. It reminds me of a new country offering sites for the hearths of men. It is cheering as the scent of the peat fire of the first settler. The farmer has improved the dry weather to burn his meadow.

[1] [Channing, p. 78.]

Vol. V

the town. The evening air is so favorable to the conveyance of sound that a sudden whistle or scream of the engine just startled me as much as it does near at hand, though I am nearly two miles distant from it. Passed two silent horses grazing in the orchard, and then a skunk prowling on the open hillside, probably probing for insects, etc. Though twenty or thirty feet off he stops repeatedly, erects his tail, and prepares to receive me. How he trusts in his weapon! Fair Haven Pond, seen now indistinctly in the moonlight, seems reduced to a shining surface of mud and slimy puddles, yet I distinguish a smoother and lighter sheen from its broad padded border. The oak leaves, as I look down this vista from the first rock, glisten in the moonlight, though not wet. Will they glisten thus in the fall?

The chief sounds now are the bullfrogs and the whip-poor-wills. The *er-er-roonk* of the bullfrog actually sounds now without a pause from one end of this river to the other, and can be heard more than a mile on each side. I hear the beat of a partridge also. Is it not a result of the white man's intrusion and a sign of the wildness of the bird, that it is compelled to employ thus the night as well as the day? Though frogs and crickets and gnats fill the air with sound, these horses, great beasts as they are, I cannot detect by any sound they make, but by their forms against the sky. The Cliff rocks are warm to the hand. It is probably after ten. I just came through a moonlit glade in the woods on the side of the hill, where an aspen (*Populus grandidentata*) trembled and betrayed a rising wind. A cuckoo

Might not rivers receive more various names? This now at length resounds with the trump of the bullfrog. Might it not be Bullfrog River, as we have "frog ponds" — it is one long frog pond — or Lily River? Those swift rivers like the Nashua have few bullfrogs or lilies, I suspect.

The moon is threatened by some mares'-tails. At Potter's sand-bank, the sand, though cold on the surface, commences to be warm two inches beneath, and the warmth reaches at least six inches deeper. The tortoise buries her eggs just deep enough to secure this greatest constant warmth. I hear a huckleberry-bird now at half past nine. In Potter's low pasture, I pass through a cold stratum full of dewy fragrance and invigorating as the springy sides of mountains, but I soon again rise out of this cool basin. You pass through these refrigerators just as you would wade through a lake or at the bottom of a sea. I passed into and along the bottom of a lake of cold and dewy evening air. Anon, rising higher, here comes a puff of warm air, trivially warm, a straggler from the sun's retinue, now buffeted about by the vanguard night breezes. Tephrosia, a day or two. Before me, southward toward the moon, on higher land than I, but springy, I saw a low film of fog like a veil reflecting the moonlight, though none on lower ground which was not springy, and, up the river beyond, a battalion of fog rising white in the moonlight in ghost-like wisps, or like a flock of scared covenanters in a recess amid the hills. The loudest sound produced by man that I hear now is that of a train of cars passing through

I just heard, an imperfect note, and a wagon going over a bridge, I know not where. It is soon over, and the horse's hoofs and the wheels are no longer heard. That small segment of the arc which the traveller described is remarkably distinguished. Might not a policeman be stationed on a central hill at night, and when any robbery was committed, be notified of it by telegraph if possible, and so hear by what bridge the rogue left the town?

The night-warbler, and again afterward. It is worth the while to walk thus in the night after a warm or sultry day to enjoy the fresh up-country, brake-like, springlike scent in low grounds. At night the surface of the earth is a cellar, a refrigerator, no doubt wholesomer than those made with ice by day.

Got home at eleven.

June 19. P. M. — To Flint's Pond.

I see large patches of blue-eyed grass in the meadow across the river from my window. The pine woods at Thrush Alley emit that hot dry scent, reminding me even of days when I used to go a-blackberrying. The air is full of the hum of invisible insects, and I hear a locust. Perhaps this sound indicates the time to put on a thin coat. But the wood thrush sings as usual far in the wood. A blue jay and a tanager come dashing into the pine under which I stand. The first flies directly away, screaming with suspicion or disgust, but the latter, more innocent, remains. The cuckoo is heard, too, in the depths of the wood. Heard my night-warbler on a solitary white pine in the Heywood

Clearing by the Peak. Discovered it at last, looking like a small ❧ piece of black bark curving partly over the limb. ❭ No fork to its tail. It appeared black beneath; was very shy, not bigger than a yellowbird, and very slender.

In the middle of the path to Wharf Rock at Flint's Pond, the nest of a Wilson's thrush, five or six inches high, between the green stems of three or four golden-rods, made of dried grass or fibres of bark, with dry oak leaves attached loosely, making the whole nine or ten inches wide, to deceive the eye. Two blue eggs. Like an accidental heap. Who taught it to do thus? *Lobelia Dortmanna*, a day or two at most. No grass balls yet. That fine-rooted green plant on bottom sends up stems with black heads three or four inches. Do they become white? Every one who has waded about the shores of a pond must have been surprised to find how much warmer the water was close to the shore, where only three or four inches deep, than a little further out. I think I saw a young crow now fully grown.

Returned by Smith's Hill and the Saw Mill Brook. Got quite a parcel of strawberries on the hill. The hellebore leaves by the brook are already half turned yellow. Plucked one blue early blueberry. The strain of the bobolink now begins to sound a little rare. It never again fills the air as the first week after its arrival. At this season we apprehend no long storm, only showers with or without thunder.

June 20. Monday. 4 A. M. — No fog ; sky mostly overcast; drought continues. I heard the robin first (before

the chip-bird) this morning. Heard the chip-bird last evening just after sunset.

10 A. M. — To Assabet Bathing-Place.

I see wood tortoises in the path; one feels full of eggs. Those great greenish-white puffs on the panicled andromeda are now decaying. On the swamp-pink they are solid. The pitchers of the comandra seeds are conspicuous. Meadow-sweet out, probably yesterday. It is an agreeable, unpretending flower. Some of the stone nests are a foot above the water now, but uninjured. I can find nothing in them. The bosky bank shows bright roses from its green recesses; the small white flowers of the panicled andromeda; beneath, yellow lilies.

Found two lilies open in the very shallow inlet of the meadow. Exquisitely beautiful, and unlike anything else that we have, is the first white lily just expanded in some shallow lagoon where the water is leaving it, — perfectly fresh and pure, before the insects have discovered it. How admirable its purity! how innocently sweet its fragrance! How significant that the rich, black mud of our dead stream produces the water-lily, — out of that fertile slime springs this spotless purity! It is remarkable that those flowers which are most emblematical of purity should grow in the mud.

There is also the exquisite beauty of the small sagittaria, which I find out, maybe a day or two, — three transparent crystalline white petals with a yellow eye and as many *small* purplish calyx-leaves, four or five inches above the same mud.

Vol. V

Coming home at twelve, I see that the white lilies are nearly shut. The river has been some days full with weeds which drape and trail from my oars — I am now on foot — (the potamogeton), as if it were Charon's boat, and this a funeral procession down the Cocytus.

8 P. M. — Up North River to Nawshawtuct.

The moon full. Perhaps there is no more beautiful scene than that on the North River seen from the rock this side the hemlocks. As we look up-stream, we see a crescent-shaped lake completely embosomed in the forest. There is nothing to be seen but the smooth black mirror of the water, on which there is now the slightest discernible bluish mist, a foot high, and thick-set alders and willows and the green woods without an interstice sloping steeply upward from its very surface, like the sides of a bowl. The river is here for half a mile completely shut in by the forest. One hemlock, which the current has undermined, has fallen over till it lies parallel with the water, a foot or two above it and reaching two thirds across the stream, its extremity curving upward to the light, now dead. Here it has been a year or two, and it has only taken the place of others which have successively fallen in and been carried away by the stream. One lies now cast up on the shore. Some wild roses, so pale now in the twilight that they look exactly like great blackberry blossoms. I think *these* would look so at midday.

Saw a little skunk coming up the river-bank in the woods at the White Oak, a funny little fellow, about

six inches long and nearly as broad. It faced me and actually compelled me to retreat before it for five minutes. Perhaps I was between it and its hole. Its broad black tail, tipped with white, was erect like a kitten's. It had what looked like a broad white band drawn tight across its forehead or top-head, from which two lines of white ran down, one on each side of its back, and there was a narrow white line down its snout. It raised its back, sometimes ran a few feet forward, sometimes backward, and repeatedly turned its tail to me, prepared to discharge its fluid like the old. Such was its instinct. And all the while it kept up a fine grunting like a little pig or a squirrel. It reminded me that the red squirrel, the woodchuck, and the skunk all make a similar sound. Now there are young rabbits, skunks, and probably woodchucks.

Walking amid the bushes and the ferns just after moonrise, I am refreshed with many sweet scents which I cannot trace to their source. How the trees shoot! The tops of young pines toward the moon are covered with fine shoots some eighteen inches long. Will they grow much more this year? There is a peculiarly soft, creamy light round the moon, now it is low in the sky. The bullfrogs begin about 8.30. They lie at their length on the surface amid the pads. I touched one's nose with my finger, and he only gave a sudden froggish belch and moved a foot or two off. How hard to imitate their note exactly, — its sonorousness. Here, close by, it is like *er er ough, er er er ough*, with a sonorous trump which these letters do not suggest. On our return, having reached the reach by Merrick's pasture, we get the best view of the moon in the southeast, reflected in the water, on account of the length of the reach. The creamy light about it is also perfectly reflected; the path of insects on the surface between us and the moon is lit up like fire. The leafy-columned elms, planted by the river at foot of Prichard's field, are exceedingly beautiful, the moon being behind them, and I see that they are not too near together, though sometimes hardly a rod apart, their branches crossing and interlacing. Their trunks look like columns of a portico wreathed with evergreens on the evening of an illumination for some great festival. They are the more rich, because in this creamy light you cannot distinguish the trunk from the verdure that drapes it.

This is the most sultry night we have had. All windows and doors are open in the village and scarcely a lamp is lit. I pass many families sitting in their yards. The shadows of the trees and houses are too extended, now that the moon is low in the heavens, to show the richest tracery.

June 21. 4.30 A. M. — Up river for lilies.

No dew even where I keep my boat. The driest night yet, threatening the sultriest day. Yet I see big crystalline drops at the tips or the bases of the ponte-deria leaves. The few lilies begin to open about 5. The nest of a brown thrasher with three eggs, on some green-briar, perfectly concealed by a grape-vine running over it; eggs greenish-brown; nest of dry sticks, lined with fibres of grape bark and with roots. Bird

scolded me much. Carpet-weed out. I have got a pan full of lilies open.

We have not had rain, except a mere sprinkling in the night of the 17th, since the 26th of May.

P. M. — To Conantum.

The warmest day yet. For the last two days I have worn nothing about my neck. This change or putting off of clothing is, methinks, as good an evidence of the increasing warmth of the weather as meteorological instruments. I thought it was hot weather perchance, when, a month ago, I slept with a window wide open and laid aside a comfortable, but by and by I found that I had got two windows open, and to-night two windows and the door are far from enough. *Hypericum perforatum* just out. This year the time when the locust was first heard was the time to put on summer clothes.

Early on the morning of the 18th the river felt lukewarm to my fingers when my paddle dipped deeper than usual. The galium with three small white petals (*G. trifidum*) has been out some time, and I find that erectish, broad-leaved, three-nerved, green-flowered one, perhaps *G. circæzans*, at Corner Spring. *Peltandra Virginica*, perhaps a week, for many of its flowers are effete and curved downward. The *Hypericum ellipticum*, by the riverside. The only violets I notice nowadays are a few white lanceolate ones in the meadows. The river has got down quite low, and the muddy shores are covered here and there with a sort of dark-brown paper, the dried filaments of

confervæ which filled the water. Now is their fall. The bright little flowers of the *Ranunculus reptans* var. *filiformis* are seen peeping forth between its interstices. Calopogon out. I think it surpasses the pogonia, though the latter is sometimes high-colored and is of a handsome form; but it is inclined to be pale, is sometimes even white.

Now see many bright red amelanchier berries and some purple or dark-blue ones amid them. They [are] mostly injured by insects or apparently pecked and deformed by birds, but, from the few perfectly sound and ripe I have eaten to-day, I should pronounce them superior to either blueberries or huckleberries. Those of the *Botryapium* have a soft skin; of the shorter bush with a stiffer leaf, a tough skin. This is a little before blueberries. The panicled cornel is the only one of the cornels or viburnums that now is noticed in flower, generally speaking. The last of our cornels — the *C. sericea*, I think it must be — is just beginning.

The farmers have commenced haying. With this the summer culminates. The most extended crop of all is ready for the harvesting. Lint still comes off the leaves and shoots. It is so hot I have to lift my hat to let the air cool my head. I notice that that low, rather rigid fern, about two feet high, on the Great Hubbard Meadow, which a month ago was yellow, but now is green and in fruit, and with a harsh-feeling fruit atop, is decidedly inclined to grow in hollow circles from one foot to six or eight feet in diameter, — often, it is true, imperfect on one side, or, if large, filled up in the middle. How to account

for it? Can it have anything to do with the hummocks deposited on the meadow? Many small stems near together in circles, *i. e.* not a single line. Is it the *Osmunda spectabilis*? Now I hear the spotted (?) flies about my head, — flies that settle and make themselves felt on the hand sometimes. The morning-glory still fresh at 3 P. M. A fine, large, delicate bell with waved border, some pure white, some reddened. The buds open perfectly in a vase. I find them open when I wake at 4 A. M. Is not this one of the eras or culminating places in the flower season? Not this till the sultry mornings come. Angelica, perhaps a day or more. Elder just opening. The four-leaved asclepias, probably some days. A rather handsome flower, with the peculiar fragrance of the milkweeds. Observed three or four sweet-briar bushes with white flowers of the usual size, by the wall under Conantum Cliff, — very slightly tinted with red or rose. In the paucity and form of prickles, at least, I make them answer to the *micrantha*, but not else. Is it intermediate? Opened at home in a vase in the shade. They are more distinctly rose-tinted. Leaves and all together in the water, they have a strong spirituous or rummy scent. There are no flowers nor flower-buds on the bass this year, though it was so full last year.

Where the other day I saw a pigeon woodpecker tapping and enlarging a hole in the dead limb of an apple tree, when as yet probably no egg was laid, to-day I see two well-grown young woodpeckers about as big as the old, looking out at the hole, showing their handsome spotted breasts and calling lustily for something to eat, or, it may be, suffering from the heat. Young birds in some situations must suffer greatly from heat these days, so closely packed in their nests and perhaps insufficiently shaded. It is a wonder they remain so long there patiently. I saw a yellowbird's nest in the willows on the causeway this afternoon and three young birds, nearly ready to fly, overflowing the nest, all holding up their open bills and keeping them steadily open for a minute or more, on noise of my approach. Still see cherry-birds in flocks.

Dogsbane and *Prinos verticillatus*. My white lilies in the pan are mostly withering the first day, the weather is so warm.

At sunset to Island.

The white anemone is withering with drought; else would probably have opened. Return while the sun is setting behind thunder-clouds, which now overshadow us. Between the heavy masses of clouds, mouse-colored, with dark-blue bases, the patches of clear sky are a glorious cobalt blue, as Sophia calls it. How happens it that the sky never appears so intensely, brightly, memorably blue as when seen between clouds and, it may be, as now in the south at sunset? This, too, is like the blue in snow. For the last two or three days it has taken me all the forenoon to wake up.

June 22. I do not remember a warmer night than the last. In my attic under the roof, with all windows and doors open, there was still not a puff of the usual

coolness of the night. It seemed as if heat which the roof had absorbed during the day was being reflected down upon me. It was far more intolerable than by day. All windows being open, I heard the sounds made by pigs and horses in the neighborhood and of children who were partially suffocated with the heat. It seemed as if it would be something to tell of, the experience of that night, as of the Black Hole of Calcutta in a degree, if one survived it.

This forenoon a smart, straight-down shower from the eastward for ten or fifteen minutes, bordered round with thunder, — the first since May 26th. It did not touch the north part of the town. Some broad-leaved dock for a few days. Is it not the *obtusifolius*, front of Conantum house and by wall front of E. Wood's barn?

5.30 p. m. — To Walden and Fair Haven Hill.

Epilobium shows some pale or pink purple flowers on its spike. *Trifolium arvense*. It is quite cool now, after the shower in the forenoon. Now is the time for young birds. You cannot go near any thicket but the old will scold at you, and you see the kingbird and the blackbird and swallows pursuing crows and hawks, as for several weeks. I looked for the nest of the Maryland yellow-throat, but could not find it. Some animal has carried it off from the tuft of sedge, but I found one little egg which had dropped out. How many tragedies of this kind in the fields! Butter-and-eggs is a handsome yellow-spiked flower which would be better appreciated if it grew less profusely.

Vol. V

The sun down, and I am crossing Fair Haven Hill, sky overcast, landscape dark and still. I see the smooth river in the north reflecting two shades of light, one from the water, another from the surface of the pads which broadly border it on both sides, and the very irregular waving or winding edge of the pads, especially perceptible in this light, makes a very agreeable border to distinguish, — the edge of the film which seeks to bridge over and inclose the river wholly. These pads are to the smooth water between like a calyx to its flower. The river at such an hour, seen half a mile away, perfectly smooth and lighter than the sky, reflecting the clouds, is a paradisaical scene. What are the rivers around Damascus to this river sleeping around Concord? Are not the Musketaquid and the Assabet, rivers of Concord, fairer than the rivers of the plain?

And then the rich warble of the blackbird may still occasionally even at this season be heard. As I come over the hill, I hear the wood thrush singing his evening lay. This is the only bird whose note affects me like music, affects the flow and tenor of my thought, my fancy and imagination. It lifts and exhilarates me. It is inspiring. It is a medicative draught to my soul. It is an elixir to my eyes and a fountain of youth to all my senses. It changes all hours to an eternal morning. It banishes all trivialness. It reinstates me in my dominion, makes me the lord of creation, is chief musician of my court. This minstrel sings in a time, a heroic age, with which no event in the village can be contemporary. How can they

be contemporary when only the latter is *temporary* at all? How can the infinite and eternal be contemporary with the finite and temporal? So there is something in the music of the cow-bell, something sweeter and more nutritious, than in the milk which the farmers drink. This thrush's song is a *ranz des vaches* to me. I long for wildness, a nature which I cannot put my foot through, woods where the wood thrush forever sings, where the hours are early morning ones, and there is dew on the grass, and the day is forever unproved, where I might have a fertile unknown for a soil about me.[1] I would go after the cows, I would watch the flocks of Admetus there forever, only for my board and clothes. A New Hampshire everlasting and unfallen.

How wonderfully moral our whole life! There is never an instant's truce between virtue and vice. Goodness is the only investment that never fails. It is sung of in the music of the harp. This it is which thrills us. The harp is the travelling patterer for the Universe Insurance Company. Our little goodness is all the assessment.[2]

All that was ripest and fairest in the wilderness and the wild man is preserved and transmitted to us in the strain of the wood thrush. It is the mediator between barbarism and civilization. It is unrepentant as Greece.

I find my clothes covered with young caterpillars these days.

How wonderfully and admirably moral is our whole

[1] [Channing, p. 71.]   [2] [*Walden*, pp. 241, 242; Riv. 340, 341.]

life! Though the youth at last grows indifferent, the laws of the universe are not indifferent; they are still and forever on the side of the most tender and sensitive.

Listen in every zephyr for some reproof. It is the sweetest strain of the music. It provokes by its proud remoteness. Its satire trembles round the world. We cannot touch a string, awake a sound, but it reproves us. Many an irksome noise in our neighborhood, go a long distance off, is heard as music and a proud sweet satire on the meanness of our life. Not a music to dance to, but to live by.

Low blueberries now begin to show on high hills. You may get a handful or two. Yet perhaps a greater proportion of the shad-berries are ripe. Blueberries always surprise us.

These are the longest days in the year. The sun rises about 4.30 o'clock [and sets] about 7.30, leaving about eight hours of night. The strawberries may perhaps be considered a fruit of the spring, for they have depended chiefly on the freshness and moisture of spring, and on high lands are already dried up, — a soft fruit, a sort of manna which falls in June, — and in the meadows they lurk at the shady roots of the grass. Now the blueberry, a somewhat firmer fruit, is beginning. Nuts, the firmest, will be the last. Is not June the month in which all trees and shrubs grow, — do far the greater part of their growing? Will the shoots add much to their length in July? Berries are ripening now, when young birds are beginning to fly generally. *Lysimachia stricta*, apparently by to-

morrow. I see froth nowadays on the panicled andromeda.

June 23. 5 A. M. — Up Union Turnpike.
The red morning-glory partly open at 5.45. Looking down on it, it is [a] regular pentagon, with sides but slightly incurved.

1.30 P. M. — To White Pond.
Sultry, dogdayish weather, with moist mists or low clouds hanging about, — the first of this kind we have had. I suspect it may be the result of a warm southwest wind met by a cooler wind from the sea. It is hard to tell if these low clouds most shade the earth or reflect its heat back upon it. At any rate a fresh, cool moisture and a suffocating heat are strangely mingled.

The *Specularia perfoliata* in flower at top of its leafy spikes for a few days, on Clamshell Hill, this side oaks. It is a rich-colored and handsome-shaped sort of lake-purple flower, — or color of a lilac violet. The lower and earlier flowers have no corollas. Perhaps one of the first-rate flowers, when many are open on the spike. Motherwort by roadside, probably yesterday. Pogonias are now very abundant in the meadow-grass, and now and then a calopogon is mixed with them. The last is broader and of more singular form, commonly with an unopened bud above on one side. Devil's-needles of various kinds abundant, now perhaps as much as ever. Some smaller ones a brilliant green with black wings. That must be the flowering fern

that grows in rings. Lupines not quite gone, though most are gone to seed. A skunk-cabbage leaf makes the best vessel to drink out of at a spring, it is so large, already somewhat dishing, oftenest entire, and grows near at hand, and, though its odor when the stem is cut off is offensive, it does not flavor the water and is not perceived in drinking.

Along Nut Meadow Brook stand now angelicas in flower, as high as your head, their great greenish umbels above their naked purple stems. Senecio is going and gone to seed. At Apple-Hollow Pond, the heart-leaf grows in small solid circles from a centre, now white with its small delicate flowers somewhat like minute water-lilies. Here are thousands of devil's-needles of all sizes hovering over the surface of this shallow pond in the woods, in pursuit of one another and their prey, and from time to time alighting on the bushes around the shore, — I hear the rustling of their wings, — while swallows are darting about in a similar manner twenty feet higher. Perhaps they descend and pick up a needle now and then. This might be called Heart-leaf Pond, if there were not so many of them. Wild radish, some time, for its jointed seed-vessels are two inches long.

The small caterpillars which I bring home on my clothes nowadays come off of the young oaks, black and probably others. Their leaves are made into sieves and riddled by them. The painted tortoise eggs which I saw being deposited by White Pond the 14th are now shrivelled shells on the surface. I every year, as to-day, observe the sweet, refreshing fragrance

of the swamp-pink, when threading the woods and swamps in hot weather. It is positively cool. Now in its prime. There is another small, shallow Heart-leaf Pond, west of White, which countless devil's-needles are hovering over with rustling wing, and swallows and pewees no doubt are on hand. That very handsome cove in White Pond at the south end, surrounded by woods. Looking down on it through the woods in middle of this sultry dogdayish afternoon, the bay being not so deep but that some reflection from the bottom affects it, the water is a misty bluish-green or glaucous color.[1] The rattlesnake and the wool grass have begun to bloom. The *e er ee er ter twee* is a pleasing wild note still pretty sure to be heard amid thick pine woods or on their edges, — rarely seen, though often heard.

After bathing I paddled to the middle in the leaky boat. The heart-leaf, which grows thinly here, is an interesting plant, sometimes floating at the end of a solitary, almost invisible, threadlike stem more than six feet long, and again many purplish stems intertwined into loose ropes, or like large skeins of silk, abruptly spreading at top, of course, into a perfectly flat shield, a foot or more [in] diameter, of small heart-shaped leaves, which rise and fall on their stems as the water is higher or lower. This perfectly horizontal disposition of the leaves in a single plane is an interesting and peculiar feature in water-plants of this kind. Leaves and flowers made to float on the dividing line between two elements. No water-bugs nor

[1] [*Walden*, p. 219; Riv. 309.]

skaters, except a very few close to the shore, though the waves do not run much. Where the water is five or six feet deep, straight sticks on the bottom are made by the undulation on the surface to look like snakes in motion. The blue flags are past their prime here. Again I saw and heard the hummingbird visit the blue flags. He announces himself by a sudden loud humming. Now, at about 5 P. M., only at long intervals is a bullfrog's trump heard. Some are white-throated, others yellow.

In the warm noons nowadays, I see the spotted small yellow eyes of the four-leaved loosestrife looking at me from under the birches and pines springing up in sandy upland fields. *Asclepias Cornuti.* Ours, I think, must be the *Cornus sericea*, not *stolonifera.* The willow by Hubbard's Bridge must be either *Salix discolor* or *eriocephala;* I think the former.

The other day I saw what I took to be a scarecrow in a cultivated field, and noticing how unnaturally it was stuffed out here and there and how ungainly its arms and legs were, I thought to myself, "Well, it is thus they make these things; they do not stand much about it;" but looking round again after I had gone by, I saw my scarecrow walking off with a real live man in it.

I was just roused from my writing by the engine's whistle, and, looking out, saw shooting through the town two enormous pine sticks stripped of their bark, just from the Northwest and going to Portsmouth Navy-Yard, they say. Before I could call Sophia, they

had got round the curve and only showed their ends on their way to the Deep Cut. Not a tree grows now in Concord to compare with them. They suggest what a country we have got to back us up that way. A hundred years ago or more perchance the wind wafted a little winged seed out of its cone to some favorable spot, and this is the result. In ten minutes they were through the township, and perhaps not half a dozen Concord eyes rested on them during their transit.

June 24. P. M. — Boated to Clamshell Hill.

My lilies in the pan have revived with the cooler weather since the rain. (It rained a little last night.) This is what they require that they may keep. Mayweed yesterday. The calopogon is a more bluish purple than the pogonia. The *Gnaphalium uliginosum* seems to be almost in blossom. Gratiola out in mud near river, — those bare, rather hard, muddy tracts on the edge of the meadow next the river, where mint grows and the mud has wide cracks, some nearly an inch wide, produced by the sun since the water went down. It is cooler and remarkably windy this afternoon, showing the under sides of the leaves and the pads, the white now red beneath and all green above. Wind northwest. Found what I take to be an Indian hoe at Hubbard Bathing-Place, sort of slate stone four or five eighths of an inch thick, semicircular, eight inches one way by four or more the other, chipped down on the edges.

At the Clamshell curve, great masses of a kind of fresh-water eel-grass have lodged against the potamo-

geton in mid-channel, as against a shore, half a foot deep, and stretch across the river, long, green, narrow, ribbon-like. It is *apparently* the *Vallisneria spiralis*, eel-grass, tape-grass. It grows at the bottom in shallow places, slanting and waving down-stream. But what has collected it here all at once? Is it this strong wind operating on shallow places at curves? Or is it that some animal — muskrat or what-not — has loosened it? Or have men been at work up-stream somewhere? Does it always happen at this season? By the botany it does not blossom till August. There were piles of dried heart-leaf on shore at the bathing-place, a foot high and more. Were they torn up and driven ashore by the wind? I suspect it is the wind in both cases. As storms at sea tear up and cast ashore the seaweeds from the rocks. These are our seaweeds cast ashore in storms, but I see only the eel-grass and the heart-leaf thus served. Our most common in the river appears to be between the *Potamogeton natans* and *pulcher;* it answers to neither, but can be no other described. See it in fruit. I do not see the ranunculus flowers *very* abundant yet — will it not be this year? Then there is that long, somewhat cylindrical, fine-capillary and bladdery leaved plant which I had wrongly thought belonged to the *Ranunculus.* Is it not a utricularia?[1] All these, but especially the *R. Purshii*, have a strong fresh-water marsh smell, rather agreeable sometimes as a bottle of salts, like the salt marsh and seaweeds, invigorating to my imagination. In our great stream of distilled water going slowly

[1] It is *Utricularia vulgaris;* now in bloom.

down to ocean to be salted. Sparganium, some time. Pontederia, just out. The lower translucent, waved leaves of the potamogeton are covered with a sort of very minute black caddis-case. The peat[?]-black petioles of these leaves are much like seaweed. There are the heart-leaf ponds, but I cannot say the potamogeton rivers on account of the tautology, and, beside, I do not like this last name, which signifies that it grows in the neighborhood of rivers, when it is not a neighbor but an indweller. You might as well describe the seaweeds as growing in the neighborhood of the sea.

The brown thrasher's nest (*vide* 21st) has been robbed, probably by some other bird. It rested on a branch of a swamp-pink and some grape-vines, effectually concealed and protected by grape-vines and greenbriar in a matted bower above it. The foundation of pretty stout twigs, eight or nine inches in diameter, surmounted by coarse strips of grape bark, giving form to the nest, and then lined with some harsh, wiry root-fibres; within rather small and shallow, and the whole fabric of loose texture, not easy to remove.

Also got a blackbird's nest whose inhabitants had flown, hung by a kind of small dried rush (?) between two button-bushes which crossed above it; of meadow-grass and sedge, dried *Mikania scandens* vine, horsetail, fish-lines, and a strip apparently of a lady's bathing-dress, lined with a somewhat finer grass; of a loose and ragged texture to look at. Green mikania running over it now.

A yellowbird's nest (*vide* 21st) in a fork of a willow on Hubbard's Causeway, resting chiefly on the leading branch; of fine grass, lined with hair, bottom outside puffing out with a fine, light, flax-like fibre, perhaps the bark of some weed, by which also it is fastened to the twigs. It is surprising that so many birds find hair enough to line their nests with. If I wish for a horsehair for my compass sights I must go to the stable, but the hair-bird, with her sharp eyes, goes to the road.

The small white (perhaps *sometimes* violet or purplish) aster-like flower of Hubbard's meadow, for some days. If an aster, then the earliest one.

June 25. Saturday. P. M. — To Assabet Bathing-Place.

Great orange lily beyond stone bridge. Found in the Glade (?) Meadows an unusual quantity of amelanchier berries, — I think of the two common kinds, — one a taller bush, twice as high as my head, with thinner and lighter-colored leaves and larger, or at least somewhat softer, fruit, the other a shorter bush, with more rigid and darker leaves and dark-blue berries, with often a sort of woolliness on them. Both these are now in their prime. These are the first berries after strawberries, or the first, and I think the sweetest, *bush* berries. Somewhat like high blueberries, but not so hard. Much eaten by insects, worms, etc. As big as the largest blueberries or peas. These are the "service-berries" which the Indians of the north and the Canadians use. *La poire* of the latter (*vide*

Indian books, No. 6, p. 13). They by a little precede the early blueberry (though Holbrook brought two quarts of the last day before yesterday), being now in their prime, while blueberries are but just *beginning*. I never saw nearly so many before. It is a very agreeable surprise. I hear the cherry-birds and others about me, no doubt attracted by this fruit. It is owing to some peculiarity in the season that they bear fruit. I have picked a quart of them for a pudding. I felt all the while I was picking them, in the low, light, wavy shrubby wood they make, as if I were in a foreign country. Several old farmers say, "Well, though I have lived seventy years, I never saw nor heard of them." I think them a delicious berry, and no doubt they require only to be more abundant every year to be appreciated.

I think it must be the purple finch, — with the crimson head and shoulders, — which I see and hear singing so sweetly and variedly in the gardens, — one or two to-day. It sits on a bean-pole or fence-pick[et]. It has a little of the martin warble and of the canary-bird.

June 26. Very cool day.

Had for dinner a pudding made of service-berries. It was very much like a rather dry cherry pudding without the stones.

A slight hail-storm in the afternoon.

Euphorbia maculata.

Our warmest night thus far this year was June 21st. It began to be cooler the 24th.

5.30 P. M. — To Cliffs.

Carrot by railroad. Mine apparently the *Erigeron strigosus*, yet sometimes tinged with purple. The tephrosia is an agreeable mixture of white, straw-color, and rose pink; unpretending. What is the result of that one leaf (or more), much and irregularly, or variously, divided and cut, with milk in it, in woods, either a lactuca or prenanthes, probably, one foot or more high?

Such is oftenest the young man's introduction to the forest and wild. He goes thither at first as a hunter and fisher, until at last the naturalist or poet distinguishes that which attracted him and leaves the gun and fishing-rod behind. The mass of men are still and always young in this respect. I have been surprised to observe that the only obvious employment which ever to my knowledge detained at Walden Pond for a whole half-day, unless it was in the way of business, any of my " fellow-citizens," whether fathers or children of the town, with just one exception, was fishing. They might go there a thousand times, perchance, before the sediment of fishing would sink to the bottom and leave their purpose pure, — before they began to angle for the pond itself. Thus, even in civilized society, the embryo man (speaking intellectually) passes through the hunter stage of development. They did not think they were lucky or well paid for their time unless they got a long string of fish, though they had the opportunity of seeing the pond all the while. They measured their success by the length of a string of fish. The Governor faintly remembers the pond, for

he went a-fishing there when he was a boy, but now he is too old and dignified to go a-fishing, and so he knows it no longer. If the Legislature regards it, it is chiefly to regulate the number of hooks to be used in fishing there; but they know nothing about the hook of hooks.[1]

At Cliffs. — The air is warmer, but wonderfully clear after the hail-storm. I do not remember when I have seen it more clear. The mountains and horizon outlines on all sides are distinct and near. Nobscot has lost all its blue, is only a more distant hill pasture, and the northwest mountains are too terrestrial a blue and firmly defined to be mistaken for clouds. Billerica is as near as Bedford commonly. I see new spires far in the south, and on every side the horizon is extended many miles. It expands me to look so much farther over the rolling surface of the earth. Where I had seen or fancied only a hazy forest outline, I see successive swelling hills and remote towns. So often to the luxurious and hazy summer in our minds, when, like Fletcher's "Martyrs in Heaven," we,

"estranged from all misery
As far as Heaven and Earth discoasted lie,
Swelter in quiet waves of immortality,"

some great chagrin succeeds, some chilling cloud comes over. But when it is gone, we are surprised to find that it has cleared the air, summer returns without its haze, we see infinitely further into the horizon on every side, and the boundaries of the world are enlarged.

[1] [*Walden*, pp. 235, 236; Riv. 331–333.]

A beautiful sunset about 7.30; just clouds enough in the west (we are on Fair Haven Hill); they arrange themselves about the western gate. And now the sun sinks out of sight just on the north side of Watatic, and the mountains, north and south, are at once a dark indigo blue, for they had been darkening for an hour or more. Two small clouds are left on the horizon between Watatic and Monadnock, their sierra edges all on fire. Three minutes after the sun is gone, there is a bright and memorable afterglow in his path, and a brighter and more glorious light falls on the clouds above the portal. His car, borne further round, brings us in the angle of excidence. Those little sierra clouds look like two castles on fire, and I see the fire through ruined windows. The low west horizon glows now, five or six minutes after sunset, with a delicate salmon-color tinged with rose, deepest where the sun disappeared, and fading off upward; and north and south are dark-blue cloud islands in it. When I invert my head these delicate salmon-colored clouds look like a celestial Sahara sloping gently upward, an inclined plane upward, to be travelled by caravans bound heavenward, with blue oases in it.

June 27. 4.30 A. M. — To Island by river.

The cuckoo's nest is robbed, or perhaps she broke her egg because I found it. Thus three out of half a dozen nests which I have revisited have been broken up. It is a very shallow nest, six or seven inches in diameter by two and a half or three deep, on a low bending willow, hardly half an inch deep within; con-

cealed by overlying leaves of a swamp white oak on the edge of the river meadow, two to three feet from ground, made of slender twigs which are prettily ornamented with much ramalina lichen, lined with hickory catkins and pitch pine needles. I have described the rest before.

Saw a little pickerel with a minnow in his mouth. It was a beautiful little silver-colored minnow, two inches long, with a broad stripe down the middle. The pickerel held [it] crosswise near the tail, as he had seized it, and as I looked down on him, he worked the minnow along in his mouth toward the head, and then swallowed it head foremost. Was this instinct? Fishermen should consider this in giving form to their bait. The pickerel does not swallow the bait at once, but first seizes it, then probably decides how it can best be swallowed, and no doubt he lets go again in disgust some baits of which he can make neither head nor tail.

The radical leaves (four?) of the floating-heart are triangularly or wedge ovate, on petioles one to two inches long. The two large potamogetons now common on river (the smaller apparently not long in flower), with ovate or elliptical floating leaves sometimes salmon-color, belong to one or two of the first three of Gray. The smaller has its immersed leaves long, narrowly linear, and semicylindrical; those of the largest are pellucid, lanceolate, and waved. That sort of ostrich feather on the bottom appears to be the *Potamogeton Robbinsii*. What is that foul, submerged, densely whorled and capillary-leaved and forked utricularia-

Vol. V

like but bladderless plant? Then there is a pinnate and cut-leafed plant on the bottom. Is it radical leaves of a proserpinaca? or a milfoil? I find a little bug between the calyx and petals of white lilies which have not opened. It has eaten holes in them.

The dogsbane is one of the more interesting little flowers.

June 28. Nettle out a few days. Pepper-grass, a week or more. Catnep, also, a few days. We have warmer weather now again.

June 29. Jersey tea, just beginning. *Asclepias obtusifolia*, a day or two. *Sericocarpus conyzoides*.

June 30. Succory on the bank under my window, probably from flowers I have thrown out within a year or two. A rainbow in the west this morning. Hot weather.

V

JULY, 1853

(ÆT. 35–36)

July 1. I am surveying the Bedford road these days, and have no time for my Journal. Saw one of those great pea-green emperor moths, like a bird, fluttering over the top of the woods this forenoon, 10 A. M., near Beck Stow's. Gathered the early red blackberry in the swamp or meadow this side of Pedrick's, where I ran a pole down nine feet. It is quite distinct from the evergreen one and is without prickles. Fruit red, middle-sized, with a few, perhaps ten or twelve, large globules. May be the *Rubus triflorus*, but not growing on hills.

July 2. Cooler to-day. *Polygonum Persicaria*. The *Ranunculus Purshii* is very rarely seen now. I hear a harsh *keow* from a bittern flying over the river. The peetweets are quite noisy about the rocks in Merrick's pasture when I approach; have eggs or young there, which they are anxious about. The tall anemone in blossom, and no doubt elsewhere much earlier, — a week or ten days before this, — but the drought has checked it here. Saw on a maple leaf floating on the Assabet a kind of large aphides, thickly covering it. It was thickly coated with a mass of down, for their tails were like swan's-down, and, as they were constantly in motion, just stirring at least, it was as if there was a wind on it. Thimble-berries probably a day or two.

July 3. Elder is now in its prime. Buttercups are almost gone. Clover is blackened. The umbelled pyrola, apparently yesterday, as well as the *P. rotundifolia* and the *P. elliptica*, or shin-leaf. The *P. secunda*, or one-sided pyrola, is already out of bloom.

The oven-bird's nest in Laurel Glen is near the edge of an open pine wood, under a fallen pine twig and a heap of dry oak leaves. Within these, on the ground, is the nest, with a dome-like top and an arched entrance of the whole height and width on one side. Lined within with dry pine-needles.

Mountain laurel lingers in the woods still. The chestnut behind my old house site is fully out, and apparently has been partly so for several days. There are no flowers on bass trees commonly this year. Smooth sumach just opening and already resounding with bees. The water-target appears to be in its prime, its flowers rising above the water. Remarkable for the thick jelly on its leaves and stem. A smaller potamogeton is in flower there, — the small globose white flower. Why is it so often already torn up by the roots? Poke a day or two in favorable places. Dogsbane and Jersey tea are among the prevailing flowers now. The *Utricularia vulgaris* now yellows low muddy water, as near the Lincoln bound by Walden. The *Vaccinium vacillans* a day or two ripe. Black huckle-

berries. Tansy on the causeway. The Canada thistle. The pinweeds have a reddish look, as if in flower.

July 4. The cotton-grass at Beck Stow's. Is it different from the early one? High blueberries begin. The oval-leaved drosera in bloom. *Campanula aparinoides.* I see now a later (?) rose in lower, wetter ground. *Polygala sanguinea.* The weeds are now so thick in the river — potamogetons, heart-leaf, *Ranunculus Purshii*, eel-grass, etc., etc. — as almost to conceal the stream and seriously to obstruct the passage of my boat. *Polygonum sagittatum.* The cymbidium now perhaps in its prime. I am attracted by the peculiar glaucous leaves of the rhodora. Noli-me-tangere. The beauty of some butterflies, — dark steel-blue with a light-blue edge. Circæa, some time, the small one, at Corner Spring. Parsnips. The bass appears now — or a few trees — to have bloomed here and there prematurely. The gall on the leaves of the slippery elm is like fruit. The greater plantain, a few days. The fine feathery tail of the *Equisetum sylvaticum* (?) nowadays in damp woods, near Corner Spring. The *Potamogeton hybridus* (?) in fruit and flower; though the spike is cylindrical like *P. heterophyllus*, yet the petioles are shorter than the floating leaves. What is the apparently wholly immersed potamogeton, upright with linear-lanceolate leaves? (No flower nor fruit now.) Also what is that small upright, round, tapering plant, three inches high, at bottom of river, with apparently bristle-formed leaves arranged alternately crosswise, visibly cellular? A

Lee's Cliff, under the slippery elm, *Parietaria Pennsylvanica*, American pellitory, in flower, and near by *Anychia dichotoma*, forked chickweed (Queria [*sic*]) also in flower.

July 5. Raspberries, some days.

Such a habit have cows in a pasture of moving forward while feeding that, in surveying on the Great Fields to-day, I was interrupted by a herd of a dozen cows, which successively passed before my line of vision, feeding forward, and I had to watch my opportunity to look between them. Sometimes, however, they were of use, when they passed behind a birch stake and made a favorable background against which to see it.

July 6. I can sound the swamps and meadows on the line of the new road to Bedford with a pole, as if they were water. It may be hard to break through the crust, but then it costs a very slight effort to force it down, sometimes nine or ten feet, where the surface is dry. Cut a straight sapling, an inch or more in [diameter]; sharpen and peel it that it may go down with the least obstruction. The larch grows in both Moore's and Pedrick's swamps. Do not the trees that grow there indicate the depth of the swamp? I drink at the black and sluggish run which rises in Pedrick's Swamp and at the clearer and cooler one at Moore's Swamp, and, as I lie on my stomach, I am surprised at the quantity of decayed wood continually borne past. It is this process which, carried on for ages,

formed this accumulation of soil. The outlets of a valley being obstructed, the decayed wood is no longer carried off but deposited near where it grew.

July 7. Very dry weather. Every traveller, horse, and cow raises a cloud of dust. It streams off from their feet, white and definite in its outline, like the steam from a locomotive. Those who walk behind a flock of sheep must suffer martyrdom. Now is that annual drought which is always spoken of as something unprecedented and out of the common course.

Is that a utricularia which fills the water at the north end of Beck Stow's? Sarsaparilla berries are ripe.

Paddled up the river this evening. It is remarkable that, in pushing a boat up a river with a sandy bottom, the sound of the oar on the sand should be communicated so distinctly through the oar to the air. It is perhaps as distinct as if no water intervened. We have cool nights now after warm days, — cooler than in June. You cannot safely wear your thin coat into evening outdoors. The *Asclepias incarnata*, or water asclepias now.

July 8. Large œnothera. Toads are still heard occasionally at evening. To-day I heard a hylodes peep (perhaps a young one), which have so long been silent.

July 10. *Galium asprellum*, probably about the 5th or 6th. The side-flowering scutellaria now. Hedge-nettle, a day or two. *Lysimachia lanceolata* var. *hybrida*,

some days. Yellow lily now common (since the 4th).
The large seed-vessels of the blue flag conspicuous.
The rainbow rush has been in bloom for some time.
Epilobium coloratum. A rough eupatorium budded
at Hubbard's burning. *Ludwigia palustris,* probably
for ten days. *Rubus Canadensis* now. The red capsules of the *Hypericum ellipticum* begin to show in
low lands. The cardinal-flower shows red. At Cardinal Shore a large *Polygonum amphibium,* seven feet
long, left by the water, creeping over the shore and
rooting in it at the joints; not yet in flower.

The bream poised over its sandy nest on waving fin
— how aboriginal! So it has poised here and watched
its ova before this New World was known to the Old.
Still I see the little cavities of their nests along the
shore.

Lycopus sinuatus, water horehound.

July 11. Rain last night.
The aromatic trichostema now springing up. *Gnaphalium uliginosum* now. Hydrocotyle, some days.
Agrimony, also, some days. Button-bush. *Centaurea
nigra,* some time, Union Turnpike, against E. Wood's,
low ground, and *Ludwigia alternifolia,* apparently
just begun, at entrance to *poke-logan* near Assabet
Bathing-Place. The small crypta already in fruit. I
find in the river, especially near the Assabet Bathing-
Place, a ranunculus some of whose leaves are capillary, others merely wedge-cut or divided. Is it not
the *R. aquatilis?* [1] But I see no flowers.

[1] I think it is the *R. Purshii.*

July 14. Heavy fog.
I see a rose, now in its prime, by the river, in the
water amid the willows and button-bushes, while
others, lower on shore, are nearly out of bloom. Is
it not the *R. Carolina?* Saw something blue, or glaucous, in Beck Stow's Swamp to-day; approached and
discovered the *Andromeda Polifolia,* in the midst of
the swamp at the north end, not long since out of
bloom. This is another instance of a common experience. When I am shown from abroad, or hear of, or
in any [way] become interested in, some plant or other
thing, I am pretty sure to find it soon. Within a week
R. W. E. showed me a slip of this in a botany, as a
great rarity which George Bradford brought from Wa-
tertown. I had long been interested in it by Linnæus's
account. I now find it in abundance. It is a neat and
tender-looking plant, with the pearly new shoots now half
a dozen inches long and the singular narrow revolute
leaves. I suspect the flower does not add much to it.

There is an abundance of the buck-bean there also.
Holly berries are beginning to be ripe. The *Polygonum Hydropiper,* by to-morrow. *Spergula arvensis*
gone to seed and in flower. A very tall ragged orchis
by the Heywood Brook, two feet high, almost like a
white fringed one. Lower ones I have seen some time.

The clematis there (near the water-plantain) will
open in a day or two. Mallows gone to seed and in
bloom. *Erigeron Canadensis,* butter-weed.

July 15. Common form of arrowhead. The *Rumex
obtusifolius* shows its single grain now. Near Loring's

July 12. White vervain. Checkerberry, maybe some
days. Spikenard, not quite yet. The green-flowered
lanceolate-leafed orchis at Azalea Brook will soon
flower. Either *Gymnadenia tridentata* or *Platanthera
flava. Circæa alpina* (?) there, but nearly eighteen
inches high. *Lycopus Virginicus,* not open in shade;
probably in a day or two. Wood horse-tail very large
and handsome there.

July 13. Purslane, probably to-day. *Chenopodium
album.* Pontederias in prime. Purple bladderwort
(*Utricularia purpurea*), not long, near Hollowell
place, the buds the deepest-colored, the stems rather
loosely leaved or branched, with whorls of five or six
leaves. On the hard, muddy shore opposite Dennis's,
in the meadow, *Hypericum Sarothra* in dense fields,
also *Canadense,* both a day or two, also ilysanthes,
sium with leaves a third of an inch wide, and the
cardinal flower, probably the 11th. *Hypericum mutilum* in the meadow, maybe a day or two. Whorled
bladderwort, for some time, even gone to seed; this,
the purple, and the common now abundant amid
the pads and rising above them. *Potamogeton com-
pressus* (?) immersed, with linear leaves. I see no
flower.

I believe it is the radical leaves of the heart-leaf,
— large, waved, transparent, — which in many places
cover the bottom of the river where five or six feet
deep, as with green paving-stones. Did not somebody
mistake these for the radical leaves of the kalmiana
lily?

Vol. V

ram that coarse mustard-like branched plant, one or
two feet high, with racemes of small yellow flowers,
— perhaps Gray's *Nasturtium palustre* or Bigelow's
Sisymbrium amphibium, — in seed and in blossom.

July 16. Rhus copallina behind Bent's, budded, not
quite open. *Solidago stricta* (?) at Cato's cellar, a day
or two. The pasture thistle, more than a week. Is
it the *Potamogeton heterophyllus* in Walden, now in
flower and for some time? Door-grass.

July 17. The common amaranth. Young toads not
half an inch long at Walden shore. The smooth sumach
resounds with the hum of bees, wasps, etc., at Water-
target Pond. I see two great devil's-needles, three
inches long, with red abdomens and bodies as big as
hummingbirds, sailing round this pond, round and
round, and ever and anon darting aside suddenly,
probably to seize some prey. Here and there the water-
targets look red, perhaps their under sides. A duck
at Goose Pond. Rank weeds begin to block up low
wood-paths, — goldenrods, asters, etc. The pearly
everlasting. *Lobelia inflata.* The *Solidago nemoralis* (?)
in a day or two, — gray goldenrod. I think we have
no *Hieracium Gronovii,* though one not veined always
and sometimes with two or more leaves on stem. No
grass balls to be seen.

July 18. Sonchus oleraceus well in bloom.
8.30 A. M. — To Sudbury meadows with W. E. C.
by boat.

Hardhack in bloom perhaps a day or two. The button-bush beginning to open generally. The late, or river, rose spots the copses over the water, — a great ornament to the river's brink now. Three utricularias and perhaps the horned also common now. Rhexia, a day or two. The pads are now much eaten. Thoroughwort. Meadow haying has commenced. There is no pause between the English and meadow haying. There are thousands of yellow butterflies on the pontederia flowers, and of various colors on the button-bush. In the Sudbury meadows are dense fields of pipes three feet high bordering the river. The common large rush, flowering at top, makes black-looking squads there. The fields of pontederia are in some places four or five rods wide and almost endless, but, crossing from side to side on shore, are the open white umbels of the hemlock, and now thesium begins to show. These meadows, with their meandering stream, through whose weeds it is hard to push a boat, are very wild. The stake-driver and the *virescens* rise and go off with sluggish flight from time to time. What is that continual dry *chucking* sound heard about the pads? The darting of a fish, or of an insect? The heart-leaves are eaten and turned dark, but the less decayed part in the centres, still green, is of the form and appearance of the less cut leaves of the *Ranunculus Purshii*, — either leading to or following after that. As they decay, such a leaf as the less divided ones of the *R. Purshii* is left, or promises to be left, — is suggested. That smaller narrow-leaved polygonum which forms the first and lower rank in the river is in many

places in blossom, rose-colored, whitish. What is that rather tall, coarse kind of aster, with a few broad rays, in the copse behind Bittern Cliff?[1] Is it *Diplopappus cornifolius?* Now are the days to go a-berrying.

July 19. Clematis has been open a day or two. The alisma will open to-morrow or next day. This morning a fog and cool. What is that small conyza-like aster, with flaccid linear leaves, in woods near Boiling Spring? Some woodbine, cultivated, apparently long since flowered. The same of some on Lee's Cliff, where it is early.

July 20. To Nawshawtuct at moonrise with Sophia, by boat.

Moon apparently fulled yesterday. A low mist incrusts the meadow, — not so perceptible when we are on the water. Now we row through a thin low mist about as high as one's head, now we come to a place where there is no mist on the river or meadow, apparently where a slight wind stirs. The gentle susurrus from the leaves of the trees on shore is very enlivening, as if Nature were freshening, awakening to some enterprise. There is but little wind, but its sound, incessantly stirring the leaves at a little distance along the shore, heard not seen, is very inspiriting. It is like an everlasting dawn or awakening of nature to some great purpose. As we go up the hill we smell the sweet-

[1] July 30th, a somewhat similar white aster with many middle-sized heads and a roughish stem in Dugan's [?] meadow.

briar. The trees are now heavy, dark masses without tracery, not as in spring or early in June; but I forgot to say that the moon was at first eclipsed by a vast black bank of cloud in the east horizon, which seemed to rise faster than it, and threatened to obscure it all the night. But suddenly she rose above it, and when, a few moments after, we thought to look again for the threatening cloud-bank, it had vanished, or a mere filmy outline could be faintly traced beneath her. It was the eclipse of her light behind it that made this evil look so huge and threatening, but now she had triumphed over it and eclipsed it with her light. It had vanished, like an ugly dream. So is it ever with evils triumphed over, which we have put behind us. What was at first a huge dark cloud in the east which threatened to eclipse the moon the livelong night is now suddenly become a filmy vapor, not easy to be detected in the sky, lit by her rays. She comes on thus, magnifying her dangers by her light, at first displaying, revealing them in all their hugeness and blackness, exaggerating, then casting them behind her into the light concealed. She goes on her way triumphing through the clear sky like a moon which was threatened by dark clouds at her rising but rose above them.[1] That black, impenetrable bank which threatened to be the ruin of all our hopes is now a filmy dash of vapor with a faint-purplish tinge, far in the orient sky.

From the hilltop we see a few distant lights in farmhouses down below, hard to tell where they are,

[1] [*Excursions*, p. 329; Riv. 405.]

yet better revealing *where* [*sic*] they are than the sun does. But cottage lights are not conspicuous now as in the autumn. As we looked, a bird flew across the disk of the moon. Saw two skunks carrying their tails about some rocks. Singular that, of all the animated creation, chiefly these skunks should be abroad in this moonlight. This is the midsummer night's moon. We have come round the east side of the hill to see the moon from amid the trees. I like best to see its light falling far in amid the trees and along the ground before me, while itself is hidden behind them or one side. It is cool, methinks with a peculiar coolness, as it were from the luxuriance of the foliage, as never in June. At any rate we have had no such sultry nights this month as in June. There is a greater contrast between night and day now, reminding me that even in Hindostan they freeze ice in shallow vessels at night in summer (?). There is a mist very generally dispersed, which gives a certain mellowness to the light, a wavingness apparently, a creaminess. Yet the light of the moon is a cold, almost frosty light, white on the ground.

There [are] a few fireflies about. Green, their light looks sometimes, and crickets are heard. You are pretty sure also to hear some human music, vocal or instrumental, far or near. The masses of the trees and bushes would be called black, if our knowledge that they are leaves did not make us call them dark-green. Here is the *Pycnanthemum lanceolatum* near the boat's place, which I scent in the dark. It has been out some days, for some flowers are quite withered. I hear from the copses or bushes along the shore, returning, a faint everlasting fine song from some small cricket, or rather locust, which it required the stillness of night to reveal. A bat hovers about us. How oily smooth the water in this moonlight! And the apparent depth where stars are reflected frightens Sophia. These Yankee houses and gardens seen rising beyond this oily moon-lit water, on whose surface the circling insects are like sparks of fire, are like Italian dwellings on the shores of Italian lakes. When we have left the boat and the river, we are surprised, looking back from the bank, to see that the water is wholly concealed under a white mist, though it was scarcely perceptible when we were in its midst. The few bullfrogs are the chief music. I do not know but walnuts are peculiarly handsome by moonlight, — seeing the moon rising through them, and the form of their leaves. I felt some nuts. They have already their size and that bracing, aromatic scent.

July 21. 2 P. M. — Went, in pursuit of boys who had stolen my boat-seat, to Fair Haven.

Plenty of berries there now, — large huckleberries, blueberries, and blackberries. My downy-leafed plant of Annursnack and under the Cliffs, now in bloom, and some days, is the *Pycnanthemum incanum*, — common mountain mint or wild basil. It is two or three feet high and very velvety-downy, while calamint is rigid. What is that small creeping plant covering the ground in the Cliff brook like a veronica, — leaf shaped like that of the small veronica on the Cliffs,

leaves opposite but far apart, rooting at base? No traces of a flower. The small purple orchis, its spikes half opened. The *Rhus copallina* is most abundant on the low knoll beneath the Cliffs, not yet blossomed. *Euphorbia hypericifolia* (?) at Bittern Cliff, how long? Horse-mint, a day or two, the earliest. *Desmodium acuminatum*, some days; it is a delicate spike of flowers on a long peduncle. The berries of the alternate cornel are beginning to ripen. I am entering Fair Haven Pond. It is now perfectly still and smooth, like dark glass. Yet the westering sun is very warm. He who passes over a lake at noon, when the waves run, little imagines its serene and placid beauty at evening, as little as he anticipates his own serenity. There is no more beautiful part of the river than the entrance to this pond. The *Asclepias incarnata* is well named water silkweed, for it grows here amid the buttonbushes and willows in the wettest places along the river. Nature is beautiful only as a place where a life is to be lived. It is not beautiful to him who has not resolved on a beautiful life. The horned utricularia appears to be in its prime, though there was none here June 16th. It yellows the shore, together with the hyssop and filiform ranunculus, not to mention the lanceolate loosestrife. The spear thistle.

The tall anemone grows by the red oak near the elms opposite the pond on Conantum and is still in flower. I am surprised by the abundance of large shining blackberries on the hillsides; every bush does its best. The river is so low and weedy that at Hubbard's bend, though there is most current at bends,

Vol. V

three rails have been lodged in different places in midchannel and have not advanced for a week or more. It rapidly grows cool toward sunset. The sun is now warm on my back, and when I turn round I have to shade my face with my hands; but some time before it sets the dews begin to fall, and a damp, cool air is felt over the water, and I want a thick coat. Ten minutes before sunset I saw large clear dewdrops at the tips, or half an inch below the tips, of the pontederia leaves.

July 22. P. M. — To Annursnack.

The *Chenopodium hybridum* (?); at least its leaves are dark-green, rhomboidal, and *heart*-shaped. The orchis and spikenard at Azalea Brook are not yet open. The early roses are now about done, — the sweetbriar quite, I think. I see sometimes houstonias still. The elodea out. Boehmeria not yet. On one account, at least, I enjoy walking in the fields less at this season than at any other; there are so many men in the fields haying now. Observed, on the wild basil on Annursnack, small reddish butterflies which looked like a part of the plant. It has a singularly soft, velvety leaf. Smooth sumach berries crimson there.

There is a kind of low blackberry which does not bear large fruit but very dense clusters, by wall-sides, shaded by the vine or other plants often, of clammy and strong-tasted berries.

Yellow butterflies in the road. I find the *Campanula Americana* of the West naturalized in our garden. Also a silene (?) without *visibly* viscid stem and with

swollen joints; apparently the snapdragon catchfly otherwise. Leaves opposite, sessile, lanceolate.

July 23. P. M. — To P. Hutchinson's.

I cannot find a single crotalaria pod there this year. Stone-crop is abundant and has now for some time been out at R. Brown's watering-place; also the waterplantain, which is abundant there. About the water further nòrth the elodea is very common, and there, too, the rhexia is seen afar on the islets, — its brilliant red like a rose. It is fitly called meadow-beauty. Is it not the handsomest and most striking and brilliant flower since roses and lilies began? Blue vervain out some days.

Bathing yesterday in the Assabet, I saw that many breams, apparently an old one with her young of various sizes, followed my steps and found their food in the water which I had muddied. The old one pulled lustily at a *Potamogeton hybridus*, drawing it off one side horizontally with her mouth full, and then swallowed what she tore off. The young pouts were two and a half inches long in Flint's Pond the 17th.

July 24. *Sunday.* 4.30 A. M. — By boat to Island.

Robins, larks, peawais, etc., as in the spring, at this hour. The mikania to-morrow or next day.[1] The zizania, some days. The low, front-rank polygonums are still imbrowned in many places; as I think, have not recovered from the effect of late frosts.

Mr. Pratt asked me to what animal a spine and

[1] July 29.

broken skull found in the wall of James Adams's shop belonged, — within the partition. I found by its having but two kinds of teeth, and they incisive and molar, that it belonged to the order *Rodentia*, which, with us, consists of the Beaver, Hare, Rat (including squirrels), and Porcupine families. From its having "incisors $\frac{2}{2}$, molars $\frac{3-3}{3-3}$" and "molars with a flat crown and zigzag plates of enamel," I knew it to be a muskrat, which probably got into the building at a time of high water. The molars appeared like one long tooth, their flat, smooth tops zigzagged with the edges of hard plates of . enamel in this wise some- what ; but after looking long and sharply with a microscope, though on the side I could not distinguish the separate teeth, I made out, by tracing about the edges of the enamel which intertwined and broke joints curiously for strength, three separate inclosures, and, with full faith in this and in science, I told Pratt it was a muskrat, and gave him my proofs ; but he could not distinguish the three molars even with a glass, or was still plainly uncertain, for he had thought them one tooth, when, taking his pincers, he pulled one out and was convinced, much to his and to my satisfaction and our confidence in science! How very hard must be the teeth of this animal whose food is clams! What keeps his incisors so sharp? Look at this strong head, with its upper jaw and incisor curved somewhat like a turtle's beak. What an apparatus for cutting, holding, crushing! What a trap to be caught in! It is amusing to think what grists have

Vol. V

come to this mill, though now the upper and nether stones fall loosely apart, and the brain-chamber above, where the miller lodged, is now empty (passing under the portcullis of the incisors), and the windows are gone.

With or without reason, I find myself associating with the idea of summer a certain cellar-like coolness, resulting from the depth of shadows and the luxuriance of foliage. I think that after this date the crops never suffer so severely from drought as in June, because of their foliage shading the ground and producing dews. We had fog this morning, and no doubt often the last three weeks, which my surveying has prevented my getting up to see.

It is the palmer-worm which has attacked the apple trees this year.

Surveying one very hot day, a week or two ago, and having occasion to strip a sapling of its bark, I was surprised to observe how cool the freshly exposed and sappy wood was, as if it extracted coolness from the cool cellars of the earth.

Sophia's *Viola pedata*, taken up in the spring, blossomed again a day or two ago. I perceive the peculiar scent of corn-fields.

Yesterday a dew-like, gentle summer rain. You scarcely know if you are getting wet.

At least two kinds of grass as tall as the zizania have preceded it along the river. One has long since gone to seed, and looks flavid or yellowish now. The other is still in blossom, its chaff (?) being remarkably and regularly on one side of the glume (?). For a week or more I have perceived that the evenings were con-

siderably longer and of some account to sit down and write in. Ate an early-harvest apple of my own raising yesterday; not quite ripe. The scent of some very early ones which I have passed in my walks, imparting some ripeness to the year, has excited me somewhat. It affects me like a performance, a poem, a thing done; and all the year is not a mere promise of Nature's.

How far behind the spring seems now, — farther off, perhaps, than ever, for this heat and dryness is most opposed to spring. Where most I sought for flowers in April and May I do not think to go now; it is either drought and barrenness or fall there now. The reign of moisture is long since over. For a long time the year feels the influence of the snows of winter and the long rains of spring, but now how changed! It is like another and a fabulous age to look back on, when earth's veins were full of moisture, and violets burst out on every hillside. Spring is the reign of water; summer, of heat and dryness; winter, of cold. Whole families of plants that lately flourished have disappeared. Now the phenomena are tropical. Let our summer last long enough, and our land would wear the aspect of the tropics. The luxuriant foliage and growth of all kinds shades the earth and is converting every copse into a jungle. Vegetation is rampant. There is not such rapid growth, it is true, but it slumbers like a serpent that has swallowed its prey. Summer is one long drought. Rain is the exception. All the signs of it fail, for it is dry weather. Though it may seem so, the current year is not peculiar in this

respect. It is a slight labor to keep count of all the showers, the rainy days, of a summer. You may keep it on your thumb nail.

P. M. — To Corner Spring and Fair Haven Hill.

Mimulus ringens at Heywood Brook, probably several days. The fruit of the skunk-cabbage is turned black. At Hubbard's Bathing-Place I tread on clams all across the river in mid-channel, flattening them down, for they are on their edges. The small linear-leaved hypericum (*H. Canadense*) shows red capsules. The black choke-berry, probably some days. The dark indigo-blue (Sophia says), waxy, and like blue china blue berries of the clintonia are already well ripe. For some time, then, though a few are yet green. They are numerous near the edge of Hubbard's lower meadow. They are in clusters of half a dozen on brittle stems eight or ten inches high, oblong or squarish round, the size of large peas with a dimple atop. Seen thus, above the handsome, regular green leaves which are still perfect in form and color and which, here growing close together, checker the ground, and also in the dense shade of the copse, there is something peculiarly celestial about them. This is the plant's true flower, for which it has preserved its leaves fresh and unstained so long. *Eupatorium pubescens* at Hubbard's burnt meadow. There is much near his grove. Also *Epilobium molle* there (put it with the *coloratum*), and *coloratum* and the common still in blossom. There is erechthites there, budded. Also *Lysimachia ciliata* and, by the causeway near, the ovate-leaved, quite distinct from the lanceolate, — I think not so early as the last. At the Corner Spring the berries of the trillium are already pink. The medeola is still in flower, though with large green berries. The swamp-pink still blooms and the morning-glory is quite fresh; it is a pure white, like a lady's morning gown.

The aspect of vegetation about the spring reminds me of fall. The angelica, skunk-cabbage, trillium, arum, and the lodged and flattened grass are all phenomena of the fall.

A spikenard just beyond the spring has already pretty large green berries, though a few flowers. Say July 10th. It is a great plant, six feet high, seven long, with the largest pinnate leaves of this kind I think of. More than two feet by two, with single leafets eleven inches by nine. The two-leaved convallaria and the *Smilacina racemosa* show ripening clusters. I hear incessantly a cricket or locust, inspired by the damp, cool shade, telling of autumn. I have not observed it more than a week. *Scutellaria galericulata*, maybe some time.

The berries of the *Vaccinium vacillans* are very abundant and large this year on Fair Haven, where I am now. Indeed these and huckleberries and blackberries are very abundant in this part of the town. Nature does her best to feed man. The traveller need not go out of the road to get as many as he wants; every bush and vine teems with palatable fruit. Man for once stands in such relation to Nature as the animals that pluck and eat as they go. The fields and hills are a table constantly spread. Wines of all kinds and qualities, of noblest vintage, are bottled up in the skins of

countless berries, for the taste of men and animals. To men they seem offered not so much for food as for sociality, that they may picnic with Nature, — diet drinks, cordials, wines. We pluck and eat in remembrance of Her. It is a sacrament, a communion. The not-forbidden fruits, which no serpent tempts us to taste.[1] Slight and innocent savors, which relate us to Nature, make us her guests and entitle us to her regard and protection. It is a Saturnalia, and we quaff her wines at every turn. This season of berrying is so far respected that the children have a vacation to pick berries, and women and children who never visit distant hills and fields and swamps on any other errand are seen making haste thither now, with half their domestic utensils in their hands. The woodchopper goes into the swamp for fuel in the winter; his wife and children for berries in the summer.

The late rose, — *R. Carolina*, swamp rose, — I think has larger and longer leaves; at any rate they are duller above (light beneath), and the bushes higher. The shaggy hazelnuts now greet the eye, always an agreeable sight to me, with which when a boy I used to take the stains of berries out of my hands and mouth. These and green grapes are found at berry time. High blueberries, when thick and large, bending the twigs, are a very handsome cool, rich, acid berry.

On Fair Haven a quarter of an hour before sunset. — How fortunate and glorious that our world is not roofed in, but open like a Roman house, — our skylight so broad and open! We do not climb the hills in vain. It is no crystal palace we dwell in. The windows of the

<hr/>

[1] [Channing, pp. 71, 72.]

Vol. V

sky are always open, and the storms blow in at them. The field sparrow sings with that varied strain. The night wind rises. On the eastern side of this hill it is already twilight. The air is cooler and clearer. The mountains which [were] almost invisible grow more distinct. The various heights of our hills are plainly shown by the more or less of the mountain bases seen from them. The atmosphere of the western horizon is impurpled, tingeing the mountains. A golden sheen is reflected from the river so brightly that it dazzles me as much as the sun. The now silver-plated river is burnished gold there, and in midst of all I see a boat ascending with regular dip of its seemingly gilt oars. That which appears a strip of smooth, light silvery water on each side of the stream, not reflecting the sky, is the reflection of light from the pads. From their edges, there stream into the smooth channel sharp blue serrations or ripples of various lengths, sometimes nearly across, where seemingly a zephyr gliding off the pads strikes it. A boy is looking after his cows, calling "ker ker ker ker," impatient to go home. The sun is passing under the portcullis of the west. The nighthawk squeaks, and the chewink jingles his strain, and the wood thrush; but I think there is no loud and general serenade from the birds. I hear no veery. How much more swiftly the sun seems to perform the morning and evening portions of his journey, when he is nearest his starting-place or goal! He is now almost ready to dip, — a round red disk shorn of his beams, — his head shaved like a captive led forth for execution.

Meanwhile the night is rapidly gathering her forces in deepening lines of shade under the east side of the willow causeway and the woods. Now the sun has dipped into the western ocean. He is one half below the horizon, and I see lines of distinct forest trees, miles and miles away on some ridge, now revealed against his disk. It takes many a western woodland — go far enough, a whole Iowa — to span it. Now only the smallest segment of its sphere, like a coal of fire rising above the forest, is seen sending a rosy glow up the horizon sky. The illustrious traveller with whom we have passed a memorable day has gone his way, and we return slowly to our castle of the night. But for some minutes the glowing portal clouds are essentially unchanged.

Pycnanthemum muticum behind Wheeler's cottages; put it with the earliest of its class.

July 25. Dodder, probably the 21st. Blue-curls. Burdock, probably yesterday.

P. M. — To Le Grosse's.

Cerasus Virginiana, — choke-cherry, — just ripe. White and red huckleberries said to be in Le Grosse's or Wetherbee's pasture. Could not find them. *Cynoglossum Morisoni*, beggar's-lice, roadside between Sam Barrett's mill and the next house east, in flower and fruiting probably ten days. Probably the same with plant found beyond the stone bridge, gone to seed, last year.

I have for years had a great deal of trouble with my shoe-strings, because they get untied continually.

They are leather, rolled and tied in a hard knot. But some days I could hardly go twenty rods before I was obliged to stop and stoop to tie my shoes. My companion and I speculated on the distance to which one tying would carry you, — the length of a shoe-tie, — and we thought it nearly as appreciable and certainly a more simple and natural measure of distance than a stadium, or league, or mile. Ever and anon we raised our feet on whatever fence or wall or rock or stump we chanced to be passing, and drew the strings once more, pulling as hard as we could. It was very vexatious, when passing through low scrubby bushes, to become conscious that the strings were already getting loose again before we had fairly started. What should we have done if pursued by a tribe of Indians? My companion sometimes went without strings altogether, but that loose way of proceeding was not [to] be thought of by me. One shoemaker sold us shoestrings made of the hide of a South American jackass, which he recommended; or rather he gave them to us and added their price to that of the shoes we bought of him. But I could not see that these were any better than the old. I wondered if anybody had exhibited a better article at the World's Fair, and whether England did not bear the palm from America in this respect. I thought of strings with recurved prickles and various other remedies myself. At last the other day it occurred to me that I would try an experiment, and, instead of tying two simple knots one over the other the same way, putting the end which fell to the right over each time, that I would reverse

Vol. V

able to get out of my way above the weeds and bushes of the low grounds, their tails not grown out to steady them. Larks, too, seen now, four or five together, sing as of yore; also the goldfinch twitters over oftener. That other kind of amaranth is apparently quite out in some places. The *Hypericum corymbosum*, which may have been out nearly as long as the *perforatum*. I see on all hands the hardhack's slender rosy pyramid spring above the walls and hedges. It is a fine coarse plant and must rank with the rhexia or near it. The broader, more cone-like meadow-sweet also. The swamp rose and the polygalas are other reds now in prime which I think of, not to include the orchis.[1] The small bluish-white berries of the trientalis appear to be ripe. *Gnaphalium polycephalum*, less downy and greener than the pearly one. I notice to-day the first purplish aster, a pretty sizable one; may have been out a day or two, near the brook beyond Hubbard's Grove, — *A. Radula* (?).

I mark again the sound of crickets or locusts about alders, etc., about this time when the first asters open, which makes you fruitfully meditative, helps condense your thoughts, like the *mel* dews in the afternoon. This the afternoon of the year. How apt we are to be reminded of lateness, even before the year is half spent! Such little objects check the diffuse tide of our thoughts and bring it to a head, which thrills us. They are such fruits as music, poetry, love, which humanity bears.

Saw one of the common wild roses (*R. lucida?*).

[1] But there are the cardinal, thistles, milkweeds, etc., etc.

the process, and put it under the other. Greatly to my satisfaction, the experiment was perfectly successful, and from that time my shoe-strings have given me no trouble, except sometimes in untying them at night.

On telling this to others I learned that I had been all the while tying what is called a granny's knot, for I had never been taught to tie any other, as sailors' children are; but now I had blundered into a square knot, I think they called it, or two running slip-nooses. Should not all children be taught this accomplishment, and an hour, perchance, of their childhood be devoted to instruction in tying knots?

Those New-Hampshire-like pastures near Asa Melvin's are covered or dotted with bunches of indigo, still in bloom, more numerously than anywhere that I remember.

July 26. I reckon that about nine tenths of the flowers of the year have now blossomed.

Dog-days, — sultry, sticky (?) weather, — now when the corn is topped out. Clouds without rain. Rains when it will. Old spring and summer signs fail.

P. M. — To Fair Haven Hill.

The lycopodium which I see is not yet out. The *Potentilla Norvegica* is common and tall, the tallest and now most flourishing of the potentillas. The xyris, some time, on Hubbard's meadow, south of the water-plantain, whose large, finely branched, somewhat pyramidal panicle of flowers is attractive. The bobolinks are just beginning to fly in flocks, and I hear their *link link*. I see the young birds also, just

The swamp blackberry ripe in open ground. The *Rhus copallina* is not yet quite out, though the *glabra* is in fruit. The smaller purple fringed orchis has not quite filled out its spike. What a surprise to detect under the dark, damp, cavernous copse, where some wild beast might fitly prowl, this splendid flower, silently standing with all its eyes on you! It has a rich fragrance withal. Rain in the evening.

July 27. 8 A. M. — Rains, still quite soakingly. June and July perhaps only are the months of drought. The drought ceases with the dog-days.

P. M. — To White Pond in rain.

The autumnal dandelion now appears more abundantly within a week. *Solidago lanceolata* also, a few days probably, though only partially open.

July 28. 7 A. M. — To Azalea Brook.

The mikania is hardly out yet;[1] like the eupatoriums, shows its color long before it opens. The vernonia not quite yet. The lilies, though a little less numerous, appear freer from insects than at first. Their pads not so much eaten as those of the nuphar. The pickerel-weed has passed its prime. The petty-morel at the brook not out, though that by the Corner Spring has berries.

P. M. — To Clematis Brook *via* Lee's with Mr. Conway.[2]

[1] *Vide* 29th.
[2] [Rev. Moncure D. Conway. See his *Autobiography*, vol. i, pp.

Tells me of a kind of apple tree with very thick leaves near the houses in Virginia called the tea-tree, under which they take tea, even through an ordinary shower, it sheds the rain so well, and there the table constantly stands in warm weather.

The *Gerardia flava* in the hickory grove behind Lee's Cliff, some days. Answers apparently in every respect to the above, yet its lower leaves are like narrow white oak leaves. Have I seen the *G. quercifolia?* Is that the *Cicuta bulbifera* just out at Clematis Brook, with decompound leaves and linear leafets fringe-toothed?[1] That low hieracium, hairy, especially the lower part, with several hairy, obovate or oblanceolate leaves, remotely, very slightly, toothed, and glandular hairs on peduncles and calyx, a few heads, some days at least. *Vide* herbarium. Saw lower leaves of the white vervain turned a reddish lake or claret. Nightshade berries begin to ripen, — to be red. Is that rather coarse flower about Mrs. Brooks's house (escaped from cultivation), called Bouncing Bet, and which has been open ten days or more, *Saponaria Vaccaria,* — cow-herb? The mullein pink is also escaped from gardens thereabouts. *Aster linariifolius.*

July 29. P. M. — To hibiscus, Beck Stow's, and Brister's Hill.

Galeopsis Tetrahit, a good while. Vernonia, just opened, a few central ones. *Polygonum hydropiper-*

141, 142, where he speaks of walking with Thoreau in the summer of 1853.]

[1] Yes.

oides. At Vernonia Meadow I notice the beds of horse-mint now in flower, — bluish whorls of flowers, — now in its prime. Now is the time to gather thoroughwort. Cardinals are in their prime. The hibiscus is barely budded, but already the meadow-hay mowers have sheared close to it.

Most fields are so completely shorn now that the walls and fence-sides, where plants are protected, appear unusually rich. I know not what aspect the flowers would present if our fields and meadows were untouched for a year, if the mower were not permitted to swing his scythe there. No doubt some plants contended long in vain with these vandals, and at last withdrew from the contest. About these times some hundreds of men with freshly sharpened scythes make an irruption into my garden when in its rankest condition, and clip my herbs all as close as they can, and I am restricted to the rough hedges and worn-out fields which had little to attract them, to the most barren and worthless pastures. I know how some fields of johnswort and goldenrod look, left in the natural state, but not much about our richest fields and meadows.

Those huckleberries near the hibiscus are remarkably glossy, fresh, and plump in the lowland, but not so sweet as some. Crossed the river there, carrying over my clothes.

The Great Meadows present a very busy scene now. There are at least thirty men in sight getting the hay, revealed by their white shirts in the distance, the farthest mere specks, and here and there great loads of hay, almost concealing the two dor-bugs that

draw them — and horse racks [*sic*] pacing regularly back and forth. It is refreshing to behold and scent even this wreck of the meadow-plants. Here is a man sedulously cocking up great heaps composed almost alone of flowering fern, yet perfectly green. Here are many owners side by side, each taking his slice of the great meadow. The mower fixes bits of newspaper to stakes in straight lines across the meadow to guide him, lest he cut over his bounds. The completion of haying might be celebrated by a farmers' festival.

The wormwood, perhaps; has hardly opened yet. Peter appears to have cut all the liatris before its time.[1] The *Solidago stricta* begins to yellow the Great Fields in front of his house, but the *nemoralis* is hardly out there yet. The crotalaria has some fully formed pods, together with flowers, a little further east than before. It must be three weeks old at least. The sight of the small rough sunflower about a dry ditch bank and hedge advances me at once further toward autumn. At the same time I hear a dry, ripe, autumnal chirp of a cricket. It is the next step to the first goldenrod. It grows where it escapes the mower, but no doubt, in our localities of plants, we do not know where they would prefer to grow if unmolested by man, but rather where they best escape his vandalism. How large a proportion of flowers, for instance, are referred to and found by hedges, walls, and fences.

I see three or four (apparently) young marsh hawks, but full grown, circling and tumbling about not much

[1] No.

above the ground and playing with one another. They are quite a reddish brown. They utter a squeak (not a shrill scream), much like a small bird or animal. I noticed that my hen-hawks screamed and circled round their old nest yesterday, though their young must be fully grown.

Butterflies of various colors are now more abundant than I have seen them before, especially the small reddish or coppery ones. I counted ten yesterday on a single *Sericocarpus conyzoides.* They were in singular harmony with the plant, as if they made a part of it. The insect that comes after the honey or pollen of a plant is necessary to it and in one sense makes a part of it. Being constantly in motion and, as they moved, opening and closing their wings to preserve their balance, they presented a very lifesome scene. To-day I see them on the early goldenrod (*Solidago stricta*).

I broke through Heywood's thick wood, north of Moore's land, going toward Beck Stow's in the Great Fields, and unexpectedly came into a long, narrow, winding, and very retired blueberry swamp which I did not know existed there. A spot seemingly untrodden, — a deep withdrawn meadow, sunk low amid the forest and filled with green waving sedge, three feet high, and low andromeda and hardhack, for the most part dry to the feet and with no print of man or beast, interspersed with islands of blueberry bushes and surrounded by a dense hedge of high blueberry bushes, panicled andromeda, high choke-berry, wild holly, with its beautiful crimson berries, etc., etc., this being the front rank to a higher wood. Thus hedged about these places are, so that it is only at some late year that you stumble upon them. Crouching you thread your way amid some dense shrub oak wood some day, descending next through the almost impenetrable hedge, and stand to your surprise on the edge of this fair open meadow with a bottom of unfathomed mud, as retired and novel as if it were a thousand miles removed from your ordinary walks. Not penetrable except in midsummer. It is as far off as Persia from Concord. I entered from this swamp to that next south, through a narrow passage hardly a foot wide, stooping close to the ground, worn by some cows once, brushing off blueberries in my passage, and then burst out into another yet larger swamp, or meadow, of a similar character. And in the first I found great blueberries as big as old-fashioned bullets or cranberries, — the ambrosial fruit. These grew side by side in singular harmony in the dense hedge with crimson holly berries and black choke-berries. Over these meadows the marsh hawk circles undisturbed. What means this profusion of berries at this season only? Beck Stow's is much frequented by cows, which burst through the thickest bushes.

Crossed over to Tuttle's. Aaron's-rod not yet. The high blackberries began to be ripe about a week ago. The *small* flowers of the *Helianthemum Canadense* (cistus). Its leaves are like the *Lechea major*, for which I took it last (?) fall, when surrounded with frost at its base (hence called frost-weed). Started a pack of

grouse two-thirds grown. *Spiranthes gracilis* in Hubbard's Wood Path, coming toward his Close. May have been out some time. *Hypopitys lanuginosa*, American pine-sap, just pushing up, — false beech-drops. Gray says from June to August. It is cream-colored or yellowish under the pines in Hubbard's Wood Path. Some near the fence east of the Close. A plant related to the tobacco-pipe. Remarkable this doubleness in nature, — not only that nature should be composed of just these individuals, but that there should be so rarely or never an individual without its kindred, — its cousin. It is allied to something else. There is not only the tobacco-pipe, but pine-sap. Moist banks covered with the nearly grown, but green, partridge-berries now. Prenanthes, almost. Tobacco-pipe, how long? Coral-root well out, — *Corallorhiza multiflora*, — at Brister's Hill. There are some beautiful glossy, firm ferns there, — *Polystichum acrostichoides* (?), — shield fern. Nature made ferns for pure leaves, to show what she could do in that line. I also see some small, umbrella-shaped (with sharp cones), shining and glossy yellow fungi, like an election cake atop, also some dead yellow and orange. Clethra, a day or two in some places. In the Poorhouse Meadow, the white orchis spike almost entirely out, some days at least. This is the best place to find the *Pycnanthemum muticum* and *lanceolatum* that I know. *Eupatorium purpureum.* We are willing this coarse plant should be called Joe-Pye-weed. *Rhus copallina* behind Bent's, out a day or two; earlier than at Cliffs. *Acalypha Virginica* probably out in

some places; not the plant I saw. Some scarlet thorn leaves are yellow-spotted now. By railroad causeway a large smooth-stemmed goldenrod (not yet out), with smooth (both sides) linear-lanceolate sharply toothed leaves.[1] Another in a meadow, smaller, downy, with broader leaves, already out, like (?) the first. That was probably the *Scirpus lacustris*, — the black rush of the Sudbury meadows, long since out; panicle just below the top.

Perchance the moon shines sometimes merely to tempt men forth to view creation by night, but soon wanes to warn them that day is the season appointed for their labors.

July 30. I have for some time noticed the emersed leaves of the *Bidens Beckii* above the river surface, and this morning find the first flower. Last year I found none. Was it owing to the high water? The river has risen some since the dog-days. Wool-grass appears now in its prime. The weeds in the river seem to be subject to more casualties than elsewhere.

Many go to Europe *to finish their education*, and when they have returned their friends remark that the most they have acquired is a correct pronunciation of English. It is a premature hardening but hollowing of the shell. They become valuable utensils of the gourd kind, but have no palatable and nutritious inside. Instead of acquiring nutritious and palatable qualities to their pulp, it is all absorbed into a prematurely hardened shell. They went away squashes,

[1] *Solidago arguta?*

and they return gourds. They are all expressed, or squeezed out; their essential oil is gone. They are pronounced for you; they are good to stand before or for a noun or man as handles; not even hollow gourds always, but the handle without the mug. They pronounce with the sharp precise report of a rifle, but the likeness is in the sound only, for they have no bullets to fire.

P. M. — To Ministerial Swamp.

Going through Dennis's and Hosmer's meadows, I see a dozen or more men at work. In almost every meadow throughout the town they are thus engaged at present. In every meadow you see far or near the lumbering hay-cart with its mountainous load and the rakers and mowers in white shirts. The bittern hardly knows where to lay its eggs. By the way, I have heard no stake-driver for some time. If the meadows were untouched, I should no doubt see many more of the rare white and the beautiful smaller purple orchis there, as I now see a few along the shaded brooks and meadow's edge.

The choke-cherries (*Cerasus Virginiana*) near Hosmer's Spring are very abundant now; the bushes, about as high as your head, are loaded with full racemes, two or three inches long, of shining dark-red berries, the size of a pea, slightly oblong or oval, but, as yet at least, very astringent, puckering the mouth for a long time. No doubt frequently mistaken at sight for the rum cherry.

The angelica has gone to seed, and its great umbels, six inches in diameter, are turned brown at the top

Butterfly on Joe-Pye-weed

The Leaning Hemlocks

of its still purple hollow stems, sometimes seven feet high, the joints two feet long, and one and one third inches in diameter. By a meandering line of tall bare stems, surmounted by dark, dry umbels, I can trace the course of Nut Meadow Brook for half a mile. Nay, I find it by their aid when concealed by the grass even within a rod of me, for they indicate every meander. They rise much above everything else in the meadow. Close at hand, also, this brook is seen to be lined with the slender *Cicuta maculata* — there is much of this poisonous plant in our meadows — and *bulbifera*, with their smaller white umbels. This is a good place to look for the latter. I suppose it is the *Rumex hydrolapathum*, or great water dock, now going to seed there, with large valves and three large glands. I find some fruit on the *Ribes hirtellum* in J. P. Brown's land. It is globular, smooth, and red, marked by internal meridian lines, and inclined to be flattened at the poles. This does not blossom so early as our earliest in garden, but its fruit is more like this in color (though more smooth and glossy), while our later one is a dark purple or blue. Rather acid and wild-tasted. Is that the *Cirsium horridulum*, now out of bloom, on the north side of T. Wheeler's meadow, with tall, downy stem and the lower leaves almost entire and downy both sides, upper clasping and cut? Apparently the same by the L. Hosmer road at Nut Meadow Brook in Brown's meadow. The painted-cup still, and there. I was correct about the alders. The *incana* has a rounder leaf; the other is more oblong and is quite smooth beneath. I have missed the veery

for some time, but the wood thrush still sings and the peawai.

The wayfarer's tree! How good a name! Who bestowed it? How did it get adopted? The mass of men are very unpoetic, yet that Adam that names things is always a poet. The boor is ready to accept the name the poet gives. How nameless is the poet among us! He is abroad, but is not recognized. He does not get crowned with the laurel.

Goodyera pubescens on hillside south of Ministerial Swamp. Its veiny leaves, a hoary green, completely cover the ground on the damp and shady hillside, like a rug, sprinkled with dry oak leaves, which it has lifted as it grew. It is just sending up its green scapes amid the sere ones of last year, and one has partly blossomed. The hunter often sits on a shady bank and muses on this beautiful leaf, wondering what rare virtues it may possess.

The tobacco-pipe has also pushed up there amid the dry leaves in the shade. It is abundant now, and here. Both stem and flowers and scales are a pure and delicate crystalline white. What to name it? Sheathed with delicate white scales. It reminded me of a maiden in her robes of purity who has always been nurtured in a shady and vault-like seclusion, — a nun of spotless purity, a daughter of Tellus and Cælum too, making her entrance into the world. Pushing aside the doorway of dry leaves, three sisters of various heights issue from their hidden convent and stand side by side in the presence of the light. We are surprised to see such pure robes come from

Vol. V

the bowels of the earth. Yet this white and crystalline purity smacks of the cellar and shade. They come forth to be proved, and stand abashed in presence of the light, with hanging heads and faces toward the ground under their pure white hoods and capes, striving at first to conceal their nakedness and tenderness. A few loose, scanty, but beautiful, pearly sheaths alone invested them, and the broader capes of their hoods. The sisters then came forth of spotless purity, but soon, exposed to light and air, their virtue dried black. I was surprised to hear that this was called the tobacco-pipe! Their untried virtue cannot long stand the light and air. These and pine-sap the plants the dog-days (?) produce.

Here, too, are clintonia berries and, with the neottia and the pyrolas, now generally almost out of bloom. *Lygodium palmatum* now apparently in bloom. It is a most beautiful slender and delicate fern, twining like [a] vine about the stem of the meadow-sweet, panicled andromeda, goldenrods, etc., to the height of three feet or more, and difficult to detach from them. The lower half, in the shade, of small leafy sterile frondlets, the upper half, exposed to the light, of the finely divided fertile frondlets. Our most beautiful fern, and most suitable for wreaths or garlands. It is rare. Round-leaved sundew for some time. Bartonia or centaurella almost out, not spread, somewhat like the former now. Tansy has been the prevailing yellow flower for some time. It precedes the goldenrods.

This month has not been so warm as June. There

have been no such *bathing* days as we had last year, two or three. Methinks our warm weather hardest to bear is the last half of June and the first half of July. Afterward the shade and the dog-days give us moisture and coolness, especially at night.

Saw some green galls on a goldenrod (?) three quarters of an inch in diameter, shaped like a fruit or an Eastern temple, with two or three little worms inside, completely changing the destiny of the plant, showing the intimate relation between animal and vegetable life. The animal signifies its wishes by a touch, and the plant, instead of going on to blossom and bear its normal fruit, devotes itself to the service of the insect and becomes its cradle and food. It suggests that Nature is a kind of gall, that the Creator stung her and man is the grub she is destined to house and feed. The plant rounds off and paints the gall with as much care and love as its own flower and fruit, admiring it perchance even more.

I see a rusty-colored shorter-wooled cotton-grass, which may be the *Eriophorum Virginicum*.

July 31. *Sunday.* P. M. — To Walden.

The bristly aralia berries in dense patches with their numerous umbels, the central ones ripe for two or three days. They are about two inches in diameter and perfect hemispheres of dark-blue or blue-black berries, size of a huckleberry, on slender peduncles of equal length, forming a dense hemispherical umbel, two inches in diameter. I counted a hundred and thirty such berries in one. Rum cherry just ripe. Purple gerardia by to-morrow or the next day; the linear-leafed gerardia. The anychia, or forked chickweed, grows larger, with spreading red stems, on the south side of Heywood Peak. The commonest *Lespideza violacea*, with small elliptical leaves, perhaps a week. *Desmodium nudiflorum*, naked-flowered tick-trefoil, some already with loments round-angled; probably more than a week; the tall, naked flowering stems, sometimes more than two feet high, appearing like separate plants, at some distance from the rest, which are much lower, about ten inches high, with a bunch of oval leaves. *Lespedeza hirta* out. I find also a trefoil plant with long, wand-like(?) panicled racemes, rising a foot or more above the leaves, with flowers turned a bluish or verdigris green, apparently wilted, and leaves below, about the simple stem, on short peti- oles, ob- longish, one to two inches. May be *Desmodium Canadense*(?) or *læviga-tum*(?) or — ? Somewhat downy-stemmed.[1] Some time — a week — out. Also in J. Hosmer's pines beyond Clamshell Hill. Also the *Gnaphalium decurrens*, to the eye much like the fragrant one near by, but a lighter green and very sticky. Pennyroyal well out for some days at least there, in large bushy tufts. White goldenrod. Bushy gerardia, showing no radical leaves yet. I see some galls on under side of hickory leaves, red like currants, hollow with a grub within. *Solidago nemoralis*. These desmodiums, etc., etc., on the south side of Heywood Peak,

[1] *Dillenii?? Vide* Aug. 14.

Vol. V

a warm dry sprout-land, where I suspect they were not to be found before the wood was cut. They are very forward there. *Goodyera repens* well out at Corallorhiza Hillside; some time out. Put it close after the *gracilis*.

I calculate that less than forty species of flowers known to me remain to blossom this year.

VI

AUGUST, 1853

(ÆT. 36)

Aug. 1. I think that that universal crowing of the chip-bird in the morning is no longer heard. Is it the *Galium circæzans* which I have seen so long on Heywood Peak and elsewhere, with four broad leaves, low and branched? Put it early in June.

Aug. 2. Heavy, long-continued, but warm rain in the night, raising the river already eight or nine inches and disturbing the meadow haymakers. John Legross brought me a quantity of red huckleberries yesterday. The less ripe are whitish. I suspect that these are the *white* huckleberries.

Sundown. — To Nawshawtuct.

The waxwork berries are yellowing. I am not sure but the bunches of the smooth sumach berries are handsomest when but partly turned, the crimson contrasting with the green, the green berries showing a velvety crimson cheek. *Geum Virginianum*, white avens (June to August, Gray), still in bloom by the sassafras hedge, south side of hill, looks as if it might be a white cinquefoil, with small hook-prickled burs. Put it in June. Mulgedium out. The green fruit of the carrion-flower forms dense, firm, spherical umbels (?) at the end of stems five or six inches long;

umbels two inches in diameter, formed, one of them, of eighty-four berries, size of peas, three to six sided, closely wedged together on peduncles three quarters of an inch long. The whole feels hard and solid in the hand.

Aug. 3. To north part of Framingham, surveying near Hopestill Brown's (in Sudbury).

He said there was a tame deer in the wood, which he saw in his field the day before. Told me of an otter killing a dog and partly killing another. He sold lately a white pine tree about four feet [in] diameter at butt, which brought twenty-three dollars, not including what was used for fuel, and they sawed eighty feet in length of it. Saw the *Solidago odora* in the woods there, but not in bloom nearly; leaves full of pellucid dots and yielding, after being in my pocket all day, a very pleasant fragrance. Many farmers are now troubled to get their meadow-hay since the rise of the river. Sand cherries, probably a good while.

Aug. 4. Rain last night and to-day again. Groundnut. The low fields which have been mown now look very green again in consequence of the rain, as if it were a second spring. Aaron's-rod, not yet. A sicyos in front of the Vose house, not quite, but probably somewhere now. *Symphytum officinale* still in bloom in front of C. Stow's, over the fence. *Polygonum Careyi*, four feet high, gigantesque, bristly-glandular, with swollen joints (*poly-gonum*), many branches from near ground.

Aug. 5. Perfect dog-days. To-day is sultry, *i. e.* hot and cloudy, the air full of mist and here and there misty clouds; and you find yourself perspiring much before you are aware of it. Farmers complain that they cannot make hay this weather. I cannot dry my red huckleberries. The sun does not shine unobstructedly.

A man mowing in the Great Meadows killed a great water adder (?) the other day, said to be four feet long and as big as a man's wrist. It ran at him. They find them sometimes when they go to open their hay. I tried to see it this morning, but some boys had chopped it up and buried it. They said that they found a *great many* young ones in it. That probably accounts for its being so large round. The clintonia berries keep a long time without wrinkling in a tumbler of water. The mower on the river meadows, when [he] comes to open his hay these days, encounters some overgrown water adder full of young (?) and bold in defense of its progeny, and tells a tale when he comes home at night which causes a shudder to run through the village, — how it came at him, and he ran, and it pursued and overtook him, and he transfixed it with a pitchfork and laid it on a cock of hay, but it revived and came at him again. This is the story he tells in the shops at evening. The big snake is a sort of fabulous animal. It is always as big as a man's arm and of indefinite length. Nobody knows exactly how deadly its bite, but nobody is known to have been bitten and recovered. Irishmen introduced into these meadows for the first time, on seeing a snake, a creature which they have seen only in pictures before, lay down their

scythes and run as if it were the evil one himself, and cannot be induced to return to their work. They sigh for Ireland, where they say there is no venomous thing that can hurt you.

Inula out (how long?), roadside just beyond Garfield's. Spikenard berries near Corner Spring just begin to turn. Collinsonia, not yet. Cohush berries not quite ripe. Pennyroyal in prime on Conantum. *Aster corymbosus* pretty plainly (a day or two) in the Miles Swamp or arboretum, — *Aster dumosus*, as I have called it also elsewhere.

Aug. 6. More dog-days. The sun, now at 9 A. M., has not yet burst through the mists. It has been warmer weather for a week than for at least three weeks before, — nights when all windows were left open, though not so warm as in June. This morning a very heavy fog. The sun has not risen clear or even handsomely for some time, nor have we had a good sunset.

P. M. — To J. Farmer's Cliff.

I see the sunflower's broad disk now in gardens, probably a few days, — a true sun among flowers, monarch of August. Do not the flowers of August and September generally resemble suns and stars? — sunflowers and asters and the single flowers of the goldenrod. I once saw one as big as a milk-pan, in which a mouse had its nest.

It is remarkable how many plants turn lake — some of their leaves I mean — in the fall. Already I notice that the lower leaves of some catnep and a white vervain (2d) have so turned. They are in fact matured,

and high-colored or wine-colored like the fruits. It suggests that the whole plant tends toward an equal richness and maturity and to become one flower. It is the blush of its evening sky. Its juices are no longer crude. I have seen some red leaves on the low choke-berry. Now begins the vintage of their juices. Nature is now a Bacchanal, drunk with the wines of a thousand plants and berries.

The rudbeckia must have been out at least a week or more; half the buds have opened. Cranberries show red cheeks, and some are wholly red, like varnished cherry wood. Yesterday I ate early summer apples. The huckleberries were many of them burst open in consequence of the copious rains. And now it begins to rain again and compels us to return.

Aug. 7. Sunday. P. M. — To Fair Haven Hill *via* Hubbard's Grove.

The krigia has bloomed again. The purple gerardia now fairly out, which I found almost out last Sunday in another place. Elder-berries begin to be ripe, bending their stems. I also see *Viburnum dentatum* berries just beginning to turn on one side. Their turning or ripening looks like decay, — a dark spot, — and so does the rarely ripe state of the naked viburnum and the sweet; but we truly regard it as a ripening still, and not falsely a decaying as when we describe the tints of the autumnal foliage.

I think that within a week I have heard the alder cricket, — a clearer and shriller sound from the leaves in low grounds, a clear shrilling out of a cool moist

shade, an autumnal sound. The year is in the grasp of the crickets, and they are hurling it round swiftly on its axle. Some wasps (I am not sure there's more than one) are building a nest in my room, of mud, these days, buzzing loudly while at work, but at no other time. Often and often I hear the cool twitter of the goldfinch passing over, — a sound one with that of the alder cricket, — and the bobolink's *link link.* How much of spring there is brought back in a young bluebird's plaintive peep!

The tall buttercup lingers still and the houstonia, not to mention the marsh speedwell and the slender bellflower.

Now for the herbs, — the various mints. The pennyroyal is out abundantly on the hills. I do not scent these things enough. Would it not be worth the while to devote a day to collecting the mountain mint, and another to the peppermint?

How trivial and uninteresting and wearisome and unsatisfactory are all employments for which men will pay you money! The ways by which you may get money all lead downward. To have done anything by which you earned money merely is to have been truly idle. If the laborer gets no more than the wages his employer pays him, he is cheated, he cheats himself. Those services which the world will most readily pay for, it is most disagreeable to render. You are paid for being something less than a man. The state will pay a genius only for some service which it is offensive to him to render. Even the poet-laureate would rather not have to celebrate the accidents of royalty.[1]

[1] [*Cape Cod, and Miscellanies,* pp. 458, 459; *Misc.,* Riv. 257, 258.]

Dangle-berries have begun. Wormwood perhaps here and not before.

It is worth the while to walk in wet weather; the earth and leaves are strewn with pearls. When I came forth it was cloudy and from time to time drizzling weather, but remarkably still (and warm enough), soothing and inducing reflection. The river is dark and smooth these days, reflecting no brightness but dark clouds, and the goldfinch is heard twittering over; though presently a thicker mist or mizzle falls, and you are prepared for rain. The river and brooks have somewhat overflown their banks, and water inundates the grass and weeds, making it look late and cool. The stillness and the shade enable you to collect and concentrate your thoughts.

I see the leaves of the two smallest johnsworts reddening. The common johnswort is quite abundant this year and still yellows the fields. I see everywhere in sandy fields the blue-curls, knocked off by the rain, strewing the ground. As I was walking along a hillside the other day, I smelled pennyroyal, but it was only after a considerable search that I discovered a single minute plant, which I had trodden on, the only one near. When, yesterday, a boy spilled his huckleberries in the pasture, I saw that Nature was making use of him to disperse her berries, and I might have advised him to pick another dishful.[1] The three kinds of

[1] ["Then there were huckleberrying parties. These were under the guidance of Thoreau, because he alone knew the precise locality of every variety of the berry. I recall an occasion when little Edward Emerson, carrying a basket of fine huckleberries, had a fall and spilt them all. Great was his distress, and our offers of berries could not

epilobium grow rankly where Hubbard burned his swamp this year, also erechthites. I think that I have observed that this last is a true fireweed.

Is it not as language that all natural objects affect the poet? He sees a flower or other object, and it is beautiful or affecting to him because it is a symbol of his thought, and what he indistinctly feels or perceives is matured in some other organization. The objects I behold correspond to my mood.

The past has been a remarkably wet week, and now the earth is strewn with fungi. The earth itself is mouldy. I see a white mould in the path. Great toadstools stand in the woods, but the mushroom growth of a night is already attacked by many worms and insects. I see in the pasture grass in many places small white roundish fungi, like eggs. Methinks the mosquitoes are not a very serious evil till the somewhat *cool* muggy dog-day nights, such as we have had of late.

I was struck by the perfect neatness, as well as elaborateness and delicacy, of a lady's dress the other day. She wore some worked lace or gauze over her bosom, and I thought it was beautiful, if it indicated an equal inward purity and delicacy, — if it was the soul she dressed and treated thus delicately.

console him for the loss of those gathered by himself. But Thoreau came, put his arm around the troubled child, and explained to him that if the crop of huckleberries was to continue it was necessary that some should be scattered. Nature had provided that little boys should now and then stumble and sow the berries. We shall have a grand lot of bushes and berries in this spot, and we shall owe them to you. Edward began to smile." — Moncure Daniel Conway, *Autobiography*, Boston, 1904, vol. i, p. 148.]

Before I came out, I saw a bee at work in a flower again in spite of mist and cloud. And here again, far in the fields by the river-bank under Fair Haven, I heard a faint but all-pervading music, while passing with care amid the dripping bushes, but did not know whether it was a distant horn or some bee about a flower near at hand. It is so still that the bees' hum is now surely heard, for they still persist in making honey. I see the tall anemone abundant and fresh yet, — both its flower and teasel-shaped bur. Mists, but not driving.

Here is the barber sailing up the still, dark, cloud-reflecting river in the long boat which he built so elaborately himself, with two large sails set. He is quite alone thus far from town, and so quiet and so sensibly employed, — bound to Fair Haven Bay, instead of meeting comrades in a shop on the Mill-Dam or sleeping away his Sabbath in a chamber, — that I think of him as having experienced religion. I know so much good of him, at least, that one dark, still Sunday he sailed alone from the village to Fair Haven Bay. What chance was there to serve the devil by that excursion? If he had had a companion I should have had some doubts, — but being alone, it seemed communion day with him.

When I see, as now climbing Fair Haven, the hills covered with huckleberry and blueberry bushes bent to the ground with fruit, — so innocent and palatable a fruit, — I think of them as fruits fit to grow on Olympus, the ambrosia of the gods, and am reminded of *Vaccinium Vitis-Idæa*. It does not occur to me at first that where such a thought is suggested is Mt.

Olympus and that I who taste these berries am a god. Why, in his only royal moments, should man abdicate his throne?

Lespedeza capitata at Lupine Bank, maybe a day or two, but I should say later than the *polystachya*. Its leaves longer and more pointed. The birds for some weeks have not sung as in the spring. Do I not already hear the jays with more distinctness, as in the fall and winter? I hear the chewink still. The narrow-leaved violet lespedeza, not yet.

In the open oak wood beneath the Cliff, in the steep path and by its side, the *Gerardia quercifolia* and also *flava*. The former is glaucous and all the leaves much cut, rather pinnate, as I remember, somewhat like Roman wormwood, but the calyx-lobes triangular and not more than a third or a fourth the length of the calyx-tube. The peduncles longer than the calyx. It differs from Gray's *G. quercifolia* in the calyx-lobes not being long and linear. I will put it with *G. flava*. These are both among the most remarkable flowers at present, so large and butter-yellow. Very rich they look, with their great trumpets. A bee has eaten a round hole in the side of an unopened flower. How few flowers and fruits blossom and ripen without being deformed by worms and insects! You must search long for perfect specimens. The panicled hieracium is abundant there, and has been open probably a few days, — two or three.

I find the *Solidago odora* out by the path to foot of cliffs beyond Hayden's, maybe twenty or thirty rods into woods about the summit level. It is said to have the odor of anise. It is somewhat like that of sassafras bark. It must be somewhat dried and then bruised. The rough goldenrod (*Solidago altissima*), a day or two. I will call that sharply serrate narrow or linear(?)-lanceolate leafed, smooth-stemmed, very *tall* goldenrod, with a large, broad, dense pyramidal head or panicle drooping every way, which grows under the railroad bank against Ebby Hubbard's land, the *S. arguta* for the present. It has been out, say one week or more.

Aug. 8. 5 A. M. — Up railroad.

The nabalus, which may have been out one week elsewhere. Also rough hawkweed, and that large aster-like flower *Diplopappus umbellatus*, a day or two. Smooth speedwell again. Erechthites. Columbine again. The first watermelon. *Aster patens* and *Aster lævis*, both a day or two.

Aug. 9. *Sedum Telephium*, garden orpine or live-for-ever, in my pitcher.

P. M. — To hibiscus and liatris and Beck Stow's.

The hibiscus which has escaped the mowers shows a little color. I am rather surprised that it escapes the mowers at all. The river is still much swollen by the rains and cooled, and the current is swifter; though it is quite hot this afternoon, with a close, melting heat. I see an empty hay-team slowly crossing the river, in the shallowest place. The oxen are half concealed, but the driver rides high and dry. The cattle must enjoy the coolness of the water. They have not got more than half the hay out of the meadows yet, and now they

are so wet I see but one team there. Much grass will be lost. If you carelessly grasp and let slip through your hand a blade of this cut-grass as you walk, it will often cut your fingers seriously. I forded the river and, for the experiment, tried swimming with one hand while I held up all my clothes with the other, for a short distance.

The *Hieracium Canadense* is out and is abundant at Peter's well. I also find one or two heads of the liatris. Perhaps I should have seen it a *few* days earlier, if it had not been for the mower. It has the aspect of a Canada thistle at a little distance. How fatally the season is advanced toward the fall! I am not surprised now to see the small rough sunflower. There is much yellow beside now in the fields. How beautiful now the early goldenrods (*Solidago stricta*), rising above the wiry grass of the Great Fields in front of Peter's where I sit (which is not worth cutting), not solid yellow like the sunflower, but little pyramidal or sheaf-like golden clouds or mists, supported by almost invisible leafy columns, which wave in the wind, like those elms which run up very tall and slender without a branch and fall over like a sheaf on every side! They give a very indefinite but rich, mellow, and golden aspect to the field. They are the more agreeable for the indistinctness of their outline, — these pillars of fire, clouds which glow only on one side. The *nemoralis*, just opening, with its one-sided, curved, and dense panicle, is more concealed by the grass. The field is ripe.

Next into Heywood's blueberry swamp. I spend the forenoon in my chamber, writing or arranging my

Vol. V

papers, and in the afternoon I walk forth into the fields and woods. I turn aside, perchance, into some withdrawn, untrodden swamp, and find these bilberries, large and fair, awaiting me in inexhaustible abundance, for I have no tame garden. They embody for me the essence and flavor of the swamp, — cool and refreshing, of various colors and flavors. I prefer the large blue, with a bloom on them, and slightly acid ones. I taste and am strengthened. This is the season of small fruits. I trust, too, that I am maturing some small fruit as palatable in these months, which will communicate my flavor to my kind. Here they hang for many weeks unchanged, in dense clusters, half a dozen touching each other, — black, blue, and intermediate colors. Our appreciation of their flavor commonly prevents our observing their beauty, though we admire the color of the holly berries which are their neighbors. If they were poisonous, we should hear more of their beauty to the eye.

You hear the peculiar scream of young hawks now-adays, — the marsh hawks, reddish beneath, which have not their perfect plumage. I plucked a great toad-stool to-day, nine inches in diameter and five high, with a stem like the bole of an oak, swelling above and below, and at the smallest one and a half inches in diameter; its top slightly curving like a great election cake. Saw pigeons the other day (August 5).

Aug. 10. 5 A. M. — I hear a warbling vireo, golden robin, red-eye, and peawais.

August, royal and rich. Green corn now, and melons

have begun. That month, surely, is distinguished when melons ripen. July could not do it. What a moist, fertile heat now! I see naked viburnum berries beginning to turn. Their whiteness faintly blushing.

Alcott spent the day with me yesterday. He spent the day before with Emerson. He observed that he had got his wine and now he had come after his venison. Such was the compliment he paid me. The question of a livelihood was troubling him. He knew of nothing which he could do for which men would pay him. He could not compete with the Irish in cradling grain. His early education had not fitted him for a clerkship. He had offered his services to the Abolition Society, to go about the country and speak for freedom as their agent, but they declined him. This is very much to their discredit; they should have been forward to secure him. Such a connection with him would confer unexpected dignity on their enterprise. But they cannot tolerate a man who stands by a head above them. They are as bad — Garrison and Phillips, etc. — as the overseers and faculty of Harvard College. They require a man who will train well *under* them. Consequently they have not in their employ any but small men, — trainers.

P. M. — To Walden and Saw Mill Brook.

These days are very warm, though not so warm as it was in June. The heat is furnace-like while I am climbing the steep hills covered with shrubs on the north of Walden, through sweet-fern as high as one's head. The goldfinch sings *er, twe, twotter twotter*. I see again the *Aster patens* (*amplexicaulis* of Bigelow), though this has no branches nor minute leaves atop. Yet it differs from the *A. undulatus*, not yet out plainly, in that the latter's lower leaves are petioled and hearted, with petioles winged at base. Find the *Arabis Canadensis*, or sickle-pod, on Heywood Peak, nearly out of bloom. Never saw it before. New plants spring up where old woods are cut off, having formerly grown here, perchance. Many such rarer plants flourish for a few years in such places before they are smothered. I have also found here, for example, round-leaved and naked-flowered desmodium and *Desmodium lævigatum* (??) and *Gnaphalium decurrens* and queria. Toadstools, which are now very abundant in the woods since the rain, are of various colors, — some red and shining, some polished white, some regularly brown-spotted, some pink, some light-blue, — buttons. The *Ranunculus repens* numerously out about Britton's Spring. A small red maple there, seven or eight feet high, all turned scarlet. It is glorious to see those great shining high blackberries, now partly ripe there, bending the bushes in moist, rocky sprout-lands, down amid the strong, bracing scented, tender ferns, which you crush with your feet. The whorled polygala in the Saw Mill Brook Path, beyond the *Desmodium paniculatum*, may have been out as long as the caducous. Is not that small narrow fern I find on Conantum about rocks ebony spleenwort? Now in fruit. The trillium fruit (varnished and stained cherry wood) now ripe. Boehmeria in prime, for long time. Cohush berries ripe. By Everett's wall beyond Cheney's, small rough sunflowers, six feet high, with many branches and flowers. Saw an

Vol. V

alder locust this morning. Hear a quail now. Of late, and for long time, only the *link, link* of bobolink.

Aug. 11. 5 A. M. — Up North Branch.

A considerable fog. The weeds still covered by the flood, so that we have no *Bidens Beckii. B. chrysanthemoides* just out. The small, dull, lead-colored berries of the *Viburnum dentatum* now hang over the water. The *Amphicarpæa monoica* appears not to have bloomed. Chickweed (*Stellaria media*) appears the most constant flower and most regardless of seasons. Cerastium blooms still. Button-bush and mikania now in prime, and cardinals. Lilies rather scarce (?), but methinks less infested with insects. The river sprinkled with meadow-hay afloat.

P. M. — To Conantum.

This is by some considered the warmest day of the year thus far; but, though the weather is melting hot, yet the river having been deepened and cooled by the rains, we have none of those bathing days of July, '52. Yesterday or day before, I heard a strange note, methought from somebody's poultry, and looking out saw, I think a bittern, go squawking over the yard — from the river southwestward. A bittern, flying over, mingles its squawk with the cackling of poultry. Did I not hear a willet yesterday? At the Swamp Bridge Brook, flocks of cow troopials now about the cows. These and other blackbirds, flying in flocks now, make a great chattering, and also the bobolinks. What a humming of insects about the sweet-scented clethra blossoms, —

honey-bees and others, and flies and various kinds of wasps!

I see some naked viburnum berries red and some purple now. There are berries which men do not use, like choke-berries, which here in Hubbard's Swamp grow in great profusion and blacken the bushes. How much richer we feel for this unused abundance and superfluity! Nature would not appear so rich, the profusion so rich, if we knew a use for everything.

Plums and grapes, about which gardeners make such an ado, are in my opinion poor fruits compared with melons.

The great rains have caused those masses of small green high blueberries, which commonly do not get ripe, to swell and ripen, so that their harvest fulfills the promise of their spring. I never saw so many, — even in swamps where a fortnight ago there was no promise.

What a helpless creature a horse is out of his element or off his true ground! Saw John Potter's horse mired in his meadow, which has been softened by the rains. His small hoofs afford no support. He is furious, as if mad, and is liable to sprain himself seriously. His hoofs go through the crust like stakes, into the soft batter beneath, though the wheels go well enough. Woodbine is reddening in some places, and ivy too. Collinsonia just begun.

Found —— rather garrulous (his breath smelled of rum). Was complaining that his sons did not get married. He told me his age when he married (thirty-odd years ago), how his wife bore him eight children and

then died, and in what respect she proved herself a true woman, etc., etc. I saw that it was as impossible to speak of marriage to such a man — to the mass of men — as of poetry. Its advantages and disadvantages are not such as they have dreamed of. Their marriage is prose or worse. To be married at least should be the one poetical act of a man's life. If you fail in this respect, in what respect will you succeed? The marriage which the mass of men comprehend is but little better than the marriage of the beasts. It would be just as fit for such a man to discourse to you on the love of flowers, thinking of them as hay for his oxen.

The difference between men affects every phase of their lives, so that at last they cannot communicate with each other. An old man of average worth, who spoke with the downrightness and frankness of age, not exaggerating aught, said he was troubled about his water, etc., — altogether of the earth.

Evening draws on while I am gathering bundles of pennyroyal on the further Conantum height. I find it amid the stubble mixed with blue-curls and, as fast as I get my hand full, tie it into a fragrant bundle. Evening draws on, smoothing the waters and lengthening the shadows, now half an hour or more before sundown. What constitutes the charm of this hour of the day? Is it the condensing of dews in the air just beginning, or the grateful increase of shadows in the landscape? Some fiat has gone forth and stilled the ripples of the lake; each sound and sight has acquired ineffable beauty. How agreeable, when the sun shines at this angle, to stand on one side and look down on flourishing sprout-lands or copses, where the cool shade is mingled in greater proportion than before with the light! Broad, shallow lakes of shadow stretch over the lower portions of the top of the woods. A thousand little cavities are filling with coolness. Hills and the least inequalities in the ground begin to cast an obvious shadow. The shadow of an elm stretches quite across the meadow. I see pigeons (?) in numbers fly up from the stubble. I hear some young bluebird's plaintive warble near me and some young hawks uttering a pulsing scream from time to time across the pond, to whom life is yet so novel. From far over the pond and woods I hear also a farmer calling loudly to his cows, in the clear still air, "Ker, ker, ker, ker."

What shall we name this season? — this very late afternoon, or very early evening, this severe and placid season of the day, most favorable for reflection, after the insufferable heats and the bustle of the day are over and before the dampness and twilight of evening! The serene hour, the Muses' hour, the season of reflection! It is commonly desecrated by being made tea-time. It begins perhaps with the very earliest condensation of moisture in the air, when the shadows of hills are first observed, and the breeze begins to go down, and birds begin again to sing. The pensive season. It is earlier than the "chaste eve" of the poet. Bats have not come forth. It is not twilight. There is no dew yet on the grass, and still less any early star in the heavens. It is the turning-point between afternoon and evening. The few sounds now heard, far or near, are delicious. It is not more dusky and obscure, but clearer than

before. The clearing of the air by condensation of mists more than balances the increase of shadows. Chaste eve is merely *preparing* with "dewy finger" to draw o'er all "the gradual dusky veil." Not yet "the plough-man homeward plods his weary way," nor owls nor beetles are abroad. It is a season somewhat earlier than is celebrated by the poets. There is not such a sense of lateness and approaching night as they describe. I mean when the first emissaries of Evening come to smooth the lakes and streams. The poet arouses himself and collects his thoughts. He postpones tea indefinitely. Thought has taken her siesta. Each sound has a broad and deep relief of silence.

Aug. 12. 9 A. M. — To Conantum by boat, berrying, with three ladies.

You now see and hear no red-wings along the river as in spring. See the blue herons opposite Fair Haven Hill, as if they had bred here. This and the last day or two *very* hot. Now at last, methinks, the most melting season of this year, though I think it is hardly last year's *bathing* time, because the water is higher. There is very little air over the water, and when I dip my head in it for coolness, I do not feel any coolness. The *Eupatorium sessilifolium* has been out a day or two on the side-hill grove at Bittern Cliff; very similar its leaves and form to the small sunflower. *Desmodium Canadense* (?), apparently a good while; perhaps with the earliest. Never saw it before. Has dense racemes of large flowers and pods. In the same place. I find, on the Cliff there, a *Gerardia quercifolia* which answers to

Vol. V

the book (Gray), though I have not perhaps the *lowest* leaves. It has the linear-lanceolate segments of calyx. My last had not, though it was glaucous and was much more cut-leaved. There are varieties of the glaucous, then. They are both less densely spiked than the *flava*. Panicled cornel berries begin. The river cornel berries just beginning in this sunny place. *Chelone glabra* also. The round-leaved desmodium, a good while, and still on the hillside beyond the elm; perhaps ten days. Was that a thistle-down over the river, without the seed? [1] Carried watermelons for drink. What more refreshing and convenient! This richest wine in a convenient cask, and so easily kept cool! No foreign wines could be so grateful. The first muskmelon to-day. If you would cool a watermelon, do not put it in water, which keeps the heat in, but cut it open and set it in a cellar or in the shade. [2] If you have carriage, carry these green bottles of wine. A good many lilies yet rested in the shade under the bridges.

Aug. 13. The last was a melting night, and a carnival for mosquitoes. Could I not write meditations under a bridge at midsummer? The last three or four days less dogdayish. We paused under each bridge yesterday, — we who had been sweltering on the quiet waves, — for the sake of a little shade and coolness, holding on by the piers with our hands. Now and then a muskrat made the water boil, which dove or came up near by. They will move so suddenly in the water when alarmed as to make quite a report.

[1] Yes.　　[2] Or in a draught.

P. M. — To hibiscus by boat.

Hibiscus just beginning to open, its large cylindrical buds, as long as your finger, fast unrolling. They look like loosely rolled pink cigars. Rowed home in haste before a black approaching storm from the northeast, which was slightly cooling the air. How grateful when, as I backed through the bridges, the breeze of the storm blew through the piers, rippling the water and slightly cooling the sultry air! How fast the black cloud came up, and passed over my head, proving all wind! Gardeners complain that their fruit is fast rotting. We have had such wet and then moist, sultry weather that apples and plums ripen and decay very fast. Sicyos well out, and probably began when I saw it before.

Aug. 14. *Sunday.* 5 A. M. — To Cliffs.

The toads probably ceased about the time I last spoke of them. Bullfrogs, also, I have not heard for a long time.

I perceive the scent of the *earliest* ripe apples in my walk. How it surpasses all their flavors! *Lespedeza violacea* var. *angustifolia* at Cliffs, *a day or two*. The bushy gerardia makes a show there now. When I came out on to the wet rock by the juniper, all green with moss and with the driving mists beneath me, — for the sun did not come out till seven, — it reminded me of mountain-tops which I have visited.

P. M. — To Walden, Saw Mill Brook, Flint's Pond.

Locust days. — sultry and sweltering. I hear them even till sunset. The usually invisible but far-heard locust. In Thrush Alley a lespedeza out of bloom, with downy stem two feet high, and oblanceolate leaves one half by one and three quarters inches, and dry pods the whole length in the axils, as if between *L. capitata* and *violacea*.

I find on Heywood Peak two similar desmodiums of apparently the same date, — one that of July 31st, which I will call for the present *D. Dillenii*, two or three feet high, curving upward, many stems from a centre, with oval-lanceolate leaves, one to two inches long, and a long, loose, open panicle of flowers, which turn blue-green in drying, stem somewhat downy and upper sides of leaves smooth and silky to the lips; the other, which I will call *D. Marylandicum*, of similar habit (and date), but a little smaller and the leaves rhombic ovate and blunt, and some of the lower round, about three quarters of an inch long, and *stem quite smooth*, or some a little roughened; also by Woodside Path to White Pond; flowers turn blue-green in drying.

In the low woodland paths full of rank weeds, there are countless great fungi of various forms and colors, the produce of the warm rains and muggy weather of a week ago, now rapidly dissolving. One great one, more than a foot in diameter, with a stem $2\frac{1}{2}+$ inches through and 5 inches high, and which has sprung up since I passed here on the 10th, is already sinking like lead into that portion already melted. The ground is covered with foul spots where they have dissolved, and for *most* of my *walk* the air is tainted with a musty, carrion-like odor, in some places very offensive, so that I at first suspected a dead horse or cow. They impress me

like humors or pimples on the face of the earth, toddy-blossoms, by which it gets rid of its corrupt blood. A sort of excrement they are. It never occurred to me before to-day that those different forms belong to one species. Some I see just pushing up in the form of blunt cones, thrusting the leaves aside, and, further along, some which are perfectly flat on top, probably the same in full bloom, and others decaying and curved up into a basin at the edges. This misty and musty dog-day weather has lasted now nearly a month, as I remember, beginning gradually from the middle of July.

The *Desmodium paniculatum*[1] which was not out on the 10th, now, say the 12th, by Saw Mill Brook Path. The *Aster acuminatus* in the copse near by. I found it last year, but where?[2] I find no grass balls yet. The dangle-berry found now, on tall glaucous-leaved bushes in low ground, is the handsomest of our gaylussacias, — smooth, round, and blue, larger than most, but with a tough skin and perhaps a slight astringency. Altogether a very handsome bush and berry. I hear no wood thrushes for a week. The pea-wai still, and sometimes the golden robin. Methinks the reign of the milkweeds is over.

Aug. 15. Rain again in the night, but now clear. Though the last week has been remarkably warm, the warmest in the year, the river, owing to the rains, has not been warm enough for perfect bathing, as in July,

[1] *Vide* August 16th.
[2] On Pack Monadnock; also near *Aster Radula* in Potter's Swamp, three feet high.

'52. It was lowest (thus far) in July this year, before these rains. It has been melting weather; hundreds sunstruck in New York. Sultry, mosquitoey nights, with both windows and door open, and scarcely a sheet to be endured. But now it is cooler at last.

P. M. — To White Pond *via* Dugan's.

The air is somewhat cooler and beautifully clear at last after all these rains. Instead of the late bluish mistiness, I see a distinct, dark shade under the edge of the woods, the effect of the luxuriant foliage seen through the clear air. The vision goes bounding buoyantly far over the plains. It is a pleasure to look at the washed woods far away. You see every feature of the white pine grove with distinctness, — the stems of the trees, then the dark shade, then their fresh sunlit outsides. The mists are washed and cleared away, and behind them is seen the offspring of the rank vegetation which they nourished, an inky darkness as of night under the edge of the woods and the hedges, now at noonday heralding the evening of the year. The fields are remarkably green with a short, firm sward, and the crickets chirp with a still more autumnal sound.

Bathed at Clamshell Hill. There are perhaps four clams there under each foot. It will be long before the native clam will be extinct, like the Wellfleet oysters. That long, ~~~~~ crinkled red gall on shrub oak ~~~~~ stems. *Bidens frondosa.* More of the *Desmodium Marylandicum* (it is pretty plainly this), in the wood-side path to White Pond. The leaves of a rubus scored by some worm or insect, *i. e.* eaten half through, leaving whitish, serpen-

tine, ribbon-like lines, doubling on themselves. Some have looked [to] find some mystic alphabet in such things. Hips are reddening.

Aug. 16. P. M. — To Flint's Pond with Mr. Conway. Started a woodcock in the woods. Also saw a large telltale, I think yellow-shanks, whose note I at first mistook for a jay's, giving the alarm to some partridges. The *Polygonum orientale*, probably some days, by Turnpike Bridge, a very rich rose-color large flowers, distinguished by its salver-shaped upper sheaths. It is a color as rich, I think, as that of the cardinal-flower. *Desmodium paniculatum* in the wood-path northeast of Flint's Pond. Its flowers turn blue-green in drying.

Yesterday also in the Marlborough woods, perceived everywhere that offensive mustiness of decaying fungi.

How earthy old people become, — mouldy as the grave! Their wisdom smacks of the earth. There is no foretaste of immortality in it. They remind me of earthworms and mole crickets.[1]

Aug. 17. Rain in forenoon.

The high blackberries are now in their prime; the richest berry we have. That wild black currant by Union Turnpike ripe (in gardens some time). The knapweed now conspicuous, like a small thistle. Did I set it down too early? Rain, rain, rain again! Good for grass and apples; said to be bad for potatoes, making them rot; makes the fruit now ripening decay, — apples, etc.

[1] [Channing, p. 327.]

Aug. 18. Rain again.

P. M. — To Great Fields.

Many leaves of the cultivated cherry are turned yellow, and a very *few* leaves of the elm have fallen, — the dead or prematurely ripe. The abundant and repeated rains since this month came in have made the last fortnight and more seem like a rainy season in the tropics, — warm, still copious rains falling straight down, contrasting with the cold, driving spring rains. Now again I am caught in a heavy shower in Moore's pitch pines on edge of Great Fields, and am obliged to stand crouching under my umbrella till the drops turn to streams, which find their way through my umbrella, and the path up the hillside is all afloat, a succession of puddles at different levels, each bounded by a ridge of dead pine-needles. An Irishman, getting out stumps and roots in Moore's Swamp, at first squatted behind a wood-pile, but, being wet to his skin, now stands up and moves about for warmth. Melons crack open before they are sweet. Is not that variety of the ambrosia going to seed by Brown's bars in Sleepy Hollow the *heterophylla?* [1] with short, pyramidal purplish spikes and dark-green entire lanceolate leaves above.

What means this sense of lateness that so comes over one now, — as if the rest of the year were down-hill, and if we had not performed anything before, we should not now? The season of flowers or of promise may be said to be over, and now is the season of fruits; but where is our fruit? The night of the year is approaching. What have we done with our talent? All nature

[1] No ; one form of the common.

prompts and reproves us. How early in the year it begins to be late! The sound of the crickets, even in the spring, makes our hearts beat with its awful reproof, while it encourages with its seasonable warning. It matters not by how little we have fallen behind; it seems irretrievably late. The year is full of warnings of its shortness, as is life. The sound of so many insects and the sight of so many flowers affect us so, — the creak of the cricket and the sight of the prunella and autumnal dandelion. They say, " For the night cometh in which no man may work."

Aug. 19. *Friday.* 9 A. M. — To Sudbury by boat with W. E. C.

Cooler weather. Last Sunday we were sweltering here and one hundred died of the heat in New York; to-day they have fires in this village. After more rain, with wind in the night, it is now clearing up cool. There is a broad, clear crescent of blue in the west, slowly increasing, and an agreeable autumnal coolness, both under the high, withdrawn clouds and the edges of the woods, and a considerable wind wafts us along with our one sail and two umbrellas, sitting in thick coats. I was going to sit and write or mope all day in the house, but it seems wise to cultivate animal spirits, to embark in enterprises which employ and recreate the whole body. Let the divine spirits like the huntsman with his bugle accompany the animal spirit that would fain range the forest and meadow. Even the gods and goddesses, Apollo and Diana, are found in the field, though they are superior to the dog and the deer.

Vol. V

The river is full and overflowing, though there are still a few lilies and pontederias left. The wind comes from the northwest and is bracing and encouraging, and we can now sail up the stream. Flocks of bobolinks go tinkling along about the low willows, and swallows twitter, and a kingbird hovers almost stationary in the air, a foot above the water. The weeds which rise above the water now bend up-stream. The rich red *Polygonum amphibium* var. *terrestre* (?), — I suppose, for it rises sometimes two feet erect and is slightly hairy and leaves not commonly heart-shaped. Also probably the variety *aquaticum* just appearing above water in midstream, where it floats.[1] Both of these probably two or three days at most; but all weeds are wholly or partially drowned. Start up three blue herons in the meadow under Fair Haven, which fly heavily like bitterns, with their breast-bones projecting like a broad keel, — or was it their necks curled up?

Mowing in Conant's meadow by Fair Haven. These mowers must often find the bittern's eggs. On entering Fair Haven with a fair wind, scare up two ducks behind the point of the Island. Saw three or four more in the afternoon. Also I hear from over the pond the clear metallic scream of young hawks, so common at this season, probably marsh hawks. Buttercups [2] are now abundant in Lee's meadow. Is it the *repens?* The pads are mostly eaten through and through and covered with water, and I see many of their wrecks drifting down the stream, and the pontederia leaves are already

[1] Doubtful if I have yet distinguished them.
[2] Were they not fall dandelions?

half of them turned brown and shrivelled dry, before any frosts! Why should they decay so soon, like skunk-cabbage leaves? The fall has come to them. Thistle-down is seen in the air sometimes. Epilobium down has been flying some time also.

The sun comes out now about noon, when we are at Rice's, and the water sparkles in the clear air, and the pads reflect the sun. The dog-days seem now fairly past. The lower rank of polygonums is nearly drowned, but the higher, the *hydropiperoides*, rises still a foot or two, with its white spike and its broader leaves bending south before the wind and reflecting the light. There is much trumpet-weed along the shore.

We have passed men at work in the water a foot or more deep, saving the grass they had cut, and now we enter the broader Sudbury meadows. How clear and bright the air! The stems of trees at a distance are absolutely black and the densest shades [*sic*]. We scare up blue herons here also. As many as half a dozen different blue herons in our voyage. They are the most common large bird we see. They have got the grass from not more than a third of the meadows here, for there is much more water on them than in Concord. We left men mowing in Conant's meadow, which is as wet as the average of ours, but here we sail across the meadow, cutting off the bends in the river. Many tons stand cocked up, blackened and lost, in the water, and probably (?) they will not get the grass now standing. Either their meadows are lower referred to the river, or the river has risen higher there, — I think the former.

There are broad fields of sium with its umbels now going to seed, exactly like carrots, half a dozen rods in width along the stream, all through this meadow. The bulrushes are turning brown and falling. I see floating or just beneath the surface, along the side of the river, masses of the *Ranunculus Purshii*,[1] four or five feet through and many rods long, as if rolled together, washed up and off. The great arundo is now green with a reddish top and blades one inch wide. Methinks it is not long out of bloom.

We landed at the first cedar hills above the causeway and ate our dinner and watermelon on them. A great reddish-brown marsh hawk circling over the meadow there. How freshly, beautifully green the landscape after all these rains! The poke-berry ripe. Hear the incessant cricket of the fall now. Found a swamp full of high blueberries there, and from the hill near by looked to Nobscot, three or four miles distant. It was seen to advantage, rising green or with a glaucous tint above the slope of a near pasture which concealed all the intervening country. The great Sudbury meadows, looking north, appear elevated. Every blade and leaf has been washed by the rains, and the landscape is indescribably bright. It is light without heat, September-ish, as if reflected from the earth, such as is common in the fall. The surface of the meadows and the whole earth is like that of a great reflector to the sun, but reflecting his light more than his heat.

It is a glorious and ever-memorable day. We observe attentively the first beautiful days in the spring, but not

[1] Is it not *Bidens Beckii?*

so much in the autumn. We might expect that the first fair days after so much rain would be remarkable. It is a day affecting the spirits of men, but there is nobody to enjoy it but ourselves. What do the laborer ox and the laborer man care for the beautiful days? Will the haymaker when he comes home to-night know that this has been such a beautiful day? This day itself has been the great phenomenon, but will it be reported in any journal, as the storm is, and the heat? It is like a great and beautiful flower unnamed. I see a man trimming willows on the Sudbury causeway and others raking hay out of the water in the midst of all this clarity and brightness, but are they aware of the splendor of this day? The mass of mankind, who live in houses or shops, or are *bent* upon their labor out of doors, know nothing of the beautiful days which are passing about and around them. Is not such a day worthy of a hymn? It is such a day as mankind might spend in praising and glorifying nature. It might be spent as a natural sabbath, if only all men would accept the hint, devoted to unworldly thoughts. The first bright day of the fall, the earth reflector. The dog-day mists are gone; the washed earth shines; the cooler air braces man. No summer day is so beautiful as the fairest spring and fall days.

Went through a potato-field overrun and concealed by Roman wormwood as high as our heads. Returning, we row all the way. On the narrow meadow in Sudbury between Sherman's Bridge and the Jenkins Bend, opposite the oaks, found a new flower, the *Coreopsis rosea*, a small purplish or pale-red flower, somewhat

like a mayweed at a distance, but with linear leaves; maybe a fortnight since, for some were gone to seed. It was now nearly covered with the water. The only coreopsis I have found; rose-flowered coreopsis. It interests me not a little from its resemblance to the coreopsis of the gardens.

Entered Fair Haven at sunset. A large hawk sat on the very top of a tall white pine in Lee's Wood, looking down at us. He looked like an eagle with his full breast, or like a great cone belonging to the tree. It is their habit thus to perch on the top of the pines, and they are not readily detected. I could see him nearly half a mile off.

As the rays of the sun fell horizontally across the placid pond, they lit up the side of Baker's Pleasant Meadow Wood, which covers a hill. The different shades of green of different and the same trees, — alders, pines, birch, maple, oak, etc., — melting into one another on their rounded bosky edges, made a most glorious soft and harmonious picture, only to be seen at this season of the day and perhaps of the year. It was a beautiful green rug with lighter shadings and rounded figures like the outlines of trees and shrubs of different shades of green. In the case of a single tree there was the dark glossy green of the lower, older leaves, — the spring growth, — which hang down, fading on every side into the silvery hoariness of the younger and more downy leaves on the edges, — the fall growth, — whose under sides are seen, which stand up, and more perhaps at this hour. This was also the case with every bush along the river, — the larger glossy

dark-green watery leaves beneath and in the recesses, the upright hoary leaves whose under sides were seen on the shoots which rose above. I never saw a forest-side look more luxuriantly and at the same time freshly beautiful. These lighter shades in the rug had the effect of watered silks, — the edges lit, the breasts dark-green, almost the cast on green crops seen by moonlight.

As toward the evening of the day the lakes and streams are smooth, so in the fall, the evening of the year, the waters are smoothed more perfectly than at any other season. The day is an epitome of the year. The smaller, or green, bittern goes over. Now, while off Conantum, we have a cool, white, autumnal twilight, and as we pass the Hubbard Bridge, see the first stars.

I have already seen the cores of white pine cones stripped by the squirrels (?).

Aug. 20. P. M. — To Great Meadows.
Bidens connata (?) by pond-hole beyond Agricultural Ground; no rays yet at least. No traces of fringed gentian can I find. The liatris now in prime, — purple with a bluish reflection. A *Desmodium Canadense* (?) with large flowers spreading ascendant in the liatris hollow. Was that *Neottia* or *Spiranthes gracilis*, fifteen inches high there, without apparent leaf?

They have got nearly all the grass from the meadow. I walk down the firm bank of the river, that broad, flat firm strip between the meadow with its poor cut-grass and the stream, on which a better but wiry kind of grass grows. There is not nearly so much water here as in Sudbury. The river is higher than it has been since spring.

This day, too, has that autumnal character. I am struck by the clearness and stillness of the air, the brightness of the landscape, or, as it were, the reflection of light from the washed earth, the darkness and heaviness of the shade, as I look now up the river at the white maples and bushes, and the smoothness of the stream. If they are between you and the sun, the trees are more black than green. It must be owing to the clearness of the air since the rains, together with the multiplication of the leaves, whose effect has not been perceived during the mists of the dog-days. But I cannot account for this peculiar smoothness of the dimpled stream — unless the air is stiller than before — nor for the peculiar brightness of the sun's reflection from its surface. I stand on the south bank, opposite the black willows, looking up the full stream, which, with a smooth, almost oily and sheeny surface, comes welling and dimpling onward, peculiarly smooth and bright now at 4 P. M., while the numerous trees seen up the stream — white maples, oaks, etc. — and the bushes look absolutely black in the clear, bright light.

Aug. 21. 6 A. M. — To Island by boat.
Aster macrophyllus. Appear not to blossom generally this year.

P. M. — To Jenny Dugan's and Conantum.

Saw one of those light-green locusts about three quarters of an inch long on a currant leaf in the garden. It kept up a steady shrilling (unlike the interrupted

creak of the cricket), with its wings upright on its shoulders, all indistinct, they moved so fast. Near at hand it made my ears ache, it was so piercing, and was accompanied by a hum like that of a factory. The wings are transparent, with marks somewhat like a letter.

That which I had mistaken for *Mentha Canadensis* at Mrs. Hosmer's brook is apparently *M. piperita*, or peppermint, naturalized. It *may* have been in bloom a fortnight. It is higher-scented, with dark leaves and dark-purplish stems, and a short spike of flowers above, and not in the axils of the leaves. What I take to be *Aster patens* is a handsome light-blue aster, now abundant on the hillside by J. Hosmer's pines. The choke-cherries, which are now, and have been for some time, as ripe as they will be, actually fur the mouth, and the juice of these taken into the mouth, mixed with the saliva, is feathered like tea into which sour cream has been poured. They are a rich, fatty-looking fruit. That must be the *Aster puniceus* (which I have falsely called *longifolius*), four or five feet high and coarse and rough, commonly with a reddish stem, filling the brook behind Dugan's; out two or three days, very *pale* purplish. I see aphides like a white mildew on the alders. The *Polygonum articulatum* not yet. The *Aster lævis* is one of the most beautiful I have seen yet, especially when there are ten or twelve in a panicle, making a small rounded bunch. The *Viburnum Lentago* berries are but just *beginning* to redden on one cheek. The *Cornus paniculata* are fairly white in some places. The polygonatum berries have been a bluish-green some time. Do they turn still?

Vol. V

Methinks I have not heard a robin sing morning or evening of late, but the peawai still, and occasionally a short note from the gold robin.

The river was as low as in July, last year at this time. It is now *perhaps* two feet higher than then. The river plants are thus subject to unusual accidents. I think it was lowest this year the latter part of July before the rains.

An aster beyond Hubbard's Grove which I should call *A. Radula*, but the calyx-scales not appressed.

Aug. 22. *Monday.* P. M. — Up Assabet to Yellow Rocket Shore.

A still afternoon with a prospect of a shower in the west. The immediate edge of the river is for the most part respected by the mowers, and many wild plants there escape from year to year, being too coarse for hay. The prevailing flowers now along the river are the mikania, polygonums, trumpet-weed, cardinal, arrowhead, *Chelone glabra*, and here and there vernonia. The button-bush is out of bloom and its balls browning. On the steep hillside where the Leaning Hemlocks grow slanted over the river and from year to year falling into it, I am surprised to see that many are leaning and falling up the hill, owing to a slide which has carried their roots forward toward the water. I hear the muttering of thunder and the first drops dimple the river.

I hear but few notes of birds these days; no singing, but merely a few hurried notes or screams or twittering or peeping. I will enumerate such as I hear or see this still louring and showery afternoon. A hurried anxious

note from a robin. Heard perhaps half a dozen afterward. They flit now, accompanied by their young. A sharp, loud *che-wink* from a ground-robin. A goldfinch twitters over; several more heard afterward. A blue jay screams, and one or two fly over, showing to advantage their handsome forms, especially their regular tails, wedge-formed. Surprised to hear a very faint *bobolink* in the air; the *link, link,* once or twice later. A yellow-bird flew over the river. Swallows twittering, but flying high, — the chimney swallows and what I take to be the bank ditto. Scared up a green bittern from an oak by the riverside. Hear a peawai whose note is more like singing — as if it were still incubating — than any other. Some of the warble of the golden robin. A kingfisher, with his white collar, darted across the river and alighted on an oak. A peetweet flew along the shore and uttered its peculiar note. Their wings appear double as they fly by you, while their bill is cumbrously carried pointing downward in front. The chipping of a song sparrow occasionally heard amid the bushes. A single duck scared up. And two nighthawks flying high over the river. At twilight many bats after the showers. These birds were heard or seen in the course of three or four hours on the river, but there were not sounds enough to disturb the general stillness.

The scarlet thorn berry has been turning some time and is now edible, — an oblong squarish fruit, scarlet with yellowish specks or spaces. The black willow has already lost some of its freshness and greenness, as if burnt; it is a little yellow or brownish. It is a tree apparently without stem, light masses of foliage resting on the water, and is badly named black willow except as descriptive of its winter and spring appearance, being one of the most buoyant and ethereal of trees.

Methinks I have seen thus far this year only the *Polygonum amphibium* var. *terrestre.* The species is not abundant, but is very interesting to me, occurring at this later cooler and darker season. There is one rarely dense bed of them in the Assabet just beyond the rock by Hosmer's bound. The smooth green leaves are surmounted by very dense rich rose-red — or a very dark shade of pink — spikes three inches or more in length, six inches to two and a half feet from the water. This little red streak is detected afar. Methinks it is the handsomest of our indigenous polygonums.

The scream of young marsh hawks sounds like some notes of the jay.

Aug. 23. 6 A. M. — To Nawshawtuct.
A very clear but cool morning, all white light. The feverwort berries are yellowing and yellowed; barberries have begun to redden, and the prinos, — some of the last quite red. The *Spiranthes gracilis,* with its leafless stalk, is very common now on grassy hillsides.

August has been thus far dog-days, rain, oppressive sultry heat, and now beginning fall weather.

P. M. — Clematis Brook *via* Conantum.
Neottia or rather *Spiranthes cernua,* a few days, bank by Hubbard's meadow, by oak beyond ivy pass. This low, with long lanceolate leaves, and in low ground compared with the taller *gracilis.* More and larger by

with its recurved standard a little more than a foot high, — marching to the Holy Land, a countless host of crusaders. That field in the woods near Well Meadow, where I once thought of squatting, is full of them. The patches of rhexia or meadow-beauty which have escaped the mowers in the low grounds, where rowen is now coming forward apace, look like a little bright purple on one side of Nature's pallet, giving place to some fresh green which Nature has ground. The traveller leaves his dog to worry the woodchuck, though he himself passes on, so little advanced has man from the savage state. Anon he will go back to save him, and legislatures perchance will pass laws for his protection. Arum berries. *Smilacina racemosa* [berries] now are reddish and minutely red speckled; its leaves are commonly eaten or decayed. The *Smilacina bifolia* in some places red. Of late I notice that saw-like grass gone to seed, — a flattened row of seeds two or three inches long under a flat, leaf-like stalk, — an autumnal sight.

Pickering, in his "Races," suggests that savages, going naked, do not disperse seeds so much as civilized men. Beggar-ticks and burs (I say) do not adhere to the bare skin. Weeds especially accompany civilization. I hesitated to collect some desmodium seeds because they looked green and the plant was still in flower, but before I had gone far I found [I] had brought away many on my clothes, which suggested to me that probably as soon as the hooked hairs were stiff enough, clinging to foreign surfaces, to overcome the adherence of the pods to their stems, it will do to pluck them for seed.

meadow path beyond swimming-place. Have we the *latifolia?* The *gracilis* has its crystalline white flowers arranged in a dense spiral cone like the thread of a screw, standing out nearly at right angles with the stem, curved downward a little.

Squirrels have commenced on hazelnuts.

Observing the blackness of the foliage, especially between me and the light, I am reminded that it begins in the spring, the dewy dawn of the year, with a silvery hoary downiness, changing to a yellowish or light green, — the saffron-robed morn, — then to a pure, spotless, glossy green with light under sides reflecting the light, — the forenoon, — and now the dark green, or early afternoon, when shadows begin to increase, and next it will turn yellow or red, — the sunset sky, — and finally sere brown and black, when the night of the year sets in.

Carrion-berries just begin to be ripe. Potato-fields are full of Roman wormwood now. I am braced and encouraged by the rank growth of this aromatic plant, concealing the potato vines which are already nearly half decayed. By path from meadow through Hubbard's rear wood and sprout-lands. The now purple naked viburnum berries — numerous drooping cymes of purple berries — are now very handsome seen against the green leaves in sprout-lands. I see to-day — and may add to yesterday's list — the blue heron launch off from an oak by the river and flap or sail away with lumbering flight; also kingbirds and crows. The red-eye may be heard *faintly* in the morning.

The *Solidago nemoralis* now yellows the dry fields

I am again struck by the perfect correspondence of a day — say an August day — and the year. I think that a perfect parallel may be drawn between the seasons of the day and of the year. Perhaps after middle age man ceases to be interested in the morning and in the spring.

I see the late flowers of the cistus again!

Poke stems are now ripe. I walked through a beautiful grove of them, six or seven feet high, on the side of Lee's Cliff, where they have ripened early. Their stems are a deep, rich purple with a bloom, contrasting with the clear green leaves. Every part but the leaves is a brilliant purple (lake (?)-purple); or, more strictly speaking, the racemes without the berries are a brilliant lake-red with crimson flame-like reflections. Hence the *lacca.* Its cylindrical racemes of berries of various hues from green to dark purple, six or seven inches long, are drooping on all sides, beautiful both with and without berries, all afire with ripeness. Its stalks, thus full of purple wine, are one of the fruits of autumn. It excites me to behold it. What a success is its! What maturity it arrives [at], ripening from leaf to root! May I mature as perfectly, root and branch, as the poke! Its stems are more beautiful than most flowers. It is the emblem of a successful life, a not premature death, — whose death is an ornament to nature. To walk amid these upright branching casks of purple wine, which retain and diffuse a sunset glow, for nature's vintage is not confined to the vine! I drink it with my eyes. Our poets have sung wine, the product of a foreign plant which they never saw, as if our own plants had no juice in them more than our poets. Here are berries enough to paint the western sky with and play the Bacchanal if you will. What flutes its ensanguined stems would make, to be used in the dance! It is a royal plant. I could spend the evening of the year musing amid the poke stems.[1]

Live in each season as it passes; breathe the air, drink the drink, taste the fruit, and resign yourself to the influences of each. Let them be your only diet drink and botanical medicines. In August live on berries, not dried meats and pemmican, as if you were on shipboard making your way through a waste ocean, or in a northern desert. Be blown on by all the winds. Open all your pores and bathe in all the tides of Nature, in all her streams and oceans, at all seasons. Miasma and infection are from within, not without. The invalid, brought to the brink of the grave by an unnatural life, instead of imbibing only the great influence that Nature is, drinks only the tea made of a particular herb, while he still continues his unnatural life, — saves at the spile and wastes at the bung. He does not love Nature or his life, and so sickens and dies, and no doctor can cure him. Grow green with spring, yellow and ripe with autumn. Drink of each season's influence as a vial, a true panacea of all remedies mixed for your especial use. The vials of summer never made a man sick, but those which he stored in his cellar. Drink the wines, not of your bottling, but Nature's bottling; not kept in goat-skins or pig-skins, but the skins of a myriad

[1] [*Excursions*, pp. 254, 255; Riv. 311–313. See also *Journal*, vol. ii, pp. 489, 490.]

fair berries. Let Nature do your bottling and your pickling and preserving. For all Nature is doing her best each moment to make us well. She exists for no other end. Do not resist her. With the least inclination to be well, we should not be sick. Men have discovered — or think they have discovered — the salutariness of a few wild things only, and not of all nature. Why, "nature" is but another name for health, and the seasons are but different states of health. Some men think that they are not well in spring, or summer, or autumn, or winter; it is only because they are not *well in* them.[1]

How handsome now the cymes of *Viburnum Lentago* berries, flattish with red cheeks! The great bidens is only partially out, by the side of the brook that comes out of Deacon Farrar's Swamp and runs under the causeway east of the Corner Bridge. The flowers are all turned toward the westering sun and are two to two and a half or more inches in diameter, like sunflowers, hieroglyphics of the seasons, only to be read by the priests of Nature. I go there as to one of autumn's favorite haunts. Most poems, like the fruits, are sweetest toward the blossom end. The milkweed leaves are already yellowing. The clematis is most interesting in its present feathery state, — light, silvery, shining green. A solidago some time out, say a week, on side of Mt. Misery, like the *S. alta*, but smooth-stemmed and commonly dark-purplish. Call it *ulmifolia* for the present, though the leaves are not so broad as the elm nearly and it is not there in low ground. Looking

[1] [See *Walden*, pp. 153, 154; Riv. 216, 217.]

Vol. V

down the river valley now from Mt. Misery, an hour before sundown, I am struck with nothing so much as the autumnal coolness of the landscape and the predominance of shade. The pale yellowish-green sidesaddle-flower, probably the var. *heterophylla*, is common enough in our meadows. A sweet-william pink at bottom of Wheildon's field. I find the pods of the amphicarpæa at last. It may have blossomed three weeks ago.

Aug. 24. Another cool, autumn-like morning, also quite foggy. Rains a little in the forenoon and cloudy the rest of the day.

P. M. — To Saw Mill Brook *via* Trillium Woods.

A cool breeze blows this cloudy afternoon, and I wear a thicker coat.

The mulgedium by railroad is seven feet high, with great panicles of a regular, somewhat elliptic-lanceolate (?) form, two and a half feet long by ten inches. The *Prinos lævigatus* berries begin to redden. The farmers are beginning to clear out their ditches now.

Blue-stemmed goldenrod, apparently a few days in some places. The goldenrods which I have observed in bloom this year are (I do not remember the order exactly): (1) *stricta*, (2) *lanceolata*, (3) *arguta* (?), (4) *nemoralis*, (5) *bicolor*, (6) *odora*, (7) *altissima*, (8) *ulmifolia* (?), (9) *cæsia*. The 4th is the prevailing one and much the most abundant now. The 1st perhaps next, though it may be getting old. The *altissima* (7th) certainly next. It is just beginning to be abundant. Its tops a foot or more broad, with numerous recurved racemes on every

side, with yellow and yellowing triangular points. It is the most conspicuous of all. The *bicolor* (5th) next, though not conspicuous. The 3d, 8th, 2d, and 6th perhaps never abundant. The *cæsia* (9th) just begun.

The asters and diplopappi are about in this order: (1) *Radula*, (2) *D. cornifolius* (?), (3) *A. corymbosus*,[1] (4) *patens*, (5) *lævis*, (6) *dumosus* (?), (7) *miser*, (8) *macrophyllus*, (9) *D. umbellatus*, (10) *A. acuminatus*, (11) *puniceus*. The *patens* (4), of various forms, *some* lilac, is the prevailing blue or bluish one now, middle-sized and very abundant on dry hillsides and by wood-paths; the *lævis* next. The 1st, or *Radula*, is not abundant. (These three are all the distinctly blue ones yet.) The *dumosus* is the prevailing white one, very abundant; *miser* mixed with it. *D. umbellatus* is conspicuous enough in some places (low grounds), and *A. puniceus* beginning to be so. But *D. cornifolius*, *A. corymbosus*, *macrophyllus*, and *acuminatus* are confined to particular localities. *Dumosus* and *patens* (and perhaps *lævis*, not common enough) are the prevailing asters now.

The common large osmunda (?) is already considerably imbrowned, but the odorous dicksonia (?), which, like most ferns, blossoms later, is quite fresh. This thin, flat, beautiful fern it is which I see green under the snow.[2] I am inclined to call it the lace fern. (Peaches fairly begun.) It is a triangular web of fine lace-work surpassing all the works of art.

Solidago latifolia not yet. I see roundish silvery slate-colored spots, surrounded by a light ring, near the base of the leaves of an aster (*miser?*), one beneath

[1] Or *cordifolius*.   [2] [A mistake. See *postea*.]

another like the dropping of a bird, or as if some tincture had fallen from above. Some of the leaves of the *A. patens* are red. The alternate cornel berries, which are particularly apt to drop off early, are a dark, dull blue, not china-like. I see those of maple-leaved viburnum merely yellowish now. There grows by Saw Mill Brook a long firmer, thimble-shaped high blackberry with small grains, with more green ones still on it, which I think like the New Hampshire kind. I see some black and some greenish light slate-colored fungi. This certainly is the season for fungi. I see on the shrub oaks now caterpillars an inch and a half or more long, black with yellowish stripes, lying along the petioles, — thick living petioles. They have stripped off the leaves, leaving the acorns bare. The *Ambrina* (*Chenopodium*, Bigelow) *Botrys*, Jerusalem-oak, a worm-seed, by R. W. E.'s heater piece. The whole plant is densely branched — branches spike-like — and appears full of seed. Has a pleasant, more distinct wormwood-like odor. In a dry sprout-land (Ministerial Lot), what I will call *Solidago puberula*[1] will open in a day or two, — upright and similar to *stricta* in leaves, with a purple stem and smooth leaves, entire above, and a regular oblong appressed panicle. *Bidens chrysanthemoides*, of a small size and earlier, by Turnpike, now in prime there. I see cattle coming down from up-country. Why? Yellow Bethlehem-star still. *A. miser* (?), with purplish disk and elliptic-lanceolate leaves, serrate in middle, may be as early as *dumosus*.

[1] *Vide* Sept. 1st.

Vol. V

white seeds in a watermelon, — an immature, ineffectual meteor.

Aug. 27. Saturday. P. M. — To Walden.

Topping corn now reveals the yellowing pumpkins. Dangle-berries very large in shady copses now; seem to love wet weather; have lost their bloom. *Aster undulatus.* The decurrent gnaphalium has not long shown yellow. Perhaps I made it blossom a little too early.

September is at hand; the first month (after the summer heat) with a *burr* to it, month of early frosts; but December will be tenfold rougher. January relents for a season at the time of its thaw, and hence that liquid *r* in its name.

Aug. 28. Sunday. P. M. — To Cliffs.

See many sparrows in *flocks* with a white feather in tail! The smooth sumach leaves are fast reddening. The berries of the dwarf sumach are not a brilliant crimson, but as yet, at least, a *dull* sort of dusty or mealy crimson. As they are later, so their leaves are more fresh and green than those of the smooth species. The acorns show now on the shrub oaks. A cool, white, autumnal evening.

Aug. 29. The 25th and 26th I was surveying Tuttle's farm. The northeast side bounds on the Mill Brook and its tributary and is very irregular. I find, after surveying accurately the windings of several brooks and of the river, that their meanders are not such regular serpentine

Aug. 25. Warmer to-day. Surveying Tuttle's farm. From the extreme eastern side of his farm, looking up the valley of the Mill Brook, in which direction it is about two miles to anything that can be called high ground (say at E. Wood's), I was surprised to see the whole outline and greater part of the base of Wachusett, though you stand in a low meadow. It is because of the great distance of the hills westward. It is a fuller view of this mountain than many of our hills afford. Seen through this lower stratum, the mountain is a very dark blue.

I am struck by the rank growth of weeds at this season. Passing over Tuttle's farm, only one field removed from the Turnpike, where various kinds of tall, rank weeds are rampant, half concealing the lusty crops, — low ground which has only been cultivated twice before, where turnips and algæ (?) contend for places, fire-weeds (senecio), thoroughwort, *Eupatorium purpureum*, and giant asters, etc., suggest a vigor in the soil, an Ohio fertility, which I was not prepared for, which on the sandy turnpike I had not suspected, — it seemed to me that I had not enough frequented and considered the products, perchance, of these fertile grounds which the farmers have enriched. He is continually selecting a virgin soil and adding the contents of his barn-yards to it.

Aug. 26. The fall dandelion is as conspicuous and abundant now in Tuttle's meadow as buttercups in the spring. It takes their place. Saw the comet in the west to-night. It made me think of those imperfect

curves as is commonly supposed, or at least represented. They flow as much in a zigzag as serpentine manner. The eye is very much deceived when standing on the brink, and one who had only surveyed a brook so would be inclined to draw a succession of pretty regular serpentine curves. But, accurately plotted, the regularity disappears, and there are found to be many straight lines and sharp turns. I want no better proof of the inaccuracy of some maps than the regular curving meanders of the streams, made evidently by a sweep of the pen. No, the Meander no doubt flowed in a very crooked channel, but depend upon it, it was as much zigzag as serpentine. This last brook I observed was doubly zigzag, or compoundly zigzag; i. e., there was a zigzag on a large scale including the lesser. To the eye this meadow is perfectly level. Probably all streams are (generally speaking) far more meandering in low and level and soft ground near their mouths, where they flow slowly, than in high and rugged ground which offers more obstacles. The meadow being so level for long distances, no doubt as high in one direction as another, how, I asked myself, did the feeble brook, with all its meandering, ever find its way to the distant lower end? What kind of instinct conducted it forward in the right direction? How unless it is the relict of a lake which once stood high over all these banks, and knew the different levels of its distant shores? How unless a flow which commenced above its level first wore its channel for it? Thus, in regard to most rivers, did not lakes first find their mouths for them, just as the tide now keeps open the mouths of sluggish rivers? And who knows to what extent the sea originally channelled the submerged globe?

Walking down the street in the evening, I detect my neighbor's ripening grapes by the scent twenty rods off; though they are concealed behind his house, every passer knows of them. So, too, ever and anon I pass through a little region possessed by the fragrance of ripe apples.

Aug. 30. Tuesday. In low ground by Turnpike, a tall aster, *A. longifolius* (?), a day or two perhaps (*salicifolius* of Bigelow).[1] Saw some by river in the afternoon with sharply serrate leaves. I think that the very small and dense-flowered white or whitish aster by roadsides and riversides, with pointed scales and disk turning purplish-brown, with very many flowers on the sides of the branches or branchlets, must be *A. Tradescanti*, sometimes quite high. I have thus far confounded it with what I have called the *dumosus*, and am not sure which is the earliest. The latter has larger flowers, not so crowded, one at the end of each branchlet, and the scales more abruptly pointed.

11 A. M. — Up river to Fair Haven.

River one or two feet higher than in July. A very little wind from the south or southwest, but the water quite smooth at first. The river foliage is slightly crisped and imbrowned; I mean the black willows, button-bushes, and polygonums. The pads are for the most part eaten, decayed, and wasted away, — the white last the longest, — and the ponderias are already

[1] Abundant in Moore's Swamp, Aug. 31st.

mostly dry and blackened. Only three or four white lilies and pontederia blossoms left. The *Polygonum hydropiperoides* and the narrow-leaved and mikania are the prevailing conspicuous flowers. Others are the trumpet-weed, yellow lilies (*Kalmiana* drowned), cardinals (rather scarce), whorled utricularia, one purple one, *Polygonum amphibium*, etc. Bathed at Hubbard's Bend. The water now cold and bracing, for it has contrived to rain more or less all the month. Men raking cranberries in the meadows. Ivy berries are crisped and whitish on the rock at Bittern Cliff. The polygonatum berries are green with a bluish bloom. *Polygonum dumetorum*, apparently not long, very abundant in Tarbell's cleared swamp by roadside, also by Peter's Path, running up a tree eight or nine feet at this Cliff. Some of the river cornel berries are almost clear white on one side, the other china-blue. These and the *Viburnum Lentago* berries are now common and handsome.

The *Solidago odora* grows abundantly behind the Minott house in Lincoln. I collected a large bundle of it. Its flower is stale for the most part and imbrowned. It grows in such thick tufts that you can easily gather it. Some haws are now edible. Grapes are already ripe; I smelled them first. As I went along from the Minott house to the Bidens Brook, I was quite bewildered by the beauty and variety of the asters, now in their prime there, — *A. lævis* (large and handsome with various leaves), *patens, linariifolius*, etc. The bidens has not yet reached its greatest profusion. Why so many asters and goldenrods now? The sun has shone on the

earth, and the goldenrod is his fruit. The stars, too, have shone on it, and the asters are their fruit.

The purple balls of the carrion-flower, now open a little beneath, standing out on all sides six or eight inches from the twining stem, are very handsome. They are covered with a blue bloom, and when this is rubbed off by leaves, are a shining blackish.

Set sail homeward about an hour before sundown. The breeze blows me glibly across Fair Haven, the last dying gale of the day. No wonder men love to be sailors, to be blown about the world sitting at the helm, to shave the capes and see the islands disappear under their sterns, — gubernators to a piece of wood. It disposes to contemplation, and is to me instead of smoking.

Saw an *Aster undulatus* (?) with a very densely [?] flowered and branched top, small, pale purple. What is the *Solidago* like an *altissima* but a simple raceme and leaves much less cut?[1] It is as early as *S. altissima*. *Galium circæzans*, the broad-leaved, is now in fruit.

Nature made a highway from southwest to northeast through this town (not to say county), broad and beautiful, which attracted Indians to dwell upon it and settlers from England at last, ten rods wide and bordered by the most fertile soil in the town, a tract most abounding in vegetable and in animal life; yet, though it passes through the centre of the town, I have been upon it the livelong day and have not met a traveller. Out of twenty-odd hundred dwellers near its banks, not one has used this highway to-day for a distance of four miles at least.

[1] Probably a variety of same?

I find at this time in fruit: (1) *Polypodium vulgare*, (2) *Struthiopteris Germanica* (ostrich fern), (3) *Pteris aquilina* (common brake) (have not looked for fruit), (4) *Adiantum pedatum* (have not looked for fruit), (5) *Asplenium Trichomanes* (dwarf spleenwort), also (6) *A. ebeneum* (ebony spleenwort), (7) *Dicksonia punctilobula*, (8) *Dryopteris marginalis* (marginal shield fern), (9) *Polystichum acrostichoides* (terminal shield fern), (10) *Onoclea sensibilis* (?) (sensitive fern) (think I saw the fruit August 12th at Bittern Cliff), (11) *Lygodium palmatum* (probably still in fruit, was when I last saw it), (12) *Osmunda spectabilis* (flowering fern) (out of fruit), (13) *Osmunda cinnamomea* (?) (tall osmunda) (also out of fruit). Nos. 1, 5, 6, and 8 common at Lee's Cliff. No. 2 behind Trillium Woods, 4 at Miles Swamp, 9 at Brister's Hill. The dwarf spleenwort grows in the sharp angles of the rocks in the side of Lee's Cliff, its small fronds spreading in curved rays, its matted roots coming away in triangular masses, moulded by the rock. The ebony spleenwort stands upright against the rocks.

Aug. 31. P. M. — To Moore's Swamp.

Bidens cernua well out, the flowering one. The asters and goldenrods are now in their prime, I think. The rank growth of flowers (commonly called weeds) in this swamp now impresses me like a harvest of flowers. I am surprised at their luxuriance and profusion. The *Solidago altissima* is now the prevailing one, *i. e.* goldenrod, in low grounds where the swamp has been cleared. It occupies acres, densely rising as high as your head, with the great white umbel-like tops of the *Diplopappus umbellatus* rising above it. There are also intermixed *Solidago stricta*, erechthites (fire-weed), *Aster puniceus* and *longifolius*, *Galium asprellum* in great beds, thoroughwort, trumpet-weed, *Polygonum Hydropiper*, *Epilobium molle*, etc., etc. There has been no such rank flowering up to this. One would think that all the poison that is in the earth and air must be extracted out of them by this rank vegetation. The ground is quite mildewy, it is so shaded by them, cellar-like.

Raspberries still fresh. I see the first dogwood turned scarlet in the swamp. Great black cymes of elderberries now bend down the bushes. Saw a great black spider an inch long, with each of his legs an inch and three quarters long, on the outside of a balloon-shaped web, within which were young and a great bag. *Viola pedata* out again. Leaves of *Hypericum mutilum* red about water. *Cirsium muticum*, in Moore's Swamp behind Indian field, going out of flower; *perhaps* out three weeks. Is that very dense-flowered small white aster with short branched racemes *A. Tradescanti?* — now begun to be conspicuous. A low aster by Brown's Ditch north of Sleepy Hollow like a *Radula*, but with narrower leaves and more numerous, and scales without herbaceous tips. An orange-colored fungus.

Baird, in Patent Office Report, says, "In all deer, except, perhaps, the reindeer, if the male be castrated when the horns are in a state of perfection, these will never be shed; if the operation be performed when the head is bare, they will never be reproduced; and if done when the secretion is going on, a stunted, ill-formed, permanent horn is the result."

VII

SEPTEMBER, 1853

(ÆT. 36)

Sept. 1. Thursday. P. M. — To Dugan Desert and Ministerial Swamp.

The character of the past month, as I remember, has been, at first, very thick and sultry, dogdayish, the height of summer, and throughout very rainy, followed by crops of toadstools, and latterly, after the dogdays and most copious of the rains, autumnal, somewhat cooler, with signs of decaying or ripening foliage. The month of green corn and melons and plums and the earliest apples, — and now peaches, — of rank weeds. As July, perchance, has its spring side, so August has its autumnal side.

Was that the cackling of hens I heard, or the clicking of a very distant hand-organ?

Methinks the silvery cinquefoil is of late much more abundant. Is there any cessation to it? The green-briar berries begin to turn. Some large maples along the river are beginning to redden. I observe the stillness of the air and the smoothness of the water of late. The *Hieracium Canadense* is, methinks, the largest and handsomest flower of its genus, large as the fall dandelion; the *paniculatum* the most delicate. To-day and yesterday quite warm, or hot, again.

I am struck again and again by the richness of the

meadow-beauty lingering, though it will last some time, in little dense purple patches by the sides of the meadows. It is so low it escapes the scythe. It is not so much distinct flowers (it is so low and dense), but a colored patch on the meadow. Yet how few observe it! How, in one sense, it is wasted! How little thought the mower or the cranberry-raker bestows on it! How few girls or boys come to see it!

That small aster which I call *A. Tradescanti*, with crowded racemes, somewhat rolled or cylindrical to appearance, of small white flowers a third of an inch in diameter, with yellow disks turning reddish or purplish, is very pretty by the low roadsides, resounding with the hum of honey-bees; which is commonly despised for its smallness and commonness, — with crowded systems of little suns. The *Polygonum articulatum*, apparently not for some time yet. The large epilobium still plenty in flower in Tarbell's cleared swamp. Hazel bushes are now browned or yellowed along wall-sides in pastures; blackberry vines also are reddening. The *Solidago nemoralis* has commonly a long, sharply triangular head of small crowded flowers, evenly convex and often, if not commonly, recurved through a quarter of a circle, very handsome, solid-looking, recurved golden spear heads. But frequently it is more erect and branched. What is that alga-like plant covering the ground in Tarbell's Swamp where lately burnt over, with close mats a rod in diameter, with fruit now two or three inches high, star-like, and little cups on the green thallus?[1] I see now puffballs, now

[1] *Marchantia polymorpha.*

four inches through, turned dark from white, and ripe, fill the air with dust four or five feet high when I kick them. Saw a red squirrel cutting off white pine cones. He had strewn the ground with them, as yet untouched, under the tree. He has a *chirrup* exactly like a partridge. Have made out *Aster multiflorus* by roadside beyond Badger house; probably not long out. It is distinguished by its hoariness, and its large herbaceous spreading calyx-tips and its crowded, somewhat rigid linear leaves, not tapering at base, low with a stout stem. A solidago by Marlborough road (*S. puberula?* or *neglecta?*), *stricta*-like, but panicle upright with short erectish racemes and lower leaves serrate, and five or six inches long; not long out. Should think it *stricta* if not for form of head; more like *puberula*, though this an imperfect one, in press.[1] I think my white daisy, which is still quite fresh in some places, must be *Erigeron strigosus*, for the hairs are minute and appressed, though the rays are not twice as long as the calyx-scales. I have seen no purplish ones since spring. *Aster undulatus* begins to be common. Johnswort, the large and common, is about done. That is the common polypody whose single fronds, six or eight inches long, stand thick in moss on the shelving rock at the Island.

The river nowadays is a permanent mirror stretching without end through the meadows, and unfailingly when I look out my window across the dusty road, I see it at a distance with the herbage of its brink reflected in it. There it lies, a mirror uncracked, unsoiled.

[1] *Vide* Aug. 24th and Sept. 11th.

Plants or weeds very widely dispersed over the globe command a certain respect, like *Sonchus oleraceus*, Oregon, New Zealand, Peru, Patagonia, etc.; *Sicyos angulatus*, New Zealand, Australia, Hawaiian Islands, etc.; *Polygonum aviculare*, *Chenopodium album*, and *Polygonum Persicaria*, Oregon and Egypt; also many others, according to Pickering.

Pickering says that "the missionaries [at the Hawaiian Islands][1] regarded as one main obstacle to improvement the extremely limited views of the natives in respect to style of living; 'a little fish and a little poi, and they were content.'" But this is putting the cart before the horse, the real obstacle being their limited views in respect to the object of living. A philosopher has equally limited views in their sense, but then he is not content with material comforts, nor is it, perhaps, quite necessary that he first be glutted with them in order to become wise. "A native, I was assured, 'could be supported for less than two cents a day.'" (They had adopted the use of coin.)

The savage lives simply through ignorance and idleness or laziness, but the philosopher lives simply through wisdom. In the case of the savage, the accompaniment of simplicity is idleness with its attendant vices, but in the case of the philosopher, it is the highest employment and development. The fact for the savage, and for the mass of mankind, is that it is better to plant, weave, and build than do nothing or worse; but the fact for the philosopher, or a nation

[1] [The bracketed portion is Thoreau's.]

loving wisdom, is that it is most important to cultivate the highest faculties and spend as little time as possible in planting, weaving, building, etc. It depends upon the height of your standard, and no doubt through manual labor as a police men are educated up to a certain level. The simple style is bad for the savage because he does worse than to obtain the luxuries of life; it is good for the philosopher because he does better than to work for them. The question is whether you can bear freedom. At present the vast majority of men, whether black or white, require the discipline of labor which enslaves them for their good. If the Irishman did not shovel all day, he would get drunk and quarrel. But the philosopher does not require the same discipline; if he shovelled all day, we should receive no elevating suggestions from him.

What a literary fame is that of Æsop, — an Æsopian fame! Pickering says: "A little to the west of Celebes, the literature of the Malay nation contains a translation of the Fables of Æsop; who, according to the unsatisfactory accounts we have of him, was one of the earliest of the Greek writers. And further, the fact may be noted, that the Æsopian style of composition is still in vogue at Madagascar. (See Ellis's Madagascar.)" A fame on its way round eastward with the Malay race to this western continent! A fame that travels round the world from west to east. P. gives California to the Malay race!

There are two kinds of simplicity, — one that is akin to foolishness, the other to wisdom. The philosopher's style of living is only outwardly simple, but inwardly

Vol. V

complex. The savage's style is both outwardly and inwardly simple. A simpleton can perform many mechanical labors, but is not capable of profound thought. It was their limited view, not in respect to *style*, but to the *object* of living. A man who has equally limited views with respect to the end of living will not be helped by the most complex and refined style of living. It is not the tub that makes Diogenes, the Jove-born, but Diogenes the tub.

Sept. 2. P. M. — Collected and brought home in a pail of water this afternoon the following asters and diplopappi, going by Turnpike and Hubbard's Close to Saw Mill Brook, and returning by Goose Pond: (1) *A. Tradescanti*, now well under way, most densely flowered, by low roadsides; (2) *dumosus*, perhaps the most prevalent of the small whitish ones, especially in wood-paths; (3) *Diplopappus linariifolius*, quite common; (4) *A. patens*, at present by far the most common of the decidedly purple asters, in dry ground; (5) *undulatus*, just begun to be common; (6) *acuminatus*, low whorl, leafy, under a shady copse, where it appears to have been rayless, scarce; (7) *longifolius*, within a few days quite common in low ground; and (8) *puniceus*, very common in like places for a good while; (9) *Radula*, now rather pale and stale in low grounds; (10) *miser*, not as yet widely dispersed, but common in Saw Mill Brook Path; (11) *Diplopappus umbellatus*, abundant in low grounds; (12) *lævis*, I did not chance to see in this walk, but found it common the next morning, on hillside by Moore's Swamp. These

twelve are all I know excepting *corymbosus*[1] in Miles Swamp and elsewhere, long time, not common; also *macrophyllus*, long since, not blooming this year; *multiflorus*, in dry roadsides, not yet (at least) common; and *Diplopappus cornifolius*, Bittern Cliff woods, probably out of bloom.

These twelve placed side by side, Sophia and I decided that, regarding only individual flowers, the handsomest was —

1st, *A. patens*, deep bluish-purple ("deep blue-purple" are Gray's very words), large!

2d, *lævis*, bright lilac-purple, large.

3d, perhaps *Radula*, pale bluish-purple, turning white, large!

4th, 5th, 6th. We could not easily decide between the next three, viz.: —

D. linariifolius, pale bluish-purple[2] ⎫

A. puniceus, purplish-pink   ⎬ some large.

and *A. longifolius*, pale purple   ⎭

But we thought afterward that perhaps the *puniceus* should take precedence of the other two.

7th, *undulatus*, pale pinkish-purple, middle size.

8th, 9th, and 10th,

dumosus, white or bluish, small;

Tradescanti, white, very small;

miser, white, very small;

and I may add *multiflorus*, white (which we had not).

11th, *Diplopappus umbellatus*, white, middle size.

[1] *Cordifolius?*

[2] Some, outdoors, have a lilac or violet tint.

12th. The *A. acuminatus* was without rays, rather large when present.

The first (*patens*) has broader rays than the second, paler within toward the large handsome yellow disk. Its rough leaves are not so handsome.

The *lævis* is more open and slender-rayed than the last, with a rather smaller disk, but, including its stem and leaves, it is altogether the most delicate and graceful, and I should incline to put it before the last.

The *Radula* has a large, coarse disk, turning brown, and at present is inclined to turn a dirty white. Its leaves are not handsome; sometimes double-rayed. Perhaps I should put this after the next two.

The *puniceus* is a very large bush full of flowers, great rounded masses, two or more feet in diameter, the very pretty pink flowers well relieved by the background of its dark-green leaves. A branch of it will, perhaps, make the greatest show of any of them at present. It has slender, rather open rays and grows upon me. It is peculiar for its color. Perhaps commonly more purplish and larger.

The *longifolius* is very densely rayed; rays too short in proportion to disk, and too pale. Some are very large bushes with a great profusion of buds now. Some are paler and have longer linear rays, split once or twice.

The *D. linariifolius* is interesting, with its commonly single flower, with very broad rays turned backward, or handsomer still when it has fifteen or twenty heads crowded together.

Vol. V

The *undulatus* has a very bushy spreading panicle of a great many middle-sized flowers of not many commonly slender and open rays. Often paler and broader than these.

The *Tradescanti* attracts attention in a vase, and carries off the palm with many, for its often perfect hollow pyramids of flowers with yellow or purplish disks.

The *dumosus*, too, is clearest white and neat. The *D. umbellatus*, a small sprig with its convex top, is a great ornament to the collection. The *miser* is like a broad-leaved and more spreading *Tradescanti* with still broader and more purplish disks, the rays turned back.

A strawberry blossoms again in meadow.

For three weeks the woods have had a strong musty smell from decaying fungi. The maple-leaved viburnum berries are a dark purple or black now. They are scarce. The red pyrus berries are ripe. The dense oval bunches of arum berries now startle the walker in swamps. They are a brilliant vermilion on a rich ground, seen where they have fallen off, which ground turns dark-purple. Saw an orange, and also a very bright yellow, slender fungus. *Solidago latifolia*, only a few out. The medeola berries are now dull glossy and almost blue-black; about three, on slender threads one inch long, arising in the midst of the cup formed by the purple bases of the whorl of three upper leaves. Hear the sharp *quivet* of pigeons at the Thrush Alley clearing. Mistook it for a jay at first, but saw the narrow, swift-flying bird soon. That low, thin, flat fern, already whitening, at Saw Mill Brook cannot be

the dicksonia, for the segments of its pinnæ are entire. *Solidago puberula* (?) just fairly begun on northwest (?) corner of Ministerial Clearing, behind Everett's; but it is not hoary and has a red stem; very neat and handsome. Found in Hubbard's Close Swamp and at Saw Mill Brook what is perhaps *Aspidium Filix-fœmina*, in fruit, and I think four other kinds which I could not make out, three in fruit. Also *Lycopodium lucidulum*, shining club-moss.

Sept. 3. Saturday. I saw this afternoon, on the chimney of the old Hunt house, in mortar filling an oblong square cavity apparently made when the chimney was, the date 1703.[1] The rafters in the garret are for the most part of oak hewn, and more slender (though sufficiently strong and quite sound) than any sawed ones I ever saw. Oak in the old houses, pine in the new.

The soapwort gentian out abundantly in Flint's Bridge Lane, apparently for a week; a surprisingly deep, *faintly* purplish blue. Crowded bunches of ten or a dozen sessile and closed narrow or oblong diamond or sharp dome shape flowers. The whole bunch like many sharp domes of an Oriental city crowded together. I have here actually drawn my pen round one. It is the flowering of the sky. The sky has descended and kissed the earth. In (at top) a whorl of clear, smooth, rich green leaves. Why come these blue flowers thus late in the year? A dome-like crowd of domelets.

[1] [See *Excursions*, p. 201; Riv. 247.]

Sophia saw last Monday morning (August 29th), going to Boston in the cars, the dew-like frost on the meadows. The hips of the sweet-briar begin to redden. Saw *Polygonum dumetorum* climbing to the top of birches and willows twelve feet high by the path to Peter's along river. It is a rampant climber.

Now is the season for those comparatively rare but beautiful wild berries which are not food for man. If we so industriously collect those berries which are sweet to the palate, it is strange that we do not devote an hour in the year to gathering those which are beautiful to the eye. It behooves me to go a-berrying in this sense once a year at least. Berries which are as beautiful as flowers, but far less known, the fruit of the flower. To fill my basket with the neglected but beautiful fruit of the various species of cornels and viburnums, poke, arum, medeola, thorns, etc.

Saw at the floral show this afternoon some splendid specimens of the sunflower, king of asters, with the disk filled with ligulate flowers.

Sept. 4. 5.30 A. M. — To Nawshawtuct by river. Roman wormwood's yellow dust on my clothes. Hear a warbling vireo, — something rare. I do not succeed in making two varieties of *Polygonum amphibium*. All mine, from three inches above water and floating to three feet high on dry land, are apparently one. The first, at any rate, must be *aquaticum*, — floating, *nearly* smooth, and leaves more heart-shaped. It appears by insensible gradations to pass into the other. See one or two lilies yet. The fragrance of a grape-vine branch, with ripe grapes on it, which I have brought home, fills the whole house. This fragrance is exceedingly rich, surpassing the flavor of any grape.

P. M. — To Cliffs *via* Hubbard's Swamp.

The skunk-cabbage fruit lies flat and black now in the meadow. The *Aster miser* is a pretty flower, with its commonly wide and loose branches, variegated or parti-colored with its white rays and broad purplish (and yellow) disks giving it a modestly parti-colored look, with green leaves of sufficient breadth to relieve the flowers.

Would it not be worth the while to devote one day each year to collecting with pains the different kinds of asters, — perhaps about this time, — and another to the goldenrods?

In Potter's dry pasture I saw the ground black with blackbirds (troopials?). As I approach, the front rank rises and flits a little further back into the midst of the flock, — it rolls up on the edges, — and, being thus alarmed, they soon take to flight, with a loud rippling rustle, but soon alight again, the rear wheeling swiftly into place like well-drilled soldiers. Instead of being an irregular and disorderly crowd, they appear to know and keep their places and wheel with the precision of drilled troops.

The lycopodium now sheds its pollen commonly. The hawks are soaring at the Cliffs. I think I never hear this peculiar, more musical scream, such as the jay appears to imitate, in the spring, only at and after midsummer when the young begin to fly. In Hubbard's

Swamp Path. Probably *Solidago speciosa*, though not yet in blossom there, very broad leaves, the radical-like plantain, covering the ground, and for the most part no more.

Carried a pail this afternoon to collect goldenrods and berries. The skunk-cabbage common. Hazels high time to gather; bushes browned. After handling some beaked hazelnuts the other day, observed my hand covered with extremely fine, shining, glass-like bristles. Arum in prime. The crowded clusters of shrub oak acorns are very handsome now, the rich, wholesome brown of the cups contrasting with the now clear green acorns, sometimes twenty-four with a breadth of three inches. China-like berries of cornel along the river now abundant, some cymes wholly white; also the panicled there and in swamps, though its little red (?) fingery stems are oftenest bare, but are pretty enough, perhaps, to take the place of the berries. The black choke-berries, as also choke-cherries, are stale. The two-leaved Solomon's-seal has just begun to redden; so the largest one. The creeping juniper berries are now a hoary green but full-grown. The scarlet thorn is in many places quite edible and now a deep scarlet. Polygonum and medeola now. Green-briar only begins to turn. *Viburnum nudum* rather stale. Clintonia probably about gone. Carrion-flower in prime. Maple viburnum fully ripe, like the *dentatum*. *Aralia hispida* getting old. Feverwort now. Rose hips generally beginning; and the two primroses beginning. Elder in prime, and cranberry. Smooth sumach stale. Celtis green.

Vol. V

There are, perhaps, four kinds of goldenrod in C. Hubbard's Swamp Path [1] which I am not certain about: one, which I have called *S. puberula*, with reddish stem; another, tall and slender, smooth, with a pyramidal panicle with four to six broad rays, leaves lanceolate, dwindling to mere bracts, appressed and entirish above, *virgata*-like, which I will call *S. virgata*, — though its leaves are not entire, — till I examine the *stricta* again; [2] also another, with thin lanceolate leaves, symmetrically tapering at each end, rough on the edges and serrate, with, I believe, six or seven rays

(specimen now withered), and this I have already named for convenience *ulmifolia*, but the leaves are not elm-like. [3] Also another, with eight to twelve (?) rays and much narrower leaves than the above three, very taper-pointed, sessile, and with margined petiole and wavy upper, entire lower, lanceolate-spatulate, and toothed slightly near end. Has the *stricta* leafets in the axils? [4]

Sept. 5. To Framingham.

Saw, in a meadow in Wayland, at a little distance,

[1] *Stricta* and *puberula*, etc., are there, August, 1859.
[2] This my early low-ground *stricta*-like.
[3] Probably form of *S. altissima*.
[4] *Vide* [p. 422].

what I have no doubt was an island of *Aster puniceus*, one rod in diameter, — one mass of flowers five feet high.

Sept. 7. R. W. E. brought from Yarmouth this week *Chrysopsis falcata* in bloom and *Vaccinium stamineum*, deerberry, or squaw huckleberry, — the last with green berries, some as large as cranberries, globular (not pear-shaped), on slender peduncles, not edible, in low ground.

Yesterday and to-day and day before yesterday, some hours of very warm weather, as oppressive as any in the year, one's thermometer at 93°.

Sept. 8. Roses, apparently *R. lucida*, abundantly out on a warm bank on Great Fields by Moore's Swamp, with *Viola pedata*.

Sept. 9. Half a bushel of handsome pears on the ground under the wild pear tree on Pedrick's land; some ripe, many more on tree. J. Wesson, who is helping me survey to-day, says that, when they dug the cellar of Stacy's shop, he saw where they cut through (with the spade) birches six inches in diameter, on which the Mill-Dam had been built; also that Nathan Hosmer, Sr., since dead, told him that he had cut meadow-grass between the bakehouse and the Middlesex Hotel. I find myself covered with green and winged lice from the birches.

Sept. 10. The pontederia and pads have already their fall look by river. It is not the work of frost. The *Aster*

Tradescanti, now in its prime, sugars the banks all along the riverside with a profusion of small white blossoms resounding with the hum of bees. It covered the ground to the depth of two feet over large tracts, looking at a little distance somewhat like a smart hoar frost or sleet or sugaring on the weeds. The banks are sugared with the *A. Tradescanti*.

Sept. 11. *Sunday.* Cool weather. Sit with windows shut, and many by fires. A great change since the 6th, when the heat was so oppressive. The air has got an autumnal coolness which it will not get rid of again.

P. M. — To Dugan's.

I think I can correct somewhat my account of the goldenrods of September 4th, [two] pages back. No. 2 may be *S. stricta*, after all. (*Vide* the one at Hosmer's ditch.) Is not the *puberula* of September 4th same with No. 2? Is not No. 3 one form of *S. altissima?* Doubt if I have seen *S. ulmifolia*. Is not No. 4 the true *S. puberula?* It is the same with that by Marlborough road, September 1st. The *speciosa* may not open for a week yet.

The present appearance of the solidago in Hosmer's ditch which may be *S. stricta*[1] is a stout erect red stem with entire, lanceolate, thick, fleshy, smooth sessile leaves above, gradually increasing in length downward till ten inches long and becoming toothed.[2] All parts very smooth. Not yet out. This apparently same with No. 2.

The *S. nemoralis* is not as fresh as a week ago. Per-

[1] *Vide* Nov. 3d and 4th.   [2] Not sharply.

haps that was the date for the goldenrods generally. Perhaps this is the time for asters. The conspicuous and handsome bluish masses of *A. puniceus*, erect or fallen, stretch in endless rows along the brook, often as high as your head; sometimes make islands in the meadow. *Polygonum articulatum* out, many of them, at the Desert. None out September 1st. Say, then, September 5th. *A. undulatus* is now in prime, very abundant along path-sides. The branches of its panicle are commonly of about equal length on different sides the stem, and as the flowers are crowded and stand vertically on the sides as well as horizontally above, they form one (or sometimes more) conical or pyramidal or cylindrical hollow panicles of middle-sized purplish flowers, roundly bunched.

Signs of frost last night in M. Miles's cleared swamp. Potato vines black. How much farther it is back to frost from the greatest heat of summer, *i. e.* from the 6th [of this month] back to the 1st of June, three months, than forward to it, four days!

Checkerberries are full-grown, but green. They must have been new mitchella berries, then, that I saw some time ago. River cornel berries have begun to disappear. In a stubble-field, I go through a very fine, diffusely branching grass now going to seed, which is like a reddish mist to my eyes, two feet deep, and trembling around me.

There is an aster in Hosmer's ditch, like *longifolius*, with linear leaves remotely toothed, red stem, smooth, three or four feet high, but scales not recurved and flowers much smaller, with many purplish disks.

Vol. V

Sept. 12. I was struck this afternoon with the beauty of the *Aster corymbosus* with its corymbed flowers, with seven or eight long slender white rays pointed at both ends, ready to curl, shaving-like, and purplish disks, — one of the more interesting asters. The *Smilacina racemosa* berries are well red now; probably with the two-leaved.

It occurred to me when I awoke this morning, feeling regret for intemperance of the day before in eating fruit, which had dulled my sensibilities, that man was to be treated as a musical instrument, and if any viol was to be made of sound timber and kept well tuned always, it was he, so that when the bow of events is drawn across him he may vibrate and resound in perfect harmony. A sensitive soul will be continually trying its strings to see if they are in tune. A man's body must be rasped down exactly to a shaving. It is of far more importance than the wood of a Cremona violin.

[Here follows an account of Thoreau's second excursion to the Maine woods, which began September 13th. As the story is told elsewhere, virtually in the language of the Journal, it is here omitted, with the exception of a few scattered sentences and paragraphs which for one reason or another were not used in the paper entitled "Chesuncook."]

Sept. 16. *Friday.* He [Joe Atean or Aitteon][1] said the stone-heaps (though we saw none) were made by chub.

[1] [In the Journal the name of the guide appears as Atean, and Thoreau "thought it might be the French Étienne, though Joe pronounced

Sept. 17. *Saturday.*

The head [of the moose],[1] measuring from the root of the ears to the end of the nose or upper lip	2 feet	2½ inches
Head and neck (from nose to breast (?) direct)	4 "	3½ "
Fore leg below level of body	4 "	9½ "
Height behind (from the tips of the hoofs to top of back)	6 "	11 "
Height from tips of hoofs to level with back above shoulders [2]	7 "	5 "
Extreme length (from nose to tail)	8 "	2 "

The ears 10 inches long.

Sept. 18. *Sunday.* One end of the log hut[3] was a camp, with the usual fir floor and log benches and a clerk's office. I measured one of the many batteaux lying about, with my two-foot ash rule made here. It was not peculiar in any respect that I noticed.

Extreme length	31	feet
Extreme width	5½	"
Width of bottom	$2\frac{2}{12}$	"
Length of "	$20\frac{9}{12}$	"
" " bow	$6\frac{10}{12}$	"
" " stern	3½	"
Depth within	17	inches.

Sept. 19. *Monday.* I looked very narrowly at the vegetation as we glided along close to the shore, and

it *At*, etc." This is probably a more correct spelling than the Aitteon of the book. Mrs. Fannie Hardy Eckstorm in *The Penobscot Man* (Boston, 1904) gives a considerable account of this man and his exploits and spells his name "Attien."]

[1] [See *Maine Woods*, p. 126; Riv. 153.]
[2] [See *ibid.*, where Thoreau says this measurement was incorrect.]
[3] [Ansell Smith's. See *Maine Woods*, pp. 137–144; Riv. 167–176.]

now and then made Joe turn aside for me to pluck a plant, that I might see what was primitive about our Concord River.

Sept. 20. Tuesday. About Hinckley's camp I saw the *Fringilla hyemalis;* also a bird a little smaller, maybe, brownish and yellowish, with some white tail-feathers, which I think makes the *tull-lull* sound, hopping on the wood-pile. Is not this the myrtle-bird? Their note interested me because I formerly had many a chase in a spring morning in the direction of this sound, in vain, to identify the bird. The lumberers said it came round the camps, and they gave it a vulgar name. Also, about the carry, a chubby sparrow with dark-brown or black stripes on the head. Saw a large and new woodpecker, probably the red-headed, making a noise like the pigeon woodpecker.

.   .   .   .

There was one woman on board, who got in at the Kineo House, who looked oddly in the one saloon for gentlemen and ladies, amid the red shirts of the lumbermen. It rained very hard while we were aboard the steamer. We had a small sloop in tow, and another stopped to speak with us, to inquire after a man who was missing. A fortnight before, he had left his horse and carriage at Sawyer's, saying that he was going to get a moose and should be back in two days. He set out in a birch alone from the south end of the lake. At length they had sent the horse home, which brought on his friends, who were now looking for him and feared that he was lost in the lake. It

was not very wise to set out in a canoe from the south end of the lake to kill a moose in two days. They thought that if he had fallen in with one Whitton, a hunter, he was safe enough.

Sept. 21. Started at 7 A. M., Wednesday. In Guilford I went into a clapboard-mill on the Piscataquis. In this town we took a new route, keeping the north side of the Piscataquis at first, through Foxcroft, Dover (quite a town), Garland, Charleston, East Corinth, Levant, Glenburn, and Hermon, to Bangor. Saw robins in flocks going south. Rode in the rain again. A few oaks near Bangor. Rained all day, which prevented the view of Ktaadn, otherwise to be seen in very many places. Stumps cut high, showing the depth of the snows. Straight roads and long hills. The country was level to the eye for twenty or thirty miles toward the Penobscot Valley. Most towns have an academy. Even away up toward the lake we saw a sort of gallows erected near one for the pupils to exercise upon.[1] I had not dreamed of such degeneracy so hard upon the primitive wilderness. The white pines near Bangor perfectly parti-colored and falling to-day. Reached Bangor at dark.

Sept. 22. Thursday. He[2] had made speeches at the Legislature. He and a companion were once put into

[1] [*Maine Woods*, p. 98; Riv. 118.]
[2] [Governor Neptune of the Penobscot tribe. See *Maine Woods*, pp. 162–165; Riv. 199–203.]

Vol. V

the bootblacks' room at the hotel in Portland, when attending the Legislature. In the morning they walked off in disgust to see the Governor of the State. He asked what was the matter. They said they could not stay there; there was too much boot there; Indians did not like boot any more than white man. The Governor saw the matter righted.

.   .   .   .

Behind one house, an Indian had nearly finished one canoe and was just beginning another, outdoors. I looked very narrowly at the process and had already carefully examined and measured our birch. We asked this Indian his name. He answered readily and pleasantly, "My name is Old John Pennyweight."[1] Said he got his bark at the head of Passadumkeag, fifty miles off. Took him two days to find one tree that was suitable; had to look very sharp to be sure the bark was not imperfect. But once he made two birches out of one tree. Took the bark off with a shovel made of rock maple, three or four inches wide. It took him a fortnight or three weeks to complete a canoe after he had got the materials ready. They sometimes made them of spruce bark, and also of skins, but they were not so good as birch. Boats of three hides were quicker made. This was the best time to get the birch bark. It would not come off in the winter. (I had heard Joe say of a certain canoe that it was made of summer bark.) They scrape all the inner bark off, and in the canoe the bark is wrong side outward.

[1] [*Maine Woods*, p. 165; Riv. 203.]

He had the ribs of a canoe, all got out of cedar, — the first step in making a canoe, after materials [have been] brought together, — and each one shaped for the particular place it was to hold in the canoe. As both ends are alike, there will be two ribs alike. These two were placed close together, and the next in succession each way were placed next on each side, and thus tied up in bundles of fourteen to sixteen till all were made. In the bundle I examined, they were two and a half inches wide in the middle and narrowing to the ends. He would untie a bundle, take out the inmost, or longest, or several, and place them on their ends in a very large iron kettle of hot water over a fire, turning them from time to time. Then, taking one of the inmost or longest ones, he bent and shaped it with much labor over his knee, giving it with his eyes the shape it was to have in the canoe. It was then tied firmly and held in that shape with the reddish cedar bark. Sometimes he was obliged to tie a straight piece of wood on tangent-wise to the rib, and, with a bark tie, draw out a side of the rib to that. Then each succeeding smaller rib in one half the bundle is forced into this. The first bundles of fourteen or sixteen making two bundles of steamed and bent and tied-up ribs; and thus all are left to dry in that shape.

I was sorry that I could not be there to witness the next step in making a canoe, for I was much struck by the *method* of this work, and the process deserves to be minutely described, — as much, at least, as most of the white man's arts, accounts of which now fill the journals. I do not know how the bark is made to hug so tightly the ribs, unless they are driven into place somewhat like a hoop. One of the next things must be to make the long, thin sheathing of cedar, less than half an inch thick, of pieces half the length of the birch, reaching each way close together beneath the ribs, and quite thin toward the edges of the canoe. However, I examined the canoe that was nearly done with minuteness. The edge or taffrail is composed first of two long strips of cedar, rather stout, one on each side. Four narrow hardwood (rock maple) cross-bars, artfully shaped so that no strength may be wasted, keep these apart, give firmness to the whole, and answer for seats. The ends of the ribs come up behind or outside this taffrail and are nailed to it with a single nail. Pennyweight said they formerly used wooden pegs.[1] The edge of the bark is brought up level with this, and a very slender triangular cleat of cedar is nailed on over it and flush with the surface of the taffrail. Then there are ties of split white spruce bark (looking like split bamboo) through the bark, between the ribs, and around these two strips of cedar, and over the two strips one flat and thin strip covering the ties, making smooth work and coming out flush with the under strips. Thus the edge of the canoe is completed. Owing to the form of the canoe, there must be some seams near the edge on the sides about eighteen inches apart, and pieces

[1] Polis canoe in '57 had them.

of bark are put under them. The edges of the bark are carefully sewed together at the ends with the same spruce roots, and, in our canoe, a strip of canvas covered with pitch was laid (doubled) over the edge. They use rosin now, but pitch formerly. Canoe is nearly straight on bottom — straight in principle — and not so rounded the other way as is supposed. *Vide* this section in middle. The sides bulge out an inch or so beyond the rail. There is an additional piece of bark, four or five inches wide, along each side in the middle for four or five feet, for protection, and a similar protecting strip for eighteen inches on each side at the ends. The canoe rises about one foot in the last five or six feet. There is an oval piece of cedar for stiffness inside, within a foot of each end, and near this the ribs are bent short to breaking. Beyond there are not ribs, but sheaths and a small keel-like piece, and the hollow is filled with shavings. Lightness, above all, is studied in the construction. Nails and rosin were all the modern things I noticed. The maker used one of those curved knives, and worked very hard at bending the knees.

. . . .

Went into a batteau manufactory. Said they made knees of almost anything; that they were about worn out in one trip up river. Were worth fourteen or sixteen dollars, lumber being high. Weigh three hundred (?) [pounds], just made, though he did n't know

exactly about it. Long spike poles, with a screw in the spike to make it hold.

Sept. 23. Friday. Walked down the riverside this forenoon to the hill where they were using a steam-shovel at the new railroad cut, and thence to a hill three quarters of a mile further. Saw *Aster undulatus, Solidago nemoralis*, fragrant everlasting, silvery cinquefoil, small white birch, *Lobelia inflata*, both kinds of primrose, low cudweed, lactuca, *Polygonum cilinode* (apparently out of bloom), yellow oxalis. I returned across the fields behind the town, and over the highest hill behind Bangor, and up the Kenduskieg, from which I saw the Ebeeme Mountains in the northwest and hills we had come by. The arbor-vitæ is the prevailing shrub.

Sept. 24. Saturday. Saw Ktaadn from a hill about two miles northwest of Bangor on the road to Pushaw. It is about eighty miles from Bangor. This was the nearest point from which we made out to see it. In the afternoon, walked up the Kenduskieg. White goldenrod, fall dandelion, hog peanut, *Solidago arguta*[1] and *altissima, Aster macrophyllus* (?), and red maple (?). Witch-hazel well out. *Epilobium coloratum, Solidago squarrosa, S. latifolia, Aster cordifolius* (?).

Sept. 25. Sunday. Dined with Lowell. Said the largest pine Goddard's men cut last winter scaled in the woods forty-five hundred feet board measure,

[1] That is, probably *gigantea*.

and was worth ninety dollars at the Bangor boom, Oldtown. They cut a road three miles and a half for this alone. They do not make much of a path, however. From L. I learned that the untouched white pine timber which comes down the Penobscot waters is to be found at the head of the East Branch and the head waters of the Allegash, about Eagle Lake and Chamberlain, etc., and Webster Stream. But Goddard had bought the stumpage in eight townships in New Brunswick. They are also buying up townships across the Canada line.

Sept. 26 and 27. Monday and Tuesday I was coming to Boston and Concord. Aboard the steamer Boston were several droves of sheep and oxen and a great crowd of passengers.

Sept. 28. Wednesday. In Concord.
The elm leaves are falling. The fringed gentian was out before Sunday; was (some of it) withered then, says Edith Emerson.

Sept. 29. Thursday. Cool and windy. Wind roars in the trees. *Viola cucullata, Aster puniceus* and *longifolius* still. *Solidago speciosa* out in Hubbard's Swamp since I went away, — say ten days ago. This must be a late one, then. *Diplopappus linariifolius, Aster undulatus*, and a few small ones. Red oak acorns fall. The witch-hazel at Lee's Cliff, in a fair situation, has but begun to blossom; has not been long out, so that I think it must be later than the gentian. Its leaves are yellowed. Barberry ripe. Sumachs and maples changed, but not trees generally. Bluets still. *Viburnum Lentago* berries yet. Lambkill blossoms again.

Sept. 30. Friday. Saw a large flock of black ducks flying northwest in the form of a harrow.

VIII

OCTOBER, 1853

(ÆT. 36)

Oct. 1. Saturday. Went a-barberrying by boat to Conantum, carrying Ellen, Edith, and Eddie. Grape-vines, curled, crisped, and browned by the frosts, are now more conspicuous than ever. Some grapes still hang on the vines. Got three pecks of barberries. Huckleberries begin to redden. Robins and blue-birds collect and flit about. Flowers are scarce.

Oct. 2. Sunday. The gentian in Hubbard's Close is frost-bitten extensively. As the [witch-] hazel is raised above frost and can afford to be later, for this reason also I think it is so. The white pines have scarcely begun at all to change here, though a week ago last Wednesday they were fully changed at Bangor. There is fully a fortnight's difference, and methinks more. The [witch-] hazel, too, was more forward there. There are but few and faint autumnal tints about Walden yet. The smooth sumach is but a dull red.

Oct. 3. Viola lanceolata in Moore's Swamp.

Oct. 4. The maples are reddening, and birches yellowing. The mouse-ear in the shade in the middle of the day, so hoary, looks as if the frost still lay on

it. Well it wears the frost. Bumblebees are on the *Aster undulatus*, and gnats are dancing in the air.

Oct. 5. The howling of the wind about the house just before a storm to-night sounds extremely like a loon on the pond. How fit!

Oct. 6 and 7. Windy. Elms bare.

Oct. 8. Found a bird's nest (?) converted into a mouse's nest in the prinos swamp, while surveying on the new Bedford road to-day, topped over with moss, and a hole on one side, like a squirrel-nest.

Oct. 9. Sunday. A high wind south of westerly. Set sail with W. E. C. down the river.

The red maples are now red and also yellow and reddening. The white maples are green and silvery, also yellowing and blushing. The birch is yellow; the black willow brown; the elms sere, brown, and thin; the bass bare. The button-bush, which was so late, is already mostly bare except the lower part, protected. The swamp white oak is green with a brownish tinge; the white ash turned mulberry. The white maples toward Ball's Hill have a burnt white appearance; the white oak a salmon-color and also red. Is that scarlet oak rosed? Huckleberries and blackberries are red. Leaves are falling; apples more distinctly seen on the trees; muskrat-houses not quite done.

This wind carried us along glibly, I think six miles an hour, till we stopped in Billerica, just below the

first bridge beyond the Carlisle Bridge, — at the Hibiscus Shore. I collected some hibiscus seeds and swamp white oak acorns, and we walked on thence, a mile or more further, over scrubby hills which with a rocky core border the western shore, still in Billerica, at last not far above the mills. At one place, opposite what I once called Grape Island (still unchanged), I smelled grapes, and though I saw no vines at first, they being bare of leaves, at last found the grapes quite plenty and ripe and fresh enough on the ground under my feet. Ah! their scent is very penetrating and memorable. Did we not see a fish hawk? We found ourselves in an extensive wood there, which we did not get out of. It took the rest of the day to row back against the wind.

Oct. 10. This morning it is very pleasant and warm. There are many small birds in flocks on the elms in Cheney's field, faintly warbling, — robins and purple finches and especially large flocks of small sparrows, which make a business of washing and pruning them-selves in the puddles in the road, as if cleaning up after a long flight and the wind of yesterday. The faint suppressed warbling of the robins sounds like a remi-niscence of the spring.

Cooler and windy at sunset, and the elm leaves come down again.

Oct. 11. Sassafras leaves are a rich yellow now and falling fast. They come down in showers on the least touching of the tree. I was obliged to cut a small one while surveying the Bedford road to-day. What singularly and variously formed leaves! For the most part three very regular long lobes, but also some simple leaves; but here is one shaped just like a hand or a mitten with a thumb. They next turn a dark cream-color.

Father saw to-day in the end of a red oak stick in his wood-shed, three and a half inches in diameter, which was sawed yesterday, something shining. It is lead, either the side of a bullet or a large buckshot just a quarter of an inch in diameter. It came from the Ministerial Lot in the southwest part of the town, and we bought the wood of Martial Miles. It is completely and snugly buried under some twelve or fifteen layers of the wood, and it appears not to have penetrated originally more than its own thickness, for there is a very close fit all around it, and the wood has closed over it very snugly and soundly, while on every other side it is killed, though snug for an eighth of an inch around it.

Oct. 12. To-day I have had the experience of borrowing money for a poor Irishman who wishes to get his family to this country. One will never know his neighbors till he has carried a subscription paper among them. Ah! it reveals many and sad facts to stand in this relation to them. To hear the selfish and cowardly excuses some make, — that *if* they help any they must help the Irishman who lives with them, — and him they are sure never to help! Others, with whom public opinion weighs, will think of it, trust-

ing you never will raise the sum and so they will not be called on again; who give stingily after all. What a satire in the fact that you are much more inclined to call on a certain slighted and so-called crazy woman in moderate circumstances rather than on the president of the bank! But some are generous and save the town from the distinction which threatened it, and *some* even who do not lend, plainly would if they could.

Oct. 14. *Friday.* A Mr. Farquhar of Maryland came to see me; spent the day and the night. Fine, clear Indian-summer weather.

Oct. 15. *Saturday.* Last night the first smart frost that I have witnessed. Ice formed under the pump, and the ground was white long after sunrise. And now, when the morning wind rises, how the leaves come down in showers after this touch of the frost! They suddenly form thick beds or carpets on the ground in this gentle air, — or without wind, — just the size and form of the tree above. Silvery cinquefoil.

Oct. 16. *Sunday.* The third pleasant day. Hunter's Moon. Walked to White Pond. The *Polygonum dumetorum* in Tarbell's Swamp lies thick and twisted, rolled together, over the loose raised twigs on the ground, as if woven over basketwork, though it is now all sere. The *Marchantia polymorpha* is still erect there. *Viola ovata* out. The *Lysimachia stricta*, with its long bulblets in the axils, how green and fresh by the shore of the pond!

Oct. 18. P. M. — With Sophia boated to Fair Haven, where she made a sketch.

The red maples have been bare a good while. In the sun and this clear air, their bare ashy branches even sparkle like silver. The woods are losing their bright colors. The muskrat-houses are more sharpened now. I find my boat all covered — the bottom and seats — with the yellow leaves of the golden willow under which it is moored, and if I empty it, it is full again to-morrow.[1] Some white oaks are salmon-red, some lighter and drier. The black oaks are a greenish yellow. Poplars (*grandidentata*) clear, rich yellow. How like some black rocks that stand in the river are these muskrat-houses! They are singularly conspicuous for the dwellings of animals.

The river is quite low now, lower than for many weeks, and accordingly the white lily pads have their stems too long, and they rise above the water four or five inches and are looped over and downward to the sunken pad with its face down. They make a singular appearance. Returning late, we see a double shadow of ourselves and boat, one, the true, quite black, the other directly above it and very faint, on the willows and high bank.

Oct. 19. *Wednesday.* Paddled E. Hoar and Mrs. King up the North Branch.

A seed of wild oat left on.

The leaves have fallen so plentifully that they quite conceal the water along the shore, and rustle pleasantly

[1] [*Excursions*, p. 266; Riv. 326, 327.]

when the wave which the boat creates strikes them. On Sunday last, I could hardly find the Corner Spring, and suspected even it had dried up, for it was completely concealed by fresh-fallen leaves, and when I swept them aside and revealed it, it was like striking the earth for a new spring. At Beck Stow's, surveying, thinking to step upon a leafy shore from a rail, I got into water more than a foot deep and had to wring my stockings out; but this is anticipating.[1]

Oct. 20. How pleasant to walk over beds of these fresh, crisp, and rustling fallen leaves, — young hyson, green tea, clean, crisp, and wholesome! How beautiful they go to their graves! how gently lay themselves down and turn to mould! — painted of a thousand hues and fit to make the beds of us living. So they troop to their graves, light and frisky. They put on no weeds. Merrily they go scampering over the earth, selecting their graves, whispering all through the woods about it. They that waved so loftily, how contentedly they return to dust again and are laid low, resigned to lie and decay at the foot of the tree and afford nourishment to new generations of their kind, as well as to flutter on high! How they are mixed up, all species, — oak and maple and chestnut and birch! They are about to add a leaf's breadth to the depth of the soil. We are all the richer for their decay. Nature is not cluttered with them. She is a perfect husbandman; she stores them all.[2]

[1] [*Excursions*, pp. 266, 267; Riv. 326, 327.]
[2] [*Excursions*, pp. 268–270; Riv. 329–331.]

While I was wringing my wet stockings (*vide* last page), sitting by the side of Beck Stow's, I heard a rush of wings, looked up, and saw three dusky ducks swiftly circling over the small water. They rounded far away, but soon returned and settled within about four rods. They first survey the spot. Wonder they did not see me. At first they are suspicious, hold up their heads and sail about. Do they not see me through the thin border of leafless bushes? At last one dips his bill, and they begin to feed amid the pads. I suddenly rise, and [they] instantly dive as at a flash, then at once rise again and all go off, with a low wiry note.

Oct. 22. A week or more of fairest Indian summer ended last night, for to-day it rains. It was so warm day before yesterday, I worked in my shirt-sleeves in the woods.

I cannot easily dismiss the subject of the fallen leaves. How densely they cover and conceal the water for several feet in width, under and amid the alders and button-bushes and maples along the shore of the river, — still light, tight, and dry boats, dense cities of boats, their fibres not relaxed by the waters, undulating and rustling with every wave, of such various pure and delicate, though fading, tints, — of hues that might make the fame of teas, — dried on great Nature's coppers. And then see this great fleet of scattered leaf boats, still tight and dry, each one curled up on every side by the sun's skill, like boats of hide, scarcely moving in the sluggish current, — like the great fleets with which you mingle on entering some great mart,

some New York which we are all approaching together. Or else they are slowly moving round in some great eddy which the river makes, where the water is deep and the current is wearing into the bank. How gently each has been deposited on the water! No violence has been used toward them yet. But next the shore, as thick as foam they float, and when you turn your prow that way, list! what a rustling of the crisped waves! Wet grounds about the edges of swamps look dry with them, and many a wet foot you get in consequence.

Consider what a vast crop is thus annually shed upon the earth. This, more than any mere grain or seed, is the great harvest of the year. This annual decay and death, this dying by inches, before the whole tree at last lies down and turns to soil. As trees shed their leaves, so deer their horns, and men their hair or nails. The year's great crop. I am more interested in it than in the English grass alone or in the corn. It prepares the virgin mould for future cornfields on which the earth fattens. They teach us how to die. How many flutterings before they rest quietly in their graves! A myriad wrappers for germinating seeds. By what subtle chemistry they will mount up again, climbing by the sap in the trees. The ground is all parti-colored with them.

For beautiful variety can any crop be compared with them? The dogwood (poison sumach) blazing its sins as scarlet, the early-blushing maple, the rich chrome (?) yellow of the poplar, the mulberry ash, the brilliant red huckleberry with which the hills'

backs are painted like sheep's, — not merely the plain flavidness of corn, but all the colors of the rainbow. The salmon-colored oaks, etc., etc. The frost touches them, and, with the slightest breath of day or jarring of earth's axle, see in what showers they come floating down, at the first earnest touch of autumn's wand. They stoop to rise, to mount higher in coming years by subtiler chemistry, and the sapling's first fruits, thus shed, transmuted at last, may adorn its crown, when, in after years, it has become the monarch of the forest.[1]

Yesterday, toward night, gave Sophia and mother a sail as far as the Battle-Ground. One-eyed John Goodwin, the fisherman, was loading into a hand-cart and conveying home the piles of driftwood which of late he had collected with his boat. It was a beautiful evening, and a clear amber sunset lit up all the eastern shores; and that man's employment, so simple and direct, — though he is regarded by most as a vicious character, — whose whole motive was so easy to fathom, — thus to obtain his winter's wood, — charmed me unspeakably. So much do we love actions that are simple. They are all poetic. We, too, would fain be so employed. So unlike the pursuits of most men, so artificial or complicated. Consider how the broker collects his winter's wood, what sport he makes of it, what is his boat and hand-cart! Postponing instant life, he makes haste to Boston in the cars, and there deals in stocks, not quite relishing his employment, — and so earns the money with which he buys his fuel. And when, by chance, I meet him about this indirect

[1] [*Excursions*, pp. 265–270; Riv. 324–331.]

and complicated business, I am not struck with the beauty of his employment. It does not harmonize with the sunset. How much more the former consults his genius, some genius at any rate! Now I should love to get my fuel so, — I have got some so, — but though I may be glad to have it, I do not love to get it in any other way less simple and direct. For if I buy one necessary of life, I cheat myself to some extent, I deprive myself of the pleasure, the inexpressible joy, which is the unfailing reward of satisfying any want of our nature simply and truly.

No *trade* is simple, but artificial and complex. It postpones life and substitutes death. It goes against the grain. If the first generation does not die of it, the third or fourth does. In face of all statistics, I will never believe that it is the descendants of tradesmen who keep the state alive, but of simple yeomen or laborers. This, indeed, statistics say of the city reinforced by the country. The oldest, wisest politician grows not more human so, but is merely a gray wharf rat at last. He makes a habit of disregarding the moral right and wrong for the legal or political, commits a slow suicide, and thinks to recover by retiring on to a farm at last. This simplicity it is, and the vigor it imparts, that enables the simple vagabond, though he does get drunk and is sent to the house of correction so often, to hold up his head among men.

"If I go to Boston every day and sell tape from morning till night," says the merchant (which we will admit is not a beautiful action), "some time or other I shall be able to buy the best of fuel without stint."

Yes, but not the pleasure of picking it up by the river-side, which, I may say, is of more value than the warmth it yields, for it but keeps the vital heat in us that we may repeat such pleasing exercises. It warms us twice, and the first warmth is the most wholesome and memorable, compared with which the other is mere coke. It is to give no account of my employment to say that I cut wood to keep me from freezing, or cultivate beans to keep me from starving. Oh, no, the greatest value of these labors is received before the wood is teamed home, or the beans are harvested (or winnowed from it). Goodwin stands on the solid earth. The earth looks solider under him, and for such as he no *political* economies, with *their* profit and loss, supply and demand, need ever be written, for they will need to use no policy. As for the complex ways of living, I love them not, however much I practice them. In as many places as possible, I will get my feet down to the earth. There is no secret in his trade, more than in the sun's. It is no mystery how he gets his living; no, not even when he steals it. But there is less double-dealing in his living than in your trade.

Goodwin is a most constant fisherman. He must well know the taste of pickerel by this time. He will fish, I would not venture to say how many days in succession. When I can remember to have seen him fishing almost daily for some time, if it rains, I am surprised on looking out to see him slowly wending his way to the river in his oilcloth coat, with his basket and pole. I saw him the other day fishing in the middle of the stream, the day after I had seen him fishing on

the shore, while by a kind of magic I sailed by him; and he said he was catching minnow for bait in the winter. When I was twenty rods off, he held up a pickerel that weighed two and a half pounds, which he had forgot to show me before, and the next morning, as he afterward told me, he caught one that weighed three pounds. If it is ever necessary to appoint a committee on fish-ponds and pickerel, let him be one of them. Surely he is tenacious of life, hard to scale.

Oct. 23. Sunday. P. M. — Down railroad to chestnut wood on Pine Hill.

A pleasant day, but breezy. I see a downy woodpecker tapping an apple tree, and hear, when I have passed, his sharp, metallic note. I notice these flowers still along the railroad causeway: fresh sprouts from the root of the *Solidago nemoralis* in bloom, one or two fall dandelions, red clover and white, yarrow, *Trifolium arvense* (perhaps not fresh), one small blue snapdragon, fresh tansy in bloom on the sunny sandbank. There are green leaves on the ends of elder twigs; blackberry vines still red; apple trees yellow and brown and partly bare; white ash bare (nearly); golden willows yellow and brown; white birches, exposed, are nearly bare; some pines still parti-colored. White, black, and red oaks still hold most of their leaves. What a peculiar red has the white! And some black have now a rich brown. The *Populus grandidentata* near railroad, bare; the *P. tremuloides*, half bare. The hickories are finely crisped, yellow, more or less browned. Several yellow butterflies in the meadow.

And many birds flit before me along the railroad, with faint notes, too large for linarias. Can they be tree sparrows? Some weeks.[1] Many phenomena remind me that now is to some extent a second spring, — not only the new-springing and blossoming of flowers, but the peeping of the hylodes for some time, and the faint warbling of their spring notes by many birds. Everywhere in the fields I see the white, hoary (ashy-colored) sceptres of the gray goldenrod. Others are slightly yellowish still. The yellow is gone out of them, as the last flake of sunshine disappears from a field when the clouds are gathering. But though their golden hue is gone, their reign is not over. Compact puffed masses of seeds ready to take wing. They will send out their ventures from hour to hour the winter through. The *Viola pedata* looking up from so low in the wood-path makes a singular impression.

I go through Brooks's Hollow. The hazels bare, only here and there a few sere, curled leaves on them. The red cherry is bare. The blue flag seed-vessels at Walden are bursting, — six closely packed brown rows.

I find my clothes all bristling as with a *chevaux-de-frise* of beggar-ticks, which hold on for many days. A storm of arrows these weeds have showered on me, as I went through their moats. How irksome the task to rid one's self of them! We are fain to let some adhere. Through thick and thin I wear some; hold on many days. In an instant a thousand seeds of the bidens fastened themselves firmly to my clothes, and

[1] Probably the white-in-tail [*i. e.* vesper sparrow, or grass finch].

I carried them for miles, planting one here and another there. They are as thick on my clothes as the teeth of a comb.

The prinos is bare, leaving red berries. The pond has gone down suddenly and surprisingly since I was here last, and this pool is left, cut off at a higher level, stagnant and drying up. This is its first decided going down since its going up a year or two ago. The red-looking water purslane is left bare, and the water-target leaves are turned brown and drying up on the bare mud. The clethra partly bare, crisped, yellowish and brown, with its fruit with persistent styles (?) in long racemes. Here are dense fields of light-colored rattlesnake grass drooping with the weight of their seeds.

The high blueberries about the pond have still a few leaves left on, turned bright scarlet red. These it is adorn the shore so, seen at a distance, small but very bright. The panicled andromeda is thinly clad with yellow and brown leaves, not sere. Alders are green. Smooth sumach bare. Chestnuts commonly bare. I now notice the round red buds of the high blueberry. The blue-stemmed, and also the white, solidago on Walden bank. Small sassafras trees bare. The *Aster undulatus* is still quite abundant and fresh on this high, sunny bank, — far more so than the *Solidago cæsia*, — and methinks it is the latest of our asters and is besides the most common or conspicuous flower now. It is in large, dense masses, two or three feet high, pale purple or whitish, and covered with humblebees. The radical leaves, now hearted and crenatish, are lake beneath. Also a hieracium quite freshly bloomed, but with white, bristly leaves and smooth stem, about twenty-flowered; peduncles and involucres glandular-hairy. Is it *Gronovii* or veiny-leaved? Almost as slender as the panicled. (In press.) No gerardias. Strawberries are red and green. It is the season of fuzzy seeds, — goldenrods, everlasting, senecio, asters, epilobium, etc., etc. *Viburnum Lentago*, with ripe berries and dull-glossy red leaves; young black cherry, fresh green or yellow; mayweed. The chestnuts have mostly fallen. One *Diplopappus linariifolius* in bloom, its leaves all yellow or red. This and *A. undulatus* the asters seen to-day.

The red oak now red, perhaps inclining to scarlet; the white, with that peculiar ingrained redness; the shrub oak, a clear thick leather-color; some dry black oak, darker brown; chestnut, light brown; hickory, yellow, turning brown. These the colors of some leaves I brought home.

Oct. 24. Early on Nawshawtuct.

Black willows bare. Golden willow with yellow leaves. Larch yellow. Most alders by river bare except at top. Waxwork shows red. Celtis almost bare, with greenish-yellow leaves at top. Some hickories bare, some with rich golden-brown leaves. Locusts half bare, with greenish-yellow leaves. Catnip fresh and green and in bloom. Barberries green, reddish, or scarlet. Cranberry beds at distance in meadows (from hill) are red, for a week or more. Lombardy poplar yellow. Red maples and elms alone very con-

spicuously bare in our landscape. White thorns bare, and berries mostly fallen, reddening the ground. Hedge-mustard still fresh and in bloom. Buttonwoods half bare. The rock maple leaves a clear yellow; now and then [one] shows some blood in its veins, and blushes. People are busy raking the leaves before their houses; some put them over their strawberries.

It has rained all day, filling the streams. Just after dark, high southerly winds arise, but very warm, blowing the rain against the windows and roof and shaking the house. It is very dark withal, so that I can hardly find my way to a neighbor's. We think of vessels on the coast, and shipwrecks, and how this will bring down the remaining leaves and to-morrow morning the street will be strewn with rotten limbs of the elms amid the leaves and puddles, and some loose chimney or crazy building will have fallen. Some fear to go to bed, lest the roof be blown off.

Oct. 25. 7 A. M. — To Hubbard's Grove.

The rain is over, the ground swept and washed. There is a high and cold west wind. Birds fly with difficulty against it (are they tree sparrows?). The brooks and the river are unexpectedly swelled with yesterday's rain. The river is a very dark blue. The wind roars in the wood. A maple is blown down. *Aster longifolius* in low ground (a *few*). This and the *Diplopappus linariifolius*, and, above all, *A. undulatus*, the only flowers of the kind seen this week.[1]

---

[1] Afterwards *A. puniceus*, *Tradescanti*, and one *lævis*! *Vide* bottom of next page.

P. M. — Sailed down river to the pitch pine hill behind Abner Buttrick's, with a strong northwest wind, and cold.

Saw a telltale on Cheney's shore, close to the water's edge. I am not quite sure whether it is the greater or lesser, but am inclined to think that all I have seen are the lesser. It was all white below and dark above, with a pure white tail prettily displayed in flying. It kept raising its head with a jerk as if it had the St. Vitus's dance. It would alight in the water and swim like a little duck. Once, when I went ashore and started it, it flew so as to bring a willow between it and me, and alighted quite near, much nearer than before, to spy me. When it went off, it uttered a sharp *te-te-te-te-te*, flying with quivering wings, dashing about. I think that the storm of yesterday and last night brought it up.

The white maples are completely bare. The tall dry grass along the shore rustles in the cold wind. The shores are very naked now. I am surprised to see how much the river has risen. The swamp white oaks in front of N. Barrett's — their leafy tops — look quite silvery at a distance in the sun, very different from near to. In *some* places along the water's edge the *Aster Tradescanti* lingers still, some flowers purple, others white. The ground is strewn with pine-needles as sunlight. The iron-wood is nearly bare (on the Flint Bridge Rock). I see one or two specimens of the *Polygonum hydropiperoides* and the smaller, nameless one in flower still. They last thus till the severe frosts. There are masses of the yellow water ranunculus

washed up by the shore after this high wind. This is one of our *river* weeds. The shepherd's-purse in bloom.

Oct. 26. I well remember the time this year when I first heard the dream of the toads. I was laying out house-lots on Little River in Haverhill. We had had some raw, cold and wet weather. But this day was remarkably warm and pleasant, and I had thrown off my outside coat. I was going home to dinner, past a shallow pool, which was green with springing grass, and where a new house was about being erected, when it occurred to me that I heard the dream of the toad. It rang through and filled all the air, though I had not heard it once. And I turned my companion's attention to it, but he did not appear to perceive it as a new sound in the air. Loud and prevailing as it is, most men do not notice it at all. It is to them, perchance, a sort of simmering or seething of all nature. That afternoon the dream of the toads rang through the elms by Little River and affected the thoughts of men, though they were not conscious that they heard it.

How watchful we must be to keep the crystal well that we were made, clear! — that it be not made turbid by our contact with the world, so that it will not reflect objects.[1] What other liberty is there worth having, if we have not freedom and peace in our minds, — if our inmost and most private man is but a sour and turbid pool? Often we are so jarred by chagrins in dealing with the world, that we cannot reflect. Everything beautiful impresses us as sufficient to itself. Many

---

[1] [Channing, p. 87.]

men who have had much intercourse with the world and not borne the trial well affect me as all resistance, all bur and rind, without any gentleman, or tender and innocent core left. They have become hedgehogs.

Ah! the world is too much with us, and our whole soul is stained by what it works in, like the dyer's hand. A man had better starve at once than lose his innocence in the process of getting his bread. This is the pool of Bethsaida [sic] which must be stilled and become smooth before we can enter to be healed. If within the old man there is not a young man, — within the sophisticated, one unsophisticated, — then he is but one of the devil's angels.

It is surprising how any reminiscence of a different season of the year affects us. When I meet with any such in my Journal, it affects me as poetry, and I appreciate that other season and that particular phenomenon more than at the time. The world so seen is all one spring, and full of beauty. You only need to make a faithful record of an average summer day's experience and summer mood, and read it in the winter, and it will carry you back to more than that summer day alone could show. Only the rarest flower, the purest melody, of the season thus comes down to us.

P. M. — To Cliffs.

As I go up the back road, some fresh sprouts in bloom on a tall rough goldenrod. I hear a faint twittering of the sparrows in the grass, like crickets. Those flitting sparrows which we have had for some weeks, are they not the sober snowbirds (tree sparrows?)? They fly in a great drifting flock, wheeling and dash-

ing about, as if preluding or acting a snow-storm, with rapid te te te. They are as dry and rustling as the grass. The Aster puniceus, with the longifolius, — a few, — on the sheltered sides of ditches. Checkerberries have now a fine, clear, fresh tint, a peculiar pink (?). Now leaves are off, or chiefly off, I begin to notice the buds of various form and color and more or less conspicuous, prepared for another season, — partly, too, perhaps, for food for birds. The tupelo is bare. The smooth speedwell in bloom, the meek-eyed flower, low or flat in the sod.

Went through the dense maple swamp against Potter's pasture. It is completely bare, and the ground is very thickly strewn with leaves, which conceal the wet places. But still the high blueberry bushes in the midst and on the edge retain a few bright-red or scarlet-red leaves. Red circles of the pitcher-plant, in the meadow beyond, are full of water to where cut evenly off by the scythe. Lambkill, being an evergreen, is now more conspicuous.

The river has risen still higher than yesterday, and flooded the meadows yet more. How long it continues to rise, before we feel the full influence of the rain that fell on the Worcester hills! The green-briar is bare except a few yellow leaves. Butter-and-eggs just ending in a sheltered place. Some Solidago nemoralis show still bright-yellow masses of flowers on bare, dead-looking stalks, the leaves having fallen or being dried up, — a constant lover of the sun. A storm appears to be thickening. The sun has been shorn of his beams all the afternoon. The clouds are not

Vol. V

distinct and handsome. It is cool, gray weather. But yet there is a little more adventure in a walk, and it better suits a pensive mood. I see the hole of the great black spider already walled about. Slate-colored snowbirds. This has been the month for acorns, — and the last half of September, — though it is now too late.

When, after feeling dissatisfied with my life, I aspire to something better, am more scrupulous, more reserved and continent, as if expecting somewhat, suddenly I find myself full of life as a nut of meat, — am overflowing with a quiet, genial mirthfulness. I think to myself, I must attend to my diet; I must get up earlier and take a morning walk; I must have done with luxuries and devote myself to my muse. So I dam up my stream, and my waters gather to a head. I am freighted with thought.

[At this point and scattered through the pages immediately succeeding, the Journal contains further matter relating to the Maine excursion of the previous month. Only the parts not included in "The Maine Woods" are here printed.]

Very small and narrow intervals on the Penobscot. Every lake and stream in the wilderness is soon made to feel the influence of the white man's dam.

At Oldtown I went on board the small river steamers which run to the Five Islands, built propeller-fashion. They lay just opposite Orono Island; had been laid up during the low stage of water, and were to start the next day on their first trip. One was properly named

the Governor Neptune. A hand told me that they drew only fourteen inches of water and could run easily in two feet of water, though they did not like to.

Why is [it] that we look upon the Indian as the man of the woods? There are races half civilized, and barbarous even, that dwell in towns, but the Indians we associate in our minds with the wilderness.

Oct. 27. 6.30 A. M. — To Island by boat.

The river still rises, — more than ever last night, owing to the rain of the 24th (which ceased in the night of the 24th). It is two feet higher than then. I hear a blackbird in the air; and these, methinks, are song sparrows flitting about, with the three spots on breast. Now it is time to look out for walnuts, last and hardest crop of the year?

I love to be reminded of that universal and eternal spring when the minute crimson-starred female flowers of the hazel are peeping forth on the hillsides, — when Nature revives in all her pores.

Some less obvious and commonly unobserved signs of the progress of the seasons interest me most, like the loose, dangling catkins of the hop-hornbeam or of the black or yellow birch. I can recall distinctly to my mind the image of these things, and that time in which they flourished is glorious as if it were before the fall of man. I see all nature for the time under this aspect. These features are particularly prominent; as if the first object I saw on approaching this planet in the spring was the catkins of the hop-hornbeam on the hillsides. As I sailed by, I saw the yellowish waving sprays.

See nowadays concave chocolate-colored fungi passing into dust on the edges, close on the ground in pastures.

Oct. 28. Rain in the night and this morning, preparing for winter.

We noticed in a great many places the narrow paths by which the moose came down to the river, and sometimes, where the bank was steep and somewhat clayey, they had slid down it. The holes made by their feet in the soft bottom in shallow water are visible for a long time. Joe told me that, though they shed their horns annually, each new pair has an additional prong. They are sometimes used as an ornament in front entries, for a hat-tree (to hang hats on).

Cedar bark appeared to be their commonest string.

.   .   .   .

These first beginnings of commerce on a lake in the wilderness are very interesting, — these larger white birds that come to keep company with the gulls, — if they only carry a few cords of wood across the lake.

.   .   .   .

Just saw in the garden, in the drizzling rain, little sparrow-sized birds flitting about amid the dry corn-stalks and the weeds, — one, quite slaty with black streaks and a bright-yellow crown and rump, which I think is the yellow-crowned warbler, but most of the others much more brown, with yellowish breasts

and no yellow on crown to be observed, which I think the young of the same. One flew up fifteen feet and caught an insect. They uttered a faint *chip.* Some of the rest were sparrows. I did not get good sight of the last. I suspect the former may be my *tull-lulls* of the Moosehead Carry.[1]

For a year or two past, my *publisher,* falsely so called, has been writing from time to time to ask what disposition should be made of the copies of "A Week on the Concord and Merrimack Rivers" still on hand, and at last suggesting that he had use for the room they occupied in his cellar. So I had them all sent to me here, and they have arrived to-day by express, filling the man's wagon, — 706 copies out of an edition of 1000 which I bought of Munroe four years ago and have been ever since paying for, and have not quite paid for yet. The wares are sent to me at last, and I have an opportunity to examine my purchase. They are something more substantial than fame, as my back knows, which has borne them up two flights of stairs to a place similar to that to which they trace their origin. Of the remaining two hundred and ninety and odd, seventy-five were given away, the rest sold. I have now a library of nearly nine hundred volumes, over seven hundred of which I wrote myself. Is it not well that the author should behold the fruits of his labor? My works are piled up on one side of my chamber half as high as my head, my *opera omnia.* This is authorship; these are the work of my brain. There was just one piece of good luck in the venture. The

[1] No, they were [*sic*].

Vol. V

unbound were tied up by the printer four years ago in stout paper wrappers, and inscribed, —

H. D. Thoreau's
Concord River
50 cops.

So Munroe had only to cross out "River" and write "Mass." and deliver them to the expressman at once. I can see now what I write for, the result of my labors.

Nevertheless, in spite of this result, sitting beside the inert mass of my works, I take up my pen to-night to record what thought or experience I may have had, with as much satisfaction as ever. Indeed, I believe that this result is more inspiring and better for me than if a thousand had bought my wares. It affects my privacy less and leaves me freer.[1]

Oct. 30. Sunday. A white frost this morning, lasting late into the day. This has settled the accounts of many plants which lingered still.

P. M. — To Hubbard's Meadow Wood.

I see tree sparrows in loose flocks, chasing one another, on the alders and willows by the brook-side. They keep up a general low and incessant twittering warble, as if suppressed, very sweet at this season, but not heard far. It is, as Wilson says, *like* a chip-bird, but this has a spot commonly on breast and a bright-chestnut crown. It is quite striped (bay and brown with dark) above and has a forked tail. I am not quite *sure* that I have seen them before. They are a chubby little bird, and have not the stripes on the

[1] [Channing, p. 84.]

breasts which the song sparrow has. The last, moreover, has not that striped bay and blackish and ash above. By the bathing-place, I see a song sparrow with his full striped breast. He drops stealthily behind the wall and skulks amid the bushes; now sits behind a post, and peeps round at me, ever restless and quirking his tail, and now and then uttering a faint *chip.* It is not so light beneath as the last.

The muskrat-houses are mostly covered with water now.

Saw a *Solidago nemoralis* in full flower yesterday. Here is the autumnal dandelion and fragrant everlasting[1] to-day.

What with the rains and frosts and winds, the leaves have fairly fallen now. You may say the fall has ended. Those which still hang on the trees are withered and dry. I am surprised at the change since last Sunday. Looking at the distant woods, I perceive that there is no yellow nor scarlet there now. They are (except the evergreens) a mere dull, dry red. The autumnal tints are gone. What life remains is merely at the foot of the leaf-stalk. The woods have for the most part acquired their winter aspect, and coarse, rustling, light-colored withered grasses skirt the river and the wood-side. This is November. The landscape prepared for winter, without snow. When the forest and fields put on their sober winter hue, we begin to look more to the sunset for color and variety.

Now, now is the time to look at the buds [of] the swamp-pink, — some yellowish, some, mixed with their

[1] [Two interrogation-points in pencil here.]

oblong seed-vessels, red, etc. The larger red maple buds have now two sets of scales, three in each. The water andromeda is still green. Along the Depot Brook, the great heads of *Aster puniceus* stand dry and fuzzy and singularly white, — like the goldenrods and other asters, — but some quite low are still green and in flower.

The prevalence of this light, dry color perhaps characterizes November, — that of bleaching withered grass, of the fuzzy gray goldenrods, harmonizing with the cold sunlight, and that of the leaves which still hang on deciduous trees.

The dead-looking fruit of the alders is now conspicuous.

Oct. 31. 7 A. M. — By river to Nawshawtuct.

Owing to the rain of the 28th, added to that of the 23d, the river has risen now probably more than three feet above where it was a week ago, yet wider over the meadows. Just at the edge, where it is mixed with grass and leaves, it is stiffened slightly this morning. On the hill, I see flocks of robins, flitting from tree to tree and peeping. It is a clear, cool, Novemberish morning, reminding me of those peculiarly pleasant mornings in winter when there is a slight vapor in the atmosphere. The same without snow or ice. There is a fine vapor, twice as high as a house, over the flooded meadows, through which I see the whiter dense smoke

above the summer level. I see many pickerel dart away, as I push my boat over the meadows. They lie up there now, and fishing is over, except spearing. You can no longer stand on the true banks to fish, and the fish are too widely dispersed over the grassy-bottomed and shallow meadow. The flood and wind have washed up great quantities of cranberries loosened by the rake, which now line the shore, mixed with the wrecked grass and weeds. We gathered five quarts, partly frost-bitten. There are already myriads of snow-fleas on the water next the shore, and on the cranberries we pick in the wreck, as if they were peppered. When we ripple the surface, the undulating light is reflected from the waves upon the bank and bushes and withered grass. Is not this already November, when the yellow and scarlet tints are gone from the forest?

It is very pleasant to float along over the smooth meadow, where every weed and each stem of coarse grass that rises above the surface has another, answering to it and even more distinct, in the water beneath, making a rhyme to it, so that the most irregular form appears regular. A few scattered dry and clean (very light straw-colored) grasses are so cheap and simple a beauty thus reflected. I see this especially on Potter's meadow. The bright hips of the meadow rose, which we brush against with our boat, — for with sallows and button-bushes it forms islands, — are handsomer thus seen than a closer inspection proves.

Tansy lingers still by Hubbard's Bridge. But methinks the flowers are disappearing earlier this season than last.

columns or streaks from the chimneys of the village, a cheerful scene. Methinks I see, far away toward the woods, a frozen mist (?) suspended against their sides.

What was that very heavy or thick, though not *very* large, hawk that sailed away from a hickory? The hemlock seeds are apparently ready to drop from their cones. The cones are mostly open. Now appears to be the very time for walnuts. I knock down showers with a stick, but all do not come out of the shells.

I believe I have not bathed since Cattle-Show. It has been rather too cold, and I have had a cold withal.

P. M. — By boat with Sophia to my grapes laid down in front of Fair Haven.

It is a beautiful, warm and calm Indian-summer afternoon. The river is so high over the meadows, and the pads and other low weeds so deeply buried, and the water is so smooth and glassy withal, that I am reminded of a calm April day during the freshets. The coarse withered grass, and the willows, and button-bushes with their myriad balls, and whatever else stands on the brink, are reflected with wonderful distinctness. This shore, thus seen from the boat, is like the ornamented frame of a mirror. The button-balls, etc., are more distinct in the reflection, if I remember, because they have there for background the reflected sky, but the actual ones are seen against the russet meadow. I even see houses a mile off, distinctly reflected in the meadow flood. The cocks crow in barn-yards as if with new lustiness. They seem to appreciate the day. The river is three feet and more

I slowly discover that this is a gossamer day. I first see the fine lines stretching from one weed or grass stem or rush to another, sometimes seven or eight feet distant, horizontally and only four or five inches above the water. When I look further, I find that they are everywhere and on everything, sometimes forming conspicuous fine white gossamer webs on the heads of grasses, or suggesting an Indian bat. They are so abundant that they seem to have been suddenly produced in the atmosphere by some chemistry, — spun out of air, — I know not for what purpose. I remember that in Kirby and Spence it is not allowed that the spider can walk on the water to carry his web across from rush to rush, but here I see myriads of spiders on the water, making some kind of progress, and one at least with a line attached to him. True they do not appear to walk well, but they stand up high and dry on the tips of their toes, and are blown along quite fast. They are of various sizes and colors, though mostly a greenish-brown or else black; some very small. These gossamer lines are not visible unless between you and the sun. We pass some black willows, now of course quite leafless, and when they are between us and the sun they are so completely covered with these fine cobwebs or lines, mainly parallel to one another, that they make one solid woof, a misty woof, against the sun. They are not drawn taut, but curved downward in the middle, like the rigging of vessels, — the ropes which stretch from mast to mast, — as if the fleets of a thousand Lilliputian nations were collected one behind another under bare poles. But when we have floated a few feet further, and thrown the willow out of the sun's range, not a thread can be seen on it.

I landed and walked up and down the causeway and found it the same there, the gossamer reaching across the causeway, though not necessarily supported on the other side. They streamed southward with the slight zephyr. As if the year were weaving her shroud out of light. It seemed only necessary that the insect have a *point d'appui;* and then, wherever you stood and brought the leeward side of its resting-place between you and the sun, this magic appeared. They were streaming in like manner southward from the railing of the bridge, parallel waving threads of light, producing a sort of flashing in the air. You saw five or six feet in length from one position, but when I moved one side I saw as much more, and found that a great many, at least, reached quite across the bridge from side to side, though it was mere accident whether they caught there, — though they were continually broken by unconscious travellers. Most, indeed, were slanted slightly upward, rising about one foot in going four, and, in like manner, they were streaming from the south rail over the water, I know not how far. And there were the spiders on the rail that produced them, similar to those on the water. Fifteen rods off, up the road, beyond the bridge, they looked like a shimmering in the air in the bare tree-tops, the finest, thinnest gossamer veil to the sun, a dim wall.

I am at a loss to say what purpose they serve, and am inclined to think that they are to some extent

attached to objects as they float through the atmosphere; for I noticed, before I had gone far, that my grape-vines in a basket in the boat had got similar lines stretching from one twig to another, a foot or two, having undoubtedly caught them as we paddled along. It might well be an electric phenomenon. The air appeared crowded with them. It was a wonder they did not get into the mouth and nostrils, or that we did not feel them on our faces, or continually going and coming amid them did not whiten our clothes more. And yet one with his back to the sun, walking the other way, would observe nothing of all this. Only stand so as to bring the south side of any tree, bush, fence, or other object between you and the sun. Methinks it is only on these very finest days late in autumn that this phenomenon is seen, as if that fine vapor of the morning were spun into these webs.

According to Kirby and Spence, "in Germany these flights of gossamer appear so constantly in autumn that they are there metaphorically called 'Der fliegender Sommer' (the flying or departing summer)." What can possess these spiders thus to run all at once to every the least elevation, and let off this wonderful stream? Harris tells me he does not know what it means. Sophia thought that thus at last they emptied themselves and wound up, or, I suggested, unwound, themselves, — cast off their mortal coil. It looks like a mere frolic spending and wasting of themselves, of their vigor, now that there is no further use for it, their prey, perchance, being killed or banished by the frost.

IX

NOVEMBER, 1853

(ÆT. 36)

Nov. 1. 6.30 A. M. — To Hubbard's Bridge to see the gossamer.

As I go up the back road (the sun rises about this hour), I am struck with [the] general stillness as far as birds are concerned. There is now no loud, cheerful effervescing with song as in the spring. Most are gone. I only hear some crows toward the woods. The road and ruts are all frosted and stiff, and the grass and clover leaves. At Swamp Bridge, I see crystals of ice six feet long, like very narrow and sharp spears, or like great window-sashes without glass between them, floating on the water. I see yarrow, autumnal dandelion, and I suppose that is turnip so freshly in flower in Hubbard's field. Now that the sun is fairly risen, I see and hear a flock of larks in Wheeler's meadow on left of the Corner road, singing [exactly as in spring and twittering also, but rather faintly or suppressedly, as if their throats had grown up or their courage were less. The white birch seeds *begin* to fall and leave the core bare. I now hear a robin, and see and hear some noisy and restless jays, and a song sparrow chips faintly; and here on the willows is a little warbler (?), with a narrow, sharp bill and a forked tail, uttering a dry chip from time to time, and, I suspect,

picking up those little spiders which I saw yesterday, which spin this gossamer.

The gossamer does not show well against this sun. There is none now streaming from the bridge or across the causeway after this frosty night; only that which was firmly fastened and comparatively short remains still on the trees and bushes. The railing is covered with frost, and I see no spiders out. Plainly the best hour to observe this phenomenon is mid-afternoon or later, when the spiders are full of activity and the sun is in the most favorable position.

But yesterday, on the willows, it was a woof, without warp, of the finest conceivable texture, as it were made to strain the air and light, — catch all the grossness of the declining year and leave us the clear, strained November air, — fall-strained. I saw no insects caught in it. As if every prominence in every twig were connected with corresponding ones in every other by a fine line, entangling the rays of light, really catching and reflecting the light alone for all prey that I could see. Or is it a despairing effort? Now that the air is so cool and clear and free of insects, what possesses these little creatures to toil and spin so? Thus Nature gathers up her trail, and finely concludes. One six feet long, and invisible but in one position, in that was seen to stream or wave and flap a foot up and down while the light flashed along it, like a ribbon blown by the wind. You could even take hold of the end and hold it still. And the number of them was beyond conception. No industry is vain, and this must have a reason. It must be a perfect day that allows of so fine a display. Any rain or a high wind and, I suspect, whatever makes a disagreeable day, would hinder it.

As I return, I notice crows flying southwesterly in a very long straggling flock, of which I see probably neither end. A small flock of red-wings singing as in spring.

P. M. — Went after pink azaleas and walnuts by boat.

Saw three of those birds (of which I saw one first on the 30th October) on the water's edge on the meadow, like the telltale. They must be either sandpipers, telltales (not the greater or lesser), or plovers (?). Or may they be the turnstone? They went off each time with a chuckling, not whistling, note. A rise of the river like this brings us new birds at once, apparently from the seaside. This locality is somewhat peculiar in this respect, that when our broad meadows are flooded, several new species of birds are added to our ordinary list. They are not so large as the other tattler I see, nor as a woodcock, quite.

It is a pleasant day but breezy, and now I can hardly detect any gossamer left on the willows. This wind, perchance, shaking the willows and the reeds, — shaking and bending their masts, — strains and breaks this fine cordage, and, moreover, the spiders cannot well walk on the surface of the water now. So, it would seem, it must not only be a perfectly fair Indian-summer day, but quite calm and the water smooth, to permit of this wonderful display, and, perchance, after one of those remarkable and memorable mornings when the air is peculiarly clear and resonant and that white

vapor as of frost-steam hangs over the earth, — after a clear, cool, calm Indian-summer morning in November. And must it not always follow the fall of the leaf, when there is least motion to the twigs? The short time in which it must be produced, and for which it endures, is remarkable.

As I paddle under the Leaning Hemlocks, the breeze rustles the boughs, and showers of their fresh winged seeds come wafted down to the water and are carried round and onward in the great eddy there.

Gathered five or six quarts of walnuts, — pignuts, — partly by clubbing the trees, thinking they might furnish entertainment some evening the coming winter. Not more than half are out of the shells, but it is pleasant shelling them to have one's fingers scented with their fine aroma. The red squirrel reproves the while. It is not true, *as I noticed to-day*, that squirrels never gnaw an imperfect and worthless nut. Many years ago I came here nutting with some boys who came to school to me; one of them climbed daringly to the top of a tall walnut to shake. He had got the nickname of Buster for similar exploits, so that some thought he was christened so. It was a true Indian name, earned for once.

A striped squirrel out yet.

While getting the azaleas, I notice the shad-bush conspicuously leafing out. Those long, narrow, pointed buds, prepared for next spring, have anticipated their time. I noticed something similar when surveying the Hunt wood-lot last winter. Remember in this connection

that at one period last spring this bud appeared the most forward.

About three weeks ago my indignation was roused by hearing that one of my townsmen, notorious for meanness, was endeavoring to get and keep a premium of four dollars which a poor Irish laborer whom he hired had gained by fifteen minutes' spading at our Agricultural Fair. To-night a free colored woman is lodging at our house, whose errand to the North is to get money to buy her husband, who is a slave to one Moore in Norfolk, Virginia. She persuaded Moore, though not a kind master, to buy him that he might not be sold further South. Moore paid six hundred dollars for him, but asks her eight hundred. My most natural reflection was that he was even meaner than my townsman. As mean as a slaveholder!

Nov. 2. What is Nature unless there is an eventful human life passing within her? Many joys and many sorrows are the lights and shadows in which she shows most beautiful.

P. M. — To Walden and Flint's.

What are those sparrows in loose flocks which I have seen two or three weeks, — some this afternoon on the railroad causeway, — with small heads and rather long necks in proportion to body, which is longish and slender, yellowish-white or olivaceous breast, striped with dark, ashy sides of neck, whitish over and beneath the eye, and some white observed in tail when they fly? I think a dark bill and legs. They utter a peculiar note, not heard here at other seasons, *somewhat* like

the linarias, a sort of shuffling or chuckling *tche-tche-tche-tche*, quickly uttered. Can they be the grass-bird? They resemble it in marking. They are much larger than the tree sparrows. Methinks it [is] a very common fall bird.[1]

C. says he saw succory yesterday, and a loon on the pond the 30th *ult.* The prinos berries are almost gone. I am somewhat surprised to find that the *Aster undulatus* at Walden is killed by the frost; only one low and obscure one has any flowers left. Therefore, though it is the latest aster that is abundant, I am not sure that it lasts absolutely longer than the *A. puniceus*, or even *Tradescanti*. I see no other flowers on the Peak. Poke berries there are still partly green, partly ripe, as usual. The leaves of the umbelled pyrola are as glossy as in the spring, which proves that they do not owe their glossiness in the spring to the influence of that season. Two ducks on Walden. The Canada snapdragon is still fresh and in flower by roadside near pond, and a sprig from root of *Solidago nemoralis*.

I gather some fine large pignuts by the wall (near the beech trees) on Baker's land. It is just the time to get these, and this seems to be quite early enough for most pignuts. I find that there have been plenty of beechnuts, and there are still some empty burs on the trees and many nuts on the ground, but I cannot find one with meat in it. The beech leaves have all fallen except some about the lower part of the trees, and they make a fine thick bed on the ground. They are very beautiful, firm, and perfect leaves, unspotted

[1] [Titlarks, perhaps.]

and not eaten by insects, of a handsome, clear leather-color, like a book bound in calf. Crisp and elastic; no wonder they make beds of them. Of a clear [space left in manuscript] or leather-color, more or less dark and remarkably free from stains and imperfections. They cover the ground so perfectly and cleanly as to tempt you to recline on it and admire the beauty of their smooth boles from that position, covered with lichens of various colors—green, etc.—which you think you never see elsewhere. They impress you as full of health and vigor, so that their bark can hardly contain their spirits but lies in folds or wrinkles about their ankles like a sock, with the embonpoint of infancy, wrinkles of fat.[1]

The pollen [*sic*] of the *Lycopodium dendroideum* falls in showers or in clouds when my foot strikes it. How long? The witch-hazel appears to be nearly out of bloom, *most* of the flowers withering or frost-bitten. The shrub oak cups which I notice to-day have lost their acorns. I examined a squirrel's nest in a tree which suggested to me (it having a foundation of twigs, coarse basketwork; above, shreds or fibres of bark and a few leaves) that *perchance* the squirrel, like the mouse, sometimes used a deserted bird's nest,—a crow's or hawk's. A red-tailed hawk.

Among the buds, etc., etc., to be noticed now, remember the alder and birch catkins, so large and conspicuous, — on the alder, pretty red catkins dangling in bunches of three or four, — the minute red buds of the panicled andromeda, the roundish plump ones

[1] [Channing, p. 290.]

---

of the common hazel, the longish sharp ones of the witch-hazel, etc.

The sun sets. We come home in the autumn twilight, which lasts long and is remarkably light, the air being purer, — clear white light, which penetrates the woods, — is seen through the woods, — the leaves being gone. When the sun is set, there is no sudden contrast, no deep darkening, but a clear, strong white light still prevails, and the west finally glows with a generally diffused and moderate saffron-golden (?). Coming home by boat the other evening, I smelled a traveller's pipe very strongly a third of a mile distant. He was crossing Wood's Bridge. The evening star is now very bright; and is that Jupiter near it?

I might put by themselves the November flowers, — flowers which survive severe frosts and the fall of the leaf. I see hedge-mustard very fresh.

Those plants which are earliest in the spring have already made the most conspicuous preparation for that season. The skunk-cabbage spathes have started, the alder catkins, as I have said, hazel, etc.; and is there anything in the double scales of the maples, the prominent scales of willow and other catkins, sometimes burst (?)? A part of the lambkill is turned dull-reddish.

The last two, this and yesterday, fine days, but not gossamer ones.

Nov. 3. 6.30 A. M. — To Swamp Bridge Brook by river.

Considerable thin mist, high as two houses.

Just as the sun is rising, many undoubtedly of the same white-in-tail sparrows described four pages back are flying high over my head west and northwest, above the thin mist, perchance to where they see the sun on the wood-side; with that peculiar shelly note. I think it was the 27th October I saw a goldfinch. There are two or three tree sparrows flitting and hopping along amid the alders and willows, with their fine silvery *tchip*, unlike the dry loud chip of the song sparrow.

The *Aster puniceus* by brook is still common, though the worse for the wear, — low and more recent ones, — so that this, though a week ago it was less prevalent, must be set down as later than the *A. undulatus*. It bears the frosts *much* better, though it has been exposed to more severe ones from its position. And with this must be included that smooth and narrower-leaved kind, in other respects the same, one of which, at least, I think I have called *A. longifolius*. They seem to run into each other. I am inclined to think it a smoother *A. longifolius*.

Now is the time to observe the radical leaves of many plants, which put forth with springlike vigor and are so unlike the others with which we are familiar that it is sometimes difficult to identify them. What is that large circular green and reddish one, flat in the grass of upland which I have seen for a fortnight?[1]

I love to see a man occasionally from whom the usnea

[1] It is the great primrose. There are none (but by chance) about the base of this year's stalks, *i. e.* perhaps unless there is an offshoot.

---

will hang as naturally as from a spruce. Cultivation exterminates the pine, but preserves the elm. Our front-yard evergreens are puny and trimmed up.

Heard a bluebird about a week ago.

There are very few phenomena which can be described indifferently as occurring at different seasons of the year, for they will occur with some essential difference.

P. M. — To Ministerial Swamp.

A warm westerly wind, the sky concealed and a storm gathering. A sober, cloudy afternoon. To-day I see yarrow, very bright; red clover; autumnal dandelion; the silvery potentilla, and one *Canadensis* and the *Norvegica*; and a dandelion; *Veronica arvensis*; and gnawel; one *Aster lœvis* (!) by the Hosmer Ditch; and, to my surprise, that solidago of September 11th, still showing some fresh yellow petals and a very fresh stem and leaves. It must be later than the *speciosa*, and this makes me doubt if it can be the *stricta*. It has a very angled stem and erect narrow pyramidal corymb. Also *S. nemoralis* by roadside. This, though it was not so prevalent as the *S. cœsia* three weeks ago, is still to be seen, while I have not seen the other for some days. It may outlast it, as the *A. puniceus* does the *A. undulatus*, though, by the way, I saw a very fresh *A. undulatus* this afternoon. I hear a few crickets and locusts (?) and see a very small brown beetle. The thistle radical leaves and fragrant everlasting not to be forgotten. Perhaps I have made the everlastings too late! A small gyrinus in Nut Meadow Brook.

Since the change and fall of the leaf a remarkable prominence is given to the evergreens; their limits are more distinctly defined as you look at distant woods, since the leaves of deciduous trees ceased to be green and fell. Very small pollywogs in pools, one and a half or two inches long. I see many white pine cones fallen and open, with a few seeds still in them. The cones of the spruce are nearly empty, hanging downward;[1] those of the larch are also open, but, being upright, appear to have a few more seeds in them.

I make it my business to extract from Nature whatever nutriment she can furnish me, though at the risk of endless iteration. I milk the sky and the earth.

The potamogeton seeds in Nut Meadow Brook have partly left the stem.

I hear the sound of the woodchopper's axe.

Nov. 4. P. M. — To Hubbard's Close.

I find no traces of the fringed gentian there, so that in low meadows I suspect it does not last very late. Hear a nuthatch. The fertile catkins of the yellow birch appear to be in the same state with those of the white, and their scales are also shaped like birds, but much larger. The great osmundas in Hubbard's Swamp have universally lost their leafets, except perhaps one or two small crisped brown ones at the extremity, and the bare midribs alone are left. They look thin and Novemberish.

[1] Probably old ones.

we attend to what is passing before us constantly, unless our genius directs our attention that way. There are these little sparrows with white in tail, perhaps the prevailing bird of late, which have flitted before me so many falls and springs, and yet they have been as it were strangers to me, and I have not inquired whence they came or whither they were going, or what their habits were. It is surprising how little most of us are contented to know about the sparrows which drift about in the air before us just before the first snows. I hear the downy woodpecker's metallic *tchip* or peep. Now I see where many a bird builded last spring or summer. These are leaves which do not fall. How similar in the main the nests of birds and squirrels and mice! I am not absolutely certain that the mice do not make the whole nest in a bush sometimes, instead of building on a bird's nest. There is in the squirrel in this respect an approach to the bird, and, beside, one of his family is partially winged. Here, too, is a sort of link between quadrupeds and birds. I perceive that the starting of the amelanchier buds is a very common phenomenon, this fall at least, and when partially unfolded they are frost-bitten. See a few robins.

Climbed the wooded hill by Holden's spruce swamp and got a novel view of the river and Fair Haven Bay through the almost leafless woods. How much handsomer a river or lake such as ours, seen thus through a foreground of scattered or else partially leafless trees, though at a considerable distance this side of it, especially if the water is open, without wooded

Nov. 5. P. M. — To Hubbard Bathing-Place for shrubs.

Most of the muskrat-cabins were lately covered by the flood, but now that it has gone down in a great measure, leaving the cranberries stranded amid the wreck of rushes, reeds, grass, etc., I notice that they have not been washed away or much injured, as a heap of manure would have been, they are so artificially constructed. Moreover, for the most part they are protected, as well as concealed, by the button-bushes, willows, or weeds about them. What exactly are they for? This is not their breeding season. I think that they are merely an artificial bank, an air-chamber near the water, houses of refuge. But why do they need them more at this season than in the summer, it may be asked. Perhaps they are constructed just before the rise of the water in the fall and winter, so that they may not have to swim so far as the flood would require in order to eat their clams.

I heard some pleasant notes from tree sparrows on the willows as I paddled by. The buds of the rhodora are among the more conspicuous now, and yet more its seed-vessels, many if not most of which are not yet dry, but purplish.

Nov. 6. *Sunday.* 2.30 P. M. — To Lee's Cliff.

I saw yesterday for a moment by the river a small olivaceous-yellow bird; possibly a goldfinch, but I think too yellow. I see *some* gossamer on the causeway this afternoon, though it is very windy; but it requires such a day as October 31st. It is remarkable how little

shores or isles! It is the most perfect and beautiful of all frames, which yet the sketcher is commonly careful to brush aside. I mean a pretty thick foreground, a view of the distant water through the near forest, through a thousand little vistas, as we are rushing toward the former, — that intimate mingling of wood and water which excites an expectation which the near and open view rarely realizes. We prefer that some part be concealed, which our imagination may navigate.

Still the Canada snapdragon, yarrow, autumnal dandelion, tansy, shepherd's-purse, silvery cinquefoil, witch-hazel. The sweet-briar hips are abundant and fresh, a dozen sometimes crowded in a space of two inches square. Their form is a handsome oval with a flat apex. Is it not somewhat like an olive-jar? The hips hold on, then, though the haws have fallen, and the prinos, too, for the most part. There are also *some* fragrant and green leaves left. These are about the prettiest red berries that we have.

Gathered some of those fine large mocker-nut (?) hickory nuts, which are now in their prime (*Carya tomentosa?*). I perceived a faint sweetness in the dry, crisp leaves on the ground (there were some also on the tree), and I perceive that Emerson speaks of their resinous-scented leaves.

The witch-hazel spray is peculiar and interesting, with little knubs at short intervals, zigzag, crinkle-crankle. How happens it? Did the leaves grow so close? The bud is long against the stem, with a neck to it. The fever-bush has small roundish buds, two or three commonly together, probably the blossom-buds. The rhodora buds are purplish, as well as the not yet dry seed-vessels, smaller but *somewhat* like the swamp-pink. The alternate cornel, small, very dark reddish buds, on forking, smooth, slender twigs at long intervals. The panicled andromeda, minute pointed red buds, hugging the curving stems. The plump, roundish, club-shaped, well-protected buds of the alders, and rich purplish or mulberry catkins, three, four, or five together. The red maple buds, showing three or more sets of scales. The remarkable roundish, plump red buds of the high blueberry. The four-sided, long (five eighths of an inch), spear-head-shaped buds of the *Viburnum Lentago*, at the end of forked twigs, probably blossom-buds, with minute leaf-buds lower on sides of twigs. Some sallow buds already burst their scales and show the woolly catkins, reddish at base. Little brownish, scale-like buds on the ends of the red cedar leaves or leafets (branchlets), probably male blossom-buds. The creeping juniper berries are yet green, with three white, swelling lips at apex and very minute buds in the axils of the leaves.

I am struck with the variety in the form and size of the walnuts in shells, — some with a slight neck and slightly club-shaped perhaps the most common; some much longer, nearly twice as long as wide; some, like the mocker-nut, slightly depressed or rather flattened above; some pignuts very large and regularly obovate, an inch and a quarter in diameter.

A sweet-briar hip; but most are more regular jar-shape.

Nov. 7. 6.15 A. M. — To Cliffs.

A clear, cold, as well as frosty, morning. I have to walk with my hands in my pockets. Hear a faint chip, probably from a tree sparrow, which I do not see in the garden.

I find the cistus or frostweed, abundantly surrounded with crystals by the Spring Path. How long? And also by the wall this side the orchard on Fair Haven the ground is spotted with it, — like little pouches [?] or fingers full of purest white cotton, tucked about the bases of their stems. These crystals are low in the withered grass, close to the ground, and fast attached to the stems, as if they grew so. They extend about an inch upward, and are from one half to one inch wide. I saw them on no other plants, and not on all the cistuses. Those which had them had their bark invariably split up a short distance at the base and thrown off, as if forced up by the frost, and the crystals were close beneath this, adhering both to stem and bark. The others were sound in this respect. It appeared as if they were a vapor which had curled up from the root and clung about the stem in the night, frozen as it ascended, — shell-like, dimpled crystals, the frozen shells of vaporous whirlpools in the air. The stems were dead, with their seed-vessels and seeds still atop, though perhaps there was a little moisture or sap in them close to the ground; and directly beneath in the earth was a little reddish-green shoot, already started, ready to

Vol. V

burst up in the spring. Oftenest it appeared as if two curls of vapor from different sides of the stem had united and frozen together at their extremities, forming little white, sugar-like horns, open upward and downward, or the crystals had the appearance of the bark of the willow-herb, cracked about the base of the stem. A section looking thus: These were very beautiful on close inspection, like the finest imaginable white silk or glass, floss-like, of the finest staple, or like asbestos of a very fine and loose grain. It is not a particularly frosty morning. Whence does this vapor come from? The cistus has thus not only its second flowering, but its third frost flowering. Will it form again about the same stem, the bark being rent? It is a sort of incense offering in behalf of the young shoot ready to spring.

The notes of one or two small birds, this cold morning, in the now comparatively leafless woods, sound like a nail dropped on an anvil, or a glass pendant tinkling against its neighbor.

The sun now rises far southward. I see westward the earliest sunlight on the reddish oak leaves and the pines. The former appear to get more than their share. How soon the sun gets above the hills, as if he would accomplish his whole diurnal journey in a few hours at this rate! But it is a long way round, and these are nothing to the hill of heaven. Whether we are idle or industrious, the sun is constantly travelling through the sky, consuming arc after arc of this great circle at this same rapid pace.

Nightshade berries still in water or over it. Great straggling flocks of crows still flying westerly.

P. M. — To Conantum by boat, nutting.

October 31st, when the river was at its height after the rains of the 24th and 28th, our first fall flood, the wreck of the river and meadow with an unusual quantity of cranberries was washed up, and is now left high and dry, forming the first water-mark of the season, an endless meandering light-brown line, further from or nearer to the river. It is now very fresh, and it is comparatively easy to distinguish the materials which compose it. But I love to see it even in midsummer, the old water-line of the last year, far away from the edge of the shrunken stream, in some meadow, perchance in the woods, reminding me of the floods and the windy days of the fall and spring, of ducks and geese and gulls, of the raw and gusty days which I have spent on the then wilderness of water, of the origin of things, as it were, when water was a prevailing element. The flood comes and takes all the summer's waste, all that lies loose, from the riverside and meadows and floats it, not to ocean, but as far toward the upland as the water reaches; there it plants again and again the seeds of fluviatile shrubs and trees and flowers. A new line of wreckage is formed every year. I looked this afternoon to see what it was composed of. Where I looked the most prominent part was different lengths of a large three-sided cellular reed (?), perchance the *Sparganium ramosum* (?),[1] for

[1] Though Gray says its leaves are one to two feet high, I saw some

the most part faded, but some still a little juicy, pieces of rushes and eel-grass, and cranberry leaves which the rake has torn off with cranberries, I believe some flags, wool-grass and various sedges, pads, potamogeton, water ranunculus, and various other weeds of the riverside and meadows, the radical leaves (?) of heart-leaf very delicate and transparent (but this is more conspicuous, at least, still floating in water along the edge); and there was a quantity of what looked like the stems of buttonwood leaves, which I now suspect were polygonum stems. There was not much, if any, pontederia where I looked, for that, though long dead, still holds to the bottom. More of this in other places, however; also small flat shells?[1]

I perceive, when I look, that some of the most enduring of the river weeds are the *Polygonum hydropiperoides* (one still in bloom), which stand withered still above the flood, and also wool-grass, and the *Scirpus lacustris* and *Juncus militaris*, both curved downward. But in other places, less open, there is an abundance of sere meadow-grasses standing. The seeds of the sweet flag are now coming off by degrees, like coarse chaff.

Under the warm south side of Bittern Cliff, where I moor my boat, I hear one cricket singing loudly and undauntedly still, in the warm rock-side.

I shook two mocker-nut trees; one just ready to drop its nuts, and most came out of the shells. But the other tree was not ready; only a part fell, and those mostly

of *this*, still greenish, in the water where I keep my boat, six feet high! It lasts longer than flags, which it resembles.

[1] *Vide* Nov. 8.

in the shells. This is the time for *our* best walnuts; the smallest, say the last of October. Got a peck and a half shelled. I did not wish to slight any of Nature's gifts. I am partial to the peculiar and wholesome sweetness of a nut, and I think that some time is profitably spent every autumn in gathering even such as our pignuts. Some of them are a very sizable, rich-looking, and palatable fruit. How can we expect to understand Nature unless we accept like children these her smallest gifts, valuing them more as her gifts than for their intrinsic value? I love to get my basket full, however small and comparatively worthless the nut. It takes very severe frosts, and sun and wind thereafter, to kill and open the shells so that the nuts will drop out. Many hold on all winter. I climbed to the tops of the trees, and then found that shaking would not do, only jarring the limbs with my feet. It is remarkable how these nuts are protected, some with an outer shell about a quarter of an inch thick, and an inner nearly as thick as the other, and when cracked open the meat is still hard to extract. I noticed, however, that the nuts on one tree, the second, notwithstanding these thick shells, were now full of fine cracks, as if, now that they were ripe, they had made themselves ready to be cracked by man or squirrels or the frost. They really crack much easier. It is a hard, tough tree, whose fruit is stones, fit to have been the food of man in the iron age. I should like to see a man whose diet was berries and nuts alone. Yet I would not rob the squirrels, who, before any man, are the true owners. I am pretty sure I heard a striped

Vol. V

squirrel in the wall near me, as if he blowed a short blast on a dry leaf. They will not be in a hurry to go into winter quarters until they have laid up some of these nuts.

The shallow pools in woods were skimmed over this morning, and there was a little ice along the riverside, which can still be detected at sundown. Three bluebirds still braving the cold winds, — Acton Blues, not gone into winter quarters. Their blue uniform makes me think of soldiers who have received orders to keep the field and not go into winter quarters.

A muskrat-house on the top of a rock, too thin round the sides for a passage beneath, yet a small cavity at top, which makes me think that they use them merely as a sheltered perch above water. They seize thus many cores to build on, as a hummock left by the ice. (Red clover.) The wads of which this muskrat-house was composed were about six inches by four, rounded and massed at one end, flaking off at the other, and were composed chiefly of a *little* green (for the most part withered dark-brown) moss-like weed, and had the strong odor of the fresh-water sponge and conferva.

Nov. 8. Mayweed and shepherd's-purse.

10 A. M. — Our first snow, the wind southerly, the air chilly and moist; a very fine snow, looking like a mist toward the woods or horizon, which at 2 o'clock has not whitened the ground. The children greet it with a shout when they come out at recess.

P. M. — To riverside as far down as near Peter's,

to look at the water-line before the snow covers it. By Merrick's pasture it is mainly a fine, still more or less green, thread-like weed or grass of the river bottom (?), sedges, utricularias (that coarse one especially, whose name I am not sure of, with tassels (?)),[1] yellow water ranunculus, potamogeton's translucent leaves, a few flags and pontederia stems. By Peter's there was much of that coarse triangular cellular stem mentioned yesterday as sparganium (?). I would not have thought it so common. There is not so much meadow grass or hay as I expected, for that has been raked and carried off. The pads, too, have wasted away and the pontederias' leaves, and the stems of the last for the most part still adhere to the bottom.

Three larks rise from the sere grass on Minott's Hill before me, the white of their outer tail-feathers very conspicuous, reminding me of arctic snowbirds by their size and form also. The snow begins to whiten the plowed ground now, but it has not overcome the russet of the grass ground. Birds generally wear the russet dress of nature at this season. They have their fall no less than the plants; the bright tints depart from their foliage or feathers, and they flit past like withered leaves in rustling flocks. The sparrow is a withered leaf.[2]

The *Stellaria media* still blooms in Cheney's garden, and the shepherd's-[purse] looks even fresher. This must be near the end of the flower season. Perchance I heard the last cricket of the season yesterday. They chirp here and there at longer and longer intervals, till

[1] *Utricularia vulgaris?*   [2] [Channing, p. 105.]

the snow quenches their song. And the last striped squirrel, too, perchance, yesterday. They, then, do not go into winter quarters till the ground is covered with snow.

The partridges go off with a whir, and then sail a long way level and low through the woods with that impetus they have got, displaying their neat forms perfectly.

The yellow larch leaves still hold on, — later than those of any of our pines.

I noticed the other day a great tangled and netted mass of an old white pine root lying upon the surface, nearly a rod across and two feet or more high, too large even to be turned up for a fence. It suggested that the roots of trees would be an interesting study. There are the small thickly interwoven roots of the swamp white oaks on the Assabet.

At evening the snow turned to rain, and the sugaring soon disappeared.

Nov. 9. High wind and rain in the night. Still more strong and gusty but remarkably warm southwest wind during the day.

P. M. — To Fair Haven Hill by boat with W. E. C.

We rowed against a very powerful wind, sometimes scarcely making any headway. It was with difficulty often that we moved our paddles through the air for a new stroke. As C. said, it seemed to blow out of a hole. We had to turn our oars edgewise to it. But we worked our way slowly upward, nevertheless, for we came to feel and hear it blow and see the waves

run. There was quite a sea running on the lee shore, — broad black waves with white crests, which made our boat toss very pleasantly. They wet the piers of the railroad bridge for eighteen inches up. I should guess that the whole height from the valley between to the top of a wave was nearer fifteen inches.

The muskrats have added a new story to their houses since the last flood which covered them; I mean that of October 31st and thereabouts. They are uncommonly high, methinks, full four feet by five or more in diameter, a heaping ox-cart load. There are at least eight such within half a mile from Clamshell Hill to Hubbard's Wood. It is remarkable how little effect the waves have on them, while a heap of manure or a haycock would be washed away or undermined at once. I opened one. It was composed of coarse grass, pontederia stems, etc., etc., not altogether in mouthfuls. This was three feet and a half above water, others quite four. After taking off a foot I came to the chamber. It was a regularly formed oval or elliptical chamber, about eighteen inches the longest way and seven or eight inches deep, shaped like a pebble, with smooth walls of the weeds, and bottomed or bedded with a very little drier grass, a mere coating of it. It would hold four or five, closely packed. The entrance, eight or nine inches wide, led directly from this to the water at an angle of 45°, and in the water there I saw some green and white stub ends of pontederia (?) stems, I think, looking like flagroot. That thick wall, a foot quite or more above and eighteen inches or two feet around, being of these damp mate-

Vol. V

rials, soon freezes and makes a tight and warm house. The walls are of such [thickness at] the bottom that the water in the gallery probably never freezes. If the height of these houses is any sign of high or low water, this winter it will be uncommonly high.

Soon after, we saw a mink swimming in the agitated water close to the shore, east side, above Nut Meadow Brook. It showed the whole top of the back and part of the tail, unlike the muskrat, and did not dive. Stopped a moment when we headed toward it, and held up its head at the end of its long neck toward us, reminding me of pictures of the otter, then turned and swam and ran the other way; dark-brown. We see no birds, unless one crow; the wind is too strong for them. I must know what that tall, coarse grass is which stands withered so abundantly amid the button-bushes all along the shore. It escapes the mower by its position. The water milkweed stands withered amid the button-bushes, the pods still erect, though open and empty.

Landed and walked over Conant's Indian rye-field, and I picked up two good arrowheads. The river with its waves has a very wild look southward, and I see the white caps of the waves in Fair Haven Bay. Went into the woods by Holden Swamp and sat down to hear the wind roar amid the tree-tops. What an incessant straining of the trees! It is a music that wears better than the opera, methinks. This reminds me how the telegraph-wire hummed coarsely in the tempest as we passed under it.

Hitherto it had only rained a little from time to time, but now it began suddenly in earnest. We hastily

rowed across to the firm ground of Fair Haven Hillside, drew up our boat and turned it over in a twinkling on to a clump of alders covered with cat-briars which kept up the lee side, and crawled under it. There we lay half an hour on the damp ground and cat-briars, hardly able to see out to the storm which we heard on our roof, through the thick alder stems, much pleased with the tightness of our roof, which we frequently remarked upon. We took immense satisfaction in the thoroughness of the protection against the rain which it afforded. Remembered that such was the origin of the Numidian architecture and, as some think, of the nave (ship) in Gothic architecture, and if we had had a dry bed beneath us, and an ugly gap under the windward side of the boat through [which] the wind drew had been stopped, we should have lain there longer. At length, as it threatened to be an all-night storm, we crawled out again and set sail homeward.

It now began to rain harder than ever, and the wind was so strong and gusty, and blew so nearly at right angles with the river, that we found it impossible to keep the stream long at a time with our sail set, sitting on one side till the water came in plentifully, that the side might act as a keel, but were repeatedly driven ashore amid the button-bushes, and then had to work our way to the other side slowly and start again. What with water in the boat and in our clothes, we were now indifferent to wet. At length it began to rain so much harder than before, the great drops seeming to flat down the waves and suppress the wind, and feeling like hail on our hands and faces, that, as we remembered, it had only sprinkled before. By this time of course we were wet quite through and through, and C. began to inquire and jest about the condition of our money — a singular prudence methought — and buried his wallet in his pocket-handkerchief and returned it to his pocket again. He thought that bank-bills would be spoiled. It had never occurred to me if a man got completely wet through how it might affect the bank-bills in his wallet, it is so rare a thing for me to have any there. At length we both took to rowing vigorously to keep ourselves warm, and so got home just after candlelight.

Nov. 11. 7 A. M. — To Hubbard Bathing-Place.

A fine, calm, frosty morning, a resonant and clear air except a slight white vapor which escaped being frozen or perchance is the steam of the melting frost. Bracing cold, and exhilarating sunlight on russet and frosty fields. I wear mittens now. Apples are frozen on the trees and rattle like stones in my pocket. *Aster puniceus* left. A little feathery frost on the dead weeds and grasses, especially about water, — springs and brooks (though now slightly frozen), — where was some vapor in the night. I notice also this little frostwork about the mouth of a woodchuck's hole, where, perhaps, was a warm, moist breath from the interior, perchance from the chuck!

9 A. M. — To Fair Haven Pond by boat.

The morning is so calm and pleasant, winter-like, that I must spend the forenoon abroad. The river

is smooth as polished silver. A little ice has formed along the shore in shallow bays five or six rods wide. It is for the most part of crystals imperfectly united, shaped like birds' tracks, and breaks with a pleasant crisp sound when it feels the undulations produced by my boat. I hear a linaria-like mew from some birds that fly over. Some muskrat-houses have received a slight addition in the night. The one I opened day before yesterday has been covered again, though not yet raised so high as before. The hips of the late rose still show abundantly along the shore, and in one place nightshade berries. I hear a faint cricket (or locust?) still, even after the slight snow. I hear the cawing of crows toward the distant wood through the clear, echoing, resonant air, and the lowing of cattle. It is rare that the water is smooth in the forenoon. It is now as smooth as in a summer evening or a September or October afternoon. There is frost on all the weeds that rise above the water or ice. The *Polygonum Hydropiper* is the most conspicuous, abundant, and enduring of those in the water. I see the spire of one white with frost-crystals, a perfect imitation at a little distance of its loose and narrow spike of white flowers, that have withered. I have noticed no turtles since October 31st, and no frogs for a still longer time. At the bathing[-place] I looked for clams, in summer almost as thick as paving-stones there, and found none. They have probably removed into deeper water and into the mud (?). When did they move?

The jays are seen and heard more of late, their plumage apparently not dimmed at all.

I counted nineteen muskrat-cabins between Hubbard Bathing-Place and Hubbard's further wood, this side the Hollowell place, from two to four feet high. They thus help materially to raise and form the river-bank. I opened one by the Hubbard Bridge. The floor of chamber was two feet or more beneath the top and one foot above the water. It was quite warm from the recent presence of the inhabitants. I heard the peculiar plunge of one close by. The instant one has put his eyes noiselessly above water he plunges like a flash, showing tail, and with a very loud sound, the first notice you have of his proximity, — that he has been there, — as loud as if he had struck a solid substance. This had a sort of double bed, the whole about two feet long by one foot wide and seven or eight inches high, floored thinly with dry meadow-grass. There were in the water green butts and roots of the pontederia, which I think they eat. I find the roots gnawed off. Do they eat flagroot? A good deal of a small green hypnum-like river-weed forms the mouthfuls in their masonry. It makes a good sponge to mop the boat with.

The wind has risen and sky overcast. I stop at Lee's Cliff, and there is a *Veronica serpyllifolia* out. Sail back. Scared up two small ducks, perhaps teal. I had not seen any of late. They have probably almost all gone south.

Nov. 12. I cannot but regard it as a kindness in those who have the steering of me that, by the want of pecuniary wealth, I have been nailed down to this

my native region so long and steadily, and made to study and love this spot of earth more and more. What would signify in comparison a thin and diffused love and knowledge of the whole earth instead, got by wandering? The traveller's is but a barren and comfortless condition. Wealth will not buy a man a home in nature, — house nor farm there. The man of business does not by his business earn a residence in nature, but is denaturalized rather. What is a farm, house and land, office or shop, but a settlement in nature under the most favorable conditions? It is insignificant, and a merely negative good fortune, to be provided with thick garments against cold and wet, an unprofitable, weak, and defensive condition, compared with being able to extract some exhilaration, some warmth even, out of cold and wet themselves, and to clothe them with our sympathy. The rich man buys woollens and furs, and sits naked and shivering still in spirit, besieged by cold and wet. But the poor Lord of Creation, cold and wet he makes to warm him, and be his garments.

Tansy is very fresh still in some places. Tasted to-day a black walnut, a spherical and corrugated nut with a large meat, but of a strong oily taste.

8 P. M. — Up river to Hubbard Bathing-Place.

Moon nearly full. A mild, almost summer evening after a very warm day, alternately clear and overcast. The meadows, with perhaps a little mist on them, look as if covered with frost in the moonlight. At first it is quite calm, and I see only where a slight wave or piece of wet driftwood along the shore reflects a flash of light, suggesting that we have come to a season of clearer air. This occasional slight sparkling on either hand along the water's edge attends me. I come out now on the water to see our little river broad and stately as the Merrimack or still larger tides, for though the shore be but a rod off, the meeting of land and water being concealed, it is as good as if a quarter of a mile distant, and the near bank is like a distant hill. There is now and of late months no smell of muskrats, which is probably confined to the spring or rutting season. While the sense of seeing is partly slumbering, that of hearing is more wide awake than by day, and, now that the wind is rising, I hear distinctly the chopping of every little wave under the bow of my boat. Hear no bird, only the loud plunge of a muskrat from time to time. The moon is wading slowly through broad squadrons of clouds, with a small coppery halo, and now she comes forth triumphant and burnishes the water far and wide, and makes the reflections more distinct. Trees stand bare against the sky again. This the first month in which they do. I hear one cricket singing still, faintly deep in the bank,[1] now after one whitening of snow. His theme is life immortal. The last cricket, full of cheer and faith, piping to himself, as the last man might. The dark squadrons of hostile clouds have now swept over the face of the moon, and she appears unharmed and riding triumphant in her chariot. Suddenly they dwindle and melt away in her mild and all-pervading light, dissipated like the mists of

[1] Was it not a frog?

the morning. They pass away and are forgotten like bad dreams.

Landed at the bathing-place. There is no sound of a frog from all these waters and meadows which a few months ago resounded so with them; not even a cricket or the sound of a mosquito. I can fancy that I hear the sound of peeping hylodes ringing in my ear, but it is all fancy. How short their year! How early they sleep! Nature is desert and iron-bound; she has shut her door. How different from the muggy nights of summer, teeming with life! That resounding life is now buried in the mud, returned into Nature's womb, and most of the birds have retreated to the warm belt of the earth. Yet still from time to time a pickerel darts away. And still the heavens are unchanged; the same starry geometry looks down on their active and their torpid state. And the first frog that puts his eye forth from the mud next spring shall see the same everlasting starry eyes ready to play at bo-peep with him, for they do not go into the mud.

However, you shall find the muskrats lively enough now at night, though by day their cabins appear like deserted cabins. When I paddle near one, I hear the sudden plunge of one of its inhabitants, and sometimes see two or three at once swimming about it. Now is their day. It is remarkable that these peculiarly aboriginal and wild animals, whose nests are perhaps the largest of any creatures' hereabouts, should still so abound in the very midst of civilization and erect their large and conspicuous cabins at the foot of our gardens. However, I notice that unless there is a strip

of meadow and water on the garden side they erect their houses on the wild side of the stream.

The hylodes, as it is the first frog heard in the spring, so it is the last in the autumn. I heard it last, methinks, about a month ago. I do not remember any hum of insects for a long time, though I heard a cricket to-day.

Nov. 13. Rain all day.

Nov. 14. Methinks I have not seen any of those white-in-tail birds for a week (?); but I see a little sparrow or two to-day, maybe a song sparrow? Mallows still in bloom, and hedge-mustard.

P. M. — To Annursnack and Cedar Swamp.

There is a clear air and a strong northwest wind drying up the washed earth after the heavy rain of yesterday. The road looks smooth and white as if washed and swept. It is surprising how rapidly our sandy soil dries up. We walk dry-shod the day after a rain which raises the river three feet. I am struck by the dark blue of the agitated river.

Saw yarrow apparently just opened and tansy still fresh, but the fringed gentian in P. Barrett's meadow has long since withered. It falls before the first severe frosts. It is remarkable how short a career it has, in our meadows at least. Its stem and leaves never conspicuous, it is not to be detected at all, perhaps, before the middle of September, and by about the middle of October with us it has already succumbed to the frosts. It came very near not being an inhabitant

of our latitude, perhaps our globe, at all. The witch-hazel lasts much longer. However, I have seen it in November on a high hillside in Weston. When the flower season is over, when the great company of flower-seekers have ceased their search, this just raises its blue face above the withering grass beside the brooks for a moment, having at the eleventh hour made up its mind to join this planet's floral exhibition.[1]

I climb Annursnack. Under this strong wind more dry oak leaves are rattling down. All winter is their fall. A distinction is to be made between those trees whose leaves fall as soon as the bright autumnal tints are gone and they are withered and those whose leaves are rustling and falling all winter even into spring.

October is the month of painted leaves, of ripe leaves, when all the earth, not merely flowers, but fruits and leaves, are ripe. With respect to its colors and its season, it is the sunset month of the year, when the earth is painted like the sunset sky. This rich glow flashes round the world. This light fades into the clear, white, leafless twilight of November, and whatever more glowing sunset or Indian summer we have then is the afterglow of the year.[2] In October the man is ripe even to his stalk and leaves; he is pervaded by his genius, when all the forest is a universal harvest, whether he possesses the enduring color of the pines, which it takes two years to ripen and wither, or the brilliant color of the deciduous trees, which fade the first fall.

From this hill I am struck with the smoothness and

[1] [*Excursions*, p. 251; Riv. 307.]   [2] [Channing, p. 105.]

washed appearance of all the landscape. All these russet fields and swells look as if the withered grass had been combed by the flowing water. Not merely the sandy roads, but the fields are swept. All waters — the rivers and ponds and swollen brooks — and many new ones are now seen through the leafless trees — are blue as indigo, reservoirs of dark indigo amid the general russet and reddish-brown and gray.[1]

October answers to that period in the life of man when he is no longer dependent on his transient moods, when all his experience ripens into wisdom, but every root, branch, leaf of him glows with maturity. What he has been and done in his spring and summer appears. He bears his fruit.

Now for the bare branches of the oak woods, where hawks have nested and owls perched, the sinews of the trees, and the brattling (?) of the wind in their midst. For, now their leaves are off, they 've bared their arms, thrown off their coats, and, in the attitude of fencers, await the onset of the wind, to box or wrestle with it. Such high winds would have done much harm six weeks ago.

The top of Annursnack has been burned, and sown with winter rye, and the green blade contrasts with the black ground there. It is the most conspicuous radical leaf.

Went through the white cedar swamp. There are white cedars, larch (now bare), spruce, etc.; cedars two feet through, the only ones I know in Concord. It was here were cut the cedar posts which Alcott

[1] [Channing, p. 108.]

Vol. V

put into Emerson's summer-house. They could not be spared even for that. It is a stout tree here, tapering with singular abruptness. Its small flattish leaves, dispersed crosswise and at other or different angles with each other, give it a peculiarly light, fantastic look. Myriads of little ones are springing in the more open parts of the swamp. They are turned a reddish green now. The large trees have a very rough bark, regularly furrowed perpendicularly, and a bright-yellow resin between the furrows. I find that the inner bark makes a good lye. Is this used by the Indians? Methinks these are flower-buds which are formed at the ends of the leafets and will open early in the spring. This swamp must be visited in midsummer. You see great shelf-shaped fungi, handsomely buttressed and perfectly horizontal, on the under side of slanting dead trees, at different stages one above another. Do lichens or fungi grow on you? Sometimes the one side of a man is pasture for fungi while the other is clothed with lichens, he being partially rotten.

Our arbor-vitæ cones are full of broadly winged seeds.

6.30 P. M. — To Baker Farm by boat.

It is full moon, and a clear night, with a strong northwest wind; so C. and I must have a sail by moonlight. The river has risen surprisingly, to a spring height, owing to yesterday's rain, higher than before since spring. We sail rapidly upward. The river apparently, almost actually, as broad as the Hudson. Venus remarkably bright, just ready to set. Not a cloud in

the sky, only the moon and a few faint unobtrusive stars here and there, and from time to time a meteor. The water washes against our bows with the same sound that one hears against a vessel's prow by night on the ocean. If you had waked up here, you would not know at first but you were there. The shore-lines are concealed; you look seemingly over an almost boundless waste of waters on either hand. The hills are dark, vast, lumpish. Some near, familiar hill appears as a distant bold mountain, for its base is indefinitely removed. It is very pleasant to make our way thus rapidly but mysteriously over the black waves, black as ink and dotted with round foam-spots with a long moonlight sheen on one side — to make one's way upward thus over the waste of waters, not knowing where you are exactly, only avoiding shores. The stars are few and faint in this bright light. How well they wear! C. thought a man could still get along with *them* who was considerably reduced in his circumstances, that they were a kind of bread and cheese that never failed.[1] Fair Haven Hill never looked more grand and mountain-like than now that all its side is dark and we only see its bold outline at an indefinite distance. Under the lee of the Holden wood we found unexpectedly smooth and pleasant water and stillness, where we heard the wind roar behind us. The night is cool but not damp, and methinks you can be abroad with more impunity than in summer nights even. The walls on Conantum are merely black streaks, inky lines running over the hill.

[1] [*Excursions*, p. 328; Riv. 403, 404.]

The wind goes down somewhat. The features of the landscape are simpler and lumped. We have the moon with a few stars above, a waste of black, dashing waves around, reflecting the moon's sheen on one side, and the distant shore in dark swelling masses, dark floating isles between the water and the sky, on either hand. Moored our boat under Fair Haven Hill.

The light is so strong that colors of objects are not much changed from the day. The water seen from the hill is still blue, and the fields are russet.

How can we omit to go forth on the water these windy days and nights, to be tossed by the waves? It is some such novelty to a landsman as an earthquake. To take the hand of Nature and be shaken. Heard one cricket to-night.

Nov. 15. P. M. — To Fair Haven Hill and by boat to witch-hazel bush.

Were they not the white-in-tail birds I saw this afternoon? Cricket still. After yesterday's clear, windy weather we have to-day less wind and much haze. It is Indian-summer-like. The river has risen yet higher than last night, so that I cut across Hubbard's meadow with ease. Took up a witch-hazel with still some fresh blossoms; also a barberry bush. What appeared to be the minute fibrous roots of the last covered one side of a rock thickly like a piece of rotten flannel. How conspicuous its bright-yellow roots in the soil!

The flood has covered most muskrat-cabins again. It has also reached and floated higher yet the last week. Just after sundown, though it had been windy before, the waters became suddenly smooth, and the clear yellow light of the western sky was handsomely reflected in the water, making it doubly light to me on the water, diffusing light from below as well as above.

Were those insects on the surface after the moon rose skaters or water-bugs?

After having some business dealings with men, I am occasionally chagrined, and feel as if I had done some wrong, and it is hard to forget the ugly circumstance. I see that such intercourse long continued would make one thoroughly prosaic, hard, and coarse. But the longest intercourse with Nature, though in her rudest moods, does not thus harden and make coarse. A hard, insensible man whom we liken to a rock is indeed much harder than a rock. From hard, coarse, insensible men with whom I have no sympathy, I go to commune with the rocks, whose hearts are comparatively soft.

I was the other night elected a curator of our Lyceum, but was obliged to decline, because I did not know where to find good lecturers enough to make a course for the winter. We commonly think that we cannot have a good journal in New England, because we have not enough writers of ability; but we do not suspect likewise that we have not good lecturers enough to make a Lyceum.

The tall wool-grass, with its stately heads, still stands above and is reflected in the smooth water.

Together with the barberry, I dug up a brake root by chance. This, too, should have gone into the witches'

caldron. It is large and black, almost like a cinder without, and within curiously black and white in parallel fibres, with a sort of mildewiness as if it were rotting; yet fresh shoots are ready for the spring with a cottony point.

Goodwin says he killed a mink the other day on a small *white pine tree*. Some years ago, about this season, he dug out fifteen muskrats in one nest in the ground at Goose Pond. He says the white rabbit does not run to his hole, but the gray one does.

This evening at sundown, when I was on the water, I heard come booming up the river what I suppose was the sound of cannon fired in Lowell to celebrate the Whig victory, the voting down the new Constitution. Perchance no one else in Concord heard them, and it is remarkable that I heard them, who was only interested in the natural phenomenon of sound borne far over water. The river is now so full and so high over the meadows, and at that hour was so smooth withal, that perchance the waves of sound flowed over the smooth surface of the water with less obstruction and further than in any other direction.

I also noticed this afternoon that, before the water generally was smoothed, those parts of the inundated meadow where spires of grass rose thinly above the surface were already quite smooth and glossy, so effectually did they break and dissipate the wavelets. A multitude of fine grass stems were a sufficient breakwater to render the surface smooth.

This afternoon has wanted no condition to make it a gossamer day, it seems to me, but a calm atmos-

Vol. V

phere. Plainly the spiders cannot be abroad on the water unless it is smooth. The one I witnessed this fall was at time of flood. May it be that they are driven out of their retreats like muskrats and snow-fleas, and spin these lines for their support? Yet they work on the causeway, too.

I see many cranberries on the vines at the bottom, making a great show. It might be worth the while, where possible, to flood a cranberry meadow as soon as they are ripe and before the frosts, and so preserve them plump and sound till spring.

Nov. 16. P. M. — To Nawshawtuct by boat with Sophia, up Assabet.

The river still higher than yesterday. I paddled straight from the boat's place to the Island. I now take notice of the green polypody on the rock and various other ferns, one the marginal (?) shield fern and one the terminal shield fern, and this other, here inserted, on the steep bank above the Hemlocks.

I admire the fine blue color of the cedar berries.

Nov. 17. I notice that many plants about this season of the year or earlier, after they have died down at top, put forth fresh and conspicuous radical leaves against another spring. So some human beings in the November of their days exhibit some fresh radical greenness, which, though the frosts may soon nip it, indicates and confirms their essential vitality. When their summer leaves have faded and fallen, they put forth fresh radical leaves which sustain the life in their

root still, against a new spring. The dry fields have for a long time been spotted with the small radical leaves of the fragrant life-everlasting, not to mention the large primrose, johnswort, etc., etc. And almost every plant, although it may show no greenness above ground, if you dig about it, will be found to have fresh shoots already pointing upward and ready to burst forth in the spring.

Are not more birds crushed under the feet of oxen than of horses?

Nov. 18. Conchologists call those shells "which are fished up from the depths of the ocean" and are never seen on the shore, which are the rarest and most beautiful, *Pelagii*, but those which are cast on shore and are never so delicate and beautiful as the former, on account of exposure and abrasion, *Littorales*. So it is with the thoughts of poets: some are fresh from the deep sea, radiant with unimagined beauty, — *Pelagii*; but others are comparatively worn, having been tossed by many a tide, — *Littorales*, — scaled off, abraded, and eaten by worms.

Nov. 19. P. M. Up river in boat to Hubbard's meadow, cranberrying.

They redden all the lee shore, the water being still apparently at the same level with the 16th. This is a very pleasant and warm Indian-summer afternoon. Methinks we have not had one like it since October 31st. This, too, is a gossamer day, though it is not particularly calm. If it were, it would be still more perfect. My boat I find to be covered with spiders, whose fine lines soon stretch from side to side. Got a bushel and a half of cranberries, mixed with chaff. Brought home one of those little shells found in the shore wreck, which look like a bugle-horn. I notice that at the bridges there is now a slight rapid, and the water is perceptibly several inches lower on the down-stream side, the piers acting as a dam, the stream being somewhat narrowed there withal by the abutments. What is the peculiarity of the Indian summer? From the 14th to the 21st October inclusive, this year, was perfect Indian summer; and this day the next? Methinks that any particularly pleasant and warmer weather after the middle of October is thus called. Has it not fine, calm spring days answering to it? Autumnal dandelion quite fresh. Tansy very fresh yesterday.

Nov. 20. 7.30 A. M. — To Hubbard's meadow, cranberrying.

Still quite warm as yesterday. I wear no greatcoat. There has been no freezing in the night. I hear a single hylodes in the wood by the water, while I am raking the cranberries. This warmth has aroused him. While raking, I disturbed two bullfrogs, one quite small. These, too, the warm weather has perhaps aroused. They appear rather stupid. Also I see one painted tortoise, but with no bright markings. Do they fade?

I observe on some muskrat-cabins much of that bleached and withered long grass, strewn as if preparatory to raising them, for almost all are covered

Vol. V

with water now. It apparently is used as a binder. I find, washed up with the cranberries and also floating over the meadow and about the cabins, many fragments of a root, often with that green, somewhat pellucid, roundish pad attached. This appears to be the muskrats' principal vegetable food now. It is not flagroot, but either yellow lily, pontederia, white lily, — or can it be heart-leaf root?

The shore is so reddened with cranberries that I perceive them fifteen rods off, tingeing it. Many of them being frost-bitten, they have now the pleasant taste of spring cranberries, which many prefer. They, as well as the wreck generally, are covered, as if peppered, with the skipping snow-fleas. In the wreck I find also the common little trumpet-shaped cockle, and some caddis-worms out of their cases. There is an abundance of chaff, *i. e.* broken meadow-grass and cranberry leaves, in it now.

Minott said he heard geese going south at daybreak the 17th, before he came out of the house, and heard and saw another large flock at 10 A. M. Those I heard this afternoon were low and far in the western horizon. I did [not] distinctly see them, but heard them farther and farther in the southwest, the sound of one which did the honking guiding my eyes. I had seen that a storm was brewing before, and low mists already gathered in the northeast. It rained soon after I got home. The 18th was also a drizzling day. Methinks the geese are wont to go south just before a storm, and, in the spring, to go north just after one, say at the end of a long April storm.

I have not seen any tree sparrows of late, nor white-in-tails. Would it not be worth the while to flood a cranberry meadow just before the frosts come, and so preserve them plump and fresh till spring?[1] I once came near speculating in cranberries. Being put to it to raise the wind to pay for "A Week on the Concord and Merrimack Rivers," and having occasion to go to New York to peddle some pencils which I had made, as I passed through Boston I went to Quincy Market and inquired the price of cranberries. The dealers took me down cellar, asked if I wanted wet or dry, and showed me them. I gave them to understand that I might want an indefinite quantity. It made a slight sensation among them and for aught I know raised the price of the berry for a time. I then visited various New York packets and was told what would be the freight, on deck and in the hold, and one skipper was very anxious for my freight. When I got to New York, I again visited the markets as a purchaser, and "the best of Eastern Cranberries" were offered me by the barrel at a cheaper rate than I could buy them in Boston. I was obliged to manufacture a thousand dollars' worth of pencils and slowly dispose of and finally sacrifice them, in order to pay an assumed debt of a hundred dollars.

What enhances my interest in dew — I am thinking of the summer — is the fact that it is so distinct from rain, formed most abundantly after bright, starlit nights, a product especially of the clear, serene air. The manna of fair weather; the upper side of rain,

[1] [See p. 508.]

as the country above the clouds. That nightly rain called dew, which gathers and falls in so low a stratum that our heads tower above it like mountains in an ordinary shower. It only consists with comparatively fair weather above our heads. Those warm volumes of air, forced high up the hillsides in summer nights, are driven thither to drop their dew there, like kine to their yards to be milked; that the moisture they hold may be condensed and so dew formed before morning on the tops of the hills. A writer in *Harper's Magazine* (vol. vii, page 505) says that the mist at evening does not rise, "but gradually forms higher up in the air." He calls it the moisture of the air become visible. Says there is most dew in clear nights, because clouds prevent the cooling down of the air; they radiate the heat of the earth back to it; and that a strong wind, by keeping the air in motion, prevents its heat from passing off. Therefore, I proceed, for a plentiful dew it must not only be clear but calm. The above writer says bad conductors of heat have always most dew on them, and that wool or swan's-down is "good for experimenting on the quantity of dew falling," — weight before and after. Thinks it not safe to walk in clear nights, especially after midnight, when the dew is most abundantly forming; better in cloudy nights, which are drier. Also thinks it not prudent to venture out until the sun begins to rise and warms the air. But methinks this prudence begets a tenderness that will catch more cold at noonday than the opposite hardiness at midnight.

Nov. 21. *Monday.* A fine misty rain all night and to-day.

Raking so many cranberries has made me quite conversant with the materials of the river wreck. There are many middle-sized living black dor-bugs in it, as well as bugle-horn shells, as I find on washing out my cranberries in the kitchen to-day. I have got about two and a half bushels of clear cranberries, and added those of Saturday afternoon makes about three and a half. I find my best way of getting cranberries is to go forth in time of flood, just before the water begins to fall and after strong winds, and, choosing the thickest places, let one, with an instrument like a large coarse dung-fork, hold down the floating grass and other coarser part of the wreck mixed with [it], while another, with a common iron garden rake, rakes them into the boat, there being just enough chaff left to enable you to get them into the boat, yet with little water. When I got them home, I filled a half-bushel basket a quarter full and set it in a tub of water, and, stirring the cranberries, the coarser part of the chaff was held beneath by the berries rising to the top. Then, raising the basket, draining it, and upsetting it into a bread-trough, the main part of the chaff fell uppermost and was cast aside. Then, draining off the water, I jarred the cranberries alternately to this end and then to that of the trough, each time removing the fine chaff — cranberry leaves and bits of grass — which adhered to the bottom, on the principle of gold-washing, except that the gold was what was thrown away, and finally I spread and dried and win-

nowed them. It would have been better if the basket had been a very coarse riddle and the trough had had a rough bottom.

The last two nights, at least, there has been no freezing.

Is not the dew but a humbler, gentler rain, the nightly rain, above which we raise our heads and unobstructedly behold the stars? The mountains are giants which tower above the rain, as we above the dew in the grass; it only wets their feet.

Nov. 22. Geese went over yesterday, and to-day also.

The drizzling rain of yesterday has not checked the fall of the river. It was raised by the rain of Sunday, the 13th, and began to fall the 20th.

P. M. — Up river by boat.

I think it must be the white lily root I find gnawed by the rats, though the leaves are pellucid. It has large roots with eyes and many smaller rootlets attached, white tinged with a bluish slate-color. The radical leaves appear to have started again. Turnip freshly in bloom in cultivated fields ; knawel still ; yarrow is particularly fresh and innocent; but I find no blossom on the *Arenaria serpyllifolia.*

If there is any one with whom we have a quarrel, it is most likely that that one makes some just demand on us which we disappoint.

I see still, here and there, a few deep-sunk yellow and decayed pads, the bleared, dulled, drowned eyes of summer.

Vol. V

I was just thinking it would be fine to get a specimen leaf from each changing tree and shrub and plant in autumn, in September and October, when it had got its brightest characteristic color, the intermediate ripeness in its transition from the green to the russet or brown state, outline and copy its color exactly with paint in a book, — a book which should be a memorial of October, be entitled October Hues or Autumnal Tints. I remember especially the beautiful yellow of the *Populus grandidentata* and the tint of the scarlet maple. What a memento such a book would be, beginning with the earliest reddening of the leaves, woodbine and ivy, etc., etc., and the lake of radical leaves, down to the latest oaks![1] I might get the impression of their veins and outlines in the summer with lampblack, and after color them.

As I was returning down the river toward night, I mistook the creaking of a plow-wheel for a flock of blackbirds passing overhead, but it is too late for them. The farmers plow considerably this month. No doubt it destroys many grubs in the earth.

Nov. 23. 6 A. M. — To Swamp Bridge Brook mouth.

The cocks are the only birds I hear, but they are a host. They crow as freshly and bravely as ever, while poets go down the stream, degenerate into science and prose. I have not seen a flock of small birds, either tree sparrows or *F. hyemalis* or white-in-tails, etc., for about a fortnight. There is now no sound of early birds on the leafless trees and bushes — willows and

[1] *[Excursions,* p. 251; Riv. 307, 308.]

alders — along this watercourse. The few that are left probably roost in the evergreen woods. Yet I hear, or seem to hear, the faintest possible lisp or creak from some sparrow, as if from a crack in the mist-clad earth, or some ox-yoke or distant wain. I suspect that the song sparrow lingers as late, here and there alone, as any migrating bird.

By 8 o'clock the misty clouds disperse, and it turns out a pleasant, calm, and springlike morning. The water, going down, but still spread far over the meadows, is seen from the window perfectly smooth and full of reflections. What lifts and lightens and makes heaven of the earth is the fact that you see the reflections of the humblest weeds against the sky, but you cannot put your head low enough to see the substance so. The reflection enchants us, just as an echo does.

If I would preserve my relation to nature, I must make my life more moral, more pure and innocent. The problem is as precise and simple as a mathematical one. I must not live loosely, but more and more continently.[1]

What an engineer this water is! It comes with its unerring level, and reveals all the inequalities of the meadow. The farmer may see now what route to take to get the driest and firmest ground for his hay-carts, how to cut his ditches, and where to drop more sand. It is an obvious piece of geometry in nature. Every peculiar curve in the limbs of the trees is doubly conspicuous seen both above and beneath, yet the

[1] *[Channing,* pp. 87, 88.]

rhyme makes even what was odd, regular what was irregular. For a week or more there has been no freezing day or night. The springs and swamps are getting filled.

The Indian summer itself, said to be more remarkable in this country than elsewhere, no less than the reblossoming of certain flowers, the peep of the hylodes, and sometimes the faint warble of some birds, is the reminiscence, or rather the return, of spring, — the year renewing its youth.

At 5 P. M. I saw, flying southwest high overhead, a flock of geese, and heard the faint honking of one or two. They were in the usual harrow form, twelve in the shorter line and twenty-four in the longer, the latter abutting on the former at the fourth bird from the front. I judged *hastily* that the interval between the geese was about double their alar extent, and, as the last is, according to Wilson, five feet and two inches, the former may safely be called eight feet. I hear they were fired at with a rifle from Bunker Hill the other day. This is the sixth flock I have seen or heard of since the morning of the 17th, *i. e.* within a week.

Vol. V

Nov. 24. At noon, after a drizzling forenoon, the weather suddenly changed to clear and wintry, freezing cold with strong wind from a northerly quarter. It seems like the beginning of winter. Ice forms in my boat at 5 P. M., and what was mud in the street is fast becoming a rigid roughness. This after more than a week of mild and much drizzly weather without frost, one or two of the fairest days being Indian-summerish.

Methinks we have had clear yellow sunsets and afterglows this month, like this to-night (not glowing red ones), with perhaps an inclination to blue and greenish clouds.

Nov. 25. Frost on the windows.

10 A. M. — To Cliffs.

A clear, cold, windy day. The water on the meadows, which are rapidly becoming bare, is skimmed over and reflects a whitish light, like silver plating, while the unfrozen river is a dark blue. In plowed fields I see the asbestos-like ice-crystals, more or less mixed with earth, frequently curled and curved like crisped locks, where the wet ground has frozen dry. By the spring under Fair Haven Hill, I see the frost about the cistus now at 11 A. M. in the sun. For some weeks I have heard occasionally the hounding of hounds, like a distant natural horn in the clear resonant air. Though the grass has but little life, even in its roots, cattle are still turned out more or less.

The landscape, seen from the side of the hill looking westward to the horizon through this clear and sparkling air, though simple to barrenness, is very

---

handsome. There is first the clean light-reflecting russet earth, the dark-blue water, the dark or dingy green evergreens, the dull reddish-brown of young oaks and shrub oaks, the gray of maples and other leafless trees, and the white of birch stems. The mountains are remarkably distinct and appear near and elevated, but there is no snow on them. The white houses of the village, also, are remarkably distinct and bare and brought very near.

Going through the orchard, I saw two birds like jays and soon heard a whistle-like note of alarm, between a robin and a downy woodpecker. Perhaps it was a butcher-bird. A heavy-shouldered hawk sails over. A *Solidago nemoralis* with flowers still at root.

Just after the sun set to-night, I observed that the northern hemisphere of the heavens was covered with fleecy clouds, which abruptly terminated in a straight line, stretching east and west from one horizon to the other directly over my head, the western end being beautifully rose-tinted. Half an hour later this cloud had advanced southward, showing clear sky behind it in the north, until its southern edge was seen at an angle of 45° by [*sic*] me, but though its line was as straight as before, it now appeared regularly curved like a segment of a melon-rind, as usual.

Nov. 27. Now a man will eat his heart, if ever,[1] now while the earth is bare, barren and cheerless, and we have the coldness of winter without the variety of ice and snow; but methinks the variety and com-

[1] [See *Journal*, vol. iv, p. 405.]

---

pensation are in the stars now. How bright they are now by contrast with the dark earth! The days are short enough now. The sun is already setting before I have reached the ordinary limit of my walk, but the 21st of next month the day will be shorter still by about twenty-five minutes. In December there will be less light than in any month in the year.

It is too cold to-day to use a paddle; the water freezes on the handle and numbs my fingers. I observe the *Lycopodium lucidulum* still of a fresh, shining green. Checkerberries and partridge-berries are both numerous and obvious now.

Nov. 28. Monday. Saw boys skating in Cambridgeport, — the first ice to bear. Settled with J. Munroe & Co., and on a new account placed twelve of my books with him on sale. I have paid him directly out of pocket since the book was published two hundred and ninety dollars and taken his receipt for it. This does not include postage on proof-sheets, etc., etc. I have received from other quarters about fifteen dollars. This has been the pecuniary value of the book. Saw at the Natural History rooms the skeleton of a moose with horns. The length of the spinal processes (?) over the shoulder was very great.[1] The hind legs were longer than the front, and the horns rose about two feet above the shoulders and spread between four and five, I judged.

Dr. Harris described to me his finding a species of cicindela at the White Mountains this fall (the same he had found there one specimen of some time ago),

[1] [*Maine Woods*, p. 127; Riv. 154.]

supposed to be very rare, found at St. Peter's River and at Lake Superior; but he proves it to be common near the White Mountains.

Nov. 29. On Saturday, the 26th, a dog on whose collar the words "Milton Hill," or equivalent ones, were engraved ran through the town, having, as the story went, bitten a boy in Lincoln. He bit several dogs in this town and was finally shot. Some of the dogs bitten have been killed, and rumor now says that the boy died yesterday. People are considerably alarmed. Some years ago a boy in Lincoln was bitten by a raccoon and died of hydrophobia. I observed to Minott to-night that I did not think that our doctors knew how to cure this disease, but he said they could cure it, he had seen a man bitten who was cured. The story is worth telling, for it shows how much trouble the passage of one mad dog through the town may produce.

It was when he was a boy and lived down below the old Ben Prescott house, over the cellar-hole on what is now Hawthorne's land. The first he remembers a couple of men had got poles and were punching at a strange dog toward night under a barn in that neighborhood. The dog, which was speckled and not very large, would growl and bite the pole, and they ran a good deal of risk, but they did not know that he was mad. At length they routed him, and he took to the road and came on towards town, and Minott, keeping his distance, followed on behind. When the dog got to the old Ben Prescott place, he turned up into the

yard, where there were a couple of turkeys, drove them into a corner, bit off the head of one, and carried the body off across the road into the meadow opposite. They then raised the cry of "Mad dog." He saw his mother and Aunt Prescott, two old ladies, coming down the road, while the dog was running the other way in the meadow, and he shouted to them to take care of themselves, for that dog was mad. The dog soon reëntered the road at some bars and held on toward town. Minott next saw Harry Hooper coming down the road after his cows, and he shouted to him to look out, for the dog was mad, but Harry, who was in the middle of the road, spread his arms out, one on each side, and, being short, the dog leaped right upon his open breast and made a pass at his throat, but missed it, though it frightened him a good deal; and Minott, coming up, exclaimed, "Why, you're crazy, Harry; if he'd 'a' bitten ye, 't would 'a' killed ye." When he got up as far as the red house or Curtis place, the dog was about in the middle of the road, and a large and stout old gentleman by the name of Fay, dressed in small-clothes, was coming down on the sidewalk. M. shouted to him also to take care of himself, for the dog was mad, and Fay said afterward that he heard him but he had always supposed that a mad dog would n't turn out for anything; but when this dog was nearly abreast of him, he suddenly inclined toward him, and then again inclined still more, and seized him by the left leg just below the knee, and Fay, giving him a kick with the other leg, tripped himself up; and when he was down, the dog bit him

in the right leg in the same place. Being by this time well frightened, and fearing that he would spring at his throat next, Fay seized the dog himself by his throat and held him fast, and called lustily for somebody to come and kill him. A man by the name of Lewis rushed out of the red house with an old axe and began to tap on the dog's nose with it, but he was afraid to strike harder, for Fay told him not to hit him. Minott saw it all, but still kept his distance. Suddenly Fay, not knowing what he did, let go, and the man, giving the dog a blow across the back, ran into the house; but, it being a dull meat axe, the dog trotted along, still toward town.

He turned and went round the pond by Bowers's and, going down to the brook by the roadside, lapped some water. Just then, Peter coming over the bridge, the dog reared up and growled at him, and he, seeing that he was mad, made haste through the bars out of his way and cut across the fields to Reuben Brown's. The dog went on, it being now between sundown and dark, to Peter Wheeler's, and bit two cows, which afterward died of hydrophobia, and next he went to where Nathan Stow now lives, and bit a goose in the wing, and so he kept on through the town. The next that was heard of him, Black Cato, that lived at the Lee place, now Sam Wheeler's, on the river, was waked up about midnight by a noise among the pigs, and, having got up, he took a club and went out to see what was the matter. Looking over into the pen, this dog reared up at him, and he knocked him back into it, and, jumping over, mauled him till he thought he was dead

and then tossed him out. In the morning he thought he [would] go out and see whose dog he had killed, but lo! he had picked himself up, and there was no dog to be found.

Cato was going out into the woods chopping that day, and as he was getting over a wall lined with brush, the same dog reared up at him once more, but this time, having heard of the mad dog, he was frightened and ran; but still the dog came on, and once or twice he knocked him aside with a large stone, till at length, the dog coming close to him, he gave him a blow which killed him; and lest he should run away again, he cut off his head and threw both head and body into the river.

In the meanwhile Fay went home (to the Dr. Heywood house), drank some spirit, then went straight over to Dr. Heywood's office and stayed there and was doctored by him for three weeks. The doctor cut out the mangled flesh and made various applications, and Fay cried like a baby, but he never experienced any further ill effects from the bite.

P. M. — To J. P. Brown's pond-hole.

J. Hosmer showed me a pestle which his son had found this summer while plowing on the plain between his house and the river. It has a rude bird's head, a hawk's or eagle's, the beak and eyes (the latter a mere prominence) serving for a knob or handle. It is affecting, as a work of art by a people who have left so few traces of themselves, a step beyond the common arrowhead and pestle and axe. Something more fanciful, a step beyond pure utility. As long as I find traces of works of convenience merely, however much skill they show, I am not so much affected as when I discover works which evince the exercise of fancy and taste, however rude. It is a great step to find a pestle whose handle is ornamented with a bird's-head knob. It brings the maker still nearer to the races which so ornament their umbrella and cane handles. I have, then, evidence in stone that men lived here who had fancies to be pleased, and in whom the first steps toward a complete culture were taken. It implies so many more thoughts such as I have. The arrowhead, too, suggests a bird, but a relation to it not in the least godlike. But here an Indian has patiently sat and fashioned a stone into the likeness of a bird, and added some pure beauty to that pure utility, and so far begun to leave behind him war, and even hunting, and to redeem himself from the savage state. In this he was leaving off to be savage. Enough of this would have saved him from extermination.

I dug for frogs at Heart-leaf Pond, but found none. The ice is two inches thick there, and already, the day being warm, is creased irregularly but agreeably on the upper surface. What is the law of these figures as on watered silks? Has it anything to do with the waves of the wind, or are they the outlines of the crystals as they originally shot, the bones of the ice? It would be worth the while to watch some water while freezing. What is that low yellowish, straw-colored sedge which is so dense in this pond now? I must look for frogs about springs, where Minott says he has dug them

out. The andromeda leaves are a rich brown color now.

It has been cloudy and milder this afternoon, but now I begin to see, under the clouds in the west horizon, a clear crescent of yellowish sky, and suddenly a glorious yellow sunlight falls on all the eastern landscape — russet fields and hillsides, evergreens and rustling oaks and single leafless trees. In addition to the clearness of the air at this season, the light is all from one side, and, none being absorbed or dissipated in the heavens, but it being reflected both from the russet earth and the clouds, it is intensely bright, and all the limbs of a maple seen far eastward rising over a hill are wonderfully distinct and lit. I think that we have some such sunsets as this, and peculiar to the season, every year. I should call it the russet afterglow of the year. It may not be warm, but must be clear and comparatively calm. I see now large insects in the calm, sunlit air over the sprout-lands.

Cattle still abroad in the fields, though there is little to be got there. They say that young cattle can stand the cold and starvation best. If I am not mistaken, their coats have less sleekness than in the spring; they have a shaggy, frowzy, and nipped look, their hair standing on end, and the sorrel color seems to predominate. Their pastures look as barren of nutriment as their own backs.

Nov. 30. 8 A. M. — To river, to examine roots.

I rake up almost everywhere from the bottom of the river that very fresh and bright green ranunculus,

the handsomely divided leaf. I ascertain this morning that that white root with eyes and slaty-tinged fibres and sharp leaves rolled up, found gnawed off and floating about muskrat-houses, is the root of the great yellow lily. The leaf-stalk is yellow, while that of the white lily is a downy or mildewy blue black. The yellow lily root is, then, a principal item, it would seem, in their vegetable diet. I find that those large triangular or rhomboidal or shell-shaped eyes or shoulders on this root are the bases of leaf-stalks which have rotted off, but toward the upper end of the root are still seen decaying. They are a sort of abutment on which the leaf-stalk rested, and the fine black dots on them are the bases of the fine threads or fibres of the leaf-stalk, which, in the still living leaf-stalk, are distinguished by their purple color. These eyes, like the leaves, of course, are arranged spirally around the roots in parallel rows, in quincunx order, so that four make a diamond figure. The slate-tinged fibres spring from the bare white intervals between the bases of the leaves. Closely packed between, and protected by the under leaf-stalk, I find already the tender club-shaped yellow flower-bud a quarter of an inch in diameter, with a stem two inches long and wider than the bud. I am surprised to find these roots, even within to the bases of the leaves about the buds, infested with white grubs nearly half an inch long and minute, threadlike reddish and speckled worms. Also on the fibres are transparent elliptical chrysalids, the color of a snail-shell, containing insects apparently just ready to fly.

The white lily roots are more enveloped in down

and fibre, a dark-blue or blackish down. I raked up one dark-brown root somewhat like a white lily, except that it was smooth and the leaf-stalks were very slender and the leaf-buds minute. Perhaps it was the kalmiana lily. I raked up one live clam in deep water, and could feel them like stones on the bottom.

All these leaves are lightly rolled up in the form of arrowheads, as thus best prepared to pierce whatever obstacles the mud or water may present. There is a vast amount of decaying vegetable matter at the bottom of the river, and what I draw up on my rake emits a very offensive odor.

P. M. — Down river by boat and inland to the Green house beyond Blood's.

A mild and summery afternoon with much russet light on the landscape.

I think it was a flock of low-warbling tree sparrows [1] which I saw amid the weeds beyond the monument, though they looked larger.

I am attracted nowadays by the various withered grasses and sedges, of different shades of straw-color and of various more or less graceful forms. That which I call fescue grass is quite interesting, gracefully bending to the zephyr, and many others are very perfect and pure. Wool-grass is one of the largest and most conspicuous. I observe it rising thinly above the water in which it is reflected, two or three feet, and all its narrow rustling leaves stream southeasterly from the stems, though it is now quite calm, proving the preva-

[1] Undoubtedly; also Dec. 3d.

lence of northwesterly winds. An abundance of withered sedges and other coarse grasses, which in the summer you scarcely noticed, now cover the low grounds, — the granary of the winter birds. A very different end they serve from the flowers which decay so early. Their rigid culms enable them to withstand the blasts of winter. Though divested of color, fairly bleached, they are not in the least decayed but seasoned and living like the heart-wood.

Now, first since spring, I take notice of the cladonia lichens, which the cool fall rains appear to have started. The *Callitriche verna* is perfectly fresh and green, though frozen in, in the pools.

We are going across the Hunt and Mason pastures. The twigs of young cedars with apparently staminate buds have even a strawberry-like fragrance, and what a heavenly blue have the berries! — a peculiar light blue, whose bloom rubs off, contrasting with the green or purplish-brown leaves.

I do not know so fine a pine grove as that of Mason's. The young second-growth white pines are peculiarly soft, thick, and bushy there. They branch directly at the ground and almost horizontally, for the most part four or five large stems springing from the ground together, as if they had been broken down by cattle originally. But the result is a very dark and dense, almost impenetrable, but peculiarly soft and beautiful grove, which any gentleman might covet on his estate.

We returned by the bridle-road across the pastures. When I returned to town the other night by the Walden

road through the meadows from Brister's Hill to the poorhouse, I fell to musing upon the origin of the meanders in the road; for when I looked straight before or behind me, my eye met the fences at a short distance, and it appeared that the road, instead of being built in a straight line across the meadows, as one might have expected, pursued a succession of curves like a cow-path. In fact, it was just such a meandering path as an eye of taste requires, and the landscape-gardener consciously aims to make, and the wonder is that a body of laborers left to themselves, without instruments or geometry, and perchance intending to make a straight road, — in short, that circumstances ordinarily, — will so commonly make just such a meandering road as the eye requires. A man advances in his walk somewhat as a river does, meanderingly, and such, too, is the progress of the race. The law that plants the rushes in waving lines along the edge of a pond, and that curves the pond-shore itself, incessantly beats against the straight fences and highways of men and makes them conform to the line of beauty which is most agreeable to the eye at last.

But to return to the walk of the day. Though there were some clouds in the west, there was a bright silver twilight before we reached our boat. C. remarked it descending into the hollows immediately after sunset. A red house could hardly be distinguished at a distance, but a white one appeared to reflect light on the landscape. At first we saw no redness in the sky, but only some peculiar dark wisp-like clouds in the west,

Vol. V

but on rising a hill I saw a few red stains like veins of red quartz on a ground of feldspar.

The river was perfectly smooth except the upwelling of its tide, and as we paddled home westward, the dusky yellowing sky was all reflected in it, together with the dun-colored clouds and the trees, and there was more light in the water than in the sky. The reflections of the trees and bushes on the banks were wonderfully dark and distinct, for though frequently we could not see the real bush in the twilight against the dark bank, in the water it appeared against the sky. We were thus often enabled to steer clear of the overhanging bushes.

It was an evening for the muskrats to be abroad, and we saw one, which dove as he was swimming rapidly, turning over like a wheel.

END OF VOLUME V

The Journal of Henry D. Thoreau

VOLUME VI

(December, 1853 — August, 1854)

The Leaning Hemlocks in Winter

CONTENTS

Vol. VI

THE JOURNAL OF
HENRY DAVID THOREAU

VOLUME VI

I

DECEMBER, 1853 (ÆT. 36)

Dec. 1. 4 P. M. — To Cliffs.

We may infer that every withered culm of grass or sedge, or weed that still stands in the fields, answers some purpose by standing.

Those trees and shrubs which retain their withered leaves through the winter — shrub oaks and young white, red, and black oaks, the lower branches of larger trees of the last-mentioned species, hornbeam, etc., and young hickories — seem to form an intermediate class between deciduous and evergreen trees. They may almost be called the ever-reds. Their leaves, which are falling all winter long, serve as a shelter to rabbits and partridges and other winter quadrupeds and birds. Even the little chickadees love to skulk amid them and peep out from behind them. I hear their faint, silvery, lisping notes, like tinkling glass, and occasionally a sprightly *day-day-day*, as they inquisitively hop nearer and nearer to me. They are our most honest and innocent little bird, drawing yet nearer to us as the

winter advances, and deserve best of any of the walker.

Dec. 2. As the stars, though spheres, present an outline of many little points of light to our eyes, like a flower of light, so I notice to-night the horns of the new moon appear split.

The skeleton which at first sight excites only a shudder in all mortals becomes at last not only a pure but suggestive and pleasing object to science. The more we know of it, the less we associate it with any goblin of our imaginations. The longer we keep it, the less likely it is that any such will come to claim it. We discover that the only spirit which haunts it is a universal intelligence which has created it in harmony with all nature. Science never saw a ghost, nor does it look for any, but it sees everywhere the traces, and it is itself the agent, of a Universal Intelligence.

A communication to a newspaper, dated Bangor, 28th (November), says of the Penobscot: " The navigation is closed here, the anchor ice with the surface ice making an obstruction of several feet thickness. There are enclosed in the ice from 60 to 80 vessels with full cargoes, besides the steamers. . . . The ice obstruction extends about five miles," etc. There is still no ice in the Concord River, or the skimming which forms along the shore in the night almost entirely disappears in the day. On the 30th I paddled on it in the afternoon, and there was not a particle of ice, and even in the morning my constantly wet hands were not cold.

The latitude of Lynn church is 42° 27′ 51″. Calling

Concord, at a venture, 42° 27′, Bangor being 44° 47′ 50″, the difference equals about 2° 21′. The length of a degree of latitude in Italy (43° 1′) being, according to Boscovich and Lemaire's measurement, 68.998 English miles, call it in this case 69 miles, and the difference of latitude in miles between B. and C. is about 162 miles.

Dec. 3. P. M. — Up river by boat to Clamshell Hill.

Saw two tree sparrows on Monroe's larch by the waterside. Larger than chip-birds, with more bay above and a distinct white bar on wings, not to mention bright-chestnut crown and obscure spot on breast; all beneath pale-ash. They were busily and very adroitly picking the seeds out of the larch cones. It would take man's clumsy fingers a good while to get at one, and then only by breaking off the scales, but they picked them out as rapidly as if they were insects on the outside of the cone, uttering from time to time a faint, tinkling chip.

I see that muskrats have not only erected cabins, but, since the river rose, have in some places dug galleries a rod into the bank, pushing the sand behind them into the water. So they dig these now as places of retreat merely, or for the same purpose as the cabins, apparently. One I explored this afternoon was formed in a low shore (Hubbard's Bathing-Place), at a spot where there were no weeds to make a cabin of, and was apparently never completed, perhaps because the shore was too low.

The ranunculus is still a fresh bright green at the

bottom of the river. It is the evergreen of the river, and indeed resembles the common running evergreen (*Lycopodium*, I think it is called).

I see along the sides of the river, two to four inches above the surface but all at one level, clear, drop-shaped crystals of ice, either held up by some twig or hanging by a dead vine of climbing mikania. They are the remains of a thin sheet of ice, which melted as the river went down, and in drops formed around and ran down these cores and again froze, and, being thicker than the surrounding ice, have outlasted it.

At J. Hosmer's tub spring, I dug out a small bullfrog (?) in the sandy mud at the bottom of the tub — it was lively enough to hop — and brought it home. Probably they lie universally buried in the mud now, below the reach of frost. In a ditch near by, under ice half an inch thick, I saw a painted tortoise moving about. The frogs then are especially to be looked for in the mud about springs.

It is remarkable how much power I can exert through the undulations which I produce by rocking my boat in the middle of the river. Some time after I have ceased I am surprised to hear the sound of the undulations which have just reached the shores acting on the thin ice there and making a complete wreck of it for a long distance up and down the stream, cracking off pieces four feet wide and more. I have stirred up the river to do this work, a power which I cannot put to rest. The secret of this power appears to lie in the extreme mobility, or, as I may say, irritability, of this element. It is the principle of the roller, or of an immense

weight moved by a child on balls, and the momentum is tremendous.

Some of the clamshells, freshly opened by the muskrats and left lying on their half-sunken cabins, where they are kept wet by the waves, show very handsome rainbow tints. I examined one such this afternoon. The hinge of the shell was not broken, and I could discover no injury to the shell, except a little broken off the edges at the broadest end, as if by the teeth of the rat in order to get hold, insert its incisors. The fish is confined to the shell by strong muscles at each end of each valve, and the rat must dissolve the union between both of these and one side of the shell before he can get it open, unless the fish itself opens it, which perhaps it cannot wide enough. I could not open one just dead without separating the muscle from the shell. The growth of the mussel's shell appears to be in somewhat concentric layers or additions to a small shell or eye.

The clam which I brought home the 30th *ult.*, and left outdoors by mistake, I now find frozen to death. J. Hosmer told me the other day that he had seen a man eat many of these clams raw and relish them. It is a somewhat saddening reflection that the beautiful colors of this shell for want of light cannot be said to exist, until its inhabitant has fallen a prey to the spoiler, and it is thus left a wreck upon the strand. Its beauty then beams forth, and it remains a splendid cenotaph to its departed tenant, symbolical of those radiant realms of light to which the latter has risen, — what glory he has gone to. And, by the way, as long as they remain in "the dark unfathomed caves of ocean,"

they are not "gems of purest ray serene," though fitted to be, but only when they are tossed up to light.

Probably the muskrat inserts his incisors between the edges of the shells (and so crumbles them) in order to pry them open. Some of these shells at Clamshell Hill, whose contents were cooked by the Indians, are still entire, but separated. Wood has spread a great many loads over his land. People would be surprised to learn what quantities of these shellfish are annually consumed by the muskrat. Their shells help convert the meadow mud or river sediment into food for plants. The Indians generally — I have particularly observed it in the case of the Penobscots — make a very extensive use of the muskrat for food, and from these heaps it would seem that they used the fresh-water clam extensively also, — these two peculiarly indigenous animals. What if it were calculated how often a muskrat rises to his stool on the surface of the ice with a mussel in his mouth and ejects the tenant, taking the roof?

It is as if the occupant had not begun to live until the light, with whatever violence, is let into its shell with these magical results. It is rather a resurrection than a death. These beaming shells, with the tints of the sky and the rainbow commingled, suggest what pure serenity has occupied it.

Look at the trees, bare or rustling with sere brown leaves, except the evergreens, their buds dormant at the foot of the leaf-stalks. Look at the fields, russet and withered, and the various sedges and weeds with dry bleached culms. Such is our relation to nature at

present; such plants are we. We have no more sap nor verdure nor color now.

I remember how cheerful it has been formerly to sit around a fire outdoors amid the snow, and, while I felt some cold, to feel some warmth also, and see the fire gradually increasing and prevailing over damp, steaming and dripping logs and making a warm hearth for me.

When I see even these humble clamshells lying open along the riverside, displaying some blue, or violet, or rainbow tints, I am reminded that some pure serenity has occupied them. (I sent two and a half bushels of my cranberries to Boston and got four dollars for them.) There the clam dwells within a little pearly heaven of its own.

But even in winter we maintain a temperate cheer and a serene inward life, not destitute of warmth and melody. Only the cold evergreens wear the aspect of summer now and shelter the winter birds.

Layard discovers sculptured on a slab at Kouyunjik (Nineveh) machines for raising water which I perceive correspond exactly to our New England well-sweeps, except that in the former case the pole is "balanced on a shaft of masonry." He observes that it is "still generally used for irrigation in the East, as well as in southern Europe, and called in Egypt a *shadoof*." [1]

Dec. 4. Sunday. The coldest day yet, clear with considerable wind, after the first cloudless morning for a week or two. Goose Pond apparently froze over last

[1] Wilkinson exhibits it from the Egyptian sculptures.

night, all but a few rods, but not thick enough to bear. I see a lizard [*sic*] on the bottom under the ice. No doubt I have sometimes mistaken them for tadpoles. (Flint's Pond only skimmed a little at the shore, like the river.) The ice of Goose Pond already has a dusty look. It shows the crystals distinctly.

Dec. 5. P. M. — Got my boat in. The river frozen over thinly in most places and whitened with snow, which was sprinkled on it this noon.

4 P. M. — To Cliffs.

Many living leaves are very dark red now, the only effect of the frost on them, — the checkerberry, andromeda, low cedar, and more or less lambkill, etc. Saw and heard a downy woodpecker on an apple tree. Have not many winter birds, like this and the chickadee, a sharp note like tinkling glass or icicles? The *chip* of the tree sparrow, also, and the whistle of the shrike, are they not wintry in the same way? And the sonorous hooting owl? But not so the jay and *Fringilla linaria*, and still less the crow. Now for the short days and early twilight, in which I hear the sound of woodchopping. The sun goes down behind a low cloud, and the world is darkened. The partridge is budding on the apple tree and bursts away from the path-side. Fair Haven Pond is skimmed completely over. The ground has been frozen more or less about a week, not very hard. Probably stiffened the 3d so as to hinder spading, but softened afterward. I rode home from the woods in a hay-rigging, with a boy who had been collecting a load of dry leaves for the hog-pen; this the

third or fourth load. Two other boys asked leave to ride, with four large empty box-traps which they were bringing home from the woods. It was too cold and late to follow box-trapping longer. They had caught five rabbits this fall, baiting with an apple.[1] Before I got home the whole atmosphere was suddenly filled with a mellow yellowish light equally diffused, so that it seemed much lighter around me than immediately after the sun sank behind the horizon cloud, fifteen minutes before. Apparently not till the sun had sunk thus far did I stand in the angle of reflection.

It is a startling thought that the Assyrian king who with so much pains recorded his exploits in stone at Nineveh, that the story might come down to a distant generation, has indeed succeeded by those means which he used. All was not vanity, quite.

Layard, at the lake of Wan, says: "Early next morning I sought the inscriptions which I had been assured were graven on the rocks near an old castle, standing on a bold projecting promontory above the lake. After climbing up a dangerous precipice by the help of two or three poles, in which large nails had been inserted to afford a footing, I reached a small natural cave in the rock. A few crosses and ancient Armenian letters were rudely cut near its entrance. There was nothing else, and I had to return as I best could, disappointed, as many a traveller has been under similar circumstances before me." They were not old enough; that was all. Wait a thousand years and you will not be disappointed.

[1] [Channing, p. 108.]

Vol. VI

Dec. 7. Wednesday. P. M. — To Trillium Woods and Hubbard's Close.

In the latter part of November [1] and now, before the snow, I am attracted by the numerous small evergreens on the forest floor, now most conspicuous, especially the very beautiful *Lycopodium dendroideum*, somewhat cylindrical, and also, *in this grove*, the variety *obscurum* of various forms, surmounted by the effete spikes, some with a spiral or screw-like arrangement of the fan-like leaves, some spreading and drooping. It is like looking down on evergreen trees. And the *L. lucidulum* of the swamps, forming broad, thick patches of a clear liquid green, with its curving fingers; also the pretty little fingers of the cylindrical *L. clavatum*, or club-moss, zigzagging amid the dry leaves; not to mention the spreading openwork umbrellas of the *L. complanatum*, or flat club-moss, all with spikes still. Also the liquid wet glossy leaves of the *Chimaphila* (winter or snow-loving) *umbellata*, with its dry fruit. Not to mention the still green *Mitchella repens* and checkerberry in shelter, both with fruit; gold-thread; *Pyrola secunda*, with drooping curled-back leaves, and other pyrolas; and, by the brooks, brooklime (?) (I mean such as at Cliff Brook and at brook in E. Hubbard's Swamp).[2] There is the mountain laurel, too. The terminal shield fern is quite fresh and green, and a common thin fern, though fallen. I observe the beds of greenish cladonia

[1] [The words "the latter part of" are crossed out in ink, but the word "retain," followed by an interrogation-point, is written over them.]

[2] Golden saxifrage. ["Brooklime" is crossed out in pencil.]

lichens. Saw a wood tortoise stirring in the now open brook in Hubbard's Swamp.

Dec. 8. 7 A. M. — How can we spare to be abroad in the morning red, to see the forms of the leafless eastern trees against the dun sky and hear the cocks crow, when a thin low mist hangs over the ice and frost in meadows? I have come along the riverside in Merrick's pasture to collect for kindling the fat pine roots and knots which the spearers dropped last spring, and which the floods have washed up. Get a heaping bushel-basketful. The thin, trembling sheets of imperfectly cemented ice or ice-crystals, loosened by the warmth of the day, now go floating down the stream, looking like dark ripples in the twilight and grating against the edges of the firm ice. They completely fill the river where it is bridged with firmer ice below.

I observed a place on the shore where a small circle of the withered grass was feathered white with frost, and, putting down my hand, felt the muskrat's hole in the bank which was concealed to my eye. I often see this, and at woodchuck-holes. Yet you may see the same over the edge of many a hole, however shallow.

At midday (3 P. M.) saw an owl fly from toward the river and alight on Mrs. Richardson's front-yard fence. Got quite near it, and followed it to a rock on the heap of dirt at Collier's cellar. A rather dark brown owl above (with a decided owl head (and eyes), though not very broad), with longitudinal tawny streaks (or the reverse), none transverse, growing lighter down the breast, and at length clear rusty yellowish or cream-color beneath and about feathered feet. Wings large and long, with a distinct large black spot beneath; bill and claws, I think, black. Saw no ears. Kept turning its head and great black eyes this way and that when it heard me, but appeared not to see me. Saw my shadow better, for I ap[proached] on the sunny side. I am inclined to think it the short-eared owl, though I could see no ears, though it reminded [me] of what I had read of the hawk owl. It was a foot or more long and spread about three feet. Flew somewhat flappingly, yet hawk-like. Went within two or three rods of it.

Walden at sunset.

The twilights, morn and eve, are very clear and light, very glorious and pure, or stained with red, and prolonged, these days. But, now the sun is set, Walden (I am on the east side) is more light than the sky, — a whiteness as of silver plating, while the sky is yellowish in the horizon and a dusky blue above.[1] Though the water is smooth enough, the trees are lengthened dimly one third in the reflection. Is this phenomenon peculiar to this season? Goose Pond now firmly frozen. It had melted since it froze before.

I see there a narrow open channel in the ice, two and a half rods long and six inches wide, leading straight to a muskrat-house by the shore, apparently kept open by them. Snow will soon come, in a measure

---

[1] The next night but one just like this, a little later. I saw from the peak the entire reflection of large white pines very distinctly against a clear white sky, though the actual tree was completely lost in night against the dark distant hillside.

broad the apex was imperfect, with many irregular rosettes of small and perfect pyramids, the largest with bases equal to two or three inches. All this appeared to advantage only while the ice (one twelfth of an inch thick, perhaps) rested on the black water.

What I write about at home I understand so well, comparatively! and I write with such repose and freedom from exaggeration.

Dec. 11. *Sunday.* P. M. — To Hayward's Pond and up brook.

Almost a complete Indian-summer day, clear and warm. I am without greatcoat. Channing says he saw larks yesterday, a painted tortoise day before yesterday under ice at White Pond, and a ground-robin (?) last week. We find Hayward's Pond frozen five inches thick. There have been some warm suns on it, and it is handsomely marbled. I find, on looking closely, that there is an indistinct and irregular crack or cleavage in the middle of each dark mark, and I have no doubt the marbling is produced thus, *viz.*, the pond, at first all dark, cracks under a change of temperature, it is expanded and cracked in a thousand directions, and at the same time it gradually grows white as the air-bubbles expand, but wherever there is a crack in it, it interferes with the rays of heat, and the ice for a short distance on each side of it retains its original color. The forms into which the ice first cracks under a higher temperature determine the character of the marbling. This pond is bordered on the northeast with much russet sedge (?) grass beneath the bushes,

to restore the equilibrium between night and day by prolonging the twilight.

I was amused by R. W. E.'s telling me that he drove his own calf out of the yard, as it was coming in with the cow, not knowing it to be his own, a drove going by at the time.

Dec. 9. The third (at least) glorious day, clear and not too cold (this morning a leaf frost on the rails a third of an inch long), with peculiarly long and clear cloudless silvery twilights morn and eve, with a stately, withdrawn after-redness.

Above all, deliver me from a city built on the site of a more ancient city, the materials of the one being the ruins of the other. There the dwellings of the living are in the cemeteries of the dead, and the soil is blanched and accursed.

Dec. 10. Another still more glorious day, if possible; Indian-summery even. These are among the finest days in the year, on account of the wholesome bracing coolness and clearness.

Paddled Cheney's boat up Assabet.

Passed in some places between shooting ice-crystals, extending from both sides of the stream. Upon the thinnest black ice-crystals, just cemented, was the appearance of broad fern leaves, or ostrich-plumes, or flat fir trees with branches bent down. The surface was far from even, rather in sharp-edged plaits or folds. The form of the crystals was oftenest that of low, flattish, three-sided pyramids; when the base was very

and the sun, now falling on the ice, seems to slide or glance off into this grass and light it up wonderfully, filling it with yellowish light. This ice being whitened and made partially opaque by heat, while the surface is quite smooth, perhaps from new freezings then, it reflects the surrounding trees, their forms and colors, distinctly like water. The white air-bubbles are the quicksilver on the back of the mirror.

R. W. E. told me that W. H. Channing conjectured that the landscape looked fairer when we turned our heads, because we beheld it with nerves of the eye unused before. Perhaps this reason is worth more for suggestion than explanation. It occurs to me that the reflection of objects in still water is in a similar manner fairer than the substance, and yet we do not employ unused nerves to behold it. Is it not that we let much more light into our eyes, — which in the usual position are shaded by the brows, — in the first case by turning them more to the sky, and in the case of the reflections by having the sky placed under our feet? *i. e.* in both cases we see terrestrial objects with the sky or heavens for a background or field. Accordingly they are not dark and terrene, but lit and elysian.

Saw a mink at Clamshell Hill on ice. They show the back in swimming.

Dec. 15. *Thursday.* Fishing through ice began on Flint's and Fair Haven yesterday. The first fishers succeed best.

9.30 A. M. — Surveying near Strawberry Hill for Smith and Brooks.

In Brooks's barn I saw twenty-two gray squirrel skins freshly tacked up. He said that as many as one hundred and fifty had been killed this fall within a mile of his barn. They had been very numerous. His brother killed sixteen in one day a month ago. There was one alive and loose in the barn, which had made a nest of husks in one corner. It could not get out, but had gnawed in many places. He had had four alive there at once, and they would not go off when they got out. You can get many more gray than red squirrels. The former often run into the ground; a dog trees the latter. October and November are the squirrel months, when the trees are bare of leaves. The red will drive the gray before it. The gray's nest always leaves; the red's grass, fibres of bark, etc. A few years ago he took one bushel and three pecks of shelled walnuts out of a hollow walnut tree, laid up by red squirrels, a dozen of them.

Nagog appears to have been frozen earlier than our ponds.

He had ten live pigeons in a cage under his barn. He used them to attract others in the spring. The reflections from their necks were very beautiful. They made me think of shells cast up on a beach. He placed them in a cage on the bed and could hear them prate at the house.

Are we not all wreckers, contriving that some treasure may be washed up on our beach and we may secure it, and do we not contract the habits of wreckers from the common modes of getting a living?

The turtle doves plagued him, for they were restless

and frightened the pigeons. He saw many white weasels. Said he had seen a blue mink, and from what he said I did not know but he had heard a whooping crane at night.

Looking from my window these bright moonlight nights, the ground being still bare, the whole landscape — fields, road, and roof — has a wintry aspect as if covered with snow. It is the frost.[1]

Dec. 16. Friday. The elms covered with hoar frost, seen in the east against the morning light, are very beautiful. These days, when the earth is still bare and the weather is so warm as to create much vapor by day, are the best for these frost works.

Would you be well, see that you are attuned to each mood of nature.

J. E. Cabot says the *lunxus* is a wolverene.

Some creature has killed ten, at least, of H. Wheeler's doves and left them together in the dove-house. I think it was my short-eared owl, which flew thither.

Dec. 17. While surveying for Daniel Weston in Lincoln to-day, saw a great many — maybe a hundred — silvery-brown cocoons, wrinkled and flattish, on young alders in a meadow, three or four inches long, fastened to the main stem and branches at same time, with dry alder and fragments of fern leaves attached to and partially concealing them; of some great moth.

[1] On the 18th, after rain in morning, there is no frost and no such appearance.

Vol. VI

Dec. 18. Sunday. P. M. — Clears off cold after rain. Cross Fair Haven Pond at sunset. The western hills, these bordering it, seen through the clear, cold air, have a hard, distinct edge against the sunset sky. The distant hills are impurpled. I have seen but one or two small birds, — chickadees and probably tree sparrows.

Young Weston said that they found, in redeeming a meadow, heaps of chestnuts under the grass, fifteen rods from the trees, without marks of teeth. Probably it was the work of the meadow mice.

Dec. 22. A slight whitening of snow last evening, the second whitening of the winter; just enough to spoil the skating, now ten days old, on the ponds. Walden skimmed over in the widest part, but some acres still open; will probably freeze entirely to-night if this weather holds.

Surveying the last three days. They have not yielded much that I am aware of. All I find is old boundmarks, and the slowness and dullness of farmers reconfirmed. They even complain that I walk too fast for them. Their legs have become stiff from toil. This coarse and hurried outdoor work compels me to live grossly or be inattentive to my diet; that is the worst of it. Like work, like diet; that, I find, is the rule. Left to my chosen pursuits, I should never drink tea nor coffee, nor eat meat. The diet of any class or generation is the natural result of its employment and locality. It is remarkable how unprofitable it is for the most part to talk with farmers. They commonly stand

on their good behavior and attempt to moralize or philosophize in a serious conversation. Sportsmen and loafers are better company. For society a man must not be too *good* or well-disposed, to spoil his natural disposition. The bad are frequently good enough to let you see how bad they are, but the good as frequently endeavor [to] get between you and themselves.

I have dined out five times and tea'd once within a week. Four times there was tea on the dinner-table, always meat, but once baked beans, always pie, but no puddings. I suspect tea has taken the place of cider with farmers. I am reminded of Haydon the painter's experience when he went about painting the nobility. I go about to the houses of the farmers and squires in like manner. This is my portrait-painting, — when I would fain be employed on higher subjects. I have offered myself much more earnestly as a lecturer than a surveyor. Yet I do not get any employment as a lecturer; was not invited to lecture once last winter, and only once (without pay) this winter. But I can get surveying enough, which a hundred others in this county can do as well as I, though it is not boasting much to say that a hundred others in New England cannot lecture as well as I on my themes. But they who do not make the highest demand on you shall rue it. It is because they make a low demand on themselves. All the while that they use only your humbler faculties, your higher unemployed faculties, like an invisible cimetar, are cutting them in twain. Woe be to the generation that lets any higher faculty in its midst go unemployed! That is to deny God and know him not, and he, accordingly, will know not of them.

P. M.— Got a white spruce [1] for a Christmas-tree for the town out of the spruce swamp opposite J. Farmer's. It is remarkable how few inhabitants of Concord can tell a spruce from a fir, and probably not two a white from a black spruce, unless they are together. The woodchopper, even hereabouts, cuts down several kinds of trees without knowing what they are. Neither do the spruce trees know the villager. The villager doesn't know a black spruce tree when he sees it. How slender his relation to the spruce tree! The white has taken refuge in swamps from him. It is nothing but so much evergreen to him. Last night's sprinkling of snow does not now whiten the ground, except that here in the swamp it whitens the ice and already I see the tracks of rabbits on it.

Dec. 24. The rain of yesterday concluded with a whitening of snow last evening, the third thus far. To-day is cold and quite windy.

P. M. — To the field in Lincoln which I surveyed for Weston the 17th.

Walden almost entirely open again. Skated across Flint's Pond; for the most part smooth but with rough spots where the rain had not melted the snow. From the hill beyond I get an arctic view northwest. The

---

[1] [" White " is crossed out and " black " written over it, evidently at a later date. In view of Thoreau's confusion of the two spruces for so many years, the next sentence may be thought amusing.]

morning. He heard Flint's Pond whooping like cannon the moment he opened the door, but sometimes he could see stars after he got to his chopping-ground. He was working with his coat off in the rain. He said he often saw gray squirrels running about and jumping from tree to tree. There was a large nest of leaves close by. That morning he saw a large bird of some kind. He took a French paper to keep himself in practice, — not for news; he said he didn't want news. He had got twenty-three or twenty-four of them, had got them bound and paid a dollar for it, and would like to have me see it. He hadn't read it half; there was a great deal of reading in it, by gorry. He wanted me to tell him the meaning of some of the hard words. How much had he cut? He wasn't a-going to kill himself. He had got money enough. He cut enough to earn his board.[1] A man could not do much more in the winter. He used the dry twigs on the trees to start his fire with, and some shavings which he brought in his pocket. He frequently found some fire still in the morning. He laid his axe by a log and placed another log the other side of it. I said he might have to dig it out of a snow-drift, but he thought it would not snow. Described a large hawk killed at Smith's (which had eaten some hens); its legs " as yellow as a sovereign;" apparently a goshawk. He has also his beetle and wedges and whetstone.

In the town hall this evening, my white spruce tree,[2] one of the small ones in the swamp, hardly a quarter the size of the largest, looked double its size, and

---

[1] [*Walden*, p. 161; Riv. 226.]   [2] [See p. 22.]

mountains are of a cold slate-color. It is as if they bounded the continent toward Behring's Straits.

In Weston's field, in springy land on the edge of a swamp, I counted thirty-three or four of those large silvery-brown cocoons within a rod or two, and probably there are many more about a foot from the ground, commonly on the main stem — though sometimes on a branch close to the stem — of the alder, sweet-fern, brake, etc., etc. The largest are four inches long by two and a half, bag-shaped and wrinkled and partly concealed by dry leaves, — alder, ferns, etc., — attached as if sprinkled over them. This evidence of cunning in so humble a creature is affecting, for I am not ready to refer it to an intelligence which the creature does not share, as much as we do the prerogatives of reason. This radiation of the brain. The bare silvery cocoons would otherwise be too obvious. The worm has evidently said to itself: " Man or some other creature may come by and see my casket. I will disguise it, will hang a screen before it." Brake and sweet-fern and alder leaves are not only loosely sprinkled over it and dangling from it, but often, as it were, pasted close upon and almost incorporated into it.

Saw Therien yesterday afternoon chopping for Jacob Baker in the rain. I heard his axe half a mile off, and also saw the smoke of his fire, which I mistook for a part of the mist which was drifting about. I asked him where he boarded. At Shannon's. He asked the price of board and said I was a *grass* boarder, *i. e.* not a regular one. Asked him what time he started in the morning. The sun was up when he got out of the house that

its top had been cut off for want of room. It was lit with candles, but the starlit sky is far more splendid to-night than any saloon.

Dec. 25. P. M. — Skated to Fair Haven and above.

At seven this morning the water had already oozed out at the sides of the river and flowed over the ice. It appears to be the result of this bridging of the river in the night and so obstructing the channel or usual outlet.

About 4 P. M. the sun sunk behind a cloud, and the pond began to boom or whoop. I noticed the same yesterday at the same hour at Flint's. It was perfectly silent before. The weather in both cases clear, cold, and windy. It is a sort of belching, and, as C. said, is somewhat frog-like. I suspect it did not continue to whoop long either night. It is a very pleasing phenomenon, so dependent on the altitude of the sun.

When I go to Boston, I go naturally straight through the city down to the end of Long Wharf and look off, for I have no cousins in the back alleys. The water and the vessels are novel and interesting. What are our maritime cities but the shops and dwellings of merchants, about a wharf projecting into the sea, where there is a convenient harbor, on which to land the produce of other climes and at which to load the exports of our own? Next in interest to me is the market where the produce of our own country is collected. Boston, New York, Philadelphia, Charleston, New Orleans, and many others are the names of wharves projecting into the sea. They are good places to take in and to discharge a cargo. Everybody in Boston lives at No. so-and-so, Long Wharf. I see a great many barrels and fig-drums and piles of wood for umbrella-sticks and blocks of granite and ice, etc., and that is Boston. Great piles of goods and the means of packing and conveying them, much wrapping-paper and twine, many crates and hogsheads and trucks, that is Boston. The more barrels, the more Boston. The museums and scientific societies and libraries are accidentals. They gather around the barrels, to save carting.[1]

Apparently the ice is held down on the sides of the river by being frozen to the shore and the weeds, and so is overflowed there, but in the middle it is lifted up and makes room for the tide. I saw, just above Fair Haven Pond, two or three places where, just before the last freezing, when the ice was softened and partly covered with sleet, there had been a narrow canal, about eight inches wide, quite across the river from meadow to meadow. I am constrained to believe, from the peculiar character of it on the meadow end, where in one case it divided and crossed itself, that it was made either by muskrats or otters or minks repeatedly crossing there. One end was for some distance like an otter trail in the soft upper part of the ice, not worn through.

Dec. 26. Monday. This forenoon it snowed pretty hard for some hours, the first snow of any consequence thus far. It is about three inches deep. I go out at 2.30, just as it ceases. Now is the time, before the

[1] [*Cape Cod*, p. 268; Riv. 324, 325.]

wind rises or the sun has shone, to go forth and see the snow on the trees. The clouds have lifted somewhat, but are still spitting snow a little. The vapor of the steam-engine does not rise high in the misty air. I go around Walden *via* the almshouse. The branches of deciduous trees, — oaks and maples, etc., — especially the gray oaks of Hubbard's Close on the side-hill, support long lightning-like arms of snow, many times their own thickness. It has fallen so gently that it forms an upright wall on the slenderest twig. The agreeable maze which the branches make is more obvious than ever. And every twig thus laden is as still as the hillside itself. The pitch pines are covered with rich globular masses. The effect of the snow is to press down the forest, confound it with the grasses, and create a new surface to the earth above, shutting us in with it, and we go along somewhat like moles through our galleries. The sight of the pure and trackless road up Brister's Hill, with branches and trees supporting snowy burdens bending over it on each side, would tempt us to begin life again. The ice is covered up, and skating gone. The bare hills are so white that I cannot see their outlines against the misty sky. The snow lies handsomely on the shrub oaks, like a coarse braiding in the air. They have so many small and zigzag twigs that it comes near to filling up with a light snow to that depth. The hunters are already out with dogs to follow the first beast that makes a track.

Saw a small flock of tree sparrows in the sprout-lands under Bartlett's Cliff. Their metallic chip is much like the lisp of the chickadee. All weeds, with

Vol. VI

their seeds, rising dark above the snow, are now remarkably conspicuous, which before were not observed against the dark earth.

I passed by the pitch pine that was struck by lightning. I was impressed with awe on looking up and seeing that broad, distinct spiral mark, more distinct even than when made eight years ago, as one might groove a walking-stick, — mark of an invisible and intangible power, a thunderbolt, mark where a terrific and resistless bolt came down from heaven, out of the harmless sky, eight years ago. It seemed a sacred spot. I felt that we had not learned much since the days of Tullus Hostilius. It at length shows the effect of the shock, and the woodpeckers have begun to bore it on one side.

Walden still open. Saw in it a small diver, probably a grebe or dobchick, dipper, or what-not, with the markings, as far as I saw, of the crested grebe, but smaller. It had a black head, a white ring about its neck, a white breast, black back, and apparently no tail. It dove and swam a few rods under water, and, when on the surface, kept turning round and round warily and nodding its head the while. This being the only pond hereabouts that is open.

Was overtaken by an Irishman seeking work. I asked him if he could chop wood. He said he was not long in this country; that he could cut one side of a tree well enough, but he had not learned to change hands and cut the other without going around it, — what we call crossing the carf. They get very small wages at this season of the year; almost give up the

ghost in the effort to keep soul and body together. He left me on the run to find a new master.

Dec. 27. High wind with more snow in the night. The snow is damp and covers the panes, darkening the room. At first I did not know that more snow had fallen, it was so drifted. Snowy ridges cross the village street and make it look as wild and bleak as a pass of the Rocky Mountains or the Sierra Nevada.

P. M. — To Fair Haven Pond up meadows and river.

The snow blows like spray, fifteen feet high, across the fields, while the wind roars in the trees as in the rigging of a vessel. It is altogether like the ocean in a storm. The snow blowing over the ice is like a vapor rising or curling from a roof. Most plowed fields are quite bare, but I am surprised to find behind the walls on the south side, like a skulking company of rangers in ambuscade or regular troops that have retreated to another parallel, a solid column of snow six or eight feet deep. The wind, eddying through and over the wall, is scooping it out in fantastic forms, — shells and troughs and glyphs of all kinds. Sometimes the drift is pierced with many holes as big as one's fist, where the fine snow-drift is passing through like steam. As it flows over, it builds out eaves to the bank of razor sharpness.

It is surprising what things the snow betrays. I had not seen a meadow mouse all summer, but no sooner does the snow come and spread its mantle over the earth than it is printed with the tracks of countless mice and larger animals. I see where the mouse has dived into a little hole in the snow, not larger than my thumb, by the side of a weed, and a yard further reappeared again, and so on alternately above and beneath. A snug life it lives. The crows come nearer to the houses, alight on trees by the roadside, apparently being put to it for food. I saw them yesterday also.

The wind has now shaken the snow from the trees, and it lies in irregular little heaps on the snow beneath, except that there is a white ridge up and down their trunks on the northwest side, showing which side the storm came from, which, better than the moss, would enable one to find his way in the night. I went to hear the pond whoop, but did not hear much. I look far, but see no rainbow flocks in the sky. It is a true winter sunset, almost cloudless, clear, cold indigo-y along the horizon. The evening (?) star is seen shining brightly, before the twilight has begun. A rosy tint suffuses the eastern horizon. The outline of the mountains is wonderfully distinct and hard, and they are a dark blue and very near. Wachusett looks like a right whale over our bow, plowing the continent, with his flukes well down. He has a vicious look, as if he had a harpoon in him.[1]

I wish that I could buy at the shops some kind of india-rubber that would rub out at once all that in my writing which it now costs me so many perusals, so many months if not years, and so much reluctance, to erase.[2]

Dec. 28. Perhaps the coldest night. The pump is slightly frozen.

    [1] [Channing, p. 107.]   [2] [Channing, p. 121.]

present winter, — disappear from the face of the earth, — would it not look to us like the end, the dissolution of the world? Such is the prospect of the Indians.

All day a driving snow-storm, imprisoning most, stopping the cars, blocking up the roads. No school to-day. I cannot see a house fifty rods off from my window through [it];[1] yet in midst of all I see a bird, probably a tree sparrow, partly blown, partly flying, over the house to alight in a field. The snow penetrates through the smallest crevices under doors and side of windows.

P. M. — Tried my snow-shoes. They sink deeper than I expected, and I throw the snow upon my back. When I returned, twenty minutes after, my great tracks were not to be seen. It is the worst snow-storm to bear that I remember. The strong wind from the north blows the snow almost horizontally, and, beside freezing you, almost takes your breath away. The driving snow blinds you, and where you are protected, you can see but little way, it is so thick. Yet in spite, or on account, of all, I see the first flock of arctic snowbirds (*Emberiza nivalis*) near the depot, white and black, with a sharp, whistle-like note. An hour after I discovered half a pint of snow in each pocket of my greatcoat.

What a contrast between the village street now and last summer! The leafy elms then resounding with the warbling vireo, robins, bluebirds, and the fiery hangbird, etc., to which the villagers, kept indoors by the heat, listen through open lattices. Now it is like a street in Nova Zembla, — if they were to have any there. I

    [1] In an ordinary snow-storm, when snowing fast, Jan. 1st, '54, I can see E. Wood's house, or about a mile.

I hear and see tree sparrows about the weeds in the garden. They seem to visit the gardens with the earliest snow; or is it that they are more obvious against the white ground? By their sharp silvery chip, perchance, they inform each other of their whereabouts and keep together.

Joe Brown owned those pigs I saw to root up the old pasture behind Paul Adams's. N. Stow tells me this morning that he has sold and brought to the butcher's three loads of pork containing twenty-five hundred pounds each, the least; at eight cents per pound amounting to more than $600.

E. W——, who got the premium on farms this year, keeps twenty-eight cows, which are milked before breakfast, or 6 o'clock, his hired men rising at 4.30 A. M.; but he gives them none of the milk in their coffee.

I noticed the other day that the ice on the river and pond was cracked very coarsely, and lay in different planes a rod or two in diameter. It being very smooth and the light differently reflected from the different surfaces, this arrangement was very obvious. In one place where the river was open yesterday, the water, tossed into waves, looked exceedingly dark and angry.

Dec. 29. We survive, in one sense, in our posterity and in the continuance of our race, but when a race of men, of Indians for instance, becomes extinct, is not that the end of the world for them? Is not the world forever beginning and coming to an end, both to men and races? Suppose we were to foresee that the Saxon race to which we belong would become extinct the

wade to the post-office as solitary a traveller as ordinarily in a wood-path in winter. The snow is mid-leg deep, while drifts as high as one's head are heaped against the houses and fences, and here and there range across the street like snowy mountains. You descend from this, relieved, into capacious valleys with a harder bottom, or more fordable. The track of one large sleigh alone is visible, nearly snowed up. There is not a track leading from any door to indicate that the inhabitants have been forth to-day, any more than there is track of any quadruped by the wood-paths. It is all pure untrodden snow, banked up against the houses now at 4 P. M., and no evidence that a villager has been abroad to-day. In one place the drift covers the frontyard fence and stretches thence upward to the top of the front door, shutting all in, and frequently the snow lies banked up three or four feet high against the front doors, and the windows are all snowed up, and there is a drift over each window, and the clapboards are all hoary with it. It is as if the inhabitants were all frozen to death, and now you threaded the desolate streets weeks after that calamity. There is not a sleigh or vehicle of any kind on the Mill-Dam, but one saddled horse on which a farmer has come into town. The cars are nowhere. Yet they are warmer, merrier than ever there within. At the post-office they ask each traveller news of the cars, — "Is there any train up or down?" — or how deep the snow is on a level.

Of the snow bunting, Wilson says that they appear in the northern parts of the United States "early in December, or with the first heavy snow, particularly if drifted by high winds." This day answers to that description exactly. The wind is northerly. He adds that "they are . . . universally considered as the harbingers of severe cold weather." They come down from the extreme north and are common to the two continents; quotes Pennant as saying that they "inhabit not only Greenland but even the dreadful climate of Spitzbergen, where vegetation is nearly extinct, and scarcely any but *cryptogamous* plants are found. It therefore excites wonder, how birds, which are graminivorous in every other than those frost-bound regions, subsist: yet are there found in great flocks both on the land and ice of Spitzbergen." P. also says that they inhabit in summer "the most naked Lapland Alps," and "descend in rigorous seasons into Sweden, and fill the roads and fields; on which account" the Uplanders call them "*hardwarsfogel*," hard-weather birds. Also P. says "they overflow [in winter] the more southern countries in amazing multitudes." W. says their colors are very variable, "and the whiteness of their plumage is observed to be greatest towards the depth of winter." Also W. says truly that they seldom sit long, "being a roving restless bird." Peabody says that in summer they are "pure white and black," but are not seen of that color here. Those I saw to-day were of that color, behind A. Wheeler's. He says they are white and rusty-brown here.

These are the true winter birds for you, these winged snowballs. I could hardly see them, the air was so full of driving snow. What hardy creatures! Where do they spend the night?

The woodchopper goes not to the wood to-day. His axe and beetle and wedges and whetstone he will find buried deep under a drift, perchance, and his fire all extinguished.

As you go down the street, you see on either hand, where erst were front yards with their parterres, rolling pastures of snow, unspotted blankness swelling into drifts. All along the path lies a huge barrow of snow raised by the arctic mound-builder. It is like a pass through the Wind River Mountains or the Sierra Nevada, — a spotless expanse of drifted snow, sloping upward over fences to the houses, deep banks all along their fronts closing the doors. It lies in and before Holbrook's piazza, dwarfing its columns, like the sand about Egyptian temples.

The windows are all sealed up, so that the traveller sees no face of inhabitant looking out upon him. The housekeeper thinks with pleasure or pain of what he has in his larder. No shovel is put to the snow this day. To-morrow we shall see them digging out. The farmer considers how much pork he has in his barrel, how much meal in his bin, how much wood in his shed. Each family, perchance, sends forth one representative before night, who makes his way with difficulty to the grocery or post-office to learn the news; *i. e.*, to hear what others say to it, who can give the best account of it, best can name it, has waded farthest in it, has been farthest out and can tell the biggest and most adequate story; and hastens back with the news.

I asked Therien yesterday if he was satisfied with himself. I was trying to get a *point d'appui* within

him, a shelf to spring an arch from, to suggest some employment and aim for life. "Satisfied!" said he; "some men are satisfied with one thing, and some with another, by George. One man, perhaps, if he has got enough, will be satisfied to sit all day with his back to the fire and his belly to the table; that will satisfy him, by gorry." When I met him the other day, he asked me if I had made any improvement. Yet I could never by any manœuvring get him to take what is called a spiritual view of things, of life. He allowed that study and education was a good thing, but for him it was too late. He only thought of its expediency; nothing answering to what many call their aspirations. He was humble, if he can be called humble who never aspires.[1]

He cut his trees very low, close to the ground, because the sprouts that came from such stumps were better.[2] Perhaps he distinguished between the red and scarlet oak; one had a pale inner bark, the other a darker or more reddish one. Without the least effort he could defend prevailing institutions which affected him, better than any philosopher, because he implicitly accepted them and knew their whole value. He gave the true reason for their prevalence, because speculation had never suggested to him any other. Looking round among the trees, he said he could enjoy himself in the woods chopping alone in a winter day; he wanted no better sport.[3] The trees were frozen, — had been sometimes, — but would frequently thaw again during the day. Split easier for it, but did not chop better.

[1] [*Walden*, pp. 163, 165, 166; Riv. 229, 233.]
[2] [*Walden*, p. 161; Riv. 227.]   [3] [*Walden*, p. 162; Riv. 228.]

The woodchopper to-day is the same man that Homer refers to, and his work the same. He, no doubt, had his beetle and wedge and whetstone then, carried his dinner in a pail or basket, and his liquor in a bottle, and caught his woodchucks, and cut and corded, the same.

The thoughts and associations of summer and autumn are now as completely departed from our minds as the leaves are blown from the trees. Some withered deciduous ones are left to rustle, and our cold immortal evergreens. Some lichenous thoughts still adhere to us.

Dec. 30. P. M. — Around Walden.

The pond not yet frozen entirely over; about six acres open, the wind blew so hard last night. I carried a two-foot rule and measured the snow of yesterday in Abiel Wheeler's wood by the railroad, near the pond. In going a quarter of a mile it varied from fourteen to twenty-four inches. Then went to Potter's wood, by Lincoln road, near Lincoln line, and paced straight through a level wood where there was no drift perceptible, measuring at every ten paces for two hundred paces, and the average was twenty and one half inches.

I see the tracks of mice, and squirrels, probably gray ones, leading straight to or from the feet of the largest pines and oaks, which they had plainly ascended. Their tracks commonly show rapidity of motion. I saw in some places a continuous trail, sometimes disappearing in the snow, between a muskrat's track and a mole's gallery, three or more inches wide. Was it a red squirrel? I think it too large.[1]

[1] A gray squirrel's. *Vide* [p. 41].

The storm being from the north, the snow is deepest just over the ridge on the south side of rising grounds, as well as houses and fences. When it has passed the ridge of the hill there is a lull and it falls, just as it is deposited behind walls because the wind does not blow there, — carries it no further.

In winter even man is to a slight extent dormant, just as some animals are but partially awake, though not commonly classed with those that hibernate. The summer circulations are to some extent stopped; the range of his afternoon walk is somewhat narrower; he is more or less confined to the highway and wood-path; the weather oftener shuts him up in his burrow; he begins to feel the access of dormancy and to assume the spherical form of the marmot; the nights are longest; he is often satisfied if he only gets out to the post-office in the course of the day. The arctic voyagers are obliged to invent and willfully engage in active amusements to keep themselves awake and alive. Most men do not now extend their walks beyond the village street. Even our experience is something like wintering in the pack.

Dec. 31. Four more inches of snow fell last night, making in all now two feet on a level.

P. M. — Down railroad to Walden and circle round to right, through Wheeler's woods out to railroad again.

It is a remarkable sight, this snow-clad landscape, with the fences and bushes half buried and the warm sun on it. The snow lies not quite level in the fields,

but in low waves with an abrupt edge on the north or wind side, as it lodges on ice.

The town and country are now so still, there being no rattle of wagons nor even jingle of sleigh-bells, every tread being as with woolen feet, I hear very distinctly from the railroad causeway the whistle of the locomotive on the Lowell road. For the same reason, in such a day as this the crowing of a cock is heard very far and distinctly. I frequently mistake at first a very distant whistle for the higher tones of the telegraph harp by my side. The telegraph and railroad are closely allied, and it is fit and to be expected that at a little distance their music should be the same. There are a few sounds still which never fail to affect me. The notes of the wood thrush and the sound of a vibrating chord, these affect me as many sounds once did often, and as almost all should. The strains of the æolian harp and of the wood thrush are the truest and loftiest preachers that I know now left on this earth. I know of no missionaries to us heathen comparable to them. They, as it were, lift us up in spite of ourselves. They intoxicate, they charm us. Where was that strain mixed into which this world was dropped but as a lump of sugar to sweeten the draught? I would be drunk, drunk, drunk, dead drunk to this world with it forever. He that hath ears, let him hear. The contact of sound with a human ear whose hearing is pure and unimpaired is coincident with an ecstasy. Sugar is not so sweet to the palate, as sound to the healthy ear;[1] the hearing of it makes men brave.

[1] [Channing, p. 78.]

(How can a poet afford to keep an account with a bookseller?) These things alone remind me of my immortality, which is else a fable. I hear it, and I realize and see clearly what at other times I only dimly remember. I get the value of the earth's extent and the sky's depth. It, as it were, takes me out of my body and gives me the freedom of all bodies and all nature. I leave my body in a trance and accompany the zephyr and the fragrance.

Walden froze completely over last night. It is, however, all snow ice, as it froze while it was snowing hard, and it looks like frozen yeast somewhat. I waded about in the woods through the snow, which certainly averaged considerably more than two feet deep where I went. It stuck to my clothes and melted, and so was more inconvenient than yesterday. Saw probably an otter's track, very broad and deep, as if a log had been drawn along. It was nearly as obvious as a man's track. It was made before last night's snow fell. The creature from time to time went beneath the snow for a few feet, to the leaves. This animal probably I should never see the least trace of, were it not for the snow, the great revealer.

I saw some squirrels' nests of oak leaves high in the trees, and, directly after, a gray squirrel tripping along the branches of an oak and shaking down the snow. It ran down the oak on the opposite side to me, over the snow and up another tall and slender oak, also on the side opposite to me, which was bare, and leapt down about four feet into a white pine, and then ran up still higher into its thick green top,

and clung behind the main stem, perfectly still, and thought itself concealed. This it did to conceal itself, though obliged to come nearer to me to accomplish it. Its fore[1] feet make but one track in the snow, about three inches broad, and its hind feet (?) another similar one,[2] a foot or more distant, and there are two sharp furrows forward and two slighter backward from each track where it has scratched along. This track it makes when running, but I am not absolutely certain that the whole four feet do not come together. There were many holes in the snow where it had gone down to the leaves and brought up acorns, which it had eaten on the nearest twig, dropping fine bits of the shell about on the snow, and also bits of lichen and of bark. I noticed the bits of acorn-shells, etc., by the holes in many places. Sometimes it made a continuous narrow trail in the snow, *somewhat* like a small musk-rat, where it had walked, or gone, several times, and it would go under a few feet and come out again.

The birds I saw were a partridge, perched on an evergreen, apparently on account of the deep snow, heard a jay, and heard and saw together white-bellied nuthatches and chickadees, the former uttering a faint *quank quank* and making a loud tapping, and the latter its usual lisping note.

[1] Four?

[2] [An interrogation-point in parenthesis is marked here in pencil.]

II

JANUARY, 1854

(ÆT. 36)

Jan. 1. Le Jeune, describing the death of a young Frenchwoman who had devoted her life to the savages of Canada, uses the expression: " Finally this beautiful soul detached itself from its body the 15th of March," etc.

The drifts mark the standstill or equilibrium between the currents of air or particular winds. In our greatest snow-storms, the wind being northerly, the greatest drifts are on the south sides of the houses and fences and accordingly on the left-hand side of the street going down it. The north track of the railroad was not open till a day or more later than the south. I notice that in the angle made by our house and shed, a southwest exposure, the snow-drift does not lie close about the pump, but is a foot off, forming a circular bowl, showing that there was an eddy about it. It shows where the wind has been, the form of the wind. The snow is like a mould, showing the form of the eddying currents of air which have been impressed on it, while the drift and all the rest is that which fell between the currents or where they counterbalanced each other. These boundary lines are mountain barriers.

The white-in-tails, or grass finches, linger pretty late, flitting in flocks before, but they come so near winter

only as the white in their tails indicates. They let it come near enough to whiten their tails, perchance, and they are off. The snow buntings and the tree sparrows are the true spirits of the snow-storm; they are the animated beings that ride upon it and have their life in it.

The snow is the great betrayer. It not only shows the tracks of mice, otters, etc., etc., which else we should rarely if ever see, but the tree sparrows are more plainly seen against its white ground, and they in turn are attracted by the dark weeds which it reveals. It also drives the crows and other birds out of the woods to the villages for food. We might expect to find in the snow the footprint of a life superior to our own, of which no zoölogy takes cognizance. Is there no trace of a nobler life than that of an otter or an escaped convict to be looked for in the snow? Shall we suppose that that is the only life that has been abroad in the night? It is only the savage that can see the track of no higher life than an otter. Why do the vast snow plains give us pleasure, the twilight of the bent and half-buried woods? Is not all there consonant with virtue, justice, purity, courage, magnanimity? Are we not cheered by the sight? And does not all this amount to the track of a higher life than the otter's, a life which has not gone by and left a footprint merely,[1] but is there with its beauty, its music, its perfume, its sweetness, to exhilarate and recreate us? Where there is a perfect government of the world according to the highest laws, is there no trace of intelligence there, whether in the snow or the earth, or in ourselves? No other trail but such

[1] But all that we see is the impress of its spirit.

Vol. VI

as a dog can smell? Is there none which an angel can detect and follow? None to guide a man on his pilgrimage, which water will not conceal? Is there no odor of sanctity to be perceived? Is its trail too old? Have mortals lost the scent? The great game for mighty hunters as soon as the first snow falls is Purity, for, earlier than any rabbit or fox, it is abroad, and its trail may be detected by curs of lowest degree. Did this great snow come to reveal the track merely of some timorous hare, or of the Great Hare, whose track no hunter has seen? Is there no trace nor suggestion of Purity to be detected? If one could detect the meaning of the snow, would he not be on the trail of some higher life that has been abroad in the night? Are there not hunters who seek for something higher than foxes, with judgment more discriminating than the senses of foxhounds, who rally to a nobler music than that of the hunting-horn? As there is contention among the fishermen who shall be the first to reach the pond as soon as the ice will bear, in spite of the cold, as the hunters are forward to take the field as soon as the first snow has fallen, so the observer, or he who would make the most of his life for discipline, must be abroad early and late, in spite of cold and wet, in pursuit of nobler game, whose traces are then most distinct. A life which, pursued, does not earth itself, does not burrow downward but upward, which takes not to the trees but to the heavens as its home, which the hunter pursues with winged thoughts and aspirations, — these the dogs that tree it, — rallying his pack with the bugle notes of undying faith, and returns with some worthier trophy than

a fox's tail, a life which we seek, not to destroy it, but to save our own. Is the great snow of use to the hunter only, and not to the saint, or him who is earnestly building up a life? Do the Indian and hunter only need snow-shoes, while the saint sits indoors in embroidered slippers?

The Indians might have imagined a large snow bunting to be the genius of the storm.

This morning it is snowing again fast, and about six inches has already fallen by 10 A. M., of a moist and heavy snow. It is about six inches in all this day. This would [be] two feet and a half in all, if it has not settled, — but it has.

I would fain be a fisherman, hunter, farmer, preacher, etc., but fish, hunt, farm, preach other things than usual.

When, in 1641, the five hundred Iroquois in force brought to Three Rivers two French prisoners (whom they had taken), seeking peace with the French, — I believe this preceded any war with them, — at the assembling for this purpose, they went through the form of tying their prisoners, that they might pass for such; then, after a speech, they broke their bonds and cast them into the river that it might carry them so far that they might never be remembered. The speaker "then made many presents, according to the custom of the country where the word for presents is speech (*où le mot de présens se nomme parole*), to signify that the present speaks more strongly than the mouth." (Le Jeune.)

Our orators might learn much from the Indians.

They are remarkable for their precision; nothing is left at loose ends. They address more senses than one, so as to preclude misunderstanding. A present accompanies each proposition. In delivering one present, the speaker said, " This is the house which we shall have at Three Rivers when we come here to treat with you," etc. This is in Paul Le Jeune's Relation for '40 and '41, page 156.

Jan. 2. The trees are white with a hoar frost this morning, small leafets, a tenth of an inch long, on every side of the twigs. They look like ghosts of trees. Took a walk on snow-shoes at 9 A. M. to Hubbard's Grove. A flock of snow buntings flew over the fields with a rippling whistle, accompanied sometimes by a tender peep and a ricochet motion.

P. M. — Up Union Turnpike.

The tints of the sunset sky are never purer and more ethereal than in the coldest winter days. This evening, though the colors are not brilliant, the sky is crystalline and the pale fawn-tinged clouds are very beautiful. I wish to get on to a hill to look down on the winter landscape. We go about these days as if we had fetters on our feet. We walk in the stocks, stepping into the holes made by our predecessors.

I noticed yesterday that the damp snow, falling gently without wind on the top of front-yard posts, had quite changed the style of their architecture, — to the dome style of the East, a four-sided base becoming a dome at top. I observe other revelations made by the snow. The team and driver have long since gone by, but I

see the marks of his whip-lash on the snow, — its recoil, — but alas! these are not a complete tally of the strokes which fell upon the oxen's back. The unmerciful driver thought perchance that no one saw him, but unwittingly he recorded each blow on the unspotted snow behind his back as in the book of life. To more searching eyes the marks of his lash are in the air.

I paced partly through the pitch pine wood and partly the open field from the Turnpike by the Lee place to the railroad, from north to south, more than a quarter of a mile, measuring at every tenth pace. The average of sixty-five measurements, up hill and down, was nineteen inches; this after increasing those in the woods by one inch each (little enough) on account of the snow on the pines. So that, apparently, it has settled about as much as the two last snows amount to. I think there has been but little over two feet at any one time. I think that one would have to pace a mile on a north and south line, up and down hill, through woods and fields, to get a quite reliable result. The snow will drift sometimes the whole width of a field, and fill a road or valley beyond. So that it would be well that your measuring included several such driftings. There is very little reliance to [be] put on the usual estimates of the depth of snow. I have heard different men set this snow at six, fifteen, eighteen, twenty-four, thirty-six, and forty-eight inches. My snow-shoes sank about four inches into the snow this morning, but more than twice as much the 29th.

On north side the railroad, above the red house crossing, the cars have cut through a drift about a quarter

of a mile long and seven to nine feet high, straight up and down. It reminds me of the Highlands, the Pictured Rocks, the side of an iceberg, etc. Now that the sun has just sunk below the horizon, it is wonderful what an amount of soft light [it] appears to be absorbing. There appears to be more day just here by its side than anywhere. I can almost see into [it] six inches. It is made translucent, it is so saturated with light.

I have heard of one precious stone found in Concord, the cinnamon stone. A geologist has spoken of it as found in this town, and a farmer has described to me one which he once found, perhaps the same referred to by the other. He said it was as large as a brick, and as thick, and yet you could distinguish a pin through it, it was so transparent. If not a mountain of light, it was a brickbatful, at any rate.

Jan. 3. Tuesday. It is now fairly winter. We have passed the line, have put the autumn behind us, have forgotten what these withered herbs that rise above the snow here and there are, what flowers they ever bore. They are fishing on Walden this P. M. The fisherman gets fifteen or twenty pounds thus, when he has pretty good luck. Two to three pounds is a common size there. From the Peak, I looked over the wintry landscape. First there is the white ground, then the dark, dulled green of evergreens, then the reddish (?) brown or leather-color of the oaks, which generally retain their leaves, then the gray of maples and other trees, which are bare. They are modest Quaker colors that are seen above the snow. The twilight appears to

linger in the snow. This it is makes the days seem suddenly longer. The sun has set, shorn of its disk [*sic*] in dun, red clouds. The young moon and the evening star are seen. The partridge has come forth to bud on some wayside apple tree. The woodchopper's task is done; he puts his axe under a log and sets out for home. For an hour the fisherman's lines have been freezing in, and now he, too, has commenced his retreat. That large round track forming nearly a straight line Goodwin thinks a fox.

A thaw appears to be commencing. We hear the eaves run in the evening.

Jan. 4. It thaws all day; the eaves drip as in a rain; the road begins to be soft and a little sloshy.

Jan. 5. Still thaws. This afternoon (as probably yesterday), it being warm and thawing, though fair, the snow is covered with snow-fleas. Especially they are sprinkled like pepper for half a mile in the tracks of a woodchopper in deep snow. These are the first since the snow came. With the first thawing weather they are [*sic*]. There is also some blueness now in the snow, the heavens being now (toward night) overcast. The blueness is more distinct after sunset.

Jan. 6. Walked Tappan[1] in P. M. down railroad to Heywood Brook, Fair Haven, and Cliffs.

At every post along the brook-side, and under almost every white pine, the snow strewn with the scales and

[1] [Doubtless William Tappan, of New York. See *Familiar Letters.*]

seeds of white pine cones left by the squirrels. They have sat on every *post* and dropped them for a great distance, also acorn-shells. The surface of the snow was sometimes strewn with the small alder scales, *i. e.* of catkins; also, here and there, the large glaucous lichens (cetrarias?). Showed Tappan a small shadbush, which interested him and reminded him of a greyhound, rising so slender and graceful with its narrow buds above the snow. To return to the squirrels, I saw where they had laid up a pitch pine cone in the fork of a rider in several places. Many marks of partridges, and disturbed them on evergreens. A winter (?) gnat out on the bark of a pine. On Fair Haven we slumped nearly a foot to the old ice. The partridges were budding on the Fair Haven orchard, and flew for refuge to the wood, twenty minutes or more after sundown. There was a low, narrow, clear segment of sky in the west at sunset, or just after (all the rest overcast), of the coppery yellow, perhaps, of some of Gilpin's pictures, all spotted coarsely with clouds like a leopard's skin. I took up snow in the tracks at dark, but could find no fleas in it then, though they were exceedingly abundant before. Do they go into the snow at night? Frequently see a spider apparently stiff and dead on snow.

In Vimont's Jesuit Relation for 1642, he describes the customs of the Iroquois. As in the case of the Hurons, everything is done by presents. The murderer and robber are restrained by the very defect of justice, and because the community (his relations or tribe) whips itself for his fault. They must appease the in-

jured with costly presents. They make that he shall involve his friends in ruin along with himself, and if he would injure any one, shall injure them too. By making it impossible for him to do an injury without doing a greater injury than he wishes, they restrain him.

Jan. 7. Saturday. Thaw ended. Cold last night; rough walking: snow crusted.

P. M. — To Ministerial Swamp.

The bare larch trees there, so slender and tall, where they grow close together, all beaded or studded with buds, or rather stubs, which look like the dry sterile blossoms. How much fuller, or denser and more flourishing, in winter is the white spruce than the white pine! It has two hues, I believe, the glaucous or bluish and the green, melting into each other. It has not shed all its seeds yet. Now that the snow has lain more than a week, it begins to be spotted and darkened in the woods, with various dry leaves and scales from the trees. The wind and thaw have brought down a fresh crop of dry pine and spruce needles. The little roundish and stemmed scales of the alder catkins spot it thickly. The bird-shaped scales of the white birch are blown more than twenty rods from the trees. I see also the wings of pine seeds, — the seed being gone, — which look exactly like the wings of ants. Also, in the pastures, the fine star-shaped fuzz of the gray goldenrod, somewhat like a spider with many legs.

The snow is still very deep in the more open parts of the swamp, where it is light, being held up by the

bushes; but in thick woods there is much less of it, beside that it has settled far more. There is also much more in sprout-lands than in woods. Is it that the ground not being frozen in the woods melts it so much faster, while in the swamp, even if the ground is equally warm, the snow, lying light, does not come in contact with it enough to melt it?

The ice has all been snow ice of late, not interesting to study. However, there are now some little pools over the snow in hollows frozen, where the thin ice is yellow and full of white bubbles and like small coins. Is this the melted snow made into tea by running amid the dead leaves and grass? I see the muddy, dripping tracks of [a] muskrat or mink that has come out of a ditch on to the snow here in the swamp. Saw a fat pitch pine stump, whose sap, four inches thick, has long been gone, but the scales of the thick bark still form a circle level with the ground four inches from the (solid or fat) wood on every side. I see at Martial Miles's house where many hundred bees lie dead on the snow close to their hives, plainly having come out during the late warmer days.

I went to these woods partly to hear an owl, but did not; but, now that I have left them nearly a mile behind, I hear one distinctly, *hoorer hoo.* Strange that we should hear this sound so often, loud and far, — a voice which we call the owl, — and yet so rarely see the bird. Oftenest at twilight. It has a singular prominence as a sound; is louder than the voice of a dear friend. Yet we see the friend perhaps daily and the owl but few times in our lives. It is a sound which

the wood or the horizon makes. I see the cars almost as often as I hear the whistle.

Jan. 8. Sunday. Gilpin, in his essay on the " Art of Sketching Landscape," says: " When you have finished your sketch therefore with Indian ink, as far as you propose, tinge the whole over with some light horizon hue. It may be the rosy tint of morning; or the more ruddy one of evening; or it may incline more to a yellowish, or a greyish cast. . . . By washing this tint over your *whole drawing*, you lay a foundation for harmony."

I have often been attracted by this harmonious tint in his and other drawings, and sometimes, especially, have observed it in nature when at sunset I inverted my head. We love not so well the landscape represented as in broad noon, but in a morning or evening twilight, those seasons when the imagination is most active, the more hopeful or pensive seasons of the day. Our mood may then possess the whole landscape, or be in harmony with it, as the hue of twilight prevails over the whole scene. Are we more than crepuscular in our intellectual and spiritual life? Have we awakened to broad noon? The morning hope is soon lost in what becomes the routine of the day, and we do not recover ourselves again until we land on the pensive shores of evening, shores which skirt the great western continent of the night. At sunset we look into the west. For centuries our thoughts fish those grand banks that lie before the newfoundland, before our spirits take up their abode in that Hesperian Continent to which these l' in the way.

P. M. — To the Spruce Swamp in front of J. Farmer's.

Can go across both rivers now. New routes are more practicable. Stood within a rod of a downy woodpecker on an apple tree. How curious and exciting the blood-red spot on its hindhead! I ask why it is there, but no answer is rendered by these snow-clad fields. It is so close to the bark I do not see its feet. It looks behind as if it had on a black cassock open behind and showing a white undergarment between the shoulders and down the back. It is briskly and incessantly tapping all round the dead limbs, but rarely twice in a place, as if to sound the tree and so see if it has any worm in it, or perchance to start them. How much he deals with the bark of trees, all his life long tapping and inspecting it! He it is that scatters those fragments of bark and lichens about on the snow at the base of trees. What a lichenist he must be! Or rather, perhaps it is fungi makes his favorite study, for he deals most with dead limbs. How briskly he glides up or drops himself down a limb, creeping round and round, and hopping from limb to limb, and now flitting with a rippling sound of his wings to another tree!

The lower two-thirds of the white spruce has its branches retraced or turned downward, and then curving upward at the extremities, as much as the white pine commonly slants upwards. Above it is so thick that you cannot see through it. All the black spruce that I know hereabouts stand on higher land than this. Saw two squirrel-nests in the thick top of a spruce.

It was a foot in diameter, of coarse grass and bark fibres, with very thick bottom and sides and a scarcely distinguishable entrance, lined with fine fibres of bark, probably inner bark of maple, very warm. Probably a red squirrel's, for I heard one winding up his clock. Many white pine cones had been eaten in the neighborhood.

Gilpin's "Essay on Picturesque Beauty" is the key to all his writings. He says in the outset that he does not mean to inquire "into the general sources of beauty," but the questions which he proposes to himself depend on the result of such an inquiry. He asks, first, "What is that quality in objects, which particularly marks them as picturesque?" and answers "*roughness*," assigning to that kind of beauty which he makes the opposite to the picturesque the quality of "*smoothness*." This last he styles, too generally or exclusively, "the beautiful." The beautiful, he says, cannot be painted; *e. g.*, "A piece of Palladian architecture may be elegant in the last degree. The proportion of its parts — the propriety of its ornaments — and the symmetry of the whole, may be highly pleasing. But if we introduce it in a picture, it immediately becomes a formal object, and ceases to please. Should we wish to give it picturesque beauty, we must use the mallet, instead of the chisel: we must beat down one half of it, deface the other, and throw its mutilated members around in heaps. In short from a *smooth* building we must turn it into a *rough* ruin."[1] I do not believe that the "beautiful" is not equally beautiful

[1] [William Gilpin. *Five Essays on Picturesque Subjects.*]

in picture, that the beautiful statue for instance, however smooth, may not appear beautiful when daguerreotyped or painted. In the case instanced he must use the mallet either because the building is not beautiful, or because he cannot catch and render the spirit of its beauty. If there is the same genius in the painter that there was in the architect, the painting will be beautiful too. The smooth may be more difficult, but is not impossible, to be represented by picture. It is not the mere roughness of the surface which makes the patriarchal head more interesting than that of a youth ever, nor is this the reason why we "admire the Laocoön more than the Antinoüs," for we do not admire it more than the Apollo Belvidere.

True, there are many reasons why the painter should select the rough. It is easier to execute; he can do it more justice. In the case of the patriarchal head, those lines and wrinkles which man's life has produced his hand can better represent than the fullness and promise of infancy; and then, on the whole, perhaps, we have more sympathy with performance than promise. The humble or sincere and true is more commonly rough and weather-beaten, so that from association we prefer it. But will Mr. Gilpin assert that the Venus and Apollo are not fit objects for painting?

So we prefer the poor man's irregular garden for its sincerity and truth to the rich man's formal and pretending parterres, and the "worn-out cart-horse" to the pampered steed for similar reasons. Indeed "he does not recommend his art," if he fails to fix the fleeting forms of the beautiful. The worn-out cart-horse is

thought to be more picturesque and admits "of being rendered with spirit," because we can far more easily enter into his spirit, whether as beholders or painters, — have more sympathy with it than with that of the free horse of the prairie. Beside, what has the pampered coach-horse done to deserve our respect and sympathy?

He defends the painter, first, by saying that "a free, bold touch is in itself pleasing," and assuming too too great an extent that the objects which he calls beautiful do not admit of being painted in this touch, — but God used a free and bold touch when he created them, and so may the creative painter do when he paints them, — secondly, by saying that "the very essence of his art requires" that he select the Picturesque for the sake of composition, variety, light and shade, and coloring.

But he is superficial. He goes not below the surface to account for the effect of form and color, etc. For instance, he thus attempts to account for the fact that the pampered steed may be a picturesque object. "Though the horse, in a *rough* state, as we have just observed, or worn down with labor, is more adapted to the pencil than when his sides shine with brushing, and high feeding; yet in this latter state also he is certainly a picturesque object. But it is not his smooth, and shining coat, that makes him so. It is the apparent interruption of that smoothness by a variety of shades, and colors, which produces the effect. Such a play of muscles appears, everywhere, through the fineness of his skin, gently swelling, and sinking into each other — he is all over so *lubricus aspici*, the reflections of light are so continually shifting upon him, and playing into each other, that the eye never considers the smoothness of the surface; but is amused with gliding up, and down, among those endless transitions, which in some degree, supply the room of *roughness*." And this is the reason why a pampered steed can be painted! Mark that there is not the slightest reference to the fact that this surface, with its lights and shades, belongs to a horse and not to a bag of wind. The same reasoning would apply equally well to one of his hind quarters hung bottom upwards in a butcher's stall. This comes of not inquiring "into the general sources of beauty."

So I should answer that "the beauty of an old head" is *not* "greatly improved by the *smoothness* of the bald pate" (if bald pates were rough they would do just as well), but it may be improved by the associations which a bald pate suggests.

He fails to show why roughness is essential to the picturesque, because he does not go beneath the surface.

To return to the horse, I should say that no arrangement of light and shade without reference to the object, actual or suggested, so lit and shaded can interest us powerfully, any more than the paint itself can charm us.

In the "Essay on Picturesque Travel," after speaking of the *objects* of such travel, he treats of the way in which "the mind is gratified by these objects." He says: "We might begin in moral style, and consider the objects of nature in a higher light than merely as amusement. We might observe, that a search after beauty should naturally lead the mind to the great origin of

all beauty," etc. "But though in theory this seems a natural climax, we insist the less upon it, as in fact we have scarce ground to hope that every admirer of *picturesque beauty* is an admirer also of the *beauty of virtue*." And he a clergyman, "vicar of Boldre!" This is to give us the play of Hamlet with Hamlet's part left out. But there is no half way in this case that is not at the same time half true.

Again, as if that were true, which G. asserts in another essay, that "the *eye*, which has nothing to do with *moral sentiments*, and is conversant only with *visible forms*, is disgusted," etc., any more than a telescope is disgusted! As if taste resided in the eye! As if the eye, which itself cannot see at all, were conversant with surfaces! Yet he adds directly that "there is a still *higher character* in landscapes than what arises from the *uniformity of objects* — and that is the power of furnishing images *analogous to the various feelings*, and *sensations of the mind*." Can good landscape have any lower aim? But he says, "To convey however ideas of this kind is the perfection of the art: it requires the splendor, and variety of colors; and is not to be attempted in such trivial sketches as these." And this is not modesty merely, but a low estimate of his own art.

I might have said some pages back that he allows that grandeur which is produced "by uniformity of color, and a long continuation of line," falls under the head of picturesque beauty, though he says that the idea of it is not easily caught.

The elegant Gilpin. I like his style and manners better than anything he says.

Vol. VI

Jan. 9. P. M. — To Heywood's Pond with Tappan.

We were looking for rainbow-tinted clouds, small whiffs of vapor which form and disperse, this clear, cold afternoon, when we saw to our surprise a star, about half past three or earlier, a mere round white dot. Is the winter then such a twilight? I wonder if the savages ever detected one by day. This was about an hour and a half before sunset. T. said he had lost fowls by the owls. They selected the roosters and took off their heads and ate their insides. Found many snow-fleas, apparently frozen, on the snow.[1]

T. has a singularly elastic step. He will run through the snow, lifting his knees like a child who enjoys the motion. When he slumped once through to water and called my attention to it, with an indescribable flash of his eye, he reminded me forcibly of Hawthorne's little son Julian. He uses the greatest economy in speech of any man I know. Speaks low, beside, and without emphasis; in monosyllables. I cannot guess what the word was for a long time. His language is different from the Algonquin.

Jan. 10. I cannot thaw out to life the snow-fleas which yesterday covered the snow like pepper, in a frozen state. How much food they must afford to small birds, — chickadees, etc. The snow went off remarkably fast in the thaw before the 7th, but it is still deep, lying light in swamps and sprout-lands, somewhat hollow beneath. The thaw produced those yellowish pools in hollows in

[1] *Vide* below [next date].

the fields, where water never stands else, and now perhaps there is a bottom of snow; and now for the last three days they have afforded good sliding. You got a start by running over the snow-crust. In one place, where the depression was inconsiderable but more extensive than usual, I found that it was mere glazed snow on which I slid, it having rapidly frozen dry.

The sportsmen chose the late thaw to go after quails. They come out at such times to pick the horse-dung in the roads, and can be traced thence to their haunts.

When we were walking last evening, Tappan admired the soft rippling of the Assabet under Tarbell's bank. One could have lain all night under the oaks there listening to it. Westward forty rods, the surface of the stream reflected a silvery whiteness, but gradually darkened thence eastward, till beneath us it was almost quite black.

What you can recall of a walk on the second day will differ from what you remember on the first day, as the mountain chain differs in appearance, looking back the next day, from the aspect it wore when you were at its base, or generally, as any view changes to one who is journeying amid mountains when he has increased the distance.

With Tappan, his speech is frequently so frugal and reserved, in monosyllables not fairly uttered clear of his thought, that I doubt if he did not cough merely, or let it pass for such, instead of asking what he said or meant, for fear it might turn out that he coughed merely.

Channing showed me last night on a map where, as

he said, he "used to walk" in Rome. He was there sixteen days.

I mistook the creaking of a tree in the woods the other day for the scream of a hawk. How numerous the resemblances of the animate to the inanimate!

Jan. 11. Thick fog in the night. The trees, accordingly, now white with hoary frost, just as the frost forms on a man's beard or about a horse's mouth.

P. M. — To Cliffs and Walden.

The north side of all stubble, weeds, and trees, and the whole forest is covered with a hoar frost a quarter to a half inch deep. It is easily shaken off. The air is still full of mist. No snow has fallen, but, as it were, the vapor has been caught by the trees like a cobweb. The trees are bright hoary forms, the ghosts of trees. In fact, the warm breath of the earth is frozen on its beard. Closely examined or at a distance, it is just like the sheaf-like forms of vegetation and the diverging crystals on the window-panes. The stiff stubble has a soft, drooping look; now feels the wind and waves like plumes. It is a *chevaux-de-frise* or armor of frost-needles, exclusively on the north side, with a myriad diverging feathery points, sheaves of darts. It covers the width of the twigs, but only a narrow and irregular strip on the larger limbs and trunk; also on the edges and protuberances of the leaves still turned toward the northern foe. Even birds' nests have a white beard.

Birches, especially, are the trees for these hoar frosts and also for glazes. They are so thickly twigged and

of such graceful forms and attitudes. I can distinguish a birch now further off than ever. As I stand by its north side (Hubbard's Grove), almost the whole forest is concealed by the hoar frost. It is as if the mist had been caught on an invisible net spread in the air. Yet the white is tinged with the ground color of reddish oak leaves and even green pine-needles. You look up and behold the hugest pine, as tall as a steeple, all frosted over. Nature is now gone into her winter palace. The trunks of the pines, greened with lichens, are now more distinct by contrast. Even the pale yellowish green of lichens speaks to us at this season, reminding us of summer.

The humblest weed is indescribably beautiful, of purest white and richest form. The hogweed becomes a fairy's wand. The blue-curls, rising from bare gray sand, is perhaps particularly beautiful. Every part of the plant is concealed. Its expression is changed or greatly enriched by this exaggeration or thickening of the mere linear original. It is an exquisitely delicate frost plant, trembling like swan's-down. As if Nature had sprinkled her breast with down this cold season. The character of each tree and weed is rendered with spirit, — the pine plumes and the cedar spires. All this you see going from north to south; but, going the other way (*perchance ?*), you might not be struck with the aspect of the woods.

Now (or a little earlier, just after the thaw, when it began to freeze) is the time to go out and see the ice organ-pipes. I walked the whole length of the Cliffs, just at the base of the rocks, for this purpose; but [it]

is rather late; no water is flowing now. These great organ-pipes are formed where the water flows over triangular  projections of the rocks. The perpendicularity of the icicles contrasts strangely with the various angles of the rocks. It is now quite cold, and in many places only a sharp spear of purest crystal, which does not reach the rock below, is left to tell of the water that has flowed here. These solid, pipe-like icicles commonly unite by their sides and form rows of pillars or irregular colonnades, run together, between which here and there you can insert your hand, revealing a peculiar internal structure, as of successive great drops. Thus when the water has fallen perpendicularly. And behind these perpendicular pipes, or congregated pillars, or colonnades run together, are formed the prettiest little aisles or triangular alcoves with lichen-clad sides. Then the ice spreads out in a thin crust over the rock, with an uneven surface as of bubbling water, and you can see the rock indistinctly through ice three or four inches thick, and so on, by successive steps or shelves down the rock.

Saw where a squirrel, probably a red one, had apparently brought up to the mouth of his hole quite a quantity of walnuts and eaten them there.

I observe that the surface of the snow under the hemlocks is now very thickly strewn with cones and scales. Was it done by the thaw? Or did the partridges help do it? The ends of the lower limbs are still under the snow.

At night a fine freezing rain begins, which turns the frost to a glaze.

Jan. 12. A. M. — It still rains very finely. The ground, etc., is covered with a black glaze, wet and shiny like water, like an invisible armor, a quarter of an inch or more thick.

Every winter the surface of the pond to the depth of a foot becomes solid so as to support the heaviest teams, and anon the snow covers it to an equal depth, so that it is not to be distinguished from a level field. Thus, like the marmots in the surrounding hills, it too closes its eyelids and becomes partially dormant.[1]

Coarse, hard rain from time to time to-day, with much mist, — thaw and rain. The cocks crow, for the ground begins to be bare in spots. Walking, or wading, very bad.

Jan. 13. Still warm and thawing, springlike; no freezing in the night, though high winds. Are we not apt to have high winds after rain?

P. M. — To Walden, Goose Pond, and Britton's Camp.

The landscape is now patches of bare ground and snow; much running water with the sun reflected from it. Lately all was clean, dry, and tight. Now, though clear and bright, all is moist and dissolving. The cocks crow with new brag. Even the telegraph harp seems to sound as with a vernal sound, heralding a new year. Those pools of greenish-yellow water with a snow bot-

---

[1] [*Walden*, pp. 312, 313; Riv. 437.]

tom, in hollows in fields and woods, are now much increased, ready to be frozen. These thawing days must have been to some extent lichen days too. I did not examine. The stumps are now richly bronzed with greenish mealy lichens. A rich scale is slowly creeping over and covering them. How the red cockscomb lichens contrast with the snow! Some of these days I have heard Therien's axe more than a mile distinctly. He has already carried it home and ground it twice, having dulled it on a stone. Walden is covered with puddles, in which you see a dim reflection of the trees and hills, as in weak soapsuds, on the grayish or light-colored snow ice.

I saw yesterday my snow-shoe tracks quite distinct, though made January 2d. Though they pressed the snow down four or five inches, they consolidated it, and it now endures and is two or three inches above the general level there, and more white.

The water on Walden has been flowing into the holes cut for pickerel and others. It has carried with it, apparently from the surface, a sort of dust that collects on the surface, which produces a dirty or grayish-brown foam. It lies sometimes several feet wide, quite motionless on the surface of the shallow water above the ice, and is very agreeably and richly figured, like the hide of some strange beast — how cheap these colors in nature ! — parts of it very much like the fur of rabbits, the tips of their tails. I stooped to pick it up once or twice, — now like bowels overlying one another, now like tripe, now like flames, *i. e.* in form, with the free, bold touch of Nature. One would not believe that the

impurities which thus color the foam could be arranged in such pleasing forms. Give any material, and Nature begins to work it up into pleasing forms.

In the deep hollow this side of Britton's Camp, I heard a singular buzzing sound from the ground, exactly like that of a large fly or bee in a spider's web. I kneeled down, and with pains traced it to a small bare spot as big as my hand, amid the snow, and searched there amid the grass stubble for several minutes, putting the grass aside with my fingers, till, when I got nearest to the spot, not knowing but I might be stung, I used a stick. The sound was incessant, like that of a large fly in agony, but though it made my ears ache, and I had my stick directly on the spot, I could find neither prey nor oppressor. At length I found that I interrupted or changed the tone with my stick, and so traced it to a few spires of dead grass occupying about a quarter of an inch in diameter and standing in the melted snow water. When I bent these one side it produced a duller and baser tone. It was a sound issuing from the earth, and as I stooped over it, the thought came over me that it might be the first puling infantine cry of an earthquake, which would ere long ingulf me. There was no bubble in the water. Perhaps it was air confined under the frozen ground, now expanded by the thaw, and escaping upward through the water by a hollow grass stem. I left it after ten minutes, buzzing as loudly as at first. Could hear it more than a rod.

Schoolcraft says, " The present name is derived from the Dutch, who called it Roode Eylant (Red Island),

from the autumnal color of its foliage." (Coll. R. I. Hist. Soc. vol. iii.)

Jan. 14. If the writers of the brazen age are most suggestive to thee, confine thyself to them, and leave those of the Augustan age to dust and the bookworms.

Was surprised this morning to see how much the river was swollen by the rain of day before yesterday. The channel, or river itself, is still covered with ice, but the meadows are broad sheets of dark-blue water, contrasting with the white patches of snow still left. The ice on the river rises with the water in this case, while it remains attached to the bottom by one edge on each side, and is heaved up and cracked in consequence along the line of the willows, thus : —

All the water on the meadows lies over ice and snow. The other day I started a partridge from a sumach bush with berries on it, and to-day from a barberry bush with berries. I suspect that they eat the berries of both.

Cato makes the vineyard of first importance to a farm; second, a well-watered garden; third, a willow plantation (*salictum*); fourth, an olive-yard (*oletum*); fifth, a meadow or grass ground (?) (*pratum*); sixth, a grain-field or tillage (?) (*campus frumentarius*); seventh, a copsewood (?) for fuel (?) (*silva caedua*) (Varro speaks of planting and cultivating this); eighth, an

arbustum (Columella says it is a plantation of elms, etc., for vines to rest on) (*arbustum*); ninth, a wood that yields mast (*glandaria silva*). He says elsewhere the *arbustum* yields *ligna et virgae*.

He says: " In earliest manhood the master of a family must study to plant his ground; as for building he must think a long time about it (*diu cogitare*); he must not think about planting, but do it. When he gets to be thirty-six years old, then let him build, if he has his ground planted. So build, that the villa may not have to seek the farm, nor the farm the villa." This contains sound advice, as pertinent now as ever.

As for farming implements, I do not see but the Romans had as great a variety as are now exhibited in the Crystal Palace.

The master of a family must have in his rustic villa " cellam oleariam, vinariam, dolia multa, uti lubeat caritatem exspectare, et rei et virtuti, et gloriae erit " (an oil and wine cellar, many casks, so that it may be pleasant to expect hard times; it will be for his advantage, and virtue and glory).

This, too, to make farmers prudent and thrifty: " Cogitato quotannis tempestates magnas venire, et oleam dejicere solere " (Consider that great tempests come every year, and the olive is wont to fall). The steward must not lend seed for sowing, etc. He may have two or three families of whom to borrow and to whom to lend and no more.

I just had a coat come home from the tailor's. Ah me! Who am I that should wear this coat? It was fitted upon one of the devil's angels about my size. Of what use that measuring of me if he did not measure my character, but only the breadth of my shoulders, as it were a peg to hang it on. This is not the figure that I cut. This is the figure the tailor cuts. That presumptuous and impertinent fashion whispered in his ear, so that he heard no word of mine. As if I had said, " Not my will, O Fashion, but thine be done." We worship not the Parcæ, nor the Graces, but Fashion, offspring of Proteus and Vanessa, of Whim and Vanity. She spins and weaves and cuts with the authority of the Fates. Oh, with what delight I could thrust a spear through her vitals or squash her under my heel! Every village might well keep constantly employed a score of knights to rid it of this monster. It changes men into bears or monkeys with a single wave of its wand. The head monkey at Paris, Count D'Orsay, put on the traveller's cap, and now all the monkeys in the world do the same thing. He merely takes the breadth of my shoulders and proceeds to fit the garment to Puck, or some other grotesque devil of his acquaintance to whom he has sold himself.

I despair of ever getting anything quite simple and honest done in this world by the help of men. They would have to be passed through a powerful press, à la cider-mill, that their old notions might be thoroughly squeezed out of them, and it would be some time before they would get upon their legs again. Then undoubtedly there would be some one with a maggot in his head, offspring of an egg deposited there nobody knows when; fire does not kill these things, and you

would have lost your labor.[1] I could cry, if it were not for laughing.

" If you have done one thing late, you will do all your work late," says Cato to the farmer. They raised a sallow (salicem) to tie vines with. Ground subject to fogs is called nebulosus. They made a cheap wine of poor grapes, called vinum praeliganeum, for the laborers to drink. (So our farmers give their men rum or weak cider.)

Oxen " must have muzzles [or little baskets, fiscellas],[2] that they may not go in quest of grass (ne herbam sectentur) when they plow."

Jan. 17. Surveying for William O. Benjamin in east part of Lincoln. Saw a red squirrel on the wall, it being thawing weather. Human beings with whom I have no sympathy are far stranger to me than inanimate matter, — rocks or earth. Looking on the last, I feel comparatively as if I were with my kindred.

Cato, prescribing a medicamentum for oxen, says, " When you see a snake's slough, take it and lay it up, that you may not have to seek it when it is wanted." This was mixed with bread, corn, etc.

He tells how to make bread and different kinds of cakes, viz., a libum, a placenta, a spira (so called because twisted like a rope, perhaps like doughnuts), scriblita (because ornamented with characters like writing), globi (globes), etc., etc. Tells how to make a vow

[1] [Walden, p. 28; Riv. 42. See also Familiar Letters, pp. 225, 226; Riv. 271, 272.]
[2] [The brackets are Thoreau's.]

for your oxen to Mars Sylvanus in a wood with an offering, no woman to be present nor know how it is done.

When the brine will float a dry maena (a fish) or an egg, then it will preserve meat. Tells how to cram hens and geese. If you wish to remove an ill savor from wine, he recommends to heat a brick and pitch it and let it down by a string to the bottom of the cask and there remain two days, the cask being stopped.

" If you wish to know if water has been added to wine, make a little vessel of ivy wood (materia ederacea). Put into it the wine which you think has water in it. If it has water, the wine will run out (effluet), the water will remain. For a vessel of ivy wood does not hold wine."

" The dogs must be shut up by day that they may be more sharp (acriores, more fierce (?)) and vigilant by night." So I might say of a moon and star gazer.

" Make a sacrificial feast for the oxen when the pear is in blossom. Afterward begin to plow in the spring." " That day is to be holy (feriae) to the oxen, and herdsmen, and those who make the feast." They offer wine and mutton to Jupiter Dapalis, also to Vesta if they choose.

When they thinned a consecrated grove (lucum conlucare) (as if [to] let in the light to a shaded place) they were to offer a hog by way of expiation and pray the god or goddess to whom it was sacred to be favorable to them, their house and family and children. Whatever god or goddess thou art to whom this grove is sacred, I pray thee be propitious. Should not all groves

be regarded as a lucus, or consecrated grove, in this sense? I wish that our farmers felt some such awe when they cut down our consecrated groves; would realize that they are sacred to some god.[1]

A lustrum, or sacrifice, of a sow, sheep, and bull (suovitaurilia) was performed every fifth year, when various things were prayed for.

Gives several charms to cure diseases, mere magician's words.

Jan. 19. Went to Cambridge to court.

Dr. Harris says that my cocoons found in Lincoln in December are of the Attacus cecropia, the largest of our emperor moths. He made this drawing[2] of the four kinds of emperor moths which he says we have. The cecropia is the largest. The cocoon must be right end uppermost when they are ready to come out. The A. Promethea is the only moth whose cocoon has a fastening wound round the petiole of the leaf, and round the shoot, the leaf partly folded round it.

That spider whose hole I found, and which I carried him, he is pretty sure is the Lycosa fatifera.

In a large and splendid work on the insects of Georgia, by Edwards and Smith (?), near end of last century, up-stairs, I found plates of the above moths, called not Attacus but Phalœna, and other species of Phalœna.

He thinks that small beetle, slightly metallic, which I saw with grubs, etc., on the yellow lily roots last fall was a Donax or one of the Donasia (?).[3]

[1] [Walden, 276, 277; Riv. 388.]
[2] [Dr. Harris's drawing is inserted here.]
[3] [Donacia is a genus of beetles. Donax is a genus of molluscs.]

In Josselyn's account of his voyage from London to Boston in 1638, he says, "June the first day in the afternoon, very thick foggie weather, we sailed by an enchanted island," etc. This kind of remark, to be found in so many accounts of voyages, appears to be a fragment of tradition come down from the earliest account of Atlantis and its disappearance.

Varro, having enumerated certain writers on agriculture, says accidentally [*sic*] that they wrote *soluta ratione, i. e.* in prose. This suggests the difference between the looseness of prose and the precision of poetry. A perfect expression requires a particular rhythm or measure for which no other can be substituted. The prosaic is always a loose expression.

Varro divides fences into four kinds, — *unum naturale, alterum agreste, tertium militare, quartum fabrile.* (Many kinds of each.) The first is the living hedge. One kind of *sepes agrestis* is our rail fence, and our other dead wooden farm fences would come under this head. The military *sepes* consists of a ditch and rampart; is common along highways; sometimes a rampart alone. The fourth is the mason's fence of stone or brick (burnt or unburnt), or stone and earth together.

Jan. 22. Saw, January 20th, some tree sparrows in the yard. Once or twice of late I have seen the mother-o'-pearl tints and rainbow flocks in the western sky. The usual time is when the air is clear and pretty cool, about an hour before sundown. Yesterday I saw a very permanent specimen, like a long knife-handle of mother-of-pearl, very pale with an interior blue and

rosaceous tinges. Methinks the summer sky never exhibits this so finely.

When I was at C.'s the other evening, he punched his cat with the poker because she purred too loud for him.

R. Rice says he saw a white owl two or three weeks since. Harris told me on the 19th that he had never found the snow-flea.

No second snow-storm in the winter can be so fair and interesting as the first. Last night was very windy, and to-day I see the dry oak leaves collected in thick beds in the little hollows of the snow-crust. These later falls of the leaf.

A fine freezing rain on the night of the 19th produced a hard crust on the snow, which was but three inches deep and would not bear.

Jan. 23. Love tends to purify and sublime itself. It mortifies and triumphs over the flesh, and the bond of its union is holiness.

The increased length of the days is very observable of late. What is a winter unless you have risen and gone abroad frequently before sunrise and by starlight? Varro speaks of what he calls, I believe, before-light (*antelucana*) occupations in winter, on the farm. Such are especially milking, in this neighborhood.[1]

[1] Speaking of the rustic villa, you must see that the kitchen is convenient, " because some things are done there in the winter before daylight (*antelucanis temporibus*); food is prepared and taken." In the study are not some things to be done before daylight, and a certain food to be prepared there ?

If one may judge from Josselyn, they began to be weather-wise very early in New England. He says: " The obscuring of the smaller stars is a certain sign of tempests approaching. . . . The resounding of the sea from the shore, and murmuring of the winds [*sic* in Josselyn] in the woods without apparent wind, sheweth wind to follow.[1] . . . The redness of the sky in the morning, is a token of winds, or rain, or both," etc., etc. " If the white hills look clear and conspicuous, it is a sign of fair weather; if black and cloudy, of rain; if yellow, it is a certain sign of snow shortly to ensue," etc. *Vide* his " Two Voyages."[2] He speaks of " the Earth-nut bearing a princely flower, the beautiful leaved Pirola,"[3] etc. Is n't this the glossy-leaved wintergreen?

At noon, go to Worcester.

Jan. 24. In Worcester.

From 9 A. M. to 4 P. M., walked about six miles northwest into Holden with Blake, returning by Stonehouse Hill. A very cold day. Less forest near Worcester than in Concord, and that hardwood. No dark pines in the horizon. The evergreen laurel is a common underwood, contrasting agreeably with the snow. Large, broad-backed hills.

De Quincey's " Historical and Critical Essays " I have not read (2 vols.). Saw a red squirrel out.

Jan. 25. At noon return to Concord.

[1] [*Cape Cod*, p. 98; Riv. 115.]
[2] [*Two Voyages to New England*, pp. 56, 57.]   [3] [*Op. cit.*, p. 59.]

A very cold day.

Saw a man in Worcester this morning who took a pride in never wearing gloves or mittens. Drives in the morning. Said he succeeded by keeping his arm and wrist well covered. He had a large hand, one of his fingers as big as three of mine. But this morning he had to give up. The 22d, 23d, 24th, and 25th of this month have been the coldest spell of weather this winter.

Clear and cold and windy.

Jan. 26. All day at court at Cambridge.

Jan. 27. I have an old account-book, found in Deacon R. Brown's garret since his death. The first leaf or two is gone. Its cover is brown paper, on which, amid many marks and scribblings, I find written: —

" Mr. Ephraim Jones
His Wast Book
Anno Domini
1742 "

It extends from November 8th, 1742, to June 20th, 1743 (inclusive). It appears without doubt from the contents of this book that he is the one of whom Shattuck writes in his history that he " married Mary Hayward, 1728, and died November 29th, 1756, aged 51; having been captain, town-clerk, and otherwise distinguished." His father's name was Ephraim, and he had a son Ephraim. The entries are made apparently by himself, or a boy, or his wife, or some other when he was out. The book is filled with familiar Concord names, the grandfathers and great-grandfathers of the present generation. Dr. Hartshorn — he lived to be ninety-two — and Dr. Temple send to the store once or twice. It is more important now what was bought than who bought it.

The articles most commonly bought were mohair (commonly with buttons) (a kind of twist to sew on buttons with), rum (often only a gill to drink at the store), — more of these than anything; salt, molasses, shalloon, fish, calico, some sugar, a castor hat, almanac, psalter (and sometimes primer and testament), paper, knee-buckles and shoe-buckles, garters and spurs by the pair, deer skins, a fan, a cart whip, various kinds of cloth and trimmings, — as half-thick, osnaburg, a very little silk, ferret, quality, serge for breeches, etc., etc., — gloves, a spring knife, an ink-horn, a gun, cap, spice, a pocket case, timber, iron, etc., earthenware; no tea (?) (I am in doubt about one or perhaps two entries), nor coffee, nor meal, nor flour. Of the last two they probably raised all they wanted. Credit is frequently given for timber and once for cloth brought to the store.

On the whole, it is remarkable how little provision was sold at the store. The inhabitants raised almost everything for themselves. Chocolate is sold once. Rum, salt, molasses, fish, a biscuit with their drink, a little spice, and the like are all that commonly come under this head that I remember.

On a loose piece of paper is a bill for "todey," "a bowl of punch," etc., and on another piece is Jonathan Dwight's (innholder's?) bill against the Estate of

Capt. Ephraim Jones for entertainment, etc., etc. (apparently he treated his company) at divers times for half a dozen years, amounting to over £146. One entry is "Dea Brown to flip & rum."

The people apparently made their own cloth and even thread, and hence for the most part bought only buttons and mohair and a few trimmings.

> Feb. 1, 1742. "Town of Concord Dr to sundry for
>   the funerel of Widow Williams daughter to 5
>   pr gloves @ 1/9 1 D P. @ 2/1 ½ . . .   0–10–10¼ "
> Jan. 10, 1742 (3). "Jonᵃ Edes to 3 Raccoon skins ⎱ 0–12– 5 "
>   @ 2/9 2 minks @ 1/6 4 musquash @ /3 ½ ·⎰
> Jan. 18, 1742 (3). "John Melven Cr by 1 Grey fox 0– 2– 3 "
> Feb. 14, 1742 (3). "Aaron Parker Cr by 100 squirell
>   skins . . . . 0– 6– 3 "[1]

Deer skins were sold at from ten to seventeen shillings. Sometimes it is written "old" or "new tenor."

Many of the customers came from as far as Harvard, or much farther.

A fan, a jack-knife, or a pair of garters are much more important relatively to the other goods sold than now.

No butter, nor rice, nor oil, nor candles are sold. They must have used candles [of their own making], made their own butter, and done without rice. There is no more authentic history of those days than this "Wast Book" contains, and, being money matters, it is more explicit than almost any other statement; something *must* be said. Each line contains and states explicitly a fact. It is the best of evidence of several facts. It tells distinctly and authoritatively who sold, who bought, the article, amount, and value, and the date. You could

[1] [*Walden*, p. 308; Riv. 432.]

not easily crowd more facts into one line. You are warned when the doctor or deacon had a new suit of clothes, by the charge for mohair, buttons, and trimmings, or a castor hat; and here also is entered the rum which ran down their very throats.

Attended the auction of Deacon Brown's effects a little while to-day, — a great proportion of old traps, rubbish, or trumpery, which began to accumulate in his father's day, and now, after lying half a century in his garret and other dust-holes, is not burned, but surviving neighbors collect and view it, and buy it, and carefully transport it to their garrets and dust-holes, to lie there till their estates are settled, when it will start again. Among his effects was a dried tapeworm and various articles too numerous and worthless to mention. A pair of old snow-shoes is almost regularly sold on these occasions, though none of this generation has seen them worn here.

I have some good friends from whom I am wont to part with disappointment, for they neither care what I think nor mind what I say. The greatest compliment that was ever paid me was when one asked me what I *thought*, and attended to my answer.

We begin to die, not in our senses or extremities, but in our divine faculties. Our members may be sound, our sight and hearing perfect, but our genius and imagination betray signs of decay. You tell me that you are growing old and are troubled to see without glasses, but this is unimportant if the divine faculty of the seer shows no signs of decay.

Cut this afternoon a cake of ice out of Walden and

brought it home in a pail, another from the river, and got a third, a piece of last year's ice from Sam Barrett's Pond, at Brown's ice-house, and placed them side by side. These lumps are not large enough to show the color. Walden ice has a green tint close by, but is distinguished by its blueness at a distance. The river ice inclines to a more opaque white.[1] Comparing the lumps, Walden ice was, you might say, more crystalline than the river, but both showed the effect of heat more than the Barrett ice of last year, the bubbles being very much elongated and advanced toward the honeycomb stage, while in the Barrett ice they were spherical and there were wide clear spaces. This looked as if it would keep best.

Varro, on grafting, says when the wood is of a close and dry texture they tie a vessel over it from which water drops slowly, that the shoot may not dry up before it coalesces; also "by the turning of some leaves you can tell what season (*tempus*) of the year it is, as the olive and white poplar, and willow. For when their leaves turn, the solstice is said to be past." They had not such a brilliant change of the leaf as we.

Speaking of the nursery, he says: "Herbaeque elidendae, et dum tenerae sunt vellendae, prius enim aridae factae rixantur, ac celerius rumpuntur, quam sequuntur (and the weeds are to be levelled and, while they are tender, pulled up, for if they have first grown tough they resist and break sooner than come up). . . . Contra herba in pratis ad spem foenisiciae nata, non modo non evellenda in nutricatu, sed etiam non cal-

[1] [*Walden*, p. 327; Riv. 457.]

canda. Quo pecus a prato ablegandum, et omne jumentum, ac etiam homines. Solum enim hominis exitium herbae, et semitae fundamentum. (On the other hand, grass in grass-ground, raised with a view to hay, not only is not to be pulled up while it is growing, but is not even to be trodden upon. Wherefore the cattle are to be driven from the mowing, and every beast of burden, and even men. For the sole (track?) of a man's foot is the destruction of the grass, and the foundation of a (foot)path.)" Even so early did the farmers raise this hue and cry about your treading down or going through their grass.

Jan. 29. A very cold morning. Thermometer, or mercury, 18° below zero.

Varro says that *gluma* seems to be *a glubendo* because the grain is shelled from its follicle (*deglubitur*). *Arista*, the beard of grain, is so called because it dries first (*quod arescit prima*). The grain, *granum*, is *a gerendo,* for this is the object of planting, that this may be borne. " But the *spica* (or ear), which the rustics call *speca*, as they have received it from their forefathers, seems to be named from *spes* (hope), since they plant because they *hope* that *this* will be hereafter (*eam enim quod sperant fore*)." [1]

The village is the place to which the roads tend, a sort of expansion of the highway, as a lake of a river, the thoroughfare and ordinary of travellers, a trivial or quadrivial place. It is the body of which roads are the arms and legs. It is from the Latin *villa*, which, together with *via* (a way), or more anciently *vea* and

[1] [*Walden*, p. 184; Riv. 258, 259.]

vella, Varro derives from *veho* (to carry), because the villa is the place to and from which things are carried. The steward or overseer of the villa was a *vilicus*, and those who got their living by teaming (?) (*vecturis*) were said *vellaturam facere.* And whence the Latin *vilis* and our word *villain* (?). The inhabitants are way-worn by the travel that goes by and over them without travelling themselves.

Jan. 30. Another cold morning. Mercury down to 13° below zero.

Frank showed me last night a white hare he had killed. It was frozen stiff, weighed four pounds, and was nearly three feet long. Its hind feet made soft brushes, which painters use in graining doors, etc. The plumage of partridges is most perfect nowadays. The white hare is a dirty white in winter, grayish (?) or brownish in summer; has peculiar puss-like expression in profile. This was frozen in the attitude of running, careering with elastic bound over the snow and amid the bushes. Now, dead, it is the symbol of that speed it was capable of. Frozen as it was, it nearly spanned one breadth of the carpet, or three feet.[1] This morning, though not so cold by a degree or two as yesterday morning, the cold has got more into the house, and the frost visits nooks never known to be visited before. The sheets are frozen about the sleeper's face; the teamster's beard is white with ice. Last night I felt it stinging cold as I came up the street at 9 o'clock; it bit my ears and face, but the stars shone all the

[1] *Vide* [p. 86].

Vol. VI

brighter. The windows are all closed up with frost, as if they were ground glass.

The greater part of last week there was no melting in the roads nor on roofs. No more yesterday and to-day. The snow is dry and squeaks under the feet, and the teams creak as if they needed greasing, — sounds associated with extremely cold weather.

P. M. — Up river on ice and snow to Fair Haven Pond.

There is a few inches of snow, perfectly level, which now for nearly a week has covered the ice. Going toward the sun, you are snow-blinded. At each clump of willows on the meadow, it looks as if there were a hillock, out of which they grow. This appearance is produced by the willow twigs holding up the ice to [the] height at which it was frozen after the last thaw, about two feet above the present level. It forms a regularly rounded hillock. We look at every track in the snow. Every little while there is the track of a fox — maybe the same one — across the river, turning aside sometimes to a muskrat's cabin or a point of ice, where he has left some traces, and frequently the larger track of a hound, which has followed his trail. It is much easier and pleasanter to walk thus on the river, the snow being shallow and level, and there is no such loud squeaking or cronching of the snow as in the road, and this road is so wide that you do not feel confined in it, and you never meet travellers with whom you have no sympathy.

The winter, cold and bound out as it is, is thrown to us like a bone to a famishing dog, and we are expected

to get the marrow out of it. While the milkmen in the outskirts are milking so many scores of cows before sunrise these winter mornings, it is our task to milk the winter itself. It is true it is like a cow that is dry, and our fingers are numb, and there is none to wake us up. Some desert the field and go into winter quarters in the city. They attend the oratorios, while the only music that we countrymen hear is the squeaking of the snow under our boots. But the winter was not given to us for no purpose. We must thaw its cold with our genialness. We are tasked to find out and appropriate all the nutriment it yields. If it is a cold and hard season, its fruit, no doubt, is the more concentrated and nutty. It took the cold and bleakness of November to ripen the walnut, but the human brain is the kernel which the winter itself matures. Not till then does its shell come off. The seasons were not made in vain. Because the fruits of the earth are already ripe, we are not to suppose that there is no fruit left for winter to ripen. It is for man the seasons and all their fruits exist. The winter was made to concentrate and harden and mature the kernel of his brain, to give tone and firmness and consistency to his thought. Then is the great harvest of the year, the harvest of thought. All previous harvests are stubble to this, mere fodder and green crop. Now we burn with a purer flame like the stars; our oil is winter-strained. We are islanded in Atlantic and Pacific and Indian Oceans of thought, Bermudas, or Friendly or Spice Islands.

Shall we take refuge in cities in November? Shall the nut fall green from the tree? Let not the year be disappointed of its crop. I knew a crazy man who walked into an empty pulpit one Sunday and, taking up a hymn-book, remarked: " We have had a good fall for getting in corn and potatoes. Let us sing Winter." So I say, " Let us sing winter." What else can we sing, and our voices be in harmony with the season?

As we walked up the river, a little flock of chickadees (apparently) flew to us from a wood-side fifteen rods off, and uttered their lively *day day day*, and followed us along a considerable distance, flitting by our side on the button-bushes and willows. It is the most, if not the only, sociable bird we have.

Now is the time to fill ice-houses, for fear they may not have another chance for solid ice. Brown filled his last week.

I will be a countryman. I will not go to the city, even in winter, any more than the sallows and sweet-gale by the river do. I see their yellow osiers and freckled, handsomely imbricated buds,[1] still rising above the ice and snow there, to cheer me.

The white rabbit is a large fellow, well furred. What does he get to eat, being a vegetable liver? He must be hardy and cunning in his way. His race have learned by long practice to find their food where a newcomer would inevitably starve.

How retired an otter manages to live! He grows to be four feet long without any mortal getting a glimpse of him, — as long as a boy.

Sometimes one·of those great cakes of green ice from Walden or Sam Barrett's Pond slips from the ice-man's

[1] Or catkins.

sled in the street and lies there like a great emerald, an object of interest to all travellers.[1]

The hips of the late rose are still abundant and perfect, amid the button-bushes.

Jan. 31. P. M. — To Great Meadows and Beck Stow's.

The wind is more southerly, and now the warmth of the sun prevails, and is felt on the back. The snow softens and melts. It is a beautiful clear and mild winter day. Our washwoman says she is proud of it. Any clear day, methinks, the sun is ready to do his part, and let the wind be right, and it will be warm and pleasant-like, at least now that the sun runs so high a course. But I do not melt; there is no thaw in me; I am bound out still.

I see the tree sparrows, one or two at a time, now and then, all winter, uttering a faint note, with their bright-chestnut crown and spot on breast and barred wings. They represent the sparrows in the winter.

Went to the Great Meadows by the Oak Island. The maples along the edge of the meadow, which all winter have been perfectly leafless, have an agreeable mixed, slightly pepper-and-salt look, spotted or barred with white lichens. It is an agreeable maze to the eye, so thick their bare and clean gray limbs.

Many tracks of partridges there along the meadow-side in the maples, and their droppings where they appear to have spent the night about the roots and between the stems of trees. I think they eat the buds of

[1] [*Walden*, p. 327; Riv. 457.]

the azalea. And now, with a mew, preluding a whir, they go off before me. Coming up, I follow her tracks to where she eased herself for lightness, and immediately after are five or six parallel cuts in the snow, where her wing struck when she lifted herself from the ground, but no trace more.

I pass the woodchoppers, busily felling trees or cutting up those which they have felled. One is measuring his lengths with his axe-helve and does not see me.

The pitch pines are yellowish, the white incline to bluish. In the winter, when there are no flowers and leaves are rare, even large buds are interesting and somewhat exciting. I go a-budding like a partridge. I am always attracted at this season by the buds of the swamp-pink, the poplars, and the sweet-gale.

A hundred years ago, as I learned from Ephraim Jones's ledger, they sold bark in our street. He gives credit for a load. Methinks my genius is coeval with that time. That is no great wildness or *selvaggia* that cannot furnish a load of bark, when the forest has lost its shagginess. This is an attempt to import this wildness into the cities in a thousand shapes. Bark is carried thither by ship and by cartloads. Bark contains the principle of tannin, by which not only the fibre of skins but of men's thoughts is hardened and consolidated. It was then that a voice was given to the dog, and a manly tone to the human voice. Ah! already I shudder for these comparatively degenerate days of the village, when you cannot collect a load of bark of good thickness.

Varro thinks that when man reached the pastoral or second stage and domesticated animals (*pecus*), " primum non sine causa putant oves assumptas, et propter utilitatem, et propter placiditatem " (they think not without reason that sheep were first taken, both on account of their usefulness and on account of their gentleness); for, as he says, they furnish milk, cheese, their fleece, and skin. It looks to me as if the sheep had been supplied with a superfluity of clothing that it might share it with man, and, as Varro suggests, did not this fleece, on account of its value, come to be called golden? was not this the origin of the fable?

We too have our thaws. They come to our January moods, when our ice cracks, and our sluices break loose. Thought that was frozen up under stern experience gushes forth in feeling and expression. There is a freshet which carries away dams of accumulated ice. Our thoughts hide unexpressed, like the buds under their downy or resinous scales; they would hardly keep a partridge from starving. If you would know what are my winter thoughts look for them in the partridge's crop. They are like the laurel buds, — some leaf, some blossom buds, — which, though food for such indigenous creatures, will not expand into leaves and flowers until summer comes.

" Et primitus oritur herba imbribus primoribus evocata," says Varro.[1]

[1] [*Walden*, p. 343; Riv. 479.]

III

FEBRUARY, 1854

(ÆT. 36)

Feb. 2. Up river on ice to Clematis Brook.

Another warm, melting day, like yesterday. You can see some softening and relenting in the sky. Apparently the vapor in the air makes a grosser atmosphere, more like that of a summer eve. We go up the Corner road and take the ice at Potter's Meadow. The Cliff Hill is nearly bare on the west side, and you hear the rush of melted snow down its side in one place. Here and there are regular round holes in the ice over the meadow, two or three feet in diameter, where the water appears to be warmer, — perchance there is a spring there, — and therein, in shallow water, is seen the cress and one or two other plants, still quite fresh. The shade of pines on the snow is in some lights quite blue.

We stopped awhile under Bittern Cliff, the south side, where it is very warm. There are a few greenish radical leaves to be seen, — primrose and johnswort, strawberry, etc., and spleenwort still green in the clefts. These sunny old gray rocks, completely covered with white and gray lichens and overrun with ivy, are a very cosy place. You hardly detect the melted snow swiftly trickling down them until you feel the drops on your cheek. The winter gnat is seen in the warm air before

the rock. In the clefts of these rocks are the latebræ of many insects, spiders, etc. Were they not sowbugs I found under the *Marchantia polymorpha* (?)? The ice is about eighteen inches thick on Fair Haven. Saw some pickerel just caught there, with a fine lustre to them. Went to the pond in the woods which has an old ditch dug from it near Clematis Brook. The red twigs of the cornels and the yellow ones of the sallows surrounding it are interesting at this season. We prize the least color now. As it is a melting day, the snow is everywhere peppered with snow-fleas, even twenty rods from the woods, on the pond and meadows.

The scream of the jay is a true winter sound. It is wholly without sentiment, and in harmony with winter. I stole up within five or six feet of a pitch pine behind which a downy woodpecker was pecking. From time to time he hopped round to the side and observed me without fear. They are very confident birds, not easily scared, but incline to keep the other side of the bough to you, perhaps.

Already we begin to anticipate spring, and this is an important difference between this time and a month ago. We begin to say that the day is springlike.

Is not January the hardest month to get through? When you have weathered that, you get into the gulf-stream of winter, nearer the shores of spring.

Feb. 3. A driving snow-storm again.

The attractions of the Hollowell Farm were: its complete retirement, being at least two miles from the village, half a mile from any neighbor, and separated

Vol. VI

from the highway by a broad field; its bounding on the river; the pleasing ruin of the house and barn; the hollow and lichen-covered apple trees gnawed by rabbits; above all the recollection I had of it from my earliest voyages up the river, when the house was concealed behind a dense grove of red maples, which then stood between it and the river, through which I once heard the house-dog bark; and in general the slight improvements that had been made upon it. These were the motives that swayed, though I did not mention them to the proprietor. To enjoy these things I was ready to carry it on and do all those things which I now see had no other motive or excuse but that I might pay for it and be unmolested in my possession of it; though I knew all the while that it would yield the most abundant crop of the kind I wanted if I could only afford to let it alone. Though it afforded no western prospect, the dilapidated fences were picturesque. I was in some haste to buy, before the proprietor finished getting out some rocks, cutting down some hollow apple trees, and grubbing up some young birches which had sprung up in the pasture, all which in my eyes very much enhanced its value.[1]

Varro speaks of two kinds of pigeons, one of which was wont to alight " on the (*columinibus villae*) columns of a villa (*a quo appellatae columbae*), from which they were called *columbae*, which on account of their natural timidity (*summa loca in tectis captant*) delight in the highest places on the roofs (?) (or under cover ?)."

[1] [*Walden*, pp. 92, 93; Riv. 131, 132.]

Feb. 4. F. Brown showed me this afternoon his game killed day before yesterday, — a gray hare, a gray squirrel, and a red squirrel. The red squirrel was peeping out of his nest in a tree. The gray was a fine large fellow in good condition; weighed one pound and a quarter, more than half as heavy as the hare, and his tail still perfectly and beautifully curved over his back. It recovered its place when you stroked it, as if it were full of electricity. All were frozen, the hare, as usual, in the attitude of running. The gray squirrel's ears were white above, edged with tawny brown. He thought that my marsh peep of the fall might [be] the ash-colored sandpiper.

John Moore and Company got about fifty weight of fish at Flint's Pond the same day. Two pickerel weighed nine pounds.

I went over to the Hemlocks on the Assabet this morning. Saw the tracks, I think of a mink, in the shallow snow along the edge of the river, looking for a hole in the ice. A clear, cold morning. The smokes from the village chimneys are quickly purified and dissipated, like vapor, in the air. They do not stream high.

Varro says *Africanae bestiae* for savage or ferocious beasts. Is this a difference of climate merely? Are not some quarters of the globe thus better fitted for the habitation of man for other reasons?

We have not much that is poetic in the accompaniments of the farmer's life. Varro speaks of the swine-herd accustoming the swine or boars to come at the sound of a horn when he fed them with acorns. I remember that my grandmother used to call her cow home at evening from a near pasture to be milked by thumping on the mortar which held her salt. The tinkling cow-bell cannot be spared. Ever what most attracts us in the farmer's life is not its profitableness. We love to go after the cow, not for the sake of her milk or her beef, or the money they yield, but perchance to hear the tinkling of the cow-bell; and we would fain keep a herd of pigs, not because of the profit there is in bacon, but because we have dreamed of hearing the swineherd's horn. We would keep hens, not for eggs, but to hear the cocks crow and the hens cackle.

As for the locality of beehives, Varro says that they must be placed near the villa, " potissimum ubi non resonent imagines, hic enim sonus harum fugae causa existimatur esse " (especially where there are no echoes, for this sound is thought to be the cause of their flight).

Feb. 5. Have two more old account-books of Ephraim Jones, running from 1741 to 1750 and further, — what are called ledgers, I think. Some of the items of the waste-book are here collected, each man's purchases and credit brought together.

I think he must have kept in the store which Goodnow & How first kept in. Some remember when an Ephraim Jones, probably his grandson, kept there. There appears to have been an Ephraim Jones keeping the jail then (probably a son of the first), in the Revolution. There is said to have been a public house with the sign of a black horse where Mr. Brooks's house stands, and hence the society that worshipped there were called the Black Horse Church.

He sold a few religious books as well as almanacs and primers. In 1745, " to Inchwoods Glimpse of Glory and Mr. (or Wm.) Row's Meditation well Bound," so much. In another place, " to Glimpse of Glory and sundry." Sometimes " a sermon book."

Whitefield was here first in 1741, and there were exciting revivals under Mr. Bliss at this time, says the History. Yet it is a dreary and ghastly life suggested, when you come upon a man's bill for a lock to the Burying Gate, and that is so nearly all that has come down. I picture to myself a rude, straggling village with a wide-open burying-ground gate.

Hezekiah Stratton has credit in 1743, " Feb. 7 by ½ a Catt skin 0–1–4½," — of course a wildcat.[1]

Gingerbread is bought several times, flour once or twice, and credit given for butter once or twice. Several times one nutmeg is bought. Credit given for weaving; also for a load of bark and tar and turpentine from Groton. The lime-kiln and iron mine are frequently named. Credit given for so much " mine," meaning apparently iron ore.

Stephen Parks has credit in 1746, " Aug 2. Cr by one wampum belt 0–15–0." To another, in 1744, " Cr by Dressing 50 squirrel skins 0–6–3." Credit is also given for fox skins and a few deer skins. But above all Jones gives credit for timber brought to the store, or, more commonly, carted to Menotomy, Mistick, Medford, or Charlestown. Some customers live in Nisstissit (?). Credit is given by " digging mine." (Probably iron, after called " mine.")

[1] [*Walden*, p. 308; Riv. 432.]

For example of the quantity of rum and the like bought, *vide* pages 128–193 of No. 2. Long columns run down the page, of nothing but flip, flip, mug flip, mug flip, todey, toddy, punch, punch, bowl of tody, brandy punch, etc., etc.; sometimes charges for the breaking of the glass, also for sugar and limes and flip for himself and company. Jones appears to have kept a public house, for he frequently charges for entertainment.

The animal merely makes him a bed, which he warms with his body in a sheltered place. He does not make a house. But man, having discovered fire, warms a spacious apartment up to the same temperature with his body, and without robbing it, so that he can divest himself of cumbersome clothing, — not keeping his bed, — maintain a kind of summer in the midst of winter, and, by means of windows, even admit the light. It was his invention to box up some air and warm it, make that his bed, and in this live and move and have his being still, and breathe as in a congenial climate or summer, without taking to his bed. Thus he goes a step or two beyond instinct and secures a little time for the fine arts.

Though I began to grow torpid when exposed a long time to the pinching winter air, — my hands and feet grew numb, and my ears and face stiffened, — when I had reached the genial atmosphere of my house, I soon recovered my faculties. I did not squat in a form, or lie in a burrow or ensconced in a nest of leaves or grass, like the squirrels, nor become quite dormant in any hole, like the woodchuck. I ameliorated the

winter climate with fire, and lengthened out the day with a lamp.[1]

Even Varro, to prove that the ancients did not shave (or that there were no barbers), is obliged to refer his readers to their bearded statues. " Olim tonsores non fuisse adsignificant antiquorum statuae, quod pleraeque habent capillum, et barbam magnam." Yet it was true of the old statues only " for the most part."

P. M. — To walk.

Begins to snow.

At Hubbard's blueberry swamp woods, near the bathing-place, came across a fox's track, which I think was made last night or since. The tracks were about two inches long, or a little less, by one and a half wide, shaped thus where the snow was only half an inch deep on ice: generally from nine to fifteen inches apart longitudinally and three to four inches apart transversely. It came from the west. I followed it back. At first it was difficult to trace, to *investigate*, it, amid some rabbit tracks, of which I did not know whether they had been made before or since. It soon led out of the woods on to the ice of the meadow to a slight prominence, then turned and followed along the side of the wood, then crossed the meadow directly to the riverside just below the mouth of Nut Meadow Brook, visited a muskrat-house there and left its mark, — watered, — for, dog-like, it turned aside to every muskrat-house or

[1] [*Walden*, p. 280; Riv. 393.]

the like prominence near its route and left its mark there. You could easily scent it there. It turned into the meadow eastward once or twice as it went up the riverside, and, after visiting another muskrat's house, where it left its manure, large and light-colored, as if composed of fir, crossed the river and John Hosmer's meadow and potato-field and the road south of Nut Meadow Bridge. (If it had been a dog it would have turned when it reached the road.) It was not lost then, but led straight across, through J. Hosmer's field and meadow again, and over ditch and up side-hill in the woods; and there, on the side of the hill, I could see where its tail had grazed the snow. It was then mixed with rabbit-tracks, but was easily unravelled. Passed out of the wood into J. P. Brown's land, over some mice or mole tracks, then over the middle of Brown's meadows westward, to Tarbell's meadows, till at last, by the brook, I found that it had had a companion up to that point, which turned off. Then I saw the large tracks of hounds on the trail. Still it held on, from straight across the road again, some way on an old dog's trail; had trodden and nosed very much about some hardhacks in the field beyond, where were a few mice-tracks, as if for food, the hound's tracks numerous with it; and so I traced it into the Ministerial Swamp, where, the snow-storm increasing I left it, having traced it back more than a mile westward in a pretty direct course. What expeditions they make in a night in search of food! No doubt the same one crosses the river many times.

Shall we not have sympathy with the muskrat which

gnaws its third leg off, not as pitying its sufferings, but through our kindred mortality, appreciating its majestic pains and its heroic virtue? Are we not made its brothers by fate? For whom are psalms sung and mass said, if not for such worthies as these? When I hear the church organ peal, or feel the trembling tones of the bass viol, I see in imagination the musquash gnawing off his leg, I offer up a note that his affliction may be sanctified to each and all of us. Prayer and praise fitly follow such exploits. I look round for majestic pains and pleasures. They have our sympathy, both in their joys and in their pains. When I think of the tragedies which are constantly permitted in the course of all animal life, they make the plaintive strain of the universal harp which elevates us above the trivial. When I think of the muskrat gnawing off his leg, it is as the plectrum on the harp or the bow upon the viol, drawing forth a majestic strain or psalm, which immeasurably dignifies our common fate. Even as the worthies of mankind are said to recommend human life by having lived it, so I could not spare the example of the muskrat.[1]

That sand foliage! It convinces me that Nature is still in her youth, — that florid fact about which mythology merely mutters, — that the very soil can fabulate as well as you or I. It stretches forth its baby fingers on every side. Fresh curls spring forth from its bald brow. There is nothing inorganic. This earth is not, then, a mere fragment of dead history, strata upon strata, like the leaves of a book, an object for a museum and an antiquarian, but living poetry, like the leaves of a tree, —

[1] [See *Journal*, vol. i, pp. 481, 482.]

Vol. VI

not a fossil earth, but a living specimen. You may melt your metals and cast them into the most beautiful moulds you can; they will never excite me like the forms which this molten earth flows out into. The very earth, as well as the institutions upon it, is plastic like potter's clay in the hands of the artist. These florid heaps lie along the bank like the slag of a furnace, showing that nature is in full blast within;[1] but there is no admittance except on business. Ye dead and alive preachers, ye have no business here. Ye will enter only to your tomb.

I fear only lest my expressions may not be extravagant enough, — may not wander far enough beyond the narrow limits of our ordinary insight and faith, so as to be adequate to the truth of which I have been convinced. I desire to speak somewhere without bounds, in order that I may attain to an expression in some degree adequate to truth of which I have been convinced. From a man in a waking moment, to men in their waking moments. Wandering toward the more distant boundaries of a wider pasture. Nothing is so truly bounded and obedient to law as music, yet nothing so surely breaks all petty and narrow bonds. Whenever I hear any music I fear that I may have spoken tamely and within bounds. And I am convinced that I cannot exaggerate enough even to lay the foundation of a true expression.[2] As for books and the adequateness of their statements to the truth, they are as the tower of Babel to the sky.

[1] [*Walden*, pp. 340, 341; Riv. 476.]
[2] [*Walden*, p. 357; Riv. 499, 500.]

In Jones's account there is a paper headed —

" funerel Charges.

4 P Shug . . .
¼ of alspice
tobackoo
11 yd Cyprus
4 goze; hankerchiefs
4 Par of women black gloves   The prices mostly
1½ yd Lutestring   cut off.
silk feret
12 pair of mens white gloves
6 yards of allomode
silk "

There was plainly much coopering done in those days.

How dangerous to the foxes and all wild animals is a light snow, accompanied and succeeded by calm weather, betraying their course to the hunters! Here was one track that crossed the road, — did not turn in it like a dog, — track of a wilder life. How distinct from the others! Such as was made before roads were, as if the road were [a] more recent track. This traveller does not turn when he strikes the trail of man. The fox that invaded the farmer's poultry-yard last night came from a great distance.

I followed on this trail so long that my thoughts grew foxy; though I was on the back track, I drew nearer and nearer to the fox each step. Strange as it may seem, I thought several times that I scented him, though I did not stoop.

Feb. 6. The weather has been very changeable for some weeks. First it is warm and thawing, sloshy weather; then the thermometer goes down to 19° below zero, and our shoes squeak on the snow; then, perhaps, it moderates and snows; then is mild and pleasant again and good sleighing; then we wake to find a drifted snow upon the last and a bleak, wintry prospect.

P. M. — To Cliffs and Walden.

It is a very light snow and, though seven or eight inches deep, but a slight obstacle to walking. Its surface in the woods is everywhere creased and scored by the flitting leaves and the snow that has fallen from the trees. For a drifting wind has followed fast upon the snow, shaking it off the trees, and there is a new fall of withered leaves. Probably these leaves decay the faster for being deposited thus in successive layers, alternating with the snow.

From the Cliff Hill the landscape looks very bleak and Nova-Zembla-like. A cold, drifting wind sweeps from the north; the surface of the snow is imbricated on a great scale, being very regularly blown into waves, alike over the high-road and the railroad, concealing the tracks and the meadow and the river and the pond. It is all one great wintry-looking snow-field, whose surface consists of great wave-like drifts, maybe twenty feet wide with an abrupt edge on the south. It is like a scaly armor drawn alike over the meadow and the pond. We need not trouble ourselves to speculate how the human race on this globe will be destroyed at last, whether by fire or otherwise. It would be so easy to cut their threads any time with a little sharper blast from the north. We go on dating from the Cold Fridays and the Great Snows and the September gales, but a little colder Friday, or greater snow, or more

violent gale would put a period to man's existence on the globe.[1]

I see great shadows on the northeast sides of the mountains, forty miles off, the sun being in the southwest. The snow is so light that few animals have been out. I see the track of a rabbit about the Cliff; there are hollows in the snow on the tops of the rocks, shaped like a milk-pan and as large, where he has squatted or whirled round. I also see the tracks of a few mice or moles. The squirrel, too, has been out. Hear the old owl at 4.30 P. M. Crossing Walden where the snow has fallen quite level, I perceive that my shadow [is of] a delicate or transparent blue rather than black.

Price on the Picturesque says, "The midsummer shoot is the first thing that gives relief to the eye, after the sameness of color which immediately precedes it; in many trees, and in none more than the oak, the effect is singularly beautiful; the old foliage forms a dark background, on which the new appears, relieved and detached in all its freshness and brilliancy: it is spring engrafted upon summer." Is not this the effect which I noticed by Fair Haven side last summer or autumn, toward night, — that watered and variously shaded foliage?

As for autumn, he speaks of "the warm haze, which, on a fine day in that season, spreads the last varnish over every part of the picture."

Gilpin talked as if there was some food for the soul in mere physical light and shadow, as if, without the suggestion of a moral, they could give a man pleasure or pain!

[1] [Walden, p. 280; Riv. 393, 394.]

Feb. 7. Under the waves of the snowy ocean yesterday, roads and rivers, pastures and cultivated fields, all traces of man's occupancy of the globe were for the most part concealed. Water and sand also assume this same form under the influence of wind. And I have seen, on the surface of the Walden ice, great sweeping, waving lines, somewhat like these. It is the track of the wind, the impress which it makes on flowing materials.

P. M. — Down river with C.

The river has not been so concealed by snow before. The snow does not merely lie level on it and on the land, so many inches deep, but great drifts, perchance beginning on the land, stretch quite across it, so that you cannot always tell where it is, for there is no greater levelness than elsewhere to betray it. In some places, where the ice is exposed, little bunches of hoar frost have formed, with perfect ribbed leaves one inch in diameter. This morning was one of the coldest in the winter. Does the whistle of the locomotive sound differently, tear the air any more, this weather? I see the prinos berries turned now a dark, coppery brown, looking blackish at a little distance. We crossed the Great Meadows lengthwise, a broad level plain, roughened only by snowy waves, about two miles long and nearly half as wide. Looking back over it made me think of what I have read of Arctic explorers travelling over snow-covered ice. Saw a few crows. Some green-briar berries quite fresh.

Made a fire on the snow-covered ice half a mile below Ball's Hill. Cut first a large bundle of green

oak twigs with leaves on them, laid them on sticks, then sprinkled on fine dead maple and alder and poplar twigs, and then dry cat-sticks of the same material. We broke up some larger pine trees by striking them on the ice, at the same time letting go to save our hands. Made a large warm fire, whose flame went up straight, there being no wind, and without smoke. Stayed half an hour, and when we took our departure, felt as if we had been in a house all the while, for we had been warm and had looked steadily at the fire instead of looking off. The fire made a large circular cavity in the snow and ice, three feet in diameter and four or five inches deep, with water at the bottom. We had often sailed over this very spot. Sticks in a circle on their ends and slanted over a common centre make a perfect fire. Such is the earliest hearth, with a hole in the roof above it. Our chimney fires are only semicircles or half-fires, or what is worse, oblong squares, or, in the case of stoves, mere boxes full of fire, without symmetry or form.

Observed in some large cakes of ice left on the river, I thought, the faintest possible tinge of green, also a white, leafy internal frostwork along the planes of the irregular flaring cleavages, — or call them deep conchoidal sometimes.

These afternoons the shadows of the woods have already a twilight length by 3 or 4 P. M. We made our fire in the shadow of a wood rather than in the sun, that the flame might show better, and the sun went down before we left it. Not till we had left our fire many rods behind did we observe the narrow column of blue smoke rising straight from it against the wood. It had appeared to us pure flame, producing merely that boiling of the air above it through which you see objects confusedly.

Feb. 8. The poets, philosophers, historians, and all writers have always been disposed to praise the life of the farmer and prefer it to that of the citizen. They have been inclined to regard trade and commerce as not merely uncertain modes of getting a living, but as running into the usurious and disreputable. And even at the present day the trader, as carrier or go-between, the speculator, the forestaller, and corporations do not escape a fling. Trade has always been regarded to some extent as a questionable mode of getting a livelihood. Cato says: "Et virum bonum cum laudabant, ita laudabant, bonum agricolam, bonumque colonum. Amplissime laudari existimabatur, qui ita laudabatur. Mercatorem autem strenuum studiosumque rei quaerendae existimo; verum . . . periculosum et calamitosum. At ex agricolis et viri fortissimi, et milites strenuissimi gignuntur, maximeque pius quaestus, stabilissimusque consequitur, minimeque invidiosus: minimeque male cogitantes sunt, qui in eo studio occupati sunt." That is: "When they [*i. e.* our ancestors][1] praised a good man, they called him a good farmer and a good husbandman (settler?). He was thought to be most amply praised who was so praised. However, I think that the merchant is energetic and studious to make money, but his business is danger-

[1] [Supplied by Thoreau.]

ous and liable to misfortunes. But from the cultivators of the soil, both the men of most fortitude and the hardiest soldiers are descended, and theirs is a gain particularly just (honest, pious) and stable, and least of all the subject of envy: and they are the least of all thinking evil who are engaged in this pursuit."

And Varro says: "Viri magni nostri majores non sine causa praeponebant rusticos Romanos urbanis. Ut ruri enim, qui in villa vivunt ignaviores, quam qui in agro versantur in aliquo opere faciundo; sic qui in oppido sederent, quam qui rura colerent, desidiosiores putabant."[1] That is: "Great men, our ancestors, preferred Romans who had lived in the country to those who lived in the city. For, as in the country, they who live in the villa are idler than they who are employed in the field doing some work, so they thought that those who sat in a town were more slothful than they who cultivated the fields." And he says that they did not need the gymnasia of the Greeks, but now one does not think that he has a villa unless he has many places with Greek names in it, and, having stolen into the city, instead of using their hands in swinging (?) a scythe or holding a plow they move them in the theatre and circus and have forgotten husbandry.[2]

And in another place V. boasts of the antiquity of rustic life, saying that "there was a time when men cultivated the fields, but had no city (fuit tempus, cum rura colerent homines, neque urbem haberent)." And again: "Immani numero annorum urbanos agricolae

[1] *Vide* [p. 111].
[2] [A free rendering of Varro's Latin.]

Vol. VI

praestant. Nec mirum, quod divina natura dedit agros, ars humana aedificavit urbes. (That is: Cultivators of the soil precede citizens by a vast number of years. Nor is it to be wondered at, for divine Nature gave fields, human art built cities.) . . . Nec sine causa Terram eandem appellabant matrem, et Cererem, et qui eam colerent, piam et utilem agere vitam credebant, atque eos solos reliquos esse ex stirpe Saturni regis. (That is: Nor without reason did they [our ancestors] call the same Earth mother and Ceres, and thought that they who cultivated it led a pious and useful life, and that they alone were left of the race of King Saturn.)"

But now, by means of railroads and steamboats and telegraphs, the country is denaturalized, the old pious, stable, and unenvied gains of the farmer are liable to all the suspicion which only the merchant's formerly excited. All milk-farms and fruit-farms, etc., are so many markets with their customs in the country.

Consider the deformities to which the farmer is liable, — the rustic, the clown (*a colono?*), the villain, etc., etc.

Josselyn, speaking of crickets, says, "The Italian who hath them cryed up and down the streets (*Grille che cantelo*) and buyeth them to put into his Gardens, if he were in New England would gladly be rid of them, they make such a dinn in an Evening."[1] I am more charmed by the Italian's taste than by Josselyn's impatience.

[1] [John Josselyn, *An Account of Two Voyages to New England*, p. 118.]

Ann, the Irishwoman who has lived with Deacon Brown so long, says that when he had taken to his bed with his last illness, she was startled by his calling, "Ann, Ann," "the bitterest Ann that you ever heard," and that was the beginning of his last illness.

On the 2d I saw the sand foliage in the Cut; pretty good. This is the frost coming out of the ground; this is spring. It precedes the green and flowery spring, as mythology does ordinary literature and poetry.[1]

P. M. — Rain, rain, rain, carrying off the snow and leaving a foundation of ice. The wind southeasterly.

Feb. 9. High wind in the night and now, the rain being over. Does it not usually follow rain-storms at this season, to dry up the water? It has cleared off very pleasant and is still quite warm.

9 A. M. — To Pine Hill.

Some of these thaws succeed suddenly to intensely cold weather, and the sky that was tense like a bow that is bent is now relaxed. There is a peculiar softness and luminousness in the air this morning, perhaps the light being diffused by vapor. It is such a warm, moist, or softened, sunlit air as we are wont to hear the first bluebird's warble in. And the brightness of the morning is increased tenfold by the sun reflected from broad sheets of rain and melted snow-water, and also, in a peculiar manner, from the snow on the sides of the Deep Cut. The crowing of cocks and the voices of the school-children sound like spring. I hear the sound of the horses' feet on the bared ice

[1] [*Walden*, p. 340; Riv. 476.]

as on pavements; and the sun is reflected from a hundred rippling sluices of snow-water finding its level in the fields. Are not both sound and light condensed or contracted by cold?

The jays are more lively than usual. That lichen with a white elastic thread for core is like a tuft of hair on the trees, sometimes springing from the centre of another, larger, flat lichen. There are snow-fleas, quite active, on the half-melted snow on the middle of Walden.

I do not hear Therien's axe far of late. The moment I came on his chopping-ground, the chickadees flew to me, as if glad to see me. They are a peculiarly honest and sociable little bird. I saw them go to his pail repeatedly and peck his bread and butter. They came and went a dozen times while I stood there. He said that a great flock of them came round him the other day while he was eating his dinner and lit on his clothes "just like flies." One roosted on his finger, and another pecked a piece of bread in his hand. They are considerable company for the woodchopper. I heard one wiry *phe-be*. They love to hop about wood freshly split. Apparently they do not leave his clearing all day. They were not scared when he threw down wood within a few feet of them. When I looked to see how much of his bread and butter they had eaten, I did not perceive that any was gone. He could afford to dine a hundred.

I see some chestnut sprouts with leaves on them still. The hollows about Walden, still bottomed with snow, are filled with greenish water like its own. I

rulers of the State are concerned, the city for the most part, instead of being a ninth-day town, gets six days, while the country gets only one day and the nights at most. We go to market every day. The city is not a ninth-day place but an every-day place, and the country is only a night or Sunday place. In a Yankee's estimation, it is perhaps the greatest satire on a New England country village to say that it has an air of quietness which reminds him of the Sabbath. He loves the bustle of a market, where things are bought and sold, and sometimes men among the rest. The boys swop jack-knives on Sunday, and their fathers, perchance, barter their own souls.

Howitt describes the harvest moon in August. Did I not put it in September? He speaks of "willow-holts on the banks of rivers." Bailey defines "holt, — a small wood or grove." Does not our "holt" on the river answer to this? It is in this case a poke-logan.[1]

My ink was frozen last month, and is now pale.

Howitt says that in Britain the law "is opposed to tracking game in a snow." I feel some pity for the wild animals when I see how their tracks betray them in calm weather after a snow-storm, and consider what risks they run of being exterminated.

Is not January alone pure winter? December belongs to the fall; is a wintry November: February, to the spring; it is a snowy March.

The water was several inches deep in the road last evening, but it has run nearly dry by morning. The illustrious farmer Romans who lived simply on their

[1] *Vide* Wright's *Dictionary of Provincialisms.*

do not find any willow catkins started, though many have lost their scales. I have brought home some alder and sweet-gale and put them in water. The black birch has a slender sharp bud, much like the shad-bush. In Stow's meadow by railroad causeway, saw many dusky flesh-colored, transparent worms, about five eighths of an inch long, in and upon the snow, crawling about. These, too, must be food for birds.

I have seen two red squirrels and heard a third since the snow covered the ground. I have seen one gray one, but traces of many.

After "putabant" in Varro, four pages back, comes "Itaque annum ita diviserunt, ut nonis modo diebus urbanas res usurparent, reliquis VII ut rura colerent. (Therefore they so divided the year as to attend to town affairs on the ninth day only, that they might cultivate the fields on the other days)." Hence *nundinae* means a fair, and *oppidum nundinarium* (a ninth-day town) is a market town, and *forum nundinarium* is the market-place.

Columella, referring to Varro, gives the same reason for the setting aside of the ninth day only, and adds: "Illis enim temporibus proceres civitatis in agris morabantur; et cum consilium publicum desiderabatur, a villis arcessebantur in senatum. Ex quo qui eos evocabant, Viatores nominati sunt. (For in those days the chief men of the state stayed on their farms; and when a public council was wanted they were sent for from their villas to the senate. Whence they who called them out were named Road-men.)" These were the times which all Romans loved to praise. But now, so far as the

land, to whom Columella refers, are Q. Cincinnatus, C. Fabricius, and Curius Dentatus.

Feb. 10. P. M. — Up railroad to Assabet and return *via* Hollowell place.

The river has risen again, and, instead of ice and snow, there is water over the ice on the meadows. This is the second freshet since the snows. The ice is cracked, and in some places heaved up in the usual manner. The sturdy white oak near the Derby railroad bridge has been cut down. It measures five feet and three inches over the stump, at eighteen inches from the ground. I observe the great well-protected buds of the balm-of-Gilead spear-head-like. There is no shine to them now, and their viscidness is not very *apparent*. A great many willow catkins show a little down peeping from under the points of the scales, but I have no doubt that all this was done last fall. I noticed it then.

Feb. 11. 7.30 A. M. — Snow-fleas lie in black patches like some of those dark rough lichens on rocks, or like ink-spots three or four inches in diameter, about the grass-stems or willows, on the ice which froze last night. When I breathe on them I find them all alive and ready to skip. Also the water, when I break the ice, arouses them. I saw yesterday, in a muddy spring in Tarbell's meadow, many cockle[*sic*]-shells on the bottom, with their feet out, and marks as if they had been moving.

When I read of the catkins of the alder and the

willow, etc., scattering their yellow pollen, they impress me as a vegetation which belongs to the earliest and most innocent dawn of nature; as if they must have preceded other trees in the order of creation, as they precede them annually in their blossoming and leafing. In the winter we so value the semblance of fruit that even the dry black female catkins of the alder are an interesting sight, not to mention, on shoots rising a foot or two above these, the red or mulberry male catkins, in little parcels, dangling at a less than right angle with the stems, and the short female ones at their bases. For how many æons did the willow shed its yellow pollen annually before man was created!

Apparently I read Cato and Varro from the same motives that Virgil did, and as I read the almanac, *New England Farmer*, or *Cultivator*, or Howitt's "Seasons."

Feb. 12. Another cold morning. The patches of snow-fleas on the ice are now much reduced, but still, when I kneel and breathe on them, they begin to skip, though the last two nights and all day yesterday have been severely cold. They look like little patches of rust on the ice.

At first, in clear cold weather, we may be walking on dry snow, which we cronch with squeaking sound under our feet. Then comes a thaw, and we slump about in slosh half a foot deep. Then, in a single night, the surface of the earth is all dried and stiffened, and we stagger over the rough, frozen ground and ice on which it is torture to walk. It becomes quite a study

how a man will shoe himself for a winter. For outdoor life in winter, I use three kinds of shoes or boots: first and chiefly, for the ordinary dry snows or bare ground, cowhide boots; secondly, for shallow thaws, half-shoe depth, and spring weather, light boots and india-rubbers; third, for the worst sloshy weather, about a week in the year, india-rubber boots.

P. M. — Skate to Pantry Brook.

Put on skates at mouth of Swamp Bridge Brook. The ice appears to be nearly two inches thick. There are many rough places where the crystals are very coarse, and the old ice on the river (for I spoke of a new ice since the freshet) is uneven and covered, more or less, with the scales of a thin ice whose water is dried up. In some places, where the wind has been strong, the foam is frozen into great concentric ridges, over which with an impetus I dash. It is hobbling and tearing work.

Just beyond the bathing-place, I see the wreck of an ice-fleet, which yesterday morning must have been very handsome. It reminds me of a vast and crowded fleet of sloops with large slanting sails all standing to the north. These sails N ⟋⟍ S are, some of them, the largest specimens of the leaf-structure in ice that I have seen, eight or nine inches long. Perhaps this structure is more apparent now they have wasted so much. Their bases can be seen continuing quite through the level ice which has formed about them, as if the wind and waves, breaking up a thin ice, had held it in that position while it froze in.

Vol. VI

One accustomed to glide over a boundless and variegated ice floor like this cannot be much attracted by tessellated floors and mosaic work. I skate over a thin ice all tessellated, so to speak, or in which you see the forms of the crystals as they shot. This is separated by two or three feet of water from the old ice resting on the meadow. The water, consequently, is not dark, as when seen against a muddy bottom, but a clear yellow, against which the white air-bubbles in and under the ice are very conspicuous.

Landed at Fair Haven Hill. I was not aware till I came out how pleasant a day it was. It was very cold this morning, and I have been putting [on] wood in vain to warm my chamber, and lo! I come forth, and am surprised to find it warm and pleasant. There is very little wind, here under Fair Haven especially. I begin to dream of summer even. I take off my mittens.

Here is a little hollow which, for a short time every spring, gives passage to the melting snow, and it was consequently wet there late into the spring. I remember well when a few little alder bushes, encouraged by the moisture, first sprang up in it. They now make a perfect little grove, fifteen feet high, and maybe half a dozen rods long, with a rounded outline, as if they were one mass of moss, with the wrecks of ferns in their midst and the sweet-fern about its edge. And so, perchance, a swamp is beginning to be formed. The shade and the decaying vegetation may at last produce a spongy soil, which will supply a constant rill. Has not something like this been the history of

the alder swamp and brook a little further along? True, the first is on a small scale and rather elevated, part way up the hill; and ere long trout begin to glance in the brook, where first was merely a course for melted snow which turned the dead grass-blades all one way, — which combed the grassy tresses down the hill.

This is a glorious winter afternoon. The clearness of a winter day is not impaired, while the air is still and you feel a direct heat from the sun. It is not like the relenting of a thaw with a southerly wind. There is a bright sheen from the snow, and the ice booms a little from time to time. On those parts of the hill which are bare, I see the radical leaves of the buttercup, mouse-ear, and the thistle.

Especially do gray rocks or cliffs with a southwest exposure attract us now, where there is warmth and dryness. The gray color is nowhere else so agreeable to us as in these rocks in the sun at this season, where I hear the trickling of water under great ice organ-pipes.

What a floor it is I glide thus swiftly over! It is a study for the slowest walker. See the shells of countless air-bubbles within and beneath it, some a yard or two in diameter. Beneath they are crowded together from the size of a dollar downward. They give the ice a white-spotted or freckled appearance. Specimens of every coin (*numismata*) from the first minting downward. I hear the pond faintly boom or mutter in a low voice, promising another spring to the fishes. I saw yesterday deeply scalloped oak leaves which had sunk nearly an inch into the ice of Walden, making a perfect impression of their forms, on account of the heat they absorbed. Their route is thus downward to dust again, through water and snow and ice and every obstacle. This thin meadow ice with yellow water under it yields a remarkable hollow sound, like a drum, as I rip over it, as if it were about to give way under me, — some of that gong-like roar which I have described elsewhere, — the ice being tense. I crossed the road at Bidens Brook. Here the smooth ice was dusty (from the road) a great distance, and I thought it would dull my skates.

To make a perfect winter day like this, you must have a clear, sparkling air, with a sheen from the snow, sufficient cold, little or no wind; and the warmth must come directly from the sun. It must not be a thawing warmth. The tension of nature must not be relaxed. The earth must be resonant if bare, and you hear the lisping tinkle of chickadees from time to time and the unrelenting steel-cold scream of a jay, unmelted, that never flows into a song, a sort of wintry trumpet, screaming cold; hard, tense, frozen music, like the winter sky itself; in the blue livery of winter's band. It is like a flourish of trumpets to the winter sky. There is no hint of incubation in the jay's scream. Like the creak of a cart-wheel. There is no cushion for sounds now. They tear our ears.

I frequently see three or four old white birches standing together on the edge of a pond or meadow, and am struck by the pleasing manner in which they will commonly be grouped, — how they spread so as

to make room for each other, and make an agreeable impression on the eye. Methinks I have seen groups of three in different places arranged almost exactly alike. I saw these near Lily Bay: The third upright one is lapped over and partly twined round the middle one at base.

Returning, I overhauled a muskrat-house by Bidens Brook. For want of other material, it was composed of grass, flags, and in a great measure (half) of twigs and sticks, mostly sweet-gale, both dead and alive, and roots, from six inches to two feet in length. These were, in fact, the principal material of it, and it was a large one, two feet above the ice. I was surprised to find that these sticks, both green and dead, had, the greater part of them, been gnawed off by the rat, — and some were nearly half an inch in diameter. They were cut off, not at a right angle with a smooth cut, but by successive cuts, smooth as with a knife, across, at the same time bending the twig down, which produced a sloping and, so to speak, terraced surface. I did not know before that they resembled the beaver in this respect also. It was chiefly the sweet-gale thus cut, commonly the top left on, two feet long, but sometimes cut off six inches long, thus: T h e bottom of its chamber was barely raised above the water, and the roof was hung with icicles from rain or frost.

The sun being low, I see as I skate, reflected from the surface of the ice, flakes of rainbow somewhat

like cobwebs, where the great slopes of the crystallization fall at the right angle, six inches or a foot across, but at so small an angle with the horizon that they had seemed absolutely flat and level before. Think of this kind of mosaic and tessellation for your floor! A floor made up of surfaces not absolutely level, — though level to the touch of the feet and to the noonday eye, — composed of crystals variously set, but just enough inclined to reflect the colors of the rainbow when the sun gets low.

See where a muskrat yesterday brought up clams through a hole in the ice over the middle of the river, and left their great violet-tinted shells on the edge of the ice. Sometimes they break the hinge.

Cold as the morning has been, I find the water, as usual, overflowing the ice along the shore and about the willows and button-bushes. Apparently when the river freezes up thus tensely, the ice compresses it, and where the ice is held down near the shore and by the bushes, not being able to rise when the sun comes to warm the water, it bursts out and overflows in such places, even in very cold weather. At last, in warmer weather still, it is difficult to get on or off on this account.

The pond does not thunder every night, and I do not know its law exactly. I cannot tell surely when to expect its thundering, for it feels scarcely perceptible changes in the weather. Who would have suspected so large and cold and thick-skinned a thing to be so sensitive? Yet it has its law to which [it] thunders

obedience when it should, as surely as the buds expand in the spring. For the earth is all alive and covered with feelers of sensation, *papillæ*. The hardest and largest rock, the broadest ocean, is as sensitive to atmospheric changes as the globule of mercury in its tube. Though you may perceive no difference in the weather, the pond does.[1] So the alligator and the turtle, with quakings of the earth, come out of the mud.[2]

Feb. 13. Monday. 7 A. M. — To Walden.

A warm morning, overcast. The ice does not ring when I strike it with an axe. Tried to drive a stake in two places outside a wood, but found it frozen. Failed also in two places within the wood, but succeeded in a third.

P. M. — It snows again, spoiling the skating, which has lasted only one day. I do not remember the winter when the ice remained uncovered a week.

Feb. 14. P. M. — Down railroad.

A moist, thawing, cloudy afternoon, preparing to rain.

The telegraph resounds at every post. It is a harp with one string, — the first strain from the American lyre. In Stow's wood, by the Deep Cut, hear the *gnah gnah* of the white-breasted, black-capped nuthatch. I went up the bank and stood by the fence. A little family of titmice gathered about me, searching for their food both on the ground and on the trees, with great industry and intentness, and now and then

[1] [*Walden*, p. 333; Riv. 465.]   [2] [*Walden*, p. 334; Riv. 467.]

pursuing each other. There were two nuthatches at least, talking to each other. One hung with his head down on a large pitch pine, pecking the bark for a long time, — leaden blue above, with a black cap and white breast. It uttered almost constantly a faint but sharp *quivet* or creak, difficult to trace home, which appeared to be answered by a baser and louder *gnah gnah* from the other. A downy woodpecker also, with the red spot on his hind head and his cassock open behind, showing his white robe, kept up an incessant loud tapping on another pitch pine. All at once an active little brown creeper makes its appearance, a small, rather slender bird, with a long tail and sparrow-colored back, and white beneath. It commences at the bottom of a tree and glides up very rapidly, then suddenly darts to the bottom of a new tree and repeats the same movement, not resting long in one place or on one tree. These birds are all feeding and flitting along together, but the chickadees are the most numerous and the most confiding. I observe that three of the four thus associated, *viz.* the chickadee, nuthatch, and woodpecker, have black crowns, at least the first two, very conspicuous black caps. I cannot but think that this sprightly association and readiness to burst into song has to do with the prospect of spring, — more light and warmth and thawing weather. The titmice keep up an incessant faint tinkling *tchip;* now and then one utters a lively *day day day*, and once or twice one commenced a gurgling strain quite novel, startling, and springlike. Beside this I heard the distant crowing of cocks and the divine harmony

of the telegraph, — all spring-promising sounds. The chickadee has quite a variety of notes. The *phebe* one I did not hear to-day.

I perceive that some of these pools by the Walden road which on the 9th looked so green have frozen blue.[1]

This greater liveliness of the birds methinks I have noticed commonly in warm, thawing days toward spring. F. Brown, who has been chasing a white rabbit this afternoon with a dog, says that they do not run off far, — often play round within the same swamp only, if it is large, and return to where they were started. Spoke of it as something unusual that one ran off so far that he could not hear the dogs, but he returned and was shot near where he started. He does not see their forms, nor marks where they have been feeding.

Feb. 16. By this time in the winter I do not look for those clear, sparkling mornings and delicate leaf frosts, which, methinks, occur earlier in the winter, as if the air of winter was somewhat tarnished and debauched, — had lost its virgin purity.

Every judgment and action of a man qualifies every other, *i. e.* corrects our estimate of every other, as, for instance, a man's idea of immortality who is a member of a church, or his praise of you coupled with his praise of those whom you do not esteem. For in this sense a man is awfully consistent, above his own consciousness. All a man's strength and all his weakness go to make up the authority of any particu-

[1] [See *Walden*, p. 327; Riv. 457.]

lar opinion which he may utter. He is strong or weak with all his strength and weakness combined. If he is your friend, you may have to consider that he loves you, but perchance he also loves gingerbread.

It must [be] the leaves of the *Chimaphila umbellata*, spotted wintergreen, which Channing left here day before yesterday.

I have not seen *F. hyemalis* since last fall, the snow buntings only during the great and severe snow-storm, no pine grosbeaks nor *F. linaria* this winter.

Snows again this morning. For the last month the weather has been remarkably changeable; hardly three days together alike.

That is an era not yet arrived, when the earth, being partially thawed, melts the slight snows which fall on it.

P. M. — To Walden and Flint's; return by Turnpike.

Saw two large hawks circling over the woods by Walden, hunting, — the first I have seen since December 15th. That Indian trail on the hillside about Walden was revealed with remarkable distinctness to me standing on the middle of the pond, by the slight snow which had lodged on it forming a clear white line unobscured by weeds and twigs. (For snow is a great revealer not only of tracks made in itself, but even in the earth before it fell.) It was quite distinct in many places where you would not have noticed it before. A light snow will often reveal a faint foot or cart track in a field which was hardly discernible before, for it reprints it, as it were, in clear white type, alto-

relievo.[1] Went to the locality of the *Chimaphila maculata* by Goose Pond.

Columella, after saying that many authors had believed that the climate ("qualitatem caeli statumque") was changed by lapse of time ("longo aevi situ"), refers to Hipparchus as having given out that the time would be when the poles of the earth would be moved from their place ("tempus fore, quo cardines mundi loco moverentur"); and, as confirmatory of this, he (C.) goes on to say that the vine and olive flourish now in some places where formerly they failed.

He gives the names of about fifty authors who had treated *de rusticis rebus* before him.

Feb. 17. P. M. — To Gowing's Swamp.

On the hill at the Deep Cut on the new road, the ground is frozen about a foot deep, and they carry off lumps equal nearly to a cartload at a time. Moore's man is digging a ditch by the roadside in his swamp. I am surprised to see that the earth there — under some snow, it is true — is frozen only about four inches. It may be owing to warm springs beneath. The hill was comparatively bare of snow (and of trees there) and was more exposed. The Irishman showed me small stumps, — larch, methinks, — which he dug and cut out *from the bottom* of the ditch, — very old ones. At Gowing's Swamp I see where some one hunted white rabbits yesterday, and perhaps the day before, with a dog. The hunter has run round and round it on firm ground, while the hare and dog

[1] [*Walden*, p. 200; Riv. 282.]

have cut across and circled about amid the blueberry bushes. The track of the white rabbit is gigantic compared with that of the gray one. Indeed few, if any (?), of *our* wild animals make a larger track with their feet alone. Where I now stand, the track of all the feet has an expanse of seven to fifteen inches, — this at intervals of from two to three feet, — and the width at the two fore feet is five inches. There is a considerable but slighter impression of the paw behind each foot.

The mice-tracks are very amusing. It is surprising how numerous they are, and yet I rarely ever see one. They must be nocturnal in their habits. Any tussocky ground is scored with them. I see, too, where they have run over the ice in the swamp, — there is a mere sugaring of snow on it, — ever trying to make an entrance, — to get beneath it. You see deep and distinct channels in the snow in some places, as if a whole colony had long travelled to and fro in them, — a highway, a well-known trail, — but suddenly they will come to an end; and yet they have not dived beneath the surface, for you see where the single traveller who did it all has nimbly hopped along as if suddenly scared, making but a slight impression, squirrel-like, on the snow. The squirrel also, though rarely, will make a channel for a short distance. These mice-tracks are of various sizes, and sometimes, when they are large and they have taken long and regular hops nine or ten inches apart in a straight line, they look at a little distance like a fox-track. I suspect that the mice sometimes build their nests in bushes from the foundation, for, in the swamp-hole on the new road,

where I found two mice-nests last fall, I find one begun with a very few twigs and some moss, close by where the others were, at the same height and also on prinos bushes, — plainly the work of mice wholly. In the open part of Gowing's Swamp I find the *Andromeda Polifolia*. Neither here nor in Beck Stow's does it grow very near the shore, in places accessible in wet weather. Some larch cones are empty, others contain seeds. In these swamps, then, you have three kinds of andromeda. The main swamp is crowded with high blueberry, panicled andromeda, prinos, swamp-pink, etc., etc. (I did not examine them particularly), and then in the middle or deepest part will be an open space, not yet quite given up to water, where the *Andromeda calyculata* and a few *A. Polifolia* reign almost alone. These are pleasing gardens.

In the early part of winter there was no walking on the snow, but after January, perhaps, when the snow-banks had settled and their surfaces, many times thawed and frozen, become indurated, in fact, you could walk on the snow-crust pretty well.

Feb. 18. P. M. — To Yellow Birch Swamp.

As I remember January, we had one (?) great thaw, succeeded by severe cold. It was harder getting about, though there may have been no more snow because it was light, and there was more continuous cold and clear sparkling weather. But the last part of January and all February thus far have been alternate thaw and freeze and snow. It has more thaws, even as the running "r" (root of ῥέω) occurs twice in it and but

once in January. I do not know but the more light and warmth plainly accounts for the difference. It does not take so much fuel to keep us warm of late. I begin to think that my wood will last. We begin to have days precursors of spring.

I see on ice by the riverside, front of N. Barrett's, very slender insects a third of an inch long, with grayish folded wings reaching far behind and two antennæ. Somewhat in general appearance like the long wasps. At the old mill-site, saw two pigeon woodpeckers dart into and out of a white oak. Saw the yellow under sides of their wings. It is barely possible I am mistaken, but, since Wilson makes them common in Pennsylvania in winter, I feel pretty sure. Such sights make me think there must be bare ground not far off south. It is a little affecting to walk over the hills now, looking at the reindeer lichens here and there amid the snow, and remember that ere long we shall find violets also in their midst. What an odds the season makes! The birds know it. Whether a rose-tinted water-lily is sailing amid the pads, or Neighbor Hobson is getting out his ice with a cross-cut saw, while his oxen are eating their stalks. I noticed that the ice which Garrison cut the other day contained the lily pads and stems within it. How different their environment now from when the queenly flower, floating on the trembling surface, exhaled its perfume amid a cloud of insects! Hubbard's wooded hill is now almost bare of trees. Barberries still hang on the bushes, but all shrivelled. I found a bird's nest of grass and mud in a barberry bush filled full with them. It must have been done by

some quadruped or bird. The curls of the yellow birch bark form more or less parallel straight lines up and down on all sides of the tree, like parted hair blown aside by the wind, or as when a vest [*sic*] bursts and blows open. Rabbit-tracks numerous there, sometimes quite a highway of tracks over and along the frozen and snow-covered brook. How pleasant the sound of water flowing with a hollow sound under ice from which it has settled away, where great white air bubbles or hollows, seen through the ice and dark water, alternately succeed each other. The *Mitchella repens* berries look very bright amid the still fresh green leaves. In the birch swamp west of this are many red (?) squirrel nests high in the birches. They are composed within of fibres of bark. I see where the squirrels have eaten walnuts along the wall and left the shells on the snow.

Channing has some microscopic reading these days. But he says in effect that these works are purely material. The idealist views things in the large.

I read some of the speeches in Congress about the Nebraska Bill, — a thing the like of which I have not done for a year. What trifling upon a serious subject! while honest men are sawing wood for them outside. Your Congress halls have an ale-house odor, — a place for stale jokes and vulgar wit. It compels me to think of my fellow-creatures as apes and baboons.

What a contrast between the upper and under side of many leaves, — the indurated and colored upper side and the tender, more or less colorless under side, — male and female, — even where they are almost equally exposed! The under side is commonly white, however, as turned away from the light toward the earth. Many in which the contrast is finest are narrow, revolute leaves, like the delicate and beautiful *Andromeda Polifolia*, the ledum, *Kalmia glauca*. De Quincey says that "the ancients had no experimental knowledge of severe climates." Neither have the English at home as compared with us of New England, nor we, compared with the Esquimaux.

This is a common form of the birch scale, — black, I think, — not white, at any rate.

The handsome lanceolate leaves of the *Andromeda Polifolia*, dark but pure and uniform dull red above, strongly revolute, and of a delicate bluish white beneath, deserve to be copied on to works of art.

Feb. 19. Many college text-books which were a weariness and a stumbling-block when *studied*, I have since read a little in with pleasure and profit. For several weeks the fall has seemed far behind, spring comparatively near. Yet I cannot say that there is any positive sign of spring yet; only we feel that we are sloping toward it. The sky has sometimes a warmth in its colors more like summer. A few birds have possibly strayed northward further than they have wintered.

P. M. — To Fair Haven by river, back by railroad.

Though the wind is cold, the earth feels the heat of the sun higher in the heavens and melts in plowed fields. The willow twigs rise out of the ice beside the river, the silvery down of each catkin just peeping

from under each scale in some places, — the work probably of last fall's sun, — like a mouse peeping from under its covert. I incline to walk now in swamps and on the river and ponds, where I cannot walk in summer. I am struck by the greenness of the greenbriar at this season, still covering the alders, etc., twelve feet high and full of shining and fresh berries. The greenness of the sassafras shoots makes a similar impression.

The large moths apparently love the neighborhood of water, and are wont to suspend their cocoons over the edge of the meadow and river, places more or less inaccessible, to men at least. I saw a button-bush with what at first sight looked like the open pods of the locust or of the water asclepias attached. They were the light ash-colored cocoons of the *A. Promethea*, four or five, with the completely withered and faded leaves wrapped around them, and so artfully and admirably secured to the twigs by fine silk wound round the leaf-stalk and the twig, — which last add nothing to its strength, being deciduous, but aid its deception, — they are taken at a little distance for a few curled and withered leaves left on. Though the particular twigs on which you find some cocoons may never or very rarely retain any leaves, — the maple, for instance, — there are enough leaves left on other shrubs and trees to warrant their adopting this disguise. Yet it is startling to think that the inference has in this case been drawn by some mind that, as most other plants retain some leaves, the walker will suspect these also to. Each and all such disguises

and other resources remind us that not some poor worm's instinct merely, as we call it, but the mind of the universe rather, which we share, has been intended upon each particular object. All the wit in the world was brought to bear on each case to secure its end. It was long ago, in a full senate of all intellects, determined how cocoons had best be suspended, — kindred mind with mine that admires and approves decided it so.[1] The hips of the late rose, though more or less shrivelled, are still red and handsome. It outlasts other hips. The sweet-briar's have lost their color and begun to decay. The former are still very abundant and showy in perfect corymbs of a dozen or so amid the button-bushes. It might be called the waterrose. The trees in the maple swamp squeak from time to time like the first fainter sounds made by the red squirrel. I have little doubt the red squirrel must lay up food, since I see them so rarely abroad. On the cherry twigs you see the shining clasp of caterpillars' eggs. The snow not only reveals a track but sometimes hands it down to the ice that succeeds it. The sled-track which I saw in the slight snow over the ice here February 2d, though we have had many snows since and now there is no snow at all, is still perfectly marked on the ice.

Much study a weariness of the flesh, eh? But did not they intend that we should read and ponder, who covered the whole earth with alphabets, — primers or bibles, — coarse or fine print? The very débris of the cliffs — the stivers [?] of the rocks — are covered

[1] [Channing, p. 122.]

with geographic lichens: no surface is permitted to be bare long. As by an inevitable decree, we have come to times at last when our very waste paper is printed. Was not He who creates lichens the abettor of Cadmus when he invented letters? Types almost arrange themselves into words and sentences as dust arranges itself under the magnet. Print! it is a closehugging lichen that forms on a favorable surface, which paper offers. The linen gets itself wrought into paper that the song of the shirt may be printed on it. Who placed us with eyes between a microscopic and a telescopic world?

There are so many rocks under Grape-vine Cliff that apparently for this reason the chopper saws instead of cuts his trees into lengths. The wood fern (*Dryopteris marginalis?*) still green there. And are they not small saxifrages so perfectly green and fresh, as if just started, in the crevices? I wait till sundown on Fair Haven to hear it boom, but am disappointed, though I hear much slight crackling. But, as for the previous cracking, it is so disruptive and produces such a commotion that it extends itself through snowdrifts six inches deep, and is even more distinct there than in bare ice, even to the sharpest angle of its forking. Saw an otter-track near Walden.

Feb. 20. Channing saw yesterday three little birds olive-green above, with yellowish-white breasts and, he thinks, bars on wings. Were they goldfinches?

P. M. — Skating to Fair Haven Pond.

Made a fire on the south side of the pond, using

canoe birch bark and oak leaves for kindlings. It is best to lay down first some large damp wood on the ice for a foundation, since the success of a fire depends very much on the bed of coals it makes, and, if these are nearly quenched in the basin of melted ice, there is danger that it will go out. How much dry wood ready for the hunter, inviting flames, is to be found in every forest, — dry bark fibres and small dead twigs of the white pine and other trees, held up high and dry as if for this very purpose! The occasional loud snapping of the fire was exhilarating. I put on some hemlock boughs, and the rich salt crackling of its leaves was like mustard to the ears, — the firing of uncountable regiments. Dead trees love the fire.

We skated home in the dusk, with an odor of smoke in our clothes. It was pleasant to dash over the ice, feeling the inequalities which we could not see, now rising over considerable hillocks, — for it had settled on the meadows, — now descending into corresponding hollows.

We have had but one [1] (and that I think was the first) of those gentle moist snows which lodge perfectly on the trees and make perhaps the most beautiful sight of any. Much more common is what we have now, i. e. —

Feb. 21. A. M. — A fine, driving snow-storm.

Have seen no good samples of the blue in snow this winter. At noon clears up.

P. M. — To Goose Pond by Tuttle Path.

[1] No more this winter.

Vol. VI

The difference between the white and black (?) birch scales (*vide* [p. 130]) is that the wings of the first are curved backward like a real bird's. The seeds of this also are broadly winged like an insect with two little antennæ. The ice in the fields by the poorhouse road — frozen puddles — amid the snow; looking westward now while the sun is about setting, in cold weather, is green.

Montanus in his account of New Netherland (Amsterdam, 1671), speaking of the beaver, says, "The wind-hairs which rise glittering above the back fall off in the summer and grow again in the fall."

Feb. 22. I measured the thickness of the frozen ground at the deep cut on the new Bedford road, about half-way up the hill. They dig under the frozen surface and then crack it off with iron wedges, with much labor, in pieces from three to six feet square. It was eighteen inches thick and more there — thicker higher up, not so thick lower down the hill.

Saw in Sleepy Hollow a small hickory stump, about six inches in diameter and six inches high, so completely, regularly, and beautifully covered by that winkle-like fungus in concentric circles and successive layers that the core was concealed and you would have taken it for some cabbage-like plant. This was the way the wound was healed. The cut surface of the stump was completely and thickly covered. Our neighbor Wetherbee was J. Moore's companion when he took that great weight of pickerel this winter. He says it was fifty-six pounds in Flint's, in

A little snow, lodged on the north side of the woods, gives them a hoary aspect, — a mere sugaring, however. The snow has just ceased falling — about two inches deep, in the woods, upon the old and on bare ground; but there is scarcely a track of any animal yet to be seen, except here and there the surface of the snow has been raised and broken interruptedly where some mouse came near the surface in its travels, and in one wood I see very numerous tracks, probably of red squirrels, leading to and from three or four holes in the earth close together, somewhat like those in an ant's nest, — quite a broad beaten path to some stumps with white pine cones on them and single tracks to the base of trees. It has now got to be such weather that after a cold morning it is colder in the house, — or we feel colder, — than outdoors, by noon, and are surprised that it is no colder when we come out. You cannot walk too early in new-fallen snow to get the sense of purity, novelty, and unexploredness. The snow has lodged more or less in perpendicular lines on the northerly sides of trees, so that I am able to tell the points of compass as well as by the sun. I guide myself accordingly. It always gladdens me to see a willow, though catkinless as well as leafless, rising above the new-fallen, untrodden snow, in some dry hollow in the woods, for then I feel nearer to spring. There are some peculiarly dry and late looking ones I see there, but it is enough that they are willows. The locust pods are open or opening. Little beans they hold. What delicate satin-like inside linings they have!

one day, and that four of them weighed eighteen pounds and seven ounces. My alder catkins in the pitcher have shed their pollen for a day or two, and the willow catkins have pushed out half an inch or more and show red and yellowish.

Feb. 23. A. M. — The snow drives horizontally from the north or northwesterly, in long waving lines like the outline of a swell or billow. The flakes do not fall perceptibly for the width of a house.

P. M. — Saw some of those architectural drifts forming. The fine snow came driving along over the field like steam curling from a roof. As the current rises to go over the wall, it produces a lull in the angle made by the wall and ground, and accordingly just enough snow is deposited there to fill the triangular calm, but the greater part passes over and is deposited in the larger calm. A portion of the wind also apparently passes through the chinks of the wall and curves upward against the main drift, appearing to carve it and perforate it in various fashion, holding many snowy particles in suspension in vertical eddies. I am not sure to what extent the drift is carved and perforated, and to what originally deposited, in these forms. How will it look behind a tight fence?

Not that ornamental beauty is to be neglected, but, at least, let it first be inward-looking and essential, like the lining of a shell, of which the inhabitant is unconscious, and not mere outside garnishing.

This forenoon a driving storm, very severe. This afternoon fair, but high wind and drifting snow.

Feb. 24. P. M. — To Walden and Fair Haven.

In Wheeler's Wood by railroad. Nuthatches are faintly answering each other, — tit for tat, — on different keys, — a faint creak. Now and then one utters a loud distinct *gnah*. This bird more than any I know loves to stand with its head downward.

Meanwhile chickadees, with their silver tinkling, are flitting high above through the tops of the pines. Measured the ice of Walden in three places, —

One about 10 rods from the shore, 16¾ inches thick
25 rods from the shore, "   "   "
In middle . . . . 17¼ "   "

Call it then 17 inches on an average. On Fair Haven, in the only place tried, it was 21 inches thick. The portion of the ice in Walden above water was *about* 1¼ inches, in Fair Haven *about* 1¾. This part then equals $\frac{1}{13}$ + and $\frac{1}{12}$ respectively.

Tried the frost in five different and very *distant* woods in my walk. Found that though the ground is frozen more than 18 inches — from 18 [inches] to 2½ feet — thick on the open hillside on the new Bedford road, notwithstanding some snow on it, I can drive a stake without any trouble in the midst of ordinary level mixed pine and oak woods where the snow is a foot deep, in *very thick* pine and oak woods where the snow is only one inch thick or none at all, and the ground does not slope to the north and east, and probably the northwest, and in sprout-lands where it is 20 inches

thick in some places, and in springy meadows. In Moore's Swamp it is frozen about 4 inches deep in open land. I think that in an average year the ice in such a pond as Fair Haven attains a greater thickness than the snow on a level. The other day I thought that I smelled a fox very strongly, and went a little further and found that it was a skunk. May not their odors differ in intensity chiefly? Observed in one of the little pond-holes between Walden and Fair Haven where a partridge had travelled around in the snow amid the bordering bushes twenty-five rods, had pecked the green leaves of the lambkill and left fragments on the snow, and had paused at each high blueberry bush, fed on its red buds and shaken down fragments of its bark on the snow. These buds appeared its main object. I finally scared the bird.

I see such mice or mole tracks as these: —

The frozen earth at the new road cut is hauled off twenty rods by chains hooked round it, and it lies like great blocks of yellow sandstone for building, cracked out exactly square by wedges. The sexton tells me that he had to dig the last grave through two feet of frozen ground. I measured a block to-day two feet five inches thick after being dragged a dozen rods.

Feb. 26. Kane, ashore far up Baffin's Bay, says, "How strangely this crust we wander over asserts its identity through all the disguises of climate!"

Speaking of the effects of refraction on the water, he says: "The single repetition was visible all around us; the secondary or inverted image sometimes above and sometimes below the primary. But it was not uncommon to see, also, the uplifted ice-berg, with its accompanying or false horizon, joined at its summit by its inverted image, and then above a second horizon, a third berg in its natural position." He refers to Agassiz at Lake Superior as suggesting "that it may be simply the reflection of the landscape inverted upon the surface of the lake, and reproduced with the actual landscape;" though there there was but one inversion.

He says that he saw sledge-tracks of Franklin's party in the neighborhood of Wellington Sound, made on the snow, six years old, which had been covered by the after-snows of five winters. This reminds me of the sled-tracks I saw this winter.

Kane says that, some mornings in that winter in the ice, they heard "a peculiar crisping or crackling sound." "This sound, as the 'noise accompanying the aurora,' has been attributed by Wrangell and others, ourselves among the rest, to changes of atmospheric temperature acting upon the crust of the snow." Kane thinks it is rather owing "to the unequal contraction and dilatation" of unequally presenting surfaces, "not to a sudden change of atmospheric temperature acting upon the snow." Is not this the same crackling I heard at Fair Haven on the 19th, and are not most of the arctic phenomena to be witnessed in our latitude on a smaller scale? At Fair Haven it seemed a slighter contraction of the ice, — not enough to make it thunder.

This morning it began with snowing, turned to a fine freezing rain producing a glaze, — the most of a glaze thus far, — but in the afternoon changed to pure rain.

P. M. — To Martial Miles's in rain.

The weeds, trees, etc., are covered with a glaze. The blue-curl cups are overflowing with icy drops. All trees present a new appearance, their twigs being bent down by the ice, — birches, apple trees, etc., but, above all, the pines. Tall, feathery white pines look like cockerels' tails in a shower. Both these and white [= pitch] pines, their branches being inclined downward, have sharpened tops like fir and spruce trees. Thus an arctic effect is produced. Very young white and pitch pines are most changed, all their branches drooping in a compact pyramid toward the ground except a single plume in the centre. They have a singularly crestfallen look. The rain is fast washing off all the glaze on which I had counted, thinking of the effect of to-morrow's sun on it. The wind rises and the rain increases. Deep pools of water have formed in the fields, which have an agreeable green or blue tint, — sometimes the one, sometimes the other. Yet the quantity of water which is fallen is by no means remarkable but, the ground being frozen, it is not soaked up. There is more water on the surface than before this winter.

Feb. 27. Morning. — Rain over; water in great part run off; wind rising; river risen and meadows flooded. The rain-water and melted snow have run swiftly over the frozen ground into the river, and raised it with the ice on it and flooded the meadows, covering the ice there which remains on the bottom; so that you have, on the male side, the narrow canal above the ice, then a floating ice everywhere bridging the river, and then a broad meadowy flood above ice again.

Those blocks of frozen earth at the new road cut are in fact a sandstone whose cement is frost. They are dragged by chains about them (and no drag), without losing any appreciable part, for twenty rods, and have preserved their form — their right-angled edges — for a month, left to thaw on the sides of the New Road embankments.

I remarked yesterday the rapidity with which water flowing over the icy ground sought its level. All that rain would hardly have produced a puddle in midsummer, but now it produces a freshet, and will perhaps break up the river.

It looks as if Nature had a good deal of work on her hands between now and April, to break up and melt twenty-one inches of ice on the ponds, — beside melting all the snow, — and before planting-time to thaw from one to two and a half or three feet of frozen ground.

They who live in the outskirts of the town do not like to have woods very near their houses, but cut them down. They are more of a bugbear than an ornament in their eyes. They who live on the village street take still more pains to rear a pine grove about their houses.

The ground being frozen, I saw the rain yesterday dripping or streaming from the edge of the bank at

Vol. VI

the edge of the river now, of the consistency of molasses or soft solder? I can think of no peculiarity in its formation unless that this water, the river rising, has flowed out over the ice in the night faster than it froze. Stirred with a stick, it shows a mass of crystals.

Probably you can study the habits of rabbits, partridges, etc., more easily in the winter, their tracks being revealed by the snow.

This is now another rise of the river. I see that the ice in hollows in the fields breaks up (partially) in the same manner with that on the river, *viz.* around the shore it is covered with water and rests on the bottom, while the middle is raised with the water, and hence a ridge is heaved up where the two ices meet. I am not certain how far this overflowing of the ice next the shore or on the meadows may be owing to the flood from the hills in the first instance running over, then under it and keeping it down, as well as to its adhesion to the bottom.

F. Brown tells me that he found a quantity of wintergreen in the crop of a partridge. I suggested that it *might* be lambkill.

the base of the wooded hill beyond William Wheeler's as from the eaves of a house, and to-day the bank is lined with icicles.

P. M. — To Flint's Pond.

Savin Wood. — Rufus Hosmer accounts for a wooden pin confining a tenon in its mortise gradually working out, — as in a gate for instance, (and this was the case on both sides of R. W. E.'s gate, to which he stepped for illustration), — by saying that, when the whole gate was wet and swelled perhaps a sixteenth of an inch, it carried the pin along with it and shrinking left it there, then swelled again and carried it a sixteenth of an inch further and left it there again, and so finally perhaps dropped it out. Among the savins I saw where rabbits had gnawed many barberry bushes, showing the yellow, and had eaten off many twigs some half an inch in diameter, also young hickories, and had gnawed off and eaten their twigs too in many places, hard as they are. They looked as if a moose had browsed them. *One* small pitch pine had lost some twigs too. I also saw where one which I scared had dropped some umbelled pyrola leaves — or it *may* have been another creature — and had eaten off some green rose-briar shoots. This gray rabbit's tail was very short, and white beneath, and curved short over his back in running. Sportsmen speak of the deer's "white flag."

Feb. 28. A pleasant morning.
What is the cause of that half ice, half water, along

IV

MARCH, 1854

(ÆT. 36)

March 1. Here is our first spring morning according to the almanac. It is remarkable that the spring of the almanac and of nature should correspond so closely. The morning of the 26th was good winter, but there came a plentiful rain in the afternoon, and yesterday and to-day are quite springlike. This morning the air is still, and, though clear enough, a yellowish light is widely diffused throughout the east, now just after sunrise. The sunlight looks and feels warm, and a *fine* vapor fills the lower atmosphere. I hear the phœbe or spring note of the chickadee, and the scream of the jay is perfectly repeated by the echo from a neighboring wood. For some days past the surface of the earth, covered with water, or with ice where the snow is washed off, has shone in the sun as it does only at the approach of spring, methinks. And are not the frosts in the morning more like the early frosts in the fall, — common white frosts?

As for the birds of the past winter: I have seen but three hawks, — one early in the winter and two lately; have heard the hooting owl pretty often late in the afternoon. Crows have not been numerous, but their cawing was heard chiefly in pleasanter mornings.

Blue jays have blown the trumpet of winter as usual, but they, as all birds, are most lively in springlike days. The chickadees have been the *prevailing* bird. The partridge common enough. One ditcher tells me that he saw two robins in Moore's Swamp a month ago. I have not seen a quail, though a few have been killed in the thaws. Four or five downy woodpeckers. The white-breasted nuthatch four or five times. Tree sparrows one or more at a time, oftener than any bird that comes to us from the north. Two pigeon woodpeckers, I think, lately. One dead shrike, and perhaps one or two live ones. Have heard of two white owls, — one about Thanksgiving time and one in midwinter. One short-eared owl in December. Several flocks of snow buntings for a week in the severest storm, and in December, last part. One grebe in Walden just before it froze completely. And two brown creepers once in middle of February. Channing says he saw a little olivaceous-green bird lately. I have not seen an *F. linaria*, nor a pine grosbeak, nor an *F. hyemalis* this winter, though the first was the prevailing bird last winter.

In correcting my manuscripts, which I do with sufficient phlegm, I find that I invariably turn out much that is good along with the bad, which it is then impossible for me to distinguish — so much for keeping bad company; but after the lapse of time, having purified the main body and thus created a distinct standard for comparison, I can review the rejected sentences and easily detect those which deserve to be readmitted.

P. M. — To Walden *via* R. W. E.'s.

I am surprised to see how bare Minott's hillside is already. It is already spring there, and Minott is puttering outside in the sun. How wise in his grandfather to select such a site for a house, the summers he has lived have been so much longer! How pleasant the calm season and the warmth — the sun is even like a burning-glass on my back — and the sight and sound of melting snow running down the hill! I look in among the withered grass blades for some starting greenness. I listen to hear the first bluebird in the soft air. I hear the dry clucking of hens which have come abroad.

The ice at Walden is softened, — the skating is gone; with a stick you can loosen it to the depth of an inch, or the first freezing, and turn it up in cakes. Yesterday you could skate here; now only close to the south shore. I notice the redness of the andromeda leaves, but not so much as once. The sand foliage is now in its prime.

March 2. A Corner man tells me that Witherell has seen a bluebird, and Martial Miles thought that he heard one. I doubt it. It may have been given to Witherell to see the first bluebird, so much has been withholden from him.

What produces the peculiar softness of the air yesterday and to-day, as if it were the air of the south suddenly pillowed amid our wintry hills? We have suddenly a different sky, — a different atmosphere. It is as if the subtlest possible soft vapor were diffused through the atmosphere. Warm air has come to us

from the south, but charged with moisture, which will yet distill in rain or congeal into snow and hail.

The sand foliage is vital in its form, reminding me [of] what are called the vitals of the animal body. I am not sure that its arteries are ever hollow. They are rather meandering channels with remarkably distinct sharp edges, formed instantaneously as by magic. How rapidly and perfectly it organizes itself! The material must be sufficiently cohesive. I suspect that a certain portion of clay is necessary. Mixed sand and clay being saturated with melted ice and snow, the most liquid portion flows downward through the mass, forming for itself instantly a perfect canal, using the best materials the mass affords for its banks. It digs and builds it in a twinkling. The less fluid portions clog the artery, change its course, and form thick stems and leaves. The lobe principle, — lobe of the ear (*labor, lapsus?*).

On the outside all the life of the earth is expressed in the animal or vegetable, but make a deep cut in it and you find it vital; you find in the very sands an anticipation of the vegetable leaf. No wonder, then, that plants grow and spring in it. The atoms have already learned the law. Let a vegetable sap convey it upwards and you have a vegetable leaf. No wonder that the earth expresses itself outwardly in leaves, which labors with the idea thus inwardly. The overhanging leaf sees here its prototype. The earth is pregnant with law.

The various shades of this sand foliage are very agreeable to the eye, including all the different colors

which iron assumes, — brown, gray, yellowish, reddish, and clay-color. Perhaps it produces the greater effect by arranging the sands of the same color side by side, bringing them together.[1]

March 4. A dull, cloudy day.

P. M. — To Walden *via* Hubbard's Wood and foot of Cliff Hill.

The snow has melted very rapidly the past week. There is much bare ground. The checkerberries are revealed, — *somewhat* shrivelled many of them. I look along the ditches and brooks for tortoises and frogs, but the ditches are still full of dirty ice, and they are not yet seen in the brooks. In Hubbard's maple swamp I see the evergreen leaves of the gold-thread as well as the mitchella and large pyrola. I begin to sniff the air and smell the ground. In the meadow beyond I see some still fresh and perfect pitcher-plant leaves, and everywhere the green and reddish radical leaves of the golden senecio, whose fragrance when bruised carries me back or forward to an incredible season. Who would believe that under the snow and ice lie still — or in midwinter — some green leaves which, bruised, yield the same odor that they do when their yellow blossoms spot the meadows in June? Nothing so realizes the summer to me now. This past winter the sphagnum (?) in swamps and meadows has been frost-bitten and blackened, but last winter it was fresh and handsome. I see nowadays, the ground being laid bare, great cracks in the earth revealed, a third of an

1 [*Walden*, pp. 337–339; Riv. 471, 472, 474.]

inch wide, running with a crinkling line for twenty rods or more through the pastures and under the walls, — frost-cracks of the past winter. Sometimes they are revealed through ice four or five inches thick over them. I observed to-day where a crack had divided a piece of bark lying over it with the same irregular and finely meandering line, *sometimes* forking. Yesterday I saw a wasp slowly stretching himself and, I think, a fly, outside of Minott's house in the sun, by his wood-shed. In the dry pasture under the Cliff Hill, the radical leaves of the johnswort are now revealed everywhere in pretty radiating wreaths flat on the ground, with leaves recurved, reddish above, green beneath, and covered with dewy drops. I can no longer get on to the river ice. I do not find any willow catkins started. A red maple which I cut bleeds somewhat, — only the upper side the cut however. Is not this the earliest distinct motion of the spring? This stood in water. Other trees were dry. Found a geiropodium (?), its globe now transparent, with the vermilion-colored remnants of others (?) lying in jelly about. In dry pastures I see that fungus — is it? — split into ten or twelve rays like a star and curved backward around a white bag or inner membrane. Were they not the seeds of rose-hips which I saw abundantly in some creature's dung? The various cladonias are now very plump and erect, not only exposed to view, the ground being bare, but flourishing on account of the abundant moisture, — some light, some dark green, and various more dusky shades.

In one or two places on the snow under the Cliffs I noticed more than a half-pint of partridge-droppings within a diameter of six inches. Were these all dropped in one night by one bird, or in the course of several nights, or by many birds? I saw that they had eaten the buds of the small blueberry *vacillans*. In their manure was what looked like woody fibres; may have been fibres of leaves. I am surprised to see how fresh and tender is the wintergreen bud, almost pure white. Was it so two months ago? It looks as if it had started under the snow. What is that gray beetle of which I found many under the bark of a large dead white pine, five eighths of an inch long, within an elliptical sort of log fort seven eighths of an inch or more in diameter piled around, of fibres of the sap-wood, perhaps one eighth or one tenth of an inch high, with some red bark chankings? Sometimes a curious chrysalis instead, like a very narrow and long bandbox with flat and parallel top and bottom, but highest at one end like a coffin. Also some white grubs stretch themselves, and some earwig-shaped creatures under the bark. I find that the ice of Walden has melted or softened so much that I sink an inch or more at every step, and hardly anywhere can I cut out a small cake, the water collects so fast in [the] hole. But at last, in a harder and drier place, I succeeded. It was now fifteen and a half inches thick, having lost about an inch and a half. Though the upper side was white and rotten and saturated with water for four or five inches, the under surface was still perfectly smooth and so far unchanged, yet ready to flake off, and did so readily in my hand, in

flakes a half-inch to an inch thick, leaving the irregular, undulating surface with which I am familiar. But this side was comparatively unchanged and hard, though for two and three quarters inches, measuring upwards, it was whitish, then for two and a half inches remarkably clear (free from air-bubbles) and hard. Then by successive layers it grew more white and soft till you reached the upper surface. I think that that slight white ice beneath the clear and dark may have been produced by the recent warmth of the water, though this is doubtful. At any rate this year the ice has melted *much* more above than beneath. Least of all between two and three quarters and five inches from the under side.

March 5. Sunday. Channing, talking with Minott the other day about his health, said, "I suppose you'd like to die now." "No," said Minott, "I've toughed it through the winter, and I want to stay and hear the bluebirds once more."

The patches of bare ground grow larger and larger, of snow less and less; even after a night you see a difference. It is a clear morning with some wind beginning to rise, and for the first time I see the water looking blue on the meadows.

Has not the johnswort two lives, in winter sending out radical shoots which creep flat on the ground under the snow, in the summer shooting upward and blossoming?

P. M. — To Upper Nut Meadow.

The river is breaking up. The meadows are already

partly bare, for it has only been cold enough to form a thin ice on them since this last freshet, and the old ice still lies concealed on the bottom. Great fields of thick ice from the channel, or between the channel and meadows, are driven by the wind against the thick ice on the channel. Hence the meadow ice *appears* to break up first. The waves dash against the edge of the ice and eat into it fast.

As I go along on the snow under Clamshell Hill I hear it sing around me, being melted next the ground. This is a spring sound. I cannot yet see the marchantia (?) in the ditches, for they are yet filled with ice or flooded. I see no horse-tail (unless one) nor flags, etc., yet started in Nut Meadow, nor any minnows out. This brook has run clear of ice a long time. Near Jenny's its sides are strewn with the wreck of angelica stems and asters. I go along looking at its deep, sometimes yellow, shelving bottom, sprinkled with red pebbles. In the upper meadow the sweet-gale grows rankly along its edges, slanted over the water almost horizontally, so as frequently to meet and conceal it altogether. It is here a dark and sluggish water, comparatively shallow, with a muddy bottom. This sweet-gale is now full of fruit. This and the water andromeda are wild plants, as it were driven to the water's edge by the white man. Saw a wood tortoise at the bottom. A reptile out of the mud before any bird, and probably quadruped. Not yet a frog, I think. The down of some willow catkins by this brook *may have* started forward this spring, though it is doubtful. Those which look most forward now will not be so a fortnight hence. It grew colder before I left. I saw some crystals beginning to shoot on the pools between the tussocks, shaped like feathers or fan-coral, — the most delicate I ever saw. Thus even ice begins with crystal leaves, and birds' feathers and wings are leaves, and trees and rivers with intervening earth are vast leaves.

Saw a small blackish caterpillar on the snow. Where do they come from? And crows, as I think, migrating northeasterly. They came in loose, straggling flocks, about twenty to each, commonly silent, a quarter to a half a mile apart, till four flocks had passed, and perhaps there were more. Methinks I see them going southwest in the fall.

March 6. A cool morning. The bare water here and there on the meadow begins to look smooth, and I look to see it rippled by a muskrat. The earth has to some extent frozen dry, for the drying of the earth goes on in the cold night as well as the warm day. The alders and hedgerows are still silent, emit no notes.

P. M. — To Goose Pond.

According to G. Emerson, maple sap sometimes begins to flow in the middle of February, but usually in the second week of March, especially in a clear, bright day with a westerly wind, after a frosty night. The brooks — the swift ones and those in swamps — open before the river; indeed some of the first have been open the better part of the winter. I saw trout glance in the Mill Brook this afternoon, though near its sources, in Hubbard's Close, it is still covered with

dark, icy snow, and the river into which it empties has not broken up. Can they have come up from the sea? Like a film or shadow they glance before the eye, and you see where the mud is roiled by them. Saw children checkerberrying in a meadow. I see the skunk-cabbage started about the spring at head of Hubbard's Close, amid the green grass, and what looks like the first probing of the skunk. The snow is now all off on meadow ground, in thick evergreen woods, and on the south sides of hills, but it is still deep in sprout-lands, on the north sides of hills, and generally in deciduous woods. In sprout-lands it is melted beneath, but upheld by the bushes. What bare ground we have now is due then not so much to the increased heat of the sun and warmth of the air as to the little frost there was in the ground in so many localities. This remark applies with less force, however, to the south sides of hills. The ponds are hard enough for skating again. Heard and saw the first blackbird, flying east over the Deep Cut, with a *tchuck, tchuck*, and finally a split whistle.

March 7. P. M. — To Annursnack.

I did not mention the drifts yesterday. Most of the snow left on bare, dry level ground consists of the remains of drifts, particularly along fences, — most on the south side. Also much that looks like snow is softened ice in the lower parts of fields. Looking from Annursnack, there is no perceptible difference as to snow between the north and south prospects, though the north one is not extensive; but the snowiest view is westward. Has this anything to do with there being

Vol. VI

most snow inland? All the sides of steep hills are likely to be bare, washed bare by rain (?). I do not know why there should be so much snow in sprout-lands and deciduous woods, unless it is because the sun has had less chance to thaw the frosts which yet have been thick there.

It is remarkable how true each plant is to its season. Why should not the fringed gentian put forth early in the spring, instead of holding in till the latter part of September? I do not perceive enough difference in the temperature. How short a time it is with us! I see many little white or dirty white puff-balls, yellowish inside, commonly less than an inch in diameter, on bare cultivated fields, and, in pastures, some great chocolate-colored ones (within). Both yield their dust. Heard the first bluebird, — something like *pe-a-wor*, — and then other slight warblings, as if farther off. Was surprised to see the bird within seven or eight rods on the top of an oak on the orchard's edge under the hill. But he appeared silent, while I heard others faintly warbling and twittering far in the orchard. When he flew I heard no more, and then I suspected that he had been ventriloquizing; as if he hardly dared open his mouth yet, while there was so much winter left. It is an overcast and moist but rather warm afternoon. He revisits the apple trees, and appears to find some worms. Probably not till now was his food to be found abundantly. Saw some fuzzy gnats in the air. Saw where a partridge had been eating many prinos berries, now black and shrivelled. I suspect that they devour a great bulk, which has but

little nutriment. The radical leaves of the pinweeds are like the johnswort with leaves reflexed, — most of them closer and finer. They appear unaffected by frost. The radical leaves of the crowfoot everywhere are the commonest green, as soon as the snow goes off. You can hardly tell when it begins to spring. Saw mountain cranberry near Brooks's pigeon-place, very flat on the pasture, raying out from a centre six feet each way, more than three quarters of an inch thick in the middle. Did not know it was so woody. This one of the *winter-reds*, perfectly fresh and glossy. The river *channel* is nearly open everywhere. Saw, on the alders by the riverside front of Hildreth's, a song sparrow, quirking its tail. It flew across the river to the willows, and soon I heard its well-known dry *tchip, tchip*. Saw, methinks, what I called ephemeræ last spring, — one on the water, three quarters of an inch long, narrow, gray-winged, several segments [?] curved on the back.

On winter-rye field, top of Annursnack, what looked like a *very large* hard core of a buttonwood ball — same color. Broke it with a stone and found it full of dark earth. Was it not my pigeon's-egg fungus turned dark and hardened?

March 8. Steady rain on the roof in the night, suggesting April-like warmth. This will help melt the snow and ice and take the frost out of the ground.

What pretty wreaths the mountain cranberry makes, curving upward at the extremity! The leaves are now a dark, glossy red, and wreath and all are of such a shape as might fitly be copied in wood or stone or architectural foliages.

I wrote a letter for an Irishman night before last, sending for his wife in Ireland to come to this country. One sentence which he dictated was, "Don't mind the rocking of the vessel, but take care of the children that they be not lost overboard."

Lightning this evening, after a day of successive rains.

March 9. A. M. — Clearing up.

Water is fast taking place of ice on the river and meadows, and morning and evening we begin to have some smooth water prospects. Saw this morning a muskrat sitting "in a round form on the ice," or, rather, motionless like the top of a stake or a mass of muck on the edge of the ice. He then dove for a clam, whose shells he left on the ice beside him.

Boiled a handful of rock-tripe (*Umbilicaria Muhlenbergii*) — which Tuckerman says "was the favorite Rock-Tripe in Franklin's Journey" — for more than an hour. It produced a *black* pulp, looking *somewhat* like boiled tea leaves, and was insipid like rice or starch. The dark water in which it was boiled had a bitter taste and was slightly gelatinous. The pulp was not positively disagreeable to the palate. The account in "The Young Voyageurs" [1] is correct.

P. M. — To Great Meadows.

Peter H. says that he saw gulls (?) and sheldrakes

[1] [By Captain Mayne Reid.]

about a month ago, when the meadow was flooded. I detect the trout minnows not an inch long by their quick motions or quirks, soon concealing themselves. The river channel is open, but there is a very *thin* ice of recent formation over the greater part of the meadows. It is a still, moist, louring day, and the water is smooth. Saw several flocks of large grayish and whitish or speckled ducks, — I suppose the same that P. calls sheldrakes. They, like ducks commonly, incline to fly in a line about an equal distance apart. I hear the common sort of quacking from them. It is pleasant to see them at a distance alight on the water with a slanting flight, launch themselves, and sail along so stately. The pieces of ice, large and small, drifting along, help to conceal them, supply so many objects on the water. There is this last night's ice on the surface, but the old ice still at the bottom of the meadows. In the spaces of still open water I see the reflection of the hills and woods, which for so long I have not seen, and it gives expression to the face of nature. The face of nature is lit up by these reflections in still water in the spring. Sometimes you see only the top of a distant hill reflected far within the meadow, where a dullgray field of ice intervenes between the water and the shore.

March 10. Misty rain, rain, — the third day of more or less rain.

P. M. — C. Miles road *via* Clamshell Hill.

Misty and mizzling. The radical leaves of the shepherd's-purse are common and fresh, also that early

thistle by Nut Meadow Brook, with much down webbed, holding the mist in drops. Each alder catkin has a clear drop at the end, though the air is filled with mist merely, which from time to time is blown in my face and I put up my umbrella. The bæomyces is very perfect and handsome to-day. It occurs to me that heavy rains and sudden meltings of the snow, such as we had a fortnight ago (February 26th), before the ground is thawed, so that all the water, instead of being soaked up by the ground, flows rapidly into the streams and ponds, is necessary to swell and break them up. If we waited for the direct influence of the sun on the ice and the influence of such water as would reach the river under other circumstances, the spring would be very much delayed. In the violent freshet there is a mechanic force added to the chemic. The willow catkins on the Miles [road] I should say had decidedly started since I was here last, and are all peeping from under their scales conspicuously. At present I should say that the vegetable kingdom showed the influence of the spring as much in the air as in the water, — that is, in the flowing of the sap, the skunk-cabbage buds, and the swelling of the willow catkins. I have detected very little, if anything, starting in brooks or ditches, for the first have far overflowed their banks and [are] full of rapid and sandy water, and the latter are still frequently full of ice. But probably that depends on the year, whether open or not. Saw a skunk in the Corner road, which I followed sixty rods or more. Out now about 4 P. M., — partly because it is a dark, foul day. It is a slender black (and white) animal, with its back re-

markably arched, standing high behind and carrying its head low; runs, even when undisturbed, with a

singular teeter or undulation, like the walking of a Chinese lady. Very slow; I hardly have to run to keep up with it. It has a long tail, which it regularly erects when I come too near and prepares to discharge its liquid. It is white at the end of the tail, and the hind head and a line on the front of the face, — the rest black, except the flesh-colored nose (and I think feet). The back is more arched and the fore and hind feet nearer together than in my sketch. It tried repeatedly to get into the wall, and did not show much cunning. Finally it steered, apparently, for an old skunk or woodchuck hole under a wall four rods off, and got into it, — or under the wall, at least, — for it was stopped up, — and there I view at leisure close to. It has a remarkably long, narrow, pointed head and snout, which enable it to make those deep narrow holes in the earth by which it probes for insects. Its eyes have an innocent, childlike, bluish-black expression. It made a singular loud patting sound repeatedly, on the frozen ground under the wall, undoubtedly with its fore feet (I saw only the upper part of the animal), which reminded me of what I have heard about your stopping and stamping in order to stop the skunk. Probably it has to do with its getting its food, — patting the earth to get the insects or worms. Though why it did so then I know not.

Its track was small, round, showing the nails, a little less than an inch in diameter, alternate five or six inches by two or two and a half, sometimes two feet together. There is something pathetic in such a sight, — next to seeing one of the human aborigines of the country. I respect the skunk as a human being in a very humble sphere. I have no doubt they have begun to probe already where the ground permits, — or as far as it does. But what have they eat all winter?

The weather is almost April-like. We always have much of this rainy, drizzling, misty weather in early spring, after which we expect to hear geese.

March 11. Fair weather after three rainy days. Air full of birds, — bluebirds, song sparrows, chickadee (phœbe notes), and blackbirds. Song sparrows toward the water, with at least two kinds or variations of their strain hard to imitate. *Ozit, ozit, ozit, psa te te̍ te te te te ter twe ter* is one; the other began *chip chip che we*, etc., etc. Bluebirds' warbling curls in elms.

Shall the earth be regarded as a graveyard, a necropolis, merely, and not also as a granary filled with the seeds of life? Is not its fertility increased by this decay? A fertile compost, not exhausted sand.

On Tuesday, the 7th, I heard the first song sparrow chirp, and saw it flit silently from alder to alder. This pleasant morning after three days' rain and mist, they

generally forthburst into sprayey song from the low trees along the river. The developing of their song is gradual but sure, like the expanding of a flower. This is the first *song* I have heard.

P. M. — To Cliffs.

River higher than any time in the winter, I think, yet, there being some ice on the meadows and the tops of reflected trees being seen along its edges, Aunt thought the river had gone down and that this was the ground. Muskrats are driven out of their holes. Heard one's loud plash behind Hubbard's. It comes up, brown striped with wet. I could detect its progress beneath in shallow water by the bubbles which came up. I believe I saw to-day, and have for some time seen, lizards in water, wiggling away more swiftly than tadpoles or frogs. From the hill the river and meadow is about equally water and ice, — rich blue water and islands or continents of white ice — no longer ice in place — blown from this side or that. The distant mountains are all white with snow while our landscape is nearly bare. Another year I must observe the alder and willow sap as early as the middle of February at least. Fair Haven covered with ice. Saw a hawk. Goodwin saw a ground squirrel a fortnight ago and heard robin this morning. He has caught skunks in traps set for minks with a piece of muskrat. Says the fox and skunk eat huckleberries, etc. Nowadays, where snow-banks have partly melted against the banks by the roadside in low ground, I see in the grass numerous galleries where the mice or moles have worked in the winter.

Vol. VI

March 12. A. M. — Up railroad to woods.

We have white frosts these mornings. This is the blackbird morning. Their sprayey notes and *conqueree* ring with the song sparrows' jingle all along the river. Thus gradually they acquire confidence to sing. It is a beautiful spring morning. I hear *my* first robin peep distinctly at a distance on some higher trees, — oaks or ? [*sic*], — on a high key. No singing yet. I hear from an apple tree a faint cricket-like chirp, and a sparrow darts away, flying far, *dashing from side to side*. I think it must be the white-in-tail, or grass finch. Saw either a large mouse or a ground squirrel on the snow near the edge of the wood, — probably the former. I hear a jay loudly screaming *phe-phay phe-phay*, — a loud, shrill chickadee's *phebe*. Now I see and hear the lark sitting with head erect, neck outstretched, in the middle of a pasture, and I hear another far off singing. Sing when they first come. All these birds do their warbling especially in the still, sunny hour after sunrise, as rivers twinkle at their sources. Now is the time to be abroad and hear them, as you detect the slightest ripple in smooth water. As with tinkling sounds the sources of streams burst their icy fetters, so the rills of music begin to flow and swell the general quire of spring. Memorable is the warm light of the spring sun on russet fields in the morning.

A new feature is being added to the landscape, and that is expanses and reaches of blue water.

C. says he saw a gull to-day.

P. M. — To Ball's Hill along river.

My companion tempts me to certain licenses of speech, *i. e.* to reckless and sweeping expressions which I am wont to regret that I have used. That is, I find that I have used more harsh, extravagant, and cynical expressions concerning mankind and individuals than I intended. I find it difficult to make to him a sufficiently moderate statement. I think it is because I have not his sympathy in my sober and constant view. He asks for a paradox, an eccentric statement, and too often I give it to him.

Saw some small ducks, black and white, — perhaps teal or widgeons. This great expanse of deep-blue water, deeper than the sky, why does it not blue my soul as of yore? It is hard to soften me now. I see no gulls myself. The time was when this great blue scene would have tinged my spirit more. Now is the season to look for Indian relics, the sandy fields being just bared. I stand on the high lichen covered and colored (greenish) hill beyond Abner Buttrick's; I go further east and look across the meadows to Bedford, and see that peculiar scenery of March, in which I have taken so many rambles, the earth just bare and beginning to be dry, the snow lying on the north sides of hills, the gray deciduous trees and the green pines soughing in the March wind — they look now as if deserted by a companion, the snow. When you walk over bare lichen-clad hills, just beginning to be dry, and look afar over the blue water on the meadows, you are beginning to break up your winter quarters and plan adventures for the new year. The scenery is like, yet unlike, November; you have the same barren russet, but now, instead of a dry, hard, cold wind, a peculiarly soft, moist air, or else a raw wind. Now is the reign of water. I see many crows on the meadow by the water's edge these days. It is astonishing how soon the ice has gone out of the river, but it still lies on the bottom of the meadow. Is it peculiar to the song sparrow to dodge behind and hide in walls and the like? Toward night the water becomes smooth and beautiful. Men are eager to launch their boats and paddle over the meadows.

The spring birds have come a little earlier this year than last, methinks, and I suspect the spring may be earlier in the air, yet there is more ice and snow and frozen ground still, because the winter has been so much more severe.

I am surprised to find that water froze pretty thick in my chamber the night of the 14th of March, '53, after a fire in the evening, and that they were at work on the ice at Loring's on the 16th. This is very different weather. The ice is all out of the river proper, and all spoiled even on Walden.

March 13. To Boston.

C. says he saw skater insects to-day. Harris tells me that those gray insects within the little log forts under the bark of the dead white pine, which I found about a week ago, are *Rhagium lineatum*. Bought a telescope to-day for eight dollars. Best military spyglass with six slides, which shuts up to about same size, fifteen dollars, and very powerful. Saw the squares

Vol. VI

of achromatic glass from Paris which Clark(e?)[1] uses; fifty-odd dollars apiece, the larger. It takes two together, one called the flint. These French glasses all one quality of glass. My glass tried by Clark and approved. Only a part of the object (?) glass available. Bring the edge of the diaphragm against middle of the light, and your nail on object glass in line with these shows what is cut off. Sometimes may enlarge the hole in diaphragm. But, if you do so, you may have to enlarge the hole in diaphragm near small end, which must be exactly as large as the pencil of light there. As the diameter of the pencil is to the diameter of the available portion of the object glass, so is the power, — so many times it magnifies. A good glass because the form of the blurred object is the same on each side of the focus, — i. e., shoved in or drawn out. C. was making a glass for Amherst College.

March 14. A. M. — Threatening rain after clear morning.

Great concert of song sparrows in willows and alders along Swamp Bridge Brook by river. Hardly hear a *distinct* strain. Couples chasing each other, and some tree sparrows with them.

R. W. E. saw a small bird in the woods yesterday which reminded him of the parti-colored warbler.

P. M. — To Great Meadows.

Raw thickening mists, as if preceding rain.

Counted over forty robins with my glass in the meadow

[Alvan Clark's name lacks the final "e."]

north of Sleepy Hollow, in the grass and on the snow. A large company of fox-colored sparrows in Heywood's maple swamp close by. I heard their loud, sweet, canary-like whistle thirty or forty rods off, sounding richer than anything yet; some on the bushes singing, *twee twee twa twa ter tweer tweer twa*,—this is the scheme of it only, there being no dental grit to it. They were shy, flitting before me, and I heard a slight susurrus where many were busily scratching amid the leaves of the swamp, without seeing them, and also saw many indistinctly. Wilson never heard but one sing, their common note there being a *cheep*. Saw fresh tracks in what looked like a woodchuck's hole. No ice visible as I look over the meadows from Peter's, though it lies at the bottom.[1] Scared up four black ducks from the flooded meadow on the right of the roadway as you go to Peter's. The water being rough on the meadows, they had apparently sought this smooth and shallow place shut in by the woods.

Alder scales are visibly loosened, their lower edges (*i. e.* as they hang) showing a line of yellowish or greenish. The pads in open warm ditches are now decidedly the greatest growth of this season, though I am not sure how much is due to last fall.

From within the house at 5.30 P. M. I hear the loud honking of geese, throw up the window, and see a large flock in disordered harrow flying more directly north or even northwest than usual. Raw, thick, misty weather.

¹ [Queried in pencil.]

March 15. Pleasant morning, unexpectedly. Hear on the alders by the river the *lill lill lill lill* of the first *F. hyemalis*, mingled with song sparrows and tree sparrows. The sound of Barrett's sawmill in the still morning comes over the water very loud. I hear that peculiar, interesting loud hollow tapping of a woodpecker from over the water.

I am sorry to think that you do not get a man's most effective criticism until you provoke him. Severe truth is expressed with some bitterness.

J. Farmer tells me his dog started up a lark last winter completely buried in the snow.

Painted my boat.

March 16. A. M. — Another fine morning.

Willows and alders along watercourses all alive these mornings and ringing with the trills and jingles and warbles of birds, even as the waters have lately broken loose and tinkle below, — song sparrows, blackbirds, not to mention robins, etc., etc. The song sparrows are very abundant, peopling each bush, willow, or alder for a quarter of a mile, and pursuing each other as if now selecting their mates. It is their song which especially fills the air, made an incessant and undistinguishable trill and jingle by their numbers. I see ducks afar, sailing on the meadow, leaving a long furrow in the water behind them. Watch them at leisure without scaring them, with my glass; observe their free and undisturbed motions. Some dark-brown partly on water, alternately dipping with their tails up, partly on land. These I think may be summer ducks.[1] Others with bright white breasts, etc., and black heads about same size or larger, which may be golden-eyes, *i. e.* brass-eyed whistlers.[2] They dive and are gone some time, and come up a rod off. At first I saw but one, then, a minute after, three. The first phœbe near the water is heard.

Saw and heard honey-bees about my boat in the yard, attracted probably by the beeswax in the grafting-wax which was put on it a year ago. It is warm weather. A thunder-storm in the evening.

March 17. Friday. A remarkably warm day for the season; too warm while surveying without my great-coat; almost like May heats.

4 P. M. — To Cliffs.

The grass is *slightly* greened on south bank-sides, — on the south side of the house. It begins to be windy. Saw a small gyrinus at the brook bridge behind Hubbard's Grove. The first tinge of green appears to be due to moisture more than to direct heat. It is not on bare dry banks, but in hollows where the snow melts last that it is most conspicuous. Fair Haven is open for half a dozen rods about the shores. If this weather holds, it will be entirely open in a day or two.

March 18. Saturday. Very high wind this forenoon; began by filling the air with a cloud of dust. Never felt it shake the house so much; filled the house with dust through the cracks; books, stove, papers covered

[1] Were they not females of the others?
[2] Probably both sheldrakes. *Vide* April 6 and 7, 1855.

with it. Blew down Mr. Frost's chimney again. Took up my boat, a very heavy one, which was lying on its bottom in the yard, and carried it two rods. The white caps of the waves on the flooded meadow, seen from the window, are a rare and exciting spectacle, — such an angry face as our Concord meadows rarely exhibit. Walked down the street to post-office. Few inhabitants out more than in a rain. Elms bending and twisting and thrashing the air as if they would come down every moment. I was cautious about passing under them. Yet scarcely a rotten limb in the street. The highest winds occur neither in summer, when the trees are covered with leaves, nor in winter, when they may be covered with ice. Saw a flattened toad on the sidewalk. Could it have been last year's?[1]

P. M. — Walked round by the west side of the river to Conantum.

Wind less violent. C. has already seen a yellow-spotted tortoise in a ditch. (Two sizable elms by river in Merrick's pasture blown down, roots being rotted off on water side.) The willow catkins this side M. Miles's five eighths of an inch long and show some red. Poplar catkins nearly as large, color somewhat like a gray rabbit. Old barn blown down on Conantum. It fell regularly, like a weak box pushed over, without moving its bottom, the roof falling upon it a little to leeward. The hay is left exposed, but does not blow away. The river was at its height last night. Before this we saw many robins and sparrows under Clamshell

[1] Guess not.

Vol. VI

Hill for shelter. Birds seek warm and sheltered places in such weather. It is very cold and freezing, this wind. The water has been blown quite across the Hubbard's Bridge causeway in some places and incrusted the road with ice. Before looking this way we had seen the whitened shore from Lupine Hill. It is blown and dashes against the willows and incrusts them with ice, sometimes to the height of three feet, with icicles shaped like bulls' horns, especially observable where many osiers stand together, and from the more horizontal osiers, etc., depend icicles, five or six inches long, very regularly, looking exactly like coarse rakes, apparently not the result of melting but of the spray and water blown or dashed upon them: only more regular. A very wintry sight.

The water is in many places blown a rod on to the shore and frozen. Saw where a woodchuck (probably) had dug out quite a pile of gravel in the side of a hill.

March 19. Sunday. Cold and windy. The meadow ice bears where shallow. William Rice 2d (?) saw a woodchuck last Sunday. Met his father in Walden Woods, who described a flock of crows he had just seen which followed him "eying down, eying down."

Saw in Mill Brook behind Shannon's three or four shiners[1] (the first), poised over the sand with a distinct longitudinal light-colored line midway along their

[1] Minnows?

sides and a darker line below it. This is a noteworthy and characteristic lineament, or cipher, or hieroglyphic, or type, of spring. You look into some clear, sandy-bottomed brook, where it spreads into a deeper bay, yet flowing cold from ice and snow not far off, and see, indistinctly poised over the sand on invisible fins, the outlines of a shiner, scarcely to be distinguished from the sands behind it, as if it were transparent, or as [if] the material of which it was builded had all been picked up from them. Chiefly distinguished by the lines I have mentioned.

Goodwin killed a pigeon yesterday.

Flint's Pond almost entirely open, — much more than Fair Haven.

March 21. Tuesday. At sunrise to Clamshell Hill.

River skimmed over at Willow Bay last night. Thought I should find ducks cornered up by the ice; they get behind this hill for shelter. Saw what looked like clods of plowed meadow rising above the ice. Looked with glass and found it to be more than thirty black ducks asleep with their heads in [sic] their backs, motionless, and thin ice formed about them. Soon one or two were moving about slowly. There was an open space, eight or ten rods by one or two. At first all within a space of apparently less than a rod [in] diameter. It was 6.30 A. M., and the sun shining on them, but bitter cold. How tough they are! I crawled far on my stomach and got a near view of them, thirty rods off. At length they detected me and quacked. Some got out upon the ice, and when I rose up all took to flight in a great straggling flock which at a distance looked like crows, in no order. Yet, when you see two or three, the parallelism produced by their necks and bodies steering the same way gives the idea of order.

March 22. Wednesday. P. M. — Launch boat and paddle to Fair Haven.

Still very cold. The most splendid show of ice chandeliers, casters, hour-glasses ($\frac{1}{2}$) that I ever saw or imagined about the piers of the bridges, surpassing any crystal, so large. Rather like the bases of columns,

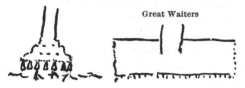

Great Waiters

— terraced pedestals, that is it, — the prototypes of the ornaments of the copings and capitals. Perfect and regular, sharp, cone-shaped drops hang from the first figure a few inches above the water. I should have described it then. It would have filled many pages. Scared up my flock of black ducks and counted forty together. See crows along the water's edge. What do they eat? Saw a small black duck with glass, — a dipper (?). Fair Haven still covered and frozen anew in part. Shores of meadow strewn with cranberries. The now silvery willow catkins (notwithstanding the severe cold) shine along the shore, over the cold water, and C. thinks some willow osiers decidedly more yellow.

Vol. VI

Is not the small duck or two I see one at a time and flying pretty high a teal? Willow osiers near Mill Brook mouth I am almost certain have acquired a fresher color; at least they surprise me at a distance by their green passing through yellowish to red at top.

March 26. River froze over at Lily Bay.[1]

March 27. Saw a hawk — probably marsh hawk — by meadow.

March 28. P. M. — To White Pond.
Coldest day for a month or more, — severe as almost any in the winter. Saw this afternoon either a snipe or a woodcock; it appeared rather small for the last.[2] Pond opening on the northeast. A flock of hyemalis drifting from a wood over a field incessantly for four or five minutes, — thousands of them, notwithstanding the cold. The fox-colored sparrow sings sweetly also. Saw a small slate-colored hawk, with wings transversely mottled beneath, — probably the sharp-shinned hawk.
Got first proof of "Walden."

March 29. Wednesday. P. M. — To Fair Haven.
Coldest night. Pump froze so as to require thawing. Saw two marsh hawks (?), white on rump. A gull of

[1] ["Lily" is crossed out in pencil and "Willow?" substituted (the interrogation-point being Thoreau's).]
[2] Probably a snipe.

March 23. Thursday. Snows and rains a little. The birds in yard active now, — hyemalis, tree sparrow, and song sparrow. The hyemalis jingle easily distinguished. Hear all together on apple trees these days. Minott confesses to me to-day that he has not been to Boston since the last war, or 1815. Aunt said that he had not been ten miles from home since; that he has not been to Acton since Miss Powers [?] lived there; but he declared that he had been there to cornwallis and musters. When I asked if he would like to go to Boston, he answered he was going to another Boston.

March 24. Fair again, the snow melting. Great flocks of hyemalis drifting about with their jingling note. The same ducks under Clamshell Hill. The elm buds were apparently expanded before this cold, which began on the 18th. Goose Pond half open. Flint's has perhaps fifteen or twenty acres of ice yet about shores. Can hardly tell when it is open this year. The black ducks — the most common that I see — are the only ones whose note I know or hear, — a hoarse, croaking quack. How shy they are!

March 25. Saturday. Cold and windy.
Down river in boat to Great Meadows.
Freezes on oars. Too cold and windy almost for ducks. They are in the smoother open water (free from ice) under the lee of hills. Got a boat-load of driftwood, — rails, bridge timber, planks, etc. White maple buds bursting, making trees look like some fruit trees with blossom-buds.

pure white, — a wave of foam in the air. How simple and wave-like its outline, the outline of the wings presenting two curves, between which the tail is merely the point of junction, — all wing like a birch scale; tail remarkably absorbed. Saw two white-throated, black-beaked divers fly off swiftly low over the water, with black tips of wings curved short downward. Afterward saw one scoot along out from the shore upon the water and dive; and that was the last I could see of him, though I watched four or five minutes. Fair Haven half open; channel wholly open. See thin cakes of ice at a distance now and then blown up on their edges and glistening in the sun. Had the experience of arctic voyagers amid the floe ice on a small scale. Think I saw a hen-hawk, — two circling over Cliffs.

March 30. 6 A. M. — To Island.
First still hour since the afternoon of the 17th. March truly came in like a lamb and went out like a lion this year. Remarkably and continuously pleasant weather from the very first day till the 18th. Apparently an early spring, — buds and birds well advanced, — then suddenly very severe cold and high winds, cold enough to skim the river over in broad places at night, and commencing with the greatest and most destructive gale for many a year, felt far and wide; and it has never ceased to blow since till this morning. Vegetation is accordingly put back. The ground these last cold (thirteen) days has been about bare of snow, but frozen. Some had peas and potatoes in before it.

First half of month very pleasant and mild spring weather, last half severe winter cold and high winds. The water at its highest, — not very high, — this month on the 17th. Ducks have been lurking in sheltered places not frozen. Robins feed along the edge of the river. At the Island I see and hear this morning the cackle of a pigeon woodpecker at the hollow poplar; had heard him tapping distinctly from my boat's place, $\frac{1}{4}$ + of a mile. Great flocks of tree sparrows and some *F. hyemalis* on the ground and trees on the Island Neck, making the air and bushes ring with their jingling. The former — some of them — say somewhat like this: *a che che, ter twee twee, tweer tweer twa.* It sounded like a new bird. The black ducks seem always to rise with that loud, hoarse croaking—quacking. The river early is partly filled with thin, floating, hardly cemented ice, occasionally turned on its edge by the wind and sparkling in the sun. If the sun had kept out of the way one day in the past fortnight, I think the river would have frozen to bear.

Read an interesting article on Étienne Geoffroy Saint-Hilaire, the friend and contemporary of Cuvier, though opposed to him in his philosophy. He believed species to be variable. In looking for anatomical resemblances he found that he could not safely be guided by function, form, structure, size, color, etc., but only by the relative position and mutual dependence of organs. Hence his *Le Principe des Connexions* and his maxim, "An organ is sooner destroyed than transposed," — "Un organ est plutôt altéré, atrophié, anéanti, que transposé." A principal formula

of his was, "Unity of Plan, Unity of Composition." (In the *Westminster Review*, January, 1854.)

March 31. Weather changes at last to drizzling.

In criticising your writing, trust your fine instinct. There are many things which we come very near questioning, but do not question. When I have sent off my manuscripts to the printer, certain objectionable sentences or expressions are sure to obtrude themselves on my attention with force, though I had not consciously suspected them before. My critical instinct then at once breaks the ice and comes to the surface.

V

APRIL, 1854

(ÆT. 36)

April 1. The tree sparrows, hyemalis, and song sparrows are particularly lively and musical in the yard this rainy and truly April day. The air rings with them. The robin now *begins* to sing sweet powerfully.

P. M. — Up Assabet to Dodge's Brook; thence to Farmer's.

April has begun like itself. It is warm and showery, while I sail away with a light southwest wind toward the Rock. Sometimes the sun seems just ready to burst out, yet I know it will not. The meadow is becoming bare. It resounds with the sprayey notes of blackbirds. The birds sing this warm, showery day after a fortnight's cold (yesterday was wet too), with a universal burst and flood of melody. Great flocks of hyemalis, etc., pass overhead like schools of fishes in the water, many abreast. The white maple stamens are beginning to peep out from the wet and weather-beaten buds. The earliest alders are just ready to bloom — to show their yellow — on the first decidedly warm and sunny day. The water is smooth at last and dark. Ice no longer forms on the oars. It is pleasant to paddle under the dripping hemlocks this dark day. They

Vol. VI

make more of a wilderness impression than pines. The lines of sawdust from Barrett's mill at different heights on the steep, wet bank under the hemlocks rather enhance the impression of freshness and wildness, as if it were a new country. Saw a painted tortoise on the bottom. The bark of poplar boughs which have been held in the ice along the sides of the river the past winter is gnawed, probably by muskrats. Saw floating a good-sized rooster without a head, — the red stump sticking out, — probably killed by an owl. Heard a bird whose note was very much like that of the purple finch, — loud and clear. First *smelled* the muskrat. Yesterday and to-day I hear the cackle of the flicker, so agreeable from association. It brings the year about. From afar, on some blasted tree, it makes all the vale ring with [?] its swelling flicker (?). Saw, at Farmer's, his snow-grubs, — the same I had seen (*vide* back). Harris, in this week's *New England Farmer*, thinks, on comparing them with English plates, that they are the larvæ of one of the species of crane-fly (*Tipula*). I saw some still in F.'s pasture. Did they not come out from the roots of the grass prematurely in the winter, and so become food for birds? The ground in Farmer's garden was in some places whitened with the droppings of the snowbirds after seeds of weeds, — *F. hyemalis* and others. The hyemalis is in the largest flocks of any at this season. You see them come drifting over a rising ground just like snowflakes before a northeast wind.

I was surprised to see how Farmer's young pears,

three or four feet high, on quince stocks, had been broken down by the snow-drifts, — broken over and over, apparently the snow freezing over them and then at last by its weight breaking them down.

I hear the jingle of the hyemalis from within the house, sounding like a trill.

April 2. P. M. — To Conantum *via* Nut Meadow Brook.

Saw black ducks in water and on land. Can see their light throats a great way with my glass. They do not dive, but dip. That liverwort [1] in the J. Hosmer ditch is now obvious. It has little green cups on its frond, with a fringed mouth ; but I saw something similar but shorter and more orbicular yesterday, under the hemlock bank, with little black dots on it. The radical leaves of some plants appear to have started, look brighter. The shepherd's-purse (?), and plainly the skunk-cabbage. In the brook there is the least possible springing yet. A little yellow lily in the ditch and sweet flag *starting* in the brook. I was sitting on the rail over the brook, when I heard something which reminded me of the song of the robin in rainy days in past springs. Why is it that not the note itself, but something which reminds me of it, should affect me most? — the ideal instead of the actual.

At Lee's Cliff the red-stemmed moss. The slippery elm is about as forward as the common, with its rusty

[1] Marchantia?

buds. The saxifrage is the most springlike plant, methinks, yet.

The tree sparrows make the alders, etc., ring. They have a metallic chirp and a short canary-like warble. They keep company with the hyemalis.

April 3. Saw from window with glass seven ducks on meadow-water, — only one or two conspicuously white, — these, black heads, white throats and breasts and along sides, — the rest of the ducks, brownish, probably young males and females. Probably the golden-eye. Jardine says it is rare to see more than one full-plumaged male in a flock.

P. M. — To Cliffs by boat.

Did I see crow blackbirds with the red-wings and hear their harsher chattering?

The water has gone down so much that I have to steer carefully to avoid the thick hummocks left here and there on the meadow by the ice. I see the deep holes they were taken out of. A muskrat has just built a small cabin, — apparently a bushel of mouthfuls on one. No clams up yet. I see a very little snow ice still, at a distance on the north sides of hills and walls. The wind is southeasterly. This is methinks the first hazy day, though not so warm as the 17th of March. The aspect of the woods reminds me of landscapes, and the sough of the wind in the pines sounds warmer, whispering of summer. I think I may say that Flint's broke up entirely on the first wet day after the cold spell, — *i. e.* the 31st of March, — though I have not been there lately. Fair Haven will last some days yet.

Vol. VI

April 4. All day surveying a wood-lot in Acton for Abel Hosmer. He says that he has seen the small slate-colored hawk pursue and catch doves, *i. e.* the sharp-shinned. Has found some trouble in driving off a large slate-colored hawk from a hen in his yard, at which he pounced again close by him, — undoubtedly a goshawk. Has also noticed the butcher-bird catching other birds. Calls him the "mock-bird." I observe that all the farmers have pretty much the same stories of this kind to tell. They will describe a large, bold slate-colored hawk (the goshawk) about here some two years ago, which caught some of their hens, and the like. The afternoon very pleasant.

April 5. This morning heard a familiar twittering over the house; looked up and saw white-bellied swallows. Another saw them yesterday.

Surveying all day for Mr. Hoar in Carlisle, near Hitchinson's and near I. [?] Green's.

See many hawks about yesterday and to-day, — marsh hawks and perhaps hen-hawks, these being pleasant days. It proved very pleasant and warm, and, while surveying in the woods with my greatcoat off, I heard a few stertorous sounds from the croaking frog. Also, as we rode along to Green's, we saw many of the large butterfly, dark with buff-edged wings, and also small reddish ones, in the dry sprout-lands. The same warm and pleasant weather brings them out to flutter along the roadside in sprout-lands, that does the hawks to sail along the meadow-side and over the wood. Saw the first frog by the roadside, — I believe a speckled,

i. e. palustris, — and, at the Green lot, heard the hyla. These days, when a soft west or southwest wind blows and it is truly warm, and an outside coat is oppressive, — these bring out the butterflies and the frogs, and the marsh hawks which prey on the last. Just so simple is every year. Whatever year it may be, I am surveying, perhaps, in the woods; I have taken off my outside coat, perhaps for the first time, and hung it on a tree; the zephyr is positively agreeable on my cheek; I am thinking what an elysian day it is, and how I seem always to be keeping the flocks of Admetus such days — that is my luck; when I hear a single, short, well-known stertorous croak from some pool half filled with dry leaves. You may see anything now — the buff-edged butterfly and many hawks — along the meadow; and hark! while I was writing down that field note, the shrill peep of the hylodes was borne to me from afar through the woods.

I rode with my employer a dozen miles to-day, keeping a profound silence almost all the way as the most simple and natural course. I treated him simply as if he had bronchitis and could not speak, just as I would a sick man, a crazy man, or an idiot. The disease was only an unconquerable stiffness in a well-meaning and sensible man.

Begin to look off hills, and see the landscape again through a slight haze, with warm wind on the cheek.

April 6. P. M. — Up Assabet.

A still warmer day than yesterday — a warm, moist rain-smelling west wind. I am surprised [to] find so much of the white maples already out. The light-colored stamens show to some rods. Probably they *began* as early as day before yesterday. They resound with the hum of honey-bees, heard a dozen rods off, and you see thousands of them about the flowers against the sky. They know where to look for the white maple and when. This susurrus carries me forward some months toward summer. I was reminded *before* of those still warm summer noons when the breams' nests are left dry, and the fishes retreat from the shallows into the cooler depths, and the cows stand up to their bellies in the river. The reminiscence came over me like a summer's dream. The alders, both kinds, just above the hemlocks, have just begun to shed their pollen. They are hardly as forward as the white maples, but these are not in so warm a position as some. I am in doubt which (alder or maple) may be earliest this year. Have not looked so closely as last year. In clearing out the Assabet Spring, disturbed two small speckled (*palustris*) frogs just beginning to move. Saw flying over what I at first thought a gull, then a fish hawk. Heard the snipe over the meadows this evening; probably to be heard for a night or two; sounds on different days as if approaching or receding ; — over the meadows recently become bare.

April 7. 6 A. M. — Down railroad to Cliffs.

The *Populus tremuloides* in a day or two. The hazel stigmas are well out and the catkins loose, but no pollen shed yet. On the Cliff I find, after long and careful search, one sedge above the rocks, low amid the with-

ered blades of last year, out, its little yellow beard amid the dry blades and few green ones, — the first *herbaceous* flowering I have detected. Fair Haven is completely open. It must have been so first either on the 5th or 6th.

April 8. Saturday. 6 A. M. — To Clamshell Hill.

Am surprised to find the skunk-cabbage out, shedding pollen (a few). This was probably the case in some places on the 5th and 6th. There has been very little growth visible in its spathes for a month. Its spring seems to be in the fall partly. This spring it has suffered more than usual, owing to the severe cold of the last half of March. Did I see a grass finch? Cheney's elm begins to show stamens. That remarkably warm first half of March appears to have advanced the plants very much, and as soon as the cold last half was past they burst out almost together. Spearers' lights two or three nights past.

P. M. — To Lee's Cliff via Clamshell.

Methinks I do not see such great and lively flocks of hyemalis and tree sparrows in the morning since the warm days, the 4th, 5th, and 6th. Perchance after the warmer days, which bring out the frogs and butterflies, the alders and maples, the greater part of them leave for the north and give place to newcomers.

At the Lyceum the other night I felt that the lecturer had chosen a theme too foreign to himself and so failed to interest me as much as formerly. He described things not in or near to his heart, but toward his ex-

tremities and superficies. The poet deals with his privatest experience. There was no *central* nor centralizing thought in the lecture.

Some southward banks and hillsides are now considerably tinged with green, not observed at a distance. I see the celandine and catnep (?) beginning to look green along the graveyard fence. The stigmas of the hazels (beyond Clamshell) are a splendid crimson star when brought between me and the light. I cannot find any of their catkins shedding pollen yet, but they may to-morrow. On the 5th saw a man sowing rye. Heard a prolonged dream from frog (?) in the river meadow; or was it a toad ? [1] See black ducks and hear their hoarse quacking. They commonly rise sixty rods off. They feed as often on the land as in the water, and look as clumsy there as the tame do. At Nut Meadow Brook saw, or rather heard, a muskrat plunge into the brook before me, and saw him endeavoring in vain to bury himself in the sandy bottom, looking like an amphibious animal. I stooped and, taking him by his tail, which projected, tossed him ashore. He did not lose the points of compass, but turned directly to the brook again, though it was toward me, and, plunging in, buried himself in the mud, and that was the last I saw of him. I see many yellow-spot tortoises to-day, — some of them quite rusty-looking. The alders are pretty generally [sic]; they are either yellowish, greenish, or reddish. At Heart-leaf Pond the croaking frogs are in full blast. I saw many on the surface, — small, ferruginous or dark brown, bodies two inches long, spread

[1] [Doubtless a toad. See *postea*.]

out on the surface and from time to time swimming about and toward each other, or diving. Most utter a short croak several times. Others use a peculiar squirming and nasal variation hard to imitate, somewhat like *er-wăh* (not broad *war* or *wor*) *er-wăh er-wăh er-wăh*, faster and faster, the nasal between the two syllables, something like *what what what what* spoken nasally. Then all will be silent. They have spells at it. Did I see their spawn? A turtle dove — went off with a slight whistling note. The willow near Miles's to-morrow or next day, *if fair*. That at the bridge equally early. The poplar catkins (*P. tremuloides*) on Conantum are beginning to curve downward, with their red anthers not yet open within the down, — mulberry-like. Apparently will open to-morrow, if warm; say the 10th. The polypody and marginal (?) shield fern and the spleenwort are evergreens at Lee's Cliff. The slippery elm, apparently in two or three days. Am surprised to find two crowfoot blossoms withered. They undoubtedly opened the 5th or 6th; say the last. They must be earlier here than at the Cliffs, where I have observed them the last two years. They are a little earlier than the saxifrage around them here, of which last I find one specimen at last, in a favorable angle of the rock, just opening. I have not allowed enough for the difference of localities. The columbine shows the most spring growth of any plant. What is that plant with narrow toothed leaves which has already shot up so straight four or five inches on the shelves of the rock? *Arabis lævigata ?*

Saw a large bird sail along over the edge of Wheeler's

Vol. VI

cranberry meadow just below Fair Haven, which I at first thought a gull, but with my glass found it was a hawk and had a perfectly white head and tail and broad or blackish wings. It sailed and circled along over the low cliff, and the crows dived at it in the field of my glass, and I saw it well, both above and beneath, as it turned, and then it passed off to hover over the Cliffs at a greater height. It was undoubtedly a white-headed eagle. It was to the eye but a large hawk.

Saw several yellow redpolls (*Sylvia petechia*) on the willows by the Hubbard Bridge. Am not sure I heard their note. May have mistaken it formerly for the pine warbler. Its chestnut crown would distinguish it.

Hazel, the very first male, open.

I find that I can criticise my composition best when I stand at a little distance from it, — when I do not see it, for instance. I make a little chapter of contents which enables me to recall it page by page to my mind, and judge it more impartially when my manuscript is out of the way. The distraction of surveying enables me rapidly to take new points of view. A day or two surveying is equal to a journey.

Pickerel have darted in shallows for nearly a week.

Some poets mature early and die young. Their fruits have a delicious flavor like strawberries, but do not keep till fall or winter. Others are slower in coming to their growth. Their fruits may be less delicious, but are a more lasting food and are so hardened by the sun of summer and the coolness of autumn that they keep sound over winter. The first are June-eatings, early

but soon withering; the last are russets, which last till June again.

April 9. I have not noticed any fox-colored sparrows for a week.[1] A large-catkined sallow (?) by the railroad, ten rods this side the jog on the west, *just* bursting out, with its pinkish-orange (before bursting) anthers. There is a little ice snow [*sic*] still under the north side of hills. Saw several more redpolls with their rich, glowing yellow breasts by the causeway sides. Saw a wren on the edge of Nathan Stow's wood and field, with some of the habits of a creeper, lurking along a fallen pine and birch, in and out in a restless manner with tail up, a snuff-colored bird with many white spots and a fine chirping note. Can it be the winter or the wood wren? Callitriche just started from bottom; pollywogs two inches long. Chrysosplenium out, — a few, — perhaps a day or two, where they rest just on the surface of the water. Cowslip in Hubbard's Close will open the first warm and sunny hour. Perhaps already at Second Division.[2] The skunk-cabbage leaves are unfolding at Brister's Hill edge, and a grass-like, groove-leaved plant three or four inches high. Nosing of skunks nowadays, and since frost out in spots. The beaked hazel stigmas out; put it just after the common. *Lycopodium lucidulum* is as green as ever.

I am surprised to find Walden completely open. When did it open? According to all accounts, it must have been between the 6th and 9th. Fair Haven must

[1] *Vide* 16th.   [2] *Vide* 16th.

have opened entirely the 5th or 6th, and Walden very nearly at the same time. This proves how steadily it has been melting, notwithstanding the severe cold of the last half of March; *i. e.*, it is less affected by transient heat or cold than most ponds.

The flowers have blossomed very suddenly this year as soon as the long cold spell was over, and almost all together. As yet the landscape generally wears its November russet.

April 10. April rain. How sure a rain is to bring the tree sparrows into the yard, to sing sweetly, canary-like!

I bought me a spy-glass some weeks since. I buy but few things, and those not till long after I begin to want them, so that when I do get them I am prepared to make a perfect use of them and extract their whole sweet.

Saw a dead sucker yesterday.

P. M. — To Great Meadows by boat, and sail back.

There are many snipes now feeding in the meadows, which you come close upon, and then they go off with hoarse *cr-r-r-ack cr-r-r-ack*. They dive down suddenly from a considerable height sometimes when they alight. A boy fired at a blue-winged teal a week ago. A great many red-wings along the water's edge in the meadow. Some of these blackbirds quite black, and some *apparently larger* than the rest. Are they all red-wings? The crimson stigmas, like the hazel, of the white maple, generally by themselves, make handsome show.

April 11. A. M. — Heard the clear, rather loud and rich warble of a purple finch and saw him on an elm. Wilson says they feed on the coverings of the blossoms. It is a distinct and peculiar note, not to be confounded with anything before it. I suspect that I heard one on the 1st of April, *q. v.*

P. M. — Surveying in Lincoln.

Large ant-hills in the woods, but no ants.

Evening on river.

Fine full moon; river smooth. Hear a slight snoring of frogs on the bared meadows. Is it not the *R. palustris*? This the first moon to walk by.

April 12. Wednesday. Surveying for Parks in Lincoln.

A white frost this morning, after the clear moonlight.

Parks says he saw a buff-edged butterfly a month ago, *i. e.* before the 17th of March. The hazels are well out to-day, and their pollen yellows my clothes, it being a warm (off-coat) day. When I went to Mr. P.'s house at noon, he addressed me, "Now, what will you have to drink?" and soon appeared stirring a glass of gin for himself.

Waited at Lincoln depot an hour and a half. Heard the telegraph harp. I perceived distinctly that man melts at the sound of music, just like a rock exposed to a furnace heat. They need not have fabled that Orpheus moved the rocks and trees, for there is nothing more insensible than man; he sets the fashion to the rocks, and it is as surprising to see him melted, as when children see the lead begin to flow in a crucible.

I observe that it is when I have been intently, and it may be laboriously, at work, and am somewhat listless or abandoned after it, reposing, that the muse visits me, and I see or hear beauty. It is from out the shadow of my toil that I look into the light. The music of the spheres is but another name for the Vulcanic force. May not such a record as this be kept on one page of the Book of Life: "A man was melted to-day."

April 13. A clear and pleasant morning. Walked down as far as Moore's at 8 A. M. and returned along the hill. Heard the first chip-bird, sitting on an apple [tree], with its head up and bill open, jingling *tche-tche-tche-tche-tche*, etc., very fast. Hear them in various parts of the town. On the hill near Moore's hear the *F. juncorum*, — *phē-phē-phē-phē-phē*, *pher-phē-ē-ē-ē-ē-ē-ē-ē*. How sweet it sounds in a clear warm morning in a wood-side pasture amid the old corn-hills, or in sprout-lands, a [*sic*] clear and distinct, "like a spoon in a cup," the last part very fast and ringing. Hear the pine warbler also, and *think I see* a female red-wing flying with some males. Did I see a bay-wing? Heard a purple finch on an elm, like a faint robin.

P. M. — Sail to Bittern Cliff.

The surface of the water, toward the sun, reflecting the light with different degrees of brilliancy, is very exhilarating to look at. The red maple in a day or two. I begin to see the anthers in some buds. So much more of the scales of the buds is now uncovered that the tops of the swamps at a distance are reddened. A couple of large ducks, which, because they flew low

over the water and appeared *black* with a little white, I thought not black ducks, — possibly velvet or a merganser. The black ducks rise at once to a considerable height and often circle about to reconnoitre. The golden-brown tassels of the alder are very rich now. The poplar (*tremuloides*) by Miles's Swamp has been out — *the earliest catkins* — maybe two or three days. On the evening of the 5th the body of a man was found in the river between Fair Haven Pond and Lee's, much wasted. How these events disturb our associations and tarnish the landscape! It is a serious injury done to a stream. One or two crowfoots on Lee's Cliff, fully out, surprise me like a flame bursting from the russet ground. The saxifrage is pretty common, ahead of the crowfoot now, and its peduncles have shot up. The slippery elm is behind the common, which is fully out beside it. It will open apparently in about two days of pleasant weather.[1] I can see the anthers plainly in its great rusty, fusty globular buds. A small brown hawk with white on rump — I think too small for a marsh hawk — sailed low over the meadow.[2] Heard now, at 5.30 P.M., that faint bullfrog-like note from the meadows, — *er-er-er*. Many of the button-bushes have been broken off about eighteen inches above the present level of the water (which is rather low), apparently by the ice. Saw a piece of meadow, twelve feet in diameter, which had been dropped on the northwest side of Willow Bay on a bare shore, thickly set with button-bushes five feet high, per-

[1] 15th, sheds pollen in chamber. Say 18th. *Vide* 23d.

[2] May it have been a young male harrier?

fectly erect, which will no doubt flourish there this summer. Thus the transplanting of fluviatile plants is carried on on a very large and effective scale. Even in one year a considerable plantation will thus be made on what had been a bare shore, and its character changed. The meadow cannot be kept smooth.

The winter-rye fields quite green, contrasting with the russet.

Saw an old log, stripped of bark, either poplar or maple, four feet long, — its whole upper half covered with that handsome winkle-like fungus.[1] They are steel-colored and of a velvety appearance, somewhat semicircular, with concentric growths (?) of different shades, passing from quite black within through a slaty-blue to (at present) a buff edge.[2] Beneath cream-color. There are many minute ones a tenth of an inch in diameter, the shell-like leaf or ear springing from one side. The full-grown are sometimes united into one leaf for eight or nine inches in one level along the log, tier above tier, with a scalloped edge. They are handsomest when two or more are opposed, meeting at their bases, and make a concentric circle. They remind you of shells, also of butterflies. The great variety and regularity of the shading are very interesting. They spring from a slight base, rising by a narrow neck. They grow on stumps and other dead wood on land, even driftwood left high, just as some marine shells, their relatives, grow on driftwood. They

[1] *Auricularia.*

[2] Saw some the 16th wholly faded out to this color on an oak stump.

are a sort of dimple. Does not the whole at last fade out to the buff of the edge?

April 14. *Friday.* 6 A. M. — To Nawshawtuct.

There is a general tinge of green now discernible through the russet on the bared meadows and the hills, the green blades just peeping forth amid the withered ones. Can they be red-wings which I have seen for some time with the red-wings, — without red or buff? They have a split note, perhaps no *gurgle-ee!* There are spider-webs on the meadow lately bared. It is difficult to find the snipe, though you stand near where he alights. Saw yellow redpolls, on Cheney's elm, — a clear metallic chip and jerks of the tail.

April 15. Morning. — Snow and snowing; four inches deep. Yesterday was very cold. Now, I trust, it will come down and out of the air. Many birds must be hard put to it. Some tree sparrows and song sparrows have got close up to the sill of the house on the south side, where there is a line of grass visible, for shelter. When Father came down this morning he found a sparrow squatting in a chair in the kitchen. Does n't know how it came there. I examined it a long time, but could not make it out. It was five or six inches long, with a somewhat finch-like bill (bluish-black above and light below); general aspect above pale brown, mottled with buffish and whitish; bay and a *little* black on the wings; the crown a faint bay, divided by an ashy line, with a broad ashy line over eye and a distincter bay or chestnut line from the angle of the mouth backward; legs *pale clear flesh-color, feet black,* claws slender; two *faint* whitish bars on wings (the tips of feathers); the breast ashy-white, with many dark or black spots edged with bay in chains; *no yellow* about it; a rounded tail, long and of a pretty uniform pale brown or bay, ashy on the inner vanes, but *no white nor black* in it; a rather slender bird. It made me *think* of the bay-wing and of the Savannah sparrow.

P. M. — This cold, moist, snowy day it is easier to see the birds and get near them. They are driven to the first bare ground that shows itself in the road, and the weather, etc., makes them more indifferent to your approach. The tree sparrows look much stouter and more chubby than usual, their feathers being puffed up and darker also, perhaps with wet. Also the robins and bluebirds are puffed up. I see the white under sides of many purple finches, busily and silently feeding on the elm blossoms within a few feet of me, and now and then their bloody heads and breasts. They utter a faint, clear chip. Their feathers are much ruffled. The yellow redpoll hops along the limbs within four or five feet of me.

Martins the 13th first. The arrival of the purple finches appears to be coincident with the blossoming of the elm, on whose blossom it feeds.

Johnson in his "Wonder-working Providence" speaks of "an army of caterpillars" in New England in 1649, so great "that the cart wheels in their passage were painted green with running over the great swarms of them."

April 16. A cold, disagreeable day, — sun not fairly out, — yet the snow of yesterday melts apace; you can almost see it melt. Each time I look out I see more of russet or green. At first the bare ground showed itself in the middle of the road and rapidly widened, giving the birds wider pasture; then the grass in the fields began to peep through and the landscape to acquire a russet hue again. The green blades under the south side of the houses and hills appear to have grown wonderfully since the snow fell, and to be several shades darker green.

P. M. — To epigæa.

Saw a fox-colored sparrow still and black ducks. There are four or five cowslips open at the Second Division Meadow, — first probably about the 11th. The buds of the shad-bush are much expanded and show considerable green or yellowish, — more than [any other] native shrub or tree that I think of.[1] The mayflower under the snow will not open for some days at least, — maybe a week. The winkle fungi are arranged either on the upper half of a prostrate log or one above another around a dead stump. Saw some to-day almost completely faded to a dark cream-color (or the buff of the edge of mine), though alternating with some faint steel-colored lines.

When I meet one of my neighbors these days who is ridiculously stately, being offended, I say in my mind: "Farewell! I will wait till you get your manners off. Why make politeness of so much consequence, when you are ready to assassinate with a word? I do not like

[1] Must be blossom-buds.

any better to be assassinated with a rapier than to be knocked down with a bludgeon. You are so grand that I cannot get within ten feet of you." Why will men so try to impose on one another? Why not be simple, and pass for what they are worth only? O such thin skins, such crockery, as I have to deal with! Do they not know that I can laugh? Some who have so much dignity that they cannot be contradicted! Perhaps somebody will introduce me one day, and then we may have some intercourse. I meet with several who cannot afford to be simple and true men, but personate, so to speak, their own ideal of themselves, trying to make the manners supply the place of the man. They are puffballs filled with dust and ashes.

April 17. Snows again.

It is remarkable how the American mind runs to statistics. Consider the number of meteorological observers and other annual phenomena. The Smithsonian Institution is a truly national institution. Every shopkeeper makes a record of the arrival of the first martin or bluebird to his box. Dodd, the broker, told me last spring that he knew when the first bluebird came to his boxes, he made a memorandum of it: John Brown, merchant, tells me this morning that the martins first came to his box on the 13th, he "made a minute of it." Beside so many entries in their day-books and ledgers, they record these things.

Did not see a linaria the past winter, though they were the prevailing bird the winter before. There are

but few *F. hyemalis* about now; they appear to have gone north mostly on the advent of warmer weather about the 5th of April. I look up, these snowy days, and see purple finches silently feeding on the elms, when I have heard no sound. They sing somewhat like a robin, continuously, with a loud, canary-like *twee twee* and *che che che*. The tree sparrow is still the prevailing bird.

April 18. For three or four days the lilac buds have looked green, — the most advanced that I have seen. The earliest gooseberry still earlier in garden (though smaller buds).

P. M. — To stone-heaps by boat.

Scared up snipes on the meadow's edge, which go off with their strange zigzag, crazy flight and a distressed sound, — *craik craik* or *cr-r-ack cr-r-rack*. One booms now at 3 P. M. They circle round and round, and zigzag high over the meadow, and finally alight again, descending abruptly from that height. Was surprised to see a wagtail thrush, the golden-crowned,[1] at the Assabet Spring, which inquisitively followed me along the shore over the snow, hopping quite near. I should say this was the golden-crowned thrush without doubt, though I saw none of the gold, if this and several more which I saw had not kept close to the water. May possibly be the *aquaticus*. Have a jerk of the forked tail. The male yellow redpoll's breast and under parts are of a peculiarly splendid and lively yellow, — glowing. It is remarkable that they too are found about willows,

[1] *Vide* April 26. Probably hermit thrush.

etc., along the water. Saw another warbler [1] (a) [2] about the same size, in the same localities, — *somewhat* creeper-like, very restless, more like the Tennessee warbler than any, methinks. Light-slate or bluish-slate head and shoulders, yellowish backward, all white beneath, and a distinct white spot on the wing; a harsh grating note (?) (b?). [3] Saw two wood ducks probably; saw a white spot behind eyes; they went off with a shriller *craik* than the black ducks.

I now feel pretty sure that they were crow blackbirds which I saw April 3d with the red-wings. They are stout fellows without any red epaulet, and go off with a hoarser *chuck chuck*, with rounded tail. They make that split singing, and, with the red-wing, feed along the water's edge. Heard a red-wing sing his *bobylee* in new wise, as if he tossed up a fourpence and it rattled on some counter in the air as it went up. Saw to-day a lesser blackbird, size of cowbird, *slatyblack*, on meadow edge. What was it?

The snow is sprinkled along the street with the large scales of buds from the trees; thus revealing what kind of *fall* is going on at this season.

April 19. Hear the tree sparrows at willow hedge-row this morning, — *ah ha ha yip yip yip yip*, or *twit-*

[1] *Vide* April 25.
[2] [This letter *a* and the *b* a few lines below are referred to on p. 220. The *b*, with the interrogation-point following it, was apparently inserted at a later date, and probably belongs only to the *note* described. Thoreau was perhaps uncertain at the time whether the note came from the bird he saw.]
[3] *Vide* April 25.

ter twitter twe twe twe, or *ch ha ha twitter twitter twe*, — very canary-like, yet clear, as if aspirated vowels alone, — no *t* or *r*.

Hear a pine warbler, — its note like the jingle of the *F. hyemalis*, — on an elm in the street.

Yesterday, as I was returning down the Assabet, paddling leisurely in the stern, the sun came out after two days of storm or louring weather and shone on the banks covered with snow. The water, which had been perfectly smooth all the afternoon, looked smoother yet, and I think that I never beheld so pure and refulgent a white as the upright snowy banks presented. Snow never looks so white in winter.

I had chosen to come to the river that afternoon, for there, the air being warm though the earth was covered with snow, there was least change. The few sparrows and warblers along the water's edge and on the twigs over the water seemed to forget the wintry prospect. I was surprised to find the river so full of sawdust from the pail-factory and Barrett's mill that I could not easily distinguish if the stone-heaps had been repaired. There was not a square three inches clear. And I saw the sawdust deposited by an eddy in one place on the bottom like a sand-bank a foot or more deep half a mile below the mill. That is a good stream to explore any summer weather, because the woods border it immediately and you can observe a greater variety of small birds. I can approach them more nearly in my boat than on foot. Melvin was inspecting his traps. From time to time masses of snow overhanging the water [fell] and floated saturated

Vol. VI

down the stream. The calm, bright hour after the sun came out was very pleasant. I first saw the crescent of clear sky widening rapidly in the north-northwestern horizon, then the cheerful sunlight on hills and houses northward, and finally it shone out on the north bank and on myself and on the south shore; and one song sparrow, when he felt its influence, sang as if with a new influx of joy. How longed for by the birds! Farmer says that he saw a man catch a bluebird yesterday which was dying in the snow. As I watched the sparrow sitting in the cold shadow while the sun was already shining on the northern bank, I wondered that he did not at once fly to it, — ay, that he had not kept pace with the sun or fair weather from the first. But thus nature rules it, and these winged creatures wait to be shined on or shaded like ourselves. It was at this time, looking down the river, that I saw the two wood ducks sailing out from the shore in the smooth water, at first suspecting that they were tame. Birds are positively curious, — *e. g.* the thrush I saw that afternoon which hopped out to the end of the overhanging alders within a few feet to reconnoitre me and my boat.

This is the fifth day that the ground has been covered with snow. There first fell about four inches on the morning of the 15th. This had two thirds melted on the evening of the 16th. Then as much more fell on the 17th, with which to-night (evening of 19th) the ground is still more than half covered. There has been sleighing. I do not remember the like. The water was slightly skimmed over along the edge of the river this morning.

P. M. — To Cliffs.

The *Populus grandidentata* will not open for a day or two. There is considerable growth in the water at the Boiling Spring. The callitriche is most forward, a foot or more long, with its delicate or pretty cup-like whorls of leaves, floating on the surface. I see no signs of a blossom. What is that narrow tooth-leafed and red-stemmed plant which has grown nearly as much in the water? crosswise. [1] Then there is the cress next under way. Yet, on the whole, I think the columbine in the most favorable places about even with these. The latter have been less checked the last four or five days. I saw yesterday, at the bottom of the water, by the sides of the river, a *yellowish, half-unfolded* pad here and there. The green tinge from new-springing grass in the wet meadow as I looked low from my boat was much more obvious and springlike. I was struck the same day with the very rigid and sharp triangular points of a kind of sedge rising four or five inches above the water, perhaps that kind that makes the wreck in the fall. As if it were prepared to contend with the ice which forms in the night after it has started. That pretty little moss in beds on the rocks, etc., at the Cliffs shows its little reddish cup-like blossoms nowadays. A man was plowing in snow this morning. Saw a bullfrog in Hayden's pond-hole and a small green grasshopper. A turtle dove flew away from the birches and lit in his stubble-field, and each time when it flew I heard a note continuously uttered

[1] *Veronica.*

like a pigeon woodpecker or a robin at a distance. *Salix humilis* (?) out, — *i. e.* the *Salix* in Stow's field, — probably before the 15th; say 14th. The sweet-gale below Emerson's *to-day*, just out, — the male, with its amber dust.

I thought yesterday that the sparrows must rejoice to sit in the sun again and dry their feathers and feel its warmth. I read to-day that a boy found twenty-six bluebirds dead in a hollow tree on the 1st of April in Great Barrington. That was just after that long cold spell.

It is remarkable how scarce and silent the birds are even in a pleasant afternoon like this, compared with the morning. Within a few days the warblers have begun to come. They are of every hue. Nature made them to show her colors with. There are as many as there are colors and shades. In certain lights, as yesterday against the snow, nothing can be more splendid and celestial than the color of the bluebird. On the creeping juniper there appear to be buds, but not blossoms yet.

Do I ever see the marsh hawk?[1] Is it not the sharp-shinned which I have mistaken for it? A man came to me yesterday to offer me as a naturalist a two-headed calf which his cow had brought forth, but I felt nothing but disgust at the idea and began to ask myself what enormity I had committed to have such an offer made to me. I am not interested in mere phenomena, though it were the explosion of a planet, only as it may have lain in the experience of a human being.

[1] I think the early large hawk was it.

April 20. A. M. — To Nawshawtuct.

Heard on the 14th a singular note on or near the hill, like a guinea-hen or other fowl, or a squeaking pump-handle. Heard [it] again this morning, and saw two large dark birds go off from a walnut with a loud squeaking *quack*. Is it a strange large woodpecker? or possibly a teal? Heard the same at starlight, — *ker-chuck ker-chuck ker-chuck.* I think it is the redwing only sings *bobylee*. Saw one pursuing a female (?). I am not sure whether these or the crow blackbirds are the earliest. Saw a small black-striped warbler or flycatcher (?) (c)[1] on a willow. Hear the *long*-drawn scold of a flicker, sounding very loud over the water.

P. M. — To Island and Hill.

A willow coming out fairly, with honey-bees humming on it, in a warm nook, — the most forward I have noticed, for the cold weather has held them in check. And now different kinds of bees and flies about them. What a sunny sight and summer sound! A striped snake on a warm, sunny bank. The painted tortoises are fairly out sunning to-day. A very pleasant and warm afternoon; the earth seems to be waking up. Frogs croak in the clear pools on the hillside where rocks have been taken out, and there is frog-spawn there, and little tadpoles are very lively in the sunny water.

I find some advantage in describing the experience of a day on the day following. At this distance it is more ideal, like the landscape seen with the head inverted, or reflections in water.

[1] [See p. 213.]

4 p. m. — To Moore's Swamp.

Red maple in a warm place shows anthers, and will open to-morrow if pleasant; say 22d. In the ditch in the Brown meadow, several yellow lily buds pushed up four or five inches. But water plants *on the whole* not decidedly ahead of land or air plants. The pine warbler on the oaks, running about somewhat creeper-like and now and then uttering a loud ringing *vetter vetter vetter vetter vetter vet* faster and faster, with its bright-yellow throat and forked tail.

At starlight by riverside a few faint stertorous sounds from the awakening meadow, and one or two faint bullfrogish notes, — *er-er-er.* The sound of the snipes, winnowing the evening air now at starlight, visible but for an instant high over the meadows, is heard far into the village, — *hoo hoo hoo hoo hoo hoo,* rising higher and higher or dying away as they circle round, — a ghostly sound. Is that bittern-like squeak made by them? I do not mean the nighthawk-like squeak.

April 21. 6 a. m. — Heard the bay-wing sparrow[1] in the redeemed meadows. None yesterday morning. At a distance hear only the end of its strain, like the ring of a small piece of steel dropped on an anvil. A few *F. hyemalis* still about. Are not those little whorls of black pointed scales the female blossom of the *Thuya occidentalis?*

Scarcely an April shower yet.

How can a man be a wise man, if he does n't know

[1] ["Bay-wing" is crossed out in pencil, and "one of the seringos" written over it.]

any better how to live than other men? — if he is only more cunning and intellectually subtle? Does Wisdom work in a treadmill? Does Wisdom fail? or does she teach how to succeed by her example? Is she merely the miller who grinds the finest logic? Did Plato get his *living* in a better way or more successfully than his contemporaries? Did he succumb to the difficulties of life like other men? Did he merely prevail over them by indifference, or by assuming grand airs? or find it easier to live because his aunt remembered him in her will?[1]

P. M. — To Saw Mill Brook.

As I was handling the arbor-vitæ to-day, an odor like strawberries came from [it]. Is that terebinthine? The lilac is beginning to open to-day. The snows go off and the lustre of the wintergreen is undiminished. The large black ants are at work on their hills. The great scalloped leaf betrays the *P. grandidentata.* How silent and deserted the woods are! I do not fairly see a chickadee even. Snow with its tracks would make it seem more inhabited. How we prize any redness on the ground! — a red stain in a stone or even a coxcomb lichen on a stump! The hellebore at the brook has shot up six or eight inches with its compact bundles and will soon catch the cabbage. It is *now* one of the most forward plants. That gooseberry at the brook is the most forward shrub or tree at present that I can find out of doors in Concord.[2] It shows more of a leaf than

[1] [*Cape Cod, and Miscellanies,* pp. 462, 463; *Misc.,* Riv. 263.]
[2] [Later:] Excepting the spiræa. [Later still:] The thimble-berry in some places equally forward, and perhaps the honeysuckle vine.

the lilac or Missouri currant, which may come next. As I go up the hill beyond the brook, while the hylodes are heard behind, I perceive the faintest possible flower-like scent as from the earth, reminding me of anemonies and houstonias. Can it be the budded mouse-ears under my feet? Downy-swaddled, they lie along flat to the earth like a child on its mother's bosom. I sit on a rock awhile just below the old trough. These are those early times when the rich golden-brown tassels of the alders tremble over the brooks — and not a leaf on their twigs. We are far north with Sir John Franklin. I see the first of that bent lake grass on the smooth surface of a flooded meadow, with a dimple at its stem. It is a warm sight. The fruit of the *O. spectabilis* (?), flowering fern, still perfect. I see on the red cedar the male blossom buds not yet quite open, and very minute hollows with whitish scales at the ends of some of the branchlets, which I take to be the female flowers.

The song of the purple finch on the elms (he also frequents firs and spruce) is rich and continuous, like, but fainter and more rapid than, that of a robin, — some of the *cherruwit* in it and a little of the warble of the martin. A martin was found dead the 18th after the snows, and many bluebirds in Brookfield.

April 23. A kingfisher with his *crack*, — *cr-r-r-rack*. Rain yesterday and to-day; yet this morning the robin sings and the blackbirds and, in the yard, the tree sparrow, hyemalis, and song sparrow. A rain is sure to bring the tree sparrow and hyemalis to the gardens.

I suppose it must be the seeds of weeds which they are so busily picking from the bare ground, which their sharp eyes detect. George Minott says that he used to shoot the red-headed woodpecker, and found their nests on the trees on his hillside. He used to steal up to the pigeon woodpeckers' holes and clap his hand over them and take out the old bird; then let her go.

The first April showers are even fuller of promise and a certain moist serenity than the sunny days. How thickly the green blades are starting up amid the russet! The tinge of green is gradually increasing in the face of the russet earth.

Now that the very earliest shrubs are beginning to unfold, — spiræa, gooseberry, honeysuckle vine, lilac, Missouri currant, — many herbaceous plants, not evergreen merely, make quite a show, as the skunk-cabbage in favorable places, nuphar in the *most favorable* places though muddy yellow and dilapidated, callitriche and the narrow tooth-leafed water plant, etc., etc., cowslip, columbine (cress and chrysosplenium, — are not both chiefly evergreen?), celandine, catnep, saxifrage, dandelion, clover, golden senecio, sweet flag, hellebore (the most forward buds begin to open), thistle, shepherd's-purse, meadow saxifrage, elder probably.

As for the birds, I have this to remark: The crows still frequent the meadows. The lark sings morning and evening. The blackbirds — red-wing and crow — have since their arrival kept up their *bobylee* and chattering and split notes on the willows and maples by the river and along the meadow's edge. They appear

Vol. VI

to depend much (as well as crows and robins) on the meadow, just left bare, for their food. They are the noisiest birds yet. Both still fly in flocks, though the male red-wings have *begun* to chase the females. Robins still frequent the meadows in flocks and sing in the rain. The song sparrows not in such flocks nor singing so tumultuously along the watercourses in the morning as in the last half of March. How wary they are! They will dodge you for half an hour behind a wall or a twig, and only a stone will make them start, looking every which way in a minute. So the blackbirds, both kinds, sidle till they bring a twig between me and them. The flock of black ducks which stayed by so long is now reduced to a quarter part their number. Before the 4th or 5th of April the *F. hyemalis* was apparently the most abundant bird of any, in great drifting flocks with their lively jingle, their light-colored bill against slate breasts; then, on the advent of warmer weather, the greater part departed. Have the fox sparrows gone also? I have not seen them of late. As for hawks, after the one or two larger (perhaps) hen-hawks in the winter and a smaller one in December (?), the first were *large* marsh (?) hawks on trees on the meadow edge or skimming along it; since which the eagle, the sharp-shinned, and the smaller brown and white-rumped over meadows, which may be the same, etc., etc. Have seen the black duck, golden-eye, merganser, blue(?)-winged teal, wood duck. The golden-eye seems to have gone. Heard a nuthatch yesterday, April 22d. The tree sparrows are the prevailing bird on ground, and most numerous of any

for the past month except one while the hyemalis. They are a chubby little bird with a clear chestnut crown, a dark spot on the otherwise clear whitish breast, and two light bars on the wings. The pigeon woodpecker now scolds long and loud morning and evening. The snipes are still feeding on the meadows. The turtle dove darts solitary about as if lost, or it had lost its mate. The yellow redpoll, with a faint clear *chip*, is the commonest *yellow* bird on hills, etc., about water. The chip sparrow does not sing much in morning yet. New kinds of warblers have begun to come within a few days. I saw yesterday the smoke of the first burning of brush which I have noticed, though the leaves cannot be very dry yet.

P. M. — To Lee's Cliff on foot.

It has cleared up. At Ivy Bridge I see the honey-bees entering the crypts of the skunk-cabbage, whose tips have been bitten by the frost and cold. The first sweet-gale, which opened a day or two ago on the sunny sides of brooks where the sun reached it above the bank, was an interesting sight, full of amber dust. Those are blossom, not leaf buds, so forward on the shad-bush. The myrtle-bird, — yellow-rumped warbler, — was not this warbler *c* of the 20th? — on the willows, alders, and the wall by Hubbard's Bridge, slate and white spotted with yellow. Its note is a *fine*, rapid, somewhat hissing or whistling *se se se se se ser riddler se*, somewhat like the common yellowbird's. The yellow redpolls are very common on the willows and alders and in the road near the bridge. They keep jerking their tails. I heard one male sing a jingle like *che ve ve ve ve vē*, very fast, and accenting the last syllable. They are quite tame. I sit awhile on the lee side of Conant's Wood, in the sun, amid the dry oak leaves, and hear from time to time the *fine* ringing note of a pine warbler, which I do not see. It reminds me of former days and indescribable things. Swarms of those little fuzzy gnats now make a faint humming about the railing of the bridge. The bay-wing has a light ring at some distance around the eye. It is also too dark for my prisoner of the 15th.

Saw my white-headed eagle again, first at the same place, the outlet of Fair Haven Pond. It was a fine sight, he is mainly — *i. e.* his wings and body — so black against the sky, and they contrast so strongly with his white head and tail. He was first flying low over the water; then rose gradually and circled westward toward White Pond. Lying on the ground with my glass, I could watch him very easily, and by turns he gave me all possible views of himself. When I observed him edgewise I noticed that the tips of his wings curved upward slightly   the more, like a stereotyped ————— undulation. He rose very high at last, till I almost lost him in the clouds, circling or rather *looping* along west-

ward, high over river and wood and farm, effectually concealed in the sky. We who live this plodding life here below never know how many eagles fly over us.

Vol. VI

twigs over the water to-day. I think, therefore, the 22d will do for the very earliest. Had a glimpse of a very small warbler (*b'*) on a pitch pine, and heard a pleasant and unusual whistle from him.[1] The slippery elm, with its dull-pinkish (?) blossoms now fully out. I think on account of the snow it could not have opened before the 18th. The sedge was abundant long before the crowfoot or saxifrage was. It must be put earlier than I have allowed. Crowfoot is not yet abundant, though it was earlier than saxifrage, which has now gone ahead. A thimble-berry under this cliff is at least as forward as any gooseberry. I find a new plant, now six or eight inches high, and which will blossom in two or three days, the *Arabis lævigata* (?).[2] The columbine is well budded. Some alders are still handsome. Here is a *common* one, — very handsome drooping clusters of three, four, or five reddish-brown and greenish-yellow catkins, two to three inches long, with the small reddish female blossoms stretched over them. How the hazel catkins elongate themselves at last!

April 24. Monday. A. M. — Up railroad.

The river slightly risen again owing to rain of yesterday morn and day before. Its greatest height this year was the 17th of March. This is the next rise of any consequence. As I stand still listening on the frosty sleepers at Wood's crossing by the lupines, I hear the loud and distinct *pump-a-gor* of a stake-driver. Thus he announces himself. I find the shepherd's-purse open in Cheney's garden at last. It has run up eight or

[1] Was it *b* of the 18th? *Vide* April 25.   [2] *Vide* May 1st.

They are concealed in the empyrean. I think I have got the worth of my glass now that it has revealed to me the white-headed eagle. Now I see him edgewise like a black ripple in the air, his white head still as ever turned to earth, and now he turns his under side to me, and I behold the full breadth of his broad black wings, somewhat ragged at the edges. I had first seen two white ducks far off just above the outlet of the pond, mistaking them for the foaming crest of a wave. These flew soon, perhaps scared by the eagle. I think they were a male and female red-breasted merganser (though I did [not] see the red of the breast), for I saw his *red bill*, and his head was not large with a crest like the golden-eye; very white on breast and sides, the female browner.[1] As ducks often do, they first flew directly and unhesitatingly up the stream, low over the water, for half a mile, then turned and came down, flying thirty or forty feet above the water, the male leading till they were out of sight. This is the way with them, I notice; they first fly in one direction and then go off to alight in another. When they came down the river, the male leading, they were a very good example of the peculiar flight of ducks. They appeared perfectly in a line one behind the other. When they are not they preserve perfect parallelism. This is because of their long necks and feet, — the wings appearing to be attached midway, — and moreover, in this case, of their perfectly level flight, as if learned from skimming over the water. Directly after rose two blue herons from the meadow.

I find but one red maple fairly in blossom on a few

[1] Certainly mergansers, probably sheldrakes.

ten inches in some places, and *may* have been open a week; but say just after the snow, or the 19th. After a very mild winter, like that of '52 and '53, it will be one of the very earliest flowers, — say second, or next after the chickweed, — but last winter it was killed down by the cold. Yet it is hardier and more forward now than the chickweed, which is still dead and bleached. Saw a black blackbird without red, with a purplish-green-black neck, and somewhat less than a red-wing, in company with two smaller slaty-black females (?). Can they be rusty grackles?[1]

P. M. — Up Assabet, and thence to Cedar Swamp.

The larch will apparently blossom in [one] or two days at least, both its low and broad purple-coned male flowers and its purple-tipped female cones.[2] Its little leaf-bundles are beginning to burst. Heard amid the white cedars the fine, clear singing warbler of yesterday, whose harsh note I *may* have heard the 18th, — *twer er te te, twer er te te, twer er te te tèr*, but very clear and fast. Go to new trees, like cedars and firs, and you hear new birds. They increase the strangeness. Also other strange plants are found there. I have also observed that the early birds are about the early trees, like maples, alders, willows, elms, etc.

The white cedar female blossoms are open, and as the brown male ones are loosened the next day in the house, I think the 25th may be called their first day. I find a raspberry (thickly clothed with bristles) in this swamp, as early as the thimble-berry. This, then,

[1] *Vide* May 9th.   [2] *Vide* May 1st.

might be put after the gooseberry among native plants, because this is not so much indebted to a favorable position, — the gooseberry not at all, — growing in a sheltered, *i. e.* covered, swamp. New plant [1] flower-budded at Cedar Swamp amid the high blueberry, panicled andromeda, clethra, etc., etc., — upright dense racemes of reddish flower-buds on reddish terminal shoots.

Saw a large thin whitish fungus or spunk, fourteen and three quarters inches by eight and a half from the tree and two or three thick, with concentric growths of various thickness, within a foot of the ground on a maple stump. There was a grape-vine and some other small plants grown directly through, which it had apparently grown round. The first red maple blossoms — so very red over the water — are very interesting. Saw a very *large* hawk, slaty above and white beneath, low over river. Was it not a goshawk? The king-fisher flies with a *crack cr-r-r-ack* and a limping or flit-ting flight from tree to tree before us, and finally, after a third of a mile, circles round to our rear. He sits rather low over the water. Now that he has come I suppose that the fishes on which he preys rise within reach. Are not they bank swallows [2] sailing so thick over the river, now at 5.30 P. M.?

April 25. A. M. — I think I hear near George Hey-wood's the *tull-lull* (?).[3] Heard and saw my war-bler (?) *b'* [4] of the 23d and 24th on Mr. Emerson's

[1] Racemed andromeda. [2] [Barn swallows.] *Vide* 29th.
[3] Yes. [4] *Vide* [p. 220].

pines. It is the smallest bird I have seen this year. Sits still amid the pines not far below the top and sings very sweetly, loud and clear, and seems further off than it is, beginning first with very *fine* wiry notes and then increasing in volume and melody till it ends with *tweeter tweeter tweeter ter twe.* Some of it a martin-like warble. Has sometimes a harsh scold-ing note. It is all light, perhaps ashy-white, beneath; has a little narrow forked tail; ashy (?) under wings, which are considerably shorter than tail; and light above and below eye; perhaps a whitish bar on wings; olivaceous (?) above. I think it may be the *golden-crested wren,* though I hardly saw the upper parts, or *possibly* the small blue-gray flycatcher. I do not find the *male* blossoms of the red cedar open yet.

P. M. — To Indian Cedar Hill.

Quite warm and the frogs are snoring on the meadow. I swelter under my greatcoat. The *Populus grandi-dentata* is fairly begun; say very first the 23d. Many shad-flies in the air and alighting on my clothes. The summer approaches by almost insensibly increasing *lieferungs* of heat, each awakening some new bird or quadruped or reptile. At first we were compelled to take off our mittens, then to unbutton our greatcoat, and now, perhaps, to take it off occasionally (I have not left it at home yet), and wear thin boots. For some time we have done with little fire, nowadays let it go out in the afternoon. (To-day, 26th, I sit without any.) Each creature awaits with confidence its proper degree of heat. I think I saw a pigeon

Vol. VI

yesterday. G. Minott says that he saw some a week ago.

Saw a golden-crested wren [1] in the woods near Goose Pond. (This must be my warblers *a* and *b* of April 18th, *b'* of April 23d and 24th.) It sounded far off and like an imitation of a robin,[2] — a long strain and often repeated. I was quite near it before I was aware of it, it sounding still like a faint imitation of a robin. Some chickadees and yellow redpolls were first ap-parent, then my wren on the pitch pines and young oaks. He appeared curious to observe me. A very interesting and active little fellow, darting about amid the tree-tops, and his song quite remarkable and rich and loud for his size. Begins with a very fine note, before its pipes are filled, not audible at a little dis-tance, then *woriter weter,* etc., etc., winding up with *teter teter,* all clear and round.[3] This was at 4 P. M., when most birds do not sing. I saw it yesterday, plum-ing itself and stretching its little wings. Our smallest bird, methinks, except the hummingbird. The snuff-colored, white-spotted wren I saw some time ago was considerably larger.

Just before this saw on the low bushes, — shrub oaks, etc., — by path, a large sparrow with ferruginous-brown and white-barred wings, — the white-throated sparrow, — uttered a faint ringing chirp. The first partridge drums in one or two places, as if the earth's pulse now beat audibly with the increased flow of life.

[1] ["Golden" crossed out in pencil and "ruby" substituted.]
[2] And of a golden robin, which later I often mistook for him.
[3] His song is comical and reminds me of the thrasher.

It slightly flutters all Nature and makes her heart palpitate. Also, as I stand listening for the wren, and sweltering in my greatcoat, I hear the woods filled with the hum of insects, as if my hearing were affected; and thus the summer's quire begins. The silent spaces have begun to be filled with notes of birds and insects and the peep and croak and snore of frogs, even as living green blades are everywhere pushing up amid the sere ones. I heard that same snoring which I hear on the river meadows, on an inland meadow this afternoon, where I think no bullfrogs are. Are they not then the *palustris,* or else the shad frog? There are now many new insects in the air. Black ducks still on Flint's. The fertile fruit-stems of the sen-sitive fern by the side of the Flint's Pond path, more than a foot high, are a rich ornament to the ground, — brown, four or five inches long, and turned to one side, contrasting with the lighter rachis (?). Saw my thrush of the 18th by the pond. It appears dark-olive, ferruginous on rump and tail, with a dark streak slanting from each cheek and flesh-colored legs. The red cedar has fairly begun to-day; maybe the first yesterday. Put the red yesterday and the white to-day. As I approach the red cedars now, I perceive a deli-cious strawberry-like fragrance in the air, like that from the arbor-vitæ. The creeping juniper apparently open, but not yet open. Though I see some amber on the sweet-fern, I am in doubt whether to say to-day or to-morrow. The wild red cherry (if that is one near Everett's), privet, and buckthorn are *beginning* to leaf out. The abele will probably blossom to-morrow.

April 26. Heard at 8 A. M. the peculiar loud and distinct ring of the first toad, at a distance. April-morning weather, threatening showeriness.

2.30 P. M. — To Lee's Cliff on foot.

A still, warm, overcast day with a southwest wind (this is what the Indians made so much of), and the finest possible dew-like rain in the air from time to time, now more of the sun. It is now so warm that I go back to leave my greatcoat for the first time, and the cooler smell of possible rain is refreshing. The toads ring more or less.

> When the toads begin to ring,
> Then thinner clothing bring,
> Or off your greatcoat fling.

It is not yet time for thin clothes. Did I hear a tree-toad to-day? As I go over Hubbard's land I see A. Wheeler burning brush, clearing up, on Fair Haven. Great volumes or clouds of white smoke are blown gently northeastward, while the bright-scarlet flame is seen here and there creeping along its edge. They begin to burn on the lee side. The farmers are now busily plowing, *some* setting out roots and planting. I seem to perceive a slight fragrance in the air.

Found part of a bird's head and bill, — I think that of the thrush I saw on the 18th and yesterday. The bill (with notch) and what part of the head is left are exactly like the hermit thrush in F. Brown's collection, except that mine is yellow inside bill (but his has probably faded); and I see that the latter's legs, which W. calls dusky, are light enough for my bird, and the colors above — olivaceous, and foxy rump

and tail — are the same, but the hermit thrush's spots on breast appear darker. I think I have seen or heard of more dead birds than usual this season, — read of bluebirds, heard of a martin (both killed by cold), also seen a dead robin or two and this thrush.

The woods are full of myrtle-birds this afternoon, more common and commonly heard than any, especially along the edge of woods on oaks, etc., — their note an oft-repeated fine jingle, *a che' che, che' che, che' che,* or a *tweedle tweedle tweedle tweedle-twe.* As I heard the *tull lull* from the same quarter from time to time, I think it came from it. Perhaps it may be written, *a tea le, tea le, tea le.* These small birds — and all small birds — seen against the sky at a little distance look black. There is not breadth enough to their colors to make any impression; they are mere motes, intercepting the light, the substance of a shadow.

Birds sing all day when it is warm, still, and overcast as now, much more than in clear weather, and the hyla too is heard, as at evening. The hylodes commonly begins early in the afternoon, and its quire increases till evening. I hear now snipes far over the meadow incessantly at 3.15 P. M. The men bogging in the meadow do not hear them, and much else.

The swamp sparrow, very dark, with chestnut and black, and quirk of the tail, flits shyly under the alders along the causeway; hides or lurks behind the trunks like song sparrow and hardly rests a moment in one place.

The lark on the top of an apple tree sings *a tchea te*

che, then perhaps *tche tchea,* only a plaintive clear round note. Hear the first chewink hopping and chewinking among the shrub oaks.

To-day the air is full of birds; they attend the opening of the buds. The trees *begin* to leaf, and the leaf-like wings of birds are in the air. The buds start, then the insects, then the birds. Saw probably a pigeon hawk skim straight and low over field and wood, and another the next day apparently dark slate-color. It is warm and still, almost sultry, as if there might be a thunder-shower before night. Now look down on Fair Haven. How pleasant in spring a still, overcast, warm day like this, when the water is smooth! The sweet-gale in blossom, forming islets surrounded by water, on the meadow, looks like sere brown leaves left on. At the Cliff the *Arabis lævigata* [1] is just out to-day; the honeysuckle will be, say, the very earliest, to-morrow. [2] A barberry bush quite forwardly leafing under the rock, and a young apple. The early gooseberry quite green.

9 P. M. — Quite a heavy thunder-shower, — the second lightning, I think.

The vivid lightning, as I walk the street, reveals the contrast between day and night. The rising cloud in the west makes it very dark and difficult to find my way, when there comes a flash which lights up the street for a moment almost as brightly as the day, far more so than moonlight, and I see a person on the sidewalk before me fifty rods off.

[1] Probably *T. stricta.*   [2] *Vide* May 1st.

April 27. 7 A. M. — To Cliffs.

Equisetum arvense on the railroad; and may have been two or three days — did not look. I am at length convinced of the increased freshness (green or yellow) of the willow bark in the spring. Some a clear yellow, others a delightful liquid green. The bark peels well now; how long? The rain of last night is helping to bring down the oak leaves. The wood thrush afar, — so superior a strain to that of other birds. I was doubting if it would affect me as of yore, but it did measurably. I did not believe there could be such differences. This is the gospel according to the wood thrush. He makes a sabbath out of a week-day. I could go to hear him, could buy a pew in his church. Did he ever practice pulpit eloquence? He is right on the slavery question. The brown thrasher, too, is along. I find a thread-like stamen now between the nutlets of the callitriche — probably three or four days. Some creature appears to have eaten this plant. The yellow redpolls still numerous; sing *chill lill lill lill lill lill.* The meadow-sweet and sweet-fern are *beginning* to leaf, and the currant in garden.

Stood on Cliffs about 7 A. M. Through a warm mistiness I see the waters with their reflections in the morning sun, while the wood thrush and huckleberry-bird, etc., are heard, — an unprofaned hour. I hear the black and white creeper's note, — *seeser seeser seeser se.* [1] What a shy fellow my hermit thrush! [2] I hear the

[1] *Vide* May 1st.
[2] [Probably it was the hermit thrush, not the wood thrush, for which the date is too early, whose song he had been praising.]

beat of a partridge and the spring hoot of an owl, now at 7 A. M. Hear a faint sort of oven-bird's (?) note.

It is only the irresolute and idle who have no leisure for their proper pursuit. Be preoccupied with this, devoted to it, and no accident can befall you, no idle engagements distract you. No man ever had the opportunity to postpone a high calling to a disagreeable *duty*. Misfortunes occur only when a man is false to his Genius. You cannot hear music and noise at the same time. We avoid all the calamities that may occur in a lower sphere by abiding perpetually in a higher. Most men are engaged in business the greater part of their lives, because the soul abhors a vacuum, and they have not discovered any continuous employment for man's nobler faculties. Accordingly they do not pine, because they are not greatly disappointed. A little relaxation in your exertion, a little idleness, will let in sickness and death into your own body, or your family and their attendant duties and distractions. Every human being is the artificer of his own fate in these respects. The well have no time to be sick. Events, circumstances, etc., have their origin in ourselves. They spring from seeds which we have sown. Though I may call it a European War, it is only a phase or trait in my biography that I wot of. The most foreign scrap of news which the journals report to me — from Turkey or Japan — is but a hue of my inmost thought.

Forbes says that the guides who crossed the Alps with him lost the skin of their faces, — apparently from the reflection from the snow.

It is remarkable that the rise and fall of Walden,

though unsteady, and whether periodical or merely occasional, are not completed but after many years. I have observed one rise and part of two falls. It attains its maximum slowly and surely, though unsteadily. It is remarkable that this fluctuation, whether periodical or not, requires many years for its accomplishment, and I expect that a dozen or fifteen years hence it will again be as low as I have ever known it.[1]

The *Salix alba* begins to leaf, and the catkins are three quarters of an inch long. The balm-of-Gilead is in bloom, about one and a half or two inches long, and some hang down straight. Quite warm to-day. In the afternoon the wind changed to east, and apparently the cool air from the sea condensed the vapor in our atmosphere, making us think it would rain every moment; but it did not till midnight.

April 28. 6 A. M. — Dug up two of half a dozen, the only black spruce suitable to transplant that I know hereabouts.

Rain all day, making the grass look green.

Nawshawtuct now in the rain looks about as green as a Roxbury russet; *i. e.*, the russet is yielding to the green. Perhaps the greenness of the landscape may be said to begin fairly now. For the last half of this month, indeed, a tinge of green has been discernible on the sides of hills. Saw yesterday some cows turned out to pasture on such a hillside; thought they would soon eat up all the grass. This is coincident, then, with the leafing of the gooseberry, or earliest native shrub.

[1] [*Walden*, p. 201; Riv. 283, 284.]

Vol. VI

First, you may say, is the starting of a few radical leaves, etc., and grass blades in favorable localities, and the blossoming of the earliest trees and herbs.

Secondly, during the last half of April the earth acquires a distinct tinge of green, which finally prevails over the russet.

Third. Then begins the leafing of the earliest shrubs and trees and the decided greenness and floweriness of the earth, in May.

Fourth. Then the decided leafiness in June and the first great crop of the year, the leaf or grass crop.

April 29. The ideal of a market is a place where all things are bought and sold. At an agricultural meeting in New York the other day, one said that he had lately heard a man inquiring for spurry seed; he wanted it to sow on drifting sand. His presumption had been that if he wanted it; *i. e.*, if there was a demand, there was a supply to satisfy that demand. He went simply to the shop instead of going to the weed itself. But the supply does not anticipate the demand.

This is the second day of rain, and the river has risen about as high as any time this year.

P M. — To Cliffs by boat in the misty rain.

The barn swallows are very numerous, flying low over the water in the rain. I think that those which I saw on the 24th were barn and not bank swallows. What an entertainment this river affords! It is subject to so great overflows, owing to its broad intervals, that a day's rain produces a new landscape. Let it rain *heavily* one whole day, and the river will be in-

creased from half a dozen rods in width to nearly a mile in some places, and, where I walked dry-shod yesterday a-maying, I sail with a smacking breeze to-day, and fancy that I am a sailor on the ocean. It is an advantage which all towns do not possess. Off the Cliffs, I met a blue heron flying slowly downstream. He flaps slowly and heavily, his long, level, straight and sharp bill projecting forward, then his keel-like neck doubled up, and finally his legs thrust out straight behind. His wings, as I looked after him, presented this outline: He alighted on a rock, and stood erect awhile.

I am surprised to find a few andromedas out, just behind the alders at the oak on Cardinal Shore. Possibly yesterday the very first, though it rained. At last I find one houstonia just out there.

The mouse-ear is now fairly in blossom in many places. It never looks so pretty as now in an April rain, covered with pearly drops. Its corymbs of five heads with one in the centre (all tinged red) look like a breast-pin set with pearls.

J. Farmer says that this rain will kill many caterpillars just hatched.

As nearly as I can remember and judge, plants were *generally* out at the following dates: —

White maple	April 7	Hazels	April 12
Alders	8	*Populus tremuloides*	14
Skunk-cabbage	9	Crowfoot	13
Sedge	11	Saxifrage	13
Earliest willows fairly begun		Slippery elm	22
(not common till April 20)	12	Common elm	12

Cowslip	April 24	Red cedar	April 26
Sweet-gale	23	White [cedar]	27 (?)
Salix humilis	23	*Populus grandidentata*	26
Red maple	26	Field horse-tail	28
Larch	28 (?)	Mouse-ear	29

VI

MAY, 1854

(ÆT. 36)

May 1. A fine, clear morning after three days of rain, — our principal rain-storm this year, — raising the river higher than it has been yet.

6 A. M. — Up railroad.

Everything looks bright and as if it were washed clean. The red maples, now fully in bloom, show red tops at a distance. Is that a black cherry so forward in the cow-killer? When I first found the saxifrage open, I observed that its leaves had been eaten considerably.

9 A. M. — To Cliffs and thence by boat to Fair Haven.

I see the scrolls of the ferns just pushed up, but yet wholly invested with wool. The sweet-fern has not yet blossomed; its anthers are green and close, but its leaves, just beginning to expand, are covered with high-scented, amber-like dots. Alder leaves begin to expand in favorable places. The viburnum (*Lentago* or *nudum*) leaves unexpectedly forward at the Cliff Brook and about Miles Swamp. I am not sure that I distinguish the *nudum* now, but suspect the other to be most forward. Snakes are now common on warm

banks. At Lee's Cliff find the early cinquefoil. I think that the columbine cannot be said to have blossomed there before to-day, — the very earliest. A choke-cherry is very strongly flower-budded and considerably leaved out there. The early rose is beginning to leaf out. At Miles Swamp, benzoin will apparently open to-morrow, before any leaves begin. The creeping juniper appears to be now just in bloom. I see only the female flower.

I sail back with a fair southwest wind. The water is strewn with myriads of wrecked shad-flies, erect on the surface, with their wings up like so many schooners all headed one way. What an abundance of food they must afford to the fishes! Now and then they try to fly, and fall on the water again. They apparently reach from one end of the river to the other, one to a square yard or two. The scleranthus is out and a tuft of that brownish-flowered kind of sedge.

P. M. — Up Assabet by boat to Cedar Swamp.

The earliest shrubs and trees to leaf have been thus far in this order: The earliest gooseberry (in garden and swamp), raspberries, thimble-berry (perhaps in favorable places only), wild red cherry (if that is one near Everett's),[1] meadow-sweet, (red currant and second gooseberry, I think, here), sweet-fern (but is *very* slow to go forward), *S. alba* (April 27), and also a small dark native willow, young black cherry (if that is one in the cow-catcher, and others are as forward), choke-cherry, young shoots, viburnum (am not sure if

[1] *Vide* May 5. It is.

Lentago is earlier than *nudum*; as both are leafing, put the *Lentago* first and *nudum* next), diervilla (if that light-stemmed plant on Island is it),[1] barberry (perhaps in favorable places only), and some young apples in like places, alders (in favorable places), early rose.

Saw two black ducks. Have seen no *F. hyemalis* for five or six days. Hear a golden-crested wren at Cedar Swamp. I think that I may have mistaken the note of the myrtle-bird for that of the creeper the other morning. A peetweet, and *methinks* I have heard it a day or two.

I have seen Goodwin and Haynes all day hunting muskrats and ducks, stealthily paddling along the riverside or by the willows and button-bushes, now the river is so high, and shooting any rat that may expose himself. In one instance a rat they had wounded looked exactly like the end of an old rider stripped of bark, as it lay just on the surface close to the shore within a few feet of them. Haynes would not at first believe it a muskrat only six or eight feet off, and the dog could not find it. How pitiful a man looks about this sport! Haynes reminded me of the Penobscots.

Early starlight by riverside.

The water smooth and broad. I hear the loud and incessant cackling of probably a pigeon woodpecker, — what some time since I thought to be a different kind. Thousands of robins are filling the air with their trills, mingling with the peeping of hylodes and ringing of frogs [*sic*]; and now the snipes have just begun

[1] *Vide* May 5.

their winnowing sounds and squeaks, and I hear Barrett's sawmill beside; and whenever a gun fires, Wheeler's peacock screams.

The flowers of the larch which I examined on the 24th *ult.* have enlarged somewhat and may now certainly be considered in blossom, *though the pollen is not quite distinct.* I am not certain whether the 26th was not too early. The crimson scales of the female cones are still more conspicuous.

May 2. The cracks in the ground made by the frost last winter are still quite distinct.

It is the young black cherry which is so forward now.

May 3. P. M. — In rain to Nawshawtuct.

The river rising still. What I have called the small pewee on the willow by my boat, — quite small, uttering a short *tchevet* from time to time. Some common cherries are quite forward in leafing; say next after the black. The *Pyrus arbutifolia,* of plants I observed, would follow the cherry in leafing. It just begins to show *minute* glossy leaves. The meadow-sweet begins to look fairly green, with its little tender green leaves, making thin wreaths of green against the bare stems of other plants (this and the gooseberry), — the next plant in this respect to the earliest gooseberry in the garden, which appears to be the same with that in the swamp. I see wood turtles which appear to be full and hard with eggs. Yesterday I counted half a dozen dead yellow-spotted turtles about Beck Stow's. There

is a small dark native willow in the meadows as early to leaf as the *S. alba,* with young catkins. *Anemone nemorosa* near the ferns and the sassafras appeared yesterday. The ferns invested with rusty wool (*cinnamomea?*) have pushed up eight or ten inches and show some of the green leaf.

May 5. P. M. — To Boiling Spring, Laurel Glen, and Hubbard's Close.

I observe the following plants, leafing in about this order, to be added to the list of May 1st: —

Elder has made shoots two or three inches long, — much more than any other shrub or tree, — but is not common enough to show. Possibly it should rank with or next to the gooseberry.

Mountain-ash, larger leaves now than any tree, and the first tree to show green at a little distance.

Cultivated cherry.

Pyrus arbutifolia.

Horse-chestnut.

Hazel just passing from buds to leaves.

Late gooseberry in gardens.

Early apples.

Probably pears.

Wild red cherry in woods.

Dwarf or sand cherry.

Hardhack.

Diervilla near Laurel Glen (comes on fast after this).[1]

Low blackberry.

Some young red maple buds begin to expand.

Against the wall in front of young Farrar's house a scroll-shaped slender fern now three inches high; stem invested with narrow shining brown scales one third

[1] May 11, is *one* of the most forward of all.

Vol. VI

of an inch long. The *Salix tristis* now out (not out May 1st), appeared the 3d. The same of the sweetfern. The red maple keys are now about three quarters of an inch long (with stems). I see no leaves on black, red, or shrub oaks now, — their buds expanding and showing a green or yellowish point, — but they still hang on the white oak.

May 3d and 4th, it rained again, — especially hard the night of the 4th, — and the river is now very high, far higher than in any other freshet this year; will reach its height probably to-morrow.

Heard what I should call the twitter and mew of a goldfinch [1] and saw the bird go over with ricochet flight. The oak leaves apparently hang on till the buds fairly expand. *Thalictrum anemonoides* by Brister's Spring on hillside. Some skunk-cabbage leaves are now eight or nine inches wide near there. These and the hellebore make far the greatest show of any herbs yet. The peculiarly beautiful clean and tender green of the grass there! Green herbs of all kinds, — tansy, buttercups, etc., etc., etc., now make more or less show. Put this with the grassy season's beginning. Have not observed a tree sparrow for four or five days. The Emerson children found blue and white violets May 1st at Hubbard's Close, probably *Viola ovata* and *blanda;* but I have not been able to find any yet. *Salix alba.*

May 6. P. M. — To epigæa *via* Clamshell Hill.

There is no such thing as pure *objective* observation.

[1] Yes, and for several days after.

Your observation, to be interesting, *i. e.* to be significant, must be *subjective.* The sum of what the writer of whatever class has to report is simply some human experience, whether he be poet or philosopher or man of science. The man of most science is the man most alive, whose life is the greatest event. Senses that take cognizance of outward things merely are of no avail. It matters not where or how far you travel, — the farther commonly the worse, — but how much alive you are. If it is possible to conceive of an event outside to humanity, it is not of the slightest significance, though it were the explosion of a planet. Every important worker will report what life there is in him. It makes no odds into what seeming deserts the poet is born. Though all his neighbors pronounce it a Sahara, it will be a paradise to him; for the desert which we see is the result of the barrenness of our experience. No mere willful activity whatever, whether in writing verses or collecting statistics, will produce true poetry or science. If you are really a sick man, it is indeed to be regretted, for you cannot accomplish so much as if you were well. All that a man has to say or do that can possibly concern mankind, is in some shape or other to tell the story of his love, — to sing; and, if he is fortunate and keeps alive, he will be forever in love. This alone is to be alive to the extremities. It is a pity that this divine creature should ever suffer from cold feet; a still greater pity that the coldness so often reaches to his heart. I look over the report of the doings of a scientific association and am surprised that there is so little life to be reported; I am put off with a parcel of dry technical terms. Anything living is easily and naturally expressed in popular language. I cannot help suspecting that the life of these learned professors has been almost as inhuman and wooden as a rain-gauge or self-registering magnetic machine. They communicate no fact which rises to the temperature of blood-heat. It does n't all amount to one rhyme.

The ducks appear to be gone (though the water is higher than any time since that greatest of all rises, I think, — reached its height yesterday; the arches are quite concealed), swept by with the spring snow and ice and wind, though to-day it has spit a little snow and is *very* windy (northwest) and cold enough for gloves. Is not that the true spring when the *F. hyemalis* and tree sparrows are with us singing in the cold mornings with the song sparrows, and ducks and gulls are about? The *Viola ovata* this end of Clamshell Hill, perhaps a day or two; let it go, then, May 1st; also dandelions, perhaps the first, yesterday. This flower makes a great show, — a sun itself in the grass. How emphatic it is! You cannot but observe it set in the liquid green grass even at a distance. I am surprised that the sight of it does not affect me more, but I look at it as unmoved as if but a day had elapsed since I saw it in the fall. As I remember, the most obvious and startling flowers as yet have been the crowfoot, cowslip, and dandelion, so much of a high color against the russet or green. We do not realize yet so high and brilliant a flower as the red lily or arethusa. Horse-mint is an inch or two high, and it

[is] refreshing to scent it again. The *Equisetum sylvaticum* has just bloomed against Hosmer's gap.

It is the young shoots of the choke-cherry which are the more forward, — those which are not blossom-budded, — and this is the case with most trees and shrubs. These are growing while the older are blossoming. Female flower of sweet-gale how long? At Ministerial Swamp, the anthers of the larch appear now effete. I am surprised to find a larch whose female cones are pure white (not rose or crimson). The bundles of larch leaves are now fairly separating. Meadow saxifrage just out at Second Division. The cowslip now makes a show there, though not elsewhere, and not there as much as it will. There is a large and dense field of a small rush there, already a foot high, whose old and dead tops look like blossoms at a distance. The mayflower is in perfection. It has probably been out more than a week.

Returned over the hill back of J. P. Brown's. Was surprised at the appearance of the flood. Seen now from the same side with the westering sun, it looks like a dark-blue liquid like indigo poured in amid the hills, with great bays making up between them, flooding the causeways and over the channel of each tributary brook, — another Musketaquid making far inland. I see in the distance the light, feathery willow rows [?] on the causeway, stretching across it, the trees just blooming and coming into leaf, and isolated red-topped maples standing far in the midst of the flood. This dark-blue water is the more interesting because it is not a permanent feature in the landscape.

Those white froth lines conform to the direction of the wind and are from four to seven or eight feet apart.

Remembering my voyage of May 1st, and Goodwin and Haynes hunting, you might have passed up and down the river three or four miles and yet not have seen one muskrat, yet they killed six at least. One in stern paddling slowly along, while the other sat with his gun ready cocked and the dog erect in the prow, all eyes constantly scanning the surface amid the button-bushes and willows, for the rats are not easy to distinguish from a bunch of dried grass or a stick. Suddenly one is seen resting on his perch, and crack goes the gun, and over the dog instantly goes to fetch him. These men represent a class which probably always exists, even in the most civilized community, and allies it to the most savage. Goodwin said in the morning that he was laying stone, but it was so muddy on account of the rain that he told Haynes he would like to take a cruise out.

May 7. I have noticed the steel-colored, velvet-like lichen on the stumps of maples especially, also on oaks and hickories. Sometimes, where a maple grove has been cut down some years, every stump will be densely clothed with them.

Our principal rain this spring was April 28th, 29th, and 30th, and again, May 3d and 4th, apparently the settling storm of the season. The great source of freshets far and wide. I observed the swallows yesterday, — barn swallows and some of those white-bellied with grayish-brown backs, — flying close to the surface

of the water near the edge of the flooded meadow. Probably they follow their insect prey.

P. M. — To Cliffs.

The causeways being flooded, I have to think before I set out on my walk how I shall get back across the river.

The earliest flowers might be called May-day flowers, — if indeed the sedge is not too far gone for one then. A white-throated sparrow still (in woods). *Viburnum Lentago* and *nudum* are both leafing, and I believe I can only put the former first because it flowers first. Cress at the Boiling Spring, one flower. As I ascend Cliff Hill, the two leaves of the Solomon's-seal now spot the forest floor, pushed up amid the dry leaves. *Vaccinium Pennsylvanicum* leafing. Flowers, *e. g.* willow and hazel catkins, are self-registering indicators of *fair* weather. I remember how I waited for the hazel catkins to become relaxed and shed their pollen, but they delayed, till at last there came a pleasanter and warmer day and I took off my greatcoat while surveying in the woods, and then, when I went to dinner at noon, hazel catkins in full flower were dangling from the banks by the roadside and yellowed my clothes with their pollen. If man is thankful for the serene and warm day, much more are the flowers.

From the Cliffs I again admire the flood, — the now green hills rising out of it. It is dark-blue, clay, slate, and light-blue, as you stand with regard to the sun. With the sun high on one side it is a dirty or clayey slate; directly in front, covered with silvery sparkles far to the right or north, dark-blue; farther to the southwest, light-blue. My eyes are attracted to the level line where the water meets the hills now, in time of flood, converting that place into a virgin or temporary shore. There is no strand, — nothing worn; but if it is calm we fancy the water slightly heaped above this line, as when it is poured gently into a goblet. (How in the spring we value any smoothness, gentleness, warmth!) It does not beat, but simply laves the hills (already the peetweet flutters and teeters along it a flight further back), submerging the blossoming flowers which I went to find. I see the sweet-gale deeply buried, and the *V. blanda*, etc., etc., and the *A. calyculata* and the cowslips. I see their deluged faces at the bottom and their wrecked petals afloat. I paddle right over Miles's meadow, where the bottom is covered with cowslips in full bloom; their lustre dimmed, they look up with tearful faces. Little promontories at Lee's Cliff, clothed with young pines, make into the water; yet they are rarely submerged; as if nature or the trees remembered even the highest floods and kept out of their way, avoiding the shore, leaving a certain neutral ground. Early strawberry just out. I found an *Amelanchier Botryapium*, with its tender reddish-green leaves already fluttering in the wind and stipules clothed with white silky hairs, and its blossom so far advanced that I thought it would open to-morrow. But a little farther there was another which did not rise above the rock, but caught all the reflected heat, which to my surprise was fully open; yet a part which did rise above the rock was not open. What indicators of warmth! No thermometer could show it better. The *Amelan-*

chier Botryapium leaves begin now to expand. The juniper branches are now tipped with yellowish and expanding leaf-buds; put it just before the larch. I begin to see cows turned out to pasture. I am inclined to think some of these are coarse, windy days, when I cannot hear any bird.

What are those small ferns under the eaves of the rocks at the Cliffs, their little balls unrolling as they ascend, now three or four inches high? How many plants have these crimson or red stigmas? Maples, hazels, sweet-gale, sweet-fern. High blackberry leafing. The leaves are now off the young oaks and shrub oaks on the plain below the Cliffs, except the white oaks, which leaf later. I noticed it elsewhere, — first May 5th, when — or a day or two before perhaps — they suddenly cast off their winter clothing; and the plain now appears thinly covered with gray stems, but in a short month they will have put on a new green coat. They wear their leaves almost all the year. The partridge and rabbit must do without their shelter now a little while. A ruby-crested wren by the Cliff Brook, — a chubby little bird. Saw its ruby crest and heard its harsh note.[1] The birds I have described as such were the same. Hellebore is the most noticeable herb now. Alders, young maples of all kinds, and ostrya, etc., now beginning to leaf. I observe the phenomena of the seashore by our riverside, now that there

[1] This was the same I have called golden-crowned; and so described by W[ilson], I should say, except that I saw its ruby crest. I did n't see the crest of the golden-crowned, and I did not hear this ruby-c. sing like the former. Have I seen the two?

Vol. VI

is quite a sea on it and the meadow, though the waves are but eight inches or a foot high. As on the sea beach, the waves are not equally high and do not break with an equally loud roar on the shore; there is an interval of four or five or half a dozen waves between the larger ones. In the middle of the meadow, where the waves run highest, only the middle and highest parts of the waves are whitened with foam, where they are thinnest and yield to the wind apparently, while their broad bases are detained by union with the water; but next the shore, where their bases are much more detained by friction on the bottom, their tops for their whole length curve over very regularly like a snow-drift, and the water is evenly poured as over a dam and falls with foam and a roar on the water and shore. It is exhilarating to stoop low and look over the rolling waves northwest. The black rolling waves remind me of the backs of waves [*sic*; = whales?]. It is remarkable how cleanly the water deposits its wreck, now spotted with cranberries. There is a bare space of clean grass, perfectly clean and about a foot wide, now left between the utmost edge of the breakers and the steep and abrupt edge of the wreck. So much it has gone down. Thus perfectly the water deposits what floats on it on the land. The oak buds — black, shrub, etc., except white oak — are now conspicuously swollen. A spreading red maple in bloom, seen against a favorable background, as water looking down from a hillside, is a very handsome object, presenting not a dense mass of color but an open, graceful and ethereal top of light crimson or scarlet, not too obvious and staring, slightly

tingeing the landscape as becomes the season, — a veil of rich workmanship and high color against the sky, or water, [or] other trees.

At sunset across the flooded meadow to Nawshawtuct. The water becoming calm. The sun is just disappearing as I reach the hilltop, and the horizon's edge appears with beautiful distinctness. As the twilight approaches or deepens, the mountains, those pillars which point the way to heaven, assume a deeper blue. As yet the aspect of the forest at a distance is not changed from its winter appearance, except where the maple-tops in blossom in low lands tinge it red. And the elm-tops are in fruit in the streets; and is there not [a] general but slight reddish tinge from expanding buds? Scared up ducks of some kind.

May 8. A. M. — To Nawshawtuct.

A female red-wing. I have not seen any before. Hear a yellowbird in the direction of the willows. Its note coarsely represented by *che-che-che-char-char-char*. No *great* flocks of blackbirds on tree-tops now, nor so many of robins. Saw a small hawk flying low, about size of a robin — tail with black bars — probably a sparrow hawk; probably the same I have seen before. Saw one at Boston next day; mine was the pigeon hawk,[1] slaty above (the male) and *coarsely* barred with black on tail. I saw these distinct bars at a distance as mine flew. It appeared hardly larger than a robin. Probably this the only hawk of this size that I

[1] No; for that is barred with white. Could mine have been the *F. fuscus* and so small?

have seen this season. The sparrow hawk is a rather reddish brown and *finely* and thickly barred above with black.[1] Missouri currant. I hear the voices of farmers driving their cows past to their up-country pastures now. The first of any consequence go by now.

P. M. — By boat to Fair Haven.

The water has fallen a foot or more, but I cannot get under the stone bridge, so haul over the road. There is a fair and strong wind with which to sail up-stream, and then I can leave my boat, depending on the wind changing to southwest soon. It is long since I have sailed on so broad a tide. How dead would the globe seem, especially at this season, if it were not for these water surfaces! We are slow to realize water, — the beauty and magic of it. It is interestingly strange to us forever. Immortal water, alive even in the superficies, restlessly heaving now and tossing me and my boat, and sparkling with life! I look round with a thrill on this bright fluctuating surface on which no man can walk, whereon is no trace of footstep, unstained as glass. When I got off this end of the Hollowell place I found myself in quite a sea with a smacking wind directly aft. I felt no little exhila-ration, mingled with a slight awe, as I drove before this strong wind over the great black-backed waves I judged to be at least twenty inches or two feet high, cutting through them, and heard their surging and felt them toss me. I was even obliged to head across them and not get into their troughs, for then I could

[1] Could the Boston pigeon hawk have been barred with black?

Vol. VI

sounded like the breakers on the seashore heard from *terra firma*.

Lee's Cliff is now a perfect natural rockery for flowers. These gray cliffs and scattered rocks, with upright faces below, reflect the heat like a hothouse. The ground is whitened with the little white cymes of the saxifrage, now shot up to six or eight inches, and more flower-like dangling scarlet columbines are seen against the gray rocks, and here and there the earth is spotted with yellow crowfoots and a few early cinque-foils (not to mention houstonias, the now mostly effete sedge, the few *Viola ovata*, — whose deep violet is another kind of *flame*, as the crowfoot is yellow, — hanging their heads low in the sod, and the as yet inconspicuous veronica); while the early *Amelanchier Botryapium* overhangs the rocks and grows in the shelves, with its loose, open-flowered racemes, curv-ing downward, of narrow-petalled white flowers, red on the back and innocently cherry-scented, — as if it had drunk cherry-bounce and you smelled its breath. To which is to be added the scent of bruised catnep and the greenness produced by many other forward herbs, and all resounding with the hum of insects. And all this while flowers are rare elsewhere. It is as if you had taken a step suddenly a month forward, or had entered a greenhouse. The rummy scent of the different cherries is remarkable. The *Veronica serpyllifolia* out, say yesterday. Not observed unless looking for it, like an infant's hood, — its pretty little blue-veined face. *Cerastium viscosum*, apparently to-day first.

hardly keep my legs. They were crested with a dirty-white foam and were ten or twelve feet from crest to crest. They were so black, — as no sea I have seen, — large and powerful, and made such a roaring around me, that I could not but regard them as gambolling monsters of the deep. They were *melainai* — what is the Greek for waves? This is our black sea. You see a *perfectly black* mass about two feet high and perhaps four or five feet thick and of indefinite length, round-backed, or perhaps forming a sharp ridge with a dirty-white crest, tumbling like a whale unceasingly before you. Only one of the epithets which the poets have applied to the color of the sea will apply to this water, — *melaina*, μέλαινα θάλασσα. I was delighted to find that our usually peaceful river could toss me so. How much more exciting than to be planting potatoes with those men in the field! What a different world! The waves increased in height till [I] reached the bridge, the impulse of wind and waves increasing with the breadth of the sea. It is remarkable that it requires a very wide expanse to produce so great an undula-tion. The length of this meadow lake in the direction of the wind is about a mile, its breadth varying from a mile to a quarter of a mile, and the great commotion is toward the southerly end. Yet after passing the bridge I was surprised to find an almost smooth ex-panse as far as I could see, though the waves were about three inches high at fifty rods' distance. I lay awhile in that smooth water, and though I heard the waves lashing the other side of the causeway I could hardly realize what a sea I [had] just sailed through. It

At I returned I saw, in the Miles meadow, on the bottom, two painted tortoises fighting. Their sternums were not particularly depressed. The smaller had got firmly hold of the loose skin of the larger's neck with his jaws, and most of the time his head was held within the other's shell; but, though he thus had the "upper hand," he had the least command of himself and was on his edge. They were very moderate, — for the most part quite still, as if weary, — and were not to be scared by me. Then they struggled a lit-tle, their flippers merely paddling the water, and I could hear the edges of their shells strike together. I took them out into the boat, holding by the smaller, which did not let go of the larger, and so raising both together. Nor did he let go when they were laid in the boat. But when I put them into the water again they instantly separated and concealed themselves.

The hornbeam has lost its leaves; in this respect put it before the white oak and, for [the] present, after the other oaks, judging from buds. Fever-bush well out now.

May 9. Tuesday. To Boston and Cambridge.

Currant in garden, but ours may be a late kind. Purple finch still here.

Looking at the birds at the Natural History Rooms, I find that I have not seen the crow blackbird at all yet this season. Perhaps I have seen the rusty-black-bird, though I am not sure what those slaty-black ones are, as large as the red-wings, nor those pure-black fellows, unless rusty blackbirds. I think that my blackbirds of the morning of the 24th may have been cow-birds.

Sat on end of Long Wharf. Was surprised to observe that so many of the men on board the shipping were pure countrymen in dress and habits, and the seaport is no more than a country town to which they come a-trading. I found about the wharves, steering the coasters and unloading the ships, men in farmer's dress. As I watched the various craft successively unfurling their sails and getting to sea, I felt more than for many years inclined to let the wind blow me also to other climes.

Harris showed me a list of plants in *Hovey's Magazine* (I think for '42 or '43) not in Bigelow's Botany, — seventeen or eighteen of them, among the rest a pine I have not seen, etc., etc., *q. v.* That early narrow curved-winged insect on ice and river which I thought an ephemera he says is a *Sialis*, or maybe rather a *Perla*. Thinks it the *Donatia palmata* I gave him. Says the shad-flies (with streamers and erect wings) are ephemeræ. He spoke of *Podura nivalis*, I think meaning ours.

Planted melons.

May 10. Now in the mornings I hear the chip-bird under my windows at and before sunrise. Warbling vireo on the elms. The chimney swallow. A peach out in yard, where it had been covered by the snow. The cultivated cherry in bloom.

8 A. M. — To Tall's Island, taking boat at Cliffs.

Had some rain about daylight, which I think makes

the weather uncertain for the day. Damp, April-like mistiness in the air. I take an umbrella with me. The *Salix alba* — and also one or two small native ones by river of similar habits — their catkins together with their leaves make the greatest show now of any trees (which are indigenous or have fairly established themselves), though a *very few* scattered *young* trembles suddenly streak the hillsides with their tender green in some places; and perhaps *young* balm-of-Gileads show in some places;[1] but with the willows it is general and from their size and being massed together they are seen afar. The *S. alba*, partly, indeed, from its commonness and growing together, is the first of *field* trees whose growth makes an impression on the careless and distant observer, — a tender yellowish green. (The mountain-ash, horse-chestnut, and perhaps some other cultivated trees, indeed, if we regard them separately and their leaves alone, which are much larger, are now ahead of the willows.) The birches of all kinds with catkins begin to show a light green.

The inquisitive *yorrick* of the Wilson's thrush, though I hear no veery note. This at entrance of Deep Cut. The oven-bird, and note loud and unmistakable, making the hollow woods ring. This is decidedly smaller than what I have taken to be the hermit thrush. The black and white creeper, unmistakable from its creeping habit. It holds up its head to sing sharp and fine *te che, te che, te che, te che, te che, te che, te chē.* The oven-bird's note is much louder, broader, and more swinging. The latter sits on a low twig quite within

[1] Not important here; rather with birches.

the wood. Yesterday was a quite warm day, and these new birds I hear directly after it.

Vaccinium Pennsylvanicum first put out, and I see a humblebee about some others which are not open, knocking at their doors, which, if open, would be too small for him to enter. *Viola pedata* already numerous — say yesterday without doubt — at Lupine Knoll, paler than the *ovata*, — their pale faces. The field sparrow resembles a more slender tree sparrow without the spot on breast, with a light-colored bill and legs and feet, ashy-white breast, and beneath eye a drab, callow look. Note, *phe phe phe phe phe phe, phe phe-e-e-e-e;* holds up its head the while. Thorns are leafing. *Viola blanda* by Corner road at brook and below Cliff Hill Spring. Canoe birch and white ditto leafing. There is a dew or rather rain drop in the centre of the sun-dial (lupine) leaf, where its seven or eight leafets meet, over the sand. Cornel (*sericea*) leafing along river. I hear the fine, wiry mew of the song sparrow. A catbird mewing.

Saw coupled on a hillock by the water two what I should have called black snakes, — a uniform very dark brown, the male much the smallest. The under side — what little I noticed of the rear of the latter — was a bluish slate; but, when they ran into *the water*, I observed dull-yellowish transverse bars on the back of the female (did not observe the other there), and, when I turned over the male, had a glimpse of a reddish or orange belly. Were they water adders or black snakes? The largest was perhaps between three and four feet.

If that is the leaf of the arrow-wood which looks

so much like a cornel, it will rank next to the *Viburnum nudum.* *Vide* plant by bridge.

In Boston yesterday an ornithologist said significantly, " If you held the bird in your hand —; " but I would rather hold it in my affections.

The wind is southwest, and I have to row or paddle up. The shad-bush in blossom is the first to show like a fruit tree, — like a pale peach, — on the hillsides, seen afar amid gray twigs, amid leafless shrub oaks, etc., before even its own leaves are much expanded. I dragged and pushed my boat over the road at Deacon Farrar's brook, carrying a roller with me. It is warm rowing with a thick coat. Heard the first regular bullfrog trump, not *very* loud, however, at the swamp white oaks southwest of Pantry. Heard the night-warbler. Saw three ducks on Sudbury meadows still, one partly white, the others all dusky, — probably black ducks. As to the first, with a large dark head and white breast and sides, I am not sure whether it was a golden-eye, or whistler.

Dined at Tall's Island. The tupelo terminates abruptly, as if mutilated at top, and the slender, straggling branches decline thence downward, often longer than the tree is high. The shores of these meadows do not invite me to land on them; they are too low. A lake requires some high land close to it. Meeting-House Hill is the most accessible hereabouts. Anemones common now; they love to grow under brush or tree-tops which the choppers have left. Shad leaves develop fast. Pitch pines started for two or three days in some places, the largest shoots now four inches.

Returning stopped at Rice's. He was feeding his chickens with Indian meal and water. While talking with him heard bobolinks. I had seen what looked like a great stake just sticking out above the surface of the water on the meadows and again covered as if it were fastened at one end. It finally disappeared and probably was a large mud turtle. Rice told me that he had hunted them. You go a little later in this month, — a calm forenoon when the water is smooth, — and "the wind must be south," — and see them on the surface. Deacon Farrar's meadow in time of flood (I had come through this) was a good place.

It began to sprinkle, and Rice said he had got "to bush that field" of grain before it rained, and I made haste back with a fair wind and umbrella for sail. Were those cowbirds in Miles's meadow, about or near the cow? Alders generally have fairly begun to leaf. I came on rapidly in a sprinkling rain, which ceased when I reached Bittern Cliff, and the water smoothed somewhat. I saw many red maple blossoms on the surface. Their keys now droop gracefully about the stems. A fresh, growing scent comes from the moistened earth and vegetation, and I perceive the sweetness of the willows on the causeway. Above the railroad bridge I saw a kingfisher twice sustain himself in one place, about forty feet above the meadow, by a rapid motion of his wings, somewhat like a devil's-needle, not progressing an inch, apparently over a fish. Heard a tree-toad.

May 11. 6 A. M. — To Laurel Hillside by Walden.

Earliest gooseberry in garden open. Heard a Maryland yellow-throat about alders at Trillium Woods, where I first heard one last year, but it finds the alders cut down in the winter. Yellow birch apparently open, its leaf as forward as the *blossom* (*comparatively* — with other birches). Many small swallows hovering over Deep Cut, — probably bank swallows (?). Hear the golden robin. It is wonderful how surely these distinguished travellers arrive when the season has sufficiently revolved. *Prunus Americana*, Canada plum, yesterday at least, at Mr. Brooks's. A common plum to-day.

To sum up leafing of trees, etc., since May 5th, add these: —

Creeping juniper.
Larch; bundles fairly separated on some trees May 6th; open slowly.
Early blueberry.
Amelanchier Botryapium. It came forward fast.
High blackberry.
Young rock maple.
    "   red   "
    "   white (?) [maple].
Alders generally.
Ostrya.
Some trembles suddenly leafed.
Balm-of-Gileads.
Some thorns.
Yellow birch.
Canoe   "
White   "
Canada plum, I think here.
Pitch pine; some shoots now four inches long.
Norway [pine]?
Cornus sericea.

P. M. — To Saw Mill Brook.

White pines have started; put them with pitch. Nepeta just out. I am in a little doubt about the wrens (I do not refer to the snuff-colored one), whether I have seen more than one. All that makes me doubt is that I saw a ruby, or perhaps it might be called fiery, crest on the last — not golden.

Amelanchier oblongifolia, say yesterday, probably the one whose fruit I gathered last year. It does not leaf till it flowers. Sweet-gale has just begun to leaf. The willows on the Turnpike now resound with the hum of bees, and I hear the yellowbird and Maryland yellow-throat amid them. These *yellow* birds are concealed by the yellow of the willows. The cornels generally have fairly started, excepting the *C. florida* (have not noticed the bunch-berry and round-leaved), and for aught I have seen yet may be placed in the order of their flowering, — alternate, panicled, sericea, putting all on the day of the sericea, *i. e.* yesterday. Wild red cherry in road near Everett's open.

The most forward oak *leafets* are, I think, in one place a red, say just started, but I see shrub oak and swamp white catkins in a few places an inch long. Some shrub oak flower-buds are yellowish, some reddish. The *Thalictrum anemonoides* is a perfect and regular white star, but methinks lacks the interesting red tinge of the other. Some young chestnuts have begun — the lower branches — and are earlier than any oaks. White birches are suddenly leafing in some places, so as to make an open veil or gauze of green against the other trees. Young hornbeams

just before cornels; the old ones just begun to leaf. Various slender ferns, without wool, springing apparently at Saw Mill Brook; some quite dark; also brake a foot high. The arrow-wood has just begun. The *young* black birch leafing with others.

While at the Falls, I feel the air cooled and hear the muttering of distant thunder in the northwest and see a dark cloud in that direction indistinctly through the wood. That distant thunder-shower very much cools our atmosphere. And I make haste through the woods homeward *via* Hubbard's Close. Hear the evergreen-forest note. The true poet will ever live aloof from society, wild to it, as the finest singer is the wood thrush, a forest bird. The shower is apparently going by on the north. There is a low, dark, blue-black arch, crescent-like, in the horizon, sweeping the distant earth there with a dusky, rainy brush, and all men, like the earth, seem to wear an aspect of expectation. There is an uncommon stillness here, disturbed only by a rush of the wind from time to time. In the village I meet men making haste to their homes, for, though the heavy cloud has gone quite by, the shower will probably strike us with its tail. Rock maple keys, etc., now two inches long, probably been out some days. Those by the path on Common not out at all. Now I have got home there is at last a still cooler wind with a rush, and at last a smart shower, slanting to the ground, without thunder.

My errand this afternoon was chiefly to look at the gooseberry at Saw Mill Brook. We have two kinds in garden, the earliest of same date to leaf with that in the swamp, but very thorny, and one later just open. The last is apparently the same with that by Everett's, also just open, and with that this side of E. Wood's. I also know one other, i. e. the one at Saw Mill Brook, plainly distinct, with long petioled and glossy heart-shaped leaves, but as yet I find no flowers. I will call this for the present the swamp gooseberry.[1] *Stellaria media*, apparently not long. Butternut beginning to leaf.

Over meadows in boat at sunset to Island, etc.

The rain is over. There is a bow in the east. The earth is refreshed; the grass is wet. The air is warm again and still. The rain has smoothed the water to a glassy smoothness. It is very beautiful on the water now, the breadth of the flood not yet essentially diminished. The ostrya will apparently shed its pollen to-morrow. High blueberry is just leafing. I see the kingbird. It is remarkable that the radical leaves of goldenrod should be already so obvious, e. g. the broad-leaved at Saw Mill Brook. What need of this haste? Now at last I see crow blackbirds without doubt. They have probably been here before, for they are put down under April in the bird book (for '37). They fly as if carrying or dragging their precious long tails, broad at the end, through the air. Their note is like a great rusty spring, and also a hoarse chuck. On the whole I think they must have been rusty grackles which I mistook for this bird, and I think I saw their

[1] May 27th, the green shoots are covered with bristly prickles, but I can find no flowers. Is it the same with that by maple swamp in Hubbard's Close with young fruit?

silvery irides; look like red-wings without the red spot. Ground-ivy *just* begins to leaf. I am surprised to find the great poplar at the Island conspicuously in leaf, — leaves more than an inch broad, from top to bottom of the tree, and are already fluttering in the wind, — and others near it — conspicuously before any other native tree, as tenderly green, wet, and glossy as if this shower had opened them. The full-grown white maples are as forward in leafing now as the young red and sugar ones are now, only their leaves are smaller than the last. Put the young, at a venture, after the low blackberry, the old just before the other maples. The balm-of-Gilead is rapidly expanding, and I scent it in the twilight twenty rods off.

The earliest of our indigenous trees, then, to leaf *conspicuously* is the early tremble. (The one or more willows which leaf when they flower, like the *Salix alba*, with their small leaves, are *shrubs*, hardly trees.) Next to it, — close upon it, — *some* white birches, and, apparently close upon this, the balm-of-Gilead and white maple. Two days, however, *may* include them all. The wild red cherry and black cherry, though earlier to begin, are not now conspicuous, but I am not sure that some of the other birches, where young in favorable places, may not be as forward as the white.[1] But the *S. alba*, etc., precede them all. It is surprising what an electrifying effect this shower appears to have had. It is like the christening of the summer, and I

[1] Probably not, to any extent. *Vide* P. M. of 17th *inst*. *Vide* list [p. 297].

suspect that summer weather may be always ushered in in a similar manner, — thunder-shower, rainbow, smooth water, and warm night. A rainbow on the brow of summer. Nature has placed this gem on the brow of her daughter. Not only the wet grass looks many shades greener in the twilight, but the old pine-needles also. The toads are heard to ring more generally and louder than before, and the bullfrogs trump regularly, though not very loudly, reminding us that they are at hand and not drowned out by the freshet. All creatures are more awake than ever. Now, some time after sunset, the robins scold and sing (but their great singing time is earlier in the season), and the Maryland yellow-throat is heard amid the alders and willows by the waterside, and the peetweet and black-birds, and sometimes a kingbird, and the tree-toad somewhat.

Sweet-briar just beginning to leaf generally (?).

May 12. 5.30 A. M. — To Nawshawtuct.

Quite a fog risen up from the river. I cannot see over it from the hill at 6 A. M. The first I have seen. The grass is now high enough to be wet. I see many perfectly geometrical cobwebs on the trees, with from twenty-six to thirty-odd rays, six inches to eighteen in diameter, but no spiders. I suspect they were spun this last warm night very generally. No insects in them yet. They are the more conspicuous for being thickly strewn with minute drops of the mist or dew, like a chain of beads. Are they not meteorologists? A robin's nest in an apple tree with three eggs, — first nest I have

seen, — also a red-wing's nest — bird about it did not look in — before the river is low enough for them to build on its brink. *Viola cucullata* apparently to-day first, near the sassafrases. A small white birch catkin. Fir balsam just begins fairly to loosen bundles. Were they blue-winged teal flew by? for there was a large white spot on the sides aft. I think I scared up the same last night. Fever-root up four or five inches.

Is not this the first day of summer, when first I sit with the window open and forget fire? and hear the golden robin and kingbird, etc., etc.? not to mention the bobolink, vireo, yellowbird, etc., and the trump of bullfrogs heard last evening.

P. M. — To climbing fern.

I have seen a little blue moth a long time. My thick sack is too much yesterday and to-day. The golden robin makes me think of a thinner coat. I see that the great thrush, — brown thrasher, — from its markings, is still of the same family with the wood thrush, etc. These genera are very curious. A shrub or bear oak beginning to leaf. Am struck with the fact that the Assabet has relieved itself of its extra waters to a much greater extent than the main branch. Woolly aphides on alder. Large black birches, not quite leafing nor in bloom. In one bunch of *Viola ovata* in Ministerial Swamp Path counted eleven, an unusual number. What are those handsome conical crimson-red buds not burst on the white [*sic*] spruce? The leaves of the larch begin to make a show. Mosquito. The climbing fern is evergreen — only the flowering top dies — and spreads by horizontal roots. I perceive no growth yet. The *Amelanchier oblongifolia* has denser and smaller racemes, more erect (?), broader petalled, and not tinged with red on the back. Its downy leaves are now less conspicuous and interesting than the other's. On the whole it is not so interesting a variety.

The bear-berry is well out, perhaps a quarter part of them. May 6th, I thought it would open in a day or two; say, then, the 8th.

At last I hear the veery strain. Why not as soon as the *yorrick?* Heard again the evergreen-forest note. It is a slender bird, about size of white-eyed vireo, with a black throat and I think some yellow above, with dark and light beneath, in the tops of pines and oaks. The only warblers at all like it are black-throated green, black-throated blue, black-poll, and golden-winged, and maybe orange-crowned.

May 13. The portion of the peach trees in bloom in our garden shows the height of the snow-drifts in the winter.

4 P. M. — To V. Muhlenbergii Brook.

The bass suddenly expanding its little round leaves; probably began about the 11th. Uvularias, amid the dry tree-tops near the azaleas, apparently yesterday. Saw the crow blackbird fly over, turning his tail in the wind into a vertical position to serve for a rudder, then sailing with it horizontal. The great red maples begin to leaf, and the young leafets of the red (?) oaks up the Assabet on Hosmer's land, and one at Rock, now begin to be conspicuous. Waxwork begins to leaf.

The sand cherry, judging from what I saw yesterday, will begin to flower to-day.

As for the birds, I have not for some time noticed crows in flocks. The voices of the early spring birds are silenced or drowned in multitude of sounds. The black ducks are probably all gone. Are the rusty grackles still here? Birds generally are now building and sitting. Methinks I heard one snipe night before last? I have not noticed the pine warbler nor the myrtle-bird for a fortnight. The chip-sparrow is lively in the morning. I suspect the purple finches are all gone within a few days. The black and white creeper is musical nowadays, and thrushes and the catbird, etc., etc. Goldfinch heard pretty often.

Insects have just begun to be troublesome.

Young *Populus grandidentata* just opening. Panicled andromeda leaf to-morrow; not for three or four days generally.

May 14. P. M. — To Hill by boat.

A St. Domingo cuckoo, black-billed with red round eye, a silent, long, slender, graceful bird, dark cinnamon (?) above, pure white beneath. It is in a leisurely manner picking the young caterpillars out of a nest (now about a third of an inch long) with its long, curved bill. Not timid. Black willows have begun to leaf, — if they are such in front of Monroe's. White ash and common elm *began* to leaf yesterday, if I have not named the elm before. The former will apparently open to-morrow. The black ash, *i. e.* that by the river, may have been open a day or two. Apple in bloom.

Swamp white oak perhaps will open to-morrow.[1] Celtis has begun to leaf. I think I may say that the white oak leaves have now fallen; saw but one or two small trees with them day before yesterday.

Sumach began to leaf, say yesterday. Pear opened, say the 12th. The leafing goes on now rapidly, these warm and moist showery days.

May 15. Judging from those in garden, the witch-hazel began to leaf yesterday, black alder to-day.

P. M. — Up Assabet.

The golden willow catkins are suddenly falling and cover my boat. High blueberry has flowered, say yesterday. Swamp-pink leafing, say yesterday. The *Amelanchier Botryapium* — some of them — have lost blossoms and show *minute* fruit. This I suspect the first *sign* of all wild edible fruit. *Cornus florida* began to leaf, say yesterday. The round-leafed cornel (at Island) is, I [think], as early as any of the cornels to leaf; put it for the present with the *alternifolia*. Gaylussacia begins to leaf to-day and is sticky. *Polygonatum pubescens* will apparently blossom to-morrow. Hickories make a show suddenly; their buds are so large, say yesterday. Young white oaks also yesterday. Old ones hardly to-day, but their catkins quite prominent. Young white oak (and black oak) leafets now very handsome, red on under side. Black oaks appear to have begun to leaf about the 13th, immediately after the red. The large *P. grandidentata* by river not leafing yet.

[1] No, no.

Looked off from hilltop. Trees generally are now bursting into leaf. The aspect of oak and other woods at a distance is somewhat like that of a very thick and reddish or yellowish mist about the evergreens. In other directions, the light, graceful, and more distinct yellowish-green forms of birches are seen, and, in swamps, the reddish or reddish-brown crescents of the red maple tops, now covered with keys. Oak leaves are as big as a mouse's ear, and the farmers are busily planting. It is suddenly very warm and looks as if there might be a thunder-shower coming up from the west. The crow blackbird is distinguished by that harsh, springlike note. For the rest, there is a sort of split whistle, like a poor imitation of the red-wing. A yellow butterfly.

Have just been looking at Nuttall's "North American Sylva." Much research, fine plates and print and paper, and unobjectionable periods, but no turpentine, or balsam, or quercitron, or salicin, or birch wine, or the aroma of the balm-of-Gilead, no gallic, or ulmic, or even malic acid. The plates are greener and higher-colored than the words, etc., etc. It is sapless, if not leafless.

May 16. *Tuesday.* Saw an arum almost open the 11th; say 16th (?), though not shedding pollen 16th at Conantum. Sugar maples, large, beginning to leaf, say 14th; also mulberry in the How garden to-day; locust the 14th; white [*sic*] spruce, the earliest to-day; buttonwood the 14th (*leafing* all).

P. M. — To Conantum by boat with S.

V. peregrina in Channing's garden, — purslane speedwell, — *some* flowers withered; some days at least. Observed all the oaks I know except the chestnut and dwarf chestnut and scarlet (?). I see anthers perhaps to all, but not yet any pollen. Apparently the most forward in respect to blossoming will be the shrub oak, which possibly is now in bloom in some places, then apparently swamp white, then red and black, then white. White oak apparently leafs with swamp white, or say next day.[1] Red and black oaks leaf about together, before swamp white and white. Earliest sassafras opened yesterday; leafs to-day. Butternut will blossom to-morrow. The great fern by sassafras begins to bloom, probably *Osmunda Claytoniana*, two feet high now, — interrupted fern, — its very dark heads soon surmounted with green. Lambkill beginning to leaf. Green-briar leaf yesterday. The rich crimson leaf-buds of the grape, yesterday globular (and some to-day), are rapidly unfolding, scattered along the vine; and the various leaves unfolding are flower-like, and taken together are more interesting than any flower. Is that a hop[2] by the path at landing on hill with shoots now five or six inches long? Pads begin to appear and spread themselves out on the surface here and there, as the water goes down, — though it is still over the meadows, — with often a scalloped edge like those tin platters on which country people sometimes bake turnovers. Their round green buds here and there look like the

[1] See forward.
[2] Probably clematis, — one of the earlier plants, then.

heads of tortoises; and I saw in the course of the afternoon three or four just begun to blossom. Golden robin building her nest. It is easy to see now that the highest part of the meadow is next the river. There is generally a difference of a foot at least. Saw around a hardhack stem on the meadow, where the water was about two feet deep, a light-brown globular mass, two inches or more in diameter, which looked like a thistle-head full of some kind of seeds, some of which were separated from it by the agitation made by the boat but returned to it again. I then saw that they were living creatures. It was a mass of gelatinous spawn filled with little light-colored pollywogs (?), or *possibly* fishes (?), all head and tail, — a long, broad light-colored and thin tail, which was vertical, appended to a head with two eyes. These were about a quarter of an inch long, and when washed off in the water wiggled back to the mass again.

Quite warm; cows already stand in water in the shade of the bridge. I stopped to get some water at the springy bank just above the railroad. I dug a little hollow with my hands so that I could dip some up with a skunk-cabbage leaf, and, while waiting for it to settle, I thought, by a squirming and wriggling movement on the bottom, that the sand was all alive with some kind of worms or insects. There were in fact some worm-skins (?) on it. Looking closer, however, I found that this motion and appearance was produced by the bursting up of the water, which not only trickled down from the bank above but burst up from beneath. The sandy bottom was speckled

Vol. VI

with hundreds of small, regularly formed orifices, like those in a pepper-box, about which the particles of sand kept in motion had made me mistake it for squirming worms. There was considerable loam or soil mixed with the sand. These orifices, separated by slight intervals like those in the nose of a water-pot, gave to the spring an unexpectedly regular appearance. It is surprising how quickly one of these springs will run clear. Also drank at what I will call Alder Spring at Clamshell Hill.

Looked into several red-wing blackbirds' nests which are now being built, but no eggs yet. They are generally hung between two twigs, say of button-bush. I noticed at one nest what looked like a tow string securely tied about a twig at each end about six inches apart, left loose in the middle. It was not a string, but I think a strip of milkweed pod, etc., — water asclepias probably, — maybe a foot long and very strong. How remarkable that this bird should have found out the strength of this, which I was so slow to find out!

The leaf-buds at last suddenly burst. It is now very difficult to compare one with another or keep the run of them. The bursting into leaf of the greater number, *including the latest*, is accomplished within a week, say from the 13th of May this year to probably the 20th; that is, within these dates they acquire minute leafets. This same is the principal planting week methinks. The clethra well leafed, say with the bass (?). *Andromeda calyculata*, leaf to-morrow.

The red or crimsoned young leaves of the black and red (?) oaks, — the former like red damask, — and

the maroon (?)-red inclining to flesh-color — salmon-red (?) — of the white oak, all arranged now like little parasols, — in white oak five leafets, — are as interesting and beautiful as flowers, downy and velvet-like. Sorrel well out in some warm places. *Ranunculus bulbosus* will flower to-morrow, under Clamshell. Yesterday, when the blossoms of the golden willow began to fall, the blossoms of the apple began to open.

Landed at Conantum by the red cherry grove above Arrowhead Field. The red cherries six inches in diameter and twenty-five or thirty [feet] high, in full bloom, with a reddish smooth bark. It is a splendid day, so clear and bright and fresh; the warmth of the air and the bright tender verdure putting forth on all sides make an impression of luxuriance and genialness, so perfectly fresh and uncankered. A sweet scent fills the air from the expanding leafets or some other source. The earth is all fragrant as one flower. And bobolinks tinkle in the air. Nature now is perfectly genial to man. I noticed the dark shadow of Conantum Cliff from the water. Why do I notice it at this season particularly? Is it because a shadow is more grateful to the sight now that warm weather has come? Or is there anything in the contrast between the rich green of the grass and the cool dark shade? As we walked along to the C. Cliff, I saw many *Potentilla Canadensis* var. *pumila* now spotting the ground. *Vaccinium vacillans* just out. *Arenaria serpyllifolia* to-morrow. *Myosotis stricta* in several places; how long? Trillium out, possibly yesterday. Maidenhair ferns some up and some starting, unclenching their little red fists. Fever-bush, say leafed about the 12th.

Returning, the water is smoother than common, — quite glassy in some places. It is getting to be difficult to cross the meadows. Float close under the edge of the wood. But the wind changes to east and blows agreeably fresh. How fair and elysian these rounded and now green Indian hills, with their cool dark shadows on the east side! There are great summer clouds in the sky, — blocked rhomboidal masses tier above tier, white, glowing above, darker beneath.

On Hubbard's meadow, saw a motion in the water as if a pickerel had darted away; approached and saw a middle-sized snapping turtle on the bottom; managed at last, after stripping off my coat and rolling up my shirt-sleeve, by thrusting in my arm to the shoulder, to get him by the tail and lift him aboard. He tried to get under the boat. He snapped at my shoe and got the toe in his mouth. His back was covered with green moss (?), or the like, mostly concealing the scales. In this were small leeches. Great, rough, but not hard, scales on his legs. He made a pretty loud hissing like a cross dog, by his breathing. It was wonderful how suddenly this sluggish creature would snap at anything. As he lay under the seat, I scratched his back, and, filling himself with air and rage, his head would suddenly fly upward, his shell striking the seat, just as a steel trap goes off, and though I was prepared for it, it never failed to startle me, it was so swift and sudden. He slowly inflated himself, and then suddenly went off like a percussion

thrusting my arm in up to the shoulder two or three times, I succeeded in getting him into the boat, where I secured him with a lever under a seat. I could get him from the landing to the house only by turning him over and drawing him by the tail, the hard crests of which afforded a good hold; for he was so heavy that I could not hold him off so far as to prevent his snapping at my legs. He weighed thirty and a half pounds.

Extreme length of shell . . . . 15½ inches
Length of shell in middle 15   "
Greatest width of shell . . . . 12¼   "
    (This was toward the rear.)
Tail (beyond shell) . . . . 11¼   "

His head and neck it was not easy to measure, but, judging from the proportions of one described by Storer, they must have been 10 inches long at least, which makes the whole length 37 inches. Width of head 4½ inches; with the skin of the neck, more than 5. His sternum, which was slightly depressed, was 10½ by 5½. Depth from back to sternum about 7 inches. There were six great scallops, or rather triangular points, on the hind edge of his shell, three on each side, the middle one of each three the longest, about ¾ of an inch. He had surprisingly stout hooked jaws, of a gray color or bluish-gray, the upper shutting over the under, ⸻ a more or less sharp triangular beak corresponding to one below; and his flippers were armed with very stout claws 1¼ inches long. He had a very ugly and spiteful face (with a vigilant gray eye, which was never shut in any position of the head), surrounded by the thick and ample

lock snapping the air. Thus undoubtedly he catches fishes, as a toad catches flies. His laminated tail and great triangular points in the rear edge of his shell. Nature does not forget beauty of outline even in a mud turtle's shell.

Rhodora well out, probably two days, and leaf as long, or yesterday. The stinkpots have climbed two or three feet up the willows and hang there. I suspect that they appear first about the same time with the snapping turtles. Far and near I see painted turtles sunning or tumbling off the little hummocks laid bare by the descending water, their shells shining in the sun.

May 17. 5.30 A. M. — To Island.

The water is now tepid in the morning to the hands (may have been a day or two), as I slip my hands down the paddle. Hear the wood pewee, the warm-weather sound. As I was returning over the meadow this side of the Island, I saw the snout of a mud turtle above the surface, — little more than an inch of the point, — and paddled toward it. Then, as he moved slowly on the surface, different parts of his shell and head just appearing looked just like the scalloped edges of some pads which had just reached the surface. I pushed up and found a large snapping turtle on the bottom. He appeared of a dirty brown there, very nearly the color of the bottom at present. With his great head, as big as an infant's, and his vigilant eyes as he paddled about on the bottom in his attempts to escape, he looked not merely repulsive, but to some extent terrible even as a crocodile. At length, after

folds of the skin about his neck. His shell was comparatively smooth and free from moss, — a dirty black. He was a *dirty* or speckled white beneath. He made the most remarkable and awkward appearance when walking. The edge of his shell was lifted about eight inches from the ground, tilting now to this side, then to that, his great scaly legs or flippers hanging with flesh and loose skin, — slowly and gravely (?) hissing the while. His walking was perfectly elephantine. Thus he stalked along, — a low conical mountain, — dragging his tail, with his head turned upward with the ugliest and most venomous look, on his flippers, half leg half fin. But he did not proceed far before he sank down to rest. If he could support a world on his back when lying down, he certainly could not stand up under it. All said that he walked like an elephant. When lying on his back, showing his *dirty* white and warty under side, with his tail curved round, he reminded you forcibly of pictures of the dragon. He could not easily turn himself back; tried many times in vain, resting betweenwhiles. Would inflate himself and convulsively spring with head and all upward, so as to lift his shell from the ground, and he would strike his head on the ground, lift up his shell, and catch at the earth with his claws. His back was of two great blunt ridges with a hollow between, down the middle of which was a slight but distinct ridge also. There was also a ridge of spines more or less hard on each side of his crested tail. Some of these spines in the crest of the tail were nearly half an inch high. Storer says that they have five *claws* on the fore legs, but only four on the hind ones. In this there was a *perfectly* distinct fifth *toe* (?) on the hind legs, though it did not pierce the skin; and on the fore legs it did not much more. S. does not say how many toes he has. These claws must be powerful to dig with.

This, then, is the season for hunting them, now that the water is warmer, before the pads are common, and the water is getting shallow on the meadows. E. Wood, Senior, speaks of two seen fighting for a long time in the river in front of his house last year. I have heard of one being found in the meadow in the winter surrounded by frozen mud. Is not this the heaviest animal found wild in this township? Certainly none but the otter approaches it. Farrar says that, when he was eleven, one which he could not lift into the boat towed him across the river; weighed twenty-nine.

Lilac is out and horse-chestnut. The female flowers — crimson cones — of the white [*sic*] spruce, but not yet the staminate.

The turtle was very sluggish, though capable of putting forth great strength. He would just squeeze into a flour barrel and would not quite lie flat in it when his head and tail were drawn in. There was [a] triangular place in the bottom of his mouth and an orifice within it through which, apparently, he breathed, the orifice opening and shutting. I hear of a man who injured his back seriously for many years by carrying one some distance at arm's length to prevent his biting him. They are frequently seen fighting and their shells heard striking together.

P. M. — To Cedar Swamp *via* Assabet.

The tupelo began to leaf apparently yesterday. The large green keys of the white maples are now conspicuous, looking like the wings of insects. *Azalea nudiflora* in woods begins to leaf now, later than the white kind. *Viola Muhlenbergii* out, say yesterday. It is a pale violet. Judging from the aspect of the *Lentago* yesterday, I should put its leafing decidedly before *Viburnum nudum*. Also apparently the late rose soon after the one observed, and the moss about same time with first. The swamp white and white oak are slow to leaf. Large maples, too, are not rapid; but the birches, aspens, and balm-of-Gileads burst out suddenly into leaf and make a great show. Also the *young* sugar maples in the street now and for some days have made a show of broad luxuriant leaves, early and rapidly. In the case of the early aspen you could almost see the leaves expand and acquire a darker green — this to be said the 12th or 13th or 14th — under the influence of the sun and genial atmosphere. Now they are only as big as a ninepence, to-morrow or sooner they are as big as a pistareen, and the next day they are as big as a dollar. So too the green veils or screens of the birches rapidly thickened. This from its far greater prevalence than the aspens, balm-of-Gilead, white maples, etc., is the first to give the woodlands anywhere generally a (fresh) green aspect. It is the first to clothe large tracts of deciduous woodlands with green, and perchance it marks an epoch in the season, the *transition* decidedly and generally from bare twigs to leaves. When the birches have put on their green sacks, then

Vol. VI

a new season has come. The light reflected from their tender yellowish green is like sunlight.

The turtle's snapping impressed me as something mechanical, like a spring, as if there were no volition about [it]. Its very suddenness seemed too great for a conscious movement. Perhaps in these cold-blooded and sluggish animals there is a near approach to the purely material and mechanical. Their very tenacity of life seems to be owing to their insensibility or small amount of life, — indeed, to be an irritation of the muscles. One man tells me of a turtle's head which, the day after it was cut off, snapped at a dog's tail and made him run off yelping, and I have witnessed something similar myself. I can think of nothing but a merely animated jaw, as it were a piece of mechanism. There is in this creature a tremendous development of the jaw, and, long after the head is cut off, this snaps vigorously when irritated, like a piece of mechanism. A naturalist tells me that he dissected one and laid its heart aside, and he found it beating or palpitating the next morning. They are sometimes baited with eels and caught with a hook. Apparently the best time to hunt them is in the morning when the water is smooth.

There is a surprising change since I last passed up the Assabet; the fields are now clothed with so dark and rich a green, and the wooded shore is all lit up with the tender, bright green of birches fluttering in the wind and shining in the light, and red maple keys are seen at a distance against the tender green of birches and other trees, tingeing them.

The wind is easterly, having changed, and produces

an agreeable raw mistiness, unlike the dry blue haze of dog-days, *just* visible, between a dew and a fog for density. I sail up the stream, but the wind is hardly powerful enough to overcome the current, and sometimes I am almost at a standstill where the stream is most contracted and swiftest, and there I sit carelessly waiting for the struggle between wind and current to decide itself. Then comes a stronger puff, and I see by the shore that I am advancing to where the stream is broader and runs less swiftly and where lighter breezes can draw me. In contracted and swift-running places, the wind and current are almost evenly matched. It is a pleasing delay, to be referred to the elements, and meanwhile I survey the shrubs on shore. The white cedar shows the least possible life in its extremities now. Put it with the arbor-vitæ, or after it. Poison dogwood beginning to leaf, say yesterday. Nemopanthes out; leafed several days ago. And the clustered andromeda leafed apparently a day or more before it. Gold-thread out. *Viola palmata.* I cannot well examine the stone-heaps, the water is so deep. Muskrats are now sometimes very bold; lie on the surface and come swimming directly toward the boat as if to reconnoitre — this in two cases within a few days. Pretty sure to see a crescent of light under their tails when they dive. The splendid rhodora now sets the swamps on fire with its masses of rich color. It is *one of the first* flowers to catch the eye at a distance in masses, — so naked, unconcealed by its own leaves.

Observed a rill emptying in above the stone-heaps, and afterward saw where it ran out of June-berry

Meadow, and I considered how surely it would have conducted me to the meadow, if I had traced it up. I was impressed as it were by the intelligence of the brook, which for ages in the wildest regions, before science is born, knows so well the level of the ground and through whatever woods or other obstacles finds its way. Who shall distinguish between the *law* by which a brook finds its river, the *instinct* [by which] a bird performs its migrations, and the *knowledge* by which a man steers his ship round the globe? The globe is the richer for the variety of its inhabitants. Saw a large gray squirrel near the split rock in the Assabet. He went skipping up the limb of one tree and down the limb of another, his great gray rudder undulating through the air, and occasionally hid himself behind the main stem. The *Salix nigra* will open to-morrow.

May 18. To Pedrick's meadow.
Viola lanceolata, two days at least. Celandine yesterday. The *V. pedata* beginning to be abundant. Chinquapin was probably a little later to leaf, and will be to flower, than the shrub oak. Its catkins, light green, remind me of those of the swamp white oak. Buttonwood balls, one third inch in diameter, have been blown off, and *some* have a dull-purplish fuzzy surface (most are solid green); apparently just beginning to blossom. Red cedar shows the least possible sign of starting. The pyrus, probably black-fruited, in bloom as much as two days. Huckleberry. Now for the tassels of the shrub oak; I can find no pollen yet about them, but, as the oak catkins in my pitcher,

plucked yesterday, shed pollen to-day, I think I may say that the bear shrub oak, red and black oaks open to-morrow.[1] I see the pincushion or crimson-tinged galls now on shrub oaks around the bases of the young shoots, — some green-shell ones on oak leaves, like large peas, and small now greenish-white fungus-like ones on swamp-pink. Thus early, before the leaves are a quarter expanded, the gall begins. I see potentillas already ascending five or six inches, but no flower on them, in the midst of low ones in flower. *Smilacina trifolia* will apparently open to-morrow in Pedrick's meadow. A large clay-brown and blotched snake; is it the chicken snake or water adder? Beach plum in full bloom by red house, apparently two or three days. It is one of the very latest plants to leaf; only a few buds just begin to show any green. One man has been a-fishing, but said the water and the wind were too high; caught a few.

High winds all day racking the young trees and blowing off blossoms.

May 19. 5.30 A. M. — To Nawshawtuct and Island.
Ranunculus Purshii will apparently open to-day. Its little green buds somewhat like a small yellow lily. The water has now fallen so much that the grass is rapidly springing up through it on the meadows. Redwing's nest with two eggs. A geranium, apparently yesterday. Celtis for several days. Button-bush began to leaf, say the 17th; *i. e.*, some of its buds began to burst. Choke-cherry out. *Aralia nudicaulis*, apparently

[1] *Vide* 22d.

yesterday. The red-eye. The early thorn looks as if it would open to-day. I hear the *sprayey*-note frog now at sunset. Now for four or five days, — though they are now for the most part large, — or since the 15th came in, the young and tender oak leaves, disposed umbrella-wise about the extremities of last year's twigs, have been very attractive from their different tints of red. Those of the black and white oaks are, methinks, especially handsome, the former already showing their minute and tender bristles, and all handsomely lobed. Some of the black oak leaves are like a rich, dark-red velvet; the white oak have a paler and more delicate tint, somewhat flesh-colored, though others are more like the black, — what S. calls a maroon red. So of the bear scrub oak; the swamp white and chinquapin are more of a downy or silvery white. The white pine shoots are now two or three inches long generally, — upright light marks on the body of dark green. Those of the pitch pine are less conspicuous. Hemlock does not show yet. The light shoots, an inch or so long, of the fir balsam spot the trees. The larch is a mass of fresh, airy, and cool green. Arbor-vitæ, red cedar, and white show no life except on the closest inspection. They are some of the latest trees. The juniper is about with the fir balsam. I have already described the oaks sufficiently. The hazel is now a pretty green bush. Butternuts, like hickories, make a show suddenly with their large buds. I have not examined the birches, except the white, this year. The alders are slow to expand their leaves, but now begin to show a mass of green along the river, and,

with the willows, afford concealment to the birds' nests. The birds appear to be waiting for this screen. The robin's nest and eggs are the earliest I see. Saw one in the midst of a green-briar over the water the other day, before the briar had put out at all, which shows some foresight, for it will be perfectly invisible, if not inaccessible, soon.

The great poplar is quite late to leaf, especially those that blossom; not yet do they show much, — a silvery leaf. The golden willow is the only tree used about here at the same time for a fence and for shade. It also prevents the causeways from being washed away. The black willow is the largest as well as the handsomest of our native willows. Young elms are leafing pretty fast, old ones are late and slow. The samaræ of the elms first make a thick top, leaf-like, before the leaves come out. Ash trees are like hickories in respect to the size of the young leaves. The young leafets of the wild holly (*Nemopanthes*) on the 17th were peculiarly thin and pellucid, yellow-green. I know of none others like them. Those of the black alder are not only late but dark. The button-bush is not only very late, but the buds are slow to expand, and methinks are very far apart, so that they do not soon make a show; for the most part at a little distance there is no appearance of life in them even yet. The sweet viburnum and also the naked are early to make a show with their substantial leaves. The andromedas are all late, — if I remember, the clustered (?) the earliest. The common swamp-pink is earlier to leaf but later to blossom than the *nudiflora*. The rhodora is late, and is *naked* flowering. The mountain laurel is one of the latest plants. The resinous dotted leaves of the huckleberry are interesting. The high blueberries are early (to bloom) and resound with the hum of bees. All the cornels begin to leaf apparently *about* the same time, though I do not know but the round-leaved is the earliest.[1] I have not observed the dwarf. The witch-hazel is rather late, and can afford to be. One kind of thorn is well leafed, the other not. The mountain-ash is the first tree which grows here, either naturally or otherwise, to show green at a little distance. Is it not true that *trees* which belong peculiarly to a colder latitude are among our earliest and those which prefer a warmer among our latest? The choke-berry's shining leaf is interesting. With what unobserved secure dispatch nature advances! The amelanchiers have bloomed, and already both kinds have shed their blossoms and show minute green fruit. There is not an instant's pause! The beach plum — such as I have observed — is the latest to begin to expand of all deciduous shrubs or trees, for aught I know. The sight of it suggests that we are near the seacoast, that even our sands are in some sense littoral, — or beaches. The cherries are all early to leaf, but only one, perhaps the wild red, and that in one place, is in mass enough to make much show. The woodbine is well advanced — shoots two or three inches long. It must have begun to leaf more than a week ago. The linden leafs suddenly and rapidly, — a round, thin, transparent-looking (?) leaf.

[1] The *C. florida* is rather late.

throat. They — these throats — come with the yellow lily. Cobwebs on grass, the first I have noticed. This is one of the *late* phenomena of spring. These little dewy nets or gauze, a faery's washing spread out in the night, are associated with the finest days of the year, days long enough and fair enough for the worthiest deeds. When these begin to be seen, then is not summer come? I notice the fir balsam sterile flowers already effete.

P. M. — To Deep Cut.

A shower, heralded only by thunder and lightning, has kept me in till late in the afternoon. The sterile *Equisetum arvense*, now well up, green the bank. Bluets begin to whiten the fields. A tanager, — the surprising red bird, — against the darkening green leaves. I see a *little* growth in the mitchella. The larger *Populus grandidentata here* are pretty well leaved out and may be put with the young ones. Trientalis, perhaps yesterday. *Smilacina bifolia*, apparently to-morrow. Hear the squeak of a nighthawk. The deciduous trees now begin to balance the evergreens. Red oaks are quite green. Young hemlocks have grown a quarter of an inch; old just started; but by to-morrow they will show their growth by contrast more than the button-bush. Lycopodiums just started, — light or yellowish green tips. *Cornus Canadensis*. The single-berry prinos leafs, say with the other. Was surprised to find a nemopanthes on the upland, — Stow's Clearing. Dangle-berry leafs, say next after the common huckleberry. Young checkerberry reddish shoots just begin to show themselves.

A washing day, — a strong rippling wind, and all things bright.

May 20. Woodbine shoots (brick house) already two or three inches long; put it, say, with the red oak. *Potentilla argentea.* White [*sic*] spruce, male flowers. White ash, apparently a day or two. Mr. Prichard's. The English hawthorn opens at same time with our earlier thorn.

Very low thunder-clouds and showers far in the north at sunset, the wind of which, though not very strong, has cooled the air. Saw the lightning, but could not hear the thunder. I saw in the northwest first rise, in the rose-tinted horizon sky, a dark, narrow, craggy cloud, narrow and projecting as no cloud on earth, seen against the rose-tinged sky, — the crest of a thunder-storm, beautiful and grand. The steadily increasing sound of toads and frogs along the river with each successive warmer night is one of the most important peculiarities of the season. Their prevalence and loudness is in proportion to the increased temperature of the day. It is the first earth-song, beginning with the croakers, (the cricket's not yet), as if the very meads at last burst into a meadowy song. I hear a few bullfrogs and but few hylodes. Methinks we always have at this time those washing winds as now, when the choke-berry is in bloom, — bright and breezy days blowing off some apple blossoms.

May 21. Sunday. Quince. A slight fog in morning. Some bullfrogs in morning, and I see a yellow swelling

Vol. VI

Twilight on river.

The reddish white lily pads here and there and the heart-leaves begin to be seen. A few pontederias, like long-handled spoons. The water going rapidly down, that often purplish bent grass is seen lying flat along it a foot or more, in parallel blades like matting. It is surprising how the grass shoots up now through the shallow water on the meadows, so fresh and tender, you can almost see it grow, for the fall of the water adds to its apparent growth; and the river weeds, too, — flags, polygonums, and potamogetons, etc., etc., — are rapidly pushing up. Sassafras is slow to leaf. A whip-poor-will.

May 22. 5.30 A. M. — Up Assabet.

Now begins the slightly sultryish morning air into which you awake early to hear the faint buzz of a fly or hum of other insect. The teeming air, deep and hollow, filled with some spiritus, pregnant as not in winter or spring, with room for imps, — good angels and bad, — many chambers in it, infinite sounds. I partially awake the first time for a month at least. As if the cope of the sky lifted, the heat stretched and swelled it as a bladder, and it remained permanently higher and more infinite for the summer. Suggesting that the night has not been, with its incidents. Naked-fl[owered] azalea in garden and wood. The dew now wets me completely each morning. Swamp white oak began to blossom apparently yesterday; the anthers completely shed their pollen at once and are effete — only a small part as yet, however. The red oak, *i. e.* at point of Island; as I did not observe it out on the 19th, say 20th. The white oak will apparently begin to-day.[1] The hemlock may have begun to bloom the 20th. *Cornus florida.* Galls, puff-like, on naked azalea and huckleberries. The later thorn is not much if any later to leaf than the other, apparently. Saw a small diving duck of some kind suddenly dash out from the side of the river above the hemlocks, like my red-breasted merganser, plowing the water with a great noise and flapping, and dive in the middle of the stream. Searching carefully, I after saw its head out amid the alders on the opposite side. When I returned, it again dived in the middle of the stream. Why should it attract my attention first by this rush? Shoots along half risen from the water, striking it with its wings. I saw one of the same family run thus a long way on the Penobscot. *Ranunculus recurvatus* out at V. Muhlenbergii Brook since the 17th; say 19th.

10 A. M. — To Fair Haven by boat.

I see many young and tender dragon-flies, both large and small, hanging to the grass-tops and weeds and twigs which rise above the water still going down. They are weak and sluggish and tender-looking, and appear to have lately crawled up these stems from the bottom where they were hatched, and to be waiting till they are hardened in the sun and air. (A few, however, are flying vigorously as usual over the water.) Where the grass and rushes are thick over the shallow water, I see their large gauze-like wings vibrating in the

[1] Some not open on the 26th.

Vol. VI

and soil without bushes. The muskrats have already taken advantage of this one to squat on and burrow under, and by raising the shore it will afford them a refuge which they had not before here.

Senecio, probably earlier still at Boiling Spring. *Rhus radicans* apparently leafs with the *Toxicodendron.* The apple bloom is chiefly passed. *Rubus sempervirens* put forth leaf soon after *R. Canadensis.* The dwarf sumach is just starting, some of them decidedly later than the button-bush! At Clamshell, the small oblong yellow heads of yellow clover, some days. Tall buttercup, a day or two. Dandelions, for some time, gone to seed. Water saxifrage, now well out. As I started away from Clamshell, it was quite warm — the seats — and the water glassy smooth, but a little wind rose afterward. Muskrats are frequently seen to dive a dozen rods from shore and not discovered again. A song sparrow's callow young in nest. A summer yellowbird close by sounded *we we we tchea tchea teche wiss wiss wiss.* I perceive some of that peculiar fragrance from the marsh at the Hubbard Causeway, though the marsh is mostly covered. Is it a particular compound of odors? It is more remarkable and memorable than the scent of any particular plant, — the fragrance, as it were, of the earth itself. The loud cawing of a crow heard echoing through a deep pine wood, — how wild! unconverted by all our preaching. Now and then the dumping sound of frogs. Large pinweed six inches high. Lupines have been out under Fair Haven Hill several days. *Viola pedata* blue the field there.

breeze and shining in the sun. It is remarkable that such tender organizations survive so many accidents.

The black oak apparently began to blossom yesterday. The bear shrub oaks apparently began to bloom with the red, though they are various. Put the chinquapin with them immediately after. Lousewort fairly out in front of geum, on Hill.

Examined the button-bush hummock. It is about eighteen feet by ten at the widest part and from one to one and a half feet thick. It consists chiefly of button-bushes, four or five feet high and now as flourishing as any, a high blueberry (killed), and some water silkweeds springing up (five or six inches) at the foot of the dry stalks, together with the grass and soil they grew in. Though these have been completely covered by the freshet for some weeks since it was deposited here, and exposed to high winds and waves, it has not sensibly washed away. These masses draw so much water that they ground commonly on the edge of the river proper, and so all things combine to make this a border bush or edging. (They are sometimes, when the water is high, dropped in the middle of the meadow, and make islands there.) They thus help to define the limits of the river and defend the edge of the meadow, and, the water being still high, I see at Fair Haven the sweeping lines formed by their broad tops mixed with willows in the midst of the flood, which mark the midsummer boundary of the pond. They not only bear but require a good deal of water for their roots. Apparently these will not feel their removal at all. Every rod or two there is a great hummock of meadow sward

I rest in the orchard, doubtful whether to sit in shade or sun. Now the springing foliage is like a sunlight on the woods. I was first attracted and surprised when I looked round and off to Conantum, at the smooth, lawn-like green fields and pasturing cows, bucolical, reminding me of new butter. The air so clear — as not in summer — makes all things shine, as if all surfaces had been washed by the rains of spring and were not yet soiled or begrimed or dulled. You see even to the mountains clearly. The grass so short and fresh, the tender yellowish-green and silvery foliage of the deciduous trees lighting up the landscape, the birds now most musical, the sorrel beginning to redden the fields with ruddy health, — all these things make earth now a paradise. How many times I have been surprised thus, on turning about on this very spot, at the fairness of the earth!

The alders (groves) begin to look like great mosses, so compact and curving to the ground at their edges, — as one system. Pairs of yellow butterflies are seen coquetting through the air higher and higher. Comandra, apparently yesterday. I am surprised, as I go along the edge of the Cliffs, at the oppressive warmth of the air from the dry leaves in the woods on the rocks. Compared with the oaks and hickories, the birches are now a dark green. The order of lightness is apparently black oak silvery (and probably large white), red oaks and hickories, *apparently* more advanced, and green white birches, and then pines. Young white oaks on plain are reddish. A pitch pine sheds pollen on Cliffs. The pines are more conspicuous now than ever, miles off, and the leaves are not yet large enough to conceal them much. It is noon, and I hear the cattle crashing their way down the Cliff, seeking the shade of the woods. They climb like goats. Others seek the water and the shade of bridges. Erigeron, a day or two. It loves moist hillsides.

Landed next at the Miles Swamp. The dense cylindrical racemes of the choke-cherry, some blasted into a puff. Caterpillars prey on this too. I do not find any arums open yet. There are many little gnats dead within them. Barberry at Lee's Cliff, two (??) days; elsewhere just beginning. Some krigias out of bloom. *Galium Aparine* (?), a day or two, but with six (?) leaves. Those scars where the woods were cut down last winter now show, for they are comparatively slow to be covered with green, — only bare dead leaves, reddish-brown spots.

First observe the creak of crickets. It is quite general amid these rocks. The song of only one is more interesting to me. It suggests lateness, but only as we come to a knowledge of eternity after some acquaintance with time. It is only late for all trivial and hurried pursuits. It suggests a wisdom mature, never late, being above all temporal considerations, which possesses the coolness and maturity of autumn amidst the aspiration of spring and the heats of summer. To the birds they say: "Ah! you speak like children from impulse; Nature speaks through you; but with us it is ripe knowledge. The seasons do not revolve for us; we sing their lullaby." So they chant, eternal, at the roots of the grass. It is heaven where

they are, and their dwelling need not be *heaved* up. Forever the same, in May and in November (?). Serenely wise, their song has the security of prose. They have drunk no wine but the dew. It is no transient love-strain, hushed when the incubating season is past, but a glorifying of God and enjoying of him forever. They sit aside from the revolution of the seasons. Their strain is unvaried as Truth. Only in their saner moments do men hear the crickets. It is balm to the philosopher. It tempers his thoughts. They dwell forever in a temperate latitude. By listening to whom, all voices are tuned. In their song they ignore our accidents. They are not concerned about the news. A quire has begun which pauses not for any news, for it knows only the eternal. I hear also *pe-a-wee pe-a-wee*, and then occasionally *pee-yu*, the first syllable in a different and higher key emphasized, — all very sweet and naïve and innocent. *Rubus Canadensis* out, on the rocks. A hummingbird dashes by like a loud humblebee.

May 23. Tuesday. P. M. — To Cedar Swamp by Assabet.

The cobwebs, apparently those I saw on the bushes the morning of the 12th, are now covered with insects, etc. (small gnats, etc.), and are much dilapidated where birds have flown through them. As I paddle up the Assabet, off the Hill, I hear a loud rustling of the leaves and see a large scared tortoise sliding and tumbling down the high steep bank a rod or more into the water. It has probably been out to lay its

Vol. VI

eggs. The old coal-pit heap is a favorite place for them. The wood pewee sings now in the woods behind the spring in the heat of the day (2 P. M.), sitting on a low limb near me, *pe-a-wee, pe-a-wee*, etc., five or six times at short and regular intervals, looking about all the while, and then, naïvely, *pee-a-oo*, emphasizing the first syllable, and begins again. The last is, in emphasis, like the scream of a hen-hawk. It flies off occasionally a few feet, and catches an insect and returns to its perch between the bars, not allowing this to interrupt their order. Scare up a splendid wood (?) duck, alternate blue and chestnut (?) forward, which flew into and lit in the woods; or was it a teal? Afterward two of them, and my diver of yesterday.

The bent grass now lies on the water (commonly light-colored) for two feet. When I first saw this on a pool this spring, with the deep dimple where the blade emerges from the surface, I suspected that the water had risen gently in calm weather and was heaped about the dry stem as against any surface before it is wetted. But now the water is rapidly falling, and there is considerable wind. Moreover, when my boat has passed over these blades, I am surprised on looking back to see the dimple still as perfect as before. I lift a blade so as to bring a part which was under water to the surface, and still there is a perfect dimple about it; the water is plainly repelled from it. I pull one up from the bottom and passing it over my lips am surprised to find that the front side is perfectly dry from the root upward and cannot be wet, but the back side is wet. It has sprung and grown in the water, and

yet one of its surfaces has never been wet. What an invaluable composition it must be coated with! The same was the case with the other erect grasses which I noticed growing in the water, and with those which I plucked on the bank and thrust into it. But the flags were wet both sides.[1] The one surface repels moisture perfectly.

The barbarea has been open several days. The first yellow dor-bug struggling in the river. The white cedar has now grown quite *perceptibly*, and is in advance of any red cedar which I have seen. Saw a hummingbird on a white oak in the swamp. It is strange to see this minute creature, fit inhabitant of a parterre, on an oak in the great wild cedar swamp. The clustered andromeda appears just ready to open; say to-morrow.[2] The smilacina is abundant and well out here now. A new warbler (?).

We soon get through with Nature. She excites an expectation which she cannot satisfy. The merest child which has rambled into a copsewood dreams of a wilderness so wild and strange and inexhaustible as Nature can never show him. The red-bird which I saw on my companion's string on election days I thought but the outmost sentinel of the wild, immortal camp, — of the wild and dazzling infantry of the wilderness, — that the deeper woods abounded with redder birds still; but, now that I have threaded all our woods and waded the swamps, I have never yet met with his compeer, still less his wilder kindred.[3] The red-

[1] *Vide* scrap-book. [2] Rather the 25th.
[3] [Cf. *Week*, pp. 56, 57; Riv. 70, 71.]

bird which is the last of Nature is but the first of God. The White Mountains, likewise, were smooth mole-hills to my expectation. We *condescend* to climb the crags of earth. It is our weary legs alone that praise them. That forest on whose skirts the red-bird flits is not of earth. I expected a fauna more infinite and various, birds of more dazzling colors and more celestial song. How many springs shall I continue to see the common sucker (*Catostomus Bostoniensis*) floating dead on our river! Will not Nature select her types from a new fount? The vignette of the year. This earth which is spread out like a map around me is but the lining of my inmost soul exposed. In me is the sucker that I see. No wholly extraneous object can compel me to recognize it. I am guilty of suckers. I go about to look at flowers and listen to the birds. There was a time when the beauty and the music were all within, and I sat and listened to my thoughts, and there was a song in them. I sat for hours on rocks and wrestled with the melody which possessed me. I sat and listened by the hour to a positive though faint and distant music, not sung by any bird, nor vibrating any earthly harp. When you walked with a joy which knew not its own origin. When you were an organ of which the world was but one poor broken pipe. I lay long on the rocks, foundered like a harp on the seashore, that knows not how it is dealt with. You sat on the earth as on a raft, listening to music that was not of the earth, but which ruled and arranged it. Man *should be* the harp articulate. When your cords were tense.

Vol. VI

greater dewy cobweb spread over the earth. It gives a wholly new aspect to the world, especially in that direction. The sun is eating up the fog. As I return down the hill, my eyes are cast toward the very dark mountains in the northwest horizon, the remnants of a hard blue scalloped rim to our saucer. As if a more celestial ware had formerly been united there to our earthen. Old china are they, worth keeping still on our side-boards, though fragmentary.

The early cinquefoil now generally yellows the banks. Put the sage willow with the black for the present. The black spruce apparently blossomed with the white [*sic*], but its leaf-buds have not yet fairly started.

P. M. — To Pedrick's meadow.

The side-flowering sandwort well out in Moore's Swamp. The pyrus has now for some days taken the place of the amelanchier, though it makes less show. How sweet and peculiar the fragrance of the different kinds of cedar! It is imparted to your hands. Lady's-slipper since the 18th; say 22d. Waded into Beck Stow's. The water was so cold at first that I thought it would not be prudent to stand long in it, but when I got further from the bank it was comparatively warm. True, it was not then shaded nor quite so deep, but I suppose there were some springs in the bank. Surprised to find the *Andromeda Polifolia* in bloom and apparently past its prime at least a week or more. It is in water a foot and a half deep, and rises but little above it. The water must have been several inches

Think of going abroad out of one's self to hear music, — to Europe or Africa! Instead of so living as to be the lyre which the breath of the morning causes to vibrate with that melody which creates worlds — to sit up late and hear Jane Lind!

You may say that the oaks (all but the chestnut oak I have seen) were in bloom yesterday; *i. e.*, shed pollen more or less. Their blooming is soon over. Water-bugs and skaters coupled. Saw in Dakin's land, near the road, at the bend of the river, fifty-nine bank swallows' holes in a small upright bank within a space of twenty by one and a half feet (in the middle), part above and part below the sand-line. This would give over a hundred birds to this bank. They continually circling about over the meadow and river in front, often in pairs, one pursuing the other, and filling the air with their twittering.

Mulberry out to-day.

May 24. 4.30 A. M. — To Cliffs.

A considerable fog, but already rising and retreating to the river. There are dewy cobwebs on the grass. The morning came in and awakened me early, — for I slept with a window open, — and the chip-bird was heard also. As I go along the causeway the [sun] rises red, with a great red halo, through the fog. When I reach the hill, the fog over the river already has its erectile feathers up. I am a little too late. But the level expanse of it far in the east, now lit by the sun, with countless tree-tops like oases seen through it, reminds of vast tracts of sand and of the seashore. It is like a

higher when it began to bloom. A timid botanist would never pluck it. Its flowers are more interesting than any of its family, almost globular, crystalline white, even the calyx, except its tips, tinged with red or rose. Properly called water andromeda: you must wade into water a foot or two deep to get it. The leaves are not so conspicuously handsome as in the winter. Also the buck-bean, apparently as old, — say a week, — in the same depth of water. The *calyculata* almost completely done, and the high blueberry getting thin. *Potentilla Canadensis* var. *simplex*, perhaps two days. I find a male juniper, with effete blossoms quite large, yet so fresh that I suspect I may have antedated it. Between Beck Stow's and Pedrick's meadow. The red cedar has grown considerably, after all. My *Rubus triflorus* (only Bigelow and Gray place it on hillsides) is nearly out of bloom. It is the same I found at the Miles Swamp; has already some green fruit as big as the *smallest* peas. Must be more than a week old. It is the only annual rubus described. May it not be a new kind?

This evening I hear the hum of dor-bugs, — a few, — but listen long in vain to hear a hylodes.

There being probably no shrub or tree which has not begun to leaf now, I sum up the order of their leafing thus (wild and a few tame).[1]

Their buds begin to burst into leaf: —

The earliest gooseberry in garden and swamp, April 20.
? Elder, longest shoots of any, in *some* places (May 5).
Raspberry in swamps.

[1] *Vide* [p. 255].

Thimble-berry (perhaps in favorable places only).

Wild red cherry in some places.

Meadow-sweet.

? Red currant, but slow to advance; observed only ours, which is late?

? Second gooseberry.

Salix alba, April 27.

?? Black currant, not seen.

Small dark native willow blossoming (?) and leafing.

?? Early willow, two-colored, not seen.

?? Muhlenberg's (?), not seen.

Young black cherry.

Choke-cherry shoots.

Viburnum Lentago } not carefully distinguished between.
?   "   *nudum* }

Diervilla, advances fast.

Barberry in favorable places.

Some young apples in favorable places.

Young alders, slow to advance, both kinds.

Early rose.

? Moss rose, not seen.

Sweet-fern, slow to advance.

Mountain-ash, May 5, larger leaves than any tree and first to show green at a distance.

Cultivated cherry.

Pyrus arbutifolia.

? Late pyrus, not seen.

Horse-chestnut.

Hazel, May 5.

? Beaked hazel, not distinguished.

Early large apples.

Late gooseberry in garden.

? Pears, not seen.

Wild red cherry generally; or let it go with the earliest.

? Dwarf or sand cherry.

Hardhack.

?? Clematis, shoots five or six inches long, May 16.

Low blackberry.

?? *Rubus triflorus*, eight inches high, May 22.

? Quince.

?? Mayflower, not seen.

Young red maples.

?? Fever-root, four or five inches high, May 12.

Creeping juniper comes forward like fir balsam.

Larch, opens slowly; makes a show, May 12.

Vaccinium Pennsylvanicum.

Amelanchier Botryapium, fast.

High blackberry.

? *Sempervirens*, not seen.

Young rock maple.

? Large white   "

Alders generally.

?? Linnæa, not seen.

Ostrya.

Amelanchier oblongifolia.

Early trembles suddenly.

?? Dwarf cassandra.

Balm-of-Gilead.

Early thorns.

? Late   "   , not seen.

Yellow birch.

? Cockspur thorn, not seen.

Canoe birch, shoots.

White   "   , shoots.

? Black, young (large not on 12th).

? Canada plum.

Pitch pine.

?? Bear-berry, not seen.

? Norway pine, not seen.

White pine.

Young hornbeam.

Cornus alternifolia.

? Round-leaved [cornel], seen late.

Panicled cornel.

Silky   "

Sweet-gale, May 11.

Red oak, May 11.

Bass, sudden.

Young chestnuts and lower limbs; full leafing of large not seen.

?? Clethra, seen late.[1]

Old hornbeam.

?? Maple-leaved arrow-wood, not seen till late.

Arrow-wood.

Butternut.

High blueberry.

Rhus Toxicodendron.

?   var. *radicans*, seen late.

Sweet-briar generally; earliest not seen.

? Swamp rose, seen late.

?? Beech, not seen.

White-ash, May 12.

Fir-balsam.

? Fever-bush, seen rather late.

?? Woodbine, not seen.

Black shrub oak.

Elm, young.

? Slippery [elm], not seen.

Great red maples, May 13.

Clustered andromeda, 13th.

Young *Populus grandidentata* (large three or four days later?).

Black oak.

Black willow.

?? Sage   "   , seen late.

? Chinquapin oak.

?? Chestnut   "   , not seen.

Celtis.

?? Cranberry.

Locust, 14th.

Nemopanthes.

? Witch-hazel, in our garden.

Swamp white oak, slow.

? Large sugar maples, not well observed.

White swamp-pink.

[1] *Vide* forward.

Buttonwood.

Cornus florida.

Panicled andromeda, not generally; several days later.

? Waxwork, seen but last place.

Pignut hickory, make a show suddenly.

? Mockernut hickory.

?? Black walnut.

Young white oak (old 15th, slow).

Prinos verticillatus, 15th.

? Single-berry prinos, seen late.

Huckleberries, black.

N. B. — Trees generally!!

Grape.

Smilax.

?? Pinweeds, seen late, six or more inches high; the large, May 22.

?? Cistus, as early at least.

Mulberry, May 16.

?? Carrion-flower, four or five feet long, the 31st of May.

White spruce,[1] slow.

Sassafras, slow.

Lambkill.

?? Mountain laurel, not seen early.

?? *Andromeda Polifolia*, seen late.

? Rhodora.

Tupelo.

Poison-dogwood.

Jersey tea.

Azalea nudiflora, 17th.

Button-bush, but does not show, being few buds.

Beach plum, 19th; *scarcely* makes any show the 24th, no more than the button-bush.

? Red cedar. } growth not obvious, and difference in trees; not
White   "   }   sure of date.
Arbor-vitæ }

Young hemlocks, 20th; old, 21st.

Checkerberry, 20th, shoots just visible.

[1] ["White" is crossed out in pencil, and "black, white **variety**" substituted.]

? Mountain sumach, 22d.[1]
? Black spruce,[2] 24th, hardly yet at Potter's.

Of *common* deciduous shrubs or trees, the button-bush is the latest to leaf, and, from the fewness of its buds, *i. e.* the great intervals between them, they appear later than other plants which leaf nearly at the same time. Their being subject to overflows at this season may have to do with this habit, as hardhacks, etc., under these circumstances are equally late.

Of *all* deciduous shrubs and trees the mountain sumach at Hubbard's field is the latest to leaf. I have not observed those under Fair Haven.[3]

The beach plum at a little distance does not make so much show of green even as the button-bush. Do the young shoots show more?

Tree-toads heard oftener, and at evening I hear a dor-bug hum past. The mouse-ear down begins to blow in fields.

May 25. 5.30 A. M. — To Hill.
Smilax. Heard and saw by the sassafras shore the rose-breasted grosbeak, a handsome bird with a loud and very rich song, in character between that of a robin and a red-eye. It sang steadily like a robin. Rose breast, white beneath, black head and above, white on shoulder and wings. The flowering ferns[4] *just begin* to light up the meadow with their yellowish green.

[1] The 31st May it is much more forward than the button-bush at Cliffs, and perhaps started first.
[2] Dark variety.   [3] *Vide* May 31.   [4] Probably onoclea.

Vol. VI

driven in an ashen wedge about three quarters of an inch thick on the outside. This made it perpendicular, and he was about filling it with clay and protecting it. In Nathan Stow's sprout-land every black cherry is completely stripped of leaves by the caterpillars, and they look *as if* dead, only their great triangular white nests being left in their forks. I see where a frost killed the young white oak leaves and some hickories in deep sprout-land hollows, apparently about a week ago, when the shoots were about an inch long and the leaves about the same. Evergreen-forest note still, — the first syllable three times repeated, er-er-er, etc., — flitting amid the tops of the pines. Some young red or scarlet (?) oaks have already grown eighteen inches, *i. e.* within a fortnight, before their leaves have two-thirds expanded. In this instance, perhaps, they have accomplished more than half their year's growth, as if, being held back by winter, their vegetative force had accumulated and now burst forth like a stream which has been dammed. They are properly called *shoots*. Gathered some small pincushion galls on a white oak. They are smaller and handsome, more colored than those I first saw on shrub oaks about a week ago. They are shaped somewhat like little bass-drum sticks with large pads, — on the end of last year's twigs. It is a globular mass composed of fine crystalline rays, somewhat like stigmas, the ground white ones, thickly sprinkled with bright-scarlet (rather than crimson) dimples. This is one of the most faery-like productions of the woods. These young white oak leaves and young leaves generally are downy, — downy-swaddled, as if for protec-

May 26. Friday. 5.30 A. M. — To climbing ivy.
Pipe-grass equisetum. Buttercups now densely spot the churchyard. Now for the fragrance of firs and spruce.

P. M. — To Walden.
Horse-radish, several days; rye four feet high. The luxuriant and rapid growth of this hardy and valuable grass is always surprising. How genial must nature be to it! It makes the revolution of the seasons seem a rapid whirl. How quickly and densely it clothes the earth! Thus early it suggests the harvest and fall. At sight of this deep and dense field all vibrating with motion and light, looking into the mass of its pale(?)-green culms, winter recedes many degrees in my memory. This the early queen of grasses with us (?). Indian corn the 2d, or later. It always impresses us at this season with a sense of genialness and bountifulness. Grasses universally shoot up like grain now, in many places deceiving with the promise of a luxuriant crop where in a few weeks they will be dry and wiry. Pastures look as if they were mowing-land. The season of grass, now everywhere green and luxuriant.

The leaves have now grown so much that it [is] difficult to see the small birds in the tree-tops, and it is too late now to survey in woods conveniently. Saw Mr. Holbrook trying an experiment on an elm this morning, which he endeavored in vain to make perpendicular last year with a brace. It was about six inches in diameter, and he had sawed it a little more than half through at about six feet from the ground and then

tion against frosts, etc. Are not the more tender the most downy? Why is the downy *Populus grandidentata* so much later than the other? The lint now *begins* to come off the young leaves.

The annular eclipse of the sun this afternoon is invisible on account of the clouds. Yet it seems to have created a strong wind by lowering the temperature? Yellow Bethlehem-star, a day or more; near the broom-rape.

May 27. P. M. — To Saw Mill Brook.
Geum rivale, a day or two at Hubbard's Close; also the *Rubus triflorus* abundant there along the brook next the maple swamp, and still in bloom. Wild pinks (*Silene*), apparently a day or two. The red-eye is an indefatigable singer, — a succession of short bars with hardly an interval long continued, now at 3 P. M. The pincushion galls on young white oaks and on shrub oaks are now in their prime. It is a kind of crystalline wool. Those which I have noticed on the shrub oaks are the largest, and are crimson-spotted, while those on the young white oaks are scarlet-spotted and for the most part about the size of a cranberry. They are either at the extremity of last year's twig or saddled on it midway. No fruit perhaps catches my eye more. It is remarkable that galls are apparently as early to form as the leaves to start, and that some of them are among the most beautiful products of the wood. Within small hard kernels in the midst of these I find minute white grubs. I see and hear the yellow-throated vireo. It is *somewhat* similar (its strain) to that of the red-eye,

prelia pre-li-ay, with longer intervals and occasionally a whistle like *tlea tlow*, or *chowy chow*, or *tully ho* (??) on a higher key. It flits about in the tops of the trees. I find the pensile nest of a red-eye between a fork of a shrub chestnut near the path. It is made, thus far, of bark and different woolly and silky materials. The arums — some of them — have bloomed probably as early as the last I saw at the Miles Swamp. *Viola pubescens* must be about out of bloom (??). *Actæa alba* fully out, the whole raceme, say two days.

I see young gooseberries as big as *small* green peas.

Is that low two or three leaved plant without stem about Saw Mill Brook a wood lettuce?

That tall swamp fern by Eb. Hubbard's Close, with fertile fronds separate and now cinnamon-colored, perhaps a little later than the interrupted, appears to be the *cinnamomea*. Is that very wide, loose-spread fern, three or four feet high, now beginning to fruit terminally, the *spectabilis*, — a large specimen?

May 28. Sunday. The *F. hyemalis*, fox-colored sparrow, rusty grackles, tree sparrows, have all gone by; also the purple finch. The snipe has ceased (?) to boom. I have not heard the phœbe of late, and methinks the bluebird and the robin are not heard so often (the former certainly not). Those tumultuous morning concerts of sparrows, tree and song, hyemalis, and grackles, like leaves on the trees, are past, and the woodland quire will rather be diminished than in-

creased henceforth. But, on the other hand, toads and frogs and insects, especially at night, all through June, betray by the sounds they make their sensitiveness to the increasing temperature, and theirs especially is the music which ushers in the summer. Each warmer night, like this, the toads and frogs sing with increased energy, and already fill the air with sound, though the bullfrogs have not yet begun to trump in earnest. To this add the hum and creak of insects. These still herald or expect the summer. The birds do not foretell that.

12 M. — By boat to Lee's Cliff.

Larch cones are now conspicuous and handsome, — dark-crimson, about half an inch long. Pitch pine cones, too, are now handsome. The larch has a little of the sweetness of the fir, etc. Pontederias, flags, *Polygonum hydropiperoides* (just showing itself), that coarse utricularia, often floating, potamogetons, etc., etc., now begin to make a conspicuous border to the river, and its summer limits begin to be defined. Pads began to be eaten by insects as soon as they appeared, though it is still so high that I am obliged to lower my mast at the bridges. Even this spring the arches of the stone bridge were completely concealed by the flood, and yet at midsummer I can sail under them without lowering my mast, which is [ ][1] feet high from the bottom of the boat. Critchicrotches have been edible some time in some places. It must be a kind of water milfoil, whose leaves I now see variously divided under water, and some nearly two feet long.[2]

[1] [A blank space left here.]   [2] Probably *Sium*.

Vol. VI

At the *old* bridge at the hill, the water being quite smooth, I saw a water-bug cross straight from the south to the north side, about six rods, furrowing the water in a waving line, there being no other insects near him on the surface. It took but about a minute. It was an interesting sight, proving that this little insect, whose eyes are hardly raised above the plane of the water, sees, or is cognizant of, the opposite shore. I have no doubt that they cross with ease and rapidity lakes a mile wide. It looked like an adventurous voyage for it. Probably he is in danger from fishy monsters, — though it must be difficult for a fish to catch one.

I see the exuviæ or cases of some insects on the stems of water plants above the surface. The large devil's-needles are revealed by the reflection in the water, when I cannot see them in the air, and at first mistake them for swallows. Broom-rape, perhaps yesterday. Thimble-berry out, — at Lee's Cliff day before yesterday at least. Distinguished by the downy under sides of its leaves. I see those large, thin, transparent radical heart (?) leaves[1] floating on the surface, as if bitten off by some creature. I see breams' nests which have been freshly cleared out and are occupied. The *red* choke-berry is fully out, and I do not know but it is as early as the black. Red clover at Clamshell, a day or two. Saw that common snake *Coluber eximius* of De Kay, — checkered adder, etc., etc., — forty-one inches long. A rather light brown above, with large dark-brown, irregularly quadrangular blotches, mar-

[1] *Nuphar Kalmiana.*

gined with black, and similar small ones, on the sides; abdomen light salmon-white, — whitest toward the head, — checkered with quadrangular blotches; very light bluish-slate in some lights and dark-slate or black in others. Abdominal plates 201, caudal scales 45. I should think from Storer's description that his specimen had lost its proper colors in spirits. He describes not the colors of a living snake, but those which alcohol might impart to it (?). It is as if you were to describe the white man as very red in the face, having seen a drunkard only.

The huckleberries, excepting the late, are now generally in blossom, their rich clear red contrasting with the light-green leaves; frequented by honey-bees, full of promise for the summer. One of the great crops of the year. The blossom of the *Vaccinium vacillans* is larger and paler, but higher-colored on one side and more transparent (?), less concealed by leaves. These are the blossoms of the *Vacciniew*, or Whortleberry Family, which affords so large a proportion of our berries. The crop of oranges, lemons, nuts, and raisins, and figs, quinces, etc., etc., not to mention tobacco and the like, is of no importance to us compared with these. The berry-promising flower of the *Vacciniew*. This crop grows wild all over the country, — wholesome, bountiful, and free, — a real ambrosia (one is called *V. Vitis-Idæa*, Vine of Mt. Ida), — and yet men — the foolish demons that they are — devote themselves to culture of tobacco, inventing slavery and a thousand other curses as the means, — with infinite pains and inhumanity go raise tobacco all their lives. Tobacco is the staple instead of huckleberries. Wreaths of tobacco smoke go up from this land, the incense of a million sensualists. With what authority can such distinguish between Christians and Mahometans?

Finding the low blackberry nearly open, I looked long and at last, where the vine ran over a rock on the south hillside, the reflected heat had caused it [to] open fully its large white blossoms. In such places, apparently yesterday. The high blackberry in similar places, at least to-day. At these rocks I hear a sharp *peep*, — methinks of a peetweet dashing away. Four pale-green (?) eggs, finely sprinkled with brown, in a brown thrasher's nest, on the ground (!!) under a barberry bush. The night-warbler, after his strain, drops down almost perpendicularly into a tree-top and is lost. The crickets, though it is everywhere an oppressively warm day (yesterday I had a fire!!) and I am compelled to take off my thinnish coat, are heard, particularly amid the rocks at Lee's Cliff. They must love warmth. As if it were already autumn there. White clover under the rocks. I see the ebony spleenwort full-grown. The pitch pines are *rather* past bloom here, — the cobwebs they contain yellowed with their dust, — probably generally in bloom elsewhere. *Turritis stricta*, apparently out of bloom. Young wild cherry under rocks, fully out two or three days; generally or elsewhere not quite out; probably will *begin* to-morrow.

It would be worth the while to ask ourselves weekly, Is our life innocent enough? Do we live *inhumanely*, toward man or beast, in thought or act? To be serene

Vol. VI

and successful we must be at one with the universe. The least conscious and needless injury inflicted on any creature is to its extent a suicide. What peace — or life — can a murderer have?

Fair Haven Cliffs.

The lint has begun to come off the young leaves. The birches are still the darkest green to be seen in large masses, except evergreens. The last begin to be less conspicuous, beginning to be lost in the sea of verdure. The shrub oak plain is now fairly greened again, only slightly tinged with redness here and there, where are the youngest white oak leaves.

As I sail down toward the Clamshell Hill about an hour before sunset, the water is smoothed like glass, though the breeze is as strong as before. How is this? Yet I have not seen much smooth water this spring. I think the fall must be the time. The rounded green hills are very fair and elysian. The low clumps of bushes on their sides, just clothed with tender verdure, look like islets half sunk and floating in a cool sea of grass. They do not stand, but float on the cool glaucous swells. Though the grass is really short and thin there. Whole schools of fishes leap out of water at once with a loud plashing, even many rods distant, scared by my sail. Cracks in the earth are still visible, and hips of the late rose still hold on under water in some places.

The inhumanity of science concerns me, as when I am tempted to kill a rare snake that I may ascertain its species. I feel that this is not the means of acquiring true knowledge.

May 29. Monday. P. M. — To Cedar Swamp by Assabet.

The white maple keys have begun to fall and float down the stream like the wings of great insects. Dandelions and mouse-ear down have been blowing for some time and are seen on water. These are interesting as methinks the first of the class of downy seeds which are more common in the fall. There are myriads of shad-flies fluttering over the dark and still water under the hill, one every yard or two, continually descending, almost falling, to the surface of the water as if to drink and then, with perhaps a little difficulty, rising again, again to fall upon it, and so on. I see the same one fall and rise five or six feet thus four or five times; others rise *much* higher; and now comes along a large dragon-fly and snatches one. This two or three times. Other smaller insects, light-colored, are fluttering low close to the water, and in some places are swarms of small black moths. *Viburnum Lentago* in a warm place. The choke-cherry is leaving off to bloom, now that the black cherry is beginning. The clustered andromeda is not yet fully, *i. e.* abundantly, out. The tall huckleberry in swamps is well out. In the longitudinal crevices of the white cedar bark there is much clear yellow resin. Raspberry, probably yesterday, side of railroad, above red house. See a purple finch and hear him, — robin-like and rich warbling. S. Barrett thinks that many chubs are killed at mills, and hence are seen floating. I see no stone-heaps distinctly formed yet.

Saw what I thought my night-warbler, — sparrow-

like with chestnut (?) stripes on breast, white or whitish below and about eyes, and perhaps chestnut (??) head.

Stellaria longifolia, apparently apetalous (!), ten or twelve inches high, will soon open on the bank near the *Ranunculus abortivus*.

These days it is left to one Mr. Loring to say whether a citizen of Massachusetts is a slave or not. Does any one think that Justice or God awaits Mr. Loring's decision? Such a man's existence in this capacity under these circumstances is as impertinent as the gnat that settles on my paper. We do not ask him to make up his mind, but to make up his pack. Why, the United States Government never performed an act of justice in its life! And this unoffending citizen is held a prisoner by the United States soldier, of whom the best you can say is that he is a fool in a painted coat. Of what use a Governor or a Legislature? they are nothing but politicians. I have listened of late to hear the voice of a Governor, Commander-in-Chief of the forces of Massachusetts. I heard only the creaking of the crickets and the hum of the insects which now fill the summer air. The Governor's exploit is to review the troops on muster-days. I have seen him on horseback, with his hat off, listening to a chaplain's prayer. That is all I have ever seen of a Governor. I think that I could manage to get along without one. When freedom is most endangered, he dwells in the deepest obscurity. A distinguished clergyman once told me that he chose the profession of a clergyman because it afforded the most leisure for literary pursuits. I would recommend to him the profession of a Governor. I see the papers full of soft speeches of the mayor and the Governor and brother editors. I see the Court-House full of armed men, holding prisoner and trying a MAN, to find out if he is not really a SLAVE. It is a question about which there is great doubt.[1]

It is really the trial of Massachusetts. Every moment that she hesitates to set this man free, she is convicted. The Commissioner on her case is God.[2] Perhaps the most saddening aspect of the matter is the tone of almost all the Boston papers, connected with the fact that they are and have been of course sustained by a majority of their readers. They are feeble indeed, but only as sin compared with righteousness and truth. They are eminently time-serving. I have seen only the *Traveller*, *Journal*, and *Post*. I never look at them except at such a time as this. Their life is abject even as that of the marines. Men in any office of government are everywhere and forever politicians. Will mankind never learn that policy is not morality, that it never secures any moral right, but always considers merely what is "expedient," — chooses the available candidate, who, when moral right is concerned, is always the devil? Witness the President of the United States. What is the position of Massachusetts? (Massachooses-it!) She leaves it to a Mr. Loring to decide whether one of her citizens is a freeman or a slave. What is the value of such a SHE 'S FREEDOM AND

[1] [*Cape Cod, and Miscellanies*, pp. 389, 390; *Misc.*, Riv. 172, 173.]
[2] [*Cape Cod, and Miscellanies*, p. 394; *Misc.*, Riv. 178.]

PROTECTION to me? Perhaps I shall so conduct that she will one day offer me the FREEDOM OF MASSACHUSETTS in a gold casket, — made of California gold in the form of a court-house, perchance. I spurn with contempt any bribe which she or her truckling men can offer. I do not vote at the polls. I wish to record my vote here. Men profess to be surprised because the devil does not behave like an angel of light. The majority of the men of the North, and of the South and East and West, are not men of principle. If they vote, they do not send men to Congress on errands of humanity; but, while their brothers and sisters are being scourged and hung for loving liberty, while (insert here all the inhumanities that pandemonium can conceive of), it is the mismanagement of wood and iron and stone and gold which concerns them. Do what you will, O Government, with my mother and brother, my father and sister, I will obey your command to the letter. It will, indeed, grieve me if you hurt them, if you deliver them to overseers to be hunted by hounds, and to be whipped to death; but, nevertheless, I will peaceably pursue my chosen calling on this fair earth, until, perhaps, one day I shall have persuaded you to relent. Such is the attitude, such are the words of Massachusetts. Rather than thus consent to establish hell upon earth, — to be a party to this establishment, — I would touch a match to blow up earth and hell together. As I love my life, I would side with the Light and let the Dark Earth roll from under me, calling my mother and my brother to follow me.[1]

[1] [*Cape Cod, and Miscellanies*, pp. 400, 401; *Misc.*, Riv. 186, 187.]

Vol. VI

May 30. *Tuesday*. Whiteweed. *Spergularia rubra*, apparently a day or two, side of railroad above red house. Yarrow.

P. M. — To Clintonia Swamp and Pond.

Saw a black snake, dead, four feet three inches long, slate-colored beneath. Saw what was called a California cat which a colored man brought home from California, — an animal at least a third smaller than a cat and shaped more like a polecat or weasel, brown-gray, with a cat-like tail of alternate black and white rings, very large ears, and eyes which were prominent, long body like a weasel, and sleeps with its head between its fore paws, curling itself about; a rank smell to it. It was lost several days in our woods, and was caught again in a tree about a crow's nest.

Ranunculus repens, perhaps a day or two; channelled peduncle and spreading calyx and conspicuously spotted leaves. The leaves of the tall buttercup are much larger and finely cut and, as it were, peltate. Pickerel are not easily detected, — such is their color, — as if they were transparent. Vetch. I see now green high blueberries, and gooseberries in Hubbard's Close, as well as shad-bush berries and strawberries. In this dark, cellar-like maple swamp are scattered at pretty regular intervals tufts of green ferns, *Osmunda cinnamomea*, above the dead brown leaves, broad, tapering fronds, curving over on every side from a compact centre, now three or four feet high. Wood frogs skipping over the dead leaves, whose color they resemble. Clintonia. Medeola. The last may be earlier. I am surprised to find arethusas abundantly out in Hub-

bard's Close, maybe two or three days, though not yet at Arethusa Meadow, probably on account of the recent freshet. It is so leafless that it shoots up unexpectedly. It is all color, a little hook of purple flame projecting from the meadow into the air. Some are comparatively pale. This high-colored plant shoots up suddenly, all flower, in meadows where it is wet walking. A superb flower. Cotton-grass here also, probably two or three days for the same reason. *Eriophorum polystachyon* var. *latifolium*, having rough peduncles.

The twigs of the dwarf willow, now gone to seed, are thickly invested with cotton, containing little green seed-vessels, like excrement of caterpillars, and the shrubs look at a little distance like sand cherries in full bloom. These are among the downy seeds that fly.

Found a ground-robin's nest, under a tuft of dry sedge which the winter had bent down, in sprout-land on the side of Heywood Peak, perfectly concealed, with two whitish eggs very thickly sprinkled with brown; made of coarse grass and weed stems and lined with a *few* hairs and *stems* of the mahogany moss.

The pink is certainly one of the finest of our flowers and deserves the place it holds in my memory. It is now in its prime on the south side of the Heywood Peak, where it grows luxuriantly in dense rounded tufts or hemispheres, raying out on every side and presenting an even and regular surface of expanded flowers. I count in one such tuft, of an oval form twelve inches by eight, some three hundred fully open and about three times as many buds, — more than a thousand in all. Some tufts consist wholly of white ones with a very faint tinge of pink. This flower is as elegant in form as in color, though it is not fragrant. It is associated in my mind with the first heats of summer, or [those] which announce its near approach. Few plants are so worthy of cultivation. The shrub oak pincushion (?) galls are larger, whiter, and less compact than those of the white oak. I find the linnæa, and budded, in Stow's Wood by Deep Cut.

Sweet flag. Waxwork to-morrow.[1] I see my umbrella toadstool on the hillside has already pierced the ground.

May 31. Old Election. Cold weather. Many go a-fishing to-day in earnest, and one gets forty pouts in river. Locust.

P. M. — To Miles Meadow by boat.

A cold southeast wind. Blue-eyed grass, apparently in pretty good season. Saw a greater telltale, and this is the only one I have seen probably; distinguished by its size. It is very watchful, but not timid, allowing me to come quite near, while it stands on the lookout at the water's edge. It keeps nodding its head with an awkward jerk, and wades in the water to the middle of its yellow legs; goes off with a loud and sharp *phe phe phe phe*, or something like that. It acts the part of the telltale, though there are no birds here, as if [it] were with a flock. Remarkable as a sentinel for other birds. I think I see a few clams come up. The

[1] June 1st.

Vol. VI

VII

JUNE, 1854

(ÆT. 36)

June 1. 4.30 A. M. — To Hill.

Fever-root. The umbrella toadstool yesterday, and now decaying. A smaller one.

It was so cold last night and still that I surely expected a frost and covered all our melons. But either the wind changed or clouds came over in the night, and there was no frost here. Here is another cool day. I sit with window shut and walk with a thick coat, as yesterday. Do we not always have these changes about the first of June?

P. M. — To Bare Hill *via* Walden road and Goose Pond.

Below the almshouse I see a small sparrow, not larger than the field sparrow, with a white line down the middle of the head, a tawny throat and breast, a yellow spot over the eye and another on the forward part of the wings, flesh-colored legs, upper mandible dusky, and wings dark with faint lines of white. Undoubtedly the *Fringilla passerina*. There were two. Its note was that of my seringo, but very faint and short, sitting on the wall or fence-post.

I see caterpillars, now full-grown, clustered upon their great nests on stripped cherry trees in the woods.

---

mountain sumach at the Cliffs is much more forward than at Hubbard's, and perhaps is earlier to leaf than the button-bush. Alternate cornel, apparently yesterday. Cockspur thorn is well out; how long?

Maidenhair fern, how handsome!

Hear my evergreen-forest note, sounding rather raspingly as usual, where there are large oaks and pines mingled, — *er-er te, te ter twee*, or *er te, te ter twe*.[1] It is very difficult to discover now that the leaves are grown, as it frequents the tops of the trees. But I get a glimpse of its black throat and, I think, yellow head. This and the red-eye and wood pewee are singing now at midday. The pincushion galls of the shrub oaks have but little color compared with those of the white oak, and are now turning brown. The shrub oak ones are larger but plainer, less spotted, and less distinctly spotted, than the others. Galls are a surprising production of nature, suggesting a union or connivance of two kingdoms, the animal and vegetable, to produce. Many, like the ordinary black oak-balls (I see some fully grown), seem as natural to the tree as its proper fruit, and plainly anticipated by its whole economy. We hesitate to pronounce them abortions. Their grub is a foster-child of the oak. I see equally if not more remarkable and regular ones on a black shrub oak, of this form, attached to a leaf, green, — a core like this: Being filled with air, they burst with a puff when pressed.

I see marks of a frost last night in sprout-land hollows; young white oaks and hickories, and some

[1] [A good rendering of the song of the black-throated green warbler.]

other oaks even, have been touched, and, though not yet black, their leaves are crisped and come off. In wood-paths and elsewhere I now see countless dragon-flies which have lately taken wing, — some of those pretty little blue ones, and various colors. One of those biting flies stabs my finger severely, wings half black, with a green front.

Within little more than a fortnight the woods, from bare twigs, have become a sea of verdure, and young *shoots* have contended with one another in the race. The leaves have unfurled all over the country like a parasol. Shade is produced, and the birds are concealed and their economies go forward uninterruptedly, and a covert is afforded to the animals generally. But thousands of worms and insects are preying on the leaves while they are young and tender. Myriads of little parasols are suddenly spread all the country over, to shield the earth and the roots of the trees from parching heat, and they begin to flutter and rustle in the breeze. Checkerberry shoots in forward places are now just fit to eat, they are so young and tender. In a long walk I have found these somewhat refreshing. From Bare Hill there is a bluish mist on the landscape, giving it a glaucous appearance.

Now I see gentlemen and ladies sitting at anchor in boats on the lakes in the calm afternoons, under parasols, making use of nature, not always accumulating money. The farmer hoeing is wont to look with scorn and pride on a man sitting in a motionless boat a whole half-day, but he does not realize that the object of his own labor is perhaps merely to add another dollar to

his heap, nor through what coarseness and inhumanity to his family and servants he often accomplishes this. He has an Irishman or a Canadian working for him by the month; and what, probably, is the lesson that he is teaching him by precept and example? Will it make that laborer more of a man? this earth more like heaven? The veiny-leaved hawkweed to-morrow. I see the sand cherry in puffs like the Canada plum in some places.

June 2. Friday. P. M. — Up Assabet to Castilleja and Annursnack.

While waiting for Mother and Sophia I look now from the yard to the waving and slightly glaucous-tinged June meadows, edged by the cool shade — gelid — of shrubs and trees, — a waving shore of shady bays and promontories, — yet different from the August shades. It is beautiful and elysian. The air has now begun to be filled with a bluish haze. These virgin shades of the year, when everything is tender, fresh and green, — how full of promise! promising bowers of shade in which heroes may repose themselves! I would fain be present at the birth of shadow. It takes place with the first expansion of the leaves.

I find sanicle just out on the Island. The black willows are already beautiful, and the hemlocks with their bead-work of new green. Are these not kingbird days, when, in clearer first June days full of light, this aërial, twittering bird flutters from willow to willow and swings on the twigs, showing his white-edged

tail? The *Azalea nudiflora* has about done, or there was apparently little of it. I see some breams' nests near my old bathing-place above the stone-heaps, with sharp, yellow, sandy edges, like a milk-pan from within,

showing considerable art (?) as well as labor. Also there are three or four small stone-heaps formed. We went near to the stone bridge and crossed direct *via* the house-leek, of which I brought home a bunch. No *Stellaria longifolia* nor *Ranunculus abortivus* to be found yet in bloom, though probably some of the first, apetalous, have opened now. Lamb-kill. The Painted-Cup Meadow is all lit up with ferns, on its springy slopes. The handsome flowering fern, now rapidly expanding and fruiting at the same time, colors these moist slopes afar with its now commonly reddish fronds. And then there are the interrupted and the cinnamon ferns in very handsome and regular tufts, and the brakes standing singly and more backward. The rue, just budded, smells remarkably like a skunk and also like a rank dog. Strange affinity! Took tea at Mrs. Barrett's.

When we returned to our boat at 7 P. M., I noticed first, to my surprise, that the river was all alive with leaping fish, their heads seen continually darted above water, and they were large fish, too. Looking up I found that the whole atmosphere over the river was full of shad-flies. It was a *great flight of ephemeræ.* It was not so when I landed an hour and a half before. They extended as high as I could see. It was like a dense snow-storm, and all (with very few exceptions) flying

as with one consent up the stream. Many coupled in the air, and many more with the bodies curved. They reached a mile or more from the stone-heaps to the mouth of the Assabet, but were densest where there were woods on both sides, whether they came out of them, or they made the air more still for them. Those I examined had three very long streamers behind, the two outside about an inch and a quarter. The fishes I saw rise for such as were struggling on the water close to the boat were, I am pretty sure, suckers. This is like what the French fishermen call "manna." There were also swarms of small black millers close above the surface, and other small ones. Several dead suckers were floating. It seemed as if the suckers were now ascending the river. In the air there was one or more at least to every foot. Apparently this phenomenon reached on this stream as far as it was wooded.

Caraway naturalized, and out apparently two or three days, in S. Barrett's front yard.

June 3. Saturday. 9 A. M. — To Fair Haven with Blake and Brown.

A very warm day, without a breeze. A kingbird's nest in a fork of a black willow. Going up Fair Haven Hill, the blossoms of the huckleberries and blueberries imparted a sweet scent to the whole hillside. The cistus is well out on the Cliffs; maybe several days. At Lee's Cliff, where we dined, the oxalis pretty early (?). Hear the first, but a faint, locust.[1] On the pond,

---

[1] Was it not a cricket?

played a long [time] with the bubbles which we made with our paddles on the smooth, perhaps unctuous, surface, in which little hemispherical cases we saw ourselves and boat, small, black and distinct, with a fainter reflection on the opposite side of the bubble (head to head). These lasted sometimes a minute before they burst. They reminded me more of Italy than of New England. Crossed to Baker Farm and Mt. Misery. To-day, having to seek a shady and the most airy place, at length we were glad when the east wind arose, ruffled the water and cooled the air, and wafted us homeward. Reflected how many times other similar bubbles, which had now burst, had reflected here the Indian, his canoe and paddle, with the same faithfulness that they now image me and my boat.

June 4. 8 A. M. — Up Assabet to Barbarea Shore with Blake and Brown.

Brown speaks of a great brown moth, — probably emperor moth, — which came out in Worcester a few days ago. I see under the window, half dead, a large sphinx-*like* moth which apparently flew last night. The surface of the still water nowadays with a kind of lint, looking like dust at a little distance. Is it the down of the leaves blown off? In many places it reaches quite across the river. It is interesting to distinguish the different surfaces, — here broken into waves and sparkling with light, there, where covered with this linty dust or film, merely undulating without breaking, and there quite smooth and stagnant. I see in one place a sharp

Vol. VI

and distinct line, as if there were a cobweb on the water, between the clear and ruffled water and the stagnant filmy part, as if it were a slightly raised seam; and particles of lint (?) are continually gliding in from the clear space and arranging themselves along the edge of the scum or film.

These warm and dry days, which put spring far behind, the sound of the cricket at noon has a new value and significance, so serene and cool. It is the *iced*-cream of song. It is modulated shade. I see now here and there deep furrows in the sandy bottom, two or three inches wide, leading from the middle of the river toward the side, and a clam on its edge at the end of each. These are distinct whiter lines. Plainly, then, about these times the clams are coming up to the shore, and I have caught them in the act. I now notice froth on the pitch and white pines. The lower and horizontal parts of the shaggy button-bushes, now left bare, are covered thickly with dry brown-paper confervæ, for the most part bleached almost white. It is very abundant, and covers these stems more thickly than clothes on a line.

P. M. — To Walden.

Now is the time [to] observe the leaves, so fair in color and so perfect in form. I stood over a sprig of choke-cherry, with fair and perfect glossy green obovate and serrate leaves, in the woods this P. M., as if it were a rare flower. Now the various forms of oak leaves in sprout-lands, wet-glossy, as if newly painted green and varnished, attract me. The chinquapin and

black shrub oak are such leaves as I fancy crowns were made of. And in the washing breeze the lighter under sides begin to show, and a new light is flashed upon the year, lighting up and enlivening the landscape. Perhaps, on the whole, as most of the under sides are of a glaucous hue, they add to the glaucous mistiness of the atmosphere, which now has begun to prevail. The mountains are hidden. Methinks the first dry spell or drought may be beginning. The dust is powdery in the street, and we do not always have dew in the night.

The cracks in the ground made by the frost in the winter are still quite distinct.

In some cases fame is perpetually false and unjust. Or rather I should say that she *never* recognizes the simple heroism of an action, but only as connected with its apparent consequence. It praises the interested energy of the Boston Tea Party, but will be comparatively silent about the more bloody and disinterestedly heroic attack on the Boston Court-House, simply because the latter was unsuccessful. Fame is not just. It never finely or discriminatingly praises, but coarsely hurrahs. The truest acts of heroism never reach her ear, are never published by her trumpet.[1]

June 5. 6 P. M. — To Cliffs.

Large yellow butterflies with black spots since the 3d. Carrion-flower, maybe a day. Dangle-berry, probably June 3d at Trillium Woods. Now, just before sundown, a nighthawk is circling, imp-like, with

[1] [*Cape Cod, and Miscellanies,* p. 403; *Misc.,* Riv. 190, 191.]

undulating, irregular flight over the sprout-land on the Cliff Hill, with an occasional squeak and showing the spots on his wings. He does not circle away from this place, and I associate him with two gray eggs somewhere on the ground beneath and a mate there sitting. This squeak and occasional booming is heard in the evening air, while the stillness on the side of the village makes more distinct the increased hum of insects. I see at a distance a kingbird or blackbird pursuing a crow lower down the hill, like a satellite revolving about a black planet. I have come to this hill to see the sun go down, to recover sanity and put myself again in relation with Nature. I would fain drink a draft of Nature's serenity. Let deep answer to deep. Already I see reddening clouds reflected in the smooth mirror of the river, a delicate tint, far off and elysian, unlike anything in the sky as yet. The evergreens now look even black by contrast with the sea of fresh and light-green foliage which surrounds them. Children have been to the Cliffs and woven wreaths or chaplets of oak leaves, which they have left, for they were unconsciously attracted by the beauty of the leaves now. The sun goes down red and shorn of his beams, a sign of hot weather, as if the western horizon or the lower stratum of the air were filled with the hot dust of the day. The dust of his chariot eclipses his beams. I love to sit here and look off into the broad deep vale in which the shades of night are beginning to prevail. When the sun has set, the river becomes more white and distinct in the landscape. The pincushion galls have mostly turned brown, especially the shrub oak ones. Perhaps the sorrel was most noticeable last week. The caterpillars are and have been very numerous this year. I see large trees (wild cherry and apple) completely stripped of leaves. Some of the latter, twenty or thirty feet high, are full of blossoms without a single leaf. I return by moonlight.

June 6. Tuesday. I perceive the sweetness of the locust blossoms fifteen or twenty rods off as I go down the street.

P. M. — To Assabet Bathing-Place and return by stone bridge.

I see now great baggy light-green puffs on the panicled andromeda, some with a reddish side, two or three inches through. The *Stellaria longifolia* has been out, apparently, a day or two. A slender rush, flowered at the top, at bathing-place, some time.

The painted tortoises are nowadays laying their eggs. I see where they have just been digging in the sand or gravel in a *hundred* places on the southerly sides of hills and banks near the river, but they have laid their eggs in *very* few. I find none whole. Here is one which has made its hole with the hind part of its shell and its tail apparently, and the ground is wet under it. They make a great deal of water at these times, apparently to soften the earth or to give it consistency, or both. They are remarkably circumspect, and it is difficult to see one working. They stop instantly and draw in their heads, and do not move till you are out of sight, and then probably try a new place.

They have dabbled in the sand and left the marks of their tails all around.

The black oaks, birches, etc., etc., are covered with ephemeræ of various sizes and colors, with one, two, three, or no streamers, ready to take wing at evening, *i. e.* about seven. I am covered with them and much incommoded. There is garlic by the wall, not yet out. The air over the river meadows is saturated with sweetness, but I look round in vain on the yellowish sensitive fern and the reddish eupatorium springing up. From time to time, at mid-afternoon, is heard the trump of a bullfrog, like a Triton's horn.

I am struck now by the large light-purple *Viola palmata* rising above the grass near the river.

There are: —

The small, firm, few-lobed, wholesome, dark-green shrub oak leaf, light beneath.

The more or less deeply cut, and more or less dark green or sometimes reddish black oak, not light beneath. These two bristle-pointed.

The very wet-glossy, obovatish, sinuate-edged swamp white oak, light beneath.

The small narrower, sinuated, and still more chestnut-like chinquapin, little lighter beneath.

All these more or less glossy, especially the swamp white and shrub.

Then the dull-green, *sometimes* reddish, more or less deeply cut or fingered, unarmed, round-lobed white oak, not light beneath. The last three without bristles.

I remember best the sort of rosettes made by the wet-glossy leaves at the ends of some swamp white

Vol. VI

oak leaves [*sic*], also the wholesome and firm dark-green shrub oak leaves, and some glossy and finely cut light-green black (?) or red (?) or scarlet (?).

I see some devil's-needles, a brilliant green, with white and black or openwork and black wings, — some with clear black wings, some white bodies and black wings, etc.

White pine.

6.30 A. M. [*sic*]. — Up Assabet.

Rhus Toxicodendron, yesterday, on Rock. *Smilacina racemosa,* probably June 4th. Beautiful the hemlock-fans, now broad at the ends of the lower branches, which slant down, seen in the shade against the dark hillside. Such is the contrast of the very light green just put forth on their edges with the old very dark, I feast my eyes on it. Pignut. A crow blackbird's nest in a white maple this side the Leaning Hemlocks, in a crotch seven or eight feet from ground; somewhat like a robin's, but larger, made of coarse weed stems, mikania, and cranberry vines (without leaves), fishlines, etc., without, and of mud lined with finer fibres or roots within; four large but blind young covered with dark down. Sphinx moths about the flowers — honeysuckles — at evening, a night or two.

June 7. Wednesday. 6 A. M. — Up railroad.

Viburnum dentatum. Grape yesterday. *Viburnum nudum,* June 5. A thick fog this morning, through which at last rain falls, — the first after a considerable and first dry spell. As yet nothing has suffered from

dryness; the grass is very green and rank, owing to the cold spring, the June-grass converting hillside pastures into mowing-land, and the seeds (or chaff?) of many grasses begin to fall on my shoes.

P. M. — To Dugan Desert *via* Linnæa Hills.

Curled dock. Linnæa abundantly out some days; say 3d or 4th. It has not rained since morning, but continues cloudy and is warm and muggy, the sun almost coming out. The birds sing now more than ever, as in the morning, and mosquitoes are very troublesome in the woods. The locusts so full of pendulous white racemes five inches long, filling the air with their sweetness and resounding with the hum of humble and honey bees, are very interesting. These racemes are strewn along the path by children. Is that the *Cratægus Crus-Galli,* roadside between Joe Hosmer's and Tarbell's? Again I am struck by the rank, doglike scent of the rue budded to blossom. Along the wood-paths and in wood-side pastures I see the golden basins of the cistus. I am surprised at the size of green berries, — shad-bush, low blueberries, choke-cherries, etc., etc. It is but a step from flowers to fruit.

As I expected I find the desert scored by the tracks of turtles, made evidently last night, though the rain of this morning has obliterated the marks of their tails. The tracks are about seven eighths of an inch in diameter, one half inch deep, two inches apart (from centre to centre) in each row, and the rows four or five inches apart; and they have dabbled in the sand in many places and made some small holes. Yesterday was hot and dusty, and this morning it rained. Did they choose such a time? Yesterday I saw the painted and the wood tortoise out. Now I see a snapping turtle, its shell about a foot long, out here on the damp sand, with its head out, disturbed by me. It had just been excavating, and its shell — especially the fore-part and sides — and especially its snout, were deeply covered with earth. It appears to use its shell as a kind of spade whose handle is within, tilting it now this way, now that, and perhaps using its head and claws as a pick. It was in a little cloud of mosquitoes, which were continually settling on its head and flippers, but which it did not mind. Its sternum was slightly depressed. It seems that they are very frequently found fighting in the water and sometimes dead in the spring, maybe killed by the ice. Some think that the suckers I see floating are killed by the ice.

The *Linaria Canadensis* well out, near Heart-leaf Pond. How long? *Œnothera pumila* in low ground. Angelica at Nut Meadow Brook. The low blackberry leaves on Dennis's lupine hill are now covered beneath with that orange rust.[1] Were those premature scarlet leaves which I saw at the Rock on the 4th the shad-bush?[2] Common iris, some days; *one withered*.

Saw again what I have pronounced the yellow-winged sparrow (*Fringilla passerina*), with white line down head and yellow over eyes and my seringo note; but this time yellow of wings not apparent; ochreous throat and breast; quite different from the bay-winged,

[1] The same on thimble-berry the 13th June.
[2] Yes; it was dying.

and smaller. Does the bay-wing make the seringo note?[1]

Now the river is reduced to summer width. It is in the spring that we observe those dark-blue lakes on our meadows. Now weeds are beginning to fill the stream.

This muggy evening I see fireflies, the first I have seen or heard of at least. This louring day has been a regular fisherman's day, and I have seen many on the river, a general turnout.

June 8. Thursday. A. M. — Gentle, steady rain-storm.

The *Rosa nitida* bud which I plucked yesterday has blossomed to-day, so that, notwithstanding the rain, I will put it down to to-day.

P. M. — On river.

Sidesaddle, apparently to-morrow (?). Earliest and common potamogeton. *Erigeron strigosus* slowly opening, perhaps to-morrow.[2] Meadow-rue, with its rank dog-like scent. Ribwort plantain is abundantly in bloom, fifteen or sixteen inches high; how long? *Utricularia vulgaris.* Young robins in nest.

Herndon, in his "Exploration of the Amazon," says that "there is wanting an industrious and active population, who know what the comforts of life are, and who have artificial wants to draw out the great resources of the country." But what are the "artificial wants" to be encouraged, and the "great resources" of a country? Surely not the love of luxuries like the tobacco and slaves of his native (?) Virginia, or that fer-

[1] No.   [2] *Vide* 14th.

tility of soil which produces these. The chief want is ever a life of deep experiences, — that is, character, — which alone draws out "the great resources" of Nature. When our wants cease to be chiefly superficial and trivial, which is commonly meant by artificial, and begin to be wants of character, then the great resources of a country are taxed and drawn out, and the result, the staple production, is poetry. Have the "great resources" of Virginia been drawn out by such "artificial wants" as there exist? Was that country really designed by its Maker to produce slaves and tobacco, or something more even than freemen and food for freemen? Wants of character, aspirations, — this is what is wanted; but what is called civilization does not always substitute this for the barren simplicity of the savage.[1]

June 9. Friday. P. M. — To Well Meadow.

The summer aspect of the river begins perhaps when the *Utricularia vulgaris* is first seen on the surface, as yesterday. As I go along the railroad causeway, I see, in the cultivated grounds, a lark flashing his white tail, and showing his handsome yellow breast, with its black crescent like an Indian locket. For a day or two I have heard the fine seringo note of the cherry-birds, and seen them flying past, the only (?) birds, methinks, that I see in small flocks now, except swallows. The willow down and seeds are blowing over the causeway. *Veronica scutellata*, apparently several days. A strawberry half turned on the sand of

[1] [*Cape Cod, and Miscellanies*, pp. 479, 480; *Misc.*, Riv. 284.]

the causeway side, — the first fruit or berry of the year that I have tasted. Ladies'-slippers are going to seed. I see some white oak pincushions, nearly two inches through.

Is that galium, out apparently some days in the woods by Deep Cut, near Linnæa, *triflorum* or *Aparine?*[1] *Vide* Maps. Compare that at Lee's. I should like to know the birds of the woods better, what birds inhabit our woods? I hear their various notes ringing through them. What musicians compose our woodland quire? They must be forever strange and interesting to me. How prominent a place the vireos hold! It is probably the yellow-throated vireo I hear now, — a more interrupted red-eye with its *prelia—prelioit* or *tully-ho*, — invisible in the tops of the trees. I see the thick, flower-like huckleberry apples. Haynes (?), Goodwin's comrade, tells me that he used to catch mud turtles in the ponds behind Provincetown with a toad on a mackerel hook thrown into the pond and the line tied to a stump or stake on shore. Invariably the turtle when hooked crawled up, following the line to the stake, and was there found waiting — Goodwin baits minks with muskrats.

Find the great fringed orchis out apparently two or three days. Two are almost fully out, two or three only budded. A large spike of peculiarly delicate pale-purple flowers growing in the luxuriant and shady swamp amid hellebores, ferns, golden senecios, etc., etc. It

[1] Call it the first, for it has less prickles or angles, has smaller and less prickly fruit, rather three separate than three couples, and is more spreading and reclining, and is later?

Great Fringed Orchis

Summer Foliage, Walden Pond

is remarkable that this, one of the fairest of all our flowers, should also be one of the rarest, — for the most part not seen at all. I think that no other but myself in Concord annually finds it. That so queenly a flower should annually bloom so rarely and in such withdrawn and secret places as to be rarely seen by man! The village belle never sees this more delicate belle of the swamp. How little relation between our life and its! Most of us never see it or hear of it. The seasons go by to us as if it were not. A beauty reared in the shade of a convent, who has never strayed beyond the convent bell. Only the skunk or owl or other inhabitant of the swamp beholds it. In the damp twilight of the swamp, where it is wet to the feet. How little anxious to display its attractions! It does not pine because man does not admire it. How independent on our race! It lifts its delicate spike amid the hellebore and ferns in the deep shade of the swamp. I am inclined to think of it as a relic of the past as much as the arrowhead, or the tomahawk I found on the 7th.

Ferns are four or five feet high there.

7 P. M. — Up Assabet.

The tupelo's stamens are loose and will perhaps shed pollen to-morrow or next day. It is twilight, and the river is covered with that dusty lint, as was the water next the shore at Walden this afternoon. Chimney and bank swallows are still hovering over the river, and cherry-birds fly past. The veery rings, and the tree-toad. The air is now pretty full of shad-flies, and there is an incessant sound made by the fishes leaping for

such as are struggling on the surface; it sounds like the *lapsing* of a swift stream, sucking amid rocks. The fishes make a business of thus getting their evening meal, dimpling the river like large drops as far as I can see, sometimes making a loud plashing. Meanwhile the kingfishers are on the lookout for the fishes as they rise, and I saw one dive in the twilight and go off uttering his *cr-r-ack, cr-r-rack*.

The mosquitoes encircle my head and torment me, and I see a great moth go fluttering over the tree-tops and the water, black against the sky, like a bat. The fishes continue to leap by moonlight. A full moon.

Covered with disgrace, this State has sat down coolly to try for their lives the men who attempted to do its duty for it. And this is called justice! They who have shown that they can behave particularly well, — they alone are put under bonds "for their good behavior!" Such a judge and court are an impertinence. Only they are guiltless who commit the crime of contempt of such a court. It behooves every man to see that his influence is on the side of justice, and let the courts make their own characters. What is any political organization worth, when it is in the service of the devil? I see that the authorities — the Governor, Mayor, Commissioner, Marshal, etc. — are either weak or unprincipled men, — *i. e.*, well disposed but not equal to the occasion, — or else of dull moral perception, with the unprincipled and servile in their pay. All sound moral sentiment is opposed to them.

I had thought that the Governor was in some sense the executive officer of the State; that it was his busi-

Vol. VI

ness to see that the laws of the State were executed; but, when there is any special use for him, he is useless, permits the laws to go unexecuted, and is not heard from. But the worst I shall say of the Governor is that he was no better than the majority of his constituents — he was not equal to the occasion. While the whole military force of the State, if need be, is at the service of a slaveholder, to enable him to carry back a slave, not a soldier is offered to save a citizen of Massachusetts from being kidnapped. Is this what all these arms, all this "training," has been for these seventy-eight years past? What is wanted is men of principle, who recognize a higher law than the decision of the majority. The marines and the militia whose bodies were used lately were not men of sense nor of principle; in a high moral sense they were not *men* at all.

Justice is sweet and musical to hear; but injustice is harsh and discordant. The judge still sits grinding at his organ, but it yields no music, and we hear only the sound of the handle. He believes that all the music resides in the handle, and the crowd toss him their coppers just the same as before.[1]

June 10. *Saturday.* P. M. — To Conantum on foot.

The bay-wing sparrow apparently is not my seringo, after all. What is the seringo? I see some with clear, dirty-yellow breasts, but others, as to-day, with white breasts, dark-streaked. Both have the yellow over eye and the white line on crown, and agree in size,

[1] [*Cape Cod, and Miscellanies*, pp. 391, 392, 404; *Misc.*, Riv. 175, 176, 191.] *Vide* 17th.

but I have seen only one with distinct yellow on wings. Both the last, *i. e.* except only the bay-wing, utter the seringo note. Are they both yellow-winged sparrows? or is the white-breasted with streaks the Savannah sparrow?

The meadows now begin to be yellow with senecio. Sidesaddle generally out; petals hang down, apparently a day or two. It is a conspicuous flower. The fragrance of the arethusa is like that of the lady's-slipper, or pleasanter. I see many dead painted tortoises, the bugs now devouring them, in the fields. The [*Viburnum*] *Lentago* is just out of bloom now that the *V. nudum* is fairly begun.

Saw probably a crow's nest high in a white pine, two crows with ragged wings circling high over it and me, not noisy.

June 11. *Sunday.* 8.30 A. M. — To Framingham with Mrs. Brown. All day cloudy and cool without rain.

At twelve walked up the Sudbury River above Frank's to Ashland, at first through the meadows, then over the high hills in the vicinity. The stream narrows suddenly in the middle of Framingham, probably about the outlet from Farm Pond and also Stony Brook. It is merely a large brook from a rod to a rod and a half wide, pursuing a serpentine course through meadows, still deep and dark and sluggish for the most part, and bordered with pads, thus preserving its character below. Diervilla abundant on bank of river at Frank's, out possibly yesterday. I see that red sugar incrustation on red maple leaves. Young song sparrows have flown some days at Frank's. Prunella well out, perhaps two or three days. From a high hill on the west of the river, about a mile from Frank's, get a good view of Farm Pond eastward, which empties into the river, with South Framingham on the southeast side of it. I did not instantly detect it, the dark hills and trees being reflected in it. How agreeable in a still, cloudy day, when large masses of clouds, equally dispersed, float across the sky, not threatening rain, but preserving a temperate air, to see a sheet of water thus revealed by its reflections, a smooth, glassy mirror, reflecting the light sky and the dark and shady woods. It is very much like a mirage. I went to a pretty high hill east of and near to Ashland, where I found an abundance of ripe strawberries, earlier, I am sure, than with us. A young man picking strawberries pointed toward Hopkinton southwesterly and said that it was four miles thither straight and six to Whitehall Pond (the source of the river), but a great deal farther by the river, that boats were used here at Ashland, and pouts and pickerel caught. Grape out. Saw in and near some woods four or five cow blackbirds, with their light-brown heads, — their strain an imperfect, milky, gurgling *conqueree*, an unsuccessful effort. It made me think, for some reason, of streams of milk bursting out a sort of music between the staves of a keg. I saw a yellow-spotted tortoise come out, — undoubtedly to lay its eggs, — which had climbed to the top of a hill as much as a hundred and thirty feet above any water. A wood tortoise had just made its hole in the damp soil of Frank's garden.

Vol. VI

the water to a tree. Mountain laurel at the pond. A narrow-leaved potamogeton well out at the bathing-place, — leaves two to three inches long. Four-leaved loosestrife.

Silene antirrhina, how long? Do I not see two birds with the seringo note, — the Savannah (?) sparrow, larger with not so bright a yellow over eye, none on wing, and white breast, and beneath former streaked with dark and perhaps a dark spot, and the smaller yellow-winged, with spot on wing also and ochreous breast and throat? The first sings *che che rar, che ra-a-a-a-a-ar*.

Sundown. — To Clamshell Hill.

Nightshade a day or two. The cracks made by cold in pastures in the winter are still quite distinct. Phleum or herd's-grass (?). I sit on the Clamshell Hill at sunset, while several kinds of swallows are playing low over it chasing each other, and occasionally alighting on the bare hillside. The level rays of the sun shine into and light up the trunk and limbs of a swamp white oak on Hubbard's meadow.

June 13. Tuesday. I hear a quail this morning.

2 P. M. — By boat to Bittern Cliff and so to Lee's Cliff.

I hear the muttering of thunder and see a dark cloud in the west-southwest horizon; am uncertain how far up-stream I shall get. The *Nuphar lutea* var. *Kalmiana*, apparently two or three days in *some* places; generally not yet. Its leaf appears to be the prevail-

Maple viburnum well out. It must come very soon after the *nudum*. The note of the cuckoo is an agreeable sound in the middle of these days. I think I saw wild radish (*Raphanus*) out, as I rode along. These days observe and admire the forms of elms.

June 12. P. M. — To Walden.

Clover now reddens the fields. Grass in its prime. Comfrey in front of Stow's well out some days apparently. With the roses now fairly begun I associate summer heats. *Galium trifidum* var. *latifolium* (?), smooth-angled, some with linear leaves. Is it *tinctorium?* Hear the evergreen-forest note, and see the bird on the top of a white pine, somewhat creeper-like, along the boughs, and golden head except a black streak from eyes, black throat, slate-colored back, forked tail, white beneath, — *er te, ter ter te.* Another bird with *yellow* throat near by may have been the other sex. Is it the golden-winged warbler?[1]

Pyrola chlorantha. *Rosa lucida*, probably yesterday, the 11th, judging from what I saw Saturday, *i. e.* the 10th. A bud in pitcher the 13th. The *R. nitida* is the most common now. The round-leaved cornel is well out at Heywood Peak, probably two or three days. Perhaps this and the maple-leaved viburnum are as early as the *V. nudum* and *V. dentatum*, only more rare. Scared a kingfisher on a bough over Walden. As he flew off, he *hovered* two or three times thirty or forty feet above the pond, and at last dove and apparently caught a fish, with which he flew off low over

[1] *Vide* June 17th.

ing pad; it is outside in the deepest water, and is smaller and narrower in proportion to its breadth than the other, with a small leaf-stem, the lobes overlapping. Now, in shallow places near the bends, the large and conspicuous spikes of the broad-leaved potamogeton rise thickly above the water. Though the plants are slanted downward by the stream, the spikes at their ends rise perpendicularly two or three inches. My boat passes over these beds of potamogetons, pressing their spikes under water. I see the yellow water ranunculus in dense fields now, in some places on the side of the stream, two or three inches above water, and many gone to seed. See a white lily bud.

The clams now lie up thickly at the Hubbard Bathing-Place, all on their edges. The small iris is budded near by. The clouds are rising up in the southwest, irregular and ragged black pillars in the form of men and bears, the northernmost with a glowing side. If it rains hard, I will run my boat ashore, turn it over, and get under it. I will not turn back; my afternoon shall not be interrupted by a thunder-shower. It is so warm that I stop to drink wherever there is a spring. The flowering fern is reddish and yellowish green on the meadows. There are bare places on the meadow, from which the surface was carried off last winter. An opposite cloud is rising fast in the east-northeast, and now the lightning crinkles down it and I hear the heavy thunder. It appears to be rising to meet the cloud in the west, and I shall surely get wet. The *Comarum palustre* well out apparently three or four days, with its small dark and dull purple petals on a dark purplish calyx ground. I paddle slowly by farmers in small parties, busily hoeing corn and potatoes. The boy rides the horse dragging the cultivator. They have a jug of sweetened water in the grass at the end of the row. The kingbird's eggs are not yet hatched. How often I see Garfield, — Uncle Daniel, — the stout broad-shouldered farmer, taking his way through the fields toward night, toward the river, with his fish-pole and basket over his shoulder! He had on a live shiner, six or seven inches long, the other day and a cork above. He wanted to see if he "could n't catch a big pickerel." At Bittern Cliff Spring, a handsomely cut petalled geranium, the whole rather elliptical in outline. Forget the number of petals. The panicled cornel by Conant's orchard wall will open in a day or two.[1] The small veronica with minute blue flowers at Lee's Cliff, how long? *V. arvensis.* Pennyroyal is four or five inches high there.

Galium circæzans well out some days at Cliff, — the broad three-nerved four leaves. The thunder-cloud in the east has disappeared southward, and that in the west has changed to a vast black sheaf falling over on all sides at top, but [it does] not rise fast. The little globular drooping reddish buds of the *Chimaphila umbellata,* — pipsissewa, — are now very pretty. It is remarkable how much the pads are eaten already. Some water-target leaves at Walden yesterday were scored as by some literal character. I see also the

[1] Probably 14th; well out the 16th elsewhere.

leaves of a columbine with light markings, being half eaten through; and, as there are eggs beneath, it may have been done to let the light through to them. The krigia seeds and down begin to fly. The common polypody and ebony spleenwort show green fruit dots. It is remarkable how many birds' nests are broken up. At least half that I examine again have been disturbed, only the broken shells left; *viz.,* a chewink's and a brown thrasher's. The last was on the ground under a barberry bush, was six or seven inches in diameter without, of dead leaves and hay, then of small twigs, then of dark root-fibres within, — no more lining. How beautiful the solid cylinders of the lamb-kill now just before sunset, — small ten-sided, rosy-crimson basins, about two inches above the recurved, drooping dry capsules of last year, — and sometimes those of the year before are two inches lower. The first rose-bug on one of these flowers. Stopped to pick strawberries on Fair Haven. When I have stayed out thus till late many miles from home, and have heard a cricket beginning to chirp louder near me in the grass, I have felt that I was not far from home after all, — began to be weaned from my village home. There is froth on alders, which comes off on to my clothes. I see over the bream nests little schools of countless minute minnows. Can they be the young breams? The breams being still in their nests. It is surprising how thickly strewn our soil is with arrowheads. I never see the surface broken in sandy places but I think of them. I find them on all sides, not only in corn and grain and potato and bean fields, but in

Vol. VI

pastures and woods, by woodchucks' holes and pigeon beds, and, as to-night, in a pasture where a restless cow has pawed the ground. I float homeward over water almost perfectly smooth, yet not methinks as in the fall, my sail so idle that I count ten devil's-needles resting along it at once.

Carpet-weed, and purslane, and sweet-briar.

Is not the rose-pink *Rosa lucida* paler than the *R. nitida?*

June 14. P. M. — To lime-kiln with Mr. Bacon of Natick.

Sisymbrium amphibium (?) of Bigelow, some days, at foot of Loring's land. Common mallows well out; how long? What is that sisymbrium or mustard-like plant at foot of Loring's? *Erigeron strigosus* (??) out earliest, say yesterday. Observed a ribwort near Simon Brown's barn by road, with elongated spikes and only pistillate flowers. Hedge-mustard, how long? Pepper-grass, how long? Some time. *Scirpus lacustris,* maybe some days. I see a black caterpillar on the black willows nowadays with red spots. Mr. Bacon thinks that cherry-birds are abundant where cankerworms are. Says that only female mosquitoes sting (not his observation alone); that there are one or two arbor-vitæs native in Natick. He has found the *Lygodium palmatum* there. There is one pure-blooded Indian woman there. Pearl [?], I think he called her. He thought those the exuviæ of mosquitoes on the river weeds under water.[1] Makes his own microscopes and uses garnets. He called

[1] Russell makes them many other creatures also.

the huckleberry-apple a parasitic plant, — pterospora, — which [has] grown on and changed the nature of the huckleberry. Observed a diseased *Andromeda paniculata* twig prematurely in blossom. Caught a locust, — properly harvest-fly (cicada), — drumming on a birch, which Bacon and Hill (of Waltham) think like the *septendecim,* except that ours has not red eyes but black ones. Harris's other kind, the dog-day cicada (*canicularis*), or harvest-fly. He says it begins to be heard invariably at the beginning of dog-days; he (Harris) heard it for many years in succession with few exceptions on the 25th of July. Bacon says he has seen pitch pine pollen in a cloud going over a hill a mile off; is pretty sure.

June 15. 5.30 A. M. — To Island and Hill.

A young painted tortoise on the surface of the water, as big as a quarter of a dollar, with a reddish or orange sternum. I suppose that my skater insect is the hydrometer. Found a nest of tortoise eggs, apparently buried last night, which I brought home, ten in all, — one lying wholly on the surface, — and buried in the garden. The soil *above* a dark virgin mould about a stump was unexpectedly hard.[1]

P. M. — Up Assabet to Garlic Wall.

That tall grass opposite the Merrick Swimming-Place is getting up pretty well, and blossoming with a broad and regular spike, for some time. This is the third afternoon that we have had a rumbling thunder-

[1] These were stinkpots and only a few feet from water's edge.

cloud arise in the east, — not to mention the west, — but all signs have failed hitherto, and I resolve to proceed on my voyage, knowing that I have a tight [roof] in my boat turned up. The froth on the alders, andromeda, etc., — not to speak of the aphides, — dirties and apparently spots my clothes, so that it is a serious objection to walking amid these bushes these days. I am covered with this spittle-like froth. At the Assabet Spring I must have been near a black and white creeper's nest. It kept up a constant chipping. Saw there also, probably, a chestnut-sided warbler. A yellow crown, chestnut stripe on sides, white beneath, and two yellowish bars on wings. A red oak there has many large twigs drooping withered, apparently weakened by some insect. May it not be the locust of yesterday? Black willow is now gone to seed, and its down covers the water, white amid the weeds. The swamp-pink apparently two or even three days in one place. Saw a wood tortoise, about two inches and a half, with a black sternum and the skin, which becomes orange, now ochreous merely, or brown. The little painted tortoise of the morning was red beneath. Both these young tortoises have a distinct dorsal ridge. The garlic not in flower yet. I observed no *Nuphar lutea* var. *Kalmiana* on the Assabet.

7 P. M. — To Cliff by railroad.

Cranberry. *Prinos lœvigatus,* apparently two days. Methinks the birds sing a little feebler nowadays. The note of the bobolink begins to sound somewhat rare. The sun has set, or is at least concealed in a low

mist. As I go up Fair Haven Hill, I feel the leaves in the sprout-land oak, hickory, etc., cold and wet to my hand with the heavy dew that is falling. They look dry, but when I rub them with my hand, they show moist or wet at once. Probably I thus spread minute drops of dew or mist on their surface. It cannot be the warmth of my hand, for when I breathe on them it has no effect. I see one or two early blueberries prematurely turning. The *Amelanchier Botryapium* berries are already reddened two thirds over, and are somewhat palatable and soft, — some of them, — not fairly ripe.

June 16. 5 A. M. — Up railroad.

As the sun went down last night, round and red in a damp misty atmosphere, so now it rises in the same manner, though there is no dense fog. Poison-dogwood yesterday, or say day before, *i. e.* 14th. *Rubus hispidus,* perhaps yesterday in the earliest place, over the sand. Mullein, perhaps yesterday.

Observed yesterday the erigeron with a purple tinge. I cannot tell whether this, which seems in other respects the same with the white, is the *strigosus* or *annuus*. The calla which I plucked yesterday sheds pollen to-day; say to-day, then. A *Hypericum perforatum* seen last night will probably open to-day. I see on the *Scirpus lacustris* and pontederia leaves black patches for some days, as if painted, of minute closely placed ova, above water. I suspect that what I took for milfoil is a sium. Is not that new mustard-like plant behind Loring's, and so on down the river, *Nasturtium hispidum,* or hairy cress? Probably the first the 19th.

Heart-leaf. *Nymphœa odorata.* Again I scent the white water-lily, and a season I had waited for is arrived. How indispensable all these experiences to make up the summer! It is the emblem of purity, and its scent suggests it. Growing in stagnant and muddy [water], it bursts up so pure and fair to the eye and so sweet to the scent, as if to show us what purity and sweetness reside in, and can be extracted from, the slime and muck of earth. I think I have plucked the first one that has opened for a mile at least. What confirmation of our hopes is in the fragrance of the water-lily! I shall not so soon despair of the world for it, notwithstanding slavery, and the cowardice and want of principle of the North. It suggests that the time may come when man's deeds will smell as sweet. Such, then, is the odor our planet emits. Who can doubt, then, that Nature is young and sound? If Nature can compound this fragrance still annually, I shall believe her still full of vigor, and that there is virtue in man, too, who perceives and loves it. It is as if all the pure and sweet and virtuous was extracted from the slime and decay of earth and presented thus in a flower. The resurrection of virtue! It reminds me that Nature has been partner to no Missouri compromise. I scent no compromise in the fragrance of the white water-lily. In it, the sweet, and pure, and innocent are wholly sundered from the obscene and baleful. I do not scent in this the time-serving irresolution of a Massachusetts Governor, nor of a Boston Mayor. All good actions have contributed to this fragrance. So behave that the odor of your actions may enhance the general sweetness of the

atmosphere, that, when I behold or scent a flower, I may not be reminded how inconsistent are your actions with it; for all odor is but one form of advertisement of a moral quality. If fair actions had not been performed, the lily would not smell sweet. The foul slime stands for the sloth and vice of man; the fragrant flower that springs from it, for the purity and courage which springs from its midst. It is these sights and sounds and fragrances put together that convince us of our immortality. No man believes against all evidence. Our external senses consent with our internal. This fragrance assures me that, though all other men fall, one shall stand fast; though a pestilence sweep over the earth, it shall at least spare one man. The genius of Nature is unimpaired. Her flowers are as fair and as fragrant as ever.[1]

Three days in succession, — the 13th, 14th, and 15th, — thunder-clouds, with thunder and lightning, have risen high in the east, threatening instant rain, and yet each time it has failed to reach us, and thus it is almost invariably, methinks, with thunder-clouds which rise in the east; they do not reach us. Perhaps they are generated along, and confined to, the seacoast.

The warmer, or at least *drier,* weather has now prevailed about a fortnight. Once or twice the sun has gone down red, shorn of his beams. There have been showers all around us, but nothing to mention here yet. Yet it is not particularly dry. I hear nowadays the anxious notes of some birds whose young have just flown, — crow blackbirds, etc., etc.

[1] [*Cape Cod, and Miscellanies,* pp. 407, 408; *Misc.,* Riv. 195, 196.]

As for birds, I think that their quire begins now to be decidedly less full and loud. I hear the phœbe note of the chickadee occasionally. I see only a stray, probably summer, duck very rarely on the river. The blue-bird is lost and somewhat rare-looking. The quail begins to be *heard*. Very few if any hawks are commonly noticed. The cow troopials have [been] seen in small flocks flitting about within a week. Along low roads, the song sparrows, bay-wings, Savannah (?), and yellow-winged (?) (*i. e.* ochreous-throated) quite commonly sing. Woodpeckers not noticeable as in spring. Rush sparrow at sundown. Methought I heard a pine warbler to-day. Many chip-birds have flown. The blue herons appear not to remain here this summer, and wood thrushes are not so numerous within my range as formerly. Kingfishers quite common, perhaps especially at Walden, where the water is clear, and on the Assabet. The black and white creeper sings much. The pine warbler, as usual, and the evergreen-forest note (golden-winged (?) warbler). Thrasher and catbird sing still; summer yellowbird and Maryland yellow-throat sing still; and oven-bird and veery. The bobolink, full strains, but further between. The red-eye incessant at midday. Goldfinches twitter over as usual. The wood pewee prominent. The nighthawk in full blast. Cherry-birds numerous, — the bold, combative-looking fellows, — etc., etc.

Since spring — say for a month or so — we have had no *tumultuous* water, — waves running with whitecaps.

Caterpillars have some time been grown on apple and cherry trees, and now the trees are leafing again.

Other caterpillars on oaks, black willows, etc. Dragon-flies of various sizes and colors are now extremely abundant, hovering just over the surface of the river and coupling there, — a blue and brown or a blue and green one united. Alighting on the least surface of a weed. One kind of cicada, at least, began a fortnight ago, — a sort of black-eyed *septendecim*. Shad-flies are *probably* disappearing. *Great* moths now abroad. Rose-bugs have just come. Various plants are frothy.

Tortoises, of all kinds, as I have seen, but *odoratus*, are laying their eggs for some time. I find their eggs dropped. Apparently young breams over nests. Frog-spawn apparently, in river; stringy, ash-color.

The effect of a good government is to make life more valuable, — of a bad government, to make it less valuable. We can afford that railroad and all merely material stock should depreciate, for that only compels us to live more simply and economically; but suppose the value of life itself should be depreciated. Every man in New England capable of the sentiment of patriotism must have lived the last three weeks with the sense of having suffered a vast, indefinite loss. I had never respected this government, but I had foolishly thought that I might manage to live here, attending to my private affairs, and forget it. For my part, my old and worthiest pursuits have lost I cannot say how much of their attraction, and I feel that my investment in life here is worth many per cent. less since Massachusetts last deliberately and forcibly restored an innocent man, Anthony Burns, to slavery. I dwelt before in the illusion that my life passed somewhere

only *between* heaven and hell, but now I cannot persuade myself that I do not dwell wholly within hell. The sight of that political organization called Massachusetts is to me morally covered with scoriæ and volcanic cinders, such as Milton imagined. If there is any hell more unprincipled than our rulers and our people, I feel curious to visit it. Life itself being worthless, all things with it, that feed it, are worthless. Suppose you have a small library, with pictures to adorn the walls, — a garden laid out around, — and contemplate scientific and literary pursuits, etc., etc., and discover suddenly that your villa, with all its contents, is located in hell, and that the justice of the peace is one of the devil's angels, has a cloven foot and a forked tail, — do not these things suddenly lose their value in your eyes? Are you not disposed to sell at a great sacrifice?

I feel that, to some extent, the State has fatally interfered with my just and proper business. It has not merely interrupted me in my passage through Court Street on errands of trade, but it has, to some extent, interrupted me and every man on his onward and upward path, on which he had trusted soon to leave Court Street far behind. I have found that hollow which I had relied on for solid.

I am surprised to see men going about their business as if nothing had happened, and say to myself, "Unfortunates! they have not heard the news;" that the man whom I just met on horseback should be so earnest to overtake his newly bought cows running away, — since all property is insecure, and if they do not

run away again, they may be taken away from him when he gets them. Fool! does he not know that his seed-corn is worth less this year, — that all beneficent harvests fail as he approaches the empire of hell? No prudent man will build a stone house under these circumstances, or engage in any peaceful enterprise which it requires a long time to accomplish. Art is as long as ever, but life is more interrupted and less available for a man's proper pursuits. It is time we had done referring to our ancestors. We have used up all our inherited freedom, like the young bird the albumen in the egg. It is not an era of repose. If we would save our lives, we must fight for them.

The discovery is what manner of men your countrymen are. They steadily worship mammon — and on the seventh day curse God with a tintamarre from one end of the *Union* to the other. I heard the other day of a meek and sleek devil of a Bishop Somebody, who commended the law and order with which Burns was given up. I would like before I sit down to a table to inquire if there is one in the company who styles himself or is styled Bishop, and he or I should go out of it. I would have such a man wear his bishop's hat and his clerical bib and tucker, that we may know him.

Why will men be such fools as [to] trust to lawyers for a *moral* reform? I do not believe that there is a judge in this country prepared to decide by the principle that a law is immoral and therefore of no force. They put themselves, or rather are by character, exactly on a level with the marine who discharges his musket in any direction in which he is ordered. They are just as much tools, and as little men.[1]

P. M. — To Baker Ditch *via* almshouse.

Autumnal dandelion, some time, in Emerson's meadow pasture. *Potentilla Norvegica*, a day or two, in low ground; very abundant at Baker Ditch with other weeds, on a cleared and ditched swamp. Veiny-leaved hawkweed at Heywood Peak appears shut up at midday, — also the autumnal dandelion. A veiny-leaved hawkweed without veins. Is not this my *Gronovii?* [2] Panicled cornel well out on Heywood Peak.

There is a cool east wind, — and has been afternoons for several days, — which has produced a very thick haze or a fog. I find a tortoise egg on this peak at least sixty feet above the pond. There is a fine ripple and sparkle on the pond, seen through the mist. But what signifies the beauty of nature when men are base? We walk to lakes to see our serenity reflected in them. When we are not serene, we go not to them. Who can be serene in a country where both rulers and ruled are without principle? The remembrance of the baseness of politicians spoils my walks. My thoughts are murder to the State; I endeavor in vain to observe nature; my thoughts involuntarily go plotting against the State. I trust that all just men will conspire.[3]

[1] [*Cape Cod, and Miscellanies*, pp. 401, 402, 405–407; *Misc.*, Riv. 187–189, 192–194.]
[2] Think not. *Vide* forward, July 1st.
[3] [*Cape Cod, and Miscellanies*, p. 407; *Misc.*, Riv. 195.]

Vol. VI

Dogsbane, apparently to-morrow. I observed yesterday that the *Viburnum dentatum* was very conspicuous and prevalent along the river, as if few other flowers were in bloom.

An abundance of *Galium trifidum* in low grounds, some smooth, some rough, with four leaves, or five or six; I do not distinguish the varieties. Am in doubt whether the polygonum which I find just opening at the ditch (say to-morrow) is *sagittatum* — a rank one — or *arifolium*.[1] The lobes of the leaves do not spread thus : ∠ ∠ but are: ∪ ∪ Three or four styles and four or five angled pods. Epilobium, probably *coloratum*, yet rather downy, to-morrow. It is worth the while to see the rank weeds which grow here on this cleared and ditched swamp, — *Potentilla Norvegica*, touch-me-not, *Polygonum sagittatum* (?), nightshade, etc., etc. The *Rosa nitida* grows along the edge of the ditches, the half-open flowers showing the deepest rosy tints, so glowing that they make an evening or twilight of the surrounding afternoon, seeming to stand in the shade or twilight. Already the bright petals of yesterday's flowers are thickly strewn along on the black mud at the bottom of the ditch.

The *R. nitida*, the earlier (?), with its narrow shiny leaves and prickly stem and its moderate-sized rose-pink petals.

The *R. lucida*, with its broader and duller leaves, but larger and perhaps deeper-colored and more purple

[1] ["Yes" is inserted after *sagittatum*, "or *arifolium*" is crossed out, and "*Vide* Aug. 19" follows.]

petals, perhaps yet higher scented, and its great yellow centre of stamens.

The smaller, lighter, but perhaps more delicately tinted *R. rubiginosa*.

One and all drop their petals the second day. I bring home the buds of the three ready to expand at night, and the next day they perfume my chamber. Add to these the white lily (just begun), also the swamp-pink, and probably morning-glory, and the great orchis, and mountain laurel (now in prime), and perhaps we must say that the fairest flowers are now to be found. Or say a few days later. (The arethusa is disappearing.)

It is eight days since I plucked the great orchis; one is perfectly fresh still in my pitcher. It may be plucked when the spike is only half opened, and will open completely and keep perfectly fresh in a pitcher more than a week. Do I not live in a garden, — in paradise? I can go out each morning before breakfast — I do — and gather these flowers with which to perfume my chamber where I read and write, all day. The note of the cherry-bird is fine and ringing, but peculiar and very noticeable. With its crest it is a resolute and combative-looking bird. The mountain laurel is remarkable for its great dense and naked (for it runs to flower now) corymbs of large and handsome flowers. And this is a prevailing underwood on many of our mountainsides! Perhaps it is more appreciated in this neighborhood, where it is comparatively rare, — rare as poetry. Whitest in the shade. Meadow-sweet to-morrow.

June 17. *Saturday.* 5 A. M. — To Hill.

A cold fog. These mornings those who walk in grass are thoroughly wetted above mid-leg. All the earth is dripping wet. I am surprised to feel how warm the water is, by contrast with the cold, foggy air. The frogs seem glad to bury themselves in it. The dewy cobwebs are very thick this morning, little napkins of the fairies spread on the grass. Whorled utricularias. A potamogeton off Dodd's with fine, grassy, thread-like leaves and stems (somewhat flattish), and small globular spikes, maybe some time? *Ranunculus reptans*, maybe a day or more. A duck, probably wood duck, which is breeding here. From the Hill I am reminded of more youthful mornings, seeing the dark forms of the trees eastward in the low grounds, partly within and against the shining white fog, the sun just risen over it. The mist fast rolling away eastward from them, their tops at last streaking the mist and dividing it into vales. All beyond them a submerged and unknown country, as if they grew on the sea-shore. Why does the fog go off always toward the sun, — is seen in the east when it has disappeared in the west? The waves of the foggy ocean divide and flow back for us Israelites of a day to march through. I hear the half-suppressed guttural sounds of a red squirrel on a tree; at length he breaks out into a sharp bark.

Slavery has produced no sweet-scented flower like the water-lily, for its flower must smell like itself. It will be a carrion-flower.[2]

[1] [*Cape Cod, and Miscellanies*, p. 408; *Misc.*, Riv. 19.]

Saw the sun reflected up from the Assabet to the hill-top, through the dispersing fog, giving to the water a peculiarly rippled, pale-golden hue, — "gilding pale streams with heavenly alchemy."

The judges and lawyers, and all men of expediency, consider not whether the Fugitive Slave Law is right, but whether it is what they call constitutional. They try the merits of the case by a very low and incompetent standard. Pray, is virtue constitutional, or vice? Is equity constitutional, or iniquity? It is as impertinent, in important moral and vital questions like this, to ask whether a law is constitutional or not, as to ask whether it is profitable or not. They persist in being the servants of man, and the worst of men, rather than the servants of God. Sir, the question is not whether you or your grandfather, seventy years ago, entered into an agreement to serve the devil, and that service is not accordingly now due; but whether you will not now, for once and at last, serve God, — in spite of your own past recreancy or that of your ancestors, — and obey that eternal and only just Constitution which he, and not any Jefferson or Adams, has written in your being. Is the Constitution a thing to live by? or die by? No, as long as we are alive we forget it, and when we die we have done with it. At most it is only to swear by. While they are hurrying off Christ to the cross, the ruler decides that he cannot *constitutionally* interfere to save him. The Christians, now and always, are they who obey the higher law, who discover it to be according to their constitution to interfere. They at least cut off the ears of the police; the others pocket the

thirty pieces of silver. This was meaner than to crucify Christ, for he could better take care of himself.[1]

P. M. — To Walden and Cliffs *via* almshouse.
Rumex obtusifolius (?), maybe some days. The evergreen-forest bird at old place in white pine and oak tops, top of Brister's Hill on right. I think it has black wings with white bars. Is it not the black-throated green warbler? The unmistakable tanager sits on the oaks at midday and sings with a *hoarse* red-eye note, *pruit, prewee, prewa, prear, preā* (often more notes), some of the latter notes clearer, without the *r*. It does not sing so continuously as the red-eye, but at short intervals repeats its half-dozen notes. *Iris Virginica* well out at Peltandra Meadow, probably a day or two, though not yet at Arum Meadow. The sorrel-fields are now turning brown.

Another remarkably hazy day; our view is confined, the horizon near, no mountains; as you look off only four or five miles, you see a succession of dark wooded ridges and vales filled with mist. It is dry, hazy June weather. We are more of the earth, farther from heaven, these days. We live in a grosser element. We [are] getting deeper into the mists of earth. Even the birds sing with less vigor and vivacity. The season of hope and promise is past; already the season of small fruits has arrived. The Indian marked the midsummer as the season when berries were ripe. We are a little saddened, because we begin to see the interval between our hopes and their fulfillment. The prospect

[1] [*Cape Cod, and Miscellanies*, pp. 401, 402; *Misc.*, Riv 188.]

Vol. VI

of the heavens is taken away, and we are presented only with a few small berries. Before sundown I reached Fair Haven Hill and gathered strawberries. I find beds of large and lusty strawberry plants in sprout-lands, but they appear to run to leaves and bear very little fruit, having spent themselves in leaves by the time the dry weather arrives. It is those still earlier and more stinted plants which grow on dry uplands that bear the *early* fruit, formed before the droughts. But the meadows produce both leaves and fruit.

I begin to see the flowering fern at a distance in the river meadows. Butter-and-eggs, some days perhaps; one or two well out, while the rest show no forwardness. Tephrosia well out, apparently some days. Lupines are going to seed. Morning-glory, apparently yesterday. Well named morning-glory. Its broad, bell- and trumpet-shaped flowers, faintly tinged with red, are like the dawn itself. The new pitcher-plant leaf is formed in some places, now free from insects. Pogonia, *perhaps* a day or two.

The sun goes down red again, like a high-colored flower of summer. As the white and yellow flowers of spring are giving place to the rose, and will soon to the red lily, etc., so the yellow sun of spring has become a red sun of June drought, round and red like a midsummer flower, production of torrid heats.

Massachusetts sits waiting his decision, as if the crime were not already committed. The crime consists first of all and chiefly in her permitting an innocent man to be tried for more than his life, — for his

liberty. They who talk about Mr. Loring's decision, and not about their own and the State's consenting that he shall be the umpire in such a case, waste time in words and are weak in the head, if not in the heart alone [*sic*].[1]

(June 9th, continued.) — The amount of it is, if the majority vote the devil to be God, the minority will live and behave accordingly, and obey the successful candidate, trusting that some time or other, by some Speaker's casting-vote, they may reinstate God again. Some men act as if they believed that they could safely slide down-hill a little way, — or a good way, — and would surely come to a place, by and by, whence they could slide up again. This is *expediency*, or choosing that course which offers the fewest obstacles to the feet (of the slider). But there is no such thing as accomplishing a moral reform by the use of expediency or policy. There is no such thing as sliding up-hill. In morals the only sliders are backsliders.

Let the judge and the jury, and the sheriff and the jailer, cease to act under a corrupt government, — cease to be tools and become men.

Certainly slavery, and all vice and iniquity, have not had power enough to create any flower thus annually to charm the senses of men. It has no life. It is only a constant decaying and a death, offensive to all healthy nostrils. The unchangeable laws of the universe, by a partial obedience to which even sin in a measure succeeds, are all on the side of the just and fair. It is his few good qualities misallied which

[1] [*Cape Cod, and Miscellanies*, p. 393; *Misc.*, Riv. 178.]

alone make the slaveholder at all to be feared; it is because he is in some respects a better man than we.

Why, who are the real opponents of slavery? The slaveholders know, and I know. Are they the governors, the judges, the lawyers, the politicians? Or are they Garrison, Phillips, Parker & Co.? The politicians do now, and always will, instinctively stand aloof from such.

And at this very time I heard the sound of a drum in our streets. There were men or boys training; and for what? With an effort I could pardon the cocks for crowing still, for they had not been beaten that morning; but I could not excuse this rubadub of the trainers.[1]

June 18. *Sunday.* P. M. — To climbing fern.

The tephrosia is interesting for the contrast of yellowish or cream-color with red. On every dry or sandy bank I see the curled egg-shells of tortoises, which the skunks have sucked. The *Rosa lucida* is pale and low on dry sunny banks like that by Hosmer's pines. The leaves of what I call *Rumex obtusifolius* are now lighter green and broader and less curled and, I think, shorter-petioled than those of the curled dock, and the root is not yellow but white at core. The great water (?) dock, with its broad but pointed leaves, is just beginning to be obvious. The flowering fern seed ripe, probably [a] good while in some places. There are many strawberries this season, in meadows now,

[1] [*Cape Cod, and Miscellanies*, pp. 392, 402, 408; *Misc.*, Riv. 176, 189, 196.]

just fairly begun there. The meadows, like this Nut Meadow, are now full of the taller grasses, just beginning to flower, and the graceful columns of the rue (*Thalictrum*), not yet generally in flower, and the large tree- or shrub-like archangelica, with its great umbels, now fairly in bloom along the edge of the brook.

What we want is not mainly to colonize Nebraska with free men, but to colonize Massachusetts with free men, — to be free ourselves. As the enterprise of a few individuals, that is brave and practical; but as the enterprise of the State, it is cowardice and imbecility. What odds where we squat, or how much ground we cover? It is not the soil that we would make free, but men.

As for asking the South to grant us the trial by jury in the case of runaway slaves, it is as if, seeing a righteous man sent to hell, we should run together and petition the devil first to grant him a trial by jury, forgetting that there is another power to be petitioned, that there is another law and other precedents.

Am surprised to find the *Cirsium horridulum*, or great yellow thistle, out, some already withering, turned a dark purple, possibly a week old.

I discover that J. Dugan found the eggs of my snapping turtle of June 7th, apparently the same day. It did not go to a new place then, after all. I opened the nest to-day. It is, perhaps, five or six rods from the brook, in the sand near its edge. The surface had been disturbed over a foot and a half in diameter

and was *slightly* concave. The nest commenced five inches beneath, and at its neck was two and a half inches across and from this nearly four inches deep,  and swelled out below to four inches in width; shaped like a short, rounded bottle with a broad mouth; and the surrounding sand was quite firm. I took out forty-two eggs, close packed, and Dugan says he had previously broken one, which made forty-three.[1] They are a dirty white and spherical, a little more than one and one sixteenth inches in diameter, — soft-shelled, so that my finger left a permanent dimple in them. It was now ten days since they had been laid, and a little more than one half of each was darker-colored (probably the lower half) and the other white and dry-looking. I opened one, but could detect no organization with the unarmed eye. The halves of the shell, as soon as emptied, curled up, as we see them where the skunks have sucked them. They must all have been laid at one time. If it were not for the skunks, and probably other animals, we should be overrun with them. Who can tell how many tortoise eggs are buried thus in this small desert?

Observed in two places golden-crowned thrushes, near whose nests I must have been, hopping on the lower branches and in the underwood, — a somewhat sparrow-like bird, with its golden-brown crest and

[1] Daniel Foster says he found forty-two this summer, in a nest in his field in Princeton.

white circle about eye, carrying the tail somewhat like a wren, and inclined to run along the branches. Each had a worm in its bill, no doubt intended for its young. That is the chief employment of the birds now, gathering food for their young. I think I heard the anxious peep of a robin whose young have just left the nest.

Examined, as well as I could with the glass, what I will call the *tweezer*-bird, — *tra-wee, shreea-shre,* — raspingly. I have heard [it] perhaps as long as the evergreen-forest. It is a slender, somewhat small, vireo-like bird, yellow and yellowish all beneath, except a chestnutish (?) crescent on breast, with apparently a white spot on the wing, and certainly a yellow or greenish-yellow back between wings. Keeping rather high in the trees, I could not see the general color of the upper parts, but thought it was dark olivaceous or maybe slaty. Can it be the blue yellow-back warbler? [1]

Small grasshoppers very abundant in some dry grass. I find the lygodium, a late fern, now from a foot to eighteen inches high and not yet flower-budded or the leaves fully expanded. *Platanthera flava* at the Harrington Bathing-Place, possibly yesterday, — an unimportant yellowish-green spike of flowers. A large fresh stone-heap eight or ten inches above water just below there, — quite sharp, like Teneriffe. *Aralia hispida. Typha latifolia* may have shed pollen two or three days. I am surprised at the abundance of its sulphur-like pollen, on the least jar covering my

[1] Probably is. *Vide* May 7, 1855.

hands and clothes, — green; at least it does not burn. The female part of the spike green and solid and apparently *immature*. *Epilobium angustifolium* up railroad, this end of high wood.

Another round red sun of dry and dusty weather to-night, — a red or red-purple helianthus. Every year men talk about the dry weather which has now begun as if it were something new and not to be expected.

Often certain words or syllables which have suggested themselves remind me better of a bird's strain than the most elaborate and closest imitation. Heard young partridges.

It is not any such free-soil party as I have seen, but a free-man party, — *i. e.* a party of free men, — that is wanted. It is not any politicians, even the truest and soundest, but, strange as it may sound, even godly men, as Cromwell discovered, who are wanted to fight this battle, — men not of policy but of probity. Politicians! I have looked into the eyes of two or three of them, but I saw nothing there to satisfy me. They will vote for my man to-morrow if I will vote for theirs to-day. They will whirl round and round, not only horizontally like weathercocks, but vertically also.

My advice to the State is simply this: to dissolve her union with the slaveholder instantly. She can find no respectable law or precedent which sanctions its continuance. And to each inhabitant of Massachusetts, to dissolve his union with the State, as long as she hesitates to do her duty.[1]

¹ [*Cape Cod, and Miscellanies*, p. 403; *Misc.*, Riv. 190.]

June 19. Monday. P. M. — Up Assabet.

A thunder-shower in the north. Will it strike us? How impressive this artillery of the heavens! It rises higher and higher. At length the thunder seems to roll quite across the sky and all round the horizon, even where there are no clouds, and I row homeward in haste. How by magic the skirts of the cloud are gathered about us, and it shoots forward over our head, and the rain comes at a time and place which baffles all our calculations! Just before it the swamp white oak in Merrick's pasture was a very beautiful sight, with its rich shade of green, its top as it were incrusted with light. Suddenly comes the gust, and the big drops slanting from the north, and the birds fly as if rudderless, and the trees bow and are wrenched. It comes against the windows like hail and is blown over the roofs like steam or smoke. It runs down the large elm at Holbrook's and shatters the house near by. It soon shines in silver puddles in the streets. This the first rain of consequence for at least three weeks.

Amelanchier berries now generally reddening. Methinks the *Botryapium* has broader, more ovate, often rounded and pointed leaves, the calyx-lobes recurved on the fruit, while the *oblongifolia* is inclined to obovate and narrower leaves and erect calyx-lobes. Flowering raspberry, perhaps yesterday.

Men may talk about measures till all is blue and smells of brimstone, and then go home and sit down and expect their measures to do their duty for them. The only measure is integrity and manhood.

Vol. VI

June 20. Tuesday. Motherwort to-morrow. Elder. A cloud of minute black pollywogs in a muddy pool. I see where the crickets are eating the wild strawberries.

P. M. — To Shad-bush Meadow.

Heard a *new* bird — *chut-cheeter-varrer-chutter-wit* — on the low bushes, about the size of Wilson's thrush apparently. Apparently olivaceous (?) above, most so on head, yellow front, dark bill, dark wings with two white bars, all yellow or yellowish breast and beneath. Perhaps never heard it before. Cow-wheat, apparently two or three days. A three-leaved *Lysimachia stricta* apparently, with reddish flower-buds, not open. Shad-berries almost, but scarce. There seems to be much variety in the *Rosa lucida*, — some to have stouter hooked prickles than the *R. Carolina*. Upland haying begun, or beginning. Common nettle.

June 21. Wednesday. We have had thick fog, and rain fell through it this morning.

P. M. — To Walden, etc.

Mitchella in Deep Cut woods, probably a day or two. Its scent is agreeable and refreshing, between the mayflower and rum cherry bark, or like peachstone meats. *Pyrola secunda* at Laurel Glen, a day or two (?). A third of the spike now out. Most hieraciums (*venosum*) are shut by day; some open this cloudy afternoon. When I see the dense, shady masses of weeds about water, — already an unexplorable maze, — I am struck with the contrast between this and the spring, [when] I wandered about in search of the first faint greenness along the borders of the brooks.

Then an inch or two of green was something remarkable and obvious afar. Now there is a dense mass of weeds along the waterside, where the muskrats lurk, and overhead a canopy of leaves conceals the birds and shuts out the sun. It is hard to realize that the seeds of all this growth were buried in that bare, frozen earth.

The glyceria is budded and drooping at the pond, but hardly in flower.

In the little meadow pool, or bay, in Hubbard's shore, I see two old pouts tending their countless young close to the shore. The former are slate-colored. The latter are about half an inch long and very black, forming a dark mass from eight to twelve inches in diameter. The old are constantly circling around them, — over and under and *through*, — as if anxiously endeavoring to keep them together, from time to time moving off five or six feet to reconnoitre. The whole mass of the young — and there must be a thousand of them at least — is incessantly moving, pushing forward and stretching out. Are often in the form of a great pout, apparently keeping together by their own instinct chiefly, now on the bottom, now rising to the top. Alone they might be mistaken for pollywogs. The old, at any rate, do not appear to be very successful in their apparent efforts to communicate with and direct them. At length they break into four parts. The old are evidently very careful parents. One has some wounds apparently. In the second part of the story of Tanner it is said: "*Ah-wa-sis-sie* — Little catfish. The Indians say this fish hatches its young in a hole in the mud, and that they accompany her for some time afterwards." Yet in Ware's Smellie it is said that fishes take no care of their young. I think also that I see the young breams in schools hovering over their nests while the old are still protecting them.

I see two varieties of *Galium trifidum*, apparently equally early, one smooth, the other rough; sometimes it grows in very dense tufts. Peltandra well out, apparently yesterday; quite abundant and pretty, raised two or three inches above the water. *Prinos verticillatus*, possibly yesterday. *Hypericum ellipticum*. Eriocaulon. Partridges drum still. The effect of the pond on its shore while standing at a great height is remarkable. Though considerably lower than it was, it appears much higher in some places, where it has worn away a barrier between itself and a meadow and so made the water deeper there.

Rambled up the grassy hollows in the sprout-lands north (?) of Goose Pond. I felt as if in a strange country, — a pleasing sense of strangeness and distance. Here, in the midst of extensive sprout-lands, are numerous open hollows more or less connected, where for some reason [1] the wood does not spring up, — and I am glad of it, — filled with a fine wiry grass, with the panicled andromeda, which loves dry places, now in blossom around the edges, and small black cherries and sand cherries straggling down into them. The woodchuck loves such places and now wabbles off with a peculiar loud squeak like the sharp bark of a red squirrel, then stands erect at the entrance of his

[1] Maybe frosts.

hole, ready to dive into it as soon as you approach. As wild and strange a place as you might find in the unexplored West or East. The quarter of a mile of sprout-land which separates it from the highway seems as complete a barrier as a thousand miles of earth. Your horizon is there all your own.

Indigo, apparently a day in *some* places. Calopogon a day or two at least in Hubbard's Close, — this handsomest of its family after the arethusa. Again I am attracted by the deep scarlet of the wild moss rose half open in the grass, all glowing with rosy light.

June 23. Friday. There has been a foggy haze, dog-day-like, for perhaps ten days, more or less. To-day it is so cold that we sit by a fire. A little skunk, a quarter or a third grown, at the edge of the North River, under hill. Birds do not sing this afternoon, though cloudy, as they did a month ago. I think they are most lively about the end of May.

P. M. — Walden and Cliffs.

I see by the railroad causeway young barn swallows on the fences learning to fly. Lactuca, maybe a day or two, but the heads not upright yet. Whiteweed now for three weeks has frosted the fields like snow; getting old. *Polygonum Convolvulus*. Wool-grass tops. *Pyrola rotundifolia* in cut woods to-morrow. A black snake in Abel Brooks's wood [?], on a warm dry side of it, his head concealed in a stump, rapidly vibrating his tail, which struck upon the leaves. Five feet one inch long; uniform coal-black above, with greenish coaly reflections; bluish or slaty beneath;

white beneath head; about 189 abdominal plates; tail more than one foot long and slender. When the head was dead, exerted great power with its body; could hardly hold it.

Early blueberries have begun on the Brown sprout-land, Fair Haven. This the third summer since the woods were cut, and the first for any quantity of berries, I think; so of Heywood's lot on Walden, which I think was cut also in '51–'52.

Lysimachia stricta, perhaps yesterday, at Lincoln bound, Walden. After one or two cold and rainy days the air is now clearer at last. From the Cliffs the air is beautifully clear, showing the glossy and light-reflecting greenness of the woods. It is a great relief to look into the horizon. There is more room under the heavens. Specularia, handsome, dark-purple, on Cliffs, how long? Disturbed three different broods of partridges in my walk this afternoon in different places. One in Deep Cut Woods, big as chickens ten days old, went flying in various directions a rod or two into the hillside. Another by Heywood's meadow, the young two and a half inches long only, not long hatched, making a fine peep. Held one in my hand, where it squatted without winking. A third near Well Meadow Field. We are now, then, in the very midst of them. Now leading forth their young broods. The old bird will return mewing and walk past within ten feet.

June 25. P. M. — To Assabet Bathing-Place and Derby Bridge.

Mayweed, say 27th. At Ludwigia Poke-logan, a cinder-like spawn in a white, frothy jelly. A green bittern, apparently, awkwardly alighting on the trees and uttering its hoarse, *zarry* note, *zskeow-xskeow-xskeow*. Shad-berry ripe. Garlic open, eighteen inches high or more. The calla fruit is curving down. I observe many kingfishers at Walden and on the Assabet, very few on the dark and muddy South Branch. *Asclepias* (the mucronate-pointed, what ?) yesterday. A raspberry on sand by railroad, ripe. Through June the song of the birds is gradually growing fainter. *Epilobium coloratum*, railroad above red house unless the one observed some time ago was a downy *coloratum*, with *lanceolate* leaves. *Trifolium arvense*.

June 26. Monday. P. M. — Up river to Purple Utricularia Shore.

Cornus sericea, yesterday at least. Small front-rank polygonum, a smut-like blast in the flower. Small form of arrowhead in Hubbard's aster meadow, apparently several days. I am struck, as I look toward the Dennis shore from the bathing-place, with the peculiar agreeable dark shade of June, a clear air, and bluish light on the grass and bright silvery light reflected from fresh green leaves. *Sparganium*, apparently *ramosum*, two or three days. The largest apparently the same, but very rarely in blossom ; found one, however, with a branched scape, but not concave leaves except below. *Gratiola. Cicuta maculata*, apparently to-morrow.

June 27. P. M. — Cliffs *via* Hubbard meadow.

Smooth sumach [1] at Texas house, two days. Hellebore in full bloom; how long? For the most part does not bloom. *Polygonum sagittatum* probably also some time at Baker Swamp. *Œnothera biennis*, two or more days. *Scutellaria galericulata*, to-morrow. *Polygonum Persicaria. Marchantia polymorpha.* Hydrocotyle, a day or two in Potter's field near Corner road by apple tree. Blueberries pretty numerously ripe on Fair Haven. P. Hutchinson says that he can remember when haymakers from Sudbury, thirty or forty years ago, used to come down the river in numbers and unite with Concord to clear the weeds out of the river in shallow places and the larger streams emptying in. The three lecheas show reddish and flower-like at top, — the second of Gray apparently a little the most forward.

June 28. A. M. — To Island.

Tall anemone. Pontederia to-morrow.

A thunder-shower in the afternoon.

June 29. Another clear morning after last evening's rain.

P. M. — To lime-kiln.

Spurry, a good while. Cichorium at Simon Brown's, three or four days (early); also catnep, about two days. Canada thistle, yesterday. Earliest cultivated cherries, a week ago. Hazelnut burs now make a show. *Veronica serpyllifolia* still. The cherry-bird's note is like the fine peep of young partridges or woodcocks.

[1] Probably staghorn; smooth not for a week probably.

VIII

JULY, 1854

(ÆT. 36–37)

July 1. Saturday. P. M. — To Cliffs.

From the hill I perceive that the air is beautifully clear after the rain of yesterday, and not hot; fine-grained. The landscape is fine as behind a glass, the horizon-edge distinct. The distant vales toward the northwest mountains lie up open and clear and elysian like so many Tempes. The shadows of trees are dark and distinct. On the river I see the two broad borders of pads reflecting the light, the dividing line between them and the water, their irregular edge, perfectly distinct. The clouds are separate glowing masses or blocks floating in the sky, not threatening rain. I see from this hill their great shadows pass slowly here and there over the top of the green forest. Later a breeze rises and there is a sparkle on the river somewhat as in fall and spring. The wood thrush and tanager sing at 4 P. M. at Cliffs. The anychia in steep path beyond springs, almost.

Some boys brought me to-night a singular kind of spawn found attached to a pole floating in Fair Haven Pond. Some of it six feet below the surface, some at top, the up-

All the large black birches on Hubbard's Hill have just been cut down, — half a dozen or more. The two largest measure two feet seven inches in diameter on the stump at a foot from the ground; the others, five or six inches less. The inner bark there about five eighths of an inch.

June 30. P. M. — Walden and Hubbard's Close.

Jersey tea. Young oak shoots have grown from one and a half to three or four feet, but now in some cases appear to be checked and a large bud to have formed. Poke, a day or two. Small crypta Elatine, apparently some days at least, at Callitriche Pool. *Rubus triflorus* berries, some time, — the earliest fruit of a rubus. The berries are very scarce, light (wine?) red, semitransparent, showing the seed, — a few (six to ten) large shining grains and rather acid. *Lobelia spicata*, to-morrow.

permost as big as a water-pail; a very *firm* and clear jelly, the surface covered with small rayed or star-shaped spawn (?). A great quantity of it.

July 2. Sunday. 4 A. M. — To Hill.

Hear the chip-bird and robin very lively at dawn. From the Hill, the sun rising, I see a fine river fog wreathing the trees — elms and maples — by the shore. I mark the outlines of the elms and *Salix Purshiana*, now so still and distinct, looking east. It is clear summer now. The cocks crow hoarsely, ushering in the long-drawn thirsty summer day. A day for cows. The morning the spring of the day. A few bullfrogs trump.

P. M. — To Flint's Pond and Smith's Hill with C.

Thimble-berries. Parsnip at Tuttle's. Tobacco-pipe well up. Spatulate or long-leaved sundew, some days. *Hypericum Canadense*, some days. *Pyrola elliptica*, apparently some days, or directly after *rotundifolia*, on east side of Smith's Hill. *Asclepias phytolaccoides*, a new plant, apparently two or three days on Smith's Hill. A blue high blueberry ripe. An abundance of red lilies in the upland dry meadow, near Smith's Spring trough; low, — from one to two feet high, — upright-flowered, more or less dark shade of red, freckled and sometimes wrinkle-edged petals; must have been some days. This has come with the intense summer heats, a torrid July heat like a red sunset threatening torrid heat. (Do we not always have a dry time just before the huckleberries turn?) I think this meadow was burnt over about a year ago.

Did that make the red lily grow? The spring now seems far behind, yet I do not remember the interval. I feel as if some broad invisible lethean gulf lay behind, between this and spring. *Geum strictum*, a new plant, apparently a week or ten days; some of the heads already five eighths of an inch in diameter; roadside at Gourgas sprout-land; aspect of a buttercup and *Potentilla Norvegica* with burs.[1] I see some *Lysimachia stricta* (?), with ends of petals coppery-reddish.

July 3. Monday. I hear the purple finch these days about the houses, — *à twitter witter weeter wee, à witter witter wee.*

P. M. — To Hubbard Bridge by boat.

On the great hummock dropped on Dennis's meadow last winter, I see now flourishing, of small plants, water milkweed, *Lysimachia stricta*, hedgehog (?) grass, horse-mint, arrowhead, onoclea, *Viola lanceolata*, gratiola, and the small-flowered hypericum, as well as meadow-grass.

The river and shores, with their pads and weeds, are now in their midsummer and hot-weather condition, now when the pontederias have just begun to bloom. The seething river is confined within two burnished borders of pads, gleaming in the sun for a mile, and a sharp snap is heard from them from time to time. Next stands the upright phalanx of dark-green pontederias. When I have left the boat a short time the seats become intolerably hot. What a luxury to bathe now! It is gloriously hot, — the first of this weather.

[1] Also near (north of) Assabet Bathing-Place, out of bloom, July 8.

mile from a cherry tree. Must have been dropped by a bird. Mulberries some time.

July 4. A sultry night the last; bear no covering; all windows open.

8 A. M. — To Framingham.

Great orange-yellow lily, some days, wild yellow lily, drooping, well out. *Asclepias obtusifolia*, also day or two. Some chestnut trees show at distance as if blossoming. Buckwheat, how long? I probably saw *Asclepias purpurascens* (??) over the walls. A very hot day.

July 5. Another very hot night, and scarcely any dew this morning. *Lysimachia lanceolata* var. *hybrida*, a day or two, at Merrick's Bathing-Place. Bass at Island.

P. M. — To White Pond.

One hundred and nine swallows on telegraph-wire at bridge within eight rods, and others flying about. *Stachys aspera*, Clamshell Ditch. The blue-curls and fragrant everlasting, with their refreshing aroma, show themselves now pushing up in dry fields, — bracing to the thought. Horse-mint under Clamshell, apparently yesterday. On Lupine Knoll, picked up a dark-colored spear-head three and a half inches long, lying on the bare sand; so hot that I could not long hold it tight in my hand. Now the earth begins to be parched, the corn curls, and the four-leaved loosestrife, etc., etc., wilt and wither. Sericocarpus. Small circæa at Corner Spring, some days. *Rosa Carolina*,

I cannot get wet enough. I must let the water soak into me. When you come out, it is rapidly dried on you or absorbed into your body, and you want to go in again. I begin to inhabit the planet, and see how I may be naturalized at last. The clams are so thick on the bottom at Hubbard's Bathing-Place that, standing up to my neck in water, I brought my feet together and lifted up between them, so as to take off in my hand without dipping my head, three clams the first time, though many more dropped off. When you consider the difficulty of carrying two melons under one arm and that this was in the water, you may infer the number of the clams. A cone-flower (new plant), — *Rudbeckia hirta* (except that I call its disk not dull brown but dull or dark purple or maroon; however, Wood calls it dark purple), — in Arethusa Meadow. Saw one plucked June 25; blossomed probably about that time. Many yesterday in meadows beyond almshouse. Probably introduced lately from West. *Pycnanthemum muticum* at Hypericum corymbosum Ditch. Proserpinaca at Skullcap Pool, apparently five or six days. Touch-me-not, good while, — ten days at least; some seeds now spring. As I return down the river, the sun westering, I admire the silvery light on the tops and extremities of the now densely leaved golden willows and swamp white oaks and maples from the under sides of the leaves. The leaves have so multiplied that you cannot see through the trees; these are solid depths of shade, on the surface of which the light is variously reflected. Saw a fresh cherry-stone (must be cultivated cherry; wild not ripe) in the spring under Clamshell Hill, nearly half a

apparently a day or two, Corner causeway; dull leaves with fine serrations, twenty-five to thirty, plus, on a side, and *narrow closed* stipules. *Asclepias incarnata* var. *pulchra*.

July 6. P. M. — To Beck Stow's.
Euphorbia maculata, good while. *Polygonum aviculare*, a day or two. Now a great show of elder blossoms. *Polygala sanguinea*, apparently a day or more. *Galium asprellum* in shade; probably earlier in sun. Partridges a third grown.

Veery still sings and toad rings.

On the hot sand of the new road at Beck Stow's, headed toward the water a rod or more off, what is probably *Cistuda Blandingii*; had *some* green conferva (?) on its shell and body. Length of upper shell, $6\frac{1}{2}$ inches; breadth behind, $4\frac{5}{8}$; tail beyond shell, $2\frac{1}{4}$. Did not see it shut its box; kept running out its long neck four inches or more; could bend it directly back to the posterior margin of the second [?] dorsal plate. Ran out its head further and oftener than usual. The spots pale-yellow or buff. Upper half of head and neck blackish, the former quite smooth for $1\frac{5}{8}$ inches and finely sprinkled with yellowish spots, the latter warty. The snout lighter, with five perpendicular black marks. Eyes large (?), irides dull green-golden. Under *jaw and throat clear chrome-yellow.* Under parts of neck and roots of fore legs duller yellow; inner parts behind duller yellow still. Fore legs with black scales, more or less yellow spotted above; at root and beneath pale-yellow and yellowish. Hind legs uniformly black above and but little lighter beneath. Tail black all round. No red or orange about the animal. No hook or notch to jaw.

Plantain, some days, and gnaphalium, apparently two or three days.

July 7. P. M. — To lygodium.

Verbena urticifolia. Ilysanthes, three or four days back, flat east of Clamshell Shore. Large form of arrowhead, two or more days. Woodcock at the spring under Clamshell. *Campanula aparinoides*, apparently three or four days. The clover heads are turned brown and dry, and whiteweed is also drying up. I think that that is the water dock just opening in J. P. Brown's meadow. Disturbed two broods of partridges this afternoon, — one a third grown, flying half a dozen rods over the bushes, yet the old, as anxious as ever, rushing to me with the courage of a hen. Columbines still.

Lygodium palmatum hardly yet in flower, I should say; for the most very green and tender atop and not much flatted out. Saw a pretty large hawk with narrow and long wings, black-tipped beneath, and white rump, light beneath, circling over the Ministerial Swamp with a loud, shuffling, jay-like and somewhat flicker-like sound.

July 8. Saturday. P. M. — To Assabet Bathing-Place.

Melilot, a day or two. *Spiranthes gracilis*, a day or two (?). A *Lysimachia stricta* (?) by birch fence in path

beyond Shad-bush Meadow, with whorls of three leaves and spike about eight inches long, about June 26th; lower half now out of bloom, one quarter in bloom, upper quarter budded. Ludwigia. The 4th and 5th were the hot bathing days thus far; thermometer at 98 and 96 respectively. Sium almost; say 9th.

8 P. M. — Full moon; by boat to Hubbard's Bend.

There is wind, making it cooler and keeping off fog, delicious on water. The moon reflected from the rippled surface like a stream of dollars. I hear a few toads still. See a bat; how long? The bullfrogs trump from time to time. It is commonly a full round *errr, err, err, err* (gutturally, and increasing in volume), and then coarsely trilled (?), *er-er-er, er-er-er, er-er-er;* occasionally varied like the looing of a bull. The whip-poor-wills are heard, and the baying of dogs.

The *Rosa nitida* I think has [been] some time done; the *lucida* generally now ceasing, and the *Carolina* (?) just begun.

The middle lechea not quite.

July 9. Sunday. P. M. — Fair Haven Hill via Hubbard's Bathing-Place.

Vaccinium vacillans berry, four or five days; common blue huckleberry. Hubbard aster, some days. Is it not *Tradescanti*-like? Begins to blossom low in the grass. *Hypericum corymbosum*, not yet. Tansy by railroad causeway, a day or more. *Chenopodium album.*

Examined a lanceolate thistle which has been

Vol. VI

pressed and laid by a year. The papers being taken off, its head sprang up more than an inch and the downy seeds began to fly off.

July 10. Monday. Took up one of the small tortoise eggs which I had buried June 15th. The eye was remarkable, developed in the colorless and almost formless head, one or two large dark circles of the full diameter; a very distinct pulsation where the heart should be and along the neck was perceptible; but there seemed to be no body but a mass of yellow yolk.

P. M. — To Hubbard's Close, spotted pyrola, and Walden.

Gaultheria, apparently two or three days in open ground. Some choke-berry leaves in dry places are now red, some locust leaves and elm leaves yellow. *Lycopus sinuatus*, a day or two. *Platanthera lacera*, in one place, apparently a week; Stow's strawberry meadow ditch. *Ludwigia palustris*, same place, apparently three or four days. *Pycnanthemum lanceolatum*, two or three days. *Polygala cruciata*, Hubbard's Close, two or three days. I find that most of the wild gooseberries are dried up and blackened. *Solidago stricta*, apparently to-morrow or next day. Northern wild red cherry ripe apparently some days. Low blackberry. A sericocarpus (?) in Poorhouse Meadow with linear, or narrow-spatulate, entire, blunt leaves.

The following are the birds I chanced to hear in this walk (did not attend much): The seringos on fences, *link* of bobolink, crow, oven-bird, tanager, chewink,

huckleberry-bird (pretty often and loud), flicker cackle, wood thrush, robin (?), before 3 P. M.; then red-eye, veery trill, catbird rigmarole, etc., etc.

This is what I think about birds now generally: —

See a few hawks about.
Have not heard owls lately, not walking at night.
Crows are more noisy, probably anxious about young.
Hear phœbe note of chickadee occasionally; otherwise inobvious.
Partridge, young one-third grown.
Lark not very common, but sings still.
Have not heard *conqueree* of blackbird for about a month, methinks.[1]
Robin still sings, and in morning; song sparrow and bay-wing.
See no downy woodpeckers nor nuthatches.
Crow blackbirds occasionally chatter.
Hear flicker rarely.
Rush sparrow, common and loud.
Saw a snipe within two or three days.[2]
Woodcock seen within two or three days.
Think I have heard pine warbler within a week.
Cuckoo and quail from time to time.
Barn swallow, bank swallow, etc., numerous with their young for a week or two.
I hear the plaintive note of young bluebirds.
Chip-sparrow in morning.
Purple finch about and sings.
Martin lively.
Warbling vireo still, and wood thrush, and red-eye, and tanager, all at midday.
Catbird's rigmarole still.
Chewink sings; and veery trill from out shade.
Whip-poor-will at evening.
Summer yellowbird and yellow-throat rarely.

[1] Heard one *conqueree* July 11th. Chattering flocks now of females and young over river.
[2] And July 11th.

Goldfinch oftener twitters over.
Oven-bird still.
Evergreen-forest note, I think, still.
Night-warbler of late.
Hardly a full bobolink.
Kingbird lively.
Cherry-bird commonly heard.
Think I saw turtle dove within a day or two.

The singing birds at present are: —

Villageous: Robin, chip-bird, warbling vireo, swallows.
Rural: Song sparrow, seringos, flicker, kingbird, goldfinch, *link* of
bobolink, cherry-bird.
Sylvan: Red-eye, tanager, wood thrush, chewink, veery, oven-bird,
— all even at midday. Catbird full strain, whip-poor-will, crows.

July 11. *Tuesday.* P. M. — By boat to Fair Haven.
White geum, probably about the 5th (not the 3d).

Pontederia now makes a handsome show. The female red-wings and their young now fly in small chattering flocks over the river. The smallest-flowered hypericum, several days; have I mentioned it? Purple utricularia well out since the 5th; say 7th. The black high blueberries are a trifle earlier, small and acid. The *Rosa lucida* still common. *Utricularia cornuta* at Fair Haven, apparently two days. The water-target is common off this shore. *Hypericum corymbosum* in front of Lee's Cliff, a day or two. The drought is very obvious on these rocks now, which are so verdurous in spring. The ivy (*Toxicodendron*), *Arenaria serpyllifolia*, etc., are quite sere and brown. Pennyroyal, thimble-berries, and ferns also are withering. Some huckleberries quite as if dried on a pan. Ampelopsis out three or

four days on the rock. Parietaria, apparently two or three days against rock. Handsome now from these rocks the bay (on the south side of Fair Haven at the inlet of river), with its spit of shining pads. *Lobelia inflata*, a day or more. *Veronica serpyllifolia* about done. There is much large bur-reed leaves afloat and lodged in the middle of the river at Clamshell Bend. Did the wind tear it up? I heard Conant's cradle cronching the rye behind the fringe of bushes in the Indian field. Reaping begun. Sun set when I was off Nut Meadow. A straight edge of massy cloud had advanced from the south-southeast and now stretched overhead from west-southwest to east-northeast, and after sunset reflected a soft fawn-colored (?) light on the landscape, lighting up with harmonious light the dry parched and shorn hillsides, the soft, mellow, fawn-colored light seeming to come from the earth itself.

July 12. P. M. — To Dodge's Brook.

The early cotton-grass is now about gone from Hubbard's Close. With this month began the reign of river-weeds obstructing the stream. Potamogetons and heart-leaves, etc., now for a *long* time covered with countless mosquito cases (?). They catch my oars and retard the boat. A rail will be detained a month by them in mid-stream, and tortoises (*Sternothærus* or *Emys*

picta), four or five or more in a row, lie along it. Many young barn (?) swallows (they have a darker crescent on the breast and long tail-feathers not grown) sit in flocks on the bared dead willows over the water and let me float within four or five feet. Birds do not distinguish a man sitting in a boat. I see a green bittern wading in a shallow muddy place, with an awkward teetering, fluttering pace. Button-bush. Observed a pickerel in the Assabet, about a foot long, headed upstream, quasi-transparent (such its color), with darker and lighter parts contrasted, very still while I float quite near. There is a constant motion of the pectoral fins and also a waving motion of the ventrals, apparently to resist the stream, and a slight waving of the anal, apparently to preserve its direction. It darted off at last by a strong sculling motion of its tail. See white maple leaves floating bottom up, covered with feathery aphides.

A *Lilium Canadense* (at Dodge Brook corner by road), approaching *superbum*, four and a half feet high, with a whorl of four flowers, and two more above, somewhat pyramidal, and petals recurved.

July 13. *Thursday.* 2 P. M. — To Bare Hill, Lincoln, by railroad.

Have heard a faint locust-like sound from crickets a week or two. In the midst of July heat and drought. The season is trivial as noon. I hear the hot-weather and noonday birds, — red-eye, tanager, wood pewee, etc. Plants are curled and withered. The leaves dry, ripe like the berries. The point of a lower leaf of a

smooth sumach is scarlet, and some geranium leaves. Many birch leaves are yellow and falling. Leaves are very much eaten (June is the time to collect perfect ones); of some kinds hard to find a perfect specimen, unless of a firm texture. The *Pyrus arbutifolia* is very thick and glossy dark green. The tupelo leaf is pretty firm and perfect, not *so* glossy, more or less winding, and the shoots are zigzag or winding. *Polygonum Hydropiper* at Baker Swamp. Thoroughwort, to-morrow or next day. *Scutellaria lateriflora*, some days at least. The chestnuts, now in full bloom, are conspicuous from the hills (Bare Hill), like a yellowish or creamy-tinged rime.

Vaccinium vacillans on Bare Hill ripe enough to pick, now considerably in advance of huckleberries; sweeter than last and grow in dense clusters. The *V. Pennsylvanicum* is soft and rather thin and tasteless, mountain and spring like, with its fine light-blue bloom, very handsome, simple and ambrosial. This *vacillans* is more earthy, like solid food. Many of the huckleberries here on the hilltop have dried black and shrivelled before ripening.

Boys go after the cows now about 5.30 o'clock. Decodon not distinctly flower-budded yet. Gnaphalium (pearly) well out, say yesterday. If there is an interregnum in the flowers, it is when berries begin. Scent the bruised leaves of the fragrant goldenrod along the Lincoln road now. What I have called *Solidago arguta* at Walden (*vide* radical leaves); also an aster, probably *Diplopappus umbellatus*, at Baker Swamp, will open in a few days.

July 14. *Friday.* Awake to day of gentle rain, — very much needed; none to speak of for nearly a month, methinks. The cooler and stiller day has a valuable effect on my spirits.

P. M. — Over the Hill to Brown's watering-place.

It holds up from time [to time], and then a fine, misty rain falls. It lies on the fine reddish tops of some grasses, thick and whitish like morning cobwebs. The stillness is very soothing. This is a summer rain. The earth is being bedewed. There is no storm or violence to it. Health is a sound relation to nature. Anychia plenty by the watering-place (with the amphicarpæa), but calyx apparently not expanded. Amphicarpæa, not yet. Penthorum, three or four days. Xyris, apparently three or four days in meadow close by. Hardhack, two or three days. A hedyotis still. Elodea to-morrow. The red capsules of the *Hypericum ellipticum*, here and there. This one of the fallward phenomena in still rainy days.

July 15. *Saturday.* P. M. — To Hubbard's Bridge causeway *via* river.

Rained still in forenoon; now cloudy. Fields comparatively deserted to-day and yesterday. Hay stands cocked in them on all sides. Some, being shorn, are clear for the walker. It is but a short time that he has to dodge the haymakers. This cooler, still, cloudy weather after the rain is very autumnal and restorative to our spirits. The robin sings still, but the goldfinch twitters over oftener, and I hear the *link link* of the bobolink (one perfect strain!), and the crickets

creak more as in the fall. All these sounds dispose our minds to serenity. Perhaps the mosquitoes are most troublesome such days in the woods, if it is warm enough. We seem to be passing, or to have passed, a dividing line between spring and autumn, and begin to descend the long slope toward winter. On the shady side of the hill I go along Hubbard's walls toward the bathing-place, stepping high to keep my feet as dry as may be. All is stillness in the fields. The calamint (*Pycnanthemum muticum*), standing by the wall with its hoary upper leaves, full of light even this cloudy day and reminding of the fragrance which I know so well, is an agreeable sight. I need not smell it; it is a balm to my mind to remember its fragrance.

I hear a bay-wing on the wall near by, sound[ing] far away, — a fainter song sparrow strain, somewhat. I see its open mouth and quivering throat, yet can hardly believe the seemingly distant strain proceeds from it, *yaw yaw, twee twee, twitter twitter, te twee twe tw tw tw*, and so ends with a short and rapid trill.

Again I am attracted by the Clamshell reach of the river, running east and west, as seen from Hubbard's fields, now beginning to be smoothed as in the fall. First, next the meadow, is the broad dark-green rank of pickerel-weeds, etc., etc. (polygonum, etc.), then the light-reflecting edging of pads, and then the smooth, still, cloud-reflecting water. My thoughts are driven inward, even as clouds and trees are reflected in the still, smooth water. There is an inwardness even in the mosquitoes' hum, while I am picking blueberries in the dank wood.

Vol. VI

Rhexia near the *Rhus copallina*, apparently yesterday. The flicker still, and the veery full, and Maryland yellow-throat, and nuthatch. Many birds begin to fly in small flocks like grown-up broods. Green grapes and cranberries also remind me of the advancing season. The former are as large as ripe cranberries, the latter as big as peas, though the vines are still full of blossoms. Cymbidiums are quite fresh and pogonias linger still. *Drosera rotundifolia*, end of Hubbard's bank wall, Corner road, some days, — perhaps a fortnight, for it was nearly out on the 2d, its lower flowers first, and now dry.

The stems and leaves of various asters and goldenrods, which ere long will reign along the way, begin to be conspicuous. *Amaranthus hybridus*, several days at least. It has come out quite fair and warm. There are many butterflies, yellow and red, about the *Asclepias incarnata* now.

July 16. *Sunday.* A thick fog began last night and lasts till late this morning; first of the kind, methinks.

P. M. — *Via* railroad and pond to Saw Mill Brook.

Many yellow butterflies and red on clover and yarrow. Is it the yellow-winged or Savannah sparrow with yellow alternating with dark streaks on throat, as well as yellow over eye, reddish flesh-colored legs, and two light bars on wings? *Solidago nemoralis* yesterday.

Woodcock by side of Walden in woods. Methinks there were most devil's-needles a month ago. *Lycopus Virginicus* by Target Meadow, a day or two; maybe

as long as the other elsewhere. *Ludwigia palustris*[1] grows there. *Goodyera repens* to-morrow. *Polygala verticillata*, apparently some days. The *Rhus Toxicodendron* leaves are turned clear light yellow in some places, in others, many dried and brown. *Mimulus ringens* at Saw Mill Brook, apparently two days. The large (?) circæa (it is the *lutetiana*, though the flowers are white), apparently two or three days. Trientalis, ash-colored fruit. After the late rains and last night's fog, it is *somewhat* dog-dayish, and there is a damp, earthy, mildewy scent to the ground in wood-paths. *Aralia nudicaulis* berries well ripe. The *Polygala sanguinea* heads in the grass look like sugar-plums.

July 17. *Monday.* Last night and this morning another thick dogdayish fog. I find my chamber full this morning. It lasts till 9 A. M.

11 A. M. — By river to Fair Haven.

I go to observe the lilies. I see a rail lodged in the weeds with seven tortoises on it, another with ten, another with eleven, all in a row sunning now at midday, hot as it is. They are mostly the painted tortoise. Apparently no weather is too hot for them thus to bask in the sun. The pontederia is in its prime, alive with butterflies, yellow and others. I see its tall blue spikes reflected beneath the edge of the pads on each side, pointing down to a heaven beneath as well as above. Earth appears but a thin crust or pellicle. The river was at its lowest thus far probably on the 13th. The rains succeeding the drought have now

¹ Box kind.

raised it a little, and this forenoon, though a little air is stirring, the water is smooth and full of reflections here and there, as if there had been oil in those rains, which smoothed it. In that hottest and driest weather about the 4th, there was yet considerable air stirring. Methinks that about *this* time the waters begin to be more glassy, dark and smooth. The cuckoo *cows* at midday.

At Purple Utricularia Shore, there are, within a circle of four or five rods' diameter, ninety-two lilies fairly open and about half a dozen which appear to have already partly closed. I have seen them far more numerous. I watch them for an hour and a half.

At 11.45...92 fairly open
At 12 ...88
At 12.15...75
At 12.30...46
At 12.45...26
At 1   ... 4 which are more or less stale

By about 1.30 they are all shut up, and no petal is to be seen up and down the river unless a lily is broken off. You may therefore say that they shut up between 11.30 and 1.30, though almost all between 12 and 1. I think that I could tell when it was 12 o'clock within half an hour by the lilies. One is about an hour about it. The petals gradually draw together, and the sepals raise themselves out of the water and follow. They do not shut up so tight but that a very little white appears at the apex. Sometimes a sepal is held back by a pad or other weed, leaving one side bare. Many fall over on their sides more or less, but none withdraw

under water as some have said. The lilies reach from the water's edge, where they are raised two or three inches above the surface, out five or six rods to where the water is four feet deep, and there succeed the *small* yellow lily.

Meanwhile large yellowish devil's-needles, coupled, are flying about and repeatedly dipping their tails in the water. Why are not all the white lily pads red beneath? On the muddy bottom, under the pads and between their stems, are countless red bugs crawling about. The birds are quite lively at this hour of noon, — the robin, red-eye, wood pewee, martins, and kingbirds, etc. The cuckoo is a very neat, slender, and graceful bird. It belongs to the nobility of birds. It is elegant. Here and there a phalanx of bluish-green *large* bulrushes rises near the shore, and all along a troop of pontederias, fronted and often surrounded by a testudo of pads. I feel an intense heat reflected from the surface of the pads. The rippled parts of the stream contrast with the dark smooth portions. They are separated as by an invisible barrier, yet, when I paddle into the smoothness, I feel the breeze the same. I see where a *Juncus militaris* has grown up through a white lily pad and stands two feet above it. Its hard, sharp point pierced it, instead of lifting it off the water. It reminds me of the Saladin's cutting a silk handkerchief in the air with his cimetar. This continual snapping of the pads which I hear appears to be made underneath and *may be* produced by minnows darting at the insects which feed on them.

At Cardinal Shore, *Lobelia cardinalis* a day or more. *Pycnanthemum incanum*, apparently several days. It also is hoary at top. Staghorn sumach in fruit. The fall of hellebore and cabbage has begun. The former lies along, yellow and black and decaying. The stinging spotted flies are very troublesome now. They settle in the hollows of the face, and pester us like imps. The clams lie on their edges or ends like buds or bulbs crowded together. *Desmodium acuminatum* at Conant Orchard Grove, perhaps two or three days. One four feet high, its leaves making a flat cricket, a foot from the ground.

Agrimony here almost done. *Diplopappus cornifolius*, a day or more. I was surprised by the loud humming of bees, etc., etc., in the bass tree; thought it was a wind rising at first. Methinks none of our trees attract so many.

I am surprised to see crossing my course in middle of Fair Haven Pond great yellowish devil's-needles, flying from shore to shore, from Island to Baker's Farm and back, about a foot above the water, some against a head wind; also yellow butterflies; suggesting that these insects see the distant shore and resolve to visit it. In fact, they move much faster than I can toward it, yet as if they were conscious that they were on a journey, flying for the most part straight forward. It shows more enterprise and a wider range than I had suspected. It looks very bold. If devil's-needles cross Fair Haven, then man may cross the Atlantic. Seeing him, I am reminded of Horace's lines about the breast of triple brass. Pasture thistle on Lee's

Cliff, three or four days. Woodbine on rocks begun to redden there. I start two green bitterns in different places amid the weeds by the shore. In Conant's meadow just behind Wheeler's, the smaller fringed orchis not quite reached by the mowers. It may have been out four or five days. It is a darker purple for being so exposed. None yet opening in the shade. *Aralia racemosa* at Spring a short time. The sarothra to-morrow. The late rose not *fairly* begun along the river, now when *lucida* is leaving off.

July 18. *Tuesday.* 5 A. M. — Up Turnpike.

A haymaking morning fog, through and above which the trees are glorious in the sun. The elm leaves appear to be drinking the moisture along the dusty, debauched highway; some of them yellowing. Whence these fogs and this increase of moisture in the air? The kingbird, song sparrows, and quail are lively. The centaurea, not yet. I think I have not heard a night-warbler for a fortnight. *Erigeron Canadensis*. *Erigeron strigosus* I must call the other.

P. M. — To Sam Barrett's by boat, and old Wheeler house.

A hot midsummer day with a sultry mistiness in the air and shadows on land and water beginning to have a peculiar distinctness and solidity. The river, smooth and still, with a deepened shade of the elms on it, like midnight suddenly revealed, its bed-curtains shoved aside, has a sultry languid look. The atmosphere now imparts a bluish or glaucous tinge to the distant trees. A certain debauched look, as the highway in the morning. This a crisis in the season. After this the foliage of some trees is almost black at a distance. I do not know why the water should be so remarkably clear and the sun shine through to the bottom of the river, making it so plain. Methinks the air is not clearer nor the sun brighter, yet the bottom is unusually distinct and obvious in the sun. There seems to be no concealment for the fishes. On all sides, as I float along, the recesses of the water and the bottom are unusually revealed, and I see the fishes and weeds and shells. I look down into the sunny water. In midsummer, when its foliage is thickest and stems most concealed, the *Salix Purshiana* is most beautiful. Its leafy sails are now all set, concealing its spars, and it appears to float in light masses buoyantly on the water.

Methinks the asters and goldenrods begin, like the early ripening leaves, with midsummer heats. Now look out for these children of the sun, when already the fall of some of the very earliest spring flowers has commenced.

The Island is now dry and shows few flowers. Where I looked for early spring flowers I do not look for midsummer ones. Such places are now parched and withering. Blue vervain, apparently a day; one circle is open a little below the top. As I go along the Joe Smith road, I see some of the lower leaves of the white vervain turned a faint mulberry-color. Brooks has let out some of his pigeons, which stay about the stands or perches to bait others. Wild ones nest in his woods quite often. He begins to catch them the middle of August.

I found so many berries on that rocky road, between and about the careless farmers' houses and walls, that the soil seemed more fertile than where I live. Every bush and bramble bears its fruit; the sides of the road are a fruit garden; blackberries, huckleberries, thimble-berries, fresh and abundant, no signs of drought; all fruits in abundance; the earth teems. What are the virtues of the inhabitants that they are thus blessed? Do the rocks hold moisture, or are there no fingers to pluck them? I seem to have wandered into a land of greater fertility, some up-country Eden. Are not these the delectable hills? It is a land flowing with milk and honey. Great shining blackberries peep out at me from under the leaves upon the rocks. There the herbage never withers. There are abundant dews.

Now comes the dews and fogs to save the berries and the transplanted trees.

Elecampane will apparently open in two or three days; begins to show some yellow. Choke-cherry, though not dark.[1] By the elecampane and the Wheeler house, to my great surprise growing abundantly in the road, the *Monarda fistulosa*, apparently a week at least, — three or more feet high with a few heads containing a whorl of large, very showy crimson flowers, with crimsoned bracts in whorls beneath, with a balm or summer savory or sweet marjoram fragrance. These things out of the heavenward northwest. Perhaps it is Wood's variety *mollis*. It cannot be the *didyma*, for the corolla is not more than one and three eighths inches long.

[1] Say a week later; ate some black, August 8th.

Vol. VI

Two common milkweeds I do not identify. First apparently *Asclepias Syriaca* of Linnæus and Bigelow; nectaries "with an oblique ridge on each side the fissure;" horns long with a slender point as high as the nectaries; leaves gradually acute. It appears to be *A. Cornuti* of Gray, but what does he mean by leaves "with a slight point"? Can he refer to the mucronate-leafed kind? Apparently *A. Cornuti* of Wood, but in his plate he gives the short, stout, recurved horn of the mucronate kind. *Vide* if the heads are spinous, as *A. Cornuti*.

Then there is a common [kind] with many thick, elliptical, short-petioled leaves (up railroad, June 25); mucronated; stout-stemmed. Is it *purpurascens* of Bigelow? It is not dark-purple. Not *purpurascens* of Gray, when he says that the pedicels are only about twice the length of the divisions of the corolla and that only the lower leaves are mucronate. Are the pods smooth?[1]

This side the sunflower house, against woods, in road, just beyond large pine, *Hedyotis longifolia*, a good while tufted, but without striæ in throat, many-flowered.

We have very few bass trees in Concord, but walk near them at this season and they will be betrayed, though several rods off, by the wonderful susurrus of the bees, etc., which their flowers attract. It is worth going a long way to hear. I was warned that I was passing one in two instances on the river, — the

[1] The pods have soft spinous projections, and it must be *A. Cornuti* of Gray (July 30th). The first kind, opposite the monarda, has no spinous projections.

only two I passed, — by this remarkable sound. At a little distance [it] is like the sound of a waterfall or of the cars; close at hand like a factory full of looms. They were chiefly humblebees, and the great globose tree was all alive with them. I heard the murmur distinctly fifteen rods off. You will know if you pass within a few rods of a bass tree at this season in any part of the town, by this loud murmur, like a waterfall, which proceeds from it.

July 19. P. M. — To Beck Stow's and Walden.

Alisma, apparently a day or more. *Polygonum Careyi* to-morrow. In Moore's Swamp I pluck cool, though not very sweet, large red raspberries in the shade, making themselves dense thickets. Wild holly berries, a day or two. The throttled sound of a cuckoo from out the shade of a grove. How lustily the poison-dogwood grows, — five feet from the ground this year and still growing, covered with a rich glaucous bloom! The more smothering, furnace-like heats are beginning, and the *locust* days. Crotalarias but few, apparently a day or two only. The tall, wand-like, large-leaved *Desmodium Canadense*, some days at least in the dry, rough sunflower field. Black choke-berry, several days. High blueberries scarce, but a few half an inch or more in diameter. Apparently a catbird's nest in a shrub oak, lined with root-fibres, with three green-blue eggs. *Erigeron annuus* perhaps fifteen rods or more beyond the Hawthorn Bridge on right hand, — a new plant, — probably last month. Thinner leaves than the *strigosus*. The white cotton-grass now (and how long?) at Beck Stow's appears to be the *Eriophorum gracile* (?). I see no rusty ones. In the maple swamp at Hubbard's Close, the great cinnamon ferns are very handsome now in tufts, falling over in handsome curves on every side, — a rank undergrowth about three feet high, completely hiding the dead leaves. Some are a foot wide and raised up six feet long. Clintonia berries in a day or two. I am surprised to see at Walden a single *Aster patens* with a dozen flowers fully open a day or more. Smooth sumach berries. The anychia shows some small pods; probably flowered about July 1st. *Lechea minor* shows stamens.

A wood thrush to-night. Veery within two or three days.

July 20. A very hot day, a bathing day. Warm days about this.

P. M. — To Hubbard Bath.

That long, narrow sparganium, which is perhaps the smaller one, growing long in our river, stands thick, with the heart-leaf and potamogeton, in the middle in shallow places. Methinks there begins to be a bluish scum on the water at this season, somewhat stagnant-looking. This may be the oil which smooths it. The large potamogeton in midstream is ten feet long. There is an immense quantity of clams there in the middle where it is four feet deep. I dived and took up four large ones in one hand at the first grip. Now and for several days I have seen, on the leaves of the red and black oaks, minute caterpillars feeding, with

thistle, apparently several days, some being withered. The larger pinweed, apparently a few days, probably same date with the *minor;* its lower leaves dull-red, those of *Lechea minor* equally red or brighter. Some *Amelanchier obovata* leaves a light dirty scarlet. Zi-zania, a day, with a handsome light-green panicle a foot or more long, a long slender stem, and corn-like leaves frequently more than an inch wide. Diervilla leaves dull red and green. The large primrose lower leaves a clear dark red. The *Epilobium coloratum* lower leaves very dark red. *Gerardia flava,* apparently two or three days, Lupine Hillside up railroad, near fence. Also *Solidago odora,* a day or two, there, and what I will call *S. puberula* (?), to-morrow. *S. altissima* on railroad, a day or two. When the flower-buds of the boehmeria, just ready to open, are touched with a pin, the stamens spring out remarkably, scattering their pollen.

July 23. Sunday. P. M. — To Walden *via* Hubbard's Grove and Fair Haven Hill.

Carrot by railroad, some time; say ten days. *Eupatorium purpureum.* There is a peculiar light reflected from the shorn fields, as later in the fall, when rain and coolness have cleared the air. *Eupatorium pubescens,* to-morrow. The white orchis at same place, four or five days at least; spike one and three quarters by three inches. I see small flocks of song sparrows, etc., rustle along the walls and fences. *Lonicera Ciliata,* apparently several days, Corner causeway, right side.

very small pearly, dewdrop-like ova near them partly hatched. Skunk-cabbage fruit some days; cut by the mowers.

A muttering thunder-cloud in northwest gradually rising and with its advanced guard hiding in the sun and now and then darting forked lightning. The wind rising ominously also drives me home again. At length down it comes upon the thirsty herbage, beating down the leaves with grateful, tender violence and *slightly* cooling the air; but all the thunder and lightning was in its van. How soon it swept over and we saw the flash in the southeast! Corn in blossom these days.

July 22. The hottest night, — the last.

It was almost impossible to pursue any work out-of-doors yesterday. There were but few men to be seen out. You were prompted often, if working in the sun, to step into the shade to avoid a sunstroke. At length a shower passing in the west slightly cooled the air. The domestic animals suffer much. Saw a dog which had crawled into a corner and was apparently dying of heat. Fogs almost every morning now. First *noticed* the dry scent of corn-fields a week ago.

Now clouds have begun to hang about all day, which do not promise rain, as it were the morning fogs elevated but little above the earth and floating through the air all day.

P. M. — To Assabet Bath.

Centaurea, one or two flowerets. There is a cool wind from east, which makes it cool walking that way while it is melting hot walking westward. Spear-leaved

Boehmeria there also. Since the 19th, have heard locusts oftener. *Aster acuminatus* at Radula Swamp, in a day or two. My three-leaved *Lysimachia stricta* (?) at Radula Swamp, common. *A. Radula* (?), a day. Saw yesterday on edge of Lee House Meadow a low blueberry (?) bush with large oblongish black berries and narrow leaves, with little or no bloom, conspicuous calyx, apparently between *Vaccinium vacillans* and *V. corymbosum.* Some elsewhere two and a half feet high. I also have seen on Fair Haven Hill-side, near west spring, a sort of larger *V. Pennsylvanicum* with oblong black berries and conspicuous calyx. *Lespedeza capitata,* Lupine Bank, a day. *Cerasus pumila* berries, some time. Hazel leaves in dry places have begun to turn yellow and brown. *Lespedeza violacea,* apparently several days. I see broods of partridges later than the others, now the size of the smallest chickens. Onoclea green fruit conspicuous. See a thunder-cloud coming up in northwest, but as I walk and wind in the woods, lose the points of compass and cannot tell whether it is travelling this way or not. At length the sun is obscured by its advance guard, but, as so often, the rain comes, leaving thunder and lightning behind.

July 24. The last four or five days it has been very hot and [we] have been threatened with thunder-showers every afternoon, which interfered with my long walk, though we had not much. Now, at 2 p. m., I hear again the loud thunder and see the dark cloud in the west. Some small and nearer clouds are float-

Shad-bush in Blossom

Ferns in Clintonia Swamp

ing past, white against the dark-blue distant one. Burdock, probably 20th.

July 25. A decided rain-storm to-day and yesterday, such as we have not had certainly since May. Are we likely ever to have two days' rain in June and the first half of July? There is considerable wind too.

P. M. — To Bare Hill, Lincoln, *via* railroad.

High blackberries, a day or two. The middle umbellet of the bristly aralia in some places, also a day or more. *Solidago bicolor*, to-morrow. I still see the cracks in the ground in old pastures, made last winter. The turtle dove dashes away with a slight note from midst of open pastures. *Diplopappus umbellatus* just beyond Baker Swamp, on right hand of road, probably about ten days; say July 15. I see some oak sprouts from the stump, six feet high. Some are now just started again after a pause, with small red leaves as in the spring. Clematis, apparently a day or two. *Hedyotis longifolia* on Bare Hill still. Decodon, not yet, but will apparently open in two or three days. The rain has saved the berries. They are plump and large. The long chestnut flowers have fallen and strew the road. *Arabis Canadensis*, sickle-pod, still in flower and with pods not quite two inches long. Pennyroyal, a day or two. Hear a wood thrush. *Desmodium nudiflorum*, a week at least. Have I not noticed it before? I now start some packs of partridges, old and young, going off together without mewing. Saw in woods a toad, dead-leaf color with black spots.

eter of five or six inches in many places. They are a greenish golden, sitting still near together, and apparently headed one way if the wind blows. At first, perhaps, you do not notice them, but, as you pass along, you disturb them, and the air is suddenly all alive with them fluttering over the road, and, when you are past, they soon settle down in a new place. How pretty these little greenish-golden spangles! Some are a very pale greenish yellow. The farmer is not aware how much beauty flutters about his wagon. I do not know what attracts them thus to sit near together, like a fleet in a haven; why they collect in groups. I see many small red ones elsewhere on the sericocarpus, etc., etc.

Rudbeckia, apparently three or four days at least; only the middle flower yet for most part. Rusty cotton-grass how long. Green grapes have for some days been ready to stew. *Diplopappus linariifolius. Aster dumosus.* Almost every bush now offers a wholesome and palatable diet to the wayfarer, — large and dense clusters of *Vaccinium vacillans*, largest in most moist ground, sprinkled with the red ones not ripe; great high blueberries, some nearly as big as cranberries, of an agreeable acid; huckleberries of various kinds, some shining black, some dull-black, some blue; and low blackberries of two or more varieties. The broods of birds just matured find thus plenty to eat. Gymnadenia [*sic*], maybe five or six days in swamp southeast of lime-kiln; one without any spurs. It is a windy day and hence worse [?] in respect to birds, like yesterday, yet almost constantly I hear borne on the wind from far, mingling with the sound of the wind, the z-ing of the

July 26. Wednesday. *Polygonum hydropiperoides* first obvious. Mikania, a day or two. Lilies open about 6 A. M. Methinks I have heard toads within a week A white mildew on ground in woods this morning.

P. M. — To lime-kiln *via* rudbeckia.

Ate an early apple from one of my own trees. Amaranthus, apparently three or four days. The under sides of its lower leaves are of a rich pale lake-color. This appears to have nothing to do with their maturity, since very young and fresh ones are so. I see these in Hosmer's onion garden, where he is weeding, and am most attracted by the weeds.

One reason why the lately shorn fields shine so and reflect so much light is that a lighter-colored and tender grass, which has been shaded by the crop taken off, is now exposed, and also a light and fresh grass is springing up there. Yet I think it is not wholly on this account, but in a great measure owing to a clearer air after rains which have succeeded to misty weather. I am going over the hill through Ed. Hosmer's orchard, when I observe this light reflected from the shorn fields, contrasting affectingly with the dark smooth Assabet, reflecting the now dark shadows of the woods. The fields reflect light quite to the edge of the stream. The peculiarity of the stream is in a certain languid or stagnant smoothness of the water, and of the bordering woods in a dog-day density of shade reflected darkly in the water. Alternate cornel berries, a day or two.

To-day I see in various parts of the town the yellow butterflies in fleets in the road, on bare damp sand (not dung), twenty or more collected within a diam-

locust, scarcely like a distinct sound. Vernonia, begun in centre a day.

July 28. Friday. Clethra. Methinks the season culminated about the middle of this month, — that the year was of indefinite promise before, but that, after the first intense heats, we postponed the fulfillment of many of our hopes for this year, and, having as it were attained the ridge of the summer, commenced to descend the long slope toward winter, the afternoon and down-hill of the year. Last evening it was much cooler, and I heard a decided fall sound of crickets.

Partridges begin to go off in packs.

Lark still sings, and robin.

Small sparrows still heard.

Kingbird lively.

Veery and wood thrush (?) not very lately, nor ovenbird.

Red-eye and chewink common.

Night-warbler[1] and evergreen-forest note not lately.

Cherry-bird common.

Turtle dove seen.

July 29. P. M. — Berrying to Brooks Clark's.

Rich-weed, how long? *Amaranthus hypochondriacus,* apparently some days, with its interesting spotted leaf, lake beneath, and purple spike; amid the potatoes.

July 30. Sunday. To lygodium.

Cuscuta, not long. *Desmodium Canadense* is to be

[1] See forward.

found at Clamshell Hill oaks. I have found the new rudbeckia in five distinct and distant parts of the town this year, — beyond almshouse, Arethusa Meadow, Sam. Wheeler meadow, Abel Hosmer meadow, and J. Hosmer meadow. Also in last place, beyond ditch, the rusty cotton-grass is now common. *Cicuta bulbifera*, apparently a week or more. Is that goose-grass near yellow thistles? Opened one of the snapping turtle's eggs at Dugan Desert, laid June 7th. There is a little mud turtle squirming in it, apparently perfect in outline, shell and all, but all *soft* and of one consistency, — a bluish white, with a mass of yellowish yolk (?) attached. Perhaps it will be [a] month more before it is hatched. There are some of what I will call the clustered low blackberries on the sand just beyond the Dugan Desert. There are commonly a few larger grains in dense clusters on very short peduncles and flat on the sand, clammy with a cool subacid taste. Small rough sunflower, apparently two days.

I have seen a *few* new fungi within a week. The tobacco-pipes are still pushing up white amid the dry leaves, sometimes lifting a canopy of leaves with them four or five inches. Bartonia, apparently some days. Bunch-berries. Mountain sumach, apparently two or three days. *Nabalus albus*, apparently three or four days. Mulgedium, apparently four or five days.

Barn swallows still.

July 31. Blue-curls. Wood thrush still sings. *Desmodium rotundifolium*. *Lespedeza hirta*, say 26th, at Heywood Peak.

Vol. VI

spare my moonlight and my mountains for the best of man I am likely to get in exchange.

I am inclined now for a pensive evening walk. Methinks we think of spring mornings and autumn evenings. I go *via* Hubbard Path. Chelone, say two days, at Conant's meadow beyond Wheeler's. July has been to me a trivial month. It began hot and continued drying, then rained some toward the middle, bringing anticipations of the fall, and then was hot again about the 20th. It has been a month of haying, heat, low water, and weeds. Birds have grown up and flown more or less in small flocks, though I notice a new sparrow's nest and eggs and perhaps a catbird's eggs lately. The woodland quire has steadily diminished in volume.

At the bass I now find that that memorable hum has ceased and the green berries are formed. Now blueberries, huckleberries, and low blackberries are in their prime. The fever-bush berries will not be ripe for two or three weeks. At Bittern Cliff the *Gerardia quercifolia* (?), apparently four or five days at least. How interesting the small alternate cornel trees, with often a flat top, a peculiar ribbed and green leaf, and pretty red stems supporting its harmless blue berries inclined to drop off! The sweet viburnum, not yet turning. I see apparently a thistle-down over the river at Bittern Cliff; it is borne toward me, but when it reaches the rock some influence raises it high above the rock out of my reach. What a fall-like look the decayed and yellow leaves of the large Solomon's-seal have in the thickets now! These, with skunk-

IX

AUGUST, 1854

(ÆT. 37)

Aug. 1. 6 A. M. On river. — *Bidens Beckii*. Bass probably out of bloom about a week. Corallorhiza, some days at Fair Haven Pond.

P. M. — To Peter's.

Sunflower. Meadow-haying begun for a week. Erechthites, begun for four or five days in Moore's Swamp. Two turtle doves in the stubble beyond. *Hieracium Canadense*, apparently a day or two. Do not see stamens of thyme-leaved pinweed, but *perhaps* petals. Ground-nut well out.

Aug. 2. *Wednesday.* Surveying in Lincoln.

Solidago lanceolata, two or three days. Decodon. *Polygonum arifolium* in swamp. *Chenopodium hybridum* probably now open. Surveyed east part of Lincoln.

5 P. M. — To Conantum on foot.

My attic chamber has compelled me to sit below with the family at evening for a month. I feel the necessity of deepening the stream of my life; I must cultivate privacy. It is very dissipating to be with people too much. As C. says, it takes the edge off a man's thoughts to have been much in society. I cannot

cabbage and hellebore, suggest that the early ripeness of leaves, etc., has somewhat normal in it, — that there is a fall already begun. *Eupatorium sessilifolium*, one or two stamens apparently for two days; its smooth leaf distinguishes it by the touch from the sunflower.

I sat on the Bittern Cliff as the still eve drew on. There was a man on Fair Haven furling his sail and bathing from his boat. A boat on a river whose waters are smoothed, and a man disporting in it! How it harmonizes with the stillness and placidity of the evening! Who knows but he is a poet in his yet obscure but golden youth? Few else go alone into retired scenes without gun or fishing-rod. He bathes in the middle of the pond while his boat slowly drifts away. As I go up the hill, surrounded by its shadow, while the sun is setting, I am soothed by the delicious stillness of the evening, save that on the hills the wind blows. I was surprised by the sound of my own voice. It is an atmosphere burdensome with thought. For the first time for a month, at least, I am reminded that thought is possible. The din of trivialness is silenced. I float over or through the deeps of silence. It is the first silence I have heard for a month. My life had been a River Platte, tinkling over its sands but useless for all great navigation, but now it suddenly became a fathomless ocean. It shelved off to unimagined depths.

I sit on rock on the hilltop, warm with the heat of the departed sun, in my thin summer clothes. Here are the seeds of some berries in the droppings of some bird on the rock. The sun has been set fifteen minutes, and a long cloudy finger, stretched along the northern horizon, is held over the point where it disappeared. I see dark shadows formed on the south side of the woods east of the river. The creaking of the crickets becomes clear and loud and shrill, — a sharp tinkling, like rills bubbling up from the ground. After a little while the western sky is suddenly suffused with a pure white light, against which the hickories further east on the hill show black with beautiful distinctness. Day does not furnish so interesting a ground. A few sparrows sing as in the morning and the spring; also a peawai and a chewink. Meanwhile the moon in her first quarter is burnishing her disk. Now suddenly the cloudy finger and the few scattered clouds glow with the parting salute of the sun; the rays of the sun, which has so long sunk below the convex earth, are reflected from each cloudy promontory with more incomparable brilliancy than ever. The hardhack leaves stand up so around the stem that now, at first starlight, I see only their light under sides a rod off. Do they as much by day?

The surface of the forest on the east of the river presents a singularly cool and wild appearance, — cool as a pot of green paint, — stretches of green light and shade, reminding me of some lonely mountainside. The nighthawk flies low, skimming over the ground now. How handsome lie the oats which have been cradled in long rows in the field, a quarter of a mile uninterruptedly! The thick stub ends, so evenly laid, are almost as rich a sight to me as the graceful tops. A few fireflies in the meadows. I am uncertain whether that so large and bright and high was a fire-

fly or a shooting star. Shooting stars are but fireflies of the firmament. The crickets on the causeway make a *steady* creak, on the dry pasture-tops an *interrupted* one. I was compelled to stand to write where a soft, faint light from the western sky came in between two willows.

Fields to-day sends me a specimen copy of my "Walden." It is to be published on the 12th *inst.*

Aug. 4. Friday. P. M. —*Via* Turnpike to Smith's Hill.

A still, cloudy day with from time to time a gentle August rain. Rain and mist contract our horizon and we notice near and small objects. The weeds — fleabane, etc. — begin to stand high in the potato-fields, overtopping the potatoes. This hardhack interests me with its bedewed pyramid. Rue is out of bloom. Sicyos, apparently in a few days. The button-woods are much improved this year and may recover. Sonchus in one place out of bloom. Purple gerardia, by brook. The autumnal dandelion is now more common. *Ranunculus aquatilis* var. *fluviatilis*, white petals with a yellow claw, small flowers on surface of Hosmer's ditch, west end, by Turnpike. A new plant. Say July 1st. Is it open in sunny weather? The lower leaves of the sharp-angled lycopus are a dull red and those of the elodea are a fine, clear, somewhat crimson red. Fragrant everlasting. The swamp blackberry on high land, ripe a day or two. I hear the pigeon woodpecker still, — *wickoff, wickoff, wickoff, wickoff,* from a neighboring oak. See a late rose still in flower. On this hill (Smith's) the bushes are black with huckle-

Vol. VI

berries. They droop over the rocks with the weight and are very handsome. Now in their prime. Some glossy black, some dull black, some blue; and patches of *Vaccinium vacillans* intermixed. *Hieracium paniculatum* in woods by Saw Mill Brook, a day or two. The leaves of some weeds, perhaps goldenrods, are eaten in a ribbon character like some strange writing apparently half-way through the leaf, often along the edge. This for some time. *Goodyera pubescens,* a day or two. *Hieracium scabrum,* apparently two or three days. It is already fall in low swampy woods where the cinnamon fern prevails. There are the sight and scent of beginning decay. I see a new growth on oak sprouts, three to six inches, with reddish leaves as in spring. Some whole trees show the lighter new growth at a distance, above the dark green. *Cannabis sativa.*

After sunset, a very low, thick, and flat white fog like a napkin, on the meadows, which ushers in a foggy night.

Aug. 5. Saturday. 8.30 A. M.— By boat to Coreopsis Bend.

A general fog in the morning, dispersed by 8 o'clock. At first the air still and water smooth, afterward a little breeze from time to time, — judging from my sail, from the north-northeast. A platoon of haymakers has just attacked the meadow-grass in the Wheeler meadow.

Methinks the river's bank is now [1] in its most in-

[1] *Vide* Aug. 15.

teresting condition. On the one hand are the light, lofty, and wide-spread umbels of the sium, pontederias already past their prime, white lilies perhaps not diminished in number, heart-leaf flowers, etc.; on the other the *Salix Purshiana*, full-foliaged, but apparently already *slightly* crisped and imbrowned or yellowed with heat, the button-bush in full blossom, and the mikania now covering it with its somewhat hoary bloom. The immediate bank is now most verdurous and florid, consisting of light rounded masses of verdure and bloom, and the river, slightly raised by the late rains, takes all rawness from the brim. Now, then, the river's brim is in perfection, after the mikania is in bloom and before the pontederia and pads and the willows are too much imbrowned, and the meadows all shorn. But already very many pontederia leaves and pads have turned brown or black. The fall, in fact, begins with the first heats of July. Skunk-cabbage, hellebores, convallarias, pontederias, pads, etc., appear to usher it in. It is one long acclivity from winter to midsummer and another long declivity from midsummer to winter. The mower's scythe, however, spares a fringe of to him useless or noxious weeds along the river's edge, such as sium, wool-grass, various sedges and bulrushes, pontederias, and polygonums. The pontederia leaves have but a short life, the spring so late and fall so early. Smaller flowers I now observe on or by the river are yellow lilies, both kinds; the larger polygonum (*hydropiperoides*), with slender white spikes, and the small front-rank rose-colored one; the *Bidens Beckii,* three to six or seven inches above the surface, on that very coarse, stout-stemmed, somewhat utricularia-like weed which makes dense beds in the water; the three water utricularias especially the purple; the cardinal-flower; water asclepias; and a few late roses. As I go past the white ash, I notice many small cobwebs on the bank, shelf above shelf, promising a fair day.

I find that we are now in the midst of the meadow-haying season, and almost every meadow or section of a meadow has its band of half a dozen mowers and rakers, either bending to their manly work with regular and graceful motion or resting in the shade, while the boys are turning the grass to the sun. I passed as many as sixty or a hundred men thus at work to-day. They stick up a twig with the leaves on, on the river's brink, as a guide for the mowers, that they may not exceed the owner's bounds. I hear their scythes cronching the coarse weeds by the river's brink as I row near. The horse or oxen stand near at hand in the shade on the firm land, waiting to draw home a load anon. I see a platoon of three or four mowers, one behind the other, diagonally advancing with regular sweeps across the broad meadow and ever and anon standing to whet their scythes. Or else, having made several bouts, they are resting in the shade on the edge of the firm land. In one place I see one sturdy mower stretched on the ground amid his oxen in the shade of an oak, trying to sleep; or I see one wending far inland with a jug to some well-known spring.

There is very little air stirring to-day, and that seems to blow which way it listeth. At Rice's Bend the river

is for a long distance clogged with weeds, where I think my boat would lodge in midstream if I did not more than guide it. The potamogeton leaves almost bridge it over, and the bur-reed blades rise a foot or more above the surface. The water weeps, or is strained, through. Though yesterday was rainy, the air to-day is filled with a blue haze. The coreopsis is (many) fairly but yet freshly out, I think not more than a week, from one foot to a foot and a half high, some quite white, commonly the petals reflexed a little, just on the edge of or in the water. The meadow-grass not yet cut there. In crossing the meadow to the Jenkins Spring at noon, I was surprised to find that the dew was not off the deep meadow-grass, but I wet the legs of my pants through. It does not get off, then, during the day. I hear these days still those familiar notes — of a vireo? — *somewhat* peawai-like, — two or more, *whe-tar che.* Near Lee's (returning), saw a large bittern, pursued by small birds, alight on the shorn meadow near the pickerel-weeds, but, though I rowed to the spot, he effectually concealed himself.

Now Lee and his men are returning to their meadow-haying after dinner, and stop at the well under the black oak in the field. I too repair to the well when they are gone, and taste the flavor of black strap on the bucket's edge. As I return down-stream, I see the haymakers now raking with hand or horse rakes into long rows or loading, one on the load placing it and treading it down, while others fork it up to him; and others are gleaning with rakes after the forkers. All farmers are anxious to get their meadow-hay as

soon as possible for fear the river will rise. On the 2d, Hagar told me he had done all his haying, having little or no meadow, and now the chief business was to kill weeds in the orchard, etc. Formerly they used to think they had nothing to do when the haying was done and might go a-fishing for three weeks.

I see very few whorled or common utricularias, but the purple ones are exceedingly abundant on both sides the river, apparently from one end to the other. The broad pad field on the southwest side of Fair Haven is distinctly purpled with them. Their color is peculiarly high for a water plant. In Sudbury the huckleberries, etc., appeared to be dried up. At Lee's Cliff, I meet in the path a woodchuck, — probably [a] this year's one, — which stood within seven feet and turned the side of its head to me as if deaf of one ear, and stood listening till I advanced. A very large flock of blackbirds, — perhaps grackles and cowbirds and maybe (?) young red-wings, — with a roar of wings, flying from this side the river to that and alighting on the sedge and willows and ground.

Aug. 6. P. M. — To Tarbell Hills by boat.
Rather cool with a strong wind, before which we glide. The rippled surface of the water and the light under sides of the white maples in rounded masses bordering the stream, and also the silvery tops of the swamp white oaks, give a pleasing breezy aspect to the shores, etc. Surprised to see the hibiscus just out nearer Flint's and also at Ball's Hill Bend. Apparently always earlier in those places. I noticed yesterday

that the fields of *Juncus militaris* on the south side of Fair Haven showed a stripe six or eight inches wide next the water and bounded by a very level line above of a different color, more or less reddish or as if wet, as if there had been a subsidence of the water to that extent. Yet it has actually risen, rather. The sun is quite hot to-day, but the wind is cool and I question if my thin coat will be sufficient. Methinks that after this date there is commonly a vein of coolness in the wind. The Great Meadows are for the most part shorn. Small light-green sensitive ferns are springing up full of light on the bank. I see some smaller white maples turned a dull red, — crimsonish, — a slight blush on them. Grape-vines, the downy under sides of their leaves turned up by the wind,[1] are methinks more conspicuous now at a distance along the edge of the meadow, where they round and mass the trees and bushes, — long, irregular bowers, here and there marked with the white, downy under sides of the leaves. The wind is very unsteady and flirts our sail about to this side and that. We prefer to sail to-day (Sunday) because there are no haymakers in the meadow.

Landed at Tarbell's Hills. I am more pleased with the form of the ground there than with anything else, — with the huckleberry hills, and hollows, the cow-paths, and perhaps the old corn-hills. There are very agreeable slopes and undulations, and the light is very agreeably reflected from the barren surface of the earth. It is at length cloudy, and still behind the hills, and very grateful is this anticipation of the fall, —

[1] *Vide* Aug. 20.

coolness and cloud, and the crickets steadily chirping in mid-afternoon. The huckleberries are somewhat shrivelled and drying up. As I look westward up the stream, the oak, etc., on Ponkawtasset are of a very dark green, almost black, which, methinks, they have worn only since midsummer. Has this anything to do with the bluish mistiness of the air? or is it an absolute deepening of their hue? We row back with two big stones in the stern. Interesting here and there the tall and slender zizania waving on the shore, with its light panicle eighteen inches or more in length.

Aug. 7. It is inspiriting at last to hear the wind whistle and moan about my attic, after so much trivial summer weather, and to feel cool in my thin pants.

Do you not feel the fruit of your spring and summer beginning to ripen, to harden its seed within you? Do not your thoughts begin to acquire consistency as well as flavor and ripeness? How can we expect a harvest of thought who have not had a seed-time of character? Already some of my small thoughts — fruit of my spring life — are ripe, like the berries which feed the first broods of birds; and other some are prematurely ripe and bright, like the lower leaves of the herbs which have felt the summer's drought.

Seasons when our mind is like the strings of a harp which is swept, and we stand and listen. A man may hear strains in his thought far surpassing any oratorio.

Sicyos.

P. M. — To Peter's, Beck Stow's, and Walden.

Liatris. Still autumnal, breezy with a cool vein in

the wind; so that, passing from the cool and breezy into the sunny and warm places, you begin to love the heat of summer. It is the contrast of the cool wind with the warm sun. I walk over the pinweed-field. It is just cool enough in my thin clothes. There is a light on the earth and leaves, as if they were burnished. It is the glistening autumnal side of summer. I feel a cool vein in the breeze, which braces my thought, and I pass with pleasure over sheltered and sunny portions of the sand where the summer's heat is undiminished, and I realize what a friend I am losing. The pinweed does not show its stamens — I mean the *L. thymifolia.* It was open probably about July 25. This off side of summer glistens like a burnished shield. The waters now are some degrees cooler. Winds show the under sides of the leaves. The cool nocturnal creak of the crickets is heard in the mid-afternoon. Tansy is apparently now in its prime, and the early goldenrods have acquired a brighter yellow. From this off side of the year, this imbricated slope, with alternating burnished surfaces and shady ledges, much more light and heat are reflected (less absorbed), methinks, than from the springward side. In mid-summer we are of the earth, — confounded with it, — and covered with its dust. Now we begin to erect ourselves somewhat and walk upon its surface. I am not so much reminded of former years, as of existence prior to years.

From Peter's I look over the Great Meadows. There are sixty or more men in sight on them, in squads of half a dozen far and near, revealed by their white

Vol. VI

shirts. They are alternately lost and reappear from behind a distant clump of trees. A great part of the farmers of Concord are now in the meadows, and toward night great loads of hay are seen rolling slowly along the river's bank, — on the firmer ground there, — and perhaps fording the stream itself, toward the distant barn, followed by a troop of tired haymakers.

The very shrub oaks and hazels now look curled and dry in many places. The bear oak acorns on the former begin to be handsome. Tansy is in *full blaze* in some warm, dry places. It must be time, methinks, to collect the hazelnuts and dry them; many of their leaves are turned. The Jersey tea fruit is blackened. The bushy gerardia is apparently out in some places. Blueberries pretty thick in Gowing's Swamp. Some have a slightly bitterish taste.

A wasp stung me at one high blueberry bush on the forefinger of my left hand, just above the second joint. It was very venomous; a white spot with the red mark of the sting in the centre, while all the rest of the finger was red, soon showed where I was stung, and the finger soon swelled much below the joint, so that I could not completely close the finger, and the next finger sympathized so much with it that at first there was a *little* doubt which was stung. These insects are effectively weaponed. But there was not enough venom to prevail further than the finger.

Trillium berry.

Aug. 8. P. M. — To Annursnack *via* Assabet.

A great spider three quarters of an inch long, with

large yellow marks on the sides, in middle of a flat web. This is a day of sunny water. As I walk along the bank of the river, I look down a rod and see distinctly the fishes and the bottom. The cardinals are in perfection, standing in dark recesses of the green shore, or in the open meadow. They are fluviatile, and stand along some river or brook, like myself. I see one *large white* maple crisped and tinged with a sort of rosaceous tinge, just above the Golden Horn. The surface is very glassy there. The foliage of most trees is now not only most dense, but a very dark green, — the swamp white oak, clethra, etc. The *Salix Purshiana* is remarkable for its *fine* and narrow leaves, — feathers, — of a very light or yellowish green, as if finely cut, against the dark green of other trees, yet not drooping or curved downward, but remarkably concealing its stems. Some silky cornel leaves are reddish next water. Very many leaves on hills are crisped and curled with drought. Black cherry ripe. The meadow-hay is sprinkled here and there on the river. On Annursnack I scare up many turtle doves from the stubble. Hear a supper horn — J. Smith's? — far away, blown with a long-drawn blast, which sounds like a strain of an æolian harp. The distance has thus refined it. I see some slight dun clouds in the east horizon, — perhaps the smoke from burning meadows.

Aug. 9. Wednesday. — To Boston.

"Walden" published. Elder-berries. Waxwork yellowing.

Aug. 10. 4.30 A. M. — To Cliffs.

A high fog. As I go along the railroad, I observe the darker green of early-mown fields. A cool wind at this hour over the wet foliage, as from over mountain-tops and uninhabited earth. The large primrose conspicuously in bloom. Does it shut by day? The woods are comparatively still at this season. I hear only the faint peeping of some robins (a few song sparrows on my way), a wood pewee, kingbird, crows, before five, or before reaching the Springs. Then a chewink or two, a cuckoo, jay, and later, returning, the *link* of the bobolink and the goldfinch. That is a peculiar and distinct hollow sound made by the pigeon woodpecker's wings, as it flies past near you. The *Aralia nudicaulis* is another plant which for some time, and perhaps more generally than any, yellows the forest floor with its early fall, or turning, as soon as its berries have ripened, along with hellebore, skunk-cabbage, convallarias, etc. Ambrosia. At length, as I return along the back road, at 6.30, the sun begins to eat through the fog.

The tinkling notes of goldfinches and bobolinks which we hear nowadays are of one character and peculiar to the season. They are not voluminous flowers, but rather nuts, of sound, — ripened seeds of sound. It is the tinkling of ripened grains in Nature's basket. It is like the sparkle on water, — a sound produced by friction on the crisped air.

For a day or two I have inclined to wear a thicker, or fall, coat.

Vol. VI

quite white. *Asclepias Cornuti* leaves begun to yellow; and brakes, etc. *Rhus Toxicodendron* along the Minott house ditch in the midst of its fall, almost all its leaves *burnt brown* and partly yellow.

First muskmelon in garden.

Mr. Loomis says that he saw a mockingbird at Fair Haven Pond to-day.

Aug. 11. P. M. — To Assabet Bath.

I have heard since the 1st of this month the *steady* creaking cricket. Some are digging early potatoes. I notice a new growth of red maple sprouts, small reddish leaves surmounting light-green ones, the old being dark-green. Green lice on birches. *Aster Tradescanti*, two or three days in low ground; flowers smaller than *A. dumosus*, densely racemed, with short peduncles or branchlets, calyx-scales narrower and more pointed. *Ammannia humilis* (?) (a new plant), perhaps three weeks at northeast end of Wheeler's brush fence meadow, like an erect isnardia, *i. e. Ludwigia palustris*, with small wrinkled yellowish petals with a purplish vein.

Aug. 12. Saturday. Watermelon.
P. M. — To Conantum by boat.

Methinks I heard a few toads till about the middle of July. To-day there is an uncommonly strong wind, against which I row, yet in shirt-sleeves, trusting to sail back. It is southwest. I see twelve painted tortoises on a rail only five feet long, and perhaps some were scared off before I observed them. The *Bidens*

P. M. — Clematis Brook *via* Conantum.

A cloudy afternoon and rather cool, but not threatening rain soon. Dangle-berries ripe how long? — one of the handsomest berries.

On the southwest side of Conant's Orchard Grove, saw from twenty rods off some patches of purple grass,[1] which painted a stripe of hillside next the woods for half a dozen rods in length. It was as high-colored and interesting, though not so bright, as the patches of rhexia. On examination I found it to be a kind of grass a little less than a foot high, with but few green blades and a fine spreading purple top in seed; but close at hand it was but a dull purple and made but little impression on the eye, was even difficult to detect where thin. But, viewed in a favorable light fifteen rods off, it was of a fine lively purple color, enriching the earth very much. It was the more surprising because grass is commonly of a sombre and humble color. I was charmed to see the grass assume such a rich color and become thus flower-like. Though a darker purple, its effect was similar to that of the rhexia.[2]

Hardly any dog-days yet. The air is quite clear now. *Aster macrophyllus* near beaked hazel by roadside, some time. That sort of sweet-william (?) pink, with viscidness below the joints, but not pubescent, against the Minott house; how long?

The *Arum triphyllum* fallen some time and turned

[1] *Poa hirsuta* according to Russell, now in bloom, abundant; in the J. Hosmer hollow.
[2] [*Excursions*, p. 252; Riv. 309. There the name of the grass appears as *Eragrostis pectinacea*.]

Beckii yellows the side of the river just below the Hubbard Path, but is hardly yet in fullest flower generally. I see goldfinches nowadays on the lanceolate thistles, apparently after the seeds. It takes all the heat of the year to produce these yellow flowers. It is the 3 o'clock P. M. of the year when they begin to prevail, — when the earth has absorbed most heat, when melons ripen and early apples and peaches. The cranberry cheeks begin to redden. *Viburnum dentatum* berries. Hazelnut husks now have a reddish edge, being ripe. Is not this a sign? It is already the yellowing year.

Viburnum nudum berries generally green, but some, higher and more exposed, of a deep, fiery pink on one cheek and light green on the other, and a very few dark purple or without bloom, black already. I put a bunch with only two or three black ones in my hat, the rest pink or green. When I got home more than half were turned black, — and ripe!! A singularly sudden chemical change. Another cluster which had no black ones was a third part turned. It is surprising how very suddenly they turn from this deep pink to a very dark purple or black, when the wine which they contain is mature. They are a very pretty, irregularly elliptical berry, one side longer than the other, and particularly interesting on account of the mixture of light-green, deep-pink, and dark-purple, and also withered berries, in the same cyme.

The wind is autumnal and at length compels me to put on my coat. I bathe at Hubbard's. The water is rather cool, comparatively. As I look down-stream from southwest to northeast, I see the red under sides of the white lily pads about half exposed, turned up by the wind to [an] angle of 45° or more. These hemispherical red shields are so numerous as to produce a striking effect on the eye, as of an endless array of forces with shields advanced; sometimes four or five rods in width. Off Holden Woods a baffling counter wind as usual (when I return), but looking up-stream I see the great undulations extending into the calm from above, where the wind blows steadily. I see no maples changed yet along this stream. There are but few haymakers left in the meadows.

On Conantum saw a cow looking steadily up into the sky for a minute. It gave to her face an unusual almost human or wood-god, faun-like expression, and reminded me of some frontispieces to Virgil's Bucolics. She was gazing upward steadily at an angle of about 45°. There were only some downy clouds in that direction. It was so unusual a sight that any one would notice it. It suggested adoration.

The woodbine on rocks in warm and dry places is now more frequently turned, a few leafets bright-scarlet.

The now quite common goldenrods fully out are what I have called *stricta* and also the more strict *puberula* (?). The *arguta* and *odora* are not abundant enough to make an impression. The *Solidago nemoralis* is not yet generally out. The common asters now are the *patens, dumosus, Radula*, and *Diplopappus umbellatus*. This is a famous year for huckleberries, etc. They are now drying up for the most part before spoiling.

The bushes on Conantum are quite black with them. They are clustered like *Vaccinium vacillans* apparently. High blackberries are in prime. And I see some great low blackberries on long peduncles, lifted above the huckleberries, composed of great grains, as large as the largest high blackberries. Poke berries, also poke stems, are purple; not yet peduncles. Plucked a small *Hieracium scabrum*, hairy, which I may have called *Gronovii*.

I think I should not notice the shadow of Conantum Cliff now; perhaps because the grass is so sere and russet. It should be a tender green.

For birds: —

I think that I begin to see a few more hawks than of late. A white-rumped to-day.

Partridges fly in packs.

Bluebirds sound oftener plaintively.

Larks are still seen.

Blackbirds fly in great flocks.

Robin peeps occasionally.

Song sparrow sings clearly in morning, etc.

Hear pigeon woodpecker's *wickoff* still occasionally.

Pigeons begin to be seen.

Hear rush sparrow still.

No seringos for some time.

Turtle doves common in small flocks in stubble.

White-bellied swallows still.

Barn swallows still.

Perhaps chip-sparrows are silent.

Have not heard a wood thrush since last week of July.

Catbird and thrasher done singing.

Chewink still heard.

Wood pewee "

No night-warbler,[1] or tweezer, or evergreen-forest note; nor veery.

[1] Hear one at evening, Aug. 14.

Vol. VI

Kingbird twitters still.

No red-eyes[1] nor tanagers heard since 5th.

Goldfinch common.

Cherry-bird heard.

Cuckoo.

Gold robin sometimes heard partially.[2]

Aug. 13. First *marked* dog-day; sultry and with misty clouds. For ten days or so we have had comparatively cool, fall-like weather.

I remember only with a pang the past spring and summer thus far. I have not been an early riser. Society seems to have invaded and overrun me. I have drank tea and coffee and made myself cheap and vulgar. My days have been all noontides, without sacred mornings and evenings. I desire to rise early henceforth, to associate with those whose influence is elevating, to have such dreams and waking thoughts that my diet may not be indifferent to me.

P. M. — To Bare Hill, Lincoln, *via* railroad.

I have not chanced to hear the bullfrogs trump much, if any, since the middle of July. This is a quite hot day again, after cooler weather. A *few* small red maples about[3] blush now a dull red. For about a month I think I have particularly noticed the light under sides of leaves, especially maples. I see small flocks of grass-birds, etc. In Macintosh's field (pasture),

[1] Hear one to-day.

[2] The nighthawk squeaks at sunset and the whip-poor-will sings, Aug. 14. The screech owl screams at evening.

[3] Pond? [This, written in pencil, evidently at a later date, seems to indicate that at the time he inserted it he had forgotten just where the trees were.]

some dwarf acalypha some time out. The erechthites down begins to fly. Some of these plants are six feet high. I see where the pasture thistles have apparently been picked to pieces (for their seeds? by the goldfinch?), and the seedless down strews the ground.

Huckleberries begin to be wormy, but are still sound on Bare Hill. Now the mountains are concealed by the dog-day haze, and the view is of dark ridges of forest, one behind the other, separated by misty valleys. Squirrels have begun to eat hazelnuts, and I see their dry husks on the ground turned reddish-brown.

The change, decay, and fall of the brakes in woods, etc., is perhaps more autumnal than any sight. They make more show than the aralia. Some are quite brown and shrivelled, others yellow, others yellow and brown, others yellow, brown, and green, making a very rich and parti-colored or checkered work, as of plaited straw, — bead or straw work or ivory; others are still green with brown spots. In respect to these and many other plants of this size and habit, it is already fall. They stand yellow and yellowing all through the woods, — none perhaps so conspicuous as the brake. At Thrush Alley, was surprised to behold how many birch leaves had turned yellow, — every other one, — while clear, fresh, leather-colored ones strewed the ground with a pretty thick bed under each tree. So far as the birches go it is a perfect autumnal scene there.

Aug. 14. No rain, — only the dusty road spotted with the few drops which fell last night, — but there is quite a high and cool wind this morning. Since August came in, we have begun to have considerable wind, as not since May, at least. The roads nowadays are covered with a light-colored, powdery dust (this yesterday), several inches deep, which also defiles the grass and weeds and bushes, and the traveller is deterred from stepping in it. The dusty weeds and bushes leave their mark on your clothes.

Mountain-ash berries orange (?), and its leaves half yellowed in some places.

3 P. M. — To climbing fern with E. Hoar.

It takes a good deal of care and patience to unwind this fern without injuring it. Sometimes same frond is half leaf, half fruit. E. talked of sending one such leaf to G. Bradford to remind him that the sun still shone in America. The uva-ursi berries beginning to turn.

6 P. M. — To Hubbard Bath and Fair Haven Hill.

I notice now that saw-like grass [1] seed where the mowers have done. The swamp blackberries are quite small and rather acid. Though yesterday was quite a hot day, I find by bathing that the river grows steadily cooler, as yet for a fortnight, though we have had no rain here. Is it owing solely to the cooler air since August came in, both day and night, or have rains in the southwest cooled the stream within a week? I now, standing on the shore, see that in sailing or floating down a smooth stream at evening it is an advantage to the fancy to be thus slightly separated from

[1] *Paspalum ciliatifolium.*

the land. It is to be slightly removed from the commonplace of earth. To float thus on the silver-plated stream is like embarking on a train of thought itself. You are surrounded by water, which is full of reflections; and you see the earth at a distance, which is very agreeable to the imagination.

I see the blue smoke of a burning meadow. The clethra must be one of the most conspicuous flowers not yellow at present. I sit three-quarters up the hill. The crickets creak strong and loud now *after sunset*. No word will spell it. It is a short, strong, regular ringing sound, as of a thousand exactly together, — though further off some alternate, — repeated regularly and in rapid time, perhaps twice in a second. Methinks their quire is much fuller and louder than a fortnight ago. Ah! I need solitude. I have come forth to this hill at sunset to see the forms of the mountains in the horizon, — to behold and commune with something grander than man. Their mere distance and unprofanedness is an infinite encouragement. It is with infinite yearning and aspiration that I seek solitude, more and more resolved and strong; but with a certain genial weakness that I seek society ever. I hear the nighthawk squeak and a whip-poor-will sing. I hear the tremulous squealing scream of a screech owl in the Holden Woods, sounding somewhat like the neighing of a horse, not like the snipe. Now at 7.45, perhaps a half-hour after sunset, the river is quite distinct and full of light in the dark landscape, — a silver strip of sky, of the same color and brightness with the sky. As I go home by Hayden's I smell the burning

meadow. I love the scent. It is my pipe. I smoke the earth.

Aug. 15. Tuesday. 5.15 A. M. — To Hill by boat.

By 5.30 the *fog* has withdrawn from the channel here and stands southward over the Texas Plain, forty or fifty feet high.

Some birds, after they have ceased to sing by day, continue to sing faintly in the morning now as in spring. I hear now a warbling vireo, a robin (half strain), a golden robin whistles, bluebirds warble, pigeon woodpecker; not to mention the tapping of a woodpecker and the notes of birds which are heard through the day, as wood peawai, song sparrow, cuckoo, etc. On the top of the Hill I see the goldfinch eating the seeds (?) of the Canada thistle. I rarely approach a bed of them or other thistles nowadays but I hear the cool twitter of the goldfinch about it. I hear a red squirrel's reproof, too, as in spring, from the hickories. Now, just after sunrise, I see the western steeples with great distinctness, — tall white lines. The fog eastward over the Great Meadows appears indefinitely far, as well as boundless. Perhaps I refer it to too great a distance. It is interesting when the fluviatile trees begin to be seen through it and the sun is shining above it. By 6 o'clock it has risen up too much to be interesting.

The button-bush is now nearly altogether out of bloom, so that it is too late to see the river's brink in its perfection. It must be seen between the blooming of the mikania and the going out of bloom of the button-

bush, before you feel this sense of lateness in the year, before the meadows are shorn and the grass of hills and pastures is thus withered and russet.

9 A. M. — Walk all day with W. E. C., northwest into Acton and Carlisle.

A dog-day, comfortably cloudy and cool as well as still. The river meadows, where no mowing, have a yellowish and autumnal look, especially the woolgrass. I see large flocks of bobolinks on the Union Turnpike. Are the darker ones with some yellowish (?) on side heads young red-wings or male bobolinks changing? Forded the Assabet at the bathing-place. Saw carrion-flower berries just begun to turn; say in a day or two. Panicled cornel berries on College Road. Many of the trees in Barrett's orchard on Annursnack touch the ground all around like a dish cover, weighed down with fruit, and the branches are no thicker over head than around. Is not this the best form for an apple tree, — a hollow hemisphere nearly resting on the earth, the branches equally dispersed over the superficies, and light and air equally admitted? Hills and pastures are now dry and slippery. They seem as completely russet as in winter. I associate the mist of this dog-day with the burning of meadows. Crossed from top of Annursnack to top of Strawberry Hill, past a pigeon-bed. Measured the great chestnut. At about seven feet from ground, the smallest place I could find, it is $14\frac{3}{4}$ feet in circumference; at six feet from ground, $15\frac{1}{12}$ feet in circumference; **at** five feet, $15\frac{4}{12}$; at one foot from ground not including some bulgings, 22 feet in circumference. It branches first at about nine feet from ground. The top has some dead limbs and is not large in proportion to trunk. There are great furrows in the bark. *Desmodium Marylandicum* on Strawberry Hill by wall, some days out. We took our dinner on the north side of the wall on top of the Hill. The dog-day haze conceals the distant hills and mountains, but some new and nearer elms, etc., stand out with new distinctness against it.

It is remarkable how far and widely the smoke of a meadow burning is visible, and how hard to locate. That in the meadow near Joe Merriam's,[1] half a dozen miles off, which has lasted some days, appears to possess the whole east horizon, as if any man who lived two or three miles east of this must smell it and know all about [it], but most who live within a mile of it may not have noticed it. It impresses me as if all who dwelt in the eastern horizon must know of it and be interested in it, — as if it were a sort of public affair and of moment to a whole town, — yet hardly the next neighbors observe it, and the other day, when I passed within half a mile of it, it did not make nearly so great a show as from this very distant eminence. The white smoke is now seen slanting upward across half a township and gradually mingled and confounded with the haze of the day, so that it may even seem to have produced the latter. West, by Nagog, is a dense dark, almost black smoke, and another less dark in the south. The owner of the meadow little thinks how

[1] It is the Brooks meadow on fire. *Vide* Aug. 23.

far the smoke of his burning is seen by the inhabitants of the country and by travellers, filling their horizon and giving a character to their day, shutting out much sky to those who dwell half a dozen miles away. So far a man's deformities are seen by and affect his fellows. They help to blot out the sky to those [who] dwell far away.

Looking from this Strawberry Hill to the long range behind William Brown's, northeast by east, I see that it and other hills are marked finely by many parallel lines, apparently the edges of so many terraces, arranging the crops and trees in dark lines, as if they were the traces of so many lake-shores. Methinks this is an almost universal phenomenon. When farthest inland we are surrounded by countless shores or beaches, terrace above terrace. It is the parallelism of green trees, bushes, and crops which betrays them at a distance. The locomotive whistle, far southwest, sounds like a bell. *Lycopodium dendroideum* pollen, apparently some days.

From this hill we steered northeast toward the east point of a wood in the direction of Hutchinson's, perhaps two miles off. Before starting on this walk I had studied the map to discover a new walk, and decided to go through a large wooded tract west and northwest of the Paul Dudley house, where there was no road, there at last to strike east across the head of Spencer Brook Meadow, perhaps to the old Carlisle road. A mile and a half northeast of Strawberry Hill, two or three large and very healthy and perfect sassafras trees (three large at least), very densely clothed

with dark-green lemon (?) or orange (?) tree shaped leaves, singularly healthy. This half a mile or so west of the Dudley house. Comparatively few of the leaves were of the common form, *i. e.* three-lobed, but rather simple. There was much mountain sumach close by, turning scarlet, and sweet-ferns also browning and yellowing. Keeping on through a somewhat swampy upland, we fell into a path, which Channing preferring, though it led us through woods widely out of our course westward, I soon corrected it, and, descending through swampy land, at length saw through the trees and bushes into a small meadow completely surrounded by woods, in which was a man haying only eight or ten rods off. We felt very much like Indians stealing upon an early settler, and naturally inclined to one side to go round the meadow through the high blueberry bushes. The high blueberries were from time to time very abundant, but have acquired a dead and flat taste, lost their raciness. Soon after, we followed an indistinct path through a dense birch wood, leading quite out of our course, *i. e.* westward. We were covered from head to foot with green lice from the birches, especially conspicuous on dark clothes, but going through other woods soon brushed them off again.

At length, when I endeavored to correct my course by compass, it pointed so that I lost my faith in it, and we continued to go out of our way, till we came out on a side-hill immediately overlooking a stream and mill and several houses and a small mill-pond undoubtedly on the Nashoba in the northern part of

Acton, on the road to Chelmsford. We were completely lost, and saw not one familiar object. At length saw steeples which we thought Westford, but the monument proved it Acton. Took their bearings, calculated a new course, and pursued it at first east-northeast, then east, and finally southeast, along rocky hillsides covered with weeds, where the fall seemed further advanced than in Concord, with more autumnal colors, through dense oak woods and scrub oak, across a road or two, over some pastures, through a swamp or two, where the cinnamon fern was as high as our heads and the dogwood, now fruiting, was avoided by C. After travelling about five miles, for the most part in woods, without knowing where we were, we came out on a hill from which we saw, far to the south, the open valley at head of Spencer Brook.

In the meanwhile we came upon another pigeon-bed, where the pigeons were being baited, a little corn, etc., being spread on the ground, and, [as?] at the first, the bower was already erected. What I call *Solidago arguta* is exceedingly handsome, a pyramidal head with rather horizontal branchlets with a convex surface of erect flowers; quite a splendid flower it would be in a garden. *Aster miser.* In Carlisle, on high land, that kind of viburnum with smaller, darker (with rusty patches), and less oblong berries and more obtuse leaves (at both ends), — a large spreading bush eight or nine feet high at least. Russell said it was the *V. prunifolium,* but the leaves are not sharply serrate but nearly entire, only crenate at most, commonly short and broad, the peduncle not half an inch long.

At evening, Mr. Russell showed his microscope at Miss Mackay's. Looked at a section of pontederia leaf. Saw what answered to the woody fibre and the cells on each side, also the starch in potato, lime in rhubarb, fern seeds (so called), and lichen ditto, of which last there were fifty or sixty in one little wart ○ ○ this size. The power of this glass was nine hundred diameters. All the objects were transparent and had a liquid look, crystalline, and reminded me of the moon seen through a telescope. They suggested the significance or insignificance of size, and that the moon itself is a microscopic object to us, so little it concerns us.

Aug. 16. 8 A. M. — To climbing fern with John Russell.

He says that my winkle fungus is a *Boletus* of Linnæus, *Polyporus* of others, *Auricularia* (ear-like) now. My beautiful purple grass, now in flower, the *Poa hirsuta.*

Peppermint has just begun. Walked along the Dennis shore. That sedge by edge of river with three-ranked linear leaves is *Dulichium spathaceum.* My wool-grass is a trichophorum. Says that in Chelmsford they rub the pigeon bait with the *Solidago odora* to attract pigeons. That fuzzy-topped sedge with slender spikes in straw-colored ovate heads, arranged umbel-like, he thought *Scirpus* (probably *Cyperus*) *strigosus. Aster puniceus,* a day or two. That saw-like spiked grass which is an autumnal

sight in the mown fields is *Paspalum ciliatifolium.* Choke-cherry leaves are now many reddened. *Scirpus capillaris,* turned yellow, only two or three inches high, now covers the sand on Lupine Hill. A bluet still. *Aster longifolius,* a day or two. A pear-formed puff-ball (*Lycoperdon*), in Yellow This-tle Meadow, now dry, buff-colored.  That concave, chocolate-colored one I have is a *Lycoperdon bovi*(something), — from being in pastures. That potamogeton in Nut Meadow Brook at the watering-place beyond Jenny's is *P. Claytoni,* with many long, linear, pellucid immersed leaves half an inch wide and some floating. My stag-horn lichen is the [*Parmelia*] *Borreri.* The former grows on the ground and is more like a cladonia. *Aster lævis,* two or three days, if I have not mentioned it before. *Hypnum riparium* in the Harrington trough. *Viola pedata* again. Uva-ursi berries reddened, but R. says not ripe or soft till spring. Saw the variolaria on the white pines on Harrington Road, and opegrapha, like Arab characters. Showed me the Prussian eagle in the stem of the brake. *Aster corymbosus* (?), some time by this road. (Russell thought it *cordifolius,* but the flowers are white and petioles not winged.) In the T. Wheeler pasture, showed me the *Cladonia rangiferina* (the common white one), the *C. sylvestris* (the green one with it), also the *furcata,* and spoke of the *alpina* as common in woods.

This day and yesterday, and when I was last on the river, the wind rose in the middle of the day, blow-

ing hardest at noon, — quite hard, — but went down toward night. Pointed out an *Erigeron strigosus* without rays. He had read of it as a variety. Some had small rays, leaves narrower. Above Rogers house, on right.

P. M. — With Russell to Fair Haven by boat.

That coarse, somewhat *B. Beckii*-looking weed, standing upright under water in the river, is hornwort (*Ceratophyllum echinatum*). That moss on the button-bushes is a fontinalis or else dichelyma. A coarser species is on the bridges. Cannot see the fruit now for some reason. On the rock at Bittern Cliff, the *Parmelia detonsa.* R. mistook a black pony in the water with a long mane behind some weeds for a heron. *Nuphar lutea* pads nearly all eaten, mere skeletons remaining. Saw where a partridge had dusted herself at a wood-chuck's hole. Methinks that for about three weeks past the light under sides of the upper leaves of maples, swamp oak, etc., etc., have been permanently conspicuous, while in June to middle of July they were observable only when there was more wind than usual. As if, owing to the dry weather and heat, those leaves were permanently held up, like those of the hard-hack, etc., — various weeds and shrubs on dry land, — perhaps had risen in the night and had not vitality enough to fall again. Now, accordingly, I see the dark-green upper sides of the lower leaves alone, and various agreeable shades of green thence upward. Now is the season to observe these various shades, especially when the sun is low in the west. At the steam-mill

sand-bank was the distinct shadow of our shadows, — first on the water, then the double one on the bank bottom to bottom, one being upside down, — three in all, — one on water, two on land or bushes. R. showed me the ginseng in my collection. Thinks that one of my Maine asters is a northern form of the *cordifolius.*

No haymakers in meadows now.

Prince's-feathers, how long? Woodcock in garden. *Polygonum dumetorum* at Bittern Cliff.

Aug. 18. Warbling vireo in morning, — one.

Russell thought it was the *Salix discolor* or else *eriocephala* which I saw, not *sericea,* which is not common; also that my cone-bearing one was *S. humilis.* Barratt the best acquainted with them. That the *Rubus triflorus* was badly described. That we had three gooseberries, — the common smooth, the prickly fruited, and the prickly branched. Said we had two straw-berries, the *Virginiana* and the *vesca,* — the last not uncommon. That the *Thalictrum dioicum* was only about a foot high. That the seed of flowering fern was heavy, and hence it fell in circles and so grew. That the *Cratægus Crus-Galli* was a variety of the white thorn. Best time for seaside flowers middle of July, for White Mountains 4th of July. Robbins of Uxbridge best acquainted now with the potamogetons. Tuckerman thought it would be impossible to arrange them at present, European specimens being inaccessible or fragmentary. That the smaller sparganium was my taller one of the river and should rather be called *minor*, being only narrower. That we had but one urtica hereabouts. Of the rose-colored water-lily in a pond-hole in Barnstable, into which Parker stripped and went; and the farmer dug it all up and sold it. The Spanish moss is a lily, — *Tillandsia*, — so named by Linnæus because it dislikes moisture as much as his friend Tillands the sea. All these spots on my collection of leaves — crimson, etc. — are fungi. The transparent globes on the hornwort are an alga, — *Nostoc*.

Almost impossible to find fishworms now it is so dry. I cannot find damp earth anywhere but where there is water on the surface or near.

P. M. — Over Great Meadows.

A great drought now for several weeks. The haymakers have been remarkably uninterrupted this year by rain. Corn and potatoes are nearly spoiled. Our melons suffer the more because there was no drought in June and they ran to vine, which now they cannot support. Hence there is little fruit formed, and that small and dying ripe. Almost everywhere, if you dig into the earth, you find it all dusty. Even wild black cherries and choke-cherries are drying before fairly ripe, all shrivelled. Many are digging potatoes half grown. Trees and shrubs recently set out, and many old ones, are dying. A good time to visit swamps and meadows. I find no flowers yet on the amphicarpæa.

In a ditch behind Peter's a small *Cistuda Blandingii* swimming off rapidly. Its shell is four and a quarter inches long by three and a quarter wide in

rear, three wide in front; and its depth is nearly two inches, with a slight dorsal ridge, which the large one has not. I distinguished it from the *Emys guttata* at first glance by its back being sculptured concentrically about the rear side, leaving a smooth space within, a half-inch in diameter. My large one is almost entirely smooth on back, being sculptured only an eighth of an inch wide on circumference of each scale. It has small, rather indistinct yellow spots, somewhat regularly arranged in the middle of each scale. Head peppered with dull-yellow spots above; head, legs, and tail black above; head light-yellow beneath, and also legs about roots, passing into a dirty white. It is a very restless and active turtle, not once inclosing itself or using its valve at all, at once walking off when put down, keeping its head, legs, and tail out, continually running out its neck to its full extent, and often bending it backward over the shell. Its neck with the loose skin about it has a squarish form. Readily turns itself over with its head when on its back. Upper shell black; sternum light-brown, with a large black blotch on the outside after part of each scale and about half its area; five claws on fore feet, four and a rudiment or concealed one on hind feet. In this small one, the sculptured part occupies nearly the whole scale and is from a half to three quarters of an inch wide, while in the large one it is only an eighth of an inch wide, — a mere border. Apparently as it grows the smooth rear is extended or shoves forward and a portion of the sculptured part scales off.

In this ditch an interesting green jelly, conferva-

Vol. VI

like at a little distance, perhaps a kind of frog-spawn, but without any *eyes* in it, of various forms, floating; often a sort of thick ring made of a hollow cylinder. Was that a proserpinaca in that ditch with all but two or three small leaves at top, pectinate? Saw there the large semipellucid, waved, heart-shaped radical leaves of a heart-leaf, green and purplish, sometimes all purplish, more delicate than the waved radical leaves of yellow lilies, etc., — a dimple of leaves. We can walk across the Great Meadows now in any direction. They are quite dry. Even the pitcher-plant leaves are empty. [The meadows] are covered with spatular sundew. Saw a snipe. There are fifteen or twenty haymakers here yet, but almost done. They and their loads loom at a distance. Men in their white shirts look taller and larger than near at hand.

I have just been through the process of killing the cistudo for the sake of science; but I cannot excuse myself for this murder, and see that such actions are inconsistent with the poetic perception, however they may serve science, and will affect the quality of my observations. I pray that I may walk more innocently and serenely through nature. No reasoning whatever reconciles me to this act. It affects my day injuriously. I have lost some self-respect. I have a murderer's experience in a degree.

The bobolinks alight on the wool-grass. Do they eat its seeds? The zizania on the north side of the river near the Holt, or meadow watering-place, is very conspicuous and abundant. Surprised to find the *Ludwigia sphærocarpa* apparently some time out (say

August 1st), in a wet place about twenty rods off the bars to the path that leads down from near Pedrick's; two to two and a half feet high, with a thick but unbroken bark about the base much like the decodon; no petals; yellowish seed-vessels. I think I saw a mockingbird on a black cherry near Pedrick's. Size of and like a catbird; bluish-black side-head, a white spot on closed wings, lighter breast and beneath; but he flew before I had fairly adjusted my glass. There were brown thrashers with it making their clicking note. The leaves of the panicled cornel are particularly curled by the heat and drought, showing their lighter under sides. Low blackberry vines generally are reddening and already give an October aspect to some dry fields where the early potentilla grows, as that plain of Pedrick's.

At Beck Stow's on new Bedford road, what I had thought a utricularia appears to be *Myriophyllum ambiguum*. One is floating, long and finely capillary leaves, with very few emersed and pectinate; another variety is on the mud, short, with linear or pectinate leaves. Perhaps they are the varieties *natans* and *limosum*. The last out some days, the first perhaps hardly yet. The green bittern there, leaving its tracks on the mud.

The *Solidago nemoralis* is now abundantly out on the Great Fields.

Aug. 19. P. M. — To Flint's Pond *via* railroad with Mr. Loomis.

The hills and fields generally have such a russet,

withered, wintry look that the meadows by the railroad appear to have got an exceedingly fresh and tender green. The near meadow is very beautiful now, seen from the railroad through this dog-day haze, which softens to velvet its fresh green of so many various shades, blending them harmoniously, — darker and lighter patches of grass and the very light yellowish-green of the sensitive fern which the mowers have left. It has an indescribable beauty to my eye now, which it could not have in a clear day. The haze has the effect both of a wash or varnish and of a harmonizing tint. It destroys the idea of definite distance which distinctness suggests. It is as if you had painted a meadow of fresh grass springing up after the mower, — here a dark green, there lighter, and there again the yellowish onoclea, — then washed it over with some gum like a map and tinted the paper of a fine misty blue. This is an effect of the dog-days.

There is now a remarkable drought, some of whose phenomena I have referred to during several weeks past, *q. v.* Of large forest trees the red maples appear to suffer most. Their leaves are very generally wilted and curled, showing the under sides. Perhaps not only because they require so much moisture, but because they are more nearly ripe, and there is less life and vigor in them. The *Populus grandidentata* perhaps suffers equally, and its leaves hang down wilted; even many willows. Many white birches long since lost the greater part of their leaves, which cover the ground, sere and brown as in autumn. I see many small trees quite dead, — birches, etc. I see amelan-

chier leaves scarlet, and black birch and willow yellowing. Various ferns are yellow and brown.

When I see at the brick-sand cutting how thin a crust of soil and darker sand, only three or four feet thick, there is above the pure white sand which appears to compose the mass of the globe itself, and this apparently perfectly dry, I am surprised that the trees are not all withered, and wonder if such a soil could sustain a large growth. After digging through ordinary soil and yellow sand three or four feet, you come to a pure white sand very evenly, abruptly, and distinctly separated from the former, and this is laid open to the depth of ten feet, — I know not how much deeper it extends, — so that the forest grows as it would in a wholly artificial soil made on a rock, perchance. I presume you would not now anywhere on these plains find any moisture in that four-feet crust, and there is never any in the sand beneath. I am surprised to see how shallow and dry all the available earth is there, in which the forest grows.

So like tinder is everything now that we passed three places within a mile where the old sleepers heaped up by the track had just been set on fire by the engine, — in one place a large pile.

Plenty of *Polygonum arifolium* in the ditch in the second field. Some barberries are red, and some thorn berries. A linear-leaved epilobium in Baker's, *i. e.* Mackintosh's, Swamp.

Flint's Pond has fallen very much since I was here. The shore is so exposed that you can walk round, which I have not known possible for several years,

and the outlet is dry. But Walden is not affected by the drought. There is such a haze we see not further than our Annursnack, which is blue as a mountain. *Lobelia Dortmanna* is still abundantly in flower, and hedge-hyssop, etc.; some clethra. There is a good deal of wind, but I see where the waves have washed ten feet further within an hour or two over the south shore. The wet sand is covered with small bird-tracks, perhaps peetweets', and is marked all over with the galleries of some small creatures, — worms or shellfish perhaps, — of various sizes, — some quite large, — which have passed under the surface like a meadow mouse. Are not these food for the water-birds? I find growing densely there on the southeast shore and at the *ball* shore, where it appears to have been covered with water recently, the *Myriophyllum tenellum*, another species of that of which I found two varieties yesterday; perhaps since August 1st. A new plant.

The *balls* again, *somewhat* stale, left high and dry apparently a month ago. Some five inches in diameter.

I find here and there, washed up, what I take to be the inner scales of a tortoise, and, in one place, where it fitted over the edge of the shell, thin and transparent like isinglass or parchment.

Plucked, about 4.30, one bunch of *Viburnum nudum* berries, *all* green, with very little pink tinge even. When

I got home at 6.30, nine were turned blue, the next morning thirty. It seems that they do not always pass through the deep-pink stage. They are quite sweet to eat, like raisins.

I noticed these birds in this walk: —

A lark, which sang.
White-bellied swallows on telegraph-wire.
Barn swallows, I think.
Nighthawks, which squeaked.
Heard a chewink *chewink*.
Saw cherry-birds flying lower over Heywood meadow like swallows, apparently for flies, and heard them, cricket-like.
Kingbirds quite common, twittering; one on telegraph-wire.
Bluebirds, saw and heard.
Chickadees, lisping note.
Jays, scream.
A woodcock, in wood-path, goes off with rattling sound.
Wilson's thrush's *yorrick*.
Saw crows.
Grouse.
Song sparrows, chirp.
Grass-bird and perhaps another sparrow.
Goldfinch, heard.

Aug. 20. Sunday. I hear no trilling of birds early. 5.15 A. M. — To Hill.

I hear a gold robin, also faint *song* of common robin. Wood pewee (fresh); red-wing blackbird with fragmentary trill; bobolinks (the males apparently darker and by themselves); kingbirds; nuthatch heard; yellow-throated vireo, heard and saw, on hickories (have I lately mistaken this for red-eye?); goldfinch; slate-colored hawk (with white rump and black wing-tips). The grape leaves even at this hour, after a dewy night, are still many of them curled upward, showing their light under sides, and feel somewhat crisped by the drought. This, I think, is one with that permanent standing up of the leaves of many trees at this season. Prinos berries have begun to redden. When the red-eye ceases generally, then I think is a crisis, — the woodland quire is dissolved. That, if I remember, was about a fortnight ago. The concert is over. The pewees sit still on their perch a long time, returning to the same twig after darting at an insect. The yellow-throated vireo is very restless, darting about. I hear a sound as of green pignuts falling from time to time, and see and hear· the chickaree thereabouts !!

P. M. — Up Assabet by boat to Bath.

A warm but breezy day, wind west by south. Water clear and sunny. I see much of my fresh-water sponge just above· the Island, attached to the bottom, rocks, or branches under water. In form it reminds me of some cladonia lichens, for it has many branches like a lichen, being a green, porous, spongy substance, with long, slender, pointed fingers or horns, pointed upward or outward, the thickest about half an inch in diameter, and emits a peculiar, penetrating, strong, rank scent like some chemicals. The whole mass perhaps eight or ten inches in diameter. When raised to the surface it slowly sinks again. The bottom of the south branch is in many places almost covered with the short cut leaves of the sium, — as I call it. On the sandy bottom in midstream (mussel shoals), a dozen rods above the Rock, I notice a small (?) green

clam which must be the same with or similar to that which Perkins showed me in Newburyport. It has bright-green rays from the eye (?) on a light-green ground. Found in pure sand. Saw three. The rays show through to the inside. It is handsomer without than the common.

Some chickadees on the pitch pines over water near the Hemlocks look longer than usual, hanging back downward. See a strange bird about size of cedarbird also on the pitch pine, perhaps greenish-olive above, whitish or ashy beneath, with a yellow vent and a dark line on side-head.[1] Saw a wood pewee which had darted after an insect over the water in this position in the air: It often utters a continuous *pe-e-e*.

The *Polygonum amphibium* at Assabet Rock, apparently several days, rising two or more feet above water. In many places I notice oaks stripped by caterpillars nowadays. Saw yesterday one of those great light-green grubs with spots. I see to-day many — more than a half-dozen — large wood tortoises on the bottom of the river, — some apparently eight to nine inches long in shell, some with their heads out. Are they particularly attracted to the water at this season? They lie quite still on the bottom.

Off Dodge's Brook, saw a fish lying on its side on the surface, with its head downward, slowly steering toward the shore with an undulating motion of the tail. Found it to be a large sucker which had apparently been struck by a kingfisher, fish hawk, or heron

[1] Could it have been the female rose-breasted grosbeak?

Vol. VI

and got away. (The mill is not a-going to-day, Sunday.) It had been seized near the tail, which for three inches was completely flayed and much torn, lacerated, a part of the caudal fin being carried off. It had also received a severe thrust midway its body, which had furrowed its side and turned down a large strip of skin. It was breathing its last when I caught it. It was evidently too powerful for the bird which had struck it. I brought it home and weighed and measured it. It weighed two pounds and two ounces and was nineteen and a quarter inches long. Above, it was a sort of blue black or slate-color, darkest on the head, with blotches of the same extending down its sides, which were of a reddish golden, passing into white beneath. There were a few small red spots on the sides, just behind the gills. It had what I should call a gibbous head, but no horns; a line of fine mucous pores above and below eye; eyes at least one and a half inches apart; great corrugated ears on the lower lip; fins all dark like the back; nostrils double; opercula not golden; irides golden; scales on lateral line sixty-five (about), those near tail gone with skin. Fin rays, as I counted: pectoral, seventeen; ventral, ten; anal, nine; dorsal, thirteen; caudal, some wanting. Looking down on it, it was very broad at base of head, tapering thence gradually to tail. It had a double bladder, nearly six inches long by one inch at widest part. I think it must have been a kingfisher, it was so much lacerated at the tail.

Now, at 4 P. M., hear a croaking frog[1] near the

[1] Mole cricket. [See *postea*.]

water's edge, sounding like the faint quacking of a duck with more of the *r* in it, — something like *crack grack grack*, rapidly repeated. Though I knew that I must be within three feet of it, as I looked from the boat upon the shore, I could see nothing, but several times I interrupted him and caused him to jump. It is surprising how perfectly they are concealed by their color, even when croaking under one's eyes. It was *Rana palustris*, though I did not see it when it croaked. I after heard them further off, just before sunset, along the edge of the river, and saw that I had often mistaken their note for that of a cricket. So similar are these two earth-sounds. The cricket-like note of this little frog in the meadow ushers in the evening.

A man tells me to-day that he once saw some black snake's eggs on the surface of a tussock in a meadow just hatching, some hatched. The old one immediately appeared and swallowed all the young. Assabet quite low. Those beds of dirty green ostrich-feather potamogetons are much exposed and dry at top.

I perceive quite a number of furrows of clams in the sand, all leading from the side toward the middle of the river, with the clams at that end. Can they be going down now? They have not moved opposite Hubbard Bath, where they are in middle as well as by shore. Their position in the furrows is on their sharp edges, with what I will call their two eyes forward.

We had a very little drizzling rain on the 4th, and I think that was the last drop.

There is so thick a bluish haze these dog-days that single trees half a mile off, seen against it as a light-colored background, stand out distinctly a dark mass, — almost black, — as seen against the more distinct blue woods. So, also, when there is less haze, the distinct wooded ridges are revealed one behind another in the horizon.

Aug. 21. P. M. — To Conantum *via* Hubbard Bath.

Leaves of small hypericums begin to be red. The river is warmer than I supposed it would become again, yet not so warm as in July. A small, wary dipper, — solitary, dark-colored, diving amid the pads. The same that lingered so late on the Assabet. Red choke-berries are dried black; ripe some time ago. In Hubbard's meadow, between the two woods, I cannot find a pitcher-plant with any water in it. Some of the Hubbard aster are still left, against the upper Hubbard Wood by the shore, which the mowers omitted. It looks like a variety of *A. Tradescanti*,[1] with longer, less rigid, and more lanceolate toothed cauline leaves, with fewer and more distant branchlets, and the whole plant more simple and wand-like. The bayonet rush has not generally blossomed this year. What has, long ago. Have noticed winged grasshoppers or locusts a week or more. Spikenard berries are now mahogany-color. Trillium berries bright-red. I see a woodchuck at a distance, cantering like a fat pig, ludicrously fat, first one end up, then the other. It runs with difficulty. The fever-bush berries are partly turned red, perhaps prematurely. Now, say, is hazel-

[1] *Vide* July 26, '56.

nut time. I think that my *Aster corymbosus* — at least the early ones — are *A. cordifolius*, since Wood makes this to vary to white and to have a flexuous stem. I see robins in small flocks and pigeon woodpeckers with them. Now see in pastures tufts of grass which have been pulled up by cattle, withered, quite thickly strewn. *Spiranthes cernua*, a day or two. Brought home a great *Eupatorium purpureum* from Miles's Swamp (made species *fistulosum* by Barratt). It is ten and a half feet high and one inch in diameter; said to grow to twelve feet. The corymb, eighteen and a half inches wide by fifteen inches deep; the largest leaves, thirteen by three inches. The stem hollow throughout. This I found, to my surprise, when I undertook to make a flute of it, trusting it was closed at the leaves; but there is no more pith there than elsewhere. It would serve many purposes, as a water-pipe, etc. Probably the Indians knew it and used. They might have blowed arrows through a straight one. It would yield an available hollow tube six feet long.

Did I see the yellow redpoll back? Head not conspicuously reddish.

Aug. 22. The haze, accompanied by much wind, is so thick this forenoon that the sun is obscured as by a cloud. I see no rays of sunlight.

A bee much like a honey-bee cutting rounded pieces out of rose leaves.

P. M. — To Great Meadows on foot along bank into Bedford meadows; thence to Beck Stow's and Gowing's Swamp.

Walking may be a science, so far as the direction of a walk is concerned. I go again to the Great Meadows, to improve this remarkably dry season and walk where in ordinary times I cannot go. There is, no doubt, a particular season of the year when each place may be visited with most profit and pleasure, and it may be worth the while to consider what that season is in each case.

This was a prairial walk. I went along the river and meadows from the first, crossing the Red Bridge road to the Battle-Ground. In the Mill Brook, behind Jones's, was attracted by one of those handsome high-colored masses of fibrous pink roots of the willow in the water. It was three or four feet long, five or six inches wide, and four or five inches thick, — long parallel roots nearly as big as a crow-quill, with innumerable short fibres on all sides, all forming a dense mass of a singular bright-pink color. There are three or four haymakers still at work in the Great Meadows, though but very few acres are left uncut. Was surprised to hear a phœbe's *pewet pewee* and see it. I perceive a dead mole in the path half-way down the meadow.

At the lower end of these meadows, between the river and the firm land, are a number of shallow muddy pools or pond-holes, where the yellow lily and pontederia, *Lysimachia stricta*, *Ludwigia sphærocarpa*, etc., etc., grow, where apparently the surface of the meadow was floated off some spring and so a permanent pond-hole was formed in which, even in this dry season, there is considerable water left. The great roots of

the yellow lily, laid bare by the floating off of the surface crust last spring, two and a half or three inches in diameter and a yard or more of visible length, look like great serpents or hydras exposed in their winter quarters. There lie now little heaps or collections of the singularly formed seed-vessels of the pontederia, as they have fallen on the mud, directly under the nodding but bare spikes.

In these shallow muddy pools, but a few inches deep and few feet in diameter, I was surprised to observe the undulations produced by pretty large fishes endeavoring to conceal themselves. In one little muddy basin where there was hardly a quart of water, caught half a dozen little breams and pickerel, only an inch long, as perfectly distinct as full grown, and in another place, where there was little else than mud left, breams two or three inches long still alive. In many dry hollows were dozens of small breams, pickerel, and pouts, quite dead and dry. Hundreds, if not thousands, of fishes had here perished on account of the drought.

Saw a blue heron — apparently a young bird, of a brownish blue — fly up from one of these pools, and a stake-driver from another, and also saw their great tracks on the mud, and the feathers they had shed, — some of the long, narrow white neck-feathers of the heron. The tracks of the heron were about six inches long. Here was a rare chance for the herons to transfix the imprisoned fish. It is a wonder that any have escaped. I was surprised that any dead were left on the mud, but I judge from what the book says that they do not touch dead fish. To these remote shallow and muddy pools, usually surrounded by reeds and sedge, far amid the wet meadows, — to these, then, the blue heron resorts for its food. Here, too, is an abundance of the yellow lily, on whose seeds they are said to feed. There, too, are the paths of muskrats.

In most of the small hollows formed by the crust being carried off in the spring, the proserpinaca grows abundantly. There are now hopping all over this meadow small *Rana palustris*, and also some more beautifully spotted *halecina* or shad frogs. There is a pretty strong wind from the north-northwest. The haze is so thick that we can hardly see more than a mile. The low blue haze around the *distant* edge of the meadow looks even like a low fog, *i. e.* at a sufficient distance. I find at length a pitcher-plant with a spoonful of water in it. It must be last night's dew. It is wonderful that in all this drought it has not evaporated. Arum berries ripe. High blueberries pretty thick, but now much wilted and shrivelled.

Thus the drought serves the herons, etc., confining their prey within narrower limits, and doubtless they are well acquainted with suitable retired pools far in the marshes to go a-fishing in. I see in Pedrick's bushy and weedy meadow dense fields of *Solidago arguta*, *stricta* or *puberula* (?), and *altissima*, etc., now in its prime. Corn-stalks begin to be cut and stacked, it is so dry.

I hear that Brooks's meadow (it is what I called the burning by Joe Merriam's) is on fire and cannot be put out. Are not most ardeas (herons and bitterns) seen at this season?

Aug. 23. Wednesday. P. M. — To Gowing's Swamp and Hadlock Meadows.

I improve the dry weather to examine the middle of Gowing's Swamp. There is in the middle an open pool, twenty or thirty feet in diameter, nearly full of sphagnum and green froth on the surface (frog-spittle), and what other plants I could not see on account of the danger in standing on the quaking ground; then a dense border, a rod or more wide, of a peculiar rush (?),

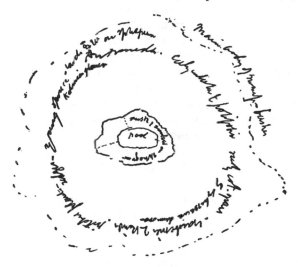

with clusters of seed-vessels, three together, now going to seed, a yellow green, forming an abrupt edge next the water, this on a dense bed of quaking sphagnum, in which I sink eighteen inches in water, upheld by its matted roots, where I fear to break through. On

Vol. VI

this the spatulate sundew abounds. This is marked by the paths of muskrats, which also extend through the green froth of the pool. Next comes, half a dozen rods wide, a dense bed of *Andromeda calyculata*, — the *A. Polifolia* mingled with it, — the rusty cottongrass, cranberries, — the common and also *V. Oxycoccus*, — pitcher-plants, sedges, and a few young spruce and larch here and there, — all on sphagnum, which forms little hillocks about the stems of the andromeda. Then ferns, now yellowing, high blueberry bushes, etc., etc., etc., — or the bushy and main body of the swamp, under which the sphagnum is now dry and white.

I find a new cranberry on the sphagnum amid the *A. calyculata*, — *V. Oxycoccus*, of which Emerson says it is the "common cranberry of the north of Europe," cranberry of commerce there, found by "Oakes on Nantucket, in Pittsfield, and near Sherburne." It has small, now purplish-dotted fruit, flat on the sphagnum, some turned scarlet partly, on terminal peduncles, with slender, thread-like stems and small leaves strongly revolute on the edges.[1]

One of the Miss Browns (of the factory quarter) speaks of the yellow-flowered asclepias in that neighborhood. Crossed the Brooks or Hadlock meadows, which have been on fire (spread from bogging) several weeks. They present a singularly desolate appearance. Much of the time over shoes in ashes and cinders. Yellowish peat ashes in spots here and there. The peat beneath still burning, as far as dry, making

[1] *Vide* Aug. 30, '56.

holes sometimes two feet deep, they say. The surface strewn with cranberries burnt to a cinder. I seemed to feel a dry heat under feet, as if the ground were on fire, where it was not.

It is so dry that I walk lengthwise in ditches perfectly dry, full of the proserpinaca, now beginning to go to seed, which usually stands in water. Its pectinate lower leaves all exposed. On the baked surface, covered with brown-paper conferva.

Aug. 24. P. M. — To Fair Haven Pond by boat.

A strong wind from the south-southwest, which I expect will waft me back. So many pads are eaten up and have disappeared that it has the effect of a rise of the river drowning them. This strong wind against which we row is quite exhilarating after the stiller summer. Yet we have no rain, and I see the blue haze between me and the shore six rods off.

The bright crimson-red under sides of the great white lily pads, turned up by the wind in broad fields on the sides of the stream, are a great ornament to the stream. It is not till August, methinks, that they are turned up conspicuously. Many are now turned over completely. After August opens, before these pads are decayed (for they last longer than the nuphars of both kinds), the stronger winds begin to blow and turn them up at various angles, turning many completely over and exposing their bright crimson(?)-red under sides with their ribs. The surface being agitated, the wind catches under their edges and turns them up and holds them commonly at an angle of 45°. It is a very wholesome color, and, after the calm summer, an exhilarating sight, with a strong wind heard and felt, cooling and condensing your thoughts. This has the effect of a ripening of the leaf on the river. Not in vain was the under side thus colored, which at length the August winds turn up.

The soft pads eaten up mostly; the pontederias crisped and considerably blackened, only a few flowers left. It is surprising how the maples are affected by this drought. Though they stand along the edge of the river, they appear to suffer more than any trees except the white ash. Their leaves — and also those of the alders and hickories and grapes and even oaks more or less — are permanently curled and turned up on the upper three quarters of the trees; so that their foliage has a singularly glaucous hue in rows along the river. At a distance they have somewhat of the same effect with the silvered tops of the swamp white oak. The sight suggests a strong wind constantly blowing. I went ashore and felt of them. They were more or less crisped and curled permanently. It suggests what to a slight extent occurs every year. On the Cliffs so many young trees and bushes are withered that from the river it looks as if a fire had run over them. At Lee's Cliff larger ash trees are completely sere and brown, — burnt up. The white pines are parti-colored there.

Now, methinks, hawks are decidedly more common, beating the bush and soaring. I see two circling over the Cliffs. See a blue heron standing on the meadow at Fair Haven Pond. At a distance before you, only

the two waving lines appear, and you would not suspect the long neck and legs.

Looking across the pond, the haze at the water's edge under the opposite woods looks like a low fog. To-night, as for at least four or five nights past, and to some extent, I think, a great many times within a month, the sun goes down shorn of his beams, half an hour before sunset, round and red, high above the horizon. There are no variegated sunsets in this dog-day weather.

Aug. 25. I think I never saw the haze so thick as now, at 11 A. M., looking from my attic window. I cannot quite distinguish J. Hosmer's house, only the dark outline of the woods behind it. There appears to be, as it were, a thick fog over the Dennis plains. Between me and Nawshawtuct is a very blue haze like smoke. Indeed many refer all this to smoke.

Tortoise eggs are nowadays dug up in digging potatoes.

P. M. — Up Assabet by boat to Bath.

I think that the *Polygonum hydropiperoides* is now in its prime. At the poke-logan opposite the bath place, the pools are nearly all dry, and many little pollywogs, an inch long, lie dead or dying together in the moist mud. Others are covered with the dry brown-paper conferva. Some swamp white oaks are yellowish and brown, many leaves. The *Viburnum nudum* berries, in various stages, — green, deep-pink, and also deep-blue, not purple or ripe, — are very abundant at Shadbush Meadow. They appear to be now in their prime

and are quite sweet, but have a large seed. Interesting for the various colors on the same bush and in the same cluster. Also the choke-berries are very abundant there, but mostly dried black. There is a large field of rhexia there now almost completely out of bloom, but its scarlet leaves, reddening the ground at a distance, supply the place of flowers.

We still continue to have strong wind in the middle of the day. The sun is shorn of his beams by the haze before 5 o'clock P. M., round and red, and is soon completely concealed, apparently by the haze alone. This blue haze is not dissipated much by the night, but is seen still with the earliest light.

Aug. 26. For a week we have had warmer weather than for a long time before, yet not so warm nearly as in July. I hear of a great many fires around us, far and near, both meadows and woods; in Maine and New York also. There *may* be some smoke in this haze, but I doubt it.

P. M. — To Dugan Desert.

I hear part of a phœbe's strain, as I go over the railroad bridge. It is the voice of dying summer. The pads now left on the river are chiefly those of the white lily. I noticed yesterday where a large piece of meadow had melted and sunk on a sandy bottom in the Assabet, and the weeds now rose above the surface where it was five feet deep around. It is so dry that I take the left of the railroad bridge and go through the meadows along the river. In the hollows where the surface of the meadow has been taken out within a year or two, spring

up pontederias and lilies, proserpinaca, polygonums, *Ludwigia palustris*, etc., etc. *Nasturtium hispidum* still in bloom, and will be for some time. I think I hear a red-eye. Rudbeckia, — the small one, — still fresh.

The *Poa hirsuta* is left on the upper edge of the meadows (as at J. Hosmer's), as too thin and poor a grass, beneath the attention of the farmers. How fortunate that it grows in such places and not in the midst of the rank grasses which are cut! With its beautiful fine purple color, its beautiful purple blush, it reminds me and supplies the place of the rhexia now about done.[1] Close by, or held in your hand, its fine color is not obvious, — it is but dull, — but [at] a distance, with a suitable light, it is exceedingly beautiful. It is at the same time in bloom. This is one of the most interesting phenomena of August.[2]

I hear these afternoons the faint, cricket-like note of the *Rana palustris* squatting by the side of the river, easily confounded with that of the interrupted cricket, only the last is more ringing and metallic.[3] How long has it been heard? The choke-cherry leaves are, some of them, from scarlet inclining to crimson. Radical leaves of the yellow thistle spot the meadow.

Opened one of my snapping turtle's eggs. The egg was not warm to the touch. The young is now larger and darker-colored, shell and all, more than a hemisphere, and the yolk which maintains it is much re-

---

[1] Leaving off, though I see some pretty handsome Sept. 4th.
[2] [*Excursions*, pp. 252, 253; Riv. 309, 310. The name of the grass appears there as *Eragrostis pectinacea*.]
[3] [See pp. 460, 461.]

duced. Its shell, very deep, hemispherical, fitting close to the shell of the egg, and, if you had not just opened the egg, you would say it could not contain so much. Its shell is considerably hardened, its feet and claws developed, and also its great head, though held in for want of room. Its eyes are open. It puts out its head, stretches forth its claws, and liberates its tail, though all were enveloped in a gelatinous fluid. With its great head it has already the ugliness of the full-grown, and is already a hieroglyphic of snappishness. It may take a fortnight longer to hatch it.

How much lies quietly buried in the ground that we wot not of! We unconsciously step over the eggs of snapping turtles slowly hatching the summer through. Not only was the surface perfectly dry and trackless there, but blackberry vines had run over the spot where these eggs were buried and weeds had sprung up above. If Iliads are not composed in our day, snapping turtles are hatched and arrive at maturity. It already thrusts forth its tremendous head, — for the first time in this sphere, — and slowly moves from side to side, — opening its small glistening eyes for the first time to the light, — expressive of dull rage, as if it had endured the trials of this world for a century. When I behold this monster thus steadily advancing toward maturity, all nature abetting, I am convinced that there must be an irresistible necessity for mud turtles. With what tenacity Nature sticks to her idea! These eggs, not warm to the touch, buried in the ground, so slow to hatch, are like the seeds of vegetable life.[1]

[1] [Channing, p. 283.]

Grapes ripe, owing to the hot dry weather.

Passing by M. Miles's, he told me he had a mud turtle in a box in his brook, where it had lain since the last of April, and he had given it nothing to eat. He wished he had known that I caught some in the spring and let them go. He would have bought them of me. He is very fond of them. He bought one of the two which Ed. Garfield caught on Fair Haven in the spring; paid him seventy-five cents for it. Garfield was out in his boat and saw two fighting on the pond. Approached carefully and succeeded in catching both and getting them into the boat. He got them both home by first carrying one along a piece, then putting him down and, while he was crawling off, going back for the other. One weighed forty-three or forty-four pounds and the other forty-seven. Miles gave me the shell of the one he bought, which weighed forty-three or forty-four. It is fifteen and six eighths inches long by fourteen and a half broad, of a roundish form, broadest backward. The smaller ones I have seen are longer in proportion to their length [sic], and the points larger also. The upper shell is more than four and a half inches deep and would make a good dish to bail out a boat with. Above it is a muddy brown, composed of a few great scales. He said he had no trouble in killing them. It was of no great use to cut off their heads. He thrust his knife through the soft thin place in their sternum and killed them at once. Told of one Artemas (?) Wheeler of Sudbury who used to keep fifteen or twenty in a box in a pond-hole, and fat them and eat them from time to time, having a great

appetite for them. Some years ago, in a January thaw, many came out on the Sudbury meadows, and, a cold snap suddenly succeeding, a great many were killed. One man counted eighty or more dead, some of which would weigh eighty to a hundred pounds. Miles himself found two shells on his river meadow of very large ones. Since then they have been scarce. Wheeler, he thought, used to go a-hunting for them the 2d (?) of May. It increases my respect for our river to see these great products of it. No wonder the Indians made much of them. Such great shells must have made convenient household utensils for them.

Miles once saw a large bullfrog jump at and catch a green snake ten inches long, which was running along the edge of the water, and hold it crosswise in its mouth, but the snake escaped at last.

Even the hinder part of a mud turtle's shell is scalloped, one would say rather for beauty than use.

Pigeons with their *quivet* dashed over the Dugan Desert.

Hear by telegraph that it rains in Portland and New York.

In the evening, some lightning in the horizon, and soon after a *little* gentle rain, which —

(*Aug. 27*) I find next day has moistened the ground about an inch down only. But now it is about as dry as ever.

P. M. — To Pine Hill *via* Turnpike and Walden.

Small *Bidens chrysanthemoides*, some time by Turnpike. The leaves of the smallest hypericum are very

many of them turned to a somewhat crimson red, sign of the ripening year. What I have called the Castile-soap gall, about one inch in diameter, handsomely variegated with a dirty white or pale tawny on a crimson ground; hard and perfectly smooth; solid and hard except a very small cavity in the centre containing some little grubs; full of crimson juice (which runs over the knife, and has stained this page [1] and blues my knife with its acid) for an eighth of an inch from the circumference, then lighter-colored.[2] Many red oak acorns have fallen.[3] The great green acorns in broad, shallow cups. How attractive these forms! No wonder they are imitated on pumps, fence and bed posts. Is not this a reason that the pigeons are about? The yellow birch is yellowed a good deal, the leaves spotted with green. The dogsbane a clear yellow. The cinnamon ferns hardly begun to turn or fall. The lice on the birches make it very disagreeable to go through them. I am surprised to find the brook and ditches in Hubbard's Close remarkably full after this long drought, when so many streams are dried up. Rice and others are getting out mud in the pond-hole opposite Breed's. They have cut down straight through clear black muck, perfectly rotted, eight feet, and it is soft yet further. Button-bushes, andromeda, proserpinaca, hardhack, etc., etc., grow atop. It looks like a great sponge. Old trees buried in it. On the Walden road some maples are yellow and some chestnuts brownish-yellow and also sere. From Heywood's

[1] [A brown stain on the page.]   [2] *Vide* [pp. 482, 483].

[3] Were they not cast down?

Peak I am surprised to see the top of Pine Hill wearing its October aspect, — yellow with changed maples and here and there faintly blushing with changed red maples. This is the effect of the drought. Among other effects of the drought I forgot to mention the fine dust, which enters the house and settles everywhere and also adds to the thickness of the atmosphere. Fences and roadside plants are thickly coated with it. I see much froth on alders. As I go up Pine Hill, gather the shrivelled *Vaccinium vacillans* berries, many as hard as if dried on a pan. They are very sweet and good, and not wormy like huckleberries. Far more abundant in this state than usual, owing to the drought. As I stand there, I think I hear a rising wind rustling the tops of the woods, and, turning, see what I think is the rear of a large flock of pigeons. Do they not eat many of these berries? Hips of the early rose changed. Some *Viburnum Lentago* berries, turned blue before fairly reddening. Blue-stemmed goldenrod, a day or two.

When I awake in the morning, I remember what I have seen and heard of snapping turtles, and am in doubt whether it was dream or reality. I slowly raise my head and peeping over the bedside see my great mud turtle shell lying bottom up under the table, showing its prominent ribs, and realize into what world I have awaked. Before I was in doubt how much prominence my good Genius would give to that fact. That the first object you see on awakening should be an empty mud turtle's shell!! Will it not make me of the earth earthy? Or does it not indicate that I am of the earth

earthy? What life, what character, this has shielded, which is now at liberty to be turned bottom upward! I can put specimens of all our other turtles into this cavity. This too was once an infant in its egg. When I see this, then I am sure that I am not dreaming, but am awake to this world. I do not know any more terrene fact. It still carries the earth on its back. Its life is between the animal and vegetable; like a seed it is planted deep in the ground and is all summer germinating. Does it not possess as much the life of the vegetable as the animal?

Would it not be well to describe some of those rough all-day walks across lots? — as that of the 15th, picking our way over quaking meadows and swamps and occasionally slipping into the muddy batter midleg deep; jumping or fording ditches and brooks; forcing our way through dense blueberry swamps, where there is water beneath and bushes above; then brushing through extensive birch forests all covered with green lice, which cover our clothes and face; then, relieved, under larger wood, more open beneath, steering for some more conspicuous trunk; now along a rocky hillside where the sweet-fern grows for a mile, then over a recent cutting, finding our uncertain footing on the cracking tops and trimmings of trees left by the choppers; now taking a step or two of smooth walking across a highway; now through a dense pine wood, descending into a rank, dry swamp, where the cinnamon fern rises above your head, with isles of poison-dogwood; now up a scraggy hill covered with shrub oak, stooping and winding one's way for half a

mile, tearing one's clothes in many places and putting out one's eyes, and find[ing] at last that it has no bare brow, but another slope of the same character; now through a corn-field diagonally with the rows; now coming upon the hidden melon-patch; seeing the back side of familiar hills and not knowing them, — the nearest house to home, which you do not know, seeming further off than the farthest which you do know; — in the spring defiled with the froth on various bushes, etc., etc., etc.; now reaching on higher land some open pigeon-place, a breathing-place for us.

I suppose that is a puffball, about two inches through (on the ground), roundish, brownish, cracked, pale wash-leather color, with a handsome, variegated slate-color within, not yet dusty, contrasting with the outside.

Aug. 28. Much cooler this morning, making us think of fire. This is gradually clearing the atmosphere, and, as it is about as dry as ever, I think that haze was not smoke; quite as dry as yesterday.

P. M. — By Great Meadows and Bedford meadows to Carlisle Bridge; back by Carlisle and Concord side across lots to schoolhouse.

Improve the continued drought to go through the meadows. There is a cool east wind (it has been east a good deal lately in this drought), which has cleared the air wonderfully, revealing the long-concealed woods and hills in the horizon and making me think of November even. And now that I am going along the path to the meadow in the woods beyond Peter's, I perceive the fall shine on the leaves and earth; *i. e.*, a great deal

of light is reflected through the clearer air, which has also a vein of coolness in it. Some crotalaria pods are now black and dry, and rattle as I walk. The farmers improve this dry spell to cut ditches and dig mud in the meadows and pond-holes. I see their black heaps in many places. I see on the Great Meadows circular patches — the stubble of a coarse light-green sedge (apparently cut-grass) — of various dimensions, which look as if they had been brought from other places and dropped there in the spring. Yet they are very numerous and extensive, running into one another, yet with a rounded or coarsely crenate edge. In fact, they probably cover the greater part of the meadow. It must be that the cut-grass merely spreads in circles. There are some in the meadow near the Kibbe Place. It makes firm ground. Between these are the dark-colored patches of cranberries, ferns, and finer grasses (?) of such singular forms as are used in lace-work, like the spaces left between circles, suggesting that this is the groundwork on which the other is dropped. Or does the cut-grass (?) incline to grow in this circular manner?

The meadow is drier than ever, and new pools are dried up. The breams, from one to two and a half inches long, lying on the sides and quirking from time to time, a dozen together where there is but a pint of water on the mud, are a handsome but sad sight, — pretty green jewels, dying in the sun. I saved a dozen or more by putting them in deeper pools. Saw a whole school of little pouts, hundreds of them one and a half inches long, many dead, all apparently fated to die, and some full-grown fishes. Several hairworms four or five inches long in this muddy water. The muddy bottom of these pools dried up is cracked into a sort of regular crystals. In the soft mud, the tracks of the great bittern and the blue heron. Scared up one of the former and saw a small dipper on the river. Just after entering the Bedford meadows (travelling north), for perhaps a mile in length and the width of the meadow, the surface on all sides had been lifted or tilted up, showing the blue edges of the soil, so that there was hardly a level square rod, — giving the aspect of waves two feet high or more with numerous holes and trenches, and making it very difficult to mow it, as well as to walk over it, and here and there permanent pools were made in it. I do not know why it should have happened there more than elsewhere. Found the *Ludwigia sphærocarpa* down that way.

It seems that the upper surface of the *Victoria regia* is " a light green " and the under "a bright crimson," according to Schomburgk, its discoverer. In this it is like our white lily pads.

We did not come to a fence or wall for about four miles this afternoon. Heard some *large* hawks whistling much like a boy high over the meadow.

Observed many of those Castile-soap galls from a tenth of an inch to an inch in diameter on a *Quercus ilicifolia*. They are attached to the outer edge of the cup, commonly filling the space between two acorns, and look as if they had merely lodged between them, dropping out readily, though they are slightly attached

to one cup. I see some not much bigger than a pin's head, in the place, and reminding me of those small abortive acorns which so often grow on the cup of the small chinquapin. May not these galls be connected with those and be also an abortive acorn? I have three, of medium size, on the edge of one acorn-cup, and not occupying more than one third its circumference, unsupported by any neighboring cup, the middle one the smallest, being apparently crowded. Apparently the insect deposits its egg in the edge of the cup, and this egg, as in all galls, is, I should say, at once the seed of vegetable and of animal life: it produces the vegetable gall, and is the seed of it, also the animal. May it not be regarded as the seed of the gall, as well as the ovum of the insect?

Moles make heaps in meadows.

In my experience, at least *of late years*, all that depresses a man's spirits is the sense of remissness, — duties neglected, unfaithfulness, — or shamming, impurity, falsehood, selfishness, inhumanity, and the like.

From the experience of late years I should say that a man's seed was the direct tax of his race. It stands for my sympathy with my race. When the brain chiefly is nourished, and not the affections, the seed becomes merely excremental.

Saw a bushel of hazelnuts in their burs, which some boy had spread on the ground to dry behind Hodgman's. Observed yesterday, in a pool in what was Heywood's peat meadow south of, but near, Turnpike, apparently a utricularia, very small with minute forked green leaves, and bladders on bare

Vol. VI

threads, rooting in mud at bottom; apparently out of bloom. Also another kind with long stems, many black bladders, and no *obviously* green leaves, filling the pools in Hubbard's Close.

Aug. 29. A cool morning with much fog, — more than yesterday. Have not had much during the warmer part of the drought, methinks.

Cattle are driven down from up-country. Hear the drovers' *whoa whoa whoa* or *whay whay whay.*

Where I walked yesterday it appeared as if the whole surface of the meadow had been at one time lifted up, but prevented by shores or bushes or ice from floating off, then broken up by wind and waves, and had finally melted and sunk irregularly, near where it rose. I repeatedly stepped into the long crack-like intervals between the cakes.

When our meadows are flooded in the spring and our river is changed to a sea, then the gulls, the sea birds, come up here to complete the scene. Or are they merely on their way eastward?

Were not those large, and often pointed, rocks occasionally seen on the meadows brought there by the floating meadow, and so dropped broad end down?

P. M. — To Derby Bridge neighborhood and front of Tarbell's.

It is a great pleasure to walk in this clearer atmosphere, though cooler. How great a change, and how sudden, from that sultry and remarkably hazy atmosphere to this clear, cool autumnal one, in which all things shine, and distance is restored to us! The wind

blew quite hard in the midst of that haze, but did not disperse it. Only this cooler weather with a steady east wind has done it. It is so cool that we are inclined to stand round the kitchen fire a little while these mornings, though we sit and sleep with open windows still. I think that the cool air from the sea has condensed the haze, not blown it off. The grass is so dry and withered that it caught fire from the locomotive four or five days ago near the widow Hosmer's, and the fire ran over forty or fifty rods, threatening the house, — grass which should have afforded some pasturage. The cymes of elder-berries, black with fruit, are now conspicuous.

Up railroad. Poison sumach berries begin to look ripe, — or dry, — of a pale straw-color. The zizania is pretty abundant in the river, in rear of Joseph Hosmer's. A small, what his father calls partridge hawk killed many chickens for him last year, but the slate-colored hawk never touches them. Very many water-plants — pontederias, lilies, zizania, etc., etc.— are now going to seed, prepared to feed the migrating water-fowl, etc. Saw a hop-hornbeam (*Ostrya*) on which every leaf was curiously marked with a small rather. triangular brown spot (eaten) in the axils of the veins next the midrib, oppositely or alternately. Under side lower leaves of *Lycopus Virginicus* lake-color. I see where the squirrels, apparently, have stripped the pitch pine cones, scattering the scales about. Many birds nowadays resort to the wild black cherry tree, as here front of Tarbell's. I see them continually coming and going directly from and to a great distance, — cherry-birds, robins, and kingbirds. I enjoy the warmth of the sun now that the air is cool, and Nature seems really more genial. I love to sit on the withered grass on the sunny side of the wall. My mistress is at a more respectful distance, for, by the coolness of the air, I am more continent in my thought and held aloof from her, while by the genial warmth of the sun I am more than ever attracted to her. I see a boy already raking cranberries. The moss rose hips will be quite ripe in a day or two. Found a new and erect euphorbia (*hypericifolia*) on the slope just east of his lizard ditches, still in bloom and pretty, probably open first in July. At Clamshell Bank the barn swallows are very lively, filling the air with their twittering now, at 6 P. M. They rest on the dry mullein-tops, then suddenly all start off together as with one impulse and skim about over the river, hill, and meadow. Some sit on the bare twigs of a dead apple tree. Are they not gathering for their migration?

Early for several mornings I have heard the sound of a flail. It leads me to ask if I have spent as industrious a spring and summer as the farmer, and gathered as rich a crop of experience. If so, the sound of my flail will be heard by those who have ears to hear, separating the kernel from the chaff all the fall and winter, and a sound no less cheering it will be. If the drought has destroyed the corn, let not all harvests fail. Have you commenced to thresh your grain? The lecturer must commence his threshing as early as August, that his fine flour may be ready for his winter customers. The fall rains will make full springs and raise his

streams sufficiently to grind his grist. We shall hear the sound of his flail all the fall, early and late. It is made of tougher material than hickory, and tied together with resolution stronger than an eel-skin. For him there is no husking-bee, but he does it all alone and by hand, at evening by lamplight, with the barn door shut and only the pile of husks behind him for warmth. For him, too, I fear there is no patent cornsheller, but he does his work by hand, ear by ear, on the edge of a shovel over a bushel, on his hearth, and after he takes up a handful of the yellow grain and lets it fall again, while he blows out the chaff; and he goes to bed happy when his measure is full.

Channing has come from Chelsea Beach this morning with *Euphorbia polygonifolia* in flower, bayberry in fruit, datura in flower, staghorn sumach fruit, chenopodium (it seems not to be made a distinct species, though very mealy), scarlet pimpernel still in flower, *Salsola Kali* (the prickly plant), and apparently *Solidago sempervirens*.

Aug. 30. Another great fog this morning, which lasts till 8.30. After so much dry and warm weather, cool weather has suddenly come, and this has produced these two larger fogs than for a long time. Is it always so?

Hear a warbling vireo faintly in the elms.

P. M. — To Conantum *via* Clamshell Hill and meadows.

The clearness of the air which began with the cool morning of the 28th makes it delicious to gaze in any

direction. *Though there has been no rain*, the valleys are emptied of haze, and I see with new pleasure to distant hillsides and farmhouses and a river-reach shining in the sun, and to the mountains in the horizon. Coolness and clarity go together. What I called *Solidago altissima*, a simple slender one with a small head, some time, — perhaps not to be distinguished. Crossed the river at Hubbard's Bath. Apparently as many clams lie up as ever. The two river polygonums may be said to be now in prime. The *hydropiperoides* has a peculiarly slender waving spike. The *Bidens Beckii* made the best show, I think, a week ago, though there may be more of them open now. They are not so widely open. Was not that a meadowhen which I scared up in two places by the riverside, — of a dark brown like a small woodcock, though it flew *straight* and low? I go along the flat Hosmer shore to Clamshell Hill. The sparganium seed balls begin to brown and come off in the hand. The *Ammannia humilis* is quite abundant on the denuded shore there and in John Hosmer's meadow, now turned red and so detected, reddening the ground. Are they not young hen-hawks which I have seen sailing for a week past, without red tails?

I go along through J. Hosmer's meadow near the river, it is so dry. I see places where the meadow has been denuded of its surface within a few years, four or five rods in diameter, forming shallow platters, in which the *Lysimachia stricta, small* hypericums, lindernia, gratiola, pipes, ammannia, etc., grow. I walk dry-shod quite to the phalanxes of bulrushes of

a handsome blue-green glaucous color. The colors of the rainbow rush are now pretty bright. The floating milfoil at Purple Utricularia Shore, with red stem. Blue-eyed grass still. Dogwood leaves have fairly begun to turn. A *few* small maples are scarlet along the meadow. A dark-brown or black shining, oval or globular, fruit of the skunk-cabbage, with prominent calyx, filaments, and style roughening it, is quite handsome like a piece of carved ebony (or dogwood?). I see its small green spathes already pushing up.

The berries are about all dried up or wormy — I am on Conantum — though I still eat the dried blueberries. There are now none to pluck in a walk, unless it be black cherries and apples. I see brown thrashers on the black cherry tree and hear their sharp click like a squirrel. Hazelnut time about a week ago, — to be in advance of the squirrels. I see the dried reddened burs and shells under every bush where they have been. The *Bidens frondosa*, some time; distinguished by its being fairly pinnate, with from three to five leafets. Notice the radical leaves of primrose. The huckleberries are so withered and brown in many places, owing to the drought, that they appear dead and as if they were some which had been broken up by the pickers, or as if burnt. Some white ash trees have suffered more than any others I have noticed, on Cliffs their leaves being quite brown and sere.

Minot Pratt here this evening. He tells me he finds a *white* hardhack, bayberry in Holden's pasture, and, on the old Carlisle road, *Cornus florida*, near Bateman's Pond, and what Russell thought a rare hedysarum somewhere. Pratt once caught a mud turtle at Brook Farm which weighed forty-six pounds.

Aug. 31. Warmer this morning and considerably hazy again. Wormwood pollen yellows my clothes commonly.

Ferris in his "Utah," crossing the plains in '52, says that, on Independence Rock near the Sweetwater, "at a rough guess, there must be 35,000 to 40,000" names of travellers.[1]

P. M. — To Lincoln.

Surveying for William Peirce. He says that several large chestnuts appear to be dying near him on account of the drought. Saw a meadow said to be still on fire after three weeks; fire had burned holes one and a half feet deep; was burning along slowly at a considerable depth. P. brought me home in his wagon. Was not quite at his ease and in his element; *i. e.*, talked with some reserve, though well-behaved, unless I approached the subject of horses. Then he spoke with a will and with authority, betraying somewhat of the jockey. He said that this dry weather was "trying to wagons; it loosened the *ties*," — if that was the word.[2] He did not use blinders nor a check-rein. Said a horse's neck must ache at night which has been reined up all day. He said that the outlet of F[lint's] Pond had not been dry before for four years, and then only two or three days; now it was a month.

Notwithstanding this unprecedented drought our

[1] [Benjamin G. Ferris, *Utah and the Mormons.* New York, 1854.]
[2] Probably "tires."

river, the main stream, has not been very low. It may have been kept up by the reservoirs. Walden is unaffected by the drought, and is still very high. But for the most part silent are the watercourses, when I walk in rocky swamps where a tinkling is commonly heard.

At nine this evening I distinctly and strongly smell smoke, I think of burning meadows, in the air in the village. There must be more smoke in this haze than I have supposed. Is not the haze a sort of smoke, the sun parching and burning the earth?

END OF VOLUME VI

Vol. VI

The Journal of Henry D. Thoreau

VOLUME VII

(September, 1854 — October, 1855)

Sam Barrett's Mill-Pond

CONTENTS

Vol. VII

Sept. 1. A misty morning followed by a still, cloudy, misty day, through which has fallen a very little rain this forenoon already. Now I notice a few faint-*chipping* sparrows, busily picking the seeds of weeds in the garden. Are they the Savannah sparrows? They show no white in tail. Yet I see no yellow on brows. Small feathers on back, centred with black and edged with pale brown (?); inner vanes of wing-quills bay; crown without chestnut; brown dash from angle of mouth backward. Do not the sparrows now commonly begin to feed on seeds of weeds in gardens?

P. M. — Along river to E. Hosmer's.

A very little mizzling. The *Aster Tradescanti* is perhaps *beginning* [1] to whiten the shores on moist banks. I see a fine (reddish) topped grass in low lands, whitened like a thin veil with what it has caught of this dewy rain. It wets my feet much.

The *Cornus sericea* berries are now in prime, of dif-

[1] *Vide* Sept. 14.

---

ferent shades of blue, lighter or darker, and bluish white. They are so abundant as to be a great ornament to our causeways and riverside. The white-berried, too, is now in prime, but drops off. The *Viburnum dentatum* berries are smaller and duller. The *Viburnum Lentago* are just fairly begun to have purple cheeks.

Even this rain or mizzling brings down many leaves of elms and willows, etc., — the first, *to notice*, since the fall of the birches which began so long ago. Saw two wild ducks go over. Another said they were large gray ducks; also that Simon Brown's boy had got a young wild duck which came home from the river with the tame ones.

Sept. 2. The second still, misty, mizzling and rainy day. We all lie abed late. Now many more sparrows in the yard, larger than chip-birds and showing ashy under sides as they fly. A *part* the same as yesterday's. Are they Savannahs, or bay-wings, or both? I see but the *slightest touch* of white in the tail of any. Those clear ashy beneath are cinereous about the shoulders above. A tree sparrow too? though I do not see the spot.[1]

Opened one of my snapping turtle's eggs. The young alive, but not very lively, with shell dark grayish-black; yolk as big as a hazelnut; tail curled round and is considerably longer than the shell, and slender; three ridges on back, one at edges of plates on each

[1] Heard a faint warble from one the next afternoon at about 6 P. M. on apple trees.

---

side of dorsal, which is very prominent. There is only the trace of a dorsal ridge in the old. Eye open.[1]

P. M. — By boat to Purple Utricularia Shore.

Still and cloudy, all shut in, but no rain. The flags are turned yellow along the river, quite an autumnal scene, with commonly a strip of green left in their centres. The sparganium not changed. The pontederias, half of them, are brown and crisp. Of pads, only the white lily are conspicuous. The button-bushes are generally yellowing, *i. e.*, are of an autumnal yellowish green. The black willows are decidedly crisped and yellowish. The interrupted fern begins to yellow. The autumnal dandelion is conspicuous on the shore.

How handsome ripe grapes with the bloom on them! This rubbed off, they show purple or black. I find some quite sweet which have ripened on a rock. They are a noble fruit to the eye. The waxwork is fairly yellow on all hands. Now is the time to gather it. Ivy leaves on some plants are yellow, scarlet, and dull-red, besides green.

I see white lilies wide open at 2.30 P. M. They are half open even at 5 P. M. in many places this moist cloudy day and thus late in their season. Still a few pontederias also. I see dogsbane still in flower. The *Bidens Beckii* is oftenest eaten (?) off just below the blossom. Saw what I think must be a solitary wood (?) duck. Started it several times, driving it before me up the river, getting within twenty rods. It uttered a shrill quacking each time. Bathed at Hubbard's. The water is surprisingly cold on account of the cool

[1] *Vide* [next page].

weather and rain, but especially since the rain of yesterday morning. It is a very important and remarkable autumnal change. It will not be warm again probably.

To my great surprise I find this morning (September 3d) that the little unhatched turtle, which I thought was sickly and dying, and left out on the grass in the rain yesterday morn, thinking it would be quite dead in a few minutes — I find the shell alone and the turtle a foot or two off vigorously crawling, with neck outstretched (holding up its head and looking round like an old one) and feet surmounting every obstacle. It climbs up the nearly perpendicular side of a basket with the yolk attached. They thus not only continue to live after they are dead, but begin to live before they are alive!

Are those large rigid green clusters the dried fertile flowers of the black ash? The keys are formed and appear ripe.

The moderate mizzling rain of yesterday and to-day is the first (excepting the slight shower in the eve of the 26th *ult.*) since that moderate one of August 4th. Yet this brings down leaves, cools the rivers and ponds, and brings back ducks and other migratory birds. I see two or three large plump sparrows hopping along on the button-bushes and eating the mikania blossoms, sometimes perching on the lower mossy stems and uttering a faint chip, with crown distinctly divided by a light line and another light line over eye, light throat and vent, ashy (?) breast and beneath, without spot. Is it not the white-throated sparrow?

Vol. VII

Observed a large clam at the Bath Place, where they have not gone down, — apparently quite old, with a sort of wart-like protuberances, as if the shell were worn into hollows while the harder parts were prominent. The shell, where worn, green, the end shaggy with a kind of moss or alga.

A sort of *Aster longifolius*, some days by Mill Brook on Lowell road, but with *not long*, loose, green-tipped scales, *i. e.* not squarrose. Call this *A. tenuifolius* for present. (It may be *carneus*.)

Two-leaved Solomon's-seal berries red.

I have not allowed enough probably for the smoke mixed with the haze in the late drought. The fires in woods and meadows have been remarkably numerous and extensive all over the country, the earth and vegetation have been so dry, especially along railroads and on mountains and pine plains. Some meadows are said to have been burned three feet deep! On some mountains it burns all the soil down to the rock. It catches from the locomotive, from sportsmen's wadding, and from burning brush and peat meadows. In all villages they smell smoke, especially at night. On Lake Champlain, the pilots of steamboats could hardly see their course, and many complained that the smoke made their eyes smart and affected their throats. Bears, it is said, have in some instances been compelled to migrate.[1]

[1] [The following appears on an inside cover page of the manuscript journal volume that ends here.]

My faults are: —

Paradoxes, — saying just the opposite, — a style which may be imitated.

Sept. 3. Sunday. Fair weather and a clear atmosphere after two days of mizzling, cloudy, and rainy weather and some smart showers at daylight and in the night. The street is washed hard and white.

P. M. — With Minot Pratt into Carlisle.

Woodbine berries purple. Even at this season I see some fleets of yellow butterflies in the damp road after the rain, as earlier. Pratt showed me a tobacco flower, long and tubular, slightly like a datura. In his yard appears a new variety of sweet-briar which he took out of the woods behind his house; larger bush and leaves, leaves less glandular and sticky beneath, the principal serrations deeper and much sharper, and the whole leaf perhaps less rounded. Saw some winged ants silvering a circular space in the pasture grass about five inches in diameter, a few *very large ones* among them. Very thick and incessantly moving, one upon another, some without wings, all running about in great excitement. It seemed the object of the winged ones to climb to the top of the grass blades, one over another, and then take to wing, which they did. In the meadow southwest of Hubbard's Hill saw

Ingenious.

Playing with words, — getting the laugh, — not always simple, strong, and broad.

Using current phrases and maxims, when I should speak for myself.

Not always earnest.

"In short," "in fact," "alas!" etc.

Want of conciseness.

Walden published, Wednesday, Aug. 9th, '54.
Sent Fields 12 copies of the *Week*, Oct. 18th, '54.

white *Polygala sanguinea*, not described. Lambkill again in Hunt Pasture. Close to the left-hand side of bridle-road, about a hundred rods south of the oak, a bayberry bush without fruit, probably a male one. It made me realize that this was only a more distant and elevated sea-beach and that we were within reach of marine influences. My thoughts suffered a sea-turn. North of the oak (four or five rods), on the left of the bridle-road in the pasture next to Mason's, tried to find the white hardhack still out, but it was too late. Found the mountain laurel out again, one flower, *close* sessile on end of this year's shoot. There were numerous blossom-buds expanding, and they may possibly open this fall. Running over the laurel an amphicarpæa in bloom, some pods nearly an inch long, out probably a week, or ten days at most. *Epilobium molle*, linear, still in flower in the spruce swamp, near my path. A white hardhack out of bloom by a pile of stones (on which I put another) in Robbins's field, and a little south of it a clump of red huckleberries.

Sept. 4. Monday. Aster multiflorus. Observed the under sides of a shrub willow by the river, lit by the rays of the rising sun, shining like silver or dewdrops. Yet, when I stood nearer and looked down on them at a different angle, they were quite dull.

I have provided my little snapping turtle with a tub of water and mud, and it is surprising how fast he learns to use his limbs and this world. He actually runs, with the yolk still trailing from him, as if he had got new vigor from contact with the mud. The insensibility and toughness of his infancy make our life, with its disease and low spirits, ridiculous. He impresses me as the rudiment of a man worthy to inhabit the earth. He is born with a shell. That is symbolical of his toughness. His shell being so rounded and sharp on the back at this age, he can turn over without trouble.

P. M. — To climbing fern.

Polygonum articulatum, apparently three or four days. In the wood-paths I find a great many of the Castile-soap galls, more or less fresh. Some are saddled on the twigs. They are now dropping from the shrub oaks. Is not Art itself a gall? Nature is stung by God and the seed of man planted in her. The artist changes the direction of Nature and makes her grow according to his idea. If the gall was anticipated when the oak was made, so was the canoe when the birch was made. Genius stings Nature, and she grows according to its idea.

7.30. — To Fair Haven Pond by boat.

Full moon; bats flying about; skaters and waterbugs (?) like sparks of fire on the surface between us and the moon. The high shore above the railroad bridge was very simple and grand, — first the bluish sky with the moon and a few brighter stars, then the near high level bank like a distant mountain ridge or a dark cloud in the eastern horizon, then its reflection in the water, making it double, and finally the glassy water and the sheen in one spot on the white lily pads.

Some willows for relief in the distance on the right. It was Ossianic.

I noticed this afternoon that bubbles would not readily form on the water, and soon burst, probably on account of the late rains, which have changed its quality. There is probably less stagnation and scum. It is less adhesive.

A fine transparent mist. Lily Bay seemed as wide as a lake. You referred the shore back to the Clamshell Hills. The mere edge which a flat shore presents makes no distinct impression on the eye and, if seen at all, appears as the base of the distant hills. Commonly a slight mist yet more conceals it. The dim low shore, but a few rods distant, is seen as the base of the distant hills whose distance you know. The low shore, if not entirely concealed by the low mist, is seen against the distant hills and passes for their immediate base. For the same reason hills near the water appear much more steep than they are. We hear a faint metallic chip from a sparrow on the button-bushes or willows now and then. Rowse was struck by the simplicity of nature now, — the sky the greater part, then a little dab of earth, and after some water near you. Looking up the reach beyond Clamshell, the moon on our east quarter, its sheen was reflected for half a mile from the pads and the rippled water next them on that side, while the willows lined the shore in indistinct black masses like trees made with India ink (without distinct branches), and it looked like a sort of Broadway with the sun reflected from its pavements. Such willows might be made with soot

or smoke merely, lumpish with fine edges. Meanwhile Fair Haven Hill, *seen blue through the transparent mist*, was as large and imposing as Wachusett, and we seemed to be approaching the *Highlands* of the river, a mountain pass, where the river had burst through mountains. A high mountain would be no more imposing.

Now I began to hear owls, screech (?) owls, at a distance up-stream; but we hardly got nearer to them, as if they retreated before us. At length, when off Wheeler's grape and cranberry meadow, we heard one near at hand. The rhythm of it was *pe-pe-ou ;* this once or twice repeated, but more of a squeal and somewhat human. Or do not all strange sounds thrill us as *human*, till we have learned to refer them to their proper source? They appeared to answer one another half a mile apart; could be heard from far woods a mile off.

The wind has risen and the echo is poor; it does not reverberate up and down the river. No sound of a bullfrog, but steadily the cricket-like *Rana palustris* [1] alongshore.

Rowse heard a whip-poor-will at Sleepy Hollow tonight. No scent of muskrats.

Sept. 5. Were those plump birds which looked somewhat like robins crossing the river yesterday afternoon golden plover? I heard the upland plover note at same time, but these were much stouter birds. The dangle-berries are now the only whortleberries which

[1] [Changed in pencil, evidently at a later date, to "mole cricket."]

are *quite* fresh. The feverwort berries began to turn about a fortnight ago. Now quite yellow.

P. M. — Up Assabet to Sam Barrett's Pond.

The river rising probably. The river weeds are now much decayed. Almost all pads but the white lily have disappeared, and they are thinned, and in midstream those dense beds of weeds are so much thinned (potamogeton, heart-leaf, sparganium, etc., etc.) as to give one the impression of the river having risen, though it is not more than six inches higher on account of the rain. As I wade, I tread on the great roots only of the yellow lily. I see now, against the edge of the pads on each side of the stream, a floating wreck of weeds, at first almost exclusively the *Sparganium minor*, which stood so thick in midstream, the first important contribution to the river wreck. These apparently become rotten or loose (though they are still green), and the wind and water wash them to one side. They form floating masses of wreck, and a few small siums and pontederias are already mixed with them. The stream must be fullest of weeds and most verdurous (potamogetons, heart-leaf, sparganium, etc.) when the brink is in perfection. The potamogetons are much decayed and washed and blown into a snarl, and no longer cover the surface with a smooth green shield, nor do the heart-leaf.

This is a fall phenomenon. The river weeds, becoming rotten, though many are still green, fall or are loosened, the water rises, the winds come, and they are drifted to the shore, and the water is cleared.

During the drought I used to see Sam Wheeler's

men carting hogsheads of water from the river to water his shrubbery. They drove into the river, and, naked all but a coat and hat, they dipped up the water with a pail. Though a shiftless, it looked like an agreeable, labor that hot weather.

Bathed at the swamp white oak, the water again warmer than I expected. One of these larger oaks is stripped nearly bare by the caterpillars. Cranberry-raking is now fairly begun. The very bottom of the river there is loose and crumbly with sawdust. I bring up the coarse *bits* of wood (water-logged) between my feet. I see much thistle-down without the seed floating on the river. Saw a hummingbird about a cardinal-flower over the water's edge. Just this side the rock, the water near the shore and pads is quite *white* for twenty rods, as with a white sawdust, with the exuviæ of small insects about an eighth of an inch long, mixed with scum and weeds, apparently like the green lice on birches, though they want the long antennæ of the last. Yet I suspect they are the same. Did not the rain destroy them? What others are so plenty? I see, as often before, a dozen doves on the rock, apparently for coolness, which fly before me. *Polygonum amphibium* var. *terrestre* apparently in prime. I find some zizania grains almost black. See a

chip-bird. See many galls thickly clustered and saddled about the twigs of some young swamp white oaks, dome-shaped; hold on all winter; with grubs in middle; reddish-green.

A pretty large tupelo on a rock behind Sam Bar-

Vol. VII

rett's; some of its leaves a very deep and brilliant scarlet, equal to any leaves in this respect. Some waxwork leaves variegated greenish-yellow and dark-green. His pond has been almost completely dry, — more than he ever knew, — and is still mostly so. The muddy bottom is exposed high and dry, half a dozen rods wide, and half covered with great drying yellow and white lily pads and stems. He improves the opportunity to skim off the fertile deposit for his compost-heap. Saw some button-bush balls going to seed, which were really quite a *rich red* over a green base, especially in this evening light. They are commonly greener and much duller reddish. Barrett shows me some very handsome pear-shaped cran-berries, not uncommon, which may be a permanent variety different from the com-

mon rounded ones. Saw two pigeons, which flew about his pond and then lit on the elms over his house. He said they had come to drink from Brooks's, as they often did. He sees a blue heron there almost every morning of late. Such is the place for them. A soap-wort gentian by river; remarkably early (?). The top has been bitten off! I hear the tree-toad to-day. Now at sundown, a blue heron flaps away from his perch on an oak over the river before me, just above the rock. Hear locusts after sundown.

Sept. 6. 6 A. M. — To Hill.

The sun is rising directly over the eastern (magnetic east) end of the street. Not yet the equinox. I hear a faint warbling vireo on the elms still, in the

morning. My little turtle, taken out of the shell September 2d, has a shell one and seven fortieths inches long, or four fortieths longer than the diameter of the egg-shell, to say nothing of head and tail. Warm weather again, and sultry nights the last two. The last a splendid moonlight and quite warm.

I am not sure that I have seen bobolinks for ten days, nor blackbirds since August 28th.

9 P. M. — There is now approaching from the west one of the heaviest thunder-showers (apparently) and with the most incessant flashes that I remember to have seen. It must be twenty miles off, at least, for I can hardly hear the thunder at all. The almost incessant flashes reveal the form of the cloud, at least the upper and lower edge of it, but it stretches north and south along the horizon further than we see. Every minute I see the crinkled lightning, intensely bright, dart to earth or forkedly along the cloud. It does not always dart *direct* to earth, but sometimes very crookedly, like the bough of a tree, or along the cloud forkedly. The forked thunderbolt of the poets. It seems like a tremendous dark battery bearing down on us, with an incessant fire kept up behind it. And each time, apparently, it strikes the earth or something on it with terrific violence. We feel the rush of the cool wind while the thunder is yet scarcely audible. The flashes are, in fact, incessant for an hour or more, though lighting up different parts of the horizon, — now the edges of the cloud, now far along the horizon, — showing a clearer golden space beneath the

cloud where rain is falling, through which stream tortuously to earth the brilliant bolts. It is a visible striking or launching of bolts on the devoted villages. It crinkles through the clear yellow portion beneath the cloud where it rains, like fiery snakes or worms, like veins in the eye. At first it was a small and very distant cloud in the southwestern horizon, revealed by its own flashes, — its rugged upper outline and its whole form revealed by the flashes, — and no thunder heard. It seemed like a ship firing broadsides, but it gradually advanced and extended itself, and united with others north and south along the horizon, and the thunder began to be heard, and wind came, etc. At last came the rain, but not heavy, nor the thunder loud, but the flashes were visible all around us.

Before this, in the afternoon, to the Hollowell place *via* Hubbard Bath, crossing the river.

A very warm day, *one* of the warmest of the year. The water is again warmer than I should have believed; say an *average* summer warmth, yet not so warm as it has been. It makes me the more surprised that only that day and a half of rain should have made it so very cold when I last bathed here. Is not all our really hot weather always contained between the 20th of May and the middle of September? The checkerberries are just beginning to redden. The cinnamon ferns along the edge of woods next the meadow are many yellow or cinnamon, or quite brown and withered. The sarsaparilla leaves, green or reddish, are spotted with yellow eyes centred with reddish, or dull-reddish eyes with yellow iris. They have a very pretty effect held over the forest floor, beautiful in their decay. The sessile-leaved bellwort is yellow, green, and brown, all together or separately. Some white oak leaves are covered with dull-yellow spots. Now apparently is the time to gather the clusters of shrub oak acorns, before they drop, to adorn a shelf with. Some, however, are ready to fall on account of the late drought. I see where the squirrels have eaten them (the *ilicifolia*) and left the shells on a stump. See galls on the chinquapin, sessile on the stem, spherical, and in appearance between that of yesterday on the swamp white oak, and the Castile-soap galls. I think I may say that large Solomon's-seal berries have begun to be red. I see no swallows now at Clamshell. They have probably migrated. Still see the cracks in the ground, and no doubt shall till snow comes. Very few of the *Aster undulatus* this year, and they late.

Some large roundish or squarish *Viburnum nudum* berries by fence between Hosmer Spring and Lupine Hill, near foot of hill, but I see no difference between the leaves, etc., and the others.

An aster, *longifolius*-like, some days at Hosmer Ditch, with smaller flowers, 27-rayed, smaller scales, leaves rough above and serrate, and purple stem rough. I will call it *A. carneus* for present. A similar, with flesh-colored blossom and longer scales, at A. Heywood Ditch. It may be a variety of what I saw by Mill Brook and called *tenuifolius;* scales alike, but that had smooth leaves.

moss- or ivy-clad, and a dark-blue cloud extends into the dun-golden sky, on which there is a little fantastic cloud like a chicken walking up the point of it, with its neck outstretched. The reflected sky is more dun and richer than the real one. Take a glorious sunset sky and double it, so that it shall extend downward beneath the horizon as much as above it, blotting out the earth, and [let] the lowest half be of the deepest tint, and every beauty more than before insisted on, and you seem withal to be floating directly into it. This seems the first autumnal sunset. The small skaters seem more active than by day, or their slight dimpling is more obvious in the lit twilight. A stray white cat sits on the shore looking over the water. This is her hour. A nighthawk dashes past, low over the water. This is what we had.

It was in harmony with this fair evening that we were not walking or riding with dust and noise through it, but moved by a paddle without a jar over the liquid and almost invisible surface, floating directly toward those islands of the blessed which we call clouds in the sunset sky. I thought of the Indian, who so many similar evenings had paddled up this stream, with what advantage he beheld the twilight sky. So we advanced without dust or sound, by gentle influences, as the twilight gradually faded away. The height of the railroad bridge, already high (more than twenty feet to the top of the rail), was doubled by the reflection, equalling that of a Roman aqueduct, for we could not possibly see where the reflection began, and the piers appeared to rise from the lowest part of the reflection

Sept. 7. Thursday. The rain of last night has brought down more leaves of elms and buttonwoods.

P. M. — To Moore's Swamp and Walden.

See some hips of the moss rose, very large and handsome, bright-scarlet, very much *flattened* globular. On the Walden road heard a somewhat robin-like clicking note. Looked round and saw one of those small slate-colored, black-tipped, white-rumped hawks skimming over the meadows with head down, at first thirty feet high, then low till he appeared to drop into the grass.[1] It was quite a loud *clicketing* sound.

Paddled to Baker Farm just after sundown, by full moon.

I suppose this is the Harvest Moon, since the sun must be in Virgo, enters Libra the 23d *inst.*

The wind has gone down, and it is a still, warm night, and no mist.

It is just after sundown. The moon not yet risen, one star, Jupiter (?), visible, and many bats over and about our heads, and small skaters creating a myriad dimples on the evening waters. We see a muskrat crossing, and pass a white cat on the shore. There are many clouds about and a beautiful sunset sky, a yellowish (dunnish?) golden sky, between them in the horizon, looking up the river. All this is reflected in the water. The beauty of the sunset is doubled by the reflection. Being on the water we have double the amount of lit and dun-colored sky above and beneath. An elm in the yellow twilight looks very rich, as if

[1] Male marsh hawk.

to the rail above, about fifty feet. We floated directly under it, between the piers, as if in mid-air, not being able to distinguish the surface of the water, and looked down more than twenty feet to the reflected flooring through whose intervals we saw the starlit sky. The ghostly piers stretched downward on all sides, and only the angle made by their meeting the real ones betrayed where was the water surface.

The twilight had now paled (lost its red and dun) and faintly illumined the high bank. I observed no firefly this evening, nor the 4th. The moon had not yet risen and there was a half-hour of dusk, in which, however, we saw the reflections of the trees. Any peculiarity in the form of a tree or other object — if it leans one side or has a pointed top, for instance — is revealed in the reflection by being doubled and so insisted on. We detected thus distant maples, pines, and oaks, and they were seen to be related to the river as mountains in the horizon are by day.

Night is the time to hear; our ears took in every sound from the meadows and the village. At first we were disturbed by the screeching of the locomotive and rumbling of the cars, but soon were left to the fainter natural sounds, — the creaking of the crickets, and the little *Rana palustris*[1] (I am not sure that I heard it the latter part of the evening), and the shrilling of other crickets (?), the occasional faint lowing of a cow and the distant barking of dogs, as in a whisper. Our ears drank in every sound. I heard once or twice a

[1] ["Mole cricket" is here substituted in pencil for "*Rana palustris.*"]

dumping frog. This was while we lay off Nut Meadow Brook waiting for the moon to rise. She burned her way slowly through the small but thick clouds, and, as fast as she triumphed over them and rose over them, they appeared pale and shrunken, like the ghosts of their former selves. Meanwhile we measured the breadth of the clear cope over our heads, which she would ere long traverse, and, while she was concealed, looked up to the few faint stars in the zenith which is ever lighted. C. thought that these few faint lights in the ever-lit sky, whose inconceivable distance was enhanced by a few downy wisps of cloud, surpassed any scene that earth could show.[1] When the moon was behind those small black clouds in the horizon, they had a splendid silver edging. At length she rose above them and shone aslant, like a ball of fire over the woods. It was remarkably clear to-night, and the water was not so remarkably broad therefore, and Fair Haven was not clothed with that blue veil like a mountain, which it wore on the 4th, but it was not till we had passed the bridge that the first sheen was reflected from the pads. The reflected shadow of the Hill was black as night, and we seemed to be paddling directly into it a rod or two before us, but we never reached it at all. The trees and hills were distinctly black between us and the moon, and the water black or gleaming accordingly. It was quite dry and warm. Above the Cliffs we heard only one or two owls at a distance, a hooting owl and a screech owl, and several whip-poor-wills. The delicious fra-

[1] [*Excursions*, p. 328; Riv. 403.]

Vol. VII

grance of ripe grapes was wafted to us by the night air, as we paddled by, from every fertile vine on the shore, and thus its locality was revealed more surely than by daylight. We knew their fragrance was better than their flavor. They perfumed the whole river for a mile, by night. You might have thought you had reached the confines of Elysium. A slight zephyr wafted us almost imperceptibly into the middle of Fair Haven Pond, while we lay watching and listening. The sheen of the moon extended quite across the pond to us in a long and narrow triangle, or rather with concave sides like a very narrow Eddystone Lighthouse, with its base on the southwest shore, and we heard the distant sound of the wind through the pines on the hilltop. Or, if we listened closely, we heard still the faint and distant barking of dogs. They rule the night. Near the south shore disturbed some ducks in the water, which slowly flew away to seek a new resting-place, uttering a distinct and alarmed *quack* something like a goose.

We walked up to the old Baker house. In the bright moonlight the character of the ground under our feet was not easy to detect, and we did not know at first but we were walking on sod and not on a field laid down and harrowed. From the upland the pond in the moonlight looked blue, — as much so as the sky. We sat on the window-sill of the old house, thought of its former inhabitants, saw our bandit shadows down the cellar-way (C. had on a red flannel shirt over his thin coat, — since he expected it would be cold and damp, — and looked like one), listened to

each sound, and observed each ray of moonlight through the cracks. Heard an apple fall in the little orchard close by, while a whip-poor-will was heard in the pines.

Returning to the boat, saw a glow-worm in the damp path in the low ground. Returning later, we experienced better the weird-like character of the night, especially perceived the fragrance of the grapes and admired the fair smooth fields in the bright moonlight. There being no mist, the reflections were wonderfully distinct; the whole of Bittern Cliff with its grove was seen beneath the waves.

Sept. 8. P. M. — To boat under Fair Haven Hill *via* Hubbard Bath, etc., a-graping.

The ivy at ivy tree is scarlet a quarter part. Saw one of my small slate-colored hawks of yesterday, sitting in the midst of the upland field beyond, like a crow. There is a great crop of *Viburnum nudum* berries this year. The green-briar berries not quite ripe. Clams still lie up.

The grapes would no doubt be riper a week hence, but I am compelled to go now before the vines are stripped. I partly smell them out. I pluck splendid great bunches of the purple ones, with a rich bloom on them and the purple glowing through it like a fire; large red ones, also, with light dots, and some clear green. Sometimes I crawl under low and thick bowers, where they have run over the alders only four or five feet high, and see the grapes hanging from a hollow hemisphere of leaves over my head. At other times I see them dark-purple or black against the silvery

undersides of the leaves, high overhead where they have run over birches or maples, and either climb or pull them down to pluck them. The witch-hazel on Dwarf Sumach Hill looks as if it would begin to blossom in a day or two.

Talked with Garfield, who was fishing off his shore. By the way, that shore might be named from him, for he is the genius of it, and is almost the only man I ever see on that part of the river. He says that the two turtles, of one of which I have the shell, weighed together eighty-nine pounds. He saw one when he was a boy, which his father caught in Fair Haven Pond, which several who saw it thought would have weighed sixty pounds. That the biggest story he could tell. Referred to the year not long since when so many were found dead. There was one rotting right on that shore where we were, "as big as a tray." Once, he and another man were digging a ditch in a meadow in Waltham. (He thought it was the last of September or first of October — and that we did not see them put their heads out much later than this.) They found two mud turtles three feet beneath the surface and no hole visible by which they entered. They laid them out on the grass, but when they went to look for them again, one was lost and the other had buried himself in the meadow all but the tip of his tail.

He heard some years ago a large flock of brant go over "yelling" very loud, flying low and in an irregular dense flock like pigeons. He says the east shore of Fair Haven under the Hill is covered with heron-tracks. One of his boys had seen marks where an otter had slid and eaten fish near the mouth of Pole Brook (my Bidens Brook). Remembered old people saying that this river used to be a great hunting-place a hundred years ago or more. A still stream with meadows, and the deer used to come out on it. Had heard an old Mr. Hosmer, who lived where E. Conant does, say that he had shot three dozen muskrats at one shot at Birch Island (the island at mouth of Fair Haven Pond).

His father caught the great turtle while fishing and sent him up to the house on Baker's farm where a Jones lived, to get an axe to cut his head off. There were two or three men — Luke Potter, who lived where Hayden does, for one — playing cards, and when they learned what he wanted the axe for, they came down to the shore to see him, and they judged that he would weigh sixty pounds. Two or three years ago he saw one caught that weighed forty-two pounds.

I saw a muskrat-cabin apparently begun on a small hummock for a core, now just before the first frost and when the river wreck had begun to wash about. Those fine mouthfuls *appear* to be gathered from the river-bottom, — fine pontederias, sium, fontinalis, etc., etc., decayed but somewhat adhesive. See fresh pontederia blossoms still. Started up ten ducks, which had settled for the night below the bath place, apparently wood ducks.

I doubt if I have distinguished the *Bidens cernua*. It may be the one I have thought a small *chrysanthemoides*. I find these last with smaller rays and larger outer involucres and more or less bristly stems, yet

equally connate and as regularly serrate, and it looks like a difference produced by growing in a drier soil.

Many green-briar leaves are very agreeably thickly spotted now with reddish brown, or fine green on a yellow or green ground, producing a wildly variegated leaf. I have seen nothing more rich. Some of these curled leaves are five inches wide with a short point. It is a leaf now for poets to sing about, a leaf to inspire poets. Now, while I am gathering grapes, I see them. It excites me to a sort of autumnal madness. They are leaves for Satyrus and Faunus to make their garlands of. My thoughts break out like them, spotted all over, yellow and green and brown. The freckled leaf. Perhaps they should be poison, to be thus spotted. I fancied these brown were blood-red spots, by contrast, but they are not. Now for the ripening year! Even leaves are *beginning* to be ripe.

Garfield says he found a hen-hawk's nest near Holden's Swamp (the old ones had got his chickens), sixty feet up a white pine. He climbed up and set a trap in it baited with a fish, with a string ten feet long attached. The young, but just hatched, faced him, and he caught the old one by the legs thus.

I have brought home a half-bushel of grapes to scent my chamber with. It is impossible to get them home in a basket with all their rich bloom on them, which, no less than the form of the clusters, makes their beauty. As I paddled home with my basket of grapes in the bow, every now and then their perfume was wafted to me in the stern, and I thought that I was passing a richly laden vine on shore. Some goldfinches twitter

Vol. VII

over, while I am pulling down the vines from the birch-tops. The ripest rattle off and strew the ground before I reach the clusters, or, while I am standing on tiptoe and endeavoring gently to break the tough peduncle, the petiole of a leaf gets entangled in the bunch and I am compelled to strip them all off loosely.

> "Yet once more . . .
> I come to pluck your berries harsh and crude,
> And with forc'd fingers rude,
> Shatter your leaves before the mellowing year." [1]

Sept. 9. This morning I find a little hole, three quarters of an inch or an inch over, above my small tortoise eggs, and find a young tortoise coming out (apparently in the rainy night) just beneath. It is the *Sternothærus odoratus* — already has the strong scent — and now has drawn in its head and legs. I see no traces of the yolk, or what-not, attached. It may have been out of the egg some days. *Only one* as yet. I buried them in the garden June 15th.

I am affected by the thought that the earth nurses these eggs. They are planted in the earth, and the earth takes care of them; she is genial to them and does not kill them. It suggests a certain vitality and intelligence in the earth, which I had not realized. This mother is not merely inanimate and inorganic. Though the immediate mother turtle abandons her offspring, the earth and sun are kind to them. The old turtle on which the earth rests takes care of them while the other waddles off. Earth was not made poisonous and deadly to them. The earth has some

[1] [Milton's *Lycidas*.]

virtue in it; when seeds are put into it, they germinate; when turtles' eggs, they hatch in due time. Though the mother turtle remained and brooded them, it would still nevertheless be the universal world turtle which, through her, cared for them as now. Thus the earth is the mother of all creatures.

Garfield said that one of his sons, while they were haying in the river meadows once, found a hundred little pickerel, an inch or inch and a half long, in [a] little hole in the meadow not bigger than a bushel basket and nearly dry. He took them out and put them into the river. Another time he himself found many hundred in a ditch, brought them home, and put them into his large tub. They there lived a spell without his feeding them, but, small as they were, lived on one another, and you could see the tails sticking out their mouths. It would seem as if their spawn was deposited in those little muddy-bottomed hollows in the meadows where we find the schools of young thus landlocked.

Sept. 10. Yesterday and to-day the first regular rain-storm, bringing down more leaves, — elms, button woods, and apple tree, — and decidedly raising the river and brooks. The still, cloudy, mizzling days, September 1st and 2d, the thunder-shower of evening of September 6th, and this regular storm are the first fall rains after the long drought. Already the grass both in meadows and on hills looks greener, and the whole landscape, this overcast rainy day, darker and more verdurous. Hills which have been russet and tawny begin to show some greenness.

On account of the drought one crop has almost entirely failed this year thus far, which the papers have not spoken of. Last year, for the last three weeks of August, the woods were filled with the strong musty scent of decaying fungi, but this year I have seen very few fungi and have not noticed that odor at all, — a failure more perceptible to frogs and toads, but no doubt serious to those whom it concerns.

As for birds: —

About *ten* days ago *especially* I saw many large hawks, probably hen-hawks and young, about.

Within a week several of the small slate-colored and black-tipped hawks.

August 20th, saw a sucker which I suppose must have been caught by a fish hawk.

Hear screech owls and hooting owls these evenings.

Have not noticed blue jays of late.

Occasionally hear the *phe-be* note of chickadees.

Partridges probably cease to mew for their young.

For about three weeks have seen one or two small dippers.

For ten days a *few* wood and probably black ducks.

Small flocks of bluebirds about apple trees.

Larks common, but have not heard them sing for some time.

Am not sure that I have seen red-wings or other blackbirds for ten days.

About three weeks ago a small flock of robins and pigeon woodpeckers.

Robins common, and still hear some faint notes of woodpeckers.

Saw a downy woodpecker as a rarity within a week.

Believe I hear no song sparrows sing nowadays.

See no *F. hyemalis;* hear no quails.

Heard my last phœbe August 26th.

See no *flocks* of white-in-tails.

Hear the nuthatch as a novelty within a week about street.

Vol. VII

Saw first tree sparrow about a week since in first rain.[1]

Have seen pigeons about a fortnight.

Have not distinguished rush sparrows for a long time, nor Savannah, nor yellow-winged.

Seen no snipe since August 16th.

Turtle doves for more than a month.

A chip-sparrow seen within a few days.

The warbling vireo still heard faintly in the morning.

For three weeks blue herons common on meadows and great bittern.

Green bittern rather earlier for most part.

Have not heard kingfisher of late, — not for three weeks methinks.

Methinks I heard a faint sound from a chewink within a week?

Seen no barn swallows for a week.

Heard no catbirds nor brown thrashers sing for long time, but seen the last at least within ten days.

Whip-poor-wills still common.

Think I saw white-throated (?) sparrows on button-bushes about a week ago, the mizzling day.

Hear no golden robins for the last fortnight.

Bats common.

Not sure I have seen bobolinks since August 20th.

Kingbirds seen within a day or two.

Hummingbird within a week.

Goldfinches common.

Nighthawks still, but have not noticed the booming lately.

Cherry-birds common.

Cuckoo not heard lately.

Meadow-hen (?) seen August 30th.

Now generally ducks and other migratory birds are returning from north and ours going south.[2]

Diplopappus linariifolius and *Aster undulatus* apparently now in prime.

[1] [Probably a mistake. The date is too early.]

[2] [It is significant that no warblers are included, even negatively, in this list. Compare entry of June 9, 1854.]

Sept. 11. Measured to-day the little *Sternothœrus odoratus* which came out the ground in the garden September 9th. Its shell is thirty-two fortieths of an inch long, by twenty-five fortieths wide. It has a distinct dorsal ridge, and its head and flippers are remarkably developed. Its raised back and dorsal ridge, as in the case of the mud turtle, enable it to turn over very easily. It may have been hatched some time before it came out, for not only there was no trace of the *yolk* (?), but its shell was much wider than the egg, when it first came out of the ground. I placed a sieve over it, and it remained in the hole it had made mostly concealed the two rainy days, — the 9th and 10th, — but to-day I found it against the edge of the sieve, its head and legs drawn in and quite motionless, so that you would have said the pulses of life had not fairly begun to beat. I put it into the tub on the edge of the mud. It seems that it does not have to learn to walk, but walks at once. It seems to have no infancy such as birds have. It is surprising how much cunning it already exhibits. It is defended both by its form and color and its instincts. As it lay on the mud, its color made it very inobvious, but, besides, it kept its head and legs drawn in and perfectly still, as if feigning death; but this was not sluggishness. At a little distance I watched it for ten minutes or more. At length it put its head out far enough to see if the coast was clear, then, with its flippers, it turned itself toward the water (which element it had never seen before), and suddenly and with rapidity launched itself into it and dove to the bottom. Its whole behavior was

calculated to enable it to reach its proper element safely and without attracting attention. Not only was it made of a color and form (like a bit of coal) which alone almost effectually concealed it, but it was made, infant as it was, to be perfectly still as if inanimate and then to move with rapidity when unobserved. The oldest turtle does not show more, if so much, cunning. I think I may truly say that it uses cunning and meditates how it may reach the water in safety. When I first took it out of its hole on the morning of the 9th, it shrunk into its shell and was motionless, feigning death. That this was not sluggishness, I have proved. When to-day it lay within half an inch of the water's edge, it knew it for a friendly element and, without deliberation or experiment, but at last, when it thought me and all foes unobservant of its motions, with remarkable precipitation it committed itself to it as if realizing a long-cherished idea. Plainly all its motions were as much the result of what is called instinct as is the act of sucking in infants. Our own subtlest [*sic*] is likewise but another kind of instinct. The wise man is a wise infant obeying his finest and never-failing instincts. It does not so much impress me as an infantile beginning of life as an epitome of all the past of turtledom and of the earth. I think of it as the result of all the turtles that have been.

The little snapping turtle lies almost constantly on the mud with its snout out of water. It does not keep under water long. Yesterday in the cold rain, however, it lay buried in the mud all day!

Surveying this forenoon, I saw a small, round,

bright-yellow gall (some are red on one side), as big as a moderate cranberry, hard and smooth, saddled on a white oak twig. So I have seen them on the swamp white, the chinquapin, and the white, not to mention the Castile-soap one on the *ilicifolia* acorn edge.

This is a *cold* evening with a white twilight, and threatens frost, the first in *these respects* decidedly autumnal evening. It makes us think of wood for the winter. For a week or so the evenings have been sensibly longer, and I am beginning to throw off my summer idleness. This twilight is succeeded by a brighter starlight than heretofore.

Sept. 12. Tuesday. A cool, overcast day threatening a storm. Yesterday, after the two days' cold rain, the air was very clear and fine-grained. This is a phenomenon we observe now after dog-days, until it is summed up in Indian summer.

P. M. — To Hubbard Bath.

Methinks these cool cloudy days are important to show the colors of some flowers, — that with an absence of light their own colors are more conspicuous and grateful against the cool, moist, dark-green earth, — the *Aster puniceus* (the most densely massed), the (now beginning to prevail) *Tradescanti*, purple gerardia, etc., etc. The river has at length risen perceptibly, and bathing I find it colder again than on the 2d, so that I stay in but a moment. I fear that it will not again be warm. The weeds in midstream are mostly drowned and are washing up to the shore, — much vallisneria and heart-leaf (with its threadlike

stems) are added to the previous wreck. (*Vide* September 5th.)

A sprinkling drove me back for an umbrella, and I started again for Smith's Hill *via* Hubbard's Close. I see plump young bluebirds in small flocks along the fences, with only the primaries and tail a bright blue, the other feathers above dusky ashy-brown, tipped with white. How much more the crickets are heard a cool, cloudy day like this! Is it not partly because the air is stiller? I see the *Epilobium molle* (?) (linear) in Hubbard's Close still out, but I cannot find a trace of the fringed gentian. I scare pigeons from Hubbard's oaks beyond. How like the creaking of trees the slight sounds they make! Thus they are concealed. Not only their *prating* or *quivet* is like a sharp creak, but I heard a sound from them like a dull grating or cracking of bough on bough. I see the small aster (?) in the woods with ink-black spots at the base of the leaves. (It looks like a *dumosus*, but has no flowers.) *White* oak acorns have many of them fallen. They are small and very neat light-green acorns, with small cups, commonly arranged two by two close together, often with a leaf growing between them; but frequently three, forming a little star with three rays,  looking very artificial. Some black scrub oak acorns have fallen, and a few black oak acorns also have fallen. The red oak began to fall first. Thorn apples are now commonly ripe and the prinos berries are conspicu-

Vol. VII

ous. Beside many white birch I now see many chestnut leaves fallen and brown in the woods. There is now at last some smell of fungi in the woods since the rains.

On a white oak beyond Everett's orchard by the road, I see quite a flock of pigeons; their blue-black droppings and their feathers spot the road. The bare limbs of the oak apparently attracted them, though its acorns are thick on the ground. These are found whole in their crops. They swallow them whole. I should think from the droppings that they had been eating berries. I hear that Wetherbee caught ninety-two dozen last week.

I see maple viburnum berries blue-black with but little bloom. No *full* cymes, and the cymes rather less spreading than the other kinds. Some time. Now, especially, the strong bracing scent of the delicate fern by the Saw Mill Brook path. Dicksonia? or a coarser? How long has the mitchella been ripe? I see many still perfectly green in the swamp. Fruit of the damp and mossy forest floor ripening amid the now mildewy and bracing fern scent of the damp wood. Medeola berries shining black (or perhaps dark blue-black?) on long peduncles; how long? The whorls of leaves now stand empty for most part like shallow saucers, with their purple centres and bare peduncles.

I hear that many upland plover have been seen on the burnt Brooks's meadow.

Marsh speedwell and yellow Bethlehem-star still out.

Sept. 13. Wednesday. P. M. — To Great Fields.

Many butternuts have dropped, — more than walnuts. A few raspberries still fresh. I find the large thistle (*Cirsium muticum*) out of bloom, seven or eight rods, perhaps, north of the potato-field and seven feet west of ditch, amid a clump of raspberry vines.

Sept. 14. Thursday. 6 A. M. — To Hill.

I hear a vireo still in the elms. The banks have now *begun* fairly to be sugared with the *Aster Tradescanti*. I get very near a small dipper behind Dodd's, which sails out from the weeds fairly before me, then scoots over the surface crosswise the river, throwing the water high, dives, and is lost. A *Viola lanceolata* out on the meadow.

The sun soon after rising has gone into a mackerel sky this morning, and, as I come down the hill, I observe a singular mirage (?). There is a large dense field of mackerel sky with a straight and distinct edge parallel with the southeast horizon and lifted above it, apparently about double the height of the highest hills there; beneath this a clear sky, and lower still some level bars of mist, which cut off the top of Pine Hill, causing it to loom. The top, fringed with pines on account of the intervening lower mist, is seen as it were above the clouds, appears much too high, being referred to a far greater distance than the reality. Our humble scenery appears on a grand scale. I see the fair forms of mighty pines standing along a mountain ridge above the clouds and overlooking from a vast distance our low valley. I think that the image is not really elevated, but the bars of mist below make me refer it to too great a distance and therefore it is seen as higher. The appearance of those fine-edged pines, a narrow strip of a mountain ridge half a mile in length, is stupendous and imposing. It is as if we lived in a valley amid the Himmalaya Mountains, a vale of Cashmere.

There was a fog last night which I think prevented a frost.

8 A. M. — To opposite Pelham's Pond by boat.

Quite cool, with some wind from east and southeast. Took a watermelon for drink. I see many new and perfect upright cobwebs on the sium gone to seed by the side of the river. Now, instead of haying, they are raking cranberries all along the river. The raker moves slowly along with a basket before him, into which he rakes (hauling) the berries, and his wagon stands one side. It is now the middle of the cranberry season. The river has risen about a foot within a week, and now the weeds in midstream have *generally* disappeared, washed away or drowned. The ranunculus stems and leaves are added to the floating wreck. Now our oars leave a broad wake of large bubbles, which are slow to burst. Methinks they are most numerous, large, and slow to burst near the end of a warm and dry spell, and that the water loses some of this tenacity in a rain. But now we have had rain. At any rate on the 4th, just after the first rains (of the 1st and 2d), they would not readily form to the hand. There is such a difference in the state of the water. As we go up the

Clamshell Reach I see the reflections of oaks very much prolonged by the fine ripple. Perhaps it is re-reflected from ripple to ripple. The rainbow portion of the bayonet rush is just covered now by the rise of the river. This cooler morning methinks the jays are heard more. Now that the pontederias have mostly fallen, the polygonums are the most common and conspicuous flowers of the river. The smaller one has not shown more before. I see a stream of small white insects in the air over the side of the river. W. Wheeler is burning his hill by the Corner road, just cut over. I see the scarlet flame licking along the ground, not in a continuous rank, but upright individual tongues of flame, undulating, flashing, forked, — narrow erect waves about the size of a man or boy; next the smoke rising perpendicularly, blue against the pines and fuscous against the sky. Not till high in the sky does it feel the southerly wind. When I look round for those light under sides of the crisped leaves, which were so conspicuous in the drought three weeks and more ago, I see none. Methinks they have not so much flattened out again since the rains, but have fallen, and that thus there are two falls every year. Those leaves which are curled by the drought of July and August apparently fall with the first fall rains, about the first week of September, and those which remain are green as usual and go on to experience their regular October change. The only difference this year will be that there will not be so many leaves for the second fall. The first fall is now over.[1]

[1] For example, on the 17th I see that all those which had changed

Crossing Fair Haven, the reflections were very fine, — not quite distinct, but prolonged by the fine ripples made by an east wind just risen. At a distance, entering the pond, we mistook some fine sparkles, probably of insects, for ducks in the water, they were so large, which when we were nearer, looking down at a greater angle with the surface, wholly disappeared. Some *large-leaved* willow bushes in the meadow southeast of Lee's reflected the light from the under sides of a part of their leaves, as if frost-covered, or as if white asters were mingled with them. We saw but two white lilies on this voyage; they are now done. About a dozen pontederia spikes, no mikania (that is now white or gray), four or five large yellow lilies, and two or three small yellow lilies. The *Bidens Beckii* is drowned or dried up, and has given place to the great bidens, *the* flower and ornament of the riversides at present, and now in its glory, especially at I. Rice's shore, where there are dense beds. It is a splendid yellow — Channing says a lemon yellow — and looks larger than it is (two inches in diameter, more or less). Full of the sun. It needs a name. I see tufts of ferns on the edge of the meadows at a little distance, handsomely tipped on edge with cinnamon brown. Like so many brown fires they light up the meadows. The button-bush everywhere *yellowing.*

We see half a dozen herons in this voyage. Their wings are so long in proportion to their bodies that

on Pine Hill have fallen and many tree-tops, maple and chestnut, are bare.

there seems to be more than one undulation to a wing as they are disappearing in the distance, and so you can distinguish them. You see another begin before the first has ended. It is remarkable how common these birds are about our sluggish and marshy river. We must attract them from a wide section of country. It abounds in those fenny districts and meadow pond-holes in which they delight. A flock of thirteen tell-tales, great yellow-legs, start up with their shrill whistle from the midst of the great Sudbury meadow, and away they *sail in a flock,* — a *sailing* (or skimming) *flock,* that is something rare methinks, — showing their white tails, to alight in a more distant place. We see some small dippers and scare up many ducks, black mostly, which probably came as soon as the earliest. The great bittern, too, rises from time to time, slowly flapping his way along at no great height above the meadow.

The small polygonum is first particularly abundant in the bend above the coreopsis, but it is [in] greatest abundance and perfection at three quarters through the great meadow, in great beds one to three rods wide, very dense and now rising but six or eight inches or so above the water. It is now apparently in perfection. See swallow *like* a barn swallow. Counted twenty haycocks in the great meadow, on staddles, of various forms, —

tied round   with hay

ropes. They are picturesque objects in the meadow. Little as the river has risen, these meadows are already wet. The phragmites is still green. Why does not that large typha above the Causeway bear fruit? [1]

Just above the Mill Village Bridge there is an interesting view of Nobscot, clad with wood, up the broad meadows on Larned Brook, which comes in there. Above the Pelham Pond Bridge, a short distance further, we dined; then went on. An interesting view and part of the river, — quite broad at the Great Chestnut house, — and a good land[ing] just before on the left. Went half a mile or more above the Chestnut house. Plenty of hibiscus out of bloom just above the Chestnut house on the west side, and some opposite some elms where we had dined, — all in Wayland.

What is that large, sharply triangular, hollow-sided sedge about four feet high on the north edge of the river in middle of the great meadow? Coarse, grass-like somewhat.[2]

We went up thirteen or fourteen miles at least, and, as we stopped at Fair Haven Hill returning, rowed about twenty-five miles to-day.

Sept. 15. P. M. — To boat under Fair Haven Hill and down river.

Desmodium (?) or lespedeza ticks cover my clothes. I know not when I get them. The witch-hazel has opened since the 8th; say 11th.[3] Its leaves, a third or a half of them, are yellow and brown. *Solidago spe-*

---

[1] It does. *Vide* July 31, 1859.   [2] *Vide* July 31, 1859.

[3] It was abundantly out the 14th (yesterday) on Wachusett Mountain, where it is probably more exposed to the sun and drier. Sophia was there.

ciosa at Clamshell out several days. Goodwin, the one-eyed fisherman, is back again at his old business (and Haynes also). He says he has been to Cape Cod a-haying. He says that their "salt grass cuts about the same with our fresh meadow."

Saw a chewink.

Mrs. Mowatt, the actress, describes a fancy ball in Paris, given by an American millionaire, at which "one lady . . . wore so many diamonds (said to be valued at two hundred thousand dollars) that she was escorted in her carriage by *gendarmes*, for fear of robbery." This illustrates the close connection between luxury and robbery, but commonly the gendarmes are further off.

Sept. 16. Sophia and mother returned from Wachusett. S. saw much bayberry in Princeton.

P. M. — To Fringed Gentian Meadow over Assabet and to Dugan Desert.

I see a wood tortoise in the woods. Why is it there now? One man thinks there are not so many pigeons as last week, that it is too cold for them. There have been a few slight frosts in some places. The clematis is feathered. One *Asclepias Cornuti* begun to discount. I see many hardhacks in the lichen pasture by Tommy Wheeler's which are *leafing* out again *conspicuously*. I see little flocks of chip-birds along the roadside and on the apple trees, showing their light under sides when they rise.

I find the mud turtle's eggs at the Desert all hatched. There is a small hole by which they have made their exit some time before the last rain (of the 14th) and

Vol. VII

since I was here on the 4th. There is, however, one still left in the nest. As the eggs were laid the 7th of June, it makes about three months before they came out of the ground. The nest was full of sand and egg-shells. I saw no tracks of the old one. I took out the remaining one, which perhaps could not get out alone, and it began slowly to crawl toward the brook about five rods distant. It went about five feet in as many minutes. At this rate it would have reached the water in a couple of hours at most. Then, being disturbed by my moving, stopped, and, when it started again, retraced its steps, crossed the hole which I had filled, and got into a rut leading toward another part of the brook, about ten rods distant. It climbed directly over some weeds and tufts of grass in its way. Now and then it paused, stretched out its head, looked round, and appeared to be deliberating, waiting for information or listening to its instinct. It seemed to be but a blundering instinct which it obeyed and as if it might be easily turned from its proper course. Yet in no case did it go wholly wrong. Whenever I took it up, it drew in its head and legs, shut its eyes, and remained motionless. It was so slow that I could not stop to watch it, and so carried it to within seven or eight inches of the water, turning its head inland. At length it put out its head and legs, turned itself round, crawled to the water, and endeavored as soon as it entered it to bury itself at the bottom, but, it being sand, it could not. I put it further into the stream, and it was at once carried down head over heels by the current. I think they come out in the night.

Another little sternothærus has come out of the ground since eight this morning (it is now 11 A. M.).[1] The first sternothærus has remained buried in the mud in the tub from the first, and the snapping turtle also for the last few days.

The locust sounds rare now. I make the oak at the southeast corner of the Agricultural Ground to be a scarlet oak, — not yellow-barked; leaf more deeply cut, lighter green, narrower at point; acorn more pointed, its upper scales not recurved off from the acorn like the black.

Sept. 18. *Monday. Viburnum nudum* in flower again. Fringed gentian near Peter's out a short time, but as there is so little, and that has been cut off by the mowers, and this is not the leading stem that blooms, it may after all be earlier than the hazel.[2] I see the potatoes all black with frosts that have occurred within a night or two in Moore's Swamp.

Sept. 19. *Tuesday.* P. M. — To Conantum.

Viburnum Lentago berries now perhaps in prime, though there are but few blue ones.

---

[1] Another, Sept. 17th, found in morning. Another the 18th, between 8 and 11 A. M. Another the 18th, between 11 A. M. and 1 P. M. Another between 1 and 8 P. M. the 18th. Another found out on the morning of the 19th. Another was dug out the 25th. (All hatched, then, but one egg which I have.)

A snapping turtle had come out on the morning of the 20th, one at least. Another on the morning of the 23d Sept. Another on the morning of the 26th.

[2] Frost-bitten in Hubbard's Close the 21st (or before).

Thinking this afternoon of the prospect of my writing lectures and going abroad to read them the next winter, I realized how incomparably great the advantages of obscurity and poverty which I have enjoyed so long (and may still perhaps enjoy). I thought with what more than princely, with what poetical, leisure I had spent my years hitherto, without care or engagement, fancy-free. I have given myself up to nature; I have lived so many springs and summers and autumns and winters as if I had nothing else to do but *live* them, and imbibe whatever nutriment they had for me; I have spent a couple of years, for instance, with the flowers chiefly, having none other so binding engagement as to observe when they opened; I could have afforded to spend a whole fall observing the changing tints of the foliage. Ah, how I have thriven on solitude and poverty! I cannot overstate this advantage. I do not see how I could have enjoyed it, if the public had been expecting as much of me as there is danger now that they will. If I go abroad lecturing, how shall I ever recover the lost winter?

It has been my vacation, my season of growth and expansion, a prolonged youth.

An upland plover goes off from Conantum top (though with a white belly), uttering a sharp *white, tu white.*

That drought was so severe that a *few* trees here and there — birch, maple, chestnut, apple, oak — have lost nearly all their leaves. I see large flocks of robins with a few flickers, the former keeping up their familiar peeping and chirping.

Many pignuts have fallen. Hardhack is very com-

monly putting forth new leaves where it has lost the old. They are half an inch or three quarters long, and green the stems well. The stone-crop fruit has for a week or more had a purplish or pinkish (?) tinge by the roadside. Fallen acorns in a few days acquire that wholesome shining dark chestnut (?) color. Did I see a returned yellow redpoll fly by?

I saw, some nights ago, a great deal of light reflected from a fog-bank over the river upon Monroe's white fence, making it conspicuous almost as by moonlight from my window.

Scarlet cup with oak acorn (commonly a broader more shelf).[1]

Sept. 20. Windy rain-storm last night.
See to-day quite a flock of what I think must be rusty grackles about the willows and button-bushes.

Sept. 21. *Thursday.* P. M. — To Flint's Pond.
The first frost in our yard last night, the grass white and stiff in the morning. The muskmelon vines are now blackened in the sun. There have been some frosts in low grounds about a week. The forenoon is cold, and I have a fire, but it is a fine clear day, as I find when I come forth to walk in the afternoon, a fine-grained air with a seething or shimmering in it, as I look over the fields, — days which remind me of the Indian summer that is to come. Do not these days always succeed the first frosty mornings?

[1] *Vide* another figure in fall of '58.

Vol. VII

The woods generally may now be said to be fairly *beginning* to turn (this with the first noticeable frost). The red maples, especially at a distance, *begin* to light their fires, some turning yellow, and within the woods many oak, *e. g.* scarlet and black and chestnut, and other leaves begin to show their colors. Those leaves of the young white oaks which have changed dull-salmon, crimson, scarlet (many incline to crimson) are mostly within the tree and partially concealed by the green leaves. They are handsomest looking up from below, the light through them.

With this bright, clear, but rather cool air the bright yellow of the autumnal dandelion is in harmony and the heads of the dilapidated goldenrods. The gentian is already frost-bitten[1] almost as soon as it is open. Those pretty little white oak acorn stars of three rays are now quite common on the ground.

Utricularia (the leafless) abundant, and *Lobelia Dortmanna* still out at Flint's Pond. That small erect milfoil is very abundant now. The pond is low near the bathing-rock.

I hear many jays since the frosts began. The nuthatch is common in woods and on street. Hear the chewink and the cluck of the thrasher.

I sometimes seem to myself to owe all my little success, all for which men commend me, to my vices. I am perhaps more willful than others and make enormous sacrifices, even of others' happiness, it may be, to gain my ends. It would seem even as if nothing good could be accomplished without some vice to aid in it.

[1] [A question-mark in pencil is inserted here.]

The leaves of the wild cherry, being sound and entire, are in some places a particularly handsome clear, uniform what you may call *cherry* red, perhaps inclining to crimson, — perhaps like the stain of cherry juice.[1]

I am surprised to see how many leaves in the woods have been apparently eaten through on the edges by some insect, leaving only a faded network of veins there, contrasting with the green centres. In some places almost every leaf of the young white oaks (and black or shrub oak) and chestnuts has this very handsome and regular pale edging as of lace-work. It is about one twelfth of an inch in diameter, and is exceedingly regular, following strictly the outline of the leaf, however cut or lobed, by nature or accident, and preserving the same width. As these leaves (of young oaks, etc.) are commonly several together in one plane disposed ray-wise, — rosettes, — the effect of this edging is enhanced. These young leaves are still of a clear and delicate and now somewhat precious green. The extreme edge is left firm and entire, and the pulp of the leaf is eaten through only just within it.

Sept. 22. *Friday.* Another hard frost this morning, notwithstanding some fog at same time, and another fine day after it.

P. M. — Over Nawshawtuct.
The river is peculiarly smooth and the water clear and sunny as I look from the stone bridge. A painted tortoise with his head out, outside of the weeds, looks as if resting in the air in that attitude, or suggests

[1] *Vide* Sept. 30.

it, — an angle of forty-five degrees, with head and flippers outstretched. I see no particular effects of frost on the pontederias; they have been falling steadily without regard to it. It would be worth the while to observe all the effects of the first frosts on vegetation, etc., etc.

Celtis berries begin to yellow. As I look off from the hilltop, I wonder if there are any finer days in the year than these. The air is so fine and more bracing, and the landscape has acquired some fresh verdure withal. The frosts come to ripen the year, the days, like fruits, — persimmons.

What if we were to walk by sunlight with equal abstraction and aloofness, yet with equally impartial observation and criticism. As if it shone not for you, nor you for it, but you had come forth into it for the nonce to admire it. By moonlight we are not of the earth earthy, but we are of the earth spiritual. So might we walk by sunlight, seeing the sun but as a moon, a comparatively faint and reflected light, and the day as a brooding night, in which we glimpse some stars still.

Some shrub oak acorns are prettily rayed, green and yellowish. Some white oak ones are turned salmon-color, or blushing like the leaves. Grape leaves in low grounds are frost-bitten and crisped before they have yellowed.[1]

Crossing the hill behind Minott's just as the sun is preparing to dip below the horizon, the thin haze in the atmosphere north and south along the west

[1] *Vide* [p. 52].

horizon reflects a purple tinge and bathes the mountains with the same, like a bloom on fruits. I wonder if this phenomenon is observed in warm weather, or before the frosts have come. Is it not another evidence of the ripe days? I saw it yesterday.

I am surprised to see balls on the scarlet oak. Its acorn and cup are peculiarly top-shaped, the point of the acorn being the bottom. The cup is broader than in the black oak, making a broader shelf about the acorn, and is more pear-shaped or prolonged at top. The acorn is not so rounded, but more tapering at point. And some scarlet oak leaves which I [see] have their two *main* veins and diverging ribs nearly opposite, while in a black oak leaf these veins, and hence lobes, are not nearly opposite.[1]

By moonlight all is simple. We are enabled to erect ourselves, our minds, on account of the fewness of objects. We are no longer distracted. It is simple as bread and water. It is simple as the rudiments of an art, — a lesson to be taken before sunlight, perchance, to prepare us for that.

Sept. 23. P. M. — To Great Meadows *via* Gowing's Swamp.

I was struck with the peculiar and interesting colors of the naked arms of the buttonwood at the brick house, delicate tints seen from the ground, — whitish, greenish, and fawn-colored (?). They look as if recently bared by the scaling off of the old bark. The buttonwoods are in a flourishing condition this year. The first time.

[1] Not general.

Vol. VII

My pink azaleas which had lost their leaves in the drought are beginning to leave out again.

The *Helianthus tuberosus* (Jerusalem artichoke) beyond Moore's shows a little yellow, but will not open there for some days yet. Low blackberry vines generally red. There are many lice on birches still, notwithstanding the frosts. The high blueberry bushes scattered here and there, the higher islands in Beck Stow's Swamp, begin to paint it bright-red. Now look out for redness on the face of the earth, such as is seen on the cheek of the sweet viburnum, or as [a] frosty morning walk imparts to a man's face. Very brilliant and remarkable now are the prinos berries, so brilliant and fresh when most things — flowers and berries — have withered. I gather pretty good wild pears near the new road, — now in prime. The *Cornus sericea* bushes along the edge of the Great Meadows are now turned mulberry, and here is an end of its berries then. The hard frosts of the 21st and 22d have put an end to several kinds of plants, and probably berries, for this year. This is the crisis when many kinds conclude their summer.

Bull says it is only the immature leaves of his new grape which are crisped by the frost as yet. Here, on the east edge of the Great Meadows, all the flowering fern is turned brown and withered (I am not sure but it began before the frost), and the common eupatoriums are a very dark brown or black for the same reason. All along the river the upper half of the button-bushes is turned brown and withered in consequence of the frost, while many other plants in their midst are un-

touched. As it began late, it falls early. Its balls are equally browned, and may now be said to be ripened by frost. After those frosts a day's sun revealed what mischief the frost had done by the withering and blackened leaves. Many plants fall with the first frosts, — grapes, button-bushes; what else? Probably some asters and goldenrods.

Monroe has shot a loon to-day.

Sept. 24. Sunday. 6 A. M. — To Hill.

Low fog-like veil on meadows.

On the large sassafras trees on the hill I see many of the handsome red club-shaped pedicels left, with their empty cups which have held fruit; and I see one or two elliptical but still green berries. Apparently the rest have ripened and fallen or been gathered by birds already, unless they fell prematurely. Gray says that the berries are dark-blue and ripen in September.

Catnep still in bloom. Hear the flicker note. See a song-sparrow-like bird singing a confused low jingle. Afterward hear from a willow by river a *clear strain* from a *song sparrow!*

Man identifies himself with earth or the material, just as he who has the least tinge of African blood in his veins regards himself as a negro and is identified with that race. Spirit is strange to him; he is afraid of ghosts.

The *Viburnum Lentago* berries now turn blue-black in pocket, as the *nudum* did, which last are now all gone, while the *Lentago* is now just in season.

P. M. — By boat to Grape Cliff.

These are the stages in the river fall: first, the two varieties of yellow lily pads begin to decay and blacken (long ago); second, the first fall rains come after dog-days and raise and cool the river, and winds wash the decaying sparganium, etc., etc., to the shores and clear the channel more or less; third, when the first harder frosts come (as this year the 21st and 22d *inst.*), the button-bushes, which before had attained only a dull mixed yellow, are suddenly bitten, wither, and turn brown, all but the protected parts.

The *first* fall is so gradual as not to make much impression, but the last suddenly and conspicuously gives a fall aspect to the scenery of the river. The button-bushes thus withered, covered still with the gray, already withered mikania, suddenly paint with a rich brown the river's brim. It is like the crust, the edging, of a boy's turnover done brown. And the black willows, slightly faded and crisped with age or heat, enhance my sense of the year's maturity. There, where the land appears to lap over the water by a mere edging, these thinner portions are first done brown. I float over the still liquid middle.

I have not seen any such conspicuous effect of frost as this sudden withering of the button-bushes. The muskrats make haste now to rear their cabins and conceal themselves.

I see still what I take to be small flocks of grackles feeding beneath the covert of the button-bushes and flitting from bush to bush. They seldom expose themselves long. The water begins to be clear of weeds,

and the fishes are exposed. It is now too cold to bathe with comfort, yet the clams have not gone down. The river is still low. I scared up a duck (wood?) (white under side wings), which circled round four times, twice (middle times) high in the air a diameter of a hundred rods, and finally alighted with a long, slanting flight near where it rose. The sumachs (though I have not observed the poison (*venenata*)) are now turned before trees. Green-briar berries ripe, blue-black, or purplish, apparently with the frosts of 21st and 22d. The red maple leaves along the river are much curled and show their whitish under sides even more than a month ago, owing probably to their age as well as the summer's drought (from which last they had partly recovered a fortnight (?) ago).

Saw a warbler which inquisitively approached me creeper-wise along some dead brush twigs. It may have been the pine-creeping warbler, though I could see no white bars on wings. I should say all yellow-olivaceous above; clear lemon-yellow throat and breast — and vent (?); narrow white ring around eye; black bill, straight; clay-colored (?) legs; edge of wings white.

Young hickories, pretty generally, and some black oaks are frost-bitten, but no young white oaks. On the shrub oak plain under Cliffs, the young white oaks are generally now tending to a dull inward red. The *ilicifolia* generally green still, with a few yellowish or else scarlet leaves. The young black oaks with many red, scarlet, or yellowish leaves. The chinquapin pretty generally a clear brilliant dark red. The same with a few twigs of the scarlet oak, but not brilliant, *i. e.*

glossy. The tupelo green, reddish, and brilliant scarlet, all together. The brightest hazel dim vermilion. Some red maple sprouts clear scarlet deepening to purplish. The panicled cornel green with a tinge of reddish purple. Only these young trees and bushes are yet conspicuously changed. The tupelo and the chinquapin the most brilliant of the above. The scarlet oak the clearest red.

But little *bright Solidago nemorosa* is left. It is generally withered or dim.

What name of a natural object is most poetic? That which he has given for convenience whose life is most nearly related to it, who has known it longest and best.

The perception of truth, as of the duration of time, etc., produces a pleasurable sensation.

Sept. 25. P. M. — To boat opposite Bittern Cliff *via* Cliffs.

I suspect that I know on what the brilliancy of the autumnal tints will depend. On the greater or less drought of the summer. If the drought has been uncommonly severe, as this year, I should think it would so far destroy the vitality of the leaf that it would attain only to a dull, dead color in autumn, that to produce a brilliant autumn the plant should be full of sap and vigor to the last.

Do I see an *F. hyemalis* in the Deep Cut? It is a month earlier than last year.

I am detained by the very bright red blackberry leaves strewn along the sod, the vine being inconspicuous. How they spot it!

On the shrub oak plain, as seen from Cliffs, the red *at least* balances the green. It looks like a rich, shaggy rug now, before the woods are changed. I see several smokes in the distance, of burning brush (?). The button-bush leaves are rapidly falling and covering the ground with a rich brown carpet. The ponte-derias, too, show decidedly the effect of the frost. The river is as low [as] ordinarily in summer, eight or nine inches below the long stone, and the stripe of the bayonet rush, now clear dark pink, eight or nine inches wide, is again exposed. Saw at a distance a fox or an otter withdrawing from the riverside. I think that if that August haze had been much of it smoke, I should have smelt it much more strongly, for I now smell strongly the smoke of this burning half a mile off, though it is scarcely perceptible in the air.

There was a splendid sunset while I was on the water, beginning at the Clamshell reach. All the lower edge of a very broad dark-slate cloud which reached up backward almost to the zenith was lit up through and through with a dun golden fire, the sun being below the horizon, like a furze plain densely on fire, a short distance above the horizon, for there was a clear, pale robin's-egg sky beneath, and some little clouds on which the light fell high in the sky but nearer, seen against the upper part of the distant uniform dark-slate one, were of a fine grayish silver color, with fine mother-o'-pearl tints unusual at sunset (?). The furze gradually burnt out on the lower edge of the cloud, changed into a smooth, hard pale pink vermilion, which gradually faded into a gray satiny pearl, a fine Quaker-color.

All these colors were prolonged in the rippled reflection to five or six times their proper length. The effect was particularly remarkable in the case of the reds, which were long bands of red perpendicular in the water.

Bats come out fifteen minutes after sunset, and then I hear some clear song sparrow strains, as from a fence-post amid snows in early spring.

Sept. 26. Took my last bath the 24th. Probably shall not bathe again this year. It was chilling cold. It is a warm and very pleasant afternoon, and I walk along the riverside in Merrick's pasture. I hear a faint jingle from some sparrows on the willows, etc., — tree or else song sparrows. Many swamp white oak acorns have turned brown on the trees. Some single red maples are very splendid now, the whole tree bright-scarlet against the cold green pines; now, when very few trees are changed, a most remarkable object in the landscape; seen a mile off. It is too fair to be believed, especially seen against the light.[1] Some are a reddish or else greenish yellow, others with red or yellow cheeks. I suspect that the yellow maples had not scarlet blossoms.

The bunches of panicled cornel are purple, though you see much of the gray under sides of the leaves. *Viburnum dentatum* berries still hold on.

Sept. 28. R. W. E.'s pines are parti-colored, preparing to fall, some of them. The sassafras trees on

[1] [*Excursions*, p. 259; Riv. 318.]

the hill are now wholly a bright orange scarlet as seen from my window, and the small ones elsewhere are also changed. Sweet-briar hips ripe.

As I complain that the voyager to arctic regions, in his description of the scenery, does not enough remind the reader directly or indirectly of the peculiar dreariness of the scene or of the perpetual twilight of the arctic night, so he whose theme is moonlight will find it difficult to illustrate it with the light of the moon alone.[1]

Sept. 29. P. M. — To Lee's Bridge *via* Mt. Misery and return by Conantum.

Yesterday was quite warm, requiring the thinnest coat. To-day is cooler. The elm leaves have in *some* places more than half fallen and strew the ground with thick rustling beds, — as front of Hubbard's, — perhaps earlier than usual.[2]

Bass berries dry and brown. Now is the time to gather barberries.

Looking from the Cliffs, the young oak plain is now probably as brightly colored as it will be. The bright reds appear here to be next the ground, the lower parts of these young trees, and I find on descending that it is commonly so as yet with the scarlet oak, which is the brightest. It is the lower half or two thirds which have changed, and this is surmounted by the slender, still green top. In many cases these

[1] [*Excursions*, p. 326; Riv. 401.]
[2] [In the margin against this paragraph the words "The dry year" are written in pencil.]

Vol. VII

leaves have only begun to be sprinkled with bloody spots and stains, — sometimes as if one had cast up a quart of blood from beneath and stained them. I now see the effect of that long drought on some young oaks, especially black oaks. Their leaves are in many instances all turned to a clear and uniform brown, having so far lost their vitality, but still plump and full-veined and not yet withered. Many are so affected and, of course, show no bright tints. They are hastening to a premature decay. The tops of many young white oaks which had turned are already withered, apparently by frost.

Saw two either pigeon or sparrow hawks, apparently male and female, the one much larger than the other. I see in *many places* the fallen leaves quite thickly covering the ground in the woods. A large flock of crows wandering about and cawing as usual at this season. I hear a very pleasant and now unusual strain on the sunny side of an oak wood from many — I think *F. hyemalis* (?), though I do not get a clear view of them. Even their slight jingling strain is remarkable at this still season. The catbird still mews. I see two ducks alternately diving in smooth water near the shore of Fair Haven Pond. Sometimes both are under at once. The milkweed down is flying at Clematis Ditch.

This evening is quite cool and breezy, with a prolonged white twilight, quite Septemberish.

When I look at the stars, nothing which the astronomers have said attaches to them, they are so simple **and remote.** *Their* knowledge is felt to be all terres-

trial and to concern the earth alone. It suggests that the same is the case with every object, however familiar; our so-called knowledge of it is equally vulgar and remote.

One might say that all views through a telescope or microscope were purely visionary, for it is only by his eye and not by any other sense — not by his whole man — that the beholder is there where he is presumed to be. It is a disruptive mode of viewing as far as the beholder is concerned.

Sept. 30. P. M. — *Via* Assabet to the monarda road.

I am surprised to see that *some* red maples, which were so brilliant a day or two ago, have already shed their leaves, and they cover the land and the water quite thickly. I see a countless fleet of them slowly carried round in the still bay by the Leaning Hemlocks.[1] I find a fine tupelo near Sam Barrett's now all turned scarlet. I find that it has borne much fruit — small oval bluish berries, those I see — and a very little not ripe is still left. Gray calls it blackish-blue. It seems to be contemporary with the sassafras. Both these trees are now particularly forward and conspicuous in their autumnal change. I detect the sassafras by its peculiar orange scarlet half a mile distant. Acorns are generally now turned brown and fallen or falling; the ground is strewn with them and in paths they are crushed by feet and wheels. The white oak ones are dark and the most glossy.

[1] [*Excursions*, p. 267; Riv. 327, 328.]

The clear bright-scarlet leaves of the smooth sumach in many places are curled and drooping, hanging straight down, so as to make a funereal impression, reminding me [of] a red sash and a soldier's funeral. They impress me quite as black crape similarly arranged, the bloody plants.[1]

The conventional acorn of art is of course of no particular species, but the artist might find it worth his while to study Nature's varieties again.

The song sparrow is still about, and the blackbird.

Saw a little bird with a distinct white spot on the wing, yellow about eye, and whitish beneath, which I think must be one of the wrens I saw last spring.

At present the river's brim is no longer browned with button-bushes, for those of their leaves which the frost had touched have already fallen entirely, leaving a thin crop of green ones to take their turn.

[1] [Channing, p. 99.]

II

OCTOBER, 1854

(ÆT. 37)

Oct. 1. The young black birches about Walden, next the south shore, are now commonly clear pale-yellow, very distinct at distance, like bright-yellow white birches, so slender amid the dense growth of oaks and evergreens on the steep shores. The black birches and red maples are the conspicuous trees changed about the pond. Not yet the oaks.

Oct. 7. Went to Plymouth to lecture and survey Watson's grounds. Returned the 15th.

The *Decodon verticillatus* (swamp loosestrife) very abundant, forming isles in the pond on Town Brook on Watson's farm, now turned (methinks it was) a somewhat orange (?) scarlet. Measured a buckthorn on land of N. Russell & Co., bounding on Watson, close by the ruins of the cotton-factory, in five places from the ground to the first branching, or as high as my head. The diameters were 4 feet 8 inches, 4–6, 4–3, 4–2, 4–6. It was full of fruit now *quite* ripe, which Watson plants. The birds eat it.

Saw a small goldenrod in the woods with four very broad rays, a new kind to me. Saw also the English oak; leaf much like our white oak, but acorns large and long, with a long peduncle, and the bark of these

Vol. VII

young trees, twenty or twenty-five feet high, quite smooth. Saw moon-seed, a climbing vine. Also the leaf of the ginkgo tree, of pine-needles run together.

Spooner's garden a wilderness of fruit trees.

Russell is not sure but Eaton has described my rare polygonum.

Oct. 16. In the streets the ash and most of the elm trees are bare of leaves; the red maples also for the most part, *apparently*, at a distance. The pines, too, have fallen.

Oct. 19. 7.15 A. M. — To Westminster by cars; thence on foot to Wachusett Mountain, four miles to Foster's, and two miles thence to mountain-top by road.

The country above Littleton (plowed ground) more or less sugared with snow, the first I have seen. We find a little on the mountain-top. The prevailing tree on this mountain, top and all, is apparently the red oak, which toward and on the top is very low and spreading. Other trees and shrubs which I remember on the top are beech, *Populus tremuliformis*, mountain-ash (looking somewhat like sumach), witch-hazel, white and yellow birch, white pine, black spruce, etc., etc. Most of the deciduous woods *look as if* dead. On the sides, beside red oak, are rock maple, yellow birch, lever-wood, beech, chestnut, shagbark, hemlock, striped maple, witch-hazel, etc., etc.

With a glass you can see vessels in Boston Harbor from the summit, just north of the Waltham hills.

Two white asters, the common ones, not yet quite out

of bloom, — *A. acuminatus* and perhaps *cordifolius* (hearted, with long sharp teeth). The *Geranium Robertianum* in bloom below the woods on the east side.

Oct. 20. Saw the sun rise from the mountain-top. This is the time to look westward. All the villages, steeples, and houses on that side were revealed; but on the east all the landscape was a misty and gilded obscurity. It was worth the while to see westward the countless hills and fields all apparently flat, now white with frost. A little white fog marked the site of many a lake and the course of the Nashua, and in the east horizon the great pond had its own fog mark in a long, low bank of cloud.

Soon after sunrise I saw the pyramidal shadow of the mountain reaching quite across the State, its apex resting on the Green or Hoosac Mountains, appearing as a deep-blue section of a cone there. It rapidly contracted, and its apex approached the mountain itself, and when about three miles distant the whole conical shadow was very distinct. The shadow of the mountain makes some minutes' difference in the time of sunrise to the inhabitants of Hubbardston, within a few miles west.

F. hyemalis, how long?

Saw some very tall and large dead chestnuts in the wood between Foster's and the mountain. Wachusett Pond appeared the best place from which to view the mountain (from a boat). Our host had picked thirty-four bushels of shagbarks last year. *For the most part* they do not rattle out yet, but it is time to gather them. On account of squirrels now is the time.

Oct. 22. This and the last two days Indian-summer weather, following hard on that sprinkling of snow west of Concord.

Pretty hard frosts these nights. Many leaves fell last night, and the Assabet is covered with their fleets. Now they rustle as you walk through them in the woods. Bass trees are bare. The redness of huckleberry bushes is past its prime. I see a snapping turtle, not yet in winter quarters. The chickadees are picking the seeds out of pitch pine cones.

Oct. 25. On Assabet.

The maples being bare, the great hornet nests are exposed. A beautiful, calm Indian-summer afternoon, the withered reeds on the brink reflected in the water.

Oct. 26. P. M. — To Conantum.

As warm as summer. Cannot wear a thick coat. Sit with windows open. I see considerable gossamer on the causeway and elsewhere. Is it the tree sparrows whose jingles I hear? As the weather grows cooler and the woods more silent, I attend to the cheerful notes of chickadees on their sunny sides. Apple trees are generally bare, as well as bass, ash, elm, maple.

Oct. 28. Saturday. The woods begin to look bare, reflected in the water, and I look far in between the stems of the trees under the bank. Birches, which be-

gan to change and fall so early, are still in many places yellow.

Oct. 29. Sunday. Detected a large English cherry in Smith's woods beyond Saw Mill Brook by the peculiar *fresh* orange-scarlet color of its leaves, now that almost all leaves are quite dull or withered. The same in gardens. The gooseberry leaves in our garden and in fields are equally and peculiarly fresh scarlet.

Oct. 31. Rain; still warm.

Ever since October 27th we have had remarkably warm and pleasant Indian summer, with frequent frosts in the morning. Sat with open window for a week.

III

NOVEMBER, 1854

(ÆT. 37)

Nov. 1. It is a little cooler.

Nov. 2. Thursday. P. M. — By boat to Clamshell.

I suspect the clams are partly gone down. May not this movement contribute to compel the muskrats to erect their cabins nearer the brink or channel, in order still to be near their food? Other things being equal, they would have to swim further than before to get the clams in the middle, but now, in addition, the water is beginning to rise and widen the river.

I see larks hovering over the meadow and hear a faint note or two, and a pleasant note from tree sparrows (?).

Sailing past the bank above the railroad, just before a clear sundown, close to the shore on the east side I see a second fainter shadow of the boat, sail, myself, and paddle, etc., directly above and upon the first on the bank. What makes the second? At length I discovered that it was the reflected sun which cast a higher shadow like the true one. As I moved to the west side, the upper shadow rose, grew larger and less perceptible; and at last when I was so near the west shore that I could not see the reflected sun, it disappeared; but then there appeared one upside down in its place!

Nov. 4. Saw a shrike in an apple tree, with apparently a worm in its mouth. The shad-bush buds have expanded into small leafets already. This while surveying on the old Colburn farm.

Nov. 5. Sunday. To White Pond with Charles Wheeler.

Passing the mouth of John Hosmer's hollow near the river, was hailed by him and Anthony Wright, sitting there, to come and see where they had dug for money. There was a hole six feet square and as many deep, and the sand was heaped about over a rod square. Hosmer said that it was dug two or three weeks before, that three men came in a chaise and dug it in the night. They were seen about there by day. Somebody dug near there in June, and then they covered up the hole again. He said they had been digging thereabouts from time to time for a hundred years. I asked him why. He said that Dr. Lee, who lived where Joe Barrett did, told him that old Mr. Wood, who lived in a house very near his (Hosmer's), told him that, one night in Captain Kidd's day, three pirates came to his house with a pair of old-fashioned deer-skin breeches, both legs full of coin, and asked leave to bury it in his cellar. He was afraid, and refused them. They then asked for some earthen pots and shovels and a lanthorn, which he let them have. A woman in the house followed the pirates at a distance down the next hollow on the south, and saw them go along the meadow-side and turn up this hollow, and then, being alone and afraid, she returned. Soon after the men returned with the tools and an old-fashioned hat full of the coin (holding about a quart), which they gave to Wood. He, being afraid, buried it in his cellar, but afterward, becoming a poor man, dug it up and used it. A bailiff made some inquiry hereabouts after the pirates.

Hosmer said that one thing which confirmed the diggers in their belief was the fact that when he was a little boy, plowing one day with his father on the hillside, they found three old-fashioned bottles bottom upward but empty under the plow. Somebody consulted Moll Pitcher, who directed to dig at a certain distance from an apple tree on a line with the bottles, and then they would find the treasure.

I think it is the fox-colored sparrow I see in flocks and hear sing now by wood-sides.

Nov. 6. Surveying on Colburn place.

It is suddenly cold. Pools frozen so as to bear, and ground frozen so that it is difficult, if not impossible, to force down a stake in plowed ground. Was that a fish hawk I saw flying over the Assabet, or a goshawk? White beneath, with slender wings.

Nov. 8. I can still rake clams near the shore, but they are chiefly in the weeds, I think. I see a snipe-like bird by riverside this windy afternoon, which goes off with a sound like creaking tackle.

Nov. 10. P. M. — Sail to Ball's Hill with W. E. C. See where the muskrats have eaten much ponte-

deria root. Got some donacia grubs for Harris, but find no chrysalids. The sight of the masses of yellow hastate leaves and flower-buds of the yellow lily, already four or six inches long, at the bottom of the river, reminds me that nature is prepared for an infinity of springs yet.

Nov. 11. Minott heard geese go over night before last, about 8 P. M. Therien, too, heard them "yelling like anything" over Walden, where he is cutting, the same evening. He cut down a tree with a flying squirrel on it; often sees them. Receive this evening a letter in French and three "ouvrages" from the Abbé Rougette in Louisiana.

Nov. 13. It has rained hard the 11th, 12th, and 13th, and the river is *at last* decidedly rising. On Friday, 10th, it was still at summer level.

Nov. 14. The river is slightly over the meadows. The willow twigs on the right of the Red Bridge causeway are bright greenish-yellow and reddish as in the spring. Also on the right railroad sand-bank at Heywood's meadow. Is it because they are preparing their catkins now against another spring? The first wreck line — of pontederia, sparganium, etc. — is observable.

Nov. 15. The first snow, a mere sugaring which went off the next morning.

Nov. 16. P. M. — Sailed to Hubbard's Bridge.

Almost every muskrat's house is covered by the flood, though they were unusually high, as well as numerous, and the river is not nearly so high as last year. I see where they have begun to raise them another story. A few cranberries begin to wash up, and rails, boards, etc., may now be collected by wreckers.

Nov. 17. Paddled up river to Clamshell and sailed back.

I think it must have been a fish hawk which I saw hovering over the meadow and my boat (a raw cloudy afternoon), now and then sustaining itself in one place a hundred feet or more above the water, intent on a fish, with a hovering or fluttering motion of the wings somewhat like a kingfisher. Its wings were very long, slender, and curved in outline of front edge. I think there was some white on rump. It alighted near the top of an oak within rifle-shot of me and my boat, afterward on the tip-top of a maple by waterside, looking very large.

Nov. 18. Saw sixty geese go over the Great Fields, in one waving line, broken from time to time by their crowding on each other and vainly endeavoring to form into a harrow, honking all the while.

Nov. 20. To Philadelphia. 7 A. M., to Boston; 9 A. M., Boston to New York, by express train, land route.

See the reddish soil (red sandstone?) all through Connecticut. Beyond Hartford a range of rocky hills

crossing the State on each side the railroad, the eastern one very precipitous, and apparently terminating at East Rock at New Haven. Pleasantest part of the whole route between Springfield and Hartford, along the river; perhaps include the hilly region this side of Springfield. Reached Canal Street at 5 P. M., or candle-light.

Started for Philadelphia from foot of Liberty Street at 6 P. M., *via* Newark, etc., etc., Bordentown, etc., etc., Camden Ferry, to Philadelphia, all in the dark. Saw only the glossy panelling of the cars reflected out into the dark, like the magnificent lit façade of a row of edifices reaching all the way to Philadelphia, except when we stopped and a lanthorn or two showed us a ragged boy and the dark buildings of some New Jersey town. Arrive at 10 P. M.; time, four hours from New York, thirteen from Boston, fifteen from Concord. Put up at Jones's Exchange Hotel, 77 Dock Street; lodgings thirty-seven and a half cents per night, meals separate; not to be named with French's in New York; next door to the fair of the Franklin Institute, then open, and over against the Exchange, in the neighborhood of the printing-offices.

Nov. 21. Looked from the cupola of the State-House, where the Declaration of Independence was declared. The best view of the city I got. Was interested in the squirrels, gray and black, in Independence and Washington Squares. Heard that they have, or have had, deer in Logan Square. The squirrels are fed, and live in boxes in the trees in the winter. Fine view from Fairmount water-works. The line of the hypothenuse of the gable end of Girard College was apparently deflected in the middle six inches or more, reminding me of the anecdote of the church of the Madeleine in Paris.

Was admitted into the building of the Academy of Natural Sciences by a Mr. Durand of the botanical department, Mr. Furness applying to him. The carpenters were still at work adding four stories (!) of galleries to the top. These four (Furness thought all of them, I am not sure but Durand referred to one side only) to be devoted to the birds. It is said to be the largest collection of birds in the world. They belonged to the son of Masséna (Prince of Essling?), and were sold at auction, and bought by a Yankee for $22,000, over all the crowned heads of Europe, and presented to the Academy.[1] Other collections, also, are added to this. The Academy has received great donations. There is Morton's collection of crania, with (I suppose a *cast* from) an Indian skull found in an Ohio mound; a polar bear killed by Dr. Kane; a male moose not so high as the female which we shot; a European elk (a skeleton) about seven feet high, with horns each about five feet long and *tremendously*

[1] [The "Yankee" referred to was Dr. Thomas B. Wilson, once president of the Academy, and the sum named includes the prices of other purchases made by him, chief of which was that of the Gould collection of Australian birds. Fifty thousand francs was the amount paid for the Masséna collection. See Dr. Wilson's amusing account of the transaction as quoted by Mr. Witmer Stone in *The Auk*, 1899, p. 174. The original owners of this collection were General Masséna and his son Victor, Duke of Rivoli and Prince of Essling.]

heavy; grinders, etc., of the *Mastodon giganteum* from Barton County, Missouri; etc., etc. Zinzinger was named as of the geological department.

In Philadelphia and also New York an ornamental tree with bunches of seed-vessels supplying the place of leaves now. I suppose it the ailanthus, or Tree of Heaven. What were those trees with long, black sickle-shaped pods? I did not see Steinhauser's Burd family[1] at St. Stephen's Church. The American Philosophical Society is described as a company of old women.

In the narrow market-houses in the middle of the streets, was struck by the neat-looking women marketers with full cheeks. Furness described a lotus identical with an Egyptian one as found somewhere down the river below Philadelphia; also spoke of a spotted chrysalis which he had also seen in Massachusetts. There was a mosquito about my head at night. Lodged at the United States Hotel, opposite the Girard (formerly United States) Bank.

Nov. 22. Left at 7.30 A. M. for New York, by boat to Tacony and rail *via* Bristol, Trenton, Princeton (near by), New Brunswick, Rahway, Newark, etc. Uninteresting, except the boat. The country very level, — red sandstone (?) sand, — apparently all New Jersey except the northern part. Saw wheat stubble and winter wheat come up like rye. Was that Jamestownweed with a prickly bur? Seen also in Connecticut.

[1] [A marble group entitled "The Angel of the Resurrection," erected to the memory of the children of Edward Shippen Burd.]

Many Dutch barns. Just after leaving Newark, an extensive marsh, between the railroad and the Kill, full of the *Arundo Phragmites*, I should say, which had been burnt over.

Went to Crystal Palace; admired the houses on Fifth Avenue, the specimens of coal at the Palace, one fifty feet thick as it was cut from the mine, in the form of a square column, iron and copper ore, etc. Saw sculptures and paintings innumerable, and armor from the Tower of London, some of the Eighth Century. Saw Greeley; Snow, the commercial editor of the *Tribune;* Solon Robinson; Fry, the musical critic, etc.; and others. Greeley carried me to the new opera-house, where I heard Grisi and her troupe. First, at Barnum's Museum, I saw the camelopards, said to be one eighteen the other sixteen feet high. I should say the highest stood about fifteen feet high at most (twelve or thirteen ordinarily). The body was only about five feet long. Why has it horns, but for ornament? Looked through his diorama, and found the houses all over the world much alike. Greeley appeared to know and be known by everybody; was admitted free to the opera, and we were led by a page to various parts of the house at different times. Saw at Museum some large flakes of cutting arrowhead stone made into a sort of wide cleavers, also a hollow stone tube, probably from mounds.

Nov. 26. What that little long-sharp-nosed mouse I found in the Walden road to-day? Brown above, gray beneath, black incisors, five toes with claws on

each foot, long snout with small blunt black extremity, many mustachios, eyes far forward, feet light or dirty white, tail 1½ inches long, whole length 3¾ inches; on causeway.

Nov. 28. Paddled to Clamshell.

Still very clear and bright as well as comfortable weather. River not so high as on the 16th.

Were those plover which just after sunset flew low over the bank above the railroad and alighted in the opposite meadow, with some white in tails like larks, gray birds, rather heavier than robins?

Nov. 30. P. M. — Sail down river.

No ice, but strong cold wind; river slightly over meadows. Was that large diver which was on the edge of the shore and scooted away down-stream as usual, throwing the water about for a quarter of a mile, then diving, some time afterward flying up-stream over our head, the goosander or red-breasted merganser? It was large, with, I should say, a white breast, long reddish bill, bright-red or pink on sides or beneath, reddish-brown crest, white speculum, upper part of throat dark, lower white with breast.

IV

DECEMBER, 1854

(ÆT. 37)

Dec. 2. Got up my boat and housed it, ice having formed about it.

Dec. 3. Sunday. The first snow of consequence fell in the evening, very damp (wind northeast); five or six inches deep in morning, after very high wind in the night.

Snowbirds in garden in the midst of the snow in the afternoon.

Dec. 4. P. M. — Down railroad to Walden.

Walden went down quite rapidly about the middle of November, leaving the isthmus to Emerson's meadow bare. Flint's has been very low all summer. The northeast sides of the trees are thickly incrusted with snowy shields, visible afar, the snow was so damp (at Boston it turned to rain). This had none of the dry delicate powdery beauties of a common first snow.

Already the bird-like birch scales dot the snow.

Dec. 5. Very cold last night. Probably river skimmed over in some places. The damp snow with water beneath (in all five or six inches deep and not drifted, notwithstanding the wind) is frozen solid, making a

crust which bears well. This, I think, is unusual at this stage of the winter.

Dec. 6. To Providence to lecture.

I see thick ice and boys skating all the way to Providence, but know not when it froze, I have been so busy writing my lecture; probably the night of the 4th.

In order to go to Blue Hill by Providence Railroad, stop at Readville Station (Dedham Low Plain once), eight miles; the hill apparently two miles east. Was struck with the Providence depot, its towers and great length of brick. Lectured in it.

Went to R. Williams's Rock on the Blackstone with Newcomb and thence to hill with an old fort atop in Seekonk, Mass., on the east side of the Bay, whence a fine view down it. At lecture spoke with a Mr. Clark and Vaughn and Eaton.

After lecturing twice this winter I feel that I am in danger of cheapening myself by trying to become a successful lecturer, *i. e.*, to interest my audiences. I am disappointed to find that most that I am and value myself for is lost, or worse than lost, on my audience. I fail to get even the attention of the mass. I should suit them better if I suited myself less. I feel that the public demand an average man, — average thoughts and manners, — not originality, nor even absolute excellence. You cannot interest them except as you are like them and sympathize with them. I would rather that my audience come to me than that I should go to them, and so they be sifted; *i. e.*, I would rather write books than lectures. That is fine, this coarse.

To read to a promiscuous audience who are at your mercy the fine thoughts you solaced yourself with far away is as violent as to fatten geese by cramming, and in this case they do not get fatter.

Dec. 7. Walked through Olneyville in Johnston, two and a half or three miles west of Providence.

Harris tells me that since he exchanged a duplicate Jesuit Relation for one he had not with the Montreal men, *all* theirs have been burnt. He has two early ones which I have not seen.

Dec. 8. P. M. — Up river and meadow on ice to Hubbard Bridge and thence to Walden.

Winter has come unnoticed by me, I have been so busy writing. This is the life most lead in respect to Nature. How different from my habitual one! It is hasty, coarse, and trivial, as if you were a spindle in a factory. The other is leisurely, fine, and glorious, like a flower. In the first case you are merely getting your living; in the second you live as you go along. You travel only on roads of the proper grade without jar or running off the track, and sweep round the hills by beautiful curves.

Here is the river frozen over in many places, I am not sure whether the fourth night or later, but the skating is hobbly or all hobbled like a coat of mail or thickly bossed shield, apparently sleet frozen in water. Very little smooth ice. How black the water where the river is open when I look from the light, by contrast with the surrounding white, the ice and

snow! A black artery here and there concealed under a pellicle of ice.

Went over the fields on the crust to Walden, over side of Bear Garden. Already foxes have left their tracks. How the crust shines afar, the sun now setting! There is a glorious clear sunset sky, soft and delicate and warm even like a pigeon's neck. Why do the mountains never look so fair as from my native fields?

Dec. 9. Surveying for T. Holden.

A cold morning. What is that green *pipes* on the *side-hill* at Nut Meadow on his land, looking at first like green-briar cut off?[1] It forms a dense bed about a dozen rods along the side of the bank in the woods, a rod in width, rising to ten or twelve feet above the swamp. White Pond mostly skimmed over. The scouring-rush is as large round as a bulrush, forming dense green beds conspicuous and interesting above the snow, an evergreen rush.

C. says he saw three larks on the 5th.

Dec. 10. P. M. — To Nut Meadow.

Weather warmer; snow softened. Saw a large flock of snow buntings (quite white against woods, at any rate), though it is quite warm. Snow-fleas in paths; first I have seen. Hear the small woodpecker's whistle; not much else; only crows and partridges else, and chickadees. How quickly the snow feels the warmer wind! The crust which was so firm and rigid is now suddenly softened and there is much water in the road.

[1] *Equisetum hyemale* (scouring-rush, shave-grass).

Dec. 11. P. M. — To Bare Hill.

C. says he found Fair Haven frozen over last Friday, *i. e.* the 8th.[1] I find Flint's frozen to-day, and how long?

We have now those early, still, clear winter sunsets over the snow. It is but mid-afternoon when I see the sun setting far through the woods, and there is that peculiar clear vitreous greenish sky in the west, as it were a molten gem. The day is short; it seems to be composed of two twilights merely;[2] the morning and the evening twilight make the whole day. You must make haste to do the work of the day before it is dark. I hear rarely a bird except the chickadee, or perchance a jay or crow. A gray rabbit scuds away over the crust in the swamp on the edge of the Great Meadows beyond Peter's. A partridge goes off, and, coming up, I see where she struck the snow first with her wing, making five or six as it were finger-marks.

Dec. 14. P. M. — With C. up north bank of Assabet to bridge.

Good sleighing still, with but little snow. A warm, thawing day. The river is open almost its whole length. It is a beautifully smooth mirror within an icy frame. It is well to improve such a time to walk by it. This strip of water of irregular width over the channel, between broad fields of ice, looks like a polished silver mirror, or like another surface of polished ice, and often is distinguished from the surrounding ice only by its reflections. I have rarely seen any reflections

[1] How much before?   [2] [Channing, p. 99.]

— of weeds, willows, and elms, and the houses of the village — so distinct, the stems so black and distinct; for they contrast not with a green meadow but clear white ice, to say nothing of the silvery surface of the water. Your eye slides first over a plane surface of smooth ice of one color to a water surface of silvery smoothness, like a gem set in ice, and reflecting the weeds and trees and houses and clouds with singular beauty. The reflections are particularly simple and distinct. These twigs are not referred to and confounded with a broad green meadow from which they spring, as in summer, but, instead of that dark-green ground, absorbing the light, is this abrupt white field of ice. We see so little open and smooth water at this season that I am inclined to improve such an opportunity to walk along the river, and moreover the meadows, being more or less frozen, make it more feasible than in summer.

I am singularly interested by the sight of the shrubs which grow along rivers, rising now above the snow, with buds and catkins, — the willows, alders, sweetgale, etc. At our old bathing-place on the Assabet, saw two ducks, which at length took to wing. They had *large* dark heads, dark wings, and clear white breasts. I think they were buffle-headed or spirit ducks.

Dec. 15. Up riverside *via* Hubbard Bath, p. m.

I see again a large flock of what I called buntings on the 10th, also another flock surely not buntings, perhaps *Fringilla linaria*. May they not all be these? How interesting a few clean, dry weeds on the shore

Vol. VII

a dozen rods off, seen distinctly against the smooth, reflecting water between ice! I see on the ice, half a dozen rods from shore, a small brown striped grub, and again a black one five eighths of an inch long. The last has apparently melted quite a cavity in the ice. How came they there?

I saw on the 11th an abundance of dried huckleberries on Bare Hill, still holding. They are such as dried ripe prematurely on account of the drought. I do not perceive any sweetness. How handsome the narrow, regularly toothed brown leaves of the sweetfern now above the snow! — handsome in their sere state! The buds of the bass are pretty now, they are a clear light red on short ash (?) twigs.

Dec. 18. P. M. — Down railroad *via* Andromeda Ponds to river.

Snowed a little finely last night and this forenoon. I see a few squirrels' tracks in the woods and, here and there in one or two places, where a mouse's gallery approached the surface. The powdery surface is broken by it. I am surprised to find in the Andromeda Ponds, especially the westernmost one, north side, an abundance of decodon, or swamp loosestrife. Where a partridge took to wing I find the round red buds of the high blueberry plucked about the swamps.

Dec. 19. P. M. — Skated a half-mile up Assabet and then to foot of Fair Haven Hill.

This is the first tolerable skating. Last night was so cold that the river closed up almost everywhere, and

made good skating where there had been no ice to catch the snow of the night before. First there is the snow ice on the sides, somewhat rough and brown or yellowish spotted where the water overflowed the ice on each side yesterday, and next, over the middle, the new dark smooth ice, and, where the river is wider than usual, a thick fine gray ice, marbled, where there was probably a thin ice yesterday. Probably the top froze as the snow fell. I am surprised to find how rapidly and easily I get along, how soon I am at this brook or that bend in the river, which it takes me so long to reach on the bank or by water. I can go more than double the usual distance before dark. It takes a little while to learn to trust the new black ice. I look for cracks to see how thick it is.

Near the island I saw a muskrat close by swimming in an open reach. He was always headed up-stream, a great proportion of the head out of water, and his whole length visible, though the root of the tail is about level with the water. Now and then he [stopped] swimming and floated down-stream, still keeping his head pointed up with his tail. It is surprising how dry he looks, as if that back was never immersed in the water.

It is apt to be melted at the bridges about the piers, and there is a flow of water over the ice there. There is a fine, smooth gray marbled ice on the bays, which apparently began to freeze when it was snowing night before last. There is a marbling of dark where there was clear water amid the snow. Now and then a crack crosses it, and the water, oozing out, has frozen on each side of it two or three inches thick, and sometimes as many feet wide. These give you a slight jolt.

Off Clamshell I heard and saw a large flock of *Fringilla linaria* over the meadow. No doubt it was these I saw on the 15th. (But I saw then, and on the 10th, a larger and whiter bird also; may have been the bunting.) Suddenly they turn aside in their flight and dash across the river to a large white birch fifteen rods off, which plainly they had distinguished so far. I afterward saw many more in the Potter swamp up the river. They were commonly brown or dusky above, streaked with yellowish white or ash, and more or less white or ash beneath. Most had a crimson crown or frontlet, and a few a crimson neck and breast, very handsome. Some with a bright-crimson crown and clear-white breasts. I suspect that these were young males. They keep up an incessant twittering, varied from time to time with some mewing notes, and occasionally, for some unknown reason, they will all suddenly dash away with that universal loud note (twitter) like a bag of nuts. They are busily clustered in the tops of the birches, picking the seeds out of the catkins, and sustain themselves in all kinds of attitudes, sometimes head downwards, while about this. Common as they are now, and were winter before last, I saw none last winter.

Dec. 20. 7 A. M. — To Hill.

Said to be the coldest morning as yet. The river appears to be frozen everywhere. Where was water

last night is a firm bridge of ice this morning. The snow which has blown on to the ice has taken the form of regular star-shaped crystals, an inch in diameter. Sometimes these are arranged in a spear three feet long quite straight. I see the mother-o'-pearl tints now, at sunrise, on the clouds high over the eastern horizon before the sun has risen above the low bank in the east. The sky in the eastern horizon has that same greenish-vitreous, gem-like appearance which it has at sundown, as if it were of perfectly clear glass, — with the green tint of a large mass of glass. Here are some crows already seeking their breakfast in the orchard, and I hear a red squirrel's reproof. The woodchoppers are making haste to their work far off, walking fast to keep warm, before the sun has risen, their ears and hands well covered, the dry, cold snow squeaking under their feet. They will be warmer after they have been at work an hour.

P. M. — Skated to Fair Haven with C.

C.'s skates are not the best, and beside he is far from an easy skater, so that, as he said, it was killing work for him. Time and again the perspiration actually dropped from his forehead on to the ice, and it froze in long icicles on his beard. Yet he kept up his spirits and his fun, said he [had] seen much more suffering than I, etc., etc.

It has been a glorious winter day, its elements so simple, — the sharp clear air, the white snow everywhere covering the earth, and the polished ice. Cold as it is, the sun seems warmer on my back even than

in summer, as if its rays met with less obstruction. And then the air is so beautifully still; there is not an insect in the air, and hardly a leaf to rustle. If there is a grub out, you are sure to detect it on the snow or ice. The shadows of the Clamshell Hills are beautifully blue as I look back half a mile at them, and, in some places, where the sun falls on it, the snow has a pinkish tinge. I am surprised to find how fast the dog can run in a straight line on the ice. I am not sure that I can beat him on skates, but I can turn much shorter. It is very fine skating for the most part. All of the river that was not frozen before, and therefore not covered with snow on the 18th, is now frozen quite smoothly; but in some places for a quarter of a mile it is uneven like frozen suds, in rounded pancakes, as when bread spews out in baking. At sundown or before, it begins to belch. It is so cold that only in one place did I see a drop of water flowing out on the ice.

Dec. 21. P. M. — To Walden and Fair Haven Ponds and down river.

It snowed slightly this morning, so as to cover the [ground] half an inch deep. Walden is frozen over, apparently about two inches thick. It must have frozen, the whole of it, since the snow of the 18th, — probably the night of the 18th. It is very thickly [covered with] what C. calls ice-rosettes, *i. e.* those small pinches of crystallized snow, — as thickly as if it had snowed in that form. I think it is a sort of hoar frost on the ice. It was all done last night, for we see them thickly clus-

tered about our skate-tracks on the river, where it was quite bare yesterday.

We are tempted to call these the finest days of the year. Take Fair Haven Pond, for instance, a perfectly level plain of white snow, untrodden as yet by any fisherman, surrounded by snow-clad hills, dark evergreen woods, and reddish oak leaves, so pure and still. The last rays of the sun falling on the Baker Farm reflect a clear pink color. I see the feathers of a partridge strewn along on the snow a long distance, the work of some hawk perhaps, for there is no track.

What a grovelling appetite for profitless jest and amusement our countrymen have! Next to a good dinner, at least, they love a good joke, — to have their sides tickled, to laugh sociably, as in the East they bathe and are shampooed. Curators of lyceums write to me: —

DEAR SIR, — I hear that you have a lecture of some humor. Will you do us the favor to read it before the Bungtown Institute?

Dec. 24. Some three inches of snow fell last night and this morning, concluding with a fine rain, which produced a slight glaze, the first of the winter. This gives the woods a hoary aspect and increases the stillness by making the leaves immovable even in considerable wind.

Dec. 25. To New Bedford *via* Cambridge.[1]

[1] [The entries for Dec. 25th and 26th are printed in *Daniel Ricketson and his Friends,* edited by Anna and Walton Ricketson, Boston, 1902.]

I think that I never saw a denser growth than the young white cedar in swamps on the Taunton & New Bedford Railroad. In most places it looked as if there was not room for a man to pass between the young trees. That part of the country is remarkably level and wooded. The evergreen prinos very common in the low ground. At New Bedford saw the casks of oil covered with seaweed to prevent fire. The weed holds moisture. Town not lively; whalers abroad at this season.

Ricketson has Bewick's "British Birds," two vols.;
"   " Æsop's Fables," one vol.;
"   " Select Fables," one vol.,
                    larger (partly the same);
"   " Quadrupeds," one vol.

Has taken some pains to obtain them. The tail-pieces were the attraction to him. He suggested to Howitt to write his "Abodes of the Poets." [1]

Dec. 26. At Ricketson's.

I do not remember to have ever seen such a day as this in Concord. There is no snow here (though there has been excellent sleighing at Concord since the 5th), but it is very muddy, the frost coming out of the ground as in spring with us. I went to walk in the woods with R. It was wonderfully warm and pleasant, and the cockerels crowed just as in a spring day at home. I felt the winter breaking up in me, and if I had been at home I should have tried to write poetry. They told me that this was not a rare day there, that they

[1] [Homes and Haunts of the British Poets.]

---

had little or no winter such as we have, and it was owing to the influence of the Gulf Stream, which was only sixty miles from Nantucket at the nearest, or one hundred and twenty miles from them. In midwinter, when the wind was southeast or even southwest, they frequently had days as warm and debilitating as in summer. There is a difference of about a degree in latitude between Concord and New Bedford, but far more in climate.

The American holly is quite common there, with its red berries still holding on, and is now their Christmas evergreen. I heard the larks sing strong and sweet, and saw robins. R. lives in that part of New Bedford three miles north of the town called the Head of the River, i. e. the Acushnet River. There is a Quaker meeting-house there. Such an ugly shed, without a tree or bush about it, which they call their meeting-house (without steeple, of course) is altogether repulsive to me, like a powder-house or grave. And even the quietness and perhaps unworldliness of an aged Quaker has something ghostly and saddening about it, as it were a mere preparation for the grave.

R. said that pheasants from England (where they are not indigenous) had been imported into Naushon and were now killed there.

Dec. 27. To Nantucket via Hyannis in misty rain.

On Cape Cod saw the hills through the mist covered with cladonias. A head wind and rather rough passage of three hours to Nantucket, the water being thirty miles over. Captain Edward W. Gardiner (where I

---

spent the evening) thought there was a beach at Barnegat similar to that at Cape Cod. Mr. Barney, formerly a Quaker minister there, who was at Gardiner's, told of one Bunker of Nantucket in old times, " who had eight sons, and steered each in his turn to the killing of a whale." Gardiner said you must have been a-whaling there before you could be married, and must have struck a whale before you could dance. They do not think much of crossing from Hyannis in a small boat, — in pleasant weather, that is, — but they can safely do it. A boy was drifted across thus in a storm in a rowboat about two years ago. By luck he struck Nantucket. The outline of the island is continually changing. The whalers now go chiefly to Behring's Straits, and everywhere between 35 N. and S. latitude and catch several kinds of whales. It was Edmund Gardiner of New Bedford (a relative of Edward's) who was carried down by a whale, and Hussey of Nantucket who, I believe, was one to draw lots to see who should be eaten. As for communication with the mainland being interrupted, Gardiner remembers when thirty-one mails were landed at once, which, taking out Sundays, made five weeks and one day. The snow ten days ago fell about two inches deep, but melted instantly.

At the Ocean House I copied from William Coffin's Map of the town (1834) this: 30,590 acres, including 3 isles beside. 1050 are fresh ponds; about 750, peat swamp. Clay in all parts. But only granite or gneiss boulders.

Dec. 28. A misty rain as yesterday. Captain Gar-

---

diner carried me to Siasconset in his carriage. He has got from forty to forty-five or fifty bushels of corn to an acre from his land. Wished to know how to distinguish guinea cocks from guinea hens. He is extensively engaged in raising pines on the island. There is not a tree to be seen, except such as are set out about houses. The land is worth commonly from a dollar to a dollar and a half. He showed me several lots of his, of different ages, — one tract of three hundred acres sown in rows with a planter, where the young trees, two years old, were just beginning to green the ground, — and I saw one of Norway pine and our pitch mixed, eight years old, which looked quite like a forest at a distance. The Norway pines had grown the fastest, with a longer shoot, and had a bluer look at a distance, more like the white pine. The American pitch pines have a reddish, crisped look at top. Some are sown in rows, some broadcast. At first he was alarmed to find that the ground moles had gone along in the furrows directly under the plants and so injured the roots as to kill many of the trees, and he sowed over again. He was also discouraged to find that a sort of spindle-worm had killed the leading shoot of a great part of his neighbors' older trees. These plantations must very soon change the aspect of the island. His common pitch pine seed, obtained from the Cape, cost him about twenty dollars a bushel at least, about a dollar a quart, with the wings, and they told him it took about eighty bushels of cones to make one such bushel of seeds. I was surprised to hear that the Norway pine seed without the wings, imported from France, had cost not quite $200 a bushel delivered at New York or Philadelphia. He has ordered eight hogsheads (! ! !) of the last, clear wingless seeds, at this rate. I *think* he said it took about a gallon to sow an acre. He had tried to get white pine seed, but in vain. The cones had not contained any of late (?). This looks as if he meant to sow a good part of the island, though he said he might sell some of the seed. It is an interesting enterprise.

Half-way to Siasconset I saw the old corn-hills where they had formerly cultivated, the authorities laying out a new tract for this purpose each year. This island must look exactly like a prairie, except that the view in clear weather is bounded by the sea. Saw crows, saw and heard larks frequently, and saw robins; but most abundant, running along the ruts or circling about just over the ground in small flocks, what the inhabitants call snowbirds, a gray bunting-like bird about the size of the snow bunting. Can it be the seaside finch? or the Savannah sparrow? or the shore lark?

Gardiner said that they had pigeon, hen, and other hawks, but there are no places for them to breed; also owls, which must breed, for he had seen their young. A few years ago some one imported a dozen partridges from the mainland, but, though some were seen for a year or two, not one had been seen for some time, and they were thought to be extinct. He thought the raccoons, which had been very numerous, might have caught them. In Harrison days some coons were imported and turned loose, and they multiplied

very fast and became quite a pest, killing hens, etc., and were killed in turn. Finally they turned out and hunted them with hounds and killed seventy-five at one time, since which he had not heard of any. There were foxes once, but none now, and no indigenous animal bigger than a "ground mole."

The nearest approach to woods that I saw was the swamps, where the blueberries, maples, etc., are higher than one's head. I saw, as I rode, high blueberry bushes and maple in the swamps, huckleberries, shrub oaks, uva-ursi (which he called mealy plum), gaultheria, beach plum, clethra, mayflower (well budded). Also withered poverty-grass, goldenrods, asters. In the swamps are cranberries, and I saw one carting the vines home to set out, which also many are doing. G. described what he made out to be "star-grass" as common.

Saw at Siasconset perhaps fifty little houses, but almost every one empty. Saw some peculiar horse-carts for conveying fish up the bank, made like a wheelbarrow, with a whole iron-bound barrel for the wheel, a rude square box for the body, resting on the shafts, and the horse to draw it after him. The barrel makes a good wheel in the sand. They may get seaweed in them. A man asked thirty-seven cents for a horse-cart-load of seaweed carried a quarter of a mile from the shore. G. pointed out the house of a singular old hermit and genealogist, over seventy years old, who, for thirty years *at least*, has lived alone and devoted his thoughts to genealogy. He knows the genealogy of the whole island, and a relative supports him by

making genealogical charts from his dictation for those who will pay for them. He at last lives in a very filthy manner, and G. helped clean his house when he was absent about two years ago. They took up three barrels of dirt in his room.

Ascended the lighthouse at Sancoty Head. The mist still prevented my seeing off and around the island. I saw the eggs (?) of some creature in dry masses as big as my fist, like the skins of so many beans, on the beach. G. told me of a boy who, a few years since, stole near to some wild geese which had alighted, and, rushing on them, seized two before they could rise, and, though he was obliged to let one go, secured the other.

Visited the museum at the Athenæum. Various South Sea implements, etc., etc., brought home by whalers.

The last Indian, not of pure blood, died this very month, and I saw his picture with a basket of huckleberries in his hand.

Dec. 29. Nantucket to Concord at 7.30 A. M.

Still in mist. The fog was so thick that we were lost on the water; stopped and sounded many times. The clerk said the depth varied from three to eight fathoms between the island and Cape. Whistled and listened for the locomotive's answer, but probably heard only the echo of our own whistle at first, but at last the locomotive's whistle and the life-boat bell.

I forgot to say yesterday that there was at one place an almost imperceptible rise not far west of Siasconset,

to a slight ridge or swell running from Tom Never's Head northward to (John) Gibbs's Swamp. This conceals the town of Nantucket. (John Gibbs was the name of the Indian Philip came after.) This, seen a mile off through the mist which concealed the relative distance of the base and summit, appeared like an abrupt hill, though an extremely gradual swell.

At the end of Obed Macy's History of Nantucket are some verses signed "Peter Folger, 1676." As for the sin which God would punish by the Indian war, —

> " Sure 't is not chiefly for those sins
>   that magistrates do name,"

but for the sin of persecution and the like, the banishing and whipping of godly men.

> " The cause of this their suffering
>   was not for any sin,
> But for the witness that they bare
>   against babes sprinkling.

>   .   .   .   .

> " The church may now go stay at home,
>   there's nothing for to do;
> Their work is all cut out by law,
>   and almost made up too.

>   .   .   .   .

> " 'T is like that some may think and say,
>   our war would not remain,
> If so be that a thousand more
>   of natives were but slain.

"Alas! these are but foolish thoughts;
    God can make more arise,
    And if that there were none at all,
    He can make war with flies."

Dec. 31. P. M. — On river to Fair Haven Pond.

A beautiful, clear, not very cold day. The shadows on the snow are indigo-blue. The pines look very dark. The white oak leaves are a cinnamon-color, the black and red (?) oak leaves a reddish brown or leather-color. I see mice and rabbit and fox tracks on the meadow. Once a partridge rises from the alders and skims across the river at its widest part just before me; a fine sight. On the edge of A. Wheeler's cranberry meadow I see the track of an otter made since yesterday morning. How glorious the perfect stillness and peace of the winter landscape !

V

JANUARY, 1855

(ÆT. 37)

Jan. 1. P. M. — Skated to Pantry Brook with C.

All the tolerable skating was a narrow strip, often only two or three feet wide, between the frozen spew and the broken ice of the middle.

Jan. 2. I see, in the path near Goose Pond, where the rabbits have eaten the bark of smooth sumachs and young locusts rising above the snow; also barberry. Yesterday we saw the pink light on the snow within a rod of us. The shadow of the bridges, etc., on the snow was a dark indigo blue.

Jan. 4. To Worcester to lecture.

Visited the Antiquarian Library of twenty-two or twenty-three thousand volumes. It is richer in pamphlets and newspapers than Harvard. One alcove contains Cotton Mather's library, chiefly theological works, reading which exclusively you might live in his days and believe in witchcraft. Old leather-bound tomes, many of them as black externally as if they had been charred with fire. Time and fire have the same effect. Haven said that the Rev. Mr. Somebody had spent almost every day the past year in that alcove.

Saw after my lecture a young negro who introduced

Vol. VII

himself as a native of Africa, Leo L. Lloyd, who lectures on "Young Africa!!" I never heard of anything but old Africa before.

Higginson told me of a simple, strong-minded man named Dexter Broad, who was at my lecture, whom I *should* see.

Jan. 5. A. M. — Walked to Quinsigamond Pond *via* Quinsigamond Village, to southerly end, and returned by Floating Bridge.

Saw the straw-built wigwam of an Indian from St. Louis (Rapids?), Canada, — apparently a half-breed. Not being able to buy straw, he had made it chiefly of dry grass, which he had cut in a meadow with his knife. It was against a bank and partly of earth all round, the straw or grass laid on horizontal poles and kept down by similar ones outside, like our thatching. Makes them of straw often in Canada. Can make one, if he has the straw, in one day. The door, on hinges, was of straw also, put on perpendicularly, pointed at top to fit the roof. The roof steep, six or eight inches thick. He was making baskets wholly of sugar maple; could find no black ash. Sewed or bound the edge with maple also. Did not look up once while [we] were there. There was a fireplace of stone, oven-like, running out one side and covered with earth. It was the nest of a large meadow mouse. Had he ever hunted moose? When he was down at Green Island. Where was that? Oh, far down, very far! Caught seals there. No books down that way.

Saw men catching minnows for fishing through

large holes in the ice of the Blackstone. At Quinsigamond Village, a Mr. Washburn showed me the wire rolling and drawing mill in which he is concerned. All sorts of scrap iron is first heated to a welding heat in masses of about two hundredweight, then rolled between vast iron rollers in successive grooves till it is reduced to long rods little more than [an] inch in diameter. These are cut up by powerful shears into lengths of about three feet, heated again, and rolled between other rollers in grooves successively of various forms, — square, oval, round, diamond, etc., which part of the work only one man in the concern fully understood and kept secret. It was here rolled and reduced to a large-sized wire maybe three eighths of an inch in diameter, of which screws are made. At this stage, first, it begins to be *drawn*, though it must be heated again in the course of the drawing to restore its ductility. Make a great deal of telegraph-wire, and for pail-bails, etc. About twenty miles of telegraph-wire in a day, of the best Swedish iron for strength. Cannot make so good iron in this country, because we cannot afford to work it over so much, labor being higher. Said they had but few competitors now in making telegraph-wire, all the mills in England being just now engaged in making wire for telegraph between England and Sevastopol. These were the first wheels turned by the Blackstone. Sometimes their great wheel breaks, yielding to the centrifugal force, though it is one man's duty to watch it, and immense masses are thrown through the roof or sides of the building. They commonly hear premonitory symptoms, when all run.

I saw a part of the glowing mass which had been heated to a welding heat, ready to be rolled, but had dropped on its way. I could still trace the outlines of the various scraps which composed it, — screws, bolts, bar iron, an old axe curiously twisted, etc., etc., — all which by mere pressure would have been rolled into a homogeneous mass. It was now in the condition of many a piece of composition, which, however, mere compression would weld together into a homogeneous mass or a continuous rod. Washburn said the workmen were like sailors; their work was exciting and they drank more spirit than other laborers. In hot weather would sometimes drink two quarts of water an hour and sweat as much. If they could not sweat, left off work. Showed me a peculiar coarse yellow sand which they imported from the shore of Long Island, whose quartz, examined by a microscope, was seen to be perfect crystals. This they used on the floor of their furnace to repair and level it when their iron bars had furrowed it. In the cavernous furnace I saw the roof *dripping* with dark stalactites from the mortar and bricks. In one place they boiled the wire in water and vitriol, which cleaned it and ate out grease and other foreign particles. Wire is hard drawn when it is rapidly reduced, *i. e.* from one size to another *much* smaller.

Higginson showed me a new translation of the Vishnu Sarma. Spoke of the autobiography of a felon older than Stephen Burroughs, one Fitch of Revolutionary days.

R. W. E. told [of] Mr. Hill, his classmate, of Bangor,

Vol. VII

who was much interested in my "Walden," but relished it merely as a capital satire and joke, and even thought that the survey and map of the pond were not real, but a caricature of the Coast Surveys. Also of Mr. Frost, the botanist, of Brattleboro, who has found five or six new species of lichens thereabouts. George Emerson is aware that he has confounded two black oaks. One is found on Nantucket. Is it not the *Quercus nigra*, and have we not got it in C. ?

Jan. 6. P. M. — To Great Meadows.

Saw one of those silver-gray cocoons which are so securely attached by the silk being wound round the leaf-stalk and the twig. This was more than a year old and empty and, having been attached to a red maple shoot, a foot or more above the meadow, it had girdled it just as a wire might, it was so unyielding, and the wood had overgrown it on each side.

What is that small insect with large, slender wings, which I see on the snow or fluttering in the air these days? Also some little black beetles on the ice of the meadow, ten rods from shore.

In many places near the shore the water has overflowed the ice to a great extent and frozen again with water between of a yellowish tinge, in which you see motes moving about as you walk. The skating is for the most part spoiled by a thin, crispy ice on top of the old ice, which is frozen in great crystals and crackles under your feet. This is apparently the puddles produced by the late thaw and rain, which froze thinly while the rest of the water was soaked up. A fine

snow is falling and drifting before the wind over the ice and lodging in shallow drifts at regular intervals.

I see where a woodpecker has drilled a hole about two inches over in a decayed white maple; quite recently, for the chippings are strewn over the ice beneath and were the first sign that betrayed it. The tree was hollow. Is it for a nest next season?[1] There was an old hole higher up.

I see that the locust pods are still closed, or but partially open, but they open wider after lying in my chamber.

Jan. 7. Sunday. P. M. — J. P. Brown road and Hubbard's Bridge.

Cloudy and misty. On opening the door I feel a very warm southwesterly wind, contrasting with the cooler air of the house, and find it unexpectedly wet in the street, and the manure is being washed off the ice into the gutter. It is, in fact, a January thaw. The channel of the river is quite open in many places, and in others I remark that the ice and water alternate like waves and the hollow between them. There are long reaches of open water where I look for muskrats and ducks, as I go along to Clamshell Hill. I hear the pleasant sound of running water. I see that black scum on the surface of water above the ice.

The delicious soft, spring-suggesting air, — how it fills my veins with life! Life becomes again credible to me. A certain dormant life awakes in me, and I begin to love nature again. Here is my Italy, my hea-

[1] [Probably for a winter lodging.]

ven, my New England. I understand why the Indians hereabouts placed heaven in the southwest, — the soft south.[1] On the slopes the ground is laid bare and radical leaves revealed, — crowfoot, shepherd's-purse, clover, etc., — a fresh green, and, in the meadow, the skunk-cabbage buds, with a bluish bloom, and the red leaves of the meadow saxifrage; and these and the many withered plants laid bare remind me of spring and of botany.

On the same bare sand is revealed a new crop of arrowheads. I pick up two perfect ones of quartz, sharp as if just from the hands of the maker.

Still birds are very rare. Here comes a little flock of titmice, plainly to keep me company, with their black caps and throats making them look top-heavy, restlessly hopping along the alders, with a sharp, clear, lisping note. There begin to be greenish pools in the fields where there is a bottom of icy snow. I saw what looked like clay-colored snow-fleas on the under side of a stone.

The bank is tinged with a most delicate pink or bright flesh-color — where the *Bœomyces roseus* grows. It is a lichen day. The ground is covered with cetrariæ, etc., under the pines. How full of life and of eyes is the damp bark! It would not be worth the while to die and leave all this life behind one.

The hillsides covered with the bear scrub oak, methinks, are of the deepest red at a distance. The pitch pine tops were much broken by the damp snow last month. I see where the birches which were weighed

[1] [Channing, p. 99.]

down and lay across the road have been cut off; and all their scales and seeds, shaken off by the sleighs, in one spot color the snow like thick sawdust. The sky, seen here and there through the wrack, bluish and greenish and, perchance, with a vein of red in the west, seems like the inside of a shell deserted of its tenant, into which I have crawled.[1]

The willow catkins *began* to peep from under their scales as early as the 26th of last month. Many buds have lost their scales.

Jan. 8. 7.30 A. M. — To river.

Still warm and cloudy, but with a great crescent of clear sky increasing in the north by west. The streets are washed bare down to the ice. It is pleasant to see the sky reflected in the open river-reach, now perfectly smooth.

10 A. M. — To Easterbrooks place via old mill site.

It is now a clear warm and sunny day. The willow osiers by the Red Bridge decidedly are not bright now.[2] There is a healthy earthy sound of cock-crowing. I hear a few chickadees near at hand, and hear and see jays further off, and, as yesterday, a crow sitting sentinel on an apple tree. Soon he gives the alarm, and several more take their places near him. Then off they flap with their *caw* of various hoarseness. I see various caterpillars and grubs on the snow and in one place a reddish ant about a third of an inch long walking off. In the swamps you see the mouths of squirrels'

[1] [Channing, pp. 99, 100.]   [2] Were too old.

holes in the snow, with dirt and leaves and perhaps pine scales about them. The fever-bush is betrayed by its little spherical buds.

Jan. 9. P. M. — To Conantum.

A cloudy day, threatening snow; wet under foot. How pretty the evergreen radical shoots of the St. John's-wort now exposed, partly red or lake, various species of it. Have they not grown since fall? I put a stone at the end of one to try it. A little wreath of green and red lying along on the muddy ground amid the melting snows. I am attracted at this season by the fine bright-red buds of the privet andromeda, sleeping couchant along the slender light-brown twigs. They look brightest against a dark ground. I notice the pink shoots of low blueberries where they are thick. How handsome now the fertile fronds of the sensitive fern standing up a foot or more on the sides of causeways, the neat pale-brown stipe clothed with rich dark-brown fruit at top, — the pinnæ on one side and slightly curved, — "a one sided spike or raceme," — still full of seed! They look quite fresh though dry and rigid. Walked up on the river a piece above the Holden Swamp, though there were very few places where I could get on to it, it has so melted along the shore and on the meadows. The ice over the channel looks dangerously dark and rotten in spots. The oak leaves are of the various leather-colors. The white oak, which is least so and most curled and withered, has to my eye a tinge of salmon-color or pink in it. The black shrub oak is particularly dark-reddish

Vol. VII

and firm. It is the black whose leaves are such a pale brown verging on yellowish, — sometimes reddish, — but well preserved.

This winter I hear the axe in almost every wood of any consequence left standing in the township.

Made a splendid discovery this afternoon. As I was walking through Holden's white spruce swamp, I saw peeping above the snow-crust some slender delicate evergreen shoots very much like the *Andromeda Polifolia*, amid sphagnum, lambkill, *Andromeda calyculata*, blueberry bushes, etc., though there was very little to be seen above the snow. It is, I have little doubt, the *Kalmia glauca* var. *rosmarinifolia* (?), with very delicate evergreen opposite linear leaves, strongly revolute, somewhat reddish-green above, slightly weather-beaten, — imbrowned or ripened by the winter, as it were, its cheeks made ruddy by the cold, — white glaucous beneath, with a yellow midrib (not veined nor mucronated nor alternate like the *Andromeda Polifolia*), on the ends of the twigs, which are sharply two-edged. The blossom-buds quite conspicuous. The whole aspect more tender and yellowish than the *Andromeda Polifolia*.[1] The pretty little blossom-buds arranged crosswise in the axils of the leaves as you look down on them.

What a strong and hearty but reckless, hit-or-miss style had some of the early writers of New England, like Josselyn and William Wood and others elsewhere in those days; as if they spoke with a relish, smacking their lips like a coach-whip, caring more to speak

[1] And green while that is mulberry now. *Vide* Jan. 10.

heartily than scientifically true. They are not to be caught napping by the wonders of Nature in a new country, and perhaps are often more ready to appreciate them than she is to exhibit them. They give you one piece of nature, at any rate, and that is themselves.[1] (Cotton Mather, too, has a rich phrase.) They use a strong, coarse, homely speech which cannot always be found in the dictionary, nor sometimes be heard in polite society, but which brings you very near to the thing itself described. The strong new soil speaks through them. I have just been reading some in Wood's "New England's Prospect." He speaks a good word for New England, indeed will come very near lying for her, and when he doubts the justness of his praise, he brings it out not the less roundly; as who cares if it is not so? we love her not the less for all that. Certainly that generation stood nearer to nature, nearer to the facts, than this, and hence their books have more life in them.

(Sometimes a lost man will be so beside himself that he will not have sense enough to trace back his own tracks in the snow.)

Expressions he uses which you now hear only in kitchens and barrooms, which therefore sound particularly fresh and telling, not book-worn. They speak like men who have backs and stomachs and bowels, with all the advantages and disadvantages that attach to them. Ready to find lions here, some having "heard such terrible roarings," "which must be either Devils or Lions; there being no other creatures which use

[1] [Channing, p. 271.]

to roar." What a gormandizing faith (or belief) he has, ready to swallow all kinds of portents and prodigies! Says the wolves have no joints from head to tail. Most admirable when they most outrage common taste and the rules of composition. Of mosquitoes he says those "that swell with their biting the first year, never swell the second." [1]

Jan. 10. P. M. — To Beck Stow's.

The swamp is suddenly frozen up again, and they are carting home the mud which was dug out last fall, in great frozen masses.

The twigs of the *Andromeda Polifolia*, with its rich leaves turned to a mulberry-color above by the winter, with a bluish bloom and a delicate bluish white, as in summer, beneath, project above the ice, the tallest twigs recurved at top, with the leaves standing up on the upper side like teeth of a rake. The intermingling shades of mulberry brown (?) and bluish bloom and glaucous white make it peculiarly rich, as it lies along the ice frozen in. The leaves uninjured by insects.

Then there is the *Andromeda calyculata*, its leaves (now (?)) appressed to the twigs, pale-brown beneath, reddish above, with minute whitish dots. As I go toward the sun now at 4 P. M., the translucent leaves are lit up by it and appear of a soft red, more or less brown, like cathedral windows, but when I look back from the sun, the whole bed appears merely gray and brown.

The leaves of the lambkill, now recurved, are more

[1] *Vide* forward.

Vol. VII

The ground, which was two thirds bare before, began to gray about Fair Haven Pond, as if it were all rocks. There were many of those grubs and caterpillars on the ice half a dozen rods from shore, some sunk deep into it. This air, thick with snowflakes, making a background, enabled me to detect a very picturesque clump of trees on an islet at Pole Brook, — a red (?) oak in midst, with birches on each side.

Jan. 12. P. M. — To Flint's Pond via Minott's meadow.

After a spitting of snow in the forenoon, I see the blue sky here and there, and the sun is coming out. It is still and warm. The earth is two thirds bare. I walk along the Mill Brook below Emerson's, looking into it for some life.

Perhaps what most moves us in winter is some reminiscence of far-off summer. How we leap by the side of the open brooks! What beauty in the running brooks! What life! What society! The cold is merely superficial; it is summer still at the core, far, far within. It is in the cawing of the crow, the crowing of the cock, the warmth of the sun on our backs. I hear faintly the cawing of a crow far, far away, echoing from some unseen wood-side, as if deadened by the springlike vapor which the sun is drawing from the ground. It mingles with the slight murmur of the village, the sound of children at play, as one stream empties gently into another, and the wild and tame are one. What a delicious sound! It is not merely crow calling to crow, for it speaks to me too. I am part of

or less reddish. The great buds of the swamp-pink, on the central twig, clustered together, are more or less imbrowned and reddened.

At European Cranberry Swamp, I saw great quantities of the seeds of that low three-celled rush or sedge, about the edge of the pool on the ice, black and elliptical, looking like the droppings of mice, this size: ⟨⟩ ⟨⟩, so thick in many places that by absorbing the sun's heat they had melted an inch or more into the ice.[1] No doubt they are the food of some creatures. Saw a thorn with long thorns and its peculiarly shining varnished twigs.

Cold and blustering as it is, the crows are flapping and sailing about and buffeting one another as usual. It is hard to tell what they would be at.

Jan. 11. P. M. — Skated to Lee's Bridge and Farrar's Swamp — call it Otter Swamp.

A fine snow had just begun to fall, so we made haste to improve the skating before it was too late. Our skates made tracks often nearly an inch broad in the slight snow which soon covered the ice. All along the shores and about the islets the water had broadly overflowed the ice of the meadows, and frequently we had to skate through it, making it fly. The snow soon showed where the water was. It was a pleasant time to skate, so still, and the air so thick with snowflakes that the outline of near hills was seen against it and not against the more distant and higher hills. Single pines stood out distinctly against it in the near horizon.

[1] *Scheuchzeria palustris.*

one great creature with him; if he has voice, I have ears.[1] I can hear when he calls, and have engaged not to shoot nor stone him if he will caw to me each spring. On the one hand, it may be, is the sound of children at school saying their a, b, ab's, on the other, far in the wood-fringed horizon, the cawing of crows from their blessed eternal vacation, out at their long recess, children who have got dismissed! While the vaporous incense goes up from all the fields of the spring — if it were spring. Ah, bless the Lord, O my soul! bless him for wildness, for crows that will not alight within gunshot! and bless him for hens, too, that croak and cackle in the yard!

Where are the shiners now, and the trout? I see none in the brook. Have the former descended to the deep water of the river? Ah, may I be there to see when they go down! Why can they not tell me? Or gone into the mud? There are few or no insects for them now.

The strong scent of this red oak, just split and corded, is a slight compensation for the loss of the tree.

How cheering the sight of the evergreens now, on the forest floor, the various pyrolas, etc., fresh as in summer!

What is that mint whose seed-vessels rubbed are so spicy to smell — minty — at the further end of the pond by the Gourgas wood-lot? [2]

On Flint's Pond I find Nat Rice fishing. He has not caught one. I asked him what he thought the best time to fish. He said, "When the wind first comes south after a cold spell, on a bright morning."

[1] [Channing, p. 100.]   [2] *Lycopus.*

Well may the tender buds attract us at this season, no less than partridges, for they are the hope of the year, the spring rolled up. The summer is all packed in them.

Observed this afternoon the following oak leaves: —

1st, the white oak, the most withered and faded and curled; many spotted with black dot lichens.

2d, the bear scrub, the most firm and fresh-colored and flat.

3d, the black, moderately firm, the darkest above, much curled.

4th, scarlet, firmest after the bear scrub, with much freshness and life; *some* conspicuously red still (unwithered); lobes remarkably distorted.

5th, red, considerably withered and lifeless and worn, thin and faded; some reddish slightly and not inclined to curl.

6th, swamp white, pretty firm and bright, but considerably curled.

7th, I suspect that the small chinquapin is deciduous, for I could not find one leaf in all my walk January 1st, though I looked along the Lupine Wall. Those on the ground are considerably withered, faded, and curled, yet pretty firm.

For color, perhaps all may be called brown, and vary into each other more or less.

The 1st, as both sides are seen, pale-brown with a salmon tinge beneath.

2d, clear reddish-brown, leather-like, above, often paler, whitish or very light beneath, silveryish.

3d, dusky-brown above (not always), clear tawny(?)-brown beneath.

4th, clear pale-brown (except the unfaded red ones), leather-like, very generally reddish, nearly the same both sides.

5th, quite pale brown or slightly reddish, nearly the same both sides; some, prematurely dead, are yellowish.

6th, deep rusty-colored brown, often bright leather-red, silveryish-white beneath.

7th, leaves on ground pale-brown, much like a withered red, but whitish beneath *like* bear shrub.

The oak leaves now resemble the different kinds of calf, sheep, Russia leather, and Morocco (a few scarlet oaks), of different ages.

Jan. 13. Warm and wet, with rain-threatening clouds drifting from southwest. Muddy, wet, and slippery. Surprised to see oak balls on a red oak.

Picked up a pitch pine cone which had evidently been cut off by a squirrel. The successive grooves made by his teeth while probably he bent it down were quite distinct. The woody stem was a quarter of an inch thick, and I counted eight strokes of his chisel.

Jan. 14. Skated to Baker Farm with a rapidity which astonished myself, before the wind, feeling the rise and fall, — the water having settled in the suddenly cold night, — which I had not time to see. Saw the intestines of (apparently) a rabbit, — betrayed by a morsel of fur, — left on the ice, probably the prey of a fox. A man feels like a new creature, a deer, perhaps,

moving at this rate. He takes new possession of nature in the name of his own majesty. There was I, and there, and there, as Mercury went down the Idæan Mountains. I judged that in a quarter of an hour I was three and a half miles from home without having made any particular exertion, — *à la volaille.*

Jan. 15. P. M. — Skated to Bedford.

It had just been snowing, and this lay in shallow drifts or waves on the Great Meadows, alternate snow and ice. Skated into a crack, and slid on my side twenty-five feet.

The river-channel dark and rough with fragments of old ice, — polygons of various forms, — cemented together, not strong.

Jan. 16. To Cambridge and Boston.

Carried to Harris the worms — brown, light-striped — and fuzzy black caterpillars (he calls the first also caterpillars); also two black beetles; all which I have found within a week or two on ice and snow; thickest in a thaw. Showed me, in a German work, plates of the larvæ of dragon-flies and ephemeræ, such as I see — or their cases — on rushes, etc., over water. Says the ant-lion is found at Burlington, Vermont, and *may* be at Concord.

I can buy Indian coats in Milk Street from three and a half to six dollars, depending on the length; also leggins from $1.50 to three or more dollars, also depending on the length.

Saw a Nantucket man, who said that their waters

were not so good as the south side of Long Island to steer in by sounding. Off Long Island it deepened a mile every fathom for at least forty miles, as he had proved, — perhaps eighty; but at Barnegat it was not so.

Jan. 19. 7 A. M. — Yesterday it rained hard all day, washing off the little snow that was left down to the ice, the gutters being good-sized mill-brooks and the water over shoes in the middle of the road.

In the night it turned to snow, which still falls, and now covers the wet ground three or four inches deep. It is a very damp snow or sleet, perhaps mixed with rain, which the strong northwest wind plasters to that side of the trees and houses. I never saw the blue in snow so bright as this damp, dark, stormy morning at 7 A. M., as I was coming down the railroad. I did not have to make a hole in it, but I saw it some rods off in the deep, narrow ravines of the drifts and under their edges or eaves, like the serenest blue of heaven, though the sky was, of course, wholly concealed by the driving snow-storm; suggesting that in darkest storms we may still have the hue of heaven in us.

At noon it is still a driving snow-storm, and a little flock of redpolls is busily picking the seeds of the pigweed, etc., in the garden. Almost all have more or less crimson; a few are very splendid, with their particularly bright crimson breasts. The white on the edge of their wing-coverts is very conspicuous.

P. M. — The damp snow still drives from the northwest nearly horizontally over the fields, while I go with C. toward the Cliffs and Walden. There is not a single fresh track on the back road, and the aspect of the road and trees and houses is very wintry. Though considerable snow has fallen, it lies chiefly in drifts under the walls. We went through the Spring Woods, over the Cliff, by the wood-path at its base to Walden, and thence by the path to Brister's Hill, and by road home. It was worth the while to see what a burden of damp snow lay on the trees notwithstanding the wind. Pitch pines were bowed to the ground with it, and birches also, and white oaks. I saw one of the last, at least twenty-five feet high, splintered near the ground past recovery. All kinds of evergreens, and oaks which retain their leaves, and birches which do not, up to twenty-five feet or more in height, were bent to the earth, and these novel but graceful curves were a new feature in the woodland scenery. Young white pines often stood draped in robes of purest white, emblems of purity, like a maiden that has taken the veil, with their heads slightly bowed and their main stems slanting to one side, like travellers bending to meet the storm with their heads muffled in their cloaks. The windward side of the wood, and the very tops of the trees everywhere, for the most part, were comparatively bare, but within the woods the whole lower two thirds of the trees were laden with the snowy burden which had sifted down on to them. The snow, a little damp, had lodged not only on the oak leaves and the evergreens, but on every twig and branch, and stood in upright walls or ruffs five or six inches high, like miniature Chinese walls, zigzag over hill and dale, making more conspicuous than ever the

Vol. VII

arrangement and the multitude of the twigs and branches; and the trunks also being plastered with snow, a peculiar soft light was diffused around, very unlike the ordinary darkness of the forest, as if you were inside a drift or snow house. This even when you stood on the windward side. In most directions you could not see more than four or five rods into this labyrinth or maze of white arms. This is to be insisted on. On every side it was like a snow-drift that lay loose to that height. They were so thick that they left no crevice through which the eye could penetrate further. The path was for the most part blocked up with the trees bent to the ground, which we were obliged to go round by zigzag paths in the woods, or carefully creep under at the risk of getting our necks filled with an avalanche of snow. In many places the path was shut up by as dense a labyrinth, high as the tree-tops and impermeable to vision, as if there had never been a path there. Often we touched a tree with our foot or shook it with our hand, and so relieved it of a part of its burden, and, rising a little, it made room for us to pass beneath. Often singular portals and winding passages were left between the pitch pines, through [which], stooping and grazing the touchy walls, we made our way. Where the path was open in the midst of the woods, the snow was about seven or eight inches deep. The trunks of the trees so uniformly covered on the northerly side, as happens frequently every winter, and sometimes continuing so for weeks, suggested that this might be a principal reason why the lichens watered by the melting snow

flourished there most. The snow lay in great continuous masses on the pitch pines and the white, not only like napkins, but great white table-spreads and counterpanes, when you looked off at the wood from a little distance. Looking thus up at the Cliff, I could not tell where it lay an unbroken mass on the smooth rock, and where on the trees, it was so massed on the last also. White pines were changed into firs by it, and the limbs and twigs of some large ones were so matted together by the weight that they looked like immense solid fungi on the side of the trees, or those nests of the social grosbeak (?)[1] of Africa which I have seen represented. Some white pine boughs hung down like fans or the webbed feet of birds. On some pitch pines it lay in fruit-like balls as big as one's head, like cocoanuts. Where the various oaks were bent down, the contrast of colors of the snow and oak leaves and the softened tints through the transparent snow — often a delicate fawn-color — were very agreeable.

As we returned over the Walden road the damp, driving snowflakes, when we turned partly round and faced them, hurt our eyeballs as if they had been dry scales.[2]

It may be that the linarias come into the gardens now not only because all nature is a wilderness to-day, but because the woods where the wind has not free play are so snowed up, the twigs are so deeply covered, that they cannot readily come at their food. In many

[1] [The sociable weaver-bird is doubtless referred to.]
[2] [Channing, p. 112.]

places single trees, or clumps of two or three drooping and massed together by the superincumbent weight, made a sort of roof, tent-like, under which you might take shelter. Under one pitch pine, which shut down to the ground on every side, you could not see the sky at all, but sat in a gloomy light as in a tent. We saw only one indistinct, snow-covered trail of an animal. Where are the crows now? I never see them at such a time. The water of yesterday is very high now on the meadows over the ice, but the snow has mingled with it so densely that it is mere slosh now. The channel ice is lifted up by the freshet, and there is dry white snow, but on each side are broad dirty or yellowish green strips of slosh. Whence comes this green color?

One of the first snows of the winter was a similar damp one which lodged on the trees and broke them down. And the sides of woodland roads were strewn with birch-tops which had obstructed the way and which travellers had been obliged to cut off.

There are plenty of those shell-like drifts along the south sides of the walls now. There are countless perforations[1] through which the fine snow drives and blinds you.

It was surprising to see what a burden of snow had lodged on the trees, especially the pitch pines in secluded dells in the woods out of the way of the wind. White oaks also, six inches in diameter and twenty-five feet high, were bent to the ground and sometimes broken or splintered by it. Maybe the white oaks are more flexible than the others, or their leaves are higher

[1] [Channing, p. 112.]

Kalmia glauca

Snow Statuary

up and they are more slender below. Some are split in the crotch. It lay on the smaller shrubs and bushes through which you walked, like lightest down, only the lightest part sifting down there.

The houses have that peculiarly wintry aspect now on the west side, being all plastered over with snow adhering to the clapboards and half concealing the doors and windows.

The trees were everywhere bent into the path like bows tautly strung, and you had only to shake them with your hand or foot, when they rose up and made way for you. You went winding between and stooping or creeping under them, fearing to touch them, lest they should relieve themselves of their burden and let fall an avalanche or shower of snow on to you. Ever and anon the wind shook down a shower from high trees. You would not have believed there were so many twigs and branches in a wood as were revealed by the snow resting on them; perfect walls of snow; no place for a bird to perch.[1]

Jan. 20. Our lesser redpoll is said to be the same with the European, which is called *Le Sizerin* by Buffon. (This in Bewick.) I heard its mew about the house early this morning before sunrise.

In many instances the snow had lodged on trees yesterday in just such forms as a white napkin or counterpane dropped on them would take, — protuberant in the middle, with many folds and dimples. An ordinary leafless bush supported so much snow

[1] *Vide* 20th and 26th *inst.*

on its twigs — a perfect maze like a whirligig, though not in one solid mass — that you could not see through it. We heard only a few *chic-a-dees*. Sometimes the snow on the bent pitch pines made me think of rams' or elephants' heads, ready to butt you. In particular places, standing on their snowiest side, the woods were incredibly fair, white as alabaster. Indeed the young pines reminded you of the purest statuary, and the stately full-grown ones towering around affected you as if you stood in a titanic sculptor's studio, so purely and delicately white, transmitting the light, their dark trunks all concealed. And in many places, where the snow lay on withered oak leaves between you and the light, various delicate fawn-colored and cinnamon tints, blending with the white, still enhanced the beauty.

A fine, clear day, not very cold.

P. M. — To Conantum and C. Miles place with Tappan.

There was a high wind last night, which relieved the trees of their burden almost entirely, but I may still see the drifts. The surface of the snow everywhere in the fields, where it is hard blown, has a fine grain with low shelves, like a slate stone that does not split well. We cross the fields behind Hubbard's and suddenly slump into dry ditches concealed by the snow, up to the middle, and flounder out again. How new all things seem! Here is a broad, shallow pool in the fields, which yesterday was slosh, now converted into a soft, white, fleecy snow ice, like bread that has spewed out and baked outside the pan. It is like the

beginning of the world. There is nothing hackneyed where a new snow can come and cover all the landscape. The snow lies chiefly behind the walls. It is surprising how much a straggling rail fence detains it, and it forms a broad, low swell beyond it, two or three rods wide, also just beyond the brow of a hill where it begins to slope to the south. You can tell by the ridges of the drifts on the south side of the walls which way the wind was. They all run from north to south; *i. e.*, the common drift is divided into ridges or plaits in this direction, frequently down to the ground between; which separate drifts are of graceful outlines somewhat like fishes, with a sharp ridge or fin gracefully curved, both as you look from one side and down on them, their sides curving like waves about to break. The thin edge of some of these drifts at the wall end, where the air has come through the wall and made an eddy, are remarkably curved, like some shells, even thus, more than once round: I would not have believed it.

The world is not only new to the eye, but is still as at creation; every blade and leaf is hushed; not a bird or insect is heard; only, perchance, a faint tinkling sleigh-bell in the distance.

As there was water on the ice of the river, which the snow converted into slosh, now, frozen, it looks like fleece.

The snow still adheres conspicuously to the northwest sides of the stems of the trees quite up to their summits, with a remarkably sharp edge in that direc-

Vol. VII

tion, — in a horizontal section like this: It would be about as good as a compass to steer   by in a cloudy day or by night. You see where the trees have deposited their load on the snow beneath, making it uneven. Saw suddenly, directly overhead, a remarkable mackerel sky, with peculiarly soft, large flakes, — polyhedrons, — showing the celestial blue between them, soft and duskyish, like new steam. This covered the greater part of the sky. In the zenith, a more leaden blue; in the crevices on the sides, a more celestial. This was just beyond the Holden Swamp. We admired the C. Miles elms, their strong branches now more conspicuous, zigzag or gracefully curved.

We came upon the tracks of a man and dog, which I guessed to be Channing's. Further still, a mile and a half from home, as I was showing to T. under a bank the single flesh-colored or pink apothecium of a bæomyces which was not covered by the snow, I saw the print of C.'s foot by its side and knew that his eyes had rested on it that afternoon. It was about the size of a pin's head. Saw also where he had examined the lichens on the rails   Now the mackerel sky was gone and all was clear again, and I could hardly realize that low, dark stratum far in the east was it, still delighting, perchance, some sailor on the Atlantic, in whose zenith it was, whose sky it occupied.

T. admired much the addition to the red house, with its steep bevelled roof. Thought he should send Mr. Upjohn to see it. The whole house, methought, was well planted, rested solidly on the earth, with its great bank (green in summer) and few stately elms before, it [was] so much simpler and more attractive than a front yard with its knickknacks. To contrast with this pleasing structure, which is painted a wholesome red, was a modern addition in the rear, perhaps no uglier than usual, only by contrast, — such an outline alone as our carpenters have learned to produce. I see that I cannot draw anything so bad as the reality. So you will often see an ugly new barn beside a pleasing old house.

Causeways are no sooner made than the swamp white oak springs up by their sides, its acorns probably washed there by the freshets.

In Sagard's History I read, "The villager did not wish to hear the Huguenot minister, saying that there was not yet any ivy on the walls of his church, and that ours were all gray with age" (*chenues de vieillesse*). The walls of the Protestant church in their turn have now got some ivy on them, and the villager does not wish to hear the preacher of any new church which has not.

In Bewick's Birds it is said of the night-jar (also called goat-sucker, dor-hawk, or fern owl) (*Caprimulgus Europeus*), — *L'Engoulevent* (Buffon): "When perched the Night-Jar sits usually on a bare twig, its head lower than its tail, and in this attitude utters its jarring note ["by which," he says elsewhere, "it is peculiarly distinguished"].[1] It is likewise distinguished by a sort of buzzing which it makes while on the wing, and which has been compared to the noise caused by the quick rotation of a spinning-wheel, from which, in

[1] [The brackets are Thoreau's.]

some places, it is called the Wheel Bird." "It is seldom seen in the daytime." This last sound is apparently the same which I hear our whip-poor-will make, and which I do not remember to have heard described.[1]

On the sides of dry hills the dried heads of the hardhack, rising above the snow, are very perfect and handsome now. I think it may be owing to the drought of the last summer, which caused them to dry up prematurely, but before they began to be brittle and to crumble. This on the first cladonia pasture of Conantum. I sit there looking up at the mackerel sky and also at the neighboring wood so suddenly relieved of its snowy burden. The pines — mostly white — have at this season a warm brown or yellowish tinge, and the oaks — chiefly young white ones — are *comparatively red*. The black oak I see is more yellowish. You have these colors of the evergreens and oaks in winter for warmth and contrast with the snow.

Seeds are still left on the birches, which, after each new snow, are sprinkled over its surface, apparently to keep the birds supplied with food.

You see where yesterday's snowy billows have broken at last in the sun or by their own weight, their curling edges fallen and crumbled on the snow beneath.

I see the tracks of countless little birds, probably redpolls, where these have run over broad pastures and visited every weed, — johnswort and coarse grasses, — whose oat-like seed-scales or hulls they have scattered about. It is surprising they did not sink deeper in the light snow. Often the impression is so

[1] [Four interrogation-points in pencil follow this.]

Vol. VII

faint that they seem to have been supported by their wings.

The pines and oaks in the deepest hollows in the woods still support some snow, but especially the low swamps are half filled with snow to the height of ten feet, resting on the bent underwood, as if affording covert to wolves.

Very musical and even sweet now, like a horn, is the hounding of a foxhound heard now in some distant wood, while I stand listening in some far solitary and silent field.

I doubt if I can convey an idea of the appearance of the woods yesterday, as you stood in their midst and looked round on their boughs and twigs laden with snow. It seemed as if there could have been none left to reach the ground. These countless zigzag white arms crossing each other at every possible angle completely closed up the view, like a light drift within three or four rods on every side. The wintriest prospect imaginable. That snow which sifted down into the wood-path was much drier and lighter than elsewhere.

Jan. 21. 2.30 P. M. — The sky has gradually become overcast, and now it is just beginning to snow. Looking against a dark roof, I detect a single flake from time to time, but when I look at the dark side of the woods two miles off in the horizon, there already is seen a slight thickness or mistiness in the air. In this way, perhaps, may it first be detected.

P. M. — To Andromeda Ponds *via* railroad; return by base of Cliffs.

The snow is turning to rain through a fine hail.

Pines and oaks seen at a distance — say two miles off — are considerably blended and make one harmonious impression. The former, if you attend, are seen to be of a blue or misty black, and the latter form commonly a reddish-brown ground out of which the former rise. These colors are no longer in strong contrast with each other.

Few twigs are conspicuous at a distance like those of the golden willow. The tree is easily distinguished at a distance by its color.

Saw in an old white pine stump, about fifteen inches from the ground, a hole pecked about an inch and a half in diameter. It was about six inches deep downward in the rotten stump and was bottomed with hypnum, rabbit's fur, and hair, and a little dry grass. Was it a mouse-nest? or a nuthatch's, creeper's, or chickadee's nest?[1] It has a slight musky smell.

Jan. 22. Heavy rain in the night and half of to-day, with very high wind from the southward, washing off the snow and filling the road with water. The roads are well-nigh impassable to foot-travellers.

P. M. — To stone bridge, Loring's Pond, Derby's, and Nut Meadow.

It is a good lichen day, for the high wind has strewn the bark over the fields and the rain has made them very bright. In some places for fifteen rods the whole road is like a lake from three to fifteen inches deep. It is very exciting to see, where was so lately only ice

[1] Probably last.

and snow, dark wavy lakes, dashing in furious torrents through the commonly dry channels under the causeways, to hear only the rush and roar of waters and look down on mad billows where in summer is commonly only dry pebbles. Great cakes of ice lodged and sometimes tilted up against the causeway bridges, over which the water pours as over a dam. After their passage under these commonly dry bridges the crowding waters are at least six or eight inches higher than those of the surrounding meadow. What a tumult at the stone bridge, where cakes of ice a rod in diameter and a foot thick are carried round and round by the eddy in circles eight or ten rods in diameter, and rarely get a chance to go down-stream, while others are seen coming up edgewise from below in the midst of the torrent!

The muskrats driven out of their holes by the water are exceedingly numerous, yet many of their cabins are above water on the south branch. Here there are none. We saw fifteen or twenty, at least, between Derby's Bridge and the Tarbell Spring, either swimming with surprising swiftness up or down or across the stream to avoid us, or sitting at the water's edge, or resting on the edge of the ice (one refreshed himself there after its cold swim regardless of us, probed its fur with its nose and scratched its ear like a dog) or on some alder bough just on the surface. They frequently swam toward an apple tree in the midst of the water in the vain hope of finding a resting-place and refuge there. I saw one, looking quite a reddish brown, busily feeding on some plant just at the water's edge, thrust-

ing his head under for it. But I hear the sound of Goodwin's gun up-stream and see his bag stuffed out with their dead bodies.

The radical leaves of the yellow thistle are now very fresh and conspicuous in Tarbell's meadow, the rain having suddenly carried off the snow.

Jan. 23. P. M. — The water is still higher than yesterday. I found [it] just over the Red Bridge road, near the bridge. The willow-row near there is not now bright, but a dull greenish below, with a yard at the ends of the twigs red. The water in many hollows in the fields has suddenly fallen away, run off, or soaked up, leaving last night's ice to mark its height around the edges and the bushes. It has fallen two feet in many cases, leaving sometimes a mere feathery crystallization to supply its place. I was pleased to see the vapor of Sam Barrett's fall and, after, the icy cases of the alder and willow stems below. But the river is higher than ever, especially the North River. I was obliged after crossing Hunt's Bridge to keep on round to the railroad bridge at Loring's before I could re-cross, it being over the road with a roar like a mill-dam this side the further stone bridge, and I could not get over dry for the feebleness and incontinuity of the fence. In front of G. M. Barrett's was a great curving bay which crossed the road between him and Heywood's, and by Fort Pond Bridge at Loring's it had been over for ten rods in the night. A great cake a foot thick stands on end against the railroad bridge. I do not quite like to see so much bare ground in mid-

winter. The radical leaves of the shepherd's-purse, seen in green circles on the water-washed plowed grounds, remind me of the internal heat and life of the globe, anon to burst forth anew.

Yesterday I met Goodwin shooting muskrats and saw the form and bloody stains of two through his game-bag. He shot such as were close to the shore where he could get them, for he had no dog, the water being too cold, he said. I saw one poor rat lying on the edge of the ice reddened with its blood, half a dozen rods from the shore, which he had shot but was unwilling to wade for.

It is surprising how much work will be accomplished in such a night as the last, so many a brook will have run itself out and now be found reduced within reasonable bounds. This settling away of the water leaves much crackling white ice in the roads.

Jan. 24. I am [reading] William Wood's "New England's Prospect." He left New England August 15th, 1633, and the last English edition referred to in this American one of 1764 is that of London, 1639.

The wild meadow-grasses appear to have grown more rankly in those days. He describes them as "thick and long, as high as a man's middle; some as high as the shoulders." (*Vide* Indian book.)[1] Strawberries too were more abundant and large before they were so cornered up by cultivation, "some being two inches about; one may gather half a bushel in a fore-

[1] [Thoreau's note-book on the Indians is doubtless referred to.]

noon;" and no doubt many other berries were far more abundant, as gooseberries, raspberries, and especially currants, which last so many old writers speak of, but so few moderns find wild. We can perhaps imagine how the primitive wood looked from the sample still left in Maine. He says, "The timber of the country grows strait, and tall, some trees being twenty, some thirty foot high, before they spread forth their branches; generally the trees be not very thick, tho' there be many that will serve for mill-posts, some being three foot and an half over." One would judge from accounts that the woods were clearer than the primitive wood that is left, on account of Indian fires, for he says you might ride a-hunting in most places. "There is no underwood, saving in swamps," which the Indian fires did not burn. (*Vide* Indian book.) "Here no doubt might be good done with saw mills; for I have seene of these stately high grown trees [he is speaking of pines particularly] ten miles together close by the river [probably Charles River][1] side." He says at first "fir and pine," as if the fir once grew in this part of the State abundantly, as now in Maine and further west. Of the oaks he says, "These trees afford much mast for hogs, especially every third year." Does not this imply many more of them than now? "The hornbound tree is a tough kind of wood, that requires so much pains in riving as is almost incredible, being the best to make bowls and dishes, not being subject to crack or leak," and [he] speaks, both in prose and verse, of the vines being particu-

[1] [The brackets are Thoreau's.]

larly inclined to run over this tree. If this is the true hornbeam it was probably larger then, but I am inclined to think it the tupelo, and that it was both larger and more abundant than commonly now, for he says it was good for bowls, and it has been so used since. Of the plums of the country he says, "They be black and yellow, about the bigness of damsons, of a reasonable good taste." Yet Emerson has not found the yellow plum, *i. e.* Canada, growing wild in Massachusetts.

Of quadrupeds no longer found in Concord, he names the lion, — that Cape Ann Lion "which some affirm that they have seen," which may have been a cougar, for he adds, "Plimouth men have traded for Lions skins in former times," — bear, moose, deer, porcupines, "the grim-fac'd Ounce, and rav'nous howling Wolf," and beaver. Martens.

"For Bears they be common, being a black kind of Bear, which be most fierce in strawberry time, at which time they have young ones; at which time likewise they will go upright like a man, and climb trees, and swim to the islands;" etc. (*Vide* Indian book.) In the winter they lie in "the clifts of rocks and thick swamps." The wolves hunt these in packs and "tear him as a Dog will tear a Kid." "They never prey upon the English cattle, or offer to assault the person of any man," unless shot. Their meat "esteemed . . . above venison."

For moose and deer see Indian book.

Complains of the wolf as the great devourer of bear, moose, and deer, which kept them from mul-

tiplying more. "Of these Deer [*i. e.* the small] [1] there be a great many, and more in the Massachusetts-Bay, than in any other place." "Some have killed sixteen Deer in a day upon this island," so called because the deer swam thither to avoid the wolves. [2]

For porcupine and raccoon *vide* Indian book.

Gray squirrels were evidently more numerous than now.

I do not know whether his ounce or wild cat is the Canada lynx [3] or wolverine. He calls it wild cat and does not describe the little wildcat. (*Vide* Indian book.) Says they are accounted "very good meat. Their skins be a very deep kind of fur, spotted white and black on the belly." Audubon and Bachman make the *Lynx rufus* black and white beneath. For wolf *vide* Indian book. He says: "These be killed daily in some places or other. . . . Yet is there little hope of their utter destruction." "Travelling in the swamp by kennels."

Says the beaver are so cunning the English "seldom or never kill any of them, being not patient to lay a long siege" and not having experience.

Eagles are probably less common; pigeons of course (*vide* Indian book); heath cocks all gone (price "four pence"); and turkeys (good cock, "four shillings"). Probably more owls then, and cormorants, etc., etc., sea-fowl generally (of humilities he "killed twelve score at two shots"), and swans. Of pigeons, "Many of them build among the pine trees, thirty miles to the north-east of our plantations; joining nest to nest,

[1] [The brackets are Thoreau's.]
[2] [Deer Island in Boston Harbor.]   [3] Probably this.

Vol. VII

and tree to tree by their nests, so that the Sun never sees the ground in that place, from whence the Indians fetch whole loads of them." And then for turkeys, tracking them in winter, or shooting them on their roosts at night. Of the crane, "almost as tall as a man," probably blue heron, — possibly the whooping crane or else the sandhill, — he says, "I have seen many of these fowls, yet did I never see one that was fat, though very sleaky;" neither did I. "There be likewise many Swans, which frequent the fresh ponds and rivers, seldom consorting themselves with ducks and geese; these be very good meat, the price of one is six shillings." Think of that! They had not only brant and common gray wild geese, but "a white Goose," probably the snow goose; "sometimes there will be two or three thousand in a flock;" continue six weeks after Michaelmas and return again north in March. Peabody says of the snow goose, "They are occasionally seen in Massachusetts Bay."

Sturgeon were taken at Cape Cod and in the Merrimack especially, "pickled and brought to England, some of these be 12, 14, and 18 feet long." An abundance of salmon, shad, and bass, —

"The stately Bass old Neptune's fleeting post,
That tides it out and in from sea to coast;"

"one of the best fish in the country," taken "sometimes two or three thousand at a set," "some four foot long," left on the sand behind the seine; sometimes used for manure. "Alewives . . . in the latter end of April come up to the fresh rivers to spawn, in such multitudes as is almost incredible, pressing up in such

shallow waters as will scarce permit them to swim, having likewise such longing desire after the fresh water ponds, that no beatings with poles, or forcive agitations by other devices, will cause them to return to the sea, till they have cast their spawn."

"The Oysters be great ones in form of a shoe-horn, some be a foot long; these breed on certain banks that are bare every spring tide. This fish without the shell is so big, that it must admit of a division before you can well get it into your mouth." For lobsters, "their plenty makes them little esteemed and seldom eaten." Speaks of "a great oyster bank" in the middle of Back Bay, just off the true mouth of the Charles, and of another in the Mistick. These obstructed the navigation of both rivers. *Vide* book of facts.

P. M. — To Walden and Andromeda Ponds.

The river is remarkably high for this season. Meeks, the carpenter, said that he could not get home to-night if he could not find Rhoades, with whom he rode into town, for the water was more than a foot deep over half the causeway. This was at 8 P. M.

But the ice is not thick enough on the meadows, so I go to Walden a-skating. Yet, to my surprise, it is thinly frozen over those parts of the river which are commonly open even in the coldest weather (as at Cheney's), probably because, it being spread over the meadows, there is not so much current there now.

On the 19th Walden was covered with slosh four or five inches deep, but the rain of the 22d turned it all to water, — or chiefly, — leaving it pretty smooth in the main, but at different levels. Under the higher levels are many handsome white figures one to two feet long, where water has flowed, now empty and white, in form of trees or cladonia lichens, very handsome. I saw a meadow full of lambkill turned reddish the other day, which looked quite handsome with the sun on it.

Those Andromeda Ponds are very attractive spots to me. They are filled with a dense bed of the small andromeda, a dull red mass as commonly seen, brighter or translucent red looking toward the sun, grayish looking from it, two feet or more high, as thick as a moss bed, springing out of a still denser bed of sphagnum beneath. Above the general level rise in clumps here and there the panicled andromeda, with brown clustered fruit, and the high blueberry. But I observe that the andromeda does not quite fill the pond, but there is an open wet place, with coarse grass, swamp loosestrife, and some button-bush, about a rod wide, surrounding the whole. Those little hummocks or paps of sphagnum, out of which the andromeda springs, as bouquets are tied up in the same to keep them fresh, are very beautiful. Now, where the frost has touched them, they are hoary protuberances, — perhaps inclining to ridges, now frozen firmly, — green beneath and within; general aspect now perhaps pale withered brownish, the green only driven in a little deeper, spotted with more or less bright reddish stars; where drier, frequently beautiful crimson stars amid the hoary portions; a beautiful soft bed, of a myriad swelling bosoms, out of which the andromeda springs.

I got a load once to stuff into the chinks in a well I was [walling up] — to keep the sand out, but, it being covered, it died, and I believe I only filled the water with motes and worms ever after. A beautiful pale-brown and hoary-red and crimson ground of swelling bosoms. Dr. Harris spoke of this andromeda as a *rare* plant in Cambridge. There was one pond-hole where he had found it, but he believed they had destroyed it now getting out the mud. What can be expected of a town where this is a rare plant? Here is Nature's parlor; here you can talk with her in the *lingua vernacula*, if you can speak it, — if you have anything to say, — her little back sitting-room, her withdrawing, her *keeping* room.

I was surprised to find the ice in the middle of the last pond a beautiful delicate rose-color for two or three rods, deeper in spots. It reminded me of red snow, and may be the same. I tried to think it the blood of wounded muskrats, but it could not be. It extended several inches into the ice, at least, and had been spread by the flowing water recently. As for vegetable pigments, there were button-bushes in and about it. It was this delicate rose tint, with internal bluish tinges like mother-o'-pearl or the inside of a conch. It was quite conspicuous fifteen rods off, and the color of spring-cranberry juice. This beautiful blushing ice! What are we coming to?

Was surprised to see oak-balls on a bear scrub oak. Have them, then, on black, scarlet, red, and bear scrub.

Saw a young (apparently) red oak (it did not taste

bitter) (another in same state has an oak-ball on it!) ten feet high, the ends of whose twigs looked at first sight as if they had been twisted off by some hungry browsing bird, leaving the fibres streaming. These I found were the strong woody fibres of last year's leaf-stalk, standing out white, in some cases two inches in all directions, from the ends of the twigs, in others rolled together like strong twine, and commonly this twine of different leaf-stalks with the flapping of the leaves twisted together; sometimes four or five leaf-stalks' fibres, with wonderful regularity, as if braided, — like braided horse-tails. On other oaks the leaves still remained with their leaf-stalks thus reduced to fibres and twisted together. It was wonderful how they could have become so wonderfully knotted or braided together, but Nature had made up in assiduity for want of skill. In one instance four leaf-stalks, reduced to fine white fibres and rolled and twisted into strong twine, had afterwards been closely braided together for half an inch in length and in the course of it tied twice round the twig. I think it must be that these leaves died (perhaps in the great drought of last year) while their fibres were still strongly united with their twigs and so preserving their flexibility without losing their connection, and so the wind flapping the leaves, which hang short down, has twisted them together and commonly worn out the leaves entirely, without loosening or breaking the tough leaf-stalk. Here is self-registered the flutterings of a leaf in this twisted, knotted, and braided twine. So fickle and

unpredictable, not to say insignificant, a motion does yet get permanently recorded in some sort. Not a leaf flutters, summer or winter, but its variation and dip and intensity are registered in THE BOOK.

Old Wood in his "New England's Prospect" says, Englishmanlike: "It is thought there can be no better water in the world, yet dare I not prefer it before good beer, as some have done, but any man will choose it before bad beer, whey, or buttermilk. Those that drink it be as healthful, fresh, and lusty, as they that drink beer."

Jan. 25. P. M. — To Andromeda Ponds.

This morning was a perfect hunter's morn, for it snowed about three quarters of an inch last evening, covering land and ice. Is not good skating a sign of snow? In the swamps, however, where there was water oozed out over the ice, there is no snow, but frozen slosh to-day, *i. e.* a rotten, roughish, dull-white ice. It is a rare day for winter, clear and bright, yet warm. The warmth and stillness in the hollows about the Andromeda Ponds are charming. You dispense with gloves. I see .. mice-tracks in the fields and meadows like this: four together, rabbit-like, four or five inches apart and one and a quarter broad. Are they the same with the ? I think so. I see rabbit-tracks, pretty large, maybe white ones, two feet apart. I suspect that in each case they are com- ing down the page.[1] In the partridge-tracks the side toes are more spread

[1] Yes.

than in crows; and I believe the hind one is not so long. Both trail the middle toe. The partridge-track looks like this: I see the tracks apparently of many hunt- ers that hastened out this morning.

I have come with basket and hatchet to get a specimen of the rose-colored ice. It is covered with snow. I push it away with my hands and feet. At first I detect no rose tint, and suspect it may have disappeared, — faded or bleached out, — or it was a dream. But the surrounding snow and the little body of the ice I had laid bare was what hindered. At length I detect a faint tinge; I cut down a young white oak and sweep bare a larger space; I then cut out a cake. The redness is all about an inch below the surface, the little bubbles in the ice there for half an inch vertically being coated interruptedly within or without with what looks like a minute red dust when seen through a microscope, as if it had dried on. Little balloons, with some old paint almost scaled off their spheres. It has no beauty nor brightness thus seen, [no] more than brick-dust. And this it is which gave the ice so delicate a tinge, seen through that inch of clear white ice. What is it? Can it be blood?

I find an abundance of the seeds of sweet-gale frozen in in windrows on the ice of the river meadows as I return, which were washed out by the freshet. I color my fingers with them. And thus they are planted, then, — somewhat, perhaps, in waving lines, as they wash up. Returning over the fields, the shallow pools made by the rain and thaw, whose water has almost

entirely settled away, — and the ice rests on the ground, — where they are bare of snow, now that the sun is about a quarter of an hour high, looking east are quite green. For a week or two the days have been sensibly longer, and it is quite light now when the five-o'clock train comes in.

Sagard says of the hares (*lièvres*) of the Huron country, "*Les sapinières* and little woods are the places of their retreat." Such is their taste now. Says the muskrats "feed on *l'herbe* on land and the white of the *joncs* at the bottom of the lakes and rivers."

A pine cone blossoms out now fully in about three days, in the house. They begin to open about halfway up. They are exceedingly regular and handsome; the scales with shallow triangular or crescent-shaped extremities, the prickle pointing downward, are most open above, and are so much recurved at the base of the cone that they lie close together and almost flat there, or at right

End of scale on side of cone.

angles with the stem, like a shield of iron scales, making a perfectly regular figure of thirteen (in one instance) curved rays, thus: — only far more regular.

There are just thirteen rays in each of the three I have!!! These vary in their roundness or the flatness of the cone; so the white pine cones in their length. I find just five such rays (the number of the needles in a fascicle) in each white pine cone I have, and each goes round once. A larch cone has five rows. Four hemlock cones have five each, like white pine, but little twisted.

Jan. 26. This morning it snows again, — a fine dry snow with no wind to speak of, giving a wintry aspect to the landscape.

What a Proteus is our weather! Let me try to remember its freaks. We had remarkably steady sleighing, on a little snow some six inches deep, from the 5th of December all through the month, and some way into January. It came damp and froze up solid. Yet there was none in Boston the while. There was, however, a little rain near the end of December, and occasional slight flurries of snow.

January 6th, after some comparatively pleasant days, there was a raw northerly wind and fine drifting or driving snow in the afternoon, as I walked over the Great Meadows, forming shallow drifts on the ice, but it soon stopped.

January 7th, I was surprised when I opened the door in the afternoon by the warm south wind and sudden softening and melting of the snow. It was a January thaw without rain, the manure beginning to wash off the ice in the streets. The winter's back was broken, and I dreamed of spring, etc., etc.

January 8th, the same. The ice in roads washed bare, the brooks full of melted snow; but it is still clear weather and warm.

January 9. A cloudy day, wet underfoot, threatening snow; difficult to get on to the river; yellow water many rods wide each side over the ice.

January 10. Suddenly cold again and blustering. All waters frozen up. Go on to the swamps, keeping ears covered.

January 11. Make haste to improve the skating in the afternoon, though it is beginning to snow, and the [ice] is soon covered half an inch. Then it stops at night.

January 12. After another slight spitting of snow in the forenoon, it clears up very pleasant and warm in the afternoon, and I walk by the brooks, looking for fish, hearing the crows caw in the horizon and thinking of spring.

January 13. Still warm. In roads, both muddy, wet, and slippery where ice; thick and misty air, threatening rain.

January 14. Clear and cold. All things frozen again. Excellent skating on meadows. Skated to Baker Farm.

January 15. In the forenoon, spit a little snow, making shallow drifts on the ice, through which I skated in the afternoon to Bedford. Stopped snowing.

January 16. Snowed a little again, spoiling the skating.

January 17. Forget.

January 18. Rained hard all day; washed off the little snow left, down to the ice. Stayed in all day. Water over shoes in the middle of the road. The gutters turned to mill-brooks. Few go out.

January 19. In the night, rain turned to damp snow, which at first made slosh, then for most part prevailed over the water, which ran off underneath; stuck to the houses and trees and made a remarkable winter scene. A driving damp snow with a strong northwest wind all day, lodging on the trees *within* the woods beyond all account. Walked in woods in midst of it to see the pines bent down and the white oaks, etc., and broken. Snowbirds, *i. e.* linarias, in yard. Making drifts by walls.

January 20. Still higher wind in night (snow over), shaking the snow from trees. Now almost bare. Snow seven or eight inches on level in woods, but almost all in drifts under the walls in fields. The sudden-frozen slosh ponds, partly run off, like spewed bread. Hardly bear yet. Not very cold. Go studying drifts. Fine clear weather.

January 21. Becomes overcast at noon. A fine snow spits, then turns to fine hail, then rain, glazing a little.

January 22. Rained all night. Walking now worse than ever this year, midleg deep in gutters. Lakes in the street. River risen,—a freshet,—breaking up ice a foot thick, flows under dry causeway, bridges a torrent; muskrats driven out by hundreds and shot; dark angry waves where was lately ice and snow. Earth washed bare. Radical leaves appear and russet hills. Still rains a *little*.

January 23. Fair weather. Water still rising over the Red Bridge road, though suddenly fallen in many

hollows in fields, leaving thin ice two feet above it around and by clumps. Great work done by brooks last night. Have to go round two or three miles to find a dry causeway. Not strong enough for skating.

January 24. Not strong enough to skate on meadows. Went to Walden. At dusk, snowed three quarters of an inch and spoiled prospect of skating.

January 25. Clear, bright, and mild. Water still higher than before; over the causeways.

January 26. A fine snow falling, spoiling all prospect of skating on this broad ice. Is not good skating the surest sign of snow or foul weather?

To continue the 26th: —

P. M. — To Walden.

A thick, driving snow, something like, but less than, that of the 19th. There is a strong easterly wind and the snow is very damp. In the deepest hollows on the Brister Hill path it has already lodged handsomely. Suppose you descend into the deepest circular one, far beneath the sweep of the blustering wind, where the flakes at last drop gently to their resting-places. There is a level, white circular floor, indicating ice beneath, and, all around, the white pines, under an accumulating snowy burthen, are hung with drooping white wreaths or fans of snow. The snow on pitch pines takes the forms of large balls, on white pines often of great rolling-pins. Already the trees are bending in all directions into the paths and hollows as here. The birches here are bowed inward to the open circle of the pond-hole, their

tops apparently buried in the old snow. Nothing can be prettier than the snow on the leafless shrub oaks, the twigs are so small and numerous, little snowy arms crossing each other at every imaginable angle, like a whirligig. It is surprising what a burden of snow already rests on little bare twigs hardly bigger than a knitting-needle, both as they stand perpendicularly and horizontally. The great damp flakes come and soon bridge across the interval, even two inches over, between the forks of such twigs where they are horizontal, one sticking to another. It rests on such horizontal twigs commonly in the form of a prism resting on one corner (vertical section where no wind). And in many places, where the wind is felt, the little walls of snow are built out at an angle with the perpendicular, in the direction whence the snow comes: (a vertical section or end). Damp as it is, it [is] like swan's-down, as if it lay as light as well as thick. As it is with these shrub oaks, so with the largest trees in the stiller parts of the woods, and even the lowest dead limbs of the white pines are not prevented by the upper from bearing their part of the burden.

I am afraid I have not described vividly enough the aspect of that Lodging Snow of the 19th and to-day partly. Imagine the innumerable twigs and boughs of the forest (as you stand in its still midst), crossing each other at every conceivable angle on every side from the ground to thirty feet in height, with each its zigzag wall of snow four or five inches high, so innumerable at different distances one behind another that they completely close up the view like

a loose-woven downy screen, into which, however, stooping and winding, you ceaselessly advance. The wintriest scene, — which perhaps can only be seen in perfection while the snow is yet falling, before wind and thaw begin. Else you miss, you lose, the delicate touch of the master. A coarse woof and warp of snowy batting, leaving no space for a bird to perch.

I see where a partridge has waddled through the snow still falling, making a continuous track. I look in the direction to which it points, and see the bird just skimming over the bushes fifteen rods off.

The plumes of pitch pines are first filled up solid, then they begin to make great snowy *casse-têtes*, or pestles. In the fields the air is thick with driving snow. You can only see a dozen rods into its woof and warp. It fills either this ear or that and your eyes with hard, cutting, blinding scales if you face it. It is forming shelly drifts behind the walls, and stretches in folds across the roads; but in deep, withdrawn hollows in the woods the flakes at last come gently and deviously down, lodging on every twig and leaf, and forming deep and downy and level beds between and on the ice of the pools. The lowermost twigs support not less snow but more.

In many places where you knew there was a thrifty young wood, there appears to be none, for all is bent down and almost completely buried in the snow, and you are stepping over them. The pitch pines are most round-headed, and the young white oaks are most leaved at top, and hence suffer most.

What changes in the aspect of the earth! one day

russet hills, and muddy ice, and yellow and greenish pools in the fields; the next all painted white, the fields and woods and roofs laid on thick. The great sloshy pools in the fields, freezing as they dried away, look like bread that has spewed in the baking, the fungi of a night, an acre in extent; but trust not your feet on it, for the under side is not done; there the principle of water still prevails.

Methinks that after any great storm in winter, whether of snow or rain, the equilibrium of the air is again disturbed and there comes a high wind shaking down the snow and drying up the water.

Jan. 27. Yesterday's driving easterly snow-storm turned to sleet in the evening, and then to rain, and this morning it is clear and pretty cold, the wind westerly, the snow settled to three or four inches on a level, with a frozen crust and some water beneath in many places. It seems as if the sky could not bear to look down on smooth ice, and so made haste to cover it up.

One is educated to believe, and would rejoice if the rising generation should find no occasion to doubt, that the State and the Church are on the side of morality, that the voice of the people is the voice of God. Harvard College was partly built by a lottery. My father tells me he bought a ticket in it. Perhaps she thus laid the foundation of her Divinity School. Thus she teaches by example. New England is flooded with the " Official Schemes of the Maryland State Lotteries," and in this that State is no less unprincipled than in

her slaveholding. Maryland, and every fool who buys a ticket of her, is bound straight to the bottomless pit. The State of Maryland is a moral fungus. Her offense is rank; it smells to heaven. Knowing that she is doing the devil's work, and that her customers are ashamed to be known as such, she advertises, as in the case of private diseases, that " the strictest confidence will be observed." "Consolidated" Deviltry!

P. M. — Up meadow to Cliffs and Walden road.

A cold, cutting southwesterly wind. The crust bears where the snow is very shallow, but lets you through to water in many places on the meadow. The river has not yet fallen much. The muskrats have added to their houses in some places. So they still use them. Started a hare among shrub oaks. It had been squatting in a slight hollow, rather concealed than sheltered. They always look poverty-stricken.

Some ice organ-pipes at the Cliffs. They appear to be formed of successive rings about half an inch thick and diameter lessening with more or less regularity to the point: Sometimes the point split in two. Then the rocks are incased with ice under which water flows, — thin sheets of rippling water frozen as it flowed, — and, with the sun, again apparently thawing beneath and giving room to a new sheet of water, for under the south side of the rocks it melts almost every day.

I came upon a fox's track under the north end of the Cliffs and followed it. It was made last night, after the sleet and probably the rain was over, before it

froze; it must have been at midnight or after. The tracks were commonly ten or twelve inches apart and each one and three quarters or two inches wide. Sometimes there was a longer interval and two feet fell nearer together, as if in a canter. It had doubled directly on its track in one place for a rod or two, then went up the north end of the Cliff where it is low and went along southward just on its edge, ascending gradually. In one place it had made water like a dog, and I perceived the peculiar rank fox odor without stooping. It did not wind round the prominent rocks, but leaped upon them as if to reconnoitre. Its route was for the most part a little below the edge of the Cliff, occasionally surmounting it. At length, after going perhaps half a mile, it turned as if to descend a dozen rods beyond the juniper, and suddenly came to end. Looking closely I found the entrance (apparently) to its hole, under a prominent rock which seemed to lie loose on the top of the ledge and about two feet from the nearest track. By stooping it had probably squeezed under this and passed into its den beneath. I could find no track leading from it.

Their tracks are larger than you would expect, as large as those of a much heavier dog, I should think. What a life is theirs, venturing forth only at night for their prey, ranging a great distance, trusting to pick up a sleeping partridge or a hare, and at home again before morning! With what relish they must relate their midnight adventures to one another there in their dens by day, if they have society! I had never associated that rock with a fox's den, though perhaps I

had sat on it many a time. There are more things in heaven and earth, Horatio, etc., etc. They are the only outlaws, the only Robin Hoods, here nowadays. Do they not stand for gypsies and all outlaws? Wild dogs, as Indians are wild men.

People will tell you of the Cold Winter, clear bright days when for six weeks the eaves did not run once.

As I went through the woods toward the railroad, the sun setting, there were many small violet-colored, *i. e.* lilac-tinted, clouds scattered along the otherwise clear western horizon.

I often see the mincing tracks of a skunk. I came upon the track of a woodchopper, who had gone to his work early this morning across Fair Haven Pond. It suggested his hard work and little pecuniary gain, but simple life and health and contentment. As I took the back track on his trail, comparing his foot and stride with mine, I was startled to detect a slight aberration, as it were sliding in his tread, or as if he had occasionally stopped and made a fresh impress not exactly coincident with the first. In short, I discovered ere long that he had had a companion; perchance they were two thieves trying to pass for one, thought I; but the truth was the second, to save his strength in this long walk to his work through the crusty snow, had stepped with more or less precision in the tracks of his predecessor. The snow was three or four inches deep. I afterwards used the track of a horse in like manner to my advantage; so that my successor might have thought that a sleigh had gone along drawn by a man.

Jan. 28. Sunday. Grew warmer toward night and snowed; but this soon turned to heavy rain in the night, which washed all the snow off the ice, leaving only bare ground and ice the county over by next morning.

Jan. 29. Not cold. Sun comes out at noon.

Jan. 30. Clear and not cold, and now fine skating, the river rising again to the height it had attained the 24th, which (with this) I think remarkable for this season. It is now about a foot lower than on the 24th (it had fallen over eighteen inches since then), but is rising. It is unusual for the river to be so much swollen in midwinter, because it is unusual to have so much rain at this season. Both these — or this whole rise — are owing to heavy rains on the frozen ground carrying off what snow there was, and now soaking up. The hills shed it all like a roof into the valleys. It is up to the hubs on the causeways, and foot-travellers have to cross on the river and meadows. Melvin and others are out after muskrats again, and [I] see them with their pouches stuffed out with their round bodies.

Minott to-day enumerates the red, gray, black, and what he calls the Sampson fox. He says, "It's a sort of yaller fox, but their pelts ain't good for much." He never *saw* one, but the hunters have told him of them. He never saw a gray nor a black one. Told how Jake Lakin lost a dog, a very valuable one, by a fox leading him on to the ice on the Great Meadows and drowning him. Said the raccoon made a track very

much like a young child's foot. He had often seen it in the mud of a ditch.

Jan. 31. Wednesday. A clear, cold, beautiful day. Fine skating. An unprecedented expanse of ice.

At 10 A. M., skated up the river to explore further than I had been. The water within ten inches of the height at which it stood April 23d, '52, as I noticed at the stone bridge.[1]

At 8 A. M., the river rising, the thin yellowish ice of last night, next the shore, is, as usual, much heaved up in ridges, as if beginning to double on itself, and here and there at 9 o'clock, being cracked thus in the lowest parts, the water begins to spurt up in some places in a stream, as from an ordinary pump, and flow along these valleys; and thus we have soon reëstablished an edging of shallow yellowish or oil-colored water all along the river and meadows, covered with floating snow-fleas.

By noon, though it was a pretty cool day, the water had generally burst through and overflowed the ice along the shore and once more stood at a level there; *i. e.*, water and ice made a level where the ice was uneven before. Before skating up-stream I tried my boat-sail on the meadow in front of the house and found that I could go well enough before the wind, resting the mast on my hip and holding by the middle with one hand, but I could not easily tack.

The country thus almost completely bare of snow, — only some ice in the roads and fields, — and the frozen

[1] *Vide* Feb. 1st.

Vol. VII

freshet at this remarkable height, I skated up as far as the boundary between Wayland and Sudbury just above Pelham's Pond, to a point which a woman called about one and a half miles from Saxonville, about twelve miles, between 10 A. M. and one, quite leisurely. There I found the river open unexpectedly, as if there were a rapid there, and as I walked up it some three quarters of a mile, it was still open before me a half-mile further at least, or probably to the falls.[1] Somewhat like this: —

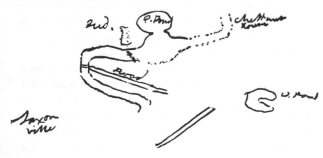

All the open part, one and a half miles at least, was pretty closely hemmed in by highlands. I skated about twelve miles and walked three quarters of a mile further. It was, all the way that I skated, a chain of meadows, with the muskrat-houses still rising above the ice, commonly on the bank of the river, and marking it like smaller haycocks amid the large ones still left. I skated past three bridges above Sherman's — or nine in all (?) — and walked to the fourth. The next, or fifth, would probably be that in middle

[1] [Three interrogation-points inserted here, evidently at a later time.]

of Saxonville. *Viz.* Causeway bridges, Mill Village Bridge at Larned Brook, Pelham Pond Bridge, and that on road from Dudley Pond to Southboro and Marlboro.

As I skated near the shore under Lee's Cliff, I saw what I took to be some scrags or knotty stubs of a dead limb lying on the bank beneath a white oak, close by me. Yet while I looked directly at them I could not but admire their close resemblance to partridges. I had come along with a rapid whir and suddenly halted right against them, only two rods distant, and, as my eyes watered a little from skating against the wind, I was not convinced that they were birds till I had pulled out my glass and deliberately examined them. They sat and stood, three of them, perfectly still with their heads erect, some darker feathers like ears, methinks, increasing their resemblance to scrabs [*sic*], as where a small limb is broken off. I was much surprised at the remarkable stillness they preserved, instinctively relying on the resemblance to the ground for their protection, *i. e.* withered grass, dry oak leaves, dead scrags, and broken twigs. I thought at first that it was a dead oak limb with a few stub ends or scrabbs [*sic*] sticking up, and for some time after I had noted the resemblance to birds, standing only two rods off, I could not be sure of their character on account of their perfect motionlessness, and it was not till I brought my glass to bear on them and saw their eyes distinctly, steadily glaring on me, their necks and every muscle tense with anxiety, that I was convinced. At length, on some signal which I did not perceive, they went with a whir, as if shot, off over the bushes.

It was quite an adventure getting over the bridge-ways or causeways, for on every shore there was either water or thin ice which would not bear. Sometimes I managed to get on to the timbers of a bridge, the end of a projecting "tie" (?), and off the same way, thus straddling over the bridges and the gulf of open water about them on to the edge of the thick ice, or else I swung myself on to the causeways by the willows, or crawled along a pole or rail, catching at a tree which stood in the water, — or got in. At the bend above the Pantry, there was [a] sort of canal or crack quite across the river and meadow, excepting a slight bridge of ice. As I passed the mouth of Larned Brook, off Wayland meeting-house, I pulled out my glass and saw that it was 12.30 o'clock. In each town I found one or two trappers come forth to shoot muskrats. As a regular thing they turned out after dinner, buttoning up their greatcoats. All along the river their cabins had been torn to pieces by them, and in one place I saw two men sitting over the hole where they had just demolished one, one with a pistol ready pointed to the water where he expected the rat to come up, the other with a gun. In this twelve miles of the river there would be two or three at least pretty sure to turn out such a day and take to the ice for muskrats. I saw again an abundance of sweet-gale seed on the ice, frozen in, near Pelham's Pond. This seed is thus dispersed regularly on a large scale. It lies as it was washed along the edge of an overflow. Beside

Vol. VII

VI

FEBRUARY, 1855

(ÆT. 37)

Feb. 1. As usual these broad fields of ice could not be left uncovered over the third day. It began to spit a little snow at noon, just enough to show on the ice, the thickness of a blanket, though not on the ground, — dissipated there both by the warmth and irregularity.

At 4 P. M., I find that the river rose last evening to within eight and a half inches of the rise of April 23d, 1852, and then began to fall. It has now fallen about four inches. Accordingly, the river falling all day, no water has burst out through the ice next the shore, and it is now one uninterrupted level white blanket of snow quite to the shore on every side. This, then, is established, — that, the river falling four inches during the day, though it has been as warm as yesterday, there has been no overflow along the shore. Apparently the thin recent ice of the night, which connects the main body with the shore, bends and breaks with the rising of the mass, especially in the morning, under the influence of the sun and wind, and the water establishes itself at a new level.

As I skated up the river so swiftly yesterday, now here now there, past the old kingdoms of my fancy, I was reminded of Landor's "Richard the First." "I

a dilapidated muskrat's house, lay the wretched carcass of its former occupant on the ice, stripped of its hide, — black, even without its skin, with veins of red. Returning, I saw a large hawk flapping and sailing low over the meadow. There was some dark color to its wings.

You were often liable to be thrown when skating fast, by the shallow puddles on the ice formed in the middle of the day and not easy to be distinguished. These detained your feet while your unimpeded body fell forward.

sailed along the realms of my family; on the right was England, on the left was France [on the right was Sudbury, on the left was Wayland;][1] little else could I discover than sterile eminences and extensive shoals. They fled behind me; so pass away generations; so shift, and sink, and die away affections." "I debark in Sicily." That was Tall's Island. "I sail again, and within a day or two [an hour or two?] I behold, as the sun is setting, the solitary majesty of Crete, mother of a religion, it is said, that lived 2000 years. [That was Nobscot surely.] Onward, and many specks bubble up along the blue Ægean [these must have been the muskrat-houses in the meadows], every one [I have no doubt] the monument of a greater man [being?] than I am."

The swelling river was belching on a high key, from ten to eleven. Quite a musical cracking, running like chain lightning of sound athwart my course, as if the river, squeezed, thus gave its morning's milk with music. A certain congealed milkiness in the sound, like the soft action of piano keys, — a little like the cry of a pigeon woodpecker, — *a-week a-week*, etc. A congealed gurgling, frog-like. As I passed, the ice forced up by the water on one side suddenly settled on another with a crash, and quite a lake was formed above the ice behind me, and my successor two hours after, to his wonder and alarm, saw my tracks disappear in one side of it and come out on the other. My seat from time to time is the springy horizontal bough of some fallen tree which is frozen into the ice, some old maple that had blown over and retained some

[1] [The brackets in this paragraph are Thoreau's.]

life for a year after in the water, covered with the great shaggy perforate parmelia. Lying flat, I quench my thirst where it is melted about it, blowing aside the snow-fleas. The great arundo in the Sudbury meadows was all level with the ice. There was a great bay of ice stretching up the Pantry and up Larned Brook. I looked up a broad, glaring bay of ice at the last place, which seemed to reach to the base of Nobscot and almost to the horizon. Some dead maple or oak saplings, laid side by side, made my bridges by which I got on to the ice along the watery shore. It was a problem to get off, and another to get on, dry-shod. You are commonly repaid for a longer excursion than usual, and being outdoors all day, by seeing some rarer bird for the season, as yesterday a great hawk.

Feb. 2. Quite clear and colder, yet it could not refrain from snowing half an inch more in the night, whitening the ground now, *as well* as the ice.

Brown is again filling his ice-house, which he commenced to do some weeks ago.

I got another skate this afternoon, in spite of the thin coating of snow. This, then, is the fourth day of this rare skating, though since yesterday noon the slight whitening of snow has hurt it somewhat.

The river at 4 P. M. has fallen some eight or ten inches. In some places there are thin flakes of ice standing on their edges within an inch or two of each other over more than a quarter of an acre, either ice blown into that position (which in this case is not likely, since there is a great deal too much for that surface)

or crystallized so while the water suddenly ran off below. There are large tracts of thin white ice, where the water ran off before it had time to freeze hard enough to bear.

This last half-inch of snow, which fell in the night, is just enough to track animals on the ice by. All about the Hill and Rock I see the tracks of rabbits which have run back and forth close to the shore repeatedly since the night. In the case of the rabbit the fore feet are further apart than the hind ones, the first say four or five inches to the outside, the last two or three.[1] They are generally not quite regular, but one of the fore feet a little in advance of the other, and so with one of the hind feet. There is an interval of about sixteen inches between each four tracks. Sometimes they are in a curve or crescent, all touching. I saw what must have been either a muskrat's or mink's track, I think, since it came out of the water, — the tracks roundish and toes much rayed, four or five inches apart in the trail, with only a trifle more between the fore and hind legs, and the mark of the tail in succes- sive curves as it struck the ice, thus: Another track puzzled me, as if a hare had been running like a dog

and touched its tail, — if it had any. This in several places.

[1] [Thoreau afterward discovered his mistake and learned that the hind feet come down outside and in front of the fore feet.]

Snowed again half an inch more in the evening, after which, at ten o'clock, the moon still obscured, I skated on the river and meadows. The water falling, the ice on the meadow occasionally settles with a crack under our weight. It is pleasant to feel these swells and valleys occasioned by the subsidence of the water, in some cases pretty abrupt. Also to hear the hollow, rumbling sound in such rolling places on the meadow where there is an empty chamber beneath, the water being entirely run out. Our skates make but little sound in this coating of snow about an inch thick, as if we had on woollen skates, and we can easily see our tracks in the night. We seem thus to go faster than before by day, not only because we do not see (but feel and imagine) our rapidity, but because of the impression which the mysterious muffled sound of our feet makes. In the meanwhile we hear the distant note of a hooting owl, and the distant rumbling of approaching or retreating cars sounds like a constant waterfall. Now and then we skated into some chippy, crackling white ice, where a superficial puddle had run dry before freezing hard, and got a tumble.

Feb. 3. This morning it is snowing again, as if a squall. The snow has thus spit on the ice four times since this last skating began on Tuesday, the 30th, *viz.* Thursday noon, Thursday evening, Friday evening, and now Saturday morning. This will deserve to be called the winter of skating. The heavens thus spit on the ice as if they had a spite against it. I even

suspect that the account of the matter may be that when an atmosphere containing more moisture than usual is wafted over this chain of broad ice lakes (especially the rest of the country being bare of snow) its moisture is suddenly condensed and frozen, and there is a spitting of snow. This last flurry lasted an hour or more, and then it grew colder and windy.

P. M. — Skating through snow.

Skated up the river with T[appa]n in spite of the snow and wind. It had cleared up, but the snow was on a level strong three quarters of an inch deep (seemingly an inch), but for the most part blown into drifts three to ten feet wide and much deeper (with bare intervals) under a strong northwesterly wind. It was a novel experience, this skating through snow, sometimes a mile without a bare spot, this blustering day. In many places a crack ran across our course where the water had oozed out, and the driving snow catching in it had formed a thick batter with a stiffish crust in which we were tripped up and measured our lengths on the ice. The few thin places were concealed, and we avoided them by our knowledge of the localities, though we sometimes saw the air-bubbles of the mid-channel through the thin ice; for, the water going down, the current is increasing and eating its way through the ice. Sometimes a thicker drift, too, threw us, or a sudden unevenness in the concealed ice; but on the whole the snow was but a slight obstruction. We skated with much more facility than I had anticipated, and I would not have missed the experience for a good deal. The water, falling rapidly, has left

a part of the ice in shelves attached to the shore and
to the alders and other trees and bushes, fifteen or
eighteen inches above the general level, with a spongy
or brittle mass of crystals suspended from its under
sides five or six inches deep, or double that of the ice,
looking like lace-work on the side and showing all
kinds of angular geometrical figures when you look down
on it turned bottom up; as if the water had sunk
away faster than it could freeze solidly. I think that
in my ice-flakes of the 2d the thin crust of the horizontal ice was blown off and had left these exposed.
Sometimes we had to face a head wind and driving
or blowing snow which concealed the prospect a few
rods ahead, and we made a tedious progress.

We went up the Pantry Meadow above the old
William Wheeler house, and came down this meadow
again with the wind and snow dust, spreading our
coat-tails, like birds, though somewhat at the risk of
our necks if we had struck a foul place. I found that
I could sail on a tack pretty well, trimming with my
skirts. Sometimes we had to jump suddenly over
some obstacle which the snow had concealed before, to
save our necks. It was worth the while for one to look
back against the sun and wind and see the other sixty
rods off coming, floating down like a graceful demon
in the midst of the broad meadow all covered and lit
with the curling snow-steam, between which you saw
the ice in dark, waving streaks, like a mighty river
Orellana braided of a myriad steaming currents, —
like the demon of the storm driving his flocks and
herds before him. In the midst of this tide of curling

snow-steam, he sweeps and surges this way and that
and comes on like the spirit of the whirlwind.

At Lee's Cliff we made a fire, kindling with white
pine cones, after oak leaves and twigs, — else we had
lost it; these saved us, for there is a resinous drop
at the point of each scale, — and then we forgot that
we were outdoors in a blustering winter day.

The drifts will probably harden by to-morrow and
make such skating impossible. I was curious to see
how my tracks looked, — what figure I cut, — and
skated back a little to look at it. That little way it
was like this somewhat: —

somewhat like the shallow snow-drifts.

Looking toward the sun and wind, you saw a broad
river half a mile or more in width, its whole surface
lit and alive with flowing streams of snow, in form
like the steam which curls along a river's surface at
sunrise, and in midst of this moving world sailed
down the skater, majestically, as if on the surface of
water while the steam curled as high as his knees.

Several broad bays open on to this, some of them,
like the Pantry and Larned Brook, two or more miles
deep.

You scarcely see a bird such a day as this.

Flash go your dry leaves like powder and leave a
few bare and smoking twigs. Then you sedulously
feed a little flame, until the fire takes hold of the solid
wood and establishes itself. What an uncertain and

negative thing, when it finds nothing to suit its appetite after the first flash! What a positive and inexpugnable thing, when it begins to devour the solid
wood with a relish, burning with its own wind! You
must study as long at last how to put it out, as you
did how to kindle it. Close up under some upright
rock, where you scorch the yellow sulphur lichens.
Then cast on some creeping juniper wreaths or hemlock boughs to hear them crackle, realizing Scripture.

Some little boys ten years old are as handsome
skaters as I know. They sweep along with a graceful
floating motion, leaning now to this side, then to that,
like a marsh hawk beating the bush.

I still recur in my mind to that skate of the 31st.
I was thus enabled to get a bird's-eye view of the river,
— to survey its length and breadth within a few hours,
connect one part (one shore) with another in my mind,
and realize what was going on upon it from end to
end, — to know the whole as I ordinarily knew a
few miles of it only. I connected the chestnut-tree
house, near the shore in Wayland, with the chimney
house[1] in Billerica, Pelham's Pond with Nutting's
Pond in Billerica. There is good skating from the
mouth to Saxonville, measuring in a straight line some
twenty-two miles, by the river say thirty now, Concord midway. It is all the way of one character, — a
meadow river, or dead stream, — Musketicook, — the
abode of muskrats, pickerel, etc., crossed within these
dozen miles each way, — or thirty in all, — by some

[1] Atkinson's?

twenty low wooden bridges, *sublicii pontes*, connected
with the mainland by willowy causeways. Thus the
long, shallow lakes divided into reaches. These long
causeways all under water and ice now, only the
bridges peeping out from time to time like a dry eyelid.
You must look close to find them in many cases. Mere
islands are they to the traveller, in the waste of water
and ice. Only two villages lying near the river, Concord and Wayland, and one at each end of this thirty
miles.

Haycocks commonly stand only in the Sudbury
meadow. You must beware when you cross the deep,
dark channel between the sunken willow rows, distinguishing it from the meadowy sea where the current
is seen eating its way through; else you may be in
overhead before you know it. I used some bits of wood
with a groove in them for crossing the causeways and
gravelly places, that I need not scratch my skate-
irons.

Minott says that the white rabbit does not make
a hole, — sits under a bunch of dry ferns and the like,
— but that the gray one does. They and the fox love
to come out and lie in the sun.

Feb. 4. Clear and cold and windy; much colder
than for some time.

Saw this afternoon a very distinct otter-track by the
Rock, at the junction of the two rivers. The separate
foot-tracks were quite round, more than two inches in
diameter, showing the five toes distinctly in the snow,
which was about half an inch deep. In one place,

where it had crossed last night to Merrick's pasture, its trail, about six inches wide and of furrows in the snow, was on one side of its foot-tracks, thus: and there was about nine inches between the fore and hind feet [*sic*]. Close by the Great Aspen I saw where it had entered or come out of the water under a shelf of ice left adhering to a maple. There it apparently played and slid on the level ice, making a broad trail as if a shovel had been shoved along, just eight inches wide, without a foot-track in it for four feet or more. And again the trail was only two inches wide and between the foot-tracks, which were

side by side and twenty-two inches apart. It had left much dung on the ice, soft, yellow, bowel-like, like a gum that has been chewed in consistency. About the edge of the hole, where the snow was all rubbed off, was something white which looked and smelt exactly like bits of the skin of pouts or eels. Minott tells of one shot once while eating an eel. Vance saw one this winter in this town by a brook eating a fish.

The water has now fallen nearly two feet, and those ice shelves I noticed yesterday, when you go into a swamp and all along the shore amid the alders, birches, and maples, look just like ample picnic tables ready set, two feet high, with often a leaf down or else a table-cloth hanging, — just like camp tables around the tent-poles, now covered with snowy napkins.

I notice my old skate-tracks like this: —

It is better skating to-day than yesterday. This is the sixth day of some kind of skating.

Feb. 5. It was quite cold last evening, and I saw the scuttle window reflecting the lamp from a myriad brilliant points when I went up to bed. It sparkled as if we lived inside of a cave, but this morning it has moderated considerably and is snowing. Already one inch of snow has fallen.

According to Webster, in Welsh a hare is "furze or gorse-cat." Also, "Chuk, a word used in calling swine. It is the original name of that animal, which our ancestors brought with them from Persia, where it is still in use. Pers. *chuk*," etc. "Sans. *sugara*. Our ancestors while in England adopted the Welsh *hwc*, hog; but *chuck* is retained in our popular name of wood-chuck, that is, wood hog."

In a journal it is important in a few words to describe the weather, or character of the day, as it affects our feelings. That which was so important at the time cannot be unimportant to remember.

Day before yesterday the fine snow, blowing over the meadow in parallel streams between which the darker ice was seen, looked just like the steam curling along the surface of a river. In the midst of this, midleg deep at least, you surged along. It was surprising how, in the midst of all this stationary and drifting snow, the skate found a smooth and level

surface over which it glided so securely, with a muffled rumble. The ice for the last week has reached quite up into the village, so that you could get on to it just in the rear of the bank and set sail on skates for any part of the Concord River valley.

Found Therien cutting down the two largest chestnuts in the wood-lot behind where my house was. On the butt of one about two feet in diameter I counted seventy-five rings. T. soon after broke his axe in cutting through a knot in this tree, which he was cutting up for posts. He broke out a piece half an inch deep. This he says often happens. Perhaps there is some frost in his axe. Several choppers have broken their axes to-day.

Feb. 6. The coldest morning this winter. Our thermometer stands at −14° at 9 A. M.; others, we hear, at 6 A. M. stood at −18°, at Gorham, N. H., −30°. There are no loiterers in the street, and the wheels of wood wagons squeak as they have not for a long time, — actually shriek. Frostwork keeps its place on the window within three feet of the stove *all day* in my chamber. At 4 P. M. the thermometer is at −10°; at six it is at −14°.

I was walking at five, and found it stinging cold. It stung the face. When I look out at the chimneys, I see that the cold and hungry air snaps up the smoke at once. The smoke is clear and light-colored and does not get far into the air before it is dissipated (?), condensed. The setting sun no sooner leaves our west windows than a solid but beautiful crystallization coats

them, except perhaps a triangularish bare spot at one corner, which perhaps the sun has warmed and dried. (I believe the saying is that by the 1st of February the meal and grain for a horse are half out.) A solid sparkling field in the midst of each pane, with broad, flowing sheaves surrounding it. It has been a very mild as well as open winter up to this. At 9 o'clock P. M., thermometer at −16°. They say it did not rise above −6° to-day.

Feb. 7. The coldest night for a long, long time was last. Sheets froze stiff about the faces. Cat mewed to have the door opened, but was at first disinclined to go out. When she came in at nine she smelt of meadow-hay. We all took her up and smelled of her, it was so fragrant. Had cuddled in some barn. People dreaded to go to bed. The ground cracked in the night as if a powder-mill had blown up, and the timbers of the house also. My pail of water was frozen in the morning so that I could not break it. Must leave many buttons unbuttoned, owing to numb fingers. Iron was like fire in the hands. Thermometer at about 7.30 A. M. gone into the bulb, − 19° at least. The cold has stopped the clock. Every bearded man in the street is a gray-beard. Bread, meat, milk, cheese, etc., etc., all frozen. See the inside of your cellar door all covered and sparkling with frost like Golconda. Pity the poor who have not a large wood-pile. The latches are white with frost, and every nail-head in entries, etc., has a white cap. The chopper hesitates to go to the woods. Yet I see S. W—— stumping past, three quarters of a mile, for his morning's dram. Neighbor Smith's thermometer stood at −26° early this morning. But this day is at length more moderate than yesterday.

R. Rice says that alewives used to go into Pelham Pond, — that you may go up Larned Brook and so into the pond by a ditch. His brother James skated from Sudbury to Billerica and by canal to Charlestown and back. He used to see where the otter had slid at Ware (Weir?) Hill, a rod down the steep bank, as if a thousand times, it was so smooth. After a thick snow had been falling in the river and formed a slosh on the surface, he could tell whether otter had been at work, by the holes in this slosh or snowy water where they had put up their heads while fishing. The surface would be all dotted with them. He had known musquash to make a canal to keep the water from freezing, a foot wide. Thinks otter make their track by drawing themselves along by the fore feet, obliterating the track of their feet. But may not the tail suffice to do this in light snow? Had seen a fox catching mice in a meadow. He would jump up and come down on a tussock, and then look round over the edge to see if he had scared any mice out of it. Two frog hawks (white rump and slaty wings, rather small hawk) have their nest regularly at his place in Sudbury. He once saw one — the male, he thinks — come along from the meadow with a frog in his claws. As he flew up toward and over the wood where the other was setting, he uttered a peculiar cry and, the other darting out, he let the frog drop two or three rods through the air, which the other caught.

Tree sparrows, two or three only at once, come into the yard, the first I have distinguished this winter. I notice that the snow-drifts on the windows, as you see the light through them, are stratified, showing undulating, equidistant strata, apparently as more or less dense (maybe more or less coarse and damp), — alternately darker and lighter strata. I was so sure this storm would bring snowbirds into the yard that I went to the window at ten to look for them, and there they were. Also a downy woodpecker — perhaps a hairy — flitted high across the street to an elm in front of the house and commenced assiduously tapping, his head going like a hammer. The snow is so light and dry that it rises like spray or foam before the legs of the horses. They dash it before them upward like water. It is a handsome sight, a span of horses at a little distance dashing through it, especially coming toward you. It falls like suds around their legs. Why do birds come into the yards in storms almost alone? Are they driven out of the fields and woods for their subsistence? Or is it that all places are wild to them in the storm? It is very dark in cellars, the windows being covered with snow.

P. M. — Up river to Hubbard's Swamp and Wood.

The river and meadow are concealed under a foot of snow. I cannot tell when I am on it. It would be dangerous for a stranger to travel across the country now. The snow is so dry that, though I go through drifts up to my middle, it falls off at once and does not adhere to and damp my clothes at all. All over this swamp I find that the ice, upheld by the trees and

He spoke of the Dunge Hole, meaning that deep hollow and swamp by the road from the Wheelers' to White Pond. This probably the same that is referred to in the Town Records. Showed me a bunching up of the twigs of a larch from his swamp, perfectly thick, two feet in diameter, forty feet up a tree. This principle extends apparently to all the evergreens. You could not begin to see through this, though all the leaves of course are off.

Though the cold has been moderate to-day compared with yesterday, it has got more into the houses and barns, and the farmers complain more of it while attending to their cattle. This, i. e. yesterday, the 6th, will be remembered as the cold Tuesday. The old folks still refer to the Cold Friday, when they sat before great fires of wood four feet long, with a fence of blankets behind them, and water froze on the mantelpiece. But they say this is as cold as that was.

Feb. 8. Commenced snowing last evening about 7 o'clock, — a fine, dry snow, — and this morning it is about six inches deep and still snows a little. Continues to snow finely all day.

Feb. 9. Snowed harder in the night and blowed considerably. It is somewhat drifted this morning. A very fine and dry snow, about a foot deep on a level. It stands on the top of our pump about ten inches deep, almost a perfect hemisphere, or half of an ellipse.

It snows finely all day, making about twice as much as we have had on the ground before this winter.

shrubs, stands some two feet above the ground, the water having entirely run out beneath, and as I go along the path, not seeing any ice in snow a foot deep, it suddenly sinks with a crash for a rod around me, snow and all, and, stooping, I look through a dry cellar from one to two feet deep, in some places pretty dark, extending over the greater part of the swamp, with a perfectly level ceiling composed of ice one to two inches thick, surmounted by a foot of snow, and from the under side of the ice there depends from four to six inches a dense mass of crystals, so that it is a most sparkling grotto. You could have crawled round under the ice and snow all over the swamp quite dry, and I saw where the rabbits, etc., had entered there. In another swamp, where the trees were larger and further apart, only about one half the ice was held up in this manner, in tables from a few feet to a rod in diameter, so that it was very difficult walking. In the first place, as I was walking along the path, the first I knew down went the whole body of the snow for a rod, and I saw into a dark cavern yawning about me. I should think this ice by its strain and fall would injure the young trees and bushes; many are barked by it. And so it melts and wastes away, tumbling down from time to time with a crash. Those crystals were very handsome, and tinkled when touched like bits of tin. I saw a similar phenomenon February 4th, on a smaller scale. The snow is so dry that but little lodges on the trees.

I saw very few tracks to-day. It must be very hard for our small wild animals to get along while the snow is

so light. Not only the legs but the whole body of some
— a skunk, for example, I think — sinks in it and leaves
its trail. They must drag themselves bodily through it.

Saw *F. linarias.*

Elsewhere we hear the snow has been much deeper
than here.

Feb. 10. P. M. — To Walden.

A fine, clear day. There is a glare of light from the
fresh, unstained surface of the snow, so that it pains
the eyes to travel toward the sun.

I go across Walden. My shadow is very blue. It
is especially blue when there is a bright sunlight on
pure white snow. It suggests that there may be something divine, something celestial, in me.

Silas Hosmer tells me that a wild deer was killed
in Northboro this winter.

In many places the edges of drifts are sharp and
curving, almost a complete circle, ⟜ reflecting a blue
color from within like blue-tinted ⟍ shells.

I hear the faint metallic chirp of a tree sparrow in
the yard from time to time, or perchance the mew of
a linaria. It is worth the while to let some pigweed
grow in your garden, if only to attract these winter
visitors. It would be a pity to have these weeds burned
in the fall. Of the former I see in the winter but three
or four commonly at a time; of the latter, large flocks.
This in and after considerable snow-storms.

Since this deeper snow, the landscape is in some respects more wintry than before; the rivers and roads
are more concealed than they have been, and billows

of snow succeed each other across the fields and roads,
like an ocean waste.

Feb. 11. P. M. — To J. Dugan's *via* Tommy
Wheeler's.

The atmosphere is very blue, tingeing the distant
pine woods. The dog scared up some partridges out
of the soft snow under the apple trees in the Tommy
Wheeler orchard.

Smith's thermometer early this morning at −22°;
ours at 8 A. M. −10°.

Feb. 12. All trees covered this morning with a hoar
frost, very handsome looking toward the sun, — the
ghosts of trees. Is not this what was so blue in the
atmosphere yesterday afternoon?

P. M. — To Walden.

A very pleasant and warm afternoon. There is a
softening of the air and snow. The eaves run fast
on the south side of houses, and, as usual in this state
of the air, the cawing of crows at a distance and the
crowing of cocks fall on the air with a peculiar softness and sweetness; they come distinct and echoing
musically through the pure air. What are those crows
about, which I see from the railroad causeway in the
middle of a field where no grass appears to rise above
the snow, — apparently feeding? I observe no mouse-
tracks in the fields and meadows. The snow is so light
and deep that they have run wholly underneath, and
I see in the fields here and there a little hole in the
crust where they have come to the surface. In Trillium

Vol. VII

Woods I see, as usual, where a squirrel has scratched
along from tree to tree. His tracks cease at the foot
of a pine, up which he has ascended within these few
hours. He may be concealed now amid the thickest
foliage. It is very pleasant to stand now in a high
pine wood where the sun shines in amid the pines and
hemlocks and maples as in a warm apartment. I see
at Warren's Crossing where, last night perhaps, some
partridges rested in this light, dry, deep snow. They
must have been almost completely buried. They
have left their traces at the bottom. They are such
holes as would be made by crowding their bodies in
backwards, slanting-wise, while perhaps their heads
were left out. The dog scared them out of similar
holes yesterday in the open orchard. I watched for
a long time two chickadee-like birds, — only, I thought,
a good deal larger, — which kept ascending the pitch
pines spirally from the bottom like the nuthatch. They
had the markings and the common faint note of the
chickadee, yet they looked so large and confined
themselves so to the trunk that I cannot but feel still
some doubt about them. They had black chins, as
well as top of head; tail, black above; back, slate;
sides, dirty-white or creamy; breast, etc., white.

Set a trap in the woods for wild mice. I saw where
they had run over the snow, making a slight impression, thus: ::‒::‒::‒::‒:: the tracks some five
inches apart, frequently with a
very distinct mark of the tail. These tracks commonly
came together soon and made one beaten trail where
two or three had passed, or one several times; as if

they had hopped along, two, three, or four in company.
The whole trail would be five or six inches wide.

Under the birches, where the snow is covered with
birch seeds and scales, I see the fine tracks, undoubtedly of linarias. The track of one of these birds in the
light surface looks like a chain, or the ova of toads.
Where a large flock has been feeding, the whole surface is scored over by them.

Feb. 13. 10 A. M. — To Walden Woods.

Not cold; sky somewhat overcast.

The tracks of partridges are more remarkable in
this snow than usual, it is so light, being at the same
time a foot deep. I see where one has waddled along
several rods, making a chain-like track about three
inches wide (or two and a half), and at the end has
squatted in the snow, making a perfectly smooth and
regular oval impression, like the bowl of a spoon,
five inches wide. Then, six inches beyond this, are the
marks of its wings where it struck the snow on each
side when it took flight. It must have risen at once
without running. In one place I see where one, after
running a little way, has left four impressions of its
wings on the snow on each side extending eighteen
or twenty inches and twelve or fifteen in width:

In one
case al-
most the
entire
wing was
distinctly

impressed, eight primaries and five or six secondaries. In one place, when alighting, the primary quills, five of them, have marked the snow for a foot. I see where many have dived into the snow, apparently last night, on the side of a shrub oak hollow. In four places they have passed quite underneath it for more than a foot; in one place, eighteen inches. They appear to have dived or burrowed into it, then passed along a foot or more underneath and squatted there, perhaps, with their heads out, and have invariably left much dung at the end of this hole. I scared one from its hole only half a rod in front of me now at 11 A. M. These holes seen sidewise look thus:—

It is evidently a hardy bird, and in the above respects, too, is like the rabbit, which squats under a brake or bush on the snow. I see the traces of the latter in hollows in the snow in such places, — their forms.

In the Journal of the Rev. William Adams (afterward settled in Dedham), written apparently in and about Cambridge, Mass. (he graduated in 1671 at Cambridge), he says under "Dece 1" (1670), "This day was the first flight of snow this winter it being hardly over shoes." And 1671, November "24. The first great snow this winter being almost knee deep." (Hist. Coll., 4th Series, vol. i.)

An English antiquarian says, "May-Flower was a very favorite name with English seamen, and given by them to vessels from almost every port in England." (*Ibid.* p. 85.)

"Hurts" is an old English word used in heraldry, where, according to Bailey, it is "certain balls resembling hurtle berries."

One of these pigweeds in the yard lasts the snowbirds all winter, and after every new storm they revisit it. How inexhaustible their granary!

To resume the subject of partridges, looking further in an open place or glade amid the shrub oaks and low pitch pines, I found as many as twenty or thirty places where partridges had lodged in the snow, apparently the last night or the night before. You could see commonly where their bodies had first struck the snow and furrowed it for a foot or two, and six inches wide, then entered and gone underneath two feet and rested at the further end, where the manure is left. Is it not likely that they remain quite under the snow there, and do not put their heads out till ready to start? In many places they walked along before they went under the snow. They do not go under deep, and the gallery they make is mostly filled up behind them, leaving only a thin crust above. Then invariably, just beyond this resting-place, you could see the marks made by their wings when they took their departure:

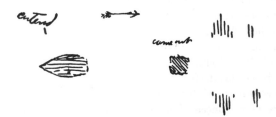

These distinct impressions made by their wings, in the pure snow, so common on all hands, though the bird that made it is gone and there is no trace beyond, affect me like some mystic Oriental symbol, — the winged globe or what-not, — as if made by a spirit. In some places you would see a furrow and hollow in the snow where there was no track for rods around, as if a large snowball or a cannon-ball had struck it, where apparently the birds had not paused in their flight. It is evidently a regular thing with them thus to lodge in the snow. Their tracks, when perfectly distinct, are seen to be almost in one straight line thus, trailing the middle toe:

about five inches apart. In one place I saw where one had evidently trailed the tips of the wings, making two distinct lines five or six inches apart, one on each side the foot-tracks; probably made by a male.

In the same place were many great tracks of the white rabbit. The earliest, made while the snow was very soft, were very large and shapeless, somewhat like the marks made by snow falling from the trees. More recent ones had settled and broken the slight crust around them, leaving a large indentation. The distinct track was like this: the front tracks, which are the largest, being about two and a half inches in diameter, and the whole track of the four feet often one foot long.[1] These impressions so slight (though distinct) it is hard to realize that so heavy an animal made them.

I see where the squirrels have been eating the pitch pine cones since the last snow.

Feb. 14. Another rather warm morning, still more overcast than yesterday's. There is also another leaf or feather frost on the trees, weeds, and rails, — slight leaves or feathers, a quarter to a half inch long by an eighth wide, standing out around the slightest core. I think it is owing to the warmer nights. At nine last evening and at nine this morning, the thermometer stood at 20°. These ghosts of trees are very handsome and fairy-like, but would be handsomer still with the sun on them, — the thickened, clubbed tansy and the goldenrods, etc., and the golden willows of the railroad causeway, with spiring tops shaped like one of the frost leaves, and the white telegraph-wire, and the hoary sides of pine woods.

That cold weather of the 6th and 7th was preceded by two days (the 4th and 5th) much colder weather than we had been having. It moderated sufficiently to snow again on the evening of the 7th and the 8th and 9th. On the morning of the 11th was down to −22°.

Aunt Louisa says that her cousin Nahum Jones, son to that Nathan whom her mother and sisters visited with her down east, carried a cat to the West Indies, sold his vessel there; and though the same vessel did not return, and he came back in another vessel without the cat, the cat got home to Gouldsboro somehow, unaccountably, about the same time that he did. Captain Woodard told her that he carried the same cat three times round the world.

I said to Therien, "You did n't live at Smith's last summer. Where did you live? At Baker's?" "Yes," said he. "Well, is that a good place?" "Oh, yes." "Is that a better place than Smith's?" "Oh, a change of pasture makes a fatter calf."

Feb. 15. Commenced a fine half snow half rain yesterday afternoon. All rain and harder in the night, and now quite a thaw, still raining finely, with great dark puddles amid the snow, and the cars detained by wet rails. Does not a thaw succeed that blue atmosphere observed on the 11th? — a thaw, as well as warmer nights and hoar frosts?

All day a steady, warm, imprisoning rain carrying off the snow, not unmusical on my roof. It is a rare time for the student and reader who cannot go abroad in the afternoon, provided he can keep awake, for we are wont to be drowsy as cats in such weather. Without, it is not walking but wading. It is so long since I have heard it that the steady, soaking, rushing sound of the rain on the shingles is musical. The fire needs no replenishing, and we save our fuel. It seems like a distant forerunner of spring. It is because I am allied to the elements that the sound of the rain is thus soothing to me. The sound soaks into my spirit, as the water into the earth, reminding me of the season when snow and ice will be no more, when the earth will be thawed and drink up the rain as fast as it falls.

Feb. 16. Still rains a little this morning. Water

at the Mill-Dam higher than ever since the new block was built — or longer. Ground half bare, but frozen and icy yet.

P. M. — To Cliff *via* Spanish Brook.

A thick fog without rain. Sounds sweet and musical through this air, as crows, cocks, and striking on the rails at a distance. In the woods by the Cut, in this soft air, under the pines draped with mist, my voice and whistling are peculiarly distinct and echoed back to me, as if the fog were a ceiling which made this hollow an apartment. Sounds are not dissipated and lost in the immensity of the heavens above you, but your voice, being confined by the fog, is distinct, and you hear yourself speak. It is a good lichen day. Every crust is colored and swollen with fruit, and C. is constantly using his knife and filling his pockets with specimens. I have caught a mouse at last, where were tracks like those of February 12th, but it is eaten half up, apparently by its fellow (?). All the flesh is eaten out and part of the skin; one fore foot eaten off, but the entrails left. No wonder we do not find their dead bodies in the woods. The rest of the trap is not moved or sprung, and there is no track of a large animal or bird in the snow. It *may* have been a weasel. The sand is flowing fast in forms of vegetation in the Deep Cut. The fog is so thick we cannot see the engine till it is almost upon us, and then its own steam, hugging the earth, greatly increases the mist. As usual, it is still more dense over the ice at the pond.

The ground is more than half bare, especially in

Vol. VII

open fields and level evergreen woods.[1] It is pleasant to see there the bright evergreens of the forest floor, undimmed by the snow, — the wintergreen, the great-leaved pyrola, the shin-leaf, the rattlesnake-plantain, and the lycopodiums. I see where probably rabbits have nibbled off the leaves of the wintergreen. It is pleasant to see elsewhere, in fields and on banks, so many green radical leaves only half killed by the winter. Are those little scratches across pallescent lichens which C. notices made by squirrels?

I find in the leavings of the partridges numerous ends of twigs. They are white with them, some half an inch long and stout in proportion. Perhaps they are apple twigs. The bark (and bud, if there was any) has been entirely digested, leaving the bare, white, hard wood of the twig. Some of the ends of apple twigs looked as if they had been bitten off. It is surprising what a quantity of this wood they swallow with their buds. What a hardy bird, born amid the dry leaves, of the same color with them, that, grown up, lodges in the snow and lives on buds and twigs! Where apple buds are just freshly bitten off they do not seem to have taken so much twig with them.

The drooping oak leaves show more red amid the pines this wet day, — agreeably so, — and I feel as if I stood a little nearer to the heart of nature.

The mouse is so much torn that I cannot get the length of the *body* and *its* markings exactly. Entire

[1] Goes on melting till there is only a little icy snow left on north of hills in woods on the 10th of March, and then is whitened again.

length, 8 inches;[1] length of head to *base* of ears, 1 inch; body, 3 (?); tail, 3½. Brown or reddish-brown above; white beneath; *fur* slate above and beneath; tail also darker above, light beneath; feet white; hind legs longest, *say* 1¼ inches long; fore ¾; hind foot more than ¾ inch long; five toes on hind feet, four on front, with rudiment of thumb without claw, with little white protuberances on the soles of all; ears *large*, almost bare, thin, slaty-colored, ⅝ inch long on outside; upper jaw ¼ + inch longer than lower; tail round, hairy, gradually tapering, dimly ringed; longest mustachios 1⅜ inches; incisors varnish or dry maple-wood color.[2] From Emmons's account I should think it the *Arvicola Emmonsii* of De Kay, or deer mouse, which is thought a connecting link between the *Arvicola* and *Gerbillus*. The *Gerbillus* is the only other described much like it, and that is a "yellowish cream color" beneath.

Where snow is left on banks I see the galleries of mice (?) or moles (?) unroofed. The mouse I caught had come up through the snow by the side of a shrub oak, run along a rod, and entered again, *i. e.* before I set the trap.

Feb. 17. It is still cloudy and a very fine rain. The river *very* high, one inch higher than the evening of January 31st. The bridge at Sam Barrett's caved in; also the *Swamp* Bridge on back road. Muskrats driven out. Heard this morning, at the new stone bridge, from the hill, that singular springlike note of a bird

[1] Probably an inch too much.   [2] *Vide* Feb. 20.

which I heard once before one year about this time (under Fair Haven Hill). The jays were uttering their unusual notes, and this made me think of a woodpecker. It reminds me of the pine warbler, *vetter vetter vetter vetter vet*, except that it is much louder, and I should say had the sound of *l* rather than *t*, — *veller*, etc., perhaps. Can it be a jay? or a pig[eon] woodpecker? Is it not the earliest springward note of a bird? In the damp misty air.

Was waked up last night by the tolling of a bell about 11 o'clock, as if a child had hold of the rope. Dressed and went abroad in the wet to see if it was a fire. It seems the town clock was out of order, and the striking part ran down and struck steadily for fifteen minutes. If it had not been so near the end of the week, it might have struck a good part of the night.

P. M. — A riparial excursion over further railroad bridge; return by Flint's Bridge.

At 2 P. M. the water at the Sam Wheeler Bridge is three inches above straight truss, or two inches higher than at 9 A. M. The ice is not broken over the channel of *this* stream, but is lifted up and also for a good distance over the meadows, but, for a broad space over the meadows on each *side*, the freshet stands over the ice, which is flat on the bottom. It rains but a trifle this afternoon, but the snow which is left is still melting. The water is just *beginning* to be over the road beyond this stone bridge. The road beyond the opposite, or Wood's, bridge is already impassable to foot-travellers.

I see no muskrats in the Assabet from the Tommy

Wheeler bank. Perhaps they provided themselves holes at the last freshet. It is running over both sides of Derby's Bridge for a dozen rods (each side), as over a dam. The ice in the middle of this stream is for the most part broken up. Great cakes of ice are wedged against the railroad bridge there, and still threaten its existence. They are about twenty feet in diameter and some twenty inches thick, of greenish ice, more or less tilted up and commonly another, if not two more, of equal size, forced directly underneath the first by the current. They stretch quite across the river, and, being partly tilted up against the spiles of the bridge, exert a tremendous power upon it. They form a dam between and over which the water falls, so that it is fully ten inches higher on the upper side of the bridge than on the lower. Two maples a little above the bridge — one a large one — have been levelled and carried off by the ice. The track-repairers have been at work here all day, protecting the bridge. They have a man on the ice with a rope round his body, — the other end in their hands, — who is cracking off the corners of the cakes with a crowbar. One great cake, as much as a dozen rods long, is slowly whirling round just above the bridge, and from time to time an end is borne against the ice which lies against the bridge. The workmen say that they had cleared the stream here before dinner, and all this had collected since. (Now 3 P. M.) If Derby's Bridge should yield to the ice which lies against it, this would surely be swept off. They say that three (?) years ago the whole of the east end of the bridge was moved some six inches,

rails and all. Waded through water in the road for eight or ten rods, beyond Loring's little bridge. It was a foot deep this morning on the short road that leads to Heywood's house. I had to go a quarter of a mile up the meadow there and down the college road. Sam Barrett's bridge is entirely covered and has slumped. They cross a broad bay in a boat there. I went over on the string-piece of the dam above. It is within eight or nine inches of the top of the little bridge this side of Flint's Bridge at 5.30 P. M. So, though it is within five and a half inches of where it was three years ago in the spring at the new stone bridge, it is not so high comparatively *here*. The fact is, the water is in each case dammed not only by the bridges and causeways but by the ice, so that it stands at as many levels as there are causeways. It is perhaps about a foot lower at Flint's Bridge now, than when it stood where it does now at the new stone bridge three years ago. So that a metre at one point alone will not enable you to compare the absolute height or quantity of water at different seasons and under different circumstances. Such a metre is the more to be relied on in proportion as a river is free from obstructions, such as ice, causeways, bridges, etc.

Everywhere now in the fields you see a green water standing over ice in the hollows. Sometimes it is a very delicate tint of green. Would this water look green on any white ground? It is commonly yellow on meadows in spring. The highway surveyor is on the alert to see what damage the freshet has done. As they could not dig in the frozen ground, they have

upset a cartload of pitch pine boughs into the hole at the Swamp Bridge.

Feb. 18. 8 A. M. — Water four and three quarters inches above truss, nearly two inches higher than yesterday at 2 P. M. It may have risen one inch higher during the day, then went down. Surface of ground and snow slightly frozen; no flowing now. At 9 A. M. sun comes out; rather warm; sunlight peculiarly yellow and spring-suggesting. Mountains in horizon dark-blue, the wooded parts, with snow below and between.

P. M. — To Great Meadows and around Beck Stow's.

A clear bright day, though with passing clouds, — the clouds darker by contrast with the bright sky, — the first since the evening of the 14th. Now for the first time decidedly there is something spring-suggesting in the air and light. Though not *particularly* warm, the light of the sun (now travelling so much higher) on the russet fields, — the ground being nearly all bare, — and on the sand and the pines, is suddenly *yellower*. It is the earliest day-breaking of the year. We now begin to look decidedly forward and put the winter behind us. We begin to form definite plans for the approaching spring and summer. I look over a parti-colored landscape of russet fields and white snow-patches, as in former spring days. Some of the frost has come out, and it is very wet and muddy crossing the plowed fields, — as filthy walking as any in the year. You have the experience of wading birds that get their living on the flats when the tide has gone down and leave their tracks there, but you are cheered by the sight of some radical greenness. The legions of light have poured into the plain in overwhelming numbers, and the winter darkness will not recover the ground it has lost. I listen ever for something springlike in the notes of birds, some peculiar tinkling notes.

Now and through the winter I am attracted by the reddish patches on the landscape where there is a dense growth of young white birches, the bark of the young shoots.

Neither the main stream nor meadows are decidedly broken up by the thaw and rise; only there are great open places in the meadows, where you observe the ripple of water still in the mornings, the cold is so much relaxed, and the ice that belonged is superimposed in great cakes upon the still firmly frozen parts. On the Great Fields I see an acre of a straw-colored feathery grass in tufts two feet high. These too reflect the yellower light.

I see pitch pine cones two years old still closed on felled trees, two to six together recurved, in the last case closely crowded and surrounding the twig in a ring, forming very rich-looking clusters eight to ten inches from the extremity, and, within two or three inches of the extremity, maybe one or two small ones of the last year. Low down on twigs around the trunks of old trees, and sometimes on the trunk itself, you see old gray cones which have only opened or blos-

somed at the apex, covered with lichens; which have lost their spines.

A man came to our house at noon and got something to eat, who set out this morning to go from Waltham to Noah Wheeler's in Nine Acre Corner. He got as far as Lee's Bridge on the edge of Lincoln, or within three quarters of a mile of Wheeler's, and could not get over the river on account of the freshet; so he came round through Concord village, — he might have come by the railroad a little nearer, — and I directed him over the railroad bridge, the first by which he could cross dry-shod down the stream, and up-stream he would have been obliged to go to Saxonville. Thus he had to go eight miles round instead of three quarters of a mile direct, and in the whole about double the usual distance from Waltham. It was probably over the road also at Nut Meadow Brook. The river thus opposes a serious obstacle to travellers from southeast to northwest for some twenty miles of its course at least, above and below Concord. No doubt hundreds have been put to great inconvenience by it within a day or two. Even travellers in wagons are stopped at many of these causeways. If they were raised two feet the trouble would be in great part, the danger wholly, obviated. There should at least be provided a ferry for foot-passengers at each causeway, at the expense of the town, and the traveller could blow a horn to call the ferryman over. You will see a man carrying a child over a causeway on his back.

After a thaw old tracks in the snow, from *basso,*

become *alto relievo.*[1] The snow which was originally compressed and hardened beneath the feet, — also, perhaps, by the influence of the sun and maybe rain, — being the last to melt, becomes protuberant, the highest part and most lasting. That part of the snow compressed and solidified under the feet remains nearly at the same level. The track becomes a raised almost icy type. How enduring these trails! How nature clings to these types. The track even of small animals like a skunk will outlast a considerable thaw.

Why do laborers so commonly turn out their feet more than the class still called gentlemen, apparently pushing themselves along by the sides of their feet? I think you can tell the track of a clown from that of a gentleman, though he should wear a gentleman's boots.

Feb. 19. Rufus Hosmer says that in the year 1820 (?) there was so smooth and strong an icy crust on a very deep snow that you could skate everywhere over the fields and for the most part over the fences. Sam Potter's father, moving into town, turned off into the fields with a four(?)-horse team as soon as he had crossed Wood's Bridge and went directly across to Deacon Hubbard's. When Wood's Bridge was carried off upstream, it was landed against Hubbard's land. Showed me where his grandfather, Nathan Hosmer, who lived in the old house still standing on Conantum, was drowned

[1] [The antithesis intended was *intaglio* and *rilievo*, of course, not low and high relief.]

when crossing the river on the ice from town, just below the bridge since built.

Many will complain of my lectures that they are transcendental. "Can't understand them." "Would you have us return to the savage state?" etc., etc. A criticism true enough, it may be, from their point of view. But the fact is, the earnest lecturer can speak only to his like, and the adapting of himself to his audience is a mere compliment which he pays them. If you wish to know how I think, you must endeavor to put yourself in my place. If you wish me to speak as if I were you, that is another affair.

I think it was about a week ago that I saw some dead honey-bees on the snow.

The water is about a foot deep on the Jimmy Miles road. E. Conant thinks that the Joe Miles causeway is rather worse than Hubbard's in respect to water. Rice and some others always say "cassey" for causeway. Conant was cutting up an old pear tree which had blown down by his old house on Conantum. This and others still standing, and a mulberry tree whose stump remains, were set anciently with reference to a house which stood in the little peach orchard near by. The only way for Conant to come to town when the water is highest is by Tarbell's and Wood's on the stone bridge, about a mile and a half round.

It is true when there is no snow we cannot so easily see the birds, nor they the weeds.

Feb. 20. I have caught another of those mice of February 16th and secured it entire, — a male.

Whole length . . . . 6½ inches
Head, from the nose to the ears . . . . 1 inch
Tail . . . . 3¼ inches
Longest of the whiskers . . . . 1⅜ "

Hind legs the longest, though only the feet, about three quarters of an inch in length, are exposed, without the fur. Of the fore legs a little more is exposed than the hands, or perhaps four to five eighths of an inch, claws concealed in tufts of white hair. The upper jaw projects about half an inch beyond the lower. The whole upper parts are brown, except the ears, from the snout to the tip of the tail, — dark-brown on the top of the head and back and upper side of the tail, reddish-brown or fawn or fox (?) colored on the sides. Tail hairy and obscurely ringed. The whole lower parts white, including the neat white feet and under side of tail. The irregular waving line along the sides, forming the boundary between the brown and the white, very sharply defined from side of the snout to the tip of the tail. Above brown, beneath white very decidedly. The brown of the sides extends down by a triangular point to the last joint or foot of the fore legs and to the same or heels of the hind ones, or you may say the white of the belly extends upward on the sides between the legs in a broad bay. The ears are large, broad and roundish, five eighths of an inch long, ash or slate-colored, thin and bare except at base. The reddish brown and the white are the striking colors. It is in the attitude of hopping, its thighs drawn up and concealed in the fur and its long hind feet in the same plane with its buttocks, while the short

fore feet appear like hands. Fur dark slate, under both brown and white hair. The droppings black, say one sixth inch long, cylindrical. Some of the whiskers are dark, some whitish. It has a rather large head, apparently curving forward or downward.[1] A very slight and delicate tinge of yellowish beneath between the fore legs.

It is undoubtedly the *Arvicola Emmonsii* of De Kay. It is a very pretty and neat little animal for a mouse, with its wholesome reddish-brown sides distinctly bounding on its pure white belly, neat white feet, large slate-colored ears which suggest circumspection and timidity, — ready to earth itself on the least sound of danger, — long tail, and *numerous* whiskers. This was caught in a dry and elevated situation, amid shrub oaks. It apparently, like the other, came up through a hole in the snow at the foot of a shrub oak (*Quercus ilicifolia*).

This tawny or reddish-brown color which belongs to the king of beasts and to the deer, singular that it should extend to this minute beast also![2]

A strong wind drying the earth which has been so very wet. The sand *begins* to be dry in spots on the railroad causeway. The northerly wind blows me along, and when I get to the cut I hear it roaring in the woods, all reminding me of March, March. The sides of the cut are all bare of snow, and the sand foliage is dried up. It is decided March weather, and I see from my window the bright-blue water here and there between the ice and on the meadow.

[1] *Vide* Mar. 12th.   [2] *Vide* [p. 202]. *Vide* Mar. 10th.

Vol. VII

The quadrupeds which I know that we have here in Concord are (*vide* Emmons, p. 5): —

Of Order	Family	
CARNIVORA. —	VESPERTILIONIDÆ.	One. Have we more of the three in the State?
	SORICIDÆ	Have we any?
	TALPIDÆ	*Condylura longicaudata*, Star-nose Mole. Have we not another of the three moles?
	URSIDÆ	*Procyon lotor*, the Raccoon.
	CANIDÆ	*Vulpes fulvus.*
	MUSTELIDÆ	*Mustela martes*, Pine Marten.
		Putorius vison, the Mink.
		Putorius vulgaris, Reddish Weasel.
		Putorius Noveboracensis, Ermine Weasel.
		Lutra Canadensis, Otter.
		Mephitis Americana.
RODENTIA	CASTORIDÆ	*Fiber zibethicus.*
	LEPORIDÆ	*Lepus Americanus.*
		Lepus Virginianus.
	MUSCIDÆ (altered to MURIDÆ on p. 59)	*Arvicola hirsutus*, Meadow Mouse, probably. (His *albo-rufescens* only a variety according

to Audubon and Bachman.)
Arvicola Emmonsii.[1]
Mus musculus, Common Mouse.
Mus rattus (?), Black Rat.
Mus decumanus, Wharf Rat, Brown Rat.
Arctomys monax, Woodchuck.
Sciurus leucotis, Little Gray Squirrel.
Sciurus Hudsonius.
Sciurus striatus.
Pteromys volucella.
Have we the *Gerbillus Canadensis*, Jumping mouse?

According to this we have at least twenty-one and perhaps twenty-six quadrupeds, — five and possibly six families of the Order *Carnivora*, and three families of the Order *Rodentia*; none of the Order *Ruminantia*. Nearly half of our quadrupeds belong to the *Muridæ*, or Rat Family, and a quarter of them to the *Mustelidæ*, or Weasel Family. Some, though numerous, are rarely seen, as the wild mice and moles. Others are very rare, like the otter and raccoon. The striped squirrel is the smallest quadruped that we commonly notice in our walks in the woods, and we do not realize, especially in summer, when their tracks are not visible, that the aisles of the wood are threaded by countless

[1] *Mus leucopus.*

wild mice, and no more that the meadows are swarming in many places with meadow mice and moles. The cat brings in a mole from time to time, and we see where they have heaved up the soil in the meadow. We see the tracks of mice on the snow in the woods, or once in a year one glances by like a flash through the grass or ice at our feet, and that is for the most part all that we see of them.

Though all the muskrat-cabins will be covered by an early rise of the river in the fall, you will yet see the greater part of them above the ice in midwinter, however high the water may be.

I frequently detect the track of a foreigner by the print of the nails in his shoes, both in snow and earth; of an india-rubber, by its being less sharply edged, and, most surely, often, by the fine diamond roughening of the sole. How much we infer from the dandy's narrow heel-tap, while we pity his unsteady tread, and from the lady's narrow slipper, suggesting corns, not to say consumption. The track of the farmer's cowhides, whose carpet-tearing tacks in the heel frequently rake the ground several inches before his foot finds a resting-place, suggests weight and impetus.

Feb. 21. Another *Arvicola Emmonsii,* a male; whole length six inches, tail three inches. This is very little reddish on the sides, but general aspect above dark-brown; though not iron-gray, yet reminding me of that; yet not the less like the hue of beasts in a menagerie. This may be a last year's mouse.

Audubon and Bachman say that when "it sheds

its hair late in spring . . . it assumes a bluish gray tint, a little lighter than that of the common mouse."

P. M. — To Fair Haven Hill *via* Cut.

A clear air, with a northwesterly, March-like wind, as yesterday. What is the peculiarity in the air that both the invalid in the chamber and the traveller on the highway say these are perfect March days? The wind is rapidly drying up earth, and elevated sands already begin to look whitish. How much light there is in the sky and on the surface of the russet earth! It is reflected in a flood from all cleansed surfaces which rain and snow have washed, — from the railroad rails and the mica in the rocks and the silvery latebræ of insects there, — and I never saw the white houses of the village more brightly white. Now look for an early crop of arrowheads, for they will shine.

When I have entered the wooded hollow on the east of the Deep Cut, it is novel and pleasant to hear the sound of the dry leaves and twigs, which have so long been damp and silent, more worn and lighter than ever, crackling again under my feet, — though there is still considerable snow about, along wall-sides, etc., — and to see the holes and galleries recently made by the mice (?) in the fine withered grass of such places, the upper aralia hollow there. I see the peculiar softened blue sky of spring over the tops of the pines, and, when I am sheltered from the wind, I feel the warmer sun of the season reflected from the withered grass and twigs on the side of this elevated hollow.

A warmth begins to be reflected from the partially

Vol. VII

dried ground here and there in the sun in sheltered places, very cheering to invalids who have weak lungs, who think they may weather it till summer now. Nature is more genial to them. When the leaves on the forest floor are dried, and begin to rustle under such a sun and wind as these, the news is told to how many myriads of grubs that underlie them! When I perceive this dryness under my feet, I feel as if I had got a new sense, or rather I realize what was incredible to me before, that there is a new life in Nature beginning to awake, that her halls are being swept and prepared for a new occupant. It is whispered through all the aisles of the forest that another spring is approaching. The wood mouse listens at the mouth of his burrow, and the chickadee passes the news along.

We now notice the snow on the mountains, because on the remote rim of the horizon its whiteness contrasts with the russet and darker hues of our bare fields. I looked at the Peterboro mountains with my glass from Fair Haven Hill. I think that there can be no more arctic scene than these mountains in the edge of the horizon completely crusted over with snow, with the sun shining on them, seen through a telescope over bare, russet fields and dark forests, with perhaps a house on some remote, bare ridge seen against them. A silver edging, or ear-like handle, to this basin of the world. They look like great loaves incrusted with pure white sugar; and I think that this must have been the origin of the name "sugar-loaf" sometimes given to mountains, and not on account of their form. We look thus from russet fields into a landscape

still sleeping under the mantle of winter. We have already forgotten snow, and think only of frosted cake. The snow on the mountains has, in this case, a singular smooth and crusty appearance, and by contrast you see even single evergreens rising here and there above it and where a promontory casts a shadow along the mountains' side. I saw what looked like a large lake of misty bluish water on the side of the further Peterboro mountain, its edges or shore very distinctly defined. This I concluded was the shadow of another part of the mountain. And it suggested that, in like manner, what on the surface of the moon is taken for water may be shadows. Could not distinguish Monadnock till the sun shone on it.

I saw a train go by, which had in front a dozen dirt-cars [from] somewhere up country, laden apparently with some kind of earth (or clay?); and these, with their loads, were thickly and evenly crusted with unspotted snow, a part of that sugary crust I had viewed with my glass, which contrasted singularly with the bare tops of the other cars, which it had hitched on this side, and the twenty miles at least of bare ground over which they had rolled. It affected me as when a traveller comes into the house with snow on his coat, when I did not know it was snowing.

How plain, wholesome, and earthy are the colors of quadrupeds generally! The commonest I should say is the tawny or various shades of brown, answering to the russet which is the prevailing color of the earth's surface, perhaps, and to the yellow of the sands beneath. The darker brown mingled with this answers to the darker-colored soil of the surface. The white of the polar bear, ermine weasel, etc., answers to the snow; the spots of the pards, perchance, to the earth spotted with flowers or tinted leaves of autumn; the black, perhaps, to night, and muddy bottoms and dark waters. There are few or no bluish animals.

Can it be true, as is said, that geese have gone over Boston, probably yesterday? It is in the newspapers.[1]

Feb. 22. P. M. — To J. Farmer's.

Remarkably warm and pleasant weather, perfect spring. I even listen for the first bluebird. I see a seething in the air over clean russet fields.[2] The westerly wind is rather raw, but in sheltered places it is deliciously warm. The water has so far gone down that I get over the Hunt Bridge causeway by going half a dozen rods on the wall in one place. This water must have moved two or three hundred cartloads of sand to the side of the road. This damage would be avoided by raising the road.

J. Farmer showed me an ermine weasel he caught in a trap three or four weeks ago. They are not very common about his barns. All white but the tip of the tail; two conspicuous canine teeth in each jaw. In summer they are distinguished from the red weasel, which is a little smaller, by the length of their tails, particularly, — six or more inches, while the red one's

[1] Henry Hosmer tells me (Mar. 17th) that he saw several flocks about this time!

[2] Also the 24th, which is very cold.

is not two inches long. He says their track is like that of the mink: —

as if they had only two legs. They go on the jump. Sometimes make a third mark. He saw one in the summer (which he called the red weasel, but, as he thought the red twice as big as the white, it may have been a white one) catch a striped squirrel thus: He was at work near the wall near his house when he saw a striped squirrel come out of the wall and jump along by the side of a large stone. When he had got two or three feet along it, as it were in the air, the weasel appeared behind him, and before he had got four feet had him by the throat. Said a man told him that he saw a weasel come running suddenly to an apple tree near which he was working, run round and round and up it, when a squirrel sitting on the end of a branch jumped off, and the weasel, jumping, had him before he touched the ground. He had no doubt that when the weasel ran round the tree he was on the track of the squirrel.

F. said he had many of the black rat, but none or very few of the wharf rats, on his premises. He had seen mice-nests twenty feet up trees. Three or four weeks ago he traced a mink by his tracks on the snow to where he had got a frog from the bottom of a ditch, — dug him out. Says that where many minnows are kept in a spring they will kill four or five hundred at once and pile them up on the bank. Showed me his spring, head of one of the sources of Dodge's Brook,

which by his mark is not a quarter of an inch higher now, when there is so much water on the surface, than it was in the midst of the great drought last summer. But the important peculiarity of it is that when, in a dry spell, this stream is dry fifteen or twenty rods from this source, it may suddenly fill again before any rain comes. This does not freeze, even for twenty rods. A pool in it, some dozen or more rods from source, where his cattle drink, he never saw frozen.

He had seen a partridge drum standing on a wall. Said it stood very upright and produced the sound by striking its wings together behind its back, as a cock often does, but did not strike the wall nor its body. This he is sure of, and declares that he is mistaken who affirms the contrary, though it were Audubon himself. Wilson says he "begins to strike with his stiffened wings" while standing on a log, but does not say what he strikes, though one would infer it was either the log or his body. Peabody says he beats his body with his wings.

The sun goes down to-night under clouds, — a round red orb, — and I am surprised to see that its light, falling on my book and the wall, is a beautiful purple, like the poke stem or perhaps some kinds of wine.

You see fresh upright green radical leaves of some plants — the dock, probably water dock, for one — in and about water now the snow is gone there, as if they had grown all winter.

Pitch pine cones must be taken from the tree at the right season, else they will not open or "blossom"

in a chamber. I have one which was gnawed off by squirrels, apparently of full size, but which does not open. Why should they thus open in the chamber or elsewhere? I suppose that under the influence of heat or dryness the upper side of each scale expands while the lower contracts, or perhaps only the one expands or the other contracts. I notice that the upper side is a lighter, almost cinnamon, color, the lower a dark (pitchy?) red.

Feb. 23. Clear, but a *very* cold north wind. I see great cakes of ice, a rod or more in length and one foot thick, lying high and dry on the bare ground in the low fields some ten feet or more beyond the edge of the thinner ice, which were washed up by the last rise (the 18th), which was some four inches higher than the former one.[1] Some of these great cakes, when the water going down has left them on a small mound, have bent as they settled, and conformed to the surface.

Saw at Walden this afternoon that that grayish ice which had formed over the large square where ice had been taken out for Brown's ice-house had a decided pink or rosaceous tinge. I see no cracks in the ground this year yet.

Mr. Loring says that he and his son George fired at white swans in Texas on the water, and, though G. shot two with ball and killed them, the others in each case gathered about them and crowded them off out of their reach.

[1] *Vide* the 26th.

Feb. 24. Clear, but very cold and windy for the season. Northerly wind; smokes blown southerly. Ground frozen harder still; but probably now and hereafter what ground freezes at night will in great part melt by middle of day. However, it is so cold this afternoon that there is no melting of the ground throughout the day.

The names of localities on the Sudbury River, the south or main branch of Concord or Musketaquid River, beginning at the mouth of the Assabet, are the Rock (at mouth), Merrick's Pasture, Lee's Hill, Bridge, Hubbard Shore, Clamshell Hill and fishing-place, Nut Meadow Brook, Hollowell Place and Bridge, Fair Haven Hill and Cliffs, Conantum opposite, Fair Haven Pond and Cliff and Baker Farm, Pole Brook, Lee's and Bridge, Farrar's or Otter Swamp, Bound Rock, Rice's Hill and   's [*sic*] Isle, the Pantry, Ware Hill, Sherman's Bridge and Round Hill, Great Sudbury Meadow and Tall's Isle, Causeway Bridges, Larned Brook, the Chestnut House, Pelham Pond, the Rapids.

I saw yesterday in Hubbard's sumach meadow a bunch of dried grass with a *few* small leaves inmixed, which had lain next the ground under the snow, probably the nest of a mouse or mole.

P. M. — To young willow-row near Hunt's Pond road.

Here is skating again, and there was some yesterday, the meadows being frozen where they had opened, though the water is fast going down. It is a thin ice

of one to two inches, one to three feet above the old, with yellowish water between. However, it is narrow dodging between the great cakes of the ice which has been broken up. The whole of the broad meadows is a rough, irregular checker-board of great cakes a rod square or more, — arctic enough to look at. The willow-row does not begin to look bright yet. The top two or three feet are red as usual at a distance, the lower parts a rather dull green. Inspecting a branch, I find that the bark is shrunk and wrinkled, and of course it will not peel. Probably when it shines it will be tense and smooth, all its pores filled.

Staples said the other day that he heard Phillips speak at the State-House. By thunder! he never heard a man that could speak like him. His words come so easy. It was just like picking up chips.

Minott says that Messer tells him he saw a striped squirrel (!) yesterday.[1] His cat caught a mole lately, not a star-nosed one, but one of those that heave up the meadow. She sometimes catches a little dark-colored mouse with a sharp nose. Tells of a Fisk of Waltham who, some thirty years ago, could go out with a club only and kill as many partridges as he could conveniently bring home. I suppose he knew where to find them buried in the snow. Both Minott and Farmer think they sometimes remain several days in the snow, if the weather is bad for them. Minott has seen twigs, he says, of apple, in their crops, three quarters of an inch long. Says he has seen them drum

[1] *Vide* Mar. 4th and 7th.

many times, standing on a log or a wall; that they strike the log or stone with their wings. He has frequently caught them in a steel trap without bait, covered with leaves and set in such places. Says that quails also eat apple buds.

I notice that, in the tracks, hens' toes are longer and more slender than partridges and more or less turned and curved one side.

The brightening of the willows or of osiers, — that is a season in the spring, showing that the dormant sap is awakened. I now remember a few osiers which I have seen early in past springs, thus brilliantly green and red (or yellow), and it is as if all the landscape and all nature shone. Though the twigs were few which I saw, I remember it as a prominent phenomenon affecting the face of Nature, a gladdening of her face. You will often fancy that they look brighter before the spring has come, and when there has been no change in them.

Thermometer at 10° at 10 P. M.

Feb. 25. Clear, cold, and windy. Thermometer at 7° at 7.30 A. M. Air filled with dust blowing over the fields. Feel the cold about as much as when it was below zero a month ago. Pretty good skating.

Feb. 26. Still clear and cold and windy. No thawing of the ground during the day. This and the last two or three days have been very blustering and unpleasant, though clear.

P. M. — To Clamshell Hill, across river.

I see some *cracks* in a plowed field, — Depot Field corn-field, — maybe recent ones. I think since this last cold snap, else I had noticed them before. Those great cakes of ice which the last freshet floated up on to uplands now lie still further from the edge of the recent ice. You are surprised to see them lying with perpendicular edges a foot thick on bare, grassy upland where there is no other sign of water, sometimes wholly isolated by bare grass there. In the last freshet the South Branch was only broken up on the meadows for a few rods in width next the shores. Where the ice did not rise with the water, but, apparently being frozen to the dry bottom, was covered by the water, — there and apparently in shallow places here, then far from the shore, the ground ice was at length broken and rose up in cakes, larger or smaller, the smaller of which were often floated up higher on to the shore by a rod or so than the ice had originally reached. Then, the water going down, when the weather became colder and froze, the new ice only reached part way up these cakes, which lay high and dry. It is therefore pretty good skating on the river itself and on a greater part of the meadows next the river, but it is interrupted by great cakes of ice rising above the general level near the shore.

Saw several of those rather small reddish-brown dor-bugs on the ice of the meadow, some frozen in. Were they washed out of their winter quarters by the freshet? Or can it be that they came forth of their own accord on the 22d? I cannot revive them by a fire.

C. says he saw a lark to-day close to him, and some other dark-colored spring bird.

Directly off Clamshell Hill, within four rods of it, where the water is three or four feet deep, I see where the musquash dived and brought up clams before the last freezing. Their open shells are strewn along close to the edge of the ice, and close together, for about three rods in one place, and the bottom under this edge of older ice, as seen through the new black ice, is perfectly white with those which sank. They may have been blown in, or the ice melted. The nacre of these freshly opened shells is very fair, — azure, or else a delicate salmon pink (?), or rosaceous, or violet. I find one not opened, but frozen, and several have one valve quite broken in two in the rat's effort to wrench them open, leaving the frozen fish half exposed. All the rest show the marks of their teeth at one end or the other, i. e., sometimes at one end, sometimes at another. You can see distinctly, also, the marks of their teeth where they have scraped off, with a scraping cut, the tough muscles which fasten the fish to its shell, also sometimes all along the nacre next the edge. One shell has apparently a little caddis-case of iron-colored sand on it. These shells look uncommonly large thus exposed; at a distance like leaves. They lie thickly around the edge of each small circle of thinner black ice in the midst of the white, showing where was open water a day or two ago. At the beginning and end of winter, when the river is partly open, the ice serves them instead of other stool. Some are reddish-brown in thick and hard layers like iron ore out-

side; some have roundish copper-colored spots on the nacre within. This shows that this is still a good place for clams, as it was in Indian days.

Examined with glass some fox-dung (?) from a tussock of grass amid the ice on the meadow. It appeared to be composed two thirds of clay, and the rest a slate-colored fur and coarser white hairs, black-tipped, — too coarse for the deer mouse. Was it that of the rabbit? This mingled with small bones. A mass as long as one's finger.

Feb. 27. Another cold, clear day, but the weather gradually moderating.

Feb. 28. Still cold and clear. Ever since the 23d inclusive a succession of clear but very cold days in which, for the most part, it has not melted perceptibly during the day. My ink has frozen, and plants, etc., have frozen in the house, though the thermometer has not indicated nearly so great a cold as before. Since the 25th it has been very slowly moderating.

The skating began again the 24th after the great freshet had gone down some two feet or more, but that part of the old ice which was broken up by the freshet and floated from its place, either on to the upland or meadow or on to the firm ice, made it remarkably broken and devious, not to be used by night. The deep bays and sides of the meadows have presented a very remarkable appearance, a stretching pack of great cakes of ice, often two or more upon each other and partly tilted up, a foot thick and one to

two or more rods broad. The westering sun reflected from their edges makes them shine finely. In short, our meadows have presented and still present a very wild and arctic scene. Far on every side, over what is usually dry land, are scattered these great cakes of ice, the water having now gone down about five feet on the South Branch.

P. M. — To further railroad bridge and Ministerial Swamp.

I see that same kind of icicle terracing about the piers of Wood's Bridge and others that I saw, I think, last spring, but not now quite so perfect, as if where the water had stood at successive levels. The lower edge now about a foot or two above water.

Examined where the white maple and the apple tree were tipped over by the ice the other day at the railroad bridge. It struck them seven or eight feet from the ground, that being the height of the water, rubbed off the bark, and then bent flat and broke them. They were about ten inches in diameter, the maple partly dead before. I see where many trees have been wounded by the ice in former years. They have a hard time of it when a cake half a dozen rods in diameter and nearly two feet thick is floated and blown against them.

Just south of Derby's Bridge lie many great cakes, some one upon another, which were stopped by the bridge and causeway, and a great many have a crust of the meadow of equal thickness — six inches to one

foot — frozen to their under surfaces. Some of these are a rod in diameter, and when the ice melts, the meadow where they are landed will present a singular appearance. I see many also freshly deposited on the Elfin Burial-Ground, showing how that was formed. The greater part of those hummocks there are probably, if not certainly, carried by the ice, though I now see a few small but thick pieces of meadow four or five feet broad without any ice or appearance of its having been attached to them. This is a powerful agent at work. Many great cakes have lodged on a ridge of the meadow west of the river here, and suggest how such a ridge may be growing from year to year.

This North River is only partially open. I see where a bright gleam from a cake of ice on the shore is reflected in the stream with remarkable brightness, in a pointed, flame-like manner. Look either side you see it. Standing here, still above the Elfin Burial-Ground, the outlines of Heywood the miller's house in the distance against the pine and oak woods come dimly out, and by their color are in very pleasing harmony with this wood. I think it is a dull-red house against the usual mixture of red oak leaves and dark pines. There is such a harmony as between the gray limbs of an overshadowing elm and the lichen-clad roof.

We crossed the river at Nut Meadow Brook. The ice was nearly worn through all along there, with wave-like regularity, in oblong (round end) or thick crescent or kidney shaped holes, as if worn by the summits of waves, — like a riddle to sift a man through. These holes are hard to detect in some lights except by shaking the water. I saw some cakes of ice, ten feet across and one foot thick, lodged with one end on the top of a fence-post and some seven or eight feet in the air, the other on the bottom. There is a fine pack of large cakes away in the bay behind Hubbard's Grove. I notice, looking at their edges, that the white or rotted part extends downward in points or triangles, alternating with the sound greenish parts, thus: —

Most, however, are a thin white, or maybe snow ice, with all beneath solid and green still.

Found a hangbird's nest fallen from the ivy maple, composed wholly of that thread they wipe the locomotive with [1] and one real thread, all as it were woven into a perfect bag.

I have a piece of a limb (alder or maple?), say five eighths of an inch in diameter, which has been cut off by a worm boring spirally, but in one horizontal plane, three times round.

I observed how a new ravine is formed in a sandhill. A new one was formed in the last thaw at Clamshell Hill thus: Much melted snow and rain being collected on the top of the hill, some apparently found its

[1] "Cotton waste."

way through the ground, frozen a foot thick, a few feet from the edge of the bank, and began with a small rill washing down the slope the unfrozen sand beneath. As the water continued to flow, the sand on each side continued to slide into it and be carried off, leaving the frozen crust above quite firm, making a bridge five or six feet wide over this cavern. Now, since the thaw, this bridge, I see, has melted and fallen in, leaving a *ravine* some ten feet wide and much longer, which now may go on increasing from year to year without limit, and thus the sand is *ravished* away. I was there just after it began.[1]

[1] Audubon and Bachman think a ravine may sometimes have been produced by the gallery of a shrew mole.

Vol. VII

VII

MARCH, 1855

(ÆT. 37)

March 1. 10 A. M. — To Derby's Bridge and return by Sam Barrett's, to see ice cakes and meadow crust.

The last day for skating. It is a very pleasant and warm day, the finest yet, with considerable coolness in the air, however, — winter still. The air is beautifully clear, and through [it] I love to trace at a distance the roofs and outlines of sober-colored farmhouses amid the woods. We go listening for bluebirds, but only hear crows and chickadees. A fine seething air over the fair russet fields. The dusty banks of snow by the railroad reflect a wonderfully dazzling white from their pure crannies, being melted into an uneven, sharp, wavy surface. This more dazzling white must be due to the higher sun. I see some thick cakes of ice where an ice-car has broken up. In one I detect a large bubble four inches in diameter about a foot beneath the upper surface and six inches from the lower.

In confirmation of my theory, the grain of the ice, as indicated by the linear bubbles within it, was converging beneath this bubble, as the rays of light under a burning-glass, and what was the under surface at that time was melted

in a concave manner to within one and a half inches of the bubble, as appeared by the curvature in the horizontal grain of the more recently formed ice beneath. I omit to draw the other horizontal grain. The situation of this bubble also suggests that ice perhaps increases more above than below the plane of its first freezing in the course of a winter, by the addition of surface water and snow ice.

Examined again the ice and meadow-crust deposited just south of Derby's Bridge. The river is almost down to summer level there now, being only three to four feet deep at that bridge. It has fallen about eight feet since February 17. The ice is piled up there three or four feet deep, and no water beneath, and most of the cakes, which are about one foot thick, have a crust of meadow of equal thickness (*i. e.* from six inches to a foot) attached beneath. I saw in one place three cakes of ice each with a crust of meadow frozen to it beneath, lying one directly upon another and all upon the original ice there, alternately ice and meadow, and the middle crust of meadow measured twenty-eight by twenty-two feet. In this case the earth was about six inches thick only for the most part, three to four feet high in all above original ice. This lay on a gentle ridge or swell between the main Derby Bridge and the little one beyond, and it suggested that that swell might have been thus formed or increased. As we went down the bank through A. Hosmer's land we saw great cakes, and even fields of ice, lying up high and dry where you would not suspect otherwise that water had been. Some have much of the withered pickerel-weed, stem and leaves, in it, causing it to melt and break up soon in the sun. I saw one cake of ice, six inches thick and more than six feet in diameter, with a cake of meadow of exactly equal dimensions attached to its under side, exactly and evenly balanced on the top of a wall in a pasture forty rods from the river, and where you would not have thought the water ever came. We saw three white maples about nine inches in diameter which had been torn up, roots and sod together, and in some cases carried a long distance. One quite sound, of equal size, had been bent flat and broken by the ice striking it some six or seven feet from the ground. Saw some very large pieces of meadow lifted up or carried off at mouth of G. M. Barrett's Bay. One measured seventy-four by twenty-seven feet. Topped with ice almost always, and the old ice still beneath. In some cases the black, peaty soil thus floated was more than one and a half feet thick, and some of this last was carried a quarter of a mile without trace of ice to buoy it, but probably it was first lifted by ice. Saw one piece more than a rod long and two feet thick of black, peaty soil brought from I know not where. The edge of these meadow-crusts is singularly abrupt, as if cut with a turf-knife. Of course a great surface is now covered with ice on each side of the river, under which there is no water, and we go constantly *getting in* with impunity. The spring sun shining on the sloping icy shores makes numerous dazzling ice-blinks, still brighter, and prolonged with rectilinear

I did well to walk in the forenoon, the fresh and inspiring half of this bright day, for now, at mid-afternoon, its brightness is dulled, and a fine stratus is spread over the sky.

Is not "the starry puff (*Lycoperdon stellatum*)" of the "Journal of a Naturalist," which "remains driving about the pastures, little altered until spring," my five-fingered fungus? The same tells of goldfinches (*Fringilla carduelis*) (Bewick calls it the "thistle-finch") "scattering all over the turf the down of the thistle, as they pick out the seed for their food." It is singular that in this particular it should resemble our goldfinch, a different bird.

March 2. Another still, warm, beautiful day like yesterday.

9 A. M. — To Great Meadows to see the ice.

Saw yesterday one of those small slender-winged insects on the ice. A. Wright says that about forty years ago an acre of meadow was carried off at one time by the ice on the Colburn place. D. Clark tells me he saw a piece of meadow, on his part of the Great Meadows, five or six rods square, which had been taken up in one piece and set down again a little distance off. I observe that where there is plowed ground much of it has been washed over the neighboring grass ground to a great distance, discoloring it.

The Great Meadows, as all the rest, are one great field of ice a foot thick to their utmost verge, far up the hillsides and into the swamps, sloping upward there, without water under it, resting almost every-

sides, in the reflection. I am surprised to find the North River more frozen than the South, and we can cross it in many places.

I think the meadow is lifted in this wise: First, you have a considerable freshet in midwinter, succeeded by severe cold before the water has run off much. Then, as the water goes down, the ice for a certain width on each side the river meadows rests on the ground, which freezes to it.[1] Then comes another freshet, which rises a little higher than the former. This gently lifts up the river ice, and that meadow ice on each side of it which still has water under it, without breaking them, but overflows the ice which is frozen to the bottom. Then, after some days of thaw and wind, the latter ice is broken up and rises in cakes, larger or smaller with or without the meadow-crust beneath it, and is floated off before the wind and current till it grounds somewhere, or melts and so sinks, frequently three cakes one upon another, on some swell in the meadow or the edge of the upland. The ice is thus with us a wonderful agent in changing the aspect of the surface of the river-valley. I think that there has been more meadow than usual moved this year, because we had so great a freshet in midwinter succeeded by severe cold, and that by another still greater freshet before the cold weather was past.

Saw a butcher-bird, as usual on top of a tree, and distinguished from a jay by black wings and tail and streak side of head.

[1] Or rather all the water freezes where it is shallow and the grass is frozen into it. *Vide* Mar. 11th.

where on the ground; a great undulating field of ice, rolling prairie-like, — the earth wearing this dry, icy shield or armor, which shines in the sun. Over brooks and ditches, perhaps, and in many other places, the ice, a foot thick in some places, is shoved (?) or *puffed* up in the form of a pent-roof, in some places three feet high and stretching twenty or thirty rods. There is certainly more ice than can lie flat there, as if the adjacent ices had been moved toward each other. Yet this general motion is not likely, and it is more probably the result of the expansion of the ice under the sun and of the warmth of the water (?) there. In many places the ice is dark and transparent, and you see plainly the bottom on which it lies. The various figures in the partially rotted ice are very interesting, — white bubbles which look like coins of various sizes overlapping each other; ⬤⬤ parallel waving lines, with sometimes very slight intervals, on the under side of sloping white ice, marking the successive levels at which the water has stood;

also countless white cleavages, perpendicular or inclined, straight and zigzag, meeting and crossing each other at all possible angles, and making all kinds of geometrical figures, checkering the whole surface, like white frills or ruffles in the ice. (At length the ice melts on the edge of these cleavages into little gutters which catch the snow.) There is the greatest noise from the ice cracking about 10 A. M., yesterday and to-day.

Where the last year's shoots or tops of the young white maples, at the *Salix Purshiana* shore, are brought together, as I walk, into a mass, a quarter of a mile off, with the sun on them, they present a fine dull-scarlet streak. Young twigs are thus more florid than the old wood, as if from their nearness to the flower, or like the complexion of children. You see thus a fine dash of red or scarlet against the distant hills, which near at hand or in their midst is wholly unobservable. I go listening, but in vain, for the warble of a bluebird from the old orchard across the river. I love to look now at the fine-grained russet hillsides in the sun, ready to relieve and contrast with the azure of the bluebirds.

I made a burning-glass of ice, which produced a slight sensation of warmth on the back of my hand, but was so untrue that it did not concentrate the rays to a sufficiently small focus.

Returning over Great Fields, found half a dozen arrowheads, one with three scallops in the base.

If we have a considerable freshet before the ice melts much, apparently much meadow crust will be moved on the South Branch. There is about six inches of frost in the swamps.

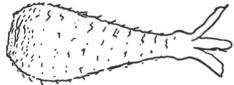

From some partially stripped I see that they begin at the base. These you find left on and about stumps where they have sat, and under the pines. Most fallen pitch pine cones show the marks of squirrels' teeth, showing they were cut off.

Day before yesterday there was good skating, and it was a beautiful warm day for it. Yesterday the ice began to be perceptibly softened. To-day it is too soft for skating.

I might have said on the 2d that though it is warm there is no trouble about getting on to the river, for, the water having fallen about six feet on the South Branch, the ice, about a foot thick, slopes upward in many places half a dozen rods or more on to the upland, like the side of an earthen milk-pan, and you do not know when you have passed the water-line.

Also I noticed yesterday that the ice, along the river-edge at the Great Meadows, still clinging to the alders and maples three or four feet from the ground, was remarkably transparent and solid, or without bubbles, like purest crystal, not rotted; probably because the rays of the sun passed through it, and there was no surface beneath to reflect them back again and so rot the ice. Of this I made my burning-glass.

I think it was yesterday morning that I first noticed

Heard two hawks scream. There was something truly March-like in it, like a prolonged blast or whistling of the wind through a crevice in the sky, which, like a cracked blue saucer, overlaps the woods. Such are the first rude notes which prelude the summer's quire, learned of the whistling March wind.

March 3. Saturday. P. M. — To Conantum.

This afternoon it is somewhat overcast for the first time since February 18th inclusive. I see a dirty-white miller fluttering about over the winter-rye patch next to Hubbard's Grove.

A few rods from the broad pitch pine beyond, I find a cone which was probably dropped by a squirrel in the fall, for I see the marks of its teeth where it was cut off; and it has probably been buried by the snow till now, for it has apparently just opened, and I shake its seeds out. Not only is this cone, resting upright on the ground, fully blossomed, a very beautiful object, but the winged seeds which half fill my hand, small triangular black seeds with thin and delicate flesh-colored wings, remind me of fishes, — alewives, perchance, — their tails more or less curved.  I do not show the curve of the tail. I see, in another place under a pitch pine, many cores of cones which the squirrels have completely stripped of their scales, excepting the (about) three at extremity which cover no seeds, cutting them off regularly at the seeds or close to the core, leaving it in this form, or more regular: —

a frost on the bare russet grass. This, too, is an early spring phenomenon. I am surprised to see that the radical johnswort leaves, which have been green all winter, are now wilted and blackened by it, and where a wood was cut off this winter on a hillside, all the rattlesnake-plantain has suffered in like manner.

Again I observe the river breaking up (from the bank). The thin and rotted ice, saturated with water, is riddled with oblong open places, whose prevailing form is curving *commonly* up-stream, though not always, — i. e. southerly *here*. Has this anything to do with the direction of the prevailing winds of winter, which make the waves bend southerly? Since the cold of a week ago — they may be of older date — I see many tracks in the earth, especially in plowed fields, which are cracked up into vast cakes in some places, apparently on the same principle that ice is.

March 4. Sunday. River *channel* fairly open.

P. M. — To Bee Tree Hill over Fair Haven Pond.

For some time, or since the ground has been bare, I have noticed the spider-holes in the plowed land. We go over the Cliffs. Though a cold and strong wind, it is very warm in the sun, and we can sit in the sun where sheltered on these rocks with impunity. It is a genial warmth. The rustle of the dry leaves on the earth and in the crannies of the rocks, and gathered in deep windrows just under their edge, midleg deep, reminds me of fires in the woods. They are almost ready to burn. I see a fly on the rock. The ice is so much rotted and softened by the sun that it looks white like snow now as I look down on the meadows. There is considerable snow on the north side of hills in the woods. At the Bee Hill-side, a striped squirrel, which quickly dives into his hole at our approach.[1] May not this season of springlike weather between the first decidedly springlike day and the first bluebird, already fourteen days long, be called the *striped squirrel spring?* In which we go listening for the bluebird, but hear him not.

Returning by the Andromeda Ponds, I am surprised to see the red ice visible still, half a dozen rods off. It is melted down to the red bubbles, and I can tinge my finger with it there by rubbing it in the rotted ice.

March 5. P. M. — To Beck Stow's.

A strong but warm southwesterly (?) wind, which has produced a remarkable haze. As I go along by Sleepy Hollow, this strong, warm wind, rustling the leaves on the hillsides, this blue haze, and the russet earth seen through it, remind me that a new season has come. There was the less thick, more remotely *blue*, haze of the 11th February, succeeded by a thaw, beginning on the 14th. Will not rain follow this much thicker haze?

March 6. To Second Division Brook.

Still stronger wind, shaking the house, and rather cool. This the third day of wind.

[1] *Vide* Mar. 7th.

It rained last evening, but not much. This the first rain or storm since February 18th inclusive, *i. e.* fifteen days. The weather began to be decidedly springlike, — air full of light, etc., — the 18th. The 20th was perfect March. The 21st and 22d were remarkably fair and warm; 23d to 28th inclusive remarkably clear and cold; March 1st and 2d remarkably clear and serene and pleasant. Since then colder, with increasing wind and some clouds, with last night some rain.

The sands are too dry and light-colored to show arrowheads so well now.

I see many places where after the late freshet the musquash made their paths under the ice, leading from the water, a rod or two, to a bed of grass above the water-level.

March 7. P. M. — To Red-Ice Pond.

A raw east wind and rather cloudy.

Methinks the buds of the early willows, the willows of the railroad bank, show more of the silvery down than ten days ago.

Did I not see crows flying northeasterly yesterday toward night?

The redness in the ice appears mostly to have evaporated, so that, melted, it does not color the water in a bottle.

Saw, about a hemlock stump on the hillside north of the largest Andromeda Pond, very abundant droppings of some kind of mice, on that common green moss (forming a firm bed about an inch high, like little pines, surmounted by a fine red stem with a green point, in

Our woods are now so reduced that the chopping of this winter has been a cutting to the quick. At least we walkers feel it as such. There is hardly a wood-lot of any consequence left but the chopper's axe has been heard in it this season. They have even infringed fatally on White Pond, on the south of Fair Haven Pond, shaved off the topknot of the Cliffs, the Colburn farm, Beck Stow's, etc., etc.

Observed a mouse or mole's nest in the Second Division Meadow, where it had been made under the snow, — a nice warm globular nest some five inches in diameter, amid the sphagnum and cranberry vines, etc., — made of dried grass and lined with a still finer grass. The hole was on one side, and the bottom was near two inches thick. There were many small paths or galleries in the meadow leading to this from the brook some rod or more distant.

The small gyrinus is circling in the brook. I see where much fur of a rabbit, which probably a fox was carrying, has caught on a moss rose twig as he leaped a ditch. It is much worse walking than it has been for ten days, the continual warmth of the sun melting the ice and snow by walls, etc., and reaching the deeper frost, unexpectedly after the surface had been dry. Pastures which look dry prove soft and full of water.

There is a peculiar redness in the western sky just after sunset. There are many great dark, slate-colored clouds floating there, seen against more distant and thin, wispy, bright-vermilion (?), almost blood-red ones. This in many places appears as the lining of the former.

all three quarters of an inch high), which they had fed on to a great extent, evidently when it was covered with snow, shearing it off level. Their droppings could be collected by the hand probably, ⬭ a light brown above, green next the earth. There were apparently many of their holes in the earth about the stump. They must have fed very extensively on this moss the past winter.[1]

It is now difficult getting on and off Walden. At Brister's Spring there are beautiful dense green beds of moss, which apparently has just risen above the surface of the water, tender and compact. I see many tadpoles of medium or full size in deep warm ditches in Hubbard's meadow. They may probably be seen as soon as the ditches are open, thus earlier than frogs. At his bridge over the brook it must have been a trout I saw glance, — rather dark, as big as my finger. To-day, as also three or four days ago, I saw a clear drop of maple sap on a broken red maple twig, which tasted very sweet. The *Pyrola secunda* is a perfect evergreen. It has lost none of its color or freshness, with its thin ovate finely serrate leaves, revealed now the snow is gone. It is more or less branched.

Picked up a very handsome white pine cone some six and a half inches long by two and three eighths near base and two near apex, perfectly blossomed. It is a very rich and wholesome brown color, of various shades as you turn it in your hand, — a light ashy or gray brown, somewhat like unpainted wood, as you look down on it, or as if the lighter brown were cov-

[1] *Vide* Mar. 14th.

ered with a gray lichen, seeing only those parts of the scales always exposed, — with a few darker streaks or marks (\\``) and a drop of pitch at the point of each scale. Within, the scales are a dark brown above (*i. e.* as it hangs) and a light brown beneath, very distinctly being marked beneath by the same darker brown, down the centre and near the apex somewhat anchorwise.

We were walking along the sunny hillside on the south of Fair Haven Pond (on the 4th), which the choppers had just laid bare, when, in a sheltered and warmer place, we heard a rustling amid the dry leaves on the hillside and saw a striped squirrel eying us from its resting-place on the bare ground. It sat still till we were within a rod, then suddenly dived into its hole, which was at its feet, and disappeared. The first pleasant days of spring come out like a squirrel and go in again.[1]

March 8. P. M. — To old Carlisle road.
Another fair day with easterly wind.

This morning I got my boat out of the cellar and turned it up in the yard to let the seams open before I calk it. The blue river, now almost completely open (*i. e.* excepting a little ice in the recesses of the shore and a good deal over the meadows), admonishes me to be swift.

I see where many young trees and bushes have been broken down by the ice after the last freshet, many of

[1] [Channing, p. 285.]

Loring's young maples, for example. The cornel and other bushes along the walls are broken like young trees by snowdrifts, the ice, sinking with them in its embrace, weighing or dragging them down. In many places, where the water rose so high as to reach the ends of the lower branches of white maples and these were afterward frozen in, the ice, sinking with the ebb, breaks off or strips down the branch.[1] There appears to be a motion to the ice (even on meadows away from the current and at Walden shore) somewhat like that of a glacier, by which it tips over the trees, etc., standing in it without breaking up, — the result, one would say, of its swelling under the influence of the sun.

Was surprised to see a cluster of those large leek buds on a rock in Clark's (?) meadow between the oak and my house that was.

Daniel Clark tells me that on his part of the Great Meadows there is a hole just about the breadth and depth of a man, commonly full of water. He does not know what made it.

I crossed through the swamp south of Boulder Field toward the old dam. Stopping in a sunny and sheltered place on a hillock in the woods, — for it was raw in the wind, — I heard the hasty, shuffling, as if frightened, note of a *robin* from a dense birch wood, — a sort of *tche tche tche tche tche*, — and then probably it dashed through the birches; and so they fetch the year about. Just from the South Shore, perchance, it alighted not in the village street, but in this remote birch wood. This sound reminds me of rainy, misty

[1] *Vide* Mar. 14th.

April days in past years. Once or twice before, this afternoon, I thought I heard one and listened, but in vain.

I still see the bluish bloom on thimble-berry vines quite fresh. I walk these days along the brooks, looking for tortoises and trout, etc. They are full of a rust-colored water, as if they flowed out of an iron mine. As the ice melts in the swamps I see the horn-shaped buds of the skunk-cabbage, green with a bluish bloom, standing uninjured, ready to feel the influence of the sun, — the most prepared for spring — to look at — of any plant. I see of late more than before of the fuzzy caterpillars, both black and reddish-brown.

March 9. A cloudy, rain-threatening day, not windy and rather warmer than yesterday.
Painted the bottom of my boat.
P. M. — To Andromeda Ponds.

Scare up a rabbit on the hillside by these ponds, which was gnawing a smooth sumach. See also where they have gnawed the red maple, sweet-fern, *Populus grandidentata*, white and other oaks (taking off considerable twigs at four or five cuts), amelanchier, and sallow; but they seem to prefer the smooth sumach to any of these. With this variety of cheap diet they are not likely to starve. I get a few drops of the sweet red maple juice which has run down the main stem where a rabbit had nibbled off close a twig. The rabbit, indeed, lives, but the sumach may be killed.

The heart-wood of the poison-dogwood, when I break it down with my hand, has a singular rotten, yellow look and a spirituous or apothecary odor.

As, on the 4th, I clambered over those great white pine masts which lay in all directions one upon another on the hillside south of Fair Haven, where the woods have been laid waste, I was struck, in favorable lights, with the jewel-like brilliancy of the sawed ends thickly bedewed with crystal drops of turpentine, thickly as a shield, as if the dryads (?), oreads (?), pine-wood nymphs had seasonably wept there the fall of the tree. The perfect sincerity of these terebinthine drops, each one reflecting the world, colorless as light, or like drops of dew heaven-distilled and trembling to their fall, is incredible when you remember how firm their consistency. And is this that pitch which you cannot touch without being defiled?

Looking from the Cliffs, the sun being as before invisible, I saw far more light in the reflected sky in the neighborhood of the sun than I could see in the heavens from my position, and it occurred to me that the reason was that there was reflected to me from the river the view I should have got if I had stood there on the water in a more favorable position.

I see that the mud in the road has crystallized as it dried (for it is not nearly cold enough to freeze), like the first crystals that shoot and set on water when freezing.

I see the minute seeds of the *Andromeda calyculata* scattered over the melting ice of the Andromeda Ponds.

C. says he saw yesterday the slate-colored hawk with a white bar across tail, — meadow hawk, *i. e.* frog hawk. Probably finds moles and mice.

An overcast and dark night.

March 10. Snowed in the night, a mere whitening. In the morning somewhat overcast still, cold and quite windy. The first clear snow to whiten the ground since February 9th.

I am not aware of growth in any plant yet, unless it be the further peeping out of willow catkins. They have crept out further from under their scales, and, looking closely into them, I detect a little redness along the twigs even now. You are always surprised by the sight of the first spring bird or insect; they seem premature, and there is no such evidence of spring as themselves, so that they literally *fetch* the year about. It is thus when I hear the first robin or bluebird or, looking along the brooks, see the first water-bugs out circling. But you think, They have come, and Nature cannot recede. Thus, when on the 6th I saw the gyrinus at Second Division Brook, I saw no peculiarity in the water or the air to remind me of them, but to-day they are here and yesterday they were not. I go looking deeper for tortoises, when suddenly my eye rests on these black circling apple-seeds in some smoother bay.

The red squirrel should be drawn with a pine cone. Those reddening leaves, as the checkerberry, lambkill, etc., etc., which at the beginning of winter were greenish, are now a deeper red, when the snow goes off. No more snow since last *night*, but a strong, cold northerly wind all day, with occasional gleams of sunshine. The whitening of snow consequently has not disappeared.

Miss Minott says that Dr. Spring told her that when the sap began to come up into the trees, *i. e.* about the middle of February (she says), then the diseases of the human body come out. The idea is that man's body sympathizes with the rest of nature, and his pent-up humors burst forth like the sap from wounded trees. This with the mass may be that languor or other weakness commonly called spring feelings.

Minott tells me that Henry Hosmer says he saw geese two or three days ago!

Jacob Farmer gave me to-day a part of the foot probably of a pine marten, which he found two or three days ago in a trap he had set in his brook for a mink, — under water, baited with a pickerel. It is clothed above with a glossy dark-brown hair, and contains but two toes (perhaps a third without the talon), armed with fine and very sharp talons, much curved. It had left thus much in the trap and departed.

Audubon and Bachman call my deer mouse "*Mus Leucopus*, Rafinesque," American White-Footed Mouse; call it "yellowish brown above" and give these synonyms: —

"*Mus Sylvaticus*, Forster, Phil. Trans., vol. lxii., p. 380.
Field-Rat, Penn., Hist. Quad., vol. ii., p. 185.
Field-Rat, Arctic Zoöl., vol. i., p. 131.
Musculus Leucopus, Rafinesque, Amer. Month. Review, Oct. 1818, p. 444.
Mus Leucopus, Desmar. Mamm., esp. 493.
Mus Sylvaticus, Harlan, Fauna, p. 151.
Mus Agrarius, Godm., Nat. Hist., vol. ii., p. 88.
Mus Leucopus, Richardson, F. B. A., p. 142.
Arvicola Nuttallii, Harlan, variety.

Vol. VII

Arvicola Emmonsii, Emm., Mass. Report, p. 61.
Mus Leucopus, Dekay, Nat. Hist. N. Y., pl. 1, p. 82."

By fur he does not mean the short inner hair only. Says they are larger in Carolina than in the Eastern States, but he does not describe any larger than mine. "Next to the common mouse, this is the most abundant and widely diffused species of mouse in North America. We have received it . . . from every State in the Union, and from Labrador, Hudson's Bay, and the Columbia River." Has found it "taking up its abode in a deserted squirrel's nest, thirty feet from the earth."

"They have been known to take possession of deserted birds' nests — such as those of the cat-bird, red-winged starling, song thrush, or red-eyed flycatcher." "We have also occasionally found their nests on bushes, from five to fifteen feet from the ground. They are in these cases constructed with nearly as much art and ingenuity as the nests of the Baltimore Oriole." Of some he has, says, "They are seven inches in length and four in breadth, the circumference measuring thirteen inches; they are of an oval shape and are outwardly composed of dried moss and a few slips of the inner bark of some wild grape-vine; other nests are more rounded, and are composed of dried leaves and moss." Thinks two pairs live in some very large ones. "The entrance in all the nests is from below, and about the size of the animal."

Female sometimes escapes with her young adhering to her teats. "Nocturnal in its habits." Only sound he has heard from them "a low squeak." Not so carniv-

orous as "most of its kindred species." Troubles trappers by getting their bait. Lays up "stores of grain and grass seeds," acorns, etc. In the North, wheat; in the South, rice. Eats out the heart of Indian corn kernels.

Thinks it produces two litters in a season in the North and three in the South. Foxes, owls, etc., destroy it. Thinks the ermine weasel its most formidable foe. Thinks it *sometimes* occupies a chipping squirrel's hole. Thinks that neither this nor the mole does much injury to garden or farm, but rather "the little pine-mouse (*Arvicola pinetorum*, Le Conte), or perhaps Wilson's meadow-mouse (*Arvicola Pennsylvanica*, Ord, *A. hirsutus*, Emmons, and Dekay)." Yet Northern farmers complain that the deer mouse gnaws young fruit trees, etc.; maybe so. Avoids houses, at least those where there are wharf rats and cats.

Observed this afternoon some celandine by Deacon Brown's fence, apparently grown about an inch. *Vide* if it is really springing.

March 11. P. M. — To Annursnack.

Clear and rather pleasant; the ground again bare; wind northerly. I am surprised to see how rapidly that ice that covered the meadows on the 1st of March has disappeared under the influence of the sun alone. The greater part of what then lay on the meadows a foot thick has melted, — two thirds at least.

On Abel Hosmer's pasture, just southeast of the stone bridge, I see where the sod was lifted up over a great space in the flood of the 17th of February. There is one bare place there, showing only the fine and now white roots of grass, seven rods long by two or three. There are other smaller ones about it. The sod carried off is from four to six inches thick commonly. Pieces of this crust, from a quarter to a third the size mentioned, are resting within ten or twenty rods. One has sunk against the causeway bridge, being too wide to go through. I see one piece of crust, twelve feet by six, turned completely topsyturvy with its ice beneath it. This has prevented the ice from melting, and on examining it I find that the ice did not settle down on to the grass after the water went down and then freeze to it, for the blades of grass penetrate one inch into the ice, showing that, the water being shallow, the whole froze, and the grass was frozen in, and thus, when the water rose again, was lifted up. The bared places I have noticed as yet were not in the low ground, but where the water was comparatively shallow, commonly at a distance from the river.[1]

A bluebird day before yesterday in Stow.[2]

Saw a cake of recent ice very handsomely marked as it decayed, with darker marks for the original crystals centred with the original white. It would be a rare pattern for a carpet, because it contains a variety of figures agreeable to the eye without regularity.

Many of those dirty-white millers or ephemeræ in the air.

As I sit at the base of Annursnack the earth appears almost completely bare, but from the top I see considerable white ice here and there. This shows that what is left is only the whitened and rotting ice, which,

[1] *Vide* [p. 245].   [2] Next page.

being confined to the lowest hollows and meadows, is only observed from a height.

At this season, — before grass springs to conceal them, — I notice those pretty little roundish shells on the tops of hills; one to-day on Annursnack.

I see pitch pine needles looking as if whitewashed, thickly covered on each of the two slopes of the needle with narrow, white, oyster-shell-like latebræ or chrysalids of an insect.

March 12. 6.30 A. M. — To Andromeda Ponds. Lesser redpolls still.[1]

Elbridge Hayden and Poland affirm that they saw a brown thrasher sitting on the top of an apple tree by the road near Hubbard's and singing after his fashion on the 5th. I suggested the shrike, which they do not know, but they say it was a *brown* bird.

Hayden saw a bluebird yesterday.

P. M. — To Great Meadows.

Comes out pleasant after a raw forenoon with a flurry of snow, already gone.

Two ducks in river, good size, white beneath with black heads, as they go over.[2] They first rise some distance down-stream, and fly by on high, reconnoitring me, and I first see them on wing; then settle a quarter of a mile above by a long slanting flight, at last opposite the swimming-elm below Flint's. I come on up the bank with the sun in my face; start them again. Again they fly down-stream by me on high, turn and

[1] *Vide* forward.   [2] Sheldrakes?

Vol. VII

come round back by me again with outstretched heads, and go up to the Battle-Ground before they alight. Thus the river is no sooner fairly open than they are back again, — before I have got my boat launched, and long before the river has worn through Fair Haven Pond. I think I heard a quack or two.

Audubon and Bachman say that Forster and Harlan refer the *Mus leucopus* "to *Mus sylvaticus* of Europe," — wrongly, for they differ in many respects. "They may always be distinguished from each other at a glance by the following mark: in more than twenty specimens we examined of *Mus sylvaticus* [in Europe][1] we have always found a yellowish line edged with dark-brown, on the breast. In many hundred specimens of *Mus leucopus* we have without a single exception found this yellow line entirely wanting, all of them being pure white on the breast, as well as on the whole under surface. We have no hesitation in pronouncing the species distinct." Now I find that I had described my specimen of February 20th, before I had read Audubon and Bachman or heard of the *Mus sylvaticus*, as having "a very slight and delicate tinge of yellowish beneath, between the fore legs," though Emmons does not mention this color. The other differences they mention certainly are not of much importance, and probably equally great ones are to be found between different specimens of *Mus leucopus*.

March 13. Northern lights last night. Rainbow in east this morning.

[1] [The brackets are Thoreau's.]

Almost all the meadow-crust now (and for a week past) lies on a cake of ice where it lodged and which, being prevented from melting any further than its edge, is of the same size with it. The crust is frozen on to this, and, the ice which first froze to it and raised it having melted some time ago, most would not know how to account for its position.

6.30 A. M. — To Hill.

Still, but with some wrack here and there. The river is low, very low for the season. It has been falling ever since the freshet of February 18th. Now, about sunrise, it is nearly filled with the thin, half-cemented ice-crystals of the night, which the warmer temperature of day apparently has loosened. They grate against the bushes and wheel round in great fields with a slight crash and piling up.

I hear the rapid tapping of the woodpecker from over the water.

P. M. — To Hubbard's Close.

For a week the more stagnant brooks and ditches have been green with conferva, a kind of green veil that conceals their bottom and invests the bubbles on the surface.

I am surprised to see, not only many pollywogs through the thin ice of the warm ditches, but, in still warmer, stagnant, unfrozen holes in this meadow, half a dozen small frogs, probably *Rana palustris*.[1] Green spires of grass stand perfectly upright in these pools, rising above water.

[1] Is it not the croaker?

Coming through the stubble of Stow's rye-field in front of the Breed house, I meet with four mice-nests in going half a dozen rods. They lie flat on the ground amid the stubble; are flattened spheres, the horizontal diameter about five inches, the perpendicular considerably less, composed of grass or finer stubble, and on taking them up you do not at once detect the entrance with your eye, but rather feel it with your finger on the side; lined with the finest of the grass. These were undoubtedly — probably — made when the snow was on the ground, for their winter residence, while they gleaned the rye-field, and when the snow went off they scampered to the woods. I think they were made by the *Mus leucopus, i. e. Arvicola Emmonsii.* Similar to that of March 6th in meadow, except that was thicker against wet.

I look into many woodchucks' holes, but as yet they are choked with leaves and there is no sign of their having come abroad.

At evening the raw, overcast day concludes with snow and hail. Two pickerel caught in Flint's Pond to-day weighed on the Mill-Dam to-night 7¾ + or nearly 8 pounds.

March 14. Three inches of snow in the morning, and it snows a little more during the day, with occasional gleams of sunshine. Winter back again in prospect, and I see a few sparrows, probably tree sparrows, in the yard.

P. M. — To Andromeda Ponds.

At one of the holes under the stump of March 7th,

caught a *Mus leucopus* (deer mouse). So this was the kind, undoubtedly, that fed on the moss, and that colored their droppings. It is in very good condition; extreme length six and a half, tail three inches. It is a less *reddish* brown on the sides and cheeks than my whole skin, and a darker brown above, mixed with a little reddish; no yellow tinge on breast. Some whiskers, as usual, are white, others black, and I count the "six tubercles on each palm." There are no tracks about the stump, for they are not abroad by day, *i. e.* since the last of this snow, but probably there will be tracks to-morrow morning. Thus it is generally. If it ceases snowing in the morning, you see few, if any, tracks in your walk, but the next morning many.

It is the first and last snows — especially the last — which blind us most, when the sun is most powerful and our eyes are unused to them.

I observe the tracks of sparrows leading to every little sprig of blue-curls amid the other weeds which (its seemingly empty pitchers) rises above the snow. There seems, however, to be a little seed left in them. This, then, is reason enough why these withered stems still stand, — that they may raise these granaries above the snow for the use of the snowbirds.

That ice of February has destroyed almost the whole of Charles Hubbard's young red maple swamp in front of the Hollowell place. Full an acre of thrifty young maples, as well as alders and birches four to seven feet high, is completely destroyed, being pulled and broken down (broken near the ground) as the ice sank after the water went down. It is all flat, and

Vol. VII

looks at a little distance as if one had gone through with a bush-whack and done his work faithfully. They [are] from half an inch to one inch thick, broken this wise: He has apparently concluded to clear it. Only the taller birches, etc., are left. I thought, as I approached, seeing some clumps still standing, all the rest flat on the ground, that without a doubt some one had been clearing the swamp, though I stood within a rod of it. Just as a snow-drift breaks down young fruit-trees. R. Rice tells me that a great many young white pines in a swamp of his in Sudbury have been barked, the bark rubbed down several inches completely bare by the ice. Thus the river from time to time asserts its authority over its swamps to a great distance.[1]

March 15. Jacob Farmer gave me to-day the foot of an otter, also of a fisher, — to put with my pine marten's foot. He cut them off of recent furs in Boston. He sells about a hundred mink skins in a year. Thinks not more than thirty or forty are caught in Concord in a year. He says (I think) a mink's skin is worth two dollars! They are sent to Europe to be worn there, not for hats.

Foul weather all day, — at first a fine snow, and finally rain. Now, at 9 P. M., a clear sky. And so the storm which began evening of 13th ends.

[1] The willows, alders, etc., all along the river where the water was deeper are commonly broken higher up, three or four feet from the ground. This Mar. 19th. *Vide* Mar. 20th.

As for the first half of this month, it began very pleasant and warm (the latter third of February had been very clear and pleasant but colder), the river opening and ice beginning to soften; then on the 4th it became windy (northerly, east, or southwest), sometimes very cold and raw, occasionally rocking the house; the 9th a little warmer, storm threatening; the 10th, ground whitened with snow; and so it goes on, more or less raw till the snow of the 14th.

Mr. Rice tells me that when he was getting mud out of the little swamp at the foot of Brister's Hill last [a blank space left for the day], he heard a squeaking and found that he was digging near the nest of what he called a "field mouse," — by his description probably the meadow mouse. It was made of grass, etc., and, while he stood over it, the mother, not regarding him, came and carried off the young, one by one, in her mouth, being gone some time in each case before she returned, and finally she took the nest itself.

He saw a bluebird about a week ago in Sudbury, and [was] surprised to observe that it had a worm in its mouth, but I am not, for the ice and snow have been sprinkled with caterpillars of several kinds all the past winter.

March 16. Cloudy in the forenoon. Sun comes out and it is rather pleasant in the afternoon.

P. M. — To Conantum End.

At the woodchuck's hole just beyond the cockspur thorn, I see several diverging and converging trails of undoubtedly a woodchuck, or several, which must have come out at least as early as the 13th. The track is about one and three quarters inches wide by two long, the five toes very distinct and much spread, and, including the *scrape* of the snow before the foot came to its bearing, is somewhat hand-like. It is simple and alternate, thus: commonly, but sometimes much like a rabbit's, and again like a mink's, somewhat thus: They had come out and run about directly from hole to hole, six in all, within a dozen rods or more. This appeared to have been all their travelling, as if they had run round a-visiting and waked each other up the first thing. At first they soiled the snow with their sandy feet. At one place they had been clearing out to-day the throats of two holes within a rod of each other, scattering the mud-like sand, made wet by the melting snow, over the pure snow around; and I saw where, between these holes, they had sat on a horizontal limb of a shrub oak (which it had tried its teeth on), about a foot from the ground, also on a rock, plainly to warm and dry themselves in the sun, having muddied it all over. I also saw where another had sunned itself on a stone at the foot of a small pitch pine and tried its teeth on a dead limb of the pine. They could not go in or out of these burrows without being completely covered with sandy mud. The path over the snow between these holes was quite covered with it.

The impression of the foot a little like this,

but not so much spread: They have but four toes on the fore feet, with rudiment of a thumb.

His first journey, then, appears to be to some neighboring hole which he remembers, a dozen or fifteen rods off, and, perchance, he goes as straight or unerringly to it as if he had not been asleep all winter. Apparently after a little gossiping there his first work is to clear out the entrance to his burrow, ejecting the leaves and sand which have there collected. None have travelled beyond these holes, except that one track leads into the swamp. But here are the tracks of foxes bound on longer journeys. They are generally ten or twelve inches apart by three to five, but are irregular, now two

at the usual distance, then two close together, three or four inches apart only. The foot is very shapely and much like a dog's.

The dirty-colored aspen down there projects an eighth of an inch, or nearly as much as the early willows.

As I stand here, some sixty rods from the river, at about 3.30 P. M., looking at the open river, toward which my shadow points at right angles with its current, that part which my shadow extended would

strike is a pale dull slate-color, but that part a dozen rods southerly from this is a distinct blue, which goes on increasing in depth southerly, till, looking at an angle of forty-five degrees from the first line, it is of a glorious, deep indigo blue. For some reason I must look much further north to see it blue.

River not yet worn through Fair Haven Pond.

You are pretty sure to see the tracks of squirrels, red ones, about the base of walnuts which they have ascended, and where they have probed the snow for a nut.

I think that a great many birds' nests are broken up in summer by weasels, minks, and skunks.

Returning, scared up two large ducks just above the bridge. One very large; white beneath, breast and neck; black head and wings and aft. The other much smaller and dark. Apparently male and female. They lit more than a hundred rods south of the bridge, and I viewed them with glass. The larger sailed about on the watch, while the smaller, dark one dived repeatedly.[1] I think there are but three ducks ever seen here anything like these, — the golden-eye or whistler, the goosander or sheldrake, and the red-breasted merganser.[2] This male I suspect was too large for the first, and, from its size and its great superiority in size to its companion, I think it the goosander or sheldrake. It did not scoot over the water as I think the red-breasted merganser[3] does.

[1] *Vide* Apr. 1st.
[2] ["Red-breasted merganser" is crossed out with pencil, and "Is it not female goosander?" written over it.]
[3] [Two interrogation-points in pencil here.]

March 17. *Saturday.* H. Hosmer says he has seen black ducks. Edmund Hosmer's meadow, *i. e.* the Hunt house meadow, is covered with great pieces of meadow, the largest thick and dense cranberry meadow. It is piled three or four feet high for several rods. Higher up on the North Branch I see where the trees, especially the swamp white oaks, have been chafed smooth and white by the ice (at that time), from the ground to three or four feet (six in some cases), as if scraped with a hoe, and the bushes all along the shore — willows, alders, etc., etc. (blueberry swamps in some places) — have been more or less broken down. I hear the lesser redpolls yet.[1] See now along the edge of the river, the ice being gone, many fresh heaps of clamshells, which were opened by the musquash when the water was higher, about some tree where the ground rises. And very many places you see where they formed new burrows into the bank, the sand being pushed out into the stream about the entrance, which is still below water, and you feel the ground undermined as you walk.

White maple blossom-buds look as if bursting; show a rusty, fusty space, perhaps a sixteenth of an inch in width, over and above the regular six scales.[2]

I see scraps of the evergreen ranunculus along the riverside.

March 18. Fair in the forenoon, but more or less cloudy and windy in the afternoon.

[1] The last.
[2] [There is an interrogation-point in the margin against this paragraph.]

P. M. — Round by Hollowell place *via* Clam-shell.

I see with my glass as I go over the railroad bridge, sweeping the river, a great gull standing far away on the top of a muskrat-cabin which rises just above the water opposite the Hubbard Bath. When I get round within sixty rods of him, ten minutes later, he still stands on the same spot, constantly turning his head to every side, looking out for foes. Like a wooden image of a bird he stands there, heavy to look at; head, breast, beneath, and rump pure white; slate-colored wings tipped with black and extending beyond the tail, — the herring gull. I can see clear down to its webbed feet. But now I advance, and he rises easily, goes off northeastward over the river with a leisurely flight. At Clamshell Hill I sweep the river again, and see, standing midleg deep on the meadow where the water is very shallow with deeper around, another of these wooden images, which is harder to scare. I do not fairly distinguish black tips to its wings. It is ten or fifteen minutes before I get him to rise, and then he goes off in the same leisurely manner, stroking the air with his wings, and now making a great circle back on its course, so you cannot tell which way it is bound. By standing so long motionless in these places they may perchance accomplish two objects, *i. e.*, catch passing fish (suckers?) like a heron and escape the attention of man. Its utmost motion was to plume itself once and turn its head about. If it did not move its head, it would look like a decoy. Our river is quite low for the season, and yet it is here without freshet

or easterly storm. It *seems* to take this course on its migrations without regard to the state of the waters.

Meanwhile a small dark-colored duck, all neck and wings, a winged rolling-pin, went over, — perhaps a teal.

For the last two or three days very wet and muddy walking, owing to the melting of the snow; which also has slightly swollen the small streams.

Some vigorous osiers about the trunk of some golden willows on the Hubbard Bridge causeway have all winter been a much brighter yellow than the rest of the trees. They cannot well be more brilliant any time.

Notwithstanding the water on the surface, it is easier crossing meadows and swamps than it will be a month hence, on account of the frost in the ground.

March 19. A fine clear and warm day for the season. Launched my boat.

P. M. — Paddled to Fair Haven Pond.

Very pleasant and warm, when the wind lulls and the water is perfectly smooth. I make the voyage without gloves. The snow of March 14th is about gone, and the landscape is once more russet. The thick ice of the meadows lies rotting on each side of the stream, white and almost soft as snow. In many places it extends still over the shallower parts of the river. As I paddle or pole up the side of the stream, the muddy bottom looks dark and dead, and no greenness is observed but on a close scrutiny. The unsightly dead leaf-stalks of the pontederia cover it in irregular whorls covered

with filth. The black stems of the polygonums here and there still rise above the surface. But on a closer scrutiny you detect here and there bits of the ever-green ranunculus (commonly floating), the cress, some reddish pads of nuphar expanded close to the bottom, and a few points of its closely rolled, unex-panded leaves, also some radical greenness in the pon-tederia. And what is that fresh green oblong, perhaps spatulate, leaf one and a half inches long, making little rosettes on a running root, in one place just this side the ash above the railroad?[1] There is this radi-cal greenness to correspond with that on the land. The muskrat-houses are for the most part flatted down, even below the present level of the water (at least five feet and more below the truss), probably by the water and ice a month ago. I see but three or four well repaired. One new one at least, however, on a piece of meadow lately lodged. It is to be inferred that they have not the same need of them as in the fall. Already Farrar is out with his boat looking for spring cranberries, and here comes, slowly paddling, the dark-faced trapper Melvin with his dog and gun.[2] I see a poor drowned gray rabbit floating, back up as in life, but three quarters submerged. I see a hawk circling over a small maple grove through this calm air, ready to pounce on the first migrating sparrow that may have arrived. As I paddle or push along by the edge of the thick ice which lines the shore, sometimes pushing against it, I observe that it is curiously worn by the

[1] It is forget-me-not.
[2] See him out here the first boating day next year also.

water into this form: the dotted line being the water's edge. The water has eaten into the edge of the ice just where its surface meets it (which may be one and a half inches beneath the top), four or five inches or more, leaving a sharp projecting eave above, while the lower part, five or six inches thick, being preserved hard by the water, slopes off to a very sharp edge from one to even four feet from the upper. The undulations made by my boat and paddle, striking under this eave, make a constant sound as I pass. I am surprised to find that the river has not yet worn through Fair Haven Pond. Getting up a weed with the paddle close to the shore under water, where five or six inches deep, I found a fishworm in the mud. Here and there, floating or on the edge of the ice, I see small pieces of nuphar root, with a few rolled, pointed leaf-buds, probably gnawed off by the musk-rats. The greater part of the Wood meadow this side Clamshell has been lifted up and settled again, and it now sounds hollow and sinks under my steps.

The wind has got round more to the east now, at 5 P. M., and is raw and disagreeable, and produces a bluish haze or mist at once in the air. It is early for such a phenomenon. *Smelled* muskrats in two places, and saw two. Saw, by their white droppings on the bottom, where ducks had fed. I hear at last the *tchuck tchuck* of a blackbird and, looking up, see him flying high over the river southwesterly, — the wrong way, — in great haste to reach somewhere; and when I reach my landing I hear my first bluebird, somewhere about Cheney's trees by the river. I hear him out of the blue deeps, but do not yet see his blue body. He comes with a warble. Now first generally heard in the village. Not a duck do I see. It is perhaps too bright and serene a day for them.

March 20. A flurry of snow at 7 A. M. I go to turn my boat up. Four or five song sparrows are flitting along amid the willows by the waterside. Probably they came yesterday with the bluebirds. From distant trees and bushes I hear a faint tinkling *te te te te té* and at last a full strain whose rhythm is *whit whit whit, ter tche, tchear tche,* deliberately sung, or measuredly, while the falling snow is beginning to whiten the ground, — not discouraged by such a reception. The bluebird, too, is in the air, and I detect its blue back for a moment upon a picket.

It is remarkable by what a gradation of days which we *call* pleasant and warm, beginning in the last of February, we come at last to real summer warmth. At first a sunny, calm, serene winter day is pronounced spring, or reminds us of it; and even the first pleasant spring day perhaps we walk with our greatcoat buttoned up and gloves on.

Trying the other day to imitate the honking of geese, I found myself flapping my sides with my elbows, as with wings, and uttering something like the syllables *mow-ack* with a nasal twang and twist in my head; and I produced their note so perfectly in the opinion of the hearers that I thought I might possibly draw a flock down.

P. M. — Up Assabet.

It soon cleared off in the morning, and proved a fair but windy day. I see a willow six inches in diameter which was broken down by the ice, and some birches up the Assabet, which had previously been bent over the stream, were broken off ten feet from the ground. I notice this havoc along the stream on making my first voyages on it. The ice either freezes to the alders, etc., one half to two thirds up them, and settling, breaks them lower down, settling upon them, or else freezes to drooping limbs and so pulls them down. As I look into the low woods or swamp on each side, I see the trees, especially rough-barked ones like the black willow, swamp white oak, and elm, chafed white to the height of three or four feet, sometimes the bark worn off, and, the maples, birches, etc., being also divested of their lichens, you see exactly the height at which the water stood when it froze. The lower twigs of swamp white oaks over the water are, as it were, nibbled off by the ice. Were those rocks by the shore this side the Leaning Hemlocks placed there by the ice?

Some willow catkins, whose limb was bent down and held in the ice, are three eighths of an inch long, *i. e.* the down beyond the scale. I see maple sap flowing and taste it sweet in many places where the branches have been stripped down. In the meadow near the stone-heaps I pace a space laid bare by the ice, — fourteen rods by one to four, nearly a quarter of an acre. The crust raised is commonly only four or five inches thick, or down to where the grass roots break; and it is taken principally from the higher parts of

a meadow, covered at the time of the freezing frequently from a longitudinal swell. We notice the color of the water especially at this season when it is recently revealed (*vide* 16th), and in the fall, because there is little color elsewhere, — when it is seen in contrast with the ice or snow or russet landscape. It shows best in a clear air contrasting with the russet shores. At my landing I hear the peculiar *tche tche, tche tche* — or somewhat like that — of the *F. hyemalis,* in company with a few tree sparrows. They take refuge from the cold wind, half a dozen in all, behind an arbor-vitæ hedge, and there plume themselves with puffed-up feathers.

March 21. 6.30 A. M. — To Swamp Bridge Brook.

Clear, but a very cold westerly wind this morning. Ground frozen very hard. Yet the song sparrows are heard from the willow and alder rows. Hear a lark far off in the meadow.

P. M. — To Bare Hill by railroad.

Early willow and aspen catkins are very conspicuous now. The silvery down of the former has in some places crept forth from beneath its scales a third of an inch at least. This increased silveriness was obvious, I think, about the first of March, perhaps earlier. It appears to be a very gradual expansion, which begins in the warm days of winter. It would be well to observe them once a fortnight through the winter. It is the first decided growth I have noticed, and is probably a month old.

The song sparrow is now seen dodging behind the wall, with a quirk of its tail, or flitting along the alders or other bushes by the side of the road, especially in low ground, and its pleasant strain is heard at intervals in spite of the cold and blustering wind. It is the most steady and resolute singer as yet, its strain being heard at intervals throughout the day, more than any as yet *peopling* the hedgerows.

There is no opening in Flint's Pond except a very little around the boat-house. The tree sparrow, flitting song-sparrow-like through the alders, utters a sharp metallic *tcheep.* In the hollow behind Britton's Camp, I see seven mouse-holes — probably *Mus leucopus* — around an old oak stump, all within a foot of it, and many of their droppings at each hole and where they have gnawed off the grass, and indistinct galleries in the grass, extending three or four feet on every side. I see red maple sap oozing out and wetting the young trees where there is no obvious wound. Crossed Goose Pond on ice.

March 22. 6.30 A. M. — To Hill.

Overcast and cold. Yet there is quite a concert of birds along the river; the song sparrows are very lively and musical, and the blackbirds already sing *o-gurgle-ee-e-e* from time to time on the top of a willow or elm or maple, but oftener a sharp, shrill whistle or a *tchuck.* I also hear a short, regular robin song, though many are flitting about with hurried note. The bluebird faintly warbles, with such ventriloquism that I thought him further off. He requires a warmer air. The jays scream. I hear the downy woodpecker's rapid tapping and *my* first distinct spring note (*phe-be*) of the chickadee.

The river has skimmed over a rod in breadth along the sides. Saw a heavy-flapping, bittern-like bird flying northeast. It was small for a fish hawk. Can it be the stake-driver?? or a gull?

A (probably meadow) mouse nest in the low meadow by stone bridge, where it must have been covered with water a month ago; probably made in fall. Low in the grass, a little dome four inches in diameter, with no sign of entrance, it being *very* low on one side. Made of fine meadow-grass.

Though there was a clear strip in the west only about three times the height of the mountains, and much less in the east, I saw the sun shining on the Peterboro mountains while we had not had a ray from him. Did the rays at this hour (seven) pass over the clouds which shaded us? They may have passed further north than the clouds reached, for there seemed a lifting in the horizon there.

P. M. — Fair Haven Pond *via* Conantum.

Caught a salamander in the spring-hole in the brook behind Hubbard's. It was lying on the mud in water as if basking. I have not yet identified it. It has no bright spots, being uniformly dark above, except to a microscope, beneath bluish-slate, beneath and sides of tail dull-golden. Three and a quarter inches long; tail alone one and a half plus; a dozen or more marks as of ribs on each side. Under microscope all above

Vol. VII

very finely sprinkled black and light brown, — hard to tell which the ground. Somewhat like *Salamandra dorsalis*, but not granulated nor ocellated with vermilion spots. Irides dull-golden. Last five-eighths inch of tail lighter-colored.

I have noticed crows in the meadows ever since they were first partially bare, three weeks ago.

I hear a song sparrow on an alder-top sing *ozit ozit oze-e-e* | (quick) *tchip tchip tchip tchip tchay* | *te tchip ter che ter tchay;* also the same shortened and *very much* varied. Heard one sing uninterruptedly, *i. e.* without a pause, almost a minute. I crossed Fair Haven Pond, including the river, on the ice, and probably can for three or four days yet.

C. says he has already seen a little dipper. How long?

Going [along] the steep side-hill on the south of the pond about 4 P. M., on the edge of the little patch of wood which the choppers have not yet levelled, — though they have felled many an acre around it this winter, — I observed a rotten and hollow hemlock stump about two feet high and six inches in diameter, and instinctively approached with my right hand ready to cover it. I found a flying squirrel in it, which, as my left hand had covered a small hole at the bottom, ran directly into my right hand. It struggled and bit not a little, but my cotton glove protected me, and I felt its teeth only once or twice. It also uttered three or four dry shrieks at first, something like *cr-r-rack cr-r-r-ack cr-r-r-ack.* I rolled it up in my handkerchief and, holding the ends tight, carried it home in my hand,

some three miles. It struggled more or less all the way, especially when my feet made any unusual or louder noise going through leaves or bushes. I could count its claws as they appeared through the handkerchief, and once it got its head out a hole. It even bit through the handkerchief.

Color, as I remember, above a chestnut ash, inclining to fawn or cream color (?), slightly browned; beneath white, the under edge of its wings (?) tinged yellow, the upper dark, perhaps black, making a dark stripe. Audubon and Bachman do not speak of any such stripe! It was a very cunning little animal, reminding me of a mouse in the room. Its very large and prominent black eyes gave it an interesting innocent look. Its very neat flat, fawn-colored, distichous tail was a great ornament. Its "sails" were not very obvious when it was at rest, merely giving it a flat appearance beneath. It would leap off and upward into the air two or three feet from a table, spreading its "sails," and fall to the floor in vain; perhaps strike the side of the room in its upward spring and endeavor to cling to it. It would run up the window by the sash, but evidently found the furniture and walls and floor too hard and smooth for it and after some falls became quiet. In a few moments it allowed me to stroke it, though far from confident.

I put it in a barrel and covered it for the night. It was quite busy all the evening gnawing out, clinging for this purpose and gnawing at the upper edge of a sound oak barrel, and then dropping to rest from time to time. It had defaced the barrel considerably by morn-

ing, and would probably have escaped if I had not placed a piece of iron against the gnawed part. I had left in the barrel some bread, apple, shagbarks, and cheese. It ate some of the apple and one shagbark, cutting it quite in two transversely.

In the morning it was quiet, and *squatted* somewhat curled up amid the straw, with its tail passing under it and the end curled over its head very prettily, as if to shield it from the light and keep it warm. I always found it in this position by day when I raised the lid.

March 23. P. M. — To Fair Haven Pond.

Carried my flying squirrel back to the woods in my handkerchief. I placed it, about 3.30 P. M., on the very stump I had taken it from. It immediately ran about a rod over the leaves and up a slender maple sapling about ten feet, then after a moment's pause sprang off and skimmed downward toward a large maple nine feet distant, whose trunk it struck three or four feet from the ground. This it rapidly ascended, on the opposite side from me, nearly thirty feet, and there clung to the main stem with its head downward, eying me. After two or three minutes' pause I saw that it was preparing for another spring by raising its head and looking off, and away it went in admirable style, more like a bird than any quadruped I had dreamed of and far surpassing the impression I had received from naturalists' accounts.[1] I marked the spot it started from and the place where it struck, and mea-

[1] *Vide* next page.

sured the height and distance carefully. It sprang off from the maple at the height of twenty-eight and a half feet, and struck the ground at the foot of a tree fifty and a half feet distant, measured horizontally. Its flight was not a *regular* descent; it varied from a direct line both horizontally and vertically. Indeed it skimmed much like a hawk and part of its flight was nearly horizontal, and it diverged from a right line eight or ten feet to the right, making a curve in that direction. There were six trees from six inches to a foot in diameter, one a hemlock, in a direct line between the two termini, and these it skimmed partly round, and passed through their thinner limbs; did not as I could perceive touch a twig. It skimmed its way like a hawk between and around the trees. Though it was a windy day, this was on a steep hillside away from the wind and covered with wood, so it was not aided by that. As the ground rose about two feet, the distance was to the absolute height as fifty and a half to twenty-six and a half, or it advanced about two feet for every one foot of descent. After its vain attempts in the house, I was not prepared for this exhibition. It did not fall heavily as in the house, but struck the ground gently enough, and I cannot believe that the mere extension of the skin enabled it to skim so far. It must be still further aided by its organization. Perhaps it fills itself with air first. Perhaps I had a fairer view than common of its flight, now at 3.30 P. M. Audubon and Bachman say *he* saw it skim "about fifty yards," curving upwards at the end and alighting on the trunk of a tree. This in a meadow

in which were scattered oaks and beeches. This near Philadelphia. Wesson [?] says he has seen them fly five or six rods.

Kicking over the hemlock stump, which was a mere shell with holes below, and a poor refuge, I was surprised to find a little nest at the bottom, open above just like a bird's nest, a mere bed. It was composed of leaves, shreds of bark, and dead pine-needles. As I remember, it was not more than an inch and a half broad when at rest, but when skimming through the air I should say it was four inches broad. This is the impression I now have. Captain John Smith says it is said to fly thirty or forty yards. Audubon and Bachman quote one Gideon B. Smith, M. D., of Baltimore, who has had much to do with these squirrels and speaks of their curving upward at the end of their flight to alight on a tree-trunk and of their "flying" into his windows. In order to perform all these flights, — to strike a tree at such a distance, etc., etc., — it is evident it must be able to steer. I should say that mine steered as a hawk that moves without flapping its wings, never being able, however, to get a new impetus after the first spring.

C. saw geese to-night.

March 24. I think that the celandine *started* as early as the 10th of March and has since been nibbled off by hens, etc., for it shows more green but [is] not longer.

P. M. — Up Assabet by boat.

A cold and blustering afternoon after a flurry of

Vol. VII

snow which has not fairly whitened the ground. I see a painted tortoise at the bottom moving slowly over the meadow. They do not yet put their heads out, but merely begin to venture forth into their calmer element. It is almost as stationary, as inert, as the pads as yet.

Passing up the Assabet, by the Hemlocks, where there has been a slide and some rocks have slid down into the river, I think I see how rocks come to be found in the midst of rivers. Rivers are continually changing their channels, — eating into one bank and adding their sediment to the other, — so that frequently where there is a great bend you see a high and steep bank or hill on one side, which the river washes, and a broad meadow on the other. As the river eats into the hill, especially in freshets, it undermines the rocks, large and small, and they slide down, alone or with the sand and soil, to the water's edge. The river continues to eat into the hill, carrying away all the lighter parts [of] the sand and soil, to add to its meadows or islands somewhere, but leaves the rocks where they rested, and thus in course of time they occupy the middle of the stream and, later still, the middle of the meadow, perchance, though it may be buried under the mud. But this does not explain how so many rocks lying in streams have been split in the direction of the current. Again, rivers appear to have travelled back and worn into the meadows of their creating, and then they become more meandering than ever. Thus in the course of ages the rivers wriggle in their beds, till it feels comfortable under them. Time is cheap and rather insignificant.

It matters not whether it is a river which changes from side to side in a geological period or an eel that wriggles past in an instant.

The scales of alders which have been broken by the ice and are lying in the water are now visibly loosened, as you look endwise at the catkins, and the catkins are much lengthened and enlarged. The white maple buds, too, show some further expansion methinks (?).

The last four days, including this, have been very cold and blustering. The ice on the ponds, which was rapidly rotting, has somewhat hardened again, so that you make no impression on it as you walk. I crossed Fair Haven Pond yesterday, and could have crossed the channel there again. The wind has been for the most part northwesterly, but yesterday was strong southwesterly yet cold. The northwesterly comes from a snow-clad country still, and cannot but be chilling. We have had several flurries of snow, when we hoped it would snow in earnest and the weather be warmer for it. It is too cold to think of those signs of spring which I find recorded under this date last year. The earliest signs of spring in vegetation noticed thus far are the maple sap, the willow catkins (and poplars? not examined early), the celandine (?), grass on south banks, and *perhaps* cowslip in sheltered places. Alder catkins loosened, and also white maple buds loosened (?).

I am not sure that the osiers are decidedly brighter yet.

March 25. P. M. — To Ministerial Lot.

Still cold and blustering. The ditches where I have seen salamanders last year before this are still frozen up. Was it not a sucker I saw dart along the brook beyond Jenny's? I see where the squirrels have fed extensively on the acorns now exposed on the melting of the snow. The ground is strewn with the freshly torn shells and nibbled meat in some places.

March 26. 6 A. M.—Still cold and blustering; wind southwest, but clear.

I see a muskrat-house just erected, two feet or more above the water and sharp; and, at the Hubbard Bath, a mink comes teetering along the ice by the side of the river. I am between him and the sun, and he does not notice me. He runs daintily, lifting his feet with a jerk as if his toes were sore. They seem to go a-hunting at night along the edge of the river; perhaps I notice them more at this season, when the shallow water freezes at night and there is no vegetation along the shore to conceal them.

The lark sings, perched on the top of an apple tree, *seel-yah seel-yah,* and then perhaps *seel-yah-see-e,* and several other strains, quite sweet and plaintive, contrasting with the cheerless season and the bleak meadow. Further off I hear one like *ah-tick-seel-yah.*

P. M. — Sail down to the Great Meadows.

A strong wind with snow driving from the west and thickening the air. The farmers pause to see me scud before it. At last I land and walk further down on the meadow-bank. I scare up several flocks of ducks. There is but little water on the meadow,

and that far down and partly frozen, but a great many acres of the meadow-crust have there been lifted and broken up by the ice and now make hundreds of slanting isles amid the shallow water, looking like waves of earth, and amid these the ducks are sailing and feeding. The nearest are two, apparently middle-sized with black heads, white breast and wings and apparently all above but the tail or tips of wings, which are black.[1] A third with them is apparently all dark. I do not know what to call them. You are much more sure to see ducks in a stormy afternoon like this than in a bright and pleasant one. Returning, I see, near the Island, two ducks which have the marks (one of them) of the wood duck (*i. e.* one or two longitudinal white stripes down the head and neck), but when they go over I hear distinctly and for a long time the whistling of their wings, fine and sharp. Are they golden-eyes, or whistlers?[2]

For several weeks, or since the ice has melted, I notice the paths made by the muskrats when the water was high in the winter, leading from the river up the bank to a bed of grass above or below the surface. When it runs under the surface I frequently slump into it and can trace it to the bed by the hollow sound when I stamp on the frozen ground. They have disfigured the banks very much in some places, only the past winter. Clams have been carried into these galleries a rod or more under the earth. The galleries kept on

[1] Probably sheldrakes.
[2] [Later:] Were they the harlequin duck? [Later still:] Probably male and female wood duck.

the surface and terminated perhaps at some stump where the earth was a little raised, where the ice still remained thick over them after the water had gone down.

I was surprised to find fishworms only four inches beneath the surface in the meadow, close against the frozen portion of the crust. A few may also be found on the bottom of brooks and ditches in the water, where they are probably food for the earliest fishes. Is that little flat moss-like or jungermannia-like plant on Cheney's shore the *Selaginella apus?* It reminds me of the finest lace-work.

March 27. 6.30 A. M. — To Island.

The ducks sleep these nights in the shallowest water which does not freeze, and there may be found early in the morning. I think that they prefer that part of the shore which is permanently covered.

Snow last evening, about one inch deep, and now it [is] fair and somewhat warmer. Again I see the tracks of rabbits, squirrels, etc. It would be a good time this forenoon to examine the tracks of woodchucks and see what they are about.

P. M. — To Hubbard's Close and down brook.

Measured a black oak just sawed down. Twenty-three inches in diameter on the ground, and fifty-four rings. It had grown twice as much on the east side as on the west. The *Fringilla linaria* still here. Saw a wood tortoise in the brook. Am surprised to see the cowslip so forward, showing so much green, in

E. Hubbard's Swamp, in the brook, where it is sheltered from the winds. The already expanded leaves rise above the water. If this is a spring growth,[1] it is the most forward herb I have seen, as forward as the celandine.

Saw my frog hawk. (C. saw it about a week ago.) Probably *Falco fuscus,* or sharp-shinned, though not well described by Wilson. Slate-colored; beating the bush; black tips to wings and white rump.[2]

March 28. P. M. — To Cliffs, along river.

It is colder than yesterday; wind strong from northwest. The mountains are still covered with snow. They have not once been bare. I go looking for meadow mice nests, but the ground is frozen so hard, except in the meadow below the banks, that I cannot come at them. That portion of the meadow next the upland, which is now thawed, has already many earthworms in it. I can dig a quantity of them,—I suspect more than in summer. Moles might already get their living there. A yellow-spotted tortoise in a still ditch, which has a little ice also. It at first glance reminds me of a bright freckled leaf, skunk-cabbage scape, perhaps. They are generally quite still at this season, or only slowly put their heads out (of their shells). I see where a skunk (apparently) has been probing the sod, though it is thawed but a few inches, and all around this spot frozen hard still. I dig up there a frozen and dead white grub, the large potato grub; this I think he was after. The skunk's nose has made

[1] Yes.   [2] No, it is the hen-harrier [*i. e.* marsh hawk], male.

small round holes such as a stick or cane would make. The river has not yet quite worn its way through Fair Haven Pond, but probably will to-morrow.

I run about these cold and blustering days, on the whole perhaps the worst to bear in the year, — partly because they disappoint expectation, — looking almost in vain for some animal or vegetable life stirring. The warmest springs hardly allow me the glimpse of a frog's heel as he settles himself in the mud, and I think I am lucky if I see one winter-defying hawk or a hardy duck or two at a distance on the water. As for the singing of birds, — the few that have come to us, — it is too cold for them to sing and for me to hear. The bluebird's warble comes feeble and frozen to my ear. We still walk on frozen ground, though in the garden I can thrust a spade in about six inches.

Over a great many acres, the meadows have been cut up into great squares and other figures by the ice of February, as if ready to be removed, sometimes separated by narrow and deep channels like musk-rat-paths, but oftener the edges have been raised and apparently stretched and, settling, have not fallen into their places exactly but lodged on their neighbors.

Even yet you see cakes of ice surmounted by a shell of meadow-crust, which has preserved it, while all around is bare meadow.

March 29. P. M. — To Flint's Pond.

Flint's Pond is entirely open; may have been a day or two. There was only a slight opening about the

boat-house on the 21st, and the weather has been very cold ever since.

Walden is more than half open, Goose Pond only a little about the shores, and Fair Haven Pond only *just* open over the channel of the river. There is washed up on the shore of Flint's some pretty little whorls of the radical leaves of the *Lobelia Dortmanna*, with its white root-fibres.

As I stand on Heywood's Peak, looking over Walden, more than half its surface already sparkling blue water, I inhale with pleasure the cold but wholesome air like a draught of cold water, contrasting it in my memory with the wind of summer, which I do not thus eagerly swallow. This, which is a chilling wind to my fellow, is decidedly refreshing to me, and I swallow it with eagerness as a panacea. I feel an impulse, also, already, to jump into the half-melted pond. This cold wind is refreshing to my palate, as the warm air of summer is not, methinks. I love to stand there and be blown on as much as a horse in July. A field of ice nearly half as big as the pond has drifted against the eastern shore and crumbled up against it, forming a shining white wall of its fragments.

March 30. 6.30 A. M. — To Island.

It is a *little* warmer than of late, though still the shallows are skimmed over.

The pickerel begin to dart from the shallowest parts not frozen. I hear many *phe-be* notes from the chickadees, as if they appreciated this slightly warmer and sunny morning.

A fine day. As I look through the window, I actually *see* a warmer atmosphere with its fine shimmer against the russet hills and the dry leaves, though the warmth has not got into the house and it is no more bright nor less windy than yesterday, or many days past. I find that the difference to the eye is a slight haze, though it is but very little warmer than yesterday.

To-day and yesterday have been bright, windy days, — west wind, cool, yet, compared with the previous colder ones, pleasantly, gratefully cool to me on my cheek. There is a very perceptible greenness on our south bank now, but I cannot detect the slightest greenness on the south side of Lee's Hill as I sail by it. It is a perfectly dead russet.

The river is but about a foot above the lowest summer level.

I have seen a few *F. hyemalis* about the house in the morning the last few days. You see a few blackbirds, robins, bluebirds, tree sparrows, larks, etc., but the song sparrow chiefly is heard these days.

He must have a great deal of life in him to draw upon, who can pick up a subsistence in November and March. Man comes out of his winter quarters this month as lean as a woodchuck. Not till late could the skunk find a place where the ground was thawed on the surface. Except for science, do not travel in such a climate as this in November and March. I tried if a fish would take the bait to-day; but in vain; I did not get a nibble. Where are they? I read that a great many bass were taken in the Merri-

mack last week. Do not the suckers move at the same time?

March 31. I see through the window that it is a very fine day, the first really warm one. I did not know the whole till I came out at 3 P. M. and walked to the Cliffs.

The slight haze of yesterday has become very thick, with a southwest wind, concealing the mountains. I can see it in the air within two or three rods, as I look against the bushes. The fuzzy gnats are in the air, and bluebirds, whose warble is thawed out. I am uncomfortably warm, gradually unbutton both my coats, and wish that I had left the outside one at home. I go listening for the croak of the first frog, or peep of a hylodes.

It is suddenly warm, and this amelioration of the weather is incomparably the most important fact in this vicinity. It is incredible what a revolution in our feelings and in the aspect of nature this warmer air alone has produced. Yesterday the earth was simple to barrenness, and dead, — *bound out*. Out-of-doors there was nothing but the wind and the withered grass and the cold though sparkling blue water, and you were driven in upon yourself. Now you would think that there was a sudden awakening in the very crust of the earth, as if flowers were expanding and leaves putting forth; but not so; I listen in vain to hear a frog or a new bird as yet; only the frozen ground is melting a little deeper, and the water is trickling down the hills in some places. No, the change is mainly in us. We feel as if we had obtained a new lease of life. Some juniper (*repens*) berries are blue now. Looking from the Cliffs I see that Walden is open to-day first, and Fair Haven Pond will open by day after to-morrow.[1]

[1] No. *Vide* Apr. 4th.

VIII

APRIL, 1855

(ÆT. 37)

April 1. The month comes in true to its reputation. We wake, though late, to hear the sound of a strong, steady, and rather warm rain on the roof, and see the puddles shining in the road. It lasts till the middle of the day, and then is succeeded by a cold northwest wind. This pattering rain and Sabbath morning combined make us all sluggards.

When I look out the window I see that the grass on the bank on the south side of the house is already much greener than it was yesterday. As it cannot have grown so suddenly, how shall I account for it? I suspect that the reason is that the few green blades are not merely washed bright by the rain, but erect themselves to imbibe its influence, and so are more prominent, while the withered blades are beaten down and flattened by it. It is remarkable how much more fatal to all superficial vegetation or greenness is a morning frost in March than a covering of snow or ice. In hollows where the ice is still melting I see the grass considerably green about its edges, though further off it shows no sign of life.

P. M. — To Conantum End.

This rain will help take the frost out of the ground.

At the first Conantum Cliff I am surprised to see how much the columbine leaves have grown in a sheltered cleft; also the cinquefoil, dandelion (?), yarrow (?), sorrel, saxifrage, etc., etc. They seem to improve the least warmer ray to advance themselves, and they hold all they get. One of the earliest-looking plants in water is the golden saxifrage.

The last half of last month was cold and windy, — excepting the 19th, — wind northwest, west, and southwest. It at last ceased to be chilling the 29th and 30th, which were fine clear, cool, but windy days; on the 30th a slight haze; then the 31st was suddenly warm with a thick haze, thawing man and earth; and this succeeded by to-day's rain.

See, resting on the edge of the ice in Fair Haven Pond, a white duck with black head, and a dark one. They take to the water when I appear on the hill a quarter of a mile off, and soon fly down the river rather low over the water. Were they not the same with those of the 16th *ult.*?

April 2. Not only the grass but the pines also were greener yesterday for being wet. To-day, the grass being dry, the green blades are less conspicuous than yesterday. It would seem, then, that this color is more vivid when wet, and perhaps all green plants, like lichens, are to some extent greener in moist weather. Green is essentially *vivid*, or the color of life, and it is therefore most brilliant when a plant is moist or most alive. A plant is said to be green in opposition to being withered and dead. The word, according to

Webster, is from the Saxon *grene*, to grow, and hence is the color of herbage when growing.

High winds all night, rocking the house, opening doors, etc. To-day also. It is wintry cold also, and ice has formed nearly an inch thick in my boat.

P. M. — Down the river-bank.

The wind is still very strong and cold from the northwest, filling the air with dust and blowing the water, which has slightly risen, over the rocks and bushes along the shore, where it freezes in the shape of bulls' horns about the osiers, making coarse rakes with its dependent icicles when the osiers are horizontal, also turtle-shells over the rocks. It is just such a wind and freezing as that of last March (18th, I think), and, if the meadow were flooded, there would probably be as much ice as then on the bushes. There may be wind enough for this phenomenon in the winter, but then there is no open water to be blown.

April 3. It is somewhat warmer, but still windy, and —

P. M. — I go to sail down to the Island and up to Hubbard's Causeway.

Most would call it cold to-day. I paddle without gloves. It is a coolness like that of March 29th and 30th, pleasant to breathe, and, perhaps, like that, presaging decidedly warmer weather. It is an amelioration, as nature does nothing suddenly. The shores are lined with frozen spray-like foam, with an abrupt edge, a foot high often on the waterside. Occasionally where there [are] twigs there is a nest of those short, thick bulls'-horn icicles, pointing in every direction. I see many hens feeding close to the river's edge, like the crows, — and robins and blackbirds later, — and I have no doubt they are attracted by a like cause. The ground being first thawed there, not only worms but other insect and vegetable life is accessible there sooner than elsewhere. See several pairs of ducks, mostly black.

Returning, when off the hill was attracted by the noise of crows, which betrayed to me a very large hawk (?), large enough for an eagle, sitting on a maple beneath them. Now and then they dived at him, and at last he sailed away low round the hill, as if hunting. The hillside was alive with sparrows, red-wings, and the first grackles [1] I have seen. I detected them first by their more rasping note, — or was that a crow blackbird? — after a short stuttering, then a fine, clear whistle.

April 4. A fine morning, still and bright, with smooth water and singing of song and tree sparrows and some blackbirds. A nuthatch is heard on the elms, and two ducks fly upward in the sun over the river.

P. M. — To Clematis Brook *via* Lee's.

A pleasant day, growing warmer; a slight haze. Now the hedges and apple trees are alive with fox-colored sparrows, all over the town, and their imperfect strains are occasionally heard. Their clear, fox-colored backs are very handsome. I get quite near to them. Stood quite near to what I called a hairy

[1] [That is, rusty grackles, or rusty blackbirds.]

woodpecker — but, seeing the downy afterward, I am in doubt about it. Its body certainly as big as a robin. It is a question of size between the two kinds. The rows of white spots near the end of the wings of the downy remind me of the lacings on the skirts of a soldier's coat. Talked with Daniel Garfield near the old house on Conantum. He was going to see if his boat was in order for fishing. Said he had been a-fishing as early as this and caught perch, etc., with a worm. He had often caught shiners in Fair Haven Pond through the ice in March, and once a trout in deep water off Baker's steep hill, which weighed two pounds, his lines having been left in over night. He had also often caught the little perch in White Pond in midwinter for bait. Sees trout and sucker running up brooks at this season and earlier, and thinks they go out of them in the fall, but not out of the river. Does not know where they go to.

I am surprised to [find] the pond, *i. e.* Fair Haven Pond, not yet fully open. There is [a] large mass of ice in the eastern bay, which will hardly melt to-morrow.[1]

It is a fine air, but more than tempered by the snow in the northwest. All the earth is bright; the very pines glisten, and the water is a bright blue. A gull is circling round Fair Haven Pond, seen white against the woods and hillsides, looking as if it would dive for a fish every moment, and occasionally resting on the ice. The water above Lee's Bridge is all alive with ducks. There are many flocks of eight or ten together,

[1] The rain of the 5th, P. M., must have finished it.

Vol. VII

their black heads and white breasts seen above the water, — more of them than I have seen before this season, — and a gull with its whole body above the water, perhaps standing where it was shallow. Not only are the evergreens brighter, but the pools, as that upland one behind Lee's, the ice as well as snow about their edges being now completely melted, have a peculiarly warm and bright April look, as if ready to be inhabited by frogs.

I can now put a spade into the garden anywhere. The rain of April 1st and the warmth of to-day have taken out the frost there; but I cannot put a spade into banks by the meadow where there is the least slope to the north.

Returning from Mt. Misery, the pond and river-reach presented a fine, warm view. The slight haze, which on a warmer day at this season softens the rough surfaces which the winter has left and fills the copses seemingly with life, — makes them appear to teem with life, — made the landscape remarkably fair. It would not be called a warm, but a pleasant day; but the water has crept partly over the meadows, and the broad border of button-bushes, etc., etc., off Wheeler's cranberry meadow, low and nearly flat, though sloping regularly from an abrupt curving edge on the riverside several rods into the meadow till it is submerged — this is isolated, but at this distance and through this air it is remarkably soft and elysian. There is a remarkable variety in the view at present from this summit. The sun feels as warm as in June on my ear. Half a mile off in front is this elysian water, high over which

two wild ducks are winging their rapid flight eastward through the bright air; on each side and beyond, the earth is clad with a warm russet, more pleasing perhaps than green; and far beyond all, in the northwestern horizon, my eye rests on a range of snow-covered mountains, glistening in the sun.

April 5. Fast-Day. 9 A. M. —To Sudbury line by boat.

A still and rather warm morning, with a very thick haze concealing the sun and threatening to turn to rain.

It is a smooth, April-morning water, and many sportsmen are out in their boats. I see a pleasure-boat, on the smooth surface away by the Rock, resting lightly as a feather in the air.

Scare up a snipe close to the water's edge, and soon after a hen-hawk from the Clamshell oaks. The last looks larger on his perch than flying. The snipe too, then, like crows, robins, blackbirds, and hens, is found near the waterside, where is the first spring (*e. g.* alders and white maples, etc., etc)., and there too especially are heard the song and tree sparrows and pewees, and even the hen-hawk at this season haunts there for his prey. Inland, the groves are almost completely silent as yet. The concert of song and tree sparrows at willow-row is now very full, and their different notes are completely mingled. See a single white-bellied swallow dashing over the river. He, too, is attracted here by the early insects that begin to be seen over the water. It being Fast-Day, we on the water hear the loud and musical sound of bells ringing for church in the surrounding towns. It is a sober, moist day, with a circle round the sun, which I can only see in the reflection in the water.

The river appears to have risen still last night, owing to the rain of the 1st, and many spring cranberries are washed together at last, and now many new seeds, apparently of sedges, are loosened and washed up. Now that for the most part it is melted quite to its edge, and there is no ice there, the water has a warmer, April look close under my eye. Now is the first time this year to get spring cranberries. In many places now the river wreck is chiefly composed of *Juncus militaris*. Was it so in fall?

There is a strong muskrat scent from many a shore. See a muskrat floating, which may have been drowned when the river was so high in midwinter, — for this is the second I have seen, — with the rabbit. I saw yesterday a yellow-spot and see to-day a painted tortoise, already out on the bank on a tuft of grass. The muskrat-hunter sits patiently with cocked gun, waiting for a muskrat to put out his head amid the button-bushes. He gets half a dozen in such a cruise. Bushed our boat with hemlock to get near some ducks, but another boat above, also bushed, scared them. Heard from one half-flooded meadow that low, general, hard, stuttering *tut tut tut* of frogs (?), — the awakening of the meadow.

Hear the cry of the peacock again.

By 4 P. M. it began to rain gently or mizzle. Saw this forenoon a great many of those little fuzzy gnats in the air.

Vol. VII

April 6. It clears up at 8 P. M. warm and pleasant, leaving flitting clouds and a little wind, and I go up the Assabet in my boat. The blackbirds have now begun to frequent the water's edge in the meadow, the ice being sufficiently out. The April waters, smooth and commonly high, before many flowers (none yet) or any leafing, while the landscape is still russet and frogs are just awakening, is [*sic*] peculiar. It began yesterday. A very few white maple stamens stand out already loosely enough to blow in the wind, and some alder catkins look almost ready to shed pollen. On the hillsides I smell the dried leaves and hear a few flies buzzing over them. The banks of the river are alive with song sparrows and tree sparrows. They now sing in advance of vegetation, as the flowers will blossom, — those slight tinkling, twittering sounds called the singing of birds; they have come to enliven the bare twigs before the buds show any signs of starting. I see a large wood tortoise just crawled out upon the bank, with three oval, low, bug-like leeches on its sternum.

You can hear all day, from time to time, in any part of the village, the sound of a gun fired at ducks. Yesterday I was wishing that I could find a dead duck floating on the water, as I had found muskrats and a hare, and now I see something bright and reflecting the light from the edge of the alders five or six rods off. Can it be a duck? I can hardly believe my eyes. I am near enough to see its green head and neck. I am delighted to find a perfect specimen of the *Mergus merganser*, or goosander, undoubtedly shot yesterday by the Fast-Day sportsmen, and I take a small flat-

tened shot from its wing, — flattened against the wing-bone, apparently. The wing is broken, and it is shot through the head.[1] It is a perfectly fresh and very beautiful bird, and as I raise it, I get sight of its long, slender vermilion bill (color of red sealing-wax) and its clean, bright-orange legs and feet, and then of its perfectly smooth and spotlessly pure white breast and belly, tinged with a faint salmon (or tinged with a delicate buff inclining to salmon).

This, according to Wilson, is one of the mergansers, or fisher ducks, of which there are nine or ten species and we have four in America. It is the largest of these four; feeds almost entirely on fin and shell fish; called water pheasant, sheldrake, fisherman diver, dun diver, sparkling fowl, harle, etc., as well as goosander. Go in April, return in November. Jardine has found seven trout in one female. Nuttall says they breed in the Russian Empire and are seen in Mississippi and Missouri in winter. He found a young brood in Pennsylvania. Yarrell says they are called also saw-bill and jack-saw; are sometimes sold in London market. Nest, according to Selby, on ground; according to others, in a hollow tree also. Found on the continent of Europe, northern Asia, and even in Japan (?). Some breed in the Orkneys and thereabouts.[2] My bird is 25⅞ inches long and 35 in alar extent; from point of wing to end of primaries, 11 inches.

[1] The chief wound was in a wing, which was broken. I afterward took three small shot from it, which were flattened against the bill's base and perhaps (?) the quills' shafts.
[2] *Vide* [p. 290].

It is a great diver and does not mind the cold. It appears admirably fitted for diving and swimming. Its body is flat, and its tail short, flat, compact, and wedge-shaped; its eyes peer out a slight slit or semi-circle in the skin of the head; and its legs are flat and thin in one direction, and the toes shut up compactly so as to create the least friction when drawing them forward, but their broad webs spread them three and a half inches when they take a stroke. The web is extended three eighths of an inch beyond the inner toe of each foot.[1] There are very conspicuous black teeth-like serrations along the edges of its bill, and this also is roughened so that it may hold its prey securely.

The breast *appeared* quite dry when I raised it from the water.

The head and neck are, as Wilson says, black, glossed with green, but the lower part of the neck pure white, and these colors bound on each other so abruptly that one appears to be sewed on to the other.

It is a perfect wedge from the middle of its body to the end of its tail, and it is only three and a quarter inches deep from back to breast at the thickest part, while the greatest breadth horizontally (at the root of the legs) is five and a half inches. In these respects it reminds me of an otter, which however I have never seen.

I suspect that I have seen near a hundred of these birds this spring, but I never got so near one before. In Yarrell's plate the depth of the male goosander

[1] *Vide* the 9th of April.

is to its length (*i. e.* from tip of tail to most forward part of breast) as thirty-seven to one hundred and three, or the depth is more than one third. This length in Yarrell's bird, calling the distance from the point of the wing to the end of the primaries eleven inches, is about fourteen and a half inches, of which my three and a quarter is not one fourth. In Nuttall's plate the proportion is thirty-two to ninety-one, also more than one third. I think they have not represented the bird flat enough.

Yarrell says it is the largest of the British mergansers; is a winter visitor, though a few breed in the north of Britain; are rare in the southern counties. But, according to Yarrell, a Mr. Low in his Natural History of Orkney says they breed there, and, after breeding, the sexes separate; and Y. quotes Selby as saying that their nest is near the edge of the water, of grass, roots, etc., lined with down, sometimes among stones, in long grass, under bushes, or in a stump or hollow tree. Y. continues, egg "a uniform buff white," two and a half inches long. Sometimes carry their young on their backs in the water. It is common in Sweden and, according to the traveller Acerbi, in Lapland they give it a hollow tree to build in and then steal its eggs. The mother, he adds, carries her young to the water in her bill. Y. says it is well known in Russia and is found in Germany, Holland, France, Switzerland, Provence, and Italy. Has been seen near the Caucasus (and is found in Japan, according to one authority). Also in North America, Hudson's Bay, Greenland, and Iceland.

April 7. In my walk in the afternoon of to-day, I saw from Conantum, say fifty rods distant, two sheldrakes, male and probably female, sailing on A. Wheeler's cranberry meadow. I saw only the white of the male at first, but my glass revealed the female. The male is easily seen a great distance on the water, being a large white mark. But they will let you come only within some sixty rods ordinarily. I observed that they were uneasy at sight of me and began to sail away in different directions. I could plainly see the vermilion bill of the male and his orange legs when he flew (but he *appeared* all white above), and the reddish brown or sorrel of the neck of the female, and, when she lifted herself in the water, as it were preparatory to flight, her white breast and belly. She had a grayish look on the sides. Soon they approached each other again and seemed to be conferring, and then they rose and went off, at first low, down-stream, soon up-stream a hundred feet over the pond, the female leading, the male following close behind, the black at the end of his curved wings very conspicuous. I suspect that about all the conspicuous white ducks I see are goosanders.

I skinned my duck yesterday and stuffed it to-day. It is wonderful that a man, having undertaken such an enterprise, ever persevered in it to the end, and equally wonderful that he succeeded. To skin a bird, drawing backward, wrong side out, over the legs and wings down to the base of the mandibles! Who would expect to see a smooth feather again? This skin was very tender on the breast. I should have done better had I stuffed it at once or turned it back before the

skin became stiff. Look out not to cut the ear and eyelid.

But what a pot-bellied thing is a stuffed bird compared even with the fresh dead one I found! It looks no longer like an otter, like a swift diver, but a mere waddling duck. How perfectly the vent of a bird is covered! There is no mark externally.

At six this morn to Clamshell. The skunk-cabbage open yesterday, — the earliest flower this season. I suspect that the spathes do not push up in the spring. This is but three inches high. I see them as high and higher in the fall, and they seem only to acquire color now and gape open. I see but one out, and that sheds pollen abundantly.

See thirty or forty goldfinches in a dashing flock, in all respects (notes and all) like lesser redpolls, on the trees by Wood's Causeway and on the railroad-bank. There is a general twittering and an occasional mew. Then they alight on the ground to feed, along with *F. hyemalis* and fox-colored sparrows. They are merely olivaceous above, dark about the base of the bill, but bright lemon-yellow in a semicircle on the breast; black wings and tails, with white bar on wings and white vanes to tail. I never saw them here so early before; or probably one or two olivaceous birds I have seen and heard of other years were this.

Clear, but a cold air.

What is [the] cockroach(?)-like black beetle with a colored edge (blue?) on pebbles, like cicindelas?

P. M. — To Hubbard's Close and Lee's Cliff.

A mouse-nest of grass, in Stow's meadow east of railroad, on the surface. Just like those seen in the rye-field some weeks ago, but this in lower ground has a distinct gallery running from it, and I think is the nest of the meadow mouse. The pool at Hubbard's Close, which was full of ice, unbroken gray ice, the 27th of March, is now warm-looking water, with the slime-covered callitriche standing a foot high in it; and already a narrow grass, the lake grass, has sprung up and lies bent nine or ten inches flat on the water. This is very early as well as sudden. In ten days there has been this change. How much had that grass grown under the ice? I see many small skaters (?) in it. Saw a trout as long as my finger, in the ditch dug from Brister's Spring, which, having no hole [or] overhanging bank where it could hide, plunged into the mud like a frog and was concealed. The female flowers of the hazel are just beginning to peep out.

At Lee's Cliff I find the radical leaves of the early saxifrage, columbine, and the tower mustard, etc., much eaten apparently by partridges and perhaps rabbits. They must have their greens in the spring, and earlier than we. Below the rocks, the most obviously forward radical leaves are the columbine, tower mustard (lanceolate and petioled and remotely toothed), and catnep, and mullein. Early crowfoot, the buttercup (*bulbosa*), is a peculiarly sappy, dark pickle-green, decided spring, and none of your sapless evergreens. The little thyme-leaved arenaria, I believe it is, which is evergreen, and some other minute leaves, also, already green the ground. The saxifrage on the rocks will apparently open in two days; it shows some white. The grass is now conspicuously green about open springs in dense tufts. The frozen sod, partly thawed in low grounds, sinks under me as I walk.

April 8. 6 A. M. — Up Assabet.

A fine clear morning. The ground white with frost, and all the meadows also, and a low mist curling over the smooth water now in the sunlight, which gives the water a silver-plated look. The frost covers the willows and alders and other trees on the sides of the river fifteen or twenty feet high. Quite a wintry sight. At first I can hardly distinguish white maple stamens from the frost spiculæ. I find some anthers effete and dark, and others still mealy with pollen. There are many in this condition. The crimson female stigmas also peeping forth. It evidently began to shed pollen yesterday. I find also at length a single catkin of the *Alnus incana*, with a few stamens near the peduncle discolored and shedding a little dust when shaken; so this must have begun yesterday, I think, but it is not so forward as the maple. Though I have looked widely, I have not found the alder out before.

I see some long cobweb lines covered with frost, hanging from tree to tree, six feet in one case, like the ropes which extend from mast to mast of a vessel. Very thin dark ice-crystals over shallowest water, showing the flat pyramids. Hear and see a pigeon woodpecker, something like *week-up week-up*. The robins now sing in full blast.

to water. The great buff-edged butterfly flutters across the river. Afterward I see a small red one over the shore.

Though the river — excepting Fair Haven Pond before the 6th — has for a week been completely free of ice, and only a little thin crystalwise forms in the night in the shallowest parts, that thick ice of the winter (February) on the meadows, covered by pieces of meadow-crust, is in many places still nearly as thick as ever, now that ice is a rather rare sight and plowing is beginning. It is remarkable how long this frozen meadow-crust lying on it has preserved it. Where the piece of meadow is only three or four feet in diameter, its edges now project over the ice, so that the whole looks like a student's four-cornered cap, — or that which the President of Harvard wears. All that mass on B.'s meadow appears to have been taken from the upper part of the meadow near the road, about thirty rods off from where it now lies. In the ditches near which it was taken up I see the coarse yellow, reddened, and sometimes already green-tipped pads of the yellow lily, partly unrolled at the bottom of the warm water, the most of a spring growth, perhaps, in the water; also two or three good-sized buds of a healthy green.

Hear at a distance in the sprout-lands the croaks of frogs from some shallow pool. Saw six muskrats' bodies, just skinned, on the bank, — two large yellowish, fatty-looking masses of (I suppose) musk on each side the lower part of the abdomen. Every part of the animal now emits a very strong scent of musk. A foot which I brought home (together with a head)

Also song sparrows and tree sparrows and *F. hyemalis* are heard in the yard. The fox-colored sparrow is also there. The tree sparrows have been very musical for several mornings, somewhat canary-like. As to which are the earliest flowers, it depends on the character of the season, and ground bare or not, meadows wet or dry, etc., etc., also on the variety of soils and localities within your reach. The columbine leaves in the clefts of Cliffs are one of the very earliest obvious growths. I noticed it the first of April. The radical leaves of the buttercup now at Lee's Cliff — a small flat dense circle — are a very different color from those evergreen leaves seen when the snow first goes off. They are emphatically a *green* green, as if a sort of green fire were kindled under them in the sod. The buds not only of lilacs, but white birches, etc., look swollen.

When taking the brain out of my duck yesterday, I perceived that the brain was the marrow of the head, and it is probably only a less sentient brain that runs down the backbone, — the spinal marrow.

Abiel Wheeler tried to plow in sandy soil yesterday, but could not go beyond a certain depth because of frost.

P. M. — Up Assabet to G. Barrett's meadow.

This forenoon it was still and the water smooth. Now there is a strong cool wind from the east. Am surprised to see a sound clam close to the shore at mouth of Dakin's Brook, in one foot of water. A school of small minnows. Already a turtle's track on sand close

scented me all over. The fore feet are small and *white* on the palm, while the hind ones are *black*. All the skin being stripped off except on the nose and feet, the fore feet look like hands clothed in gauntlets of fur.

This evening, about 9 P. M., I hear geese go over, now there in the south, now southeast, now east, now northeast, low over the village, but not seen. The first *I* have heard.

April 9. 5.15 A. M. — To Red Bridge just before sunrise.

Fine clear morning, but still cold enough for gloves. A slight frost, and mist as yesterday curling over the smooth water. I see half a dozen crows on an elm within a dozen rods of the muskrats' bodies, as if eying them. I see thus often crows very early in the morning near the houses, which soon after sunrise take their way across the river to the woods again. It is a regular thing with them.

Hear the hoarse rasping *chuck* or chatter of crow blackbirds and distinguish their long broad tails. Wilson says that the only note of the rusty grackle is a *chuck*, though he is told that at Hudson's Bay, at the breeding-time, they sing with a fine note.[1] Here they utter not only a *chuck*, but a *fine* shrill whistle. They cover the top of a tree now, and their concert is of this character: They all seem laboring together to get out a clear strain, as it were wetting their whistles

[1] [The only song they are known to possess is the whistle that Thoreau here describes.]

against their arrival at Hudson's Bay. They begin as it were by disgorging or spitting it out, like so much tow, from a full throat, and conclude with a clear, fine, shrill, ear-piercing whistle. Then away they go, all chattering together.

Hear a phœbe near the river. The golden willow is, methinks, a little livelier green and begins to peel a little, but I am not sure the bark is any smoother yet.

Heard a loud, long, dry, tremulous shriek which reminded me of a kingfisher, but which I found proceeded from a woodpecker which had just alighted on an elm; also its clear whistle or *chink* afterward. It is probably the hairy woodpecker, and I am not so certain I have seen it earlier this year. Wilson does not allow that the downy one makes exactly such a sound. Did I hear part of the note of a golden-crowned (?) wren this morning? It was undoubtedly a robin, the last part of his strain.

Some twenty minutes after sundown I hear the first *booming* of a snipe.

The forenoon was cloudy and in the afternoon it rained, but the sun set clear, lighting up the west with a yellow light, which there was no green grass to reflect, in which the frame of a new building is distinctly seen, while drops hang on every twig, and producing the first rainbow I have seen or heard of except one long ago in the morning. With April showers, methinks, come rainbows. Why are they so rare in the winter? Is the fact that the clouds are then of snow commonly, instead of rain, sufficient to account for it?

At sunset after the rain, the robins and song sparrows fill the air along the river with their song.

MacGillivray says that divers, mergansers, and cormorants actually fly under water, using their wings fully expanded. He had seen them pursuing sand eels along the shores of the Hebrides. Had seen the water-ouzel fly in like manner.

Several flocks of geese went over this morning also. Now, then, the main body are moving. Now first are they generally seen and heard.

April 10. Another fine clear morning with, as usual, a little frost.

6 A. M. — To river.

I see afar, more than one hundred rods distant, sailing on Hubbard's meadow, on the smooth water in the morning sun, conspicuous, two male sheldrakes and apparently one female. They glide along, a rod or two apart in shallow water, alternately passing one another and from time to time plunging their heads in the water, but the female (whom only the glass reveals) almost alone diving. I think I saw one male drive the other back. One male with the female kept nearly together, a rod or two ahead of the other.

Therien says James Baker sold his wood-lot south of Fair Haven Pond, about twenty-five acres, chiefly white pine, for one hundred and twenty dollars an acre, and that there was one hemlock whose top and branches alone yielded two and a half cords.[1]

The buds of the earliest gooseberry in garden now

[1] *Vide* next page.

first begin to show a little green on a close inspection.

P. M. — To Fair Haven Pond by boat.

A strong south wind and overcast. There is the slightest perceptible green on the hill now. No doubt in a rain it would be pretty obvious. Saw a tolerably fresh sucker floating. Have seen two halves two days before which looked very ancient, as if they had died in the winter. There are three or four small scallops in the dorsal fin. Another dead muskrat, equally old with the two others I have seen this spring, — as if they had died at the time of the great freshet in February.

At Lee's the early sedge; one only sheds pollen. The saxifrage there to-morrow; one flower is partly expanded.

I measured the hemlock mentioned on the last page [above]. The circumference at the butt, a foot from the ground, was $9\frac{10}{12}$ feet, at ten feet from the ground $8\frac{10}{12}$, at the small end, where it was cut off, $1\frac{1}{2}$ feet. Length, 40 feet. Its diameter diminished very regularly the first twenty-five feet.

As for the early sedge, who would think of looking for a flower of any kind in those dry tufts whose withered blades almost entirely conceal the springing green ones? I patiently examined one tuft after another, higher and higher up the rocky hill, till at last I found one little yellow spike low in the grass which shed its pollen on my finger. As for the saxifrage, when I had given it up for to-day, having, after a long search in the warmest clefts and recesses, found only three or four

buds which showed some white, I at length, on a still warmer shelf, found one flower partly expanded, and its common peduncle had shot up an inch. These few earliest flowers in these situations have the same sort of interest with the arctic flora, for they are remote and unobserved and often surrounded with snow, and most have not begun to think of flowers yet.

Early on the morning of the 8th I paddled up the Assabet looking for the first flowers of the white maple and alder. I held on to the low curving twigs of the maple where the stream ran swiftly, the round clusters of its bursting flower-buds spotting the sky above me, and on a close inspection found a few which (as I have said) must have blossomed the day before. I also paddled slowly along the riverside looking closely at the alder catkins and shaking the most loose, till at length I came to a bush which had been weighed down by the ice and whose stem curved downward, passing through the water, and on this was one looser and more yellowish catkin, which, as I have said, on a close examination showed some effete anthers near the peduncle.

The morning of the 6th, when I found the skunk-cabbage out, it was so cold I suffered from numbed fingers, having left my gloves behind. Since April came in, however, you have needed gloves only in the morning.

Under some high bare bank sloping to the south on the edge of a meadow, where many springs, issuing from the bank, melt the snow early, — there you find the first skunk-cabbage in bloom.

I see much yellow lily root afloat, which the musk-rats have dug up and nibbled.

April 11. Rained in the night. Awake to see the ground white with snow, and it is still snowing, the sleet driving from the north at an angle of certainly not more than thirty or thirty-five degrees with the horizon, as I judge by its course across the window-panes. By mid-afternoon the rain has so far prevailed that the ground is bare. As usual, this brings the tree sparrows and *F. hyemalis* into the yard again.

April 12. Still falls a little snow and rain this morning, though the ground is not whitened. I hear a purple finch, nevertheless, on an elm, steadily warbling and uttering a sharp chip from time to time.

P. M. — To Cliffs and Hubbard's Close.

Fair with drifting clouds, but cold and windy. At the spring brook I see some skunk-cabbage leaves already four or five inches high and partly unrolled. From the Cliff Hill the mountains are again thickly clad with snow, and, the wind being northwest, this coldness is accounted for. I hear it fell fourteen or fifteen inches deep in Vermont.

As I sit in a sheltered place on the Cliffs, I look over the pond with my glass, but see no living thing. Soon after, I saw a boat on Lee's meadow just inside the button-bushes on the west of the pond, about a mile distant, and, raising my glass, I saw one man paddling in the stern and another in white pantaloons standing up in the bow, ready to shoot. Presently I saw the

last raise his gun, take aim, and fire into the bushes, though I heard no sound from over the dashing waves, but merely saw the smoke as in a picture. There was a strong wind from the northwest, while I was looking southwest. The gunner then pointed out the course while his companion paddled and struck the game in the water with a paddle, and I distinctly saw him lift up a muskrat by the tail. In a few moments, very nearly the same actions were repeated, though this time I did not see the rat raised. Then, turning my glass down the stream, I saw, on the Miles meadow shore about half a mile distant, a man whom I knew emptying his boat of fat pine roots which he had got for spearing, while his dog was digging at a woodchuck's hole close by.

For a week past I have frequently seen the tracks of woodchucks in the sand.

Golden saxifrage out at Hubbard's Close, — one, at least, effete. It may have been the 10th.

The grass has within ten days shot up very perceptibly in shallow water and about springs. In the last place it forms dense moss-like tufts in some cases; also some warm southward banks are considerably greened, and some hollows where the ice has recently melted, but *generally* there is no *obvious* greening as yet. It is at most a mere radical greenness, which you must seek to find.

Cowslip will apparently open in two days at Hubbard's Close.[1]

[1] Not 16th, but apparently touched by frost, but probably some by Second Division. *Vide* 18th.

April 13. P. M. — To Second Division cowslips.

A fair day, but a cool wind still, from the snow-covered country in the northwest. It is, however, pleasant to sit in the sun in sheltered places.

The small croaking frogs are now *generally* heard in all those stagnant ponds or pools in woods floored with leaves, which are mainly dried up in the summer. At first, perhaps, you hear but one or two dry croaks, but, if you sit patiently, you may hear quite a concert of them at last, — *er-wah er-wah er-wah*, with a nasal twang and twist, — and see them dimpling the surface here and there by their movements. But if you approach the pond-side, they suddenly cease. We hear them at J. P. Brown's Pond, which is edged with ice still on the north. The water must be smooth and the weather pretty warm.

There is still some icy snow in hollows under the north sides of woods.

I see the feathers, apparently of a fox-colored sparrow, completely covering a stump, where some creature has devoured it. At a great ant-hill, the common half-red, half-black ants are stirring, apparently clearing out rubbish from their nest. Great quantities of odoriferous sweet-gale seed are collected with the scum at the outlet of Nut Meadow, for they float. The *Alnus incana* blossoms begin generally to show. The *serrulata* will undoubtedly blossom to-morrow in some places.[1]

The pine on the Marlborough road which I saw

[1] Or probably not till 15th? Did I not take the *incana* for this in '54?

from my window has been sawed down the past winter. I try to count its circles; count sixty-one from centre to sap, but there the pitch conceals the rest completely. I guessed there were fifteen more, at least. The tree was probably quite eighty years old. It was about two and a quarter feet in diameter.

The common hazel just out. It is perhaps the prettiest flower of the *shrubs* that have opened. A little bunch of (in this case) half a dozen catkins, one and three quarters inches long, trembling in the wind, shedding golden pollen on the hand, and, close by, as many minute, but clear crystalline crimson stars at the end of a bare and seemingly dead twig. For two or three days in my walks, I had given the hazel catkins a fillip with my finger under their chins to see if they were in bloom, but in vain; but here, on the warm south side of a wood, I find one bunch fully out and completely relaxed. They know when to trust themselves to the weather. At the same time I hear through the wood the sharp peep of the first hylodes I have chanced to hear. Many cowslip buds show a little yellow, but they will not open there for two or three days. The road is paved with solid ice there.

Returning by the steep side-hill just south of Holden's wood-lot and some dozen or fourteen rods west of the open land, I saw, amid the rattlesnake-plantain leaves, what I suspect to be the *Polygala paucifolia*, — some very beautiful oval leaves of a dull green (green turned dark) above, but beneath — and a great many showed the under side — a clear and brilliant purple (or lake??), growing and looking like checkerberry leaves, but more flaccid. It is three or four inches high, with the oval and revolute leaves at top and a few remote small bract-like leaves on the (three-sided) stem. This polygala is sometimes called flowering wintergreen, and, indeed, it is not only an evergreen but somewhat pyrola-like to the eye.

See a sparrow without marks on throat or breast, running peculiarly in the dry grass in the open field beyond, and hear its song, and then see its white feathers in tail; the baywing.

A small willow by the roadside beyond William Wheeler's, to-morrow.

April 14. 6 A. M. — To Island.

An overcast and moist day, but truly April — no sun all day — like such as began methinks on Fast-Day, or the 5th. You cannot foretell how it will turn out. The river has been steadily rising since the first of April, though you would not think there had been rain enough to cause it. It now covers the meadows pretty respectably. It is perhaps because the warm rain has been melting the frost in the ground. This may be the great cause of the regular spring rise. I see half a dozen crow blackbirds uttering their coarse rasping *char char*, like great rusty springs, on the top of an elm by the riverside; and often at each *char* they open their great tails. They also attain to a clear whistle with some effort, but seem to have some difficulty in their throats yet.

The *Populus tremuloides* by the Island shed pollen — a very few catkins — yesterday at least; for some

anthers are effete and black this morning, though it [*sic*] is hardly curved down yet an is but an inch and a half long at most. White maples are now generally in bloom. The musk tortoise stirring on the bottom. Most of the stellaria has been winter-killed, but I find a few flowers on a protected and still green sprig, probably not blossomed long.

At 8 A. M. — Took caterpillars' eggs from the apple trees at the Texas house and found about thirty.

It being completely overcast, having rained a little, the robins, etc., sing at 4.30 as at sundown usually. The waters, too, are smooth and full of reflections.

April 15. 9 A. M. — To Atkins's boat-house.

No sun till setting. Another still, moist, overcast day, without sun, but all day a crescent of light, as if breaking away in the north. The waters smooth and full of reflections. A still cloudy day like this is perhaps the best to be on the water. To the clouds, perhaps, we owe both the stillness and the reflections; for the light is in great measure reflected from the water. Robins sing now at 10 A. M. as in the morning, and the phoebe; and pigeon woodpecker's cackle is heard, and many martins (with white-bellied swallows) are skimming and twittering above the water, perhaps catching the small fuzzy gnats with which the air is filled. The sound of church bells, at various distances, in Concord and the neighboring towns, sounds very sweet to us on the water this still day. It is the song of the villages heard with the song of the birds.

Vol. VII

The Great Meadows are covered, except a small island in their midst, but not a duck do we see there. On a low limb of a maple on the edge of the river, thirty rods from the present shore, we saw a fish hawk eating a fish. Sixty rods off we could [see] his white crest. We landed, and got nearer by stealing through the woods. His legs looked long as he stood up on the limb with his back to us, and his body looked black against the sky and by contrast with the white of his head. There was a dark stripe on the side of the head. He had got the fish under his feet on the limb, and would bow his head, snatch a mouthful, and then look hastily over his right shoulder in our direction, then snatch another mouthful and look over his left shoulder. At length he launched off and flapped heavily away. We found at the bottom of the water beneath where he sat numerous fragments of the fish he had been eating, parts of the fins, entrails, gills, etc., and some was dropped on the bough. From one fin which I examined, I judged that it was either a sucker or a pout. There were small leeches adhering to it.

In the meanwhile, as we were stealing through the woods, we heard the pleasing note of the pine warbler, bringing back warmer weather, and we heard one honk of a goose, and, looking up, saw a large narrow harrow of them steering northeast. Half a mile further we saw another fish hawk, upon a dead limb midway up a swamp white oak over the water, at the end of a small island. We paddled directly toward him till within thirty rods. A crow came scolding to the tree and lit within three feet, looking about as large, compared

with the hawk, as a crow blackbird to a crow, but he paid no attention to him. We had a very good view of him, as he sat sidewise to us, and of his eagle-shaped head and beak. The white feathers of his head, which were erected somewhat, made him look like a copple-crowned hen. When he launched off, he uttered a clear whistling note, — *phe phe, phe phe, phe phe,* — somewhat like that of a telltale, but more round and less shrill and rapid, and another, perhaps his mate, fifty rods off, joined him. They flew heavily, as we looked at them from behind, more like a blue heron and bittern than I was aware of, their long wings undulating slowly to the tip, like the heron's, and the bodies seeming sharp like a gull's and unlike a hawk's.

In the water beneath where he was perched, we found many fragments of a pout, — bits of red gills, entrails, fins, and some of the long flexible black feelers, — scattered for four or five feet. This pout appeared to have been quite fresh, and was probably caught alive. We afterward started one of them from an oak over the water a mile beyond, just above the boat-house, and he skimmed off very low over the water, several times striking it with a loud sound heard plainly sixty rods off at least; and we followed him with our eyes till we could only see faintly his undulating wings against the sky in the western horizon. You could probably tell if any were about by looking for fragments of fish under the trees on which they would perch.

We had scared up but few ducks — some apparently black, which quacked — and some small rolling-pins, probably teal.

Returning, we had a fine view of a blue heron, standing erect and open to view on a meadow island, by the great swamp south of the bridge, looking as broad as a boy on the side, and then some sheldrakes sailing in the smooth water beyond. These soon sailed behind points of meadow. The heron flew away, and one male sheldrake flew past us low over the water, reconnoitring, large and brilliant black and white. When the heron takes to flight, what a change in size and appearance! It is *presto change!* There go two great undulating wings pinned together, but the body and neck must have been left behind somewhere.

Before we rounded Ball's Hill, — the water now beautifully smooth, — at 2.30 P. M., we saw three gulls sailing on the glassy meadow at least half a mile off, by the oak peninsula, — the plainer because they were against the reflection of the hills. They looked larger than afterward close at hand, as if their whiteness was reflected and doubled. As we advanced into the Great Meadows, making the only ripples in their broad expanse, there being still not a ray of sunshine, only a subdued light through the thinner crescent in the north, the reflections of the maples, of Ponkawtasset and the poplar hill, and the whole township in the southwest, were as perfect as I ever saw. A wall which ran down to the water on the hillside, without any remarkable curve in it, was exaggerated by the reflection into the half of an ellipse. The meadow was expanded to a large lake, the shore-line being referred to the sides of the hills reflected in it. It was a scene worth many such voyages to see. It was remarkable

how much light those white gulls, and also a bleached post on a distant shore, absorbed and reflected through that sombre atmosphere, — conspicuous almost as candles in the night. When we got near to the gulls, they rose heavily and flapped away, answering a more distant one, with a remarkable, deliberate, melancholy, squeaking scream, mewing, or piping, almost a squeal. It was a *little* like the loon. Is this sound the origin of the name sea-mew? Notwithstanding the smoothness of the water, we could not easily see black ducks against the reflection of the woods, but heard them rise at a distance before we saw them. The birds were still in the middle of the day, but began to sing again by 4.30 P. M., probably because of the clouds. Saw and heard a kingfisher — do they not come with the smooth waters of April? — hurrying over the meadow as if on urgent business.

That general *tut tut tut tut*, or snoring, of frogs on the shallow meadow heard first slightly the 5th. There is a very faint *er er er* now and then mixed with it.

April 16. 5 A. M. — To Hill.

Clear and cool. A frost whitens the ground; yet a mist hangs over the village. There is a thin ice, reaching a foot from the water's edge, which the earliest rays will melt. I scare up several snipes feeding on the meadow's edge. It is remarkable how they conceal themselves when they alight on a bare spit of the meadow. I look with my glass to where one alighted four rods off, and at length detect its head rising amid the

cranberry vines and withered grass blades, — which last it closely resembles in color, — with its eye steadily fixed on me. The robins, etc., blackbirds, song sparrows sing now on all hands just before sunrise, perhaps quite as generally as at any season. Going up the hill, I examined the tree-tops for hawks. What is that little hawk about as big as a turtle dove on the top of one of the white oaks on top of the hill? It appears to have a reddish breast. Now it flies to the bare top of a dead tree. Now some crows join, and it pursues one, diving at it repeatedly from above, down a rod or more, as far as I can see toward the hemlocks. Returning that way, I came unexpectedly close to this hawk perched near the top of a large aspen by the river right over my head. He seemed neither to see nor hear me. At first I thought it a new woodpecker. I had a fair view of all its back and tail within forty feet with my glass. Its back was, I should say, a rather dark ash, spotted, and so barred, wings and back, with large white spots, woodpecker-like (not well described in books), probably on the inner vanes of the feathers, both secondaries and primaries, and probably coverts. The tail conspicuously barred with black, three times beyond the covering and feathers and once at least under them. Beneath and under tail, mainly a dirty white with long and conspicuous femoral feathers, unlike sparrow hawk. Head darker and bill dark. It was busily pruning itself, and suddenly pitched off downward. What I call a pigeon hawk.[1] In the meanwhile heard the quivet through the wood, and,

[1] Probably sharp-shinned. *Vide* May 4th.

looking, saw through an opening a small compact flock of pigeons flying low about.

From the Hill-top looked to the Great Meadows with glass. They were very smooth, with a slight mist over them, but I could see very clearly the pale salmon of the eastern horizon reflected there and contrasting with an intermediate streak of skim-milk blue, — now, just after sunrise.

P. M. — To Flint's Pond.

A perfectly clear and very warm day, a little warmer than the 31st of March or any yet, and I have not got far before, for the first time, I regret that I wore my greatcoat. Noticed the first wasp, and many cicindelæ on a sandy place. Have probably seen the latter before in the air, but this warmth brings them out in numbers. The gray of Hubbard's oaks looks drier and more like summer, and it is now drier walking, the frost in most places wholly out. I got so near a grass-bird as to see the narrow circle of white round the eye. The spots on the *Emys guttata*, in a still, warm leafy-paved ditch which dries up, are exceedingly bright now. Does it last? At Callitriche Pool (I see no flowers on it), I see what looks like minnows an inch long, with a remarkably forked tail-fin; probably larvæ of dragon-flies. The eyed head conspicuous, and something like a large dorsal fin. They dart about in this warm pool and rest at different angles with the horizon. The water ranunculus was very forward here. This pool dries up in summer. The very pools, the receptacles of all kinds of rubbish, now, soon after the ice has melted, so transparent and of glassy smoothness and full of animal and vegetable life, are interesting and beautiful objects. Stow's cold pond-hole is still full of ice though partly submerged, — the only pool in this state that I see. The orange-copper vanessa, middle-sized, is out, and a great many of the large buff-edged are fluttering over the leaves in wood-paths this warm afternoon. I am obliged to carry my greatcoat on my arm. A striped snake rustles down a dry open hillside where the withered grass is long.

I could not dig to the nest of the deer mouse in Britton's Hollow, because of the frost about six inches beneath the surface. (Yet, though I have seen no plowing in fields, the surveyors plowed in the road on the 14th.) As far as I dug, their galleries appeared at first to be lined with a sort of membrane, which I found was the bark or skin of roots of the right size, their galleries taking the place of the decayed wood. An oak stump.

At Flint's, sitting on the rock, we see a great many ducks, mostly sheldrakes, on the pond, which will hardly abide us within half a mile. With the glass I see by their reddish heads that all of one party — the main body — are females. You see little more than their heads at a distance and not much white but on their throats, perchance. When they fly, they look black and white, but not so large nor with that brilliant contrast of black and white which the male exhibits. In another direction is a male by himself, conspicuous, perhaps several. Anon alights near us a flock of golden-eyes — *surely*, with their great black (looking) heads and a white patch on the side; short

stumpy bills (after looking at the mergansers); much clear black, contrasting with much clear white. Their heads and bills look ludicrously short and parrot-like after the others. Our presence and a boat party on the pond at last drove nearly all the ducks into the deep easterly cove.

We stole down on them carefully through the woods, at last crawling on our bellies, with great patience, till at last we found ourselves within seven or eight rods — as I measured afterward — of the great body of them, and watched them for twenty or thirty minutes with the glass through a screen of cat-briar, alders, etc. There were twelve female sheldrakes close together, and, nearest us, within two rods of the shore, where it was very shallow, two or more constantly moving about within about the diameter of a rod and keeping watch while the rest were trying to sleep, — to catch a nap with their heads in their backs; but from time to time one would wake up enough to plume himself. It seemed as if they must have been broken of their sleep and were trying to make it up, having an arduous journey before them, for we had seen them all disturbed and on the wing within half an hour. They were headed various ways. Now and then they seemed to see or hear or smell us, and uttered a low note of alarm, something like the note of a tree-toad, but very faint, or perhaps a little more wiry and like that of pigeons, but the sleepers hardly lifted their heads for it. How fit that this note of alarm should be made to resemble the croaking of a frog and so not betray them to the gunners! They appeared to sink

about midway in the water, and their heads were all a rich reddish brown, their throats white. Now and then one of the watchmen would lift his head and turn his bill directly upward, showing his white throat.

There were some black or dusky ducks in company with them at first, apparently about as large as they, but more alarmed. Their throats looked straw-colored, somewhat like a bittern's, and I saw their shovel bills. These soon sailed further off.

At last we arose and rushed to the shore within three rods of them, and they rose up with a din, — twenty-six mergansers (I think all females), ten black ducks, — and five golden-eyes from a little further off, also another still more distant flock of one of these kinds. The black ducks alone uttered a sound, their usual hoarse *quack*. They all flew in loose array, but the three kinds in separate flocks. We were surprised to find ourselves looking on a company of birds devoted to slumber after the alarm and activity we had just witnessed.

Returning, at Goose Pond, which many water-bugs (gyrinus) were now dimpling, we scared up two black ducks. The shore was strewn with much fresh eel-grass and the fine, now short eriocaulon with its white roots, apparently all pulled up by them and drifted in.

The spearer's light to-night, and, after dark, the sound of geese honking all together very low over the houses and apparently about to settle on the Lee meadow.

Have not noticed fox-colored sparrows since April 13th.

I am startled sometimes these mornings to hear the sound of doves alighting on the roof just over my head; they come down so hard upon it, as if one had thrown a heavy stick on to it, and I wonder it does not injure their organizations. Their legs must be cushioned in their sockets to save them from the shock?

When we reached Britton's clearing on our return this afternoon, at sunset, the mountains, after this our warmest day as yet, had got a peculiar soft mantle of blue haze, pale blue as a blue heron, ushering in the long series of summer sunsets, and we were glad that we had stayed out so late and felt no need to go home now in a hurry.

April 17. 5 A. M. — Up Assabet.

Very little frost; a clear morning. The oars still cold to the hand at this hour. Did I not hear an *F. juncorum* at a distance??[1] Saw some crow blackbirds inspecting that old nest of theirs. I believe I see a tree sparrow still, but I do not remember an *F. hyemalis* for two days.[2] Geese went over at noon, when warm and sunny.

P. M. — To Lee's Cliff.

I leave off my greatcoat, though the wind rises rather fresh before I return. It is worth the while to walk so free and light, having got off both boots and greatcoat. Great flocks of grackles and red-wings about the Swamp Bridge Brook willows, perching restlessly on an apple tree all at once, and then, with a sweeping

[1] Yes.   [2] *Vide* 18th.

or curving flight, alighting on the ground. Many robins flit before me in flocks these days. I rarely find a nest (of the right species) near the river but it has a piece of a fish-line in it. The yellow-spot tortoises are very common now in the ditches, tumbling in and crawling off, and perhaps burying themselves at your approach. Many are outside. The second sallow catkin (or any willow) I have seen in blossom — there are three or four catkins on the twig partly open — I am about to clutch, but find already a bee curved close on each half-opened catkin, intoxicated with its early sweet, — one perhaps a honey-bee, — so intent on its sweets or pollen that they do not dream of flying. Various kinds of bees — some of the honey-bees — have little yellow masses of pollen (?) on their thighs; some seem to be taking [it] into their mouths. So quickly and surely does a bee find the earliest flower, as if he had slumbered all winter at the root of the plant. No matter what pains you take, probably — undoubtedly — an insect will have found the first flower before you.

Yesterday I saw several larger frogs out. Perhaps some were small bullfrogs. That warmth brought them out on to the bank, and they jumped in before me. The general stirring of frogs. To-day I see a *Rana palustris* — I think the first — and a middling-sized bullfrog, I think. I suspect that those first seen in Hubbard's Close were the little croakers.

I see by their droppings that many birds — perhaps robins — have lately roosted in that wine-glass apple scrub on Conantum, an excellent covert from the hawks,

Vol. VII

and there are three old nests in it, though it is only six or eight feet in diameter. I also see where birds have roosted in a thick white pine in Lee's Wood. It is easy to detect their roosting-places now, because they are in flocks.

Saw a woodchuck. His deep reddish-brown rear, somewhat grizzled about, looked like a ripe fruit mellowed by winter. C. saw one some time ago. They have several holes under Lee's Cliff, where they have worn bare and smooth sandy paths under the eaves of the rock, and I suspect that they nibble the early leaves there. (The arabis is half exterminated by some creature.) They, or the partridges or rabbits, there and at Middle Conantum Cliff, make sad havoc with the earliest radical leaves and flowers which I am watching, and in the village I have to contend with the hens, who also love an early salad.

Sat at the wall corner to see an eagle's white head and tail against the red hillside, but in vain. The distant white pines over the Spanish Brook seem to flake into tiers; the whole tree looks like an open cone. A sudden warm day, like yesterday and this, takes off some birds and adds others. It is a crisis in their career. The fox-colored sparrows seem to be gone, and I suspect that *most* of the tree sparrows and *F. hyemalis*, at least, went yesterday. So the pleasanter weather seems not an unmixed benefit. The flowers of the common elm at Lee's are now loose and dangling, apparently well out a day or two in advance of Cheney's, but I see no pollen. Walking under the Cliff, I am struck by the already darker, healthier green of early

weeds there — *e. g.* the little thyme-flowering sand-wort — before there is any green to speak of elsewhere.

Did I not see the yellow redpoll on an apple tree with some robins, by chance in the same place where I saw one last year?[1] Yet I see no chestnut on head, but bright-yellow breast and blackish further extremity.

The early aspen catkins are now some of them two and a half inches long and white, dangling in the breeze. The earliest gooseberry leaves are fairly unfolding now, and show some green at a little distance.

April 18. 6 A. M. — See and hear tree sparrows, and hear hyemalis still. Rained last evening and was very dark. Fair this morning and warm. White-bellied swallow's and martin's twitter now at 9 A. M.

P. M. — To Cliffs and Walden and Hubbard's Close.

The hillside and especially *low* bank-sides are now conspicuously green. Almost did without a fire this morning. Coming out, I find it very warm, warmer than yesterday or any day yet. It is a reminiscence of past summers. It is perfectly still and almost sultry, with wet-looking clouds hanging about, and from time to time hiding the sun. First weather of this kind. And as I sit on Fair Haven Hill-side, the sun actually burns my cheek; yet I left some fire in the house, not knowing behind a window how warm it was. The flooded meadows and river are smooth, and just enough in shadow for reflections. The rush sparrows tinkle now at 3 P. M. far over the bushes, and hylodes are

[1] Yes.

peeping in a distant pool. Robins are singing and peeping, and jays are screaming. I see one or two smokes in the horizon. I can still see the mountains slightly spotted with snow. The frost is out enough for plowing probably in most open ground.

When I reach the top of the hill, I see suddenly all the southern horizon (east or south from Bear Hill in Waltham to the river) full of a mist, like a dust, already concealing the Lincoln hills and producing distinct wreaths of vapor, the rest of the horizon being clear. Evidently a sea-turn, — a wind from over the sea, condensing the moisture in our warm atmosphere and putting another aspect on the face of things. All this I see and say long before I feel the change, while still sweltering on the rocks, for the heat was oppressive. Nature cannot abide this sudden heat, but calls for her fan. In ten minutes I hear a susurrus in the shrub oak leaves at a distance, and soon an agreeable fresh air washes these warm rocks, and some mist surrounds me.

A low blackberry on the rocks is now expanding its leaves just after the gooseberry. A little sallow, about two feet high and apparently intermediate between *tristis* and the next, with reddish anthers not yet burst, will bloom to-morrow in Well Meadow Path. The shad-bush flower-buds, beginning to expand, look like leaf-buds bursting now. Male sweet-gale. One cowslip fully expanded, but no pollen; probably is at Second Division.[1] Some are plowing. Am overtaken

[1] Some fully open May 4th, but no pollen till next morning in chamber!!

by a sudden sun-shower, after which a rainbow. Elm (American) in tumbler and probably at Cliffs probably a day [or] two before Cheney's.

In the evening hear far and wide the ring of toads, and a thunder-shower with its lightning is seen and heard in the west.

April 19. 5 A. M. — Up Assabet.

Warm and still and somewhat cloudy. Am without greatcoat. The guns are firing and bells ringing. I hear a faint *honk* and, looking up, see going over the river, within fifty rods, thirty-two geese in the form of a hay-hook, only two in the hook, and they are at least six feet apart. Probably the whole line is twelve rods long. At least three hundred have passed over Concord, or rather within the breadth of a mile, this spring (perhaps twice as many); for I have seen or heard of a dozen flocks, and the two I counted had about thirty each. Many tortoises have their heads out. The river has fallen a little. Going up the Assabet, two or three tortoises roll down the steep bank with a rustle. One tumbles on its edge and rolls swiftly like a disk cast by a boy, with its back to me, from eight or ten feet into the water. I hear no concert of tree sparrows. Hear the *tull-lull* of myrtle-bird [1] in street, and the jingle of the chip-bird.

This forenoon, sit with open window.

Now plowing and planting will begin generally.

P. M. — To Walden.

[1] White-throated sparrow.

Some golden willows will now just peel fairly, though on this one the buds have not started. (Another sudden change in the wind to northeast and a freshness with some mist from the sea at 3.30 P. M.) These osiers to my eye have only a little more liquid green than a month ago. A shad frog on the dry grass. The wild red cherry will begin to leaf to-morrow.

From Heywood's Peak I thought I saw the head of a loon in the pond, thirty-five or forty rods distant. Bringing my glass to bear, it seemed sunk very low in the water, — all the neck concealed, — but I could not tell which end was the bill. At length I discovered that it was the whole body of a little duck, asleep with its head in its back, exactly in the middle of the pond. It had a moderate-sized black head and neck, a white breast, and *seemed* dark-brown above, with a white spot on the side of the head, not reaching to the outside, from base of mandibles, and another, perhaps, on the end of the wing, with some black there. It sat drifting round a little, but with ever its breast toward the wind, and from time to time it raised its head and looked round to see if it were safe. I think it was the smallest duck I ever saw. Floating buoyantly asleep on the middle of Walden Pond. Was it not a female of the buffle-headed or spirit duck? I believed the wings looked blacker when it flew, with some white beneath. It floated like a little casket, and at first I doubted a good while if it possessed life, until I saw it raise its head and look around. It had chosen a place for its nap exactly equidistant between the two shores there, and, with its breast to the wind, swung

Vol. VII

round only as much as a vessel held by its anchors in the stream. At length the cars scared it.

Goodwin had caught twenty-five pouts and one shiner at the Walden meadow, but no perch.

Slippery elm in tumbler to-day; probably to-morrow at Cliffs.

A partridge drums.

April 20. Rains all day, taking out the frost and imprisoning me. You cannot set a post yet on account of frost.

April 21. 5 A. M. — To Cliffs.

Fair and still. There is a fog over the river, which shows at a distance more than near by. Not much. The frost conceals the green of the gooseberry leaves just expanding. The shallow puddles left by yesterday's rain in the fields are skimmed over.

Hear the first seringo. The duskyish crown is divided by a lighter line. Above it is ashy-brown and drab (?), a streak of lemon yellow over the eye; some brownish drab or bay making a spot on wings; white lines diverging from throat; reddish legs against sun; breast and sides dashed. It has not the note of Nuttall's Savannah, nor, methinks, the blackness of Wilson's. Is it the *passerina*, which Nuttall does not describe? [1]

[1] Yes. He calls it *F. savanarum* (p. 494); says they arrive about the middle of May "occasionally." "On these occasions they perch in sheltered trees in pairs, and sing in an agreeable voice somewhat like that of the Purple Finch, though less vigorously." Thinks they go

At Cliffs, I hear at a distance a wood thrush.[1] It affects us as a part of our unfallen selves. The *Populus grandidentata* there may open to-morrow. The frost saves my feet a wetting probably. As I sit on the Cliffs, the sound of the frost and frozen drops melting and falling on the leaves in the woods below sounds [*sic*] like a gentle but steady rain all the country over, while the sun shines clear above all.

Aunt Maria has put into my hands to-day for safe-keeping three letters from Peter Thoreau, dated Jersey (the first July 1st, 1801, the second April 22d, 1804, and the third April 11th, 1806) and directed to his niece "Miss Elizabeth Thoreau, Concord, Near Boston," etc.; also a "Vue de la Ville de St. Helier," etc., accompanying the first. She is not certain that any more were received from him.

The first is in answer to one from Elizabeth announcing the death of her father (my grandfather). He states that *his* mother died the 26th of June, 1801, — the day before he received E.'s letter, — though not till after he had heard from another source of the death of his brother, which was not communicated to his mother. "She was in the 79th year of her age, and retained her memory to the last. . . . She lived with my two sisters, who took the greatest care of her." He says that he had written to E.'s father about his oldest brother, who died about a year before, but had

north to breed. [It would be hard to describe the grasshopper sparrow's song more inaccurately.]

[1] [The singer must have been a hermit thrush. The date is conclusive.]

had no answer; had written that he left his children, two sons and a daughter, in a good way. "The eldest son and daughter are both married, and have children, the youngest is about eighteen. I am still a widower of four children. . . . I have but two left, Betsy and Peter, James and Nancy are both at rest." He adds that he sends a view "of our native town," etc.

The second of these letters is sent by Captain John Harvey of Boston, then at Guernsey. He says that on the 4th of February previous he sent her a copy [1] of the last letter he had written, which was in answer to her second, since he feared she had not received it. Says they are still at war with the French; that they received the day before a letter from her "Uncle and Aunt Le Cappelain of London." Complains of not receiving letters. "Your Aunts Betsy and Peter join with me," etc.

According to the third letter, he received an answer to that he sent by Captain Harvey, by Captain Touzel, and will forward this by the last, who is going *via* Newfoundland to Boston. "He expects to go to Boston every year." Several vessels from Jersey go there every year. His nephew had told him some time before that he "met a gentleman from Boston who told him he [saw or knew? (torn out)] [2] Thoreau & Hayse there," and he (Peter Thoreau) therefore thinks the children must have kept up the name of the firm. Says Captain Harvey was an old friend of his. "Your cousin John is a Lieutenant in the British service, he has been already a campaign on the continent, he

[1] Where is it?   [2] [The brackets are Thoreau's.]

is very fond of it." "Your aunts Betsy and Peter join," etc.

Aunt Maria thinks the correspondence ceased at Peter's death, because he was the one who wrote English.[1]

P. M. — Sail to meadow near Carlisle Bridge.

A fine, clear, and pleasant day with a little west wind. Saw a painted turtle not two inches in diameter. This must be more than one year old. A female red-wing. I see yellow redpolls on the bushes near the water, — handsome birds, — but hear no note. Watched for some time a dozen black ducks on the meadow's edge in a retired place, some on land and some sailing. Fifty rods off and without the glass, they looked like crows feeding on the meadow's edge, with a scarcely perceptible tinge of brown. Examining the ground afterward, found that the whitish lichen thallus (which formed a crust, a sort of scurfy bald place, here and there in the meadow where the water had just risen) was loosened up and floating over the bare spaces mixed with a few downy feathers. I thought the flat meadow islets showed traces of having been probed by them. *All* the button-bushes, etc., etc., in and about the water are now swarming with those minute fuzzy gnats about an eighth of an inch long. The insect youth are on the wing. The whole shore resounds with their hum wherever we approach it, and they cover our boat and persons. They are in countless myriads the whole length of the river. A peep, peetweet

[1] [Sanborn, pp. 2-4.]

on the shore. There is some gossamer on the willows. The river has risen considerably, owing to yesterday's rain, and new drift is brought down. The greater fullness of the Assabet is perceptible at the junction.

The New York *Tribune* said on the 19th, "The caterpillar-blossoms, and the slightest peeping of green leaves among the poplars and willows, and a tolerable springing of grass, are the only vegetable proofs yet to be seen." I should think they were just with our gooseberry.

April 22. 5.30 A. M. — To Assabet stone bridge.

Tree sparrows still. See a song sparrow getting its breakfast in the water on the meadow like a wader. Red maple yesterday, — an early one by further stone bridge. Balm-of-Gilead probably to-morrow. The black currant is just begun to expand leaf — probably yesterday elsewhere — a little earlier than the red. Though my hands are cold this morning I have not worn gloves for a few *mornings* past, — a week or ten days. The grass is now become rapidly green by the sides of the road, promising dandelions and buttercups.

P. M. — To Lee's Cliff.

Fair, but windy. Tree sparrows about with their buntingish head and faint chirp. The leaves of the skunk-cabbage, unfolding in the meadows, make more show than any green yet. The yellow willow catkins pushing out begin to give the trees a misty, downy appearance, dimming them. The bluish band

on the breast of the kingfisher leaves the pure white beneath in the form of a heart. The blossoms of the sweet-gale are now on fire over the brooks, contorted like caterpillars. The female flowers also out like the hazel, with more stigmas, — out at same time with the male. I first nóticed my little mud turtles in the cellar out of their [*sic*], one of them, some eight days ago. I suspect those in the river begin to stir about that time? Antennaria probably yesterday, Skull-cap Meadow Ditch. Many yellow redpolls on the willows now. They jerk their tails constantly like phœbes, but I hear only a faint chip. Could that have been a female with them, with an ash head and merely a yellow spot on each side of body, white beneath (?), and forked tail? [1] Red-stemmed moss now. Goosanders, male and female. They rise and fly, the female leading. They afterward show that they can get out of sight about as well by diving as by flying. At a distance you see only the male, alternately diving and sailing, when the female may be all the while by his side. Getting over the wall under the middle Conantum Cliff, I heard a loud and piercingly sharp whistle of two notes, — *phe-phe*, like a peep somewhat. Could it have been a woodchuck? Heard afterward under Lee's Cliff a similar fainter one, which at one time *appeared* to come from a pigeon woodpecker. Cowbirds on an apple tree. Crowfoot on Cliff. Johnswort radical leaves have grown several inches and angelica shows.

Elder leaves have grown one and a half inches, and thimble-berry is forward under rocks. Meadow-

[1] Probably a myrtle-bird.

sweet in some places begins to open to-day; also barberry under Cliffs and a moss rose to-morrow. Say earliest gooseberry, then elder, raspberry, thimbleberry, and low blackberry (the last two under rocks), then wild red cherry, then black currant (yesterday), then meadow-sweet, and barberry under Cliff, to-day. A moss rose to-morrow and hazel under Cliffs to-morrow

April 23. River higher than before since winter. Whole of Lee Meadow covered. Saw two pigeon woodpeckers approach and, I think, put their bills together and utter that *o-week, o-week.* The currant and second gooseberry are bursting into leaf.

P. M. — To Cedar Swamp *via* Assabet.

Warm and pretty still. Even the riversides are quiet at this hour (3 p. m.) as in summer; the birds are neither seen nor heard. The anthers of the larch are conspicuous, but I see no pollen. White cedar to-morrow.[1] See a frog hawk beating the bushes regularly. What a peculiarly formed wing! It should be called the kite. Its wings are very narrow and pointed, and its form in front is a remarkable curve, and its body is not heavy and buzzard-like. It occasionally hovers over some parts of the meadow or hedge and circles back over it, only rising enough from time to time to clear the trees and fences. Soon after I see hovering over Sam Barrett's, high sailing, a more buzzard-like brown hawk, black-barred beneath and on tail, with short, broad, ragged wings and perhaps a

[1] In house the 24th.

white mark on under side of wings. The chickens utter a note of alarm. Is it the broad-winged hawk (*Falco Pennsylvanicus*)?[1] But why should the other be called *F. fuscus?* I think this is called the partridge hawk. The books are very unsatisfactory on these two hawks. Apparently barn swallows over the river. And do I see bank swallows also?

C. says he has seen a yellow-legs.

I have seen also for some weeks occasionally a brown hawk with white rump, flying low, which I have thought the frog hawk in a different stage of plumage; but can it be at this season? and is it not the marsh hawk? Yet it is not so heavy nearly as the hen-hawk.[2]

April 24. P. M. — To Flint's Pond.

Warm and quite a thick haze. Cannot see distant hills, nor use my glass to advantage. The *Equisetum arvense* on the causeway sheds its green pollen, which looks like lint on the hand abundantly, and may have done so when I *first* saw it upon the 21st. Young caterpillars' nests are just hatched on the wild cherry. Some are an inch in diameter, others just come out. The little creatures have crawled at once to the extremity of the twigs and commenced at once on the green buds just about to burst, eating holes into them. They do not come forth till the buds are about to burst. I see on the pitch pines at Thrush Alley that golden-crested wren or the other, ashy-olive above and whitish beneath, with a white bar on wings, restlessly darting

[1] Probably not. *Vide* May 2d.

[2] Probably female hen-harrier [*i. e.* marsh hawk].

at insects like a flycatcher, — into the air after them. It is quite tame. A very neat bird, but does not sing now. I see a bee like a small bumble-bee go into a little hole under a leaf in the road, which apparently it has made, and come out again back foremost. That fine slaty-blue butterfly, bigger than the small red, in wood-paths. I see a cone-bearing willow in dry woods, which will begin to leaf to-morrow, and apparently to show cones. *Pyrus arbutifolia* will begin to leaf to-morrow. Its buds are red while those of the shad-bush are green. I can find no red cedar in bloom, but it will undoubtedly shed pollen to-morrow. It is on the point of it. I am not sure that the white cedar is any earlier. The sprigs of red cedar, now full of the buff-colored staminate flowers, like fruit, are very rich. The next day they shed an abundance of pollen in the house. It is a clear buff color, while that of the white cedar is very different, being a faint salmon. It would be very pleasant to make a collection of these powders, — like dry ground paints. They would be the right kind of chemicals to have. I see the black birch stumps, where they have cut by Flint's Pond the past winter, completely covered with a greasy-*looking* pinkish-colored cream, yet without any particular taste or smell, — what the sap has turned to. The *Salix alba* begins to leaf. Have not seen the *F. hyemalis* for a week.

April 25. A moist April morning. A small native willow leafing[1] and showing catkins to-day; also the

[1] Or say May 1st, if they are bracts.

black cherry in some places. The common wild rose to-morrow. Balm-of-Gilead will not shed pollen apparently for a day or more. Shepherd's-purse will bloom to-day, — the first I have noticed which has sprung from the ground this season, or of an age. Say lilac begins to leaf with common currant.

P. M. — To Beck Stow's.

Hear a faint cheep and at length detect the white-throated sparrow, the handsome and well-marked bird, the largest of the sparrows, with a yellow spot on each side of the front, hopping along under the rubbish left by the woodchopper. I afterward hear a faint *cheep* very rapidly repeated, making a faint sharp jingle, — no doubt by the same.[1] Many sparrows have a similar faint metallic *cheep*, — the tree sparrow and field sparrow, for instance. I first saw the white-throated sparrow at this date last year. Hear the peculiar *squeaking* notes of a pigeon woodpecker. Two black ducks circle around me three or four times, wishing to alight in the swamp, but finally go to the river meadows. I hear the whistling of their wings. Their bills point downward in flying.

The *Andromeda calyculata* is out in water, in the little swamp east of Beck Stow's, some perhaps yesterday; and C. says he saw many bluets yesterday, and also that he saw two *F. hyemalis* yesterday.

I have noticed three or four upper jaws of muskrats on the meadow lately, which, added to the dead bodies floating, make more than half a dozen perhaps drowned out last winter.

[1] Probably by field sparrows; this their common low note.

After sunset paddled up to the Hubbard Bath. The bushes ringing with the evening song of song sparrows and robins, and the evening sky reflected from the surface of the rippled water like the *lake* grass on pools. A spearers' fire seems three times as far off as it is.

April 26. A cloudy, still, damp, and at length drizzling day.

P. M. — To Bayberry and Black Ash Cellar.

Wheildon's arbor-vitæ well out, maybe for a week. The silvery abele, probably to-day or yesterday, but I do not see pollen. The blossoms of the red maple (some a yellowish green) are now most generally conspicuous and handsome scarlet crescents over the swamps. Going over Ponkawtasset, hear a golden-crested (?) wren, — the robin's note, etc., — in the tops of the high wood; see myrtle-birds and half a dozen pigeons. The *prate* of the last is much like the creaking of a tree. They lift their wings at the same moment as they sit. There are said to be many about now. See their warm-colored breasts. I see pigeon woodpeckers billing on an oak at a distance. Young apple leafing, say with the common rose, also some early large ones. Bayberry not started much. Fever-bush out apparently a day or two, between Black Birch Cellar and Easterbrook's. It shows plainly now, before the leaves have come out on bushes, twenty rods off. See and hear chewinks, — all their strains; the same date with last year, by accident. Many male and female white-throated sparrows feeding on the pasture with the song sparrow. The

male's white is buff in the female. A brown thrasher (?) seen at a little distance.[1]

We see and hear more birds than usual this mizzling and still day, and the robin sings with more vigor and promise than later in the season.

April 27. 5 A. M. — S. tristis Path around Cliffs.

Cold and windy, but fair. The earliest willow by railroad begins to leaf and is out of bloom. Few birds are heard this cold and windy morning. Hear a partridge drum before 6 A. M., also a golden-crested (?) wren. *Salix tristis*, probably to-day, the female more forward than the male. Heard a singular sort of screech, somewhat like a hawk, under the Cliff, and soon some pigeons flew out of a pine near me. The black and white creepers running over the trunks or main limbs of red maples and uttering their fainter oven-bird-like notes. The principal singer on this walk, both in wood and field away from town, is the field sparrow. I hear the sweet warble of a tree sparrow in the yard.

Cultivated cherry is beginning to leaf. The balm-of-Gilead catkins are well loosened and about three inches long, but I have seen only fertile ones. Say male the 25th, 26th, or 27th.

April 28. A second cold but fair day. Good fires are required to-day and yesterday.

P. M. — Sail to Ball's Hill.

The *chimney swallow*, with the white-bellied and barn swallows, over the river. The red maples, now

[1] Heard May 4th.

in bloom, are quite handsome at a distance over the flooded meadow beyond Peter's. The abundant wholesome gray of the trunks and stems beneath surmounted by the red or scarlet crescents. Are not they sheldrakes which I see at a distance on an islet in the meadow? The wind is strong from the northwest.

Landed at Ball's Hill to look for birds under the shelter of the hill in the sun. There were a great many myrtle-birds there, — they have been quite common for a week, — also yellow redpolls, and some song sparrows, tree sparrows, field sparrows, and one *F. hyemalis*. In a cold and windy day like this you can find more birds than in a serene one, because they are collected under the wooded hillsides in the sun. The myrtle-birds flitted before us in great numbers, yet quite tame, uttering commonly only a *chip*, but sometimes a short trill or *che che, che che, che che.* Do I hear the *tull-lull* in the afternoon? It is a bird of many colors, — slate, yellow, black, and white, — singularly spotted. Those little gnats of the 21st are still in the air in the sun under this hill, but elsewhere the cold strong wind has either drowned them or chilled them to death. I saw where they had taken refuge in a boat and covered its bottom with large black patches.

I noticed on the 26th (and also to-day) that since this last rise of the river, which reached its height the 23d, a great deal of the young flag, already six inches to a foot long, though I have hardly observed it growing yet, has washed up all along the shore, and as to-day I find a piece of flag-root with it gnawed by a muskrat, I think that they have been feeding very exten-

sively on the white and tender part of the young blades. They, and not ducks, for it is about the bridges also as much as anywhere. I think that they desert the clams now for this vegetable food. In one place a dead muskrat scents the shore, probably another of those drowned out in the winter. Saw the little heaps of dirt where worms had come out by river.

April 29. This morning it snows, but the ground is not yet whitened. This will probably take the cold out of the air. Many chip-birds are feeding in the yard, and one bay-wing. The latter incessantly scratches like a hen, all the while looking about for foes. The bay on its wings is not obvious except when it opens them. The white circle about the eye is visible afar. Now it makes a business of pluming itself, doubling prettily upon itself, now touching the root of its tail, now thrusting its head under its wing, now between its wing and back above, and now between its legs and its belly; and now it drops flat on its breast and belly and spreads and shakes its wings, now stands up and repeatedly shakes its wings. It is either cleaning itself of dirt acquired in scratching and feeding, — for its feet are black with mud, — or it is oiling its feathers thus. It is rather better concealed by its color than the chip-bird with its chestnut crown and light breast. The chip-bird scratches but slightly and rarely; it finds what it wants on the surface, keeps its head down more steadily, not looking about. I see the bay-wing eat some worms.

For two or three days the *Salix alba*, with its catkins

(not yet open) and its young leaves, or bracts (?), has made quite a show, before any other *tree*, — a pyramid of tender yellowish green in the russet landscape.

The water now rapidly going down on the meadows, a bright-green grass is springing up.

P. M. — By boat to Lupine Hill.

It did not whiten the ground. Raw, overcast, and threatening rain. A few of the cones within reach on F. Monroe's larches shed pollen; say, then, yesterday. The crimson female flowers are now handsome but small.

That lake grass — or perhaps I should call it *purple grass* — is now apparently in perfection on the water. Long and slender blades (about an eighth of an inch wide and six to twelve inches long, the part exposed) lie close side by side straight and parallel on the surface, with a dimple at the point where they emerge. Some are a very rich purple, with apparently a bloom, and very suggestive of placidity. It is a true *bloom*, at any rate, — the first blush of the spring caught on these little standards elevated to the light. By the water they are left perfectly smooth and flat and straight, as well as parallel, and thus, by their mass, make the greater impression on the eye. It has a strong marshy, somewhat fishy, almost seaweed-like scent when plucked. Seen through a glass the surface is finely grooved.

The scrolls of the interrupted fern are already four or five inches high.

I see a woodchuck on the side of Lupine Hill, eight or ten rods off. He runs to within three feet of his hole; then stops, with his head up. His whole body makes

an angle of forty-five degrees as I look sideways at it. I see his shining black eyes and black snout and his little erect ears. He is of a light brown forward at this distance (hoary above, yellowish or sorrel beneath), gradually darkening backward to the end of the tail, which is dark-brown. The general aspect is grizzly, the ends of most of the hairs being white. The yellowish brown, or rather sorrel, of his throat and breast very like the sand of his burrow, over which it is slanted.[1] No glaring distinctions to catch the eye and betray him. As I advance, he crawls a foot nearer his hole, as if to make sure his retreat while he satisfies his curiosity. Tired of holding up his head, he lowers it at last, yet waits my further advance.

The snout of the little sternothærus is the most like a little black stick seen above the water of any of the smaller tortoises. I was almost perfectly deceived by it close at hand; but it moved.

Choke-cherry begins to leaf. Dandelions out yesterday, at least. Some young alders begin to leaf. *Viola ovata* will open to-morrow. Mountain-ash began to leaf, say yesterday. Makes a show with leaves alone before any tree.

Paddling slowly along, I see five or six snipes within four or five rods, feeding on the meadow just laid bare, or in the shallow and grassy water. This dark, damp, cold day they do not mind me. View them with my glass. How the ends of their wings curve upward! They do not thrust their bills clear down com-

[1] Four nails on fore feet and five behind. The hind feet are also longer. Are the first not hands partly?

monly, but wade and nibble at something amid the grass, apparently on the surface of the water. Sometimes it seems to be the grass itself, sometimes on the surface of the bare meadow. They are not now thrusting their bills deep in the mud. They have dark-ash or slate-colored breasts. At length they take a little alarm and rise with a sort of rippling whistle or peep, a little like a robin's peep, but faint and soft, and then alight within a dozen rods. I hear often at night a very different harsh squeak from them, and another squeak much like the nighthawk's and also the booming.

April 30. Horse-chestnut begins to leaf, — one of them.

Another, more still, cloudy, almost drizzling day, in which, as the last three, I wear a greatcoat.

P. M. — To Lee's Cliff.

Privet begins to leaf. (*Viburnum nudum* and *Lentago* yesterday.)

I observed yesterday that the barn swallows confined themselves to one place, about fifteen rods in diameter, in Willow Bay, about the sharp rock. They kept circling about and flying up the stream (the wind easterly), about six inches above the water, — it was cloudy and almost raining, — yet I could not perceive any insects there. Those myriads of little fuzzy gnats mentioned on the 21st and 28th must afford an abundance of food to insectivorous birds. Many new birds should have arrived about the 21st. There were plenty of myrtle-birds and yellow redpolls where the gnats

were. The swallows were confined to this space when I passed up, and were still there when I returned, an hour and a half later. I saw them nowhere else. They uttered only a slight twitter from time to time and when they turned out for each other on meeting. Getting their meal seemed to be made a social affair. Pray, how long will they continue to circle thus without resting?

The early willow by Hubbard's Bridge has not begun to leaf. This would make it a different species from that by railroad, which has.

Hear a short, rasping note, somewhat tweezer-bird-like, I think from a yellow redpoll. Yellow dor-bug.

I hear from far the scream of a hawk circling over the Holden woods and swamp. This accounts for those two men with guns just entering it. What a dry, shrill, angry scream! I see the bird with my glass resting upon the topmost plume of a tall white pine. Its back, reflecting the light, looks white in patches; and now it circles again. It is a red-tailed hawk. The tips of its wings are curved upward as it sails. How it scolds at the men beneath! I see its open bill. It must have a nest there. Hark! there goes a gun, and down it tumbles from a rod or two above the wood. So I thought, but was mistaken. In the meanwhile, I learn that there is a nest there, and the gunners killed one this morning, which I examined. They are now getting the young. Above it was brown, but not at all reddish-brown except about head. Above perhaps I should call it brown, and a dirty white beneath; wings above

thickly barred with darker, and also wings beneath. The
tail of twelve reddish feathers, once black-barred near
the end. The feet pale-yellow and very stout, with
strong, sharp black claws. The head and neck were
remarkably stout, and the beak short and curved from
the base. Powerful neck and legs. The claws pricked
me as I handled it. It measured one yard and three
eighths plus from tip to tip, *i. e.* four feet and two inches.[1]
Some ferruginous on the neck; ends of wings nearly
black.

Columbine just out; one anther sheds. Also turritis
will to-morrow apparently; many probably, if they had
not been eaten. Crowfoot and saxifrage are now in
prime at Lee's; they yellow and whiten the ground.
I see a great many little piles of dirt made by the worms
on Conantum pastures.

The woodchuck has not so much what I should call
a musky scent, but exactly that peculiar rank scent
which I perceive in a menagerie. The musky at length
becomes the regular wild-beast scent.

Red-wing blackbirds now fly in large flocks, covering the tops of trees — willows, maples, apples, or
oaks — like a black fruit, and keep up an incessant
gurgling and whistling, — all for some purpose; what
is it? White pines now show the effects of last year's
drought in our yard and on the Cliffs, the needles faded
and turning red to an alarming extent. I now see
many *Juniperus repens* berries of a handsome light blue
above, being still green beneath, with three hoary
pouting lips. The Garfields had found a burrow of

[1] *Vide* forward. *More.*

IX

MAY, 1855

(ÆT. 37)

May 1. Rained some in the night; cloudy in the
forenoon; clears up in the afternoon.

P. M. — By boat with Sophia to Conantum, a may-
ing.

The water has gone down very fast and the grass
has sprung up. There is a strong, fresh marsh scent
wafted from the meadows, much like the salt marshes.
We sail with a smart wind from the northeast, yet it
is warm enough. Horse-mint is seen springing up,
and for two or three days at the bottom of the river
and on shore. At Hill Shore the *Anemone nemoralis*
to-morrow. See none wide open. The myrtle-bird is
one of the commonest and tamest birds now. It catches
insects like a pewee, darting off from its perch and
returning to it, and sings something like *a-chill chill,
chill chill, chill chill, a-twear, twill twill twee,* or it
may be all *tw* — not loud; a little like the *F. hyemalis,*
or more like pine warbler, — rapid, and more and
more intense as it advances. There is an unaccountable sweetness as of flowers in the air, — a true May-
day. Raw and drizzling in the morning. The grackle
still. What various brilliant and evanescent colors
on the surface of this agitated water, now, as we are
crossing Willow Bay, looking toward the half-con-

young foxes. How old?[1] I see the black feathers of
a blackbird by the Miles Swamp side, and this single
bright-scarlet one shows that it belonged to a red-
wing, which some hawk or quadruped devoured.

[1] Saw the old and tracks of young; thinks they may be one
month old.

cealed sun over the foam-spotted flood! It reminds
me of the sea.

At Clamshell, the *Viola blanda.* I do not look for
pollen. I find a clamshell five inches long (wanting
one sixteenth) and more than two and a half inches
broad and two inches thick. What that little dusky-
colored lichen on the ground at Clamshell end ditch,
with a sort of triangular green fruit? or marchantia?
The maples of Potter's Swamp, seen now nearly half
a mile off against the russet or reddish hillside, are a
very dull scarlet, like Spanish brown, but one against
a green pine wood is much brighter. *Thalictrum
anemonoides* at Conant Cliff. Did not look for pollen.

Why have the white pines at a distance that silvery
(dewy?) look around their edges or thin parts? Is it
owing to the wind showing the under sides of the
needles? Methinks you do not see it in the winter.

Went to Garfield's for the hawk of yesterday. It was
nailed to the barn *in terrorem* and as a trophy. He
gave it to me with an egg. He called it the female,
and probably was right, it was so large. He tried in
vain to shoot the male, which I saw circling about
just out of gunshot and screaming, while he robbed
the nest. He climbed the tree when I was there yesterday afternoon, the tallest white pine or other tree
in its neighborhood, over a swamp, and found two
young, which he thought not more than a fortnight
old, — with only down, at least no feathers, — and
one addled egg, also three or four white-bellied or
deer mouse (*Mus leucopus*), a perch, and a sucker,[1]

[1] I think these must have been dead fish they found.

and a gray rabbit's skin. He had seen squirrels, etc., in other nests. These fishes were now stale. I found the remains of a partridge under the tree. The reason I did not see my hawks at Well Meadow last year was that he found and broke up their nest there, containing five eggs.

The hawk measures exactly 22½ inches in length and 4 feet 4½ inches in alar extent, and weighs 3¼ pounds. The ends of closed wings almost two inches short of end of tail. General color *above* of wings and back an olivaceous brown, thickly barred with waving lines of very dark brown, there being a much broader bar next to the tip of the secondaries and tertiaries; and the first five primaries are nearly black toward the ends. A little white appears, especially on the tertiaries. The wing-coverts and scapulars glossed with purple reflections. The twelve tail-feathers (which MacGillivray says is the number in all birds of prey, *i. e.* the *Falconinæ* and *Striginæ*) showing five and three quarters inches a clear brown red, or rather foxcolor, above, with a narrow dark band within half an inch of the end, which is tipped with dirty white. A slight inclination to dusky bars near the end of one side feather. Lower tail-coverts for nearly an inch white, barred with fox-color. Head and neck a paler, inclining to ferruginous, brown. *Beneath*, breast and wing-linings brown and white, the feathers of first centred with large dark-brown hastate spots, and the wing-linings streaked with ferruginous. Wings white, barred with dusky. "Vent and femorals," as Nuttall says, "pale ochreous." Tail white, softened by the

superior color. I do not perceive that the abdomen is barred.

Bill very *blue* black, with a *short, stout* curved tip, — curving from the cere more than a quarter of a circle, extends not quite a quarter of an inch beyond the lower mandible, — and is proportionally stouter *at tip* than in any of *his Falconinæ*, judging from plates of heads; whole visible, including cere, 1⅛ inches long, and 1 inch deep at base; cere yellowish-green.

Tarsus and toes very pale yellow; claws blue-black. As MacGillivray says of *Buteo*, claws flattened beneath, "that of the middle toe with an inner sharp edge." (He says, as I *gather*, that all the diurnal birds of prey of Great Britain, *i. e. Falconinæ*, have claws either flattened or concave beneath, except *Pandion*, the inner edge of the middle one being more or less sharp, but least so in *Circus*, or harrier.) Tarsus feathered in front one third the way down. The toes for length stand in this order, — the first (or hind), second, fourth, third, the first being the shortest; for stoutness thus, — one, two, three, four. Claws for stoutness follow the same order with the toes. Utmost spread of toes and claws 4½ inches. A considerable web between third and fourth toes.[1] Toes with papillæ not rigid beneath.

The wing extends nearly two feet from the body, and is 10¾ inches wide; from flexure is 15¾ inches. When fully expanded it has a rounded outline and a

[1] In this respect *Circus* and *Falco* much the same; *Aquila* and *Pernis* and *Milvus* have several short webs; *Haliaëtus, Pandion,* and *Accipiter* are free.

ragged appearance owing to the separation of the first five or six primaries, as I noticed the male bird while resting. The first primary short; they stand, first and eighth, seventh, sixth, second, fifth, third, fourth. The fifth and third are about the same length, and the fourth only a quarter of an inch longer than the third. As in the *Buteo vulgaris* of MacGillivray, found in Europe and in our north, the four first primaries "abruptly cut out on the inner web;" the second, third, fourth, and fifth, but *not* the first and sixth, "slightly so on the outer." There are ten primaries and there are fourteen secondaries. (MacGillivray says the primaries of the *Falconinæ* are ten, the secondaries from thirteen to eighteen.) The wing, I see, naturally opens at the primaries.

This is evidently very closely allied to the *Buteo vulgaris*, but apparently the wings are not so long compared with the tail, and there is a difference in the comparative length and stoutness of the toes; the feet of this are not "*bright* yellow," and the upper mandible is much stouter and more recurved at tip, judging from his plate of the head and his description. It is recurved as much as his osprey's.

The ear looked like a large round hole in the side of the head behind the eye.

The egg is a very dirty brownish white, with brown spots about the smaller end, though one end is about as large as the other. It is larger than a hen's egg, — 2⅜ inches by 2.

MacGillivray describes the *Buteo*, as "body full, broad and muscular anteriorly;" "wings long, broad,

rounded, the third or fourth quill longest, the first very short." Of *Haliaëtus* he says, "wings very long, broad, rounded, the fourth and fifth quills longest;" *Aquila*, like last, omitting the "very;" *Pandion*, "wings very long, comparatively narrow, rounded, with thirty quills, the third primary longest, the second nearly equal, the fourth not much shorter, the first longer than the fifth;" *Falco*, "wings very long, pointed, the second quill longest, the first almost as long; primaries ten;" *Accipiter*, "wings long, much rounded; primary quills ten, fourth and fifth longest, first very short;" *Pernis*, "wings very long, broad, rounded, the third quill longest, the first about the length of the sixth;" *Milvus*, "wings extremely long, broad, and pointed, the fourth quill longest . . . first much shorter;" *Circus*, "wings long, much rounded; primary quills ten, the fourth and third longest, the first about equal to the seventh." These the genera of Great Britain.

Says of *Buteo*: "In form and plumage they are very intimately allied to the eagles and sea-eagles, as well as in the form of the bill, which is, however, shorter and less deep towards the end, and of the feet, which differ, notwithstanding, in being proportionally less robust, and in having the claws smaller. . . . Usually fly low, and with less rapidity than the falcons and hawks; sail in circles, like the eagles and some other species, and prey on heavy-flying birds, small quadrupeds, reptiles, and even insects." He says the *Buteo vulgaris* "greatly resembles the golden eagle in his mode of flying," so that he has mistaken them for it at a distance; that he "rarely gives chase to a bird on wing."

Neither he, in this case, nor Wilson nor Nuttall, in the case of the red-tail, speaks of their feeding on fishes.

MacGillivray says the *Falconinæ* lay from two to five eggs, and their cries are "seldom heard except during the breeding season." "When the young have longitudinal spots on the breast, the old have them transverse."

I do not find much in MacGillivray about the breeding-season of the *Falconinæ*. He says the white-tailed sea eagle (*Haliaëtus albicilla*) begins to prepare a nest some time in March, and the kestrel near the end of March, and the young of the golden eagle "are fledged about the end of July." Nuttall says the white-headed eagle begins to lay early in February, that with *Falco peregrinus* incubation "commences in winter, or very early in the spring," and that the osprey begins to lay early in May. This is all to the purpose about the season of incubation of hawks and eagles.

Early in spring I occasionally see hen-hawks perched about river, and approach quite near them, but never at any other time.

This hawk's flesh had a very disagreeable rank scent, as I was cutting it up, though fresh, — cutting off the wings, etc., etc.

I found the feathers of a partridge under the tree where the nest was.

What I have called the frog hawk is probably the male hen-harrier, Nuttall's *Circus cyaneus*, which he says is the same with the European. MacGillivray

refers to *C. Americanus* (?) and says the question of identity is undecided, and the large brown bird with white rump is the female.[1]

(Probably my small brown hawk is the *Falco fuscus*, or sharp-shinned.)

MacGillivray says the harrier occasionally eats dead fish and also will catch a chicken, not a hen. *Sometimes* catches its prey in open flight. Will hunt on the same beat at the same hour, for many days, according to Jardine (MacGillivray says that the golden eagle "seeks for *live* prey at a small height over the surface"); sail in circles. "The male, after the first autumnal moult, acquires in a considerable degree the plumage of the adult." "The change of plumage is effected in the autumn of the year after it leaves the nest, and not in the same year." The female used to be regarded as a distinct species called the "Ring-tail. Country people name it Blue Kite, Blue Hawk, Ring-tail, Brown Kite, or Gled; and the Highlanders call it Breid-air-toin (rag-on-rump), on account of the white tail-coverts conspicuous in both sexes."

May 2. P. M. — By boat up Assabet.

Quince begins to leaf, and pear; perhaps some of last earlier. Aspen leaves of young trees — or twenty to twenty-five feet high — an inch long suddenly; say yesterday began; not till the 11th last year. Leafing, then, is differently affected by the season from flowering. The leafing is apparently comparatively earlier this year than the flowering. The young aspens

[1] *Vide* Wilson.

are the first of indigenous trees conspicuously leafed. Diervilla, say began to leaf with viburnums. *Amelanchier Botryapium* yesterday leafed. That small native willow now in flower, or say yesterday, just before leaf, — for the first seem to be bracts, — two to seven or eight feet high, very slender and curving. Apparently has three or four lanceolate toothed bracts at base of petioled catkin; male three quarters and female one inch long; scales black and silky-haired; ovary oblong-oval, stalked, downy, with a small yellowish gland not so long as its stalk. See leaf by and by. Saw many crow blackbirds day before yesterday. Vigorous look the little spots of triangular sedge (?) springing up on the river-banks, five or six inches high, yellowish below, glaucous and hoary atop, straight and rigid. Many clamshells have round brassy-colored spots as big as a fourpence. Found one opened by rats last winter, almost entirely the color of tarnished brass within. Open the Assabet spring. The anemone is well named, for see now the *nemorosa*, amid the fallen brush and leaves, trembling in the wind, so fragile. Hellebore seems a little later than the cabbage.

Was that a harrier seen at first skimming low then soaring and circling, with a broad whiteness on the wings beneath?

May 3. P. M. — To Assabet Bath.

Small pewee; *tchevet*, with a jerk of the head. Hardhack leafed two or maybe three days in one place. Early pyrus leafed yesterday or day before, if I have not named it. The skull of a horse, — not a mare,

for I did not see the two small canine teeth in the upper jaw, nor in the under, — six molars on each side, above and below, and six incisors to each jaw. I first observed the stillness of birds, etc., at noon, with the increasing warmth, on the 23d of April. Sitting on the bank near the stone-heaps, I see large suckers rise to catch insects, — sometimes leap. A butterfly one inch in alar extent, dark velvety brown with slate-colored tips, on dry leaves. On the north of Groton Turnpike beyond Abel Hosmer's, three distinct terraces to river; first annually overflowed, say twenty-five or thirty rods wide, second seven or eight feet higher and forty or sixty wide, third forty feet higher still. Sweet-fern opened apparently yesterday. *Vaccinium Pennsylvanicum* began to leaf yesterday. Young red maple leaf to-morrow; also some white birch, and perhaps sugar maple.

Humphrey Buttrick, one of eight who alone returned from Texas out of twenty-four, says he can find woodcock's eggs; now knows of several nests; has seen them setting with snow around them; and that Melvin has seen partridges' eggs some days ago. He has seen crows building this year. Found in a hen-hawk's nest once the legs of a cat. Has known of several goshawks' nests (or what he calls some kind of eagle; Garfield called it the Cape eagle); one in a shrub oak, with eggs. Last year his dog caught seven black ducks so far grown that he got sixty cents a pair for them; takes a pretty active dog to catch such. He frequently finds or hears of them. Knew of a nest this year. Also finds wood ducks' nests. Has very often seen partridges drum close to him. Has watched one for an hour. They strike the body with their wings. He shot a white-headed eagle from Carlisle Bridge. It fell in the water, and his dog was glad to let it alone. He suggested that my fish hawks found pouts in holes made by ice.

May 4. A robin sings when I, in the house, cannot distinguish the earliest dawning from the full moonlight. His song first advertised me of the daybreak, when I thought it was night, as I lay looking out into the full moonlight. I heard a robin begin his strain, and yielded the point to him, believing that he was better acquainted with the springs of the day than I, — with the signs of day.

5 A. M. — To Hill.

Many red-wings and grackles feeding together on meadows. They still fly in flocks. Some dark-ash; are they female grackles? Hear a brown thrasher. Yellow lily pads are just beginning to show themselves on the surface, the first noticeable on the water. All kinds of young maples, and some limbs of large white, begin to leaf. Red maple blossoms begin to cover ground. Ostrya will leaf to-morrow. The second amelanchier, sweet-fern, and early thorn begin to leaf to-day. Small white-barked shrub (andromeda?) on Island Neck begins to leaf to-morrow.[1] I think I hear a warbling vireo.[2]

Birds. Still see three or four crows together, though some at least are building. Jays do not scream as

[1] Or say 7th, and then slow.   [2] Certainly the 10th.

early. Chickadee, spring notes still. Partridges setting. Have noticed no ducks for some days. All the *black* blackbirds as plenty as ever, and in flocks. Have not noticed robins in flocks for two or three days. See no gulls, nor *F. hyemalis*[1] nor tree sparrows now. Red-tail hawk young fourteen days old. Snipes feeding in numbers on the 29th April. Yellow redpolls in numbers May 1st. Woodcocks setting. Purple finch sings steadily. Myrtle-birds numerous, and sing their *tea lee, tea lee* in morning. White-throated sparrows here, and numerous. No goldfinches for long time. The water is now generally off the meadows.

P. M. — To beeches.

In cut woods a small thrush, with crown inclining to rufous, tail foxy, and edges of wings dark-ash; clear white beneath. I think the golden-crowned? See more white-throated sparrows than any other bird to-day in various parts of our walk, generally feeding in numbers on the ground in open dry fields and meadows next to woods, then flitting through the woods. Hear only that sharp, lisping *chip* (?) from them. A partridge's grayish tail - feather, with a subterminal dark band. Several larger thrushes on low limbs and on ground, with a dark eye (not the white around it of the wood thrush) and, I think, the nankeen spot on the secondaries. A hermit thrush?

Sitting in Abel Brooks's Hollow, see a small hawk go over high in the air, with a long tail and distinct from wings. It advanced by a sort of limping flight yet

[1] Think I saw one to-day.

rapidly, not circling nor tacking, but flapping briskly at intervals and then gliding straight ahead with rapidity, controlling itself with its tail. It seemed to be going a journey. Was it not the sharp-shinned, or *Falco fuscus?* I think that what I have called the sparrow hawk falsely, and latterly pigeon hawk, is also the sharp-shinned (*vide* April 26th and May 8th, 1854, and April 16th, 1855),[1] for the pigeon hawk's tail is white-barred.

Found a black snake's skeleton. Remarked the globular protuberance on which the vertebræ revolve, and the four (?) sharp, recurved teeth in the lower jaw.

Red cherry not *generally* leafing before yesterday. Sand cherry yesterday leafs. See where a skunk has probed last night, and large black dung with apparently large ants' heads and earth or sand and stubble or insects' wings in it; probably had been probing a large ants' hill. Was that a ⌇⌇ cerasus or prunus on Pine Hill, thus from ⌇⌇ wood-pile? AB two rods west. The beech ⌇⌇ leaf-buds are very handsome reddish-brown now, some nearly an inch and a half long and very slender, not more than a sixth of an inch in diameter and regularly swelling from each end; will open, apparently, in three or four days. The blossom-buds are still larger; may bloom in eight days. Potentilla out.

What that plant in Baker's Pool, with sessile spatulate leaves toothed at end, now four or five inches high?

Noticed a perfectly regular circular concavity in

[1] And July, 1858.

a sandy soil in a hollow in birch woods, where apparently a partridge had dusted herself.

Yesterday a great many spotted and wood tortoises in the Sam Wheeler birch-fence meadow pool, which dries up. One of the former gradually settled itself into the sod by turning round and round and scratching with its claws.

A shower.

May 5. P. M. — To Beck Stow's.

Cold weather for several days. Canada plum and cultivated cherry and Missouri currant look as if they would bloom to-morrow. The sugar maples on the Common have just begun to show their stamens peeping out of the bud, but that by Dr. Barrett's has them an inch and a half long or more.

The trees and shrubs which I observe to make a show now with their green, without regard to the time when they began, are (to put them in the order of their intensity and generalness): —

Gooseberry, both kinds
Raspberry
Meadow-sweet
Choke-cherry *shoots*
Some young trembles
Very young apples
Red currant, and probably black
Pyrus, probably *arbutifolia*
Young black cherry
Thimble-berry
Probably wild red cherry in *some* places
Salix alba with bracts (?)
Some small native willows

Cultivated cherry
Some mountain-ash (*i. e.* European)
Some horse-chestnut

Excepting the *S. alba*, I am inclined to stop with the *Pyrus arbutifolia*.

The *Andromeda Polifolia* will apparently open about the 10th. High blueberry began to leaf in some places yesterday. Larch began to leaf, say when it opened, the 28th of April, but not noticeably till to-day. I find one bundle with needles a quarter of an inch long and spreading.

The small andromeda has lost its reddish leaves, probably about the time it blossomed, and I can neither get the red cathedral-window light looking toward the now westering sun in a most favorable position, nor the gray colors in the other direction, but it is all a grayish green. But the patches of cranberry in the swamp, seen at some distance toward the sun, are a beautiful crimson, which travels with you, keeping between you and the sun, like some rare plant in bloom there densely. I could not believe it was cranberry.

Looking over my book, I found I had done my errands, and said to myself I would find a crow's nest. (I had heard a crow scold at a passing hawk a quarter of an hour before.) I had hardly taken this resolution when, looking up, I saw a crow wending his way across an interval in the woods towards the highest pines in the swamp, on which he alighted. I directed my steps to them and was soon greeted with an angry *caw*, and, within five minutes from my resolve, I detected a new nest close to the top of the tallest white pine in the swamp.

A crow circled cawing about it within gunshot, then over me surveying, and, perching on an oak directly over my head within thirty-five feet, cawed angrily. But suddenly, as if having taken a new resolution, it flitted away, and was joined by its mate and two more, and they went off silently a quarter of a mile or more and lit in a pasture, as if they had nothing to concern them in the wood.

May 6. The young sugar maples leafing are more conspicuous now than any maples. Black oak buds are large and silvery. Peach leafed yesterday.

P. M. — To epigæa.

Salix alba opened yesterday. Gilead not leafing yet, but perhaps to-morrow? A robin's nest with two eggs, betrayed by peeping. On the 30th of April a phœbe flew out from under the arched bridge; probably building.

Saw again a slender vireo-like bird (seen yesterday, near R. Brown's); head somewhat crested behind; made me think of small pewee, — catches insects somewhat like it. *As I remember*, maybe ashy-white beneath, dusky-olive above, with two whitish bars on wings and dusky tail. Can it be the solitary vireo? *Equisetum sylvaticum*, probably yesterday or day before. Strawberry. That low sedge-like plant under Clamshell very common, with brownish, somewhat umbelled spikes, probably *Luzula campestris* (?), one of the wood rushes. *Viola lanceolata*, yesterday at least. High blackberry has begun to leaf; say two days. Hear near Second Division the *er er twe*,

ter ter twe, evergreen-forest note. Bright-yellow head and shoulders and beneath, and dark legs and bill-catching insects along base of pitch pine plumes, some, what creeper-like; very active and restless, darting from tree to tree; darted at and drove off a chickadee. I find I have thus described its colors last year at various times, *viz.*: black throat, this often with dark and light beneath; again, black streak from eyes, slate-colored back (?), forked tail, white beneath (?); another bird with yellow throat near by, perhaps female; again, June 17, black wings with white bars (?). Is it black-throated green, or Latham's yellow-fronted, or the golden-winged warbler? From Wilson I should think it the last, which he thinks the same with Pennant and Latham's yellow-front.

The small juncus at Second Division shows a field of dark green with reddish top, the flower just beginning to peep out; this the earliest plant of this kind to make a show; more than a foot high. Epigæa in full bloom.

Myrtle-birds very numerous just beyond Second Division. They sing like an instrument, *teee teee te, t t t, t t t*, on very various keys, *i. e.* high or low, sometimes beginning like *phe-be*. As I sat by roadside one drew near, perched within ten feet, and dived once or twice with a curve to catch the little black flies about my head, coming once within three feet, not minding me much. I could not tell at first what attracted it toward me. It saw them from twenty-five feet off. There was a little swarm of small flies, regularly fly-like with large shoulders, about my head. Many white-throated sparrows there.

Road full of cattle going up country.

Heard at a distance a ruby(?)-crowned wren, so robin-like and spirited. After saw one within ten or fifteen feet. Dark bill and legs, apparently dark olivaceous ashy head, a *little* whitish before and behind the full black eyes, ash breast, olive-yellow on primaries, with a white bar, dark tail and ends of wings, white belly and vent. Did not notice vermilion spot on hindhead. It darted off from apple tree for insects like a pewee, and returned to within ten feet of me as if curious. I think this the only *Regulus* I have ever seen.

Near Jenny Dugan's, perceive that unaccountable fugacious fragrance, as of all flowers, bursting forth in air, not near a meadow, which perhaps I first perceived on May 1st. It is the general fragrance of the year. I am almost afraid I shall trace it to some particular plant. It surpasses all particular fragrances. I am not sitting near any flower that I can perceive.

Two or three rods this side of John Hosmer's pitch pines, beyond Clamshell, some white *Viola ovata*, some with a faint bluish tinge.

A beautiful sunset, the sun behind a gilt-edged cloud, with a clear bright crimson space beneath.

May 7. 5 A. M. — To Island.

Finger-cold and windy. The sweet-flags showed themselves about in the pads. Hear Maryland yellow-throat. Many grackles still in flocks singing on trees, male and female, the latter a very dark or black ash, but with silvery eye. I suspect the red-wings are building. Large white maples began to leaf yesterday at least, generally; one now shows considerably across the river. The aspen is earlier. *Viburnum dentatum* yesterday leafed. Bass to-morrow (some shoots sheltered now).

A crow's nest near the top of a pitch pine about twenty feet high, just completed, betrayed by the birds' cawing and alarm.[1] As on the 5th, *one* came and sat on a bare oak within forty feet, cawed, reconnoitred; and then both flew off to a distance, while I discovered and climbed to the nest within a dozen rods. One comes near to spy you first. It was about sixteen inches over, of the pitch pine dead twigs laid across the forks, and white oak leaves and bark fibres laid copiously on them; the cavity deep, and more than half covered and concealed with a roof of leaves; a long, sloping approach or declivity left on one side the nest.

Red currant out.

P. M. — To Lee's Cliff *via* Hubbard's Bath.

Viola cucullata apparently a day or two. A ladybug and humblebee, the last probably some time. A lily wholly above water, and yellow, in Skull-Cap Meadow, ready to open.[2] See *Rana fontinalis*.

Climbed to two crows' nests, — or maybe one of them a squirrel's, — in Hubbard's Grove. Do they not sometimes use a squirrel's nest for a foundation? A ruby-crested wren is apparently attracted and eyes me. It is wrenching and fatiguing, as well as dirty,

[1] A mistake.
[2] On the 12th I observed it sunk beneath the water.

work to climb a tall pine with nothing, or maybe only dead twigs and stubs, to hold by. You must proceed with great deliberation and see well where you put your hands and your feet. Saw probably a female *Falco fuscus* sail swift and low close by me and alight on a rail fence. It was a rich, very dark, perhaps reddish slate brown. I saw some white under the head; no white on rump. Wings thickly barred with dark beneath. It then flew and alighted on a maple. Did not fly so irregularly as the last one I called by this name. The early willow on the left beyond the bridge has begun to leaf, but by no means yet the one on the right. Scared up two gray squirrels in the Holden wood, which ran glibly up the tallest trees on the opposite side to me, and leaped across from the extremity of the branches to the next trees, and so on very fast ahead of me. Remembering — aye, aching with — my experience in climbing trees this afternoon and morning, I could not but admire their exploits. To see them travelling with so much swiftness and ease that road over which I climbed a few feet with such painful exertion!

A partridge flew up from within three or four feet of me with a loud whir, and betrayed one cream-colored egg in a little hollow amid the leaves. Hear the tweezer-bird. It looks like a bluish slate above, with a greenish(?)-yellow back and bright orange-yellow throat and breast, forked tail, two white bars on wings, whitish vent. Another, probably female, paler bluish, with fainter yellow and a conspicuous black crescent on breast. This is undoubtedly the parti-colored warbler,

Vol. VII

i. e. Brewer's blue yellow-back (*Sylvia Americana* of Latham and Audubon, *pusilla* of Wilson). *Vide* June 18th, 1854 and May 9th, 1853. I believe the yellow-rumped warbler has a note somewhat like the tweezer's.

Climbed a hemlock to a very large and complete, probably gray squirrel's, nest, eighteen inches [in] diameter, — a foundation of twigs, on which a body of leaves and some bark fibres, lined with the last, and the whole covered with many fresh green hemlock twigs one foot or more long with the leaves on, — which had been gnawed off, — and many strewed the ground beneath, having fallen off. Entrance one side.

A short distance beyond this and the hawk's-nest pine, I observed a middling-sized red oak standing a little aslant on the side-hill over the swamp, with a pretty large hole in one side about fifteen feet from the ground, where apparently a limb on which a felled tree lodged had been cut some years before and so broke out a cavity. I thought that such a hole was too good a one not to be improved by some inhabitant of the wood. Perhaps the gray squirrels I had just seen had their nest there. Or was not the entrance big enough to admit a screech owl? So I thought I would tap on it and put my ear to the trunk and see if I could hear anything stirring within it, but I heard nothing. Then I concluded to look into it. So I shinned up, and when I reached up one hand to the hole to pull myself up by it, the thought passed through my mind perhaps something may take hold my fingers, but nothing did. The first limb was nearly opposite to the hole, and, resting on this, I looked in, and, to my great surprise,

there squatted, filling the hole, which was about six inches deep and five to six wide, a salmon-brown bird not so big as a partridge, seemingly asleep within three inches of the top and close to my face. It was a minute or two before I made it out to be an owl. It was a salmon-brown or fawn (?) above, the feathers shafted with small blackish-brown somewhat hastate (?) marks, *grayish* toward the ends of the wings and tail, as far as I could see. A large white circular space about or behind eye, banded in rear by a pretty broad (one third of an inch) and quite conspicuous perpendicular *dark*-brown stripe. Egret, say one and a quarter inches long, sharp, triangular, reddish-brown without mainly. It lay crowded in that small space, with its tail somewhat bent up and one side of its head turned up with one egret, and its large dark eye open only by a long slit about a sixteenth of an inch wide; visible breathing. After a little while I put in one hand and stroked it repeatedly, whereupon it reclined its head a little lower and closed its eye entirely. Though curious to know what was under it, I disturbed it no farther at that time.

In the meanwhile, the crows were making a great cawing amid and over the pine-tops beyond the swamp, and at intervals I heard the scream of a hawk, probably the surviving male hen-hawk, whom they were pestering (unless they had discovered the male screech owl), and a part of them came cawing about me. This was a very fit place for hawks and owls to dwell in, — the thick woods just over a white spruce swamp, in which the glaucous kalmia grows; the gray squirrels, partridges, hawks, and owls, all together. It was probably these screech owls which I heard in moonlight nights hereabouts last fall. *Vide* end of this day.

Birch leafs to-day; probably some yesterday, with white maple. The Conantum thorn (cockspur?) leafs with earliest. That little red-stemmed (?) moss has now yellow-green oval fruit hanging densely in the sod. Sweet-briar shoots two inches long; this one of the earlier roses to leaf. Put it with early rose. The *Rubus triflorus* up two inches or more. Put it next after raspberry for present.

Polygonatum pubescens at Lee's, in three or four days. *Amelanchier Botryapium* on rocks, partly open; will probably shed pollen to-morrow. The long, narrow unfolded flower-buds, *rose-pink* without, are very pretty with the dark-*purplish* leaves, — prettier than the open ones, — like little cigarettes, to compare fair with foul. The dark-purple fruit-like fascicles of the staminate flowers of the ash on the rocks are now very remarkable, about the size of pignuts, and looking somewhat like them against the sky on the perfectly bare tree, or like dry alder scales or cones; will shed pollen in a day or two. Oftener one *pedicelled* anther and stamen than two together in the very minute calyx, — if it is one. Young bass from seed an inch high, the two leaves remarkably cut.

Returning by owl's nest, about one hour before sunset, I climbed up and looked in again. The owl was gone, but there were four nearly round *dirty brownish white*[1] eggs, quite warm, on nothing but the

[1] MacGillivray describes no eggs of this color, — only white, —

bits of rotten wood which made the bottom of the hole. The eggs were very nearly as large at one end as the other, slightly oblong, $1\frac{3}{8}$ inches by $1\frac{2}{8}$, as nearly as I could measure. I took out one. It would probably have hatched within a week, the young being considerably feathered and the bill remarkably developed. Perhaps she heard me coming, and so left the nest. My bird corresponds in color, as far as I saw it, with Wilson's *Strix asio*, but not his *nævia*, which Nuttall and others consider a young (?) bird, though the egg was not pure white. I do not remember that my bird was barred or *mottled* at all.[1]

Nuttall says, Little Screech-Owl: Greenland to Florida; chiefly prey on mice; also small birds, beetles, crickets, etc.; nest in May and June, and lined with etc., etc., eggs four to six; several bluebirds, blackbirds, and song sparrows in one. In cloudy weather come out earlier. Wilson's thrush attacked one. Note in autumn, " hō, hŏ hŏ hŏ hŏ hŏ hŏ, proceeding from high and clear to a low guttural shake or trill."

Was not that an owl's feather which I found half a mile beyond, downy more than half, and with base and separate white *points* beyond a dark band at the end?

Was not mine a bird of last year? But MacGillivray says of owls that the young differ very little from the old; "the older the individual becomes, the more simple is the colouring; the dark markings diminish

and the same with Nuttall, except the great gray owl. [Screech owl's eggs, *when clean*, are always white.]

[1] *Vide* the 12th.

in extent, and the finer mottlings are gradually obliterated." *Rhus Toxicodendron* under rocks leafs.

May 8. 5 A. M. — To Gilead.[1]
Still finger-cold. Think I saw bank swallows.[2]

At noon begins a cold, drizzling rain, which continues at intervals through the next day. A cold May storm, wind easterly. Grackle here still. Cultivated cherry opened flower yesterday. The rock maples (such sized as we *generally* have) come on faster and show more now than the red.

May 9. P. M. — To Annursnack.
The black currant will not bloom for five or six days. A *large* red maple just begun to leaf — its keys an inch and a half long — by Assabet Bridge. Castilleja show red, — *one*, — but will not bloom under a week probably. The same of erigeron. *Cornus alternifolia* and *paniculata* begin to leaf. Scared up three quails in the stubble in G. M. Barrett's orchard. They go off partridge-like from within two rods, with a sharp, whistling whir. Heard, methinks, a whitethroated sparrow (?) sing very much like the beginning of a catbird's song. Could see no other bird. Thought it a catbird at first. See several of these sparrows yet.

May 10. Canada plum opens petals to-day and leafs. Domestic plum only leafs. Summer yellowbird.
P. M. — To Beeches.

[1] Began to leaf yesterday.   [2] Not at all certain.

Young red maples are *generally* later to leaf than young sugar maples; hardly began before yesterday; and large white are not so forward as young sugar. Muhlenberg's willow leafed four or five days. Young yellow birch leaf, say two days. In Callitriche Pool hear a bullfrog belch or dump. Is that a proserpinaca with finely divided leaves in this pool? Hear a treetoad, — or, maybe, a woodpecker tapping. A juncus in Hubbard's Close two feet high and big as a crow's quill. Round-leafed cornel leaf to-morrow; also pignut leaf to-day in some places. The beech leaf-buds are more back[ward], apparently, than chestnut, but some leaves are expanding with the flower-buds, which are now opened so as to show the separate buds. *Vaccinium Pennsylvanicum*, early blueberry, in bloom; probably may shed pollen. A yellow redpoll still.

May 11. A. M. — To Island.
Only the lower limbs of bass begin to leaf yet, — yesterday. A crow blackbird's nest, about eight feet up a white maple over water, — a large, loose nest without, some eight inches high, between a small twig and main trunk, composed of coarse bark shreds and dried last year's grass, without mud; within deep and size of robin's nest; with four pale-green eggs, streaked and blotched with black and brown. Took one. Young bird not begun to form. Hear and see yellow-throat vireo. See oat-seed spawn — a mass as big as fist — on bottom; of brown jelly composed of smaller globules, each with a fish-like tadpole, color of a seed.

P. M. — To *Andromeda Polifolia*.

Some young elms begin to leaf. Butternut leafs apparently to-morrow. Larger rock maples not yet begun to leaf, — later considerably than large white maples, and somewhat than large red. Apparently andromeda will not open before the 15th or 16th, and the buck-bean, now just budded above the water, not before the 20th. *Juniperus repens* will not open, apparently, before the 14th or 15th. Canoe birch just sheds pollen. Very handsome drooping golden catkins, sometimes two or three together, some five and a quarter inches long. The leaves of some young sprouts already three-quarters inch over, but of the trees not started. The second amelanchier just sheds pollen, in a swamp.

I trod on a large black snake, which, as soon as I stepped again, went off swiftly down the hill toward the swamp, with head erect like a racer. Looking closely, I found another left behind, partly concealed by the dry leaves. They were lying amid the leaves in this open wood east of Beck Stow's, amid the sweet-fern and huckleberry bushes. The remaining one ran out its tongue at me, and vibrated its tail swiftly, making quite a noise on the leaves; then darted forward, passed round an oak, and *whipped* itself straight down into a hole at its base one and a half inches over. After its head had entered, its tail was not long in following.

You can hardly walk in a thick pine wood now, especially a swamp, but presently you will have a crow or two over your head, either silently flitting over, to spy what you would be at and if its nest is in danger,

or angrily cawing. It is most impressive when, looking for their nests, you first detect the presence of the bird by its shadow.

Was not that a bay-wing which I heard sing, — *ah, twar twe twar, twit twit twit twit, twe?* *Viola pedata* sheds pollen,[1] — the first I have chanced to see.

I hear some kind of owl partially hooting now at 4 P. M., I know not whether far off or near.

May 12. Cold enough for a fire this many a day.

6 A. M. — To Hill.

I hear the myrtle-bird's[2] *te-e-e, te-e-e, t t t, t t t,* clear flute-like whistle, and see eight or ten crow blackbirds together.

P. M. — To Lee's Cliff.

C. says he saw upland plover two or three nights ago. The sweet-gale begins to leaf. I perceive the fragrance of the *Salix alba*, now in bloom, more than an eighth of a mile distant. They now adorn the causeways with their yellow blossoms and resound with the hum of bumblebees, etc., etc. I have found half a dozen robins' nests with eggs already, — one in an elm, two in a *Salix alba*, one in a *Salix nigra*, one in a pitch pine, etc., etc. I find the partridge-nest of the 7th partially covered with dry oak leaves, and two more eggs only, three in all, cold. Probably the bird is killed.

As I approached the owl's nest, I saw her run past the hole up into that part of the hollow above it, and

[1] A *great many* out on the 13th.   [2] White-throat sparrow's.

Vol. VII

probably she was there when I thought she had flown on the 7th. I looked in, and at first did not know what I saw. One of the three remaining eggs was hatched, and a little downy *white* young one, two or three times as long as an egg, lay helpless between the two remaining eggs. Also a dead white-bellied mouse (*Mus leucopus*) lay with them, its tail curled round one of the eggs. Wilson says of his red owl (*Strix asio*), — with which this apparently corresponds, and not with the mottled, though my egg is not "pure white," — that "the young are at first covered with a whitish down." *Heard* an oven-bird.

Passing on into the Miles meadow, was struck by the interesting tender green of the just springing foliage of the aspens, apples, cherries (more reddish), etc. It is now especially interesting while you can see through it, and also the tender yellowish-green grass shooting up in the bare river meadows and prevailing over the dark and sere.

Watched a black and white creeper from Bittern Cliff, a very neat and active bird, exploring the limbs on all sides and looking three or four ways almost at once for insects. Now and then it raises its head a *little*, opens its bill, and, without closing it, utters its faint *seeser seeser seeser*.

From beyond the orchard saw a large bird far over the Cliff Hill, which, with my glass, I soon made out to be a fish hawk advancing. Even at that distance, half a mile off, I distinguished its gull-like body, — pirate-like fishing body fit to dive, — and that its wings did not curve upward at the ends like a hen-hawk's

(at least I could not see that they did), but rather hung down. It came on steadily, bent on fishing, with long and *heavy* undulating wings, with an easy, sauntering flight, over the river to the pond, and hovered over Pleasant Meadow a long time, hovering from time to time in one spot, when more than a hundred feet high, then making a very short circle or two and hovering again, then sauntering off against the woodside. At length he reappeared, passed downward over the shrub oak plain and alighted on an oak (of course now bare), standing this time apparently lengthwise on the limb. Soon took to wing again and went to fishing down the stream a hundred feet high. When just below Bittern Cliff, I observed by its motions that it observed something. It made a broad circle of observation in its course, lowering itself somewhat; then, by one or two steep sidewise flights, it reached the water, and, as near as intervening trees would let me see, skimmed over it and endeavored to clutch its prey in passing. It failed the first time, but probably succeeded the second. Then it leisurely winged its way to a tall bare tree on the east end of the Cliffs, and there we left it apparently pluming itself. It had a very white belly, and indeed appeared all white beneath its body. I saw broad black lines between the white crown and throat.

The brown thrasher is a powerful singer; he is a quarter of a mile off across the river, when he sounded within fifteen rods. Hear the night-warbler.

Slippery elm leaf more forward than the common; say yesterday; only young common yet. White ash begins to shed pollen at Lee's; yesterday, or possibly day before, but no leaves on the same. Hear the first creak of a cricket beneath the rocks there, so serene and composing. Methinks it surpasses the song of all birds; sings from everlasting to everlasting. Apparently a thousand little slender catchflies shooting up on the top of the cliff. The red oak there leafed a day or two, or one day earlier than hickory, and the black near it not yet. *Rhus radicans* leafed there a day or two. See one white-throat sparrow still.

The hearing of the cricket whets my eyes. I see one or two long lighter and smoother streaks across the rippled pond from west to east, which preserve their form remarkably, only are bent somewhat at last. The zephyr does not strike the surface from over the broad button-bush row till after a rod or so, leaving a perfectly smooth border, with a fine, irregular shaded edge where the rippling begins. I now begin to distinguish where at a distance the *Amelanchier Botryapium*, with its white against the russet, is waving in the wind.

Under Lee's Cliff, about one rod east of the ash, am surprised to find some pale-yellow columbines, — not a tinge of scarlet, — the leaves and stem also not purplish, but a yellowish and light green, with leaves differently shaped from the common, the parts, both flower and leaves, more slender, and the leaves not so flat, but inclining to fold. One flower of the *Polygonatum pubescens* open there; probably may shed pollen to-morrow.

Returning over Conantum, I directed my glass

Vol. VII

toward the dead tree on Cliffs, and was surprised to see the fish hawk still sitting there, about an hour after he first alighted; and now I found that he was eating a fish, which he had under his feet on the limb and ate as I have already described. At this distance his whole head looked white with his breast.

Just before sundown, took our seats before the owl's nest and sat perfectly still and awaited her appearance. We sat about half an hour, and it was surprising what various distinct sounds we heard there deep in the wood, as if the aisles of the wood were so many eartrumpets, — the cawing of crows, the peeping of hylas in the swamp and perhaps the croaking of a tree-toad, the oven-bird, the *yorrick* of Wilson's thrush, a distant stake-driver, the night-warbler and black and white creeper, the lowing of cows, the late supper horn, the voices of boys, the singing of girls, — not all together but separately, distinctly, and musically, from where the partridge and the red-tailed hawk and the screech owl sit on their nests.

May 13. P. M. — Down river and to Yellow Birch Swamp.

Yesterday was the first warm day for a week or two, and to-day it is much warmer still and hazy — as much like summer as it can be without the trees being generally leafed. I saw a *Fringilla hyemalis* this morning and heard the golden robin, now that the elms are beginning to leaf, also the myrtle-bird's *tealee*. The earliest gooseberry in garden has opened.

As we float down the river through the still and hazy

air, enjoying the June-like warmth, see the first kingbirds on the bare black willows with their broad white breasts and white-tipped tails; and the sound of the first bobolink was floated to us from over the meadows; now that the meadows are lit by the tender yellow green of the willows and the silvery-green fruit of the elms. I heard from a *female* red-wing that peculiar rich screwing warble — not *o gurgle ee* — made with *r*, not with *l*. The whole air too is filled with the ring of toads louder than heretofore. Some men are already fishing, indistinctly seen through the haze. Under the hop-hornbeam below the monument, observed a large pellet, apparently dropped by some bird of prey, consisting of mouse-hair, with an oat or two in it undigested, which probably the mouse had swallowed. This reminded me that I had read this kind of birds digested the flesh of the animals they swallowed, but not the vegetable food in the stomachs of the latter. The air is filled with the song of birds, — warbling vireo, gold robin, yellowbirds, and occasionally the bobolink. The gold robin, just come, is heard in all parts of the village. I see both male and female. It is a remarkable difference between this day and yesterday, that yesterday this and the bobolink were not heard and now the former, at least, is so musical and omnipresent. Even see boys a-bathing, though they must find it cold. I saw yesterday some of that common orange rust-like fungus already on a *Potentilla simplex* leaf. Hear the first catbird, more clear and tinkling than the thrasher. Left the boat below N. Barrett's and walked inland. Saw several handsome red-winged grass-

hoppers in different parts of our walk; but though we saw where they alighted, yet several times we could not find them in the grass for all that. The bayberry apparently will not open under a week. There are now a great many *Viola pedata*. The brook in Yellow Birch Swamp is very handsome now — broad and full, with the light-green hellebore eighteen inches high and the small two-leaved Solomon's-seal about it, in the open wood. Only a part of the yellow birches are leafing, but not yet generally the large ones. I notice no catkins. One white birch sheds pollen. The white birches on the side of Ponkawtasset are beginning to show faint streaks of yellowish green here and there.

A cooler and stronger wind from the east by midafternoon.

The large bass trees now begin to leaf.

Now, about two hours before sunset, the brown thrashers are particularly musical. One seems to be contending in song with another. The chewink's strain sounds quite humble in comparison.

At 9.30 P. M. I hear from our gate my night-warbler. Never heard it in the village before.

I doubt if we shall at any season hear more birds singing than now.[1]

Saw an amelanchier with downy leaf (apparently *oblongifolia*) on the southeast edge of Yellow Birch Swamp, about eighteen feet high and five or six inches in diameter, — a clump of them about as big as an apple tree.

[1] [This sentence is queried in the margin.]

May 14. Our peaches begin to bloom; others probably earlier. Domestic plums open; some *maybe* yesterday. Missouri currant open yesterday or day before. One apple on a roof open. The beech blossom in house opens; say to-morrow in woods, and probably will leaf generally by the next day. Second gooseberry in garden open. White ash begins to leaf; and waxwork. Clethra leafs. High blueberry open by Hubbard's Bath. Black scrub oak leafs, and chinquapin. Red choke-berry leafed, *say* two days later than black.

P. M. — To Cliffs *via* Hubbard's Bath.

See a male hen-harrier skimming low along the side of the river, often within a foot of the muddy shore, looking for frogs, with a very compact flock of small birds, probably swallows, in pursuit. Occasionally he alights and walks or hops flutteringly a foot or two over the ground. The Lombardy poplar and silvery white leafed at least two days ago. *Vaccinium vacillans* leafed, and perhaps flower opened, if that is one near West Fair Haven Spring. Some hickories, just opening their leaves, make quite a show with the red inner sides of the bud-scales turned back. All the oak leaves off the shrub oak plain, except apparently a few white oaks. Some gaylussacias leafed. Uva-ursi at Cliffs out some time, and some new shoots leafing.

Under the dead pine on which the fish hawk sat on the 12th *inst.*, a half-mile from the river, I find a few fish bones — one, I am pretty sure from comparison, the jaw of a pout. So that in three instances, the only ones observed this year, they were feeding on pouts. Probably the mice, etc., had picked up the rest of his

droppings. Thus these inhabitants of the interior get a taste of fish from time to time, — crumbs from the fish hawk's table.

Prinos verticillatus leafs.

May 15. P. M. — To Beck Stow's.

Suddenly very warm. Hear a hummingbird in the garden. Pear blossomed, — some perhaps yesterday. Locust, black and scarlet oak, and *some* buttonwoods leaf. A yellow butterfly. I hear from the top of a pitch pine in the swamp that loud, clear, familiar whistle which I have sometimes wrongly referred to the wood pewee, — *whip-ter-phe-ee*. Is it the whip-tom-kelly note which Soane and Wilson gave to the red-eye, but which Nuttall says he never heard from it? Sometimes *ter-phee-e*. This is repeated at considerable intervals, the bird sitting quite still a long time. I saw it dart out once, catch an insect, and return to its perch muscicapa-like.[1] As near as I could see it had a white throat, was whitish, streaked with dark, beneath, darker tail and wings, and maybe olivaceous shoulders; bright-yellow within bill.

Andromeda calyculata begins to leaf — separate twigs from blossoming ones. *Andromeda Polifolia* just open. Buck-bean, apparently in three days (in house the 18th).

The 13th, saw large water-bugs (*Gyrinus*) crawled up high on rocks. Watch a pine warbler on a pitch pine, slowly and faithfully searching it creeper-like. It encounters a black and white creeper on the same

[1] Probably *M. Cooperi*. *Vide* June 10th.

Vol. VII

tree; they fly at each other, and the latter leaves, apparently driven off by the first. This warbler shuts its bill each time to produce its peculiar note. Rhodora will apparently open in two or three days. See and hear for a moment a small warbler-like bird in Nemopanthes Swamp which sings somewhat like *tchut a-worieter-worieter-worieter-woo*.

The greater part of the large sugar maples on the Common leaf. Large red maples generally are late to leaf.

Minott says that some years ago, maybe ten or fifteen, a man in Bedford climbed to an owl's nest (probably a cat owl's), and the owl took out one of his eyes and nearly killed him. He read it in the papers.

May 16. P. M. — Up Assabet.

Trees generally leafing. Black willow leafs. Bass leaf is an inch over; probably began about the 14th. Panicled andromeda leafed in some places, probably a day or two. Grape buds begin to open. Swamp white oak leaf, probably yesterday. Silky cornel leaf, two days or three. A woodcock, near river. A blue heron-like bird on a tree over river, but with uniformly fawn-colored throat and breast and *red* feet. We hear these last two or three warm days the loud sound of toads borne on or amid the rippling wind. A green bittern with its dark-green coat and crest, sitting watchful, goes off with a limping peetweet flight.

May 17. Waked up at 2.30 by the peep of robins, which were aroused by a fire at the pail-factory about

two miles west. I hear that the air was full of birds singing thereabouts. It rained gently at the same time, though not steadily.

May 18. P. M. — Boat to Nut Meadow.

Large devil's-needle. Sassafras well open. How long? Celtis will probably shed pollen to-morrow; shoots already an inch long. Sorrel pollen. First veery strain. Green-briar leafed several days. *Veronica serpyllifolia* well out (how long?) at Ash Bank Spring. Saw the yellow-legs feeding on shore.[1] Legs *not* bright-yellow. Goes off with the usual whistle; also utters a long monotonous call as it were [*sic*] standing on the shore, not so whistling. Am inclined to think it the lesser yellow-legs (though I think the only one we see). Yet its bill appears quite two inches long. Is it curved up? Observed a blackbird's (red-wing's) nest finished.[2] At Clamshell a bay-wing sparrow's nest, four eggs (young half hatched) — some *black*-spotted, others not.[3] These last warmer days a great many fishes dart away from close to the shore, where they seem to lie now more than ever. I see some darting about and rippling the water there with large back fins out, either pouts or suckers (not pickerel certainly). Apparently their breeding-season arrived. Is not this where the fish hawks get them? Rhodora; probably some yesterday. Black scrub oak pollen. Fir balsam pollen; say begins to leaf at same time. The clump of golden willows

[1] C. now thinks he has not seen it before.
[2] Four eggs in it on the 25th.
[3] Three young partly (slightly) fledged the 26th.

west of new stone bridge is very handsome now seen from hill, with its light-yellowish foliage; because the stems of the trees are seen through it.

May 19. Put my little turtles into the river. They had not noticeably increased in size, — or hardly. Three had died within a week for want of attention, — two mud turtles and one musk turtle. Two were missing, — one mud and one musk. Five musk were put into the river.

May 20. Rains a little.

May 21. P. M. — To Island.
Salix nigra leafs. Is that plump blue-backed, *rufous-rumped* swallow the cliff swallow, flying with barn swallows, etc., over the river? Nuttall apparently so describes it, — 5½ by 12. It dashes within a foot of me. Lambkill leaf, a day or two. Choke-berry pollen; perhaps a day or more elsewhere. *Viola palmata* pretty common, apparently two or three days. *Some* button-bush begins to leaf. Cranberry well started; shoots three quarters of an inch. Bluets whiten the fields, and violets are now perhaps in prime.

Very cold to-day; cold weather, indeed, from the 20th to 23d inclusive. Sit by fires, and *sometimes* wear a greatcoat and expect frosts.

May 22. *Cerasus pumila* in full bloom. How long? Bank swallows — ashy-brown above — have holes at Deep Cut. Have not surely distinguished them before,

this season. Sage willow may have begun to leaf a week or ten days ago or more. Cuckoo. Scared up a nighthawk — from the white on wings — amid the dry leaves on the edge of a copse on Fair Haven Hill, where apparently it had been scratching, the leaves looking as if they had been turned up. *Linaria Canadensis* on Cliffs open. The deciduous trees leafing begin to clothe or invest the evergreens. The oaks are a *little* more than in the gray. Huckleberry open, possibly yesterday. Fringed polygala, how long? Herd's-grass (?) on Channing's bank, pollen.[1] Harris tells Emerson my cicada is the *Noveboracensis* (?), known to New-Yorkers. Lupine not open yet for two or three days. Not yet chinquapin oak.

May 23. A. M. — To bayberry *via* river.
Myrica, not quite. Lousewort pollen, how long?

May 24. A. M. — To Beck Stow's.
Buttonwood not open. Celandine pollen. Butternut pollen, apparently a day or two. Black oak pollen yesterday, at least. Scarlet oak the same, but a little later. The staminate flowers of the first are on long and handsome tassels for three or four inches along the extremities of last year's shoots, depending five inches (sometimes six) by four in width and quite dense and thick. The scarlet oak tassels are hardly half as long; the leaves, much greener and smoother and now somewhat wilted, emit a sweet odor, which those of the black do not. Both these oaks are appar-

[1] [See May 24, where this grass apparently is called foxtail grass.]

ently more forward at top, where I cannot see them. Mountain-ash open apparently yesterday. In woods by *Andromeda Polifolia* the chestnut-sided warbler, with clear yellow crown and yellow on wings and chestnut sides. It is exploring low trees and bushes, often along stems about young leaves, and frequently or after short pauses utters its somewhat summer-yellowbird-like note, say, *tchip tchip, chip chip* (quick), *tche tche ter tchéa*, — spray[ey] and rasping and faint. Another, further off.

Andromeda Polifolia now in prime, but the leaves are apt to be blackened and unsightly, and the flowers, though delicate, have a feeble and sickly look, rose-white, somewhat crystalline. Its shoots or new leaves, unfolding, say when it flowered or directly after, now one inch long. Buck-bean just fairly begun, though probably first the 18th; a handsome flower, but already when the raceme is only half blown, some of the lowest flowers are brown and withered, deforming it. What a pity! *Juniperus repens* pollen not even yet; apparently to-morrow. Apparently put back by the cold weather. Beach plum pollen probably several days in some places; and leaves begun as long.

Hear a rose-breasted grosbeak. At first thought it a tanager, but soon I perceived its more *clear* and instrumental — should say whistle, if one could whistle like a flute; a noble singer, reminding me also of a robin; clear, loud and flute-like; on the oaks, hillside south of Great Fields. Black all above except white on wing, with a triangular red mark on breast but, as I saw, all white beneath this. Female quite

different, yellowish olivaceous above, more like a muscicapa. Song not so sweet as clear and strong. Saw it fly off and catch an insect like a flycatcher.

An early thorn pollen (not *Crus-Galli*) apparently yesterday.

Picked up a pellet in the wood-path, of a small bird's feathers, one inch in diameter and loose; nothing else with them; some slate, some yellow. Young robins some time hatched. Heard a purple finch sing more than one minute without pause, loud and rich, on an elm over the street. Another singing very faintly on a neighboring elm.

Conant fever-bush had not begun to leaf the 12th. I seem to have seen, among sedges, etc., (1) the *Carex Pennsylvanica;* also (2) another similar, but later and larger, in low ground with many more pistillate flowers nearly a foot high, three-sided and rough culm (the first is smooth); also (3) an early sedge at Lee's Cliff with striped and pretty broad leaves not rigid, perhaps on 554th page of Gray; (4) the rigid tufted are common in meadows, with cut-grass-like leaves. Call it *C. stricta*, though not yet more than a foot high or eighteen inches.

Of *Juncaceæ*, perhaps *Luzula campestris*, the early umbelled purple-leaved, low.

And, apparently, of grasses, foxtail grass, on C.'s bank.

Naked azalea shoots more than a week old, and other leaves, say a week at least.

P. M. — To Cliffs.

Wind suddenly changed to south this forenoon, and for first time I think of a thin coat. It is very hazy in consequence of the sudden warmth after cold, and I cannot see the mountains. Chinquapin pollen. Lupine not yet. Black scrub oak tassels, some reddish, some yellowish. Just before six, see in the northwest the first summer clouds, methinks, piled in cumuli with silvery edges, and westward of them a dull, rainy-looking cloud advancing and shutting down to the horizon; later, lightning in west and south and a little rain. Another kind of frog spawn at Beck Stow's.

May 25. A rather warm night the last; window slightly open. Hear buzz of flies in the *sultryish* morning air on awaking.

8 A. M. — To Hill.

Late rose shoots, two inches, say a fortnight since. *Salix nigra* pollen, a day at least. Wood pewee. Apparently yellowbirds' nests just completed — one by stone bridge causeway,[1] another on birch by mud turtle meadow. *Veronica peregrina* in Mackay's strawberries, how long? Most of the robins' nests I have examined this year had three eggs, clear bluish green.

A chip-bird's nest on a balm-of-Gilead, eight feet high, between the main stem and a twig or two, with four very pale blue-green eggs with a sort of circle of brown-black spots about larger end.

Red-wing's nest with four eggs — white, very faintly tinged with (perhaps) green and curiously and neatly

[1] One egg in it the next morning. Also a red-wing's nest opposite Dodd's (one egg in it next morning, *i. e.* 26th).

marked with brown-black spots and lines on the large end. Red-wings now *generally* beginning to lay.

Fever-root one foot high and more, say a fortnight or three weeks. Scared a screech owl out of an apple tree on hill; flew swiftly off at first like a pigeon woodpecker and lit near by facing me; was instantly visited and spied at by a brown thrasher; then flew into a hole high in a hickory near by, the thrasher following close to the tree. It was reddish or ferruginous. Chokecherry pollen on island, apparently two or three days. Hemlock pollen, probably to-morrow; some in house to-day; say to-day; not yet leafing. *Aralia nudicaulis*, perhaps two days pollen. *Cornus florida*, no bloom. Was there year before last? Does it not flower every other year? Its leaf, say, just after *C. sericea*. Tupelo leaf before button-bush; maybe a week now. Red oak pollen, say a day or two before black. Swamp white oak pollen.

River at summer level, four inches below long stone. Grass patches conspicuous, and flags and *Equisetum limosum* and pontederia (eight inches high), and white lily pads now (after yellow) red above, and purplish polygonum leaves in beds above water. For some days the handsome phalanxes of the *Equisetum limosum* have attracted me. The button-bush hardly yet *generally* begun to leaf. Critchicrotches in prime.

Heard the first regular bullfrog's trump on the 18th; none since.[1]

Juniper, plucked yesterday, sheds pollen in house to-day, and probably in field.

[1] One in the evening.

Vol. VII

Is our white willow Gray's var. 2d, *cœrulea?*

The golden robin keeps whistling something like *Eat it, Potter, eat it!*

Carex exilis (??), river-shore opposite Wheeler's gate, six inches high, but the culm smooth — some time.

Is that sweet-scented vernal grass just begun to bloom at celtis shore?

Fir balsam begun to leaf — with flower.

Cottony aphides on white pines. Hear a quail and the summer spray frog,[1] amid the ring of toads.

May 26. 8 A. M. — By boat to *Kalmia glauca* and thence to scouring-rush.

Again a strong cold wind from the north by west, turning up the new and tender pads. The young white lily pads are now red and crimson above, while greenish beneath. Nightshade dark-green shoots are eight inches long. Button-bush would commonly·be said to begin to leaf.

At Clamshell. *Ranunculus acris* and *bulbosus* pollen apparently about two or three days. Comandra pollen apparently two days there. *Arenaria serpyllifolia* and scleranthus, how long? White oak pollen. The oaks apparently shed pollen about four days later than last year; may be owing to the recent cold weather. Interrupted fern pollen the 23d; may have been a day or two. Cinnamon fern to-day. Checkerberry shoots one inch high. *Carex stipata?* Close-spiked sedge in Clamshell Meadow some time. Early willow on right

[1] Or toad?

beyond Hubbard's Bridge leafed since 12th; say 19th or *generally* before button-bush.

At Kalmia Swamp. — Nemopanthes, apparently several days, and leaf say before tupelo. White spruce pollen one or two days at least, and now begins to leaf.

To my surprise the *Kalmia glauca* almost all out; perhaps began with rhodora. A very fine flower, the more interesting for being early. The leaf say just after the lambkill. I was wading through this white spruce swamp just to look at the leaves. The more purple rhodora rose here and there above the small andromeda, so that I did not at first distinguish the *K. glauca*. When I did, probably my eyes at first confounded it with the lambkill, and I did not remember that this would not bloom for some time. There were a few leaves just faintly started. But at last my eyes and attention both were caught by those handsome umbels of the *K. glauca*, rising, one to three together, at the end of bare twigs, six inches or more above the level of the andromeda, etc., together with the rhodora.[1] Umbels, one and one half inches [in] diameter, of five to eighteen flowers on red threads three quarters to an inch long, at first deep rose-color, after pale rose. Twigs bare except two or three small old leaves close to the end of the dry-looking twigs. Flowers not arranged in whorls about the twig, but rising quite above it. The larger flowers about nine-sixteenths inch diameter. Flowers somewhat larger, methinks, and more terminal than lambkill. The whole about two feet

[1] The rhodora did not accompany it into the more open and level and wet parts, where was andromeda almost alone.

high in sphagnum. The lambkill is just beginning to be flower-budded.

What that neat song-sparrow-like nest of grass merely, in the wet sphagnum under the andromeda there, with three eggs, — in that very secluded place, surrounded by the watery swamp and andromeda, — — from which the bird stole like a mouse under the andromeda? *Vide* egg. It is narrower and more pointed at one end and lighter, a little, — the brown less confluent, — than that of the song sparrow with one spot on breast which took from ivy tree tuft. The last is bluish-white very thickly spotted and blotched with brown. Four eggs first seen, I think, the 22d.

Swamp-pink leaf before lambkill. A mosquito. Lupine in house from Fair Haven Hill, and probably in field.

At the screech owl's nest I now find two young slumbering, almost uniformly gray above, about five inches long, with little dark-grayish tufts for incipient horns (?). Their heads about as broad as their bodies. I handle them without their stirring or opening their eyes. There are the feathers of a small bird and the leg of the *Mus leucopus* in the nest.

The partridge which on the 12th had left three cold eggs covered up with oak leaves is now sitting on eight. She apparently deserted her nest for a time and covered it. Already the mouse-ear down begins to blow in the fields and whiten the grass, together with the bluets. In Conant's thick wood on the White-Pond-ward lane, hear the evergreen-forest note, but commonly, at a distance, only the last notes — a fine sharp *té té*. The

mountain laurel near scouring-rush apparently just begun to leaf. Trientalis open. Do I not hear a tanager? See a beautiful blue-backed and long-tailed pigeon sitting daintily on a low white pine limb.

I perceive no new life in the pipes (*Equisetum hyemale*), except that some are flower-budded at top and *may* open in a week, and on pulling them up I find a new one just springing from the base at root. The flower-bud is apparently on those dry-looking last year's plants which I thought had no life in them.

Returning, I lay on my back again in Conant's thick wood. Saw a redstart over my head there; black with a sort of brick red on sides [of] breast, spot on wing, and under root of tail. Note heard once next day, at Kalmia Swamp, somewhat like *aveet aveet aveet aveet*. In the meanwhile hear another note, very *smart* and somewhat sprayey, rasping, *tshrip tshrip tshrip tshrip*, or five or six times with equal force each time. The bird hops near, directly over my head. It is black, with a large white mark forward on wings and a fiery orange throat, above and below eye, and line on crown, yellowish beneath, white vent, forked tail, dusky legs and bill; holds its wings (which are light beneath) loosely. It inclines to examine about the lower branches of the white pines or midway up. The Blackburnian warbler very plainly; whose note Nuttall knows nothing about.

Two-leaved Solomon's-seal pollen not long in most places. *Ranunculus recurvatus* at Corner Spring up several days at least; pollen. Trillium pollen maybe several days. Arum, how long? The *Ranunculus*

Purshii in that large pool in the Holden Swamp Woods makes quite a show at a little distance now.

See to-day (and saw the 23d) a larger peetweet-like bird on the shore, with longer, perhaps more slender, wings, black or blackish without white spots; all white beneath; and when it goes off it flies higher. Is it not the *Totanus solitarius*, which Brown found at Goose Pond?

I think that the red-fruited choke-berry has shed pollen about a day, though I have not examined. The leaves are a little downy beneath and the common peduncle and the pedicels stout and quite hairy, while the black-fruited is smooth and gloossy.

May 27. P. M. — To Fair Haven Pond, taking boat opposite Puffer's.

Still a very strong wind from northerly, and hazy and rather cool for season. The fields now begin to wear the aspect of June, their grass just beginning to wave; the light-colored withered grass seen between the blades, foliage thickening and casting darker shadows over the meadows, elm-tree-tops thick in distance, deciduous trees rapidly investing evergreens, haze with the strong wind. How important the dark evergreens now seen through the haze in the distance and contrasting with the gauze-like, as yet thin-clad deciduous trees! They are like solid protuberances of earth. A thrasher's nest on the bare open ground with four eggs which were seen three days ago. The nest is as open and exposed as it well can be, lined with roots, on a slight ridge where a rail fence has been, some rods

from any bush. Saw the yellow-legs on one side flying over the meadow *against* the strong wind and at first mistook it for a hawk. It appeared now quite brown, with its white rump; and, excepting [for] its bill and head, I should have taken it for a hawk; between the size of male harrier and the male pigeon hawk, or say the size of a dove. It alighted on the shore. And now again I think it must be the large one.

The blue yellow-back or parti-colored warbler still, with the chestnut crescent on breast, near my Kalmia Swamp nest. See a painted turtle on a hill forty or fifty feet above river, probably laying eggs. Some mountain sumach has grown one inch, some not started; some button-bush three inches, some not started. The first must be put after the last. *Myosotis stricta* under Cliffs, how long? The meadow fragrance to-day. How interesting the huckleberries now generally in blossom on the knoll below the Cliff — countless wholesome red bells, beneath the fresh yellow-green foliage! The berry-bearing vaccinium! It is a rich sight. Geranium at Bittern Cliff, apparently several days, and *Arabis rhomboidea* there in meadow, apparently still longer — say seven or eight days; but I am doubtful about the "slender style tipped with a conspicuous stigma." Carrion-flower a foot high. Crimson gall on a shrub oak. A loose-spiked sedge at Bittern Cliff Meadow, — forgot to bring, — a foot high.

May 28. How's morus not yet, apparently, for two or three days, though the stigmas are obvious. Button-wood stigmas are now brown, since the 24th.

P. M. — To Middle Conantum Cliff.

Yesterday left my boat at the willow opposite this Cliff, the wind northwest. Now it is southeast, and I can sail back. *Our* quince open this morning, possibly yesterday; and some others, I believe, much earlier. Do I not hear a short snappish, rasping note from a yellow-throat vireo? I see a tanager, the most brilliant and tropical-looking bird we have, bright-scarlet with black wings, the scarlet appearing on the rump again between wing-tips. He brings heat, or heat him. A remarkable contrast with the green pines. At this distance he has the aspect and manners of a parrot, with a fullness about the head and throat and beak, indolently inspecting the limbs and twigs — leaning over to it — and sitting still a long time. The female, too, is a neat and handsome bird, with the same indolent ways, but very differently colored from the male; all yellow below with merely dusky wings, and a sort of clay(?)-color on back.

While we sit by the path in the depths of the woods three quarters of a mile beyond Hayden's, confessing the influence of almost the first summer warmth, the wood thrush sings steadily for half an hour, now at 2.30 P. M., amid the pines, — loud and clear and sweet. While other birds are warbling betweenwhiles and catching their prey, he alone appears to make a business of singing, like a true minstrel. Is that one which I see at last in the path, above dusky olive-brown becoming *ferruginous* on base of tail, eye not very prominent with a white line around it, some dark-colored feathers apparently on outer wing-coverts, very light-

colored legs, with dashes on breast which I do not see clearly? I should say that it had not the large black eye of the hermit thrush, and I cannot see the yellowish spot on the wings; yet it may have been this.

I find the feathers apparently of a brown thrasher in the path, plucked since we passed here last night. You can generally find all the tail and quill feathers in such a case. The apple bloom is very rich now. Fever-bush shoots are now two inches long; say begin to leaf just before late willow. Black ash shoots three inches long; say with late willow. White pine and pitch pine shoots from two to five inches long. *Rubus triflorus* at Miles Swamp will apparently open to-morrow. *Some* krigia done some days. *Silene antirrhina.* Barberry open (probably two or more days at Lee's). C. says he has seen a green snake. Examined my two yellowbirds' nests of the 25th. Both are destroyed, — pulled down and torn to pieces probably by some bird, — though they [had] but just begun to lay. Large yellow and black butterfly. The leaves of kalmiana lily obvious.

I have seen within three or four days two or three new warblers which I have not identified; one to-day, in the woods, all pure white beneath, with a full breast, and greenish-olive-yellow (?) above, with a duskier head and a slight crest muscicapa-like, on pines, etc., high; very small.[1]

Also one all lemon-yellow beneath, except whitish vent, and apparently bluish above.

[1] Perhaps young and female redstarts.

Vol. VII

May 29. P. M. — To Island Neck.

That willow by the rock south of Island (of May 2d) appears to be without doubt the *Salix sericea*, — the leaves beginning to turn black quite soon, and the bark is *very* bitter.[1] There is, then, another small willow or sallow with narrower and shining leaves, very common along river, with longer catkins and very long tapering smooth pods, — I mean the one I have associated with the *S. alba.*

Azalea nudiflora in garden.

There are a great many birds now on the Island Neck. The red-eye, its clear loud song in bars continuously repeated and varied; all tempered white beneath and dark yellow olive above and on edge of wings, with a dark line on side-head or from root of bill; dusky claws, and a very long bill. The long bill and the dark line on the side of the head, with the white above and beneath, or in the midst of the white, giving it a certain oblong, swelled-cheek look, would distinguish on a side view. There is also the warbling vireo, with its smooth-flowing, continuous, one-barred, shorter strain, with methinks a dusky side-head. Also the yellow-throated vireo — its head and shoulders as well as throat yellow (apparently olive-yellow above), and its strain but little varied and short, not continuous. It has dusky legs and two very distinct white bars on wings (the male).

I see the first swamp sparrow of the season, and probably heard its loud song; clear, broad, undivided

[1] June 6th. — The leaves answer well to the account, and the bitter bark and brittle twig at base.

chestnut or bay (?) crown and clear *dark-ash* throat and breast, and light, perhaps yellowish, line over eye, dark bill, and much bay (?) on wings. Low, amid the alders.

But what is that bird I hear much like the first part of the yellowbird's strain, only two thirds as long and varied at end, and not so loud, — *a-che che che, che-á,* or *tche tche tche, tche-a,* or *ah tche tche tche, chit-i-vet?*

It is very small, not timid, but incessantly changing its position on the pitch pines, etc. Some a pure dull white, some tawny-white, beneath; some cinereous, others more dusky still, above; with a flycatcher or muscicapa bill and head (head rounded?), but — what is most remarkable — a very deeply forked or divided tail with a broad black tip beneath, and toward the roots a fire-brick-color, this last color much brighter on the sides of the breast, and some of it on the wings in a broad bar, though some perhaps have not the last mark. Did I see some of the yellowish on rump? Dark-ash above and some reddish-brown (?). One is very inquisitive; hops down toward me lower and lower on the pitch pine twigs, while I hold out my hand till within five feet, but in such a light that I cannot distinguish its colors. There are at least half a dozen of them about; continually flitting about, sometimes in a circle of a few rods' diameter, one pursuing another, both male and female, back to near the same spot, but I can hardly bring my glass to bear on them before they change their position. It is undoubtedly young males and the females of the redstart, described by Wilson, — very different from the full-plumaged black males.

I see on the first limb of a white oak, close to the trunk and about eight feet from the ground, squatting as if asleep, a chipping squirrel two thirds grown. The hole it came out of, apparently, is four or five feet from the base of the tree. When I am about to put my hand on it, it runs feebly up the tree and rests again as much higher in a similar place. When C. climbs after, it runs out quite to the end of a limb, where it can hardly hold on, and I think it will drop every moment with the shaking of the tree.

May 30. Saw bird's nest on an apple by roadside, seven feet high; one egg.

Cherry-bird on a cherry; also pecking at the apple blossoms. Minott says that within two or three days a stream of winged ants came out from under his door-sill, and the hens and countless swallows and the kingbirds came and fed on them. Buttonwood flowers now effete; fertile flowers were not brown on the 24th, but were the 28th; say, then, about the 26th.

Nuttall thus describes the note of the white-eyed vireo: It is much varied; in March in Florida, "*ss't* (with a whistle) *wá wĭtte wĭtte wē-wá* (the first part very quick);" in June at Fresh Pond, "'*tshĭppewee-wá-say tshippewee-wée-was-say*, sweetly whistled," with great compass of voice and loudness, etc., etc.; other variations. Also "'*whĭp te woĭ wee*, the last syllable but one considerably lengthened and clearly whistled." [1]

Lepidium virginicum, roadside bank at Minott's.

[1] [*A Manual of the Ornithology of the United States and of Canada*, second edition, vol. i, p. 348.]

Vol. VII

ends of last year's shoots, which are three to six feet from ground.

Hear a familiar warbler not recognized for some years, in the thick copse in Dennis's Swamp, south of railroad; considerably yellowbird-like (the note) — *tshe tshe tshar tshar tchit, tchit tit te vet.* It has apparently a yellow head, bluish or slaty wings with two white bars, tail even, wings dusky at tips, legs light, bill dark, beneath all bright-yellow, remarkably striped lengthwise with dusky, more or less dark in different specimens. Can it be the *S. maculosa*, or black and yellow warbler, seen formerly? I did not see the black — nor indeed the back at all well. It may have been a female, not described by Wilson. Frequents the tops of trees.

Ladies' slipper, apparently.

May 31. Another windy, washing day, but warm. See a yellowbird building a nest on a white oak on the Island. She goes to a fern for the wool. In evening hear distinctly a *tree-toad*.[1]

[1] And again the 4th of June.

The myrica, bayberry, plucked on the 23d, now first sheds pollen in house, the leaf being but little more expanded on the flowering shoot. Gray says, "somewhat preceding the flowers." The catkins about a quarter of an inch long, erect, sterile, oval, on the sides of last year's twigs.

P. M. — Up railroad.

A strong west wind and much haze. Silvery potentilla, four or five days at least. In the thick of the wood between railroad and Turnpike, hear the evergreen-forest note, and see probably the bird, — black throat, greenish-yellow or yellowish-green head and back, light-slate (?) wings with two white bars. Is it not the black-throated green warbler? I find close by a small fresh egg on the forest floor, with a slight perforation, white (with perhaps a tinge of flesh-color (?) when full), and brown spots and black marks at the larger end. In Brewer's synopsis the egg of the black-throat is described as "light flesh-color with purple spots." But these spots are not purple. I could find no nest.

Senecio in open meadows, say yesterday. See a small black snake run along securely through thin bushes (alders and willows) three or four feet from the ground, passing intervals of two feet easily, — very readily and gracefully, — ascending or descending. *Cornus Canadensis* out, how long?

Green lice from birches (?) get on my clothes.

Is it not summer now when the creak of the crickets begins to be general?

Poison-dogwood has grown three or four inches at

X

JUNE, 1855

(ÆT. 37)

June 1. A *very* windy day, the third, drowning the notes of birds, scattering the remaining apple blossoms. Rye, to my surprise, three or four feet high and glaucous. Cloudy and rain, threatening withal. Surveying at Holden wood-lot, I notice the *Equisetum hyemale*, its black-scaled flowerets now in many cases separated so as to show the green between, but not yet in open rings or whorls like the *limosum*.

I find the *Linnæa borealis* growing near the end of the ridge in this lot toward the meadow, near a large white pine stump recently cut. C. has found the arethusa out at Hubbard's Close; say two or three days at a venture, there being considerable.

June 2. Still windier than before, and yet no rain. It is now very dry indeed, and the grass is suffering. Some springs commonly full at this season are dried up. The wind shakes the house night and day. From that cocoon of the *Attacus cecropia* which I found — I think it was on the 24th of May — on a red maple shrub, three or four feet from the ground, on the edge of the meadow by the new Bedford road just this side of Beck Stow's, came out this forenoon a splendid moth. I had pinned the cocoon to the sash at the upper part of my window and quite forgotten it. About the middle of the forenoon Sophia came in and exclaimed that there was a moth on my window. At first I supposed that she meant a cloth-eating moth, but it turned out that my *A. cecropia* had come out and dropped down to the window-sill, where it hung on the *side* of a slipper (which was inserted into another) to let its wings hang down and develop themselves. At first the wings were not only not unfolded laterally, but not longitudinally, the thinner ends of the forward ones for perhaps three quarters of an inch being very feeble and occupying very little space. It was surprising to see the creature unfold and expand before our eyes, the wings gradually elongating, as it were by their own gravity; and from time to time the insect assisted this operation by a slight shake. It was wonderful how it waxed and grew, revealing some new beauty every fifteen minutes, which I called Sophia to see, but never losing its hold on the shoe. It looked like a young emperor just donning the most splendid ermine robes that ever emperor wore, the wings every moment acquiring greater expansion and their at first wrinkled edge becoming more tense. At first its wings appeared double, one within the other. At last it advanced so far as to spread its wings completely but feebly when we approached. This occupied several hours. It continued to hang to the shoe, with its wings ordinarily closed erect behind its back, the rest of the day; and at dusk, when apparently it was waving its wings preparatory to its evening flight, I gave it ether and so saved it in a perfect state. As it lies, not

spread to the utmost, it is five and nine tenths inches by two and a quarter.

P. M. — To Hill.

Equisetum limosum pollen — a few — apparently two or three days. The late cratægus on the hill is in full bloom while the other is almost entirely out of bloom.

Three yellowbirds' nests, which I have marked since the 25th of May, the only ones which I have actually inspected, have now all been torn to pieces, though they were in places (two of them, at least) where no boy is at all likely to have found them.

I see in the meadow-grass a fine cobweb or spider's nest three or four inches [in] diameter and, within it, on two twigs, two collections of little yellowish spiders containing a thousand or more, about half as big as a pin-head, like minute fruit-buds or kernels clustered on the twig.  One of the clusters disperses when I stoop over it and spreads over the nest on the fine lines.

Hemlock leafed two or three days, the earliest young plants. The black spruce beyond the hill has apparently just begun to leaf, but not yet to blossom. *Pinus rigida* pollen a day or two or three on the plain. Sweet-flag pollen about two days.

Mr. Hoar tells me that Deacon Farrar's son tells him that a white robin has her nest on an apple tree near their house. Her mate is of the usual color. All the family have seen her, but at the last accounts she has not been seen on the nest.

Vol. VII

Silene, or wild pink, how long?

The *Azalea nudiflora* now in its prime. What splendid masses of pink! with a few glaucous green leaves sprinkled here and there — just enough for contrast.

June 3. A rainy day at last. Caraway in garden apparently three days out.

June 4. P. M. — To Hubbard's Close.

Clears up in forenoon. Some of the scouring-rush gathered the 1st begins to open its whorls or stages in the chamber; say sheds pollen to-morrow. Not quite yet the How mulberry pollen. White clover out probably some days, also red as long.

It has just cleared off after this first rain of consequence for a long time, and now I observe the shadows of massive clouds still floating here and there in the peculiarly blue sky; which dark shadows on field and wood are the more remarkable by contrast with the light yellow-green foliage now, and when they rest on evergreens they are doubly dark, like dark rings about the eyes of June. Great white-bosomed clouds, darker beneath, float through the cleared sky and are seen against the deliciously blue sky, such a sky as we have not had before. Thus it is after the first important rain at this season. The song of birds is more lively and seems to have a new character; a new season has commenced. In the woods I hear the tanager and chewink and red-eye. It is fairly summer, and mosquitoes begin to sting *in earnest*. I see the dandelions now generally gone to seed amid the grass — their

downy spheres. There are now many potentillas ascendant, and the *Erigeron bellidifolius* is sixteen inches high and quite handsome, by the railroad this side of turn-off.

Redstarts still very common in the Trillium Woods (yesterday on Assabet also). Note *tche tche, tche vit*, etc. I see some dark on the breast.

The *Lycopodium dendroideum* now shows fresh green tips like the hemlock. Greenish puffs on panicled andromedas. Lint comes off on to clothes from the tender leaves, but it is clean dirt and all gone when you get home; and now the crimson velvety leafets of the black oak, showing also a crimson edge on the downy under sides, are beautiful as a flower, and the more salmon white oak. The *Linnæa borealis* has grown an inch. But are not the flowers winter-killed? I see dead and blackened flower-buds. Perhaps it should have opened before. Wintergreen has grown two inches.

See a warbler much like the black and white creeper, but perched warbler-like on trees; streaked slate, white, and black, with a large white and black mark on wing, crown divided by a white line and then chestnut (?) or slate or dark, and then white above and below eye, breast and throat streaked downward with dark, rest beneath white. Can it be the common black and white creeper? Its note hardly reminds me of that. It is somewhat like *pse pse pse pse, psa psa, weese weese weese*, or longer. It did not occur to me that it was the same till I could not find any other like this in the book.

Cotton-grass apparently two or three days out.

Geum, apparently some days. In the clintonia swamp I hear a smart, brisk, loud and clear whistling warble, quite novel and remarkable, something like *te chit a wit, te chit a wit, tchit a wit, tche tche*. It is all bright-yellow or ochreous orange (?) below except vent, and a dark or black crescent on breast, with a white line about eye. Above it appears a nearly uniform dark blue slate, legs light, bill dark (?), tail long and forked. I think it must be the Canada warbler, seen in '37,[1] though that seems *short* for this. It is quite different from the warbler of May 30.

The recent high winds have turned the edges of young leaves by beating and killing them.

Ellen Emerson finds the *Viola pubescens* scarce to-day, but the *Actæa alba* in full bloom. Eddy has brought a great polygonatum from Medford, which he says grew in the woods there. I do not find a satisfactory account of it. It differs from the *pubescens* of Gray, in that the leaves can hardly be called downy beneath and are clasping, the peduncles are two to five flowered (instead of one to two) and the perianth is four fifths of an inch long (instead of a half). Perianth white or whitish with green lobes. It differs from the *canaliculatum* in not being channelled obviously (though angled *between the leaves*), the filaments not being smooth nor inserted in the middle of the tube.

Carex scoparia (?) in meadows some days.

June 5. P. M. — To Clamshell by river.

[1] [A surprising entry, the Canada warbler being a common migrant, brilliantly marked, and from its habits eminently observable.]

Yellow Bethlehem-star in prime. Aphyllon, or orobanche, well out apparently several days. *Nuphar Kalmiana* budded above water. Green-briar flower out apparently two or three days. Low blackberry out in low ground. That very early (or in winter green radical leaf) plant by ash is the *Myosotis laxa*, open since the 28th of May, say June 1st. *Ranunculus reptans*, say two days out, river being very low. Common cress well out along river. Side-flowering sandwort apparently three days out in Clamshell *flat* meadow. Some oxalis done, say two or three days, on ditch bank. *Ranunculus repens* in prime. Yellow clover well out some days. Flowering ferns, reddish-green, show on meadows. Green oak-balls.

Walking along the upper edge of the flat Clamshell meadow, a bird, probably a song sparrow (for I saw two chipping about immediately after), flew up from between my feet, and I soon found its nest remarkably concealed. It was under the thickest of the dry river wreck, with an entry low on one side, full five inches long and very obscure. On looking close I detected the eggs from above by looking down through some openings in the wreck about as big as sparrows' eggs, through which I saw the eggs, five in number. I never saw the nest so perfectly concealed.

I am much interested to see how Nature proceeds to heal the wounds where the turf was stripped off this meadow. There are large patches where nothing remained but pure black mud, nearly level or with slight hollows like a plate in it. This the sun and air had cracked into irregular polygonal figures, a foot,

more or less, in diameter. The whole surface of these patches here is now covered with a short, soft, and pretty dense moss-like vegetation springing up and clothing it. The little hollows and the cracks are filled with a very dense growth of reddish grass or sedge, about one inch high, the growth in the cracks making pretty regular figures as in a carpet, while the intermediate spaces are very evenly but much more thinly covered with minute sarothra and whitish *Gnaphalium uliginosum*. Thus the wound is at once scarred over. Apparently the seeds of that grass were heavier and were washed into the hollows and cracks. Is it likely that the owner has sprinkled seed here?[1]

June 6. P. M. — Up Assabet by boat to survey Hosmer's field.

On the Island I hear still the redstart — *tsip tsip tsip tsip, tsit-i-yet*, or sometimes *tsip tsip tsip tsip, tse vet*. A young male. It repeats this at regular intervals for a long time, sitting pretty still now. Waxwork open and pollen one or two days. I notice a clam lying up, and two or three cleared or light-colored places, apparently bream-nests commenced.

You see the dark eye and shade of June on the river as well as on land, and a dust-like tint on river, apparently from the young leaves and bud-scales, covering the waters, which begin to be smooth, and imparting a sense of depth. Blue-eyed grass maybe several days in some places. One thimble-berry blossom done — probably several days. There are now those large

[1] No.

swarms of black-winged millers (?) a half-inch long, with two long streamers ahead, fluttering three to six inches over the water; not long, methinks; also other insects. I see a yellow-spotted tortoise twenty rods from river, and a painted one four rods from it which has just made a hole for her eggs. Two catbirds' nests in the thickest part of the thicket on the edge of Wheeler's meadow near Island. One done laying (I learn after); four eggs, green, — much darker green than the robin's and more slender in proportion. This is *loosely* placed in the forks of a broad alternate or silky cornel bush, about five feet from the ground, and is composed of dead twigs and a little stubble, then grape-vine bark, and is lined with dark root-fibres. Another, eight rods beyond, rests still more loosely on a *Viburnum dentatum* and birch; has some dry leaves with the twigs, and one egg, — about six feet high. The bird hops within five feet.[1]

The white maple keys are about half fallen. It is remarkable that this happens at the time the emperor moth (cecropia) comes out. *Carex crinita* (?), a few days, along bank of Assabet. Whiteweed, Merrick's pasture shore, these two or three days.

The *Salix cordata* (which apparently blossomed some days after the *S. sericea*) is very common on Prichard's shore and also Whiting's. Also at the last place is a small shrub, — a little of it, — perhaps *S. lucida*, which apparently blossomed about same time [as], or a day or two after, the *sericea*.

[1] This egg gone on the 9th.

June 7. Rain.

In afternoon — mizzling weather — to Abel Hosmer Woods.

Cistus, apparently yesterday, open. A yellowbird's nest on a willow bough against a twig, ten feet high, four eggs. I have heard no musical *gurgle-ee* from blackbirds for a fortnight. They are now busy breeding.

June 8. P. M. — Goose Pond.

High blueberry. A crow two thirds grown tied up for a scarecrow. A tanager's (?) nest in the topmost forks of a pitch pine about fifteen feet high, by Thrush Alley; the nest very slight, apparently of pine-needles, twigs, etc.; can see through it; bird on.

In that pitch pine wood see two rabbit forms (?), very snug and well-roofed retreats formed by the dead pine-needles falling about the base of the trees, where they are upheld on the dead stubs from the butt at from six inches to a foot from the ground, as if the carpet [of the] forest floor were puffed up there. Gnawed acorn-shells in them. Two *Fringilla pusilla* nests in my old potato-field, at the foot of little white pines each; made of dried grass lined with hair, snug in the sod. Four eggs to each; one lot nearly hatched; with reddish-brown spots, especially toward larger end, but a light opening quite at that end; smaller, slenderer, and less spotted than the song sparrow's. The bird is ash side-head, ferruginous above, mahogany bill and legs, two whitish bars. Eggs do not agree with account? Nuttall says this bird's eggs are so thick with ferruginous as to appear almost wholly of that color! A jay's nest

with three young half fledged in a white pine, six feet high (in it), by the Ingraham cellar, made of coarse sticks. Hear, I am pretty sure, a rose-breasted grosbeak sing. See apparently a summer duck in Goose Pond. C. says he saw two other *dark* ducks here yesterday. A great many devil's-needles in woods within a day or two. G. Brooks told me on June 1st that a few evenings before he saw as many as a thousand chimney swallows pour down into Goodnow's chimney.

A catbird's nest on the peninsula of Goose Pond — four eggs — in a blueberry bush, four feet from ground, close to water; as usual of sticks, dry leaves, and bark lined with roots.

What was that little nest on the ridge near by, made of fine grass lined with a few hairs and containing five small eggs (two hatched the 11th), nearly as broad as long, yet pointed, white with fine dull-brown spots especially on the large end — nearly hatched? The nest in the dry grass under a shrub, remarkably concealed.[1]

Found in this walk, of nests, one tanager, two bay-wing, one blue jay, one catbird, and the last named.

June 9. P. M. — To Wheeler's azalea swamp, across meadow.

Early primrose done, say two days. An orchis, probably yellowish, will be common in Wheeler's meadow.[2]

[1] June 11. — It is a Maryland yellow-throat; *runs* and *flies* along *the ground* away like a nighthawk. Can't trace it off, it goes so low in the grass, etc., at first. Very shy it is.

[2] [A marginal query here.]

Vol. VII

Sidesaddle, apparently a day or two; petals hang down. A song sparrow's nest low in Wheeler's meadow, with five eggs, made of grass lined with hair. *Rhus Toxicodendron* on Island Rock.

The nest probably of the small pewee — looking from the ground like a yellowbird's, showing reddish wool of ferns — against a white birch, on a small twig, eighteen feet from ground. Four little eggs, all pale cream-color before blowing, white after — fresh. A yellowbird's nest eight feet from ground in crotch of a very slender maple. A chip-bird's in a white thorn on the Hill; one egg.

A catbird's nest, three eggs, in a high blueberry, four feet from ground, with rather more dry leaves than usual, above Assabet Spring. Lambkill out. Catbird's nest, one egg, on a blueberry bush, three feet from ground, of (as usual) sticks, leaves, bark, roots. Another near same (also in V. Muhlenbergii Swamp) on a bent white birch and andromeda, eighteen inches from ground; three eggs; stubble of weeds mainly instead of twigs, otherwise as usual. A chewink's nest sunk in ground under a bank covered with ferns, dead and green, and huckleberry bushes; composed of dry leaves, then grass stubble, and lined with a very few slender, reddish moss stems; four eggs, rather fresh; merely enough moss stems to indicate its choice. Fever-root, *perhaps* several days.

See very few hawks for several weeks.

Found to-day, of nests, one song sparrow, one small pewee (?), one yellowbird, one chip-bird, three cat-

birds, one chewink, one robin (the last on a black willow, two feet from ground, one egg).

I think I have hardly heard a bobolink for a week or ten days.

June 10. P. M. — To owl's nest.

A remarkably strong wind from the southwest all day, racking the trees very much and filling the air with dust. I do not remember such violent and incessant gusts at this season. Many eggs, if not young, must have been shaken out of birds' nests, for I hear of some fallen. It is almost impossible to hear birds — or to keep your hat on. The waves are like those of March.

That common grass,[1] which was in blossom a fortnight since, and still on our bank, began a week ago to turn white here and there, killed by worms. *Veronica scutellata*, apparently a day or two. *Iris versicolor*, also a day or two. A red maple leaf with those crimson spots. Clintonia, apparently four or five days (not out at Hubbard's Close the 4th).

A catbird's nest of usual construction, one egg, two feet high on a swamp-pink; an old nest of same near by on same.

Some *Viola cucullata* are now nine inches high, and leaves nearly two inches wide. Archangelica staminiferous umbellets, say yesterday, but some, apparently only pistilliferous ones, look some days at least older; seed-vessel pretty large.

[1] June-grass.

Oven-bird's nest with four eggs two thirds hatched, under dry leaves, composed of pine-needles and dry leaves and a hair or two for lining, about six feet southwest of a white oak which is six rods southwest of the hawk pine. The young owls are gone. The *Kalmia glauca* is done before the lambkill is begun here; apparently was done some days ago. A very few rhodoras linger.

Nest of a kingbird or wood pewee [1] on a white [*sic*] spruce in the Holden Swamp, about fifteen feet high, on a small branch near the top, of a few twigs and pine-needles, and an abundance of usnea mainly composing and lining and overflowing from it, very open beneath and carelessly built, with a small concavity; with three eggs pretty fresh, but apparently all told, cream-color before blowing, with a circle of brown spots about larger end. The female (?) looked darker beneath than a kingbird and uttered that clear plaintive *till tilt*, like a robin somewhat, sitting on a spruce.

C. finds an egg to-day, somewhat like a song sparrow's, but a little longer and slenderer, or with less difference between the ends in form, and more finely and regularly spotted *all over* with pale brown. It was in a pensile nest of grape-vine bark, on the low branch of a maple. Probably a cowbird's; fresh-laid.

He has found in nests of grass in thick bushes near river what he thought red-wing's eggs,[2] but they are pale-blue with large black blotches — one with a very

[1] Probably of *Muscicapa Cooperi* or pe-pe, disc[overed] by Nuttall (?). *Vide* May 15.

[2] Yes.

Vol. VII

'phŭ of the Fish Hawk. The male, however, besides this note, at long intervals, had a call of *'eh 'phèbēē*, or *'h'phebéā*, almost exactly in the tone of the circular tin whistle, or bird-call." [1]

June 11. How's morus, staminate flowers apparently only a day or two (pollen); the pistillate a long time. The locust apparently two or three days open.

When I would go a-visiting I find that I go off the fashionable street — not being inclined to change my dress — to where man meets man and not polished shoe meets shoe.

According to Holland's "History of Western Massachusetts," in Westfield, "In 1721, it was voted that the pews next the pulpit should be highest in dignity. The next year it was voted that persons should be seated in the meeting house according to their age and estate, and that so much as any man's estate is increased by his negroes, '*that shall be left out.*' If a man lived on a hired farm, 'or hath obtained his property by marrying a widow, it shall be reckoned only one-third,' that is, he shall have only one-third as much dignity as if he owned his farm, or had acquired his money by his own industry." [2]

What if we feel a yearning to which no breast answers? I walk alone. My heart is full. Feelings impede the current of my thoughts. I knock on the earth

[1] [*A Manual of the Ornithology of the United States and of Canada,* second edition, vol. i, pp. 298–302.]

[2] [Josiah Gilbert Holland, *History of Western Massachusetts,* vol. ii, pp. 142, 143.]

large black spot on one side. Can they be bobolinks? or what? [1]

My partridge still sits on seven eggs.

The black spruce which I plucked on the 2d expanded a loose, rather light brown cone on the 5th, say. Can that be the pistillate flower? The white spruce cones are now a rich *dark* purple, more than a half-inch long.

Nuttall thus describes the *Muscicapa Cooperi,* olive-sided flycatcher, or pe-pe: —

"SPEC. CHARACT. — Dusky brown; head darker, without discolored spot; sides olive grey; lateral space beneath the wing white; lower mandible purplish horn color; tail nearly even and extending but little beyond the closed wings."

No white on tail; secondaries and coverts edged with whitish; "rictus bright yellow, as well as the inside of the mouth and tongue." "Chin white." "Sides dusky olive, a broad line down the middle of the breast, with the abdomen and rump yellowish white; a broadish white space on the side, beneath the wing towards the back." "This species, though of the size of the King-bird, is nearly related to the Wood Pewee, yet perfectly distinct."

Of note, her "oft repeated, whining call of *'pŭ 'pŭ,* then varied to *'pŭ pĭp,* and *'pĭp pŭ,* also at times *'pĭp 'pĭp 'pŭ, 'pĭp 'pĭp 'pĭp, 'pŭ 'pŭ pĭp,* or *'tŭ 'tŭ 'tŭ,* and *'tŭ 'tŭ.* This shrill, pensive, and quick whistle sometimes dropped almost to a whisper, or merely *'pŭ.* The tone was in fact much like that of the *'phŭ 'phŭ*

[3] Probably red-wings.

for my friend. I expect to meet him at every turn; but no friend appears, and perhaps none is dreaming of me. I am tired of frivolous society, in which silence is forever the most natural and the best manners. I would fain walk on the deep waters, but my companions will only walk on shallows and puddles. I am naturally silent in the midst of twenty from day to day, from year to year. I am rarely reminded of their presence. Two yards of politeness do not make society for me. One complains that I do not take his jokes. I took them before he had done uttering them, and went my way. One talks to me of his apples and pears, and I depart with my secret untold. His are not the apples that tempt me.

Now (September 16, '55), after four or five months of invalidity and worthlessness, I begin to feel some stirrings of life in me.

Is not that carex, *Pennsylvanica*-like, with a long spike (one inch long by one half-inch wide), *C. bullata?*

What a difference between one red-wing blackbird's egg and another's! C. finds one long as a robin's, but narrow, with large black spots on larger end and on side, on or between the bushes by riverside; another much shorter, with a large black spot on the side. Both pale-blue ground.

The early willows at the bridge are apparently either *S. discolor* or *eriocephala,* or both.

I have noticed the green oak-balls some days. Now observe the dark *evergreen* of June.

The target leaf is eaten above.

In order to get the deserted tanager's nest at the top

[of] a pitch pine which was too weak to climb, we carried a rope in our pockets and took three rails a quarter of a mile into the woods, and there rigged a derrick, by which I climbed to a level with the nest, and I could see if there were eggs in it. I have the nest. Tied the three tops together and spread the bottoms.

Carex cephalophora (?) on Heywood's Peak. That fine, dry, wiry wild grass in hollows in woods and sprout-lands, never mown, is apparently the *C. Pennsylvanica*, or early sedge. There are young bluebirds.

June 12. Tuesday. Down river to swamp east of Poplar Hill.

I hear the toad, which I have called "spray *frog*" falsely, *still*. He sits close to the edge of the water and is hard to find — hard to tell the direction, though you may be within three feet. I detect him chiefly by the motion of the great swelling bubble in his throat. A peculiarly rich, sprayey dreamer, now at 2 P. M.! How serenely it ripples over the water! What a luxury life is to him! I have to use a little geometry to detect him. Am surprised at my discovery at last, while C. sits by incredulous. Had turned our prow to shore to search. This rich, sprayey note possesses all the shore. It diffuses itself far and wide over the water and enters into every crevice of the noon, and you cannot tell whence it proceeds.

Young red-wings now begin to fly feebly amid the button-bushes, and the old ones chatter their anxiety. At mouth of Mill Brook, a red-wing's nest tied on to that thick, high grass and some low willow, eighteen

inches from ground, with four eggs variously marked, full of young.

In a hedge thicket by meadow near Peter's Path, a catbird's nest, one egg; as usual in a high blueberry, in the thickest and darkest of the hedge, and very loosely built beneath on joggle-sticks.

In the thick swamp behind the hill I look at the vireo's nest which C. found on the 10th, within reach on a red maple forked twig, eight feet from ground. He took one cowbird's egg from it, and I now take the other, which he left. There is no vireo's egg, and it is said they always desert their nest when there are two cowbird's eggs laid in it. I saw a red-eye lurking near. Have the nest. Near by, in a part of the swamp which had been cleared and then burnt apparently by accident, we find the nest of a veery on a tussock eight inches high, which like those around has been burnt all off close and black. The nest is directly in the top, the outside burnt. It contains three eggs, which have been scorched, discolored, and cooked, — one cracked by the heat, though fresh. Some of the sedge has since sprung up green, eight inches high, around here and there. All the lower part of the nest is left, an inch thick with dead leaves, — maple, etc., — and well lined with moss stems (??). It is a dry swamp.

In a high blueberry bush, on the Poplar Hill-side, four feet from ground, a catbird's nest with four eggs, forty feet high up the hill. They even follow the blueberry up-hill.

A field sparrow's nest with three young, on a *Vac-*

Vol. VII

cinium vacillans, rose, and grass, *six inches from ground*, made of grass and hair.

A *Carya tomentosa* hickory on the hill well out, *and froth on the nuts*, almost all out and black; perhaps three or four days.

A hawthorn grows near by, just out of bloom, twelve feet high — *Cratægus Oxyacantha*. A veronica at Peetweet Rock; forget which kind. A crow blackbird's nest high in an elm by riverside just below the Island. C. climbed to it and got it. I have it. There were eggs. Bottom of mud and coarse grass and sedge, lined with finer grass and dry weed stems. Another in an elm rear of Loring's, in a recess where a limb was once broken off, open on one side, eighteen feet high. Young with heads out almost ready to fly.

Nuttall says of the cowbird's egg, "If the egg be deposited in the nest alone, it is uniformly forsaken;" has seen "sometimes 2 of these eggs in the same nest, but in this case one of them commonly proves abortive." "Is almost oval, scarcely larger than that of the Bluebird." He says it is "thickly sprinkled with points and confluent touches of olive brown, of two shades, somewhat more numerous at the greater end, on a white ground tinged with green. But in some of these eggs the ground is almost pure white, and the spots nearly black." [1]

June 13. C. finds a pigeon woodpecker's nest in an apple tree, five of those pearly eggs, about six feet from the ground; could squeeze your hand in. Also

[1] [*Op. cit.*, pp. 193–195.]

a peetweet's, with four eggs, in Hubbard's meadow beyond the old swamp oak site; and two kingbirds' nests with eggs in an apple and in a willow by riverside.

June 14. Thursday. Up river.

See young red-wings; like grizzly-black vultures, they are still so bald. See many empty red-wing nests now amid the *Cornus sericea*. The bluebird's nest high in the black willow at Sassafras Shore has five eggs. The gold robin's nest, which I could pull down within reach, just beyond, has three eggs. I have one. I told C. to look into an old mortise-hole in Wood's Bridge for a white-bellied swallow's nest, as we were paddling under; but he laughed, incredulous. I insisted, and when he climbed up he scared out the bird. Five eggs. "You see the feathers about, do you not?" "Yes," said he.

Kalmiana lily, several days. The little galium in meadow, say one day. A song sparrow's (?) nest in ditch bank under Clamshell, of coarse grass lined with fine, and five eggs nearly hatched and a peculiar dark end to them. Have one or more and the nest. The bird evidently deserted the nest when two eggs had been taken. Could not see her return to it, nor find her on it again after we had flushed her. A kingbird's nest with four eggs on a large horizontal stem or trunk of a black willow, four feet high, over the edge of the river, amid small shoots from the willow; outside of mikania, roots, and knotty sedge, well lined with root-fibres and wiry weeds. *Viburnum dentatum*, apparently not long, say two days, and carrion-flower the same.

Looked at the peetweet's nest which C. found yesterday. It was very difficult to find again in the broad open meadow; no nest but a mere hollow in the dead cranberry leaves, the grass and stubble ruins, under a little alder. The old bird went off at last from under us; low in the grass at first and with *wings up*, making a worried sound which attracted other birds. I frequently noticed others afterward flying low over the meadow and alighting and uttering this same note of alarm. There [were] only four eggs in this nest yesterday, and to-day, to C.'s surprise, there are the two eggs which he left and a young peetweet beside; a gray pinch of down with a black centre to its back, but already so old and precocious that it runs with its long legs swiftly off from squatting beside the two eggs, and hides in the grass. We have some trouble to catch it. How came it here with these eggs, which will not be hatched for some days? C. saw nothing of it yesterday. J. Farmer says that young peetweets run at once like partridges and quails, and that they are the only birds he knows that do. These eggs were not addled (I had opened one, C. another). Did this bird come from another nest, or did it belong to an earlier brood? Eggs white, with black spots here and there all over, dim at great end.

A cherry-bird's nest and two eggs in an apple tree fourteen feet from ground.[1] One egg, round black spots and a few oblong, about equally but thinly dispersed over the whole, and a dim, internal, purplish tinge about the large end. It is difficult to see anything of

[1] *Vide* 16th.

the bird, for she steals away early, and you may neither see nor hear anything of her while examining the nest, and so think it deserted. Approach very warily and look out for them a dozen or more rods off.

It suddenly began to rain with great violence, and we in haste drew up our boat on the Clamshell shore, upset it, and got under, sitting on the paddles, and so were quite dry while our friends thought we were being wet to our skins. But we had as good a roof as they. It was very pleasant to lie there half an hour close to the edge of the water and see and hear the great drops patter on the river, each making a great bubble; the rain seemed much heavier for it. The swallows at once and numerously began to fly low over the water in the rain, as they had not before, and the toads' spray rang in it. After it began to hold up, the wind veered a little to the east and apparently blew back the rear of the cloud, and blew a second rain somewhat in upon us.

As soon as the rain was over I crawled out, straightened my legs, and stumbled at once upon a little patch of strawberries within a rod, — the sward red with them. These we plucked while the last drops were thinly falling.

Silene antirrhina out on Clamshell, how long?

June 15. Friday. To Moore's Swamp.

Robin's nest in apple tree, twelve feet high — young nearly grown. Hair-bird's nest on main limb of an apple tree, horizontal, ten feet high. Many pollywogs an inch long. In the swamp a catbird's nest in the

darkest and thickest part, in a high blueberry, five feet from ground, two eggs; bird comes within three feet while I am looking.

Viburnum nudum, how long? Not long.

Wool(?)-grass.

I see a strange warbler still in this swamp. A chestnut and gray backed bird, five or six inches long, with a black throat and yellow crown; note, *chit chit chill le le*, or *chut chut a wutter chut a wut, che che*.

Crimson frosting on maple leaves. The swamp pyrus twigs are in some places curving over and swollen, and curling up at ends, forming bunches of leaves.

June 16. Saturday. The cherry-bird's egg was a satin color, or very pale slate, with an internal or what would be called black-and-blue ring about large end.

P. M. — To Hubbard's Grove, on river.

A sparrow's nest with four gray eggs in bank beyond ivy tree. Four catbirds half fledged in the green-briar near bathing-place, hung three feet from ground.

Examined a kingbird's nest found before (13th) in a black willow over edge of river, four feet from ground. Two eggs. West of oak in Hubbard's meadow. Catbird's nest in an alder, three feet from ground, three fresh eggs.

See young and weak striped squirrels nowadays, with slender tails, asleep on horizontal boughs above their holes, or moving feebly about; might catch them. Redstarts in the swamp there. Also see there a blue yellow-green-backed warbler, with an orange breast

and throat, white belly and vent, and forked tail — indigo-blue head, etc.

Ground-nut, how long?

A painted tortoise just burying three flesh-colored eggs in the dry, sandy plain near the thrasher's nest. It leaves no trace on the surface. Find near by four more about this business. When seen they stop stock-still in whatever position, and stir not nor make any noise, just as their shells may happen to be tilted up.

June 18. To Hemlocks.

Sparganium. A yellowbird feigns broken wings. Woodcock.

At 3 p. m., as I walked up the bank by the Hemlocks, I saw a painted tortoise just beginning its hole; then another a dozen rods from the river on the bare barren field near some pitch pines, where the earth was covered with cladonias, cinquefoil, sorrel, etc. Its hole was about two thirds done. I stooped down over it, and, to my surprise, after a slight pause it proceeded in its work, directly under and within eighteen inches of my face. I retained a constrained position for three quarters of an hour or more for fear of alarming it. It rested on its fore legs, the front part of its shell about one inch higher than the rear, and this position was not changed essentially to the last. The hole was oval, broadest behind, about one inch wide and one and three quarters long, and the dirt already removed was quite wet or moistened. It made the hole and removed the dirt with its hind legs only, not using its tail or shell, which last of course could not enter the hole, though there was some dirt on it. It first scratched two or three times with one hind foot; then took up a pinch of the loose sand and deposited it directly behind that leg, pushing it backward to its full length and then deliberately opening it and letting the dirt fall; then the same with the other hind foot. This it did rapidly, using each leg alternately with perfect regularity, standing on the other one the while, and thus tilting up its shell each time, now to this side, then to that. There was half a minute or a minute between each change. The hole was made as deep as the feet could reach, or about two inches. It was very neat about its work, not scattering the dirt about any more than was necessary. The completing of the hole occupied perhaps five minutes.

It then without any pause drew its head completely into its shell, raised the rear a little, and protruded and dropped a wet flesh-colored egg into the hole, one end foremost, the red skin of its body being considerably protruded with it. Then it put out its head again a little, slowly, and placed the egg at one side with one hind foot. After a delay of about two minutes it again drew in its head and dropped another, and so on to the fifth — drawing in its head each time, and pausing somewhat longer between the last. The eggs were placed in the hole without any *particular* care, — only well down flat and [each] out of the way of the next, — and I could plainly see them from above.

After these ten minutes or more, it without pause or turning began to scrape the moist earth into the hole with its hind legs, and, when it had half filled it, it

carefully pressed it down with the edges of its hind feet, dancing on them alternately, for some time, as on its knees, tilting from side to side, pressing by the whole weight of the rear of its shell. When it had drawn in thus all the earth that had been moistened, it stretched its hind legs further back and to each side, and drew in the dry and lichen-clad crust, and then danced upon and pressed that down, still not moving the rear of its shell more than one inch to right or left all the while, or changing the position of the forward part at all. The thoroughness with which the covering was done was remarkable. It persevered in drawing in and dancing on the dry surface which had never been disturbed, long after you thought it had done its duty, but it never moved its fore feet, nor once looked round, nor saw the eggs it had laid. There were frequent pauses throughout the whole, when it rested, or ran out its head and looked about circumspectly, at any noise or motion. These pauses were especially long during the covering of its eggs, which occupied more than half an hour. Perhaps it was hard work.

When it had done, it immediately started for the river at a pretty rapid rate (the suddenness with which it made these transitions was amusing), pausing from time to time, and I judged that it would reach it in fifteen minutes. It was not easy to detect that the ground had been disturbed there. An Indian could not have made his cache more skillfully. In a few minutes all traces of it would be lost to the eye.

The object of moistening the earth was perhaps to enable it to take it up in its hands (?), and also to pre-

vent its falling back into the hole. Perhaps it also helped to make the ground more compact and harder when it was pressed down.[1]

June 19. *Tuesday.* P. M. — Up Assabet.

A pewee's nest (bird apparently small pewee, nest apparently wood pewee's) on a white maple's nearly horizontal bough, eighteen feet above water, opposite Hemlocks; externally of lichens from the maple trunk, and hemlock (?) twigs, very inconspicuous, like a lichen-covered knot.[2] I hear many wood pewees about here.

Young song sparrows flutter about.

A yellowbird's nest saddled on a horizontal (or slanting down amid twigs) branch of a swamp white oak, within reach, six feet high, of fern down and lint; a sharp cone bottom; four eggs, just laid, pale flesh-color with brown spots; have one.

There are a great many glaucous and also hoary and yellowish-green puffs on the *Andromeda paniculata* now, some four inches in diameter. Wood tortoises united, with heads out of water.

Did I enumerate the sharp-shinned hawk among ours?

Mr. Bull found in his garden this morning a snapping turtle about twenty rods from the brook, which had there just made a round hole (apparently with head) $2\frac{1}{2}$ inches in diameter and $5+$ deep, in a slanting direction. I brought her home and put her into a pen in the garden that she might lay (she weighed seven pounds five ounces), but she climbed over an

[1] *Vide* September 10th.   [2] Empty on July 25th.

upright fence of smooth stakes twenty-two inches high.

June 20. A catbird's nest eight feet high on a pitch pine in Emerson's heater piece, partly of paper. A summer yellowbird's, saddled on an apple, of cotton-wool, lined with hair and feathers, three eggs, white with flesh-colored tinge and purplish-brown and black spots. Two hair-birds' nests fifteen feet high on apple trees at R. W. E.'s (one with two eggs). A robin's nest with young, which was lately, in the great wind, blown down and somehow lodged on the lower part of an evergreen by arbor, — without spilling the young!

June 21. Saw a white lily in Everett's Pond.

Sparrow's nest, four eggs, deep in the moist bank beyond cherry-bird's nest (have three), of peculiar color. She deserted the nest after one was taken. Outside of stubble, scantily lined with fibrous roots. Clams abundant within three feet of shore, and bream-nests. The early grass is ripe or browned, and clover is drying. Peetweets make quite a noise calling to their young with alarm.

On an apple at R. W. E.'s a small pewee's nest, on a horizontal branch, seven feet high, almost wholly of hair, cotton without, not incurved at edge; four eggs, pale cream-color.

June 22. At 6 P. M. the temperature of the air is 77°, of river one rod from shore 72°. Warmest day yet.

June 23. Probably a redstart's nest (?) on a white oak sapling, twelve feet up, on forks against stem. Have it. See young redstarts about.

Hear of flying squirrels now grown.

June 25. Under E. Wood's barn, a phœbe's nest, with two birds ready to fly; also barn swallow's nest lined with feathers, hemisphere or cone against side of sleeper; five eggs, delicate, as well as white-bellied swallow's.

June 26. C. has found a wood pewee's nest on a horizontal limb of a small swamp white oak, ten feet high, with three fresh eggs, cream-colored with spots of two shades in a ring about large end. Have nest and an egg.

June 28. On river.

Two red-wings' nests, four eggs and three — one without any black marks. Hear and see young golden robins which have left the nest, now peeping with a peculiar tone. Shoals of minnows a half-inch long. Eel-grass washed up.

June 30. 2 P. M. — Thermometer north side of house, 95°; in river where one foot deep, one rod from shore, 82°.

XI

JULY, 1855

(ÆT. 37–38)

July 2. Young bobolinks are now fluttering over the meadow, but I have not been able to find a nest, so concealed in the meadow-grass.

At 2 P. M. — Thermometer north side of house . 93°
Air over river at Hubbard's Bath . . . . . 88°
Water six feet from shore and one foot deep . 84½°
  " near surface in middle, where up to neck . 83½°
  " at bottom in same place, pulling it up quickly 83½°

Yet the air on the wet body, there being a strong southwest wind, feels colder than the water.

July 3. 4 P. M. — Air out-of-doors generally, 86°. On the sand between rails in the Deep Cut, 103°. Near the surface of Walden, fifteen rods from shore, 80°. Three feet below the surface there, and everywhere nearer shore (and probably further from it), 78°.

July 4. To Boston on way to Cape Cod with C.

The schooner Melrose was advertised to make her first trip to Provincetown this morning at eight. We reached City (?) Wharf at 8.30. "Well, Captain Crocker, how soon do you start?" "To-morrow morning at 9 o'clock." "But you have advertised to leave at 8

Vol. VII

this morning." "I know it, but we are going to lay over till to-morrow." ! ! ! So we had to spend the day in Boston, — at Athenæum gallery, Alcott's, and at the regatta. Lodged at Alcott's, who is about moving to Walpole.

July 5. In middle of the forenoon sailed in the Melrose. We hugged the Scituate shore as long as possible on account of wind. The great tupelo on the edge of Scituate is very conspicuous for many miles about Minot's Rock. Scared up a flock of young ducks on the Bay, which have been bred hereabouts. Saw the petrel.[1]

Went to Gifford's Union House (the old Tailor's Inn) in Provincetown. They have built a town-house since I was here — the first object seen in making the port. Talked with Nahum Haynes, who is making fisherman's boots there. He came into the tavern in the evening. I did not know him — only that he was a Haynes. He remembered two mud turtles caught in a seine with shad on the Sudbury meadows forty years ago, which would weigh a hundred pounds each. Asked me, "Who was that man that used to live next to Bull's, — acted as if he were crazy or out?"[2]

Talked with a man who has the largest patch of cranberries here, — ten acres, — and there are fifteen or twenty acres in all.

The fishermen sell lobsters fresh for two cents apiece.

July 6. Rode to North Truro very early in the stage

[1] [*Cape Cod*, p. 264; Riv. 320.]
[2] [Nathaniel Hawthorne lived next to Mr. Bull for some years.]

or covered wagon, on the new road, which is just finished as far as East Harbor Creek. Blackfish on the shore. Walked from post-office to lighthouse. Fog till eight or nine, and short grass very wet. Board at James Small's, the lighthouse, at $3.50 the week.

Polygala polygama well out, flat, ray-wise, all over the fields. *Cakile Americana*, sea-rocket, the large weed of the beach, some time and going to seed, on beach. Pasture thistle (*Cirsium pumilum*), out some time. A great many white ones. The boy, Isaac Small, got eighty bank swallows' eggs out of the clay-bank, *i. e.* above the clay. Small says there are a few great gulls here in summer. I see small (?) yellow-legs. Many crow blackbirds in the dry fields hopping about. Upland plover near the lighthouse breeding. Small once cut off one's wing when mowing in the field next the lighthouse as she sat on her eggs. Many seringo-birds, apparently like ours. They say mackerel have just left the Bay, and fishermen have gone to the eastward for them. Some, however, are catching cod and halibut on the back side. Cape measures two miles in width here on the great chart.[1]

July 7. *Smilax glauca* in blossom, running over the shrubbery. *Honkenya peploides*, sea sandwort, just out of bloom on beach. The thick-leaved and dense-tufted, upright plant *Salsola Kali*, saltwort, prickly and glaucous, in bloom. Beach pea (*Lathyrus maritimus*) going out of bloom.[2]

[1] [*Cape Cod*, pp. 164, 167; Riv. 196, 200.]
[2] [*Cape Cod*, p. 167; Riv. 200.]

Barn Swallows

Provincetown

C. says he saw in the catalogue of the Mercantile Library, New York, "Peter Thoreau on Book-keeping, London."

The piping plover running and standing on the beach, and a few mackerel gulls skimming over the sea and fishing. Josh (?) pears [1] ("*juicy*," suggests Small) just begun; few here compared with Provincetown; do not cook them.

Seaside goldenrod (*Solidago sempervirens*) not nearly yet.

Xanthium echinatum, sea cocklebur or sea-burdock, not yet.[2]

What that smilacina-like plant very common in the shrubbery, a foot high, with now green fruit big as peas at end of spike, with reddish streaks? Uncle Sam calls it snake-corn.[3] Brought home some fruit.

Just south of the lighthouse near the bank on a steep hillside, the savory-leaved aster (*Diplopappus linariifolius*) and mouse-ear (*Gnaphalium plantaginifolium*) form a dense sward, being short and thick; [the aster] not yet out.[4] Scarlet pimpernel, or poor-man's weather-glass (*Anagallis arvensis*), in bloom some time, very common on sandy fields and sands, and very pretty, with a peculiar scarlet.[5]

July 8. A northeasterly storm. A great part of beach bodily removed and a rock five feet high exposed

[1] [The fruit of the shad-bush. See *Cape Cod*, p. 203; Riv. 244.]
[2] I saw its burs early in October in New Bedford.
[3] It is *Smilacina racemosa*.
[4] Out July 10th. [*Cape Cod*, p. 135; Riv. 160.]
[5] [*Cape Cod*, p. 167; Riv. 200.]

— before invisible — opposite lighthouse. The black-throated bunting common among the shrubbery. Its note much like the Maryland yellow-throat's, — *wittichee te tchea, tche te tchea, tche.*[1]

The *Corema Conradii*, broom crowberry, is quite common at edge of higher bank just south of the light-house. It is now full of small green fruit, small pin-head size. It spreads from a centre, raying out and rooting every four or five inches. It forms peculiar handsome-shaped mounds, four or five feet in diam-eter by nine inches or a foot high, very soft springy beds to lie on, — a woodman's bed already spread.[2]

I am surprised at the number of large light-colored toads everywhere hopping over these dry and sandy fields.

Went over to Bay side. That pond at Pond Village three eighths of a mile long and densely filled with cat-tail flag seven feet high. Many red-wing black-birds in it. Small says there are two kinds of cat-tail there, one the barrel flag for coopers, the other shorter for chairs; he used to gather them.[3]

See the killdeer a dozen rods off in pasture, anxious about its eggs or young, with its shrill squeaking note, its ring of white about its neck and two black crescents on breast. They are not so common and noisy as in June. A milkweed out some days.[1]

Hudsonia tomentosa, the downy, still lingering, and *ericoides* even yet up to 17th. The last is *perhaps* the most common.

[1] [*Cape Cod*, p. 131; Riv. 156.]   [2] [*Cape Cod*, p. 167; Riv. 200.]
[3] [*Cape Cod*, p. 142; Riv. 169.]

Vol. VII

Euphorbia polygonifolia, seaside spurge, small and flat on pure sand. Did n't notice flower. *Lemna minor*, duckweed, duck-meat, covering the surface at the pond, — scale-like. See a nighthawk at 8 A. M., sitting length-wise on a rail. Asked Small if a quarter of the fuel of North Truro was driftwood. He thought it was, beside some lumber. None of the *Mya arenaria* on back side, but a small thicker-shelled clam, *Mesodesma arctata*, with a golden-yellow epidermis, very common on the flats, which S. said was good to eat. The shells washed up were commonly perforated; could dig them with your hands.[1]

S. said that nineteen small yellow birds (probably goldfinches) were found dead under the light in the spring early.[2]

July 9. Peterson brings word of blackfish. I went over and saw them. The largest about fourteen feet long. Nineteen years ago three hundred and eighty at this (Great) Hollow in one school. Sometimes eat them. Small says they generally come about the last of July; some yield five barrels, average one barrel.[3]

A kind of artemisia or sea wormwood by Bay-side on sand-hills, not out. Bay-wings here.

I find the edible mussel generally in bunches as they were washed off the rocks thirty or forty together, held together by the twine-like byssus. Many little mussels on the rocks exposed at high tide.

[1] [*Cape Cod*, p. 110; Riv. 130.]
[2] [*Cape Cod*, p. 170; Riv. 204.]
[3] [See *Cape Cod*, pp. 142–146; Riv. 170–174.]

Uncle Sam Small, half blind, sixty-six years old, re-members the building of the lighthouse and their pro-phecies about the bank wasting. Thought the now over-hanging upper solid parts *might* last ten years. His path had sometimes lasted so long (??). Saw him making a long diagonal slanting path with a hoe, in order to get up a small pile of stuff on his back. (There lay his hooked pike-staff on the bank ready for immediate use.) But this path was destroyed before we left. Told of a large rock which was carried along the shore half a mile.[1] He gets all his fuel on the beach. At flood-tide there is a strong inshore current to north. We saw some (perhaps) bales of grass, or else dried bits of marsh, six feet long carried along thus very fast a quarter of a mile out. Told us of man-eating sharks, one twelve feet long, which he killed and drew up with his oxen.

No quahogs on this side.

Now, with a clear sky and bright weather, we see many dark streaks and patches where the surface of the ocean is rippled by fishes, mostly menhaden, far and wide, in countless myriads, such the populousness of the sea. Occasionally, when near, can see their shin-ing sides appear — and the mackerel gulls dive. Also see bass, whiting, cod, etc., turn up their bellies, near the shore.[2] The distant horizon a narrow blue line from distance (?) like mountains. They call peetweets shore-birds here. Small thought the waves never ran less than seven or eight feet up the shore here, though

[1] [*Cape Cod*, p. 155; Riv. 186.]
[2] [*Cape Cod*, p. 120; Riv. 142, 143.]

these might be perfectly smooth.[1] Speaks of mackerel gulls breeding on islands in Wellfleet Harbor.

July 10. The sea, like Walden, is greenish within half a mile of shore, then blue. The purple tinges near the shore run far up and down. Walked to marsh head of East Harbor Creek. Marsh rosemary (*Statice Limonium*), "meadow root," rays small, out some time, with five reddish petals. Also see there samphire of two kinds, *herbacea* and *mucronata*. *Juncus Gerardii*, black grass, in bloom. The pigweed about seashore is remarkably white and mealy. Great devil's-needles above the bank, apparently catching flies. I see a brood of young peeps running on the beach under the sand-hills ahead of me. Indigo out. Heard a cannon from the sea, which echoed under the bank dully, as if a part of the bank had fallen; then saw a pilot-boat standing down and the pilot looking through his glass toward the distant outward-bound vessel, which was putting back to speak with him. The latter sailed many a mile to meet her. She put her sails aback and communicated alongside.

July 11. See *young* piping plover running in a troop on the beach like peetweets. Patches of shrub oaks, bayberry, beach plum, and early wild roses, overrun with woodbine. What a splendid show of wild roses, whose sweetness is mingled with the aroma of the bayberry! ! Small made three thousand shingles of a mast, worth six dollars a thousand.

[1] [*Cape Cod*, p. 156; Riv. 186.]

Vol. VII

and beach pea. Fog wets your beard till twelve o'clock.[1]

Long slender seaside plantain leaf (?) at East Harbor head. *Solanum* (with white flowers) *nigrum* (?) in marsh. *Spergularia rubra* var. *marina*. Great many little shells by edge of marsh — *Auricula bidentata* (?) and *Succinea avara* (?).

Great variety of beetles, dor-bugs, etc., on beach. I have one green shining one. Also butterflies over bank. Small thought the pine land was worth twenty-five cents an acre. I was surprised to see great spider-holes in pure sand and gravel, with a firm edge, where man could not make a hole without the sand sliding in, — in tunnel form.

They are gone off for mackerel and cod; also catching mackerel, halibut, and lobsters about here for the market.

The upland plover begins with a quivering note somewhat like a tree-toad and ends with a long, clear, somewhat plaintive (?) or melodious (?) hawk-like scream. I never heard this very near to me, and when I asked the inhabitants about it they did not know what I meant. Frank Forester, in "Manual for Young Sportsmen," 1856, page 308, says, "This bird has a soft plaintive call or whistle of two notes, which have something of a ventriloquial character and possess this peculiarity, that when uttered close to the ear, they appear to come from a distance, and when the bird is really two or three fields distant, sound as if near at hand." It hovers on quivering wing, and alights by a steep dive.

[1] [*Cape Cod*, p. 165; Riv. 198.]

A bar wholly made within three months; first exposed about first of May; as I paced, now seventy-five rods long and six or eight rods wide at high water, and bay within six rods wide. The bay has extended twice as far, but is filled up.

Lespedeza Stuvei (?) or *procumbens* (?).

I see five young swallows dead on the sand under their holes. Fell out and died in the storm?

The upland plover hovers almost stationary in the air with a quivering note of alarm. Above, dark-brown interspersed with white, darkest in rear; gray-spotted breast, white beneath; bill dark above, yellowish at base beneath, and legs yellowish. *Totanus Bartramius* — "gray," "grass," "field" plover.

Bank at lighthouse one hundred and seventy feet on the slope, perpendicular one hundred and ten; say shelf slopes four and ordinary tide-fall is nine, makes one hundred and twenty-three in all. Saw sandbank south fifteen to twenty-five feet higher.

Small says *cantle* for quintal. Mackerel-fishing not healthy like cod-fishing; hard work packing the mackerel, stooping over.

July 12. Peterson says he dug one hundred and twenty-six dollars' worth of small clams near his house in Truro one winter, — twenty-five bucketfuls at one time. One man forty. Says they are scarce because they feed pigs on them. I measure a horseshoe on the back side twenty-two inches by eleven. The low sand-downs between East Harbor head and sea are thinly covered with beach-grass, seaside goldenrod,

My paper so damp in this house I can't press flowers without mildew, nor dry my towel for a week.[1]

Small thought there was no stone wall west of Orleans. Squid the bait for bass. Small said the blackfish ran ashore in pursuit of it. Hardly use pure salt at Small's. Do not drink water.[2] S. repeats a tradition that the back side was frozen over one mile out in 1680 (?). Often is on Bay, but never since on Atlantic.

July 13. About $33,000 has been appropriated for the protection of Provincetown Harbor. Northeast winds the strongest. Caught a box tortoise. It appeared to have been feeding on insects, — their wing-cases, etc., in its droppings, — also leaves. No undertow on the bars because the shore is flat.

July 14. The sea has that same streaked look that our meadows have in a gale.

Go to Bay side. Stench of blackfish. The lobster holds on to the pot himself. Throw away the largest. Find French crown. I was walking close to the water's edge just after the tide had begun to fall, looking for shells and pebbles, and observed on the still wet sand, under the abrupt caving edge of the bank, this dark-colored round, flat — old button? I cheated my companion by holding up round *Scutella parma* on the bars, between my fingers.[3] High hill — where town-house? — in Provincetown; according to big map, 109 feet high.

[1] [*Cape Cod*, p. 165; Riv. 198.]   [2] [*Cape Cod*, p. 165; Riv. 198.]
[3] [*Cape Cod*, p. 161; Riv. 193.]

When numerous you may count about eighty vessels at once. A little kelp and rockweed grow offshore here. Nest of grass-bird (?), — grass stubble, lined with grass and root-fibres, three eggs half hatched, under a tuft of beach-grass, a quarter of a mile inland. Have an egg. Measured apple trees at Uncle Sam's.

They say the keeper of Billingsgate Light a few days ago put his initials in [a] thousand dollars' worth of blackfish in one morning, and got that of Province-town for them.[1] Another, some years ago, got one hundred in a morning, and sold them for fifteen hundred dollars. Got a fox's skull. Thirty-six feet from base to centre of this light. Light called in book one hundred and seventy-one feet above sea?

Found washed up, and saw swimming in the cove where we bathed, young mackerel two inches long.

Uncle Sam says there is most drift in the spring; so in our river. He calls his apple trees "he."

July 16. Why not have one large reflector instead of many small ones, for a strong light? Uva-ursi berries begin to redden. Beach-grass grows on the highest land here. Uncle Sam tells of sea-turtles, which he regarded as natives, as big as a barrel, found on the marsh; of more than one kind.[2] Call the fishing captains skippers. The oak wood north of Rich's or Dyer's Hollow, say twenty years old, nine feet high. Red (?) oaks, etc. Can see soil on edge of bank covered five feet deep with sand which has blown up, on the

[1] [*Cape Cod*, pp. 145, 146; Riv. 173, 174.]
[2] [*Cape Cod*, p. 202; Riv. 243.]

highest part of bank. See three black snakes on sand just behind edge of bank. Blueberries only one inch high.

July 18. Leave Small's. Corn-cockle, or rose-campion, a handsome flower, by East Harbor Marsh. *Lychnis Githago*, how long? Perfect young horseshoe crab shells there. Goosefoot by marsh very spreading, with entire, obovate leaves. Came up in the Olata, Captain Freeman, a fine yacht. Little wind; were from half past eight into candle-light on water. Melrose and another, which started with us, were ten miles astern when we passed light-boat. Kept pace awhile with a steamer towing one of Train's ships far in the north. The steamer looked very far from ship, and some wondered that the interval continued the same for hours. Smoke stretched perfectly horizontal for miles over the sea, and, by its direction, warned me of a change in the wind before we felt it.[1]

July 19. In Concord.

Young bobolinks; one of the first autumnalish notes. The early meadow aster out.

July 21. A red-eyed vireo nest on a red maple on Island Neck, on meadow-edge, ten feet from ground; one egg half hatched and one cowbird's egg, nearly fresh (!), a trifle larger. The first white (the minute brown dots washing off), sparsely black-dotted at the large end. Have them.

[1] [*Cape Cod*, pp. 264, 265; Riv. 320, 321.]

Vol. VII

July 22. I hear that many of those balls have been found at Flint's Pond within a few days. See small flocks of red-wings, young and old, now, over the willows. The pigeon woodpeckers have flown. Dog-day weather begins.

July 25. Many little toads about.

That piece of hollow kelp stem which I brought from the Cape is now shrivelled up and is covered and all white with crystals of salt a sixth of an inch long, like frost, on all sides.[1]

Morrhua vulgaris is the cod of Europe and New-foundland. Those caught off our coast are the *M. Americana.*

July 30. Saw the lightning on the telegraph battery and heard the shock about sundown from our window, — an intensely bright white light.

July 31. Our dog-days seem to be turned to a rainy season. Mr. Derby, whose points of compass I go to regulate, tells me that he remembers when it rained for three weeks in haying time every day but Sundays.

Rode to J. Farmer's. He says that on a piece of an old road on his land, discontinued forty years ago, for a distance of forty rods which he plowed, [he found] two or three dollars in small change. Among the rest he showed me an old silver piece about as big as a ten-cent-piece, with the word *skilli*, etc., etc., on it, apparently a Danish shilling?

[1] [*Cape Cod*, p. 69; Riv. 79.]

His boy has a republican swallow's egg, long and much spotted; a dove's egg. Found a bay-wing's nest and got an egg; three half hatched, with dark *spots*, not *lines;* low in grass; of stubble, lined with root-fibres and then horsehair; in a dry field of his. He gave me what he called the seringo's egg. (He calls it chick-le-see.)[1] Pointed out the bird to me. Says that she enters to her nest by a long gallery, sometimes two or three feet long, under the grass, and the nest is very hard to find. Gave me a small pure white egg. The boy thought it a small pewee's (?).

Farmer showed me that every wilted or diseased pigweed had green lice on its root. He says he sometimes finds the marsh wren's nest in meadows, hung to the grass, and hole on one side. Hears it almost every night near the brook beyond Dr. Bartlett's. Has found lark's nest covered over.

Found lately on his sand two arrowheads, and, close by, a rib and a shoulder-blade and kneepan (?), he thinks of an Indian.

His son Edward gave me a blue jay's egg as well as the seringo's above named, also another, rounder and broader egg found in that open field without any nest, *maybe* the same kind, somewhat singularly marked, but whiter at one end and browner at the other.

Mr. Samuel Hoar tells me that about forty-eight years ago, or some two or three years after he came to Concord, where he had an office in the yellow store, there used to be a great many bullfrogs in the mill-pond, which, by their trumping in the night, disturbed the

[1] Does he mean whittiche, Maryland yellow-throat?

apprentices of a Mr. Joshua Jones who built and lived in the brick house near by and soon after set up the trip-hammer. But, as Mr. H. was going one day to or from his office (he boarded this side the Mill-Dam), he found that the apprentices had been round the pond in a boat knocking the frogs on the head; got a good-sized tub nearly full of them. After that scarcely any were heard, and, the trip-hammer being set up soon after, they all disappeared as if frightened away by the sound. But perhaps the cure was worse than the disease, for I know of one, then a young minister studying divinity, who boarded in that very brick house, who was so much disturbed by that trip-hammer that, out of compassion, he was taken in at the old parsonage.

Mr. H. remembers that blackfish oil, which was used at the tan-yards, was sold to put on horses and keep the flies off.

Tree-toads sing more than before. Have observed the twittering over of goldfinches for a week.

XII

AUGUST, 1855

(ÆT. 38)

Aug. 1. P. M. — To Conantum by boat.

Squirrels have eaten and stripped pitch pine cones. Small rough sunflower a day or two. *Diplopappus cornifolius* (how long?) at Conant Orchard Grove. In the spring there, which has not been cleared out lately, I find a hairworm, eight or nine inches long and big as a pin-wire; is biggest in the middle and tapers thence to tail; at head is abruptly cut off; curly in your fingers like the tendril of a vine. I spent half an hour overhauling the heaps of clamshells under the rocks there. Was surprised to find the anodon and the green-rayed clams there.

Pennyroyal and alpine enchanter's-nightshade well out, how long?.

Young Adams of Waltham tells me he has been moose-hunting at Chesuncook. Hunted with a guide in evening without horn, it being too early to call them out. Heard the water dropping from their muzzles when they lifted their heads from feeding on the pads, as they stood in the river.

Aug. 2. Silas Hosmer tells me of his going a-spearing in Concord River up in Southboro once with some friends of his. It is a mere brook there, and they went

along the bank without any boat, one carrying a large basket of pine and another the crate and a third the spear. It was hard work. He afterward showed them how they did here, by going in *midsummer* with them and catching a great many.

Aug. 4. Just after bathing at the rock near the Island this afternoon, after sunset, I saw a flock of thousands of barn swallows and some white-bellied, and perhaps others, for it was too dark to distinguish them. They came flying over the river in loose array, wheeled and flew round in a great circle over the bay there, about eighty feet high, with a loud twittering as if seeking a resting-place, then flew up the stream. I was very much surprised at their numbers. Directly after, hearing a buzzing sound, we found them all alighted on the dense golden willow hedge at Shat-tuck's shore, parallel with the shore, quite densely leaved and eighteen feet high. They were generally perched five or six feet from the top, amid the thick leaves, filling it for eight or ten rods. They were very restless, fluttering from one perch to another and about one another, and kept up a loud and remarkable buzz-ing or squeaking, breathing or hum, with only occa-sionally a regular twitter, now and then flitting along-side from one end of the row to the other. It was so dark we had to draw close to see them. At intervals they were perfectly still for a moment, as if at a signal. At length, after twenty or thirty minutes of bustle and hum, they all settled quietly to rest on their perches, I supposed for the night. We had rowed up within a

rod of one end of the row, looking up so as to bring the birds between us and the sky, but they paid not the slightest attention to us. What was remarkable was: first, their numbers; second, their perching on densely leaved willows; third, their buzzing or hum-ming, like a hive of bees, even squeaking notes; and fourth, their disregarding our nearness. I supposed that they were preparing to migrate, being the early broods.

Aug. 5. 4 A. M. — On river to see swallows.

They are all gone; yet Fay saw them there last night after we passed. Probably they started very early. I asked Minott if he ever saw swallows migrating, not telling him what I had seen, and he said that [he] used to get up and go out to mow very early in the morning on his meadow, as early as he could see to strike, and once, at that hour, hearing a noise, he looked up and could just distinguish high overhead fifty thou-sand swallows. He thought it was in the latter part of August.

What I saw is like what White says of the swallows, in the autumn, roosting "every night in the osier beds of the aits" of the river Thames; and his editor, Jesse, says, "Swallows in countless numbers still assemble every autumn on the willows growing on the aits of the river Thames." And Jardine, in his notes to Wil-son, says that a clergyman of Rotherham describes in an anonymous pamphlet their assembling (in the words of the pamphlet) "at the willow ground, on the banks of the canal, preparatory to their migration," early in September, 1815, daily increasing in numbers until there were tens of thousands. Divided into bands every morning and sought their food. They finally left R. the 7th October.

As I was paddling back at 6 A. M., saw, nearly half a mile off, a blue heron standing erect on the topmost twig of the great buttonwood on the street in front of Mr. Prichard's house, while perhaps all within were abed and asleep. Little did they think of it, and how they were presided over. He looked at first like a spiring twig against the sky, till you saw him flap his wings. Presently he launched off and flew away over Mrs. Brooks's house.

It seems that I used to tie a regular granny's knot in my shoe-strings, and I learned of myself — rediscovered — to tie a true square knot, or what sailors sometimes call a reef-knot. It needed to be as secure as a reef-knot in any gale, to withstand the wringing and twisting I gave it in my walks.

The common small violet lespedeza out, ellipticleaved, one inch long. The small white spreading polygala, twenty rods behind Wyman site, some time. Very common this year.

It is the wet season, and there is a luxuriant dark foliage. Hear a yellow-legs flying over, — *phe' phe phe, phe' phe phe*.

8 P. M. — On river to see swallows.

At this hour the robins fly to high, thick oaks (as this swamp white oak) to roost for the night. The wings of the chimney swallows flying near me make a whis-

tling sound like a duck's. Is not this peculiar among the swallows? They flutter much for want of tail. I see martins about. Now many swallows in the twilight, after circling eight feet high, come back two or three hundred feet high and then go down the river.

Aug. 6. P. M. — Down river to Tarbell Hill with C. Saw a *Sternothærus odoratus*, caught by the neck and hung in the fork between a twig and main trunk of a black willow, about two feet above water, — apparently a month or two, being nearly dry. Probably in its haste to get down had fallen and was caught. I have noticed the same thing once or twice before. Hear the autumnal crickets.

At Ball's Hill see five summer ducks, a brood now grown, feeding amid the pads on the opposite side of the river, with a whitish ring, perhaps nearly around neck. A rather shrill squeaking quack when they go off. It is remarkable how much more game you will see if you are in the habit of *sitting* in the fields and woods. As you pass along with a noise it hides itself, but presently comes forth again.

The *Ludwigia sphærocarpa* out maybe a week. I was obliged to wade to it all the way from the shore, the meadow-grass cutting my feet above and making them smart. You must wear boots here. The lespedeza with short heads, how long? These great meadows through which I wade have a great abundance of hedge-hyssop now in bloom in the water. Small St. John's-worts and elodeas, lanceolate loosestrife, arrow-

Vol. VII

heads, small climbing bellflower, also horse-mint on the drier clods. These all over the meadow.

I see seven or eight nighthawks together; dull-buff breasts, with tails short and black beneath. The mole cricket creaks along the shore.

Meadow-haying on all hands.

Aug. 7. To Tarbell Hill again with the Emersons, a-berrying.

Very few berries this year.

Aug. 8. Blue-curls, how long? Not long.

Aug. 9. Elecampane, apparently several days. River is risen and fuller, and the weeds at bathing-place washed away somewhat. Fall to them.

Dana says a sprit is the diagonal boom or gaff, and hence a spritsail. Most fore-and-aft sails have a gaff and boom.

Aug. 10. P. M. — To Nagog.

Middle of huckleberrying.

Aug. 19. See painted tortoise shedding scales, — half off and loose.[1]

Aug. 22. I hear of some young barn swallows in the nest still in R. Rice's barn, Sudbury.

Aug. 24. Scare up a pack of grouse.

[1] Again Sept. 10 and 15.

Aug. 25. In Dennis's field this side the river, I count about one hundred and fifty cowbirds about eight cows, running before their noses and in odd positions, awkwardly walking with a straddle, often their heads down and tails up a long time at once, occasionally flying to keep up with a cow, over the heads of the others, and following off after a single cow. They keep close to the cow's head and feet, and she does not mind them; but when all went off in a whirring (rippling?) flock at my approach, the cow (about whom they were all gathered) *looked off after them* for some time, as if she felt deserted.

Aug. 29. Saw two green-winged teal, somewhat pigeon-like, on a flat low rock in the Assabet.

Aug. 31. First frost in our garden. Passed in boat within fifteen feet of a great bittern, standing perfectly still in the water by the riverside, with the point of its bill directly up, as if it knew that from the color of its throat, etc., it was much less likely to be detected in that position, near weeds.

XIII

SEPTEMBER, 1855

(ÆT. 38)

Sept. 2. Small locusts touched by frost, probably of the 31st August; nothing else in the woodland hollows.

Sept. 5. *Wednesday.* A stream of black ants a sixth of an inch long in the steep path beyond the Springs, some going, others returning, diagonally across the path two rods, and an inch or more wide, their further course obscured by leaves in the woods.

Sept. 10. I can find no trace of the tortoise-eggs of June 18, though there is no trace of their having been disturbed by skunks. They must have been hatched earlier. C. says he saw a painted tortoise a third grown, with a freshly killed minnow in his mouth as long as himself, eating it.

Thinking over the tortoises, I gave these names: rough tortoise, scented ditto, vermilion (rainbow, rail ?), yellow box, black box, and yellow-spotted.

Sept. 11. Loudly the mole cricket creaks by mid-afternoon. Muskrat-houses begun.

Sept. 12. A few clams freshly eaten. Some grapes ripe.

Vol. VII

the wall and down the road, quite gray, and does not see me in the road a rod off. He stops a rod off when I move in front of him. Short legs and body flat toward the ground, *i. e.* flattened out at sides.

Sept. 19. Up Assabet.

Do I see wood tortoises on this branch only? About a week since, Mr. Thurston told me of his being carried by a brother minister to hear some music on the shore of a pond in Harvard, produced by the lapse of the waves on some stones.

Sept. 20. First decisive frost, killing melons and beans, browning button-bushes and grape leaves.

P. M. — Up main stream.

The great bittern, as it flies off from near the railroad bridge, filthily drops its dirt and utters a low hoarse *kwa kwa;* then runs and hides in the grass, and I land and search within ten feet of it before it rises. See larks in flocks on meadow. See blackbirds (grackle or red-wing or crow blackbird ?).

Tried to trace by the sound a mole cricket, — thinking it a frog, — advancing from two sides and looking where our courses intersected, but in vain.

Opened a new and pretty sizable muskrat-house with no hollow yet made in it. Many tortoise-scales upon it. It is a sort of tropical vegetation at the bottom of the river. The palm-like potamogeton, — or ostrich-plumes.

Sept. 21. Stopped at the old Hunt house with Ricket-

Sept. 14. P. M. — To Hubbard's Close.

I scare from an oak by the side of the Close a young hen-hawk, which, launching off with a scream and a heavy flight, alights on the topmost plume of a large pitch pine in the swamp northward, bending it down, with its back toward me, where it might be mistaken for a plume against the sky, the light makes all things so black. It has a red tail; black primaries; scapulars and wing-coverts gray-brown; back showing much white and whitish head. It keeps looking round, first this side then that, warily.

I see no fringed gentian yet.

It costs so much to publish, would it not be better for the author to put his manuscripts in a safe?

Sept. 15. P. M. — Up Assabet.

See many painted tortoise scales being shed, half erect on their backs. An *Emys insculpta* which I mistook for dead, under water near shore; head and legs and tail *hanging down straight.* Turned it over, and to my surprise found it coupled with another. It was at first difficult to separate them with a paddle. I see many scales from the sternum of tortoises.

Three weeks ago saw many brown thrashers, catbirds, robins, etc., on wild cherries. They are worth raising for the birds about you, though objectionable on account of caterpillars.

Sept. 16. As I go up the Walden road, at Breed's, Hubbard, driving his cows through the weed-field, scares a woodchuck, which comes running through

son and C. The rafters are very slender, of oak, yet quite sound; the laths of split cedar (?), yet long and straight and as thin or thinner than our sawed ones. Between the boards and plastering, in all the lower story, at least, large-sized bricks are set on their edges in clay. Was it not partly to make it bullet-proof? They had apparently been laid from within after boarding, — from the fresh marks of the boards on the clay. An Egyptian-shaped fireplace or frame in the chamber and painted or spotted panels to the door. Large old-fashioned latches and bolts, blacksmith-made? The upper story projects in front and at ends seven or eight inches over the lower, and the gables above a foot over this. No weather-boards at the corners.

Sept. 22. Many tortoise-scales about the river now. Some of my driftwood — floating rails, etc. — are scented with muskrats; have been their perches; and also covered with a thick clear slime or jelly.

Sept. 23. Small sparrows, with yellow on one side above eye in front and white belly, erectile (?) crown divided by a light line. Those weeds, etc., on the bared meadow come up spontaneously.

8 P. M. — I hear from my chamber a screech owl about Monroe's house this bright moonlight night, — a loud, piercing scream, much like the whinner of a colt perchance, a rapid trill, then subdued or smothered a note or two.

A little wren-like (or female goldfinch) bird on a

willow at Hubbard's Causeway, eating a miller; with bright-yellow rump when wings open, and white on tail. Could it have been a yellow-rump warbler?

Sept. 24. P. M. — Up river to Conantum with C.

A very bright and pleasant fall day. The button-bushes pretty well browned with frost (though the maples are but just beginning to blush), their pale-yellowish season past. Nowadays remark the more the upright and fresh green phalanxes of bulrushes when the pontederias are mostly prostrate. The river is perhaps as low as it has been this year. Hardly can I say a bird sings, except a slight warble, perhaps, from some kind of migrating sparrow. Was it a tree sparrow, not seen?[1] The slender white spikes of the *Polygonum hydropiperoides* and the rose-colored ones of the front-rank kind, and rarely of the *P. amphibium*, look late and cool over the water. See some kalmiana lilies still freshly bloomed.

Above the Hubbard Bridge we see coming from the south in loose array some twenty apparently black ducks, with a silveriness to the under sides of their wings in the light. At first they were in form like a flock of blackbirds, then for a moment assumed the outline of a fluctuating harrow.

Some still raking, others picking, cranberries.

I suppose it was the solitary sandpiper (*Totanus solitarius*) which I saw feeding at the water's edge on Cardinal Shore, like a snipe. It was very tame; we did not scare it even by shouting. I walked along

[1] Probably a song sparrow.

the shore to within twenty-five feet of it, and it still ran toward me in feeding, and when I flushed it, it flew round and alighted between me and C., who was only three or four rods off. It was about as large as a snipe; had a bluish dusky bill about an inch and a quarter long, apparently straight, which it kept thrusting into the shallow water with a nibbling motion, a perfectly white belly, dusky-green legs; bright brown and black above, with duskier wings. When it flew, its wings, which were uniformly dark, hung down much, and I noticed no white above, and heard no note.

Brought home quite a boat-load of fuel, — one oak rail, on which fishers had stood in wet ground at Bittern Cliff, a white pine rider (?) with a square hole in [it] made by a woodpecker anciently, so wasted the sap as to leave the knots projecting, several chestnut rails; and I obtained behind Cardinal Shore a large oak stump which I know to have been bleaching there for more than thirty years, with three great gray prongs sprinkled with lichens. It bore above the marks of the original burning. There was a handful of hazel-nuts under it emptied by the ground (?) squirrel, a pretty large hole in the rough and thin stem end of each, where the bur was attached. Also, at Clamshell Hill Shore, a chestnut boat-post with a staple in it, which the ice took up last winter, though it had an arm put through it two feet underground. Some much decayed perhaps old red maple stumps at Hubbard's Bath Place. It would be a triumph to get all my winter's wood thus. How much better than to buy a

Vol. VII

cord coarsely from a farmer, seeing that I get my money's worth! Then it only affords me a momentary satisfaction to see the pile tipped up in the yard. Now I derive a separate and peculiar pleasure from every stick that I find. Each has its history, of which I am reminded when I come to burn it, and under what circumstances I found it. Got home late. C. and I supped together after our work at wooding, and talked it over with great appetites.

Dr. Aikin, in his "Arts of Life," says that "the acorns of warm climates are fit for human food."

Sept. 25. A very fine and warm afternoon after a cloudy morning. Carry Aunt and Sophia a-barberry-ing to Conantum. Scare up the usual great bittern above the railroad bridge, whose hoarse *qua qua*, as it flies heavily off, a pickerel-fisher on the bank imitates. Saw two marsh hawks skimming low over the meadows and another, or a hen-hawk, sailing on high.

Saw where the moles had been working in Conant's meadow, — heaps of fresh meadow mould some eight inches in diameter on the green surface, and now a little hoary.

We got about three pecks of barberries from four or five bushes, but I filled my fingers with prickles to pay for them. With the hands well defended, it would be pleasant picking, they are so handsome, and beside are so abundant and fill up so fast. I take hold the end of the drooping twigs with my left hand, raise them, and then strip downward at once as many clusters as my hand will embrace, commonly bring-

ing away with the raceme two small green leaves or bracts, which I do not stop to pick out. When I come to a particularly thick and handsome wreath of fruit, I pluck the twig entire and bend it around the inside of the basket. Some bushes bear much larger and plumper berries than others. Some also are comparatively green yet. Meanwhile the catbird mews in the alders by my side, and the scream of the jay is heard from the wood-side.

When returning, about 4.30 P. M., we observed a slight mistiness, a sea-turn advancing from the east, and soon after felt the raw east wind, — quite a contrast to the air we had before, — and presently all the western woods were partially veiled with the mist. Aunt thought she could smell the salt marsh in it. At home, after sundown, I observed a long, low, and uniformly level slate-colored cloud reaching from north to south throughout the western horizon, which I supposed to be the sea-turn further inland, for we no longer felt the east wind here.

In the evening went to Welch's (?) circus with C. Approaching, I perceived the peculiar scent which belongs to such places, a certain sourness in the air, suggesting trodden grass and cigar smoke. The curves of the great tent, at least eight or ten rods in diameter, — the main central curve and wherever it rested on a post, — suggested that the tent was the origin of much of the Oriental architecture, the Arabic perhaps. There was the pagoda in perfection. It is remarkable what graceful attitudes feats of strength and agility seem to require.

Sept. 26. Went up Assabet for fuel. One old piece of oak timber looks as if it had been a brace in a bridge. I get up oak rails here and there, almost as heavy as lead, and leave them to dry somewhat on the bank. Stumps, partially burned, which were brought by the freshet from some newly cleared field last spring; bleached oak trees which were once lopped for a fence; alders and birches which the river ice bent and broke by its weight last spring. It is pretty hard and dirty work. It grieves me to see how rapidly some great trees which have fallen or been· felled waste away when left on the ground. There was the large oak by the Assabet, which I remember to have been struck by lightning, and afterward blown over, being dead. It used to lie with its top down-hill and partly in the water and its butt far up. Now there is no trace of its limbs, and the very core of its trunk is the only solid part, concealed within a spongy covering. Soon only a richer mould will·mark the spot.

Sept. 27. Collecting fuel again this afternoon, up the Assabet.

Yesterday I traced the note of what I have falsely thought the *Rana palustris*, or cricket frog, to its true source. As usual it sounded loud and incessant above all ordinary crickets and led me at once to a bare and soft sandy shore. After long looking and listening, with my head directly over the spot from which the sound still came at intervals (as I had often done before), I concluded, as no creature was visible, that it must issue from the mud, or rather slimy sand. I noticed that the

shore near the water was upheaved and cracked as by a small mole-track and, laying it open with my hand, I found a *mole cricket* (*Gryllotalpa brevipennis*). Harris says that their burrows "usually terminate beneath a stone or clod of turf." They live on the roots of grass and other vegetables, and in Europe the corresponding species does a great deal of harm. They "avoid the light of day, and are active chiefly during the night." Have their burrows "in moist and soft ground, particularly about ponds." "There are no house crickets in America."

Among crickets "the males only are musical." The "shrilling" is produced by shuffling their wing-covers together lengthwise. French call crickets *cri-cri*. Most crickets die on approach of winter, but a few survive under stones.

See furrows made by many clams now moving into deep water.

Some single red maples now fairly make a show along the meadow. I see a blaze of red reflected from the troubled water.

Sept. 29. Go to Daniel Ricketson's, New Bedford.

At Natural History Library saw Dr. Cabot, who says that he has heard either the hermit, or else the olivaceous, thrush sing, — very like a wood thrush, but softer. Is sure that the hermit thrush sometimes breeds hereabouts.

De Kay, in the New York Reports, thus describes the blackfish:[1] —

[1] [The quotation is somewhat abridged.]

Vol. VII

"FAMILY DELPHINIDÆ.
Genus *Globicephalus*. Lesson.
The Social Whale.
Globicephalus melas.
Delphinus melas. Trail, Nicholson's Journal.
D. globiceps. Cuvier, Mem. Mus. Vol. 19.
D. deductor. Scoresby, Arct. Regions.
D. intermedius. Harlan.
Phocena globiceps. Sampson, Am. Journal."

"Length 15 to 20 feet;" "shining, bluish black above;" a narrow light-gray stripe beneath; "remarkable for its loud cries when excited."

"Black Whale-fish," "Howling Whale," "Social Whale," and "Bottle-head."[1] Often confounded with the grampus. Not known why they are stranded. In 1822 one hundred stranded in one herd at Wellfleet. First described in a History of Greenland. In the Naturalists' Library, Jardine, I find *Globicephalus deductor* or *melas*, "The Deductor or Ca'ing Whale." First *accurately* described by Trail in 1809. Sixteen to twenty-four feet long. In 1799 two hundred ran ashore on one of the Shetland Isles. In the winter of 1809–10, one thousand one hundred and ten "approached the shore of Hvalfiord, Iceland, and were captured."[2] In 1812 were used as food by the poor of Bretagne.[3] They visit the neighborhood of Nice in May and June.

Get out at Tarkiln Hill, or Head of the River Station, three miles this side of New Bedford. Recognized an old Dutch barn. R.'s sons Arthur and **Walton** were

[1] [*Cape Cod*, p. 142; Riv. 170.]   [2] [*Cape Cod*, p. 146; Riv. 174.]
[3] [*Cape Cod*, p. 144; Riv. 171.]

just returning from tautog-fishing in Buzzard's Bay, and I tasted one at supper. Singularly curved from snout to tail.[1]

Sept. 30. Sunday. Rode with R. to Sassacowens Pond, in the north part of New Bedford on the Taunton road, called also Toby's Pond, from Jonathan Toby, who lives close by, who has a famous lawsuit about a road he built to Taunton years ago, which he has not got paid for; in which suit, he told us, he had spent thirty thousand dollars; employed Webster. Toby said the pond was called from the last of the Indians who lived there one hundred or one hundred and fifty years ago, and that you can still see his cellar-hole, etc., on the west side of the pond. We saw floating in the pond the bottom of an old log canoe — the sides rotted off — and some great bleached trunks of trees washed up. Found two quartz arrowheads on the neighboring fields. Noticed the ailanthus, or trees of heaven, about Toby's house, giving it a tropical look.

Thence we proceeded to Long Pond, stopping at the south end, which is in Freetown, about eight miles from R.'s. The main part is in Middleborough. It is about four (a man near by said five) miles long by seven eighths wide, measuring on the map of Middleborough and of the State, and fifteen feet deep, or twenty [in] some places, with at least three islands in it. This and the neighboring ponds were remarkably low. We first came out on to a fine, soft, white sandy beach,

[1] [*Daniel Ricketson and his Friends*, p. 337.]

two rods wide, near the southeast end, and walked westerly. It was very wild, and not a boat to be seen. The sandy bottom in the shallow water from the shore to three or four rods out, or as far as we could see, was thickly furrowed by clams, chiefly the common unio, and a great many were left dead or dying, high and dry, within a few feet of the water. These furrows, with each its clam at the end, though headed different ways, — all ways, — described various figures on the bottom; some pretty perfect circles, figure 6's and 3's, whip-lashes curling to snap, bow-knots, serpentine lines, and often crossing each other's tracks like the paths of rockets or bombshells. I never saw these furrows so numerous. Soon we came to a stony and rocky shore abutting on a meadow fringed with wood, with quite a primitive aspect. With the stones the clams ceased. Saw two places where invisible inhabitants make fires and do their washing on the shore, — some barrels or firkins, etc., still left. Some of the rocks at high-water mark were very large and wild, which the water had undermined on the edge of the woods. Here, too, were some great bleached trunks of trees, high and dry. Saw a box tortoise which had been recently killed on the rocky shore.

After walking in all about a third or half a mile, came again to a sandy shore, where the sand-bars lately cast up and saturated with water sank under us. There we saw, washed up dead, a great pickerel twenty-three inches long (we marked it on a cane), and there was projecting from its mouth the tail of another pickerel. As I wished to ascertain the size of the last, but could

not pull it out, — for I found it would part first at the tail, it was so firmly fixed, — I cut into the large one, though it was very offensive, and found that the head and much more was digested and that the smaller fish had been at least fifteen inches long. The big one had evidently been choked by trying to swallow too large a mouthful. Such was the penalty it had paid for its voracity. There were several suckers and some minnows also washed up near by.

They get no iron from these ponds now.

Went to a place easterly from the south end of this pond, called Joe's Rock, just over the Rochester line, where a cousin of Marcus Morton told us that one Joe Ashly secreted himself in the Revolution amid the fissures of the rocks, and, being supplied with food by his friends, could not be found, though he had enlisted in the army.

Returning, we crossed the Acushnet River where it took its rise, coming out of a swamp. Looked for arrowheads in a field where were many quahog, oyster, scallop, clam, and winkle (*Pyrula*) shells, probably brought by the whites, four or five miles, from the salt water. Also saw these in places which Indians had frequented.

Went into an old deserted house, the Brady house, where two girls who had lived in the family of R. and his mother had been born and bred, their father Irish, their mother Yankee. R. said that they were particularly bright girls and lovers of nature; had read my "Walden." Now keep school. Have still an affection for their old house. We visited the spring they had

Vol. VII

used. Saw the great willow tree at the corner of the house, in which one of the girls, an infant in the cradle, thought that the wind began as she looked out the window, and heard the wind sough through it. Saw how the chimney in the garret was eked out with flat stones, bricks being dear.

Arthur Ricketson showed me in his collection what was apparently (?) an Indian mortar, which had come from Sampson's in Middleborough. It was a dark granite-like stone, some ten inches long by eight wide and four thick, with a regular round cavity worn in it four inches in diameter and one and one half deep, also a smaller one opposite on the other side.

He also showed me the perfect shell of an *Emys guttata*, with some of the internal bones, which had been found between the plastering and boarding of a meeting-house at the Head of the River (in New Bedford), which was seventy-five or eighty years old and was torn down fifteen or twenty years ago. Supposed to have crawled in when the meeting-house was built, though it was not very near water. It had lost no scales, but was bleached to a dirty white, sprinkled with spots still yellow.[1]

[1] [*Daniel Ricketson and his Friends*, pp. 337–340.]

XIV

OCTOBER, 1855

(ÆT. 38)

Oct. 1. Among R.'s books is Bewick's "Æsop's Fables." On a leaf succeeding the title-page is engraved a facsimile of B.'s handwriting to the following effect:

"Newcastle, January, 1824.

To Thomas Bewick & Son Dr.

£   s   d

To a Demy Copy of Æsop's Fables   "   18   "

Received the above with thanks

Thomas Bewick   Robert Elliot Bewick."

Then there was some fine red sea-moss adhering to the page just over the view of a distant church and windmill (probably Newcastle) by moonlight, and at the bottom of the page: —

"No. 809

Thomas Bewick

his   mark"

It being the impression of his thumb.[1]

[1] [An inky thumb-mark, doubtless Thoreau's own, precedes this rude sketch.]

A cloudy, somewhat rainy day. Mr. R. brought me a snail, apparently *Helix albolabris*, or possibly *thyroidus*, which he picked from under a rock where he was having a wall built. It had put its stag- or rather giraffe-like head and neck out about two inches, the whole length to the point behind being about three, — mainly a neck of a somewhat buffish-white or grayish-buff color or buff-brown, shining with moisture, with a short head, deer-like, and giraffe-like horns or tentacula on its top black at tip, five eighths of an inch long, and apparently two short horns on snout. Its neck, etc., flat beneath, by which surface it draws or slides itself along in a chair. It is surprisingly long and large to be contained in that shell, which moves atop of it. It moves at the rate of an inch or half an inch a minute over a level surface, whether horizontal or perpendicular, and holds quite tight to it, the shell like a whorled dome to a portion of a building. Its foot (?) extends to a point behind. It *commonly* touches by an inch of its flat under side, flatting out by as much of its length as it touches. Shell rather darker mottled (?) than body. The tentacula become all dark as they are drawn in, and it can draw them or contract them straight back to naught. No *obvious* eyes (?) or mouth.

P. M. — Rode to New Bedford and called on Mr. Green, a botanist, but had no interview with him. Walked through Mrs. Arnold's arboretum. Rode to the beach at Clark's Cove where General Gray landed his four thousand troops in the Revolution. Found there in abundance *Anomia ephippium* (?), their ir-

regular golden-colored shells; *Modiola plicatula* (rayed mussel); *Crepidula fornicata* (?), worn; *Pecten concentricus*, alive; and one or two more.

Returned by the new Point road, four miles long, and R. said eighty feet wide (I should think from recollection more), and cost $50,000. A magnificent road, by which New Bedford has appropriated the sea. Passed salt works still in active operation, windmills going; a series of frames, with layers of bushes one above another to a great height, apparently for filtering. Went into a spermaceti candle and oil factory.

Arthur R. has a soapstone pot (Indian), about nine inches long, more than an inch thick, with a kind of handle at the ends, — or protuberances.[1] A. says he uses fresh-water clams for bait for perch, etc., in ponds. I think it was to-day some one saw geese go over here, so they said.

Oct. 2. A cloudy day. Rode to "Sampson's" in Middleborough, thirteen miles. Many quails in road. Passed over a narrow neck between the two Quitticus ponds, after first visiting Great Quitticus on right of road and gathering clamshells there, as I had done at Long Pond and intend to do at Assawampsett. These shells labelled will be good mementos of the ponds. It was a great, wild pond with large islands in it.

Saw a loon on Little or West Quitticus from road, an old bird with a black bill. The bayonet or rainbow rush was common along the shore there.

[1] [*Daniel Ricketson and his Friends*, pp. 341, 342.]

Vol. VII

In Backus's Account of Middleborough, Historical Collections, vol. iii, First Series: "Philip once sent an army to waylay Capt. Church in Assowamset Neck; which is in the south part of Middleborough." Perhaps this was it.

Just beyond this neck, by the roadside, between the road and West Quitticus Pond, is an old Indian burying-ground. R. thought it was used before the whites came, though of late by the "praying Indians." This was the old stage road from New Bedford to Boston. It occupies a narrow strip between the road and the pond, about a dozen rods wide at the north end, and narrower at the south, and is thirty or forty feet above the water. Now covered with a middling growth of oak, birch, hickory, etc. Chestnut oaks (perhaps *Quercus montana*) grow near there. I gathered some leaves and one large acorn, from the buggy.

There were two stones with inscriptions. R. copied one as follows: —

> In memory of Jean Squeen
> who died April 13th 1794 in
> her 23 year. Also of Benj:
> who died at sea April 22 1799
> in his 26th year children of
> Lydia Squeen a native[1]
> When earth was made when time began
> Death was decreed the fate of man

The purport of the other was that Lydia Squeen died in 1812, aged seventy-five. The other graves were only faintly marked with rough head and foot stones. All amid the thick wood. There were one or

[1] [*Daniel Ricketson and his Friends*, pp. 343, 344.]

two graves without any stones, apparently not more than five or six years old.

We soon left the main road and turned into a path on the right, leading to Assawampsett Pond, a mile distant. There, too, was a fine sandy beach, the south shore of the pond, three or four rods wide. We walked along the part called Betty's Neck. This pond is, by the map of Middleborough, a little more than three miles long in a straight line northwest and southeast across Pocksha, and nearly two wide. We saw the village of Middleborough Four Corners far across it, yet no village on the shore. As we walked easterly, the shore became stony. On one large slate (?) rock with a smooth surface, sloping toward the pond at high-water mark, were some inscriptions or sculptures which R. had copied about ten years since, thus: —

1749   B. Hill   Israel felix

The "B. Hill" is comparatively modern. R. said that Israel Felix was an old Indian preacher. According to Backus in Historical Collections, vol. iii, First Series, Thomas Felix was an Indian teacher in Middleborough once. The foot appeared very ancient, though pecked in only half an inch. It has squarish form and broad at the toes, like the representation of some sculptured in rocks at the West. For a long time we could discern only 1749 and B. Hill. At length we detected the foot, and after my companion had given up, concluding that the water and the ice had obliterated the rest within ten years, I at last rather felt with my fingers than saw with my eyes the faintly graven and lichen-covered letters of Israel Felix's name. We had looked on that surface full fifteen minutes in vain, yet I felt out the letters after all with certainty.

In a description of Middleborough in the Historical Collections, vol. iii, 1810, signed "Nehemiah Bennet, Middleborough, 1793," it is said, "There is on the easterly shore of Assawampsitt Pond, on the shore of Betty's-neck, two rocks which have curious marks thereon (supposed to be done by the Indians) which appear like the steppings of a person with naked feet, which settled into the rocks; likewise the prints of a hand on several places, with a number of other marks; also, there is a rock on a high hill, a little to the eastward of the old stone fishing wear, where there is the print of a person's hand in said rock." [1]

Perhaps we might have detected more on these same rocks, had we read this before, for we saw that there was something on the next rock. We did not know of the "wear."

The same writer speaks of a settlement of Indians at "Betty's-neck (which place took its name from an ancient Indian woman by the name of Betty Sasemore, who owned that neck) where there is now eight Indian houses and eight families," between thirty and forty souls.

I was interested by some masses of pudding-stone further along the shore. There were also a few large flat, sloping slate (?) rocks. I saw a small *Emys picta;* and a young snapping turtle, apparently hatched this

[1] [*Familiar Letters*, pp. 264, 265; Riv. 313.]

summer, the *whole* length when swimming about three inches. It was larger than mine last April and had ten very distinct points to its shell behind. I first saw it in the water next the shore. The same Bennet quoted above adds in a postscript: —

"In the year 1763, Mr. Shubael Thompson found a land turtle in the north-east part of Middleborough, which by some misfortune had lost one of its feet, and found the following marks on its shell, viz. I. W. 1747. He marked it S. T. 1763, and let it go. It was found again in the year 1773, by Elijah Clap, who marked it E. C. 1773, and let it go. It was found again in the year 1775, by Captain William Shaw, in the month of May, who marked it W. S. 1775. It was found again by said Shaw the same year, in September, about one hundred rods distance from the place where he let it go.

"It was found again in the year 1784, by Jonathan Soule, who marked it J. S. 1784, and let it go. It was found again in the year 1790, by Joseph Soule, who marked it J. S. 1790, and let it go. It was found again in the year 1791, by Zenas Smith, who marked it Z. S. 1791, and let it go; it being the last time it was found; 44 years from the time the first marks were put on."

We saw five loons diving near the shore of Betty's Neck, which, instead of swimming off, approached within ten rods as if to reconnoitre us. Only one had a black bill, and that not entirely so; another's was turning. Their throats were all very white. I was surprised to see the usnea hanging *thick* on many apple

trees and some pears in the neighborhood of this and the other ponds, as on spruce. Sheep are pastured hereabouts.

Returning along the shore, we saw a man and woman putting off in a small boat, the first we had seen. The man was black. He rowed, and the woman steered. R. called to them. They approached within a couple of rods in the shallow water. "Come nearer," said R. "Don't be afraid; I ain't a-going to hurt you." The woman answered, "I never saw the man yet that I was afraid of." The man's name was Thomas Smith, and, in answer to R.'s very direct questions as to how much he was of the native stock, said that he was one-fourth Indian. He then asked the woman, who sat unmoved in the stern with a brown dirt-colored dress on, a regular countrywoman with half an acre of face (squaw-like), having first inquired of Tom if she was his woman, how much Indian blood she had in her. She did not answer directly so home a question, yet at length as good as acknowledged to one-half Indian, and said that she came from Carver, where she had a sister; the only half-breeds about here. Said her name was Sepit, but could not spell it. R. said, "Your nose looks rather Indiany." Where will you find a Yankee and his wife going a-fishing thus? They lived on the shore. Tom said he had seen turtles in the pond that weighed between fifty and sixty; had caught a pickerel that morning that weighed four or five pounds; had also seen them washed up with another in their mouths.

Their boat was of peculiar construction, and T. said

it was called a sharper [*sic*]; [1] with very high sides and a remarkable run on the bottom aft, and the bottom boards were laid across, com-  ing out flush, and the sides set on them. An ugly model. [2]

Tom said that Assawampsett was fifteen to twenty feet deep in deepest part. A Mr. Sampson, good authority, told me nine or ten on an average, and the deepest place said to be thirty or more.

R. told the squaw that we were interested in those of the old stock, now they were so few. "Yes," said she, "and you'd be glad if they were all gone." This boat had a singular "wooden grapple," as Tom called it, made in form of a cross, thus: with a stone within.

The stones on which we walked about all the ponds were covered, now the water was low, with a hoary sort of moss which I do not remember to have seen in Concord; very fine and close to the rock.

Great shallow lakes, the surrounding country hardly rising anywhere to more than a hundred feet above them. According to Bourne's map there are in Middleborough: —

[1] [Probably a sharp, or sharpie, a boat used by oystermen.]
[2] [*Daniel Ricketson and his Friends*, pp. 344-348.]

57,937½ acres of land
5,250   "   " water
63,187½   total

Backus says that iron was discovered at the bottom of Assawampsett Pond about 1747. (Historical Collections, vol. iii, First Series.) "Men go out with boats, and make use of instruments much like those with which oysters are taken, to get up the ore from the bottom of the pond." "It became the main ore that was used in the town." Once one man got two tons a day; in 1794, half a ton. Yet there was then (in 1794) plenty of it in an adjacent pond which was twenty feet deep. Much of it was better than the bog ore they had been using. Dr. Thacher says that Assawampsett Pond once afforded annually six hundred tons of ore. A man afterward discovered it in a pond in Carver, by drawing up some with a fish-line accidentally, and it was extensively used. I did not hear of any being obtained now.

There were three Praying Indian villages in Middleborough — Namassekett, Assawomsit, and Ketchiquut (Titicut), — the last in the northwest part, on Taunton River, where was an Indian weir. Winslow and company on a visit to Massasoit in June, 1621, stopped at Nemasket, fifteen miles, the first night before "conceived by us to be very near, because the inhabitants flocked so thick upon every slight occasion amongst us," etc., etc., q. v.

R. is a man of feeling. As we were riding by a field in which a man was shackling a sheep, which struggled,

R. involuntarily shouted to him and asked, "What would you do?"

We left our horse and buggy at John Kingman's and walked by Sampson's to a hill called King Philip's Lookout, from which we got a good view of Assawampsett and Long Ponds. There was a good-sized sailboat at Sampson's house, now kept by a Barrows. The shores were now surrounded with pale wine-colored foliage, of maples, etc., and inland were seen the very *fresh* green and yellow of pines, contrasting with the red (*Rubus*) blackberry. The highest land appears to be about the northwest end of the ponds.

I saw at Kingman's long-handled but small scoop nets for taking young alewives for pickerel bait. They think the white perch one of the best fish, like a cod.

Elder's Pond, a little further north, is said to be the deepest and clearest.[1] Walking along the north end of Long Pond, while R. bathed, I found amid the rainbow rush, pipewort (*Eriocaulon*), etc., on the now broad flat shore, a very beautiful flower, pinkish rose-color, new to me, and still quite fresh, the *Sabbatia chloroides*, referred to Plymouth; ten stamens and petal divisions, about one foot high. I also observed there the very broad and distinct trail of an otter in the wet sand, to and from the water, with the mark of its tail, though Kingman did not know of any now hereabouts.

The arrowheads hereabouts are commonly white quartz.

R. says "gamble-roof." This should be "gambrel,"

[1] Not so deep as said.

Vol. VII

apparently from the hind leg of a horse, — crooked like it.

Oct. 3. Copied the map of Middleborough.

Somewhat rainy. Walked along shore of Acushnet looking for shells. R. pointed out to me the edible mushroom, which he says he loves raw even. It is common. The shore was all alive with fiddler crabs, carrying their fiddles on one side, and their holes, nearly an inch over, were very common and earth heaped up. The samphire was turned red in many places, yielding to the autumn. Atkinson, in his Siberian and steppe travels, speaks of the "Salsola plant" turned a bright crimson. On the Kirghis Steppes, he says, "in the distance I could see salt lakes: I knew them to be salt by the crimson margins which encircled them." (Page 425.)

Got some quahogs and *Modiola plicatula* (rayed mussel); the last was very abundant; also some pyrulas, which are dug up alive by sand [?]-diggers. Gathered there apparently wild germander (*Teucrium*), out of bloom, and *Iva frutescens*, or high-water shrub, ditto. Sailed back up the river in Arthur's whale-boat with three sails. Her side drank water through a crack. He gave three dollars for her and spent ten more in repairs. Twenty feet long, and worth originally perhaps $75. If I had stayed longer we should probably have gone to Cuttyhunk in this.

P. M. — Rode to see some old houses in Fairhaven, etc., etc. How beautiful the evergreen leaf of the *Prinos glaber*, slightly toothed toward end!

The old Woods place, a quarter of a mile off the road, looked like this: —

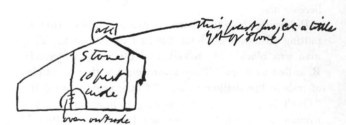

The end showed the great stone chimney, all stone to top, except about hearth. The upper story overlapped about eighteen inches, with   t h e
ornamental points of timbers drop-   ping
from it. Above this, in front, the   shingles were rounded, scale-like.   There
was one half of a diamond window left in front, set in lead, very thin lead, with a groove in each side for sash, and a narrow slit-window for firing through, also another on farther end. Chimney mortared. The old latch to front door was primitive, apparently made by village blacksmith.

Also an old house in the village of Fairhaven, said to have been standing in Philip's War; a small house, a ten-footer, with one end and chimney wholly of stone. The chimney quite   handsome,   of this form, looking down on it:

Visited the studio in Fair-   haven of a young marine painter, built over the water, the dashing and gurgling of it coming up through a grating in the floor.

He was out, but we found there painting Van Best, a well-known Dutch painter of marine pieces whom he has attracted to him. He talked and looked particularly Dutchman-like. Then visited Fort Nobscot [1] on a rocky point.

Oct. 4. Rode to Westport, where R. wished to consult the Proprietors' Records of Dartmouth to find the names, etc., of his ancestors. Passed through Smith's Mills village, the older settlement in Dartmouth, on the stream which comes from Sassacowens Pond, then Westport, about three miles beyond, and crossed the Westport River to Gifford's, a mile beyond, where the Records were.

Returning, lunched by Westport Pond in Dartmouth, said to contain sixty acres but to [be] only about two feet deep. Saw a blue heron in it some rods from the shore, where the water did not come up to its body. Perhaps it might have waded anywhere in it. It stood with the *side* of its head towards us, being wary of us. When it moved, walked with a peculiar stooping and undulating gait in the water. At length thrust its bill in as if feeding. That must be a rare place for it to catch frogs and perhaps minnows in, though we were told that there [were] only turtles, snakes, and pouts in it.

The vanes on this ride were often a whale, rather a lumpish form, but reminding us that the farmer had, perhaps, been a whaler.

[1] [The fort at Fairhaven is called Fort Phœnix.]

Oct. 5. Rode to Plymouth with R., in his buggy.

In the north part of Rochester, went into an old uninhabited house which once belonged to John Shearman. It had the date 1753 engraved on an oblong square stone in the stone chimney, though the chimney-top had been rebuilt with the old stone. The house had a singular musty scent when we opened it. The bare joists above in the kitchen all black with smoke. In the cellar grew the apple-of-Peru, *Nicandra physalodes,* then in bloom; a *short* datura-like blossom with a large fruit-like capsule.

After passing the Neck between the two Quitticus Ponds, we turned to the right and passed by the Point road between the Great Quitticus and Pocksha Ponds. This was a mere bar, half a mile long, two or three rods wide, and built up above high water with larger stones. We rode with one wheel in the water. There was in one place a stream crossing it and two or more bridges prepared for high water. Scared up five apparently black ducks. Continued on towards Carver by small winding country roads *via* where was once Nelson's meeting-house and along the east side of Tispaquin Pond, — this was the name of the old sachem of Nemasket, — near which in a field R. picked up a young *Emys picta's* (?) shell, which I have. Beyond this the country was almost uniformly level, sandy, — oak wood, with few dwellings. Lunched near the boundary of Carver. Passed Johns Pond and Wenham Pond and others in Carver, passing a mile or more south of Carver Green, and afterward Clear Pond in Plymouth. We heard the blasting at

the Quincy quarries (so Watson told us) during this ride, I think even as far back as New Bedford township, very distinctly.

According to Bennet, writing 1793 (*vide* Historical Collections), Snipatuet Pond in Rochester has one stream emptying into the sea at Mattapoisett Harbor and another, three quarters of a mile long, emptying into East Quitiquos Pond. "So that the alewife fish come into Snipatuet pond from both streams."

In a description of Carver in the Fourth Volume, Second Series, of the Historical Collections, I read: "The cast iron tea kettle was first cast at Plympton (now Carver) between 1760 and 1765. So modern is this very common utensil in New England. Wrought iron imported tea kettles were used before a copper tea kettle was first used at Plymouth, 1702." Also, "A place called 'Swan Holt' by the first planters, a little southeast of Wenham Pond, denotes the former visits of that bird, the earliest harbinger of spring; for before the ice is yet broken up, the swan finds an open resting place among the ozier holts, while the kildee, flying over the land from the sea shore, soon after confirms the vernal promise." A note adds: "A species of plover, probably the 'que ce qu'il dit' of the French. It may be added that kildee is the Danish word for a spring."

Lodged at Olney's (the old Hedge) House in Plymouth.

Oct. 6. Return to Concord *via* Natural History Library.

De Kay calls the pine marten the American sable.

Oct. 8. On river. — Flocks of tree sparrows by river, slightly warbling. Hear a song sparrow sing. See apparently white-throated sparrows hopping under covert of the button-bushes. Found my boat yesterday full of willow leaves after the rain. See no tortoises now on the rocks and boards. It is too cold.

Oct. 10. A young man has just shown me a small duck which he shot in the river from my boat. I thought it a blue-winged teal, but it has no distinct beauty-spot. The bill broad and, I should say from remembrance, bluish-black, as are the legs and feet, not red or yellow or flesh-color, webbed thus: Above black and brown with no bright colors or distinct white; neck brown beneath and breast; secondaries pale-bluish, tipped with white; a little greenish perhaps on the scapulars.

Mr. William Allen, now here, tells me that when, some years ago, a stream near his house in East Bridgewater, emptying into the Taunton River, was drained, he found a plant on the bottom very similar to a sponge — of the same form and color — and say six inches wide.

Oct. 12. P. M. — Up Assabet.

The leaves fallen apparently last night now lie thick on the water next the shore, concealing it, — fleets of dry boats, blown with a rustling sound. [1] I see a painted

[1] Probably maple chiefly, — the Leaf Harvest, call it.

tortoise still out on shore. Three of his back scales are partly turned up and show fresh black ones ready beneath. When I try to draw these scales off they tear first in my hand. They are covered, as are all the posterior ones, with a thick shaggy muddy fleece of moss (?). No wonder they must shed their scales to get rid of this. And now I see that the six main anterior scales have already been shed. They are fresh black and bare of moss. Apparently no fresh scales on the sternum. Is not this the only way they get rid of the moss, etc., which adhere to them?

Carried home a couple of rails which I fished out of the bottom of the river and left on the bank to dry about three weeks ago. One was a chestnut which I have noticed for some years on the bottom of the Assabet, just above the spring on the east side, in a deep hole. It looked as if it had been there a hundred years. It was so heavy that C. and I had as much as we could do to lift it, covered with mud, on to the high bank. It was scarcely lighter to-day, and I amused myself with asking several to lift one half of it after I had sawed it in two. They failed at first, not being prepared to find it so heavy, though they could easily lift it afterward. It was a regular segment of a log, and though the thin edge was comparatively firm and solid, the sap-wood on the broad and rounded side, now that it had been lying in the air, was quite spongy and had opened into numerous great chinks, five eighths of an inch wide by an inch deep. The whole was of a rusty brown externally, having imbibed some iron from the water. When split up it was of a dark blue

black, if split parallel with the layers, or alternately black and light brown, if split across them. There were concentric circles of black, as you looked at the end, coinciding nearly with the circles of pores, perhaps one sixteenth of an inch wide. When you looked at these on the side of a stick split across the circles, they reminded you of a striped waistcoat or sheepskin. But after being exposed to the air a little while, the whole turned to an almost uniform pale slate-color,[1] the light brown turning slate and the dark stripes also paling into slate. It had a strong dye-stuff-like scent, etc.

The other was a round oak stick, and, though it looked almost as old as the first, was quite sound even to the bark, and evidently quite recent comparatively, though full as heavy. The wood had acquired no peculiar color. Some farmers load their wood with gunpowder to punish thieves. There's no danger that mine will be loaded.

Pieces of both of these sank at once in a pail of water.[2]

Oct. 13. P. M. — To Conantum.

The maples now stand like smoke along the meadows. The bass is bare. A thick carpet of white pine needles lies now lightly, half an inch or more in thickness, above the dark-reddish ones of last year. Larks in flocks in the meadows, showing the white in their tails as they fly, sing sweetly as in spring. Methinks I have seen one or two myrtle-birds, sparrow-like.

[1] After a few weeks it became quite uniform.
[2] On the 18th they floated, after drying in my chamber.

Oct. 14. Some sparrow-like birds with yellow on rump flitting about our wood-pile. One flies up against the house and alights on the window-sill within a foot of me inside. Black bill and feet, yellow rump, brown above, yellowish-brown on head, cream-colored chin, two white bars on wings, tail black, edged with white, — the yellow-rump warbler or myrtle-bird without doubt. They fly to several windows, though it is not cold.

P. M. — Up Assabet.

The muskrats eat a good many clams now and leave their pearly shells open on the shore. Sometimes I find a little one which they have brought ashore in the night but left entire and alive. The green-rayed ones, — are they not a peculiar light blue within?

I still see the *Emys insculpta* coupled, the upper holding with its claws under the edge of the lower shell.

Oct. 15. P. M. — Go to look for white pine cones, but see none.

Saw a striped squirrel on a rail fence with some kind of weed in his mouth. Was it milkweed seed? At length he scud swiftly along the middle rail past me, and, instead of running over or around the posts, he glided through the little hole in the post left above the rails, as swiftly as if there had been no post in the way. Thus he sped through five posts in succession in a straight line, incredibly quick, only stooping and straightening himself at the holes.

The hornets' nests are exposed, the maples being bare, but the hornets are gone. I see one a very per-

fect cone, like a pitch pine cone, uninjured by the birds, about twelve feet from the ground, by a swamp, three feet from the end of a maple twig and upheld by it alone passing through its top, about an inch deep, seven and a half inches wide, by eight long. A few sere maple leaves adorn and partly conceal the crown, at the ends of slight twigs which are buried in it. What a wholesome color! somewhat like the maple bark (and so again concealed) laid on in successive layers in arcs of circles a tenth of an inch wide, eyebrow-wise, gray or even white or brown of various shades, with a few dried maple leaves sticking out the top of it.

Oct. 16. P. M. — To the white pine grove beyond Beck Stow's.

What has got all the cones? How evenly the freshly fallen pine-needles are spread on the ground! quite like a carpet. Throughout this grove no square foot is left bare. I dug down with a stick and found that the layers of three or four years could be distinguished with considerable ease, and much deeper the old needles were raised in flakes or layers still. The topmost, or this year's, were fawn-colored; last year's, dark dull reddish; and so they went on, growing darker and more decayed, till, at the depth of three inches, where, perhaps, the needles were fifteen or twenty years old, they began to have the aspect of a dark loose-lying virgin mould, mixed with roots (pine cones and sticks a little higher). The freshly fallen needles lay as evenly strewn as if sifted over the whole surface, giving it a uniform neat fawn-color, tempting one to stretch himself on it. They rested alike on the few green leaves of weeds and the fallen cones and the cobwebs between them, in every direction across one another like joggle-sticks. In course of years they are beaten by rain and snow into a coarse, thick matting or felt to cover the roots of the trees with.

I look at a grass-bird on a wall in the dry Great Fields. There is a dirty-white or cream-colored line above the eye and another from the angle of the mouth beneath it and a white ring close about the eye. The breast is streaked with this creamy white and dark brown in streams, as on the cover of a book.

Oct. 17. P. M. — Up river.

A fine Indian-summer afternoon. There is much gossamer on the button-bushes, now bare of leaves, and on the sere meadow-grass, looking toward the sun, in countless parallel lines, like the ropes which connect the masts of a vessel.

I see the roots of the great yellow lily lying on the mud where they have made a ditch in John Hosmer's meadow for the sake of the mud, gray-colored when old and dry. Some are three and a half inches in diameter, with their great eyes or protuberant shoulders where the leaf-stalks stood in quincunx order around them. What rank vigor they suggest! like serpents winding amid the mud of the meadow. You see where the ditcher's spade has cut them into masses about as thick as long. What are those clusters of cuplike cavities between the eyes, some nearly a quarter of

an inch in diameter, with a pistil-like prominence within?

I saw behind (or rather *in front of*) me as I rowed home a little dipper appear in mid-river, as if I had passed right over him. It dived while I looked, and I could not see it come up anywhere.

Oct. 18. Last night I was reading Howitt's account of the Australian gold-diggings, and had in my mind's eye the numerous valleys with their streams all cut up with foul pits, ten to a hundred feet deep and half a dozen feet across, as close as they can be dug, and half full of water, where men furiously rushed to probe for their fortunes, uncertain where they shall break ground, not knowing but the gold is under their camp itself; sometimes digging a hundred and sixty feet before they strike the vein, or then missing it by a foot; turned into demons and regardless of each other's rights in their thirst after riches; whole valleys for thirty miles suddenly honeycombed by the pits of the miners, so that hundreds are drowned in them. Standing in water and covered with mud and clay, they work night and day, dying of exposure and disease. Having read this and partly forgotten it, I was thinking of my own unsatisfactory life, doing as others do without any fixed star habitually in my eye, my foot not planted on any blessed isle. Then, with that vision of the diggings before me, I asked myself why I might not be washing some gold daily, though it were only the finest particles, or might not sink a shaft down to the gold within me and work that mine. There

is a Ballarat or Bendigo for you. What though it were a "Sulky Gully"? Pursue some path, however narrow and crooked, in which you can walk with love and reverence. Wherever a man separates from the multitude and goes his own way, there is a fork in the road, though the travellers along the highway see only a gap in the paling.[1]

P. M. — To Great Meadows to observe the hummocks left by the ice.

They are digging the pond at the new cemetery. I go by Peter's path. How charming a footpath! *Nihil humanum*, etc. I was delighted to find a new footpath crossing this toward Garfield's. The broad and dusty roads do not remind me of man so much as of cattle and horses. There are a great many crows scattered about on the meadow. What do they get to eat there? Also I scare up a dozen larks at once. A large brown marsh hawk comes beating the bush along the river, and ere long a slate-colored one (male), with black tips, is seen circling against a distant wood-side. I scare up in midst of the meadows a great many dark-colored sparrows, one or two at a time, which go off with a note somewhat like the lesser redpoll's, — some migrating kind, I think.[2]

There is a hummock in the lower part of the meadows near the river every two or three rods, where they appeared as thick last year, sometimes consisting of that coarse meadow-grass or sedge but quite as often

[1] [*Cape Cod, and Miscellanies*, pp. 465, 466; *Misc.*, Riv. 266, 267.] *Vide* [4] pages forward.

[2] Probably what I think must be shore larks in fall of '58.

of the common meadow sod. Very often it has lodged on one of those yellowish circles of the sedge, it being higher. Last winter's hummocks are not much flattened down yet. I am inclined to think that the coarse sedgy hummocks do not fall so round at first, but are wont to grow or spread in that wise when a fragment has been dropped. Perhaps the sedge is oftenest lifted because it is so coarse.

There is no life perceptible on this broad meadow except what I have named. The crows are very conspicuous, black against the green. The maple swamps, bare of leaves, here and there about the meadow, look like smoke blown along the edge of the woods. Some distinct maples, wholly stripped, look very wholesome and neat, nay even ethereal.

To-day my shoes are whitened with the gossamer which I noticed yesterday on the meadow-grass.

I find the white fragments of a tortoise-shell in the meadow, — thirty or forty pieces, straight-sided polygons, — which apparently a hay-cart passed over. They look like broken crockery. I brought it home and amused myself with putting it together. It is a painted tortoise. The variously formed sections or component parts of the shell are not broken, but only separated. To restore them to their places is like the game which children play with pieces of wood completing a picture. It is surprising to observe how these different parts are knitted together by countless minute teeth on their edges. Then the scales, which are not nearly so numerous, and therefore larger commonly, are so placed over the former as to break joints always, as appears by the indented lines at their edges and the serrations of the shell. These scales, too, *slightly* overlap each other, *i. e.* the foremost over the next behind, so that they may not be rubbed off. Thus the whole case is bound together like a very stout band-box. The bared shell is really a very interesting study. The sternum in its natural position looks like a well-contrived drag, turned up at the sides in one solid piece.

Noticed a single wreath of a blood-red blackberry vine on a yellow sand slope, very conspicuous by contrast.

When I was surveying for Legross, as we went to our work in the morning, we passed by the Dudley family tomb, and Legross remarked to me, all in good faith, "Wouldn't you like to see old Daddy Dudley? He lies in there. I'll get the keys if you'd like. I sometimes go in and look at him."

The upper shell of this tortoise is formed of curved rafters or ribs, which are flatted out to half an inch or five eighths in width, but the rib form appears in an elevated ridge along the middle and in a spine at the lower end, fitting firmly into a deep hole in an edge bone, and also a projection (or process?) to meet the spinal column at the upper end. Some of these plates (?) I fitted together far more closely and wonderfully, considering the innumerable sharp serrations, than any child's wooden sections of a picture. Yet it is impossible to put the whole together again, so perfectly do the plates interlock and dovetail into each other at different angles, and they could only have grown together and shrunk apart. It is an admirable system of breaking joints, both in the arrangement of the

Vol. VII

parts of the shell and in that of the scales which overlap the serrations of the former. The sternum consists of nine parts, there being an extra trigonal or pentagonal piece under the head or throat. The two middle pieces on each side curve upward to meet the edge bones, without any serration or joint at the lower edge of the sternum there; nor is there any joint in the scales there. In the upper shell there *appear to be* eight or nine small dorsal pieces, about sixteen rib pieces, and about twenty-two edge or marginal pieces; but of the parts of the upper shell I am not quite certain.

The sternums of the box turtles and the stinkpot are much flatter, *i. e.* not so much curved up at the sides, and are nearer to the upper shell. The painted tortoise has the flattest back; the *Cistudo Carolina*, the highest and fullest (with a ridge); the stinkpot, the sharpest. The *C. Blandingii* is very regularly arched. The *Emys insculpta* is of moderate elevation (with a ridge).

Those bright-red marks on the marginal scales of the painted tortoise remind me of some Chinese or other Oriental lacquer-work on waiters (?). This color fades to a pale yellow. The color is wholly in the scale above the bone. Of the bright colors, the yellow marks on tortoise-shells are the fastest.

How much beauty in decay! I pick up a white oak leaf, dry and stiff, but yet mingled red and green, October-like, whose pulpy part some insect has eaten beneath, exposing the delicate network of its veins. It is very beautiful held up to the light, — such work

as only an insect eye could perform. Yet, perchance, to the vegetable kingdom such a revelation of ribs is as repulsive as the skeleton in the animal kingdom. In each case it is some little gourmand, working for another end, that reveals the wonders of nature. There are countless oak leaves in this condition now, and also with a submarginal line of network exposed.

Men rush to California and Australia as if the true gold were to be found in that direction; but that is to go to the very opposite extreme to where it lies. They go prospecting further and further away from the true lead, and are most unfortunate when most successful. Is not our native soil auriferous? Does not a stream from the golden mountains flow through our native valley? and has it not for more than geologic ages been bringing down the shining particles and the nuggets? Yet, strange to tell, if a digger steal away prospecting for this true gold into the unexplored solitudes, there is no danger, alas, that any will dog his steps and endeavor to supplant him. He may claim and undermine the whole valley, even the cultivated and uninhabited portions, his whole life long in peace, and no one will ever dispute his claim. They will not mind his cradles or his toms. He is not confined to a claim twelve feet square, as at Ballarat, but may mine anywhere, and wash the whole wide world in his tom.[1]

To rebuild the tortoise-shell is a far finer game than any geographical or other puzzle, for the pieces

[1] [*Cape Cod, and Miscellanies*, p. 466; *Misc.*, Riv. 267, 268.] *Vide* [4] pages forward.

do not merely make part of a plane surface, but you have got to build a roof and a floor and the connecting walls. These are not only thus dovetailed and braced and knitted and bound together, but also held together by the skin and muscles within. It is a *band*-box.

Oct. 19. P. M. — To Pine Hill for chestnuts.

It is a very pleasant afternoon, quite still and cloudless, with a thick haze concealing the distant hills. Does not this haze mark the Indian summer?

I see Mrs. Riordan and her little boy coming out of the woods with their bundles of fagots on their backs. It is surprising what great bundles of wood an Irishwoman will contrive to carry. I confess that though I could carry one I should hardly think of making such a bundle of them. They are first regularly tied up, and then carried on the back by a rope, — somewhat like the Indian women and their straps. There is a strange similarity; and the little boy carries his bundle proportionally large. The sticks about four feet long. They make haste to deposit their loads before I see them, for they do not know how pleasant a sight it is to me. The Irishwoman does the squaw's part in many respects. Riordan also buys the old railroad sleepers at three dollars a hundred, but they are much decayed and full of sand.

Therien tells me, when I ask if he has seen or heard any large birds lately, that he heard a cock crow this morning, a wild one, in the woods. It seems a dozen fowls (chickens) were lost out of the cars here a fortnight ago. Poland has caught some, and they have one at the shanty, but this cock, at least, is still abroad and can't be caught. If they could survive the winter, I suppose we should have had wild hens before now. Sat and talked with Therien at the pond, by the railroad. He says that James Baker told the story of the perch leaping into a man's throat, etc., of his father or uncle (Amos ?).

The woods about the pond are now a perfect October picture; yet there *have been* no very bright tints this fall. The young white and the shrub oak leaves were withered before the frosts came, perhaps by the late drought after the wet spring.

Walking in E.'s path west of the pond, I am struck by the conspicuous wreaths of waxwork leaves about the young trees, to the height of twelve or fifteen feet. These broad and handsome leaves are still freshly green, though drooping or hanging now closely about the vine, but contrast remarkably with the bare trunks and the changed leaves above and around.

I hear many crickets by this path and see many warily standing on the *qui vive* in awkward positions, or running their heads under a chip, or prying into a hole, but I can see none creaking. I see at last a few white pine cones open on the trees, but almost all appear to have fallen. The chestnuts are scarce and small and apparently have but just begun to open their burs.

That globular head of pale-yellow spheres of seed-parachutes along the wood road is the rough hawkweed. The single heads of savory-leaved aster are of the same color now.

When, returning at 5 o'clock, I pass the pond in the road, I see the sun, which is about entering the grosser hazy atmosphere above the western horizon, brilliantly reflected in the pond, — a dazzling sheen, a bright golden shimmer. His broad sphere extended stretches the whole length of the pond toward me. First, in the extreme distance, I see a few sparkles of the gold on the dark surface; then begins a regular and solid column of shimmering gold, straight as a rule, but at one place, where a breeze strikes the surface from one side, it is remarkably spread or widened, then recovers its straightness again, thus: Again it is remarkably curved, say thus: then broken into several pieces, then straight and entire again, then spread or blown aside at the point like smoke from a chimney, thus: Of course, if there were eyes enough to occupy all the east shore, the whole pond would be seen as one dazzling shimmering lake of melted gold. Such beauty and splendor adorns our walks!

I measured the depth of the needles under the pitch pines east of the railroad (behind the old shanties), which, as I remember, are about thirty years old. In one place it is three quarters of an inch in all to the soil, in another one and a quarter, and in a hollow under a larger pine about four inches. I think the thickness of the needles, old and new, is not more than one inch there on an average. These pines are only four or five inches thick.

Vol. VII

See slate-colored snowbirds.

Talking with Bellew this evening about Fourierism and communities, I said that I suspected any enterprise in which two were engaged together. "But," said he, "it is difficult to make a stick stand unless you slant two or more against it." "Oh, no," answered I, "you may split its lower end into three, or drive it single into the ground, which is the best way; but most men, when they start on a new enterprise, not only figuratively, but really, *pull up stakes*. When the sticks prop one another, none, or only one, stands erect."

He showed me a sketch of Wachusett. Spoke of his life in Paris, etc. I asked him if he had ever visited the Alps and sketched there. He said he had not. Had he been to the White Mountains? "No," he answered, "the highest mountains I have ever seen were the Himalayas, though I was only two years old then." It seems that he was born in that neighborhood.

He complains that the Americans have attained to bad luxuries, but have no comforts.

Howitt says of the man who found the great nugget which weighed twenty-eight pounds at the Bendigo diggings in Australia: "He soon began to drink; got a horse, and rode all about, generally at full gallop, and when he met people, called out to inquire if they knew who he was, and then kindly informed them that he was 'the bloody wretch that had found the nugget.' At last he rode full speed against a tree, and nearly knocked his brains out. He is a hopelessly ruined man." In my opinion there was no danger, for he had already

knocked his brains out against the nugget. But he is a type of the class. They are all fast men. Hear some of the names of the places where they dig: "Jackass Flat," — "Sheep's-Head Gully," — "Sulky Gully," — "Murderer's Bar," etc.[1]

Oct. 20. P. M. — To Nawshawtuct.

Agreeable to me is the scent of the withered and decaying leaves and pads, pontederias, on each side as I paddle up the river this still cloudy day, with the faint twittering or chirping of a sparrow still amid the bare button-bushes. It is the scent of the year, passing away like a decaying fungus, but leaving a rich mould, I trust.

On the 18th I found the Great Meadows wet, yet Beck Stow's was remarkably dry. Last summer the case was reversed.

I find, here and there on the hill, apples, sometimes three or four, carried to the mouth of a striped squirrel's hole, four or five rods from the tree, with the marks of his teeth in them, by which he carried them, and the chankings or else fragments of the skin of others there. There is no heap of sand to betray these little holes, but they descend perpendicularly in the midst of a clean sod. I was at first admiring the beauty of the wild apples, — now is the time, — some freckled with blood-red spots and perhaps also touched with a greenish rust here and there, like a fine lichen or fungus.[2]

[1] [*Cape Cod, and Miscellanies*, p. 467; *Misc.*, Riv. 268.]
[2] [*Excursions*, p. 315; Riv. 386.]

I see on the dead top of a hickory, twittering very much like swallows, eighteen and more bluebirds, perhaps preparing to migrate.

I have collected and split up now quite a pile of driftwood, — rails and riders and stems and stumps of trees, — perhaps half or three quarters of a tree. It is more amusing, not only to collect this with my boat and bring [it] up from the river on my back, but to split it also, than it would be to speak to a farmer for a load of wood and to saw and split that. Each stick I deal with has a history, and I read it as I am handling it, and, last of all, I remember my adventures in getting it, while it is burning in the winter evening. That is the most interesting part of its history. It has made part of a fence or a bridge, perchance, or has been rooted out of a clearing and bears the marks of fire on it. When I am splitting it, I study the effects of water on it, and, if it is a stump, the curiously winding grain by which it separates into so many prongs, — how to take advantage of its grain and split it most easily. I find that a dry oak stump will split pretty easily in the direction of its diameter, but not at right angles with it or along its circles of growth. I got out some good knees for a boat. Thus one half the value of my wood is enjoyed before it is housed, and the other half is equal to the whole value of an equal quantity of the wood which I buy.

Some of my acquaintances have been wondering why I took all this pains, bringing some nearly three miles by water, and have suggested various reasons for it. I tell them in my despair of making them under-

stand me that it is a profound secret, — which it has proved, — yet I did hint to them that one reason was that I wanted to get it. I take some satisfaction in eating my food, as well as in being nourished by it. I feel well at dinner-time as well as after it. The world will never find out why you don't love to have your bed tucked up for you, — why you will be so perverse. I enjoy more drinking water at a clear spring than out of a goblet at a gentleman's table. I like best the bread which I have baked, the garment which I have made, the shelter which I have constructed, the fuel which I have gathered.

It is always a recommendation to me to know that a man has ever been poor, has been regularly born into this world, knows the language. I require to be assured of certain philosophers that they have once been barefooted, footsore, have eaten a crust because they had nothing better, and know what sweetness resides in it.

I have met with some barren accomplished gentlemen who seemed to have been to school all their lives and never had a vacation to live in. Oh, if they could only have been stolen by the Gypsies! and carried far beyond the reach of their guardians! They had better have died in infancy and been buried under the leaves, their lips besmeared with blackberries, and Cock Robin for their sexton.

Oct. 21. It began to rain about 10 o'clock last evening after a cloudy day, and it still rains, gently but steadily, this morning. The wind must be east,

for I hear the church bell very plainly; yet I sit with an open window, it is so warm.

Looking into the yard, I see the currant bushes all bare of leaves, as they have been some time; but the gooseberries at the end of their row are covered with reddened leaves. This gradualness in the changing and falling of the leaves produces agreeable effects and contrasts. The currant row is bare, but the gooseberries at the end are full of scarlet leaves still.

I have never liked to have many rich fruits ripening at the same season. When Porter apples, for instance, are ripe, there are also other early apples and pears and plums and melons, etc. Nature by her bounteousness thus disgusts us with a sense of repletion — and uncleanness even. Perhaps any one of these fruits would answer as well as all together. She offers us too many good things at once.

I enjoyed getting that large oak stump from Fair Haven some time ago, and bringing it home in my boat. I tipped it in with the prongs up, and they spread far over the sides of the boat. There was no passing amidships. I much enjoyed this easy carriage of it, floating down the Musketaquid from far. It was a great stump and sunk my boat considerably, and its prongs were so in the way that I could take but a short stroke with my paddle. I enjoyed every stroke of my paddle, every rod of my progress, which advanced me so easily nearer to my port. It was as good as to sit by the best oak wood fire. I still enjoy such a conveyance, such a victory, as much as boys do riding on a rail. All the upper part of this, when I came to split it, I

found to be very finely honeycombed, reduced to a coarse cellular mass, apparently by shrinkage and wasting; but it made excellent fuel, nevertheless, as if all the combustible part remained. Only the earthy had returned to earth.

When Allen was here the other day, I found that I could not take two steps with him. He taught school in Concord seventeen [?] years ago, and has not been here since. He wished much to see the town again, but nothing living and fair in it. He had, I should say, a very musty recollection of it. He called on no living creature among all his pupils, but insisted on going [to] the new burying-ground and reading all the epitaphs. I waited at the gate, telling him that that ground did not smell good. I remembered when the first body was placed in it. He did, however, ask after one or two juvenile scamps and one idiotic boy who came to school to him, — how they had turned out, — and also after a certain caged fool, dead since he was here, who had lived near where he boarded; also after a certain ancient tavern, now pulled down. This at odd intervals, for he improved all the rest of his time while he was here in attending a Sabbath-school convention.

I have been thinking over with Father the old houses in this street. There was the Hubbard (?) house at the fork of the roads; the Thayer house (now Garrison's); Sam Jones's (now Channing's); Willoughby Prescott's (a bevel-roof, which I do not remember), where Loring's is (Hoar's was built by a Prescott); Ma'm Bond's; the Jones Tavern (Bigelow's); the old Hurd (or Cumming's?) house; the Dr. Hurd house;

the old mill; and the Richardson Tavern (which I do not remember). On this side, the Monroe house, in which we lived; the Parkman house, which William Heywood told me twenty years ago that he helped raise the rear of sixty years before (it then sloping to one story behind), and that then it was called an old house (Dr. Ripley said that a Bond built it); the Merrick house; a rough-cast house where Bates's is (Betty ?); and all the south side of the Mill-Dam. Still further from the centre the old houses and sites are about as numerous as above. Most of these houses slanted to one story behind.

P. M. — Up Assabet.

A damp cloudy day only, after all, and scarcely any rain; a good day for all *hunters* to be out, especially on the water.

The yellowish leaves of the black oak incline soon to a decayed and brown look. The red oak is more red. But the scarlet is very bright and conspicuous. How finely its leaves are cut against the sky with sharp points, especially near the top of the tree! They look somewhat like double or treble crosses.[1] The squirrels appear to have stripped this tree entirely, and I find the fragments of nutshells beneath it. They have also eaten the white and red and black oak acorns very generally, but there are more of the last left.

Further up, on the big red maple in Wheeler's Swamp, I see two gray squirrels chasing each other round and round the trunk of the tree, now close to each other, now

[1] [*Excursions*, p. 278; Riv. 341.]

far apart, one stealing off behind a limb, and now resting on opposite sides of the trunk, — where they might not be noticed, being of the same color with the bark, — indifferently with their heads down or up. Then away goes one out on a twig, and leaps into the next tree, and the other swiftly follows, and sometimes, when the twig is slight or chiefly leaves they leap into, they have to make a swinging somerset of it, to save themselves while they cling to it.

At length they separate to feed, and I see them running up to the very tops of the swamp white oaks and out to the extremities of the boughs, and jumping at the extreme twig which bears acorns, which they cut off, and devour, sitting on a firmer limb. It is surprising how rapidly they devour one after another, dropping the cups and scales and bits of the meat. It is surprising also to observe, when one wishes to reach a certain part of a neighboring tree, how surely he runs back to the trunk and then selects the right limb by which to reach it, without any hesitation, as if he knew the road.

You see, around the muskrat-houses, a clear space, where they have cut off the pontederias of which they are built; and now, after last night's rain, the river is risen some, and the pontederia roots, etc., which have been eaten by them, are washed up together next the shore.

That apparently shell-less snail or slug which is so common this damp day under apple trees, eating the apples, is evidently one of the naked *Mollusca*, the Division *Gasteropoda*, a *Limax*, perhaps the *Limax*

Vol. VII

tunicata of Gould. He describes but one other species.

Almost all wild apples are handsome. Some are knurly and peppered all over or on the stem side with fine crimson spots on a yellowish-white ground; others have crimson blotches or eyes, more or less confluent and fiery when wet, — for apples, like shells and pebbles, are handsomest in a wet day. Taken from under the tree on the damp sward, they shrivel and fade. Some have these spots beneath a reddened surface with obscure rays. Others have hundreds of fine blood-red rays, running regularly, though broken, from the stem dimple to the blossom, like meridian lines, on a straw-colored ground, — perfect spheres. Others are a deep, dark red, with very obscure yet darker rays; others a uniform clear, bright red, approaching to scarlet.[1]

Oct. 22. Another cloudy day without rain.

P. M. — To Fair Haven Hill *via* Hubbard's Grove.

How welcome this still, cloudy day! An inward sunniness more than makes up for the want of an external one. As I pass this grove, I see the open ground strewn and colored with yellow leaves, which have been wafted from a large black birch ten rods within the wood. I see at a distance the scattered birch-tops, like yellow flames amid the pines, also, in another direction, the red of oaks in the bosom of a pine wood, and, in sprout-lands on Fair Haven, the deep and uniform red of young oaks.

[1] [*Excursions*, pp. 314, 315; Riv. 385–387.]

I sat on a bank at the brook crossing, beyond the grove, to watch a flock of *seringos*, perhaps Savannah sparrows, which, with some *F. hyemalis* and other sparrows, were actively flitting about amid the alders and dogwood. At last I saw one resting a moment to prune himself, and in this operation he opened his plumage very thoroughly to me. Distinct yellow eyebrows, extending round beneath the bill; tail blackish or dusky; primaries bay or chestnut; secondaries (?) edged with white; some white lines on shoulders; *pale* flesh-colored bill and legs; toward vent beneath, pure white. Suddenly a pigeon hawk[1] dashed over the bank very low and within a rod of me, and, striking its wings against the twigs with a clatter close to a sparrow, which escaped, it alighted amid the alders in front, within four rods of me. It was attracted by the same objects which attracted me. It sat a few moments, balancing itself and spreading its tail and wings, — a chubby little fellow. Its back appeared a sort of deep chocolate-brown. Every sparrow at once concealed itself, apparently deep in the bushes next the ground. Once or twice he dashed down there amid the alders and tried to catch one. In a few minutes he skimmed along the hedge by the path and disappeared westward. But presently, hearing the sound of his wings amid the bushes, I looked up and saw him dashing along through the willows and then out and upward high over the meadow in pursuit of a sparrow (perhaps a seringo). The sparrow flew pretty high and kept doubling. When it flew

[1] Was I sure?

direct, the hawk gained, and got within two or three feet of it; but when it doubled, it gained on the hawk; so the latter soon gave up the chase, and the little bird flew off high over my head, with a panting breath and a rippling ricochet flight, toward the high pine grove. When I passed along the path ten minutes after, I found that all those sparrows were still hid under the bushes by the ditch-side, close to the ground, and I saw nothing of them till I scared them out by going within two or three feet. No doubt they warned each other by a peculiar note. What a corsair the hawk is to them! — a little fellow hardly bigger than a quail.

Birds certainly are afraid of man. They [allow] all other creatures, — cows and horses, etc., — excepting only one or two kinds, birds or beasts of prey, to come near them, but not man. What does this fact signify? Does it not signify that man, too, is a beast of prey to them? Is he, then, a true lord of creation, whose subjects are afraid of him, and with reason? They know very well that he is not humane, as he pretends to be.

In Potter's pasture, as you go to Fair Haven Hill, where he had grain in the summer, the great mullein leaves are strewn as thick as turnips that have been sown. This the first year. The next I suppose they will blossom. They have felled and carted off that middling-sized white oak just beyond. I count about one hundred and twenty rings of growth. In Potter's maple swamp, where the red maple leaves lie in thick beds on the ground, what a strong mustiness, even sourness in some places! Yet I like this scent. With

the present associations, sweet to me is the mustiness of the grave itself. I hear a hyla.

The swamp pyrus (*Amelanchier*) is leafing again. One opening **leafet** is an inch long, while the reddish-yellow leaves still hold on at the end of the twig above. Its green swollen buds are generally conspicuous, curving round the stems. There is a twig full of those dead black leaves on one. It is a new spring there. I hear the sound of the first flail from William Wheeler's barn. I mark the gray diverging stems of the dogwood, which is now bare, topped with the long, recurved, dry panicles like loose barbs.

I think that the trees generally have not worn very brilliant colors this month, but I find to-day that many small shrubs which have been protected by the forest are remarkably fair and bright. They, perhaps, have not felt the drought nor been defaced by insects. They are the best preserved and the most delicately tinted. I see the maple viburnum leaves a dark, dull spotted crimson toward the edges, like some wild apples. I distinguish it from the red maple at first only by its downy feeling beneath and the simple form of some leaves. These have also a short petiole and not a sharp sinus. Then there is the more or less crimson *nudum* viburnum, passing from scarlet through crimson to black-spotted and crimson in its decay. The blackness spreads very fast in one night. The glossy scarlet blueberries and the redder huckleberries; the scarlet choke-berry, or vermilion; some red maples which are yellow with only scarlet eyes. But still, in the shade and shelter of the woods as fair as anything,

the leaves of the wild cherry, so clear of injury from insects, passing from green through yellow or a cherry red to the palest and purest imaginable cherry-color, the palest fawn with a mere tinge of cherry, with their fine overlapping serrations. Those great twisted yellow leaves of hickory sprouts, yellow and green, from which I used to drink. And here is a very handsome orange-red high blackberry leaf, with its five leafets all perfect; most are dark-red. But all these, like shells and pebbles must be seen on their own seashore. There are two seasons when the leaves are in their glory, their green and perfect youth in June and this their ripe old age. Some of the very young oak leaves have the deepest lustreless or inward scarlet of any. Most of the reddish oak leaves now in the woods are spotted, mildewed as it were, by the drip from above.

Brought home the three kinds of lechea, whose pretty whorls of radical shoots or branches are now, methinks, more conspicuous than before. I should distinguish the two lesser by the one having larger pods and being more slender, taller, and more simple every way, the other low, bushy, spreading, the branches making a larger angle with the stems, fine-leaved, small and few pods, and the radical shoots (alone of the three specimens I have) very densely *branched* and leafed. Those of the other two are simple. All have a part of the radical leafets above recurved.

The Plymouth fishermen have just come home from the Banks, except one.

Oct. 23. P. M. — To Saw Mill Brook.

The streets are strewn with buttonwood leaves, which rustle under your feet, and the children are busy raking them into heaps, some for bonfires. The large elms are bare; not yet the buttonwoods. The sugar maples on the Common stand dense masses of rich yellow leaves with a deep scarlet blush, — far more than blush. They are remarkably brilliant this year on the exposed surfaces. The last are as handsome as any trees in the street.[1] I am struck with the handsome form and clear, though very pale, say lemon, yellow of the black birch leaves on sprouts in the woods, finely serrate and distinctly *plaited* from the midrib. I plucked three leaves from the end of a red maple shoot, an underwood, each successively smaller than the last, the brightest and clearest scarlet that I ever saw. These and the birch attracted universal admiration when laid on a sheet of white paper and passed round the supper table, and several inquired particularly where I found them. I never saw such colors painted. They were without spot;[2] ripe leaves. The small willows two or three feet high by the roadside in woods have some rich, deep chrome-yellow leaves with a gloss. The sprouts are later to ripen and richer-colored.

The pale whitish leaves of horehound in damp grassy paths, with its spicy fruit in the axils, are tinged with purple or lake more or less.

Going through what was E. Hosmer's muck-hole

[1] [*Excursions*, p. 271; Riv. 332, 333.]
[2] Yet some spots appeared and they were partly wilted the next morning, so delicate are they.

pond, now almost entirely dry, the surface towards the shore is covered with a dry crust more or less cracked, which crackles under my feet. I strip it up like bark in long pieces, three quarters of an inch thick and a foot wide and two long. It appears to be composed of fine mosses and perhaps utricularia and the like, such as grow in water. A *little* sphagnum is quite conspicuous, *erect* but dry, in it.

Now is the time for chestnuts. A stone cast against the trees shakes them down in showers upon one's head and shoulders. But I cannot excuse myself for using the stone. It is not innocent, it is not just, so to maltreat the tree that feeds us. I am not disturbed by considering that if I thus shorten its life I shall not enjoy its fruit so long, but am prompted to a more innocent course by motives purely of humanity. I sympathize with the tree, yet I heaved a big stone against the trunks like a robber, — not too good to commit murder. I trust that I shall never do it again. These gifts should be accepted, not merely with gentleness, but with a certain humble gratitude. The tree whose fruit we would obtain should not be too rudely shaken even. It is not a time of distress, when a little haste and violence even might be pardoned. It is worse than boorish, it is criminal, to inflict an unnecessary injury on the tree that feeds or shadows us. Old trees are our parents, and our parents' parents, perchance. If you would learn the secrets of Nature, you must practice more humanity than others. The thought that I was robbing myself by injuring the tree did not occur to me, but I was affected as if I had

cast a rock at a sentient being, — with a duller sense than my own, it is true, but yet a distant relation. Behold a man cutting down a tree to come at the fruit! What is the moral of such an act?

Faded white ferns now at Saw Mill Brook. They press yellow or straw-color.

Ah! we begin old men in crime. Would that we might grow innocent at last as the children of light!

A downy woodpecker on an apple tree utters a sharp, shrill, rapid *tea te t, t, t, t t t t t.*

Is that tall weed in Mrs. Brooks's yard *Cacalia suaveolens* ? ? Yet stem more angled than grooved; four or five feet high. Some time ago.

Cousin Charles writes that his horse drew 5286 pounds up the hill from Hale's factory, at Cattle-Show in Haverhill the other day.

Oct. 24. Rained last night and all this day for the most part, bringing down the leaves, buttonwoods and sugar maples, in the street. The rich yellow and scarlet leaves of the sugar maple on the Common, which now thickly cover the grass in great circles about the trees, half having fallen, look like the reflection of the trees in water, and light up the Common, reflecting light even to the surrounding houses. The gentle touch of the rain brings down more leaves than the wind.

Looked at the old picture of Concord at Mrs. Brooks's, — she says by a Minott, an uncle (or granduncle?) of hers. There are the British marching into town in front of the meeting-house and facing about

Vol. VII

in front of where the tavern now stands, scattered Britons going up Main Street and about the town, and two officers on the Burying Hill looking west with a spy-glass.

The meeting-house stands as I remember it, but with three stories of windows, door in front toward Common, and no porches or spire; horse-sheds and noon (?) house behind and one side. The Jarvis house; then Wright's Tavern very plain; a bevel-roofed house endwise to the road where the Middlesex House is, which Mrs. B. calls Dr. Minott's house;[1] then a little hut; then the old court-house about where the brick schoolhouse is (this the extreme right). Left of the bevel-roofed house is a small house where the stable and sheds are, — some say Betty Hartshorne's; then a small building on the Mill-Dam; then the old mill; the Vose house, plain, three stories; another house *just* beyond and apparently in front of it; E. Hubbard's plain, and a small house back and towards the Vose house, and a dozen or fifteen provincials there; then some houses, probably Peter Wheeler's three or four storehouses, whence redcoats are rolling barrels into the pond, — and maybe partly from E. Hubbard's; and perhaps that is the Timothy, and after Peter, Wheeler house seen a little further east, where N. Stow's house is now. A large house apparently where the brick house is, and a row seen behind it up the street; Dr. Hurd's house, and four small buildings far behind it; and others seen up street behind Hurd

[1] Yes, and President Langdon lived there. The same, altered, was the tavern I knew.

house. But we see no further up *in* the street than where N. Brooks now lives. Beyond, the town appears well wooded. Lee's Hill also on this side. Great and Little Wachusett are seen in the horizon, and Nobscot.

Oct. 25. Quite cold it has cleared up after the rain. P. M. — I row up the river, which has risen eight or nine inches After these pleasant and warm days it is suddenly cold and windy, and the risen waters have an angry look. It is uncomfortable rowing with wet hands in this wind. The muskrats must now prepare for winter in earnest. I see many places where they have left clamshells recently. Now gather all your apples, if you have not before, or the frost will have them. The willows along the river now begin to look faded and somewhat bare and wintry. The dead wool-grass, etc., characterizes the shore. The meadows look sere and straw-colored.

Oct. 26. P. M. — To Conantum.

Another clear cold day, though not so cold as yesterday. The light and sun come to us directly and freely, as if some obstruction had been removed, — the windows of heaven had been washed.

The old house on Conantum is fast falling down. Its chimney, laid in clay, measures, on the lower floor, twelve and a half feet in breadth across the hearth, oven, and a small fireplace, parallel with the end of the house. On a level with the chamber floor it measures on the front side eight feet. The mantel-tree of a *small* fireplace in a chamber is an oak joist with the inside corner sloped off thus: That of the great kitchen fireplace is a pine timber, ten inches by thirteen, also with a great sloped surface within, showing traces of fire. The small girders (?) of the roof overlap a foot or more on the rafters (?).

I see some farmers now cutting up their corn. The sweet viburnum leaves hang thinly on the bushes and are a dull crimsonish red. What apples are left out now, I presume that the farmers do not mean to gather. The witch-hazel is still freshly in flower, and near it I see a houstonia in bloom. The hillside is slippery with new-fallen white pine leaves. The leaves of the oaks and hickories have begun to be browned, — lost their brilliancy.

I examine some frostweed there near the hazel. It is still quite alive, — the leaves now a purplish brown, — indeed just out of bloom, and its bark at the ground is quite tight and entire. Pulling it up, I find bright-pink shoots to have put forth half an inch long and starting even at the surface of the sod. Is not this, as well as its second blossoming, somewhat peculiar to this plant? And may it not be that, when at last the cold is severe, the sap is frozen and bursts the bark and the breath of the dying plant is frozen about it?

I return by way of the mocker-nut trees. The squirrels have already begun on them, though the trees are still covered with yellow and brown leaves, and the nuts do not fall. It is surprising to see how they have gnawed in two and made wrecks of the great, hard

Vol. VII

hunting, fishing, wigwam-building, making garments of skins, and collecting wood wherever you find it, than for butchering, farming, carpentry, working in a factory, or going to a wood market.

Oct. 27. P. M. — A-chestnutting down the Turnpike.

There are *many* fringed gentians, now considerably frost-bitten, in what was E. Hosmer's meadow between his dam and the road. It is high time we came a-nutting, for the nuts have nearly all fallen, and you must depend on what you can find on the ground, left by the squirrels, and cannot shake down any more to speak of. The trees are nearly all bare of leaves as well as burs. The wind comes cold from the northwest, as if there were snow on the earth in that direction. Larches are yellowing.

I try one of the wild apples in my desk. It is remarkable that the wild apples which I praise as so spirited and racy when eaten in the fields and woods, when brought into the house have a harsh and crabbed taste. As shells and pebbles must be beheld on the seashore, so these October fruits must be tasted in a bracing walk amid the somewhat bracing airs of late October. To appreciate their wild and sharp flavors, it seems necessary that you be breathing the sharp October or November air. The outdoor air and exercise which the walker gets give a different tone to his palate, and he craves a fruit which the sedentary would call harsh and crabbed even. The palate rejects a wild apple eaten in the house — so of haws and

nuts, not stopping to take any advantage. A little this side I see a red squirrel dash out from the wall, snatch an apple from amid many on the ground, and, running swiftly up the tree with it, proceed to eat it, sitting on a smooth dead limb, with its back to the wind and its tail curled close over its back. It allows me to approach within eight feet. It holds the apple between its two fore paws and scoops out the pulp, mainly with its lower incisors, making a saucer-like cavity, high and thin at the edge, where it bites off the skin and lets it drop. It keeps its jaws a-going very fast, from time to time turning the apple round and round with its paws (as it eats), like a wheel in a plane at right angles to its body. It holds it up and twirls it with ease. Suddenly it pauses, having taken alarm at something, then drops the remainder of the apple in [the hollow] of the bough and glides off by short snatches, uttering a faint, sharp bird-like note.

The song sparrow still sings on a button-bush.

A columbine leaf curiously marked by the eating of an insect, — a broad white trail, corresponding mainly to the lobes of the leaf. That little grayish-green and rigid moss-like plant on top of Lee's Cliff, now dropping fine orange-colored pellets or spores (?), seems to be the *Selaginella rupestris?*

I sometimes think that I must go off to some wilderness where I can have a better opportunity to play life, — can find more suitable materials to build my house with, and enjoy the pleasure of collecting my fuel in the forest. I have more taste for the wild sports of

acorns — and demands a tamed one, for here you miss that October air which is the wine it is eaten with. I frequently pluck wild apples of so rich and spicy a flavor that I wonder all orchardists do not get a scion from them, but when I have brought home my pockets full, and taste them in the house, they are unexpectedly harsh, crude things. They must be eaten in the fields, when your system is all aglow with exercise, the frosty weather nips your fingers (in November), the wind rattles the bare boughs and rustles the leaves, and the jay is heard screaming around.

So there is one thought for the field, another for the house. I would have my thoughts, like wild apples, to be food for walkers, and will not warrant them to be palatable if tasted in the house.

To appreciate the flavor of those wild apples requires vigorous and healthy senses, papillæ firm and erect on the tongue and palate, not easily tamed and flattened. Some of those apples might be labelled, "To be eaten in the wind." [1]

Oct. 28. P. M. — By boat to Leaning Hemlocks.

I think it was the 18th that I first noticed snow-fleas on the surface of the river amid the weeds at its edge. Green leaves are now so scarce that the polypody at the Island rock is more conspicuous, and the terminal shield fern (?) further up. As I paddle under the Hemlock bank this cloudy afternoon, about 3 o'clock, I see a screech owl sitting on the edge of a hollow hemlock stump about

[1] [*Excursions*, pp. 311–314; Riv. 382, 383, 385.]

three feet high, at the base of a large hemlock. It sits
with its head drawn in, eying me, with its eyes partly
open, about twenty feet off. When it hears me move, it
turns its head toward me, perhaps one eye only open,
with its great glaring golden iris. You see two whitish
triangular lines above the eyes meeting at the bill, with
a sharp reddish-brown triangle between and a narrow
curved line of black under each eye. At this distance
and in this light, you see only a black spot where the
eye is, and the question is whether the eyes are open
or not. It sits on the lee side of the tree this raw and
windy day. You would say that this was a bird without
a neck. Its short bill, which rests upon its breast,
scarcely projects at all, but in a state of rest the whole
upper part of the bird from the wings is rounded off
smoothly, excepting the horns, which stand up conspicuously or are slanted back. After watching it ten
minutes from the boat, I landed two rods above, and,
stealing quietly up behind the hemlock, though from
the windward, I looked carefully around it, and, to
my surprise, saw the owl still sitting there. So I sprang
round quickly, with my arm outstretched, and caught
it in my hand. It was so surprised that it offered no
resistance at first, only glared at me in mute astonishment with eyes as big as saucers. But ere long it began
to snap its bill, making quite a noise, and, as I rolled
it up in my handkerchief and put it in my pocket, it
bit my finger slightly. I soon took it out of my pocket
and, tying the handkerchief, left it on the bottom of
the boat. So I carried it home and made a small cage
in which to keep it, for a night. When I took it up,

it clung so tightly to my hand as to sink its claws into
my fingers and bring blood.

When alarmed or provoked most, it snaps its bill
and hisses. It puffs up its feathers to nearly twice its usual
size, stretches out its neck, and, with wide-open eyes,
stares this way and that, moving its head slowly and
undulatingly from side to side with a curious motion.
While I write this evening, I see that there is ground
for much superstition in it. It looks out on me from
a dusky corner of its box with its great solemn eyes,
so perfectly still itself. I was surprised to find that
I could imitate its note as I remember it, by a *guttural*
whinnering.

A remarkably squat figure, being very broad in proportion to its length, with a short tail, and very cat-
like in the face with its horns and great eyes. Remarkably large feet and talons, legs thickly clothed
with whitish down, down to the talons. It brought
blood from my fingers by clinging to them. It would
lower its head, stretch out its neck, and, bending it
from side to side, peer at you with laughable circumspection; from side to side, as if to catch or absorb
into its eyes every ray of light, strain at you with complacent yet earnest scrutiny. Raising and lowering its
head and moving it from side to side in a slow and
regular manner, at the same time snapping its bill
smartly perhaps, and faintly hissing, and puffing itself up more and more, — cat-like, turtle-like, both in
hissing and swelling. The slowness and gravity, not
to say solemnity, of this motion are striking. There
plainly is no jesting in this case.

Vol. VII

I saw yesterday at Saw Mill Brook a common salamander on a rock close to the water, not long dead,
with a wound in the top of its head.

General color of the owl a rather pale and perhaps
slightly reddish brown, the feathers centred with black.
Perches with two claws above and two below the perch.
It is a slight body, covered with a mass of soft and
light-lying feathers. Its head muffled in a great hood.
It must be quite comfortable in winter. Dropped a
pellet of fur and bones (?) in his cage. He sat, not
really moping but trying to sleep, in a corner of his
box all day, yet with one or both eyes slightly open
all the while. I never once caught him with his eyes
shut. Ordinarily stood rather than sat on his perch.

Oct. 29. P. M. — Up Assabet.

Carried my owl to the hill again. Had to shake
him out of the box, for he did not go of his own accord.
(He had learned to alight on his perch, and it was surprising how lightly and noiselessly he would hop upon
it.) There he stood on the grass, at first bewildered,
with his horns pricked up and looking toward me. In
this strong light the pupils of his eyes suddenly contracted and the iris expanded till they were two great
brazen orbs with a centre spot merely. His attitude
expressed astonishment more than anything. I was
obliged to toss him up a little that he might feel his
wings, and then he flapped away low and heavily to a
hickory on the hillside twenty rods off. (I had let him
out in the plain just east of the hill.) Thither I followed and tried to start him again. He was now on

the *qui vive*, yet would not start. He erected his head,
showing some neck, narrower than the round head
above. His eyes were broad brazen rings around bullets of black. His horns stood quite an inch high, as
not before. As I moved around him, he turned his
head always toward me, till he looked *directly* behind
himself as he sat crosswise on a bough. He behaved
as if bewildered and dazzled, gathering all the light
he could and ever straining his great eyes toward [you]
to make out who you are, but not inclining to fly. I
had to lift him again with a stick to make him fly,
and then he only rose to a higher perch, where at last
he seemed to seek the shelter of a thicker cluster
of the sere leaves, partly crouching there. He never
appeared so much alarmed as surprised and astonished.

When I first saw him yesterday, he sat on the edge
of a hollow hemlock stump about three feet high, at
the bottom of a large hemlock, amid the darkness of
the evergreens that cloudy day. (It threatened to rain
every moment.) At the bottom of the hollow, or eighteen inches beneath him, was a very soft bed of the
fine green moss (hypnum) which grows on the bank
close by, probably his own bed. It had been recently
put there.

When I moved him in his cage he would cling to the
perch, though it was in a perpendicular position, one
foot above another, suggesting his habit of clinging
to and climbing the inside of hollow trees. I do not
remember any perpendicular line in his eyes, as in those
of the cat.

I see many aphides very thick and long-tailed on the alders. Soapwort gentian and pasture thistle still. There are many fresh election-cake toadstools amid the pitch pines there, and also very regular higher hemispherical ones with a regularly warted or peppered surface.

As I was passing Merrick's pasture, I saw and counted about a hundred crows advancing in a great rambling flock from the southeast and crossing the river on high, and cawing.

There is a wild apple on the hill which has to me a peculiarly pleasant bitter tang, not perceived till it is three quarters tasted. It remains on the tongue. As you cut it, it smells exactly like a squash-bug. I like its very acerbity. It is a sort of triumph to eat and like it, an ovation. In the fields alone are the sours and bitters of nature appreciated; just as the woodchopper eats his meal in a sunny glade in middle of a winter day, with contentment, in a degree of cold which, experienced in the house, would make the student miserable, — basks in a sunny ray and dreams of summer, in a degree of cold which, felt in a chamber, would make a student wretched. They who are abroad at work are not cold; it is they who sit shivering in houses. As with cold and heat, so with sweet and sour. This natural raciness, sours and bitters, etc., which the diseased palate refuses, are the true casters and condiments. What is sour in the house a bracing walk makes sweet. Let your condiments be in the condition of your senses. Apples which the farmer neglects and leaves out as unsalable, and unpalatable to those

Vol. VII

who frequent the markets, are choicest fruit to the walker.[1] When the leaves fall, the whole earth is a cemetery pleasant to walk in. I love to wander and muse over them in their graves, returning to dust again. Here are no lying nor vain epitaphs. The scent of their decay is pleasant to me. I buy no lot in the cemetery which my townsmen have just *consecrated* with a poem and an auction, paying so much for a choice. *Here* is room enough for me.[2] The swamp white oak has a fine, firm, leathery leaf with a silver under side, half of them now turned up. Oaks are now fairly brown; very few still red. Water milkweed discounts.

I have got a load of great hardwood stumps. For sympathy with my neighbors I might about as well live in China. They are to me barbarians, with their committee-works and gregariousness.

Returning, I scare up a blue heron from the bathing-rock this side the Island. It is whitened by its droppings, in great splotches a foot or more wide. He has evidently frequented it to watch for fish there. Also a flock of blackbirds fly eastward over my head from the top of an oak, either red-wings or grackles.

Oct. 30. Wednesday. Going to the new cemetery, I see that the scarlet oak leaves have still some brightness; perhaps the latest of the oaks.

[1] [*Excursions*, pp. 311–313; Riv. 382–385.]
[2] [*Excursions*, p. 270; Riv. 331, 332.]

END OF VOLUME VII